W9-DJP-056

THE BANTAM NEW COLLEGE FRENCH & ENGLISH DICTIONARY

COMPREHENSIVE: More than 70,000 words and phrases in education, business, travel, science, history, literature, art and music, social sciences, law, medicine, diplomacy, international affairs, and everyday life.

AUTHORITATIVE: Based on reliable spoken and written sources and organized to achieve the utmost clarity, precision, and convenience.

EASY TO USE: All words are found in one single alphabet for each language, including proper names and abbreviations.

**A NEW LANDMARK IN FRENCH-ENGLISH DICTIONARIES
FOR THE MODERN USER OF WORDS!**

THE BANTAM NEW
COLLEGE DICTIONARY SERIES

Roger J. Steiner, Author

Roger J. Steiner, A.B., A.M., Ph.D., has done extensive linguistic research in France, where he has traveled widely and taught for two years at the University of Bordeaux. Now a member of the French faculty at the University of Delaware, he is the author of a book dealing with the origin and development of bilingual dictionaries. TWO CENTURIES OF SPANISH AND ENGLISH LEXICOGRAPHY (The Hague and Paris, 1970), and has contributed articles and reviews to learned journals.

Edwin B. Williams, General Editor

Edwin B. Williams, A.B., A.M., Ph.D., Doct. d'Univ., LL.D., L.H.D., has been Chairman of the Department of Romance Languages, Dean of the Graduate School, and Provost of the University of Pennsylvania. He is a member of the American Philosophical Society and the Hispanic Society of America and the author of the Holt SPANISH AND ENGLISH DICTIONARY, THE BANTAM NEW COLLEGE SPANISH AND ENGLISH DICTIONARY and many other works on the Spanish, French and Portuguese languages.

THE BANTAM NEW COLLEGE
FRENCH & ENGLISH
DICTIONARY

DICTIONNAIRE
ANGLAIS et FRANÇAIS

BY ROGER J. STEINER
University of Delaware

BANTAM BOOKS
TORONTO · NEW YORK · LONDON · SYDNEY

THE BANTAM NEW COLLEGE
FRENCH & ENGLISH DICTIONARY

A Bantam Book / published April 1972

2nd printing	.... July 1973	6th printing	.. December 1977
3rd printing	...... January 1974	7th printing	...... March 1979
4th printing	. December 1975	8th printing	.... April 1980
5th printing	.... July 1976	9th printing	.... February 1981

All rights reserved.
Copyright © 1972 by Bantam Books, Inc.
This book may not be reproduced in whole or in part, by
mimeograph or any other means, without permission.
For information address: Bantam Books, Inc.

ISBN 0–553–14890–7

Published simultaneously in the United States and Canada

Bantam Books are published by Bantam Books, Inc. Its trade-
mark, consisting of the words "Bantam Books" and the por-
trayal of a bantam, is Registered in U.S. Patent and Trademark
Office and in other countries. Marca Registrada. Bantam
Books, Inc., 666 Fifth Avenue, New York, New York 10103.

PRINTED IN THE UNITED STATES OF AMERICA

18 17 16 15 14 13 12 11 10

CONTENTS

PREFACE

Inasmuch as the basic function of a bilingual dictionary is to provide semantic equivalences, syntactical constructions are shown in both the source and target languages on both sides of the Dictionary. In performing this function, a bilingual dictionary must fulfill six purposes. For example, a French and English bilingual dictionary must provide (1) French words which an English-speaking person wishes to use in speaking and writing (by means of the English-French part), (2) English meanings of French words which an English-speaking person encounters in listening and reading (by means of the French-English part), (3) the spelling, pronunciation, and inflection of French words and the gender of French nouns which an English-speaking person needs in order to use French words correctly (by means of the French-English part), (4) English words which a French-speaking person wishes to use in speaking and writing (by means of the French-English part), (5) French meanings of English words which a French-speaking person encounters in listening and reading (by means of the English-French part), and (6) the spelling, pronunciation, and inflection of English words which a French-speaking person needs in order to use English words correctly (by means of the English-French part).

It may seem logical to provide the pronunciation and inflection of English words and the pronunciation and inflection of French words and the gender of French nouns where these words appear as target words inasmuch as target words, according to (1) and (4) above, are sought for the purpose of speaking and writing. Thus the user would find not only the words he seeks but all the information he needs about them at one and the same place. But this technique is impractical because target words are not alphabetized and could, therefore, be found only by the

PRÉFACE

La mission essentielle d'un dictionnaire bilingue étant de fournir à l'usager des équivalences sémantiques, les constructions syntaxiques sont données à la fois dans la langue source et dans la langue cible dans les deux parties de l'ouvrage. En s'acquittant de cette mission, le dictionnaire bilingue doit viser six buts; c'est ainsi qu'un dictionnaire bilingue français et anglais doit donner: (1) dans la partie anglais-français, les mots français que la personne anglophone désire utiliser pour parler et pour écrire; (2) dans la partie français-anglais, les acceptions anglaises des mots français que cette même personne entend dans la langue parlée et rencontre dans la lecture des textes; (3) dans la partie français-anglais, l'orthographe, la prononciation figurée, l'inflexion des mots français et le genre des noms français indispensables à l'anglophone pour l'utilisation correcte de la langue française; (4) dans la partie français-anglais, les mots anglais que la personne francophone désire utiliser pour parler et pour écrire; (5) dans la partie anglais-français, les acceptions françaises des mots anglais que cette même personne entend dans la langue parlée et rencontre dans la lecture des textes; (6) dans la partie anglais-français, l'orthographe, la prononciation figurée et l'inflexion des mots anglais indispensables au francophone pour l'utilisation correcte de la langue anglaise.

A première vue, il paraît logique que la prononciation et l'inflexion des mots anglais et la prononciation et l'inflexion des mots français et le genre des noms français soient indiqués à la suite des traductions puisqu'on recherche ces traductions, selon (1) et (4) ci-dessus, pour parler et pour écrire. Ainsi, l'usager trouverait au même endroit, non seulement les mots qu'il cherche, mais également tous les renseignements dont il aurait besoin. Cependant, ce procédé n'est pas pratique parce que les traductions ne sont pas présentées dans l'ordre alphabétique et l'on ne pourrait

roundabout and uncertain way of seeking them through their translations in the other part of the dictionary. And this would be particularly inconvenient for persons using the dictionary for purposes (2) and (5) above. It is much more convenient to provide immediate alphabetized access to pronunciation and inflection where the words appear as source words. Showing the gender of nouns takes so little space that this information is provided with both source and target words.

trouver qu'avec difficulté. Cela entraînerait surtout des inconvénients pour les personnes qui utilisent le dictionnaire dans les cas (2) et (5) ci-dessus. L'ordre alphabétique permet un accès immédiat et plus commode à la prononciation et à l'inflexion quand les mots se présentent comme mots-souches. Néanmoins, l'indication du genre des noms prend si peu de place qu'elle figure aussi bien après les traductions qu'après les mots-souches.

All words are treated in a fixed order according to the parts of speech and the functions of verbs, as follows: article, adjective, substantive, pronoun, adverb, preposition, conjunction, transitive verb, intransitive verb, impersonal verb, auxiliary verb, reflexive verb, impersonal reflexive verb, interjection.

Tous les mots-souches sont traités suivant un ordre fixe—selon les parties du discours et les fonctions des verbes —qui est le suivant: article, adjectif, substantif, pronom, adverbe, préposition, conjonction, verbe transitif, verbe intransitif, verbe impersonnel, verbe auxiliaire, verbe pronominal (réfléchi ou réciproque), verbe à la fois impersonnel et réfléchi, interjection.

Meanings with subject and usage labels come after more general meanings. Subject and usage labels (printed in roman and in parentheses) refer to the preceding entry or phrase (printed in boldface). However, when labels come immediately, i.e., without any intervening punctuation mark, after a target word, they refer to that target word and the preceding word or words separated from it only by commas, e.g.,

Les sens d'un mot suivis des rubriques qui indiquent le sujet ou l'usage du mot viennent à la suite des sens d'emploi normal. Les rubriques qui indiquent le sujet ou l'usage du mot (imprimées en caractères romains et entre parenthèses) s'appliquent au mot-souche ou à la locution précédente (imprimés en caractères gras). Cependant, lorsque la rubrique suit immédiatement la traduction, c'est-à-dire sans aucun signe de ponctuation, elle s'applique à la traduction elle-même ou aux traductions précédentes qui n'en sont séparées que par une virgule, par ex.,

optometrist [ɑpˈtɑmɪtrɪst] *s* opticien *m*; optométriste *mf* (Canad)

English adjectives are always translated by the French masculine form regardless of whether the translation of the exemplary noun modified would be masculine or feminine, e.g.,

Les adjectifs anglais sont toujours traduits en français au masculin, quel que soit le genre des traductions des noms donnés en exemple et auxquelles ils se rapportent, par ex.,

close [klos] *adj* . . . ; (*friendship*) étroit; (*room*) renfermé

In order to facilitate the finding of the meaning and use sought for, changes within a vocabulary entry in part of speech and function of verb, in irregular inflection, in the gender of French nouns, and in the pronunciation of

Afin de faciliter le repérage de l'acception cherchée, les traductions sont groupées selon la partie du discours, la fonction du verbe, l'inflexion irrégulière, le genre du nom français, et la prononciation des mots français et des

French and English words are marked with parallels: ||, instead of the usual semicolons.

Since vocabulary entries are not determined on the basis of etymology, homographs are included in a single entry. When the pronunciation of a homograph changes, this is shown in the proper place after parallels.

Note, however, that plurals and words spelled with capitals are shown as run-on entries. They must be preceded by parallels only when there is a change in part of speech, in pronunciation, or in inflection.

Peculiarities in the pronunciation of the plural of nouns and of run-on entries are generally indicated, e.g.,

mouth [mauθ] *s* (*pl* **mouths** [mauðz])
house [haus] *s* (*pl* **houses** ['hauziz])
œil [œj] *m* . . . ; **entre quatre yeux** [ãtrəkatzjø]
guet-apens [gɛtapã] *m* (*pl* **guets-apens** [gɛtapã])

Periods are omitted after labels and grammatical abbreviations and at the end of vocabulary entries.

Proper nouns and abbreviations are listed in their alphabetical position in the main body of the Dictionary. Thus **Algérie** and **algérien** or **Suède** and **suédois** do not have to be looked up in two different parts of the book. And all subentries are listed in strictly alphabetical order.

The feminine form of a French adjective used as a noun (or a French feminine noun having identical spelling with the feminine form of an adjective) which falls alphabetically in a separate position from the adjective is treated in that position and is listed again as a cross reference under the adjective.

mots anglais. Ces groupes sont séparés par deux barres: ||, au lieu du point-virgule habituel.

Etant donné que l'étymologie n'entre pas dans la séparation des articles, tous les homographes sont incorporés dans le même article. Quand la pronon-ciation d'un homographe change, cette prononciation figurée est placée entre crochets à la suite des deux barres ||.

On remarquera cependant que les pluriels et les mots qui commencent par une majuscule sont présentés parmi les locutions dans l'ordre alphabétique et ne sont séparés de celles-ci que par un point-virgule. Ils ne sont précédés des deux barres || qu'en cas de changement dans la partie du discours, dans la prononciation, ou dans l'inflexion.

Les caractéristiques spéciales de la prononciation du pluriel des noms et des locutions sont généralement indi-quées, ex.:

Les points sont omis après les ru-briques, les abréviations d'ordre gram-matical et à la fin des articles.

Les noms propres et les abréviations se présentent toujours dans l'ordre alphabétique de la nomenclature du Dictionnaire. Par exemple, il n'est pas nécessaire de chercher **Algérie** et **algé-rien** ou **Suède** et **suédois** dans deux parties du livre. Toutes les locutions se présentent rigoureusement dans l'ordre alphabétique.

Lorsque la forme féminine d'un ad-jectif français ne suit pas immédiate-ment la forme masculine alphabétique-ment (ou lorsqu'il s'agit d'un nom féminin français qui aurait une ortho-graphe identique à la forme féminine de l'adjectif), et lorsqu'elle est prise substantivement, sa position comme mot-souche substantif est strictement alphabétique; mais un renvoi se trouve alors après le mot-souche adjectif.

cber chère [ʃɛr] adj . . . ‖ f see chère ‖ . . .
chère [ʃɛr] f fare, food and drink; . . .

The centered period is used in vocabulary entries of inflected words to mark off, according to standard orthographic principles in the two languages, the final syllable that has to be detached before the syllable showing the inflection is added, e.g.,	Quand les mots-souches sont des vocables à flexions, on emploie le point centré · pour séparer, selon les principes reconnus de l'orthographe des deux langues, la syllabe finale qui doit être détachée avant que la syllabe de la désinence ne soit attachée, ex.:

heu·reux [œrø] **-reuse** [røz]
satis·fy ['sætɪs ˌfaɪ] v (pret & pp **-fied**)

Since the orthographic break coming in French words (a) between the two l's of liquid l, (b) between s and c followed by e, i, or y, and (c) between the two elements of any double consonant pronounced as a single consonant does not correspond to the phonetic break, the centered period is used as usual but the full form of the inflected variant is shown, also with the centered period, and the full phonetic transcription of both forms is shown without a break, e.g.,	Puisque la séparation orthographique qui se trouve dans les mots français (a) entre les deux l de l'l mouillé, (b) entre s et c suivi de e, i, ou y et (c) entre les deux éléments de n'importe quelle consonne doublée prononcée comme simple consonne, ne répond pas à la séparation phonétique, on présente la forme entière de toute variante, imprimée également avec le point centré; et la transcription phonétique complète des deux formes se présente sans séparation, ex.:

(a) **merveil·leux** [mɛrvejø] **merveil·leuse** [mɛrvejøz]
(b) **évanes·cent** [evanesɑ̃] **évanes·cente** [evanesɑ̃t]
(c) **éton·nant** [etɔnɑ̃] **éton·nante** [etɔnɑ̃t]
    miel·leux [mjelø] **miel·leuse** [mjeløz]

Where the orthographic break, according to some authorities,* is not permitted, for example, between a y and a following vowel, the centered period is not used, e.g.,	Lorsque selon l'avis de certains spécialistes,* la séparation orthographique n'est pas permise, par exemple, entre un y et la voyelle suivante, on n'utilisera pas le point centré, ex.:

croyant [krwajɑ̃] **croyante** [krwajɑ̃t]
métayer [meteje] **métayère** [metejɛr]

* V. Maurice Grevisse, *Le Bon Usage*, 8th ed., 1964, §89, p. 52.

If the two components of an English solid compound are not separated by an accent mark, a centered period is used to mark off the division between them, e.g., **la′dy·bird′**.	Dans les cas où les deux éléments d'un mot composé anglais écrit comme mot simple, ne seraient pas séparés par un accent, on utilisera un point centré pour montrer la division entre les deux, par ex., **la′dy·bird′**.

Numbers referring to the model tables of French verbs (p. 7 ff.) are placed before the abbreviation indicating the part of speech. Numbers referring to the model tables of other French parts of speech (p. 21 ff.) are placed	Les numéros qui renvoient aux tableaux des verbes français à partir de la p. 7, précèdent l'abréviation qui indique la partie du discours. Les numéros qui renvoient aux tableaux des autres parties

after the French word on both sides of the Dictionary.

Il y a certains verbes français transitifs qui sous la forme pronominale régissent le pronom réfléchi comme complément d'attribution. Cependant, sous cette forme pronominale ils sont également transitifs et peuvent se traduire par des verbes transitifs anglais. Inversement, ces verbes pronominaux français peuvent traduire des verbes transitifs anglais. Cette équation est indiquée dans la partie français-anglais à la suite de l'abréviation *ref* par l'insertion de (with *dat* of *reflex pron*). Elle n'est pas indiquée dans la partie anglais-français, puisque l'abréviation *tr* indique nettement la relation syntaxique.

There are some French transitive verbs which, when used reflexively, take the reflexive pronoun in the dative. As reflexive verbs they may still take a direct object and may, accordingly, be translated by English transitive verbs. And they may in turn be used to translate English transitive verbs. This equation is shown on the French-English side after the abbreviation *ref* by the insertion of (with *dat* of *reflex pron*). It is not shown on the English-French side, as the abbreviation *tr* indicates unmistakably the syntactical relationship.

du discours, à partir de la p. 21, sont placés à la suite du mot français dans chaque partie du Dictionnaire.

The author wishes to express his gratitude to many persons who helped him in the production of this book and particularly to Dr. Edwin B. Williams, whose efforts were unstinting in the attempt to make this a useful dictionary, to his dear wife Kathryn, whose patience carried through the ten years of research and compilation, and to René Coulet du Gard and to Claud J. Pujolle for their constant help, as well as to the following: Jean Béranger, Brigitte Callay, Paul Dumestre, Maurice Jonas, Marc and Philomena Lampe, Daniel Pralus, Wayne and Paule Ready, and André Vincent.

Labels and Grammatical Abbreviations
Rubriques et abréviations grammaticales

abbr abbreviation—abréviation
(acronym) word formed from the initial letters or syllables of a series of words—mot formé de la suite des lettres initiales ou des syllabes initiales d'une série de mots
adj adjective—adjectif
adv adverb—adverbe
(aer) aeronautics—aéronautique
(agr) agriculture—agriculture
(alg) algebra—algèbre
(anat) anatomy—anatomie
(archaic) archaïque
(archeol) archeology—archéologie
(archit) architecture—architecture
(arith) arithmetic—arithmétique
art article—article
(arti) artillery—artillerie
(astr) astronomy—astronomie
(astrol) astrology—astrologie
(aut) automobile—automobile
aux auxiliary verb—verbe auxiliaire
(bact) bacteriology—bactériologie
(baseball) base-ball
(bb) bookbinding—reliure
(Bib) Biblical—biblique
(billiards) billard
(biochem) biochemistry—biochimie
(biol) biology—biologie
(bk) bookkeeping—comptabilité
(bot) botany—botanique
(bowling) jeu de quilles, jeu de boules
(boxing) boxe
(Brit) British—britannique
(Canad) Canadian—canadien
(cap) capital—majuscule
(cards) cartes
(carpentry) charpenterie
(checkers) jeu de dames
(chem) chemistry—chimie
(chess) échecs
(coll) colloquial—familier
(com) commercial—commercial
comp comparative—comparatif
(comp) computers—ordinateurs
(complimentary close) formule de politesse
cond conditional—conditionnel
conj conjunction—conjonction; conjunctive—atone
(culin) cooking—cuisine
dat dative—datif
def definite—défini
dem demonstrative—démonstratif
(dentistry) art dentaire
(dial) dialectal—dialectal

(dipl) diplomacy—diplomatie
disj disjunctive—tonique
(eccl) ecclesiastical—ecclésiastique
(econ) economics—économique
(educ) education—éducation, pédagogie e.g. par ex.
(elec) electricity—électricité
(electron) electronics—électronique
(embryol) embryology—embryologie
(eng) engineering—profession de l'ingénieur, génie
(ent) entomology—entomologie
(equit) horseback riding—équitation
(escr) fencing—escrime
f feminine noun—nom féminin
(fa) fine arts—beaux-arts
fem feminine—féminin
(feudal) feudalism—féodalité
(fig) figurative—figuré
(fishing) pêche
fpl feminine noun plural—nom féminin pluriel
fut future—futur
(game) jeu
(geog) geography—géographie
(geol) geology—géologie
(geom) geometry—géométrie
ger gerund—gérondif
(govt) government—gouvernement
(gram) grammar—grammaire
(gymnastics) gymnastique
(heral) heraldry—héraldique, blason
(hist) history—histoire
(hort) horticulture—horticulture
(hum) humorous—humoristique
(hunting) chasse
(ichth) ichthyology—ichtyologie
i.e. c.-à-d.
imperf imperfect—imparfait
impers impersonal verb—verbe impersonnel
impv imperative—impératif
ind indicative—indicatif
indef indefinite—indéfini
inf infinitive—infinitif
(ins) insurance—assurance
interj interjection—interjection
interr interrogative—interrogatif
intr intransitive—intransitif
invar invariable—invariable
(ironical) ironique
(jewelry) bijouterie
(journ) journalism—journalisme
(Lat) Latin—latin
(law) droit
(l.c.) lower case—bas de casse

xii

(letterword) word in the form of an abbreviation which is pronounced by sounding the names of its letters in succession and which functions as a part of speech—mot en forme d'abréviation qu'on prononce en faisant sonner le nom de chaque lettre consécutivement et qui fonctionne comme partie du discours

(lit) literary—littéraire

(logic) logique

m masculine noun—nom masculin

(mach) machinery—machinerie

(mas) masonry—maçonnerie

masc masculine—masculin

(Masonry) franc-maçonnerie

(math) mathematics—mathématiques

(mech) mechanics—mécanique

(med) medicine—médecine

(metallurgy) métallurgie

(meteo) meteorology—météorologie

mf masculine or feminine noun according to sex—nom masculin ou nom féminin selon le sexe

[for *m* & *f* see abbreviation following (mythol)]

(mil) military—militaire

(min) mining—travail des mines

(mineral) mineralogy—minéralogie

(mountaineering) alpinisme

(mov) moving pictures—cinéma

mpl masculine noun plural—nom masculin pluriel

(mus) music—musique

(mythol) mythology—mythologie

m & *f* masculine and feminine noun without regard to sex—nom masculin et féminin sans distinction de sexe

(naut) nautical—nautique

(nav) naval—naval

neut neuter—neutre

(nucl) nuclear physics—physique nucléaire

(obs) obsolete—vieilli, vieux

(obstet) obstetrics—obstétrique

(opt) optics—optique

(orn) ornithology—ornithologie

(painting) peinture

(parl) parliamentary procedure—usages parlementaires

(pathol) pathology—pathologie

(pej) pejorative—péjoratif

perf perfect—parfait

pers personal—personnel; person—personne

(pharm) pharmacy—pharmacie

(phila) philately—philatélie

(philos) philosophy—philosophie

(phonet) phonetics—phonétique

(phot) photography—photographie

(phys) physics—physique

(physiol) physiology—physiologie

pl plural—pluriel

(poetic) poetical—poétique

(pol) politics—politique

poss possessive—possessif

pp past participle—participe passé

prep preposition—préposition

pres present—présent

pret preterit—prétérit, passé simple

pron pronoun—pronom

(pros) prosody—métrique, prosodie

(psychoanal) psychoanalytic—psychanalytique

(psychol) psychology—psychologie

(psychopathol) psychopathology—psychopathologie

(public sign) affiche, écriteau

q.ch. or *q.ch.* quelque chose—something

qn or *qn* quelqu'un—someone

(rad) radio—radio

ref reflexive verb—verbe pronominal, réfléchi ou réciproque

reflex reflexive—réfléchi

rel relative—relatif

(rel) religion—religion

(rhet) rhetoric—rhétorique

(rok) rocketry—fusées

(rowing) canotage

(rr) railroad—chemin de fer

s substantive—substantif

(sculp) sculpture—sculpture

(seismol) seismology—sismologie

(sewing) couture

sg singular—singulier

(slang) populaire, argotique

s.o. or *s.o.* someone—quelqu'un

spl substantive plural—substantif pluriel

(sports) sports

s.th. or *s.th.* something—quelque chose

subj subjunctive—subjonctif

super superlative—superlatif

(surg) surgery—chirurgie

(surv) surveying—topographie

(swimming) nage

(taur) bullfighting—tauromachie

(telg) telegraphy—télégraphie

(telp) telephony—téléphonie

(telv) television—télévision

(tennis) tennis

(tex) textile—textile

(theat) theater—théâtre

(theol) theology—théologie

tr transitive verb—verbe transitif

(trademark) marque déposée

(turf) horse racing—courses de chevaux

(typ) printing—imprimerie

(U.S.A.) U.S.A., E.-U.A.

v verb—verbe

var variant—variante

(vet) veterinary medicine—médecine vétérinaire

(vulg) vulgar—grossier

(wrestling) lutte, catch

(zool) zoology—zoologie

PART ONE

French-English

French Pronunciation

The following phonetic symbols represent all the sounds of the French language.

VOWELS

SYMBOL	SOUND	EXAMPLE
[a]	A little more open than the a in English hat.	patte [pat]
[ɑ]	Like a in English father.	pâte [pɑt] phase [fɑz]
[ɛ]	Like e in English met.	sec [sek] fer [fer] fête [fɛt] aile [ɛl] parallèle [paralɛl]
[e]	Like a in English fate, but without the glide the English sound sometimes has.	été [ete] fée [fe] et [e] créer [kree]
[ə]	Like a in English comma or like o in English pardon.	le [lə] petit [pəti]
[i]	Like i in English machine or like e in English she.	si [si]
[ɔ]	A little more open and rounded than aw in English law.	donne [dɔn] joli [jɔli]
[o]	Like o in English note but without the glide the English sound sometimes has.	mot [mo] eau [o] faute [fot]
[u]	Like u in English rude.	sou [su] four [fur]
[y]	The lips are rounded for [u] and held without moving while the sound [i] is pronounced.	su [sy] sûr [syr]
[ø]	The lips are rounded for [o] and held without moving while the sound [e] is pronounced.	peu [pø] eux [ø] feutre [føtr]
[œ]	The lips are rounded for [ɔ] and held without moving while the sound [e] is pronounced.	peur [pœr] seul [sœl]

NASAL VOWELS

To produce the nasal vowels, sound is emitted through both nose and mouth by means of a lowering of the velum. The orthographic m or n has no consonantal value.

SYMBOL	SOUND	EXAMPLE
[ɑ̃]	Like a in English father and nasalized.	en [ɑ̃] tant [tɑ̃] temps [tɑ̃] paon [pɑ̃]
[ɔ̃]	More close than aw in English law and nasalized.	on [ɔ̃] pont [pɔ̃] comte [kɔ̃t]
[ɛ̃]	Like e in English met and nasalized.	pin [pɛ̃] pain [pɛ̃] faim [fɛ̃] teint [tɛ̃]
[œ̃]	Like [œ] of French bœuf and nasalized. There has been a tendency in this century to assimilate the nasal sound [œ̃] to the nasal sound [ɛ̃], making brun [brœ̃] and brin [brɛ̃] sound much the same.	un [œ̃] parfum [parfœ̃]

3

The sounds [j], [ɥ], and [w] are used to form diphthongs.

SYMBOL	SOUND	EXAMPLE
[j]	Like y in English year or like y in English toy.	hier [jer] ail [aj]
[ɥ]	Like the letter u [y] pronounced with consonantal value preceding a vowel.	lui [lɥi] situation [sitɥasjɔ̃] nuage [nɥaʒ] écuelle [ekɥel]
[w]	Like w in English water.	oie [wa] jouer [ʒwe] jouir [ʒwir]

CONSONANTS

The speaker of French characteristically keeps the tip of his tongue down behind his lower teeth and arches the back of the tongue at the same time. Thus, sounds such as [t], [d], [n], [s], [z], [l], and [r] must in French be articulated with the tongue tip and blade in the proximity of the back surface of the teeth.

SYMBOL	SOUND	EXAMPLE
[b]	Like b in English baby.	basse [bɑs]
[d]	Like d in English dead.	doux [du]
[f]	Like f in English face.	fou [fu]
[g]	Like g in English go.	gare [gar]
[k]	Like k in English kill, but without the aspiration which normally accompanies k in English.	cas [kɑ] kiosque [kjɔsk]
[l]	Like l in English like or in English slip—pronounced toward the front of the mouth. Not like l in old.	lit [li] houle [ul]
[m]	Like m in English more.	masse [mas]
[n]	Like n in English nest.	nous [nu]
[ɲ]	Like ny in English canyon or like ni in English onion.	signe [siɲ] agneau [aɲo]
[ŋ]	Like ng in English parking.	parking [parkiŋ]
[p]	Like p in English pen, but without the aspiration which normally accompanies p in English.	passe [pɑs]
[r]	Sometimes the uvular r but for some decades now usually a friction r with the point of articulation between the rounded back of the tongue and the hard palate. It resembles the Spanish aspirate in jota, the German aspirate in ach, and the g in the modern Greek gamma more than it resembles the modern American retroflex r. The tip of the tongue must point down near the back of the lower teeth and must not move during the utterance of the French [r].	rire [rir] caractère [karakter] roi [rwa] roue [ru]
[s]	Like s in English send.	sot [so] leçon [ləsɔ̃] place [plas] lassitude [lɑsityd] attention [atɑ̃sjɔ̃]
[ʃ]	Like sh in English shall or ch in English machine.	cheval [ʃval] mèche [meʃ]
[t]	Like t in English ten, but without the aspiration which normally accompanies t in English.	toux [tu] thé [te]

SYMBOL	SOUND	EXAMPLE
[v]	Like **v** in English **vest**.	**verre** [vɛr]
[z]	Like **z** in English **zeal**.	**zèle** [zɛl] **oser** [oze]
[ʒ]	Like **s** in English **pleasure**.	**joue** [ʒu] **rouge** [ruʒ] **mangeur** [mãʒœr]

FRENCH STRESS

Stress is not shown on French words in this Dictionary because stress is not a fixed characteristic of the pronunciation of French words. It depends on the position of the word in the sentence and it falls on the last syllable of the word that terminates a rhythmic or sense grouping unless the vowel of that syllable is a mute **e** [ə], in which case it falls on the immediately preceding syllable.

VOWEL LENGTH

Vowel length is not shown in the phonetic transcription of French words in this Dictionary because it, like stress, is not a fixed characteristic of the pronunciation of French words. The following vowel sounds in the positions indicated are long when stressed: 1) all when followed by [r], [z], [v], [ʒ], or [vr]; 2) all spelled with a circumflex accent and followed by a consonant sound; and 3) [ã], [ɔ̃], [ɛ̃], [œ̃], [ɑ], [o], and [ø] followed by a consonant sound. When these conditions are not fulfilled, all vowel sounds are normal in length (or sometimes they may be short in length, even when stressed, if followed by [k], [p], [t], [kt], [rk], [rp], or [rt]).

ELISION AND LIAISON

Elision and liaison are usually made with words beginning with a vowel or a mute **h**. Elision and liaison are made with some words beginning with **y**, such as: **yèbe, yeuse, yeux, Yonne**, and **York**.

However, there are words which begin with a vowel or an **h** with which elision and liaison are not made. Most of these words begin with **h**, called aspirate **h**, although it has not been pronounced for centuries. In this Dictionary these words are indicated by an asterisk placed before the opening bracket of the phonetic symbols, e.g., **hameau** *[amo], **onze** *[ɔ̃z], **a** *[ɑ], **s** *[es].

TABLE OF FRENCH REGULAR VERBS

The letters standing before the names of the tenses in this table correspond to the designation of the tenses shown on the following page. The forms printed in boldface correspond to the key forms described likewise on the following page.

TENSE	FIRST CONJUGATION	SECOND CONJUGATION	THIRD CONJUGATION
inf	**DONNER**	**FINIR**	**VENDRE**
ger	donnant	finissant	vendant
pp	donné	fini	vendu
a) *impv*	donne donnons donnez	finis finissons finissez	vends vendons vendez
b) *pres ind*	**donne** donnes donne **donnons** donnez **donnent**	**finis** finis finit **finissons** finissez **finissent**	vends vends vend **vendons** vendez **vendent**
c) *pres subj*	donne donnes donne donnions donniez donnent	finisse finisses finisse finissions finissiez finissent	vende vendes vende vendions vendiez vendent
d) *imperf ind*	donnais donnais donnait donnions donniez donnaient	finissais finissais finissait finissions finissiez finissaient	vendais vendais vendait vendions vendiez vendaient
e) *fut ind*	**donnerai** donneras donnera donnerons donnerez donneront	**finirai** finiras finira finirons finirez finiront	**vendrai** vendras vendra vendrons vendrez vendront
pres cond	donnerais donnerais donnerait donnerions donneriez donneraient	finirais finirais finirait finirions finiriez finiraient	vendrais vendrais vendrait vendrions vendriez vendraient
f) *pret ind*	**donnai** donnas donna donnâmes donnâtes donnèrent	**finis** finis finit finîmes finîtes finirent	**vendis** vendis vendit vendîmes vendîtes vendirent
imperf subj	donnasse donnasses donnât donnassions donnassiez donnassent	finisse finisses finît finissions finissiez finissent	vendisse vendisses vendît vendissions vendissiez vendissent

6

MODEL VERBS

ORDER OF TENSES

(a) imperative
(b) present indicative
(c) present subjunctive

(d) imperfect indicative
(e) future indicative
(f) preterit indicative

In addition to the infinitive, gerund, and past participle, all simple tenses are shown in these tables if they contain one irregular form or more, except the conditional (which can always be derived from the stem of the future indicative) and the imperfect subjunctive (which can always be derived from the preterit indicative). Those forms are considered irregular which deviate morphologically and/or orthographically in root, stem, or ending from the paradigms of regular verbs which appear on page 6. The infinitive is printed in boldface capital letters. And the following forms are printed in boldface: (1) key forms (that is, irregular forms from which other irregular forms can be derived, but not the derived forms), e.g., **buvons**, (2) individual irregular forms which occupy the place of key forms but cannot function as key forms because other irregular forms cannot be derived from them, e.g., **sommes**, and (3) individual irregular forms which cannot be derived from key forms, e.g., **dites**. The names of the key forms and the forms derived from each of them are listed below.

KEY FORM	DERIVED FORMS
1st sg pres ind	*2d & 3d sg pres ind & 2d sg impv**
1st pl pres ind	*2d pl pres ind, 1st & 2d pl pres subj, whole imperf ind, 1st & 2d pl impv, & ger*
3d pl pres ind	*whole sg & 3d pl pres subj*
1st sg fut ind	*rest of fut ind & whole conditional*
1st sg pret ind	*rest of pret ind & whole imperf subj*

* Some irregular verbs of the third conjugation which end in s, not preceded by d, in the *1st sg pres ind*, end in s also in the *2d sg pres ind* and the *2d sg impv*, and in t in the *3d sg pres ind*, e.g., **crains, crains, craint** and **bois, bois, boit.** And three verbs, namely, **pouvoir, valoir,** and **vouloir,** which end in x in the *1st sg pres ind*, end in x also in the *2d sg pres ind* and the *2d sg impv*, and in t in the *3d sg pres ind*, e.g., **veux, veux, veut.**

1st sg pres subj of **faire,**   rest of *pres subj*
   pouvoir, & **savoir**
1st sg pres subj of **aller,**   *2d & 3d sg & 3d pl pres subj*
   valoir, & **vouloir**

§1 ABRÉGER—abrégeant—abrégé   Combination of §10 and §38
   (a) abrège, abrégeons, abrégez
   (b) **abrège,** abrèges, abrège, **abrégeons,** abrégez, **abrègent**
   (c) abrège, abrèges, abrège, abrégions, abrégiez, abrègent
   (d) abrégeais, abrégeais, abrégeait, abrégions, abrégiez, abré-
      geaient
   (f) **abrégeai,** abrégeas, abrégea, abrégeâmes, abrégeâtes, abré-
      gèrent

§2 ACHETER—achetant—acheté
   (a) achète, achetons, achetez
   (b) **achète,** achètes, achète, achetons, achetez, **achètent**
   (c) achète, achètes, achète, achetions, achetiez, achètent
   (e) **achèterai,** achèteras, achètera, achèterons, achèterez, achè-
      teront

§3 ACQUÉRIR—acquérant—**acquis**
   (a) acquiers, acquérons, acquérez
   (b) **acquiers,** acquiers, acquiert, **acquérons,** acquérez, **acquiè-**
      rent
   (c) acquière, acquières, acquière, acquérions, acquériez,
      acquièrent
   (d) acquérais, acquérais, acquérait, acquérions, acquériez,
      acquéraient
   (e) **acquerrai,** acquerras, acquerra, acquerrons, acquerrez,
      acquerront
   (f) **acquis,** acquis, acquit, acquîmes, acquîtes, acquirent

§4 ALLER—allant—allé
   (a) **va,** allons, allez
   (b) **vais** [ve], **vas, va,** allons, allez, **vont**
   (c) **aille** [aj], ailles, aille, allions, alliez, aillent
   (e) **irai,** iras, ira, irons, irez, iront

§5A ASSEOIR—asseyant—**assis**
   (a) assieds, asseyons, asseyez
   (b) **assieds,** assieds, assied, **asseyons,** asseyez, **asseyent**
   (c) asseye, asseyes, asseye, asseyions, asseyiez, asseyent
   (d) asseyais, asseyais, asseyait, asseyions, asseyiez, asseyaient
   (e) **assiérai,** assiéras, assiéra, assiérons, assiérez, assiéront
   (f) **assis,** assis, assit, assîmes, assîtes, assirent

§5B ASSEOIR—assoyant—**assis**
- (a) assois, assoyons, assoyez
- (b) **assois**, assois, assoit, **assoyons**, assoyez, **assoient**
- (c) assoie, assoies, assoie, assoyions, assoyiez, assoient
- (d) assoyais, assoyais, assoyait, assoyions, assoyiez, assoyaient
- (e) **assoirai**, assoiras, assoira, assoirons, assoirez, assoiront
- (f) **assis**, assis, assit, assîmes, assîtes, assirent

§6 AVOIR—**ayant**—**eu** [y]
- (a) **aie** [e], **ayons**, ayez
- (b) **ai** [e], as, a, **avons**, avez, **ont**
- (c) **aie**, **aies**, **ait**, **ayons**, **ayez**, **aient**
- (d) avais, avais, avait, avions, aviez, avaient
- (e) **aurai**, auras, aura, aurons, aurez, auront
- (f) **eus** [y], eus, eut, eûmes, eûtes, eurent

§7 BATTRE—battant—battu
- (a) bats, battons, battez
- (b) **bats**, bats, bat, battons, battez, **battent**

§8 BOIRE—buvant—**bu**
- (a) bois, buvons, buvez
- (b) bois, bois, boit, **buvons**, buvez, **boivent**
- (c) boive, boives, boive, buvions, buviez, boivent
- (d) buvais, buvais, buvait, buvions, buviez, buvaient
- (f) **bus**, bus, but, bûmes, bûtes, burent

§9 BOUILLIR—bouillant—bouilli
- (a) bous, bouillons, bouillez
- (b) **bous**, bous, bout, **bouillons**, bouillez, **bouillent**
- (c) bouille, bouilles, bouille, bouillions, bouilliez, bouillent
- (d) bouillais, bouillais, bouillait, bouillions, bouilliez, bouillaient

§10 CÉDER—cédant—cédé
- (a) cède, cédons, cédez
- (b) **cède**, cèdes, cède, cédons, cédez, **cèdent**
- (c) cède, cèdes, cède, cédions, cédiez, cèdent

§11 CONCLURE—concluant—**conclu**
- (f) **conclus**, conclus, conclut, conclûmes, conclûtes, conclurent

§12 CONNAÎTRE—connaissant—**connu**
- (a) connais, connaissons, connaissez
- (b) **connais**, connais, connaît, **connaissons**, connaissez, **connaissent**
- (c) connaisse, connaisses, connaisse, connaissions, connaissiez, connaissent

- (d) connaissais, connaissais, connaissait, connaissions, connaissiez, connaissaient
- (f) **connus**, connus, connut, connûmes, connûtes, connurent

§13 COUDRE—cousant—**cousu**
- (a) couds, cousons, cousez
- (b) couds, couds, coud, **cousons**, cousez, **cousent**
- (c) couse, couses, couse, cousions, cousiez, cousent
- (d) cousais, cousais, cousait, cousions, cousiez, cousaient
- (f) **cousis**, cousis, cousit, cousîmes, cousîtes, cousirent

§14 COURIR—courant—**couru**
- (a) cours, courons, courez
- (b) **cours**, cours, court, **courons**, courez, **courent**
- (c) coure, coures, coure, courions, couriez, courent
- (d) courais, courais, courait, courions, couriez, couraient
- (e) **courrai**, courras, courra, courrons, courrez, courront
- (f) **courus**, courus, courut, courûmes, courûtes, coururent

§15 CRAINDRE—craignant—**craint**
- (a) crains, craignons, craignez
- (b) **crains**, crains, craint, **craignons**, craignez, **craignent**
- (c) craigne, craignes, craigne, craignions, craigniez, craignent
- (d) craignais, craignais, craignait, craignions, craigniez, craignaient
- (f) **craignis**, craignis, craignit, cragnîmes, craignîtes, craignirent

§16 CROIRE—croyant—**cru**
- (a) crois, croyons, croyez
- (b) crois, crois, croit, **croyons**, croyez, croient
- (c) croie, croies, croie, croyions, croyiez, croient
- (d) croyais, croyais, croyait, croyions, croyiez, croyaient
- (f) **crus**, crus, crut, crûmes, crûtes, crurent

§17 CROÎTRE—croissant—**crû, crue**
- (a) croîs, croissons, croissez
- (b) **croîs**, croîs, croît, **croissons**, croissez, **croissent**
- (c) croisse, croisses, croisse, croissions, croissiez, croissent
- (d) croissais, croissais, croissait, croissions, croissiez, croissaient
- (f) **crûs**, crûs, crût, crûmes, crûtes, crûrent

§18 CUEILLIR—cueillant—**cueilli**
- (a) cueille, cueillons, cueillez
- (b) **cueille**, cueilles, cueille, **cueillons**, cueillez, **cueillent**
- (c) cueille, cueilles, cueille, cueillions, cueilliez, cueillent

(d) cueillais, cueillais, cueillait, cueillions, cueilliez, cueillaient
(e) **cueillerai,** cueilleras, cueillera, cueillerons, cueillerez, cueilleront

§19 CUIRE—cuisant—**cuit**
(a) cuis, cuisons, cuisez
(b) cuis, cuis, cuit, **cuisons,** cuisez, **cuisent**
(c) cuise, cuises, cuise, cuisions, cuisiez, cuisent
(d) cuisais, cuisais, cuisait, cuisions, cuisiez, cuisaient
(f) **cuisis,** cuisis, cuisit, cuisîmes, cuisîtes, cuisirent

§20 DÉPECER—dépeçant—dépecé   Combination of §2 and §51
(a) dépèce, dépeçons, dépecez
(b) **dépèce,** dépèces, dépèce, **dépeçons,** dépecez, **dépècent**
(c) dépèce, dépèces, dépèce, dépecions, dépeciez, dépècent
(d) dépeçais, dépeçais, dépeçait, dépecions, dépeciez, dépeçaient
(e) **dépècerai,** dépèceras, dépècera, dépècerons, dépècerez, dépèceront
(f) **dépeçai,** dépeças, dépeça, dépeçâmes, dépeçâtes, dépecèrent

§21 DEVOIR—devant—**dû, due**
(a) missing
(b) **dois,** dois, doit, **devons,** devez, **doivent**
(c) doive, doives, doive, devions, deviez, doivent
(d) devais, devais, devait, devions, deviez, devaient
(e) **devrai,** devras, devra, devrons, devrez, devront
(f) **dus,** dus, dut, dûmes, dûtes, durent

§22 DIRE—disant—**dit**
(a) dis, disons, **dites**
(b) dis, dis, dit, **disons, dites, disent**
(c) dise, dises, dise, disions, disiez, disent
(d) disais, disais, disait, disions, disiez, disaient
(f) **dis,** dis, dit, dîmes, dîtes, dirent

§23 DORMIR—dormant—dormi
(a) dors, dormons, dormez
(b) **dors,** dors, dort, **dormons,** dormez, **dorment**
(c) dorme, dormes, dorme, dormions, dormiez, dorment
(d) dormais, dormais, dormait, dormions, dormiez, dormaient

§24 ÉCLORE—éclosant—**éclos**
(a) éclos
(b) éclos, éclos, **éclôt, éclosent**
(c) éclose, écloses, éclose, **éclosions, éclosiez,** éclosent
(d) missing
(f) missing

11

§25 ÉCRIRE—écrivant—écrit
- (a) écris, écrivons, écrivez
- (b) écris, écris, écrit, **écrivons**, écrivez, **écrivent**
- (c) écrive, écrives, écrive, écrivions, écriviez, écrivent
- (d) écrivais, écrivais, écrivait, écrivions, écriviez, écrivaient
- (f) **écrivis**, écrivis, écrivit, écrivîmes, écrivîtes, écrivirent

§26 ENVOYER—envoyant—envoyé
- (a) envoie, envoyons, envoyez
- (b) **envoie**, envoies, envoie, envoyons, envoyez, **envoient**
- (c) envoie, envoies, envoie, envoyions, envoyiez, envoient
- (e) **enverrai**, enverras, enverra, enverrons, enverrez, enverront

§27 ESSUYER—essuyant—essuyé
- (a) essuie, essuyons, essuyez
- (b) **essuie**, essuies, essuie, essuyons, essuyez, **essuient**
- (c) essuie, essuies, essuie, essuyions, essuyiez, essuient
- (e) **essuierai**, essuieras, essuiera, essuierons, essuierez, essuieront

§28 ÊTRE—étant—été
- (a) **sois, soyons, soyez**
- (b) **suis, es, est, sommes, êtes, sont**
- (c) **sois, sois, soit, soyons, soyez, soient**
- (d) **étais, étais, était, étions, étiez, étaient**
- (e) **serai**, seras, sera, serons, serez, seront
- (f) **fus**, fus, fut, fûmes, fûtes, furent

§29 FAIRE—faisant—fait
- (a) fais, faisons, **faites**
- (b) fais, fais, fait, **faisons, faites, font**
- (c) **fasse**, fasses, fasse, fassions, fassiez, fassent
- (d) faisais, faisais, faisait, faisions, faisiez, faisaient
- (e) **ferai**, feras, fera, ferons, ferez, feront
- (f) **fis**, fis, fit, fîmes, fîtes, firent

§30 FALLOIR—missing—fallu
- (a) missing
- (b) **faut**
- (c) **faille**
- (d) **fallait**
- (e) **faudra**
- (f) **fallut**

§31 FUIR—fuyant—fui
- (a) fuis, fuyons, fuyez
- (b) fuis, fuis, fuit, **fuyons**, fuyez, **fuient**

12

(c) fuie, fuies, fuie, fuyions, fuyiez, fuient
(d) fuyais, fuyais, fuyait, fuyions, fuyiez, fuyaient

§32 GRASSEYER—grasseyant—grasseyé
(regular, unlike other verbs with stem ending in **y**)

§33 HAÏR—haïssant—**haï**
(a) hais [ɛ], haïssons, haïssez
(b) **hais** [ɛ], hais, hait, **haïssons**, haïssez, **haïssent**
(c) haïsse, haïsses, haïsse, haïssions, haïssiez, haïssent
(d) haïssais, haïssais, haïssait, haïssions, haïssiez, haïssaient
(f) haïs, haïs, haït, **haïmes**, **haïtes**, haïrent

§34 JETER—jetant—jeté
(a) jette, jetons, jetez
(b) **jette**, jettes, jette, jetons, jetez, **jettent**
(c) jette, jettes, jette, jetions, jetiez, jettent
(e) **jetterai**, jetteras, jettera, jetterons, jetterez, jetteront

§35 JOINDRE—joignant—**joint**
(a) joins, joignons, joignez
(b) **joins**, joins, joint, **joignons**, joignez, **joignent**
(c) joigne, joignes, joigne, joignions, joigniez, joignent
(d) joignais, joignais, joignait, joignions, joigniez, joignaient
(f) **joignis**, joignis, joignit, joignîmes, joignîtes, joignirent

§36 LIRE—lisant—**lu**
(a) lis, lisons, lisez
(b) lis, lis, lit, **lisons**, lisez, **lisent**
(c) lise, lises, lise, lisions, lisiez, lisent
(d) lisais, lisais, lisait, lisions, lisiez, lisaient
(f) **lus**, lus, lut, lûmes, lûtes, lurent

§37 LUIRE—luisant—**lui**
(a) luis, luisons, luisez
(b) luis, luis, luit, **luisons**, luisez, **luisent**
(c) luise, luises, luise, luisions, luisiez, luisent
(d) luisais, luisais, luisait, luisions, luisiez, luisaient
(f) archaic

§38 MANGER—mangeant—mangé
(a) mange, mangeons, mangez
(b) mange, manges, mange, **mangeons**, mangez, mangent
(d) mangeais, mangeais, mangeait, mangions, mangiez, mangeaient
(f) **mangeai**, mangeas, mangea, mangeâmes, mangeâtes, mangèrent

§39 MAUDIRE—maudissant—**maudit**
- (a) maudis, maudissons, maudissez
- (b) maudis, maudis, maudit, **maudissons**, maudissez, **maudissent**
- (c) maudisse, maudisses, maudisse, maudissions, maudissiez, maudissent
- (d) maudissais, maudissais, maudissait, maudissions, maudissiez, maudissaient
- (f) **maudis**, maudis, maudit, maudîmes, maudîtes, maudirent

§40 MÉDIRE—médisant—**médit**
- (a) médis, médisons, médisez
- (b) médis, médis, médit, **médisons**, médisez, **médisent**
- (c) médise, médises, médise, médisions, médisiez, médisent
- (d) médisais, médisais, médisait, médisions, médisiez, médisaient
- (f) **médis**, médis, médit, médîmes, médîtes, médirent

§41 MENTIR—mentant—**menti**
- (a) mens, mentons, mentez
- (b) **mens**, mens, ment, **mentons**, mentez, **mentent**
- (c) mente, mentes, mente, mentions, mentiez, mentent
- (d) mentais, mentais, mentait, mentions, mentiez, mentaient

§42 METTRE—mettant—**mis**
- (a) mets, mettons, mettez
- (b) **mets**, mets, met, mettons, mettez, mettent
- (f) **mis**, mis, mit, mîmes, mîtes, mirent

§43 MOUDRE—moulant—**moulu**
- (a) mouds, moulons, moulez
- (b) mouds, mouds, moud, **moulons**, moulez, **moulent**
- (c) moule, moules, moule, moulions, mouliez, moulent
- (d) moulais, moulais, moulait, moulions, mouliez, moulaient
- (f) **moulus**, moulus, moulut, moulûmes, moulûtes, moulurent

§44 MOURIR—mourant—**mort**
- (a) meurs, mourons, mourez
- (b) **meurs**, meurs, meurt, **mourons**, mourez, **meurent**
- (c) meure, meures, meure, mourions, mouriez, meurent
- (d) mourais, mourais, mourait, mourions, mouriez, mouraient
- (e) **mourrai**, mourras, mourra, mourrons, mourrez, mourront
- (f) **mourus**, mourus, mourut, mourûmes, mourûtes, moururent

§45 MOUVOIR—mouvant—**mû, mue, mus, mues**
- (a) meus, mouvons, mouvez
- (b) **meus**, meus, meut, **mouvons**, mouvez, **meuvent**

(c) meuve, meuves, meuve, mouvions, mouviez, meuvent
(d) mouvais, mouvais, mouvait, mouvions, mouviez, mouvaient
(e) **mouvrai**, mouvras, mouvra, mouvrons, mouvrez, mouvront
(f) **mus**, mus, mut, mûmes, mûtes, murent

§46 NAÎTRE—naissant—né
(a) nais, naissons, naissez
(b) **nais**, nais, naît, **naissons**, naissez, **naissent**
(c) naisse, naisses, naisse, naissions, naissiez, naissent
(d) naissais, naissais, naissait, naissions, naissiez, naissaient
(f) naquis, naquis, naquit, naquîmes, naquîtes, naquirent

§47 NETTOYER—nettoyant—nettoyé
(a) nettoie, nettoyons, nettoyez
(b) **nettoie**, nettoies, nettoie, nettoyons, nettoyez, **nettoient**
(c) nettoie, nettoies, nettoie, nettoyions, nettoyiez, nettoient
(e) **nettoierai**, nettoieras, nettoiera, nettoierons, nettoierez, nettoieront

§48 PAÎTRE—paissant—pu
(a) pais, paissez
(b) **pais**, pais, paît, **paissons**, paissez, **paissent**
(c) paisse, paisses, paisse, paissions, paissiez, paissent
(d) paissais, paissais, paissait, paissions, paissiez, paissaient
(f) missing

§49 PAYER—payant—payé
(a) paie or paye, payons, payez
(b) **paie**, paies, paie, payons, payez, **paient** or paye, payes, paye, payons, payez, payent
(c) paie, paies, paie, payions, payiez, paient or paye, payes, paye, payions, payiez, payent
(e) **paierai**, paieras, paiera, paierons, paierez, paieront or payerai, payeras, payera, payerons, payerez, payeront

§50 PEINDRE—peignant—peint
(a) peins, peignons, peignez
(b) **peins**, peins, peint, **peignons**, peignez, **peignent**
(c) peigne, peignes, peigne, peignions, peigniez, peignent
(d) peignais, peignais, peignait, paignions, peigniez, peignaient
(f) **peignis**, peignis, peignit, peignîmes, peignîtes, peignirent

§51 PLACER—plaçant—placé
(a) place, plaçons, placez
(b) place, places, place, **plaçons**, placez, placent
(d) plaçais, plaçais, plaçait, placions, placiez, plaçaient
(f) **plaçai**, plaças, plaça, plaçâmes, plaçâtes, placèrent

§52 PLAIRE—plaisant—plu
- (a) plais, plaisons, plaisez
- (b) plais, plais, **plaît, plaisons,** plaisez, **plaisent**
- (c) plaise, plaises, plaise, plaisions, plaisiez, plaisent
- (d) plaisais, plaisais, plaisait, plaisions, plaisiez, plaisaient
- (f) **plus,** plus, plut, plûmes, plûtes, plurent

§53 PLEUVOIR—pleuvant—plu
- (a) **pleus, pleuvons, pleuvez** (fig & rare)
- (b) **pleut, pleuvent**
- (c) pleuve, pleuvent
- (d) **pleuvait, pleuvaient**
- (e) **pleuvra, pleuvront**
- (f) **plut, plurent**

§54 POURVOIR—pourvoyant—**pourvu**
- (a) pourvois, pouvoyons, pourvoyez
- (b) **pourvois,** pourvois, pourvoit, **pourvoyons,** pourvoyez, **pourvoient**
- (c) pourvoie, pourvoies, pourvoie, pourvoyions, pourvoyiez, pourvoient
- (d) pourvoyais, pourvoyais, pourvoyait, pourvoyions, pourvoyiez, pourvoyaient
- (f) **pourvus,** pourvus, pourvut, pourvûmes, pourvûtes, pourvurent

§55 POUVOIR—pouvant—**pu**
- (a) missing
- (b) **peux** or **puis,** peux, peut, **pouvons,** pouvez, **peuvent**
- (c) **puisse,** puisses, puisse, puissions, puissiez, puissent
- (d) pouvais, pouvais, pouvait, pouvions, pouviez, pouvaient
- (e) **pourrai,** pourras, pourra, pourrons, pourrez, pourront
- (f) **pus,** pus, put, pûmes, pûtes, purent

§56 PRENDRE—prenant—**pris**
- (a) prends, prenons, prenez
- (b) prends, prends, prend, **prenons,** prenez, **prennent**
- (c) prenne, prennes, prenne, prenions, preniez, prennent
- (d) prenais, prenais, prenait, prenions, preniez, prenaient
- (f) **pris,** pris, prit, prîmes, prîtes, prirent

§57 PRÉVOIR—prévoyant—**prévu**
- (a) prévois, prévoyons, prévoyez
- (b) **prévois,** prévois, prévoit, **prévoyons,** prévoyez, **prévoient**
- (c) prévoie, prévoies, prévoie, prévoyions, prévoyiez, prévoient
- (d) prévoyais, prévoyais, prévoyait, prévoyions, prévoyiez, prévoyaient
- (f) **prévis,** prévis, prévit, prévîmes, prévîtes, prévirent

§58 RAPIÉCER—rapiéçant—rapiécé Combination of §10 and §51
- (a) rapièce, rapiéçons, rapiécez
- (b) **rapièce**, rapièces, rapièce, **rapiéçons**, rapiécez, **rapiècent**
- (c) rapièce, rapièces, rapièce, rapiécions, rapiéciez, rapiècent
- (d) rapiéçais, rapiéçais, rapiéçait, rapiécions, rapiéciez, rapié-çaient
- (f) **rapiéçai**, rapiéças, rapiéça, rapiéçâmes, rapiéçâtes, rapiécè-rent

§59 RECEVOIR—recevant—**reçu**
- (a) reçois, recevons, recevez
- (b) **reçois**, reçois, reçoit, **recevons**, recevez, **reçoivent**
- (c) reçoive, reçoives, reçoive, recevions, receviez, reçoivent
- (d) recevais, recevais, recevait, recevions, receviez, recevaient
- (e) **recevrai**, recevras, recevra, recevrons, recevrez, recevront
- (f) **reçus**, reçus, reçut, reçûmes, reçûtes, reçurent

§60 RÉSOUDRE—résolvant—**résolu; résout** (invar)
- (a) résous, résolvons, résolvez
- (b) **résous**, résous, résout, **résolvons**, résolvez, **résolvent**
- (c) résolve, résolves, résolve, résolvions, résolviez, résolvent
- (d) résolvais, résolvais, résolvait, résolvions, résolviez, résol-vaient
- (f) **résolus**, résolus, résolut, résolûmes, résolûtes, résolurent

§61 RIRE—riant—**ri**
- (f) **ris**, ris, rit, rîmes, rîtes, rirent

§62 SAVOIR—sachant—**su**
- (a) **sache, sachons, sachez**
- (b) **sais**, sais, sait, **savons**, savez, **savent**
- (c) **sache**, saches, sache, sachions, sachiez, sachent
- (d) savais, savais, savait, savions, saviez, savaient
- (e) **saurai**, sauras, saura, saurons, saurez, sauront
- (f) **sus**, sus, sut, sûmes, sûtes, surent

§63 SERVIR—servant—servi
- (a) sers, servons, servez
- (b) **sers**, sers, sert, **servons**, servez, **servent**
- (c) serve, serves, serve, servions, serviez, servent
- (d) servais, servais, servait, servions, serviez, servaient

§64 SORTIR—sortant—sorti
- (a) sors, sortons, sortez
- (b) **sors**, sors, sort, **sortons**, sortez, **sortent**
- (c) sorte, sortes, sorte, sortions, sortiez, sortent
- (d) sortais, sortais, sortait, sortions, sortiez, sortaient

17

§65 SOUFFRIR—souffrant—**souffert**
  (a) souffre, souffrons, souffrez
  (b) **souffre**, souffres, souffre, **souffrons**, souffrez, **souffrent**
  (c) souffre, souffres, souffre, souffrions, souffriez, souffrent
  (d) souffrais, souffrais, souffrait, souffrions, souffriez, souffraient

§66 SUFFIRE—suffisant—**suffi**
  (a) suffis, suffisons, suffisez
  (b) suffis, suffis, suffit, **suffisons**, suffisez, **suffisent**
  (c) suffise, suffises, suffise, suffisions, suffisiez, suffisent
  (d) suffisais, suffisais, suffisait, suffisions, suffisiez, suffisaient
  (f) **suffis**, suffis, suffit, suffîmes, suffîtes, suffirent

§67 SUIVRE—suivant—**suivi**
  (a) suis, suivons, suivez
  (b) **suis**, suis, suit, suivons, suivez, suivent

§68 TRAIRE—trayant—**trait**
  (a) trais, trayons, trayez
  (b) trais, trais, trait, **trayons**, trayez, traient
  (c) traie, traies, traie, trayions, trayiez, traient
  (d) trayais, trayais, trayait, trayions, trayiez, trayaient
  (f) missing

§69 TRESSAILLIR—tressaillant—**tressailli**
  (a) tressaille, tressaillons, tressaillez
  (b) **tressaille**, tressailles, tressaille, **tressaillons**, tressaillez, **tressaillent**
  (c) tressaille, tressailles, tressaille, tressaillions, tressailliez, tressaillent
  (d) tressaillais, tressaillais, tressaillait, tressaillions, tressailliez, tressaillaient
  (e) **tressaillirai**, tressailliras, tressaillira, tressaillirons, tressaillirez, tressailliront, or **tressaillerai**, tressailleras, tressaillera, tressaillerons, tressaillerez, tressailleront

§70 VAINCRE—vainquant—**vaincu**
  (a) vaincs [vɛ̃], vainquons, vainquez
  (b) vaincs, vaincs, vainc, **vainquons**, vainquez, **vainquent**
  (c) vainque, vainques, vainque, vainquions, vainquiez, vainquent
  (d) vainquais, vainquais, vainquait, vainquions, vainquiez, vainquaient
  (f) **vainquis**, vainquis, vainquit, vainquîmes, vainquîtes, vainquirent

§71 VALOIR—valant—**valu**
  (a) vaux, valons, valez
  (b) **vaux**, vaux, vaut, **valons**, valez, **valent**

(c) **vaille** [vaj], vailles, vaille, valions, valiez, vaillent
(d) valais, valais, valait, valions, valiez, valaient
(e) **vaudrai**, vaudras, vaudra, vaudrons, vaudrez, vaudront
(f) **valus**, valus, valut, valûmes, valûtes, valurent

§72 VENIR—venant—**venu**
(a) viens, venons, venez
(b) **viens**, viens, vient, **venons**, venez, **viennent**
(c) vienne, viennes, vienne, venions, veniez, viennent
(e) **viendrai**, viendras, viendra, viendrons, viendrez, viendront
(f) **vins**, vins, vint, vînmes [vɛ̃m], vîntes [vɛ̃t], vinrent [vɛ̃r]

§73 VÊTIR—vêtant—**vêtu**
(a) vêts, vêtons, vêtez
(b) **vêts**, vêts, vêt, **vêtons**, vêtez, **vêtent**
(c) vête, vêtes, vête, vêtions, vêtiez, vêtent
(d) vêtais, vêtais, vêtait, vêtions, vêtiez, vêtaient

§74 VIVRE—vivant—**vécu**
(a) vis, vivons, vivez
(b) **vis**, vis, vit, vivons, vivez, vivent
(f) **vécus**, vécus, vécut, vécûmes, vécûtes, vécurent

§75 VOIR—voyant—**vu**
(a) vois, voyons, voyez
(b) **vois**, vois, voit, **voyons**, voyez, **voient**
(c) voie, voies, voie, voyions, voyiez, voient
(d) voyais, voyais, voyait, voyions, voyiez, voyaient
(e) **verrai**, verras, verra, verrons, verrez, verront
(f) **vis**, vis, vit, vîmes, vîtes, virent

§76 VOULOIR—voulant—**voulu**
(a) veux, voulons, voulez
(b) **veux**, veux, veut, **voulons**, voulez, **veulent**
(c) veuille, veuilles, veuille, voulions, vouliez, veuillent
(d) voulais, voulais, voulait, voulions, vouliez, voulaient
(e) **voudrai**, voudras, voudra, voudrons, voudrez, voudront
(f) **voulus**, voulus, voulut, voulûmes, voulûtes, voulurent

GRAMMATICAL TABLES

§77 le *art def* the. The following table shows the forms of the definite article, the combination of **le** with **à** and **de**, and the combinations of **les** with **à**, **de**, and **en**.

		masc	fem
	sg	le; l' before a vowel or mute h	la; l' before a vowel or mute h
	pl	les	les
with à	sg	au; à l' before a vowel or mute h	à la; à l' before a vowel or mute h
with à	pl	aux	aux
with de	sg	du; de l' before a vowel or mute h	de la; de l' before a vowel or mute h
with de	pl	des	des
with en	pl	ès, e.g., maître ès arts	ès, e.g., docteur ès lettres

§78 lequel *pron rel* who, whom; which ‖ *pron interr* which, which one. The following table shows all the forms of the word **lequel** and their combinations with the prepositions **à** and **de**.

		masc	fem
	sg	lequel	laquelle
	pl	lesquels	lesquelles
with à	sg	auquel	à laquelle
with à	pl	auxquels	auxquelles
with de	sg	duquel	de laquelle
with de	pl	desquels	desquelles

The forms combined with **de** and used as relative pronouns sometimes mean: whose, e.g., **l'étudiant avec la sœur duquel j'ai dansé** the student with whose sister I danced

§79 dont *rel pron* of whom; of which; from which; with which; on which; at which; which; whose. The relative pronoun **dont** may be: a) the complement of the subject of the dependent verb, e.g., **cette malheureuse dont la jambe droite était brisée** that wretched woman whose right leg was broken; b) the complement of the object of the dependent verb, e.g., **sa grande chambre dont on avait fermé les volets** his large bedroom the shutters of which they had closed;

21

c) the complement of the verb itself, e.g., **les termes dont il se servait** the expressions which he used.

If the antecedent is one of point of origin, **d'où** is used, e.g., **la porte d'où il est sorti** the door from which he went out, unless the point of origin is one of ancestry or extraction having to do with a person, e.g., **la famille distinguée dont il sortait** the distinguished family from which he came.

The relative pronoun **dont** cannot be the complement of a noun which is the object of a preposition but must be replaced by a form of **lequel** combined with **de** (see §78), or by **de qui**, e.g., **l'étudiante avec le frère de laquelle (or de qui) j'ai dansé** the student with whose brother I danced.

§80 quel *adj* what; what sort of; which; what a, e.g., **quelle belle ville!** what a beautiful city!; **n'importe quel** any ‖ *adj interr* what, e.g., **quel est le but de la vie?** what is the purpose of life?; who, e.g., **quel est cet homme?** who is that man? ‖ *adj indef*—**quel que** whoever, e.g., **quel que soit l'homme** whoever the man may be; whatever, e.g., **quelles que soient les difficultés** whatever difficulties there may be; whichever, e.g., **quel que soit le pied sur lequel il s'appuie** whichever foot he leans on. The following table shows all the forms of the word **quel.**

	masc	*fem*
sg	quel	quelle
pl	quels	quelles

§81 quelqu'un *pron indef* someone, somebody; anyone, anybody; **quelques-uns** some; any, a few. The following table shows all the forms of the word **quelqu'un.**

	masc	*fem*
sg	quelqu'un	quelqu'une
pl	quelques-uns	quelques-unes

§82A ce *adj dem* this; that; **ces** these; those. The following table shows all the forms of this word.

	masc	*fem*
sg	ce; cet before a vowel or mute h	cette
pl	ces	ces

This word has two meanings as exemplified by the following example:

cet homme this man; that man

However, the particles **-ci** and **-là** are attached to the noun modified by the forms of **ce** to distinguish what is near the person speaking

22

(i.e., the first person) from what is near the person spoken to (i.e., the second person) or what is remote from both (i.e., the third person), for example:

> cet homme-ci this man (*not that man*)
> cet homme-là that man (*not this man*)
> cet homme-là that man (*yonder*)

---

§82B ce *pron dem*

it, e.g., **c'est un bon livre** it is a good book;
he, e.g., **c'est un bon professeur** he is a good professor;
she, e.g., **c'est une belle femme** she is a beautiful woman;
they, e.g., **ce sont des élèves** they are students

---

§83 celui *pron dem* this one; that one.

The following table shows all the forms of the demonstrative pronoun with their translations into English.

	masc	*fem*
sg	**celui** this one; that one; he	**celle** this one; that one; she
pl	**ceux** these; those	**celles** these; those

This word in all its forms is generally used with a following **de** or the relative pronouns **que** and **qui**:

> celui de
> celle de
> ceux de } 's, e.g., celui de Marie Mary's
> celles de

celui que	he whom; the one that; the one which	
celle que	she whom; the one that; the one which	whomever;
ceux que	those whom; the ones whom; the ones which	whichever
celles que	those whom; the ones whom; the ones which	

celui qui	he who; the one that; the one which	
celle qui	she who; the one that; the one which	whoever;
ceux qui	those who; the ones who; the ones which	whichever
celles qui	those who; the ones who; the ones which	

§84 celui-ci *pron dem* this one; he; the latter.

The particles **-ci** and **-là** are attached to the forms of **celui** to distinguish what is near the person speaking (i.e., the first person) from what is near the person spoken to (i.e., the second person) or remote from both (i.e., the third person). The following table shows all the forms of this word with particles attached and with their translations into English.

	masc	*fem*
sg	**celui-ci** this one	**celle-ci** this one
	celui-là that one	**celle-là** that one
pl	**ceux-ci** these	**celles-ci** these
	ceux-là those	**celles-là** those

23

The forms of **celui-ci** also mean the latter; and the forms of **celui-là**, the former, e.g., **Henri était roi et Catherine était reine. Celle-ci était espagnole et celui-là anglais.** Henry was a king and Catherine was a queen. The former was English and the latter Spanish. (The English word order requires the inversion.)

§85 Disjunctive personal and reflexive pronouns.

This table shows all the forms of the disjunctive personal and reflexive pronouns with their translations into English.

moi	me; myself; I	**nous**	we, us; ourselves
toi	you, thee; yourself	**vous**	you; yourselves
lui	he, him, it; himself	**eux**	they, them *masc*; themselves *masc*
elle	she, her, it; herself	**elles**	they, them *fem*; themselves *fem*
soi	oneself; himself, herself, itself	**soi**	themselves

A) The disjunctive personal pronouns are used:

1) as the object of a preposition, e.g., **Jean a été invité chez elle** John was invited to her house; e.g., **il est très content de lui** he is very satisfied with himself

   Disjunctive pronouns especially as objects of prepositions rarely stand for things. Prepositional phrases which would include them are generally expressed by **y** (see §87), e.g., **je m'y suis avancé** I walked up to it, as contrasted with **je me suis avancé vers lui** I walked up to him; or are expressed by one of the adverbs **là-dessus, là-dessous, là-dedans,** etc., e.g., **voilà mon nom; écrivez le vôtre là-dessous** there is my name; write yours under it, as contrasted with **il n'a pas d'argent sur lui** he has no money with him.

2) after the preposition **à** in phrases which are used to clarify or to stress the meaning of a conjunctive personal pronoun, e.g., **il lui a parlé, à elle** he spoke to her (or, he spoke to *her*)

3) after the preposition **à** in phrases which are used to clarify the meaning of a preceding possessive adjective, e.g., **son chapeau à elle** her hat

4) as predicate pronouns after the verb **être**, especially after **c'est** and **ce sont:**

c'est moi	it is I	**c'est nous**	it is we
c'est toi	it is you, it is thee	**c'est vous**	it is you
c'est lui	it is he	**ce sont eux**	it is they *masc*
c'est elle	it is she	**ce sont elles**	it is they *fem*

5) after **que** (than, as) in comparisons, e.g., **nous y allons plus souvent qu'eux** we go there more often than they; e.g., **nous y allons aussi souvent que vous** we go there as often as you

6) when the verb is not expressed, e.g., **qui a fait cela? Lui** who did that? He did

24

7) to stress the subject or object of the sentence, e.g., **lui, il a raison** he is right
8) in compound subjects and objects, e.g., **lui et moi, nous sommes médecins** he and I are doctors
9) when an adverb separates the subject pronoun from the verb, e.g., **lui toujours arrive en retard** he always arrives late
10) after **être + à** to contrast ownership, e.g., **ce stylo est à lui mais ce papier est à elle** this pen is his but this paper is hers.

B) The disjunctive indefinite reflexive pronoun **soi** corresponds to **on** and is used mainly as the object of a preposition, that is, according to **A, 1** above, e.g., **on doit parler rarement de soi** one should seldom talk about oneself. But it may also be used in the predicate after the verb **être**, according to **A, 4** above, e.g., **on a plus confiance quand c'est soi qui conduit** one has more confidence when it is oneself who drives.

§86 The following table shows all the forms of the intensive personal pronouns. They are made by combining the disjunctive personal pronouns with the forms of **même**.

moi-même	myself; I myself	**nous-mêmes**	ourselves; we ourselves
toi-même	yourself, thyself; you yourself	**vous-même**	yourself; you yourself
		vous-mêmes	yourselves; you yourselves
lui-même	himself; he himself; itself		
elle-même	herself; she herself; itself	**eux-mêmes**	themselves; they themselves
soi-même	oneself; itself		
		elles-mêmes	themselves; they themselves

§87 Conjunctive personal and reflexive pronouns.

person	1 subject	2 negative	3 direct & indirect object	4 direct object	5 indirect object
1	je (j')—I		me (m')—me, to me; myself, to myself		
2	tu—you, thou		te (t')—you, to you; thee, to thee; thyself, to thyself		
3	il—he; it elle—she; it on—one, they	ne (n')—not §90B	se (s')—himself, herself, itself, oneself; to himself, to herself, to itself, to oneself	le (l')—him; it la (l')—her; it	lui—to him; to her
4	nous—we		nous—us, to us; ourselves, to ourselves		
5	vous—you		vous—you, to you; yourself, to yourself; yourselves, to yourselves		
6	ils—they elles—they		se—themselves; to themselves	les—them	leur—to them

This table shows all the forms of the conjunctive personal and reflexive pronouns with their translations into English and their positions (reading horizontally, not vertically) with respect to each other and with respect to the verb; and in negative declarative sentences, with respect to **ne** and **pas** and **personne**. All of the elements in this table except the verb and **pas** and **personne** (and the other negative words listed in §90) are unstressed.

In affirmative and negative interrogative sentences, the subject pronouns in column 1 are placed after the verb or auxiliary in column 8 and attached to it with a hyphen. A **t**, preceded and followed by hyphens, is intercalated between third-singular forms ending in a vowel and the subject pronoun. The interrogative forms of the first singular present indicative whose final sound is a nasal vowel or a consonant are not used, while those whose final sound is an oral vowel are, e.g., où vais-je? where am I going?; e.g., que dirai-je? what shall I say?. And the ending **-e** of the first singular

26

person	6	7	8	9	10	11
				negative		*negative*
1						
2						
3						
	y—there; to it; to them	en—some; of it; of them	VERB or AUXILIARY	pas—not §90B	past participle	personne—no one §90B
4						
5						
6						

present indicative of verbs of the first conjugation is changed to -é, e.g., donné-je? do I give?, but these forms are not in current use in prose. All the forms not used are replaced by the affirmative forms introduced by est-ce que in affirmative interrogative sentences and by n'est-ce pas que in negative interrogative sentences. And est-ce que and n'est-ce pas que may be thus used in any person of any tense of the indicative. The ending -e of the first singular imperfect subjunctive of some verbs is likewise changed to -é in conditional clauses without si in literary usage, e.g., dussé-je if I should.

In affirmative imperative sentences, the subject pronouns are not expressed and the pronouns in columns 3, 4, 5, 6, and 7 are placed after the verb and attached to it and to each other with hyphens except where elision occurs, and the pronouns in column 4 precede those in column 3. And unless followed by en or y, me is replaced by moi and te is replaced by toi; and moi and toi are stressed.

In negative imperative sentences, the subject pronouns are not expressed either and columns 2, 3, 4, 5, 6, 7, 8, and 9 have the same order as in negative declarative sentences.

A pronoun of column 5 cannot be used with a pronoun of column 3 but is replaced by a disjunctive pronoun preceded by the preposition à.

§88 The following table shows all the forms of possessive adjectives with their translations into English.

masc sg	fem sg	masc & fem pl	
mon	ma*	mes	my
ton	ta*	tes	your, thy, thine
son	sa*	ses	his, her, its
notre	notre	nos	our
votre	votre	vos	your
leur	leur	leurs	their

* The forms **mon, ton,** and **son** are used instead of **ma, ta,** and **sa** respectively before feminine nouns and adjectives beginning with a vowel or mute **h,** e.g., **Marie a fait un cadeau à son aïeule** Mary gave a present to her grandmother; e.g., **elle y est venue avec son aimable tante** she came with her nice aunt.

The possessive adjectives:
1) agree in gender and number with the thing possessed rather than with the possessor, e.g., **Marie lit son livre** Mary is reading her book
2) must be repeated before each noun in a series, e.g., **Marie apporte son stylo et son crayon** Mary is bringing her pen and pencil

§89 The following table shows all the forms of possessive pronouns with their translations into English.

	sg	pl	
masc	le mien	les miens	mine
fem	la mienne	les miennes	
masc	le tien	les tiens	yours, thine
fem	la tienne	les tiennes	
masc	le sien	les siens	his, hers, its
fem	la sienne	les siennes	
masc	le nôtre	les nôtres	ours
fem	la nôtre		
masc	le vôtre	les vôtres	yours
fem	la vôtre		
masc	le leur	les leurs	theirs
fem	la leur		

The possessive pronouns:
1) agree in gender and number with the thing possessed rather than with the possessor, e.g., **donnez votre livre à Marie, elle a perdu le sien** give your book to Mary; she has lost hers
2) are preceded by a definite article, e.g., **tu dois obéir à son ordre et au mien** you must obey his order and mine
3) are sometimes used without antecedent: a) **le mien** mine, my own (i.e., property); **le sien** his, his own (i.e., property); hers her own (i.e., property); etc.; b) **les miens** my folks, my family

my friends; my men; **les siens** his folks, his family; his friends; his men; her folks, etc.; c) **faire des siennes** (coll) to be up to one's (his, etc.) old tricks.

§90 The adverb **ne** is a conjunctive particle, that is, it always precedes a verb and, like conjunctive pronouns, is unstressed. Because of its weakness, it is generally accompanied by another word, which follows the verb (or auxiliary) in most cases, is stressed, and gives force or added meaning to the negation, e.g., **il n'est pas ici** he is not here.

A) The following table shows **ne** with the various words with which it is associated. (For more detail, see each expression under the second word in the body of the Dictionary, e.g., s.v. **aucun;** e.g., s.v. **aucunement;** etc.)

ne . . . aucun	no, none; no one, nobody	ne . . . ni . . . ni	neither . . . nor
		ne . . . nul	no, none
ne . . . aucunement	by no means	ne . . . nullement	not at all
ne . . . brin (archaic)	not a bit, not a single	ne . . . pas	not, no
		ne . . . pas un	not one
ne . . . davantage	no more	ne . . . personne	no one, nobody
ne . . . goutte (archaic)	not a drop, nothing	ne . . . plus	no more, no longer
ne . . . guère	hardly, scarcely; hardly ever	ne . . . plus jamais	never any more
		ne . . . plus que	now only
ne . . . jamais	never	ne . . . point	not, no, not at all
ne . . . mie (archaic)	not a crumb, not	ne . . . que	only, but
ne . . . mot (archaic)	not a word, nothing	ne . . . rien	nothing

B) The position of **ne** in the sentence is that of column 2 of §87. The position of **pas** and all the other like words, with the exception of **aucun, ni . . . ni, nul, personne,** and **que** is that of column 9. The position of **aucun, nul, personne,** and **que** is that of column 11. And the position of the first **ni** of **ni . . . ni** is that of column 11 unless the past participle is one of the correlatives, in which case its position is that of column 9.

Aucun, nul, pas un, personne, and rien may be used as subjects of the verb; they then precede **ne** and the verb, e.g., **personne n'est ici** no one is here. And **aucun, nul,** and **pas un** may be used as adjectives in the same position, e.g., **nul péril ne l'arrête** no danger stops him.

Usually when an infinitive is in the negative, **pas** immediately follows **ne,** e.g., **il m'a dit de ne pas y aller** he told me not to go there; e.g., **il regrette de ne pas me l'avoir dit** he regrets not having told me it.

C) The adverb **ne** is often used without **pas** or a similar word with the verbs **bouger, cesser, oser, pouvoir,** and **savoir,** e.g., **je ne saurais vous le dire** I can't tell you. And it is not translated (1) with a compound tense after **il y a . . . que, voilà . . . que,** and **depuis que,** e.g., **il y a trois jours que je ne l'ai vu** it is three days since I saw him or

29

(2) with the verb of a clause introduced by a) **à moins que, avant que, empêcher ... que,** and **éviter ... que,** e.g., **à moins que je ne sois retenu** unless I am detained; b) **si** meaning unless, e.g., **si je ne me trompe** unless I am mistaken; c) a comparative + **que,** e.g., **vous étiez plus occupé qu'il ne l'était** you were busier than he was; d) a verb or expression of fear such as **avoir peur que, craindre que, redouter que,** e.g., **je crains qu'il ne soit malade** I am afraid that he is sick; e) a negative verb or expression of doubt, denial, despair such as **ne pas désespérer que, ne pas disconvenir que, ne pas douter que, ne pas nier que,** e.g., **je ne doute pas qu'il ne vienne** I do not doubt that he will come.

§91 *adj & adv comp & super* The comparative of superiority of adjectives and adverbs is formed by placing **plus** before the positive, e.g., **heureux** happy, **plus heureux** happier. The superlative of superiority of adjectives and adverbs is the same as the comparative, e.g., **heureux** happy, **plus heureux** happier and happiest. It is to be observed that the superlative is generally used in both French and English with the definite article or the possessive pronoun, e.g., **le plus heureux** the happiest, **son plus heureux** his happiest.

Some adjectives and adverbs have irregular comparatives and superlatives.

ADJECTIVES		ADVERBS	
positive	*comp and super*	*positive*	*comp and super*
bon good	**meilleur** better; best	**beaucoup** much	**plus** more; most
mauvais bad	**pire** worse; worst	**bien** well	**mieux** better; best
petit small	**moindre** lesser, less; least	**mal** badly	**pis** worse; worst
		peu little	**moins** less; least

30

A

A, a [α], *[α] *m invar* first letter of the French alphabet

à [a] *prep* to, into; at; by, e.g., **à l'année** by the year; from, e.g., **arracher à** to snatch from; in, e.g., **à l'italienne** in the Italian manner; on, e.g., **à temps** on time; with, e.g., **la jeune fille aux yeux bleus** the girl with the blue eyes

abaisse-langue [abeslɑ̃g] *m invar* tongue depressor

abaissement [abesmɑ̃] *m* lowering; drop; humbling

abaisser [abese] *tr* to lower; to humble || *ref* to go down; to humble oneself; to condescend

abandon [abɑ̃dɔ̃] *m* abandon; abandonment; desertion; neglect

abandonner [abɑ̃dɔne] *tr* to abandon; to forsake; to give up || *ref* to neglect oneself, become slovenly; **s'abandonner à** to give way to

abasourdir [abazurdir] *tr* to dumfound, flabbergast; to deafen

abasourdis-sant [abazurdisɑ̃] **abasourdis-sante** [abazurdisɑ̃t] *adj* astounding

abâtardir [abɑtardir] *tr* to debase || *ref* to deteriorate, to degenerate

abâtardissement [abɑtardismɑ̃] *m* debasement; deterioration, degeneration

abat-jour [abaʒur] *m invar* lampshade; eyeshade, sun visor; skylight

abats [aba] *mpl* giblets

abattage [abataʒ] *m* slaughtering (*of animals*); felling (*of trees*); demolition (*of a building*); bag, bagging (*of game*)

abattant [abatɑ̃] *m* drop leaf

abattement [abatmɑ̃] *m* dejection, despondency; prostration; tax deduction

abatteur [abatœr] *m* slaughterer; woodcutter; **abatteur de besogne** hard worker

abattis [abati] *m* felling (*of trees*); clearing (*of woods*); (mil) abatis; **abattis** *mpl* giblets; (slang) arms and legs

abattoir [abatwar] *m* slaughterhouse

abattre [abatr] §7 *tr* to pull down, to demolish; to fell; to slaughter; to overthrow; to discourage; to shoot down, to bring down (*a bird, airplane, etc.*); to lay (*dust*); (cards) to lay down (*one's hand*) || *ref* to abate, subside; to be dejected; to swoop down; to pounce; to crash (*said of airplane*)

abat-tu -tue [abaty] *adj* dejected, downcast

abat-vent [abavɑ̃] *m invar* chimney pot

abbaye [abei] *f* abbey

abbé [abe] *m* abbot; abbé, father

abbesse [abes] *f* abbess

a b c [abese] *m* (letterword) ABC's; speller

abcès [apse] *m* abscess

abdiquer [abdike] *tr & intr* to abdicate

abdomen [abdomen] *m* abdomen

abécédaire [abesedɛr] *m* speller

abeille [abej] *f* bee

abêtir [abetir] *tr* to make stupid || *intr & ref* to become stupid

abhorrer [abɔre] *tr* to abhor

abîme [abim] *m* abyss; depth

abîmer [abime] *tr* to spoil; to damage || *ref* to sink; to be sunk; to get spoiled

ab-ject -jecte [abʒekt] *adj* abject

abjurer [abʒyre] *tr* to abjure

abla-tif [ablatif] **-tive** [tiv] *adj & m* ablative

aboiement [abwamɑ̃] *m* barking; yelp, cry, outcry

abois [abwa] *mpl* desperate straits; **aux abois** at bay; hard pressed

abolir [abɔlir] *tr* to abolish; to annul

abomination [abɔminasjɔ̃] *f* abomination

abondamment [abɔ̃damɑ̃] *adv* abundantly

abondance [abɔ̃dɑ̃s] *f* abundance, plenty; wealth; flow (*of words*); **parler d'abondance** to ad-lib

abon-dant [abɔ̃dɑ̃] **-dante** [dɑ̃t] *adj* abundant, plentiful; wordy

abon-né -née [abɔne] *mf* subscriber; season-ticket holder; consumer (*of gas, electricity, etc.*); commuter (*on railroad*)

abonnement [abɔnmɑ̃] *m* subscription

abonner [abɔne] *tr* to take out a subscription for (*s.o.*) || *ref* to subscribe, take out a subscription

abord [abɔr] *m* approach; **abords** outskirts, surroundings; **d'abord** at first; **d'un abord facile** easy to approach; **tout d'abord** first of all

abordable [abɔrdabl] *adj* approachable, accessible; reasonable (*price*)

abordage [abɔrdaʒ] *m* (naut) boarding; (naut) collision

aborder [abɔrde] *tr* to approach, to accost; to board; to collide with, run afoul of || *intr* to land, to go ashore

aborigène [abɔriʒen] *adj & m* native, aboriginal

abor-tif [abɔrtif] **-tive** [tiv] *adj* abortive

aboucher [abuʃe] *tr* to join; to bring together || *ref* to have an interview

aboutir [abutir] *intr* to end; to come to an end

aboutissement [abutismã] *m* outcome, result

aboyer [abwaje] §47 *intr* to bark; to bay

abracada•brant [abrakadabrã] **-brante** [brãt] *adj* amazing, breath-taking

abra•sif [abrazif] **-sive** [ziv] *adj & m* abrasive

abrégé [abreʒe] *m* abridgment, summary

abrégement [abreʒmã] *m* abridgment

abréger [abreʒe] §1 *tr* to abridge; to shorten, curtail

abreuvage [abrœvaʒ] *m* watering

abreuver [abrœve] *tr* to water; to soak; to overwhelm, to shower || *ref* to drink

abreuvoir [abrœvwar] *m* drinking trough, watering trough, horsepond

abréviation [abrevjɑsjɔ̃] *f* abbreviation; abridgment, curtailment

abri [abri] *m* shelter, refuge, cover; air-raid shelter; **à l'abri de** protected from

abricot [abriko] *m* apricot

abricotier [abrikɔtje] *m* apricot tree

abri-promenade [abriprɔmnad] *m* hurricane deck, shelter deck

abriter [abrite] *tr* to shelter, protect, shield, screen || *ref* to take shelter

abroger [abrɔʒe] §38 *tr* to abrogate, repeal

a•brupt -brupte [abrypt] *adj* abrupt, steep; rough, crude; blunt

abru•ti -tie [abryti] *adj* sottish

abrutir [abrytir] *tr* to brutalize; to besot; to overwhelm

abrutis•sant [abrytisã] **abrutis•sante** [abrytisãt] *adj* stupefying; deadening

absence [apsɑ̃s] *f* absence

ab•sent -sente [apsɑ̃ -sɑ̃t] *adj* absent; absent-minded || *mf* absentee

absenter [apsɑ̃te] *ref* to absent oneself, be absent, stay away

abside [apsid] *f* apse

absinthe [apsɛ̃t] *f* absinthe, wormwood; absinthe (*liqueur*)

abso•lu -lue [apsɔly] *adj* absolute

absolument [apsɔlymã] *adv* absolutely

absor•bant [apsɔrbɑ̃] **-bante** [bɑ̃t] *adj* absorbent; absorbing || *m* absorbent

absorber [apsɔrbe] *tr* to absorb, to soak up; to eat up; to drink || *ref* to become absorbed, be deeply interested

absoudre [apsudr] §60 (*pp* absous, absoute; no *pret* or *imperf subj*) *tr* to absolve; to forgive; to acquit

abstenir [apstənir] §72 *ref* to abstain, refrain

absti•nent [apstinã] **-nente** [nɑ̃t] *adj* abstinent; abstemious || *mf* moderate eater or drinker

abstraction [apstraksjɔ̃] *f* abstraction; **faire abstraction de** to leave out, to disregard

abstraire [apstrɛr] §68 (no *pret* or *imperf subj*) *tr* to abstract || *ref* to become engrossed

abs•trait [apstrɛ] **-traite** [trɛt] *adj* abstract

abs•trus [apstry] **-truse** [tryz] *adj* abstruse

absurde [apsyrd] *adj* absurd

absurdité [apsyrdite] *f* absurdity

abus [aby] *m* abuse

abuser [abyze] *tr* to deceive || *intr* to exaggerate; **abuser de** to take advantage of, to impose upon; to indulge unwisely in || *ref* to be mistaken

abu•sif [abyzif] **-sive** [ziv] *adj* abusive, wrong

acacia [akasja] *m* locust tree; **faux acacia** black locust tree

académicien [akademisjɛ̃] *m* academician

académie [akademi] *f* academy

académique [akademik] *adj* academic

acagnarder [akaɲarde] *tr* to make lazy || *ref* to grow lazy; to lounge

acajou [akaʒu] *m* mahogany; mahogany tree; **acajou à pommes** (bot) cashew

acariâtre [akarjɑtr] *adj* grumpy

acca•blant [akɑblɑ̃] **-blante** [blɑ̃t] *adj* overwhelming

accabler [akɑble] *tr* to overwhelm; to weigh down

accalmie [akalmi] *f* lull, standstill

accaparer [akapare] *tr* to corner (*the market*); to monopolize

accéder [aksede] §10 *intr* to accede; to acquiesce; to have access

accéléra•teur [akseleratœr] **-trice** [tris] *adj* accelerating || *m* accelerator

accélérer [akselere] §10 *tr, intr, & ref* to accelerate

accent [aksɑ̃] *m* accent; **accent de hauteur** pitch accent; **accent d'insistance** emphasis; **accent d'intensité** stress accent; **accent tonique** tonic accent

accentuer [aksɑ̃tɥe] *tr* to accent || *ref* to become more marked

acceptable [aksɛptabl] *adj* acceptable

acceptation [aksɛptɑsjɔ̃] *f* acceptance

accepter [aksɛpte] *tr* to accept || *intr*— **accepter de** to agree to

acception [aksɛpsjɔ̃] *f* sense, meaning; preference, partiality

accès [aksɛ] *m* access; outburst; (pathol) attack, bout; **accès aux quais** (public sign) to the docks

accessible [aksesibl] *adj* accessible; susceptible

accession [aksesjɔ̃] *f* accession

accessit [aksesit] *m* honorable mention

accessoire [akseswar] *adj* accessory || **accessoires** *mpl* accessories; (theat) properties

accident [aksidɑ̃] *m* accident; unevenness (*of ground*); (mus) accidental

acciden•té -tée [aksidɑ̃te] *adj* rough, uneven; bumpy (*road*); eventful (*life*); (coll) wrecked (*car*) || *mf* (coll) casualty, victim

acciden•tel -telle [aksidɑ̃tɛl] *adj* accidental

accidenter [aksidɑ̃te] *tr* to make uneven; to vary; to injure

accise [aksiz] *f* excise tax

acclamer [aklame] *tr* to acclaim

acclimater [aklimate] *tr* to acclimate || *ref* to become acclimated

accolade [akɔlad] *f* embrace; accolade; (mus, typ) brace

accoler [akɔle] *tr* to hug; to join side by side; to couple (*names*); (typ) to brace

accommo·dant [akɔmɔdɑ̃] **-dante** [dɑ̃t] *adj* accommodating, obliging

accommodation [akɔmɔdɑsjɔ̃] *f* accommodation

accommodement [akɔmɔdmɑ̃] *m* settlement, compromise; arrangement

accommoder [akɔmɔde] *tr* to accommodate; to conciliate; to arrange (*furniture*); to prepare (*food*)

accompagna·teur [akɔ̃paɲatœr] **-trice** [tris] *mf* accompanist

accompagnement [akɔ̃paɲmɑ̃] *m* accompaniment

accompagner [akɔ̃paɲe] *tr* to accompany

accom·pli -plie [akɔ̃pli] *adj* completed; polished; accomplished

accomplir [akɔ̃plir] *tr* to accomplish; to complete; to fulfill (*a promise*) ‖ *ref* to come to pass

accomplissement [akɔ̃plismɑ̃] *m* accomplishment, performance

accord [akɔr] *m* accord, agreement, consent; harmony; settlement, bargain; (mus) chord; (mus) tuning; **d'accord** in accord; **d'accord!** O.K.!, check!; **d'un commun accord** by common consent

accordage [akɔrdaʒ] *m* tuning

accordéon [akɔrdeɔ̃] *m* accordion; **en accordéon** squashed; accordion-pleated

accorder [akɔrde] *tr* to grant; to reconcile; (mus, rad) to tune ‖ *intr*—**accorder à qn de** to allow s.o. to ‖ *ref* to harmonize; to tally; to agree

ac·cort ac·corte [akɔr] [akɔrt] *adj* sprightly, engaging (*e.g., young lady*)

accoster [akɔste] *tr* to approach ‖ *intr* to dock, to berth

accotement [akɔtmɑ̃] *m* shoulder (*of a road*)

accoter [akɔte] *tr* to shore up ‖ *ref* to lean

accouchement [akuʃmɑ̃] *m* childbirth

accoucher [akuʃe] *tr* to deliver ‖ *intr* (*aux:* ÊTRE) to be confined, be delivered ‖ *intr* (*aux:* AVOIR)—**accoucher de** to give birth to

accou·cheur [akuʃœr] **-cheuse** [ʃøz] *mf* obstetrician

accouder [akude] *ref* to lean on one's elbows

accoudoir [akudwar] *m* armrest

accouple [akupl] *f* leash

accouplement [akuplǝmɑ̃] *m* coupling; **accouplement consanguin** inbreeding

accoupler [akuple] *tr* to couple; to yoke; to bring together for breeding; to link; (elec) to hook up ‖ *ref* to mate

accourir [akurir] §14 *intr* (*aux:* AVOIR or ÊTRE) to run up

accoutrement [akutrǝmɑ̃] *m* togs, getup

accoutrer [akutre] *tr* to rig out ‖ *ref* to dress ridiculously

accoutu·mé -mée [akutyme] *adj* accustomed; **à l'accoutumée** as usual ‖ *mf* regular customer; frequent visitor

accoutumer [akutyme] *tr* to accustom ‖ *ref* to become accustomed

accouvage [akuvaʒ] *m* artificial incubation

accouver [akuve] *tr* to set (*a hen*) ‖ *intr* to set (*said of a hen*) ‖ *ref* to begin to set

accréditer [akredite] *tr* to accredit; to win a hearing for; **accrédité auprès de** accredited to ‖ *ref* to gain credence or favor

accréditeur [akreditœr] *m* bondsman

accroc [akro] *m* tear (*in a dress*); (fig) snag, hitch

accrochage [akrɔʃaʒ] *m* hanging; hooking; clinch (*in boxing*); collision; (mil) encounter; (rad) receiving; (coll) squabble

accroche [akrɔʃ] *m* hanger

accrocher [akrɔʃe] *tr* to hang, to hang up; to hook; to catch; (mil) to come to grips with; (rad) to pick up; (coll) to buttonhole ‖ *ref* (coll) to come to blows; to cling; to catch; to get caught

accroire [akrwar] (used only in *inf* after **faire**) *tr*—**faire accroire** (with *dat*) to make (*s.o.*) believe ‖ *ref*—**s'en faire accroire** to get a swelled head

accroissement [akrwasmɑ̃] *m* growth; accumulation (*of capital*); increment

accroître [akrwatr] §17 (*pp* accru; *pres ind* accrois; *pret* accrus, etc.) *tr & ref* to increase

accroupir [akrupir] *ref* to squat, to crouch

accu [aky] *m* storage battery

accueil [akœj] *m* reception, welcome

accueil·lant [akœjɑ̃] **accueil·lante** [akœjɑ̃t] *adj* hospitable, gracious

accueillir [akœjir] §18 *tr* to welcome; to honor (*a bill*)

acculer [akyle] *tr* to corner

accumulateur [akymylatœr] *m* storage battery

accumuler [akymyle] *tr, intr, & ref* to accumulate

accusa·teur [akyzatœr] **-trice** [tris] *adj* incriminating ‖ *mf* accuser

accusatif [akyzatif] *m* accusative

accusation [akyzɑsjɔ̃] *f* accusation; charge

accu·sé -sée [akyze] *adj* marked; prominent (*features*) ‖ *mf* defendant ‖ *m* acknowledgment (*of receipt*)

accuser [akyze] *tr* to accuse; to acknowledge (*receipt*)

acerbe [aserb] *adj* sour; sharp; caustic (*remark*)

acé·ré -rée [asere] *adj* keen (*edge*); sharp (*tongue*)

acétate [asetat] *m* acetate

acétique [asetik] *adj* acetic

acétone [asetɔn] *f* acetone

achalander [aʃalɑ̃de] *tr* to attract customers to ‖ *ref* to get customers

achar·né -née [aʃarne] *adj* fierce; relentless (*pursuit*); inveterate (*gambler*); bitter (*enemy*); **acharné à** bent on, set on

acharnement [aʃarnəmɑ̃] m fierceness, fury; stubbornness; eagerness

acharner [aʃarne] tr to set, to sic (dogs); to bait (a trap) || ref to fight bitterly; s'acharner to work away at; to be bent on, to persist in; s'acharner contre to attack fiercely; s'acharner sur to light into; to swoop down upon; to bear down on; to be dead set against

achat [aʃa] m purchase; achat à terme installment buying; aller aux achats to go shopping

ache [aʃ] f wild celery

acheminement [aʃminmɑ̃] m forwarding; progress

acheminer [aʃmine] tr to direct || ref to proceed

acheter [aʃte] §2 tr to buy; acheter à to buy from; to buy for; acheter de to buy from; acheter pour to buy for

achèvement [aʃevmɑ̃] m completion

achever [aʃve] §2 tr to complete; to finish off, kill || intr to end; to be just finishing || ref to come to an end

Achille [aʃil] m Achilles

achoppement [aʃɔpmɑ̃] m obstacle; impact

achopper [aʃɔpe] intr & ref to stumble

achromatique [akromatik] adj achromatic

acide [asid] adj & m acid; acide phénique carbolic acid

acidité [asidite] f acidity

acidu·lé -lée [asidyle] adj acid; fruit-flavored

aciduler [asidyle] tr to acidulate

acier [asje] m steel; (fig) sword; acier inoxydable stainless steel

aclérie [asjeri] f steelworks, steel mill

acmé [akme] f acme; (pathol) crisis

acolyte [akolit] m acolyte; accomplice

acompte [akɔ̃t] m installment; deposit, down payment; acompte provisionnel payment on estimated income tax

Açores [asɔr] fpl Azores

à-côté [akote] m (pl -côtés) sidelight; path (beside road); kickback

à-coup [aku] m (pl -coups) jerk; par à-coups by fits and starts

acoustique [akustik] adj acoustic, acoustical || f acoustics

acquéreur [akerœr] m buyer

acquérir [akerir] §3 tr to acquire, to get

acquiescement [akjesmɑ̃] m acquiescence

acquiescer [akjese] §51 intr to acquiesce

ac·quis [aki] -quise [kiz] adj established || m know-how

acquisition [akizisjɔ̃] f acquisition

acquit [aki] m receipt; pour acquit paid in full

acquit-à-caution [akitakosjɔ̃] m (pl acquits-à-caution) permit to transport in bond

acquittement [akitmɑ̃] m acquittal

acquitter [akite] tr to acquit; to receipt (a bill); to pay, discharge (a debt); s'acquitter de to fulfill, to perform

âcre [ɑkr] adj acrid

acrimo·nieux [akrimonjø] -nieuse [njøz] adj acrimonious

acrobate [akrobat] mf acrobat

acrobatie [akrobasi] f acrobatics

acropole [akropol] f acropolis

acrostiche [akrostiʃ] m acrostic

acte [akt] m action; bill; act; certificate, deed; acte de présence personal appearance; acte de vente bill of sale; actes minutes; faire acte to make a declaration; prendre acte to take minutes

acteur [aktœr] m actor

ac·tif [aktif] -tive [tiv] adj active; full (citizen) || m credit side (of an account); assets; (gram) active voice

action [aksjɔ̃] f action; share (of stock); action de grâces thanksgiving

actionnaire [aksjoner] mf stockholder

actionner [aksjone] tr to actuate; to drive; to sue

activer [aktive] tr to activate; to hasten || ref to hasten

activité [aktivite] f activity; active service; en pleine activité in full swing

actrice [aktris] f actress

actuaire [aktɥer] mf actuary

actualisation [aktɥalizasjɔ̃] f modernization

actualiser [aktɥalize] tr to modernize, to bring up to date

actualité [aktɥalite] f present condition; actualités current events; newsreel; d'actualité newsworthy

ac·tuel -tuelle [aktɥel] adj present, present-day, current

actuellement [aktɥelmɑ̃] adv now, at the present time

acuité [akɥite] f acuity

adage [adaʒ] m adage

Adam [adɑ̃] m Adam

adapta·teur [adaptatœr] -trice [tris] mf adapter || m (mov) adapter

adaptation [adaptasjɔ̃] f adaptation

adapter [adapte] tr & ref to adapt

addenda [adɛ̃da] m invar addendum

addi·tif [aditif] -tive [tiv] adj & m additive

addition [adisjɔ̃] f addition; check (for a restaurant meal)

additionner [adisjone] tr to add up; to add; to dilute, mix

adénoïde [adenoid] adj adenoid

adent [adɑ̃] m dovetail

adepte [adept] mf adept

adé·quat [adekwa] -quate [kwat] adj adequate

adhérence [aderɑ̃s] f adherence; traction; (pathol) adhesion

adhé·rent [aderɑ̃] -rente [rɑ̃t] adj & mf adherent

adhérer [adere] §10 intr to adhere; to stick; adhérer à la route to hold the road

adhé·sif [adezif] -sive [ziv] adj & m adhesive

adhésion [adezjɔ̃] f adhesion

adieu [adjø] m (pl adieux) farewell || interj adieu!, bon voyage!; good riddance!; sans adieu! see you later!

adja·cent [adʒasɑ̃] -cente [sɑ̃t] adj adjacent

adjec·tif [adʒɛktif] **-tive** [tiv] *adj & m* adjective

adjoindre [adʒwɛdr] §35 *tr & ref* to join

ad·joint [adʒwɛ̃] **-jointe** [ʒwɛ̃t] *adj & mf* assistant, stand-by

adjudant [adʒydɑ̃] *m* warrant officer; sergeant major; (pej) martinet

adjudication [adʒydikɑsjɔ̃] *f* auction; awarding (*of a contract*)

adjuger [adʒyʒe] §38 *tr* to adjudge, award; to knock down (*at auction*)

admettre [admɛtr] §42 *tr* to admit

administra·teur [administratœr] **-trice** [tris] *mf* administrator, director

administration [administrɑsjɔ̃] *f* administration; **administration des ponts et chaussées** highway department

administrer [administre] *tr* to administer

admira·teur [admiratœr] **-trice** [tris] *mf* admirer

admira·tif [admiratif] **-tive** [tiv] *adj* admiring; amazed

admiration [admirɑsjɔ̃] *f* admiration; wonder

admirer [admire] *tr* to admire; to wonder at

admissible [admisibl] *adj* admissible; eligible

admission [admisjɔ̃] *f* admission; (aut) intake

admonester [admɔneste] *tr* to admonish

adolescence [adɔlesɑ̃s] *f* adolescence

adoles·cent [adɔlesɑ̃] **adoles·cente** [adɔlesɑ̃t] *adj & mf* adolescent

adonner [adɔne] *ref* to devote oneself; **s'adonner à** to give oneself up to

adopter [adɔpte] *tr* to adopt

adop·tif [adɔptif] **-tive** [tiv] *adj* adopted; adoptive

adoption [adɔpsjɔ̃] *f* adoption

adorable [adɔrabl] *adj* adorable

adora·teur [adɔratœr] **-trice** [tris] *mf* adorer; worshiper

adoration [adɔrɑsjɔ̃] *f* adoration

adorer [adɔre] *tr* to adore, worship

adosser [adɔse] *tr*—**adosser q.ch. à** to turn the back of s.th. against || *ref*—**s'adosser à** to lean back against

adouber [adube] *tr* to dub

adoucir [adusir] *tr* to soften || *ref* to soften; to grow milder

adrénaline [adrenalin] *f* adrenalin

adresse [adrɛs] *f* address; skill, dexterity; neatness; expertness, expertise; **adresse particulière** home address

adresser [adrese] *tr* to address || *ref* to apply

Adriatique [adriatik] *adj & f* Adriatic

a·droit [adrwa] **-droite** [drwat] *adj* adroit, clever; neat

aduler [adyle] *tr* to adulate

adulte [adylt] *adj & mf* adult

adultère [adyltɛr] *adj* adulterous || *m* adultery; adulterer || *f* adulteress

adultérer [adyltere] §10 *tr* to adulterate; to falsify (*a text*)

adulté·rin [adyltɛrɛ̃] **-rine** [rin] *adj* born in adultery

advenir [advənir] §72 (used only in *inf*; *pp*; 3d *pers sg & pl*) *intr* (*aux*: ÊTRE)

to come to pass; **advienne que pourra** come what may

adventice [advɑ̃tis] *adj* adventitious

adverbe [advɛrb] *m* adverb

adversaire [advɛrsɛr] *mf* adversary

adverse [advɛrs] *adj* adverse; opposite (*side*)

adversité [advɛrsite] *f* adversity

aérer [aere] §10 *tr* to aerate; to ventilate; to air

aé·rien [aerjɛ̃] **-rienne** [rjɛn] *adj* aerial || *m* elevated railway

aéro [aero] *m* airplane

aérodynamique [aerɔdinamik] *adj* aerodynamic; streamlined || *f* aerodynamics

aérogare [aerɔgar] *f* air terminal

aéroglisseur [aerɔglisœr] *m* hydrofoil

aérogramme [aerɔgram] *m* air letter

aérolite or **aérolithe** [aerɔlit] *m* meteorite, aerolite

aéronef [aerɔnef] *m* aircraft

aérophare [aerɔfar] *m* air beacon

aéroport [aerɔpɔr] *m* airport

aéropor·té **-tée** [aerɔpɔrte] *adj* airborne

aéros·tal **-tale** [aerɔpostal] *adj* (*pl* **-taux** [to]) air-mail

aérosol [aerɔsɔl] *m* aerosol

aérospa·tial **-tiale** [aerɔspasjal] *adj* (*pl* **-tiaux** [sjo]) aerospace

A.F. *abbr* **(allocations familiales)** family (social security) allotments

affable [afabl] *adj* affable

affadir [afadir] *tr & ref* to stale

affaiblir [afɛblir] *tr & ref* to weaken

affaire [afɛr] *f* affair; job; business; trouble; (law) case; (coll) belongings; **affaire à saisir** bargain; **affaire d'or** (fig) gold mine; **affaire en instance** unfinished business; **affaires** business; **bonne affaire** bargain; **cela fait mon affaire** that is just what I want

affai·ré **-rée** [afere] *adj* busy, bustling

affairiste [aferist] *m* slicker, operator

affaissement [afesmɑ̃] *m* sagging; cave-in, collapse

affaisser [afese] *tr* to weigh down; to depress || *ref* to sag; to cave in, to collapse

affaler [afale] *tr* to haul down || *ref* to drop, sink, flop

affa·mé **-mée** [afame] *adj* famished, starved

affamer [afame] *tr* to starve

affectable [afɛktabl] *adj* impressionable; mortgageable

affectation [afɛktɑsjɔ̃] *f* affectation; assignment; allotment

affec·té **-tée** [afɛkte] *adj* affected; assigned

affecter [afɛkte] *tr* to affect; to assign; to assume (*various shapes or manners*) || *ref* to grieve

affec·tif [afɛktif] **-tive** [tiv] *adj* affective, emotional

affection [afɛksjɔ̃] *f* affection; mental state; disease, affection

affection·né **-née** [afɛksjɔne] *adj* loving, fond, devoted

affectionner [afɛksjɔne] *tr* to be fond of ‖ *ref* to become attached

affectueusement [afɛktɥøzmɑ̃] *adv* affectionately

affec•tueux [afɛktɥø] **-tueuse** [tɥøz] *adj* affectionate

affé•rent [aferɑ̃] **-rente** [rɑ̃t] *adj* due, accruing

affermer [afɛrme] *tr* to lease, to rent

affermir [afɛrmir] *tr* to strengthen, harden ‖ *ref* to become stronger, sounder

affichage [afiʃaʒ] *m* billposting

affiche [afiʃ] *f* poster, bill; (theat) playbill

afficher [afiʃe] *tr* to post, to post up; to display; (theat) to bill ‖ *ref* to seek the limelight; **s'afficher avec** to hang around with

afficheur [afiʃœr] *m* billposter

affi•lé -lée [afile] *adj* sharpened; sharp (*tongue*) ‖ *adv*—**d'affilée** in a row

affiler [afile] *tr* to sharpen, to whet; to hone, to strop; to set (*a saw*)

affi•lié -liée [afilje] *adj* & *mf* affiliate

affilier [afilje] *tr* & *ref* to affiliate

affiloir [afilwar] *m* sharpener; whetstone; hone, strop

affiner [afine] *tr* to improve; to refine; to sift ‖ *ref* to improve; to mature, ripen

affinité [afinite] *f* affinity; in-law relationship

affirma•tif [afirmatif] **-tive** [tiv] *adj* & *f* affirmative

affirmer [afirme] *tr* to affirm ‖ *ref* to assert oneself; **s'affirmer comme** to take one's place as

affixe [afiks] *m* affix

affleurer [aflœre] *tr* to level; to come up to the level of ‖ *intr* to come to the surface

affliction [afliksjɔ̃] *f* affliction

affli•gé -gée [afliʒe] *adj* sorrowful

affli•geant [afliʒɑ̃] **-geante** [ʒɑ̃t] *adj* sorrowful (*news*)

affliger [afliʒe] §38 *tr* to afflict ‖ *ref* to grieve, to sorrow; **s'affliger de** to sorrow for

affluence [aflyɑ̃s] *f* crowd

af•fluent [aflyɑ̃] **af•fluente** [aflyɑ̃t] *adj* & *m* tributary

affluer [aflye] *intr* to flow; to throng, crowd, flock

afflux [afly] *m* afflux, flow; rush

affo•lé -lée [afole] *adj* panic-stricken

affolement [afɔlmɑ̃] *m* distraction, panic; infatuation; unsteadiness (*of a compass*)

affoler [afɔle] *tr* to distract, to panic; to infatuate; to disturb (*compass*) ‖ *ref* to be distracted; to stampede; to become infatuated; to spin (*as a compass*)

affran•chi -chie [afrɑ̃ʃi] *adj* emancipated; postpaid ‖ *mf* freethinker

affranchir [afrɑ̃ʃir] *tr* to emancipate, free; to pay the postage for

affranchissement [afrɑ̃ʃismɑ̃] *m* emancipation; payment of postage; cancellation (*of mail*); **affranchissement insuffisant** postage due

affres [afr] *fpl* pangs

affrètement [afrɛtmɑ̃] *m* chartering (*of a boat*)

affréter [afrete] §10 *tr* to charter (*a boat*)

af•freux [afrø] **af•freuse** [afrøz] *adj* frightful

affront [afrɔ̃] *m* affront

affronter [afrɔ̃te] *tr* to confront; to face

affût [afy] *m* hunting blind; mount (*for cannon*); **être à l'affût de** to lie in wait for

affûter [afyte] *tr* to sharpen

afin [afɛ̃] *adv*—**afin de** in order to; **afin que** in order that, so that

afri•cain [afrikɛ̃] **-caine** [kɛn] *adj* African ‖ (*cap*) *mf* African

Afrique [afrik] *f* Africa; **l'Afrique** Africa

agacement [agasmɑ̃] *m* irritation, annoyance

agacer [agase] §51 *tr* to irritate, annoy; to tease; to set on edge

agape [agap] *f* agape; **agapes** banquet

âge [ɑʒ] *m* age; **d'un certain âge** middle-aged; **quel âge avez-vous?** how old are you?

â•gé -gée [aʒe] *adj* old, aged; old, e.g., **âgé de seize ans** sixteen years old

agence [aʒɑ̃s] *f* agency, office, service, bureau; **agence de location** rental service; real-estate office; **agence de voyages** travel bureau; **agence immobilière** real-estate office

agencement [aʒɑ̃smɑ̃] *m* arrangement; furnishing (*of a house*); construction (*of a sentence*); **agencements** fixtures

agencer [aʒɑ̃se] §51 *tr* to arrange

agenda [aʒɛ̃da] *m* engagement book

agenouiller [aʒnuje] *ref* to kneel

agent [aʒɑ̃] *m* agent; policeman; **agent comptable** accountant; **agent de change** stockbroker; **agent de location** realtor

agglomération [aglɔmerɑsjɔ̃] *f* agglomeration; metropolitan area; built-up area

aggloméré -rée [aglɔmere] *adj* compressed ‖ *m* briquette; adobe

agglomérer [aglɔmere] §10 *tr* & *ref* to agglomerate

aggraver [agrave] *tr* to aggravate ‖ *ref* to become more serious

agile [aʒil] *adj* agile, nimble

agilité [aʒilite] *f* agility

agio•teur [aʒjɔtœr] **-teuse** [tøz] *mf* speculator

agir [aʒir] *intr* to act; to take action ‖ *ref*—**il s'agit de** it is a question of

agis•sant [aʒisɑ̃] **agis•sante** [aʒisɑ̃t] *adj* active

agissements [aʒismɑ̃] *mpl* machinations

agita•teur [aʒitatœr] **-trice** [tris] *mf* agitator (*person*) ‖ *m* stirrer

agi•té -tée [aʒite] *adj* restless; rough (*sea*)

agiter [aʒite] *tr* to agitate; to stir; to wave; to discuss ‖ *ref* to move about

a•gneau [aɲo] *m* (*pl* **-gneaux**) lamb

agnostique [agnɔstik] *adj* & *mf* agnostic

agonie [agɔni] *f* agony, death throes

agrafe [agraf] *f* clasp, pin; paper clip; staple (*for papers*); belt buckle; snap, hook; (med) clamp

agrafer [agrafe] *tr* to clasp, pin; to buckle; to snap; to hook; to fasten, to clip; to staple; (med) to clamp

agrafeuse [agrafǿz] *f* stapler

agraire [agrer] *adj* agrarian

agrandir [agrãdir] *tr* to enlarge ‖ *ref* to grow, become larger

agrandissement [agrãdismã] *m* enlargement

agréable [agreabl] *adj* agreeable, pleasant; neighborly

agréé agréée [agree] *adj* approved ‖ *m* attorney

agréer [agree] *tr* to accept, approve; **veuillez agréer l'expression de mes sentiments distingués** (complimentary close) sincerely yours ‖ *intr* (with *dat*) to agree with, to please

agrégat [agrega] *m* aggregate

agrégation [agregasjɔ̃] *f* aggregation; admittance (*as a member of an organization*); competitive teacher's examination

agré-gé -gée [agreʒe] *adj* aggregate ‖ *mf* one who has passed his *agrégation*

agréger [agreʒe] §1 *tr* to attach, to add ‖ *ref*—**s'agréger (à)** to join

agrément [agremã] *m* approval; pleasantness; pleasure, pastime; **agréments** adornments

agrès [agre] *mpl* rigging; gym equipment

agresseur [agresœr] *adj & m* aggressor

agres-sif [agresif] **agres-sive** [agresiv] *adj* aggressive

agression [agresjɔ̃] *f* aggression; (law) assault

agreste [agrest] *adj* rustic, rural

agricole [agrikɔl] *adj* agricultural

agriculture [agrikyltyr] *f* agriculture

agrumes [agrym] *mpl* citrus fruit

aguerrir [agerir] *tr* to season, inure ‖ *ref* to become seasoned, inured

aguets [age] *mpl* watch, look-out; **être aux aguets** to be on the look-out

agui-chant -chante [agi/ɑ̃] *adj* alluring ‖ *adj fem* sexy

ah [a] *interj* ah!; **ah çà!** now then!

ahu-ri -rie [ayri] *adj* dumfounded

ahurir [ayrir] *tr* to dumfound

ahurissement [ayrismã] *m* stupefaction

aide [ed] *mf* aid, assistant, helper ‖ *f* aid, assistance, help; **aide sociale** welfare department

aider [ede] *tr* to aid, help; **aider + inf** to help to **+ inf** ‖ *intr* to help ‖ *ref* —**s'aider de** to use

aïe [aj] *interj* ouch!

aïeul aïeule [ajœl] *mf* grandparent ‖ *m* grandfather ‖ *m* (*pl* **aïeux** [ajǿ]) ancestor ‖ *f* grandmother

aigle [egl] *mf* eagle; **aigle de mer** eagle ray; **aigle pêcheur, grand aigle de mer** osprey, fish hawk; **grand aigle** spread eagle

aiglefin [eglǝfɛ̃] *m* haddock

ai·glon [eglɔ̃] **-glonne** [glɔn] *mf* eaglet

aigre [egr] *adj* sour, tart, bitter; harsh (*voice*)

aigre-doux [egrǝdu] **-douce** [dus] *adj* bittersweet

aigrefin [egrǝfɛ̃] *m* crook

aigre·let [egrǝle] **-lette** [let] *adj* tart

aigrir [egrir] *tr* to turn (*s.th.*) sour ‖ *intr & ref* to turn sour

ai·gu -guë [egy] *adj* sharp; acute; shrill, high-pitched ‖ *m* (mus) treble

aigue-marine [egmarin] *f* (*pl* **aigues-marines**) aquamarine

aiguille [egɥij] *f* needle; peak; spire (*of steeple*); hand (*of clock*); (rr) switch

aiguiller [egɥije] *tr* to switch, shunt ‖ *ref* to be switched, shunted

aiguilleur [egɥijœr] *m* (aer, rr) towerman

aiguillon [egɥijɔ̃] *m* goad; sting

aiguiser [egɥize] *tr* to sharpen; to whet (*appetite*)

ail [aj] *m* (*pl* **ails** or **aulx** [o]) garlic

aile [el] *f* wing; flank (*of army*); fender (*of auto*); brim (*of hat*); blade (*of propeller*); vane, arm (*of windmill*); **aile en flèche** (aer) backswept wing

aileron [elrɔ̃] *m* aileron

ailleurs [ajœr] *adv* elsewhere; **d'ailleurs** moreover, besides; from somewhere else; **par ailleurs** furthermore

aimable [emabl] *adj* kind, likeable; **voulez-vous être assez aimable de** will you be good enough to

aimant [emã] *m* magnet

aimanter [emãte] *tr* to magnetize

aimer [eme], [eme] *tr* to love; to like; to like to; **aimer à** to like to; **aimer bien** to like, to be fond of; to like to; **aimer mieux** to prefer; to prefer to

aine [en] *f* groin

aî·né -née [ene] *adj & mf* elder, eldest, oldest; senior

aînesse [enes] *f* seniority

ainsi [ɛ̃si] *adv* thus; **ainsi de suite** and so forth; **ainsi nommé** so-called; **ainsi que** as well as; **ainsi soit-il** amen

air [er] *m* air; look, appearance; air de famille family resemblance; **avoir l'air de** to seem to; **en l'air** empty, idle (*threats, talk*)

airain [erɛ̃] *m* brass; bronze

aire [er] *f* area; threshing floor; eyrie; **aire de lancement** launching pad

airelle [erel] *f* huckleberry; blueberry

aisance [ezãs] *f* ease, comfort

aise [ez] *adj*—**bien aise** glad, content ‖ *f* ease; **aises** comforts; **à son aise** well-to-do

ai·sé -sée [eze] *adj* easy; natural; well-to-do

aisément [ezemã] *adv* easily

aisselle [esel] *f* armpit

ajonc [aʒɔ̃] *m* furze

ajou·ré -rée [aʒure] *adj* openwork, perforated

ajourer [aʒure] *tr* to cut openings in

ajournement [aʒurnǝmã] *m* adjournment, postponement; subpoenaing; rejection (*of a candidate*)

ajourner [aʒurne] *tr* to postpone; to subpoena; to reject (*a candidate in an examination*)

ajouter [aʒute] *tr & intr* to add ‖ *ref* to be added

ajus·té -tée [aʒyste] *adj* tight-fitting

ajuster [aʒyste] *tr* to adjust; to arrange; to fit; to aim at

ajusteur [aʒystœr] *m* fitter

alacrité [alakrite] *f* gaiety, vivacity

alambic [alɑ̃bik] *m* still

alambi·qué -quée [alɑ̃bike] *adj* fine-spun, far-fetched

alanguir [alɑ̃gir] *tr* to weaken ‖ *ref* to languish

alar·mant [alarmɑ̃] **-mante** [mɑ̃t] *adj* alarming

alarme [alarm] *f* alarm

alarmer [alarme] *tr* to alarm ‖ *ref* to be alarmed

alba·nais [albanɛ] **-naise** [nez] *adj* Albanian ‖ *m* Albanian (*language*) ‖ (*cap*) *mf* Albanian (*person*)

albâtre [albɑtr] *m* alabaster

albatros [albatros] *m* albatross

albi·geois [albiʒwa] **-geoise** [ʒwaz] *adj* Albigensian ‖ (*cap*) *mf* Albigensian

albinos [albinos] *adj & m* albino

album [albɔm] *m* album; scrapbook

albumen [albymen] *m* albumen

alcali [alkali] *m* alkali

alca·lin [alkalɛ̃] **-line** [lin] *adj* alkaline

alchimie [alʃimi] *f* alchemy

alcool [alkɔl] *m* alcohol; **alcool à friction** rubbing alcohol; **alcool dénaturé** denatured alcohol

alcoolique [alkɔlik], [alkɔlik] *adj & mf* alcoholic

alcôve [alkov] *f* alcove; **d'alcôve** amatory, gallant

ale [ɛl] *f* ale

aléa [alea] *m* risk

aléatoire [aleatwar] *adj* risky; aleatory

alène [alɛn] *f* awl

alentour [alɑ̃tur] *adv* round about ‖ **alentours** *mpl* neighborhood

alerte [alɛrt] *adj & f* alert; **alerte aérienne** air-raid alarm

alerter [alɛrte] *tr* to alert

alésage [alezaʒ] *m* bore (*of cylinder*)

aléser [aleze] §10 *tr* to ream; to bore

ale·zan [alzɑ̃] **-zane** [zan] *adj* chestnut (*colored*)

algarade [algarad] *f* altercation

algèbre [alʒɛbr] *f* algebra

Alger [alʒe] *m* Algiers

Algérie [alʒeri] *f* Algeria

algé·rien [alʒerjɛ̃] **-rienne** [rjen] *adj* Algerian ‖ (*cap*) *mf* Algerian

algé·rois [alʒerwa] **-roise** [rwaz] *adj of* Algiers; Algerian ‖ (*cap*) *mf* native of Algiers; Algerian

algues [alg] *fpl* algae

alias [aljas] *adv* alias

alibi [alibi] *m* (*law*) alibi

alié·né -née [aljene] *adj* alienated; insane ‖ *mf* insane person

aliéner [aljene] §10 *tr* to transfer, alienate ‖ *ref* (with *dat of reflex pron*) to alienate (*s.o.*); (with *dat of reflex pron*) to lose (*e.g., s.o.'s sympathy*)

alignement [alinmɑ̃] *m* alignment

aligner [aline] *tr* to align; **aligner ses phrases** to choose one's words with care ‖ *ref* to line up

aliment [alimɑ̃] *m* aliment, food; **aliments** (*law*) necessities

alimentaire [alimɑ̃ter] *adj* alimentary; subsistence, e.g., **pension alimentaire** subsistence allowance

alimentation [alimɑ̃tɑsjɔ̃] *f* nourishment; supplying; feeding (*a fire, a machine*)

alimenter [alimɑ̃te] *tr* to nourish; to supply; to feed (*a fire, a machine*)

alinéa [alinea] *m* indentation (*of the first line of a paragraph*); paragraph

aliter [alite] *tr* to keep in bed ‖ *ref* to be confined to bed

alizés [alize] *mpl* trade winds

allaiter [alete] *tr* to nurse

al·lant [alɑ̃] **al·lante** [alɑ̃t] *adj* active ‖ *m*—**allants et venants** passers-by; **beaucoup d'allant** (coll) a lot of pep

allé·chant [aleʃɑ̃] **-chante** [ʃɑ̃t] *adj* enticing, tempting

allécher [aleʃe] §10 *tr* to allure

allée [ale] *f* walk, path; going; city street, boulevard; aisle (*of theater*)

allégeance [aleʒɑ̃s] *f* allegiance; lightening (*of care*); handicapping (*of a race*)

alléger [aleʒe] §1 *tr* to lighten; to alleviate, mitigate, relieve

allégorie [alegɔri] *f* allegory

allègre [alegr] *adj* lively, cheerful

alléguer [alege] §10 *tr* to allege as an excuse; to cite (*an authority*)

Allemagne [alman] *f* Germany; **l'Allemagne** Germany

alle·mand [almɑ̃] **-mande** [mɑ̃d] *adj* German ‖ *m* German (*language*) ‖ (*cap*) *mf* German (*person*)

aller [ale] *m* going; go; **aller (et) retour** round trip; round-trip ticket; **au pis aller** at the worst ‖ §4 *intr* (*aux:* ÊTRE) to go; to work, function; (with *dat*) to suit, fit, become, e.g., **la robe lui va bien** the dress becomes her; **aller + inf** to be going to + *inf*, e.g., **je vais au magasin acheter des souliers** I am going to the store to buy some shoes; **allez!, allons!**, **allons donc!** well!, come on!, all right!; **allez-y doucement!** take it easy!; **ça va?, comment allez-vous?** how are you? ‖ *ref*—**s'en aller** to go away ‖ *aux*—**aller + inf** to be going to + *inf* (to express futurity), e.g., **il va se marier** he is going to get married

allergie [alerʒi] *f* allergy

aller-retour [aleretur] *m*—**faire l'aller-retour** to go and come back

alliage [aljaʒ] *m* alloy

alliance [aljɑ̃s] *f* alliance; marriage; wedding ring; **ancienne alliance** Old Covenant; **nouvelle alliance** New Covenant

al·lié -liée [alje] *adj* allied (*by treaty*); united (*in marriage*) ‖ *mf* ally; kin, in-law

allier [alje] *tr* to ally; to alloy ‖ *ref* to become allied, to ally oneself

allô [alo] *interj* hello!

allocation [allɔkɑsjɔ̃] *f* allocation, allotment; **allocations familiales** family (social security) allotments

allocution [allɔkysjɔ̃] *f* short speech

allonger [alɔ̃ʒe] §38 *tr, intr,* & *ref* to lengthen

allouer [alwe] *tr* to allow, allocate

allumage [alymaʒ] *m* lighting; switching on (*of a light*); kindling (*of a fire*); ignition

allume-feu [alymfø] *m invar* kindling

allumer [alyme] *tr* to ignite; to light (*a cigarette*); to light up (*a room*); to put on, switch on (*a light; a radio; a heater*); to provoke (*anger*) ‖ *ref* to go on (*said of a light*); to light up (*said of eyes*); to catch fire

allumette [alymɛt] *f* match; **allumette de sûreté** safety match

allumette-gaz [alymɛtgɑz] *m* pilot light

allumeur [alymœr] *m* ignition system; **allumeur de réverbères** lamplighter

allumeuse [alymøz] *f* (coll) vamp

allure [alyr] *f* speed, pace; gait, bearing, aspect; **à l'allure de l'escargot** at a snail's pace; **à toute allure** at top speed

allusion [allyzjɔ̃] *f* allusion

almanach [almana] *m* almanac; yearbook

aloès [alɔɛs] *m* aloe

aloi [alwa] *m* legal alloy; quality; **de bon aloi** genuine

alors [alɔr] *adv* then; **alors même que** even though; **alors que** whereas

alose [aloz] *f* shad

alouette [alwɛt] *f* lark, skylark; **alouette sans tête** rolled veal

alourdir [alurdir] *tr* to weigh down, to make heavy ‖ *ref* to become heavy

aloyau [alwajo] *m* (*pl* **aloyaux**) sirloin

Alpes [alp] *fpl*—**les Alpes** the Alps

alphabet [alfabe] *m* alphabet

alpinisme [alpinism] *m* mountain climbing

alpiniste [alpinist] *mf* mountain climber

alpiste [alpist] *m* birdseed

alsa-cien [alzasjɛ̃] **-cienne** [sjɛn] *adj* Alsatian ‖ *M* Alsatian (*dialect*) ‖ (*cap*) *mf* Alsatian (*person*)

alté-rant [alterɑ̃] **-rante** [rɑ̃t] *adj* thirst-provoking

altération [alterɑsjɔ̃] *f* alteration, falsification; deterioration; heavy thirst; (mus) accidental

altérer [altere] §10 *tr* to alter, falsify; to ruin (*one's health*); to weaken, impair; to make thirsty ‖ *ref* to undergo a change for the worse; to become thirsty

alternance [alternɑ̃s] *f* alternation; (agr) rotation

alterna-tif [alternatif] **-tive** [tiv] *adj* alternative; alternating; alternate ‖ *f* alternative, dilemma; alternation

alterne [altern] *adj* alternate (*angles*)

alterner [alterne] *tr* to rotate (*crops*) ‖ *intr* to alternate

al-tier [altje] **-tière** [tjer] *adj* haughty

altitude [altityd] *f* altitude

alto [alto] *m* alto; viola

altruiste [altrɥist] *adj* & *mf* altruist

aluminium [alyminjɔm] *m* aluminum

alun [alœ̃] *m* alum

alunir [alynir] *intr* to land on the moon

alunissage [alynisaʒ] *m* landing on the moon

alvéole [alveɔl] *m* & *f* alveolus; cavity; cell (*of honeycomb*); socket (*of tooth*)

amadou [amadu] *m* punk, tinder

amadouer [amadwe] *tr* to wheedle

amaigrir [amegrir] *tr* to emaciate; to make thin ‖ *ref* to grow thin

amalgame [amalgam] *m* amalgam

amalgamer [amalgame] *tr* & *ref* to amalgamate

aman [amɑ̃] *m*—**demander l'aman** to give in

amande [amɑ̃d] *f* almond; kernel; **amande de Malaga** Jordan almond

amandier [amɑ̃dje] *m* almond tree

a·mant [amɑ̃] **-mante** [mɑ̃t] *mf* lover

amareyeur [amarejœr] *m* oysterman

amariner [amarine] *tr* to season (*a crew*); to impress (*a ship*)

amarre [amar] *f* hawser

amarrer [amare] *tr* & *ref* to moor

amas [amɑ] *m* mass; heap; cluster (*of stars*); **amas de neige** snowdrift

amasser [amase] *tr* to amass; to gather ‖ *intr* to hoard ‖ *ref* to pile up, to crowd

amateur [amatœr] *adj* amateur ‖ *m* amateur; (coll) prospective buyer

amatir [amatir] *tr* to mat, dull (*metal or glass*)

amazone [amazon] *f* amazon; horsewoman; riding habit; **monter en amazone** to ride sidesaddle ‖ (*cap*) *f* Amazon

ambages [ɑ̃baʒ] *fpl* circumlocutions; **sans ambages** without beating around the bush

ambassade [ɑ̃basad] *f* embassy

ambassadeur [ɑ̃basadœr] *m* ambassador

ambassadrice [ɑ̃basadris] *f* ambassadress; wife of ambassador; emissary

ambiance [ɑ̃bjɑ̃s] *f* environment, milieu; atmosphere, tone

ambidextre [ɑ̃bidɛkstrə] *adj* ambidextrous ‖ *mf* ambidextrous person

ambi·gu -guë [ɑ̃bigy] *adj* ambiguous ‖ *m* ambiguousness; buffet lunch; odd mixture

ambiguïté [ɑ̃biguite] *f* ambiguity

ambi·tieux [ɑ̃bisjø] **-tieuse** [sjøz] *adj* ambitious

ambition [ɑ̃bisjɔ̃] *f* ambition

amble [ɑ̃bl] *m* amble

ambler [ɑ̃ble] *intr* (equit) to amble

ambre [ɑ̃brə] *m*—**ambre gris** ambergris; **ambre** (**jaune** or **succin**) amber

ambulance [ɑ̃bylɑ̃s] *f* ambulance

ambulan·cier [ɑ̃bylɑ̃sje] **-cière** [sjer] *mf* ambulance driver or attendant

ambu·lant [ɑ̃bylɑ̃] **-lante** [lɑ̃t] *adj* ambulant ‖ *m* railway mail clerk

ambulatoire [ɑ̃bylatwar] *adj* ambulatory; itinerant

âme [ɑm] *f* soul; spirit, heart, mind;

core (of cable); bore (of cannon); web (of rail); sound post (of violin); **âme damnée** evil genius; **rendre l'âme** to give up the ghost

améliorer [ameljɔre] tr & ref to ameliorate, to improve

amen [amen] m invar Amen

aménagement [amenaʒmɑ̃] m arrangement, equipping; preparation, development (of land); adjustment (of taxes); **aménagements** furnishings

aménager [amenaʒe] §38 tr to arrange, equip; to remodel; to parcel out; to grade (a roadbed); to feed (a machine); to harness (a waterfall)

amende [amɑ̃d] f fine; forfeit (in a game); **faire amende honorable** (coll) to apologize

amendement [amɑ̃dmɑ̃] m amendment; fertilizer

amender [amɑ̃de] tr to amend; to manure || ref to mend one's ways, to amend

amène [amen] adj pleasant

amener [amne] §2 tr to bring; to lead; to bring on; to furnish (proof); (naut) to lower; **amener pavillon** to surrender || ref (coll) to arrive; **amenez-vous!** (slang) get a move on!

aménité [amenite] f amenity; **aménités** cutting remarks

amenuiser [amənɥize] tr to whittle || ref to be whittled down

a·mer -mère [amer] adj bitter || m bitters; seamark; gall (of animal)

améri·cain -caine [amerikɛ̃] -kɛn] adj American || m American English || f phaeton; bicycle relay || (cap) mf American (person)

américanisme [amerikanism] m Americanism; American studies

Amérique [amerik] f America; **l'Amérique** America

amerrir [amerir] intr to land, alight on water

amerrissage [amerisaʒ] m landing (on water); (rok) splashdown; **amerrissage forcé** ditching; **faire un amerrissage forcé** to ditch

amertume [amertym] f bitterness

améthyste [ametist] f amethyst

ameublement [amœbləmɑ̃] m furnishings; furniture, suite

ameublir [amœblir] tr (agr) to soften, to mellow (soil)

ameuter [amøte] tr to rouse (the pack) || ref to riot

a·mi -mie [ami] adj friendly || mf friend || f mistress

amiable [amjabl] adj amicable; **à l'amiable** privately, out of court

amiante [amjɑ̃t] m asbestos

amibe [amib] f amoeba

ami·bien [amibjɛ̃] **-bienne** [bjen] adj amoebic

ami·cal -cale [amikal] adj (pl -caux [ko]) amicable || f professional club

amidon [amidɔ̃] m starch

amidonner [amidɔne] tr to starch

amincir [amɛ̃sir] tr to make more slender, to attenuate || ref to grow thinner

ami·ral [amiral] m (pl -raux [ro]) admiral

amirale [amiral] f admiral's wife

amirauté [amirote] f admiralty

amitié [amitje] f friendship; **amitiés** (complimentary close) cordially yours; **faites mes amitiés à** give my regards to; **faites-moi l'amitié de** do me the favor of

ammo·niac -niaque [amɔnjak] adj ammoniacal || m ammonia (gas) || f ammonia (gas dissolved in water)

amnésie [amnezi] f amnesia

amnistie [amnisti] f amnesty

amnistier [amnistje] tr to amnesty

amoindrir [amwɛ̃drir] tr to lessen || ref to diminish

amollir [amɔlir] tr & ref to soften

amollissement [amɔlismɑ̃] m softening

amonceler [amɔ̃sle] §34 tr to pile up, to gather || ref to pile up, to gather; to drift (said of snow)

amont [amɔ̃] m upper waters; **en amont** upstream; **en amont de** above

amorçage [amɔrsaʒ] m baiting; priming

amorce [amɔrs] f bait, lure; fuse, percussion cap; beginning; leader (of strip of film); (mov) preview

amorcer [amɔrse] §51 tr to bait; to prime; to entice; to begin

amorphe [amɔrf] adj amorphous

amortir [amɔrtir] tr to absorb (shock); to subdue (color; pain; passions); to damp (waves); to amortize

amortissement [amɔrtismɑ̃] m absorption (of shock, sound, etc.); amortization

amortisseur [amɔrtisœr] m shock absorber

amour [amur] m love; love affair; **premières amours** puppy love || (cap) m Cupid

amou·reux -reuse [amurø] [røz] adj amorous; loving; fond, devoted; **amoureux de** in love with || m lover || f sweetheart

amour-propre [amurprɔpr] m (pl amours-propres) self-esteem; vanity

amovible [amɔvibl] adj removable; detachable; (jur) revocable

ampère [ɑ̃per] m ampere

ampèremètre [ɑ̃permetr] m ammeter

amphibie [ɑ̃fibi] adj amphibious, amphibian || m amphibian

amphibien [ɑ̃fibjɛ̃] m amphibian

amphithéâtre [ɑ̃fiteatr] m amphitheater; auditorium (with raised seats)

amphitryon [ɑ̃fitrijɔ̃] m host at dinner || (cap) m Amphitryon

ample [ɑ̃pl] adj ample; long (speech); liberal (reward)

amplifica·teur [ɑ̃plifikatœr] **-trice** [tris] adj amplifying || mf exaggerator || m amplifier; (phot) enlarger

amplifier [ɑ̃plifje] tr to amplify, to enlarge

amplitude [ɑ̃plityd] f amplitude

ampoule [ɑ̃pul] f ampule; (elec) bulb; (pathol) blister

ampu·té -tée [ɑ̃pyte] mf amputee

amputer [ãpyte] *tr* to amputate; to cut (*an article, speech*)

amuïr [amɥir] *ref* to become silent

amuïssement [amɥismã] *m* (phonet) silencing

amulette [amylet] *f* amulet

amure [amyr] *f* tack (*of sail*)

amuse-gueule [amyzgœl] *m* (*pl* **-gueule** or **-gueules**) (coll) appetizer, snack

amusement [amyzmã] *m* amusement

amuser [amyze] *tr* to amuse; to mislead ‖ *ref* to have a good time; to sow one's wild oats; **s'amuser à** to pass the time by; **s'amuser de** to play with; to make fun of

amygdale [amigdal] *f* tonsil

an [ã] *m* year; **l'an de grâce** the year of Our Lord

anacarde [anakard] *m* cashew nut

anachronisme [anakrɔnism] *m* anachronism

analogie [analɔʒi] *f* analogy

analogue [analɔg] *adj* analogous; similar

analphabète [analfabet] *adj* & *mf* illiterate

analphabétisme [analfabetism] *m* illiteracy

analyse [analiz] *f* analysis; **analyse des renseignements** data processing

analyser [analize] *tr* to analyze

analyseur [analizœr] *m* analyzer, tester

analyste [analist] *mf* analyst

analytique [analitik] *adj* analytic(al)

ananas [anana] *m* pineapple

anarchie [anarʃi] *f* anarchy

anarchiste [anarʃist] *mf* anarchist

anathème [anatem] *m* anathema

anatife [anatif] *m* barnacle

anatomie [anatɔmi] *f* anatomy

anatomique [anatɔmik] *adj* anatomic(al)

ances·tral **-trale** [ãsestral] *adj* (*pl* **-traux** [tro]) ancestral

ancêtre [ãsetr] *m* ancestor

anche [ãʃ] *f* (mus) reed

anchois [ãʃwa] *m* anchovy

an·cien [ãsjɛ̃] **-cienne** [sjen] *adj* ancient, old, long-standing; antiquated; antique ‖ (when standing before noun) *adj* former, previous, old; retired (*businessman*); ancient (*Greece, Rome*) ‖ *mf* senior (*in rank*); oldster; **les Anciens** the Ancients

anciennement [ãsjenmã] *adv* formerly

ancienneté [ãsjente] *f* antiquity; seniority (*in rank*)

ancre [ãkr] *f* anchor; **ancres levées** anchors aweigh

ancrer [ãkre] *tr* & *intr* to anchor ‖ *ref* to become established

andain [ãdɛ̃] *m* swath; row of shocks

andouille [ãduj] *f* (coll) fool, sap

andouiller [ãduje] *m* antler

âne [ɑn] *m* ass, donkey

anéantir [aneãtir] *tr* to annihilate; to prostrate ‖ *ref* to disappear; to humble oneself (*before God*)

anéantissement [aneãtismã] *m* annihilation; prostration

anecdote [anegdɔt] *f* anecdote

anémie [anemi] *f* anemia

ânesse [anes] *f* she-ass

anesthésie [anestezi] *f* anesthesia

anesthésier [anestezje] *tr* to anesthetize

anesthésique [anestezik] *adj* & *m* anesthetic

anesthésiste [anestezist] *mf* anesthetist

anévrisme [anevrism] *m* aneurysm

anfractuosité [ãfraktɥozite] *f* rough outline (*of coast*); ruggedness, cragginess

ange [ãʒ] *m* angel; **ange gardien, ange tutélaire** guardian angel; **être aux anges** to walk on air

angélique [ãʒelik] *adj* angelic(al)

angélus [ãʒelys] *m* Angelus

angine [ãʒin] *f* tonsillitis, quinsy; **angine de poitrine** angina pectoris

an·glais [ãgle] **-glaise** [glez] *adj* English; **à l'anglaise** in the English manner; **filer à l'anglaise** to take French leave ‖ *m* English (*language*) ‖ (*cap*) *m* Englishman; **les Anglais** the English ‖ *f* Englishwoman

angle [ãgl] *m* angle; corner

Angleterre [ãglətɛr] *f* England; **l'Angleterre** England

angois·sant [ãgwasã] **angois·sante** [ãgwasãt] *adj* agonizing

angoisse [ãgwas] *f* anguish

anguille [ãgij] *f* eel; **anguille de mer** conger eel

angulaire [ãgylɛr] *adj* angular

angu·leux [ãgylø] **-leuse** [løz] *adj* angular, sharp

anicroche [anikrɔʃ] *f* (coll) hitch, snag

ani·mal **-male** [animal] (*mo*) *adj* animal ‖ *m* animal, brute, beast; (coll) blockhead

anima·teur [animatœr] **-trice** [tris] *adj* animating ‖ *mf* animator, moving spirit; master of ceremonies; **animateur de théâtre** theatrical producer

animation [animasjɔ̃] *f* animation

animer [anime] *tr* to animate; to encourage ‖ *ref* to become alive, liven up

animosité [animozite] *f* animosity

anion [anjɔ̃] *m* anion

anis [ani] *m* anise

annales [anal] *fpl* annals

an·neau [ano] *m* (*pl* **-neaux**) ring

année [ane] *f* year; **année bissextile** leap year; **année de lumière** lightyear; **bonne année** Happy New Year

année-lumière [anelymjɛr] *f* (*pl* **années-lumière**) light-year

annexe [aneks] *adj* annexed ‖ *f* annex

annexer [anekse] *tr* to annex

annexion [aneksjɔ̃] *f* annexation

annihiler [aniile] *tr* to annihilate

anniversaire [aniverser] *adj* & *m* anniversary; **anniversaire de naissance** birthday

annonce [anɔ̃s] *f* announcement; advertisement; (cards) bid; **petites annonces** classified ads

annoncer [anɔ̃se] §51 *tr* to announce; to advertise ‖ *ref* to augur; to promise to be

annonceur [anɔ̃sœr] *m* advertiser

annoncia·teur [anɔ̃sjatœr] **-trice** [tris] *adj* betokening, foreboding ‖ *m* harbinger annoter [anɔte] *tr* to annotate

annuaire [anɥɛr] *m* annual, yearbook, directory; catalog, bulletin (*e.g.*, *of a school*)

an·nuel -nuelle [anɥɛl] *adj* annual

annuité [anɥite] *f* annuity

annuler [anɥle] *tr* to annul

ano·din [anɔdɛ̃] -dine [din] *adj* & *m* anodyne

ânon [ɑnɔ̃] *m* foal of an ass

anonner [anɔne] *tr* to recite in a stumbling manner

anonymat [anɔnima] *m* anonymity

anonyme [anɔnim] *adj* anonymous; incorporated; (fig) colorless, drab ‖ *mf* unidentified person

anor·mal -male [anɔrmal] (*pl* -maux [mo]) *adj* abnormal ‖ *mf* abnormal person

anse [ɑ̃s] *f* handle; **faire danser l'anse du panier** to pad the bill

antagonisme [ɑ̃tagɔnism] *m* antagonism

antan [ɑ̃tɑ̃] *m* yesteryear

Antarctique [ɑ̃tarktik] *adj* & *m* Antarctic ‖ *f* Antarctic (*region*); **l'Antarctique** Antarctica

antécé·dent [ɑ̃tesedɑ̃] -dente [dɑ̃t] *adj* & *m* antecedent

antenne [ɑ̃tɛn] *f* antenna (*feeler*; *aerial*); outpost; (naut) lateen yard; **porter à l'antenne** to put on the air

antépénultième [ɑ̃tepenyltjɛm] *adj* antepenultimate ‖ *f* antepenult

anté·rieur -rieure [ɑ̃terjœr] *adj* anterior; former; previous, preceding; earlier; front

antériorité [ɑ̃terjɔrite] *f* priority

anthologie [ɑ̃tɔlɔʒi] *f* anthology

anthropoïde [ɑ̃trɔpɔid] *adj* & *m* anthropoid

anthropophage [ɑ̃trɔpɔfaʒ] *adj* & *mf* cannibal

antiaé·rien [ɑ̃tiaerjɛ̃] -rienne [rjɛn] *adj* antiaircraft

antialcoolique [ɑ̃tialkɔɔlik] *adj* antialcoholic ‖ *mf* teetotaler; temperance worker

antibiotique [ɑ̃tibjɔtik] *adj* & *m* antibiotic

antichambre [ɑ̃tiʃɑ̃br] *f* antechamber, anteroom

antichar [ɑ̃tiʃar] *adj* antitank

anticipation [ɑ̃tisipasjɔ̃] *f* anticipation; **anticipations** prophecies (*of science fiction*); **d'anticipation** science fiction (*stories*, *films*, etc.); **par anticipation** in advance

antici·pé -pée [ɑ̃tisipe] *adj* anticipated, advanced, ahead of time; premature (*e.g.*, *death*)

anticiper [ɑ̃tisipe] *tr* to anticipate; to advance ‖ *intr* to act ahead of time; **anticiper sur** to encroach on; to pay ahead of time; to spend ahead of time

anticléri·cal -cale [ɑ̃tiklerikal] *adj* (*pl* -caux [ko]) anticlerical

anticonception·nel -nelle [ɑ̃tikɔ̃sepsjɔnɛl] *adj* contraceptive

anticorps [ɑ̃tikɔr] *m* antibody

antidéra·pant [ɑ̃tiderapɑ̃] -pante [pɑ̃t] *adj* nonskid ‖ *m* nonskid tire

antidéto·nant [ɑ̃tidetɔnɑ̃] -nante [nɑ̃t] *adj* & *m* antiknock

antidote [ɑ̃tidɔt] *m* antidote

antienne [ɑ̃tjen] *f* antiphon, anthem; **chanter toujours la même antienne** to harp on the same subject

antigel [ɑ̃tiʒɛl] *m* antifreeze

antigi·vrant [ɑ̃tiʒivrɑ̃] -vrante [vrɑ̃t] *adj* deicing, defrosting ‖ *m* deicer

antigivre [ɑ̃tiʒivr] *m* deicer, defroster

Antilles [ɑ̃tij] *fpl* West Indies

antilope [ɑ̃tilɔp] *f* antelope

antimite [ɑ̃timit] *adj* mothproof ‖ *m* moth killer

antimoine [ɑ̃timwan] *m* antimony

antiparasite [ɑ̃tiparazit] *adj* (rad) static-eliminating ‖ *m* (rad) static eliminator; insecticide

antipathie [ɑ̃tipati] *f* antipathy

antiquaire [ɑ̃tiker] *m* antique dealer

antique [ɑ̃tik] *adj* antique, classic; old-fashioned ‖ *m* antique

antiquité [ɑ̃tikite] *f* antiquity; **antiquités** antiques

antisémite [ɑ̃tisemit] *adj* anti-Semitic ‖ *mf* anti-Semite

antisémitique [ɑ̃tisemitik] *adj* anti-Semitic

antiseptique [ɑ̃tiseptik] *adj* & *m* antiseptic

antiso·cial -ciale [ɑ̃tisɔsjal] *adj* (*pl* -ciaux [sjo]) antisocial

antispor·tif [ɑ̃tispɔrtif] -tive [tiv] *adj* unsportsmanlike

antithèse [ɑ̃titez] *f* antithesis

antitoxine [ɑ̃titɔksin] *f* antitoxin

antitranspirant [ɑ̃titrɑ̃spirɑ̃] *m* antiperspirant

antonyme [ɑ̃tɔnim] *m* antonym

antre [ɑ̃tr] *m* den, lair; cave

anxiété [ɑ̃ksjete] *f* anxiety

anxieux [ɑ̃ksjø] anxieuse [ɑ̃ksjøz] *adj* anxious, worried

aorte [aɔrt] *f* aorta

août [u], [ut] *m* August

A.P. *abbr* (assistance publique) welfare department

apache [apaʃ] *m* apache, hoodlum

apaisement [apezmɑ̃] *m* appeasement

apaiser [apeze] *tr* to appease ‖ *ref* to quiet down

apanage [apanaʒ] *m* attribute

aparté [aparte] *m* stage whisper, aside; **en aparté** privately

apathie [apati] *f* apathy

apathique [apatik] *adj* apathetic

apatride [apatrid] *adj* stateless ‖ *mf* stateless person

apercevoir [apersəvwar] §59 *tr* to perceive ‖ *ref* to notice; to realize; **s'apercevoir de** to notice, realize, be aware of

aperçu [apersy] *m* glimpse; view, look; outline

apéri·tif [aperitif] -tive [tiv] *adj* appetizing ‖ *m* appetizer

aperture [apertyr] *f* (phonet) aperture

apesanteur [apəzɑ̃tœr] *f* weightlessness

à-peu-près [apøprɛ] *m invar* approximation, rough estimate

apeu·ré -rée [apœre] *adj* frightened

aphorisme [afɔrism] *m* aphorism

aphrodisiaque [afrɔdizjak] *adj* & *m* aphrodisiac

aphte [aft] *m* mouth canker, cold sore

apiculteur [apikyltœr] *m* beekeeper

apiculture [apikyltyr] *f* beekeeping

apitoiement [apitwamɑ̃] *m* compassion

apitoyant [apitwajɑ̃] **apitoyante** [apitwajɑ̃t] *adj* piteous, pitiful

apitoyer [apitwaje] §47 *tr* to move (*s.o.*) to pity ‖ *ref*—s'apitoyer sur to feel compassion for

ap. J.-C. *abbr* (après Jésus-Christ) A.D.

aplanir [aplanir] *tr* to even off; to iron out (*difficulties*)

aplatir [aplatir] *tr* to flatten ‖ *ref* to go flat; to grovel

aplomb [aplɔ̃] *m* aplomb; hang (*of gown*); (coll) cheek, rudeness; **aplombs** stand (*of horse*); **d'aplomb** plumb; steadily

apocalyptique [apɔkaliptik] *adj* apocalyptic

apocryphe [apɔkrif] *adj* apocryphal ‖ **Apocryphes** *mpl* Apocrypha

apogée [apɔʒe] *m* apogee

Apollon [apɔllɔ̃] *m* Apollo

apologie [apɔlɔʒi] *f* apology

apophonie [apɔfɔni] *f* ablaut

apoplectique [apɔplɛktik] *adj* & *mf* apoplectic

apoplexie [apɔplɛksi] *f* apoplexy

apostille [apɔstij] *f* endorsement

apostiller [apɔstije] *tr* to endorse

apostolat [apɔstɔla] *m* apostleship

apostrophe [apɔstrɔf] *f* apostrophe; sharp reprimand

apostropher [apɔstrɔfe] *tr* to apostrophize; to reprimand sharply

apothicaire [apɔtiker] *m* apothecary

apôtre [apotr] *m* apostle; **faire le bon apôtre** to play the hypocrite

apparaître [aparetr] §12 *intr* (*aux:* AVOIR or ÊTRE) to appear, come into view; to become evident

apparat [apara] *m* pomp, ostentation

apparaux [aparo] *mpl* rigging

appareil [aparej] *m* apparatus, machine, appliance; apparel; radio set; airplane; pomp, show, display; camera; telephone; (archit) bond; **à l'appareil!** speaking!; **appareil à sous** slot machine; **appareil plâtré** plaster cast

appareiller [apareje] *tr* to prepare; to bond (*stones*); to pair, match; (naut) to rig ‖ *intr* to set sail

apparemment [aparamɑ̃] *adv* apparently

apparence [aparɑ̃s] *f* appearance

appa·rent [aparɑ̃] **-rente** [rɑ̃t] *adj* apparent

apparenter [aparɑ̃te] *tr* to relate by marriage ‖ *ref* to become related

apparier [aparje] *tr* to pair off, to match

apparition [aparisjɔ̃] *f* apparition; appearance

apparoir [aparwar] (used only in: *inf;* 3d *sg pres ind* appert) *impers*—il appert de it follows from; il appert que it is evident that

appartement [apartəmɑ̃] *m* apartment

appartenance [apartənɑ̃s] *f* appurtenance

appartenir [apartənir] §72 *intr*—appartenir à to belong to; to pertain to ‖ *impers*—il appartient à qn de it behooves s.o. to ‖ *ref* to be one's own master

appas [apɑ] *mpl* charms; bosom

appât [apɑ] *m* bait

appâter [apate] *tr* to lure; to fatten up (*fowl*)

appauvrir [apovrir] *tr* to impoverish ‖ *ref* to become impoverished

ap-peau [apo] *m* (*pl* -peaux) decoy; bird call

appel [apel] *m* call; appeal; summons; roll call; ring (*on telephone*); (mil) draft; **appel interurbain** long-distance call; **appel nominal** roll call; **faire l'appel** to call the roll

appe·lant [aplɑ̃] **-lante** [lɑ̃t] *adj* appellant ‖ *mf* appellant ‖ *m* decoy

appelé [aple] *m* draftee

appeler [aple] §34 *tr* to call; to name; to summon; to subpoena; to require; to call up, to draft ‖ *intr* to call; to appeal (*in court*); **en appeler à** to appeal to ‖ *ref* to be named, e.g., **elle s'appelle Marie** she is named Mary, her name is Mary

appendice [apɛ̃dis] *m* appendix

appendicectomie [apɛ̃disektɔmi] *f* appendectomy

appendicite [apɛ̃disit] *f* appendicitis

appentis [apɑ̃ti] *m* lean-to

appesantir [apzɑ̃tir] *tr* to weigh down; to slow down (*e.g., bodily activity*); to make (*a burden*) heavier ‖ *ref* to be weighed down; **s'appesantir sur** to dwell on, to expatiate on

appétis·sant [apetisɑ̃] **appétis·sante** [apetisɑ̃t] *adj* appetizing, tempting

appétit [apeti] *m* appetite

applaudir [aplodir] *tr* to applaud; **applaudir qn de** to commend, applaud s.o. for ‖ *intr* to applaud; **applaudir à** to approve, commend, applaud ‖ *ref*—s'applaudir de to congratulate oneself on, to pat oneself on the back for

applaudissement [aplodismɑ̃] *m* round of applause; **applaudissements** applause

applicable [aplikabl] *adj* applicable

application [aplikasjɔ̃] *f* application

applique [aplik] *f* appliqué; sconce

appli·qué -quée [aplike] *adj* industrious, studious; applied (*science*)

appliquer [aplike] *tr* to apply ‖ *ref* to apply; to apply oneself

appoint [apwɛ̃] *m* addition; balance; aid, help; **faire l'appoint** to have the right change

appointements [apwɛ̃tmɑ̃] *mpl* salary

appointer [apwɛ̃te] *tr* to point, sharpen; to pay a salary to

appontage [apɔ̃taʒ] *m* deck-landing

appontement [apɔ̃təmɑ̃] *m* jetty (*landing pier*)

apponter [apɔ̃te] *intr* to deck-land

apport [apɔr] *m* contribution

apporter [apɔrte] *tr* to bring

apposer [apoze] *tr* to affix; to insert (*a clause in a contract*)

appréciable [apresjabl] *adj* appreciable

appréciation [apresjɑsjɔ̃] *f* appreciation, appraisal

apprécier [apresje] *tr* to appreciate

appréhender [apreɑ̃de] *tr* to apprehend; to be apprehensive about

appréhension [apreɑ̃sjɔ̃] *f* apprehension

apprendre [aprɑ̃dr] §56 *tr* to learn; **apprendre à vivre à qn** to teach s.o. manners; **apprendre q.ch. à qn** to inform s.o. of s.th.; to teach s.o. s.th. ‖ *intr* to learn

appren·ti -tie [aprɑ̃ti] *mf* apprentice; beginner, learner

apprentissage [aprɑ̃tisaʒ] *m* apprenticeship

apprêt [apre] *m* preparation, finishing touches; **sans apprêt** unaffectedly

apprêter [aprete] *tr & ref* to prepare

apprivoi·sé -sée [aprivwaze] *adj* tame, domesticated

apprivoiser [aprivwaze] *tr* to tame; to contain (*sorrow*) ‖ *ref* to become tame; to become sociable

approba·teur [aprɔbatœr] **-trice** [tris] *adj* approving ‖ *m* (slang) yes man

approbation [aprɔbasjɔ̃] *f* approbation, approval, consent

appro·chant -chante [aprɔʃɑ̃] **-chante** [ʃɑ̃t] *adj* similar ‖ **approchant** *adv* thereabouts

approche [aprɔʃ] *f* approach

approcher [aprɔʃe] *tr* to approach; to draw up (*e.g., a chair*) ‖ *intr* to approach; **approcher de** to approach, approximate ‖ *ref* to approach, to come near; **s'approcher de** to approach, to come near to, to go up to

approfon·di -die [aprɔfɔ̃di] *adj* thorough, deep

approfondir [aprɔfɔ̃dir] *tr* to deepen; to go deep into, get to the bottom of

appropriation [aprɔprijɑsjɔ̃] *f* appropriation; adaptation

appro·prié -priée [aprɔprije] *adj* appropriate

approprier [aprɔprije] *tr* to fit, adapt ‖ *ref* to appropriate, preempt

approuver [apruve] *tr* to approve, to approve of

approvisionnement [aprɔvizjɔnmɑ̃] *m* provisioning, stocking; **approvisionnements** supplies

approvisionner [aprɔvizjɔne] *tr* to provision, to stock ‖ *ref* to lay in supplies

approxima·tif [aprɔksimatif] **-tive** [tiv] *adj* approximate

appui [apɥi] *m* support; endorsement

appui-bras [apɥibra] *m* (*pl* **appuis-bras**) armrest

appui-livres [apɥilivr] *m* (*pl* **appuis-livres**) book end

appui-main [apɥimɛ̃] *m* (*pl* **appuis-main**) maulstick

appui-tête [apɥitet] *m* (*pl* **appuis-tête**) headrest

appuyer [apɥije] §27 *tr* to support; to prop; to rest, lean; to endorse (*a candidate*); **appuyer le doigt sur** to push (*a button, a lever, a switch*) with the finger ‖ *intr*—**appuyer sur** to lean on; to press (*a button*); to move (*a lever*); to pull (*a trigger*); to bear down on (*a pen or pencil*); to stress (*a syllable*) ‖ *ref*—**s'appuyer sur** to lean on; to be based on; to rely on; (slang) to put up with

âpre [ɑpr] *adj* harsh, rough; bitter; greedy (*for gain*)

après [apre] *adv* after, afterward; behind; **après que** after ‖ *prep* after; behind; **après Jésus-Christ** (ap. J.-C.) after Christ (A.D.); **d'après** after, from; by, according to

après-demain [apredəmɛ̃] *adv & m* the day after tomorrow

après-guerre [apreger] *m & f* (*pl* **-guerres**) postwar period

après-midi [apremidi] *m & f invar* afternoon

âpreté [ɑprəte] *f* harshness; bitterness

à-propos [aprɔpo] *m* opportuneness, aptness

apte [apt] *adj* apt; **apte à** suitable for

aptitude [aptityd] *f* aptitude; proficiency

apurement [apyrmɑ̃] *m* audit, check

apurer [apyre] *tr* to audit, to check

apyre [apir] *adj* fireproof

aquafortiste [akwafɔrtist] *mf* etcher

aquaplane [akwaplan] *m* aquaplane

aquarelle [akwarel] *f* watercolor

aquarium [akwarjɔm] *m* aquarium

aquatique [akwatik] *adj* aquatic

aqueduc [akdyk] *m* aqueduct

aquilin [akilɛ̃] *adj masc* aquiline

aquilon [akilɔ̃] *m* north wind

ara [ara] *m* (orn) macaw

arabe [arab] *adj* Arabian, Arab ‖ *m* Arabic; Arab (*horse*) ‖ (*cap*) *mf* Arabian, Arab

arachide [araʃid] *f* peanut

araignée [areɲe] *f* spider; grapnel; **araignée de mer** spider crab; **avoir une araignée dans le plafond** (coll) to have bats in the belfry

aratoire [aratwar] *adj* agricultural

arbitrage [arbitraʒ] *m* arbitration

arbitraire [arbitrer] *adj* arbitrary ‖ *m* arbitrariness, despotism

arbitre [arbitr] *m* arbiter; arbitrator; umpire, judge; **libre arbitre** free will

arbitrer [arbitre] *tr & intr* to arbitrate; to umpire

arborer [arbɔre] *tr* to hoist (*a flag*); to show off (*new clothes*)

arbouse [arbuz] *f* arbutus berry

arbousier [arbuzje] *m* arbutus

arbre [arbr] *m* tree; (mach) arbor, shaft; **arbre de Noël** Christmas tree; **arbre généalogique** family tree

arbris·seau [arbriso] *m* (*pl* **-seaux**) bushy tree

arbuste [arbyst] *m* shrub

arc [ark] *m* bow; arch; (elec, geom) arc

arcade [arkad] *f* arcade, archway

arcanes [arkan] *mpl* mysteries, secrets

arcanson [arkɑ̃sɔ̃] *m* rosin

arc-boutant [arkbutɑ̃] *m* (*pl* **arcs-boutants**) flying buttress

arc-en-ciel [arkɑ̃sjel] *m* (*pl* **arcs-en-ciel** [arkɑ̃sjel]) rainbow

archaïque [arkaik] *adj* archaic
archaïsme [arkaism] *m* archaism
archange [arkɑ̃ʒ] *m* archangel
arche [arʃ] *f* arch (*of bridge*); Ark
archéologie [arkeɔlɔʒi] *f* archaeology
archéologue [arkeɔlɔg] *mf* archaeologist
archer [arʃe] *m* archer, bowman
archet [arʃe] *m* bow
archétype [arketip] *m* archetype
archevêque [arʃəvɛk] *m* archbishop
archiduc [arʃidyk] *m* archduke
archipel [arʃipɛl] *m* archipelago
archiprêtre [arʃiprɛtr] *m* archpriest
architecte [arʃitɛkt] *m* architect
architecture [arʃitɛktyr] *f* architecture
archives [arʃiv] *fpl* archives
arçon [arsɔ̃] *m* saddletree
Arctique [arktik] *adj* & *m* Arctic || *f* Arctic (*region*)
ardemment [ardamɑ̃] *adv* ardently
ar•dent [ardɑ̃] -dente [dɑ̃t] *adj* ardent; burning; bright-red (*hair*)
ardeur [ardœr] *f* ardor; intense heat
ardoise [ardwaz] *f* slate
ardoi•sier [ardwazje] -sière [zjɛr] *adj* slate || *m* slate-quarry worker || *f* slate quarry
ar•du•due [ardy] *adj* steep; arduous
arène [arɛn] *f* arena; sand; (fig) arena; arènes arena, coliseum, amphitheater
arête [arɛt] *f* fishbone; beard (*of wheat*); angle, ridge
argent [arʒɑ̃] *m* silver; money; argent comptant cash
argenter [arʒɑ̃te] *tr* to silver || *ref* to turn silvery (*i.e., gray*)
argenterie [arʒɑ̃tri] *f* silver plate, silverware
argentier [arʒɑ̃tje] *m* silverware cabinet; (hist) Treasurer
argen•tin [arʒɑ̃tɛ̃] -tine [tin] *adj* silvery (*voice*); Argentinian || (*cap*) *mf* Argentinian (*person*) || l'Argentine *f* Argentina
argile [arʒil] *f* clay
argot [argo] *m* slang; jargon, cant
argotique [argɔtik] *adj* slangy
arguer [argɥe] (many authorities write: j'argüe, tu argües, etc.) *tr* to argue, imply; arguer de faux to doubt the authenticity of (*a document*) || *intr* to draw a conclusion; arguer de to use as a pretext
argument [argymɑ̃] *m* argument
argumentation [argymɑ̃tɑsjɔ̃] *f* argument
argumenter [argymɑ̃te] *intr* to argue
argus [argys] *m* look-out, spy; price list, book (*e.g., for used cars*); argus de la presse clipping service
aria [arja] *m* (coll) fuss, bother || *f* aria
aride [arid] *adj* arid; (*subject, speaker, etc.*) dry
aridité [aridite] *f* aridity; (fig) dryness, dullness
aristocrate [aristɔkrat] *adj* aristocratic || *mf* aristocrat
aristocratie [aristɔkrasi] *f* aristocracy
Aristote [aristɔt] *m* Aristotle
arithméti•cien [aritmetisjɛ̃] -cienne [sjɛn] *mf* arithmetician

arithmétique [aritmetik] *f* arithmetic
arlequin [arləkɛ̃] *m* goulash; wrench || (*cap*) *m* Harlequin
armateur [armatœr] *m* ship outfitter; shipowner
armature [armatyr] *f* framework; keeper (*of a horseshoe magnet*); (mus) key signature
arme [arm] *f* arm; weapon; arme blanche cold steel; steel blade; armes portatives small arms; faire ses premières armes to make one's début
armée [arme] *f* army
armement [armǝmɑ̃] *m* armament; fire power; (naut) outfitting
armé•nien [armenjɛ̃] -nienne [njɛn] *adj* Armenian || *m* Armenian (*language*) || (*cap*) *mf* Armenian (*person*)
armer [arme] *tr* to arm; to cock (*a gun*); to reinforce (*concrete*); armer chevalier to knight || *ref* to arm oneself, to arm
armistice [armistis] *m* armistice
armoire [armwar] *f* wardrobe, closet; armoire à pharmacie medicine cabinet; armoire frigorifique freezer
armoiries [armwari] *fpl* arms, coat of arms
armoise [armwaz] *f* sagebrush
armorier [armɔrje] *tr* to emblazon
armure [armyr] *f* armor; (tex) weave
aromatique [arɔmatik] *adj* aromatic
arôme [arom] *m* aroma
aronde [arɔ̃d] *f* swallow
arpège [arpɛʒ] *m* arpeggio
arpent [arpɑ̃] *m* acre
arpentage [arpɑ̃taʒ] *m* surveying
arpenter [arpɑ̃te] *tr* to survey; (coll) to pace (*the floor*)
arpenteur [arpɑ̃tœr] *m* surveyor
ar•qué -quée [arke] *adj* arched, bowed; cambered (*beam*); hooked (*nose*)
arquer [arke] *tr* to arch, to bow || *ref* to arch, to be bowed
arraché [araʃe] *m* (sports) lift
arrache-clou [araʃklu] *m* (*pl* -clous) claw hammer
arrache-pied [araʃpje] *adv*—d'arrache-pied at a stretch, without stopping
arracher [araʃe] *tr* to dig up, uproot, tear out, pull out; to wheedle (*money; a confession*); arracher q.ch. à qn to take away, snatch, or pry s.th. from s.o.; arracher q.ch. de q.ch. to pull s.th. off, from, or out of s.th.; to strip s.th. of s.th.; arracher qn à to deliver s.o. from (*evil; temptation; death*); arracher qn de to make s.o. get out of (*e.g., bed*) || *ref* to tear oneself away
arra•cheur [araʃœr] -cheuse [ʃøz] *mf* puller || *f* (mach) picker
arraisonnement [arɛzɔnmɑ̃] *m* port inspection
arraisonner [arɛzɔne] *tr* to inspect (*a ship*)
arrangement [arɑ̃ʒmɑ̃] *m* arrangement
arranger [arɑ̃ʒe] §38 *tr* to arrange; to settle (*a difficulty*); to fix (*to repair; to punish*) || *ref* to be arranged; to get ready; to agree
arrérages [areraʒ] *mpl* arrears
arrestation [arɛstɑsjɔ̃] *f* arrest

arrêt [arɛ] *m* stop; stopping; arrest; decree; **arrêt complet** standstill; **arrêt facultatif** whistle stop; **mettre aux arrêts** to house, to confine to quarters

arrê-té -tée [arete] *adj* stopped, standing; decided, fixed || *m* decree; authorization; (com) closing out (*of an account*); **arrêté de police** police ordinance; **prendre un arrêté** to pass a decree

arrêter [arete] *tr* to stop; to arrest; to fix (*one's gaze*); to settle, decide upon; to hire, engage; to point (*game, as hunting dog does*) || *intr* to stop; to point (*said of hunting dog*) || *ref* to stop; **s'arrêter à** to decide on; **s'arrêter de** + *inf* to stop + *ger*

arrhes [ar] *fpl* deposit, down payment

arriération [arjerasjɔ̃] *f* retardation

arrière [arjɛr] *adj invar* back, rear; tail (*wind*) || *m* back, rear; stern; **à l'arrière** in back; astern; **en arrière** backward; **en arrière de** behind || *adv* back

arrié-ré -rée [arjere] *adj* backward; delinquent (*in payment*); back (*pay, taxes, etc.*); old-fashioned || *mf* backward child || *m* arrears; back pay; back payment; backlog

arrière-boutique [arjɛrbutik] *f* (*pl* -**boutiques**) back room (*of a shop*)

arrière-cour [arjɛrkur] *f* (*pl* -**cours**) backyard

arrière-garde [arjɛrgard] *f* (*pl* -**gardes**) rear guard

arrière-goût [arjɛrgu] *m* (*pl* -**goûts**) aftertaste

arrière-grand-mère [arjɛrgrɑ̃mɛr] *f* (*pl* -**grand-mères**) great-grandmother

arrière-grand-père [arjɛrgrɑ̃pɛr] *m* (*pl* -**grands-pères**) great-grandfather

arrière-pays [arjɛrpei] *m invar* back country

arrière-pensée [arjɛrpɑ̃se] *f* (*pl* -**pensées**) mental reservation, ulterior motive

arrière-plan [arjɛrplɑ̃] *m* (*pl* -**plans**) background

arriérer [arjere] §10 *tr* to delay || *ref* to fall behind (*in payment*)

arrière-train [arjɛrtrɛ̃] *m* (*pl* -**trains**) rear (*of a vehicle*); hindquarters

arrimage [arimaʒ] *m* stowage; docking (*of space vehicle*)

arrimer [arime] *tr* to stow

arrimeur [arimœr] *m* stevedore

arrivage [arivaʒ] *m* arrival (*of goods or ships*)

arrivée [arive] *f* arrival; intake; (sports) finish, goal; **arrivée en douceur** (rok) soft landing

arriver [arive] *intr* (*aux:* ÊTRE) to arrive; to succeed; to happen; **arriver à** to attain, reach; **en arriver à** + *inf* to be reduced to + *ger*

arriviste [arivist] *mf* upstart, parvenu

arrogance [arɔgɑ̃s] *f* arrogance

arro·gant [arɔgɑ̃] -**gante** [gɑ̃t] *adj* arrogant

arroger [arɔʒe] §38 *ref* to arrogate to oneself

arrondir [arɔ̃dir] *tr* to round, round off, round out || *ref* to become round

arrondissement [arɔ̃dismɑ̃] *m* district

arrosage [arozaʒ] *m* sprinkling, irrigation; (mil) heavy bombing

arroser [aroze] *tr* to sprinkle, to water; to irrigate; to flow through (*e.g., a city*); to wash down (*a meal*); (coll) to bribe; (coll) to drink to (*a success*)

arro·seur [arozœr] -**seuse** [zøz] *mf* sprinkler (*person*) || *f* street sprinkler

arrosoir [arozwar] *m* sprinkling can

arse·nal [arsənal] *m* (*pl* -**naux** [no]) shipyard, navy yard; (fig) storehouse; (archaic) arsenal, armory

arsenic [arsənik] *m* arsenic

art [ar] *m* art; **arts d'agréments** music, drawing, dancing, etc.; **arts ménagers** home economics; **le huitième art** television; **les arts du spectacle** the performing arts; **le septième art** the cinema

artère [artɛr] *f* artery

arté·riel -rielle [arterjɛl] *adj* arterial

artérioscléreux [arterjoskleɾø] -**reuse** [røz] *adj & mf* arteriosclerotic

arté·sien [artezjɛ̃] -**sienne** [zjɛn] *adj* of Artois; artesian (*well*)

arthrite [artrit] *f* arthritis

artichaut [artiʃo] *m* artichoke

article [artikl] *m* article; entry (*in a dictionary*); **à l'article de la mort** on the point of death; **article de fond** leader; editorial; **article de tête** front-page story; **articles divers** sundries

articuler [artikyle] *tr & ref* to articulate

artifice [artifis] *m* artifice; craftsmanship

artifi·ciel -cielle [artifisjɛl] *adj* artificial

artificier [artifisje] *m* fireworks maker; soldier in charge of ammunition supply

artifi·cieux [artifisjø] -**cieuse** [sjøz] *adj* artful, cunning

artillerie [artijəri] *f* artillery

artilleur [artijœr] *m* artilleryman

arti·san [artizɑ̃] -**sane** [zan] *mf* artisan, artificer || *m* craftsman

artiste [artist] *adj* artistic; artist, of art, e.g., **le monde artiste** the world of art || *mf* artist; actor

artistique [artistik] *adj* artistic

ar·yen [arjɛ̃] -**yenne** [jɛn] *adj* Aryan || (*cap*) *mf* Aryan (*person*)

as [as] *m* ace; **as du volant** speed king

A.S. *abbr* (**assurances sociales**) social security

a/s *abbr* (**aux bons soins de**) c/o

asbeste [asbɛst] *m* asbestos

ascendance [asɑ̃dɑ̃s] *f* lineal ancestry; rising (*of air; of star*)

ascenseur [asɑ̃sœr] *m* elevator

ascension [asɑ̃sjɔ̃] *f* ascension; **Ascension** *f* Ascension Day

ascèse [asɛz] *f* asceticism

ascète [asɛt] *mf* ascetic

ascétique [asetik] *adj* ascetic

ascétisme [asetism] *m* asceticism

aseptique [aseptik] *adj* aseptic

Asie [azi] *f* Asia; **Asie Mineure** Asia Minor; **l'Asie** Asia; **l'Asie Mineure** Asia Minor asile [azil] m asylum, shelter, home

aspect [aspɛ], [aspɛk] m aspect

asperge [aspɛrʒ] f asparagus; des asperges asparagus (stalks and tips used as food)

asperger [aspɛrʒe] §38 tr to sprinkle

aspérité [asperite] f roughness; harshness; gruffness

aspersion [aspɛrsjɔ̃] f sprinkling

asphalte [asfalt] m asphalt

asphyxier [asfiksje] tr to asphyxiate || ref to be asphyxiated

aspic [aspik] m asp

aspi·rant [aspirɑ̃] -rante [rɑ̃t] adj aspirant, aspiring; suction (pump) || mf candidate (for a degree) || m midshipman

aspirateur [aspiratœr] m vacuum cleaner; aspirateur de buée kitchen fan

aspi·ré -rée [aspire] adj & m (phonet) aspirate

aspirer [aspire] tr to inhale; to suck in || intr—aspirer à to aspire to

aspirine [aspirin] f aspirin

assagir [asaʒir] tr to make wiser || ref to become wiser

assail·lant [asajɑ̃] assail-lante [asajɑ̃t] adj attacking || mf assailant

assaillir [asajir] §69 tr to assail, to assault

assainir [asenir] tr to purify, to clean up; to drain (a swamp)

assainissement [asenismɑ̃] m purification; draining

assaisonnement [asezɔnmɑ̃] m seasoning

assaisonner [asezɔne] tr to season, to flavor

assas·sin [asasɛ̃] assas·sine [asasin] adj murderous || m assassin

assassinat [asasina] m assassination

assassiner [asasine] tr to assassinate; (coll) to bore to death

assaut [aso] m assault

assèchement [asɛʃmɑ̃] m drainage, drying; dryness

assécher [aseʃe] §10 tr to drain, to dry up

assemblage [asɑ̃blaʒ] m assemblage; assembling (e.g., of printed pages); (woodworking) joint, joining

assemblée [asɑ̃ble] f assembly, meeting

assembler [asɑ̃ble] tr to assemble || ref to assemble, convene, meet

assener [asne] §2 tr to land (a blow)

assentiment [asɑ̃timɑ̃] m assent, consent

asseoir [aswar] §5 tr to seat, sit, place; to base (an opinion) || ref to sit down

assermen·té -tée [asɛrmɑ̃te] adj under oath

assertion [asɛrsjɔ̃] f assertion

asser·vi -vie [asɛrvi] adj subservient

asservir [asɛrvir] tr to enslave; to subdue (e.g., passions) || ref to submit (to convention; to tyranny)

asservissement [asɛrvismɑ̃] m enslavement; subservience

assesseur [asesœr] adj & m assistant; associate (judge)

assez [ase] adv enough; fairly, rather; assez de enough; en voilà assez!

that's enough!, cut it out! || interj enough!, stop!

assi·du -due [asidy] adj assiduous; attentive

assidûment [asidymɑ̃] adv assiduously

assié·geant [asjeʒɑ̃] -geante [ʒɑ̃t] adj besieging || mf besieger

assiéger [asjeʒe] §1 tr to besiege

assiette [asjɛt] f plate, dish; plateful; seat (of a rider on horseback); position, condition; assiette anglaise, assiette de viandes froides cold cuts; assiette au beurre (fig) gravy train; assiette creuse soup plate

assignation [asiɲasjɔ̃] f assignation; subpoena, summons

assi·gné -gnée [asiɲe] mf appointee; assigné à résidence permanent appointee; assigné intérim temporary appointee

assigner [asiɲe] tr to assign, allot; to fix (a date); to subpoena, summon

assimilable [asimilabl] adj assimilable; comparable

assimilation [asimilasjɔ̃] f assimilation

assimiler [asimile] tr to assimilate; to compare; to identify with || ref to assimilate

as·sis [asi] as·sise [asiz] adj seated, sitting; firmly established || f foundation; stratum; assises assizes

assistance [asistɑ̃s] f assistance; audience, persons present; presence; assistance judiciaire public defender; assistance publique welfare department; assistance sociale social service

assis·tant [asistɑ̃] -tante [tɑ̃t] adj assistant || mf assistant; bystander, spectator; assistante sociale public health nurse

assister [asiste] tr to assist, help || intr —assister à to attend, be present at

association [asɔsjasjɔ̃] f association; (sports) soccer; association des spectateurs theater club

asso·cié -ciée [asɔsje] adj & mf associate

associer [asɔsje] tr to associate || ref to go into partnership

assoif·fé -fée [aswafe] adj thirsty

assolement [asɔlmɑ̃] m rotation (of crops)

assombrir [asɔ̃brir] tr & ref to darken

assom·mant [asɔmɑ̃] assom·mante [asɔmɑ̃t] adj (coll) boring, fatiguing

assommer [asɔme] tr to kill with a heavy blow; to beat up; to stun; (coll) to heckle; (coll) to bore

assommoir [asɔmwar] m bludgeon; (coll) gin mill, dive, clip joint

Assomption [asɔ̃psjɔ̃] f Assumption

assonance [asɔnɑ̃s] f assonance

assor·ti -tie [asɔrti] adj assorted (e.g., cakes); well-matched (couple); stocked, supplied (store); to match, e.g., une cravate assortie a necktie to match

assortiment [asɔrtimɑ̃] m assortment; matching (of colors); set (of dishes); platter (of cold cuts)

assortir [asɔrtir] tr to assort, match;

to stock || *ref* to match, harmonize; **s'assortir de** to be accompanied with

assoupir [asupir] *tr* to make drowsy, to lull; to deaden (*pain*) || *ref* to doze off; to lessen (*with time*)

assoupissement [asupismɑ̃] *m* drowsiness; lethargy

assouplir [asuplir] *tr* to make supple, flexible; to break in (*a horse*) || *ref* to become supple, manageable

assouplissement [asuplismɑ̃] *m* suppleness, flexibility; limbering up; relaxation (*of a rule*)

assourdir [asurdir] *tr* to deafen; to tone down, muffle

assouvir [asuvir] *tr* to assuage, appease, satiate; to satisfy (*e.g., a thirst for vengeance*)

assouvissement [asuvismɑ̃] *m* assuagement, appeasement, satisfying

assujet·ti -tie [asyʒeti] *adj* fastened, subject, liable || *mf* taxpayer; contributor (*e.g., to social security*)

assujettir [asyʒetir] *tr* to subjugate; to subject; to fasten, secure || *ref* to submit

assujettis·sant [asyʒetisɑ̃] **assujettis·sante** [asyʒetisɑ̃t] *adj* demanding

assujettissement [asyʒetismɑ̃] *m* subjugation, subduing; submission (*to a stronger force*); fastening, securing

assumer [asyme] *tr* to assume, take upon oneself

assurance [asyrɑ̃s] *f* assurance; insurance; **assurances sociales** social security

assu·ré -rée [asyre] *adj* assured, satisfied; insured || *mf* insured

assurément [asyremɑ̃] *adv* assuredly

assurer [asyre] *tr* to assure; to secure; to insure || *ref* to be assured, to make sure; to be insured

astate [astat] *m* astatine

aster [aster] *m* (bot) aster

astérie [asteri] *f* starfish

astérisque [asterisk] *m* asterisk

asthénie [asteni] *f* debility

asthme [asm] *m* asthma

asticot [astiko] *m* maggot

astiquer [astike] *tr* to polish

as·tral -trale [astral] *adj* (*pl* -traux [tro]) astral

astre [astrə] *m* star, heavenly body; leading light; **astre de la nuit** moon; **astre du jour** sun

astreindre [astrɛ̃dr] §50 *tr* to force, compel, subject || *ref* to force oneself; to be subjected

astrologie [astrɔlɔʒi] *f* astrology

astrologue [astrɔlɔg] *m* astrologer

astronaute [astrɔnot] *mf* astronaut

astronautique [astrɔnotik] *f* astronautics

astronef [astrɔnef] *m* spaceship

astronome [astrɔnɔm] *mf* astronomer

astronomie [astrɔnɔmi] *f* astronomy

astronomique [astrɔnɔmik] *adj* astronomical

astuce [astys] *f* slyness, guile; tricks (*of a trade*)

astu·cieux [astysjø] **-cieuse** [sjøz] *adj* astute, crafty

atelier [atəlje] *m* studio; workshop

atermoiement [atermwamɑ̃] *m* procrastination; extension of a loan

athée [ate] *adj* atheistic || *mf* atheist

athéisme [ateism] *m* atheism

Athènes [aten] *f* Athens

athlète [atlɛt] *mf* athlete

athlétique [atletik] *adj* athletic

athlétisme [atletism] *m* athletics

Atlantique [atlɑ̃tik] *adj & m* Atlantic || *(cap) m* Atlantic

atlas [atlɑs] *m* atlas || *(cap) m* Atlas

atmosphère [atmɔsfɛr] *f* atmosphere

atome [atom] *m* atom

atomique [atomik] *adj* atomic

atomi·sé -sée [atomize] *adj* afflicted with radiation sickness

atomiser [atomize] *tr* to atomize

atone [atɔn] *adj* dull, expressionless; drab (*life*); (phonet) unaccented

atours [atur] *mpl* finery

atout [atu] *m* trump; **sans atout** no-trump

atrabilaire [atrabilɛr] *adj & mf* hypochondriac

âtre [ɑtr] *m* hearth

atroce [atrɔs] *adj* atrocious

atrocité [atrɔsite] *f* atrocity

atrophie [atrɔfi] *f* atrophy

atrophier [atrɔfje] *tr & ref* to atrophy

atta·chant [ata/ɑ̃] **-chante** [ʃɑ̃t] *adj* appealing, attractive

attache [ataʃ] *f* attachment, tie; paper clip; (anat) joint; **attache parisienne** paper clip

attachement [ataʃmɑ̃] *m* attachment

attacher [ataʃe] *tr* to attach; to tie up || *intr* (culin) to stick || *ref* to be fastened, tied; **s'attacher à** to stick to; to become devoted to

attaque [atak] *f* attack; (pathol) stroke; **attaque brusque** or **attaque brusquée** surprise attack; **attaque de nerfs** case of nerves

attaquer [atake] *tr & intr* to attack || *ref*—**s'attaquer à** to attack

attar·dé -dée [atarde] *adj* retarded; behind the times; belated, delayed || *mf* mentally retarded person; lover of the past

attarder [atarde] *tr* to delay, retard || *ref* to be delayed; to stay, remain

atteindre [atɛ̃dr] §50 *tr* to attain; to reach || *intr*—**atteindre à** to attain; to reach; to attain to

at·teint [atɛ̃] **at·teinte** [atɛ̃t] *adj* stricken || *f* reaching; injury; harm; **hors d'atteinte** out of reach; **porter atteinte à** to endanger; **premières atteintes** first signs (*of illness*)

attelage [atlaʒ] *m* harnessing; coupling

atteler [atle] §34 *tr* to harness; to hitch; to couple (*cars on a railroad*) || *ref*—**s'atteler à** (coll) to buckle down to

attelle [atel] *m* splint; **attelles** hames

atte·nant [atnɑ̃] **-nante** [nɑ̃t] *adj* adjoining

attendre [atɑ̃dr] *tr* to wait for, await; to expect || *intr* to wait || *ref*—**s'attendre à** to expect; to rely on; **s'attendre à** + *inf* to expect to + *inf*; **s'attendre à ce que** + *subj* to expect (*s.o.*) to + *inf*, e.g., **il s'attend à ce que je lui raconte toute l'affaire** he expects me to tell him the whole story; **s'y attendre** to expect it or them

attendrir [atɑ̃drir] *tr* to tenderize; to soften || *ref* to become tender; to be deeply touched or moved

attendrissement [atɑ̃drismɑ̃] *m* softening; compassion

atten·du -due [atɑ̃dy] *adj* expected || **attendus** *mpl* (law) grounds || *adv*—**attendu que** whereas, inasmuch as || **attendu** *prep* in view of

attentat [atɑ̃ta] *m* attempt, assault; outrage (*to decency*); offense (*against the state*)

attente [atɑ̃t] *f* wait; expectation

attenter [atɑ̃te] *intr*—**attenter à** to attempt (*e.g., s.o.'s life*); **attenter à ses jours** to attempt suicide

atten·tif -tive [atɑ̃tif] (tiv] *adj* attentive

attention [atɑ̃sjɔ̃] *f* attention; **attentions** attention, care, consideration || *interj* attention!, be careful!

attention·né -née [atɑ̃sjɔne] *adj* considerate

atténuation [atenɥasjɔ̃] *f* attenuation

atténuer [atenɥe] *tr* to subdue, soften (*color; pain; passions*); to attenuate (*words; bacteria*); to extenuate (*a fault*) || *ref* to soften; to lessen

atterrer [atere] *tr* to dismay

atterrir [aterir] *intr* (*aux:* AVOIR *or* ÊTRE) to land

atterrissage [aterisaʒ] *m* landing; **atterrissage forcé** forced landing; **atterrissage sur le ventre** pancake landing

attestation [atestasjɔ̃] *f* attestation; **attestation d'études** transcript

attester [ateste] *tr* to attest, to attest to; **attester qn de q.ch.** to call s.o. to witness to s.th.

attiédir [atjedir] *tr & ref* to cool off; to warm up

attifer [atife] *tr & ref* to spruce up

attirail [atiraj] *m* gear, tackle, outfit; (coll) paraphernalia

attirance [atirɑ̃s] *f* attraction, lure, attractiveness

atti·rant -rante [atirɑ̃] (rɑ̃t] *adj* appealing, attractive

attirer [atire] *tr* to attract || *ref* to be attracted; to attract each other; to call forth (*criticism*)

attiser [atize] *tr* to stir, stir up, to poke

atti·tré -trée [atitre] *adj* appointed; regular (*dealer*)

attitude [atityd] *f* attitude

attrac·tif -tive [atraktif] (tiv] *adj* attractive (*force*)

attraction [atraksjɔ̃] *f* attraction; les **attractions** vaudeville

attrait [atre] *m* attraction, attractiveness, appeal; **attraits** charms

attrape [atrap] *f* trap; (coll) trick, joke

attrape-mouche [atrapmuʃ] *m* (*pl* **-mouche** *or* **-mouches**) flypaper; Venus's-flytrap

attrape-nigaud [atrapnigo] *m* (*pl* **-nigauds**) booby trap

attraper [atrape] *tr* to catch; to snare,

trap; to trick || *ref* to trick each other; to hang on

attrayant [atrejɑ̃] **attrayante** [atrejɑ̃t] *adj* attractive

attribuer [atribɥe] *tr* to ascribe, attribute; to assign (*a share*) || *ref* to claim, assume

attribut [atriby] *m* attribute; predicate

attribu·tif [atribytif] **-tive** [tiv] *adj* (gram) predicative

attribution [atribysjɔ̃] *f* attribution; assignment, assignation

atris·té -tée [atriste] *adj* sorrowful

attrister [atriste] *tr* to sadden || *ref* to become sad

attrition [atrisjɔ̃] *f* attrition

attroupement [atrupmɑ̃] *m* mob

attrouper [atrupe] *tr* to bring together in a mob || *ref* to flock together in a mob

au [o] §77

aubaine [oben] *f* windfall, godsend, bonanza

aube [ob] *f* dawn

aubépine [obepin] *f* hawthorn

auberge [oberʒ] *f* inn; **auberge de la jeunesse** youth hostel

aubergine [oberʒin] *f* eggplant

auburn [obœrn] *adj invar* auburn

au·cun [okœ̃] **-cune** [kyn] *adj*—**aucun . . . ne** *or* **ne . . . aucun** §90 no, none, not any || *pron indef*—**aucun ne** §90B no one, nobody; **d'aucuns** some, some people

aucunement [okynmɑ̃] §90 *adv*—**ne . . . aucunement** not at all, by no means

audace [odas] *f* audacity

auda·cieux [odasjø] **-cieuse** [sjøz] *adj* audacious

au-deçà [odəsa] *adv* (obs) on this side; **au-deçà de** (obs) on this side of

au-dedans [odədɑ̃] *adv* inside; **au-dedans de** inside, inside of

au-dehors [odəɔr] *adv* outside; **au-dehors de** outside, outside of

au-delà [odəla] *m*—**l'au-delà** the beyond || *adv* beyond; **au-delà de** beyond

au-dessous [odəsu] *adv* below; **au-dessous de** under

au-dessus [odəsy] *adv* above; **au-dessus de** above

au-devant [odəvɑ̃] *adv*—**aller au devant de** to go to meet; to anticipate (*s.o.'s wishes*); to court (*defeat*)

audience [odjɑ̃s] *f* audience

audio-fréquence [odjofrekɑ̃s] *f* audio frequency

audiomètre [odjometr] *m* audiometer

audi·teur [oditœr] **-trice** [tris] *mf* listener; auditor (*in class*); **auditeur libre** auditor (*in class*)

audi·tif [oditif] **-tive** [tiv] *adj* auditory

audition [odisjɔ̃] *f* audition; public hearing; musical recital

auditionner [odisjɔne] *tr & intr* to audition

auditoire [oditwar] *m* audience; courtroom

auditorium [oditɔrjɔm] *m* auditorium; concert hall; projection room

auge [oʒ] *f* trough

augmentation [ɔgmɑ̃tɑsjɔ̃] *f* augmentation; raise (*in salary*)

augmenter [ɔgmɑ̃te] *tr* to augment; to increase or supplement (*income*); to raise (*prices*); to raise the salary of (*an employee*) || *intr* to augment, increase; **augmenter de** to increase by (*a stated amount*)

augure [ɔgyr] *m* augur; augury

augurer [ɔgyre] *tr & intr* to augur

auguste [ɔgyst] *adj* august

aujourd'hui [oʒurdɥi], [oʒɔrdɥi] *m & adv* today; **d'aujourd'hui en huit** a week from today; **d'aujourd'hui en quinze** two weeks from today

aumône [omon] *f* alms; **faire l'aumône** to give alms; **faire l'aumône de** (fig) to hand out

aumônier [omonje] *m* chaplain

aune [on] *m* alder || *f* ell

auparavant [oparavɑ̃] *adv* before, previously

auprès [opre] *adv* close by, in the neighborhood; **auprès de** near, close to; at the side of; to; **auprès de** at the side of; to (*a king, a government*); with; compared with

auquel [okel] (*pl* **auxquels**) §78

auréole [ɔreɔl] *f* aureole, halo

auréomycine [ɔreɔmisin] *f* aureomycin

auriculaire [ɔrikyler] *adj* firsthand (*witness*); auricular (*confession*) || *m* little finger

auricule [ɔrikyl] *f* auricle

aurifier [ɔrifje] *tr* to fill (*a tooth*) with gold

aurore [ɔrɔr] *f* aurora, dawn

ausculter [ɔskylte] *tr* to auscultate

auspice [ɔspis] *m* omen; **sous les auspices de** under the auspices of

aussi [osi] *adv* also, too; therefore, and so; so; **aussi ... que** as ... as

aussitôt [osito] *adv* right away, immediately; **aussitôt dit, aussitôt fait** no sooner said than done; **aussitôt que** as soon as

austère [ɔster] *adj* austere

Australie [ɔstrali] *f* Australia; **l'Australie** Australia

austra·lien [ɔstraljɛ̃] -**lienne** [ljɛn] *adj* Australian || (*cap*) *mf* Australian

autant [otɑ̃] *adv* as much, as many; as far, as long; **autant de** so many; **autant que** as much as, as far as; **d'autant** by so much; **d'autant plus** all the more; **d'autant plus (or moins) ... que ... plus (or moins)** all the more (*or* less) ... as (*or* in proportion as) ... more (*or* less); **d'autant que** inasmuch as

autel [otel], [ɔtel] *m* altar

auteur [otœr] *adj*—**une femme auteur** an authoress || *m* author

authentifier [otɑ̃tifje] *tr* to authenticate

authentique [otɑ̃tik] *adj* authentic; genuine (*antique*); notarized

authentiquer [otɑ̃tike] *tr* to notarize

auto [oto], [ɔto] *f* auto

auto-allumage [otoalymaʒ] *m* preignition

autobiographie [otɔbjɔgrafi] *f* autobiography

auto-buffet [otobyfe] *m* drive-in; curb service

autobus [otobys] *m* bus, city bus

autocar [otokar] *m* interurban bus

autochenille [otoʃənij] *f* caterpillar (*tractor*)

autochtone [otokton] *adj & mf* native

autoclave [otoklav] *m* pressure cooker; autoclave, sterilizer

autocopie [otokɔpi] *f* duplicating, multicopying; duplicated copy

autocopier [otokɔpje] *tr* to run off, to duplicate, to ditto

auto-couchette [otokuʃet] *f*—**en auto-couchette** piggyback

autocrate [otokrat] *mf* autocrat

autocratique [otokratik] *adj* autocratic

autocritique [otokritik] *f* self-criticism

autocuiseur [otokɥizœr] *m* pressure cooker

autodétermination [otodeterminasjɔ̃] *f* self-determination

autodidacte [otodidakt] *adj* self-taught || *mf* self-taught person

autodrome [otodrom] *m* race track; test strip

auto-école [otoekɔl] *f* (*pl* -**écoles**) driving school

autogare [otogar] *f* bus station

autographe [otograf] *adj & m* autograph

autographie [otografi] *f* multicopying

autographier [otografje] *tr* to duplicate

autogreffe [otogref] *f* skin grafting

auto-grue [otogry] *f* (*pl* -**grues**) tow truck

autoguidage [otogidaʒ] *m* automatic piloting

auto-intoxication [otoɛ̃tɔksikasjɔ̃] *f* autointoxication

automate [otomat] *m* automaton

automation [otomasjɔ̃] *f* automation

automatique [otomatik] *adj* automatic || *m* dial telephone

automatisation [otomatizasjɔ̃] *f* automation

automatiser [otomatize] *tr* to automate

automitrailleuse [otomitrajøz] *f* armored car mounting machine guns

automn·al -**nale** [otomnal] *adj* (*pl* -**naux** [no]) autumnal

automne [oton], [otɔn] *m* fall, autumn; **à l'automne, en automne** in the fall

automobile [otomɔbil], [otɔmɔbil] *adj* automotive || *f* automobile

automobilisme [otomɔbilism] *m* driving, motoring

automobiliste [otomɔbilist] *mf* motorist

automo·teur [otomɔtœr] -**trice** [tris] *adj* self-propelling, automatic || *m* self-propelled river barge || *f* rail car

autonome [otonom] *adj* autonomous, independent

autonomie [otonomi] *f* autonomy; cruising radius, range (*of ship, plane, or tank*)

autoplastie [otoplasti] *f* plastic surgery

autoportrait [otopɔrtre] *m* self-portrait

auto-propul·sé -**sée** [otopropylse] *adj* self-propelled

autopsie [otopsi] *f* autopsy

autopsier [otopsje] *tr* to perform an autopsy on

autorail [otoraj] m rail car

autorisation [otorizasjɔ̃] f authorization

autoriser [otorize] tr to authorize || ref —s'autoriser de to take as authority, to base one's opinion on

autoritaire [otoriter] adj authoritarian, bossy

autorité [otorite] f authority

autoroute [otorut] f superhighway

auto-stop [otostop] m hitchhiking; faire de l'auto-stop to hitchhike

auto-stop·peur [otostopœr] -stop·peuse [stopøz] mf (pl -stop·peurs -stop·peuses) hitchhiker

autostrade [otostrad] f superhighway

autour [otur] m goshawk || adv around; autour de around; about

autre [otr] adj indef other; autre chose (coll) something else; nous autres we, e.g., nous autres Américains we Americans; vous autres you || pron indef other; d'autres others; j'en ai vu bien d'autres I have seen worse than that; un autre another

autrefois [otrəfwa] adv formerly, of old; d'autrefois of yore

autrement [otrəmɑ̃] adv otherwise

Autriche [otriʃ] f Austria; l'Autriche Austria

autri·chien [otriʃjɛ̃] -chienne [ʃjen] adj Austrian || (cap) mf Austrian

autruche [otryʃ] f ostrich

autrui [otrɥi] pron indef others

auvent [ovɑ̃] m canopy (over door); flap (of tent)

aux [o] §77

auxiliaire [oksiljer] adj auxiliary, standby; ancillary || m (gram) auxiliary || f noncombatant unit

aux·quels ·quelles [okel] §78

aval [aval] m lower waters; en aval downstream; en aval de below || m (pl avals) endorsement

avalanche [avalɑ̃ʃ] f avalanche

avaler [avale] tr to swallow || intr to go downstream

ava·leur [avalœr] -leuse [løz] mf swallower; avaleur de sabres sword swallower

avaliser [avalize] tr to endorse

avance [avɑ̃s] f advance; en avance fast (clock)

avan·cé -cée [avɑ̃se] adj advanced; overripe; tainted (meat)

avancement [avɑ̃smɑ̃] m advancement

avancer [avɑ̃se] §51 tr, intr, & ref to advance

avanie [avani] f snub, insult; essuyer une avanie to swallow an affront

avant [avɑ̃] adj invar front || m front; (aer) nose; (naut) bow; d'avant previous; en avant forward; en avant de in front of, ahead of || adv before; avant de (with inf) before; avant que before; bien (or très) avant late into; far into; deep into; plus avant farther on || prep before; avant Jésus-Christ (av. J.-C.) before Christ (B.C.)

avantage [avɑ̃taʒ] m advantage; (tennis) add; avantages en nature payment in kind

avanta·geux [avɑ̃taʒø] -geuse [ʒøz] adj advantageous; bargain (price); becoming (e.g., hairdo); conceited (manner)

avant-bras [avɑ̃bra] m invar forearm

avant-cour [avɑ̃kur] f (pl -cours) front yard

avant-coureur [avɑ̃kurœr] (pl -coureurs) adj masc presaging (signs) || m forerunner, precursor, harbinger

avant-goût [avɑ̃gu] m (pl -goûts) foretaste

avant-guerre [avɑ̃ger] m & f (pl -guerres) prewar period

avant-hier [avɑ̃tjer], [avɑ̃jer] adv & m the day before yesterday

avant-port [avɑ̃por] m (pl -ports) outer harbor

avant-poste [avɑ̃post] m (pl -postes) outpost; avant-postes front lines

avant-première [avɑ̃prəmjer] f (pl -premières) review (of a play); premiere (for the drama critics); preview

avant-projet [avɑ̃prɔʒe] m (pl -projets) rough draft; draft (of a law)

avant-propos [avɑ̃prɔpo] m invar foreword

avant-scène [avɑ̃sen] f (pl -scènes) forestage, proscenium

avant-toit [avɑ̃twa] m (pl -toits) eave

avant-train [avɑ̃trɛ̃] m (pl -trains) front end, front assembly (of vehicle)

avant-veille [avɑ̃vej] f (pl -veilles) two days before

avare [avar] adj avaricious, miserly; saving, economical || mf miser

avarice [avaris] f avarice

avari·cieux [avarisjø] -cieuse [sjøz] adj avaricious

avarie [avari] f damage; breakdown; spoilage; (naut) average

avarier [avarje] tr to damage; to spoil || ref to spoil

avatar [avatar] m avatar; avatars vicissitudes

avec [avek] adv (coll) with it; (coll) along, with me, etc. || prep with

aveline [avlin] f filbert

ave·nant [avnɑ̃] -nante [nɑ̃t] adj gracious, charming; à l'avenant keeping, to match; à l'avenant de in accord with || m (ins) endorsement

avènement [avenmɑ̃] m Advent; accession (to the throne)

avenir [avnir] m future; à l'avenir in the future

Avent [avɑ̃] m Advent

aventure [avɑ̃tyr] f adventure; à l'aventure at random; aimlessly; d'aventure by chance; la bonne aventure fortunetelling; par aventure by chance

aventurer [avɑ̃tyre] tr to venture || ref to take a chance; s'aventurer à to venture to

aventu·reux [avɑ̃tyrø] -reuse [røz] adj adventurous

aventurier [avɑ̃tyrje] m adventurer

aventurière [avɑ̃tyrjer] f adventuress

avenue [avny] f avenue

avé·ré -rée [avere] adj established, authenticated

avérer [avere] §10 tr to aver || ref to prove to be (e.g., difficult)

avers [aver] *m* heads (*of coin*), face (*of medal*)

averse [avers] *f* shower

aversion [aversjɔ̃] *f* aversion

avertir [avertir] *tr* to warn; **avertir qn de** + *inf* to warn s.o. to + *inf*

avertissement [avertismɑ̃] *m* warning; notification; foreword

avertisseur [avertisœr] *adj masc* warning ‖ *m* alarm; (aut) horn; (theat) callboy; **avertisseur d'incendie** fire alarm

a·veu [avø] *m* (*pl* **-veux**) avowal, confession; consent; **sans aveu** unscrupulous

aveu·glant [avœglɑ̃] **-glante** [glɑ̃t] *adj* blinding

aveugle [avœgl] *adj* blind ‖ *mf* blind person; **en aveugle** without thinking

aveuglement [avœgləmɑ̃] *m* (fig) blindness

aveuglément [avœglemɑ̃] *adv* blindly

aveugler [avœgle] *tr* to blind; to dazzle; to stop up, to plug; to board up (*a window*) ‖ *ref*—**s'aveugler sur** to shut one's eyes to

aveuglette [avœglet] *adv*—**à l'aveuglette** blindly

aveulir [avølir] *tr* to enervate, deaden ‖ *ref* to become limp, enervated

aveulissement [avølismɑ̃] *m* enervation

aviateur [avjatœr] *m* aviator

aviation [avjasjɔ̃] *f* aviation

aviatrice [avjatris] *f* aviatrix

avide [avid] *adj* avid, eager; greedy; voracious; **avide de** avid for

avidité [avidite] *f* avidity, eagerness; greed; voracity

avilir [avilir] *tr* to debase, dishonor; (com) to lower the price of ‖ *ref* to debase oneself; (com) to deteriorate

avilis·sant [avilisɑ̃] **avilis·sante** [avilisɑ̃t] *adj* debasing

avilissement [avilismɑ̃] *m* debasement; (com) depreciation

avi·né -née [avine] *adj* drunk

aviner [avine] *tr* to soak (*a new barrel*) with wine ‖ *ref* (coll) to booze

avion [avjɔ̃] *m* airplane; **avion à réaction** jet; **avion de chasse** fighter plane; **avion long-courrier** long-range plane; **en avion** by plane; **par avion** air mail

avion-cargo [avjɔ̃kargo] *m* (*pl* **avions-cargos**) cargo liner, freighter

avion-taxi [avjɔ̃taksi] *m* (*pl* **avions-taxis**) taxiplane

aviron [avirɔ̃] *m* oar; **aviron de couple** scull

avis [avi] *m* opinion; advice; notice, warning; decision; **à mon avis** in my opinion; **avis au lecteur** note to the reader; **changer d'avis** to change one's mind

avi·sé -sée [avize] *adj* prudent, shrewd; **bien avisé** well-advised

aviser [avize] *tr* to glimpse, descry; to advise, inform, warn ‖ *intr* to decide; **aviser à** to think of, look into; to deal with ‖ *ref*—**s'aviser de** to contrive, to think up; to be on the look-out for; **s'aviser de** + *inf* to take it into one's head to + *inf*

aviso [avizo] *m* dispatch boat, sloop

avivage [avivaʒ] *m* brightening; polishing

aviver [avive] *tr* to revive, to stir up (*fire; passions*); to brighten (*colors*); (med & fig) to open (*a wound*)

av. J.-C. *abbr* (**avant Jésus-Christ**) B.C.

avo·cat [avɔka] **-cate** [kat] *mf* lawyer; advocate; barrister (Brit); **avocat du diable** devil's advocate ‖ *m* avocado

avoine [avwan] *f* oats

avoir [avwar] *m* wealth; credit side (*of ledger*) ‖ §6 *tr* to have; to get; **avoir ... ans** to be ... years old, e.g., **mon fils a dix ans** my son is ten years old; **avoir beau** + *inf* to be useless for (*s.o.*) to + *inf*, e.g., **j'ai beau travailler** it is useless for me to work; for expressions like **avoir froid** to be cold, **avoir raison** to be right, see the noun ‖ *intr*—**avoir à** to have to; **en avoir à** or **contre** to be angry with ‖ *impers*—**il y a** there is, there are, e.g., **il n'y a pas d'espoir** there is no hope ‖ *aux* to have, e.g., **j'ai couru trop vite** I have run too fast

avoisiner [avwazine] *tr* to neighbor, to be near

avortement [avɔrtəmɑ̃] *m* abortion; miscarriage

avorter [avɔrte] *intr* to abort; to miscarry

avorton [avɔrtɔ̃] *m* runt; (biol) stunt

avoué [avwe] *m* lawyer (*doing notarial work*); solicitor (Brit)

avouer [avwe] *tr* to avow, to admit; to claim, to acknowledge authorship of ‖ *ref* to be admitted; **s'avouer vaincu** to admit defeat

avril [avril] *m* April

axe [aks] *m* axis

axer [akse] *tr* to set on an axis; to orient

axiomatique [aksjɔmatik] *adj* axiomatic

axiome [aksjom] *m* axiom

axonge [aksɔ̃ʒ] *f* lard

ayant-droit [ɛjɑ̃drwa] *m* (*pl* **ayants-droit**) claimant; beneficiary

azalée [azale] *f* azalea

azimut or **azimuth** [azimyt] *m* azimuth

azote [azɔt] *m* nitrogen

azo·té -tée [azɔte] *adj* nitrogenous

Aztèques [aztɛk] *mpl* Aztecs

azur [azyr] *adj & m* azure

azyme [azim] *adj* unleavened ‖ *m* unleavened bread

B, b [be] *m invar* second letter of the French alphabet

baba [baba] *adj* (coll) flabbergasted, wide-eyed ‖ *m* baba

babeurre [babœr] *m* buttermilk

babil [babil], [babi] *m* babble, chatter; **babil enfantin** baby talk

babillage [babijaȝ] *m* babbling

babil·lard [babijar] **babil·larde** [babijard] *adj* babbling ‖ *mf* babbler ‖ *f* (slang) letter

babiller [babije] *intr* to babble, to chatter

babine [babin] *f* chop (*mouth*); **s'essuyer or se lécher les babines** to lick one's chops

babiole [babjɔl] *f* (coll) bauble

bâbord [babɔr] *m* (naut) port, portside; **à bâbord** port; **bâbord armures** port sail

babouche [babuʃ] *f* babouche, slipper

babouin [babwɛ̃] *m* baboon; pimple on the lips; brat

bac [bak] *m* ferryboat; tub, vat; box, bin; tray (*for ice cubes*); drawer (*of refrigerator*); case (*of battery*); (slang) baccalaureate

baccalauréat [bakalɔrea] *m* baccalaureate, bachelor's degree

bacchanale [bakanal] *f* bacchanal

bâche [baʃ] *f* tarpaulin; hot-water tank

bache·lier [baʃəlje] **-lière** [ljer] *mf* bachelor (*holder of degree*) ‖ *m* (hist) bachelor (*young knight*)

bâcher [baʃe] *tr* to cover with a tarpaulin

bachique [baʃik] *adj* bacchanalian, bacchic; drinking (*song*)

bachot [baʃo] *m* dinghy, punt; (coll) baccalaureate

bachotage [baʃɔtaȝ] *m* (coll) cramming (*for an exam*)

bachoter [baʃɔte] *intr* (coll) to cram

bacille [basil] *m* bacillus

bâclage [baklaȝ] *m* blocking up (*of harbor*); (slang) botching (*of work*)

bâcle [bakl] *f* bolt (*of door*)

bâcler [bakle] *tr* to bolt (*a door*); to close up (*a harbor*); (coll) to botch, to hurry through carelessly

bâ·cleur [baklœr] **-cleuse** [kløz] *mf* (coll) botcher

bacon [bakɔ̃] *m* bacon

bactéricide [bakterisid] *adj* bactericidal ‖ *m* bactericide

bactérie [bakteri] *f* bacterium; **bactéries** bacteria

bactériologie [bakterjɔlɔȝi] *f* bacteriology

ba·daud [bado] **-daude** [dod] *mf* rubberneck, gawk, idler

badauder [badode] *intr* to stand and stare

badigeon [badiȝɔ̃] *m* whitewash

badigeonner [badiȝɔne] *tr* to whitewash; (med) to paint (*e.g., the throat*)

ba·din [badɛ̃] **-dine** [din] *adj* sprightly, playful, teasing ‖ *mf* tease ‖ *m* (aer) air-speed indicator ‖ *f* cane, switch

badinage [badinaȝ] *m* banter; **badinage amoureux** necking

badiner [badine] *intr* to joke, to tease; to trifle, to be flippant

badinerie [badinri] *f* teasing; childishness

bafouer [bafwe] *tr* to heckle, to humiliate

bafouiller [bafuje] *intr* (coll) to stammer, mumble, babble

bâfrer [bafre] *tr & intr* (slang) to guzzle

bagage [bagaȝ] *m* baggage; **bagages** baggage, luggage; **bagages non accompagnés** baggage sent on ahead; **menus bagages** hand luggage; **plier bagage** to pack one's bags; (coll) to scram; (coll) to kick the bucket

bagarre [bagar] *f* brawl, row, riot; **chercher la bagarre** (coll) to be looking for a fight

bagarrer [bagare] *intr & ref* to riot; (coll) to brawl, scrap, scuffle

bagar·reur [bagarœr] **bagar·reuse** [bagarøz] *mf* (coll) rioter, brawler

bagatelle [bagatel] *f* trifle, bagatelle, frivolity ‖ *interj* nonsense!

bagnard [baɲar] *m* convict

bagne [baɲ] *m* penitentiary, penal colony; (nav) prison ship; (slang) sweatshop

bagnole [baɲɔl] *f* (slang) jalopy

bagou [bagu] *m* (coll) gift of gab

bague [bag] *f* ring; cigar band; (mach) collar, sleeve; **bague de fiançailles** engagement ring

baguenauder [bagnode] *intr* to waste time, to fool around ‖ *ref* (coll) to wander about

baguer [bage] *tr* to band (*a tree*); to baste (*cloth*)

baguette [baget] *f* stick, switch, rod; baton; long thin loaf of bread; chopstick; **baguette de fée** fairy wand; **baguettes de tambour** drumsticks; **mener qn à la baguette** (coll) to lead s.o. by the nose; **passer par les baguettes** to run the gauntlet

baguier [bagje] *m* jewel box

bahut [bay] *m* trunk, chest; cupboard; (slang) high school

bai baie [bɛ] *adj* bay (*horse*) ‖ *f* bay; berry; bayberry; bay window

baignade [bɛɲad] *f* bathing, swimming; swimming hole, bathing spot

baigner [beɲe] *tr* to bathe; to wash (*the coast*) ‖ *intr* to be immersed, to soak ‖ *ref* to bathe; to go bathing

bai·gneur [beɲœr] **-gneuse** [ɲøz] *mf* bather; vacationist at a spa or seaside resort; bathhouse attendant ‖ *m* doll

baignoire [beɲwar] *f* bathtub; (theat) orchestra box

bail [baj] *m* (*pl* **baux** [bo]) lease; **passer un bail** to sign a lease; **prendre à bail** to lease

bâillement [bajmɑ̃] *m* yawn

bâiller [baje] *tr*—**vous me la baillez belle** (coll) you're pulling my leg

bâiller [baje] *intr* to yawn; to be ajar, to be half open

bail·leur [bajœr] **bail·leresse** [bajɛres] *mf* lessor; **bailleur de fonds** lender

bailli [baji] *m* bailiff

bailliage [baja3] *m* bailiwick

bâillon [bajɔ̃] *m* gag, muzzle

bâillonner [bajone] *tr* to gag; (fig) to muzzle

bain [bɛ̃] *m* bath; **bain de soleil** sun bath; **bains** watering place, spa; bathing establishment; **être dans le bain** (coll) to be in hot water

baïonnette [bajonet] *f* bayonet

baiser [beze], [bɛze] *m* kiss || *tr* (vulgar) to have sex with; (archaic) to kiss

baisoter [bezote] *tr* (coll) to keep on kissing || *ref* (coll) to bill and coo

baisse [bes] *f* fall; **jouer à la baisse** (com) to bear the market

baissement [besmɑ̃] *m* lowering

baisser [bese] *m* lowering; **baisser du rideau** curtain fall || *tr* to lower; to take in (*sail*) || *intr* to fall, drop, sink || *ref* to bend, stoop

baissier [besje] *m* bear (*on the stock exchange*)

bajoue [ba3u] *f* jowl

bal [bal] *m* (*pl* **bals**) ball, dance; **bal travesti** fancy-dress ball

balade [balad] *f* stroll; **balade en auto** joy ride

balader [balade] *ref* to go for a stroll; **se balader en auto** to go joy-riding

bala·deur [baladœr] **-deuse** [døz] *adj* strolling || *mf* stroller || *m* gear || *f* cart (*of street vendor*); lamp with long cord

baladin [baladɛ̃] *m* mountebank, showman; oaf

balafre [balafr] *f* gash, scar

balafrer [balafre] *tr* to gash, to scar

balai [bale] *m* broom; **balai à laver** mop; **balai de sorcière** witches'-broom; **balai électrique** vacuum cleaner; **balai mécanique** carpet sweeper; **donner un coup de balai à** to make a clean sweep of (*s.th.*); to kick (*s.o.*) out

balai-éponge [baleepɔ̃3] *m* (*pl* **balais-éponges**) mop

balance [balɑ̃s] *f* balance; scales; **faire la balance de** (bk) to balance

balancement [balɑ̃smɑ̃] *m* swaying, teetering; (fig) indecision, wavering; (fig) harmony (*of phrase*)

balancer [balɑ̃se] §51 *tr* to balance; to move (*arms or legs*) in order to balance; to balance (*an account*); to weigh (*the pros and cons*); to swing, rock; (coll) to fire (*s.o.*) || *intr* to swing, rock; to hesitate, waver || *ref* to swing or to seesaw; to sway, rock; to ride (*at anchor*)

balancier [balɑ̃sje] *m* pendulum; balance wheel; pole (*of tightrope walker*)

balançoire [balɑ̃swar] *f* swing; seesaw, teeter-totter; (slang) nonsense

balayage [baleja3] *m* sweeping; (telv) scanning

balayer [baleje], [baleje] §49 *tr* to sweep, to sweep up; to sweep out; to scour (*the sea*); (telv) to scan

balayeur [balejœr] **balayeuse** [balejøz] *mf* sweeper, scavenger || *f* street-cleaning truck

balayures [balejyr] *fpl* sweepings

balbutiement [balbysimɑ̃] *m* stammering, mumbling; initial effort

balbutier [balbysje] *tr* to stammer out || *intr* to stammer, to mumble

balbuzard [balbyzar] *m* osprey, bald buzzard, sea eagle

balcon [balkɔ̃] *m* balcony; (theat) dress circle

baldaquin [baldakɛ̃] *m* canopy, tester

Baléares [balear] *fpl* Balearic Islands

baleine [balen] *f* right whale, whalebone whale; whalebone; rib (*of umbrella*); stay (*of a corset*)

baleinier [balenje] *m* whaling vessel

baleinière [balenjer] *f* whaleboat; lifeboat

balisage [baliza3] *m* (aer) ground lights; (naut) buoys

balise [baliz] *f* buoy, marker; ground light, beacon; landing signal

baliser [balize] *tr* to furnish with markers, buoys, landing lights, beacons, or radio signals

balistique [balistik] *adj* ballistic || *f* ballistics

baliverne [balivern] *f* nonsense, humbug

balkanique [balkanik] *adj* Balkan

ballade [balad] *f* ballade

bal·lant [balɑ̃] **bal·lante** [balɑ̃t] *adj* waving, swinging, dangling || *m* oscillation, shaking

balle [bal] *f* ball; bullet; hull, chaff; bale; (tennis) match point; **balle traçante** tracer bullet; **prendre** or **saisir la balle au bond** to seize time by the forelock

ballerine [balrin] *f* ballerina

ballet [bale] *m* ballet

ballon [balɔ̃] *m* balloon; ball; football, soccer ball; round-bottom flask; rounded mountaintop; **ballon d'essai** trial balloon

ballonner [balone] *tr*, *intr*, & *ref* to balloon

ballot [balo] *m* pack; bundle; (slang) blockhead, chump

ballottage [balota3] *m* tossing, shaking; second ballot

ballotter [balote] *tr* & *intr* to toss about

balnéaire [balneer] *adj* seaside

ba·lourd [balur] **-lourde** [lurd] *adj* awkward, lumpish || *mf* blockhead, bumpkin || *m* wobble

balte [balt] *adj* Baltic || (*cap*) *mf* Balt

Baltique [baltik] *f* Baltic (*sea*)

balustrade [balystrad] *f* balustrade, banisters

balustre [balystr] *m* baluster, banister

bal·zan [balzɑ̃] **-zane** [zan] *adj* white-footed (*horse*) || *f* white spot (*on horse's foot*)

bam·bin [bɑ̃bɛ̃] **-bine** [bin] *mf* (coll) babe

bambo·chard [bɑ̃bɔʃar] **-charde** [ʃard] *adj* (coll) carousing || *mf* (coll) carouser

bamboche [bãbɔʃ] *f* (slang) jag, bender
bambocher [bãbɔʃe] *intr* (coll) to carouse, to go on a spree
bambo·cheur [bãbɔʃœr] **-cheuse** [ʃøz] *adj* (coll) carousing || *mf* (coll) carouser
bambou [bãbu] *m* bamboo
ban [bã] *m* ban; cadenced applause; **ban de mariage** banns; **convoquer le ban et l'arrière-ban** to invite everyone and his brother; **mettre au ban** to banish, to ban
ba·nal -nale [banal] *adj* (*pl* **-nals -nales**) banal, trite, commonplace || *adj* (*pl* **-naux** [no] **-nales**) (archaic) common, public, in common
banaliser [banalize] *tr* to vulgarize, to make commonplace
banalité [banalite] *f* banality; triteness
banane [banan] *f* banana
bananier [bananje] *m* banana tree
banc [bã] *m* bench; shoal; school (*of fish*); pew (*reserved for church officials*); (hist) privy council; **être sur les bancs** to go to high school
bancaire [bãker] *adj* banking, of banks
ban·cal -cale [bãkal] *adj* (*pl* **-cals -cales**) bowlegged, bandy-legged
bandage [bãdaʒ] *m* bandage; bandaging; truss; tire (*of metal or rubber*)
bande [bãd] *f* band; movie film; recording tape; cushion (*in billiards*); wrapper (*of a newspaper*); **bande magnétique** recording tape; tape recording; **bande sonore** or **parlante** sound track; **donner de la bande** to heel, to list; **faire bande à part** to keep to oneself
ban·deau [bãdo] *m* (*pl* **-deaux**) blindfold; headband; bending (*of a bow*); **bandeau royal** diadem; **bandeaux** hair parted in the middle
bander [bãde] *tr* to band, to put a band on; to bandage; to blindfold; to bend (*a bow*); to put a tire on; to draw taut || *ref* to band together; to put up resistance
banderole [bãdrɔl] *f* pennant, streamer; strap (*of gun*)
bandière [bãdjer] *f* battle, e.g., **front de bandière** battle front
bandit [bãdi] *m* bandit ||
bandoulière [bãduljer] *f* shoulder strap, sling; **en bandoulière** slung over the shoulder
banlieue [bãljø] *f* suburbs; **de banlieue** suburban
banlieu·sard [bãljøzar] **-sarde** [zard] *mf* suburbanite (*especially of a Parisian suburb*)
banne [ban] *f* awning (*of store*)
ban·ni -nie [bani] *adj* banished, exiled || *mf* exile
bannière [banjer] *f* banner, flag
bannir [banir] *tr* to banish
bannissement [banismã] *m* banishment
banque [bãk] *f* bank; **banque des yeux** eye bank; **banque du sang** blood bank; **faire sauter la banque** to break the bank
banqueroute [bãkrut] *f* bankruptcy (*with blame for negligence or fraud*)

banquerou·tier [bãkrutje] **-tière** [tjer] *adj & mf* bankrupt (*with culpability*)
banquet [bãke] *m* banquet
banqueter [bãkte] §34 *intr* to banquet
banquette [bãket] *f* seat (*in a train, bus, automobile*); bunker (*of earth or sand*); bunker (*in a golf course*); **banquette arrière** back seat; **banquette de tir** (mil) emplacement for shooting; **jouer devant les banquettes** to play to an empty house
ban·quier [bãkje] **-quière** [kjer] *mf* banker
banquise [bãkiz] *f* pack ice
banquiste [bãkist] *m* charlatan, quack
baptême [batem] *m* baptism; christening; **baptême de la ligne, baptême des tropiques** or **du tropique** polliwog initiation
baptiser [batize] *tr* to baptize; to christen; (slang) to dilute (*wine*) with water
baptis·mal -male [batismal] *adj* (*pl* **-maux** [mo]) baptismal
baptistaire [batister] *adj* baptismal (*certificate*)
baptiste [batist] *mf* Baptist
baptistère [batister] *m* baptistery
baquet [bake] *m* wooden tub, bucket; (aut) bucket seat
bar [bar] *m* bar; (ichth) bass, perch
baragouin [baragwɛ̃] *m* (slang) gibberish
baragouiner [baragwine] *tr* (coll) to murder (*a language*); (coll) to stumble through (*a speech*) || *intr* (coll) to jabber
baraque [barak] *f* booth, stall; shanty, hovel
baraterie [baratri] *f* barratry
baratin [baratɛ̃] *m* (slang) blah-blah, hokum
baratte [barat] *f* churn
baratter [barate] *tr* to churn
Barbade [barbad] *f* Barbados; **la Barbade** Barbados
barbare [barbar] *adj* barbarous, barbaric, savage || *mf* barbarian
barbaresque [barbaresk] *adj* of Barbary
barbarie [barbari] *f* barbarity, barbarism || (*cap*) *f* Barbary
barbarisme [barbarism] *m* barbarism (*in speech or writing*)
barbe [barb] *f* beard; bristle; whiskers (*of an animal*); barbel; **barbes** vane (*of a feather*); deckle edge; **faire q.ch. à la barbe de qn** to do s.th. right under the nose of s.o.; **rire dans sa barbe** to laugh up one's sleeve; **se faire la barbe** to shave || *interj*—**la barbe!** shut up!
bar·beau [barbo] *m* (*pl* **-beaux**) cornflower; (ichth) barbel; (slang) pimp
barbe·lé -lée [barbale] *adj* barbed || **barbelés** *mpl* barbed wire
bar·bet [barbe] **-bette** [bet] *mf* water spaniel
barbiche [barbiʃ] *f* goatee
barbier [barbje] *m* barber
barbillon [barbijɔ̃] *m* barb
barbiturique [barbityrik] *m* barbiturate
barbon [barbɔ̃] *m* (pej) old fogy

barboter [barbɔte] *intr* to paddle (*like ducks*); to wallow (*like pigs*); to bubble (*like carbonated water*); (coll) to splutter; (slang) to steal

barbo·teur [barbɔtœr] **-teuse** [tøz] *mf* (slang) muddler ‖ *m* duck; wash bottle ‖ *f* rompers

barbouiller [barbuje] *tr* to smear, blur; to daub; (coll) to scribble; **barbouiller le cœur à** to nauseate

barbouil·leur [barbujœr] **barbouil·leuse** [barbujøz] *mf* dauber; messy person; scribbler

bar·bu ·bue [barby] *adj* bearded

bard [bar] *m* handbarrow

bardane [bardan] *f* burdock

barde [bard] *m* bard ‖ *f* blanket of bacon

bar·deau [bardo] *m* (*pl* **-deaux**) shingle; lath

barder [barde] *tr* to carry with a handbarrow; to armor (*a horse*); to blanket (*a roast*)

bardot [bardo] *m* hinny

barème [barem] *m* schedule (*of rates, taxes, etc.*)

baréter [barete] §10 *intr* to trumpet (*like an elephant*)

barge [barʒ] *f* barge; haystack; godwit, black-tailed godwit

barguigner [bargiɲe] *intr* to shilly-shally, to have trouble deciding

bargui·gneur [bargiɲœr] **-gneuse** [ɲøz] *mf* shilly-shallyer, procrastinator

baricaut [bariko] *m* small cask, keg

baril [baril], [bari] *m* small barrel, cask, keg

barillet [barije] *m* small barrel; revolver cylinder; spring case

bariolage [barjɔlaʒ] *m* (coll) motley, mixture of colors

bario·lé ·lée [barjɔle] *adj* speckled, multicolored, variegated

barioler [barjɔle] *tr* to variegate

bariolure [barjɔlyr] *f* clashing colors, motley

bar·man [barman] *m* (*pl* **-men** [men] or **-mans**) bartender

baromètre [barɔmetr] *m* barometer

barométrique [barɔmetrik] *adj* barometric

baron [barɔ̃] *m* baron

baronne [barɔn] *f* baroness

baroque [barɔk] *adj* & *m* baroque

barque [bark] *f* boat

barrage [baraʒ] *m* dam; barrage, cordon (*of police*); tollgate; barricade, roadblock, checkpoint; (sports) play-off

barre [bar], [bar] *f* bar; crossbar (*of a t*); tiller, helm; bore (*tidal flood*); **barre de justice** rod to hold shackles; **barre du gouvernail** helm; **barres** (typ) parallels; **jouer aux barres** to play prisoner's base

bar·reau [baro] *m* (*pl* **-reaux**) bar, crossbar, rail; rung (*of ladder or chair*); (law) bar

barrer [bare] *tr* to cross out, strike out, cancel; to cross (*a t; a check in a British bank*); to bar (*the door; the way*); to block off (*a street*); to dam (*a stream*); to steer (*a boat*)

barrette [baret], [baret] *f* biretta; bar; slide; pin

barreur [barœr] *m* helmsman

barricade [barikad] *f* barricade

barricader [barikade] *tr* to barricade

barrière [barjer] *f* barrier; gate (*of a town; of a grade crossing*); tollgate; neighborhood shopping district

barrique [barik] *f* cask; hogshead, large barrel

barrir [barir] *intr* to trumpet (*like an elephant*)

barrot [baro] *m* beam (*of a ship*)

baryton [baritɔ̃] *m* baritone; alto (*saxhorn*)

baryum [barjɔm] *m* barium

bas [ba] **basse** [bas] *adj* low; base, vile; cloudy (*weather*); *adj* low; (when standing before noun) *adj* low; base, vile; early (*age*) ‖ *m* stocking; lower part, bottom; **à bas . . . !** down with . . . !; **bas de casse** (typ) lower case; **bas de laine** nest egg, savings; **en bas** at the bottom; downstairs ‖ *f* see **basse** ‖ *bas adv* softly; down, low

ba·sal ·sale [bazal] *adj* (*pl* **-saux** [zo]) basic; basal (*metabolism*)

basalte [bazalt] *m* basalt

basa·né ·née [bazane] *adj* tanned, sunburned

basaner [bazane] *tr* to tan, to sunburn

bas-bleu [bablø] *m* (*pl* **-bleus**) bluestocking

bas-côté [bakote] *m* (*pl* **-côtés**) aisle (*of a church*); footpath (*beside a road*)

bascule [baskyl] *f* scale; rocker; seesaw

basculement [baskylmɑ̃] *m* rocking, seesawing, tipping; dimming

basculer [baskyle] *tr* to tip over ‖ *intr* to tip over; to seesaw, rock, swing; **faire basculer** to dim (*the headlights*)

bas-dessus [badəsy] *m* mezzo-soprano

base [baz] *f* base; basis; **à la base** at heart, to the core; **de base** basic

base-ball [bezbol] *m* baseball

baser [baze] *tr* to base; to ground, found (*an opinion*) ‖ *ref* to be based

bas-fond [bafɔ̃] *m* (*pl* **-fonds**) lowland; shallows; **bas-fonds** dregs, underworld; slums

basilic [bazilik] *m* basil

basilique [bazilik] *f* basilica

basin [bazɛ̃] *m* dimity

basique [bazik] *adj* basic, alkaline

basket [basket] *m* basketball

basoche [bazɔʃ] *f* law, legal profession

basque [bask] *adj* Basque ‖ *m* Basque (*language*) ‖ *f* coattail ‖ (*cap*) *mf* Basque (*person*)

basse [bas] *f* shoal; tuba; (mus) bass; **basse chiffrée** (mus) figured bass

basse-contre [baskɔ̃tr] *f* (*pl* **basses-contre**) basso profundo

basse-cour [baskur] *f* (*pl* **basses-cours**) barnyard, farmyard; barnyard animals; poultry yard

bassesse [bases] *f* baseness; base act

basset [base] *m* basset hound

bassin [basɛ̃] *m* basin; dock; artificial lake; collection plate; pelvis; **bassin**

de lit bedpan; **bassin de radoub** dry dock; **bassin hygiénique** bedpan

bassine [basin] *f* dishpan

bassinoire [basinwar] *f* bedwarmer

basson [bɑsɔ̃] *m* bassoon

baste [bast] *m* ace of clubs; saddle basket ‖ *interj* enough!

bastille [bastij] *f* small fortress

bastion [bastjɔ̃] *m* bastion

bastonnade [bɑstɔnad] *f* beating

bas-ventre [bɑvɑ̃tr] *m* abdomen, lower part of the belly

bât [bɑ] *m* packsaddle

bataclan [batɑklɑ̃] *m—***tout le bataclan** (slang) the whole caboodle

bataille [batɑj], [bataj] *f* battle, fight

batailler [batɑje], [bataje] *intr* to battle, to fight

batail·leur [batajœr] **batail·leuse** [batajøz] *adj* belligerent ‖ *mf* fighter

bataillon [batɑjɔ̃] *m* battalion

bâ·tard [bɑtar] **-tarde** [tard] *adj & mf* mongrel; bastard ‖ *m* one-pound loaf of short-length type of bread ‖ *f* cursive handwriting

bâtar·deau [bɑtardo] *m* (*pl* **-deaux**) cofferdam, caisson

ba·teau [bato] *m* (*pl* **-teaux**) boat; **bateau automobile** motorboat, motor launch; **bateau à vapeur** steamboat; **bateau à voiles** sailboat; **bateau de guerre** warship; **bateau de pêche** fishing boat; **bateau de sauvetage** lifeboat; **monter un bateau à qn** (slang) to pull s.o.'s leg; **par (le) bateau** by boat

bateau-citerne [batositern] *m* (*pl* **bateaux-citernes**) tanker

bateau-feu [batofø] *m* (*pl* **bateaux-feux**) lightship

bateau-maison [batomezɔ̃] *m* (*pl* **bateaux-maisons**) houseboat

bateau-mouche [batomuʃ] *m* (*pl* **bateaux-mouches**) excursion boat

bateau-pompe [batopɔ̃p] *m* (*pl* **bateaux-pompes**) fireboat

batelage [batlaʒ] *m* lighterage; juggling; tumbling

batelée [batle] *f* boatload

bateler [batle] §34 *tr* to lighter ‖ *intr* to juggle; to tumble

bate·leur [batlœr] **-leuse** [løz] *mf* juggler; tumbler

bate·lier [batlje] **-lière** [ljer] *mf* skipper ‖ *m* boatman; ferryman

batellerie [batelri] *f* lighterage

bâter [bɑte] *tr* to packsaddle

bath [bat] *adj* (slang) A-one, swell

bâ·ti -tie [bɑti] *adj* built; **bien bâti** well-built (*person*) ‖ *m* frame; basting (*thread*); basted garment

batifoler [batifɔle] *intr* (coll) to frolic

bâtiment [bɑtimɑ̃] *m* building; ship

bâtir [bɑtir] *tr* to build; to baste, to tack ‖ *ref* to be built

bâtisse [bɑtis] *f* masonry, construction; building, edifice; ramshackle house

bâtis·seur [bɑtisœr] **bâtis·seuse** [batisøz] *mf* builder

bâton [bɑtɔ̃] *m* stick; baton; staff, cane; rung (*of a chair*); stroke (*of a pen*); stick (*of gum*); **à bâtons rompus** by fits and starts; impromptu;

(archit) with zigzag molding; **bâton de reprise** (mus) repeat bar; **bâton de rouge à lèvres** lipstick; **bâton de vieillesse** helper or nurse for the aged; **mettre des bâtons dans les roues** to throw a monkey wrench into the works

bâtonner [bɑtɔne] *tr* to cudgel; to cross out

bâtonnet [bɑtɔne] *m* rod (*in the retina*); chopstick

battage [bataʒ] *m* beating; threshing; churning; (slang) ballyhoo

bat·tant [batɑ̃] **bat·tante** [batɑ̃t] *adj* beating; pelting, driving; swinging (*door*) ‖ *m* flap; clapper (*of bell*); **à deux battants** double (*door*)

batte [bat] *f* mallet, beater; dasher, plunger; bench for beating clothes; wooden sword (*for slapstick comedy*); (sports) bat; **batte de l'or** goldbeating

battement [batmɑ̃] *m* beating, beat; throbbing, pulsing; clapping (*of hands*); dance step; wait (*e.g.*, *between trains*)

batterie [batri] *f* (elec, mil, mus) battery; train service (*in one direction*); ruse, scheming; **batterie de cuisine** kitchen utensils

batteur [batœr] *m* beater; thresher; (sports) batter; **batteur de grève** beachcomber; **batteur de pieux** piledriver; **batteur électrique** electric mixer

batteuse [batøz] *f* threshing machine

battoir [batwar] *m* bat, beetle (*for washing clothes*); tennis racket

battre [batr] §7 *tr* to beat; to clap (*one's hands*); to flap, flutter; to wink; to bang; to pound (*the sidewalk*); to search; to shuffle (*the cards*); **battre la mesure** to beat time; **battre monnaie** to mint money ‖ *intr* to beat ‖ *ref* to fight

bau [bo] *m* (*pl* **baux**) beam (*of a ship*)

baudet [bode] *m* ass, donkey; stallion ass; sawhorse; (slang) jackass, idiot

baudrier [bodrije] *m* shoulder belt

bauge [boʒ] *f* lair, den; clay and straw mortar; (coll) pigsty

baume [bom] *m* balsam; (*consolation*) balm

ba·vard [bavar] **-varde** [vard] *adj* talkative, loquacious; tattletale ‖ *mf* chatterer; tattletale; gossip

bavardage [bavardaʒ] *m* chattering; gossiping

bavarder [bavarde] *intr* to chatter; to gossip

bava·rois [bavarwa] **-roise** [rwaz] *adj* Bavarian ‖ (*cap*) *mf* Bavarian (*person*)

bave [bav] *f* dribble, froth, spittle; (fig) slander

baver [bave] *intr* to dribble, to drool; to run (*like a pen*); **baver sur** to besmirch

bavette [bavet] *f* bib

ba·veux [bavø] **-veuse** [vøz] *adj* drooling; tendentious, wordy; undercooked

Bavière [bavjɛr] *f* Bavaria; **la Bavière** Bavaria

bavocher [bavɔʃe] *intr* to smear

bavochure [bavɔʃyr] *f* smear

bavure [bavyr] *f* bur (*of metal*); smear

bayer [baje] §49 *intr*—**bayer aux corneilles** to gawk, to stargaze

bazar [bazar] *m* bazaar; five-and-ten; **tout le bazar** (slang) the whole shebang

béant [beã] **béante** [beãt] *adj* gaping, wide-open

béat [bea] **béate** [beat] *adj* smug, complacent, sanctimonious

béatifier [beatifje] *tr* to beatify

béatitude [beatityd] *f* beatitude

beau [bo] (or **bel** [bɛl] before vowel or mute h) **bel** [bɛl] (*pl* **beaux belles**) *adj* beautiful; handsome; **bel et bien** truly, for sure; **de plus belle** more than ever; **il fait beau** it is nice out, we are having fair weather; **tout beau!** steady!, easy does it! || (*when standing before noun*) *adj* beautiful; handsome; fine, good; considerable, large, long; fair (*weather*); odd-numbered or recto (*page*) || *mf* fair one; **faire le beau, faire la belle** to strut, swagger; to sit up and beg (*said of a dog*); **la belle** the deciding match; **la Belle au bois dormant** Sleeping Beauty || **beau** *adv*—**il a beau parler** it is no use for him to speak || **belle** *adv*—**la bailler belle** (slang) to tell a whopper; **l'échapper belle** to have a narrow escape

beaucoup [boku] §91 *adv* much, many; **beaucoup de** much, many; **de beaucoup** by far

beau-fils [bofis] *m* (*pl* **beaux-fils**) son-in-law; stepson

beau-frère [bofrɛr] *m* (*pl* **beaux-frères**) brother-in-law

beau-père [bopɛr] *m* (*pl* **beaux-pères**) father-in-law; stepfather

beau-petit-fils [bopətifis] *m* (*pl* **beaux-petits-fils**) son of a stepson or of a stepdaughter

beaupré [bopre] *m* bowsprit

beauté [bote] *f* beauty; **beauté du diable** bloom of youth; **se faire une beauté** (coll) to doll up

beaux-arts [bozar] *mpl* fine arts

beaux-parents [boparã] *mpl* in-laws

bébé [bebe] *m* baby

bec [bɛk] *m* beak; nozzle, jet, burner; point (*of a pen*); (mus) mouthpiece; (slang) beak, face, mouth; **avoir bon bec** to be gossipy; **claquer du bec** (coll) to be hungry; **clore, clouer le bec à qn** (coll) to shut s.o. up; **tomber sur un bec** (coll) to encounter an unforeseen obstacle

bécane [bekan] *f* (coll) bike, bicycle

bécarre [bekar] *m* (mus) natural

bécasse [bekas] *f* woodcock; (slang) stupid woman

bécas·seau [bekaso] *m* (*pl* **bécas·seaux**) sandpiper

bec-de-cane [bɛkdəkan] *m* (*pl* **becs-de-cane**) door handle; flat-nosed pliers

bec-de-corbeau [bɛkdəkɔrbo] *m* (*pl* **becs-de-corbeau**) wire cutters

bec-de-corbin [bɛkdəkɔrbɛ̃] *m* (*pl* **becs-de-corbin**) crowbar

bec-de-lièvre [bɛkdəljɛvr] *m* (*pl* **becs-de-lièvre**) harelip

bêche [bɛʃ] *f* spade

bêcher [beʃe] *tr* to dig; (slang) to run (*s.th.*) down, to give (*s.o.*) a dig

bê·cheur [beʃœr] **-cheuse** [ʃøz] *mf* (coll) detractor, critic; (slang) stuffed shirt

bêchoir [beʃwar] *m* hoe

bécoter [bekɔte] *tr* to give (*s.o.*) a peck or little kiss on the cheek

becqueter [bɛkte] §34 *tr* to peck at; (coll) to eat || *ref* to bill and coo

bedaine [bədɛn] *f* paunch, beer belly

bédane [bedan] *m* cold chisel

be·deau [bədo] *m* (*pl* **-deaux**) beadle

bé·douin [bedwɛ̃] **-douine** [dwin] *adj* Bedouin || (*cap*) *mf* Bedouin (*person*)

bée [be] *adj*—**bouche bée** mouth agape, flabbergasted || *f* penstock

beffroi [befrwa] *m* belfry

bégaiement [begemã] *m* stammering, stuttering

bégayer [begeje] §49 *tr & intr* to stammer, stutter

bègue [bɛg] *adj* stammering, stuttering || *mf* stammerer

bégueter [begte] §2 *intr* to bleat

bégueule [begœl] *adj* (coll) prudish || *f* (coll) prudish woman

béguin [begɛ̃] *m* hood, cap; sweetheart; (coll) infatuation

béguine [begin] *f* Beguine; sanctimonious woman

beige [bɛʒ] *adj & m* beige

beignet [bɛɲe] *m* fritter

béjaune [beʒon] *m* nestling; greenhorn, novice, ninny

bêlement [bɛlmã] *m* bleat, bleating

bêler [bɛle] *intr* to bleat

belette [bəlɛt] *f* weasel

belge [bɛlʒ] *adj* Belgian || (*cap*) *mf* Belgian (*person*)

Belgique [bɛlʒik] *f* Belgium; **la Belgique** Belgium

bélier [belje] *m* ram; battering ram

bélière [beljɛr] *f* sheepbell

bélinogramme [belinɔgram] *m* Wirephoto (*trademark*)

bélinographe [belinɔgraf] *m* Wirephoto transmitter

bélître [belitr] *m* scoundrel

belladone [beladɔn] *f* belladonna

bellâtre [belɑtr] *adj* foppish || *m* fop

belle-dame [bɛldam] *f* belladonna

belle-de-jour [bɛldəʒur] *f* (*pl* **belles-de-jour**) morning glory

belle-de-nuit [bɛldənɥi] *f* (*pl* **belles-de-nuit**) marvel-of-Peru

belle-d'un-jour [bɛldœ̃ʒur] *f* (*pl* **belles-d'un-jour**) day lily

belle-fille [bɛlfij] *f* (*pl* **belles-filles**) daughter-in-law; stepdaughter

belle-mère [bɛlmɛr] *f* (*pl* **belles-mères**) mother-in-law; stepmother

belle-petite-fille [bɛlpətitfij] *f* (*pl* **belles-petites-filles**) daughter of a stepson or of a stepdaughter

belles-lettres [bɛllɛtr] *fpl* belles-lettres, literature

belle-sœur [bɛlsœr] *f* (*pl* **belles-sœurs**) sister-in-law

belliciste [belisist] *mf* warmonger

belligé·rant [beliʒerɑ̃] **-rante** [rɑ̃t] *adj & m* belligerent

belli·queux [belikø] **-queuse** [køz] *adj* bellicose, warlike

bel·lot [belo] **bel·lote** [belɔt] *adj* pretty, cute; dapper

bémol [bemɔl] *adj invar & m* (mus) flat

bémoliser [bemɔlize] *tr* to flat (*a note*); to provide (*a key signature*) with flats

ben [bɛ̃] *interj* (slang) well!

bénédicité [benedisite] *m* grace (*before a meal*)

bénédic·tin [benediktɛ̃] **-tine** [tin] *adj & m* Benedictine || (*cap*) *f* Benedictine (*liqueur*)

bénédiction [benediksjɔ̃] *f* benediction; manna from heaven

bénéfice [benefis] *m* profit; benefit; benefice; parsonage, rectory; **à bénéfice** benefit (*performance*); **sous bénéfice d'inventaire** with grave reservations

bénéficiaire [benefisjɛr] *adj* profit, e.g., **marge bénéficiaire** profit margin || *mf* beneficiary

bénéficier [benefisje] *intr* to profit, benefit

benêt [bənɛ] *adj masc* simple-minded || *m* simpleton, numskull

bé·nin [benɛ̃] **-nigne** [niɲ] *adj* benign; mild, slight; benignant, accommodating

béni-oui-oui [beniwiwi] *mpl* yes men

bénir [benir] *tr* to bless, to consecrate

bé·nit [beni] **-nite** [nit] *adj* consecrated (*bread*); holy (*water*)

bénitier [benitje] *m* font (*for holy water*)

benja·min [bɛ̃ʒamɛ̃] **-mine** [min] *mf* baby (*the youngest child*) || (*cap*) *m* Benjamin

benne [bɛn] *f* bucket, bin, hopper; dumper; cage (*in mine*); **benne preneuse** (mach) scoop, jaws (*of crane*)

be·noît [bənwa] **-noîte** [nwat] *adj* indulgent; sanctimonious || (*cap*) *m* Benedict

benzène [bɛ̃zɛn] *m* (chem) benzene

benzine [bɛ̃zin] *f* benzine

béquille [bekij] *f* crutch

béquiller [bekije] *intr* to walk with a crutch or crutches

bercail [bɛrkaj] *m* fold, bosom (*of church or family*)

ber·ceau [bɛrso] *m* (*pl* **-ceaux**) cradle; bower; **berceau de verdure** or **de chèvrefeuille** arbor

bercelonnette [bɛrsəlɔnɛt] *f* bassinet

bercer [bɛrse] §51 *tr* to cradle, rock; to beguile; to assuage (*grief, pain*) || *ref* to rock, swing; to delude oneself (*with vain hopes*)

ber·ceur [bɛrsœr] **-ceuse** [søz] *adj* rocking, cradling || *f* rocking chair; cradle song, lullaby

berge [bɛrʒ] *f* bank, steep bank

berger [bɛrʒe] *m* shepherd; shepherd dog

bergère [bɛrʒer] *f* shepherdess; wing chair

bergerie [bɛrʒəri] *f* sheepfold; pastoral poem

berle [bɛrl] *f* water parsnip

Berlin [bɛrlɛ̃] *m* Berlin; **Berlin-Est** East Berlin; **Berlin-Ouest** West Berlin

berline [bɛrlin] *f* sedan (*automobile*); berlin (*carriage*)

berlingot [bɛrlɛ̃go] *m* caramel candy; milk carton

berli·nois [bɛrlinwa] **-noise** [nwaz] *adj* Berlin || *mf* Berliner (*person*)

berlue [bɛrly] *f*—**avoir la berlue** (coll) to be blind to what is going on

Bermudes [bɛrmyd] *fpl*—**les Bermudes** Bermuda

bernacle [bɛrnakl] *f* (orn) anatid; (zool) barnacle

berne [bɛrn] *f* hazing; **en berne** at half-mast

berner [bɛrne] *tr* to toss in a blanket; to ridicule; to fool

bernique [bɛrnik] *interj* (coll) shucks!, heck!, what a shame!

berthe [bɛrt] *f* corsage; cape

béryllium [beriljɔm] *m* beryllium

besace [bəzas] *f* beggar's bag; mendicancy

besicles [bəzikl] *fpl* (archaic) spectacles; **prenez donc vos besicles!** (coll) put your specs on!

besogne [bəzɔɲ] *f* work, task; **abattre de la besogne** to accomplish a great deal of work; **aller vite en besogne** to work too hastily

besogner [bəzɔɲe] *intr* to drudge, slave

beso·gneux [bəzɔɲø] **-gneuse** [ɲøz] *adj* needy || *m* needy person

besoin [bəzwɛ̃] *m* need; poverty, distress; **au besoin** if necessary; **avoir besoin de** to need; **si besoin est** if need be

bes·son [besɔ̃] **bes·sonne** [besɔn] *mf* (dial) twin

bestiaire [bɛstjɛr] *m* bestiary

bes·tial -tiale [bɛstjal] (*pl* **-tiaux** [tjo]) *adj* bestial || *mpl* see **bestiaux**

bestialité [bɛstjalite] *f* bestiality

bestiaux [bɛstjo] *mpl* livestock, cattle and horses

bestiole [bɛstjɔl] *f* bug, vermin

bê·ta [beta] **-tasse** [tas] *adj* (coll) silly || *mf* (coll) sap, dolt

bétail [betaj] *m invar* grazing animals (*on a farm*); **gros bétail** cattle and horses; **menu bétail** or **petit bétail** sheep, goats, pigs, etc.

bête [bɛt] *adj* stupid, foolish || *f* animal; beast; **bête à bon Dieu** (ent) ladybird; **bête de charge**, **bête de somme** pack animal; **bonne bête** harmless fool

bêtifier [betifje], [betifje] *tr* to make stupid || *intr* to play the fool, to talk foolishly

bêtise [betiz], [betiz] *f* foolishness, stupidity, nonsense; trifle; **faire des bêtises** to blunder, do stupid things; to throw money around

béton [betɔ̃] *m* concrete; **béton armé** reinforced concrete

bétonner [betɔne] *tr* to make of concrete

bétonnière [betɔnjɛr] *f* cement mixer

bette [bɛt] *f* Swiss chard; **bette à carde** Swiss chard

betterave [betrav] *f* beet; **betterave sucrière** sugar beet

beuglement [bøgləmã] *m* bellow, bellowing, lowing

beugler [bøgle] [bœgle] *tr* (slang) to bawl out (*a song*) || *intr* to bellow (*like a bull*); to low (*like cattle*)

beurre [bœr] *m* butter; **faire son beurre** (coll) to feather one's nest

beurrée [bœre] *f* slice of bread and butter

beurrer [bœre] *tr* to butter

beur·rier [bœrje] **beur·rière** [bœrjer] *adj* butter || *m* butter dish

beuverie [bœvri] *f* drinking party

bévue [bevy] *f* blunder, slip, boner

biais [bje] **biaise** [bjɛz] *adj* bias, oblique, slanting; skew (*arch*) || *m* bias, slant; skew (*of an arch*); **de biais** or **en biais** aslant, askew

biaiser [bjeze] *intr* to slant; (fig) to be evasive

bibelot [biblo] *m* curio, trinket, knickknack

bibeloter [bibləte] *intr* to buy or collect curios

bibe·ron [bibrɔ̃] **-ronne** [rɔn] *adj* addicted to the bottle || *mf* heavy drinker || *m* nursing bottle

Bible [bibl] *f* Bible

bibliobus [bibliɔbys] *m* bookmobile

bibliographe [bibliɔgraf] *m* bibliographer

bibliographie [bibliɔgrafi] *f* bibliography

bibliomane [bibliɔman] *mf* book collector

bibliothécaire [bibliɔteker] *mf* librarian

bibliothèque [bibliɔtɛk] *f* library; bookstand; **bibliothèque vivante** walking encyclopedia

biblique [biblik] *adj* Biblical

biceps [bisɛps] *m* biceps

biche [biʃ] *f* hind; doe; **ma biche** (coll) my darling

bicher [biʃe] *intr*—**ça biche!** (slang) fine!, it's fine!

bichlamar [biʃlamar] *m* pidgin

bichof [biʃɔf] *m* spiced wine

bi·chon [biʃɔ̃] **-chonne** [ʃɔn] *mf* lap dog

bichonner [biʃɔne] *tr* to curl (*one's hair*); to doll up || *ref* to doll up

bicoque [bikɔk] *f* shack, ramshackle house

bicorne [bikɔrn] *adj* two-cornered || *m* cocked hat

bicot [biko] *m* (coll) kid (*goat*); (pej) North African, Arab

bicyclette [bisiklɛt] *f* bicycle

bident [bidã] *m* two-pronged fork

bidet [bidɛ] *m* bidet; nag (*horse*)

bidon [bidɔ̃] *m* drum (*for liquids*); canteen, water bottle

bidonville [bidɔ̃vil] *m* shantytown

bidule [bidyl] *m* (slang) gadget

bief [bjɛf] *m* millrace; reach, level (*of a stream or canal*)

bielle [bjɛl] *f* connecting rod, tie rod

bien [bjɛ̃] *m* good; welfare; estate, fortune; **biens** property, possessions; **biens consomptibles** consumer goods; **biens immeubles** real estate; **biens meubles** personal property || *adv* §91 well; rightly, properly, quite; indeed, certainly; fine, e.g., **je vais bien** I'm fine; **bien de** + *art* much, e.g., **bien de l'eau** much water; many, e.g., **bien des gens** many people; **bien entendu** of course; **bien que** although; **eh bien!** so!; **si bien que** so that; **tant bien que mal** so-so, as well as possible || *interj* good!; all right!; that's enough!

bien-ai·mé -mée [bjɛ̃neme] *adj & mf* beloved, darling

bien-dire [bjɛ̃dir] *m* gracious speech, eloquent delivery; **être sur son bien-dire** to be on one's best behavior

bien-di·sant [bjɛ̃dizã] **-sante** [zãt] *adj* smooth-spoken, smooth-tongued

bien-être [bjɛ̃nɛtr] *m* well-being, welfare

bienfaisance [bjɛ̃fəzãs] *f* charity, beneficence

bienfai·sant [bjɛ̃fəzã] **-sante** [zãt] *adj* charitable, beneficent

bienfait [bjɛ̃fɛ] *m* good turn, good deed, favor; **bienfaits** benefits

bienfai·teur [bjɛ̃fɛtœr] **-trice** [tris] *mf* benefactor || *f* benefactress

bien-fondé [bjɛ̃fɔ̃de] *m* cogency

bien-fonds [bjɛ̃fɔ̃] *m* (*pl* biens-fonds) real estate

bienheu·reux [bjɛ̃nœrø] **-reuse** [røz] *adj & mf* blessed

bien·nal -nale [bjɛnnal] *adj* (*pl* -naux [no]) biennial || *f* biennial exposition

bienséance [bjɛ̃seãs] *f* propriety

bienséant [bjɛ̃seã] **bienséante** [bjɛ̃seãt] *adj* fitting, proper, appropriate

bientôt [bjɛ̃to] *adv* soon; **à bientôt!** so long!

bienveillance [bjɛ̃vɛjãs] *f* benevolence, kindness

bienveil·lant [bjɛ̃vɛjã] **bienveil·lante** [bjɛ̃vɛjãt] *adj* benevolent, kindly, kind

bienvenir [bjɛ̃vnir] *intr*—**se faire bienvenir** to make oneself welcome

bienve·nu -nue [bjɛ̃vny] *adj* welcome || *m*—**soyez le bienvenu!** welcome! || *f* welcome; **souhaiter la bienvenue à** to welcome

bière [bjɛr] *f* beer; coffin; **bière à la pression** draft beer

biffer [bife] *tr* to cross out, to cancel, to erase; (slang) to cut (*class*)

biffin [bifɛ̃] *m* (slang) ragman; (slang) doughboy, G.I. Joe

bifo·cal -cale [bifɔkal] *adj* (*pl* -caux [ko]) bifocal

bifteck [biftɛk] *m* beefsteak

bifurquer [bifyrke] *tr* to bifurcate, divide into two branches || *intr & ref* to bifurcate, fork; to branch off

bigame [bigam] *adj* bigamous || *mf* bigamist

bigamie [bigami] *f* bigamy

bigar·ré -rée [bigare] *adj* mottled, variegated; motley (*crowd*)

bigar·reau [bigaro] *m* (*pl* **-reaux**) white-heart cherry

bigarrer [bigare] *tr* to mottle, to variegate, to streak

bigarrure [bigaryr] *f* variegation, medley, mixture

bigle [bigl] *adj* cross-eyed || *m* beagle

bigler [bigle] *intr* to squint; to be cross-eyed

bigorne [bigɔrn] *f* two-horn anvil

bigorner [bigɔrne] *tr* to form on the anvil; (slang) to smash

bi·got [bigo] **-gote** [gɔt] *adj* sanctimonious || *mf* religious bigot

bigoterie [bigɔtri] *f* religious bigotry

bigoudi [bigudi] *m* hair curler, roller

bihebdomadaire [biebdɔmader] *adj* semiweekly

bi·jou [biʒu] *m* (*pl* **-joux**) jewel

bijouterie [biʒutri] *f* jewelry; jewelry shop; jewelry business

bijou·tier [biʒutje] **-tière** [tjer] *mf* jeweler

bilan [bilɑ̃] *m* balance sheet; balance; petition of bankruptcy; **faire le bilan** to tabulate the results

bilboquet [bilbɔke] *m* job printing

bile [bil] *f* bile; **se faire de la bile** (coll) to worry, fret

bi·lieux [biljø] **-lieuse** [ljøz] *adj* bilious; irascible, grouchy

bilingue [bilɛ̃g] *adj* bilingual

billard [bijar] *m* billiards; billiard table; billiard room

bille [bij] *f* ball; ball bearing; billiard ball; marble; log; **à bille** ball-point (*pen*)

billet [bije] *m* note; ticket; bill (*currency*); **billet à ordre** promissory note; **billet d'abonnement** season ticket; **billet d'aller et retour** round-trip ticket; **billet de banque** bank note; **billet de correspondance** transfer; **billet de faire-part** announcement, notification (*of birth, wedding, death*); **billet de logement** billet; **billet doux** love letter; **billet simple** one-way ticket

billette [bijet] *f* billet

billevesée [bijvəze], [bilvəze] *f* nonsense

billion [biljɔ̃] *m* trillion (U.S.A.); billion (Brit)

billot [bijo] *m* block, chopping block; executioner's block

biloquer [bilɔke] *tr* to plow deeply

bimen·suel -suelle [bimɑ̃sɥel] *adj* semimonthly

bimes·triel -trielle [bimestriel] *adj* bimonthly (*every two months*)

bimoteur [bimɔtœr] *adj* twin-motor || *m* twin-motor plane

binaire [biner] *adj* binary

biner [bine] *tr* to hoe; to cultivate, to work over (*the soil*) || *intr* to say two masses the same day

binette [binet] *f* hoe; (hist) wig; (slang) phiz

bineur [binœr] *m* or **bineuse** [binøz] *f* cultivator (*implement*)

binocle [binɔkl] *m* lorgnette

binoculaire [binɔkyler] *adj* & *f* binocular

binôme [binom] *adj* & *m* binomial

biochimie [bjɔ/imi] *f* biochemistry

biographe [bjɔgraf] *mf* biographer

biographie [bjɔgrafi] *f* biography

biographique [bjɔgrafik] *adj* biographical

biologie [bjɔlɔʒi] *f* biology

biologiste [bjɔlɔʒist] *mf* biologist

biophysique [bjɔfizik] *f* biophysics

biopsie [bjɔpsi] *f* biopsy

bioxyde [biɔksid] *m* dioxide

bipar·ti -tie [biparti] *adj* bipartite

bipartisme [bipartism] *m* bipartisanship

bipartite [bipartit] *adj* bipartite; bipartisan

bipède [biped] *adj* & *mf* biped || *m* pair of legs of a horse

biplan [biplɑ̃] *m* biplane

bique [bik] *f* nanny goat

bir·man [birmɑ̃] **-mane** [man] *adj* Burmese || (*cap*) *mf* Burmese (*person*)

Birmanie [birmani] *f* Burma; **la Birmanie** Burma

bis [bi] **bise** [biz] *adj* gray-brown || [bis] *m*—**un bis** an encore || *f* see **bise** || **bis** [bis] *adv* twice; (mus) repeat; **sept bis** seven A, seven and a half || **bis** [bis] *interj* encore!

bisaïeul bisaïeule [bizajœl] *mf* great-grand-parent || *m* great-grandfather || *f* great-grandmother

bisan·nuel -nuelle [bizanɥel] *adj* biennial

bisbille [bisbij] *f* (coll) squabble

biscaïen [biskajɛ̃] **biscaïenne** [biskajen] *adj* Biscayan || (*cap*) *mf* Biscayan (*person*)

biscor·nu -nue [biskɔrny] *adj* misshapen, distorted

biscotin [biskɔtɛ̃] *m* hardtack

biscotte [biskɔt] *f* zwieback

biscuit [biskɥi] *m* hardtack; cracker; cookie; unglazed porcelain; **biscuit soda** soda cracker

bise [biz] *f* north wind; (fig) winter; (slang) kiss

bi·seau [bizo] *m* (*pl* **-seaux**) bevel, chamfer; **en biseau** beveled, chamfered

biseauter [bizote] *tr* to bevel, chamfer; to mark (*cards*)

biser [bize] *tr* to redye || *intr* to blacken

bi·son [bizɔ̃] **-sonne** [zɔn] *mf* bison, buffalo

bisque [bisk] *f* bisque

bisquer [biske] *intr* (coll) to be resentful

bissac [bisak] *m* bag, sack

bisser [bise] *tr* to encore; to repeat

bissextile [bisekstil] *adj* bissextile, leap, e.g., **année bissextile** leap year

bissexué bissexuée [biseksɥe] *adj* bisexual

bissexuel bissexuelle [biseksɥel] *adj* bisexual

bistouri [bisturi] *m* scalpel

bistournage [bisturnaʒ] *m* castration

bistre [bistr] *adj invar* soot-brown || *m* bister, soot-brown

bis·tré -trée [bistre] *adj* swarthy

bisulfate [bisylfat] *m* bisulfate
bisulfite [bisylfit] *m* bisulfite
bitter [biter] *m* bitters
bitume [bitym] *m* bitumen
bitumer [bityme] *tr* to asphalt
bitumi·neux [bityminø] **-neuse** [nøz] *adj* bituminous
bivouac [bivwak] *m* bivouac
bivouaquer [bivwake] *intr* to bivouac
bizarre [bizar] *adj* bizarre, strange
bizutage [bizyta3] *m* (slang) initiation, hazing
bizuth [bizyt] *m* (slang) freshman
blackbouler [blakbule] *tr* to blackball; (coll) to flunk
bla·fard [blafar] **-farde** [fard] *adj* pallid, pale, wan; lambent (*flame*)
blague [blag] *f* tobacco pouch; (coll) yarn, tall story, blarney; **blague à part** (coll) all joking aside; **faire une blague** (coll) to play a trick; **sale blague** (coll) dirty trick; **sans blague!** (coll) no kidding!
blaguer [blage] *tr* (coll) to kid; **blaguer qn** (coll) to pull s.o.'s leg || *intr* (coll) to kid, to tell tall stories
bla·gueur [blagœr] **-gueuse** [gøz] *adj* (coll) kidding, tongue-in-cheek || *mf* (coll) kidder, joker
blai·reau [blero] *m* (*pl* **-reaux**) badger; shaving brush
blâmable [blamabl] *adj* blameworthy
blâme [blam] *m* blame; **s'attirer un blâme** to receive a reprimand
blâmer [blame] *tr* to blame; to disapprove of
blanc [blã] **blanche** [blãʃ] *adj* white; blank; clean; sleepless (*night*); expressionless (*voice*); **blanc comme un linge** white as a sheet || *m* white; blank; white meat; white man; white goods; chalk; bull's-eye; **à blanc** with blank cartridges; **blanc de baleine** spermaceti; **blanc de chaux** whitewash; **en blanc** blank; **en blanc et noir** in black and white
blanc-bec [blãbɛk] *m* (*pl* **blancs-becs**) (coll) greenhorn, callow youth
blanchâtre [blãʃatr] *adj* whitish
blanchir [blãʃir] *tr* to whiten; to wash or bleach; to whitewash; to blanch (*almonds*) || *intr* to blanch, whiten; to grow old
blanchissage [blãʃisa3] *m* laundering; sugar refining
blanchisserie [blãʃisri] *f* laundry
blanchis·seur [blãʃisœr] **blanchis·seuse** [blãʃisøz] *mf* launderer || *m* laundryman || *f* laundress, washerwoman
blanc-manger [blãmã3e] *m* (*pl* **blancs-manger**) blancmange
blanc-seing [blãsɛ̃] *m* (*pl* **blancs-seings**) carte blanche
bla·sé -sée [blaze] *adj* blasé, jaded
blaser [blaze] *tr* to cloy, to blunt
blason [blazɔ̃] *m* (heral) blazon
blasonner [blazɔne] *tr* (heral) to blazon
blasphéma·teur [blasfematœr] **-teuse** [tøz] *adj* blasphemous, blaspheming || *mf* blasphemer
blasphématoire [blasfematwar] *adj* blasphemous
blasphème [blasfɛm] *m* blasphemy

blasphémer [blasfeme] §10 *tr & intr* to blaspheme
blatte [blat] *f* cockroach
blé [ble] *m* wheat; **blé à moudre** grist; **blé de Turquie** corn; **blé froment** wheat; **blé noir** buckwheat; **manger son blé en herbe** to spend one's money before one has it
bled [blɛd] *m* (coll) backwoods, hinterland
blême [blɛm] *adj* pale; livid, sallow, wan; ghastly
blêmir [blemir] *intr* to turn pale or livid, to blanch; to grow dim
blennorragie [blenɔra3i] *f* gonorrhea
blèse [blɛz] *adj* lisping || *mf* lisper
blèsement [blɛzmã] *m* lisping
bléser [bleze] §10 *intr* to lisp
bles·sé -sée [blese] *adj* wounded || *mf* injured person; victim; casualty
blesser [blese], *tr* to wound; to injure
blessure [blesyr] *f* wound; injury
blet blette [blɛt] *adj* overripe || *f* chard
blettir [bletir] *intr* to overripen
bleu bleue [blø] (*pl* **bleus bleues**) *adj* blue; fairy (*stories*); violent (*anger*); rare (*meat*) || *m* blue; bluing; bruise; sauce for cooking fish; telegram or pneumatic letter; (coll) raw recruit, greenhorn; **bleu barbeau** light blue; **bleu marine** navy blue; **bleus** coveralls, dungarees; **passer au bleu** to avoid, elude (*a question*); **petit bleu** bad wine
bleuâtre [bløatr] *adj* bluish
bleuet [bløɛ] *m* bachelor's-button
bleuir [bløir] *tr & intr* to turn blue
bleu·té -tée [bløte] *adj* bluish
blindage [blɛ̃da3] *m* armor plate; armor plating; (elec) shield
blin·dé -dée [blɛ̃de] *adj* armored; armor-plated; (elec) shielded || *m* (mil) tank
blinder [blɛ̃de] *tr* to armor-plate; (elec) to shield
bloc [blɔk] *m* block; blocking; tablet, pad (*of paper*); (cars, mach) unit; **à bloc** tight; **en bloc** all together, in a lump; **envoyer** or **mettre au bloc** (slang) to throw (*s.o.*) in the jug; **serrer le frein à bloc** to jam on the brakes
blocage [blɔka3] *m* blockage, blocking; lumping together; rubble; freezing (*of prices; of wages*); application (*of brakes*)
blocaille [blɔkaj] *f* rubble
bloc-diagramme [blɔkdjagram] *m* (*pl* **blocs-diagrammes**) cross section
bloc-moteur [blɔkmɔtœr] *m* (aut) motor and transmission system
bloc-notes [blɔknɔt] *m* (*pl* **blocs-notes**) scratch pad, note pad
blocus [blɔkys] *m* blockade
blond blonde [blɔ̃d] *adj* blond || *m* blond || *f* see **blonde**
blondasse [blɔ̃das] *adj* washed-out blond
blonde [blɔ̃d] *f* blonde; blond lace; **blonde platinée** platinum blonde
blon·din [blɔ̃dɛ̃] **-dine** [din] *adj* fair-

haired ‖ *mf* blond ‖ *m* cableway; hopper for concrete; (obs) fop

blondir [blɔ̃dir] *tr* to bleach ‖ *intr* to turn yellow, become blond

bloquer [bloke] *tr* to blockade; to block up; to fill with rubble; to jam on (*the brakes*); to stop (*a car*) by jamming on the brakes; to pocket (*a billiard ball*); to run on (*two paragraphs*); to tighten (*a nut or bolt*) as much as possible; to freeze (*wages*)

blottir [blotir] *ref* to cower; to curl up

blouse [bluz] *f* smock; billiard pocket

blouser [bluze] *tr* to deceive, take in ‖ *intr* to pucker around the waist ‖ *ref* to be mistaken

blouson [bluzɔ̃] *m* jacket

blouson-noir [bluzɔ̃nwar] *m* (*pl* **blousons-noirs**) juvenile delinquent

blue-jean [bludʒin] *m* blue jeans

bluet [blye] *m* bachelor's-button; (Canad) blueberry

bluette [blyet] *f* piece of light fiction; spark, flash

bluffer [blyfe] *tr & intr* to bluff

bluf·feur [blyfœr] **bluf·feuse** [blyføz] *mf* bluffer

blutage [blytaʒ] *m* bolting, sifting; boltings, siftings

bluter [blyte] *tr* to bolt, to sift

blutoir [blytwar] *m* bolter, sifter

B.N. *abbr* (**Bibliothèque Nationale**) National Library

boa [bɔa] *m* boa

bobard [bɔbar] *m* (coll) fish story, tall tale

bobèche [bɔbeʃ] *f* bobeche (*disk to catch drippings of candle*)

bobine [bɔbin] *f* bobbin; spool, reel; (elec) coil; **bobine d'allumage** (aut) ignition coil

bobiner [bɔbine] *tr* to spool, wind

bocage [bɔkaʒ] *m* grove

boca·ger [bɔkaʒe] **-gère** [ʒer] *adj* wooded

bo·cal [bɔkal] *m* (*pl* **-caux** [ko]) jar, bottle, globe; fishbowl

boche [bɔʃ] *adj & mf* (slang & pej) German

bock [bɔk] *m* beer glass (*half pint*); glass of beer; enema; douche

boëte [bwet] *f* fish bait

bœuf [bœf] *m* (*pl* **bœufs** [bø]) beef; head of beef; steer; ox; **bœuf en conserve** corned beef

boggle [bɔʒi] *m* (rr) truck

bogue [bɔgi] *f* chestnut bur

Bohême [bɔem] *f* Bohemia; **la Bohême** Bohemia

bohème [bɔem] *adj & mf* Bohemian (*artist*) ‖ *f*—**la bohème** Bohemia (*of the artistic world*)

bohé·mien [bɔemjɛ̃] **-mienne** [mjen] *adj* Bohemian; gypsy ‖ (cap) *mf* Bohemian; gypsy

boire [bwar] *m* drink; drinking; **le boire et le manger** food and drink ‖ §8 *tr* to drink; to swallow (*an affront*) ‖ *intr* to drink; **boire à la santé de** to drink to the health of; **boire à** (**même**) to drink out of (*a bottle*); **boire comme un trou** to

drink like a fish; **boire dans** to drink out of (*a glass*)

bois [bwa] *m*, [bwa] *m* wood; woods; horns, antlers; **bois de chauffage** firewood; **bois de lit** bedstead; **bois flotté** driftwood; **bois fondu** plastic wood; **les bois** (mus) the woodwinds

boisage [bwazaʒ] *m* timbering

boi·sé **-sée** [bwaze] *adj* wooded; paneled

boiser [bwaze] *tr* to panel, to wainscot; to timber (*a mine*); to reforest

boiserie [bwazri] *f* woodwork, paneling, wainscoting

bois·seau [bwaso] *m* (*pl* **bois·seaux**) bushel

boisson [bwasɔ̃] *f* drink, beverage; **boissons hygiéniques** light wines, beer, and soft drinks

boîte [bwat] *f* box; can; canister; (slang) joint, dump; **boîte aux lettres** mailbox; **boîte de nuit** night club; **boîte d'essieu** (mach) journal box; **boîte de vitesses** transmission-gear box; **boîte postale** post-office box; **en boîte** boxed; canned; **ferme ta boîte!** (slang) shut up!; **mettre en boîte** to box; to can; (slang) to make fun of

boiter [bwate] *intr* to limp

boi·teux [bwatø] **-teuse** [tøz] *adj* lame, limping; unsteady, wobbly (*chair*) ‖ *mf* lame person

boî·tier [bwatje] **-tière** [tjer] *mf* box-maker; mail collector (*from mailboxes*) ‖ *m* box, case; kit; medicine kit; (mach) housing; **boîtier de montre** watchcase

boitte [bwat] *f* fish bait

bol [bɔl] *m* bowl, basin; cud; bolus, pellet

bolchevique [bɔlʃəvik] *adj* Bolshevik ‖ (cap) *mf* Bolshevik

bolcheviste [bɔlʃəvist] *adj* Bolshevik ‖ (cap) *mf* Bolshevik

bolduc [bɔldyk] *m* colored ribbon

bolée [bɔle] *f* bowlful

bolide [bɔlid] *m* meteorite, fireball; racing car

bombance [bɔ̃bɑ̃s] *f* (coll) feast; **faire bombance** (coll) to have a blowout

bombardement [bɔ̃bardəmɑ̃] *m* bombing; bombardment

bombarder [bɔ̃barde] *tr* to bomb; to bombard; (coll) to appoint at the last minute

bombardier [bɔ̃bardje] *m* bomber; bombardier

bombe [bɔ̃b] *f* bomb; **bombe à hydrogène** hydrogen bomb; **bombe atomique** atomic bomb; **bombe glacée** molded ice cream; **bombe volante** buzz bomb; **faire la bombe** (slang) to go on a spree

bom·bé -bée [bɔ̃be] *adj* convex, bulging

bomber [bɔ̃be] *tr* to bend, to arch; to stick out (*one's chest*); **bomber le torse** (fig) to stick one's nose up ‖ *intr & ref* to bulge

bon [bɔ̃] **bonne** [bɔn] *adj* §91 good; **à quoi bon?** what's the use?; **sentir bon** to smell good; **tenir bon** to hold fast

|| (when standing before noun) *adj*
§91 good; fast (*color*) || *m* coupon;
bon de commande order blank; **pour
de bon** or **pour tout de bon** for good,
really || *f* see **bonne** || **bon** *interj*
good!; what!

bonace [bɔnas] *f* calm (*of the sea*)

bonasse [bɔnas] *adj* simple, naïve

bon-bec [bɔbɛk] *m* (*pl* **bons-becs**) fast
talker

bonbon [bɔbɔ] *m* bonbon, piece of
candy

bonbonne [bɔbɔn] *f* demijohn

bonbonnière [bɔbɔnjɛr] *f* candy dish;
candy box

bond [bɔ] *m* bound, bounce; leap,
jump; **faire faux bond** to miss an appointment; **faux bond** misstep

bonde [bɔd] *f* plug; bunghole; sluice
gate

bon-dé -dée [bɔde] *adj* crammed

bondir [bɔdir] *intr* to bound, to bounce;
to leap, to jump; **faire bondir** to
make (*s.o.*) hit the ceiling

bondissement [bɔdismɑ] *m* bouncing,
leaping

bondon [bɔdɔ] *m* bung

bonheur [bɔnœr] *m* happiness; good
luck; **au petit bonheur** by chance, at
random; **par bonheur** luckily

bonheur-du-jour [bɔnœrdyʒur] *m* (*pl*
bonheurs-du-jour) escritoire

bonhomie [bɔnɔmi] *f* good nature; cre-
dulity

bonhomme [bɔnɔm] *adj* good-natured,
simple-minded || *m* (*pl* **bonshommes**
[bɔzɔm]) fellow, guy; old fellow;
bonhomme de neige snowman; **Bonhomme Hiver** Jack Frost; **faux bonhomme** humbug; **petit bonhomme**
little man (*child*)

boni [bɔni] *m* bonus; discount coupon;
surplus (*over estimated expenses*)

bonification [bɔnifikasjɔ] *f* improvement; discount; bonus; advantage

bonifier [bɔnifje] *tr* to improve; to give
a discount to

boniment [bɔnimɑ] *m* sales talk,
smooth talk

bonimenteur [bɔnimɑtœr] *m* huckster,
charlatan

bonjour [bɔʒur] *m* good day, good
morning, good afternoon, hello

bonne [bɔn] *f* maid; **bonne à tout faire**
maid of all work

bonne-maman [bɔnmamɑ] *f* (*pl* **bon-
nes-mamans**) grandma

bonnement [bɔnmɑ] *adv* honestly,
plainly

bonnet [bɔnɛ] *m* bonnet; stocking cap;
cup (*of a brassière*); (mil) undress
hat; **bonnet d'âne** dunce cap; **bonnet
de nuit** nightcap; **gros bonnet** (coll)
VIP

bonneterie [bɔnɛtri] *f* hosiery; knit-
wear

bon-papa [bɔpapa] *m* (*pl* **bons-papas**)
grandpa

bonsoir [bɔswar] *m* good evening;
(coll) good night

bonté [bɔte] *f* goodness; kindness

booster [bustœr] *m* (rok) booster

borborygme [bɔrbɔrigm] *m* rumbling
(*in the stomach*)

bord [bɔr] *m* edge, border; rim, brim;
side (*of a ship*); **à bord** on board; **à
pleins bords** overflowing; without
hindrance; **à ras bords** full to the
brim; **être du (même) bord de** to be
of the same mind as; **faux bord** list
(*of ship*); **jeter par-dessus bord** to
throw overboard

bordage [bɔrdaʒ] *m* edging (*of dress*);
planking (*of ship*)

bordé [bɔrde] *m* border, edging

bordée [bɔrde] *f* broadside, volley;
(naut) tack; **bordée de bâbord** port
watch; **bordée de tribord** starboard
watch; **courir une bordée** to go sky-
larking on shore leave; **tirer une bordée** to jump ship

bordel [bɔrdɛl] *m* (vulgar) brothel

borde-lais [bɔrdəlɛ] **-laise** [lɛz] *adj* of
Bordeaux || *f* Bordeaux cask || (*cap*)
mf native or inhabitant of Bordeaux

border [bɔrde] *tr* to border; to hem;
to sail along (*the coast*); **border un
lit** to make a bed

borde-reau [bɔrdəro] *m* (*pl* **-reaux**)
itemized account, memorandum

bordure [bɔrdyr] *f* border

bore [bɔr] *m* boron

boréal boréale [bɔreal] *adj* (*pl* **boréaux**
[bɔreo]) or **boréals**) boreal; northern

borgne [bɔrɲ] *adj* one-eyed; blind in
one eye; disreputable (*bar, house,
etc.*) || *mf* one-eyed person

borne [bɔrn] *f* landmark; boundary
stone; milestone; (elec) binding post,
terminal; (slang) kilometer; **bornes**
bounds, limits

bor-né -née [bɔrne] *adj* limited, narrow; dull (*mind*)

borner [bɔrne] *tr* to mark out the
boundary of; to set limits to || *ref* to
restrain oneself

bosquet [bɔskɛ] *m* grove

bosse [bɔs] *f* hump; bump; (coll) flair

bosseler [bɔsle] §34 *tr* to emboss; to
dent

bossoir [bɔswar] *m* davit; bow (*of
ship*)

bos·su -sue [bɔsy] *adj* hunchbacked ||
mf hunchback; **rire comme un bossu**
to split one's sides laughing

botanique [bɔtanik] *adj* botanical || *f*
botany

botte [bɔt] *f* boot; bunch (*e.g., of
radishes*); sword thrust; **lécher les
bottes à qn** (coll) to lick s.o.'s boots

botteler [bɔtle] §34 *tr* to tie in bunches

botter [bɔte] *tr* to boot, to boot out;
cela me botte that suits me || *ref* to
put on one's boots

bottier [bɔtje] *m* custom shoemaker

Bottin [bɔtɛ] *m* business directory

bottine [bɔtin] *f* high button shoe

boubouler [bubule] *intr* to hoot like an
owl

bouc [buk] *m* billy goat; goatee; **bouc
émissaire** scapegoat

boucan [bukɑ] *m* smokehouse; (coll)
uproar

boucaner [bukane] *tr* to smoke (*meat*)

boucanier [bukanje] *m* buccaneer

boucharde [buʃard] *f* bushhammer

bouche [buʃ] *f* mouth; muzzle (*of gun*); door (*of oven*); entrance (*to subway*); **bouche close!** mum's the word!; **bouche d'incendie** fire hydrant; **bouches mouth** (*of river*); **faire la petite bouche à** to turn up one's nose at

bouchée [buʃe] *f* mouthful; patty; chocolate cream (*candy*)

boucher [buʃe] *m* butcher ‖ *tr* to stop up, to plug; to wall up; to cut off (*the view*); to bung (*a barrel*); to cork (*a bottle*); **bouché à l'émeri** (coll) completely dumb ‖ *ref* to be stopped up

boucherie [buʃri] *f* butcher shop; **boucherie chevaline** horsemeat butcher shop

bouche-trou [buʃtru] *m* (*pl* **-trous**) stopgap

bouchon [buʃɔ̃] *m* cork, stopper; bob (*on a fishline*); **bouchon de circulation** traffic jam

bouclage [buklaʒ] *m* closing of circuit; (mil) encirclement

boucle [bukl] *f* buckle; earring; curl; (aer) loop; **boucler la boucle** to loop the loop

boucler [bukle] *tr* to buckle; to curl (*the hair*); to lock up (*prisoners*); to put a nose ring on (*a bull*); **boucler son budget** (coll) to make ends meet; **la boucler** (slang) to shut up, to button one's lip ‖ *intr* to curl

bouclier [buklije] *m* shield; **bouclier antithermique** heat shield

bouddhisme [budism] *m* Buddhism

bouddhiste [budist] *adj* & *mf* Buddhist

bouder [bude] *tr* to be distant toward ‖ *intr* to pout, sulk

bou·deur [budœr] **-deuse** [døz] *adj* pouting ‖ *mf* sullen person

boudin [budɛ̃] *m* blood sausage; **à boudin** spiral

boudiner [budine] *tr* to twist

boue [bu] *f* mud

bouée [bwe] *f* buoy; **bouée de sauvetage** life preserver

boueur [bwœr] *m* garbage collector; scavenger

bou·eux [bwø] **boueuse** [bwøz] *adj* muddy; grimy; (typ) sharp

bouf·fant [bufɑ̃] **bouf·fante** [bufɑ̃t] *adj* puffed (*sleeves*); baggy (*trousers*)

bouffe [buf] *adj* comic (*opera*) ‖ *f* (slang) grub

bouffée [bufe] *f* puff, gust

bouffer [bufe] *tr* (slang) to gobble up ‖ *intr* to puff out

bouf·fi -fie [bufi] *adj* puffed up or out

bouffir [bufir] *tr* & *intr* to puff up

bouffissure [bufisyr] *f* swelling

bouf·fon [bufɔ̃] **bouf·fonne** [bufɔn] *adj* & *m* buffoon, comic

bouffonnerie [bufɔnri] *f* buffoonery

bouge [buʒ] *m* bulge; hovel, dive

bougeoir [buʒwar] *m* flat candlestick

bougeotte [buʒɔt] *f* (coll) wanderlust

bouger [buʒe] §38 *tr*—**ne bougez rien!** (coll) don't move a thing! ‖ *intr* to budge, stir

bougie [buʒi] *f* candle; candlepower; spark plug

bou·gon [bugɔ̃] **-gonne** [gɔn] *adj* grumbling ‖ *mf* grumbler

bougran [bugrɑ̃] *m* buckram

bou·gre [bugr] **-gresse** [grɛs] *mf* (slang) customer; **bougre d'âne** (slang) perfect ass ‖ *m* (slang) guy; **bon bougre** (slang) swell guy ‖ *f* (slang) wench

bougrement [bugrəmɑ̃] *adv* (slang) awfully, darned

bouillabaisse [bujabɛs] *f* bouillabaisse, fish stew, chowder

bouil·lant [bujɑ̃] **bouil·lante** [bujɑ̃t] *adj* boiling; fiery, impetuous

bouilleur [bujœr] *m* distiller (*of brandy*); boiler tube; small nuclear reactor

bouilli [buji] *m* beef stew

bouillir [bujir] §9 *tr* & *intr* to boil; **faire bouillir la marmite** (coll) to bring home the bacon

bouilloire [bujwar] *f* kettle

bouillon [bujɔ̃] *m* broth, bouillon; bubble; bubbling; cheap restaurant; **à gros bouillons** gushing; **boire un bouillon** (coll) to gulp water; (coll) to suffer business losses; **bouillon de culture** (bact) broth; **bouillon d'onze heures** poisoned drink; **bouillons unsold** copies, remainders

bouillonnement [bujɔnmɑ̃] *m* boiling; effervescence

bouillonner [bujɔne] *tr* to put puffs in (*a dress*) ‖ *intr* to boil up; to have copies left over

bouillotte [bujɔt] *f* hot-water bottle

boulanger [bulɑ̃ʒe] *m* baker ‖ §38 *intr* to bake bread

boulangerie [bulɑ̃ʒri] *f* bakery

boule [bul] *f* ball; (slang) nut, head; **boule d'eau chaude** hot-water bottle; **boule de neige** snowball; **boule noire** blackball; **boules** bowling; **en boule** (fig) tied in a knot, on edge; **perdre la boule** (slang) to go off one's rocker; **se mettre en boule** (coll) to get mad

bou·leau [bulo] *m* (*pl* **-leaux**) birch

boule-de-neige [buldənɛʒ] *f* (*pl* **boules-de-neige**) guelder-rose; meadow mushroom

bouledogue [buldɔg] *m* bulldog

bouler [bule] *tr* to pad (*a bull's horn*) ‖ *intr* to roll like a ball; **envoyer bouler** (slang) to send (*s.o.*) packing

boulet [bulɛ] *m* cannonball; (coll) cross to bear

boulette [bulɛt] *f* ball, pellet

boulevard [bulvar] *m* boulevard; **boulevard périphérique** belt road

boulevar·dier [bulvardje] **-dière** [djɛr] *adj* fashionable ‖ *m* boulevardier, man about town

bouleversement [bulvɛrsəmɑ̃] *m* upset

bouleverser [bulvɛrse] *tr* to upset; to overthrow

boulier [bulje] *m* abacus (*for scoring billiards*)

bouline [bulin] *f* (naut) bowline

boulingrin [bulɛ̃grɛ̃] *m* bowling green

bouliste [bulist] *mf* bowler

boulodrome [bulɔdrɔm] *m* bowling alley

boulon [bulɔ̃] *m* bolt; **boulon à œil** eyebolt

boulonner [bulɔne] *tr* to bolt || *intr* (slang) to work

bou·lot [bulo] **-lotte** [lɔt] *adj* (coll) dumpy, squat || *m* (slang) cylindrical loaf of bread; (slang) work

boulotter [bulɔte] *tr* (slang) to eat

boum [bum] *interj* boom!

bouquet [buke] *m* bouquet; clump (*of trees*); prawn; jack rabbit; **le bouquet** (coll) it's tops; (coll) that's the last straw

bouquetière [buktjer] *f* flower girl

bouquin [bukɛ̃] *m* (coll) book; (coll) old book

bouquiner [bukine] *intr* to shop around for old books; (coll) to read

bouquinerie [bukinri] *f* secondhand books; secondhand bookstore

bouqui·neur [bukinœr] **-neuse** [nøz] *mf* collector of old books; browser in bookstores

bouquiniste [bukinist] *mf* secondhand bookdealer

bourbe [burb] *f* mire

bour·beux [burbø] **-beuse** [bøz] *adj* miry, muddy

bourbier [burbje] *m* quagmire

bourbillon [burbijɔ̃] *m* core (*of boil*)

bourde [burd] *f* (coll) boner

bourdon [burdɔ̃] *m* bumblebee; big bell; (mus) bourdon; **avoir le bourdon** (slang) to have the blues; **faux bourdon** drone

bourdonnement [burdɔnmɑ̃] *m* buzzing

bourdonner [burdɔne] *tr* (coll) to hum (*a tune*) || *intr* to buzz

bourg [bur] *m* market town

bourgade [burgad] *f* small town

bour·geois [burʒwa] **-geoise** [ʒwaz] *adj* bourgeois, middle-class || *mf* commoner, middle-class person; Philistine; **gros bourgeois** solid citizen || *m* businessman; **en bourgeois** in civies || *f* (slang) old woman (*wife*)

bourgeoisie [burʒwazi] *f* middle class; **haute bourgeoisie** upper middle class; **petite bourgeoisie** lower middle class

bourgeon [burʒɔ̃] *m* bud; pimple

bourgeonnement [burʒɔnmɑ̃] *m* budding

bourgeonner [burʒɔne] *intr* to bud; to break out in pimples

bourgeron [burʒərɔ̃] *m* jumper, overalls; sweat shirt

bourgogne [burgɔɲ] *m* Burgundy (*wine*) || (cap) *f* Burgundy (*province*); **la Bourgogne** Burgundy

bourgui·gnon [burgiɲɔ̃] **-gnonne** [ɲɔn] *adj* Burgundian || *m* Burgundian (*dialect*) || (cap) *mf* Burgundian

bourlinguer [burlɛ̃ge] *intr* to labor (*in high seas*); (coll) to travel, to venture forth

bourrade [burad] *f* sharp blow; poke

bourrage [buraʒ] *m* cramming; **bourrage de crâne** (coll) ballyhoo

bourre [bur] *f* stuffing, animal hair

bour·reau [buro] *m* (*pl* **-reaux**) executioner; torturer; **bourreau des cœurs** lady-killer; **bourreau de travail** glutton for work

bourrée [bure] *f* fagot of twigs

bourreler [burle] §34 *tr* to torment

bourrelet [burle] *m* weather stripping; roll (*of fat*); contour pillow

bourrer [bure] *tr* to stuff, cram; **bourrer de coups** to pummel, slug; **bourrer le crâne à** (coll) to hand (*s.o.*) a line, to take (*s.o.*) in || *ref* to stuff

bourriche [burif] *f* hamper

bourrique [burik] *f* she-ass; (coll) ass

bour·ru -rue [bury] *adj* rough; grumpy; unfermented (*wine*)

bourse [burs] *f* purse; scholarship, fellowship; stock exchange, bourse; **bourse du travail** labor union hall; **bourses** scrotum

bourse-à-pasteur [bursapastœr] *f* (*pl* **bourses-à-pasteur** [bursapastœr]) (bot) shepherd's-purse

boursicaut or **boursicot** [bursiko] *m* little purse; nest egg

boursicoter [bursikɔte] *intr* to dabble in the stock market

bour·sier [bursje] **-sière** [sjer] *adj* scholarship (*student*); stock-market (*operation*) || *mf* scholar (*holder of scholarship*); speculator

boursoufler [bursufle] *tr* to puff up

bousculer [buskyle] *tr* to jostle

bouse [buz] *f*—**bouse de vache** cow dung

bouseux [buzø] *m* (slang) peasant

bousillage [buzijaʒ] *m* cob (*mixture of clay and straw*); (coll) botched job

bousiller [buzije] *tr* (coll) to bungle; (slang) to smash up || *intr* to build with cob

boussole [busɔl] *f* compass; **perdre la boussole** (coll) to go off one's rocker

boustifaille [bustifaj] *f* (slang) feasting; (slang) good food

bout [bu] *m* end; piece, scrap, bit; **à bout** exhausted; **à bout de bras** at arm's length; **à bout portant** point-blank; **à tout bout de champ** at every turn, repeatedly; **au bout du compte** after all; **bout de fil** (telp) (coll) ring, call; **bout de l'an** watch night; **bout d'essai** screen test; **bout d'homme** wisp of a man; **bout filtre** filter tip; **de bout en bout** from start to finish; **montrer le bout de l'oreille** to show one's true colors; **rire du bout des dents** to force a laugh; **sur le bout du doigt** or **sur le bout des doigts** at one's fingertips; **venir à bout de** to succeed in, to triumph over

boutade [butad] *f* sally, quip; whim

bout-dehors [budəɔr] *m* (*pl* **bouts-dehors**) (naut) boom

boute-en-train [butɑ̃trɛ̃] *m invar* life of the party

boute-feu [butfø] *m* (*pl* **-feux**) firebrand

bouteille [butej] *f* bottle; **bouteille isolante** vacuum bottle

bouteiller [buteje] *m* (hist) cupbearer

bouterolle [butrɔl] *f* ward (*of lock*); rivet snap

boute-selle [butsɛl] *m* boots and saddles (*trumpet call*)

boutique [butik] *f* shop; stock, goods; workshop; set of tools; **boutique cadeaux, boutique de souvenirs** gift shop; **boutique de modiste** millinery shop; **quelle boutique!** (coll) what a hellhole!, what an awful place!

boutiquier [butikje] *m* shopkeeper

bouton [butɔ̃] *m* button; pimple; doorknob; bud; **bouton de puissance** volume control

bouton-d'argent [butɔ̃darʒã] *m* (*pl* **boutons-d'argent**) sneezewort

bouton-d'or [butɔ̃dɔr] *m* (*pl* **boutonsd'or**) buttercup

boutonner [butɔne] *tr* to button || *intr* to bud

bouton·neux [butɔnø] **bouton-neuse** [butɔnøz] *adj* pimply

boutonnière [butɔnjɛr] *f* buttonhole

bouton-pression [butɔ̃presjɔ̃] *m* (*pl* **boutons-pression**) snap fastener

bouture [butyr] *f* cutting (*from a plant*)

bouturer [butyre] *tr* to propagate (*plants*) by cuttings || *intr* to shoot suckers

bouverie [buvri] *f* cowshed

bou·vier [buvje] **-vière** [vjɛr] *mf* cowherd

bouvillon [buvijɔ̃] *m* steer, young bullock

bouvreuil [buvrœj] *m* bullfinch; **bouvreuil cramoisi** scarlet grosbeak

box [bɔks] *m* (*pl* **boxes**) stall

boxe [bɔks] *f* boxing

boxer [bɔksœr] *m* boxer (*dog*) || [bɔkse] *tr* & *intr* to box

boxeur [bɔksœr] *m* (sports) boxer

boy [bɔj] *m* houseboy; chorus boy

boyau [bwajo] *m* (*pl* **boyaux**) intestine, gut; inner tube; (mil) communication trench

boycottage [bɔjkɔtaʒ] *m* boycott

boycotter [bɔjkɔte] *tr* to boycott

boy-scout [bɔjskut] *m* (*pl* **-scouts**) boy scout

b. p. f. *abbr* (**bon pour francs**) value in francs

bracelet [braslɛ] *m* bracelet; wristband; **bracelet de caoutchouc** rubber band; **bracelet de cheville** anklet

bracelet-montre [braslɛmɔ̃tr] *m* (*pl* **bracelets-montres**) wrist watch

braconnage [brakɔnaʒ] *m* poaching

braconner [brakɔne] *intr* to poach

bracon·nier [brakɔnje] **bracon·nière** [brakɔnjɛr] *mf* poacher

brader [brade] *tr* to sell off

braderie [bradri] *f* clearance sale

braguette [bragɛt] *m* fly (*of trousers*)

brahmane [braman] *m* Brahman

brai [brɛ] *m* resin, pitch

braille [braj] *m* braille

brailler [braje] *tr* & *intr* to bawl

brail·leur [brajœr] **brail·leuse** [brajøz] *adj* loudmouthed || *mf* loudmouth

braiment [brɛmã] *m* bray

braire [brɛr] §68 (usually used in: *inf*; *ger*; *pp*; 3d *sg* & *pl*) *intr* to bray

braise [brɛz] *f* embers, coals

braiser [brɛze] *tr* to braise

braisière [brɛzjɛr] *f* braising pan

bramer [brame] *intr* to bell

bran [brã] *m* bran; (slang) dung; **bran de scie** sawdust

brancard [brãkar] *m* stretcher; shaft (*of carriage*)

brancardier [brãkardje] *m* stretcher-bearer

branche [brãʃ] *f* branch

brancher [brãʃe] *tr* to branch, fork; to hook up, connect; (elec) to plug in || *intr* to perch

brande [brãd] *f* heather; heath

brandir [brãdir] *tr* to brandish

brandon [brãdɔ̃] *m* torch; firebrand; **brandon de discorde** mischief-maker

bran·lant [brãlã] **-lante** [lãt] *adj* shaky, tottering, unsteady

branle [brãl] *m* oscillation; impetus; **mener le branle** to lead the dance; **mettre en branle** to set in motion

branle-bas [brãləba] *m invar* call to battle stations; bustle, commotion

branler [brãle] *tr* to shake (*the head*) || *intr* to shake; to oscillate; to be loose (*said of tooth*); **branler dans le manche** to be about to fall

braque [brak] *adj* (coll) featherbrained || *mf* (coll) featherbrain || *m* pointer (*dog*)

braquer [brake] *tr* to aim, point; to fix (*the eyes*); to turn (*a steering wheel*); **braquer contre** to turn (*e.g., an audience*) against || *intr* to steer

bras [bra] *m* arm; handle; shaft; à **bras raccourcis** violently; **bras de mer** sound (*passage of water*); **bras de pick-up** pickup arm, tone arm; **bras dessus bras dessous** arm in arm; **en bras de chemise** in shirt sleeves; **manquer de bras** to be short-handed

braser [braze] *tr* to braze

brasero [brazero] *m* brazier

brasier [brazje] *m* glowing coals; blaze

bras-le-corps [bralkɔr] *m*—à **bras-le-corps** around the waist

brassage [brasaʒ] *m* brewing

brasse [bras], [bras] *f* fathom; breast stroke

brassée [brase] *f* armful; stroke (*in swimming*)

brasser [brase] *tr* to brew

brasserie [brasri] *f* brewery; restaurant, lunchroom

bras·seur [brasœr] **bras·seuse** [brasøz] *mf* brewer; swimmer doing the breast stroke; **brasseur d'affaires** person with many irons in the fire

brassière [brasjer] *f* sleeved shirt (*for an infant*); shoulder strap; **brassière de sauvetage** life preserver

bravache [bravaʃ] *adj* & *m* braggart

bravade [bravad] *f* bravado

brave [brav] *adj* brave || (when standing before noun) *adj* worthy, honest || *m* brave man

braver [brave] *tr* to brave

bravoure [bravur] *f* bravery, gallantry

break [brɛk] *m* station wagon

brebis [brəbi] *f* ewe; sheep, lamb; **brebis galeuse** black sheep

brèche [brɛʃ] *f* breach (*in a wall*); gap (*between mountains*); nick (*e.g., on china*); (fig) dent (*in a fortune*);

battre en brèche to batter; (fig) to disparage; mourir sur la brèche to go down fighting

bredouille [brəduj]—rentrer or revenir bredouille to return empty-handed

bredouiller [brəduje] tr to stammer out (an excuse) || intr to mumble

bref [brɛf] brève [brɛv] adj brief, short; curt || m papal brief || f short syllable; brèves et longues dots and dashes || bref adv briefly, in short

brelan [brəlɑ̃] m (cards) three of a kind

breloque [brələk] f trinket, charm; battre la breloque to sound the all clear; to keep irregular time; (coll) to have a screw loose somewhere

brème [brɛm] f (ichth) bream

Brésil [brezil] m—le Brésil Brazil

brési·lien -lienne [breziljɛ̃] -lienne [ljɛn] adj Brazilian || (cap) mf Brazilian

Bretagne [brətaɲ] f Brittany; la Bretagne Brittany

bretelle [brətɛl] f strap, sling; access route; bretelles suspenders

bre·ton [brətɔ̃] -tonne [tɔn] adj Breton || m Breton (language) || (cap) mf Breton (person)

bretteur [brɛtœr] m swashbuckler

bretzel [brɛtzɛl] m pretzel

breuvage [brœvaʒ] m beverage, drink

brevet [brəvɛ] m diploma; license; (mil) commission; brevet d'invention patent

breve·té -tée [brəvte] adj commissioned; patented; non breveté noncommissioned || m commissioned officer

breveter [brəvte] §34 tr to patent

bréviaire [brevjɛr] m (eccl) breviary

bribe [brib] f hunk of bread; bribes scraps, leavings, fragments

bric [brik] m—de bric et de broc with odds and ends; somehow

bric-à-brac [brikabrak] m invar secondhand merchandise; junk shop

brick [brik] m brig (kind of ship)

bricolage [brikɔlaʒ] m do-it-yourself

bricoler [brikɔle] intr to do odd jobs; to putter around

brico·leur [brikɔlœr] -leuse [løz] mf jack-of-all-trades || m handyman

bride [brid] f bridle; strap; clamp; à toute bride or à bride abattue full speed ahead

bridge [bridʒ] m (cards, dentistry) bridge

bridger [bridʒe] intr to play bridge

brid·geur [bridʒœr] -geuse [ʒøz] mf bridge player

briefing [brifiŋ] m briefing

brièvement [brijɛvmɑ̃] adv briefly

brièveté [brijɛvte] f brevity

brigade [brigad] f brigade

brigadier [brigadje] m corporal; police sergeant; noncom

brigand [brigɑ̃] m brigand

brigantin [brigɑ̃tɛ̃] m brigantine

brigue [brig] f intrigue, lobbying

briguer [brige] tr to influence underhandedly; to lobby for (s.th.); to court (favor, votes)

brigueur [brigœr] m schemer

bril·lant [brijɑ̃] bril·lante [brijɑ̃t] adj brilliant, bright || m brilliancy, luster; fingernail polish

briller [brije] intr to shine; to sparkle; faire briller to show (s.o.) off

brimade [brimad] f hazing

brimborion [brɛ̃bɔrjɔ̃] m mere trifle

brimer [brime] tr to haze

brin [brɛ̃] m blade; sprig, shoot; staple (of hemp, linen); strand (of rope); belt (of pulley); (coll) (little) bit, e.g., un brin d'air a (little) bit of air; ne . . . brin §90 (archaic) not a bit, not a single; un beau brin de fille (coll) a fine figure of a girl

brinde [brɛ̃d] f (archaic) toast

brindille [brɛ̃dij] f twig, sprig

brioche [brijɔʃ] f brioche, breakfast roll

brique [brik] f brick

briquer [brike] tr (coll) to polish up, scour

briquet [brikɛ] m lighter

briquetage [briktaʒ] m brickwork

briqueter [brikte] §34 tr to brick (up)

briqueterie [briktri] f brickyard

briqueteur [briktœr] m bricklayer

brisant [brizɑ̃] m breakers; brisants surf

brise [briz] f breeze

bri·sé -sée [brize] adj broken; folding (door) || fpl see brisées

brise-bise [brizbiz] m invar weather stripping; café curtain

brisées [brize] fpl track, footsteps

brise-glace [brizglas] m invar (naut) icebreaker

brise-jet [brizʒɛ] m invar (anti)splash attachment (for water faucet), spray filter

brise-lames [brizlam] m invar breakwater

brisement [brizmɑ̃] m breaking

briser [brize] tr, intr, & ref to break

brise-tout [briztu] m invar (coll) butterfingers, clumsy person

bri·seur [brizœr] -seuse [zøz] mf breaker (person); briseur de grève strikebreaker

brise-vent [brizvɑ̃] m invar windbreak

brisque [brisk] f service stripe

bristol [bristɔl] m Bristol board, pasteboard; visiting card

brisure [brizyr] f break; joint

britannique [britanik] adj British || (cap) mf Briton

broc [bro] m pitcher, jug

brocanter [brɔkɑ̃te] tr to buy, sell, or trade (secondhand articles) || intr to deal in secondhand articles

brocan·teur [brɔkɑ̃tœr] -teuse [tøz] mf secondhand dealer

brocard [brɔkar] m lampoon, brickbat; (zool) brocket; lancer des brocards to make sarcastic remarks, to gibe

brocart [brɔkar] m brocade

broche [brɔʃ] f brooch; pin; (culin) spit, skewer

bro·ché -chée [brɔʃe] adj paperback, paperbound

brocher [brɔʃe] tr to brocade; to sew (book bindings); (coll) to hurry through

brochet [brɔʃɛ] m (ichth) pike

brochette [brɔʃet] *f* skewer; skewerful; string (*of decorations*)

bro·cheur [brɔʃœr] **-cheuse** [ʃøz] *mf* bookbinder ‖ *f* stapler

brochure [brɔʃyr] *f* brochure, pamphlet

brocoli [brɔkɔli] *m* broccoli

brodequin [brɔdkɛ̃] *m* buskin

broder [brɔde] *tr & intr* to embroider

broderie [brɔdri] *f* embroidery

brome [brom] *m* (chem) bromine

bromure [brɔmyr] *m* bromide

bronche [brɔ̃ʃ] *f* bronchial tube

broncher [brɔ̃ʃe] *intr* to stumble; to flinch; to grumble

bronchique [brɔ̃ʃik] *adj* bronchial

bronchite [brɔ̃ʃit] *f* bronchitis

bronze [brɔ̃z] *m* bronze

bron·zé -zée [brɔ̃ze] *adj* bronze; suntanned

bronzer [brɔ̃ze] *tr & ref* to bronze; to sun-tan

brook [bruk] *m* (turf) water jump

broquette [brɔket] *f* brad, tack

brossage [brɔsaʒ] *m* brushing

brosse [brɔs] *f* brush; **brosse à cheveux** hairbrush; **brosse à dents** toothbrush; **brosse à habits** clothesbrush; **brosse de chiendent** scrubbing brush; **brosses** shrubs, bushes

brosser [brɔse] *tr* to brush; to paint the broad outlines of (*a picture*); (fig) to sketch; (slang) to beat, conquer ‖ *ref* to brush one's clothes; (coll) to skimp, to scrimp

brouet [brue] *m* gruel, broth

brouette [bruet] *f* wheelbarrow

brouetter [bruete] *tr* to carry in a wheelbarrow

brouhaha [bruaa] *m* (coll) babel, hubbub

brouillage [brujaʒ] *m* (rad) jamming

brouillamini [brujamini] *m* (coll) mess

brouillard [brujar] *adj masc* blotting (*paper*) ‖ *m* fog, mist; (com) daybook

brouillasse [brujas] *f* (coll) drizzle

brouillasser [brujase] *intr* (coll) to drizzle

brouille [bruj] *f* discord, misunderstanding

brouiller [bruje] *tr* to mix up; to jam (*a broadcast*); to scramble (*eggs*); **brouiller mes (ses, etc.) pistes** to cover my (his, etc.) tracks ‖ *ref* to quarrel; to cloud over

brouil·lon [brujɔ̃] **-lonne** [brujɔn] *adj* crackpot; blundering; at loose ends ‖ *mf* crackpot ‖ *m* scratch pad; draft; outline

broussailles [brusaj] *fpl* underbrush, brushwood; **en broussailles** disheveled

broussail·leux [brusajø] **broussail·leuse** [brusajøz] *adj* bushy

broussard [brusar] *m* (coll) bushman, colonist

brousse [brus] *f* veldt, bush

broutage [brutaʒ] *m* grazing (*of animal*); ratatat (*of a machine*)

brouter [brute] *intr* to browse, graze; to jerk, to grab (*said of clutch, cutting tool, brake*)

broutille [brutij] *f* twig; trifle, bauble

broyage [brwajaʒ] *m* grinding, crushing

broyer [brwaje] §47 *tr* to grind, crush; **broyer du noir** (coll) to be down in the dumps

broy·eur [brwajœr] **broyeuse** [brwajøz] *adj* grinding, crushing ‖ *mf* grinder, crusher ‖ *f* (mach) grinder

bru [bry] *f* daughter-in-law

bruant [bryɑ̃] *m* (orn) bunting; **bruant jaune** yellowhammer

brucelles [brysel] *fpl* tweezers

brugnon [bryɲɔ̃] *m* nectarine

bruine [brɥin] *f* drizzle

bruiner [brɥine] *intr* to drizzle

bruire [brɥir] (usually used in: **inf**; 3d sg pres ind **bruit**; 3d sg & pl imperf ind **bruyait** or **bruissait**, **bruyaient** or **bruissaient**) *intr* to rustle; to hum, buzz; to splash

bruissement [brɥismɑ̃] *m* rustling

bruit [brɥi] *m* noise; stir, fuss; **le bruit court que** it is rumored that

bruitage [brɥitaʒ] *m* sound effects

brû·lant [brylɑ̃] **-lante** [lɑ̃t] *adj* burning; ardent; ticklish (*question*)

brû·lé -lée [bryle] *adj* burned ‖ *m* smell of burning; burned taste ‖ *f* (slang) beating

brûle-gueule [brylgœl] *m invar* (slang) short pipe (*for smoking*)

brûle-parfum [brylparfœ̃] *m invar* incense burner

brûle-pourpoint [brylpurpwɛ̃]—**à brûle-pourpoint** point-blank

brûler [bryle] *tr* to burn; to burn out (*a fuse*); to go through (*a red light*); to pass (*another car*); to roast (*coffee*); to distill (*liquor*); **brûler la cervelle à qn** to blow s.o.'s brains out ‖ *intr* to burn, burn up ‖ *ref* to burn up, to be burned

brû·leur [brylœr] **-leuse** [løz] *mf* arsonist; distiller ‖ *m* (mach) burner; **brûleur à café** coffee roaster

brûloir [brylwar] *m* roaster

brûlure [brylyr] *f* burn

brume [brym] *f* fog, mist

brumer [bryme] *intr* to be foggy

bru·meux [brymø] **-meuse** [møz] *adj* foggy, misty

brun [brœ̃] **brune** [bryn] *adj* dark-brown; dark ‖ *m* brunet; dark brown ‖ *f* see **brune**

brunâtre [brynɑtr] *adj* brownish

brune [bryn] *f* brunette; twilight

bru·net [bryne] **-nette** [net] *adj* black-haired ‖ *m* dark-haired man, brunet ‖ *f* brunette

bru·ni -nie [bryni] *adj* burnished, polished ‖ *m* burnishing, polish

brunir [brynir] *tr* to brown; to burnish, polish ‖ *intr* to turn brown

brunissoir [bryniswar] *m* (mach) buffer

brusque [brysk] *adj* brusque; sudden; surprise (*attack*); quick (*movements; decision*)

brusquer [bryske] *tr* to hurry, rush through; to be blunt with

brusquerie [bryskri] *f* brusqueness; suddenness

brut [bry] **brute** [bryt] *adj* crude, unpolished, unrefined, uncivilized; uncut (*diamond*); raw (*material*); dry (*champagne*); brown (*sugar*); gross (*weight*) ‖ *f* see **brute** ‖ **brut** *adv*—**peser brut** to have a gross weight of

bru·tal -tale [brytal] (*pl* **-taux** [to]) *adj* brutal, rough; outspoken; coarse, beastly ‖ *mf* brute, bully

brutaliser [brytalize] *tr* to bully; to mistreat

brutalité [brytalite] *f* brutality; **brutalité policière** police brutality

brute *f* brute

Bruxelles [brysel] *f* Brussels

bruxel·lois [bryselwa] **bruxel·loise** [bryselwaz] *adj* of Brussels ‖ (*cap*) *mf* native or inhabitant of Brussels

bruyamment [bryijamã] *adv* noisily

bruyant [bruijã] **bruyante** [bruijãt] *adj* noisy

bruyère [bruijer] *f* heather; heath

buanderie [byãdɔri] *f* laundry room

buan·dier [byãdje] **-dière** [djer] *mf* laundry worker ‖ *f* laundress

bubonique [bybɔnik] *adj* bubonic

bûche [byʃ] *f* log; (slang) dunce; **bûche de Noël** yule log; cake decorated as a yule log; **ramasser une bûche** (slang) to take a tumble

bûcher [byʃe] *m* woodshed; pyre; stake (*e.g.*, *for burning witches*) ‖ *tr* to rough-hew; (slang) to bone up on ‖ *intr* (slang) to keep on working; to slave away ‖ *ref* (slang) to fight

bûche·ron [byʃrɔ̃] **-ronne** [rɔn] *mf* woodcutter ‖ *m* lumberjack

bûchette [byʃet] *f* stick of wood

bû·cheur [byʃœr] **-cheuse** [ʃøz] *mf* (coll) eager beaver

budget [bydʒe] *m* budget; **boucler son budget** (coll) to make ends meet

budgétaire [bydʒeter] *adj* budgetary

buée [bye] *f* steam; mist

buffet [byfe] *m* buffet; snack bar; station restaurant; **danser devant le buffet** to miss a meal

buf·fle [byfl] **buf·flonne** [byflɔn] *mf* water buffalo; Cape buffalo

bugle [bygl] *m* (mus) saxhorn, bugle ‖ *f* (bot) bugle

building [bildiŋ] *m* large office building, skyscraper

buire [buir] *f* ewer

buis [bui] *m* boxwood

buisson·neux [buisɔnø] **buisson·neuse** [buisɔnøz] *adj* bushy

buisson·nier [buisɔnje] **buisson·nière** [buisɔnjer] *adj*—**faire l'école buissonnière** (coll) to play hooky

bulbe [bylb] *m* bulb

bul·beux [bylbø] **-beuse** [bøz] *adj* bulbous

bulgare [bylgar] *adj* Bulgarian ‖ *m* Bulgarian (*language*) ‖ (*cap*) *mf* Bulgarian (*person*)

Bulgarie [bylgari] *f* Bulgaria; **la Bulgarie** Bulgaria

bulle [byl] *m* wrapping paper ‖ *f* bubble; blister; (eccl) bull

bulletin [byltɛ̃] *m* bulletin; ballot; **bulletin de bagages** baggage check; **bulletin de commande** order blank;

bulletin de naissance birth certificate; **bulletin scolaire** report card

bul·leux [bylø] **bul·leuse** [byløz] *adj* blistery

bure [byr] *m* mine shaft ‖ *f* drugget, sackcloth

bu·reau [byro] *m* (*pl* **-reaux**) desk; office; **bureau à cylindre** roll-top desk; **bureau ambulant** post-office car; **bureau d'aide sociale** welfare department; **Bureau de l'état civil** Bureau of Vital Statistics; **bureau de location** box office; **bureau de placement** employment agency; **bureau de poste** post office; **bureau des objets trouvés** lost-and-found department; **bureau de tabac** tobacco shop; **bureau directoire** cabinet, committee; **deuxième bureau** intelligence division

bureaucrate [byrokrat] *mf* bureaucrat

bureaucratie [byrokrasi] *f* bureaucracy

bureaucratique [byrokratik] *adj* bureaucratic

burette [byret] *f* cruet; oilcan

burin [byrɛ̃] *m* engraving; burin (*tool*)

burlesque [byrlesk] *adj* & *m* burlesque

busard [byzar] *m* harrier, marsh hawk

busc [bysk] *m* whalebone

buse [byz] *f* buzzard

business [biznes] *m* (slang) work; (slang) complicated business

bus·qué -quée [byske] *adj* arched

buste [byst] *m* bust

but [by], [byt] *m* mark, goal, target; aim, end, purpose; point (*scored in game*); **aller droit au but** to come straight to the point; **de but en blanc** point-blank

bu·té -tée [byte] *adj* obstinate, headstrong ‖ *f* abutment

buter [byte] *tr* to prop up; (slang) to bump off, kill ‖ *intr*—**buter contre** to bump into, to stumble on ‖ *ref*—**se buter à** to butt up against; (fig) to be dead set on

buteur [bytœr] *m* scorekeeper

butin [bytɛ̃] *m* booty; profits, savings

butiner [bytine] *tr* to pillage; to gather honey from ‖ *intr* to pillage; to gather honey (*said of bees*); **butiner dans** to browse among (*books*)

butoir [bytwar] *m* buffer, stop, catch

bu·tor -torde [tɔrd] *mf* (slang) lout, good-for-nothing

butte [byt] *f* butte, knoll; **butte de tir** butt, mound (*for target practice*); **être en butte à** to be exposed to

butter [byte] *tr* to hill (*plants*)

buttoir [bytwar] *m* (agr) hiller

buty·reux [bytirø] **-reuse** [røz] *adj* buttery

buvable [byvabl] *adj* drinkable; (pharm) to be taken by mouth

buvard [byvar] *adj* blotting (*paper*) ‖ *m* blotter

buvette [byvet] *f* bar, fountain

buvette-buffet [byvetbyfe] *f* (coll) snack bar

bu·veur [byvœr] **-veuse** [vøz] *mf* drinker; **buveur d'eau** abstainer; vacationist at a spa

byzan·tin [bizɑ̃tɛ̃] **-tine** [tin] *adj* Byzantine

C

C, c [se] *m invar* third letter of the French alphabet

C/ *abbr* (**compte**) account

ça [sa] *pron indef* (coll) that; **ah ça non!** no indeed!; **avec ça!** tell me another!; **ça y est** that's that; that's it, that's right; **comment ça!** how so?; **et avec ça?** what else?; **où ça,** where?

çà [sa] *adv*—**ah çà!** now then! **çà et là** here and there

cabale [kabal] *f* cabal, intrigue

cabaler [kabale] *intr* to cabal, intrigue

caban [kabã] *m* (naut) peacoat

cabane [kaban] *f* cabin, hut

cabanon [kabanɔ̃] *m* hut; padded cell

cabaret [kabare] *m* tavern; cabaret, night club; liquor closet

cabas [kabɑ] *m* basket

cabestan [kabestã] *m* capstan

cabillaud [kabijo] *m* haddock; (coll) fresh cod

cabine [kabin] *f* cabin (*of ship or airplane*); bathhouse; car (*of elevator*); cab (*of locomotive or truck*); **cabine téléphonique** telephone booth

cabinet [kabine] *m* (ministry) cabinet; study (*of scholar*); office (*of professional man*); clientele; staff (*of a cabinet officer*); toilet; storeroom closet; **cabinet d'aisance** rest room; **cabinet de débarras** storeroom closet; **cabinet de toilette** powder room; **cabinets** rest rooms

câble [kɑbl] *m* cable

câbler [kable] *tr & intr* to cable

câblier [kablije] *m* cable ship

câblogramme [kɑblɔgram] *m* cablegram

cabo‧chard [kabɔʃar] **-charde** [ʃard] *adj* obstinate, pigheaded

caboche [kabɔʃ] *f* hobnail; (coll) noodle (*head*)

cabochon [kabɔʃɔ̃] *m* uncut gem; stud, upholstery nail

cabot [kabo] *m* (ichth) miller's-thumb, bullhead; (coll) ham (actor)

cabotage [kabotaʒ] *m* coastal navigation, coasting trade

cabo‧tin [kabotɛ̃] **-tine** [tin] *mf* barnstormer; (coll) ham actor; **cabotin de la politique** (coll) corny politician, political orator given to histrionics

cabotinage [kabotinaʒ] *m* barnstorming; (coll) ham acting

cabotiner [kabotine] *intr* to barnstorm; (coll) to play to the grandstand

cabrer [kabre] *tr* to make (*a horse*) rear; to nose up (*a plane*) ‖ *ref* to rear; to kick over the traces; (aer) to nose up

cabri [kabri] *m* (zool) kid

cabriole [kabrijɔl] *f* caper

cabrioler [kabrijɔle] *intr* to caper

cacahouète [kakawet] or **cacahuète** [kakaɥet] *f* peanut

cacao [kakao] *m* cocoa; cocoa bean

cacaotier [kakaɔtje] *m* (bot) cacao

cacaoyer [kakaɔje] *m* (bot) cacao

cacarder [kakarde] *intr* to cackle

cacatoès [kakatɔes] or **cacatois** [kakatwa] *m* cockatoo

cachalot [kaʃalo] *m* sperm whale

cache [kaʃ] *m* masking tape ‖ *f* hiding place

cache-cache [kaʃkaʃ] *m invar* hide-and-seek

cache-col [kaʃkɔl] *m invar* scarf

cachemire [kaʃmir] *m* cashmere

cache-nez [kaʃne] *m invar* muffler

cache-poussière [kaʃpusjer] *m invar* duster (*overgarment*)

cacher [kaʃe] *tr* to hide; **cacher q.ch. à qn** to hide s.th. from s.o. ‖ *ref* to hide; **se cacher à** to hide from; **se cacher de q.ch.** to make a secret of s.th.

cache-radiateur [kaʃradjatœr] *m invar* radiator cover

cache-sexe [kaʃseks] *m invar* G-string

cachet [kaʃe] *m* seal; postmark; fee; price of a lesson; meal ticket; (pharm, phila) cachet; (fig) seal; stylishness; **payer au cachet** to pay a set fee

cacheter [kaʃte] §34 *tr* to seal, to seal up; to seal with wax

cachette [kaʃet] *f* hiding place; **en cachette** secretly

cachot [kaʃo] *m* dungeon; prison

cacophonie [kakɔfɔni] *f* cacophony

cactier [kaktje] or **cactus** [kaktys] *m* cactus

c.-à-d. *abbr* (**c'est-à-dire**) that is

cadastre [kadastr] *m* land-survey register

cadavre [kadɑvr] *m* corpse, cadaver; (slang) dead soldier (*bottle*)

ca‧deau [kado] *m* (*pl* **-deaux**) gift

cadenas [kadna] *m* padlock

cadenasser [kadnase] *tr* to padlock

cadence [kadãs] *f* cadence, rhythm, time; output (*of worker, of factory, etc.*); **cadence de tir** rate of firing

cadencer [kadãse] §51 *tr* to cadence ‖ *intr* to call out cadence

ca‧det [kade] **-dette** [det] *adj* younger ‖ *mf* youngest; junior; (sports) player fifteen to eighteen years old; **le cadet de mes soucis** (coll) the least of my worries ‖ *m* caddy; (mil) cadet; younger brother; younger son ‖ *f* younger sister; younger daughter

cadmium [kadmjɔm] *m* cadmium

cadrage [kadraʒ] *m* (mov, telv) framing; (phot) centering

cadran [kadrã] *m* dial; **cadran d'appel** telephone dial; **cadran solaire** sundial; **faire le tour du cadran** to sleep around the clock

cadre [kadr] *m* frame; framework; setting; outline, framework (*of a literary work*); limits, scope (*of activities or duties*); (mil) cadre; (naut) cot; **cadres** officials; (mil) regulars; **cadres sociaux** memorable dates or events

cadrer [kadre] *tr* to frame (*film*) ‖ *intr* to conform, tally

ca‧duc **-duque** [kadyk] *adj* decrepit,

frail; outlived (*custom*); deciduous (*leaves*); lapsed (*insurance policy*); (law) null and void

caducée [kadyse] *m* caduceus

C.A.F. *abbr* (coût, assurance, fret) **C.I.F.** (*cost, insurance, and freight*)

ca·fard [kafar] **-farde** [fard] *adj* sanctimonious || *mf* hypocrite; (coll) squealer || *m* (coll) cockroach; (coll) blues

café [kafe] *adj invar* tan || *m* coffee; café; coffeehouse; **café chantant** music hall (*with tables*); **café complet** coffee, hot milk, rolls, butter, and jam; **café nature, café noir** black coffee

café-concert [kafekɔ̃ser] *m* (*pl* **cafés-concerts**) music hall (*with tables*), cabaret

caféier [kafeje] *m* coffee plant

caféière [kafejer] *f* coffee plantation

caféine [kafein] *f* caffeine

cafe·tier [kaftje] **-tière** [tjer] *mf* café owner || *f* coffeepot

cafouiller [kafuje] *intr* (slang) to miss (*said of engine*); (slang) to flounder around

cage [kaʒ] *f* cage; **cage d'un ascenseur** elevator shaft; **cage d'un escalier** stairwell; **cage thoracique** thoracic cavity; **en cage** (coll) in the clink, in the pen

cageot [kaʒo] *m* crate

ca·gnard [kaɲar] **-gnarde** [ɲard] *adj* indolent, lazy || *m* (coll) sunny spot

ca·gneux [kaɲø] **-gneuse** [ɲøz] *adj* knock-kneed; pigeon-toed

cagnotte [kaɲɔt] *f* kitty, pool

ca·got [kago] **-gotte** [gɔt] *adj* hypocritical || *mf* hypocrite

cagoule [kagul] *f* cowl; hood (*with eyeholes*)

cahier [kaje] *m* notebook; **cahier à feuilles mobiles** loose-leaf notebook; **cahier des charges** (com) specifications

cahin-caha [kaɛ̃kaa] *adv* (coll) so-so

cahot [kao] *m* jolt, bump

cahoter [kaɔte] *tr & intr* to jolt

caho·teux [kaotø] **-teuse** [tøz] *adj* bumpy (*road*)

cahute [kayt] *f* hut, shack

caille [kaj] *f* quail

cail·lé **-lée** [kaje] *adj* curdled || *m* curd

caillebotis [kajbɔti] *m* boardwalk; (mil) duckboard; (naut) grating

caillebotte [kajbɔt] *f* curds

caillebotter [kajbɔte] *tr & intr* to curdle

cailler [kaje] *tr & ref* to clot, curdle, curd

caillot [kajo] *m* clot; blood clot

cail·lou [kaju] *m* (*pl* **-loux**) pebble; (coll) bald head; **caillou du Rhin** rhinestone

caillou·teux [kajutø] **-teuse** [tøz] *adj* stony (*road*); pebbly (*beach*)

cailloutis [kajuti] *m* crushed stone, gravel

Caïn [kaɛ̃] *m* Cain

Caire [ker] *m*—**Le Caire** Cairo

caisse [kes] *f* chest, box; case (*for packing; of a clock or piano*); chest-

ful, boxful; till, cash register, coffer, safe; cashier, cashier's window; desk (*in a hotel*); **caisse à eau** water tank; **caisse claire** snare drum; **caisse d'épargne** savings bank; **caisse des écoles** scholarship fund; **grosse caisse** bass drum; bass drummer; **petite caisse** petty cash

caisson [kesɔ̃] *m* caisson

cajoler [kaʒɔle] *tr* to cajole, wheedle

cajolerie [kaʒɔlri] *f* cajolery

cajou [kaʒu] *m* cashew nut

cake [kek] *m* fruit cake

cal [kal] *m* (*pl* **cals**) callus, callosity; **cal vicieux** badly knitted bone

calage [kalaʒ] *m* wedging, chocking; stalling (*of motor*)

calamité [kalamite] *f* calamity

calami·teux [kalamitø] **-teuse** [tøz] *adj* calamitous

calandre [kalɑ̃dr] *f* mangle (*for clothes*); calender (*for paper*); grill (*for car radiator*); (ent) weevil; (orn) lark

calandrer [kalɑ̃dre] *tr* to calender

calcaire [kalker] *adj* calcareous; chalky; hard (*water*) || *m* limestone

calcifier [kalsifje] *tr & ref* to calcify

calciner [kalsine] *tr & ref* to burn to a cinder

calcium [kalsjɔm] *m* calcium

calcul [kalkyl] *m* calculation; (math, pathol) calculus; **calcul biliaire** gallstone; **calcul mental** mental arithmetic; **calcul rénal** kidney stone

calcula·teur [kalkylatœr] **-trice** [tris] *adj* calculating || *mf* calculator (*person*) || *m* (mach) calculator || *f* (mach) computer

calculer [kalkyle] *tr & intr* to calculate

cale [kal] *f* wedge, chock; hold (*of ship*); **cale de construction** stocks; **cale sèche** dry dock

ca·lé **-lée** [kale] *adj* stalled; (coll) well-informed; (slang) involved, difficult; **calé en** (coll) strong in, up on

calebasse [kalbas] *f* calabash

calèche [kalɛʃ] *f* open carriage

caleçon [kalsɔ̃] *m* drawers, shorts; **caleçon de bain** swimming trunks

calembour [kalɑ̃bur] *m* pun

calendes [kalɑ̃d] *fpl* calends; **aux calendes grecques** (coll) when pigs fly

calendrier [kalɑ̃drije] *m* calendar

calepin [kalpɛ̃] *m* notebook

caler [kale] *tr* to wedge, to chock; to jam; to stall; to lower (*sail*); (naut) to draw || *intr* to stall (*said of motor*); (coll) to give in || *ref* to stall; to get nicely settled

calfater [kalfate] *tr* to caulk

calfeutrer [kalføtre] *tr* to stop up || *ref* to shut oneself up

calibre [kalibr] *m* caliber

calibrer [kalibre] *tr* to calibrate

calice [kalis] *m* chalice; (bot) calyx

calicot [kaliko] *m* calico; sign, banner; (slang) sales clerk

califat [kalifa] *m* caliphate

calife [kalif] *m* caliph

Californie [kaliforni] *f* California; **la basse Californie** Lower California; **la Californie** California

califourchon [kalifurʃõ]—**à califourchon** astride, astraddle; **s'asseoir à califourchon** to straddle

câ·lin [kɑlɛ̃] **-line** [lin] *adj* coaxing; caressing

câliner [kaline] *tr* to coax; to caress

cal·leux [kalø] **cal·leuse** [kaløz] *adj* callous, calloused

callisthénie [kalisteni] *f* calisthenics

cal·mant [kalmã] **-mante** [mãt] *adj* calming ‖ *m* sedative

calmar [kalmar] *m* squid

calme [kalm] *adj & m* calm

calmement [kalməmã] *adv* calmly

calmer [kalme] *tr* to calm ‖ *ref* to become calm, to calm down

calmir [kalmir] *intr* to abate

calomnie [kalɔmni] *f* calumny, slander

calomnier [kalɔmnje] *tr* to calumniate

calorie [kalɔri] *f* calory

calorifère [kalɔrifɛr] *adj* heating, heat-conducting ‖ *m* heater; **calorifère à air chaud** hot-air heater; **calorifère à eau chaude** hot-water heater

calorifuge [kalɔrifyʒ] *adj* insulating ‖ *m* insulator

calorifuger [kalɔrifyʒe] §38 *tr* to insulate

calorique [kalɔrik] *adj* caloric

calot [kalo] *m* policeman's hat, kepi

calotte [kalɔt] *f* skullcap; dome; (coll) box on the ear; (coll) clergy; **calotte des cieux** vault of heaven; **flanquer une calotte à** (coll) to box on the ear

calotter [kalɔte] *tr* (coll) to box on the ear, to cuff; (slang) to snitch

calque [kalk] *m* tracing; decal; word-for-word correspondence (*between two languages*); slavish imitation; spitting image

calquer [kalke] *tr* to trace; to imitate slavishly

calumet [kalyme] *m* calumet; **calumet de paix** peace pipe

calvados [kalvados] *m* applejack

calvaire [kalver] *m* calvary

calviniste [kalvinist] *adj & mf* Calvinist

calvitie [kalvisi] *f* baldness

camarade [kamarad] *mf* comrade; **camarade de chambre** roommate; **camarade de travail** fellow worker; **camarade d'étude** schoolmate

camaraderie [kamaradri] *f* comradeship; camaraderie, fellowship

ca·mard [kamar] **-marde** [mard] *adj* snub-nosed

cambouis [kãbwi] *m* axle grease

cambrer [kãbre] *tr* to curve, arch

cambrioler [kãbrijɔle] *tr* to break into, to burglarize

cambrio·leur [kãbrijɔlœr] **-leuse** [løz] *mf* burglar

cambrure [kãbryr] *f* curve, arch

cambuse [kãbyz] *f* (naut) storeroom between decks

came [kam] *f* cam

camée [kame] *m* cameo

caméléon [kameleõ] *m* chameleon

camélia [kamelja] *m* camellia

camelot [kamlo] *m* cheap woolen cloth; huckster; newsboy

camelote [kamlɔt] *f* shoddy merchandise, rubbish, junk

caméra [kamera] *f* (mov, telv) camera

camion [kamjõ] *m* truck; paint bucket; **camion à remorque** trailer truck (truck); **camion à semi-remorque** semitrailer; **camion d'enregistrement** (mov) sound truck

camion-benne [kamjõbɛn] *m* (*pl* **camions-bennes**) dump truck

camion-citerne [kamjõsitɛrn] *m* (*pl* **camions-citernes**) tank truck

camion-grue [kamjõgry] *m* (*pl* **camions-grues**) tow truck

camionnage [kamjɔnaʒ] *m* trucking

camionner [kamjɔne] *tr* to truck

camionnette [kamjɔnet] *f* van; **camionnette de police** police wagon; **camionnette sanitaire** mobile health unit

camionneur [kamjɔnœr] *m* trucker; truckdriver, teamster

camisole [kamizɔl] *f* camisole; **camisole de force** strait jacket

camouflage [kamuflaʒ] *m* camouflage

camoufler [kamufle] *tr* to camouflage

camp [kã] *m* camp

campa·gnard [kãpaɲar] **-gnarde** [ɲard] *adj & mf* rustic

campagne [kãpaɲ] *f* campaign; country

cam·pé **-pée** [kãpe] *adj* encamped; **bien campé** well-built (*man*); clearly presented (*story*); firmly fixed

campement [kãpmã] *m* encampment; camping

camper [kãpe] *tr* to camp; (coll) to clap (*e.g., one's hat on one's head*); **camper là qn** (coll) to run out on s.o. ‖ *intr & ref* to camp

cam·peur [kãpœr] **-peuse** [pøz] *mf* camper

camphre [kãfr] *m* camphor

camping [kãpiŋ] *m* campground; trailer; camping

campos [kãpo] *m* (coll) vacation, day off

campus [kãpys] *m* campus

ca·mus [kamy] **-muse** [myz] *adj* snub-nosed, pug-nosed, flat-nosed

Canada [kanada] *m*—**le Canada** Canada

cana·dien [kanadjɛ̃] **-dienne** [djɛn] *adj* Canadian ‖ *f* sheepskin jacket; station wagon ‖ (*cap*) *mf* Canadian

canaille [kanaj] *adj* vulgar, coarse ‖ *f* rabble, riffraff; scoundrel

ca·nal [kanal] *m* (*pl* **-naux** [no]) canal; tube, pipe; ditch, drain; (rad, telv) channel; **canal de Panama** Panama Canal; **canal de Suez** Suez Canal; **par le canal de** through the good offices of

canapé [kanape] *m* sofa, davenport; (culin) canapé; **canapé à deux places** settee

canapé-lit [kanapeli] *m* (*pl* **canapés-lits**) sofa bed, day bed

canard [kanar] *m* duck; sugar soaked in coffee, brandy, etc.; (mus) false note; (coll) hoax; (coll) rag, paper; **canard mâle** drake; **canard publicitaire** publicity stunt; **canard sauvage** wild duck

canarder [kanarde] *tr* to snipe at ‖ *intr* to snipe

canari [kanari] *m* canary

cancan [kɑ̃kɑ̃] *m* cancan (*dance*); (coll) gossip

cancaner [kɑ̃kane] *intr* to quack; (coll) to gossip

canca·nier [kɑ̃kanje] **-nière** [njɛr] *adj* (coll) catty ‖ *mf* (coll) gossip

cancer [kɑ̃sɛr] *m* cancer

cancé·reux [kɑ̃serø] **-reuse** [røz] *adj* cancerous

cancre [kɑ̃kr] *m* (coll) dunce, lazy student; (coll) tightwad; (zool) crab

candélabre [kɑ̃delabr] *m* candelabrum; espaliered fruit tree; cactus; lamp-post

candeur [kɑ̃dœr] *f* naïveté

candi [kɑ̃di] *adj* candied (*fruit*) ‖ *m* rock candy

candi·dat [kɑ̃dida] **-date** [dat] *mf* candidate; nominee

candidature [kɑ̃didatyr] *f* candidacy

candide [kɑ̃did] *adj* naïve

candir [kɑ̃dir] *intr*—**faire candir** to candy, to crystallize (*sugar*) ‖ *ref* to candy, to crystallize

cane [kan] *f* duck, female duck

caner [kane] *intr* (slang) to chicken out

caneton [kantɔ̃] *m* duckling

canette [kanet] *f* female duckling; beer bottle; **canette de bière** can of beer

canevas [kanva] *m* canvas (*cloth*); outline (*of novel, story, etc.*); embroidery netting; (*in artillery, in cartography*) triangulation

canezou [kanzu] *m* sleeveless lace blouse

caniche [kaniʃ] *m* poodle

canicule [kanikyl] *f* dog days

canif [kanif] *m* penknife, pocketknife

ca·nin [kanɛ̃] **-nine** [nin] *adj* canine ‖ *f* canine (*tooth*)

canitie [kanisi] *f* grayness (*of hair*)

cani·veau [kanivo] *m* (*pl* **-veaux**) gutter; (elec) conduit

cannaie [kane] *f* sugar plantation

canne [kan] *f* cane; reed; cane, walking stick; **canne à pêche** fishing rod; **canne à sucre** sugar cane

canneberge [kanbɛrʒ] *f* cranberry

canneler [kanle] §34 *tr* to groove; to corrugate; to flute (*a column*)

cannelle [kanel] *f* cinnamon; spout

cannelure [kanlyr] *f* groove, channel, corrugation; fluting (*of column*)

canner [kane] *tr* to cane (*a chair*)

cannibale [kanibal] *adj* & *mf* cannibal

canoë [kanɔe] *m* canoe

canoéiste [kanɔeist] *mf* canoeist

canon [kanɔ̃] *m* canon; cannon; gun barrel; tube; nozzle, spout; **canon à électrons** electron gun

cañon [kaɲɔ̃] *m* canyon

cano·nial -niale [kanɔnjal] *adj* (*pl* **-niaux** [njo]) canonical

canonique [kanɔnik] *adj* canonical

canoniser [kanɔnize] *tr* to canonize

canonnade [kanɔnad] *f* cannonade

canonner [kanɔne] *tr* to cannonade

canonnier [kanɔnje] *m* cannoneer

canonnière [kanɔnjer] *f* gunboat; popgun

canot [kano] *m* rowboat, launch; **canot automobile** speedboat, motorboat; **canot de sauvetage** lifeboat

canotage [kanɔtaʒ] *m* boating

canoter [kanɔte] *intr* to go boating

canotier [kanɔtje] *m* rower; skimmer

cant [kɑ̃] *m* cant

cantaloup [kɑ̃talu] *m* cantaloupe

cantate [kɑ̃tat] *f* cantata

cantatrice [kɑ̃tatris] *f* singer

cantilever [kɑ̃tilevœr] *adj* & *m* cantilever

cantine [kɑ̃tin] *f* canteen (*restaurant*); **cantine d'officier** officer's kit

cantique [kɑ̃tik] *m* canticle, ode; **cantique de Noël** (eccl) Christmas carol; **Cantique des Cantiques** (Bib) Song of Songs

canton [kɑ̃tɔ̃] *m* canton, district; **Cantons de l'Est** Eastern Townships (*in Canada*)

cantonade [kɑ̃tɔnad] *f* (theat) wings; **à la cantonade** (theat) offstage; **crier à la cantonade** to yell out (*s.th.*); **parler à la cantonade** to seem to be talking to oneself; (theat) to speak toward the wings

cantonnement [kɑ̃tɔnmɑ̃] *m* billeting

cantonner [kɑ̃tɔne] *tr* to billet

cantonnier [kɑ̃tɔnje] *m* road laborer; (rr) section hand

canular [kanylar] *m* (coll) practical joke, hoax, canard

canule [kanyl] *f* nozzle (*of syringe or injection needle*)

canuler [kanyle] *tr* (slang) to bother

caoutchouc [kautʃu] *m* rubber; **caoutchouc mousse** foam rubber; **caoutchoucs** rubbers, overshoes

caoutchouter [kautʃute] *tr* to rubberize

caoutchou·teux [kautʃutø] **-teuse** [tøz] *adj* rubbery

cap [kap] *m* cape, headland; bow, head (*of ship*); **Cap de Bonne Espérance** Cape of Good Hope; **mettre le cap sur** (coll) to set a course for

capable [kapabl] *adj* capable

capacité [kapasite] *f* capacity; ability

cape [kap] *f* cape; hood; derby; outer leaf, wrapper (*of cigar*); **à la cape** (naut) hove to; **de cape et d'épée** cloak-and-dagger (*novel, movie, etc.*); **rire sous cape** to laugh up one's sleeve; **vendre sous cape** (coll) to sell under the counter

C.A.P.E.S. [kapes] *m* (acronym) (**certificat d'aptitude au professorat de l'enseignement du second degré**) secondary-school teachers certificate

capillaire [kapiller] *adj* capillary ‖ *m* (bot) maidenhair (*fern*)

capitaine [kapiten] *m* captain

capi·tal -tale [kapital] (*pl* **-taux** [to] **-tales**) *adj* capital, principal, essential; capital (*city; punishment; crime; letter*); death (*sentence*); deadly (*sins*) ‖ *m* capital, assets; principal (*main sum*); **avec de minces capitaux** on a shoestring; **capitaux** capital ‖ *f* capital (*city; letter*)

capitalisation [kapitalizɑsjɔ̃] *f* capitalization; hoarding (*of money*)

capitaliser [kapitalize] *tr* to capitalize (*an income*); to compound (*interest*) || *intr* to hoard

capitalisme [kapitalism] *m* capitalism

capitaliste [kapitalist] *adj* capitalist || *mf* capitalist; investor

capi·teux [kapitø] **-teuse** [tøz] *adj* heady (*wine, champagne, etc.*)

Capitole [kapitɔl] *m* Capitol

capitonner [kapitɔne] *tr* to upholster

capituler [kapityle] *intr* to capitulate; to parley

ca·pon [kapɔ̃] **-ponne** [pɔn] *adj* cowardly || *mf* coward; sneak; tattletale

capo·ral [kapɔral] *m* (*pl* **-raux** [ro]) corporal; shag, caporal (*tobacco*); **Caporal a dit . . .** Simon says . . .

caporalisme [kapɔralism] *m* militarism; dictatorial government

capot [kapo] *adj invar* speechless, confused; (cards) trickless || *m* cover; hood (*of automobile*); (naut) hatch

capotage [kapotaʒ] *m* overturning

capote [kapɔt] *f* coat with a hood; hood (*of baby carriage*); **capote rebattable** (aut) folding top

capoter [kapɔte] *intr* to capsize; to overturn, upset

câpre [kɑpr] *f* (bot) caper

caprice [kapris] *m* caprice, whim

capri·cieux [kaprisjø] **-cieuse** [sjøz] *adj* capricious, whimsical

capsule [kapsyl] *f* capsule; bottle cap; percussion cap; (bot) capsule, pod; (rok) capsule; **capsules surrénales** adrenal glands

capsuler [kapsyle] *tr* to cap

capter [kapte] *tr* to win over; to harness (*a river*); to tap (*electric current; a water supply*); (rad, telv) to receive, pick up

cap·tieux [kapsjø] **-tieuse** [sjøz] *adj* captious, insidious; specious

cap·tif [kaptif] **-tive** [tiv] *adj & mf* captive

captiver [kaptive] *tr* to captivate

captivité [kaptivite] *f* captivity

capture [kaptyr] *f* capture

capturer [kaptyre] *tr* to capture

capuce [kapys] *m* (eccl) pointed hood

capuchon [kapyʃɔ̃] *m* hood (*of coat*); cap (*of pen*); (aut) valve cap; (eccl) cowl

capucine [kapysin] *f* nasturtium

caque [kak] *f* keg, barrel

caquet [kake] *m* cackle

caqueter [kakte] §34 *intr* to cackle; to gossip

car [kar] *m* bus, sightseeing bus, interurban; **car de police** patrol wagon; **car sonore** loudspeaker truck || *conj* for, because

carabe [karab] *m* ground beetle

carabine [karabin] *f* carbine

carabi·né -née [karabine] *adj* (coll) violent (*wind, cold, criticism*)

caraco [karako] *m* loose blouse

caractère [karakter] *m* character; **caractères gras** (typ) boldface

caractériser [karakterize] *tr* to characterize

caractéristique [karakteristik] *adj & f* characteristic

carafe [karaf] *f* carafe; **rester en carafe** (slang) to be left out in the cold

carafon [karafɔ̃] *m* small carafe

caraïbe [karaib] *adj* Caribbean, Carib || (*cap*) *mf* Carib (*person*)

carambolage [karɑ̃bɔlaʒ] *m* jostling; (coll) bumping (*e.g., of autos*)

caramboler [karɑ̃bɔle] *tr* (coll) to strike, bump into || *intr* (billiards) to carom

caramel [karamel] *m* caramel

carapace [karapas] *f* turtle shell, carapace

carapater [karapate] *ref* (slang) to beat it

carat [kara] *m* carat

caravane [karavan] *f* caravan; house trailer; group (*of tourists*)

caravaning [karavaniŋ] *m* trailer camping

caravansérail [karavãseraj] *m* caravansary; (fig) world crossroads

caravelle [karavel] *f* caravel

carbonade [karbɔnad] *f* see **carbonnade**

carbone [karbɔn] *m* carbon

carbonique [karbɔnik] *adj* carbonic

carboniser [karbɔnize] *tr* to carbonize, char

carbonnade [karbɔnad] *f* charcoal-grilled steak (ham, etc.); beef and onion stew (*in northern France*); **à la carbonnade** charcoal-grilled

carburant [karbyrã] *m* motor fuel

carburateur [karbyratœr] *m* carburetor

carbure [karbyr] *m* carbide

carburéacteur [karbyreaktœr] *m* jet fuel

carcan [karkã] *m* pillory

carcasse [karkas] *f* skeleton; framework; (coll) carcass

cardan [kardã] *m* (mach) universal joint

carde [kard] *f* card; leaf rib; teasel head

carder [karde] *tr* to card

cardiaque [kardjak] *adj & mf* cardiac

cardi·nal -nale [kardinal] *adj & m* (*pl* **-naux** [no]) cardinal

cardiogramme [kardjɔgram] *m* cardiogram

carême [karem] *m* Lent; **de carême** Lenten

carême-prenant [karɛmprənã] *m* (*pl* **carêmes-prenants**) Shrovetide

carence [karãs] *f* lack, deficiency; failure

carène [karen] *f* hull

caréner [karene] §10 *tr* to streamline; (naut) to careen

caren·tiel -tielle [karãsjel] *adj* deficiency (*disease*)

cares·sant [karesã] **cares·sante** [karesãt] *adj* caressing; lovable; nice to pet; soothing (*e.g., voice*)

caresse [kares] *f* caress; endearment

caresser [karese] *tr* to caress; to pet; to nourish (*a hope*)

cargaison [kargezɔ̃] *f* cargo

cargo [kargo] *m* freighter; **cargo mixte** freighter carrying passengers

carl [karl] *m* curry

caricature [karikatyr] *f* caricature; cartoon

caricaturer [karikatyre] *tr* to caricature

caricaturiste [karikatyrist] *mf* caricaturist; cartoonist

carie [kari] *f* caries; **carie sèche** dry rot

carillon [karijɔ̃] *m* carillon

carillonner [karijɔne] *tr & intr* to carillon, to chime

carlingue [karlɛ̃g] *f* (aer) cockpit

carmin [karmɛ̃] *adj & m* carmine

carnage [karnaʒ] *m* carnage

carnas·sier [karnasje] **carnas·sière** [karnasjɛr] *adj* carnivorous ‖ *m* carnivore ‖ *f* game bag

carnation [karnɑsjɔ̃] *f* flesh tint

carna·val [karnaval] *m* (*pl* **-vals**) carnival; parade dummy

car·né -née [karne] *adj* flesh-colored; meat (*diet*)

carnet [karne] *m* notebook, address book; memo pad; book (*of tickets, checks, stamps, etc.*); **carnet à feuilles mobiles** loose-leaf notebook

carnier [karnje] *m* hunting bag

carotte [karɔt] *f* carrot; (min) core sample; **tirer une carotte à** (coll) to cheat

carotter [karɔte] *tr* (coll) to cheat

carpe [karp] *m* (anat) wrist bones ‖ *f* carp; **être muet comme une carpe** to be still as a mouse

carpette [karpet] *f* rug, mat

carquois [karkwa] *m* quiver

carre [kar] *f* thickness (*of board*); crown (*of hat*); edge (*of ice skate*); square toe (*of shoe*); **d'une bonne carre** broad-shouldered (*man*)

car·ré -rée [kare] *adj* square; forth-right ‖ *m* square; landing (*of staircase*); patch (*in garden*); (cards) four of a kind; (naut) wardroom ‖ *f* (slang) room, pad

car·reau [karo] *m* (*pl* **-reaux**) tile, flagstone; windowpane; stall (*in market*); pithead (*of mine*); goose (*of tailor*); quarrel (*square-headed arrow*); (cards) diamond; (cards) diamonds; **à carreaux** checked (*design*); **rester sur le carreau** (coll) to be left out of the running; **se garder à carreau** (coll) to be on one's guard

carrefour [karfur] *m* crossroads; square (*in a city*)

carrelage [karlaʒ] *m* tiling

carreler [karle] §34 *tr* to tile

carrément [karemã] *adv* squarely; frankly

carrer [kare] *tr* to square ‖ *ref* (coll) to plunk oneself down; (coll) to strut

carrier [karje] *m* quarryman

carrière [karjɛr] *f* career; course (*e.g., of the sun*); quarry; **donner carrière à** to give free rein to

carriole [karjɔl] *f* light cart, trap; (coll) jalopy

carrossable [karɔsabl] *adj* passable

carrosse [karɔs] *m* carriage, coach

carrosserie [karɔsri] *f* (aut) body

carrossier [karɔsje] *m* coachmaker

carrousel [karuzel] *m* carrousel; parade ground; tiltyard

carrure [karyr] *f* width (*of shoulders, garment, etc.*); **d'une belle carrure** broad-shouldered (*man*)

cartable [kartabl] *m* briefcase

cartayer [karteje] §49 *intr* to avoid the ruts

carte [kart] *f* card; map, chart; bill (*to pay*); bill of fare, menu; **carte d'abonnement** commutation ticket; season ticket; **carte d'entrée** pass, ticket of admission; **carte des vins** wine list; **carte grise** automobile registration; **carte postale** post card; **cartes truquées** marked cards, stacked deck; **tirer les cartes à qn** to tell s.o.'s fortunes with cards

cartel [kartel] *m* cartel; wall clock; challenge (*to a duel*)

carte-lettre [kartəlɛtr] *f* (*pl* **cartes-lettres**) gummed letter-envelope

carter [karter] *m* housing; bicycle chain guard; (aut) crankcase

cartilage [kartilaʒ] *m* cartilage, gristle

cartographe [kartɔgraf] *m* cartographer

cartomancie [kartɔmɑ̃si] *f* fortunetelling with cards

carton [kartɔ̃] *m* pasteboard, cardboard; cardboard box, carton; carton (*of cigarettes*); cartoon (*preliminary sketch*); (typ) cancel; **carton à chapeau** hatbox; **carton à dessin** portfolio for drawings and plans

carton-pâte [kartɔ̃pat] *m* papier-mâché

cartouche [kartuʃ] *m* (archi) cartouche, tablet ‖ *f* cartridge; carton (*of cigarettes*); canister (*of gas mask*); refill (*of pen*); **cartouche à blanc** blank cartridge

cartouchière [kartuʃjer] *f* cartridge belt, cartridge case

carvi [karvi] *m* caraway

cas [kɑ] *m* case; **cas urgent** emergency; **en cas de** in the event of, in a time of; **en cas d'imprévu** in case of emergency; **en cas que, au cas que, au cas où, dans le cas où** in the event that; **faire cas de** to esteem, to make much of; **le cas échéant** should the occasion arise, if necessary; **selon le cas** as the case may be

casa·nier -nière [njer] *adj* home-loving ‖ *mf* homebody

casaque [kazak] *f* jockey coat; blouse; **tourner casaque** to be a turncoat

cascade [kaskad] *f* cascade; jerk; spree; **prendre à la cascade** to ad-lib

cascader [kaskade] *intr* to cascade; (slang) to lead a wild life

casca·deur [kaskadœr] **-deuse** [døz] *mf* (mov) double ‖ *m* stunt man ‖ *f* stunt girl

case [kaz] *f* compartment; pigeonhole; square (*e.g., of checkerboard or ledger*); box (*to be filled out on a form*); hut, cabin; **case postale** post-office box

caséine [kazein] *f* casein

caser [kaze] *tr* to put away (*e.g., in a drawer*); to arrange (*e.g., a counter display in a store*); (coll) to place, to find a job for ‖ *ref* (coll) to get settled

caserne [kazɛrn] *f* barracks; **de caserne** off-color (*jokes*); regimented

caserner [kazɛrne] *tr & intr* to barrack

ca·sher -shère [kaʃɛr] *adj* kosher

casier [kasje] *m* rack (*for papers, magazines, letters, bottles*); cabinet; **casier à homards** lobster pot; **casier à tiroirs** music cabinet; **casier judiciaire** police record

casque [kask] *m* helmet; earphones, headset; comb (*of rooster*); **casque à mèche** nightcap; **casque à pointe** spiked helmet; **casque blindé** crash helmet

casquer [kaske] *intr* to fall into a trap; (slang) to shell out

casquette [kaskɛt] *f* cap

cas·sant [kasã] **cas·sante** [kasãt] *adj* brittle; abrupt, curt

casse [kas] *m* (slang) burglarizing || *f* breakage || [kas], [kas] *f* ladle, scoop; crucible; (bot) cassia; (pharm) senna; (typ) case; (coll) scrap heap, junk

cas·sé -sée [kase] *adj* broken-down; shaky, weak (*voice*)

casse-cou [kasku] *m invar* (coll) daredevil; (coll) stunt man; (coll) danger spot || *interj* look out!

casse-croûte [kaskrut] *m invar* snack

casse-gueule [kasgœl] *adj invar* (slang) risky || *m invar* (coll) risky business

casse-noisettes [kasnwazɛt] *m invar* nutcracker

casse-noix [kasnwa], [kasnwa] *m invar* nutcracker

casse-pieds [kaspje] *m invar* (coll) pain in the neck

casser [kase] *tr* to break; to crack, to shatter; (law) to break (*a will*); (mil) to break, to bust; (coll) to split (*one's eardrums*); **casser sa pipe** (coll) to kick the bucket || *réf* to break; (coll) to rack (*one's brains*); **se casser le nez** (coll) to fail

casserole [kasrɔl] *f* saucepan

casse-tête [kastɛt] *m invar* truncheon; din; brain teaser, puzzler; **casse-tête chinois** jigsaw puzzle

cassette [kasɛt], [kasɛt] *f* strongbox, coffer; casket (*for jewels*)

cassis [kasi], [kasis] *m* black currant; cassis (*liqueur*); gutter

cassolette [kasɔlɛt] *f* incense burner

cassonade [kasɔnad] *f* brown sugar

cassoulet [kasulɛ] *m* pork and beans

cassure [kasyr] *f* break; crease; rift

castagnettes [kastaɲɛt] *fpl* castanets

caste [kast] *f* caste; **hors caste** outcast

castil·lan [kastijã] **castil·lane** [kastijan] *adj* Castilian || *m* Castilian (*language*) || (*cap*) *mf* Castilian (*person*)

Castille [kastij] *f* Castile; **la Castille** Castile

castor [kastɔr] *m* beaver

castrat [kastra] *m* castrato

castrer [kastre] *tr* to castrate

ca·suel -suelle [kazɥɛl] *adj* casual; (coll) brittle || *m* perquisites

cataclysme [kataklism] *m* cataclysm

catacombes [katakɔ̃b] *fpl* catacombs

catafalque [katafalk] *m* catafalque

cataire [katɛr] *f* catnip

Catalogne [katalɔɲ] *f* Catalonia; **la Catalogne** Catalonia

catalogue [katalɔg] *m* catalogue

cataloguer [kataloge] *tr* to catalogue

catalyseur [katalizœr] *m* catalyst

cataplasme [kataplasm] *m* poultice

catapulte [katapylt] *f* catapult

catapulter [katapylte] *tr* to catapult

cataracte [katarakt] *f* cataract

catarrhe [katar] *m* catarrh; bad cold

catastrophe [katastrɔf] *f* catastrophe

catch [katʃ] *m* wrestling

catcheur [katʃœr] *m* wrestler

catéchiser [kateʃize] *tr* to catechize; to reason with

catéchisme [kateʃism] *m* catechism

catégorie [kategɔri] *f* category

catégorique [kategɔrik] *adj* categorical

catgut [katgyt] *m* (surg) catgut

cathédrale [katedral] *f* cathedral

cathéter [kateter] *m* (med) catheter

cathode [katɔd] *f* cathode

catholicisme [katɔlisism] *m* Catholicism

catholicité [katɔlisite] *f* catholicity; Catholicism; Catholics

catholique [katɔlik] *adj* catholic; Catholic; orthodox; **pas très catholique** (coll) questionable || *mf* Catholic

cati [kati] *m* glaze, gloss

catimini [katimini]—**en catimini** (coll) on the sly

catir [katir] *tr* to glaze

cauca·sien [kokazjɛ̃] **-sienne** [zjɛn] *adj* Caucasian || (*cap*) *mf* Caucasian

caucasique [kokazik] *adj* Caucasian

cauchemar [koʃmar] *m* nightmare

cause [koz] *f* cause; (law) case; **à cause de** because of, on account of, for the sake of; **et pour cause** with good reason; **hors de cause** irrelevant, beside the point; **mettre q.ch. en cause** to question s.th.; **mettre qn en cause** to implicate s.o.

causer [koze] *tr* to cause || *intr* to chat

causerie [kozri] *f* chat; informal lecture

causette [kozɛt] *f*—**faire la causette** (coll) to chat

cau·seur [kozœr] **-seuse** [zøz] *adj* talkative, chatty || *mf* speaker, conversationalist || *f* love seat

caustique [kostik] *adj* caustic

cante·leux [kotlø] **-leuse** [løz] *adj* crafty, wily; cunning (*mind*)

cautériser [koterize] *tr* to cauterize

caution [kosjɔ̃] *f* security, collateral; guarantor, bondsman; **mettre en liberté sous caution** to let out on bail; **se porter caution pour qn** to put up bail for s.o.; **sujet à caution** unreliable; **verser une caution** to make a deposit

cautionnement [kosjɔnmã] *m* surety bond, guaranty; bail; deposit

cautionner [kosjɔne] *tr* to bail out; to guarantee

cavalcade [kavalkad] *f* cavalcade

cavalerie [kavalri] *f* cavalry

cava·lier [kavalje] **-lière** [ljɛr] *adj* cavalier; bridle (*path*) || *mf* horseback rider; dance partner || *m* cavalier, horseman; escort; (chess) knight || *f* horsewoman

cave [kav] *adj* hollow (*cheeks*) || *f* cellar; liquor cabinet; liquor store; night club; bank (*in game of chance*); stake (*in gambling*); **cave à vin** wine cellar

ca·veau [kavo] *m* (*pl* **-veaux**) small cellar; vault, crypt; rathskeller

caver [kave] *tr* to hollow out || *intr* to ante || *ref* to become hollow (*said of eyes*); to wager

caverne [kavern] *f* cave, cavern; (pathol) cavity (*e.g., in lung*)

caver·neux [kavernø] **-neuse** [nøz] *adj* cavernous; hollow (*voice*)

caviar [kavjar] *m* caviar

caviarder [kavjarde] *tr* to censor

cavité [kavite] *f* cavity, hollow

caw·cher·chère [kaʃer] *adj* kosher

Cayes [kaj] *fpl*—**Cayes de la Floride** Florida Keys

C.C.P. *abbr* (**Compte chèques postaux**) postal banking account

ce [sə] (*or* **cet** [set] *before vowel or mute* h) **cette** [set] *adj dem* (*pl* **ces** [se]) §82A || **ce** *pron* §82B, §85A4

C.E.A. *abbr* (**Commissariat à l'Énergie atomique**) Atomic Energy Commission

céans [seɑ̃] *adv* herein

ceci [səsi] *pron dem indef* this, this thing, this matter

cécité [sesite] *f* blindness

céder [sede] §10 *tr* to cede, transfer; to yield, give up; **ne le céder à personne** to be second to none || *intr* to yield, succumb, give way

cédille [sedij] *f* cedilla

cédrat [sedra] *m* citron

cèdre [sedr] *m* cedar

cédule [sedyl] *f* rate, schedule; (law) notification

C.E.E. *abbr* (**Communauté économique européenne**) Common Market

cégétiste [seʒetist] *mf* unionist

ceindre [sɛ̃dr] §50 *tr* to buckle on, to gird; to encircle; to wreathe (*one's head*); **ceindre la couronne** to assume the crown || *ref*—**se ceindre de** to gird on

ceinture [sɛ̃tyr] *f* belt; waist, waistline; sash, waistband; girdle; **ceinture de sauvetage** life belt; **ceinture de sécurité** safety belt; **se mettre la ceinture** or **se serrer la ceinture** to tighten one's belt

ceinturer [sɛ̃tyre] *tr* to girdle, to belt; to encircle, to belt; (wrestling) to grip around the waist

cela [səla] *pron dem indef* that, that thing; that matter; **à cela près** with that one exception; **et avec cela?** what else?

célébrant [selebrɑ̃] *m* (eccl) celebrant

célébration [selebrasjɔ̃] *f* celebration

célèbre [selebr] *adj* famous

célébrer [selebre] §10 *tr* to celebrate

célébrité [selebrite] *f* celebrity

celer [səle] §2 *tr* to hide, conceal

céleri [selri], [selri] *m* celery

céleste [selest] *adj* celestial

célibat [seliba] *m* celibacy

célibataire [selibater] *adj* single || *mf* celibate || *m* bachelor || *f* spinster

celle [sel] §83

celle-ci [selsi] §84

celle-là [sella] §84

cellier [selje] *m* wine cellar; fruit cellar

cellophane [selɔfan] *f* cellophane

cellule [selyl], [selyl] *f* cell

celluloïd [selyloid] *m* celluloid

celte [selt] *adj* Celtic || (*cap*) *mf* Celt

celtique [seltik] *adj & m* Celtic

celui [səlɥi] **celle** [sel] (*pl* **ceux** [sø] **celles**) §83

celui-ci [səlɥisi] **celle-ci** [selsi] (*pl* **ceux-ci** [søsi] **celles-ci**) §84

celui-là [səlɥila] **celle-là** [sella] (*pl* **ceux-là** [søla] **celles-là**) §84

cémentation [semɑ̃tasjɔ̃] *f* casehardening

cendre [sɑ̃dr] *f* cinder; **cendres** ashes

cendrée [sɑ̃dre] *f* shot; buckshot; (sports) cinder track

cendrer [sɑ̃dre] *tr* to cinder

cendrier [sɑ̃drije] *m* ashtray

Cendrillon [sɑ̃drijɔ̃] *f* Cinderella

cène [sen] *f* (eccl) Holy Communion || (*cap*) *f* (eccl) Last Supper

cens [sɑ̃s] *m* census; poll tax

cen·sé -sée [sɑ̃se] *adj* supposed to, e.g., **je ne suis pas censé le savoir** I am not supposed to know it; reputed to be, e.g., **il est censé juge infaillible** he is reputed to be an infallible judge

censément [sɑ̃semɑ̃] *adv* supposedly, apparently, allegedly

censeur [sɑ̃sœr] *m* censor; census taker; critic; auditor; proctor

censure [sɑ̃syr] *f* censure; censorship; (psychoanal) censor

censurer [sɑ̃syre] *tr* to censure; to censor

cent [sɑ̃] *adj & pron* (*pl* **cents** in multiples when standing before modified noun, e.g., **trois cents œufs** three hundred eggs) one hundred, a hundred, hundred; **cent pour cent** one hundred percent; **cent un** [sɑ̃œ̃] one hundred and one, a hundred and one, hundred and one; **l'an dix-neuf cent** the year nineteen hundred; **page deux cent** page two hundred || *m* hundred, one hundred || [sɛ̃t] *m* cent

centaine [sɑ̃ten] *f* hundred; **par centaines** by the hundreds; **une centaine de** about a hundred

centaure [sɑ̃tor] *m* centaur

centenaire [sɑ̃tner] *adj* centenary || *mf* centenarian || *m* centennial

centen·nal -nale [sɑ̃tennal] *adj* (*pl* **-naux** [no]) centennial

centième [sɑ̃tjem] *adj, pron* (*masc, fem*), *& m* hundredth || *f* hundredth performance

centigrade [sɑ̃tigrad] *adj & m* centigrade

centime [sɑ̃tim] *m* centime

centimètre [sɑ̃timetr] *m* centimeter; tape measure

centrage [sɑ̃traʒ] *m* centering

cen·tral -trale [sɑ̃tral] *adj* (*pl* **-traux** [tro]) central; main (*office*) || *m* (telp) central || *f* powerhouse; labor union; **centrale atomique** or **nucléaire** atomic generator

centralisation [sãtralizɑsjɔ̃] *f* centralization

centraliser [sãtralize] *tr & ref* to centralize

centre [sãtr] *m* center; **centre commercial** shopping district; **centre de dépression** storm center; **centre de triage** (rr) switchyard; **centre d'études** college; **centre de villégiature** resort; **centre social des étudiants** student center, student union

centrer [sãtre] *tr* to center

centrifuge [sãtrify ʒ] *adj* centrifugal

centuple [sãtypl] *adj & m* hundredfold; **au centuple** hundredfold

cep [sɛp] *m* vine stock

cépage [sepaʒ] *m* (bot) vine

cèpe [sɛp] *f* cepe mushroom

cependant [səpãdã] *adv* meanwhile; however, but, still; **cependant que** while, whereas; **et cependant** and yet

céramique [seramik] *adj* ceramic || *f* (art of) ceramics; ceramic piece; **céramiques** ceramics (*objects*)

cerbère [sɛrber] *m* (coll) watchdog || (*cap*) *m* Cerberus

cer·ceau [sɛrso] *m* (*pl* -**ceaux**) hoop; **cerceaux** pinfeathers

cercle [sɛrkl] *m* circle; circle, club, society; clubhouse; hoop; **en cercle** in the cask

cercler [sɛrkle] *tr* to ring, encircle; to hoop

cercueil [sɛrkœj] *m* coffin

céréale [sereal] *adj & f* cereal

céré·bral -brale [serebral] *adj* (*pl* -**braux** [bro]) cerebral

cérémo·nial -niale [seremɔnjal] *adj & m* ceremonial

cérémonie [seremɔni] *f* ceremony; **faire des cérémonies** to stand on ceremony

cérémo·niel -nielle [seremɔnjɛl] *adj* ceremonial

cérémo·nieux -nieuse [seremɔnjø] [njøz] *adj* ceremonious, formal, stiff

cerf [sɛr] *m* deer, red deer; stag, buck

cerf-volant [sɛrvɔlã] *m* (*pl* **cerfs-volants**) kite

cerisaie [sərize] *f* cherry orchard

cerise [səriz] *f* cherry

cerisier [sərizje] *m* cherry tree

cerne [sɛrn] *m* annual ring (*of tree*); ring (*around moon, black eye, wound*)

cer·neau [sɛrno] *m* (*pl* -**neaux**) unripe nutmeat

cerner [sɛrne] *tr* to ring, encircle; to hem in, besiege; to shell (*nuts*)

cer·tain -taine [sɛrtɛ̃] [tɛn] *adj* certain, sure || § (when standing before noun) *adj* certain, some; **certain auteur** a certain author; **depuis un certain temps** for some time; **d'un certain âge** middle-aged || **certains** *pron indef pl* certain people

certainement [sɛrtɛnmã] *adv* certainly

certes [sɛrt] *adv* indeed, certainly

certificat [sɛrtifika] *m* certificate

certifier [sɛrtifje] *tr* to certify

certitude [sɛrtityd] *f* certainty

cérumen [serymɛn] *m* earwax

céruse [seryz] *f* white lead

cer·veau [sɛrvo] *m* (*pl* -**veaux**) brain; mind; **cerveau brûlé** (coll) hothead

cervelas [sɛrvəla] *m* salami

cervelet [sɛrvəle] *m* cerebellum

cervelle [sɛrvel] *f* brains; **brûler la cervelle à qn** (coll) to shoot s.o.'s brains out

ces [se] §82A

césa·rien -rienne [sezarjɛ̃] [rjɛn] *adj* Caesarean || *f* Caesarean section

cesse [ses] *f* cessation, ceasing; **sans cesse** unceasingly, incessantly

cesser [sese] *tr* to stop, to cease, to leave off (*e.g., work*) || *intr* to cease, stop; **cesser de** + *inf* to stop, cease, quit + *ger*

cessez-le-feu [seselfø] *m invar* cease-fire

cession [sesjɔ̃] *f* ceding, surrender; (law) transfer

c'est-à-dire [setadir] *conj* that is, namely

césure [sezyr] *f* caesura

cet [set] §82A

cette [set] §82A

ceux [sø] §83

ceux-ci [søsi] §84

ceux-là [søla] §84

Ceylan [selã] *m* Ceylon

C.G.T. [seʒete] *f* (letterword) (**confédération générale du travail**) national labor union || *abbr* (Cie Générale transatlantique) French Line

cha·cal [ʃakal] *m* (*pl* -**cals**) jackal

cha·cun -cune [ʃakœ̃] [kyn] *pron indef* each, each one, every one; everybody, everyone; **chacun pour soi** every man for himself; **chacun son goût** every man to his own taste; **tout chacun** (coll) every Tom, Dick, and Harry

chadburn [tʃadbœrn] *m* (naut) public-address system

chadouf [ʃaduf] *m* well sweep

cha·grin -grine [ʃagrɛ̃] [grin] *adj* sad, downcast || *m* grief, sorrow

chagriner [ʃagrine] *tr* to grieve, distress; to make into shagreen leather || *intr* to grieve, worry

chah [ʃa] *m* shah

chahut [ʃay] *m* (coll) horseplay, row

chahuter [ʃayte] *tr* (coll) to upset; (coll) to boo, heckle || *intr* (coll) to create a disturbance

chai [ʃe] *m* wine cellar

chaîne [ʃen] *f* chain; warp (*of fabric*); necklace; (archit) pier; (archit) tie; (naut) cable; (rad, telv) network; (telv) channel; **chaîne de fabrication** or **chaîne de montage** assembly line; **faire la chaîne** to form a bucket brigade

chaînon [ʃenɔ̃] *m* link

chair [ʃer] *f* flesh; pulp (*of fruits*); meat (*of animals*); **chair de poule** gooseflesh; **chair de sa chair** one's flesh and blood; **chairs** (painting, sculpture) nude parts; **en chair et en os** in the flesh; **ni chair ni poisson** neither fish nor fowl

chaire [ʃer] *f* pulpit; lectern; chair (*held by university professor*)

chaise [ʃez] *f* chair; bowline knot; (mach) bracket; **chaise à bascule** rocking chair; **chaise à porteurs** sedan chair; **chaise berceuse** rocking chair; **chaise brisée** folding chair; **chaise d'enfant** high chair; **chaise électrique** electric chair; **chaise percée** commode, toilet; **chaise pliante** folding chair

cha·land [ʃalɑ̃] **-lande** [lɑ̃d] *mf* customer ‖ *m* barge; **chaland de débarquement** (mil) landing craft

châle [ʃɑl] *m* shawl

chalet [ʃale] *m* chalet, cottage, summer home; **chalet de nécessité** public rest room

chaleur [ʃalœr] *f* heat; warmth; **les grandes chaleurs de l'été** the hot weather of summer

chaleu·reux [ʃalœrø] **-reuse** [røz] *adj* warm, heated

châlit [ʃɑli] *m* bedstead

chaloupe [ʃalup] *f* launch

chalu·meau [ʃalymo] *m* (*pl* **-meaux**) reed; blowtorch; (mus) pipe; **chalumeau oxhydrique** or **chalumeau oxyacétylénique** acetylene torch

chalut [ʃaly] *m* trawl

chalutier [ʃalytje] *m* trawler

chamade [ʃamad] *f*—**battre la chamade** to beat wildly (*said of the heart*)

chamailler [ʃamaje] *ref* to squabble

chamarrer [ʃamare] *tr* to decorate, to ornament; to bedizen, to bedeck; (slang) to cover (*s.o.*) with ridicule

chambarder [ʃɑ̃barde] *tr* (slang) to upset, to turn upside down

chambellan [ʃɑ̃belɑ̃] *m* chamberlain

chambouler [ʃɑ̃bule] *tr* (slang) to upset, to turn topsy-turvy

chambranle [ʃɑ̃brɑ̃l] *m* frame (*of a door or window*); mantelpiece

chambre [ʃɑ̃br] *f* chamber; room; **chambre à air** inner tube; **chambre à coucher** bedroom; **chambre d'ami** guest room; **chambre de compensation** clearing house; **chambre noire** darkroom

chambrée [ʃɑ̃bre] *f* dormitory, barracks; bunkmates

chambrer [ʃɑ̃bre] *tr* to keep under lock and key; to keep (*wine*) at room temperature

cha·meau [ʃamo] **-melle** [mel] *mf* (*pl* **-meaux**) camel ‖ *m* (slang) bitch (*person*)

chamois [ʃamwa] *adj & m* chamois

champ [ʃɑ̃] *m* field; **aux champs** salute (*played on trumpet or drum*); **champ clos** lists, dueling field; **champ de courses** race track; **champ de repos** cemetery; **champ de tir** firing range; **champ libre** clear field; **champs Élysées** Elysian Fields; **Champs-Élysées** Champs Elysées (*street*)

champagne [ʃɑ̃paɲ] *m* champagne; **champagne brut** extra dry champagne; **champagne d'origine** vintage champagne ‖ (*cap*) *f* Champagne; **la Champagne** Champagne

champe·nois [ʃɑ̃pənwa] **-noise** [nwaz] *adj* Champagne ‖ *m* Champagne

dialect ‖ (*cap*) *mf* inhabitant of Champagne

champêtre [ʃɑ̃petr] *adj* rustic, rural

champignon [ʃɑ̃piɲɔ̃] *m* mushroom; fungus; (slang) accelerator pedal; **champignon de couche** cultivated mushroom; **champignon vénéneux** toadstool

champignonner [ʃɑ̃piɲɔne] *intr* to mushroom

cham·pion [ʃɑ̃pjɔ̃] **-pionne** [pjɔn] *mf* champion ‖ *f* championess

championnat [ʃɑ̃pjɔna] *m* championship

champlever [ʃɑ̃lve] §2 *tr* to chase out, to gouge out

chan·çard [ʃɑ̃sar] **-çarde** [sard] *adj* (slang) in luck ‖ *mf* (slang) lucky person

chance [ʃɑ̃s] *f* luck; good luck; **avoir de la chance** to be lucky; **bonne chance** good luck; **chance moyenne** off chance; **chances** chances, risks, probability, possibility

chance·lant [ʃɑ̃slɑ̃] **-lante** [lɑ̃t] *adj* shaky, unsteady, tottering; delicate (*health, constitution*)

chanceler [ʃɑ̃sle] §34 *intr* to stagger, to totter, to teeter; to waver

chancelier [ʃɑ̃səlje] *m* chancellor

chancellerie [ʃɑ̃selri] *f* chancellery

chan·ceux [ʃɑ̃sø] **-ceuse** [søz] *adj* lucky; risky

chanci [ʃɑ̃si] *m* manure pile for mushroom growing

chancir [ʃɑ̃sir] *intr* to grow moldy

chancre [ʃɑ̃kr] *m* chancre; ulcer, canker

chandail [ʃɑ̃daj] *m* sweater; **chandail à col roulé** turtleneck sweater

chandeleur [ʃɑ̃dlœr] *f*—**la chandeleur** Candlemas

chandelier [ʃɑ̃dəlje] *m* candlestick; chandler

chandelle [ʃɑ̃del] *f* tallow candle; prop, stay (*used in construction*); **chandelle de glace** icicle; **en chandelle** vertically; **voir trente-six chandelles** to see stars (*on account of a blow*)

chanfrein [ʃɑ̃frɛ̃] *m* forehead (*of a horse*); chamfer, beveled edge

chanfreiner [ʃɑ̃frene] *tr* to chamfer, to bevel

change [ʃɑ̃ʒ] *m* exchange; rate of exchange; **de change** in reserve, extra; **donner le change à** to throw off the trail; **prendre le change** to let one self be duped; **rendre le change à qn** to give s.o. a taste of his own medicine

changeable [ʃɑ̃ʒabl] *adj* changeable

chan·geant [ʃɑ̃ʒɑ̃] **-geante** [ʒɑ̃t] *adj* changeable, changing, fickle; iridescent

changement [ʃɑ̃ʒmɑ̃] *m* change; shift; shifting; **changement de propriétaire** under new ownership; **changement de vitesse** gearshift

changer [ʃɑ̃ʒe] §38 *tr* to change; **changer contre** to exchange for ‖ *intr* to change; **changer d'avis** to change one's mind; **changer de place** to change one's seat; **changer de ton**

(coll) to change one's tune; **changer de visage** to blush; to change color || *ref* to change, change clothes

chanoine [ʃanwan] *m* (eccl) canon

chanson [ʃɑ̃sɔ̃] *f* song; **chanson bachique** drinking song; **chanson de geste** medieval epic; **chanson de Noël** Christmas carol; **chanson du terroir** folk song; **chanson sentimentale** torch song

chansonner [ʃɑ̃sɔne] *tr* to lampoon in a satirical song

chansonneur [ʃɑ̃sɔnœr] *m* lampooner (*who writes satirical songs*)

chanson·nier [ʃɑ̃sɔnje] **chanson·nière** [ʃɑ̃sɔnjɛr] *mf* songwriter || *m* chansonnier; song book

chant [ʃɑ̃] *m* singing; song, chant; canto; crowing (*of rooster*); side (*e.g., of a brick*); **chant du cygne** swan song; **chant de Noël** Christmas carol; **chant national** national anthem; **chants** poetry; **de chant** on end, edgewise

chantage [ʃɑ̃taʒ] *m* blackmail

chan·tant [ʃɑ̃tɑ̃] **-tante** [tɑ̃t] *adj* singable, melodious; singsong (*accent*); musical (*evening*)

chan·teau [ʃɑ̃to] *m* (*pl* **-teaux**) chunk (*of bread*); remnant

chantepleure [ʃɑ̃tplœr] *f* wine funnel; tap (*of cask*); sprinkler; weep hole

chanter [ʃɑ̃te] *tr* to sing || *intr* to sing; to crow (*as a rooster*); to pay blackmail; **chanter faux** to sing out of tune; **chanter juste** to sing in tune; **faire chanter** to blackmail

chanterelle [ʃɑ̃trɛl] *f* first string (*of violin*); decoy bird; mushroom; **appuyer sur la chanterelle** (coll) to rub it in

chan·teur [ʃɑ̃tœr] **-teuse** [tøz] *adj* singing; song (*bird*) || *mf* singer; **chanteur de charme** crooner; **chanteur de rythme** jazz singer

chantier [ʃɑ̃tje] *m* shipyard; stocks, slip; workshop, yard; gantry, stand (*for barrels*); (public sign) men at work; **chantier de démolition** junkyard, scrap heap; **mettre en** or **sur le chantier** to start work on

chantilly [ʃɑ̃tiji] *m* whipped cream

chantonner [ʃɑ̃tɔne] *tr & intr* to hum

chantoung [ʃɑ̃tuŋ] *m* shantung

chantourner [ʃɑ̃turne] *tr* to jigsaw

chantre [ʃɑ̃tr] *m* cantor, chanter; precentor; songster; bard, poet

chanvre [ʃɑ̃vr] *m* hemp; **en chanvre** hempen; flaxen (*color*)

chan·vrier [ʃɑ̃vrije] **-vrière** [vrijɛr] *adj* hemp (*industry*) || *mf* dealer in hemp; hemp dresser

chaos [kao] *m* chaos

chaotique [kaɔtik] *adj* chaotic

chaparder [ʃaparde] *tr* (coll) to pilfer, to filch

chape [ʃap] *f* cover, covering; tread (*of tire*); coping (*of bridge*); frame, shell (*of pulley block*); (eccl) cope

cha·peau [ʃapo] *m* (*pl* **-peaux**) hat; head (*of mushroom*); lead (*of magazine or newspaper article*); cap (*of fountain pen; of valve*); cowl (*of*

chimney); **chapeau à cornes** cocked hat; **chapeau bas** hat in hand; **chapeau bas!** hats off!; **chapeau chinois** Chinese bells; **chapeau de roue** hubcap; **chapeau haut de forme** top hat; **chapeau melon** derby; **chapeau mou** fedora

chapeau-cloche [ʃapoklɔʃ] *m* (*pl* **chapeaux-cloches**) cloche (*hat*)

chapeauter [ʃapote] *tr* (coll) to put a hat on (*e.g., a child*)

chapelain [ʃaplɛ̃] *m* chaplain (*of a private chapel*)

chapeler [ʃaple] §34 *tr* to scrape the crust off of (*bread*)

chapelet [ʃaplɛ] *m* chaplet, rosary; string (*of onions; of islands; of insults*); chain (*of events; of mountains*); series (*e.g., of attacks*); (mil) stick (*of bombs*); **chapelet hydraulique** bucket conveyor; **défiler son chapelet** (coll) to speak one's mind; **dire son chapelet** to tell one's beads; **en chapelet** (elec) in series

chape·lier [ʃaplje] **-lière** [ljɛr] *mf* hatter || *f* Saratoga trunk

chapelle [ʃapɛl] *f* chapel; clique, coterie; **chapelle ardente** mortuary chamber lighted by candles; hearse

chapellerie [ʃapɛlri] *f* hatmaking; millinery; hat shop; millinery shop

chapelure [ʃaplyr] *f* bread crumbs

chaperon [ʃaprɔ̃] *m* chaperon; hood; cape with a hood; coping (*of wall*); **le Petit Chaperon rouge** Little Red Ridinghood

chaperonner [ʃaprɔne] *tr* to chaperon

chapi·teau [ʃapito] *m* (*pl* **-teaux**) capital (*of column*); circus tent

chapitre [ʃapitr] *m* chapter; **commencer un nouveau chapitre** to turn over a new leaf

chapon [ʃapɔ̃] *m* capon; (culin) crust rubbed with garlic

chaque [ʃak] *adj indef* each, every || *pron indef* (coll) each, each one

char [ʃar] *m* chariot; float (*in parade*); (mil) tank; **char d'assaut** or **char de combat** (mil) tank; **char funèbre** hearse

charabia [ʃarabja] *m* gibberish

charançon [ʃarɑ̃sɔ̃] *m* weevil

charbon [ʃarbɔ̃] *m* coal; soft coal; charcoal; carbon (*of an electric cell or arc*); cinder (*in the eye*); **charbon ardent** live coal; **charbon de bois** charcoal; **charbon de terre** coal; **être sur les charbons ardents** to be on pins and needles

charbonnage [ʃarbɔnaʒ] *m* coal mining; coal mine

charbonner [ʃarbɔne] *tr* to char; to draw (*a picture*) with charcoal || *intr & ref* to char, to carbonize

charbon·neux [ʃarbɔnø] **charbon·neuse** [ʃarbɔnøz] *adj* sooty; anthrax-carrying

charbon·nier [ʃarbɔnje] **charbon·nière** [ʃarbɔnjɛr] *adj* coal (*e.g., industry*) || *mf* coal dealer || *m* charcoal burner; coaler || *f* coal scuttle; charcoal kiln; (orn) coal titmouse

charcuter [ʃarkyte] *tr* to butcher, mangle

charcuterie [ʃarkytri] *f* delicatessen; pork butcher shop

charcu·tier [ʃarkytje] **-tière** [tjɛr] *mf* pork butcher; (coll) sawbones

chardon [ʃardɔ̃] *m* thistle

chardonneret [ʃardɔnrɛ] *m* (orn) goldfinch

charge [ʃarʒ] *f* charge; load, burden; caricature; public office; **à charge de** on condition of, with the proviso of; **à charge de revanche** on condition of getting the same thing in return; **charges de famille** dependents; **être à charge** to be dependent upon; **être à la charge de** to be supported by; **faire la charge de** to do a takeoff of

char·gé -gée [ʃarʒe] *adj* loaded; full; overcast (*sky*); registered (*letter*) ∥ *m* assistant, deputy, envoy; **chargé de cours** assistant professor

chargement [ʃarʒəmɑ̃] *m* charging; loading; cargo

charger [ʃarʒe] §38 *tr* to charge; to drive, to take (*s.o. in one's car*) ∥ *intr* (mil) to charge; (naut) to load ∥ *ref* to be loaded; **se charger de** to take charge of; to take up (*a question*)

chargeur [ʃarʒœr] *m* loader; stoker; shipper; clip (*of gun*); (elec) charger

chariot [ʃarjo] *m* wagon, cart; typewriter carriage; **chariot d'enfant** walker; **chariot élévateur** fork-lift truck; **Grand Chariot, Chariot de David** Big Dipper; **Petit Chariot** Little Dipper

charitable [ʃaritabl] *adj* charitable

charité [ʃarite] *f* charity; **faire la charité** to give alms; **faites la charité de** or **ayez la charité de** have the goodness to; **par charité** for charity's sake

charlatan [ʃarlatɑ̃] *m* charlatan

charlemagne [ʃarləmaɲ] *m* (cards) king of hearts; **faire charlemagne** to quit while winning

char·mant [ʃarmɑ̃] **-mante** [mɑ̃t] *adj* charming

charme [ʃarm] *m* charm; (*Carpinus betulus*) hornbeam; **se porter comme un charme** to be fit as a fiddle

charmer [ʃarme] *tr* to charm

char·meur [ʃarmœr] **-meuse** [møz] *adj* charming ∥ *mf* charmer

charmille [ʃarmij] *f* bower, arbor

char·nel -nelle [ʃarnɛl] *adj* carnal

charnière [ʃarnjɛr] *f* hinge

char·nu -nue [ʃarny] *adj* fleshy; plump; pulpy

charogne [ʃarɔɲ] *f* carrion

charpentage [ʃarpɑ̃taʒ] *m* carpentry

charpente [ʃarpɑ̃t] *f* framework; scaffolding; frame, build (*of body*)

charpenter [ʃarpɑ̃te] *tr* to square (*timber*); to outline, map out, plan (*a novel, speech, etc.*); **être solidement charpenté** to be well built or well constructed ∥ *intr* to carpenter

charpenterie [ʃarpɑ̃tri] *f* carpentry; structure (*of building*)

charpentier [ʃarpɑ̃tje] *m* carpenter

charpie [ʃarpi] *f* lint; **en charpie in shreds**

charrée [ʃare] *f* lye

charre·tier [ʃartje] **-tière** [tjɛr] *mf* teamster; **jurer comme un charretier** to swear like a trooper

charrette [ʃarɛt] *f* cart

charriage [ʃarjaʒ] *m* cartage; drifting (*of ice*); (slang) exaggeration

charrier [ʃarje] *tr* to cart, to transport; to carry away (*sand, as the river does*); (slang) to poke fun at ∥ *intr* to be full of ice (*said of river*); (slang) to exaggerate

charroi [ʃarwa], [ʃarwa] *m* cartage

charron [ʃarɔ̃], [ʃarɔ̃] *m* wheelwright, cartwright

charroyer [ʃarwaje] §47 *tr* to cart

charrue [ʃary] *f* plow; **mettre la charrue devant les bœufs** to put the cart before the horse

charte [ʃart] *f* charter; title deed; fundamental principle

chas [ʃa] *m* eye (*of needle*)

chasse [ʃas] *f* hunt, hunting; hunting song; chase; bag (*game caught*); **aller à la chasse** to go hunting; **chasse à courre** riding to the hounds; **chasse aux appartements** house hunting; **chasse aux fauves** big-game hunting; **chasse d'eau** flush; **chasse gardée** game preserve; **chasse réservée** (public sign) no shooting; **tirer la chasse** to pull the toilet chain

châsse [ʃɑs] *f* reliquary; frame (*e.g., for eyeglasses*) ∥ **châsses** *mpl* (slang) blinkers, eyes

chasse-bestiaux [ʃasbɛstjo] *m invar* cowcatcher

chasse-clou [ʃasklu] *m* (*pl* **-clous**) punch, nail set

chassé-croisé [ʃasekrwaze] *m* (*pl* **chassés-croisés**) futile efforts

chasselas [ʃasla] *m* white table grape

chasse-mouches [ʃasmuʃ] *m invar* fly swatter; fly net

chasse-neige [ʃasnɛʒ] *m invar* snowplow

chasse-pierres [ʃaspjɛr] *m invar* (rr) cowcatcher

chasser [ʃase] *tr* to hunt; to chase; to chase away, to put to flight; to drive (*e.g., a herd of cattle*); (coll) to fire (*e.g., a servant*) ∥ *intr* to hunt; to skid; to come, e.g., **le vent chasse du nord** the wind is coming from the north; **chasser de race** (coll) to be a chip off the old block

chasseresse [ʃasrɛs] *f* huntress

chas·seur [ʃasœr] **-seuse** [ʃasøz] *mf* hunter; bellhop ∥ *m* chasseur; fighter pilot; **chasseur à réaction** jet fighter; **chasseur d'assaut** fighter plane; **chasseur de chars** antitank tank; **chasseur de sous-marins** submarine chaser

chasseur-bombardier [ʃasœrbɔ̃bardje] *m* fighter-bomber

chassie [ʃasi] *f* gum (*on eyelids*)

chas·sieux [ʃasjø] **chas·sieuse** [ʃasjøz] *adj* gummy (*eyelids*)

châssis [ʃasi] *m* chassis; window frame; chase (*for printing*); **châssis à**

demeure or dormant sealed window frame; **châssis couche** (hort) hotbed; **châssis mobile** movable sash

châssis-presse [ʃɑsipres] *m* (*pl* -**presses**) printing frame

chaste [ʃast] *adj* chaste

chasteté [ʃastəte] *f* chastity

chat [ʃa] **chatte** [ʃat] *mf* cat || *m* tom-cat; **à bon chat bon rat** tit for tat; **acheter chat en poche** (coll) to buy a pig in a poke; **appeler un chat un chat** (coll) to call a spade a spade; **chat à neuf queues** cat-o'-nine-tails; **chat dans la gorge** (coll) frog in the throat; **chat de gouttière** alley cat; **chat sauvage** wildcat; **d'autres chats à fouetter** (coll) other fish to fry; **il ne faut pas réveiller le chat qui dort** let sleeping dogs lie; **le Chat botté** Puss in Boots; **mon petit chat!** darling!; **pas un chat** (coll) not a soul || *f* see **chatte**

châtaigne [ʃatɛɲ] *f* chestnut

châtaignier [ʃatɛɲe] *m* chestnut tree

chataire [ʃatɛr] *f* catnip

châ-teau [ʃato] *m* (*pl* -**teaux**) cha-teau; palace; estate, manor; **château d'eau** water tower; **château de cartes** house of cards; **château fort** castle, fort, citadel; **châteaux en Espagne** castles in the air; **mener une vie de château** to live like a prince

châteaubriand or **châteaubriant** [ʃatobriã] *m* grilled beefsteak

châte·lain [ʃatlɛ̃] -**laine** [lɛn] *mf* pro-prietor of a country estate || *f* wife of the lord of the manor; bracelet

châtelet [ʃatlɛ] *m* small chateau

chat-huant [ʃayã] *m* (*pl* **chats-huants** [ʃayã]) screech owl

châtier [ʃatje] *tr* to chasten, chastise; to correct; to purify (*style*)

chatière [ʃatjɛr] *f* ventilation hole; cathole

châtiment [ʃatimã] *m* punishment

chatoiement [ʃatwamã] *m* glisten, sparkle, sheen, shimmer; play of colors

chaton [ʃatɔ̃] *m* kitten; setting (*of ring*); (bot) catkin

chatonner [ʃatɔne] *tr* to set (*a gem*) || *intr* to have kittens

chatouillement [ʃatujmã] *m* tickle; tickling sensation

chatouiller [ʃatuje] *tr* to tickle; (fig) to excite, arouse || *intr* to tickle

chatouil·leux [ʃatujø] **chatouil·leuse** [ʃatujøz] *adj* ticklish; touchy

chatoyer [ʃatwaje] §47 *intr* to glisten, to sparkle; to shimmer

chat-pard [ʃapar] *m* (*pl* **chats-pards**) ocelot

châtrer [ʃatre] *tr* to castrate

chatte [ʃat] *adj fem* kittenish || *f* cat, female cat

chatterie [ʃatri] *f* cajoling; sweets

chatterton [ʃatertɔn] *m* friction tape

chaud [ʃo] **chaude** [ʃod] *adj* hot, warm; last-minute (*news flash*); **il fait chaud** it is warm (weather); **pleurer à chaudes larmes** to cry one's eyes out || *m* heat, warmth; **à chaud** emergency (*operation*); (med) in the acute stage; **avoir chaud** to be warm, to be hot (*said of person*); **il a eu chaud** (coll) he had a narrow escape || *adv*—**coûter chaud** (coll) to cost a pretty penny; **servir chaud** to serve (*s.th.*) piping hot

chaudière [ʃodjɛr] *f* boiler

chaudron [ʃodrɔ̃] *m* cauldron

chaudron·nier [ʃodrɔnje] **chaudron·nière** [ʃodrɔnjɛr] *mf* coppersmith; boilermaker

chauffage [ʃofaʒ] *m* heating; stoking; (coll) coaching

chauffard [ʃofar] *m* road hog, Sunday driver

chauffe [ʃof] *f* stoking; furnace

chauffe-assiettes [ʃofasjet] *m invar* hot plate

chauffe-bain [ʃofbɛ̃] *m* (*pl* -**bains**) bathroom water heater

chauffe-eau [ʃofo] *m invar* water heater

chauffe-lit [ʃofli] *m* (*pl* -**lits**) bed-warmer

chauffe-pieds [ʃofpje] *m invar* foot warmer

chauffe-plats [ʃofpla] *m invar* chafing dish

chauffer [ʃofe] *tr* to heat; to warm up; to limber up; (coll) to coach; (slang) to snitch, filch || *intr* to heat up; to get up steam; to overheat; **ça va chauffer!** (coll) watch the fur fly! || *ref* to warm oneself; to heat up

chaufferette [ʃofret] *f* foot warmer; space heater; car heater

chauffeur [ʃofœr] *m* driver; chauffeur; (rr) stoker, fireman

chauffeuse [ʃoføz] *f* fireside chair

chaume [ʃom] *m* stubble; thatch

chaumière [ʃomjɛr] *f* thatched cottage

chaussée [ʃose] *f* pavement, road; causeway

chausse-pied [ʃospje] *m* (*pl* -**pieds**) shoehorn

chausser [ʃose] *tr* to put on (*shoes, skis, glasses, tires, etc.*); to shoe; to fit || *intr* to fit (*said of shoe*); **chausser de** to wear (*a certain size shoe*) || *ref* to put one's shoes on

chausses [ʃos] *fpl* hose (*in medieval dress*); **aux chausses de** on the heels of; **c'est elle qui porte les chausses** (coll) she wears the pants

chausse-trape [ʃostrap] *f* (*pl* -**trapes**) trap

chaussette [ʃoset] *f* sock

chausseur [ʃosœr] *m* shoe salesman

chausson [ʃosɔ̃] *m* pump, slipper, savate; **chausson aux pommes** apple turnover

chaussure [ʃosyr] *f* footwear, shoes; shoe; **trouver chaussure à son pied** to find what one needs

chauve [ʃov] *adj* bald

chauve-souris [ʃovsuri] *f* (*pl* **chauves-souris**) (zool) bat

chau·vin [ʃovɛ̃] -**vine** [vin] *adj* chau-vinistic || *mf* chauvinist

chauvir [ʃovir] *intr*—**chauvir de l'oreil-le** or **chauvir des oreilles** to prick up the ears (*said of horse, mule, donkey*)

chaux [ʃo] *f* lime

chavirement [ʃavirmã] m capsizing, overturning

chavirer [ʃavire] tr & intr to tip over, to capsize

chef [ʃɛf] m head, chief, leader; boss; scoutmaster; **chef de bande** ringleader, gang leader; **chef de cuisine** chef; **chef de file** leader, standard-bearer; **chef de gare** stationmaster; **chef de l'exécutif** chief executive; **chef de musique** bandmaster; **chef de rayon** floorwalker; **chef de tribu** chieftain; **chef d'orchestre** conductor; bandleader; **de son propre chef** by one's own authority, on one's own

chef-d'œuvre [ʃɛdœvr] m (pl **chefs-d'œuvre**) masterpiece

chef-lieu [ʃɛfljø] m (pl **chefs-lieux**) county seat, capital city

cheftaine [ʃɛftɛn] f Girl Scout unit leader

cheik [ʃɛk] m sheik

chelem [ʃlɛm] m slam (at bridge); **être chelem** (cards) to be shut out

chemin [ʃmɛ̃] m way; road; **chemin battu** beaten path; **chemin de la Croix** (eccl) Way of the Cross; **chemin de fer** railroad; **chemin des écoliers** (coll) long way around; **chemin de table** table runner; **chemin de traverse** side road; shortcut; **chemin de velours** primrose path; **n'y pas aller par quatre chemins** (coll) to come straight to the point

chemi·neau [ʃmino] m (pl **-neaux**) hobo, tramp; deadbeat

cheminée [ʃmine] f chimney, stack, smokestack; fireplace; (naut) funnel

cheminer [ʃmine] intr to trudge, tramp; to make headway

cheminot [ʃmino] m railroader

chemise [ʃmiz] f shirt; dust jacket (of book); folder, file; jacket, shell, metal casing; **chemise de mailles** coat of mail; **chemise de nuit** nightgown

chemiser [ʃmize] tr (mach) to case, to jacket

chemiserie [ʃmizri] f haberdashery

chemisette [ʃmizɛt] f short-sleeved shirt

chemi·sier [ʃmizje] **-sière** [zjɛr] mf haberdasher ‖ m shirtwaist

che·nal [ʃnal] m (pl **-naux** [no]) channel; millrace

chenapan [ʃnapã] m rogue, scoundrel

chêne [ʃɛn] m oak

ché·neau [ʃeno] m (pl **-neaux**) rain spout

chêne-liège [ʃɛnljɛʒ] m (pl **chênes-lièges**) cork oak

chenet [ʃnɛ] m andiron

chènevis [ʃɛnvi] m hempseed, birdseed

chenil [ʃni] m kennel

chenille [ʃnij] f caterpillar; chenille; caterpillar tread

chenil·lé -lée [ʃnije] adj with a caterpillar tread

che·nu -nue [ʃny] adj hoary

cheptel [ʃɛptɛl], [ʃɛtɛl] m livestock; **cheptel mort** implements and buildings

chèque [ʃɛk] m check; **chèque de voyage** traveler's check; **chèque prescrit** lapsed check; **chèque sans provision** worthless check

chéquier [ʃekje] m checkbook

cher chère [ʃɛr] adj expensive, dear ‖ (when standing before noun) adj dear, beloved ‖ f see **chère** ‖ **cher** adv dear(ly); **coûter cher** to cost a great deal

chercher [ʃɛrʃe] tr to look for, search for, seek, hunt; to try to get; **aller chercher** to go and get; **envoyer chercher** to send for ‖ intr to search; **chercher à** to try to, to endeavor to ‖ ref to look for each other; to feel one's way

cher·cheur [ʃɛrʃœr] **-cheuse** [ʃøz] adj inquiring (mind); homing (device) ‖ mf seeker; researcher, scholar; investigator; prospector (for gold, uranium, etc.)

chère [ʃɛr] f fare, food and drink; **faire bonne chère** to live high

ché·ri -rie [ʃeri] adj & mf darling

chérir [ʃerir] tr to cherish

cherry [ʃeri] m cherry cordial

cherté [ʃɛrte] f high price; **cherté de la vie** high cost of living

chérubin [ʃerybɛ̃] m cherub

ché·tif -tive [ʃetif], [tiv] adj puny, sickly; poor, wretched

che·val [ʃəval] m (pl **-vaux** [vo]) horse; metric or French horsepower (735 watts); **à cheval** on horseback; **à cheval sur** astride; insistent upon; **cheval de bois** or **cheval d'arçons** horse (for vaulting); **cheval de course** race horse; **cheval de race** thoroughbred; **cheval de retour** (coll) jailbird; **cheval entier** stallion; **monter sur ses grands chevaux** (fig) to get up on one's high horse

chevalement [ʃəvalmã] m support, shoring; (min) headframe

chevaler [ʃəvale] tr to shore up

chevaleresque [ʃəvalrɛsk] adj knightly, chivalrous

chevalerie [ʃəvalri] f chivalry

chevalet [ʃəvalɛ] m easel; sawhorse; stand, frame; bridge (of violin)

chevalier [ʃəvalje] m knight; (orn) sandpiper; **chevalier d'industrie** manipulator, swindler; **chevalier errant** knight-errant; **Chevaliers du taste-vin** wine-tasting club

chevalière [ʃəvaljɛr] f signet ring

cheva·lin -line [ʃəvalɛ̃] **-line** [lin] adj equine

cheval-vapeur [ʃəvalvapœr] m (pl **che-vaux-vapeur**) metric or French horsepower (735 watts)

chevauchée [ʃəvoʃe] f ride

chevaucher [ʃəvoʃe] tr to straddle ‖ intr to ride horseback; to overlap

cheve·lu -lue [ʃəvly] adj hairy; long-haired

chevelure [ʃəvlyr] f hair, head of hair; tail (of a comet)

chevet [ʃəvɛ] m headboard; bolster; **de chevet** bedside (lamp, table, book)

che·veu [ʃəvø] m (pl **-veux**) hair; **avoir mal aux cheveux** (coll) to have a hangover; **cheveux nus** (of the head); hairs; **cheveux en brosse** crew cut; **couper les cheveux en quatre** (coll) to split hairs; **en cheveux** hatless; **faire dresser les cheveux** (coll) to make one's hair stand on end; **ne tenir qu'à un cheveu** (coll) to hang by a thread; **saisir l'occasion aux cheveux** (coll) to take time by the forelock; **se faire des cheveux** (coll) to worry oneself gray; **tiré par les cheveux** (coll) far-fetched

chevillard [ʃəvijar] *m* wholesale cattle dealer or jobber

cheville [ʃəvij] *f* peg; pin; bolt; padding (*of verse*); ankle; **cheville ouvrière** (mach) kingbolt; (fig) mainspring (*of an enterprise*); **être en cheville avec** (coll) to be in cahoots with; **ne pas arriver à la cheville de qn** (coll) not to hold a candle to s.o.

chèvre [ʃɛvr] *f* goat; nanny goat

che·vreau [ʃəvro] *m* (*pl* **-vreaux**) kid

chèvrefeuille [ʃɛvrəfœj] *m* honeysuckle

chevrette [ʃəvrɛt] *f* kid; doe (*roe deer*); shrimp; tripod

chevreuil [ʃəvrœj] *m* roe deer; roebuck

chevron [ʃəvrɔ̃] *m* rafter; chevron, hash mark; **en chevron** in a herringbone pattern

chevron·né -née [ʃəvrone] *adj* wearing chevrons; experienced, oldest

chevronner [ʃəvrone] *tr* to put rafters on; to give chevrons to

chevroter [ʃəvrote] *intr* to bleat; to sing or speak in a quavering voice

chewing-gum [ʃwiŋɡɔm], [tʃuwiŋɡɔm] *m* chewing gum

chez [ʃe] *prep* at the house, home, office, etc., of, e.g., **chez mes amis** at my friends' house; e.g., **chez le boulanger** at the baker's; in the country of, among, e.g., **chez les Français** among the French; in the time of, e.g., **chez les anciens Grecs** in the time of the ancient Greeks; in the work of, e.g., **chez Homère** in Homer's works; with, e.g., **c'est chez lui une habitude** it's a habit with him

chez-soi [ʃeswa] *m invar* home

chialer [ʃjale] *intr* (slang) to cry

chiasse [ʃjas] *f* flyspecks; (metallurgy) dross; (coll) loose bowels

chic [ʃik] *adj invar* stylish, chic; **un chic type** (coll) a good egg ‖ *m* style; skill, knack; (coll) smartness, elegance; (slang) ovation; **de chic** from memory ‖ *interj* (coll) fine!, good!

chicane [ʃikan] *f* chicanery; shady lawsuit; baffle, baffle plate; **chercher chicane à** to engage in a petty quarrel with; **en chicane** staggered, zigzag; curved (*tube*)

chicaner [ʃikane] *tr* to pick a fight with; **chicaner q.ch. à qn** to quibble over s.th. with s.o. ‖ *intr* to quibble

chicanerie [ʃikanri] *f* chicanery

chiche [ʃiʃ] *adj* stingy; small, dwarf ‖ *interj* (coll) I dare you!

chicon [ʃikɔ̃] *m* (coll) romaine

chicorée [ʃikɔre] *f* chicory; **chicorée frisée** endive

chicot [ʃiko] *m* stump (*of tree*); (coll) stump, stub (*of tooth*)

chien [ʃjɛ̃] **chienne** [ʃjɛn] *mf* dog ‖ *m* hammer (*of gun*); glamour; **à la chien**

(coll) with bangs; **chien couchant** setter; (slang) apple polisher; **chien d'arrêt** pointer; **chien d'aveugle** Seeing Eye dog; **chien de** or **chienne de** (coll) dickens of a; **chien de garde** watchdog; **chien du jardinier** (coll) dog in the manger; **chien savant** performing dog; **de chien** (coll) miserable (*weather, life, etc.*); **en chien de fusil** (coll) curled up (*e.g., to sleep*); **entre chien et loup** (coll) at dusk; **les chiens écrasés** (slang) the accident page (*of newspaper*); **petit chien** pup; **se regarder en chiens de faïence** (coll) to glare at one another ‖ *f* see **chienne**

chiendent [ʃjɛ̃dɑ̃] *m* couch grass; (coll) trouble

chienlit [ʃjɑ̃li] *mf* (vulgar) person who soils his bed ‖ *m* carnival mask; masquerade, fantastic costume

chien-loup [ʃjɛ̃lu] *m* (*pl* **chiens-loups**) wolfhound

chienne [ʃjɛn] *f* bitch

chienner [ʃjene] *intr* to whelp

chiennerie [ʃjenri] *f* stinginess, meanness

chiffe [ʃif] *f* rag; (coll) weakling

chiffon [ʃifɔ̃] *m* rag; scrap of paper; **chiffons** (coll) fashions

chiffonnade [ʃifɔnad] *f* salad greens

chiffonner [ʃifɔne] *tr* to rumple, crumple; to make (*a dress*); (coll) to ruffle (*tempers*), to bother ‖ *intr* to pick rags; to make dresses

chiffon·nier [ʃifɔnje] **chiffon·nière** [ʃifɔnjɛr] *mf* scavenger, ragpicker ‖ *m* chiffonier

chiffre [ʃifr] *m* figure, number; cipher, code; sum total; combination (*of lock*); monogram; **chiffre d'affaires** turnover; **chiffres romains** roman numerals

chiffrer [ʃifre] *tr* to number; to monogram; to figure the cost of; to cipher, code ‖ *intr* to calculate; to mount up; to cipher, code ‖ *ref*—**se chiffrer par** to amount to

chignole [ʃiɲɔl] *f* breast drill, hand drill; (coll) jalopy

chignon [ʃiɲɔ̃] *m* chignon, bun, knot

Chili [ʃili] *m*—**le Chili** Chile

chimère [ʃimɛr] *f* chimera; **se forger des chimères** to indulge in wishful thinking

chimie [ʃimi] *f* chemistry

chimique [ʃimik] *adj* chemical

chimiste [ʃimist] *mf* chemist

chimpanzé [ʃɛ̃pɑ̃ze] *m* chimpanzee

Chine [ʃin] *f* China; **la Chine** China

chi·né -née [ʃine] *adj* mottled, figured

chiner [ʃine] *tr* to mottle (*cloth*); (coll) to make fun of

chi·nois -noise [nwaz] *adj* Chinese ‖ *m* Chinese (*language*) ‖ (*cap*) *mf* Chinese (*person*)

chinoiserie [ʃinwazri] *f* Chinese curio; **chinoiseries administratives** (coll) red tape

chiot [ʃjo] *m* puppy

chiourme [ʃjurm] *f* chain gang

chiper [ʃipe] *tr* (slang) to swipe

chipie [ʃipi] *f* (coll) shrew

chipoter [ʃipɔte] *intr* to haggle

chips [ʃips] *mpl* potato chips

chique [ʃik] *f* chew, quid (*of tobacco*); (ent) chigger

chiqué [ʃike] *m* (slang) sham, bluff

chiquenaude [ʃiknod] *f* fillip, flick

chiquer [ʃike] *tr* to chew (*tobacco*) || *intr* to chew tobacco

chiromancie [kirɔmɑ̃si] *f* palmistry

chiroman-cien [kirɔmɑ̃sjɛ̃] **-cienne** [sjɛn] *mf* palm reader

chiropracteur [kirɔpraktœr] *m* chiropractor

chirurgi-cal -cale [ʃiryrʒikal] *adj* (*pl* **-caux** [ko]) surgical

chirurgie [ʃiryrʒi] *f* surgery

chirur-gien [ʃiryrʒjɛ̃] **-gienne** [ʒjɛn] *mf* surgeon

chirurgien-dentiste [ʃiryrʒjɛ̃dɑ̃tist] *m* (*pl* **chirurgiens-dentistes**) dental surgeon

chiure [ʃjyr] *f* flyspeck

chlore [klɔr] *m* chlorine

chlo-ré -rée [klɔre] *adj* chlorinated

chlorhydrique [klɔridrik] *adj* hydrochloric

chloroforme [klɔrɔfɔrm] *m* chloroform

chloroformer [klɔrɔfɔrme] *tr* to chloroform

chlorophylle [klɔrɔfil] *f* chlorophyll

chlorure [klɔryr] *m* chloride; **chlorure de soude** sodium chloride

choc [ʃɔk] *m* shock; clash; bump; clink (*of glasses*)

chocolat [ʃɔkɔla] *adj invar* & *m* chocolate

chocolaterie [ʃɔkɔlatri] *f* chocolate factory

chœur [kœr] *m* choir, chorus

choir [ʃwar] (usually used only in *inf* and *pp* **chu**; sometimes used in *pres ind* **chois**, etc.; *pret* **chus**, etc.; *fut* **choirai**, etc.) *intr* (*aux:* ÊTRE *or* AVOIR) to fall; **se laisser choir** to drop, to flop

choi-si -sie [ʃwazi] *adj* choice, select; chosen; selected (*works*)

choisir [ʃwazir] *tr* & *intr* to choose

choix [ʃwa] *m* choice; **au choix** at one's discretion; **de choix** choice

choléra [kɔlera] *m* cholera

cholérique [kɔlerik] *mf* cholera victim

cholestérol [kɔlesterɔl] *m* cholesterol

chômage [ʃomaʒ] *m* unemployment; **en chômage** unemployed

chô-mé -mée [ʃome] *adj* closed for business, off, e.g., **jour chômé** day off

chômer [ʃome] *tr* to take (*a day*) off; to observe (*a holiday*) || *intr* to take off (*from work*); to be unemployed

chô-meur [ʃomœr] **-meuse** [møz] *mf* unemployed worker

chope [ʃɔp] *f* stein, beer mug

chopine [ʃɔpin] *f* half-liter measure; (slang) bottle

chopper [ʃɔpe] *intr* to stumble; to blunder

choquer [ʃɔke] *tr* to shock; to bump; to clink (*glasses*); (elec) to shock || *ref* to collide; to take offense

cho-ral -rale [kɔral] *adj* (*pl* **-raux** [ro]) choral || *m* (*pl* **-rals**) chorale || *f* choral society, glee club

chorégraphie [kɔregrafi] *f* choreography

choriste [kɔrist] *mf* chorister

chorus [kɔrys] *m*—**faire chorus** to repeat in unison; to chime in; to approve unanimously

chose [ʃoz] *adj invar* (coll) odd; **être tout chose** (coll) to feel funny || *m* thingamajig; **Monsieur Chose** (coll) Mr. what's-his-name || *f* thing || *pron indef masc*—**autre chose** something else; **quelque chose** something

chou [ʃu] **choute** [ʃut] *mf*—**ma choute, mon chou** (coll) sweetheart || *m* (*pl* **choux**) cabbage; **chou à la crème** cream puff; **chou de Bruxelles** Brussels sprouts; **de chou** (coll) of little value; **faire chou blanc** (coll) to draw a blank; **finir dans le chou** (coll) to come in last

choucas [ʃuka] *m* jackdaw

choucroute [ʃukrut] *f* sauerkraut; **choucroute garnie** sauerkraut with ham or sausage

chouette [ʃwet] *adj* (coll) swell; **chouette alors!** (coll) oh boy! || *f* owl; (coll) radio; **chouette épervière** hawk owl

chou-fleur [ʃuflœr] *m* (*pl* **choux-fleurs**) cauliflower

chou-rave [ʃurav] *m* (*pl* **choux-raves**) kohlrabi

chow-chow [ʃuʃu] *m* (*pl* **-chows**) chow (*dog*)

choyer [ʃwaje] §47 *tr* to pamper, coddle; to cherish (*a hope*); to entertain (*an idea*)

chrestomatie [krestɔmati], [krestɔmasi] *f* chrestomathy

chré-tien [kretjɛ̃] **-tienne** [tjɛn] *adj* & *mf* Christian

chrétiennement [kretjɛnmɑ̃] *adv* in the faith

chrétienté [kretjɛ̃te] *f* Christendom

christ [krist] *m* crucifix || (*cap*) *m* Christ; **le Christ** Christ

christianiser [kristjanize] *tr* to Christianize

christianisme [kristjanism] *m* Christianity

chromatique [krɔmatik] *adj* chromatic

chrome [krom] *m* chrome, chromium

chromer [krome] *tr* to chrome

chromosome [krɔmozom] *m* chromosome

chronique [krɔnik] *adj* chronic || *f* chronicle; column (*in newspaper*); **chronique financière** financial page; **chronique mondaine** society news; **chronique théâtrale** theater page

chroniqueur [krɔnikœr] *m* chronicler; columnist; **chroniqueur dramatique** drama critic

chrono [krɔno] *m*—**faire du 60 chrono** (coll) to do 60 by the clock

chronologie [krɔnɔlɔʒi] *f* chronology

chronologique [krɔnɔlɔʒik] *adj* chronological

chronomètre [krɔnometr] *m* chronometer; stopwatch

chronométrer [krɔnɔmetre] §10 *tr* to clock, to time

chronométreur [krɔnɔmetrœr] *m* time-keeper

chrysalide [krizalid] *f* chrysalis

chrysanthème [krizɑ̃tem] *m* chrysanthemum

chuchotement [ʃyʃɔtmɑ̃] *m* whisper, whispering

chuchoter [ʃyʃɔte] *tr & intr* to whisper

chuinter [ʃɥɛ̃te] *intr* to hoot (*said of owl*); to make a swishing sound, to hiss (*said of escaping gas*); to pronounce [ʃ] instead of [s] and [ʒ] instead of [z]

chut [ʃyt] *interj* sh!

chute [ʃyt] *f* fall; downfall; drop (*in prices, voltage, etc.*); **chute d'eau** waterfall

chuter [ʃyte] *tr* to hush; to hiss (*an actor*) ‖ *intr* (coll) to fall; (cards) to be down

Chypre [ʃipr] *f* Cyprus

ci [si] *pron indef*—**comme ci comme ça** so-so ‖ *adv*—**entre ci et là** between now and then

-ci [si] §82, §84

ci-après [siapre] *adv* hereafter, below, further on

ci-bas [sibɑ] *adv* below

cible [sibl] *f* target

ciboule [sibul] *f* scallion

ciboulette [sibulet] *f* chive, chives

cicatrice [sikatris] *f* scar

cicatriser [sikatrize] *tr* to heal; to scar ‖ *ref* to heal

Cicéron [siserɔ̃] *m* Cicero

cicérone [siserɔn] *m* guide

ci-contre [sikɔ̃tr] *adv* opposite, on the opposite page; in the margin

ci-dessous [sidəsu] *adv* further on, below, hereunder

ci-dessus [sidəsy] *adv* above

ci-devant [sidəvɑ̃] *mf invar* (hist) aristocrat; (coll) back number ‖ *adv* previously, formerly

cidre [sidr] *m* cider

Cie *abbr* (**Compagnie**) Co.

ciel [sjel] *m* (*pl* **cieux** [sjø]) sky, heavens (*firmament*); heaven (*state of great happiness*) ‖ *m* (*pl* **ciels**) heaven (*abode of the blessed*); sky (*upper atmosphere, especially with reference to meteorological conditions; representation of sky in a painting*); canopy (*of a bed*) ‖ *m* (*pl* **cieux** or **ciels**) clime, sky

cierge [sjerʒ] *m* wax candle; cactus; **droit comme un cierge** straight as a ramrod; **en cierge** straight up

cigale [sigal] *f* cicada, grasshopper

cigare [sigar] *m* cigar

cigarette [sigaret] *f* cigarette

ci-gît [siʒi] see **gésir**

cigogne [sigɔɲ] *f* stork

ciguë [sigy] *f* hemlock (*herb and poison*)

ci-in-clus [siɛ̃kly] **-cluse** [klyz] *adj* enclosed ‖ **ci-inclus** *adv* enclosed

ci-joint [siʒwɛ̃] **-jointe** [ʒwɛ̃t] *adj* enclosed ‖ **ci-joint** *adv* enclosed

cil [sil] *m* eyelash; **cils** eyelash (*fringe of hair*)

cilice [silis] *m* hair shirt

ciller [sije] *tr & intr* to blink

cime [sim] *f* summit, top

ciment [simɑ̃] *m* cement; **ciment armé** reinforced concrete

cimentation [simɑ̃tasjɔ̃] *f* cementing

cimenter [simɑ̃te] *tr* to cement

cimeterre [simter] *m* scimitar

cimetière [simtjer] *m* cemetery

cinéaste [sineast] *mf* film producer; movie director; scenarist; movie technician

cinégraphiste [sinegrafist] *mf* scenarist

cinéma [sinema] *m* movies; moving-picture theater; cinema; **cinéma auto** drive-in movie; **cinéma d'essai** preview theater; **cinéma muet** silent movie

cinémathèque [sinematek] *f* film library

cinématographique [sinematɔgrafik] *adj* motion-picture, film

cinéphile [sinefil] *mf* movie fan

cinéprojecteur [sineprɔʒektœr] *m* motion-picture projector

ciné-roman [sinerɔmɑ̃] *m* (*pl* **-romans**) published story (*of a film*)

cinétique [sinetik] *adj* kinetic ‖ *f* kinetics

cin-glant [sɛ̃glɑ̃] **-glante** [glɑ̃t] *adj* scathing

cin-glé -glée [sɛ̃gle] *adj* (slang) screwy ‖ *mf* (slang) screwball

cingler [sɛ̃gle] *tr* to whip; to cut to the quick ‖ *intr* to go full sail

cinq [sɛ̃(k)] *adj & pron* five; the Fifth, e.g., **Jean cinq** John the Fifth; **cinq heures** five o'clock ‖ *m* five; fifth (*in dates*); **il était moins cinq** (coll) it was a close shave

cinquantaine [sɛ̃kɑ̃ten] *f* about fifty; age of fifty, fifty mark, fifties

cinquante [sɛ̃kɑ̃t] *adj, pron, & m* fifty; **cinquante et un** fifty-one; **cinquante et unième** fifty-first

cinquantième [sɛ̃kɑ̃tjem] *adj, pron* (*masc, fem*), & *m* fiftieth

cinquième [sɛ̃kjem] *adj, pron* (*masc, fem*), & *m* fifth

cintre [sɛ̃tr] *m* arch; coat hanger; bend; **plein cintre** semicircular arch

cin-tré -trée [sɛ̃tre] *adj* (slang) crazy

cintrer [sɛ̃tre] *tr* to arch, to bend

cirage [siraʒ] *m* waxing; shoe polish; **dans le cirage** (coll) in the dark

circoncire [sirkɔ̃sir] §66 (*pp* **circoncis**) *tr* to circumcise

circoncision [sirkɔ̃sizjɔ̃] *f* circumcision

circonférence [sirkɔ̃ferɑ̃s] *f* circumference

circonflexe [sirkɔ̃fleks] *adj & m* circumflex

circonscription [sirkɔ̃skripsjɔ̃] *f* circumscription; ward, district

circonscrire [sirkɔ̃skrir] §25 *tr* to circumscribe

circons-pect [sirkɔ̃spe], [sirkɔ̃spek(t)] **-pecte** [pekt] *adj* circumspect

circonstance [sirkɔ̃stɑ̃s] *f* circumstance; **circonstances et dépendances** appurtenances; **de circonstance** proper for the occasion, topical; emergency (*measure*); guest, e.g., **orateur de circonstance** guest speaker

circonstan·cié -ciée [sirkɔ̃stãsje] *adj* circumstantial, in detail

circonstan·ciel -cielle [sirkɔ̃stãsjel] *adj* (gram) adverbial

circonvenir [sirkɔ̃vnir] §72 *tr* to circumvent

circonvoi·sin [sirkɔ̃vwazɛ̃] **-sine** [zin] *adj* nearby, neighboring

circuit [sirkɥi] *m* circuit; circumference; detour; tour

circulaire [sirkyler] *adj & f* circular

circulation [sirkylasjɔ̃] *f* circulation; traffic; **circulation interdite** (public sign) no thoroughfare

circuler [sirkyle] *intr* to circulate

cire [sir] *f* wax; **cire à cacheter** sealing wax; **cire molle** (fig) wax in one's hands

ci·ré -rée [sire] *adj* waxed ‖ *m* waterproof garment; raincoat

cirer [sire] *tr* to wax; to polish

ci·reur [sirœr] **-reuse** [røz] *mf* waxer, polisher (*person*); shoeblack, bootblack ‖ *f* floor waxer (*machine*)

ci·reux -reuse [sirø] **-reuse** [røz] *adj* waxy

ciron [sirɔ̃] *m* mite

cirque [sirk] *m* circus; amphitheater

cirrhose [siroz] *f* cirrhosis

cisaille [sizaj] *f* metal clippings, scissel; **cisailles** clippers, shears; wire cutter

cisailler [sizaje] *tr* to shear

ci·seau [sizo] *m* (*pl* **-seaux**) chisel; **ciseau à froid** cold chisel; **ciseaux** scissors; **ciseaux à ongles** nail scissors; **ciseaux à raisin** pruning shears; **ciseaux à tondre** sheep shears

ciseler [sizle] §2 *tr* to chisel; to chase; to cut, shear; to prune

ciseleur [sizlœr] *m* chaser, tooler

citadelle [sitadel] *f* citadel

cita·din [sitadɛ̃] **-dine** [din] *adj* urban ‖ *mf* city dweller

citation [sitasjɔ̃] *f* citation, quotation; citation, summons

cité [site] *f* housing development; (hist) fortified city, citadel; **cité ouvrière** low-cost housing development; **cité sainte** Holy City; **cité universitaire** university dormitory complex; **la Cité** the City (*district within ancient boundaries*)

citer [site] *tr* to cite, quote; to summon, subpoena

citerne [sitern] *f* cistern; tank; **citerne flottante** tanker

cithare [sitar] *f* cither, zither

citoyen [sitwajɛ̃] **citoyenne** [sitwajen] *mf* citizen; (coll) individual, person; **citoyens** citizenry

citoyenneté [sitwajente] *f* citizenship; citizenry

citrique [sitrik] *adj* citric

citron [sitrɔ̃] *adj & m* lemon

citronnade [sitrɔnad] *f* lemonade

citron·né -née [sitrɔne] *adj* lemon-flavored

citronnelle [sitrɔnel] *f* citronella

citronner [sitrɔne] *tr* to flavor with lemon

citronnier [sitrɔnje] *m* lemon tree

citrouille [sitruj] *f* pumpkin, gourd

cive [siv] *f* scallion

civet [sive] *m* stew

civette [sivet] *f* civet; civet cat; chive, chives

civière [sivjer] *f* stretcher, litter

ci·vil -vile [sivil] *adj* civil; civilian; secular ‖ *m* civilian; layman; **en civil** plain-clothes (*man*); in civies

civilisation [sivilizasjɔ̃] *f* civilization

civiliser [sivilize] *tr* to civilize ‖ *ref* to become civilized

civilité [sivilite] *f* civility; **civilités** kind regards; amenities

civique [sivik] *adj* civic; civil (*rights*); national (*guard*)

civisme [sivism] *m* good citizenship

clabauder [klabode] *intr* to clamor

claie [kle] *f* wickerwork; trellis

clair claire [kler] *adj* clear, bright; evident, plain; light, pale ‖ *m* light, brightness; **clair de lune** moonlight; **clairs** highlights ‖ *f* oyster bed

clai·ret [klere] **-rette** [ret] *adj* light-red; thin, high-pitched (*voice*) ‖ *m* light, red wine ‖ *f* light sparkling wine

claire-voie [klervwa] *f* (*pl* **claires-voies**) latticework, slats; clerestory; **à claire-voie** with open spaces

clairière [klerjer] *f* clearing, glade

clairon [klerɔ̃] *m* bugle; bugler

claironner [klerɔne] *tr* to announce ‖ *intr* to sound the bugle

clairse·mé -mée [klersəme] *adj* scattered, sparse; thin, thinned out

clairvoyance [klervwajãs] *f* clear-sightedness, clairvoyance

clairvoyant [klervwajã] **clairvoyante** [klervwajãt] *adj* clear-sighted, clairvoyant

clamer [klame] *tr & intr* to cry out

clameur [klamœr] *f* clamor, outcry

clamp [klã] *m* (med) clamp

clampin [klãpɛ̃] *m* (mil) straggler

clan [klã] *m* clan, clique

clandes·tin [klãdestɛ̃] **-tine** [tin] *adj* clandestine

clapet [klape] *m* valve; **ferme ton clapet!** (slang) shut your trap!

clapier [klapje] *m* rabbit hutch

clapoter [klapɔte] *intr* to splash; to be choppy

claque [klak] *m* opera hat ‖ *f* slap, smack; claque, paid applauders

cla·qué -quée [klake] *adj* dog-tired; sprained

claquement [klakmã] *m* clapping; slam (*of a door*); chattering (*of teeth*)

claquemurer [klakmyre] *tr* to shut in ‖ *ref* to shut oneself up at home

claquer [klake] *tr* to slap; to clap; to smack (*the lips*); to slam (*the door*); to crack (*the whip*); to click (*the heels*); to snap (*the fingers*); (coll) to tire out; (coll) to waste ‖ *intr* to clap, snap, slam; to crack; (slang) to fail; (slang) to die ‖ *ref* (with *dat* of *reflex pron*) to sprain; (slang) to work oneself to death

claquettes [klaket] *fpl* tap-dancing

claqueur [klakœr] *m* applauder, member of a claque

clarifier [klarifje] *tr* to clarify ‖ *ref* to become clear

clarine [klarin] *f* cowbell

clarinette [klarinet] *f* clarinet

clarté [klarte] *f* clarity; brightness; **clarté du soleil** sunshine

classe [klɑs] *f* class; classroom; **classe de rattrapage** refresher course (*for backward children*); **classe de travaux pratiques** lab class

clas·sé -sée [klɑse] *adj* pigeonholed, tabled; standard (*literary work*); listed; **non classé** (sports) also-ran

classer [klɑse] *tr* to class; to sort out, to file; to pigeonhole, to table

classeur [klɑsœr] *m* file (*for letters, documents*); filing cabinet

classicisme [klasisism] *m* classicism

classification [klasifikasjɔ̃] *f* classification

classifier [klasifje] *tr* to classify; to sort out

classique [klasik] *adj* classic, classical; standard (*author, work*) ‖ *mf* classicist ‖ *m* classic; standard work

claudication [klodikasjɔ̃] *f* limping

clause [kloz] *f* clause, stipulation, provision; **clause additionnelle** rider; **clause ambiguë** joker clause; **clause de style** unwritten provision

claustration [klostrasjɔ̃] *f* confinement; cloistering

clavecin [klavsɛ̃] *m* harpsichord

claveciniste [klavsinist] *mf* harpsichordist

clavette [klavet] *f* pin, cotter pin; key

clavicule [klavikyl] *f* collarbone

clavier [klavje] *m* keyboard; key ring; range (*e.g., of the voice*); **clavier universel** standard keyboard

clayère [klejer] *f* oyster bed

clé [kle] *f* see **clef**

clef [kle] *adj invar* key ‖ *f* key; wrench; (wrestling) lock; **clef anglaise** monkey wrench; **clef à tube** socket wrench; **clef crocodile** alligator wrench; **clef des champs** vacation; **clef de voûte** keystone; **sous clef** under lock and key

clémence [klemɑ̃s] *f* clemency

clé·ment -mente [klemɑ̃] -[mɑ̃t] *adj* mild, clement

clenche [klɑ̃ʃ] *f* latch

cleptomane [kleptɔman] *mf* kleptomaniac

clerc [kler] *m* cleric, clergyman; scholar; clerk

clergé [klerʒe] *m* clergy

clergie [klerʒi] *f* learning, scholarship; clergy

cléri·cal -cale [klerikal] *adj & mf* (*pl* -caux [ko]) clerical

cliché [kliʃe] *m* cliché; (phot) negative; (typ) plate, stereotype; **prendre un cliché** (phot) to make an exposure

clicher [kliʃe] *tr* (typ) to stereotype

client [klijɑ̃] **cliente** [kljɑ̃t] *mf* client; patient; customer; guest (*of a hotel*)

clientèle [klijɑ̃tel] *f* clientele; adherents

cligner [kliɲe] *tr* to squint (*one's eyes*) ‖ *intr* to squint, to blink; **cligner de l'œil à** to wink at

cligno·tant -tante [kliɲɔtɑ̃] -[tɑ̃t] *adj* blinking ‖ *m* (aut) directional signal

clignotement [kliɲɔtmɑ̃] *m* blinking; twinkling; flickering

clignoter [kliɲɔte] *intr* to blink; to twinkle; to flicker

clignoteur [kliɲɔtœr] *m* (aut) directional signal

climat [klimɑ], [klima] *m* climate

climatisation [klimatizɑsjɔ̃] *f* air conditioning

climati·sé -sée [klimatize] *adj* air-conditioned

climatiseur [klimatizœr] *m* air conditioner

clin [klɛ̃] *m*—**à clin** (carpentry) overlapping, covering; **clin d'œil** wink; **en un clin d'œil** in the twinkling of an eye

clinicien [klinisjɛ̃] *adj masc* clinical ‖ *m* clinician

clinique [klinik] *adj* clinical ‖ *f* clinic; private hospital

clinquant [klɛ̃kɑ̃] *m* foil, tinsel; flashiness, tawdriness

clip [klip] *m* clip, brooch

clique [klik] *f* drum and bugle corps; (coll) gang; **cliques** wooden shoes

cliquet [klike] *m* (mach) pawl, catch

cliqueter [klikte] §34 *intr* to click, to clink, to clank, to jangle

cliquetis [klikti] *m* click, clink, clank, jangle

cliquette [kliket] *f* castanets; (fishing) sinker

clisse [klis] *f* draining rack, wicker bottleholder

clivage [klivaʒ] *m* cleavage

cliver [klive] *tr* to cleave; to cut

cloaque [klɔak] *m* cesspool

clo·chard [klɔʃar] **-charde** [ʃard] *mf* beggar, tramp

cloche [klɔʃ] *adj* bell (*skirt*) ‖ *f* bell; bell glass; blister (*on skin*); **cloche à plongeurs** diving bell; **cloche de sauvetage** escape hatch (*on submarine*); **déménager à la cloche de bois** (coll) to skip out without paying; **la cloche** (slang) beggars

clochement [klɔʃmɑ̃] *m* limp, limping

cloche-pied [klɔʃpje]—**à cloche-pied** on one foot, hopping

clocher [klɔʃe] *m* steeple; belfry; parish, home town; **de clocher** local (politics) ‖ *intr* to limp; **quelque chose cloche** something jars, is not right

clocheton [klɔʃtɔ̃] *m* little steeple

clochette [klɔʃet] *f* little bell; (bot) bellflower

cloison [klwazɔ̃] *f* partition; division, barrier (*e.g., between classes*); (anat, bot) septum, dividing membrane; (naut) bulkhead; **cloison étanche** (naut) watertight compartment

cloisonner [klwazɔne] *tr* to partition

cloître [klwatr] *m* cloister

cloîtrer [klwatre] *tr* to cloister; to confine

clopin-clopant [klɔpɛ̃klɔpɑ̃] *adv* (coll) so-so; **aller clopin-clopant** (coll) to go hobbling along

clopiner [klɔpine] *intr* to hobble

cloque [klɔk] *f* blister

cloquer [klɔke] *tr & intr* to blister

clore [klɔr] §24 *tr & intr* to close

clos [klo] **close** [kloz] *adj* closed || *m* enclosure; **clos de vigne** vineyard

clôture [klotyr] *f* fence; wall; cloistered life; closing of an account

clôturer [klotyre] *tr* to enclose, to wall in; to close out (*an account*); to conclude (*a discussion*)

clou [klu] *m* nail; (coll) boil; (coll) jalopy; (coll) feature attraction; (slang) pawnshop; **clou de girofle** clove; **clous** pedestrian crossing; **des clous!** (slang) nothing at all!

clouer [klue] *tr* to nail; to immobilize, rivet; **clouer le bec à qn** (coll) to shut s.o.'s mouth

clouter [klute] *tr* to stud; to trim or border with studs, e.g., **passage clouté** pedestrian crossing (bordered with studs)

clown [klun] *m* clown; **faire le clown** to clown (around)

clownerie [klunri] *f* high jinks, clowning

club [klyb] *m* (literary) society; (political) association || [klœb] *m* club (*for social and athletic purposes, etc.*); clubhouse; (golf) club; armchair

clubiste [klybist] *mf* (coll) club member; (coll) joiner

clubman [klœbman] *m* club member

coaccu·sé -sée [koakyze] *mf* codefendant

coaguler [koagyle] *tr & ref* to coagulate

coaliser [koalize] *tr* to form into a coalition || *ref* to form a coalition

coalition [koalisjɔ̃] *f* coalition

coassement [koasmɑ̃] *m* croak, croaking

coasser [koase] *intr* to croak

coasso·cié -ciée [koasosje] *mf* copartner

coauteur [kootœr] *m* coauthor

cobalt [kobalt] *m* cobalt

cobaye [kobaj] *m* guinea pig

cocaïne [kokain] *f* cocaine

cocarde [kokard] *f* cockade; rosette of ribbons; **avoir sa cocarde** (coll) to be tipsy; **prendre la cocarde** (coll) to enlist

cocasse [kokas] *adj* (coll) funny, ridiculous

coccinelle [koksinɛl] *f* ladybug

coche [kɔʃ] *m* coach, stagecoach; twodoor sedan; barge || *f* notch, score; (zool) sow

cocher [koʃe] *m* coachman, driver || *tr* to notch, to score; to check off

cochère [koʃɛr] *adj* carriage (*entrance*)

co·chon [koʃɔ̃] **-chonne** [ʃɔn] *mf* (coll) skunk, slob || *m* pig, hog; **cochon de lait** suckling pig; **cochon de mer** porpoise; **cochon d'Inde** guinea pig

cochonnerie [koʃɔnri] *f* (slang) dirty trick; (slang) filthy speech, smut

cocker [kokɛr] *m* cocker spaniel

cockpit [kokpit] *m* (aer) cockpit

cocktail [koktɛl] *m* cocktail; cocktail party

coco [koko], [koko] *m* coconut; licorice water; **mon coco** (coll) my darling; **un joli coco** (coll) a stinker || *f* (slang) cocaine

cocon [kokɔ̃] *m* cocoon

cocorico [kokoriko] *m* cockcrow || *interj* cock-a-doodle-doo!

cocotier [kokotje] *m* coconut tree

cocotte [kokot] *f* saucepan; cocotte, floozy; **ma cocotte** (coll) my little chick, my baby doll

co·cu -cue [koky] *adj & m* cuckold

cocufier [kokyfje] *tr* (slang) to cuckold

code [kod] *m* code; **code de la route** traffic regulations; **code pénal** criminal code; **codes** (slang) dimmers; **se mettre en code** to dip one's headlights

codex [kodeks] *m* pharmacopoeia

codicille [kodisil] *m* codicil

codifier [kodifje] *tr* to codify

coéducation [koedykasjɔ̃] *f* coeducation

coefficient [koefisjɑ̃] *m* coefficient

coéqui·pier [koekipje] **-pière** [pjɛr] *mf* teammate

coercition [koersisjɔ̃] *f* coercion

cœur [kœr] *m* heart; core; courage, spirit; bosom, breast; depth (*of winter*); (cards) heart; (cards) hearts; **à cœur joie** to one's heart's content; **avoir du cœur** to be kind-hearted; **avoir du cœur au ventre** (coll) to have guts; **avoir le cœur sur la main** (coll) to be open-handed; **avoir le cœur sur les lèvres** to wear one's heart on one's sleeve; **cœur de bronze** heart of stone; **de bon cœur** willingly, heartily; **de mauvais cœur** reluctantly; **en avoir le cœur net** to get to the bottom of it; **épancher son cœur à** to open one's heart to; **fendre le cœur à** to break the heart of; **le cœur gros** with a heavy heart; **mal au cœur** or **mal de cœur** stomach ache; nausea; **par cœur** by heart; **prendre à cœur** to take to heart; **se ronger le cœur** to eat one's heart out; **soulever le cœur** to turn the stomach

coexistence [koegzistɑ̃s] *f* coexistence

coexister [koegziste] *intr* to coexist

coffre [kofr] *m* chest; coffer, bin; safe-deposit box; trunk (*of car*); buoy (*for mooring*); cofferdam

coffre-fort [kofrəfor] *m* (*pl* **coffres-forts**) safe, strongbox, vault

coffret [kofrɛ] *m* gift box

cognac [koɲak] *m* cognac

cognat [koɲa] *m* blood kin

cognée [koɲe] *f* ax, hatchet

cogner [koɲe] *tr, intr, & ref* to knock, bump

cohabiter [koabite] *intr* to cohabit

cohé·rent [koerɑ̃] **-rente** [rɑ̃t] *adj* coherent

cohériter [koerite] *intr* to inherit jointly

cohéri·tier [koeritje] **-tière** [tjɛr] *mf* coheir

cohésion [koezjɔ̃] *f* cohesion

cohorte [koort] *f* cohort

cohue [koy] *f* crowd, throng, mob

coi [kwa] **coite** [kwat] *adj* quiet; **demeurer** or **se tenir coi** to keep still

coiffe [kwaf] *f* cap; headdress; caul

coif·fé -fée [kwafe] *adj*—**coiffé de** wearing (*a hat*); (fig) crazy about (*a person*); **être coiffé** to be wearing a

hairdo; **être né coiffé** (fig) to be
lucky

coiffer [kwafe] *tr* to put a hat or cap
on (*s.o.*); to dress or do the hair of;
(mil) to reach (*an objective*) || *intr*—
coiffer de to wear (*a certain size hat*)
|| *ref* to do one's hair; **se coiffer de**
(coll) to set one's cap for

coif·feur [kwafœr] **coif·feuse** [kwaføz]
mf hairdresser; barber; **coiffeur pour
dames** coiffeur || *f* dresser, dressing
table

coiffure [kwafyr] *f* coiffure; headdress;
coiffure en brosse crew cut

coin [kwɛ̃] *m* corner; angle; nook;
wedge, coin; stamp, die (*for coining
money*); (typ) quoin; **le petit coin**
(coll) the powder room

coinçage [kwɛ̃saʒ] *m* wedging

coincer [kwɛ̃se] §51 *tr* to wedge, jam;
(coll) to pinch, arrest || *ref* to jam

coïncidence [kɔɛ̃sidɑ̃s] *f* coincidence

coïncider [kɔɛ̃side] *intr* to coincide

coin-coin [kwɛ̃kwɛ̃] *m invar* quack (*of
duck*); toot (*of horn*)

coing [kwɛ̃] *m* quince

coït [kɔit] *m* coition

coke [kɔk] *m* coke

cokéfier [kɔkefje] *tr & ref* to coke

col [kɔl] *m* neck (*of bottle; of womb*);
collar (*of dress*); mountain pass;
(coll) head (*on beer*); **col de fourrure**
neckpiece; **col roulé** turtleneck; **faux
col** detachable collar

colback [kɔlbak] *m* busby

colère [kɔler] *f* anger; **en colère** angry; **se mettre en colère** to become
angry

colé·reux [kɔlerø] **-reuse** [røz] *adj*
irascible, choleric

colérique [kɔlerik] *adj* choleric

colibri [kɔlibri] *m* hummingbird

colimaçon [kɔlimasɔ̃] *m* snail; **en colimaçon** spiral

colin [kɔlɛ̃] *m* hake

colin-maillard [kɔlɛ̃majar] *m* blind-
man's buff

colique [kɔlik] *f* colic

colis [kɔli] *m* piece of baggage, package, parcel; **colis postal** parcel post

colisée [kɔlize] *m* coliseum

collabora·teur [kɔlabɔratœr] **-trice**
[tris] *mf* collaborator; contributor

collaborationniste [kɔlabɔrasjɔnist] *mf*
collaborationist

collaborer [kɔlabɔre] *intr* to collaborate; **collaborer à** to contribute to

collage [kɔlaʒ] *m* pasting, mounting;
collage; sizing; clarifying (*of wine*);
(coll) common-law marriage

col·lant [kɔlɑ̃] **col·lante** [kɔlɑ̃t] *adj*
sticky; tight, close-fitting || *m* tights

collapsus [kɔllapsys] *m* (pathol) collapse

collaté·ral -rale [kɔllateral] (*pl* -raux
[ro]) *adj* collateral; parallel; inter-
mediate (*points of the compass*) ||
mf collateral (relative) || *m* side aisle
of a church

collation [kɔllasjɔ̃] *f* conferring (*of
titles, degrees, etc.*); collation (*of
texts*) || [kɔlasjɔ̃] *f* snack

collationner [kɔllasjɔne] *tr* to collate,

to compare; **faire collationner un
télégramme** to request a copy of a
telegram || *intr* to have a snack

colle [kɔl] *f* paste, glue; (coll) brain-
teaser, stickler; (slang) detention;
(slang) oral exam; (slang) flunking;
colle forte glue; **poser une colle**
(slang) to ask a hard one

collecte [kɔlekt] *f* collection (*for charitable cause*); (eccl) collect

collecteur [kɔlektœr] *adj & noun m, e.g.,
égout collecteur** main sewer || *m* col-
lector; commutator (*of motor or
dynamo*); (aut) manifold; **collecteur
d'ondes** aerial

collec·tif [kɔlektif] **-tive** [tiv] *adj* collective

collection [kɔleksjɔ̃] *f* collection

collectionner [kɔleksjɔne] *tr* to collect

collection·neur [kɔleksjɔnœr] **collec-
tion·neuse** [kɔleksjɔnøz] *mf* collector

collège [kɔleʒ] *m* high school; preparatory school; college (*of cardinals,
electors, etc.*); **collège universitaire**
junior college

collé·gial -giale [kɔleʒjal] (*pl* -giaux
[ʒjo]) *adj* collegiate || *f* collegiate
church

collé·gien [kɔleʒjɛ̃] **-gienne** [ʒjen] *adj*
high-school || *m* schoolboy || *f*
schoolgirl; coed

collègue [kɔlleg] *mf* colleague

coller [kɔle] *tr* to paste, stick, glue; to
clarify (*wine*); to mat (*e.g., with
blood*); (coll) to floor, to stump;
(coll) to punish (*a pupil*); (coll) to
flunk; (coll) to sock (*e.g., on the
jaw*) || *intr* to cling, to fit tightly
(*said of dress*); (coll) to stick close;
ça colle! (slang) O.K.! || *ref* (slang)
to have a common-law marriage; **se
coller contre** to stand close to; to
cling to

collet [kɔle] *m* collar; neck (*of person;
of tooth*); neck, scrag (*e.g., of mutton*); cape; snare; stalk and roots;
lasso, noose; **collet monté** (coll)
stuffed shirt

colleter [kɔlte] §34 *tr* to collar || *ref* to
fight, scuffle

collier [kɔlje] *m* necklace; collar; dog
collar; horse collar; **à collier** ring-
necked; **reprendre le collier** (coll) to
get back into harness

colliger [kɔlliʒe] §38 *tr* to make a collection of

colline [kɔlin] *f* hill

collision [kɔllizjɔ̃] *f* collision

colloï·dal -dale [kɔlloidal] *adj* (*pl* -daux
[do]) colloid, colloidal

colloïde [kɔlloid] *m* colloid

colloque [kɔllɔk] *m* colloquy, symposium

colloquer [kɔllɔke] *tr* to classify (*creditors' claims*); **colloquer q.ch. à qn**
(coll) to palm off s.th. on s.o.

collusion [kɔllyzjɔ̃] *f* collusion

collyre [kɔllir] *m* (med) eyewash

Cologne [kɔlɔɲ] *f* Cologne

Colomb [kɔlɔ̃] *m* Columbus

colombe [kɔlɔ̃b] *f* dove

Colombie [kɔlɔ̃bi] *f* Colombia; **la Colombie** Colombia

colombier [kɔlɔ̃bje] *m* dovecote; large-size paper

colom·bin [kɔlɔ̃bɛ̃] **-bine** [bin] *adj* columbine || *m* stock dove; lead ore || *f* bird droppings; (bot) columbine

colon [kɔlɔ̃] *m* colonist; tenant farmer; summer camper

côlon [kolɔ̃] *m* (anat) colon

colonel [kɔlɔnel] *m* colonel

colonelle [kɔlɔnel] *f* colonel's wife; (theat) performance for the press

colonie [kɔlɔni] *f* colony; **colonie de déportation** penal settlement; **colonie de vacances** summer camp

coloniser [kɔlɔnize] *tr* to colonize

colonnade [kɔlɔnad] *f* colonnade

colonne [kɔlɔn] *f* column; pillar; **cinquième colonne** fifth column; **colonne vertébrale** spinal column

colophane [kɔlɔfan] *f* rosin

colophon [kɔlɔfɔ̃] *m* colophon

colo·rant [kɔlɔrɑ̃] **-rante** [rɑ̃t] *adj* coloring || *m* dye, stain

colorer [kɔlɔre] *tr & ref* to color

colorier [kɔlɔrje] *tr* to paint, color

coloris [kɔlɔri] *m* hue; brilliance

colos·sal -sale [kɔlɔsal] *adj* (*pl* **colossaux** [kɔlɔso]) colossal

colosse [kɔlɔs] *m* colossus

colporter [kɔlpɔrte] *tr* to peddle

colporteur [kɔlpɔrtœr] *m* peddler

coltiner [kɔltine] *tr* to lug on one's back or on one's head

coma [kɔma] *m* (pathol) coma

coma·teux [kɔmatø] **-teuse** [tøz] *adj* comatose || *mf* person in a coma

combat [kɔ̃ba] *m* combat; **combat tournoyant** (aer) dogfight; **hors de combat** disabled

comba·tif [kɔ̃batif] **-tive** [tiv] *adj* combative

combat·tant [kɔ̃batɑ̃] **combat·tante** [kɔ̃batɑ̃t] *adj & mf* combatant; **anciens combattants** veterans

combattre [kɔ̃batr] §7 *tr & intr* to combat

combien [kɔ̃bjɛ̃] *adv* how much, how many; how far; how long; how, e.g., **combien il était brave!** how brave he was! || *m invar*—**du combien chaussez-vous?** what size shoes do you wear?; **du combien coiffez-vous?** what size hat do you wear?; **le combien?** which one (*in a series*)?; **le combien êtes-vous?** (coll) what rank do you have?; **le combien sommes-nous?** (coll) what day of the month is it?; **tous les combien?** how often?

combinaison [kɔ̃binezɔ̃] *f* combination; coveralls; slip, undergarment

combi·né -née [kɔ̃bine] *adj* combined || *m* French telephone, handset; radio phonograph

combiner [kɔ̃bine] *tr* to combine; to arrange, group; to concoct (*a scheme*) || *ref* (chem) to combine

comble [kɔ̃bl] *adj* full, packed || *m* summit; roof, coping; **au comble de** at the height of; **c'est le comble!**, **c'est un comble!** (coll) that's the limit!, that takes the cake!; **sous les combles** in the attic

combler [kɔ̃ble] *tr* to heap up; to fill to the brim; to overwhelm; **combler d'honneurs** to shower honors upon

combustible [kɔ̃bystibl] *adj & m* combustible, fuel

combustion [kɔ̃bystjɔ̃] *f* combustion

comédie [kɔmedi] *f* comedy; play; sham

comé·dien [kɔmedjɛ̃] **-dienne** [djen] *mf* comedian; actor; hypocrite; **comédien ambulant** strolling player || *f* comedienne; actress

comédon [kɔmedɔ̃] *m* blackhead

comestible [kɔmestibl] *adj* edible || **comestibles** *mpl* foodstuffs

comète [kɔmet] *f* comet

comique [kɔmik] *adj & m* comic

comité [kɔmite] *m* committee

commandant [kɔmɑ̃dɑ̃] *m* commandant, commander; major

commande [kɔmɑ̃d] *f* order (*for goods or services*); control, command; **à la commande** (paid) down; **commande postale** mail order; **de commande** operating; **(fait) sur commande** (made) to order

commandement [kɔmɑ̃dmɑ̃] *m* command, order; commandment

commander [kɔmɑ̃de] *tr* to order (*goods or services*); to command, order à + *inf* (mil) to command; **commander à** to control, to have command over; **commander à qn de** + *inf* to order s.o. to + *inf* || *ref* to control oneself

commanditaire [kɔmɑ̃diter] *adj* sponsoring || *mf* (com) sponsor, backer

commandite [kɔmɑ̃dit] *f* joint-stock company

commanditer [kɔmɑ̃dite] *tr* to back, to finance; (rad, telv) to sponsor

comme [kɔm] *adv* as; how; **comme ci comme ça** so-so || *prep* as, like || *conj* as; since

commémorer [kɔmmemɔre] *tr* to commemorate

commen·çant [kɔmɑ̃sɑ̃] **-çante** [sɑ̃t] *mf* beginner

commencement [kɔmɑ̃smɑ̃] *m* beginning

commencer [kɔmɑ̃se] §51 *tr & intr* to begin; **commencer à** to begin to

comment [kɔmɑ̃] *m invar* how; wherefore || *adv* how; why; **mais comment donc!** by all means!; **n'importe comment** any way || *interj* what!; indeed!

commentaire [kɔmɑ̃ter] *m* commentary; unfriendly comment

commenta·teur [kɔmɑ̃tatœr] **-trice** [tris] *mf* commentator

commenter [kɔmɑ̃te] *tr* to comment on; to make a commentary on; to criticize

commérage [kɔmeraʒ] *m* (coll) gossip

commer·çant [kɔmersɑ̃] **-çante** [sɑ̃t] *adj* commercial, business || *mf* merchant, dealer

commerce [kɔmers] *m* commerce, trade

commercer [kɔmerse] §51 *intr* to trade

commer·cial -ciale [kɔmersjal] *adj* (*pl* **-ciaux** [sjo]) **-ciales** commercial || *m* station wagon

commercialisation [kɔmersjalizasjɔ̃] *f* marketing

commercialiser [kɔmersjalize] *tr* to commercialize

commère [kɔmer] *f* (coll) busybody, gossip

commettre [kɔmetr] §42 *tr* to commit; to compromise || *ref* to compromise oneself

commis [kɔmi] *m* clerk; **commis voyageur** traveling salesman

commisération [kɔmizerasjɔ̃] *f* commiseration

commissaire [kɔmiser] *m* commissioner; commissary

commissaire-priseur [kɔmiserprizœr] *m* (*pl* **commissaires-priseurs**) appraiser; auctioneer

commissariat [kɔmisarja] *m* commissariat; **commissariat de police** police station

commission [kɔmisjɔ̃] *f* commission; errand; committee

commissionnaire [kɔmisjɔner] *m* agent, broker; messenger

commissionner [kɔmisjɔne] *tr* to commission

commissure [kɔmisyr] *f* corner (*of lips*)

commode [kɔmɔd] *adj* convenient; comfortable; easygoing || *f* chest of drawers, bureau

commodité [kɔmɔdite] *f* comfort, accommodation; **à votre commodité** at your convenience; **commodités** comfort station

commotion [kɔmɔsjɔ̃] *f* commotion; concussion; shock

commotionner [kɔmɔsjɔne] *tr* to shake up, injure, shock

commuer [kɔmɥe] *tr* (law) to commute

com·mun -mune [kɔmœ̃] **com·mune** [kɔmyn] *adj* common || *m* common run || *f* see **commune**

commu·nal -nale [kɔmynal] (*pl* **-naux** [no]) *adj* communal, common || *mpl* common property, commons

communautaire [kɔmynoter] *adj* communal

communauté [kɔmynote] *f* community; **Communauté économique européenne** Common Market

commune [kɔmyn] *f* commune; **communes** Commons

commu·niant -niante [kɔmynjã] **-niante** [njãt] *mf* communicant

communicable [kɔmynikabl] *adj* communicable

communi·cant [kɔmynikã] **-cante** [kãt] *adj* communicating

communica·teur [kɔmynikatœr] **-trice** [tris] *adj* connecting (*wire*)

communica·tif [kɔmynikatif] **-tive** [tiv] *adj* communicative; infectious (*laughter*)

communication [kɔmynikasjɔ̃] *f* communication; telephone call; (telp) connection; **communication avec avis d'appel** (telp) messenger call; **communication avec préavis** person-to-person call; **communication payable à l'arrivée** collect call; **en communication** in touch; **fausse communication** (telp)

wrong number; **vous avez la communication!** (telp) go ahead!

communier [kɔmynje] *intr* to take communion; to have a common bond of sympathy, to be in accord

communion [kɔmynjɔ̃] *f* communion

communiqué [kɔmynike] *m* communiqué

communiquer [kɔmynike] *tr & intr* to communicate

communi·sant [kɔmynizã] **-sante** [zãt] *adj* fellow-traveling || *mf* fellow traveler

communisme [kɔmynism] *m* communism

communiste [kɔmynist] *adj & mf* communist

commutateur [kɔmytatœr] *m* (elec) changeover switch, two-way switch

commutation [kɔmytasjɔ̃] *f* commutation

commutatrice [kɔmytatris] *f* (elec) rotary converter

com·pact -pacte [kɔ̃pakt] *adj* compact

compagne [kɔ̃paɲ] *f* companion; helpmate.

compagnie [kɔ̃paɲi] *f* company; **de compagnie** or **en compagnie** together; **fausser compagnie à** to give (*s.o.*) the slip; **tenir compagnie à** to keep (*s.o.*) company

compagnon [kɔ̃paɲɔ̃] *m* companion; **compagnon d'armes** comrade in arms; **compagnon de jeu** playmate; **compagnon de route** fellow traveler; **compagnon d'infortune** fellow sufferer; **joyeux compagnon** good fellow

comparaison [kɔ̃parezɔ̃] *f* comparison; **en comparaison de** compared to; **par comparaison** in comparison; **sans comparaison** beyond comparison

comparaître [kɔ̃paretr] §12 *intr* (law) to appear in (out) court

compara·tif [kɔ̃paratif] **-tive** [tiv] *adj & m* comparative

compa·ré -rée [kɔ̃pare] *adj* comparative

comparer [kɔ̃pare] *tr* to compare

comparoir [kɔ̃parwar] (used only in: *inf*; *ger* **comparant**) *intr* (law) to appear in court

comparse [kɔ̃pars] *mf* (theat) walk-on; (fig) nobody, unimportant person

compartiment [kɔ̃partimã] *m* compartment

comparution [kɔ̃parysjɔ̃] *f* appearance in court

compas [kɔ̃pa] *m* compasses (*for drawing circles*); calipers; (naut) compass; **avoir le compas dans l'œil** to have a sharp eye

compas·sé -sée [kɔ̃pase] *adj* stiff, studied

compasser [kɔ̃pase] *tr* to measure out, to lay off; **compasser ses discours** to speak like a book

compassion [kɔ̃pasjɔ̃] *f* compassion

compatibilité [kɔ̃patibilite] *f* compatibility

compatir [kɔ̃patir] *intr*—**compatir à** to take pity on, to feel for; to be indulgent toward; to share in (*s.o.'s* *bereavement*); **ne pouvoir compatir** to be unable to agree

compatis·sant [kɔ̃patisɑ̃] **compatis·sante** [kɔ̃patisɑ̃t] *adj* compassionate, sympathetic, indulgent

compatriote [kɔ̃patriɔt] *mf* compatriot

compensa·teur [kɔ̃pɑ̃sɑtœr] **-trice** [tris] *adj* compensating, equalizing

compensation [kɔ̃pɑ̃sɑsjɔ̃] *f* compensation

compenser [kɔ̃pɑ̃se] *tr* to compensate; to compensate for ‖ *ref* to balance each other

compérage [kɔ̃peraʒ] *m* complicity

compère [kɔ̃per] *m* accomplice; comrade; stooge (*for a clown*)

compétence [kɔ̃petɑ̃s] *f* competence, proficiency; (law) jurisdiction

compé·tent [kɔ̃petɑ̃] **-tente** [tɑ̃t] *adj* competent, proficient; (law) having jurisdiction, expert

compéter [kɔ̃pete] §10 *intr*—**compéter à** to belong to by right; to be within the competency of (*a court*)

compéti·teur [kɔ̃petitœr] **-trice** [tris] *mf* rival, competitor

compétition [kɔ̃petisjɔ̃] *f* competition

compilation [kɔ̃pilasjɔ̃] *f* compilation

compiler [kɔ̃pile] *tr* to compile

complainte [kɔ̃plɛ̃t] *f* sad ballad; (law) complaint

complaire [kɔ̃pler] §52 *intr* (with *dat*) to please, gratify ‖ *ref*—**se complaire à** to take pleasure in

complaisance [kɔ̃plezɑ̃s] *f* compliance; courtesy; complacency; **auriez-vous la complaisance de . . . ?** would you be so kind as to . . . ?; **de complaisance** out of kindness

complai·sant [kɔ̃plezɑ̃] **-sante** [zɑ̃t] *adj* complaisant, obliging; complacent

complément [kɔ̃plemɑ̃] *m* complement; (gram) object; **complément d'attribution** (gram) indirect object

com·plet [kɔ̃ple] **-plète** [plɛt] *adj* complete, full; **c'est complet!** that's the last straw! ‖ *m* suit (*of clothes*); **au complet** full (*house*); **au grand complet** at full strength

compléter [kɔ̃plete] §10 *tr* to complete ‖ *ref* to be completed; to complement one another

complet-veston [kɔ̃plevestɔ̃] *m* (*pl* **complets-veston**) man's suit

complexe [kɔ̃pleks] *adj & m* complex; **complexe de culpabilité** guilt complex

complexé complexée [kɔ̃plekse] *adj* (coll) timid, withdrawn ‖ *mf* person with complexes

complexion [kɔ̃pleksjɔ̃] *f* constitution, disposition

complication [kɔ̃plikasjɔ̃] *f* complication

complice [kɔ̃plis] *adj* accessory, abetting ‖ *mf* accomplice; **complice d'adultère** corespondent

complicité [kɔ̃plisite] *f* complicity

compliment [kɔ̃plimɑ̃] *m* compliment

complimenter [kɔ̃plimɑ̃te] *tr* to compliment; to congratulate

complimen·teur [kɔ̃plimɑ̃tœr] **-teuse** [tøz] *adj* complimentary ‖ *mf* flatterer, yes man

compli·qué -quée [kɔ̃plike] *adj* complicated

compliquer [kɔ̃plike] *tr* to complicate ‖ *ref* to become complicated; to have complications

complot [kɔ̃plo] *m* plot, conspiracy

comploter [kɔ̃plɔte] *tr & intr* to plot, conspire

comploteur [kɔ̃plɔtœr] *m* conspirator

comportement [kɔ̃pɔrtəmɑ̃] *m* behavior

comporter [kɔ̃pɔrte] *tr* to permit; to include ‖ *ref* to behave

compo·sant [kɔ̃pozɑ̃] **-sante** [zɑ̃t] *adj* constituent ‖ *m* (chem) component ‖ *f* (mech) component

compo·sé -sée [kɔ̃poze] *adj & m* compound

composer [kɔ̃poze] *tr* to compose; to compound; to dial (*a telephone number*) ‖ *intr* to take an exam; to come to terms ‖ *ref*—**se composer de** to be composed of

composi·teur [kɔ̃pozitœr] **-trice** [tris] *mf* composer; compositor; **amiable compositeur** (law) arbitrator

composition [kɔ̃pozisjɔ̃] *f* composition; compound; dialing (*of telephone number*); term paper; **de bonne composition** easygoing, reasonable; **entrer en composition** to reach an agreement

composteur [kɔ̃pɔstœr] *m* composing stick; dating and numbering machine, dating stamp

compote [kɔ̃pɔt] *f* compote; **compote de pommes** applesauce

compotier [kɔ̃pɔtje] *m* compote (*dish*)

compréhensible [kɔ̃preɑ̃sibl] *adj* comprehensible

compréhen·sif [kɔ̃preɑ̃sif] **-sive** [siv] *adj* understanding; comprehensive

compréhension [kɔ̃preɑ̃sjɔ̃] *f* comprehension, understanding

comprendre [kɔ̃prɑ̃dr] §56 *tr* to understand; to comprehend, to include, to comprise ‖ *intr* to understand ‖ *ref* to be understood; to be included

compresse [kɔ̃pres] *f* (med) compress

compresseur [kɔ̃presœr] *m* compressor

compression [kɔ̃presjɔ̃] *f* compression; repression; reduction

compri·mé -mée [kɔ̃prime] *adj* compressed ‖ *m* (pharm) tablet, lozenge

comprimer [kɔ̃prime] *tr* to compress; to repress

com·pris [kɔ̃pri] **-prise** [priz] *adj* understood; included, including, e.g., **la ferme comprise** or **y compris la ferme** the farm included, including the farm

compromet·tant [kɔ̃prɔmetɑ̃] **compromet·tante** [kɔ̃prɔmetɑ̃t] *adj* compromising, incriminating

compromettre [kɔ̃prɔmetr] §42 *tr* to compromise ‖ *intr* to submit to arbitration ‖ *ref* to compromise oneself

compromis [kɔ̃prɔmi] *m* compromise

comptabiliser [kɔ̃tabilize] *tr* (com) to enter into the books comptabilité [kɔ̃tabilite] f bookkeeping, accounting; accounting department, accounts; **comptabilité à partie double** double-entry bookkeeping; **comptabilité simple** single-entry bookkeeping; **tenir la comptabilité** to keep the books

comptable [kɔ̃tabl] adj accountable, responsible; accounting (machine) || mf bookkeeper; **comptable agréé** or **expert comptable** certified public accountant; **comptable contrôleur** auditor

comp·tant [kɔ̃tɑ̃] -tante [tɑ̃t] adj spot (cash); down, e.g., **argent comptant** cash down || m—**au comptant** cash, for cash || **comptant** adv cash (down), e.g., **payer comptant** to pay cash

compte [kɔ̃t] m account; accounting; (sports) count; **à bon compte** cheap; **à ce compte** in that case; **à compte** on account; **au bout du compte** or **en fin de compte** when all is said and done; **compte à rebours** countdown; **compte courant** current account; charge account; **compte de dépôt** checking account; **compte de profits et pertes** profit and loss statement; **compte en banque** bank account; **compte rendu** report, review; **compte rond** round numbers; **donner son compte à** to give the final paycheck to, to discharge; **être en compte à demi** to go fifty-fifty; **loin de compte** wide of the mark; **rendre compte de** to review; **se rendre compte de** to realize, to be aware of; **tenir compte de** to bear in mind

compte-fils [kɔ̃tfil] m invar cloth prover

compte-gouttes [kɔ̃tgut] m invar dropper; **au compte-gouttes** in driblets

compter [kɔ̃te] tr to count; to number, have; **compter + inf** to count on + ger; **sans compter** not to mention || intr to count; **à compter de** starting from; **compter avec** to reckon with; **compter sur** to count on

compte-tours [kɔ̃tatur] m invar tachometer, r.p.m. counter

comp·teur [kɔ̃tœr] -teuse [tøz] mf counter, checker (person) || m meter; counter; speedometer; **compteur de gaz** gas meter; **compteur de Geiger** Geiger counter; **compteur de stationnement** parking meter; **relever le compteur** to read the meter

compteur-indicateur [kɔ̃tœrɛ̃dikatœr] m (pl **compteurs-indicateurs**) speedometer

comptine [kɔ̃tin] f counting-out rhyme

comptoir [kɔ̃twar] m counter; branch bank; bank; **comptoir postal** mail-order house

compulser [kɔ̃pylse] tr to go through, examine (books, papers, etc.)

computer [kɔ̃pyte] tr to compute

comte [kɔ̃t] m count

comté [kɔ̃te] m county

comtesse [kɔ̃tes] f countess

concasser [kɔ̃kase] tr to crush, pound

concasseur [kɔ̃kasœr] adj masc crushing || m (mach) crusher

concave [kɔ̃kav] adj concave

concéder [kɔ̃sede] §10 tr & intr to concede

concen·tré -trée [kɔ̃sɑ̃tre] adj concentrated; condensed (milk); reserved (person)

concentrer [kɔ̃sɑ̃tre] tr to concentrate; to repress, hold back

concentrique [kɔ̃sɑ̃trik] adj concentric

concept [kɔ̃sɛpt] m concept

conception [kɔ̃sɛpsjɔ̃] f conception

concerner [kɔ̃sɛrne] tr to concern; **en ce qui concerne** concerning

concert [kɔ̃sɛr] m concert; **de concert** together, in concert

concer·tant [kɔ̃sɛrtɑ̃] -tante [tɑ̃t] adj performing together || mf (mus) performer

concerter [kɔ̃sɛrte] tr & ref to concert, to plan

concertiste [kɔ̃sɛrtist] mf concert performer

concession [kɔ̃sɛsjɔ̃] f concession

concessionnaire [kɔ̃sɛsjɔnɛr] mf grantee, licensee; dealer (in automobiles); agent (for insurance)

concetti [kɔ̃t/eti] mpl conceits

concevable [kɔ̃səvabl] adj conceivable

concevoir [kɔ̃səvwar] §59 tr to conceive; to compose (a letter, telegram)

concierge [kɔ̃sjɛrʒ] mf concierge, building superintendent

concile [kɔ̃sil] m (eccl) council

concilia·teur [kɔ̃siljatœr] -trice [tris] adj conciliating || mf conciliator

conciliatoire [kɔ̃siljatwar] adj conciliatory

concilier [kɔ̃silje] tr to reconcile (two parties, two ideas, etc.); to win (e.g., favor) || ref to win over, gain (e.g., esteem); to agree

con·cis [kɔ̃si] -cise [siz] adj concise

concitoyen [kɔ̃sitwajɛ̃] concitoyenne [kɔ̃sitwajɛn] mf fellow citizen

concluant [kɔ̃klyɑ̃] concluante [kɔ̃klyɑ̃t] adj conclusive

conclure [kɔ̃klyr] §11 tr to conclude || intr to conclude; **conclure à** to decide on, to decide in favor of

conclusion [kɔ̃klyzjɔ̃] f conclusion

concombre [kɔ̃kɔ̃br] m cucumber

concomi·tant [kɔ̃kɔmitɑ̃] -tante [tɑ̃t] adj concomitant

concordance [kɔ̃kɔrdɑ̃s] f agreement; concordance (of Bible)

concorde [kɔ̃kɔrd] f concord

concorder [kɔ̃kɔrde] intr to agree

concourir [kɔ̃kurir] §14 intr to compete; to cooperate; to converge, concur

concours [kɔ̃kur] m crowd; cooperation; contest, competition, meet; competitive examination; **concours de beauté** beauty contest; **concours de créanciers** meeting of creditors; **concours hippique** horse show; **hors concours** not competing; in a class by itself

con·cret [kɔ̃krɛ] -crète [krɛt] adj & m concrete

concrétiser [kɔ̃kretize] *tr* to put in concrete form

concubine [kɔ̃kybin] *f* concubine

concurrence [kɔ̃kyrɑ̃s] *f* competition; competitors; **jusqu'à concurrence de** to the amount of; **libre concurrence** free enterprise

concurrencer [kɔ̃kyrɑ̃se] §51 *tr* to rival, to compete with

concur·rent [kɔ̃kyrɑ̃] **concur·rente** [kɔ̃kyrɑ̃t] *adj* competitive ‖ *mf* competitor; contestant

concurren·tiel -tielle [kɔ̃kyrɑ̃sjɛl] *adj* competitive

concussion [kɔ̃kysjɔ̃] *f* extortion; embezzlement

condamnable [kɔ̃danabl] *adj* blameworthy

condamnation [kɔ̃danasjɔ̃] *f* condemnation

condamner [kɔ̃dane] *tr* to condemn; to give up (*an incurable patient*); to forbid the use of; to board up (*a window*); to batten down (*the hatches*)

condensateur [kɔ̃dɑ̃satœr] *m* (elec) condenser

condenser [kɔ̃dɑ̃se] *tr & ref* to condense

condenseur [kɔ̃dɑ̃sœr] *m* condenser

condescendance [kɔ̃desɑ̃dɑ̃s] *f* condescension

condescen·dant [kɔ̃desɑ̃dɑ̃] **-dante** [dɑ̃t] *adj* condescending

condescendre [kɔ̃desɑ̃dr] *intr* to condescend; to yield, comply

condiment [kɔ̃dimɑ̃] *m* condiment

condisciple [kɔ̃disipl] *mf* classmate

condition [kɔ̃disjɔ̃] *f* condition; **à condition, sous condition** conditionally; on approval; **à condition que** on condition that; **dans de bonnes conditions** in good condition; **sans conditions** unconditional

condition·nel -nelle [kɔ̃disjɔnɛl] *adj & m* conditional

conditionner [kɔ̃disjɔne] *tr* to condition; (com) to package

condoléances [kɔ̃dɔleɑ̃s] *fpl* condolence

conduc·teur [kɔ̃dyktœr] **-trice** [tris] *adj* conducting; driving; (elec) power (*line*); (elec) lead (*wire*) ‖ *adj masc* (elec, phys) (in predicate after **être**, it may be translated by a noun) conductor, e.g., **les métaux sont bons conducteurs de l'électricité** metals are good conductors of electricity ‖ *mf* guide; leader; driver ‖ *m* motorman; foreman; pressman; (elec, phys) conductor

conduire [kɔ̃dɥir] §19 *tr* to conduct; to lead; to drive; to see (*s.o. to the door*) ‖ *intr* to drive ‖ *ref* to conduct oneself

conduit [kɔ̃dɥi] *m* conduit; **conduit auditif** auditory canal; **conduits lacrymaux** tear ducts

conduite [kɔ̃dɥit] *f* conduct, behavior; management, command; driving (*of a car; of cattle*); pipe line; duct, flue; **avoir de la conduite** to be well behaved; **conduite d'eau** water main; **conduite intérieure** closed car; **faire la conduite à** to escort; **faire une conduite de Grenoble à qn** (coll) to kick s.o. out

cône [kon] *m* cone

confection [kɔ̃fɛksjɔ̃] *f* manufacture; construction (*e.g., of a machine*); ready-made clothes; **de confection** ready-made (*suit, dress, etc.*)

confectionner [kɔ̃fɛksjɔne] *tr* to manufacture; to prepare (*a dish*)

confection·neur [kɔ̃fɛksjɔnœr] **confection·neuse** [kɔ̃fɛksjɔnøz] *mf* manufacturer (*esp. of ready-made clothes*)

confédération [kɔ̃federasjɔ̃] *f* confederation, confederacy

confédérer [kɔ̃federe] §10 *tr & ref* to confederate

conférence [kɔ̃ferɑ̃s] *f* conference; lecture, speech; **conférence au sommet** summit conference; **conférence de presse** press conference

conféren·cier [kɔ̃ferɑ̃sje] **-cière** [sjɛr] *mf* lecturer, speaker

conférer [kɔ̃fere] §10 *tr* to confer, award; to administer (*a sacrament*); to collate, compare ‖ *intr* to confer

confesse [kɔ̃fɛs] *f*—**à confesse** to confession; **de confesse** from confession

confesser [kɔ̃fese] *tr* to confess; (coll) to pump (*s.o.*) ‖ *ref* to confess

confesseur [kɔ̃fesœr] *m* confessor

confession [kɔ̃fesjɔ̃] *f* confession; (eccl) denomination

confessionnal [kɔ̃fesjɔnal] *m* confessional

confession·nel -nelle [kɔ̃fesjɔnɛl] *adj* denominational

confiance [kɔ̃fjɑ̃s] *f* confidence; **confiance en soi** self-confidence; **de confiance** reliable; confidently; **en confiance** with confidence

con·fiant [kɔ̃fjɑ̃] **-fiante** [fjɑ̃t] *adj* confident; confiding, trusting

confidence [kɔ̃fidɑ̃s] *f* confidence, secret

confi·dent [kɔ̃fidɑ̃] **-dente** [dɑ̃t] *mf* confident

confiden·tiel -tielle [kɔ̃fidɑ̃sjɛl] *adj* confidential

confier [kɔ̃fje] *tr* to entrust; to confide, disclose; to commit (*to memory*); to consign; **confier à** to put (*seed*) in (*the ground*) ‖ *ref*—**se confier à** to confide in, to trust; **se confier en** to put one's trust in

confinement [kɔ̃finmɑ̃] *m* imprisonment

confiner [kɔ̃fine] *tr* to confine ‖ *intr*—**confiner à** to border on, to verge on ‖ *ref* to confine oneself; **se confiner dans** to confine oneself to

confins [kɔ̃fɛ̃] *mpl* confines

confire [kɔ̃fir] §66 (*pp* **confit**) *tr* to preserve; to pickle; to candy; to can (*goose, chicken, etc.*); to dip (*skins*) ‖ *ref* to become immersed (*in work, prayer, etc.*)

confirmer [kɔ̃firme] *tr* to confirm

confiserie [kɔ̃fizri] *f* confectionery

confi·seur [kɔ̃fizœr] **-seuse** [zøz] *mf* confectioner, candymaker

confisquer [kɔ̃fiske] *tr* to confiscate

con·fit [kɔ̃fi] **-fite** [fit] *adj* preserved; pickled; candied; steeped (*e.g., in* *piety*); incrusted (*in bigotry*) ‖ *m* canned chicken, goose, etc.

confiture [kɔ̃fityr] *f* preserves, jam

confitu-rier [kɔ̃fityrje] **-rière** [rjɛr] *mf* manufacturer of jams ‖ *m* jelly glass, jam jar

conflagration [kɔ̃flagrasjɔ̃] *f* conflagration, turmoil

conflit [kɔ̃fli] *m* conflict

confluer [kɔ̃flye] *intr* to meet, come together (*said of two rivers*)

confondre [kɔ̃fɔ̃dr] *tr* to confuse, mix up, mingle; to confound ‖ *ref* to become bewildered, mixed up; se **confondre en excuses** to fall all over oneself apologizing

conforme [kɔ̃fɔrm] *adj* corresponding; certified, e.g., **pour copie conforme** certified copy; **conforme à** conformable to, consistent with; **conforme à l'échantillon** identical with sample; **conforme aux normes** according to specifications; **conforme aux règles** in order

confor-mé -mée [kɔ̃fɔrme] *adj* shaped, built; **bien conformé** well-built; **mal conformé** misshapen

conformément [kɔ̃fɔrmemã] *adv*—**conformément à** in compliance with

conformer [kɔ̃fɔrme] *tr & ref* to conform

conformiste [kɔ̃fɔrmist] *mf* conformist

conformité [kɔ̃fɔrmite] *f* conformity, conformance

confort [kɔ̃fɔr] *m* comfort; convenience; **pneu confort** balloon tire

confortable [kɔ̃fɔrtabl] *adj* comfortable ‖ *m* comfort; easy chair

confrère [kɔ̃frɛr] *m* confrere, colleague

confrérie [kɔ̃freri] *f* brotherhood

confronter [kɔ̃frɔ̃te] *tr* to confront; to compare, collate

con-fus -fuse [kɔ̃fy] [fyz] *adj* confused; vague, blurred; embarrassed

confusion [kɔ̃fyzjɔ̃] *f* confusion

congé [kɔ̃ʒe] *m* leave; vacation; dismissal; **congé libérable** military discharge; **congé payé** vacation with pay; **donner congé à** to lay off; **donner son congé à** to give notice to; **prendre congé de** to take leave of

congédiement [kɔ̃ʒedimã] *m* dismissal, discharge; paying off (*of crew*)

congédier [kɔ̃ʒedje] *tr* to dismiss

congélateur [kɔ̃ʒelatœr] *m* freezer (*for frozen foods*)

congélation [kɔ̃ʒelasjɔ̃] *f* freezing

congeler [kɔ̃ʒle] §2 *tr & ref* to freeze; to congeal; **congeler à basse température** to deep-freeze

congéni-tal -tale [kɔ̃ʒenital] *adj* (*pl* **-taux** [to]) congenital

congère [kɔ̃ʒɛr] *f* snowdrift

congestion [kɔ̃ʒɛstjɔ̃] *f* congestion; **congestion cérébrale** stroke; **congestion pulmonaire** pneumonia

congestionner [kɔ̃ʒɛstjɔne] *tr & ref* to congest

conglomération [kɔ̃glɔmerasjɔ̃] *f* conglomeration

conglomérer [kɔ̃glɔmere] §10 *tr & ref* to conglomerate

congratulation [kɔ̃gratylasjɔ̃] *f* congratulation

congratuler [kɔ̃gratyle] *tr* to congratulate

congre [kɔ̃gr] *m* conger eel

congréer [kɔ̃gree] *tr* to worm (*rope*)

congrégation [kɔ̃gregasjɔ̃] *f* (eccl) congregation

congrès [kɔ̃grɛ] *m* congress, convention

congressiste [kɔ̃gresist] *mf* delegate ‖ *m* congressman ‖ *f* congresswoman

con-gru -grue [kɔ̃gry] *adj* precise, suitable; scanty; (math) congruent

conifère [kɔnifɛr] *adj* coniferous ‖ *m* conifer

conique [kɔnik] *adj* conical ‖ *f* conic section

conjecture [kɔ̃ʒɛktyr] *f* conjecture

conjecturer [kɔ̃ʒɛktyre] *tr & intr* to conjecture, to surmise

conjoindre [kɔ̃ʒwɛ̃dr] §35 *tr* to join in marriage

con-joint [kɔ̃ʒwɛ̃] **-jointe** [ʒwɛ̃t] *adj* united, joint ‖ *mf* spouse, consort

conjoncteur [kɔ̃ʒɔ̃ktœr] *m* automatic switch

conjonction [kɔ̃ʒɔ̃ksjɔ̃] *f* conjunction

conjugaison [kɔ̃ʒygɛzɔ̃] *f* conjugation

conju-gal -gale [kɔ̃ʒygal] *adj* (*pl* **-gaux** [go]) conjugal, connubial

conjuguer [kɔ̃ʒyge] *tr* to combine (*e.g.*, *forces*); to conjugate

conjuration [kɔ̃ʒyrasjɔ̃] *f* conjuration; conspiracy; **conjurations** entreaties

conju-ré -rée [kɔ̃ʒyre] *mf* conspirator

conjurer [kɔ̃ʒyre] *tr* to conjure; to conjure away; to conjure up; to conspire for, to plot; **conjurer qn de** + *inf* to entreat s.o. to + *inf* ‖ *intr* to hatch a plot ‖ *ref* to plot together, conspire

connaissance [kɔnɛsɑ̃s] *f* knowledge; acquaintance; consciousness; attention; **connaissance des temps** nautical almanac; **connaissances** knowledge; **en connaissance de** with full knowledge of; **faire connaissance avec** to become acquainted with; **faire la connaissance de** to meet; **parler en connaissance de cause** to know what one is talking about; **perdre connaissance** to lose consciousness; **sans connaissance** unconscious

connaissement [kɔnɛsmã] *m* bill of lading

connais-seur [kɔnɛsœr] **connais-seuse** [kɔnɛsøz] *mf* connoisseur; expert

connaître [kɔnɛtr] §12 *tr* to know; to be acquainted with ‖ *intr*—**connaître de** (law) to have jurisdiction over ‖ *ref* to be acquainted; to become acquainted; **se connaître à** or **en** to know a lot about; **s'y connaître** to know what one is talking about; **s'y connaître en** to know a lot about

connecter [kɔnɛkte] *tr* to connect

connétable [kɔnetabl] *m* constable

connexe [kɔnɛks] *adj* connected

connexion [kɔnɛksjɔ̃] *f* connection

connexité [kɔnɛksite] *f* connection

con-nu -nue [kɔny] *adj* well-known ‖ *m*—**le connu** the known

conque [kɔ̃k] *f* conch
conqué·rant [kɔ̃kerɑ̃] **-rante** [rɑ̃t] *adj* (coll) swaggering || *mf* conqueror
conquérir [kɔ̃kerir] §3 *tr* to conquer
conquête [kɔ̃kɛt] *f* conquest
consa·cré -crée [kɔ̃sakre] *adj* accepted, time-honored, stock
consacrer [kɔ̃sakre] *tr* to consecrate; to devote, dedicate (*time, energy, effort*); to give, to spare (*e.g., time*); to sanction, confirm || *ref*—**se consacrer à** to devote or dedicate oneself to
consan·guin [kɔ̃sɑ̃gɛ̃] **-guine** [gin] *adj* consanguineous; on the father's side || *mf* blood relation
consciemment [kɔ̃sjamɑ̃] *adv* consciously
conscience [kɔ̃sjɑ̃s] *f* conscience; conscientiousness; consciousness; **avoir la conscience large** to be broadminded; **en conscience** conscientiously
conscien·cieux [kɔ̃sjɑ̃sjø] **-cieuse** [sjøz] *adj* conscientious
cons·cient [kɔ̃sjɑ̃] **cons·ciente** [kɔ̃sjɑ̃t] *adj* conscious, aware, knowing
conscription [kɔ̃skripsjɔ̃] *f* draft, conscription
conscrit [kɔ̃skri] *m* draftee, conscript
consécration [kɔ̃sekrɑsjɔ̃] *f* consecration; confirmation
consécu·tif [kɔ̃sekytif] **-tive** [tiv] *adj* consecutive; dependent (*clause*); **consécutif à** resulting from
conseil [kɔ̃sɛj] *m* advice, counsel; counselor; council, board, committee; **conseil d'administration** board of directors; **conseil de guerre** court-martial; staff meeting of top brass; **conseil de prud'hommes** arbitration board; **conseil de révision** draft board; **conseils** advice; **un conseil a** piece of advice
conseil·ler [kɔ̃seje] **conseil·lère** [kɔ̃sejɛr] *mf* councilor; counselor, adviser || *f* councilor's wife; counselor's wife || **conseiller** *tr* to advise, to counsel (*s.o. or s.th.*); **conseiller q.ch. à qn** to recommend s.th. to s.o. || *intr* to advise, to counsel; **conseiller à qn de** + *inf* to advise s.o. to + *inf*
conseil·leur [kɔ̃sejœr] **conseil·leuse** [kɔ̃sejøz] *mf* adviser; know-it-all
consensus [kɔ̃sɛ̃sys] *m* consensus
consentement [kɔ̃sɑ̃tmɑ̃] *m* consent
consentir [kɔ̃sɑ̃tir] §41 *tr* to grant, allow; to accept, recognize; **consentir que** + *subj* to permit (*s.o.*) to + *inf* || *intr* to consent; **consentir à** to consent to, to agree to, to approve of
conséquemment [kɔ̃sekamɑ̃] *adv* consequently; consistently
conséquence [kɔ̃sekɑ̃s] *f* consequence; consistency; **en conséquence** accordingly
consé·quent [kɔ̃sekɑ̃] **-quente** [kɑ̃t] *adj* consequent; consistent; important || *m* (logic, math) consequent; **par conséquent** consequently
conserva·teur [kɔ̃sɛrvatœr] **-trice** [tris] *adj* conservative || *mf* conservative;

curator, keeper; warden, ranger; registrar
conservation [kɔ̃sɛrvɑsjɔ̃] *f* conservation, preservation; curatorship; curator's office
conservatisme [kɔ̃sɛrvatism] *m* conservatism
conservatoire [kɔ̃sɛrvatwar] *m* conservatory (*of music*); museum, academy
conserve [kɔ̃sɛrv] *f* canned food, preserves; escort, convoy; **conserves** dark glasses; **conserves au vinaigre** pickles; **mettre en conserve** to can; **voler de conserve avec** to fly alongside of
conserver [kɔ̃sɛrve] *tr* to conserve; to preserve; to keep (*one's health; one's equanimity; a secret*); to escort, to convoy (*a ship*) || *ref* to stay in good shape; to take care of oneself
conserverie [kɔ̃sɛrvəri] *f* canning factory; canning
considérable [kɔ̃siderabl] *adj* considerable; important; large, great
considérant [kɔ̃siderɑ̃] *m* motive, grounds; **considérant que** whereas
considération [kɔ̃siderɑsjɔ̃] *f* consideration
considérer [kɔ̃sidere] §10 *tr* to consider, examine; to esteem, consider
consignataire [kɔ̃siɲatɛr] *m* consignee, trustee
consignation [kɔ̃siɲasjɔ̃] *f* consignment; **en consignation** on consignment
consigne [kɔ̃siɲ] *f* password; baggage room, checkroom; checking fee; confinement to barracks, detention; deposit; (mil) orders, instructions; **en consigne à la douane** held up in customs; **être de consigne** to be on duty; **manquer à la consigne** to disobey orders
consigner [kɔ̃siɲe] *tr* to consign; to check (*baggage*); to put down in writing, to enter in the record; to confine to barracks, to keep (*a student*) in; to put out of bounds (*e.g., for military personnel*); to close (*a port*); **consigner sa** (or **la**) **porte** to be at home to no one
consistance [kɔ̃sistɑ̃s] *f* consistency; stability (*of character*); credit, reality, standing; **en consistance de** consisting of
consis·tant [kɔ̃sistɑ̃] **-tante** [tɑ̃t] *adj* consistent; stable (*character*); **consistant en** consisting of
consister [kɔ̃siste] *intr*—**consister à** + *inf* to consist in + *ger*; **consister dans** or **en** to consist in; to consist of
consistoire [kɔ̃sistwar] *m* consistory
consola·teur [kɔ̃sɔlatœr] **-trice** [tris] *adj* consoling || *mf* comforter
consolation [kɔ̃sɔlasjɔ̃] *f* consolation
console [kɔ̃sɔl] *f* console; console table; bracket
consoler [kɔ̃sɔle] *tr* to console
consolider [kɔ̃sɔlide] *tr* to consolidate; to fund (*a debt*)
consomma·teur [kɔ̃sɔmatœr] **-trice**

[tris] *mf* consumer; customer (*in a restaurant or bar*)

consommation [kɔsɔmɑsjɔ̃] *f* consummation (*e.g., of a marriage*); perpetration (*e.g., of a crime*); consumption, use; drink (*e.g., in a café*)

consom·mé **-mée** [kɔsɔme] *adj* consummate; skilled (*e.g., technician*); consumed, used up ‖ *m* consommé

consommer [kɔsɔme] *tr* to consummate, complete; to perpetrate (*e.g., a crime*); to consume

consomp·tif [kɔsɔ̃ptif] **-tive** [tiv] *adj* wasting away

consomption [kɔsɔ̃psjɔ̃] *f* wasting away, decline

conso·nant [kɔsɔnɑ̃] **-nante** [nɑ̃t] *adj* consonant, harmonious

consonne [kɔsɔn] *f* consonant

consorts [kɔsɔr] *mpl* partners, associates; (*pej*) confederates

conspira·teur [kɔspiratœr] **-trice** [tris] *mf* conspirator

conspiration [kɔspirasjɔ̃] *f* conspiracy

conspirer [kɔspire] *tr & intr* to conspire

conspuer [kɔspɥe] *tr* to boo, hiss

constamment [kɔstamɑ̃] *adv* constantly

constance [kɔstɑ̃s] *f* constancy

cons·tant [kɔstɑ̃] **-tante** [tɑ̃t] *adj* constant; true; established, evident ‖ *f* constant

constat [kɔsta] *m* affidavit

constatation [kɔstatasjɔ̃] *f* authentication; declaration; claim

constater [kɔstate] *tr* to certify; to find out; to prove, establish

constellation [kɔstellasjɔ̃] *f* constellation

consteller [kɔstelle] *tr* to spangle

consterner [kɔsterne] *tr* to dismay

constipation [kɔstipasjɔ̃] *f* constipation

constiper [kɔstipe] *tr* to constipate

consti·tuant [kɔstitɥɑ̃] **-tuante** [tɥɑ̃t] *adj & m* constituent

constituer [kɔstitɥe] *tr* to constitute; to settle (*a dowry*); to form (*a cabinet; a corporation*); to empanel (*a jury*); to appoint (*a lawyer*) ‖ *ref* to be formed; **se constituer prisonnier** to give oneself up

constitu·tif [kɔstitytif] **-tive** [tiv] *adj* constituent

constitution [kɔstitysjɔ̃] *f* constitution; settlement (*of a dowry*); **constitution en société** incorporation

construc·teur [kɔstryktœr] **-trice** [tris] *adj* constructive, building ‖ *mf* constructor, builder

construc·tif [kɔstryktif] **-tive** [tiv] *adj* constructive

construction [kɔstryksjɔ̃] *f* construction; **construction mécanique** mechanical engineering

construire [kɔstrɥir] §19 *tr* to construct, to build; to draw (*e.g., a triangle*); (*gram*) to construe

consul [kɔsyl] *m* consul

consulaire [kɔsyler] *adj* consular

consulat [kɔsyla] *m* consulate

consul·tant [kɔsyltɑ̃] **-tante** [tɑ̃t] *adj* consulting ‖ *mf* consultant

consulta·tif [kɔsyltatif] **-tive** [tiv] *adj* advisory

consultation [kɔsyltasjɔ̃] *f* consultation; **consultation externe** outpatient clinic; **consultation populaire** poll, referendum

consulte [kɔsylt] *f* (eccl, law) consultation

consulter [kɔsylte] *tr* to consult ‖ *intr* to consult, to give consultations ‖ *ref* to deliberate

consumer [kɔsyme] *tr* to consume, use up, destroy ‖ *ref* to burn out; to waste away; to fail

contact [kɔtakt] *m* contact; **mettre en contact** to put in touch, to connect; **prendre contact** to make contact

contacter [kɔtakte] *tr* (coll) to contact

conta·gieux [kɔtaʒjø] **-gieuse** [ʒjøz] *adj* contagious

contagion [kɔtaʒjɔ̃] *f* contagion

contamination [kɔtaminasjɔ̃] *f* contamination

contaminer [kɔtamine] *tr* to contaminate

conte [kɔt] *m* tale, story; **conte à dormir debout** cock-and-bull story, baloney; **conte de fées** fairy tale

contemplation [kɔtɑ̃plasjɔ̃] *f* contemplation

contempler [kɔtɑ̃ple] *tr* to contemplate

contempo·rain [kɔtɑ̃porɛ̃] **-raine** [rɛn] *adj & m* contemporary

contemp·teur [kɔtɑ̃ptœr] **-trice** [tris] *mf* scoffer

contenance [kɔtnɑ̃s] *f* capacity; area; countenance; **faire bonne contenance** to put up a bold front

conte·nant [kɔtnɑ̃] **-nante** [nɑ̃t] *adj* containing ‖ *m* container

contenir [kɔtnir] §72 *tr* to contain; to restrain ‖ *ref* to contain oneself, to hold oneself back

con·tent [kɔtɑ̃] **-tente** [tɑ̃t] *adj* content; happy, glad, pleased; **content de** satisfied with ‖ *m* fill, e.g., **avoir son content** to have one's fill

contentement [kɔtɑ̃tmɑ̃] *m* contentment

contenter [kɔtɑ̃te] *tr* to content, satisfy ‖ *ref* to satisfy one's desires; **se contenter de** to be content or satisfied with

conten·tieux [kɔtɑ̃sjø] **-tieuse** [sjøz] *adj* contentious ‖ *m* contention, litigation; claims department

contention [kɔtɑ̃sjɔ̃] *f* application, intentness

conte·nu **-nue** [kɔtny] *adj* contained, restrained, stifled ‖ *m* contents

conter [kɔte] *tr* to relate, tell; **en conter à** (coll) to take (*s.o.*) in; **en conter (de belles)** (coll) to tell tall tales ‖ *intr* to narrate, to tell a story

contestation [kɔtestasjɔ̃] *f* argument, dispute; **sans contestation** without opposition

conteste [kɔtest] *f*—**sans conteste** incontestably, unquestionably

contester [kɔteste] *tr & intr* to contest

con·teur [kɔtœr] **-teuse** [tøz] *mf* storyteller

contexte [kɔtɛkst] *m* context

conti·gu -guë [kɔ̃tigy] *adj* contiguous; **contigu à** adjoining

continence [kɔ̃tinɑ̃s] *f* continence

conti·nent [kɔ̃tinɑ̃] **-nente** [nɑ̃t] *adj* & *m* continent

continen·tal -tale [kɔ̃tinɑ̃tal] *adj* (*pl* **-taux** [to]) continental

contingence [kɔ̃tɛ̃ʒɑ̃s] *f* contingency

contin·gent [kɔ̃tɛ̃ʒɑ̃] **-gente** [ʒɑ̃t] *adj* contingent || *m* contingent; quota

conti·nu -nue [kɔ̃tiny] *adj* continuous; direct (*current*) || *m* continuum

continuation [kɔ̃tinɥasjɔ̃] *f* continuation

conti·nuel -nuelle [kɔ̃tinɥel] *adj* continual

continuité [kɔ̃tinɥite] *f* continuity

continûment [kɔ̃tinymɑ̃] *adv* continuously

contorsion [kɔ̃tɔrsjɔ̃] *f* contortion

contour [kɔ̃tur] *m* contour

contourner [kɔ̃turne] *tr* to contour; to go around, to skirt; to get around (*the law*); to twist, distort

contrac·tant [kɔ̃traktɑ̃] **-tante** [tɑ̃t] *adj* contracting (*parties*) || *mf* contracting party

contracter [kɔ̃trakte] *tr* to contract; to float (*a loan*) || *ref* to contract; to be contracted

contraction [kɔ̃traksjɔ̃] *f* contraction

contradiction [kɔ̃tradiksjɔ̃] *f* contradiction

contradictoire [kɔ̃tradiktwar] *adj* contradictory

contraindre [kɔ̃trɛ̃dr] §15 *tr* to compel, force, constrain; to restrain, to curb || *ref* to restrain oneself

con·traint [kɔ̃trɛ̃] **-trainte** [trɛ̃t] *adj* constrained, forced; stiff (*person*) || *f* constraint; restraint; exigencies (*e.g., of the rhyme*)

contraire [kɔ̃trer] *adj* contrary; opposite (*e.g., direction*); injurious (*e.g., to health*) || *m* contrary, opposite; antonym; **au contraire** on the contrary

contrairement [kɔ̃trermɑ̃] *adv* contrary

contrarier [kɔ̃trarje] *tr* to thwart; to vex, annoy; to contrast (*e.g., colors*)

contrariété [kɔ̃trarjete] *f* vexation, annoyance; clashing (*e.g., of colors*)

contraste [kɔ̃trast] *m* contrast

contraster [kɔ̃traste] *tr* & *intr* to contrast

contrat [kɔ̃tra] *m* contract

contravention [kɔ̃travɑ̃sjɔ̃] *f* infraction; **dresser une contravention** to write out a (traffic) ticket; **recevoir une contravention** to get a ticket

contre [kɔ̃tr] *m* opposite, con; (cards) double; **par contre** on the contrary || *adv* against; nearby; **contre à contre** alongside || *prep* against; contrary to; to, e.g., **dix contre un** ten to one; for, e.g., **échanger contre** to exchange for; e.g., **remède contre la toux** remedy for a cough; (sports) versus; **contre remboursement** (com) collect on delivery

contre-allée [kɔ̃trale] *f* (*pl* **-allées**) parallel walk

contre-amiral [kɔ̃tramiral] *m* (*pl* **-amiraux** [amiro]) rear admiral

contre-appel [kɔ̃trapel] *m* (*pl* **-appels**) second roll call; double-check

contre-attaque [kɔ̃tratak] *f* (*pl* **-attaques**) counterattack

contre-attaquer [kɔ̃tratake] *tr* to counterattack

contrebalancer [kɔ̃trəbalɑ̃se] §51 *tr* to counterbalance

contrebande [kɔ̃trəbɑ̃d] *f* contraband; smuggling; **faire la contrebande** to smuggle

contreban·dier [kɔ̃trəbɑ̃dje] **-dière** [djer] *adj* smuggled, contraband || *mf* smuggler

contrebas [kɔ̃trəba]—**en contrebas** downwards

contrebasse [kɔ̃trəbas] *f* contrabass

contre-biais [kɔ̃trəbje]—**à contre-biais** the wrong way, against the grain

contre-boutant [kɔ̃trəbutɑ̃] *m* (*pl* **-boutants**) shore

contrecarrer [kɔ̃trəkare] *tr* to stymie, to thwart

contre-chant [kɔ̃trəʃɑ̃] *m* (*pl* **-chants**) counter melody

contrecœur [kɔ̃trəkœr] *m* smoke shelf; **à contrecœur** unwillingly

contrecoup [kɔ̃trəku] *m* rebound, recoil, backlash; repercussion

contre-courant [kɔ̃trəkurɑ̃] *m* (*pl* **-courants**) countercurrent; **à contre-courant** upstream; behind the times

contredire [kɔ̃trədir] §40 *tr* to contradict || *ref* to contradict oneself

contrée [kɔ̃tre] *f* region, countryside

contre-écrou [kɔ̃trekru] *m* (*pl* **-écrous**) lock nut

contre-espion [kɔ̃trespjɔ̃] *m* (*pl* **-espions**) counterspy

contre-espionnage [kɔ̃trespjonaʒ] *m* (*pl* **-espionnages**) counterespionage

contrefaçon [kɔ̃trəfasɔ̃] *f* infringement (*of patent or copyright*); forgery; counterfeit; plagiarism

contrefacteur [kɔ̃trəfaktœr] *m* forger; counterfeiter; plagiarist

contrefaction [kɔ̃trəfaksjɔ̃] *f* forgery; counterfeiting

contrefaire [kɔ̃trəfer] §29 *tr* to forge; to counterfeit; to imitate, to mimic; to disguise

contre-fait [kɔ̃trəfe] **-faite** [fet] *adj* counterfeit; deformed

contre-fenêtre [kɔ̃trəfnetr] *f* (*pl* **-fenêtres**) inner sash; storm window

contre-feu [kɔ̃trəfø] *m* (*pl* **-feux**) backfire (*in fire fighting*)

contreficher [kɔ̃trəfiʃe] *ref* (slang) to not give a rap

contre-fil [kɔ̃trəfil] *m* (*pl* **-fils**) opposite direction, wrong way; **à contre-fil** upstream; against the grain

contre-filet [kɔ̃trəfile] *m* short loin (*club and porterhouse steaks*)

contrefort [kɔ̃trəfɔr] *m* buttress, abutment; foothills

contre-haut [kɔ̃trəo]—**en contre-haut** on a higher level; from top to bottom

contre-interrogatoire [kɔ̃trɛ̃terogatwar] *m* cross-examination

contre-interroger [kɔ̃trɛ̃terɔʒe] §38 *tr* to cross-examine

contre-jour [kɔ̃trəʒur] *m invar* back-lighting; **à contre-jour** against the light

contremaî·tre [kɔ̃trəmetr] **-tresse** [tres] *mf* overseer ‖ *m* foreman; (naut) boatswain's mate; (nav) petty officer ‖ *f* forewoman

contremander [kɔ̃trəmɑ̃de] *tr* to countermand; to call off

contremarche [kɔ̃trəmarʃ] *f* countermarch; riser (*of stair step*)

contremarque [kɔ̃trəmark] *f* countersign; pass-out check

contremarquer [kɔ̃trəmarke] *tr* to countersign

contre-mesure [kɔ̃trəməzyr] *f (pl -mesures)* countermeasure

contre-offensive [kɔ̃trɔfɑ̃siv] *f (pl -offensives)* counteroffensive

contrepartie [kɔ̃trəparti] *f* counterpart; (bk) duplicate entry; **en contrepartie** as against this

contre-pas [kɔ̃trəpɑ] *m invar* half step (*taken in order to get in step*)

contre-pente [kɔ̃trəpɑ̃t] *f (pl -pentes)* reverse slope

contre-performance [kɔ̃trəpɛrfɔrmɑ̃s] *f (pl -performances)* unexpected defeat

contrepèterie [kɔ̃trəpetri] *f* spoonerism

contre-pied [kɔ̃trəpje] *m (pl -pieds)* backtrack; opposite opinion; **à contre-pied** off balance

contre-plaqué [kɔ̃trəplake] *m (pl -plaqués)* plywood

contre-plaquer [kɔ̃trəplake] *tr* to laminate

contrepoids [kɔ̃trəpwa] *m invar* counterweight, counterbalance

contre-poil [kɔ̃trəpwal] *m* wrong way (*e.g., of fur*); **à contre-poil** the wrong way; at the wrong end

contrepoint [kɔ̃trəpwɛ̃] *m* counterpoint

contre-pointe [kɔ̃trəpwɛ̃t] *f (pl -pointes)* false edge (*of sword*); tailstock (*of lathe*)

contre-pointer [kɔ̃trəpwɛ̃te] *tr* to quilt

contrepoison [kɔ̃trəpwazɔ̃] *m* antidote

contrer [kɔ̃tre] *tr & intr* (cards) to double; (coll) to counter

contreseing [kɔ̃trəsɛ̃] *m* countersignature

contresens [kɔ̃trəsɑ̃s] *m invar* misinterpretation; mistranslation; wrong way; **à contresens** in the wrong sense; in the wrong direction

contresigner [kɔ̃trəsiɲe] *tr* to countersign

contretemps [kɔ̃trətɑ̃] *m*—**à contretemps** at the wrong moment; syncopated

contre-torpilleur [kɔ̃trətɔrpijœr] *m (pl -torpilleurs)* (nav) torpedo-boat destroyer

contreve·nant [kɔ̃trəvnɑ̃] **-nante** [nɑ̃t] *mf* lawbreaker, delinquent

contrevenir [kɔ̃trəvnir] §72 *intr* (with *dat*) to contravene, to break (*a law*)

contrevent [kɔ̃trəvɑ̃] *m* shutter, window shutter

contre-voie [kɔ̃trəvwa] *f (pl -voies)* parallel route; **à contre-voie** in reverse (*of the usual direction*); on the side opposite the platform

contribuable [kɔ̃tribɥabl] *adj* taxpaying ‖ *mf* taxpayer

contribuer [kɔ̃tribɥe] *intr* to contribute

contribution [kɔ̃tribysjɔ̃] *f* contribution; tax

contrister [kɔ̃triste] *tr* to sadden

con·trit [kɔ̃tri] **-trite** [trit] *adj* contrite

contrôlable [kɔ̃trolabl] *adj* verifiable

contrôle [kɔ̃trol] *m* inspection, verification, check; supervision, observation; auditing; inspection booth, ticket window; (mil) muster roll; **contrôle des naissances** birth control; **contrôle de soi** self-control; **contrôle par sondage** spot check

contrôler [kɔ̃trole] *tr* to inspect, verify, check; to supervise, to put under observation; to audit; to criticize ‖ *ref* to control oneself

contrô·leur [kɔ̃trolœr] **-leuse** [løz] *mf* inspector, checker; supervisor, observer; auditor, comptroller; conductor, ticket collector ‖ *m* gauge; **contrôleur de vitesse** speedometer; **contrôleur de vol** flight indicator

controversable [kɔ̃trɔversabl] *adj* controversial

controverse [kɔ̃trɔvers] *f* controversy

controverser [kɔ̃trɔverse] *tr* to controvert

contumace [kɔ̃tymas] *f* contempt of court

con·tus [kɔ̃ty] **-tuse** [tyz] *adj* bruised

contusion [kɔ̃tyzjɔ̃] *f* contusion, bruise

contusionner [kɔ̃tyzjɔne] *tr* to bruise

convain·cant [kɔ̃vɛ̃kɑ̃] **-cante** [kɑ̃t] *adj* convincing

convaincre [kɔ̃vɛ̃kr] §70 *tr* to convince; to convict ‖ *ref* to be satisfied

convain·cu **-cue** [kɔ̃vɛ̃ky] *adj* convinced, dyed-in-the-wool; convicted

convalescence [kɔ̃valesɑ̃s] *f* convalescence

convales·cent [kɔ̃valesɑ̃] **convales·cente** [kɔ̃valesɑ̃t] *adj & mf* convalescent

convenable [kɔ̃vnabl] *adj* suitable, proper; opportune (*moment*)

convenance [kɔ̃vnɑ̃s] *f* suitability, propriety; conformity; **convenances** conventions

convenir [kɔ̃vnir] §72 *intr* to agree; (with *dat*) to fit, suit; **convenir de** to admit, to admit to, to admit the truth of; to agree on ‖ *ref* to agree with one another ‖ *impers*—**il convient** it is fitting, it is appropriate

convention [kɔ̃vɑ̃sjɔ̃] *f* convention

convention·nel **-nelle** [kɔ̃vɑ̃sjɔnel] *adj* conventional

conve·nu **-nue** [kɔ̃vny] *adj* settled; stipulated (*price*); appointed (*time, place*); trite, stereotyped (*language*)

converger [kɔ̃verʒe] §38 *intr* to converge

conversation [kɔ̃versɑsjɔ̃] *f* conversation

converser [kɔ̃verse] *intr* to converse

conversion [kɔ̃versjɔ̃] *f* conversion; turning

conver·ti -tie [kɔ̃vɛrti] *adj* converted ‖ *mf* convert

convertible [kɔ̃vɛrtibl] *adj* convertible

convertir [kɔ̃vɛrtir] *tr* to convert ‖ *ref* to convert, to be converted; to change one's mind

convertissable [kɔ̃vɛrtisabl] *adj* convertible

convertisseur [kɔ̃vɛrtisœr] *m* converter; (elec) converter

convexe [kɔ̃vɛks] *adj* convex

conviction [kɔ̃viksjɔ̃] *f* conviction

convier [kɔ̃vje] *tr* to invite

convive [kɔ̃viv] *mf* dinner guest; table companion

convocation [kɔ̃vɔkasjɔ̃] *f* convocation; summoning

convoi [kɔ̃vwa] *m* convoy; funeral procession

convoiter [kɔ̃vwate] *tr* to covet

convoi·teur [kɔ̃vwatœr] **-teuse** [tøz] *adj* covetous ‖ *mf* covetous person

convoitise [kɔ̃vwatiz] *f* covetousness, cupidity

convoquer [kɔ̃vɔke] *tr* to convoke; to summon

convoyer [kɔ̃vwaje] §47 *tr* to convoy

convoyeur [kɔ̃vwajœr] *adj* convoying ‖ *m* (mach) conveyor; (nav) escort

convulser [kɔ̃vylse] *tr* to convulse

convulsion [kɔ̃vylsjɔ̃] *f* convulsion

convulsionner [kɔ̃vylsjɔne] *tr* to convulse

coordon·né -née [kɔɔrdɔne] *adj & f* coordinate

coordonner [kɔɔrdɔne] *tr* to coordinate

co·pain [kɔpɛ̃] **-pine** [pin] *mf* (coll) pal, chum

co·peau [kɔpo] *m* (*pl* **-peaux**) chip, shaving

copie [kɔpi] *f* copy; exercise, composition (*at school*); paper; **pour copie conforme** true copy

copier [kɔpje] *tr & intr* to copy

co·pieux [kɔpjø] **-pieuse** [pjøz] *adj* copious

copilote [kɔpilɔt] *m* copilot

copiste [kɔpist] *mf* copyist; copier

coposséder [kɔpɔsede] §10 *tr* to own jointly

copropriété [kɔprɔprijete] *f* joint ownership

copula·tif [kɔpylatif] **-tive** [tiv] *adj* (gram) coordinating

copulation [kɔpylasjɔ̃] *f* copulation

copule [kɔpyl] *f* (gram) copula

coq [kɔk] *adj* bantam ‖ *m* cock rooster; (naut) cook

coq-à-l'âne [kɔkalɑn] *m invar* cock-and-bull story

coque [kɔk] *f* shell; cocoon; hull; **coque de noix** coconut

coquelicot [kɔkliko] *m* poppy

coqueluche [kɔkly ʃ] *f* whooping cough; (coll) rage, vogue

coquemar [kɔkmar] *m* teakettle

coquerie [kɔkri] *f* (naut) galley

coqueriquer [kɔkrike] *intr* to crow

co·quet [kɔkɛ] **-quette** [kɛt] *adj* coquettish; stylish; considerable (*sum*)

coqueter [kɔkte] §34 *intr* to flirt

coquetier [kɔktje] *m* eggcup; egg man

coquetterie [kɔkɛtri] *f* coquetry

coquillage [kɔkijaʒ] *m* shellfish; shell

coquille [kɔkij] *f* shell; typographical error (*of transposed letters*); pat (*of butter*); **coquille de noix** nutshell; **coquille Saint-Jacques** scallop

co·quin [kɔkɛ̃] **-quine** [kin] *adj* deceitful; roguish ‖ *mf* scoundrel; rogue

cor [kɔr] *m* horn; corn (*on foot*); prong (*of antler*); horn player; **à cor et à cri** with hue and cry; **cor anglais** English horn; **cor de chasse** hunting horn; **cor d'harmonie** French horn

co·rail [kɔraj] *m* (*pl* **-raux** [ro]) coral

cor·beau [kɔrbo] *m* (*pl* **-beaux**) crow, raven

corbeille [kɔrbɛj] *f* basket; flower bed; (theat) dress circle; **corbeille à papier** wastebasket; **corbeille de mariage** wedding present

corbillard [kɔrbijar] *m* hearse

corbillon [kɔrbijɔ̃] *m* small basket; word game

cordage [kɔrdaʒ] *m* cordage, rope; (naut) rigging

corde [kɔrd] *f* rope, cord; tightrope; inside track; (geom) chord; **corde à** or **de boyau** catgut (*for, e.g., violin*); **corde à linge** wash line; **corde à nœuds** knotted rope; **cordes vocales** vocal cords; **être sur la corde raide** to be out on a limb; **les cordes** (mus) the strings; **toucher la corde sensible** to touch a sympathetic chord; **usé jusqu'à la corde** threadbare

cor·dé -dée [kɔrde] *adj* heart-shaped ‖ *f* cord (*of wood*); roped party (*of mountain climbers*)

cor·deau [kɔrdo] *m* (*pl* **-deaux**) tracing line; tracing thread; mine fuse; **tiré au cordeau** in a straight line

cordelier [kɔrdəlje] *m* Franciscan friar

corder [kɔrde] *tr* to twist; to string (*a tennis racket*)

cor·dial -diale [kɔrdjal] *adj & m* (*pl* **-diaux** [djo]) cordial

cordialité [kɔrdjalite] *f* cordiality

cordier [kɔrdje] *m* ropemaker; tailpiece (*of violin*)

cordon [kɔrdɔ̃] *m* cordon; cord; latchstring; **cordon de sonnette** bellpull; **cordon de soulier** shoestring

cordon-bleu [kɔrdɔ̃blø] *m* (*pl* **cordons-bleus**) cordon bleu

cordonnerie [kɔrdɔnri] *f* shoemaking; shoe repairing; shoe store; shoemaker's

cordon·nier [kɔrdɔnje] **cordon·nière** [kɔrdɔnjer] *mf* shoemaker

Corée [kɔre] *f* Korea; **la Corée** Korea

coré·en [kɔreɛ̃] **-enne** [kɔreen] *adj* Korean ‖ *m* Korean (*language*) ‖ (*cap*) *mf* Korean (*person*)

coriace [kɔrjas] *adj* tough, leathery; (coll) stubborn

coricide [kɔrisid] *m* corn remover

cormoran [kɔrmɔrɑ̃] *m* cormorant

cornac [kɔrnak] *m* mahout

cor·nard [kɔrnar] **-narde** [nard] *adj* horned; (slang) cuckold; (*of horse*) wheezing ‖ *m* (slang) cuckold

corne [kɔrn] *f* horn; dog-ear (*of page*); hoof; shoehorn; **corne d'abondance**

horn of plenty; **faire les cornes à** (coll) to make a face at

cor·né -née [kɔrne] *adj* horny || *f* cornea

corneille [kɔrnɛj] *f* crow, rook; **corneille d'église** jackdaw

cornemuse [kɔrnəmyz] *f* bagpipe

cornemuseur [kɔrnəmyzœr] *m* bagpiper

corner [kɔrne] *tr* to dog-ear; to give (*s.o.*) the horn; (coll) to trumpet (*news*) about || *intr* to blow the horn, to honk; to ring (*said of ears*); (mus) to blow a horn; **cornez!** sound your horn!

cornet [kɔrne] *m* cornet; horn; dicebox; cornetist; mouthpiece (*of microphone*); receiver (*of telephone*); **cornet acoustique** ear trumpet; **cornet à pistons** cornet; **cornet de glace** icecream cone

cornette [kɔrnɛt] *m* (mil) cornet || *f* (*headdress*) cornet

cornettiste [kɔrnetist] *mf* cornetist

corniche [kɔrniʃ] *f* cornice

cornichon [kɔrniʃɔ̃] *m* pickle, gherkin; (*fool*) (coll) dope, drip

cor·nier -nière [kɔrnje] -nière [njɛr] *adj* corner || *f* valley (*joining roofs*); angle iron

corniste [kɔrnist] *mf* horn player

Cornouailles [kɔrnwaj] *f* Cornwall

cornouiller [kɔrnuje] *m* dogwood

cor·nu -nue [kɔrny] *adj* horned; preposterous (*ideas*) || *f* (chem) retort

corollaire [kɔrɔllɛr] *m* corollary

coronaire [kɔrɔnɛr] *adj* coronary

coroner [kɔrɔnœr] *m* coroner

corporation [kɔrpɔrasjɔ̃] *f* association, guild

corpo·rel -relle [kɔrpɔrɛl] *adj* corporal, bodily

corps [kɔr] *m* body; corps; **à corps perdu** without thinking; **à mon** (**ton,** etc.) **corps défendant** in self-defense; reluctantly; **corps à corps** hand-to-hand; in a clinch; **corps céleste** heavenly body; **corps composé** (chem) compound; **corps de garde** guardhouse, guardroom; **corps de logis** main part of the building; **corps du délit** corpus delicti; **corps enseignant** faculty; **corps simple** (chem) simple substance; **prendre corps** to take shape; **saisir au corps** (law) to arrest

corps-à-corps [kɔrakɔr] *m* hand-to-hand combat; (boxing) infighting

corpulence [kɔrpylɑ̃s] *f* corpulence

corpuscule [kɔrpyskyl] *m* (phys) corpuscle

corral [kɔral] *m* corral

cor·rect -recte [kɔrrɛkt] *adj* correct

correc·teur [kɔrrɛktœr] **-trice** [tris] *mf* corrector; proofreader

correc·tif [kɔrrɛktif] **-tive** [tiv] *adj & m* corrective

correction [kɔrrɛksjɔ̃] *f* correction; correctness; proofreading

corrélation [kɔrrelasjɔ̃] *f* correlation

correspondance [kɔrɛspɔ̃dɑ̃s] *f* correspondence; transfer, connection

correspon·dant [kɔrɛspɔ̃dɑ̃] **-dante** [dɑ̃t] *adj* corresponding, correspondent || *mf* correspondent; party (*person who gets a telephone call*)

correspondre [kɔrɛspɔ̃dr] *intr* to correspond; **correspondre à** to correspond to, to correlate with; **correspondre avec** to correspond with (*a letter writer*); to connect with (*e.g., a train*)

corridor [kɔridɔr] *m* corridor

corriger [kɔriʒe] §38 *tr* to correct; to proofread

corroborer [kɔrrɔbɔre] *tr* to corroborate

corroder [kɔrrɔde] *tr & ref* to corrode; to erode

corrompre [kɔrɔ̃pr] (3d *sg pres ind* **corrompt**) *tr* to corrupt; to rot; to bribe; to seduce; to spoil

corro·sif [kɔrrozif] **-sive** [ziv] *adj & m* corrosive

corrosion [kɔrrozjɔ̃] *f* corrosion; erosion

corroyer [kɔrwaje] §47 *tr* to weld; to plane (*wood*); to prepare (*leather*)

corruption [kɔrrypsjɔ̃] *f* corruption; bribery; seduction

corsage [kɔrsaʒ] *m* blouse, corsage

corsaire [kɔrsɛr] *m* corsair; **corsaire de finance** ruthless businessman, robber baron

corse [kɔrs] *adj* Corsican || *m* Corsican (*language*) || (*cap*) *f* Corsica; **la Corse** Corsica || (*cap*) *mf* Corsican (*person*)

cor·sé -sée [kɔrse] *adj* full-bodied, heavy; spicy, racy

corser [kɔrse] *tr* to spike, to give body to (*wine*); to spice up (*a story*) || *ref* to become serious; **ça se corse** the plot thickens

corset [kɔrse] *m* corset

cortège [kɔrtɛʒ] *m* cortege; parade; **cortège funèbre** funeral procession

cortisone [kɔrtizɔn] *f* cortisone

corvée [kɔrve] *f* chore; forced labor; work party

coryphée [kɔrife] *m* coryphée; (fig) leader

cosaque [kɔzak] *adj* Cossack || (*cap*) *mf* Cossack

cosmétique [kɔsmetik] *adj* cosmetic || *m* cosmetic; hair set, hair spray || *f* beauty culture

cosmique [kɔsmik] *adj* cosmic

cosmonaute [kɔsmɔnot] *mf* cosmonaut

cosmopolite [kɔsmɔpɔlit] *adj & mf* cosmopolitan

cosmos [kɔsmos], [kɔsmɔs] *m* cosmos; outer space

cosse [kɔs] *f* pod; **avoir la cosse** (slang) to be lazy

cos·su -sue [kɔsy] *adj* rich; well-to-do

cos·taud [kɔsto] **-taude** [tod] *adj* (slang) husky, strapping || *m* (slang) muscleman

costume [kɔstym] *m* costume; suit; **costume sur mesure** custom-made or tailor-made suit; **costume tailleur** lady's tailor-made suit

costumer [kɔstyme] *tr & ref* to dress up (*for a fancy-dress ball*); **se costumer en** to come dressed as a

costu·mier [kɔstymje] **-mière** [mjɛr] *mf* costumer

cote [kɔt] *f* assessment, quota; identification mark, letter, or number; call number (of book); altitude (above sea level); bench mark; book value (of, e.g., used cars); racing odds; (telv) rating; **avoir la cote** (coll) to be highly thought of; **cote d'alerte** danger point; **cote d'amour** moral qualifications; **cote de la Bourse** stock-market quotations; **cote mal taillée** rough compromise

côte [kot] f rib; chop; coast; slope; **à côtes** ribbed, corded; **aller** or **se mettre à la côte**, **faire côte** to run aground; **avoir les côtes en long** (coll) to feel lazy; **côte à côte** side by side; **côte d'Azur** French Riviera; **côtes découvertes**, **plates côtes** spareribs; **en côte** uphill; **être à la côte** to be broke; **faire côte** to run aground

co·té -tée [kɔte] adj listed (on the stock market); (fig) esteemed

côté [kote] m side; **à côté** in the next room; near; **à côté de** beside; **côté cour** (theat) stage right; **côté jardin** (theat) stage left; **d'à côté** next-door; **de côté** sideways; sidelong; aside; **de mon côté** for my part; **donner**, **passer**, or **toucher à côté** to miss the mark; **du côté de** in the direction of, toward; on the side of; **d'un côté . . . de l'autre côté** or **d'un autre côté** on the one hand . . . on the other hand; **répondre à côté** to miss the point

co·teau [kɔto] m (pl **-teaux**) knoll; slope

Côte-de-l'Or [kotdəlɔr] f Gold Coast

côte·lé -lée [kotle] adj ribbed, corded

côtelette [kotlɛt] f cutlet, chop; **côtelettes découvertes** spareribs

coter [kɔte] tr to assess; to mark; to number; to esteem; (com) to quote, to give a quotation on; (geog) to mark the elevations on

coterie [kɔtri] f coterie, clique

cothurne [kɔtyrn] m buskin

cô·tier -tière [tjer] adj coastal

cotir [kɔtir] tr to bruise (fruit)

cotisation [kɔtizɑsjɔ̃] f dues; assessment

cotiser [kɔtize] tr to assess (each member of a group) || intr to pay one's dues || ref to club together

coton [kɔtɔ̃] m cotton; **c'est coton** (slang) it's difficult; **coton de verre** glass wool; **coton hydrophile** absorbent cotton; cotton batting; **élever dans le coton** to coddle; **filer un mauvais coton** (coll) to be in a bad way

cotonnade [kɔtɔnad] f cotton cloth

cotonner [kɔtɔne] tr to pad or stuff with cotton || ref to become fluffy; to become spongy or mealy

cotonnerie [kɔtɔnri] f cotton field; cotton mill

coton·neux [kɔtɔnø] **coton·neuse** [kɔtɔnøz] adj cottony; spongy, mealy

coton·nier [kɔtɔnje] **-nière** [njer] adj cotton || mf cotton picker || m cotton plant

côtoyer [kotwaje] §47 tr to skirt (the edge); to hug (the shore); to border on (the truth, the ethics, etc.)

cotre [kɔtr] m (naut) cutter

cotte [kɔt] f petticoat; peasant skirt; overalls; **cotte de mailles** coat of mail

cou [ku] m neck; **sauter au cou de** to throw one's arms around

couard [kwar] **couarde** [kward] adj mf coward

couardise [kwardiz] f cowardice

couchage [kuʃaʒ] m bedding; bed for the night

cou·chant [kuʃɑ̃] **-chante** [ʃɑ̃t] adj setting || m west; decline, old age

couche [kuʃ] f layer, stratum; coat (of paint); diaper; (hort) hotbed; **couche de fond** primer, prime coat; **couches** strata; childbirth, e.g., **une femme en couches** a woman in childbirth; **fausse couche** miscarriage

coucher [kuʃe] m setting (of sun); going to bed; **coucher du soleil** sunset; **le coucher et la nourriture** room and board || tr to put to bed; to put down, lay down; to bend down, flatten; to mention (one's will); **coucher en joue** to aim at; **coucher par écrit** to set down in writing || intr to spend the night; (naut) to heel over || ref to go to bed, to lie down; to set (said of sun); to bend; **allez vous coucher!** (coll) go to blazes!

couchette [kuʃet] f berth; crib

couci-couça [kusikusa] or **couci-couci** [kusikusi] adv so-so

coucou [kuku] m cuckoo; cuckoo clock; (coll) marsh marigold

coude [kud] m elbow; angle, bend, turn; **coude à coude** shoulder to shoulder; **jouer des coudes à travers** to elbow one's way through (a crowd)

coudée [kude] f cubit; **avoir ses coudées franches** to have a free hand; to have elbowroom

cou-de-pied [kudpje] m (pl **cous-de-pied**) instep

couder [kude] tr to bend like an elbow

coudoiement [kudwamɑ̃] m elbowing

coudoyer [kudwaje] §47 tr to elbow, to jostle; to rub shoulders with

coudraie [kudre] f hazel grove

coudre [kudr] §13 tr & intr to sew

coudrier [kudrije] m hazel tree

couenne [kwan] f pigskin; rind, crackling; mole, birthmark

couette [kwet] f feather bed; (little) tail; (mach) bearing; **couette de lapin** scut; **couettes** (naut) slip

cougouar or **couguar** [kugwar] m cougar

couiner [kwine] intr to send Morse code; (coll) to squeak (said of animal)

coulage [kulaʒ] m flow; leakage; casting (of metal); pouring (of concrete); (naut) scuttling; (coll) wasting

cou·lant [kulɑ̃] **-lante** [lɑ̃t] adj flowing, running; accommodating (person) || m sliding ring; (bot) runner

coule [kul] f cowl; **être à la coule** (slang) to know the ropes

cou·lé -lée [kule] adj cast; sunken;

(coll) sunk ‖ *m* (mus) slur ‖ *f* casting; run (*of wild beasts*); **coulée volcanique** outflow of lava

couler [kule] *tr* to pour; to cast (*e.g., a statue*); to scuttle; to pass (*e.g. many happy hours*); (mus) to slur ‖ *intr* to flow; to run; to leak; to sink; to slip (away) ‖ *ref* to slip, slide; (coll) to be done for, to be sunk; **se la couler douce** (coll) to take it easy

couleur [kulœr] *f* color; policy (*of newspaper*); (cards) suit; **de couleur** colored; **les trois couleurs** the tricolor; **sous couleur de** with the pretext of, with a show of

couleuvre [kulœvr] *f* snake; **avaler des couleuvres** (coll) to swallow insults; (coll) to be gullible; **couleuvre à collier** grass snake

coulis [kuli] *m*—**coulis de tomates** tomato sauce

coulisse [kulis] *f* groove; slide (*of trombone*); (com) curb exchange; (pol) lobby; **à coulisse** sliding; **coulisses** (theat) wings; (theat) backstage; **dans les coulisses** behind the scenes, out of sight; **travailler dans les coulisses** to pull strings

coulis-seau [kuliso] *m* (*pl* **-seaux**) slide, runner

couloir [kulwar] *m* corridor; hallway; lobby

couloire [kulwar] *f* strainer

coup [ku] *m* blow; stroke; blast (*of whistle*); jolt; **à coup de** with the aid of; **à coup sûr** certainly; **après coup** when it is too late; **à tout coup** each time; **boire à petits coups** to sip; **coup de bélier** water hammer (*in pipe*); **coup de coude** nudge; **coup de dés** throw of the dice; risky business; **coup de fer** pressing, ironing; **coup de feu**, **coup de fusil** shot, gunshot; **coup de fion** (slang) finishing touch; **coup de foudre** thunderbolt; love at first sight; bolt from the blue; **coup de fouet** whiplash; stimulus; **coup de froid** cold snap; **coup de grâce** last straw; deathblow; **coup de Jarnac** [ʒarnak] stab in the back; **coup de patte** expert stroke (*e.g., of the brush*); (coll) dig, insult; **coup de pied** kick; **coup d'épingle** pinprick; **coup de poing** punch; **coup de sang** (pathol) stroke; **coup de semonce** warning shot; **coup de sifflet** whistle, toot; **coup de soleil** sunburn; (coll) sunstroke; **coup de téléphone** telephone call; **coup de tête** butt; sudden impulse; **coup de théâtre** dramatic turn of events; **coup de tonnerre** thunderclap; **coup d'œil** glance, look; **coup manqué**, **coup raté** miss; **coup monté** put-up job, frame-up; **coups et blessures** assault and battery; **coup sur coup** one right after the other; **donner un coup de main** (à) to lend a helping hand (to); **encore un coup** once again; **en venir aux coups** to come to blows; **être dans le coup** (coll) to be in on it; **faire coup double** to kill two birds with one stone; **faire les quatre coups** (coll) to

live it up, to dissipate; **faire un coup de main** to go on a raid; **manquer son coup** to miss one's chance; **se faire donner un coup de piston** (coll) to pull wires, to use influence; **sous le coup de** under the (immediate) influence of; **sur le coup** on the spot, outright; **tout à coup** suddenly; **tout d'un coup** at one shot, at once

coupable [kupabl] *adj* guilty ‖ *mf* culprit

cou·pant [kupɑ̃] **-pante** [pɑ̃t] *adj* cutting, sharp ‖ *m* (cutting) edge

coup-de-poing [kudpwɛ̃] *m* (*pl* **coups-de-poing**) brass knuckles

coupe [kup] *f* champagne glass; loving cup, trophy; cup competition; cutting; cross section; wood acreage to be cut; cut (*of cloth; of clothes; of playing cards*); division (*of verse*); **coupe claire** cutover forest; **coupe de cheveux** haircut; **coupe sombre** harvested forest; **être sous la coupe de qn** (coll) to be under s.o.'s thumb; **il y a loin de la coupe aux lèvres** there is many a slip between the cup and the lip; **mettre en coupe réglée** (coll) to fleece

cou·pé -pée [kupe] *adj* cut, cut off; interrupted (*sleep*); diluted (*wine*) ‖ *m* coupé ‖ *f* gangway

coupe-circuit [kupsirkɥi] *m invar* (elec) fuse

coupe-coupe [kupkup] *m invar* machete

coupe-feu [kupfø] *m invar* firebreak

coupe-fil [kupfil] *m invar* wire cutter

coupe-file [kupfil] *m invar* police pass (*for emergency vehicles*)

coupe-gorge [kupgɔrʒ] *m invar* deathtrap, dangerous territory

coupe-jarret [kupʒarɛ] *m* (*pl* **-jarrets**) cutthroat

coupe-ongles [kupɔ̃gl] *m invar* nail clippers

coupe-papier [kuppapje] *m invar* paper knife, letter opener

couper [kupe] *tr* to cut; to cut off; to cut out; to break off, interrupt; to cut, water down; to turn off; to trump; to castrate, geld; **ça te la coupe!** (coll) top that! **couper la file** (aut) to leave one's lane; **couper la parole à** to interrupt; **couper menu** to mince ‖ *intr* to cut; to trump; **couper court à** to cut (*s.o. or s.th.*) short ‖ *ref* to cut oneself; to intersect; (coll) to contradict oneself; (coll) to give oneself away

couperet [kupre] *m* cleaver; guillotine blade

couperose [kuproz] *f* (pathol) acne

cou·peur [kupœr] **-peuse** [pøz] *mf* cutter; **coupeur de bourses** (coll) purse snatcher; **coupeur d'oreilles** (coll) hatchet man, hired thug

couplage [kuplaʒ] *m* (mach) coupling

couple [kupl] *m* couple (*e.g., of friends, cronies, thieves, etc.; man and wife*); pair (*e.g., of pigeons*); (mech) couple, torque; **couple thermo-électrique** thermoelectric couple;

maître couple (naut) midship frame || f yoke (of oxen); couple; leash

coupler [kuple] tr to couple; to pair

coupleur [kuplœr] m (mach) coupler

coupole [kupɔl] f cupola

coupon [kupɔ̃] m coupon; remnant (of cloth); theater ticket

coupon-réponse [kupɔ̃repɔ̃s] m—**coupon-réponse international** international (postal) reply coupon; **coupon-réponse postal** return-reply post card or letter

coupure [kupyr] f cut, incision, slit; cut, deletion; newspaper clipping; small note; interruption, break; drain (e.g., through a marsh)

cour [kur] f court; courtyard; courtship; **bien en cour** in favor; **cour anglaise** courtyard or court (of apartment building); **cour d'appel** appellate court; **cour d'assises** criminal court; **cour de cassation** supreme court of appeals; **cour d'école** school playground; **faire la cour à** to court; **mal en cour** out of favor

courage [kuraʒ] m courage; **reprendre courage** to take heart; **travailler avec courage** to work hard || interj buck up!, cheer up!

coura·geux [kuraʒø] **-geuse** [ʒøz] adj courageous; hard-working

courailler [kuraje] intr to gallivant

couramment [kuramɑ̃] adv currently; fluently, easily

cou·rant [kurɑ̃] **-rante** [rɑ̃t] adj current; running (water); present-day (language, customs, etc.) || m current; flow; shift (of opinion, population, etc.); **courant alternatif** alternating current; **courant continu** direct current; **courant d'air** draft; **Courant du Golfe** Gulf Stream; **dans le courant du mois** (de la semaine, etc.) in the course of the month (of the week, etc.); **être au courant de** to be informed about

courba·tu -tue [kurbaty] adj stiff in the joints, aching all over

courbature [kurbatyr] f stiffness, aching

courbaturer [kɔrbatyre] tr to make stiff; to exhaust (the body)

courbe [kurb] adj curved || f curve; **courbe de niveau** contour line

cour·bé -bée [kurbe] adj curved, bent, crooked

courber [kurbe] tr to bend, curve || intr & ref to bend, curve; to give in

courbure [kurbyr] f curve, curvature; **double courbure** S-curve

courette [kuret] f small courtyard

cou·reur [kurœr] **-reuse** [røz] mf runner; **coureur cycliste** bicycle racer; **coureur de cotillons** (coll) wolf; **coureur de dot** fortune hunter; **coureur de filles** Casanova, Don Juan; **coureur de girls** stage-door Johnny; **coureur de spectacles** playgoer; **coureur de vitesse** sprinter

courge [kurʒ] f gourd, squash

courir [kurir] §14 tr to run; to run after; to roam; to frequent || intr to run; **le bruit court que** rumor has it

that; **par le temps qui court** at the present time

courlis [kurli] m curlew

couronne [kurɔn] f crown; wreath; coronet; rim (of atomic structures)

couronnement [kurɔnmɑ̃] m crowning; coronation; coping

couronner [kurɔne] tr to crown; to top, cap; to reward || ref to be crowned; to be covered (with flowers)

courrier [kurje] m courier; mail; **courrier du cœur** advice to the lovelorn; **courrier mondain** gossip column; **courrier théâtral** theater section

courriériste [kurjerist] mf columnist

courroie [kurwa] f strap; belt

courroucer [kuruse] §51 tr (lit) to anger

courroux [kuru] m (lit) wrath, anger

cours [kur] m course; current (of river); tree-lined walk; rate (of exchange); market quotation; style, vogue; **au cours de** in the course of; **avoir cours** to be in circulation; to be legal tender; to have classes; **cours d'eau** stream, river; **cours d'été** or **cours de vacances** summer school; **cours du soir** night school; **de cours** in length (said of a river); **de long cours** long-range; **suivre un cours** to take a course (in school)

course [kurs] f running; race; errand; trip; ride (e.g., in a taxi); course, path; privateering; stroke (of a piston); **course à pied** foot race; **course attelée** harness race; **course au trot** trotting race; **course aux armements** arms race; **course de chevaux** horse race; **course de côte** hill climb; **course de taureaux** bullfight; **course de vitesse** sprint; **course d'obstacles** steeplechase; **courses sur route** road racing; **de course** at a run; racing (car; track; crowd); (mil) on the double; **en pleine course** in full swing; **faire des courses** to go shopping

cour·sier [kursje] **-sière** [sjer] mf messenger || m errand boy; steed

coursive [kursiv] f (naut) alleyway, gangway (connecting staterooms)

court [kur] **courte** [kurt] adj short; brief; concise; choppy (sea); thick (sauce, gravy); **à court** short; **de court** by surprise; **prendre le plus court** to take a shortcut; **tenir de court** to hold on a short leash || (when standing before noun) adj short, brief (interval, time, life) || m court (for tennis) || court adv short; **demeurer court** to forget what one wanted to say; **tourner court** to turn sharp; to stop short, to change the subject; **tout court** simply, merely; plain

courtage [kurtaʒ] m brokerage; broker's commission

cour·taud [kurto] **-taude** [tod] adj stocky, short and stocky

court-circuit [kursirkɥi] m (pl **courts-circuits**) short circuit

court-circuiter [kursirkɥite] tr to short-circuit

courtepointe [kurtəpwɛ̃t] f counterpane

cour·tier [kurtje] **-tière** [tjer] *mf* broker; agent; **courtier électoral** canvasser

courtisan [kurtizã] *m* courtier

courtisane [kurtizan] *f* courtesan

cour·tiser [kurtize] *tr* to court

cour·tois [kurtwa] **-toise** [twaz] *adj* courteous; courtly

courtoisie [kurtwazi] *f* courtesy

court-vê·tu -tue [kurvety] *adj* short-skirted

cou·ru -rue [kuru] *adj* sought after, popular; **c'est couru** (coll) it's a sure thing

cou·seur [kuzœr] **-seuse** [zøz] *mf* sewer ‖ *f* seamstress; (mach) stitcher

cou·sin [kuzɛ̃] **-sine** [zin] *mf* cousin; **cousin germain** first cousin; **cousins issus de germains** first cousins once removed ‖ *m* mosquito

cousinage [kuzinaʒ] *m* cousinship; (coll) relatives

coussin [kusɛ̃] *m* cushion

coussinet [kusine] *m* little cushion; (mach) bearing

coût [ku] *m* cost; **coût de la vie** cost of living

cou·teau [kuto] *m* (*pl* **-teaux**) knife; **couteau à cran d'arrêt** clasp knife with safety catch; switchblade knife; **couteau à découper** carving knife; **couteau à ressort** switchblade knife; **couteau pliant, couteau de poche** jackknife

coutelas [kutla] *m* cutlass; butcher knife

coutellerie [kutelri] *f* cutlery

coûter [kute] *tr* to cost; **coûte que coûte** cost what it may; **il m'en coûte de + inf** it's hard for me to + *inf*

coû·teux [kutø] **-teuse** [tøz] *adj* costly, expensive

coutil [kuti] *m* duck (*cloth*); mattress ticking

coutume [kutym] *f* custom; habit; common law; **de coutume** ordinarily

coutu·mier [kutymje] **-mière** [mjer] *adj* customary; common (*law*); accustomed ‖ *m* book of common law

couture [kutyr] *f* needlework; sewing; seam; suture; scar; **battre qn à plate couture** (coll) to beat s.o. hollow; **examiner sur toutes les coutures** to examine inside and out or from every angle; **haute couture** fashion designing, haute couture; **sans couture** seamless

couturer [kutyre] *tr* to scar

coutu·rier [kutyrje] **-rière** [rjer] *mf* dressmaker ‖ *m* dress designer ‖ *f* seamstress

couvaison [kuvezɔ̃] *f* incubation period

couvée [kuve] *f* brood

couvent [kuvã] *m* convent; monastery; convent school

couver [kuve] *tr* to brood, hatch ‖ *intr* to brood; to smolder

couvercle [kuverkl] *m* cover, lid

cou·vert [kuver] **-verte** [vert] *adj* covered; dressed; clothed; cloudy (*weather*); wooded (*countryside*) ‖ *m* cover; setting (*of table*); service (*fork and spoon*); cover charge; room, lodging;

authority (*given by a superior*); **à couvert** sheltered; **mettre le couvert** to set the table; **sous le couvert de** under cover of; **sous les couverts** under cover (*of trees*) ‖ *f* glaze

couverture [kuvertyr] *f* cover; coverage; covering; wrapper; blanket, bedspread

couveuse [kuvøz] *f* brood hen; incubator

couvre-chef [kuvrəʃef] *m* (*pl* **-chefs**) (coll) headgear

couvre-feu [kuvrəfø] *m* (*pl* **-feux**) curfew

couvre-lit [kuvrəli] *m* (*pl* **-lits**) bedspread

couvre-livre [kuvrəlivr] *m* (*pl* **-livres**) dust jacket

couvre-pieds [kuvrəpje] *m invar* bedspread; quilt

couvre-plat [kuvrəpla] *m* (*pl* **-plats**) dish cover

couvre-théière [kuvrətejer] *m* (*pl* **-théières**) tea cozy

couvreur [kuvrœr] *m* roofer

couvrir [kuvrir] §65 *tr* to cover ‖ *ref* to cover; to cover oneself; to get cloudy; to put one's hat on

cow-boy [kaubɔj], [kobɔj] *m* (*pl* **-boys**) cowboy

C.P. *abbr* (**case postale**) post-office box

C.R. [seer] *adv* (letterword) (**contre remboursement**) C.O.D.; **envoyez-le-moi C.R.** send it to me C.O.D.

crabe [krab], [krab] *m* crab; caterpillar (tractor)

crachat [kraʃa] *m* sputum, spit

cra·ché -chée [kraʃe] *adj* (coll) spitting (*image*)

cracher [kraʃe] *tr & intr* to spit

crachin [kraʃɛ̃] *m* light drizzle

crachoir [kraʃwar] *m* spittoon; **tenir le crachoir** (slang) to have the floor, to speak

crachoter [kraʃɔte] *intr* to keep on spitting; to sputter

crack [krak] *m* favorite (*the horse favored to win*); (coll) champion, ace; (coll) crackerjack

cracking [krakiŋ] *m* cracking (*of oil*)

craie [kre] *f* chalk; piece of chalk

crailler [kraje] *intr* to caw

craindre [krɛ̃dr] §15 *tr* to fear, to be afraid of, to dread; to respect ‖ *intr* to be afraid

crainte [krɛ̃t] *f* fear, dread; **dans la crainte que** or **de crainte que** for fear that

crain·tif [krɛ̃tif] **-tive** [tiv] *adj* fearful; timid

cramoi·si -sie [kramwazi] *adj & m* crimson

crampe [krãp] *f* cramp (*in a muscle*)

crampon [krãpɔ̃] *m* clamp; cleat (*on a shoe*); (coll) pest, bore

cramponner [krãpone] *tr* to clamp together; (coll) to pester ‖ *ref* to hold fast, hang on, cling

cran [krã] *m* notch; cog, catch, tooth; **avoir du cran** (coll) to be game (*for anything*); **baisser un cran** to come down a peg; **être à cran** (coll) to be exasperated, cross

crâne [krɑn] *adj* bold, daring ‖ *m* skull, cranium; **bourrer le crâne à qn** (coll) to hand s.o. a line

crâner [krɑne] *intr* (coll) to swagger

cra·neur [krɑnœr] **-neuse** [nøz] *adj & mf* (coll) braggart

crapaud [krapo] *m* toad; baby grand; flaw (*in diamond*); low armchair; (coll) brat; **avaler un crapaud** (coll) to put up with a lot

crapule [krapyl] *f* underworld, scum; bum, punk; **vivre dans la crapule** to live in debauchery

crapu·leux [krapylø] **-leuse** [løz] *adj* debauched, lewd, filthy

craquage [krakaʒ] *m* cracking (*of petroleum*)

craquement [krakmɑ̃] *m* crack, crackle

craquer [krake] *intr* to crack; to burst; (coll) to crash, fail

craqueter [krakte] §34 *intr* to crackle

crash [kraʃ] *m* crash landing

crasse [kras] *adj* gross; crass (*ignorance*) ‖ *f* filth, squalor; avarice; dross; **faire une crasse à qn** (slang) to play a dirty trick on s.o.

cras·seux [krasø] **cras·seuse** [krasøz] *adj* filthy, squalid; (coll) stingy

crassier [krasje] *m* slag heap

cratère [krater] *m* crater; ewer

cravache [kravaʃ] *f* riding whip, horsewhip

cravacher [kravaʃe] *tr* to horsewhip

cravate [kravat] *f* necktie, cravat; scarf; sling (*for unloading goods*); **cravate de chanvre** (coll) noose; **cravate de drapeau** pennant

cravater [kravate] *tr* to tie a necktie on (*s.o.*) ‖ *intr* (slang) to tell a fish story

crawl [krol] *m* crawl (*in swimming*)

crayeux [krejø] **crayeuse** [krejøz] *adj* chalky

crayon [krejɔ̃] *m* pencil; **crayon de pastel** wax crayon; **crayon de rouge à lèvres** lipstick

crayonner [krejone] *tr* to crayon, to pencil, to sketch

créance [kreɑ̃s] *f* belief, credence; **créances gelées** frozen assets; **créances véreuses** bad debts

créan·cier [kreɑ̃sje] **-cière** [sjer] *mf* creditor; **créancier hypothécaire** mortgage holder

créa·teur [kreatœr] **-trice** [tris] *adj* creative ‖ *mf* creator; originator

création [kreasjɔ̃] *f* creation

créature [kreatyr] *f* creature

crécelle [kresel] *f* rattle; chatterbox; **de crécelle** rasping

crèche [kreʃ] *f* manger; crèche; day nursery

crédence [kredɑ̃s] *f* buffet, sideboard, credenza

crédibilité [kredibilite] *f* credibility

crédit [kredi] *m* credit; (govt) appropriation

créditer [kredite] *tr* (com) to credit

crédi·teur [kreditœr] **-trice** [tris] *adj* credit (*side, account*) ‖ *mf* creditor

credo [kredo] *m invar* credo, creed

crédule [kredyl] *adj* credulous

créer [kree] *tr* to create

crémaillère [kremajer] *f* pothook;

rack; rack rail; **crémaillère et pignon** rack and pinion; **pendre la crémaillère** to have a housewarming

crémation [kremasjɔ̃] *f* cremation

crématoire [krematwar] *adj & m* crematory

crème [krem] *f* cream; **crème chantilly** whipped cream; **crème de démaquillage** cleansing cream; **crème fouettée** whipped cream; **crème glacée** ice cream

crémer [kreme] §10 *intr* to cream

crémerie [kremri] *f* dairy; milkhouse (*on a farm*); dairy luncheonette

cré·meux [kremø] **-meuse** [møz] *adj* creamy

crémier [kremje] *m* dairyman

crémière [kremjer] *f* dairymaid; cream pitcher

crémone [kremɔn] *f* casement bolt

cré·neau [kreno] *m* (*pl* **-neaux**) crenel; loophole; **créneaux** battlements

créneler [krenle] §34 *tr* to crenelate; to tooth (*a wheel*); to mill (*a coin*)

créole [kreɔl] *adj* Creole ‖ *m* Creole (*language*) ‖ (*cap*) *mf* Creole (*person*)

crêpe [krep] *m* crepe ‖ *f* pancake

crépitation [krepitasjɔ̃] *f* crackle

crépitement [krepitmɑ̃] *m* crackling

crépiter [krepite] *intr* to crackle

cré·pu -pue [krepy] *adj* crimped, frizzly, crinkled

crépuscule [krepyskyl] *m* twilight

cresson [kresɔ̃] *m* cress; **cresson de fontaine** watercress

crête [kret] *f* crest; **crête de coq** cockscomb

Crète [kret] *f* Crete; **la Crète** Crete

crête-de-coq [kretdəkɔk] *f* (*pl* **crêtes-de-coq**) (bot) cockscomb

cré·tin [kretɛ̃] **-tine** [tin] *mf* cretin; (coll) jackass, fathead

cré·tois [kretwa] **-toise** [twaz] *adj* Cretan ‖ (*cap*) *mf* Cretan

creuser [krøze] *tr* to dig, excavate; to hollow out; to furrow; to go into thoroughly ‖ *ref*—**se creuser la tête** (coll) to rack one's brains

creuset [krøze] *m* crucible

creux [krø] **creuse** [krøz] *adj* hollow; concave, sunken, deep-set; empty (*stomach*); deep (*voice*); off-peak (*hours*); **songer creux** to dream idle dreams; **sonner creux** to sound hollow ‖ *m* hollow (*of hand*); hole (*in ground*); pit (*of stomach*); trough (*of wave*); **creux de l'aisselle** armpit; **creux des reins** small of the back

crevaison [krəvezɔ̃] *f* blowout

crevasse [krəvas] *f* crevice; crack (*in skin*); rift (*in clouds*); flaw (*in metal*)

crevasser [krəvase] *tr* to chap ‖ *intr & ref* to crack, to chap

crève-cœur [krevkœr] *m invar* heartbreak, keen disappointment

crever [krəve] §2 *tr* to burst; to work to death (*e.g., a horse*) ‖ *intr* to burst; to split; to burst, go flat (*said of a tire*); (slang) to die, kick the bucket ‖ *ref* to work oneself to death

crevette [krəvet] *f* shrimp; **crevette**

grise shrimp; **crevette rose, crevette bouquet** prawn

C.-R.F. *abbr* (Croix-Rouge française) French Red Cross

cri [kri] *m* cry; shout; whine, squeal; **dernier cri** last word, latest thing

criailler [kriaje] *intr* to honk (*said of goose*); (coll) to whine, complain, grouse; **criailler après, criailler contre** (coll) to nag at

criaillerie [kriajri] *f* (coll) shouting; (coll) whining, complaining; (coll) nagging

criant [krijɑ̃] **criante** [krijɑ̃t] *adj* crying (*shame*); obvious (*truth*); flagrant (*injustice*)

criard [krijar] **criarde** [krijard] *adj* complaining; shrill (*voice*); loud (*color*); pressing (*debts*) ‖ *mf* complainer ‖ *f* scold, shrew

crible [kribl] *m* sieve; screen; **crible à gravier** gravel screen; **crible à minerai** jig; **passer au crible** to sift or screen

cri·blé -blée [krible] *adj* riddled (*with*, e.g., *debts*); pitted (*by*, e.g., *small-pox*)

cribler [krible] *tr* to sift, screen; to riddle; **cribler de ridicule** to cover with ridicule

cric [krik] *m* (aut) jack ‖ *interj* crack!, snap!

cricket [kriket] *m* (sports) cricket

cricri [krikri] *m* (ent) cricket

crier [krije] *tr* to cry; to cry out; to shout; to cry for (*revenge*); **crier misère** to complain of being poor; to cry poverty (*said of clothing, furniture, etc.*) ‖ *intr* to cry; to cry out; to shout; to creak; to squeak; to squeal; **crier à** to cry out against (*scandal, injustice, etc.*); to cry for (*help*); **crier après** to yell at, to bawl out; **crier contre** to cry out against; **crier contre** to cry out against; to rail at

crieur [krijœr] **crieuse** [krijøz] *mf* crier; hawker, peddler; **crieur public** town crier

crime [krim] *m* crime; felony

crimi·nel -nelle [kriminɛl] *adj* & *mf* criminal

crin [krɛ̃] *m* horsehair (*on mane and tail*); **à tous crins** out-and-out, hardcore (*e.g., revolutionist*)

crinière [krinjɛr] *f* mane

crique [krik] *f* cove

criquet [krikɛ] *m* locust; weak wine; (coll) shrimp (*person*)

crise [kriz] *f* crisis; **crise d'appendicite** appendicitis attack; **crise de foi** shaken faith; **crise de main-d'œuvre** labor shortage; **crise de nerfs** fit of hysterics; **crise du foie** liver upset; **crise du logement** housing shortage; **crise économique** (com) depression

cris·pant -pante [krispɑ̃] **-pante** [pɑ̃t] *adj* irritating, annoying

crispation [krispasjɔ̃] *f* contraction, shriveling up; (coll) fidgeting

crisper [krispe] *tr* to contract, clench; (coll) to make fidgety ‖ *ref* to contract, to curl up

crisser [krise] *tr* to grind or grit (*one's teeth*) ‖ *intr* to grate, crunch

cris·tal [kristal] *m* (*pl* **-taux** [to]) crystal; **cristal de roche** rock crystal; **cristal taillé** cut glass; **cristaux** glassware; **cristaux de soude** washing soda

cristal·lin [kristalɛ̃] **cristal·line** [kristalin] *adj* crystalline ‖ *m* crystalline lens (*of the eye*)

cristalliser [kristalize] *tr, intr, & ref* to crystallize

critère [kritɛr] *m* criterion

critérium [kriterjɔm] *m* championship game

critiquable [kritikabl] *adj* open to criticism, questionable

critique [kritik] *adj* critical ‖ *mf* critic ‖ *f* criticism; critics; **critiques** censure

critiquer [kritike] *tr* to criticize, find fault with ‖ *intr* to find fault

critiqueur [kritikœr] *m* critic, faultfinder

croassement [krɔasmɑ̃] *m* croak, caw, croaking (*of raven*)

croasser [krɔase] *intr* to croak, to caw

croate [krɔat] *adj* Croatian ‖ *m* Croat, Croatian (*language*) ‖ (cap) *mf* Croatian (*person*)

croc [kro] *m* hook; fang (*of dog*); tusk (*of walrus*)

croc-en-jambe [krɔkɑ̃ʒɑ̃b] *m* (*pl* **crocs-en-jambes** [krɔkɑ̃ʒɑ̃b])—**faire un croc-en-jambe à qn** to trip s.o. up

croche [krɔʃ] *f* (mus) quaver

crochet [krɔʃɛ] *m* hook; fang (*of snake*); crochet work; crochet needle; picklock; **crochet radiophonique** talent show; **crochets** (typ) brackets; **faire un crochet** to swerve; **vivre aux crochets de** to live on or at the expense of

crocheter [krɔʃte] §2 *tr* to pick (*a lock*)

crocheteur [krɔʃtœr] *m* picklock; porter

cro·chu -chue [krɔʃy] *adj* hooked (*e.g., nose*); crooked; **avoir les mains crochues** to be light-fingered

crocodile [krɔkɔdil] *m* crocodile

crocus [krɔkys] *m* crocus

croire [krwar] §16 *tr* to believe; **croire** + *inf* to think that + *ind*; **croire qn** + *adj* to believe s.o. to be + *adj*; **croire que non** to think not; **croire que oui** to think so; **je crois bien** or **je le crois bien** I should say so ‖ *intr* to believe; **croire à** to believe in; **croire en Dieu** to believe in God; **j'y crois** I believe in it ‖ *ref* to believe oneself to be

croisade [krwazad] *f* crusade

croi·sé -sée [krwaze] *adj* crossed; twilled (*cloth*); double-breasted (*suit*); alternate (*rhymes*) ‖ *m* Crusader ‖ *f* crossing, crossroads

croisement [krwazmɑ̃] *m* crossing; intersection; meeting, passing (*of two vehicles*); cross-breeding; **croisement en trèfle** cloverleaf, cloverleaf intersection

croiser [krwaze] *tr* to cross; to fold over; to meet; to pass ‖ *intr* to fold over, to lap; to cruise ‖ *ref* to cross, intersect; to go on a crusade

croiseur [krwazœr] *m* cruiser; **croiseur de bataille** battle cruiser

croisière [krwazjer] *f* cruise; **en croisière** cruising

croissance [krwasɑ̃s] *f* growth

crois·sant [krwasɑ̃] **crois·sante** [krwasɑ̃t] *adj* growing, increasing, rising ‖ *m* crescent; crescent roll; billhook

croître [krwatr] §17 *intr* to grow; to increase, to rise

croix [krwa] *f* cross; (typ) dagger; **croix gammée** swastika; **en croix** crossed, crosswise

Croix-Rouge [krwaruʒ] *f* Red Cross

cro·quant [krɔkɑ̃] **-quante** [kɑ̃t] *adj* crisp, crunchy ‖ *m* wretch

croque-mitaine [krɔkmiten] *m* (*pl* **-mitaines**) bugaboo, bogeyman

croque-monsieur [krɔkməsjø] *m invar* grilled ham-and-cheese sandwich

croque-mort [krɔkmɔr] *m* (*pl* **-morts**) (coll) funeral attendant

croquer [krɔke] *tr* to munch; to sketch; to dissipate (*a fortune*) ‖ *intr* to crunch

croquet [krɔke] *m* croquet; almond cookie

croquis [krɔki] *m* sketch; draft, outline; **croquis coté** diagram, sketch

crosse [krɔs] *f* crosier; butt (*of gun*); hockey stick; lacrosse stick; golf club; **chercher des crosses à** (slang) to pick a fight with; **mettre la crosse en l'air** to show the white flag, to surrender

crotale [krɔtal] *m* rattlesnake

crotte [krɔt] *f* dung; mud; **crotte de chocolat** chocolate cream (candy)

crotter [krɔte] *tr* to dirty ‖ *ref* to get dirty; to commit a nuisance (*said of dog*)

crottin [krɔtɛ̃] *m* horse manure

crouler [krule] *intr* to collapse

croup [kru] *m* (pathol) croup

croupe [krup] *f* croup, rump; ridge, brow; **en croupe** behind the rider

croupetons [kruptɔ̃]—**à croupetons** squatting

croupier [krupje] *m* croupier; financial partner

croupière [krupjer] *f* crupper; **tailler des croupières à** (coll) to make it hard for

croupion [krupjɔ̃] *m* rump

croupir [krupir] *intr* to stagnate; to wallow (*in vice, filth*); to remain (*e.g., in ignorance*)

croustil·lant [krustijɑ̃] **croustil·lante** [krustijɑ̃t] *adj* crisp, crunchy; spicy (*story*)

croustille [krustij] *f* piece of crust; snack; **croustilles** potato chips

croustiller [krustije] *intr* to munch, to nibble

croustil·leux [krustijø] **croustil·leuse** [krustijøz] *adj* spicy (*story*)

croûte [krut] *f* crust; pastry shell (*of meat pie*); scab (*of wound*); (coll) daub, worthless painting; **casser la croûte** (coll) to have a snack

croû·teux [krutø] **-teuse** [tøz] *adj* scabby

croûton [krutɔ̃] *m* crouton; heel (*of bread*); **vieux croûton** (coll) old dodo

croyable [krwajabl], [krwajabl] *adj* believable

croyance [krwajɑ̃s] *f* belief

croyant [krwajɑ̃] **croyante** [krwajɑ̃t] *adj* believing ‖ *mf* believer

C.R.S. [seeres] *fpl* (letterword) (**Compagnies républicaines de sécurité**) state troopers

cru crue [kry] *adj* raw, uncooked; indigestible; crude (*language; art*); glaring, harsh (*light*); hard (*water*); plain (*terms*); **à cru** directly; bareback ‖ *m* region (*in which s.th. is grown*); vineyard; vintage; **de son cru** of his own invention; **du cru** local, at the vineyard ‖ *see* **crue**

cruauté [kryote] *f* cruelty

cruche [kryʃ] *f* pitcher, jug

cruchon [kryʃɔ̃] *m* small pitcher or jug

cru·cial -ciale [krysjal] *adj* (*pl* **-ciaux** [sjo]) crucial; cross-shaped

crucifiement [krysifimɑ̃] *m* crucifixion

crucifier [krysifje] *tr* to crucify

crucifix [krysifi] *m* crucifix

crucifixion [krysifiksjɔ̃] *f* crucifixion

crudité [krydite] *f* crudity; indigestibility; rawness (*of food*); harshness (*of light*); hardness (*of water*); **crudités** raw fruits and vegetables; off-color remarks

crue [kry] *f* overflow (*of river*); growth

cruel cruelle [kryel] *adj* cruel

cruellement [kryelmɑ̃] *adv* cruelly; sorely

crû·ment [krymɑ̃] *adv* crudely; roughly

crustacé [krystase] *m* crustacean

crypte [kript] *f* crypt

CᵗᵉCᵗ *abbr* (**compte courant**) current account

cubage [kybaʒ] *m* volume

cu·bain [kybɛ̃] **-baine** [ben] *adj* Cuban ‖ (*cap*) *mf* Cuban

cube [kyb] *adj* cubic ‖ *m* cube

cuber [kybe] *tr* to cube

cubique [kybik] *adj* cubic

cueillaison [kœjezɔ̃] *f* picking, gathering; harvest time

cueil·leur [kœjœr] **cueil·leuse** [kœjøz] *mf* picker; fruit picker

cueillir [kœjir] §18 *tr* to pick; to pluck; to gather; to win (*laurels*); to steal (*a kiss*); (coll) to nab (*a thief*); (coll) to pick up (*a friend*)

cuiller *or* **cuillère** [kɥijer] *f* spoon; ladle (*for molten metal*); scoop (*of dredger*); **cuiller à bouche** table spoon; **cuiller à café** teaspoon; **cuiller à pot** ladle; **cuiller à soupe** soup spoon; **cuiller et fourchette** fork and spoon

cuillerée [kɥijre] *f* spoonful

cuilleron [kɥijrɔ̃] *m* bowl (*of spoon*)

cuir [kɥir] *m* leather; hide; **cuir chevelu** scalp; **cuir verni** patent leather; **cuir vert** rawhide; **faire des cuirs** to make mistakes in liaison

cuirasse [kɥiras] *f* cuirass, breastplate, armor

cuiras·sé -sée [kɥirase] *adj* armored ‖ *m* battleship

cuirasser [kɥirase] *tr* to armor ‖ *ref* to steel oneself

cuire [kɥir] §19 *tr* to cook; to ripen ‖ *intr* to cook; to sting, smart; **faire cuire** to cook; **il vous en cuira** you'll suffer for it

cui·sant [kɥizɑ̃] **-sante** [zɑ̃t] *adj* stinging, smarting

cuisine [kɥizin] *f* kitchen; cooking; cuisine; (coll) skulduggery; **cuisine roulante** chuck wagon, field kitchen; **faire la cuisine** to cook

cuisiner [kɥizine] *tr* to cook; (coll) to grill (*a suspect*); (coll) to fix (*an election*) ‖ *intr* to cook

cuisi·nier [kɥizinje] **-nière** [njer] *mf* cook ‖ *f* kitchen stove, cookstove

cuisse [kɥis] *f* thigh; (culin) drumstick; **cuisses de grenouille** frogs' legs; **il se croit sorti de la cuisse de Jupiter** (coll) he thinks he is the Lord God Almighty

cuis·seau [kɥiso] *m* (*pl* **-seaux**) leg of veal

cuisson [kɥisɔ̃] *f* baking, cooking; (fig) burning sensation, smarting; **en cuisson** on the stove, on the grill, in the oven

cuissot [kɥiso] *m* leg (*of game*)

cuistre [kɥistr] *m* pedant, prig

cuit [kɥi] **cuite** [kɥit] *adj* cooked; **nous sommes cuits** (coll) our goose is cooked ‖ *f* firing (*in a kiln*); **prendre une cuite** (slang) to get soused

cuivre [kɥivr] *m* copper; **cuivre jaune** brass; **les cuivres** (mus) the brasses

cui·vré **-vrée** [kɥivre] *adj* coppercolored, bronzed; brassy, metallic (*sound or voice*)

cuivrer [kɥivre] *tr* to copper; to bronze, tan; to make (*a sound or one's voice*) brassy or metallic ‖ *ref* to become copper-colored

cui·vreux [kɥivrø] **-vreuse** [vrøz] *adj* (chem) cuprous

cul [ky] *m* bottom (*of bottle, bag*); (slang) ass, hind end, rump; **faire cul sec** (slang) to chug-a-lug

culasse [kylas] *f* breechblock; (mach) cylinder head

cul-blanc [kyblɑ̃] *m* (*pl* **culs-blancs**) wheatear, whitetail

culbute [kylbyt] *f* somersault; tumble, bad fall; (coll) failure; (coll) fall (*of a cabinet*); **faire la culbute** to sell at double the purchase price

culbuter [kylbyte] *tr* to overthrow; to overwhelm (*the enemy*) ‖ *intr* to tumble, to fall backwards; to somersault

culbuteur [kylbytœr] *m* (mach) rocker arm

cul-de-basse-fosse [kydbasfos] *m* (*pl* **culs-de-basse-fosse**) dungeon

cul-de-jatte [kydəʒat] *mf* (*pl* **culs-de-jatte**) legless person

cul-de-sac [kydəsak] *m* (*pl* **culs-de-sac**) dead end; (public sign) no outlet

culée [kyle] *f* abutment

culer [kyle] *intr* to back water

culinaire [kyliner] *adj* culinary

culmi·nant [kylminɑ̃] **-nante** [nɑ̃t] *adj* culminating; highest (*point*)

culmination [kylminasjɔ̃] *f* (astr) culmination

culminer [kylmine] *intr* to rise high, to tower; (astr) to culminate

culot [kylo] *m* base, bottom; (coll) baby of the family; **avoir du culot** (slang) to have a lot of nerve

culotte [kylɔt] *f* breeches, pants; forked pipe; panties (*feminine undergarment*); (culin) rump; **culotte de golf** plus fours; **culotte de peau** (slang) old soldier; **culotte de sport** shorts; **porter la culotte** (coll) to wear the pants; **prendre une culotte** (slang) to lose one's shirt; (slang) to have a jag on

culot·té **-tée** [kylote] *adj* (coll) nervy, fresh

culotter [kylɔte] *tr* to cure (*a pipe*) ‖ *ref* to put out one's pants on

culte [kylt] *m* worship; cult; divine service, ritual; religion, creed; **avoir un culte pour** to worship (*e.g., one's parents*)

cul-terreux [kyterø] *m* (*pl* **culs-terreux**) (coll) clodhopper, hayseed

cultivable [kyltivabl] *adj* arable, tillable

cultiva·teur [kyltivatœr] **-trice** [tris] *adj* farming ‖ *mf* farmer ‖ *m* (mach) cultivator

cultiver [kyltive] *tr* to cultivate; to culture

cultu·ral **-rale** [kyltyral] *adj* (*pl* **-raux** [ro]) agricultural

culture [kyltyr] *f* culture; cultivation

cultu·rel **-relle** [kyltyrɛl] *adj* cultural

cumula·tif [kymylatif] **-tive** [tiv] *adj* cumulative

cunéiforme [kyneiform] *adj* cuneiform

cupide [kypid] *adj* greedy

cupidité [kypidite] *f* cupidity

Cupidon [kypidɔ̃] *m* Cupid

curage [kyraʒ] *m* cleansing, cleaning out; unstopping (*of a drain*)

curatelle [kyratel] *f* guardianship, trusteeship

cura·teur [kyratœr] **-trice** [tris] *mf* guardian, trustee

cura·tif [kyratif] **-tive** [tiv] *adj* curative

cure [kyr] *f* treatment, cure; vicarage, rectory; parish; sun porch; **n'avoir cure de rien** or **n'en avoir cure** not to care

curé [kyre] *m* parish priest

cure-dent [kyrdɑ̃] *m* (*pl* **-dents**) toothpick

curée [kyre] *f* quarry (*given to the hounds*); scramble, mad race (*for gold, power, recognition, etc.*)

cure-oreille [kyrɔrej] *m* (*pl* **-oreilles**) earpick

cure-pipe [kyrpip] *m* (*pl* **-pipes**) pipe cleaner

curer [kyre] *tr* to clean out; to dredge ‖ *ref* (with *dat* of *reflex pron*) to pick (*one's nails, one's teeth, etc.*)

cu·rieux [kyrjø] **-rieuse** [rjøz] *adj* curious

curiosité [kyrjozite] *f* curiosity; curio; connoisseurs, *e.g.*, **le langage de la curiosité** the jargon of connoisseurs;

curiosités sights; **visiter les curiosités** to go sightseeing
curseur [kyrsœr] *m* slide, runner
cur·sif -sive [kyrsif] [siv] *adj* cursory; cursive (*handwriting*) ‖ *f* cursive
cuta·né -née [kytane] *adj* cutaneous
cuticule [kytikyl] *f* cuticle
cuve [kyv] *f* vat, tub, tank
cu·veau [kyvo] *m* (*pl* **-veaux**) small vat or tank
cuver [kyve] *tr* to leave to ferment; **cuver son vin** (coll) to sleep it off ‖ *intr* to ferment in a wine vat
cuvette [kyvet] *f* basin, pan; bulb (*of a thermometer*); (chem, phot) tray
cuvier [kyvje] *m* washtub
C.V. [seve] *m* (letterword) (**cheval-vapeur**) hp, horsepower
cyanamide [sjanamid] *f* cyanamide
cyanose [sjanoz] *f* cyanosis
cyanure [sjanyr] *m* cyanide
cyclable [siklabl] *adj* reserved for bicycles
cycle [sikl] *m* cycle
cyclique [siklik] *adj* cyclic(al)

cycliste [siklist] *mf* cyclist
cyclomoteur [siklomotœr] *m* motorbike
cyclone [siklon] *m* cyclone
cyclope [siklɔp] *m* cyclops
cyclotron [siklotrɔ̃] *m* cyclotron
cygne [siɲ] *m* swan
cylindrage [silɛ̃draʒ] *m* rolling (*of roads, gardens, etc.*); calendering, mangling
cylindre [silɛ̃dr] *m* cylinder; roller (*e.g., of rolling mill*); steam roller
cylindrée [silɛ̃dre] *f* piston displacement
cylindrer [silɛ̃dre] *tr* to roll (*a road, garden, etc.*); to calender, to mangle
cylindrique [silɛ̃drik] *adj* cylindrical
cymbale [sɛ̃bal] *f* cymbal
cynique [sinik] *adj* & *m* cynic
cynisme [sinism] *m* cynicism
cyprès [sipre] *m* cypress
cyrillique [sirilik] *adj* Cyrillic
cytoplasme [sitoplasm] *m* cytoplasm
czar [ksar] *m* czar
czarine [ksarin] *f* czarina

D

D, d [de] *m invar* fourth letter of the French alphabet
d' = de before vowel or mute **h**
d'abord [dabɔr] see **abord**
dactylo [daktilo] *mf* (coll) typist
dactylographe [daktilograf] *mf* typist
dactylographier [daktilografje] *tr* to type
dactyloscopie [daktiloskɔpi] *f* finger-printing
dada [dada] *m* hobby-horse; hobby, fad, pet subject; **enfourcher son dada** to ride one's hobby
dague [dag] *f* dagger; first antler; tusk
dahlia [dalja] *m* dahlia
daigner [deɲe] *intr*—**daigner** + *inf* to deign to, to condescend to + *inf*; **daignez** please
d'ailleurs [dajœr] see **ailleurs**
daim [dɛ̃] *m* fallow deer; suede
daine [den] *f* doe
dais [de] *m* canopy
dalle [dal] *f* flagstone, slab, paving block; **se rincer la dalle** (slang) to wet one's whistle
daller [dale] *tr* to pave with flagstones
dalto·nien [daltɔnjɛ̃] **-nienne** [njen] *adj* color-blind ‖ *mf* color-blind person
dam [dɑ̃] *m*—**au dam de** to the detriment of
damas [damɑ] *m* damask ‖ (*cap*) [damɑs] *f* Damascus
damasquiner [damaskine] *tr* to dama-scene
damas·sé -sée [damase] *adj* & *m* damask
dame [dam] *f* dame; lady; tamp, tamper; rowlock; (cards, chess) queen; (checkers) king; **aller à dame** (checkers) to crown a man king; (chess) to

queen a pawn; **dames** (public sign) ladies ‖ *interj* for heaven's sake!
damer [dame] *tr* to tamp (*the earth*); (checkers) to crown (*a checker*); (chess) to queen (*a pawn*); **damer le pion à qn** to outwit s.o.
damier [damje] *m* checkerboard
damnation [dɑnasjɔ̃] *f* damnation
dam·né -née [dɑne] *adj* & *mf* damned
damner [dɑne] *tr* to damn
damoi·seau [damwazo] **-selle** [zel] *mf* (*pl* **-seaux**) (archaic) young member of the nobility ‖ *m* lady's man ‖ *f* (archaic) damsel
dancing [dɑ̃siŋ] *m* dance hall
dandiner [dɑ̃dine] *tr* to dandle ‖ *ref* to waddle along
dandy [dɑ̃di] *m* dandy
Danemark [danmark] *m*—**le Danemark** Denmark
danger [dɑ̃ʒe] *m* danger
dange·reux [dɑ̃ʒrø] **-reuse** [røz] *adj* dangerous
da·nois [danwa] **-noise** [nwaz] *adj* Danish ‖ *m* Danish (*language*) ‖ (*cap*) *mf* Dane
dans [dɑ̃] *prep* in; into; **boire dans un verre** to drink out of a glass; **dans la suite** later
danse [dɑ̃s] *f* dance; **danse guerrière** war dance
danser [dɑ̃se] *tr* & *intr* to dance; **faire danser** to mistreat
dan·seur [dɑ̃sœr] **-seuse** [søz] *mf* dancer; **danseur de corde** tightrope walker; **en danseuse** in a standing position (*taken by cyclist*)
Danube [danyb] *m* Danube
d'après [dapre] see **après**
dard [dar] *m* dart; sting; snake's tongue; harpoon

darder [darde] *tr* to dart, to hurl

dare-dare [dardar] *adv* (coll) on the double

darse [dars] *f* wet dock

date [dat] *f* date; **de fraîche date recent; de longue date** of long standing; **en date de** from; **faire date** to mark an epoch; **prendre date** to make an appointment

dater [date] *tr* & *intr* to date; **à dater de** dating from

datif [datif] *m* dative

datte [dat] *f* date

dattier [datje] *m* date palm

daube [dob] *f* braised meat; **en daube** braised

dauber [dobe] *tr* to braise; to heckle; to slander; (coll) to pummel || *intr*—**dauber sur qn** to heckle s.o., to slander s.o.

dau·beur [dobœr] **-beuse** [bøz] *mf* heckler

dauphin [dofɛ̃] *m* dolphin; dauphin

dauphine [dofin] *f* dauphiness

dauphinelle [dofinɛl] *f* delphinium

davantage [davɑ̃taʒ] §90 *adv* more; any more; any longer; **ne . . . davantage** no more; **pas davantage** no longer

de [də] §77, §78, §79 *prep* of, from; with, e.g., **frapper d'une épée** to strike with a sword; (to indicate the agent with the passive voice) by, e.g., **ils sont aimés de tous** they are loved by all; (to indicate the point of departure) from, e.g., **de Paris à Madrid** from Paris to Madrid; (to indicate the point of arrival) for, e.g., **le train de Paris** the train for Paris; (with a following infinitive after certain verbs) to, e.g., **il essaie d'écrire la lettre** he is trying to write the letter; (with a following infinitive after an adjective used with the impersonal expression **il est**) to, e.g., **il est facile de chanter cette chanson** it is easy to sing that song; (after **changer, se souvenir, avoir besoin,** etc.), e.g., **changer de vêtements** to change clothes; (after a comparative and before a numeral) than, e.g., **plus de quarante** more than forty; (to express the indefinite plural or partitive idea), e.g., **de l'eau** water, some water; (to form prepositional phrases with some adverbs), e.g., **auprès de vous** near you; (with the historical infinitive), e.g., **et chacun de pleurer** and everyone cried

dé [de] *m* die (*singular of dice*); thimble; domino; golf tee; **dés** dice

déambuler [deɑ̃byle] *intr* to stroll

débâcle [debɑkl] *m* debacle; breakup (*of ice*)

débâcler [debɑkle] *intr* to break up (*said of ice in a river*)

déballage [debalaʒ] *m* unpacking; cut-rate merchandise (*sold by street vendor*)

déballer [debale] *tr* to unpack (*merchandise*); to display (*merchandise*)

débandade [debɑ̃dad] *f* rout, stampede; **à la débandade** in confusion, helter-skelter

débander [debɑ̃de] *tr* to rout, to stampede; to slacken (*s.th. under tension*); to unwind; **débander les yeux à qn** to take the blindfold from s.o.'s eyes || *intr* to flee, to stampede

débaptiser [debatize] *tr* to change the name of, to rename

débarbouiller [debarbuje] *tr* to wash the face of

débarcadère [debarkader] *m* wharf, dock, landing platform

débarder [debarde] *tr* to unload

débardeur [debardœr] *m* stevedore, longshoreman

débar·qué ·quée [debarke] *adj* disembarking || *mf* new arrival || *m* disembarkment; **au débarqué** on arrival

débarquement [debarkəmɑ̃] *m* disembarkation

débarquer [debarke] *m*—**au débarquer de qn** at the moment of s.o.'s arrival || *tr* to unload; to lower (*a lifeboat, seaplane, etc.*); (coll) to sack (*s.o.*) || *intr* to disembark, get off

débarras [debara] *m* catchall

débarrasser [debarase] *tr* to disencumber, to disentangle; to clear (*the table*); to rid (*of* || *ref*—**se débarrasser de** to get rid of

débarrer [debare] *tr* to unbar

débat [deba] *m* debate; dispute; **débats** discussion (*in a meeting*); proceedings (*in a court*)

débâter [debate] *tr* to unsaddle

débattre [debatr] §7 *tr* to debate, argue, discuss; to haggle over (*a price*); to question (*items in an account*) || *ref* to struggle; to be debated

débauche [deboʃ] *f* debauch, debauchery; riot (*e.g., of colors*); overeating; striking, quitting work

débaucher [deboʃe] *tr* to debauch; to induce (*a worker*) to strike; to lay off (*workers*); to steal (*a worker*) from another employer || *ref* to become debauched

débile [debil] *adj* weak || *mf* mental defective

débilité [debilite] *f* debility

débiliter [debilite] *tr* to debilitate

débiner [debine] *tr* (slang) to run (*s.o.*) down || *ref* (slang) to fly the coop

débit [debi] *m* debit; retail sale; shop; cutting up (*of wood*); output; way of speaking

débiter [debite] *tr* to debit; to cut up in pieces; to retail; to produce; to speak (*one's part*); to repeat thoughtlessly

débi·teur [debitœr] **-trice** [tris] *adj* debit (*account, balance*); delivery (*spool*) || *mf* debtor || **-teur** [tœr] **-teuse** [tøz] *mf* gossip, talebearer; salesclerk

déblai [deble] *m* excavation; **déblais** rubble, fill

déblaiement [deblemɑ̃] *m* clearing away

déblatérer [deblatere] §10 *tr* to bluster or fling (*threats, abuse*) || *intr*—**déblatérer contre** to rail at

déblayer [debleje] §49 *tr* to clear, to clear away

débloquer [deblɔke] *tr* to unblock; to unfreeze (*funds, credits, etc.*)

déboire [debwar] *m* unpleasant after-taste; disappointment

déboisement [debwazmɑ̃] *m* deforestation

déboîter [debwate] *tr* to disconnect (*pipe*); to dislocate (*a shoulder*) ‖ *intr* to move into another lane (*said of automobile*); (naut) to haul (*out of a line*)

débonder [debɔ̃de] *tr* to unbung

débonnaire [debɔner] *adj* good-natured, easygoing; (Bib) meek

débor·dant -dante [debɔrdɑ̃] [dɑ̃t] *adj* overflowing

débor·dé -dée [debɔrde] *adj* overwhelmed

déborder [debɔrde] *tr* to extend beyond, to jut out over; to trim the border from; to overwhelm; to untuck (*a bed*); (mil) to outflank ‖ *intr* to overflow; (naut) to shove off

débotté [debɔte] *m*—**au débotté** immediately upon arrival, at once

débouché [debuʃe] *m* outlet; opening (*for trade; of an attack*)

déboucher [debuʃe] *tr* to free from obstruction; to uncork ‖ *intr*—**déboucher dans** to empty into (*said of river*); **déboucher sur** to open onto, to emerge into

déboucler [debukle] *tr* to unbuckle; to take the curls out of

débouler [debule] *tr* to fly down (*e.g., a stairway*) ‖ *intr* to run suddenly out of cover (*said of rabbits*); to dash; **débouler dans** to roll down (*a stairway*)

déboulonner [debulone] *tr* to unbolt; (coll) to ruin, have fired; (coll) to debunk

débourber [deburbe] *tr* to clear of mud, to clean

débourrer [debure] *tr* to unhair (*a hide*); to remove the stuffing from (*a chair*); to knock (*a pipe*) clean

débours [debur] *m* disbursement; **rentrer dans ses débours** to recover one's investment

déboursement [debursmɑ̃] *m* disbursing

débourser [deburse] *tr* to disburse

debout [dəbu] *adv* upright, on end; standing; up (*out of bed*)

déboutonner [debutone] *tr* to unbutton; **à ventre déboutonné** immoderately ‖ *ref* (coll) to get something off one's chest

débrail·lé -lée [debraje] *adj* untidy, mussed up, unkempt; loose (*morals*); vulgar (*speech*) ‖ *m* untidiness

débrancher [debrɑ̃ʃe] *tr* to switch (*railroad cars*) to a siding; (elec) to disconnect

débrayage [debrejaʒ] *m* (aut) clutch release; (coll) walkout

débrayer [debreje] §49 *tr* to disengage, throw out (*the clutch*) ‖ *intr* to throw out the clutch; (coll) to walk out (*said of strikers*)

débri·dé -dée [debride] *adj* unbridled

débris [debri] *mpl* debris; remains

débrouil·lard [debrujar] **débrouil·larde** [debrujard] *adj* (coll) resourceful ‖ *mf* (coll) smart customer

débrouiller [debruje] *tr* to disentangle, to unravel; to clear up (*a mystery*); to make out (*e.g., a signature*); (coll) to teach (*s.o.*) to be resourceful ‖ *ref* to clear (*said of sky*); (coll) to manage to get along, to take care of oneself; (coll) to extricate oneself (*from a difficult situation*)

débucher [debyʃe] *tr* to flush out (*game*) ‖ *intr* to run out of cover (*said of game*)

débusquer [debyske] *tr* to flush out (*game; the enemy*)

début [deby] *m* debut; beginning, commencement; opening play

débu·tant [debytɑ̃] **-tante** [tɑ̃t] *adj* beginning ‖ *mf* beginner; newcomer (*e.g., to stage or screen*) ‖ *f* debutante

débuter [debyte] *intr* to make one's debut, to begin; to start up a business; to make the opening play; **en deçà de** on this side of

deçà [dəsa] *adv*—**deçà delà** here and there; **en deçà de** on this side of

décacheter [dekaʃte] §34 *tr* to unseal

décade [dekad] *f* period of ten days; (hist, lit) decade

décadence [dekadɑ̃s] *f* decadence

déca·dent [dekadɑ̃] **-dente** [dɑ̃t] *adj* & *mf* decadent

décaféi·né -née [dekafeine] *adj* decaffeinated, caffeine-free

décagénaires [dekaʒener] *mfpl* teenagers

décaisser [dekese] *tr* to uncrate; to disburse, pay out

décalage [dekalaʒ] *m* unkeying; shift; slippage; (aer) stagger

décalcomanie [dekalkɔmani] *f* decal

décaler [dekale] *tr* to unkey; to shift

décalquage [dekalkaʒ] or **décalque** [dekalk] *m* decal

décalquer [dekalke] *tr* to transfer (*a decal*) onto paper, canvas, metal, etc.; **décalquer sur** to transfer (*a decal*) onto (*e.g., paper*)

décamper [dekɑ̃pe] *intr* to decamp

décanat [dekana] *m* deanship

décanter [dekɑ̃te] *tr* to decant

décapant [dekapɑ̃] *m* scouring agent

décaper [dekape] *tr* to scour, scale

décapiter [dekapite] *tr* to behead, to decapitate; to top (*a tree*)

décapotable [dekapɔtabl] *adj* & *f* (aut) convertible

déca·ti -tie [dekati] *adj* haggard, worn-out, faded

décatir [dekatir] *tr* to steam (*cloth*)

décaver [dekave] *tr* (coll) to fleece

décéder [desede] §10 *intr* (aux: ÊTRE) to die (*said of human being*)

décèlement [deselmɑ̃] *m* disclosure

déceler [desle] §2 *tr* to uncover, detect; to betray (*confusion*)

décélération [deselerasjɔ̃] *f* deceleration

décembre [desɑ̃br] *m* December

décennie [deseni] *f* decade

dé·cent [desã] **-cente** [sãt] *adj* decent

décentraliser [desãtralize] *tr* to decentralize

déception [desɛpsjɔ̃] *f* disappointment

décernement [desɛrnəmã] *m* awarding

décerner [desɛrne] *tr* to award (*a prize*); to confer (*an honor*); to issue (*a writ*)

décès [desɛ] *m* decease, demise

déce·vant [desvã] **-vante** [vãt] *adj* disappointing; deceptive

décevoir [desvwar] §59 *tr* to disappoint; to deceive

déchaînement [deʃɛnmã] *m* unchaining, unleashing; outburst, wave

déchaîner [deʃene] *tr* to unchain, let loose || *ref* to fly into a rage; to break out (*said of storm*)

déchanter [deʃãte] *intr* (coll) to sing a different tune

décharge [deʃarʒ] *f* discharge; drain; rubbish heap; storeroom, shed; **à décharge** for the defense

déchargement [deʃarʒəmã] *m* unloading

décharger [deʃarʒe] §38 *tr* to discharge; to unload; to unburden; to exculpate (*a defendant*) || *ref* to vent one's anger; to go off (*said of gun*); to run down (*said of battery*); **se décharger de q.ch. sur qn** to shift the responsibility for s.th. on s.o.

déchargeur [deʃarʒœr] *m* porter (*e.g., in a market*); dock hand

déchar·né **-née** [deʃarne] *adj* emaciated, skinny, bony

décharner [deʃarne] *tr* to strip the flesh from; to emaciate || *ref* to waste away

déchaus·sé·sée [deʃose] *adj* barefoot

déchausser [deʃose] *tr* to take the shoes off of (*s.o.*); to expose the roots of (*a tree, a tooth*) || *ref* to take off one's shoes; to shrink (*said of gums*)

déchéance [deʃeãs] *f* downfall; lapse, forfeiture (*of a right*); expiration, term (*of a note or loan*)

déchet [deʃɛ] *m* loss, decrease; **déchet de route** loss in transit; **déchets** waste products

décheveler [deʃəvle] §34 *tr* to dishevel, to muss (*s.o.'s hair*)

déchiffonner [deʃifone] *tr* to iron (*wrinkled material*)

déchiffrable [deʃifrabl] *adj* legible; decipherable

déchiffrement [deʃifrəmã] *m* deciphering, decoding; sight-reading

déchiffrer [deʃifre] *tr* to decipher; to sight-read (*music*)

déchif·freur [deʃifrœr] **déchif·freuse** [deʃifrøz] *mf* decipherer, decoder; sight-reader

déchique·té·tée [deʃikte] *adj* jagged, torn

déchiqueter [deʃikte] §34 *tr* to cut into strips; to shred; to slash

déchi·rant **-rante** [deʃirã] *adj* heartrending

déchi·ré·rée [deʃire] *adj* torn; sorry

déchirer [deʃire] *tr* to tear, to tear up; to split (*a country; one's eardrums*);

to pick (*s.o.'s character*) to pieces || *ref* (with *dat* of *reflex pron*) to skin (*e.g., one's knee*)

déchirure [deʃirur] *f* tear, rent; sprain

déchoir [deʃwar] (usually used only in: *inf*; *pp* **déchu**; sometimes used in: *pres ind* **déchois**, etc.; *fut* **déchoirai**, etc.; *cond* **déchoirais**, etc.) *intr* (aux: AVOIR or ÊTRE) to fall (*from high estate*); to decline, to fail

dé·chu·chue [deʃy] *adj* fallen; deprived (*of rights*); expired (*insurance policy*)

décider [deside] *tr* to decide, to decide on; **décider qn à** + *inf* to persuade s.o. to + *inf* || *intr* to decide; **décider de** to decide, determine the outcome of, e.g., **le coup a décidé de la partie** the trick decided the (outcome of the) game; **décider de** + *inf* to decide to + *inf* || *ref* to decide, to make up one's mind, to resolve; **se décider à** + *inf* to decide to + *inf*

déci·mal·male [desimal] *adj* (*pl* **-maux** [mo]) decimal || *f* decimal

décimer [desime] *tr* to decimate

déci·sif [desizif] **-sive** [ziv] *adj* decisive

décision [desizjɔ̃] *f* decision; decisiveness

déclama·teur [deklamatœr] **-trice** [tris] *adj* bombastic || *mf* declaimer

déclamatoire [deklamatwar] *adj* declamatory

déclamer [deklame] *tr* to declaim || *intr* to rant; **déclamer contre** to inveigh against

déclara·tif [deklaratif] **-tive** [tiv] *adj* declarative

déclaration [deklarasjɔ̃] *f* declaration; **déclaration de revenus** income-tax return

déclarer [deklare] *tr & intr* to declare || *ref* to declare oneself; to arise, break out, occur

déclassement [deklasmã] *m* disarrangement; drop in social status; transfer to another class (*on ship, train, etc.*); dismantling; demoting

déclasser [deklase] *tr* to disarrange; to dismantle; to demote

déclenchement [deklãʃmã] *m* releasing; launching (*of an attack*)

déclencher [deklãʃe] *tr* to unlatch, disengage; to release (*the shutter*); to open (*fire*); to launch (*an attack*)

déclencheur [deklãʃœr] *m* (mach, phot) release

déclic [deklik] *m* pawl, catch; hair trigger

déclin [deklɛ̃] *m* decline

déclinaison [deklinɛzɔ̃] *f* (astr) declination; (gram) declension

décliner [dekline] *tr & intr* to decline

déclive [dekliv] *adj* sloping || *f* slope

déclivité [deklivite] *f* declivity

dé·clos [deklo] **-close** [kloz] *adj* in bloom

décocher [dekɔʃe] *tr* to let fly; to flash (*a smile*)

décoder [dekɔde] *tr* to decode

décoiffer [dekwafe] *tr* to loosen or muss the hair of; to uncap (*a bottle*)

|| *ref* to muss one's hair; to take one's hair down

décoincer [dekwɛ̃se] §51 *tr* to unwedge, to loosen (*a jammed part*)

décolérer [dekɔlere] §10 *intr* to calm down

décollage [dekɔlaʒ] *m* unsticking, ungluing; takeoff (*of airplane*)

décoller [dekɔle] *tr* to unstick, detach || *intr* (aer) to take off

décolletage [dekɔltaʒ] *m* low-cut neck; screw cutting; topping

décolle‧té -tée [dekɔlte] *adj* décolleté || *m* low-cut neckline; bare neck and shoulders

décolleter [dekɔlte] §34 *tr* to cut the neck of (*a dress*) low; to bare the neck and shoulders of || *ref* to wear a low-necked dress

décoloration [dekɔlɔrasjɔ̃] *f* discoloration

décolorer [dekɔlɔre] *tr & ref* to bleach; to fade

décombres [dekɔ̃br] *mpl* debris, ruins

décommander [dekɔ̃mɑ̃de] *tr* to cancel an order for; to call off (*a dinner*); to cancel the invitation to (*a guest*) || *ref* to cancel a meeting

décompléter [dekɔ̃plete] §10 *tr* to break up (*a set*)

décomposer [dekɔ̃poze] *tr & ref* to decompose

décomposition [dekɔ̃pozisjɔ̃] *f* decomposition

décompression [dekɔ̃presjɔ̃] *f* decompression

décomprimer [dekɔ̃prime] *tr* to decompress

décompte [dekɔ̃t] *m* itemized statement; discount (*to be deducted from total*); disappointment

décompter [dekɔ̃te] *tr* to deduct (*a sum from an account*) || *intr* to strike the wrong hour

déconcerter [dekɔ̃serte] *tr* to disconcert

décon‧fit [dekɔ̃fi] **-fite** [fit] *adj* discomfited, baffled, confused

déconfiture [dekɔ̃fityr] *f* discomfiture; downfall, rout; business failure

décongeler [dekɔ̃ʒle] §2 *tr* to thaw; to defrost

décongestionner [dekɔ̃ʒɛstjɔne] *tr* to relieve congestion in

déconseiller [dekɔ̃seje] *tr* to dissuade; **déconseiller q.ch. à qn** to advise s.o. against s.th. || *intr*—**déconseiller à qn de** + *inf* to advise s.o. against + *ger*

déconsidération [dekɔ̃siderasjɔ̃] *f* disrepute

déconsidérer [dekɔ̃sidere] §10 *tr* to bring into disrepute, to discredit

déconsigner [dekɔ̃siɲe] *tr* to take (*one's baggage*) out of the checkroom; to free (*soldiers*) from detention

décontenancer [dekɔ̃tnɑ̃se] §51 *tr* to discountenance, abash || *ref* to lose one's self-assurance

décontrac‧té -tée [dekɔ̃trakte] *adj* relaxed, at ease; indifferent

décontracter [dekɔ̃trakte] *tr* to loosen

up (*one's muscles*) || *intr* to stretch one's muscles; to relax

déconvenue [dekɔ̃vny] *f* disappointment, mortification

décor [dekɔr] *m* décor, decoration; (theat) setting; **décor découpé** cutout; **décors** (theat) set, stage setting

décora‧teur [dekɔratœr] **-trice** [tris] *mf* interior decorator; stage designer

décora‧tif [dekɔratif] **-tive** [tiv] *adj* decorative, ornamental

décoration [dekɔrasjɔ̃] *f* decoration

décorum [dekɔrɔm] *m invar* decorum

découcher [dekuʃe] *intr* to sleep away from home

découdre [dekudr] §13 *tr* to unstitch, to rip up; to gore || *intr*—**en découdre** to cross swords || *ref* to come unsewn, to rip at the seam

découler [dekule] *intr* to trickle; to proceed, arise, be derived

découpage [dekupaʒ] *m* shooting script

découper [dekupe] *tr* to carve (*e.g., a turkey*); to cut out (*a design*); to indent (*the coast*) || *ref*—**se découper sur** to stand out against (*the horizon*)

décou‧plé -plée [dekuple] *adj* well-built, brawny

découpler [dekuple] *tr* to unleash

découpure [dekupyr] *f* cutting out; ornamental cutout; indentation (*in coast*)

découragement [dekuraʒmɑ̃] *m* discouragement

décourager [dekuraʒe] §38 *tr* to discourage || *ref* to become discouraged

décours [dekur] *m* wane

décou‧su -sue [dekuzy] *adj* unsewn; disjointed, unsystematic; incoherent (*words*); desultory (*remarks*)

décou‧vert [dekuver] **-verte** [vert] *adj* uncovered, open, exposed || *m* deficit; overdraft || *f* uncovering; discovery

décou‧vreur [dekuvrœr] **-vreuse** [vrøz] *mf* discoverer

découvrir [dekuvrir] §65 *tr* to discover; to discern (*in the distance*); to pick out (*with a searchlight*); to uncover || *intr* to become visible (*said of rocks at low tide*) || *ref* to take off one's hat; to lower one's guard; to clear up (*said of the sky*); to say what one is thinking; to come to light, to be revealed

décrasser [dekrase] *tr* to clean; to polish up

décré‧pit [dekrepi] **-pite** [pit] *adj* decrepit

décret [dekre] *m* decree

décrier [dekrije] *tr* to decry, disparage, run down

décrire [dekrir] §25 *tr* to describe

décrocher [dekrɔʃe] *tr* to unhook, take down; (coll) to wangle; **décrocher la timbale** (coll) to hit the jackpot || *intr* to withdraw

décrochez-moi-ça [dekrɔʃemwasa] *m invar* (coll) secondhand clothing store

décroît [dekrwa] *m* last quarter (*of moon*)

décroître [dekrwatr] §17 (*pp* **décru**; *pres ind* **décrois**, etc.; *pret* **décrus**, etc.) *intr* to decrease; to shorten (*said of days*); to fall (*said of river*)

décrotter [dekrɔte] *tr* to remove mud from; (coll) to teach how to behave

décrotteur [dekrɔtœr] *m* shoeshine boy

décrottoir [dekrɔtwar] *m* doormat; scraper (*for shoes*)

décrue [dekry] *f* fall, drop, subsiding

décrypter [dekripte] *tr* to decipher

déculotter [dekylɔte] *tr* to take the pants off of || *ref* to take off one's pants

décuple [dekypl] *adj & m* tenfold

décupler [dekyple] *tr & intr* to increase tenfold

dédaigner [dedɛɲe] *tr* to disdain; to reject (*e.g., an offer*); **dédaigner de** + *inf* not to condescend to + *inf*

dédai·gneux [dedɛɲø] **-gneuse** [ɲøz] *adj* disdainful

dédain [dedɛ̃] *m* disdain

dedans [dɑdɑ̃] *m* inside; **en dedans** inside || *adv* inside, within; **mettre dedans** (coll) to take in, to fool

dédicace [dedikas] *f* dedication

dédicacer [dedikase] §51 *tr* to dedicate, to autograph

dédicatoire [dedikatwar] *adj* dedicatory

dédier [dedje] *tr* to dedicate; to offer (*e.g., a collection to a museum*)

dédire [dedir] §41 *tr*—**dédire qn** to disavow s.o.'s words or actions || *ref* to make a retraction, to back down; **se dédire de** to go back on, to fail to keep

dédit [dedi] *m* penalty (*for breaking a contract*); breach of contract

dédommagement [dedɔmaʒmɑ̃] *m* compensation, damages, indemnity

dédommager [dedɔmaʒe] §38 *tr* to compensate for a loss, to indemnify

dédouaner [dedwane] *tr* to clear through customs; to rehabilitate (*a politician, statesman, etc.*)

dédoublement [dedublǝmɑ̃] *m* splitting; subdivision; unfolding

dédoubler [deduble] *tr* to divide or split in two; to remove the lining from; to unfold; to put on another section of (*a train*)

déduction [dedyksjɔ̃] *f* deduction

déduire [dedɥir] §19 *tr* to deduce; to infer; (com) to deduct

déesse [dees] *f* goddess

défaillance [defajɑ̃s] *f* failure, failing; faint (*of memory*); lapse (*of memory*); nonappearance (*of witness*); **défaillance cardiaque** heart failure; **sans défaillance** unflinching

défail·lant [defajɑ̃] **défail·lante** [defajɑ̃t] *adj* failing, faltering

défaillir [defajir] §69 *intr* to fail; to falter, weaken, flag; to faint

défaire [defer] §29 *tr* to undo; to untie, unwrap, unpack; to rearrange; to let down (*one's hair*); to rid; to defeat, to rout; to wear (*s.o.*) down, to tire (*s.o.*) out || *ref* to come undone; **se défaire de** to get rid of

dé·fait [defe] **-faite** [fet] *adj* undone, untied; loose; disheveled; drawn

(*countenance*) || *f* defeat; disposal, turnover; (fig) loophole

défaitisme [defetism] *m* defeatism

défaitiste [defetist] *mf* defeatist

défalcation [defalkasjɔ̃] *f* deduction

défalquer [defalke] *tr* to deduct

défaufiler [defofile] *tr* to untack

défausser [defose] *tr* to straighten || *ref*—**se défausser (de)** to discard

défaut [defo] *m* defect, fault; lack (*of knowledge, memory, etc.*); flaw; chink (*in armor*); **à défaut de** in default of, lacking; **faire défaut à** to abandon, fail (*e.g., one's friends*); (law) to default; **mettre en défaut** to foil

défaveur [defavœr] *f* disfavor

défavorable [defavɔrabl] *adj* unfavorable

défavoriser [defavɔrize] *tr* to handicap, to put at a disadvantage

défécation [defekasjɔ̃] *f* defecation

défec·tif [defektif] **-tive** [tiv] *adj* (gram) defective

défection [defeksjɔ̃] *f* defection; **faire défection** to defect

défec·tueux [defektɥø] **-tueuse** [tɥøz] *adj* defective, faulty

défectuosité [defektɥozite] *f* imperfection

défen·deur [defɑ̃dœr] **-deresse** [dres] *mf* defendant

défendre [defɑ̃dr] *tr* to defend; to protect (*e.g., against the cold*); **à son corps défendant** in self-defense; against one's will; **défendre q.ch. à qn** to forbid s.o. s.th. || *intr*—**défendre à qn de** + *inf* to forbid s.o. to + *inf* || *ref* to defend oneself; (coll) to hold one's own; **se défendre de** to deny (*e.g., having said s.th.*); to refrain from, to keep from

défen·du·due [defɑ̃dy] *adj* forbidden

défense [defɑ̃s] *f* defense; tusk; **défense passive** civil defense (*against air raids*); (public signs): **défense d'afficher** post no bills; **défense de dépasser** no passing; **défense de déposer les ordures** no dumping, no littering; **défense de doubler** no passing; **défense de faire des ordures** commit no nuisance; **défense de fumer** no smoking; **défense d'entrer** private, keep out, no admittance

défenseur [defɑ̃sœr] *m* defender; lawyer for the defense; stand-by

défen·sif [defɑ̃sif] **-sive** [siv] *adj & f* defensive

déférence [deferɑ̃s] *f* deference

défé·rent [deferɑ̃] **-rente** [rɑ̃t] *adj* deferential

déférer [defere] §10 *tr* to confer, award; to refer (*a case to a court*); **déférer en justice** to haul into court || *intr* to comply; **déférer à** to defer to, to comply with

déferler [deferle] *tr* to unfurl; to set (*the sails of a ship*) || *intr* to spread out (*said of a crowd*); to break (*said of waves*)

défeuiller [defœje] *tr* to defoliate || *ref* to lose its leaves

défi [defi] *m* challenge, dare; **défi à**

l'autorité defiance of authority; **porter un défi à** to defy; **relever un défi** to take a dare

défiance [defjãs] *f* distrust

dé·fiant [defjã] **-fiante** [fjãt] *adj* distrustful

déficeler [defisle] §34 *tr* to untie

déficience [defisjãs] *f* deficiency

défi·cient [defisjã] **-ciente** [sjãt] *adj* deficient

déficit [defisit] *m* deficit

déficitaire [defisiter] *adj* deficit; meager (*crop*); lean (*year*)

défier [defje] §38 *tr* to challenge; to defy (*death, time, etc.*); **défier qn de** to dare s.o. to || *ref*—**se défier de** to mistrust

défiger [defiʒe] §38 *tr* to liquefy

défiguration [defigyrasjõ] *f* disfigurement; defacement

défigurer [defigyre] *tr* to disfigure; to deface; to distort

défilé [defile] *m* defile (*in mountains*); parade, procession, line of march

défilement [defilmã] *m* (mil) defilade, cover

défiler [defile] *tr* to unstring; (mil) to put under cover || *intr* to march by, to parade, to defile || *ref* to come unstrung; to take cover; (coll) to gold-brick

défi·ni **-nie** [defini] *adj* definite; defined

définir [definir] *tr* to define || *ref* to be defined

définissable [definisabl] *adj* definable

défini·tif [definitif] **-tive** [tiv] *adj* definitive; standard (*edition*); **en définitive** in short, all things considered

définition [definisjõ] *f* definition

définitivement [definitivmã] *adv* definitively, for good, permanently

déflation [deflasjõ] *f* deflation (*of currency*); sudden drop (*in wind*)

défleurir [deflœrir] *tr* to deflower, to strip of flowers || *intr & ref* to lose its flowers

déflexion [defleksjõ] *f* deflection

défloraison [deflɔrezõ] *f* dropping of petals

déflorer [deflɔre] *tr* to deflower

défon·cé **-cée** [defõse] *adj* battered, smashed, crumpled; bumpy

défoncer [defõse] §51 *tr* to batter in; to stave in (*a cask*); to remove the seat of (*a chair*); to break up (*ground; a road*) || *ref* to be broken up (*said of road*)

déformation [defɔrmasjõ] *f* deformation, distortion; **déformation professionnelle** narrow professionalism

défor·mé **-mée** [defɔrme] *adj* out of shape; rough (*road*)

déformer [defɔrme] *tr* to deform, distort || *ref* to become deformed

défoulement [defulmã] *m* (psychoanal) insight, recall; (coll) relief

défrai·chi **-chie** [defreʃi] *adj* dingy, faded

défraîchir [defreʃir] *tr* to make stale, to fade

défrayer [defreje] §49 *tr* to defray the

expenses of (*s.o.*); **défrayer la conversation** to be the subject of the conversation

défricher [defriʃe] *tr* to reclaim; to clear up (*a puzzler*)

défricheur [defriʃœr] *m* pioneer, explorer

défriser [defrize] *tr & ref* to uncurl

défroncer [defrõse] §51 *tr* to remove the wrinkles from

défroque [defrɔk] *f* piece of discarded clothing

défroquer [defrɔke] *tr* to unfrock || *ref* to give up the frock

dé·funt [defœ̃] **-funte** [fœ̃t] *adj & mf* deceased

déga·gé **-gée** [degaʒe] *adj* breezy, jaunty, nonchalant; free, detached

dégagement [degaʒmã] *m* disengagement; clearing, relieving of congestion; liberation (*e.g., of heat*); exit; retraction (*of promise*); redemption, taking out of hock

dégager [degaʒe] §38 *tr* to disengage; to free, clear, release; to draw, extract (*the moral or essential points*); to give off, liberate; to take back (*one's word*); to redeem, to take out of hock

dégaine [degen] *f* (coll) awkward bearing; ridiculous posture

dégainer [degene] *tr* to unsheathe || *intr* to take up a sword

dégar·ni **-nie** [degarni] *adj* empty, depleted, stripped

dégarnir [degarnir] *tr* to clear (*a table*); to withdraw soldiers from (*a sector*); to prune || *ref* to thin out

dégât [dega] *m* damage, havoc

dégauchir [degoʃir] *tr* to smooth out the rough edges of (*stone, wood; an inexperienced person*)

dégel [deʒel] *m* thaw

dégeler [deʒle] §2 *tr* to thaw, to defrost; to loosen up, relax || *intr* to thaw out; **il dégèle** it is thawing

dégéné·ré **-rée** [deʒenere] *adj & mf* degenerate

dégénérer [deʒenere] §10 *intr* to degenerate

dégénérescence [deʒeneresãs] *f* degeneration

dégingan·dé **-dée** [deʒẽgãde] *adj* gangling, ungainly

dégivrage [deʒivraʒ] *m* defrosting

dégivrer [deʒivre] *tr* to defrost, to deice

dégivreur [deʒivrœr] *m* defroster, deicer

déglacer [deglase] §51 *tr* to deice; to remove the glaze from (*paper*)

dégommer [degɔme] *tr* to ungum; (coll) to fire (*s.o.*)

dégon·flé **-flée** [degõfle] *adj* flat (*tire*)

dégonflement [degõflemã] *m* deflation

dégonfler [degõfle] *tr* to deflate || *ref* to go flat; to go down, to subside (*said of swelling*); (slang) to lose one's nerve

dégorger [degɔrʒe] §38 *tr* to disgorge; to unstop, open (*a pipe*); to scour (*e.g., wool*) || *intr* to discharge, to overflow

dégour·di -die [degurdi] *adj* limbered up, lively, sharp, adroit ‖ *mf* smart aleck

dégourdir [degurdir] *tr* to remove stiffness or numbness from (*e.g., legs*); to stretch (*one's limbs*); to take the chill off; to teach (*s.o.*) the ropes, to polish (*s.o.*) ‖ *ref* to limber up

dégoût [degu] *m* distaste, dislike

dégoû·tant -tante [degutɑ̃] **-tante** [tɑ̃t] *adj* disgusting, distasteful

dégoû·té -tée [degute] *adj* fastidious, hard to please ‖ *mf* finicky person

dégoûter [degute] *tr* to disgust; **dégoûter qn de** to make s.o. dislike ‖ *ref* to become fed up

dégoutter [degute] *intr* to drip, trickle

dégradation [degradasjɔ̃] *f* degradation; defacement; shading off, graduation; worsening (*of a situation*); (mil) demotion; **dégradation civique** loss of civil rights

dégrader [degrade] *tr* to degrade, to bring down; to deface; to shade off, to graduate; (mil) to demote, to break ‖ *ref* to debase oneself; to become dilapidated

dégrafer [degrafe] *tr* to unhook, to unclasp

dégraissage [degrɛsaʒ] *m* dry cleaning

dégraisser [degrese] *tr* to remove grease from; to dry-clean

dégrais·seur [degrɛsœr] **dégrais·seuse** [degrɛsøz] *mf* dry cleaner, cleaner and dyer

degré [dəgre] *m* degree; step (*of stairs*); **monter d'un degré** to take a step up (*on the ladder of success*)

dégringolade [degrɛ̃gɔlad] *f* (coll) tumble; (coll) comedown, collapse, downfall

dégringoler [degrɛ̃gɔle] *tr* to bring down (*a government*) ‖ *intr* (coll) to tumble, to tumble down

dégriser [degrize] *tr & ref* to sober up

dégrossir [degrosir] *tr* to rough-hew; to make the preliminary sketches of; to refine or polish (*a hick*)

déguenil·lé -lée [degənije] *adj* ragged, in tatters ‖ *mf* ragamuffin

déguerpir [degɛrpir] *intr* (coll) to clear out, to beat it; **faire déguerpir** to evict

déguisement [degizmɑ̃] *m* disguise

déguiser [degize] *tr* to disguise

dégusta·teur [degystatœr] **-trice** [tris] *mf* winetaster

dégustation [degystasjɔ̃] *f* tasting, art of tasting; consumption (*of beverages*)

déguster [degyste] *tr* to taste discriminatingly; to sip, drink; to consume

déhancher [deɑ̃ʃe] *tr* to dislocate the hip of ‖ *intr* to swing one's hips

déharnacher [dearnaʃe] *tr* to unsaddle, unharness ‖ *ref* (coll) to throw off one's heavy clothing

dehors [dəɔr] *m* outside; **dehors** *mpl* outward appearance; **du dehors** from without, foreign, external; **en dehors** outside; **en dehors de** outside of; beyond ‖ *adv* outside, out; out-of-doors

déification [deifikɑsjɔ̃] *f* deification

déifier [deifje] *tr* to deify

déiste [deist] *adj & mf* deist

déité [deite] *f* deity

déjà [deʒa] *adv* already

déjanter [deʒɑ̃te] *tr* to take (*a tire*) off the rim ‖ *ref* to come off

déjection [deʒɛksjɔ̃] *f* excretion; volcanic debris

déjeter [deʒte] §34 *tr & ref* to warp, to spring

déjeuner [deʒœne] *m* lunch; breakfast; breakfast set; **petit déjeuner** breakfast ‖ *intr* to have lunch; to have breakfast

déjouer [deʒwe] *tr* to foil, thwart

déjucher [deʒyʃe] *tr* to unroost ‖ *intr* to come off the roost (*said of fowl*)

déjuger [deʒyʒe] §38 *ref* to change one's mind

delà [dəla] *adv*—**au delà de** beyond; **par delà** beyond

délabrement [delabrəmɑ̃] *m* decay, dilapidation; impairment (*of health*)

délabrer [delabre] *tr* to ruin, wreck ‖ *ref* to become dilapidated

délacer [delase] §51 *tr* to unlace

délai [delɛ] *m* term, duration, period (*of time*); postponement, extension; **à bref délai** at short notice; **dans le plus bref délai** in the shortest possible time; **dans un délai de** within; **dans un délai record** in record time; **dernier délai** deadline; **sans délai** without delay

délais·sé -sée [delese] *adj* forsaken, forlorn, neglected

délaissement [delɛsmɑ̃] *m* abandonment

délaisser [delese] *tr* to abandon, desert; to relinquish (*a right*)

délassement [delɑsmɑ̃] *m* relaxation

délasser [delɑse] *tr* to rest, refresh, relax ‖ *ref* to rest up

déla·teur [delatœr] **-trice** [tris] *mf* informer

délation [delɑsjɔ̃] *f* paid informing

déla·vé -vée [delave] *adj* washed-out, weak

délayer [deleje] §49 *tr* to add water to, to dilute; **délayer un discours** to stretch out a speech

deleatur [deleatyr] *m* dele

délébile [delebil] *adj* erasable

délectable [delektabl] *adj* delectable

délectation [delɛktɑsjɔ̃] *f* pleasure

délecter [delekte] *ref*—**se délecter à** to find pleasure in

délégation [delegɑsjɔ̃] *f* delegation

délé·gué -guée [delege] *adj* delegated ‖ *mf* delegate, spokesman

déléguer [delege] §10 *tr* to delegate

délester [deleste] *tr* to unballast; to unburden, relieve

délétère [deleter] *adj* deleterious

délibération [deliberɑsjɔ̃] *f* deliberation

délibé·ré -rée [delibere] *adj* deliberate, firm, decided

délibérer [delibere] §10 *tr & intr* to deliberate

déli·cat [delika] **-cate** [kat] *adj* delicate; fine, sensitive (*ear, mind, taste*); touchy; tactful; scrupulous, honest

délicatesse [delikatɛs] *f* delicacy; refinement, fineness; fastidiousness; fragility, weakness

délice [delis] *m* great pleasure ‖ **délices** *fpl* delights, pleasures

déli·cieux [delisjǿ] **-cieuse** [sjǿz] *adj* delicious; delightful, charming

dé·lié -liée [delje] *adj* slender (*figure*); nimble (*mind*); fine (*handwriting*); glib (*tongue*) ‖ *m* upstroke, thin stroke

délier [delje] *tr* to untie, to loosen, to release ‖ *ref* to come loose

délinéament [delineamã] *m* delineation

délinéer [deline] *tr* to delineate

délinquance [delɛ̃kãs] *f* delinquency; **délinquance juvénile** juvenile delinquency

délin·quant [delɛ̃kã] **-quante** [kãt] *adj* & *mf* delinquent; **délinquant primaire** first offender

déli·rant [delirã] **-rante** [rãt] *adj* delirious, raving

délire [delir] *m* delirium; **en délire** delirious, in a frenzy

délirer [delire] *intr* to be delirious, to rave

délit [deli] *m* offense, wrong, crime; **en flagrant délit** in the act

délivrance [delivrãs] *f* delivrance; delivery

délivre [delivr] *m* afterbirth, placenta

délivrer [delivre] *tr* to deliver

déloger [deloʒe] §38 *tr* to dislodge; (coll) to oust, to evict ‖ *intr* to move out (*of a house*)

déloyal déloyale [delwajal] *adj* (*pl* **déloyaux** [delwajo]) disloyal; unfair, dishonest

déloyauté [delwajote] *f* disloyalty; disloyal act; dishonesty

delta [delta] *m* delta

déluge [delyʒ] *m* deluge, flood

délu·ré -rée [delyre] *adj* smart, clever; smart-alecky, forward

délurer [delyre] *tr* & *ref* to wise up

délustrer [delystre] *tr* to take the gloss off of

démagnétiser [demaɲetize] *tr* to demagnetize

démagogie [demagɔʒi] *f* demagogy

démagogique [demagɔʒik] *adj* demagogic

démagogue [demagɔg] *adj* demagogic ‖ *mf* demagogue

démaigrir [demegrir] *tr* to thin down

démailler [demaje] *tr* to unshackle (*a chain*); to unravel (*e.g., a knitted sweater*); to make a run in (*a stocking*) ‖ *ref* to run (*said of stocking*)

démailloter [demajɔte] *tr* to take the diaper off of

demain [dəmɛ̃] *adv* & *m* tomorrow; **à demain** until tomorrow; so long; **de demain en huit** a week from tomorrow; **de demain en quinze** two weeks from tomorrow; **demain matin** tomorrow morning

démancher [demɑ̃ʃe] *tr* to remove the handle of; (coll) to dislocate

demande [dəmɑ̃d] *f* request; application (*for a position*); inquiry; demand (*by buyers for goods*)

demander [dəmɑ̃de] *tr* to ask (*a favor; one's way*); to ask for (*a package; a porter*); to require, to need (*attention*); **demander q.ch. à qn** to ask s.o. for s.th. ‖ *intr*—**demander à** or **de** + *inf* to ask permission to + *inf*; to insist upon + *ger*; **demander après** to ask about, ask for (*s.o.*); **demander à qn de** + *inf* to ask s.o. to + *inf*; **je ne demande pas mieux** I wish I could ‖ *ref* to be needed; to wonder

deman·deur [dəmɑ̃dœr] **-deuse** [døz] *mf* asker; buyer ‖ **-deur** [dœr] **-deresse** [drɛs] *mf* plaintiff

démangeaison [demɑ̃ʒɛzɔ̃] *f* itch

démanger [demɑ̃ʒe] §38 *tr* & *intr* to itch ‖ *intr* (with *dat*) to itch; **la langue lui démange** he is itching to speak

démanteler [demɑ̃tle] §2 *tr* to dismantle (*a fort or town*); to uncover (*a spy ring*)

démaquillage [demakijaʒ] *m* removal of paint or make-up

démaquillant [demakijã] *m* cleansing cream, make-up remover

démaquiller [demakije] *tr* & *ref* to take the paint or make-up off

démarcation [demarkasjɔ̃] *f* demarcation

démarche [demarʃ] *f* gait, step, bearing; method; step, move, action

démarier [demarje] *tr* to thin out (*plants*)

démarque [demark] *f* (com) markdown

démarquer [demarke] *tr* to remove the identification marks from; to plagiarize; to mark down

démarrage [demaraʒ] *m* start

démarrer [demare] *tr* to unmoor ‖ *intr* to cast off (*said of ship*); to start (*said of train or car*); to spurt (*said of racing contestant; said of economy*); **démarrer trop tôt** to jump the gun; **faire démarrer** to start (*a car*); **ne démarrez pas!** don't stir!

démarreur [demarœr] *m* starter (*of car*)

démasquer [demaske] *tr* & *ref* to unmask

démâter [demɑte] *tr* to dismast ‖ *intr* to lose her masts (*said of ship*)

démêlé [demele] *m* quarrel, dispute; **avoir des démêlés avec** to be at odds with, to run afoul of

démêler [demele] *tr* to disentangle, unravel; to bring to light, uncover (*a plot*); to make out, discern

démembrement [demɑ̃brəmɑ̃] *m* dismemberment

déménagement [demenaʒmɑ̃] *m* moving

déménager [demenaʒe] §38 *tr* to move (*household effects*) to another residence; to move the furniture from (*a house*) ‖ *intr* to move, to change one's residence; (coll) to become childish; **tu déménages!** (coll) you're out of your mind!

déménageur [demenaʒœr] *m* mover

démence [demɑ̃s] f madness, insanity; **en démence** demented

démener [demne] §2 ref to struggle, to be agitated; to take great pains

dé·ment [demɑ̃] **-mente** [mɑ̃t] adj & mf lunatic

démenti [demɑ̃ti] m contradiction, denial; proof to the contrary; (coll) shame (on account of a failure)

démentir [demɑ̃tir] §41 tr to contradict, to deny; to give the lie to, to belie || intr to go back on one's word; to be inconsistent

démériter [demerite] intr to lose esteem, to become unworthy

démesure [demǝzyr] f lack of moderation, excess

démesu·ré -rée [demǝzyre] adj measureless, immense; immoderate, excessive

démettre [demetr] §42 tr to dismiss (from a job or position); to dislocate (an arm) || ref to resign, retire

démeubler [demœble] tr to remove the furniture from

demeurant [demœrɑ̃]—**au demeurant** all things considered, after all

demeure [demœr] f home, abode, dwelling; **à demeure** permanently; **dernière demeure** final resting place; **en demeure** in arrears; **mettre qn en demeure de** to oblige s.o. to; **sans plus longue demeure** without further delay

demeurer [demœre] intr to live, dwell || intr (aux: ÊTRE) to stay, remain; **en demeurer à** to leave off; **en demeurer là** to stop, rest there; to leave it at that

demi [dǝmi] m half; (sports) center; (sports) halfback; **à demi** half; **et demi and a half**, e.g., **un centimètre et demi** a centimeter and a half; (after **midi** or **minuit**) half past, e.g., **midi et demi** half past twelve

demi-bas [dǝmiba] m half hose

demi-botte [dǝmibɔt] f (pl **-bottes**) half boot

demi-cercle [dǝmiserkl] m (pl **-cercles**) semicircle

demi-clef [dǝmikle] f (pl **-clefs**) half hitch; **demi-clef à capeler** clove hitch; **deux demi-clefs** two half hitches

demi-congé [dǝmikɔ̃ʒe] m (pl **-congés**) half-holiday

demi-deuil [dǝmidœj] m (pl **-deuils**) half mourning

demi-dieu [dǝmidjø] m (pl **-dieux**) demigod

demie [dǝmi] f half hour; **et demie** half past, e.g., **deux heures et demie** half past two

demi-finale [dǝmifinal] f (pl **-finales**) semifinal

demi-frère [dǝmifrɛr] m (pl **-frères**) half brother; stepbrother

demi-heure [dǝmiœr] f (pl **-heures**) half-hour; **toutes les demi-heures à la demi-heure juste** every half-hour on the half-hour

demi-jour [dǝmiʒur] m invar twilight, half-light

demi-journée [dǝmiʒurne] f (pl **-journées**) half-day; **à demi-journée** half-time

démilitariser [demilitarize] tr to demilitarize

demi-longueur [dǝmilɔ̃gœr] f half-length

demi-lune [dǝmilyn] f (pl **-lunes**) half-moon

demi-mondaine [dǝmimɔ̃dɛn] f (pl **-mondaines**) demimondaine

demi-monde [dǝmimɔ̃d] m demimonde

demi-mot [dǝmimo] m (pl **-mots**) understatement, euphemism; **comprendre à demi-mot** to get the drift of; to take the hint

déminer [demine] tr to clear of mines

demi-pause [dǝmipoz] f (pl **-pauses**) (mus) half rest

demi-pension [dǝmipɑ̃sjɔ̃] f (pl **-pensions**) breakfast and one meal

demi-place [dǝmiplas] f (pl **-places**) half fare; half-price seat

demi-reliure [dǝmiraljyr] f (pl **-reliures**) quarter binding; **demi-reliure à petits coins** half binding

demi-saison [dǝmisezɔ̃] f in-between season; **de demi-saison** spring-and-fall (coat)

demi-sang [dǝmisɑ̃] m invar half-bred horse

demi-sœur [dǝmisœr] f (pl **-sœurs**) half sister; stepsister

demi-solde [dǝmisɔld] m invar pensioned officer || f (pl **-soldes**) army pension, half pay

demi-soupir [dǝmisupir] m (pl **-soupirs**) (mus) eighth rest

démission [demisjɔ̃] f resignation

démissionnaire [demisjɔner] adj outgoing || mf former incumbent

démissionner [demisjɔne] tr (coll) to fire || intr to resign

demi-tasse [dǝmitɑs] f (pl **-tasses**) half-cup; small cup, demitasse

demi-teinte [dǝmitɛ̃t] f (pl **-teintes**) halftone

demi-ton [dǝmitɔ̃] m (pl **-tons**) (mus) half tone

demi-tour [dǝmitur] m (pl **-tours**) about-face; half turn; **demi-tour, (à) droite!** about face!; **au demi-tour, au rear!**; **faire demi-tour** to do an about-face; to turn back

démobiliser [demɔbilize] tr to demobilize

démocrate [demɔkrat] mf democrat

démocratie [demɔkrasi] f democracy

démocratique [demɔkratik] adj democratic

démo·dé -dée [demɔde] adj old-fashioned, out-of-date, outmoded

démoder [demɔde] ref to be outmoded

demoiselle [dǝmwazɛl] f single girl, young lady, miss; dragonfly; (slang) girl; **demoiselle de magasin** salesgirl; **demoiselle d'honneur** maid of honor, bridesmaid; lady-in-waiting

démolir [demɔlir] tr to demolish; to overturn (a cabinet or government)

démolition [demɔlisjɔ̃] f demolition; **démolitions** scrap, rubble

démon [demɔ̃] m demon

démoniaque [demɔnjak] *adj* demonic, demoniac(al) ‖ *mf* demoniac

démonstra·teur [demɔ̃stratœr] **-trice** [tris] *mf* demonstrator

démonstra·tif [demɔ̃stratif] **-tive** [tiv] *adj & m* demonstrative

démontable [demɔ̃tabl] *adj* collapsible, detachable; knockdown

démonte-pneu [demɔ̃tpnø] *m* (*pl* **-pneus**) tire iron

démonter [demɔ̃te] *tr* to dismount; to dismantle ‖ *ref* to come apart; to go to pieces (*while taking an exam*)

démontrable [demɔ̃trabl] *adj* demonstrable

démontrer [demɔ̃tre] *tr* to demonstrate

démoraliser [demɔralize] *tr* to demoralize

démouler [demule] *tr* to remove from a mold

dému·ni -nie [demyni] *adj* out of money; **démuni de** out of; devoid of

démunir [demynir] *tr* to strip, deprive; to deplete (*a garrison*) ‖ *ref* to deprive oneself

démystifier [demistifje] *tr* to debunk

dénationaliser [denasjɔnalize] *tr* to denationalize

dénaturaliser [denatyralize] *tr* to denaturalize

dénatu·ré -rée [denatyre] *adj* denatured; unnatural, perverse

dénaturer [denatyre] *tr* to denature; to pervert; to distort

dénégation [denegasjɔ̃] *f* denial

déni [deni] *m* refusal; (law) denial

dénicher [denife] *tr* to dislodge; to take out of the nest; to make (*s.o.*) move; to search out ‖ *intr* to leave the nest

déni·cheur [denifœr] **-cheuse** [ʃøz] *mf* hunter (*of rare books, antiques, etc.*); **dénicheur de vedettes** talent scout

denier [dənje] *m* (fig) penny, farthing; **denier à Dieu** gratuity; **deniers** money, funds; **de ses deniers** with his own money

dénier [denje] *tr* to deny, refuse

dénigrer [denigre] *tr* to disparage

déniveler [denivle] §34 *tr* to make uneven, to change the level of

dénivellation [denivelasjɔ̃] *f* or **dénivellement** [denivelmɑ̃] *m* unevenness; depression, settling

dénombrement [denɔ̃brəmɑ̃] *m* census, enumeration

dénombrer [denɔ̃bre] *tr* to take a census of, to enumerate

dénomination [denɔminasjɔ̃] *f* denomination, appellation, designation

dénommer [denɔme] *tr* to denominate, to name

dénoncer [denɔ̃se] §51 *tr* to renounce; to indicate, reveal ‖ *ref* to give oneself up

dénonciation [denɔ̃sjasjɔ̃] *f* denunciation; declaration

dénoter [denɔte] *tr* to denote

dénouement [denumɑ̃] *m* outcome, denouement; untying

dénouer [denwe] *tr* to untie; to unravel

dénoyer [denwaje] §47 *tr* to pump out

denrée [dɑ̃re] *f* commodity; **denrées** provisions, products

dense [dɑ̃s] *adj* dense

densité [dɑ̃site] *f* density

dent [dɑ̃] *f* tooth; cog; scallop (*of an edge*); **dent d'éléphant** tusk; **dents de lait** baby teeth; **dents de sagesse** wisdom teeth; **sur les dents** on one's toes

dentaire [dɑ̃ter] *adj* dental

den·tal -tale [dɑ̃tal] *adj & f* (*pl* **-taux** [to] **-tales**) dental

dent-de-chien [dɑ̃dəʃjɛ̃] *f* (*pl* **dents-de-chien**) dogtooth violet

dent-de-lion [dɑ̃dəljɔ̃] *f* (*pl* **dents-de-lion**) dandelion

denteler [dɑ̃tle] §34 *tr* to notch, to indent

dentelle [dɑ̃tel] *f* lace; lacework

dentelure [dɑ̃tlyr] *f* notching; serration; scalloping; (phila) perforation

denter [dɑ̃te] *tr* to furnish with cogs or teeth

dentier [dɑ̃tje] *m* false teeth, denture

dentifrice [dɑ̃tifris] *m* dentifrice

dentiste [dɑ̃tist] *mf* dentist

denture [dɑ̃tyr] *f* denture; **denture artificielle** false teeth

dénuder [denyde] *tr* to strip, denude

dénuement [denymɑ̃] *m* destitution

dénuer [denɥe] *tr* to deprive, strip

déontologie [deɔtɔlɔʒi] *f* study of ethics; **déontologie médicale** (med) code of medical ethics

dépannage [depanaʒ] *m* emergency service, repairs

dépanner [depane] *tr* to give emergency service to; (coll) to get (*s.o.*) out of a scrape

dépan·neur [depanœr] **dépan·neuse** [depanøz] *adj* repairing ‖ *m* serviceman, repairman ‖ *f* tow truck, wrecker

dépaqueter [depakte] §34 *tr* to unpack, unwrap

dépareil·lé -lée [depareje] *adj* incomplete, broken (*set*); odd (*sock*)

dépareiller [depareje] *tr* to break (*a set*)

déparer [depare] *tr* to mar, to spoil the beauty of; to strip of ornaments

déparier [deparje] *tr* to break, split up the pair of

départ [depar] *m* departure; beginning; division; sorting out; **départ usine** F.O.B.; **faux départ** false start

département [departəmɑ̃] *m* (govt) department

départir [departir] §64 (or sometimes like **finir**) *tr* to divide up, to distribute ‖ *ref*—**se départir de** to give up; to depart from

dépassement [depasmɑ̃] *m* passing

dépasser [depase] *tr* to pass, overtake; to go beyond; to overshoot (*the mark*); to exceed; to extend beyond; to be longer than; (coll) to surprise ‖ *intr* to pass; to stick out; to overlap, to show

dépayser [depeize] *tr* to take out of one's familiar surroundings; to bewilder ‖ *ref* to leave one's country

dépecer [depəse] §20 tr to carve, to cut up

dépêche [depeʃ] f dispatch; telegram

dépêcher [depeʃe] tr to dispatch || ref to hurry

dépeigner [depeɲe] tr to tousle, to muss up (the hair)

dépeindre [depɛ̃dr] §50 tr to depict

dépendance [depɑ̃dɑ̃s] f dependence; **dépendances** outbuildings, annex; dependencies, possessions

dépen•dant [depɑ̃dɑ̃] **-dante** [dɑ̃t] adj dependent

dépendre [depɑ̃dr] tr to take down || intr to depend; **dépendre de** to depend on; to belong to; **il dépend de vous de** it is for you to

dépens [depɑ̃] mpl expenses, costs; **aux dépens de** at the expense of

dépense [depɑ̃s] f expense; pantry; dispensary (of hospital); flow (of water); consumption (of fuel)

dépenser [depɑ̃se] tr to spend, expend || ref to exert oneself, to spend one's energy

dépen•sier [depɑ̃sje] **-sière** [sjɛr] adj & mf spendthrift

dépérir [deperir] intr to waste away, decline

dépêtrer [depetre] tr to get (s.o.) out of a jam

dépeupler [depœple] tr to depopulate; to unstock (a pond)

dépha•sé -sée [defaze] adj out of phase

dépiauter [depjote] tr to skin

dépiécer [depjese] §58 tr to dismember

dépiler [depile] tr to remove the hair from

dépister [depiste] tr to track down

dépit [depi] m spite, resentment; **en dépit de** in spite of

dépiter [depite] tr to spite, to vex || ref to take offense

dépla•cé -cée [deplase] adj displaced (person); misplaced, out of place

déplacement [deplasmɑ̃] m displacement; movement; travel; transfer (of an official); shift (in votes); change (in schedule); (naut) displacement

déplacer [deplase] §51 tr to displace; to move; **déplacer la question** to stray from the subject || ref to move

déplaire [depler] §52 intr (with dat) to displease; (with dat) to dislike, e.g., **le lait lui déplaît** he dislikes milk; **ne vous en déplaise** if you have no objection, by your leave || ref to be displeased, e.g., **ils se sont déplu** they were displeased; **se déplaire à** not to like it in, e.g., **je me déplais à la campagne** I don't like it in the country

déplai•sant [deplezɑ̃] **-sante** [zɑ̃t] adj unpleasant, disagreeable

déplaisir [deplezir] m displeasure

déplanter [deplɑ̃te] tr to dig up for transplanting

déplantoir [deplɑ̃twar] m garden trowel

dépliant [deplijɑ̃] m folder, brochure

déplier [deplije] tr & ref to unfold

déplisser [deplise] tr to unpleat

déploiement [deplwamɑ̃] m unfolding,

unfurling; display, array; (mil) deployment

déplorable [deplorabl] adj deplorable

déplorer [deplore] tr to deplore; to grieve over

déployer [deplwaje] §47 tr to unfold, to unfurl; to display; (mil) to deploy || ref (mil) to deploy

déplumer [deplyme] tr to pluck (a chicken) || ref (coll) to lose one's hair

dépolariser [depolarize] tr to depolarize

dépo•li -lie [depoli] adj ground (glass)

dépolir [depolir] tr to remove the polish from; to frost (glass)

déport [depor] m disqualification of oneself; (com) commission; **sans déport** without delay

déportation [deportasjɔ̃] f deportation; internment in a concentration camp

dépor•té -tée [deporte] mf deported criminal, convict; prisoner in a concentration camp

déportement [deportəmɑ̃] m swerve; **déportements** misconduct, immoral conduct, bad habits

déporter [deporte] tr to deport; to send to a concentration camp; to make (an automobile) swerve; to deflect (an airplane) from its course || intr to swerve

dépo•sant [depozɑ̃] **-sante** [zɑ̃t] adj testifying; depositing || mf deponent, witness; depositor

dépose [depoz] f removal

déposer [depoze] tr to deposit; to depose; to drop, leave off; to register (a trademark); to lodge (a complaint); to file (a petition) || intr & ref to depose; to settle, to form a deposit

dépositaire [depoziter] mf trustee, holder; dealer

déposséder [deposede] §10 tr to dispossess

dépôt [depo] m deposit; depository, depot; warehouse; delivery, handing in; **dépôt d'autobus** carbarn; **dépôt de locomotives** roundhouse; **dépôt de mendicité** poorhouse; **dépôt d'épargne** savings account; **dépôt des bagages** baggage room; **dépôt d'essence** filling station; **dépôt de vivres** commissary; **dépôt d'ordures** dump

dépouille [depuj] f castoff skin; hide (taken from animal); **dépouille mortelle** mortal remains; **dépouilles** spoils (of war)

dépouillement [depujmɑ̃] m gathering, selection, sifting; despoilment; counting (of votes); **dépouillement volontaire** relinquishing

dépouiller [depuje] tr to skin; to strip; to gather, select, sift; to count (votes) || ref to shed one's skin (said of insects and reptiles); to strip oneself, to divest oneself

dépour•vu -vue [depurvy] adj destitute; **au dépourvu** unaware; **dépourvu de** devoid of, lacking in

dépoussiérer [depusjere] §10 tr to vacuum

dépravation [depravɑsjɔ̃] *f* depravity

dépraver [deprave] *tr* to deprave

déprécation [deprekɑsjɔ̃] *f* supplication

dépréciation [depresjɑsjɔ̃] *f* depreciation

déprécier [depresje] *tr & ref* to depreciate

déprédation [depredɑsjɔ̃] *f* depredation; embezzlement, misappropriation

déprendre [deprɑ̃dr] §56 *ref* to detach oneself; to come loose; to melt

dépres·sif [depresif] dépres·sive [depresiv] *adj* depressive

dépression [depresjɔ̃] *f* depression

déprimer [deprime] *tr* to depress, to lower ‖ *ref* to be depressed

dépriser [deprize] *tr* to undervalue

depuis [dəpɥi] *adv* since; depuis que since ‖ *prep* since, for, e.g., je suis à Paris depuis trois jours I have been in Paris for three days; depuis . . . jusqu'à from . . . to

dépurer [depyre] *tr* to purify

députation [depytɑsjɔ̃] *f* deputation

député [depyte] *m* deputy

députer [depyte] *tr* to deputize

der [der] *f*—la der des der (coll) the war to end all wars

déraci·né -née [derasine] *adj* uprooted ‖ *mf* uprooted person, wanderer

déraciner [derasine] *tr* to uproot, to root out; to eradicate

déraillement [derɑjmɑ̃] *m* derailment

dérailler [derɑje] *intr* to jump the track; (coll) to get off the track

déraison [derezɔ̃] *f* unreasonableness, irrationality

déraisonnable [derezɔnabl] *adj* unreasonable

déraisonner [derezɔne] *intr* to talk nonsense

dérangement [derɑ̃ʒmɑ̃] *m* derangement; breakdown; disturbance, bother

déranger [derɑ̃ʒe] §38 *tr* to derange, to put out of order; to disturb, trouble ‖ *ref* to move, to change jobs; to become disordered, upset; ne vous dérangez pas! don't get up!; don't bother!

déraper [derape] *intr* to skid, to sideslip; to weigh anchor

dératé [derate] *m*—courir comme un dératé to run like a jack rabbit

dératiser [deratize] *tr* to derat

derby [derbi] *m* derby (*race*)

derechef [dərəʃef] *adv* (lit) once again

déré·glé -glée [deregle] *adj* out of order; irregular (*pulse*); disorderly, excessive

dérégler [deregle] §10 *tr* to put out of order, upset ‖ *ref* to get out of order; to run wild

dérider [deride] *tr* to smooth, unwrinkle; to cheer up ‖ *ref* to cheer up

dérision [derizjɔ̃] *f* derision

dérisoire [derizwar] *adj* derisive

dérivation [derivɑsjɔ̃] *f* derivation; drift; by-pass; diversion (*of river, stream, etc.*); en dérivation shunted (*circuit*)

dérive [deriv] *f* drift; (aer) fin; (naut) centerboard; à la dérive adrift

déri·vé -vée [derive] *adj* drifting; shunted (*current*) ‖ *m* derivative

dériver [derive] *tr* to derive; to divert (*e.g., a river*); to unrivet ‖ *intr* to derive; to be derived; to result; to drift

dermatologie [dermatɔlɔʒi] *f* dermatology

der·nier [dernje] -nière [njer] *adj* last; latest; latter; final; last (*just elapsed*), e.g., la semaine dernière last week ‖ (when standing before noun) *adj* last (*in a series*), e.g., la dernière semaine de la guerre the last week of the war

dernièrement [dernjermɑ̃] *adv* lately

dernier-né [dernjene] dernière-née [dernjerne] *mf* (*pl* -nés -nées) lastborn child

déro·bé -bée [derɔbe] *adj* secret; à la dérobée stealthily, on the sly

dérober [derɔbe] *tr* to steal; to hide; dérober à to steal from; to rescue from (*e.g., death*) ‖ *ref* to steal away, disappear; to hide; to shy away, balk; to shirk; to give way (*said of knees or one's footing*); se dérober à to slip away from; to escape from

dérogation [derɔgɑsjɔ̃] *f*—dérogation à departure from (*custom*); waiving of (*principle*); deviation from (*instructions*); par dérogation à notwithstanding

déroger [derɔʒe] §38 *intr*—déroger à to depart from (*custom*); to waive (a *principle*); to derogate from (*dignity*, *one's rank*)

dérouiller [deruje] *tr* to remove the rust from; to polish (*s.o.*); (coll) to limber up; (coll) to brush up on ‖ *ref* to lose its rust; to brush up; to limber up

dérouler [derule] *tr & ref* to unroll, unfold

dérou·tant [derutɑ̃] -tante [tɑ̃t] *adj* baffling, misleading

déroute [derut] *f* rout, downfall

dérouter [derute] *tr* to steer off the course; to reroute; to disconcert, baffle ‖ *ref* to go astray; to become confused

derrick [derik] *m* oil derrick

derrière [derjer] *m* rear, backside ‖ *adv & prep* behind

derviche [derviʃ] *m* dervish

des [de] §77

dès [dɛ] *prep* by (a *certain time*); from (a *certain place*); as early as, as far back as; from, beginning with; dès lors from that time, ever since; dès lors que since, inasmuch as; dès que as soon as

désabonner [dezabɔne] *tr* to cancel the subscription of ‖ *ref* to cancel one's subscription

désabu·sé -sée [dezabyze] *adj* disillusioned

désabuser [dezabyze] *tr* to disabuse, disillusion ‖ *ref* to have one's eyes opened

désaccord [dezakɔr] *m* disagreement, discord

désaccorder [dezakɔrde] *tr* to put (*an instrument*) out of tune ‖ *ref* to get out of tune

désaccoupler [dezakuple] *tr* to unpair; to uncouple

désaccoutumer [dezakutyme] *tr* to break (*s.o.*) of a habit ‖ *ref* to break oneself of a habit

désaffecter [dezafekte] *tr* to turn from its intended use

désagréable [dezagreabl] *adj* disagreeable; unpleasant

désagréger [dezagreʒe] §1 *tr* to break up, to dissolve, to disintegrate

désagrément [dezagremã] *m* unpleasantness, annoyance

désaimanter [dezɛmɑ̃te] *tr* to demagnetize

désalté·rant [dezaltɛrã] **-rante** [rãt] *adj* thirst-quenching, refreshing

désaltérer [dezaltere] §10 *tr* to quench the thirst of; to refresh with a drink ‖ *ref* to quench one's thirst

désamorcer [dezamɔrse] §51 *tr* to deactivate, to disconnect the fuse of; to unprime

désappointement [dezapwɛ̃tmã] *m* disappointment

désappointer [dezapwɛ̃te] *tr* to disappoint; to break the point of, to blunt

désapprendre [dezaprɑ̃dr] §56 *tr* to unlearn, to forget

désapproba·teur [dezaprɔbatœr] **-trice** [tris] *adj* disapproving ‖ *mf* critic

désapprouver [dezapruve] *tr* to disapprove of, to disapprove

désarçonner [dezarsɔne] *tr* to unhorse, buck off; (coll) to dumfound

désarmement [dezarməmã] *m* disarmament; disarming; dismantling (*of ship*)

désarmer [dezarme] *tr* to disarm; to deactivate; to dismantle; to appease ‖ *intr* to disarm; to slacken, let up (*said of hostility*)

désarroi [dezarwa] *m* disorder, disarray, confusion

désarticulation [dezartikylasjɔ̃] *f* dislocation

désassembler [dezasɑ̃ble] *tr* to disassemble

désastre [dezastr] *m* disaster

désas·treux [dezastrø] **-treuse** [trøz] *adj* disastrous

désavantage [dezavɑ̃taʒ] *m* disadvantage

désavantager [dezavɑ̃taʒe] §38 *tr* to put at a disadvantage, to handicap

désavanta·geux [dezavɑ̃taʒø] **-geuse** [ʒøz] *adj* disadvantageous

désa·veu [dezavø] *m* (*pl* **-veux**) disavowal, denial, repudiation

désavouer [dezavwe] *tr* to disavow, to deny, to repudiate, to disown

désaxé [dezakse] *adj* unbalanced, out of joint

desceller [desele] *tr* to unseal

descendance [desɑ̃dɑ̃s] *f* descent

descendeur [desɑ̃dœr] *m* ski jumper

descendre [desɑ̃dr], [desɑ̃dr] *tr* to descend, to go down (*a hill, street,*

stairway); to take down, to lower (*a picture*); (coll) to bring down (*an airplane; luggage*); (coll) to drop off, let off at the door ‖ *intr* (*aux:* ÊTRE) to descend; to go down, to go downstairs; to stay, to stop (*at a hotel*); **descendre** + *inf* to go down to + *inf*; to stop off to + *inf*; **descendre court** to undershoot (*said of airplane*); **descendre de** to come down from (*a mountain, ladder, tree*); to be descended from

descente [desɑ̃t] *f* descent; invasion, raid; stay (*at a hotel*); stop (*en route*); **descente à terre** (nav) shore leave; **descente de lit** bedside rug

descriptible [deskriptibl] *adj* describable

descrip·tif [deskriptif] **-tive** [tiv] *adj* descriptive

description [deskripsjɔ̃] *f* description

déségrégation [desegregasjɔ̃] *f* desegregation

désempa·ré -rée [dezɑ̃pare] *adj* disconcerted; disabled (*ship*)

désemparer [dezɑ̃pare] *tr* to disable (*a ship*) ‖ *intr*—**sans désemparer** continuously, without intermission

désemplir [dezɑ̃plir] *intr*—**ne pas désemplir** to be always full

désenchaîner [dezɑ̃ʃene] *tr* to unchain

désenchantement [dezɑ̃ʃɑ̃tmã] *m* disenchantment

désenchanter [dezɑ̃ʃɑ̃te] *tr* to disenchant

désencombrer [dezɑ̃kɔ̃bre] *tr* to disencumber, to clear, to free

désengager [dezɑ̃gaʒe] §38 *tr* to release from a promise

désengorger [dezɑ̃gɔrʒe] §38 *tr* to unstop

désengrener [dezɑ̃grəne] §2 *tr* to disengage, to throw out of gear

désenivrer [dezɑ̃nivre] *tr & intr* to sober up

désenlacer [dezɑ̃lase] §51 *tr* to unbind

désennuyer [dezɑ̃nɥije] §27 *tr* to divert, cheer up ‖ *ref* to find relief from boredom

désensabler [dezɑ̃sable] *tr* to free (*a ship*) from the sand; to dredge the sand from (*a canal*)

désensibiliser [dezɑ̃sibilize] *tr* to desensitize

désensorceler [dezɑ̃sɔrsəle] §34 *tr* to remove the spell from

désentortiller [dezɑ̃tɔrtije] *tr* to straighten out

désenvelopper [dezɑ̃vlɔpe] *tr* to unwrap

déséquilibre [dezekilibr] *m* mental instability

déséquili·bré -brée [dezekilibre] *adj* mentally unbalanced ‖ *mf* unbalanced person

déséquilibrer [dezekilibre] *tr* to unbalance

dé·sert [dezer] **-serte** [zert] *adj & m* desert

déserter [dezerte] *tr & intr* to desert

déserteur [dezertœr] *m* deserter

désertion [dezersjɔ̃] *f* desertion

désespérance [dezesperɑ̃s] *f* despair

désespé·ré -rée [dezespere] adj desperate, hopeless || mf desperate person

désespérer [dezespere] §10 tr to be the despair of || ref to lose hope

désespoir [dezespwar] m despair; **en désespoir de cause** as a last resort

déshabillage [dezabijaʒ] m striptease

déshabillé [dezabije] m morning wrap

déshabiller [dezabije] tr & ref to undress; **déshabiller saint Pierre pour habiller saint Paul** to rob Peter to pay Paul

déshabituer [dezabitɥe] tr to break (s.o.) of a habit

déshéri·té -tée [dezerite] adj underprivileged; **les déshérités** the underprivileged

déshériter [dezerite] tr to disinherit; to disadvantage

déshonnête [dezɔnet] adj improper, immodest

déshonnêteté [dezɔnetəte] f impropriety, immodesty, indecency

déshonneur [dezɔnœr] m dishonor

déshono·rant [dezɔnɔrɑ̃] **-rante** [rɑ̃t] adj dishonorable, discreditable

déshonorer [dezɔnɔre] tr to dishonor

déshydratation [dezidratɑsjɔ̃] f dehydration

déshydrater [dezidrate] tr to dehydrate

désignation [dezinɑsjɔ̃] f designation; appointment, nomination

dési·gné -gnée [desine] mf nominee

désigner [desine] tr to designate; to indicate, point out; to appoint, nominate; to signify, mean; to set (the hour of an appointment) || ref—se **désigner à l'attention de** to bring oneself to the attention of

désillusion [dezilyzjɔ̃] f disillusion; disappointment

désillusionner [dezilyzjɔne] tr to disillusion; to disappoint

désinence [dezinɑ̃s] f (gram) ending

désinfecter [dezɛ̃fekte] tr to disinfect

désintégration [dezɛ̃tegrɑsjɔ̃] f disintegration

désintégrer [dezɛ̃tegre] §10 tr & ref to disintegrate

désintéres·sé -sée [dezɛ̃terese] adj disinterested, impartial; unselfish

désintéressement [dezɛ̃teresmɑ̃] m disinterestedness, impartiality; payment, satisfaction (of a debt); paying off (of a creditor)

désintéresser [dezɛ̃terese] tr to pay off; to buy out || ref—se **désintéresser de** to lose interest in

désintoxication [dezɛ̃tɔksikɑsjɔ̃] f treatment for alcoholism, drug addiction, or poisoning; disintoxification

désinvolte [dezɛ̃vɔlt] adj free and easy, casual; offhanded, impertinent

désinvolture [dezɛ̃vɔltyr] f free and easy manner, offhandedness; impertinence

désir [dezir] m desire

désirable [dezirabl] adj desirable

désirer [dezire] tr to desire, wish

dési·reux -reuse [dezirø] **-reuse** [røz] adj desirous

désister [deziste] ref to desist; to withdraw from a runoff election; se dé-

sister de to waive (a claim); to drop (a lawsuit)

désobéir [dezɔbeir] intr to disobey; (with dat) to disobey; **être désobéi** to be disobeyed

désobli·geant [dezɔbliʒɑ̃] **-geante** [ʒɑ̃t] adj disagreeable, ungracious

désobliger [dezɔbliʒe] §38 tr to offend, displease, disoblige

désodori·sant [dezɔdɔrizɑ̃] **-sante** [zɑ̃t] adj & m deodorant

désodoriser [dezɔdɔrize] tr to deodorize

désœu·vré -vrée [dezœvre] adj idle, unoccupied, out of work; **les désœuvrés** the unemployed

désœuvrement [dezœvrəmɑ̃] m idleness, unemployment

déso·lant [dezɔlɑ̃] **-lante** [lɑ̃t] adj distressing, sad

désolation [dezɔlɑsjɔ̃] f desolation; grief, distress

déso·lé -lée [dezɔle] adj desolate; distressed

désoler [dezɔle] tr to desolate, destroy; to distress || ref to be distressed

désopi·lant [dezɔpilɑ̃] **-lante** [lɑ̃t] adj hilarious, sidesplitting

désordon·né -née [dezɔrdɔne] adj disordered; untidy; disorderly

désordonner [dezɔrdɔne] tr to upset, confuse

désordre [dezɔrdr] m disorder, confusion; moral laxity

désorganisa·teur [dezɔrganizatœr] **-trice** [tris] adj disorganizing || mf troublemaker

désorganisation [dezɔrganizɑsjɔ̃] f disorganization

désorganiser [dezɔrganize] tr to disorganize

désorien·té -tée [dezɔrjɑ̃te] adj disoriented, bewildered

désorienter [dezɔrjɑ̃te] tr to disorient; to mislead; to disconcert || ref to become confused; to lose one's bearings

désormais [dezɔrme] adv henceforth

désosser [dezɔse] tr to bone

despote [despɔt] m despot

despotique [despɔtik] adj despotic

despotisme [despɔtism] m despotism

des·quels -quelles [dekel] §78

dessaisir [desezir] tr to dispossess; to let go, to release || ref—se **dessaisir de** to relinquish

dessalement [desalmɑ̃] m desalinization

dessaler [desale] tr to desalt, to desalinate || ref (coll) to wise up

dessécher [dese/e] §10 tr to dry up, wither; to drain (a pond); to dehydrate (the body); to sear (the heart) || ref to dry up; to waste away

dessein [desɛ̃] m design, plan, intent; **à dessein** on purpose

desseller [desele] tr to unsaddle

desserrer [desere] tr to loosen; **ne pas desserrer les dents** to keep mum

dessert [deser] m dessert, last course

desserte [desert] f buffet, sideboard; branch (of railroad or bus line); ministry (of a substituting clergyman)

dessertir [desertir] *tr* to remove (*a gem*) from its setting

desservant [deservã] *m* parish priest

desservir [deservir] §63 *tr* to clear (*the table*); to be of disservice to, to harm; (aer, aut, rr) to stop at (*a town or station*); (aer, aut, eccl, rr) to serve (*a locality*); (elec) to supply (*a region*)

dessiller [desije] *tr*—**dessiller les yeux à qn** or **de qn** to open s.o.'s eyes, to undeceive s.o.

dessin [desẽ] *m* drawing, sketch, design; profile (*of face*); **dessins animés** (mov) animated cartoons

dessina·teur [desinatœr] **-trice** [tris] *mf* designer; cartoonist

dessiner [desine] *tr* to draw, sketch, design; to delineate, outline || *ref* to stand out, to be outlined

dessoûler or **dessouler** [desule] *tr & intr* to sober up

dessous [dəsu] *m* underpart; reverse side, wrong side; coaster (*underneath a glass*); seamy side, machinations behind the scenes; **au dessous de** below; **avoir le dessous** to get the short end of the deal; **du dessous** below; **en dessous** underneath; **les dessous** lingerie, undergarments || *adv & prep* under, underneath, below

dessous-de-bouteille [dəsudəbutej] *m invar* coaster

dessous-de-bras [dəsudəbra] *m invar* underarm pad

dessous-de-carafe [dəsudəkaraf] *m invar* coaster

dessous-de-plat [dəsudəpla] *m invar* hot pad

dessous-de-table [dəsudətabl] *m invar* under-the-counter money

dessus [dəsy] *m* upper part; back (*of the hand*); right side (*of material*); (mus) treble part; **au dessus de** beyond, above; **avoir le dessus** to have the upper hand; **le dessus du panier** the cream of the crop || *adv* above || *prep* on, above, over

dessus-de-cheminée [dəsydə∫mine] *m invar* mantelpiece

dessus-de-lit [dəsydəli] *m invar* bedspread

dessus-de-porte [dəsydəpɔrt] *m invar* overdoor

dessus-de-table [dəsydətabl] *m invar* table cover

destin [destẽ] *m* destiny, fate

destinataire [destinater] *mf* addressee; payee; **destinataire inconnu** or **absent** (formula stamped on envelope) not at this address

destination [destinasjõ] *f* destination; **à destination de** to, bound for

destinée [destine] *f* destiny

destiner [destine] *tr* to destine; to set aside, to reserve; **destiner q.ch. à qn** to mean or intend s.th. for s.o.

destituer [destitɥe] *tr* to remove from office

destitution [destitysjõ] *f* dismissal, removal from office

destrier [destrije] *m* (hist) steed, charger

destroyer [destrɔjœr] *m* (nav) destroyer

destruc·teur [destryktœr] **-trice** [tris] *adj* destroying, destructive || *mf* destroyer

destruc·tif [destryktif] **-tive** [tiv] *adj* destructive

destruction [destryksjõ] *f* destruction

dé·suet [dezɥe] **-suète** [zɥet] *adj* obsolete, antiquated, out-of-date

désuétude [dezɥetyd] *f* desuetude, disuse

désu·ni -nie [dezyni] *adj* at odds, divided against itself; uncoordinated

désunion [dezynjõ] *f* dissension

désunir [dezynir] *tr* to disunite, divide; to estrange

déta·ché -chée [deta∫e] *adj* detached; clean; spare (*parts*); acting, temporary (*official*); staccato (*note*)

détachement [deta∫mã] *m* detachment; (mil) detail

détacher [deta∫e] *tr* to detach; to let loose; to clean; to make (*s.th.*) stand out in relief || *ref* to come loose; to break loose; to stand out in relief

détacheur [deta∫œr] *m* spot remover

détail [detaj] *m* detail; retail; item (*of an account*); **au détail** at retail; **en détail** detailed

détail·lant [detajã] **détail·lante** [detajãt] *adj* retail || *mf* retailer

détailler [detaje] *tr* to detail; to cut up into pieces; to retail; to itemize (*an account*)

détartrer [detartre] *tr* to remove the scale from (*a boiler*); to remove the tartar from (*teeth*)

détaxation [detaksɑsjõ] *f* lowering or removal of taxes

détaxer [detakse] *tr* to lower or remove the tax from

détecter [detekte] *tr* to detect

détecteur [detektœr] *m* detector; **détecteur de mines** mine detector

détection [deteksjõ] *f* detection

détective [detektiv] *m* detective, private detective; box camera

déteindre [detẽdr] §50 *tr* to fade, bleach || *intr* to fade, run

dételer [detle] §34 *tr* to unharness || *intr* to let up; to settle down

détendre [detãdr] *tr* to relax; to stretch out (*one's legs*); to lower (*the gas*) || *ref* to relax, to enjoy oneself

détenir [detnir] §72 *tr* to detain (*in prison*); to hold, withhold; to own

détente [detãt] *f* trigger; relaxation, easing (*of tension*); relaxation of tension (*in international affairs*)

déten·teur [detãtœr] **-trice** [tris] *mf* holder (*of stock; of a record*); keeper (*of a secret*)

détention [detãsjõ] *f* detention, custody; possession; **détention préventive** pretrial imprisonment, custody

déte·nu -nue [detny] *adj* detained, imprisoned || *mf* prisoner

déterger [deterʒe] §38 *tr* to clean

détérioration [deterjɔrɑsjõ] *f* deterioration

détériorer [deterjɔre] *tr* to damage || *intr* to deteriorate

détermination [determinɑsjɔ̃] *f* determination

déterminer [determine] *tr* to determine || *ref* to decide

déter·ré -rée [detere] *adj* disinterred || *mf* (fig) corpse, ghost

déterrer [detere] *tr* to dig up; to exhume

déter·sif [detεrsif] **-sive** [siv] *adj & m* detergent

détester [deteste] *tr* to detest, to hate

déto·nant [detɔnɑ̃] **-nante** [nɑ̃t] *adj & m* explosive

détoner [detɔne] *intr* to detonate, to explode

détonner [detɔne] *intr* to sing or play off key; to clash (*said of colors*)

détordre [detɔrdr] *tr* to untwist

détortiller [detɔrtije] *tr* to untangle

détour [detur] *m* turn, curve, bend; roundabout way, detour; **sans détour** frankly, honestly

détour·né -née [deturne] *adj* off the beaten track, isolated; indirect, roundabout; twisted (*meaning*)

détourner [deturne] *tr* to divert; to deter; to embezzle; to lead astray; to distort, twist

détrac·teur [detraktœr] **-trice** [tris] *adj* disparaging || *mf* detractor

détra·qué -quée [detrake] *adj* out of order; broken (*in health*); unhinged, deranged || *mf* nervous wreck

détraquer [detrake] *tr* to put out of commission; (coll) to upset, unhinge || *ref* to break down

détrempe [detrɑ̃p] *f* distemper (*painting*); annealing (*of steel*)

détremper [detrɑ̃pe] *tr* to soak; to dilute; to anneal (*steel*)

détresse [detrεs] *f* distress

détriment [detrimɑ̃] *m* detriment

détritus [detritys] *m* debris, rubbish, refuse

détroit [detrwa] *m* strait, sound

détromper [detrɔ̃pe] *tr* to undeceive, to enlighten

détrôner [detrone] *tr* to dethrone

détrousser [detruse] *tr* to let down (*e.g.*, one's sleeves); to hold up (*s.o.*) in the street || *ref* to let down a garment

détrousseur [detrusœr] *m* highwayman

détruire [detrɥir] §19 *tr* to destroy; to put an end to || *ref* (coll) to commit suicide

dette [dεt] *f* debt; **dette active** asset; **dette passive** liability

deuil [dœj] *m* mourning; grief, sorrow; bereavement; funeral procession; **deuil de veuve** widow's weeds; **faire son deuil de** (coll) to say good-by to

deux [dø] *adj & pron* two; the Second, e.g., **Charles deux** Charles the Second; **deux heures** two o'clock || *m* two; second (*in dates*)

deuxième [døzjεm] *adj & m* second

deux-pièces [døpjεs] *m invar* two-piece suit

deux-points [døpwε̃] *m invar* colon

deux-ponts [døpɔ̃] *m invar* (aer, naut) double-decker

dévaler [devale] *tr* to descend (*a slope*) || *intr* to descend quickly

dévaluation [devalɥɑsjɔ̃] *f* devaluation

dévaluer [devalɥe] *tr* to devaluate

devant [dəvɑ̃] *m* front; **par devant** in front; **prendre les devants** to make the first move; to get ahead; to take precautions || *adv* before, in front || *prep* before, in front of

devanture [dəvɑ̃tyr] *f* show window; display; storefront

dévasta·teur [devastatœr] **-trice** [tris] *adj* devastating

dévastation [devastɑsjɔ̃] *f* devastation

dévaster [devaste] *tr* to devastate

déveine [devεn] *f* bad luck

développé [devlɔpe] *m* press (*in weight lifting*)

développement [devlɔpmɑ̃] *m* development; unwrapping (*of package*); expansion

développer [devlɔpe] *tr* to develop; to unwrap (*a package*); to reveal, show (*e.g.*, a card); to spread out, open out; to expand (*an algebraic expression*) || *ref* to develop

devenir [dəvnir] §72 *intr* (aux: ÊTRE) to become; **qu'est devenu Robert?** what has become of Robert?

dévergondage [devεrgɔ̃daʒ] *m* profligacy

dévergon·dé -dée [devεrgɔ̃de] *adj & mf* profligate

dévergonder [devεrgɔ̃de] *ref* to become dissolute

dévernir [devεrnir] *tr* to remove the varnish from

déverrouiller [devεruje] *tr* to unbolt

dé·vers [devεr] **-verse** [vεrs] *adj* warped; out of alignment || *m* inclination, slope; banking

déverser [devεrse] *tr* to pour out; to slope, bank || *intr* to pour out; to lean, to become lopsided || *ref* to empty, flow (*said of river*)

dévêtir [devetir] §73 *tr & ref* to undress

déviation [devjɑsjɔ̃] *f* deviation; detour

dévider [devide] *tr* to unwind, to reel off

dévier [devje] *tr* to deflect, to by-pass || *intr* to deviate, to swerve

de·vin [dəvε̃] **-vineresse** [vinrεs] *mf* fortuneteller

deviner [dəvine] *tr* to guess

devinette [dəvinεt] *f* riddle

dévirer [devire] *tr* to turn back; to bend back; to feather (*an oar*)

devis [dəvi] *m* estimate

dévisager [devizaʒe] §38 *tr* to stare at, to stare down

devise [dəviz] *f* motto, slogan; heraldic device; name of a ship; currency; **devise forte** strong currency

deviser [dəvize] *intr* to chat

dévisser [devise] *tr* to unscrew

dévitaliser [devitalize] *tr* to kill the nerve of (*a tooth*)

dévoiler [devwale] *tr* to unveil; to straighten (*e.g.*, a bent wheel) || *ref* to unveil; to come to light

devoir [dəvwar] *m* duty; exercise,

homework; **devoirs** respects; homework || **§21** *tr* to owe || *aux* used to express 1) necessity, e.g., **il doit s'en aller** he must go away; **il devra s'en aller** he will have to go away; **il a dû s'en aller** he had to go away; 2) obligation, e.g., **il devrait s'en aller** he ought to go away, he should go away; **il aurait dû s'en aller** he ought to have gone away, he should have gone away; 3) conjecture, e.g., **il doit être malade** he must be ill; **il a dû être malade** he must have been ill; 4) what is expected or scheduled, e.g., **que dois-je faire maintenant?** what am I to do now?; **le train devait arriver à six heures** the train was to arrive at six o'clock

dévo·lu -lue [devɔly] *adj*—**dévolu à** devolving upon, vested in || *m*—**jeter son dévolu sur** to fix one's choice upon

dévora·teur [dévɔratœr] **-trice** [tris] *adj* devouring

dévorer [devɔre] *tr* to devour, eat up

dévo·reur [devɔrœr] **-reuse** [røz] *mf* devourer; (fig) glutton

dé·vot [devo] **-vote** [vɔt] *adj* devout, pious || *mf* devout, pious person; **devotee; faux dévot** hypocrite

dévotion [devosjɔ̃] *f* devotion, devoutness; **à votre dévotion** at your service, at your disposal; **être à la dévotion de qn** to be at s.o.'s beck and call

dé·voué -vouée [devwe] *adj* devoted; **dévoué à vos ordres** (complimentary close) at your service; **votre dévoué** (complimentary close) yours truly

dévouement [devumɑ̃] *m* devotion

dévouer [devwe] *tr* to dedicate, sacrifice || *ref* to devote oneself

dévoyé dévoyée [devwaje] *adj* || *mf* delinquent (*young person*) || *mf* delinquent

dévoyer [devwaje] **§47** *tr* to lead astray

dextérité [dɛksterite] *f* dexterity

dextrose [dɛkstroz] *m* dextrose

diabète [djabɛt] *m* diabetes

diabétique [djabetik] *adj* & *mf* diabetic

diable [djɑbl] *m* · devil; hand truck, dolly; (coll) fellow; **à la diable** haphazardly; **c'est là le diable** (coll) there's the rub; **diable à ressort** jack-in-the-box; **du diable** extreme; **en diable** extremely; **faire le diable à quatre** (coll) to raise Cain; **tirer le diable par la queue** (coll) to be hard up

diablerie [djɑbləri] *f* deviltry

diabolique [djabɔlik] *adj* diabolic(al)

diaconesse [djakɔnes] *f* deaconess

diacre [djakr] *m* deacon

diacritique [djakritik] *adj* diacritical

diadème [djadɛm] *m* diadem; (*woman's headdress*) tiara, coronet

diagnose [djagnoz] *f* diagnostics, diagnosis

diagnostic [djagnɔstik] *m* diagnosis

diagnostiquer [djagnɔstike] *tr* to diagnose

diago·nal -nale [djagɔnal] *adj* & *f* (*pl* **-naux** [no] **-nales**) diagonal

diagonalement [djagɔnalmɑ̃] *adv* diagonally, cater-cornered

diagramme [djagram] *m* diagram

dialecte [djalɛkt] *m* dialect

dialogue [djalɔg] *m* dialogue

diamant [djamɑ̃] *m* diamond

diamantaire [djamɑ̃ter] *adj* diamondbright || *m* dealer in diamonds

diamé·tral -trale [djametral] *adj* (*pl* **-traux** [tro]) diametric(al)

diamètre [djametr] *m* diameter

diane [djan] *f* reveille

diantre [djɑ̃tr] *interj* the dickens!

diapason [djapazɔ̃] *m* range (*of voice or instrument*); pitch, standard pitch; tuning fork

diaphane [djafan] *adj* diaphanous

diaphragme [djafragm] *m* diaphragm

diapo [djapo] *f* (coll) slide

diapositive [djapozitiv] *f* (phot) transparency, slide

diaprer [djapre] *tr* to variegate

diarrhée [djare] *f* diarrhea

diastole [djastɔl] *f* diastole

diathermie [djatermi] *f* diathermy

diatribe [djatrib] *f* diatribe

dichotomie [dikɔtɔmi] *f* dichotomy; split fee (*between physicians*)

dictaphone [diktafɔn] *m* dictaphone

dictateur [diktatœr] *m* dictator

dictature [diktatyr] *f* dictatorship

dictée [dikte] *f* dictation; **écrire sous la dictée de** to take dictation from

dicter [dikte] *tr* & *intr* to dictate

diction [diksjɔ̃] *f* diction

dictionnaire [diksjɔner] *m* dictionary; **dictionnaire vivant** (coll) walking encyclopedia

dicton [diktɔ̃] *m* saying, proverb

didactique [didaktik] *adj* didactic(al)

dièdre [djedr] *adj* & *m* dihedral

diérèse [djerez] *f* diaeresis

dièse [djez] *adj* & *m* (mus) sharp

diesel [dizel] *m* Diesel motor

diéser [djeze] **§10** *tr* (mus) to sharp

diète [djet] *f* diet

diététi·cien [djetetisjɛ̃] **-cienne** [sjen] *mf* dietitian

diététique [djetetik] *adj* dietetic || *f* dietetics

dieu [djø] *m* (*pl* **dieux**) god || (*cap*) *m* God; **Dieu merci!** thank heavens!; **mon Dieu!** good gracious!

diffamation [difamasjɔ̃] *f* defamation

diffamer [difame] *tr* to defame

diffé·ré -rée [difere] *adj* deferred; delayed (*action*) || *m* (rad, telv) prerecording; **en différé** (rad, telv) prerecorded

différemment [diferamɑ̃] *adv* differently

différence [diferɑ̃s] *f* difference; **à la différence de** unlike, contrary to

différencier [diferɑ̃sje] *tr* & *ref* to differentiate

différend [diferɑ̃] *m* dispute, disagreement, difference; **partager le différend** to split the difference

diffé·rent [diferɑ̃] **-rente** [rɑ̃t] *adj* different

différen·tiel -tielle [diferɑ̃sjel] *adj* differential ‖ *m* (mach) differential ‖ *f* (math) differential

différer [difere] §10 *tr* to defer, to put off ‖ *intr* to differ; to disagree

difficile [difisil] *adj* difficult, hard; hard to please, crotchety; **faire le difficile** to be hard to please

difficulté [difikylte] *f* difficulty

difforme [difɔrm] *adj* deformed

difformité [difɔrmite] *f* deformity

dif·fus [dify] **dif·fuse** [difyz] *adj* diffuse, verbose, windy

diffuser [difyze] *tr* to broadcast ‖ *ref* to diffuse

diffuseur [difyzœr] *m* spreader (*of news*); loudspeaker; nozzle

digérer [diʒere] §10 *tr* & *intr* to digest ‖ *ref* to be digested

digeste [diʒest] *adj* (coll) easy to digest ‖ *m* (law) digest

digestible [diʒestibl] *adj* digestible

diges·tif [diʒestif] **-tive** [tiv] *adj* digestive

digestion [diʒestjɔ̃] *f* digestion

digi·tal -tale [diʒital] *adj* (pl **-taux** [to]) digital ‖ *f* digitalis, foxglove

digitaline [diʒitalin] *f* (pharm) digitalis

digne [diɲ] *adj* worthy; dignified; haughty, uppish

dignitaire [diɲiter] *mf* dignitary

dignité [diɲite] *f* dignity

digression [digresjɔ̃] *f* digression

digue [dig] *f* dike; breakwater; (fig) barrier

dilacérer [dilasere] §10 *tr* to lacerate

dilapider [dilapide] *tr* to squander; to embezzle

dilater [dilate] *tr* & *ref* to dilate

dilatoire [dilatwar] *adj* dilatory

dilemme [dilem] *m* dilemma

dilettante [diletɑ̃t] *mf* dilettante

diligemment [diliʒamɑ̃] *adv* diligently

diligence [diliʒɑ̃s] *f* diligence; **à la diligence de** at the request of

dili·gent [diliʒɑ̃] **-gente** [ʒɑ̃t] *adj* diligent

diluer [dilɥe] *tr* to dilute

dilution [dilysjɔ̃] *f* dilution

dimanche [dimɑ̃ʃ] *m* Sunday; **du dimanche** (coll) Sunday (*driver*); (coll) amateur (*painter*); **le dimanche des Rameaux** Palm Sunday

dîme [dim] *f* tithe

dimension [dimɑ̃sjɔ̃] *f* dimension

diminuer [diminɥe] *tr* & *intr* to diminish

diminu·tif [diminytif] **-tive** [tiv] *adj* & *m* diminutive

dinde [dɛ̃d] *f* turkey; (culin) turkey; (coll) silly girl

dindon [dɛ̃dɔ̃] *m* turkey

dindonner [dɛ̃dɔne] *tr* to dupe, take in

dîner [dine] *m* dinner; **dîner de garçons** stag dinner; **dîner prié** formal dinner ‖ *intr* to dine

dînette [dinet] *f* family meal; children's playtime meal

dî·neur [dinœr] **-neuse** [nøz] *mf* diner, dinner guest

dinosaure [dinozɔr] *m* dinosaur

diocèse [djosez] *m* diocese

diode [djod] *f* diode

dionée [djone] *f* Venus's-flytrap

diphtérie [difteri] *f* diphtheria

diphtongue [diftɔ̃g] *f* diphthong

diplomate [diplɔmat] *adj* diplomatic ‖ *mf* diplomat

diplomatie [diplɔmasi] *f* diplomacy

diplomatique [diplɔmatik] *adj* diplomatic

diplôme [diplom] *m* diploma

dire [dir] *m* statement; **au dire de** according to ‖ §22 *tr* to say, tell, relate; **à l'heure dite** at the appointed time; **à qui le dites-vous?** (coll) you're telling me!; **autrement dit** in other words; **dire que . . .** to think that; **dites-lui bien des choses de ma part** say hello for me; **tu l'as dit!** (coll) you said it! ‖ *intr* to say; **à vrai dire** to tell the truth; **cela va sans dire** it goes without saying; **c'est beaucoup dire** (coll) that's going rather far; **c'est pas peu dire** (slang) that's saying a lot; **comme on dit** as the saying goes; **dites donc!** hey!, say!; **il n'y a pas à dire** make no mistake about it ‖ *ref* to be said; to say to oneself or to each other; to claim to be, to call oneself

di·rect -recte [direkt] *adj* direct ‖ *m* (boxing) solid punch; **en direct** (rad, telv) live

direc·teur [direktœr] **-trice** [tris] *adj* directing, guiding; principal; driving (*rod, wheel*) ‖ *mf* director ‖ *f* directress

direction [direksjɔ̃] *f* direction; administration, management, board; head office; (aut) steering

direction·nel -nelle [direksjɔnel] *adj* directional

directorat [direktɔra] *m* directorship

dirigeable [diriʒabl] *adj* & *m* dirigible

diri·geant [diriʒɑ̃] **-geante** [ʒɑ̃t] *adj* governing, ruling ‖ *mf* ruler, leader, head, executive

diriger [diriʒe] §38 *tr* to direct, control, manage; to steer ‖ *ref* to go; **se diriger vers** to head for

dirigisme [diriʒism] *m* government economic planning and control

discernable [disernabl] *adj* discernible

discernement [disernamɑ̃] *m* discernment, perception

discerner [diserne] *tr* to discern

disciple [disipl] *m* disciple

disciplinaire [disipliner] *adj* disciplinary ‖ *m* military policeman

discipline [disiplin] *f* discipline; scourge

discipliner [disipline] *tr* to discipline

disconti·nu -nue [diskɔ̃tiny] *adj* discontinuous

discontinuer [diskɔ̃tinɥe] *tr* to discontinue

disconvenir [diskɔ̃vnir] §72 *tr* to deny ‖ *intr* (with *dat*) to not suit, displease ‖ *intr* (*aux*: ÊTRE)—**ne pas disconvenir de** to admit, agree

discophile [diskɔfil] *mf* record collector

discord [diskɔr] *adj masc* out of tune ‖ *m* instrument out of tune

discordance [diskɔrdɑ̃s] *f* discordance

discor·dant [diskɔrdɑ̃] **-dante** [dɑ̃t] *adj* discordant

discorde [diskɔrd] f discord
discorder [diskɔrde] intr to be discordant, to jar
discothèque [diskɔtek] f record cabinet; record library; discotheque
discourir [diskurir] §14 intr to discourse
discours [diskur] m discourse; speech
discour·tois [diskurtwa] **-toise** [twaz] adj discourteous
discourtoisie [diskurtwazi] f discourtesy
discrédit [diskredi] m discredit
discréditer [diskredite] tr to discredit
dis·cret [diskre] **-crète** [kret] adj discreet; discrete
discrétion [diskresjɔ̃] f discretion; à discrétion as much as one wants
discrimination [diskriminɑsjɔ̃] f discrimination
discriminatoire [diskriminatwar] adj discriminatory
discriminer [diskrimine] tr to discriminate
disculper [diskylpe] tr to clear, exonerate || ref to clear oneself
discur·sif [diskyrsif] **-sive** [siv] adj discursive
discussion [diskysjɔ̃] f discussion
discuter [diskyte] tr & intr to discuss; to question, debate
di·sert [dizer] **-serte** [zert] adj eloquent, fluent
disertement [dizertəmɑ̃] adv eloquently, fluently
disette [dizet] f shortage, scarcity; famine
di·seur [dizœr] **-seuse** [zøz] mf talker, speaker; monologuist; **diseuse de bonne aventure** fortuneteller
disgrâce [disgrɑs] f disfavor; misfortune; surliness, gruffness
disgra·cié -ciée [disgrɑsje] adj out of favor; ill-favored, homely; unfortunate
disgracier [disgrɑsje] tr to deprive of favor
disgra·cieux [disgrɑsjø] **-cieuse** [sjøz] adj awkward; homely, ugly; disagreeable
disjoindre [disʒwɛ̃dr] §35 tr to sever, to separate
disjoncteur [disʒɔ̃ktœr] m circuit breaker
dislocation [dislɔkɑsjɔ̃] f dislocation; separation; dismemberment
disloquer [dislɔke] tr to dislocate; to disperse; to dismember || ref to break up, disperse
disparaître [disparetr] §12 intr to disappear
disparate [disparat] adj incongruous || f incongruity; clash (of colors)
disparité [disparite] f disparity
disparition [disparisjɔ̃] f disappearance
dispa·ru -rue [dispary] adj disappeared; missing (in battle) || mf missing person; **le disparu** the deceased
dispen·dieux [dispɑ̃djø] **-dieuse** [djøz] adj expensive
dispensaire [dispɑ̃ser] m dispensary, outpatient clinic

dispensa·teur [dispɑ̃satœr] **-trice** [tris] mf dispenser
dispense [dispɑ̃s] f dispensation, exemption
dispenser [dispɑ̃se] tr to dispense; **dispensé du timbrage** (label on envelope) mailing permit
disperser [disperse] tr & ref to disperse
dispersion [dispersjɔ̃] f dispersion, dissipation
disponibilité [dispɔnibilite] f availability; **disponibilités** liquid assets; **en disponibilité** in the reserves
disponible [dispɔnibl] adj available; vacant (seat); (govt, mil) subject to call
dis·pos [dispo] **-pose** [poz] adj alert, fit, in good condition
dispo·sé -sée [dispoze] adj disposed; arranged; **disposé d'avance** predisposed; **peu disposé** reluctant
disposer [dispoze] tr to dispose || intr to dispose; **disposer de** to dispose of, to have at one's disposal; to have at hand; to make use of; **disposer pour** to provide for (e.g., the future); **vous pouvez disposer** you may leave || ref —se disposer à to be disposed to; to plan on
dispositif [dispozitif] m apparatus, device; (mil) disposition
disposition [dispozisjɔ̃] f disposition; disposal; **dispositions** arrangements; aptitude; provisions (of a legal document)
disproportion·né -née [disprɔpɔrsjɔne] adj disproportionate, incompatible
dispute [dispyt] f dispute
disputer [dispyte] tr to dispute; (coll) to bawl out || ref to dispute
disquaire [disker] m record dealer
disqualification [diskalifikɑsjɔ̃] f disqualification
disqualifier [diskalifje] tr & ref to disqualify
disque [disk] m disk; record, disk; (sports) discus; **changer de disque** (coll) to change the subject; **disque de longue durée** long-playing record
dissection [diseksjɔ̃] f dissection
dissemblable [disɑ̃blabl] adj dissimilar
dissemblance [disɑ̃blɑs] f dissimilarity
disséminer [disemine] tr to disseminate
dissension [disɑ̃sjɔ̃] f dissension
dissentiment [disɑ̃timɑ̃] m dissent
disséquer [diseke] §10 tr to dissect
dissertation [disertɑsjɔ̃] f dissertation; (in school) essay, term paper
dissidence [disidɑs] f dissent
dissi·dent -dente [disidɑ̃] adj dissenting || mf dissenter, dissident
dissimiler [disimile] tr (phonet) to dissimilate
dissimulation [disimylɑsjɔ̃] f dissemblance
dissimuler [disimyle] tr & intr to dissemble; **dissimuler q.ch. à qn** to conceal s.th. from s.o. || ref to hide, skulk
dissipation [disipɑsjɔ̃] f dissipation
dissi·pé -pée [disipe] adj dissipated; pleasure-seeking; unruly (schoolboy)
dissiper [disipe] tr & ref to dissipate

dissocier [disɔsje] *tr & ref* to dissociate
disso·lu -lue [disɔly] *adj* dissolute | *mf* profligate
dissolution [disɔlysjɔ̃] *f* dissolution; dissoluteness; rubber cement
dissol·vant [disɔlvɑ̃] **-vante** [vɑ̃t] *adj & m* solvent
dissonance [disɔnɑ̃s] *f* dissonance
dissoudre [disudr] §60 (*pp* dissous, dissoute; no *pret* or *imperf subj*) *tr & ref* to dissolve
dissuader [disɥade] *tr* to dissuade
distance [distɑ̃s] *f* distance; **à distance** at a distance
distancer [distɑ̃se] §51 *tr* to outdistance; to distance (*a race horse*)
dis·tant [distɑ̃] **-tante** [tɑ̃t] *adj* distant
distendre [distɑ̃dr] *tr & ref* to distend; to strain (*a muscle*)
distillation [distilɑsjɔ̃] *f* distillation
distiller [distile] *tr* to distill
distillerie [distilri] *f* distillery; distilling industry
dis·tinct [distɛ̃], [distɛ̃kt] **-tincte** [tɛ̃kt] *adj* distinct
distinc·tif [distɛ̃ktif] **-tive** [tiv] *adj* distinctive
distinction [distɛ̃ksjɔ̃] *f* distinction
distin·gué -guée [distɛ̃ge] *adj* distinguished; famous; sincere, e.g., **veuillez accepter nos sentiments distingués** (*complimentary close*) please accept our sincere regards
distinguer [distɛ̃ge] *tr* to distinguish || *ref* to be distinguished; to distinguish oneself
distordre [distɔrdr] *tr* to twist, to sprain
dis·tors [distɔr] **-torse** [tɔrs] *adj* twisted
distorsion [distɔrsjɔ̃] *f* sprain; convulsive twist; (electron, opt) distortion
distraction [distraksjɔ̃] *f* distraction; heedlessness, lapse; embezzlement; appropriation (*of a sum of money*)
distraire [distrer] §68 *tr* to distract, amuse; to separate, set aside (*e.g., part of one's savings*) || *ref* to amuse oneself
dis·trait [distre] **-traite** [tret] *adj* absent-minded
distribuer [distribɥe] *tr* to distribute; to arrange the furnishings of (*an apartment*)
distribu·teur [distribytœr] **-trice** [tris] *mf* distributor (*person*) || *m* (mach) distributor; **distributeur automatique** vending machine; **distributeur de musique** jukebox
distribution [distribysjɔ̃] *f* distribution; mail delivery; supply system (*of gas, water, or electricity*); valve gear (*of steam engine*); timing gears (*of internal-combustion engine*); (theat) cast
district [distrik], [distrikt] *m* district
dit [di] **dite** [dit] *adj* agreed upon, stated || *m* saying
dito [dito] *adv* ditto
diva [diva] *f* diva
divaguer [divage] *intr* to ramble
divan [divɑ̃] *m* divan

diverger [diverʒe] §38 *intr* to diverge
di·vers [diver] **-verse** [vers] *adj* changing, varied || **di·vers -verses** *adj pl* diverse, different, several
diversifier [diversifje] *tr & ref* to diversify
diversion [diversjɔ̃] *f* diversion
diversité [diversite] *f* diversity
divertir [divertir] *tr* to divert, amuse || *ref* to be diverted, amused
dividende [dividɑ̃d] *m* dividend
di·vin [divɛ̃] **-vine** [vin] *adj* divine
divination [divinɑsjɔ̃] *f* divination
divinité [divinite] *f* divinity
diviser [divize] *tr & ref* to divide
diviseur [divizœr] *m* (math) divisor; (fig) troublemaker
divisible [divizibl] *adj* divisible
division [divizjɔ̃] *f* division
divisionnaire [divizjɔner] *adj* divisional || *m* division head
divorce [divɔrs] *m* divorce
divor·cé -cée [divɔrse] *mf* divorced person || *f* divorcee
divorcer [divɔrse] §51 *tr* to divorce (*a married couple*) || *intr* to divorce, to get a divorce; **divorcer avec** to withdraw from (*the world*); **divorcer d'avec** to get a divorce from; to be divorced from, to divorce (*husband or wife*); to withdraw from (*the world*)
divulguer [divylge] *tr* to divulge
dix [di(s)] *adj & pron* ten; the Tenth, e.g., **Jean dix** John the Tenth; **dix heures** ten o'clock || *m* ten; tenth (*in dates*)
dix-huit [dizɥi], [dizɥit] *adj & pron* eighteen; the Eighteenth, e.g., **Jean dix-huit** John the Eighteenth || *m* eighteen; eighteenth (*in dates*)
dix-huitième [dizɥitjem] *adj & m* eighteenth
dixième [dizjem] *adj, pron (masc, fem), & m* tenth
dix-neuf [diznœf] *adj & pron* nineteen; the Nineteenth, e.g., **Jean dix-neuf** John the Nineteenth || *m* nineteen; nineteenth (*in dates*)
dix-neuvième [diznœvjem] *adj & m* nineteenth
dix-sept [disset] *adj & pron* seventeen; the Seventeenth, e.g., **Jean dix-sept** John the Seventeenth || *m* seventeen; seventeenth (*in dates*)
dix-septième [dissetjem] *adj & m* seventeenth
djinn [dʒin] *m* jinn
do° *abbr* (**dito**) do. (ditto)
docile [dɔsil] *adj* docile
dock [dɔk] *m* dock; warehouse; **dock flottant** floating dry dock
docker [dɔker] *m* dock worker
docte [dɔkt] *adj* learned, scholarly || *mf* scholar || *m* learned man
doc·teur [dɔktœr] **-toresse** [tɔres] *mf* doctor
docto·ral -rale [dɔktɔral] *adj* (*pl* **-raux** [ro]) doctoral
doctorat [dɔktɔra] *m* doctorate
doctrine [dɔktrin] *f* doctrine
document [dɔkymɑ̃] *m* document

documentaire [dɔkymãtɛr] *adj & m* documentary

documentation [dɔkymãtasjɔ̃] *f* documentation; literature (*about a region, business, etc.*)

documenter [dɔkymãte] *tr* to document ‖ *ref* to gather documentary evidence

dodeliner [dɔdline] *tr & intr* to sway, rock

dodo [dodo] *m* (orn) dodo; **aller au dodo** (*baby talk*) to go to bed; **faire dodo** to sleep

do·du ‑due [dɔdy] *adj* (coll) plump

dogmatique [dɔgmatik] *adj* dogmatic ‖ *mf* dogmatic person ‖ *f* dogmatics

dogmatiser [dɔgmatize] *intr* to dogmatize

dogme [dɔgm] *m* dogma

dogue [dɔg] *m* bulldog

doigt [dwa] *m* finger; **à deux doigts de** a hairbreadth away from; **doigt annulaire** ring finger; **doigt de Dieu** hand of God; **doigt du pied** toe; **mettre le doigt dessus** to hit the nail on the head; **mon petit doigt m'a dit** (coll) a little bird told me; **montrer du doigt** to single out (*for ridicule*); to point at; **petit doigt** little finger; **se mettre le doigt dans l'œil** (coll) to put one's foot in one's mouth; **se mordre les doigts** to be sorry

doigté [dwate] *m* touch; adroitness, skillfulness; fingering

doigter [dwate] *m* fingering ‖ *tr & intr* to finger

doigtier [dwatje] *m* fingerstall

doit [dwa] *m* debit

doléances [dɔleãs] *fpl* grievances

do·lent ‑lente [dɔlã] [lãt] *adj* doleful

dollar [dɔlar] *m* dollar

domaine [dɔmɛn] *m* domain

dôme [dom] *m* dome; cathedral

domestication [dɔmɛstikasjɔ̃] *f* domestication

domesticité [dɔmɛstisite] *f* domestication; staff of servants

domestique [dɔmɛstik] *adj & mf* domestic

domestiquer [dɔmɛstike] *tr* to domesticate

domicile [dɔmisil] *m* residence

domicilier [dɔmisilje] *tr* to domicile ‖ *ref* to take up residence

dominance [dɔminãs] *f* (genetics) dominance

domi·nant [dɔminã] **‑nante** [nãt] *adj* dominant ‖ *f* dominating trait; (mus) dominant

domina·teur [dɔminatœr] **‑trice** [tris] *adj* domineering, overbearing ‖ *mf* ruler, conqueror

domination [dɔminasjɔ̃] *f* domination

dominer [dɔmine] *tr & intr* to dominate ‖ *ref* to control oneself

domini·cal ‑cale [dɔminikal] *adj* (pl **‑caux** [ko]) Sunday; dominical

domino [dɔmino] *m* domino

dommage [dɔmaʒ] *m* loss; injury; **c'est dommage!** that's too bad! **dommages et intérêts** (law) damages; **quel dommage!** what a pity!

dommageable [dɔmaʒabl] *adj* injurious

dommages‑intérêts [dɔmaʒetere] *mpl* (law) damages

dompter [dɔ̃te] *tr* to tame; to train (*animals*); to subdue

domp·teur [dɔ̃tœr] **‑teuse** [tøz] *mf* tamer, trainer; conquerer

don [dɔ̃] *m* gift; don (*Spanish title*)

donataire [dɔnatɛr] *mf* legatee

dona·teur [dɔnatœr] **‑trice** [tris] *mf* (law) donor, legator

donation [dɔnasjɔ̃] *f* donation, gift, grant

donc [dɔ̃k], [dɔ̃] *adv* therefore, then; thus; now, of course; (often used for emphasis), e.g., **entrez donc!** do come in!

donjon [dɔ̃ʒɔ̃] *m* keep, donjon; (nav) turret

don·nant [dɔnã] **don·nante** [dɔnãt] *adj* generous, open-handed; **donnant donnant** tit for tat; cash down; **peu donnant** closefisted

donne [dɔn] *f* (cards) deal; doña (*Spanish title*); **fausse donne** misdeal

don·né ‑née [dɔne] *adj* given; **étant donné que** whereas, since ‖ *f* datum; **données** data, facts

donner [dɔne] *tr* to give; (cards) to deal ‖ *intr* to give; **donner sur** to open onto, to look out on; **donner sur les doigts** to rap one's knuckles

don·neur [dɔnœr] **don·neuse** [dɔnøz] *mf* donor; **donneur universel type‑O** blood donor ‖ *m* (cards) dealer

dont [dɔ̃] §79

donzelle [dɔ̃zɛl] *f* woman of easy virtue

doper [dɔpe] *tr* to dope

doping [dɔpiŋ] *m* dope, pep pill

dorade [dɔrad] *f* gilthead

dorénavant [dɔrenavã] *adv* henceforth

dorer [dɔre] *tr* to gild; (fig) to sugar-coat

d'ores [dɔr] see ores

dorlotement [dɔrlɔtmã] *m* coddling

dorloter [dɔrlɔte] *tr* to coddle

dor·mant [dɔrmã] **‑mante** [mãt] *adj* stagnant, immovable ‖ *m* doorframe

dor·meur [dɔrmœr] **‑meuse** [møz] *adj* sleeping ‖ *mf* sleeper ‖ *f* earring

dormir [dɔrmir] §23 *intr* to sleep; to lie dormant; **à dormir debout** boring, dull; **dormir debout** to sleep standing up; **dormir sur les deux oreilles** to feel secure

dortoir [dɔrtwar] *m* dormitory

dorure [dɔryr] *f* gilding; gilt; icing

dos [do] *m* back; bridge (*of nose*); **dans le dos de** behind the back of; **en dos d'âne** saddle-backed, hog-backed; **se mettre qn à dos** to make an enemy of s.o.; **voir au dos** see other side

dosage [dozaʒ] *m* dosage

dose [doz] *f* dose

doser [doze] *tr* to dose out, to measure out, to proportion

dossier [dosje] *m* chair back; dossier

dot [dɔt] *f* dowry

dotation [dɔtasjɔ̃] *f* endowment

doter [dɔte] *tr* to endow; to dower; to give a dowry to

douaire [dwɛr] *m* dower

douairière [dwɛrjɛr] *f* dowager

douane [dwan] *f* customs, duty; customhouse

doua·nier [dwanje] **-nière** [njer] *adj* customs ‖ *m* customs officer

doublage [dubla3] *m* doubling; metal plating of a ship; lining (*act of lining*); dubbing (*on tape or film*)

double [dubl] *adj & adv* double; **à double face** two-faced ‖ *m* double; duplicate, copy; **au double** twice; **double au carbone** carbon copy; **en double** in duplicate

doublement [dubləmã] *m* doubling ‖ *adv* doubly

doubler [duble] *tr* to double; to parallel, to run alongside; to pass (*s.o., s.th. going in the same direction*); to line (*a coat*); to dub (*a film*); to copy, dub (*a sound tape*); to replace (*an actor*); to gain one lap on (*another contestant*); (coll) to cheat ‖ *intr* to double; to pass (*on highway*)

doublure [dublyr] *f* lining; (theat) understudy, replacement

douce-amère [dusamer] *f* (*pl* **douces-amères**) (bot) bittersweet

douceâtre [dusɑtr] *adj* sweetish; mawkish

doucement [dusmã] *adv* softly; slowly ‖ *interj* easy now!, just a minute!

douce·reux [dusrø] **-reuse** [røz] *adj* unpleasantly sweet, cloying; mealymouthed

douceur [dusœr] *f* sweetness; softness, gentleness; **douceurs** sweets

douche [du∫] *f* shower bath; douche; (coll) dressing down; (coll) shock, disappointment

doucher [du∫e] *tr* to give a shower bath to; (coll) to reprimand; (coll) to disappoint ‖ *ref* to take a shower bath

doucir [dusir] *tr* to polish, rub

doué douée [dwe] *adj* gifted, endowed

douer [dwe] *tr* to endow; **douer de** to endow or gift (*s.o.*) with

douille [duj] *f* cartridge case; sconce (*of candlestick*); bushing; (elec) socket

douil·let [dujɛ] **douil·lette** [dujɛt] *adj* soft, delicate; oversensitive ‖ *f* child's padded coat

douleur [dulœr] *f* pain; sorrow; soreness

doulou·reux [dulurø] **-reuse** [røz] *adj* painful; sad; sore

doute [dut] *m* doubt; **sans doute** no doubt

douter [dute] *tr* to doubt, e.g., **je doute qu'il vienne** I doubt that he will come ‖ *intr* to doubt; **à n'en pas douter** beyond a doubt; **douter de** to doubt; to distrust ‖ *ref*—**se douter de** to suspect; **se douter que** to suspect that

dou·teur [dutœr] **-teuse** [tøz] *adj* doubting ‖ *mf* doubter

dou·teux [dutø] **-teuse** [tøz] *adj* doubtful; dubious

Douvres [duvr] Dover

doux [du] **douce** [dus] *adj* sweet; soft; pleasing, suave; quiet; new (*wine*) fresh (*water*); gentle (*slope*); mild

(*weather, climate*); **en douce** on the sly, on the q.t. ‖ **doux** *interj*—**tout doux!** easy there!

douzain [duzɛ̃] *m* twelve-line verse

douzaine [duzɛn] *f* dozen; **à la douzaine** by the dozen; **une douzaine de** a dozen

douze [duz] *adj & pron* twelve; the Twelfth, e.g., **Jean douze** John the Twelfth ‖ *m* twelve; twelfth (*in dates*)

douzième [duzjɛm] *adj, pron* (*masc, fem*), *& m* twelfth

doyen [dwajɛ̃] **doyenne** [dwajɛn] *mf* dean; **doyen d'âge** oldest member

doyenneté [dwajɛnte] *f* seniority

D′ *abbr* (**Docteur**) Dr.

drachme [drakm] *m* drachma; dram

dragage [draga3] *m* dredging

dragée [draʒe] *f* sugar-coated almond; (pharm) pill; (coll) bitter pill; **tenir la dragée haute à qn** to make s.o. pay through the nose; to be highhanded with s.o.

drageon [draʒɔ̃] *m* (bot) sucker

dragon [dragɔ̃] *m* (bot) dragon; dragoon; shrew; **dragon de vertu** prude

dragonne [dragɔn] *f* tassel, sword knot

drague [drag] *f* dredge; minesweeping apparatus

draguer [drage] *tr* to dredge, drag; to sweep for mines

dragueur [dragœr] *adj* minesweeping ‖ *m* dredger; **dragueur de mines** minesweeper

drain [drɛ̃] *m* drainpipe; (med) drain

drainage [drena3] *m* drainage

drainer [drene], [drene] *tr* to drain

draisine [drezin] *f* (rr) handcar

dramatique [dramatik] *adj* dramatic

dramatiser [dramatize] *tr* to dramatize

dramaturge [dramatyrʒ] *mf* playwright

dramaturgie [dramatyrʒi] *f* dramatics

drame [dram] *m* drama; tragic event

drap [dra] *m* cloth; sheet; **être dans de beaux draps** to be in a pretty pickle

dra·peau [drapo] *m* (*pl* **-peaux**) flag; **au drapeau!** colors (*bugle call*)!; **drapeau parlementaire** flag of truce; **être sous les drapeaux** to be a serviceman

draper [drape] *tr* to drape ‖ *ref* to drape oneself

draperie [drapri] *f* drapery; drygoods business; textile industry

dra·pier [drapje] **-pière** [pjɛr] *mf* draper; textile manufacturer

drastique [drastik] *adj* (med) drastic

drêche [drɛ∫] *f* draff, residue of malt

drège [drɛʒ] *f* dragnet

drelin [drəlɛ̃] *m* ting-a-ling

dressage [dresa3] *m* training (*of animals*); erection

dresser [drese] *tr* to raise, to hold erect; to train; to put up; to erect; to set (*the table; a trap*); to draw up, to draft; to plane, smooth; **dresser l'oreille** to prick up one's ears ‖ *ref* to stand or sit up straight; **se dresser contre** to be dead set against

dressoir [dreswar] *m* sideboard, buffet, dish closet

dribble [dribl] *m* (sports) dribble

dribbler [drible] *tr & intr* (sports) to dribble

drille [drij] *m*—**joyeux drille** gay blade || *f* jeweler's drill brace; **drilles** rags (*for papermaking*)

drisse [dris] *f* halyard, rope

drogue [drɔg] *f* drug; chemical; nostrum, concoction; narcotic; (coll) trash, rubbish

droguer [drɔge] *tr* to drug or dope (*with too much medicine*) || *intr* (coll) to cool one's heels || *ref* to drug or dope oneself

droguerie [drɔgri] *f* drysaltery (Brit)

droguiste [drɔgist] *mf* drysalter (Brit)

droit [drwa], [drwa] **droite** [drwat], [drwat] *adj* right; honest, sincere; fair, just || *m* law; right, justice; tax; right angle; **à bon droit** with reason; **de (plein) droit** rightfully, by rights, incontestably; **droit coutumier** common law; **droit de cité** key to the city; acceptability; **droits** duties, customs; rights; **droits civils** rights to manage property; **droits civiques, droits politiques** civil rights; **droits d'auteur** royalty; **droits de reproduction réservés** copyrighted; **tous droits réservés** all rights reserved, copyrighted || *f* right, right-hand side; right hand; straight line; **à droite** to or on the right || **droit** *adv* —**droit au** but straight to the point; **tout droit** straight ahead

droi•tier [drwatje], [drwatje] **-tière** [tjer] *adj* right-handed || *mf* right-handed person; rightist

droiture [drwatyr], [drwatyr] *f* integrity

drolatique [drɔlatik] *adj* droll, comic

drôle [drol] *adj* droll, funny, strange; **drôle de** funny, e.g., **une drôle d'idée** a funny idea; **drôle de guerre** phony war; **drôle d'homme, de corps, de pistolet,** or **de pierrot** (coll) queer duck || *mf* (coll) queer duck, strange person

drôlerie [drolri] *f* drollery

drôlesse [droles] *f* wench, hussy

dromadaire [drɔmader] *m* dromedary

dronte [drɔt] *m* (orn) dodo

droppage [drɔpaʒ] *m* airdrop

drosser [drɔse] *tr* to drive, carry (*as the wind drives a ship ashore*)

dru drue [dry] *adj* thick, dense; fine (*rain*) || **dru** *adv* thickly, heavily

druide [drɥid] *m* druid

du [dy] §77

dû due [dy] *adj & m* due

duc [dyk] *m* duke; horned owl

ducat [dyka] *m* ducat

duché [dyʃe] *m* duchy, dukedom

duchesse [dyʃes] *f* duchess

duègne [dɥɛɲ] *f* duenna

duel [dɥel] *m* duel; dual number; **duel oratoire** verbal battle

duelliste [dɥelist] *m* duelist

dulcifier [dylsifje] *tr* to sweeten

dûment [dymɑ̃] *adv* duly

dune [dyn] *f* dune

dunette [dynet] *f* (naut) poop

Dunkerque [dœ̃kerk] *f* Dunkirk

duo [dɥo] *m* duet; duo; **duo d'injures** exchange of words, insults

duodénum [dɥodenɔm] *m* duodenum

dupe [dyp] *f* dupe

duper [dype] *tr* to dupe

duperie [dypri] *f* deception, trickery

duplicata [dyplikata] *m* duplicate

duplicateur [dyplikatœr] *m* duplicating machine

duplication [dyplikasjɔ̃] *f* duplication

duplicité [dyplisite] *f* duplicity

duquel [dykel] §78

dur dure [dyr] *adj* hard; tough; difficult; **coucher sur la dure** to sleep on the bare ground or floor; **dur à la détente** tight-fisted; **dur d'oreille** hard of hearing; **élever un enfant à la dure** to give a child a strict upbringing || *mf* (coll) tough customer || *m* hard material, concrete || **dur** *adv* hard, e.g., **travailler dur** to work hard

durable [dyrabl] *adj* durable

durant [dyrɑ̃] *prep* during; (sometimes stands after noun), e.g., **sa vie durant** during his life

durcir [dyrsir] *tr, intr & ref* to harden

durcissement [dyrsismɑ̃] *m* hardening

durée [dyre] *f* duration; wear

durer [dyre] *intr* to last, endure

dureté [dyrte] *f* hardness; cruelty

durillon [dyrijɔ̃] *m* callus, corn

duvet [dyve] *m* down, fuzz; nap (*of cloth*)

duve•té -tée [dyvte] *adj* downy

duve•teux [dyvtø] **-teuse** [tøz] *adj* fuzzy

dynamique [dinamik] *adj* dynamic || *f* dynamics

dynamite [dinamit] *f* dynamite

dynamiter [dinamite] *tr* to dynamite

dynamo [dinamo] *f* dynamo

dynaste [dinast] *m* dynast

dynastie [dinasti] *f* dynasty

dysenterie [disɑ̃tri] *f* dysentery

dyspepsie [dispɛpsi] *f* dyspepsia

E

E, e [ə], ***** [ə] *m invar* fifth letter of the French alphabet

eau [o] *f* (*pl* **eaux**) water; wake (*of ship*); **à l'eau de rose** maudlin; **de la plus belle eau** of the first water; **eau calcaire** hard water; **eau de cale** bilge water; **eau de Javel** bleach; **eau dentifrice** mouthwash; **eau douce** soft water; fresh water; **eau dure** hard water; **eau lourde** heavy water;

eau oxygénée hydrogen peroxide; eau vive running water; eaux waters; waterworks; eaux juvéniles mineral waters; eaux thermales hot springs; eaux usées, eaux résiduelles polluted water; eaux vives swift current; être en eau to sweat; faire de l'eau to take in water; faire eau to leak; grandes eaux fountains; nager entre deux eaux to float under the surface; to play both sides of the street; pêcher en eau trouble to fish in troubled waters; porter de l'eau à la rivière or à la mer to carry coals to Newcastle; tomber à l'eau to fizzle out

eau-de-vie [odvi] f (pl **eaux-de-vie**) brandy; spirits

eau-forte [ofɔrt] f (pl **eaux-fortes**) aqua fortis; etching

éba·hi ·hie [ebai] adj dumfounded

ébattre [ebatr] §7 ref to frolic, to gambol

ébauche [eboʃ] f rough sketch or draft; suspicion (of a smile)

ébaucher [eboʃe] tr to sketch, to make a rough draft of

ébène [eben] f ebony

ébénier [ebenje] m ebony (tree)

ébéniste [ebenist] m cabinetmaker

ébénisterie [ebenistri] f cabinetmaking

éberluer [eberlɥe] tr to astonish

éblouir [ebluir] tr to dazzle, blind

éblouissement [ebluismɑ̃] m dazzle; glare; (pathol) dizziness

éboueur [ebwœr] m street cleaner, trash man; garbage collector

ébouillanter [ebujɑ̃te] tr to scald

éboulement [ebulmɑ̃] m cave-in, landslide

ébouler [ebule] tr & ref to cave in

ébouri·fant [eburifɑ̃] **ébouri·fante** [eburifɑ̃t] adj (coll) astounding

ébouriffer [eburife] tr to ruffle; (coll) to astound

ébouter [ebute] tr to cut off the end of

ébranchage [ebrɑ̃ʃaʒ] m pruning

ébrancher [ebrɑ̃ʃe] tr to prune

ébranlement [ebrɑ̃lmɑ̃] m shaking; shock

ébranler [ebrɑ̃le] tr to shake, jar || ref to start out; to be shaken

ébrécher [ebreʃe] §10 tr to nick, chip; to make a dent in (e.g., a fortune) || ref to be nicked, chipped; (with dat of reflex pron) to break off (a tooth)

ébriété [ebrijete] f inebriation

ébrouer [ebrue] ref to snort (said of horse); to splash about; to shake the water off oneself

ébruiter [ebrɥite] tr to noise about, to blab || ref to get around (said of news); to leak out (said of secret)

ébullition [ebylisjɔ̃] f boiling; ebullience, ferment

ébur·né ·née [ebyrne] adj ivory

écaille [ekaj] f scale (of fish, snake); shell; tortoise shell

écail·ler [ekaje] **écail·lère** [ekajer] mf oyster opener || m oysterman || f oysterwoman || **écailler** tr & ref to scale

écale [ekal] f shell, husk, hull

écaler [ekale] tr to shell, husk, hull

écarlate [ekarlat] adj & f scarlet

écarquiller [ekarkije] tr (coll) to open wide, to spread apart

écart [ekar] m swerve, side step; digression, flight (of imagination); difference, gap, spread; error (in range); lapse (in good conduct); (cards) discard; à l'écart aside; aloof; à l'écart de far from; faire le grand écart to do the splits; faire un écart to shy (said of horse); to swerve (said of car); to step aside (said of person)

écar·té ·tée [ekarte] adj lonely, secluded; wide-apart

écartèlement [ekartelmɑ̃] m quartering

écarteler [ekartəle] §2 tr to quarter

écartement [ekartəmɑ̃] m removal, separation; spreading; space between; spark gap; gauge (of rails)

écarter [ekarte] tr to put aside; to keep away; to ward off; to draw aside; to spread; (cards) to discard || ref to turn away; to stray

ecchymose [ekimoz] f black-and-blue mark

ecclésiastique [eklezjastik] adj & m ecclesiastic

écerve·lé ·lée [eservəle] adj scatterbrained || mf scatterbrain

échafaud [eʃafo] m scaffold

échafaudage [eʃafodaʒ] m scaffolding

échafauder [eʃafode] tr to pile up; to lay the groundwork for || intr to erect a scaffolding

échalasser [eʃalase] tr to stake

échalote [eʃalɔt] f shallot

échancrer [eʃɑ̃kre] tr to make a V-shaped cut in (the neck of a dress); to cut (a dress) low in the neck; to indent; to hollow out

échange [eʃɑ̃ʒ] m exchange

échanger [eʃɑ̃ʒe] §38 tr to exchange; **échanger pour** or **contre** to exchange (s.th.) for

échangeur [eʃɑ̃ʒœr] m interchange

échanson [eʃɑ̃sɔ̃] m cupbearer

échantillon [eʃɑ̃tijɔ̃] m sample; **comparer à l'échantillon** to spot-check

échantillonnage [eʃɑ̃tijɔnaʒ] m sampling; spot check

échantillonner [eʃɑ̃tijɔne] tr to cut samples of; to spot-check; to select (a sampling to be polled)

échappatoire [eʃapatwar] f loophole, way out

échap·pé ·pée [eʃape] mf escapee || f escape; short period; glimpse; (sports) spurt; à l'échappée stealthily

échappement [eʃapmɑ̃] m escape, leak; exhaust; escapement (of watch); **échappement libre** cutout

échapper [eʃape] tr—**l'échapper belle** to have a narrow escape || intr to escape; **échapper à** to escape from; **échapper de** to slip out of || ref to escape

écharde [eʃard] f splinter

écharpe [eʃarp] f scarf; sash; sling; **en écharpe** diagonally, crosswise; in a sling; across the shoulder

écharper [eʃarpe] tr to slash, cut up

échasse [eʃɑs] *f* stilt

échauder [eʃode] *tr* to scald; to whitewash; to gouge (*a customer*)

échauffement [eʃofmɑ̃] *m* heating; overexcitement

échauffer [eʃofe] *tr* to heat; to warm; **échauffer les oreilles à qn** to get s.o.'s dander up || *ref* to heat up; to become excited

échauffourée [eʃofure] *f* skirmish; rash undertaking

èche [ɛʃ] *f* bait

échéance [eʃeɑ̃s] *f* due date, expiration

échec [eʃɛk] *m* check; chessman; failure; **échec et mat** checkmate; **échecs** [eʃɛ] chess; chess set; **être échec** to be in check; **jouer aux échecs** to play chess

échelle [eʃɛl] *f* ladder; scale; **échelle de sauvetage** fire escape; **échelle mobile** sliding scale; **échelle pliante** stepladder; **monter à l'échelle** (coll) to bite, be fooled

échelon [eʃlɔ̃] *m* echelon; rung (*of ladder*)

échelonner [eʃlone] *tr* to spread out, to space out

écheniller [eʃnije] *tr* to remove caterpillars from; to exterminate (*pests*); to eradicate (*corruption*)

éche·veau [eʃvo] *m* (*pl* **-veaux**) skein

écheve·lé -lée [eʃəvle] *adj* disheveled; wild (*dance, race*)

écheveler [eʃəvle] §34 *tr* to dishevel

échevin [eʃvɛ̃] *m* (hist) alderman

échine [eʃin] *f* spine, backbone; **avoir l'échine souple** (coll) to be a yes man

échiner [eʃine] *tr* to break the back of; to beat, kill || *ref* to tire oneself out

échiquier [eʃikje] *m* chessboard; exchequer

écho [eko] *m* echo; piece of gossip; **échos** gossip column; **faire écho** to echo

échoir [eʃwar] (usually used only in: *inf*; *ger* **échéant**; *pp* **échu**; 3d *sg*: *pres ind* **échoit**; *pret* **échut**; *cond* **échoirait**) *intr* (*aux*: AVOIR or ÊTRE) to fall, devolve; to fall due

échoppe [eʃɔp] *f* burin; (com) stand, booth; workshop

échopper [eʃɔpe] *tr* to scoop out

échotier [eʃotje] *m* gossip columnist, society editor

échouer [eʃwe] *tr* to ground, to beach || *intr* to sink; to run aground; to fail || *ref* to run aground

é·chu -chue [eʃy] *adj* due, payable

écimer [esime] *tr* to top

éclaboussement [eklabusmɑ̃] *m* splash

éclabousser [eklabuse] *tr* to splash

éclair [ekler] *adj* lightning (*e.g., speed*); flash (*bulb*) || *m* flash (*of light, of lightning, of the eyes, of wit*); (culin) éclair; **éclairs** lightning; **éclairs de chaleur** heat lightning; **éclairs en nappe** sheet lightning; **il fait des éclairs** it is lightening; **passer comme un éclair** to flash by

éclairage [ekleraʒ] *m* lighting; **sous cet éclairage** (fig) in this light

éclaircie [eklersi] *f* break, clearing; spell of good weather

éclaircissement [eklersismɑ̃] *m* explanation, clearing up

éclairement [eklermɑ̃] *m* illumination

éclairer [eklere] *tr* to light; to enlighten; **éclairer sa lanterne** (fig) to ring a bell for s.o. || *intr* to light up, to glitter; **il éclaire** it is lightening || *ref* to be lighted

éclai·reur [eklerœr] **-reuse** [røz] *mf* scout || *m* boy scout || *f* girl scout

éclat [ekla] *m* splinter; ray (*of sunshine*); peal (*of thunder*); burst (*of laughter*); brightness, splendor

éclatement [eklatmɑ̃] *m* explosion; blowout (*of tire*); (fig) split

éclater [eklate] *intr* to splinter; to sparkle, glitter; to burst; to break out; to blow up

éclateur [eklatœr] *m* spark gap (*of induction coil*)

éclectique [eklektik] *adj* eclectic

éclipse [eklips] *f* eclipse; **à éclipses** flashing, blinking

éclipser [eklipse] *tr* to eclipse || *ref* to be eclipsed; (coll) to vanish; (coll) to sneak off

éclisse [eklis] *f* splinter; (med) splint; (rr) fishplate

éclisser [eklise] *tr* to splint

éclo·pé -pée [eklope] *adj* lame || *mf* cripple

éclore [eklɔr] §24 *intr* (*aux*: ÊTRE) to hatch; to blossom out

éclosion [eklozjɔ̃] *f* hatching; blooming

écluse [eklyz] *f* lock (*of canal, river, etc.*); floodgate

écluser [eklyze] *tr* to close (*a canal*) by a lock; to pass (*a boat*) through a lock

écœurer [ekœre] *tr* to sicken; to dishearten

école [ekɔl] *f* school; **école à tir** artillery practice; **école d'application** model school; **école d'arts et métiers** trade school; **école dominicale**, **école du dimanche** Sunday School; **école libre** private school; **école maternelle** nursery school; **école mixte** coeducational school; **être à bonne école** to be in good hands; **faire école** to set a fashion; to form a school (*to set up a doctrine, gain adherents*); **faire l'école buissonnière** (coll) to play hooky

éco·lier [ekɔlje] **-lière** [ljer] *adj* schoolboy || *mf* pupil, scholar; novice || *m* schoolboy || *f* schoolgirl

écologie [ekɔlɔʒi] *f* ecology

éconduire [ekɔ̃dɥir] §19 *tr* to show out

économat [ekɔnɔma] *m* comptroller's office; commissary, company or co-op store; **économats** chain stores

économe [ekɔnɔm] *adj* economical || *mf* treasurer; housekeeper || *m* bursar

économie [ekɔnɔmi] *f* economy; **économie de marché** free enterprise; **économies** savings

économique [ekɔnɔmik] *adj* economic; economical || *f* economics

économiser [ekɔnɔmize] *tr & intr* to economize, save

écope [ekɔp] f scoop (for bailing)
écoper [ekɔpe] tr to bail out ‖ intr (coll) to get a bawling out
écorce [ekɔrs] f bark (of tree); peel, rind; crust (of earth)
écorcer [ekɔrse] §51 tr to peel, to strip off
écorcher [ekɔrʃe] tr to peel; to chafe; to fleece, overcharge; to grate on (the ears); to burn (the throat); to murder (a language) ‖ ref (with dat of reflex pron) to skin (e.g., one's arm)
écor·cheur [ekɔrʃœr] **-cheuse** [ʃøz] mf skinner; fleecer, swindler
écorchure [ekɔrʃyr] f scratch, abrasion
écorner [ekɔrne] tr to poll, break the horns of; to dog-ear; to make a hole in (e.g., a fortune)
écornifler [ekɔrnifle] tr to cadge; **écornifler un dîner à qn** to bum a dinner off s.o.
écorni·fleur [ekɔrnifloer] **-fleuse** [fløz] mf sponger, moocher
écos·sais [ekɔsɛ] **écos·saise** [ekosɛz] adj Scotch, Scottish ‖ m Scotch, Scottish (language); Scotch plaid ‖ (cap) mf Scot; **les Écossais** the Scotch ‖ m Scotchman
Écosse [ekɔs] f Scotland; **l'Écosse** Scotland
écosser [ekɔse] tr to shell, hull, husk
écot [eko] m share; tree stump; **payer son écot** to pay one's share
écoulement [ekulmɑ̃] m flow; (com) sale, turnover; (pathol) discharge; **écoulement d'eau** drainage
écouler [ekule] tr to sell, dispose of ‖ ref to run (said, e.g., of water); to flow; to drain; to leak; to elapse, go by
écourter [ekurte] tr to shorten (a dress, coat, etc.); to crop (the tail, ears, etc.); to cut short, curtail
écoute [ekut] f listening post; monitoring; (naut) sheet; **écoutes** wild boar's ears; **être aux écoutes** to eavesdrop, to keep one's ears to the ground; **se mettre à l'écoute** to listen to the radio
écouter [ekute] tr to listen to; **écouter parler** to listen to (s.o.) speaking ‖ intr to listen; **écouter aux portes** to eavesdrop ‖ ref to coddle oneself; **s'écouter parler** to be pleased with the sound of one's own voice
écou·teur [ekutœr] **-teuse** [tøz] mf listener; **écouteur aux portes** eavesdropper ‖ m telephone receiver; earphone
écoutille [ekutij] f hatchway
écouvillon [ekuvijɔ̃] m swab, mop
écrabouiller [ekrabuje] tr (coll) to squash
écran [ekrɑ̃] m screen; (phot) filter; **écran de cheminée** fire screen; **écran de protection aérienne** air umbrella; **le petit écran** television screen; **porter à l'écran** to put on the screen
écra·sant [ekrazɑ̃] **-sante** [zɑ̃t] adj crushing
écraser [ekraze] tr to crush; to overwhelm; to run over ‖ ref to be crushed; to crash

écrémer [ekreme] §10 tr to skim; (fig) to skim the cream off
écrémeuse [ekremøz] f cream separator
écrevisse [ekrəvis] f crayfish
écrier [ekrije] ref to cry out, exclaim
écrin [ekrɛ̃] m jewel case
écrire [ekrir] §25 tr to write; to spell ‖ intr to write ‖ ref to write to each other; to be written; to be spelled
é·crit [ekri] **-crite** [krit] adj written; **c'était écrit** it was fate ‖ m writing, written word; written examination; **écrits** writings, works; **par écrit** in writing
écriteau [ekrito] m (pl **-teaux**) sign, placard
écritoire [ekritwar] f desk set
écriture [ekrityr] f handwriting; writing (style of writing); **écriture de chat** scrawl; **écritures** accounts; **Écritures** Scriptures; **écritures publiques** government documents
écrivailleur [ekrivɑjœr] m (coll) scribbler, hack writer
écrivain [ekrivɛ̃] adj—**femme écrivain** woman writer ‖ m writer; **écrivain public** public letter writer
écrivasser [ekrivase] intr (coll) to scribble
écrou [ekru] m nut (with internal thread); register (on police blotter); **écrou à oreille** thumb nut
écrouer [ekrue] tr to jail, to book
écrouler [ekrule] ref to collapse; to crumble; to flop (in a chair)
é·cru -crue [ekry] adj raw; unbleached
écu [eky] m shield; crown (money); **écus** money
écubier [ekybje] m (naut) hawsehole
écueil [ekœj] m reef, sandbank; stumbling block
écuelle [ekɥɛl] f bowl
éculer [ekyle] tr to wear down at the heel
écu·mant [ekymɑ̃] **-mante** [mɑ̃t] adj foaming, fuming (with rage)
écume [ekym] f foam; froth; lather; dross; scum (on liquids; on metal; of society); **écume de mer** meerschaum
écumer [ekyme] tr to skim, scum; to pick up (e.g., gossip); to scour (the seas) ‖ intr to foam; to scum; to fume (with anger)
écu·meur [ekymœr] **-meuse** [møz] mf drifter; **écumeur de marmite** hanger-on; **écumeur de mer** pirate
écu·meux [ekymø] **-meuse** [møz] adj foamy, frothy
écumoire [ekymwar] f skimmer
écurage [ekyraʒ] m scouring; cleaning out
écurer [ekyre] tr to scour; to clean out
écureuil [ekyrœj] m squirrel
écurie [ekyri] f stable (for horses, mules, etc.); string of horses
écusson [ekysɔ̃] m escutcheon; bud (for grafting); (mil) identification tag
écuyer [ekɥije] **écuyère** [ekɥijɛr] mf horseback rider ‖ m horseman; squire; riding master ‖ f horsewoman
eczéma [ɛkzema], [ɛgzema] m eczema

edelweiss [edəlvɑjs], [edelves] *m* edelweiss

éden [eden] *m* Eden || (*cap*) *m* Garden of Eden

éden·té -tée [edɑ̃te] *adj* toothless

E.D.F. *abbr* (**Électricité de France**) French national electric company

édicter [edikte] *tr* to decree, to promulgate

édicule [edikyl] *m* kiosk; street urinal

édi·fiant [edifjɑ̃] **-fiante** [fjɑ̃t] *adj* edifying

édification [edifikɑsjɔ̃] *f* edification; construction, building

édifice [edifis] *m* edifice, building

édifier [edifje] *tr* to edify; to inform, enlighten; to construct, to build; to found

édit [edi] *m* edict

éditer [edite] *tr* to publish; to edit (*a manuscript*)

édi·teur [editœr] **-trice** [tris] *mf* publisher; editor (*of a manuscript*)

édition [edisjɔ̃] *f* edition; publishing

édito·rial -riale [editɔrjal] *adj & m* (*pl* **-riaux** [rjo]) editorial

édredon [edrədɔ̃] *m* eiderdown

éduca·teur [edykatœr] **-trice** [tris] *adj* educational || *mf* educator

éduca·tif [edykatif] **-tive** [tiv] *adj* educational

éducation [edykɑsjɔ̃] *f* education, bringing-up, nurture

éduquer [edyke] *tr* to bring up (*children*); to educate, train

éfaufiler [efofile] *tr* to unravel

effacement [efasmɑ̃] *m* effacement, erasing; self-effacement

effacer [efase] §51 *tr* to efface; to erase || *ref* to efface oneself; to stand aside

effarement [efarmɑ̃] *m* fright, scare

effaroucher [efaru/e] *tr* to frighten, scare off

effec·tif [efɛktif] **-tiv** [tiv] *adj* actual, real || *m* personnel, manpower; strength (*of military unit*); complement (*of ship*); size (*of class*)

effectivement [efɛktivmɑ̃] *adv* actually, really, sure enough

effectuer [efɛktɥe] *tr* to effect

effémi·né -née [efemine] *adj* effeminate

efféminer [efemine] *tr* to make a sissy of; to unman || *ref* to become effeminate

effervescence [efervesɑ̃s] *f* effervescence; excitement, ferment

efferves·cent [efervesɑ̃] **efferves·cente** [efervesɑ̃t] *adj* effervescent

effet [efɛ] *m* effect; (billiards) english; **à cet effet** for that purpose; **en effet** indeed, actually, sure enough; **effet de commerce** bill of exchange; **effets publics** government bonds; **faire de l'effet** to be striking; **faire l'effet de** to give the impression of

effeuillage [efœjaʒ] *m* thinning of leaves

effeuillaison [efœjezɔ̃] *f* fall of leaves

effeuiller [efœje] *tr* to thin out the leaves of, to pluck off the petals of || *ref* to shed its leaves

effeuilleuse [efœjøz] *f* (coll) stripteaser

efficace [efikas] *adj* effective

efficacement [efikasmɑ̃] *adv* effectively

efficacité [efikasite] *f* efficacy, efficiency

efficience [efisjɑ̃s] *f* efficiency

effi·cient [efisjɑ̃] **-ciente** [sjɑ̃t] *adj* efficient

effigie [efiʒi] *f* effigy

effiler [efile] *tr* to unravel; to taper

effilocher [efilɔ/e] *tr* to unravel

efflan·qué -quée [eflɑ̃ke] *adj* skinny

effleurer [eflœre] *tr* to graze; to touch on

effluve [eflyv] *m* effluvium, emanation

effondrement [efɔ̃drəmɑ̃] *m* collapse

effondrer [efɔ̃dre] *tr* to break open; to break (*ground*) || *ref* to collapse, cave in; to sink

efforcer [eforse] §51 *ref*—**s'efforcer à** or **de** to try hard to, to strive to

effort [efɔr] *m* effort; (med) hernia, rupture; **effort de rupture** breaking stress; **effort de tension** torque; **faire effort sur soi-même** to get a hold of oneself

effraction [efraksjɔ̃] *f* housebreaking

effraie [efre] *f* screech owl

effranger [efrɑ̃ʒe] §38 *tr & ref* to fray

effrayant [efrejɑ̃] **effrayante** [efrejɑ̃t] *adj* frightful, dreadful

effrayer [efreje] §49 *tr* to frighten || *ref* to be frightened

effré·né -née [efrene] *adj* unbridled

effritement [efritmɑ̃] *m* crumbling

effriter [efrite] *tr & ref* to crumble

effroi [efrwa] *m* fright

effron·té -tée [efrɔ̃te] *adj* impudent; shameless; (slang) saucy, sassy

effronterie [efrɔ̃tri] *f* effrontery

effroyable [efrwajabl] *adj* frightful

effusion [efyzjɔ̃] *f* effusion; shedding (*of blood*); (fig) gushing

égailler [egaje] *ref* to scatter

é·gal -gale [egal] (*pl* **-gaux** [go]) *adj* equal; level; (coll) indifferent; **ça m'est égal** (coll) it's all the same to me, it's all right || *mf* equal; **à l'égal de** as much as, no less than

également [egalmɑ̃] *adv* equally, likewise, also

égaler [egale] *tr* to equal, match

égaliser [egalize] *tr* to equalize; to equate

égalitaire [egaliter] *adj & mf* equalitarian

égalité [egalite] *f* equality; evenness; **être à égalité** to be tied

égard [egar] *m* respect; **à l'égard de** with regard to; **à tous (les) égards** in all respects; **eu égard à** in consideration of

éga·ré -rée [egare] *adj* stray, lost

égarement [egarmɑ̃] *m* wandering (*of mind, senses, etc.*); frenzy (*of sorrow, anger, etc.*)

égarer [egare] *tr* to mislead; to misplace; to bewilder || *ref* to get lost, to stray; to be on the wrong track

égayer [egeje] §49 *tr & ref* to cheer up; to brighten

égide [eʒid] f aegis
églefin [egləfɛ̃] m haddock
église [egliz] f church
églogue [eglog] f eclogue
égoïne [egɔin] f handsaw
égoïsme [egɔism] m egoism
égoïste [egɔist] adj selfish ‖ mf egoist
égorgement [egɔrʒəmɑ̃] m slaughter
égorger [egɔrʒe] §38 tr to cut the throat of; (coll) to overcharge
égosiller [egɔzije] ref to shout oneself hoarse
égotisme [egɔtism] m egotism
égotiste [egɔtist] adj egotistical ‖ mf egotist
égout [egu] m drainage; sewer; sink, cesspool (e.g., of iniquity)
égoutier [egutje] m sewer worker
égoutter [egute] tr to drain; to let drip ‖ ref to drip
égouttoir [egutwar] m drainboard
égrapper [egrape] tr to pick off from the cluster
égratigner [egratiɲe] tr to scratch; to take a dig at, to tease
égratignure [egratiɲyr] f scratch; gibe, dig
égrener [egrəne] §2 tr to shell (e.g., peas); to gin (cotton); to pick off (grapes); to unstring (pearls); to tell (beads) ‖ ref to drop one by one; to be strung out
égril·lard [egrijar] égril·larde [egrijard] adj spicy, lewd ‖ mf shameless, unblushing person
égrugeoir [egryʒwar] m mortar (for pounding or grinding)
égruger [egryʒe] §38 tr to pound (in a mortar)
égueuler [egœle] tr to break the neck of (e.g., a bottle)
Égypte [eʒipt] f Egypt; l'Égypte Egypt
égyp·tien [eʒipsjɛ̃] -tienne [sjɛn] adj Egyptian ‖ (cap) mf Egyptian
éhon·té -tée [eɔ̃te] adj shameless
eider [ejder] m eider duck
éjaculation [eʒakylɑsjɔ̃] f ejaculation; (eccl) short, fervent prayer
éjaculer [eʒakyle] tr & intr to ejaculate
éjecter [eʒɛkte] tr to eject; (coll) to oust
éjection [eʒɛksjɔ̃] f ejection
élabo·ré -rée [elabɔre] adj elaborated; prepared, elaborate
élaborer [elabɔre] tr to elaborate; to work out, develop
élaguer [elage] tr to prune
élan [elɑ̃] m dash; impulse, outburst; spirit, glow; (zool) elk, moose; avec élan with enthusiasm
élan·cé -cée [elɑ̃se] adj slender, slim
élancement [elɑ̃smɑ̃] m throbbing, twinge; yearning (e.g., for God)
élancer [elɑ̃se] §51 intr to throb, to twinge ‖ ref to rush, spring, dash; to spurt out
élargir [elarʒir] tr to widen; to broaden; to release (a prisoner) ‖ ref to widen; to become more lax
élasticité [elastisite] f elasticity
élastique [elastik] adj elastic ‖ m elastic; rubber band

élec·teur [elɛktœr] -trice [tris] adj voting ‖ mf voter, constituent; (hist) elector; électeurs electorate
élec·tif [elɛktif] -tive [tiv] adj elective
élection [elɛksjɔ̃] f election; choice
électorat [elɛktɔra] m right to vote; (hist) electorate
électri·cien [elɛktrisjɛ̃] -cienne [sjɛn] adj electrical (worker) ‖ mf electrician
électricité [elɛktrisite] f electricity
électrifier [elɛktrifje] tr to electrify
électrique [elɛktrik] adj electric(al)
électriser [elɛktrize] tr to electrify
électro [elɛktro] m electromagnet
électro-aimant [elɛktroɛmɑ̃] m (pl -aimants) electromagnet
électrochoc [elɛktroʃɔk] m (med) electric shock treatment
électro-culinaire [elɛktrokylinɛr] adj electric kitchen (appliances)
électrocuter [elɛktrɔkyte] tr to electrocute
électrode [elɛktrɔd] f electrode
électrolyse [elɛktrɔliz] f electrolysis
électrolyte [elɛktrɔlit] m electrolyte
électromagnétique [elɛktrɔmaɲetik] adj electromagnetic
électroména·ger [elɛktrɔmenaʒe] -gère [ʒɛr] adj household-electric
électromo·teur [elɛktrɔmɔtœr] -trice [tris] adj electromotive ‖ m electric motor
électron [elɛktrɔ̃] m electron
électronique [elɛktrɔnik] adj electronic ‖ f electronics
électron-volt [elɛktrɔvɔlt] m (pl électrons-volts) electron-volt
électrophone [elɛktrɔfɔn] m electric phonograph
électrotype [elɛktrɔtip] m electrotype
électrotyper [elɛktrɔtipe] tr to electrotype
élégance [elegɑ̃s] f elegance
élé·gant [elegɑ̃] -gante [gɑ̃t] adj elegant
élégiaque [eleʒjak] adj elegiac ‖ mf elegist
élégie [eleʒi] f elegy
élément [elemɑ̃] m element; (of an electric battery) cell, element; (elec, mach) unit; élément standard standard part
élémentaire [elemɑ̃tɛr] adj elementary
éléphant [elefɑ̃] m elephant
éléphantesque [elefɑ̃tɛsk] adj (coll) gigantic, elephantine
élevage [elvaʒ], [elvaʒ] m rearing, raising, breeding; ranch
éléva·teur [elevatœr] -trice [tris] adj lifting ‖ m elevator; hoist
élévation [elevɑsjɔ̃] f elevation; promotion; increase; (rok) lift-off
élève [elɛv] mf pupil, student; ancien élève alumnus; élève externe day student; élève interne boarding student ‖ f breeder (animal); (hort) seedling
éle·vé -vée [elve] adj high, elevated; lofty, noble; bien élevé well-bred; mal élevé ill-bred
élever [elve] §2 tr to raise; to raise,

bring up, nurture; to erect || *ref* to rise; to arise; to be built, to stand

éle·veur [ɛlvœr] **-veuse** [vøz] *mf* breeder, rancher

elfe [ɛlf] *m* elf

élider [elide] *tr* to elide

éligible [eliʒibl] *adj* eligible

élimer [elime] *tr & ref* to wear threadbare

éliminatoire [eliminatwar] *adj* (sports) preliminary || *f* (sports) preliminaries

éliminer [elimine] *tr* to eliminate

élire [elir] §36 *tr* to elect

élision [elizjɔ̃] *f* elision

élite [elit] *f* elite

elle [ɛl] *pron disj* §85 || *pron conj* §87

elle-même [ɛlmɛm] §86

ellipse [elips] *f* (gram) ellipsis; (math) ellipse

elliptique [eliptik] *adj* elliptic(al)

élocution [elɔkysjɔ̃] *f* elocution; choice and arrangement of words

éloge [elɔʒ] *m* eulogy; praise

élo·gieux [elɔʒjø] **-gieuse** [ʒjøz] *adj* full of praise

éloi·gné -gnée [elwaɲe] *adj* distant

éloignement [elwaɲəmã] *m* remoteness; aversion; postponement

éloigner [elwaɲe] *tr* to move away; to remove; to drive away; to postpone || *ref* to move away; to digress, deviate; to become estranged

élongation [elɔ̃gasjɔ̃] *f* stretching

élonger [elɔ̃ʒe] §38 *tr* to lay (*e.g., a cable*); **élonger la terre** to skirt the coast

éloquence [elɔkãs] *f* eloquence

élo·quent [elɔkã] **-quente** [kãt] *adj* eloquent

é·lu -lue [ely] *adj* elected || *mf* chosen one; **les élus** the elect

élucider [elyside] *tr* to elucidate

éluder [elyde] *tr* to elude, avoid

éma·cié -ciée [emasje] *adj* emaciated

émacier [emasje] *ref* to become emaciated

é·mail [emaj] *m* (*pl* **-maux** [mo]) enamel || *m* (*pl* **-mails**) nail polish; car or bicycle paint

émaillage [emajaʒ] *m* enameling

émailler [emaje] *tr* to enamel; to sprinkle (*e.g., with quotations, metaphors, etc.*); to dot (*e.g., the fields, as flowers do*)

émanation [emanasjɔ̃] *f* emanation; manifestation (*e.g., of authority*)

émanciper [emãsipe] *tr* to emancipate || *ref* to be emancipated; (coll) to get out of hand

émaner [emane] *intr* to emanate

émarger [emarʒe] §38 *tr* to trim (*e.g., a book*); to initial (*a document*) || *intr* to get paid; **émarger à** to be paid from

émasculer [emaskyle] *tr* to emasculate

embâcle [ãbakl] *m* pack ice, ice floe

emballage [ãbalaʒ] *m* packing, wrapping

emballer [ãbale] *tr* to wrap up, to pack; to race (*a motor*); (coll) to thrill; (coll) to bawl out || *ref* to bolt, to run away; (mach) to race; (coll) to get worked up

embal·leur [ãbalœr] **embal·leuse** [ãbaløz] *mf* packer

embarbouiller [ãbarbuje] *tr* to besmear; (coll) to muddle, confuse || *ref* (coll) to get tangled up

embarcadère [ãbarkader] *m* wharf; (rr) platform

embarcation [ãbarkasjɔ̃] *f* small boat

embardée [ãbarde] *f* lurch; (aut) swerve; (aer, naut) yaw

embarder [ãbarde] *intr* (aut) to swerve; (aer, naut) to yaw

embargo [ãbargo] *m* embargo

embarquement [ãbarkəmã] *m* embarkation; shipping; loading

embarquer [ãbarke] *tr* to embark; to ship (*a sea*); to load (*in car, plane, etc.*); (coll) to put in the clink || *ref* to embark; to board; to get into a car

embarras [ãbara] *m* embarrassment; trouble, inconvenience; encumbrance, obstruction; perplexity; financial difficulties; **embarras de voitures** traffic jam; **embarras du choix** too much to choose from; **faire des embarras** (coll) to put on airs

embarrasser [ãbarase] *tr* to embarrass; to hamper, to obstruct; to stump, to perplex || *ref*—**s'embarrasser de** to take an interest in; to bother with

embaucher [ãboʃe] *tr* to hire, to sign on; (coll) to entice (*soldiers*) to desert || *intr* to hire; **on n'embauche pas** (public sign) no help wanted

embauchoir [ãboʃwar] *m* shoetree

embaumement [ãboməmã] *m* embalming; perfuming

embaumer [ãbome] *tr* to embalm; to perfume || *intr* to smell good

embaumeur [ãbomœr] *m* embalmer

embellir [ãbelir] *tr* to embellish || *intr* to clear up (*said of weather*); to improve in looks || *ref* to grow more beautiful

embellissement [ãbelismã] *m* embellishment

embêtement [ãbetmã] *m* (coll) annoyance

embêter [ãbete], [ãbete] *tr* (coll) to annoy

emblave [ãblav] *f* grainfield

emblaver [ãblave] *tr* to sow

emblée [ãble]—**d'emblée** then and there, right off; without difficulty

emblématique [ãblematik] *adj* emblematic(al)

emblème [ãblem] *m* emblem

embobeliner [ãbɔbline] *tr* (coll) to bamboozle

embobiner [ãbɔbine] *tr* to wind up (*e.g., on a reel*); (coll) to bamboozle

emboîter [ãbwate] *tr* to encase; to nest (*boxes, boats, etc.*); (mach) to interlock, joint; **emboîter le pas** to fall into step

embolie [ãbɔli] *f* (pathol) embolism

embonpoint [ãbɔ̃pwɛ̃] *m* portliness; **prendre de l'embonpoint** to put on flesh

embouche [ãbuʃ] *f* pasture

embou·ché -chée [ɑ̃buʃe] *adj*—mal embouché foul-mouthed

emboucher [ɑ̃buʃe] *tr* to blow, sound

embouchoir [ɑ̃buʃwar] *m* mouthpiece

embouchure [ɑ̃buʃyr] *f* mouth (*of a river*); mouthpiece

embourber [ɑ̃burbe] *tr* to stick in the mud; to vilify, to implicate

embout [ɑ̃bu] *m* tip, ferrule; rubber tip (*for chair*)

embouteillage [ɑ̃butejaʒ] *m* bottling; bottleneck, traffic jam

emboutir [ɑ̃butir] *tr* to stamp, emboss; to smash (*e.g., a fender*) ‖ *ref* to bump

embranchement [ɑ̃brɑ̃ʃmɑ̃] *m* branching (off); branch; branch line; junction (*of roads, track, etc.*)

embrasement [ɑ̃brazmɑ̃] *m* conflagration; illumination, glow

embraser [ɑ̃braze] *tr* to set aflame or aglow ‖ *ref* to flame up; to glow

embrassade [ɑ̃brasad] *m* embrace; kissing

embrasse [ɑ̃brɑs] *f* curtain tieback

embrassement [ɑ̃brɑsmɑ̃] *m* embrace

embrasser [ɑ̃brase] *tr* to embrace; to kiss; to join; to undertake; to take in (*at a glance*); to take (*the opportunity*) ‖ *ref* to embrace; to neck

embras·seur [ɑ̃brasœr] **embras·seuse** [ɑ̃brasøz] *mf* smoocher

embrasure [ɑ̃brazyr] *f* embrasure, loophole; opening (*for door or window*)

embrayage [ɑ̃brejaʒ] *m* coupling, engagement; (aut) clutch

embrayer [ɑ̃breje], [ɑ̃breje] §49 *tr* to engage, connect; to throw into gear ‖ *intr* to throw the clutch in

embrocher [ɑ̃broʃe] *tr* to put on a spit

embrouiller [ɑ̃bruje] *tr* to embroil ‖ *ref* to become embroiled

embroussail·lé -lée [ɑ̃brusaje] *adj* bushy; tangled; complicated, complex

embrasure *see above*

embru·mé -mée [ɑ̃bryme] *adj* foggy, misty

embruns [ɑ̃brœ̃] *mpl* spray

embryologie [ɑ̃brijɔlɔʒi] *f* embryology

embryon [ɑ̃brijɔ̃] *m* embryo

embryonnaire [ɑ̃brijɔnɛr] *adj* embryonic

em·bu -bue [ɑ̃by] *adj* lifeless, dull ‖ *m* dull tone (*of a painting*)

embûche [ɑ̃byʃ] *f* snare, trap

embuer [ɑ̃bɥe] *tr* to cloud with steam; embué de larmes dimmed with tears

embuscade [ɑ̃byskad] *f* ambush

embus·qué -quée [ɑ̃byske] *adj* in ambush; se tenir embusqué to lie in ambush ‖ *m* (mil) goldbricker, shirker

embusquer [ɑ̃byske] *tr* to ambush, trap ‖ *ref* to lie in ambush; (mil) to get a safe assignment

émé·ché -chée [emeʃe] *adj* (coll) tipsy, high

émender [emɑ̃de] *tr* to amend (*a sentence, decree, etc.*)

émeraude [emrod] *f* emerald

émergence [emɛrʒɑ̃s] *f* emergence

émerger [emɛrʒe] §38 *intr* to emerge

émeri [emri] *m* emery

émerillon [emrijɔ̃] *m* swivel; (orn) merlin

émerillon·né -née [emrijɔne] *adj* lively, gay

émérite [emerit] *adj* experienced; distinguished, remarkable; confirmed (*smoker*); (obs) retired, emeritus

émersion [emɛrsjɔ̃] *f* emersion

émerveillement [emɛrvɛjmɑ̃] *m* wonderment

émerveiller [emɛrveje] *tr* to astonish, amaze

émétique [emetik] *adj & m* emetic

émet·teur [emetœr] **émet·trice** [emetris] *adj* issuing; transmitting ‖ *mf* maker (*of check, draft*); issuer ‖ *m* broadcasting station; (rad) transmitter

émetteur-récepteur [emetœrrɛseptœr] *m* (*pl* **émetteurs-récepteurs**) (rad) walkie-talkie

émettre [emɛtr] §42 *tr* to emit; to express (*an opinion*); to issue (*stamps, bank notes, etc.*); to transmit (*a radio signal*) ‖ *intr* to transmit, broadcast

é·meu [emø] *m* (*pl* **-meus**) (zool) emu

émeute [emøt] *f* riot

émeutier [emøtje] *m* rioter

émietter [emjete] *tr* to crumble; to break up (*an estate*)

émi·grant -grante [emigrɑ̃ -grɑ̃t] *adj & mf* emigrant; migrant

émi·gré -grée [emigre] *adj* emigrating ‖ *mf* emigrant; émigré

émigrer [emigre] *intr* to emigrate; to migrate

émincer [emɛ̃se] §51 *tr* to cut in thin slices

éminemment [eminamɑ̃] *adv* eminently

éminence [eminɑ̃s] *f* eminence

émi·nent -nente [eminɑ̃ -nɑ̃t] *adj* eminent

émissaire [emisɛr] *m* emissary; outlet (*of lake, basin, etc.*)

émission [emisjɔ̃] *f* emission; utterance; issue (*of stamps, bank notes, etc.*); (rad) transmission, broadcast

emmagasiner [ɑ̃magazine] *tr* to put in storage; to store up; to stockpile

emmailloter [ɑ̃majɔte] *tr* to swathe; to bandage

emmancher [ɑ̃mɑ̃ʃe] *tr* to put a handle on ‖ *ref* (coll) to begin; s'emmancher bien (coll) to get off to a good start; s'emmancher mal (coll) to get off to a bad start

emmêler [ɑ̃mele], [ɑ̃mele] *tr* to tangle up; to mix up

emménagement [ɑ̃menaʒmɑ̃] *m* moving in; installation

emménager [ɑ̃menaʒe] §38 *tr & intr* to move in

emmener [ɑ̃mne] §2 *tr* to take or lead away; to take out (*e.g., to dinner*); to take (*on a visit*)

emmenthal [emɛ̃tal], [emɛ̃tal] *m* Swiss cheese

emmiel·lé -lée [ɑ̃mjele], [ɑ̃mjele] *adj* honeyed (*e.g., words*)

emmitoufler [ɑ̃mitufle] *tr & ref* to bundle up (*in warm clothing*)

emmurer [ɑ̃myre] *tr* to wall in, immure

émoi [emwa] *m* agitation, alarm

émolument [emɔlymɑ̃] *m* share; **émoluments** emolument, fee, salary

émonder [emɔ̃de] *tr* to prune, trim

émo·tif [emɔtif] **-tive** [tiv] *adj* emotional ‖ *mf* emotional person

émotion [emosjɔ̃] *f* emotion; commotion

émotionnable [emosjɔnabl] *adj* emotional

émotion·nant [emosjɔnɑ̃] **émotion·nante** [emosjɔnɑ̃t] *adj* stirring, moving

émotionner [emosjɔne] *tr* to move deeply, thrill, affect ‖ *ref* to get excited, flustered

émoucher [emuʃe] *tr* to chase flies away from

émouchet [emuʃɛ] *m* sparrow hawk

émouchoir [emuʃwar] *m* whisk, fly swatter

émoudre [emudr] §43 *tr* to grind, sharpen

émoulage [emulaʒ] *m* grinding, sharpening

émou·lu -lue [emuly] *adj*—**frais émoulu de** (fig) fresh from, just back from

émous·sé -sée [emuse] *adj* blunt

émousser [emuse] *tr* to dull, blunt

émoustiller [emustije] *tr* (coll) to exhilarate, to rouse

émouvoir [emuvwar] §45 (*pp* ému) *tr* to move; to excite ‖ *ref* to be moved; to be excited

empailler [ɑ̃paje] *tr* to stuff (*animals*); to cane (*a chair*)

empail·leur [ɑ̃pajœr] **empail·leuse** [ɑ̃pajøz] *mf* taxidermist; caner

empaler [ɑ̃pale] *tr* to impale

empan [ɑ̃pɑ̃] *m* span (*of hand*)

empanacher [ɑ̃panaʃe] *tr* to plume

empaquetage [ɑ̃paktaʒ] *m* packaging, package

empaqueter [ɑ̃pakte] §34 *tr* to package

emparer [ɑ̃pare] *ref*—**s'emparer de** to seize, take hold of

empâter [ɑ̃pate] *tr* to make sticky; to fatten up (*chickens, turkeys, etc.*); to coat (*the tongue*); (typ) to over-ink ‖ *ref* to put on weight; to become coated (*said of tongue*); to become husky (*said of voice*)

empattement [ɑ̃patmɑ̃] *m* foundation, footing; (aut) wheelbase

empaumer [ɑ̃pome] *tr* to catch in the hand; to hit with a racket; to palm (*a card*); (coll) to hoodwink

empêchement [ɑ̃peʃmɑ̃] *m* impediment, bar; hindrance, obstacle

empêcher [ɑ̃peʃe] *tr* to hinder; **empêcher qn de** + *inf* to prevent or keep s.o. from + *ger*; **n'empêche que** all the same, e.g., **n'empêche qu'il est très poli** he's very polite all the same ‖ *ref*—**ne pouvoir s'empêcher de** + *inf* not to be able to help + *ger*, e.g., **je n'ai pu m'empêcher de rire** I could not help laughing

empê·cheur [ɑ̃peʃœr] **-cheuse** [ʃøz] *mf*—**empêcheur de danser en rond** (coll) wet blanket

empeigne [ɑ̃pɛɲ] *f* upper (*of shoe*)

empennage [ɑ̃pennaʒ] *m* feathers (*of arrow*); fins, vanes; (aer) empennage

empereur [ɑ̃prœr] *m* emperor

emperler [ɑ̃pɛrle] *tr* to ornament with pearls; to cover with drops; **la sueur emperlait son front** his forehead was covered with beads of perspiration

empe·sé -sée [ɑ̃pəze] *adj* starched; stiff, wooden (*style*)

empeser [ɑ̃pəze] §2 *tr* to starch

empes·té -tée [ɑ̃peste] *adj* pestilential; stinking, reeking; depraved

empester [ɑ̃peste] *tr* to stink; to corrupt ‖ *intr* to stink

empêtrer [ɑ̃petre] *tr* to hamper; to involve, entangle ‖ *ref* to become involved, entangled

emphase [ɑ̃faz] *f* overemphasis; bombast, pretentiousness

emphatique [ɑ̃fatik] *adj* overemphasized; bombastic, pretentious

emphysème [ɑ̃fizem] *m* emphysema

empiècement [ɑ̃pjesmɑ̃] *m* yoke (*of shirt, blouse, etc.*)

empierrer [ɑ̃pjere] *tr* to pave with stones; (rr) to ballast

empiétement [ɑ̃pjetmɑ̃] *m* encroachment, incursion

empiéter [ɑ̃pjete] §10 *intr* to encroach

empiffrer [ɑ̃pifre] *tr* (coll) to stuff, fatten ‖ *ref* (coll) to stuff oneself, to guzzle

empiler [ɑ̃pile] *tr* to pile up, stack; (slang) to dupe ‖ *ref* to pile up; **se faire empiler** (slang) to be had

empire [ɑ̃pir] *m* empire; control, supremacy

empirer [ɑ̃pire] *tr* to make worse, to aggravate ‖ *intr* (*aux:* AVOIR or ÊTRE) to grow worse

empirique [ɑ̃pirik] *adj* empiric(al) ‖ *m* empiricist; charlatan, quack

emplacement [ɑ̃plasmɑ̃] *m* emplacement; location, site

emplâtre [ɑ̃platr] *m* patch (*on tire*); (med) plaster; (coll) boob

emplette [ɑ̃plɛt] *f* purchase; **aller faire des emplettes** to go shopping

emplir [ɑ̃plir] *tr & ref* to fill up

emploi [ɑ̃plwa] *m* employment, job; employment, use; (theat) type (*of role*); **double emploi** useless duplication; **emploi du temps** schedule

employé employée [ɑ̃plwaje] *mf* employee; clerk

employer [ɑ̃plwaje] §47 *tr* to employ; to use ‖ *ref* to be employed; **s'employer à** to try to, to do one's best to

employeur [ɑ̃plwajœr] **employeuse** [ɑ̃plwajøz] *mf* employer

empocher [ɑ̃pɔʃe] *tr* (coll) to pocket

empoi·gnant [ɑ̃pwaɲɑ̃] **-gnante** [ɲɑ̃t] *adj* exciting, arresting, thrilling

empoigner [ɑ̃pwaɲe] *tr* to grasp; to collar (*a crook*); to grip, move (*an audience*)

empois [ɑ̃pwa] *m* starch

empoisonnement [ɑ̃pwazɔnmɑ̃] *m* poisoning; **avoir des empoisonnements** (coll) to be annoyed

empoisonner [ɑ̃pwazɔne] *tr* to poison; to infect (*the air*); to corrupt; (coll) to bother || *intr* to reek || *ref* to be poisoned

empoison·neur [ɑ̃pwazɔnœr] **empoi·son·neuse** [ɑ̃pwazɔnøz] *adj* poisoning || *mf* poisoner; corrupter

empoissonner [ɑ̃pwasɔne] *tr* to stock with fish

empor·té -tée [ɑ̃pɔrte] *adj* quick-tempered, impetuous

emportement [ɑ̃pɔrtəmɑ̃] *m* anger, temper

emporte-pièce [ɑ̃pɔrtəpjɛs] *m* (*pl* **-pièces**) punch; **à l'emporte-pièce** trenchant, cutting, biting (*style, words, etc.*)

emporter [ɑ̃pɔrte] *tr* to take away; to carry off; to remove; **à emporter** to take out, to go (*e.g., said of food to take out of the restaurant*); **l'emporter** to have the upper hand over || *ref* to be carried away; to lose one's temper; to run away

empo·té -tée [ɑ̃pɔte] *adj* (coll) clumsy || *mf* (coll) butterfingers

empoter [ɑ̃pɔte] *tr* to pot (*a plant*)

empourprer [ɑ̃purpre] *tr* to set aglow || *ref* to turn crimson; to flush

empoussiérer [ɑ̃pusjere] §10 *tr* to cover with dust

empreindre [ɑ̃prɛ̃dr] §50 *tr* to imprint, stamp

empreinte [ɑ̃prɛ̃t] *f* imprint, stamp; **empreinte des roues** wheel tracks; **empreinte digitale** fingerprint; **empreinte du pied** or **empreinte de pas** footprint

empres·sé -sée [ɑ̃prese] *adj* eager

empressement [ɑ̃presmɑ̃] *m* haste, alacrity; eagerness; readiness

empresser à to be anxious to; **s'empresser à** to be anxious to; **s'empresser auprès de** to be attentive to, make a fuss over; to press around; **s'empresser de** to hasten to

emprise [ɑ̃priz] *f* expropriation; control, ascendancy

emprisonnement [ɑ̃prizɔnmɑ̃] *m* imprisonment

emprisonner [ɑ̃prizɔne] *tr* to imprison

emprunt [ɑ̃prœ̃] *m* loan; loan word; **d'emprunt** feigned, assumed

emprunter [ɑ̃prœ̃te] *tr* to borrow; to take (*a road, a route*); to take on (*false appearances*); **emprunter q.ch. à** to borrow s.th. from; to get s.th. from

empuantir [ɑ̃pyɑ̃tir] *tr* to stink up

empyème [ɑ̃pjɛm] *m* empyema

empyrée [ɑ̃pire] *m* empyrean

é·mu -mue [emy] *adj* moved, touched; tender (*memory*); **ému de** alarmed by

émulation [emylɑsjɔ̃] *f* emulation, rivalry

émule [emyl] *mf* emulator, rival

émulsion [emylsjɔ̃] *f* emulsion

émulsionner [emylsjɔne] *tr* to emulsify

en [ɑ̃] *pron indef* & *adv* §87 || *prep* in; into; to, e.g., **aller en France** to go to France; e.g., **de mal en pis** from bad to worse; at, e.g., **en mer** at sea; e.g., **en guerre** at war; on, e.g., **en congé** on leave; by, e.g., **en chemin**

de fer by rail; of, made of, e.g., **en bois** (made) of wood

enamourer [ɑ̃namure] *ref* to become enamored, to fall in love

encabaner [ɑ̃kabane] *ref* (Canad) to hole up, to dig in (*e.g., for the winter*)

encablure [ɑ̃kablyr] *f* cable's length (*unit of measure*)

encadrement [ɑ̃kadrəmɑ̃] *m* framing; frame; framework; window frame; doorframe; border, edge; staffing; officering (*furnishing with officers*)

encadrer [ɑ̃kadre] *tr* to frame; to staff (*an organization*); to officer (*troops*); to incorporate (*recruits*) into a unit

encadreur [ɑ̃kadrœr] *m* framer (*person*)

encager [ɑ̃kaʒe] §38 *tr* to cage

encaisse [ɑ̃kɛs] *f* cash on hand, cash balance; **encaisse métallique** bullion

encais·sé -sée [ɑ̃kese] *adj* deeply embanked, sunken

encaissement [ɑ̃kesmɑ̃] *m* cashing (*e.g., of check*); boxing, crating; embankment

encaisser [ɑ̃kese], [ɑ̃kɛse] *tr* to cash; to box, to crate; to receive (*a blow*); to embank (*a river*); (coll) to put up with || *ref* to be steeply embanked

encaisseur [ɑ̃kesœr] *m* collector; payee; cashier

encan [ɑ̃kɑ̃] *m* auction

encanailler [ɑ̃kanaje] *tr* to debase || *ref* to acquire bad habits; to keep low company

encapuchonner [ɑ̃kapyʃɔne] *tr* to hood

encaquer [ɑ̃kake] *tr* to barrel; to pack (*sardines*); (coll) to pack in like sardines

encart [ɑ̃kar] *m* inset, insert

encarter [ɑ̃karte] *tr* to card (*buttons, pins, etc.*); (bb) to tip in

en-cas [ɑ̃kɑ̃] *m invar* snack; reserve, emergency supply

encasernement [ɑ̃kazernəmɑ̃] *m*—**encasernement de conscience** thought control, regimentation

encaserner [ɑ̃kazerne] *tr* to quarter, to barrack (*troops*)

encastrement [ɑ̃kastrəmɑ̃] *m* groove; fitting

encastrer [ɑ̃kastre] *tr* & *ref* to fit

encaustique [ɑ̃kostik] *f* furniture polish; floor wax; encaustic painting

encaustiquer [ɑ̃kostike] *tr* to wax

encaver [ɑ̃kave] *tr* to cellar (*wine*)

enceindre [ɑ̃sɛ̃dr] §50 *tr* to enclose, to encircle

enceinte [ɑ̃sɛ̃t] *adj fem* pregnant || *f* enclosure; walls, ramparts; precinct, compass; (boxing) ring

encens [ɑ̃sɑ̃] *m* incense; flattery

encenser [ɑ̃sɑ̃se] *tr* to incense, perfume with incense; to flatter

encensoir [ɑ̃sɑ̃swar] *m* censer

encéphalite [ɑ̃sefalit] *f* encephalitis

encercler [ɑ̃serkle] *tr* to encircle

enchaînement [ɑ̃ʃenmɑ̃] *m* chaining up; chain, sequence

enchaîner [ɑ̃ʃene], [ɑ̃ʃene], *tr* to chain; to connect || *intr* to go on speaking || *ref* to be connected

enchan·té -tée [ɑ̃ʃɑ̃te] *adj* delighted, pleased

enchantement [ɑ̃ʃɑ̃tmɑ̃] *m* enchantment

enchanter [ɑ̃ʃɑ̃te] *tr* to enchant

enchan·teur [ɑ̃ʃɑ̃tœr] **-teresse** [tres] *adj* enchanting, bewitching || *m* enchanter, magician || *f* enchantress

enchâsser [ɑ̃ʃɑse] *tr* to enshrine; to insert; to set, chase (*a gem*)

enchère [ɑ̃ʃɛr] *f* bid, bidding; **folle enchère** bid that cannot be made good; folly

enchérir [ɑ̃ʃerir] *tr* to bid on; to raise the price of || *intr* to bid; to rise in price; **enchérir sur** to improve on; to outbid

enchérisseur [ɑ̃ʃerisœr] *m* bidder; **dernier enchérisseur** highest bidder

enchevêtrement [ɑ̃ʃvetrəmɑ̃] *m* entanglement; network; jumble

enchevêtrer [ɑ̃ʃvetre] *tr* to tangle up; to halter (*a horse*) || *ref* to become complicated or confused

enchifre·né -née [ɑ̃ʃifrəne] *adj* stuffed-up (*with a cold*)

enclave [ɑ̃klav] *f* enclave

enclaver [ɑ̃klave] *tr* to enclose; to dovetail

enclencher [ɑ̃klɑ̃ʃe] *tr & ref* to interlock

en·clin [ɑ̃klɛ̃] **-cline** [klin] *adj* inclined, prone

encliquetage [ɑ̃kliktaʒ] *m* ratchet

encliqueter [ɑ̃klikte] §34 *tr* to cog, to mesh

enclitique [ɑ̃klitik] *adj & m & f* enclitic

enclore [ɑ̃klɔr] §24 (has also 1st & 2d *pl pres ind* **enclosons, enclosez**) *tr* to close in, to wall in

enclos [ɑ̃klo] *m* enclosure, close

enclume [ɑ̃klym] *f* anvil; **se trouver entre l'enclume et le marteau** (coll) to be between the devil and the deep blue sea

encoche [ɑ̃kɔʃ] *f* notch, nick; slot; thumb index

encocher [ɑ̃kɔʃe] *tr* to notch, to nick; to slot

encoignure [ɑ̃kɔɲyr] *f* corner; corner piece; corner cabinet

encollage [ɑ̃kɔlaʒ] *m* gluing; sizing

encoller [ɑ̃kɔle] *tr* to glue; to size

encolure [ɑ̃kɔlyr] *f* collar size; neck line; neck and withers (*of horse*); **gagner par une encolure** to win by a neck

encombre [ɑ̃kɔ̃br] *m*—**sans encombre** without a hitch, without hindrance

encombrement [ɑ̃kɔ̃brəmɑ̃] *m* encumbrance, congestion

encombrer [ɑ̃kɔ̃bre] *tr* to encumber; to crowd, congest; to block up, to jam; to litter; to load down || *ref*—**s'encombrer de** (coll) to be saddled with

encontre [ɑ̃kɔ̃tr]—**à l'encontre de** counter to, against; contrary to

encore [ɑ̃kɔr] *adv* still, e.g., **il est encore ici** he is still here; yet, e.g., **encore mieux** better yet; e.g., **encore** not yet; only, e.g., **si encore vous m'en aviez parlé!** if only you had told me!; **encore que** although;

encore une fois once more, once again; **en voulez-vous encore?** do you want some more? || *interj* again!, oh no, not again! (*expressing impatience or astonishment*)

encorner [ɑ̃kɔrne] *tr* to gore, to toss

encouragement [ɑ̃kuraʒmɑ̃] *m* encouragement

encourager [ɑ̃kuraʒe] §38 *tr* to encourage

encourir [ɑ̃kurir] §14 *tr* to incur

encrasser [ɑ̃krase] *tr* to soil, to dirty; to soot (*a chimney*); to foul (*a gun*) || *ref* to get dirty; to stop up, clog; to soot up

encre [ɑ̃kr] *f* ink; **encre de Chine** India ink; **encre sympathique** invisible ink

encrer [ɑ̃kre] *tr* to ink

encreur [ɑ̃krœr] *adj* inking (*ribbon, roller*) || *m* ink roller

encrier [ɑ̃krije] *m* inkwell

encroûter [ɑ̃krute] *tr* to encrust; to plaster (*walls*) || *ref* to become encrusted; to get rusty; to become hidebound, prejudiced

encyclique [ɑ̃siklik] *adj & f* encyclical

encyclopédie [ɑ̃siklɔpedi] *f* encyclopedia

encyclopédique [ɑ̃siklɔpedik] *adj* encyclopedic

endauber [ɑ̃dobe] *tr* to braise

endémie [ɑ̃demi] *f* endemic

endémique [ɑ̃demik] *adj* endemic

endenter [ɑ̃dɑ̃te] *tr* to tooth, to cog; to mesh (*gears*); **bien endenté** (coll) with plenty of teeth; (coll) with a hearty appetite

endetter [ɑ̃dete] *tr & ref* to run into debt

endêver [ɑ̃deve] *intr*—**faire endêver** to bedevil, to drive wild

endia·blé -blée [ɑ̃djɑble] *adj* devilish, reckless; full of pep

endiguement [ɑ̃digmɑ̃] *m* damming up; embankment

endiguer [ɑ̃dige] *tr* to dam up

endimancher [ɑ̃dimɑ̃ʃe] *tr & ref* to put on Sunday clothes, to dress up

endive [ɑ̃div] *f* endive

endocrine [ɑ̃dɔkrin] *adj* endocrine

endoctriner [ɑ̃dɔktrine] *tr* to indoctrinate; to win over

endolo·ri -rie [ɑ̃dɔlɔri] *adj* painful, sore

endommagement [ɑ̃dɔmaʒmɑ̃] *m* damage

endommager [ɑ̃dɔmaʒe] §38 *tr* to damage || *ref* to suffer damage

endor·mi -mie [ɑ̃dɔrmi] *adj* asleep, sleeping; sluggish, apathetic; dormant; numb (*arm or leg*)

endormir [ɑ̃dɔrmir] §23 *tr* to put to sleep; to lull, to put off guard || *ref* to go to sleep; to slack off; to let down one's guard

endos [ɑ̃do] *m* endorsement

endosse [ɑ̃dos] *f* responsibility

endossement [ɑ̃dɔsmɑ̃] *m* endorsement

endosser [ɑ̃dose] *tr* to endorse; to take on the responsibility of

endosseur [ɑ̃dosœr] *m* endorser

endroit [ɑ̃drwa], [ɑ̃drwa] *m* place, spot; right side (*of cloth*); **à l'endroit**

right side out; **à l'endroit de** with regard to; **le petit endroit** (coll) the toilet; **mettre à l'endroit** to put on right side out

enduire [ãdɥir] §19 *tr* to coat, smear

enduit [ãdɥi] *m* coat, coating

endurance [ãdyrãs] *f* endurance

endu·rant [ãdyrã] **-rante** [rãt] *adj* untiring; meek, patient

endur·ci -cie [ãdyrsi] *adj* hardened; tough, calloused; inveterate

endurcir [ãdyrsir] *tr* to harden; to inure, to toughen ‖ *ref* to harden; **s'endurcir à** to become accustomed to, to become inured to

endurcissement [ãdyrsismã] *m* hardening

endurer [ãdyre] *tr* to endure

énergétique [enerʒetik] *adj* energy, power

énergie [enerʒi] *f* energy

énergique [enerʒik] *adj* energetic

énergumène [energymɛn] *mf* ranter, wild person, nut

éner·vant [enervã] **-vante** [vãt] *adj* annoying, nerve-racking

énerver [enerve] *tr* to enervate; to unnerve ‖ *ref* to get nervous; to be exasperated

enfance [ãfãs] *f* childhood; infancy; dotage, second childhood; **c'est l'enfance de l'art** (coll) it's child's play; **enfance délinquante** juvenile delinquents; **première enfance** infancy

enfant [ãfã] *adj invar* childish, childlike; **bon enfant** good-natured ‖ *mf* child; **enfant de chœur** altar boy; **enfant de la balle** child who follows in his father's footsteps; **enfant en bas âge** infant; **enfant terrible** (fig) stormy petrel; **enfant trouvé** foundling; **mon enfant!** my boy!; **petit enfant** infant

enfantement [ãfãtmã] *m* childbirth

enfanter [ãfãte] *tr* to give birth to

enfantillage [ãfãtijaʒ] *m* childishness

enfan·tin [ãfãtɛ̃] **-tine** [tin] *adj* childish, infantile

enfari·né -née [ãfarine] *adj* smeared with flour

enfer [ãfer] *m* hell

enfermer [ãferme] *tr* to enclose; to shut up, to lock up ‖ *ref* to shut oneself in; to closet oneself

enferrer [ãfere] *tr* to pierce, to run through ‖ *ref* to run oneself through with a sword; to bite (*said of fish*); (fig) to be caught in one's own trap

enfiévrer [ãfjevre] §10 *tr* to inflame, to make feverish

enfilade [ãfilad] *f* row, string, series; (mil) enfilade; **en enfilade** connecting, e.g., **chambres en enfilade** connecting rooms

enfile-aiguille [ãfilegɥij] *m invar* threader, needle threader

enfiler [ãfile] *tr* to pierce; to thread (*a needle*); to string (*beads*); to start down (*a street*); (coll) to put on (*clothes*)

enfin [ãfɛ̃] *adv* finally, at last; in short; after all, anyway

enflam·mé -mée [ãflame], [ãflame] *adj* flaming; bright red; inflamed

enflammer [ãflame], [ãflame] *tr* to inflame ‖ *ref* to be inflamed; to flare up

enfler [ãfle] *tr* to swell; to puff up or out; to exaggerate ‖ *intr & ref* to swell, to puff up

enflure [ãflyr] *f* swelling; (fig) exaggeration

enfon·cé -cée [ãfõse] *adj* sunken, deep; deep-set; broken (*ribs*); (coll) taken, had (*bested*)

enfoncement [ãfõsmã] *m* driving in; breaking open; hollow, recess

enfoncer [ãfõse] §51 *tr* to drive in; to push in, break open; (coll) to get the better of ‖ *intr* to sink to the bottom ‖ *ref* to sink, plunge; to give way; to disappear; to penetrate (*said of root, bullet, etc.*)

enforcir [ãforsir] *tr* to reinforce ‖ *intr & ref* to become stronger; to grow

enfouir [ãfwir] *tr* to bury; to hide ‖ *ref* to burrow; to bury oneself (*e.g., in an out-of-the-way locality*)

enfourcher [ãfurʃe] *tr* to stick a pitchfork into; to mount, straddle

enfourchure [ãfurʃyr] *f* crotch

enfourner [ãfurne] *tr* to put in the oven; (coll) to gobble down

enfreindre [ãfrɛ̃dr] §50 *tr* to violate, break (*e.g., a law*)

enfuir [ãfɥir] §31 *ref* to run away; to escape; to elope

enfu·mé -mée [ãfyme] *adj* blackened; smoky (*color*)

enfumer [ãfyme] *tr* to smoke up, blacken; to smoke out

enfutailler [ãfytaje] *tr* to cask, to barrel

enga·gé -gée [ãgaʒe] *adj* committed; hocked ‖ *m* (mil) enlisted man

engagement [ãgaʒmã] *m* engagement; hocking; obligation; promise; (mil) enlistment; (mil) engagement

engager [ãgaʒe] §38 *tr* to engage; to hock; to enlist, urge, involve; to open, to begin (*negotiations, the conversation, etc.*) ‖ *ref* to commit oneself; to promise, to pledge; to enter a contest; to become engaged to be married; (mil) to enlist; **s'engager dans** to begin (*battle; a conversation*); to plunge into; to fit into

engainer [ãgene], [ãgene] *tr* to sheathe, to envelop

engazonner [ãgazone] *tr* to sod

engeance [ãʒãs] *f* (pej) breed, brood

engelure [ãʒlyr] *f* chilblain

engendrer [ãʒãdre] *tr* to engender

engin [ãʒɛ̃] *m* device; **engin balistique** ballistic missile; **engin guidé** or **engin spécial** guided missile; **engins de pêche** fishing tackle

englober [ãglobe] *tr* to put together, to unite; to embrace, to comprise

engloutir [ãglutir] *tr* to gobble down; to swallow up, to engulf

engluer [ãglye] *tr* to lime (*a trap*); to catch; to take in, hoodwink ‖ *ref* to be caught; to fall into a trap, to be taken in

engommer [ãgɔme] *tr* to gum

engon·cé -cée [ãgɔ̃se] *adj* awkward, stiff (*air*)

engoncer [ãgɔ̃se] §51 *tr* to bundle up; to cramp

engorgement [ãgɔrʒəmã] *m* obstruction, blocking

engorger [ãgɔrʒe] §38 *tr* to obstruct, block

engouement [ãgumã] *m* infatuation; (*pathol*) obstruction

engouer [ãgwe] *tr* to obstruct || *ref*—**s'engouer de** (coll) to be infatuated with, to be wild about

engouffrer [ãgufre] *tr* to engulf; to gobble up; to eat up (*e.g., a fortune*) || *ref* to be swallowed up; to dash; to surge

engour·di ·die [ãgurdi] *adj* numb

engourdir [ãgurdir] *tr* to numb; to dull || *ref* to grow numb

engourdissement [ãgurdismã] *m* numbness; dullness, torpidity

engrais [ãgrɛ] *m* fertilizer; manure; fodder; **mettre à l'engrais** to fatten

engraisser [ãgrese], [ãgrɛse] *tr* to fatten; to fertilize; to enrich || *intr* (*aux:* AVOIR or ÊTRE) to fatten up, to get fat || *ref* to become fat; to become rich

engranger [ãgrãʒe] §38 *tr* to garner; to get in, to put in the barn

engraver [ãgrave] *tr, intr,* & *ref* to silt up; (*naut*) to run aground

engrenage [ãgrənaʒ] *m* gear; gearing; (coll) mesh, toils; **engrenage à vis sans fin** worm gear; **engrenages de distribution** timing gears

engrener [ãgrəne] §2 *tr* to feed (*a hopper, a thresher; a fowl*); to put into gear, to mesh || *intr* & *ref* (*mach*) to mesh, engage

engrenure [ãgrənyr] *f* engaging (*of toothed wheels*)

engrumeler [ãgrymle] §34 *tr* & *ref* to clot, to curdle

engueuler [ãgœle] *tr* (slang) to bawl out

enguirlander [ãgirlãde] *tr* to garland; to adorn; (coll) to bawl out

enhardir [ãardir] *tr* to embolden || *ref*—**s'enhardir à** to be so bold as to

énième [enjem] *adj* nth

énigmatique [enigmatik] *adj* enigmatic(al), puzzling

énigme [enigm] *f* enigma, riddle, puzzle

enivrement [ãnivrəmã] *m* intoxication

enivrer [ãnivre] *tr* to intoxicate; to elate || *ref* to get drunk

enjambée [ãʒãbe] *f* stride

enjambement [ãʒãbmã] *m* enjambment

enjamber [ãʒãbe] *tr* to stride over, to span || *intr* to stride along; to run on (*said of line of poetry*); **enjamber sur** to project over; to encroach on

en·jeu [ãʒø] *m* (*pl* -**jeux**) stake, bet

enjoindre [ãʒwɛdr] §35 *tr* to enjoin

enjôler [ãʒole] *tr* (coll) to cajole

enjô·leur [ãʒolœr] -**leuse** [løz] *adj* cajoling || *mf* cajoler, wheedler

enjoliver [ãʒɔlive] *tr* to embellish

enjoli·veur [ãʒɔlivœr] -**veuse** [vøz] *mf* embellisher || *m* hubcap

en·joué -jouée [ãʒwe] *adj* sprightly

enjouement [ãʒumã] *m* playfulness

enlacement [ãlasmã] *m* embrace, hug; lacing, interweaving

enlacer [ãlase] §51 *tr* & *ref* to enlace, to entwine; to embrace

enlaidir [ãledir], [ãlɛdir] *tr* to disfigure || *intr* to grow ugly || *ref* to disfigure oneself

enlèvement [ãlɛvmã] *m* removal; kidnaping, abduction

enlever [ãlve] §2 *tr* to take away, take off, remove; to carry off; to lift, lift up; to send up (*a balloon*); (fig) to carry away (*an audience*); **enlever le couvert** to clear the table; **enlever q.ch. à** to take s.th. from, remove s.th. from || *ref* to come off, wear off; to rise; to boil over; (fig) to flare up

enliasser [ãljase] *tr* to tie up in bundles

enliser [ãlize] *ref* to get stuck

enluminer [ãlymine] *tr* to illuminate; to make colorful

enluminure [ãlyminyr] *f* illuminated drawing; (painting) illumination

enneiger [ãneʒe], [ãnɛʒe] §38 *tr* to cover with snow

enne·mi -mie [ɛnmi] *adj* hostile, inimical; enemy, e.g., **en pays ennemi** in enemy country || *mf* enemy

ennoblir [ãnɔblir] *tr* to ennoble

ennui [ãnɥi] *m* ennui, boredom; nuisance, bother; worry, trouble

ennuyer [ãnɥije] §27 *tr* to bore; to bother || *ref* to be bored

énon·cé -cée [enõse] *m* statement; wording (*of a document*); terms (*of a theorem*)

énoncer [enõse] §51 *tr* to state, enunciate; to utter

enorgueillir [ãnɔrgœjir] *tr* to make proud or boastful || *ref*—**s'enorgueillir de** to pride oneself on, to boast of, to glory in

énorme [enɔrm] *adj* enormous; (coll) shocking; (coll) outrageous

énormément [enɔrmemã] *adv* enormously, tremendously; (coll) awfully; **énormément de** lots of

énormité [enɔrmite] *f* enormity; (coll) nonsense; (coll) blunder

enquérir [ãkerir] §3 *ref*—**s'enquérir de** to ask or inquire about

enquête [ãkɛt] *f* investigation, inquiry; inquest; **enquête par sondage** public-opinion poll

enquêter [ãkete] *intr* to conduct an investigation

enraciner [ãrasine] *tr* to root; to instill || *ref* to take root

enra·gé -gée [ãraʒe] *adj* enraged, hotheaded; mad (*dog*); rabid (*communist*); out-and-out (*socialist*); inveterate (*gambler*); enthusiastic (*sportsman*) || *mf* enthusiast, fan; fanatic, fiend

enrager [ãraʒe] §38 *intr* to be mad; **faire enrager** to enrage

enrayer [ãreje], [ãrɛje] §49 *tr* to put

spokes to; to jam, lock; to stem, halt || *ref* to jam

enrayure [ārejyr] *f* (mach) skid, shoe

enrégimenter [ārezimāte] *tr* to regiment

enregistrement [ārəʒistrəmã] *m* recording; registration; transcription; checking (*of baggage*); **enregistrement sur bande** or **sur ruban** tape recording

enregistrer [ārəʒistre] *tr* to record; to register; to transcribe; to check (*baggage*)

enregis·treur [ārəʒistrœr] **-treuse** [trøz] *adj* recording || *mf* recorder

enrhumer [āryme] *tr* to give a cold to || *ref* to catch cold

enrichir [āri/ir] *tr* to enrich || *ref* to become rich

enrichissement [āri/ismã] *m* enrichment

enrober [ārobe] *tr* to coat; to wrap

enrôlement [ārolmã] *m* enrollment; enlistment

enrôler [ārole] *tr & ref* to enroll, enlist

enrouement [ārumã] *m* hoarseness, huskiness

enrouer [ārwe] *tr* to make hoarse || *ref* to become hoarse

enrouiller [āruje] *tr & ref* to rust

enroulement [ārulmã] *m* coil; (archit) volute; (elec) winding

enrouler [ārule] *tr & ref* to wind, coil; to roll up

ensabler [āsable] *tr & ref* to run aground on the sand

ensacher [āsa/e] *tr* to bag

ensanglanter [āsāglāte] *tr* to stain with blood; to steep in blood

ensei·gnant [āseɲā] **-gnante** [ɲāt] *adj* teaching || *mf* teacher

enseigne [āseɲ] *m* (nav) ensign || *f* flag, ensign; sign (*on tavern, store*)

enseignement [āseɲəmã] *m* teaching, instruction, education; **enseignement confessionnel** parochial school education; **enseignement libre** or **privé** private-school education; **enseignement supérieur** higher education

enseigner [āseɲe] *tr* to teach; to show; **enseigner q.ch. à qn** to teach s.o. s.th. || *intr* to teach; **enseigner à qn à + *inf*** to teach s.o. to + *inf*

ensemble [āsãbl] *m* ensemble; **avec ensemble** in harmony, with one mind; **dans son ensemble** as a whole; **d'ensemble** general, comprehensive, overall; **grand ensemble** housing development || *adv* together

ensemencement [āsmãsmã] *m* sowing

ensemencer [āsmãse] §51 *tr* to seed, sow; to culture (*microorganisms*)

enserrer [āsere] *tr* to enclose; to squeeze, clasp

ensevelir [āsəvlir] *tr* to bury; to shroud

ensevelissement [āsəvlismã] *m* burial; shrouding

ensilage [āsila3] *m* storing in a pit or silo

ensiler [āsile] *tr* to ensilage

ensoleiller [āsəleje] *tr* to make sunny, to brighten

ensommeil·lé **-lée** [āsɔmeje], [āsɔmeje] *adj* drowsy

ensorceler [āsɔrsəle] §34 *tr* to bewitch, to enchant

ensorce·leur [āsɔrsəlœr] **-leuse** [løz] *adj* bewitching, enchanting || *m* sorcerer, wizard; charmer || *f* witch; enchantress

ensorcellement [āsɔrsɛlmã] *m* sorcery, enchantment; spell, charm

ensuite [āsɥit] *adv* then, next; afterwards, after; **ensuite?** what then?, what next?; anything else?

ensuivre [āsɥivr] §67 (used only in 3d *sg & pl*) *ref* to ensue; **il s'ensuit que . . .** it follows that . . .

entacher [āta/e] *tr* to blemish; **entaché de nullité** null and void

entaille [ātaj] *f* notch, nick; gash

entailler [ātaje] *tr* to notch, to nick; to gash

entame [ātam] *f* top slice, first slice, end slice

entamer [ātame] *tr* to cut the first slice of; to begin; to engage in, to start (*a conversation*); to make a break in (*the skin; a battle line*); to cast a slur upon; to open (*a bottle; negotiations; a card suit*); (coll) to make a dent in (*e.g., one's savings*)

entartrer [ātartre] *tr & ref* to scale, fur

entassement [ātasmã] *m* piling up

entasser [ātase] *tr & ref* to pile up, to accumulate; to crowd

ente [āt] *f* paintbrush handle; (hort) graft, scion

entendement [ātãdmã] *m* understanding; consciousness

entendre [ātãdr] *tr* to hear; to understand; to mean; **entendre chanter** to hear (*s.o.*) singing, to hear (*s.o.*) sing; to hear (*s.th.*) sung; **entendre dire que** to hear that; **entendre parler de** to hear of or about; **entendre raison** to listen to reason; **il entend que je le fasse** he expects me to do it, he insists that I do it || *intr* to hear || *ref* to understand one another; to get along; **s'entendre à** to be skilled in, to know

enten·du **-due** [ātãdy] *adj* agreed; **bien entendu** of course; **c'est entendu!** all right!

enténébrer [ātenebre] §10 *tr* to plunge into darkness

entente [ātāt] *f* understanding, agreement, pact; **à double entente** with a double meaning, e.g., **expression à double entente** expression with a double meaning, double entendre; **entente industrielle** (com) combine

enter [āte] *tr* to graft; to splice (*pieces of wood*)

entérinement [āterinmã] *m* ratification

entériner [āterine] *tr* to ratify

enterrement [ātermã] *m* burial, interment; funeral procession; funeral; funeral expenses; pigeonholing

enterrer [ātere] *tr* to bury, inter; to pigeonhole, sidetrack; (coll) to attend the funeral services of; **enterrer sa vie de garçon** (coll) to give a farewell stag party || *ref* to bury oneself; (mil) to dig oneself in

en-tête [ɑ̃tɛt] *m* (*pl* **-têtes**) headline; chapter heading; letterhead

enté·té -tée [ɑ̃tete] *adj* obstinate, stubborn

entêtement [ɑ̃tɛtmɑ̃] *m* obstinacy, stubbornness

entêter [ɑ̃tete] *tr* to give a headache to; to make giddy || *intr* to go to one's head || *ref* to persist

enthousiasme [ɑ̃tuzjasm] *m* enthusiasm

enthousiasmer [ɑ̃tuzjasme] *tr & ref* to enthuse

enthousiaste [ɑ̃tuzjast] *adj* enthusiastic || *mf* enthusiast, fan, buff

entichement [ɑ̃ti∫mɑ̃] *m* infatuation

enticher [ɑ̃ti∫e] *tr* to infatuate || *ref* to become infatuated

en·tier -tière [ɑ̃tje] [tjɛr] *adj* entire, whole, full; obstinate || *m* whole, entirety; **en entier** in full

entièrement [ɑ̃tjɛrmɑ̃] *adv* entirely

entité [ɑ̃tite] *f* entity, being

entoiler [ɑ̃twale] *tr* to put a backing on, to mount

entomologie [ɑ̃tɔmɔlɔʒi] *f* entomology

entonner [ɑ̃tɔne] *tr* to barrel; to intone, start off (*a song*); to sing (*s.o.'s praises*) || *ref* to rush up and down (*said of wind*)

entonnoir [ɑ̃tɔnwar] *m* funnel; shell hole

entorse [ɑ̃tɔrs] *f* sprain; infringement (*of a rule*); stretching (*of the truth*)

entortiller [ɑ̃tɔrtije] *tr & ref* to twist

entour [ɑ̃tur] *m*—**à l'entour** in the vicinity; **à l'entour de** around; **entours** surroundings

entourage [ɑ̃turaʒ] *m* setting, surroundings; entourage; (mach) casing

entourer [ɑ̃ture] *tr* to surround

entourloupette [ɑ̃turlupɛt] *f* (coll) double cross; **faire une entourloupette à** (coll) to double-cross

entournure [ɑ̃turnyr] *f* armhole; **gêné dans les entournures** ill at ease

entraccuser [ɑ̃trakyze] *ref* to accuse one another

entracte [ɑ̃trakt] *m* intermission

entraide [ɑ̃trɛd] *f* mutual assistance

entrailles [ɑ̃traj] *fpl* entrails; tenderness, pity; bowels (*of the earth*); **sans entrailles** (fig) heartless

entr'aimer [ɑ̃treme], [ɑ̃trɛme] *ref* to love each other

entrain [ɑ̃trɛ̃] *m* spirit, gusto, pep

entraînement [ɑ̃trɛnmɑ̃] *m* training; enthusiasm

entraîner [ɑ̃trene] *tr* to carry along or away, to entrain; to involve, entail; to pull (*railroad cars*); to work (*a pump*); to train (*an athlete*) || *ref* (sports) to train

entraîneur [ɑ̃trɛnœr] *m* trainer, coach

entraîneuse [ɑ̃trɛnøz] *f* B-girl

entr'apercevoir [ɑ̃trapɛrsəvwar] §59 *tr* to catch a glimpse of

entrave [ɑ̃trav] *f* shackle; hindrance

entra·vé -vée [ɑ̃trave] *adj* impeded, hampered; checked (*vowel*)

entraver [ɑ̃trave] *tr* to shackle; to hinder, impede

entre [ɑ̃tr] *prep* between; among; in or into, e.g., **entre les mains de** in or into the hands of; **d'entre** among; from among, out of; of, e.g., **l'un d'entre eux** one of them; **entre deux eaux** under the surface of the water

entrebâillement [ɑ̃trəbajmɑ̃] *m* chink, slit, crack

entrebâiller [ɑ̃trəbaje] *tr* to leave ajar

entrechat [ɑ̃trə∫a] *m* caper; entrechat

entrechoquer [ɑ̃trə∫ɔke] *tr & ref* to bump together || *ref* to clash

entrecôte [ɑ̃trəkot] *f* sirloin steak, loin of beef; top chuck roast

entrecouper [ɑ̃trəkupe] *tr* to interrupt; to intersect || *ref* to intersect

entrecroiser [ɑ̃trəkrwaze] *tr & ref* to interlace; to intersect

entre-deux [ɑ̃trədø] *m invar* space between; interval; partition; (sports) jump ball

entre-deux-guerres [ɑ̃trədøgɛr] *m & f invar* period between the wars (*the First and Second World War*)

entrée [ɑ̃tre] *f* entrance, entry; admission, admittance; beginning; customs duty; (culin) entree; **avoir ses entrées à, chez,** or **dans** to have the entree into; **d'entrée** at the start, right off; **entrée de serrure** keyhole; **entrée d'un chapeau** hat size; **entrée interdite** (public sign) keep out, no admittance

entrefaites [ɑ̃trəfɛt] *fpl*—**sur ces entrefaites** meanwhile

entrefer [ɑ̃trəfɛr] *m* (elec) air gap

entrefermer [ɑ̃trəfɛrme] *tr* to close part way

entrefilet [ɑ̃trəfilɛ] *m* short feature, special item

entregent [ɑ̃trəʒɑ̃] *m* tact, diplomacy, savoir-faire; **avoir de l'entregent** to be a good mixer

entrejambe [ɑ̃trəʒɑ̃b] *m* crotch

entrelacer [ɑ̃trəlase] §51 *tr & ref* to interlace, to entwine, intertwine

entrelarder [ɑ̃trəlarde] *tr* to lard; to interlard

entre-ligne [ɑ̃trəliɲ] *m* (*pl* **-lignes**) space (*between the lines*); insertion (*written between the lines*); **à l'entre-ligne** double-spaced

entremêler [ɑ̃trəmele] *tr* to mix, mingle; to intersperse

entremets [ɑ̃trəmɛ] *m* side dish; dessert

entremet·teur [ɑ̃trəmɛtœr] **entremet·teuse** [ɑ̃trəmɛtøz] *mf* go-between || *m* (pej) pimp

entremettre [ɑ̃trəmɛtr] §42 *ref* to intervene, to intercede

entremise [ɑ̃trəmiz] *f* intervention; **par l'entremise de** through the medium of

entre-nuire [ɑ̃trənɥir] §19 (*pp* nui) (with *dat* of *reflex pron*) to hurt each other

entrepont [ɑ̃trəpɔ̃] *m* (naut) betweendecks

entreposer [ɑ̃trəpoze] *tr* to place in a warehouse, to store; to bond

entrepôt [ɑ̃trəpo] *m* warehouse; **en entrepôt** in bond

entrepre·nant [ɑ̃trəprənɑ̃] **-nante** [nɑ̃t]

adj enterprising; bold, audacious; gallant

entreprendre [ātrəprādr] §56 *tr* to undertake; to contract for; to enter upon; (coll) to try to win over ‖ *intr*—**entreprendre sur** to encroach upon

entrepre·neur [ātrəprənœr] **-neuse** [nøz] *mf* contractor; **entrepreneur de camionnage** trucker; **entrepreneur de pompes funèbres** undertaker

entreprise [ātrəpriz] *f* undertaking; business, firm; contract

entrer [ātre] *tr* to introduce, bring in ‖ *intr* (*aux*: ÊTRE) to enter; to go in, to come in; **entrer à, dans,** or **en** to enter; to enter into; to begin; **entrer pour** to enter into, to be an ingredient of

entre-rail [ātrəraj] *m* (rr) gauge

entre-regarder [ātrərəgarde] *ref* to exchange glances

entresol [ātrəsɔl] *m* mezzanine

entre-temps [ātrətā] *m invar* interval; **dans l'entre-temps** in the meantime ‖ *adv* meanwhile

entreteneur [ātrətnœr] *m* keeper of a mistress

entretenir [ātrətnir] §72 *tr* to maintain, keep up; to carry on (*a conversation*); to keep (*a mistress*); to entertain, harbor ‖ *ref* to converse, talk

entrete·nu -nue [ātrətny] *adj* kept (*woman*); continuous, undamped (*waves*)

entretien [ātrətjē] *m* maintenance, upkeep; support (*of family, army, etc.*); interview

entretoise [ātrətwaz] *f* strut, brace, crosspiece

entre-tuer [ātrətɥe] *ref* to kill each other, to fight to the death

entre-voie [ātrəvwa] *f* (rr) gauge

entrevoir [ātrəvwar] §75 *tr* to glimpse; to foresee

entre·vu -vue [ātrəvy] *adj* half-seen; vaguely foreseen ‖ *f* interview

entrouvrir [ātruvrir] §65 *tr & ref* to open part way

enture [ātyr] *f* splice (*of pieces of wood*)

énumérer [enymere] §10 *tr* to enumerate

envahir [āvair] *tr* to invade

envahissement [āvaismā] *m* invasion

envaser [āvaze] *tr* to fill with mud; to stick in the mud

enveloppe [āvlɔp] *f* envelope; **enveloppe à fenêtre** window envelope

envelopper [āvlɔpe] *tr* to envelop; to wrap up

envenimer [āvnime] *tr* to inflame, make sore; (fig) to envenom, embitter

envergure [āvergyr] *f* span; wingspread; spread of sail; span, scope

envers [āver] *m* wrong side, reverse, back; **à l'envers** inside out; upside down; back to front; topsy-turvy; **mettre à l'envers** to put on backwards ‖ *prep* towards; with regard to; **envers et contre tous** in spite of everyone else

envi [āvi]—**à l'envi** vying with each other; **à l'envi de** vying with

enviable [āvjabl] *adj* enviable

envie [āvi] *f* desire, longing; envy; birthmark; hangnail; **avoir envie de** to feel like, to have a notion to

envier [āvje] *tr* to envy; to desire; **envier q.ch. à qn** to begrudge s.o. s.th.

en·vieux [āvjø] **-vieuse** [vjøz] *adj* envious ‖ *mf* envious person

environ [āvirɔ̄] *m* outlying section; **aux environs de** in the vicinity of; around, about; **environs** surroundings ‖ *adv* about, approximately

environnement [āvirɔnmā] *m* environment

environner [āvirɔne] *tr* to surround

envisager [āvizaʒe] §38 *tr* to envisage ‖ *intr*—**envisager + inf** to plan to + *inf*, to expect to + *inf*

envoi [āvwa] *m* consignment; remittance; envoy (*of ballad*)

envol [āvɔl] *m* flight; (aer) takeoff

envolée [āvɔle] *f* flight; (aer) takeoff

envoler [āvɔle] *ref* to fly (*said of time*); (aer) to take off

envoûtement [āvutmā] *m* spell, voodoo

envoûter [āvute] *tr* to cast a spell on

envoyer envoyée [āvwaje] *mf* envoy; messenger; **envoyé spécial** special correspondent (*of newspaper*)

envoyer [āvwaje] §26 *tr* to send; to send out; to throw (*e.g., a stone*); to give (*a kick*); **envoyer promener** to send (*s.o.*) about his business; **envoyer qn + inf** to send s.o. to + *inf*; **envoyer qn chercher q.ch.** or **qn** to send s.o. for s.th. or *s.o.* ‖ *intr*—**envoyer chercher** to send for (*s.o. or s.th.*) ‖ *ref* (coll) to gulp down

enzyme [āzim] *m & f* enzyme

épa·gneul -gneule [epaɲœl] *mf* spaniel

épais [epe] **épaisse** [epes] *adj* thick ‖ **épais** *adv* thickly

épaisseur [epesœr] *f* thickness

épaissir [epesir] *tr, intr, & ref* to thicken

épanchement [epā̃ʃmā] *m* outpouring, effusion; (pathol) discharge

épancher [epā̃ʃe] *tr* to pour out; to unburden (*e.g., one's feelings*) ‖ *ref* to pour out; **s'épancher auprès de** to unbosom oneself to; **s'épancher de q.ch.** to get s.th. off one's chest

épandre [epā̃dr] *tr & ref* to spread; to scatter

épanouir [epanwir] *tr* to make (*flowers*) bloom; to light up (*the face*) ‖ *ref* to bloom; to beam (*said of face*)

épanouissement [epanwismā] *m* blossoming; brightening up (*of a face*)

épar·gnant [eparɲā] **-gnante** [ɲāt] *adj* thrifty ‖ *mf* depositor

épargne [eparɲ] *f* saving, thrift; **épargnes** savings

épargner [eparɲe] *tr* to save; to spare; to husband

éparpillement [eparpijmā] *m* scattering

éparpiller [eparpije] *tr* to scatter; to dissipate (*e.g., one's efforts*)

épars [epar] **éparse** [epars] *adj* scattered, sparse; in disorder

épa·tant [epatã] **-tante** [tãt] *adj* (coll) wonderful, terrific

épate [epat] *f*—**faire de l'épate** (slang) to make a big show, to splurge

épa·té -tée [epate] *adj* flattened; (slang) flabbergasted

épater [epate] *tr* (coll) to shock, amaze

épaulard [epolar] *m* killer whale

épaule [epol] *f* shoulder; **donner un coup d'épaule à qn** (coll) to give s.o. a hand; **par-dessus l'épaule** (fig) contemptuously

épaulé-jeté [epoleʒte] *m* clean and jerk (*in weight lifting*)

épaulement [epolmã] *m* breastworks

épauler [epole] *tr* to back, support ‖ *intr* to take aim

épaulette [epolet] *f* epaulet

épave [epav] *f* wreck, derelict, stray; **épaves** wreckage

épée [epe] *f* sword

épéiste [epeist] *m* swordsman

épeler [eple] **§34** *tr* to spell, to spell out; to read letter by letter

épellation [epellasjõ] *f* spelling

éper·du -due [eperdy] *adj* bewildered; desperate (*resistance*); mad (*with pain*); wild (*with joy*)

éperdument [eperdymã] *adv* desperately, madly, wildly

éperlan [eperlã] *m* smelt

éperon [eperõ] *m* spur

éperonner [eperɔne] *tr* to spur

épervier [epervje] *m* sparrow hawk; fish net

éphémère [efemer] *adj* ephemeral ‖ *m* mayfly

épi [epi] *m* ear, cob, spike; cowlick

épice [epis] *f* spice

épicéa [episea] *m* Norway spruce

épicer [epise] **§51** *tr* to spice

épicerie [episri] *f* grocery store; canned goods

épi·cier [episje] **-cière** [sjer] *mf* grocer

épidémie [epidemi] *f* epidemic

épidémiologie [epidemjɔlɔʒi] *f* epidemiology

épidémique [epidemik] *adj* epidemic; contagious (*e.g.*, laughter)

épiderme [epiderm] *m* epidermis

épier [epje] *tr* to spy upon; to be on the lookout for ‖ *intr* to ear, to head

épieu [epjø] *m* (*pl* **épieux**) pike

épiglotte [epiglɔt] *f* epiglottis

épigramme [epigram] *f* epigram

épigraphe [epigraf] *f* epigraph

épilepsie [epilepsi] *f* epilepsy

épileptique [epileptik] *adj & mf* epileptic

épiler [epile] *tr* to pluck (*one's eyebrows*); to remove hair from

épilogue [epilɔg] *m* epilogue

épiloguer [epilɔge] *intr* to split hairs; **épiloguer sur** to carp at

épinard [epinar] *m* spinach; **des épinards** spinach (*leaves used as food*)

épine [epin] *f* thorn; **épine dorsale** backbone; **épine noire** blackthorn; **être sur les épines** to be on pins and needles

épinette [epinet] *f* spinet; hencoop

épi·neux [epinø] **-neuse** [nøz] *adj* thorny; ticklish (*question*)

épingle [epɛ̃gl] *f* pin; **épingle à chapeau** hatpin; **épingle à cheveux** hairpin; **épingle à linge** clothespin; **épingle anglaise** safety pin; **épingle dans une meule de foin** needle in a haystack; **épingle de cravate** stickpin; **épingle de sûreté** safety pin; **monter en épingle** (coll) to make much of; **tiré à quatre épingles** (coll) spic-and-span; (coll) all dolled up; **tirer son épingle du jeu** (coll) to get out by the skin of one's teeth

épingler [epɛ̃gle] *tr* to pin; (coll) to pin down (*s.o.*)

épinière [epinjer] *adj fem* spinal (*cord*)

Épiphanie [epifani] *f* Epiphany, Twelfth-night

épique [epik] *adj* epic

épisco·pal -pale [episkɔpal] (*pl* **-paux** [po]) *adj* episcopal; Episcopalian ‖ *mf* Episcopalian

épisode [epizɔd] *m* episode

épisodique [epizɔdik] *adj* episodic

épisser [epise] *tr* to splice

épissure [episyr] *f* splice

épistémologie [epistemɔlɔʒi] *f* epistemology

épitaphe [epitaf] *f* epitaph

épithète [epitet] *f* epithet

épitoge [epitɔʒ] *f* shoulder band (*worn by French lawyers and holders of French degrees*)

épitomé [epitɔme] *m* epitome

épître [epitr] *f* epistle

éplo·ré -rée [eplɔre] *adj* in tears

épluchage [eplyʃaʒ] *m* peeling; examination

éplucher [eplyʃe] *tr* to peel, pare; to clean, pick; (fig) to find fault with, to pick holes in

éplu·cheur [eplyʃœr] **-cheuse** [ʃøz] *mf* (coll) faultfinder ‖ *m* potato peeler, orange peeler, peeling knife ‖ *f*—**éplucheuse électrique** electric peeler

épluchure [eplyʃyr] *f* peelings; **épluchure de maïs** cornhusks

épointer [epwɛ̃te] *tr* to dull the point of

éponge [epõ ʒ] *f* sponge

éponger [epõʒe] **§38** *tr* to sponge off, to mop up

épopée [epɔpe] *f* epic

époque [epɔk] *f* epoch; time; period; **à l'époque de** at the time of; **d'époque** a real antique; **faire époque** to be epoch-making

épouiller [epuje] *tr* to delouse

époumoner [epumɔne] *ref* to shout oneself out of breath

épousailles [epuzaj] *fpl* wedding

épouser [epuze] *tr* to marry; to espouse; **épouser la forme de** to take the exact shape of

époussetage [epustaʒ] *m* dusting

épousseter [epuste] **§34** *tr* to dust

époussette [epuset] *f* duster

épouvantable [epuvãtabl] *adj* frightful, terrible

épouvantail [epuvãtaj] *m* scarecrow

épouvante [epuvãt] *f* fright, terror

épouvanter [epuvɑ̃te] *tr* to frighten, terrify
époux [epu] **épouse** [epuz] *mf* spouse || *m* husband; **les époux** husband and wife || *f* wife
éprendre [eprɑ̃dr] §56 *ref*—**s'éprendre de** to fall in love with; to hold fast to (*liberty, justice, etc.*)
épreuve [eprœv] *f* proof, test, trial; ordeal; examination; (phot, typ) proof
épris [epri] **éprise** [epriz] *adj* infatuated; **épris de** in love with
éprouver [epruve] *tr* to prove, test, try; to experience, to feel; to put to the test
éprouvette [epruvɛt] *f* test tube; specimen; (med) probe
epsomite [epsɔmit] *f* Epsom salts
épucer [epyse] §51 *tr* to clean of fleas, to delouse
épui·sé -sée [epɥize] *adj* exhausted, tired out; sold out
épuisement [epɥizmɑ̃] *m* exhaustion; diminution; draining off
épuiser [epɥize] *tr* to exhaust, use up; to wear out; to tire out || *ref* to run out; to wear out
épuration [epyrɑsjɔ̃] *f* purification; refining (*e.g., of petroleum*); (pol) purge
épure [epyr] *f* working drawing
épurement [epyrmɑ̃] *m* expurgation
épurer [epyre] *tr* to purify; to expurgate; to weed out, to purge
équanimité [ekwanimite] *f* equanimity
équarrir [ekarir] *tr* to cut up, quarter (*an animal*); to square off
équateur [ekwatœr] *m* equator; **l'Équateur** Ecuador
équation [ekwɑsjɔ̃] *f* equation
équato·rial -riale [ekwatɔrjal] *adj* (*pl* **-riaux** [rjo]) equatorial
équerrage [ekerɑʒ] *m* bevel; beveling
équerre [eker] *f* square (*L- or T-shaped instrument*); **d'équerre** square, true; **mettre d'équerre** to square, to true
équerrer [ekere] *tr* to bevel
équestre [ekɛstr] *adj* equestrian
équilaté·ral -rale [ekɥilateral] *adj* (*pl* **-raux** [ro]) equilateral
équilibre [ekilibr] *m* equilibrium, balance; equipoise
équilibrer [ekilibre] *tr & ref* to balance
équilibriste [ekilibrist] *mf* balancer, ropedancer
équinoxe [ekinɔks] *m* equinox
équipage [ekipaʒ] *m* crew; retinue, suite; attire
équipe [ekip] *f* team; crew; gang, work party; (naut) train of boats; **équipe de jour** day shift; **équipe de nuit** night shift; **équipe de secours** rescue squad
équipée [ekipe] *f* escapade, lark; crazy project
équipement [ekipmɑ̃] *m* equipment
équiper [ekipe] *tr* to equip
équi·pier [ekipje] **-pière** [pjer] *mf* teammate; crew member
équitable [ekitabl] *adj* equitable
équitation [ekitɑsjɔ̃] *f* horseback riding
équité [ekite] *f* equity

équiva·lent [ekivalɑ̃] **-lente** [lɑ̃t] *adj & m* equivalent
équivaloir [ekivalwar] §71 *intr*—**équivaloir à** to be equivalent to; to be tantamount to
équivoque [ekivɔk] *adj* equivocal; questionable (*e.g., reputation*) || *f* double entendre; uncertainty; **sans équivoque** without equivocation
équivoquer [ekivɔke] *intr* to equivocate, quibble; to pun
érable [erabl] *m* maple; **érable à sucre** sugar maple
érafler [erafle] *tr* to graze, scratch
éraflure [eraflyr] *f* graze, scratch
érail·lé -lée [eraje] *adj* bloodshot (*eyes*); hoarse (*voice*)
érailler [eraje] *tr* to fray
ère [er] *f* era
érection [erɛksjɔ̃] *f* erection
érein·té -tée [erɛ̃te] *adj* all in, worn out, tired out
éreinter [erɛ̃te] *tr* to exhaust, tire out; (coll) to criticize unmercifully, to run down (*an author, play, etc.*) || *ref* to wear oneself out; to drudge
erg [ɛrg] *m* erg
ergot [ergo] *m* spur (*of rooster*); **monter** or **se dresser sur ses ergots** (fig) to get up on a high horse
ergotage [ergotaʒ] *m* (coll) quibbling
ergoter [ergote] *tr* (coll) to quibble
ériger [eriʒe] §38 *tr* to erect || *ref*—**s'ériger en** to set oneself up as
ermitage [ermitaʒ] *m* hermitage
ermite [ermit] *m* hermit
éroder [erode] *tr* to erode
érosion [erozjɔ̃] *f* erosion
érotique [erotik] *adj* erotic
érotisme [erotism] *m* eroticism
er·rant [erɑ̃] **er·rante** [erɑ̃t] *adj* wandering, stray; errant
erratique [eratik] *adj* intermittent, irregular, erratic
erre [ɛr] *f* (naut) headway; **erres** track (*e.g., of deer*)
errements [ermɑ̃] *mpl* ways, methods; (pej) erring ways, bad habits
errer [ere] *intr* to wander; to err; to play (*said of smile*)
erreur [erœr] *f* error, mistake; **erreur de frappe** typing error
erro·né -née [erone] *adj* erroneous
éructation [eryktɑsjɔ̃] *f* belch
éructer [erykte] *tr* (fig) to belch forth || *intr* to belch
éru·dit -dite [erydi] [dit] *adj* erudite, learned || *mf* scholar, erudite
érudition [erydisjɔ̃] *f* erudition
éruption [erypsjɔ̃] *f* eruption
ès [es] *prep* §77
esc. *abbr* (escompte) discount
esca·beau [eskabo] *m* (*pl* **-beaux**) stool; stepladder
escadre [eskadr] *f* squadron; fleet
escadron [eskadrɔ̃] *m* (mil) squadron
escalade [eskalad] *f* scaling, climbing
escalader [eskalade] *tr* to scale, to climb; to clamber over or up
escalator [eskalator] *m* escalator
escale [eskal] *f* port of call, stop; **faire escale** to make a stop; **sans escale** nonstop

escalier [ɛskalje] *m* stairway; **escalier à vis** circular stairway; **escalier de sauvetage** fire escape; **escalier en colimaçon** spiral staircase; **escalier mécanique** or **roulant** escalator

escalope [ɛskalɔp] *f* scallop

escamotable [ɛskamɔtabl] *adj* retractable (*e.g., landing gear*); concealable (*piece of furniture*)

escamotage [ɛskamɔtaʒ] *m* sleight of hand; side-stepping, avoiding; theft

escamoter [ɛskamɔte] *tr* to palm (*a card*); to pick (*a wallet*); to dodge (*a question*); to slur (*a word*); to hush up (*a scandal*); (aer) to retract (*landing gear*)

escamo·teur [ɛskamɔtœr] -teuse [tøz] *mf* prestidigitator; pickpocket

escapade [ɛskapad] *f* escapade, escape

escarbille [ɛskarbij] *f* cinder, clinker

escarbot [ɛskarbo] *m* beetle

escarboucle [ɛskarbukl] *f* (mineral) carbuncle

escargot [ɛskargo] *m* snail

escarmouche [ɛskarmuʃ] *f* skirmish

escarmoucher [ɛskarmuʃe] *intr* to skirmish

escarpe [ɛskarp] *m* ruffian, bandit ‖ *f* escarpment (*of a fort*)

escar·pé -pée [ɛskarpe] *adj* steep

escarpement [ɛskarpəmã] *m* escarpment

escarpin [ɛskarpɛ̃] *m* pump, dancing shoe

escarpolette [ɛskarpɔlɛt] *f* swing

escarre [ɛskar] *f* scab

escarrifier [ɛskarifje] *tr* to form a scab on

esche [ɛʃ] *f* bait

Eschyle [ɛsʃil], [ɛʃil] *m* Aeschylus

escient [ɛsjã]—**à bon escient** knowingly, wittingly; **à mon (ton, etc.) escient** to my (your, etc.) certain knowledge

esclaffer [ɛsklafe] *ref* to burst out laughing

esclandre [ɛsklɑ̃dr] *m* scandal

esclavage [ɛsklavaʒ] *m* slavery

esclavagiste [ɛsklavaʒist] *adj* pro-slavery ‖ *mf* advocate of slavery

esclave [ɛsklav] *adj & mf* slave

escompte [ɛskɔ̃t] *m* discount, rebate; **escompte de caisse** cash discount; **escompte en dehors** bank discount; **prendre à l'escompte** to discount

escompter [ɛskɔ̃te] *tr* to discount (*a premature note*); to anticipate

escompteur [ɛskɔ̃tœr] *adj* discounting (*banker*) ‖ *m* discount broker

escopette [ɛskɔpɛt] *f* blunderbuss

escorte [ɛskɔrt] *f* escort

escorter [ɛskɔrte] *tr* to escort

escouade [ɛskwad] *f* infantry section; gang (*of laborers*)

escrime [ɛskrim] *f* fencing

escrimer [ɛskrime] *intr & ref* to fence; **s'escrimer à** to work with might and main at; **s'escrimer contre** to fence with

escri·meur [ɛskrimœr] -meuse [møz] *mf* fencer

escroc [ɛskro] *m* crook, swindler

escroquer [ɛskrɔke] *tr* to swindle

escroquerie [ɛskrɔkri] *f* swindling, cheating; racket, swindle

ésotérique [ɛzɔterik] *adj* esoteric

espace [ɛspas] *m* space; room; **espace cosmique** outer space ‖ *f* (typ) space

espacement [ɛspasmã] *m* spacing

espacer [ɛspase] §51 *tr* to space

espadon [ɛspadɔ̃] *m* swordfish

espadrille [ɛspadrij] *f* tennis shoe; beach sandal; esparto sandal

Espagne [ɛspaɲ] *f* Spain; **l'Espagne** Spain

espa·gnol -gnole [ɛspaɲɔl] *adj* Spanish ‖ *m* Spanish (*language*) ‖ (*cap*) *mf* Spaniard (*person*); **les Espagnols** the Spanish

espagnolette [ɛspaɲɔlɛt] *f* espagnolette (*door fastener for French casement window*)

espalier [ɛspalje] *m* espalier

espèce [ɛspɛs] *f* species; sort, kind; **en espèces** in specie; **en l'espèce** in the matter; **espèces sonnantes** hard cash; **sale espèce** cad, bounder ‖ *mf*— **espèce de** (coll) damn, e.g., **cet espèce d'idiot** that damn fool

espérance [ɛsperãs] *f* hope; **espérances** expectations; prospects

espérer [ɛspere] §10 *tr* to hope, to hope for; (coll) to wait for; **espérer + inf** to hope to + *inf* ‖ *intr* to trust; (coll) to wait

espiègle [ɛspjɛgl] *adj* mischievous ‖ *mf* rogue

espièglerie [ɛspjɛgləri] *f* mischievousness; prank

es·pion [ɛspjɔ̃] -pionne [pjɔn] *mf* spy ‖ *m* concealed microphone; busybody (*mirror*)

espionnage [ɛspjɔnaʒ] *m* espionage

espionner [ɛspjɔne] *tr* to spy on

espoir [ɛspwar] *m* hope; promise

esprit [ɛspri] *m* spirit; mind; intelligence; wit; spirits (*of wine*); **à l'esprit clair** clearheaded; **avoir l'esprit de l'escalier** to think of what to say too late; **bel esprit** man of letters; **esprit d'équipe** teamwork; **esprit de système** love of order; (pej) pigheadedness; **esprit fort** freethinker; **rendre l'esprit** to give up the ghost

esquif [ɛskif] *m* skiff

esqui·mau [ɛskimo] -maude [mod] (*pl* -maux) *adj* Eskimo ‖ *m* husky, Eskimo dog; Eskimo (*language*) ‖ (*cap*) *mf* Eskimo (*person*)

esquinter [ɛskɛ̃te] *tr* (coll) to tire out; (coll) to wear out; (coll) to run down, knock, criticize

esquisse [ɛskis] *f* sketch; outline, draft; beginning (*e.g., of a smile*)

esquisser [ɛskise] *tr* to sketch; to outline, draft; to begin

esquiver [ɛskive] *tr* to dodge, to sidestep; **esquiver de la tête** to duck ‖ *ref* to sneak away

essai [ɛse] *m* essay; trial, test; **à l'essai** on trial; **essais** first attempts (*of artist, writer, etc.*); **faire l'essai de** to try out

essaim [ɛsɛ̃] *m* swarm

essaimer [ɛseme] *intr* to swarm

essarter [ɛsarte] *tr* to clear (*brush*)

essarts [esar] *mpl* clearings

essayage [eseja3] *m* fitting, trying on

essayer [eseje], [eseje] §49 *tr* to try on or try out; to assay (*ore*) || *intr* to try; **essayer de** to try to || *ref*—**s'essayer à** to try one's skill at

essayeur [esejœr] **essayeuse** [esejøz] *mf* assayer

essayiste [esejist] *mf* essayist

esse [es] *f* S-hook; sound hole (*of violin*)

essence [esɑ̃s] *f* essence; gasoline; kind, species; **par essence** by definition

essen·tiel -tielle [esɑ̃sjɛl] *adj & m* essential

esseu·lé -lée [escle] *adj* abandoned

es·sieu [esjø] *m* (*pl* -**sieux**) axle

essor [esɔr] *m* flight; development; boom (*in business*); **donner libre essor à** to give vent to; to give full scope to; **prendre son essor** to take wing

essorer [esɔre] *tr* to spin-dry; to wring; to centrifuge

essoreuse [esɔrøz] *f* spin-drier; wringer; centrifuge

essouf·flé -flée [esufle] *adj* breathless, out of breath

essuie-glace [esɥiglas] *m* (*pl* -**glaces**) windshield wiper

essuie-mains [esɥimɛ̃] *m invar* towel

essuie-plume [esɥiplym] *m* (*pl* -**plumes**) penwiper

essuyer [esɥije], [esɥije] §27 *tr* to wipe; to wipe off; to wipe away; to suffer, endure; to undergo; to weather (*a storm*); **essuyer les plâtres** (coll) to be the first to occupy a house

est [est] *adj invar & m* east

estacade [estakad] *f* breakwater; pier; boom (*barrier of floating logs*); railway trestle

estafette [estafet] *f* messenger

estaminet [estamine] *m* bar, café

estampe [estɑ̃p] *f* print, engraving; (*tool*) stamp

estamper [estɑ̃pe] *tr* to stamp (*with a design*); to engrave; to overcharge, to fleece

estampille [estɑ̃pij] *f* identification mark; trademark; hallmark

ester [ester] *m* ester || [este] *intr*—**ester en justice** to go to law, to sue

esthète [estɛt] *mf* aesthete

esthéti·cien [estetisjɛ̃] **-cienne** [sjen] *mf* aesthetician || *f* beautician

esthétique [estetik] *adj* aesthetic || *f* aesthetics

estimable [estimabl] *adj* estimable

estimateur [estimatœr] *m* estimator, appraiser

estimation [estimɑsjɔ̃] *f* estimation, appraisal

estime [estim] *f* esteem; **à l'estime** by guesswork; (naut) by dead reckoning

estimer [estime] *tr* to esteem; to estimate, to assess; **estimer + inf** to think that + *ind*, e.g., **j'estime avoir fait mon devoir** I think that I did my duty

esti·val -vale [estival] *adj* (*pl* -**vaux** [vo]) summer

esti·vant [estivɑ̃] **-vante** [vɑ̃t] *mf* summer vacationist, summer resident

estiver [estive] *intr* to summer

estocade [estɔkad] *f* thrust (*in fencing*); unexpected attack

estomac [estɔma] *m* stomach

estomaquer [estɔmake] *tr* (coll) to astound || *ref* (coll) to be angered

estomper [estɔ̃pe] *tr* to shade off, to rub away (*a drawing*); to blur || *ref* to be blurred

Estonie [estɔni] *f* Estonia; **l'Estonie** Estonia

estrade [estrad] *f* platform

estragon [estragɔ̃] *m* tarragon

estro·pié -piée [estrɔpje] *adj* crippled || *mf* cripple

estuaire [estɥer] *m* estuary

estudian·tin [estydjɑ̃tɛ̃] **-tine** [tin] *adj* student

esturgeon [estyrʒɔ̃] *m* sturgeon

et [e] *conj* and; **et . . . et** both . . . and

Établ. *abbr* (**Établissement**) company, establishment

étable [etabl] *f* stable, cowshed

établer [etable] *tr* to stable

établi [etabli] *m* workbench

établir [etablir] *tr* to establish || *ref* to settle down; to set up headquarters

établissement [etablismɑ̃] *m* establishment

étage [etaʒ] *m* floor, story; tier, level; rank, social level; (rok) stage; **de bas étage** lower-class; **dernier étage** top floor; **premier étage** first floor above ground floor

étager [etaʒe] §38 *tr* to arrange in tiers; to stagger; to perform in stages

étagère [etaʒer] *f* rack, shelf

étai [ete] *m* prop, stay

étain [etɛ̃] *m* tin; pewter

étal [etal] *m* (*pl* **étals** or **étaux** [eto]) stall, stand; butcher's block

étalage [etalaʒ] *m* display

étalager [etalaʒe] §38 *tr* to display

étalagiste [etalaʒist] *mf* window dresser, display artist; demonstrator

étaler [etale] *tr* to display; to spread out || *ref* (coll) to sprawl

étalon [etalɔ̃] *m* stallion; monetary standard

étalonner [etalɔne] *tr* to verify, control; to standardize; to graduate, calibrate

étalon-or [etalɔ̃ɔr] *m* gold standard

étambot [etɑ̃bo] *m* (naut) sternpost

étamer [etame] *tr* to tin-plate; to silver (*a mirror*)

étamine [etamin] *f* stamen; sieve; cheesecloth

étampe [etɑ̃p] *f* stamp, die, punch

étamper [etɑ̃pe] *tr* to stamp, punch

étanche [etɑ̃ʃ] *adj* watertight, airtight

étancher [etɑ̃ʃe] *tr* to check, stanch the flow of; to quench (*one's thirst*); to make watertight or airtight

étang [etɑ̃] *m* pond

étape [etap] *f* stage; stop, halt; day's march; (sports) lap; **brûler les étapes** to go straight through

état [eta] *m* state; statement, record; trade, occupation; government; (hist) estate; **en tout état de cause** at all costs; **in any case; état civil** marital status; **état tampon** buffer state; **être dans tous ses états** to stew; **être en état de** to be in a position to; **faire état de** to take into account; to expect to; **hors d'état** out of order, unfit; **tenir en état** to keep in shape, to repair

étatisation [etatizɑsjɔ̃] f nationalization

étatiser [etatize] tr to nationalize

étatisme [etatism] m statism

état-major [etamaʒɔr] m (pl **états-majors**) headquarters, staff

état-providence [etaprɔvidɑ̃s] m welfare state

États-Unis [etazyni] mpl United States

étau [eto] m (pl **étaux**) vise

étayer [eteje] §49 tr to prop, stay

et Cⁱᵉ abbr (**et Compagnie**) & Co.

été [ete] m summer

éteignoir [etɛɲwar] m candle snuffer; (coll) kill-joy, wet blanket

éteindre [etɛ̃dr] §50 tr to extinguish, put out; to turn off; to wipe out; to appease (e.g., one's thirst); to dull (a color) || intr to put out the light || ref to go out; (fig) to die, pass away

éteint [etɛ̃] **éteinte** [etɛ̃t] adj extinguished; extinct; dull, dim

étendard [etɑ̃dar] m flag, banner

étendoir [etɑ̃dwar] m clothesline; drying rack

étendre [etɑ̃dr] tr to extend, spread out || ref to stretch out; to spread

éten·du -due [etɑ̃dy] adj outspread; extensive; vast; diluted, adulterated || f stretch; range, scope

éter·nel -nelle [etɛrnɛl] adj eternal

éterniser [etɛrnize] tr to perpetuate (a name); to drag out || ref (coll) to drag on; **s'éterniser chez qn** (coll) to overstay an invitation

éternité [etɛrnite] f eternity

éternument [etɛrnymɑ̃] m sneeze; sneezing

éternuer [etɛrnɥe] intr to sneeze

étêter [etete] tr to top (a tree); to take the head off (a fish, nail, etc.)

éteule [etœl] f stubble

éther [etɛr] m ether

éthé·ré -rée [etere] adj ethereal

Éthiopie [etjɔpi] f Ethiopia; **l'Éthiopie** Ethiopia

éthio·pien [etjɔpjɛ̃] **-pienne** [pjɛn] adj Ethiopian || m Ethiopian (language) || (cap) mf Ethiopian (person)

éthique [etik] adj ethical || f ethics

ethnique [etnik] adj ethnic(al)

ethnographie [etnɔgrafi] f ethnography

ethnologie [etnɔlɔʒi] f ethnology

éthyle [etil] m ethyl

éthylène [etilɛn] m ethylene

étiage [etjaʒ] m low-water mark

étince·lant [etɛ̃slɑ̃] **-lante** [lɑ̃t] adj sparkling, glittering

étinceler [etɛ̃sle] §34 intr to sparkle, glitter

étincelle [etɛ̃sɛl] f spark; (fig) flash

étiolement [etjɔlmɑ̃] m wilting

étioler [etjɔle] tr & ref to wilt

étique [etik] adj lean, emaciated

étiqueter [etikte] §34 tr to label

étiquette [etikɛt] f etiquette; label; **étiquette gommée** sticker

étirer [etire] tr to stretch, lengthen, elongate || ref (coll) to stretch one's limbs

étoffe [etɔf] f stuff; material, fabric; quality, worth

étoile [etwal] f star; traffic circle; **à la belle étoile** out of doors; **étoile de mer** starfish; **étoile filante** shooting or falling star; **étoile polaire** pole-star

étoi·lé -lée [etwale] adj star-spangled, starry

étole [etɔl] f stole

éton·nant [etɔnɑ̃] **éton·nante** [etɔnɑ̃t] adj astonishing

étonnement [etɔnmɑ̃] m surprise, astonishment; fissure, crack

étonner [etɔne] tr to surprise, astonish; to shake or crack (masonry) || ref to be surprised

étouf·fant [etufɑ̃] **étouf·fante** [etufɑ̃t] adj suffocating; sweltering

étouffée [etufe] f braising; **cuire à l'étouffée** to braise

étouffer [etufe] tr, intr, & ref to suffocate; to stifle; to choke

étoupe [etup] f oakum, tow

étourderie [eturdri] f thoughtlessness

étour·di -die [eturdi] adj scatterbrained || mf scatterbrain

étourdir [eturdir] tr to stun, daze; to numb; to deafen (with loud noise) || ref to try to forget, get in a daze

étourdissement [eturdismɑ̃] m dizziness; numbing

étour·neau [eturno] m (pl **-neaux**) starling

étrange [etrɑ̃ʒ] adj strange

étran·ger [etrɑ̃ʒe] **-gère** [ʒɛr] adj foreign; irrelevant; unknown, strange; **être étranger à** to be unacquainted with || mf foreigner; stranger; **à l'étranger** abroad, in a foreign country

étrangeté [etrɑ̃ʒte] f strangeness

étrangler [etrɑ̃gle] tr & intr to strangle || ref to choke; to narrow (said of passageway, valley, etc.)

étran·gleur [etrɑ̃glœr] **-gleuse** [gløz] mf strangler

étrave [etrav] f (naut) stempost; **de l'étrave à l'étambot** from stem to stern

être [etr] m being || §28 intr to be; **en être pour sa peine** to have nothing for one's trouble; **être à** + pron (disj) to be + pron poss, e.g., **le livre est à moi** the book is mine; **n'est-ce pas** see ne || aux (used with some intransitive verbs and all reflexive verbs) to have, e.g., **elles sont arrivées** they have arrived; (used to form the passive voice) to be, e.g., **il est aimé de tout le monde** he is loved by everybody

étrécir [etresir] tr & ref to shrink

étreindre [etrɛ̃dr] §50 tr to embrace; to grip, seize

étreinte [etrɛ̃t] f embrace; hold, grasp

étrenne [etren] f first sale of the day;

avoir l'étrenne de to have the first use of; étrennes New-Year gifts

étrenner [etrene] tr to put on for the first time; to be the first to wear || intr (coll) to be the first to catch it

étrier [etrije] m stirrup

étrille [etrij] f currycomb

étriller [etrije] tr to curry; (coll) to thrash, to tan the hide of; (coll) to overcharge, to fleece

étriper [etripe] tr to gut, disembowel

étri·qué ·quée [etrike] adj skimpy, tight; narrow, cramped

étriquer [etrike] tr to make too tight; to shorten (e.g., a speech)

étroit [etrwa] étroite [etrwat] adj narrow; strict; tight; close; à l'étroit confined, cramped

étroitesse [etrwɑtɛs] f narrowness; étroitesse d'esprit narrow-mindedness

étude [etyd] f study; law office; law practice; spadework, planning; à l'étude under consideration; mettre à l'étude to study; terminer ses études to finish one's courses

étu·diant ·diante [etydjɑ̃] mf student

étu·dié ·diée [etydje] adj studied; set (speech); artificial, affected

étudier [etydje] tr to study; to practice, rehearse; to learn by heart; to design || intr to study || ref to be overly introspective; s'étudier à to take pains to, to make a point of

étui [etɥi] m case, box

étuve [etyv] f steam bath or room; drying room; steam sterilizer; incubator (for breeding cultures)

étuver [etyve] tr to stew; to steam; to dry

étymologie [etimɔlɔʒi] f etymology

étymon [etimɔ̃] m etymon

eucalyptus [økaliptys] m eucalyptus

Eucharistie [økaristi] f Eucharist

eunuque [ønyk] m eunuch

euphémique [øfemik] adj euphemistic

euphémisme [øfemism] m euphemism

euphonie [øfoni] f euphony

euphonique [øfonik] adj euphonic

euphorie [øfori] f euphoria

Europe [ørɔp] f Europe; l'Europe Europe

européen [ørɔpeɛ̃] européenne [ørɔpeɛn] adj European || (cap) mf European

eux [ø] §85

eux-mêmes [ømɛm] §86

évacuer [evakɥe] tr & ref to evacuate

éva·dé ·dée [evade] mf escapee

évader [evade] ref to escape, evade

évaluer [evalɥe] tr to evaluate, appraise; to estimate

évanes·cent [evanesɑ̃] évanes·cente [evanesɑ̃t] adj evanescent

évangélique [evɑ̃ʒelik] adj evangelic(al)

évangéliste [evɑ̃ʒelist] m evangelist

évangile [evɑ̃ʒil] m gospel

évanouir [evanwir] ref to faint; to lose consciousness; to vanish; (rad) to fade

évanouissement [evanwismɑ̃] m fainting; disappearance

évapo·ré ·rée [evapore] adj flighty, fickle, giddy

évaporer [evapore] tr & ref to evaporate

évaser [evɑze] tr & ref to widen

éva·sif [evɑzif] ·sive [ziv] adj evasive

évasion [evɑzjɔ̃] f evasion; escape; d'évasion escapist (literature)

Ève [ev] f Eve; je ne le connais ni d'Ève ni d'Adam (coll) I don't know him from Adam

évêché [eveʃe] m bishopric

éveil [evej] m awakening; alarm, warning

éveil·lé ·lée [eveje] adj alert, lively; sharp, intelligent

éveiller [eveje] tr & ref to wake up

événement [evenmɑ̃], [evenmɑ̃] m event; outcome, development; faire événement to cause quite a stir

évent [evɑ̃] m vent; staleness

éventail [evɑ̃taj] m fan; range, spread; screen

éventaire [evɑ̃ter] m tray (carried by flower girl, cigarette girl, etc.); sidewalk display

éventer [evɑ̃te] tr to fan; to ventilate; to get wind of (a secret); éventer la mèche (coll) to let the cat out of the bag || ref to fan oneself; to fade away (said of odor); to go stale or flat

éventrer [evɑ̃tre] tr to disembowel; to smash open

éventualité [evɑ̃tɥalite] f eventuality; possibility

éven·tuel ·tuelle [evɑ̃tɥel] adj eventual; possible, contingent; forthcoming || m eventuality; possibility; possibilities (e.g., of a job)

éventuellement [evɑ̃tɥelmɑ̃] adv eventually; possibly; if need be

évêque [evek] m bishop

évertuer [evertɥe] ref—s'évertuer à or pour + inf to strive to + inf

éviction [eviksjɔ̃] f eviction, removal; éviction scolaire quarantine

évidement [evidmɑ̃] m hollowing out

évidemment [evidamɑ̃] adv evidently

évidence [evidɑ̃s] f evidence, obviousness; conspicuousness; de toute évidence by all appearances; se mettre en évidence to come to the fore

évi·dent [evidɑ̃] -dente [dɑ̃t] adj evident

évider [evide] tr to hollow out

évier [evje] m sink

évincer [evɛ̃se] §51 tr to evict, to oust; to discriminate against

éviter [evite] tr to avoid, escape

évoca·teur [evɔkatœr] -trice [tris] adj evocative, suggestive

évocation [evɔkɑsjɔ̃] f evocation

évoluer [evɔlɥe] intr to evolve; to change one's mind

évolution [evɔlysjɔ̃] f evolution

évoquer [evɔke] tr to evoke; to recall, to call to mind

exact [egza], [egzakt] exacte [egzakt] adj exact

exactitude [egzaktityd] f exactness; punctuality

exagérer [egzaʒere] §10 tr to exaggerate; to overdo

exal·té ·tée [egzalte] adj impassioned;

high-strung, wrought-up ‖ *mf* hot-head, fanatic

exalter [ɛgzalte] *tr* to exalt; to excite (*e.g., the imagination*) ‖ *ref* to get excited

examen [ɛgzamɛ̃] *m* examination; à l'examen under consideration; on approval; examen de fin d'études or examen de fin de classe final examination; examen probatoire placement exam; libre examen free inquiry; se présenter à, passer, or subir un examen to take an examination

examina·teur [ɛgzaminatœr] **-trice** [tris] *mf* examiner

examiner [ɛgzamine] *tr* to examine

exaspération [ɛgzasperɑsjɔ̃] *f* exasperation; crisis, aggravation

exaspérer [ɛgzaspere] §10 *tr* to exasperate; to make worse

exaucer [ɛgzose] §51 *tr* to answer the prayer of; to fulfill (*a wish*)

excava·teur [ɛkskavatœr] **-trice** [tris] *m & f* excavator, steam shovel

excaver [ɛkskave] *tr* to excavate

excé·dant [ɛksedɑ̃] **-dante** [dɑ̃t] *adj* excess; tiresome

excédent [ɛksedɑ̃] *m* excess, surplus

excédentaire [ɛksedɑ̃ter] *adj* excess

excéder [ɛksede] §10 *tr* to exceed; to tire out; to overtax

excellence [ɛkselɑ̃s] *f* excellence; Votre Excellence Your Excellency

exceller [ɛksele] *intr* to excel

excentricité [ɛksɑ̃trisite] *f* eccentricity

excentrique [ɛksɑ̃trik] *adj* eccentric; remote, outlying ‖ *mf* eccentric ‖ *m* (mach) eccentric

excep·té -tée [ɛksepte] *adj* excepted ‖ excepté *adv*—excepté que except that ‖ excepté *prep* except, except for

exception [ɛksepsjɔ̃] *f* exception; à l'exception de with the exception of

exception·nel -nelle [ɛksepsjɔnel] *adj* exceptional

excès [ɛksɛ] *m* excess; excès de pose (phot) overexposure; excès de vitesse speeding

exces·sif [ɛksesif] **exces·sive** [ɛksesiv] *adj* excessive

exciper [ɛksipe] *intr*—exciper de (law) to offer a plea of, to allege

excitable [ɛksitabl] *adj* excitable

exci·tant [ɛksitɑ̃] **-tante** [tɑ̃t] *adj* stimulating ‖ *m* stimulant

exciter [ɛksite] *tr* to excite, stimulate; to stir, incite; to provoke (*e.g., laughter*)

exclamation [ɛksklamɑsjɔ̃] *f* exclamation

exclamer [ɛksklame] *ref* to exclaim

exclure [ɛksklyr] §11 *tr* to exclude

exclu·sif [ɛksklyzif] **-sive** [ziv] *adj* exclusive

exclusion [ɛksklyzjɔ̃] *f* exclusion; à l'exclusion de exclusive of, excluding

exclusivité [ɛksklyzivite] *f* exclusiveness; exclusive rights; newsbeat; en exclusivité (public sign in front of a theater) exclusive showing

excommunication [ɛkskɔmynikɑsjɔ̃] *f* excommunication

excommunier [ɛkskɔmynje] *tr* to excommunicate

excorier [ɛkskɔrje] *tr* to scratch, skin

excrément [ɛkskremɑ̃] *m* excrement

excroissance [ɛkskrwasɑ̃s] *f* growth, tumor

excursion [ɛkskyrsjɔ̃] *f* excursion; tour, trip; outing

excursionner [ɛkskyrsjɔne] *intr* to go on an excursion

excusable [ɛkskyzabl] *adj* excusable

excuse [ɛkskyz] *f* excuse; des excuses apologies

excuser [ɛkskyze] *tr* to excuse ‖ *ref* to excuse oneself, to apologize; Je m'excuse! (coll) excuse me!

exécrer [ɛgzekre] §10 *tr* to execrate

exécu·tant [ɛgzekytɑ̃] **-tante** [tɑ̃t] *mf* performer

exécuter [ɛgzekyte] *tr* to execute; to perform; to make (*copies*) ‖ *ref* to comply

exécuteur [ɛgzekytœr] *m*—exécuteur testamentaire executor; exécuteur des hautes œuvres hangman

exécu·tif [ɛgzekytif] **-tive** [tiv] *adj & m* executive

exécution [ɛgzekysjɔ̃] *f* execution; performance; fulfillment; mettre à exécution to carry out

exécutrice [ɛgzekytris] *f* executrix

exemplaire [ɛgzɑ̃pler] *adj* exemplary ‖ *m* exemplar, model; sample, specimen; copy (*e.g., of book*); en double exemplaire with carbon copy; exemplaire dédicacé autographed copy; exemplaires de passe extra copies

exemple [ɛgzɑ̃pl] *m* example; à l'exemple de after the example of; par exemple for example; par exemple! the idea!, well I never!; prêcher d'exemple to practice what one preaches; sans exemple unprecedented

exempt [ɛgzɑ̃] **exempte** [ɛgzɑ̃t] *adj* exempt ‖ *m* (hist) police officer

exempter [ɛgzɑ̃te] *tr* to exempt

exemption [ɛgzɑ̃psjɔ̃] *f* exemption

exer·cé -cée [ɛgzerse] *adj* practiced, experienced

exercer [ɛgzerse] §51 *tr* to exercise; to exert; to practice (*e.g., medicine*) ‖ *ref* to exercise; to practice, to drill

exercice [ɛgzersis] *m* exercise; drill; practice; exercice budgétaire fiscal year

exhalaison [ɛgzalɛzɔ̃] *f* exhalation (*of gas, vapors, etc.*)

exhalation [ɛgzalɑsjɔ̃] *f* exhalation (*of air from lungs*)

exhaler [ɛgzale] *tr, intr, & ref* to exhale

exhaure [ɛgzɔr] *f* pumping out (*of a mine*); drain pumps

exhaussement [ɛgzosmɑ̃] *m* raising; rise

exhausser [ɛgzose] *tr* to raise, to increase the height of ‖ *ref* to rise

exhaus·tif [ɛgzostif] **-tive** [tiv] *adj* exhaustive

exhiber [ɛgzibe] *tr* to exhibit; to show (*a ticket, passport, etc.*) || *ref* to make an exhibition of oneself

exhibition [ɛgzibisjɔ̃] *f* exhibition

exhorter [ɛgzɔrte] *tr* to exhort

exhumer [ɛgzyme] *tr* to exhume

exi·geant [ɛgziʒɑ̃] **-geante** [ʒɑ̃t] *adj* exigent, exacting; unreasonable

exigence [ɛgziʒɑ̃s] *f* demand, claim; requirement; unreasonableness; **exigences** exigencies

exiger [ɛgziʒe] §38 *tr* to demand, require, exact

exigible [ɛgziʒibl] *adj* required; due, on demand

exi·gu -guë [ɛgzigy] *adj* tiny; insufficient

exiguïté [ɛgzigɥite] *f* smallness; insufficiency

exil [ɛgzil] *m* exile

exi·lé -lée [ɛgzile] *adj & mf* exile

exiler [ɛgzile] *tr* to exile

existence [ɛgzistɑ̃s] *f* existence

exister [ɛgziste] *intr* to exist

exode [ɛgzɔd] *m* exodus; flight (*of capital; of emigrants, refugees, etc.*)

exonération [ɛgzɔnerasjɔ̃] *f* exemption, exoneration

exonérer [ɛgzɔnere] §10 *tr* to exempt, exonerate || *ref* to pay up a debt

exorbi·tant [ɛgzɔrbitɑ̃] **-tante** [tɑ̃t] *adj* exorbitant

exorciser [ɛgzɔrsize] *tr* to exorcise

exotique [ɛgzɔtik] *adj* exotic

expan·sif [ɛkspɑ̃sif] **-sive** [siv] *adj* expansive

expansion [ɛkspɑ̃sjɔ̃] *f* expansion; expansiveness; spread (*of a belief*)

expa·trié -triée [ɛkspatrije] *adj & mf* expatriate

expatrier [ɛkspatrije] *tr* to expatriate

expectorer [ɛkspɛktɔre] *tr & intr* to expectorate

expé·dient -diente [djɑ̃t] *adj* expedient || *m* expedient; (coll) makeshift; **expédient provisoire** emergency measure; **vivre d'expédients** to live by one's wits

expédier [ɛkspedje] *tr* to expedite; to ship; to make a certified copy of; (coll) to dash off, do hurriedly

expédi·teur [ɛkspeditœr] **-trice** [tris] *adj* forwarding (*station, agency, etc.*) || *mf* sender, shipper

expédi·tif [ɛkspeditif] **-tive** [tiv] *adj* expeditious

expédition [ɛkspedisjɔ̃] *f* expedition; shipping; shipment; certified copy

expéditionnaire [ɛkspedisjɔner] *adj* expeditionary || *mf* sender; clerk

expérience [ɛksperjɑ̃s] *f* experience; experiment

expérimen·té -tée [ɛksperimɑ̃te] *adj* experienced

expérimenter [ɛksperimɑ̃te] *tr* to try out, to test || *intr* to conduct experiments

ex·pert [ɛkspɛr] **-perte** [pɛrt] *adj* expert || *m* expert; connoisseur; appraiser

expert-comptable [ɛkspɛrkɔ̃tabl] *m* (*pl* **experts-comptables**) certified public accountant

expertise [ɛkspɛrtiz] *f* expert appraisal

expertiser [ɛkspɛrtize] *tr* to appraise

expier [ɛkspje] *tr* to expiate, to atone for

expirer [ɛkspire] *tr & intr* to expire; to exhale

explicable [ɛksplikabl] *adj* explicable, explainable

explica·tif [ɛksplikatif] **-tive** [tiv] *adj* explanatory

explication [ɛksplikasjɔ̃] *f* explanation; interpretation (*of a text*); **avoir une explication avec qn** to have it out with s.o.

explicite [ɛksplisit] *adj* explicit

expliciter [ɛksplisite] *tr* to make explicit

expliquer [ɛksplike] *tr* to explain; to give an interpretation of || *ref* to explain oneself; to understand

exploit [ɛksplwa] *m* exploit; **exploit d'ajournement** subpoena; **signifier un exploit** to serve a summons

exploi·tant [ɛksplwatɑ̃] **-tante** [tɑ̃t] *adj* operating, working || *mf* operator (*of enterprise*); developer; cultivator; (mov) exhibitor

exploitation [ɛksplwatasjɔ̃] *f* exploitation; management, development, cultivation; land under cultivation

exploiter [ɛksplwate] *tr* to exploit; to manage, develop, cultivate || *intr* to serve summonses

explora·teur [ɛksplɔratœr] **-trice** [tris] *mf* explorer

exploration [ɛksplɔrasjɔ̃] *f* exploration

explorer [ɛksplɔre] *tr* to explore; (telv) to scan

exploser [ɛksploze] *intr* to explode

explosible [ɛksplozibl] *adj* explosive

explo·sif [ɛksplozif] **-sive** [ziv] *adj & m* explosive

explosion [ɛksplozjɔ̃] *f* explosion; **à explosion** internal-combustion (*engine*)

exporta·teur [ɛkspɔrtatœr] **-trice** [tris] *adj* exporting || *mf* exporter

exportation [ɛkspɔrtasjɔ̃] *f* export; exportation

exporter [ɛkspɔrte] *tr & intr* to export

expo·sant [ɛkspozɑ̃] **-sante** [zɑ̃t] *mf* exhibitor; petitioner || *m* (math) exponent

exposé [ɛkspoze] *m* exposition, account, statement; report (*given by a student in class*)

exposer [ɛkspoze] *tr* to expose; to explain, expound; to exhibit, display

exposition [ɛkspozisjɔ̃] *f* exposition; exposure (*to one of the points of the compass*); introduction (*of a book*); lying in state; **exposition canine** dog show; **exposition d'horticulture** flower show; **exposition hippique** horse show

ex·près [ɛkspre] **-presse** [pres] *adj* express || **exprès** *adj invar* special-delivery (*letter, package, etc.*) || *m* express; **par exprès** by special delivery || **exprès** *adv* expressly, on purpose

express [ɛkspres] *adj & m* express (*train*)

expressément [ɛkspresemã] adv expressly
expres·sif [ɛkspresif] expres·sive [ɛks-
presiv] adj expressive
expression [ɛkspresjɔ̃] f expression;
d'expression française native French-
speaking
exprimer [ɛksprime] tr to express; to
squeeze out
exproprier [ɛksprɔprije] tr to expropriate
expul·sé -sée [ɛkspylse] adj deported ||
mf deportee
expulser [ɛkspylse] tr to expel; to
evict; to throw out
expulsion [ɛkspylsjɔ̃] f expulsion
expurger [ɛkspyrʒe] §38 tr to expurgate
ex·quis [ɛkski] -quise [kiz] adj exquisite; sharp (pain)
exsangue [ɛksãg] adj bloodless, anemic
exsuder [ɛksyde] tr & intr to exude
extase [ɛkstaz] f ecstasy
exta·sié -siée [ɛkstazje] adj enraptured,
ecstatic, in ecstasy
extasier [ɛkstazje] ref to be enraptured
extatique [ɛkstatik] adj & mf ecstatic
extempora·né -née [ɛkstãpɔrane] adj
(law) unpremeditated; (pharm) ready
for use
exten·sif [ɛkstãsif] -sive [siv] adj wide
(meaning); (mech) tensile
extension [ɛkstãsjɔ̃] f extension
exténuer [ɛkstenɥe] tr to exhaust, tire
out || ref to tire oneself out
exté·rieur -rieure [ɛksterjœr] adj exterior; external; outer, outside; for-
eign (policy) || m exterior; outside;
(mov) location shot; à l'extérieur
outside; abroad; en extérieur (mov)
on location
extérieurement [ɛksterjœrmã] adv ex-
ternally; superficially; on the outside
extérioriser [ɛksterjɔrize] tr to reveal,
to show || ref to open one's heart
exterminer [ɛkstermine] tr to exterminate
externat [ɛksterna] m day school
externe [ɛkstern] adj external || m day
student; outpatient; (med) nonresident intern
extinc·teur [ɛkstɛ̃ktœr] -trice [tris]
adj extinguishing || m fire extinguisher
extinction [ɛkstɛ̃ksjɔ̃] f extinction; ex-
tinguishing; loss (of voice); l'extinction des feux (mil) lights out, taps
extirper [ɛkstirpe] tr to extirpate

extorquer [ɛkstɔrke] tr to extort
extor·queur [ɛkstɔrkœr] -queuse [køz]
mf extortionist
extorsion [ɛkstɔrsjɔ̃] f extortion
extra [ɛkstra] adj invar (coll) extra-
special, extra || m invar extra
extraction [ɛkstraksjɔ̃] f extraction
extrader [ɛkstrade] tr to extradite
extradition [ɛkstradisjɔ̃] f extradition
extra-fin [ɛkstrafɛ̃] -fine [fin] adj
high-quality
extraire [ɛkstrɛr] §68 tr to extract; to
excerpt; to get out || ref to extricate
oneself
extrait [ɛkstrɛ] m extract; excerpt;
abstract; certified copy; extrait de
baptême baptismal certificate; extrait
de naissance birth certificate; ex-
traits selections (e.g., in an anthology)
extra-muros [ɛkstramyros] adj invar
extramural; suburban || adv outside
the town
extraordinaire [ɛkstraɔrdiner], [ɛks-
trɔrdiner] adj extraordinary
extrapoler [ɛkstrapɔle] tr to extrapolate
extra-sensoriel -sensorielle [ɛkstrasãsɔr-
jel] adj extrasensory
extravagance [ɛkstravagãs] f extrava-
agance; excess; absurdity, wildness
extrava·gant [ɛkstravagã] -gante [gãt]
adj excessive, extravagant; absurd,
wild, eccentric || mf eccentric, screw-
ball
extraver·ti -tie [ɛkstraverti] adj & mf
extrovert
extrême [ɛkstrem] adj & m extreme
extrêmement [ɛkstremmã] adv extremely
extrême-onction [ɛkstremɔ̃ksjɔ̃] f extreme unction
Extrême-Orient [ɛkstremɔrjã] m Far
East
extrémiste [ɛkstremist] adj & mf extremist
extrémité [ɛkstremite] f extremity; en
venir à des extrémités to resort to
violence; être à toute extrémité to
be at death's door
extrinsèque [ɛkstrɛ̃sɛk] adj extrinsic
exubé·rant [ɛgzyberã] -rante [rãt] adj
exuberant
exulter [ɛgzylte] intr to exult
ex-voto [ɛksvɔto] m invar votive inscription or tablet

F

F, f [ɛf], *[ɛf] m invar sixth letter of
the French alphabet
F abbr (franc) franc
fable [fabl] f fable; laughingstock
fabri·cant [fabrikã] -cante [kãt] mf
manufacturer

fabrica·teur [fabrikatœr] -trice [tris]
mf fabricator (e.g., of lies); forger;
counterfeiter
fabrication [fabrikasjɔ̃] f manufacture; forging; counterfeiting
fabrique [fabrik] f factory; factory

workers; mill hands; (obs) church trustees; (obs) church revenue; **fabrique de papier** paper mill

fabriquer [fabrike] *tr* to manufacture; to fabricate; to forge; to counterfeit

fabu·leux [fabylø] **-leuse** [løz] *adj* fabulous

façade [fasad] *f* façade; frontage; **en façade sur** facing, overlooking

face [fas] *f* face; side (*of a diamond; of a phonograph record*); surface; heads (*of coin*); **de face** full-faced (*portrait*); **en face (de)** opposite, facing; **faire face à** to face; to face up to; to meet (*an obligation*); **perdre la face** to lose face; **sauver la face** to save face

face-à-main [fasamɛ̃] *m* (*pl* **faces-à-main**) lorgnette

facétie [fasesi] *f* off-color joke; practical joke

facé·tieux [fasesjø] **-tieuse** [sjøz] *adj* droll, funny || *mf* wag

facette [faset] *f* facet

fâ·ché -chée [faʃe] *adj* angry; sorry; **fâché avec** at odds with; **fâché contre** angry with (*a person*); **fâché de** angry at (*a thing*); sorry for

fâcher [faʃe] *tr* to anger || *ref* to get angry; to be sorry

fâ·cheux [faʃø] **-cheuse** [ʃøz] *adj* annoying, tiresome; unfortunate || *mf* nuisance, bore

fa·cial -ciale [fasjal] *adj* (*pl* **-ciaux** [sjo]) facial; face (*value*)

facile [fasil] *adj* easy; easygoing; facile, glib

facilité [fasilite] *f* facility; opportunity (*e.g., to meet s.o.*); **facilités de paiement** installments; easy terms

faciliter [fasilite] *tr* to facilitate

façon [fasɔ̃] *f* fashion; fashioning; way, manner; fit (*of clothes*); **à façon** job (*work; workman*); **à la façon de** like; **de façon à** so as to; **de façon que** or **de telle façon que** so that, e.g., **parlez de telle façon qu'on vous comprenne** speak so that you can be understood; **de toute façon** in any event; **façons** manners; **faire des façons** to stand on ceremony; **sans façon** informal

faconde [fakɔ̃d] *f* glibness, gift of gab

façonner [fasone] *tr* to fashion, shape; to work (*the land*); to accustom

façon·nier [fasɔnje] **façon·nière** [fasɔnjɛr] *adj* jobbing; fussy || *mf* pieceworker; stuffed shirt

fac-similé [faksimile] *m* (*pl* **-similés**) facsimile

factage [faktaʒ] *m* delivery service; home delivery

facteur [faktœr] *m* factor; mailman; expressman; auctioneer (*at a market*); maker (*of musical instruments*)

factice [faktis] *adj* imitation, artificial

fac·tieux [faksjø] **-tieuse** [sjøz] *adj* factious, seditious || *mf* troublemaker, agitator

faction [faksjɔ̃] *f* faction; **être de faction** to be on sentry duty

factionnaire [faksjɔnɛr] *m* sentry

factorerie [faktɔrəri] *f* trading post

factotum [faktɔtɔm] *m* factotum; meddler; jack-of-all-trades

factum [faktɔm] *m* political pamphlet; (law) brief

facturation [faktyrɑsjɔ̃] *f* billing, invoicing

facture [faktyr] *f* invoice; bill; workmanship; **établir une facture** to make out an invoice; **suivant facture** as per invoice

facturer [faktyre] *tr* to bill

factu·rier [faktyrje] **-rière** [rjɛr] *mf* billing clerk || *m* invoice book

faculta·tif [fakyltatif] **-tive** [tiv] *adj* optional

faculté [fakylte] *f* faculty; school, college (*of law, medicine, etc.*); **la Faculté** medical men

fadaise [fadez] *f* piece of nonsense; **fadaises** drivel

fade [fad] *adj* tasteless, flat; insipid, namby-pamby

fader [fade] *tr* (coll) to beat; (coll) to share the swag with; **il est fadé** (coll) he's done for

fadeur [fadœr] *f* insipidity; pointlessness; **fadeurs** platitudes

fagot [fago] *m* faggot; **fagot d'épines** ill-tempered person; **sentir le fagot** to smell of heresy

fagoter [fagɔte] *tr* to tie up in bundles, to faggot; (coll) to dress like a scarecrow

faible [febl] *adj* feeble, weak; low (*figure; moan*); poor (*harvest*); slight (*difference*) || *mf* weakling || *m* weakness, foible, weak spot; **faible d'esprit** feeble-minded person

faiblesse [febles] *f* feebleness, weakness, frailty

faiblir [feblir] *intr* to weaken; to diminish

faïence [fajɑ̃s] *f* earthenware, pottery

faille [faj] *f* (geol) fault; (tex) faille; (fig) defect; (fig) rift

fail·li -lie [faji] *adj* & *mf* bankrupt

faillible [fajibl] *adj* fallible

faillir [fajir] *intr* to fail, to go bankrupt || (used only in: *inf*; *ger* **faillant**; *pp* & compound tenses; *pret*; *fut*; *cond*) *intr* to fail; to give way; (with *dat*) to fail, let (*s.o.*) down; **faillir à** to fail in (*a duty*); to fail to keep (*a promise*); **faillir à** + *inf* to fail to + *inf*; **sans faillir** without fail || (used only in *pret* and *past indef*) *intr*—nearly, almost, e.g., **il a failli être écrasé** he was nearly run over

faillite [fajit] *f* bankruptcy; **faire faillite** to go bankrupt

faim [fɛ̃] *f* hunger; **avoir faim** to be hungry; **avoir une faim de loup** to be hungry as a bear; **manger à sa faim** to eat one's fill

fainéant [feneɑ̃] **fainéante** [feneɑ̃t] *adj* lazy || *mf* loafer, do-nothing

fainéanter [feneɑ̃te] *intr* (coll) to loaf

faire [fer] *m* making, doing || §29 *tr* to make; to do; to give (*an order; a lecture; alms, a gift; thanks*); to take (*a walk, a step*); to pack (*a trunk*); to clean (*the room, the shoes, etc.*); to follow (*a trade*); to keep (*silence*);

to perform (*a play; a miracle*); to play the part of; to charge for, e.g., **combien faites-vous ces souliers?** how much do you charge for these shoes?; to say, e.g., **oui, fit-il** yes, said he; (coll) to estimate the cost of; for expressions like **il fait chaud** it is warm, see the noun; **cela ne fait rien** it doesn't matter; **faire** + *inf* to have + *inf*, e.g., **je le ferai aller** I shall have him go; **faire** + *inf* to make + *inf*, e.g., **je le ferai parler** I will make him talk; **faire** + *inf* to have + *pp*, e.g., **je vais faire faire un complet** I am going to have a suit made; **il n'en fait pas d'autres** that's just like him; **ne faire que** + *inf* to keep on + *ger*, e.g., **il ne fait que crier** he keeps on yelling ‖ *intr* to go, e.g., **la cravate fait bien avec la chemise** the tie goes well with the shirt; to act; **comment faire?** what shall I do?; **faire dans** to make a mess in; **ne faire que de** + *inf* to have just + *pp*, e.g., **il ne fait que d'arriver** he has just arrived ‖ *ref* to become (*a doctor, lawyer, etc.*); to grow (*e.g., old*); to improve; to happen; to pretend to be; **se faire à** to get accustomed to, to adjust to; **s'en faire** to worry, e.g., **ne vous en faites pas!** don't worry!

faire-part [ferpar] *m invar* announcement (*of birth, marriage, death*)
faire-valoir [fervalwar] *m invar* turning to account; **faire-valoir direct** farming by the owner
faisable [fəzabl] *adj* feasible
fai·san [fəzã] **-sane** [zan] or **-sande** [zãd] *mf* pheasant
faisander [fəzãde] *tr* to jerk (*game*) ‖ *intr* to become gamy, to get high
fais·ceau [feso] *m* (*pl* **-ceaux**) bundle, cluster; beam (*of light*); pencil (*of rays*); **faisceaux** fasces; **faisceaux de preuves** cumulative evidence; **former les faisceaux** to stack or pile arms
fai·seur [fəzœr] **-seuse** [zøz] *mf*—**bon faiseur** first-rate workman; **faiseur de mariages** matchmaker; **faiseur de vers** versifier, poetaster ‖ *m* bluffer; schemer
fait [fɛ] **faite** [fɛt] *adj* well-built, shapely; full-grown; made-up (*with cosmetics*); **fait à la main** hand-made; **tout fait** ready-made ‖ *m* deed, act; fact; **dire son fait à qn** (coll) to give s.o. a piece of one's mind; **prendre fait et cause pour** to take up the cudgels for; **si fait** yes, indeed; **sur le fait** redhanded, in the act; **tout à fait** entirely ‖ [fɛt] *m*—**au fait** to the point; after all; **de fait** de facto; **du fait que** owing to the fact that; **en fait** as a matter of fact
faîtage [fɛtaʒ] *m* ridgepole; roofs; roofing
fait-divers [fediver] *m* (*pl* **faits-divers**) news item
faîte [fɛt] *m* peak; top (*of tree*); ridge (*of roof*)
faîtière [fɛtjɛr] *adj fem* ridge ‖ *f* ridge tile; skylight

fait-tout [fetu] *m invar* stewpan, casserole
faix [fɛ] *m* load, burden; (archit) settling; (physiol) fetus and placenta
falaise [falɛz] *f* cliff, bluff
falla·cieux [falasjø] **-cieuse** [sjøz] *adj* fallacious
falloir [falwar] §30 *impers* to be necessary; **c'est plus qu'il n'en faut** that's more than enough; **comme il faut** proper; properly; the right kind of, e.g., **un chapeau comme il faut** the right kind of hat; **il fallait le dire!** why didn't you say so!; **il faut** + *inf* it is necessary to + *inf*, one must + *inf*; **il faut qu'il** + *subj* it is necessary that he + *subj*, it is necessary for him to + *inf*; he must + *inf* (expressing conjecture), e.g., **il n'est pas venu, il faut qu'il soit malade** he did not come, he must be sick; **il faut qu'il ne** + *subj* + **pas** he must not + *inf*, e.g., **il faut qu'il ne vienne pas** he must not come; **il faut une connaissance des affaires à ce travail** the work requires business experience; **il faut une heure** it takes an hour; **il leur a fallu trois jours** it took them three days; **il leur faut** + *inf* they have to + *inf*, they must + *inf*; **il leur faut du repos** they need rest; **il leur faut sept dollars** they need seven dollars; **il ne faut pas** + *inf* one must or should not + *inf*, e.g., **il ne faut pas se fier à ce garçon** one must not trust that boy; **il ne faut pas qu'il** + *subj* he must not + *inf*; **que leur faut-il?** what do they need?, what do they require?; **qu'il ne fallait pas** wrong, e.g., **la police a arrêté l'homme qu'il ne fallait pas** the police arrested the wrong man ‖ *ref*—**il s'en faut de beaucoup** not by a long shot, far from it, not by any means; **il s'en faut de dix dollars** there is a shortage of ten dollars; **peu m'en est fallu que . . .** it very nearly happened that . . . ; **peu s'en faut** very nearly; **tant s'en faut que** far from, e.g., **tant s'en faut qu'il soit artiste** he is far from being an artist
fa·lot [falo] **-lotte** [lɔt] *adj* wan, colorless; quaint, droll ‖ *m* lantern
falsification [falsifikasjɔ̃] *f* falsification; adulteration; debasement (*of coin*)
falsifier [falsifje] *tr* to falsify; to adulterate; to debase (*coin*)
fa·mé -mée [fame] *adj*—**mal famé** disreputable
famélique [famelik] *adj* famished
fa·meux [famø] **-meuse** [møz] *adj* famous ‖ (when standing before noun) *adj* (coll) notorious; well-known
fami·lial -liale [familjal] *adj* (*pl* **-liaux** [ljo]) family, domestic ‖ *f* station wagon
familiariser [familjarize] *tr* to familiarize ‖ *ref* to become familiar
familiarité [familjarite] *f* familiarity
fami·lier [familje] **-lière** [ljɛr] *adj*

familiar, intimate; household (*gods*); pet (*animal*) || *mf* familiar, intimate; pet animal

famille [famij] *f* family; **en famille** in the family circle, at home; (Canad) pregnant

famine [famin] *f* famine

fa·nal [fanal] *m* (*pl* **-naux** [no]) lantern; (naut) running light

fanatique [fanatik] *adj* fanatic(al) || *mf* fanatic; enthusiast, fan

fanatisme [fanatism] *m* fanaticism

faner [fane] *tr & ref* to fade

fanfare [fɑ̃far] *f* fanfare; brass band

fanfa·ron [fɑ̃farɔ̃] **-ronne** [rɔn] *adj* bragging || *mf* braggart

fanfaronner [fɑ̃farɔne] *intr* to brag

fange [fɑ̃ʒ] *f* mire, mud; (fig) mire, gutter

fan·geux [fɑ̃ʒø] **-geuse** [ʒøz] *adj* muddy; (fig) dirty, soiled

fanion [fanjɔ̃] *m* pennant, flag

fanon [fanɔ̃] *m* dewlap (*of ox*); whalebone; fetlock; wattle

fantaisie [fɑ̃tezi] *f* imagination; fantasy, fancy, whim; **de fantaisie** fanciful; fancy, e.g., **pain de fantaisie** fancy bread

fantaisiste [fɑ̃tezist] *adj* fantastic, whimsical || *mf* whimsical person; singing comedian

fantasque [fɑ̃task] *adj* fantastic; whimsical, temperamental

fantassin [fɑ̃tasɛ̃] *m* foot soldier

fantastique [fɑ̃tastik] *adj* fantastic

fantoche [fɑ̃tɔʃ] *m* puppet

fantôme [fɑ̃tom] *adj* shadow (*government*) || *m* phantom, ghost

fanum [fanɔm] *m* hallowed ground

faon [fɑ̃] *m* fawn

faonner [fane] *intr* to bring forth young (*said especially of deer*)

faquin [fakɛ̃] *m* rascal

fa·raud [faro] **-raude** [rod] *adj* (coll) swanky || *mf* (coll) fop, bumpkin; **faire le faraud** (coll) to show off

farce [fars] *f* farce; trick, joke; (culin) stuffing

far·ceur [farsœr] **-ceuse** [søz] *mf* practical joker; phony

farcir [farsir] *tr* to stuff

fard [far] *m* make-up; **parler sans fard** to speak plainly, to tell the unvarnished truth; **piquer un fard** (coll) to blush

far·deau [fardo] *m* (*pl* **-deaux** [do]) load, burden; weight (*of years*)

farder [farde] *tr* to make up (*an actor*); to disguise (*the truth*) || *ref* to weigh heavily; (archit) to sink; (theat) to make up

fardier [fardje] *m* dray, cart

farfe·lu -lue [farfəly] *adj* (coll) harebrained, cockeyed, bizarre

farfouiller [farfuje] *tr* (coll) to rummage about in || *intr* (coll) to rummage about; **farfouiller dans** (coll) to rummage about in

farine [farin] *f* flour, meal; **farine de froment** whole-wheat flour; **farine de riz** ground rice; **farine lactée** malted milk

fariner [farine] *tr* (culin) to flour

fari·neux [farinø] **-neuse** [nøz] *adj* white with flour; mealy; starchy

farouche [faruʃ] *adj* wild, savage; unsociable; shy; stubborn (*resistance*); fierce (*look*)

fascicule [fasikyl] *m* fascicle; **fascicule de mobilisation** marching orders

fascina·teur [fasinatœr] **-trice** [tris] *adj* fascinating || *mf* spellbinder

fasciner [fasine] *tr* to fascinate; to spellbind

fascisme [faʃism] *m* fascism

fasciste [faʃist] *adj & mf* fascist

faste [fast] *adj* auspicious; feast (*day*) || *m* pomp; **fastes** annals

fasti·dieux [fastidjø] **-dieuse** [djøz] *adj* tedious, wearisome

fas·tueux [fastɥø] **-tueuse** [tɥøz] *adj* pompous, ostentatious

fat [fat] *adj masc* conceited, foppish || *m* fop

fa·tal -tale [fatal] *adj* (*pl* **-tals**) fatal; fateful; inevitable

fatalisme [fatalism] *m* fatalism

fataliste [fatalist] *adj* fatalistic || *mf* fatalist

fatalité [fatalite] *f* fatality; fatalism; fate; curse, misfortune

fatidique [fatidik] *adj* fateful; prophetic

fati·gant [fatigɑ̃] **-gante** [gɑ̃t] *adj* fatiguing; tiresome (*person*)

fatigue [fatig] *f* fatigue

fati·gué -guée [fatige] *adj* fatigued; worn-out (*clothing*); well-thumbed (*book*)

fatiguer [fatige] *tr* to fatigue; to wear out; to weary || *intr* to strain, labor; to pull (*said of engine*); to bear a heavy strain (*said of beam*) || *ref* to get tired

fatras [fatra] *m* jumble, hodgepodge

fatuité [fatɥite] *f* conceit; foppishness

faubert [fober] *m* (naut) swab

faubourg [fubur] *m* suburb; outskirts; quarter, district (*especially of Paris*)

faubou·rien [fuburjɛ̃] **-rienne** [rjɛn] *adj* working-class, vulgar || *mf* resident of the outskirts of a city; local inhabitant

fau·ché -chée [foʃe] *adj* (coll) broke (*without money*)

faucher [foʃe] *tr* to mow, reap; (coll) to swipe

fau·cheur [foʃœr] **-cheuse** [ʃøz] *mf* reaper || *m* (ent) daddy-longlegs || *f* (mach) reaper, mower

faucheux [foʃø] *m* (ent) daddy-longlegs

faucille [fosij] *f* sickle

faucon [fokɔ̃] *m* falcon

fauconnier [fokɔnje] *m* falconer

faufil [fofil] *m* basting thread

faufiler [fofile] *tr* to baste || *ref* to thread one's way, to worm one's way

faune [fon] *m* faun || *f* fauna

faunesse [fones] *f* female faun

faussaire [foser] *mf* forger

fausser [fose] *tr* to falsify, distort; to bend, twist; to warp (*the judgment*); to force (*a lock*); to strain (*the voice*); **fausser compagnie à qn** (coll) to give s.o. the slip || *intr* to sing or play out of tune ‖ *ref* to bend, buckle; to crack (*said of voice*)

fausset [fosɛ] *m* falsetto; plug (*for wine barrel*)

fausseté [fostе] *f* falsity; double-dealing

faute [fot] *f* fault; mistake; blame; lack, need, want; (sports) foul; (sports) error; **faire faute** to be lacking; **faute de** for want of; **faute de copiste** clerical error; **faute de frappe** typing error; **faute d'impression** misprint; **sans faute** without fail

fauter [fote] *intr* (coll) to go wrong (*said of a woman*)

fauteuil [fotœj] *m* armchair, easy chair; seat (*of member of an academy*); chair (*of presiding officer; presiding officer himself*); **fauteuil à bascule** or **à balançoire** rocking chair; **fauteuil à oreilles** wing chair; **fauteuil d'orchestre** orchestra seat; **fauteuil pliant** folding chair; **fauteuil roulant pour malade** wheelchair; **siéger au fauteuil présidentiel** to preside

fau·teur [fotœr] **-trice** [tris] *mf* instigator, agitator

fau·tif [fotif] **-tive** [tiv] *adj* faulty

fauve [fov] *adj* fawn (*color*); musky (*odor*); wild (*beast*) ‖ *m* fawn color; wild beast; **fauves** big game

fauvette [fovɛt] *f* warbler

faux [fo] **fausse** [fos] *adj* false; counterfeit; wrong, e.g., **fausse date** wrong date; e.g., **fausse note** wrong note ‖ *m* imitation; forgery; **à faux** wrongly ‖ **faux** *f* scythe ‖ **faux** *adv* out of tune, off key

faux-bourdon [foburdɔ̃] *m* (*pl* **-bourdons**) *m* (ent) drone

faux-col [fokɔl] *m* (*pl* **-cols**) collar, detachable collar

faux-filet [fofilɛ] *m* (*pl* **-filets**) sirloin

faux-fuyant [fofɥijɑ̃] *m* (*pl* **-fuyants**) subterfuge, pretext

faux-jour [foʒur] *m* (*pl* **-jours**) half-light

faux-monnayeur [fomɔnɛjœr] *m* (*pl* **-monnayeurs**) counterfeiter

faux-pas [fopɑ] *m invar* faux pas, slip, blunder

faux-semblant [fosɑ̃blɑ̃] *m* (*pl* **-semblants**) false pretense

faveur [favœr] *f* favor; **à la faveur de** under cover of; **en faveur de** in favor of; on behalf of

favorable [favɔrabl] *adj* favorable

favo·ri [favɔri] **-rite** [rit] *adj & mf* favorite ‖ **favoris** *mpl* sideburns ‖ *f* mistress

favoriser [favɔrize] *tr* to favor; to encourage, promote

Fᶜᵒ or **fᶜᵒ** *abbr* (**franco**) postpaid

fébrile [febril] *adj* feverish

fèces [fɛs] *fpl* feces

fé·cond [fekɔ̃] **-conde** [kɔ̃d] *adj* fecund, fertile

féconder [fekɔ̃de] *tr* to impregnate

fécondité [fekɔ̃dite] *f* fecundity, fertility

fécule [fekyl] *f* starch; **fécule de maïs** cornstarch

fécu·lent [fekylɑ̃] **-lente** [lɑ̃t] *adj* starchy ‖ *m* starchy food

fédé·ral -rale [federal] *adj & m* (*pl* **-raux** [ro]) federal

fédéra·tif [federatif] **-tive** [tiv] *adj* federated, federative

fédération [federasjɔ̃] *f* federation

fédérer [federe] §10 *tr & ref* to federate

fée [fe] *f* fairy; **de fée** fairy; meticulous (*work*); **vieille fée** old hag

féerie [feri] *f* fairyland; fantasy

féerique [ferik] *adj* fairy, magic(al)

feindre [fɛ̃dr] §50 *tr* to feign ‖ *intr* to feign; to limp (*said of horse*)

feinte [fɛ̃t] *f* feint

feinter [fɛ̃te] *tr* (coll) to trick ‖ *intr* to feint

feldspath [feldspat], [felspat] *m* feldspar

fê·lé -lée [fele] *adj* (coll) cracked, crazy

fêler [fele] *tr* to crack

félicitations [felisitɑsjɔ̃] *fpl* congratulations

féliciter [felisite] *tr* to congratulate; **féliciter qn de** + *inf* to congratulate s.o. for + *ger*; **féliciter qn de** or **pour** to congratulate s.o. for ‖ *ref*—**se féliciter de** to congratulate oneself on, to be pleased with oneself because of

fé·lon [felɔ̃] **-lonne** [lɔn] *adj* disloyal, treasonable

félonie [feloni] *f* disloyalty, treason

fêlure [felyr] *f* crack, chink

femelle [fəmɛl] *adj & f* female

fémi·nin [feminɛ̃] **-nine** [nin] *adj & m* feminine

féminisme [feminism] *m* feminism

femme [fam] *f* woman; wife; bride; **bonne femme** (coll) simple, good-natured woman; **femme agent** (*pl* **femmes agents**) policewoman; **femme auteur** (*pl* **femmes auteurs**) authoress; **femme de chambre** chambermaid; **femme de charge** housekeeper; **femme de journée** cleaning woman; **femme de ménage** cleaning woman; **femme d'intérieur** homebody; **femme docteur** woman doctor (*e.g., with Ph.D. degree*); **femme juge** woman judge; **femme médecin** woman doctor (*physician*); **femme pasteur** woman preacher

fendiller [fɑ̃dije] *tr & ref* to crack

fendoir [fɑ̃dwar] *m* cleaver, chopper

fendre [fɑ̃dr] *tr* to crack; to split (*e.g., wood*); to cleave (*e.g., the air*); to break (*one's heart*); to elbow one's way through (*a crowd*) ‖ *ref* to crack; (escr) to lunge

fenêtre [fənɛtr] *f* window; **fenêtre à battants** casement window, French window; **fenêtre à guillotine** sash window; **fenêtre en saillie** bay window

fenil [fənil], [fəni] *m* hayloft

fenouil [fənuj] *m* fennel; **fenouil bâtard** dill

fente [fɑ̃t] *f* crack, split, fissure; notch; slot (*e.g., in a coin telephone*); (escr) lunge

féo·dal -dale [feɔdal] *adj* (*pl* **-daux** [do]) feudal

féodalisme [feɔdalism] *m* feudalism

fer [fɛr] *m* iron; head (*of tool*); point (*of weapon*); **croiser le fer avec** to cross swords with; **fer à cheval** horseshoe; **fer à friser** curling iron; **fer à marquer** or **flétrir** branding iron; **fer à repasser** iron, flatiron; **fer à souder** soldering iron; **fer de fonte** cast iron; **fer forgé** wrought iron; **fers** irons, chains, fetters; **marquer au fer** to brand; **remuer le fer dans la plaie** (coll) to rub it in

ferblanterie [fɛrblɑ̃tri] *f* tinware; tinwork, sheet-metal work; tinsmith's shop

ferblantier [fɛrblɑ̃tje] *m* tinsmith

fé·rié -riée [ferje] *adj* feast (*day*)

férir [ferir] *tr*—**sans coup férir** without striking a blow

ferler [fɛrle] *tr* (naut) to furl

fermage [fɛrmaʒ] *m* tenant farming; rent

ferme [fɛrm] *adj* firm || *f* farm, tenant farm; farmhouse || *adv* firmly, fast

fer·mé -mée [fɛrme] *adj* exclusive, restricted; inscrutable (*countenance*)

ferment [fɛrmɑ̃] *m* ferment

fermenter [fɛrmɑ̃te] *intr* to ferment

fermer [fɛrme] *tr* to close, to shut; to turn off; **fermer à clef** to lock; **fermer au verrou** to bolt; **la ferme!** (slang) shut up!, shut your trap! || *intr & ref* to close, to shut

fermeté [fɛrmate] *f* firmness

fermeture [fɛrmatyr] *f* closing; fastening; **fermeture éclair** zipper

fer·mier [fɛrmje] **-mière** [mjɛr] *adj* farming || *m* farmer; tenant farmer; lessee || *f* farmer's wife

fermoir [fɛrmwar] *m* snap, clasp

féroce [feros] *adj* ferocious

férocité [ferosite] *f* ferocity

ferraille [fɛrɑj] *f* scrap iron; (coll) small change; **mettre à la ferraille** to junk

ferrailleur [fɛrɑjœr] *m* dealer in scrap iron; sword rattler

fer·ré -rée [fere] *adj* ironclad; hobnailed (*shoe*); paved (*road*); **ferré sur** well versed in

ferrer [fere] *tr* to shoe (*a horse*)

ferret [fere] *m* tag (*of shoelace*); (geol) hard core

ferronnerie [fɛrɔnri] *f* ironwork; hardware

ferron·nier [fɛrɔnje] **ferron·nière** [fɛrɔnjɛr] *mf* ironworker; hardware dealer

ferrotypie [ferɔtipi] *f* tintype

ferroviaire [fɛrɔvjɛr] *adj* railway

ferrure [fɛryr] *f* horseshoeing; **ferrures** hardware; metal trim

ferry-boat [feribot] *m* (*pl* **-boats**) train ferry

fertile [fɛrtil] *adj* fertile

fertiliser [fɛrtilize] *tr* to fertilize

fertilité [fɛrtilite] *f* fertility

fé·ru -rue [fery] *adj*—**féru de** wrapped up in (*an idea, an interest*)

fer·vent [fɛrvɑ̃] **-vente** [vɑ̃t] *adj* fervent || *mf* devotee

ferveur [fɛrvœr] *f* fervor

fesse [fɛs] *f* buttock

fessée [fese] *f* spanking

fesse-mathieu [fesmatjø] *m* (*pl* **-mathieux**) usurer; skinflint

fesser [fese] *tr* to spank

fes·su -sue [fesy] *adj* broad-bottomed

festin [fɛstɛ̃] *m* feast, banquet

festi·val [fɛstival] *m* (*pl* **-vals**) music festival

festivité [fɛstivite] *f* festivity

feston [fɛstɔ̃] *m* festoon

festonner [fɛstɔne] *tr* to festoon; to scallop

festoyer [fɛstwaye] §47 *tr* to fete, to regale || *intr* to feast

fê·tard [fetar] **-tarde** [tard] *mf* merrymaker

fête [fɛt] *f* festival; feast day, holiday; name day; party, festivity; **être à la fête** (coll) to be very pleased or gratified; **faire fête à** to receive with open arms; **faire la fête** (coll) to carouse; **fête foraine** carnival; **fête légale** or **fête nationale** legal holiday; **la fête des Mères** Mother's Day; **la fête des Morts** All Souls' Day; **la fête des Rois** Twelfth-night; **se faire une fête de** to look forward with pleasure to; **souhaiter une bonne fête à qn** to wish s.o. many happy returns

Fête-Dieu [fɛtdjø] *f* (*pl* **Fêtes-Dieu**)— **la Fête-Dieu** Corpus Christi

fêter [fete] *tr* to fete; to celebrate (*a special event*)

fétiche [fetiʃ] *m* fetish

fétu [fety] *m* straw; trifle

feu feue [fø] *adj* (*pl* **feus**) (standing before noun) late, deceased, e.g., **la feue reine** the late queen || *adj invar* (standing before article and noun) late, deceased, e.g., **la reine** the late queen || *m* (*pl* **feux**) fire; flame; traffic light; burner (*of stove*); **à petit feu** by inches; **du feu** a light (*to ignite a cigar, etc.*); **être sous les feux de la rampe** to be in the limelight; **faire du feu** to light a fire; **faire long feu** to hang fire; to fail; (arti) to miss; **feu d'artifice** fireworks; **feu de joie** bonfire; **feu de paille** (fig) flash in the pan; **feu follet** will-o'-the-wisp; **feux de position, feux de stationnement** parking lights; **mettre le feu à** to set on fire; **prendre feu** to catch fire || **feu** *interj* fire! (*command to fire*); **au feu!** fire! (*warning*)

feuillage [fœjaʒ] *m* foliage; **feuillages** fallen branches

feuille [fœj] *f* leaf; sheet; form (*to be filled out*); **feuille de chou** (coll) rag (*newspaper of little value*); **feuille de présence** time sheet; **feuille d'étain** tin foil; **feuille de température** temperature chart; **feuille d'imposition** income-tax blank

feuil·lé feuil·lée [fœje] *adj* leafy, foliaged || *f* bower; **feuillées** (mil) camp latrine

feuiller [fœje] *intr* to leaf

feuille·té -tée [fœjte] *adj* foliated; in flaky layers

feuilleter [fœjte] §34 *tr* to leaf through; to foliate; (culin) to roll into thin layers

feuilleton [fœjtɔ̃] *m* newspaper serial (*printed at bottom of page*); (rad, telv) serial

feuil·lu feuil·lue [fœjy] *adj* leafy || *m* foliage

feuillure [fœjyr] *f* groove

feuler [fœle] *intr* to growl (*said of cat*)

feutre [føtr] *m* felt

feu·tré -trée [føtre] *adj* velvetlike; muffled (*steps*)

feutrer [føtre] *tr* to felt

fève [fev] *f* bean; **fève des Rois** bean or figurine baked in the Twelfth-night cake; **fèves au lard** pork and beans

février [fevrie] *m* February

fi [fi] *interj* fie!; **faire fi de** to scorn

fiacre [fjakr] *m* horse-drawn cab

fiançailles [fjɑ̃saj] *fpl* engagement, betrothal

fian·cé -cée [fjɑ̃se] *mf* betrothed || *m* fiancé || *f* fiancée

fiancer [fjɑ̃se] §51 *tr* to betroth || *ref* to become engaged

fiasco [fjasko] *m* (coll) fiasco, failure; **faire fiasco** to flop, fail

fibre [fibr] *f* fiber; (fig) feeling, sensibility; **avoir la fibre sensible** to be easily moved

fi·breux [fibrø] **-breuse** [brøz] *adj* fibrous

ficeler [fisle] §34 *tr* to tie up

ficelle [fisel] *adj* (coll) knowing || *f* string; **connaître les ficelles** (fig) to know the ropes; **tenir** or **tirer les ficelles** (fig) to pull strings; **vieille ficelle** (coll) old hand

fiche [fiʃ] *f* peg; slip, form, blank; filing card, index card; membership card; (cards) chip, counter; (elec) plug; **fiche de consolation** booby prize; **fiche femelle** (elec) jack; **fiche perforée** punch card; **fiche scolaire** report card

ficher [fiʃe] *tr* to drive in (*a stake*); to take down (*information on a form*); to fasten, fix, stick; **ficher qn à la porte** (coll) to kick s.o. out; **ficher une gifle à qn** (coll) to box s.o. on the ear; **fichez-moi le camp!** (slang) beat it! || *ref*—**se ficher de** (slang) to make fun of

fichier [fiʃje] *m* card catalogue; cabinet, file (*for cards or papers*)

fichtre [fiʃtrə] *interj* (coll) gosh!

fi·chu -chue [fiʃy] *adj* (coll) wretched, ugly; **fichu de** capable of || *m* scarf, shawl

fic·tif [fiktif] **-tive** [tiv] *adj* fictitious

fiction [fiksjɔ̃] *f* fiction

fidéicommis [fideikɔmi] *m* (law) trust

fidèle [fidel] *adj* faithful || *mf* supporter; **les fidèles** (eccl) the congregation, the faithful

fidélité [fidelite] *f* fidelity, faithfulness; **haute fidélité** high fidelity

fief·fé fief·fée [fjefe] *adj* (coll) downright, real, regular (*liar, coward, etc.*)

fiel [fjel] *m* bile; gall

fiel·leux [fjelø] **fiel·leuse** [fjeløz] *adj* galling

fiente [fjɑ̃t] *f* droppings

fier fière [fjer] *adj* proud; haughty

fier [fje] *tr* (archaic) to entrust || *ref*—**se fier à** or **en** to trust, to have confidence in, to rely upon; **se fier à qn de** to entrust s.o. with; **s'y fier** to trust it

fier-à-bras [fjerabra] *m* (*pl* **fier-à-bras** or **fiers-à-bras** [fjerabra]) braggart

fierté [fjerte] *f* pride

fièvre [fjevr] *f* fever; **fièvre aphteuse** foot-and-mouth disease

fifre [fifr] *m* fife; fife player

fi·gé -gée [fiʒe] *adj* curdled; fixed, set; frozen (*smile*); **figé sur place** rooted to the spot

figement [fiʒmɑ̃] *m* clotting, coagulation

figer [fiʒe] §38 *tr* to curdle; to stop dead || *ref* to curdle; to set, to freeze (*said, e.g., of smile*)

fignoler [fiɲɔle] *tr* to work carefully at || *intr* to be finicky

figue [fig] *f* fig; **figue de Barbarie** prickly pear

figuier [figje] *m* fig tree

figu·rant [figyrɑ̃] **-rante** [rɑ̃t] *mf* (theat) supernumerary, extra

figura·tif [figyratif] **-tive** [tiv] *adj* figurative, emblematic

figure [figyr] *f* figure; face (*of a person*); face card; **faire figure** to cut a figure; **figure de proue** (naut) figurehead; **prendre figure** to take shape

figu·ré -rée [figyre] *adj* figurative; figured || *m* figurative sense

figurer [figyre] *tr* to figure || *intr* to figure, take part; (theat) to walk on || *ref* to imagine, believe

fil [fil] *m* thread; wire; edge (*e.g., of knife*); grain (*of wood*); **au fil de l'eau** with the stream; **droit fil** with the grain; **elle lui a donné du fil à retordre** (fig) she gave him more than he bargained for; **fil à plomb** plumb line; **fil de fer barbelé** barbed wire; **fil de lin** yarn; **fil d'or** spun gold; **fils de la vierge** gossamer; **passer au fil de l'épée** to put to the sword; **plein de fils** stringy; **sans fil** wireless

filament [filamɑ̃] *m* filament

filamen·teux [filamɑ̃tø] **-teuse** [tøz] *adj* stringy

filan·dreux [filɑ̃drø] **-dreuse** [drøz] *adj* stringy (*meat*); long, drawn-out

fi·lant [filɑ̃] **-lante** [lɑ̃t] *adj* ropy (*liquid*); shooting (*star*)

filasse [filas] *f* tow, oakum

filature [filatyr] *f* manufacture of thread; spinning mill; shadowing (*of a suspect*)

fil-de-fériste [fildəferist] *mf* tightwire walker

file [fil] *f* file, row, lane; **à la file** one after another, in a row; **file d'attente** waiting line; **marcher en file indienne** to walk Indian file

filer [file] *tr* to spin; to pay out (*rope, cable*); to prolong; to shadow (*a suspect*) || *intr* to ooze; to smoke (*said of lamp*); (coll) to go fast; **filer à**

l'anglaise (coll) to take French leave; **filer doux** (coll) to back down, to give in; **filez!** (coll) get out!

filet [file] *m* net; trickle (*of water*); streak (*of light*); thread (*of screw or nut*); (culin) fillet; (typ) rule; **faux filet** sirloin; **filet à bagage** baggage rack; **filet à cheveux** hair net; **filet à provisions** string bag, mesh bag

fileter [filte] §2 *tr* to thread (*a screw*); to draw (*wire*)

fi·leur [filœr] **-leuse** [løz] *mf* spinner

fi·lial -liale [filjal] *adj* (*pl* **-liaux** [ljo]) filial ǁ *f* (com) branch, subsidiary

filiation [filjasjɔ̃] *f* filiation

filière [filjɛr] *f* (mach) die; (mach) drawplate; **filière administrative** official channels; **passer par la filière** (coll) to go through channels; (coll) to work one's way up

filigrane [filigran] *m* filigree; watermark (*in paper*)

filigraner [filigrane] *tr* to filigree

filin [filɛ̃] *m* (naut) rope

fille [fij] *f* daughter; unmarried girl; servant; (pej) tart; **fille de joie, des rues,** or **de vie, fille publique** prostitute; **fille de salle** nurse's aid; **fille d'honneur** bridesmaid; **jeune fille** girl; **vieille fille** old maid

fillette [fijɛt] *f* young girl, little lass

fil·leul fil·leule [fijœl] *mf* godchild ǁ *m* godson ǁ *f* goddaughter

film [film] *m* film; (fig) train (*of events*); **film sonore** sound film

filmage [filmaʒ] *m* filming

filmer [filme] *tr* to film

filmique [filmik] *adj* film

filon [filɔ̃] *m* vein, lode; (coll) soft job; (coll) bonanza, strike; **filon guide** leader vein

filoselle [filozɛl] *f* floss silk

filou [filu] *m* sneak thief; cheat, sharper

filouter [filute] *tr* (coll) to swindle, cheat; **filouter q.ch. à qn** (coll) to do s.o. out of s.th. ǁ *intr* to cheat at cards

fils [fis] *m* son; (when following proper name) junior; **fils à papa** (coll) rich man's son, playboy; **fils de ses œuvres** (fig) self-made man

filtrage [filtraʒ] *m* filtering; surveillance (*by the police*)

fil·trant [filtrɑ̃] **-trante** [trɑ̃t] *adj* filterable; filter, e.g., **papier filtrant** filter paper

filtre [filtr] *m* filter

filtrer [filtre] *tr & intr* to filter

fin [fɛ̃] **fine** [fin] *adj* fine ǁ (when standing before noun) *adj* clever, sly, smart; secret, hidden ǁ *m* fine linen; smart person; **le fin du fin** the finest of the fine ǁ **fin** *f* end; **à la fin** at last; **à seule fin de** for the sole purpose of; **à toutes fins utiles** for your information; **c'est la fin des haricots** (slang) that takes the cake; **en fin de compte** in the end; to get to the point; **fin d'interdiction de dépasser** (public sign) end of no passing; **mot de la fin** clincher; **sans**

fin endless ǁ **fin** *adv* absolutely; finely (*ground*); small, e.g., **écrire fin** to write small

fi·nal -nale [final] (*pl* **-nals** or **-naux** [no]) *adj* final ǁ *m* finale ǁ *f* last syllable or letter; (mus) keynote; (sports) finals

finalement [finalmɑ̃] *adv* finally

finaliste [finalist] *mf* finalist

financement [finɑ̃smɑ̃] *m* financing

financer [finɑ̃se] §51 *tr* to finance

finan·cier [finɑ̃sje] **-cière** [sjɛr] *adj* financial; spicy (*sauce for vol-au-vent*) ǁ *m* financier

finasser [finase] *intr* (coll) to use finesse, to finagle

finasserie [finasri] *f* shrewdness

fi·naud [fino] **-naude** [nod] *adj* wily, sly ǁ *mf* sly fox; smart aleck

finesse [fines] *f* finesse; fineness; **savoir les finesses** to know the fine points or niceties

fi·ni -nie [fini] *adj* finished; finite; ruined (*in health, financially, etc.*); arrant (*rogue*) ǁ *m* finish; finite

finir [finir] *tr & intr* to finish; **en finir avec** to have done with; **finir de** + *inf* to finish + *ger*; **finir par** + *inf* to finish by + *inf*

finissage [finisaʒ] *m* finishing touch, final step

finition [finisjɔ̃] *f* finish; **finitions** finishing touches

finlan·dais [fɛ̃lɑ̃dɛ] **-daise** [dɛz] *adj* Finnish ǁ *m* Finnish (*language*) ǁ (cap) *mf* Finn

Finlande [fɛ̃lɑ̃d] *f* Finland; **la Finlande** Finland

fin·nois [finwa] **fin·noise** [finwaz] *adj* Finnish ǁ *m* Finnish (*language*; Finnic (*branch of Uralic*) ǁ (cap) *mf* Finn

fiole [fjɔl] *f* phial

fioriture [fjɔrityr] *f* flourish, curlicue

firmament [firmamɑ̃] *m* firmament

firme [firm] *f* firm, house, company

fisc [fisk] *m* bureau of internal revenue, tax-collection agency

fis·cal -cale [fiskal] *adj* (*pl* **-caux** [ko]) fiscal; revenue, taxation

fiscaliser [fiskalize] *tr* to subject to tax

fiscalité [fiskalite] *f* tax collections; fiscal policy

fissile [fisil] *adj* fissionable

fission [fisjɔ̃] *f* fission

fissure [fisyr] *f* fissure, crack

fissurer [fisyre] *tr & ref* to fissure

fiston [fistɔ̃] *m* (slang) sonny

fixation [fiksɑjsɔ̃] *f* fixation; fixing

fixe [fiks] *adj* fixed; permanent (*ink*); glassy (*stare*); regular (*time*); set (*price*); standing (*rule*) ǁ *m* fixed income ǁ *interj* (mil) eyes front!

fixe-chaussette [fiksəʃozɛt] *m* (*pl* **-chaussettes**) garter (*for men's socks*)

fixement [fiksəmɑ̃] *adv* fixedly

fixer [fikse] *tr* to fix; to appoint; (coll) to stare at; **fixer son choix sur** to fix on; **pour fixer les idées** for the sake of argument ǁ *ref* to be fastened; to establish residence; to make up one's mind

flacon [flakɔ̃] *m* small bottle; flask

flageller [flaʒelle] *tr* to flagellate
flageoler [flaʒɔle] *intr* to quiver
flageolet [flaʒɔle] *m* flageolet; kidney bean
flagorner [flagɔrne] *tr* to flatter
fla·grant [flagrã] **-grante** [grãt] *adj* flagrant, glaring, obvious
flair [fler] *m* scent, sense of smell; (*discernment*) flair, keen nose
flairer [flere] *tr* to smell, to sniff; to scent, to smell out
fla·mand [flamã] **-mande** [mãd] *adj* Flemish || *m* Flemish (*language*) || (*cap*) *mf* Fleming (*person*)
flamant [flamã] *m* flamingo
flam·bant [flãbã] **-bante** [bãt] *adj* flaming; **flambant neuf** (coll) brand-new
flam·beau [flãbo] *m* (*pl* **-beaux**) torch; candlestick; large wax candle; (fig) light
flambée [flãbe] *f* blaze
flamber [flãbe] *tr* to singe; to sterilize; **être flambé** (coll) to be all washed up, ruined || *intr* to flame
flamberge [flãberʒ] *f* (archaic) sword, blade; **mettre flamberge au vent** to unsheathe the sword
flamboiement [flãbwamã] *m* glow, flare
flamboyant [flãbwajã] **flamboyante** [flãbwajãt] *adj* flaming, blazing; (archit) flamboyant
flamboyer [flãbwaje] §47 *intr* to flame
flamme [flam], [flɑm] *f* flame; pennant
flammèche [flameʃ] *f* ember, large spark
flan [flã] *m* custard; blank (*coin, medal, record*); **à la flan** (slang) happy-go-lucky; botched (*job*); **c'est du flan** (slang) it's ridiculous
flanc [flã] *m* flank; side (*of ship, mountain, etc.*); **battre du flanc** to pant; **être sur le flanc** (coll) to be laid up; **flancs** (archaic) womb; bosom; **prêter le flanc à** to lay oneself open to; **se battre les flancs** to go to a lot of trouble for nothing; **tirer au flanc** (coll) to gold-brick, to malinger
flancher [flãʃe] *intr* (coll) to give in; (coll) to weaken, give way
flanchet [flãʃe] *m* flank (*of beef*)
Flandre [flãdr] *f* Flanders; **la Flandre** Flanders
flanelle [flanel] *f* flannel
flâner [flɑne] *intr* to stroll, saunter; to loaf
flânerie [flɑnri] *f* strolling; loafing
flâ·neur [flɑnœr] **-neuse** [nøz] *mf* stroller; loafer
flanquer [flãke] *tr* to flank; (coll) to throw, fling; **flanquer à la porte** (coll) to kick out; **flanquer un coup à** (coll) to take a swing at
fla·pi ·pie [flapi] *adj* (coll) tired out, fagged out
flaque [flak] *f* puddle, pool
flash [flaʃ] *m* (*pl* **flashes**) news flash; (phot) flash attachment; (phot) flash bulb

flasque [flask] *adj* flabby || *m* metal trim || *f* flask; powder horn
flatter [flate] *tr* to flatter; to stroke; to delight; to cater to; to delude || *intr* to flatter || *ref*—**se flatter de** to flatter oneself on
flatterie [flatri] *f* flattery
flat·teur [flatœr] **flat·teuse** [flatøz] *adj* flattering || *mf* flatterer
flatulence [flatylãs] *f* (pathol) flatulence
flatuosité [flatɥozite] *f* (pathol) flatulence
fléau [fleo] *m* (*pl* **fléaux**) flail; beam (*of balance*); (fig) scourge, plague
flèche [fleʃ] *f* arrow; spire (*of church*); boom (*of crane*); flitch (*of bacon*); **en flèche** like an arrow; in tandem; **faire flèche de tout bois** to leave no stone unturned; **flèche d'eau** (bot) arrowhead
fléchette [fleʃet] *f* dart (*used in game*)
fléchir [fleʃir] *tr* to bend; to move (*e.g., to pity*) || *intr* to bend, give way; to weaken, to flag; to go down, to sag (*said of prices*)
flegmatique [flegmatik] *adj* phlegmatic, stolid
flegme [flegm] *m* phlegm
flemme [flem] *f* (slang) sluggishness; **tirer sa flemme** (slang) to not lift a finger
flet [fle] *m* flounder
flétan [fletã] *m* halibut
flétrir [fletrir] *tr & ref* to fade, wither; to weaken
flétrissure [fletrisyr] *f* fading, withering; branding (*of criminals*); blot, stigma
fleur [flœr] *f* flower; blossom; **à fleur de** level with, even with; on the surface of; **à fleur de peau** skin-deep; **à fleur de tête** bulging (*eyes*); **en fleur** in bloom; **en fleurs** in bloom (*said of group of different varieties*); **fleur de farine** fine white flour; **fleur de l'âge** prime of life; **fleur de lis** [flœrdəlis] fleur-de-lis; **fleur des pois** (coll) pick of the lot; **fleurs** mold (*on wine, cider, etc.*)
fleurer [flœre] *intr* to exhale or give off an odor; **fleurer bon** to smell good
fleuret [flœre] *m* fencing foil
fleurette [flœret] *f* little flower; **conter fleurette** to flirt
fleu·ri ·rie [flœri] *adj* in bloom; flowery; florid (*complexion; style*)
fleurir [flœrir] *tr* to decorate with flowers || *intr* to flower, bloom || *intr* (*ger* **florissant**; *imperf* **florissais**, etc.) to flourish
fleuriste [flœrist] *mf* florist; floral gardener; maker or seller of artificial flowers
fleuron [flœrõ] *m* floret; (archit) finial; **fleuron à sa couronne** feather in his cap
fleuve [flœv] *m* river (*flowing directly to the sea*); (fig) river (*of tears, blood, etc.*)
flexible [fleksibl] *adj* flexible; (fig) pliant

flexion [flɛksjɔ̃] *f* bending, flexion; (gram) inflection

flibuster [flibyste] *tr* to rob, to snitch ‖ *intr* to filibuster

flibustier [flibystje] *m* filibuster (*pirate*)

flic [flik] *m* (slang) copper, fuzz

flirt [flœrt] *m* flirt; flirtation

flirter [flœrte] *intr* to flirt

flir•teur [flœrtœr] **-teuse** [tøz] *adj* flirtatious ‖ *mf* flirt

flocon [flɔkɔ̃] *m* flake; snowflake; tuft (*e.g., of wool*); **flocons d'avoine** oatmeal; **flocons de maïs** cornflakes; **flocons de neige** snowflakes

floconner [flɔkɔne] *intr* to form flakes; to become fleecy

flocon•neux [flɔkɔnø] **flocon•neuse** [flɔkɔnøz] *adj* flaky; fleecy

floraison [flɔrɛzɔ̃] *f* flowering, blooming

flo•ral -rale [flɔral] *adj* (*pl* **-raux** [ro]) floral

floralies [flɔrali] *fpl* flower show

flore [flɔr] *f* flora

floren•tin [flɔrɑ̃tɛ̃] **-tine** [tin] *adj* Florentine; **à la florentine** with spinach ‖ (*cap*) *mf* Florentine (*native or inhabitant of Florence*)

Floride [flɔrid] *f* Florida; **la Floride** Florida

florilège [flɔrilɛʒ] *m* anthology

floris•sant [flɔrisɑ̃] **floris•sante** [flɔrisɑ̃t] *adj* flourishing

floss [flɔs] *m* (coll) dental floss

flot [flo] *m* wave; tide; flood, multitude; **à flot** afloat; **à flots** in torrents, abundantly; **flots waters** (*of a lake, the sea, etc.*); **flots de** lots of

flottabilité [flɔtabilite] *f* buoyancy

flottable [flɔtabl] *adj* buoyant; navigable (*for rafts*)

flottage [flɔtaʒ] *m* log driving

flottaison [flɔtɛzɔ̃] *f* water line

flot•tant [flɔtɑ̃] **flot•tante** [flɔtɑ̃t] *adj* floating; vacillating, undecided

flotte [flɔt] *f* fleet; buoy; float (*on fishline*); (slang) water, rain

flottement [flɔtmɑ̃] *m* floating; hesitation, vacillation; undulation

flotter [flɔte] *intr* to float; to waver, hesitate; to fly (*said of flag*); **il flotte** (slang) it is raining

flotteur [flɔtœr] *m* log driver; float (*of fishline, carburetor, etc.*); pontoon, float (*of seaplane*)

flottille [flɔtij] *f* flotilla; **flottille de pêche** fishing fleet

flou floue [flu] *adj* blurred, hazy; fluffy (*hair*); loose-fitting (*dress*); light and soft (*tones, lines in a painting*) ‖ *m* blur, fuzziness; dressmaking

fluctuation [flyktɥasjɔ̃] *f* fluctuation

fluctuer [flyktɥe] *intr* to fluctuate

fluet fluette [flɥe] [flɥet] *adj* thin, slender

fluide [flɥid] *adj & m* fluid

fluidifier [flɥidifje] *tr* to liquefy

fluor [flyɔr] *m* fluorine

fluores•cent [flyɔresɑ̃] **fluores•cente** [flyɔresɑ̃t] *adj* fluorescent

fluoridation [flyɔridasjɔ̃] *f* fluoridation

fluorider [flyɔride] *tr & intr* to fluoridate

fluorure [flyɔryr] *m* fluoride

flûte [flyt] *f* flute; long thin loaf of French bread; tall champagne glass; **flûte à bec** recorder; **flûte de Pan** Pan's pipes; **flûtes** (slang) legs; **grande flûte** concert flute; **jouer** or **se tirer des flûtes** (slang) to run for it; **petite flûte** piccolo ‖ *interj* shucks!, rats!

flûtiste [flytist] *mf* flutist

flux [fly] *m* flow; flood tide; (cards) flush; (chem, elec, med, metallurgy) flux; **flux de sang** flush, blush; dysentery; **flux de ventre** diarrhea; **flux et reflux** ebb and flow

fluxion [flyksjɔ̃] *f* inflammation

foc [fɔk] *m* (naut) jib

fo•cal -cale [fɔkal] *adj* (*pl* **-caux** [ko]) focal

fœtus [fetys] *m* fetus

foi [fwa] *f* faith; word (*of a gentleman*); **ajouter foi à** to give credence to; **bonne foi** good faith, sincerity; **de bonne foi** sincere; sincerely; **de mauvaise foi** dishonest; dishonestly; **en foi de quoi** in witness whereof; **faire foi de** to be evidence of; **ma foi!** upon my word; **manquer de foi à** to break faith with; **mauvaise foi** bad faith, insincerity; **sur la foi de** on the strength of

foie [fwa] *m* liver; **avoir les foies** (slang) to be scared stiff; **foie gras** goose liver

foin [fwɛ̃] *m* hay; **avoir du foin dans ses bottes** (coll) to be well heeled; **faire du foin** (slang) to kick up a fuss

foire [fwar] *f* fair; market; (coll) chaos, mess; **foire d'empoigne** free-for-all

foirer [fware] *intr* (slang) to flop, fail; (slang) to hang fire; (slang) to be stripped (*said of screw, nut, etc.*)

fois [fwa] *f* time, e.g., **visiter trois fois par semaine** to visit three times a week; times, e.g., **deux fois deux font quatre** two times two is four; **à la fois** at the same time, together; **deux fois** twice; twofold; **encore une fois** once more, again; **il y avait une fois** once upon a time there was; **maintes et maintes fois** time and time again; **une fois** one time, once; **une fois pour toutes** or **une bonne fois** once and for all

foison [fwazɔ̃] *f*—**à foison** in abundance

foison•nant [fwazɔnɑ̃] **foison•nante** [fwazɔnɑ̃t] *adj* abundant, plentiful

foisonner [fwazɔne] *intr* to abound

folâtre [fɔlatr] *adj* frisky, playful

folâtrer [fɔlatre] *intr* to frolic, romp

folie [fɔli] *f* madness, insanity; folly, piece of folly; country lodge, hideaway (*for romantic trysts*); **à la folie** madly, passionately; **faire une folie** to do something crazy; **folie de la persécution** persecution complex

folio [fɔljo] *m* folio

folioter [fɔljɔte] *tr* to folio

folle [fɔl] *f* crazy woman

follement [fɔlmɑ̃] *adv* madly

fol·let [fɔlɛ] **fol·lette** [fɔlɛt] _adj_ merry, playful; elfish

follicule [fɔlikyl] _m_ follicle

fomenta·teur [fɔmɑ̃tatœr] **-trice** [tris] _mf_ agitator, troublemaker

fomenter [fɔmɑ̃te] _tr_ to foment

fon·cé -cée [fɔ̃se] _adj_ dark; deep

foncer [fɔ̃se] §51 _tr_ to darken; to dig (_a well_); to fit a bottom to (_a cask_) || _intr_ to charge, to rush

fon·cier [fɔ̃sje] **-cière** [sjɛr] _adj_ landed (_property_); property (_tax_); fundamental, natural || _m_ real-estate tax

foncièrement [fɔ̃sjɛrmɑ̃] _adv_ fundamentally, naturally

fonction [fɔ̃ksjɔ̃] _f_ function; duty; **faire fonction de** to function as

fonctionnaire [fɔ̃ksjɔnɛr] _mf_ civil servant; officeholder

fonctionnarisme [fɔ̃ksjɔnarism] _m_ bureaucracy

fonction·nel -nelle [fɔ̃ksjɔnɛl] _adj_ functional

fonctionner [fɔ̃ksjɔne] _intr_ to function, to work

fond [fɔ̃] _m_ bottom; back, far end; background; foundation; dregs; core, inner meaning, main issue; **à fond** thoroughly; **à fond de train** at full speed; **au fond, dans le fond,** or **par le fond** actually, really, basically; **de fond** fundamental, main; **de fond en comble** from top to bottom; **faire fond sur** to rely on; **fond sonore** background noise; **râcler les fonds du tiroir** to scrape the bottom of the barrel; **sans fond** bottomless; **y aller au fond** to go the whole way || see **fonds**

fondamen·tal -tale [fɔ̃damɑ̃tal] _adj_ (_pl_ -**taux** [to]) fundamental, basic

fon·dant [fɔ̃dɑ̃] **-dante** [dɑ̃t] _adj_ melting; juicy, luscious || _m_ fondant (_candy_); (metallurgy) flux

fonda·teur [fɔ̃datœr] **-trice** [tris] _mf_ founder

fondation [fɔ̃dɑsjɔ̃] _f_ foundation; founding; endowment

fon·dé -dée [fɔ̃de] _adj_ founded; justified; authorized; **bien fondé** well-founded || _m_—**fondé de pouvoir** proxy, authorized agent

fondement [fɔ̃dmɑ̃] _m_ foundation, basis; (coll) behind; **sans fondement** unfounded

fonder [fɔ̃de] _tr_ to found

fonderie [fɔ̃dri] _f_ foundry; smelting

fondeur [fɔ̃dœr] _m_ founder, smelter

fondre [fɔ̃dr] _tr_ to melt, dissolve; to smelt; to cast (_metal_); to blend (_colors_); to merge (_companies_) || _intr_ to melt; (coll) to lose weight; **fondre en larmes** to burst into tears; **fondre sur** to pounce on

fondrière [fɔ̃drijɛr] _f_ quagmire; mudhole, rut, pothole

fonds [fɔ̃] _m_ land (_of an estate_); business, good will; fund; **bon fonds** good nature; **fonds** _mpl_ capital; **fonds de commerce** business house; **fonds de prévoyance** reserve fund; **fonds d'État** _mpl_ government bonds

fon·du -due [fɔ̃dy] _adj_ melted; molten || _m_ blending (_of colors_); (mov, telv) dissolve, fade-out

fontaine [fɔ̃tɛn] _f_ fountain; spring; well; cistern; **fontaine de Jouvence** Fountain of Youth

fonte [fɔ̃t] _f_ melting; casting; cast iron; holster; (typ) font; **venir de fonte avec** to be cast in one piece with

fonts [fɔ̃] _mpl_—**fonts baptismaux** baptismal font

football [futbol] _m_ soccer

footing [futiŋ] _m_ walking

for [fɔr] _m_—**dans son for intérieur** in his heart of hearts; **for intérieur** conscience

forage [fɔraʒ] _m_ drilling

fo·rain [fɔrɛ̃] **-raine** [rɛn] _adj_ traveling, itinerant || **forains** _mpl_ carnival people

forban [fɔrbɑ̃] _m_ pirate

forçage [fɔrsaʒ] _m_ (agr) forcing

forçat [fɔrsa] _m_ convict; (hist) galley slave; (fig) drudge

force [fɔrs] _f_ force; strength; **à force de** by dint of, as a result of; **à toute force** at all costs; **de première force** foremost (_musician, artist, scientist, etc._); **de toutes ses forces** with all one's might; **force de frappe** striking force; **force m'est de . . .** (lit) I am obliged to . . . ; **force majeure** (law) act of God; **forces** sheep shears; **force vive** (phys) kinetic energy; **la force de l'âge** the prime of life || _adj invar_ (archaic) many

forcément [fɔrsemɑ̃] _adv_ inevitably, necessarily

force·né -née [fɔrsəne] _adj_ frenzied, frantic || _m_ madman || _f_ crazy woman

forceps [fɔrsɛps] _m_ (obstet) forceps

forcer [fɔrse] §51 _tr_ to force; to do violence to; to bring to bay; to increase (_the dose_); to strain (_a muscle_); to mark up (_a receipt_); **forcer la main à qn** to force s.o.'s hand; **forcer la note** (coll) to overdo it; **forcer le respect de qn** to compel respect from s.o.; **forcer qn à** or **de + inf** to force s.o. to + _inf_ || _ref_ to overdo; to do violence to one's feelings

forclore [fɔrklɔr] (used only in _inf_ and _pp_ **forclos**) _tr_ to foreclose

forclusion [fɔrklyzjɔ̃] _f_ foreclosure

forer [fɔre] _tr_ to drill, to bore

fores·tier [fɔrɛstje] **-tière** [tjɛr] _adj_ forest || _m_ forester

foret [fɔrɛ] _m_ drill

forêt [fɔrɛ] _f_ forest

fo·reur [fɔrœr] **-reuse** [røz] _adj_ drilling || _mf_ driller || _f_ drill, machine drill

forfaire [fɔrfɛr] §29 (used only in _inf;_ 1st, 2d, & 3d _sg pres ind;_ compound tenses) _intr_—**forfaire à** to forfeit (_one's honor_); to fail in (_a duty_)

forfait [fɔrfɛ] _m_ heinous crime; contract; package deal; (turf) forfeit; **à forfait** for a lump sum

forfaitaire [fɔrfɛtɛr] _adj_ contractual

forfaiture [fɔrfɛtyr] _f_ malfeasance

forfanterie [fɔrfɑ̃tri] _f_ bragging

forge [fɔrʒ] *f* forge; steel mill

forger [fɔrʒe] §38 *tr* to forge

forgeron [fɔrʒərɔ̃] *m* blacksmith

forgeur [fɔrʒœr] *m* forger, smith; coiner (*e.g., of new expressions*); fabricator (*of false stories*)

formaliser [formalize] *ref* to take offense

formaliste [formalist] *adj* formalistic, conventional || *mf* formalist

formalité [formalite] *f* formality, convention

format [forma] *m* size, format

formation [formɑsjɔ̃] *f* formation; education, training

forme [fɔrm] *f* form; **en forme** fit, in shape; **en forme, en bonne forme,** or **en bonne et due forme** in order, in due form; **pour la forme** for appearances

for·mel -melle [fɔrmɛl] *adj* explicit; strict; formal, superficial

formellement [fɔrmɛlmɑ̃] *adv* absolutely, strictly

former [fɔrme] *tr & ref* to form

formidable [fɔrmidabl] *adj* formidable; (coll) tremendous, terrific

formulaire [fɔrmylɛr] *m* formulary; form (*with spaces for answers*)

formule [fɔrmyl] *f* formula; form, blank; format; **formule de politesse** complimentary close

formuler [fɔrmyle] *tr* to formulate; to draw up

fort [fɔr] **forte** [fɔrt] *adj* strong; fortified (*city*); **c'est fort!** it's hard to believe! || (when standing before noun) *adj* high (*fever*); large (*sum*); hard (*task*) || *m* fort; strong man; forte; height (*of summer*) || **fort** *adv* exceedingly; loud; hard

forteresse [fɔrtərɛs] *f* fortress, fort

forti·fiant -fiante [fɔrtifjɑ̃] **-fiante** [fjɑ̃t] *adj & m* tonic

fortification [fɔrtifikɑsjɔ̃] *f* fortification

fortifier [fɔrtifje] *tr* to fortify; to confirm (*one's opinions*)

fortin [fɔrtɛ̃] *m* small fort

for·tuit -tuite [fɔrtɥi] **-tuite** [tɥit] *adj* fortuitous, accidental

fortune [fɔrtyn] *f* fortune; **faire fortune** to make a fortune

fortu·né -née [fɔrtyne] *adj* fortunate; rich

fosse [fos] *f* pit; grave; **fosse aux lions** lions' den; **fosse commune** pauper's grave; **fosse d'aisances** cesspool; **fosse septique** septic tank

fossé [fose] *m* ditch, trench; moat; **sauter le fossé** to take the plunge

fossette [fosɛt] *f* dimple

fossile [fosil] *adj & m* fossil || *mf* fossil (*person*)

fossoyeur [foswajœr] *m* gravedigger

fou [fu] *or* **fol** [fɔl] **folle** [fɔl] (*pl* **fous folles**) *adj* mad, insane; foolish; extravagant; unsteady; loose (*pulley*); (coll) tremendous (*success*); **être fou à lier** to be raving mad; **être fou de** to be wild about; to be wild with (*joy, pain, etc.*) || **fou** *m* madman; fool; jester; (cards) joker; (chess) bishop || *f* see **folle**

foucade [fukad] *f* whim, impulse

foudre [fudr] *m* thunderbolt (*of Zeus*); large cask; **foudre de guerre** great captain; **foudre d'éloquence** powerful orator || *f* lightning; **foudres** displeasure (*e.g., of a prince*); **foudres de l'Église** excommunication

foudroyant [fudrwajɑ̃] **foudroyante** [fudrwajɑ̃t] *adj* lightning-like; crushing, overwhelming

foudroyer [fudrwaje] §47 *tr* to strike with lightning; to strike suddenly; to dumfound; **foudroyer d'un regard** to cast a withering glance at || *intr* to hurl thunderbolts

fouet [fwɛ] *m* whip; (culin) beater

fouetter [fwete] *tr & intr* to whip

fougère [fuʒɛr] *f* fern

fougue [fug] *f* spirit, ardor

fou·gueux [fugø] **-gueuse** [gøz] *adj* spirited, fiery, impetuous

fouille [fuj] *f* excavation; search

fouiller [fuje] *tr* to excavate; to search, comb, inspect

fouillis [fuji] *m* jumble, disorder

fouine [fwin] *f* beech marten; pitchfork; harpoon

fouiner [fwine] *intr* (coll) to pry, meddle

fouir [fwir] *tr* to dig, burrow

foulard [fular] *m* scarf, neckerchief

foule [ful] *f* crowd, mob; **en foule** in great numbers

fouler [fule] *tr* to tread on, to press; to sprain || *ref* (with *dat of reflex pron*) to sprain; (slang) to put oneself out, to tire oneself out

foulque [fulk] *f* (zool) coot

foulure [fulyr] *f* sprain

four [fur] *m* oven; kiln, furnace; (coll) flop, turkey; **faire cuire au four** to bake; to roast; **faire four** (coll) to flop; **four à briques** brickkiln; **four à chaux** limekiln; **petit four** teacake

fourbe [furb] *adj* deceiving, cheating || *mf* deceiver, cheat

fourberie [furbəri] *f* deceit, cheating

fourbir [furbir] *tr* to furbish, polish

fourbissage [furbisaʒ] *m* furbishing, polishing

four·bu -bue [furby] *adj* broken-down (*horse*); (coll) dead tired, all in

fourche [furʃ] *f* fork; pitchfork; **fourche avant** front fork (*of bicycle*); **fourches patibulaires** (hist) gallows

fourcher [furʃe] *tr & intr* to fork; **la langue lui a fourché** (coll) he made a slip of the tongue

fourchette [furʃɛt] *f* fork; wishbone

four·chu -chue [furʃy] *adj* forked, cloven

fourgon [furgɔ̃] *m* truck; poker; (rr) baggage car; (rr) boxcar; **fourgon bancaire** armored car; **fourgon de queue** caboose; **fourgon funèbre** hearse

fourmi [furmi] *f* ant; **fourmi blanche** white ant, termite

fourmilier [furmilje] *m* anteater

fourmilière [furmiljɛr] *f* ant hill

fourmiller [furmije] *intr* to swarm; to tingle (*said, e.g., of foot*); **fourmiller de** to teem with

fournaise [furnez] *f* furnace; (fig) oven

four·neau [furno] *m* (*pl* **-neaux**) furnace; cooking stove; **haut fourneau** blast furnace

fournée [furne] *f* batch

four·ni -nie [furni] *adj* bushy, thick; **bien fourni** well-stocked

fourniment [furnimã] *m* (mil) kit

fournir [furnir] *tr* to furnish, to supply, to provide; to follow (*a suit in cards*) ‖ *intr* (with *dat*) to supply (*s.o.'s* needs); (with *dat*) to defray (*expenses*); (with *dat*) (cards) to follow (*suit*) ‖ *ref* to grow thick; to be a customer

fournissement [furnismã] *m* contribution, holdings (*of each shareholder*); statement of holdings

fournisseur [furnisœr] *m* supplier, dealer

fourniture [furnityr] *f* furnishing, supplying; (culin) seasoning; **fournitures** supplies

fourrage [furaʒ] *m* fodder

fourrager [furaʒe] §38 *tr* to forage; to rummage, to rummage through ‖ *intr* to rummage (about), to forage

fourragère [furaʒer] *f* lanyard; tailboard

four·ré -rée [fure] *adj* lined with fur; furred (*tongue*); stuffed (*dates*); filled (*candies*); sham, hollow (*peace*) ‖ *m* thicket

four·reau [furo] *m* (*pl* **-reaux**) sheath; scabbard; tight skirt; **coucher dans son fourreau** (coll) to sleep in one's clothes

fourrer [fure] *tr* to line with fur; (coll) to cram, stuff; (coll) to shut up (*in prison*); (coll) to stick, poke ‖ *ref* (coll) to turn, go; (coll) to curl up (*in bed*); **se fourrer dans** (coll) to stick one's nose in

fourre-tout [furtu] *m invar* catchall; duffel bag

fourreur [furœr] *m* furrier

fourrier [furje] *m* quartermaster

fourrière [furjer] *f* pound (*for automobiles*; *for stray dogs*)

fourrure [furyr] *f* fur

fourvoyer [furvwaje] §47 *tr* to lead astray

fox [foks] *m* fox terrier

fox-terrier [foksterje] *m* fox terrier

fox-trot [fokstrot] *m invar* fox trot

foyer [fwaje] *m* foyer, lobby; hearth, fireside; firebox; focus; home; greenroom; center (*of learning; of infection*); **à double foyer** bifocal; **foyer des étudiants** student center; **foyer du soldat** service club; **foyers** native land

frac [frak] *m* cutaway coat

fracas [fraka] *m* crash; roar (*of waves*); peal (*of thunder*)

fracasser [frakase] *tr & ref* to break; to shatter, break to pieces

fraction [fraksjɔ̃] *f* fraction; breaking (*e.g., of bread*)

fractionnaire [fraksjɔner] *adj* fractional

fractionnement [fraksjɔnmã] *m* cracking (*of petroleum*)

fractionner [fraksjɔne] *tr* to divide into fractions

fracture [fraktyr] *f* fracture; breaking open

fracturer [fraktyre] *tr* to fracture; to break open

fragile [fraʒil] *adj* fragile

fragment [fragmã] *m* fragment

fragmenter [fragmãte] *tr* to fragment

frai [fre] *m* spawning; spawn, roe

fraîche [freʃ] *f* cool of the day

fraîchement [freʃmã] *adv* in the open air; recently; (coll) cordially

fraîcheur [freʃœr] *f* coolness; freshness; newness

fraîchir [freʃir] *intr* to become cooler; to freshen (*said of wind*)

frais [fre] **fraîche** [freʃ] *adj* cool; fresh; wet (*paint*); **il fait frais** it is cool out ‖ (when standing before noun) *adj* recent (*date*) ‖ *m* cool place; fresh air; **aux frais de** at the expense of; **de frais** just, freshly; **faire les frais de la conversation** (coll) to take the lead in the conversation; to be the subject of the conversation; **frais** *mpl* expenses; **se mettre en frais** (coll) to go to a great deal of expense or trouble ‖ *f* see **fraîche** ‖ **frais** *adv*—**boire frais** to have a cool drink ‖ **frais fraîche** *adv* (agrees with following *pp*) just, freshly, e.g., **garçon frais arrivé de l'école** boy just arrived from school; e.g., **roses fraîches cueillies** freshly gathered roses

fraise [frez] *f* strawberry; wattle (*of turkey*); (mach) countersink

fraiser [freze] *tr* (mach) to countersink

fraisier [frezje] *m* strawberry plant

framboise [frãbwaz] *f* raspberry

framboisier [frãbwazje] *m* raspberry bush

franc [frã] **franche** [frãʃ] *adj* free; frank, sincere; complete ‖ (when standing before noun) *adj* arrant (*knave*); downright (*fool*) ‖ **franc** **franque** [frãk] *adj* Frankish ‖ **franc** (unit of currency) ‖ (*cap*) *m* Frank (*medieval German*) ‖ **franc** *adv* frankly

fran·çais [frãse] **-çaise** [sez] *adj* French ‖ *m* French (*language*); **en bon français** in correct French ‖ (*cap*) *m* Frenchman; **les Français** the French ‖ *f* Frenchwoman

franc-alleu [frãkalø] *m* (*pl* **francs-alleux** [frãkalø]) (hist) freehold

France [frãs] *f* France; **la France** France

franchement [frãʃmã] *adv* frankly, sincerely; without hesitation

franchir [frãʃir] *tr* to cross, to go over or through; to jump over; to overcome (*an obstacle*)

franchise [frãʃiz] *f* exemption; frankness; freedom; **franchise postale** frank

francique [frãsik] *m* Frankish

franciser [frãsize] *tr* to make French

franc-maçon [frãmasɔ̃] *m* (*pl* **francs-maçons**) Freemason

franc-maçonnerie [frãmɑsɔnri] *f* Freemasonry

franco [frãko] *adv* free, without shipping costs; **franco de bord** free on board; **franco de port** postpaid

franco-cana·dien [frãkɔkanadjɛ̃] **-dienne** [djen] *adj* French-Canadian || **Franco-Cana·dien -dienne** *mf* French Canadian

francophone [frãkɔfɔn] *adj* French-speaking || *mf* French speaker

franc-parler [frãparle] *m*—**avoir son franc-parler** to be free-spoken

franc-tireur [frãtirœr] *m* (*pl* **francs-tireurs**) free lance; sniper

frange [frãʒ] *f* fringe; **à frange** fringed

franger [frãʒe] §38 *tr* to fringe

franquette [frãket] *f*—**à la bonne franquette** (coll) simply, without fuss

frap·pant [frapã] **frap·pante** [frapãt] *adj* striking, surprising

frappe [frap] *f* minting, striking; stamp (*on coins, medals, etc.*); touch (*in typing*)

frap·pé frap·pée [frape] *adj* struck; iced; (slang) crazy || *m* (mus) downbeat

frapper [frape] *tr* to strike, hit, knock; to mint (*coin*); to stamp (*cloth*); to ice (*e.g., champagne*) || *intr* to strike, hit, knock || *ref* (coll) to become panic-stricken

frasque [frask] *f* escapade

frater·nel -nelle [fraternel] *adj* fraternal, brotherly

fraterniser [fraternize] *intr* to fraternize

fraternité [fraternite] *f* fraternity, brotherhood

fraude [frod] *f* fraud; smuggling; **en fraude** fraudulently; **faire la fraude** to smuggle; **fraude fiscale** tax evasion

fraudu·leux [frodylø] **-leuse** [løz] *adj* fraudulent

frayer [freje], [freje] §49 *tr* to mark out (*a path*) || *intr* to spawn; **frayer avec** to associate with

frayeur [frejœr] *f* fright, scare

fredaine [frəden] *f* (coll) escapade, prank, spree

fredon [frədɔ̃] *m* (cards) three of a kind

fredonnement [frədɔnmã] *m* hum, humming

fredonner [frədɔne] *tr & intr* to hum

frégate [fregat] *f* frigate

frein [frɛ̃] *m* bit (*of bridle*); brake (*of car*); **frein à main** hand brake; **frein à pied** foot brake; **mettre le frein** to put the brake on; **mettre un frein à** to curb, check; **ronger son frein** to champ at the bit

freiner [frene] *tr & intr* to brake

frelater [frəlate] *tr* to adulterate

frêle [frel] *adj* frail

frelon [frəlɔ̃] *m* hornet

frémir [fremir] *intr* to shudder

frémissement [fremismã] *m* shudder

frêne [fren] *m* ash tree

frénésie [frenezi] *f* frenzy

frénétique [frenetik] *adj* frenzied

fréquemment [frekamã] *adv* frequently

fréquence [frekãs] *f* frequency; **basse fréquence** low frequency; **fréquence du pouls** pulse rate; **haute fréquence** high frequency

fré·quent [frekã] **-quente** [kãt] *adj* frequent; rapid (*pulse*)

fréquenter [frekãte] *tr* to frequent; to associate with; (coll) to go steady with (*a boy or girl*)

frère [frer] *m* brother; **frère consanguin** half brother (*by the father*); **frère convers** (eccl) lay brother; **frère de lait** foster brother; **frère germain** whole brother; **frère jumeau** twin brother; **frères siamois** Siamese twins; **frère utérin** half brother (*by the mother*)

fresque [fresk] *f* fresco

fréter [frete] §10 *tr* to charter (*a ship*); to rent (*a car*)

fréteur [fretœr] *m* shipowner

frétiller [fretije] *intr* to wriggle; to quiver; **frétiller de** to wag (*its tail*)

fretin [frətɛ̃] *m*—**le menu fretin** small fry

frette [fret] *f* hoop, iron ring

freudisme [frødism] *m* Freudianism

freux [frø] *m* rook, crow

friand [frijã] **friande** [frijãd] *adj* tasty; fond (*of food, praise, etc.*) || *m* sausage roll

friandise [frijãdiz] *f* candy, sweet; delicacy, tidbit

fric [frik] *m* (slang) jack, money

fricasser [frikase] *tr* to fricassee; to squander

friche [friʃ] *f* fallow land; **en friche** fallow

friction [friksjɔ̃] *f* friction; massage

frictionner [friksjɔne] *tr* to rub, massage

frigide [friʒid] *adj* frigid

frigidité [friʒidite] *f* frigidity

frigorifier [frigɔrifje] *tr* to refrigerate

frigorifique [frigɔrifik] *adj* refrigerating || *m* cold-storage plant

fri·leux [frilø] **-leuse** [løz] *adj* chilly, shivery

frimas [frima] *m* icy mist, rime

frime [frim] *f* (coll) sham, fake, hoax

frimousse [frimus] *f* (coll) little face, cute face

fringale [frɛ̃gal] *f* (coll) mad hunger

frin·gant [frɛ̃gã] **-gante** [gãt] *adj* dashing, spirited

fringuer [frɛ̃ge] *tr* (slang) to dress || *intr* (obs) to frisk about

fringues [frɛ̃g] *fpl* (slang) duds

fri·pé -pée [fripe] *adj* rumpled, mussed, worn, tired (*face*)

friper [fripe] *tr* to wrinkle, rumple

friperie [fripri] *f* secondhand clothes; secondhand furniture

fri·pier [fripje] **-pière** [pjer] *mf* old-clothes dealer; junk dealer

fri·pon [fripɔ̃] **-ponne** [pɔn] *adj* roguish || *mf* rogue, rascal

friponnerie [fripɔnri] *f* rascality, cheating

fripouille [fripuj] *f* (coll) scoundrel

frire [frir] §22 (used in *inf; pp;* 1st, 2d, 3d *sg pres ind; sg imperv;* rarely used

in *fut; cond*) *tr* to fry; to deep-fry;
être frit (coll) to be done for ‖ *intr*
to fry
frise [friz] *f* frieze
friselis [frizli] *m* soft rustling; gentle
lapping (*of water*)
friser [frize] *tr* to curl; to border on;
to graze ‖ *intr* to curl
frisoir [frizwar] *m* curling iron
fri·son [frizɔ̃] **-sonne** [zɔn] *adj* Frisian
‖ *m* wave, curl; Frisian (*language*)
‖ (*cap*) *mf* Frisian
fris·quet [friskɛ] **-quette** [kɛt] *adj*
(coll) chilly
frisson [frisɔ̃] *m* shiver; shudder, thrill;
frissons shivering
frissonner [frisɔne] *intr* to shiver
frisure [frizyr] *f* curling; curls
frites [frit] *fpl* French fries
frittage [frita3] *m* (metallurgy) sintering
friture [frityr] *f* frying; deep fat; fried
fish; (rad, telv) static
frivole [frivɔl] *adj* frivolous, trifling
froc [frɔk] *m* (eccl) frock
froid [frwa] **froide** [frwad] *adj* cold;
chilly (*manner*) ‖ *m* cold; coolness
(*between persons*); **avoir froid** to be
cold; **il fait froid** it is cold; **jeter un
froid sur** (fig) to put a damper on
froideur [frwadœr] *f* coldness; coolness
froissement [frwasmɑ̃] *m* bruising;
rumpling, crumpling; clash (*of interests*); ruffling (*of feelings*)
froisser [frwase] *tr* to bruise; to rumple, crumple ‖ *ref* to take offense
frôlement [frolmɑ̃] *m* grazing; rustle
frôler [frole] *tr* to graze, to brush
against; (coll) to have a narrow
escape from
fromage [frɔma3] *m* cheese; (coll) soft
job; **fromage blanc** cream cheese;
fromage de tête headcheese
froma·ger [frɔma3e] **-gère** [3er] *adj*
cheese (*industry*) ‖ *m* cheesemaker;
(bot) silk-cotton tree
fromagerie [frɔma3ri] *f* cheese factory;
cheese store
froment [frɔmɑ̃] *m* wheat
fronce [frɔ̃s] *f* crease, fold; **à fronces**
shirred
froncement [frɔ̃smɑ̃] *m* puckering;
froncement de sourcils frown
froncer [frɔ̃se] §51 *tr* to pucker;
froncer les sourcils to frown, to
wrinkle one's brow
frondaison [frɔ̃dɛzɔ̃] *f* foliation; foliage
fronde [frɔ̃d] *f* slingshot
fronder [frɔ̃de] *tr* to scoff at
fron·deur [frɔ̃dœr] **-deuse** [døz] *adj*
bantering, irreverent ‖ *mf* scoffer
front [frɔ̃] *m* forehead; impudence;
brow (*of hill*); (geog, mil, pol) front;
de front abreast; frontal; at the same
time; **faire front à** to face up to
fronta·lier [frɔ̃talje] **-lière** [ljer] *adj*
frontier ‖ *m* frontiersman ‖ *f* frontier
woman
frontière [frɔ̃tjer] *adj & f* frontier
frontispice [frɔ̃tispis] *m* frontispiece;
title page

frottement [frɔtmɑ̃] *m* rubbing, friction
frotter [frɔte] *tr* to rub; to polish; to
strike (*a match*); **frotter les oreilles
à qn** (coll) to box s.o.'s ears ‖ *ref*—
se frotter à (coll) to attack, to challenge; (coll) to rub shoulders with
froufrou [frufru] *m* rustle, swish
frousse [frus] *f* (slang) jitters
fructifier [fryktifje] *intr* to bear fruit
fruc·tueux [fryktɥø] **-tueuse** [tɥøz] *adj*
fruitful, profitable
fru·gal -gale [frygal] *adj* (*pl* **-gaux**
[go]) temperate; frugal (*meal*)
fruit [frɥi] *m* fruit; **des fruits** fruit;
fruits civils income (*from rent, interest, etc.*); **fruits de mer** seafood;
fruit sec (fig) flop, failure
fruiterie [frɥitri] *f* fruit store
frui·tier [frɥitje] **-tière** [tjer] *adj* fruit;
fruit-bearing ‖ *mf* fruit vendor
fruste [fryst] *adj* worn; rough, uncouth
frustrer [frystre] *tr* to frustrate, disappoint; to cheat, defraud
fugace [fygas] *adj* fleeting, evanescent
fugi·tif [fyʒitif] **-tive** [tiv] *adj & m*
fugitive
fugue [fyg] *f* sudden disappearance;
(mus) fugue
fuir [fɥir] §31 *tr* to flee, to run away
from ‖ *intr* to flee; to leak; to recede
(*said of forehead*)
fuite [fɥit] *f* flight; leak
fulgu·rant [fylgyrɑ̃] **-rante** [rɑ̃t] *adj*
flashing; vivid; stabbing (*pain*)
fulguration [fylgyrasjɔ̃] *f* sheet lightning
fulgurer [fylgyre] *intr* to flash
fuligi·neux [fyliʒinø] **-neuse** [nøz] *adj*
sooty
fumage [fyma3] *m* smoking (*of meat*);
manuring (*of fields*)
fume-cigare [fymsigar] *m invar* cigar
holder
fume-cigarette [fymsigaret] *m invar*
cigarette holder
fumée [fyme] *f* smoke; steam; **fumées**
fumes
fumer [fyme] *tr & intr* to smoke; to
fume; to manure
fumerie [fymri] *f* opium den; smoking
room
fumet [fyme] *m* aroma; bouquet (*of
wine*)
fu·meur [fymœr] **-meuse** [møz] *mf*
smoker; **fumeur à la file** chain smoker
fu·meux [fymø] **-meuse** [møz] *adj*
smoky, foggy, hazy (*ideas*)
fumier [fymje] *m* manure; dunghill;
(slang) skunk, scoundrel
fumiger [fymi3e] §38 *tr* to fumigate
fumiste [fymist] *m* heater man; (coll)
practical joker
fumisterie [fymistri] *f* heater work;
heater shop; (coll) hooey
fumoir [fymwar] *m* smoking room;
smokehouse
funambule [fynɑ̃byl] *mf* tightrope
walker
funèbre [fynɛbr] *adj* funereal; funeral
(*march, procession, service*)
funérailles [fyneraj] *fpl* funeral
funéraire [fynerer] *adj* funeral
funeste [fynɛst] *adj* baleful, fatal

funiculaire [fynikylɛr] *adj & m* funicular

fur [fyr] *m*—**au fur et à mesure** progressively, gradually; **au fur et à mesure de** in proportion to; **au fur et à mesure que** as, in proportion as

furet [fyrɛ] *m* ferret; snoop; ring-in-the-circle (*parlor game*)

fureter [fyrte] §2 *intr* to ferret

fureur [fyrœr] *f* fury; **à la fureur** passionately; **faire fureur** to be the rage

furi·bond [fyribɔ̃] **-bonde** [bɔ̃d] *adj* furious; withering (*look*) ‖ *mf* irascible individual

furie [fyri] *f* fury; termagant

fu·rieux [fyrjø] **-rieuse** [rjøz] *adj* furious; angry (*wind*)

furoncle [fyrɔ̃kl] *m* boil

fur·tif [fyrtif] **-tive** [tiv] *adj* furtive, stealthy

fusain [fyzɛ̃] *m* charcoal; charcoal drawing; spindle tree

fu·seau [fyzo] *m* (*pl* **-seaux**) spindle; **à fuseau** tapering; **fuseau horaire** time zone (*between two meridians*)

fusée [fyze] *f* rocket; spindleful; spindle (*of axle*); (coll) ripple, burst (*of laughter*); **fusée à retard** delayed-action fuse; **fusée d'artifice** or **fusée volante** skyrocket; **fusée éclairante** flare; **fusée engin** rocket engine; **fusée fusante** time fuse; **fusée percutante** percussion fuse

fuselage [fyzlaʒ] *m* fuselage

fuse·lé -lée [fyzle] *adj* spindle-shaped; tapering, slender (*fingers*); streamlined

fuseler [fyzle] §34 *tr* to taper; to streamline

fuser [fyze] *intr* to melt; to run (*said of colors*); to fizz, to spurt; to stream in or out (*said of light*)

fusible [fyzibl] *adj* fusible ‖ *m* fuse

fusil [fyzi] *m* gun, rifle; whetstone; rifleman; **fusil à deux coups** double-barreled gun; **fusil de chasse** shotgun; **fusil mitrailleur** light machine gun; **un bon fusil** a good shot (*person*)

fusillade [fyzijad] *f* fusillade

fusiller [fyzije] *tr* to shoot, to execute by a firing squad

fusion [fyzjɔ̃] *f* fusion

fusionner [fyzjɔne] *tr & intr* to blend, to fuse; (com) to merge

fustiger [fystiʒe] §38 *tr* to thrash, flog; to castigate

fût [fy] *m* cask, keg; barrel (*of drum*); stock (*of gun*); trunk (*of tree*); shaft (*of column*); stem (*of candelabrum*)

futaie [fytɛ] *f* stand of timber; **de haute futaie** full-grown

futaille [fytaj] *f* cask, barrel

futaine [fytɛn] *f* fustian

fu·té -tée [fyte] *adj* (coll) cunning, shrewd ‖ *f* mastic, filler

futile [fytil] *adj* futile

futilité [fytilite] *f* futility; **futilités** trifles

fu·tur -ture [fytyr] *adj* future ‖ *m* future; husband-to-be ‖ *f* future wife

fuyant [fɥijɑ̃] **fuyante** [fɥijɑ̃t] *adj* fleeting; receding (*forehead*)

fuyard [fɥijar] **fuyarde** [fɥijard] *adj & mf* runaway

G

G, g [ʒe] *m invar* seventh letter of the French alphabet

gabardine [gabardin] *f* gabardine

gabare [gabar] *f* barge

gabarit [gabari] *m* templet; (rr) maximum structure; (coll) size

gabelle [gabɛl] *f* (hist) salt tax

gâche [gɑʃ] *f* catch (*at a door*); trowel; wooden spatula

gâcher [gɑʃe] *tr* to mix (*cement*); to spoil, bungle; to squander

gâchette [gɑʃɛt] *f* trigger; pawl, spring catch

gâ·cheur [gɑʃœr] **-cheuse** [ʃøz] *adj* bungling ‖ *mf* bungler

gâchis [gɑʃi] *m* wet cement; mud, slush; (coll) mess, muddle

gaélique [gaelik] *adj & m* Gaelic

gaffe [gaf] *f* gaff; (coll) social blunder, faux pas

gaffer [gafe] *tr* to hook with a gaff ‖ *intr* (coll) to make a blunder

gaga [gaga] *adj* (coll) doddering ‖ *mf* (coll) dotard

gage [gaʒ] *m* pledge, pawn; forfeit (*in a game*); **gages** wage, wages; **prêter sur gages** to pawn

gager [gaʒe] §38 *tr* to wager, to bet; to pay wages to

ga·geur [gaʒœr] **-geuse** [ʒøz] *mf* bettor

gageure [gaʒyr] *f* wager, bet

gagiste [gaʒist] *mf* pledger; wage earner; (theat) extra

ga·gnant [gaɲɑ̃] **-gnante** [ɲɑ̃t] *adj* winning ‖ *mf* winner

gagne-pain [gaɲpɛ̃] *m invar* breadwinner; livelihood, bread and butter

gagne-petit [gaɲpəti] *m invar* cheapjack, low-salaried worker

gagner [gaɲe] *tr* to gain; to win; to earn; to reach; to save (*time*) ‖ *intr* to improve; to gain; to spread ‖ *ref* to be catching (*said of disease*)

ga·gneur [gaɲœr] **-gneuse** [ɲøz] *mf* winner; earner

gai gaie [ge] *adj* gay; (coll) tipsy

gaiement [gemɑ̃] *adv* gaily

gaieté [gete] *f* gaiety; **de gaieté de cœur** of one's own free will

gail·lard [gajar] **gail·larde** [gajard] *adj*

healthy, hearty; merry; ribald, spicy ‖ *m* sturdy fellow; tricky fellow; **gaillard d'arrière** quarter-deck; **gaillard d'avant** forecastle ‖ *f* bold young lady; husky young woman

gaillardise [gajardiz] *f* cheerfulness; **gaillardises** spicy stories

gain [gɛ̃] *m* gain; earnings; winning (*e.g.*, *of bet*); **avoir gain de cause** to win one's case

gaine [gɛn] *f* sheath; case, covering; girdle (*corset*); **gaine d'aération** ventilation shaft

gainer [gene] *tr* to sheath, to encase

gaité [gete] *f* gaiety

gala [gala] *m* gala; state dinner

galamment [galamã] *adv* gallantly

ga·lant [galã] **-lante** [lãt] *adj* gallant; amorous; kept (*woman*) ‖ *m* gallant; **vert galant** gay old blade

galanterie [galãtri] *f* gallantry; libertinism

galaxie [galaksi] *f* galaxy

galbe [galb] *m* curve, sweep, graceful outline

gale [gal] *f* mange; (coll) backbiter, cad

galée [gale] *f* (typ) galley

galéjade [galeʒad] *f* joke, far-fetched story

galère [galɛr] *f* galley; drudgery; mason's hand truck

galerie [galri] *f* gallery; cornice, rim; baggage rack; **galerie marchande** shopping center

galérien [galerjɛ̃] *m* galley slave

galet [galɛ] *m* pebble; (mach) roller

galetas [galta] *m* hovel

galette [galɛt] *f* cake; buckwheat pancake; hardtack; (slang) dough, money; **galette des Rois** twelfth-cake (*eaten at Epiphany*)

ga·leux [galø] **-leuse** [løz] *adj* mangy

galimatias [galimatja] *m* nonsense, gibberish

galion [galjɔ̃] *m* galleon

Galles [gal]—**le pays de Galles** Wales; **prince de Galles** Prince of Wales

gal·lois [galwa] **gal·loise** [galwaz] *adj* Welsh ‖ *m* Welsh (*language*) ‖ (*cap*) *m* Welshman; **les Gallois** the Welsh ‖ (*cap*) *f* Welshwoman

gallon [galɔ̃] *m* gallon (*imperial or American*)

galoche [galɔʃ] *f* clog (*shoe*); **de** or **en galoche** pointed (*chin*)

galon [galɔ̃] *m* galloon, braid; (mil) stripe, chevron; **prendre du galon** to move up

galonner [galɔne] *tr* to trim with braid

galop [galo] *m* gallop; **petit galop** canter

galoper [galɔpe] *tr & intr* to gallop

galopin [galɔpɛ̃] *m* (coll) urchin

galvaniser [galvanize] *tr* to galvanize

galvauder [galvode] *tr* (coll) to botch; (coll) to waste (*e.g.*, *one's talent*); (coll) to sully (*a name*) ‖ *intr* (slang) to walk the streets ‖ *ref* (slang) to go bad

gambade [gãbad] *f* gambol

gambader [gãbade] *intr* to gambol

gambit [gãbi] *m* gambit

gamelle [gamɛl] *f* mess kit

ga·min [gamɛ̃] **-mine** [min] *mf* street urchin; youngster

gaminerie [gaminri] *f* mischievousness

gamme [gam] *f* gamut, range; set (*of tools*); (mus) scale, gamut

Gand [gã] *m* Ghent

ganglion [gãglijɔ̃] *m* ganglion

gangrène [gãgrɛn] *f* gangrene

gangrener [gãgrəne] §2 *tr & ref* to gangrene

ganse [gãs] *f* braid, piping

gant [gã] *m* glove; **jeter le gant** to throw down the gauntlet; **prendre des gants pour** to put on kid gloves to; **relever le gant** to take up the gauntlet; **se donner des gants** to take all the credit

gantelet [gãtlɛ] *m* protective glove

ganter [gãte] *tr* to put gloves on (*s.o.*); to fit, to become (*s.o.*; *said of gloves*); **cela me gante** (coll) that suits me ‖ *intr*—**ganter de** to wear, to take (*a certain size of glove*) ‖ *ref* to put on one's gloves

garage [garaʒ] *m* garage; turnout

garagiste [garaʒist] *m* garageman, mechanic

ga·rant [garã] **-rante** [rãt] *adj* guaranteeing ‖ *mf* guarantor, warrantor; **se porter garant de** to guarantee ‖ *m* guarantee, warranty

garantie [garãti] *f* guarantee

garantir [garãtir] *tr* to guarantee; to vouch for; to shelter, protect

garce [gars] *f* (coll) wench; (coll) bitch

garçon [garsɔ̃] *m* boy; young man; bachelor; apprentice; waiter; **garçon de courses** errand boy; **garçon de recette** bank messenger; **garçon de salle** orderly; **garçon d'honneur** best man; **garçon manqué** tomboy; **vieux garçon** old bachelor

garçonne [garsɔn] *f* bachelor girl

garçonnet [garsɔnɛ] *m* little boy

garçon·nier [garsɔnje] **garçon·nière** [garsɔnjɛr] *adj* bachelor; tomboyish ‖ *f* bachelor apartment; tomboy

garde [gard] *m* guard, guardsman; keeper, custodian; **garde champêtre** constable; **garde de nuit** night watchman; **garde forestier** ranger ‖ *f* guard; custody; nurse; flyleaf; **de garde** on duty; **garde à vous!** (mil) attention!; **garde civique** national guard; **monter la garde** to go on guard duty; **prendre garde à** to look out for, to take notice of; **prendre garde de** to take care not to; to be careful to; **prendre garde que** to notice that; **prendre garde que . . . ne + *subj*** to be careful lest, to be careful that . . . not; **sur ses gardes** on one's guard

garde-à-vous [gardavu] *m invar* (*military position*) attention

garde-à-vue [gardavy] *f* custody, imprisonment

garde-barrière [gardəbarjɛr] *mf* (*pl* **gardes-barrière** or **gardes-barrières**) crossing guard

garde-bébé [gardəbebe] *mf* (*pl* **-bébés**) baby-sitter

garde-boue [gardəbu] *m invar* mud-guard

garde-chasse [gardə/as] *m* (*pl* **gardes-chasse** or **gardes-chasses**) game-keeper

garde-corps [gardəkɔr] *m invar* guard-rail; (naut) life line

garde-côte [gardəkot] *m* (*pl* -**côtes**) coast-guard cutter || *m* (*pl* **gardes-côtes**) (obs) coastguardsman; (obs) coast guard

garde-feu [gardəfø] *m invar* fire screen

garde-fou [gardəfu] *m* (*pl* -**fous**) guard-rail

garde-frein [gardəfrɛ̃] *m* (*pl* **gardes-frein** or **gardes-freins**) brakeman

garde-magasin [gardəmagazɛ̃] *m* (*pl* **gardes-magasin** or **gardes-magasins**) warehouseman

garde-malade [gardəmalad] *mf* (*pl* **gardes-malades**) nurse

garde-manger [gardəmɑ̃ʒe] *m invar* icebox; larder

garde-meuble [gardəmœbl] *m* (*pl* -**meuble** or **meubles**) furniture ware-house

garde-nappe [gardənap] *m* (*pl* -**nappe** or **nappes**) table mat, place mat

garde-pêche [gardəpɛ/] *m* (*pl* **gardes-pêche**) fish warden || *m invar* fishery service boat

garder [garde] *tr* to guard; to keep; **garder à vue** to hold in custody; **garder jusqu'à l'arrivée** (formula on envelope) hold for arrival; **garder la chambre** to stay in one's room; **garder la ligne** to keep one's figure || *ref* to keep (*to stay free of deterioration*); **se garder de** to protect oneself from; to watch out for; to take care not to

garde-rats [gardəra] *m invar* rat guard

garderie [gardəri] *f* nursery; forest re-serve

garde-robe [gardərɔb] *f* (*pl* -**robes**) wardrobe

gar·deur [gardœr] -**deuse** [døz] *mf* keeper, herder

garde-voie [gardəvwa] *m* (*pl* **gardes-voie** or **gardes-voies**) trackwalker

garde-vue [gardəvy] *m invar* eyeshade, visor

gar·dien [gardjɛ̃] -**dienne** [djen] *adj* guardian (*angel*) || *mf* guard, guardian; keeper; caretaker; attendant (*at a garage*); **gardien de but** goalkeeper; **gardien de la paix** policeman

gare [gar] *f* station; **gare aérienne** airport; **gare de triage** switch-yard; **gare maritime** port, dock; **gare routière** or **gare d'autobus** bus station || [gar] *interj* look out!

garer [gare] *tr* to park; to put in the garage; (naut) to dock; (rr) to shunt; (coll) to secure (*e.g., a fortune*) || *ref* to get out of the way; to park, park one's car; **se garer de** to look out for

gargariser [gargarize] *ref* to gargle

gargarisme [gargarism] *m* gargle

gargote [gargɔt] *f* (coll) hash house, beanery

gargouille [garguj] *f* gargoyle

gargouillement [gargujmɑ̃] *m* gurgling; rumbling (*in stomach*)

gargouiller [garguje] *intr* to gurgle

garnement [garnəmɑ̃] *m* scamp, bad boy

gar·ni -**nie** [garni] *adj* furnished (*room*) || *m* furnished room; furnished house

garnir [garnir] *tr* to garnish, adorn; to furnish; to strengthen; to line (*a brake*) || *ref* to fill up (*said of crowded room, theater seats, etc.*)

garnison [garnizɔ̃] *f* garrison

garniture [garnityr] *f* garniture, decoration; fittings; accessories; complete set; (culin) garnish; **garniture de feu** fire irons; **garniture de lit** bedding

garrot [garo] *m* garrote (*instrument of torture*); (med) tourniquet; (zool) withers

garrotte [garɔt] *f* garrote (*torture*)

garrotter [garɔte] *tr* to garrote; to pinion

gars [ga] *m* (coll) lad

Gascogne [gaskɔɲ] *f* Gascony; **la Gascogne** Gascony

gasconnade [gaskɔnad] *f* gasconade; insincere invitation

gas-oil [gazwal] *m* diesel oil

Gaspésie [gaspezi] *f* Gaspé Peninsula

gaspiller [gaspije] *tr* to waste, squander

gastrique [gastrik] *adj* gastric

gastronomie [gastrɔnɔmi] *f* gastronomy

gâ·teau [gato] *adj invar* (coll) fond (*papa*); (coll) fairy (*godmother*) || *m* (*pl* -**teaux**) cake; (coll) booty, loot; **gâteau de miel** honeycomb; **gâteau des Rois** twelfth-cake

gâte-métier [gatmetje] *m invar* under-cutter

gâte-papier [gatpapje] *m invar* hack writer

gâter [gate] *tr & ref* to spoil

gâte-sauce [gatsos] *m invar* poor cook; kitchen boy

gâ·teux [gatø] -**teuse** [tøz] *adj* (coll) senile || *mf* (coll) dotard

gâtisme [gatism] *m* senility

gauche [go/] *adj* left; left-hand; crooked; awkward || *f* left hand; left side; (pol) left wing; **à gauche** to the left; **à gauche, gauche!** (mil) left, face!

gau·cher [go/e] -**chère** [/ɛr] *adj* left-handed || *mf* left-hander

gauchir [go/ir] *tr & intr* to warp

gauchiste [go/ist] *adj & m* leftist

gaudriole [godrijɔl] *f* broad joke

gaufre [gofr] *f* waffle; **gaufre de miel** honeycomb

gaufrer [gofre] *tr* to emboss, figure; to flute; to corrugate

gaufrette [gofret] *f* wafer

gaufrier [gofrije] *m* waffle iron

gaule [gol] *f* pole; **la Gaule** Gaul

gauler [gole] *tr* to bring down (*e.g., fruit*) with a pole

gau·lois [golwa] -**loise** [waz] *adj* Gaulish, Gallic; broad (*humor*) || *m* Gaulish (*language*) || (*cap*) *mf* Gaul || (*cap*) *f* gauloise (*cigarette*)

gauloiserie [golwazri] *f* racy joking

gaulthérie [goteri] *f* (bot) wintergreen

gausser [gose] *ref*—**se gausser de** (coll) to poke fun at

gaver [gave] *tr & ref* to cram

gavroche [gavrɔʃ] *mf* street urchin

gaz [gɑz] *m* gas; gaslight; gas company; **gaz d'échappement** exhaust; **gaz d'éclairage** illuminating gas; **gaz de combat** poison gas; **gaz en cylindre** bottled gas; **gaz hilarant** laughing gas; **gaz lacrimogène** tear gas; **mettre les gaz** (aut) to step on the gas

gaze [gɑz] *f* gauze; cheesecloth

ga·zé -zée [gɑze] *adj* gassed ‖ *mf* gas casualty

gazéifier [gɑzeifje] *tr* to gasify; to carbonate, charge

gazelle [gazɛl] *f* gazelle

gazer [gɑze] *tr* to gas; to cover with gauze; to tone down ‖ *intr* (coll) to go full steam ahead; **ça gaze?** (coll) how goes it?

ga·zeux [gɑzø] **-zeuse** [zøz] *adj* gaseous; carbonated

ga·zier [gɑzje] **-zière** [zjɛr] *adj* gas ‖ *m* gasman; gas fitter

gazoduc [gɑzɔdyk] *m* gas pipe line

gazogène [gɑzɔʒɛn] *m* gas producer

gazoline [gɑzɔlin] *f* petroleum ether

gazomètre [gɑzɔmɛtr] *m* gasholder, gas tank

gazon [gɑzɔ̃] *m* lawn; turf, sod

gazonner [gɑzɔne] *tr* to sod

gazouiller [gazuje] *intr* to chirp, twitter; to warble; to babble

gazouillis [gazuji] *m* chirping; warbling; babbling

geai [ʒɛ] *m* jay

géant [ʒeɑ̃] **géante** [ʒeɑ̃t] *adj* gigantic ‖ *m* giant ‖ *f* giantess

Gédéon [ʒedeɔ̃] *m* (Bib) Gideon

gei·gnard [ʒɛɲar] **-gnard** [ɲard] *adj* (coll) whining ‖ *mf* (coll) whiner

geignement [ʒɛɲmɑ̃] *m* whining, whimper

geindre [ʒɛ̃dr] §50 *intr* to whine, whimper; (coll) to complain

gel [ʒɛl] *m* frost, freezing; (chem) gel

gélatine [ʒelatin] *f* gelatin

gelée [ʒəle] *f* frost; (culin) jelly; **gelée blanche** hoarfrost

geler [ʒəle] §2 *tr, intr & ref* to freeze; to congeal

gelure [ʒəlyr] *f* frostbite

gémi·né -née [ʒemine] *adj* twin; coeducational (*school*)

gémir [ʒemir] *intr* to groan, moan

gémissement [ʒemismɑ̃] *m* groaning, moaning

gemme [ʒɛm] *f* gem; bud; pine resin

gemmer [ʒɛme] *tr* to tap for resin ‖ *intr* to bud

gê·nant [ʒenɑ̃] **-nante** [nɑ̃t] *adj* troublesome, embarrassing

gencive [ʒɑ̃siv] *f* (anat) gum

gendarme [ʒɑ̃darm] *m* policeman; rock pinnacle; flaw (*of gem*); (coll) virago; (slang) red herring

gendarmerie [ʒɑ̃darmri] *f* police headquarters

gendre [ʒɑ̃dr] *m* son-in-law

gêne [ʒɛn] *f* discomfort, embarrassment; **être dans la gêne** to be hard

up; **être sans gêne** (coll) to be rude, casual

gène [ʒɛn] *m* (biol) gene

généalogie [ʒenealɔʒi] *f* genealogy

gêner [ʒene] *tr* to embarrass; to inconvenience; to hinder; to embarrass financially; to pinch (*the feet*)

géné·ral -rale [ʒeneral] *adj & m* (*pl* **-raux** [ro]) general; **en général** in general; **général de brigade** brigadier general; **général de corps d'armée** lieutenant general; **général de division** major general ‖ *f* general's wife; (theat) opening night; **battre la générale** (mil) to sound the alarm

généralat [ʒenerala] *m* generalship

généraliser [ʒeneralize] *tr & intr* to generalize

généralissime [ʒeneralisim] *m* generalissimo

généralité [ʒeneralite] *f* generality; **la généralité de** the general run of

généra·teur [ʒeneratœr] **-trice** [tris] *adj* generating ‖ *m* boiler ‖ *f* generator

génération [ʒenerasjɔ̃] *f* generation

générer [ʒenere] §10 *tr* to generate

géné·reux [ʒenerø] **-reuse** [røz] *adj* generous; full (*bosom*); rich, full (*wine*)

générique [ʒenerik] *adj* generic ‖ *m* (mov) credit line

générosité [ʒenerozite] *f* generosity; **générosités** acts of generosity

Gênes [ʒɛn] *f* Genoa

genèse [ʒənɛz] *f* genesis

genet [ʒəne] *m* jennet (*horse*)

genêt [ʒəne] *m* (bot) broom; **genêt épineux** furze

génétique [ʒenetik] *adj* genetic ‖ *f* genetics

gê·neur [ʒenœr] **-neuse** [nøz] *mf* intruder, spoilsport

Genève [ʒənɛv] *f* Geneva

gene·vois [ʒənvwa], [ʒɛnvwa] **-voise** [vwaz] *adj* Genevan ‖ (*cap*) *mf* Genevan (*person*)

genévrier [ʒenevrije] *m* juniper

gé·nial -niale [ʒenjal] *adj* (*pl* **-niaux** [njo]) brilliant, ingenious; geniuslike, of genius

génie [ʒeni] *m* genius; bent, inclination; genie; engineer corps; **génie civil** civil engineering; **génie industriel** industrial engineering; **génie maritime** naval construction

genièvre [ʒənjɛvr] *m* juniper; juniper berry; gin

génisse [ʒenis] *f* heifer

géni·tal -tale [ʒenital] *adj* (*pl* **-taux** [to]) genital

géni·teur [ʒenitœr] **-trice** [tris] *adj* engendering ‖ *m* sire ‖ *f* genetrix

géni·tif [ʒenitif] **-tive** [tiv] *adj & m* genitive

génocide [ʒenɔsid] *m* genocide

gé·nois [ʒenwa] **-noise** [nwaz] *adj* Genoese ‖ (*cap*) *mf* Genoese

ge·nou [ʒənu] *m* (*pl* **-noux**) knee; (mach) joint

genouillère [ʒənujɛr] *f* kneecap; kneepad

genre [ʒɑ̃r] *m* genre; genus; kind, sort;

manner, way; fashion, taste; (gram) gender; **de genre** (fa) genre; **faire du genre** (coll) to put on airs; **genre humain** humankind

gens [ʒã] *mpl* (an immediately preceding adjective that varies in its feminine form is put in that form, and so are **certain, quel, tel,** and **tout** that precede that preceding adjective, but the noun remains masculine for pronouns that stand for it, for past participles that agree with it, and for adjectives in all other positions, e.g., **toutes ces vieilles gens sont intéressants** all these old people are interesting) people; nations, e.g., **droit des gens** law of nations; men, e.g., **gens de lettres** men of letters; **gens d'affaires** businessmen; **gens d'Église** clergy; **gens de la presse** newsmen; **gens de mer** seamen; **gens de robe** bar; **jeunes gens** young people (*men and women*); young men

gent [ʒã] *f* (obs) nation, race

gentiane [ʒãsjan] *f* gentian

gen·til [ʒãti] **-tille** [tij] *adj* nice, kind || (*cap*) *m* pagan, gentile

gentilhomme [ʒãtijɔm] *m* (*pl* **gentils-hommes** [ʒãtizɔm]) nobleman

gentillesse [ʒãtijes] *f* niceness, kindness; **gentillesses** nice things, kind words

gentil·let [ʒãtije] **gentil·lette** [ʒãtijet] *adj* rather nice

gentiment [ʒãtimã] *adv* nicely; gracefully

géographie [ʒeɔgrafi] *f* geography

geôle [ʒol] *f* jail

geô·lier [ʒolje] **-lière** [ljer] *mf* jailer

géologie [ʒeɔlɔʒi] *f* geology

géologique [ʒeɔlɔʒik] *adj* geologic(al)

géomé·tral -trale [ʒeɔmetral] *adj* (*pl* **-traux** [tro]) flat (*projection*)

géométrie [ʒeɔmetri] *f* geometry

géométrique [ʒeɔmetrik] *adj* geometric(al)

géophysique [ʒeɔfizik] *f* geophysics

géopolitique [ʒeɔpɔlitik] *f* geopolitics

Georges [ʒɔrʒ] *m* George

gérance [ʒerãs] *f* management; board of directors

géranium [ʒeranjɔm] *m* geranium

gé·rant [ʒerã] **-rante** [rãt] *mf* manager; **gérant d'une publication** managing editor

gerbe [ʒerb] *f* sheaf; spray (*of flowers; of water; of bullets*); shower (*of sparks*)

gerbée [ʒerbe] *f* straw

gerber [ʒerbe] *tr* to sheave; to stack

gerce [ʒers] *f* crack, split; clothes moth

gercer [ʒerse] §51 *tr, intr, & ref* to crack, to chap

gerçure [ʒersyr] *f* crack, chap

gérer [ʒere] §10 *tr* to manage, to run

gériatrie [ʒerjatri] *f* geriatrics

ger·main -maine [men] *adj* german, first (*cousin*)

germe [ʒerm] *m* germ

germer [ʒerme] *intr* to germinate

germicide [ʒermisid] *adj* germicidal || *m* germicide

gérondif [ʒerɔ̃dif] *m* gerund

gérontologie [ʒerɔ̃tɔlɔʒi] *f* gerontology

gésier [ʒesje] *m* gizzard

gésir [ʒezir] (used only in *inf*; *ger* **gisant**; 3d *sg pres ind* **gît**; 1st, 2d, 3d *pl pres ind* **gisons, gisez, gisent**; *imperf ind* **gisais, gisait, gisions, gisiez, gisaient**) *intr* to lie; **ci-gît** here lies (*buried*)

gesse [ʒes] *f* vetch; **gesse odorante** sweet pea

gestation [ʒestasjɔ̃] *f* gestation

geste [ʒest] *m* gesture || *f* medieval epic poem

gesticuler [ʒestikyle] *intr* to gesticulate

gestion [ʒestjɔ̃] *f* management, administration

gestionnaire [ʒestjɔner] *adj* managing || *mf* manager, administrator

geyser [ʒezer], [ʒejzer] *m* geyser

ghetto [geto], [getto] *m* ghetto

gib·beux [ʒibø] **gib·beuse** [ʒibøz] *adj* humped, hunchbacked

gibecière [ʒibsjer] *f* game bag; sack (*for papers, books, etc.*)

gibelotte [ʒiblɔt] *f* rabbit stew

gibet [ʒibe] *m* gibbet, gallows

gibier [ʒibje] *m* game; **gibier à plume** feathered game; **gibier de potence** gallows bird

giboulée [ʒibule] *f* shower; hailstorm

gi·boyeux [ʒibwajø] **giboyeuse** [ʒibwajøz] *adj* full of game

gibus [ʒibys] *m* opera hat

giclée [ʒikle] *f* spurt

gicler [ʒikle] *intr* to spurt

gicleur [ʒiklœr] *m* atomizer; (aut) spray nozzle (*of carburetor*)

gifle [ʒifl] *f* slap in the face

gifler [ʒifle] *tr* to slap in the face

gigantesque [ʒigãtesk] *adj* gigantic

gigogne [ʒigɔɲ] *adj*—**table gigogne** nest of tables || (*cap*) *f*—**la mère Gigogne** the old woman who lived in a shoe

gigolo [ʒigolo] *m* (coll) gigolo

gigot [ʒigo] *m* leg of lamb, leg of mutton; **à gigot** leg-of-mutton (*sleeve*)

gigue [ʒig] *f* jig; haunch (*of venison*); (coll) leg; (slang) long-legged gawky girl

gilet [ʒile] *m* vest; **gilet de sauvetage** life jacket; **gilet pare-balles** bulletproof vest; **pleurer dans le gilet de qn** (coll) to cry on s.o.'s shoulder

gingembre [ʒɛ̃ʒãbr] *m* ginger

girafe [ʒiraf] *f* giraffe

giration [ʒirasjɔ̃] *f* gyration

girl [gœrl] *f* chorus girl

girofle [ʒirɔfl] *m* clove

giroflée [ʒirɔfle] *f* gillyflower

giron [ʒirɔ̃] *m* lap; bosom (*of the Church*)

girouette [ʒirwet] *f* weather vane

gisement [ʒizmã] *m* deposit; lode, seam; (naut) bearing; **gisement de pétrole** oil field

gi·tan -tane [tan] *adj & mf* gypsy

gîte [ʒit] *m* lodging; lair, cover; deposit (*of ore*); **gîte à la noix** round steak || *f* (naut) list; **donner de la gîte** to heel

gîter [ʒite] *intr* to lodge; to lie, couch;

to perch; (naut) to list, heel ‖ *ref* to find shelter

givre [ʒivr] *m* rime, hoarfrost

givrer [ʒivre] *tr* to frost

glabre [glɑbr] *adj* beardless

glaçage [glasaʒ] *m* icing (*on cake*)

glace [glas] *f* ice; ice cream; mirror; plate glass; car window; glaze, icing; flaw (*of gem*); **être de glace** (fig) to be hard as stone; **glace au sirop sundae**; **glace panachée** Neapolitan ice cream; **rompre la glace** (fig) to break the ice

gla·cé -cée [glase] *adj* frozen; iced, chilled; icy, frosty; glazed, glossy

glacer [glase] §51 *tr* to freeze; to chill; to glaze; to ice (*a cake*)

glacerie [glasri] *f* glass factory

glaciaire [glasjer] *adj* glacial

gla·cial -ciale [glasjal] *adj* (*pl* -**cials**) glacial

glacier [glasje] *m* glacier; ice-cream man

glacière [glasjer] *f* icehouse; icebox; freezer

glacis [glasi] *m* slope; ramp; (mil) glacis; (painting) glaze

glaçon [glasɔ̃] *m* icicle; ice cube; ice floe; (fig) cold fish, iceberg

glaçure [glasyr] *f* (ceramics) glaze

gladiateur [gladjatœr] *m* gladiator

glaïeul [glajœl] *m* gladiola

glaire [gler] *f* white of egg; mucus

glaise [glez] *f* clay, loam

glaisière [glezjer] *f* clay pit

glaive [glev] *m* (lit) sword

gland [glɑ̃] *m* acorn; tassel

glande [glɑ̃d] *f* gland

glane [glan] *f* gleaning; cluster

glaner [glane] *tr* to glean

glanure [glanyr] *f* gleaning

glapir [glapir] *intr* to yelp, yap

glas [glɑ] *m* knell, tolling

glauque [glok] *adj & m* blue-green

glèbe [gleb] *f* clod (*sod*); soil (*land*)

glène [glen] *f* (anat) socket; (naut) coil of rope

glissade [glisad] *f* slip; sliding; (dancing) glide; **glissade de terre** landslide; **glissade sur l'aile** (aer) sideslip; **glissade sur la queue** (aer) tail dive

glis·sant [glisɑ̃] **glis·sante** [glisɑ̃t] *adj* slippery

glissement [glismɑ̃] *m* sliding; gliding

glisser [glise] *tr* to slip; to drop (*a word into s.o.'s ear*) ‖ *intr* to slip; to slide; to skid; to glide ‖ *ref* to slip

glissière [glisjer] *f* slide, groove; **à glissière** sliding; zippered

glissoire [gliswar] *f* slide (*on ice or snow*)

glo·bal -bale [glɔbal] *adj* (*pl* -**baux** [bo]) global; lump (*sum*)

globe [glɔb] *m* globe; **globe de feu** fireball; **globe de l'œil** eyeball

globule [glɔbyl] *f* globule; (physiol) corpuscle

gloire [glwar] *f* glory; pride; halo; **pour la gloire** for fun, for nothing; **se faire gloire de** to glory in

gloriette [glɔrjet] *f* arbor, summerhouse

glo·rieux [glɔrjø] **-rieuse** [rjøz] *adj* glorious; blessed; vain

glorifier [glɔrifje] *tr* to glorify ‖ *ref*— **se glorifier de** to glory in

gloriole [glɔrjɔl] *f* vainglory

glose [gloz] *f* gloss; (coll) gossip

gloser [gloze] *intr* (coll) to gossip

glossaire [glɔser] *m* glossary

glotte [glɔt] *f* glottis

glouglou [gluglu] *m* gurgle, glug; gobble-gobble; coo (*of dove*)

glouglouter [gluglute] *intr* to gurgle; to gobble (*said of turkey*)

glousser [gluse] *intr* to cluck; to chuckle

glou·ton [glutɔ̃] **-tonne** [tɔn] *adj* gluttonous ‖ *mf* glutton ‖ *m* (zool) glutton, wolverine

gloutonnerie [glutɔnri] *f* gluttony

glu [gly] *f* birdlime; (coll) trap

gluant [glyɑ̃] **gluante** [glyɑ̃t] *adj* sticky, gummy; (fig) tenacious

glucose [glykoz] *m* glucose

glycérine [gliserin] *f* glycerine

gnognote [ɲɔɲɔt] *f* (coll) junk

gnome [gnom] *m* gnome

gnomon [gnomɔ̃] *m* sundial

gnon [ɲɔ̃] *m* (slang) blow, punch

go [go]—**tout de go** (coll) straight off, at once

goal [gol] *m* goalkeeper

gobelet [gɔble] *m* cup, tumbler, mug; **gobelets utilisés** (public sign) used paper drinking cups

gobe-mouches [gɔbmuʃ] *m invar* (zool) flycatcher; (fig) sucker, gull

gober [gɔbe] *tr* to gulp down, to gobble; to suck (*an egg*); (coll) to swallow, to be a sucker for

goberger [gɔberʒe] §38 *ref* (coll) to guzzle; (coll) to live in comfort

gobeter [gɔbte] §34 *tr* to plaster, to fill in the cracks of

go·beur [gɔbœr] **-beuse** [bøz] *mf* (coll) sucker, gullible person

godet [gɔde] *m* cup; basin; bucket (*of water wheel*); (bot) calyx; **à godets** flared

godille [gɔdij] *f* scull, oar

godiller [gɔdije] *intr* to scull

godillot [gɔdijo] *m* (slang) clodhopper (*shoe*)

goéland [gɔelɑ̃] *m* sea gull

goélette [gɔelet] *f* (naut) schooner

goémon [gɔemɔ̃] *m* seaweed

gogo [gogo] *m* (coll) sucker, gull; **à gogo** (coll) galore

gogue·nard [gɔgnar] **-narde** [nard] *adj* jeering, mocking

goguenarder [gɔgnarde] *intr* to jeer

goguette [gɔget] *f*—**en goguette** (coll) tipsy

goinfre [gwɛ̃fr] *m* glutton, guzzler

goitre [gwatr] *m* goiter

golf [gɔlf] *m* golf

golfe [gɔlf] *m* gulf

gomme [gɔm] *f* gum; eraser; **gomme à mâcher** chewing gum; **gomme d'épinette** spruce gum; **gomme de sapin** balsam; **gomme élastique** India rubber; **mettre la gomme** (slang) to speed it up

gomme-laque [gɔmlak] *f* (*pl* **gommes-laques**) shellac

gommelaquer [gɔmlake] *tr* to shellac

gommer [gɔme] *tr* to gum; to erase ǁ *intr* to stick, to gum up

gond [gɔ̃] *m* hinge; **sortir de ses gonds** (coll) to fly off the handle

gondole [gɔ̃dɔl] *f* gondola

gondoler [gɔ̃dɔle] *intr & ref* to buckle up

gondolier [gɔ̃dɔlje] *m* gondolier

gonfalon [gɔ̃falɔ̃] *m* pennant

gonflement [gɔ̃fləmɑ̃] *m* swelling

gonfler [gɔ̃fle] *tr* to swell, inflate ǁ *intr* to swell up, puff up ǁ *ref* to become inflated; (coll) to swell up with pride

gonfleur [gɔ̃flœr] *m* tire pump

gong [gɔ̃g] *m* gong

goret [gɔre] *m* piglet; (coll) slob

gorge [gɔrʒ] *f* throat; bust, breasts (*of woman*); gorge; **à pleine gorge** or **à gorge déployée** at the top of one's voice; **avoir la gorge serrée** to have a lump in one's throat; **faire des gorges chaudes de** (coll) to scoff at; to gloat over; **rendre gorge** to make restitution

gorger [gɔrʒe] §38 *tr & ref* to gorge, stuff

gorille [gɔrij] *m* gorilla; (slang) strongarm man, bodyguard; (slang) bouncer (*in a night club*)

gosier [gozje] *m* throat, gullet; **à plein gosier** loudly, lustily; **gosier serré** with one's heart in one's mouth; **s'humecter** or **se rincer le gosier** (slang) to wet one's whistle

gosse [gɔs] *mf* (coll) kid, youngster

gothique [gɔtik] *adj* Gothic ǁ *m* Gothic (*language*); Gothic art ǁ *f* black letter, Old English

gouailler [gwaje] *tr* to jeer at ǁ *intr* to jeer

gouape [gwap] *f* (slang) hoodlum, blackguard

gouaper [gwape] *intr* (slang) to lead a disreputable life

goudron [gudrɔ̃] *m* tar

goudronner [gudrɔne] *tr* to tar

gouffre [gufr] *m* gulf, abyss; whirlpool

gouge [guʒ] *f* gouge; harlot

gouger [guʒe] §38 *tr* to gouge

goujat [guʒa] *m* boor, cad

goujon [guʒɔ̃] *m* gudgeon, pin; pintle (*of hinge*); dowel; (ichth) gudgeon; **taquiner le goujon** to go fishing

goulasch [gula∫] *m & f* goulash

goule [gul] *f* ghoul

goulet [gule] *m* narrows, sound; **goulet d'étranglement** bottleneck

goulot [gulo] *m* neck (*of bottle*); **boire au goulot** to drink right out of the bottle

gou·lu -lue [guly] *adj* gluttonous

goupil [gupi] *m* (obs) fox

goupille [gupij] *f* pin; **goupille fendue** cotter pin

goupiller [gupije] *tr* to cotter; (slang) to contrive, wangle

goupillon [gupijɔ̃] *m* bottle brush; sprinkler (*for holy water*); **goupillon nettoie-pipes** pipe cleaner

gourd [gur] **gourde** [gurd] *adj* numb (*with cold*) ǁ *adj fem* (coll) dumb ǁ

f gourd; canteen, metal flask; (coll) dumbbell

gourdin [gurdɛ̃] *m* cudgel

gourgandine [gurgɑ̃din] *f* (hist) low-necked bodice; (coll) trollop

gour·mand -mande [gurmɑ̃] -[mɑ̃d] *adj & mf* gourmand, gourmet

gourmander [gurmɑ̃de] *tr* to bawl out

gourmandise [gurmɑ̃diz] *f* gluttony; love of good food; **gourmandises** delicacies

gourme [gurm] *f* impetigo; **jeter sa gourme** (coll) to sow one's wild oats

gour·mé -mée [gurme] *adj* stiff, stuck-up

gourmet [gurme] *m* gourmet

gourmette [gurmet] *f* curb (*of harness*); curb watch chain

gousse [gus] *f* pod; clove (*of garlic*)

gousset [guse] *m* vest pocket; fob, watch pocket (*in trousers*)

goût [gu] *m* taste; flavor; sense of taste; **au goût du jour** up to date

goûter [gute] *m* afternoon snack ǁ *tr* to taste; to sample; to relish, enjoy ǁ *intr* to have a bite to eat; **goûter à** to sample, try; **goûter de** (coll) to try out (*e.g., a trade*)

goutte [gut] *f* drop, drip; (pathol) gout; **boire la goutte** (coll) to take a nip of brandy; **la goutte d'eau qui a fait déborder le vase** the straw which broke the camel's back; **ne ... goutte** §90 (used only with **comprendre, connaître, entendre,** and **voir**) (archaic & hum) not at all, e.g., **je n'y vois goutte** I don't see at all; **tomber goutte à goutte** to drip

goutte-à-goutte [gutagut] *m invar* (med) dropping bottle (*for intravenous drip*)

gouttelette [gutlet] *f* droplet

goutter [gute] *intr* to drip

gouttière [gutjer] *f* eavestrough, gutter; (med) splint

gouvernail [guvernaj] *m* rudder, helm; **gouvernail de profondeur** (aer) elevator

gouver·nant -nante [guvernɑ̃] -[nɑ̃t] *adj* governing ǁ **gouvernants** *mpl* powers that be, rulers ǁ *f* governess; housekeeper

gouverne [guvern] *f* guidance; **gouvernes** (aer) controls; **pour votre gouverne** for your guidance

gouvernement [guvernəmɑ̃] *m* government; **gouvernement fantoche** puppet government

gouvernemen·tal -tale [guvernəmɑ̃tal] *adj* (*pl* -**taux** [to]) governmental

gouverner [guverne] *tr* to govern, to control; to steer; to manage with care ǁ *intr* to govern; (naut) to answer to the helm

gouverneur [guvernœr] *m* governor; tutor; director (*e.g., of a bank*)

goyave [gɔjav] *f* guava

goyavier [gɔjavje] *m* guava tree

Graal [gral] *m* Grail

grabat [graba] *m* pallet, straw bed

grâce [gras] *f* grace; de **bonne grâce** willingly; **de grâce** for mercy's sake; **de mauvaise grâce** unwillingly; **faire**

grâce à to pardon; to spare; **faites-moi la grâce de** be kind enough to; **grâce!** mercy!; **grâce à** thanks to

gracier [grasje] *tr* to reprieve

gra·cieux [grasjø] **-cieuse** [sjøz] *adj* gracious; graceful

gracile [grasil] *adj* slender, slim

gradation [gradasjɔ̃] *f* gradation

grade [grad] *m* grade; rank; degree (*in school*); **en prendre pour son grade** (coll) to get called down

gra·dé -dée [grade] *adj* noncommissioned ‖ *mf* noncommissioned officer

gradient [gradjɑ̃] *m* gradient

gradin [gradɛ̃] *m* tier

graduation [graduɑsjɔ̃] *f* graduation

gra·dué -duée [gradɥe] *adj* graduated (*scale*); graded (*lessons*) ‖ *mf* graduate

gra·duel -duelle [gradɥɛl] *adj & m* gradual

graduer [gradɥe] *tr* to graduate

grailler [graje] *intr* to speak hoarsely; to sound the horn to recall the dogs

grain [grɛ̃] *m* grain; particle, speck; bean; squall; **grain de beauté** beauty spot, mole; **grain de raisin** grape; **grains** grain, cereals; **veiller au grain** (fig) to be on one's guard

graine [grɛn] *f* seed; **graine d'anis** aniseed; **mauvaise graine** (coll) shady character; **monter en graine** to run to seed; to soon be on the shelf (*said of young girl*); (coll) to grow; **prendre de la graine de** (coll) to follow the example of

graissage [grɛsaʒ] *m* (aut) lubrication

graisse [grɛs] *f* grease; fat; mother (*of wine*)

graisser [grɛse], [grese] *tr* to grease; to lubricate; to get grease stains on; **graisser la patte à qn** (coll) to grease s.o.'s palm

grais·seux [grɛsø] **grais·seuse** [grɛsøz] *adj* greasy

grammaire [gramɛr] *f* grammar

grammai·rien [gramɛrjɛ̃] **-rienne** [rjɛn] *mf* grammarian

grammati·cal -cale [gramatikal] *adj* (*pl* **-caux** [ko]) grammatical

gramme [gram] *m* gram

grand grande [grɑ̃d] *adj* tall ‖ (when standing before noun) *adj* large; great; important; high (*priest; mass; society; explosive*); vain, empty (*words*); broad (*daylight*); grand (*dignitary; officer; lady*); main (*road*); (fig) big (*heart*) ‖ *m* adult, grownup; grandee, noble; **en grand** life-size; on a grand scale; enlarged (*copy*); wide (*open*); **grands et petits** young and old ‖ **grand** *adv*—**voir grand** to see big, to envisage great projects

grand-chose [grɑ̃ʃoz] *mf invar*—**pas grand-chose** (coll) nobody, person of no importance ‖ *adv*—**pas grand-chose** not much

grand-duc [grɑ̃dyk] *m* (*pl* **grands-ducs**) grand duke

grand-duché [grɑ̃dyʃe] *m* (*pl* **grands-duchés**) grand duchy

Grande-Bretagne [grɑ̃dbrətaɲ] *f* Great Britain; **la Grande-Bretagne** Great Britain

grande-duchesse [grɑ̃dədyʃɛs] *f* (*pl* **grandes-duchesses**) grand duchess

grande-let [grɑ̃dlɛ] **-lette** [lɛt] *adj* tall for his or her age

grandement [grɑ̃dmɑ̃] *adv* highly; handsomely; **se tromper grandement** to be very mistaken

grand-erre [grɑ̃tɛr] *adv* at full speed

gran·det [grɑ̃dɛ] **-dette** [dɛt] *adj* rather big; rather tall

grandeur [grɑ̃dœr] *f* size; height; greatness; (astr) magnitude

grandiose [grɑ̃djoz] *adj* grandiose

grandir [grɑ̃dir] *tr* to enlarge; to increase ‖ *intr* to grow; to grow up

grandissement [grɑ̃dismɑ̃] *m* magnification, enlargement; growth

grand-livre [grɑ̃livr] *m* (*pl* **grands-livres**) ledger

grand-maman [grɑ̃mamɑ̃] *f* (*pl* **-mamans**) grandma

grand-mère [grɑ̃mɛr] *f* (*pl* **-mères** or **grands-mères**) grandmother; (coll) old lady

grand-messe [grɑ̃mɛs] *f* (*pl* **-messes**) high mass

grand-oncle [grɑ̃tɔ̃kl] *m* (*pl* **grands-oncles**) granduncle

Grand-Orient [grɑ̃tɔrjɑ̃] *m* grand lodge

grand-papa [grɑ̃papa] *m* (*pl* **grands-papas**) grandpa

grand-peine [grɑ̃pɛn]—**à grand-peine** with great difficulty

grand-père [grɑ̃pɛr] *m* (*pl* **grands-pères**) grandfather

grand-route [grɑ̃rut] *f* (*pl* **-routes**) highway

grand-rue [grɑ̃ry] *f* (*pl* **-rues**) main street

Grands Lacs [grɑ̃lak] *mpl* Great Lakes

grands-parents [grɑ̃parɑ̃] *mpl* grandparents

grand-tante [grɑ̃tɑ̃t] *f* (*pl* **-tantes**) grandaunt

grange [grɑ̃ʒ] *f* barn

granit [grani], [granit] *m* granite

granite [granit] *m* granite

granulaire [granylɛr] *adj* granular

granule [granyl] *m* granule

granu·lé -lée [granyle] *adj* granulated ‖ *m* little pill; medicine in granulated form

granuler [granyle] *tr & ref* to granulate

graphie [grafi] *f* spelling

graphique [grafik] *adj* graphic(al) ‖ *m* graph

graphite [grafit] *m* graphite

grappe [grap] *f* bunch, cluster; string (*of onions*); **une grappe humaine** a bunch of people

grappillage [grapijaʒ] *m* gleaning; (coll) graft

grappiller [grapije] *tr & intr* (in vineyard) to glean; (coll) to pilfer

grappillon [grapijɔ̃] *m* little bunch

grappin [grapɛ̃] *m* grapnel; **jeter or mettre le grappin sur qn** (coll) to get one's hooks into s.o.

gras grasse [grɑs] *adj* fat; greasy; rich (*soil*); carnival (*days*); smutty (*stories*); (typ) bold-faced ‖ *m* fatty part; calf (*of leg*); foggy weather; **au gras** with meat sauce; **faire gras** to eat meat ‖ **gras** *adv*—**parler gras** to speak with uvular r; to tell smutty stories

gras-double [gradubl] *m* (*pl* **-doubles**) tripe

grassement [grɑsmɑ̃] *adv* comfortably; generously

grasseyer [grɑseje] §32 *tr* to make (*one's r's*) uvular ‖ *intr* to speak with uvular r

grassouil·let [grɑsuje] **grassouil·lette** [grɑsujɛt] *adj* plump, chubby

gratification [gratifikɑsjɔ̃] *f* tip, gratuity

gratifier [gratifje] *tr* to favor, reward; **gratifier qn de q.ch.** to bestow s.th. upon s.o.

gratin [gratɛ̃] *m* (culin) crust; (coll) upper crust; **au gratin** breaded

gratiner [gratine] *tr* to cook au gratin ‖ *intr* to brown, to crisp

gratis [gratis] *adv* gratis

gratitude [gratityd] *f* gratitude

gratte [grat] *f* scraper; (coll) graft

gratte-ciel [gratsjɛl] *m invar* skyscraper

gratte-cul [gratky] *m invar* (bot) hip

gratte-dos [gratdo] *m invar* back scratcher

gratte-papier [gratpapje] *m invar* (coll) pencil pusher, office drudge

gratte-pieds [gratpje] *m invar* shoescraper

gratter [grate] *tr* to scratch; to scratch out; to scrape up, scrape together; to itch; (coll) to pocket ‖ *intr* to knock gently ‖ *ref* to scratch; (with *dat of reflex pron*) to scratch (*e.g., one's arm*)

grattoir [gratwar] *m* scraper; knife eraser

gra·tuit [gratɥi] **-tuite** [tɥit] *adj* free of charge; gratuitous; unfounded

gratuité [gratɥite] *f* gratuity

grave [grav], [grɑv] *adj* grave; low (*frequency*) ‖ (mus) bass; (mus) flat

grave·leux [gravlø] **-leuse** [løz] *adj* gravelly, gritty; smutty, licentious

gravelle [gravɛl] *f* (pathol) gravel

graver [grave] *tr* to engrave; to cut (*a phonograph record*)

graveur [gravœr] *m* engraver; etcher

gravier [gravje] *m* gravel

gravir [gravir] *tr* to climb, climb up

gravitation [gravitɑsjɔ̃] *f* gravitation

gravité [gravite] *f* gravity

graviter [gravite] *intr* to gravitate

gravure [gravyr] *f* engraving; etching; cutting (*of phonograph record*)

gré [gre] *m* will; **à son gré** to one's liking; **bon gré mal gré** willy-nilly; **de bon gré** willingly; **de gré à gré** by mutual consent; **de gré ou de force** willy-nilly; **savoir (bon) gré de** to be grateful for; **savoir mauvais gré de** to be displeased with

grec grecque [grek] *adj* Greek; classic (*profile*) ‖ *m* Greek (*language*) ‖ *f* Greek fret ‖ (*cap*) *mf* Greek

Grèce [gres] *f* Greece; **la Grèce** Greece

gre·din [grədɛ̃] **-dine** [din] *mf* scoundrel

gréement [gremɑ̃] *m* (naut) rigging

gréer [gree] *tr* (naut) to rig

greffe [gref] *m* (jur) office of the court clerk ‖ *f* grafting; (hort, med) graft; **greffe du cœur** heart transplant

greffer [grefe] *tr* to graft; to add ‖ *ref* to be added

greffier [grefje] *m* clerk of court, recorder; court reporter

greffon [grefɔ̃] *m* (hort) graft; (surg) transplant

grégaire [greger] *adj* gregarious

grège [grɛʒ] *adj* raw (*silk*) ‖ *f* raw silk

grégo·rien [gregorjɛ̃] **-rienne** [rjɛn] *adj* Gregorian

grêle [grɛl] *adj* slender, slim; thin, high-pitched ‖ *f* hail; (fig) shower

grê·lé -lée [grele] *adj* pockmarked

grêler [grele] *tr* to damage by hail; to pockmark ‖ *intr* (fig) to rain down thick; **il grêle** it is hailing

grêlon [grelɔ̃] *m* hailstone

grelot [grəlo] *m* sleigh bell

grelottement [grəlɔtmɑ̃] *m* shivering, trembling; jingle, jingling

grelotter [grəlɔte] *intr* to shiver, tremble; to jingle

grenade [grənad] *f* grenade; (bot) pomegranate; **grenade à main** hand grenade; **grenade éclairante** flare; **grenade lacrymogène** tear bomb; **grenade sous-marine** depth charge

grenadier [grənadje] *m* pomegranate tree; (mil) grenadier

grenadine [grənadin] *f* grenadine

grenaille [grənaj] *f* shot; **grenaille de plomb** buckshot

grenailler [grənaje] *tr* to granulate

grenat [grəna] *adj invar* & *m* garnet

grenier [grənje] *m* attic, loft; granary

grenouille [grənuj] *f* frog; **grenouille mugissante** or **taureau** bullfrog; **manger la grenouille** (coll) to make off with the money, to abscond

grenouillère [grənujer] *f* marsh

gre·nu -nue [grəny] *adj* full of grain; grainy (*leather*); granular (*marble*) ‖ *m* graininess; granularity

grès [gre] *m* gritstone, sandstone; stoneware; terra cotta (*for drainpipes*)

grésil [grezil] *m* sleet

grésillement [grezijmɑ̃] *m* sizzling; chirping (*of cricket*)

grésiller [grezije] *tr* to scorch, to shrivel up ‖ *intr* to sizzle, to sputter; **il grésille** it is sleeting

grève [grev] *f* beach; strike; (armor) greave; **faire (la) grève** to strike; **faire la grève de la faim** to go on a hunger strike; **grève de solidarité** sympathy strike; **grève du zèle** slowdown (*caused by rigid application of rules*); **grève improvisée**, **grève inattendue**, **grève surprise** walkout; **grève perlée** slowdown; **grève sauvage**, **grève spontanée** wildcat strike; **grève sur le tas** sitdown strike; **grève tournante** strike in one industry at a time or for several hours at a time; **se met-tre en grève** to go on strike

grever [grəve] §2 *tr* to burden; to assess (*property*); **grever de** to burden with

gréviste [grevist] *mf* striker

gribouillage [gribuja3] *m* (coll) scribble, scrawl; (coll) daub (*in painting*)

gribouiller [gribuje] *tr* (coll) to scribble off (*a note*) || *intr* (coll) to scribble, scrawl; (coll) to daub

grief [grijef] *m* grievance, complaint; **faire grief de q.ch. à qn** to complain to s.o. about s.th.

grièvement [grijɛvmɑ̃] *adv* seriously, badly

griffe [grif] *f* claw, talon; signature stamp; (bot) tendril; (mach) hook, grip; **faire ses griffes** to sharpen its claws (*said of cat*); **griffe à papiers** paper clip; **porter la griffe de** to carry the stamp of; **tomber sous la griffe de** (coll) to fall into the clutches of

griffer [grife] *tr* to claw, scratch

griffon [grifɔ̃] *m* griffin

griffonner [grifone] *tr* to scrawl; (coll) to scribble off (*a letter*)

grignoter [griɲɔte] *tr* to nibble on or at; to wear down (*e.g., the enemy*) || *intr* (coll) to make a little profit, to get a cut

gril [gril] *m* gridiron, grid, grill; (theat) upper flies; **être sur le gril** (coll) to be on tenterhooks

grillade [grijad] *f* grilled meat; broiling

grillage [grija3] *m* grating, latticework, trellis; broiling; roasting; toasting; burning out (*of a light bulb*); (tex) singeing

grille [grij] *f* grille; grating, bars; railing; gate; squares (*of crossword puzzle*); grid (*of storage battery and vacuum tube*); **grille des salaires** salary schedule

grille-pain [grijpɛ̃] *m invar* toaster

griller [grije] *tr* to grill, broil; to put a grill on; to roast (*coffee*); to toast (*bread*); to burn out (*a fuse, lamp, electric iron, etc.*); to singe, scorch; to nip (*a bud, as the frost does*) || *intr* to grill; to toast; to burn out; **griller de** to long to

grilloir [grijwar] *m* roaster; (culin) broiler

grillon [grijɔ̃] *m* cricket

grimace [grimas] *f* grimace; **faire des grimaces** to make faces; to smirk, simper; to be full of wrinkles

grimacer [grimase] §51 *intr* to grimace; to make wrong creases

grime [grim] *m* dotard, old fogey

grimer [grime] *tr* to make up (*an actor*) || *ref* to make up

grimper [grɛ̃pe] *tr* to climb || *intr* to climb; **grimper à or sur** to climb up on

grimpe·reau [grɛ̃pro] *m* (*pl* -reaux) (orn) tree creeper

grim·peur [grɛ̃pœr] -peuse [pøz] *adj* climbing || *m* climber

grincement [grɛ̃smɑ̃] *m* grating

grincer [grɛ̃se] §51 *tr* to gnash, grit (*the teeth*) || *intr* to grate, grind, creak; to scratch (*said of pen*)

grin·cheux [grɛ̃/ø] -cheuse [/øz] *adj* grumpy || *mf* grumbler, sorehead

gringa·let [grɛ̃galɛ] -lette [lɛt] *adj* weak, puny || *m* (coll) weakling, shrimp

griot [grijo] **griotte** [grijɔt] *mf* witch doctor || *m* seconds (*in milling grain*) || *f* sour cherry

grippe [grip] *f* grippe; **prendre en grippe** to take a dislike to

grippeminaud [gripmino] *m* (coll) smoothy, hypocrite

gripper [gripe] *tr* to snatch; (slang) to steal || *intr* (mach) to jam || *ref* to get stuck

grippe-sou [gripsu] *m* (*pl* -sou or -sous) (coll) tightwad, skinflint

gris [gri] **grise** [griz] *adj* gray; cloudy; brown (*paper*); (coll) tipsy

grisailler [grizaje] *tr* to paint gray || *intr* to turn gray

grisâtre [grizatr] *adj* grayish

griser [grize] *tr* to paint gray; (coll) to intoxicate; **les succès l'ont grisé** (coll) success has gone to his head || *ref* to get tipsy; **se griser de** (coll) to revel in

griserie [grizri] *f* intoxication

grisette [grizet] *f* gay working girl

gris-gris [grigri] *m* lucky charm

grisonner [grizone] *intr* to turn gray

grisotte [grizot] *f* clock (*in stocking*)

grisou [grizu] *m* firedamp

grive [griv] *f* thrush; **grive mauvis** song thrush; **grive migratoire** (*Turdus migratorius*) robin

grive·lé -lée [grivle] *adj* speckled

grivèlerie [grivelri] *f* sneaking out without paying the check

gri·vois [grivwa] -voise [vwaz] *adj* spicy, off-color

grizzly [grizli] *m* grizzly bear

Groënland [grɔenlɑ̃d] *m*—**le Groënland** Greenland

grog [grɔg] *m* grog

gro·gnard [grɔɲar] -gnarde [ɲard] *adj* grumbling || *mf* grumbler

grogner [grɔɲe] *intr* to grunt, to growl; to grumble, to grouch

gro·gnon [grɔɲɔ̃] -gnonne [ɲɔn] *adj* grouchy, grumbling || *mf* grouch, grumbler

grognonner [grɔɲɔne] *intr* to grunt; to be a complainer, to whine

groin [grwɛ̃] *m* snout; (coll) ugly mug

grommeler [grɔmle] §34 *tr* & *intr* to mutter, grumble; to growl

grondement [grɔ̃dmɑ̃] *m* growl; rumble

gronder [grɔ̃de] *tr* to scold || *intr* to scold; to growl; to grumble

gron·deur [grɔ̃dœr] -deuse [døz] *adj* scolding; grumbling || *mf* grumbler

groom [grum] *m* bellhop, pageboy

gros [gro] **grosse** [gros] *adj* big (*with child*); heavy (*heart*); (when standing before noun) *adj* big, large, bulky; course; plain (*common sense*); main (*walls*); high (*stakes*); rich (*merchant*); booming (*voice*); bad (*weather*); heavy, rough (*sea*); swear (*words*) || *m* bulk, main part; **en gros**

wholesale; roughly, without going into detail; **faire le gros et le détail** to
deal in wholesale and retail || *f* see
grosse || **gros** *adv* much, a great deal;
(fig) probably

gros-bec [grobɛk] *m* (*pl* **-becs**) grosbeak

groseille [grozej] *f* currant; **groseille à
maquereau** gooseberry

groseillier [grozeje] *m* currant bush

Gros-Jean [groʒã] *m*—**être Gros-Jean
comme devant** to be in the same fix
again

grosse [gros] *f* fat woman; (com)
gross; (law) engrossed copy

grosserie [grosri] *f* silver dishes

grossesse [groses] *f* pregnancy

grosseur [grosœr] *f* size; swelling, tumor

gros-sier [grosje] **gros-sière** [grosjer]
adj coarse; crude, rude; vulgar, ribald; glaring (*error*)

grossièrement [grosjɛrmã] *adv* grossly

grossièreté [grosjerte] *f* coarseness,
grossness, vulgarity

grossir [grosir] *tr* to enlarge; to in-
crease || *intr* to grow larger; to put
on weight

grossis-sant [grosisã] **grossis-sante**
[grosisãt] *adj* swelling; magnifying
(*glasses*)

grossiste [grosist] *m* wholesaler, jobber

grotesque [grotesk] *adj* grotesque || *mf*
grotesque person || *m* grotesque || *f*
grotesque (*ornament*)

grotte [grot] *f* grotto

grouillement [grujmã] *m* swarming;
rumbling

grouiller [gruje] *intr* to swarm; **grouil-
ler de** to teem with || *ref* (slang) to
get a move on

groupe [grup] *m* group; (mach & mil)
unit; **groupe franc** (mil) commando;
groupe sanguin blood type

groupement [grupmã] *m* grouping;
organization

grouper [grupe] *tr & ref* to group

gruau [gryo] *m* (*pl* **gruaux**) groats;
(culin) gruel; (orn) small crane

grue [gry] *f* crane; (orn) crane; (coll)
tart

gruger [gryʒe] §38 *tr* to sponge on,
exploit; to crunch

grume [grym] *f* bark; **en grume** rough
(*timber*)

gru-meau [grymo] *m* (*pl* **-meaux**) gob;
curd

grumeler [grymle] §34 *intr* to curdle,
clot

gruyère [gryjer] *m* Gruyère cheese

guatémaltèque [gwatemaltɛk] *adj* Gua-
temalan || (*cap*) *mf* Guatemalan

gué [ge] *m* ford, crossing; **sonder le
gué** (coll) to see how the land lies
|| *interj* hurrah!

guéable [geabl] *adj* fordable

guéer [gee] *tr* to ford; to water (*a
horse*)

guelte [gɛlt] *f* commission, percentage

guenille [gənij] *f* ragged garment; **en
guenilles** in tatters

guenon [gənõ] *f* female monkey; long-
tailed monkey; (coll) hag, old bag

guépard [gepar] *m* cheetah

guêpe [gɛp] *f* wasp

guère [ger] §90 *adv* hardly ever; **ne . . .
guère** hardly, scarcely; hardly ever;
not very; **ne . . . guère de** hardly any;
ne . . . guère que hardly any but;
hardly anyone but; **ne . . . plus guère**
hardly ever any more; not much
longer

guères [ger] *adv* (poetic) var of **guère**

guéret [gere] *m* fallow land

guéridon [geridõ] *m* pedestal table

guérilla [gerija] *f* guerrilla warfare

guérillero [gerijero] *m* guerrilla

guérir [gerir] *tr* to cure || *intr* to get
well; to get better; to heal || *ref* to
cure oneself; to recover

guérison [gerizõ] *f* cure, healing; recovery

guérissable [gerisabl] *adj* curable

guéris-seur [gerisœr] **guéris-seuse** [ge-
risøz] *mf* healer; quack

guérite [gerit] *f* sentry box; (rr) signal
box; **guérite téléphonique** call box

guerre [ger] *f* war; **de guerre lasse** for
the sake of peace and quiet; **être de
bonne guerre** to be fair, to be cricket;
guerre à outrance all-out war;
Guerre de Troie Trojan War; **guerre
d'usure** war of attrition; **guerre éclair**
blitzkrieg; **guerre froide** cold war;
guerre presse-bouton push-button
war

guer-rier [gerje] **guer-rière** [gerjer] *adj*
warlike, martial || *m* warrior || *f*
amazon

guerroyant [gerwajã] **guerroyante** [ger-
wajãt] *adj* warlike, bellicose

guerroyer [gerwaje] §47 *intr* to make
war

guerroyeur [gerwajœr] **guerroyeuse**
[gerwajøz] *adj* fighting (*spirit*) || *mf*
fighter

guet [ge] *m* watch, lookout

guet-apens [getapã] *m* (*pl* **guets-apens**
[getapã]) ambush, trap

guêtre [getr] *f* gaiter, legging

guêtrer [getre] *tr & ref* to put gaiters
on

guetter [gete] *tr* to watch; to watch
for; (coll) to lie in wait for

guetteur [getœr] *m* lookout, sentinel

gueu-lard [gœlar] **-larde** [lard] *adj*
(slang) loud-mouthed; (slang) fond
of good eating || *mf* gourmet; (slang)
loud-mouth || *m* mouth (*of blast fur-
nace; of cannon*); (naut) megaphone

gueule [gœl] *f* mouth (*of animal; of
furnace, cannon, etc.*); (slang) mouth,
mug (*of person*); **avoir de la gueule**
(coll) to have a certain air; **avoir la
gueule de bois** (coll) to have a hangover; **fine gueule** (coll) gourmet;
gueule cassée (coll) disabled veteran;
gueule noire (coll) miner; **ta gueule!**
(slang) shut up!

gueule-de-loup [gœldəlu] *f* (*pl* **gueules-
de-loup**) (bot) snapdragon

gueuler [gœle] *tr & intr* (slang) to bellow

gueuleton [gœltõ] *m* (slang) big feed

gueux [gø] **gueuse** [gøz] *adj* beggarly,
wretched || *mf* beggar; scamp || *f*

pig iron; pig (mold); woolen jacket; (coll) whore; **courir la gueuse** (coll) to go whoring

gugusse [gygys] m clown

gui [gi] m mistletoe; (naut) boom

guichet [giʃe] m window (in post office, bank, box office, etc.); counter (e.g., in bank); wicket

guidage [gidaʒ] m (rok) guidance

guide [gid] m guide; guidebook ‖ f rein; **mener la vie à grandes guides** to live extravagantly

guide-âne [gidɑn] m (pl -âne or -ânes) manual, guide

guider [gide] tr to guide

guidon [gidɔ̃] m handlebars; sight, bead (of gun); (naut) pennant

guigne [giɲ] f heart cherry; (coll) jinx

guigner [giɲe] tr to steal a glance at; (coll) to covet ‖ intr to peep

guignol [giɲɔl] m Punch (puppet); Punch and Judy show; (aer) king post

guignolet [giɲɔle] m cherry brandy

guillaume [gijom] m rabbet plane; **Guillaume** William

guilledou [gijdu] m—**courir le guilledou** (coll) to make the rounds

guillemet [gijme] m quotation mark; **fermer les guillemets** to close quotes; **ouvrir les guillemets** to quote

guillemeter [gijmøte] §34 tr to put in quotes

guiller [gije] intr to ferment

guille·ret [gijre] -**rette** [ret] adj chipper, lively, gay

guillotine [gijɔtin] f guillotine; à guillotine sliding; sash (window)

guillotiner [gijɔtine] tr to guillotine

guimauve [gimov] f (bot) marshmallow

guimbarde [gɛ̃bard] f (mus) jew's-harp; (coll) jalopy

guimpe [gɛ̃p] f wimple

guin·dé -dée [gɛ̃de] adj affected, stiff

guin·deau [gɛ̃do] m (pl -deaux) windlass

guinder [gɛ̃de] tr to hoist ‖ ref to put on airs

guinée [gine] f guinea (coin); **Guinée** Guinea; **la Guinée** Guinea

guingan [gɛ̃gɑ̃] m gingham

guingois [gɛ̃gwa] m—**de guingois** askew; lopsidedly

guinguette [gɛ̃get] f roadside inn, roadside park

guipage [gipaʒ] m wrapping, lapping

guiper [gipe] tr to wind; to cover (a wire)

guipure [gipyr] f pillow lace

guirlande [girlɑ̃d] f garland, wreath

guirlander [girlɑ̃de] tr to garland

guise [giz] f manner; à sa guise as one pleases; **en guise de** by way of

guitare [gitar] f guitar

guitariste [gitarist] mf guitarist

guppy [gypi] m guppy

gustation [gystasjɔ̃] f tasting; drinking

guttu·ral -rale [gytyral] (pl -raux [ro] -rales) adj & f guttural

Guyane [gɥijan] f Guiana; **la Guyane** Guiana

gymnase [ʒimnɑz] m gymnasium

gymnaste [ʒimnast] mf gymnast

gymnote [ʒimnɔt] m electric eel

gynécologie [ʒinekɔlɔʒi] f gynecology

gypse [ʒips] m gypsum

gyrocompas [ʒirokɔ̃pa] m gyrocompass

gyroscope [ʒirɔskɔp] m gyroscope

H

H, h [aʃ], *[aʃ] m invar eighth letter of the French alphabet

habile [abil] adj skillful; clever

habileté [abilte] f skill; cleverness

habiliter [abilite] tr to qualify, entitle

habillement [abijmɑ̃] m clothing; clothes

habiller [abije] tr to dress; to clothe; to put together ‖ intr to be becoming, e.g., **robe qui habille bien** becoming dress ‖ ref to dress; to get dressed; **s'habiller chez** to buy one's clothes at or from

habit [abi] m dress suit; habit, frock; **habit de cérémonie** or **soirée, habit à queue de pie, habit à queue de morue** tails; **habits** clothes

habitacle [abitakl] m (aer) cockpit; (naut) binnacle; (poetic) dwelling

habi·tant [abitɑ̃] -**tante** [tɑ̃t] mf inhabitant

habitat [abita] m habitat; living conditions, housing

habitation [abitasjɔ̃] f habitation;

dwelling; residence; **habitation à bon marché** or **à loyer modéré** low-rent apartment

habi·té -tée [abite] adj inhabited; (rok) manned

habiter [abite] tr to live in, to inhabit ‖ intr to live, reside

habitude [abityd] f habit, custom; **comme d'habitude** as usual; **d'habitude** usually

habi·tuel -tuelle [abitɥel] adj habitual

habituer [abitɥe] tr to accustom

hâbler *[able] intr to brag, to boast

hâblerie *[abləri] f bragging

hâ·bleur *[ablœr] -**bleuse** [bløz] adj boastful ‖ mf braggart, boaster

hache *[aʃ] f ax, hatchet

ha·ché -chée *[aʃe] adj ground, chopped; hachured; choppy (sea); jerky (style); dotted (line)

hacher *[aʃe] tr to hack; to grind, chop up; **hacher menu** to mince

hache·reau *[aʃro] m (pl -reaux) hatchet

hachette * [aʃɛt] f hatchet
hachis * [aʃi] m hash, forcemeat
hachisch * [aʃiʃ] m hashish
hachoir * [aʃwar] m cleaver; chopping board
hachure * [aʃyr] f shading
hachurer * [aʃyre] tr to shade, hatch
haddock * [adɔk] m finnan haddie
ha·gard * [agar] -garde [gard] adj haggard
haie * [e] f hedge; hurdle; line, row
haie * [aj] interj giddap!
haillon * [ajɔ̃] m old piece of clothing; en haillons in rags and tatters
haillon·neux * [ajɔnø] haillon·neuse * [ajɔnøz] adj ragged, tattered
haine * [en] f hate
hai·neux * [enø] -neuse [nøz] adj full of hate, spiteful, malevolent
hair * [air] §33 tr to hate, to detest || intr—hair de to hate to
haire * [ɛr] f hair shirt
haïssable * [aisabl] adj hateful
Haïti [aiti] f Haiti
haï·tien [aisjɛ̃] -tienne [sjɛn] adj Haitian || (cap) mf Haitian
halcyon [alsjɔ̃] m (orn) kingfisher
hâle * [ɑl] m sun tan
haleine [alɛn] f breath; avoir l'haleine courte to be short-winded; (fig) to have little inspiration; de longue haleine hard, arduous (work); en haleine in good form; hors d'haleine out of breath; perdre haleine to get out of breath; reprendre haleine to catch one's breath; tenir en haleine to hold (e.g., an audience) breathless
halenée [alne] f whiff; strong breath
haler * [ale] tr to haul, to tow
hâler * [ale] tr to tan
hale·tant * [altɑ̃] -tante [tɑ̃t] adj breathless, panting
haleter * [alte] §2 intr to pant, puff
hall * [ol] m lobby; hall, auditorium
halle * [al] f market, marketplace; exchange
hallebarde * [albard] f halberd; il pleut des hallebardes (coll) it's raining cats and dogs
hallier * [alje] m thicket
hallucination * [allysinɑsjɔ̃] f hallucination
halo * [alo] m halo
halogène [alɔʒɛn] m halogen
halte * [alt] f halt; stop; (rr) flag stop, way station; faire faire halte à to halt || interj halt!
halte-là * [altla] interj (mil) halt!
haltère * [altɛr] m dumbbell
haltérophile [alterɔfil] m weight lifter
haltérophilie [alterɔfili] f weight lifting
hamac * [amak] m hammock
ha·meau * [amo] m (pl -meaux) hamlet
hameçon [amsɔ̃] m hook, fishhook; (fig) bait
hammam * [ammam] m Turkish bath
hampe * [ɑ̃p] f staff, pole; shaft; downstroke; (culin) flank
hamster * [amster] m hamster
han * [ɑ̃], [hɑ̃] m grunt
hanap * [anap] m hanap, goblet
hanche * [ɑ̃ʃ] f hip; haunch

hancher * [ɑ̃ʃe] intr to lean on one leg || ref (mil) to stand at ease
handball * [ɑ̃bol] m handball
handicap * [ɑ̃dikap] m handicap
handicaper * [ɑ̃dikape] tr to handicap
hangar * [ɑ̃gar] m hangar; shed
hanneton * [antɔ̃] m June bug, chafer
hanter * [ɑ̃te] tr to haunt
hantise * [ɑ̃tiz] f obsession
happe * [ap] f crucible tongs; (carp) cramp, staple
happer * [ape] tr to snap up; (coll) to nab || intr to stick
haquenée * [akne] f palfrey
haquet * [ake] m dray; haquet à main pushcart
harangue * [arɑ̃g] f harangue
haranguer * [arɑ̃ge] tr & intr to harangue
haras * [arɑ] m stud farm
harasser * [arase] tr to tire out
harceler * [arsəle] §2 or §34 tr to harass, to harry; to pester; to dun
harde * [ard] f herd; leash; set (of dogs); hardes old clothes
har·di -die * [ardi] adj bold || hardi interj up and at them!
hardiesse * [ardjes] f boldness
harem * [arem] m harem
hareng * [arɑ̃] m herring; hareng fumé kipper; hareng saur red herring; sec comme un hareng (coll) long and thin; serrés comme des harengs (coll) packed like sardines
harengère * [arɑ̃ʒer] f fishwife; (coll) shrew
harenguet * [arɑ̃ge] m sprat
hargne * [arɲ] f bad temper
har·gneux * [arɲø] -gneuse [ɲøz] adj bad-tempered, peevish, surly
haricot * [ariko] m bean; haricot beurre lima bean, butter bean; haricot de Lima lima bean; haricot de mouton haricot (stew); haricot de Soissons kidney bean; haricot vert string bean
harmonica [armɔnika] m mouth organ
harmonie [armɔni] f harmony; (mus) band
harmo·nieux [armɔnjø] -nieuse [njøz] adj harmonious
harmonique [armɔnik] adj harmonic
harmoniser [armɔnize] tr & ref to harmonize
harnachement * [arnaʃmɑ̃] m harness; harnessing
harnacher * [arnaʃe] tr to harness; to rig out
harnais * [arne] m harness
haro * [aro] m—crier haro sur (coll) to make a hue and cry against
harpagon [arpagɔ̃] m scrooge
harpe * [arp] f harp
harpie * [arpi] f harpy
harpiste * [arpist] mf harpist
harpon * [arpɔ̃] m harpoon
harponner * [arpɔne] tr to harpoon; (coll) to nab (e.g., a thief)
hart * [ar] f noose
hasard * [azar] m hazard, chance; à tout hasard just in case, come what may; au hasard at random; par hasard by chance

hasar·dé -dée *[azarde] adj hazardous
hasar·deux *[azardø] -deuse [døz] adj risky, uncertain
hase *[az] f doe hare
hâte *[ɑt] f haste; à la hâte hastily; avoir hâte de to be eager to; en hâte, en toute hâte posthaste
hâter *[ɑte] tr & ref to hasten
hâ·tif *[ɑtif] -tive [tiv] adj premature; (hort) early
hauban *[obã] m (naut) shroud; (naut) guy
haubert *[ober] m coat of mail
hausse *[os] f rise, increase; block, wedge, prop; (mil) elevation, range; jouer à la hausse to bull the market
haussement *[osmã] m shrug
hausser *[ose] tr to raise, to lift; to shrug (one's shoulders) || intr to rise
haussier *[osje] m bull (on the stock exchange)
haussière *[osjer] f (naut) hawser
haut *[o] haute *[ot] adj high; loud; high and mighty || (when standing before noun) adj high; loud; upper, higher; extra (pay); early (antiquity, Middle Ages, etc.) || m top; height; de haut en bas from top to bottom; en haut up; upstairs; haut de casse (typ) upper case; haut des côtes sparerib; le prendre de haut to get on one's high horse; traiter de haut en bas to high-hat || f see haute || haut adv high; up high; loudly; haut les bras! start working!; haut les cœurs! lift up your hearts!; haut les mains! hands up!
hau·tain *[otɛ̃] -taine [tɛn] adj haughty
hautbois *[obwa] m oboe
haut-de-chausses *[odəʃos] m (pl hauts-de-chausses) trunk hose, breeches
haut-de-forme *[odəfɔrm] m (pl hauts-de-forme) top hat
haute *[ot] f high society
hautement *[otmã] adv loudly; openly, clearly; highly (qualified); proudly
hauteur *[otœr] f height; hill, upland; altitude; nobility; haughtiness; (phys) pitch (of sound); à la hauteur de equal to, up to; (naut) off
haut-fond *[ofɔ̃] m (pl hauts-fonds) shoal, shallows
haut-le-cœur *[oləkœr] m invar nausea
haut-le-corps *[oləkɔr] m invar jump, sudden start
haut-parleur *[oparlœr] m (pl haut-parleurs) loudspeaker
hautu·rier *[otyrje] -rière [rjer] adj deep-sea
havage *[avaʒ] m (min) cutting
havane *[avan] adj invar tan, brown || m Havana cigar || (cap) f—La Havane Havana
hâve *[ɑv] adj haggard, peaked
havir *[avir] tr (culin) to sear
havre *[ɑvr] m haven, harbor
havresac *[ɑvrəsak] m haversack, knapsack; tool bag
hawaïen or hawaiien [awajɛ̃], [avajɛ̃] hawaïenne or hawaiienne [awajɛn],

[avajɛn] adj Hawaiian || (cap) mf Hawaiian
Haye *[ɛ] f—La Haye The Hague
H.B.M. [aʃbeem] f (letterword) (habitation à bon marché) low-rent apartment
he *[e], [he] interj hey!
heaume *[om] m helmet
hebdomadaire [ɛbdɔmader] adj & m weekly
héberger [eberʒe] §38 tr to lodge
hébé·té -tée [ebete] adj dazed
hébéter [ebete] §10 tr to daze, stupefy
hébraïque [ebraik] adj Hebrew
hébraï·sant [ebraizɑ̃] -sante [zɑ̃t] mf Hebraist
hébraïser [ebraize] tr & intr to Hebraize
hé·breu [ebrø] (pl -breux) adj masc Hebrew || m Hebrew (language); c'est de l'hébreu pour moi it's Greek to me || (cap) m Hebrew (man)
hécatombe [ekatɔ̃b] f hecatomb
hein *[ɛ̃] interj (coll) eh!, what!
hélas [elɑs] interj alas!
Hélène [elen] f Helen
héler *[ele] §10 tr to hail, to call
hélice [elis] f (aer) propeller; (math) helix, spiral; (naut) screw
hélicoptère [elikɔpter] m helicopter
héliport [elipɔr] m heliport
hélium [eljɔm] m helium
hélix [eliks] m helix
hellène [elɛn] adj Hellenic || (cap) mf Hellene
helvétique [elvetik] adj Swiss
hématie [emati] f red blood corpuscle
hémisphere [emisfer] m hemisphere
hémistiche [emisti] m hemistich
hémoglobine [emoɡlobin] f hemoglobin
hémophilie [emofili] f hemophilia
hémorragie [emoraʒi] f hemorrhage
hémorroïdes [emoroid] fpl hemorrhoids
hémostatique [emostatik] adj hemostatic || m hemostatic, hemostat
henné [enne] m henna
hennir *[enir] intr to neigh, whinny
hennissement *[enismã] m neigh, whinny
Henri [ɑ̃ri], *[ɑ̃ri] m Henry
héraldique [eraldik] adj heraldic
héraut *[ero] m herald
herbe [erb] f grass; lawn; herb; couper l'herbe sous le pied de qn (coll) to pull the rug from under s.o.'s feet; en herbe unripe; budding; fines herbes herbs for seasoning; herbe à la puce (Canad) poison ivy; herbe aux chats catnip; herbes médicinales or officinales (pharm) herbs; herbes potagères potherbs; mauvaise herbe weed
her·beux [erbø] -beuse [bøz] adj grassy
herboristerie [erbɔristri] f herb shop
her·bu -bue [erby] adj grassy
herculéen [erkyleɛ̃] herculéenne [erkyleen] adj herculean
hère *[er] m wretch
héréditaire [erediter] adj hereditary
hérédité [eredite] f heredity
hérésie [erezi] f heresy
hérétique [eretik] adj & mf heretic

héris·sé héris·sée *[erise] *adj* bristly; shaggy; prickly; surly
hérisser *[erise] *tr & intr* to bristle
hérisson *[erisɔ̃] *m* hedgehog
héritage [eritaʒ] *m* heritage; inheritance
hériter [erite] *tr* to inherit || *intr* to inherit; **hériter de** to become the heir of; to inherit, to come into
héri·tier [eritje] **-tière** [tjɛr] *mf* heir || *f* heiress
hermétique [ermetik] *adj* hermetic(al), airtight; (fig) obscure
hermine [ermin] *f* ermine
herminette [erminet] *f* adze
hernie [erni] *f* hernia
her·nieux *[ernjø] **-nieuse** [njøz] *adj* ruptured
héroïne [erɔin] *f* heroine; (*drug*) heroin
héroïque [erɔik] *adj* heroic
héroïsme [erɔism] *m* heroism
héron *[erɔ̃] *m* heron
héros *[ero] *m* hero
herse *[ers] *f* harrow; portcullis; **les herses** (theat) stage lights
herser *[erse] *tr* to harrow
hési·tant [ezitɑ̃] **-tante** [tɑ̃t] *adj* hesitant
hésitation [ezitasjɔ̃] *f* hesitation
hésiter [ezite] *intr* to hesitate
hétéroclite [eterɔklit] *adj* unusual, odd
hétérodoxe [eterɔdɔks] *adj* heterodox
hétérodyne [eterɔdin] *adj* heterodyne
hétérogène [eterɔʒen] *adj* heterogeneous
hêtre *[etr] *m* beech, beech tree
heur *[œr] *m* pleasure; **heur et malheur** joys and sorrows
heure [œr] *f* hour; time (*of day*); o'clock; **à la bonne heure!** fine!; **à l'heure on time;** by the hour, per hour; **à l'heure juste, à l'heure sonnante on the hour; à tout à l'heure!** see you later!; **à toute heure** at any time; **de bonne heure** early; **heure d'été** daylight-saving time; **heure H** zero hour; **heure légale** twelve-month daylight time (standard time); **heure militaire** sharp, e.g., **huit heures, heure militaire** eight hours sharp; **heures d'affluence** rush hours; **heures de consultation** office hours; **heures de pointe** rush hours; **heures d'ouverture** business hours; **heures supplémentaires** overtime; **l'heure du déjeuner** lunch hour; **tout à l'heure** in a little while; a little while ago
heu·reux *[œrø], [ørø] **-reuse** [røz] *adj* happy, pleased; lucky, fortunate
heurt *[œr] *m* knock, bump; clash; bruise; **sans heurt** without a hitch
heur·té -tée *[œrte] *adj* clashing (*colors*); abrupt (*style*)
heurter [œrte] *tr* to knock against, to bump into; to antagonize || *intr*—**heurter contre** to bump into || *ref* to clash, to collide; **se heurter à** to come up against
heurtoir *[œrtwar] *m* door knocker; (rr) buffer
hi *[i] *m invar*—**hi hi hi!** ho ho ho!;

pousser des hi et des ha to sputter in amazement
hiatus [jatys], *[jatys] *m* hiatus
hiberner [iberne] *intr* to hibernate
hibiscus [ibiskys] *m* hibiscus
hi·bou *[ibu] *m* (*pl* **-boux**) owl
hic *[ik] *m*—**voilà le hic!** (coll) there's the rub!
hi·deux *[idø] **-deuse** [døz] *adj* hideous
hie *[i] *f* pile driver
hièble [jebl] *f* (bot) elder
hié·mal -male [jemal] *adj* (*pl* **-maux** [mo]) winter
hier [jer] *adv & m* yesterday; **hier soir** last evening, last night
hiérarchie *[jerarʃi] *f* hierarchy
hiéroglyphe [jerɔglif] *m* hieroglyphic
hiéroglyphique [jerɔglifik] *adj* hieroglyphic
hila·rant [ilarɑ̃] **-rante** [rɑ̃t] *adj* hilarious; laughing (*gas*)
hilare [ilar] *adj* hilarious
hin·dou -doue *[ɛ̃du] *adj* Hindu || (*cap*) *mf* Hindu
hippique [ipik] *adj* horse (*race, show*)
hippisme [ipism] *m* horse racing
hippodrome [ipɔdrom] *m* hippodrome, race track
hippopotame [ipɔpɔtam] *m* hippopotamus
hirondelle [irɔ̃del] *f* (orn) swallow; (coll) bicycle cop
hispanique [ispanik] *adj* Hispanic
hispani·sant [ispanizɑ̃] **-sante** [zɑ̃t] *mf* Hispanist
hisser *[ise] *tr* to hoist, to raise
histoire [istwar] *f* history; story; **faire des histoires à** (coll) to make trouble for; **histoire à dormir debout** (coll) tall tale; **histoire de rire** (coll) just for fun; **histoire de s'informer** (coll) out of curiosity; **pas d'histoires** (coll) no fuss
histologie [istɔlɔʒi] *f* histology
histo·rien [istɔrjɛ̃] **-rienne** [rjen] *mf* historian
historier [istɔrje] *tr* to illustrate, adorn
historique [istɔrik] *adj* historic(al) || *m* historical account
histrion [istrijɔ̃] *m* ham actor
hiver [iver] *m* winter
hiver·nal -nale [ivernal] *adj* (*pl* **-naux** [no]) winter
hiverner [iverne] *intr* to winter
H.L.M. [aʃelem] *m* (letterword) (habitation à loyer modéré) low-rent apartment
ho *[o], [ho] *interj* hey there!; what!
hobe·reau *[ɔbro] *m* (*pl* **-reaux**) (orn) hobby; (coll) squire
hoche *[ɔʃ] *f* nick on a blade
hochement *[ɔʃmɑ̃] *m* shake, toss
hochepot *[ɔʃpo] *m* (culin) hotchpotch
hochequeue *[ɔʃkø] *m* (orn) wagtail
hocher *[ɔʃe] *tr* to shake; to nod
hochet *[ɔʃe] *m* rattle (*toy*); bauble
hockey *[ɔke] *m* hockey; **hockey sur glace** ice hockey
hoirie [wari] *f* legacy
holà *[ɔla], [hɔla] *m invar*—**mettre le**

holà à (coll) to put a stop to || *interj* hey!; stop!

holding *[ɔldiŋ] *m* holding company

hold-up *[ɔldœp] *m invar* holdup

hollan·dais *[ɔlɑ̃dɛ] -daise [dez] *adj* Dutch || *m* Dutch (*language*) || (*cap*) *mf* Hollander (*person*)

hollande *[ɔlɑ̃d] *m* Edam cheese || *f* Holland (*linen*) || (*cap*) *f* Holland; la Hollande Holland

holocauste [ɔlɔkost] *m* holocaust

homard *[ɔmar] *m* lobster

home *[om] *m* home

homélie [ɔmeli] *f* homily

homéopathie [ɔmeɔpati] *f* homeopathy

homicide [ɔmisid] *adj* homicidal || *mf* homicide (*person*) || *m* homicide (*act*)

hommage [ɔmaʒ] *m* homage; hommage de l'auteur (formula in presenting complimentary copies) with the compliments of the author; hommages respects, compliments

hommasse [ɔmas] *adj* mannish (*woman*)

homme [ɔm] *m* man; brave homme fine man, honest man; être homme à to be the man to, to be capable of; homme à tout faire jack-of-all-trades; handyman; homme d'affaires businessman; homme d'armes man-at-arms; homme de droite rightist; homme de gauche leftist; homme d'église churchman; homme de guerre or d'épée military man; homme de la rue man in the street, first comer; homme de l'espace spaceman; homme de lettres man of letters; homme de paille figurehead, stooge; homme de peine working-man; homme des bois orang-utan; homme d'État statesman; homme de troupe (*pl* hommes des troupes) (mil) enlisted man, private; homme d'expédition go-getter; homme d'intérieur homebody; homme du monde man of the world; homme galant ladies' man; hommes de bien men of good will; honnête homme upright man; man of culture, gentleman; jeune homme young man; teen-age boy; le vieil homme (Bib) the old Adam; un homme à la mer! man overboard!

homme-grenouille [ɔmgrənuj] *m* (*pl* hommes-grenouilles) frogman

homme-sandwich [ɔmsɑ̃dwit ʃ], [ɔmsɑ̃dwiʃ] *m* (*pl* hommes-sandwichs) sandwich man

homogène [ɔmɔʒɛn] *adj* homogeneous

homogénéiser [ɔmɔʒeneize] *tr* to homogenize

homologation [ɔmɔlɔgasjɔ̃] *f* validation

homologue [ɔmɔlɔg] *adj* homologous || *mf* (fig) opposite number

homologuer [ɔmɔlɔge] *tr* to confirm, endorse; to probate (*e.g., a will*)

homonyme [ɔmɔnim] *adj* homonymous || *m* homonym; namesake

homosexuel homosexuelle [ɔmɔseksɥel] *adj & mf* homosexual

hongre *[ɔ̃gr] *adj* gelded || *m* gelding

hongrer *[ɔ̃gre] *tr* to geld

Hongrie *[ɔ̃gri] *f* Hungary; la Hongrie Hungary

hon·grois *[ɔ̃grwa] -groise [grwaz] *adj* Hungarian || *m* Hungarian (*language*) || (*cap*) *mf* Hungarian (*person*)

honnête [ɔnɛt] *adj* honest, honorable

honnêteté [ɔnɛtəte] *f* honesty, uprightness

honneur [ɔnœr] *m* honor; faire honneur à sa parole to keep one's word

honnir *[ɔnir] *tr* to shame

honorabilité [ɔnɔrabilite] *f* respectability

honorable [ɔnɔrabl] *adj* honorable

honoraire [ɔnɔrer] *adj* honorary, emeritus || honoraires *mpl* honorarium, fee

honorer [ɔnɔre] *tr* to honor || *ref*—s'honorer de to pride oneself on

honorifique [ɔnɔrifik] *adj* honorific

honte *[ɔ̃t] *f* shame; avoir honte to be ashamed; faire honte à qn to make s.o. ashamed; faire honte à ses parents to be a disgrace to one's parents; fausse honte bashfulness; sans honte unashamedly

hon·teux *[ɔ̃tø] -teuse [tøz] *adj* ashamed; shameful

hop *[ɔp] *interj* go!, off with you!

hôpi·tal *[ɔpital] *m* (*pl* -taux [to]) hospital; charity hospital

hoquet *[ɔke] *m* hiccough

hoqueter *[ɔkte] §34 *intr* to hiccough

horaire [ɔrer] *adj* hourly, by hour || *m* timetable; schedule

horde *[ɔrd] *f* horde

horion *[ɔrjɔ̃] *m* punch, clout

horizon [ɔrizɔ̃] *m* horizon

horizon·tal [ɔrizɔ̃tal] *m* (*pl* -taux [to] -tales) *adj & f* horizontal

horloge [ɔrlɔʒ] *f* clock

horlo·ger [ɔrlɔʒe] -gère [ʒer] *adj* clockmaking, watchmaking || *mf* clockmaker, watchmaker

horlogerie [ɔrlɔʒri] *f* clockmaking, watchmaking; d'horlogerie clockwork

hormis *[ɔrmi] *prep* (lit) except for

hormone [ɔrmɔn] *f* hormone

horoscope [ɔrɔskɔp] *m* horoscope; tirer l'horoscope de qn to cast s.o.'s horoscope

horreur [ɔrœr] *f* horror; avoir horreur de to have a horror of; commettre des horreurs to commit atrocities; dire des horreurs to say obscene things; dire des horreurs de to say shocking things about

horrible [ɔribl] *adj* horrible

horrifier [ɔrifje] *tr* to horrify

horripi·lant [ɔrripilɑ̃] -lante [lɑ̃t] (coll) *adj* hair-raising

horripilation [ɔrripilasjɔ̃] *f* gooseflesh; (coll) exasperation

horripiler [ɔrripile] *tr* to give gooseflesh to; (coll) to exasperate

hors *[ɔr] *prep* out, beyond, outside; except, except for, save; hors de out of, outside of; hors de soi beside oneself, frantic; **hors d'ici!** get out!; **hors tout** overall

hors-bord *[ɔrbɔr] *m invar* outboard (*motor or motorboat*)

hors-caste *[ɔrkast] *mf invar* outcaste

hors-concours *[ɔrkɔ̃kur] *adj invar* excluded from competition || *m invar* contestant excluded from competition

hors-d'œuvre *[ɔrdœvr] *m invar* hors-d'œuvre

hors-jeu *[ɔrʒø] *m invar* offside position

hors-la-loi *[ɔrlalwa] *m invar* outlaw

hors-ligne *[ɔrliɲ] *adj invar* (coll) exceptional || *m invar* roadside

hors-texte *[ɔrtɛks] *m invar* (bb) insert

hortensia [ɔrtɑ̃sja] *m* hydrangea

horticole [ɔrtikɔl] *adj* horticultural

horticulture [ɔrtikyltyr] *f* horticulture

hospice [ɔspis] *m* hospice; home (*for the old, infirm, orphaned, etc.*)

hospita•lier [ɔspitalje] **-lière** [ljer] *adj* hospitable; hospital || *mf* hospital employee

hospitaliser [ɔspitalize] *tr* to hospitalize

hospitalité [ɔspitalite] *f* hospitality

hostie [ɔsti] *f* (eccl) Host

hostile [ɔstil] *adj* hostile

hostilité [ɔstilite] *f* hostility

hôte [ot] *m* host; guest

hôtel [otel], [ɔtel] *m* hotel; mansion; **hôtel des Monnaies** mint; **hôtel des Postes** main post office; **hôtel de ville** city hall; **hôtel meublé** rooming house, residential hotel

hôtel-Dieu [oteldjø], [ɔteldjø] *m* (*pl* **hôtels-Dieu**) city hospital

hôte•lier [otalje], [ɔtalje] **-lière** [ljer] *adj* hotel (*business*) || *mf* hotel manager

hôtellerie [otelri], [ɔtelri] *f* hotel business; fine restaurant; hostelry, hotel

hôtesse [otes] *f* hostess; **hôtesse de l'air** air hostess, stewardess

hotte *[ɔt] *f* basket (*carried on back*); hod (*of mason*); hood (*of chimney*)

hou *[u] *interj* oh oh!

houache *[waʃ] *f* wake (*of ship*)

houblon *[ublɔ̃] *m* hop (*vine*); hops (*dried flowers*)

houe *[u] *f* hoe

houer *[we] *tr* to hoe

houille *[uj] *f* coal; **houille blanche** water power; **houille bleue** tide power; **houille d'or** energy from the sun; **houille grasse** or **collante** soft coal; **houille incolore** wind power; **houille maigre** or **éclatante** hard coal; **houille rouge** energy from the heat of the earth

houil•ler [uje] **houil•lère** [ujer] *adj* coal-bearing, carboniferous; coal (*industry*) || *f* coal mine

houilleur *[ujœr] *m* coal miner

houle *[ul] *f* swell

houlette *[ulet] *f* crook (*of shepherd*); (hort) trowel

hou•leux [ulø] **-leuse** [løz] *adj* swelling (*sea*); (fig) stormy, turbulent

houp *[up], [hup] *interj* go to it!

houppe *[up] *f* tuft; crest; tassel; **houppe à poudre** powder puff

houppelande *[uplɑ̃d] *f* greatcoat

houppette *[upet] *f* tuft; powder puff

hourra *[ura], [hura] *m*—**pousser trois hourras** to give three cheers || *interj* hurrah!

hourvari *[urvari] *m* call to the hounds; (coll) uproar

houspiller *[uspije] *tr* to jostle, knock around; to rake over the coals, to tell off

housse *[us] *f* slipcover; cover (*e.g., for typewriter*); garment bag; housing, horsecloth; (aut) seat cover

housser *[use] *tr* to dust (*with feather duster*)

houssine *[usin] *f* rug beater; switch

houssoir *[uswar] *m* feather duster; whisk broom

houx *[u] *m* holly

hoyau *[wajo] *m* (*pl* **hoyaux**) mattock; pickax

hublot *[yblo] *m* porthole

huche *[yʃ] *f* hutch; bin

hucher *[yʃe] *tr* to call, to shout to

hue *[y] *interj* gee!; gee up! **tirer à hue et à dia** (fig) to pull in opposite directions

huée *[ɥe] *f* hoot, boo

huer *[ɥe] *tr & intr* to hoot, to boo

hugue•not *[ygno] **-note** [nɔt] *adj* Huguenot || *f* pipkin || (*cap*) *mf* Huguenot (*person*)

huile *[ɥil] *f* oil; big shot; **d'huile calm,** e.g., **mer d'huile** calm sea; **huile de coude** elbow grease; **huile de foie de morue** cod-liver oil; **huile de freins** brake fluid; **huile de ricin** castor oil; **huile lourde** diesel fuel; **huile solaire** suntan oil; **les huiles** (coll) the VIP's; **sentir l'huile** (fig) to smell of midnight oil; **verser de l'huile sur le feu** (fig) to add fuel to the fire

huiler [ɥile] *tr* to oil; to grease

hui•leux [ɥilø] **-leuse** [løz] *adj* oily; greasy

huis [ɥi] *m* (archaic) door; **à huis clos** behind closed doors; (law) in camera; **à huis ouvert** spectators admitted || [ɥi] *m*—**demander le huis clos** to request a closed-door session

huisserie [ɥisri] *f* doorframe

huissier [ɥisje] *m* doorman; usher (*before a person of rank*); **huissier audiencier** bailiff; **huissier exploitant** process server

huit *[ɥi(t)] *adj & pron* eight; **the Eighth,** e.g., **Jean huit** John the Eighth; **huit heures** eight o'clock || *m* eight; eighth (*in dates*); **faire des huit** to cut figures of eight (*in figure skating*)

huitain *[ɥitɛ̃] *m* eight-line verse

huitaine *[ɥiten] *f* (grouping of) eight; week; **à huitaine** the same day next week; **une huitaine de** about eight

huitième *[ɥitjem] *adj, pron* (*masc, fem*), *& m* eighth

huître [ɥitr] *f* oyster

huit-reflets *[ɥirafle] *m invar* top hat

hui•trier *[ɥitrije] **-trière** [trijer] *adj* oyster (*industry*) || *m* (orn) oyster-catcher || *f* oyster bed

hulotte *[ylɔt] *f* hoot owl

hululer *[ylyle] *intr* to hoot

hum *[œm], [hœm] *interj* hum!

hu·main [ymɛ̃] **-maine** [mɛn] *adj* human; humane

humaniste [ymanist] *adj & m* humanist

humanitaire [ymaniter] *adj & mf* humanitarian

humanité [ymanite] *f* humanity; **humanités (classiques)** humanities (*Greek & Latin classics*); **humanités modernes** humanities, belles-lettres; **humanités scientifiques** liberal studies (*concerned with the observation and classification of facts*)

humble [œ̃bl] *adj* humble

humecter [ymekte] *tr* to moisten ‖ *ref* to become damp; **s'humecter le gosier** (slang) to wet one's whistle

humer *[yme] *tr* to suck, to suck up; to sip; to inhale, to breathe in

humérus [ymerys] *m* humerus

humeur [ymœr] *f* humor, body fluid; humor, mood, spirits; **avec humeur** testily; **avoir de l'humeur** to be in a bad mood; **être de bonne humeur** to be in a good humor

humide [ymid] *adj* humid, damp; wet

humidifier [ymidifje] *tr* to humidify

humidité [ymidite] *f* humidity

humi·liant [ymiljɑ̃] **-liante** [ljɑ̃t] *adj* humiliating

humiliation [ymiljɑsjɔ̃] *f* humiliation

humilier [ymilje] *tr* to humiliate, to humble ‖ *ref* to humble oneself

humilité [ymilite] *f* humility

humoriste [ymɔrist] *adj* humorous (*writer*) ‖ *mf* humorist

humoristique [ymɔristik] *adj* humorous

humour [ymur] *m* humor; **humour noir** macabre humor, sick humor

humus [ymys] *m* humus

hune *[yn] *f* (naut) top; **hune de vigie** (naut) crow's-nest

huppe *[yp] *f* tuft, crest (*of bird*); (orn) hoopoe

hup·pé -pée *[ype] *adj* tufted, crested; (coll) smart, stylish

hure *[yr] *f* head (*of boar, salmon, etc.*); (culin) headcheese

hurlement *[yrlmɑ̃] *m* howl, roar; howling, roaring (*e.g., of wind*)

hurler *[yrle] *tr* to cry out, yell ‖ *intr* to howl, to roar

hur·leur *[yrlœr] **-leuse** [løz] *adj* howling ‖ *mf* howler ‖ *m* (zool) howler

hurluberlu [yrlyberly] *m* (coll) scatterbrain

hu·ron *[yrɔ̃] **-ronne** [rɔn] *adj* (coll) boorish, uncouth ‖ *mf* (coll) boor

hurricane *[urikan], *[œriken] *m* hurricane

hutte *[yt] *f* hut, cabin

hyacinthe [jasɛ̃t] *f* hyacinth (*stone*)

hya·lin [jalɛ̃] **-line** [lin] *adj* glassy

hybride [ibrid] *adj & m* hybrid

hydrate [idrat] *m* hydrate

hydrater [idrate] *tr & ref* to hydrate

hydraulique [idrolik] *adj* hydraulic ‖ *f* hydraulics

hydravion [idravjɔ̃] *m* hydroplane

hydre [idr] *f* hydra

hydrocarbure [idrɔkarbyr] *m* hydrocarbon

hydro-électrique [idroelektrik] *adj* hydroelectric

hydrofoil [idrɔfɔjl] *m* hydrofoil

hydrofuge [idrɔfyʒ] *adj* waterproof

hydrofuger [idrɔfyʒe] §38 *tr* to waterproof

hydrogène [idrɔʒɛn] *m* hydrogen

hydroglisseur [idrɔglisœr] *m* speedboat

hydromètre [idrɔmɛtr] *m* hydrometer ‖ *f* (ent) water spider

hydrophile [idrɔfil] *adj* absorbent ‖ *m* —**hydrophile brun** (ent) water devil

hydrophobie [idrɔfɔbi] *f* hydrophobia

hydropisie [idrɔpizi] *f* dropsy

hydroscope [idrɔskɔp] *m* dowser

hydroxyde [idrɔksid] *m* hydroxide

hyène [jɛn] *f* hyena

hygiène [iʒjɛn] *f* hygiene

hygiénique [iʒjenik] *adj* hygienic

hymnaire [imner] *m* hymnal

hymne [imnə], [im] *m* hymn, ode, anthem; **hymne national** national anthem ‖ *f* (eccl) hymn, canticle

hyperacidité [iperasidite] *f* hyperacidity

hyperbole [iperbɔl] *f* (math) hyperbola; (rhet) hyperbole

hypersensible [ipersɑ̃sibl] *adj* hypersensitive, supersensitive

hypersensi·tif [ipersɑ̃sitif] **-tive** [tiv] *adj* hypersensitive, supersensitive

hypertension [ipertɑ̃sjɔ̃] *f* high blood pressure, hypertension

hypnose [ipnoz] *f* hypnosis

hypnotique [ipnɔtik] *adj & m* hypnotic

hypnotiser [ipnɔtize] *tr* to hypnotize ‖ *ref*—**s'hypnotiser sur** (fig) to be hypnotized by

hypnoti·seur [ipnɔtizœr] **-seuse** [zøz] *mf* hypnotist

hypnotisme [ipnɔtism] *m* hypnotism

hypocondriaque [ipokɔ̃drijak] *adj & mf* hypochondriac

hypocrisie [ipɔkrizi] *f* hypocrisy

hypocrite [ipɔkrit] *adj* hypocritical ‖ *mf* hypocrite

hypodermique [ipɔdermik] *adj* hypodermic

hyposulfite [ipɔsylfit] *m* hyposulfite

hypotension [ipɔtɑ̃sjɔ̃] *f* low blood pressure

hypoténuse [ipɔtenyz] *f* hypotenuse

hypothèque [ipɔtek] *f* mortgage; **prendre une hypothèque sur** to put a mortgage on; **purger une hypothèque** to pay off a mortgage

hypothéquer [ipɔteke] §10 *tr* to mortgage

hypothèse [ipɔtez] *f* hypothesis

hypothétique [ipɔtetik] *adj* hypothetic(al)

hystérie [isteri] *f* hysteria

hystérique [isterik] *adj* hysteric(al)

I

I, i [i], *[i] *m invar* ninth letter of the French alphabet
iambique [jãbik] *adj* iambic
ibé·rien [iberjẽ] **-rienne** [rjen] *adj* Iberian || (*cap*) *mf* Iberian
ibérique [iberik] *adj* Iberian
iceberg [isberg] *m* iceberg
ichtyologie [iktjɔlɔʒi] *f* ichthyology
ici [isi] *adv* here; this is, e.g., **ici Paris** (rad, telv) this is Paris; e.g., **ici Robert** (telp) this is Robert; **d'ici** hereabouts; from today; **d'ici demain** before tomorrow; **d'ici là** between now and then, in the meantime; **d'ici peu** before long; **jusqu'ici** up to now, hitherto; **par ici** this way, through here
ici-bas [isiba] *adv* here below, on earth
icône [ikon] *f* icon
iconoclaste [ikɔnɔklast] *adj* iconoclastic || *mf* iconoclast
iconographie [ikɔnɔgrafi] *f* iconography; pictures, pictorial material
iconoscope [ikɔnɔskɔp] *m* iconoscope
ictère [ikter] *m* jaundice
ictérique [ikterik] *adj* jaundiced
idéal idéale [ideal] *adj & m* (*pl* **idéaux** [ideo] or **idéals**) ideal
idéaliser [idealize] *tr* to idealize
idéaliste [idealist] *adj & mf* idealist
idée [ide] *f* idea; mind, head; opinion, esteem; (coll) shade, touch; **changer d'idée** to change one's mind
identification [idãtifikasjɔ̃] *f* identification
identifier [idãtifje] *tr* to identify
identique [idãtik] *adj* identic(al)
identité [idãtite] *f* identity
idéologie [ideɔlɔʒi] *f* ideology; (pej) utopianism
idéologique [ideɔlɔʒik] *adj* ideologic(al); conceptual
ides [id] *fpl* ides
idiomatique [idjɔmatik] *adj* idiomatic
idiome [idjom] *m* idiom, language
idiosyncrasie [idjɔsɛ̃krazi] *f* idiosyncrasy
i·diot [idjo] **-diote** [djɔt] *adj* idiotic || *mf* idiot
idiotie [idjɔsi] *f* idiocy
idiotisme [idjɔtism] *m* idiom, idiomatic expression
idolâtrer [idɔlatre] *tr* to idolize
idolâtrie [idɔlatri] *f* idolatry
idole [idɔl] *f* idol
idylle [idil] *f* idyll; romance, love affair
idyllique [idilik] *adj* idyllic
if [if] *m* yew
IGAME [igam] *m* (acronym) (**Inspecteur Général de l'Administration en Mission Extraordinaire**) head prefect
igname [iɲam], [iɲam] *f* yam
ignare [iɲar] *adj* ignorant
ig·né -née [igne] *adj* igneous
ignifuge [iɲifyʒ] *adj* fireproof || *m* fireproofing
ignifuger [iɲifyʒe] §38 *tr* to fireproof

ignition [ignisjɔ̃] *f* ignition; red heat (*of metal*)
ignoble [iɲɔbl] *adj* ignoble; disgusting
ignomi·nieux [iɲɔminjø] **-nieuse** [njøz] *adj* ignominious
ignorance [iɲɔrɑ̃s] *f* ignorance
igno·rant [iɲɔrɑ̃] **-rante** [rɑ̃t] *adj* ignorant || *mf* ignoramus
ignorer [iɲɔre] *tr* not to know, to be ignorant of; to be unacquainted with
il [il] §87
île [il] *f* island, isle; **les îles Normandes** the Channel Islands
illé·gal -gale [illegal] *adj* (*pl* **-gaux** [go]) illegal
illégitime [illeʒitim] *adj* illegitimate; unjustified
illet·tré -trée [illetre] *adj & mf* illiterate
illicite [illisit] *adj* illicit; foul (*blow*)
illimi·té -tée [illimite] *adj* unlimited
illisible [illizibl] *adj* illegible; unreadable (*book*)
illogique [illɔʒik] *adj* illogical
illumination [illyminasjɔ̃] *f* illumination
illumi·né -née [illymine] *adj & mf* fanatic, visionary
illuminer [illymine] *tr* to illuminate
illusion [illyzjɔ̃] *f* illusion; **illusion de la vue** optical illusion; **se faire des illusions** to indulge in wishful thinking
illusionner [illyzjɔne] *tr* to delude || *ref* to delude oneself
illusionniste [illyzjɔnist] *mf* magician
illusoire [illyzwar] *adj* illusory, illusive
illustra·teur [illystratœr] *m* illustrator
illustration [illystrasjɔ̃] *f* illustration; glorification; glory; celebrity
illustre [illystr] *adj* illustrious, renowned
illus·tré -trée [illystre] *adj* illustrated || *m* illustrated magazine
illustrer [illystre] *tr* to illustrate || *ref* to distinguish oneself
îlot [ilo] *m* small island, isle; block (*of houses*)
ils [il] §87
image [imaʒ] *f* image; picture; **images** imagery
imager [imaʒe] §38 *tr* to embellish with metaphors, to color
imagerie [imaʒri] *f*—**imagerie d'Épinal** cardboard cutouts
imaginaire [imaʒiner] *adj* imaginary
imagination [imaʒinasjɔ̃] *f* imagination
imaginer [imaʒine] *tr* to imagine; to invent || *intr* to imagine; **imaginer de** + *inf* to have the idea of + *ger* || *ref* to imagine oneself; (with *dat* of *reflex pron*) to imagine
imbattable [ɛ̃batabl] *adj* unbeatable
imbat·tu -tue [ɛ̃baty] *adj* unbeaten
imbécile [ɛ̃besil] *adj & mf* imbecile
imbécillité [ɛ̃besilite] *f* imbecility
imberbe [ɛ̃berb] *adj* beardless
imbiber [ɛ̃bibe] *tr & ref* to soak; **s'imbiber de** to soak up; to be imbued with

imbri·qué -quée [ɛ̃brike] *adj* overlapping
imbrisable [ɛ̃brizabl] *adj* unbreakable
imbrûlable [ɛ̃brylabl] *adj* fireproof
im·bu -bue [ɛ̃by] *adj*—imbu de imbued with, steeped in
imita·teur [imitatœr] **-trice** [tris] *mf* imitator
imitation [imitɑsjɔ̃] *f* imitation
imiter [imite] *tr* to imitate
immacu·lé -lée [immakyle] *adj* immaculate
immangeable [ɛ̃mɑ̃ʒabl] *adj* inedible
immanquable [ɛ̃mɑ̃kabl] *adj* infallible; inevitable
immaté·riel -rielle [immaterjɛl] *adj* immaterial
immatriculation [immatrikylɑsjɔ̃] *f* registration; enrollment
immatriculer [immatrikyle] *tr* to register
immature [immatyr] *adj* unmatured
immé·diat -diate [immedja] [djat] *adj* immediate
immédiatement [immedjatmɑ̃] *adv* immediately
immémo·rial -riale [immemɔrjal] *adj* (*pl* -riaux [rjo]) immemorial
immense [immɑ̃s] *adj* immense
immensurable [immɑ̃syrabl] *adj* immeasurable, immensurable
immerger [immerʒe] §38 *tr* to immerse, to dip; to throw overboard; to lay (*a cable*)
imméri·té -tée [immerite] *adj* undeserved
immersion [immersjɔ̃] *f* immersion
immettable [ɛ̃metabl] *adj* unwearable
immeuble [immœbl] *adj* real, e.g., **biens immeubles** real estate ‖ *m* building, apartment building
immi·grant -grante [immigrɑ̃] [grɑ̃t] *adj* & *mf* immigrant
immigration [immigrɑsjɔ̃] *f* immigration
immi·gré -grée [immigre] *adj* & *mf* immigrant
immigrer [immigre] *intr* to immigrate
immi·nent -nente [imminɑ̃] [nɑ̃t] *adj* imminent, impending
immiscer [immise] §51 *ref*—s'immiscer dans to interfere with, to meddle with
immixtion [immiksjɔ̃] *f* interference
immobile [immɔbil] *adj* motionless; immobile (*resolute*); dead (*typewriter key*)
immobi·lier -lière [immɔbilje] [ljer] *adj* real-estate, property; real, e.g., **biens immobiliers** real estate
immobiliser [immɔbilize] *tr* to immobilize; to tie up ‖ *ref* to come to a stop
immodé·ré -rée [immɔdere] *adj* immoderate
immonde [immɔ̃d] *adj* foul, filthy; (*eccl*) unclean
immondices [immɔ̃dis] *fpl* garbage, refuse
immo·ral -rale [immɔral] *adj* (*pl* -raux [ro]) immoral
immortaliser [immɔrtalize] *tr* to immortalize

immor·tel -telle [immɔrtɛl] *adj* & *mf* immortal ‖ *f* (bot) everlasting
immoti·vé -vée [immɔtive] *adj* groundless
immuable [immɥabl] *adj* changeless
immuniser [immynize] *tr* to immunize
immunité [immynite] *f* immunity
im·pair -paire [ɛ̃per] *adj* odd, uneven ‖ *m* (coll) blunder
impardonnable [ɛ̃pardɔnabl] *adj* unpardonable
impar·fait -faite [ɛ̃parfe] [fet] *adj* & *m* imperfect
imparité [ɛ̃parite] *f* inequality, disparity
impar·tial -tiale [ɛ̃parsjal] *adj* (*pl* -tiaux [sjo]) impartial
impartir [ɛ̃partir] *tr* to grant
impasse [ɛ̃pas] *f* blind alley, dead-end street; impasse, deadlock; (cards) finesse; **faire l'impasse à** (cards) to finesse
impassible [ɛ̃pasibl] *adj* impassible; impassive (*look, face, etc.*)
impatience [ɛ̃pasjɑ̃s] *f* impatience; **impatiences** (coll) attack of nerves
impa·tient -tiente [ɛ̃pasjɑ̃] [sjɑ̃t] *adj* impatient
impatienter [ɛ̃pasjɑ̃te] *tr* to make impatient ‖ *ref* to lose patience
impatroniser [ɛ̃patrɔnize] *ref* to take charge; to take hold
impavide [ɛ̃pavid] *adj* fearless
impayable [ɛ̃pejabl] *adj* (coll) priceless, very funny
impayé impayée [ɛ̃peje] *adj* unpaid
impeccable [ɛ̃pekabl] *adj* impeccable
impénétrable [ɛ̃penetrabl] *adj* impenetrable
impéni·tent -tente [ɛ̃penitɑ̃] [tɑ̃t] *adj* impenitent, obdurate, inveterate
impensable [ɛ̃pɑ̃sabl] *adj* unthinkable
imper [ɛ̃per] *m* (coll) raincoat
impéra·tif -tive [ɛ̃peratif] [tiv] *adj* & *m* imperative
impératrice [ɛ̃peratris] *f* empress
imperceptible [ɛ̃perseptibl] *adj* imperceptible; negligible
imperdable [ɛ̃perdabl] *adj* unlosable
imperfection [ɛ̃perfeksjɔ̃] *f* imperfection, defect
impé·rial -riale [ɛ̃perjal] *adj* (*pl* -riaux [rjo]) imperial ‖ *f* goatee; upper deck (*of bus, coach, etc.*)
impérialiste [ɛ̃perjalist] *adj* & *mf* imperialist
impé·rieux -rieuse [ɛ̃perjø] [rjøz] *adj* imperious, haughty; imperative, urgent
impérissable [ɛ̃perisabl] *adj* imperishable
impéritie [ɛ̃perisi] *f* incompetence
imperméabiliser [ɛ̃permeabilize] *tr* to waterproof
imperméable [ɛ̃permeabl] *adj* waterproof; impervious ‖ *m* raincoat
imperson·nel -nelle [ɛ̃persɔnɛl] *adj* impersonal; commonplace; ordinary
imperti·nent -nente [ɛ̃pertinɑ̃] [nɑ̃t] *adj* impertinent ‖ *mf* impertinent person
impé·trant -trante [ɛ̃petrɑ̃] [trɑ̃t] *mf* holder (*of a title or degree*)

impé·tueux [ɛ̃petɥø] -tueuse [tɥøz] adj impetuous

impie [ɛ̃pi] adj impious, ungodly; blasphemous || mf unbeliever; blasphemer

impiété [ɛ̃pjete] f impiety; disrespect

impitoyable [ɛ̃pitwajabl] adj unmerciful

implanter [ɛ̃plɑ̃te] tr to implant; to introduce || ref to take root; s'implanter chez (coll) to thrust oneself upon

implication [ɛ̃plikɑsjɔ̃] f implication

implicite [ɛ̃plisit] adj implicit

impliquer [ɛ̃plike] tr to implicate; to imply

implorer [ɛ̃plɔre] tr to implore

imployable [ɛ̃plwajabl] adj pitiless; inflexible

impo·li -lie [ɛ̃pɔli] adj impolite

impolitique [ɛ̃pɔlitik] adj ill-advised

impondérable [ɛ̃pɔ̃derabl] adj & m imponderable

impopulaire [ɛ̃pɔpyler] adj unpopular

impopularité [ɛ̃pɔpylarite] f unpopularity

importance [ɛ̃pɔrtɑ̃s] f importance; size; d'importance large, of consequence; thoroughly, very hard

impor·tant [ɛ̃pɔrtɑ̃] -tante [tɑ̃t] adj important; large, considerable || m main thing; faire l'important (coll) to act big

importa·teur [ɛ̃pɔrtatœr] -trice [tris] mf importer

importer [ɛ̃pɔrte] tr to import || intr to matter; to be important; n'importe no matter, never mind; n'importe comment any way; n'importe où anywhere; n'importe quand anytime; n'importe quel . . . any . . . ; n'importe qui anybody; n'importe quoi anything; peu m'importe it doesn't matter to me; qu'importe? what does it matter?

impor·tun [ɛ̃pɔrtœ̃] -tune [tyn] adj bothersome || mf pest, nuisance

importuner [ɛ̃pɔrtyne] tr to importune

imposable [ɛ̃pozabl] adj taxable

impo·sant [ɛ̃pozɑ̃] -sante [zɑ̃t] adj imposing

impo·sé -sée [ɛ̃poze] adj taxed; fixed (price) || mf taxpayer

imposer [ɛ̃poze] tr to impose; to levy a tax on || intr —en imposer à to make an impression on; to impose on || ref to assert oneself; to be indispensable; s'imposer à to force itself upon; s'imposer chez to foist oneself upon

imposition [ɛ̃pozisjɔ̃] f imposition; taxation; laying on, levying

impossible [ɛ̃pɔsibl] adj impossible

imposte [ɛ̃pɔst] f transom; (archit) impost

imposteur [ɛ̃pɔstœr] m impostor

imposture [ɛ̃pɔstyr] f imposture

impôt [ɛ̃po] m tax; impôt du sang military duty; impôt foncier property tax; impôt indirecte sales tax; impôt retenu à la source withholding tax; impôt sur le revenu income tax

impotence [ɛ̃pɔtɑ̃s] f lameness, infirmity

impo·tent [ɛ̃pɔtɑ̃] -tente [tɑ̃t] adj crippled; bedridden || mf cripple

impraticable [ɛ̃pratikabl] adj impracticable; impassable (e.g., road)

impré·cis [ɛ̃presi] -cise [siz] adj vague, hazy

imprégner [ɛ̃preɲe] §10 tr to impregnate

imprenable [ɛ̃prənabl] adj impregnable

impréparation [ɛ̃preparɑsjɔ̃] f unpreparedness

imprésario [ɛ̃presarjo] m impresario

impression [ɛ̃presjɔ̃] f impression; printing

impression·nant [ɛ̃presjɔnɑ̃] impression·nante [ɛ̃presjɔnɑ̃t] adj impressive

impressionner [ɛ̃presjɔne] tr to impress, to affect; (phot) to expose

imprévisible [ɛ̃previzibl] adj unforeseeable

imprévision [ɛ̃previzjɔ̃] f lack of foresight

imprévoyant [ɛ̃prevwajɑ̃] imprévoyante [ɛ̃prevwajɑ̃t] adj improvident, shortsighted

impré·vu -vue [ɛ̃prevy] adj & m unforeseen, unexpected; sauf imprévu unless something unforeseen happens

impri·mé -mée [ɛ̃prime] adj printed || m print, calico; printed work, book; printing (as opposed to script); imprimés printed matter

imprimer [ɛ̃prime] tr to print; to imprint; to impress; to impart (e.g., movement)

imprimerie [ɛ̃primri] f printing; printing office, print shop

imprimeur [ɛ̃primœr] m printer

imprimeur-éditeur [ɛ̃primœreditœr] m (pl imprimeurs-éditeurs) printer and publisher

imprimeur-libraire [ɛ̃primœrlibrer] m (pl imprimeurs-libraires) printer and publisher

imprimeuse [ɛ̃primøz] f printing press

improbable [ɛ̃prɔbabl] adj improbable

improba·tif [ɛ̃prɔbatif] -tive [tiv] adj disapproving

improbité [ɛ̃prɔbite] f dishonesty

improduc·tif [ɛ̃prɔdyktif] -tive [tiv] adj unproductive

impromp·tu -tue [ɛ̃prɔ̃pty] adj impromptu || m impromptu play; (mus) impromptu || impromptu adv impromptu

impropre [ɛ̃prɔpr] adj improper (not right); impropre à unfit for

impropriété [ɛ̃prɔprjete] f incorrectness

improviser [ɛ̃prɔvize] tr & intr to improvise

improviste [ɛ̃prɔvist]—à l'improviste unexpectedly, impromptu; prendre à l'improviste to catch napping

impru·dent [ɛ̃prydɑ̃] -dente [dɑ̃t] adj imprudent

impubère [ɛ̃pyber] adj under the age of puberty

impubliable [ɛ̃pybljabl] adj unpublishable, not fit to print

impu·dent [ɛ̃pydɑ̃] -dente [dɑ̃t] adj impudent

impudeur [ɛ̃pydœr] f immodesty

impudicité [ɛ̃pydisite] *f* indecency

impudique [ɛ̃pydik] *adj* immodest

impuissance [ɛ̃pɥisɑ̃s] *f* impotence; **être dans l'impuissance de faire q.ch.** to be powerless to do s.th.

impuis·sant [ɛ̃pɥisɑ̃] **impuis·sante** [ɛ̃pɥisɑ̃t] *adj* impotent, powerless, helpless; (pathol) impotent

impul·sif [ɛ̃pylsif] **-sive** [siv] *adj* impulsive ‖ *mf* impulsive person

impulsion [ɛ̃pylsjɔ̃] *f* impulse; **donner l'impulsion à** to give an impetus to; **sous l'impulsion du moment** on the spur of the moment

impunément [ɛ̃pynemɑ̃] *adv* with impunity

impu·ni -nie [ɛ̃pyni] *adj* unpunished

impunité [ɛ̃pynite] *f* impunity

im·pur -pure [ɛ̃pyr] *adj* impure

impureté [ɛ̃pyrte] *f* impurity

imputation [ɛ̃pytɑsjɔ̃] *f* imputation; (com) charge; (com) deduction

imputer [ɛ̃pyte] *tr* to impute, ascribe; (com) **imputer q.ch. à** to charge s.th. to

inaccessible [inaksesibl] *adj* inaccessible

inac·tif [inaktif] **-tive** [tiv] *adj* inactive

inaction [inaksjɔ̃] *f* inaction

inactivité [inaktivite] *f* inactivity

inadaptation [inadaptɑsjɔ̃] *f* maladjustment

inadap·té -tée [inadapte] *adj* maladjusted ‖ *mf* misfit

inadvertance [inadvertɑ̃s] *f*—**par inadvertance** inadvertently

inalté·ré -rée [inaltere] *adj* unspoiled

inani·mé -mée [inanime] *adj* inanimate

inappréciable [inapresjabl] *adj* inappreciable, imperceptible; invaluable

inapprivoisable [inaprivwazabl] *adj* untamable

inapte [inapt] *adj* inept; **inapte à** unfit for, unsuitable for ‖ *mf* dropout, washout; **les inaptes** the unfit; the unemployable

inaptitude [inaptityd] *f* unfitness

inarticu·lé -lée [inartikyle] *adj* inarticulate

inassou·vi -vie [inasuvi] *adj* unsatisfied

inattaquable [inatakabl] *adj* unquestionable; unassailable; **inattaquable par** unaffected by, resistant to

inatten·du -due [inatɑ̃dy] *adj* unexpected

inatten·tif [inatɑ̃tif] **-tive** [tiv] *adj* inattentive; careless

inattention [inatɑ̃sjɔ̃] *f* inattentiveness, carelessness

inaudible [inodibl] *adj* inaudible

inaugu·ral -rale [inogyral] *adj* (*pl* **-raux** [ro]) inaugural

inauguration [inogyrɑsjɔ̃] *f* inauguration

inaugurer [inogyre] *tr* to inaugurate; to unveil (*a statue*)

inauthentique [inotɑ̃tik] *adj* unauthentic

inavouable [inavuabl] *adj* shameful

ina·voué -vouée [inavwe] *adj* unacknowledged

Inca [ɛ̃ka] *adj invar* Inca ‖ (*cap*) *m* Inca

incandes·cent [ɛ̃kɑ̃desɑ̃] **incandes·cente** [ɛ̃kɑ̃desɑ̃t] *adj* incandescent; wild, stirred up (*crowd*)

incapable [ɛ̃kapabl] *adj* incapable; (law) incompetent ‖ *mf* (law) incompetent person

incapacité [ɛ̃kapasite] *f* incapacity; disability

incarcérer [ɛ̃karsere] §10 *tr* to incarcerate

incar·nat -nate [ɛ̃karna] **-nate** [nat] *adj* flesh-colored; rosy ‖ *m* flesh color

incarnation [ɛ̃karnɑsjɔ̃] *f* incarnation

incar·né -née [ɛ̃karne] *adj* incarnate; ingrowing (*nail*)

incarner [ɛ̃karne] *tr* to incarnate, to embody ‖ *ref* to become incarnate; (pathol) to become ingrown; **s'incarner dans** to become the embodiment of

incartade [ɛ̃kartad] *f* indiscretion; prank

incassable [ɛ̃kasabl] *adj* unbreakable

incendiaire [ɛ̃sɑ̃djer] *adj & mf* incendiary

incendie [ɛ̃sɑ̃di] *m* fire, conflagration; **incendie volontaire** arson

incen·dié -diée [ɛ̃sɑ̃dje] *adj* burnt down ‖ *mf* fire victim

incendier [ɛ̃sɑ̃dje] *tr* to set on fire; to burn down; (fig) to fire, inflame; (slang) to give a tongue-lashing to

incer·tain [ɛ̃sertɛ̃] **-taine** [ten] *adj* uncertain; indistinct; unsettled (*weather*)

incertitude [ɛ̃sertityd] *f* incertitude, uncertainty; **dans l'incertitude** in doubt

incessamment [ɛ̃sesamɑ̃] *adv* incessantly; without delay, at any moment

inces·sant [ɛ̃sesɑ̃] **inces·sante** [ɛ̃sesɑ̃t] *adj* incessant

inceste [ɛ̃sest] *m* incest

inces·tueux [ɛ̃sestɥø] **-tueuse** [tɥøz] *adj* incestuous

inchan·gé -gée [ɛ̃ʃ/ɑʒe] *adj* unchanged

incidemment [ɛ̃sidamɑ̃] *adv* incidentally

incidence [ɛ̃sidɑ̃s] *f* incidence

inci·dent [ɛ̃sidɑ̃] **-dente** [dɑ̃t] *adj & m* incident

incinérer [ɛ̃sinere] §10 *tr* to incinerate; to cremate

incirconcis [ɛ̃sirkɔ̃si] *adj masc* uncircumcised

inciser [ɛ̃size] *tr* to make an incision in; to tap (*a tree*); (med) to lance

inci·sif [ɛ̃sizif] **-sive** [ziv] *adj* incisive ‖ *f* incisor

incision [ɛ̃sizjɔ̃] *f* incision

incitation [ɛ̃sitɑsjɔ̃] *f* incitement

inciter [ɛ̃site] *tr* to incite

inci·vil -vile [ɛ̃sivil] *adj* uncivil

incivili·sé -sée [ɛ̃sivilize] *adj* uncivilized

inclassable [ɛ̃klasabl] *adj* unclassifiable

inclé·ment [ɛ̃klemɑ̃] **-mente** [mɑ̃t] *adj* inclement

inclinaison [ɛ̃klinezɔ̃] *f* inclination; slope

inclination [ɛ̃klinɑsjɔ̃] *f* inclination; bow; love, affection

incliner [ɛ̃kline] *tr & ref* to incline; to bend; to bow

inclure [ɛklyr] §11 (*pp* **inclus**) *tr* to include; to enclose

in·clus [ɛkly] **-cluse** [klyz] *adj* including, e.g., **jusqu'à la page dix incluse** up to and including page ten; inclusive, e.g., **de mercredi à samedi inclus** from Wednesday to Saturday inclusive

inclu·sif [ɛklyzif] **-sive** [ziv] *adj* inclusive

inclusivement [ɛklyzivmɑ̃] *adv* inclusively, inclusive

incognito [ɛkɔɲito] *m & adv* incognito

incohé·rent [ɛkoerɑ̃] **-rente** [rɑ̃t] *adj* incoherent; inconsistent, illogical

incolore [ɛkɔlɔr] *adj* colorless

incomber [ɛkɔ̃be] *intr*—**incomber à** to devolve on, to fall upon; **il incombe à qn de** it behooves s.o. to

incombustible [ɛkɔ̃bystibl] *adj* incombustible; fireproof

incommode [ɛkɔmɔd] *adj* inconvenient; unwieldy

incommoder [ɛkɔmɔde] *tr* to inconvenience

incommodité [ɛkɔmɔdite] *f* inconvenience

incomparable [ɛkɔ̃parabl] *adj* incomparable

incompatible [ɛkɔ̃patibl] *adj* incompatible; conflicting

incompétence [ɛkɔ̃petɑ̃s] *f* incompetence; lack of jurisdiction

incompé·tent [ɛkɔ̃petɑ̃] **-tente** [tɑ̃t] *adj* incompetent; lacking jurisdiction

incom·plet [ɛkɔ̃plɛ] **-plète** [plɛt] *adj* incomplete

incompréhensible [ɛkɔ̃preɑ̃sibl] *adj* incomprehensible

incom·pris [ɛkɔ̃pri] **-prise** [priz] *adj* misunderstood

inconcevable [ɛkɔ̃svabl] *adj* inconceivable

inconciliable [ɛkɔ̃siljabl] *adj* irreconcilable

incondition·nel -nelle [ɛkɔ̃disjɔnɛl] *adj* unconditional

inconduite [ɛkɔ̃dɥit] *f* misconduct

inconfort [ɛkɔ̃fɔr] *m* discomfort

incon·gru -grue [ɛkɔ̃gry] *adj* incongruous

incon·nu -nue [ɛkɔny] *adj* unknown; **inconnu à cette adresse** address unknown ‖ *mf* unknown (*person*) ‖ *m* unknown (*what is not known*) ‖ *f* (*math*) unknown

inconsciemment [ɛkɔ̃sjamɑ̃] *adv* subconsciously; unconsciously

inconscience [ɛkɔ̃sjɑ̃s] *f* unconsciousness; unawareness

incons·cient [ɛkɔ̃sjɑ̃] **incons·ciente** [ɛkɔ̃sjɑ̃t] *adj* unconscious, unaware, oblivious; thoughtless; subconscious ‖ *mf* dazed person ‖ *m* unconscious

inconséquence [ɛkɔ̃sekɑ̃s] *f* inconsistency; thoughtlessness, inconsiderateness

inconsé·quent [ɛkɔ̃sekɑ̃] **-quente** [kɑ̃t] *adj* inconsistent; thoughtless, inconsiderate

inconsidé·ré -rée [ɛkɔ̃sidere] *adj* inconsiderate

inconsistance [ɛkɔ̃sistɑ̃s] *f* inconsistency; flimsiness, instability

inconsis·tant [ɛkɔ̃sistɑ̃] **-tante** [tɑ̃t] *adj* inconsistent; flimsy, unstable

inconsolable [ɛkɔ̃sɔlabl] *adj* inconsolable

incons·tant [ɛkɔ̃stɑ̃] **-tante** [tɑ̃t] *adj* inconstant

inconstitution·nel -nelle [ɛkɔ̃stitysjɔnɛl] *adj* unconstitutional

inconti·nent [ɛkɔ̃tinɑ̃] **-nente** [nɑ̃t] *adj* incontinent ‖ **incontinent** *adv* at once, forthwith

incontrôlable [ɛkɔ̃trolabl] *adj* unverifiable

incontrô·lé -lée [ɛkɔ̃trole] *adj* unverified; unchecked, uncontrollable

inconvenance [ɛkɔ̃vnɑ̃s] *f* impropriety

inconve·nant [ɛkɔ̃vnɑ̃] **-nante** [nɑ̃t] *adj* improper, indecent

inconvénient [ɛkɔ̃venjɑ̃] *m* inconvenience, disadvantage; **voir un inconvénient à** to have an objection to

incorporation [ɛkɔrpɔrɑsjɔ̃] *f* incorporation; (mil) induction

incorpo·ré -rée [ɛkɔrpɔre] *adj* built-in

incorpo·rel -relle [ɛkɔrpɔrɛl] *adj* incorporeal; intangible (*property*)

incorporer [ɛkɔrpɔre] *tr* to incorporate; (mil) to induct ‖ *ref* to incorporate

incor·rect -recte [ɛkɔrɛkt] *adj* incorrect; unfair

incrédule [ɛkredyl] *adj* incredulous; unbelieving ‖ *mf* unbeliever, freethinker

incrédulité [ɛkredylite] *f* incredulity; disbelief

increvable [ɛkrəvabl] *adj* punctureproof; (slang) untiring

incriminer [ɛkrimine] *tr* to incriminate

incrochetable [ɛkrɔʃtabl] *adj* burglarproof (*lock*)

incroyable [ɛkrwajabl] *adj* unbelievable

incroyant [ɛkrwajɑ̃] **incroyante** [ɛkrwajɑ̃t] *adj* unbelieving ‖ *mf* unbeliever

incrustation [ɛkrystɑsjɔ̃] *f* incrustation; inlay; (sewing) insert

incruster [ɛkryste] *tr* to incrust; to inlay ‖ *ref* to take root, to become ingrained

incubateur [ɛkybatœr] *m* incubator

incuber [ɛkybe] *tr* to incubate

inculpation [ɛkylpɑsjɔ̃] *f* indictment; **sous l'inculpation de** on a charge of

incul·pé -pée [ɛkylpe] *adj* indicted; **inculpé de** charged with, accused of ‖ *mf* accused, defendant

inculper [ɛkylpe] *tr* to indict, to charge

inculquer [ɛkylke] *tr* to inculcate

inculte [ɛkylt] *adj* uncultivated; uncouth

incunables [ɛkynabl] *mpl* incunabula

incurable [ɛkyrabl] *adj & mf* incurable

incurie [ɛkyri] *f* carelessness

incursion [ɛkyrsjɔ̃] *f* incursion, foray

Inde [ɛd] *f* India; **Indes Occidentales** West Indies; **Indes Orientales Néerlandaises** Dutch East Indies; **l'Inde** India

indébrouillable [ɛdebrujabl] *adj* inextricable, hopelessly involved

indécence [ɛ̃desɑ̃s] *f* indecency

indé·cent [ɛ̃desɑ̃] **-cente** [sɑ̃t] *adj* indecent

indéchiffrable [ɛ̃deʃifrabl] *adj* undecipherable; incomprehensible; illegible

indé·cis [ɛ̃desi] **-cise** [siz] *adj* indecisive; uncertain, undecided; blurred

indéclinable [ɛ̃deklinabl] *adj* indeclinable

indécrottable [ɛ̃dekrɔtabl] *adj* (coll) incorrigible, hopeless

indéfectible [ɛ̃defektibl] *adj* everlasting; unfailing

indéfendable [ɛ̃defɑ̃dabl] *adj* indefensible

indéfi·ni -nie [ɛ̃defini] *adj* indefinite

indéfinissable [ɛ̃definisabl] *adj* indefinable

indéfrisable [ɛ̃defrizabl] *adj* permanent (*wave*) ‖ *f* permanent wave

indélébile [ɛ̃delebil] *adj* indelible

indéli·cat [ɛ̃delika] **-cate** [kat] *adj* indelicate; dishonest

indémaillable [ɛ̃demajabl] *adj* runproof

indemne [ɛ̃demn] *adj* undamaged, unharmed

indemnisation [ɛ̃demnizɑsjɔ̃] *f* indemnification, compensation

indemniser [ɛ̃demnize] *tr* to compensate

indemnité [ɛ̃demnite] *f* indemnity; allowance, grant; compensation; **indemnité journalière** workmen's compensation; **indemnité parlementaire** salary of members (*of parliamentary body*)

indéniable [ɛ̃denjabl] *adj* undeniable

indépendance [ɛ̃depɑ̃dɑ̃s] *f* independence

indépen·dant [ɛ̃depɑ̃dɑ̃] **-dante** [dɑ̃t] *adj & mf* independent

indéréglable [ɛ̃dereglabl] *adj* foolproof

indescriptible [ɛ̃deskriptibl] *adj* indescribable

indésirable [ɛ̃dezirabl] *adj* undesirable

indestructible [ɛ̃destryktibl] *adj* indestructible

indétermi·né -née [ɛ̃determine] *adj* indeterminate

indétraquable [ɛ̃detrakabl] *adj* foolproof

index [ɛ̃dɛks] *m* index; forefinger; index number; **Index** (eccl) Index

indica·teur [ɛ̃dikatœr] **-trice** [tris] *adj* indicating ‖ *mf* informer ‖ *m* gauge; indicator, pointer; timetable; road sign; guidebook; street guide

indica·tif [ɛ̃dikatif] **-tive** [tiv] *adj* indicative, suggestive ‖ *m* (gram) indicative; (rad) station identification; **indicatif d'appel** (rad, telg) call letters or number

indication [ɛ̃dikɑsjɔ̃] *f* indication; **fausse indication** wrong piece of information; **indications** directions; **sauf indication contraire** unless otherwise directed; **sur l'indication de** at the suggestion of

indice [ɛ̃dis] *m* indication, sign; clue; **indice des prix** price index; **indice d'octane** octane number; **indice du coût de la vie** cost-of-living index

indicible [ɛ̃disibl] *adj* inexpressible

in·dien [ɛ̃djɛ̃] **-dienne** [djen] *adj* Indian ‖ *f* calico, chintz ‖ (cap) *mf* Indian

indifféremment [ɛ̃diferamɑ̃] *adv* indiscriminately

indiffé·rent [ɛ̃diferɑ̃] **-rente** [rɑ̃t] *adj* indifferent; unimportant; **cela m'est indifférent** it's all the same to me

indigence [ɛ̃diʒɑ̃s] *f* indigence, poverty

indigène [ɛ̃diʒen] *adj* indigenous, native ‖ *mf* native

indi·gent [ɛ̃diʒɑ̃] **-gente** [ʒɑ̃t] *adj* indigent ‖ *mf* pauper; **les indigents** the poor

indigeste [ɛ̃diʒest] *adj* indigestible; heavy, stodgy; undigested, mixed up

indigestion [ɛ̃diʒestjɔ̃] *f* indigestion

indignation [ɛ̃diɲɑsjɔ̃] *f* indignation

indigne [ɛ̃diɲ] *adj* unworthy; shameful

indi·gné -gnée [ɛ̃diɲe] *adj* indignant

indigner [ɛ̃diɲe] *tr* to outrage ‖ *ref* to be indignant

indignité [ɛ̃diɲite] *f* unworthiness; indignity, outrage

indigo [ɛ̃digo] *adj invar & m* indigo

indi·qué -quée [ɛ̃dike] *adj* advisable, appropriate; **être tout indiqué pour** to be just the thing for; to be just the man for

indiquer [ɛ̃dike] *tr* to indicate; to name; **indiquer du doigt** to point to, to point out

indi·rect -recte [ɛ̃dirɛkt] *adj* indirect

indisciplinable [ɛ̃disiplinabl] *adj* unruly

indiscipline [ɛ̃disiplin] *f* lack of discipline, disobedience

indiscipli·né -née [ɛ̃disipline] *adj* undisciplined

indis·cret [ɛ̃diskre] **-crète** [kret] *adj* indiscreet

indiscrétion [ɛ̃diskresjɔ̃] *f* indiscretion; **sans indiscrétion...** if I may ask...

indiscutable [ɛ̃diskytabl] *adj* unquestionable

indiscu·té -tée [ɛ̃diskyte] *adj* unquestioned

indispensable [ɛ̃dispɑ̃sabl] *adj & m* indispensable, essential

indisponible [ɛ̃dispɔnibl] *adj* unavailable; out of commission (*said of car, machine, etc.*)

indispo·sé -sée [ɛ̃dispoze] *adj* indisposed (*slightly ill*); ill-disposed

indisposer [ɛ̃dispoze] *tr* to indispose

indissoluble [ɛ̃disɔlybl] *adj* indissoluble

indis·tinct [ɛ̃distɛ̃], [ɛ̃distɛ̃kt] **-tincte** [tɛ̃kt] *adj* indistinct

indistinctement [ɛ̃distɛ̃ktəmɑ̃] *adv* indistinctly; indiscriminately

individu [ɛ̃dividy] *m* individual; (coll) fellow, guy

individualiser [ɛ̃dividɥalize] *tr* to individualize

individualité [ɛ̃dividɥalite] *f* individuality

indivi·duel -duelle [ɛ̃dividɥel] *adj* individual; separate

indi·vis -vise [ɛ̃divi] **-vise** [viz] *adj* joint; **par indivis** jointly

indivisible [ɛ̃divizibl] *adj* indivisible

Indochine [ɛ̃dɔʃin] *f* Indochina; **l'Indochine** Indochina

indocile [ɛ̃dɔsil] *adj* rebellious, unruly

indo-européen [ɛ̃dɔørɔpeɛ̃] **-européenne** [ørɔpeen] *adj* Indo-European ‖ *m* Indo-European (*language*) ‖ (*cap*) *mf* Indo-European

indo·lent [ɛ̃dɔlɑ̃] **-lente** [lɑ̃t] *adj* indolent; apathetic; painless (*e.g., tumor*) ‖ *mf* idler

indolore [ɛ̃dɔlɔr] *adj* painless

indomptable [ɛ̃dɔ̃tabl] *adj* indomitable

indomp·té -tée [ɛ̃dɔ̃te] *adj* untamed

Indonésie [ɛ̃dɔnezi] *f* Indonesia; **l'Indonésie** Indonesia

indoné·sien [ɛ̃dɔnezjɛ̃] **-sienne** [zjɛn] *adj* Indonesian ‖ *m* Indonesian (*language*) ‖ (*cap*) *mf* Indonesian (*person*)

in-douze [ɛ̃duz] *adj invar* & *m invar* duodecimo

in·du -due [ɛ̃dy] *adj* unseemly (*e.g., hour*); undue (*haste*); unwarranted (*remark*) ‖ *m* something not due

inducteur [ɛ̃dyktœr] *m* (elec) field

induction [ɛ̃dyksjɔ̃] *f* (elec, logic) induction

induire [ɛ̃dɥir] §19 *tr* to induce; **induire en** to lead into (*temptation, error, etc.*)

in·duit -duite [ɛ̃dɥi] **-duite** [dɥit] *adj* induced ‖ *m* (elec) armature

indulgence [ɛ̃dylʒɑ̃s] *f* indulgence

indul·gent [ɛ̃dylʒɑ̃] **-gente** [ʒɑ̃t] *adj* indulgent

indûment [ɛ̃dymɑ̃] *adv* unduly

indurer [ɛ̃dyre] *tr* & *ref* to harden

industrialiser [ɛ̃dystrijalize] *tr* to industrialize ‖ *ref* to become industrialized

industrie [ɛ̃dystri] *f* industry; trickery; (obs) occupation, trade; **l'industrie du spectacle** show business

industrie-clef [ɛ̃dystriklɛ] *f* (*pl* **industries-clefs**) key industry

indus·triel -trielle [ɛ̃dystrijel] *adj* industrial ‖ *m* industrialist

indus·trieux [ɛ̃dystrijø] **-trieuse** [trijøz] *adj* industrious; skilled

inébranlable [inebrɑ̃labl] *adj* unshakable

inéchangeable [ineʃɑ̃ʒabl] *adj* unexchangeable

iné·dit [inedi] **-dite** [dit] *adj* unpublished; new, novel

inéducable [inedykabl] *adj* unteachable

ineffable [inefabl] *adj* ineffable

ineffaçable [inefasabl] *adj* indelible

inefficace [inefikas] *adj* ineffective, inefficient

iné·gal -gale [inegal] *adj* (*pl* **-gaux** [go]) unequal; uneven

inégalité [inegalite] *f* inequality; unevenness

inéligible [ineliʒibl] *adj* ineligible

inéluctable [inelyktabl] *adj* unavoidable

inénarrable [inenarabl] *adj* beyond words, too funny for words

inepte [inept] *adj* inept, inane

ineptie [inepsi] *f* ineptitude, inanity; inane remark

inépuisable [inepɥizabl] *adj* inexhaustible

inerme [inerm] *adj* thornless

inertie [inersi] *f* inertia

inescomptable [ineskɔ̃tabl] *adj* not subject to discount

inespé·ré -rée [inespere] *adj* unhoped-for, unexpected

inévitable [inevitabl] *adj* inevitable

inexact inexacte [inegzakt] *adj* inexact, inaccurate; unpunctual

inexactitude [inegzaktityd] *f* inexactness, inaccuracy; unpunctuality

inexau·cé -cée [inegzose] *adj* unfulfilled, unanswered

inexcitable [ineksitabl] *adj* unexcitable

inexcusable [inekskyzabl] *adj* inexcusable

inexécutable [inegzekytabl] *adj* impracticable

inexécution [inegzekysjɔ̃] *f* nonfulfillment

inexer·cé -cée [inegzerse] *adj* untried; untrained

inexhaustible [inegzostibl] *adj* inexhaustible

inexigible [inegziʒibl] *adj* uncollectable

inexis·tant [ineksistɑ̃] **-tante** [tɑ̃t] *adj* nonexistent

inexorable [inegzɔrabl] *adj* inexorable

inexpérience [ineksperjɑ̃s] *f* inexperience

inexpérimen·té -tée [ineksperimɑ̃te] *adj* inexperienced; untried

inex·pié -piée [inekspje] *adj* unexpiated

inexplicable [ineksplikabl] *adj* inexplicable, unexplainable

inexpli·qué -quée [ineksplike] *adj* unexplained

inexploi·té -tée [ineksplwate] *adj* untapped

inexplo·ré -rée [ineksplɔre] *adj* unexplored

inexpres·sif [inekspresif] **inexpres·sive** [inekspresiv] *adj* expressionless

inexprimable [ineksprimabl] *adj* inexpressible

inexpri·mé -mée [ineksprime] *adj* unexpressed

inexpugnable [inekspygnabl] *adj* impregnable

inextinguible [inekstɛ̃gibl], [inekstɛ̃gɥibl] *adj* inextinguishable; uncontrollable; unquenchable

infaillible [ɛ̃fajibl] *adj* infallible

infaisable [ɛ̃fəzabl] *adj* unfeasible

infa·mant [ɛ̃famɑ̃] **-mante** [mɑ̃t] *adj* opprobrious

infâme [ɛ̃fɑm] *adj* infamous; squalid

infamie [ɛ̃fami] *f* infamy; **dire des infamies à** to hurl insults at; **noter d'infamie** to brand as infamous

infant [ɛ̃fɑ̃] *m* infante

infante [ɛ̃fɑ̃t] *f* infanta

infanterie [ɛ̃fɑ̃tri] *f* infantry; **infanterie de l'air, infanterie aéroportée** parachute troops; **infanterie de marine** overseas troops; **infanterie portée, infanterie motorisée** motorized troops

infantile [ɛ̃fɑ̃til] *adj* infantile

infatigable [ɛ̃fatigabl] *adj* indefatigable

infatuation [ɛ̃fatɥɑsjɔ̃] *f* conceit, false pride

infa·tué -tuée [ɛ̃fatɥe] *adj* infatuated with oneself, conceited infé·cond [ɛ̃fekɔ̃] -conde [kɔ̃d] adj sterile, barren

in·fect -fecte [ɛ̃fɛkt] adj stinking; foul, vile

infecter [ɛ̃fɛkte] tr to infect; to pollute; to stink up

infec·tieux [ɛ̃fɛksjø] -tieuse [sjøz] adj infectious

infection [ɛ̃fɛksjɔ̃] f infection; stench

inférer [ɛ̃fere] §10 tr to infer, conclude

infé·rieur -rieure [ɛ̃ferjœr] adj lower; inferior; inférieur à below; less than || mf subordinate, inferior

infériorité [ɛ̃ferjɔrite] f inferiority

infer·nal -nale [ɛ̃fɛrnal] adj (pl -naux [no]) infernal

infester [ɛ̃fɛste] tr to infest

infidèle [ɛ̃fidɛl] adj infidel; unfaithful || mf infidel || m unfaithful husband || f unfaithful wife

infidélité [ɛ̃fidelite] f infidelity; inaccuracy, unfaithfulness

infiltration [ɛ̃filtrasjɔ̃] f infiltration

infiltrer [ɛ̃filtre] ref to infiltrate; to seep, percolate; s'infiltrer à travers or dans to infiltrate

infime [ɛ̃fim] adj very small, infinitesimal; very low; trifling, negligible

infi·ni -nie [ɛ̃fini] adj infinite || m infinite; (math) infinity; à l'infini infinitely

infiniment [ɛ̃finimɑ̃] adv infinitely; (coll) greatly, deeply, terribly

infinité [ɛ̃finite] f infinity

infini·tif [ɛ̃finitif] -tive [tiv] adj & m infinitive

infirme [ɛ̃firm] adj infirm, crippled, disabled || mf invalid, cripple

infirmer [ɛ̃firme] tr (law) to invalidate

infirmerie [ɛ̃firməri] f infirmary; (nav) sick bay

infir·mier [ɛ̃firmje] -mière [mjɛr] mf nurse; infirmière bénévole volunteer nurse; infirmière diplômée registered nurse || m male nurse; orderly, attendant

infirmière-major [ɛ̃firmjɛrmaʒɔr] f head nurse

infirmité [ɛ̃firmite] f infirmity

infixe [ɛ̃fiks] m infix

inflammable [ɛ̃flamabl] adj inflammable

inflammation [ɛ̃flamasjɔ̃] f inflammation

inflammatoire [ɛ̃flamatwar] adj inflammatory

inflation [ɛ̃flasjɔ̃] f inflation

inflationniste [ɛ̃flasjɔnist] adj inflationary

infléchir [ɛ̃fleʃir] tr to inflect, bend || ref to bend, curve

inflexible [ɛ̃flɛksibl] adj inflexible

inflexion [ɛ̃flɛksjɔ̃] f inflection; change; bend, curve; metaphony

infliger [ɛ̃fliʒe] §38 tr to inflict; infliger q.ch. à to inflict s.th. on

influence [ɛ̃flyɑ̃s] f influence

influencer [ɛ̃flyɑ̃se] §51 tr to influence

influ·ent [ɛ̃flyɑ̃] influente [ɛ̃flyɑ̃t] adj influential

influenza [ɛ̃flyɑ̃za] f influenza

influer [ɛ̃flye] intr—influer sur to influence

in-folio [ɛ̃fɔljo] adj & m (pl -folio or -folios) folio

informa·teur [ɛ̃fɔrmatœr] -trice [tris] mf informant

information [ɛ̃fɔrmasjɔ̃] f information; piece of information; (law) investigation; aller aux informations to make inquiries; information génétique genetic characteristics; informations news; information; informations de presse press reports

informatique [ɛ̃fɔrmatik] adj informational || f information storage

informe [ɛ̃fɔrm] adj formless, shapeless

informer [ɛ̃fɔrme] tr to inform, advise || intr—informer contre to inform on ref to inquire, to keep oneself informed

infortune [ɛ̃fɔrtyn] f misfortune

infortu·né -née [ɛ̃fɔrtyne] adj unfortunate

infraction [ɛ̃fraksjɔ̃] f infraction

infranchissable [ɛ̃frɑ̃ʃisabl] adj insuperable; impassable (e.g., mountain)

infrarouge [ɛ̃fraruʒ] adj & m infrared

infrason [ɛ̃frasɔ̃] m infrasonic vibration

infrastructure [ɛ̃frastryktyr] f infrastructure; (rr) roadbed

infroissable [ɛ̃frwasabl] adj creaseless, wrinkleproof

infruc·tueux [ɛ̃fryktyø] -tueuse [tyøz] adj unfruitful, fruitless

in·fus [ɛ̃fy] -fuse [fyz] adj inborn, innate, intuitive

infuser [ɛ̃fyze] tr to infuse; to brew; infuser un sang nouveau à to put new blood or life into || intr to steep

infusion [ɛ̃fyzjɔ̃] f steeping; brew

ingambe [ɛ̃gɑ̃b] adj spry, nimble, alert

ingénier [ɛ̃ʒenje] ref to strive hard

ingénierie [ɛ̃ʒeniri] or ingénierie [ɛ̃ʒɛnjeri] f engineering

ingénieur [ɛ̃ʒenjœr] m engineer; ingénieur des ponts et chaussées civil engineer

ingé·nieux [ɛ̃ʒenjø] -nieuse [njøz] adj ingenious

ingéniosité [ɛ̃ʒenjozite] f ingenuity

ingé·nu -nue [ɛ̃ʒeny] adj ingenuous, artless || mf naïve person || f ingénue

ingénuité [ɛ̃ʒenɥite] f ingenuousness

ingérer [ɛ̃ʒere] §10 tr to ingest || ref to meddle

ingouvernable [ɛ̃guvɛrnabl] adj unruly, unmanageable

in·grat [ɛ̃gra] -grate [grat] adj ungrateful; disagreeable; thankless (task); unprofitable (work); barren (soil); awkward (age) || mf ingrate

ingratitude [ɛ̃gratityd] f ingratitude

ingrédient [ɛ̃gredjɑ̃] m ingredient

inguérissable [ɛ̃gerisabl] adj & mf incurable

ingurgiter [ɛ̃gyrʒite] tr to swallow; to gulp down

inhabile [inabil] adj unskilled; unfitted, unqualified

inhabileté [inabilte] f inability; clumsiness; unfitness

inhabitable [inabitabl] adj uninhabitable

inhabi·té -tée [inabite] adj uninhabited

inhabi·tuel -tuelle [inabituɛl] *adj* unusual

inhé·rent [inerɑ̃] -rente [rɑ̃t] *adj* inherent

inhiber [inibe] *tr* to inhibit

inhibition [inibisjɔ̃] *f* inhibition

inhospita·lier [inɔspitalje] -lière [ljɛr] *adj* inhospitable

inhu·main [inymɛ̃] -maine [mɛn] *adj* inhuman

inhumanité [inymanite] *f* inhumanity

inhumation [inymɑsjɔ̃] *f* burial

inhumer [inyme] *tr* to bury, to inter

inimitié [inimitje] *f* enmity

intelli·gent [inɛteliʒɑ̃] -gente [ʒɑ̃t] *adj* unintelligent

inintéres·sant [inɛteresɑ̃] inintéres·sante [inɛteresɑ̃t] *adj* uninteresting

ininterrom·pu -pue [inɛterɔ̃py] *adj* uninterrupted

inique [inik] *adj* iniquitous, unjust

iniquité [inikite] *f* iniquity

ini·tial -tiale [inisjal] (*pl* -tiaux [sjo] -tiales) *adj* & *f* initial

initia·teur [inisjatœr] -trice [tris] *adj* initiating ‖ *mf* initiator

initiation [inisjɑsjɔ̃] *f* initiation

initiative [inisjativ] *f* initiative

initier [inisje] *tr* to initiate; to introduce ‖ *ref* to become initiated

injecter [inʒɛkte] *tr* to inject; to impregnate ‖ *ref* to become bloodshot

injec·teur [inʒɛktœr] -trice [tris] *adj* injecting ‖ *m* injector; nozzle (*in motor*)

injection [inʒɛksjɔ̃] *f* injection; impregnation; redness (*of eyes*); (geog) intrusion

injonction [inʒɔ̃ksjɔ̃] *f* injunction, order

injouable [inʒwabl] *adj* unplayable

injure [inʒyr] *f* insult; wrong; l'injure des ans the ravages of time

injurier [inʒyrje] *tr* to insult, to abuse

inju·rieux [inʒyrjø] -rieuse [rjøz] *adj* insulting, abusive; harmful, offensive

injuste [inʒyst] *adj* unjust

injustice [inʒystis] *f* injustice

injusti·fié -fiée [inʒystifje] *adj* unjustified

inlassable [inlɑsabl] *adj* untiring

in·né -née [inne] *adj* innate, inborn

innocence [inɔsɑ̃s] *f* innocence

inno·cent [inɔsɑ̃] -cente [sɑ̃t] *adj* & *mf* innocent

innocenter [inɔsɑ̃te] *tr* to exonerate

innocuité [inɔkɥite] *f* innocuousness

innombrable [inɔ̃brabl] *adj* innumerable

innova·teur [inɔvatœr] -trice [tris] *adj* innovating ‖ *mf* innovator

innovation [inɔvɑsjɔ̃] *f* innovation

innover [inɔve] *tr* & *intr* to innovate

inoccu·pé -pée [inɔkype] *adj* unoccupied; unemployed, idle ‖ *mf* idler

in-octavo [inɔktavo] *adj* & *m* (*pl* -octavo *or* -octavos) octavo

inoculation [inɔkylɑsjɔ̃] *f* inoculation

inoculer [inɔkyle] *tr* to inoculate

inodore [inɔdɔr] *adj* odorless

inoffen·sif [inɔfɑ̃sif] -sive [siv] *adj* inoffensive

inondation [inɔ̃dɑsjɔ̃] *f* flood

inonder [inɔ̃de] *tr* to flood

inopi·né -née [inɔpine] *adj* unexpected

inoppor·tun [inɔpɔrtœ̃] -tune [tyn] *adj* untimely, inconvenient

inopportunité [inɔpɔrtynite] *f* untimeliness

inorganique [inɔrganik] *adj* inorganic

inorgani·sé -sée [inɔrganize] *adj* unorganized (*workers*), nonunion

inoubliable [inublijabl] *adj* unforgettable

inouï inouïe [inwi] *adj* unheard-of

inoxydable [inɔksidabl] *adj* inoxidizable, stainless, rustproof

inqualifiable [ɛ̃kalifjabl] *adj* unspeakable

in·quiet [ɛ̃kje] -quiète [kjɛt] *adj* anxious, worried, uneasy; restless

inquié·tant [ɛ̃kjetɑ̃] -tante [tɑ̃t] *adj* disquieting, worrisome

inquiéter [ɛ̃kjete] §10 *tr* & *intr* to worry

inquiétude [ɛ̃kjetyd] *f* uneasiness, worry

inquisi·teur [ɛ̃kizitœr] -trice [tris] *adj* inquisitorial; searching (*e.g., look*) ‖ *m* inquisitor

inquisition [ɛ̃kizisjɔ̃] *f* inquisition; investigation

inracontable [ɛ̃rakɔ̃tabl] *adj* untellable

insaisissable [ɛ̃sezisabl] *adj* hard to catch; elusive

insalubre [ɛ̃salybr] *adj* unhealthy

insane [ɛ̃san] *adj* insane, crazy

insanité [ɛ̃sanite] *f* insanity; piece of folly

insatiable [ɛ̃sasjabl] *adj* insatiable

insatisfaction [ɛ̃satisfaksjɔ̃] *f* dissatisfaction

inscription [ɛ̃skripsjɔ̃] *f* inscription; registration, enrollment; inscription de *or* en faux (law) plea of forgery; prendre ses inscriptions to register at a university

inscrire [ɛ̃skrir] §25 *tr* to inscribe; to register; to record ‖ *ref* to register, enroll; s'inscrire à to join; s'inscrire en faux contre to deny; s'inscrire pour to sign up for

ins·crit [ɛ̃skri] -crite [krit] *adj* inscribed; registered, enrolled ‖ *mf* registered student; (sports) entry; inscrit maritime naval recruit

insecte [ɛ̃sɛkt] *m* insect, bug

insecticide [ɛ̃sɛktisid] *adj* insecticidal ‖ *m* insecticide

insen·sé -sée [ɛ̃sɑ̃se] *adj* senseless, insane, crazy ‖ *m* madman ‖ *f* madwoman

insensible [ɛ̃sɑ̃sibl] *adj* insensitive; imperceptible

inséparable [ɛ̃separabl] *adj* inseparable ‖ *m* lovebird

insérer [ɛ̃sere] §10 *tr* to insert

insertion [ɛ̃sɛrsjɔ̃] *f* insertion

insi·dieux [ɛ̃sidjø] -dieuse [djøz] *adj* insidious

insigne [ɛ̃sin] *adj* signal, noteworthy; notorious ‖ *m* badge, mark; insignes insignia

insigni·fiant [ɛ̃sinifjɑ̃] -fiante [fjɑ̃t] *adj* insignificant

insincère [ɛ̃sɛ̃ser] *adj* insincere

insinuation [ɛ̃sinɥasjɔ̃] *f* insinuation

insinuer [ɛ̃sinɥe] *tr* to insinuate; to

hint, hint at; to work in, introduce ‖ *ref*—s'**insinuer dans** to worm one's way into

insipide [ɛsipid] *adj* insipid, tasteless; insipid, dull

insister [ɛsiste] *intr* to insist; (coll) to continue, persevere; **insister pour** to insist on; **insister sur** to stress

insociable [ɛsɔsjabl] *adj* unsociable

insolation [ɛsɔlɑsjɔ̃] *f* exposure to the sun; sunstroke

insolence [ɛsɔlɑ̃s] *f* insolence

inso·lent [ɛsɔlɑ̃] **-lente** [lɑ̃t] *adj* insolent; extraordinary, unexpected

insolite [ɛsɔlit] *adj* bizarre

insoluble [ɛsɔlybl] *adj* insoluble

insolvabilité [ɛsɔlvabilite] *f* insolvency

insolvable [ɛsɔlvabl] *adj* insolvent

insomnie [ɛsɔmni] *f* insomnia

insondable [ɛsɔ̃dabl] *adj* unfathomable

insonore [ɛsɔnɔr] *adj* soundproof; noiseless

insonoriser [ɛsɔnɔrize] *tr* to soundproof

insouciance [ɛsusjɑ̃s] *f* carefreeness; indifference, carelessness

insou·ciant [ɛsusjɑ̃] **-ciante** [sjɑ̃t] *adj* carefree, unconcerned

insou·cieux [ɛsusjø] **-cieuse** [sjøz] *adj* carefree, unmindful

insou·mis [ɛsumi] **-mise** [miz] *adj* unruly; unsubjugated ‖ *mf* rebel ‖ *m* (mil) A.W.O.L.

insoumission [ɛsumisjɔ̃] *f* insubordination, rebellion; (mil) absence without leave

insoupçonnable [ɛsupsɔnabl] *adj* above suspicion

insoupçon·né -née [ɛsupsɔne] *adj* unsuspected

insoutenable [ɛsutnabl] *adj* untenable; unbearable

inspecter [ɛspekte] *tr* to inspect

inspec·teur [ɛspektœr] **-trice** [tris] *mf* inspector

inspection [ɛspeksjɔ̃] *f* inspection; inspectorship

inspiration [ɛspirɑsjɔ̃] *f* inspiration

inspirer [ɛspire] *tr* to inspire; to breathe in; **inspirer à qn de** to inspire s.o. to; **inspirer q.ch. à** to inspire s.o. with s.th. ‖ *ref*—s'**inspirer de** to be inspired by

instable [ɛstabl] *adj* unstable

installateur [ɛstalatœr] *m* heater man; fitter, plumber

installation [ɛstalɑsjɔ̃] *f* installation; equipment, outfit; appointments, fittings

installer [ɛstale] *tr* to install; to equip, furnish; **être bien installé** to be comfortably settled ‖ *ref* to settle down, to set up shop; **s'installer chez** to foist oneself on

instamment [ɛstamɑ̃] *adv* urgently, earnestly

instance [ɛstɑ̃s] *f* insistence; **avec instance** earnestly; **en instance** pending; **en instance de** on the point of; **en seconde instance** on appeal; **instances** entreaties; **introduire une instance** to start proceedings

ins·tant [ɛstɑ̃] **-tante** [tɑ̃t] *adj* urgent, pressing ‖ *m* instant, moment; **à cha-** que **instant, à tout instant** continually; **à l'instant** at once, right away; just now; at the moment; **par instants** from time to time

instanta·né -née [ɛstɑ̃tane] *adj* instantaneous ‖ *m* snapshot

instantanément [ɛstɑ̃tanemɑ̃] *adv* instantaneously; instantly

instar [ɛstar]—**à l'instar de** in the manner of

instauration [ɛstɔrɑsjɔ̃] *f* establishment

instaurer [ɛstɔre] *tr* to establish

instigation [ɛstigɑsjɔ̃] *f* instigation

instiller [ɛstile] *tr* to instill

instinct [ɛstɛ̃] *m* instinct; **d'instinct, par instinct** by instinct

instinc·tif [ɛstɛ̃ktif] **-tive** [tiv] *adj* instinctive

instituer [ɛstitɥe] *tr* to found; to institute (*e.g., proceedings*)

institut [ɛstity] *m* institute; **institut de beauté** beauty parlor; **institut de coupe** tonsorial parlor; **institut dentaire** dental school

institu·teur [ɛstitytœr] **-trice** [tris] *mf* schoolteacher; founder

institution [ɛstitysjɔ̃] *f* institution

instructeur [ɛstryktœr] *m* instructor

instruc·tif [ɛstryktif] **-tive** [tiv] *adj* instructive

instruction [ɛstryksjɔ̃] *f* instruction; education; **instruction judiciaire** (law) preliminary investigation; **instructions permanentes** standing orders

instruire [ɛstrɥir] §19 *tr* to instruct; **instruire qn de** to inform s.o. of ‖ *ref* to improve one's mind

instrument [ɛstrymɑ̃] *m* instrument; **instrument à anche** reed instrument; **instrument à cordes** stringed instrument; **instrument à vent** wind instrument; **instrument en bois** woodwind; **instrument en cuivre** brass

instrumen·tal -tale [ɛstrymɑ̃tal] *adj* (*pl* **-taux** [to]) instrumental

instrumenter [ɛstrymɑ̃te] *tr* to instrument

instrumentiste [ɛstrymɑ̃tist] *mf* instrumentalist

insu [ɛsy] *m*—**à l'insu de** unknown to; **à mon insu** unknown to me

insubmersible [ɛsybmersibl] *adj* unsinkable

insubordon·né -née [ɛsybɔrdɔne] *adj* insubordinate

insuccès [ɛsyksɛ] *m* failure

insuffi·sant [ɛsyfizɑ̃] **-sante** [zɑ̃t] *adj* insufficient

insulaire [ɛsyler] *adj* insular ‖ *mf* islander

insuline [ɛsylin] *f* insulin

insulte [ɛsylt] *f* insult

insulter [ɛsylte] *tr* to insult ‖ *intr* (with *dat*) to offend, outrage

insupportable [ɛsypɔrtabl] *adj* unbearable

insur·gé -gée [ɛsyrʒe] *adj* & *mf* insurgent

insurger [ɛsyrʒe] §38 *ref* to revolt, rebel

insurmontable [ɛsyrmɔ̃tabl] *adj* insurmountable

insurrection [ɛ̃syrɛksjɔ̃] *f* insurrection

in·tact -tacte [ɛ̃takt] *adj* intact, untouched

intangible [ɛ̃tɑ̃ʒibl] *adj* intangible

intarissable [ɛ̃tarisabl] *adj* inexhaustible

inté·gral -grale [ɛ̃tegral] *adj* (*pl* -graux [gro]) integral; complete (*e.g.*, edition); full (*e.g.*, payment) ‖ *f* complete works; (math) integral

inté·grant -grante [ɛ̃tegrɑ̃] -grante [grɑ̃t] *adj* integral

intégration [ɛ̃tegrasjɔ̃] *f* integration

intègre [ɛ̃tegr] *adj* honest, upright

intégrer [ɛ̃tegre] §10 *tr* to integrate ‖ *ref* to form an integral part; (slang) to be accepted (*at an exclusive school*)

intégrité [ɛ̃tegrite] *f* integrity

intellect [ɛ̃telɛkt] *m* intellect

intellec·tuel -tuelle [ɛ̃telɛktɥel] *adj & mf* intellectual

intelligence [ɛ̃teliʒɑ̃s] *f* intelligence; intellect (*person*); **en bonne intelligence avec** on good terms with; **être d'intelligence** to be in collusion

intelli·gent -gente [ɛ̃teliʒɑ̃] -gente [ʒɑ̃t] *adj* intelligent

intelligible [ɛ̃teliʒibl] *adj* intelligible

intempé·rant -rante [ɛ̃tɑ̃perɑ̃] -rante [rɑ̃t] *adj* intemperate

intempéries [ɛ̃tɑ̃peri] *fpl* bad weather

intempes·tif -tive [ɛ̃tɑ̃pestif] -tive [tiv] *adj* untimely

intenable [ɛ̃tnabl] *adj* untenable

intendance [ɛ̃tɑ̃dɑ̃s] *f* stewardship; controllership, office of bursar; **Intendance** (mil) Quartermaster Corps

inten·dant [ɛ̃tɑ̃dɑ̃] -dante [dɑ̃t] *mf* steward, superintendent; controller, bursar; **intendant militaire** quartermaster

intense [ɛ̃tɑ̃s] *adj* intense

inten·sif -sive [ɛ̃tɑ̃sif] -sive [siv] *adj* intensive

intensifier [ɛ̃tɑ̃sifje] *tr & ref* to intensify

intensité [ɛ̃tɑ̃site] *f* intensity

intenter [ɛ̃tɑ̃te] *tr* to start (*a suit*); to bring (*an action*)

intention [ɛ̃tɑ̃sjɔ̃] *f* intention, intent; **à l'intention de** for (the sake of)

intention·né -née [ɛ̃tɑ̃sjɔne] *adj* motivated; **bien intentionné** well-meaning; **mal intentionné** ill-disposed

intention·nel -nelle [ɛ̃tɑ̃sjɔnel] *adj* intentional

inter [ɛ̃ter] *m* (coll) long distance

interaction [ɛ̃teraksjɔ̃] *f* interaction, interplay

intercaler [ɛ̃terkale] *tr* to intercalate; to insert, to sandwich

intercéder [ɛ̃tersede] §10 *intr* to intercede

intercepter [ɛ̃tersepte] *tr* to intercept

intercepteur [ɛ̃terseptœr] *m* interceptor

interchangeable [ɛ̃terʃɑ̃ʒabl] *adj* interchangeable

interclasse [ɛ̃terklɑs] *m* (educ) break between classes

intercourse [ɛ̃terkurs] *f* (naut) free entry

interdépen·dant [ɛ̃terdepɑ̃dɑ̃] -dante [dɑ̃t] *adj* interdependent

interdiction [ɛ̃terdiksjɔ̃] *f* interdiction; suspension; **interdiction de séjour** forbidden entry

interdire [ɛ̃terdir] §40 *tr* to prohibit, to forbid; to confound, to abash; to interdict; to suspend; **interdire q.ch. à qn** to forbid s.o. s.th.

inter·dit [ɛ̃terdi] -dite [dit] *adj* prohibited, forbidden; dumfounded, abashed; deprived of rights; (mil) off limits ‖ *m* interdict

intéres·sant [ɛ̃teresɑ̃] **intéres·sante** [ɛ̃teresɑ̃t] *adj* interesting; attractive (*offer*)

intéres·sé -sée [ɛ̃terese] *adj* interested; self-seeking ‖ *mf* interested party

intéresser [ɛ̃terese] *tr* to interest; to involve ‖ *ref*—**s'intéresser à** or **dans** to be interested in

intérêt [ɛ̃tere] *m* interest; **intérêts composés** compound interest

interférence [ɛ̃terferɑ̃s] *f* interference

interférer [ɛ̃terfere] §10 *intr* (phys) to interfere ‖ *ref* to interfere with each other

inté·rieur -rieure [ɛ̃terjœr] *adj* interior; inner, inside ‖ *m* interior; inside; house, home

intérieurement [ɛ̃terjœrmɑ̃] *adv* inwardly, internally; to oneself

intérim [ɛ̃terim] *m invar* interim; **dans l'intérim** in the meantime; **par intérim** acting, pro tem, interim

intérimaire [ɛ̃terimer] *adj* temporary, acting

interjection [ɛ̃terʒeksjɔ̃] *f* interjection

interligne [ɛ̃terliɲ] *m* space between the lines; writing in the space between the lines; **à double interligne** double-spaced ‖ *f* lead

interligner [ɛ̃terliɲe] *tr* to interline; (typ) to lead out

interlocu·teur [ɛ̃terlɔkytœr] -trice [tris] *mf* interlocutor; intermediary; party (*with whom one is conversing*)

interlope [ɛ̃terlɔp] *adj* illegal, shady ‖ *m* (naut) smuggling vessel

interloquer [ɛ̃terlɔke] *tr* to disconcert

interlude [ɛ̃terlyd] *m* interlude

intermède [ɛ̃termed] *m* (theat & fig) interlude

intermédiaire [ɛ̃termedjer] *adj* intermediate, intermediary ‖ *mf* intermediary ‖ *m* (com) middleman; **par l'intermédiaire de** by means of, by the medium of

interminable [ɛ̃terminabl] *adj* interminable

intermit·tent [ɛ̃termitɑ̃] **intermit·tente** [ɛ̃termitɑ̃t] *adj* intermittent

internat [ɛ̃terna] *m* boarding school; boarding-school life; (med) internship

internatio·nal -nale [ɛ̃ternasjɔnal] *adj* (*pl* -naux [no]) international

interne [ɛ̃tern] *adj* inner; (math) interior ‖ *mf* boarder (*at a school*); (med) intern

inter·né -née [ɛ̃terne] *mf* internee

internement [ɛ̃ternəmɑ̃] *m* internment; confinement (*of a mental patient*)

interner [ɛterne] *tr* to intern
interpeller [ɛterpele] *tr* to question, to interrogate; to yell at; to heckle
interphone [ɛterfɔn] *m* intercom
interplanétaire [ɛterplaneter] *adj* interplanetary
interpoler [ɛterpɔle] *tr* to interpolate
interposer [ɛterpoze] *tr* to interpose
interprétation [ɛterpretasjɔ̃] *f* interpretation
interprète [ɛterpret] *mf* interpreter
interpréter [ɛterprete] §10 *tr* to interpret; **mal interpréter** to misinterpret
interrogation [ɛterɔgasjɔ̃] *f* interrogation
interroger [ɛterɔʒe] §38 *tr* to interrogate, to question
interrompre [ɛterɔ̃pr] (3d *sg pres ind* **interrompt** [ɛterɔ̃]) *tr* to interrupt; to heckle ‖ *ref* to break off, to be interrupted
interrup·teur [ɛteryptœr] **-trice** [tris] *adj* interrupting; circuit-breaking ‖ *m* switch; **interrupteur à couteau** knife switch; **interrupteur à culbuteur** or **à bascule** toggle switch; **interrupteur d'escalier** two-way switch; **interrupteur encastré** flush switch; **interrupteur olive** pear switch
interruption [ɛterypsjɔ̃] *f* interruption
intersection [ɛtersɛksjɔ̃] *f* intersection
intersigne [ɛtersiɲ] *m* omen, portent
interstellaire [ɛtersteler] *adj* interstellar
interstice [ɛterstis] *m* interstice
interur·bain [ɛteryrbɛ̃] **-baine** [ben] *adj* interurban; (telp) long-distance ‖ *m* (telp) long distance
intervalle [ɛterval] *m* interval
intervenir [ɛtervnir] §72 (*aux:* ÊTRE) *intr* to intervene; to take place, happen; (med) to operate; **faire intervenir** to call in
intervention [ɛtervãsjɔ̃] *f* intervention; (med) operation
intervertir [ɛtervertir] *tr* to invert, to transpose
interview [ɛtervju] *f* (journ) interview
interviewer [ɛtervjuvœr] *m* interviewer ‖ [ɛtervjuve] *tr* to interview
intestat [ɛtesta] *adj & mf invar* intestate
intes·tin [ɛtestɛ̃] **-tine** [tin] *adj* intestine, internal ‖ *m* intestine; **gros intestin** large intestine; **intestin grêle** small intestine
intimation [ɛtimasjɔ̃] *f* (law) summons
intime [ɛtim] *adj & mf* intimate
inti·mé -mée [ɛtime] *mf* (law) defendant
intimer [ɛtime] *tr* to notify; to give (*an order*)
intimider [ɛtimide] *tr* to intimidate
intimité [ɛtimite] *f* intimacy; privacy; depths (*of one's being*)
intituler [ɛtityle] *tr* to entitle
intolérable [ɛtɔlerabl] *adj* intolerable
intolé·rant [ɛtɔlerã] **-rante** [rãt] *adj* intolerant
intonation [ɛtɔnasjɔ̃] *f* intonation
intouchable [ɛtuʃabl] *adj & mf* untouchable
intoxication [ɛtɔksikasjɔ̃] *f* poisoning
intoxiquer [ɛtɔksike] *tr* to poison

intraitable [ɛtretabl] *adj* intractable
intransi·geant [ɛtrãziʒã] **-geante** [ʒãt] *adj* intransigent ‖ *mf* diehard, standpatter
intransi·tif [ɛtrãzitif] **-tive** [tiv] *adj* intransitive
intravei·neux [ɛtravenø] **-neuse** [nøz] *adj* intravenous
intrépide [ɛtrepid] *adj* intrepid; persistent
intri·gant [ɛtrigã] **-gante** [gãt] *adj* intriguing ‖ *mf* plotter, schemer
intrigue [ɛtrig] *f* intrigue, plot; love affair; **intrigues de couloir** lobbying
intriguer [ɛtrige] *tr & intr* to intrigue
intrinsèque [ɛtrɛ̃sek] *adj* intrinsic
introduction [ɛtrɔdyksjɔ̃] *f* introduction; admission
introduire [ɛtrɔdɥir] §19 *tr* to introduce, to bring in; to show in; to interject (*e.g., a remark*) ‖ *ref* to be introduced; **s'introduire dans** to slip in
intronisation [ɛtrɔnizasjɔ̃] *f* investiture, inauguration
introniser [ɛtrɔnize] *tr* to enthrone
introspec·tif [ɛtrɔspektif] **-tive** [tiv] *adj* introspective
introuvable [ɛtruvabl] *adj* unfindable
introver·ti -tie [ɛtrɔverti] *adj & mf* introvert
in·trus [ɛtry] **-truse** [tryz] *adj* intruding ‖ *mf* intruder
intrusion [ɛtryzjɔ̃] *f* intrusion
intuition [ɛtɥisjɔ̃] *f* intuition
inusable [inyzabl] *adj* durable, wearproof
inusi·té -tée [inyzite] *adj* obsolete
inutile [inytil] *adj* useless, unnecessary
inutilement [inytilmã] *adv* in vain, uselessly; unnecessarily
inutilité [inytilite] *f* uselessness
invain·cu -cue [ɛ̃vɛ̃ky] *adj* unconquered
invalide [ɛ̃valid] *adj* invalid ‖ *mf* invalid, cripple; **invalide de guerre** disabled veteran
invalider [ɛ̃valide] *tr* to invalidate
invalidité [ɛ̃validite] *f* invalidity; disability
invariable [ɛ̃varjabl] *adj* invariable
invasion [ɛ̃vazjɔ̃] *f* invasion
invective [ɛ̃vektiv] *f* invective
invectiver [ɛ̃vektive] *tr* to rail at ‖ *intr* to inveigh
invendable [ɛ̃vãdabl] *adj* unsalable
inven·du -due [ɛ̃vãdy] *adj* unsold ‖ *m* —**les invendus** the unsold copies; the unsold articles
inventaire [ɛ̃vãter] *m* inventory
inventer [ɛ̃vãte] *tr* to invent
inven·teur [ɛ̃vãtœr] **-trice** [tris] *mf* inventor; (law) finder
inven·tif [ɛ̃vãtif] **-tive** [tiv] *adj* inventive
invention [ɛ̃vãsjɔ̃] *f* invention
inventorier [ɛ̃vãtɔrje] *tr* to inventory
inversable [ɛ̃versabl] *adj* untippable, uncapsizable
inverse [ɛ̃vers] *adj & m* inverse; **faire l'inverse de** to do the opposite of
inverser [ɛ̃verse] *tr* to invert, to reverse ‖ *intr* (elec) to reverse

inverseur [ɛ̃versœr] m reversing device; inverseur des phares (aut) dimmer

inversion [ɛ̃versjɔ̃] f inversion

inverté·bré -brée [ɛ̃vertebre] adj & m invertebrate

inver·ti ·tie [ɛ̃verti] mf invert

invertir [ɛ̃vertir] tr to invert, reverse

investiga·teur [ɛ̃vestigatœr] -trice [tris] adj investigative; searching || mf investigator

investigation [ɛ̃vestigɑsjɔ̃] f investigation

investir [ɛ̃vestir] tr to invest; to vest; investir qn de sa confiance to place one's confidence in s.o.

investissement [ɛ̃vestismɑ̃] m investment

investiture [ɛ̃vestityr] f investiture; nomination (as a candidate for election)

invété·ré -rée [ɛ̃vetere] adj inveterate

invétérer [ɛ̃vetere] ref to become inveterate

invincible [ɛ̃vɛ̃sibl] adj invincible

invisible [ɛ̃vizibl] adj invisible; (coll) hiding, keeping out of sight

invitation [ɛ̃vitɑsjɔ̃] f invitation

invite [ɛ̃vit] f invitation, inducement; répondre à l'invite de qn (cards) to return s.o.'s lead; (fig) to respond to s.o.'s advances

invi·té -tée [ɛ̃vite] adj invited || mf guest

inviter [ɛ̃vite] tr to invite

involontaire [ɛ̃vɔlɔ̃ter] adj involuntary

invoquer [ɛ̃vɔke] tr to invoke

invraisemblable [ɛ̃vresɑ̃blabl] adj improbable, unlikely, hard to believe; (coll) strange, weird

invraisemblance [ɛ̃vresɑ̃blɑ̃s] f improbability, unlikelihood; (coll) queerness

invulnérable [ɛ̃vylnerabl] adj invulnerable

iode [jɔd] m iodine

iodure [jɔdyr] m iodide

ion [jɔ̃] m ion

ioniser [jɔnize] tr to ionize

iota [jɔta] m iota

Irak [irak] m—l'Irak Iraq

ira·kien [irakjɛ̃] -kienne [kjen] adj Iraqi || (cap) mf Iraqi

Iran [irɑ̃] m—l'Iran Iran

ira·nien [iranjɛ̃] -nienne [njen] adj Iranian || m Iranian (language) || (cap) mf Iranian (person)

iris [iris] m iris

irlan·dais [irlɑ̃de] -daise [dez] adj Irish || m Irish (language) || (cap) m Irishman; les Irlandais the Irish || (cap) f Irishwoman

Irlande [irlɑ̃d] f Ireland; l'Irlande Ireland

ironie [irɔni] f irony

ironique [irɔnik] adj ironic(al)

ironiser [irɔnize] tr to say ironically || intr to speak ironically, to jeer

irradier [iradje] tr & ref to irradiate

irraison·né -née [irezɔne] adj unreasoning

irration·nel -nelle [irɑsjɔnel] adj irrational

irréalisable [irealizabl] adj impractical, unattainable

irréalité [irealite] f unreality

irrécouvrable [irekuvrabl] adj uncollectible

irrécupérable [irekyperabl] adj irretrievable

irrécusable [irekyzabl] adj unimpeachable, incontestable, indisputable

irréel irréelle [ireel] adj unreal

irréflé·chi -chie [irefleʃi] adj rash, thoughtless

irréfutable [irefytabl] adj irrefutable

irrégu·lier [iregylje] -lière [ljer] adj & m irregular

irréli·gieux [irelizjø] -gieuse [zjøz] adj irreligious

irrémédiable [iremedjabl] adj irremediable

irremplaçable [irɑ̃plasabl] adj irreplaceable

irréparable [ireparabl] adj irreparable; irretrievable (loss, mistake, etc.)

irrépressible [irepresibl] adj irrepressible

irréprochable [ireproʃabl] adj irreproachable

irrésistible [irezistibl] adj irresistible

irréso·lu -lue [irezɔly] adj irresolute

irrespect [irespe] m disrespect

irrespec·tueux [irespektɥø] -tueuse [tɥøz] adj disrespectful

irrespirable [irespirabl] adj unbreathable

irresponsable [irespɔ̃sabl] adj irresponsible

irrétrécissable [iretresisabl] adj preshrunk, unshrinkable

irrévéren·cieux [ireverɑ̃sjø] -cieuse [sjøz] adj irreverent

irréversible [ireversibl] adj irreversible

irrévocable [irevɔkabl] adj irrevocable

irrigation [irigɑsjɔ̃] f irrigation

irriguer [irige] tr to irrigate

irri·tant [iritɑ̃] -tante [tɑ̃t] adj irritating || m irritant

irritation [iritɑsjɔ̃] f irritation

irriter [irite] tr to irritate || ref to become irritated

irruption [irypsjɔ̃] f irruption; invasion; faire irruption to burst in

isabelle [izabel] m dun or light-bay horse || (cap) f Isabel

Isaïe [izai] m Isaiah

Islam [islam] m—l'Islam Islam

islan·dais [islɑ̃de] -daise [dez] adj Icelandic || m Icelandic (language) || (cap) mf Icelander

Islande [islɑ̃d] f Iceland; l'Islande Iceland

isocèle [izɔsel] adj isosceles

iso·lant [izɔlɑ̃] -lante [lɑ̃t] adj insulating || m insulator

isolateur [izɔlatœr] m insulator

isolation [izɔlɑsjɔ̃] f insulation; isolation phonique soundproofing

isolationniste [izɔlɑsjɔnist] adj & mf isolationist

iso·lé -lée [izɔle] adj isolated; independent; insulated

isolement [izɔlmɑ̃] m isolation; insulation

isolément [izɔlemɑ̃] adv separately, independently

isoler [izɔle] *tr* to isolate; to insulate ‖ *ref* to cut oneself off

isoloir [izɔlwar] *m* polling booth

isotope [izɔtɔp] *m* isotope

Israël [israel] *m*—l'Israël Israel

israé·lien [israeljɛ̃] **-lienne** [ljen] *adj* Israeli ‖ *(cap) mf* Israeli

israélite [israelit] *adj* Israelite ‖ *(cap) mf* Israelite

is·su is·sue [isy] *adj*—issu de descended from, born of ‖ *f* exit, way out; outlet; outcome, issue; **à l'issue de** on the way out from; at the end of; issues sharps, middlings (*in milling flour*); offal (*in butchering*); **sans issue** without exit; without any way out

isthme [ism] *m* isthmus

Italie [itali] *f* Italy; **l'Italie** Italy

ita·lien [italjɛ̃] **-lienne** [ljen] *adj* Ital-ian ‖ *m* Italian (*language*) ‖ *(cap) mf* Italian (*person*)

italique [italik] *adj* Italic; (typ) italic ‖ *m* (typ) italics

item [item] *m* question (*in a test*) ‖ *adv* ditto

itinéraire [itinerer] *adj & m* itinerary

itiné·rant [itinerã] **-rante** [rãt] *adj & mf* itinerant

itou [itu] *adv* (slang) also, likewise

ivoire [ivwar] *m* ivory

ivraie [ivre] *f* darnel, cockle; (Bib) tares

ivre [ivr] *adj* drunk, intoxicated

ivresse [ivres] *f* drunkenness; ecstasy, rapture

ivrogne [ivrɔɲ] *adj* hard-drinking ‖ *m* drunkard

ivrognerie [ivrɔɲri] *f* drunkenness

ivrognesse [ivrɔɲes] *f* drinking woman

J

J, j [ʒi] *m invar* tenth letter of the French alphabet

jabot [ʒabo] *m* jabot; crop (*of bird*)

jabotage [ʒabotaʒ] *m* jabbering

jaboter [ʒabote] *tr & intr* to jabber

jacasse [ʒakas] *f* magpie; chatterbox

jacasser [ʒakase] *intr* to chatter, to jabber

jacasserie [ʒakasri] *f* chatter, jabber

jachère [ʒaʃer] *f* fallow ground

jacinthe [ʒasɛ̃t] *f* hyacinth; **jacinthe des bois** bluebell

Jacques [ʒak] *m* James, Jacob; **Jacques Bonhomme** the typical Frenchman

jactance [ʒaktãs] *f* bragging

jade [ʒad] *m* jade

jadis [ʒadis] *adv* formerly, of yore

jaguar [ʒagwar] *m* jaguar

jaillir [ʒajir] *intr* to gush, to burst forth

jaillissement [ʒajismã] *m* gush

jais [ʒe] *m* jet

jalon [ʒalɔ̃] *m* stake; landmark; surveying staff

jalonner [ʒalɔne] *tr* to stake out; to mark (*a way, a channel*)

jalousie [ʒaluzi] *f* jealousy; awning; Venetian blind

ja·loux [ʒalu] **-louse** [luz] *adj* jealous

jamais [ʒame] *adv* ever; never; **jamais de la vie!** not on your life!; **jamais plus** never again; **ne . . . jamais** §90 never; **pour jamais** forever

jambe [ʒãb] *f* leg; à **toutes jambes** as fast as possible; **prendre ses jambes à son cou** to take to one's heels

jambon [ʒãbɔ̃] *m* ham; **jambon d'York** boiled ham

jambon·neau [ʒãbɔno] *m* (*pl* **-neaux**) ham knuckle

jamboree [ʒãbɔre], [dʒãbɔri] *m* jamboree

jante [ʒãt] *f* felloe; rim (*of auto wheel*)

janvier [ʒãvje] *m* January

Japon [ʒapɔ̃] *m*—**le Japon** Japan

japo·nais [ʒapone] **-naise** [nez] *adj* Japanese ‖ *m* Japanese (*language*) ‖ *(cap) mf* Japanese (*person*)

japper [ʒape] *intr* to yap, to yelp

jaquemart [ʒakmar] *m* jack (*figurine striking the time on a bell*)

jaquette [ʒaket] *f* coat, jacket; cutaway coat, morning coat; book jacket

jardin [ʒardɛ̃] *m* garden; **jardin d'acclimatation** zoo; **jardin d'enfants** kindergarten; **jardin d'hiver** greenhouse

jardiner [ʒardine] *tr* to clear out, to trim ‖ *intr* to garden

jardi·nier [ʒardinje] **-nière** [njer] *adj* garden ‖ *mf* gardener ‖ *m* flower stand; mixed vegetables; spring wagon ‖ *f* kindergartner (*teacher*)

jargon [ʒargɔ̃] *m* jargon

jarre [ʒar] *f* earthenware jar

jarret [ʒare] *m* hock, gambrel; shin (*of beef or veal*); back of the knee

jarretelle [ʒartel] *f* garter

jarretière [ʒartjer] *f* garter

jars [ʒar] *m* gander

jaser [ʒaze] *intr* to babble, prattle; to blab, gossip

jasmin [ʒasmɛ̃] *m* jasmine

jaspe [ʒasp] *m* jasper; (bb) marbling

jasper [ʒaspe] *tr* to marble, speckle

jatte [ʒat] *f* bowl

jauge [ʒoʒ] *f* gauge; dipstick; (agr) trench; (naut) tonnage

jauger [ʒoʒe] §38 *tr* to gauge, measure; (naut) to draw

jaunâtre [ʒonatr] *adj* yellowish; sallow

jaune [ʒon] *adj* yellow ‖ *mf* yellow

person (*Oriental*) ‖ *m* yellow; yolk (*of egg*); scab, strikebreaker
jaunir [ʒonir] *tr & intr* to yellow
jaunisse [ʒonis] *f* jaundice
Javel [ʒavɛl] *f*—**eau de Javel** bleach
javelle [ʒavɛl] *f* swath (*of grain*); bunch (*of twigs*)
javelliser [ʒavelize] *tr* to chlorinate (*water*)
javelot [ʒavlo] *m* javelin
jazz [dʒaz] *m* jazz
je [ʒə] §87
Jean [ʒɑ̃] *m* John
Jeanne [ʒɑn] *f* Jane, Jean, Joan
jeannette [ʒanɛt] *f* gold cross (*ornament*); sleevebreaker
Jeannot [ʒano] *m* (coll) Johnny, Jack
jeep [dʒip] *f* jeep
Jéhovah [ʒeova] *m* Jehovah
je-m'en-fichisme [ʒmɑ̃fiʃism] *m* (slang) what-the-hell attitude
je-ne-sais-quoi [ʒənsekwa] *m invar* what-you-call-it
Jérôme [ʒerom] *m* Jerome
jerrycan [dʒerikan] *m* gasoline can
jersey [ʒerse] *m* jersey, sweater
Jérusalem [ʒeryzalem] *f* Jerusalem
Jésuite [ʒezɥit] *m* Jesuit
Jésus [ʒezy] *m* Jesus
Jésus-Christ [ʒezykri] *m* Jesus Christ
jet [ʒɛ] *m* throw, cast; jet; spurt, gush; flash (*of light*); **du premier jet** at the first try; **jet à la mer** jettison; **jet d'eau** fountain; **jet de pierre** stone's throw
jetée [ʒəte] *f* breakwater, jetty
jeter [ʒəte] §34 *tr* to throw; to throw away; to throw down; to hurl, fling; to toss; to cast (*a glance*); to shed (*the skin*); to pour forth; to utter; to drop (*anchor*); to lay (*the foundations*) ‖ *intr* to sprout ‖ *ref* to throw oneself; to rush; to empty (*said of a river*)
jeton [ʒətɔ̃] *m* token, counter; slug
jeu [ʒø] *m* (*pl* **jeux**) play, game, sport; gambling; pack, deck (*of cards*); set (*of chessmen; of tools*); playing; acting; execution, performance; **en jeu** in gear; at stake; **franc jeu** fair play; **gros jeu** high stakes; **jeu d'eau** dancing waters; **jeu de dames** checkers; **jeu de hasard** game of chance; **jeu de massacre** hit-the-baby (*game at fair*); **jeu de mots** pun, play on words; **jeu d'enfant** child's play; **jeu de patience** jigsaw puzzle; **jeu de puce** tiddlywinks; **jeu de société** parlor game; **jeu d'orgue** organ stop; **jouer un jeu d'enfer** to play for high stakes; **vieux jeu** old hat
jeudi [ʒødi] *m* Thursday; **jeudi saint** Maundy Thursday
jeun [ʒœ̃]—**à jeun** fasting; on an empty stomach
jeune [ʒœn] *adj* young; youthful; junior, younger ‖ *m* young man; **jeunes délinquants** juvenile delinquents; **les jeunes** young people; the young (*of an animal*)
jeûne [ʒøn] *m* fast, fasting

jeûner [ʒøne] *intr* to fast; to abstain; to eat sparingly
jeunesse [ʒœnes] *f* youth; youthfulness; boyhood, girlhood; **jeunesse dorée** young people of wealth and fashion
jeu·net [ʒœne] **-nette** [net] *adj* youngish
jeû·neur [ʒœnœr] **-neuse** [nøz] *mf* faster
joaillerie [ʒoajri] *f* jewelry; jewelry business; jewelry shop
joail·lier [ʒoaje] **joail·lière** [ʒoajer] *mf* jeweler
jobard [ʒobar] *m* (coll) dupe
jobarderie [ʒobardri] *f* gullibility
jockey [ʒoke] *m* jockey
jodler [ʒodle] *tr & intr* to yodel
joie [ʒwa] *f* joy; **joies** pleasures
joindre [ʒwɛ̃dr] §35 *tr* to join; to add; to adjoin; to catch up with; **joindre les deux bouts** to make both ends meet ‖ *intr* to join ‖ *ref* to join, unite; to be adjacent, to come together
joint [ʒwɛ̃] **jointe** [ʒwɛ̃t] *adj* joined; joint (*effort*); **joint** à added to ‖ *m* joint; **joint de cardan** (mach) universal joint; **joint de culasse** (aut) gasket (*of cylinder head*); **joint de dilatation thermique** expansion joint; **trouver le joint** (coll) to hit on the solution
jointure [ʒwɛ̃tyr] *f* knuckle; joint
joker [ʒoker] *m* joker
jo·li -lie [ʒoli] *adj* pretty; tidy (*income*)
joliment [ʒolimɑ̃] *adv* nicely; (coll) extremely, awfully
Jonas [ʒonas], [ʒonɑ] *m* Jonah
jonc [ʒɔ̃] *m* rush; **jonc d'Inde** rattan
jonchée [ʒɔ̃ʃe] *f* litter (*things strewn about*); cottage cheese
joncher [ʒɔ̃ʃe] *tr* to strew; to litter
jonction [ʒɔ̃ksjɔ̃] *f* junction
jongler [ʒɔ̃gle] *intr* to juggle
jonglerie [ʒɔ̃glɔri] *f* jugglery
jongleur [ʒɔ̃glœr] *m* juggler; jongleur
jonque [ʒɔ̃k] *f* (naut) junk
jonquille [ʒɔ̃kij] *adj invar* pale-yellow ‖ *m* pale yellow ‖ *f* jonquil
Jordanie [ʒordani] *f* Jordan; **la Jordanie** Jordan
joue [ʒu] *f* cheek; **se caler les joues** (slang) to stuff oneself
jouer [ʒwe] *tr* to play; to gamble away; to feign; to act (*a part*) ‖ *intr* to play; to gamble; to feign; **faire jouer** to spring (*a lock*); **jouer à** to play (*a game*); **jouer à la baisse** to bear the market; **jouer à la hausse** to bull the market; **jouer de** to play (*a musical instrument*) ‖ *ref* to frolic; **se jouer de** to make fun of; to be independent of; to make light of
jouet [ʒwe] *m* toy, plaything
joueur [ʒwœr] **joueuse** [ʒwøz] *mf* player (*of games; of musical instruments*); gambler; **beau joueur** good sport; **joueur à la baisse** bear; **joueur à la hausse** bull; **mauvais joueur** poor sport
jouf·flu -flue [ʒufly] *adj* chubby
joug [ʒu] *m* yoke

jouir [ʒwir] *intr* to enjoy oneself, enjoy life; **jouir de** to enjoy

jouissance [ʒwisɑ̃s] *f* enjoyment; use, possession

jouis•seur [ʒwisœr] **jouis•seuse** [ʒwisøz] *adj* pleasure-loving || *mf* pleasure lover

jou•jou [ʒuʒu] *m* (*pl* **-joux**) toy, plaything

jour [ʒur] *m* day; daylight; light, window, opening; **à jour** openwork; up to date; **de nos jours** nowadays; **grand jour** broad daylight; **huit jours** a week; **il fait jour** it is getting light; **jour chômé** day off; **jour de ma fête** my birthday; **jour férié** legal holiday; **jour ouvrable** workday; **le jour de l'An** New Year's day; **le jour J** D-Day; **quinze jours** two weeks; **sous un faux jour** in a false light; **vivre au jour le jour** to live from hand to mouth

Jourdain [ʒurdɛ̃] *m* Jordan (*river*)

jour•nal [ʒurnal] *m* (*pl* **-naux** [no]) newspaper; journal; diary; (naut) logbook, journal; **journal parlé** newscast; **journal télévisé** telecast

journa•lier [ʒurnalje] **-lière** [ljɛr] *adj* daily || *m* day laborer

journalisme [ʒurnalism] *m* journalism

journaliste [ʒurnalist] *mf* journalist

journée [ʒurne] *f* day; day's journey; day's pay; day's work; **journée d'accueil** open house; **toute la journée** all day long

journellement [ʒurnɛlmɑ̃] *adv* daily

joute [ʒut] *f* joust

jouter [ʒute] *intr* to joust

jo•vial -viale [ʒovjal] *adj* (*pl* **-vials** or **-viaux** [vjo]) **-viales** jovial, jocose

joyau [ʒwajo] *m* (*pl* **joyaux**) jewel

joyeux [ʒwajø] **joyeuse** [ʒwajøz] *adj* joyful, cheerful; jocose

jubi•lant -lante [ʒybilɑ̃] [lɑ̃t] *adj* jubilant

jubilé [ʒybile] *m* jubilee; golden-wedding anniversary

jucher [ʒyʃe] *tr & intr* to perch || *ref* to go to roost

judaïque [ʒydaik] *adj* Jewish

judaïsme [ʒydaism] *m* Judaism

Judas [ʒyda] *m* peephole || (*cap*) *m* Judas

judicature [ʒydikatyr] *f* judiciary

judiciaire [ʒydisjɛr] *adj* legal, judicial

judi•cieux [ʒydisjø] **-cieuse** [sjøz] *adj* judicious, judicial

juge [ʒyʒ] *m* judge; umpire; **juge assesseur** associate judge

jugement [ʒyʒmɑ̃] *m* judgment

juger [ʒyʒe] §38 *tr & intr* to judge

jugulaire [ʒygylɛr] *adj* jugular || *f* chin strap

juif [ʒɥif] **juive** [ʒɥiv] *adj* Jewish || (*cap*) *mf* Jew

juillet [ʒɥije] *m* July

juin [ʒɥɛ̃] *m* June

Jules [ʒyl] *m* Julius; (coll) Mack; (slang) pimp; (slang) chamber pot

ju•lien [ʒyljɛ̃] **-lienne** [ljen] *adj* Julian || *f* (*soup*) julienne; (bot) rocket

ju•meau [ʒymo] **-melle** [mel] (*pl* **-meaux -melles**) *adj & mf* twin || *f* see **jumelles**

jumelage [ʒymlaʒ] *m* twinning

jume•lé -lée [ʒymle] *adj* double; twin (*cities*); semidetached (*house*); bilingual (*text*)

jumeler [ʒymle] §34 *tr* to couple, to join; to pair

jumelles [ʒymɛl] *fpl* opera glasses; field glasses; **jumelles de manchettes** cuff links

jument [ʒymɑ̃] *f* mare

jungle [ʒɔ̃gl] *f* jungle

jupe [ʒyp] *f* skirt

jupon [ʒypɔ̃] *m* petticoat

juré [ʒyre] *m* juror; member of an examining board

jurer [ʒyre] *tr* to swear || *intr* to swear; to clash

juridiction [ʒyridiksjɔ̃] *f* jurisdiction

juridique [ʒyridik] *adj* legal, judicial

juriste [ʒyrist] *m* writer on legal matters

juron [ʒyrɔ̃] *m* oath

jury [ʒyri] *m* jury; examining board

jus [ʒy] *m* juice; gravy; (slang) drink (*body of water*)

jusqu'au-boutiste [ʒyskobutist] *mf* (coll) bitterender, diehard

jusque [ʒysk(ə)] *adv* even; **jusqu'à** as far as, down to, up to; until; even; **jusqu'à ce que** until; **jusqu'après** until after; **jusqu'à quand** how long || *prep* as far as; until; **jusques et y compris** [ʒyskəzeikɔ̃pri] up to and including; **jusqu'ici** this far; until now; **jusqu'où** how far

jusqu-.-là [ʒyskəla] *adv* that far; until then

jusquiame [ʒyskjam] *f* henbane

juste [ʒyst] *adj* just, righteous; accurate; just enough; sharp, e.g., **à six heures justes** at six o'clock sharp; (mus) in tune, on key || *adv* justly; correctly, exactly

justement [ʒystəmɑ̃] *adv* just; justly; exactly; as it happens

juste-milieu [ʒystəmiljø] *m* happy medium, golden mean

justesse [ʒystes] *f* justness; precision, accuracy; **de justesse** barely

justice [ʒystis] *f* justice; **faire justice de** to mete out just punishment to; to make short work of

justiciable [ʒystisjabl] *adj*—**justiciable de** accountable to; subject to

justifier [ʒystifje] *tr* to justify || *intr*— **justifier de** to account for, to prove || *ref* to clear oneself

jute [ʒyt] *m* jute

ju•teux [ʒytø] **-teuse** [tøz] *adj* juicy

juvénile [ʒyvenil] *adj* juvenile, youthful

juxtaposer [ʒykstapoze] *tr* to juxtapose

K

K, k [ka] *m invar* eleventh letter of
the French alphabet
kaki [kaki] *adj invar* & *m* khaki
kaléidoscope [kaleidɔskɔp] *m* kaleidoscope
kangourou [kãguru] *m* kangaroo
keepsake [kipsɛk] *m* giftbook, keepsake
képi [kepi] *m* kepi
kermesse [kɛrmɛs] *f* charity bazaar
kérosène [kerozɛn] *m* kerosene
ketchup [ketʃœp] *m* ketchup
khan [kã] *m* khan
kidnapper [kidnape] *tr* to kidnap
kidnap·peur [kidnapœr] **kidnap·peuse**
[kidnapøz] *mf* kidnaper
kif [kif] *m* (coll) pot, marijuana
kif-kif [kifkif] *adj invar* (coll) all the
same; **c'est kif-kif** (coll) it's fifty-fifty
kilo [kilo] *m* kilo, kilogram
kilocycle [kilɔsikl] *m* kilocycle
kilogramme [kilɔgram] *m* kilogram
kilomètre [kilɔmɛtr] *m* kilometer, kilo
kilowatt [kilowat] *m* kilowatt
kilowatt-heure [kilowatœr] *m* (*pl* kilo-
watts-heures) kilowatt-hour

kilt [kilt] *m* kilt
kimono [kimɔno] *m* kimono
kinescope [kineskɔp] *m* kinescope
kiosque [kjɔsk] *m* newsstand; band-
stand; summerhouse
kipper [kipœr], [kipɛr] *m* kipper
klaxon [klaksɔn] *m* (aut) horn
klaxonner [klaksɔne] *intr* to sound the
horn
kleptomane [klɛptɔman] *adj* & *mf*
kleptomaniac
km/h *abbr* (**kilomètres-heure, kilomètres à l'heure**) kilometers per hour
knock-out [nɔkaut], [knɔkut] *adj invar*
(boxing) knocked out, groggy ‖ *m*
(boxing) knockout
k.o. [kao] (letterword) (**knock-out**)
adj k.o., knocked out; **mettre k.o.** to
knock out ‖ *m* k.o., knockout
kraft [kraft] *m* strong wrapping paper
krak [krak] *m* crash (*e.g., on stock
market*)
kyrielle [kirjɛl] *f* rigmarole, string
kyste [kist] *m* cyst

L

L, l [ɛl], *[el] m invar* twelfth letter of
the French alphabet
la [la] *art* §77 ‖ *m* (mus) la ‖ *pron* §87
là [la] *adv* there; here, e.g., **je suis là**
I am here; in, e.g., **est-il là?** is he
in?; **il n'était pas là** he was out; **là,
là!** there, there! (*it's not as bad as
that!*)
-là [la] §82, §84
là-bas [laba] *adv* yonder, over there
label [label] *m* union label
labeur [labœr] *m* labor, toil
la·bial -biale [labjal] (*pl* **-biaux** [bjo]
-biales) *adj* & *f* labial
laboran·tin [labɔrãtɛ̃] **-tine** [tin] *mf*
laboratory assistant
laboratoire [labɔratwar] *m* laboratory
labo·rieux [labɔrjø] **-rieuse** [rjøz]
adj laborious; arduous; industrious;
working (*classes*); **c'est laborieux!**
(coll) it's endless!
labour [labur] *m* tilling, plowing
labourable [laburabl] *adj* arable, tillable
labourer [labure] *tr* to till, to plow; to
furrow (*the brow*); to scratch
laboureur [laburœr] *m* farm hand,
plowman
Labrador [labradɔr] *m*—**le Labrador**
Labrador
labyrinthe [labirɛ̃t] *m* labyrinth, maze
lac [lak] *m* lake; **Grands Lacs** Great
Lakes
lacer [lase] §51 *tr* to lace; to tie (*one's
shoes*)

lacération [laserɑsjɔ̃] *f* tearing
lacérer [lasere] §10 *tr* to lacerate; to
tear up
lacet [lase] *m* lace; snare, noose; bow-
string (*for strangling*); hairpin curve;
en lacet winding (*road*); **lacet de
soulier** shoelace
lâche [laʃ] *adj* slack, loose; lax, careless; cowardly ‖ *mf* coward
lâcher [laʃe] *tr* to loosen; to let go, to
release; to turn loose; to blurt out (*a
word*); to fire (*a shot*); (coll) to drop
(*one's friends*); **lâcher pied** to give
ground; **lâcher prise** to let go
lâcheté [laʃte] *f* cowardice
lâ·cheur [laʃœr] **-cheuse** [ʃøz] *mf*
fickle friend, turncoat
lacis [lasi] *m* network (*of threads,
nerves*)
laconique [lakɔnik] *adj* laconic
lacrymogène [lakrimɔʒɛn] *adj* tear
(*gas*)
lacs [la] *m* noose, snare; **lacs d'amour**
love knot
lac·té -tée [lakte] *adj* milky; milk
(*diet*)
lacune [lakyn] *f* lacuna, gap, blank
lad [lad] *m* stableboy
là-dedans [ladadã] §85A *adv* in it,
within, in that, in there
là-dessous [ladəsu] §85A *adv* under it,
under that, under there
là-dessus [ladəsy] §85A *adv* on it, on
that; thereupon

ladre [ladr] *adj* stingy, niggardly ‖ *mf* miser
ladrerie [ladrəri] *f* miserliness
lagon [lagɔ̃] *m* lagoon
lagune [lagyn] *f* lagoon
lai laie [le] *adj* lay ‖ *m* lay (*poem*) ‖ *f* see **laie**
laïc laïque [laik] *adj* lay, secular ‖ *mf* layman ‖ *f* laywoman
laiche [lɛ] *f* (bot) sedge, reed grass
laïcisation [laisizasjɔ̃] *f* secularization
laïciser [laisize] *tr* to secularize
laid [le] **laide** [led] *adj* ugly; plain, homely; mean, low-down
laide·ron [ledrɔ̃] **-ronne** [rɔn] *adj* homely, ugly ‖ **laideron** *m* or *f* ugly wench
laideur [ledœr] *f* ugliness; meanness
laie [le] *f* (zool) wild sow
lainage [lena3] *m* woolens
laine [len] *f* wool; **laine d'acier** steel wool; **manger** or **tondre la laine sur le dos à** (fig) to fleece
lainer [lene] *tr* to teasel, to nap
lai·neux [lenø] **-neuse** [nøz] *adj* wooly; downy
lai·nier [lenje] **-nière** [njer] *adj* wool (*industry*) ‖ *mf* dealer in wool; worker in wool
laïque [laik] *adj* lay, secular ‖ *mf* layman ‖ *f* laywoman
laisse [les] *f* leash; foreshore; laisse
laissé-pour-compte laissée-pour-compte [lesepurkɔ̃t] *adj* returned (*merchandise*) ‖ *m* (*pl* laissés-pour-compte) reject; leftover merchandise
laisser [lese], [lɛse] *tr* to leave, to quit; to let, to allow; to let go (*at a low price*); to let have, e.g., **il me l'a laissé pour trois dollars** he let me have it for three dollars; **laisser +** *inf* + **qn** to let s.o. + *inf*, e.g., **il a laissé Marie aller au théâtre** he let Mary go to the theater; e.g., **il me l'a laissé peindre** or **il m'a laissé le peindre** he let me paint it ‖ *intr*—**ne pas laisser de** to not fail to, to not stop ‖ *ref* to let oneself, e.g., **se laisser aller** to let oneself go; **se laisser aller à** to give way to
laisser-aller [leseale] *m* abandon, easy-goingness; slovenliness, negligence
laisser-passer [lesepase] *m invar* permit, pass
lait [le] *m* milk; **lait de chaux** whitewash; **lait de poule** eggnog; **lait écrémé** skim milk; **se mettre au lait** to go on a milk diet
laitage [leta3] *m* dairy products
laitance [letɑ̃s] *f* milt
laiterie [letri] *f* dairy, creamery; dairy farming
lai·tier [letje] **-tière** [tjer] *adj* dairy; milch (*cow*) ‖ *m* milkman; (metallurgy) slag, dross ‖ *f* dairymaid; milch cow
laiton [letɔ̃] *m* brass
laitonner [letone] *tr* to plate with brass
laitue [lety] *f* lettuce; **laitue romaine** romaine
laïus [lajys] *m* (coll) speech, impromptu remarks; (coll) hot air

laïus·seur [lajysœr] **laïus·seuse** [lajysøz] *mf* (coll) windbag
laize [lez] *f* width (*of cloth*)
lamanage [lamana3] *m* harborage
lamaneur [lamanœr] *m* harbor pilot
lam·beau [lɑ̃bo] *m* (*pl* -beaux) scrap, bit; rag; **en lambeaux** in tatters, in shreds
lam·bin [lɑ̃bɛ̃] **-bine** [bin] *adj* (coll) slow ‖ *mf* (coll) slowpoke
lambiner [lɑ̃bine] *intr* (coll) to dawdle
lambris [lɑ̃bri] *m* paneling, wainscoting; plaster (*of ceiling*); **lambris dorés** (fig) palatial home
lambrisser [lɑ̃brise] *tr* to panel, to wainscot; to plaster
lame [lam] *f* blade; slat (*of blinds*); runner (*of skate*); wave; lamina, thin plate; sword; (fig) swordsman; **lame de fond** ground swell
la·mé -mée [lame] *adj* gold-trimmed, silver-trimmed, spangled ‖ *m*—**de lamé**, e.g., **une robe de lamé** a spangled dress
lamelle [lamel] *f* lamella, thin strip; slide (*of microscope*)
lamentable [lamɑ̃tabl] *adj* lamentable
lamentation [lamɑ̃tasjɔ̃] *f* lamentation, lament
lamenter [lamɑ̃te] *intr & ref* to lament
laminer [lamine] *tr* to laminate; to roll (*a metal*)
laminoir [laminwar] *m* rolling mill; calender
lampadaire [lɑ̃pader] *m* lamppost; floor lamp
lampe [lɑ̃p] *f* lamp; (electron) tube; **lampe à pétrole** kerosene lamp; **lampe à rayons ultraviolets** sun lamp; **lampe à souder** blowtorch; **lampe au néon** neon light; **lampe de chevet** bedlamp; **lampe de poche** flashlight; **lampe survoltée** photoflood bulb; **s'en mettre plein la lampe** (slang) to fill one's belly
lampée [lɑ̃pe] *f* (coll) gulp, swig
lamper [lɑ̃pe] *tr* (coll) to gulp down, to guzzle
lampe-tempête [lɑ̃ptɑ̃pet] *f* (*pl* lampes-tempête) hurricane lamp
lampion [lɑ̃pjɔ̃] *m* Chinese lantern
lampiste [lɑ̃pist] *m* lightman; (coll) scapegoat; (coll) underling
lamproie [lɑ̃prwa] *f* lamprey
lampyre [lɑ̃pir] *m* glowworm
lance [lɑ̃s] *f* lance; nozzle (*of hose*); **rompre une lance avec** to cross swords with
lan·cé -cée [lɑ̃se] *adj* flying (*start*); in the swim
lance-bombes [lɑ̃sbɔ̃b] *m invar* trench mortar; (aer) bomb release
lancée [lɑ̃se] *f* impetus
lance-flammes [lɑ̃sflam] *m invar* flamethrower
lance-fusées [lɑ̃sfyze] *m invar* rocket launcher
lancement [lɑ̃smɑ̃] *m* launching, throwing; (of ship; of new product on the market) launching; (aer) airdrop; (aer) release; (baseball) pitching
lance-mines [lɑ̃smin] *m invar* minelayer

lance-pierres [lãspjɛr] *m invar* slingshot

lancer [lãse] §51 *tr* to throw, fling, cast; to launch (*e.g., a ship, a new product*); to issue (*e.g., an appeal*); (baseball) to pitch ‖ *ref* to rush, dash; **se lancer dans** to launch out into, to take up

lance-roquettes [lãsrɔkɛt] *m invar* (arti) bazooka

lance-torpilles [lãstɔrpij] *m invar* torpedo tube

lancette [lãsɛt] *f* (surg) lancet

lan·ceur [lãsœr] **-ceuse** [søz] *mf* promoter; (baseball) pitcher; (sports) hurler, thrower ‖ *m* (rok) booster

lanci·nant [lãsinã] **-nante** [nãt] *adj* shooting, throbbing (*pain*); gnawing (*regret*)

lanciner [lãsine] *tr* to torment ‖ *intr* to shoot; to throb

lan·dau [lãdo] *m* (*pl* **-daus**) landau; baby carriage

lande [lãd] *f* moor, heath

landier [lãdje] *m* kitchen firedog with pothangers

langage [lãgaʒ] *m* language, speech

lange [lãʒ] *m* diaper

langer [lãʒe] §38 *tr* to swaddle, diaper

langou·reux [lãgurø] **-reuse** [røz] *adj* languorous

langouste [lãgust] *f* spiny lobster, crayfish

langous·tier [lãgustje] **-tière** [tjɛr] *m & f* lobster net ‖ *m* lobster boat

langoustine [lãgustin] *f* prawn

langue [lãg] *f* tongue; language; speech; **avoir la langue bien pendue** (coll) to have the gift of gab; **donner sa langue au chat** (coll) to give up; **langue cible** target language; **langue source** source language; **langues vivantes** modern languages; **langue verte** slang; **mauvaise langue** backbiter, gossip; **prendre langue avec** to open up a conversation with; **tirer la langue à** to stick out one's tongue at

langue-de-chat [lãgdəʃa] *f* (*pl* **langues-de-chat**) (culin) ladyfinger

languette [lãgɛt] *f* tongue (*e.g., of shoe*); pointer (*of scale*); flap, strip

langueur [lãgœr] *f* languor

languir [lãgir] *intr* to languish; to pine away

languis·sant [lãgisã] **languis·sante** [lãgisãt] *adj* languid; languishing; long-drawn-out, tiresome

lanière [lanjɛr] *f* strap, strip, thong

lanoline [lanɔlin] *f* lanolin

lanterne [lãtɛrn] *f* lantern; (aut) parking light; (obs) street lamp; **conter des lanternes** (coll) to talk nonsense; **lanterne d'agrandissement** (phot) enlarger; **lanterne de projection, lanterne à projections** slide projector, filmstrip projector; **lanterne rouge** (slang) tail end, last to arrive; **lanterne sourde** dark lantern; **lanterne vénitienne** Japanese lantern; **oublier d'éclairer** or **d'allumer sa lanterne** (coll) to leave out the most important point

lanterner [lãterne] *tr* (coll) to string along, to put off ‖ *intr* to loaf around, to dawdle; **faire lanterner qn** to keep s.o. waiting

lapider [lapide] *tr* to stone; to vilify

la·pin [lapɛ̃] **-pine** [pin] *mf* rabbit; **lapin de garenne** wild rabbit; **lapin russe** albino rabbit; **poser un lapin à qn** (coll) to stand s.o. up

la·pon [lapɔ̃] **-pone** [pɔn] *adj* Lappish ‖ *m* Lapp, Lappish (*language*) ‖ (*cap*) *mf* Lapp, Laplander (*person*)

Laponie [laponi] *f* Lapland; **la Laponie** Lapland

lapsus [lapsys] *m* slip (*of tongue, pen, etc.*)

laquais [lakɛ] *m* lackey, footman

laque [lak] *m & f* lacquer ‖ *m* lacquer ware ‖ *f* lac; shellac; hair spray

laquelle [lakɛl] §78

laquer [lake] *tr* to shellac; to lacquer

larcin [larsɛ̃] *m* petty larceny; plagiarism

lard [lar] *m* bacon, side pork; (coll) fat (*of a person*); (slang) fat slob; **se faire du lard** (coll) to get fat

larder [larde] *tr* to lard; to pierce, riddle

large [larʒ] *adj* wide, broad; generous; ample; large, *e.g.,* **pour une large part** to a large extent ‖ *m* width, breadth; open sea; room, *e.g.,* **donner du large à qn** to give s.o. room; **au large** in the offing; **au large de** off, *e.g.,* **au large du Havre** off Le Havre; **prendre le large** (coll) to shove off; **calculer large** *adv* boldly; **calculer large** to figure roughly; **habiller large** to dress in loose-fitting clothes; **il n'en mène pas large** (fig) he gets rattled in a tight spot; **voir large** (fig) to think big

largement [larʒəmã] *adv* widely; abundantly; fully; plenty, *e.g.,* **vous avez largement le temps** you have plenty of time

largesse [larʒɛs] *f* largess

largeur [larʒœr] *f* width, breadth; (naut) beam

larguer [large] *tr* to let go, to release

larme [larm] *f* tear; (coll) drop; **fondre en larmes** to burst into tears; **pleurer à chaudes larmes** to shed bitter tears

larmoyant [larmwajã] **larmoyante** [larmwajãt] *adj* tearful; watery (*eyes*)

larmoyer [larmwaje] §47 *intr* to water (*said of eyes*); to snivel, to blubber

lar·ron [larɔ̃] **lar·ronnesse** [larɔnɛs] *mf* thief; **s'entendre comme larrons en foire** to be as thick as thieves

larve [larv] *f* larva

laryn·gé·gée [larɛ̃ʒe] *adj* laryngeal

laryn·gien [larɛ̃ʒɛ̃] **-gienne** [ʒjɛn] *adj* laryngeal

laryngite [larɛ̃ʒit] *f* laryngitis

laryngoscope [larɛ̃gɔskɔp] *m* laryngoscope

larynx [larɛ̃ks] *m* larynx

las [lɑ] **lasse** [lɑs] *adj* weary ‖ **las** [lɑs], [la] *interj* alas!

las·cif [lasif] **las·cive** [lasiv] *adj* lascivious

lasciveté [lasivte] *f* lasciviousness

laser [lazer] m laser

las·sant [lɑsɑ̃] las·sante [lɑsɑ̃t] adj tiring, tedious

lasser [lɑse] tr to tire, to weary; to wear out (s.o.'s patience) || ref—sans se lasser unceasingly; se lasser de + inf to tire of + ger; to tire oneself out + ger

lassitude [lɑsityd] f lassitude, weariness

lasso [lɑso] m lasso

latence [latɑ̃s] f latency

la·tent [latɑ̃] -tente [tɑ̃t] adj latent

laté·ral -rale [lateral] adj (pl -raux) lateral

la·tin [latɛ̃] -tine [tin] adj Latin || m Latin (language) || (cap) mf Latin (person)

latino-améri·cain [latinoɑmerikɛ̃] -caine [kɛn] (pl -américains) adj Latin-American || (cap) mf Latin American

latitude [latityd] f latitude

latrines [latrin] fpl latrine

latte [lat] f lath; broadsword

latter [late] tr to lath

lattis [lati] m lathing, laths

laudanum [lodanɔm] m laudanum

lauda·tif [lodatif] -tive [tiv] adj laudatory

lauréat [lɔrea] lauréate [lɔreat] adj laureate || mf winner, laureate

laurier [lɔrje] m laurel, sweet bay; laurier rose rosebay; s'endormir sur ses lauriers to rest on one's laurels

lavable [lavabl] adj washable

lavabo [lavabo] m washbowl; washroom; lavabos toilet, lavatory

lavage [lavaʒ] m washing; lavage de cerveau (coll) brainwashing; lavage des titres wash sale; lavage de tête (coll) dressing down

lavallière [lavaljer] f loosely tied bow

lavande [lavɑ̃d] f lavender

lavandière [lavɑ̃djer] f washerwoman

lave [lav] f lava

lave-glace [lavglas] m (pl -glaces) (aut) windshield washer

lavement [lavmɑ̃] m enema

laver [lave] tr to wash; laver le cerveau à (coll) to brainwash || intr to wash || ref to wash oneself, wash; (with dat of reflex pron) to wash (e.g., one's hands)

laverie [lavri] f (min) washery; laverie automatique, laverie libre-service self-service laundry

lavette [lavet] f dishcloth

la·veur [lavœr] -veuse [vøz] mf washer; laveur de vaisselle dishwasher (person); laveur de vitres window washer (person) || f washerwoman; washing machine

lavoir [lavwar] m place for washing clothes

lavure [lavyr] f dishwater; (coll) swill, hogwash

laxa·tif [laksatif] -tive [tiv] adj & m laxative

layer [leje] §49 tr to blaze a trail through; to blaze (trees to mark a trail)

layette [lejet] f layette; packing case

lazzi [lazi] mpl jeers

le [lə] art §77 || pron §87

leader [lidœr] m leader

lèche [leʃ] f (coll) thin slice (e.g., of bread); faire de la lèche à qn (slang) to lick s.o.'s boots

lèche-carreaux [leʃkaro] m invar (slang) window-shopping

lèchefrite [leʃfrit] f dripping pan

lécher [leʃe] §10 tr to lick; to overpolish (one's style)

lé·cheur [leʃœr] -cheuse [ʃøz] mf (coll) bootlicker, flatterer

lèche-vitrines [leʃvitrin] m invar window-shopping; faire du lèche-vitrines to go window-shopping

leçon [ləsɔ̃] f lesson; reading (of manuscript); faire la leçon à to lecture, sermonize; to prime on what to say

lec·teur [lektœr] -trice [tris] mf reader; lecturer (of university rank) || m playback

lecture [lektyr] f reading; playback; lecture sur les lèvres lip reading

ledit [lədi] ladite [ladit] adj (pl lesdits [ledi] lesdites [ledit]) the aforesaid

lé·gal -gale [legal] adj (pl -gaux [go]) legal; statutory

légaliser [legalize] tr to legalize

légalité [legalite] f legality

légat [lega] m papal legate

légataire [legater] mf legatee; légataire universel residual heir

légation [legasjɔ̃] f legation

légendaire [leʒɑ̃der] adj legendary

légende [leʒɑ̃d] f legend; caption

lé·ger [leʒe] -gère [ʒer] adj light; slight (accent, difference, pain, mistake, etc.); faint (sound, tint, etc.); delicate (odor, perfume, etc.); mild, weak (drink); scanty (dress); graceful (figure); empty (stomach); agile, active; frivolous, carefree; à la légère lightly; without due consideration

légèreté [leʒerte] f lightness; gracefulness; frivolity; fickleness

leggings [legins] mpl & fpl leggings

leghorn [legɔrn] f leghorn (chicken)

légiférer [leʒifere] §10 intr to legislate

légion [leʒjɔ̃] f legion

législa·teur [leʒislatœr] -trice [tris] mf legislator

législa·tif [leʒislatif] -tive [tiv] adj legislative

législation [leʒislasjɔ̃] f legislation

législature [leʒislatyr] f legislative session; legislature

légiste [leʒist] m jurist

légitime [leʒitim] adj legitimate || f (slang) lawful spouse; ma légitime (slang) my better half

légitimer [leʒitime] tr to legitimate; to justify

légitimité [leʒitimite] f legitimacy

legs [le], [leg] m legacy

léguer [lege] §10 tr to bequeath

légume [legym] m vegetable; legume (pod) || f—grosse légume (slang) bigwig, big wheel

légu·mier [legymje] -mière [mjer] adj vegetable (garden, farming, etc.) || m vegetable dish

léndemain [lɑ̃dmɛ̃] m next day; results,

outcome, e.g., **avoir d'heureux lende-mains** to have happy results or a happy outcome; **au lendemain de** the day after; **le lendemain matin** the next morning; **sans lendemain** short-lived

lénifier [lenifje] *tr* (med) to soothe

lent [lɑ̃] **lente** [lɑ̃t] *adj* slow ‖ *f* nit

lentement [lɑ̃tmɑ̃] *adv* slowly; deliberately

lenteur [lɑ̃tœr] *f* slowness, sluggishness; **lenteurs** delays, dilatoriness

lentille [lɑ̃tij] *f* lens; (bot) lentil; **lentilles** freckles

léopard [leɔpar] *m* leopard

lèpre [lepr] *f* leprosy

lé·preux [leprø] **-preuse** [prøz] *adj* leprous ‖ *mf* leper

lequel [ləkɛl] §78

les [le] *art* §77 ‖ *pron* §87 ‖ *prep* near (*in place names*)

les·bien [lesbjɛ̃] **-bienne** [bjɛn] *adj* Lesbian ‖ *f* lesbian ‖ (cap) *mf* Lesbian

lèse-majesté [lezmaʒeste] *f*—**crime de lèse-majesté** lese majesty, high treason

léser [leze] §10 *tr* to injure

lésine [lezin] *f* stinginess

lésiner [lezine] *intr* to haggle, to be stingy

lésion [lezjɔ̃] *f* lesion, wrong, damage

les·quels -quelles [lekɛl] §78

lessivage [lesivaʒ] *m* washing; **lessivage de crâne** (coll) brainwashing

lessive [lesiv] *f* washing (*of clothes*); wash; washing soda, lye; **faire la lessive** to do the wash

lessiver [lesive] *tr* to wash; to scrub (*with a cleaning agent*); (slang) to clean out (*e.g., another poker player*); **être lessivé** (slang) to be exhausted

lessiveuse [lesivøz] *f* washing machine

lest [lest] *m* ballast

leste [lest] *adj* nimble, quick; suggestive, broad; flippant

lestement [lestəmɑ̃] *adv* nimbly, deftly

lester [leste] *tr* to ballast; (coll) to fill (*one's stomach, pockets, etc.*) ‖ *ref* (coll) to stuff oneself

léthargie [letarʒi] *f* lethargy

léthargique [letarʒik] *adj* lethargic ‖ *mf* lethargic person

Lettonie [letɔni] *f* Latvia; **la Lettonie** Latvia

lettrage [letraʒ] *m* lettering

lettre [letr] *f* letter; **à la lettre, au pied de la lettre** to the letter; **avant la lettre** before complete development; **en toutes lettres** in full; in so many words; **lettre de change** bill of exchange; **lettre de faire-part** announcement; **lettre de voiture** bill of lading; **lettre d'imprimerie** printed letter; **lettre majuscule** capital letter; **lettres numérales** roman numerals; **mettre une lettre à la poste** to mail a letter

let·tré -trée [letre] *adj* lettered, literate ‖ *mf* learned person

lettre-morte [letrəmɔrt] *f* letter returned to sender

lettrine [letrin] *f* catchword; initial letter

leu [lø] *m*—**à la queue leu leu** in single file

leucémie [løsemi] *f* leukemia

leucorrhée [løkɔre] *f* leucorrhea

leur [lœr] *adj poss* §88 ‖ *pron poss* §89 ‖ *pron pers* §87

leurre [lœr] *m* lure; delusion

leurrer [lœre] *tr* to lure; to trick, delude ‖ *ref* to be deceived

levain [ləvɛ̃] *m* leaven

levant [ləvɑ̃] *adj masc* rising (*sun*) ‖ *m* east ‖ (cap) *m* Levant

levan·tin [ləvɑ̃tɛ̃] **-tine** [tin] *adj* Levantine ‖ (cap) *mf* Levantine

le·vé -vée [ləve] *adj* rising (*sun*); raised (*e.g., hand*); up, e.g., **le soleil est levé** the sun is up ‖ *m* (mus) upbeat; (surv) survey ‖ *f* levee, embankment; collection (*of mail*); levying (*of troops, taxes, etc.*); raising (*of siege*); lifting (*of embargo*); striking (*of camp*); breaking (*of seals*); upstroke (*of piston*); **faire une levée** (cards) to take a trick; **levée de boucliers** public protest, outcry; **levée d'écrou** discharge (*from prison*); **levée de séance** adjournment; **levée du corps** removal of the body; funeral service (*in front of the coffin*); **levées manquantes** (cards) undertricks

lever [ləve] *m* rising; (surv) survey; **lever du rideau** rise of the curtain; curtain raiser; **lever du soleil** sunrise ‖ §2 *tr* to lift; to raise; to collect, to pick up (*the mail*); to levy (*troops, taxes, etc.*); to strike (*camp*); to adjourn (*a meeting*); to weigh (*anchor*); to relieve (*a guard*); to remit (*a punishment*); to flush (*e.g., a partridge*); to effect (*a survey*); to break (*the seals*) ‖ *intr* to come up (*said of plants*); to rise (*said of dough*) ‖ *ref* to get up; to stand up; to rise; to heave (*said of sea*); to clear up (*said of weather*)

léviathan [levjatɑ̃] *m* leviathan

levier [ləvje] *m* lever; crowbar; **être aux leviers de commande** (aer) to be at the controls; (fig) to be in control; **levier de changement de vitesse** gearshift lever

lévitation [levitɑsjɔ̃] *f* levitation

levraut [ləvro] *m* young hare, leveret

lèvre [levr] *f* lip; rim; **du bout des lèvres** half-heartedly, guardedly; **embrasser sur les lèvres** to kiss; **serrer les lèvres** to purse one's lips

lévrier [levrije] *m* greyhound

levure [ləvyr] *f* yeast; **levure anglaise** or **chimique** baking powder; **levure de bière** brewer's yeast

lexi·cal -cale [leksikal] *adj* (*pl* **-caux** [ko]) lexical

lexicographe [leksikɔgraf] *mf* lexicographer

lexicographie [leksikɔgrafi] *f* lexicography

lexicographique [leksikɔgrafik] *adj* lexicographic(al)

lexicologie [leksikɔlɔʒi] *f* lexicology

lexique [lɛksik] *m* lexicon, vocabulary; abridged dictionary

lez [le] *prep* near (*in place names*)

lézard [lezar] *m* lizard; **faire le lézard** (coll) to sun oneself, to loaf

lézarde [lezard] *f* crack, split, crevice; gimp (*of furniture*); braid; (mil) gold braid

lézarder [lezarde] *tr & ref* to crack, to split || *intr* (coll) to bask in the sun

liaison [ljezɔ̃] *f* liaison

liant [ljɑ̃] **liante** [ljɑ̃t] *adj* flexible, supple; sociable, affable || *m* flexibility; sociability; binder, binding material; **avoir du liant** to be a good mixer

liard [ljar] *m* (fig) farthing

liasse [ljas] *f* packet, bundle (*e.g., of letters*); wad (*of bank notes*)

Liban [libɑ̃] *m*—**le Liban** Lebanon

liba·nais [libane] **-naise** [nez] *adj* Lebanese || (*cap*) *mf* Lebanese

libation [libasjɔ̃] *f* libation

libelle [libɛl] *m* lampoon

libellé [libelle] *m* wording

libeller [libele], [libɛle] *tr* to word; to draw up (*e.g., a contract*); to make out (*a check*)

libellule [libellyl] *f* dragonfly

libé·ral -rale [liberal] *adj & mf* (*pl* **-raux** [ro]) liberal

libéralisme [liberalism] *m* liberalism

libéralité [liberalite] *f* liberality

libéra·teur [liberatœr] **-trice** [tris] *adj* liberating || *mf* liberator

libération [liberasjɔ̃] *f* liberation

libérer [libere] §10 *tr* to liberate || *ref* to free oneself; to pay up

liberté [liberte] *f* liberty, freedom; **liberté d'association** or **liberté de réunion** right of assembly; **liberté de langage** freedom of speech; **liberté de la presse** freedom of the press; **liberté de la propriété** right to own private property; **liberté du commerce et de l'industrie** free enterprise; **liberté du culte** freedom of worship

liber·tin [libertɛ̃] **-tine** [tin] *adj* libertine; (archaic) freethinking || *mf* libertine; (archaic) freethinker

libidi·neux [libidinø] **-neuse** [nøz] *adj* libidinous

libido [libido] *f* libido

libraire [librer] *mf* bookseller; publisher

libraire-éditeur [librereditœr] *m* (*pl* **libraires-éditeurs**) publisher and bookseller

librairie [libreri] *f* bookstore; book trade; publishing house

libre [libr] *adj* free; **je suis libre de mon temps** my time is my own; **libre arbitre** free will; **libre de** free to, at liberty to

libre-échange [libreʃɑʒ] *m* free trade

libre-échangiste [libreʃɑʒist] *m* (*pl* **-échangistes**) free trader

libre-pen·seur [librəpɑ̃sœr] **-seuse** [søz] *mf* (*pl* **libres-penseurs**) freethinker

libre-service [librəsɛrvis] *m* (*pl* **libres-services**) self-service; self-service store

lice [lis] *f* enclosure or fence (*of race track, fairground, tiltyard, etc.*); (zool) hound bitch; **de basse lice** (tex) low-warp; **de haute lice** (tex) high-warp; **entrer en lice** to enter the lists

licence [lisɑ̃s] *f* license; **licence ès lettres** advanced liberal-arts degree, master of arts; **prendre des licences avec** to take liberties with

licen·cié -ciée [lisɑ̃sje] *mf* holder of a master's degree

licenciement [lisɑ̃simɑ̃] *m* discharge, layoff

licencier [lisɑ̃sje] *tr* to discharge, lay off

licen·cieux [lisɑ̃sjø] **-cieuse** [sjøz] *adj* licentious

lichen [liken] *m* lichen

licher [liʃe] *tr* (slang) to gulp down

licite [lisit] *adj* lawful, licit

licorne [likɔrn] *f* unicorn

licou [liku] *m* halter

lie [li] *f* dregs, lees; (fig) dregs, scum

lie-de-vin [lidvɛ̃] *adj invar* maroon

liège [ljeʒ] *m* cork

lien [ljɛ̃] *m* tie, bond, link

lier [lje] *tr* to tie, to bind, to link || *ref* to bind together; to make friends; **lier conversation avec** to fall into conversation with; **se lier d'amitié avec** to become friends with

lierre [ljer] *m* ivy

liesse [ljes] *f*—**en liesse** in festive mood, gay

lieu [ljø] *m* (*pl* **lieux**) place; **au lieu de** instead of, in lieu of; **avoir lieu** to take place; **avoir lieu de** to have reason to; **donner lieu à** to give rise to; **en aucun lieu** nowhere; **en dernier lieu** finally; **en haut lieu** high up, in responsible circles; **en premier lieu** first of all; **en quelque lieu que** wherever; **en tous lieux** everywhere; **il y a lieu à** there is room for; **lieu commun** commonplace; platitude; **lieu de villégiature** resort; **lieu géométrique** locus; **lieux** premises; **lieux d'aisances** rest rooms; **lieux payants** comfort station, public lavatory; **sur les lieux** on the spot; on the premises; **tenir lieu** to take place; **tenir lieu de** to take the place of

lieu-dit [ljødi] *m* (*pl* **lieux-dits**)—**le lieu-dit . . .** the place called . . .

lieue [ljø] *f* league

lieur [ljœr] **lieuse** [ljøz] *mf* binder || *f* (mach) binder

lieutenant [ljøtnɑ̃] *m* lieutenant; (merchant marine) mate; **lieutenant de port** harbor master; **lieutenant de vaisseau** (nav) lieutenant commander

lieutenant-colonel [ljøtnɑ̃kɔlɔnɛl] *m* (*pl* **lieutenants-colonels**) lieutenant colonel

lièvre [ljevr] *m* hare; **c'est là que gît le lièvre** there's the rub; **lever un lièvre** (fig) to raise an embarrassing question; **prendre le lièvre au gîte** (fig) to catch s.o. napping

ligament [ligamɑ̃] *m* ligament

ligature [ligatyr] *f* ligature

ligaturer [ligatyre] *tr* to tie up

ligne [liɲ] *f* line; figure, waistline; (of an automobile) lines; **aller à la ligne** to begin a new paragraph; **avoir de la ligne** to have a good figure; **en première ligne** of the first importance; on the firing line; **garder sa ligne** to keep one's figure; **grande ligne** (rr) main line; **grandes lignes** broad outline; **hors ligne** unrivaled, outstanding; **ligne à postes groupés** (telp) party line; **ligne de changement de date** international date line; **ligne de flottaison** water line; **ligne de mire** (arti) line of sight; **ligne de partage des eaux** watershed; **ligne partagée** (telp) party line; **ligne pointillée** or **hachée** dotted line

lignée [liɲe] *f* lineage, offspring

li·gneux -gneuse [liɲø] [ɲøz] *adj* woody

lignifier [liɲifje] *tr & ref* to turn into wood

ligot [ligo] *m* firewood (in tied bundle)

ligoter [ligɔte] *tr* to tie up, to bind

ligue [lig] *f* league

liguer [lige] *tr & ref* to league

lilas [lila] *adj invar & m* lilac

li·lial -liale [liljal] *adj* (*pl* -liaux [ljo]) lily-white, lily-like

lilliput·tien -tienne [lilipysjɛ̃] -**tienne** [sjɛn] *adj & mf* Lilliputian

limace [limas] *f* (zool) slug; (coll) slowpoke; (slang) shirt

limaçon [limasɔ̃] *m* snail; **en limaçon** spiral

limaille [limaj] *f* filings

limbe [lɛ̃b] *m* (astr, bot) limb; **limbes** limbo

lime [lim] *f* file; (*Citrus limetta*) sweet lime; **dernier coup de lime** finishing touches; **enlever à la lime** to file off; **lime à ongles** nail file; **lime émeri** emery board

limer [lime] *tr* to file; to fray; (fig) to polish

limette [limɛt] *f* (*Citrus limetta*) sweet lime

limier [limje] *m* bloodhound; (coll) sleuth

liminaire [liminɛr] *adj* preliminary

limitation [limitasjɔ̃] *f* limitation

limite [limit] *f* limit; maximum, e.g., **vitesse limite** maximum speed; **dernière limite** deadline

limiter [limite] *tr* to limit || *ref* to be limited; to limit oneself

limitrophe [limitrɔf] *adj* frontier; **limitrophe de** adjacent to

limogeage [limɔʒaʒ] *m* (coll) removal from office

limoger [limɔʒe] §838 *tr* (coll) to remove from office, to relieve of a command

limon [limɔ̃] *m* silt; clay; mud; shaft (of wagon)

limonade [limɔnad] *f* lemon soda

limona·dier -dière [limɔnadje] -**dière** [djɛr] *mf* soft-drink manufacturer; café manager

limo·neux -neuse [limɔnø] -**neuse** [nøz] *adj* silty; muddy

limousine [limuzin] *f* heavy cloak; (aut) limousine

limpide [lɛ̃pid] *adj* limpid

lin [lɛ̃] *m* flax; linen

linceul [lɛ̃sœl] *m* shroud; cover (of snow)

linéament [lineamɑ̃] *m* lineament

linge [lɛ̃ʒ] *m* linen (sheets, tablecloths, underclothes, etc.); piece of linen; **laver le linge** to do the wash; **linge de corps** underclothes

lingère [lɛ̃ʒɛr] *f* linen maid; linen closet

lingerie [lɛ̃ʒri] *f* linen (sheets, tablecloths, underclothes, etc.); linen closet; **lingerie de dame** lingerie; **lingerie d'homme** men's underwear

lingot [lɛ̃go] *m* ingot

lin-gual -guale [lɛ̃gwal] (*pl* -guaux [gwo] -guales) *adj & f* lingual

linguiste [lɛ̃gɥist] *mf* linguist

linguistique [lɛ̃gɥistik] *adj* linguistic || *f* linguistics

liniment [linimɑ̃] *m* liniment

linoléum [linɔleɔm] *m* linoleum

linon [linɔ̃] *m* lawn (sheer linen)

linotte [linɔt] *f* (orn) linnet

linotype [linɔtip] *f* linotype

linotypiste [linɔtipist] *mf* linotype operator

lin-teau [lɛ̃to] *m* (*pl* -teaux) lintel

lion [ljɔ̃] **lionne** [ljɔn] *mf* lion || *f* lioness

lion·ceau [ljɔ̃so] *m* (*pl* -ceaux) lion cub

lippe [lip] *f* thick lower lip, blubber lip

lip·pu -pue [lipy] *adj* thick-lipped

liquéfier [likefje] *tr* to liquefy

liqueur [likœr] *f* liqueur; liquid; (chem, pharm) liquor

liquidation [likidɑsjɔ̃] *f* liquidation; settlement; clearance sale

liquide [likid] *adj & m* liquid || *f* liquid (consonant)

liquider [likide] *tr* to liquidate; to settle (a score); to wind up (a piece of business); (coll) to get rid of; to put an end to

liquidité [likidite] *f* liquidity

liquo·reux -reuse [likɔrø] -**reuse** [røz] *adj* sweet

lire [lir] §36 *tr & intr* to read; **lire à haute voix** to read aloud; **lire à vue** to sight-read; **lire sur les lèvres** to lip-read || *ref* to read; to show, e.g., **la surprise se lit sur votre visage** your face shows surprise

lis [lis] *m* lily; **lis blanc** lily; **lis jaune** day lily

Lisbonne [lizbɔn] *f* Lisbon

liséré [lizere] or **liséré** [lizere] *m* braid, border, strip

li·seur -seuse [lizœr] -**seuse** [zøz] *mf* reader || *f* bookmark; reading lamp; book jacket; bed jacket

lisibilité [lizibilite] *f* legibility

lisible [lizibl] *adj* legible; readable

lisière [lizjɛr] *f* edge, border; list, selvage; **tenir en lisières** to keep in leading strings

lisse [lis] *adj* smooth, polished, sleek || *f* (naut) handrail

lisser [lise] *tr* to smooth, to polish, to

sleek; to glaze (*paper*) || *ref* to become smooth; **se lisser les plumes** to preen its feathers

liste [list] *f* list

lit [li] *m* bed; layer; stratum; **dans le lit de la marée in the tideway; dans le lit du vent** in the wind's eye; **du premier lit** by or of the first marriage; **lit de mort** deathbed; **lit d'époque** period bed; **lit de sangle, lit de camp** folding cot, camp bed; **lit en portefeuille** apple-pie bed; **lit pliant, lit escamotable, lit à rabattement** foldaway bed; **lits jumeaux** twin beds

litanie [litani] *f* litany; tale of woe

lit-cage [likaʒ] *m* (*pl* **lits-cages**) foldaway bed

litée [lite] *f* litter (*of animals*)

literie [litri] *f* bedding, bedclothes

lithine [litin] *f* lithia

lithium [litjɔm] *m* lithium

lithographe [litɔgraf] *mf* lithographer

lithographie [litɔgrafi] *f* lithography; lithograph

lithographier [litɔgrafje] *tr* to lithograph

litière [litjɛr] *f* litter (*bedding for animals*); **faire litière de** to trample

litige [litiʒ] *m* litigation

liti·gieux [litiʒjø] **-gieuse** [ʒjøz] *adj* litigious

litre [litr] *m* liter

littéraire [literɛr] *adj* literary || *mf* teacher of literature; belletrist

litté·ral -rale [literal] *adj* (*pl* **-raux** [ro]) literal; literary, written

littérature [literatyr] *f* literature

litto·ral -rale [litɔral] *adj* (*pl* **-raux** [ro]) littoral, coastal || *m* coast, coastline

Lituanie [litɥani] *f* Lithuania; **la Lituanie** Lithuania

litua·nien [litɥanjɛ̃] **-nienne** [njɛn] *adj* Lithuanian || *m* Lithuanian (*language*) || (*cap*) *mf* Lithuanian (*person*)

liturgie [lityrʒi] *f* liturgy

liturgique [lityrʒik] *adj* liturgic(al)

livide [livid] *adj* livid

Livourne [livurn] *f* Leghorn

livrable [livrabl] *adj* ready for delivery

livraison [livrɛzɔ̃] *f* delivery; installment; **livraison contre remboursement** cash on delivery

livre [livr] *m* book; **à livre ouvert** at sight; **faire un livre** to write a book; (*racing*) to make book; **feuilleter un livre** to glance through a book; **grand livre** (bk) ledger; **livre de bord** (aer, naut) logbook; **livre de classe** textbook; **livre de cuisine, livre de recettes** cookbook; **livre d'or** blue book; testimonial volume; **livre jaune** white book; **petit livre** (bk) journal, day book; **porter au grand livre** (bk) to post || *f* pound (*weight; currency*)

livrée [livre] *f* livery; appearances; coat (*of horse, deer, etc.*)

livrer [livre] *tr* to deliver; to surrender; to betray || *ref* **—se livrer à** to surrender oneself to; to give way to; to indulge in

livresque [livresk] *adj* bookish

livret [livre] *m* booklet; (mus) libretto; **livret de caisse d'épargne** bankbook; **livret de famille** marriage certificate; **livret militaire** military record; **livret scolaire** transcript (*of grades*)

li·vreur [livrœr] **-vreuse** [vrøz] *mf* deliverer (*of parcels, packages, etc.*) || *m* deliveryman || *f* woman who makes deliveries; delivery truck

lobe [lɔb] *m* lobe

lo·cal -cale [lɔkal] (*pl* **-caux** [ko]) *adj* local || *m* place, premises, quarters; headquarters; **locaux** (sports) home team; **locaux commerciaux** office space

localiser [lɔkalize] *tr* to locate; to localize

localité [lɔkalite] *f* locality

locataire [lɔkatɛr] *mf* tenant, renter

location [lɔkɑsjɔ̃] *f* rental; reservation

loch [lɔk] *m* (naut) log (*to determine speed*)

locomotive [lɔkɔmɔtiv] *f* locomotive; (fig) mover

locuste [lɔkyst] *f* (ent) locust

locu·teur [lɔkytœr] **-trice** [tris] *mf* speaker

locution [lɔkysjɔ̃] *f* locution; phrase

lof [lɔf] *m* windward side; **aller or venir au lof** to sail into the wind

logarithme [lɔgaritm] *m* logarithm

loge [lɔʒ] *f* lodge; circus cage; concierge's room; chamber, cell; (theat) dressing room; (theat) box

logeabilité [lɔʒabilite] *f* spaciousness

logeable [lɔʒabl] *adj* livable, inhabitable

logement [lɔʒmã] *m* lodging, lodgings

loger [lɔʒe] §38 *tr, intr, & ref* to lodge

lo·geur [lɔʒœr] **-geuse** [ʒøz] *mf* proprietor of a boardinghouse || *m* landlord || *f* landlady

logi·cien [lɔʒisjɛ̃] **-cienne** [sjɛn] *mf* logician

logique [lɔʒik] *adj* logical || *f* logic

logis [lɔʒi] *m* abode

logistique [lɔʒistik] *adj* logistic(al) || *f* logistics

loi [lwa] *f* law; **faire des lois** to legislate; **faire la loi** to lay down the law; **loi exceptionnelle** emergency legislation

loin [lwɛ̃] *adv* far; far away, far off; **au loin** in the distance; **d'aussi loin que, du plus loin que** as soon as; as far back as; **de loin** from afar; far from; far be it from (*e.g., me*); **de loin en loin** now and then; **il y a loin** de it is a far cry from

loin·tain [lwɛ̃tɛ̃] **-taine** [tɛn] *adj* faraway, distant, remote; early (*e.g., memories*) || *m* distance, background; **le lointain** (theat) upstage

loir [lwar] *m* dormouse; **dormir comme un loir** to sleep like a log

loisible [lwazibl] *adj*—**il m'est** (**lui est,** etc.) **loisible de** I am (he is, etc.) free to or entitled to, it is open for me (him, etc.) to

loisir [lwazir] *m* leisure, spare time; **loisirs** diversions

lolo [lolo] *m* (coll) milk (*in baby talk*)

lombes [lɔ̃b] *mpl* loins

londo‧nien [lɔ̃dɔnjɛ̃] **-nienne** [njɛn] *adj* London || (*cap*) *mf* Londoner

Londres [lɔ̃dr] *m* London

londrès [lɔ̃drɛs] *m* Havana cigar

long [lɔ̃] **longue** [lɔ̃g] *adj* long; lengthy (*speech*); long (*syllable, vowel*); thin, weak (*sauce, gravy*); slow (*to understand, to decide*) || (when standing before noun) *adj* long; de longue main de long standing || *m* length; extent; **au long** at length; **de long** lengthwise; **de long en large** up and down, back and forth; **le long de** along || *f see* **longue** || **long** *adv* much; **en dire long** to talk a long time; to speak volumes; **en savoir long sur** to know a great deal about; **en savoir plus long** to know more about it

longanimité [lɔ̃ganimite] *f* long-suffering

long-courrier [lɔ̃kurje] (*pl* **-courriers**) *adj* long-range || *m* airliner; liner, ocean liner

longe [lɔ̃ʒ] *f* tether, leash; (culin) loin

longer [lɔ̃ʒe] §38 *tr* to walk along, to go beside; to extend along, to skirt

longeron [lɔ̃ʒrɔ̃] *m* crossbeam, girder

longévité [lɔ̃ʒevite] *f* longevity

longitude [lɔ̃ʒityd] *f* longitude

longtemps [lɔ̃tɑ̃] *m* a long time; **avant longtemps** before long; **depuis longtemps** for a long time; long since; **ne . . . plus longtemps** no . . . longer || *adv* long; for a long time

longue [lɔ̃g] *f* long syllable; long vowel; long suit (*in cards*); **à la longue** in the long run

longuement [lɔ̃gmɑ̃] *adv* at length, a long time

lon‧guet [lɔ̃gɛ] **-guette** [gɛt] *adj* (coll) longish, rather long

longueur [lɔ̃gœr] *f* length; lengthiness; **de longueur, dans la longueur** lengthwise; **d'une longueur** by a length, by a head; **longueur d'onde** wavelength

longue-vue [lɔ̃gvy] *f* (*pl* **longues-vues**) telescope, spyglass

looping [lupiŋ] *m* loop-the-loop

lopin [lɔpɛ̃] *m* patch of ground, plot

loquace [lɔkwas], [lɔkas] *adj* loquacious

loque [lɔk] *f* rag; **être comme une loque** to feel like a dishrag; **être en loques** to be in tatters

loquet [lɔkɛ] *m* latch

loque‧teux [lɔktø] **-teuse** [tøz] *adj* in tatters || *mf* tatterdemalion

lorgner [lɔrɲe] *tr* to cast a sidelong glance at; to ogle; to have one's eyes on (*a job, an inheritance, etc.*)

lorgnette [lɔrɲɛt] *f* opera glasses

lorgnon [lɔrɲɔ̃] *m* pince-nez; lorgnette

loriot [lɔrjo] *m* golden oriole

lorry [lɔri] *m* lorry, small flatcar

lors [lɔr] *adv*—**lors de** at the time of; **lors même que** even if

lorsque [lɔrsk] *conj* when

losange [lozɑ̃ʒ] *m* (geom) lozenge; **en losange** diamond-shaped; oval-shaped

lot [lo] *m* lot; prize (*e.g., in lottery*); **gagner le gros lot** to hit the jackpot

loterie [lɔtri] *f* lottery

lo‧ti -tie [lɔti] *adj*—**bien loti** well off; **mal loti** badly off

lotion [losjɔ̃] *f* lotion; **lotion capillaire** hair tonic

lotionner [losjɔne] *tr* to bathe (*a wound*)

lotir [lɔtir] *tr* to parcel out; **lotir qn de qch.** to allot s.th. to s.o.

lotissement [lɔtismɑ̃] *m* allotment, apportionment; building lot

louable [lwabl] *adj* praiseworthy; for hire

louage [lwaʒ] *m* hire

louange [lwɑ̃ʒ] *f* praise; **à la louange de** in praise of

louanger [lwɑ̃ʒe] §38 *tr* to praise, extol

louan‧geur [lwɑ̃ʒœr] **-geuse** [ʒøz] *adj* laudatory, flattering

louche [luʃ] *adj* ambiguous; suspicious, shady; cross-eyed; cloudy (*e.g., wine*) || *f* ladle; basting spoon

loucher [luʃe] *intr* to be cross-eyed, to squint; **faire loucher qn de jalousie** (coll) to turn s.o. green with envy; **loucher sur** (coll) to cast longing eyes at

louchet [luʃɛ] *m* spade (*for digging*)

louer [lwe] *tr* to praise, hire; to reserve (*a seat*); to rent || *ref* to be rented; to hire oneself out; **se louer de** to be satisfied with

loueur [lwœr] **loueuse** [lwøz] *mf* operator of a rental service; flatterer

loufoque [lufɔk] *adj* (slang) cracked || *m* (slang) crackpot

lougre [lugr] *m* (naut) lugger

Louisiane [lwizjan] *f* Louisiana; **la Louisiane** Louisiana

lou‧lou [lulu] **-loute** [lut] *mf* (coll) darling, pet || *m*—**loulou de Poméranie** Pomeranian, spitz

loup [lu] *m* wolf; mask; flaw; **avoir vu le loup** to have lost one's innocence; **crier au loup** to cry wolf; **loup de mer** (ichth) wolf eel; (coll) old salt; **mon petit loup** (coll) my pet

loup-cervier [luservje] *m* (*pl* **loups-cerviers**) lynx

loupe [lup] *f* magnifying glass; gnarl (*on tree*); (pathol) wen

lou‧pé -pée [lupe] *adj* bungled; defective || *m* defect

louper [lupe] *tr* (coll) to goof up, to muff; (coll) to miss (*e.g., one's train*) || *intr* (coll) to fail, to goof

loup-garou [lugaru] *m* (*pl* **loups-garous**) werewolf

lou‧piot [lupjo] **-piotte** [pjɔt] *mf* (coll) kid, child; **loupiots** (coll) small fry

lourd [lur] **lourde** [lurd] *adj* heavy; hefty; clumsy; sultry (*weather*); off-color (*joke*); dull (*mind*); (agr) hard to cultivate || (when standing before noun) *adj* heavy; grave; clumsy (*e.g., compliments*); off-color (*joke*) || **lourd** *adv* heavy, heavily

lour·daud [lurdo] **-daude** [dod] *adj* clumsy, loutish, dull ‖ *mf* lout, oaf
lourdement [lurdəmã] *adv* heavily; clumsily; **avancer** or **rouler lourdement** to lumber along
lourdeur [lurdœr] *f* heaviness; clumsiness; sultriness; dullness
loustic [lustik] *m* wag, clown; (coll) screwball, character
loutre [lutr] *f* otter
louve [luv] *f* she-wolf
louve·teau [luvto] *m* (*pl* **-teaux**) wolf cub; cub scout
louvoyer [luvwaje] §47 *intr* to be evasive; (naut) to tack
lovelace [lɔvlas] *m* seducer, Don Juan
lover [lɔve] *tr & ref* to coil
loyal loyale [lwajal] *adj* (*pl* **loyaux** [lwajo]) loyal; honest; fair, just
loyaliste [lwajalist] *mf* loyalist
loyauté [lwajote] *f* loyalty; honesty; fairness
loyer [lwaje] *m* rent
lubie [lybi] *f* whim
lubricité [lybrisite] *f* lubricity, lewdness
lubri·fiant [lybrifjã] **-fiante** [fjãt] *adj & m* lubricant
lubrifier [lybrifje] *tr* to lubricate
lucarne [lykarn] *f* dormer window; skylight
lucide [lysid] *adj* lucid
luciole [lysjɔl] *f* firefly
lucra·tif [lykratif] **-tive** [tiv] *adj* lucrative
lucre [lykr] *m* lucre
luette [lɥet] *f* uvula
lueur [lɥœr] *f* glimmer, gleam; flash, blink
luge [lyʒ] *f* sled
lugubre [lygybr] *adj* gloomy
lui [lɥi] *pron disj* §85 ‖ *pron conj* §87
lui-même [lɥimem] §86
luire [lɥir] §37 *intr* to shine; to gleam, glow, glisten; to dawn
lui·sant [lɥizã] **-sante** [zãt] *adj* shining
lulu [lyly] *m* (orn) tree pipit
lumbago [lɔ̃bago] *m* lumbago
lumière [lymjer] *f* light; aperture; (*person*) luminary; **avoir des lumières de** to have knowledge of
lumignon [lymiɲɔ̃] *m* feeble light
luminaire [lyminer] *m* luminary
lumines·cent [lyminesã] **lumines·cente** [lyminesãt] *adj* luminescent
lumi·neux [lyminø] **-neuse** [nøz] *adj* luminous; light (*e.g.*, spot); bright (*idea*)
lunaire [lyner] *adj* lunar ‖ *f* (bot) honesty
lunatique [lynatik] *adj* whimsical, eccentric ‖ *mf* whimsical person, eccentric
lunch [lœntʃ], [lœ̃ʃ] *m* buffet lunch
lundi [lœ̃di] *m* Monday
lune [lyn] *f* moon; **être dans la lune** to be daydreaming; **lune de miel** honeymoon; **lune des moissons** harvest moon; **vieilles lunes** good old days, bygone days
lu·né -née [lyne] *adj* moon-shaped;

bien luné in a good mood; **mal luné** in a bad mood
lune·tier [lyntje] **-tière** [tjer] *mf* optician
lunette [lynet] *f* telescope, spyglass; toilet seat; hole (*in toilet seat*); wishbone (*of turkey, chicken*); (archit) lunette; (aut) rear window; **lunettes** eyeglasses, spectacles; goggles; **lunettes de lecture, lunettes pour lire** reading glasses; **lunettes de soleil** sunglasses; **lunettes noires** dark glasses
lurette [lyret] *f*—**il y a belle lurette** (coll) ages ago
luron [lyrɔ̃] *m* (coll) playboy
luronne [lyrɔn] *f* (coll) hussy
lustre [lystr] *m* luster; five-year period; chandelier
lus·tré -trée [lystre] *adj* lustrous, glossy
lustrine [lystrin] *f* cotton satin
lut [lyt] *m* (chem) lute
luth [lyt] *m* (mus) lute
lutherie [lytri] *f* violin making
luthé·rien [lyterjɛ̃] **-rienne** [rjen] *adj* Lutheran ‖ (*cap*) *mf* Lutheran
luthier [lytje] *m* violin maker
lu·tin [lytɛ̃] **-tine** [tin] *adj* impish ‖ *m* imp
lutiner [lytine] *tr* to tease
lutrin [lytrɛ̃] *m* lectern
lutte [lyt] *f* struggle, fight; wrestling; **de bonne lutte** aboveboard; **de haute lutte** by force; in open competition; hard-won; **lutte à la corde de traction** tug of war; **lutte libre** catch-as-catch-can
lutter [lyte] *intr* to fight, to struggle; to wrestle
lut·teur [lytœr] **lut·teuse** [lytøz] *mf* wrestler; (fig) fighter
luxation [lyksasjɔ̃] *f* dislocation
luxe [lyks] *m* luxury
Luxembourg [lyksãbur] *m*—**le Luxembourg** Luxembourg
luxer [lykse] *tr* to dislocate
luxueux [lyksɥø] **luxueuse** [lyksɥøz] *adj* luxurious
luxure [lyksyr] *f* lechery, lust
luxu·riant [lyksyrjã] **-riante** [rjãt] *adj* luxuriant
luxu·rieux [lyksyrjø] **-rieuse** [rjøz] *adj* lecherous, lustful
luzerne [lyzern] *f* alfalfa
lycée [lise] *m* high school; lyceum
lycéen [liseɛ̃] **lycéenne** [liseen] *mf* high-school student
lymphatique [lɛ̃fatik] *adj* lymphatic
lymphe [lɛ̃f] *f* lymph
lynchage [lɛ̃ʃaʒ] *m* lynching
lyncher [lɛ̃ʃe] *tr* to lynch
lynx [lɛ̃ks] *m* lynx
Lyon [ljɔ̃] *m* Lyons
lyon·nais [lione] **lyon·naise** [ljonez] *adj* Lyonese; **à la lyonnaise** lyonnaise
lyre [lir] *f* lyre
lyrique [lirik] *adj* lyric(al) ‖ *m* lyric poet ‖ *f* lyric poetry
lyrisme [lirism] *m* lyricism
lys [lis] *m* lily; **lys blanc** lily; **lys jaune** day lily
lysimaque [lizimak] *f* loosestrife

M

M, m [em], *[em] *m invar* thirteenth letter of the French alphabet

M. *abbr* (**Monsieur**) Mr.

ma [ma] §88

ma·boul -boule [mabul] *adj* (slang) nuts, balmy || *mf* (slang) nut

macabre [makabr] *adj* macabre

macadam [makadam] *m* macadam

macadamiser [makadamize] *tr* to macadamize

macaron [makarɔ̃] *m* macaroon

macchabée [makabe] *m* (slang) stiff (*corpse*)

macédoine [masedwan] *f* macédoine, medley; **macédoine de fruits** fruit salad; **macédoine de légumes** mixed vegetables

macérer [masere] §10 *tr* to macerate; to mortify (*the flesh*); to soak, to steep || *intr* to soak, to steep

mâcher [mɑʃe] *m* clinker

mâcher [mɑʃe] *tr* to chew; **mâcher la besogne à qn** to do all one's work for one; **ne pas mâcher ses mots** to not mince words

machin [maʃɛ̃] *m* (coll) what-do-you-call-it; (coll) what's-his-name, so-and-so

machi·nal -nale [maʃinal] *adj* (*pl* -naux [no]) mechanical

machination [maʃinasjɔ̃] *f* machination

machine [maʃin] *f* machine; engine; **faire machine arrière** to go into reverse; **machine à calculer** adding machine; **machine à coudre** sewing machine; **machine à écrire** typewriter; **machine à laver** washing machine; **machine à laver la vaisselle** dishwasher; **machine à vapeur** steam engine; **machines** machinery

machine-outil [maʃinuti] *f* (*pl* **machines-outils**) machine tool

machinerie [maʃinri] *f* machinery; engine room

machiniste [maʃinist] *m* (theat) stage-hand

mâchoire [mɑʃwar] *f* jaw; jawbone; lower jaw

mâchonner [mɑʃone] *tr* to chew, munch; to mumble (*e.g., the end of a sentence*)

mâchurer [mɑʃyre] *tr* to crush; to smudge

maçon [masɔ̃] *m* mason

maçonner [masone] *tr* to mason, to wall up

maçonnerie [masonri] *f* masonry

macule [makyl] *f* spot, blotch; inkblot; birthmark

maculer [makyle] *tr* to soil, spot; (typ) to smear

madame [madam] *f* (*pl* **mesdames** [medam]) madam; Mrs.; (not translated), *e.g.,* **madame votre femme** your wife

Madeleine [madlɛn] *f* Madeleine, Magdalen; sponge cake; **pleurer comme une Madeleine** to weep bitterly

mademoiselle [madmwazɛl] *f* (*pl* **mesdemoiselles** [medmwazɛl]) Miss; eldest daughter; (not translated), *e.g.,* **mademoiselle votre fille** your daughter

Madone [madɔn] *f* Madonna

ma·dré -drée [madre] *adj* sly, cagey || *mf* sly one

madrier [madrije] *m* beam

maf·flu -flue [mafly] *adj* heavy-jowled

magasin [magazɛ̃] *m* store; warehouse; magazine (*of gun or camera; for munitions or powder*); **avoir en magasin** to have in stock; **grands magasins** department store; **magasin à libre service** self-service store; **magasin à succursales multiples** chain store; **magasin d'antiquités** antique shop; **magasin de modes** dress shop

magasinage [magazinaʒ] *m* storage, warehousing; storage charges; (Canad) shopping

magasinier [magazinje] *m* warehouseman

magazine [magazin] *m* magazine; (mov, telv) hour, program, *e.g.,* **magazine féminin** woman's hour

mages [maʒ] *mpl* Magi

magi·cien -cienne [maʒisjɛ̃] [sjɛn] *mf* magician

magie [maʒi] *f* magic

magique [maʒik] *adj* magic

magis·tral -trale [maʒistral] *adj* (*pl* -traux [tro]) masterful, masterly; magisterial; (pharm) magistral

magistrat [maʒistra] *m* magistrate

magnanime [maɲanim] *adj* magnanimous

magnat [maɲa] *m* magnate

magnésium [maɲezjɔm] *m* magnesium

magnétique [maɲetik] *adj* magnetic; hypnotic

magnétiser [maɲetize] *tr* to magnetize; to hypnotize; to spellbind

magnétisme [maɲetism] *m* magnetism

magnéto [maɲeto] *f* magneto

magnétophone [maɲetofon] *m* tape recorder

magnétoscope [maɲetoskop] *m* video tape recorder; video tape recording

magnifier [magnifje] *tr* to extol, glorify

magnifique [maɲifik] *adj* magnificent; lavishly generous

magnitude [magnityd] *f* (astr) magnitude

magot [mago] *m* Barbary ape; figurine; (coll) hoard, pile (*of money*)

Mahomet [maɔme] *m* Mahomet

mahomé·tan [maɔmetɑ̃] **-tane** [tan] *adj & m* Mohammedan

mai [me] *m* May; Maypole

maie [me] *f* bread bin; kneading trough

maigre [megr] *adj* lean; thin; meager; meatless (*day*); **faire maigre** to abstain from meat

maigreur [megrœr] *f* leanness; meagerness

maigri·chon [megriʃɔ̃] **-chonne** [ʃɔn] *adj* (coll) skinny

maigrir [megrir] *tr* to slim; to make (s.o.) look thinner || *intr* to lose weight

mail [maj] *m* mall

maille [maj] *f* link; stitch; mesh, loop; **avoir maille à partir avec qn** to have a bone to pick with s.o.; **mailles** mail

maillet [maje] *m* mallet

maillon [majɔ̃] *m* link (of a chain)

maillot [majo] *m* swimming suit; jersey; **maillot de bain** swimming suit; **maillot de corps** undershirt; **maillot de danseur** tights; **maillot des acrobates** tights

main [mɛ̃] *f* hand; quire; **à la main** by hand; **à main levée** in one stroke; **avoir la haute main sur** to control; **avoir la main, être la main** (cards) to be the dealer; **battre des mains** to applaud; **de la main à la main** privately; **de longue main** carefully; for a long time; **de main à main** from one person to another; **de première main** firsthand; **donner les mains à q.ch.** to be in favor of s.th.; **en venir aux mains** to come to blows; **faire main basse sur** to grab, to steal; **haut les mains!** hands up!; **passer la main dans le dos à qn** to soft-soap s.o.; **serrer la main à** to shake hands with; **sous main** secretly; **tout main** handmade

main-d'œuvre [mɛ̃dœvr] *f* (*pl* **mains-d'œuvre**) labor; laborers, manpower

maint [mɛ̃] **mainte** [mɛ̃t] *adj* many a; **à maintes reprises** time and again

maintenant [mɛ̃tnɑ̃] *adv* now

maintenir [mɛ̃tnir] §72 *intr* to maintain; to hold up || *ref* to keep on; to keep up

maintien [mɛ̃tjɛ̃] *m* maintenance; bearing

maire [mɛr] *m* mayor

mairesse [mɛrɛs] *f* (coll) mayor's wife

mairie [meri] *f* town hall, city hall

mais [mɛ] *m* but || *adv* why, well; **mais non** certainly not || *conj* but

maïs [mais] *m* corn, maize

maison [mezɔ̃] *f* house; home; household, family; house, firm, business; **à la maison** at home; home; **fait à la maison** homemade; **maison centrale** state or federal prison; **maison close, borgne, publique, mal famée, de débauche, de passe, de rendez-vous, de tolérance** house of ill fame; **maison d'accouchement** lying-in hospital; **maison d'antiquités, de meubles d'époque,** or **d'originaux** antique shop; **maison de commerce** firm; **maison de confiance** (com) trustworthy firm; **maison de correction** reform school; **maison de couture** dressmaking establishment; **maison de fous** madhouse; **maison de jeux** gambling house; **maison de plaisance** or **de campagne** cottage, summer home; **maison de rapport** apartment house; **maison de repos** rest home; **maison de retraite** old-people's home; **maison de santé** nursing home; **maison jumelée** semi-detached house; **maison mère** head office; **maison mortuaire** home of the deceased; **maison religieuse** convent

maisonnée [mezone] *f* household

maisonnette [mezɔnɛt] *f* little house, cottage

maî·tre [metr] **-tresse** [trɛs] *adj* expert, capable, basic, key; main (*beam, girder*); utter (*fool*); arrant (*knave*); high (*card*) || *m* master; Mr. (*when addressing a lawyer*); (naut) mate; (naut) petty officer; **être passé maître en** to be a past master of or in; **maître chanteur** blackmailer; **maître d'armes** fencing master; **maître de chapelle** choirmaster; **maître d'école** schoolmaster; **maître de conférences** associate professor; **maître de forges** ironmaster; **maître de maison** man of the house, householder; **maître d'équipage** boatswain; **maître d'études** monitor, supervisor; **maître d'hôtel** headwaiter; butler; **maître d'œuvre** foreman; **maître Jacques** jack-of-all-trades; **maître mécanicien** chief engineer; **maître mineur** mine foreman; **maître queue chef;** **passer maître** to know one's trade || *f* see **maîtresse**

maître-autel [metrotel] *m* (*pl* **maîtres-autels**) high altar

maîtresse [metrɛs] *f* mistress; **maîtresse d'école** schoolmistress; **maîtresse de maison** lady of the house

maîtrise [metriz] *f* mastery, command; master's degree; **maîtrise de soi** self-control

maîtriser [metrize] *tr* to master, control; to subdue

maj. abbr (**majuscule**) cap.

majesté [maʒɛste] *f* majesty

majes·tueux [maʒɛstɥø] **-tueuse** [tɥøz] *adj* majestic

ma·jeur [maʒœr] **-jeure** [ʒøz] *adj & m* major

major [maʒɔr] *m* regimental quartermaster; army doctor; **être le major de sa promotion** to be at the head of one's class

majordome [maʒɔrdɔm] *m* major-domo

majorer [maʒore] *tr* to increase the price of; to overprice; to raise (*the price*)

majoritaire [maʒoriter] *adj* majority

majorité [maʒorite] *f* majority

Majorque [maʒɔrk] *f* Majorca

major·quin [maʒɔrkɛ̃] **-quine** [kin] *adj* Majorcan || (*cap*) *mf* Majorcan

majuscule [maʒyskyl] *adj* capital (*letter*) || *f* capital letter

mal [mal] *adj*—**de mal bad,** e.g., **dire q.ch. de mal** to say s.th. bad; **pas mal** not bad, quite good-looking || *m* (*pl* **maux** [mo]) evil; trouble; hurt; pain; wrong; **avoir du mal à** + *inf* to have a hard time + *ger*, to have difficulty in + *ger*; **avoir mal à la tête** to have a headache; **avoir mal au cœur** to be nauseated; **avoir mal aux dents** to have a toothache; **avoir mal de gorge** to have a sore throat; **dire du mal de qn** to speak ill of s.o.; **faire mal à, faire du mal à** to hurt, to harm; **le Mal** Evil; **mal aux reins**

backache; **mal blanc** whitlow; **mal de l'air** airsickness; **mal de la route** carsickness; **mal de mer** seasickness; **mal des rayons** radiation sickness; **mal du pays** homesickness; **mal du siècle** Weltschmerz, romantic melancholy; **se donner du mal** to take pains ‖ *adv* §91 badly, bad; **de mal en pis** from bad to worse; **être mal avec qn** to be on bad terms with s.o.; **pas mal** not bad; **pas mal de** a lot of, quite a few

malade [malad] *adj* sick, ill ‖ *mf* patient, sick person

maladie [maladi] *f* disease, sickness; distemper; **elle va en faire une maladie** (coll) she'll be terribly upset over it; **maladie de carence** or **par carence** deficiency disease; **maladie de cœur** heart trouble; **maladie des caissons** bends; **maladie diplomatique** malingering; **revenir de maladie** to convalesce

mala·dif [maladif] **-dive** [div] *adj* sickly; morbid

maladresse [maladres] *f* awkwardness; blunder

mala·droit [maladrwa] **-droite** [drwat] *adj* clumsy, awkward

ma·lais [male] **-laise** [lez] *adj* Malay ‖ *m* Malay (*language*) ‖ see **malaise** *m* ‖ (*cap*) *mf* Malay (*person*)

malaise [malez] *m* malaise, discomfort

malai·sé -sée [maleze] *adj* difficult

malap·pris [malapri] **malap·prise** [malapriz] *adj* uncouth, ill-bred ‖ *mf* ill-bred person

malard [malar] *m* (orn) mallard

malaria [malarja] *f* malaria

malavi·sé -sée [malavize] *adj* ill-advised, indiscreet

malaxer [malakse] *tr* to knead; to churn (*butter*); to massage

malaxeur [malaksœr] *m* churn; (mach) mixer

malchance [mal/ãs] *f* bad luck; **par malchance** unluckily; **une malchance** a piece of bad luck

malchan·ceux [mal/ãsø] **-ceuse** [søz] *adj* unlucky

malcommode [malkɔmɔd] *adj* inconvenient; unsuitable, impracticable

maldonne [maldɔn] *f* misdeal

mâle [mɑl] *adj* male; energetic, virile ‖ *m* male

malédiction [malediksjɔ̃] *f* curse

maléfice [malefis] *m* evil spell

maléfique [malefik] *adj* baleful

malencon·treux [malãkɔ̃trø] **-treuse** [trøz] *adj* untimely, unfortunate

malentendu [malãtãdy] *m* misunderstanding

malfaçon [malfasɔ̃] *f* defect

malfai·sant [malfəzã] **-sante** [zãt] *adj* mischievous, harmful

malfaiteur [malfetœr] *m* malefactor

malfa·mé -mée [malfame] *adj* ill-famed

malgra·cieux [malgrasjø] **-cieuse** [sjøz] *adj* ungracious

malgré [malgre] *prep* in spite of; **malgré que** in spite of the fact that, although

malhabile [malabil] *adj* inexperienced, clumsy

malheur [malœr] *m* misfortune; unhappiness; bad luck; **faire un malheur** to commit an act of violence; **jouer de malheur** to be unlucky

malheu·reux [malœrø] **-reuse** [røz] *adj* unfortunate; unhappy; unlucky; paltry ‖ *m* poor man, wretch; **les malheureux** the unfortunate ‖ *f* poor woman, wretch

malhonnête [malɔnet] *adj* dishonest; (slang) rude, uncivil

malhonnêteté [malɔnette] *f* dishonesty

malice [malis] *f* mischievousness

mali·cieux [malisjø] **-cieuse** [sjøz] *adj* malicious, mischievous

malignité [malinite] *f* malignancy

ma·lin [malɛ̃] **-line** [lin] *adj* cunning, sly, smart; mischievous; malignant (*e.g., tumor*); **ce n'est pas malin** (coll) it's easy ‖ *mf* sly one; **Le Malin** the Evil One

malingre [malɛ̃gr] *adj* weakly, puny

malintention·né -née [malɛ̃tãsjone] *adj* evil-minded, ill-disposed

mal-jugé [malʒyʒe] *m* miscarriage (*of justice*)

malle [mal] *f* trunk; mailboat; **faire ses malles** to pack

malléable [maleabl] *adj* malleable; compliant, pliable

mallette [malet] *f* suitcase; small trunk

malmener [malməne] §2 *tr* to rough up

malodo·rant [malɔdɔrã] **-rante** [rãt] *adj* malodorous; bad (*breath*)

malo·tru -true [malɔtry] *adj* coarse, uncouth ‖ *mf* ill-bred person, oaf

malpropre [malprɔpr] *adj* dirty; improper; crude, clumsy (*workmanship*)

mal·sain [malsɛ̃] **-saine** [sɛn] *adj* unhealthy

malséant [malseã] **malséante** [malseãt] *adj* improper

malson·nant [malsɔnã] **malson·nante** [malsɔnãt] *adj* offensive, objectionable

malt [malt] *m* malt

maltraiter [maltrete] *tr* to mistreat

malveil·lant [malvejã] **malveil·lante** [malvejãt] *adj* malevolent

malve·nu -nue [malvəny] *adj* ill-advised, out of place; poorly developed

malversation [malversasjɔ̃] *f* embezzlement

maman [mamã] *f* mamma

mamelle [mamel] *f* breast; udder

mamelon [mamlɔ̃] *m* nipple, teat; knoll

mamie [mami] *f* (coll) my dear

mammifère [mamifer] *adj* mammalian ‖ *m* mammal

mammouth [mamut] *m* mammoth

mamours [mamur] *mpl* (coll) caresses

mam'selle or **mam'zelle** [mamzel] *f* (coll) Miss

manant [manã] *m* hick, yokel

manche [mã/] *m* handle; stick, stock; neck (*of violin*); (culin) knuckle; **branler au manche** or **dans le manche** to be shaky; **manche à balai** broomstick; (aer) joy stick; **manche à gigot** holder (*for carving*) ‖ *f* sleeve; hose; channel; game, heat, round; shaft, chute; (baseball) inning; (bridge) game; (tennis) set; **en manches de chemise** in shirt sleeves; **la Manche** the English Channel; **manche à air** windsock; **manche à manche** neck and neck, even up; **manches à gigot** leg-of-mutton sleeves

manchette [mɑ̃ʃɛt] *f* cuff; (journ) headline

manchon [mɑ̃ʃɔ̃] *m* muff; (*of gaslight*) mantle; (mach) casing, sleeve

man·chot [mɑ̃ʃo] **-chote** [ʃɔt] *adj* one-armed; one-handed; (coll) clumsy || *mf* one-armed person; one-handed person || *m* (orn) penguin

mandarine [mɑ̃darin] *f* mandarin orange

mandat [mɑ̃da] *m* mandate; term of office; money order; power of attorney; proxy; **mandat d'arrêt** warrant; **mandat de perquisition** search warrant

mandataire [mɑ̃dater] *mf* representative; proxy; defender

mandat-carte [mɑ̃dakart] *m* (*pl* **mandats-carte**) postal-card money order

mandat-poste [mɑ̃dapɔst] *m* (*pl* **mandats-poste**) postal money order

Mandchourie [mɑ̃t/uri] *f* Manchuria; **la Mandchourie** Manchuria

mander [mɑ̃de] *tr* to summon

mandoline [mɑ̃dɔlin] *f* mandolin

mandragore [mɑ̃dragɔr] *f* mandrake

mandrin [mɑ̃drɛ̃] *m* (mach) punch; (mach) chuck

manécanterie [manekɑ̃tri] *f* choir school

manège [manɛʒ] *m* horsemanship; riding school; trick, little game; **manège de chevaux de bois** merry-go-round

mânes [mɑn] *mpl* shades, spirits (*of ancestors*)

maneton [mantɔ̃] *m* crank handle; pin (*of crankshaft*)

manette [manet] *f* lever, switch

manganèse [mɑ̃ganez] *m* manganese

mangeable [mɑ̃ʒabl] *adj* edible; barely fit to eat

mangeaille [mɑ̃ʒaj] *f* swill; (coll) grub, chow

mangeotter [mɑ̃ʒɔte] *tr* to pick at (*one's food*)

manger [mɑ̃ʒe] *m* food, e.g., **le boire et le manger** food and drink; (slang) meal || **§38** *tr* to eat; to eat up; to mumble (*one's words*); **manger du bout des lèvres** to nibble at || *intr* to eat

mangerie [mɑ̃ʒri] *f* (coll) big meal

mange-tout [mɑ̃ʒtu] *m invar* sugar pea

man·geur [mɑ̃ʒœr] **-geuse** [ʒøz] *mf* eater; wastrel, spendthrift; **mangeur d'hommes** man-eater

mangouste [mɑ̃gust] *f* mongoose

maniable [manjabl] *adj* maneuverable, easy to handle, supple

maniaque [manjak] *adj & mf* maniac

manie [mani] *f* mania

maniement [manimɑ̃] *m* handling

manier [manje] *tr* to handle || *ref* (coll) to get a move on

manière [manjer] *f* manner; **à la ma-**

nière de in the manner of; **de manière à** so as to; **de manière que** so that; **de toute manière** in any case; **d'une manière ou d'une autre** one way or another; **en aucune manière** by no means; **faire des manières** to pretend to be indifferent, to want to be coaxed; **manière de voir** point of view; **manières** manners

manié·ré -rée [manjere] *adj* mannered, affected

maniérisme [manjerism] *m* mannerism

ma·nieur [manjœr] **-nieuse** [njøz] *mf* handler; **grand manieur d'argent** tycoon

manifes·tant [manifestɑ̃] **-tante** [tɑ̃t] *mf* demonstrator

manifestation [manifestasjɔ̃] *f* demonstration, manifestation

manifeste [manifest] *adj* manifest || *m* manifesto; (naut) manifest

manifester [manifeste] *tr* to manifest || *intr* to demonstrate || *ref* to reveal oneself

maniganee [manigɑ̃s] *f* trick, intrigue

manipuler [manipyle] *tr* to manipulate; to handle (*e.g., packages*); to arrange (*equipment*) for an experiment

manitou [manitu] *m* manitou; (coll) bigwig

manivelle [manivel] *f* crank

manne [man] *f* manna

mannequin [mankɛ̃] *m* mannequin; scarecrow

manœuvre [manœvr] *m* hand, laborer || *f* maneuver; (naut) handling, maneuvering; (rr) shifting; **fausse manœuvre** wrong move; **manœuvres** rigging

manœuvrer [manœvre] *tr & intr* to maneuver; (rr) to shift

manoir [manwar] *m* manor, manor house

man·quant [mɑ̃kɑ̃] **-quante** [kɑ̃t] *adj* missing || *mf* absentee || *m* missing article; **manquants** shortages

manque [mɑ̃k] *m* lack; shortage; insufficiency; **manque à gagner** lost opportunity; **manque de parole** breach of faith; **par manque de** for lack of || *f*—**à la manque** (coll) rotten, poor, dud

man·qué -quée [mɑ̃ke] *adj* missing, unsuccessful; broken (*engagement*); (with abilities which were not professionally developed), e.g., **le docteur est un cuisinier manqué** the doctor could have been a cook by profession

manquement [mɑ̃kmɑ̃] *m* breach, lapse

manquer [mɑ̃ke] *tr* to miss; to flunk || *intr* to misfire; to be missing, e.g., **il en manque trois** three are missing; to be missed, e.g., **vous lui manquez beaucoup** you are very much missed by him, he misses you very much; to be short, e.g., **il lui manque cinq francs** he is five francs short; **manquer à** to break (*one's word*); to disobey (*an order*); to fail to observe (*a rule*); to fail, e.g., **le cœur lui a manqué** his heart failed him; **manquer de** to lack, to be short of, to

run out of; **manquer de** + *inf* to
nearly + *inf*, e.g., **il a manqué de se
noyer** he nearly drowned; **sans man-
quer** without fail || *ref* to miss each
other; to fail
mansarde [mãsard] *f* mansard roof;
mansard
manse [mãs] *m & f* (hist) small manor
mante [mãt] *f* mantle; **mante religieuse**
(ent) praying mantis
man-teau [mãto] *m* (*pl* **-teaux**) overcoat; mantle, cloak; mantelpiece;
sous le manteau sub rosa
mantille [mãtij] *f* mantilla
manucure [manykyr] *mf* manicurist
ma-nuel -nuelle [manɥɛl] *adj* manual
|| *mf* laborer, blue-collar worker ||
m manual, handbook
manufacture [manyfaktyr] *f* factory,
plant
manufacturer [manyfaktyre] *tr* to manufacture
manus-crit [manyskri] **-crite** [krit]
adj & m manuscript
manutention [manytãsjɔ̃] *f* handling
(*of merchandise*)
manutentionner [manytãsjɔne] *tr* to
handle (*merchandise*)
mappemonde [mapmɔ̃d] *f* world map;
mappemonde céleste map of the
heavens
maque-reau [makro] **-relle** [rɛl] (*pl*
-reaux -relles) *mf* (slang) procurer ||
m mackerel; (slang) pimp || *f* (slang)
madam (*of a brothel*)
maquette [makɛt] *f* maquette, model;
dummy (*of book*); rough sketch
maquignon [makiɲɔ̃] *m* horse trader;
wholesale cattle dealer; (coll) go-
between
maquignonnage [makiɲɔnaʒ] *m* horse
trading
maquignonner [makiɲɔne] *intr* to
horse-trade
maquillage [makijaʒ] *m* make-up;
fakery
maquiller [makije] *tr* to make up; to
fake, to distort || *ref* to make up
maquil-leur [makijœr] **maquil-leuse**
[makijøz] *mf* make-up artist || *m*
make-up man
maquis [maki] *m* bush; maquis;
prendre le maquis to go underground
maraî-cher [marɛʃe] **-chère** [ʃɛr] *adj*
truck-farming || *mf* truck farmer
marais [marɛ] *m* marsh; truck farm;
marais salant saltern
marasme [marasm] *m* depression;
doldrums, standstill
marathon [maratɔ̃] *m* marathon
marâtre [maratr] *f* stepmother; cruel
mother
maraude [marod] *f* marauding; **en
maraude** cruising (*taxi*)
marauder [marode] *intr* to maraud;
to cruise (*said of taxi*)
marau-deur [marodœr] **-deuse** [døz]
adj marauding || *mf* marauder
marbre [marbr] *m* marble; (typ) stone
marbrer [marbre] *tr* to marble; to
mottle, vein; to bruise, blotch
marc [mar] *m* mark (*old coin*); marc,
pulp; **marc de café** coffee grounds;

marc de thé tea leaves || [mark]
(*cap*) *m* Mark
marcassin [markasɛ̃] *m* young wild
boar
mar-chand [marʃɑ̃] **-chande** [ʃɑ̃d] *adj*
marketable; sale (*value*); trading
(*center*); wholesale (*price*); merchant
(*marine*) || *mf* merchant; **marchand
ambulant** peddler; **marchand de
canons** munitions maker; **marchand
de couleurs** paint dealer, dealer in
household articles; **marchand de
ferraille** junk dealer; **marchand de
journaux** newsdealer; **marchand des
quatre-saisons** fruit vendor; **marchand en gros** wholesaler; **marchand
forain** hawker || *f* **marchande
d'amour** or **de plaisir** prostitute
marchandage [marʃɑ̃daʒ] *m* bargain-
ing; haggling; deal, underhanded arrangement
marchander [marʃɑ̃de] *tr* to bargain
over; to haggle over; to be stingy
with (*e.g., one's compliments*) || *intr*
to haggle
marchan-deur [marʃɑ̃dœr] **-deuse**
[døz] *mf* bargainer; haggler
marchandise [marʃɑ̃diz] *f* merchandise;
marchandises goods
mar-chant [marʃɑ̃] **-chante** [ʃɑ̃t] *adj*
marching; militant (*wing of political
party*); (mil) wheeling (*flank*)
marche [marʃ] *f* march; step (*of stairway*); walking; movement; progress,
course; (aut) gear; **à dix minutes de
marche** ten minutes walk from here;
attention à la marche! watch your
step!; **en marche** in motion, running,
operating; **faire marche arrière** to
back up, to reverse; **fermer la marche**
to bring up the rear; **marche funèbre**
funeral march; **ouvrir la marche** to
lead off the procession
marché [marʃe] *m* market; marketing;
shopping; deal, bargain; **à bon
marché** cheap; cheaply; **à meilleur
marché** cheaper; more cheaply; **bon
marché** cheapness; cheap; cheaply;
faire bon marché de to set little store
by; **faire son marché** to do the marketing; **lancer, mettre**, or **vendre sur
le marché** to market; **marché noir**
black market; **par-dessus le marché**
into the bargain
marchepied [marʃəpje] *m* footstool;
little stepladder; running board; (fig)
stepping stone
marcher [marʃe] *intr* to walk; to run,
operate; to march; **marcher à grands
pas** to stride; **marcher au pas** to
walk in step; **marcher dans l'espace**
to take a space walk; **marcher sur**
to tread on, to walk on; **marchez au
pas** (public sign) drive slowly
mar-cheur [marʃœr] **-cheuse** [ʃøz] *mf*
walker
mardi [mardi] *m* Tuesday; **mardi gras**
Shrove Tuesday; Mardi gras
mare [mar] *f* pool, pond
marécage [marekaʒ] *m* marsh, swamp
maréca-geux [marekaʒø] **-geuse** [ʒøz]
adj marshy, swampy
maré-chal [mareʃal] *m* (*pl* **-chaux**

[ʃo]) marshal; blacksmith; **maréchal des logis** artillery or cavalry sergeant

maréchale [mare/al] *f* marshal's wife

maréchal-ferrant [mare/alferɑ̃] *m* (*pl* **maréchaux-ferrants**) blacksmith, farrier

marée [mare] *f* tide; fresh seafood; **marée descendante** ebb tide; **marée montante** flood tide

marelle [marel] *f* hopscotch

marémo·teur [maremotœr] **-trice** [tris] *adj* tide-driven

margarine [margarin] *f* margarine

marge [marʒ] *f* margin; border, edge; leeway, room; **en marge de** on the fringe of; a footnote to; **marge bénéficiaire** margin of profit; **marge de sécurité** margin of safety

margelle [marʒel] *f* curb, edge (*of well, fountain, etc.*)

margeur [marʒœr] *m* margin stop

margi·nal -nale [marʒinal] *adj* (*pl* **-naux** [no]) marginal

margot [margo] *f* (coll) magpie; (coll) chatterbox; **Margot** (coll) Maggie

margotin [margotɛ̃] *m* kindling

margouillis [marguji] *m* (coll) rotten stinking mess

margou·lin [margulɛ̃] **-line** [lin] *mf* sharpster, shyster

marguerite [margərit] *f* daisy; **Marguerite** Margaret

marguillier [margije] *m* churchwarden

mari [mari] *m* husband

mariable [marjabl] *adj* marriageable

mariage [marjaʒ] *m* marriage; wedding; blend, combination

Marianne [marjan] *f* Marian; Marianne (*symbol of the French Republic*)

ma·rié -riée [marje] *adj* married || *m* bridegroom; **jeunes mariés** newlyweds; **les mariés** the bride and groom || *f* bride

marier [marje] *tr* to marry, join in wedlock; to marry off; to blend, harmonize || *ref* to get married; **se marier avec** to marry

marie-salope [marisalɔp] *f* (*pl* **maries-salopes**) dredger; (slang) slut

ma·rieur [marjœr] **-rieuse** [rjøz] *mf* (coll) matchmaker

marihuana [mariɥana] or **marijuana** [mariʒuana] *f* marijuana

ma·rin [marɛ̃] **-rine** [rin] *adj* marine; seagoing; sea, e.g., **brise marine** sea breeze || *m* sailor, seaman; **marin suit** || *f* navy; seascape; **marine marchande** merchant marine

mariner [marine] *tr & intr* to marinate

mari·nier [marinje] **-nière** [njer] *adj* naval; petty (*officer*); **à la marinière** cooked in gravy with onions || *m* waterman || *f* blouse; (swimming) sidestroke

marionnette [marjɔnet] *f* marionette; (fig) puppet

mari·tal -tale [marital] *adj* (*pl* **-taux** [to]) of the husband

maritime [maritim] *adj* maritime

maritorne [maritɔrn] *f* slut

marivaudage [marivodaʒ] *m* playful flirting; sophisticated conversation

marjolaine [marʒɔlen] *f* marjoram

marlou [marlu] *m* (slang) pimp

marmaille [marmɑj] *f* (coll) brats

marmelade [marmәlad] *f* marmalade; (coll) mess

marmite [marmit] *f* pot, pan; (geol) pothole; (mil) shell, heavy shell; **marmite autoclave**, **marmite sous pression** pressure cooker; **marmite norvégienne** double boiler

marmiton [marmitɔ̃] *m* cook's helper

marmonner [marmɔne] *tr & intr* to mumble

marmot [marmo] *m* (coll) lad; (coll) grotesque figurine (*on knocker*); **croquer le marmot** (coll) to cool one's heels; **marmots** (coll) urchins, kids

marmotte [marmɔt] *f* woodchuck; **dormir comme une marmotte** to sleep like a log; **marmotte d'Amérique** groundhog; **marmotte de commis voyageur** traveling salesman's sample case

marmouset [marmuze] *m* grotesque figurine; little man

marner [marne] *tr* to marl

marner [marne] *tr* to marl

Maroc [marɔk] *m*—**le Maroc** Morocco

maro·cain [marɔkɛ̃] **-caine** [ken] *adj* Moroccan || (*cap*) *mf* Moroccan

maronner [marɔne] *intr* (coll) to grumble

maroquin [marɔkɛ̃] *m* morocco leather

maroquinerie [marɔkinri] *f* leather goods

marotte [marɔt] *f* fad; whim; dummy head (*of milliner*); jester's staff

mar·quant [markɑ̃] **-quante** [kɑ̃t] *adj* remarkable, outstanding; purple (*passages*)

marque [mark] *f* mark; brand, make; hallmark; token, sign; **de marque** distinguished; **marque déposée** trademark

marquer [marke] *tr* to mark; to brand; to score; to indicate, show || *intr* to make a mark, to leave an impression

marqueterie [markәtri], [marketri] *f* marquetry, inlay

mar·queur [markœr] **-queuse** [køz] *mf* marker || *m* scorekeeper; scorer || *f* (mach) stenciler

marquis [marki] *m* marquis

marquise [markiz] *f* marchioness, marquise; marquee, awning; (rr) roof (*over platform*)

marraine [maren] *f* godmother, sponsor; christener; **marraine de guerre** war mother

mar·rant [marɑ̃] **mar·rante** [marɑ̃t] *adj* (slang) sidesplitting; (slang) funny, queer

marre [mar] *adv*—**en avoir marre** (coll) to be fed up

marrer [mare] *ref* (slang) to have a good laugh

mar·ron [marɔ̃] **mar·ronne** [marɔn] *adj* quack (*doctor*); shyster (*lawyer*) || **marron** *adj invar* reddish-brown, chestnut || *m* chestnut; **marron d'Inde** horse chestnut

marronnier [marɔnje] *m* chestnut tree; **marronnier d'Inde** horse-chestnut tree

mars [mars] m March; **Mars** Mars

Marseille [marsɛj] f Marseilles

marsouin [marswɛ̃] m porpoise

marte [mart] f (zool) marten

mar·teau [marto] (pl -teaux) adj (coll) cracked; balmy ‖ m hammer; (ichth) hammerhead; **marteau de porte** knocker

marteau-pilon [martopilɔ̃] m (pl marteaux-pilons) drop hammer

marteler [martəle] §2 tr to hammer; to hammer at; to hammer out

Marthe [mart] f Martha

mar·tial -tiale [marsjal] adj (pl -tiaux [sjo]) martial

martinet [martinɛ] m triphammer; scourge, cat-o'-nine-tails; (orn) martin, swift

martin-pêcheur [martɛ̃peʃœr] m (pl martins-pêcheurs) (orn) kingfisher

martre [martr] f (zool) marten

mar·tyr -tyre [martir] adj & mf martyr ‖ **martyre** m martyrdom

martyriser [martirize] tr to martyr

marxiste [marksist] adj & mf Marxist

maryland [marilā] f choice tobacco ‖ (cap) m—**le Maryland** Maryland

mas [ma], [mas] m farmhouse or farm (in Provence)

mascarade [maskarad] f masquerade

mascaret [maskarɛ] m bore

mascaron [maskarɔ̃] m mask, mascaron

mascotte [maskɔt] f mascot

mascu·lin -line [maskylɛ̃] [lin] adj & m masculine

masque [mask] m mask; **masque à gaz** gas mask; **masque mortuaire** death mask

masquer [maske] tr & ref to mask

massacre [masakr] m massacre; botched job

massacrer [masakre] tr to massacre; to botch

massage [masaʒ] m massage

masse [mas] f mass; sledge hammer; mace; pool, common fund; (elec) ground (e.g., of an automobile); **masse d'air froid** cold front; **mettre à la masse** (elec) to ground; **une masse de** (coll) a lot of

massepain [maspɛ̃] m marzipan

masser [mase] tr to mass; to massage ‖ ref to mass; to massage oneself

massette [masɛt] f sledge hammer (of stonemason); (bot) bulrush

mas·seur [masœr] **mas·seuse** [masøz] mf masseur ‖ m massager (instrument)

mas·sif [masif] **mas·sive** [masiv] adj massive; heavyset; solid (e.g., gold) ‖ m massif, high plateau; clump (of flowers, trees, etc.)

massue [masy] f club, bludgeon

mastic [mastik] m putty

mastiquer [mastike] tr to masticate; to putty

mastoc [mastɔk] adj invar heavy, massive

masturber [mastyrbe] tr & ref to masturbate

m'as-tu-vu -vue [matyvy] (pl -vu -vue) adj (coll) stuck-up ‖ mf (coll) show-

off, smart aleck; (coll) bragging actor

masure [mazyr] f hovel, shack, shanty

mat mate [mat] adj dull, flat ‖ **mat** adj invar checkmate ‖ m checkmate ‖ **mat** adv dull

mât [ma] m mast; pole

matamore [matamɔr] m braggart

match [matʃ] m match, contest, game

matelas [matla] m mattress; (coll) roll (of bills)

matelasser [matlase] tr to pad, to cushion

matelot [matlo] m sailor, seaman

matelote [matlɔt] f fish stew in wine

mater [mate] tr to dull; to checkmate; to subdue

matérialiser [materjalize] ref to materialize

matérialiste [materjalist] adj materialistic ‖ mf materialist

maté·riau [materjo] m (pl -riaux) material

maté·riel -rielle [materjel] adj material; materialistic ‖ m material; equipment; (mil) matériel; **matériel roulant** (rr) rolling stock ‖ f (slang) living

mater·nel -nelle [maternel] adj maternal ‖ f nursery school

maternité [maternite] f maternity; maternity hospital

math or **maths** [mat] fpl (coll) math

mathémati·cien [matematisjɛ̃] **-cienne** [sjen] mf mathematician

mathématique [matematik] adj mathematical ‖ **mathématiques** fpl mathematics

matière [matjɛr] f matter; subject matter; material; **matière première** raw material

matin [matɛ̃] m morning; early part of the morning; **au petit matin** in the wee hours of the morning; **de bon matin, de grand matin** very early; **du matin** in the morning, A.M., e.g., **onze heures du matin** eleven o'clock in the morning, eleven A.M. ‖ adv early

mâ·tin [matɛ̃] **-tine** [tin] mf (coll) sly one ‖ m (zool) mastiff ‖ **mâtin** adv indeed!, well I'll be!

mati·nal -nale [matinal] adj (pl -naux [no]) morning; early-rising

mâti·né -née [matine] adj crossbred; **mâtiné de** mixed with, crossbred with

matinée [matine] f morning; matinée; **faire la grasse matinée** to sleep late

mâtiner [matine] tr to crossbreed

matines [matin] fpl matins

matité [matite] f dullness

ma·tois -toise [matwa] [twaz] adj sly, cunning ‖ mf sly dog

matou [matu] m tomcat

matraque [matrak] f bludgeon; club, billy

matraquer [matrake] tr to club, bludgeon

matriarcat [matrijarka] m matriarchy

matrice [matris] f matrix

matricide [matrisid] mf matricide (person) ‖ m matricide (action)

matricule [matrikyl] adj serial (num-

ber) || *m* serial number || *f* roll, register

matrimo·nial -niale [matrimɔnjal] *adj* (*pl* **-niaux** [njo]) matrimonial, marital

matrone [matrɔn] *f* matron; matriarch; old hag; midwife; abortionist

mâture [matyr] *f* masts (*of ship*)

maudire [modir] §39 *tr* to curse, to damn

mau·dit [modi] **-dite** [dit] *adj* cursed

maugréer [mogree] *intr* to grumble, gripe

maure [mɔr] *adj* Moorish || (*cap*) *m* Moor

mauresque [mɔresk] *adj* Moorish || (*cap*) *f* Moorish woman

mausolée [mozɔle] *m* mausoleum

maussade [mosad] *adj* sullen, gloomy

mau·vais [move], [move] **-vaise** [vez] *adj* §91 bad; evil; wrong; **il fait mauvais** the weather is bad; **sentir mauvais** to smell bad || *mf* wicked person; **le Mauvais** the Evil One || *m* evil

mauve [mov] *adj* mauve || *f* (bot) mallow

mauviette [movjet] *f* (orn) lark; (coll) milquetoast

mauvis [movi] *m* (orn) redwing

maxillaire [maksiller] *m* jawbone

maxime [maksim] *f* maxim

maximum [maksimɔm] *adj & m* maximum

mayonnaise [majɔnez] *f* mayonnaise

mazette [mazet] *f* duffer || *interj* gosh!

mazout [mazut] *m* fuel oil

mazouter [mazute] *intr* to fuel up

Me *abbr* (**Maître**) Mr.

me [mə] §87

méandre [meɑ̃dr] *m* meander

mec [mek] *m* (slang) guy; (slang) tough egg

mécanicien [mekanisjɛ̃] *m* mechanic; machinist; engineer (*of locomotive*)

mécanicienne [mekanisjen] *f* sewing-machine operator

mécanique [mekanik] *adj* mechanical || *f* mechanism; mechanics

mécaniser [mekanize] *tr* to mechanize

mécanisme [mekanism] *m* mechanism

mécano [mekano] *m* (coll) mechanic

mécène [mesen] *m* patron, Maecenas

méchanceté [meʃɑ̃ste] *f* malice, wickedness; nastiness

mé·chant [meʃɑ̃] **-chante** [ʃɑ̃t] *adj* malicious, wicked; nasty; naughty (*child*) || *mf* mean person; **faire le méchant** to threaten; (coll) to strike back; **les méchants** the wicked; **méchant!** naughty boy!

mèche [meʃ] *f* wick; fuse; lock (*of hair*); bit (*of drill*); **être de mèche avec** (coll) to be in cahoots with; **éventer** or **découvrir la mèche** to discover the plot; **il n'y a pas mèche** (coll) it's no go, nothing doing; **vendre la mèche** (coll) to let the cat out of the bag

mécompte [mekɔ̃t] *m* miscalculation; disappointment

méconnaissable [mekɔnesabl] *adj* unrecognizable

méconnaître [mekɔnetr] §12 *tr* to ignore; to underestimate

mécon·nu -nue [mekɔny] *adj* underestimated, misunderstood

mécon·tent [mekɔ̃tɑ̃] **-tente** [tɑ̃t] *adj* dissatisfied, displeased || *mf* grumbler

mécontentement [mekɔ̃tɑ̃tmɑ̃] *m* dissatisfaction, displeasure

mécontenter [mekɔ̃tɑ̃te] *tr* to displease

Mecque [mek] *f*—**La Mecque** Mecca

mécréant [mekreɑ̃] **mécréante** [mekreɑ̃t] *adj* unbelieving || *mf* unbeliever

médaille [medaj] *f* medal

médaillon [medajɔ̃] *m* medallion; locket; thin round slice (*e.g., of meat*); pat (*of butter*)

médecin [medsɛ̃], [metsɛ̃] *m* doctor; **femme médecin** woman doctor

médecine [medsin], [metsin] *f* medicine (*science and art*)

mé·dian [medjɑ̃] **-diane** [djan] *adj & f* median

média·teur [medjatœr] **-trice** [tris] *mf* mediator

médiation [medjɑsjɔ̃] *f* mediation

médi·cal -cale [medikal] *adj* (*pl* **-caux** [ko]) medical

médicament [medikamɑ̃] *m* (pharm) medicine

médicamenter [medikamɑ̃te] *tr* to dose

médicamen·teux [medikamɑ̃tø] **-teuse** [tøz] *adj* medicinal

médici·nal -nale [medisinal] *adj* (*pl* **-naux** [no]) medicinal

médié·val -vale [medjeval] *adj* (*pl* **-vaux** [vo]) medieval

médiéviste [medjevist] *mf* medievalist

médiocre [medjɔkr] *adj* mediocre, poor; average

médiocrité [medjɔkrite] *f* mediocrity

médire [medir] §40 *intr* to backbite; **médire de** to run down, to disparage

médisance [medizɑ̃s] *f* disparagement, backbiting

médi·sant [medizɑ̃] **-sante** [zɑ̃t] *adj* disparaging, backbiting || *mf* slanderer

méditation [meditɑsjɔ̃] *f* meditation

méditer [medite] *tr & intr* to meditate

méditerra·né -née [mediterane] *adj* Mediterranean; inland || (*cap*) *f* Mediterranean (Sea)

méditerranéen [mediteraneɛ̃] **méditerranéenne** [mediteraneen] *adj* Mediterranean

médium [medjɔm] *m* medium (*in spiritualism*); range (*of voice*)

médiumnique [medjɔmnik] *adj* psychic

médius [medjys] *m* middle finger

méduse [medyz] *f* jellyfish, medusa || (*cap*) *f* Medusa

méduser [medyze] *tr* to petrify (*with terror*)

meeting [mitiŋ] *m* rally, meet, meeting

méfait [mefe] *m* misdeed; **méfaits** ravages

méfiance [mefjɑ̃s] *f* mistrust

mé·fiant [mefjɑ̃] **-fiante** [fjɑ̃t] *adj* mistrustful

méfier [mefje] *ref* to beware; **se méfier de** to guard against, to mistrust

mégacycle [megasikl] *m* megacycle

mégaphone [megafɔn] *m* megaphone

mégarde [megard] *f*—**par mégarde** inadvertently

mégère [meʒer] *f* shrew

mégohm [megom] *m* megohm

mégot [mego] *m* butt (*of cigarette or cigar*)

meil·leur -leure [mejœr] §91 *adj comp & super* better; best; **meilleur marché** cheaper

mélancolie [melɑ̃kɔli] *f* melancholy, melancholia

mélancolique [melɑ̃kɔlik] *adj* melancholy

mélange [melɑ̃ʒ] *m* mixing, blending; mixture, blend

mélanger [melɑ̃ʒe] §38 *tr* to mix, to blend

mélan·geur [melɑ̃ʒœr] **-geuse** [ʒøz] *m & f* mixer

mélasse [melas] *f* molasses; **dans la mélasse** (coll) in the soup

mê·lé -lée [mele] *adj* mixed ‖ *f* melee

mêler [mele] *tr* to mix; to tangle; to shuffle (*the cards*) ‖ *ref* to mix; **se mêler à** to mingle with; to join in; **se mêler de** to meddle with, to interfere with

mélèze [melez] *m* (bot) larch

mélodie [melɔdi] *f* melody

mélo·dieux [melɔdjø] **-dieuse** [djøz] *adj* melodious

mélodique [melɔdik] *adj* melodic

mélodramatique [melɔdramatik] *adj* melodramatic

mélomane [melɔman] *adj* music-loving ‖ *mf* music lover

melon [məlɔ̃] *m* melon; derby; **melon d'eau** watermelon

mélopée [melɔpe] *f* singsong, chant

membrane [mɑ̃bran] *f* membrane; **membrane vibrante** (elec) diaphragm

membre [mɑ̃br] *m* member; limb, member; **membre de phrase** clause

membrure [mɑ̃bryr] *f* frame, limbs

même [mem] *adj indef* very, e.g., **le jour même** on that very day ‖ (*when standing before noun*) *adj indef* same, e.g., **en même temps** at the same time ‖ *pron indef* same, same one; **à même de** + *inf* up to + *ger*, in a position to + *inf*; **à même la** (la, etc.) straight out of the (*e.g., bottle*); flush with the (*e.g., pavement*); next to one's (*e.g., skin*); on the bare (*ground, sand, etc.*); **cela revient au même** that amounts to the same thing; **de même** likewise; **de même que** in the same way as; **tout de même** nevertheless ‖ *adv* even; **même quand** even when; **même si** even if

-même [mem] §86

mémento [memɛ̃to] *m* memento; memo book

mémère [memer] *f* (coll) granny; (coll) blowsy dame

mémoire [memwar] *m* memorandum; statement, account; term paper; treatise; petition; **mémoires** memoirs ‖ *f* memory; **de mémoire** from memory; **de mémoire d'homme** within memory; **pour mémoire** for the record

mémorandum [memɔrɑ̃dɔm] *m* memorandum; **mémorandum de combat** battle orders

mémo·rial [memɔrjal] *m* (*pl* **-riaux** [rjo]) memorial; (dipl) memorandum; memoirs

menace [mənas] *f* menace, threat

menacer [mənase] §51 *tr & intr* to menace, to threaten

ménage [menaʒ] *m* household; family; married couple; furniture; **de ménage** homemade; **faire bon ménage** to get along well; **faire des ménages** to do housework (*for hire*); **faire le ménage** to do the housework; **se mettre en ménage** to set up housekeeping; (coll) to live together (*without being married*)

ménagement [menaʒmɑ̃] *m* discretion; consideration

ména·ger [menaʒe] **-gère** [ʒer] *adj* household; **ménager de** thrifty with ‖ *f* housewife, homemaker; silverware; silverware case ‖ **ménager** §38 *tr* to be careful with, to spare; to save (*money; one's strength*); to husband (*one's resources, one's strength*); to be considerate of, to handle with kid gloves; to arrange, to bring about; to install, to provide; to make (*e.g., a hole*) ‖ *intr* to save ‖ *ref* to take good care of oneself

ménagerie [menaʒri] *f* menagerie

men·diant [mɑ̃djɑ̃] **-diante** [djɑ̃t] *adj & mf* beggar; **des mendiants** dessert (*of dried fruits and nuts*)

mendier [mɑ̃dje] *tr & intr* to beg

menées [məne] *fpl* intrigues, schemes

mener [məne] §2 *tr* to lead; to take; to manage; to draw (*e.g., a line*) ‖ *intr* to lead

ménestrel [menestrel] *m* wandering minstrel

ménétrier [menetrije] *m* fiddler

me·neur [mənœr] **-neuse** [nøz] *mf* leader; ringleader; **meneur de jeu** master of ceremonies; narrator; moving spirit

menotte [mənɔt] *f* tiny hand; **menottes** handcuffs; **mettre** or **passer les menottes à** to handcuff

mensonge [mɑ̃sɔ̃ʒ] *m* lie; **pieux mensonge** white lie

menson·ger [mɑ̃sɔ̃ʒe] **-gère** [ʒer] *adj* lying, false; illusory, deceptive

menstrues [mɑ̃stry] *fpl* menses

mensualité [mɑ̃sɥalite] *f* monthly installment; monthly salary

men·suel -suelle [mɑ̃sɥel] *adj* monthly

men·tal -tale [mɑ̃tal] *adj* (*pl* **-taux** [to]) mental

mentalité [mɑ̃talite] *f* mentality

men·teur [mɑ̃tœr] **-teuse** [tøz] *adj* lying ‖ *mf* liar

menthe [mɑ̃t] *f* mint; **menthe poivrée** peppermint; **menthe verte** spearmint

mention [mɑ̃sjɔ̃] *f* mention; **avec mention** with honors; **biffer les mentions inutiles** to cross out the questions which do not apply; **être reçu sans mention** to receive just a passing grade

mentionner [mɑ̃sjɔne] *tr* to mention

mentir [mãtir] §41 *intr* to lie
menton [mãtɔ̃] *m* chin
mentonnière [mãtɔnjer] *f* chin rest; chin strap
me·nu -nue [məny] *adj* small, little; tiny, fine ‖ *m* menu; minute detail
menuet [mənɥɛ] *m* minuet
menuiserie [mənɥizri] *f* carpentry; woodwork
menuisier [mənɥizje] *m* carpenter
méprendre [meprãdr] §56 *ref* to be mistaken; **à s'y méprendre** enough to take one for the other; **il n'y a pas à s'y méprendre** there's no mistake about it
mépris [mepri] *m* contempt, scorn
méprisable [meprizabl] *adj* contemptible, despicable
mépri·sant [meprizɑ̃] **-sante** [zɑ̃t] *adj* contemptuous, scornful
méprise [mepriz] *f* mistake
mépriser [meprize] *tr* to despise, scorn
mer [mer] *f* sea; **basse mer** low tide; **de haute mer** seagoing; **haute mer, pleine mer** high seas; high tide; **mer des Indes** Indian Ocean; **sur mer** afloat
mercanti [merkãti] *m* profiteer
mercantile [merkãtil] *adj* profiteering, mercenary
mercenaire [mersəner] *adj & mf* mercenary
mercerie [mersəri] *f* notions
merci [mersi] *m* thanks, thank you; **merci de** + *inf* thank you for + *ger*; **merci de** or **pour** thank you for ‖ *f*—**à la merci de** at the mercy of; **Dieu merci!** thank heavens! ‖ *interj* thanks!, thank you!; no thanks!, no thank you!
mercredi [merkrədi] *m* Wednesday; **mercredi des Cendres** Ash Wednesday
mercure [merkyr] *m* mercury
mercuriale [merkyrjal] *f* reprimand; market quotations; mercury (*weed*)
merde [merd] *f* excrement; **merde alors!** (coll) well I'll be!
mère [mer] *f* mother; **la mère Gigogne** the old woman who lived in a shoe
méri·dien [meridjɛ̃] **-dienne** [djen] *adj & m* meridian ‖ *f* meridian line; couch, sofa; siesta
méridio·nal -nale [meridjɔnal] (*pl* **-naux** [no]) *adj* meridional, southern ‖ (*cap*) *mf* inhabitant of the Midi
meringue [mərɛ̃g] *f* meringue
merise [məriz] *f* wild cherry
merisier [mərizje] *m* wild cherry (tree)
méri·tant [meritɑ̃] **-tante** [tɑ̃t] *adj* deserving, worthy
mérite [merit] *m* merit
mériter [merite] *tr* to merit, to deserve; to win, earn ‖ *intr*—**mériter bien de** to deserve the gratitude of
méritoire [meritwar] *adj* deserving, meritorious
merlan [merlɑ̃] *m* (ichth) whiting
merle [merl] *m* (orn) blackbird; **merle blanc** (fig) rara avis; **vilain merle** (fig) dirty dog
merlin [merlɛ̃] *m* ax; poleax; (naut) marline

merluche [merlyʃ] *f* (ichth) hake, cod
merveille [mervej] *f* marvel, wonder; **à merveille** marvelously, wonderfully
merveil·leux [mervejø] **merveil·leuse** [mervejøz] *adj* marvelous, wonderful
mes [me] §88
mésalliance [mezaljɑ̃s] *f* misalliance, mismatch
mésallier [mezalje] *tr* to misally ‖ *ref* to marry beneath one's station
mésange [mezɑ̃ʒ] *f* (orn) chickadee, titmouse
mésaventure [mezavɑ̃tyr] *f* misadventure
mésentente [mezɑ̃tɑ̃t] *f* misunderstanding
mésestimer [mezɛstime] *tr* to underestimate
mésintelligence [mezɛ̃teliʒɑ̃s] *f* misunderstanding, discord
mes·quin [mɛskɛ̃] **-quine** [kin] *adj* mean; stingy; petty
mess [mes] *m* officer's mess
message [mesaʒ] *m* message
messa·ger [mesaʒe] **-gère** [ʒer] *mf* messenger
messagerie [mesaʒri] *f* express; messageries express company
messe [mes] *f* (eccl) Mass; **dire** or **faire des messes basses** (coll) to speak in an undertone; **messe basse, petite messe** Low Mass; **première messe, messe du début** early Mass
Messie [mesi] *m* Messiah
messieurs-dames [mesjødam] *interj* ladies and gentlemen!
mesure [məzyr] *f* measure; measurement; (mus, poetic) measure; **à mesure** successively, one by one; **à mesure que** as; according as, proportionately as; **battre la mesure** to keep time; **dans la mesure de** insofar as; **dans une certaine mesure** to a certain extent; **être en mesure de** to be in a position to; **faire sur mesure** to make (*clothing*) to order; (fig) to tailor-make; **mesure de circonstance** emergency measure; **mesure en ruban** tape measure; **prendre des mesures de** to take measures to; **prendre la mesure de** to size up; **prendre les mesures de** to measure
mesurer [məzyre] *tr* to measure; to measure off or out ‖ *ref* to measure; **se mesurer avec** to measure swords with
métairie [meteri] *f* farm (*of a sharecropper*)
mé·tal [metal] *m* (*pl* **-taux** [to]) metal
métallique [metalik] *adj* metallic
métalloïde [metalɔid] *m* nonmetal
métallurgie [metalyrʒi] *f* metallurgy
métamorphose [metamɔrfoz] *f* metamorphosis
métaphore [metafɔr] *f* metaphor
métaphorique [metafɔrik] *adj* metaphorical
métathèse [metatez] *f* metathesis
métayage [metejaʒ] *m* sharecropping, tenant farming
métayer [meteje] **métayère** [metejer] *mf* sharecropper

méteil [metej] *m* wheat and rye

météo [meteo] *adj invar* meteorological ‖ *m* weatherman ‖ *f* meteorology; weather bureau; weather report

météore [meteɔr] *m* meteor (*atmospheric phenomenon*)

météorite [meteɔrit] *m & f* meteorite

météorologie [meteɔrɔlɔʒi] *f* meteorology; weather bureau; weather report

métèque [metɛk] *m* (pej) foreigner

méthane [metan] *m* methane

méthode [metɔd] *f* method

méthodique [metɔdik] *adj* methodic(al)

méthodiste [metɔdist] *adj & mf* Methodist

méticu·leux [metikylø] **-leuse** [løz] *adj* meticulous

métier [metje] *m* trade, craft; loom; **faites votre métier!** mind your own business!; **sur le métier** on the stocks

mé·tis ·tisse [metis] *adj & mf* half-breed

métisser [metise] *tr* to crossbreed

métrage [metraʒ] *m* length in meters; length (*of remnant, film, etc.*); (mov) length of film in meters (*in English: footage, i.e., length of film in feet*); **court métrage** (mov) short subject, short; **long métrage** (mov) full-length movie, feature

mètre [mɛtr] *m* meter; **mètre à ruban** tape measure; **mètre pliant** folding rule

métrer [metre] §10 *tr* to measure out by the meter

métrique [metrik] *adj* metric(al) ‖ *f* metrics

métro [metro] *m* subway

métronome [metrɔnɔm] *m* metronome

métropole [metrɔpɔl] *f* metropolis; mother country

métropoli·tain [metrɔpɔlitɛ̃] **-taine** [tɛn] *adj* metropolitan ‖ *m* subway; (eccl) metropolitan

mets [mɛ] *m* dish, food

mettable [metabl] *adj* wearable

met·teur [metœr] **met·teuse** [metøz] *mf*—**metteur au point** mechanic; **metteur en œuvre** setter; (fig) promoter; **metteur en ondes** (rad) director, producer; **metteur en pages** (typ) make-up man; **metteur en scène** (mov, theat) director, producer

mettre [metr] §42 *tr* to put, lay, place; to put on (*clothes*); to set (*the table*); to take (*time*); **mettre à feu** (rok) to fire; **mettre au point** to carry out, complete; to tune up, adjust; (opt) to focus; (rad) to tune; **mettre au rancart** to pigeonhole; **mettre en accusation** to indict; **mettre en marche** to start; **mettre en œuvre** to put into action; **mettre en valeur** to develop, improve; to set off, enhance; **mettre en vigueur** to enforce; **mettre feu à** to set fire to; **mettre que** (coll) to suppose that ‖ *intr*—**mettre bas** (zool) to litter ‖ *ref* to sit or stand; to go; **se mettre à** to begin to; **se mettre à table** to sit down to eat; (slang) to confess; **se mettre en colère** to get angry; **se**

mettre en route to set out; **se mettre mal avec** to quarrel with

meuble [mœbl] *adj* uncemented; loose (*ground*); personal (*property*) ‖ *m* piece of furniture; **meubles** furniture; **meubles d'occasion** secondhand furniture

meubler [mœble] *tr* to furnish

meuglement [møgləmã] *m* lowing (*of cow*)

meugler [møgle] *intr* to low

meule [møl] *f* millstone; grindstone; stack (*e.g., of hay*)

meuler [møle] *tr* to grind

meu·nier [mønje] **-nière** [njer] *adj* milling (*e.g., industry*) ‖ *m* miller ‖ *f* miller's wife; **à la meunière** sautéed in butter

meurt-de-faim [mœrdəfɛ̃] *mf invar* starving, poor; **de meurt-de-faim** starvation (*wages*)

meurtre [mœrtr] *m* manslaughter; (fig) shame, crime; **meurtre commis avec préméditation** murder

meur·trier [mœrtrije] **-trière** [trijer] *adj* murderous, deadly ‖ *m* murderer ‖ *f* murderess; gun slit, loophole

meurtrir [mœrtrir] *tr* to bruise

meute [møt] *f* pack, band

mévente [mevãt] *f* slump (*in sales*)

mexi·cain [meksikɛ̃] **-caine** [kɛn] *adj* Mexican ‖ (*cap*) *mf* Mexican

Mexico [meksiko] Mexico City

Mexique [meksik] *m*—**le Mexique** Mexico

mezzanine [medzanin] *m & f* (theat) mezzanine ‖ *f* mezzanine; mezzanine window

miaou [mjau] *m* meow

miaulement [mjolmã] *m* meow; caterwauling; catcall

miauler [mjole] *intr* to meow

mi-bas [miba] *m invar* half hose

mica [mika] *m* mica

miche [miʃ] *f* round loaf of bread

mi-chemin [miʃmɛ̃] *m*—**à mi-chemin** halfway

mi-clos [miklo] **-close** [kloz] *adj* (pl **-clos -closes**) half-shut

micmac [mikmak] *m* (coll) underhand dealing

mi-corps [mikɔr] *m*—**à mi-corps** to the waist

mi-côte [mikot] *m*—**à mi-côte** halfway up the hill

microbe [mikrɔb] *m* microbe

microbicide [mikrɔbisid] *adj & m* germicide

microbiologie [mikrɔbjɔlɔʒi] *f* microbiology

microfilm [mikrɔfilm] *m* microfilm

microfilmer [mikrɔfilme] *tr* to microfilm

micro-onde [mikrɔɔ̃d] *f* (pl **-ondes**) microwave

microphone [mikrɔfɔn] *m* microphone

microscope [mikrɔskɔp] *m* microscope

microscopique [mikrɔskɔpik] *adj* microscopic

microsillon [mikrɔsijɔ̃] *adj & m* microgroove

midi [midi] *m* noon; south; twelve, e.g., **midi dix** ten minutes after twelve; **chercher midi à quatorze heures** (fig) to look for difficulties where there are none; **Midi** south of France

midinette [midinɛt] *f* dressmaker's assistant; working girl

mie [mi] *f* soft part, crumb; female friend; **ne . . . mie** §90 (archaic) not a crumb, not, e.g., **je n'en veux mie** I don't want any

miel [mjɛl] *m* honey

miel·leux [mjɛlø] **miel·leuse** [mjɛløz] *adj* honeyed, unctuous

mien [mjɛ̃] **mienne** [mjɛn] §89

miette [mjɛt] *f* crumb

mieux [mjø] §91 *adv comp & super* better; **aimer mieux** to prefer; **à qui mieux mieux** trying to outdo each other; **de mieux en mieux** better and better; **être mieux, aller mieux** to feel better; **tant mieux** so much the better; **valoir mieux** to be better

mieux-être [mjøzɛtr] *m* improved well-being

mièvre [mjɛvr] *adj* dainty, affected

mi-figue [mifig] *f*—**mi-figue mi-raisin** half one way half the other; half in jest half in earnest

mi·gnard [miɲar] **-gnarde** [ɲard] *adj* affected, mincing

mi·gnon [miɲɔ̃] **-gnonne** [ɲɔn] *adj* cute, darling || *mf* darling

mignon·net [miɲɔnɛ] **mignon·nette** [miɲɔnɛt] *adj* dainty || *f* fine lace; pepper; (bot) pink

mignoter [miɲɔte] *tr* (coll) to pet (*a child*)

migraine [migrɛn] *f* migraine; headache

migratoire [migratwar] *adj* migratory

mi-jambe [miʒɑ̃b] *f*—**à mi-jambe** up to one's knee

mijoter [miʒɔte] *tr* to simmer; (coll) to cook up, to brew || *intr* to simmer

mil [mil] *adj* one thousand, e.g., **l'an mil neuf cent soixante-six** the year one thousand nine hundred and sixty-six || *m* Indian club; millet

milan [milɑ̃] *m* (orn) kite

milice [milis] *f* militia

mi·lieu [miljø] *m* (*pl* **-lieux**) middle; milieu; **milieu de table** centerpiece

militaire [militɛr] *adj* military || *m* soldier; **le militaire** the military

mili·tant [militɑ̃] **-tante** [tɑ̃t] *adj & mf* militant

militariser [militarize] *tr* to militarize

militarisme [militarism] *m* militarism

militer [milite] *intr* to militate

mille [mil] *adj & pron* thousand || *m* thousand; mile; **mettre dans le mille** to hit the bull's-eye; **mille marin** international nautical mile

millefeuille [milfœj] *m* napoleon (*pastry*)

mille-feuille [milfœj] *f* (*pl* **-feuilles**) (bot) yarrow

millénaire [milenɛr] *adj* millennial || *m* millennium

mille-pattes [milpat] *m invar* centipede

millésime [milezim] *m* date, vintage

millet [mijɛ] *m* millet; birdseed

milliard [miljar] *m* billion

milliardaire [miljardɛr] *mf* billionaire

millième [miljɛm] *adj, pron* (*masc, fem*) thousandth || *m* thousandth; mill (*thousandth part of a dollar*)

millier [milje] *m* thousand; about a thousand; **par milliers** by the thousands; **un millier de** a thousand

milligramme [miligram] *m* milligram

millimètre [milimɛtr] *m* millimeter

million [miljɔ̃] *m* million; **un million de** a million

millionième [miljɔnjɛm] *adj, pron* (*masc, fem*), & *m* millionth

millionnaire [miljɔnɛr] *adj & m* millionaire

mime [mim] *mf* mime; mimic

mimer [mime] *tr & intr* to mime; to mimic

mimique [mimik] *adj* sign (*language*) || *f* mimicry

minable [minabl] *adj* wretched, shabby; (coll) pitiful (*performance, existence, etc.*) || *mf* unfortunate

minaret [minarɛ] *m* minaret

minauder [minode] *intr* to simper, smirk

minau·dier [minodje] **-dière** [djɛr] *adj* mincing

mince [mɛ̃s] *adj* thin, slim, slight; **mince!** or **mince alors!** golly!

mine [min] *f* mine; lead (*of pencil*); look, face; looks; (fig) mine (*of information*); **avoir bonne mine** to look well; **avoir la mine d'être** to look to be; **avoir mauvaise mine** to look badly; **faire bonne mine à** to be nice to; **faire des mines** to simper; **faire la mine à** to pout at; **faire mauvaise mine à** to be unpleasant to; **faire mine de** to make as if to

miner [mine] *tr* to mine; to undermine; to wear away

minerai [minrɛ] *m* ore

miné·ral -rale [mineral] (*pl* **-raux** [ro]) *adj & m* mineral

minéralogie [mineralɔʒi] *f* mineralogy

mi·net [minɛ] **-nette** [nɛt] *mf* (coll) kitty, pussy; (coll) darling

mi·neur -neure [minœr] *adj & mf* minor || *m* miner

miniature [minjatyr] *f* miniature

miniaturisation [minjatyrizasjɔ̃] *f* miniaturization

miniaturiser [minjatyrize] *tr* to miniaturize

minijupe [miniʒyp] *f* miniskirt

mini·mal -male [minimal] *adj* (*pl* **-maux** [mo]) minimum (*temperature*)

minime [minim] *adj* tiny, derisory (*salary*)

minimiser [minimize] *tr* to minimize

minimum [minimɔm] *adj & m* minimum; **minimum vital** minimum wage

ministère [ministɛr] *m* ministry; **ministère des Affaires étrangères** Department of State

ministé·riel -rielle [ministerjɛl] *adj* ministerial

ministre [ministr] *m* minister; **ministre des Affaires étrangères** secretary of state; **premier ministre** premier, prime minister

minium [minjɔm] *m* red lead

minois [minwa] *m* (coll) pretty little face

minoritaire [minɔriter] *adj* minority

minorité [minɔrite] *f* minority

Minorque [minɔrk] *f* Minorca

minoterie [minɔtri] *f* flour mill; flour industry

minotier [minɔtje] *m* miller

minuit [minɥi] *m* midnight; twelve, e.g., **minuit et demi** twelve thirty

minuscule [minyskyl] *adj* tiny; small (*letter*) || *f* small letter

minus habens [minysabɛ̃s] *mf invar* (coll) moron, idiot

minutage [minytaʒ] *m* timing

minute [minyt] *f* minute; moment, instant; **à la minute** that very moment || *interj* (coll) just a minute!

minuter [minyte] *tr* to itemize; to time

minuterie [minytri] *f* delayed-action switch; (mach) timing mechanism

minutie [minysi] *f* minute detail; great care; **minuties** minutiae

minu·tieux [minysjø] **-tieuse** [sjøz] *adj* meticulous, thorough

mioche [mjɔʃ] *mf* (coll) brat

mi-pente [mipɑ̃t]—**à mi-pente** halfway up or halfway down

mirabilis [mirabilis] *m* (bot) marvel-of-Peru

miracle [mirɑkl] *m* miracle; wonder, marvel; miracle play; **crier au miracle** to go into ecstasies

miracu·leux [mirakylø] **-leuse** [løz] *adj* miraculous; wonderful, marvelous

mirador [miradɔr] *m* watchtower

mirage [miraʒ] *m* mirage

mire [mir] *f* sight (*of gun*); surveyor's pole; (telv) test pattern

mire-œufs [mirø] *m invar* candler

mirer [mire] *tr* to candle (*eggs*) || *ref* to look at oneself; to be reflected

mirifique [mirifik] *adj* (coll) marvelous

mirobo·lant [mirɔbɔlɑ̃] **-lante** [lɑ̃t] *adj* (coll) astounding

miroir [mirwar] *m* mirror; **miroir à alouettes** decoy

miroiter [mirwate] *intr* to sparkle, gleam; **faire miroiter q.ch. à qn** to lure s.o. with s.th.

miroton [mirɔtɔ̃] *m* Irish stew

misaine [mizɛn] *f* foresail

misanthrope [mizɑ̃trɔp] *mf* misanthrope

miscellanées [miselane], [misellane] *fpl* miscellany

mise [miz] *f* placing, putting; dress, attire; (cards) stake, ante; **de mise** acceptable, proper; **mise à feu** firing (*e.g., of missile*); **mise à l'eau** launching; **mise à prix** opening bid; **mise au point** carrying out, completion; tuning up, adjustment; (opt) focusing; (rad) tuning; **mise au rancart** pigeonholing; **mise bas** delivery (*of litter*); **mise de fonds** investment; **mise en accusation** indictment; **mise en demeure** (law) injunction; **mise en marche** starting; **mise en œuvre** putting into action; **mise en scène** (theat) direction; (theat & fig) staging; **mise**

en valeur development, improvement; **mise en vigueur** enforcement

miser [mize] *tr & intr* to ante; to stake, bet; to bid (*e.g., at auction*)

misérable [mizerabl] *adj* miserable || *mf* wretch

misère [mizer] *f* misery, wretchedness; poverty; worry; (coll) trifle; **crier misère** to make a poor mouth; to look forsaken; **faire des misères à** to pester

misé·reux [mizerø] **-reuse** [røz] *adj* destitute, wretched || *mf* pauper

miséricorde [mizerikɔrd] *f* mercy

miséricor·dieux [mizerikɔrdjø] **-dieuse** [djøz] *adj* merciful

missel [misel] *m* missal

missile [misil] *m* guided missile

mission [misjɔ̃] *f* mission

missionnaire [misjɔner] *adj & m* missionary

missive [misiv] *adj & f* missive

mitaine [miten] *f* mitt

mite [mit] *f* (ent) mite; (ent) clothes moth

mi·té -tée [mite] *adj* moth-eaten; (coll) shabby

mi-temps [mitɑ̃] *f invar* (sports) half time; **à mi-temps** half time

miter [mite] *ref* to become moth-eaten

mi·teux [mitø] **-teuse** [tøz] *adj* shabby || *mf* (coll) shabby-looking person

mitiger [mitiʒe] §38 *tr* to mitigate

mitonner [mitɔne] *tr* to simmer; to pamper; (coll) to contrive, devise || *intr* to simmer

mitoyen [mitwajɛ̃] **mitoyenne** [mitwajen] *adj* midway, intermediate, dividing; jointly owned, common

mitraille [mitraj] *f* scrap iron; grapeshot; artillery fire

mitrailler [mitraje] *tr* to machine-gun; to pepper (*with gunfire, flash bulbs, etc.*)

mitraillette [mitrajet] *f* submachine gun, Tommy gun

mitrail·leur [mitrajœr] **mitrail·leuse** [mitrajøz] *adj* repeating, automatic (*firearm*) || *m* machine gunner || *f* machine gun

mitre [mitr] *f* miter; chimney pot

mitron [mitrɔ̃] *m* baker's boy

mi-voix [mivwa]—**à mi-voix in** a low voice, under one's breath

mixte [mikst] *adj* mixed; coeducational; composite; joint (*e.g., commission*); (rr) freight-and-passenger

mixtion [mikstjɔ̃] *f* mixing; mixture

mixture [mikstyr] *f* mixture

Mlle *abbr* (**Mademoiselle**) Miss

MM. *abbr* (**Messieurs**) Messrs.

Mme *abbr* (**Madame**) Mrs.; Mme

mobile [mɔbil] *adj* mobile || *m* motive; (fa) mobile

mobi·lier [mɔbilje] **-lière** [ljer] *adj* personal || *m* furniture

mobilisable [mɔbilizabl] *adj* (mil) subject to call

mobilisation [mɔbilizasjɔ̃] *f* mobilization

mobiliser [mɔbilize] *tr & intr* to mobilize

mobilité [mɔbilite] *f* mobility

moche [mɔʃ] *adj* (coll) ugly; (coll) lousy

modalité [mɔdalite] *f* modality, manner, method; **modalités** terms

mode [mɔd] *m* kind, method, mode; (gram) mood; (mus) mode; **mode d'emploi** directions for use ‖ *f* fashion; **à la mode** in style, fashionable; **à la mode de** in the manner of; **modes** fashions; millinery

modèle [mɔdɛl] *adj & m* model

modeler [mɔdle] §2 *tr* to model; to shape, mold ‖ *ref*—**se modeler sur** to take as a model

modéliste [mɔdelist] *mf* model-airplane designer, etc.; dress designer

modéra·teur [mɔderatœr] **-trice** [tris] *adj* moderating ‖ *mf* moderator; regulator; moderator (*for slowing down neutrons*); **modérateur de son** volume control

modé·ré -rée [mɔdere] *adj* moderate

modérer [mɔdere] §10 *tr & ref* to moderate

moderne [mɔdern] *adj* modern

moderniser [mɔdernize] *tr* to modernize

modeste [mɔdɛst] *adj* modest

modestie [mɔdɛsti] *f* modesty

modicité [mɔdisite] *f* paucity (*of resources*); lowness (*of price*)

modifica·teur [mɔdifikatœr] **-trice** [tris] *adj* modifying ‖ *m* modifier

modifier [mɔdifje] *tr* to modify

modique [mɔdik] *adj* moderate, reasonable

modiste [mɔdist] *f* milliner

modulation [mɔdylɑsjɔ̃] *f* modulation; **modulation d'amplitude** amplitude modulation; **modulation de fréquence** frequency modulation

module [mɔdyl] *m* module; **module lunaire** (rok) lunar module

moduler [mɔdyle] *tr & intr* to modulate

moelle [mwal] *f* marrow; (bot) pith; **moelle épinière** spinal cord

moel·leux [mwalø] **moel·leuse** [mwaløz] *adj* soft; mellow; flowing (*brush stroke*)

moellon [mwalɔ̃] *m* building stone

mœurs [mœr], [mœrs] *fpl* customs, habits; morals

mohair [mɔɛr] *m* mohair

moi [mwa] §85, §87

moignon [mwaɲɔ̃] *m* stump

moi-même [mwamɛm] §86

moindre [mwɛ̃dr] §91 *adj comp & super* less; lesser; least, slightest

moine [mwan] *m* monk

moi·neau [mwano] *m* (*pl* **-neaux**) sparrow

moins [mwɛ̃] *m* less; minus; **au moins** or **du moins** at least; **(le) moins** (the) least; **moins de fewer** ‖ *adv comp & super* §91 less; fewer; **à moins de** + *inf* without + *ger*, unless + *ind*; **à moins que** unless; **de moins en moins** less and less; **en moins de rien** in no time at all; **moins de** (followed by numeral) less than; **moins que** less than; **rien moins que** anything but ‖

prep minus; to, e.g., **dix heures moins le quart** a quarter to ten

moire [mwar] *f* moire; **moire de soie** watered silk

moi·ré -rée [mware] *adj* watered (*silk*) ‖ *m* wavy sheen

mois [mwa] *m* month

Moïse [mɔiz] *m* Moses

moi·si -sie [mwazi] *adj* moldy ‖ *m* mold; **sentir le moisi** to have a musty smell

moisir [mwazir] *tr* to mold ‖ *intr* to become moldy, to mold; (fig) to vegetate ‖ *ref* to mold

moisissure [mwazisyr] *f* mold

moisson [mwasɔ̃] *f* harvest

moissonner [mwasɔne] *tr* to harvest, reap

moisson·neur [mwasɔnœr] **moisson·neuse** [mwasɔnøz] *mf* reaper ‖ *f* (mach) reaper

moite [mwat] *adj* moist, damp; clammy

moiteur [mwatœr] *f* moistness, dampness; **moiteur froide** clamminess

moitié [mwatje] *f* half; (coll) better half (*wife*); **à moitié, la moitié** half; **à moitié chemin** halfway; **à moitié prix** at half price; **de moitié** by half ‖ *adv* half

moka [mɔka] *m* mocha coffee; mocha cake

molaire [mɔler] *adj & f* molar

môle [mol] *m* mole, breakwater ‖ *f* (ichth) sunfish

molécule [mɔlekyl] *f* molecule

moleskine [mɔleskin] *f* (*fabric*) moleskin; imitation leather

molester [mɔleste] *tr* to molest

moleter [mɔlte] §34 *tr* to knurl, to mill

mollas·son [mɔlasɔ̃] **mollas·sonne** [mɔlasɔn] *mf* (coll) softy

mollement [mɔlmɑ̃] *adv* flabbily; listlessly

mollesse [mɔles] *f* flabbiness; apathy; softness (*of contour*); mildness (*of climate*)

mol·let [mɔle] **mol·lette** [mɔlet] *adj* soft, downy; soft-boiled (*egg*) ‖ *m* (anat) calf

molletière [mɔltjer] *f* puttee, legging

molleton [mɔltɔ̃] *m* flannel

mollir [mɔlir] *intr* to weaken

mollusque [mɔlysk] *m* mollusk

molosse [mɔlɔs] *m* watchdog

molybdène [mɔlibdɛn] *m* molybdenum

môme [mom] *adj* (slang) little ‖ *mf* (coll) kid ‖ *f* (slang) babe

moment [mɔmɑ̃] *m* moment; **à aucun moment** at no time; **à ce moment-là** then, at that time; **à tout moment, à tous moments** continually; **au moment où** just when; **c'est le moment** now is the time; **d'un moment à l'autre** at any moment; **en ce moment** now; at this moment; **par moments** now and then; **sur le moment** at the very moment; **un petit moment** a little while

momenta·né -née [mɔmɑ̃tane] *adj* momentary

momerie [mɔmri] *f* mummery

momie [mɔmi] *f* mummy

mon [mɔ̃] §88

Mon *abbr* (**Maison**) (com) House

mona·cal -cale [mɔnakal] *adj* (*pl* **-caux** [ko]) monastic, monkish

monachisme [mɔnaʃism], [mɔnakism] *m* monasticism

monarchique [mɔnarʃik] *adj* monarchic

monarque [mɔnark] *m* monarch

monastère [mɔnaster] *m* monastery

monastique [mɔnastik] *adj* monastic

mon·ceau [mɔ̃so] *m* (*pl* **-ceaux**) heap, pile

mon·dain [mɔ̃dɛ̃] **-daine** [den] *adj* worldly; social (*life, functions, etc.*); sophisticated ‖ *mf* worldly-minded person; socialite

mondanité [mɔ̃danite] *f* worldliness; **mondanités** social events; (journ) social news

monde [mɔ̃d] *m* world; people; **avoir du monde chez soi** to have company; **il y a du monde, il y a un monde fou** there is a big crowd; **le beau monde, le grand monde** high society, fashionable society; **mettre au monde** to give birth to; **tout le monde** everybody, everyone

monder [mɔ̃de] *tr* to hull; to blanch; to stone

mon·dial -diale [mɔ̃djal] *adj* (*pl* **-diaux** [djo]) world; world-wide

monétaire [mɔneter] *adj* monetary

mon·gol -gole [mɔ̃gɔl] *adj* Mongol ‖ *m* Mongol (*language*) ‖ (*cap*) *mf* Mongol (*person*)

moni·teur [mɔnitœr] **-trice** [tris] *mf* coach, trainer, instructor; monitor (*at school*)

monnaie [mɔne] *f* change, small change; money (*legal tender of a country*); **fausse monnaie** counterfeit money; **la Monnaie** the Mint; **monnaie forte** hard currency; **payer en monnaie de singe** to give lip service to

monnayer [mɔneje] §49 *tr* to mint, to coin; to convert into cash; to cash in on

monnayeur [mɔnejœr] *m*—**faux monnayeur** counterfeiter

monocle [mɔnɔkl] *m* monocle

monogamie [mɔnɔgami] *f* monogamy

monogramme [mɔnɔgram] *m* monogram

monographie [mɔnɔgrafi] *f* monograph

monolithique [mɔnɔlitik] *adj* monolithic

monologue [mɔnɔlɔg] *m* monologue

monologuer [mɔnɔlɔge] *tr* to soliloquize

monomanie [mɔnɔmani] *f* monomania

monôme [mɔnom] *m* single file (*of students*); (math) monomial

monoplan [mɔnɔplɑ̃] *m* monoplane

monopole [mɔnɔpɔl] *m* monopoly

monopoliser [mɔnɔpɔlize] *tr* to monopolize

monorail [mɔnɔrɑj] *m* monorail

monosyllabe [mɔnɔsilab] *m* monosyllable

monothéiste [mɔnɔteist] *adj* & *mf* monotheist

monotone [mɔnɔtɔn] *adj* monotonous

monotonie [mɔnɔtɔni] *f* monotony

monotype [mɔnɔtip] *adj* monotypic ‖

m monotype ‖ *f* Monotype (*machine to set type*)

monseigneur [mɔ̃seɲœr] *m* (*pl* **messeigneurs** [meseɲœr]) monseigneur

monsieur [məsjø] *m* (*pl* **messieurs** [mesjø]) gentleman; sir; mister; Mr.

monstre [mɔ̃str] *adj* huge, monster ‖ *m* monster; freak; **monstres sacrés** (fig) sacred cows, idols

mons·trueux [mɔ̃stryø] **-trueuse** [tryøz] *adj* monstrous

mont [mɔ̃] *m* mount; mountain; **par monts et par vaux** over hill and dale; **passer les monts** to cross the Alps

montage [mɔ̃taʒ] *m* hoisting; setting up (*of a machine*); (elec) hookup; (mov) cutting, editing

monta·gnard [mɔ̃taɲar] **-gnarde** [ɲard] *adj* mountain ‖ *mf* mountaineer

montagne [mɔ̃taɲ] *f* mountain; **montagnes russes** roller coaster

monta·gneux [mɔ̃taɲø] **-gneuse** [ɲøz] *adj* mountainous

mon·tant [mɔ̃tɑ̃] **-tante** [tɑ̃t] *adj* rising, ascending; uphill; vertical; high-necked (*dress*) ‖ *m* upright, riser; gatepost; total (*sum*); allure; (culin) tang; **montants** gate posts; (slang) pair of trousers

mont-de-piété [mɔ̃dpjete] *m* (*pl* **monts-de-piété**) pawnshop

mon·té -tée [mɔ̃te] *adj* mounted; organized; equipped, well-provided; worked-up, angry ‖ *f* climb; slope

monte-charge [mɔ̃tʃarʒ] *m invar* freight elevator

monte-plats [mɔ̃tpla] *m invar* dumbwaiter

monter [mɔ̃te] *tr* to go up, to climb; to mount; to set up; to carry up, take up, bring up ‖ *intr* (*aux:* ÊTRE) to go up, to come up; to come upstairs; to rise; to come in (*said of tide*); **monter** + *inf* to go up to + *inf*; **monter à** or **en** to go up, to climb, to ascend, to mount; **monter sur** to mount (*the throne*); to go on (*the stage*) ‖ *ref*—**se monter à** to amount to; **se monter en** to lay in a supply of; **se monter la tête** to get excited

montre [mɔ̃tr] *f* show, display; watch; **en montre** in the window, on display; **faire montre de** to show off, to parade; **montre à remontoir** stem-winder; **montre à répétition** repeater

montre-bracelet [mɔ̃trabrasle] *f* (*pl* **montres-bracelets**) wrist watch

montrer [mɔ̃tre] *tr* to show; **montrer du doigt** to point out or at ‖ *ref* to appear; to show oneself to be (*e.g.*, *patient*)

mon·treur [mɔ̃trœr] **-treuse** [trøz] *mf* showman, exhibitor

mon·tueux [mɔ̃tɥø] **-tueuse** [tɥøz] *adj* rolling, hilly

monture [mɔ̃tyr] *f* mounting; assembling; mount (*e.g.*, *horse*)

monument [mɔnymɑ̃] *m* monument; **monument aux morts** memorial monument

moquer [mɔke] *tr* & *ref* to mock; **se moquer de** to make fun of, to laugh at

moquerie [mɔkri] *f* mockery
moquette [mɔkɛt] *f* pile carpet
mo·ral -rale [mɔral] (*pl* **-raux** [ro]) *adj* moral || *m* morale || *f* ethics; moral (*of a fable*); **faire la morale à qn** to lecture s.o.
moralité [mɔralite] *f* morality; moral (*e.g., of a fable*)
morasse [mɔras] *f* final proof (*of newspaper*)
moratoire [mɔratwar] *m* moratorium
moratorium [mɔratɔrjɔm] *m* moratorium
morbide [mɔrbid] *adj* morbid
morbleu [mɔrblø] *interj* (obs) zounds!
mor·ceau [mɔrso] *m* (*pl* **-ceaux**) piece, bit; morsel; **bas morceaux** (culin) cheap cuts; **en morceaux** in cubes (*of sugar*); **morceaux choisis** selected passages
morceler [mɔrsəle] §34 *tr* to parcel out
morcellement [mɔrsɛlmɑ̃] *m* parceling out, division
mordancer [mɔrdɑ̃se] §51 *tr* to size
mor·dant [mɔrdɑ̃] **-dante** [dɑ̃t] *adj* mordant, caustic || *m* mordant; cutting edge; fighting spirit; (mus) mordent
mordicus [mɔrdikys] *adv* (coll) stoutly, tenaciously
mordiller [mɔrdije] *tr & intr* to nibble; to nip
mordo·ré -rée [mɔrdɔre] *adj* golden-brown, bronze-colored
mordre [mɔrdr] *tr* to bite || *intr* to bite; **mordre à** to bite on; to take to, to find easy; **mordre dans** to bite into; **mordre sur** to encroach upon || *ref* to bite
mor·du -due [mɔrdy] *adj* bitten, smitten || *mf* (coll) fan (*person*)
morelle [mɔrɛl] *f* nightshade
morfondre [mɔrfɔ̃dr] *tr* to chill to the bone || *ref* to be bored waiting
morgue [mɔrg] *f* morgue; haughtiness
mori·caud [mɔriko] **-caude** [kod] *adj* (coll) dark-skinned, dusky
morigéner [mɔriʒene] §10 *tr* to scold
morillon [mɔrijɔ̃] *m* rough emerald; duck; **morillon à dos blanc** canvasback
mor·mon [mɔrmɔ̃] **-mone** [mɔn] *adj & mf* Mormon
morne [mɔrn] *adj* dismal, gloomy || *m* hillock, knoll
mornifle [mɔrnifl] *f* (coll) slap
morose [mɔroz] *adj* morose
morphine [mɔrfin] *f* morphine
morphologie [mɔrfɔlɔʒi] *f* morphology
morpion [mɔrpjɔ̃] *m* tick-tack-toe; (*youngster*) (slang) squirt; (*Phthirius pubis*) (slang) crab louse
mors [mɔr] *m* bit; jaw (*of vise*)
morse [mɔrs] *m* Morse code; walrus
morsure [mɔrsyr] *f* bite
mort [mɔr] **morte** [mɔrt] *adj* dead; spent (*bullet*); (aut) neutral || *mf* dead person, corpse || *m* (bridge) dummy; **faire le mort** to play dead || **mort** *f* death; **attraper la mort** to catch one's death of cold
mortadelle [mɔrtadɛl] *f* bologna

mortaise [mɔrtɛz] *f* mortise
mortaiser [mɔrtɛze] *tr* to mortise
mortalité [mɔrtalite] *f* mortality
mort-aux-rats [mɔrtora], [mɔrora] *f invar* rat poison
mort-bois [mɔrbwa] *m* deadwood
morte-eau [mɔrto] *f* (*pl* **mortes-eaux** [mɔrtəzo]) low tide
mor·tel -telle [mɔrtɛl] *adj & mf* mortal
morte-saison [mɔrtəsɛzɔ̃] *f* (*pl* **mortes-saisons**) off-season
mortier [mɔrtje] *m* mortar; round judicial cap
mortifier [mɔrtifje] *tr* to mortify; to tenderize (*meat*)
mort-né -née [mɔrne] (*pl* **-nés**) *adj* stillborn || *mf* stillborn child
mortuaire [mɔrtɥɛr] *adj* mortuary; funeral (*e.g., service*); death (*notice*)
morue [mɔry] *f* cod
morve [mɔrv] *f* snot
mor·veux [mɔrvø] **-veuse** [vøz] *adj* snotty || *mf* (coll) young snot, brat, whippersnapper
mosaïque [mɔzaik] *adj* mosaic; Mosaic || *f* mosaic
Moscou [mɔsku] *m* Moscow
mosquée [mɔske] *f* mosque
mot [mo] *m* word; answer (*to riddle*); **à mots couverts** guardedly; **au bas mot** at least; **avoir toujours le mot pour rire** to be always cracking jokes; **bon mot** witticism; **gros mots** foul words; **le mot à mot** the word-for-word translation; **mot à double sens** double entendre; **mot de passe** password; **mot d'ordre** slogan; **mot pour mot** word for word; **mots croisés** crossword puzzle; **ne . . . mot** §90 (archaic) not a word, nothing; **placer un mot** to put in a word; **prendre qn au mot** to take s.o. at his word; **sans mot dire** without a word
motard [mɔtar] *m* (coll) motorcyclist; (coll) motorcycle cop
mot-clé [mɔkle] *m* (*pl* **mots-clés**) key word
motel [mɔtɛl] *m* motel
mo·teur [mɔtœr] **-trice** [tris] *adj* driving (*wheel*); drive (*shaft*); motive (*power*); power (*brake*); motor (*nerve*) || *m* motor, engine; prime mover; instigator; **moteur à deux temps** two-cycle engine; **moteur à explosion** internal-combustion engine; **moteur à quatre temps** four-cycle engine; **moteur à réaction** jet engine; **moteur hors bord** outboard motor
moteur-fusée *m* (*pl* **moteurs-fusées**) rocket engine
motif [mɔtif] *m* motive; (fa, mus) motif
motion [mosjɔ̃] *f* (parl) motion
motiver [mɔtive] *tr* to motivate
moto [mɔto] *f* motorcycle
motoriser [mɔtɔrize] *tr* to motorize
mot-outil [mɔuti] *m* (*pl* **mots-outils**) link word
mot-piège [mɔpjɛʒ] *m* (*pl* **mots-pièges**) tricky word

mots-croisés [mokrwaze] *mpl* cross-word puzzle

mot-souche [mosuʃ] *m* (*pl* **mots-souches**) entry word; (typ) catch-word

motte [mɔt] *f* clod, lump; slab (*of butter*); **motte de gazon** turf

motus [mɔtys] *interj* mum's the word!

mou [mu] (*m* [mɔl] **mol**) before vowel or mute h) **molle** [mɔl] (*pl* **mous molles**) *adj* soft; limp, flabby, slack; spineless, listless || *m* slack; lights, lungs; (coll) softy

mou•chard [muʃar] **-charde** [ʃard] *mf* (coll) stool pigeon, squealer

moucharder [muʃarde] *tr* (coll) to spy on; (coll) to squeal on || *intr* (coll) to squeal

mouche [muʃ] *f* fly; beauty spot; **faire d'une mouche un éléphant** to make a mountain out of a molehill; **faire la mouche** to fly into a rage; **faire mouche** to hit the bull's-eye; **mouche à miel** honeybee; **mouche d'Espagne** (pharm) Spanish fly; **mouche du coche** busybody

moucher [muʃe] *tr* to blow (*one's nose*); to snuff, to trim; (coll) to scold || *ref* to blow one's nose

moucherolle [muʃrɔl] *f* (orn) fly-catcher

moucheron [muʃrɔ̃] *m* gnat; snuff (*of candle*)

moucheter [muʃte] §34 *tr* to speckle

mouchoir [muʃwar] *m* handkerchief

moudre [mudr] §43 *tr* to grind

moue [mu] *f* wry face; **faire la moue** to pout

mouette [mwet] *f* gull, sea gull; **mouette rieuse** black-headed gull

mouffette [mufet] *f* skunk

moufle [mufl] *m* & *f* pulley block || *f* mitten

mouillage [mujaʒ] *m* anchorage; wetting; watering, diluting

mouil•lé -lée [muje] *adj* wet; at anchor; palatalized; liquid (*l*)

mouiller [muje] *tr* to wet; to water, dilute; to palatalize; to drop (*anchor*) || *intr* to drop anchor || *ref* to get wet; to water; (coll) to become involved

moulage [mulaʒ] *m* molding, casting; mold, cast; grinding, milling

moule [mul] *m* mold, form || *f* mussel; (slang) fleabrain; (slang) jellyfish

mouler [mule] *tr* to mold; to outline, e.g., **corsage qui moule le buste** blouse which outlines the bosom

moulin [mulɛ̃] *m* mill; **moulin à café** coffee grinder; **moulin à paroles** (coll) windbag; **moulin à vent** windmill

moulinet [muline] *m* winch; reel (*of casting rod*); turnstile; pinwheel (*child's toy*); **faire le moulinet avec** to twirl

moult [mult] *adv* (obs) much, many

mou•lu -lue [muly] *adj* ground; (coll) done in

moulure [mulyr] *f* molding

mou•rant [murɑ̃] **-rante** [rɑ̃t] *adj* dying || *mf* dying person

mourir [murir] §44 *intr* (aux: ÊTRE) to die || *ref* to be dying

mouron [murɔ̃] *m* (bot) starwort, stitchwort; (bot) pimpernel

mousquetaire [muskəter] *m* musketeer

mousse [mus] *adj* dull || *m* cabin boy || *f* moss; froth, foam; lather, suds; whipped cream

mousseline [muslin] *f* muslin; **mousseline de soie** chiffon

mousser [muse] *intr* to froth, to foam; to lather; **faire mousser** (coll) to crack up, to build up; (slang) to enrage

mous•seux [musø] **mous•seuse** [musøz] *adj* mossy, frothy, foamy; sudsy; sparkling (*wine*)

mousson [musɔ̃] *f* monsoon

moustache [mustaʃ] *f* moustache; **moustaches** whiskers (*of, e.g., cat*); **moustaches en croc** handle-bar mustache

moustiquaire [mustiker] *f* mosquito net

moustique [mustik] *m* mosquito

moût [mu] *m* must; wort

moutard [mutar] *m* (slang) kid

moutarde [mutard] *f* mustard

moutier [mutje] *m* (obs) monastery

mouton [mutɔ̃] *m* sheep; mutton; (slang) stool pigeon; **doux comme un mouton** gentle as a lamb; **moutons** whitecaps; **moutons de Panurge** (fig) chameleons, yes men; **revenons à nos moutons** let's get back to our subject

mouton•né -née [mutone] *adj* fleecy; frothy (*sea*); mackerel (*sky*)

moutonner [mutone] *tr* to curl || *intr* to break into whitecaps

mouton•neux [mutonø] **mouton•neuse** [mutonøz] *adj* frothy; fleecy (*e.g., cloud*)

mouture [mutyr] *f* grinding; mixture of wheat, rye, and barley; (fig) reworking

mouvement [muvmɑ̃] *m* movement; motion; **mouvement d'horlogerie** clockwork; **mouvement d'humeur** fit of bad temper; **mouvement ondulatoire** wave motion

mouvemen•té -tée [muvmɑ̃te] *adj* lively; eventful; hilly, broken (*terrain*)

mouvementer [muvmɑ̃te] *tr* to enliven

mouvoir [muvwar] §45 *tr* to move; to set in motion, to drive || *ref* to move, stir

moyen [mwajɛ̃] **moyenne** [mwajen] *adj* average; ordinary; middle, intermediate; medium || *m* way, manner; **au moyen de** by means of; **moyens** means || *f* average; mean; passing mark; **en moyenne** on an average

moyen-âge [mwajenaʒ] *m* Middle Ages

moyen-courrier [mwajɛ̃kurje] *m* (*pl* **moyens-courriers**) medium-range plane

moyennant [mwajenɑ̃] *prep* in exchange for || *conj* provided that

Moyen-Orient [mwajenɔrjɑ̃] *m* Middle East

moyeu [mwajø̃] *m* (*pl* **moyeux**) hub

mû mue [my] *adj* driven, propelled ‖ *f* see **mue**

mucosité [mykozite] *f* mucus

mucus [mykys] *m* mucus

mue [my] *f* molt, shedding

muer [mɥe] *intr* to molt; to shed; (*said of voice*) to break, change

muet [mɥe] **muette** [mɥet] *adj* mute; silent; non-speaking (*rôle*); blank; dead (*key*) ‖ *mf* mute ‖ *m* silent movie

mufle [myfl] *m* muzzle, snout; (coll) cad, skunk

mugir [myʒir] *intr* to bellow

mugissement [myʒismã] *m* bellow

muguet [myge] *m* lily of the valley

mulâ·tre [mylɑtr] **-tresse** [tres] *mf* mulatto

mule [myl] *f* mule

mulet [myle] *m* mule; (ichth) mullet

mule·tier [myltje] **-tière** [tjer] *adj* mule (*e.g., trail*) ‖ *m* muleteer

mulette [mylet] *f* fresh-water clam

mulot [mylo] *m* field mouse

multilaté·ral **-rale** [myltilateral] *adj* (*pl* **-raux** [ro]) multilateral

multiple [myltipl] *adj & m* multiple

multiplicité [myltiplisite] *f* multiplicity

multiplier [myltiplije] *tr & ref* to multiply

multitude [myltityd] *f* multitude

munici·pal **-pale** [mynisipal] *adj* (*pl* **-paux** [po]) municipal

municipalité [mynisipalite] *f* municipality; city officials; city hall

munifi·cent [mynifisã] **-cente** [sãt] *adj* munificent

munir [mynir] *tr* to provide, equip ‖ *ref*—**se munir de** to provide oneself with

munitions [mynisjɔ̃] *fpl* munitions

mu·queux [mykø] **-queuse** [køz] *adj* mucous ‖ *f* mucous membrane

mur [myr] *m* wall; **mettre au pied du mur** to corner; **mur de soutènement** retaining wall; **mur sonique, mur du son** sound barrier

mûr mûre [myr] *adj* ripe, mature ‖ *f* see **mûre**

muraille [myraj] *f* wall, rampart

mu·ral **-rale** [myral] *adj* (*pl* **-raux** [ro]) mural

mûre [myr] *f* mulberry; blackberry

murer [myre] *tr* to wall up or in ‖ *ref* to shut oneself up

mûrier [myrje] *m* mulberry tree

mûrir [myrir] *tr & intr* to ripen, mature

murmure [myrmyr] *m* murmur

murmurer [myrmyre] *tr & intr* to murmur

musaraigne [myzareɲ] *f* (zool) shrew

musarder [myzarde] *intr* to dawdle

musc [mysk] *m* musk

muscade [myskad] *f* nutmeg; **passez muscade!** presto!

muscardin [myskardɛ̃] *m* dormouse

muscat [myska] *m* muscatel

muscle [myskl] *m* muscle

mus·clé **-clée** [myskle] *adj* muscular; (coll) powerful (*e.g., drama*); (slang) difficult

musculaire [myskyler] *adj* muscular

muscu·leux [myskylø] **-leuse** [løz] *adj* muscular

muse [myz] *f* muse; **les Muses** the Muses

mu·seau [myzo] *m* (*pl* **-seaux**) snout; (coll) mug, face

musée [myze] *m* museum

museler [myzle] §34 *tr* to muzzle

muselière [myzəljer] *f* muzzle

muser [myze] *intr* to dawdle

musette [myzet] *f* feed bag; kit bag; haversack

muséum [myzeɔm] *m* museum of natural history

musi·cal **-cale** [myzikal] *adj* (*pl* **-caux** [ko]) musical

music-hall [myzikol] *m* (*pl* **-halls**) vaudeville; vaudeville house; music hall (Brit)

musi·cien [myzisjɛ̃] **-cienne** [sjen] *mf* musician

musicologie [myzikɔlɔʒi] *f* musicology

musique [myzik] *f* music; band; **toujours la même musique** (coll) the same old song

mus·qué **-quée** [myske] *adj* musk-scented

musul·man [myzylmã] **-mane** [man] *adj & mf* Mussulman

mutation [mytasjɔ̃] *f* mutation; transfer; (biol) mutation, sport

muter [myte] *tr* to transfer

muti·lé **-lée** [mytile] *mf* disabled veteran

mutiler [mytile] *tr* to mutilate; to deface; to disable; to garble (*e.g., the truth*)

mu·tin [mytɛ̃] **-tine** [tin] *adj* roguish ‖ *mf* mutineer

muti·né **-née** [mytine] *adj* mutinous ‖ *mf* mutineer

mutiner [mytine] *ref* to mutiny

mutualité [mytɥalite] *f* mutual insurance

mu·tuel **-tuelle** [mytɥel] *adj* mutual ‖ *f* mutual benefit association

myope [mjɔp] *adj* near-sighted ‖ *mf* near-sighted person

myriade [mirjad] *f* myriad

myrrhe [mir] *f* myrrh

myrte [mirt] *m* myrtle

myrtille [mirtij] *f* blueberry

mystère [mister] *m* mystery

mysté·rieux [misterjø] **-rieuse** [rjøz] *adj* mysterious

mysticisme [mistisism] *m* mysticism

mystification [mistifikasjɔ̃] *f* mystification; hoax

mystifier [mistifje] *tr* to mystify; to hoax

mystique [mistik] *adj & mf* mystic

mythe [mit] *m* myth

mythique [mitik] *adj* mythical

mythologie [mitɔlɔʒi] *f* mythology

mythologique [mitɔlɔʒik] *adj* mythological

N

N, n [en], *[en] *m invar* fourteenth letter of the French alphabet

na·bot [nabo] **-bote** [bɔt] *adj* dwarfish || *mf* dwarf, midget

nacelle [nasɛl] *f* (aer) nacelle; (naut) wherry, skiff; (fig) boat

nacre [nakr] *f* mother-of-pearl

na·cré -crée [nakre] *adj* pearly

nage [naʒ] *f* swimming; rowing, paddling; **être (tout) en nage** to be wet with sweat; **nage à la pagaie** paddling; **nage de côté** sidestroke; **nage en couple** sculling; **nage en grenouille** breaststroke

nagée [naʒe] *f* swimming stroke

nageoire [naʒwar] *f* fin; flipper (*of seal*); float (*for swimmers*)

nager [naʒe] §38 *intr* to swim; to float; to row; **nager à culer** (naut) to back water; **nager debout** to tread water; **nager standing up; nager entre deux eaux** to swim under water; (fig) to carry water on both shoulders

na·geur [naʒœr] **-geuse** [ʒøz] *adj* swimming; floating || *mf* swimmer; rower

naguère or **naguères** [nager] *adv* lately, just now

naïf [naif] **naïve** [naiv] *adj* naïve || *mf* simple-minded person

nain [nɛ̃] **naine** [nen] *adj* & *mf* dwarf

naissain [nesɛ̃] *m* seed oysters

naissance [nesɑ̃s] *f* birth; lineage; descent; beginning; (archit) springing line; **de basse naissance** lowborn; **de haute naissance** highborn; **de naissance** by birth; **donner naissance à** to give birth to; to give rise to; **naissance de la gorge** bosom, throat; **naissance des cheveux** hairline; **naissance du jour** daybreak; **prendre naissance** to arise, originate

nais·sant [nesɑ̃] **nais·sante** [nesɑ̃t] *adj* nascent, rising, budding

naître [netr] §46 *intr* (aux: ÊTRE) to be born; to bud; to arise, originate; to dawn; **faire naître** to give birth to; to give rise to

naïveté [naivte] *f* naïveté; artlessness

nanan [nanɑ̃], [nɑ̃nɑ̃] *m* (coll) goody; **du nanan** (coll) nice

nantir [nɑ̃tir] *tr* to give security or a pledge to; **nantir de** to provide with || *intr* to stock up; to feather one's nest || *ref*—**se nantir de** to provide oneself with

nantissement [nɑ̃tismɑ̃] *m* security

napée [nape] *f* wood nymph

napel [napel] *m* monkshood, wolfsbane

naphte [naft] *m* naphtha

napoléo·nien [napoleonjɛ̃] **-nienne** [njen] *adj* Napoleonic

nappage [napaʒ] *m* table linen

nappe [nap] *f* tablecloth; sheet (*of water, flame*); net (*for fishing; for bird catching*); **mettre la nappe** to set the table; **nappe d'autel** altar cloth; **ôter la nappe** to clear the table

napperon [naprɔ̃] *m* tablecloth cover; **petit napperon** doily

narcisse [narsis] *m* narcissus; **narcisse des bois** daffodil; **Narcisse** Narcissus

narcotique [narkɔtik] *adj* & *m* narcotic

narcotiser [narkɔtize] *tr* to dope

nargue [narg] *f* scorn, contempt; **faire nargue de** to defy; **nargue de . . . !** fie on . . . !

narguer [narge] *tr* to flout, to snap one's fingers at

narguilé [argile] *m* hookah

narine [narin] *f* nostril

nar·quois [narkwa] **-quoise** [kwaz] *adj* sly, cunning; sneering

narra·teur [naratœr] **-trice** [tris] *mf* narrator, storyteller

narra·tif [naratif] **-tive** [tiv] *adj* narrative

narration [narasjɔ̃] *f* narration; narrative

narrer [nare] *tr* to narrate, relate

na·sal -sale [nazal] *adj* (*pl* **-saux** [zo]) nasal || *f* nasal (*vowel*)

nasaliser [nazalize] *tr* & *intr* to nasalize

nasarde [nazard] *f* fillip on one's nose (*in contempt*); snub, insult

na·seau [nazo] *m* (*pl* **-seaux**) nostril (*of horse, etc.*); **naseaux** (coll) snout

nasil·lard [nazijar] **nasil·larde** [nazijard] *adj* nasal

nasiller [nazije] *intr* to talk through one's nose; to squawk, quack

nasse [nas] *f* fish trap; (sports) basket

na·tal -tale [natal] *adj* (*pl* **-tals**) natal, of birth, native

natalité [natalite] *f* birth rate

natation [natasjɔ̃] *f* swimming

na·tif [natif] **-tive** [tiv] *adj* & *mf* native

nation [nasjɔ̃] *f* nation; **Nations Unies** United Nations

natio·nal -nale [nasjɔnal] *adj* & *mf* (*pl* **-naux** [no] **-nales**) national

nationaliser [nasjɔnalize] *tr* to nationalize

nationalité [nasjɔnalite] *f* nationality

nativité [nativite] *f* nativity; nativity scene; **Nativité** Nativity

natte [nat] *f* mat, matting; braid

natter [nate] *tr* to weave; to braid

naturalisation [natyralizɑsjɔ̃] *f* naturalization

naturaliser [natyralize] *tr* to naturalize

naturalisme [natyralism] *m* naturalism

naturaliste [natyralist] *adj* & *mf* naturalist

nature [natyr] *adj invar* raw; black (*coffee*) || *f* nature; **nature morte** (painting) still life

natu·rel -relle [natyrel] *adj* natural; native || *m* naturalness; native, citizen

naturellement [natyrelmɑ̃] *adv* naturally; of course

naufrage [nofraʒ] *m* shipwreck

naufra·gé -gée [nofraʒe] *adj* shipwrecked || *mf* shipwrecked person

nauséa·bond [nozeabɔ̃] **-bonde** [bɔ̃d] *adj* nauseating

nausée [noze] *f* nausea

nauséeux [nozeø] **nauséeuse** [nozeøz] *adj* nauseous

nautique [notik] *adj* nautical

nautisme [notism] *m* yachting

nauto·nier [notɔnje] **-nière** [njɛr] *mf* pilot

na·val -vale [naval] *adj* (*pl* **-vals**) naval; nautical, maritime

navel [navɛl] *f* navel orange

navet [navɛ] *m* turnip

navette [navɛt] *f* shuttle; shuttle train; **faire la navette** to shuttle, to ply back and forth

navigable [navigabl] *adj* navigable (*river*); seaworthy (*ship*)

naviga·teur [navigatœr] **-trice** [tris] *adj* seafaring || *m* navigator

navigation [navigasjɔ̃] *f* navigation; sailing; **navigation de plaisance** (*sports*) sailing

naviguer [navige] *intr* to navigate, sail; **naviguer sur** to navigate, sail (*the sea*)

navire [navir] *m* ship; **navire de débarquement** landing craft; **navire marchand** merchantman

navire-citerne [navirsitern] *m* (*pl* **navires-citernes**) tanker

navire-école [navirekɔl] *m* (*pl* **navires-écoles**) training ship

navire-jumeau [navirʒymo] *m* (*pl* **navires-jumeaux**) sister ship

na·vrant [navrɑ̃] **-vrante** [vrɑ̃t] *adj* distressing, heartrending

na·vré -vrée [navre] *adj* sorry, grieved

navrer [navre] *tr* to distress, grieve

nazaréen [nazareɛ̃] **nazaréenne** [nazareɛn] *adj* Nazarene || (*cap*) *mf* Nazarene

N.-D. *abbr* (**Notre-Dame**) Our Lady

ne [nə] §87, §90; **n'est-ce pas?** isn't that so? La traduction précédente est généralement remplacée par diverses locutions. Si l'énoncé est négatif, la question qui équivaut à **n'est-ce pas?** sera affirmative, par ex., **Vous ne travaillez pas. N'est-ce pas?** You are not working. Are you? Si l'énoncé est affirmatif, la question sera négative, par ex., **Vous travaillez. N'est-ce pas?** You are working. Are you not? ou **Aren't you?** Si l'énoncé contient un auxiliaire, la question contiendra cet auxiliaire moins l'infinitif ou moins le participe passé, par ex., **Il arrivera demain. N'est-ce pas?** He will arrive tomorrow. Won't he?; par ex., **Paul est déjà arrivé. N'est-ce pas?** Paul has already arrived. Hasn't he? Si l'énoncé ne contient un auxiliaire ni forme de la copule "to be," la question contiendra l'auxiliaire "do" ou "did" moins l'infinitif, par ex., **Marie parle anglais. N'est-ce pas?** Mary speaks English. Doesn't she?

né née [ne] *adj* born; by birth; **bien né** highborn; **né pour** cut out for

néanmoins [neɑ̃mwɛ̃] *adv* nevertheless

néant [neɑ̃] *m* nothing, nothingness; worthlessness; obscurity; none (*as a response on the appropriate blank of an official form*)

nébu·leux [nebylø] **-leuse** [løz] *adj* nebulous; gloomy (*facial expression*); worried (*brow*) || *f* nebula

nécessaire [neseser] *adj* necessary, needful; **nécessaire à** required for || *m* necessities; kit, dressing case

nécessairement [nesesermɑ̃] *adv* necessarily

nécessité [nesesite] *f* necessity; need; **nécessité préalable** prerequisite

nécessiter [nesesite] *tr* to necessitate

nécessi·teux [nesesitø] **-teuse** [tøz] *adj* needy || *mf* needy person; **les nécessiteux** the needy

nécrologie [nekrɔlɔʒi] *f* necrology, obituary

nectar [nektar] *m* nectar

néerlan·dais [neerlɑ̃dɛ] **-daise** [dɛz] *adj* Dutch || *m* Dutch (*language*) || (*cap*) *mf* Netherlander

nef [nɛf] *f* nave; (*archaic*) ship; **nef latérale** aisle

néfaste [nefast] *adj* ill-starred, unlucky

nèfle [nɛfl] *f* medlar

néflier [neflije] *m* medlar tree

néga·teur [negatœr] **-trice** [tris] *adj* negative

néga·tif [negatif] **-tive** [tiv] *adj* negative || *m* (phot) negative || *f* negative (*side of a question*)

négation [negasjɔ̃] *f* negation; (gram) negative

négli·gé -gée [negliʒe] *adj* careless; unadorned, unstudied || *m* carelessness; negligee, dressing gown

négligeable [negliʒabl] *adj* negligible

négligence [negliʒɑ̃s] *f* negligence; **avec négligence** slovenly

négli·gent [negliʒɑ̃] **-gente** [ʒɑ̃t] *adj* negligent || *mf* careless person

négliger [negliʒe] §38 *tr* to neglect || *ref* to neglect oneself

négoce [negos] *m* trade, commerce; (com) company

négociable [negosjabl] *adj* negotiable

négo·ciant [negosjɑ̃] **-ciante** [sjɑ̃t] *mf* wholesaler, dealer

négocia·teur [negosjatœr] **-trice** [tris] *mf* negotiator

négociation [negosjasjɔ̃] *f* negotiation

négocier [negosje] *tr* to negotiate || *intr* to negotiate; to deal

nègre [nɛgr] *adj* Negro; dark brown || *m* Negro; ghost writer; **petit nègre** pidgin, Creole

négrerie [negrəri] *f* slave quarters

négrier [negrije] *adj masc* slave || *m* slave driver; slave ship

neige [nɛʒ] *f* snow

neiger [neʒe] §38 *intr* to snow

Némésis [nemezis] *f* Nemesis

nenni [nani], [nɛni], [nɛni] *adv* (archaic) no, not

nénuphar [nenyfar] *m* water lily

néologisme [neɔlɔʒism] *m* neologism

néon [neɔ̃] *m* neon

néophyte [neɔfit] *mf* neophyte, convert

neptunium [nɛptynjɔm] *m* neptunium

nerf [nɛr] *m* nerve; tendon, sinew; (archit, bb) rib; (fig) backbone, sinew; **avoir du nerf** to have nerves of steel; **avoir les nerfs à fleur de peau** to be on edge; **nerf de bœuf**

scourge; **porter sur les nerfs à qn** to get on s.o.'s nerves

Néron [nerɔ̃] *m* Nero

ner·veux [nervø] **-veuse** [vøz] *adj* nervous; nerve; jittery; sinewy, muscular; forceful (*style*)

nervure [nervyr] *f* rib

net nette [nɛt] *adj* clean; clear, sharp, distinct; neat; **net d'impôt** tax-exempt || *m*—**mettre au net** to make a fair copy of || **net** *adv* flatly, point-blank, outright

netteté [nɛtəte] *f* neatness; clearness, sharpness

nettoiement [netwamã] *m* cleaning

nettoyage [netwajaʒ] *m* cleaning; **nettoyage à sec** dry cleaning

nettoyer [netwaje] §47 *tr* to clean; to wash up or out; **nettoyer à sec** to dry-clean || *ref* to wash up, to clean oneself

nettoyeur [netwajœr] **nettoyeuse** [netwajøz] *mf* cleaner

neuf [nœf] **neuve** [nœv] *adj* new; flambant neuf, tout neuf brand-new || **neuf** *adj & pron* nine; the Ninth, e.g., **Jean neuf** John the Ninth; **neuf heures** nine o'clock || *m* nine; ninth (*in dates*)

neutraliser [nøtralize] *tr* to neutralize

neutralité [nøtralite] *f* neutrality

neutre [nøtr] *adj & m* neuter; neutral

neuvième [nœvjem] *adj, pron* (*masc, fem*), & *m* ninth

ne·veu [nəvø] *m* (*pl* -**veux**) nephew; **nos neveux** our posterity

névralgie [nevralʒi] *f* neuralgia

névrose [nevroz] *f* neurosis

névro·sé -sée [nevroze] *adj & mf* neurotic

New York [nujɔrk], [nœjɔrk] *m* New York

newyor·kais [nœjɔrkɛ] **-kaise** [kɛz] *adj* New York || (*cap*) *mf* New Yorker

nez [ne] *m* nose; cape, headland; **nez à nez** face to face

ni [ni] §90 *conj*—**ne . . . ni . . .** ni neither . . . nor, e.g., **elle n'a ni papier ni stylo** she has neither paper nor pen; **ni . . . ni** neither . . . nor; **ni . . . non plus** nor . . . either

niable [njabl] *adj* deniable

niais [nje] **niaise** [njez] *adj* foolish, silly, simple-minded || *mf* fool, simpleton

niaiserie [njezəri] *f* foolishness, silliness, simpleness

niche [niʃ] *f* niche; alcove; prank; **niche à chien** doghouse

nichée [niʃe] *f* brood

nicher [niʃe] *tr* to niche, to lodge || *intr* to nestle; to nest; to hide || *ref* to nest

nickeler [nikle] §34 *tr* to nickel-plate

nickelure [niklyr] *f* nickel plate

nicotine [nikɔtin] *f* nicotine

nid [ni] *m* nest; **en nid d'abeilles** honeycombed; **nid de pie** crow's-nest

nièce [njes] *f* niece

nième [njem] *adj* nth

nier [nje] *tr* to deny || *intr* to plead not guilty

ni·gaud [nigo] **-gaude** [god] *adj* silly || *mf* nincompoop

nigauderie [nigodri] *f* silliness

nihilisme [niilism] *m* nihilism

Nil [nil] *m* Nile

nimbe [nɛ̃b] *m* halo, nimbus

nimber [nɛ̃be] *tr* to halo

nimbus [nɛ̃bys] *m* (meteo) nimbus

nipper [nipe] *tr* (coll) to tog || *ref* (coll) to tog oneself out

nippes [nip] *fpl* (coll) worn-out clothes; (slang) duds

nique [nik] *f*—**faire la nique à** to turn up one's nose at

nitrate [nitrat] *m* nitrate

nitre [nitr] *m* niter, nitrate

ni·treux [nitrø] **-treuse** [trøz] *adj* nitrous

nitrière [nitrijer] *f* saltpeter bed

nitrique [nitrik] *adj* nitric

nitrogène [nitrɔʒen] *m* nitrogen

nitroglycérine [nitrɔgliserin] *f* nitroglycerin

ni·veau [nivo] *m* (*pl* -**veaux**) level; **au niveau de** on a par with; **niveau à bulle d'air** spirit level; **niveau à lunettes** surveyor's level; **niveau d'essence** gasoline gauge; **niveau de vie** standard of living; **niveau d'huile** oil gauge; **niveau mental** I.Q.

niveler [nivle] §34 *tr* to level; to survey

nive·leur [nivlœr] **-leuse** [løz] *mf* leveler || *m* harrow || *f* (agr) leveler

nivellement [nivelmã] *m* leveling; surveying

No, n° *abbr* (**numéro**) No.

noble [nɔbl] *adj & mf* noble

noblesse [nɔbles] *f* nobility; nobleness

noce [nɔs] *f* wedding; wedding party; **faire la noce** to go on a spree; **ne pas être à la noce** to be in trouble; **noces** wedding

no·ceur [nɔsœr] **-ceuse** [søz] *adj* (coll) bacchanalian, reveling || *mf* (coll) reveler, debauchee

no·cif [nɔsif] **-cive** [siv] *adj* noxious

noctambule [nɔktãbyl] *mf* nighthawk; sleepwalker

nocturne [nɔktyrn] *adj* nocturnal; night; nightly || *m* (mus) nocturne || *f* open night (*of store*)

nodosité [nɔdozite] *f* nodule (*of root*); node, wart

Noé [nɔe] *m* Noah

noël [nɔel] *m* Christmas carol; (coll) Christmas present; **Noël** Christmas

nœud [nø] *m* knot; rosette; finger joint; Adam's apple; tie, alliance; crux (*of question, plot, crisis*); node; (naut) knot; **nœud de vache** granny knot; **nœud plat** square knot; **nœuds** coils (*of snake*); **nœud vital** nerve center

noir noire [nwar] *adj* black; noir **comme poix** pitch-black || *mf* Negro || *m* black; bruise; **broyer du noir** to be blue, down in the dumps; **noir de fumée** lampblack || *f* (mus) quarter note

noirâtre [nwaratr] *adj* blackish

noi·raud [nwaro] **-raude** [rod] *adj* swarthy

noirceur [nwarsœr] *f* blackness; black spot

noircir [nwarsir] *tr* to blacken || *intr & ref* to burn black; to turn dark

noircissure [nwarsisyr] *f* black spot, smudge

noise [nwaz] *f* squabble; **chercher noise à** to pick a quarrel with

noisetier [nwaztje] *m* hazelnut tree

noisette [nwazet] *adj invar* reddish-brown || *f* hazelnut

noix [nwɑ], [nwa] *f* walnut; nut; **à la noix** (slang) trifling; **noix d'acajou, noix de cajou** cashew nut; **noix du Brésil** Brazil nut; **noix de coco** coconut; **noix de galle** nutgall; **noix de muscade** nutmeg; **noix de veau** round of veal

nolis [nɔli] *m* freight

noliser [nɔlize] *tr* to charter (*a ship*)

nom [nɔ̃] *m* name; noun; **de nom** by name; **nom à rallonges, nom à tiroirs** (coll) word made up of several parts; **nom commercial** trade name; **nom de baptême** baptismal name, Christian name; **nom de demoiselle** maiden name; **nom de famille** surname; **nom de guerre** fictitious name, assumed name; **nom de jeune fille** maiden name; **nom d'emprunt** assumed name; **nom de théâtre** stage name; **nom marchand** trade name; **petit nom** first name; **petit nom d'amitié** pet name; **sans nom** nameless; **sous le nom de** by the name of

nomade [nɔmad] *adj & mf* nomad

nombre [nɔ̃br] *m* number, quantity

nombrer [nɔ̃bre] *tr* to number

nom·breux [nɔ̃brø] **-breuse** [brøz] *adj* numerous; rhythmic, harmonious (*e.g., prose*)

nombril [nɔ̃bri] *m* navel

nomenclature [nɔmɑ̃klatyr] *f* nomenclature; vocabulary; body (*of dictionary*)

nomi·nal -nale [nɔminal] *adj* (*pl* **-naux** [no]) nominal; **appel nominal** roll call

nomina·tif [nɔminatif] **-tive** [tiv] *adj* nominative; registered (*stocks, bonds, etc.*) || *m* nominative

nomination [nɔminɑsjɔ̃] *f* appointment

nom·mé -mée [nɔme] *adj* named; appointed; called || *m*—**le nommé . . .** the man called . . .

nommément [nɔmemɑ̃] *adv* namely, particularly

nommer [nɔme] *tr* to name, call; to appoint || *ref* to be named, e.g., **je me nomme . . .** my name is . . .

non [nɔ̃] *m invar* no || *adv* no, not; **non pas** not so; **non plus** neither, not, nor . . . either, e.g., **moi non plus** nor I either; **non point!** by no means!; **que non!** no indeed!

non-belligé·rant [nɔ̃belliʒerɑ̃] **-rante** [rɑ̃t] *adj & mf* nonbelligerent

nonce [nɔ̃s] *m* nuncio

noncha·lant [nɔ̃ʃalɑ̃] **-lante** [lɑ̃t] *adj* nonchalant

non-com·bat·tant [nɔ̃kɔ̃batɑ̃] **non-com-bat·tante** [nɔ̃kɔ̃batɑ̃t] *adj & mf* noncombatant

non-conformiste [nɔ̃kɔ̃fɔrmist] *adj & mf* nonconformist

non-enga·gé -gée [nɔnɑ̃gaʒe] *adj* unaligned, uncommitted

nonnain [nɔnɛ̃] *f* (pej) nun

nonne [nɔn] *f* nun

nonobstant [nɔnɔpstɑ̃] *adv* notwithstanding; **nonobstant que** although || *prep* in spite of

non-pesanteur [nɔ̃pəzɑ̃tœr] *f* weightlessness

non-rési·dent [nɔ̃rezidɑ̃] **-dente** [dɑ̃t] *adj & mf* nonresident

non-réussite [nɔ̃reysit] *f* failure

non-sens [nɔ̃sɑ̃s] *m* absurdity, nonsense

non-usage [nɔnyzaʒ] *m* disuse

non-violence [nɔ̃vjɔlɑ̃s] *f* nonviolence

nord [nɔr] *adj invar* north, northern || *m* north; **du nord** northern; **faire le nord** to steer northward; **vers le nord** northward

nord-est [nɔrest] *adj invar & m* northeast

nord-ouest [nɔrwest] *adj invar & m* northwest

nor·mal -male [nɔrmal] *adj* (*pl* **-maux** [mo]) normal; regular, standard; perpendicular || *f* normal; perpendicular

norma·lien [nɔrmaljɛ̃] **-lienne** [ljen] *mf* student at a teachers college

nor·mand [nɔrmɑ̃] **-mande** [mɑ̃d] *adj* Norman || *m* Norman (*dialect*) || (*cap*) *mf* Norman (*person*)

Normandie [nɔrmɑ̃di] *f* Normandy; **la Normandie** Normandy

norme [nɔrm] *f* norm; specifications

nor·rois [nɔrwa] **nor·roise** [nɔrwaz] *adj* Norse || *m* Norse (*language*) || (*cap*) *mf* Norseman

Norvège [nɔrvɛʒ] *f* Norway; **la Norvège** Norway

norvé·gien [nɔrveʒjɛ̃] **-gienne** [ʒjen] *adj* Norwegian || *m* Norwegian (*language*) || *f* round-stemmed rowboat || (*cap*) *mf* Norwegian (*person*)

nos [no] §88

nostalgie [nɔstalʒi] *f* nostalgia, homesickness

nostalgique [nɔstalʒik] *adj* nostalgic, homesick

notable [nɔtabl] *adj* notable, noteworthy || *m* notable

notaire [nɔter] *m* notary; lawyer

notamment [nɔtamɑ̃] *adv* especially

notation [nɔtɑsjɔ̃] *f* notation

note [nɔt] *f* note; bill (*to be paid*); grade, mark (*in school*); footnote; **être dans la note** to be in the swing of things; **note de rappel** reminder; **prendre note de** to note down

noter [nɔte] *tr* to note; to note down; to notice; to mark (*a student*); to write down (*a tune*)

notice [nɔtis] *f* notice (*review, sketch*)

notification [nɔtifikɑsjɔ̃] *f* notification, notice

notifier [nɔtifje] *tr* to report on; to serve (*a summons*)

notion [nɔsjɔ̃] *f* notion

notoire [nɔtwar] *adj* well-known

notoriété [nɔtɔrjete] *f* fame

notre [nɔtr] §88

nôtre [notr] §89; **serez-vous des nôtres?** will you join us?

noue [nu] *f* pasture land; roof gutter

noué nouée [nwe] *adj* afflicted with rickets

nouer [nwe] *tr* to knot; to tie; to form; to cook up (*a plot*) || *ref* to form knots; to be tied; (*hort*) to set

noueux [nwø] **noueuse** [nwøz] *adj* knotty, gnarled

nouille [nuj] *f* noodle

nounou [nunu] *f* nanny

nour·ri -rie [nuri] *adj* heavy, sustained; rich (*style*)

nourrice [nuris] *f* wet nurse; can; (aut) reserve tank

nourricerie [nurisri] *f* baby farm; stock farm; silkworm farm

nourri·cier [nurisje] **-cière** [sjer] *adj* nutritive; nourishing; foster

nourrir [nurir] *tr* to nourish; to suckle; to feed (*a fire*); to nurse (*plants; hopes*) || *intr* to be nourishing || *ref* to feed; to thrive

nourrisseur [nurisœr] *m* stock raiser, dairyman

nourrisson [nurisɔ̃] *m* nursling, suckling; foster child

nourriture [nurityr] *f* nourishment, food; nourishing; nursing; breast-feeding; **nourriture du feu** firewood

nous [nu] §85, §87; **nous autres Américains** we Americans

nous-mêmes [numem] §86

nou·veau [nuvo] (or **-vel** [vel] before vowel or mute h) **-velle** [vel] (*pl* **-veaux -velles**) *adj* new (*recent*) || (when standing before noun) *adj* new (*other, additional, different*) || *m* freshman; **à nouveau** anew; **de nouveau** again; **du nouveau** something new; **le nouveau** the new || *f* see **nouvelle**

nouveau-né -née [nuvone] *adj & mf* (*pl* -**nés**) newborn

nouveauté [nuvote] *f* newness, novelty

nouvelle [nuvel] *f* piece of news; novelette, short story; **donnez-moi de vos nouvelles** let me hear from you; **nouvelles** news

Nouvelle-Angleterre [nuvelɑ̃gləter] *f* New England; **la Nouvelle-Angleterre** New England

Nouvelle-Écosse [nuvelekɔs] *f* Nova Scotia; **la Nouvelle-Écosse** Nova Scotia

Nouvelle-Orléans [nuvelɔrleɑ̃] *f*—**la Nouvelle-Orléans** New Orleans

nouvelliste [nuvelist] *mf* short-story writer

nova·teur [nɔvatœr] **-trice** [tris] *adj* innovating || *mf* innovator

novembre [nɔvɑ̃br] *m* November

novice [nɔvis] *adj* inexperienced, new || *mf* novice, neophyte

noviciat [nɔvisja] *m* novitiate

novocaïne [nɔvokain] *f* novocaine

noyade [nwajad] *f* drowning

noyau [nwajo] *m* (*pl* **noyaux**) nucleus; stone, kernel; pit (*of fruit*); core (*of electromagnet*); newel; hub; (fig) cell (*of conspirators*); (fig) bunch (*of*

card players); **noyau d'atome** atomic nucleus

noyautage [nwajotaʒ] *m* infiltration (*e.g., of communists*)

noyer [nwaje] *m* walnut tree; **en noyer** in walnut (*wood*) || §47 *tr & ref* to drown

nu nue [ny] *adj* naked, nude; bare; barren; uncarpeted; unharnassed; unsaddled (*horse*); (aut) stripped || *m* nude; **à nu** exposed; bareback || *f* see **nue**

nuage [nɥaʒ] *m* cloud

nua·geux [nɥaʒø] **-geuse** [ʒøz] *adj* cloudy

nuance [nɥɑ̃s] *f* hue, shade, tone, nuance

nucléaire [nykleer] *adj* nuclear

nucléole [nykleɔl] *m* nucleolus

nucléon [nykleɔ̃] *m* nucleon

nudiste [nydist] *adj & mf* nudist

nudité [nydite] *f* nakedness; nudity; plainness (*of style*); nude

nue [ny] *f* clouds; sky; **mettre** or **porter aux nues** to praise to the skies

nuée [nɥe] *f* cloud, storm cloud; flock

nuire [nɥir] §19 (*pp* **nui**) *intr* (with *dat*) to harm, to injure

nuisible [nɥizibl] *adj* harmful

nuit [nɥi] *f* night; **à la nuit close** after dark; **bonne nuit** good night; **cette nuit** last night; **nuit blanche** sleepless night

nuitamment [nɥitamɑ̃] *adv* at night

nu-jambes [nyʒɑ̃b] *adj invar* barelegged

nul nulle [nyl] *adj indef* no; **ne . . . nul** or **nul . . . ne** §90 no; **nul et non avenu, nulle et non avenue** [nylenɔnavny] null and void || *f* dummy word or letter || **nul** *pron indef*—**nul ne** §90B no one, nobody

nullement [nylmɑ̃] §90 *adv* not at all

nullité [nylite] *f* nonentity, nobody

nûment [nymɑ̃] *adv* candidly, frankly

numé·ral -rale [nymeral] *adj & m* (*pl* -**raux** [ro]) numeral

numération [nymerasjɔ̃] *f* numeration; **numération globulaire** blood count

numérique [nymerik] *adj* numerical

numéro [nymero] *m* numeral; number; issue, number (*of a periodical*), e.g., **dernier numéro** current issue; e.g., **numéro ancien** back number; (slang) queer duck; **faire un numéro** to dial; **numéro de vestiaire** check (*of checkroom*); **numéro d'ordre** serial number

numéroter [nymerɔte] *tr* to number

numismatique [nymismatik] *adj* numismatic || *f* numismatics

nu-pieds [nypje] *adj invar* barefooted

nup·tial -tiale [nypsjal] *adj* (*pl* -**tiaux** [sjo]) nuptial

nuque [nyk] *f* nape, scruff

nurse [nœrs] *f* children's nurse

nu-tête [nytet] *adj invar* bareheaded

nutri·tif [nytritif] **-tive** [tiv] *adj* nutritive; nutritious

nutrition [nytrisjɔ̃] *f* nutrition

nylon [nilɔ̃] *m* nylon

nymphe [nɛ̃f] *f* nymph

O

O, o [o], *[o] *m invar* fifteenth letter of the French alphabet

oasis [ɔazis] *f* oasis

obéir [ɔbeir] *intr* to obey; (with *dat*) to obey, yield to; (with *dat*) to be subject to; **être obéi** to be obeyed; **obéir au doigt et à l'œil** to obey blindly

obéissance [ɔbeisɑ̃s] *f* obedience

obéis‧sant [ɔbeisɑ̃] **obéis‧sante** [ɔbeisɑ̃t] *adj* obedient

obélisque [ɔbelisk] *m* obelisk

obérer [ɔbere] §10 *tr* to burden with debt || *ref* to run into debt

obèse [ɔbɛz] *adj* obese

obésité [ɔbezite] *f* obesity

objecter [ɔbʒɛkte] *tr* to object, e.g., **objecter que . . .** to object that . . . ; to bring up, e.g., **objecter q.ch. à qn** to bring up s.th. against s.o.; to put forward (*in opposition*), e.g., **objecter de bonnes raisons à** or **contre un** argument to put forward good reasons against an argument

objecteur [ɔbʒɛktœr] *m*—**objecteur de conscience** conscientious objector

objec‧tif [ɔbʒɛktif] **-tive** [tiv] *adj* objective || *m* objective; object lens; (mil) target

objection [ɔbʒɛksjɔ̃] *f* objection; **faire des objections** to object

objectivité [ɔbʒɛktivite] *f* objectivity

objet [ɔbʒɛ] *m* object; **menus objets** notions; **objet d'art** work of art; **objet de risée** laughingstock; **objets de première nécessité** articles of everyday use; **remplir son objet** to attain one's end

obligation [ɔbligasjɔ̃] *f* obligation; (com) bond, debenture; **être dans l'obligation de** to be obliged to

obligatoire [ɔbligatwar] *adj* required, obligatory; (coll) inevitable

obli‧gée [ɔbliʒe] *adj* obliged, compelled; necessary, indispensable; **bien obligé** much obliged; **c'est obligé** (coll) it has to be; **être obligé de** to be obliged to

obli‧geant [ɔbliʒɑ̃] **-geante** [ʒɑ̃t] *adj* obliging

obliger [ɔbliʒe] §38 *tr* to oblige || *ref*—**s'obliger à** + *inf* to undertake to + *inf*; **s'obliger pour qn** to stand surety for s.o.

oblique [ɔblik] *adj* oblique

oblitération [ɔbliterasjɔ̃] *f* obliteration; cancellation (*of postage stamp*); (pathol) occlusion

oblitérer [ɔblitere] §10 *tr* to obliterate; to cancel (*a postage stamp*); to obstruct (*e.g., a vein*)

o‧blong [ɔblɔ̃] **-blongue** [blɔ̃g] *adj* oblong

obnubiler [ɔbnybile] *tr* to cloud, befog

obole [ɔbɔl] *f* widow's mite

obscène [ɔpsɛn] *adj* obscene

obscénité [ɔpsenite] *f* obscenity

obs‧cur -cure [ɔpskyr] *adj* obscure

obscurcir [ɔpskyrsir] *tr* to obscure; to dim || *ref* to grow dark; to grow dim

obscurité [ɔpskyrite] *f* obscurity

obséder [ɔpsede] §10 *tr* to obsess; to importune, to harass

obsèques [ɔpsɛk] *fpl* obsequies, funeral rites

obsé‧quieux [ɔpsekjø] **-quieuse** [kjøz] *adj* obsequious

observance [ɔpsɛrvɑ̃s] *f* observance

observa‧teur [ɔpsɛrvatœr] **-trice** [tris] *adj* observant || *mf* observer

observation [ɔpsɛrvasjɔ̃] *f* observation

observatoire [ɔpsɛrvatwar] *m* observatory

observer [ɔpsɛrve] *tr* to observe || *ref* to watch oneself; to watch each other

obsession [ɔpsesjɔ̃] *f* obsession

obsolète [ɔpsɔlɛt] *adj* obsolete

obstacle [ɔpstakl] *m* obstacle

obstétrique [ɔpstetrik] *adj* obstetrical || *f* obstetrics

obstination [ɔpstinasjɔ̃] *f* obstinacy

obsti‧né -née [ɔpstine] *adj* obstinate

obstruction [ɔpstryksjɔ̃] *f* obstruction; (sports) blocking; (pol) to filibuster; **obstruction systématique** filibustering

obstruer [ɔpstrye] *tr* to obstruct

obtempérer [ɔptɑ̃pere] §10 *intr* (with *dat*) to comply with, to obey

obtenir [ɔptənir] §72 *tr* to obtain, get

obtention [ɔptɑ̃sjɔ̃] *f* obtaining

obtura‧teur [ɔptyratœr] **-trice** [tris] *adj* stopping, closing || *m* (mach) stopcock; (phot) shutter

obturation [ɔptyrasjɔ̃] *f* stopping up; filling (*of tooth*); **obturation des lumières** blackout

obturer [ɔptyre] *tr* to stop up; to fill (*a tooth*)

ob‧tus [ɔpty] **-tuse** [tyz] *adj* obtuse

obus [ɔby] *m* (mil) shell; plunger (*of tire valve*); **obus à balles** shrapnel; **obus à mitraille** shrapnel; **obus de rupture** armor-piercing shell

obvier [ɔbvje] *intr* (with *dat*) to obviate, to prevent

oc [ɔk] *adv* (Old Provençal) yes

occasion [ɔkazjɔ̃], [ɔkazjɔ̃] *f* occasion; opportunity; bargain; à l'occasion on occasion; **à l'occasion de** for (*e.g., s.o.'s birthday*); **d'occasion** second-hand (*clothing*); used (*car*)

occasion‧nel -nelle [ɔkazjɔnɛl] *adj* occasional; chance (*meeting*); determining (*cause*)

occasionnellement [ɔkazjɔnɛlmɑ̃] *adv* occasionally; by chance, accidentally

occasionner [ɔkazjɔne] *tr* to occasion

occident [ɔksidɑ̃] *m* occident, west

occiden‧tal -tale [ɔksidɑtal] *adj & mf* (*pl* **-taux** [to]) occidental

occlu‧sif [ɔklyzif] **-sive** [ziv] *adj & f* occlusive

occlusion [ɔklyzjɔ̃] *f* occlusion

occulte [ɔkylt] *adj* occult

occu‧pant [ɔkypɑ̃] **-pante** [pɑ̃t] *adj* occupying || *mf* occupant

occupation [ɔkypasjɔ̃] *f* occupation

occu‧pé -pée [ɔkype] *adj* occupied; **occupé** (public sign) in use

occuper [ɔkype] *tr* to occupy ‖ *ref* to find something to do; **s'occuper de** to be occupied with, to be busy with; to take care of, to handle

occurrence [ɔkyrɑ̃s] *f* occurrence; **en l'occurrence** under the circumstances; **être en occurrence** to occur; **selon l'occurrence** as the case may be

océan [ɔseɑ̃] *m* ocean; **océan glacial arctique** Arctic Ocean; **océan Indien** Indian Ocean

océanique [ɔseanik] *adj* oceanic

ocre [ɔkr] *f* ochre

octane [ɔktan] *m* octane

octave [ɔktav] *f* octave

octa·von [ɔktavɔ̃] **-vonne** [vɔn] *mf* octoroon

octobre [ɔktɔbr] *m* October

octroi [ɔktrwa] *m* granting (*of a favor*); tax on provisions being brought into town

octroyer [ɔktrwaje] §47 *tr* to grant, concede; to bestow

oculaire [ɔkyler] *adj* ocular, eye ‖ *m* ocular, eyepiece

oculariste [ɔkylarist] *mf* optician (*who specializes in glass eyes*)

oculiste [ɔkylist] *mf* oculist

ode [ɔd] *f* ode

odeur [ɔdœr] *f* odor, scent

o·dieux [ɔdjø] **-dieuse** [djøz] *adj* odious ‖ *m* odium, odiousness

odo·rant [ɔdɔrɑ̃] **-rante** [rɑ̃t] *adj* fragrant

odorat [ɔdɔra] *m* (sense of) smell

Odyssée [ɔdise] *f* Odyssey

œcuménique [ekymenik] *adj* ecumenical

œdème [edem] *m* (pathol) edema

Œdipe [edip] *m* Oedipus

œil [œj] *m* (*pl* **yeux** [jø] **les yeux** [lezjø]) eye; typeface, font; bud; **avoir l'œil (américain)** (coll) to be observant; **coûter les yeux de la tête** (coll) to cost a fortune; **donner de l'œil à** to give a better appearance to; **entre quatre yeux** [ɑ̃trəkatzjø] (coll) between you and me; **faire les gros yeux à** (coll) to glare at; **faire les yeux doux à** to make eyes at; **ne pas avoir les yeux dans la poche** (coll) to keep one's eyes peeled; (coll) to be no shrinking violet; **œil au beurre noir** (coll) black eye; **œil de pie** (naut) eyelet; **œil de verre** glass eye; **œil électrique** electric eye; **pocher un œil à qn** to give s.o. a black eye; **sale œil** disapproving or dirty look; **sauter aux yeux, crever les yeux** to be obvious; **se mettre le doigt dans l'œil** (coll) to put one's foot in one's mouth; **se rincer l'œil** (slang) to get an eyeful; **taper dans l'œil à** or **de qn** (coll) to take s.o.'s fancy; **voir d'un mauvais œil** to take a dim view of

œil-de-bœuf [œjdəbœf] *m* (*pl* **œils-de-bœuf**) bull's-eye, small oval window

œil-de-chat [œjdəʃa] *m* (*pl* **œils-de-chat**) cat's-eye (*gem*)

œil-de-perdrix [œjdəperdri] *m* (*pl* **œils-de-perdrix**) (pathol) soft corn

œillade [œjad] *f* glance, leer, wink;

lancer, **jeter**, or **décocher une œillade à** to ogle

œillère [œjer] *f* eyecup; blinker; **avoir des œillères** to be biased

œillet [œje] *m* eyelet; eyelet hole; carnation, clove pink; **œillet d'Inde** (*Tagetes*) marigold

œilleton [œjtɔ̃] *m* eye, bud; eyepiece; sight (*of rifle, camera, etc.*)

œillette [œjet] *f* opium poppy

œnologie [enɔlɔʒi] *f* science of viniculture, oenology

œsophage [ezɔfaʒ] *m* esophagus

œstres [estr] *mpl* botflies, nose flies

œuf [œf] *m* (*pl* **œufs** [ø]) egg; **marcher sur des œufs** to walk on thin ice; **œuf à la coque** soft-boiled egg; **œuf à repriser** darning egg; **œuf de Colomb** ingenious, though obvious, solution to a problem; **œuf de Pâques** or **œuf rouge** Easter egg; **œuf dur** hard-boiled egg; **œuf mollet** soft-boiled egg; **œuf poché** poached egg; **œufs** spawn, roe; **œufs au lait** custard; **œufs au miroir** fried eggs; **œufs brouillés** scrambled eggs; **œuf sur le plat** fried egg; **plein comme un œuf** chock-full; **tondre un œuf** to squeeze blood out of a turnip; **tuer, écraser**, or **étouffer dans l'œuf** to nip in the bud

œuvre [œvr] *m* works (*of a painter*); **dans œuvre** inside (*measurements*); **hors d'œuvre** out of alignment; **le grand œuvre** the philosopher's stone; **le gros œuvre** (archit) the foundation, walls, and roof ‖ *f* work; piece of work; **bonnes œuvres** good works; **mettre en œuvre** to implement, to use; **mettre qn à l'œuvre** to set s.o. to work; **mettre tout en œuvre** to leave no stone unturned; **œuvres complètes** collected works; **œuvres mortes** (naut) topsides; **œuvre pie** good deed, good work; **œuvres vives** (naut) hull below water line; **se mettre à l'œuvre** to get to work

offen·sant [ɔfɑ̃sɑ̃] **-sante** [sɑ̃t] *adj* offensive

offense [ɔfɑ̃s] *f* offense; **faire offense à qn** to offend s.o.; **soit dit sans offense** with all due respect

offenser [ɔfɑ̃se] *tr* to offend ‖ *ref* to be offended

offen·sif [ɔfɑ̃sif] **-sive** [siv] *adj & f* offensive

office [ɔfis] *m* office; (eccl) office, service; **d'office** ex officio; **faire l'office de** to act as; **office d'ami** friendly turn; **remplir son office** (fig) to do its job ‖ *f* pantry

offi·ciel -cielle [ɔfisjɛl] *adj & mf* official

officier [ɔfisje] *m* officer; (naut) mate; **officier de service** (mil) officer of the day; **officier ministériel** notary public; **officier supérieur** (mil) field officer ‖ *intr* to officiate

offi·cieux [ɔfisjø] **-cieuse** [sjøz] *adj* unofficial, off-the-cuff; zealous; well-meant (*lie*); **faire l'officieux** to be officious

offrant [ɔfrɑ̃] *m*—**le plus offrant** the highest bidder

offre [ɔfr] *f* offer; **l'offre et la demande** supply and demand; **offres d'emploi** (formula in want ads) help wanted

offrir [ɔfrir] §65 *tr* to offer ‖ *ref* to offer oneself; to offer itself, to occur

offset [ɔfsɛt] *m invar* offset

offusquer [ɔfyske] *tr* to obfuscate, obscure; to irritate, displease ‖ *ref*—**s'offusquer de** to take offense at

ogive [ɔʒiv] *f* ogive; (rok) nose cone

ogre [ɔgr] **ogresse** [ɔgrɛs] *mf* ogre; **manger comme un ogre** (coll) to eat like a horse

ohé [ɔe] *interj* hey!; **ohé du navire!** ship ahoy!

ohm [om] *m* ohm

• **oie** [wa] *f* goose; simpleton; **oie blanche** simple little goose (*naïve girl*); **oie sauvage** wild goose

oignon [ɔɲɔ̃] *m* onion; (hort) bulb; (pathol) bunion; (coll) turnip, pocket watch; **aux petits oignons** (coll) perfect; **occupe-toi de tes oignons** (coll) mind your own business

oil [ɔil], [ɔj] *adv* (Old French) yes

oindre [wɛ̃dr] §35 *tr* to anoint

oi·seau [wazo] *m* (*pl* **-seaux**) bird; hod (*of mason*); (coll) character; **être comme l'oiseau sur la branche** to be here today and gone tomorrow; **oiseau de paradis, oiseau des îles** bird of paradise; **oiseau des tempêtes** stormy petrel; **oiseaux domestiques, oiseaux de basse-cour** poultry

oiseau-mouche [wazomuʃ] *m* (*pl* **-mouches**) hummingbird

oiseler [wazle] §34 *tr* to train (*hawks*) ‖ *intr* to trap birds

oiselet [wazlɛ] *m* little bird

oiseleur [wazlœr] *m* fowler

oise·lier [wazəlje] **-lière** [ljɛr] *mf* bird fancier

oi·seux [wazø] **-seuse** [zøz] *adj* useless

oi·sif [wazif] **-sive** [ziv] *adj* idle ‖ *mf* idler

oisillon [wazijɔ̃] *m* fledgling

oisiveté [wazivte] *f* idleness

oison [wazɔ̃] *m* gosling; (coll) ninny

O.K. [oke] *interj* (letterword) O.K.!

oléagi·neux [ɔleaʒinø] **-neuse** [nøz] *adj* oily

olfac·tif [ɔlfaktif] **-tive** [tiv] *adj* olfactory

olibrius [ɔlibrijys] *m* pedant; pest; braggart (*in medieval plays*)

oligarchie [ɔligarʃi] *f* oligarchy

olivaie [ɔlivɛ] *f* olive grove

olivâtre [ɔlivɑtr] *adj* olive (*complexion*)

olive [ɔliv] *adj invar* & *f* olive

olivette [ɔlivɛt] *f* olive grove

olivier [ɔlivje] *m* olive tree; olive wood; **Olivier** Oliver

olympiade [ɔlɛ̃pjad] *f* olympiad

olym·pien [ɔlɛ̃pjɛ̃] **-pienne** [pjɛn] *adj* Olympian

olympique [ɔlɛ̃pik] *adj* Olympic

ombilic [ɔbilik] *m* umbilicus

ombili·cal -cale [ɔbilikal] *adj* (*pl* **-caux** [ko]) umbilical

ombrage [ɔbraʒ] *m* shade; **porter om-** brage à to offend; **prendre ombrage (de)** to take offense (at)

ombrager [ɔbraʒe] §38 *tr* to shade

ombra·geux [ɔbraʒø] **-geuse** [ʒøz] *adj* shy, skittish; touchy; distrustful

ombre [ɔbr] *f* shadow; shade; **ombres (chinoises)** shadow play, shadowgraph; **une ombre au tableau** (coll) a fly in the ointment

ombrelle [ɔbrɛl] *f* parasol; (aer) umbrella

ombrer [ɔbre] *tr* to shade; to apply eye shadow to

om·breux [ɔbrø] **-breuse** [brøz] *adj* shady

omelette [ɔmlɛt] *f* omelet

omettre [ɔmɛtr] §42 *tr* to omit

omission [ɔmisjɔ̃] *f* omission

omnibus [ɔmnibys] *adj* omnibus; local (*train*) ‖ *m* omnibus; local (train)

omnipo·tent [ɔmnipɔtɑ̃] **-tente** [tɑ̃t] *adj* omnipotent

omnis·cient [ɔmnisjɑ̃] **omnis·ciente** [ɔmnisjɑ̃t] *adj* omniscient

omnium [ɔmnjɔm] *m* (com) holding company, general trading company; (sports) open race

omnivore [ɔmnivɔr] *adj* omnivorous

omoplate [ɔmɔplat] *f* shoulder blade

on [ɔ̃] §87 *pron indef* one, they, people; (coll) we, e.g., **y va-t-on?** are we going there?; (coll) I, e.g., **on est fatigué** I am tired; (often translated by passive forms), e.g., **on sait que** it is generally known that

once [ɔ̃s] *f* ounce

oncle [ɔ̃kl] *m* uncle

onction [ɔ̃ksjɔ̃] *f* unction; eloquence

onc·tueux [ɔ̃ktɥø] **-tueuse** [tɥøz] *adj* unctuous; greasy; bland

onde [ɔ̃d] *f* wave; watering (*of silk*); (poetic) water; **les petites ondes** (rad) shortwave; **mettre en ondes** to put on the air; **onde de choc** (aer) shock wave; **onde porteuse** (rad) carrier wave; **ondes amorties** (rad) damped waves; **ondes entretenues** (rad) continuous waves; **ondes radiophoniques** airwaves; **onde sonore** sound wave

ondée [ɔ̃de] *f* shower

on-dit [ɔ̃di] *m invar* gossip, scuttlebutt

ondoyant [ɔ̃dwajɑ̃] **ondoyante** [ɔ̃dwajɑ̃t] *adj* undulating, wavy; wavering (*person*)

ondoyer [ɔ̃dwaje] §47 *tr* to baptize in an emergency ‖ *intr* to undulate, wave

ondulation [ɔ̃dylɑsjɔ̃] *f* undulation, waving; flowing (*e.g., of drapery*); wave (*of hair*); **à ondulations** rolling (*ground*); **ondulation permanente** permanent wave

ondu·lé -lée [ɔ̃dyle] *adj* wavy; corrugated

onduler [ɔ̃dyle] *tr* to wave (*hair*) ‖ *intr* to wave, to undulate

oné·reux [ɔnerø] **-reuse** [røz] *adj* onerous

ongle [ɔ̃gl] *m* nail, fingernail; **jusqu'au bout des ongles** to or at one's fingertips; **ongle des pieds** toenail

onglée [ɔ̃gle] *f* numbness in the fingertips

onglet [ɔ̃glɛ] *m* nail hole, groove (*in blade*); thimble; **à onglets** thumb-indexed; **monter sur onglet** (bb) to insert (*a page*)

onguent [ɔ̃gɑ̃] *m* ointment, salve

O.N.U. [ɔny] (acronym) or [ɔɛny] (letterword) (**Organisation des Nations Unies**) *f* UN

onyx [ɔniks] *m* onyx

onzain * [ɔ̃zɛ̃] *m* eleven-line verse

onze * [ɔ̃z] *adj & pron* eleven; the Eleventh, e.g., **Jean onze** John the Eleventh; **onze heures** eleven o'clock || *m* eleven; eleventh (*in dates*), e.g., **le onze mai** the eleventh of May

onzième * [ɔ̃zjɛm] *adj, pron* (*masc, fem*), & *m* eleventh

opale [ɔpal] *f* opal

opaque [ɔpak] *adj* opaque

opéra [ɔpera] *m* opera; opera house; **grand opéra**, **opéra sérieux** grand opera; **opéra bouffe** comic opera, **opéra bouffe**

opéra-comique [ɔperakɔmik] *m* (*pl* **opéras-comiques**) light opera

opéra·teur [ɔperatœr] **-trice** [tris] *mf* operator || *m* cameraman

opération [ɔperasjɔ̃] *f* operation

opé·ré -rée [ɔpere] *mf* surgical patient

opérer [ɔpere] §10 *tr* to operate on; **opérer à chaud** to perform an emergency operation on (*s.o.*); **opérer qn de q.ch.** (med) to operate on s.o. for s.th. || *intr* to operate; to work || *ref* to occur, take place

opérette [ɔperɛt] *f* operetta, musical comedy

opia·cé -cée [ɔpjase] *adj* opiate

opiner [ɔpine] *intr* to opine; **opiner du bonnet** (coll) to be a yes man

opiniâtre [ɔpinjɑtr] *adj* stubborn

opiniâtreté [ɔpinjɑtrəte] *f* stubbornness

opinion [ɔpinjɔ̃] *f* opinion; public opinion; **avoir bonne opinion de** to think highly of; **avoir une piètre opinion de** to take a dim view of

opium [ɔpjɔm] *m* opium

oponce [ɔpɔ̃s] *m* prickly pear

opossum [ɔpɔsɔm] *m* opossum

oppor·tun [ɔpɔrtœ̃] **-tune** [tyn] *adj* opportune, timely, expedient

opportuniste [ɔpɔrtynist] *adj* opportunistic || *mf* opportunist

opportunité [ɔpɔrtynite] *f* opportuneness

oppo·sant -sante [ɔpozɑ̃] [zɑ̃t] *adj* opposing || *mf* opponent

oppo·sé -sée [ɔpoze] *adj & m* opposite, contrary; **à l'opposé de** contrary to

opposer [ɔpoze] *tr* to raise (*an objection*); **opposer q.ch. à** to set up s.th. against; to place s.th. opposite; to contrast s.th. with || *ref*—**s'opposer à** to oppose, object to

opposite [ɔpozit] *m*—**à l'opposite (de)** opposite

opposition [ɔpozisjɔ̃] *f* opposition; contrast

oppresser [ɔprese] *tr* to oppress; to impede (*respiration*); to weigh upon (*one's heart*)

oppresseur [ɔpresœr] *m* oppressor

oppres·sif [ɔpresif] **oppres·sive** [ɔpresiv] *adj* oppressive

oppression [ɔpresjɔ̃] *f* oppression; difficulty in breathing

opprimer [ɔprime] *tr* to oppress

opprobre [ɔprɔbr] *m* opprobrium, shame

opter [ɔpte] *intr* to opt, to choose

opticien [ɔptisjɛ̃] *m* optician

optimisme [ɔptimism] *m* optimism

optimiste [ɔptimist] *adj* optimistic || *mf* optimist

option [ɔpsjɔ̃] *f* option

optique [ɔptik] *adj* optic(al) || *f* optics; perspective; **sous cette optique** from that point of view

opu·lent -lente [ɔpylɑ̃] [lɑ̃t] *adj* opulent

opuscule [ɔpyskyl] *m* opuscule, treatise; brochure, pamphlet

or [ɔr] *m* gold; **rouler sur l'or** to be rolling in money || *adv* now; therefore

oracle [ɔrakl] *m* oracle

orage [ɔraʒ] *m* storm

ora·geux [ɔraʒø] **-geuse** [ʒøz] *adj* stormy

oraison [ɔrezɔ̃] *f* prayer; **oraison dominicale** Lord's Prayer; **oraison funèbre** funeral oration; **prononcer l'oraison funèbre de** (coll) to write off (*a custom, institution, etc.*)

o·ral -rale [ɔral] *adj* (*pl* **-raux** [ro]) oral

orange [ɔrɑ̃ʒ] *adj invar* orange (*color*) || *m* orange (*color*) || *f* orange (*fruit*)

oran·gé -gée [ɔrɑ̃ʒe] *adj & m* orange (*color*)

orangeade [ɔrɑ̃ʒad] *f* orangeade

oranger [ɔrɑ̃ʒe] *m* orange tree

orangeraie [ɔrɑ̃ʒrɛ] *f* orange grove

orangerie [ɔrɑ̃ʒri] *f* orangery; orange grove

orang-outan [ɔrɑ̃utɑ̃] *m* (*pl* **orangs-outans**) orang-outang

ora·teur [ɔratœr] **-trice** [tris] *mf* orator; speaker

oratoire [ɔratwar] *adj* oratorical || *m* (eccl) oratory

oratorio [ɔratɔrjo] *m* oratorio

orbite [ɔrbit] *f* orbit; socket (*of eye*); **placer sur son orbite**, **mettre en orbite** to orbit; **sur orbite** in orbit

orchestre [ɔrkɛstr] *m* orchestra; band; **orchestre de typique** rumba band

orchestrer [ɔrkɛstre] *tr* to orchestrate

orchidée [ɔrkide] *f* orchid

ordalie [ɔrdali] *f* (hist) ordeal

ordinaire [ɔrdiner] *adj* ordinary || *m* ordinary; regular bill of fare; (mil) mess; **d'ordinaire**, **à l'ordinaire** ordinarily

ordi·nal -nale [ɔrdinal] *adj & m* (*pl* **-naux** [no]) ordinal

ordinateur [ɔrdinatœr] *m* (electron) computer

ordination [ɔrdinasjɔ̃] *f* ordination

ordonnance [ɔrdɔnɑ̃s] *f* ordinance; order, arrangement; (pharm) prescription

ordonna·teur [ɔrdɔnatœr] **-trice** [tris]

mf organizer; marshal; **ordonnateur des pompes funèbres** funeral director

ordon·né -née [ɔrdɔne] *adj* orderly

ordonner [ɔrdɔne] *tr* to arrange, put in order; to order; to prescribe (*e.g., medicine*); (eccl) to ordain; **ordonner à qn de + inf** to order s.o. to + *inf*; **ordonner q.ch. à qn** to order s.o. to do s.th.

ordre [ɔrdr] *m* order; **avoir de l'ordre** to be neat, orderly; **à vos ordres** at your service; **dans l'ordre d'entrée en scène** (theat) in order of appearance; **en ordre** in order; **jusqu'à nouvel ordre** until further notice; **as things stand; les ordres** (eccl) orders; **ordre du jour** (mil) order of the day; (parl) agenda; **ordre public** law and order; **payez à l'ordre de** (com) pay to the order of; **sous les ordres de** under the command of

ordure [ɔrdyr] *f* rubbish, filth; **ordures ménagères** garbage

ordu·rier [ɔrdyrje] **-rière** [rjɛr] *adj* lewd, filthy

orée [ɔre] *f* edge (*of a forest*)

oreille [ɔrɛj] *f* ear; **avoir l'oreille basse** to be humiliated; **dormir sur les deux oreilles** to sleep soundly; **dresser** or **tendre l'oreille** to prick up one's ears; **échauffer les oreilles à qn** to rile s.o. up; **faire la sourde oreille** to turn a deaf ear; **rompre les oreilles à qn** (coll) to talk s.o.'s head off; **se faire tirer l'oreille** (coll) to play hard to get

oreiller [ɔreje] *m* pillow

oreillette [ɔrejet] *f* earflap (*of cap*); (anat) auricle

oreillons [ɔrejɔ̃] *mpl* mumps

ores [ɔr] *adv*—**d'ores et déjà** [dɔrzedeʒa] from now on

Orfée [ɔrfe] *m* Orpheus

orfèvre [ɔrfɛvr] *m* goldsmith; silversmith; **être orfèvre en la matière** (coll) to know one's onions

orfèvrerie [ɔrfɛvrəri] *f* goldsmith's shop; goldsmith's trade; gold plate; gold or silver jewelry

orfraie [ɔrfrɛ] *f* osprey, fish hawk

organdi [ɔrgɑ̃di] *m* organdy

organe [ɔrgan] *m* organ; part (*of a machine*)

organique [ɔrganik] *adj* organic

organisa·teur [ɔrganizatœr] **-trice** [tris] *adj* organizing ‖ *mf* organizer

organisation [ɔrganizasjɔ̃] *f* organization

organiser [ɔrganize] *tr* to organize

organisme [ɔrganism] *m* organism; organization

organiste [ɔrganist] *mf* organist

orgasme [ɔrgasm] *m* orgasm

orge [ɔrʒ] *f* barley

orgelet [ɔrʒəle] *m* (pathol) sty

orgie [ɔrʒi] *f* orgy

orgue [ɔrg] *m* organ; **orgue de Barbarie** hand organ; **orgue de cinéma** theater organ ‖ *f*—**les grandes orgues** the pipe organ

orgueil [ɔrgœj] *m* pride, conceit; **avoir l'orgueil de** to take pride in

orgueil·leux [ɔrgœjø] **orgueil·leuse** [ɔrgœjøz] *adj* proud, haughty

orient [ɔrjɑ̃] *m* orient; east; **Orient** Orient, East

orien·tal -tale [ɔrjɑ̃tal] (*pl* **-taux** [to]) *adj* oriental; eastern, east ‖ (*cap*) *mf* Oriental (*person*)

orientation [ɔrjɑ̃tasjɔ̃] *f* orientation; **orientation professionnelle** vocational guidance

orienter [ɔrjɑ̃te] *tr* to orient; to guide ‖ *ref* to take one's bearings

orien·teur [ɔrjɑ̃tœr] **-teuse** [tøz] *mf* guidance counselor

orifice [ɔrifis] *m* orifice, hole, opening

origan [ɔrigɑ̃] *m* marjoram

originaire [ɔriziner] *adj* native; original, first

origi·nal -nale [ɔriʒinal] *adj* (*pl* **-naux** [no]) original; eccentric, peculiar ‖ *m* antique (*piece of furniture*); eccentric, card (*person*); (typ) copy, original

originalité [ɔriʒinalite] *f* originality; eccentricity

origine [ɔriʒin] *f* origin

origi·nel -nelle [ɔriʒinel] *adj* original (*sin; meaning*); primitive, early

ori·gnal [ɔriɲal] *m* (*pl* **-gnaux** [ɲo]) moose, elk

orillon [ɔrijɔ̃] *m* ear, handle; (archit) projection

ori·peau [ɔripo] *m* (*pl* **-peaux**) tinsel; **oripeaux** cheap finery

Orléans [ɔrleɑ̃] *f* Orléans; **la Nouvelle Orléans** New Orleans

orme [ɔrm] *m* elm; **attendez-moi sous l'orme** (coll) I won't be there

or·né -née [ɔrne] *adj* ornate

ornement [ɔrnəmɑ̃] *m* ornament

ornemen·tal -tale [ɔrnəmɑ̃tal] *adj* (*pl* **-taux** [to]) ornamental

orner [ɔrne] *tr* to ornament, to adorn

ornière [ɔrnjɛr] *f* rut, groove

ornithologie [ɔrnitɔlɔʒi] *f* ornithology

orphe·lin [ɔrfəlɛ̃] **-line** [lin] *adj & mf* orphan

orphelinat [ɔrfəlina] *m* orphanage (*asylum*)

orphéon [ɔrfeɔ̃] *m* male choir, glee club; brass band

orteil [ɔrtej] *m* toe; big toe; **gros orteil** big toe

O.R.T.F. [ɔɛrteɛf] *m* (letterword) (**office de radio-télévision française**) French radio and television system

orthodoxe [ɔrtɔdɔks] *adj* orthodox

orthographe [ɔrtɔgraf] *f* spelling, orthography

orthographier [ɔrtɔgrafje] *tr* to spell

ortie [ɔrti] *f* nettle

orviétan [ɔrvjetɑ̃] *m* nostrum

os [ɔs] *m* (*pl* **os** [o]) bone; **à gros os** big-boned; **os à moelle** marrowbone; **trempé jusqu'aux os** soaked to the skin

osciller [ɔsile] *intr* to oscillate; to waver, hesitate

o·sé -sée [oze] *adj* daring, bold; risqué, off-color

oseille [ozɛj] *f* sorrel; (slang) dough

oser [oze] *tr & intr* to dare

osier [ozje] *m* osier; **d'osier** wicker

osmose [ɔsmoz] f osmosis

ossature [ɔsatyr] f bone structure; framework, skeleton

ossements [ɔsmɑ̃] mpl bones, remains

os·seux [ɔsø] os·seuse [ɔsøz] adj bony

ossifier [ɔsifje] tr & ref to ossify

os·su -sue [ɔsy] adj bony; big-boned

ostensible [ɔstɑ̃sibl] adj conspicuous, ostensible; ostentatious

ostensoir [ɔstɑ̃swar] m monstrance

ostentatoire [ɔstɑ̃tatwar] adj ostentatious

ostracisme [ɔstrasism] m ostracism

otage [ɔtaʒ] m hostage

otalgie [ɔtalʒi] f earache

O.T.A.N. or OTAN [ɔtan], [otan], [otɑ̃] f (acronym) (Organisation du traité de l'Atlantique Nord)—l'O.T.A.N. NATO

otarie [ɔtari] f sea lion

OTASE [ɔtaz] f (acronym) (Organisation du traité de l'Asie du Sud-Est)—l'OTASE SEATO

ôter [ote] tr to remove, to take away; to take off; to tip (one's hat); ôter q.ch. à qn to remove or take away s.th. from s.o.; ôter q.ch. de q.ch. to take s.th. away from s.th. ‖ ref to withdraw, to get out of the way

otto·man [ɔtɔmɑ̃] -mane [man] adj Ottoman ‖ m ottoman (corded fabric) ‖ f ottoman (divan) ‖ (cap) mf Ottoman (person)

ou [u] conj or; ou . . . ou either . . . or

où [u] adv where; d'où from where, whence; où que wherever; par où which way ‖ conj where; when; d'où from where, whence; par où through which; partout où wherever

ouailles [waj] fpl (eccl) flock

ouais [we] interj (coll) oh yeah!

ouate *[wat] f cotton batting, wadding

ouater *[wate] tr to pad, to wad

oubli [ubli] m forgetfulness; omission, oversight; tomber dans l'oubli to fall into oblivion

oublier [ublije] tr & intr to forget ‖ ref to forget oneself; to be forgotten

oubliettes [ublijet] fpl dungeon of oblivion

ou·blieux [ublijø] -blieuse [blijøz] adj forgetful, oblivious, unmindful

ouche [uʃ] f orchard; vegetable garden

ouest [west] adj invar & m west

ouest-alle·mand [westalmɑ̃] -mande [mɑ̃d] adj West German ‖ (cap) mf West German

ouf *[uf] interj whew!

oui *[wi] m invar yes; les oui l'emportent the ayes have it ‖ adv yes; je crois que oui I think so; oui madame yes ma'am; oui monsieur yes sir; oui mon capitaine (mon général, etc.) yes sir

ouï-dire [widir] m invar hearsay; simples ouï-dire (law) hearsay evidence

ouïe [wi] f hearing; être tout ouïe [tutwi] to be all ears; ouïes gills; sound holes (of violin) ‖ interj oh my!

ouïr [wir] (used only in: inf, compound tenses with pp ouï, and 2d pl impv oyez) tr to hear; oyez . . . ! hear ye . . . !

ouragan [uragɑ̃] m hurricane

ourdir [urdir] tr to warp (cloth before weaving); to hatch (e.g., a plot)

ourler [urle] tr to hem; ourler à jour to hemstitch

ourlet [urle] m hem; ourlet de la jupe hemline

ours [urs] m bear; (fig) lone wolf; ours en peluche teddy bear; ours mal léché unmannerly boor; ours marin (zool) seal; vendre la peau de l'ours avant de l'avoir tué to count one's chickens before they are hatched

ourse [urs] f she-bear; la Grande Ourse the Big Dipper, the Great Bear; la Petite Ourse the Little Dipper, the Little Bear

oursin [ursɛ̃] m sea urchin

ourson [ursɔ̃] m bear cub

ouste [ust] interj (coll) out!, out you go!

outarde [utard] f (orn) bustard

outil [uti] m tool, implement

outillage [utijaʒ] m tools; equipment

outil·lé -lée [utije] adj equipped with tools; tooled-up (factory)

outiller [utije] tr to equip with tools; to tool up (a factory) ‖ ref to supply oneself with equipment; to tool up

outilleur [utijœr] m toolmaker

outrage [utraʒ] m outrage, affront; ravages (of time); contempt of court; faire outrage à qn to outrage s.o.; outrage aux bonnes mœurs traffic in pornography; outrage public à la pudeur indecent exposure

outrager [utraʒe] §38 tr to outrage, to affront

outra·geux [utraʒø] -geuse [ʒøz] adj outrageous, insulting

outrance [utrɑ̃s] f excess; exaggeration; à outrance to the limit

outran·cier [utrɑ̃sje] -cière [sjɛr] adj extreme, excessive, out-and-out ‖ mf extremist, out-and-outer

outre [utr] f goatskin canteen ‖ adv further; d'outre en d'outre right through; en outre besides, moreover; passer outre à to ignore (e.g., an order) ‖ prep in addition to, apart from; beyond

ou·tré -trée [utre] adj overdone, exaggerated; exasperated

outrecui·dant [utrəkɥidɑ̃] -dante [dɑ̃t] adj self-satisfied; insolent, presumptuous

outre-Manche [utrəmɑ̃ʃ] adv across the Channel

outremer [utrəmer] m ultramarine, lapis lazuli (color)

outre-mer [utrəmer] adv overseas

outre-monts [utrəmɔ̃] adv over the mountains (i.e., the Alps)

outrepasser [utrəpase] tr to go beyond, to exceed

outrer [utre] tr to overdo, to exaggerate; to exasperate

outre-tombe [utrətɔ̃b] adv—d'outre-tombe posthumous

ou·vert [uver] -verte [vert] adj open;

exposed; frank, candid; on (said of meter, gas, etc.)

ouverture [uvertyr] f opening; hole, gap; (mus) overture; (phot) aperture

ouvrable [uvrabl] adj working, e.g., **jour ouvrable** working day

ouvrage [uvraʒ] m work, handiwork; piece of work; work, treatise

ouvrager [uvraʒe] §38 tr to work (e.g., iron); to turn (wood)

ou·vré -vrée [uvre] adj worked, wrought; finished (product)

ouvre-boîtes [uvrəbwat] m invar can opener

ouvre-bouteilles [uvrəbutej] m invar bottle opener

ouvreur [uvrœr] m opener (in poker)

ouvreuse [uvrøz] f usher

ou·vrier [uvrije] **-vrière** [vrijer] adj working, worker; worker's, working-man's ‖ mf worker ‖ m workman, laborer; **workingman** ‖ f working-woman

ouvrir [uvrir] §65 tr to open; to turn on (the light; the radio or television; the gas); **ouvrir boutique** to set up shop ‖ intr to be open; to open (said of store, school, etc.; said of card player) ‖ ref to open; to be opened; **s'ouvrir à** to open up to, confide in

ouvroir [uvrwar] m workroom

ovaire [over] m ovary

ovale [ɔval] adj & m oval

ovation [ɔvasjɔ̃] f ovation

ovationner [ɔvasjɔne] tr to give an ovation to

Ovide [ɔvid] m Ovid

oxford [ɔksfɔr] m oxford cloth

oxyde [ɔksid] m oxide

oxyder [ɔkside] tr & ref to oxidize

oxygène [ɔksiʒɛn] m oxygen

oxygéner [ɔksiʒene] §10 tr to oxygenate; to bleach (hair) ‖ ref—**s'oxygéner les poumons** (coll) to fill one's lungs full of ozone

oxyton [ɔksitɔ̃] adj & m oxytone

ozone [ozɔn] m ozone

P

P, p [pe] m invar sixteenth letter of the French alphabet

pacage [pakaʒ] m pasture

pacifica·teur [pasifikatœr] **-trice** [tris] mf pacifier

pacifier [pasifje] tr to pacify

pacifique [pasifik] adj pacific ‖ **Pacifique** adj & m Pacific

pacifisme [pasifism] m pacifism

pacifiste [pasifist] mf pacifist

pacotille [pakɔtij] f junk; **de pacotille** shoddy; junky

pacte [pakt] m pact, covenant

pactiser [paktize] intr to compromise; to traffic (with the enemy)

paf [paf] adj (slang) tipsy, tight ‖ interj bang!

pagaie [page] f paddle

pagaïe or **pagaille** [pagaj] f disorder; **en pagaïe** (coll) in great quantity; (coll) in a mess

paganisme [paganism] m paganism

pagayer [pageje] §49 tr & intr to paddle

page [paʒ] m page ‖ f page (of a book); **être à la page** to be up to date

paginer [paʒine] tr to page

pagne [paɲ] m loincloth

paie [pe] f pay, wages

paiement [pemɑ̃] m payment

païen [pajɛ̃] **païenne** [pajɛn] adj & mf pagan

pail·lard [pajar] **pail·larde** [pajard] adj ribald ‖ mf debauchee

paillasse [pajas] m buffoon ‖ f straw mattress; (slang) whore

paillasson [pajasɔ̃] m doormat

paille [pɑj] f straw; flaw; (Bib) mote; **paille de fer** iron shavings

pail·lé -lée [paje] adj rush-bottomed (chair)

pailler [paje] m straw stack ‖ tr to bottom (a chair) with straw; to mulch

pailleter [pajte] §34 tr to spangle

paillette [pajɛt] f spangle; flake (of mica; of soap); grain (of gold); flaw (in a diamond)

pain [pɛ̃] m bread; loaf (of bread, of sugar); cake (of soap); pat (of butter); **avoir du pain sur la planche** (coll) to have a lot to do; **pain à cacheter** sealing wafer; **pain aux raisins** raisin roll; **pain bis** brown bread; **pain complet** whole-wheat bread; **pain de fantaisie** bread sold by the loaf (instead of by weight); **pain de mie** sandwich bread; **pain d'épice** gingerbread; **pain grillé** toast; **pain perdu** French toast; **petit pain** roll; **se vendre comme des petits pains** (coll) to sell like hot cakes

pair paire [per] adj even (number) ‖ m peer; equal; (com) par; **hors de pair, hors pair** unrivaled; **marcher de pair avec** to keep abreast of; **travailler au pair** (coll) to work for one's keep; **au pair** at par ‖ f pair; couple; brace (of dogs, pistols, etc.); yoke (of oxen)

pairesse [peres] f peeress

pairie [peri], [peri] f peerage

paisible [pezibl] adj peaceful

paître [petr] §48 tr & intr to graze; **envoyer paître** (coll) to send packing

paix [pe] f peace

Pakistan [pakistɑ̃] m—**le Pakistan** Pakistan

pakista·nais [pakistane] **-naise** [nez] adj Pakistani ‖ (cap) mf Pakistani

pal [pal] *m* (*pl* **paux** [po] *or* **pals**) pale, stake
palabre [palabr] *m & f* palaver
palace [palas] *m* luxury hotel
palais [pale] *m* palace; palate; courthouse, law courts
palan [palã] *m* block and tackle
palanque [palãk] *f* stockade
pala·tal -tale [palatal] (*pl* **-taux** [to] **-tales**) *adj & f* palatal
pale [pal] *f* blade (*of, e.g., oar*); stake; sluice gate; (eccl) pall
pâle [pɑl] *adj* pale
palefrenier [palfrənje] *m* groom; (coll) hick, oaf
palefroi [palfrwa] *m* palfrey
paleron [palrɔ̃] *m* bottom chuck roast
palet [pale] *m* disk, flat stone; puck
paletot [palto] *m* topcoat
palette [palet] *f* palette; paddle
pâleur [pɑlœr] *f* pallor; paleness
palier [palje] *m* landing (*of stairs*); plateau (*of curve of a graph*); (mach) bearing; **en palier** on the level; **palier à billes** ball bearing; **par paliers** graduated (*e.g., tax*)
pâlir [pɑlir] *tr & intr* to pale, turn pale
palis [pali] *m* picket fence
palissade [palisad] *f* palisade; fence
palissandre [palisɑ̃dr] *m* rosewood
pallier [palje] *tr* to palliate; to mitigate || *intr* (with *dat*) to mitigate
palmarès [palmares] *m* list of winners
palme [palm] *f* (bot) palm
palmeraie [palmərɛ] *f* palm grove
palmier [palmje] *m* palm tree
palmipède [palmiped] *adj* webfooted || *m* webfoot
palombe [palɔ̃b] *f* ringdove
palourde [palurd] *f* clam
palpable [palpabl] *adj* palpable; plain, obvious
palper [palpe] *tr* to feel; to palpate; (coll) to pocket (*money*)
palpiter [palpite] *intr* to palpitate
palsambleu [palsɑ̃blø] *interj* zounds!
paltoquet [paltɔke] *m* nonentity
palu·déen [palydeẽ] **-déenne** [deen] *adj* marsh (*plant*); swamp (*fever*)
paludisme [palydism] *m* malaria
pâmer [pame] *ref* to swoon
pâmoison [pamwazɔ̃] *f* swoon
pamphlet [pɑ̃fle] *m* lampoon
pamplemousse [pɑ̃pləmus] *m & f* grapefruit
pan [pɑ̃] *m* tail (*of shirt or coat*); section; side, face; patch (*of sky*); **Pan** || *interj* bang!
panacée [panase] *f* panacea
panachage [panaʃaʒ] *m* mixing; **faire du panachage** to split one's vote
panache [panaʃ] *m* plume; wreath (*of smoke*); **aimer le panache** to be fond of show; **avoir son panache** (coll) to be tipsy; **faire panache** to somersault, to turn over
pana·ché -chée [panaʃe] *adj* variegated; mixed (*salad*); motley (*crowd*)
panacher [panaʃe] *tr* to variegate; to plume; to split (*one's vote*) || *ref* to become variegated
panais [pane] *m* parsnip
panama [panama] *m* panama hat; **le**

Panama Panama; **Panama** Panama City
panaris [panari] *m* (pathol) whitlow, felon
pancarte [pɑ̃kart] *f* placard; poster, sign
panchromatique [pɑ̃krɔmatik] *adj* panchromatic
pancréas [pɑ̃kreas] *m* pancreas
pandémonium [pɑ̃demɔnjɔm] *m* den of iniquity; pandemonium
pa·né -née [pane] *adj* breaded
panetière [pantjɛr] *f* breadbox
panier [panje] *m* basket; hoop (*of skirt*); creel (*trap*); **être dans le même panier** to be in the same boat; **panier à ouvrage** work basket; **panier à papier** wastepaper basket; **panier à provisions** shopping basket; **panier à salade** wire salad washer; (coll) paddy wagon; **panier percé** spendthrift
panier-repas [panjerəpa] *m* (*pl* **paniers-repas**) box lunch
panique [panik] *adj & f* panic
panne [pan] *f* breakdown, trouble; plush; fat (*of pig*); peen (*of hammer*); tip (*of soldering iron*); bank (*of clouds*); purlin (*of roof*); daub; (theat) small part; (em) **panne sèche** (public sign) out of gas; **être dans la panne** (coll) to be hard up; **être en panne** (coll) to be unable to continue; **être en panne de** (coll) to be deprived of; **laisser en panne** to leave in the lurch; **mettre en panne** (naut) to heave to; **panne fendue** claw (*of hammer*); **rester en panne** to come to a standstill; **tomber en panne** to have a breakdown
pan·né -née [pane] *adj* (slang) hard up
pan·neau [pano] *m* (*pl* **-neaux**) panel; snare, net; **condamner les panneaux** (naut) to batten down the hatches; **donner dans le panneau** to walk into the trap; **panneau d'affichage** billboard; **panneau de tête** headboard (*of bed*); **panneaux paneling**; **panneaux de signalisation** traffic signs; **tomber** *or* **donner dans le panneau** to be taken in, to fall into a trap
panoplie [panɔpli] *f* panoply
panorama [panɔrama] *m* panorama
panoramiquer [panɔramike] *intr* (mov, telv) to pan
panse [pɑ̃s] *f* belly; rumen, first stomach
pansement [pɑ̃smɑ̃] *m* (surg) dressing
panser [pɑ̃se] *tr* to dress, bandage; to groom (*an animal*)
pan·su -sue [pɑ̃sy] *adj* potbellied
pantalon [pɑ̃talɔ̃] *m* trousers, pair of trousers; panties; slacks; **pantalon à pattes d'éléphant** bell-bottomed trousers; **pantalon corsaire** pedal pushers; **pantalon de coutil** ducks; blue jeans; **pantalon de golf** knickers; **pantalon de ski** ski pants
pante [pɑ̃t] *m* (slang) guy
panteler [pɑ̃tle] §34 *intr* to pant
panthéisme [pɑ̃teism] *m* pantheism
panthéon [pɑ̃teɔ̃] *m* pantheon
panthère [pɑ̃ter] *f* panther

pantin [pɑ̃tɛ̃] *m* puppet; jumping jack; **pantin articulé** string puppet
pantomime [pɑ̃tɔmim] *f* pantomime
pantou·flard [pɑ̃tuflar] **-flarde** [flard] *mf* (coll) homebody
pantoufle [pɑ̃tufl] *f* slipper
pantoufler [pɑ̃tufle] *intr* to leave government service
paon [pɑ̃] *m* peacock, peafowl; **peacock butterfly**
paonne [pan] *f* peahen
papa [papa] *m* papa; **à la papa** (coll) cautiously; **de papa** (coll) outmoded; **papa gâteau** (coll) sugar daddy
papas [papɑs] *m* pope (*in Orthodox Church*)
papauté [papote] *f* papacy
pape [pap] *m* pope
pape·lard [paplar] **-larde** [lard] *adj* hypocritical ‖ *mf* hypocrite ‖ *m* scrap of paper
paperasse [papras] *f* old paper
paperasserie [paprasri] *f* red tape
paperas·sier [paprasje] **paperas·sière** [paprasjɛr] *adj* fond of red tape ‖ *mf* bureaucrat
papeterie [paptri] *f* paper mill; stationery store
pape·tier [paptje] **-tière** [tjɛr] *mf* stationer
papier [papje] *m* paper; newspaper article; document; piece of paper; **être dans les petits papiers de** (coll) to be in the good graces of; **gratter du papier** to scribble; **papier à calquer, papier végétal** tracing paper; **papier à en-tête** letterhead; **papier à lettres** writing paper; **papier à machine** typewriter paper; **papier à musique** staff paper; **papier bible, indien,** or **pelure** Bible paper, onionskin; **papier buvard** blotting paper; **papier carbone** carbon paper; **papier collant** Scotch tape; **papier d'emballage** wrapping paper; **papier de soie** tissue paper; **papier d'étain** tin foil; **papier de verre** sandpaper; **papier hygiénique** toilet paper; **papier journal** newsprint; **papier kraft** cardboard (*for packing*); **papier mâché** papier-maché; **papier ministre** foolscap; **papier paraffiné** wax paper; **papier peint** wallpaper; **papier rayé** lined paper; **papier sensible** photographic paper; **papier tue-mouches** flypaper; **rayez cela de vos papiers!** (coll) don't count on it!
papier-filtre [papjefiltra] *m* filter paper
papier-monnaie [papjemɔnɛ] *m* paper money
papier-pierre [papjepjɛr] *m* (*pl* **papiers-pierre**) papier-mâché
papille [papij, papil] *f* papilla; **papille gustative** taste bud
papillon [papijɔ̃] *m* butterfly; flier; handbill; inset; form, application; thumbscrew, wing nut; butterfly valve; rider (*to document*); (coll) parking ticket; **papillon de nuit** moth; **papillons noirs** gloomy thoughts
papillonner [papijɔne] *intr* to flit about

papillote [papijɔt] *f* curlpaper; (culin) paper wrapper
papilloter [papijɔte] *intr* to blink; to flicker
papoter [papote] *intr* to chitchat
paprika [paprika] *m* paprika
papyrus [papirys] *m* papyrus
pâque [pɑk] *f* Passover; **la pâque russe** Russian Easter; **Pâque** Passover
paquebot [pakbo] *m* liner
pâquerette [pakrɛt] *f* white daisy
Pâques [pɑk] *m* Easter ‖ *fpl* Easter; **faire ses pâques** or **Pâques** to take Easter Communion; **Pâques fleuries** Palm Sunday
paquet [pakɛ] *m* packet, bundle; package; parcel; pack (*of cigarettes*); dressing down; **être un paquet d'os** [dɔs] to be nothing but skin and bones; **faire son paquet** (coll) to pack up; **mettre le paquet** (coll) to shoot the works; **paquet de mer** heavy sea; **petit paquet** parcel (*under a kilogram*); **petits paquets** parcel post; **un paquet de** a lot of
par [par] *prep* by; through; out of, e.g., **par la fenêtre** out of the window; per, a, e.g., **huit dollars par jour** eight dollars per day, eight dollars a day; on, e.g., **par une belle matinée** on a beautiful morning; in, e.g., **par temps de brume** in foggy weather; **de par la loi** in the name of the law; **par avion** (formula on envelope) air mail; **par delà** beyond; **par derrière** at the back, the back way; **par devant** in front, before; **par exemple** for example; **par ici** this way; **par là** that way; **par où?** which way?
para [para] *m* (coll) paratrooper
parabole [parabɔl] *f* parable; (*curve*) parabola
parachever [para/ve] §2 *tr* to finish off
parachutage [para/ytaʒ] *m* airdrop, airdropping
parachute [para/yt] *m* parachute
parachuter [para/yte] *tr* to airdrop; (coll) to appoint in haste
parachutisme [para/ytism] *m* parachuting; (sports) skydiving
parachutiste [para/ytist] *mf* parachutist; (sports) skydiver ‖ *m* paratrooper
parade [parad] *f* show; parry; sudden stop (*of horse*); come-on (*in front of sideshow*); (mil) inspection, parade; **à la parade** on parade; **faire parade de** to show off, to display
parader [parade] *intr* to show off
paradis [paradi] *m* paradise; (theat) peanut gallery
paradoxal paradoxale [paradɔksal] *adj* (*pl* **paradoxaux** [paradɔkso]) paradoxical
paradoxe [paradɔks] *m* paradox
parafe [paraf] *m* flourish; initials
parafer [parafe] *tr* to initial
paraffine [parafin] *f* paraffin
paraffiner [parafine] *tr* to paraffin
parages [paraʒ] *mpl* region, vicinity; **dans ces parages** in these parts
paragraphe [paragraf] *m* paragraph

Paraguay [parage] *m*—le **Paraguay** Paraguay

paraguayen [paragejɛ̃] **paraguayenne** [paragejen] *adj* Paraguayan ‖ (*cap*) *mf* Paraguayan

paraître [paretr] §12 *intr* to appear; to seem; to come out; to show (off); **à ce qu'il paraît** from all appearances; **faire paraître** to publish; **vient de paraître** just out

parallèle [paralel] *adj* parallel ‖ *m* parallel, comparison; (geog) parallel ‖ *f* (geom) parallel

paralyser [paralize] *tr* to paralyze

paralysie [paralizi] *f* paralysis

paralytique [paralitik] *adj & mf* paralytic

parangon [parɑ̃gɔ̃] *m* paragon

paranoïaque [paranɔjak] *adj & mf* paranoiac

parapet [parapɛ] *m* railing, parapet; (mil) parapet

paraphe [paraf] *m* flourish; initials

parapher [parafe] *tr* to initial

paraphrase [parafrɑz] *f* circumlocution, paraphrase; commentary

paraphraser [parafrɑze] *tr* to paraphrase

parapluie [paraplɥi] *m* umbrella

parasite [parazit] *adj* parasitic(al) ‖ *m* parasite; **parasites** (rad) static

parasiter [parazite] *tr* to live as a parasite on or in (*a host*); (fig) to sponge on

parasol [parasɔl] *m* parasol; beach umbrella

paratonnerre [paratɔner] *m* lightning rod

parâtre [parɑtr] *m* stepfather; cruel father

paravent [paravɑ̃] *m* folding screen

parbleu [parblø] *interj* rather!, by Jove!, you bet!

parc [park] *m* park; sheepfold; corral, pen; playpen; grounds, property; (mil) supply depot; (rr) rolling stock; **parc à huîtres** oyster bed; **parc automobile** motor pool; **parc de stationnement** (**payant**) parking lot

parcage [parkaʒ] *m* parking

parcelle [parsel] *f* particle; plot

parce que [pars(ə)kə] *conj* because

parchemin [parʃəmɛ̃] *m* parchment; (coll) sheepskin (*diploma*)

parchemi·né **-née** [parʃəmine] *adj* wrinkled

parcheminer [parʃəmine] *tr* to parchmentize ‖ *ref* to shrivel up

par-ci [parsi] *adv*—**par-ci par-là** here and there

parcimo·nieux [parsimɔnjø] **-nieuse** [njøz] *adj* parsimonious

parcomètre [parkɔmetr] *m* parking meter

parcourir [parkurir] §14 *tr* to travel through, to tour; to wander about; to cover (*a distance*); to scour (*the country*); to glance through

parcours [parkur] *m* run, trip; route, distance covered; round (*e.g., of golf*); stroke (*of piston*)

par-delà [pardəla] *adv & prep* beyond

par-derrière [parderjer] *adv & prep* behind

par-dessous [pardəsu] *adv & prep* underneath

pardessus [pardəsy] *m* overcoat

par-dessus [pardəsy] *adv* on top, over ‖ *prep* on top of, over

par-devant [pardəvɑ̃] *adv* in front ‖ *prep* in front of, before

par-devers [pardəver] *prep* in the presence of; **par-devers soi** in one's own possession

pardi [pardi] *interj* of course!

pardon [pardɔ̃] *m* pardon; Breton pilgrimage ‖ *adv* (to contradict a negative statement or question) yes, e.g., **Vous ne parlez pas français, n'est-ce pas? Pardon, je le parle très bien** You don't speak French, do you? Yes, I speak it very well ‖ *interj* pardon me!; (slang) oh boy!

pardonnable [pardɔnabl] *adj* pardonable

pardonner [pardɔne] *tr* to pardon; **pardonner q.ch. à qn** to pardon s.o. for s.th. ‖ *intr* (with *dat*) to pardon, to forgive; **ne pas pardonner** to be fatal (*said of illness, mistake, etc.*)

pare-balles [parbal] *adj invar* bulletproof

pare-boue [parbu] *m invar* mudguard

pare-brise [parbriz] *m invar* windshield

pare-chocs [parʃɔk] *m invar* (aut) bumper

pare-étincelles [paretɛ̃sel] *m invar* fire screen

pa·reil -reille [parej] *adj* identical, the same; such, such a ‖ *mf* equal, match; **sans pareil, sans pareille** without parallel, unequaled ‖ *m*—**c'est du pareil au même** (coll) it's six of one and half dozen of the other ‖ *f* same (thing); **rendre la pareille à qn** to pay s.o. back in his own coin

pareillement [parejmɑ̃] *adv* likewise

parement [parmɑ̃] *m* cuff; facing; trimming; (eccl) parament

pa·rent [parɑ̃] **-rente** [rɑ̃t] *adj* like ‖ *mf* relative; **parents** parents; relatives; ancestors; **plus proche parent** next of kin

parenté [parɑ̃te] *f* relationship; relations

parenthèse [parɑ̃tez] *f* parenthesis; **entre parenthèses** in parentheses

parer [pare] *tr* an adorn; to parry; to prepare ‖ *intr*—**parer à** to provide for ‖ *ref* to show off

pare-soleil [parsɔlej] *m invar* sun visor

paresse [pares] *f* laziness

paresser [parese] *intr* (coll) to loaf

pares·seux [paresø] **-seuse** [paresøz] *adj* lazy ‖ *mf* lazy person, lazybones; malingerer ‖ *m* (zool) sloth

par ex. *abbr* (**par exemple**) e.g.

parfaire [parfer] §29 *tr* to perfect; to make up (*e.g., a sum of money*)

par·fait [parfɛ] **-faite** [fet] *adj & m* perfect ‖ **parfait** *interj* fine!, excellent!

parfaitement [parfetmɑ̃] *adv* perfectly; completely; certainly, of course

parfois [parfwa] *adv* sometimes

parfum [parfœ̃] *m* perfume; aroma; bouquet (*of wines*); flavor (*of ice cream*)

parfumer [parfyme] *tr* to perfume; to flavor ‖ *ref* to use perfume

pari [pari] *m* bet, wager

paria [parja] *m* pariah

parier [parje] *tr & intr* to bet, wager

Paris [pari] *m* Paris

pari·sien [parizjɛ̃] **-sienne** [zjen] *adj* Parisian ‖ (*cap*) *mf* Parisian

parité [parite] *f* parity; likeness; evenness (*of numbers*)

parjure [parʒyr] *adj* perjured ‖ *mf* perjurer ‖ *m* perjury

parking [parkiŋ] *m* parking lot

par·lant [parlɑ̃] **-lante** [lɑ̃t] *adj* speaking; talking (*e.g., picture*); eloquent, expressive

parlement [parləmɑ̃] *m* parliament

parlementaire [parləmɑ̃ter] *adj* parliamentary ‖ *mf* peace envoy; member of a parliament, legislator

parlementer [parləmɑ̃te] *intr* to parley

parler [parle] *m* speech, way of speaking; dialect ‖ *tr & intr* to speak, to talk

par·leur [parlœr] **-leuse** [løz] *mf*—**beau parleur** good talker; windbag

parloir [parlwar] *m* reception room

parlote [parlɔt] *f* (coll) talk, gossip, rumor

parmi [parmi] *prep* among

Parnasse [parnas] *m*—**le Parnasse** Parnassus (*poetry*); Mount Parnassus

parodie [parɔdi] *f* parody, travesty

parodier [parɔdje] *tr* to parody, to travesty

paroi [parwa] *f* partition, wall; inner side; (anat) wall

paroisse [parwas] *f* parish

parois·sial -siale [parwasjal] *adj* (*pl* **parois·siaux** [parwasjo]) parochial, parish

parois·sien [parwasjɛ̃] **parois·sienne** [parwasjen] *mf* parishioner ‖ *m* prayer book; (coll) fellow

parole [parɔl] *f* word; speech; word, promise; **avoir la parole** to have the floor; **donner la parole à** to recognize, to give the floor to; **sur parole** on one's word

paro·lier [parɔlje] **-lière** [ljer] *mf* lyricist; librettist

parpaing [parpɛ̃] *m* concrete block; building block

parquer [parke] *tr* to park; to pen in ‖ *intr* to be penned in ‖ *ref* to park

Parques [park] *fpl* Fates

parquet [parke] *m* parquet, floor; floor (*of stock exchange*); public prosecutor's office

parqueter [parkəte] §34 *tr* to parquet, to floor

parrain [parɛ̃] *m* godfather; sponsor

parricide [parisid] *mf* parricide, patricide (*person*) ‖ *m* parricide, patricide (*act*)

parsemer [parsəme] §2 *tr* to sprinkle; to spangle

part [par] *m* newborn child; dropping (*of young by animal in labor*) ‖ *f* part, share; **aller quelque part** (coll)

to go to the toilet; **à part** aside; aside from; **à part entière** with full privileges; **autre part** elsewhere; **avoir part au gâteau** (coll) to have a slice in the pie; **d'autre part** besides; **de la part de** on the part of, from; **de part en part** through and through; **de toutes parts** on all sides; **d'une part . . . d'autre part**; on the one hand . . . on the other hand; **faire la part de** to make allowance for; **faire part de** to announce; **faire part de q.ch. à qn** to inform s.o. of s.th.; **nulle part** nowhere; **nulle part ailleurs** nowhere else; **pour ma part** as for me, for my part; **prendre en bonne part** to take good-naturedly; **prendre en mauvaise part** to take offense at; **prendre part à** to take part in; **quelque part** somewhere

partage [partaʒ] *m* division, partition; sharing; share; tie vote; **échoir en partage à qn** to fall to s.o.'s lot

partager [partaʒe] §38 *tr* to share; to divide

partance [partɑ̃s] *f* departure; **en partance** leaving; **en partance pour** bound for

partant [partɑ̃] *m* (sports) starter; **partants** departing guests, departing travelers, etc. ‖ *adv* (lit) consequently

partenaire [partəner] *mf* partner; sparring partner

parterre [parter] *m* orchestra circle; flower bed

parti [parti] *m* party; side; match, good catch; **faire un mauvais parti à** to rough up, to mistreat; **parti pris** fixed opinion; prejudice; **prendre le parti de** to decide to; **prendre le parti de qn** to take s.o.'s side; **prendre parti** to take sides; **prendre son parti** to make up one's mind; **prendre son parti de** to resign oneself to; **tirer parti de** to take advantage of

par·tial -tiale [parsjal] *adj* (*pl* **-tiaux** [sjo]) partial, biased

partici·pant [partisipɑ̃] **-pante** [pɑ̃t] *adj & mf* participant

participation [partisipasjɔ̃] *f* participation

participe [partisip] *m* participle

participer [partisipe] *intr*—**participer à** to participate in; **participer de** to partake of

particulariser [partikylarize] *tr* to specify ‖ *ref* to make oneself conspicuous

particularité [partikylarite] *f* peculiarity; detail

particule [partikyl] *f* particle

particu·lier [partikylje] **-lière** [ljer] *adj* particular; special; private ‖ *mf* private citizen; (coll) odd person ‖ *m* particular

partie [parti] *f* part; line, specialty; game, winning score; contest; party (*diversion*); (law) party; **avoir partie liée avec** to be in league with; **faire partie de** to belong to; **faire partie intégrante de** to be part and parcel of; **partie civile** plaintiff; **partie de chasse** hunting party; **partie de plai-**

sir outing, picnic; **partie nulle** tie game; **prendre à partie** to take to task

par·tiel -tielle [parsjɛl] *adj* partial

partir [partir] (used only in *inf*) *tr*— **avoir maille à partir** to have a bone to pick ‖ §64 *intr* (*aux*: ÊTRE) to leave; to go off (*said of firearm*); to begin; **à partir de** from; from . . . on, e.g., **à partir de maintenant** from now on; **faire partir** to send off; to remove (*a spot*); to set off (*an explosive*); to fire (*a gun*); **partir** + *inf* to leave in order to + *inf*; **partir de** to come from; to start with; **partir pour** or **à** to leave for

parti·san [partizɑ̃] **-sane** [zan] *adj* & *mf* partisan

partition [partisjɔ̃] *f* (mus) score

partout [partu] *adv* everywhere; **partout ailleurs** anywhere else; everywhere else; **partout où** wherever; everywhere

parure [paryr] *f* ornament; set; finery; necklace

parution [parysjɔ̃] *f* appearance, publication

parvenir [parvənir] §72 *intr* (*aux*: ÊTRE) —**parvenir à** to reach; **parvenir à** + *inf* to succeed in + *ger*

parve·nu -nue [parvəny] *adj* & *mf* upstart

parvis [parvi] *m* square (*in front of a church*)

pas [pɑ] *m* step; pace; footprint; footfall; pass; straits; pitch (*of screw*); **allonger le pas** to quicken one's pace; to put one's best foot forward; **à pas comptés** with measured tread; **à pas de loup**, **à pas feutrés** stealthily; **à pas de tortue** at a snail's pace; **à quatre pas** nearby; **au pas** at a walk; **céder le pas (à)** to stand aside (for); to keep clear (*in front of a driveway*); **de ce pas** at once; **être au pas** to be in step; **faire le premier pas** to make the first move; **faire les cent pas** to come and go; **faux pas** misstep; blunder; **marcher sur les pas de** to follow in the footsteps of; **marquer le pas** to mark time; **mauvais pas** tight squeeze, fix; **pas à pas** little by little, cautiously; **pas d'armes** passage at arms; **Pas de Calais** Straits of Dover; **pas de cheval** hoofbeat; **pas de clerc** blunder; **pas de deux** two-step; **pas de la porte** doorstep; **pas de l'oie** goosestep; **pas de porte** (com) price paid for good will; **prendre le pas sur** to get ahead of ‖ *adv* — **pas** §90 not, e.g., **je ne sais pas** I do not know; e.g., **ne pas signer** to not sign; (used with **non**), e.g., **non pas** no; (used without **ne**) (slang) not, e.g., **je fais pas de politique** I don't meddle in politics; **n'est-ce pas?** see **ne; pas?** (coll) not so?; **pas de no; pas du tout** not at all; **pas encore** not yet

pas·cal -cale [paskal] *adj* (*pl* -**caux** [ko]) Passover; Easter

passable [pɑsabl] *adj* passable, fair; mediocre, so-so

passade [pɑsad] *f* passing fancy

passage [pɑsaʒ] *m* passage; crossing; pass; **barrer le passage** to block the way; **livrer passage à** to let through; **passage à niveau** grade crossing; **passage au-dessous de la voie**, **passage souterrain** underpass; **passage au-dessus de la voie** overpass; **passage clouté**, **passage zébré** pedestrian crossing; **passage de vitesses** gear shifting; **passage interdit** (public sign) do not enter; (public sign) no thoroughfare; **passage protégé** arterial crossing (*vehicles intersecting highway must stop*)

passa·ger [pɑsaʒe] **-gère** [ʒɛr] *adj* passing, fleeting; migratory; busy (*road*) ‖ *mf* passenger; **passager clandestin**, **passager de cale** stowaway; **passager d'entrepont** steerage passenger

pas·sant [pɑsɑ̃] **pas·sante** [pɑsɑ̃t] *adj* busy (*street*) ‖ *mf* passer-by

passation [pɑsasjɔ̃] *f* handing over

passavant [pɑsavɑ̃] *m* permit; (naut) gangway

passe [pɑs] *m* master key ‖ *f* pass; channel; **être en bonne passe de** to be in a fair way to; **être en passe de** to be about to; **mauvaise passe** tight spot

pas·sé -sée [pɑse] *adj* past; faded; overripe; last (*week*) ‖ *m* past; past tense ‖ **passé** *prep* past, beyond, after

passe-bouillon [pɑsbujɔ̃] *m invar* soup strainer

passe-droit [pɑsdrwa] *m* (*pl* -**droits**) illegal favor; injustice

passe-lacet [pɑslasɛ] *m* (*pl* -**lacets**) bodkin

passe-lait [pɑslɛ] *m invar* milk strainer

passe-lettres [pɑslɛtr] *m* (*pl* -**lettres**) letter drop

passement [pɑsmɑ̃] *m* braid, trimming

passementer [pɑsmɑ̃te] *tr* to trim

passementerie [pɑsmɑ̃tri] *f* trimmings

passe-montagne [pɑsmɔ̃taɲ] *m* (*pl* -**montagnes**) storm hood, ski mask

passe-partout [pɑspartu] *m invar* master key; slip mount

passe-passe [pɑspas] *m invar* legerdemain

passepoil [pɑspwal] *m* piping, braid

passeport [pɑspɔr] *m* passport

passer [pɑse] *tr* to pass; to ferry; to get across (*e.g., a river*); to spend, to pass (*e.g., the evening*); to take (*an exam*); to slip on (*e.g., a dressing gown*); to show (*a film*); to make (*a telephone call*); to go on (*one's way*); **passer q.ch. à qn** to hand or lend s.o. s.th.; to forgive s.o. s.th. ‖ *intr* (*aux*: AVOIR or ÊTRE) to pass; to pass away; to become; **en passer par là** to knuckle under; **faire passer** to get (*e.g., a message*) through; to while away (*the time*); **passer à** to pass over; **passer chez** or **passer voir** to drop in on; **passer outre à** to override; **passer par** to pass through, to go through; **passer pour** to pass for or as; **passons!** let's skip it! ‖ *ref* to happen, to take place; **se passer de** to do without

passe·reau [pasro] m (pl -reaux) sparrow

passerelle [pasrel] f footbridge; gangplank; (naut) bridge

passe-temps [pastɑ̃] m invar pastime, hobby

passe-thé [paste] m invar tea strainer

pas·seur [pasœr] **pas·seuse** [pasøz] mf smuggler ‖ m ferryman

passible [pasibl] adj—**passible de** liable for, subject to

pas·sif [pasif] **pas·sive** [pasiv] adj passive ‖ m passive; debts, liabilities

passiflore [pasiflɔr] f passionflower

passion [pasjɔ̃], [pɑsjɔ̃] f passion

passion·nant [pasjɔnɑ̃] **passion·nante** [pasjɔnɑ̃t] adj thrilling, fascinating

passion·né -née [pasjɔne] adj passionate; impassioned; **passionné de** or **pour** passionately fond of ‖ mf enthusiast, fan

passion·nel -nelle [pasjɔnel] adj of passion, of jealousy

passionner [pasjɔne] tr to excite the interest of, to arouse ‖ ref—**se passionner pour** or **à** to be passionately fond of

passoire [paswar] f colander; strainer; (fig) sieve

pastel [pastel] m pastel; (bot) woad

pastèque [pastek] f watermelon

pasteur [pastœr] m pastor, minister; shepherd

pasteuriser [pastœrize] tr to pasteurize

pastiche [pastiʃ] m pastiche; parody

pastille [pastij] f lozenge, drop; tire patch; polka dot; **pastille pectorale** cough drop

pasto·ral -rale [pastɔral] (pl -raux [ro] -rales) adj & f pastoral

pastorat [pastɔra] m pastorate

pat [pat] adj invar (chess) in stalemate; **faire pat** to stalemate ‖ m (chess) stalemate

patache [pataʃ] f police boat; (coll) rattletrap

patachon [pataʃɔ̃] m—**mener une vie de patachon** to lead a wild life

patapouf [patapuf] m (coll) roly-poly ‖ interj flop!

pataquès [patakes] m faulty liaison; blooper, goof

patate [patat] f sweet potato; (coll) spud

patati [patati]—**et patati et patata!** (coll) and so on and on!

patatras [patatra] interj bang!, crash!

pa·taud [pato] **-taude** [tod] adj clumsy, loutish ‖ mf lout

patauger [patɔʒe] §38 intr to splash; (coll) to flounder

pâte [pat] f paste; dough, batter; **en pâte** (typ) pied; **mettre la main à la pâte** to put one's shoulder to the wheel; **pâte à papier** wood pulp; **pâte brisée**, **pâte feuilletée** puff paste; **pâte dentifrice** toothpaste; **pâte molle** spineless person; **pâtes alimentaires** pastas (macaroni, noodles, spaghetti, etc.); **peindre à la pâte** to paint with a full brush; **une bonne pâte d'homme** (coll) a good sort

pâté [pate] m blot, splotch; (typ) pi;

pâté de foie gras minced goose livers; **pâté de maisons** block of houses; **pâté en croûte** meat or fish pie; **pâté maison** chef's-special pâté

pâtée [pate] f dog food, cat food; chicken feed

pate·lin [patlɛ̃] **-line** [lin] adj fawning, wheedling ‖ m wheedler; (coll) native village

patenôtre [patnotr] f prayer; (archaic) mumbo jumbo

pa·tent [patɑ̃] **-tente** [tɑ̃t] adj patent ‖ f license; tax; **patente (de santé)** (naut) bill of health

paten·té -tée [patɑ̃te] adj licensed ‖ mf licensed dealer

patenter [patɑ̃te] tr to license

Pater [pater] m invar Lord's Prayer

patère [pater] f clothes hook; curtain hook

paterne [patern] adj mawkish, mealymouthed

pater·nel -nelle [paternel] adj paternal; fatherly ‖ m (slang) pop, dad

paternité [paternite] f paternity; fatherhood; authorship

pâ·teux [patø] **-teuse** [tøz] adj pasty; thick; coated (tongue)

pathétique [patetik] adj pathetic ‖ m pathos

pathologie [patɔlɔʒi] f pathology

pathos [patos] m bathos

patibulaire [patibyler] adj hangdog (look)

patience [pasjɑ̃s] f patience

pa·tient [pasjɑ̃] **-tiente** [sjɑ̃t] adj & mf patient

patienter [pasjɑ̃te] intr to be patient

patin [patɛ̃] m skate; runner; sill, sleeper; (sole) patten; (aer) skid; (rr) base, flange (of rails); **patin à glace** ice skate; **patin à roulettes** roller skate; **patin de frein** brake shoe

patiner [patine] intr to skate; to slide; to skid

patinette [patinet] f scooter

pati·neur [patinœr] **-neuse** [nøz] mf skater

patinoire [patinwar] f skating rink

patio [patjo], [pasjo] m patio

pâtir [patir] intr—**pâtir de** to suffer from

pâtisserie [patisri] f pastry; pastry shop; pastry making

pâtis·sier [patisje] **pâtis·sière** [patisjer] mf pastry cook; proprietor of a pastry shop

patois [patwa] m patois; jargon, lingo

patouiller [patuje] tr (coll) to paw, maul ‖ intr (coll) to splash

patraque [patrak] adj in bad shape ‖ f (coll) turnip (old watch)

pâtre [patr] m herdsman

patriarche [patrijarʃ] m patriarch

patrice [patris] m patrician; **Patrice** Patrick

patri·cien [patrisjɛ̃] **-cienne** [sjɛn] adj & mf patrician

patrie [patri] f native land, fatherland

patrimoine [patrimwan] m patrimony

patrio·tard [patrijɔtar] **-tarde** [tard] adj flag-waving, chauvinistic

patriote [patrijɔt] *adj* patriotic ‖ *mf* patriot

patriotique [patrijɔtik] *adj* patriotic

patriotisme [patrijɔtism] *m* patriotism

pa-tron [patrɔ̃] **-tronne** [trɔn] *mf* patron saint; proprietor; boss; sponsor ‖ *m* pattern, model; captain, skipper; coxswain; master, lord; medium size; **grand patron** large size; **patron à jours** stencil; **patron de thèse** thesis sponsor ‖ *f* mistress of the house; (slang) better half

patronage [patrɔnaʒ] *m* patronage, protection; sponsorship; (eccl) social center

patronat [patrɔna] *m* management

patronner [patrɔne] *tr* to patronize, to protect; to sponsor; to stencil

patrouille [patruj] *f* patrol

patrouiller [patruje] *intr* to patrol

patte [pat] *f* paw; foot (*of bird*); leg (*of insect*); flap, tab; hook; (coll) hand, foot, or leg (*of person*); **à pattes d'éléphant** bell-bottom (*trousers*); **à quatre pattes** on all fours; **faire patte de velours** to pull in one's claws; **graisser la patte à** (coll) to grease the palm of; **patte d'épaule** shoulder strap; **pattes de mouche** (coll) scrawl

patte-d'oie [patdwa] *f* (*pl* **pattes-d'oie**) crow's-foot; crossroads; (bot) goose-foot

pattemouille [patmuj] *f* damp cloth

pâturage [pɑtyraʒ] *m* pasture; pasturage; pasture rights

pâture [pɑtyr] *f* fodder; pasture; (fig) food

paume [pom] *f* palm; (archaic) tennis

pau-mé -mée [pome] *adj* (coll) lost

paupière [popjɛr] *f* eyelid

pause [poz] *f* pause; (mus) full rest; **pause café** coffee break

pauvre [povr] *adj* poor; **pauvre de moi!** woe is me!; **pauvre d'esprit** (coll) dim-witted ‖ (when standing before noun) *adj* poor, wretched; late (*deceased*) ‖ *mf* pauper; **les pauvres** the poor

pauvreté [povrəte] *f* poverty

P.A.V. [peave] *adj* (letterword) (**payable avec préavis**) person-to-person (*telephone call*)

pavaner [pavane] *ref* to strut

pavé [pave] *m* pavement, street; paving stone; paving block; (culin) slab; **sur le pavé** pounding the streets, out of work

pavement [pavmɑ̃] *m* paving (*act*); mosaic or marble flooring

paver [pave] *tr* to pave

pavillon [pavijɔ̃] *m* pavilion; tent, canopy; lodge, one-story house; wing, pavilion; flag; bell (*of trumpet*); **amener son pavillon** to strike one's colors; **baisser pavillon** to knuckle under

pavois [pavwa] *m* shield; **élever sur le pavois** to extol

pavoiser [pavwaze] *tr* to deck out with bunting, to decorate

pavot [pavo] *m* poppy

payable [pejabl] *adj* payable

payant [pejɑ̃] **payante** [pejɑ̃t] *adj* paying

paye [pej] *f* pay, wages

payement [pejmɑ̃] *m* payment

payer [peje] §49 *tr* to pay; to pay for; **payer comptant** to pay cash for; **payer de retour** to pay back; **payer q.ch. à qn** to pay s.o. for s.th.; to pay for s.th. for s.o.; **payer qn de q.ch.** to pay s.o. for s.th.; **payer rubis sur l'ongle** to pay down on the nail ‖ *intr* to pay ‖ *ref* to treat oneself to; to take what is due; **pouvoir se** (*dat*) **payer** to be able to afford; **se payer de** to be satisfied with

pays [pei] *m* country; region; town; (coll) fellow countryman; **du pays** local; **le pays de** the land of; **pays de cocagne** land of milk and honey

paysage [peizaʒ] *m* landscape, scenery; (painting) landscape

paysagiste [peizaʒist] *m* landscape painter

pay-san [peizɑ̃] **-sane** [zan] *adj* & *mf* peasant

Pays-Bas [peiba], [peibɑ] *mpl*—**les Pays-Bas** The Netherlands

payse [peiz] *f* countrywoman

P.C. [pese] *m* (letterword) (**parti communiste**) Communist party; (**poste de commandement**) command post

P.c.c. *abbr* (**pour copie conforme**) certified copy

p.c.v. or **P.C.V.** [peseve] *m* (letterword) (**payable chez vous**) or (**à percevoir**)—**téléphoner en p.c.v.** to telephone collect

péage [peaʒ] *m* toll

peau [po] *f* (*pl* **peaux**) skin; pelt; hide; film (*on milk*); (slang) bag, whore; **entrer dans la peau d'un personnage** (theat) to get right inside a part; **faire peau neuve** to turn over a new leaf; **la peau!** (slang) nothing doing!; **peau d'âne** (coll) sheepskin; **peau de tambour** drumhead; **vendre la peau de l'ours avant de l'avoir tué** to count one's chickens before they are hatched

peau-rouge [poruʒ] *mf* (*pl* **peaux-rouges**) redskin

pêche [pɛʃ] *f* peach; fishing; **pêche à la mouche noyée** fly casting; **pêche au coup** fishing with hook, line, and pole; **pêche au lancer** casting; **pêche sous-marine** deep-sea fishing; **pêche sportive** fishing with a fly rod or casting rod

péché [peʃe] *m* sin

pécher [peʃe] §10 *intr* to sin

pêcher [peʃe] *m* peach tree ‖ *tr* to fish, fish for; (coll) to get ‖ *intr* to fish; **pêcher à la mouche** to fly-fish

pêcherie [peʃri] *f* fishery

pé-cheur [peʃœr] **-cheresse** [ʃres] *mf* sinner

pê-cheur [peʃœr] **-cheuse** [ʃøz] *mf* fisher; **pêcheur de perles** pearl diver ‖ *m* fisherman

pécore [pekɔr] *f* (coll) silly goose

pecque [pek] *f* (coll) silly affected woman

péculat [pekyla] *m* embezzlement

pécule [pekyl] *m* nest egg

pédagogie [pedagɔʒi] *f* pedagogy, education

pédagogue [pedagɔg] *adj* pedagogical ‖ *mf* pedagogue; teacher

pédale [pedal] *f* pedal; treadle; (vulg) pederast; **pédale d'embrayage** (aut) clutch pedal

pédaler [pedale] *intr* to pedal

pédalier [pedalje] *m* pedal keyboard; pedal and sprocket-wheel assembly

pédalo [pedalo] *m* water bicycle

pé·dant [pedɑ̃] **-dante** [dɑ̃t] *adj* pedantic ‖ *mf* pedant

pédanterie [pedɑ̃tri] *f* pedantry

pédantesque [pedɑ̃tɛsk] *adj* pedantic

pédestre [pedɛstr] *adj* on foot

pédiatrie [pedjatri] *f* pediatrics

pédicure [pedikyr] *mf* chiropodist

pedigree [pedigri] *m* pedigree

Pégase [pegaz] *m* Pegasus

pègre [pɛgr] *f* underworld

peigne [pɛɲ] *m* comb; card (for wool); reed (of loom); (zool) scallop

peigner [peɲe] *tr* to comb; to card ‖ *ref* to comb one's hair

peignoir [peɲwar] *m* bathrobe; dressing gown; peignoir

peindre [pɛ̃dr] §50 *tr & intr* to paint

peine [pɛn] *f* pain; trouble; difficulty; penalty; **à peine** hardly, scarcely; **en être pour sa peine** to have nothing to show for one's trouble; **faire (de la) peine à** to grieve; **faire peine à voir** to be pathetic; **peine capitale** capital punishment; **peine de cœur** heartache; **peine de mort** death penalty; **peine pécuniaire** financial distress; **purger sa peine** to serve one's sentence; **valoir la peine** to be worth while; **veuillez vous donner la peine de** please be so kind as to

peiner [pene] *tr* to pain, grieve; to fatigue ‖ *intr* to labor

peintre [pɛ̃tr] *m* painter

peinture [pɛ̃tyr] *f* paint; painting; attention à la peinture (public sign) wet paint; **je ne peux pas le voir en peinture** (coll) I can't stand him

peinturer [pɛ̃tyre] *tr* to lay a coat of paint on; to daub

peinturlurer [pɛ̃tyrlyre] *tr* (coll) to paint in all the colors of the rainbow

péjora·tif [peʒɔratif] **-tive** [tiv] *adj & m* pejorative

pékin [pekɛ̃] *m* pekin; **en pékin** (slang) in civies; **Pékin** Peking

péki·nois [pekinwa] **-noise** [nwaz] *adj* Pekingese ‖ *m* Pekingese (language; dog) ‖ (cap) *mf* Pekingese (inhabitant)

pelage [pəlaʒ] *m* coat (of animal)

pe·lé ·lée [pəle] *adj* bald; bare

pêle-mêle [pɛlmɛl] *m invar* jumble ‖ *adv* pell-mell

peler [pəle] §2 *tr, intr, & ref* to peel, to peel off

pèle·rin [pɛlrɛ̃] **-rine** [rin] *mf* pilgrim ‖ *m* peregrine falcon; basking shark ‖ *f* see **pèlerine**

pèlerinage [pɛlrinaʒ] *m* pilgrimage

pèlerine [pɛlrin] *f* pelerine, cape; hooded cape

péliade [peljad] *f* adder

pélican [pelikɑ̃] *m* pelican

pellagre [pelagr] *f* pellagra

pelle [pɛl] *f* shovel; scoop; **pelle à poussière** dustpan; **pelle à vapeur** steam shovel; **pelle mécanique** power shovel; **ramasser à la pelle** to shovel, to shovel up

pelletée [pɛlte] *f* shovelful

pelleter [pɛlte] §34 *tr* to shovel

pelleterie [pɛltri] *f* fur trade; skin, pelt

pelleteuse [pɛltøz] *f* power shovel

pellicule [pelikyl], [pɛllikyl] *f* film; pellicle; speck of dandruff; (phot) film; **pellicules** dandruff

pelote [pəlɔt] *f* ball (of string, of snow, etc.); **faire sa pelote** (coll) to make one's pile; **pelote basque** pelota; **pelote d'épingles** pincushion

peloter [pəlɔte] *tr* to wind into a ball; (fig) to flatter; (slang) to feel up, to paw ‖ *intr* to bat the ball back and forth

pelo·teur [pəlɔtœr] **-teuse** [tøz] *adj* flattering, ingratiating; (coll) fresh, amorous, spoony ‖ *mf* (coll) masher, spooner

peloton [pəlɔtɔ̃] *m* little ball (e.g., of wool); group (of racers); (mil) platoon, troop, detachment; **peloton d'exécution** firing squad

pelotonner [pəlɔtɔne] *tr* to wind into a ball ‖ *ref* to curl up, to snuggle

pelouse [pluz] *f* lawn; (golf) green

peluche [plyʃ] *f* plush

pelure [plyr] *f* peel, peeling, skin; rind; (coll) coat

pénaliser [penalize] *tr* to penalize

pénalité [penalite] *f* penalty

pe·naud [pəno] **-naude** [nod] *adj* bashful, shy; shamefaced; crestfallen

penchant [pɑ̃ʃɑ̃] *m* penchant, bent

pen·ché -chée [pɑ̃ʃe] *adj* leaning; stooping, bent over

pencher [pɑ̃ʃe] *tr, intr, & ref* to lean, to bend, to incline; **se pencher sur** to make a close study of

pendable [pɑ̃dabl] *adj* outrageous; (archaic) hangable

pendaison [pɑ̃dezɔ̃] *f* hanging

pen·dant [pɑ̃dɑ̃] **-dante** [dɑ̃t] *adj* hanging; pending ‖ *m* pendant; counterpart; **pendant d'oreille** eardrop; **se faire pendant** to make a pair ‖ **pendant** *adv*—**pendant que** while ‖ **pendant** *prep* during

pendeloque [pɑ̃dlɔk] *f* pendant; jewel (of eardrop)

pendentif [pɑ̃dɑ̃tif] *m* pendant; eardrop; lavaliere

penderie [pɑ̃dri] *f* clothes closet

pendoir [pɑ̃dwar] *m* meat hook

pendre [pɑ̃dr] *tr* to hang; to hang up; **être pendu à** to hang on on (e.g., the telephone) ‖ *intr* to hang; to hang down; to sag; **ça lui pend au nez** he's got it coming to him ‖ *ref* to hang oneself; **se pendre à** to hang on to

pen·du -due [pɑ̃dy] *adj* hanging; hanged ‖ *mf* hanged person

pendule [pɑ̃dyl] *m* pendulum ‖ *f* clock; **pendule à pile** battery clock

pêne [pen] *m* bolt; latch
pénétration [penetrɑsjɔ̃] *f* penetration; permeation
pénétrer [penetre] §10 *tr* to penetrate, to permeate ‖ *intr* to penetrate; to enter ‖ *ref* to mix; **se pénétrer de** to become imbued with
pénible [penibl] *adj* hard, painful
péniche [peniʃ] *f* barge; houseboat; **péniche de débarquement** landing craft
pénicilline [penisilin] *f* penicillin
péninsulaire [penɛ̃syler] *adj* peninsular
péninsule [penɛ̃syl] *f* large peninsula
pénitence [penitɑ̃s] *f* penitence; penalty (*in games*); punishment; **en pénitence** in disgrace; **faire pénitence** to do penance
pénitencier [penitɑ̃sje] *m* penitentiary; penal colony
péni-tent [penitɑ̃] **-tente** [tɑ̃t] *adj & mf* penitent
penne [pen] *f* quill, feather
Pennsylvanie [pensilvani] *f* Pennsylvania; **la Pennsylvanie** Pennsylvania
pénombre [penɔ̃br] *f* penumbra; half-light; **dans la pénombre** out of the limelight
pense-bête [pɑ̃sbet] *m* (*pl* **-bêtes**) (coll) reminder
pensée [pɑ̃se] *f* thought; thinking; (bot) pansy
penser [pɑ̃se] *tr* to think; **penser de** to think of (*to have an opinion of*); **penser + inf** to intend to + *inf* ‖ *intr* to think; **penser à** to think of (*to direct one's thoughts toward*); **y penser** to think of it, e.g., **pendant que j'y pense** while I think of it
penseur [pɑ̃sœr] *m* thinker
pen-sif [pɑ̃sif] **-sive** [siv] *adj* pensive; absent-minded
pension [pɑ̃sjɔ̃] *f* pension (*annuity; room and board; boardinghouse*); **avec pension complète** with three meals; **pension de famille** residential hotel; **pension de retraite, pension viagère** annuity; **prendre pension** to board; **sans pension** without meals
pensionnaire [pɑ̃sjɔner] *mf* boarder; guest (*in hotel*); resident student ‖ *f* naïve girl
pensionnat [pɑ̃sjɔna] *m* boarding school
pension-né **-née** [pɑ̃sjɔne] *adj* pensioned ‖ *mf* pensioner
pensionner [pɑ̃sjɔne] *tr* to pension
pensum [pɛ̃sɔm] *m* thankless task
Pentagone [pɛ̃tagɔn] *m* Pentagon
pente [pɑ̃t] *f* slope; inclination, bent; fall (*of river*); **en pente** sloping
Pentecôte [pɑ̃tkot] *f*—**la Pentecôte** Pentecost, Whitsunday
pénultième [penyltjem] *adj* next to the last ‖ *f* penult
pénurie [penyri] *f* lack, shortage
pépé [pepe] *m* (slang) grandpa
pépée [pepe] *f* doll; (slang) doll
pépère [peper] *adj* (coll) easygoing ‖ *m* grandpa; (coll) old duffer; (coll) overgrown boy
pépètes [pepet] *fpl* (slang) dough

pépie [pepi] *f* (vet) pip; **avoir la pépie** (coll) to be thirsty
pépiement [pepimɑ̃] *m* chirp
pépier [pepje] *intr* to chirp
pépin [pepɛ̃] *m* pip, seed; (coll) umbrella; **avoir un pépin** (coll) to strike a snag
pépinière [pepinjer] *f* (hort) nursery; (fig) training school; (fig) hotbed
pépiniériste [pepinjerist] *m* nurseryman
pépite [pepit] *f* nugget
péque-naud [pekno] **-naude** [nod] *adj & mf* (slang) peasant
péquenot [pekno] *m* (slang) peasant
perçage [persaʒ] *m* drilling, boring
per-çant [persɑ̃] **-çante** [sɑ̃t] *adj* piercing, penetrating
perce [pers] *f* drill, bore; **en perce** on tap
perce-neige [persɛneʒ] *m invar* (bot) snowdrop
percepteur [perseptœr] *m* tax collector
perception [persepsjɔ̃] *f* perception; tax collection; tax; tax department, bureau of internal revenue
percer [perse] §51 *tr* to pierce; to drill; to tap (*a barrel*); to break through ‖ *intr* to come through or out; to burst (*said, e.g., of abscess*); to make a name for oneself
perceuse [persøz] *f* drill; machine drill
percevoir [persəvwar] §59 *tr* to perceive; to collect
perche [perʃ] *f* pole; (ichth) perch; (coll) beanpole; **perche à sauter** vaulting pole; **perche à son micro-phone** stand; **tendre la perche à** to lend a helping hand to
percher [perʃe] *tr* to perch ‖ *intr* to perch, to roost
perchoir [perʃwar] *m* perch
per-clus [perkly] **-cluse** [klyz] *adj* crippled, paralyzed
percolateur [perkɔlatœr] *m* large coffee maker
percuter [perkyte] *tr* to strike; to crash into; to percuss ‖ *intr* to crash
percuteur [perkytœr] *m* firing pin
per-dant [perdɑ̃] **-dante** [dɑ̃t] *adj* losing ‖ *mf* loser
perdition [perdisjɔ̃] *f* perdition; **en perdition** (naut) in distress
perdre [perdrə] *tr* to lose; to ruin ‖ *intr* to lose; to leak; to deteriorate ‖ *ref* to get lost; to disappear
per-dreau [perdro] *m* (*pl* **-dreaux**) young partridge
perdrix [perdri] *f* partridge
per-du -due [perdy] *adj* lost; spare (*time*); stray (*bullet*); remote (*locality*); advance (*sentry*)
père [per] *m* father; senior, e.g., **M. Martin père** Mr. Martin, senior; **père de famille** head of the household; **père spirituel** father confessor
péréquation [perekwɑsjɔ̃] *f* equalizing
perfection [perfeksjɔ̃] *f* perfection
perfectionner [perfeksjɔne] *tr* to perfect ‖ *ref* to improve
perfide [perfid] *adj* perfidious ‖ *mf* treacherous person
perfidie [perfidi] *f* perfidy

perforation [perfɔrasjɔ̃] *f* perforation

perforatrice [perfɔratris] *f* pneumatic drill; perforator; keypunch (machine)

perforer [perfɔre] *tr* to perforate; to drill, bore; to punch (*a card*)

performance [perfɔrmãs] *f* (sports) performance

péricliter [periklite] *intr* to fail

péril [peril] *m* peril

péril·leux [perijø] **péril·leuse** [perijøz] *adj* perilous

péri·mé -mée [perime] *adj* expired, elapsed; out-of-date

périmer [perime] *intr* & *ref* to lapse

période [perjɔd] *f* period; (phys) cycle

périodique [perjɔdik] *adj* periodic(al)

péripétie [peripesi] *f* vicissitude

périphérie [periferi] *f* periphery

périphérique [periferik] *adj* peripheral

périple [peripl] *m* journey

périr [perir] *intr* to perish

périscope [periskɔp] *m* periscope

périssable [perisabl] *adj* perishable

perle [perl] *f* pearl; bead

perler [perle] *tr* to pearl; to do to perfection || *intr* to form beads

permanence [permanãs] *f* permanence; headquarters, station; **en permanence** at all hours

perma·nent [permanã] **-nente** [nãt] *adj* permanent; standing; continuous, nonstop || *f* permanent

perme [perm] *f* (coll) furlough

permettre [permetr] §42 *tr* to permit; **permettre q.ch. à qn** to allow s.o. s.th. || *intr*—**permettez!** excuse me!; **permettre à qn de** + *inf* to permit s.o. to or let s.o. + *inf*; **vous permettez?** may I? || *ref*—**se permettre de** to take the liberty of

permis [permi] *m* permit, license; **permis de conduire** driver's license

permission [permisjɔ̃] *f* permission; (mil) furlough, leave

permissionnaire [permisjɔner] *m* soldier on leave

permutation [permytasjɔ̃] *f* permutation; exchange of posts; transposition

permuter [permyte] *tr* to permute; to exchange || *intr* to change places

perni·cieux [pernisjø] **-cieuse** [sjøz] *adj* pernicious

péroné [perɔne] *m* (anat) fibula

pérorer [perɔre] *intr* to hold forth

Pérou [peru] *m*—**le Pérou** Peru

peroxyde [perɔksid] *m* peroxide

perpendiculaire [perpãdikyler] *adj* & *f* perpendicular

perpète [perpet]—**à perpète** (slang) forever

perpétrer [perpetre] §10 *tr* to perpetrate

perpé·tuel -tuelle [perpetɥel] *adj* perpetual; life (*imprisonment*); constant, continual

perpétuer [perpetɥe] *tr* to perpetuate || *ref* to be perpetuated

perpétuité [perpetɥite] *f* perpetuity; **à perpétuité** forever; for life

perplexe [perpleks] *adj* perplexed; **rendre perplexe** to perplex

perplexité [perpleksite] *f* perplexity

perquisition [perkizisjɔ̃] *f* search

perquisitionner [perkizisjɔne] *intr* to make a search

perron [perɔ̃] *m* front-entrance stone steps

perroquet [perɔke] *m* parrot

perruche [peryʃ] *f* parakeet; hen parrot

perruque [peryk] *f* wig; **vieille perruque** (coll) old fogey

per·san [persã] **-sane** [san] *adj* Persian || *m* Persian (*language*) || (*cap*) *mf* Persian (*person*)

perse [pers] *adj* Persian || (*cap*) *mf* Persian || (*cap*) *f* Persia; **la Perse** Persia

persécuter [persekyte] *tr* to persecute

persécution [persekysjɔ̃] *f* persecution

persévérer [persevere] §10 *intr* to persevere

persienne [persjen] *f* Persian blind, slatted shutter

persil [persi] *m* parsley

persis·tant [persistã] **-tante** [tãt] *adj* persistent

persister [persiste] *intr* to persist; **persister à** to persist in

personnage [persɔnaʒ] *m* personage; (theat) character

personnalité [persɔnalite] *f* personality

personne [persɔn] *f* person; self; appearance; lady, e.g., **belle personne** beautiful lady; e.g., **jolie personne** pretty lady; **grande personne** grown-up; **par personne** per person; **payer de sa personne** to not spare one's efforts; **s'assurer de la personne de** to arrest; **une tierce personne** a third party || *pron indef* no one, nobody; **personne ne or ne . . . personne** §90B no one, nobody, not anyone

person·nel -nelle [persɔnel] *adj* personal || *m* personnel

personnifier [persɔnifje] *tr* to personify

perspective [perspektiv] *f* perspective; outlook; **en perspective** in view

perspicace [perspikas] *adj* perspicacious

persuader [persɥade] *tr* to persuade; **persuader q.ch. à qn or persuader qn de q.ch.** to persuade s.o. of s.th. || *intr*—**persuader à qn de** to persuade s.o. to || *ref* to be convinced

persuasion [persɥazjɔ̃] *f* persuasion

perte [pert] *f* loss; ruin, downfall; **à perte de vue** as far as the eye can see; **en pure perte** uselessly

perti·nent [pertinã] **-nente** [nãt] *adj* pertinent

perturba·teur [pertyrbatœr] **-trice** [tris] *adj* disturbing || *mf* troublemaker

perturber [pertyrbe] *tr* to perturb

péru·vien [peryvjɛ̃] **-vienne** [vjen] *adj* Peruvian || (*cap*) *mf* Peruvian

pervenche [pervãʃ] *f* periwinkle

per·vers [perver] **-verse** [vers] *adj* perverted || *mf* pervert

perversion [perversjɔ̃] *f* perversion

perversité [pɛrversite] *f* perversity, depravity

pervertir [pɛrvertir] *tr* to pervert

pesage [pəzaʒ] *m* weigh-in; paddock

pe·sant [pəzɑ̃] **-sante** [zɑ̃t] *adj* heavy ‖ *m*—valoir son pesant d'or to be worth one's weight in gold

pesanteur [pəzɑ̃tœr] *f* heaviness; weight; (phys) gravity

pèse-bébé [pɛzbebe] *m* (*pl* **-bébés**) baby scale

pesée [pəze] *f* weighing; leverage

pèse-lettre [pɛzlɛtr] *m* (*pl* **-lettres**) letter scale

pèse-personne [pɛzpɛrsɔn] *m* (*pl* **-personnes**) bathroom scale

peser [pəze] §2 *tr* to weigh ‖ *intr* to weigh; **peser à** to hang heavy on; **peser sur** to bear down on; to lie down on; to lie heavy on; to stress ‖ *ref* to weigh oneself; to weigh in

peson [pəzɔ̃] *m* spring scale

pessimisme [pesimism] *m* pessimism

pessimiste [pesimist] *adj* pessimistic ‖ *mf* pessimist

peste [pɛst] *f* plague; pest, nuisance ‖ *interj* gosh!

pester [pɛste] *intr* to grouse; **pester contre** to rail at

pestiféré·ré -rée [pɛstifere] *adj* plague-ridden ‖ *mf* victim of the plague

pestilence [pɛstilɑ̃s] *f* pestilence

pet [pɛ] *m* (slang) scandal; (vulgar) wind; **ça ne vaut pas un pet (de lapin)** (coll) it's not worth a wooden nickel ‖ *interj* (coll) look out!

pétale [petal] *m* petal

pétarade [petarad] *f* series of explosions; backfire

pétard [petar] *m* firecracker; blast; (slang) gat, revolver; (slang) backside; **faire du pétard** (coll) to kick up a fuss; **lancer un pétard** (coll) to drop a bombshell

pet-de-loup [pɛdlu] *m* (*pl* **pets-de-loup**) absent-minded professor

pet-de-nonne [pɛdnɔn] *m* (*pl* **pets-de-nonne**) fritter

pet-en-l'air [pɛtɑ̃lɛr] *m invar* short jacket

péter [pete] §10 *tr*—**péter du feu** (coll) to be a live wire ‖ *intr* (coll) to go bang; (vulg) to break wind

pètesec [pɛtsɛk] *adj invar* (coll) bossy, despotic ‖ *m invar* (coll) martinet, bossy fellow

pétil·lant [petijɑ̃] **pétil·lante** [petijɑ̃t] *adj* crackling; sparkling

pétiller [petije] *intr* to crackle; to sparkle

pe·tiot [pətjo] **-tiote** [tjɔt] *adj* (coll) tiny, wee ‖ *mf* (coll) tot

pe·tit [pəti] **-tite** [tit] *adj* §91 small, little; short; minor, lower; en petit shortened; miniature; **petit à petit** little by little, bit by bit ‖ *mf* youngster; young (*of an animal*); poor little thing ‖ *m* little boy ‖ *f* little girl

petit-beurre [pətibœr] *m* (*pl* **petits-beurre**) cookie

petit-cou·sin [pətikuzɛ̃] **-sine** [zin] *mf* (*pl* **petits-cousins**) second cousin

petite-fille [pətitfij] *f* (*pl* **petites-filles**) granddaughter

petite-nièce [pətitnjɛs] *f* (*pl* **petites-nièces**) great-niece

petitesse [pətites] *f* smallness

petit-fils [pətifis] *m* (*pl* **petits-fils**) grandson; grandchild

petit-gris [pətigri] *m* (*pl* **petits-gris**) miniver; snail

pétition [petisjɔ̃] *f* petition; **faire une pétition de principe** to beg the question

petit-lait [pətilɛ] *m* (*pl* **petits-laits**) whey

petit-neveu [pətinvø] *m* (*pl* **petits-neveux**) great-nephew

petits-enfants [pətizɑ̃fɑ̃] *mpl* grandchildren

petit-suisse [pətisɥis] *m* (*pl* **petits-suisses**) cream cheese

peton [pətɔ̃] *m* (coll) tiny foot

pétoncle [petɔ̃kl] *m* scallop

Pétrarque [petrark] *m* Petrarch

pétrifier [petrifje] *tr & ref* to petrify

pétrin [petrɛ̃] *m* kneading trough; (coll) mess, jam

pétrir [petrir] *tr* to knead; to mold

pétrole [petrɔl] *m* petroleum; **à pétrole** kerosene (*lamp*); **pétrole brut** crude oil; **pétrole lampant** kerosene

pétro·lier [petrɔlje] **-lière** [ljɛr] *adj* oil ‖ *m* tanker; oil baron

P et T [peete] *fpl* (letterword) (**Postes et télécommunications**) post office, telephone, and telegraph

pétu·lant [petylɑ̃] **-lante** [lɑ̃t] *adj* lively, frisky

peu [pø] *m* bit, little; **peu de** few; not much; not many; **peu de chose** not much ‖ *adv* §91 little; not very; **à peu près** about, practically; **depuis peu** of late; **peu ou prou** more or less; **peu probable** improbable; **peu s'en faut** very nearly; **pour peu que**, **si peu que** however little; **quelque peu** somewhat; **sous peu** before long; **tant soit peu** ever so little

peuplade [pœplad] *f* tribe

peuple [pœpl] *adj* plebeian, common ‖ *m* people

peuplement [pœpləmɑ̃] *m* populating; planting; stocking (*e.g., with fish*)

peupler [pœple] *tr* to people; to plant; to stock ‖ *intr* to multiply, to breed

peuplier [pøplje] *m* poplar

peur [pœr] *f* fear; **avoir peur (de)** to be afraid (of); **de peur que** lest, for fear that; **une peur bleue** (coll) an awful fright

peu·reux [pœrø] **-reuse** [røz] *adj* fearful, timid

peut-être [pøtɛtr] *adv* perhaps; **peut-être que non** perhaps not

p. ex. *abbr* (**par exemple**) e.g.

phalange [falɑ̃ʒ] *f* phalanx

phalène [falɛn] *m & f* moth

Pharaon [faraɔ̃] *m* Pharaoh

phare [far] *m* lighthouse; beacon; (aut) headlight; **phares code** dimmers

phari·sien [farizjɛ̃] **-sienne** [zjɛn] *adj* pharisaic ‖ *mf* pharisee

pharmaceutique [farmasøtik] *adj* pharmaceutical || *f* pharmaceutics

pharmacie [farmasi] *f* drugstore, pharmacy; medicine chest; drugs

pharma·cien [farmasjẽ] **-cienne** [sjen] *mf* pharmacist

pharynx [farẽks] *m* pharynx

phase [faz] *f* phase

Phébé [febe] *f* Phoebe

Phénicie [fenisi] *f* Phoenicia; **la Phénicie** Phoenicia

phéni·cien [fenisjẽ] **-cienne** [sjen] *adj* Phoenician || (*cap*) *mf* Phoenician

phénix [feniks] *m* phoenix

phénomé·nal -nale [fenɔmenal] *adj* (*pl* **-naux** [no]) phenomenal

phénomène [fenɔmen] *m* phenomenon; (*coll*) monster, freak

philanthrope [filãtrɔp] *mf* philanthropist

philanthropie [filãtrɔpi] *f* philanthropy

philatélie [filateli] *f* philately

philatéliste [filatelist] *mf* philatelist

philip·pin [filipẽ] **-pine** [pin] *adj* Philippine || (*cap*) *mf* Filipino

Philippines [filipin] *fpl* Philippines

philistin [filistẽ] *adj masc & m* Philistine

philologie [filɔlɔʒi] *f* philology

philologue [filɔlɔg] *mf* philologist

philosophe [filɔzɔf] *adj* philosophic || *mf* philosopher

philosophie [filɔzɔfi] *f* philosophy

philosophique [filɔzɔfik] *adj* philosophic(al)

philtre [filtr] *m* philter

phlébite [flebit] *f* phlebitis

phobie [fɔbi] *f* phobia

phonétique [fɔnetik] *adj* phonetic || *f* phonetics

phoniatrie [fɔnjatri] *f* speech therapy

phono [fɔno] *m* (*coll*) phonograph

phonographe [fɔnɔgraf] *m* phonograph

phonologie [fɔnɔlɔʒi] *f* phonology

phonothèque [fɔnɔtek] *f* record library

phoque [fɔk] *m* seal

phosphate [fɔsfat] *m* phosphate

phosphore [fɔsfɔr] *m* phosphorus

phosphores·cent [fɔsfɔresã] **phosphores·cente** [fɔsfɔresãt] *adj* phosphorescent

photo [fɔto] *f* photo, snapshot

photocopier [fɔtɔkɔpje] *tr* to photocopy, to photostat

photogénique [fɔtɔʒenik] *adj* photogenic

photographe [fɔtɔgraf] *mf* photographer

photographie [fɔtɔgrafi] *f* photography; photograph

photographier [fɔtɔgrafje] *tr* to photograph

photogravure [fɔtɔgravyr] *f* photoengraving

photostat [fɔtɔsta] *m* photostat

phrase [fraz] *f* sentence; (*mus*) phrase; **phrase de choc** punch line

phrénologie [frenɔlɔʒi] *f* phrenology

physi·cien [fizisjẽ] **-cienne** [sjen] *mf* physicist

physiologie [fizjɔlɔʒi] *f* physiology

physiologique [fizjɔlɔʒik] *adj* physiological

physionomie [fizjɔnɔmi] *f* physiognomy

physique [fizik] *adj* physical; material || *m* physique; appearance || *f* physics

piaffer [pjafe] *intr* to paw the ground; to fidget, fume

piailler [pjaje] *intr* (*coll*) to cheep; (*coll*) to squeal

pianiste [pjanist] *mf* pianist

piano [pjano] *m* piano; **piano à queue** grand piano; **piano droit** upright piano || *adv* (*coll*) quietly

pianoter [pjanɔte] *intr* to strum; to drum, to thrum; to rattle away

piastre [pjastr] *f* (Canad) dollar

piauler [pjole] *intr* to peep; to screech (*said of pulley*); (*coll*) to whine

pic [pik] *m* peak; (*tool*) pick; (*orn*) woodpecker; **à pic** sheer, steep; (*coll*) in the nick of time; **couler à pic** to sink like a stone

picaillons [pikajõ] *mpl* (slang) dough

picaresque [pikaresk] *adj* picaresque

piccolo [pikɔlo] *m* piccolo

pichet [pi/e] *m* pitcher, jug

pick-up [pikœp] *m invar* pickup; record player; pickup truck

picoler [pikɔle] *intr* (slang) to get pickled

picorer [pikɔre] *tr & intr* to peck

picoter [pikɔte] *tr* to prick; to peck at; to sting

picotin [pikɔtẽ] *m* peck (*measure*)

pictu·ral -rale [piktyral] *adj* (*pl* **-raux** [ro]) pictorial

pie [pi] *adj invar* piebald || *f* magpie

pièce [pjes] *f* piece; patch; room; play; document; coin; wine barrel; **à la pièce** separately; **donner la pièce** to tip; **faire pièce à** to play a trick on; to put a check on; **inventé de toutes pièces** made up out of the whole cloth; **la pièce** apiece; **pièce à conviction** (law) exhibit; **pièce comptable** voucher; **pièce d'eau** ornamental pond; **pièce de rechange, pièce détachée** spare part; **pièce de résistance** pièce de résistance; (culin) entree; **tout d'une pièce** in one piece; (*coll*) rigid; (*coll*) stiffly || *adv* apiece

pied [pje] *m* foot; foothold; **à pied** on foot; **au pied de la lettre** literally; **au pied levé** offhand; **de pied en cap** from head to toe; **faire le pied de grue** (*coll*) to cool one's heels, to stand around waiting; **faire les pieds à** (*coll*) to give what's coming to; **faire un pied de nez** (*coll*) to thumb one's nose; **lever le pied** to abscond; **mettre à pied** to dismiss, fire; **mettre les pieds dans le plat** (*coll*) to put one's foot in one's mouth; **mettre pied à terre** to dismount; **pied équin** clubfoot; **travailler comme un pied** (*coll*) to botch one's work

pied-à-terre [pjetater] *m invar* hangout, temporary base

pied-bot [pjebo] *m* (*pl* **pieds-bots**) clubfooted person

pied-d'alouette [pjedalwet] *m* (*pl* **pieds-d'alouette**) delphinium

pied-droit [pjedrwa] *m* (*pl* **pieds-droits**) (archit) pier

piédes·tal -tale [pjedestal] *m* (*pl* **-taux** [to]) pedestal

pied-noir [pjenwar] *m* (*pl* **pieds-noirs**) Algerian of European descent

piège [pjɛʒ] *m* trap, snare

piéger [pjeʒe] §1 *tr* to trap, to snare; to booby-trap

pie-grièche [pigrijɛʃ] *f* (*pl* **pies-grièches**) shrike; shrew

pierraille [pjɛrɑj] *f* rubble

pierre [pjer] *f* stone; **faire d'une pierre deux coups** to kill two birds with one stone; **Pierre** Peter; **pierre à aiguiser** whetstone; **pierre à briquet** flint; **pierre à chaux, pierre à plâtre** gypsum; **pierre à feu, pierre à fusil** gunflint; **pierre angulaire** cornerstone; **pierre à rasoir** hone; **pierre calcaire** limestone; **pierre d'achoppement** stumbling block; **pierre de gué** stepping stone; **pierre de touche** touchstone; **pierre tombale** tombstone

pierreries [pjɛrri] *fpl* precious stones

pier·reux [pjɛrø] **pier·reuse** [pjɛrøz] *adj* stony || *f* (coll) streetwalker

pierrot [pjero] *m* clown; sparrow; (coll) oddball; (coll) greenhorn

piété [pjete] *f* piety; devotion

piéter [pjete] §10 *intr* to toe the line || *ref* to stand firm

piétiner [pjetine] *tr* to trample on || *intr* to stamp; to mark time

piéton [pjetɔ̃] *m* pedestrian

piètre [pjetr] *adj* poor, wretched

pieu [pjø] *m* (*pl* **pieux**) post, stake; (archit) pile

pieuvre [pjœvr] *f* octopus; (coll) leech

pieux [pjø] **pieuse** [pjøz] *adj* pious; dutiful; white (*lie*)

pif [pif] *m* (slang) snout (*nose*) || *interj* bang!

pige [piʒ] *f* (slang) year; **à la pige** (journ) so much a line; **faire la pige à** (slang) to outdo

pigeon [piʒɔ̃] *m* pigeon; **pigeon voyageur** homing pigeon

pigeonner [piʒɔne] *tr* (coll) to dupe

pigeonnier [piʒɔnje] *m* dovecote

piger [piʒe] §38 *tr* (slang) to look at; (slang) to get || *intr*—**tu piges?** (slang) do you get it?

pigment [pigmã] *m* pigment

pignocher [piɲɔʃe] *intr* to pick at one's food

pignon [piɲɔ̃] *m* gable; (mach) pinion; **avoir pignon sur rue** (coll) to have a home of one's own; (coll) to be well off; **pignon de chaîne** sprocket wheel

pile [pil] *f* stack, pile; pier; (elec) battery (*primary cell*); (coll) thrashing; **pile atomique** atomic pile; **pile ou face** heads or tails; **pile sèche** dry cell || *adv* (coll) short; (coll) exactly

piler [pile] *tr* to grind, to crush

pilier [pilje] *m* pillar; **pilier de cabaret** barfly

pillage [pijaʒ] *m* looting

pil·lard [pijar] **pil·larde** [pijard] *adj* looting || *mf* looter

piller [pije] *tr* & *intr* to loot; to plagiarize

pil·leur [pijœr] **pil·leuse** [pijøz] *mf* pillager

pilon [pilɔ̃] *m* pestle; (coll) drumstick (*of chicken*); (coll) wooden leg; **pilon à vapeur** steam hammer

pilonnage [pilɔnaʒ] *m* crushing; **pilonnage aérien** saturation bombing

pilonner [pilɔne] *tr* to crush; to bomb

pilori [pilɔri] *m* pillory

pilot [pilo] *m* pile (*in piling*); rags (*for paper*)

pilotage [pilɔtaʒ] *m* piloting; **pilotage sans visibilité** blind flying

pilote [pilɔt] *m* pilot; **pilote de ligne** airline pilot; **pilote d'essai** test pilot

piloter [pilɔte] *tr* to pilot; to guide; to drive piles into || *intr* to pilot; to be a guide

pilotis [pilɔti] *m* piles

pilule [pilyl] *f* pill; (coll) bitter pill; **dorer la pilule** to gild the lily

piment [pimã] *m* allspice (*berry*); (fig) spice; **piment doux** sweet pepper; **piment rouge** red or hot pepper

pimenter [pimãte] *tr* to season with red pepper; (fig) to spice

pim·pant [pɛ̃pã] **-pante** [pãt] *adj* smart, spruce

pin [pɛ̃] *m* pine; **pin de Weymouth** (*Pinus strobus*) white pine; **pin sylvestre** (*Pinus sylvestris*) Scotch pine

pinacle [pinakl] *m* pinnacle

pince [pɛ̃s] *f* tongs; pliers; forceps; crowbar; gripper; grip; pleat; claw (*of crab*); **aller à pinces** (slang) to hoof it; **petites pinces, pince à épiler** tweezers; **pince à linge** clothespin; **pince à sucre** sugar tongs; **pince hémostatique** hemostat; **pinces** tongs; pincers, pliers; **pinces de cycliste** bicycle clips; **serrer la pince à** (slang) to shake hands with

pin·cé -cée [pɛ̃se] *adj* prim, tight-lipped; thin, pinched || *f* see **pincée**

pin·ceau [pɛ̃so] *m* (*pl* **-ceaux**) paintbrush; pencil (*of light*)

pincée [pɛ̃se] *f* pinch

pincement [pɛ̃smã] *m* pinching; plucking

pince-monseigneur [pɛ̃smɔ̃sɛɲœr] *f* (*pl* **pinces-monseigneur**) jimmy

pince-nez [pɛ̃sne] *m invar* nose glasses

pincer [pɛ̃se] §51 *tr* to pinch; to grip; to nip off; to pluck; to top (*plants*); to purse (*the lips*); to pleat; (coll) to nab, to catch || *intr* to bite (*said of cold*); **en pincer pour** (slang) to have a crush on; **pincer de** (mus) to strum on

pince-sans-rire [pɛ̃ssãrir] *adj invar* deadpan || *mf invar* deadpan comic

pincette [pɛ̃set] *f* tweezers; **pincettes** tweezers; fire tongs

pinçon [pɛ̃sɔ̃] *m* bruise (*from pinch*)

pinède [pined] *f* pine grove

pingouin [pɛ̃gwɛ̃] *m* (*family:* Alcidae) auk

pingre [pɛ̃gr] *adj* (coll) stingy ‖ *mf* (coll) tightwad

pinson [pɛ̃sõ] *m* (orn) finch

pintade [pɛ̃tad] *f* guinea fowl

pin up [pinœp] *f invar* (coll) pinup girl

pioche [pjɔʃ] *f* pickax

piocher [pjɔʃe] *tr & intr* to dig, to pick; (coll) to cram

pio•cheur [pjɔʃœr] **-cheuse** [ʃøz] *mf* digger; (coll) grind ‖ *f* (mach) cultivator

piolet [pjɔlɛ] *m* ice ax

pion [pjõ] *m* (checkers) man; (chess & fig) pawn; (slang) proctor; **damer le pion à** (coll) to get the better of

pionnier [pjɔnje] *m* pioneer

pipe [pip] *f* pipe; **casser sa pipe** (slang) to kick the bucket

pi•peau [pipo] *m* (*pl* **-peaux**) bird call; shepherd's pipe; lime twig

piper [pipe] *tr* to snare, to catch; to load (*the dice*); to mark (*the cards*) ‖ *intr*—**ne pipe pas!** (coll) not a peep out of you!

pi•quant [pikã] **-quante** [kãt] *adj* piquant, intriguing; racy, spicy ‖ *m* sting; prickle; quill (*of porcupine*); piquancy, pungency; point (*of story*); (fig) bite

pique [pik] *m* (cards) spade; (cards) spades ‖ *f* pike; pique

pi•qué -quée [pike] *adj* stung; sour; (mus) staccato; (coll) batty; **piqué de** studded with ‖ *m* quilt; **descendre en piqué** to nose-dive

pique-assiette [pikasjɛt] *mf* (*pl* **-assiettes**) (coll) sponger

pique-feu [pikfø] *m invar* poker

pique-nique [piknik] *m* (*pl* **-niques**) picnic

pique-niquer [piknike] *intr* to picnic

piquer [pike] *tr* to sting; to prick; to pique; to stimulate; to quilt; to spur; to give a shot to; (mus) to play staccato; (slang) to filch; (slang) to pinch, to nab ‖ *intr* to turn sour; (aer) to nose-dive ‖ *ref* to be piqued; to spot; to give oneself a shot; **se piquer de** to take pride in; **se piquer pour** to take a fancy to

piquet [pikɛ] *m* peg, stake; picket; **piquet de grève** picket line

piqueter [pikte] §34 *tr* to stake out; to spot, dot

piquette [pikɛt] *f* poor wine; (coll) crushing defeat

pi•queur [pikœr] **-queuse** [køz] *mf* stitcher ‖ *m* huntsman; outrider

piqûre [pikyr] *f* sting, bite; prick; injection, shot; stitching; puncture; **piqûre de ver** moth hole

pirate [pirat] *m* pirate; **pirate de l'air** hijacker

pirater [pirate] *intr* to pirate

piraterie [piratri] *f* piracy; **piraterie aérienne** hijacking

pire [pir] §91 *adj comp & super* worse; worst ‖ *m* (the) worst

pirouette [pirwɛt] *f* pirouette

pirouetter [pirwete] *intr* to pirouette

pis [pi] *adj comp & super* worse;

worst ‖ *m* udder; **au pis aller** at worst; **de pis en pis** worse and worse; **(le) pis** (the) worst; **qui pis est** what's worse; **tant pis** so much the worse ‖ *adv comp & super* §91 worse; worst

pis-aller [pizale] *m invar* makeshift

piscine [pisin] *f* swimming pool

pissenlit [pisãli] *m* dandelion

pisser [pise] *tr* (coll) to spout (*water*); (coll) to leak; (slang) to pass (*e.g., blood*); **pisser de la copie** (slang) to be a hack writer ‖ *intr* (slang) to urinate

pisse-vinaigre [pisvinɛgr] *m invar* (coll) skinflint

pissoir [piswar] *m* (coll) urinal

pissotière [pisɔtjɛr] *f* (coll) street urinal

pistache [pistaʃ] *f* pistachio

piste [pist] *f* track; trail; ring (*of, e.g., circus*); rink; lane (*of highway*); **à double piste** four-lane (*highway*); **piste cavalière** bridle path; **piste cyclable** bicycle path; **piste d'atterrissage** landing strip; **piste de danse** dance floor; **piste d'envoi** runway; **piste pour skieurs** ski run; **piste sonore** sound track

pister [piste] *tr* to track, trail

pistolet [pistɔlɛ] *m* pistol; spray gun; (coll) card; **pistolet à bouchon** popgun; **pistolet d'arçon** horse pistol; **pistolet mitrailleur** submachine gun

piston [pistõ] *m* piston; (coll) pull

pistonner [pistɔne] *tr* (coll) to push, to back

pitance [pitãs] *f* ration; food

pi•teux [pitø] **-teuse** [tøz] *adj* pitiful, sorry, sad

pitié [pitje] *f* pity; **à faire pitié** (coll) very badly; **par pitié!** for pity's sake!; **quelle pitié!** how awful

piton [pitõ] *m* screw eye; peak

pitou [pitu] *m* (Canad) dog; (Canad) tyke

pitoyable [pitwajabl] *adj* pitiful

pitre [pitr] *m* clown

pittoresque [pitɔrɛsk] *adj* picturesque

pivoine [pivwan] *f* peony

pivot [pivo] *m* pivot

pivoter [pivɔte] *intr* to pivot

P.J. [peʒi] *f* (letterword) **(police judiciaire)** (coll) police (*dealing with criminal cases*)

placage [plakaʒ] *m* veneering; plating

placard [plakar] *m* cupboard; closet; placard, poster; (typ) galley

placarder [plakarde] *tr* to placard; (typ) to print in galleys

place [plas] *f* place; city square; room; seat; job, position; fare; **sur place** on the spot

placement [plasmã] *m* placement; investment; **de placement** employment (*agency*)

placer [plase] §51 *tr* to place; to invest; to slip in ‖ *ref* to seat oneself; to rank; to get a job; to take place

pla•ceur [plasœr] **-ceuse** [søz] *mf* employment agent ‖ *m* usher

placide [plasid] *adj* placid

pla·cier [plasje] -cière [sjɛr] mf agent, representative

plafond [plafɔ̃] m ceiling

plafonner [plafɔne] intr—plafonner (à) to hit the top (at)

plafonnier [plafɔnje] m ceiling light; (aut) dome light

plage [plaʒ] f beach; band (of record); (poetic) clime

plagiaire [plaʒjɛr] mf plagiarist

plagiat [plaʒja] m plagiarism

plagier [plaʒje] tr & intr to plagiarize

plagiste [plaʒist] mf beach concessionaire

plaider [plede] tr to argue (a case); to plead (e.g., ignorance) || intr to plead; to go to law

plai·deur [pledœr] -deuse [døz] mf litigant

plaidoirie [pledwari] f pleading

plaidoyer [pledwaje] m appeal (of lawyer to judge or jury)

plaie [ple] f wound, sore; plague; plaie en séton flesh wound

plai·gnant [plɛɲɑ̃] -gnante [ɲɑ̃t] mf plaintiff

plain [plɛ̃] m high tide

plaindre [plɛ̃dr] §15 tr to pity || ref to complain

plaine [plen] f plain

plain-pied [plɛ̃pje] m—de plain-pied on the same floor; (fig) on an equal footing

plainte [plɛ̃t] f complaint; moan

plain·tif [plɛ̃tif] -tive [tiv] adj plaintive

plaire [plɛr] §52 intr (with dat) to please; (with dat) to like, e.g., le lait lui plaît he likes milk; s'il vous plaît please || ref to be pleased; to enjoy oneself; to like one another; se plaire à to like it in, e.g., je me plais à la campagne I like it in the country

plaisance [plezɑ̃s] f—de plaisance pleasure (e.g., boat)

plai·sant [plezɑ̃] -sante [zɑ̃t] adj pleasant; funny || m—mauvais plaisant practical joker

plaisanter [plezɑ̃te] tr to poke fun at || intr to joke

plaisanterie [plezɑ̃tri] f joke; joking

plaisantin [plezɑ̃tɛ̃] adj masc roguish, waggish || m wag

plaisir [plezir] m pleasure; à plaisir without cause; at one's pleasure; au plaisir (de vous revoir) good-by; faire plaisir à to please, give pleasure to

plan [plɑ̃] plane [plan] adj even, flat; plane (angle) || m plan; design; (geom) plane; au deuxième plan in the background; au premier plan in the foreground; downstage; au troisième plan far in the background; gros plan (mov) close-up; laisser en plan (coll) to leave stranded; (coll) to put off, delay; lever un plan to survey; plan de travail work schedule; rester en plan (coll) to remain in suspense; sur le plan de from the point of view of || f see plane

planche [plɑ̃ʃ] f board; plank; (hort) bed; (typ) plate; (slang) blackboard; faire la planche to float on one's back; planche de bord instrument panel; planche de débarquement gangplank; planche de salut sheet anchor

planchéier [plɑ̃ʃeje] tr to floor; to board

plancher [plɑ̃ʃe] m floor; le plancher des vaches (coll) terra firma

plane [plan] f drawknife

planer [plane] tr to plane || intr to hover; to glide; to float; planer sur to overlook, to sweep (e.g., a landscape with one's eyes); (fig) to hover over

planète [planɛt] f planet

planeur [planœr] m glider

planeuse [planøz] f planing machine

planification [planifikasjɔ̃] f planning

planifier [planifje] tr to plan

planning [planiŋ] m detailed plan; planning familial birth control

plan-plan [plɑ̃plɑ̃] adv (coll) quietly, without hurrying

planque [plɑ̃k] f (coll) soft job; (slang) hideout

planquer [plɑ̃ke] tr to hide || ref (mil) to take cover; (slang) to hide out

plant [plɑ̃] m planting; bed, patch; seedling, sapling

plantation [plɑ̃tasjɔ̃] f planting; plantation; plantation de cheveux hairline; head of hair

plante [plɑ̃t] f plant; sole

plan·té·tée [plɑ̃te] adj set, situated

planter [plɑ̃te] tr to plant; to set; planter là to give the slip to || ref to stand

planteur [plɑ̃tœr] m planter

plantoir [plɑ̃twar] m (hort) dibble

planton [plɑ̃tɔ̃] m (mil) orderly

plantu·reux [plɑ̃tyrø] -reuse [røz] adj abundant; fertile; (coll) buxom

plaque [plak] f plate; plaque; splotch; plaque à crêpes pancake griddle; plaque croûteuse scab; plaque d'immatriculation, plaque minéralogique (aut) license plate; plaque tournante (rr) turntable; (fig) hub (of a city)

plaquer [plake] tr to plate; to veneer; to plaster down (one's hair); to strike (a chord); (football) to tackle; (coll) to jilt; plaquer à l'électricité to electroplate || ref to lie flat; (aer) to pancake

plaquette [plakɛt] f plaque; pamphlet; (histology) platelet

plastic [plastik] m plastic bomb

plastique [plastik] adj plastic || m plastics || f plastic art

plastron [plastrɔ̃] m shirt front; breastplate; hostile contingent (in war games)

plastronner [plastrone] intr (fig) to throw out one's chest

plat [pla] plate [plat] adj flat; even; smooth (sea); dead (calm); corny (joke); à plat run-down; flat || m dish; platter; course (of meal); flat (of hand); blade (of oar); face (of hammer); plat cuisiné platter, short-order meal; **plat de côtes** sparerib; **plat du jour** today's special, chef's special; **plat principal, plat de résistance** entree; **plats** (bb) boards

platane [platan] *m* plane tree; **faux platane** sycamore

pla·teau [plato] *m* (*pl* **-teaux**) plateau; tray; shelf; platform; plate; pan (*of scale*); (mov, telv) set; (rr) flatcar; (theat) stage; **plateau porte-disque** turntable (*of phonograph*); **plateau tournant** revolving stage

plate-bande [platbãd] *f* (*pl* **plates-bandes**) flower bed

plate-forme [platfɔrm] *f* (*pl* **plates-formes**) platform; (rr) flatcar

platine [platin] *m* platinum || *f* plate; platen; lock (*of gun*); stage (*of microscope*)

plati·né -née [platine] *adj* platinum-plated; platinum

platitude [platityd] *f* platitude; flatness; obsequiousness

Platon [platɔ̃] *m* Plato

plâtre [plɑtr] *m* plaster; plaster cast; **essuyer les plâtres** to be the first occupant of a new house; **plâtre à mouler** plaster of Paris

plâtrer [plɑtre] *tr* to plaster; to put in a cast; to fertilize || *ref* (coll) to pile on the make-up or face powder

plausible [plozibl] *adj* plausible

plébéien [plebejɛ̃] **plébéienne** [plebejɛn] *adj & mf* plebeian

plein [plɛ̃] **pleine** [plɛn] *adj* full; round, plump; solid (*bar, wheel, wire, etc.*); continuous (*line*); heavy (*heart*); in foal, with calf, etc.; (coll) drunk; **plein aux as** (coll) well-heeled; **plein de** full of; covered with; preoccupied with; **plein de soi** self-centered || (when standing before noun) *adj* full; high (*tide*); **en plein + noun** in the midst of the + *noun*, right in the + *noun*; at the height of the (*season*); in the open (*air*); out at (*sea*), on the high (*seas*); in broad (*daylight*); in the dead of (*winter*) || *m* full (*of the moon*); bull's-eye; downstroke; **battre son plein** to be in full swing; **en plein** plumb, plump, squarely; **faire le plein (de)** to fill up the tank (with) || **plein** *adv* full; **tout plein** very much

plein-emploi [plɛ̃nãplwa] *m* full employment

pleu·rard [plœrar] **-rarde** [rard] *adj* (coll) whimpering || *mf* (coll) whimperer

pleurer [plœre] *tr* to weep over; **pleurer misère** to complain of being poor || *intr* to cry, weep; **pleurer à chaudes larmes** to weep bitterly

pleurésie [plœrezi] *f* pleurisy

pleu·reur [plœrœr] **-reuse** [røz] *adj* weeping || *f* paid mourner

pleurnicher [plœrniʃe] *intr* to whimper, snivel

pleurs [plœr] *mpl* tears

pleutre [pløtr] *adj* (coll) cowardly || *m* (coll) coward

pleuvasser [pløvase] *intr* (coll) to drizzle

pleuvoir [pløvwar] §53 *intr & impers* to rain; **pleuvoir à verse, à flots, or à seaux** to rain buckets

pli [pli] *m* fold; pleat; bend (*of arm or leg*); hollow (*of knee*); letter; envelope; undulation (*of ground*); (cards) trick; **faux pli** crease, wrinkle; **petit pli** tuck; **sous ce pli** enclosed, herewith; **sous pli cacheté** in a sealed envelope; **sous pli distinct** or **séparé** under separate cover

pliage [plijaʒ] *m* folding

pliant [plijã] **pliante** [plijãt] *adj* folding; collapsible; pliant || *m* campstool, folding chair

plier [plije] *tr* to fold; to bend; to force || *intr* to fold; to bend; to yield; **ne pas plier,** s.v.p. (formula on envelope) please do not bend || *ref* to fold; to yield; to fall back (*said of army*)

plisser [plise] *tr* to pleat; to crease; to wrinkle; to squint (*the eyes*) || *intr* to fold || *ref* to wrinkle; to pucker up (*said of mouth*)

plomb [plɔ̃] *m* lead; shot; seal; plumb; sinker (*of fishline*); (elec) fuse; **à plomb** plumb, vertical; straight down, directly; **faire sauter un plomb** to burn or blow out a fuse

plombage [plɔ̃baʒ] *m* filling (*of tooth*); sealing (*e.g., at customs*)

plombagine [plɔ̃baʒin] *f* graphite

plom·bé -bée [plɔ̃be] *adj* leaden; in bond, sealed; filled (*tooth*); livid (*hue*)

plomber [plɔ̃be] *tr* to cover with lead; to seal; to plumb; to fill (*a tooth*); to make livid; to roll (*the ground*)

plomberie [plɔ̃bri] *f* plumbing; plumbing-supply store; leadwork

plombeur [plɔ̃bœr] *m* (mach) roller

plombier [plɔ̃bje] *m* plumber; worker in lead

plonge [plɔ̃ʒ] *f* dishwashing

plon·geant [plɔ̃ʒã] **-geante** [ʒãt] *adj* plunging; from above

plongée [plɔ̃ʒe] *f* plunge; dive; dip, slope; **en plongée** submerged

plongeoir [plɔ̃ʒwar] *m* diving board

plongeon [plɔ̃ʒɔ̃] *m* plunge; dive; (football) tackle; **plongeon de haut vol** high dive

plonger [plɔ̃ʒe] §38 *tr* to plunge; to thrust, to stick || *intr* to plunge; to dive; (coll) to have a good view; **plonger raide** to crash-dive || *ref*—se **plonger dans** to immerse oneself in; to give oneself over to

plon·geur [plɔ̃ʒœr] **-geuse** [ʒøz] *adj* diving || *mf* diver; dishwasher (*in restaurant*) || *m* (mach) plunger; (orn) diver

plot [plo] *m* (elec) contact point

ployer [plwaje] §47 *tr & intr* to bend

pluches [plyʃ] *fpl* (mil) K.P.

pluie [plɥi] *f* rain; shower; **pluies radioactives** fallout

plumage [plymaʒ] *m* plumage

plumard [plymar] *m*—**aller au plumard** (slang) to hit the hay

plume [plym] *f* feather; pen; penpoint

plu·meau [plymo] *m* (*pl* **-meaux**) feather duster

plumer [plyme] *tr* to pluck; (coll) to fleece ‖ *intr* to feather one's oar

plumet [plyme] *m* plume

plu·meux [plymø] **-meuse** [møz] *adj* feathery

plumier [plymje] *m* pencil box

plupart [plypar] *f*—**la plupart** most; the most; for the most part; **la plupart de** most; the most; most of, the majority of; **la plupart d'entre nous (eux)** most of us (them); **pour la plupart** for the most part

plu·riel -rielle [plyrjɛl] *adj & m* plural; **au pluriel** in the plural

plus [ply] ([plyz] before vowel; [plys] in final position) *m* plus; **au plus, tout au plus** at the most, at best; at the latest; at the outside; **d'autant plus** all the more so; **de plus** more, moreover, besides; **de plus en plus** more and more; **en plus** besides, en **plus de** in addition to, besides; **le plus, la plus, les plus** (the) most; **le plus de** the most; **le plus que** as much as, as fast as; **ni . . . non plus** nor . . . either, e.g., **ni moi non plus** nor I either; **ni plus ni moins** neither more nor less; **non plus** neither, not . . . either, e.g., **plus de** more, e.g., **plus de chaleur** more heat; no more, e.g., **plus de potage** no more soup; **qui plus est** what is more, moreover ‖ *adv comp & super* §91 more; **des plus** + *adj* most + *adj*, extremely + *adj*; **(le) plus . . .** (the) most . . . , e.g., **ce que j'aime le plus** what I like (the) most; **le** (or **son, etc.**) **plus** + *adj* the (or his, etc.) most; **ne . . . plus** §90 no more, no longer; **ne . . . plus que** §90 now only, e.g., **il n'y a plus que mon oncle** there is now only my uncle; **on ne peut plus** + *adj* or *adv* extremely + *adj* or *adv*; **plus de** (followed by numeral) more than; **plus jamais** never more; **plus . . . plus** (or **moins**) the more . . . the more (or the less); **plus que** more than; **plus tôt** sooner ‖ *prep* plus

plusieurs [plyzjœr] *adj & pron indef* several

plus-que-parfait [plyskəparfɛ] *m* pluperfect

plus-value [plyvaly] *f* (*pl* **-values**) appreciation; increase; surplus; extra cost; surplus value (*in Marxian economics*)

Plutarque [plytark] *m* Plutarch

Pluton [plytɔ̃] *m* Pluto

plutonium [plytɔnjɔm] *m* plutonium

plutôt [plyto] *adv* rather; instead; **plutôt . . . que** rather . . . than

pluvier [plyvje] *m* (orn) plover

plu·vieux [plyvjø] **-vieuse** [vjøz] *adj* rainy

pneu [pnø] *m* (*pl* **pneus**) tire; express letter (*by Parisian tube*); **pneu ballon**

or **confort** balloon tire; **pneu de secours** spare tire

pneumatique [pnømatik] *adj* pneumatic ‖ *m* tire; express letter (*by Parisian tube*)

pneumonie [pnømɔni] *f* pneumonia

pochade [pɔʃad] *f* sketch

po·chard [pɔʃar] **-charde** [ʃard] *mf* (coll) boozer, guzzler

poche [pɔʃ] *f* pocket; bag, pouch; crop (*of bird*)

po·ché -chée [pɔʃe] *adj* poached; black (*eye*)

pocher [pɔʃe] *tr* to poach; to dash off (*a sketch*)

pochette [pɔʃɛt] *f* folder; book (*of matches*); kit; fancy handkerchief; **pochette à disque** record jacket; **pochette surprise** surprise package

pocheuse [pɔʃøz] *f* egg poacher

pochoir [pɔʃwar] *m* stencil

poêle [pwal] *m* stove; pall; canopy ‖ *f* frying pan

poêlon [pwalɔ̃] *m* saucepan

poème [pɔem] *m* poem; **poème symphonique** tone poem

poésie [pɔezi] *f* poetry; poem

poète [pɔet] *mf* poet

poétesse [pɔetes] *f* poetess

poétique [pɔetik] *adj* poetic(al) ‖ *f* poetics

pogrom [pɔgrɔm] *m* pogrom

poids [pwa], [pwɑ] *m* weight; **poids lourd** truck

poi·gnant [pwaɲɑ̃] **-gnante** [ɲɑ̃t] *adj* poignant

poignard [pwaɲar] *m* dagger

poignarder [pwaɲarde] *tr* to stab

poigne [pwaɲ] *f* grip, grasp; **à poigne** strong, energetic

poignée [pwaɲe] *f* handful; handle; grip; hilt; **poignée de main** handshake

poignet [pwaɲe] *m* wrist; cuff; **poignet mousquetaire** French cuff

poil [pwal] *m* hair; bristle; nap, pile; coat (*of animals*); **à long poil** shaggy; **à poil** naked; bareback; **au poil** (slang) peachy; **avoir un poil dans la main** (coll) to be lazy; **de mauvais poil** (coll) in a bad mood; **de tout poil** (coll) of every shade and hue; **poil follet** down; **reprendre du poil de la bête** (coll) to be one's own self again; **se mettre à poil** to strip to the skin

poi·lu -lue [pwaly] *adj* hairy ‖ *m* (mil) doughboy

poinçon [pwɛ̃sɔ̃] *m* punch; stamp; hallmark; **poinçon à glace** ice pick

poinçonner [pwɛ̃sɔne] *tr* to punch; to stamp; to prick; to hallmark

poinçonneuse [pwɛ̃sɔnøz] *f* stamping machine; ticket punch

poindre [pwɛ̃dr] §35 *intr* to dawn; to sprout

poing [pwɛ̃] *m* first; **dormir à poings fermés** to sleep like a log

point [pwɛ̃] *m* point; stitch; period (*used also in French to mark the divisions of whole numbers*); hole (*in a strap*); mark (*on a test*); (aer, naut) position; (typ) point; **à point** at the right moment; to a turn, medium; **à point nommé** in the nick of time; **à tel point que** to such a degree that; **au dernier point** to the utmost degree; **de point en point** exactly to the letter; **de tout point, en tout point** entirely; **deux points** colon; **faire le point** to take stock, to get one's bearings; **mettre au point** to focus; to adjust, to tune up; to develop, to perfect; **mettre les points sur les i** to dot one's i's; **point d'appui** fulcrum; base of operations; **point de bâti** (sewing) tack; **point de départ** starting point; **point de repère** point of reference, guide; (surv) bench mark; (fig) landmark; **point d'estime** dead reckoning; **point d'exclamation** exclamation point; **point d'interrogation** question mark; **point d'orgue** (mus) pause; **point du jour** break of day; **point et virgule** semicolon; **point mort** dead center; (aut) neutral; **points et traits** dots and dashes || *adv*—**ne . . . point** §90 not; not at all

pointage [pwɛ̃taʒ] *m* checking; check mark; aiming

pointe [pwɛ̃t] *f* point; tip; peak; head (*of* arrow); nose (*e.g., of bullet*); toe (*of shoe*); twinge (*of pain*); dash (*of, e.g., vanilla*); suggestion, touch; witty phrase, quip; (geog) cape, point; (mil) spearhead; **à pointes** spiked (*shoes*); **de pointe** peak (*e.g., hours*); **discuter sur les pointes d'épingle** to split hairs; **en pointe** tapering; **faire des pointes** to toe-dance; **pointe d'aiguille** needlepoint; **pointe de Paris** wire nail; **pointe de vitesse** spurt; **pointe du jour** daybreak; **sur la pointe des pieds** on tiptoe

poin·teau [pwɛ̃to] *m* (*pl* -teaux) checker; needle

pointer [pwɛ̃tœr] *m* pointer (*dog*) || [pwɛ̃te] *tr* to check off; to check in; to prick up (*the ears*); to dot || *intr* to rise, to soar skywards; to stand out; to sprout || *ref* to check in, to show up

poin·teur [pwɛ̃tœr] **-teuse** [tøz] *mf* checker; scorer; timekeeper; gunner; (dog) pointer

pointillé [pwɛ̃tije] *m* perforated line

pointil·leux [pwɛ̃tijø] **pointil·leuse** [pwɛ̃tijøz] *adj* punctilious; touchy; captious

poin·tu -tue [pwɛ̃ty] *adj* pointed; shrill; (fig) touchy

pointure [pwɛ̃tyr] *f* size

poire [pwar] *f* pear; bulb (*of camera, syringe, horn, etc.*); (slang) mug; (slang) sucker, sap; **couper la poire en deux** to split the difference; **garder une poire pour la soif** to put something aside for a rainy day; **poire à poudre** powder flask; **poire électrique** pear-shaped switch

poi·reau [pwaro] *m* (*pl* -reaux) (bot) leek

poirée [pware] *f* (bot) Swiss chard

poirier [pwarje] *m* pear tree

pois [pwa], [pwɑ] *m* pea; polka dot; **petits pois, pois verts** peas; **pois cassés** split peas; **pois chiche** chickpea; **pois de senteur** sweet pea

poison [pwazɔ̃] *m* poison

pois·sard [pwasar] **pois·sarde** [pwasard] *adj* vulgar || *f* fishwife

poisser [pwase] *tr* to coat with wax or pitch || *intr* to be sticky

pois·seux [pwasø] **pois·seuse** [pwasøz] *adj* sticky

poisson [pwasɔ̃] *m* fish; **poisson d'avril** April Fool (*joke, trick*); **poisson rouge** goldfish

poisson-chat [pwasɔ̃ʃa] *m* (*pl* poissons-chats) catfish

poissonnerie [pwasɔnri] *f* fish market

poisson·nier [pwasɔnje] **poisson·nière** [pwasɔnjer] *mf* dealer in fish || *f* fishwife; fish kettle

poitrail [pwatraj] *m* breast

poitrinaire [pwatriner] *adj & mf* (pathol) consumptive

poitrine [pwatrin] *f* chest; breast; bosom

poivre [pwavr] *m* pepper

poivrer [pwavre] *tr* to pepper

poivrier [pwavrije] *m* pepper plant; pepper shaker

poivrière [pwavrijer] *f* pepper shaker; pepper plantation

poivron [pwavrɔ̃] *m* pepper; sweet pepper plant

poix [pwa], [pwɑ] *f* pitch; **poix sèche** resin

poker [pɔker] *m* poker; four of a kind

polaire [pɔler] *adj* pole, polar

polariser [pɔlarize] *tr* to polarize

pôle [pol] *m* pole

po·li -lie [pɔli] *adj* polished; polite || *m* polish, gloss

police [pɔlis] *f* police; policy; **police d'assurance** insurance policy

policer [pɔlise] §51 *tr* to civilize; (obs) to police

Polichinelle [pɔliʃinel] *m* Punch; **de polichinelle** open (*secret*)

poli·cier [pɔlisje] **-cière** [sjer] *adj* police (*investigation, dog, etc.*); detective (*e.g., story*) || *m* plain-clothes man, detective

polio [pɔljo] *mf* (coll) polio victim || *f* (coll) polio

polir [pɔlir] *tr* to polish

polissoir [pɔliswar] *m* polisher

polis·son [pɔlisɔ̃] **polis·sonne** [pɔlisɔn] *adj* smutty || *mf* scamp, rascal

politesse [pɔlites] *f* politeness; **politesses** civilities, compliments

politicard [pɔlitikar] *m* unscrupulous politician

politi·cien [pɔlitisjɛ̃] **-cienne** [sjen] *adj* short-sighted; insincere || *mf* politician

politique [pɔlitik] *adj* political; prudent, wise || *m* politician; statesman || *f* politics; policy; cunning, shrewdness

pollen [pɔlɛn] *m* pollen

polluer [pɔllɥe] *tr* to pollute

polo [pɔlo] *m* polo

Pologne [pɔlɔɲ] *f* Poland; **la Pologne** Poland

polo·nais [pɔlɔne] **-naise** [nez] *adj* Polish ‖ *m* Polish (*language*) ‖ (*cap*) *mf* Pole

polonium [pɔlɔnjɔm] *m* polonium

pol·tron [pɔltrɔ̃] **-tronne** [trɔn] *adj* cowardly ‖ *mf* coward

polycopie [pɔlikɔpi] *f* mimeographing; **tiré à la polycopie** mimeographed

polycopié [pɔlikɔpje] *m* mimeographed university lectures

polycopier [pɔlikɔpje] *tr* to mimeograph

polygame [pɔligam] *adj* polygamous ‖ *mf* polygamist

polyglotte [pɔliglɔt] *adj* polyglot ‖ *mf* polyglot, linguist

polygone [pɔligɔn] *m* polygon; shooting range

polynôme [pɔlinom] *m* polynomial

polype [pɔlip] *m* polyp

polythéiste [pɔliteist] *adj* polytheistic ‖ *mf* polytheist

pom [pɔ̃] *interj* bang!

pommade [pɔmad] *f* pomade; **passer de la pommade à** (coll) to soft-soap

pomme [pɔm] *f* apple; ball, knob; head (*of lettuce*); **pomme de discorde** bone of contention; **pomme de pin** pine cone; **pomme de terre** potato; **pommes chips** potato chips; **pommes de terre au four** baked potatoes; scalloped potatoes; **pommes de terre en robe de chambre, en robe des champs,** or **en chemise** potatoes in their jackets; **pommes de terre sautées** fried potatoes; **pommes frites** French fried potatoes; **pommes soufflées** potato puffs; **pommes vapeur** boiled potatoes; steamed potatoes

pom·meau [pɔmo] *m* (*pl* **-meaux**) pommel; butt (*of fishing pole*)

pomme·lé -lée [pɔmle] *adj* dappled; fleecy (*clouds*); mackerel (*sky*)

pommette [pɔmet] *f* cheekbone

pommier [pɔmje] *m* apple tree

pompe [pɔ̃p] *f* pomp; pump; **à la pompe** on draught; **pompe à incendie** fire engine; **pompe aspirante** suction pump; **pompes funèbres** funeral

pomper [pɔ̃pe] *tr* to pump; to suck in

pompette [pɔ̃pet] *adj* (coll) tipsy

pom·peux [pɔ̃pø] **-peuse** [pøz] *adj* pompous; high-flown

pom·pier [pɔ̃pje] **-pière** [pjer] *adj* conventional; pretentious ‖ *mf* fitter ‖ *m* fireman

pompiste [pɔ̃pist] *mf* filling-station attendant

pomponner [pɔ̃pɔne] *tr & ref* to dress up

ponçage [pɔ̃saʒ] *m* sandpapering; pumicing

ponce [pɔ̃s] *f* pumice stone

pon·ceau [pɔ̃so] (*pl* **-ceaux**) *adj* poppy-red ‖ *m* rude bridge; culvert

poncer [pɔ̃se] §51 *tr* to sandpaper; to pumice

poncho [pɔ̃tʃo] *m* poncho

poncif [pɔ̃sif] *m* banality

ponctualité [pɔ̃ktɥalite] *f* punctuality

ponctuation [pɔ̃ktɥasjɔ̃] *f* punctuation

ponc·tuel -tuelle [pɔ̃ktɥel] *adj* punctual

ponctuer [pɔ̃ktɥe] *tr* to punctuate

pondération [pɔ̃derasjɔ̃] *f* balance; weighting

pondé·ré -rée [pɔ̃dere] *adj* moderate, well-balanced; weighted

pondérer [pɔ̃dere] §10 *tr* to balance; to weight

pondeuse [pɔ̃døz] *f* layer (*hen*); (coll) prolific woman

pondre [pɔ̃dr] *tr* to lay (*an egg*); (coll) to turn out (*a book*); (slang) to bear (*a child*) ‖ *intr* to lay

poney [pɔne] *m* pony

pont [pɔ̃] *m* bridge; (naut) deck; **faire le pont** (coll) to take the intervening day or days off; **pont aérien** airlift; **pont arrière** (aut) rear-axle assembly; **pont cantilever, pont à consoles** cantilever bridge; **ponts et chaussées** [pɔ̃zeʃose] highway department; **pont suspendu** suspension bridge

ponte [pɔ̃t] *f* egg laying; eggs

pontet [pɔ̃te] *m* trigger guard

pontife [pɔ̃tif] *m* pontiff

pont-levis [pɔ̃lvi] *m* (*pl* **ponts-levis**) drawbridge

ponton [pɔ̃tɔ̃] *m* pontoon; landing stage

pont-promenade [pɔ̃prɔmnad] *m* (*pl* **ponts-promenades**) promenade deck

pool [pul] *m* pool (*combine*)

pope [pɔp] *m* Orthodox priest

popeline [pɔplin] *f* poplin

popote [pɔpɔt] *adj invar* (coll) stay-at-home ‖ *f* (mil) mess; (coll) cooking; **faire la popote** (coll) to do the cooking oneself

populace [pɔpylas] *f* populace, rabble

populaire [pɔpyler] *adj* popular; vulgar, common

populariser [pɔpylarize] *tr* to popularize

popularité [pɔpylarite] *f* popularity

population [pɔpylasjɔ̃] *f* population

popu·leux [pɔpylø] **-leuse** [løz] *adj* populous; crowded

populo [pɔpylo] *m* (coll) rabble

porc [pɔr] *m* pig, hog; pork

porcelaine [pɔrsəlen] *f* porcelain; china

porcelet [pɔrsəle] *m* piglet

porc-épic [pɔrkepik] *m* (*pl* **porcs-épics** [pɔrkepik]) porcupine

porche [pɔrʃ] *m* porch, portico

porcher [pɔrʃe] *m* swineherd

porcherie [pɔrʃəri] *f* pigpen

pore [pɔr] *m* pore

po·reux [pɔrø] **-reuse** [røz] *adj* porous

pornographie [pɔrnɔgrafi] *f* pornography

porphyre [pɔrfir] *m* porphyry

port [pɔr] *m* port; carrying; wearing; bearing; shipping charges; **arriver à bon port** to arrive safe; **port d'attache** home port; **port d'escale** port of call; **port franc** duty-free; free port; **port payé** postpaid

portable [pɔrtabl] *adj* portable; wearable

portail [pɔrtaj] *m* portal, gate

por·tant [pɔrtɑ̃] **-tante** [tɑ̃t] *adj* bearing; lifting; **être bien portant** to be in good health ‖ *m* handle

porta·tif [pɔrtatif] **-tive** [tiv] *adj* portable

porte [pɔrt] *f* door; doorway; gate; **fausse porte** blind door; **porte à deux battants** double door; **porte à tambour** revolving door; **porte battante** swinging door; **porte cochère** covered carriage entrance

porte-à-faux [pɔrtafo] *m invar*—**en porte-à-faux** out of line; (fig) in an untenable position

porte-aiguilles [pɔrtegɥij] *m invar* needle case

porte-allumettes [pɔrtalymɛt] *m invar* matchbox

porte-assiette [pɔrtasjɛt] *m* (*pl* **-assiette** or **-assiettes**) place mat

porte-avions [pɔrtavjɔ̃] *m invar* aircraft carrier

porte-bagages [pɔrtbagaʒ] *m invar* baggage rack

porte-bannière [pɔrtbanjɛr] *mf* (*pl* **-bannière** or **-bannières**) colorbearer

porte-bonheur [pɔrtbɔnœr] *m invar* good-luck charm

porte-carte [pɔrtkart] *m* (*pl* **-carte** or **-cartes**) card case

porte-chapeaux [pɔrtʃapo] *m invar* hatrack

porte-cigarette [pɔrtsigarɛt] *m invar* cigarette holder

porte-cigarettes [pɔrtsigarɛt] *m invar* cigarette case

porte-clés or **porte-clefs** [pɔrtəkle] *m invar* key ring

porte-disques [pɔrtdisk] *m invar* record case

porte-documents [pɔrtdɔkymɑ̃] *m invar* letter case, portfolio

porte-drapeau [pɔrtdrapo] *m* (*pl* **-drapeau** or **-drapeaux**) standard-bearer

portée [pɔrte] *f* range, reach; import, significance; litter; (mus) staff; **à la portée de** within reach of; **à portée de la voix** within speaking distance; **à portée de l'oreille** within hearing distance; **hors de la portée de** out of reach of

portefaix [pɔrtəfɛ] *m* porter; dock hand

porte-fenêtre [pɔrtfənɛtr], [pɔrtəfnɛtr] *f* (*pl* **portes-fenêtres**) French window, French door

portefeuille [pɔrtəfœj] *m* portfolio; wallet, billfold

porteman·teau [pɔrtmɑ̃to] *m* (*pl* **-teaux**) clothes tree; **en portemanteau** square (*shoulders*)

porte-mine [pɔrtəmin] *m* (*pl* **-mine** or **mines**) mechanical pencil

porte-monnaie [pɔrtmɔne] *m invar* change purse

porte-parapluies [pɔrtparaplɥi] *m invar* umbrella stand

porte-parole [pɔrtparɔl] *m invar* spokesman, mouthpiece

porte-plume [pɔrtəplym] *m invar* penholder; **porte-plume réservoir** fountain pen

porter [pɔrte] *tr* to carry; to bear; to wear; to propose (*a toast*); **être porté à** to be inclined to; **être porté sur** to have a weakness for; **porter à l'écran** (mov) to put on the screen ‖ *intr* to carry; **porter sur** to bear down on, to emphasize; to be aimed at ‖ *ref* to be worn; to proceed, to go; to be, e.g., **comment vous portez-vous?** how are you?; **se porter à** to indulge in; **se porter candidat** to run as a candidate

porte-savon [pɔrtsavɔ̃] *m* (*pl* **-savon** or **-savons**) soap dish

porte-serviettes [pɔrtservjɛt] *m invar* towel rack

por·teur [pɔrtœr] **-teuse** [tøz] *mf* porter; bearer; holder

porte-vêtement [pɔrtəvetmɑ̃] *m invar* clothes hanger

porte-voix [pɔrtəvwa] *m invar* megaphone; **mettre les mains en porte-voix** to cup one's hands

por·tier [pɔrtje] **-tière** [tjɛr] *mf* concierge ‖ *m* doorman ‖ *f* door (*of car*); portiere

portillon [pɔrtijɔ̃] *m* gate; (rr) side gate (*at crossing*); **refouler du portillon** (slang) to have bad breath

portion [pɔrsjɔ̃] *f* portion; share

portique [pɔrtik] *m* portico

porto [pɔrto] *m* port wine

portori·cain [pɔrtorikɛ̃] **-caine** [ken] *adj* Puerto Rican ‖ (*cap*) *mf* Puerto Rican

Porto Rico [pɔrtoriko] *f* Puerto Rico

portrait [pɔrtre] *m* portrait; **être tout le portrait de** to be the very image of; **portrait à mi-corps** half-length portrait; **portrait de face** full-faced portrait

portraitiste [pɔrtretist] *mf* portrait painter

portu·gais [pɔrtyge] **-gaise** [gez] *adj* Portuguese ‖ *m* Portuguese (*language*) ‖ (*cap*) *mf* Portuguese (*person*)

Portugal [pɔrtygal] *m*—**le Portugal** Portugal

pose [poz] *f* pose; laying, setting in place; (phot) exposure

po·sé **-sée** [poze] *adj* poised, steady; trained (*voice*)

posément [pozemɑ̃] *adv* calmly, steadily, carefully

posemètre [pozmetr] *m* (phot) light meter, exposure meter

poser [poze] *tr* to place; to arrange; to ask (*a question*); to set up (*a principle*) ‖ *intr* to pose ‖ *ref* to pose; to alight; to land; **se poser en** to set oneself up as

po·seur [pozœr] **-seuse** [zøz] *mf* layer; poseur; phony; **poseur d'affiches** billposter

posi·tif [pozitif] **-tive** [tiv] *adj* & *m* positive

position [pozisjɔ̃] *f* position

posséder [pɔsede] §10 *tr* to possess, own; to have a command of, to know perfectly ‖ *ref* to control oneself

possession [pɔsesjɔ̃] *f* possession

possibilité [pɔsibilite] *f* possibility

possible [pɔsibl] *adj & m* possible

postage [pɔstaʒ] *m* mailing

pos·tal -tale [pɔstal] *adj (pl -taux* [to]) postal

postdate [pɔstdat] *f* postdate

postdater [pɔstdate] *tr* to postdate

poste [pɔst] *m* post; station; set; position, job; **poste de douane** port of entry; **poste d'émetteur** broadcasting station; **poste de radio** radio set; **poste de repérage** tracking station; **poste de secours** first-aid station; **poste des malades** (nav) sick bay; **poste d'essence** gas station; **poste d'incendie** fire station; **poste supplémentaire** (telp) extension ‖ *f* post, mail; **mettre à la poste** to mail; **poste restante** general delivery; **postes** post office department

poster [pɔste] *tr* to post ‖ *ref* to lie in wait

postérité [pɔsterite] *f* posterity

posthume [pɔstym] *adj* posthumous

postiche [pɔstiʃ] *adj* false; detachable ‖ *m* toupee; switch, false hair

pos·tier -tière [pɔstje] [tjer] *mf* postal clerk

postscolaire [pɔstskɔler] *adj* adult (*education*); extension (*courses*)

post-scriptum [pɔstskriptɔm] *m invar* postscript

postu·lant -lante [pɔstylã] [lãt] *mf* applicant, candidate; postulant

postuler [pɔstyle] *tr* to apply for ‖ *intr* to apply; **postuler pour** to represent (*a client*)

posture [pɔstyr] *f* posture; situation

pot [po] *m* pot; pitcher, jug; jar; can; **découvrir le pot aux roses** (coll) to discover the secret; **payer les pots cassés** (coll) to pay the piper; **pot à bière** beer mug; **pot à fleurs** flowerpot; **pot d'échappement** (aut) muffler; **pot de noir** cloudy weather; **pot d'étain** pewter tankard; **tourner autour du pot** (coll) to beat about the bush

potable [pɔtabl] *adj* drinkable; (coll) acceptable, passable

potache [pɔtaʃ] *m* (coll) schoolboy

potage [pɔtaʒ] *m* soup; **potage de maïs** hominy; **pour tout potage** (lit) all told

pota·ger -gère [pɔtaʒe] [ʒer] *adj* vegetable ‖ *m* vegetable garden

potasse [pɔtas] *f* potash

potasser [pɔtase] *tr* (coll) to bone up on ‖ *intr* (coll) to grind away

potas·seur potas·seuse [pɔtasœr] [pɔtasøz] *mf* (coll) grind

potassium [pɔtasjɔm] *m* potassium

pot-au-feu [pɔtofø] *adj invar* (coll) home-loving ‖ *m invar* beef stew

pot-de-vin [pɔdvɛ̃] *m (pl* **pots-de-vin**) bribe, money under the table

po·teau [pɔto] *m (pl* **-teaux**) post, pole; **poteau de but** goal post; **poteau indicateur** signpost

pote·lé -lée [pɔtle] *adj* chubby

potence [pɔtãs] *f* gallows; bracket

potentat [pɔtãta] *m* potentate

poten·tiel -tielle [pɔtãsjel] *adj & m* potential

poterie [pɔtri] *f* pottery; metalware; **poterie mordorée** lusterware

poterne [pɔtern] *f* postern

potiche [pɔtiʃ] *f* large Oriental vase; (fig) figurehead

potin [pɔtɛ̃] *m* piece of gossip; racket; **faire du potin** (coll) to raise a row; **potins** gossip

potiner [pɔtine] *intr* to gossip

potion [posjɔ̃] *f* potion

potiron [pɔtirɔ̃] *m* pumpkin; **potiron lumineux** jack-o'-lantern

pou [pu] *m (pl* **poux**) louse

poubelle [pubel] *f* garbage can

pouce [pus] *m* thumb; big toe; inch; **manger sur le pouce** (coll) to eat on the run

poudre [pudr] *f* powder; face powder; **en poudre** powdered; granulated (*sugar*); **il n'a pas inventé la poudre** (coll) he's not so smart; **jeter de la poudre aux yeux de** to deceive; **poudre dentifrice** tooth powder; **se mettre de la poudre** to powder one's nose

poudrer [pudre] *tr* to powder

poudrerie [pudrəri] *f* powder mill

pou·dreux -dreuse [pudrø] [drøz] *adj* powdery; dusty ‖ *f* sugar shaker

poudrier [pudrije] *m* compact

poudrière [pudrijer] *f* powder magazine; (fig) powder keg

poudroyer [pudrwaje] §47 *intr* to raise the dust; to shine through the dust

pouf [puf] *m* hassock, pouf ‖ *interj* plop!; **faire pouf** (slang) to flop

pouffer [pufe] *intr* to burst out laughing

pouil·leux -leuse [pujø] [pujøz] *adj* lousy; sordid ‖ *mf* person covered with lice

pouillot [pujo] *m* (orn) warbler

poulailler [pulaje] *m* henhouse; (theat) peanut gallery

poulain [pulɛ̃] *m* colt, foal

poule [pul] *f* hen; chicken; (*in games*) pool; jackpot; (turf) sweepstakes; (coll) skirt, dame; (slang) tart, mistress; **ma poule** (coll) my pet; **poule au pot** chicken stew; **poule d'Inde** turkey hen; **poule mouillée** (coll) milksop; **tuer la poule aux œufs d'or** to kill the goose that lays the golden eggs

poulet [pule] *m* chicken, (coll) love letter; **mon petit poulet** (coll) my pet; **poulet d'Inde** turkey cock

poulette [pulet] *f* pullet; (coll) gal; **ma poulette** (coll) darling

pouliche [puliʃ] *f* filly

poulie [puli] *f* pulley; block

poulpe [pulp] *m* octopus

pouls [pu] *m* pulse; **tâter le pouls à** to feel the pulse of

poumon [pumɔ̃] *m* lung

poupe [pup] *f* (naut) stern, poop

poupée [pupe] *f* doll; dummy; sore finger; (mach) headstock

pou·pon [pupɔ̃] **-ponne** [pɔn] *mf* baby; chubby-faced youngster

pouponnière [pupɔnjɛr] f nursery

pour [pur] m—**le pour et le contre** the pros and the cons ‖ adv—**pour lors** then; **pour peu que** however little; **pour que** in order that; **pour . . . que** however, e.g., **pour charmante qu'elle soit** however charming she may be ‖ prep for; in order to; **pour ainsi dire** so to speak; **pour cent** per cent

pourboire [purbwar] m tip

pour·ceau [purso] m (pl **-ceaux**) swine, hog, pig

pourcentage [pursɑ̃taʒ] m percentage

pourchasser [purʃase] tr to hound

pourlécher [purleʃe] §10 ref to smack one's lips

pourparlers [purparle] mpl talks, parley, conference

pourpoint [purpwɛ̃] m doublet

pourpre [purpr] adj purple ‖ m purple (violescent) ‖ f purple (deep red, crimson)

pourquoi [purkwa] m why; **le pourquoi et le comment** the why and the wherefore ‖ adv & conj why; **pourquoi pas?** why not?

pour·ri -rie [puri] adj rotten; spoiled ‖ m rotten part

pourrir [purir] tr, intr, & ref to rot; to spoil; to corrupt

pourriture [purityr] f rot; decay; corruption

poursuite [pursɥit] f pursuit; (law) action, suit; (coll) spotlight

poursui·vant [pursɥivɑ̃] **-vante** [vɑ̃t] mf pursuer; (law) plaintiff

poursuivre [pursɥivr] §67 tr to pursue, chase; to proceed with; to persecute; to sue ‖ intr to continue ‖ ref to be continued

pourtant [purtɑ̃] adv however, nevertheless, yet

pourtour [purtur] m circumference

pourvoi [purvwa] m (law) appeal

pourvoir [purvwar] §54 tr—**pourvoir de** to supply with, to provide with; to favor with ‖ intr—**pourvoir à** to provide for, to attend to ‖ ref (law) to appeal

pourvoyeur [purvwajœr] **pourvoyeuse** [purvwajøz] mf provider, supplier; caterer; **pourvoyeurs** gun crew

pourvu que [purvykə] conj provided that

pousse [pus] f shoot, sprout

pous·sé -sée [puse] adj elaborate; searching, exhaustive ‖ f push, shove; thrust; rise; pressure; (rok) thrust

pousse-café [puskafe] m invar liqueur

pousser [puse] tr to push, to shove, to egg on, to urge; to utter (a cry); to heave (a sigh); **pousser plus loin** to carry further ‖ intr to push, shove; to grow; to push on ‖ ref to push oneself forward

poussette [puset] f baby carriage

poussier [pusje] m coal dust

poussière [pusjɛr] f dust; powder; **poussière d'eau** spray; **une pous-**

sière a trifle; **une poussière de a lot of**

poussié·reux [pusjerø] **-reuse** [røz] adj dusty; powdery

pous·sif [pusif] **pous·sive** [pusiv] adj wheezy

poussin [pusɛ̃] m chick

poussoir [puswar] m push button

poutre [putr] f beam; joist; girder

poutrelle [putrɛl] f small girder

pouvoir [puvwar] m power; **pouvoir d'achat** purchasing power ‖ §55 tr to be able to do; **je n'y puis rien** I can't or cannot help it, I can do nothing about it ‖ intr to be able; **on ne peut mieux** couldn't be better; **on ne peut plus** I (we, they, etc.) can do no more; I'm (we're, they're, etc.) all in ‖ aux used to express 1) ability, e.g., **elle peut prédire l'avenir** she is able to predict the future, she can predict the future; 2) permission, e.g., **vous pouvez partir** you may go; e.g., **puis-je partir?** may I go?; 3) possibility, e.g., **il peut pleuvoir** it may rain; e.g., **il a pu oublier son parapluie** he may have forgotten his umbrella; 4) optative, e.g., **puisse-t-il venir!** may he come! ‖ impers ref—**il se peut que** it is possible that, e.g., **il se peut qu'il vienne ce soir** it is possible that he may come this evening, he may come this evening; **il se pourrait bien que** it might well be that, e.g., **il se pourrait bien qu'il vînt ce soir** it might well be that he will come this evening, he might come this evening ‖ ref to be possible; **cela ne se peut pas** that is not possible

pragmatique [pragmatik] adj pragmatic(al)

prairie [preri], [prɛri] f meadow; **les Prairies** the prairie

praticable [pratikabl] adj practicable; passable ‖ m practicable stage property; (mov, telv) camera platform

prati·cien [pratisjɛ̃] **-cienne** [sjɛn] mf practitioner

prati·quant [pratikɑ̃] **-quante** [kɑ̃t] adj practicing (e.g., Catholic); churchy ‖ mf churchgoer

pratique [pratik] adj practical ‖ f practice; contact, company; customer; **libre pratique** freedom of worship; (naut) freedom from quarantine

pratiquement [pratikmɑ̃] adv practically, in practice

pratiquer [pratike] tr to practice; to cut, make (e.g., a hole); to frequent; to read a great deal of ‖ intr to practice (said, e.g., of doctor); to practice one's religion ‖ ref to be practiced, done; to rule, prevail (said of prices)

pré [pre] m meadow; **sur le pré** on the field of honor (dueling ground)

préalable [prealabl] adj previous; preliminary ‖ m prerequisite; **au préalable** before, in advance

préambule [preɑ̃byl] m preamble

préau [preo] m (pl **préaux**) yard

préavis [preavi] m advance warning;

avec **préavis** person-to-person (*telephone call*)

précaire [preker] *adj* precarious

précaution [prekosjɔ̃] *f* precaution

précautionner [prekosjɔne] *tr* to caution ‖ *intr* to be on one's guard

précaution·neux [prekosjonø] **précaution·neuse** [prekosjonøz] *adj* precautious

précé·dent [presedɑ̃] **-dente** [dɑ̃t] *adj* preceding ‖ *m* precedent

précéder [presede] §10 *tr & intr* to precede

précepte [presɛpt] *m* precept

précep·teur [preseptœr] **-trice** [tris] *mf* tutor

prêche [prɛʃ] *m* sermon

prêcher [preʃe] *tr* to preach; to preach to ‖ *intr* to preach; **prêcher d'exemple** to practice what one preaches

prê·cheur [preʃœr] **-cheuse** [ʃøz] *adj* preaching ‖ *mf* sermonizer

pré·cieux [presjø] **-cieuse** [sjøz] *adj* precious; valuable; affected

préciosité [presjozite] *f* preciosity (*French literary style corresponding to English euphuism*)

précipice [presipis] *m* precipice

précipi·té -tée [presipite] *adj* hurried, precipitous ‖ *m* precipitate

précipiter [presipite] *tr* to hurl ‖ *ref* to hurl oneself; to precipitate; to hurry, rush

pré·cis [presi] **-cise** [siz] *adj* precise; sharp, e.g., **trois heures précises** three o'clock sharp ‖ *m* abstract, summary

préciser [presize] *tr* to specify ‖ *intr* to be precise ‖ *ref* to become clear; to take shape, to jell

précision [presizjɔ̃] *f* precision; **précisions** data

préci·té -tée [presite] *adj* aforementioned

précoce [prekɔs] *adj* precocious; (*bot*) early

précon·çu -çue [prekɔsy] *adj* preconceived

préconiser [prekɔnize] *tr* to advocate, recommend

précurseur [prekyrsœr] *adj masc* precursory ‖ *m* forerunner, harbinger

prédateur [predatœr] *adj masc* predatory ‖ *m* predatory animal

prédécesseur [predesesœr] *m* predecessor

prédicateur [predikatœr] *m* preacher

prédiction [prediksjɔ̃] *f* prediction

prédire [predir] §40 *tr* to predict

prédisposer [predispoze] *tr* to predispose

prédomi·nant [predɔminɑ̃] **-nante** [nɑ̃t] *adj* predominant

préémi·nent [preeminɑ̃] **-nente** [nɑ̃t] *adj* preeminent

préfabri·qué -quée [prefabrike] *adj* prefabricated

préface [prefas] *f* preface

préfacer [prefase] §51 *tr* to preface

préfecture [prefektyr] *f* prefecture; **préfecture de police** police headquarters

préférable [preferabl] *adj* preferable

préférence [preferɑ̃s] *f* preference

préférer [prefere] §10 *tr* to prefer

préfet [prefɛ] *m* prefect; **préfet de police** police commissioner

préfixe [prefiks] *m* prefix

préfixer [prefikse] *tr* to prefix

préhistorique [preistɔrik] *adj* prehistoric

préjudice [preʒydis] *m* prejudice, detriment; **porter préjudice à** to injure, to harm; **sans préjudice de** without affecting

préjudiciable [preʒydisjabl] *adj* detrimental

préjudicier [preʒydisje] *intr* (with *dat*) to harm, damage

préjugé [preʒyʒe] *m* prejudice

préjuger [preʒyʒe] §38 *tr* to foresee ‖ *intr*—**préjuger de** to prejudge

prélart [prelar] *m* tarpaulin

prélasser [prelase] *ref* to lounge

prélat [prela] *m* prelate

prélèvement [prelɛvmɑ̃] *m* deduction; sample; levy

prélever [prelve] §2 *tr* to set aside, deduct; to take (*a sample*); to levy; **prélever à** to take from

préliminaire [preliminer] *adj & m* preliminary

prélude [prelyd] *m* prelude

préluder [prelyde] *intr* to warm up (*said of singer, musician, etc.*); **préluder à** to prelude

prématu·ré -rée [prematyre] *adj* premature

préméditer [premedite] *tr* to premeditate

prémices [premis] *fpl* first fruits; beginning

pre·mier [prəmje] **-mière** [mjer] *adj* first; raw (*materials*); prime (*number*); the First, e.g., **Jean premier** John the First ‖ (*when standing before noun*) *adj* first; prime (*minister*); maiden (*voyage*); early (*infancy*) ‖ *m* first; **jeune premier** leading man; **premier de cordée** leader ‖ *f* first; first class; (*theat*) première; **jeune première** leading lady ‖ *pron* (*masc & fem*) first

premier-né [prəmjene] **première-née** [prəmjerne] (*pl* **premiers-nés**) *adj & mf* first-born

prémisse [premis] *f* premise

prémonition [premɔnisjɔ̃] *f* premonition

prémunir [premynir] *tr* to forewarn ‖ *ref*—**se prémunir contre** to protect oneself against

pre·nant [prənɑ̃] **-nante** [nɑ̃t] *adj* sticky; winning, pleasing

prendre [prɑ̃dr] §56 *tr* to take; to take on; to take up; to catch; to get (*obtain and bring*); to steal (*a kiss*); to buy (*a ticket*); to make (*an appointment*); **à tout prendre** all things considered; **prendre de l'âge** to be getting old; **prendre la mer** to take to sea; **prendre l'eau** to leak; **prendre le large** to take to the open sea; **prendre q.ch. à qn** to take s.th. from s.o.; to charge s.o. s.th. (*i.e., a cer-*

tain sum of money); **prendre son temps** to take one's time ‖ *intr* to catch (*said of fire*); to take root; to form (*said of ice*); to set (*said of mortar*); to stick (*to a pan or dish*); to catch on (*said of a style*); to turn (*right or left*); **prendre à droite** to bear to the right; **qu'est-ce qui lui prend?** what's come over him? ‖ *ref* to get caught, to catch (*e.g., on a nail*); to congeal; to clot; to curdle; to jam; to take from each other; **pour qui se prend-il?** who does he think he is?; **s'en prendre à qn de q.ch.** to blame s.o. for s.th.; **se prendre à** to begin to; **se prendre d'amitié** to strike up a friendship; **se prendre de vin** to get drunk; **s'y prendre** to go about it

pre·neur [prənœr] **-neuse** [nøz] *mf* taker; buyer; payee; lessee

prénom [prenɔ̃] *m* first name

prénommer [prenɔme] *tr* to name ‖ *ref* —**il (elle, etc.) se prénomme** his (her, etc.) first name is

préoccupation [preɔkypɑsjɔ̃] *f* preoccupation

préoccuper [preɔkype] *tr* to preoccupy ‖ *ref*—**se préoccuper de** to pay attention to; to be concerned about

prépara·teur [preparatœr] **-trice** [tris] *mf* laboratory assistant

préparatifs [preparatif] *mpl* preparations

préparation [preparɑsjɔ̃] *f* preparation; notice, warning

préparatoire [preparatwar] *adj* preparatory

préparer [prepare] *tr, intr,* & *ref* to prepare

prépondé·rant [prepɔ̃derɑ̃] **-rante** [rɑ̃t] *adj* preponderant

prépo·sé -sée [prepoze] *mf* employee, clerk; **préposé de la douane** customs officer; **préposée au vestiaire** hatcheck girl

préposer [prepoze] *tr*—**préposer qn à q.ch.** to put s.o. in charge of s.th.

préposition [prepozisjɔ̃] *f* preposition

prérogative [prerogativ] *f* prerogative

près [pre] *adv* near; **à beaucoup près** by far; **à cela près** except for that; **à peu d'exceptions près** with few exceptions; **à peu près** about, practically; **à . . . près** except for; within, *e.g.*, **je peux vous dire l'heure à cinq minutes près** I can tell you what time it is within five minutes; **au plus près** to the nearest point; **de près** close; closely; **ici près** near here; **près de** near; nearly, about; alongside, at the side of; **près de** + *inf* about to + *inf;* **tout près** nearby, right here ‖ *prep* near; to, at

présage [prezaʒ] *m* presage, foreboding

présager [prezaʒe] §38 *tr* to presage, forebode; to anticipate

pré-salé [presale] *m* (*pl* **prés-salés**) salt-meadow sheep; salt-meadow mutton

presbyte [presbit] *adj* far-sighted ‖ *mf* far-sighted person

presbytère [presbiter] *m* presbytery

presbyté·rien [presbiterjɛ̃] **-rienne** [rjen] *adj* & *mf* Presbyterian

presbytie [presbisi] *f* far-sightedness

prescription [preskripsjɔ̃] *f* prescription

prescrire [preskrir] §25 *tr* to prescribe ‖ *ref* to be prescribed

préséance [preseɑ̃s] *f* precedence

présence [prezɑ̃s] *f* presence; attendance; **en présence** face to face

pré·sent [prezɑ̃] **-sente** [zɑ̃t] *adj* present ‖ *m* present, gift; (*gram*) present; **les présents** those present

présentable [prezɑ̃tabl] *adj* presentable

présenta·teur [prezɑ̃tatœr] **-trice** [tris] *mf* (*rad*) announcer; **présentateur de disques** disk jockey

présentation [prezɑ̃tɑsjɔ̃] *f* presentation; introduction; appearance; look, form (*of a new product*)

présentement [prezɑ̃tmɑ̃] *adv* right now

présenter [prezɑ̃te] *tr* to present; to introduce; to offer; to pay (*one's respects*) ‖ *ref* to present oneself; to present itself; **se présenter à** to be a candidate for

présérie [preseri] *f* (*com*) trial run, sample run

préservatif [prezervatif] *m* preventive; condom

préserver [prezerve] *tr* to preserve

présidence [prezidɑ̃s] *f* presidency; chairmanship; presidential mansion

prési·dent [prezidɑ̃] **-dente** [dɑ̃t] *mf* president; chairman; presiding judge ‖ *f* president's wife; chairwoman; **madame la présidente** madam chairman

présiden·tiel -tielle [prezidɑ̃sjel] *adj* presidential

présider [prezide] *tr* to preside over ‖ *intr* to preside; **présider à** to preside over

présomp·tif [prezɔ̃ptif] **-tive** [tiv] *adj* presumptive, presumed

présomption [prezɔ̃psjɔ̃] *f* presumption

présomp·tueux [prezɔ̃ptɥø] **-tueuse** [tɥøz] *adj* presumptuous

presque [presk(ə)] *adv* almost, nearly; **presque jamais** hardly ever; **presque personne** scarcely anybody

presqu'île [preskil] *f* peninsula

pres·sant [presɑ̃] **pres·sante** [presɑ̃t] *adj* pressing, urgent

presse [pres] *f* press; hurry, rush; crowd; hand screw, clamp; **mettre sous presse** to go to press

pres·sé -sée [prese] *adj* pressed; pressing, urgent; squeezed

presse-bouton [presbutɔ̃] *adj invar* push-button (*warfare*)

presse-citron [presitrɔ̃] *m invar* lemon squeezer

pressentiment [presɑ̃timɑ̃] *m* presentiment, foreboding

pressentir [presɑ̃tir] §41 *tr* to have a foreboding of; to sound out

presse-papiers [prespapje] *m invar* paperweight

presse-purée [prespyre] *m invar* potato masher

presser [prese], [prese] *tr* to press; to squeeze; to hurry, hasten || *intr* to be urgent || *ref* to hurry; **se presser à** to crowd around

pressing [presiŋ] *m* dry cleaner's, tailor shop

pression [presjɔ̃] *f* pressure; snap fastener; **à la pression** on draught; **pression artérielle** blood pressure

pressoir [preswar] *m* press

pressurer [presyre] *tr* to press, squeeze; to bleed white, to wring money out of

pressuriser [presyrize] *tr* to pressurize

prestance [prestɑ̃s] *f* commanding appearance, dignified bearing

prestation [prestasjɔ̃] *f* taking (*of oath*); tax; allotment, allowance, benefit

preste [prest] *adj* nimble

prestidigita·teur [prestidiʒitatœr] **-trice** [tris] *mf* magician

prestidigitation [prestidiʒitasjɔ̃] *f* sleight of hand, legerdemain

prestige [prestiʒ] *m* prestige; illusion, magic

presti·gieux [prestiʒjø] **-gieuse** [ʒjøz] *adj* prestigious, famous; marvelous

présumer [prezyme] *tr* to presume; to presume to be || *intr* to presume; **présumer de** to presume upon

présupposer [presypoze] *tr* to presuppose

présure [prezyr] *f* rennet

prêt [pre] **prête** [pret] *adj* ready; **prêt à porter** ready-to-wear, ready-made; **prêt à tout** ready for anything || *m* loan

prêt-à-porter [pretaporte] *m* (*pl* **prêts-à-porter** [pretaporte]) ready-to-wear, ready-made clothes

prêt-bail [prebaj] *m invar* lend-lease

préten·dant [pretɑ̃dɑ̃] **-dante** [dɑ̃t] *mf* pretender || *m* suitor

prétendre [pretɑ̃dr] *tr* to claim; to require || *intr*—**prétendre à** to aspire to; to lay claim to

préten·du·due [pretɑ̃dy] *adj* so-called, alleged || *m* fiancé || *f* fiancée

prête-nom [pretnɔ̃] *m* (*pl* **-noms**) dummy, figurehead, straw man

prétentaine [pretɑ̃ten] *f*—**courir la prétentaine** (coll) to be on the loose; (coll) to have many love affairs

préten·tieux [pretɑ̃sjø] **-tieuse** [sjøz] *adj* pretentious

prétention [pretɑ̃sjɔ̃] *f* pretention, pretense; claim, pretensions

prêter [prete], [prete] *tr* to lend; to give (*e.g., help*); to pay (*attention*); to take (*an oath*); to impart (*e.g., luster*); to attribute, ascribe || *intr* to lend; to stretch; **prêter à** to lend itself to || *ref*—**se prêter à** to lend itself to; to be a party to, to countenance; to indulge in

prê·teur [pretœr] **-teuse** [tøz] *mf* lender; **prêteur sur gages** pawnbroker

prétexte [pretekst] *m* pretext

prétexter [pretekste] *tr* to give as a pretext

prétonique [pretɔnik] *adj* pretonic

prêtre [pretr] *m* priest

prêtresse [pretres] *f* priestess

prêtrise [pretriz] *f* priesthood

preuve [prœv] *f* proof, evidence

preux [prø] *adj masc* valiant || *m* doughty knight

prévaloir [prevalwar] §71 (*subj* **prévale**, etc.) *intr* to prevail || *ref*—**se prévaloir de** to avail oneself of; to pride oneself on

prévarication [prevarikasjɔ̃] *f* breach of trust

prévariquer [prevarike] *intr* to betray one's trust

prévenance [prevnɑ̃s] *f* kindness, thoughtfulness

préve·nant [prevnɑ̃] **-nante** [nɑ̃t] *adj* attentive, considerate; prepossessing

prévenir [prevnir] §72 *tr* to anticipate; to avert, forestall; to ward off, to prevent; to notify, inform; to bias, to prejudice

préven·tif [prevɑ̃tif] **-tive** [tiv] *adj* preventive; pretrial (*detention*)

prévention [prevɑ̃sjɔ̃] *f* bias, prejudice; custody, imprisonment; prevention (*of accidents*); **prévention routière** traffic police; road safety

préve·nu·nue [prevny] *adj* biased, prejudiced; forewarned; accused || *mf* prisoner, accused, defendant

prévision [previzjɔ̃] *f* anticipation, estimate; **prévision du temps** weather forecast; **prévisions** expectations

prévoir [prevwar] §57 *tr* to foresee, anticipate; to forecast

prévoyance [prevwajɑ̃s] *f* foresight

prévoyant [prevwajɑ̃] **prévoyante** [prevwajɑ̃t] *adj* far-sighted, provident

prie-dieu [pridjø] *m invar* prie-dieu || *f* praying mantis

prier [prije] *tr* to ask, to beg; to pray (*God*); **je vous en prie!** I beg your pardon!; by all means!; you are welcome!; please have some!; **je vous prie!** please!; **prier qn de** + *inf* to ask, to beg s.o. to + *inf* || *intr* to pray

prière [prijer] *f* prayer; **prière de . . . please . . . ; prière d'insérer** publisher's insert for reviewers

primaire [primer] *adj* primary; first (*offender*); (coll) narrow-minded || *m* (elec) primary; (coll) primitive

primat [prima] *m* (eccl) primate

primate [primat] *m* (zool) primate

primauté [primote] *f* supremacy

prime [prim] *adj* early (*youth*); (math) prime || *f* premium; bonus; free gift; (eccl) prime; **prime de transport** traveling expenses

primer [prime] *tr* to excel; to take priority over; to award a prize to

primerose [primroz] *f* hollyhock

primesau·tier [primsotje] **-tière** [tjer] *adj* impulsive, quick

primeur [primœr] *f* freshness; first fruit; early vegetable; (journ) beat;

scoop; **primeurs** fruits and vegetables out of season

primevère [primver] f primrose

primi·tif [primitif] **-tive** [tiv] adj primitive; original, early; primary (colors; tense) || mf primitive

primo [primo] adv firstly

primor·dial -diale [primordjal] adj (pl **-diaux** [djo]) primordial; fundamental, prime, primary

prince [prɛ̃s] m prince; **prince de Galles** Prince of Wales

princesse [prɛ̃ses] f princess

prin·cier [prɛ̃sje] **-cière** [sjer] adj princely

princi·pal ·pale [prɛ̃sipal] adj & m (pl **-paux** [po]) principal, chief

principauté [prɛ̃sipote] f principality

principe [prɛ̃sip] m principle; beginning; source

printa·nier [prɛ̃tanje] **-nière** [njer] adj spring; springlike

printemps [prɛ̃tɑ̃] m spring; springtime; **au printemps** in the spring

priorité [prijorite] f priority; right of way; **de priorité** preferred (stock); main (road); **priorité à droite, priorité à gauche** (public sign) yield

pris [pri] **prise** [priz] adj set, frozen; **être pris** to be busy; **pris de vin** drunk || f capture, seizure; taking; hold; setting; tap, faucet; (med) dose; (naut) prize; **donner prise à** to lay oneself open to; **être aux prises avec** to be struggling with; **hors de prise** out of gear; **lâcher prise** to let go; **prise d'air** ventilator; **prise d'antenne** (rad) lead-in; **prise d'armes** military parade; **prise d'eau** water faucet; hydrant; **prise de bec** (coll) quarrel; **prise de conscience** awakening, awareness; **prise de courant** (elec) plug; (elec) tap, outlet; **prise de position** statement of opinion; **prise de sang** blood specimen; **prise de son** recording; **prise de tabac** pinch of snuff; **prise de terre** (elec) ground connection; **prise de vue(s)** (phot) shot, picture taking; **prise de vue directe** (telv) live broadcast; **prise directe** high gear

prisée [prize] f appraisal

priser [prize] tr to value; to snuff up || intr to take snuff

pri·seur [prizœr] **-seuse** [zøz] mf snuffer || m appraiser

prisme [prism] m prism

prison [prizɔ̃] f prison

prison·nier [prizɔnje] **prison·nière** [prizɔnjer] mf prisoner

privautés [privote] fpl liberties

pri·vé ·vée [prive] adj private; tame, pet || m private life

priver [prive] tr to deprive || ref to deprive oneself; **se priver de** to do without, to abstain from

privilège [privilɛʒ] m privilege

privilé·gié ·giée [privileʒje] adj privileged; preferred (stock)

prix [pri] m price; prize; value; **à aucun prix** not at any price; by no means; **à tout prix** at all costs; **au prix de** at the price of; at the rate of; compared with; **dans mes prix** within my means; **grand prix** championship race; **hors de prix** at a prohibitive cost; **prix courant** list price; **prix de départ** upset price; **prix de détail** retail price; **prix de fabrique** factory price; **prix de gros** wholesale price; **prix de la vie** cost of living; **prix de location** rent; **prix de revient** cost price; **prix de vente** selling price; **prix fixe** table d'hôte

probabilité [probabilite] f probability

probable [probabl] adj probable, likely

pro·bant [probɑ̃] **-bante** [bɑ̃t] adj convincing; conclusive (evidence)

probe [prob] adj honest, upright

problème [problem] m problem

procédé [prosede] m process; procedure; tip (of cue); **procédés** proceedings; behavior

procéder [prosede] §10 intr to proceed; (with dat) to perform, carry out; **procéder de** to arise from

procédure [prosedyr] f procedure; proceedings

procès [prose] m lawsuit, case; trial; **intenter un procès à** to sue; to prosecute; **sans autre forme de procès** then and there, without appeal

proces·sif [prosesif] **proces·sive** [prosesiv] adj litigious

procession [prosesjɔ̃] f procession

processus [prosesys] m process

procès-verbal [proseverbal] m (pl **-verbaux** [verbo]) report; minutes; ticket (e.g., for speeding)

pro·chain [proʃɛ̃] **-chaine** [ʃen] adj next; impending; (lit) nearest, immediate; **la prochaine semaine** the next week; **la semaine prochaine** next week || m neighbor, fellow-man || f—**à la prochaine!** (coll) so long!

prochainement [proʃɛnmɑ̃] adv shortly

proche [proʃ] adj near; nearby; close (relative) || **proches** mpl close relatives || adv—**de proche en proche** little by little

proclamer [proklame] tr to proclaim

proclitique [proklitik] adj & m proclitic

procuration [prokyrasjɔ̃] f power of attorney; **par procuration** by proxy

procurer [prokyre] tr & ref to procure, to get

procureur [prokyrœr] m attorney; **procureur de la république** district attorney; **procureur général** attorney general

prodige [prodiʒ] m prodigy; wonder

prodi·gieux [prodiʒjø] **-gieuse** [ʒjøz] adj prodigious, wonderful; terrific

prodigue [prodig] adj prodigal, lavish || mf prodigal, spendthrift

prodiguer [prodige] tr to squander, waste; to lavish || ref to not spare oneself; to show off

prodrome [prodrom] m harbinger; introduction

produc·teur [prodyktœr] **-trice** [tris] adj productive || mf producer

produc·tif [prɔdyktif] **-tive** [tiv] *adj* productive; producing

production [prɔdyksjɔ̃] *f* production

produire [prɔdɥir] §19 *tr* to produce; to create; to introduce || *ref* to take place; to be produced; to show up

produit [prɔdɥi] *m* product; proceeds; offspring; **produit de luxe** luxury item; **produit pharmaceutique** patent medicine, drug; **produits agricoles** agricultural produce; **produits de beauté** cosmetics

proémi·nent [prɔeminã] **-nente** [nãt] *adj* prominent, protuberant

profane [prɔfan] *adj* profane; lay, uninformed || *mf* profane; layman

profaner [prɔfane] *tr* to profane; (fig) to prostitute

proférer [prɔfere] §10 *tr* to utter

professer [prɔfese] *tr* to profess; to teach || *intr* to teach

professeur [prɔfesœr] *m* teacher; professor

profession [prɔfesjɔ̃] *f* profession; occupation, trade

profession·nel -nelle [prɔfesjɔnel] *adj & mf* professional

profil [prɔfil] *m* profile; side face; cross section; skyline (*of city*)

profi·lé -lée [prɔfile] *adj* streamlined, aerodynamic

profiler [prɔfile] *tr* to profile || *ref* **se profiler sur** to stand out against

profit [prɔfi] *m* profit; **mettre à profit** to take advantage of; **profits et pertes** profit and loss

profitable [prɔfitabl] *adj* profitable

profiter [prɔfite] *intr* to profit; to grow; (with *dat*) to profit; **profiter à, dans,** or **en** to profit from

profi·teur [prɔfitœr] **-teuse** [tøz] *mf* profiteer

pro·fond [prɔfɔ̃] **-fonde** [fɔ̃d] *adj* profound; deep; low (*bow; voice*); **peu profond** shallow || *m* depths § *f* (slang) pocket || **profond** *adv* deep

profondément [prɔfɔ̃demã] *adv* profoundly, deeply; soundly; deep

profondeur [prɔfɔ̃dœr] *f* depth

progéniture [prɔʒenityr] *f* progeny; offspring, child

programma·teur [prɔgramatœr] **-trice** [tris] *mf* (mov, rad, telv) programmer

programmation [prɔgramasjɔ̃] *f* programming

programme [prɔgram] *m* program; **programme de prévoyance** retirement program; **programme des études** curriculum

programmer [prɔgrame] *tr* to program

program·meur [prɔgramœr] **programmeuse** [prɔgramøz] *mf* (comp) programmer

progrès [prɔgrɛ] *m* progress; **faire des progrès** to make progress

progresser [prɔgrese] *intr* to progress

progres·sif [prɔgresif] **progres·sive** [prɔgresiv] *adj* progressive

progressiste [prɔgresist] *adj & mf* progressive

prohiber [prɔibe] *tr* to prohibit

prohibition [prɔibisjɔ̃] *f* prohibition

proie [prwa], [prwɑ] *f* prey; **de proie** predatory; **en proie à** a prey to

projecteur [prɔʒɛktœr] *m* projector; searchlight; (mov) projection machine

projectile [prɔʒɛktil] *m* projectile; **projectile téléguidé** guided missile

projection [prɔʒɛksjɔ̃] *f* projection

projet [prɔʒɛ] *m* project; draft; sketch, plan; **faire des projets** to make plans; **projet de loi** bill

projeter [prɔʒte] §34 *tr* to project; to pour forth (*smoke*); to cast (*a shadow*); to plan || *intr* to plan

prolétaire [prɔletɛr] *m* proletarian

prolétariat [prɔletarja] *m* proletariat

proléta·rien [prɔletarjɛ̃] **-rienne** [rjɛn] *adj* proletarian

proliférer [prɔlifere] §10 *intr* to proliferate

prolifique [prɔlifik] *adj* prolific

prolixe [prɔliks] *adj* prolix

prologue [prɔlɔg] *m* prologue; preface

prolonger [prɔlɔ̃ʒe] §38 *tr* to prolong; to extend || *ref* to be prolonged; to continue, extend

promenade [prɔmnad] *f* promenade; walk; ride; drive; sail; **faire une promenade (en auto, à cheval, à motocyclette, en bateau,** etc.) to take a ride

promener [prɔmne] §2 *tr* to take for a walk or drive; to walk (*e.g., a dog*); to take along; **envoyer promener qn** (coll) to send s.o. packing; **promener ... sur** to run (*e.g., one's hand, eyes*) over || *ref* to stroll; to go for a walk, ride, drive, or sail; **allez vous promener!** get out of here!

prome·neur [prɔmnœr] **-neuse** [nøz] *mf* walker, stroller

promenoir [prɔmnwar] *m* ambulatory, cloister; (theat) standing room

promesse [prɔmes] *f* promise

promettre [prɔmetr] §42 *tr* to promise; **promettre q.ch. à qn** to promise s.th. to s.o. || *intr* to look promising; **promettre à qn de + inf** to promise s.o. to + *inf* || *ref* to promise oneself; (with *dat of reflex pron*) to promise oneself (*e.g., a vacation*); **se promettre de** to resolve to

pro·mis [prɔmi] **-mise** [miz] *adj* promised; **promis à** headed for

promiscuité [prɔmiskɥite] *f* indiscriminate mixture; lack of privacy

promontoire [prɔmɔ̃twar] *m* promontory

promo·teur [prɔmɔtœr] **-trice** [tris] *mf* promoter; originator

promotion [prɔmɔsjɔ̃] *f* promotion; uplift; class (*in school*)

promouvoir [prɔmuvwar] §45 (*pp* **promu**) *tr* to promote

prompt [prɔ̃] **prompte** [prɔ̃t] *adj* prompt, ready, quick

promptitude [prɔ̃tityd] *f* promptness

promulguer [prɔmylge] *tr* to promulgate

prône [pron] *m* homily

prôner [prone] *tr* to extol

pronom [prɔnɔ̃] *m* pronoun

pronomi·nal -nale [prɔnɔminal] *adj* (*pl*

-naux [no]) pronominal; reflexive (*verb*)

pronon·cé -cée [prɔnɔ̃se] *adj* marked; sharp (*curve*); prominent (*nose*)

prononcer [prɔnɔ̃se] §51 *tr* to pronounce; to utter; to deliver (*a speech*); to pass (*judgment*) ‖ *intr* to decide ‖ *ref* to be pronounced; to express an opinion

prononciation [prɔnɔ̃sjɑsjɔ̃] *f* pronunciation

pronostic [prɔnɔstik] *m* prognosis

pronostiquer [prɔnɔstike] *tr* to prognosticate

propagande [prɔpagɑ̃d] *f* propaganda; publicity, advertising

propager [prɔpaʒe] §38 *tr* to propagate; to spread ‖ *ref* to be propagated; to spread

propédeutique [prɔpedøtik] *f* (educ) preliminary study

propension [prɔpɑ̃sjɔ̃] *f* propensity

prophète [prɔfɛt] *m* prophet

prophétesse [prɔfetɛs] *f* prophetess

prophétie [prɔfesi] *f* prophecy

prophétiser [prɔfetize] *tr* to prophesy

prophylactique [prɔfilaktik] *adj* prophylactic

propice [prɔpis] *adj* propitious; lucky (*star*)

proportion [prɔpɔrsjɔ̃] *f* proportion; **en proportion de** in proportion to

proportion·né -née [prɔpɔrsjɔne] *adj* proportionate

proportion·nel -nelle [prɔpɔrsjɔnɛl] *adj* proportional

proportionner [prɔpɔrsjɔne] *tr* to proportion

propos [prɔpo] *m* remark; purpose; **à ce propos** in this connection; **à propos** by the way; timely, fitting; at the right moment; **à propos de** with regard to, concerning; **à tout propos** at every turn; **changer de propos** to change the subject; **de propos délibéré** on purpose; **des propos en l'air** idle talk; **hors de propos** out of place; irrelevant

proposer [prɔpoze] *tr* to propose; to nominate; to recommend (*s.o.*) ‖ *ref* to have in mind; to apply (*for a job*); **se proposer de** to intend to

proposition [prɔpozisjɔ̃] *f* proposition; proposal; clause

propre [prɔpr] *adj* clean, neat; original (*meaning*); proper (*name*); literal (*meaning*); **propre à** fit for, suited to ‖ (when standing before noun) *adj* own ‖ *m* characteristic; **au propre** in the literal sense; **c'est du propre!** (coll) what a dirty trick!; **en propre** in one's own right

pro·pret [prɔprɛ] **-prette** [prɛt] *adj* (coll) clean, bright

propreté [prɔprəte] *f* cleanliness, neatness

propriétaire [prɔprijetɛr] *mf* proprietor, owner; landowner ‖ *m* landlord ‖ *f* proprietress; landlady

propriété [prɔprijete] *f* property; propriety, appropriateness

propulseur [prɔpylsœr] *m* engine, motor; outboard motor; (rok) booster

propulsion [prɔpylsjɔ̃] *f* propulsion; **propulsion à réaction** jet propulsion

prorata [prɔrata] *m invar*—**au prorata de** in proportion to

proroger [prɔrɔʒe] §38 *tr* to postpone; to extend; to adjourn ‖ *ref* to be adjourned

prosaïque [prɔzaik] *adj* prosaic

prosateur [prɔzatœr] *m* prose writer

proscrire [prɔskrir] §25 *tr* to proscribe; to banish, outlaw

pros·crit [prɔskri] **-crite** [krit] *adj* banished ‖ *mf* outlaw

prose [proz] *f* prose; (coll) style (*of writing*)

prosélyte [prɔzelit] *mf* proselyte

prosodie [prɔzɔdi] *f* prosody

prospecter [prɔspɛkte] *tr* & *intr* to prospect

prospec·teur [prɔspɛktœr] **-trice** [tris] *mf* prospector

prospectus [prɔspɛktys] *m* prospectus; handbill

prospère [prɔspɛr] *adj* prosperous

prospérer [prɔspere] §10 *intr* to prosper, to thrive

prospérité [prɔsperite] *f* prosperity

prosternation [prɔstɛrnɑsjɔ̃] *f* prostration; groveling

prosterner [prɔstɛrne] *tr* to bend over ‖ *ref* to prostrate oneself; to grovel

prostituée [prɔstitɥe] *f* prostitute

prostituer [prɔstitɥe] *tr* to prostitute

prostration [prɔstrɑsjɔ̃] *f* prostration

pros·tré -trée [prɔstre] *adj* prostrate

protagoniste [prɔtagɔnist] *m* protagonist

prote [prɔt] *m* (typ) foreman

protection [prɔtɛksjɔ̃] *f* protection; **protection civile** civil defense

proté·gé -gée [prɔteʒe] *adj* guarded; arterial (*crossing*) ‖ *mf* protégé, dependent; pet

protège-cahier [prɔtɛʒkaje] *m* (*pl* -**cahiers**) notebook cover

protège-livre [prɔtɛʒlivr] *m* (*pl* -**livres**) dust jacket

protéger [prɔteʒe] §1 *tr* to protect; to be a patron of

protéine [prɔtein] *f* protein

protes·tant [prɔtɛstɑ̃] **-tante** [tɑ̃t] *adj* & *mf* Protestant; protestant

protestation [prɔtɛstɑsjɔ̃] *f* protest

protester [prɔtɛste] *tr* & *intr* to protest; **protester de** to protest

protêt [prɔtɛ] *m* (com) protest

protocole [prɔtɔkɔl] *m* protocol

proton [prɔtɔ̃] *m* proton

protoplasme [prɔtɔplasm] *m* protoplasm

prototype [prɔtɔtip] *m* prototype

protozoaire [prɔtɔzɔɛr] *m* protozoan

protubérance [prɔtyberɑ̃s] *f* protuberance

proue [pru] *f* prow, bow

prouesse [prɥɛs] *f* prowess

prouver [prɥve] *tr* to prove

provenance [prɔvnɑ̃s] *f* origin; **en provenance de** from

proven·çal -çale [prɔvɑ̃sal] (*pl* -**çaux** [so]) *adj* Provençal ‖ *m* Provençal (*language*) ‖ (*cap*) *mf* Provençal (*person*)

provenir [prɔvnir] §72 *intr (aux:* ÊTRE)
—**provenir de** to come from
proverbe [prɔvɛrb] *m* proverb
providence [prɔvidɑ̃s] *f* providence
providen•tiel -tielle [prɔvidɑ̃sjɛl] *adj*
providential
province [prɔvɛ̃s] *adj invar* (coll) pro-
vincial || *f* province; **la province** the
provinces (*all of France outside of
Paris*)
proviseur [prɔvizœr] *m* headmaster
provision [prɔvizjɔ̃] *f* stock, store; deposit; **aller aux provisions** to go
shopping; **faire provision de** to stock
up on; **provisions** provisions, food-
stuffs; **sans provision** bad (*check*)
provisoire [prɔvizwar] *adj* provisional,
temporary; emergency
provo•cant [prɔvɔkɑ̃] **-cante** [kɑ̃t] *adj*
provocative
provoquer [prɔvɔke] *tr* to provoke; to
cause, bring about; to arouse
proxénète [prɔksenet] *mf* procurer || *m*
pimp
proximité [prɔksimite] *f* proximity; **à
proximité de** near
prude [pryd] *adj* prudish || *f* prude
prudence [prydɑ̃s] *f* prudence
pru•dent [prydɑ̃] **-dente** [dɑ̃t] *adj* prudent
pruderie [prydri] *f* prudery
prud'homme [prydɔm] *m* arbitrator;
(obs) solid citizen
prudhommesque [prydɔmesk] *adj* pompous
pruine [prɥin] *f* bloom
prune [pryn] *f* plum; **des prunes!**
(slang) nuts!; **pour des prunes** (coll)
for nothing
pru•neau [pryno] *m* (*pl* **-neaux**) prune;
(slang) bullet
prunelle [prynel] *f* pupil (*of eye*); sloe;
sloe gin; **jouer de la prunelle** (coll)
to ogle; **prunelle de ses yeux** apple
of his (one's, etc.) eye
prunellier [prynelje] *m* sloe, blackthorn
prunier [prynje] *m* plum tree
prus•sien [prysjɛ̃] **prus•sienne** [pry-
sjen] *adj* Prussian || (*cap*) *mf* Prus-
sian
P.-S. [pees] *m* (letterword) (**post-
scriptum**) P.S.
psalmodier [psalmɔdje] *tr & intr* to
speak in a singsong
psaume [psom] *m* psalm
psautier [psotje] *m* psalter
pseudonyme [psødɔnim] *adj* pseudony-
mous || *m* pseudonym; nom de plume
psitt [psit] *interj* (coll) hist!
P.S.V. [peesve] *m* (letterword) (**pilotage sans visibilité**) blind flying
psychanalyse [psikanaliz] *f* psychoanalysis
psychanalyser [psikanalize] *tr* to psychoanalyze
psyché [psife] *f* psyche; cheval glass
psychiatre [psikjatr] *mf* psychiatrist
psychiatrie [psikjatri] *f* psychiatry
psychique [psifik] *adj* psychic
psychologie [psikɔlɔʒi] *f* psychology
psychologique [psikɔlɔʒik] *adj* psycho-
logic(al)

psychologue [psikɔlɔg] *mf* psychologist
psychopathe [psikɔpat] *mf* psychopath
psychose [psikoz] *f* psychosis
psychotique [psikɔtik] *adj & mf* psychotic
ptomaine [ptɔmain] *f* ptomaine
P.T.T. [petete] *fpl* (letterword) (**Postes, télégraphes, et téléphones**) post
office, telephone, and telegraph
puant [pɥɑ̃] **puante** [pɥɑ̃t] *adj* stinking
puanteur [pɥɑ̃tœr] *f* stench, stink
puberté [pyberte] *f* puberty
pu•blic -blique [pyblik] *adj* public;
notorious || *m* public; audience
publication [pyblikasjɔ̃] *f* publication;
proclamation
publicitaire [pyblisiter] *adj* advertising
|| *m* advertising man
publicité [pyblisite] *f* publicity; advertising; **publicité aérienne** skywriting
publier [pyblije] *tr* to publish; to publicize, proclaim
puce [pys] *f* flea; **mettre la puce à
l'oreille à qn** (fig) to put a bug in
s.o.'s ear
pu•ceau [pyso] **-celle** [sel] (*pl* **-ceaux**)
adj & mf (coll) virgin || *f* maid
puceron [pysrɔ̃] *m* plant louse
pudding [pudtŋ] *m* plum pudding
puddler [pydle] *tr* to puddle
pudeur [pydœr] *f* modesty
pudi•bond [pydibɔ̃] **-bonde** [bɔ̃d] *adj*
prudish
pudibonderie [pydibɔ̃dri] *f* false modesty
pudique [pydik] *adj* modest, chaste
puer [pɥe] *tr* to reek of || *intr* to stink
pué•ril -rile [pɥeril] *adj* puerile
puérilité [pɥerilite] *f* puerility
pugilat [pyʒila] *m* fight, brawl
pugiliste [pyʒilist] *m* pugilist
pugnace [pygnas] *adj* pugnacious
puî•né -née [pɥine] *adj* younger || *mf*
younger child
puis [pɥi] *adv* then; next; **et puis besides; et puis après?** (coll) what
next?
puisard [pɥizar] *m* drain, cesspool;
sump
puisatier [pɥizatje] *m* well digger
puiser [pɥize] *tr* to draw (*water*);
puiser à or **dans** to draw (s.th.) from
|| *intr*—**puiser à** or **dans** to draw
from or on; to dip or reach into
puisque [pɥisk(ə)] *conj* since, as, seeing that
puissamment [pɥisamɑ̃] *adv* power-
fully; exceedingly
puissance [pɥisɑ̃s] *f* power
puis•sant [pɥisɑ̃] **puis•sante** [pɥisɑ̃t]
adj powerful
puits [pɥi] *m* well; pit; (min) shaft;
(naut) locker; **puits absorbant, puits
perdu** cesspool; **puits de pétrole** oil
well; **puits de science** fountain of
knowledge
pull-over [pulɔvœr], [pylɔvœr] *m* (*pl*
-overs) sweater, pullover
pulluler [pylyle] *intr* to swarm, to teem
pulmonaire [pylmɔner] *adj* pulmonary
|| *f* (bot) lungwort

pulpe [pylp] f pulp
pulsation [pylsɑsjɔ̃] f pulsation, beat; pulse
pulsion [pylsjɔ̃] f (psychoanal) impulse
pulvérisateur [pylverizatœr] m spray, atomizer
pulvériser [pylverize] tr to pulverize; to spray
punaise [pynez] f bug; bedbug; thumbtack
punch [pɔ̃ʃ] m punch (drink) || [pœnʃ] m (boxing) punch
punching-ball [pœnʃiŋbol] m punching bag
punir [pynir] tr & intr to punish
punition [pynisjɔ̃] f punishment
pupille [pypil], [pypij] mf ward || f pupil (of eye)
pupitre [pypitr] m desk; stand, rack; lectern; console, controls; pupitre à musique music stand
pur pure [pyr] adj pure || mf diehard; les purs the pure in heart
purée [pyre] f purée; mashed potatoes; (coll) wretch; être dans la purée (coll) to be broke; purée de pois (culin, fig) pea soup || interj (slang) how awful!
pureté [pyrte] f purity
purga•tif [pyrgatif] -tive [tiv] adj & m purgative
purgatoire [pyrgatwar] m purgatory
purge [pyrʒ] f purge
purger [pyrʒe] §38 tr to purge; to pay off (e.g., a mortgage); to serve (a sentence)

purifier [pyrifje] tr to purify
puri•tain [pyritɛ̃] -taine [ten] adj & mf puritan; Puritan
pur-sang [pyrsɑ̃] adj & m invar thoroughbred
pus [py] m pus
pusillanime [pyzilanim] adj pusillanimous
pustule [pystyl] f pimple
putain [pytɛ̃] adj invar (coll) amiable, agreeable || f (vulg) whore
putois [pytwa] m skunk, polecat
putréfier [pytrefje] tr & ref to decompose, to rot
putride [pytrid] adj putrid
puy [pɥi] m volcanic peak
puzzle [pœzl] m jigsaw puzzle
p.-v. [peve] m (letterword) (procès-verbal) (coll) ticket, e.g., attraper un p.-v. to get a ticket
pygargue [pigarg] m osprey, fish hawk
pygmée [pigme] m pygmy
pygméen [pigmeɛ̃] pygméenne [pigmeen] adj pygmy
pyjama [piʒama] m pajamas; un pyjama a pair of pajamas
pylône [pilon] m pylon; tower
pyramide [piramid] f pyramid
Pyrénées [pirene] fpl Pyrenees
pyrite [pirit] f pyrites
pyrotechnie [pirotekni] f pyrotechnics
pyrotechnique [piroteknik] adj pyrotechnical
python [pitɔ̃] m python
pythonisse [pitonis] f pythoness
pyxide [piksid] f pyx

Q

Q, q [ky] m invar seventeenth letter of the French alphabet
quadrant [kwadrɑ̃], [kadrɑ̃] m (math) quadrant
quadrilatère [kwadrilater] m quadrilateral
quadrupède [kwadryped] m quadruped
quadruple [kwadrypl] adj & m quadruple
quadrupler [kwadryple] tr & intr to quadruple
quadru•plés -plées [kwadryple] mfpl quadruplets
quai [ke] m quay, wharf; platform (e.g., in a railroad station); embankment, levee; amener à quai to berth; le Quai d'Orsay the French foreign office
qua•ker [kwekœr], [kwaker] -keresse [kres] mf Quaker
qualifiable [kalifjabl] adj describable
quali•fié -fiée [kalifje] adj qualified; qualifying; aggravated (crime)
qualifier [kalifje] tr & intr to qualify
qualité [kalite] f quality; title, capacity; avoir qualité pour to be authorized to; en qualité de in the capacity of

quand [kɑ̃] adv when; how soon; n'importe quand anytime; quand même though, just the same || conj when; quand même even if
quant [kɑ̃] adv—quant à as for, as to, as far as; quant à cela for that matter
quant-à-soi [kɑ̃taswa] m dignity, reserve; rester or se tenir sur son quant-à-soi to keep one's distance
quantique [kwɑ̃tik] adj quantum
quantité [kɑ̃tite] f quantity
quan•tum [kwɑ̃təm] m (pl -ta [ta]) quantum
quarantaine [karɑ̃ten] f age of forty, forty mark, forties; quarantine; une quarantaine de about forty
quarante [karɑ̃t] adj, pron, & m forty; quarante et un forty-one; quarante et unième forty-first
quarante-deux [karɑ̃tdø] adj, pron, & m forty-two
quarante-deuxième [karɑ̃tdøzjem] adj, pron (masc, fem), & m forty-second
quarantième [karɑ̃tjem] adj, pron (masc, fem), & m fortieth
quart [kar] m quarter; fourth (in fractions); quarter of a pound; quarter

of a liter; **bon quart!** (naut) all's well!; **passer un mauvais quart d'heure** to have a trying time; **petit quart** (naut) dogwatch; **prendre le quart** (naut) to come on watch; **quart de cercle** quadrant; **quart de soupir** (mus) sixteenth-note rest; **quart d'heure de Rabelais** day of reckoning; **tous les quarts d'heure au quart d'heure juste** every quarter-hour on the quarter-hour; **un petit quart d'heure** a quarter of an hour or so

quarte [kart] *adj* quartan (*fever*) ‖ *f* half-gallon; (escr) quarte; (mus) fourth

quarte·ron [kartərɔ̃] **-ronne** [rɔn] *mf* quadroon ‖ *m* handful (*e.g., of people*)

quartette [kwartet] *m* combo (*four-some*)

quartier [kartje] *m* quarter; neighborhood; section (*of orange*); portion; **à quartier** aloof; apart; **avoir quartier libre** (mil) to have a pass; to be off duty; **les beaux quartiers** the upper-class residential district; **mettre en quartiers** to dismember; **quartier d'affaires** business district; **quartier général** (mil) headquarters; **quartier réservé** red-light district; **quartiers** quarters, barracks

quartier-maître [kartjemetr] *m* (*pl* **quartiers-maîtres**) quartermaster

quartz [kwarts] *m* quartz

quasar [kwazar], [kazar] *m* quasar

quasi [kazi] *m* butt (*of a loin cut*) ‖ *adv* almost

quasiment [kazimã] *adv* (coll) almost

quatorze [katɔrz] *adj & pron* fourteen; the Fourteenth, e.g., **Jean quatorze** John the Fourteenth ‖ *m* fourteen; fourteenth (*in dates*)

quatorzième [katɔrzjem] *adj, pron* (*masc, fem*), *& m* fourteenth

quatrain [katrɛ̃] *m* quatrain

quatre [katr] *adj & pron* four; the Fourth, e.g., **Jean quatre** John the Fourth; **quatre à quatre** four at a time; **quatre heures** four o'clock ‖ *m* four; fourth (*in dates*); **se mettre en quatre pour** to fall all over oneself for; **se tenir à quatre** to keep oneself under control

quatre-épices [katrepis] *m & f invar* allspice (*plant*); **des quatre-épices** allspice (*spice*)

quatre-saisons [katrəsezɔ̃], [katsezɔ̃] *f invar* everbearing small strawberry

quatre-temps [katrətã] *mpl* Ember days

quatre-vingt-dix [katrəvẽdi(s)] *adj, pron, & m* ninety

quatre-vingt-dixième [katrəvẽdizjem] *adj, pron* (*masc, fem*), *& m* ninetieth

quatre-vingtième [katrəvẽtjem] *adj, pron* (*masc, fem*), *& m* eightieth

quatre-vingt-onze [katrəvẽɔ̃z] *adj, pron, & m* ninety-one

quatre-vingt-onzième [katrəvẽɔ̃zjem] *adj, pron* (*masc, fem*), *& m* ninety-first

quatre-vingts [katrəvẽ] *adj & pron*

eighty; **quatre-vingt** eighty, e.g., **page quatre-vingt** page eighty ‖ *m* eighty

quatre-vingt-un [katrəvẽœ̃] *adj, pron, & m* eighty-one

quatre-vingt-unième [katrəvẽynjem] *adj, pron* (*masc, fem*), *& m* eighty-first

quatrième [katrijem] *adj, pron* (*masc, fem*), *& m* fourth

quatuor [kwatɥɔr] *m* (mus) quartet

que [kə] (or **qu'** [k] before a vowel or mute h) *pron rel* whom; which, that; **ce que** that which, what; ‖ *pron interr* what; **qu'est-ce que . . . ?** what (as direct object) . . . ?; **qu'est-ce qui . . . ?** what (as subject) . . . ? ‖ *adv* why, e.g., **qu'avez-vous besoin de tant de livres?** why do you need so many books?; how!, e.g., **que cette femme est belle!** how beautiful that woman is!; **que de** what a lot of, e.g., **que de difficultés!** what a lot of difficulties! ‖ *conj* that; when, e.g., **un jour que je suis allé chez le dentiste** once when I went to the dentist; since, e.g., **il y a trois jours qu'il est arrivé** it is three days since he came; until, e.g., **attendez qu'il vienne** wait until he comes; than, e.g., **plus grand que moi** taller than I; as, e.g., **aussi grand que moi** as tall as I; but, e.g., **personne que vous** no one but you; whether, e.g., **qu'il parte ou qu'il reste** whether he leaves or stays; (in a conditional sentence without **si**, to introduce the conditional in a dependent clause which represents the main clause of the corresponding sentence in English), e.g., **il ferait faillite que cela ne m'étonnerait pas** if he went bankrupt it would not surprise me; (as a repetition of another conjunction), e.g., **si elle chante et que la salle soit comble** if she sings and there is a full house; e.g., **comme il avait soif et que le vin était bon** as he was thirsty and the wine was good; (in a prayer or exhortation), e.g., **que Dieu vous bénisse!** may God bless you!, God bless you!; (in a command), e.g., **qu'il parle** (aille, parte, etc.) let him speak (go, leave, etc.); **ne . . . que** §90 only, but

quel quelle [kel] §80

quelconque [kelkɔ̃k] *adj indef* any; any, whatever; any at all, some kind of ‖ (when standing before noun) *adj indef* some, some sort of ‖ *adj* ordinary, nondescript, mediocre

quelque [kelkə] *adj indef* some, any; **quelque chose** (always *masc*) something; **quelque chose de bon** something good; **quelque part** somewhere; **quelque . . . qui** or **quelque . . . que** whatever . . . ; whichever . . . ; **quelques** a few ‖ *adv* some, about; **quelque peu** somewhat; **quelque + adj** or **adv . . . que** however + adj or adv

quelquefois [kelkəfwa] *adv* sometimes

quel·qu'un [kelkœ̃] **-qu'une** [kyn] §81

quémander [kemãde] *tr* to beg for ‖ *intr* to beg

qu'en-dira-t-on [kɑ̃diratɔ̃] *m invar* what other people will say, gossip

quenotte [kənɔt] *f* (coll) baby tooth

quenouille [kənuj] *f* distaff; distaff side

querelle [kərɛl] *f* quarrel; **chercher querelle à** to pick a quarrel with; **une querelle d'Allemand, une mauvaise querelle** a groundless quarrel

quereller [kərele] *tr* to nag, scold || *ref* to quarrel

querel•leur [kərelœr] **querel•leuse** [kərelØz] *adj* quarrelsome || *mf* wrangler || *f* shrew

quérir [kerir] (used only in *inf*) *tr* to go for, to fetch

question [kɛstjɔ̃] *f* question

questionnaire [kɛstjɔner] *m* questionnaire

questionner [kɛstjɔne] *tr* to question

question•neur [kɛstjɔnœr] **question-neuse** [kɛstjɔnØz] *adj* inquisitive || *mf* inquisitive person || *m* (rad, telv) quizmaster

quête [kɛt] *f* quest; **faire la quête** to take up the collection

quêter [kete] *tr* to beg or fish for (*votes, praise, etc.*); to hunt for (*game*); to collect (*contributions*) || *intr* to take up a collection

quetsche [kwɛt∫] *f* quetsch

queue [kØ] *f* tail; queue; billiard cue; train (*of dress*); handle (*of pan*); bottom (*of class*); stem, stalk; **à la queue leu leu** in single file; **faire la queue** to line up, to queue up; **fausse queue miscue; queue de cheval** (bot) horsetail; **queue de loup** (bot) purple foxglove; **queue de poisson** (aut) fishtail; **queue de vache** cat's-tail (*cirrus*); **sans queue ni tête** without head or tail; **venir en queue** to bring up the rear

queue-d'aronde [kØdarɔ̃d] *f* (*pl* **queues-d'aronde**) dovetail; **assembler à queue-d'aronde** to dovetail

queue-de-morue [kØdmɔry] *f* (*pl* **queues-de-morue**) tails, swallow-tailed coat; (painting) flat brush

queue-de-rat [kØdəra] *f* (*pl* **queues-de-rat**) rat-tail file; taper

qui [ki] *pron rel* who, whom; which, that; **ce qui** that which, what; **n'importe qui** anyone; **qui que** anyone, no one; whoever, e.g., **qui que vous soyez** whoever you are || *pron interr* who, whom; **qui est-ce que . . . ?** whom . . . ?; **qui est-ce qui . . . ?** who . . . ?

quia [kɥija]—**mettre** or **réduire qn à quia** (obs) to stump or floor s.o.

quiconque [kikɔ̃k] *pron indef* whoever, whosoever; whomever; anyone

quidam [kɥidam], [kidam] *m* individual, person

quiétude [kɥijetyd], [kjetyd] *f* peace of mind; quiet, calm

quignon [kiɲɔ̃] *m* hunk (*of bread*)

quille [kij] *f* keel; pin (*for bowling*); **quilles** ninepins

quincaillerie [kɛ̃kajri] *f* hardware; hardware store

quincail•lier [kɛ̃kaje] **quincail•lière** [kɛ̃kajer] *mf* hardware dealer

quinconce [kɛ̃kɔ̃s] *m* quincunx; **en quinconce** quincuncially

quinine [kinin] *f* quinine

quinquen•nal -nale [kɥɛ̃kɥennal] *adj* (*pl* -naux [no]) five-year

quinquet [kɛ̃ke] *m*—**allume tes quinquets!** (slang) open your eyes!

quinquina [kɛ̃kina] *m* cinchona

quin•tal [kɛ̃tal] *m* (*pl* -taux [to]) hundredweight; one hundred kilograms

quinte [kɛ̃t] *f* whim; (cards) sequence of five; (mus) fifth; **quinte de toux** fit of coughing

quintessence [kɛ̃tesɑ̃s] *f* quintessence

quintette [kɥɛ̃tet], [kɛ̃tet] *m* (mus) quintet; (coll) five-piece combo; **quintette à cordes** string quintet

quin•teux [kɛ̃tØ] **-teuse** [tØz] *adj* crotchety, fitful, restive

quintu•plés -plées [kɛ̃typle] *mfpl* quintuplets

quinzaine [kɛ̃zen] *f* (group of) fifteen; two weeks, fortnight; **une quinzaine de** about fifteen

quinze [kɛ̃z] *adj & pron* fifteen; the Fifteenth, e.g., **Jean quinze** John the Fifteenth || *m* fifteen; fifteenth (*in dates*)

quinzième [kɛ̃zjem] *adj, pron* (*masc, fem*), & *m* fifteenth

quiproquo [kiproko] *m* mistaken identity, misunderstanding

quiscale [kɥiskal] *m* (orn) purple grackle

quittance [kitɑ̃s] *f* receipt

quitte [kit] *adj* free (*from obligation*); clear (*of debts*); **(en) être quitte pour** to get off with; **être quitte de** to be quits; **tenir qn quitte de** to release s.o. from || *m*—**jouer (à) quitte ou double** to play double or nothing || *adv*—**quitte à** even if one has to, e.g., **commençons par en rire, quitte à en pleurer plus tard** let us begin by laughing, even if we have to cry later on

quitter [kite] *tr* to leave; to take off (*e.g., a coat*) || *intr* to leave, go away; **ne quittez pas!** (telp) hold the line! || *ref* to part, separate

quitus [kɥitys] *m* discharge, acquittance

qui-vive [kiviv] *m invar*—**sur le qui-vive** on the qui vive || *interj* (mil) who goes there?

quoi [kwa] *pron indef* what, which; **à quoi bon?** what's the use?; **de quoi** enough; **moyennant quoi** in exchange for which; **n'importe quoi** anything; **quoi que** whatever; **quoi qu'il en soit** be that as it may; **sans quoi** otherwise

quoique [kwakə] *conj* although, though

quolibet [kɔlibɛ] *m* gibe, quip

quorum [kwɔrɔm], [kɔrɔm] *m* quorum

quota [kwɔta], [kɔta] *m* quota

quote-part [kɔtpar] *f invar* quota, share

quoti•dien [kɔtidjɛ̃] **-dienne** [djɛn] *adj* daily || *m* daily newspaper

quotient [kɔsjɑ̃] *m* quotient

quotité [kɔtite] *f* share, amount

R

R, r [er], *[er] *m invar* eighteenth letter of the French alphabet

rabâcher [rabɑʃe] *tr* to harp on ‖ *intr* to harp on the same thing

rabais [rabɛ] *m* reduction, discount

rabaisser [rabɛse] *tr* to lower; to disparage

rabat [raba] *m* flap (*vestment*)

rabat-joie [rabaʒwa] *m invar* kill-joy

rabattre [rabatr] §7 *tr* to lower; to discount; to turn down; to fold up; to pull down; to cut back; to flush (*game*) ‖ *intr* to turn; **en rabattre** to come down a peg or two; **rabattre de** to reduce (*a price*) ‖ *ref* to fold; to drop down; to turn the other way; **se rabattre sur** to fall back on

rabat·tu -tue [rabaty] *adj* turndown

rabbin [rabɛ̃] *m* rabbi

rabibocher [rabibɔʃe] *tr* (coll) to patch up ‖ *ref* (coll) to make up

rabiot [rabjo] *m* overtime; extra bit; (mil) extra service; (coll) graft

rabioter [rabjɔte] *tr & intr* to graft

râ·blé -blée [rɑble] *adj* husky

rabot [rabo] *m* plane

raboter [rabɔte] *tr* to plane

rabo·teux -teuse [rabɔtø] [-tøz] *adj* rough, uneven ‖ *f* (mach) planer

rabou·gri -grie [rabugri] *adj* scrub, scrawny

rabrouer [rabrue] *tr* to snub

racaille [rakɑj] *f* riffraff

raccommodage [rakɔmɔdaʒ] *m* mending; darning; patching

raccommodement [rakɔmɔdmɑ̃] *m* (coll) reconciliation

raccommoder [rakɔmɔde] *tr* to mend; to darn; to patch; (coll) to patch up

raccompagner [rakɔ̃paɲe] *tr* to see back, to see home

raccord [rakɔr] *m* connection; coupling; joint; adapter; **faire un raccord à** to touch up

raccordement [rakɔrdəmɑ̃] *m* connecting, linking, joining

raccorder [rakɔrde] *tr & ref* to connect

raccour·ci -cie [rakursi] *adj* shortened; abridged; squat, dumpy; bobbed (*hair*) ‖ *m* abridgment; shortcut, cutoff; foreshortening; **en raccourci** in miniature; in a nutshell

raccourcir [rakursir] *tr* to shorten; to abridge; to foreshorten ‖ *intr* to grow shorter

raccourcissement [rakursismɑ̃] *m* shortening; abridgment; shrinking

raccroc [rakro] *m* fluke

raccrocher [rakrɔʃe] *tr & intr* to hang up ‖ *ref*—**se raccrocher à** to hang on to

race [ras] *f* race; **de race** thoroughbred

ra·cé -cée [rase] *adj* thoroughbred

rachat [raʃa] *m* repurchase; redemption; ransom

racheter [raʃte] §2 *tr* to buy back; to redeem; to ransom

rachitique [raʃitik] *adj* rickety

rachitisme [raʃitism] *m* rickets

ra·cial -ciale [rasjal] *adj* (*pl* -**ciaux** [sjo]) race, racial

racine [rasin] *f* root; **racine carrée** square root; **racine cubique** cube root

racket [rakɛt] *m* (coll) racket

racketter or **racketteur** [rakɛtœr] *m* racketeer

raclée [rakle] *f* beating

racler [rakle] *tr* to scrape

raclette [raklɛt] *f* scraper; hoe; (phot) squeegee

racloir [raklwar] *m* scraper

raclure [raklyr] *f* scrapings

racolage [rakɔlaʒ] *m* soliciting

racoler [rakɔle] *tr* (coll) to solicit; (archaic) to shanghai

raco·leur [rakɔlœr] -**leuse** [løz] *mf* recruiter ‖ *f* (coll) hustler, streetwalker

racontar [rakɔ̃tar] *m* (coll) gossip

raconter [rakɔ̃te] *tr* to tell, narrate; to describe

racon·teur [rakɔ̃tœr] -**teuse** [tøz] *mf* storyteller

racornir [rakɔrnir] *tr & intr* to harden; to shrivel

radar [radar] *m* radar

rade [rad] *f* roadstead; **en rade** (coll) abandoned

ra·deau [rado] *m* (*pl* -**deaux**) raft

ra·diant [radjɑ̃] -**diante** [djɑ̃t] *adj* (astr, phys) radiant

radiateur [radjatœr] *m* radiator

radiation [radjɑsjɔ̃] *f* radiation; striking off

radi·cal -cale [radikal] *adj & mf* (*pl* -**caux** [ko]) radical ‖ *m* (chem, gram, math) radical

radier [radje] *tr* to cross out, to strike out or off

ra·dieux [radjø] -**dieuse** [djøz] *adj* radiant

radin [radɛ̃] *adj masc & fem* (slang) stingy

radio [radjo] *m* radiogram; radio operator ‖ *f* radio; radio set; X ray

radioac·tif [radjɔaktif] -**tive** [tiv] *adj* radioactive

radio-crochet [radjokrɔʃɛ] *m* (*pl* -**crochets**) talent show

radiodiffuser [radjɔdifyze] *tr* to broadcast

radiodiffusion [radjɔdifyzjɔ̃] *f* broadcasting

radiofréquence [radjɔfrekɑ̃s] *f* radiofrequency

radiogramme [radjɔgram] *m* radiogram

radiographier [radjɔgrafje] *tr* to X-ray

radio-journal [radjɔʒurnal] *m* (*pl* -**journaux** [ʒurno]) radio newscast

radiologie [radjɔlɔʒi] *f* radiology

radiophare [radjɔfar] *m* radio beacon

radioreportage [radjɔrəpɔrtaʒ] *m* news broadcast; sports broadcast

radioscopie [radjɔskɔpi] *f* radioscopy, fluoroscopy

radiotélévi·sé -sée [radjɔtelevize] *adj* broadcast over radio and television

radis [radi] *m* radish

radium [radjɔm] *m* radium

radius [radjys] *m* (anat) radius

radotage [radɔtaʒ] *m* drivel, twaddle

radoter [radɔte] *intr* to talk nonsense, to ramble

radoub [radu] *m* (naut) graving

radouber [radube] *tr* (naut) to grave

radoucir [radusir] *tr & ref* to calm down

rafale [rafal] *f* squall, gust; burst of gunfire

raffermir [rafɛrmir] *tr & ref* to harden

raffinage [rafinaʒ] *m* refining

raffinement [rafinmã] *m* refinement

raffiner [rafine] *tr* to refine ‖ *intr* to be subtle; **raffiner sur** to overdo

raffinerie [rafinri] *f* refinery

raffoler [rafɔle] *intr*—**raffoler de** to dote on, to be wild about

raffut [rafy] *m* (coll) uproar

rafistolage [rafistɔlaʒ] *m* (coll) patching up

rafistoler [rafistɔle] *tr* (coll) to patch up

rafle [rafl] *f* raid, mass arrest; stalk; corncob

rafler [rafle] *tr* (coll) to carry away, to make a clean sweep of

rafraîchir [rafreʃir] *tr & ref* to cool; to refresh; to freshen up; to trim (*the hair*) ‖ *intr* to cool ‖ *ref* to cool off; to refresh oneself

rafraîchissement [rafreʃismã] *m* refreshment; cooling off

ragaillardir [ragajardir] *tr* to cheer up

rage [raʒ] *f* rage; rabies; **à la rage** madly; **faire rage** to rage

rager [raʒe] §38 *intr* (coll) to be enraged

ra·geur [raʒœr] **-geuse** [ʒøz] *adj* bad-tempered

ragot [rago] *m* (coll) gossip

ragoût [ragu] *m* stew, ragout; (obs) spice, relish

ragoû·tant [ragutã] **-tante** [tãt] *adj* tempting, inviting; pleasing; **peu ragoûtant** not very appetizing

rai [re] *m* ray; spoke

raid [red] *m* raid; air raid; endurance test

raide [red] *adj* stiff; tight, taut; steep; (coll) incredible ‖ *adv* suddenly

raideur [redœr] *f* stiffness

raidillon [redijɔ̃] *m* short steep path

raidir [redir] *tr & ref* to stiffen

raie [re] *f* stripe, streak; stroke; line (*of spectrum*); part (*of hair*); (ichth) ray, skate

raifort [refɔr] *m* horseradish

rail [raj] *m* rail; **rail conducteur** third rail; **remettre sur les rails** (fig) to put back on the track; **sortir des rails** to jump the track

railler [raje] *tr* to make fun of ‖ *intr* to joke ‖ *ref*—**se railler de** to make fun of

raillerie [rajri] *f* raillery, banter

rail·leur [rajœr] **rail·leuse** [rajøz] *adj* teasing, bantering ‖ *mf* teaser

rainette [renet] *f* tree frog

rainure [renyr] *f* groove

raisin [rezɛ̃] *m* grapes; grape; **raisin d'ours** (bot) bearberry; **raisins de Corinthe** currants; **raisins de mer** cuttlefish eggs; **raisins de Smyrne** seedless raisins; **raisins secs** raisins

raisiné [rezine] *m* grape jelly; (slang) blood

raison [rezɔ̃] *f* reason; ratio, rate; **à raison de** at the rate of; **avoir raison** to be right; **avoir raison de** to get the better of; **donner raison à** to back, support; **en raison de** because of; **raison sociale** trade name; **se faire une raison** to resign oneself

raisonnable [rezɔnabl] *adj* reasonable; rational

raison·né -née [rezɔne] *adj* rational; detailed

raisonnement [rezɔnmã] *m* reasoning; argument

raisonner [rezɔne] *tr* to reason out; to reason with ‖ *intr* to reason; to argue ‖ *ref* to reason with oneself

raison·neur [rezɔnœr] **raison·neuse** [rezɔnøz] *adj* rational; argumentative ‖ *mf* reasoner; arguer

rajeunir [raʒœnir] *tr* to rejuvenate ‖ *intr* to grow young again ‖ *ref* to pretend to be younger than one is

rajeunissement [raʒœnismã] *m* rejuvenation

rajouter [raʒute] *tr* to add again; (coll) to add more

rajuster [raʒyste] *tr* to readjust; to adjust ‖ *ref* to adjust one's clothes

râle [rɑl] *m* rale; death rattle; (orn) rail

ralen·ti -tie [ralãti] *adj* slow ‖ *m* slowdown; **au ralenti** slowdown (*work*); go-slow (*policy*); slow-motion (*moving picture*); idling (*motor*); **tourner au ralenti** (aut) to idle

ralentir [ralãtir] *tr, intr, & ref* to slow down; **ralentir** (public sign) slow

ralliement [ralimã] *m* rally

rallier [ralje] *tr & ref* to rally

rallonge [ralɔ̃ʒ] *f* extra piece; leaf (*of table*); (coll) under-the-table payment; **à rallonges** extension (*table*)

rallonger [ralɔ̃ʒe] §38 *tr & intr* to lengthen

rallumer [ralyme] *tr* to relight; (fig) to rekindle ‖ *intr* to put on the lights again ‖ *ref* to be rekindled

rallye [rali] *m* rallye

ramage [ramaʒ] *m* floral design; warbling

ramas [ramɑ] *m* heap; pack (*e.g., of thieves*)

ramassage [ramɑsaʒ] *m* gathering; **ramassage scolaire** school-bus service

ramas·sé -sée [ramɑse] *adj* stocky; compact (*style*)

ramasser [ramɑse] *tr* to gather; to gather together; to pick up; (coll) to catch (*a scolding; a cold*) ‖ *ref* to gather; to gather oneself together

rambarde [rãbard] *f* handrail

rame [ram] *f* prop, stick; oar, pole; ream (*of paper*); string (*e.g., of barges*); (rr) train, section; **rame de métro** subway train

ra·meau [ramo] *m* (*pl* -meaux) branch; sprig

ramée [rame] *f* boughs

ramener [ramne] §2 *tr* to lead back; to bring back; to reduce; to restore

ramer [rame] *tr* to stake (*a plant*) ‖ *intr* to row

ra·meur [ramœr] **-meuse** [møz] *mf* rower

ramier [ramje] *m* wood pigeon

ramifier [ramifje] *tr & ref* to ramify, to branch out

ramol·li -lie [ramɔli] *adj* sodden; (coll) half-witted ‖ *mf* (coll) half-wit

ramollir [ramɔlir] *tr & ref* to soften

ramoner [ramɔne] *tr* to sweep (*a chimney*)

ramoneur [ramɔnœr] *m* chimney sweep

ram·pant [rɑ̃pɑ̃] **-pante** [pɑ̃t] *adj* crawling, creeping; (hum) ground (*crew*)

rampe [rɑ̃p] *f* ramp; grade, gradient; banister; flight (*of stairs*); (aer) runway lights; (theat) footlights; **rampe de lancement** launching pad

ramper [rɑ̃pe] *intr* to crawl; to grovel; (bot) to creep

ramure [ramyr] *f* branches; antlers

rancart [rɑ̃kar] *m* (slang) rendezvous; **mettre au rancart** (coll) to scrap, to shelve

rance [rɑ̃s] *adj* rancid

ranch [rɑ̃tʃ] *m* ranch

rancir [rɑ̃sir] *intr & ref* to turn rancid

rancœur [rɑ̃kœr] *f* rancor

rançon [rɑ̃sɔ̃] *f* ransom

rançonner [rɑ̃sɔne] *tr* to ransom

rancune [rɑ̃kyn] *f* grudge

rancu·nier [rɑ̃kynje] **-nière** [njer] *adj* vindictive

randonnée [rɑ̃dɔne] *f* long walk; long ride

rang [rɑ̃] *m* rank; **au premier rang** in the first row; ranking; **en rang d'oignons** in a line

ran·gé -gée [rɑ̃ʒe] *adj* orderly; pitched (*battle*); steady (*person*)

ranger [rɑ̃ʒe] §38 *tr* to range; to rank ‖ *ref* to take one's place; to get out of the way; to mend one's ways; **se ranger à** to adopt, take (*e.g., a suggestion*)

ranimer [ranime] *tr & ref* to revive

raout [raut] *m* reception

rapace [rapas] *adj* rapacious ‖ *m* bird of prey

rapatriement [rapatrimɑ̃] *m* repatriation

rapatrier [rapatrije] *tr* to repatriate

râpe [rɑp] *f* rasp; grater

râ·pé -pée [rɑpe] *adj* grated; threadbare ‖ *m* (coll) grated cheese

râper [rɑpe] *tr* to rasp, to grate

rapetasser [raptase] *tr* (coll) to patch up

rapetisser [raptise] *tr, intr, & ref* to shrink, shorten

râ·peux [rɑpø] **-peuse** [pøz] *adj* raspy, grating

ra·piat [rapja] **-piate** [pjat] *adj* (coll) stingy ‖ *mf* (coll) skinflint

rapide [rapid] *adj* rapid; steep ‖ *m* rapids; (rr) express; **rapides** rapids

rapidité [rapidite] *f* rapidity; steepness

rapiéçage [rapjesaʒ] *m* patching

rapiécer [rapjese] §58 *tr* to patch

rapière [rapjer] *f* rapier

rapin [rapɛ̃] *m* dauber; (coll) art student

rapine [rapin] *f* rapine, pillage

rappel [rapel] *m* recall; reminder; call-up; recurrence; booster (*shot*); (theat) curtain call; **battre le rappel** to call to arms; **rappel au règlement** point of order; **rappel de chariot** backspacer

rappeler [raple] §34 *tr* to recall; to remind; to call back; to call up ‖ *ref* to remember

rapport [rapɔr] *m* yield, return; report; connection, bearing; (math) ratio; **en rapport avec** in touch with; in keeping with; **par rapport à** in comparison with; **rapports** relations; sexual relations; **sous tous les rapports** in all respects

rapporter [rapɔrte] *tr* to bring back; to yield; to report; to relate; to repeal, call off; to attach; to retrieve (*game*); (bk) to post ‖ *intr* to yield; (coll) to squeal ‖ *ref*—**s'en rapporter à** to leave it up to; **se rapporter à** to be related to, to refer to

rappor·teur [rapɔrtœr] **-teuse** [tøz] *mf* tattletale ‖ *m* recorder; (geom) protractor

rapprochement [raprɔʃmɑ̃] *m* bringing together; parallel; rapprochement

rapprocher [raprɔʃe] *tr* to bring closer; to reconcile; to compare ‖ *ref* to draw closer, to approach; **se rapprocher de** to approximate, to resemble

rapt [rapt] *m* kidnapping

raquette [raket] *f* racket; snowshoe; tennis player; (bot) prickly pear

rare [rar] *adj* rare; scarce; sparse, thin (*hair*)

rarement [rarmɑ̃] *adv* rarely, seldom

rareté [rarte] *f* rarity; scarcity; rareness

ras [rɑ] **rase** [rɑz] *adj* short (*hair, nap, etc.*); level; close-cropped; close-shaven; open (*country*) ‖ *m*—**à ras de, au ras de** flush with; **ras d'eau** water line; **ras du cou** crew neck; **voler au ras du sol** to skim along the ground

rasade [rɑzad] *f* bumper, glassful

rasage [rɑzaʒ] *m* shearing; shaving

ra·sant [rɑzɑ̃] **-sante** [zɑ̃t] *adj* level; grazing; close to the ground; (coll) boring

rase-mottes [rɑzmɔt] *m invar*—**faire du rase-mottes** or **voler en rase-mottes** to hedgehop

raser [rɑze] *tr* to shave; to raze; to graze ‖ *ref* to shave

ra·seur [rɑzœr] **-seuse** [zøz] *adj* (coll) boring ‖ *mf* (coll) bore

rasoir [rɑzwar] *adj invar* (slang) boring ‖ *m* razor; (slang) bore; **rasoir à manche** straight razor; **rasoir de sûreté** safety razor

rassasiement [rasazimɑ̃] *m* satiation

rassasier [rasazje] *tr* to satisfy; to satiate ‖ *ref* to have one's fill

rassemblement [rasɑ̃bləmɑ̃] *m* assembling; crowd; muster; (*trumpet call*) assembly; **rassemblement!** (mil) fall in!

rassembler [rasãmble] *tr & ref* to gather together

rasseoir [raswar] §5 *tr* to reseat; to set in place again ‖ *ref* to sit down again

rasséréner [raserene] §10 *tr & ref* to calm down

rassir [rasir] *intr & ref* (coll) to get stale

ras·sis [rasi] **ras·sise** [rasiz] *adj* level-headed; stale (*bread*)

rassortir [rasɔrtir] *tr* to restock ‖ *ref* to lay in a new stock

rassurer [rasyre] *tr* to reassure ‖ *ref* to be reassured

rastaquouère [rastakwer] *m* (coll) flashy stranger

rat [ra] *m* rat; (coll) tightwad; **fait comme un rat** caught like a rat in a trap; **mon rat** (coll) my turtledove; **rat à bourse** gopher; **rat de bibliothèque** bookworm; **rat de cale** stowaway; **rat de cave** thin candle; tax collector; **rat d'égout** sewer rat; **rat des champs** field mouse; **rat d'hôtel** hotel thief; **rat d'Opéra** ballet girl; **rat musqué** muskrat

ratatiner [ratatine] *ref* to shrivel up

ratatouille [ratatuj] *f* (coll) stew; (coll) bad cooking; (coll) blows

rate [rat] *f* spleen; female rat

ra·té -tée [rate] *adj* miscarried; bad (*shot, landing, etc.*) ‖ *mf* failure, dropout

râ·teau [rɑto] *m* (*pl* -teaux) rake

râteler [rɑtle] §34 *tr* to rake

râtelier [rɑtəlje] *m* rack; set of false teeth; **manger à deux râteliers** (coll) to play both sides of the street; **râtelier d'armes** gun rack

rater [rate] *tr* to miss ‖ *intr* to miss, to misfire; to fail

ratiboiser [ratibwaze] *tr* (coll) to take to the cleaners; **ratiboiser q.ch. à qn** (coll) to clean s.o. out of s.th.

ratifier [ratifje] *tr* to ratify

ration [rɑsjɔ̃] *f* ration

ration·nel -nelle [rasjɔnel] *adj* rational

rationnement [rasjɔnmã] *m* rationing

rationner [rasjɔne] *tr* to ration

ratisser [ratise] *tr* to rake; to rake in; to search with a fine-tooth comb; (coll) to fleece

ratissoire [ratiswar] *f* hoe

raton [ratɔ̃] *m* little rat; **raton laveur** raccoon

rattacher [rataʃe] *tr* to tie again; to link; to unite ‖ *ref* to be connected

rattrapage [ratrapaʒ] *m* catch-up; (typ) catchword

rattraper [ratrape] *tr* to catch up to; to recover; to recapture ‖ *ref* to catch up; **se rattraper à** to catch hold of; **se rattraper de** to make good, to recoup

rature [ratyr] *f* erasure

raturer [ratyre] *tr* to cross out

rauque [rok] *adj* hoarse, raucous

ravage [ravaʒ] *m* ravage

ravager [ravaʒe] §38 *tr* to ravage

ravalement [ravalmã] *m* trimming down; resurfacing; disparagement

ravaler [ravale] *tr* to choke down; to disparage; to drag down; to resurface; to eat (*one's words*) ‖ *ref* to lower oneself

ravaudage [ravodaʒ] *m* mending; darning; (fig) patchwork

ravauder [ravode] *tr* to mend; to darn

ravier [ravje] *m* hors-d'oeuvre dish

ravigoter [ravigɔte] *tr* (coll) to revive

ravilir [ravilir] *tr* to debase

ravin [ravɛ̃] *m* ravine

ravine [ravin] *f* mountain torrent

raviner [ravine] *tr* to furrow

ravir [ravir] *tr* to ravish; to kidnap, abduct; to delight, entrance; **ravir q.ch. à qn** to snatch or take s.th. from s.o. ‖ *intr*—**à ravir** marvelously

raviser [ravize] *ref* to change one's mind

ravis·sant [ravisã] **ravis·sante** [ravisãt] *adj* ravishing, entrancing

ravis·seur [raviscer] **ravis·seuse** [ravisøz] *mf* kidnaper

ravitaillement [ravitajmã] *m* supplying; supplies

ravitailler [ravitaje] *tr* to supply; to fill up the gas tank of (*a vehicle*) ‖ *ref* to lay in supplies; to fill up (*to get gas*)

raviver [ravive] *tr* to revive; to brighten up; to reopen (*an old wound*) ‖ *ref* to revive; to break out again

ravoir [ravwar] (used only in *inf*) *tr* to get back again

rayer [reje] §49 *tr* to cross out, to strike out; to rule; to line; to stripe; to rifle (*a gun*)

rayon [rejɔ̃] *m* ray; radius; spoke; shelf; honeycomb; department (*in a store*); point (*of star*); **ce n'est pas mon rayon** (coll) that's not in my line; **rayon de lune** moonbeam; **rayons X** X rays; **rayon visuel** line of sight

rayon·nant [rejɔnã] **rayon·nante** [rejɔnãt] *adj* radiant; radiating; radioactive; (rad) transmitting

rayonne [rejɔn] *f* rayon

rayonner [rejɔne] *intr* to radiate

rayure [rejyr] *f* stripe; scratch; rifling

raz [rɑ] *m* race (*channel and current of water*); **raz de marée** tidal wave; landslide (*in an election*)

razzia [razja] *f* raid

razzier [razje] *tr* to raid

réacteur [reaktœr] *m* reactor; **réacteur nucléaire** nuclear reactor

réactif [reaktif] *m* (chem) reagent

réaction [reaksjɔ̃] *f* reaction; kick (*of rifle*); **à réaction** jet; **réaction en chaîne** chain reaction

réactionnaire [reaksjɔner] *adj & mf* reactionary

réadaptation [readaptasjɔ̃] *f* rehabilitation; **réadaptation fonctionnelle** occupational therapy

réadapter [readapte] *tr* to rehabilitate ‖ *ref* to be rehabilitated

réaffirmer [reafirme] *tr* to reaffirm

réagir [reaʒir] *intr* to react

réalisable [realizabl] *adj* feasible; (com) saleable

réalisa·teur [realizatœr] **-trice** [tris]

adj producing || *mf* achiever; producer || *m* (mov, rad, telv) director

réalisation [realizɑsjɔ̃] *f* accomplishment; work; (mov, rad, telv) production; (com) liquidation

réaliser [realize] *tr* to realize; to accomplish; to sell out; (mov) to produce || *ref* to come to pass, to be realized

réalisme [realism] *m* realism

réaliste [realist] *adj* realistic || *mf* realist

réalité [realite] *f* reality

réanimer [reanime] *tr* to revive

réapparaître [reaparetr] §12 *intr* to reappear

réapparition [reaparisjɔ̃] *f* reappearance

réarmement [rearməmɑ̃] *m* rearmament

réassortir [reasɔrtir] *tr* to restock || *ref* to lay in a new stock

réassurer [reasyre] *tr* to reinsure

rébarba·tif [rebarbatif] **-tive** [tiv] *adj* forbidding, repulsive

rebâtir [rɑbatir] *tr* to rebuild

rebattre [rɑbatr] §7 *tr* to beat; to reshuffle; to repeat over and over again

rebat·tu -tue [rɑbaty] *adj* hackneyed

rebelle [rɑbɛl] *adj* rebellious || *mf* rebel

rebeller [rɑbele], [rɑbɛlle] *ref* to rebel

rébellion [rebeljɔ̃] *f* rebellion

rebiffer [rɑbife] *ref* to kick over the traces

reboisement [rɑbwazmɑ̃] *m* reforestation

rebond [rɑbɔ̃] *m* rebound

rebon·di -die [rɑbɔ̃di] *adj* plump, buxom; paunchy

rebondir [rɑbɔ̃dir] *intr* to bounce; (fig) to come up again

rebord [rɑbɔr] *m* edge, border; sill, ledge; hem; brim (*of hat*); rim (*of saucer*); lip (*of cup*)

reboucher [rɑbuʃe] *tr* to recork; to stop up || *ref* to be stopped up

rebours [rɑbur] *m*—**à rebours** backwards; against the grain; the wrong way; backhanded (*compliment*); **à** or **au rebours de** contrary to

rebouter [rɑbute] *tr* to set (*a bone*)

rebrousse-poil [rɑbruspwal]—**à rebrousse-poil** against the grain, the wrong way

rebrousser [rɑbruse] *tr* to brush up; **rebrousser chemin** to turn back; **rebrousser qn** (coll) to rub s.o. the wrong way || *ref* to turn up, to bend back

rebuffade [rɑbyfad] *f* rebuff; **essuyer une rebuffade** to be snubbed

rebut [rɑby] *m* castoff; waste; scum (*of society*); rebuff; **de rebut** castoff; waste; unclaimed (*letter*); **mettre au rebut** to discard

rebu·tant -tante [rɑbytɑ̃] **-tante** [tɑ̃t] *adj* dull, tedious; repugnant

rebuter [rɑbyte] *tr* to rebuff; to bore; to be repulsive to

recaler [rɑkale] *tr* (coll) to flunk

récapitulation [rekapitylɑsjɔ̃] *f* recapitulation

recéder [rɑsede] §10 *tr* to give or sell back

recel [rɑsel] *m* concealment (*of stolen goods; of criminals*)

receler [rɑsle] §2 *tr* to conceal; to receive (*stolen goods*); to harbor (*a criminal*) || *intr* to hide

rece·leur [rɑslœr] **-leuse** [løz] *mf* fence, receiver of stolen goods

récemment [resamɑ̃] *adv* recently, lately

recensement [rɑsɑ̃smɑ̃] *m* census; **recensement du contingent** draft registration

recenser [rɑsɑ̃se] *tr* to take the census of; to take a count of

recenseur [rɑsɑ̃sœr] *m* census taker

ré·cent [resɑ̃] **-cente** [sɑ̃t] *adj* recent

récépissé [resepise] *m* receipt

réceptacle [reseptakl] *m* receptacle

récep·teur [reseptœr] **-trice** [tris] *adj* receiving || *m* receiver

récep·tif [reseptif] **-tive** [tiv] *adj* receptive

réception [resepsjɔ̃] *f* reception; receipt; approval; admission (*to a club*); registration desk (*of hotel*); landing (*of, e.g., a parachutist*); (sports) catch; **accuser réception de** to acknowledge receipt of

réceptionnaire [resepsjɔner] *mf* consignee; chief receptionist

récession [resesjɔ̃] *f* recession

recette [rɑset] *f* receipt; collection (*of debts, taxes, etc.*); (culin) recipe; **faire recette** to be a box-office attraction; **recettes de métier** tricks of the trade

recevable [rɑsvabl] *adj* acceptable; admissible

rece·veur [rɑsvœr] **-veuse** [vøz] *mf* collector; conductor (*of bus, streetcar, etc.*); blood recipient; **receveur des postes** postmaster; **receveur universel** recipient of blood from a universal donor

recevoir [rɑsvwar] §59 *tr* to receive; to accommodate; to admit (*to a school, club, etc.*); **être reçu** to be admitted; to pass || *intr* to receive

rechange [rɑʃɑ̃ʒ] *m* replacement, change; **de rechange** spare (*e.g., parts*)

rechaper [rɑʃape] *tr* to recap, to retread

réchapper [reʃape] *intr*—**en réchapper** to get away with it; to get well; **réchapper à** or **de** to escape from

recharge [rɑʃarʒ] *f* refill; recharging; reloading

recharger [rɑʃarʒe] §38 *tr* to recharge; to refill; to reload; to ballast (*a roadbed*)

réchaud [reʃo] *m* hot plate

réchauffer [reʃofe] *tr* & *ref* to warm up

rêche [reʃ] *adj* rough, harsh

recherche [rɑʃerʃ] *f* search; quest; investigation, piece of research; refinement; **recherches** research

recher·ché [rɑʃerʃe] *adj* sought-after, in demand; elaborate; studied, affected

rechercher [rəʃerʃe] *tr* to seek, to look for

rechigner [rəʃiɲe] *intr*—**rechigner à** to balk at

rechute [rəʃyt] *f* relapse

rechuter [rəʃyte] *intr* to relapse

récidive [residiv] *f* recurrence; second offense

récidiver [residive] *intr* to recur; to relapse

récif [resif] *m* reef

récipiendaire [resipjɑ̃der] *m* new member, inductee; initiate

récipient [resipjɑ̃] *m* recipient, vessel

réciprocité [resiprɔsite] *f* reciprocity

réciproque [resiprɔk] *adj* reciprocal || *f* converse

récit [resi] *m* recital, account

réci·tal -tale [resital] *m* (*pl* **-tals**) recital

récitation [resitɑsjɔ̃] *f* recitation

réciter [resite] *tr* to recite

récla·mant [reklamɑ̃] **-mante** [mɑ̃t] *mf* claimant

réclamation [reklamɑsjɔ̃] *f* complaint; demand

réclame [reklam] *f* advertising; advertisement; (theat) cue; (typ) catchword; **faire de la réclame** to advertise, to ballyhoo; **réclame à éclipse** flashing sign; **réclame lumineuse** illuminated sign

réclamer [reklame] *tr* to claim; to clamor for; to demand || *intr* to lodge a complaint; to intercede || *ref* —**se réclamer de** to appeal to; to claim kinship with; **se réclamer de qn** to use s.o.'s name as a reference

reclassement [rəklɑsmɑ̃] *m* reclassification

reclasser [rəklɑse] *tr* to reclassify

re·clus [rəkly] **-cluse** [klyz] *adj & mf* recluse

recoin [rəkwɛ̃] *m* nook, cranny

récollection [rekɔleksjɔ̃] *f* religious meditation

recoller [rəkɔle] *tr* to paste again

récolte [rekɔlt] *f* harvest

récolter [rekɔlte] *tr* to harvest

recommander [rəkɔmɑ̃de] *tr* to recommend; to register (*a letter*) || *ref*—**se recommander à** to seek the protection of; **se recommander de** to ask (*s.o.*) for a reference

recommencer [rəkɔmɑ̃se] §51 *tr & intr* to begin again

récompense [rekɔ̃pɑ̃s] *f* recompense, reward; award

récompenser [rekɔ̃pɑ̃se] *tr* to recompense

réconcilier [rekɔ̃silje] *tr* to reconcile

reconduire [rəkɔ̃dɥir] §19 *tr* to escort; (coll) to kick out, to send packing

réconfort [rekɔ̃fɔr] *m* comfort

réconfor·tant [rekɔ̃fɔrtɑ̃] **-tante** [tɑ̃t] *adj* consoling; stimulating

réconforter [rekɔ̃fɔrte] *tr* to comfort; to revive || *ref* to recuperate; to cheer up

reconnaissance [rəkɔnesɑ̃s] *f* recognition; gratitude; (mil) reconnaissance; **aller en reconnaissance** to reconnoiter; **reconnaissance de** or **pour** gratitude for

reconnais·sant [rəkɔnesɑ̃] **reconnaissante** [rəkɔnesɑ̃t] *adj* grateful; **être reconnaissant de** + *inf* to be grateful for + *ger*; **être reconnaissant de** or **pour** to be grateful for

reconnaître [rəkɔnetr] §12 *tr* to recognize; (mil) to reconnoiter || *ref* to recognize oneself; to know where one is; to acknowledge oneself (*e.g., guilty*); **s'y reconnaître** to know where one is

reconquérir [rəkɔ̃kerir] §3 *tr* to reconquer

reconquête [rəkɔ̃ket] *f* reconquest

reconsidérer [rəkɔ̃sidere] §10 *tr* to reconsider

reconstituant [rəkɔ̃stitɥɑ̃] *m* tonic

reconstituer [rəkɔ̃stitɥe] *tr* to reconstruct; to restore

reconstruire [rəkɔ̃strɥir] §19 *tr* to reconstruct

record [rəkɔr] *adj invar & m* record

recordman [rəkɔrdman] *m* record holder

recoudre [rəkudr] §13 *tr* to sew up

recouper [rəkupe] *tr* to cut again; to blend (*wines*)

recourir [rəkurir] §14 *intr* to run again; **recourir à** to resort to; to appeal to

recours [rəkur] *m* recourse; **recours en grâce** petition for pardon

recouvrement [rəkuvrəmɑ̃] *m* recovery

recouvrer [rəkuvre] *tr* to recover

recouvrir [rəkuvrir] §65 *tr* to cover; to cover up; to mask; to resurface (*e.g., a road*) || *ref* to overlap

récréation [rekreasjɔ̃] *f* recreation; recess (*at school*)

recréer [rəkree] *tr* to re-create

récréer [rekree] *tr & ref* to relax

récrier [rekrije] *ref* to cry out

récrire [rekrir] §25 *tr* to rewrite; to write again

recroquevil·lé -lée [rəkrɔkvije] *adj* shriveled up, curled up; huddled up

recroqueviller [rəkrɔkvije] *tr & ref* to shrivel up, to curl up

re·cru -crue [rəkry] *adj* exhausted

recrue [rəkry] *f* recruit

recruter [rəkryte] *tr* to recruit || *ref* to be recruited

rectangle [rektɑ̃gl] *m* rectangle

rectificateur [rektifikatœr] *m* rectifier

rectifier [rektifje] *tr* to rectify; to true up; to grind (*a cylinder*)

rectum [rektɔm] *m* rectum

reçu [rəsy] *m* receipt

recueil [rəkœj] *m* collection; compilation

recueillement [rəkœjmɑ̃] *m* meditation

recueillir [rəkœjir] §18 *tr* to collect, to gather; to take in (*a needy person*); to receive (*a legacy*) || *ref* to collect oneself, to meditate

recuire [rəkɥir] §19 *tr* to anneal, to temper; to cook over again || *intr* (fig) to stew

recul [rəkyl] *m* backing, backward movement; kick, recoil; **être en recul** to be losing ground; **prendre du recul** to consider in perspective

reculer [rəkyle] *tr* to move back; to put off (*e.g., a decision*) || *intr* to move back; to back out; to recoil; **reculer devant** to shrink from || *ref* to move back

reculons [rəkylɔ̃]—**à reculons** backwards

récupération [rekyperasjɔ̃] *f* recovery

récupérer [rekypere] §10 *tr* to salvage, to recover; to recuperate; to make up (*e.g., lost hours*); to find another job for || *intr* to recuperate

récurer [rekyre] *tr* to scour

récur·rent [rekyrɑ̃] **récur·rente** [rekyrɑ̃t] *adj* recurrent

récuser [rekyze] *tr* to take exception to || *ref* to refuse to give one's opinion

rédac·teur [redaktœr] **-trice** [tris] *mf* editor; **rédacteur en chef** editor in chief; **rédacteur gérant** managing editor; **rédacteur publicitaire** copywriter; **rédacteur sportif** sports editor

rédaction [redaksjɔ̃] *f* editorial staff; editorial office; edition; editing

reddition [redisjɔ̃] *f* surrender

redécouvrir [rədekuvrir] §65 *tr* to rediscover

rédemp·teur [redɑ̃ptœr] **-trice** [tris] *adj* redemptive || *mf* redeemer

rédemption [redɑ̃psjɔ̃] *f* redemption

redevable [rədvabl] *adj* indebted

redevance [rədvɑ̃s] *f* dues, fees; rent; tax (*on radio sets*)

rédiger [rediʒe] §38 *tr* to edit; to draft; to write up

redingote [rədɛ̃gɔt] *f* frock coat

redire [rədir] §22 *tr* to repeat; to give away (*a secret*) || *intr*—**trouver à redire à** to find fault with

redon·dant [rədɔ̃dɑ̃] **-dante** [dɑ̃t] *adj* redundant

redoutable [rədutabl] *adj* frightening

redoute [rədut] *f* redoubt

redouter [rədute] *tr* to dread

redressement [rədresmɑ̃] *m* straightening out; redress; (elec) rectifying

redresser [rədrese] *tr* to straighten; to hold up (*e.g., the head*); to redress; (elec) to rectify || *ref* to straighten up

redresseur [rədresœr] *m* (elec) rectifier; **redresseur de torts** knight-errant; (coll) reformer

réduction [redyksjɔ̃] *f* reduction

réduire [reduir] §19 *tr* to reduce; to set (*a bone*)

réduit [redui] *m* retreat, nook; redoubt

rééditer [reedite] *tr* to reedit

réel réelle [reel] *adj & m* real, actual

réélection [reeleksjɔ̃] *f* reelection

réellement [reelmɑ̃] *adv* really

réescompte [reeskɔ̃t] *m* rediscount

réexamen [reegzamɛ̃] *m* reexamination

réexpédier [reekspedje] *tr* to reship; to return to sender

réexpédition [reekspedisjɔ̃] *f* reshipment; return

refaire [rəfer] §29 *tr* to redo || *intr*—**à refaire** to be done over; to be dealt over || *ref* to recover; to make good one's losses

référence [referɑ̃s] *f* reference

référendum or **referendum** [referɛ̃dɔm] *m* referendum

référer [refere] §10 *intr*—**en référer à** to appeal to || *ref*—**s'en référer à** to leave it up to; **se référer à** to refer to

refermer [rəferme] *tr & ref* to close again, to close

refiler [rəfile] *tr*—**refiler à qn** (slang) to palm off on s.o.

réfléchir [reflefir] *tr & intr* to reflect || *ref* to be reflected

reflet [rəfle] *m* reflection; glint, gleam

refléter [rəflete] §10 *tr* to reflect || *ref* to be mirrored

réflexe [refleks] *adj & m* reflex

réflexion [refleksjɔ̃] *f* reflection

refluer [rəflye] *intr* to ebb

reflux [rəfly] *m* ebb

refonte [rəfɔ̃t] *f* recasting

réforma·teur [reformatœr] **-trice** [tris] *mf* reformer

réformation [reformasjɔ̃] *f* reformation

réforme [reform] *f* reform; **la Réforme** the Reformation

réfor·mé -mée [reforme] *adj* (eccl) Reformed; (mil) disabled

reformer [rəforme] *tr & ref* to regroup

réformer [reforme] *tr* to reform; (mil) to discharge || *ref* to reform

refou·lé -lée [rəfule] *adj* (coll) inhibited

refoulement [rəfulmɑ̃] *m* driving back; (psychoanal) repression

refouler [rəfule] *tr* to drive back; to choke back (*a sob*); to sail against (*the current*); to compress, stem; (psychoanal) to repress || *intr* to flow back

réfractaire [refrakter] *adj* refractory; rebellious || *mf* insubordinate

réfraction [refraksjɔ̃] *f* refraction

refrain [rəfrɛ̃] *m* refrain; hum; **le même refrain** the same old tune

réfréner [refrene] §10 *tr* to curb

réfrigérateur [refriʒeratœr] *m* refrigerator

réfrigérer [refriʒere] §10 *tr* to refrigerate; (coll) to chill to the bone

refroidir [rəfrwadir] *tr* to cool; (slang) to rub out || *intr* to cool || *ref* to cool; to catch cold

refroidissement [rəfrwadismɑ̃] *m* cooling

refuge [rəfyʒ] *m* refuge; shelter; safety zone

réfu·gié -giée [refyʒje] *mf* refugee

réfugier [refyʒje] *ref* to take refuge

refus [rəfy] *m* refusal; **refus seulement** regrets only (*to invitation*)

refuser [rəfyze] *tr* to refuse; to refuse to recognize; to flunk; to decline || *intr* to refuse; **refuser de** or **à** to refuse to || *ref* to be refused; **se refuser à** to refuse to accept

réfuter [refyte] *tr* to refute

regagner [rəgaɲe] *tr* to regain

regain [rəgɛ̃] *m* second growth; (fig) aftermath; **regain de** new lease on

ré·gal [regal] *m* (*pl* **-gals**) treat

régaler [regale] *tr* to treat; to level || *intr* to treat

regard [rəgar] *m* look, glance; **couver du regard** to gloat over; to look fondly at; to look greedily at; **en regard** facing, opposite

regar·dant [rəgardɑ̃] **-dante** [dɑ̃t] *adj* (coll) penny-pinching

regarder [rəgarde] *tr* to look at; to face; to concern ‖ *intr* to look; **regarder à** to pay attention to; to watch (*one's money*); to mind (*the price*); **y regarder à deux fois** to watch one's step, think twice ‖ *ref* to face each other

régate [regat] *f* regatta

régence [rezɑ̃s] *f* regency

régénérer [rezenere] §10 *tr & ref* to regenerate

ré·gent [rezɑ̃] **-gente** [zɑ̃t] *mf* regent

régenter [rezɑ̃te] *tr & intr* to boss

régicide [rezisid] *mf* regicide (*person*) ‖ *m* regicide (*act*)

régie [rezi] *f* commission, administration; excise tax; stage management; **en régie** state owned or operated

regimber [rəzɛ̃be] *intr & ref* to revolt; to balk

régime [rezim] *m* government, form of government; administration; system; diet; performance, working conditions; rate (*of speed; of flow; of charge or discharge of a storage battery*); bunch, cluster; stem (*of bananas*); (gram) complement; (gram) government; **en régime permanent** under steady working conditions

régiment [rezimɑ̃] *m* regiment

régimentaire [rezimɑ̃tɛr] *adj* regimental

région [rezjɔ̃] *f* region

régir [rezir] *tr* to govern

régisseur [rezisœr] *m* manager; stage manager

registre [rezistr] *m* register; damper; throttle valve

réglable [reglabl] *adj* adjustable

réglage [reglaz] *m* setting, adjusting; lines (*on paper*); (mach, rad, telv) tuning

règle [regl] *f* rule; ruler; **en règle** in order; **en règle générale** as a general rule; **règle à calcul** slide rule; **règles** menstrual period

ré·glé -glée [regle] *adj* regulated; adjusted, tuned; well-behaved, orderly; ruled (*paper*); finished, decided

règlement [rɛgləmɑ̃] *m* regulation, rule; settlement; **règlement intérieur** by-laws

réglementaire [rɛgləmɑ̃tɛr] *adj* regular; regulation

réglementer [rɛgləmɑ̃te] *tr* to regulate, to control

régler [regle] §10 *tr* to regulate, to put in order; to set (*a watch*); to settle (*an account*); to rule (*paper*); (aut, rad, telv) to tune ‖ *intr* to pay

réglisse [reglis] *m & f* licorice

règne [rɛɲ] *m* reign; (biol) kingdom

régner [reɲe] §10 *intr* to reign

regorger [rəgɔrze] §38 *intr* to overflow; **regorger de** to abound in

regratter [rəgrate] *tr* to scrape ‖ *intr* to pinch pennies

regret [rəgrɛ] *m* regret; **à regret** regretfully

regrettable [rəgrɛtabl] *adj* regrettable

regretter [rəgrɛte] *tr* to regret; to long for, to miss ‖ *intr* to be sorry

régulariser [regylarize] *tr* to regularize; to adjust, regulate

régularité [regylarite] *f* regularity

régula·teur [regylatœr] **-trice** [tris] *adj* regulating ‖ *m* (mach) governor

régulation [regylasjɔ̃] *f* regulation

régu·lier [regylje] **-lière** [ljɛr] *adj* regular; (coll) aboveboard, fair ‖ *m* regular

réhabiliter [reabilite] *tr* to rehabilitate

rehausser [rəose] *tr* to heighten; to enhance

Reims [rɛ̃s] *m* Rheims

rein [rɛ̃] *m* kidney

réincarnation [reɛ̃karnɑsjɔ̃] *f* reincarnation

reine [ren] *f* queen

reine-claude [renklod] *f* (*pl* **-claudes** or **reines-claudes**) greengage

reine-des-prés [rendepre] *f* (*pl* **reines-des-prés**) meadowsweet

reine-marguerite [renmargərit] *f* (*pl* **reines-marguerites**) aster

réintégrer [reɛ̃tegre] §10 *tr* to reinstate; to return to

réitérer [reitere] §10 *tr* reiterate

rejaillir [rəzajir] *intr* to spurt out; to bounce; to splash; **rejaillir sur** to reflect on

rejet [rəze] *m* casting up; rejection; enjambment; (bot) shoot

rejeter [rəzte] §34 *tr* to reject; to throw back; to throw up; to shift (*responsibility*) ‖ *ref* to fall back

rejeton [rəztɔ̃] *m* shoot; offshoot, offspring; (coll) child

rejoindre [rəzwɛ̃dr] §35 *tr* to rejoin; to overtake ‖ *ref* to meet

réjouir [rezwir] *tr* to gladden, cheer ‖ *ref* to rejoice, to be delighted

réjouissance [rezwisɑ̃s] *f* rejoicing; **réjouissances** festivities

réjouis·sant [rezwisɑ̃] **-sante** [rezwisɑ̃t] *adj* cheery; amusing

relâche [rɑlɑʃ] *m & f* respite, letup ‖ *f* (naut) stop; **faire relâche** (naut) to make a call; (theat) to close (*for a day or two*); **relâche** (public sign) no performance today

relâ·ché -chée [rɑlɑʃe] *adj* lax; loose

relâchement [rɑlɑʃmɑ̃] *m* relaxation; letting up

relâcher [rɑlɑʃe] *tr* to loosen; to relax; to release ‖ *intr* (naut) to make a call ‖ *ref* to loosen; to become lax

relais [rɑlɛ] *m* relay; shift

relance [rɑlɑ̃s] *f* raise (*e.g., in poker*); outbreak

relancer [rɑlɑ̃se] §51 *tr* to start up again; to harass, to hound; to return (*the ball*); to raise (*the ante*) ‖ *intr* (cards) to raise

re·laps -lapse [rɑlaps] *mf* backslider

relater [rɑlate] *tr* to relate

rela·tif [rɑlatif] **-tive** [tiv] *adj* relative

relation [rɑlasjɔ̃] *f* relation; **en relation avec, en relations avec** in touch with; **relations** connections

relativité [rɑlativite] *f* relativity

relaxation [rɑlaksɑsjɔ̃] *f* relaxation

relaxer [rəlakse] *tr* to relax; to free ‖ *ref* to relax

relayer [rəleje] §49 *tr* to relay; to relieve ‖ *ref* to work in relays or shifts

reléguer [rələge] §10 *tr* to relegate

relent [rəlɑ̃] *m* musty smell

relève [rəlɛv] *f* relief; change (*of the guard*); **prendre la relève** to take over

rele·vé -vée [rələve] *adj* lofty, elevated; turned up; graded (*curve*); spicy ‖ *m* check list; tuck (*in dress*); (culin) next course; **faire le relevé de** to survey; to check off; **relevé de compte** bank statement; **relevé de compteur** meter reading; **relevé de notes des écoles** transcript of grades

relèvement [rələvmɑ̃] *m* raising; recovery, improvement; picking up (*e.g., of wounded*); (naut) bearing

relever [rələve] §2 *tr* to raise; to turn up; to restore; to relieve, enhance; to pick out; to take a reading of; to season; (mil) to relieve ‖ *intr*—**relever de** to recover from; to depend on ‖ *ref* to rise; to recover; to right itself; to take turns

relief [rəljɛf] *m* relief; **en relief** in relief; **reliefs** leavings

relier [rəlje] *tr* to bind; to link

re·lieur [rəljœr] **-lieuse** [ljøz] *mf* bookbinder

reli·gieux [rəliʒjø] **-gieuse** [ʒjøz] *adj* religious ‖ *m* monk ‖ *f* nun; cream puff

religion [rəliʒjɔ̃] *f* religion

reliquat [rəlika] *m* remainder

relique [rəlik] *f* relic

relire [rəlir] §36 *tr* to read again; to read over again

reliure [rəljyr] *f* binding; bookbinding

reloger [rələʒe] §38 *tr* to find a new home for, to relocate

reluire [rəlɥir] §37 *intr* to shine, gleam, sparkle

relui·sant [rəlɥizɑ̃] **-sante** [zɑ̃t] *adj* shiny, gleaming; **peu reluisant** unpromising, not brilliant

reluquer [rəlyke] *tr* to have an eye on

remâcher [rəmɑʃe] *tr* (coll) to stew over

remailler [rəmaje] *tr* to mend the meshes of

remanier [rəmanje] *tr* to revise, revamp; to reshuffle

remarier [rəmarje] *tr & ref* to remarry

remarquable [rəmarkabl] *adj* remarkable

remarquer [rəmarke] *tr & intr* to remark, to notice; **faire remarquer** to point out ‖ *ref*—**se faire remarquer** to make oneself conspicuous

remballer [rɑ̃bale] *tr* to repack

rembarquer [rɑ̃barke] *tr, intr, & ref* to reembark

rembarrer [rɑ̃bare] *tr* to snub, rebuff

remblai [rɑ̃blɛ] *m* fill; embankment

remblayer [rɑ̃bleje] §49 *tr* to fill

rembobiner [rɑ̃bɔbine] *tr* to rewind

remboîter [rɑ̃bwate] *tr* to reset (*a bone*); to recase (*a book*)

rembourrer [rɑ̃bure] *tr* to upholster; to stuff; to pad

rembourrure [rɑ̃buryr] *f* stuffing

remboursement [rɑ̃bursəmɑ̃] *m* reimbursement

rembourser [rɑ̃burse] *tr* to reimburse

rembrunir [rɑ̃brynir] *tr* to darken; to sadden ‖ *ref* to cloud over

remède [rəmɛd] *m* remedy

remédier [rəmedje] *intr* (with *dat*) to remedy

remembrement [rəmɑ̃brəmɑ̃] *m* regrouping

remémorer [rəmemɔre] *tr*—**remémorer q.ch. à qn** to remind s.o. of s.th. ‖ *ref* to remember

remerciement [rəmɛrsimɑ̃] *m* thanking; **remerciements** thanks; **mille remerciements de** or **pour** a thousand thanks for

remercier [rəmɛrsje] *tr* to thank; to dismiss (*an employee*); to refuse with thanks; **remercier qn de** + *inf* to thank s.o. for + *ger*; **remercier qn de** or **pour** to thank s.o. for

remettre [rəmɛtr] §42 *tr* to remit, to deliver; to put back; to put back on; to give back; to put off; to reset ‖ *ref* to resume; to recover; to pull oneself together; (*said of weather*) to clear; **s'en remettre à** to leave it up to, to depend on

remise [rəmiz] *f* remittance; discount; delivery; postponement; surrender, return; garage; cover (*for game*); **de remise** rented (*car*)

remiser [rəmize] *tr* to put away; to park ‖ *ref* to take cover

rémission [remisjɔ̃] *f* remission

remmailler [rɑ̃maje] *tr* to darn

remmener [rɑ̃mne] §2 *tr* to take back

remon·tant [rəmɔ̃tɑ̃] **-tante** [tɑ̃t] *adj* fortifying; remontant (*rose*) ‖ *m* tonic

remonte [rəmɔ̃t] *f* ascent

remontée [rəmɔ̃te] *f* climb; surfacing; comeback

remonte-pente [rəmɔ̃tpɑ̃t] *m* (pl **-pentes**) ski lift

remonter [rəmɔ̃te] *tr* to remount; to pull up; to wind (*a clock*); to pep up; (theat) to put on again ‖ *intr* (aux: ÊTRE) to go up again; to date back ‖ *ref* to pep up

remontoir [rəmɔ̃twar] *m* knob (*of stem-winder*)

remontrance [rəmɔ̃trɑ̃s] *f* remonstrance

remontrer [rəmɔ̃tre] *tr* to show again; to point out ‖ *intr*—**en remontrer à** to outdo, to best

remords [rəmɔr] *m* remorse

remorque [rəmɔrk] *f* tow rope; trailer; **à la remorque** in tow

remorquer [rəmɔrke] *tr* to tow; to haul

remorqueur [rəmɔrkœr] *m* tugboat

rémouleur [remulœr] *m* knife grinder, scissors grinder

remous [rəmu] *m* eddy; wash (*of boat*); agitation

rempailler [rɑ̃paje] *tr* to cane

rempart [rɑ̃par] *m* rampart

remplaçable [rɑ̃plasabl] *adj* replaceable

rempla·çant [rɑ̃plasɑ̃] **-çante** [sɑ̃t] *mf* replacement, substitute

remplacement [rãplasmã] *m* replacement

remplacer [rãplase] §51 *tr* to replace; to take the place of; **remplacer par** to replace with

rem·pli -plie [rãpli] *adj* full ‖ *m* tuck

remplir [rãplir] *tr* to fill; to fill up; to fill out or in; to fulfill ‖ *ref* to fill up

remplissage [rãplisaʒ] *m* filling up

remplumer [rãplyme] *ref* (coll) to put on flesh again; (coll) to make a comeback

remporter [rãpɔrte] *tr* to take back; to carry off; to win

remue-ménage [rəmymenaʒ] *m invar* stir, bustle, to-do

remuer [rəmɥe] *tr* to move; to stir; to remove (*e.g., a piece of furniture*) ‖ *intr* to move ‖ *ref* to move; to hustle

rémunération [remynerasjɔ̃] *f* remuneration

renâcler [rənakle] *intr* to snort; **renâcler à** (coll) to shrink from, to bridle at

renaissance [rənesãs] *f* renascence, rebirth; renaissance

renais·sant [rənesã] **renais·sante** [rənesãt] *adj* renascent, reviving; Renaissance

renaître [rənetr] §46 *tr* to be reborn; to revive; to grow again

re·nard [rənar] **-narde** [nard] *mf* fox

renché·ri -rie [rãʃeri] *adj* fastidious

renchérir [rãʃerir] *tr* to make more expensive ‖ *intr* to go up in price; **renchérir sur** to improve on

rencontre [rãkɔ̃tr] *f* meeting, encounter; clash; collision; **aller à la rencontre de** to go to meet

rencontrer [rãkɔ̃tre] *tr* to meet, encounter ‖ *ref* to meet; to collide; to occur

rendement [rãdmã] *m* yield; (mech) output, efficiency

rendez-vous [rãdevu] *m* appointment, date; rendezvous; **sur rendez-vous** by appointment

rendre [rãdr] *tr* to render; to yield; to surrender; to make; to translate; to vomit ‖ *intr* to bring in, yield ‖ *ref* to surrender; **se rendre à** to go to; **se rendre compte de** to realize

ren·du -due [rãdy] *adj* arrived; translated; all in, exhausted ‖ *m* rendering; returned article

rêne [ren] *f* rein

réné·gat [rənega] **-gate** [gat] *mf* renegade

renfer·mé -mée [rãferme] *adj* closemouthed, stand-offish ‖ *m* close smell; **sentir le renfermé** to smell stuffy

renfermer [rãferme] *tr* to contain; to include ‖ *ref—*se renfermer dans to withdraw into; to confine oneself to

renfler [rãfle] *ref* to swell up

renflouer [rãflue] *tr* to keep afloat; to salvage

renfoncement [rãfɔ̃smã] *m* recess; hollow; dent

renfoncer [rãfɔ̃se] §51 *tr* to recess; to dent; to pull down (*e.g., one's hat*) ‖ *ref* to recede; to draw back

renforcement [rãfɔrsəmã] *m* reinforcement

renforcer [rãfɔrse] §51 *tr* to reinforce

renforcir [rãfɔrsir] *tr* (slang) to strengthen ‖ *intr* (slang) to grow stronger

renfort [rãfɔr] *m* reinforcement

renfro·gné -gnée [rãfrɔɲe] *adj* sullen, glum

renfrogner [rãfrɔɲe] *ref* to scowl

rengager [rãgaʒe] §38 *tr* to rehire ‖ *intr & ref* to reenlist

rengaine [rãgen] *f*—**la même rengaine** the same old story; **vieille rengaine** old refrain

rengorger [rãgɔrʒe] §38 *ref* to strut

reniement [rənimã] *m* denial

renier [rənje] *tr* to deny; to repudiate

renifler [rənifle] *tr & intr* to sniff

renne [ren] *m* reindeer

renom [rənɔ̃] *m* renown, fame

renom·mé -mée [rənɔme] *adj* renowned, well-known ‖ *f* fame; reputation

renommer [rənɔme] *tr* to reelect; to reappoint

renoncement [rənɔ̃smã] *m* renunciation

renoncer [rənɔ̃se] §51 *tr* to renounce, repudiate ‖ *intr* to give up; (cards) to renege; (with *dat*) to renounce; (with *dat*) to give up, to abandon; **y renoncer** to give it up

renonciation [rənɔ̃sjasjɔ̃] *f* renunciation; waiver

renoncule [rənɔ̃kyl] *f* buttercup; **renoncule double** bachelor's-button; **renoncule langue** spearwort

renouer [rənwe] *tr* to tie again; to resume (*e.g., a conversation*) ‖ *intr* to renew a friendship

renou·veau [rənuvo] *m* (*pl* **-veaux**) springtime; revival

renouvelable [rənuvlabl] *adj* renewable

renouveler [rənuvle] §34 *tr & ref* to renew

renouvellement [rənuvelmã] *m* renewal

rénover [renɔve] *tr* to renew; to renovate

renseignement [rãsɛɲmã] *m* piece of information; **de renseignements** (mil) intelligence; **renseignements** information

renseigner [rãsɛɲe] *tr* to inform ‖ *ref* to find out; **se renseigner auprès de qn** to inquire of s.o.

rentable [rãtabl] *adj* profitable

rente [rãt] *f* revenue, income; annuity; dividend, return; **rente viagère** life annuity

ren·té -tée [rãte] *adj* well-off

renter [rãte] *tr* to endow

ren·tier -tière [rãtje] *mf* person of independent means

ren·tré -trée [rãtre] *adj* sunken (*eyes*); suppressed (*feelings*) ‖ *f* return; reopening (*of school*); yield

rentrer [rãtre] *tr* to bring in or back; to put in; to hold back (*e.g., one's tears*); to draw in (*claws*) ‖ *intr* (aux: ÊTRE) to return, to reenter; to go or come home; to be paid or collected; **rentrer dans** to fit into; to come back to; to get back, recover; **rentrer en soi-même** to take stock of oneself

renverse [rɑ̃vɛrs] *f* shift, turn; **à la renverse** backwards

renversement [rɑ̃vɛrsəmɑ̃] *m* reversal, shift; upset, overturn; overthrow

renverser [rɑ̃vɛrse] *tr* to reverse; to overthrow || *intr & ref* to capsize

renvoi [rɑ̃vwa] *m* dismissal; postponement; reference; return; belch

renvoyer [rɑ̃vwaje] §26 *tr* to dismiss; to fire (*an employee*); to postpone; to refer; to send back

réorganiser [reɔrganize] *tr & ref* to reorganize

réouverture [reuvɛrtyr] *f* reopening

repaire [rəpɛr] *m* den

repaître [rəpɛtr] §12 *tr* to graze; **repaître de** to feast (*e.g., one's eyes*) on || *ref* to eat one's fill (*said of only animals*); **se repaître de** to indulge in, to wallow in

répandre [repɑ̃dr] *tr* to spread; to strew, scatter; to spill; to shed || *ref* to spread; **se répandre en** to be profuse in

répan-du -due [repɑ̃dy] *adj* widespread; widely known

reparaître [rəparɛtr] §12 *intr* to reappear

répara-teur [reparatœr] **-trice** [tris] *adj* restorative || *m* repairman

réparation [reparasjɔ̃] *f* repair; reparation; restoration

réparer [repare] *tr* to repair; to mend, patch; to make up (*a loss*); to redress (*a wrong*); to restore (*one's strength*)

repartie [rəparti], [reparti] *f* repartee

repartir [rəpartir] §64 *tr* to retort || *intr* (*aux:* ÊTRE) to start again; to leave again

répartir [repartir] *tr* to distribute

répartiteur [repartitœr] *m* distributor; assessor

répartition [repartisjɔ̃] *f* distribution; apportionment; range (*of words*)

repas [rəpa] *m* meal, repast; **dernier repas** (rel) last supper; **repas champêtre** picnic; **repas de noce** wedding breakfast; **repas froid** cold snack; **repas sur le pouce** takeout meal

repassage [rəpasaʒ] *m* recrossing; ironing; stropping; whetting

repasser [rəpase] *tr* to pass again; to go over, to review; to iron; to strop; to whet || *intr* to pass by again; to drop in again

repêcher [rəpeʃe] *tr* to fish out; to give another chance to; (coll) to get (*s.o.*) out of a scrape

repentance [rəpɑ̃tɑ̃s] *f* repentance

repen-tant [rəpɑ̃tɑ̃] **-tante** [tɑ̃t] *adj* repentant

repen-ti -tie [rəpɑ̃ti] *adj* repentant

repentir [rəpɑ̃tir] *m* repentance || §41 *ref* to repent; **se repentir de** to be sorry for, to repent

repérage [reperaʒ] *m* spotting, locating; tracking; marking with a reference mark; (mov) synchronization

répercussion [repɛrkysjɔ̃] *f* repercussion

répercuter [repɛrkyte] *tr* to reflect || *ref* to reverberate; to have repercussions

repère [rəpɛr] *m* mark, reference

repérer [rəpere] §10 *tr* to locate, spot; to mark with a reference mark; (mov) to synchronize

répertoire [repɛrtwar] *m* repertory; index; **répertoire à onglets** thumb index; **répertoire d'adresses** address book; **répertoire vivant** walking encyclopedia

répéter [repete] §10 *tr & ref* to repeat

répéti-teur [repetitœr] **-trice** [tris] *mf* assistant teacher; coach, tutor

répétition [repetisjɔ̃] *f* repetition; private lesson, tutoring; rehearsal; **répétition des couturières** next to last dress rehearsal; **répétition générale** final dress rehearsal

repeupler [rəpœple] *tr* to repeople; to restock

repiquer [rəpike] *tr* to plant out (*seedlings*); to repave; to restitch; to rerecord; (phot) to retouch || *intr—* **repiquer à** (slang) to come back to

répit [repi] *m* respite, letup

replacement [rəplasmɑ̃] *m* replacement; reinvestment

replacer [rəplase] §51 *tr* to replace; to find a new job for; to reinvest || *ref* to find a new job

replâtrage [rəplɑtraʒ] *m* replastering; makeshift; (fig) patchwork

re-plet [rəplɛ] **-plète** [plɛt] *adj* fat, plump

repli [rəpli] *m* crease, fold; dip, depression; (mil) falling back

replier [rəplije] *tr* to refold; to turn up; to close (*e.g., an umbrella*) || *ref* to curl up, to coil up; (mil) to fall back

réplique [replik] *f* reply, retort; replica; **donner la réplique à qn** to answer s.o.; (theat) to give s.o. his cue; (theat) to play the straight man or stooge for s.o.

répliquer [replike] *tr & intr* to reply

replonger [rəplɔ̃ʒe] §38 *tr* to plunge again || *intr* to dive again || *ref—se* **replonger dans** to get back into

répon-dant [repɔ̃dɑ̃] **-dante** [dɑ̃t] *mf* guarantor; (eccl) server; **avoir du répondant** (coll) to have money behind one

répondre [repɔ̃dr] *tr* to answer (*e.g., yes or no*); to assure || *intr* to answer, reply; to answer back, be saucy; to reecho; **répondre à** to answer (*e.g., a question, a letter*); to correspond to; **répondre de** to answer for (*a person*); to guarantee (*a thing*) || *ref* to answer each other; to correspond to each other; to be in harmony

réponse [repɔ̃s] *f* answer, response; **réponse normande** evasive answer

report [rəpɔr] *m* carrying forward or over; carry-over

reportage [rəpɔrtaʒ] *m* reporting

reporter [rəpɔrtɛr] *m* reporter || [rəpɔrte] *tr* to carry back; to postpone; (math) to carry forward || *intr* (com) to carry stock; **à reporter** carried forward || *ref*—**se reporter à** to be carried back to (*e.g., childhood days*); to refer to

reporteur [rǝpɔrtœr] *m* broker

repos [rǝpo] *m* rest, repose; **au repos** not running, still; **de tout repos** reliable; **en repos** at rest; **repos!** (mil) at ease!

repo·sé -sée [rǝpoze] *adj* refreshed, relaxed

reposer [rǝpoze] *tr* to rest || *intr* to rest; **ici repose . . . here lies . . .** || *ref* to rest; **s'en reposer sur** to rely on

repous·sant [rǝpusɑ̃] **repous·sante** [rǝpusɑ̃t] *adj* repulsive

repousser [rǝpuse] *tr* to push, shove; to repulse, repel; to reject, refuse; to postpone; to emboss || *intr* to grow again; to be offensive; (arti) to recoil

repoussoir [rǝpuswar] *m* foil; contrast; (mach) driving bolt

reprendre [rǝprɑ̃dr] §56 *tr* to take back; to resume; to regain (*consciousness*); to find fault with; to take in (*e.g., a dress*); to catch (*one's breath*); (theat) to put on again || *intr* to start again; to pick up, to improve; to criticize || *ref* to pull oneself together; to correct oneself in speaking

représailles [rǝprezaj] *fpl* reprisal

représentant [rǝprezɑ̃tɑ̃] *m* representative

représenta·tif [rǝprezɑ̃tatif] **-tive** [tiv] *adj* representative

représentation [rǝprezɑ̃tɑsjɔ̃] *f* representation; performance; remonstrance

représenter [rǝprezɑ̃te] *tr* to represent; to put on, to perform || *intr* to make a good showing

répression [represjɔ̃] *f* repression

réprimande [reprimɑ̃d] *f* reprimand

réprimander [reprimɑ̃de] *tr* to reprimand

réprimer [reprime] *tr* to repress

re·pris [rǝpri] **-prise** [priz] *adj* recaptured; **être repris de** to suffer from a recurrence of || *m*—**repris de justice** hardened criminal, habitual offender || *f* see **reprise**

reprisage [rǝprizaʒ] *m* darning

reprise [rǝpriz] *f* recapture; resumption; darning; pickup (*acceleration of motor*); (theat) revival; **à plusieurs reprises** several times; **faire une reprise à** to darn; **par reprises** a little at a time

repriser [rǝprize] *tr* to darn; to mend

réproba·teur [reprɔbatœr] **-trice** [tris] *adj* reproving

reproche [rǝprɔʃ] *m* reproach

reprocher [rǝprɔʃe] *tr* to reproach; to begrudge; (law) to take exception to (*a witness*); **reprocher q.ch. à qn** to reproach s.o. for s.th.; to begrudge s.o. s.th.; to remind s.o. reproachfully of s.th.

reproduction [rǝprɔdyksjɔ̃] *f* reproduction

reproduire [rǝprɔdɥir] §19 *tr & ref* to reproduce

réprou·vé -vée [repruve] *adj & mf* outcast; damned

réprouver [repruve] *tr* to disapprove

reptile [reptil] *m* reptile

re·pu -pue [rǝpy] *adj* satiated

républi·cain [repyblikɛ̃] **-caine** [kɛn] *adj & mf* republican

république [repyblik] *f* republic

répudier [repydje] *tr* to repudiate

répu·gnant [repyɲɑ̃] **-gnante** [ɲɑ̃t] *adj* repugnant

répugner [repyɲe] *intr* (with *dat*) to disgust; to balk at; **répugner à + inf** to be loath to + *inf*

répul·sif [repylsif] **-sive** [siv] *adj* repulsive

réputation [repytɑsjɔ̃] *f* reputation

répu·té -tée [repyte] *adj* of high repute; **être réputé** to be reputed to be

requérir [rǝkerir] §3 *tr* to demand; to ask; to require; to summon; to requisition

requête [rǝket] *f* petition, appeal

requiem [rekɥijem] *m* requiem

requin [rǝkɛ̃] *m* shark

réquisition [rekizisjɔ̃] *f* requisition

réquisitionner [rekizisjɔne] *tr* to requisition

réquisitoire [rekizitwar] *m* indictment

res·capé -capée [reskape] *adj* rescued || *mf* survivor

rescinder [resɛ̃de] *tr* to rescind

rescousse [reskus] *f* rescue

ré·seau [rezo] *m* (*pl* **-seaux**) net; network, system; **réseau de barbelés** barbed wire entanglement

réséda [rezeda] *m* mignonette

réservation [rezervɑsjɔ̃] *f* reservation

réserve [rezerv] *f* reserve; reservation; **de réserve** emergency, reserve (*rations, fund, etc.*); **sous réserve que** on condition that; **sous toutes réserves** without committing oneself

réserver [rezerve] *tr* to reserve; to set aside || *ref* to set aside for oneself; to wait and see, to hold off

réserviste [rezervist] *m* reservist

réservoir [rezervwar] *m* reservoir, tank; **réservoir de bombes** bomb bay

résidence [rezidɑ̃s] *f* residence

rési·dent [rezidɑ̃] **-dente** [dɑ̃t] *mf* alien, foreigner; (dipl) resident

résiden·tiel -tielle [rezidɑ̃sjɛl] *adj* residential

résider [rezide] *intr* to reside

résidu [rezidy] *m* residue; refuse

résignation [reziɲɑsjɔ̃] *f* resignation

résigner [reziɲe] *tr* to resign || *ref* to be or become resigned

résilier [rezilje] *tr* to cancel

résille [rezij] *f* hair net

résine [rezin] *f* resin

résistance [rezistɑ̃s] *f* resistance

résis·tant [rezistɑ̃] **-tante** [tɑ̃t] *adj* resistant; strong; fast (*color*)

résister [reziste] *intr* to be fast, not run (*said of colors or dyes*); (with *dat*) to resist, to withstand, to hold out against; (with *dat*) to weather (*e.g., a storm*); **résister à + inf** to resist + *ger*

réso·lu -lue [rezɔly] *adj* resolute, resolved

résolution [rezɔlysjɔ̃] f resolution; canceling

résonance [rezɔnɑ̃s] f resonance

résonner [rezɔne] intr to resound; to re-echo

résorber [rezɔrbe] tr to absorb ‖ ref to become absorbed

résoudre [rezudr] §60 tr to resolve; to decide; to solve; to persuade; to cancel; **être résolu à** to be resolved to ‖ intr—**résoudre de** to decide to ‖ ref—**se résoudre à** to decide to; to reconcile oneself to; **se résoudre en** to turn into

respect [respe] m respect; **présenter ses respects (à)** to pay one's respects (to); **respect de soi** or **soi-même** self-respect; **respect humain** [respekymɛ̃] fear of what people might say; **sauf votre** (**mon**, etc.) **respect** with all due respect; **pardon the language**

respectable [respektabl] adj respectable

respecter [respekte] tr to respect ‖ ref to keep one's self-respect

respec•tif [respektif] **-tive** [tiv] adj respective

respec•tueux [respektɥø] **-tueuse** [tɥøz] adj respectful

respirer [respire] tr to breathe ‖ intr to breathe; to catch one's breath

resplendis•sant [resplãdisã] **resplendis•sante** [resplãdisãt] adj resplendent

responsabilité [respɔ̃sabilite] f responsibility

responsable [respɔ̃sabl] adj responsible; **responsable de** responsible for; **responsable envers** accountable to ‖ mf person responsible, person in charge

resquiller [reskije] tr (coll) to obtain by fraud ‖ intr (coll) to crash the gate

resquil•leur [reskijœr] **resquil•leuse** [reskijøz] mf (coll) gate-crasher

ressac [rəsak] m surf; undertow

ressaisir [rəsezir] tr to recapture ‖ ref to regain one's self-control

ressasser [rəsase] tr to go over and over again

ressaut [rəso] m projection; sharp rise

ressemblance [rəsãblãs] f resemblance

ressembler [rəsãble] intr (with dat) to resemble, look like ‖ ref to resemble one another; to be alike, to look alike

ressemeler [rəsəmle] §34 tr to resole

ressentiment [rəsãtimã] m resentment

ressentir [rəsãtir] §41 tr to feel keenly, to be hurt by (an insult); to experience (joy, pain, surprise) ‖ ref—**se ressentir de** to feel the aftereffects of

resserre [rəser] f shed, storeroom

resserrer [rəsere] tr to tighten; to contract; to close; to lock up (e.g., valuables) again ‖ ref to tighten; to contract

ressort [rəsɔr] m spring; springiness; motive; **du ressort de** within the jurisdiction of; **en dernier ressort** without appeal; as a last resort; **ressort à boudin** coil spring; **sans ressort** slack

ressortir [rəsɔrtir] intr—**ressortir à** to come under the jurisdiction of; to

fall under the head of ‖ §64 intr (aux: ÊTRE) to go out again; to stand out, to be evident; **faire ressortir** to set off; **il ressort de** it follows from; **il ressort que** it follows that

ressortis•sant [rəsɔrtisã] **ressortis•sante** [rəsɔrtisãt] adj—**ressortissant à** under the jurisdiction of ‖ mf national

ressource [rəsurs] f resource

ressouvenir [rəsuvnir] §72 ref to reminisce; **se ressouvenir de** to recall

ressusciter [resysite] tr to resuscitate; to resurrect ‖ intr (aux: ÊTRE) to rise from the dead; to get well

res•tant [restã] **-tante** [tãt] adj remaining ‖ m remainder

restaurant [restɔrã] m restaurant; **restaurant libre-service** self-service restaurant

restauration [restɔrasjɔ̃] f restoration; restaurant business

restaurer [restɔre] tr to restore ‖ ref (coll) to take some nourishment

reste [rest] m rest, remainder; remnant; relic; **au reste**, **du reste** moreover; **de reste** spare; **restes** remains; leftovers

rester [reste] intr (aux: ÊTRE) to remain, to stay; to be left over; **en rester** to stop, to leave off; **en rester là** to stop right there; **il me** (**te**, **leur**, etc.) **reste q.ch.** I (you, they, etc.) have s.th. left

restituer [restitɥe] tr to restore; to give back

restitution [restitysjɔ̃] f restitution; restoration

restoroute [restɔrut] m drive-in restaurant

restreindre [restrɛ̃dr] §50 tr to restrict; to curtail ‖ ref to become limited; to cut down expenses

res•treint [restrɛ̃] **-treinte** [trɛ̃t] adj limited

restriction [restriksjɔ̃] f restriction

résultat [rezylta] m result

résulter [rezylte] intr to result; **il en résulte que** it follows that

résumé [rezyme] m summary, recapitulation; **en résumé** in short, in a word

résumer [rezyme] tr to summarize ‖ ref to be summed up

résurrection [rezyreksjɔ̃] f resurrection

rétablir [retablir] tr to restore ‖ ref to recover

rétablissement [retablismã] m restoration; recovery

retailler [rətaje] tr to resharpen

retape [rətap] f (slang) streetwalking

retaper [rətape] tr (coll) to straighten up; (coll) to give a lick and a promise to ‖ ref (coll) to perk up

retard [rətar] m delay; **en retard** late; slow (clock); **en retard sur** behind

retardataire [rətardater] adj tardy; retarded ‖ mf latecomer, straggler

retarder [rətarde] tr to delay; to put off; to set back ‖ intr to go slow, to be behind

retenir [rətnir] §72 tr to hold or keep back; to detain; to remember, note; to reserve; to retain (a lawyer); to carry (a number) || ref—se retenir à to cling to; se retenir de to refrain from

retentir [rətɑ̃tir] intr to resound

rete·nu -nue [rətny] adj reserved; held back || f withholding; reserve; **retenue à la source** withholding tax

réticence [retisɑ̃s] f evasiveness, concealment; hesitation; reservation, misgiving

réti·cent [retisɑ̃] **-cente** [sɑ̃t] adj evasive; hesitant; reserved, withdrawn

réticule [retikyl] m handbag

ré·tif [retif] **-tive** [tiv] adj restive

rétine [retin] f retina

retirement [rətirmɑ̃] m contraction

retirer [rətire] tr to withdraw; to take off; to fire again || intr to fire again || ref to withdraw; to retire

retombée [rətɔ̃be] f fall; hang (of cloth); **retombées radioactives** fallout

retomber [rətɔ̃be] intr (aux: ÊTRE) to fall again; to fall; to fall back; to hang, hang down; to relapse

retordre [rətɔrdrə] tr to twist; to wring out

rétorquer [retɔrke] tr to retort

re·tors [rətɔr] **-torse** [tɔrs] adj twisted; wily; curved (beak) || mf rascal

retouche [rətuʃ] f retouch; (phot) retouching; **retouches** alterations

retoucher [rətuʃe] tr to retouch; to make alterations on

retour [rətur] m return; turn, bend; reversal (e.g., of opinion); **en retour d'équerre** at right angles; **être de retour** to be back; **par retour du courrier** by return mail; **retour à la masse** (elec) ground (on chassis of auto, radio, etc.); **retour à la terre** (elec) ground; **retour d'âge** change of life; **retour de flamme** backfire; **retour de manivelle** kick (of the crank); (fig) backlash; **retour en arrière** flashback

retourner [rəturne] tr to send back, to return; to upset; to turn over (e.g., the soil); to turn inside out || intr (aux: ÊTRE) to go back, to return || ref to turn around, to look back; to turn over; (fig) to veer, to shift; **s'en retourner** to go back; **se retourner contre** to turn against

retracer [rətrase] §51 tr to retrace; to bring to mind, to recall || ref to come to mind again; to recall

rétracter [retrakte] tr & ref to retract

rétraction [retraksjɔ̃] f contraction

retrait [rətrɛ] m withdrawal; shrinkage; running out (of tide); **en retrait** set back, recessed; (typ) indented; **retrait de permis** suspension of driver's license

retraite [rətrɛt] f retreat; retirement; pension; **battre en retraite** to retreat; **en retraite** retired; **prendre sa retraite** to retire; **toucher sa retraite** to draw one's pension

retrai·té -tée [rətrete] adj pensioned, retired || mf pensioner

retranchement [rətrɑ̃ʃmɑ̃] m retrenchment; cutting out

retrancher [rətrɑ̃ʃe] tr to cut off or

out, to retrench || ref to become entrenched

retransmettre [rətrɑ̃smetr] §42 tr to retransmit; to rebroadcast

retransmission [rətrɑ̃smisjɔ̃] f retransmission; rebroadcast

rétré·ci -cie [retresi] adj narrow; shrunk

rétrécir [retresir] tr to shrink; to take in (a garment) || intr & ref to shrink; to narrow

retremper [rətrɑ̃pe] tr to soak again; to retemper; to give new strength or life to || ref to take another dip; to get new vigor

rétribuer [retribɥe] tr to remunerate

rétribution [retribysjɔ̃] f retribution; salary, fee

rétroaction [retrɔaksjɔ̃] f feedback; retroaction

rétrofusée [retrɔfyze] f retrorocket

rétrograder [retrɔgrade] intr to retrogress

rétrospection [retrɔspeksjɔ̃] f retrospection

retrousser [rətruse] tr to roll up, to turn up; to curl up (one's lip) || ref to turn up or pull up one's clothes

retrouver [rətruve] tr to find again; to recover || ref to be back again; to meet again; to get one's bearings

rétroviseur [retrɔvizœr] m rear-view mirror

rets [rɛ] m—**prendre dans des rets** to snare

réunification [reynifikɑsjɔ̃] f reunification

réunion [reynjɔ̃] f reunion; meeting

réunir [reynir] tr to unite, join; to reunite; to call together, convene || ref to meet; to reunite

réus·si -sie [reysi] adj successful

réussir [reysir] tr to make a success of, to be good at || intr to succeed; **réussir à** to succeed in; to pass (an exam)

réussite [reysit] f success; **faire une réussite** (cards) to play solitaire

revaloir [rəvalwar] §71 tr—**revaloir q.ch. à qn** to pay s.o. back for s.th.

revan·chard [rəvɑ̃ʃar] **-charde** [ʃard] adj (coll) vengeful || mf (coll) avenger

revanche [rəvɑ̃ʃ] f revenge; return bout or engagement, return match; **en revanche** on the other hand; **prendre sa revanche** to get even with

revancher [rəvɑ̃ʃe] ref to get even

rêvasser [revase] intr to daydream

rêvasserie [revasri] f fitful dreaming; daydreaming

rêve [rev] m dream

revêche [rəvɛʃ] adj sullen, crabbed

réveil [revej] m awakening; alarm clock; (mil) reveille

réveille-matin [revejmatɛ̃] m invar alarm clock

réveiller [reveje] tr & ref to wake up

réveillon [revejɔ̃] m Christmas Eve supper; New Year's Eve party

réveillonner [revejɔne] intr to celebrate Christmas Eve or New Year's Eve

révéla·teur [revelatœr] **-trice** [tris] adj

revealing; telltale || *mf* informer || *m* (phot) developer
révélation [revelasjɔ̃] *f* revelation
révéler [revele] §10 *tr* to reveal; (phot) to develop
revenant [rəvnɑ̃] *m* ghost
reven·deur [rəvɑ̃dœr] **-deuse** [døz] *mf* retailer; secondhand dealer
revendication [rəvɑ̃dikɑsjɔ̃] *f* claim
revendiquer [rəvɑ̃dike] *tr* to claim; to insist upon; to assume (*a responsibility*)
revendre [rəvɑ̃dr] *tr* to resell
revenez-y [rəvnezi] *m invar* (coll) return; **un goût de revenez-y** (coll) a taste like more
revenir [rəvnir] §72 *intr* (aux: ÊTRE) to return, come back; (with *dat*) to suit, to please; **en revenir** to have a narrow escape; **faire revenir** (culin) to brown; **n'en pas revenir** to not get over it; **revenir à** to come to, amount to; to come to (*e.g.*, *mind*); **revenir à soi** to come to; **revenir bredouille** to come back empty-handed; **revenir de** to recover from; to realize (*a mistake*); **revenir de loin** to have been at death's door; **revenir sur** to go back on (*e.g.*, *one's word*) || *ref*—**s'en revenir** to come back
revente [rəvɑ̃t] *f* resale
revenu [rəvny] *m* revenue, income
revenue [rəvny] *f* new growth (*of trees*)
rêver [reve] *tr* to dream || *intr* to dream; **rêver à** to dream of (*think about*); **rêver de** to dream of (*in sleep; to long to*)
réverbère [reverber] *m* streetlight
réverbérer [reverbere] §10 *tr* to reflect (*light, heat, etc.*) || *ref* to be reflected
reverdir [rəverdir] *tr* to make green || *intr* to grow green; to become young again
révérence [reverɑ̃s] *f* reverence; curtsy; **révérence parler** (coll) pardon the language; **tirer sa révérence** to bow out
révéren·cieux [reverɑ̃sjø] **-cieuse** [sjøz] *adj* obsequious
révé·rend [reverɑ̃] **-rende** [rɑ̃d] *adj & m* reverend
révérer [revere] §10 *tr* to revere
rêverie [revri] *f* reverie
revers [rəver] *m* reverse; lapel; (tennis) backhand; **à revers** from behind; **revers de main** slap with the back of the hand
reverser [rəverse] *tr* to pour back; to pour out again
réversible [reversibl] *adj* reversible
revêtement [rəvɛtmɑ̃] *m* surfacing; facing; lining; casing
revêtir [rəvetir] §73 *tr* to put on; to clothe, to dress up; to invest; to surface; to line; to face; to assume (*a form; an aspect*)
rê·veur [revœr] **-veuse** [vøz] *adj* dreamy || *mf* dreamer; **cela me laisse rêveur** that leaves me puzzled
revirement [rəvirmɑ̃] *m* sudden reversal; (naut) tack
réviser [revize] *tr* to revise; to review; to overhaul; to recondition

réviseur [revizœr] *m* proofreader
révision [revizjɔ̃] *f* revision; review; overhauling; proofreading
révisionniste [revizjɔnist] *adj & mf* revisionist
revivre [rəvivr] §74 *tr* to live again, relive || *intr* to live again
révocation [revɔkɑsjɔ̃] *f* dismissal; revocation
revoici [rəvwasi] *prep*—**me (vous, etc.)** **revoici** (coll) here I am (you are, etc.) again
revoilà [rəvwala] *prep*—**le (la, etc.)** **voilà** (coll) there it, he (she, etc.) is again
revoir [rəvwar] *m*—**au revoir** good-by || §75 *tr* to see again; to review; to revise || *ref* to meet again
révol·tant [revɔltɑ̃] **-tante** [tɑ̃t] *adj* revolting
révolte [revɔlt] *f* revolt, rebellion
révol·té -tée [revɔlte] *adj & mf* rebel
révolter [revɔlte] *tr & ref* to revolt; **se révolter devant** to be revolted by
révo·lu -lue [revɔly] *adj* completed; elapsed; bygone
révolution [revɔlysjɔ̃] *f* revolution
révolutionnaire [revɔlysjɔner] *adj & mf* revolutionary
revolver [revɔlver] *m* revolver
révoquer [revɔke] *tr* to revoke; to countermand; to dismiss; to recall
re·vu -vue [rəvy] *adj* revised || *f* see revue
revue [rəvy] *f* review; magazine, journal; (theat) revue; **passer en revue** to review (*past events; troops*)
rez-de-chaussée [red/ose] *m invar* first floor, ground floor
R.F. *abbr* (**République Française**) French Republic
rhabiller [rabije] *tr* to repair; to dress again; to refurbish || *ref* to change one's clothes; **va te rhabiller!** (pej) get out!
rhapsodie [rapsɔdi] *f* rhapsody
Rhénanie [renani] *f* Rhineland
rhéostat [reɔsta] *m* rheostat
Rhin [rɛ̃] *m* Rhine
rhinocéros [rinɔserɔs] *m* rhinoceros
rhubarbe [rybarb] *f* rhubarb
rhum [rɔm] *m* rum
rhumati·sant [rymatizɑ̃] **-sante** [zɑ̃t] *adj & mf* rheumatic
rhumatis·mal -male [rymatismal] *adj* (*pl* **-maux** [mo]) rheumatic
rhumatisme [rymatism] *m* rheumatism
rhume [rym] *m* cold; **rhume des foins** hay fever
riant [rjɑ̃] **riante** [rjɑ̃t] *adj* smiling; cheerful, pleasant
ribambelle [ribɑ̃bɛl] *f* (coll) long string, swarm, lot
ri·baud [ribo] **-baude** [bod] *adj* licentious || *mf* camp follower; debauchee
ricanement [rikanmɑ̃] *m* snicker
ricaner [rikane] *intr* to snicker
ri·chard [ri/ar] **-charde** [/ard] *mf* (coll) moneybags
riche [ri/] *adj* rich || *m* rich man; **nouveaux riches** newly rich

riche·lieu [riʃəljø] *m* (*pl* -lieu or -lieus) oxford

richesse [riʃes] *f* wealth; richness; **richesses** riches; **richesses naturelles** natural resources

ricin [risɛ̃] *m* castor-oil plant; castor bean

ricocher [rikɔʃe] *intr* to ricochet, rebound

ricochet [rikɔʃɛ] *m* ricochet; **faire des ricochets** to play ducks and drakes; **par ricochet** indirectly

rictus [riktys] *m* rictus; grin

ride [rid] *f* wrinkle; ripple

ri·deau [rido] *m* (*pl* -deaux) curtain; **rideau d'arbres** line of trees; **rideau de fer** iron curtain; safety blind (*of a store*); (theat) fire curtain; **rideau de feu** (mil) cover of artillery fire; **rideau de fumée** smoke screen

ridelle [ridɛl] *f* rave, side rails (*of wagon*)

rider [ride] *tr* to wrinkle; to ripple

ridicule [ridikyl] *adj* ridiculous ‖ *m* ridicule

ridiculiser [ridikylize] *tr* to ridicule

rien [rjɛ̃] *m* trifle; **comme un rien** with no trouble at all; **un rien de** just a little (bit) of; **un rien de temps** no time at all ‖ *pron indef*—**de rien** don't mention it, you're welcome; of no importance; **il n'en est rien** such is not the case; **rien ne** or **ne ... rien** §90B nothing, not anything; **rien de moins (que)** nothing less (than); **rien que** nothing but

rieur [rjœr] **rieuse** [rjøz] *adj* laughing ‖ *mf* laugher, mocker ‖ *f* (orn) black-headed gull

riflard [riflar] *m* coarse file; jack plane; paring chisel

rigide [riʒid] *adj* rigid; stiff; strict

rigolade [rigɔlad] *f* (coll) good time, fun; (coll) big joke

rigole [rigɔl] *f* drain; ditch

rigoler [rigɔle] *intr* (slang) to laugh, to joke

rigo·lo [rigɔlo] **-lote** [lɔt] *adj* (coll) comical; (coll) queer, funny ‖ *mf* (coll) card ‖ *m* (slang) rod, gat

rigou·reux [rigurø] **-reuse** [røz] *adj* rigorous; severe

rigueur [rigœr] *f* rigor, strictness; **à la rigueur** to the letter; as a last resort; **de rigueur** compulsory, de rigueur

rillons [rijɔ̃] *mpl* cracklings

rimail·leur [rimajœr] **rimail·leuse** [rimajøz] *mf* (coll) rhymester

rime [rim] *f* rhyme; **rimes croisées** alternate rhymes; **rimes plates** couplets of alternate masculine and feminine rhymes

rimer [rime] *tr & intr* to rhyme

rinçage [rɛ̃saʒ] *m* rinse

rince-bouche [rɛ̃sbuʃ] *m invar* mouthwash

rince-bouteilles [rɛ̃sbutej] *m invar* (mach) bottle-washing machine

rince-doigts [rɛ̃sdwa] *m invar* fingerbowl

rincer [rɛ̃se] §51 *tr* to rinse; (slang) to ruin, to take to the cleaners

rinçure [rɛ̃syr] *f* rinsing water

ring [riŋ] *m* ring (*for, e.g., boxing*)

ringard [rɛ̃gar] *m* poker (*for fire*)

ripaille [ripaj] *f* (coll) blowout; **faire ripaille** (coll) to carouse

ripe [rip] *f* scraper

riper [ripe] *tr* to scrape; (naut) to slip ‖ *intr* to slip; to skid

riposte [ripɔst] *f* riposte, retort

riposter [ripɔste] *tr* to riposte, to retort

rire [rir] *m* laugh; laughter; laughing ‖ §61 *intr* to laugh; to joke; to smile; **pour rire** for fun, in jest; **rire dans sa barbe, rire sous cape** to laugh up one's sleeve; **rire de** to laugh at or over; **rire du bout des lèvres, rire du bout des dents** to titter; **rire jaune** to force a laugh ‖ *ref*—**se rire de** to laugh at

ris [ri] *m* (naut) reef; (obs) laughter; **ris d'agneau** or **de veau** sweetbread

risée [rize] *f* scorn; laughingstock; light squall

risible [rizibl] *adj* laughable

risque [risk] *m* risk

ris·qué -quée [riske] *adj* risky; risqué

risquer [riske] *tr* to risk; to hazard (*e.g., a remark*) ‖ *intr*—**risquer de** + *inf* to risk + *ger*; to have a good chance of + *ger*

risque-tout [riskətu] *mf invar* daredevil

rissoler [risɔle] *tr & intr* to brown

ristourne [risturn] *f* rebate, refund; dividend

ristourner [risturne] *tr* to refund

ritournelle [riturnɛl] *f*—**c'est toujours la même ritournelle** it's always the same old story; **ritournelle publicitaire** advertising jingle or slogan

ri·tuel -tuelle [ritɥɛl] *adj & m* ritual

rivage [rivaʒ] *m* shore; bank

ri·val -vale [rival] (*pl* -vaux [vo] -vales) *adj & mf* rival

rivaliser [rivalize] *intr* to compete; **rivaliser avec** to compete with, to rival

rivalité [rivalite] *f* rivalry

rive [riv] *f* shore; bank

river [rive] *tr* to rivet

rive·rain [rivrɛ̃] **-raine** [ren] *adj* waterfront; bordering ‖ *mf* riversider; dweller along a street or road

riveraineté [rivrɛnte] *f* riparian rights

rivet [rive] *m* rivet

rivière [rivjɛr] *f* river, stream, tributary; (turf) water jump; **rivière de diamants** diamond necklace

rixe [riks] *f* brawl

riz [ri] *m* rice; **riz au lait** rice pudding; **riz glacé** polished rice

rizière [rizjɛr] *f* rice field

robe [rɔb] *f* dress; gown; robe; wrapper (*of cigar*); skin (*of onion, sausage, etc.*); husk (*of, e.g., bean*); **robe de chambre** dressing gown; **robe d'intérieur** housecoat

rober [rɔbe] *tr* to husk, to skin; to wrap (*a cigar*)

roberts [rɔber] *mpl* (slang) breasts

robin [rɔbɛ̃] *m* (coll) judge; (pej) shyster

robinet [rɔbine] *m* faucet, tap; cock;

robinet d'eau tiède (coll) bore; **robinet mélangeur** mixing faucet
robinier [rɔbinje] m (bot) locust tree
robot [rɔbo] m robot
robre [rɔbr] m rubber (in bridge)
robuste [rɔbyst] adj robust; firm
roc [rɔk] m rock
rocaille [rɔkaj] adj rococo || f stones; rocky ground; stonework
rocail·leux [rɔkajø] **rocail·leuse** [rɔkajøz] adj rocky, stony; harsh
roche [rɔʃ] f rock; boulder
rocher [rɔʃe] m rock; crag
rochet [rɔʃe] m ratchet; bobbin
ro·cheux [rɔʃø] **-cheuse** [ʃøz] adj rocky
rodage [rɔdaʒ] m grinding; breaking in; **en rodage** being broken in, new
roder [rɔde] tr to grind (a valve); to break in (a new car); to polish up (a new play)
rôder [rɔde] intr to prowl
rô·deur [rɔdœr] **-deuse** [døz] adj prowling || mf prowler
rogatons [rɔgatɔ̃] mpl (coll) scraps
rogne [rɔɲ] f (coll) anger; **mettre qn en rogne** (coll) to make s.o. see red
rogner [rɔɲe] tr to pare, to trim
rognon [rɔɲɔ̃] m kidney
rogomme [rɔgɔm] m—**de rogomme** (coll) husky, beery (voice)
rogue [rɔg] adj arrogant
roi [rwa], [rwɑ] m king; **tirer les rois** to gather to eat the Twelfth-night cake
roitelet [rwatle] m kinglet; (orn) king-let
rôle [rol] m role; roll, muster
ro·main [rɔmɛ̃] **-maine** [men] adj Roman; roman (type); romaine (lettuce) || m (typ) roman || f romaine (lettuce) || (cap) mf Roman (person)
ro·man [rɔmɑ̃] **-mane** [man] adj Romance (language); (archit) Romanesque || m novel; **roman d'anticipation** science-fiction novel; **roman policier** detective story
romance [rɔmɑ̃s] f ballad
romanche [rɔmɑ̃ʃ] m Romansh
roman·cier [rɔmɑ̃sje] **-cière** [sjer] mf novelist; **romancier d'anticipation** science-fiction writer
ro·mand [rɔmɑ̃] **-mande** [mɑ̃d] adj French-speaking (Switzerland)
romanesque [rɔmanesk] adj romanesque, romantic, fabulous
roman-feuilleton [rɔmɑ̃fœjtɔ̃] m (pl **romans-feuilletons**) newspaper serial
roman-fleuve [rɔmɑ̃flœv] m (pl **romans-fleuves**) saga novel
romani·chel **-chelle** [rɔmaniʃel] mf gypsy, vagrant
romantique [rɔmɑ̃tik] adj & mf romantic
romantisme [rɔmɑ̃tism] m romanticism
romarin [rɔmarɛ̃] m (bot) rosemary
Rome [rɔm] f Rome
rompre [rɔ̃pr] (3d sg pres ind **rompt** [rɔ̃]) tr to break; to burst; to break in, train; to break off || intr & ref to break
romsteck [rɔmstek] m rump steak
ronce [rɔ̃s] f bramble; curly grain (of

wood); **en ronces artificielles** barbed-wire (fence)
ronchonner [rɔ̃ʃɔne] intr (coll) to bellyache, grumble
rond [rɔ̃] **ronde** [rɔ̃d] adj round; rounded; plump; straightforward; (slang) tight, drunk || m ring, circle; round slice; (coll) dough, money; **en rond** in a circle; **rond de fumée** smoke ring; **rond de serviette** napkin ring || f round; beat, round; round dance; radius; round hand; (mus) whole note; **à la ronde** around; **s'amuser à la ronde, faire la ronde** to go ring-around-a-rosy || **rond** adv —**tourner rond** to work or go smoothly
rond-de-cuir [rɔ̃dkɥir] m (pl **ronds-de-cuir**) leather seat; (pej) bureaucrat
ron·deau [rɔ̃do] m (pl **-deaux**) rondeau; field roller
ronde·let [rɔ̃dle] **-lette** [let] adj plump; tidy (sum)
rondelle [rɔ̃del] f disk; slice; washer (of faucet, bolt, etc.)
rondement [rɔ̃dmɑ̃] adv briskly; **mener rondement** to make short work of; **parler rondement** to be blunt
rondeur [rɔ̃dœr] f roundness; plumpness; frankness
rond-point [rɔ̃pwɛ̃] m (pl **ronds-points**) intersection, crossroads; traffic circle; circus, roundabout (Brit)
ronéo [rɔneo] f Mimeograph machine
ronéotyper [rɔneotipe] tr to mimeograph
ron·flant [rɔ̃flɑ̃] **-flante** [flɑ̃t] adj snoring; roaring; whirring, humming; (pej) high-sounding, pretentious
ronflement [rɔ̃fləmɑ̃] m snore; roar; whirr, hum
ronfler [rɔ̃fle] intr to snore; to roar; to whirr, to hum
ron·fleur [rɔ̃flœr] **-fleuse** [fløz] mf snorer || m vibrator (replacing bell)
ronger [rɔ̃ʒe] §38 tr to gnaw, nibble; to eat away; to bite (one's nails); to corrode; to torment || ref to be worn away; to be eaten away; to eat one's heart out, to fret
ron·geur [rɔ̃ʒœr] **-geuse** [ʒøz] adj gnawing || m rodent
ronron [rɔ̃rɔ̃] m purr; drone
ronronnement [rɔ̃rɔnmɑ̃] m purring
ronronner [rɔ̃rɔne] intr to purr
roquer [rɔke] intr (chess) to castle
roquet [rɔke] m cur, yapper; (breed of dog) pug
roquette [rɔket] f (plant; missile) rocket
rosace [rɔzas] f rose window; (archit) rosette
rosa·cé -cée [rɔzase] adj roselike || f skin eruption
rosaire [rɔzer] m rosary
rosâtre [rɔzɑtr] adj dusty-pink
rosbif [rɔsbif] m roast beef
rose [roz] adj & m rose, pink (color) || f rose; rose window; **dire la rose** to box the compass; **rose des vents** compass card; **rose d'Inde** (Tagetes) marigold
ro·sé -sée [roze] adj rose, rose-colored || m rosé wine || f see **rosée**

ro·seau [rozo] *m (pl* -seaux) reed

rosée [roze] *f* dew

roséole [rozeɔl] *f* rash; rose rash

roseraie [rozrɛ] *f* rose garden

rosette [rɔzɛt] *f* bowknot; rosette; red ink; red chalk

rosier [rozje] *m* rosebush; **rosier églantier** sweetbrier

rosse [rɔs] *adj* nasty, mean; strict, stern; cynical || *f* (coll) beast, stinker; (coll) nag; **sale rosse** (coll) dirty bitch

rossée [rɔse] *f* (coll) thrashing

rosser [rɔse] *tr* to beat up, thrash; (coll) to beat, to best

rossignol [rɔsiɲɔl] *m* skeleton key; (orn) nightingale; (coll) piece of junk, drug on the market

rot [ro] *m* (slang) burp, belch

rota·tif [rɔtatif] -tive [tiv] *adj* rotary || *f* rotary press

rotation [rɔtasjɔ̃] *f* rotation; turnover (*of merchandise*)

rotatoire [rɔtatwar] *adj* rotary

roter [rɔte] *intr* (slang) to burp

rô·ti -tie [roti] *adj* roasted || *m* roast || *f* piece of toast; **rôtie à l'anglaise** Welsh rarebit

rotin [rɔtɛ̃] *m* rattan; de or en rotin cane (*chair*); **pas un rotin!** not a penny!

rôtir [rotir] *tr*, *intr*, & *ref* to roast; to toast; to scorch

rôtisserie [rotisri] *f* rotisserie shop (*where roasted fowl is sold*); grillroom (*restaurant*)

rôtissoire [rotiswar] *f* rotisserie

rotonde [rɔtɔ̃d] *f* rotunda; (rr) roundhouse

rotor [rɔtɔr] *m* rotor

rotule [rɔtyl] *f* kneecap

roture [rɔtyr] *f* common people

rotu·rier [rɔtyrje] -rière [rjɛr] *adj* plebeian, of the common people || *mf* commoner

rouage [rwaʒ] *m* cog; **rouages** movement (*of a watch*)

rou·blard [rublar] -blarde [blard] *adj* (coll) wily || *mf* (coll) schemer

roublardise [rublardiz] *f* (coll) cunning

roucoulement [rukulmɑ̃] *m* cooing; billing and cooing

roucouler [rukule] *tr* & *intr* to coo

roue [ru] *f* wheel; **faire la roue** to turn cartwheels; to strut; **roue de secours** spare wheel (*with tire*)

roué rouée [rwe] *adj* slick; knocked out || *mf* slicker || *m* rake

rouelle [rwɛl] *f* fillet (*of veal*)

rouer [rwe] *tr* to break upon the wheel; **rouer de coups** to thrash, beat up

rouerie [ruri] *f* trickery; trick

rouet [rwɛ] *m* spinning wheel

rouge [ruʒ] *adj* red || *m* red; rouge; blush; **porter au rouge** to heat redhot; **rouge à lèvres** lipstick || *adv* red

rou·geaud [ruʒo] -geaude [ʒod] *adj* ruddy || *mf* ruddy-faced person

rouge-gorge [ruʒgɔrʒ] *m* (*pl* rougesgorges) robin (*Erithacus rubecula*)

rougeole [ruʒɔl] *f* measles

rougeur [ruʒœr] *f* redness; blush; **rougeurs** red spots

rougir [ruʒir] *tr* to redden || *intr* to turn red; to blush

rouille [ruj] *f* rust

rouil·lé -lée [ruje] *adj* rusty; (*out of practice; blighted*) rusty

rouiller [ruje] *tr*, *intr*, & *ref* to rust

roulade [rulad] *f* trill; (mus) run

rou·lant [rulɑ̃] -lante [lɑ̃t] *adj* rolling; (coll) funny

rou·leau [rulo] *m* (*pl* -leaux) roller; roll; spool; rolling pin; **rouleau compresseur** road roller

roulement [rulmɑ̃] *m* roll; rotation; rattle, clatter; exchange; **par roulement** in rotation; **roulement à billes** ball bearing

rouler [rule] *tr* to roll; (coll) to take in, cheat || *intr* to roll; to roll along; **rouler sur** to roll in (*wealth*); to turn on || *ref* to roll; to roll up; to toss and turn; (with *dat* of *reflex pron*) to twiddle (*one's thumbs*); **se les rouler** (coll) to not turn a hand

roule-ta·bille [rultabij] *m invar* (coll) rolling stone

roulette [rulɛt] *f* small wheel; castor; roulette; **aller comme sur des roulettes** to go well, to work smoothly

rou·leur [rulœr] -leuse [løz] *mf* drifter (*from one job to another*) || *m* freight handler || *f* streetwalker

roulis [ruli] *m* (naut) roll

roulotte [rulɔt] *f* trailer; gypsy wagon

rou·main [rumɛ̃] -maine [mɛn] *adj* Rumanian || *m* Rumanian (*language*) || (*cap*) *mf* Rumanian (*person*)

roupiller [rupije] *intr* to take a snooze

rou·quin [rukɛ̃] -quine [kin] *adj* (coll) red-headed; || *mf* (coll) redhead || *m* (slang) red wine; **Rouquin** Red (*nickname*)

rouspéter [ruspete] §10 *intr* (coll) to bellyache, to kick

rouspé·teur [ruspetœr] -teuse [tøz] *mf* (coll) bellyacher, complainer

roussâtre [rusatr] *adj* auburn

rousse [rus] *f* redhead, auburn-haired woman; (slang) cops

rousseur [rusœr] *f* reddishness; freckle

roussir [rusir] *tr* to scorch; to singe || *intr* to become brown; **faire roussir** (culin) to brown

route [rut] *f* road; route, itinerary; **bonne route!** happy motoring!; **en route!** let's go!; **faire fausse route** to take the wrong road; (fig) to be on the wrong track; **mettre en route** to start; **route déformée** rough road; **route déviée** detour

rou·tier [rutje] -tière [tjɛr] *adj* road (*e.g., map*) || *m* trucker; bicycle racer; Explorer, Rover (*boy scout*); (naut) track chart; **vieux routier** veteran, old hand

routine [rutin] *f* routine

routi·nier [rutinje] -nière [njɛr] *adj* routine; one-track (*mind*)

rouvieux [ruvjø] *adj masc* mangy || *m* mange

rouvrir [ruvrir] §65 *tr* & *intr* to reopen

roux [ru] **rousse** [rus] *adj* russet, red-

dish; red, auburn (*hair*); browned
(*butter*) ‖ *mf* redhead ‖ *m* russet,
reddish brown, auburn (*color*);
brown sauce ‖ *f* see **rousse**

royal royale [rwajal] *adj* (*pl* **royaux**
[rwajo]) royal ‖ *f* imperial, goatee

royaliste [rwajalist] *adj & mf* royalist

royaume [rwajom] *m* kingdom

royauté [rwajote] *f* royalty

R.S.V.P. [eresvepe] *m* (letterword)
(**répondez, s'il vous plaît**) R.S.V.P.

R.T.F. [erteef] *f* (letterword) (**radio-
diffusion-télévision française**) French
radio and television

ruade [rɥad] *f* kick, buck

ruban [rybɑ̃] *m* ribbon; tape; **ruban
adhésif** adhesive tape; **ruban adhésif
transparent** transparent tape; **ruban
de chapeau** hatband; **ruban de frein**
brake lining; **ruban encreur** typewriter ribbon; **ruban magnétique** recording tape

rubéole [rybeɔl] *f* German measles

rubis [rybi] *m* ruby; jewel (*of watch*);
payer rubis sur l'ongle to pay down
on the nail

rubrique [rybrik] *f* rubric; caption,
heading; label (*in a dictionary*)

ruche [ry] *f* beehive

rude [ryd] *adj* rude, rough; rugged;
hard; steep; (*coll*) amazing

rudement [rydmɑ̃] *adv* roughly; (*coll*)
awfully, mighty

rudesse [rydes] *f* rudeness, roughness;
harshness

rudiment [rydimɑ̃] *m* rudiment

rudoyer [rydwaje] §47 *tr* to bully,
browbeat; to abuse, treat roughly

rue [ry] *f* street; **rue barrée** (public
sign) no thoroughfare; (public sign)
closed for repairs; **rue sans issue**
(public sign) no outlet

ruée [rɥe] *f* rush; **ruée vers l'or** gold
rush

ruelle [rɥel] *f* alley, lane; space between bed and wall

ruer [rɥe] *intr* to kick, to buck; **ruer
dans les brancards** to kick over the
traces ‖ *ref*—**se ruer sur** to rush at

rugir [ryʒir] *intr* to roar, bellow

rugissement [ryʒismɑ̃] *m* roar

ru·gueux [rygø] **-gueuse** [gøz] *adj*
rough, rugged

ruine [rɥin] *f* ruin

ruiner [rɥine] *tr* to ruin

ruis·seau [rɥiso] *m* (*pl* **-seaux**) stream,
brook; (fig) gutter

ruisseler [rɥisle] §34 *intr* to stream; to
drip, to trickle

ruisselet [rɥisle] *m* little stream

ruissellement [rɥiselmɑ̃] *m* streaming;
(*e.g., of light*) flood

rumeur [rymœr] *f* rumor; hum (*e.g., of
voices*); roar (*of the sea*); **rumeur
publique** public opinion

ru·pin [rypɛ̃] **-pine** [pin] *adj* (slang)
rich ‖ *mf* (slang) swell

rupiner [rypine] *tr & intr* (coll) to do
well

rupteur [ryptœr] *m* (elec) contact
breaker

rupture [ryptyr] *f* rupture; breach;
break; breaking off

ru·ral -rale [ryral] (*pl* **-raux** [ro]) *adj*
rural ‖ *mf* farmer; **ruraux** country
people

ruse [ryz] *f* ruse

ru·sé -sée [ryze] *adj* cunning, crafty ‖
mf sly one

russe [rys] *adj* Russian ‖ *m* Russian
(*language*) ‖ (*cap*) *mf* Russian (*person*)

Russie [rysi] *f* Russia; **la Russie** Russia

rus·taud [rysto] **-taude** [tod] *adj* rustic, clumsy ‖ *mf* bumpkin

rustique [rystik] *adj* rustic; hardy

rustre [rystr] *adj* oafish ‖ *m* bumpkin,
oaf; (obs) peasant

rut [ryt] *m* (zool) rut

ruti·lant [rytilɑ̃] **-lante** [lɑ̃t] *adj* bright-
red; gleaming

rutiler [rytile] *intr* to gleam, to glow

rythme [ritm] *m* rhythm; rate (*of production*)

ryth·mé -mée [ritme] *adj* rhyth-
mic(al); cadenced

rythmer [ritme] *tr* to cadence; to mark
with a rhythm

rythmique [ritmik] *adj* rhythmic(al)

S

S, s [es], *[es] *m invar* nineteenth
letter of the French alphabet

S. *abbr* (**saint**) St.

sa [sa] §88

S.A. [esa] *f* (letterword) (**Société
anonyme**) Inc.

sabbat [saba] *m* Sabbath; witches'
Sabbath; racket, uproarious gaiety;
sabbat des chats caterwauling

sabir [sabir] *m* pidgin

sable [sɑbl] *m* sand; sable; **sable
mouvant** quicksand

sabler [sable] *tr* to sandblast; to drink

in one gulp; to toss off (*some champagne*)

sa·bleux [sɑblø] **-bleuse** [bløz] *adj*
sandy ‖ *f* sandblast; sandblaster

sablier [sɑblije] *m* hourglass; (*for drying ink*) sandbox; dealer in sand

sablière [sɑblijer] *f* sandpit; wall plate;
(rr) sandbox

sablon·neux [sɑblɔnø] **sablon·neuse**
[sɑblɔnøz] *adj* sandy

sablonnière [sɑblɔnjer] *f* sandpit

sabord [sabɔr] *m* porthole

saborder [sabɔrde] *tr* to scuttle

sabot [sabo] *m* wooden shoe; hoof; whipping top; bungled work; ferrule; caster cup; **dormir comme un sabot** to sleep like a top; **sabot de frein** brake shoe; **sabot d'enrayage** wedge, block, scotch

sabotage [sabɔtaʒ] *m* sabotage

saboter [sabɔte] *tr* to sabotage; to bungle || *intr* (coll) to make one's wooden shoes clatter

sabo·teur [sabɔtœr] **-teuse** [tøz] *mf* saboteur; bungler

sabo·tier [sabɔtje] **-tière** [tjer] *mf* maker and seller of wooden shoes || *f* clog dance

sabre [sabr] *m* saber

sabrer [sabre] *tr* to saber; (coll) to botch; (coll) to cut, condense

sac [sak] *m* sack, bag; **être un sac d'os** [dɔs] to be nothing but skin and bones; **sac à main** handbag; **sac à malice** bag of tricks; **sac à provisions** shopping bag; **sac de couchage** sleeping bag

saccade [sakad] *f* jerk

sacca·dé -dée [sakade] *adj* jerky

saccager [sakaʒe] §38 *tr* to sack; (coll) to upset, to turn topsy-turvy

saccha·rin [sakarɛ̃] **-rine** [rin] *adj* saccharine || *f* saccharin

saccharose [sakaroz] *m* sucrose

sacerdoce [saserdɔs] *m* priesthood

sacerdo·tal -tale [saserdɔtal] *adj* (*pl* **-taux** [to]) sacerdotal, priestly

sachet [saʃe] *m* sachet; packet (*of needles, medicine, etc.*); powder charge

sacoche [sakɔʃ] *f* satchel

sacramen·tel -telle [sakramɑ̃tel] *adj* sacramental

sacre [sakr] *m* crowning, consecration

sa·cré -crée [sakre] *adj* sacred; (anat) sacral || (when standing before noun) *adj* (coll) darned, blasted

sacrement [sakrəmɑ̃] *m* sacrament

sacrer [sakre] *tr* to crown, to consecrate || *intr* to curse

sacrifice [sakrifis] *m* sacrifice

sacrifier [sakrifje] *tr* to sacrifice

sacrilège [sakrilɛʒ] *adj* sacrilegious || *mf* sacrilegious person || *m* sacrilege

sacristain [sakristɛ̃] *m* sexton

sadique [sadik] *adj* sadistic || *mf* sadist

safran [safrɑ̃] *m* saffron

sagace [sagas] *adj* sagacious, shrewd

sage [saʒ] *adj* wise; well-behaved; modest (*woman*); good (*child*); **soyez sage!** be good! || *mf* sage

sage-femme [saʒfam] *f* (*pl* **sages-femmes**) midwife

sagesse [saʒes] *f* wisdom; good behavior

sai·gnant [seɲɑ̃] **-gnante** [ɲɑ̃t] *adj* bleeding; (*wound*) fresh; (*meat*) rare

saignée [seɲe] *f* bloodletting; bend of the arm, small of the arm; (fig) drain on the purse

saignement [seɲmɑ̃] *m* bleeding; **saignement de nez** nosebleed

saigner [seɲe], [seɲe] *tr & intr* to bleed; **saigner à blanc, saigner aux quatre veines** to bleed white

sail·lant [sajɑ̃] **sail·lante** [sajɑ̃t] *adj* prominent, salient; projecting; high (*cheekbones*)

saillie [saji] *f* projection; spurt; sally, outburst; **faire saillie** to jut out, project

saillir [sajir] (used only in *inf, ger,* & 3d *sg & pl*) *tr* (agr) to cover || §69 *intr* to protrude, to project; to spurt

sain [sɛ̃] **saine** [sen] *adj* healthy; **sain d'esprit** sane; **sain et sauf** safe and sound

saindoux [sɛ̃du] *m* lard

sainement [senmɑ̃] *adv* soundly

saint [sɛ̃] **sainte** [sɛ̃t] *adj* saintly; sacred, holy || *mf* saint

sainteté [sɛ̃təte] *f* holiness

saisie [sezi] *f* seizure; foreclosure

saisie-arrêt [seziare] *f* (*pl* **-arrêts**) attachment, garnishment

saisir [sezir] *tr* to seize; to sear (*meat*); to grasp (*to understand*); to strike, startle; to overcome; **saisir un tribunal de** to lay before a court || *ref* **—se saisir de** to take possession of

saisissement [sezismɑ̃] *m* chill; shock

saison [sezɔ̃] *f* season

salace [salas] *adj* salacious

salade [salad] *f* salad; (fig) mess; **salade russe** mixed vegetable salad with mayonnaise

saladier [saladje] *m* salad bowl

salaire [saler] *m* salary, wage; recompense, punishment

salariat [salarja] *m* salaried workers, employees; salary (*fixed wage*)

sala·rié -riée [salarje] *adj* salaried, hired || *mf* wage earner; employee

sa·laud [salo] **-laude** [lod] *adj* (coll) slovenly || *mf* (slang) skunk, scoundrel

sale [sal] *adj* dirty; dull (*color*) || *mf* dirty person

sa·lé -lée [sale] *adj* salty, salted; dirty (*joke*); padded (*bill*); (slang) exaggerated || *m* salt pork

saler [sale] *tr* to salt

saleté [salte] *f* dirtiness; piece of dirt; (slang) dirty trick; (slang) dirt

salière [saljer] *f* saltcellar

salir [salir] *tr & ref* to soil

salive [saliv] *f* saliva

salle [sal] *f* room; hall; auditorium; ward (*in a hospital*); (theat) audience, house; **salle à manger** dining room; **salle d'armes** fencing room; **salle d'attente** waiting room; **salle de bains** bathroom; **salle d'écoute** language laboratory; **salle de police** (mil) guardhouse; **salle des accouchées** maternity ward; **salle de séjour** living room; **salle des machines** engine room; **salle des pas perdus** lobby, waiting room; **salle de rédaction** city room; **salle de spectacle** movie house; **salle des ventes** salesroom, showroom; **salle de travail** delivery room; **salle d'exposition** showroom

salon [salɔ̃] *m* living room, parlor; exposition; saloon (*ship's lounge*); **salon de beauté** beauty parlor; **salon de l'automobile** automobile show; **salon de thé** tearoom

salon·nard [salɔnar] **salon·narde** [salɔnard] *mf* sycophant

saloperie [salɔpri] *f* (slang) trash

salopette [salɔpɛt] *f* coveralls, overalls; bib; smock

salpêtre [salpetr] *m* saltpeter

salsepareille [salsəparɛj] *f* sarsaparilla

saltimbanque [saltɛ̃bɑ̃k] *mf* tumbler; mountebank, charlatan

salubre [salybr] *adj* salubrious, healthful

saluer [salɥe] *tr* to salute; to greet, to bow to, to wave to

salut [saly] *m* health; safety; salvation; salute; greeting, bow; nod; **salut!** (coll) hi!, howdy!; **salut les gars!, salut les copains!** hi, fellows!

salutation [salytɑsjɔ̃] *f* greeting; salutations distinguées, or sincères salutations (complimentary close) yours truly

salve [salv] *f* salvo, salute

samari·tain [samaritɛ̃] **-taine** [ten] *adj* Samaritan ‖ (*cap*) *mf* Samaritan

samedi [samdi] *m* Saturday

sanatorium [sanatɔrjɔm] *m* sanitarium

sanctifier [sɑ̃ktifje] *tr* to sanctify

sanction [sɑ̃ksjɔ̃] *f* sanction; penalty

sanctionner [sɑ̃ksjɔne] *tr* to sanction; to penalize

sanctuaire [sɑ̃ktɥer] *m* sanctuary

sandale [sɑ̃dal] *f* sandal; gym shoe

sandwich [sɑ̃dwit/], [sɑ̃dwi/] *m* (*pl* **sandwiches, sandwichs**) sandwich

sang [sɑ̃] *m* blood; **avoir le sang chaud** (coll) to be a go-getter; **bon sang!** (coll) darn it!; **sang et tripes** blood and guts; **se faire du mauvais sang** to get all stewed up

sang-froid [sɑ̃frwa], [sɑ̃frwɑ] *m* self-control

san-glant [sɑ̃glɑ̃] **-glante** [glɑ̃t] *adj* bloody; cruel

sangle [sɑ̃gl] *f* cinch

sanglier [sɑ̃glije] *m* wild boar

sanglot [sɑ̃glo] *m* sob

sangloter [sɑ̃glɔte] *intr* to sob

sang-mêlé [sɑ̃mele] *m invar* half-breed

sangsue [sɑ̃sy] *f* bloodsucker, leech

san-guin [sɑ̃gɛ̃] **-guine** [gin] *adj* sanguine ‖ *f* (fa) sanguine

sanitaire [saniter] *adj* sanitary; hospital, e.g., **avion sanitaire** hospital plane

sans [sɑ̃] *adv*—**sans que** without; **sans quoi** or else ‖ *prep* without; **sans cesse** ceaselessly; **sans façon** informally; **sans fil** wireless

sans-abri [sɑ̃zabri] *mf invar* homeless person

sans-cœur [sɑ̃kœr] *mf invar* heartless person

sans-filiste [sɑ̃filist] *mf* (*pl* **-filistes**) radio operator; radio amateur

sans-gêne [sɑ̃ʒen] *adj invar* offhanded ‖ *mf invar* offhanded person ‖ *m* offhandedness

sansonnet [sɑ̃sɔne] *m* starling; blackbird

sans-travail [sɑ̃travaj] *mf invar* unemployed worker

san·tal [sɑ̃tal] *m* (*pl* **-taux** [to]) (bot) sandalwood

santé [sɑ̃te] *f* health; sanity; **santé publique** public health service

sape [sap] *f* sap (*undermining*)

saper [sape] *tr* to sap, to undermine

sapeur [sapœr] *m* (mil) sapper; **fumer comme un sapeur** (coll) to smoke like a chimney

sapeur-pompier [sapœrpɔ̃pje] *m* (*pl* **sapeurs-pompiers**) fireman; **sapeurs-pompiers** fire department

saphir [safir] *m* sapphire; sapphire needle

sapin [sapɛ̃] *m* fir

sapristi [sapristi] *interj* hang it!

saquer [sake] *tr* (slang) to fire, to sack

sarbacane [sarbakan] *f* blowgun

sarcasme [sarkasm] *m* sarcasm

sarcler [sarkle] *tr* to weed, root out

sarcloir [sarklwar] *m* hoe

Sardaigne [sardeɲ] *f* Sardinia; **la Sardaigne** Sardinia

sarde [sard] *adj* Sardinian ‖ *m* Sardinian (*language*) ‖ (*cap*) *mf* Sardinian (*person*)

sardine [sardin] *f* sardine

S.A.R.L. *abbr* (**Société à responsabilité limitée**) corporation

sarment [sarmɑ̃] *m* vine; vine shoot

sarra·sin [sarazɛ̃] **-sine** [zin] *adj* Saracen ‖ *m* buckwheat ‖ *f* portcullis ‖ (*cap*) *mf* Saracen

sar·rau [saro] *m* (*pl* **-raus**) smock

sarriette [sarjet] *f* (bot) savory

sas [sɑ], [sɑs] *m* sieve; lock (*of canal, submarine, etc.*); air lock (*of caisson, spaceship, etc.*); **sas d'évacuation** (aer) escape hatch

sasser [sɑse] *tr* to sift, screen; to pass through a lock

satelliser [satelize] *tr* to make a satellite; (rok) to put into orbit

satellite [satelit] *adj & m* satellite

satin [satɛ̃] *m* satin

satinette [satinet] *f* sateen

satire [satir] *f* satire

satirique [satirik] *adj* satiric(al)

satiriser [satirize] *tr* to satirize

satisfaction [satisfaksjɔ̃] *f* satisfaction

satisfaire [satisfer] §29 *tr* to satisfy ‖ *intr* to satisfy; (with *dat*) to fulfill; (with *dat*) to meet (a need) ‖ *ref* to be satisfied

satisfai·sant [satisfəzɑ̃] **-sante** [zɑ̃t] *adj* satisfactory; satisfying

saturer [satyre] *tr* to saturate

Saturne [satyrn] *m* Saturn

saturnisme [satyrnism] *m* lead poisoning

sauce [sos] *f* sauce; gravy; drawing pencil; (tech) solution

saucer [sose] §51 *tr* to dip in sauce or gravy; (coll) to soak to the skin; (coll) to reprimand severely

saucière [sosjer] *f* gravy bowl

saucisse [sosis] *f* sausage; frankfurter

saucisson [sosisɔ̃] *m* bologna, sausage

sauf [sof] **sauve** [sov] *adj* safe ‖ **sauf** *prep* save, except; barring; subject to (*e.g.*, correction)

sauf-conduit [sofkɔ̃dɥi] *m* (*pl* **-conduits**) safe-conduct

sauge [soʒ] *f* (bot) sage, salvia

saugre·nu -nue [sogrəny] *adj* absurd, silly

saule [sol] *m* willow

saumâtre [somɑtr] *adj* brackish

saumon [som5] *m* salmon; pig (*of crude metal*)

saumure [somyr] *f* brine

sauner [sone] *intr* to make salt

saupoudrer [sopudre] *tr* to sprinkle (*with powder, sugar; citations*)

saurer [sɔre] *tr* to kipper

saut [so] *m* leap, jump; falls, waterfall; **au saut du lit** on getting out of bed; **faire le saut** to take the fatal step; **faire un saut chez** to drop in on; **par sauts et par bonds** by fits and starts; **saut à la perche** pole vault; **saut de carpe** jackknife; **saut de l'ange** swan dive; **saut en chute libre** skydiving; **saut périlleux** somersault

saut-de-lit [sodli] *m invar* wrap

saut-de-mouton [sodmut5] *m* (*pl* **sauts-de-mouton**) cloverleaf (*intersection*)

saute [sot] *f* change in direction, shift

saute-mouton [sotmut5] *m* leapfrog

sauter [sote] *tr* to leap over; to skip ‖ *intr* to leap, jump; to blow up; **faire sauter** to sauté; to flip (*a pancake*); to fire (*an employee*); **sauter à cloche-pied** to hop on one foot; **sauter à pieds joints** to do a standing jump; **sauter aux nues** to get mad

sauterelle [sotrɛl] *f* grasshopper

sauterie [sotri] *f* (coll) hop (*dancing party*)

sau·teur -teuse [sotœr] [tøz] *adj* jumping ‖ *mf* jumper ‖ *m* jumper, jumping horse ‖ *f* frying pan

sautiller [sotije] *intr* to hop

sautoir [sotwar] *m* St. Andrew's cross; **en sautoir** crossways

sauvage [sovaʒ] *adj* savage; wild; shy ‖ *mf* savage

sauvagerie [sovaʒri] *f* savagery; wildness; shyness

sauvegarde [sovgard] *f* safeguard

sauvegarder [sovgarde] *tr* to safeguard

sauve-qui-peut [sovkipø] *m invar* panic, stampede, rout

sauver [sove] *tr* to save; to rescue ‖ *intr*—**sauve qui peut!** every man for himself! ‖ *ref* to run away; to escape; (theat) to exit; **sauve-toi!** (coll) scram!

sauvetage [sovtaʒ] *m* salvage; lifesaving, rescue

sauveteur [sovtœr] *adj masc* lifesaving ‖ *m* lifesaver

sauveur [sovœr] *adj masc* Saviour ‖ *m* savior; **Le Sauveur** the Saviour

savamment [savamɑ̃] *adv* knowingly; skillfully

savane [savan] *f* prairie, savanna

sa·vant -vante [savɑ̃] [vɑ̃t] *adj* scholarly, learned ‖ *mf* scientist, scholar, savant; **savant atomiste** nuclear physicist

savate [savat] *f* old slipper; foot boxing; (coll) butterflyer; **traîner la savate** to be down at the heel

saveur [savœr] *f* savor, taste

savoir [savwar] *m* learning ‖ §62 *tr* & *intr* to know; to know how to; **à**

savoir namely, to wit; **à savoir que** with the understanding that; **en savoir long** to know all about it; **pas que je sache** not that I know of

savoir-faire [savwarfer] *m invar* know-how

savon [sav5] *m* soap; (slang) sharp reprimand; **savon en paillettes** soap flakes

savonnage [savonaʒ] *m* soaping

savonner [savone] *tr* to soap

savonnerie [savonri] *f* soap factory

savonnette [savonet] *f* toilet soap

savon·neux -neuse [savonø] [savonøz] *adj* soapy

savourer [savure] *tr* to savor

savou·reux -reuse [savurø] [røz] *adj* savory, tasty

saxon [saks5] **saxonne** [saksɔn] *adj* Saxon ‖ *m* Saxon (*language*) ‖ (*cap*) *mf* Saxon (*person*)

saxophone [saksofon] *m* saxophone

saynète [senet] *f* sketch, playlet

sca·bieux -bieuse [skabjø] [bjøz] *adj* scabby ‖ *f* scabious

sca·breux -breuse [skabrø] [brøz] *adj* rough (*road*); risky (*business*); scabrous (*remark*)

scalpel [skalpɛl] *m* scalpel

scalper [skalpe] *tr* to scalp

scandale [skɑ̃dal] *m* scandal; disturbance

scanda·leux -leuse [skɑ̃dalø] [løz] *adj* scandalous

scandaliser [skɑ̃dalize] *tr* to lead astray; to scandalize ‖ *ref* to take offense

scander [skɑ̃de] *tr* to scan (*verses*)

scandinave [skɑ̃dinav] *adj* Scandinavian ‖ *m* Scandinavian (*language*) ‖ (*cap*) *mf* Scandinavian (*person*); **Scandinaves** Scandinavian countries

scaphandre [skafɑ̃dr] *m* diving suit; spacesuit; **scaphandre autonome** aqualung

scaphandrier [skafɑ̃drije] *m* diver

scarlatine [skarlatin] *f* scarlet fever

scarole [skarɔl] *f* escarole

sceau [so] *m* (*pl* **seaux**) seal

scélé·rat [selera] **-rate** [rat] *adj* villainous ‖ *mf* villain

scellé [sele] *m* seal

sceller [sele] *tr* to seal

scénario [senarjo] *m* scenario

scène [sen] *f* scene; stage; theater

scénique [senik] *adj* scenic

scepticisme [septisism] *m* skepticism

sceptique [septik] *adj* & *mf* skeptic

sceptre [septr] *m* scepter

schah [ʃa] *m* shah

schelem [ʃlem] *m* slam (*at bridge*)

schéma [ʃema] *m* diagram

schisme [ʃism] *m* schism

schizophrène [skizofren] *adj* & *mf* schizophrenic

schlague [ʃlag] *f* flogging

schooner [skunœr] [ʃunœr] *m* schooner

sciatique [sjatik] *adj* sciatic ‖ *f* (pathol) sciatica

scie [si] *f* saw; (coll) bore, nuisance; **scie à découper** jig saw

sciemment [sjamɑ̃] *adv* knowingly

science [sjɑ̃s] *f* science; learning, knowledge

science-fiction [sjɑ̃sfiksjɔ̃] *f* science fiction

scientifique [sjɑ̃tifik] *adj* scientific || *mf* scientist

scier [sje] *tr* to saw; (coll) to bore || *intr* (naut) to row backwards

scierie [siri] *f* sawmill

scieur [sjœr] *m* sawyer

scinder [sɛ̃de] *tr* to divide || *ref* to be divided

scintil·lant [sɛ̃tijɑ̃] **scintil·lante** [sɛ̃tijɑ̃t] *adj* scintillating; twinkling

scintillation [sɛ̃tijɑsjɔ̃] *f* twinkling, twinkle; (phys) scintillation

scintillement [sɛ̃tijmɑ̃] *m* twinkling

scintiller [sɛ̃tije] *intr* to scintillate; to twinkle

scion [sjɔ̃] *m* scion; tip (*of fishing rod*)

scission [sisjɔ̃] *f* schism; (biol & phys) fission

sciure [sjyr] *f* sawdust

sclérose [skleroz] *f* sclerosis

scolaire [skɔler] *adj* school

scolastique [skɔlastik] *adj* & *m* scholastic || *f* scholasticism

sconse [skɔ̃s] *m* skunk fur; skunk

scories [skɔri] *fpl* slag, dross

scorpion [skɔrpjɔ̃] *m* scorpion

scout scoute [skut] *adj* & *m* scout

scoutisme [skutism] *m* scouting

scribe [skrib] *m* scribe

script [skript] *m* scrip; (typ) script

scripturaire [skriptyrer] *adj* Scriptural || *m* fundamentalist

scrofule [skrɔfyl] *f* scrofula

scrotum [skrɔtɔm] *m* scrotum

scrupule [skrypyl] *m* scruple

scrupu·leux [skrypylø] **-leuse** [løz] *adj* scrupulous

scruter [skryte] *tr* to scrutinize

scrutin [skrytɛ̃] *m* ballot; balloting, voting, poll; **dépouiller le scrutin** to count the votes; **scrutin de ballottage** runoff election

scrutiner [skrytine] *intr* to ballot

sculpter [skylte] *tr* to sculpture; to carve (*wood*)

sculpteur [skyltœr] *m* sculptor

sculpture [skyltyr] *f* sculpture

s.d. *abbr* (**sans date**) n.d.

S.D.N. [esdeen] *f* (letterword) (**Société des Nations**) League of Nations

se [sə] §87

séance [seɑ̃s] *f* session, sitting; seat (*in an assembly*); performance, showing; séance; **séance tenante** on the spot

séant [seɑ̃] **séante** [seɑ̃t] *adj* fitting, decent; sitting (*as a king or a court in session*) || *m* buttocks, bottom; **se mettre sur son séant** to sit up (*in bed*)

seau [so] *m* (*pl* **seaux**) bucket, pail; **il pleut à seaux** it's raining cats and dogs; **seau à charbon** coal scuttle

sébile [sebil] *f* wooden bowl

sec [sek] **sèche** [sɛʃ] *adj* dry; sharp; rude; unguarded (*card*); total (*loss*); **en cinq sec** in a jiffy; **sec comme un hareng** (coll) long and thin; **tout sec** and **nothing more** || *m* dryness; **à sec** dry; (coll) broke || *f* see **sèche** || *adv*—**aussi sec** (slang) on the spot;

boire sec to drink one's liquor straight; **frapper sec** to land a hard fast punch; **parler sec** to talk tough

sécession [sesesjɔ̃] *f* secession

sèche [sɛʃ] *f* (slang) fag, cigarette

sèche-cheveux [sɛʃəvø] *m invar* hair drier

sécher [seʃe] §10 *tr* to dry; to season; to cut (*a class*) || *intr* to become dry

sécheresse [seʃrɛs] *f* dryness; drought; baldness (*of style*); curtness; (fig) coldness

séchoir [seʃwar] *m* drier; drying room; clotheshorse

se·cond [səgɔ̃] **-conde** [gɔ̃d] *adj* & *pron* second; **en second** next in rank || *m* second || *f* see **seconde**

secondaire [səgɔ̃der] *adj* & *m* secondary

seconde [səgɔ̃d] *f* second (*in time*; *musical interval*; *of angle*); second class

seconder [səgɔ̃de] *tr* to help, second

secouer [səkwe] *tr* to shake; to shake off or down || *ref* to pull oneself together

secourable [səkurabl] *adj* helpful

secourir [səkurir] §14 *tr* to help, aid

secourisme [səkurism] *m* first aid

secouriste [səkurist] *mf* first-aider; first-aid worker

secours [səkur] *m* help, aid; **au secours!** help!; **de secours** emergency; spare (*tire*); **des secours** supplies, relief

secousse [səkus] *f* shake, jolt; (elec) shock

se·cret [səkre] **-crète** [kret] *adj* secret; secretive || *m* secret; secrecy; **au secret** in solitary confinement || *f* see **secrète**

secrétaire [səkreter] *mf* secretary || *m* secretary (*desk*)

secrète [səkret] *f* central intelligence

sécréter [sekrete] §10 *tr* to secrete

sectaire [sekter] *adj* & *mf* sectarian

secte [sekt] *f* sect

secteur [sektœr] *m* sector; (elec) house current, local supply circuit; **secteur postal** postal zone; (mil) A.P.O. number

section [seksjɔ̃] *f* section; cross section

sectionner [seksjone] *tr* to section; to cut || *ref* to break apart

séculaire [sekyler] *adj* secular

sécu·lier [sekylje] **-lière** [ljer] *adj* & *m* secular

sécurité [sekyrite] *f* security

séda·tif [sedatif] **-tive** [tiv] *adj* & *m* sedative

sédation [sedɑsjɔ̃] *f* sedation

sédentaire [sedɑ̃ter] *adj* sedentary

sédiment [sedimɑ̃] *m* sediment

sédi·tieux [sedisjø] **-tieuse** [sjøz] *adj* seditious

sédition [sedisjɔ̃] *f* sedition

séduc·teur [sedyktœr] **-trice** [tris] *adj* seducing, bewitching || *mf* seducer || *f* vamp

séduction [sedyksjɔ̃] *f* seduction

séduire [sedɥir] §19 *tr* to seduce; to charm, to bewitch; to bribe

sédui·sant [sedɥizɑ̃] **-sante** [zɑ̃t] *adj* seductive, tempting

segment [segmã] *m* segment; **segment de piston** piston ring

ségrégation [segregasjɔ̃] *f* segregation

ségrégationniste [segregasjɔnist] *adj* segregationist

seiche [sɛʃ] *f* cuttlefish

séide [seid] *m* henchman

seigle [sɛgl] *m* rye

seigneur [sɛɲœr] *m* lord

sein [sɛ̃] *m* breast; bosom; womb; **au sein de** in the heart of

seine [sɛn] *f* dragnet

seing [sɛ̃] *m* signature; **sous seing privé** privately witnessed

seize [sez] *adj & pron* sixteen; the Sixteenth, e.g., **Jean seize** John the Sixteenth ‖ *m* sixteen; sixteenth (*in dates*)

seizième [sezjɛm] *adj, pron* (*masc, fem*), & *m* sixteenth

séjour [seʒur] *m* stay, visit

séjourner [seʒurne] *intr* to reside; to stay, to visit

sel [sɛl] *m* salt; **gros sel** coarse salt; (fig) dirty joke; **sel ammoniac** sal ammoniac; **sel gemme** rock salt

sélec·tif [selektif] **-tive** [tiv] *adj* selective

sélection [seleksjɔ̃] *f* selection

sélectionner [seleksjɔne] *tr* to select

self [sɛlf] *f* (elec) coil, spark coil

self-service [selfsɛrvis] *m* self-service

selle [sɛl] *f* saddle; seat (*of bicycle, motorcycle, etc.*); sculptor's tripod; stool, movement; (culin) saddle; **aller à la selle** to go to the toilet

seller [sele] *tr* to saddle

sellier [selje] *m* saddler

selon [səlɔ̃] *adv*—**c'est selon** that depends; **selon que** according as ‖ *prep* according to; after (*e.g., my own heart*)

semailles [səmɑj] *fpl* sowing, seeding

semaine [səmɛn] *f* week; week's wages; set of seven; **à la petite semaine** day-to-day, hand-to-mouth; short-sighted; **de semaine** on duty during the week; **la semaine des quatre jeudis** (coll) never; **semaine anglaise** five-day workweek

semai·nier [səmenje] **-nière** [njɛr] *mf* week worker ‖ *m* highboy; office calendar

sémantique [semɑ̃tik] *adj* semantic ‖ *f* semantics

sémaphore [semafɔr] *m* semaphore

semblable [sɑ̃blabl] *adj* similar, like ‖ *m* fellow-man, equal

semblant [sɑ̃blɑ̃] *m* semblance, appearance; **faire semblant** to pretend

sembler [sɑ̃ble] *intr* to seem; to seem to

semelle [səmɛl] *f* sole; foot (*of stocking*); tread (*of tire*); bed (*of concrete*)

semence [səmɑ̃s] *f* seed; semen; brad; **semence de perles** seed pearls

semer [səme] §2 *tr* to seed, to sow; to scatter, strew; to lay (*mines*); (slang) to outdistance; (slang) to drop (*an acquaintance*)

semestre [səmɛstr] *m* semester; six-month period

semes·triel **-trielle** [səmestrijel] *adj* six-month; semester

se·meur [səmœr] **-meuse** [møz] *mf* sower; spreader of gossip ‖ *f* seeder, drill

semi-chenillé [səmi/nije] *m* half-track

semi-conduc·teur [səmikɔ̃dyktœr] **-trice** [tris] *adj* semiconductive ‖ *m* semiconductor

semifi·ni **-nie** [səmifini] *adj* unfinished

sémil·lant [semijɑ̃] **sémil·lante** [semi-jɑ̃t] *adj* sprightly, lively

séminaire [seminer] *m* seminary; seminar; conference

semi-remorque [səmirəmɔrk] *f* (*pl* **-remorques**) semitrailer

semis [səmi] *m* sowing; seedling; seedbed

sémite [semit] *adj* Semitic ‖ (*cap*) *mf* Semite

sémitique [semitik] *adj* Semitic

semoir [səmwar] *m* seeder, drill

semonce [səmɔ̃s] *f* reprimand; (naut) order to heave to

semoncer [səmɔ̃se] §51 *tr* to reprimand; (naut) to order to heave to

semoule [səmul] *f* (culin) semolina

sénat [sena] *m* senate

sénateur [senatœr] *m* senator

sénile [senil] *adj* senile

sens [sɑ̃s] *m* sense, meaning; opinion; direction; **en sens inverse** in the opposite direction; **sens dessus dessous** [sɑ̃dəsydəsu] upside down; **sens devant derrière** [sɑ̃dəvɑ̃derjer] back to front; **sens interdit** (public sign) no entry; **sens obligatoire** (public sign) right way, this way; **sens unique** (public sign) one way

sensation [sɑ̃sasjɔ̃] *f* sensation

sensation·nel **-nelle** [sɑ̃sasjɔnel] *adj* sensational

sen·sé **-sée** [sɑ̃se] *adj* sensible

sensibiliser [sɑ̃sibilize] *tr* to sensitize

sensibilité [sɑ̃sibilite] *f* sensibility; sensitivity

sensible [sɑ̃sibl] *adj* sensitive; sensible; appreciable, perceptible

sensi·tif [sɑ̃sitif] **-tive** [tiv] *adj* sensory; sensitive, touchy

senso·riel **-rielle** [sɑ̃sɔrjel] *adj* sensory

sen·suel **-suelle** [sɑ̃syel] *adj* sensual

sent-bon [sɑ̃bɔ̃] *m invar* odor, perfume

sentence [sɑ̃tɑ̃s] *f* proverb; (law) sentence

senteur [sɑ̃tœr] *f* odor, perfume

sentier [sɑ̃tje] *m* path; **hors des sentiers battus** off the beaten track

sentiment [sɑ̃timɑ̃] *m* sentiment, feeling

sentimen·tal **-tale** [sɑ̃timɑ̃tal] *adj* (*pl* **-taux** [to]) sentimental

sentine [sɑ̃tin] *f* bilge

sentinelle [sɑ̃tinel] *f* sentinel

sentir [sɑ̃tir] §41 *tr* to feel; to smell; to smell like, smell of; to taste of; to have all the earmarks of; to show the effects of; **ne pas pouvoir sentir qn** to be unable to stand s.o. ‖ *intr* to smell; to smell bad ‖ *ref* to feel; to be felt; **se sentir de** to feel the effects of

seoir [swar] §5A (3d *pl pres ind* **sléent;**

used only in 3d *sg* & *pl* of most simple tenses) *intr* (with *dat*) to be suitable to, to become; to be fitting to, to be proper for ‖ (used only in *inf* and 2d *sg* & *pl* and 1st *pl impv*) *ref* (coll & poetic) to sit down, have a seat

séparation [separɑsjɔ̃] *f* separation

séparer [separe] *tr* & *ref* to separate, to divide

sept [sɛt] *adj* & *pron* seven; the Seventh, e.g., **Jean sept** John the Seventh; **sept heures** seven o'clock ‖ *m* seven; seventh (*in dates*)

septembre [sɛptɑ̃br] *m* September

septième [sɛtjɛm] *adj, pron (masc, fem),* & *m* seventh

septique [sɛptik] *adj* septic

sépulcre [sepylkr] *m* sepulcher

sépulture [sepyltyr] *f* grave, tomb, burial place; burial

séquelle [sekel] *f* gang; (pathol) complications; **séquelles** aftermath

séquence [sekɑ̃s] *f* sequence; (*in poker*) straight

séquestrer [sekɛstre] *tr* to sequester

séraphin [serafɛ̃] *m* seraph; (coll) angel

serbe [sɛrb] *adj* Serb ‖ (*cap*) *mf* Serb

se·rein [sərɛ̃] **-reine** [rɛn] *adj* serene ‖ *m* night dew

sérénade [serenad] *f* serenade

sérénité [serenite] *f* serenity

serf [sɛr], [sɛrf] **serve** [sɛrv] *mf* serf

serge [sɛrʒ] *f* serge

sergent [sɛrʒɑ̃] *m* sergeant

série [seri] *f* series, string, set; (elec) series; **de série** standard; stock (*car*); **en série** in (a) series; mass, e.g., **fabrication en série** mass production; **hors série** outsize (*wearing apparel*); discontinued (*as an item of manufacture*); custom-built; almost unheard of; **série noire** run of bad luck

sé·rieux [serjø] **-rieuse** [rjøz] *adj* serious

serin [sərɛ̃] *m* canary; (coll) simpleton

seringa [sərɛ̃ga] *m* mock orange

seringue [sərɛ̃g] *f* syringe; (hort) spray gun; **seringue à graisse** grease gun; **seringue à injections** hypodermic syringe; **seringue à instillations** nasal spray

serment [sɛrmɑ̃] *m* oath; **prêter serment** to take oath

sermon [sɛrmɔ̃] *m* sermon

sermonner [sɛrmɔne] *tr* to sermonize

serpe [sɛrp] *f* billhook

serpent [sɛrpɑ̃] *m* snake, serpent; **serpent à sonnettes** rattlesnake; **serpent caché sous les fleurs** snake in the grass

serpenter [sɛrpɑ̃te] *intr* to wind

serpen·tin [sɛrpɑ̃tɛ̃] **-tine** [tin] *adj* serpentine ‖ *m* coil; worm (*of still*); paper streamer

serpillière [sɛrpijɛr] *f* floorcloth; sacking, burlap

serpolet [sɛrpɔle] *m* thyme

serre [sɛr] *f* greenhouse; **serres** claws, talons

ser·ré -rée [sere] *adj* tight; narrow; compact; close ‖ **serré** *adv*—**jouer serré** to play it close to the vest

serre-fils [sɛrfil] *m invar* (elec) binding post

serre-freins [sɛrfrɛ̃] *m invar* brakeman

serre-livres [sɛrlivr] *m invar* book end

serrement [sɛrmɑ̃] *m* squeezing, pressing; (min) partition (*to keep out water*); (pathol) pang; **serrement de cœur** heaviness of heart; **serrement de main** handshake

serrer [sere] *tr* to press; to squeeze; to wring; to tighten; to close up (*ranks*); to clasp, shake, e.g., **serrer la main à** to shake hands with; to grit (*one's teeth*); to put on (*the brakes*) ‖ *intr*—**serrez à droite** (public sign) squeeze to right ‖ *ref* to squeeze together, to be close together

serre-tête [sɛrtɛt] *m invar* headband; kerchief; crash helmet; (telp) headset

serrure [seryr] *f* lock; **serrure de sûreté** safety lock

serrurier [seryrje] *m* locksmith

sertir [sɛrtir] *tr* to set (*a stone*)

sérum [serɔm] *m* serum

servage [sɛrvaʒ] *m* serfdom

ser·veur [sɛrvœr] **-veuse** [vøz] *mf* (tennis) server ‖ *m* waiter; barman ‖ *f* waitress; barmaid; extra maid; (mach) coffee maker

serviable [sɛrvjabl] *adj* obliging

service [sɛrvis] *m* service; agency; **être de service** to be on duty; **service compris** tip included; **service de garde** twenty-four-hour service; **service des abonnés absents** telephone answering service; **service des renseignements téléphoniques** information service; **service sanitaire** ambulance corps

serviette [sɛrvjɛt] *f* napkin; towel; brief case; **serviette de bain** bath towel; **serviette éponge** washcloth; Turkish towel; **serviette hygiénique** sanitary napkin

servile [sɛrvil] *adj* servile

servir [sɛrvir] §63 *tr* to serve; to deal (*cards*) ‖ *intr* to serve; **servir à** to be useful for, to serve as; **servir à qn de** to serve s.o. as; **servir de** to serve as, to function as ‖ *ref* to help oneself; **se servir chez** to patronize; **se servir de** to use

serviteur [sɛrvitœr] *m* servant

servitude [sɛrvityd] *f* servitude; (law) easement

servofrein [sɛrvofrɛ̃] *m* power brake

ses [se] §88

sésame [sezam] *m* sesame

session [sesjɔ̃] *f* session

seuil [sœj] *m* threshold

seul seule [sœl] *adj* alone; lonely ‖ (when standing before noun) *adj* sole, single, only ‖ *pron indef* single one, only one; single person, only person ‖ **seul** *adv* alone

seulement [sœlmɑ̃] *adv* only, even ‖ *conj* but

sève [sɛv] *f* sap; vim

sévère [sever] *adj* severe; stern; strict

sévices [sevis] *mpl* cruelty, brutality

sévir [sevir] *intr* to rage

sevrage [səvraʒ] *m* weaning

sevrer [səvre] §2 *tr* to wean

sexe [sɛks] *m* sex; **le beau sexe** the fair sex; **le sexe fort** the sterner sex

sextant [sɛkstɑ̃] *m* sextant

sextuor [sɛkstɥɔr] *m* (mus) sextet

sexuel sexuelle [sɛksɥɛl] *adj* sexual

seyant [sejɑ̃] **seyante** [sejɑ̃t] *adj* becoming

shampooing [ʃɑ̃pwɛ̃] *m* shampoo

shérif [ʃerif] *m* sheriff

short [ʃɔrt] *m* shorts

si [si] *m invar* if; **des si et des car** ifs and buts || *adv* so; as; (to contradict a negative statement or question) yes, e.g., **Vous ne le saviez pas. Si!** You didn't know. Yes, I did!; **si bien que** so that, with the result that; **si peu que** so little that; **si peu que ce soit** however little it may be; **si** + *adj* or *adv* + **que** + *subj* however + *adj* or *adv* + *ind*, e.g., **si vite qu'il s'en aille** however fast he goes away || *conj* if; whether; **si . . . ne** unless, e.g., **si je ne me trompe** unless I am mistaken; **si ce n'est** unless; **si tant est que** if it is true that

sia·mois [sjamwa] **-moise** [mwaz] *adj* Siamese || (*cap*) *mf* Siamese

sibé·rien [siberjɛ̃] **-rienne** [rjɛn] *adj* Siberian || (*cap*) *mf* Siberian

sibylle [sibil] *f* sibyl

Sicile [sisil] *f* Sicily; **la Sicile** Sicily

sici·lien [sisiljɛ̃] **-lienne** [ljɛn] *adj* Sicilian || (*cap*) *mf* Sicilian

sidé·ral -rale [sideral] *adj* (*pl* **-raux** [ro]) sidereal

sidérer [sidere] §10 *tr* (coll) to flabbergast

sidérurgie [sideryrʒi] *f* iron-and-steel industry

sidérurgique [sideryrʒik] *adj* iron-and-steel

siècle [sjɛkl] *m* century; age; (eccl) world

siège [sjɛʒ] *m* seat; headquarters; (eccl) see; (mil) siege; **siège à glissière** glider; **siège baquet** (*pl* **sièges baquets**) bucket seat; **siège éjectable** ejection seat

siéger [sjeʒe] §1 *intr* to sit, to be in session; (*said of malady*) to be seated

sien [sjɛ̃] **sienne** [sjɛn] §89

sieste [sjɛst] *f* siesta; **faire la sieste** to take a siesta

sifflement [sifləmɑ̃] *m* whistle; hiss; swish, whiz

siffler [sifle] *tr* to whistle (*e.g., a tune*); to hiss, boo; to whistle to || *intr* to whistle; to hiss; to swish, to whiz

sifflet [siflɛ] *m* whistle

sif·fleur [siflœr] **sif·fleuse** [sifløz] *mf* whistler

sigle [sigl] *m* abbreviation; word formed by literation; acronym

si·gnal [siɲal] *m* (*pl* **-gnaux** [ɲo]) signal; sign; (telp) busy signal

signa·lé -lée [siɲale] *adj* signal, noteworthy

signalement [siɲalmɑ̃] *m* description

signaler [siɲale] *tr* to signal; to point out || *ref* to distinguish oneself

signalisation [siɲalizasjɔ̃] *f* signs

signataire [siɲatɛr] *adj* & *mf* signatory

signature [siɲatyr] *f* signature; signing

signe [siɲ] *m* sign; **faire signe à** to motion to, to signal; **signe de ponctuation** punctuation mark; **signe de tête** nod

signer [siɲe] *tr* to sign || *ref* to cross oneself

signet [siɲɛ], [siɲe] *m* bookmark

significa·tif [siɲifikatif] **-tive** [tiv] *adj* significant

signifier [siɲifje] *tr* to signify; to mean

silence [silɑ̃s] *m* silence

silen·cieux [silɑ̃sjø] **-cieuse** [sjøz] *adj* silent || *m* (aut) muffler

silex [silɛks] *m* flint

silhouette [silwɛt] *f* silhouette

silhouetter [silwete] *tr* to silhouette

silicium [silisjɔm] *m* silicon

silicone [silikɔn] *f* silicone

sillage [sijaʒ] *m* wake

sillet [sijɛ] *m* (mus) nut

sillon [sijɔ̃] *m* furrow; groove; **sillon sonore** sound track

sillonner [sijɔne] *tr* to furrow; to groove; to cross, to streak

silo [silo] *m* silo

silure [silyr] *m* catfish

simagrée [simagre] *f* pretense

similaire [similɛr] *adj* similar

similigravure [similigravyr] *f* halftone

similitude [similityd] *f* similarity

similor [similɔr] *m* ormolu

simple || [sɛ̃pl] *adj* simple; **passer en simple police** to go to police court; **simple particulier** private citizen; **simple soldat** private || *mf* simpleminded person || *m* simple (*herb*); (tennis) singles

sim·plet [sɛ̃plɛ] **-plette** [plɛt] *adj* artless

simplifier [sɛ̃plifje] *tr* to simplify

simpliste [sɛ̃plist] *adj* oversimple

simulacre [simylakr] *m* sham; **simulacre de combat** sham battle

simuler [simyle] *tr* to simulate

simulta·né -née [simyltane] *adj* simultaneous

sinapisme [sinapism] *m* mustard plaster

sincère [sɛ̃sɛr] *adj* sincere

sincérité [sɛ̃serite] *f* sincerity

sinécure [sinekyr] *f* sinecure

singe [sɛ̃ʒ] *m* monkey; (slang) boss; **grimacer comme un vieux singe** to grin like a Cheshire cat

singer [sɛ̃ʒe] §38 *tr* to ape

singerie [sɛ̃ʒri] *f* monkeyshine; grimace; monkey cage

singulariser [sɛ̃gylarize] *tr* to draw attention to || *ref* to stand out

singu·lier [sɛ̃gylje] **-lière** [ljɛr] *adj* & *m* singular

sinistre [sinistr] *adj* sinister || *m* disaster

sinis·tré -trée [sinistre] *adj* damaged, ruined; homeless; shipwrecked || *mf* victim

sinon [sinɔ̃] *adv* if not; perhaps even; **sinon que** except for the fact that || *prep* except for, except to || *conj* except, unless; or else, else, otherwise

si·nueux [sinɥø] **-nueuse** [nɥøz] *adj* sinuous, winding

sinus [sinys] *m* sinus; (trig) sine

sionisme [sjɔnism] *m* Zionism

siphon [sifɔ̃] *m* siphon; siphon bottle; trap (*double-curved pipe*)

siphonner [sifɔne] *tr* to siphon

sirène [siren] *f* siren; foghorn

sirop [siro] *m* syrup; **sirop pectoral** cough syrup

siroter [sirɔte] *tr & intr* (coll) to sip

sis [si] **sise** [siz] *adj* located

sismographe [sismɔgraf] *m* seismograph

sismologie [sismɔlɔʒi] *f* seismology

site [sit] *m* site; lay of the land

sitôt [sito] *adv* immediately; **sîtot dit, sitôt fait** no sooner said than done; **sitôt que** as soon as

sittelle [sitɛl] *f* (orn) nuthatch

situation [sitɥasjɔ̃] *f* situation; **situation sans issue** deadlock, impasse

situer [sitɥe] *tr* to situate, to locate

six [si(s)] *adj & pron* six; the Sixth, e.g., **Jean six** John the Sixth; **six heures** six o'clock || *m* six; sixth (*in dates*)

sixième [sizjɛm] *adj, pron* (*masc, fem*), & *m* sixth

six-quatre-deux [siskatdø]—**à la six-quatre-deux** (coll) slapdash

sizain [sizɛ̃] *m* six-line verse; pack (*of cub scouts*)

sizerin [sizrɛ̃] *m* (orn) redpoll

ski [ski] *m* ski; skiing; **faire du ski** to go skiing; **ski nautique** water-skiing

skier [skje] *intr* to ski

skieur [skjœr] **skieuse** [skjøz] *mf* skier

slalom [slalɔm] *m* slalom

slave [slav] *adj* Slav; Slavic || *m* Slavic (*language*) || (*cap*) *mf* Slav (*person*)

slogan [slɔgã] *m* (com) slogan

slovaque [slɔvak] *adj* Slovak || *m* Slovak (*language*) || (*cap*) *mf* Slovak (*person*)

smoking [smɔkiŋ] *m* tuxedo

snack [snak] *m* snack bar

S.N.C.F. [esenseef] *f* (letterword) (**Société nationale des Chemins de fer français**) French railroad

snob [snɔb] *adj invar* snobbish || *mf* (*pl* **snob** or **snobs**) snob

snober [snɔbe] *tr* to snub

snobisme [snɔbism] *m* snobbery

sobre [sɔbr] *adj* sober, moderate; simple (*ornamentation*)

sobriété [sɔbrijete] *f* sobriety; moderation (*in eating, speaking*)

sobriquet [sɔbrike] *m* nickname

soc [sɔk] *m* plowshare

sociable [sɔsjabl] *adj* sociable, neighborly; social (*creature*)

so‧cial ‑ciale [sɔsjal] *adj* (*pl* **‑ciaux** [sjo]) social

sociali‧sant ‑sante [sɔsjalizã] *adj* socialistic || *mf* socialist sympathizer

socialiser [sɔsjalize] *tr* to socialize

socialisme [sɔsjalism] *m* socialism

socialiste [sɔsjalist] *adj & mf* socialist

sociétaire [sɔsjeter] *mf* stockholder; member (*as, of an acting company*)

société [sɔsjete] *f* society; company; firm, partnership; **société anonyme** stock company, corporation; **société de prévoyance** benefit society; **Société des Nations** League of Nations

sociologie [sɔsjɔlɔʒi] *f* sociology

socle [sɔkl] *m* pedestal; footing, socle

socque [sɔk] *m* clog, sabot; (theat) comedy

socquette [sɔket] *f* anklet

Socrate [sɔkrat] *m* Socrates

soda [sɔda] *m* soda water

sodium [sɔdjɔm] *m* sodium

sœur [sœr] *f* sister; **et ta sœur!** (slang) knock it off!; **ma sœur** (eccl) sister

sofa [sɔfa] *m* sofa

soi [swa] §85, §85B; **à part soi** to oneself (himself, etc.); **de soi, en soi** in itself

soi-disant [swadizã] *adj invar* so-called, self-styled || *adv* supposedly

soie [swa] *f* silk; bristle

soierie [swari] *f* silk goods; silk factory

soif [swaf] *f* thirst; **avoir soif** to be thirsty

soi‧gné ‑gnée [swaɲe] *adj* well-groomed, trim; polished (*speech*)

soigner [swaɲe] *tr* to nurse, take care of; to groom; to polish (*one's style*)

soigneur [swaɲœr] *m* (sports) trainer

soi‧gneux ‑gneuse [swaɲø] **‑gneuse** [ɲøz] *adj* careful, meticulous

soi-même [swamem] §86

soin [swɛ̃] *m* care, attention; treatment; **aux bons soins de** in care of (*c/o*); **être aux petits soins auprès de** to wait on (*s.o.*) hand and foot; **premiers soins** first aid; **soins d'urgence** first aid

soir [swar] *m* evening, night; **hier soir** last night; **le soir** in the evening, at night

soirée [sware] *f* evening; evening party; **en soirée** evening (*performance*); **soirée dansante** dance

soit [swa], [swat] *conj* take for instance, e.g., **soit quatre multiplié par deux** take for instance four multiplied by two; say, e.g., **bien des hommes étaient perdus, soit un million** many men were lost, say a million; **soit . . . soit** either . . . or, whether . . . or; **soit que . . . soit que** whether . . . or || [swat] *interj* so be it!, all right!

soixante [swasãt] *adj, pron, & m* sixty; **soixante et onze** seventy-one; **soixante et onzième** seventy-first; **soixante et un** sixty-one; **soixante et unième** sixty-first

soixante-dix [swasãtdi(s)] *adj, pron, & m* seventy

soixante-dixième [swasãtdizjem] *adj, pron* (*masc, fem*) & *m* seventieth

soixantième [swasãtjem] *adj, pron* (*masc, fem*), & *m* sixtieth

soja [sɔʒa] *m* soybean

sol [sɔl] *m* soil; ground; floor

solaire [sɔler] *adj* solar

soldat [sɔlda] *m* soldier

soldatesque [sɔldatesk] *adj* barrack-room (*humor; manners*) || *f* rowdies

solde [sɔld] *m* balance (*of an account*); remnant; clearance sale; **en solde** reduced (*in price*) || *f* (mil) pay

solder [sɔlde] *tr* to settle (*an account*); to sell out; (mil) to pay || *intr* to sell out

sol·deur [sɔldœr] **-deuse** [døz] *mf* dealer in seconds and remnants

sole [sɔl] *f* sole (*fish*); field (*used for crop rotation*)

soleil [sɔlɛj] *m* sun; sunshine, sunlight; sunflower; pinwheel; **il fait du soleil** or **il fait soleil** it is sunny

solen·nel -nelle [sɔlanel] *adj* solemn

solénoïde [sɔlenɔid] *m* solenoid

solfège [sɔlfɛʒ] *m* sol-fa

solidage [sɔlidaʒ] *f* goldenrod

solidaire [sɔlider] *adj* interdependent; jointly binding; **solidaire de** responsible for; answerable to; integral with, in one piece with

solidariser [sɔlidarize] *ref* to join together

solidarité [sɔlidarite] *f* solidarity, interdependence

solide [sɔlid] *adj & m* solid

solidité [sɔlidite] *f* solidity; soundness; strength (*e.g., of a fabric*)

soliloque [sɔlilɔk] *m* soliloquy

soliste [sɔlist] *mf* soloist

solitaire [sɔliter] *adj* solitary; lonely ‖ *m* solitary, anchorite; old wild boar; solitaire

solitude [sɔlityd] *f* solitude

solive [sɔliv] *f* joist

soli·veau [sɔlivo] *m* (*pl* **-veaux**) small joist; (coll) nobody

sollicitaire [sɔllisite] *tr* to solicit; to apply for; to incite; to attract (*attention; iron*); to induce ‖ *intr* to seek favors

sollici·teur [sɔllisitœr] **-teuse** [tøz] *mf* solicitor; office seeker, petitioner, lobbyist

solo [sɔlo] *adj invar & m* solo

solstice [sɔlstis] *m* solstice

soluble [sɔlybl] *adj* soluble; solvable

solution [sɔlysjɔ̃] *f* solution

solutionner [sɔlysjɔne] *tr* to solve

solvabilité [sɔlvabilite] *f* solvency

solvable [sɔlvabl] *adj* solvent

solvant [sɔlvã] *m* solvent

sombre [sɔbr] *adj* somber; sullen

sombrer [sɔ̃bre] *intr* to sink; to vanish (*as a fortune*)

sommaire [sɔmer] *adj & m* summary

sommation [sɔmasjɔ̃] *f* summons; sentry challenge; **faire les trois sommations** to read the riot act

somme [sɔm] *m* nap ‖ *f* sum; **en somme, somme toute** in short, when all is said and done

sommeil [sɔmɛj] *m* sleep; **avoir sommeil** to be sleepy

sommeiller [sɔmeje] *intr* to doze; to lie dormant

sommelier [sɔməlje] *m* wine steward

sommer [sɔme] *tr* to add up; to summon, to issue a legal writ to

sommet [sɔme] *m* summit, top; apex (*of a triangle*); vertex (*of an angle*); (fig) acme

sommier [sɔmje] *m* bedspring; ledger; crossbeam; (archaic) pack animal; **sommier élastique** spring mattress

sommité [sɔmite] *f* pinnacle, crest; leader, authority

somnambule [sɔmnãbyl] *adj* sleepwalking ‖ *mf* sleepwalker

somnifère [sɔmnifer] *adj & m* soporific

somnolence [sɔmnɔlãs] *f* drowsiness; indolence, laziness

somno·lent [sɔmnɔlã] **-lente** [lãt] *adj* somnolent, drowsy; indolent

somnoler [sɔmnɔle] *intr* to doze

somptuaire [sɔ̃ptɥer] *adj* luxury (*tax*)

somp·tueux [sɔ̃ptɥø] **-tueuse** [tɥøz] *adj* sumptuous

son [sɔ̃] *adj poss* §88 ‖ *m* sound; bran

sonate [sɔnat] *f* sonata

sondage [sɔ̃daʒ] *m* sounding, probing; **sondage de l'opinion** public-opinion poll; **sondage d'exploration** wildcat (*well*)

sonde [sɔ̃d] *f* lead, probe; borer, drill

sonder [sɔ̃de] *tr* to sound, probe, bore, fathom; to explore, reconnoiter; to poll (*e.g., public opinion*); to sound out (*s.o.*)

son·deur [sɔ̃dœr] **-deuse** [døz] *mf* prober, sounder

songe [sɔ̃ʒ] *m* dream

songe-creux [sɔ̃ʒkrø] *m invar* visionary, pipe dreamer

songer [sɔ̃ʒe] §38 *tr* to dream up ‖ *intr* to dream; to think; to intend to; **songer à** to think of; to imagine, to dream of; **songez-y!** think it over!

songerie [sɔ̃ʒri] *f* reverie, daydreaming

son·geur [sɔ̃ʒœr] **-geuse** [ʒøz] *adj* dreamy, preoccupied ‖ *mf* daydreamer

sonique [sɔnik] *adj* sonic, of sound

sonnaille [sɔnaj] *f* cowbell, sheepbell

sonnailler [sɔnaje] *m* bellwether ‖ *intr* to ring often and without cause

son·nant [sɔnã] **son·nante** [sɔnãt] *adj* striking (*clock*); metal (*money*); at the stroke of, e.g., **à huit heures sonnantes** at the stroke of eight

son·né -née [sɔne] *adj* past, e.g., **deux heures sonnées** past two o'clock; over, e.g., **il a soixante ans sonnés** he is over sixty; (slang) cuckoo, nuts; (slang) stunned

sonner [sɔne] *tr* to ring; to ring for; to sound ‖ *intr* to ring; to strike; to sound

sonnerie [sɔnri] *f* chimes, chiming; set of bells, carillon; fanfare; ring (*of a telephone, doorbell, etc.*); alarm or striking mechanism (*of clock*)

sonnet [sɔne] *m* sonnet

sonnette [sɔnet] *f* doorbell; pile driver

sonneur [sɔnœr] *m* bellringer; trumpeter

sonore [sɔnɔr] *adj* sonorous; sound (*wave, track*); echoing (*hall, cathedral, etc.*); (phonet) voiced ‖ *f* voiced consonant

sonoriser [sɔnɔrize] *tr* to record sound effects on (*a film*); to equip (*an auditorium*) with loudspeakers

sonorité [sɔnɔrite] *f* sonority, resonance

sonotone [sɔnɔton] *m* hearing aid

sophistication [sɔfistikasjɔ̃] *f* adulteration

sophisti·qué -quée [sɔfistike] *adj* adulterated; artificial, counterfeit

sophistiquer [sɔfistike] *tr* to adulterate; to subtilize

Sophocle [sɔfɔkl] *m* Sophocles

sopraniste [sɔpranist] *m* male soprano

sopra·no [sɔprano] *mf* (*pl* **-ni** [ni] or **-nos**) soprano ‖ *m* soprano (*voice*)

sorbet [sɔrbɛ] *m* sherbet

sorbetière [sɔrbɛtjɛr] *f* ice-cream freezer

sorbon·nard [sɔrbɔnar] **sorbon·narde** [sɔrbɔnard] *mf* (coll) Sorbonne student; (coll) Sorbonne professor

sorcellerie [sɔrsɛlri] *f* sorcery

sor·cier [sɔrsje] **-cière** [sjɛr] *adj* sorcerer's; **cela n'est pas sorcier** there's no trick to that ‖ *m* sorcerer, wizard ‖ *f* sorceress, witch; **vieille sorcière** old hag

sordide [sɔrdid] *adj* sordid

sornette [sɔrnɛt] *f* nonsense

sort [sɔr] *m* fate, destiny; fortune, lot; spell, charm

sortable [sɔrtabl] *adj* suitable, acceptable; presentable

sor·tant [sɔrtɑ̃] **-tante** [tɑ̃t] *adj* retiring (*congressman*); winning (*number*) ‖ *mf* person leaving

sorte [sɔrt] *f* sort, kind; state, condition; way, manner; **de la sorte** this way, thus; **de sorte que** so that, with the result that; **en quelque sorte** in a certain way; **en sorte que** in such a way that

sortie [sɔrti] *f* exit, way out; outing, jaunt; quitting time; outburst, tirade; (mil) sortie; **sortie de bain** bathrobe; **sortie de bal** evening wrap; **sortie de secours** emergency exit; **sortie de voiture(s)** driveway

sortilège [sɔrtilɛʒ] *m* spell, charm

sortir [sɔrtir] §64 *tr* to take out, to bring out; to publish ‖ *intr* (aux: ÊTRE) to go out, to come out; to come forth; to stand out; **au sortir de** on coming out of; **sortir de** + *inf* (coll) to have just + *pp*

S.O.S. [ɛsoɛs] *m* (letterword) S.O.S.

sosie [sɔzi] *m* double

sot [so] **sotte** [sɔt] *adj* stupid, silly ‖ *mf* fool, simpleton

sottise [sɔtiz] *f* stupidity, silliness, foolishness

sou [su] *m* sou; (fig) penny, farthing; **sans le sou** penniless; **sou à sou** or **sou par sou** a penny at a time

soubassement [subasmɑ̃] *m* subfoundation, infrastructure

soubresaut [subraso] *m* sudden start, jerk; palpitation, jump (*of the heart*)

soubrette [subrɛt] *f* (theat) soubrette; (coll) attractive chambermaid

souche [suʃ] *f* stump; stock; stack (*of fireplace*); strain (*of virus*); (coll) dolt

souci [susi] *m* care; marigold; **sans souci** carefree

soucier [susje] *ref* to care, concern oneself

soucieusement [susjøzmɑ̃] *adv* uneasily, anxiously; with concern

sou·cieux [susjø] **-cieuse** [sjøz] *adj* solicitous, concerned; uneasy, anxious

soucoupe [sukup] *f* saucer; **soucoupe volante** flying saucer

soudage [sudaʒ] *m* soldering; welding

sou·dain [sudɛ̃] **-daine** [dɛn] *adj* sudden ‖ **soudain** *adv* suddenly

soudainement [sudɛnmɑ̃] *adv* suddenly

soudaineté [sudɛnte] *f* suddenness

souda·nais [sudanɛ] **-naise** [nez] *adj* Sudanic ‖ *m* Sudanic (*language*) ‖ (*cap*) *mf* Sudanese (*person*)

soude [sud] *f* (chem) soda

souder [sude] *tr* to solder; to weld ‖ *ref* to knit (*as bones do*)

soudeur [sudœr] *m* welder

soudoyer [sudwaje] §47 *tr* to bribe; to hire (*assassins*)

soudure [sudyr] *f* solder; soldering; soldered joint; knitting (*of bones*); **faire la soudure** to bridge the gap; **soudure autogène** welding

soue [su] *f* pigsty

soufflage [suflaʒ] *m* blowing; glass blowing

souffle [sufl] *m* breath; breathing

souf·flé -flée [sufle] *adj* puffed up ‖ *m* soufflé

souffler [sufle] *tr* to blow; to blow out (*a candle*); to blow up (*a balloon*); to prompt (*an actor*); to huff (*a checker*); to suggest (*an idea*); **ne pas souffler mot** to not breathe a word; **souffler à l'oreille** to whisper; **souffler q.ch. à qn** to take s.th. from s.o. ‖ *intr* to blow; to pant, puff; to take a breather, to catch one's breath

soufflerie [sufləri] *f* bellows; wind tunnel

soufflet [suflɛ] *m* slap in the face; affront, insult; bellows; gore (*of dress*); (rr) flexible cover (*between two cars*)

souffleter [suflɔte] §34 *tr* to slap in the face; to affront

souf·fleur [suflœr] **souf·fleuse** [sufløz] *mf* (théat) prompter ‖ *m* glass blower ‖ *f* (mach) blower

soufflure [suflyr] *f* blister, bubble

souffrance [sufrɑ̃s] *f* suffering; **en souffrance** unfinished (*business*); outstanding (*bill*); unclaimed (*parcel*); at a standstill, suspended

souf·frant [sufrɑ̃] **souf·frante** [sufrɑ̃t] *adj* suffering; sick, ailing

souffre-douleur [sufrədulœr] *m invar* butt (*of a joke*), laughingstock

souffre·teux [sufrətø] **-teuse** [tøz] *adj* sickly; destitute, half-starved

souffrir [sufrir] §65 *tr* to suffer; to stand, bear, tolerate; to permit ‖ *intr* to suffer ‖ *ref* to put up with each other

soufre [sufr] *m* sulfur

soufrer [sufre] *tr* to sulfurate

souhait [swɛ] *m* wish; **à souhait** to one's liking, to perfection; **à vos souhaits!** (salutation) gesundheit!; **souhaits** good wishes; **souhaits de bonne année** New Year's greetings

souhaitable [swɛtabl] *adj* desirable

souhaiter [swɛte] *tr* to wish; to wish for; to wish to; **je vous la souhaite bonne et heureuse** I wish you a happy New Year

souille [suj] *f* wallow

souiller [suje] *tr* to dirty, spot, stain, soil, sully

souillon [sujɔ̃] *f* (coll) scullery maid

souillure [sujyr] *f* spot, stain

soûl [su] **soûle** [sul] *adj* drunk; sottish ‖ *m* fill, e.g., **manger son soûl** to eat one's fill

soulagement [sulaʒmã] *m* relief; comfort

soulager [sulaʒe] §38 *tr* to relieve; to comfort

soûler [sule] *tr* (slang) to cram down one's throat; (slang) to get (*s.o.*) drunk ‖ *ref* (fig) to have one's fill; (slang) to get drunk

soulèvement [sulɛvmã] *m* upheaval; uprising; surge; **soulèvement de cœur** nausea

soulever [sulve] §2 *tr* to raise, heave, lift (up); to stir up ‖ *ref* to rise; to raise oneself; to revolt

soulier [sulje] *m* shoe

soulignement [suliɲəmã] *m* underlining

souligner [suliɲe] *tr* to underline; to emphasize

soulte [sult] *f* balance due

soumettre [sumetr] §42 *tr* to submit; to subject; to overcome, subdue ‖ *ref* to submit, surrender

sou·mis [sumi] **-mise** [miz] *adj* submissive, subservient; subject; amenable (*to a law*)

soumission [sumisjɔ̃] *f* submission, surrender; bid (*to perform a service*); guarantee

soumissionnaire [sumisjɔnɛr] *mf* bidder

soupape [supap] *f* valve; **soupape à réglage** or **à papillon** damper; **soupape de sûreté** safety valve; **soupape électrique** rectifier

soupçon [supsɔ̃] *m* suspicion; misgiving; dash, touch (*small amount*)

soupçonner [supsɔne] *tr* & *intr* to suspect

soupçon·neux [supsɔnø] **soupçon·neuse** [supsɔnøz] *adj* suspicious

soupe [sup] *f* vegetable soup; sop (*bread*); (mil) mess; **de soupe** on K.P.; **soupe au lait** (coll) meantempered person; **soupe populaire** soup kitchen; **trempé comme une soupe** soaking wet

soupente [supãt] *f* attic

souper [supe] *m* supper ‖ *intr* to have supper

soupeser [supəze] §2 *tr* to heft, to weigh (*e.g., a package*) in one's hand

soupière [supjɛr] *f* soup tureen

soupir [supir] *m* sigh; breath; (mus) quarter rest

soupi·rail [supiraj] *m* (*pl* **-raux** [ro]) cellar window

soupirant [supirã] *m* suitor

soupirer [supire] *intr* to sigh; **soupirer après** or **pour** to long for

souple [supl] *adj* supple; flexible, pliant; versatile, adaptable

souplesse [suples] *f* suppleness, flexibility

souquer [suke] *tr* to haul taut ‖ *intr* to pull hard (*on the oars*)

source [surs] *f* source; spring, fountain; **source de pétrole** oil well; **source jaillissante** gusher

sourcier [sursje] *m* dowser

sourcil [sursi] *m* eyebrow

sourciller [sursije] *intr* to knit one's brows; **sans sourciller** without batting an eye

sourcil·leux [sursijø] **sourcil·leuse** [sursijøz] *adj* supercilious

sourd [sur] **sourde** [surd] *adj* deaf; quiet; dull (*sound, color*); deep (*voice*); undeclared (*war*); (phonet) unvoiced; **sourd comme un pot** (coll) stone-deaf ‖ *mf* deaf person ‖ *f* unvoiced consonant

sourdement [surdəmã] *adv* secretly; heavily; dully

sourdine [surdin] *f* (mus) mute; **à la sourdine** muted; **en sourdine** on the sly

sourd-muet [surmɥɛ] **sourde-muette** [surdəmɥɛt] (*pl* **sourds-muets**) *adj* deaf and dumb, deaf-mute ‖ *mf* deaf-mute

sourdre [surdr] (used in: *inf*; 3d *sg* & *pl pres ind* **sourd, sourdent**) *intr* to spring, well up

souricier [surisje] *m* mouser

souricière [surisjer] *f* mousetrap; (fig) trap

sourire [surir] *m* smile ‖ §61 *intr* to smile; **sourire à** to smile at; to smile on; to look good to

souris [suri] *m* (obs) smile ‖ *f* mouse

sour·nois [surnwa] **-noise** [nwaz] *adj* sly, cunning, artful

sous [su] *prep* under; on (*a certain day; certain conditions*); **sous caoutchouc** rubber-covered; **sous clef** under lock and key; **sous la main** at hand; **sous les drapeaux** in the army; **sous main** underhandedly; **sous peu** shortly; **sous un certain angle** from a certain point of view

sous-alimentation [suzalimãtasjɔ̃] *f* undernourishment

sous-bois [subwa] *m* underbrush, undergrowth

sous-chef [suʃɛf] *m* (*pl* **-chefs**) assistant (*to the head man*), deputy, second-in-command

souscripteur [suskriptœr] *m* subscriber (*to a loan or charity*); signer (*of a commercial paper*)

souscription [suskripsjɔ̃] *f* signature; subscription; **souscription de soutien** sustaining membership

souscrire [suskrir] §25 *tr* & *intr* to subscribe

sous-cuta·né ·née [sukytane] *adj* subcutaneous

sous-dévelop·pé ·pée [sudevlɔpe] *adj* underdeveloped

sous-diacre [sudjakr] *m* subdeacon

sous-direc·teur [sudirektœr] **-trice** [tris] *mf* (*pl* **-directeurs**) second-in-command

sous-entendre [suzãtãdr] *tr* to understand (*what is not expressed*); to imply

sous-entendu [suzãtãdy] *m* inference, implication, innuendo, double meaning, double entendre

sous-entente [suzãtãt] *f* mental reservation; hidden, cryptic meaning

sous-entrepreneur [suzãtrəprənœr] *m* (*pl* **-entrepreneurs**) subcontractor

sous-estimer [suzɛstime] *tr* to underestimate

sous-fifre [sufifr] *m* (*pl* **-fifres**) (coll) underling

sous-garde [sugard] *f* trigger guard

sous-lieutenant [suljøtnã] *m* (*pl* **-lieutenants**) second lieutenant

sous-location [suləkasjɔ̃] *f* sublease

sous-louer [sulwe] *tr* to sublet, sublease

sous-main [sumɛ̃] *m invar* desk blotter; **en sous-main** underhandedly

sous-marin [sumarɛ̃] **-marine** [marin] *adj & m* (*pl* **-marins**) submarine

sous-marinier [sumarinje] *m* (*pl* **-mariniers**) submarine crewman

sous-mentonnière [sumɑ̃tɔnjər] *f* (*pl* **-mentonnières**) chin strap

sous-nappe [sunap] *f* (*pl* **-nappes**) table pad

sous-off [suzɔf] *m* (*pl* **-offs**) noncom

sous-officier [suzɔfisje] *m* (*pl* **-officiers**) noncommissioned officer

sous-ordre [suzɔrdr] *m* (*pl* **-ordres**) underling, subordinate; (biol) suborder; **en sous-ordre** subordinate; subordinately

sous-production [suprɔdyksjɔ̃] *f* underproduction

sous-produit [suprɔdɥi] *m* (*pl* **-produits**) by-product

sous-secrétaire [suskreter] *m* (*pl* **-secrétaires**) undersecretary

sous-secrétariat [suskretarja] *m* undersecretaryship

sous-seing [susɛ̃] *m invar* privately witnessed document

soussi·gné -gnée [susiɲe] *adj & mf* undersigned

sous-sol [susɔl] *m* (*pl* **-sols**) subsoil; basement

sous-titre [sutitr] *m* (*pl* **-titres**) subtitle

sous-titrer [sutitre] *tr* to subtitle

soustraction [sustraksjɔ̃] *f* subtraction; (law) purloining

soustraire [sustrer] §68 *tr* to remove; take away; to subtract; to deduct; **soustraire de** to subtract from; **soustraire q.ch. à qn** to take s.th. away from s.o.; to steal s.th. from s.o. || *ref* to withdraw; **se soustraire à** to escape from

sous-traitant [sutretã] *m* (*pl* **-traitants**) subcontractor; sublessee

sous-traité [sutrete] *m* (*pl* **-traités**) subcontract

sous-traiter [sutrete] *tr & intr* to subcontract

sous-ventrière [suvãtrijer] *f* (*pl* **-ventrières**) girth

sous-verre [suver] *m invar* passe-partout; coaster

sous-vêtement [suvetmã] *m* (*pl* **-vêtements**) undergarment

soutache [sutaʃ] *f* braid

soutacher [sutaʃe] *tr* to trim with braid

soutane [sutan] *f* soutane, cassock

soutanelle [sutanel] *f* frock coat; choir robe

soute [sut] *f* (naut) storeroom; **soute à charbon** coal bunker

soutenable [sutnabl] *adj* supportable, tenable

soutenance [sutnɑ̃s] *f* defense (*of an academic thesis*)

soutènement [sutenmã] *m* support

souteneur [sutnœr] *m* pimp

soutenir [sutnir] §72 *tr* to support, bear; to sustain; to insist, claim; to defend (*a thesis*) || *ref* to stand up; to keep afloat

soute·nu -nue [sutny] *adj* sustained; elevated (*style*); steady (*market*); true (*colors*)

souter·rain [suterɛ̃] **souter·raine** [suteren] *adj* subterranean, underground; underhanded || *m* tunnel, subway (*for pedestrians*)

soutien [sutjɛ̃] *m* support; stand-by

soutien-gorge [sutjɛ̃gɔrʒ] *m* (*pl* **soutiens-gorge**) brassiere

soutirage [sutiraʒ] *m* racking

soutirer [sutire] *tr* to rack (*wine*); **soutirer q.ch. à qn** to get s.th. out of s.o., to sponge on s.o. for s.th.

souvenir [suvnir] *m* memory, remembrance; souvenir || §72 *intr*—**faire souvenir qn de q.ch.** to remind s.o. of s.th. || *ref* to remember; **se souvenir de** to remember

souvent [suvã] *adv* often

souve·rain [suvrɛ̃] **-raine** [ren] *adj & mf* sovereign || *m* sovereign (*coin*)

souveraineté [suvrente] *f* sovereignty

soviet [sɔvjɛt] *m* soviet

soviétique [sɔvjetik] *adj* Soviet || (*cap*) *mf* Soviet Russian

soya [sɔja] *m* soybean

soyeux [swajø] **soyeuse** [swajøz] *adj* silky

S.P. *abbr* (**sapeurs-pompiers**) fire department

spa·cieux [spasjø] **-cieuse** [sjøz] *adj* spacious, roomy

spadassin [spadasɛ̃] *m* hatchet man, hired thug

spaghetti [spagetti] *m* spaghetti

sparadrap [sparadra] *m* adhesive tape

spartiate [sparsjat] *adj* Spartan || (*cap*) *mf* Spartan

spasme [spasm] *m* spasm

spasmodique [spasmɔdik] *adj* spasmodic; (pathol) spastic

spath [spat] *m* (mineral) spar

spa·tial -tiale [spasjal] *adj* (*pl* **-tiaux** [sjo]) spatial

spatule [spatyl] *f* spatula; (orn) spoonbill

spea·ker [spikœr] **-kerine** [krin] *mf* (rad, telv) announcer || *m* speaker (*presiding officer*)

spé·cial -ciale [spesjal] *adj* (*pl* **-ciaux** [sjo]) special

spécialiser [spesjalize] *tr & ref* to specialize

spécialiste [spesjalist] *mf* specialist; expert

spécialité [spesjalite] *f* specialty; specialization; patent medicine

spé·cieux [spesjø] **-cieuse** [sjøz] *adj* specious

spécifier [spesifje] *tr* to specify

spécifique [spesifik] *adj* & *m* specific

spécimen [spesimɛn] *adj* & *m* specimen

spectacle [spektakl] *m* spectacle, sight; show; play; **à grand spectacle** spectacular (*production*)

specta·teur [spektatœr] **-trice** [tris] *mf* spectator

spectre [spɛktr] *m* ghost; spectrum; (fig) specter

spécula·teur [spekylatœr] **-trice** [tris] *mf* speculator

spéculer [spekyle] *tr* to speculate

spéléologie [speleɔlɔʒi] *f* speleology

sperme [sperm] *m* sperm

sphère [sfer] *f* sphere

sphérique [sferik] *adj* spherical

sphinx [sfɛks] *m* sphinx

spider [spider] *m* (aut) rumble seat

spi·nal -nale [spinal] *adj* (*pl* **-naux** [no]) spinal

spi·ral -rale [spiral] (*pl* **-raux** [ro]) *adj* spiral || *m* hairspring (*of watch*) || *f* spiral; **en spirale** spiral

spire [spir] *f* turn (*in a wire*); whorl (*of a shell*)

spirée [spire] *f* (bot) spirea

spirite [spirit] *adj* & *mf* spiritualist

spiri·tuel -tuelle [spirituɛl] *adj* spiritual; sacred (*music*); witty || *m* ecclesiastical power

spiri·tueux [spirituø] **-tueuse** [tyøz] *adj* spirituous || *m* spirituous liquor

spleen [splin] *m* boredom, melancholy

splendeur [splɑ̃dœr] *f* splendor

splendide [splɑ̃did] *adj* splendid; bright, brilliant

spolia·teur [spɔljatœr] **-trice** [tris] *adj* despoiling || *mf* despoiler

spolier [spɔlje] *tr* to despoil

spon·gieux [spɔ̃ʒjø] **-gieuse** [ʒjøz] *adj* spongy

sponta·né -née [spɔ̃tane] *adj* spontaneous

sporadique [spɔradik] *adj* sporadic(al)

sport [spɔr] *adj invar* sport, sporting; sportsmanlike || *m* sport

spor·tif [spɔrtif] **-tive** [tiv] *adj* sport, sporting || *mf* athlete, player || *m* sportsman

spot [spɔt] *m* spotlight; (radar) blip

spoutnik [sputnik] *m* sputnik

spu·meux [spymø] **-meuse** [møz] *adj* frothy, foamy

squale [skwal] *m* (ichth) dogfish

squelette [skəlɛt] *m* skeleton

squelettique [skeletik] *adj* skeletal

S.R. *abbr* (**Service de renseignements**) information desk or bureau

stabiliser [stabilize] *tr* to stabilize

stabilité [stabilite] *f* stability

stable [stabl] *adj* stable

stade [stad] *m* stadium; (fig) stage (*of development*)

stage [staʒ] *m* probationary period, apprenticeship

stagiaire [staʒjer] *adj* & *mf* apprentice

stag·nant [stagnɑ̃] **-nante** [nɑ̃t] *adj* stagnant

stalle [stal] *f* stall

stance [stɑ̃s] *f* stanza

stand [stɑ̃d] *m* stands; shooting gallery; pit (*for motor racing*)

standard [stɑ̃dar] *adj invar* standard || *m* standard; switchboard

standardiser [stɑ̃dardize] *tr* to standardize

standardiste [stɑ̃dardist] *mf* switchboard operator, telephone operator

standing [stɑ̃diŋ] *m* status, standing; standard of living; **de grand standing** luxury (*apartments*)

star [star] *f* (mov, theat) star

starter [starter], [startœr] *m* (aut) choke; (sports) starter

station [stasjɔ̃] *f* station; resort; (rr) flag station; **station d'écoute** monitoring station; **station d'émission** broadcasting station; **station de repérage** tracking station; **station de taxis** taxi stand; **station orbitale** space station

stationnaire [stasjɔner] *adj* stationary || *m* gunboat

stationnement [stasjɔnmɑ̃] *m* parking; **stationnement interdit** (public sign) no parking

stationner [stasjɔne] *intr* to stop; to park

station-service [stasjɔ̃servis] *f* (*pl* **stations-service**) service station

statique [statik] *adj* static

statisti·cien [statistisjɛ̃] **-cienne** [sjen] *mf* statistician

statistique [statistik] *adj* statistical || *f* statistics

statuaire [statyer] *adj* statuary || *mf* sculptor || *f* statuary

statue [staty] *f* statue

statuer [statye] *tr* to hand down (*a ruling*) || *intr* to hand down a ruling

statu quo [statykwo], [statuko] *m* status quo

stature [statyr] *f* stature

statut [staty] *m* statute; legal status

statutaire [statyter] *adj* statutory

Ste *abbr* (**Sainte**) St. (*female saint*)

Sté *abbr* (**Société**) Inc.

sténo [steno] *f* stenographer; stenography

sténodactylo [stenɔdaktilo] *f* shorthand typist; shorthand typing

sténogramme [stenɔgram] *m* shorthand notes

sténographe [stenɔgraf] *mf* stenographer

sténographie [stenɔgrafi] *f* stenography

sténographier [stenɔgrafje] *tr* to take down in shorthand

stéréo [stereo] *adj invar* stereo || *f*—**en stéréo** (electron) in stereo

stéréophonie [stereɔfɔni] *f* stereophonic sound system; **en stéréophonie** stereophonic (*e.g., broadcast*)

stéréoscopique [stereɔskɔpik] *adj* stereo, stereoscopic

stéréoty·pé -pée [stereɔtipe] *adj* stereotyped

stérile [steril] *adj* sterile

stériliser [sterilize] *tr* to sterilize

stérilité [sterilite] *f* sterility

sterling [sterliŋ] *adj invar* sterling

stéthoscope [stetɔskɔp] *m* stethoscope

stick [stik] *m* walking stick

stigmate [stigmat] *m* stigma

stigmatiser [stigmatize] *tr* to stigmatize

stimu·lant [stimylɑ̃] -lante [lɑ̃t] *adj* &
  m stimulant
stimuler [stimyle] *tr* to stimulate
stimu·lus [stimylys] *m* (*pl* -li [li])
  (physiol) stimulus
stipendier [stipɑ̃dje] *tr* to hire (*e.g., an
  assassin*); to bribe
stipuler [stipyle] *tr* to stipulate
stock [stɔk] *m* goods, stock; hoard
stocker [stɔke] *tr* & *intr* to stockpile
stockiste [stɔkist] *m* authorized dealer
  (*carrying parts, motors, etc.*)
stoi·cien [stɔisjɛ̃] -cienne [sjɛn] *adj* &
  mf Stoic
stoïque [stɔik] *adj* stoical ‖ *mf* stoic
stop [stɔp] *m* stop; stoplight; **du stop**
  (coll) hitchhiking ‖ *interj* stop!
stoppage [stɔpaʒ] *m* reweaving, invisible mending
stopper [stɔpe] *tr* to reweave; to stop ‖
  intr to stop
store [stɔr] *m* blind; window awning;
  outside window shade
strabique [strabik] *adj* squint-eyed
strabisme [strabism] *m* squint
strapontin [strapɔ̃tɛ̃] *m* jump seat;
  (theat) attached folding seat
strass [stras] *m* paste (*jewelry*)
stratagème [strataʒɛm] *m* stratagem
strate [strat] *f* (geol) stratum
stratège [strateʒ] *m* strategist
stratégie [strateʒi] *f* strategy
stratégique [strateʒik] *adj* strategic(al)
stratégiste [strateʒist] *m* strategist
stratifier [stratifje] *tr* & *ref* to stratify
stratosphère [stratɔsfɛr] *f* stratosphere
strict stricte [strikt] *adj* strict
stri·dent [stridɑ̃] -dente [dɑ̃t] *adj* strident
strie [stri] *f* streak; stripe
strier [strije] *tr* to streak; to score,
  groove
strontium [strɔ̃sjɔm] *m* strontium
strophe [strɔf] *f* verse, stanza; strophe
structu·ral -rale [stryktyral] *adj* (*pl*
  -raux [ro]) structural
structure [stryktyr] *f* structure
strychnine [striknin] *f* strychnine
stuc [styk] *m* stucco; **enduire de stuc**
  to stucco
stu·dieux [stydjø] -dieuse [djøz] *adj*
  studious
studio [stydjo] *m* studio
stupé·fait [stypefɛ] -faite [fɛt] *adj*
  dumfounded, amazed
stupé·fiant [stypefjɑ̃] -fiante [fjɑ̃t] *adj*
  astounding ‖ *m* drug, narcotic
stupéfier [stypefje] *tr* to astound; to
  stupefy (*as with a drug*)
stupeur [stypœr] *f* stupor; amazement
stupide [stypid] *adj* stupid
stupidité [stypidite] *f* stupidity
stuquer [styke] *tr* to stucco
style [stil] *m* style; stylus
styler [stile] *tr* to train
stylet [stile] *m* stiletto
styliser [stilize] *tr* to stylize
stylo [stilo] *m* pen, fountain pen; **stylo
  à bille** ball-point pen
styptique [stiptik] *adj* & *m* styptic
suaire [sɥɛr] *m* shroud, winding sheet

suave [sɥav] *adj* sweet (*perfume, music, etc.*); bland (*food*); suave
subcons·cient [sypkɔsjɑ̃] subcons·ciente
  [sypkɔsjɑ̃t] *adj* & *m* subconscious
subdiviser [sybdivize] *tr* to subdivide
subir [sybir] *tr* to submit to; to undergo; to feel, experience; to take (*an
  exam*); to serve (*a sentence*)
su·bit [sybi] -bite [bit] *adj* sudden
subjec·tif [sybʒɛktif] -tive [tiv] *adj*
  subjective
subjonc·tif [sybʒɔ̃ktif] -tive [tiv] *adj*
  & *m* subjunctive
subjuguer [sybʒyge] *tr* to dominate; to
  spellbind
sublime [syblim] *adj* sublime
sublimer [syblime] *tr* to sublimate
submerger [sybmɛrʒe] §38 *tr* to submerge
submersible [sybmɛrsibl] *adj* & *m* submersible
submersion [sybmɛrsjɔ̃] *f* submersion
subodorer [sybɔdɔre] *tr* to scent
  (*game*); (fig) to scent (*a plot*)
subordon·né -née [sybɔrdɔne] *adj* & *mf*
  subordinate
subordonner [sybɔrdɔne] *tr* to subordinate
suborner [sybɔrne] *tr* to bribe
subrécargue [sybrekarg] *m* supercargo
subreptice [sybreptis] *adj* surreptitious
subsé·quent [sypsekɑ̃] -quente [kɑ̃t]
  adj subsequent
subside [sypsid], [sybzid] *m* subsidy
subsidiaire [sypsidjɛr] *adj* subsidiary
subsistance [sybzistɑ̃s], [sypsistɑ̃s] *f*
  subsistence; (mil) rations
subsister [sybziste], [sypsiste] *intr* to
  subsist
substance [sypstɑ̃s] *f* substance; **en
  substance** briefly
substan·tiel -tielle [sypstɑ̃sjɛl] *adj* substantial
substan·tif [sypstɑ̃tif] -tive [tiv] *adj* &
  m substantive
substituer [sypstitɥe] *tr*—**substituer qn
  or q.ch. à** to substitute s.o. or s.th.
  for, e.g., **une biche fut substituée à
  Iphigénie** a hind was substituted for
  Iphigenia ‖ *ref*—**se substituer à** to
  take the place of
substitut [sypstity] *m* substitute
substitution [sypstitysjɔ̃] *f* substitution
substrat [sypstra] *m* substratum
subterfuge [sypterfyʒ] *m* subterfuge
sub·til -tile [syptil] *adj* subtle; fine
  (*powder, dust, etc.*); quick (*poison*);
  delicate (*scent*); clever (*crook*)
subtiliser [syptilize] *tr* to pick (*a purse*)
  ‖ *intr* to split hairs
subtilité [syptilite] *f* subtlety
subur·bain [sybyrbɛ̃] -baine [bɛn] *adj*
  suburban
subvenir [sybvənir] §72 *intr* (with *dat*)
  to supply, provide, satisfy
subvention [sybvɑ̃sjɔ̃] *f* subsidy, subvention
subventionner [sybvɑ̃sjɔne] *tr* to subsidize
subver·sif [sybvɛrsif] -sive [siv] *adj*
  subversive
subvertir [sybvertir] *tr* to subvert

suc [syk] *m* juice; sap; (fig) essence

succéda·né -née [syksedane] *adj & m* substitute

succéder [syksede] §10 *intr* to happen; (with *dat*) to succeed, follow; **succéder à** to succeed to (*the throne, a fortune*) || *ref* to follow one after the other, to follow one another

succès [sykse] *m* success; outcome; **avoir du succès** to be a success

succes·sif [syksesif] **succes·sive** [syksesiv] *adj* successive

succession [syksesjɔ̃] *f* succession; inheritance; heirs

suc·cinct [syksɛ̃] **-cincte** [sɛ̃t] *adj* succinct; scanty; meager

succion [syksjɔ̃] *f* suction

succomber [sykɔ̃be] *intr* to succumb

succursale [sykyrsal] *f* branch

sucer [syse] §51 *tr* to suck

sucette [syset] *f* pacifier; lollipop, sucker

su·ceur [sysœr] **-ceuse** [søz] *adj* sucking || *m* nozzle

suçoter [sysɔte] *tr* to suck away at

sucre [sykr] *m* sugar; **sucre brut** brown sugar; **sucre candi** rock candy; **sucre de canne** cane sugar; **sucre glace** confectioners' sugar

su·cré -crée [sykre] *adj* sugary; with sugar, e.g., **du café sucré** coffee with sugar || *f*—**faire la sucrée** to be mealy-mouthed

sucrer [sykre] *tr* to sugar; (slang) to take away, to cut out || *ref* (slang) to grab the lion's share

sucrerie [sykrəri] *f* sugar refinery; **sucreries** candy

su·crier [sykrije] **-crière** [krijer] *adj* sugar || *m* sugar bowl

sud [syd] *adj invar & m* south

sud-améri·cain [sydamerikɛ̃] **-caine** [ken] *adj* South American || (*cap*) *mf* (*pl* **Sud-Américains**) South American

sudation [sydasjɔ̃] *f* sweating

sud-est [sydest] *adj invar & m* southeast

sudiste [sydist] *mf* Southerner (*in U.S.A.*)

sud-ouest [sydwest] *adj invar & m* southwest

sud-vietna·mien [sydvjetnamjɛ̃] **-mienne** [mjen] *adj* South Vietnamese || (*cap*) *mf* (*pl* **Sud-Vietnamiens**) South Vietnamese

suède [sɥed] *m* suede || (*cap*) *f* Sweden; **la Suède** Sweden

sué·dois [sɥedwa] **-doise** [dwaz] *adj* Swedish || *m* Swedish (*language*) || (*cap*) *mf* Swede

suée [sɥe] *f* sweating

suer [sɥe] *tr & intr* to sweat

sueur [sɥœr] *f* sweat

suffire [syfir] §66 *intr* to suffice; (with *dat*) to suffice; **il suffit de** + *inf* it suffices to + *inf*; **suffire à** + *inf* to suffice to + *inf*; **suffit!** enough! || *ref* to be sulf-sufficient

suffisance [syfizɑ̃s] *f* sufficiency; self-sufficiency, smugness

suffi·sant [syfizɑ̃] **-sante** [zɑ̃t] *adj* sufficient; smug, sophomoric; impudent || *mf* prig

suffixe [syfiks] *m* suffix

suffoquer [syfɔke] *tr & intr* to suffocate, choke, stifle, smother

suffrage [syfraʒ] *m* suffrage, vote; public approval; **au suffrage universel** by popular vote; **suffrage capacitaire** suffrage contingent upon literacy tests; **suffrage censitaire** suffrage upon payment of taxes

suggérer [sygʒere] §10 *tr* to suggest

sugges·tif [sygʒestif] **-tive** [tiv] *adj* suggestive

suggestion [sygʒestjɔ̃] *f* suggestion

suggestionner [sygʒestjɔne] *tr* to influence by means of suggestion

suicide [sɥisid] *adj* suicidal || *m* suicide (*act*)

suici·dé -dée [sɥiside] *adj* dead by suicide || *mf* suicide (*person*)

suicider [sɥiside] *ref* to commit suicide

suie [sɥi] *f* soot

suif [sɥif] *m* tallow

suint [sɥɛ̃] *m* wool fat, wool grease

suinter [sɥɛ̃te] *intr* to seep, to ooze; to sweat (*said of wall*); to run (*said of wound*)

suisse [sɥis] *adj* Swiss; **faire suisse** to eat or drink by oneself; to go Dutch || *m* Swiss guard; uniformed usher; **petit suisse** cream cheese || (*cap*) *f* Switzerland; **la Suisse** Switzerland || **Suisse Suissesse** [sɥises] *mf* Swiss (*person*)

suite [sɥit] *f* suite; consequence; continuation, sequel (*of literary work*); sequence, series; **à la suite de** after; **de suite** in succession; in a row; **par la suite** later on; **par suite** consequently; **par suite de** because of

sui·vant [sɥivɑ̃] **-vante** [vɑ̃t] *adj* next, following, subsequent || *mf* follower; next (person) || *f* servant, confidante || **suivant** *adv*—**suivant que** according as || **suivant** *prep* according to

sui·veur [sɥivœr] **-veuse** [vøz] *adj* follow-up (*e.g., car*) || *mf* follower

sui·vi -vie [sɥivi] *adj* connected, coherent; popular

suivre [sɥivr] §67 *tr* to follow; to take (*a course in school*); **suivre la mode** (fig) to follow suit || *intr* to follow; **à suivre** to be continued || *ref* to follow in succession; to follow one after the other

su·jet [syʒe] **-jette** [ʒet] *adj* subject; apt, liable; inclined || *mf* subject (*of a government*); **mauvais sujet** ne'er-do-well || *m* subject, topic; (gram) subject; **au sujet de** about, concerning

sujétion [syʒesjɔ̃] *f* subjection

sulfamide [sylfamid] *m* sulfa drug

sulfure [sylfyr] *m* sulfide

sulfurique [sylfyrik] *adj* sulfuric

sultan [syltɑ̃] *m* sultan

sumac [symak] *m* sumac; **sumac vénéneux** poison ivy

super [syper] *m* (coll) high-test gas

superbe [syperb] *adj* superb; proud ‖ *m* proud person ‖ *f* pride

supercarburant [syperkarbyrã] *m* high-test gasoline

supercherie [syperʃəri] *f* hoax, swindle

superfétatoire [syperfetatwar] *adj* redundant

superficie [syperfisi] *f* surface, area

superfi·ciel -cielle [syperfisjel] *adj* superficial

super·flu -flue [syperfly] *adj* superfluous ‖ *m* superfluity, excess

supé·rieur -rieure [syperjœr] *adj* superior; higher; upper (*e.g., story*); supérieur à above; more than ‖ *mf* superior

supérieurement [syperjœrmã] *adv* superlatively, exceptionally

supériorité [syperjorite] *f* superiority

superla·tif [syperlatif] **-tive** [tiv] *adj* & *m* superlative; au superlatif superlatively; in the superlative

supermarché [sypermarʃe] *m* supermarket

superposer [syperpoze] *tr* to superimpose ‖ *ref* to intervene

supersonique [sypersonik] *adj* supersonic

supersti·tieux [syperstisjø] **-tieuse** [sjøz] *adj* superstitious

superstition [syperstisjɔ̃] *f* superstition

superstrat [syperstra] *m* superstratum

superviser [sypervize] *tr* to inspect; to revise; to correct; to supervise

supplanter [syplãte] *tr* to supplant

suppléance [sypleãs] *f* substituting; temporary post

suppléant [sypleã] **suppléante** [sypleãt] *adj* substituting ‖ *mf* substitute (*e.g., a teacher, judge*)

suppléer [syplee] *tr* to supply; to take the place of; to make up for (*what is lacking*); to fill in (*the gaps*); to substitute for (*s.o.*); to fill (*a vacancy*) ‖ *intr*—suppléer à to make up for (*s.th.*)

supplément [syplemã] *m* supplement

supplé·tif [sypletif] **-tive** [tiv] *adj* & *m* (mil) auxiliary

suppliant [syplijã] **suppliante** [syplijãt] *adj* & *mf* suppliant, supplicant

supplice [syplis] *m* torture; punishment; être au supplice to be in agony

supplicier [syplisje] *tr* to torture to death; to torment

supplier [syplije] *tr* to beseech, implore, supplicate; je vous en supplie I beg you; supplier qn de to implore s.o. to

supplique [syplik] *f* petition

support [sypor] *m* support, prop, pillar, bracket, strut; standard (*e.g., for a lamp*)

support-chaussette [syporʃoset] *m* (*pl* supports-chaussette) garter (*for men*)

supporter [syportœr], [syporter] *m* fan, devotee, supporter, partisan ‖ [syporte] *tr* to support, to prop up; to bear; to endure; to stand; to tolerate, to put up with ‖ *intr*—supporter de + *inf* to tolerate or stand for + *ger* ‖ *ref* to be tolerated; to put up with each other

suppo·sé -sée [sypoze] *adj* supposed, admitted; spurious, assumed ‖ supposé *prep* supposing, admitting, granting

supposer [sypoze] *tr* to suppose; to imply; à supposer que . . . suppose that . . . ; supposer un testament to palm off a forged will

supposition [sypozisjɔ̃] *f* supposition; forgery, fraudulent substitution or alteration; supposition de part or supposition d'enfant false claim of maternity and maternal rights

suppositoire [sypozitwar] *m* suppository

suppôt [sypo] *m* henchman, tool, agitator, hireling; suppôt de Bacchus drunkard; suppôt du diable imp

suppression [sypresjɔ̃] *f* suppression; elimination (*of a job*); discontinuance (*of a festival*); killing (*of a person*); suppression de part or suppression d'enfant concealment of a child's birth or death

supprimer [syprime] *tr* to suppress, to cancel, to abolish; to cut out, to omit; (slang) to eliminate, liquidate ‖ *ref* to kill oneself

suppurer [sypyre] *intr* to suppurate

supputation [sypytasjɔ̃] *f* calculation, evaluation, reckoning

supputer [sypyte] *tr* to calculate (*e.g., forthcoming profits, expenses*)

suprême [syprem] *adj* supreme; last

sur sure [syr] *adj* sour ‖ **sur** *prep* on, over; about; concerning; with (*on the person or*); out of, in, e.g., un jour sur quatre one day out of four, one day in four; after, e.g., page sur page page after page; sur ce, sur quoi whereupon; sur le fait in the act

sûr sûre [syr] *adj* sure; trustworthy; safe; certain; à coup sûr, pour sûr for sure, without fail

surabon·dant [syrabɔ̃dã] **-dante** [dãt] *adj* superabundant

surabonder [syrabɔ̃de] *intr* to superabound; surabonder de or en to be glutted with

surajouter [syraʒute] *tr* to add on

suralimentation [syralimãtasjɔ̃] *f* forced feeding; (aut) supercharging

suran·né -née [syrane] *adj* outmoded, out-of-date, superannuated; expired (*driver's license, passport, etc.*)

surboum [syrbum] *f* (slang) dance, hop

surcharge [syrʃarʒ] *f* surcharge; overwriting; (sports) handicap (*of weight on a horse*)

surcharger [syrʃarʒe] §38 *tr* to surcharge; to write a word over (*another word*); to write a word over a crossed-out word on (*a document*)

surchauffe [syrʃof] *f* superheating; overheating (*of the economy*)

surchauffer [syrʃofe] *tr* to superheat (*steam; an oven*); to overheat (*an oven, iron, etc.*)

surchoix [syrʃwa] *m* finest quality

surclasser [syrklɑse] *tr* to outclass
surcompo·sé -sée [syrkɔ̃poze] *adj* (gram) double-compound
surcompression [syrkɔ̃presjɔ̃] *f* pressurization, high compression
surcompri·mé -mée [syrkɔ̃prime] *adj* high-compression (*engine*)
surcomprimer [syrkɔ̃prime] *tr* to supercharge; to pressurize
surcontrer [syrkɔ̃tre] *tr* (cards) to redouble
surcouper [syrkupe] *tr* (cards) to overtrump
surcroît [syrkrwɑ], [syrkrwa] *m* addition, increase; **de surcroît** or **par surcroît** in addition, extra
surdi-mutité [syrdimɥtite] *f* deaf-muteness
surdité [syrdite] *f* deafness
su·reau [syro] *m* (*pl* **-reaux**) elderberry
surélévation [syrelevasjɔ̃] *f* escalation, excessive increase; extra story (*added to a building*)
surélever [syrelve] §2 *tr* to raise, raise up; to drive up; to jack up
surenchère [syrɑ̃ʃer] *f* higher bid; **surenchère électorale** campaign promise, political outbidding
surenchérir [syrɑ̃ʃerir] *intr* to make a higher bid; **surenchérir sur qn** to outbid s.o.
surestimer [syrestime] *tr* to overestimate
su·ret -rette [ret] *adj* tart
sûreté [syrte] *f* safety, security; sureness (*of touch; of taste*); surety; **en sûreté** out of harm's way; in custody, confined (*e.g., in prison*); **sûreté individuelle** legal protection (*e.g., against arbitrary arrest*); **Sûreté nationale** or **la Sûreté** central intelligence; **sûretés** precautions; guarantees, security (*for a loan*)
surévaluer [syrevalɥe] *tr* to overvalue
surexciter [syreksite] *tr* to overexcite
surexposer [syrekspoze] *tr* (phot) to overexpose
surexposition [syrekspozisjɔ̃] *f* (phot) overexposure
surface [syrfas] *f* surface; financial backing; **faire surface** to surface (*said of a submarine*)
surfaire [syrfer] §29 *tr & intr* to overprice; to overrate
sur·fin -fine [syrfɛ̃] **-fine** [fin] *adj* superfine
surge·lé -lée [syrʒəle] *adj* frozen (*foods*)
surgeon [syrʒɔ̃] *m* offshoot, sucker
surgir [syrʒir] *intr* to spring up; arise, appear; to arrive, reach port
surglacer [syrglase] §51 *tr* to glaze; to ice (*cake*)
surhaussement [syrosmɑ̃] *m* heightening, raising; banking (*of road*)
surhausser [syrose] *tr* to heighten, to raise; to force up (*prices*); to force up the price of (*s.th.*); to bank (*a road*)
surhomme [syrɔm] *m* superman
surhu·main [syrymɛ̃] **-maine** [men] *adj* superhuman

surimpression [syrɛ̃presjɔ̃] *f* superimposition; (mov) montage
surintendant [syrɛ̃tɑ̃dɑ̃] *m* superintendent, administrator
surir [syrir] *intr* to turn sour
sur-le-champ [syrlɑ̃] *adv* on the spot, immediately
surlendemain [syrlɑ̃dmɛ̃] *m*—**le surlendemain** the second day after, two days later
surlier [syrlje] *tr* to whip (*a rope*)
surmenage [syrmənaʒ] *m* overworking, fatigue
surmener [syrməne] §2 *tr & ref* to overwork
sur-moi [syrmwa] *m* superego
surmonter [syrmɔ̃te] *tr* to surmount ‖ *intr* to come to the top (*said of oil in water*)
surmouler [syrmule] *tr* to cast from another mold
surmultiplication [syrmyltiplikɑsjɔ̃] *f* (aut) overdrive
surnager [syrnaʒe] §38 *intr* to float; to survive
surnatu·rel -relle [syrnatyrel] *adj & m* supernatural
surnom [syrnɔ̃] *m* nickname, sobriquet
surnombre [syrnɔ̃br] *m* excess number; **en surnombre** supernumerary; spare; **rester en surnombre** to be odd man; **surnombre des habitants** overpopulation
surnommer [syrnɔme] *tr* to name, call, nickname
surnuméraire [syrnymerer] *adj* supernumerary, extra ‖ *mf* substitute, supernumerary
suroffre [syrɔfr] *f* better or higher offer
suroît [syrwa] *m* southwest wind
surpasser [syrpɑse] *tr* to surpass; to astonish ‖ *ref* to outdo oneself
surpaye [syrpej] *f* extra pay
surpayer [syrpeje] §49 *tr* to pay too much to; to pay too much for
surpeu·plé -plée [syrpœple] *adj* overpopulated
surpeuplement [syrpœpləmɑ̃] *m* overpopulation
surplis [syrpli] *m* surplice
surplomber [syrplɔ̃be] *tr & intr* to overhang
surplus [syrply] *m* surplus; **au surplus** moreover
surpopulation [syrpɔpylɑsjɔ̃] *f* overpopulation
surprendre [syrprɑ̃dr] §56 *tr* to surprise; to come upon by chance; to detect; to overtake, catch
surprise [syrpriz] *f* surprise
surprise-party or **surprise-partie** [syrprizparti] *f* (*pl* **surprises-parties**) private dancing party
surproduction [syrprɔdyksjɔ̃] *f* overproduction
surréalisme [syrealism] *m* surrealism
sursaut [syrso] *m* sudden start; **en sursaut** with a start
sursauter [syrsote] *intr* to give a jump, to start, to jerk

surseoir [syrswar] §5B *(fut* **surseoirai,** etc.) *tr* to postpone, defer, put off ‖ *intr*—**surseoir** (with *dat*) to stay *(an investigation; an execution)*

sursis [syrsi] *m* suspension *(of penalty);* postponement, deferment, stay; **en sursis, avec sursis** suspended *(sentence)*

surtaxe [syrtaks] *f* surtax, surcharge; **surtaxe postale** postage due

surtaxer [syrtakse] *tr* to surtax

surtension [syrtɑ̃sjɔ̃] *f* (elec) surge

surtout [syrtu] *m* topcoat; centerpiece, epergne ‖ *adv* especially, particularly

surveillance [syrvejɑ̃s] *f* supervision; *(by the police)* surveillance

surveil·lant [syrvejɑ̃] **surveil·lante** [syrvejɑ̃t] *mf* supervisor, superintendent, overseer; **surveillant d'études** study-hall proctor

surveiller [syrveje] *tr* to inspect, to put under surveillance; to supervise, watch over, monitor

survenir [syrvənir] §72 *intr (aux:* ÊTRE) to arrive unexpectedly, to happen suddenly, to crop up

survenue [syrvəny] *f* unexpected arrival

survêtement [syrvetmɑ̃] *m* track suit, sweat shirt

survie [syrvi] *f* survival; afterlife; (law) survivorship

survivance [syrvivɑ̃s] *f* survival

survi·vant [syrvivɑ̃] **-vante** [vɑ̃t] *adj* surviving ‖ *mf* survivor

survivre [syrvivr] §74 *intr* to survive; (with *dat*) to survive, outlive

survoler [syrvole] *tr* to fly over; to skim over *(e.g., a problem)*

survol·té -tée [syrvolte] *adj* electrified, charged with emotion

sus [sys], [sy] *adv*—**en sus de** in addition to ‖ *interj* up and at it (them)!

susceptible [syseptibl] *adj* susceptible; **susceptible de** capable of

susciter [sysite] *tr* to stir up, evoke, rouse; (lit) to raise up

sus·dit [sysdi] **-dite** [dit] *adj* aforesaid

susmention·né -née [sysmɑ̃sjone] *adj* aforementioned

sus·pect [syspe], [syspekt] **-pecte** [pekt] *adj* suspect, suspicious ‖ *mf* suspect

suspecter [syspekte] *tr* to suspect

suspendre [syspɑ̃dr] *tr* to suspend; to hang, to hang up; **être suspendu aux lèvres de qn** to hang on s.o.'s every word ‖ *ref* to be hung; to hang on

suspen·du -due [syspɑ̃dy] *adj* suspended; hanging

suspens [syspɑ̃] *m* suspense; **en suspens** suspended; in abeyance; outstanding

suspension [syspɑ̃sjɔ̃] *f* suspension

suspi·cieux [syspisjø] **-cieuse** [sjøz] *adj* suspicious

suspicion [syspisjɔ̃] *f* suspicion

sustenter [systɑ̃te] *tr* to sustain ‖ *ref* to sustain oneself

susurrer [sysyre] *tr & intr* to murmur, to whisper

susvi·sé -sée [sysvize] *adj* above-mentioned

suture [sytyr] *f* suture

suturer [sytyre] *tr* to suture

suze·rain [syzrɛ̃] **-raine** [rɛn] *adj & mf* suzerain

svastika [svastika] *m* swastika

svelte [svelt] *adj* slender, lithe, willowy

S.V.P. [ɛsvepe] *m* (letterword) **(s'il vous plaît)** if you please, please

sweater [switœr] *m* sweater

sycophante [sikofɑ̃t] *m* informer

syllabe [silab] *f* syllable

syllogisme [silɔʒism] *m* syllogism

sylphe [silf] *m* sylph

sylvestre [silvɛstr] *adj* sylvan

symbole [sɛ̃bɔl] *m* symbol; **Symbole des apôtres** Apostles' Creed

symbolique [sɛ̃bɔlik] *adj* symbolic(al)

symboliser [sɛ̃bɔlize] *tr* to symbolize

symbolisme [sɛ̃bɔlism] *m* symbolism

symétrie [simetri] *f* symmetry

symétrique [simetrik] *adj* symmetric(al)

sympathie [sɛ̃pati] *f* fondness, liking; sympathy

sympathique [sɛ̃patik] *adj* likable, attractive; sympathetic

sympathi·sant [sɛ̃patizɑ̃] **-sante** [zɑ̃t] *adj* sympathetic ‖ *mf* sympathizer

sympathiser [sɛ̃patize] *intr* to get along well; **sympathiser avec** to be drawn toward

symphonie [sɛ̃fɔni] *f* symphony

symptôme [sɛ̃ptom] *m* symptom

synagogue [sinagɔg] *f* synagogue

synchrone [sɛ̃krɔn] *adj* synchronous

synchroniser [sɛ̃krɔnize] *tr* to synchronize

syncope [sɛ̃kɔp] *f* faint, swoon, syncope; syncopation

syndicat [sɛ̃dika] *m* labor union; **syndicat d'initiative** chamber of commerce; **syndicat patronal** employers' association

syndicats-patrons [sɛ̃dikapatrɔ̃] *adj invar* labor-management

syndiquer [sɛ̃dike] *tr & ref* to syndicate

synonyme [sinɔnim] *adj* synonymous ‖ *m* synonym

synopsis [sinɔpsis] *m & f* (mov) synopsis

syntaxe [sɛ̃taks] *f* syntax

synthèse [sɛ̃tez] *f* synthesis

synthétique [sɛ̃tetik] *adj* synthetic

synthétiser [sɛ̃tetize] *tr* to synthesize

syntonisation [sɛ̃tɔnizasjɔ̃] *f* tuning *(of radio)*

syntoniser [sɛ̃tɔnize] *tr* to tune in

syphilis [sifilis] *f* syphilis

Syrie [siri] *f* Syria; **la Syrie** Syria

sy·rien [sirjɛ̃] **-rienne** [rjɛn] *adj* Syrian ‖ *(cap) mf* Syrian *(person)*

systématique [sistematik] *adj* systematic

systématiser [sistematize] *tr* to systematize

système [sistem] *m* system; **courir, porter,** or **taper sur le système à qn** (slang) to get on s.o.'s nerves; **système D** (coll) resourcefulness

systole [sistɔl] *f* systole

T

T, t [te] *m invar* twentieth letter of the French alphabet

t. *abbr* (**tome**) vol.

ta [ta] §88

tabac [taba] *m* tobacco; tobacco shop; **avoir le gros tabac** (slang) to be a hit; **passer qn à tabac** (coll) to give s.o. the third degree; **tabac à chiquer** chewing tobacco; **tabac à priser** snuff

tabagie [tabaʒi] *f* smoke-filled room

tabasser [tabase] *tr* (slang) to give a licking to, to shellac

tabatière [tabatjer] *f* snuffbox; skylight, dormer window

tabernacle [tabernakl] *m* tabernacle

table [tabl] *f* table; **aimer la table** to like good food; **à table!** dinner is served!; **dresser** *or* **mettre la table** to set the table; **faire table rase** to make a clean sweep; **sainte table** altar rail; **se mettre à table** (slang) to tell all, to confess, to squeal; **table à abattants** gate-leg table; **table à ouvrage** worktable; **table à rallonges** extension table; **table de chevet, table de nuit** bedside table; **table d'écoute** wiretap; **table de jeu** card table; **table des matières** table of contents; **table de toilette** dressing table; **table d'hôte** table d'hôte; chef's special; **table d'opération** operating table; **table gigogne** nest of tables; **table interurbaine** long-distance switchboard; **table roulante** serving cart; **tenir table ouverte** to keep open house

ta·bleau [tablo] *m* (*pl* **-bleaux**) painting, picture; scoreboard; board; table, catalogue; panel (*of jurors*); **tableau d'affichage** bulletin board; **tableau d'avancement** senority list; **tableau de bord** dashboard; instrument panel; **tableau de distribution** switchboard; **tableau d'honneur** honor roll; **tableau noir** blackboard; **tableau vivant** tableau

tabler [table] *intr*—**tabler sur** to count on; to use as a base

tablette [tablet] *f* shelf; mantelpiece; bar (*e.g., of chocolate*); **rayez cela de vos tablettes** don't count on it; **tablettes** pocket notebook

table-valise [tablavaliz] *f* (*pl* **tables-valises**) folding table

tablier [tablije] *m* apron; roadway (*of bridge*); hood (*of chimney*); **tablier de fer** protective shutter (*on store window*)

ta·bou -bou *or* **boue** [tabu] *adj* & *m* taboo

tabouret [taburε] *m* stool; footstool

tabulaire [tabyler] *adj* tabular

tabulateur [tabylatœr] *m* tabulator

tac [tak] *m* click, clack; **du tac au tac** tit for tat; **tac tac tac tac!** rat-a-tat-tat!

tache [taʃ] *f* spot, stain; blemish, flaw; blot, smear; speck; **faire tache** to be out of place; **faire tache d'huile** to

spread; **sans tache** spotless, unblemished; **tache de rousseur, tache de son** freckle; **tache de vin** birthmark; **tache originelle** original sin; **tache solaire** sunspot

tâche [taʃ] *f* task, job; **prendre à tâche de** to try to; **travailler à la tâche** to do piecework

tacher [taʃe] *tr* & *ref* to spot, stain

tâcher [taʃe] *tr*—**tâcher que** to see to it that ‖ *intr*—**tâcher de** to try to; **y tâcher** to try

tâcheron [taʃrɔ̃] *m* small jobber; pieceworker; hard worker; wage slave

tacheter [taʃte] §34 *tr* to spot, to speckle

tacite [tasit] *adj* tacit

taciturne [tasityrn] *adj* taciturn

tacot [tako] *m* (coll) jalopy

tact [takt] *m* tact; sense of touch

tacticien [taktisjε̃] *m* tactician

tactique [taktik] *adj* tactical ‖ *f* tactics

taffetas [tafta] *m* taffeta; **taffetas gommé** adhesive tape

Tage [taʒ] *m* Tagus

taïaut [tajo] *interj* tallyho!

taie [tε] *f* (pathol) leukoma; **avoir une taie sur l'œil** (fig) to be blinded by prejudice; **taie d'oreiller** pillowcase

taillader [tajade] *tr* & *ref* to slash, cut

taille [taj] *f* cutting (*e.g., of diamond*); trimming (*e.g., of hedge*); height, stature; waist, waistline; size; cut (*of garment*); **à la taille de, de la taille de** to the measure of, suitable for; **avoir la taille fine** to have a slim waist; **de taille** big enough, strong enough; (coll) big; **être de taille à** to be up to, to be big enough to; **taille de guêpe** wasp waist; **taille en dessous** next size smaller; **taille en dessus** next size larger

tail·lé -lée [taje] *adj* cut; trimmed; **bien taillé** well-built; **taillé pour** cut out for

taille-crayon [tajkrεjɔ̃] *m* (*pl* **-crayon** *or* **-crayons**) pencil sharpener

taille-douce [tajdus] *f* (*pl* **tailles-douces**) copperplate

taille-pain [tajpε̃] *m invar* bread knife; bread slicer

tailler [taje] *tr* to cut; to sharpen (*a pencil*); to prune, trim (*a tree*); to carve (*stone*); to clip (*hair*) ‖ *intr* (cards) to deal ‖ *ref* to carve out (*a path; a career*); (coll) to beat it

tailleur [tajœr] *m* tailor; woman's suit; (cards) dealer; **en tailleur** squatting (*while tailoring*); **tailleur de diamants** diamond cutter; **tailleur de pierre** stonecutter; **tailleur sur mesure** lady's tailor-made suit

taillis [taji] *m* thicket, copse

tain [tε̃] *m* silvering (*of mirror*)

taire [ter] §52 (3d *sg pres ind* **tait**) *tr* to hush up, to hide; **la tairas-tu?** (slang) will you shut your trap?; **taire q.ch. à qn** to keep s.th. from s.o. ‖ *intr*—**faire taire** to silence ‖ *ref* to keep quiet, keep still; **se taire sur** to say nothing about; **tais-toi!** shut up!

talent [talɑ̃] *m* talent

talen·tueux [talɑ̃tɥø] **-tueuse** [tɥøz] *adj* talented

taloche [talɔʃ] *f* plastering trowel; (coll) clout, smack

talon [talɔ̃] *m* heel; stub

talonner [talɔne] *tr* to tail; to harass; to dig one's spurs into ‖ *intr* to bump

talus [taly] *m* slope; embankment

tambour [tɑ̃bur] *m* drum; drummer; entryway; spool (*of reel*); **tambour battant** (coll) roughly; (coll) quickly; **tambour cylindrique** revolving door; **tambour de basque** tambourine; **tambour de freins** brake drum; **tambour de ville** town crier

tambouriner [tɑ̃burine] *tr* to drum; to broadcast far and wide ‖ *intr* to beat a tattoo; to drum

tambour-major [tɑ̃burmaʒɔr] *m* (*pl* **tambours-majors**) drum major

tamis [tami] *m* sieve; **passer au tamis** to sift; **tamis à farine** flour sifter

Tamise [tamiz] *f* Thames

tamiser [tamize] *tr & intr* to sift

tampon [tɑ̃pɔ̃] *m* plug; bung; swab; rubber stamp; buffer; cancellation, postmark; (surg) tampon; **tampon buvard** hand blotter; **tampon encreur** stamp pad

tamponner [tɑ̃pɔne] *tr* to swab, to dab; to bump, to bump into; (surg) to tampon

tan [tɑ̃] *adj invar* tan ‖ *m* tanbark

tancer [tɑ̃se] §51 *tr* to scold

tandem [tɑ̃dem] *m* tandem; **en tandem** tandem

tandis que [tɑ̃dikə], [tɑ̃diskə] *conj* while; whereas

tangage [tɑ̃gaʒ] *m* (naut) pitching

Tanger [tɑ̃ʒe] *m* Tangier

tangible [tɑ̃ʒibl] *adj* tangible

tanguer [tɑ̃ge] *intr* to pitch (*said of ship*)

tanière [tanjɛr] *f* den, lair

tanker [tɑ̃kɛr] *m* oil tanker

tan·nant [tanɑ̃] **tan·nante** [tanɑ̃t] *adj* (coll) boring

tanne [tan] *f* spot (*on leather*); blackhead

tanner [tane] *tr* to tan; (coll) to pester

tannerie [tanri] *f* tannery

tanneur [tanœr] *m* tanner

tan-sad [tɑ̃sad] *m* (*pl* **-sads**) rear seat (*of motorcycle*)

tant [tɑ̃] *adv* so, so much; so long; **en tant que** as; in so far as; **si tant est que** if it is true that; **tant bien que mal** somehow or other; **tant de** so many; so much; **tant mieux** so much the better; **tant pis** so much the worse; never mind; **tant qu'à faire** while we're (you've, etc.) at it; **tant que** as well as; as long as; **tant s'en faut** far from it; **tant soit peu** ever so little; **vous m'en direz tant** (coll) you've just said a mouthful

tante [tɑ̃t] *f* aunt; (slang) fairy; **ma tante** (coll) the hockshop

tantième [tɑ̃tjɛm] *m* percentage

tantine [tɑ̃tin] *f* (coll) auntie

tantôt [tɑ̃to] *m* (coll) afternoon ‖ *adv* in a little while; a little while ago; (coll) in the afternoon; **à tantôt** see you soon; **tantôt . . . tantôt** sometimes . . . sometimes

taon [tɑ̃] *m* horsefly

tapage [tapaʒ] *m* uproar

tapa·geur [tapaʒœr] **-geuse** [ʒøz] *adj* loud

tape [tap] *f* tap, slap

ta·pé -pée [tape] *adj* dried (*fruit*); rotten in spots; (coll) crazy; (slang) worn (*with age or fatigue*); **bien tapé** (coll) well done; (coll) nicely served; (coll) to the point

tape-à-l'œil [tapalœj] *adj* gaudy, showy ‖ *m invar* mere show

taper [tape] *tr* to tap, to slap; to type; (coll) to hit (*s.o. for money*) ‖ *intr* to tap, to slap; to type; (coll) to go to the head (*said of wine*); **ça tape ici** (slang) it hurts here; **taper dans** (coll) to use; **taper dans le mille** (coll) to succeed; **taper dans l'œil de qn** (coll) to make a hit with s.o.; **taper de** to hit (*e.g., 100 m.p.h.*); **taper des pieds** to stamp one's feet; **taper sur** (coll) to get on (*s.o.'s nerves*); **taper sur le ventre de qn** (coll) to give s.o. a poke in the ribs; **taper sur qn** (coll) to run down s.o., to give s.o. a going-over

tapette [tapɛt] *f* carpet beater; fly swatter; handball; (slang) fairy; **avoir une fière tapette** (coll) to be a chatterbox

tapin [tapɛ̃] *m* (coll) drummer boy; (slang) solicitation (*by a prostitute*)

tapinois [tapinwa]—**en tapinois** stealthily

tapir [tapir] *ref* to crouch, to squat; to hide

tapis [tapi] *m* carpet; rug; game of chance; **mettre sur le tapis** to bring up for discussion; **tapis de bain** bath mat; **tapis de sol** ground cloth; **tapis de table** table covering; **tapis roulant** conveyor belt; moving sidewalk

tapis-brosse [tapibrɔs] *m* (*pl* **-brosses**) doormat

tapisser [tapise] *tr* to upholster; to tapestry; to wallpaper

tapisserie [tapisri] *f* upholstery; tapestry; **faire tapisserie** to be a wallflower

tapis·sier [tapisje] **tapis·sière** [tapisjɛr] *mf* upholsterer; tapestry maker; paperhanger

tapoter [tapɔte] *tr & intr* to tap

taquet [take] *m* wedge, peg; (mach) tappet; (naut) cleat; **taquet d'arrêt** (rr) scotch, wedge

ta·quin [takɛ̃] **-quine** [kin] *adj* teasing ‖ *mf* tease

taquiner [takine] *tr* to tease

taquinerie [takinri] *f* teasing

taraud [taro] *m* (mach) tap

tarauder [tarode] *tr* (mach) to tap; (coll) to pester

taraudeuse [tarodøz] *f* tap wrench

tard [tar] *m*—**sur le tard** late in the day; late in life ‖ *adv* late; **pas plus tard que** no later than; **plus tard** later on

tarder [tarde] *intr* to delay; **tarder à** to be long in ‖ *impers*—**il tarde** (with *dat*) de long to, e.g., **il lui tarde de vous voir** he longs to see you

tar·dif [tardif] **-dive** [div] *adj* late; backward; tardy

tardivement [tardivmɑ̃] *adv* belatedly

tare [tar] *f* defect, blemish; taint; loss in value; tare (*weight*)

tarer [tare] *tr* to damage; to taint; to tare ‖ *ref* to spoil

targette [tarʒet] *f* latch

targuer [targe] *ref*—**se targuer de** to pride oneself on

tarière [tarjer] *f* auger, drill

tarif [tarif] *m* price list; rate, tariff; **plein tarif** full fare; **tarifs postaux** postal rates

tarifaire [tarifer] *adj* tariff

tarifer [tarife] *tr* to price; to rate

tarir [tarir] *tr* to drain, exhaust, dry up ‖ *intr* to dry up, to run dry; **ne pas tarir** to never run out ‖ *ref* to dry up; to be exhausted

tarse [tars] *m* tarsus; instep

tartare [tartar] *adj* tartar (*sauce*); Tartar ‖ (*cap*) *mf* Tartar

tarte [tart] *adj* (coll) silly, stupid; (coll) ugly ‖ *f* pie, tart; (slang) slap

tartine [tartin] *f* slice of bread and butter or jam; (coll) long-winded speech; (coll) rambling article

tartiner [tartine] *tr* to spread

tartre [tartr] *m* tartar; scale

tartuferie [tartyfri] *f* hypocrisy

tas [tɑ] *m* heap, pile; **mettre en tas** to pile up; **prendre sur le tas** to catch red-handed; **tas de foin** haystack; **un tas de** (coll) a lot of

tasse [tɑs] *f* cup; **tasse à café** coffee cup; **tasse à thé** teacup; **tasse de café** cup of coffee

tas·seau [tɑso] *m* (*pl* **-seaux**) bracket; cleat; lug (*on casting*)

tasser [tɑse] *tr* to cram; to tamp; **bien tassé** (coll) brimful ‖ *intr* to grow thick ‖ *ref* to settle; to huddle; (coll) to go back to normal

taste-vin [tastəvɛ̃] *m invar* wine taster (*cup*); sampling tube

tata [tata] *f* (slang) auntie

tâter [tate] *tr* to feel, to touch; to test, to feel out; **tâter le pouls à qn** to feel s.o.'s pulse ‖ *intr*—**tâter de** to taste; to experience; to try one's hand at ‖ *ref* to stop to think, to ponder

tâte-vin [tatvɛ̃] *m invar* wine taster (*cup*); sampling tube

tatil·lon [tatijɔ̃] **tatil·lonne** [tatijɔn] *adj* fussy, hairsplitting ‖ *mf* hair-splitter

tâtonner [tatɔne] *intr* to grope

tâtons [tatɔ̃]—**à tâtons** gropingly

tatouage [tatwaʒ] *m* tattoo

tatouer [tatwe] *tr* to tattoo

taudis [todi] *m* hovel; **taudis** *mpl* slums

taule [tol] *f* (slang) fleabag; **faire de la taule** (slang) to do a stretch

taupe [top] *f* mole; moleskin

taupin [topɛ̃] *m* (mil) sapper; (coll) engineering student

taupinière [topinjer] *f* molehill

tau·reau [toro] *m* (*pl* **-reaux**) bull

taux [to] *m* rate; **taux d'escompte** discount rate

taveler [tavle] §34 *tr* to spot ‖ *ref* to become spotted

taverne [tavern] *f* inn, tavern

taxation [taksasjɔ̃] *f* fixing (*of prices, wages, etc.*); assessment; taxation

taxe [taks] *f* fixed price; rate; tax; **taxe à la valeur ajoutée** value-added tax; **taxe de luxe** luxury tax; **taxe de séjour** nonresident tax; **taxe directe** sales tax; **taxe perçue** postage paid; **taxe supplémentaire** postage due; **taxe sur les spectacles** entertainment tax

taxer [takse] *tr* to fix the price of; to regulate the rate of; to assess; to tax; **taxer qn de** to tax or charge s.o. with ‖ *ref* to set an offering price; **se taxer de** to accuse oneself of

taxi [taksi] *m* taxi; (coll) cabdriving; **hep taxi!** taxi! ‖ *mf* (coll) cabdriver

taxidermie [taksidermi] *f* taxidermy

taxiphone [taksifon] *m* pay phone

Tchécoslovaquie [tʃekɔslɔvaki] *f* Czechoslovakia; **la Tchécoslovaquie** Czechoslovakia

tchèque [tʃek] *adj* Czech ‖ *m* Czech (*language*) ‖ (*cap*) *mf* Czech (*person*)

te [tə] §87

techni·cien [teknisjɛ̃] **-cienne** [sjɛn] *mf* technician; engineer

technique [teknik] *adj* technical ‖ *f* technique; engineering

teck [tek] *m* teak

teigne [teɲ] *f* moth; ringworm; (fig) pest, nuisance

teindre [tɛ̃dr] §50 *tr* to dye; to tint ‖ *ref* to be tinted; to dye or tint one's hair; (with *dat* of *reflex pron*) to dye or tint (*one's hair*)

teint [tɛ̃] **teinte** [tɛ̃t] *adj* dyed; with dyed hair ‖ *m* dye; complexion; **bon teint** fast color ‖ *f* tint, shade; (fig) tinge

teinter [tɛ̃te] *tr* to tint; to tinge

teinture [tɛ̃tyr] *f* dye; dyeing; tincture; (fig) smattering; **teinture d'iode** (pharm) iodine

teinturerie [tɛ̃tyrri] *f* dry cleaner's; dyer's; dyeing

teintu·rier [tɛ̃tyrje] **-rière** [rjer] *mf* dry cleaner; dyer

tel telle [tel] *adj* such; like, e.g., **tel père tel fils** like father like son; **de telle sorte que** so that; **tel ou tel** such and such; **tel que** such as, the same as, as; **tel quel** as is ‖ *mf*—**un tel** or **une telle** so-and-so ‖ *pron* such a one, such

télé [tele] *f* (coll) TV; (coll) TV set

télécommander [telekɔmɑ̃de] *tr* to operate by remote control; (fig) to inspire, influence

téléférique [teleferik] *m* skyride, cableway

télégramme [telegram] *m* telegram

télégraphe [telegraf] *m* telegraph

télégraphier [telegrafje] *tr & intr* to telegraph

télégraphiste [telegrafist] *mf* telegrapher

téléguider [telegide] *tr* to guide (*e.g.*, *a missile*); (coll) to influence

téléimprimeur [teleɛ̃primœr] *m* teletype, teleprinter

télémètre [telemetr] *m* telemeter; range finder

téléobjectif [teleɔbʒektif] *m* telephoto lens

télépathie [telepati] *f* telepathy

téléphérique [teleferik] *m* skyride, cableway

téléphone [telefɔn] *m* telephone

téléphoner [telefɔne] *tr & intr* to telephone

téléphoniste [telefɔnist] *mf* telephone operator ‖ *m* lineman ‖ *f* telephone girl

télescope [teleskɔp] *m* telescope

télescoper [teleskɔpe] *tr & ref* to telescope

télescopique [teleskɔpik] *adj* telescopic

téléscripteur [teleskriptœr] *m* teletype, teletypewriter

télésiège [telesjɛʒ] *m* chair lift

téléski [teleski] *m* ski lift

téléspecta·teur [telespektatœr] **-trice** [tris] *mf* (television) viewer

télétype [teletip] *m* teletype

téléviser [televize] *tr* to televise

téléviseur [televizœr] *m* television set; **téléviseur à servo-réglage** remote-control television set

télévision [televizjɔ̃] *f* television; (coll) television set

télévi·suel -suelle [televizɥel] *adj* television

tellement [telmɑ̃] *adv* so much, so; **tellement de** so much, so many; **tellement que** to such an extent that

téméraire [temerer] *adj* rash, reckless, foolhardy

témérité [temerite] *f* temerity, rashness

témoignage [temwaɲaʒ] *m* testimony, witness; **en témoignage de quoi** in witness whereof; **rendre témoignage à** or **pour** to testify in favor of

témoigner [temwaɲe] *tr* to show; to testify ‖ *intr* to testify; **témoigner de** to give evidence of; to bear witness to

témoin [temwɛ̃] *adj invar* type, model; pilot ‖ *m* witness; control (*in scientific experiment*); second (*in duel*); **prendre à témoin** to call to witness; **témoin à charge** witness for the prosecution; **témoin à décharge** witness for the defense; **témoin oculaire** eyewitness

tempe [tɑ̃p] *f* (anat) temple

tempérament [tɑ̃peramɑ̃] *m* temperament; amorous nature; **à tempérament** on the installment plan

tempérance [tɑ̃perɑ̃s] *f* temperance

tempé·rant [tɑ̃perɑ̃] **-rante** [rɑ̃t] *adj* temperate

température [tɑ̃peratyr] *f* temperature

tempé·ré -rée [tɑ̃pere] *adj* temperate; tempered; restrained

tempérer [tɑ̃pere] §10 *tr* to temper ‖ *ref* to moderate

tempête [tɑ̃pet] *f* tempest, storm; **affronter la tempête** (fig) to face the music; **tempête dans un verre d'eau** tempest in a teapot; **tempête de neige**

blizzard; **tempête de poussière** dust storm; **tempête de sable** sandstorm

tempêter [tɑ̃pete] *intr* to storm

tempé·tueux [tɑ̃petɥø] **-tueuse** [tɥøz] *adj* tempestuous

temple [tɑ̃pl] *m* temple; chapel, church

tempo [tempo], [tɛpo] *m* tempo

temporaire [tɑ̃pɔrer] *adj* temporary

tempo·ral -rale [tɑ̃pɔral] *adj* (*pl* **-raux** [ro]) (anat) temporal

tempo·rel -relle [tɑ̃pɔrel] *adj* temporal

temporiser [tɑ̃pɔrize] *intr* to temporize, to stall

temps [tɑ̃] *m* time; times; cycle (*of internal-combustion engine*); position, movement (*in gymnastics, fencing, carrying of arms*); weather, e.g., **quel temps fait-il?** what is the weather like?; (gram) tense; (mus) beat, measure; **à temps** in time; **avoir fait son temps** to have seen better days; **dans le temps** formerly; **de temps en temps** from time to time; **en même temps** at the same time; **en temps et lieu** in due course; **en temps utile** in due course; **faire son temps** to do time (*in prison*); **gagner du temps** to save time; **le bon vieux temps** the good old days; **Le Temps** Father Time; **temps atomique** atomic era; **temps d'arrêt** pause, halt

tenable [tənabl] *adj*—**pas tenable** untenable; unbearable

tenace [tənas] *adj* tenacious

ténacité [tenasite] *f* tenacity

tenailler [tənaje] *tr* to torture

tenailles [tənaj] *fpl* pincers

tenan·cier [tənɑ̃sje] **-cière** [sjer] *mf* sharecropper; lessee; keeper (*e.g., of a dive*)

te·nant [tənɑ̃] **-nante** [nɑ̃t] *adj* attached (*collar*) ‖ *mf* (sports) holder (*of a title*) ‖ *m* champion, supporter; **connaître les tenants et les aboutissants** to know the ins and outs; **d'un seul tenant** in one piece

tendance [tɑ̃dɑ̃s] *f* tendency

tendan·cieux [tɑ̃dɑ̃sjø] **-cieuse** [sjøz] *adj* tendentious, slanted

ten·deur -deuse [døz] *mf* paperhanger; layer (*of traps*) ‖ *m* stretcher

tendoir [tɑ̃dwar] *m* clothesline

tendon [tɑ̃dɔ̃] *m* tendon

tendre [tɑ̃dr] *adj* tender ‖ *tr* to stretch; to hang; to bend (*a bow*); to lay (*a trap*); to strain (*one's ear*); to hold out, to reach out ‖ *intr*—**tendre à** to aim at; to tend toward ‖ *ref* to become strained

tendresse [tɑ̃dres] *f* tenderness, love, affection; (coll) partiality; **mille tendresses** (*closing of letter*) fondly

tendreté [tɑ̃drəte] *f* tenderness

ten·du -due [tɑ̃dy] *adj* tense, taut; strained; stretched out; **tendu de** hung with

ténèbres [tenebr] *fpl* darkness

téné·breux [tenebrø] **-breuse** [brøz] *adj* dark; somber (*person*); shady (*deal*); obscure (*style*)

te·neur [tənœr] **-neuse** [nøz] *mf* holder; **teneur de livres** bookkeeper

‖ **teneur** *f* tenor, gist; text; grade (*e.g., of ore*)

ténia [tenja] *m* tapeworm

tenir [tənir] §72 *tr* to hold; to keep; to take up (*space*); **être tenu à** to be obliged to; **être tenu de** to be responsible for ‖ *intr* to hold; **il ne tient qu'à vous** it's up to you; **tenez!** here!; **tenir à** to insist upon; to care for, to value; to be caused by; **tenir de** to take after, to resemble; **tenir debout** (fig) to hold water, to ring true; **tenir q.ch. de qn** to have s.th. from s.o., to learn s.th. from s.o.; **tiens!** well!, hey! ‖ *ref* to stay, remain; to sit up; to stand up; to behave; to contain oneself; **à quoi s'en tenir** what to believe; **s'en tenir à** to limit oneself to; to abide by

tennis [tenis] *m* tennis; tennis court

ténor [tenɔr] *adj masc* tenor ‖ *m* tenor; star performer

tension [tɑ̃sjɔ̃] *f* tension; blood pressure; **avoir de la tension** to have high blood pressure; **haute tension** (elec) high tension; **tension artérielle** blood pressure

tentacule [tɑ̃takyl] *m* tentacle

tenta‧teur [tɑ̃tatœr] **‧trice** [tris] *mf* tempter

tentation [tɑ̃tɑsjɔ̃] *f* temptation

tentative [tɑ̃tativ] *f* attempt

tente [tɑ̃t] *f* tent; awning

tente-abri [tɑ̃tabri] *f* (*pl* **tentes-abris** [tɑ̃tabri]) pup tent

tenter [tɑ̃te] *tr* to tempt; to attempt ‖ *intr*—**tenter de** to attempt to

tenture [tɑ̃tyr] *f* drape; hangings; wallpaper

te‧nu ‧nue [təny] *adj* firm (*securities, market, etc.*); **bien tenu** well-kept ‖ *f* see **tenue**

té‧nu ‧nue [təny] *adj* tenuous; thin

tenue [təny] *f* holding; managing; up-keep, maintenance; behavior; bearing; dress, costume; uniform; session; (mus) hold; **avoir de la tenue** to have good manners; **avoir une bonne tenue** (horsemanship) to have a good seat; **en tenue** in uniform; **grande tenue** (mil) full dress; **petite tenue** (mil) undress; **tenue des livres** bookkeeping; **tenue de soirée** evening clothes; **tenue de ville** street clothes

térébenthine [terebɑ̃tin] *f* turpentine

tergiverser [terʒiverse] *intr* to duck, equivocate, vacillate

terme [term] *m* term; end, limit; quarterly payment; **avant terme** prematurely; **terme fatal** last day of grace

terminaison [terminezɔ̃] *f* ending, termination

termi‧nal ‧nale [terminal] *adj* (*pl* **‧naux** [no]) terminal

terminer [termine] *tr & ref* to terminate

terminus [terminys] *m* terminal ‖ *interj* the end has come!

termite [termit] *m* termite

terne [tern] *adj* dull, drab

ternir [ternir] *tr & ref* to tarnish

terrain [terɛ̃] *m* ground; terrain; playing field; dueling field; **ne pas être**

sur son **terrain** to be out of one's depth; **tâter le terrain** to find out the lay of the land; **terrain à bâtir** or **à lotir** building plot; **terrain brûlant** (fig) unsafe ground; **terrain d'atterrissage** landing field; **terrain d'aviation** airfield; **terrain de courses** race track; **terrain de jeux** playground; **terrain de manœuvres** parade ground; **terrain vague** vacant lot

terrasse [teras] *f* terrace; sidewalk café; **terrasse en plein air** outdoor café

terrasser [terase] *tr* to embank; to floor, to knock down

terre [ter] *f* earth; land; (elec) ground; **descendre à terre** to go ashore; **la Terre Sainte** the Holy Land; **mettre pied à terre** to dismount; **par terre** on the floor; on the ground; **terre cuite** terra cotta; **Terre de Feu** Tierra del Fuego; **terre ferme** terra firma; **terre franche** loam

ter‧reau [tero] *m* (*pl* **-reaux**) compost

terre-neuve [ternœv] *m invar* Newfoundland dog ‖ **—Terre-Neuve** *f* Newfoundland

terre-plein [terplɛ̃] *m* (*pl* **-pleins**) median, divider (*of road*); fill, embankment; earthwork, rampart; terrace; (rr) roadbed

terrer [tere] *tr* to earth up (*e.g., a tree*); to earth over (*seed*) ‖ *ref* to burrow; to entrench oneself

terrestre [terestr] *adj* land; terrestrial

terreur [terœr] *f* terror; **la Terreur** the Reign of Terror

ter‧reux [terø] **ter‧reuse** [terøz] *adj* earthy; dirty; sallow (*complexion*)

terrible [teribl] *adj* terrible; terrific

ter‧rien [terjɛ̃] **ter‧rienne** [terjen] *adj* landed (*gentry*) ‖ *mf* landowner; landlubber ‖ *m* earthman

terrier [terje] *m* hole, burrow; (*dog*) terrier

terrifier [terifje] *tr* to terrify

terrir [terir] *intr* to come close to shore (*said of fish*)

territoire [teritwar] *m* territory

terroir [terwar] *m* soil; homeland

terroriser [terorize] *tr* to terrorize

tertiaire [tersjer] *adj* tertiary

tertre [tertr] *m* mound, knoll

tes [te] §88

tesson [tesɔ̃] *m* shard; broken glass

test [test] *m* test; (zool) shell; **test de niveau** placement test

testament [testamɑ̃] *m* testament; will

testa‧teur [testatœr] **‧trice** [tris] *mf* testator

tester [teste] *tr* to test ‖ *intr* to make one's will

testicule [testikyl] *m* testicle

tétanos [tetanos] *m* tetanus

têtard [tetar] *m* tadpole; (bot) pollard

tête [tet] *f* head; heading (*e.g., of chapter*); **à la tête de** in charge of, at the head of; **à tête reposée** at (one's) leisure; **avoir la tête près du bonnet** (coll) to be quick-tempered; **avoir une bonne tête** to have a pleasant look or expression; **de tête** in one's mind's eye, mentally; capable, *e.g.,* **une femme de tête** a capable woman;

en avoir par-dessus la tête (coll) to be fed up with it; en tête foremost, at the front, leading; en tête à tête avec alone with; faire la tête à to frown at, to give a dirty look to; faire une tête to wear a long face; forte tête strong-minded person; jeter à la tête à qn (fig) to cast in s.o.'s face; la tête en bas head downwards, upside down; la tête la première headfirst, headlong; laver la tête à qn (coll) to give s.o. a dressing down; mauvaise tête troublemaker; monter à la tête de qn to go to s.o.'s head; n'en faire qu'à sa tête to be a law unto oneself; par tête per capita, per head; piquer une tête to take a header, to dive; saluer de la tête to nod; se mettre en tête de to take it into one's head to; se payer la tête de qn (coll) to pull s.o.'s leg; tenir tête à to face up to, to stand up to; tête baissée headlong, heedless; tête brûlée daredevil; tête chercheuse homing head (of missile); tête d'affiche (theat) headliner; tête de bois blockhead; tête de cuvée choice wine; tête de lecture (elec) playback head; tête de ligne truck terminal; tête de linotte scatterbrain; tête de pont (mil) bridgehead, beachhead; tête de Turc butt, scapegoat, fall guy; tête morte excitable person; tête morte et tibias skull and crossbones; tomber sur la tête (coll) to be off one's rocker

tête-à-queue [tetakø] m invar about-face, slue

tétée [tete] f sucking; feeding time

téter [tete] §10 tr & intr to suck

tétine [tetin] f nipple; teat

téton [tet5] m (coll) tit

tétras [tetra] m grouse

tette [tɛt] f (coll) tit

tê-tu -tue [tety] adj stubborn

teuf-teuf [tœftœf] m (pl teuf-teuf or teufs-teufs) (coll) jalopy || interj chug!, chug!

tévé [teve] f (acronym) (télévision) TV

texte [tɛkst] m text; apprendre son texte (theat) to learn one's lines

textile [tɛkstil] adj & m textile

tex•tuel -tuelle [tɛkstyɛl] adj textual; verbatim

texture [tɛkstyr] f texture

thaï [taj] adj invar & m Thai

thaïlan•dais [tajlɑ̃dɛ] -daise [dɛz] adj Thai || (cap) mf Thai

Thaïlande [tajlɑ̃d] f Thailand

thaumaturge [tomatyrʒ] m miracle worker, magician

thé [te] m tea

théâ•tral -trale [teatral] adj (pl -traux [tro]) theatrical

théâtre [teatr] m theater; stage, boards; scene (e.g., of the crime)

théier [teje] théière [tejɛr] adj tea || m tea (shrub) || f see théière

théière [tejɛr] f teapot

thème [tɛm] m theme; translation (into a foreign language)

théologie [teɔlɔʒi] f theology

théorème [teɔrɛm] m theorem

théorie [teɔri] f theory; procession

théorique [teɔrik] adj theoretical

thérapeutique [terapøtik] adj therapeutic || f therapeutics

thérapie [terapi] f therapy

Thérèse [terɛz] f Theresa

ther•mal -male [tɛrmal] adj (pl -maux [mo]) thermal

thermique [tɛrmik] adj thermal

thermocouple [tɛrmɔkupl] m thermocouple

thermodynamique [tɛrmɔdinamik] adj thermodynamic || f thermodynamics

thermomètre [tɛrmɔmɛtr] m thermometer

thermonucléaire [tɛrmɔnyklɛɛr] adj thermonuclear

Thermopyles [tɛrmɔpil] fpl—les Thermopyles Thermopylae

thermos [tɛrmɔs] f thermos bottle

thermosiphon [tɛrmɔsifɔ̃] m hot-water heater

thermostat [tɛrmɔsta] m thermostat

thésauriser [tezɔrize] tr & intr to hoard

thésauri•seur [tezɔrizœr] -seuse [zøz] mf hoarder

thèse [tɛz] f thesis

thon [tɔ̃] m tuna

thorax [tɔraks] m thorax

thrène [trɛn] m threnody

thuriféraire [tyriferɛr] m incense bearer; flatterer

thym [tɛ̃] m thyme

thyroïde [tiroid] adj & f thyroid

tiare [tjar] f tiara (papal miter); papacy

tibia [tibja] m tibia; shin; tibias croisés et tête de mort skull and crossbones

tic [tik] m (pathol) tic; tic tac ticktock

ticket [tikɛ] m ticket (of bus, subway, etc.); check (for article in baggage room); ration stamp; sans tickets unrationed; ticket de quai platform ticket

tic-tac [tiktak] m invar tick

tiède [tjɛd] adj lukewarm; mild

tiédeur [tjedœr] f lukewarmness; mildness

tiédir [tjedir] tr to take the chill off || intr to become lukewarm

tien [tjɛ̃] tienne [tjɛn] §89

tiens [tjɛ̃] interj welll, hey!

tiers [tjɛr] tierce [tjɛrs] adj third; tertian (fever) || m third (in fractions); le tiers a third; the third party; le tiers et le quart (coll) everybody and anybody || f (typ) press proof

tige [tiʒ] f stem; trunk; shaft; shank; piston rod; leg (of boot); stock (of genealogy)

tignasse [tiɲas] f shock, mop (of hair)

tigre [tigr] m tiger

ti-gré -grée [tigre] adj striped; speckled, spotted

tigresse [tigrɛs] f tigress

tillac [tijak] m top deck (of old-time ships)

tilleul [tijœl] m linden

timbale [tɛ̃bal] f metal cup, mug; (culin) mold; (mus) kettledrum; décrocher la timbale (coll) to carry off the prize

timbalier [tɛ̃balje] m kettledrummer

timbrage [tɛ̃braʒ] *m* stamping; cancellation (*of mail*)

timbre [tɛ̃br] *m* bell; doorbell; buzzer; seal, stamp; postage stamp; postmark; snare (*of drum*); (phonet, phys) timbre

tim·bré ·brée [tɛ̃bre] *adj* stamped; ringing (*voice*); (coll) cracked, crazy

timbre-poste [tɛ̃brəpɔst] *m* (*pl* **timbres-poste**) postage stamp

timbrer [tɛ̃bre] *tr* to stamp; to postmark

timbres-prime [tɛ̃mbrəprim] *mpl* trading stamps

timide [timid] *adj* timid, shy

timon [timɔ̃] *m* pole (*of carriage*); beam (*of plow*); (naut) helm

timonier [timɔnje] *m* helmsman; wheel horse

timo·ré ·rée [timɔre] *adj* timorous

tin [tɛ̃] *m* chock

tinette [tinet] *f* firkin (*tub*); bucket (*for fecal matter*)

tintamarre [tɛ̃tamar] *m* uproar

tintement [tɛ̃tmɑ̃] *m* tolling (*of bell*); tinkle (*of bell*); ringing (*in ears*)

tinter [tɛ̃te] *tr* to toll || *intr* to toll; to tinkle; to jingle, to clink; to ring (*said of ears*)

tintin [tɛ̃tɛ̃] *m*—**faire tintin** (slang) to do without || *interj* (slang) nothing doing!

tintouin [tɛ̃twɛ̃] *m* (coll) trouble

tique [tik] *f* (ent) tick

tiquer [tike] *intr* to twitch; (coll) to wince; **sans tiquer** (coll) without turning a hair

tir [tir] *m* shooting; firing; aim; shooting gallery; **tir à la cible** target practice; **tir à l'arc** archery; **tir au fusil** gunnery; **tir au pigeon** trapshooting

tirade [tirad] *f* (theat) long speech

tirage [tiraʒ] *m* drawing; towing; draft (*of chimney*); printing; circulation (*of newspaper*); (coll) tension, friction; **tirage à part** offprint; **tirage au sort** lottery drawing; **tirage de luxe** deluxe edition

tiraillement [tirajmɑ̃] *m* pain, cramp; conflict, tension

tirailler [tiraje] *tr* to pull about, to tug at; to pester || *intr* to blaze away; **tirailler sur** to snipe at || *ref* to have a misunderstanding

tirailleur [tirajœr] *m* sharpshooter; sniper; (fig) free lance

tirant [tirɑ̃] *m* string; strap; **tirant d'eau** draft (*of ship*)

tire [tir] *f* (heral) row (*of vair*); (slang) car, auto; (Canad) taffy pull

ti·ré ·rée [tire] *adj* drawn; printed || *m* shooting preserve; payee; **tiré à part** offprint

tire-au-flanc [tiroflɑ̃] *m invar* malingerer, shirker

tire-botte [tirbɔt] *m* (*pl* **-bottes**) bootjack

tire-bouchon [tirbuʃɔ̃] *m* (*pl* **-bouchons**) corkscrew; corkscrew curl

tire-bouchonner [tirbuʃɔne] *tr* to twist in a spiral

tire-bouton [tirbutɔ̃] *m* (*pl* **-boutons**) buttonhook

tire-clou [tirklu] *m* (*pl* **-clous**) nail puller

tire-d'aile [tirdel]—**à tire-d'aile** with wings outspread, swiftly

tire-fond [tirfɔ̃] *m invar* spike; screw eye

tire-larigot [tirlarigo]—**boire à tire-larigot** to drink like a fish

tire-ligne [tirliɲ] *m* (*pl* **-lignes**) ruling pen

tirelire [tirlir] *f* piggy bank; (*face*) (coll) mug; (*head*) (coll) noggin; (slang) belly

tire-l'œil [tirlœj] *m invar* eye catcher

tirer [tire] *tr* to draw; to pull, to tug; to shoot, to fire; to run off, to print; to take out; to take, to get; to stick out (*one's tongue*); **tirer au clair** to bring out into the open; **tirer parti de** to turn to account || *intr* to pull; to shoot; to draw (*e.g., to a close*); to draw (*said of chimney*); **tirer à, vers, or sur** to border on || *ref* to extricate oneself; **s'en tirer** to manage; **se tirer d'affaire** to pull through, to get along

tiret [tire] *m* dash; blank (*to be filled in*)

tirette [tiret] *f* slide (*of desk*); damper (*of chimney*)

tireur [tirœr] *m* marksman; drawer, payer (*of check*); printer; **tireur de bois flotté** log driver; **tireur d'élite** sharpshooter; **tireur d'épée** fencer; **tireur isolé** sniper

tireuse [tirøz] *f* markswoman; **tireuse de cartes** fortuneteller

tiroir [tirwar] *m* drawer; (mach) slide valve; **à tiroirs** episodic (*play, novel, etc.*)

tiroir-caisse [tirwarkes] *m* (*pl* **tiroirs-caisses**) cash register

tisane [tizan] *f* tea, infusion; (coll) bad champagne; (slang) slap

tison [tizɔ̃] *m* ember; (fig) firebrand

tisonner [tizɔne] *tr* to poke

tisonnier [tizɔnje] *m* poker

tissage [tisaʒ] *m* weaving

tisser [tise] *tr & intr* to weave

tisse·rand [tisrɑ̃] **-rande** [rɑ̃d] *mf* weaver

tis·seur [tisœr] **tis·seuse** [tisøz] *mf* weaver

tissu [tisy] *m* tissue; cloth; fabric, material; pack (*of lies*)

tissu-éponge [tisyepɔ̃ʒ] *m* (*pl* **tissus-éponges**) toweling, terry cloth

tissure [tisyr] *f* texture; (fig) framework

titane [titan] *m* titanium

titi [titi] *m* (slang) street urchin

Titien [tisjɛ̃] *m*—**le Titien** Titian

titre [titr] *m* title; title page; heading; fineness (*of coinage*); claim; right; concentration (*of a solution*); **à juste titre** rightly so; **à titre de** in the capacity of; by virtue of; **à titre d'emprunt** as a loan; **à titre d'essai** on trial; **à titre gratuit** or **gracieux** free of charge; **titres** qualifications; (com) securities

titrer [titre] *tr* to title; to subtitle (*films*)

tituber [titybe] *intr* to stagger
titulaire [tityler] *adj* titular ‖ *mf* incumbent; holder (*of passport, license, degree, post*)
titulariser [titylarize] *tr* to confirm the appointment of
toast [tost] *m* toast; **porter un toast à** to toast
toboggan [tɔbɔgɑ̃] *m* toboggan; toboggan run; slide, chute
toc [tɔk] *adj invar* (coll) worthless; (coll) crazy ‖ *m* (mach) chuck; (coll) imitation; **en toc** (coll) worthless; **toc, toc!** knock, knock!
tohu-bohu [tɔybɔy] *m* hubbub
toi [twa] §85, §87
toile [twal] *f* cloth; linen; canvas, painting; (theat) curtain; **toile à coton** calico; **toile à laver** dishrag; **toile à matelas** ticking; **toile à voile** sailcloth; **toile cirée** oilcloth; **toile d'araignée** cobweb; **toile de fond** backdrop
toilette [twalet] *f* toilet; dressing table; dress, outfit (*of a woman*); **aimer la toilette** to be fond of clothing; **faire la toilette de** to lay out (*a corpse*)
toi-même [twamem] §86
toise [twaz] *f* fathom; **passer à la toise** to measure the height of
toiser [twaze] *tr* to size up
toison [twazɔ̃] *f* fleece; mop (*of hair*); **Toison d'or** Golden Fleece
toit [twa] *m* roof; rooftop; home, house; **crier sur les toits** to shout from the housetops
toiture [twatyr] *f* roofing
tôle [tol] *f* sheet metal; tole (*decorative metalware*); **tôle de blindage** armor plate; **tôle étamée** tin plate; **tôle galvanisée** galvanized iron; **tôle noire** sheet iron; **tôle ondulée** corrugated iron
tolérable [tɔlerabl] *adj* tolerable, bearable
tolérance [tɔlerɑ̃s] *f* tolerance
tolérer [tɔlere] §10 *tr* to tolerate
tôlerie [tolri] *f* sheet metal; rolling mill
tolet [tɔle] *m* oarlock
tomaison [tɔmezɔ̃] *f* volume number
tomate [tɔmat] *f* tomato
tombe [tɔ̃b] *f* tomb; grave; tombstone
tom-beau [tɔ̃bo] *m* (*pl* **-beaux**) tomb; **à tombeau couvert** lickety-split
tombée [tɔ̃be] *f* fall (*of rain, snow, etc.*); **tombée de la nuit** nightfall
tomber [tɔ̃be] *tr* to throw (*a wrestler*); (coll) to remove (*a piece of clothing*); (slang) to seduce (*a woman*) ‖ *intr* (*aux:* ÊTRE) to fall, to drop; **tomber amoureux** to fall in love; **tomber bien** to happen just in time; **tomber en panne** to have a breakdown; **tomber sur** to run into, chance upon; to turn to (*said of conversation*)
tombe-reau [tɔ̃bro] *m* (*pl* **-reaux**) dump truck; dumpcart; load
tombola [tɔ̃bɔla] *m* raffle
tome [tɔm] *m* tome, volume
ton [tɔ̃] *adj poss* §88 ‖ *m* tone; (mus) key

to-nal -nale [tɔnal] *adj* (*pl* **-nals**) tonal
ton-deur [tɔ̃dœr] **-deuse** [dØz] *mf* shearer ‖ *f* shears; **tondeuse à cheveux** hair clippers; **tondeuse à gazon** lawn mower; **tondeuse (à gazon) à moteur** power mower; **tondeuse électrique** electric clippers; **tondeuse mécanique** cropper; power mower
tondre [tɔ̃dr] *tr* to clip; to shear; to mow
toni-fiant [tɔnifjɑ̃] **-fiante** [fjɑ̃t] *adj* & *m* tonic
tonifier [tɔnifje] *tr* to tone up
tonique [tɔnik] *adj* & *m* tonic
toni-truant [tɔnitryɑ̃] **-truante** [tryɑ̃t] *adj* (coll) thunderous
tonne [tɔn] *f* ton; tun
ton-neau [tɔno] *m* (*pl* **-neaux**) barrel; cart; roll (*of automobile, airplane, etc.*); (naut) ton; **au tonneau** on draught; **tonneau de poudre** powder keg
tonnelet [tɔnle] *m* keg
tonnelier [tɔnəlje] *m* cooper
tonnelle [tɔnel] *f* arbor
tonner [tɔne] *intr* to thunder
tonnerre [tɔner] *m* thunder
tonte [tɔ̃t] *f* clipping; shearing; mowing
tonton [tɔ̃tɔ̃] *m* (slang) uncle
top [tɔp] *m* beep
topaze [tɔpaz] *f* topaz
toper [tɔpe] *intr* to shake hands on it; **tope là!** it's a deal!
topinambour [tɔpinɑ̃bur] *m* Jerusalem artichoke
topique [tɔpik] *adj* local, regional
topographie [tɔpɔgrafi] *f* topography
toquade [tɔkad] *f* (coll) infatuation
toquante [tɔkɑ̃t] *f* (coll) ticker (*watch*)
toque [tɔk] *f* toque; cap (*of chef; of judge*)
to-qué -quée [tɔke] *adj* (coll) crazy, cracked ‖ *mf* (coll) nut
toquer [tɔke] *tr* to infatuate ‖ *intr* (coll) to rap, tap ‖ *ref*—**se toquer de** to be infatuated with
torche [tɔrʃ] *f* torch; **se mettre en torche** to fail to open (*said of parachute*); **torche électrique** flashlight
torcher [tɔrʃe] *tr* to wipe clean; to rush through, to botch; to daub with clay and straw
torchère [tɔrʃer] *f* candelabrum; floor lamp
torchis [tɔrʃi] *m* adobe
torchon [tɔrʃɔ̃] *m* dishcloth; rag; (coll) scribble; **le torchon brûle** they're squabbling
torchonner [tɔrʃone] *tr* (coll) to botch
tor-dant -dante [tɔrdɑ̃] **-dante** [dɑ̃t] *adj* (coll) sidesplitting
tord-boyaux [tɔrbwajo] *m invar* (coll) rotgut
tordeuse [tɔrdØz] *f* moth
tordoir [tɔrdwar] *m* wringer; rope-making machine
tordre [tɔrdr] *tr* to twist; to wring ‖ *ref* to twist; to writhe; **se tordre de rire** to split one's sides laughing
tornade [tɔrnad] *f* tornado
toron [tɔrɔ̃] *m* strand (*of rope*)
torpédo [tɔrpedo] *f* (archaic) open touring car

torpeur [tɔrpœr] *f* torpor
torpille [tɔrpij] *f* torpedo; (arti) mine
torpiller [tɔrpije] *tr* to torpedo
torpilleur [tɔrpijœr] *m* torpedo boat; torpedoman
torque [tɔrk] *f* coil of wire; twist (*of tobacco*)
torréfaction [tɔrefaksjɔ̃] *f* roasting
torréfier [tɔrefje] *tr* to roast
torrent [tɔrɑ̃] *m* torrent
torride [tɔrid] *adj* torrid
tors [tɔr] **torse** [tɔrs] *adj* twisted; crooked || *m* twist || see **torse** *m*
torsade [tɔrsad] *f* twisted cord; coil (*of hair*); **à torsades** fringed
torsader [tɔrsade] *tr* to twist
torse [tɔrs] *m* torso, trunk
torsion [tɔrsjɔ̃] *f* twisting, torsion
tort [tɔr] *m* wrong; harm; **à tort** wrongly; **à tort et à travers** at random, wildly; carelessly, inconsiderately; **à tort ou à raison** rightly or wrongly; **avoir tort** to be wrong; **donner tort à** to lay the blame on; **faire tort à** to wrong
torticolis [tɔrtikɔli] *m* stiff neck
tortillard [tɔrtijar] *adj masc* knotty || *m* (coll) jerkwater train
tortiller [tɔrtije] *tr* to twist, to twirl; (slang) to gulp down || *intr* to wriggle; (coll) to beat about the bush || *ref* to wriggle, squirm; to writhe, twist
tor·tu -tue [tɔrty] *adj* crooked || *f* turtle, tortoise
tor·tueux [tɔrtɥø] **-tueuse** [tɥøz] *adj* winding; devious, underhanded
torture [tɔrtyr] *f* torture
torturer [tɔrtyre] *tr* to torture
torve [tɔrv] *adj* menacing
tos·can -cane [kan] *adj* Tuscan || *m* Tuscan (*dialect*) || (cap) *mf* Tuscan (*person*)
tôt [to] *adv* soon; early; **au plus tôt** as soon as possible; at the earliest; **le plus tôt possible** as soon as possible; **pas de si tôt** not soon; **tôt ou tard** sooner or later
to·tal -tale [tɔtal] *adj & m* (*pl* **-taux** [to]) total
totaliser [tɔtalize] *tr* to total
totalitaire [tɔtaliter] *adj* totalitarian
totem [tɔtɛm] *m* totem
toton [tɔtɔ̃] *m* teetotum
toubib [tubib] *m* (coll) medical officer; (coll) doctor, physician
tou·chant [tuʃɑ̃] **-chante** [ʃɑ̃t] *adj* touching || **touchant** *prep* touching, concerning
touche [tuʃ] *f* touch; key (*of piano or typewriter*); stop (*of organ*); fret (*of guitar*); fingerboard (*of violin*); hit (*in fencing*); bite (*on fishline*); goad (*for cattle*); tab (*of file index*); thumb index; (elec) contact; (coll) look, appearance; **touche de blocage** shift lock; **touche de manœuvre** shift key
touche-à-tout [tuʃatu] *m invar* (coll) busybody
toucher [tuʃe] *m* touch, sense of touch || *tr* to touch; to concern; to cash (*a check*); to draw out (*money*); to goad

(*cattle*); (mus) to pluck (*the strings*) || *intr* to touch; **toucher à** to touch (*one's food, capital, etc.*); to touch on; to call at (*a port*); to be about to achieve (*one's aim*); **toucher de** to play (*e.g., the piano*) || *ref* to touch
touer [twe] *tr* to warp, to kedge
touffe [tuf] *f* tuft; clump (*of trees*)
touffeur [tufœr] *f* suffocating heat
touf·fu -fue [tufy] *adj* bushy; (fig) dense
touille [tuj] *m* dogfish, shark
touiller [tuje] *tr* (coll) to stir; (coll) to mix; (coll) to shuffle
toujours [tuʒur] *adv* always; still; anyhow; **M. Toujours** (coll) yes man; **pour toujours** forever
toupet [tupe] *m* tuft (*of hair*); forelock (*of horse*); (coll) nerve, brass
toupie [tupi] *f* top; molding board; silly woman
tour [tur] *m* turn; tour; trick; lathe; **à tour de bras** with all one's might; **à tour de rôle** in turn; **en un tour de main** in a jiffy; **faire le tour de** to tour, to visit; to walk or ride around; **faire un tour de** to take a walk or ride in; **tour à tour** by turns; **tour de bâton** (coll) rake-off, killing; **tour de main** sleight of hand; **tour d'adresse** sleight of hand; **tour de poitrine** chest size; **tour de taille** waist measurement; **tour de tête** hat size; **tours et retours** twists and turns || *f* tower; (chess) castle, rook; (mil) turret; **tour de contrôle** control tower; **tour de guet** lookout tower
tourbe [turb] *f* peat; mob
tourbillon [turbijɔ̃] *m* whirl; whirlpool; whirlwind
tourbillonner [turbijɔne] *intr* to whirl, to swirl
tourelle [turɛl] *f* turret
tourillon [turijɔ̃] *m* axle; trunnion
touriste [turist] *adj & mf* tourist
tourment [turmɑ̃] *m* torment
tourmente [turmɑ̃t] *f* storm
tourmenter [turmɑ̃te] *tr* to torment || *ref* to fret
tour·nant [turnɑ̃] **-nante** [nɑ̃t] *adj* turning, revolving || *m* turn; turning point; water wheel
tourne-à-gauche [turnagoʃ] *m invar* wrench; saw set; diestock
tournebroche [turnəbrɔʃ] *m* roasting jack, turnspit
tourne-disque [turnədisk] *m* (*pl* **-disques**) record player
tournedos [turnədo] *m* filet mignon
tournée [turne] *f* round; **en tournée** (theat) on tour; **faire une tournée** to take a trip; **tournée électorale** political campaign
tournemain [turnəmɛ̃] **—en un tournemain** in a split second
tourne-pierre [turnəpjɛr] *m* (*pl* **-pierres**) (orn) turnstone
tourner [turne] *tr* to turn; to turn over; to shoot (*a moving picture; a scene*); to outflank; **tourner et retourner** to turn over and over || *intr* to turn; (mov) to shoot a picture; (theat) to tour; **la tête me (lui, etc.) tourne** my

(his, etc.) head is turning, I feel (he feels, etc.) dizzy; **silence, on tourne!** quiet on the set!; **tourner à** or **en to** turn into; **tourner autour du pot** (coll) to beat about the bush; **tourner bien** to turn out well; **tourner en rond** to go around in circles, to spin; **tourner mal** to go bad || *ref* to turn

tournesol [turnəsɔl] *m* litmus; sunflower

tournevis [turnəvis] *m* screwdriver

tourniquet [turnike] *m* turnstile; revolving door; revolving display stand; (surg) tourniquet; **passer au tourniquet** (slang) to be court-martialed

tournoi [turnwa] *m* tournament

tournoyer [turnwaje] §47 *intr* to turn, to wheel; to twirl; to tourney

tournure [turnyr] *f* turn, course (*of events*); wording, phrasing, turn (*of phrase*); expression; shape, figure

tourte [turt] *adj* stupid || *f* (coll) dolt; **tourte à la viande** meat pie

tour·teau [turto] *m* (*pl* **-teaux**) oil cake; crab

tourte·reau [turtəro] *m* (*pl* **-reaux**) turtledove, young lover

tourterelle [turtərɛl] *f* turtledove

tourtière [turtjɛr] *f* pie pan

toussailler [tusaje] *intr* to keep on coughing

Toussaint [tusɛ̃] *f* All Saints' Day; **la Toussaint** All Saints' Day

tousser [tuse] *intr* to cough; to clear one's throat

tousserie [tusri] *f* constant coughing

toussotement [tusɔtmɑ̃] *m* slight coughing

toussoter [tusɔte] *intr* to cough slightly

tout [tu] **toute** [tut] *adj* (*pl* **tous** [tus]) any, every, all; **tous les** all, all of, e.g., **tous les hommes** all men, all of the men; whole, entire, e.g., **toute la journée** the whole day; **à tout coup** every time; **à toute heure** at any time; **tous les deux** both || *m* (*pl* **touts**) whole, all; everything; sum; **du tout** (coll) not at all; **en tout** wholly, in all; **pas du tout** not at all || **tout toute** (*pl* **tous** [tus] **toutes**) *pron* all, everything, anything; **à tout prendre** on the whole; **tout compté** all things considered || **tout** *adv* all, quite, completely; very, e.g., **un des tout premiers** one of the very foremost; **tout à côté de** right next to; **tout à coup** suddenly; **tout à fait** quite; **tout à l'heure** in a little while; a little while ago; **tout au plus** at most; **tout de même** however, all the same; **tout de suite** at once, immediately; **tout en** while, e.g., **tout en parlant** while talking; **tout éveillé** wide awake; **tout fait** ready-made; **tout haut** aloud; **tout neuf** brand-new; **tout nu** stark-naked; **tout près** nearby; **tout . . . que** despite the fact that, e.g., **tout vieux qu'il était** despite the fact that he was old || **toute toutes** *adv* (before a feminine word beginning with a consonant or an aspirate **h**) all, quite, completely, e.g., **elles sont toutes seules** they are all (or quite or completely) alone

tout-à-l'égout [tutalegu] *m invar* sewerage

toute-épice [tutepis] *f* (*pl* **toutes-épices** [tutepis]) allspice (*berry*)

toutefois [tutfwa] *adv* however

toute-puissance [tutpɥisɑ̃s] *f* omnipotence

toutou [tutu] *m* (coll) doggie

Tout-Paris [tupari] *m invar* high society, smart set (*in Paris*)

tout-petit [tupəti] *m* (*pl* **-petits**) toddler

tout-puissant [tupɥisɑ̃] **toute-puissante** [tutpɥisɑ̃t] (*pl* **tout-puissants toutes-puissantes**) *adj* almighty || **le Tout-Puissant** the Almighty

tout-venant [tuvnɑ̃] *m invar* all comers; run-of-the-mine coal; run-of-the-mill product; ordinary run of people

toux [tu] *f* cough

toxicomane [tɔksikɔman] *adj* addicted || *mf* drug addict

toxicomanie [tɔksikɔmani] *f* drug addiction

toxique [tɔksik] *adj* toxic || *m* poison

trac [trak] *m* (coll) stage fright; **avoir le trac** (coll) to lose one's nerve; **tout à trac** without thinking

tracas [traka] *m* worry, trouble

tracasser [trakase] *tr & ref* to worry

tracasserie [trakasri] *f* bother; **tracasseries** interference

tracassin [trakasɛ̃] *m* (coll) worry

trace [tras] *f* trace; track, trail; sketch; footprint; **marcher sur les traces de** to follow in the footsteps of

tracé [trase] *m* tracing; **faire le tracé de** to lay out; (math) to plot

tracer [trase] §51 *tr* to trace, draw

tra·ceur [trasœr] **-ceuse** [søz] *mf* tracer || *m* tracer (*radioactive substance*)

trachée [traʃe] *f* trachea, windpipe

trachée-artère [traʃearter] *f* (*pl* **trachées-artères**) windpipe

tract [trakt] *m* tract

tractation [traktɑsjɔ̃] *f* underhanded deal

tracteur [traktœr] *m* tractor

traction [traksjɔ̃] *f* traction; **faire des tractions** to do chin-ups; **traction avant** front-wheel drive

tradition [tradisjɔ̃] *f* tradition

tradition·nel -nelle [tradisjɔnel] *adj* traditional

traduc·teur [tradyktœr] **-trice** [tris] *mf* translator

traduction [tradyksjɔ̃] *f* translation

traduire [tradɥir] §19 *tr* to translate; **traduire en justice** to haul into court

trafic [trafik] *m* traffic, trade; **trafic d'influence** influence peddling; **trafic routier** highway traffic

trafi·quant [trafikɑ̃] **-quante** [kɑ̃t] *mf* racketeer; **trafiquant en stupéfiants** dope peddler

trafiquer [trafike] *tr* to traffic in || *intr* to traffic; **trafiquer de** to traffic in or on

trafi·queur [trafikœr] **-queuse** [køz] *mf* racketeer

tragédie [traʒedi] f tragedy

tragé·dien [traʒedjɛ̃] **-dienne** [djen] mf tragedian

tragique [traʒik] adj tragic

trahir [trair] tr to betray

trahison [traizɔ̃] f betrayal; treason

train [trɛ̃] m pace, speed; manner, way; series; raft (of logs); (rr) train; (coll) row, racket; **être en train de +** inf to be in the act or process of + ger; (translated by a progressive form of the verb), e.g., **je suis en train d'écrire** I am writing; **mettre en train** to start; **train arrière** (aut) rear-axle assembly; (rr) rear car; **train avant** (aut) front-axle assembly; **train d'atterrissage** landing gear; **train de banlieue** suburban train; **train de marchandises** freight train; **train de vie** way of life; standard of living; **train direct** through train; **train omnibus** local train; **train sanitaire** military hospital train

traî·nant [trenɑ̃] **-nante** [nɑ̃t] adj trailing; creeping; drawling; languid

traî·nard [trenar] **-narde** [nard] mf straggler

traîne [tren] f train (of dress); dragnet; **à la traîne** dragging; straggling; in tow

traî·neau [treno] m (pl **-neaux**) sleigh; sled; sledge; dragnet

traînée [trene] f trail, train; (coll) streetwalker

traîner [trene] tr to drag, to lug; to drawl; to shuffle (the feet) || intr to drag; to straggle; to lie around || ref to crawl; to creep; to limp

traî·neur [trenœr] **-neuse** [nøz] mf straggler; loiterer

train-train [trɛ̃trɛ̃] m routine

traire [trer] §68 tr to milk

trait [tre] m arrow, dart; dash; stroke; feature (of face); trait, characteristic; trace (of harness); **avoir trait à** to refer to; **de trait** draft (horse); **d'un trait** in one gulp; **partir comme un trait** to be off like a shot; **tracer à grands traits** to trace in broad outlines; **trait d'esprit** witticism; **trait d'héroïsme** heroic deed; **trait d'union** hyphen; **trait pour trait** exactly

traitable [tretabl] adj tractable

traite [tret] f trade, traffic; milking; (com) draft; **tout d'une traite** at a single stretch

traité [trete] m treatise; treaty

traitement [tretmɑ̃] m treatment; salary; **mauvais traitements** affront, mistreatment

traiter [trete] tr to treat; to receive; **traiter qn de** to call s.o. (a name) || intr to negotiate; **traiter de** to deal with

traiteur [tretœr] m caterer; (obs) restaurateur

traî·tre [tretr] **-tresse** [tres] adj traitorous; treacherous; (coll) single || mf traitor; (theat) villain || f traitress

traîtrise [tretriz] f treachery

trajectoire [traʒektwar] f trajectory

trajet [traʒe] m distance, trip, passage; (aer) flight

tralala [tralala] m (coll) fuss

trame [tram] f weft; web (of life); conspiracy

tramer [trame] tr to weave; to hatch (a plot) || ref to be plotted

traminot [tramino] m traction-company employee

tramontane [tramɔ̃tan] f north wind; **perdre la tramontane** to lose one's bearings

tramp [trɑp] m tramp steamer

tramway [tramwe] m streetcar

tran·chant [trɑ̃ʃɑ̃] **-chante** [ʃɑ̃t] adj cutting; glaring; trenchant || m cutting edge; knife; side (of hand); **à double tranchant** or **à deux tranchants** two-edged

tranche [trɑ̃ʃ] f slice; section; portion, installment; group (of figures); cross section; **doré sur tranches** (bb) giltedged; (coll) gilded (e.g., youth); **une tranche de vie** a slice of life

tranchée [trɑ̃ʃe] f trench; **tranchées** colic

trancher [trɑ̃ʃe] tr to cut off; to slice; to decide, settle || intr to decide once and for all; to stand out; **trancher avec** to contrast with; **trancher dans le vif** to cut to the quick; (fig) to take drastic measures; **trancher de** (lit) to affect the manners of

tranquille [trɑ̃kil] adj quiet, tranquil; **laissez-moi tranquille** leave me alone; **soyez tranquille** don't worry

tranquilli·sant [trɑ̃kilizɑ̃] **-sante** [zɑ̃t] adj tranquilizing || m tranquilizer

tranquilliser [trɑ̃kilize] tr to tranquilize; to reassure || ref to calm down

tranquillité [trɑ̃kilite] f tranquillity

transaction [trɑ̃zaksjɔ̃] f transaction; compromise

transat [trɑ̃zat] m (coll) transatlantic liner; (coll) deck chair || **la Transat** (coll) the French Line

transatlantique [trɑ̃zatlɑ̃tik] adj & m transatlantic

transbordement [trɑ̃sbɔrdəmɑ̃] m transshipment, transfer

transborder [trɑ̃sbɔrde] tr to transship, to transfer

transbordeur [trɑ̃sbɔrdœr] m transporter bridge

transcender [trɑ̃sɑ̃de] tr & ref to transcend

transcription [trɑ̃skripsjɔ̃] f transcription

transcrire [trɑ̃skrir] §25 tr to transcribe; **transcrire en clair** to decode

transe [trɑ̃s] f apprehension, anxiety; trance; **être dans des transes** to be quaking in one's boots

transept [trɑ̃sept] m transept

transférer [trɑ̃sfere] §10 tr to transfer; to convey

transfert [trɑ̃sfer] m transfer, transference

transfo [trɑ̃sfo] m (coll) transformer

transforma·teur [trɑ̃sfɔrmatœr] **-trice** [tris] adj (elec) transforming || m (elec) transformer; **transformateur abaisseur (de tension)** step-down transformer; **transformateur de sonnerie** doorbell transformer; **transfor-**

mateur élévateur (de tension) step-up transformer

transformer [trãsfɔrme] tr & ref to transform

transfuge [trãsfyʒ] m turncoat

transfuser [trãsfyze] tr to transfuse; to instill

transfusion [trãsfyzjɔ̃] f transfusion

transgresser [trãsgrese] tr to transgress

transgression [trãsgresjɔ̃] f transgression

transhumer [trãzyme] tr & intr to move from winter to summer pasture

tran·si ·sie [trãzi], [trãsi] adj chilled to the bone; numb, transfixed (with fright)

transiger [trãziʒe] §38 intr to compromise

transistor [trãzistɔr] m transistor

transit [trãzit] m transit

transi·tif [trãzitif] -tive [tiv] adj transitive

transition [trãzisjɔ̃] f transition

transitoire [trãzitwar] adj transitory; transitional

translation [trãslɑsjɔ̃] f transfer, translation

translitérer [trãslitere] §10 tr to transliterate

translucide [trãslysid] adj translucent

transmetteur [trãsmɛtœr] adj masc transmitting || m (telg, telp) transmitter; transmetteur d'ordres (naut) engine-room telegraph

transmettre [trãsmɛtr] §42 tr to transmit; to transfer; (sports) to pass

transmission [trãsmisjɔ̃] f transmission; broadcast; transmission en différé recorded broadcast; transmission en direct live broadcast; transmissions (mil) signal corps

transmuer [trãsmɥe] tr to transmute

transmuter [trãsmyte] tr to transmute

transparaître [trãsparetr] §12 intr to show through

transpa·rent [trãsparã] -rente [rãt] adj transparent

transpercer [trãsperse] §51 tr to transfix

transpiration [trãspirɑsjɔ̃] f perspiration

transpirer [trãspire] tr to sweat || intr to sweat, perspire; to leak out (said of news)

transplanter [trãsplãte] tr to transplant

transport [trãspɔr] m transport; transportation; transport au cerveau cerebral hemorrhage

transpor·té -tée [trãspɔrte] adj enraptured, carried away

transporter [trãspɔrte] tr to transport

transposer [trãspoze] tr to transpose

transver·sal -sale [trãsversal] adj (pl -saux [so]) transversal; cross (street)

trapèze [trapez] m trapeze; trapezoid

trappe [trap] f trap door; pitfall, trap; Trappist monastery; Trappe Trappist order

trappeur [trapœr] m trapper

tra·pu -pue [trapy] adj stocky, squat

traque [trak] f driving of game

traquenard [traknar] m trap, booby trap, pitfall

traquer [trake] tr to hem in, to bring to bay

traumatique [tromatik] adj traumatic

tra·vail [travaj] m (pl -vaux [vo]) work; workmanship; en travail in labor; Travail Labor; travail à la pièce, travail à la tâche piecework; travail d'équipe teamwork; travail de Romain herculean task; travaux forcés hard labor; travaux ménagers housework || m (pl -vails) stocks (for horses)

travail·lé -lée [travaje] adj finely wrought, elaborate; labored

travailler [travaje] tr to work; to worry || intr to work; to warp (said of wood)

travail·leur [travajœr] travail·leuse [travajøz] adj hardworking || mf worker, toiler

travailliste [travajist] adj & mf Labourite (Brit)

travée [trave] f span (of bridge); row of seats; (archit) bay

traveling [travliŋ] m (mov, telv) dolly (for camera)

travers [traver] m breadth; fault, failing; à travers across, through; de travers awry; en travers de across; par le travers de abreast of

traverse [travers] f crossbeam; cross street; setback; rung (of ladder); (rr) tie; de traverse cross (e.g., street); mettre à la traverse de to oppose

traversée [traverse] f crossing

traverser [traverse] tr to cross; to cut across

traver·sier [traversje] -sière [sjer] adj cross, crossing

traversin [traversē] m bolster (of bed)

traves·ti ·tie [travesti] adj disguised; costume (ball) || m fancy costume, disguise; transvestite; female impersonator

travestir [travestir] tr to travesty; to disguise

travestissement [travestismã] m travesty; disguise

trébucher [trebyʃe] intr to stumble

tréfiler [trefile] tr to wiredraw

trèfle [trefl] m clover; trefoil; cloverleaf (intersection); (cards) club; (cards) clubs

tréfonds [trefɔ̃] m secret depths

treillage [trejaʒ] m trellis

treillager [trejaʒe] §38 tr to trellis

treille [trej] f grape arbor

treillis [treji] m latticework; iron grating; denim; treillis métallique wire netting

treillisser [trejise] tr to trellis

treize [trez] adj & pron thirteen; the Thirteenth, e.g., Jean treize John the Thirteenth || m thirteen; thirteenth (in dates); treize à la douzaine baker's dozen

treizième [trezjem] adj, pron (masc, fem), & m thirteenth

tréma [trema] m dieresis

tremble [trãbl] m aspen (tree)

tremblement [trãblemã] m trembling; tremblement de terre earthquake

trembler [trãble] intr to tremble

trembleur [trãblœr] *m* vibrator, buzzer; (rel) Shaker; (rel) Quaker

trembloter [trãblɔte] *intr* to quiver; to quaver

trémie [tremi] *f* hopper

trémoussement [tremusmã] *m* fluttering, flutter; jiggling, jiggle

trémousser [tremuse] *ref* to flutter; to jiggle; (coll) to bustle

trempage [trãpaʒ] *m* soaking

trempe [trãp] *f* temper; soaking; (slang) scolding

trempée [trãpe] *f* tempering

tremper [trãpe] *tr* to temper; to dilute; to dunk ‖ *intr* to soak; to become involved (*in, e.g., a crime*)

trempette [trãpɛt] *f*—**faire la trempette** to dunk; **faire trempette** to take a dip

tremplin [trãplɛ̃] *m* springboard, diving board; trampoline; ski jump; (fig) springboard

trentaine [trãten] *f* age of thirty; **une trentaine de** about thirty

trente [trãt] *adj & pron* thirty; **sur son trente et un** (coll) all spruced up; **trente et un** thirty-one; **trente et unième** thirty-first ‖ *m* thirty; thirtieth (*in dates*); **trente et un** thirty-one; thirty-first (*in dates*); **trente et unième** thirty-first

trente-deux [trãtdø] *adj, pron, & m* thirty-two

trente-deuxième [trãtdøzjem] *adj, pron (masc, fem), & m* thirty-second

trente-six [trãtsi(s)] *adj, pron, & m* thirty-six; **tous les trente-six du mois** (coll) once in a blue moon

trentième [trãtjem] *adj, pron (masc, fem), & m* thirtieth

trépas [trepɑ] *m* (lit) death; **passer de vie à trépas** (lit) to pass away

trépasser [trepase] *intr* (lit) to die

trépied [trepje] *m* tripod

trépigner [trepiɲe] *intr* to stamp one's feet

très [tre] *adv* very; **le très honorable** the Right Honorable

trésor [trezɔr] *m* treasure; **Trésor** Treasury

trésorerie [trezɔrri] *f* treasury

tréso·rier [trezɔrje] **-rière** [rjer] *mf* treasurer

tressaillement [tresajmã] *m* start, quiver

tressaillir [tresajir] §69 *intr* to give a start, to quiver

tressauter [tresote] *intr* to start

tresse [tres] *f* tress

tresser [trese] *tr* to braid, to plait; to weave (*e.g., a basket*)

tré·teau [treto] *m* (*pl* **-teaux**) trestle; **sur les tréteaux** (theat) on the boards

treuil [trœj] *m* windlass; winch

trêve [trev] *f* truce; respite; **trêve de . . .** that's enough . . .

tri [tri] *m* sorting

triage [trijaʒ] *m* sorting, selection; classification; (rr) shifting

triangle [trijãgl] *m* triangle

tribord [tribɔr] *m* starboard

tribu [triby] *f* tribe

tribu·nal [tribynal] *m* (*pl* **-naux** [no]) tribunal, court; **en plein tribunal** in open court; **tribunal de police** police court; **tribunaux pour enfants** juvenile courts

tribune [tribyn] *f* rostrum, tribune; gallery; grandstand; **monter à la tribune** to take the floor; **tribune des journalistes** press box; **tribune d'orgue** organ loft; **tribune libre** open forum

tribut [triby] *m* tribute

tributaire [tribyter] *adj & m* tributary; **être tributaire de** to be dependent upon

tricher [triʃe] *tr & intr* to cheat

tricherie [triʃri] *f* cheating

tri·cheur [triʃœr] **-cheuse** [ʃøz] *mf* cheater; **tricheur professionnel** card-sharper

tricolore [trikɔlɔr] *adj & m* tricolor

tricot [triko] *m* knitting; knitted garment

tricotage [trikɔtaʒ] *m* knitting

tricoter [trikɔte] *tr & intr* to knit

trier [trije] *tr* to pick out, to screen; **trier sur le volet** to hand-pick

trieur [trijœr] **trieuse** [trijøz] *mf* sorter ‖ *m & f* (mach) sorter

trigonométrie [trigɔnɔmetri] *f* trigonometry

trille [trij] *m* trill

triller [trije] *tr & intr* to trill

trillion [triljɔ̃] *m* quintillion (U.S.A.); trillion (Brit)

trilogie [trilɔʒi] *f* trilogy

trimbaler [trɛ̃bale] *tr* to cart around

trimer [trime] *intr* to slave

trimestre [trimestr] *m* quarter (*of a year*); quarter's salary; quarter's rent; (educ) term

tringle [trɛ̃gl] *f* rod; **tringle de rideau** curtain rod

trinité [trinite] *f* trinity

trinquer [trɛ̃ke] *intr* to clink glasses, to toast; (slang) to drink; **trinquer avec** to hobnob with

trio [trijo] *m* trio

triom·phant [trijɔ̃fɑ̃] **-phante** [fɑ̃t] *adj* triumphant

triomphe [trijɔ̃f] *m* triumph; **faire triomphe à** to welcome in triumph

tripar·ti **-tie** [triparti] *adj* tripartite

tripartit [tripartit] *adj* tripartite

tripatouiller [tripatuje] *tr* (coll) to tamper with

tripette [tripet] *f*—**ça ne vaut pas tripette** it's not worth a wooden nickel

triple [tripl] *adj & m* triple

tri·plé **-plée** [triple] *mf* triplet

tripler [triple] *tr & intr* to triple

triplicata [triplikata] *m invar* triplicate

tripot [tripo] *m* gambling den; house of ill repute

tripoter [tripɔte] *tr* to finger, toy with ‖ *intr* to dabble, to potter around; to rummage

trique [trik] *f* (coll) cudgel

triste [trist] *adj* sad

tristesse [tristes] *f* sadness, sorrow

triturer [trityre] *tr* to pulverize, to grind ‖ *ref*—**se triturer la cervelle** to rack one's brain

tri·vial **-viale** [trivjal] *adj* (*pl* **-viaux** [vjo]) trivial; vulgar, coarse

trivialité [trivjalite] ƒ triviality; vulgarity, coarseness

troc [trɔk] m barter; swap; **troc pour troc** even up

troglodyte [trɔglɔdit] m cave dweller; (orn) wren

trognon [trɔɲɔ̃] m core; (slang) darling, pet

Troie [trwa], [trwa] ƒ Troy

trois [trwa] adj & pron three; the Third, e.g., **Jean trois** John the Third; **trois heures** three o'clock || m three; third (in dates)

troisième [trwazjɛm] adj, pron (masc, fem), & m third

trolley [trɔle] m trolley

trolleybus [trɔlebys] m trackless trolley

trombe [trɔ̃b] ƒ waterspout; **entrer en trombe** to dash in; **trombe d'eau** deluge

trombone [trɔ̃bɔn] m trombone; paper clip

trompe [trɔ̃p] ƒ horn; trunk (of elephant); beak (of insect); **trompe d'Eustache** Eustachian tube

trompe-la-mort [trɔ̃plamɔr] mƒ invar daredevil

trompe-l'œil [trɔ̃plœj] m invar dummy effect; (coll) bluff, fake; **en trompe-l'œil** in perspective

tromper [trɔ̃pe] tr to deceive, to cheat || ref to be wrong; **se tromper de** to be mistaken about

tromperie [trɔ̃pri] ƒ deceit; fraud; illusion

trompeter [trɔ̃pte] §34 tr & intr to trumpet

trompette [trɔ̃pet] m trumpeter || ƒ trumpet; **en trompette** turned up

trom·peur [trɔ̃pœr] **-peuse** [pøz] adj false, lying || mƒ deceiver

tronc [trɔ̃] m trunk; (slang) head; **tronc des pauvres** poor box

tronche [trɔ̃ʃ] ƒ (slang) noodle

tronçon [trɔ̃sɔ̃] m stump; section (e.g., of track)

trône [tron] m throne

trôner [trone] intr to sit in state || ref —**se trôner sur** to lord it over

tronquer [trɔ̃ke] tr to truncate, to cut off; to mutilate

trop [tro] m excess; too much; **de trop** too much; to excess; in the way, e.g., **il est de trop ici** he is in the way here; **par trop** altogether, excessively; **trop de . . .** too much . . . ; too many . . . || adv too; too much; **trop lourd** overweight

trophée [trofe] m trophy

tropi·cal -cale [trɔpikal] adj (pl -caux [ko]) tropical

trop-plein [trɔplɛ̃] m (pl -pleins) overflow

troquer [trɔke] tr to barter; **troquer contre** to swap for

trot [tro] m trot; **au trot** at a trot; (coll) on the double, quickly

trotte [trɔt] ƒ (coll) quite a distance to walk

trotter [trɔte] intr to trot

trot·teur [trɔtœr] **-teuse** [trɔtøz] mƒ (turf) trotter || ƒ second hand; **trotteuse centrale** sweep-second

trottin [trɔtɛ̃] m errand girl

trottinette [trɔtinet] ƒ scooter

trottoir [trɔtwar] m sidewalk; **faire le trottoir** to walk the streets (said of prostitute); **trottoir roulant** escalator

trou [tru] m hole; pothole; eye (of needle); gap; jerkwater town; **faire son trou** to feather one's nest; **faire un trou à la lune** to fly the coop; **trou d'air** air pocket; **trou de clef** keyhole (of clock); **trou de la serrure** keyhole; **trou d'obus** shell hole; **trou du souffleur** prompter's box; **trou individuel** (mil) foxhole

trouble [trubl] adj muddy, cloudy, turbid (liquid); murky (sky); misty (glass); blurred (image; sight); dim (light); vague, disquieting || m disquiet; unrest; trouble (illness)

trouble-fête [trublfet] mƒ invar wet blanket, kill-joy

troubler [truble] tr to upset, trouble; to make muddy; to disturb; to make cloudy; to blur || ref to become muddy or cloudy; to lose one's composure

trouée [true] ƒ gap, breach; (mil) breakthrough

trouille [truj] ƒ—**avoir la trouille** (slang) to get cold feet

troupe [trup] ƒ troop; band, party; (theat) troupe

trou·peau [trupo] m (pl -peaux) flock; herd; **attention aux troupeaux** (public sign) cattle crossing

troupier [trupje] m (coll) soldier; **jurer comme un troupier** to swear like a trooper

trousse [trus] ƒ case, kit; **avoir qn à ses trousses** to have s.o. at one's heels; **trousse de première urgence** first-aid kit

trous·seau [truso] m (pl -seaux) trousseau; outfit; bunch (of keys)

troussequin [truskɛ̃] m cantle

trousser [truse] tr to turn up; to tuck up; to polish off; (culin) to truss || ref to lift one's skirts

trouvaille [truvaj] ƒ find

trouver [truve] tr to find || ref to be found; to find oneself; to be, e.g., **où se trouve-t-il?** where is he?; **il se trouve que . . .** it happens that . . . ; **se trouver mal** to feel ill

troyen [trwajɛ̃] **troyenne** [trwajen] adj Trojan || (cap) m Trojan

truand [tryɑ̃] **truande** [tryɑ̃d] adj & m good-for-nothing

truc [tryk] m gadget, device; (coll) trick, gimmick; (coll) thing; (coll) what's-his-name

truchement [tryʃmɑ̃] m spokesman; interpreter; **par le truchement de** thanks to, through

trucu·lent [trykylɑ̃] **-lente** [lɑ̃t] adj truculent

truelle [tryel] ƒ trowel

truffe [tryf] ƒ truffle

truie [trɥi] ƒ sow

truisme [tryism] m truism

truite [trɥit] ƒ trout

tru·meau [trymo] m (pl -meaux) trumeau (mirror with painting above in same frame)

truquage [tryka3] *m* faking
truquer [tryke] *tr* to fake; to cook (*the accounts*); to stack (*the deck*); to load (*the dice*); to fix (*the outcome of a fight*) || *intr* to resort to fakery
trust [trœst] *m* trust, holding company
T.S.F. [teesef] *f* (letterword) (**télégraphie sans fil**) wireless; radio
t. s. v. p. *abbr* (**tournez s'il vous plaît**) over (*please turn the page*)
tu [ty] §87; **être à tu et à toi avec** to hobnob with
T.U. [tey] *m* (letterword) (**temps universel**) universal time, Greenwich Mean Time
tube [tyb] *m* tube; pipe; (anat) duct; (slang) hit
tubercule [tyberkyl] *m* tubercle; tuber
tuberculose [tyberkyloz] *f* tuberculosis
tue-mouches [tymu] *m invar* flypaper
tuer [tɥe] *tr* to kill || *ref* to be killed; to kill oneself
tuerie [tyri] *f* slaughter
tue-tête [tytet]—**à tue-tête** at the top of one's voice
tuile [tɥil] *f* tile; (coll) nasty blow
tuilerie [tɥilri] *f* tileworks
tulipe [tylip] *f* tulip
tumeur [tymœr] *f* tumor
tumulte [tymylt] *m* tumult, hubbub
tungstène [tœksten] *m* tungsten
tunique [tynik] *f* tunic
tunnel [tynel] *m* tunnel; **passer sous un tunnel** to go through a tunnel; **tunnel aérodynamique** wind tunnel
turban [tyrbã] *m* turban
turbine [tyrbin] *f* turbine
turbu‧lent [tyrbylã] **-lente** [lãt] *adj* turbulent
turc turque [tyrk] *adj* Turkish || *m* Turkish (*language*) || (*cap*) *mf* Turk (*person*)

turf [tyrf] *m*—**le turf** the turf, the track
turfiste [tyrfist] *m* turfman, racegoer
turlututu [tyrlytyty] *interj* fiddlesticks!, nonsense!
Turquie [tyrki] *f* Turkey; **la Turquie** Turkey
turquoise [tyrkwaz] *m* turquoise (*color*) || *f* turquoise (*stone*)
tutelle [tytel] *f* guardianship, tutelage; trusteeship
tu‧teur [tytœr] **-trice** [tris] *mf* guardian || *m* (hort) stake, prop
tutoyer [tytwaje] §47 *tr* to thou, to address familiarly || *ref* to thou each other, to be on a first-name basis
tuyau [tɥijo], [tyjo] *m* (*pl* **tuyaux**) pipe, tube; fluting; (coll) tip; **tuyau d'arrosage** garden hose; **tuyau d'échappement** exhaust; **tuyau d'incendie** fire hose
tuyauter [tɥijote], [tyjote] *tr* to flute; (coll) to tip off || *intr* (coll) to crib
tuyauterie [tɥijotri] *f* pipe mill; piping; (aut) manifold; **tuyauterie d'admission** intake manifold; **tuyauterie d'échappement** exhaust manifold
tympan [tẽpã] *m* eardrum; (archit, mus) tympanum
type [tip] *m* type; (coll) fellow, character
typer [tipe] *tr* to type
typhoïde [tifɔid] *adj & f* typhoid
typhon [tifɔ̃] *m* typhoon
typique [tipik] *adj* typical; South American (*music*)
typographie [tipɔgrafi] *f* typography
typographique [tipɔgrafik] *adj* typographic(al)
tyran [tirã] *m* tyrant; (orn) kingbird
tyrannie [tirani] *f* tyranny
tyrannique [tiranik] *adj* tyrannic(al)

U

U, u [y], *[y] *m invar* twenty-first letter of the French alphabet
Ukraine [ykren] *f* Ukraine
ukrai‧nien [ykrenjẽ] **-nienne** [njen] *adj* Ukrainian || *m* Ukrainian (*language*) || (*cap*) *mf* Ukrainian (*person*)
ulcère [ylser] *m* ulcer, sore
ulcérer [ylsere] §10 *tr* to ulcerate; to embitter || *ref* to ulcerate; to fester
ulté‧rieur -rieure [ylterjœr] *adj* ulterior; subsequent
ultimatum [yltimatɔm] *m* ultimatum
ultime [yltim] *adj* ultimate, final
ultra-court [yltrakur] **-courte** [kurt] *adj* (electron) ultrashort
ultravio‧let [yltravjɔle] **-lette** [let] *adj & m* ultraviolet
ululer [ylyle] *intr* to hoot
un [œ̃] **une** [yn] *adj & pron* one; **l'un à l'autre** to each other, to one another; **l'un et l'autre** both; **l'un l'autre** each other, one another; ni

l'un ni l'autre neither, neither one; **un à un** one by one; **une heure une** o'clock || *art indef* a || *m* one || *f*—**la une** the front page
unanime [ynanim] *adj* unanimous
unanimité [ynanimite] *f* unanimity
Unesco [ynesko] *f* (acronym) (**Organisation des Nations Unies pour l'Éducation, la Science et la Culture**) —**l'Unesco** UNESCO
u‧ni -nie [yni] *adj* united; smooth; level; uneventful; plain; solid (*color*); together (*said, e.g., of the hands of a clock*) || *m* plain cloth
unicorne [ynikɔrn] *m* unicorn
unification [ynifikasjɔ̃] *f* unification
unifier [ynifje] *tr* to unify || *ref* to consolidate, merge; to become unified
uniforme [ynifɔrm] *adj & m* uniform
uniformiser [ynifɔrmize] *tr* to make uniform
uniformité [ynifɔrmite] *f* uniformity

unijambiste [yniʒãbist] *adj* one-legged ‖ *mf* one-legged person

unilaté·ral -rale [ynilateral] *adj* (*pl* **-raux** [ro]) unilateral

union [ynjɔ̃] *f* union; **union libre** common-law marriage

unique [ynik] *adj* only, single; unique

unir [ynir] *tr & ref* to unite

unisson [ynisɔ̃] *m* unison

unitaire [yniter] *adj* unit

unité [ynite] *f* unity; unit; battleship; (coll) one million old francs

univers [yniver] *m* universe

univer·sel -selle [yniversɛl] *adj & m* universal

universitaire [yniversiter] *adj* university

université [yniversite] *f* university

uranium [yranjɔm] *m* uranium

ur·bain -baine [yrbɛ̃] **-baine** [ben] *adj* urban; urbane

urbaniser [yrbanize] *tr* to urbanize

urbanisme [yrbanism] *m* city planning

urbaniste [yrbanist] *adj* zoning (*ordinance*) ‖ *mf* city planner

urbanité [yrbanite] *f* urbanity

urètre [yretr] *m* urethra

urgence [yrʒãs] *f* urgency; emergency; emergency case; **d'urgence** emergency (*e.g., hospital ward*); rush away, without delay

ur·gent [yrʒã] **-gente** [ʒãt] *adj* urgent; emergency (*case*); (formula on letter or envelope) rush ‖ *m* urgent matter

urinaire [yriner] *adj* urinary

uri·nal [yrinal] *m* (*pl* **-naux** [no]) urinal (*for use in bed*)

urine [yrin] *f* urine

uriner [yrine] *tr & intr* to urinate

urinoir [yrinwar] *m* urinal (*place*)

urne [yrn] *f* urn; ballot box; **aller aux urnes** to go to the polls

urologie [yrɔlɔʒi] *f* urology

U.R.S.S. [yereses] *f* (letterword) (**Union des Républiques Socialistes Soviétiques**) U.S.S.R.

Ursse [yrs] *f* (acronym) (**Union des Républiques Socialistes Soviétiques**) U.S.S.R.

urticaire [yrtiker] *f* hives

urubu [yryby] *m* turkey vulture

us [ys] *mpl*—**les us et (les) coutumes** the manners and customs

U.S. [yes] *adj* (letterword) (**United States**) U.S., e.g., **l'aviation U.S.** U.S. aviation

U.S.A. [yesa] *mpl* (letterword) (**United States of America**) U.S.A.

usage [yzaʒ] *m* usage; custom; use; **faire de l'usage** to wear well; **hors d'usage** outmoded; (gram) obsolete; **manquer d'usage** to lack good breeding; **usage du monde** good breeding, savoir-vivre

usa·gé -gée [yzaʒe] *adj* secondhand; worn-out, used

usa·ger [yzaʒe] **-gère** [ʒer] *mf* user

usant [yzã] **usante** [yzãt] *adj* exhausting, wearing

u·sé -sée [yze] *adj* worn-out; trite, commonplace

user [yze] *tr* to wear out; to wear away; to ruin (*e.g., health*) ‖ *intr*—**en user bien avec** to treat well; **user de** to use ‖ *ref* to wear out

usine [yzin] *f* factory, mill, plant; **usine à gaz** gasworks

usiner [yzine] *tr* to machine, to tool

usi·nier [yzinje] **-nière** [njer] *adj* manufacturing; factory (*town*) ‖ *m* manufacturer

usi·té -tée [yzite] *adj* used, in use; **peu usité** out of use, rare

ustensile [ystãsil] *m* utensil, implement

u·suel -suelle [yzɥel] *adj* usual

usure [yzyr] *f* usury; wear; wear and tear

usurper [yzyrpe] *tr* to usurp

utérus [yterys] *m* uterus, womb

utilisable [ytilizabl] *adj* usable

utilisa·teur [ytilizatœr] **-trice** [tris] *mf* user

utilitaire [ytiliter] *adj* utilitarian; utility (*vehicle, goods, etc.*)

utilité [ytilite] *f* utility, usefulness, use; (theat) support; (theat) supporting rôle; **jouer les utilités** (fig) to play second fiddle; **utilités** (theat) small parts

utopique [ytɔpik] *adj* utopian

utopiste [ytɔpist] *mf* utopian

V

V, v [ve] *m invar* twenty-second letter of the French alphabet

v. *abbr* (**voir**) see; (**volume**) vol.

vacance [vakãs] *f* vacancy, opening; **vacances** vacation

vacancier [vakãsje] *m* vacationist

va·cant [vakã] **-cante** [kãt] *adj* vacant

vacarme [vakarm] *m* din, racket

vacation [vakasjɔ̃] *f* investigation; **vacations** fee; recess

vaccin [vaksɛ̃] *m* vaccine

vaccination [vaksinasjɔ̃] *f* vaccination

vaccine [vaksin] *f* cowpox

vacciner [vaksine] *tr* to vaccinate

vache [vaʃ] *adj* embarrassing (*question*); cantankerous (*person*) ‖ *f* cow; cowhide; (*woman*) (slang) bitch; (*man*) (slang) swine, rat; (*policeman*) (slang) flatfoot, bull; **en vache leather** (*e.g., suitcase*); **manger de la vache enragée** (coll) not to have a red cent to one's name; **oh, la vache!** damn it!; **parler français comme une vache espagnole** (coll) to murder the French language; **vache à eau** canvas bucket (*for camping*); **vache à lait** milch cow; (coll) gull, sucker

vachement [vaʃmã] *adv* (slang) tremendously

va·cher [vaʃe] **-chère** [ʃer] *mf* cowherd

vacherie [vaʃri] *f* cowshed; dairy farm; (coll) dirty trick

vachette [vaʃet] *f* young calf; calf (*leather*)

vaciller [vasije] *intr* to vacillate, waver; to flicker; to totter

vacuité [vakuite] *f* vacuity, emptiness

vacuum [vakyɔm] *m* vacuum

vade-mecum [vademekɔm] *m invar* handbook, vade mecum

vadrouille [vadruj] *f* (naut) mop, swab; (slang) bender, spree

vadrouiller [vadruje] *intr* (slang) to ramble around, to gad about

vadrouil·leur [vadrujœr] **vadrouil·leuse** [vadrujøz] *mf* (slang) rounder

va-et-vient [vaevjɛ̃] *m invar* backward-and-forward motion; hurrying to and fro; comings and goings; ferryboat; (elec) two-way switch

vaga·bond [vagabɔ̃] **-bonde** [bɔ̃d] *adj* vagabond || *mf* vagabond, tramp

vagabondage [vagabɔ̃daʒ] *m* vagrancy; **vagabondage interdit** (public sign) no loitering, no begging

vagabonder [vagabɔ̃de] *intr* to wander about, to roam, to tramp

vagir [vaʒir] *intr* to cry, wail

vague [vag] *adj* vague; vacant (*look; lot*); waste (*land*) || *m* vagueness; (fig) space, thin air || *f* wave; **la nouvelle vague** the wave of the future; **vague de fond** ground swell

vaguemestre [vagmestr] *m* (mil, nav) mail clerk

vaguer [vage] *intr* to wander

vaillance [vajɑ̃s] *f* valor

vail·lant [vajɑ̃] **vail·lante** [vajɑ̃t] *adj* valiant; up to scratch

vain [vɛ̃] **vaine** [ven] *adj* vain; **en vain** in vain

vaincre [vɛ̃kr] §70 *tr* to defeat, conquer; to overcome (*fear, instinct, etc.*) || *intr* to conquer || *ref* to control oneself

vain·cu **-cue** [vɛ̃ky] *adj* defeated, beaten, conquered || *mf* loser

vainqueur [vɛ̃kœr] *adj masc* victorious || *m* victor, winner

vairon [verɔ̃] *adj masc* whitish (*eye*); **vairons** of different colors (*said of eyes*) || *m* (ichth) minnow

vais·seau [veso] *m* (*pl* **-seaux**) vessel; nave (*of church*); **vaisseau amiral** flagship; **vaisseau sanguin** blood vessel; **vaisseau spatial** spaceship

vaisseau-école [vesoekɔl] *m* (*pl* **vaisseaux-écoles**) (nav) training ship

vaisselier [vesəlje] *m* china closet

vaisselle [vesel] *f* dishes; **faire la vaisselle** to wash the dishes; **vaisselle plate** plate (*of gold or silver*)

val [val] *m* (*pl* **vaux** [vo] or **vals**) (obs) valley; **à val** going down the valley; **à val de** (obs) down from

valable [valabl] *adj* valid; worthwhile (*e.g., experience*)

valence [valɑ̃s] *f* (chem) valence

valen·tin [valɑ̃tɛ̃] **-tine** [tin] *mf* valentine (*sweetheart*)

valet [vale] *m* valet; holdfast, clamp; (cards) jack; **valet de chambre** valet; **valet de ferme** hired man; **valet de pied** footman

valeur [valœr] *f* value, worth, merit; valor; (*person, thing, or quality worth having*) asset; (com) security, stock; **de valeur** able; valuable; (Canad) too bad, unfortunate; **envoyer en valeur déclarée** to insure (*a package*); **mettre en valeur** to develop (*e.g., a region*); to set off, enhance

valeu·reux [valœrø] **-reuse** [røz] *adj* valorous, brave

validation [validɑsjɔ̃] *f* validation

valide [valid] *adj* valid; fit, able-bodied

valider [valide] *tr* to validate

validité [validite] *f* validity

valise [valiz] *f* suitcase; **faire ses valises** to pack, to pack one's bags; **valise diplomatique** diplomatic pouch

vallée [vale] *f* valley

vallon [valɔ̃] *m* vale, dell

valoir [valwar] §71 *tr* to equal; **un service en vaut un autre** one good turn deserves another; **valoir q.ch. à qn** to get or bring s.o. s.th., e.g., **cela lui a valu une amélioration** that got him a raise; e.g., **la condamnation lui a valu cinq ans de prison** the verdict brought him five years in prison || *intr* to be worth; **autant vaut y renoncer** might as well give up; **cela ne vaut rien** it's worth nothing; **faire valoir** to set off to advantage; to use to advantage; to develop (*one's land*); to invest (*funds, capital*); to put forward (*one's reasons*); **faire valoir que . . .** to argue that . . . || *impers*—**il vaut mieux** it would be better to, e.g., **il vaut mieux attendre** it would be better to wait; **mieux vaut tard que jamais** better late than never || *ref*—**les deux se valent** one is as good as the other

valse [vals] *f* waltz

valser [valse] *tr & intr* to waltz

valve [valv] *f* (anat, bot, zool) valve; (elec) vacuum tube

valvule [valvyl] *f* valve

vamp [vãp] *f* vamp

vamper [vãpe] *tr* (coll) to vamp

vampire [vãpir] *m* vampire

van [vã] *m* van (*for moving horses*)

vandale [vãdal] *adj* vandal; Vandal || *m* vandal || (*cap*) *mf* Vandal

vandalisme [vãdalism] *m* vandalism

vanille [vanij] *f* vanilla

vani·teux [vanitø] **-teuse** [tøz] *adj* vain, conceited

vanne [van] *f* sluice gate, floodgate; butterfly valve; (slang) gibe

van·neau [vano] *m* (*pl* **-neaux**) (orn) lapwing

vanner [vane] *tr* to winnow; to tire out

vannerie [vanri] *f* basketry

vannier [vanje] *m* basket maker

van·tail [vãtaj] *m* (*pl* **-taux** [to]) leaf (*of door, shutter, sluice gate, etc.*)

van·tard [vɑ̃tar] **-tarde** [tard] *adj* bragging, boastful || *mf* braggart

vantardise [vɑ̃tardiz] *f* bragging, boasting

vanter [vɑ̃te] *tr* to praise; to boost, to push (*a product on the market*) || *ref* to brag, to boast

va-nu-pieds [vanypje] *mf invar* (coll) tramp

vapeur [vapœr] *m* steamship || *f* steam; vapor, mist; **à la vapeur** steamed (*e.g., potatoes*); under steam; (coll) at full speed; **à vapeur** steam (*e.g., engine*); **vapeurs** low spirits

vaporisateur [vaporizatœr] *m* atomizer, spray

vaporiser [vaporize] *tr & ref* to vaporize; to spray

vaquer [vake] *intr* to take a recess; **vaquer à** to attend to || *impers*—**il vaque** there is vacant

varappe [varap] *f* cliff; rock climbing

varech [varek] *m* wrack, seaweed

vareuse [varøz] *f* (mil) blouse; (nav) peacoat

variable [varjabl] *adj & f* variable

va·riant [varjɑ̃] **-riante** [rjɑ̃t] *adj & f* variant

variation [varjɑsjɔ̃] *f* variation

varice [varis] *f* varicose veins

varicelle [varisel] *f* chicken pox

va·rié -riée [varje] *adj* varied

varier [varje] *tr & intr* to vary

variété [varjete] *f* variety; **variétés** selections (*from literary works*); vaudeville

variole [varjɔl] *f* smallpox

vari·queux [varikø] **-queuse** [køz] *adj* varicose

Varsovie [varsɔvi] *f* Warsaw

vase [vɑs] *m* vase; vessel; **en vase clos** shut up; in an airtight chamber; **vase de nuit** chamber pot || *f* mud, slime

vaseline [vazlin] *f* vaseline

va·seux [vazø] **-seuse** [zøz] *adj* muddy, slimy; (coll) all in, tired; (coll) fuzzy, obscure

vasistas [vazistɑs] *m* transom

vasouiller [vazuje] *tr* (coll) to make a mess of || *intr* (coll) to go badly

vasque [vask] *f* basin (*of fountain*)

vas·sal -sale [vasal] (*pl* **vas·saux** [vaso] **-sales**) *adj & mf* vassal

vaste [vast] *adj* vast

vastement [vastəmɑ̃] *adv* (coll) very

Vatican [vatikɑ̃] *m* Vatican

vaticane [vatikan] *adj fem* Vatican

va-tout [vatu] *m*—**jouer son va-tout** to stake one's all

vaudeville [vodvil] *m* vaudeville (*light theatrical piece interspersed with songs*); (obs) satirical song

vaudou [vodu] *adj invar & m* voodoo

vau-l'eau [volo]—**à vau-l'eau** downstream; **s'en aller à vau-l'eau** (fig) to go to pot

vau·rien [vorjɛ̃] **-rienne** [rjɛn] *mf* good-for-nothing

vautour [votur] *m* vulture

vautrer [votre] *ref* to wallow

veau [vo] *m* (*pl* **veaux**) calf; veal; calfskin; (coll) lazybones, dope; **pleurer comme un veau** to cry like a baby; **veau marin** seal

vé·cu -cue [veky] *adj* true to life

vedette [vədɛt] *f* patrol boat; scout; lead, star; **en vedette** in the limelight; **mettre en vedette** to headline, to highlight; **vedette de l'écran** movie star; **vedette du petit écran** television star

végé·tal -tale [veʒetal] (*pl* **-taux** [to]) *adj* vegetable, vegetal || *m* vegetable

végéta·rien [veʒetarjɛ̃] **-rienne** [rjɛn] *adj & mf* vegetarian

végétation [veʒetɑsjɔ̃] *f* vegetation; **végétations (adénoïdes)** adenoids

végéter [veʒete] §10 *intr* to vegetate

véhémence [veemɑ̃s] *f* vehemence

véhé·ment [veemɑ̃] **-mente** [mɑ̃t] *adj* vehement

véhicule [veikyl] *m* vehicle

veille [vej] *f* watch, vigil; wakefulness; **à la veille de** on the eve of; just before; on the verge or point of; **la veille de** the eve of; the day before; **la Veille de Noël** Christmas Eve; **la Veille du jour de l'An** New Year's Eve; **veilles** sleepless nights, late nights; night work

veillée [veje] *f* evening; social evening; **veillée funèbre, veillée du corps** wake

veiller [veje] *tr* to sit up with, to watch over || *intr* to sit up, to stay up; to keep watch; **veiller à** to look after, to see to

veil·leur [vejœr] **veil·leuse** [vejøz] *mf* watcher || *m* watchman; **veilleur de nuit** night watchman || *f see* **veilleuse**

veilleuse [vejøz] *f* night light; rushlight; pilot light; **mettre en veilleuse** to turn down low; to dim (*the headlights*); to slow down (*production in a factory*)

vei·nard [venar] **-narde** [nard] *adj* (coll) lucky || *mf* (coll) lucky person

veine [ven] *f* vein; luck; **veine alors!** (coll) swell!

veiner [vene] *tr* to vein

vei·neux [venø] **-neuse** [nøz] *adj* veined; venous

vélaire [veler] *adj & f* velar

vêler [vele] *intr* to calve

vélin [velɛ̃] *m* vellum

velléitaire [veleiter] *adj & mf* erratic

velléité [veleite] *f* stray impulse, fancy; **velléité de sourire** slight smile

vélo [velo] *m* bike; **faire du vélo** to go bicycle riding

vélocité [velɔsite] *f* velocity; speed; agility

vélomoteur [velɔmɔtœr] *m* motorbike

velours [vəlur] *m* velvet; **velours côtelé** corduroy

velou·té -tée [vəlute] *adj* velvety || *m* velvetiness

velouter [vəlute] *tr* to make velvety

ve·lu -lue [vəly] *adj* hairy

vélum [veləm] *m* awning

velvet [velvet] *m* velveteen

venaison [vənezɔ̃] *f* venison

ve·nant [vənɑ̃] **-nante** [nɑ̃t] *adj* coming; thriving || *mf* comer; **à tout venant** to all comers

vendange [vãdãʒ] *f* grape harvest; vintage

vendanger [vãdãʒe] §38 *tr* to pick (*the grapes*) ‖ *intr* to harvest grapes

ven·deur [vãdœr] **-deuse** [døz] *mf* seller, vendor; salesclerk; **vendeur ambulant** peddler ‖ *m* salesman ‖ *f* salesgirl, saleslady

vendre [vãdr] *tr* to sell; to sell out, to betray; **à vendre** for sale; **vendre au détail** to retail; **vendre aux enchères** to auction off; **vendre en gros** to wholesale ‖ *ref* to sell; to sell oneself, to sell out

vendredi [vãdrədi] *m* Friday; **vendredi saint** Good Friday

ven·du -due [vãdy] *adj* sold; corrupt ‖ *mf* traitor

véné·neux [venenø] **-neuse** [nøz] *adj* poisonous

vénérable [venerabl] *adj* venerable

vénérer [venere] §10 *tr* to venerate

véné·rien [venerjɛ̃] **-rienne** [rjen] *adj* venereal ‖ *mf* person with venereal disease

vengeance [vãʒãs] *f* vengeance, revenge

venger [vãʒe] §38 *tr* to avenge ‖ *ref* to get revenge

ven·geur [vãʒœr] **-geuse** [ʒøz] *adj* avenging ‖ *mf* avenger

veni·meux [vønimø] **-meuse** [møz] *adj* venomous

venin [vønɛ̃] *m* venom

venir [vønir] §72 *intr* to come; **à venir** forthcoming; **faire venir** to send for; **où voulez-vous en venir?** what are you getting at?; **venez avec** (coll) come along; **venir de** to have just, e.g., **il vient de partir** he has just left ‖ *impers*—**il me (nous, etc.) vient à l'esprit que** it occurs to me (to us, etc.) that

Venise [vøniz] *f* Venice

véni·tien [venisjɛ̃] **-tienne** [sjen] *adj* Venetian ‖ (*cap*) *mf* Venetian

vent [vã] *m* wind; **avoir le vent en poupe** to be in luck; **avoir vent de** to get wind of; **contre vents et marées** through thick and thin; **en plein vent** in the open air; **être dans le vent** to be up to date; **il fait du vent** it is windy; **les vents** (mus) the woodwinds; **vent arrière** tailwind; **vent coulis** draft; **vent debout** headwind; **vent en poupe** (naut) tailwind

vente [vãt] *f* sale; felling (*of timber*); **en vente** on sale; **en vente libre** (pharm) on sale without a prescription; **jeunes ventes** new overgrowth; **vente amiable** private sale; **vente à tempérament** installment selling; **vente à terme** sale on time; **vente au détail** retailing; **vente en gros** wholesaling

ventilateur [vãtilatœr] *m* ventilator; fan; electric fan

ventiler [vãtile] *tr* to ventilate; to value separately; (bk) to apportion

ventouse [vãtuz] *f* sucker; suction cup; suction grip; nozzle (*of vacuum cleaner*); vent

ventre [vãtr] *m* belly; stomach; womb;

à plat ventre prostrate; **à ventre déboutonné** (coll) excessively; (coll) with all one's might; **avoir q.ch. dans le ventre** (coll) to have s.th. on the ball; **bas ventre** (fig) genitals; **ventre à terre** (coll) lickety-split

ventricule [vãtrikyl] *m* ventricle

ventriloque [vãtrilɔk] *mf* ventriloquist

ventriloquie [vãtrilɔki] *f* ventriloquism

ventripo·tent [vãtripɔtã] **-tente** [tãt] *adj* (coll) potbellied

ven·tru -true [vãtry] *adj* potbellied

ve·nu -nue [vøny] *adj*—**bien venu** successful; welcome ‖ *mf*—**le premier venu** the first comer; just anyone; **les nouveaux venus** the newcomers ‖ *f* coming, advent

Vénus [venys] *f* Venus

vénusté [venyste] *f* charm, grace

vêpres [vepr] *fpl* vespers

ver [ver] *m* worm; **tirer les vers du nez** à to worm secrets out of, to pump; **ver à soie** silkworm; **ver de terre** earthworm; **ver luisant** glowworm

véracité [verasite] *f* veracity

véranda [verãda] *f* veranda

ver·bal -bale [verbal] *adj* (*pl* -baux [bo]) verbal; (gram) verb

verbaliser [verbalize] *intr* to write out a report or summons; **verbaliser contre qn** to give s.o. a ticket (*e.g., for speeding*)

verbe [verb] *m* verb; **avoir le verbe haut** to talk loud; **Verbe** (eccl) Word

ver·beux [verbø] **-beuse** [bøz] *adj* verbose, wordy

verbiage [verbjaʒ] *m* verbiage

verdâtre [verdatr] *adj* greenish

verdeur [verdœr] *f* greenness; vigor, spryness; crudeness (*of speech*)

verdict [verdik], [verdikt] *m* verdict

verdir [verdir] *tr & intr* to turn green

verdoyer [verdwaje] §47 *intr* to become green

verdure [verdyr] *f* verdure; greens

vé·reux [verø] **-reuse** [røz] *adj* wormy

verge [verʒ] *f* rod; shank (*of anchor*); penis

verger [verʒe] *m* orchard

verglas [vergla] *m* glare ice; sleet

vergogne [vergɔɲ] *f*—**sans vergogne** immodest, brazen; immodestly, brazenly

véridique [veridik] *adj* veracious

vérifica·teur [verifikatœr] **-trice** [tris] *mf* inspector, examiner; **vérificateur comptable** auditor

vérification [verifikɑsjɔ̃] *f* verification; auditing; ascertainment

vérifier [verifje] *tr* to verify; to audit; to ascertain

véritable [veritabl] *adj* veritable; real, genuine

vérité [verite] *f* truth; **à la vérité** to tell the truth; **dire à qn ses quatre vérités** (coll) to give s.o. a piece of one's mind; **en vérité** truly, in truth

ver·meil -meille [vermej] *adj* rosy

vermillon [vermijɔ̃] *adj invar & m* vermilion

vermine [vermin] *f* vermin

vermou·lu -lue [vɛrmuly] *adj* worm-eaten

vermout or **vermouth** [vɛrmut] *m* vermouth

vernaculaire [vɛrnakyler] *adj* vernacular

vernir [vɛrnir] *tr* to varnish; **être verni** (coll) to be lucky

vernis [vɛrni] *m* varnish; (fig) veneer

vernissage [vɛrnisaʒ] *m* varnishing; private viewing (*of pictures*)

vernisser [vɛrnise] *tr* to glaze

vérole [verɔl] *f* (slang) syphilis; **petite vérole** smallpox

verre [vɛr] *m* glass; crystal (*of watch*); **verre à vitre** windowpane; **verre consigné** bottle with deposit; **verre de contact** contact lens; **verre de lamp** lamp chimney; **verre dépoli** frosted glass; **verre perdu** disposable bottle (*no deposit*); **verres eyeglasses; verres de soleil** sunglasses; **verres grossissants** magnifying glasses; **verre taillé** cut glass

verrière [vɛrjer] *f* stained-glass window

verrou [vɛru] *m* bolt; **être sous le verrous** to be locked up

verrouiller [vɛruje] *tr* to bolt; to lock up || *ref* to lock oneself in

verrue [vɛry] *f* wart

vers [vɛr] *m* verse; **les vers** verse, poetry || *prep* toward; about, e.g., **vers les cinq heures** about five o'clock

Versailles [vɛrsaj] *f* Versailles

versant [vɛrsɑ̃] *m* slope, side

versatile [vɛrsatil] *adj* fickle

verse [vɛrs] *f*—**pleuvoir à verse** to pour

ver·sé -sée [vɛrse] *adj*—**versé dans** versed in

versement [vɛrsəmɑ̃] *m* deposit; installment; **versement anticipé** payment in advance

verser [vɛrse] *tr* to pour; to upset; to tip over; to deposit || *intr* to overturn

verset [vɛrse] *m* (Bib) verse

versification [vɛrsifikɑsjɔ̃] *f* versification

versifier [vɛrsifje] *tr & intr* to versify

version [vɛrsjɔ̃] *f* version; translation from a foreign language

verso [vɛrso] *m* verso; **au verso** on the back

vert [vɛr] **verte** [vɛrt] *adj* green; verdant; vigorous (*person*); new (*wine*); raw (*leather*); sharp (*scolding*); spicy (*story*); **ils sont trop verts!** sour grapes! || *m* green; greenery; **mettre au vert** to put out to pasture; **se mettre au vert** to take a rest in the country

vert-de-gris [vɛrdəgri] *m invar* verdigris

vertèbre [vɛrtebr] *f* vertebra

verté·bré -brée [vɛrtebre] *adj & m* vertebrate

verti·cal -cale [vɛrtikal] (*pl* **-caux** [ko] **-cales**) *adj* vertical || *m* (astr) vertical circle || *f* vertical

vertige [vɛrtiʒ] *m* vertigo, dizziness

vertigo [vɛrtigo] *m* staggers (*of horse*); caprice

vertu [vɛrty] *f* virtue

ver·tueux [vɛrtɥø] **-tueuse** [tɥøz] *adj* virtuous

verve [vɛrv] *f* verve

ver·veux [vɛrvø] **-veuse** [vøz] *adj* lively, animated || *m* fishnet

vésanie [vezani] *f* madness

vesce [ves] *f* vetch

vésicule [vezikyl] *f* vesicle; blister; **vésicule biliaire** gall bladder

vespasienne [vespazjen] *f* street urinal

vessie [vesi] *f* bladder; **vessie à glace** ice bag

veste [vest] *f* coat, suit coat; **remporter une veste** (coll) to suffer a setback; **retourner sa veste** (coll) to do an about-face; **veste croisée** double-breasted coat; **veste de pyjama** pajama top; **veste de sport** sport coat; **veste d'intérieur, veste d'appartement** lounging robe; **veste droite** single-breasted coat

vestiaire [vestjer] *m* checkroom, cloakroom

vestibule [vestibyl] *m* vestibule

vestige [vestiʒ] *m* vestige; footprint

veston [vestɔ̃] *m* coat

Vésuve [vezyv] *m*—**le Vésuve** Vesuvius

vêtement [vɛtmɑ̃] *m* garment; **vêtements** clothes

vétéran [veterɑ̃] *m* veteran

vétérinaire [veteriner] *adj & mf* veterinary

vétille [vetij] *f* trifle

vétiller [vetije] *intr* to split hairs

vêtir [vetir] §73 *tr & ref* to dress

veto [veto] *m* veto; **mettre** or **opposer son veto à** to veto

vétuste [vetyst] *adj* decrepit, rickety

veuf [vœf] **veuve** [vœv] *adj* widowed || *m* widower || *f* see **veuve**

veule [vøl] *adj* (coll) feeble, weak

veuvage [vœvaʒ] *m* widowhood; widowerhood

veuve [vœv] *f* widow

vexation [veksɑsjɔ̃] *f* vexation

vexer [vekse] *tr* to vex

via [vja] *prep* via

viaduc [vjadyk] *m* viaduct

via·gère [vjaʒe] **-gère** [ʒer] *adj* life, for life || *m* life annuity

viande [vjɑ̃d] *f* meat; **amène ta viande!** (slang) get over here!

vibration [vibrɑsjɔ̃] *f* vibration

vibrer [vibre] *intr* to vibrate

vicaire [viker] *m* vicar

vice [vis] *m* vice; defect; **vice de conformation** physical defect; **vice de forme** (law) irregularity, flaw; **vice versa** vice versa

vice-amiral [visamiral] *m* (*pl* **-amiraux** [amiro]) vice-admiral

vice-président [visprezidɑ̃] **-présidente** [prezidɑ̃t] *mf* (*pl* **-présidents**) vice-president

vice-roi [visrwa] *m* (*pl* **-rois**) viceroy

vice-versa [viseversa], [visversa] *adv* vice versa

vi·cié -ciée [visje] *adj* foul, polluted; poor, thin (*blood*)

vicier [visje] *tr* to foul, to pollute; to taint, to spoil

vi·cieux [visjø] **-cieuse** [sjøz] *adj* vicious; wrong (*use*)

vici·nal -nale [visinal] *adj (pl* **-naux** [no]) local, side *(road)*

vicissitude [visisityd] *f* vicissitude

vicomte [vikɔ̃t] *m* viscount

victime [viktim] *f* victim

victoire [viktwar] *f* victory

victo·rieux [viktɔrjø] **-rieuse** [rjøz] *adj* victorious

victuailles [viktɥaj] *fpl* victuals, foods

vidange [vidɑ̃ʒ] *f* draining; night soil; drain *(of pipe, sink, etc.)*

vidanger [vidɑ̃ʒe] §38 *tr* to drain

vide [vid] *adj* empty; blank; vacant ‖ *m* emptiness, void; vacuum

vi·dé -dée [vide] *adj* cleaned *(fish, fowl, etc.)*; played out, exhausted

vide-bouteille [vidbutɛj] *m (pl* **-bouteilles)** siphon

vide-cave [vidkav] *m invar* sump pump

vide-citron [vidsitrɔ̃] *m (pl* **-citrons)** lemon squeezer

vide-gousset [vidgusɛ] *m (pl* **-goussets)** (hum) thief

vide-ordures [vidɔrdyr] *m invar* garbage shoot

vide-poches [vidpɔʃ] *m invar* dresser; pin tray; (aut) glove compartment

vider [vide] *tr* to empty; to drain; to clean *(fish, fowl, etc.)*; to settle *(a question)*; **se faire vider de** (coll) to get thrown out of; to be fired from; to be expelled from

vi·deur [vidœr] **-deuse** [døz] *mf* (coll) bouncer *(in a night club)*

viduité [vidɥite] *f* widowhood

vidure [vidyr] *f* guts *(e.g., of cleaned fish)*; **vidures de poubelle** garbage

vie [vi] *f* life; livelihood, living; **à vie** for life; **de ma** (sa, etc.) **vie** in my (his, etc.) life, e.g., **je ne l'ai jamais vu de ma vie** I have never seen it in my life; **jamais de la vie!** not on your life!; **vie de bâton de chaise** disorderly life; **vie de château** life of ease

vieillard [vjejar] *m* old man; **les vieillards** old people

vieille [vjej] *f* old woman

vieilleries [vjejri] *fpl* old things; old ideas

vieillesse [vjejɛs] *f* old age

vieil·li -lie [vjeji] *adj* aged; out-of-date, antiquated

vieillir [vjejir] *tr* to age; to make *(s.o.)* look older ‖ *intr* to age, to grow old ‖ *ref* to make oneself look older

vieil·lot [vjejo] **vieil·lotte** [vjejɔt] *adj* (coll) oldish, quaint

vielle [vjɛl] *f* (hist) hurdy-gurdy

Vienne [vjen] *f* Vienna; Vienne *(city in France)*

vien·nois [vjenwa] **vien·noise** [vjenwaz] *adj* Viennese ‖ *(cap) mf* Viennese

vierge [vjɛrʒ] *adj* virginal; virgin; blank; unexposed *(film)* ‖ *f* virgin

Vietnam [vjetnam] *m*—**le Vietnam** Vietnam

vietna·mien [vjetnamjɛ̃] **-mienne** [mjen] *adj* Vietnamese ‖ *(cap) mf* Vietnamese

vieux [vjø] (or **vieil** [vjej] before vowel or mute **h**) **vieille** [vjej] *adj* old *(wine)* ‖ (when standing before noun) *adj* old; old-fashioned; obsolete *(word, meaning, etc.)* ‖ *mf* old person ‖ *m* old man; **les vieux** old people; **mon vieux** (coll) my boy ‖ *f* see **vieille**

vif [vif] **vive** [viv] *adj* alive, living; lively, quick; bright, intense; hearty, heartfelt; sharp *(criticism)*; keen *(pleasure)*; spring *(water)* ‖ *m* quick; **couper dans le vif** to take drastic measures; **entrer dans le vif de** to get to the heart of; **peindre au vif** to paint from life; **piqué au vif** stung to the quick

vif-argent [vifarʒɑ̃] *m* quicksilver; *(person)* live wire

vigie [viʒi] *f* lookout

vigilance [viʒilɑ̃s] *f* vigilance

vigi·lant [viʒilɑ̃] **-lante** [lɑ̃t] *adj* vigilant ‖ *m* night watchman

vigile [viʒil] *m* night watchman ‖ *f* (eccl) vigil

vigne [viɲ] *f* vine; vineyard; **vigne blanche** clematis; **vigne de Judas** bittersweet; **vigne vierge** Virginia creeper

vigne·ron [viɲrɔ̃] **-ronne** [rɔn] *mf* vinegrower; vintner

vignette [viɲɛt] *f* vignette; tax stamp; gummed tab

vignoble [viɲɔbl] *m* vineyard

vigou·reux [vigurø] **-reuse** [røz] *adj* vigorous

vigueur [vigœr] *f* vigor; **entrer en vigueur** to go into effect

vil vile [vil] *adj* vile; cheap

vi·lain [vilɛ̃] **-laine** [len] *adj* nasty; ugly; naughty ‖ *mf* nasty person

vilebrequin [vilbrəkɛ̃] *m* brace *(of brace and bit)*; crankshaft

vilenie [vilni] *f* villainy; abuse

villa [vila] *f* villa; cottage, small one-story home

village [vilaʒ] *m* village

villa·geois [vilaʒwa] **-geoise** [ʒwaz] *mf* villager

ville [vil] *f* city; town; **aller en ville** to go downtown; **la Ville Lumière** the City of Light *(Paris)*; **ville champignon** boom town; **ville satellite** suburban town; **villes jumelées** twin cities; **villes réunies** twin cities

villégiature [vileʒjatyr] *f* vacation

vin [vɛ̃] *m* wine; **avoir le vin gai** to be hilariously drunk; **être entre deux vins** to be tipsy; **vin d'honneur** reception *(at which toasts are offered)*; **vin d'orange** sangaree; **vin mousseux** sparkling wine; **vin ordinaire** table wine

vinaigre [vinegr] *m* vinegar

vinaigrette [vinegret] *f* French dressing, vinaigrette sauce

vindica·tif [vɛ̃dikatif] **-tive** [tiv] *adj* vindictive

vingt [vɛ̃] *adj & pron* twenty; the Twentieth, e.g., **Jean vingt** John the Twentieth; **vingt et un** [vɛ̃teœ̃] twenty-one; twenty-first, e.g., **Jean vingt et un** John the Twenty-first; **vingt et unième** twenty-first ‖ *m* twenty; twentieth *(in dates)*; **vingt et**

un twenty-one; twenty-first (*in dates*); **vingt et unième** twenty-first

vingtaine [vɛ̃ten] *f* score; **une vingtaine de** about twenty

vingt-deux [vɛ̃tdø] *adj & pron* twenty-two; the Twenty-second, e.g., **Jean vingt-deux** John the Twenty-second ‖ *m* twenty-two; twenty-second (*in dates*) ‖ *interj* (slang) beware!; cheese it!

vingt-deuxième [vɛ̃tdøzjem] *adj, pron* (*masc, fem*), & *m* twenty-second

vingt-et-un [vɛ̃teœ̃] *m* (cards) twenty-one

vingtième [vɛ̃tjem] *adj, pron* (*masc, fem*), & *m* twentieth

vinyle [vinil] *m* vinyl

viol [vjɔl] *m* rape

violation [vjɔlɑsjɔ̃] *f* violation

violence [vjɔlɑ̃s] *f* violence

vio·lent [vjɔlɑ̃] **-lente** [lɑ̃t] *adj* violent

violenter [vjɔlɑ̃te] *tr* to do violence to

violer [vjɔle] *tr* to violate; to break (*the faith*); to rape, ravish

vio·let [vjɔle] **-lette** [let] *adj & m* violet (*color*) ‖ *f* (bot) violet

violon [vjɔlɔ̃] *m* violin; (slang) calaboose, jug; **payer les violons** (coll) to pay the piper; **violon d'Ingres** hobby

violoncelle [vjɔlɔ̃sel] *m* violoncello

violoniste [vjɔlɔnist] *mf* violinist

vipère [viper] *f* viper

virage [viraʒ] *m* turning; turn, e.g., **pas de virage à gauche** no left turn; (aer) bank; (phot) toning; **virage en épingle à cheveux** hairpin curve; **virages** (public sign) winding road; **virage sur place** U-turn

virago [virago] *f* mannish woman

virée [vire] *f* (coll) spin (*in a car*); (coll) round (*of bars*)

virement [virmɑ̃] *m* transfer (*of funds*); (naut) tacking

virer [vire] *tr* to transfer (*funds*); (phot) to tone ‖ *intr* to turn; (aer) to bank; **virer à** to turn (*sour, red, etc.*); **virer de bord** (naut) to tack

virevolte [virvɔlt] *f* turn; about-face

virevolter [virvɔlte] *intr* to make an about-face; to go hither and thither

virginité [virʒinite] *f* virginity, maidenhood

virgule [virgyl] *f* (gram) comma; (*used in French to set off the decimal fraction from the integer*) decimal point

virilité [virilite] *f* virility

virole [virɔl] *f* ferrule

virologie [virɔlɔʒi] *f* virology

vir·tuel -tuelle [virtɥel] *adj* potential; (mech, opt, phys) virtual

virtuose [virtɥoz] *mf* virtuoso

virtuosité [virtɥozite] *f* virtuosity

virulence [virylɑ̃s] *f* virulence

viru·lent [virylɑ̃] **-lente** [lɑ̃t] *adj* virulent

virus [virys] *m* virus

vis [vis] *f* screw; thread (*of screw*); spiral staircase; **fermer à vis** to screw shut; **serrer la vis à** (fig) to put the screws on; **vis à métaux** machine screw; **vis de blocage** setscrew

visa [viza] *m* visa; (fig) approval

visage [vizaʒ] *m* face; **à deux visages** two-faced; **faire bon visage à** to pretend to be friendly to; **trouver visage de bois** to find the door closed; **visages pâles** palefaces; **voir qn sous son vrai visage** to see s.o. in his true colors

visagiste [vizaʒist] *mf* beautician

vis-à-vis [vizavi] *adv* vis-à-vis; **vis-à-vis de** vis-à-vis; towards; in the presence of ‖ *m* vis-à-vis; **en vis-à-vis** facing

viscère [viser] *m* organ; **viscères** viscera

visée [vize] *f* aim

viser [vize] *tr* to aim; to aim at; to concern; to visa ‖ *intr* to aim; **viser à** to aim at; to aim to

viseur [vizœr] *m* viewfinder; sight (*of gun*); **viseur de lancement** bombsight

visibilité [vizibilite] *f* visibility; **sans visibilité** blind (*flying*)

visible [vizibl] *adj* visible; obvious; (coll) at home, free; (coll) open to the public

visière [vizjer] *f* visor; sight (*of gun*); **rompre en visière à** to take a stand against

vision [vizjɔ̃] *f* vision

visionnaire [vizjɔner] *adj & mf* visionary

visionner [vizjɔne] *tr* to view, inspect

visionneuse [vizjɔnøz] *f* viewer

visite [vizit] *f* visit; inspection; **en, de visite** visiting; **faire, rendre visite à** to visit

visiter [vizite] *tr* to visit; to inspect

visi·teur [vizitœr] **-teuse** [tøz] *adj* visiting (*e.g., nurse*) ‖ *mf* visitor; inspector

vison [vizɔ̃] *m* mink

vis·queux [viskø] **-queuse** [køz] *adj* viscous

visser [vise] *tr* to screw; to screw on; (coll) to put the screws on

visualiser [vizɥalize] *tr* to visualize

vi·suel -suelle [vizɥel] *adj* visual

vi·tal -tale [vital] *adj* (*pl* **-taux** [to]) vital

vitaliser [vitalize] *tr* to vitalize

vitalité [vitalite] *f* vitality

vitamine [vitamin] *f* vitamin

vite [vit] *adj* fast, swift ‖ *adv* fast, quickly; **faites vite!** hurry up!

vitesse [vites] *f* speed, velocity; rate; **à toute vitesse** at full speed; **changer de vitesse** (aut) to shift gears; **en grande vitesse** (rr) by express; **en petite vitesse** (rr) by freight; **en première (seconde, etc.) vitesse** (aut) in first (second, etc.) gear; **vitesse acquise** momentum

viticole [vitikɔl] *adj* wine

vitrage [vitraʒ] *m* glasswork; small window curtain; sash; glazing

vi·trail [vitraj] *m* (*pl* **-traux** [tro]) stained-glass window

vitre [vitr] *f* windowpane, pane; (aut) window; **casser les vitres** (coll) to kick up a fuss

vi·tré -trée [vitre] *adj* glazed; vitreous (*humor*); glassed-in

vi•treux [vitrø] **-treuse** [trøz] *adj* glassy; vitreous

vitrier [vitrije] *m* glazier

vitrine [vitrin] *f* show window; show-case; glass cabinet; **lécher les vitrines** (coll) to go window-shopping

vitupérer [vitypere] §10 *tr* to vituperate, abuse ‖ *intr*—**vitupérer contre** (coll) to vituperate

vivace [vivas] *adj* hardy, vigorous; long-lived; (bot) perennial

vivacité [vivasite] *f* vivacity

vivan•dier [vivɑ̃dje] **-dière** [djer] *mf* sutler ‖ *f* camp follower

vi•vant [vivɑ̃] **-vante** [vɑ̃t] *adj* living, alive; lively; modern (*language*) ‖ *m*—**bon vivant** high liver, jolly companion; **du vivant de** during the life-time of; **les vivants et les morts** the quick and the dead

vivat [viva] *m* viva ‖ *interj* viva!

vivement [vivmɑ̃] *adv* quickly; warmly; deeply; sharply, briskly

viveur [vivœr] *m* pleasure seeker, rounder

vivier [vivje] *m* fish preserve, fishpond

vivifier [vivifje] *tr* to vivify, vitalize

vivisection [viviseksjɔ̃] *f* vivisection

vivoir [vivwar] *m* (Canad) living room

vivoter [vivɔte] *intr* (coll) to live from hand to mouth

vivre [vivr] *m*—**le vivre et le couvert** room and board; **le vivre et le vêtement** food and clothing; **vivres** provisions; (mil) rations, supplies ‖ §74 *tr* to live (*one's life, faith, art*); to live through, to experience ‖ *intr* to live; **être difficile à vivre** to be difficult to live with; **qui vive?** (mil) who is there?; **qui vivra verra** time will tell; **vive!, vivent! viva!,** long live!; **vivre au jour le jour** to live from hand to mouth; **vivre de** to live on

vizir [vizir] *m* vizier

vlan [vlɑ̃] *interj* whack!

vocable [vɔkabl] *m* word

vocabulaire [vɔkabyler] *m* vocabulary

vo•cal -cale [vɔkal] *adj* (*pl* -**caux** [ko]) vocal

vocaliser [vɔkalize] *tr, intr, & ref* to vocalize

vocatif [vɔkatif] *m* vocative

vocation [vɔkasjɔ̃] *f* vocation, calling; **vocation pédagogique** teaching career

vociférer [vɔsifere] §10 *tr* to shout (*e.g., insults*) ‖ *intr* to vociferate

vœu [vø] *m* (*pl* **vœux**) vow; wish; resolution; **meilleurs vœux!** best wishes!; **tous mes vœux!** my best wishes!

vogue [vɔg] *f* vogue, fashion; **en vogue** in vogue, in fashion

voguer [vɔge] *intr* to sail; **vogue la galère!** let's chance it, here goes!

voici [vwasi] *prep* here is, here are; for, e.g., **voici quatre jours qu'elle est partie** she has been gone for four days; **le voici** here he is; **nous voici** here we are; **voici** here, e.g., **mon frère que voici va vous accompagner** my brother here is going to accompany you

voie [vwa] *f* way; road; lane (*of high-*

way); (anat) tract; (rr) track; **en voie de** on the road to, nearing; **être en bonne voie** to be doing well; **voie d'eau** leak; **voie de garage** driveway; **voie d'évitement** siding; **Voie lactée** Milky Way; **voie maritime** seaway; **voie(s) de fait** (law) assault and battery; **voie surface** surface mail

voilà [vwala] *prep* there is, there are; here is, here are; that's, e.g., **voilà pourquoi** that's why; ago, e.g., **voilà quatre jours qu'elle est partie** she left four days ago; **voilà, monsieur** there you are, sir

voile [vwal] *m* veil; (phot) fog (*on negative*); **voile du palais** soft palate; **voile noir** (pathol) blackout ‖ *f* sail; sailboat; **faire voile** sur to set sail for

voi•lé -lée [vwale] *adj* veiled; overcast; muffled; warped; husky (*voice*); (phot) fogged; **peu voilé** thinly veiled, broad (*e.g., hint*)

voiler [vwale] *tr* to veil; (phot) to fog ‖ *ref* to cloud over; to become warped

voi•lier [vwalje] **-lière** [ljer] *adj* sailing ‖ *m* sailboat; sailmaker; migratory bird

voilure [vwalyr] *f* sails; warping

voir [vwar] §75 *tr* to see; **faire voir** to show; **voir jouer** to see (*s.o.*) playing, to see (*s.th.*); **voir** qn **qui vient** to see s.o. coming, to see s.o. come; **voir venir** qn to see s.o. coming, to see s.o. come; (fig) to see through s.o. ‖ *intr* to see; **faites voir!** let's see it!, let me see it!; **j'en ai vu bien d'autres** I have seen worse than that; **n'avoir rien à voir avec, à,** or **dans** to have nothing to do with; **voir à** + *inf* to see that + *ind*, e.g., **voir à nous loger** to see that we are housed; **voir au dos** see other side, turn the page; **voyons!** see here!, come now! ‖ *ref* to see oneself; to see one another; to be obvious; to be seen, to be found

voire [vwar] *adv* nay, indeed; **voire même** or even, and even

voirie [vwari] *f* highway department; garbage collection; dump

voi•sé -sé [vwaze] *adj* voiced

voi•sin [vwazɛ̃] **-sine** [zin] *adj* neighboring; adjoining; **voisin de** near ‖ *mf* neighbor

voisinage [vwazinaʒ] *m* neighborhood; neighborliness

voisiner [vwazine] *intr* to visit one's neighbors; **voisiner avec** to be placed next to

voiture [vwatyr] *f* vehicle; carriage; (aut, rr) car; **en voiture!** all aboard!; **petite voiture** (coll) wheelchair; **voiture à bras** handcart; **voiture d'enfant** baby carriage; **voiture de pompier** fire engine; **voiture de remise** rented car; **voiture de série** stock car; **voiture de tourisme** pleasure car; **voiture d'infirme** wheelchair; **voiture d'occasion** used car

voiture-bar [vwatyrbar] *f* (*pl* **voitures-bars**) club car

voiture-lit [vwatyrli] *f* (*pl* **voitures-lits**) sleeping car

voiturer [vwatyre] *tr* to transport, to convey

voiture-restaurant [vwatyrrestorɑ̃] *f* (*pl* **voitures-restaurants**) dining car

voiture-salon [vwatyrsalɔ̃] *f* (*pl* **voitures-salons**) parlor car

voix [vwa], [vwɑ] *f* voice; vote; **à haute voix** aloud; in a loud voice; **à pleine voix** at the top of one's voice; **à voix basse** in a low voice; **à voix haute** in a loud voice; **de vive voix** by word of mouth; **voix de tête, voix de fausset** falsetto

vol [vɔl] *m* theft, robbery; flight; flock; **au vol** in flight; in passing; **à vol d'oiseau** as the crow flies; **de haut vol** high-flying; big-time (*crook*); **vol avec effraction** burglary; **vol cosmique** space flight; **vol plané** volplane; **vol sans visibilité** blind flying

volage [vɔlaʒ] *adj* fickle, changeable

volaille [vɔlaj] *f* fowl; (slang) hens (*women*); (slang) gal

vo·lant [vɔlɑ̃] **-lante** [lɑ̃t] *adj* flying ǁ *m* steering wheel; flywheel; shuttlecock; sail (*of windmill*); flounce (*of dress*); leaf (*attached to stub*); **volant de sécurité** safety margin, reserve

vola·til -tile [vɔlatil] *adj* volatile ǁ *m* bird; fowl

volatiliser [volatilize] *tr* & *ref* to volatilize

volcan [vɔlkɑ̃] *m* volcano

volcanique [vɔlkanik] *adj* volcanic

vole [vɔl] *f*—**faire la vole** to take all the tricks

volée [vɔle] *f* volley; flight (*of birds; of stairs*); flock; **à la volée** on the wing; at random; **à toute volée** loud and clear; **de haute volée** upperclass; **de la première volée** first-class, crack; **sonner à toute volée** to peal out

voler [vɔle] *tr* to rob; to steal; to fly at; **ne l'avoir pas volé** to deserve all that is coming; **voler à** to steal from ǁ *intr* to rob; to steal; to fly

volet [vɔle] *m* shutter; inside flap; end paper; (aer) flap; **trier sur le volet** to choose with care

voleter [vɔlte] §34 *intr* to flutter

vo·leur [vɔlœr] **-leuse** [løz] *adj* thievish ǁ *mf* thief; **au voleur!** stop thief!; **voleur à la tire** pickpocket; **voleur à l'étalage** shoplifter; **voleur de grand chemin** highwayman

volition [vɔlisjɔ̃] *f* volition

volley-ball [vɔlebol] *m* volleyball

volontaire [vɔlɔ̃ter] *adj* voluntary; headstrong, willful; determined (*chin*) ǁ *mf* volunteer

volonté [vɔlɔ̃te] *f* will; wishes; **à volonté** at will; **bonne volonté** good will; **faire ses quatre volontés** (coll) to do just as one pleases; **mauvaise volonté** ill will

volontiers [vɔlɔ̃tje] *adv* gladly, willingly

volt [vɔlt] *m* volt

voltage [vɔltaʒ] *m* voltage

volte-face [vɔltafas] *f invar* volte-face

voltige [vɔltiʒ] *f* acrobatics

voltiger [vɔltiʒe] §38 *intr* to flit about; to flutter

voltmètre [vɔltmetr] *m* voltmeter

volubile [vɔlybil] *adj* voluble

volume [vɔlym] *m* volume; **faire du volume** (coll) to put on airs

volumi·neux [vɔlyminø] **-neuse** [nøz] *adj* voluminous

volupté [vɔlypte] *f* voluptuousness, ecstasy

volup·tueux [vɔlyptɥø] **-tueuse** [tɥøz] *adj* voluptuous ǁ *mf* voluptuary

vomir [vɔmir] *tr* & *intr* to vomit

vomissure [vɔmisyr] *f* vomit

vorace [vɔras] *adj* voracious

voracité [vɔrasite] *f* voracity

vos [vo] §88

vo·tant [vɔtɑ̃] **-tante** [tɑ̃t] *mf* voter

vote [vɔt] *m* vote; **passer au vote** to vote on; **vote affirmatif** yea; **vote négatif** nay; **vote par correspondance** absentee ballot; **vote par procuration** proxy

voter [vɔte] *tr* to vote; to vote for ǁ *intr* to vote; **voter à mains levées** to vote by show of hands; **voter par assis et levé** to give one's vote by standing or by remaining seated

vo·tif [vɔtif] **-tive** [tiv] *adj* votive

votre [vɔtr] §88

vôtre [votr] §89

vouer [vwe] *tr* to vow, to dedicate; to doom, to condemn; **voué à** headed for; doomed to ǁ *ref*—**se vouer à** to dedicate oneself to

vouloir [vulwar] *m* will ǁ §76 *tr* to want, to wish; to require; **je voudrais** I would like; I would like to; **veuillez** + *inf* please + *inf*; **voulez-vous vous taire?** will you be quiet?; **vouloir bien** to be glad to, to be willing to; **vouloir dire** to mean ǁ *intr*—**en vouloir à** to bear a grudge against; **je veux!** (slang) and how!; **je veux bien** I'm quite willing; **si vous voulez bien** if you don't mind ǁ *ref*—**s'en vouloir** to have it in for each other

vou·lu -lue [vuly] *adj* required; deliberate

vous [vu] §85, §87; **vous autres Américains** you Americans

vous-même [vumem] §86

voussoir [vuswar] *m* (archit) arch stone

voussure [vusyr] *f* arch, arching

voûte [vut] *f* vault; **voûte céleste** canopy of heaven

voûter [vute] *tr* to vault; to bend ǁ *ref* to become round-shouldered

vouvoyer [vuvwaje] §47 *tr* to address with the pronoun **vous** (*instead of* **tu**)

voy. *abbr* (**voyez**) see

voyage [vwajaʒ] *m* trip, journey, voyage; ride (*in car, train, plane, etc.*); **voyage à forfait** all-expense tour; **voyage aller et retour** round trip; **voyage de noces** honeymoon

voyager [vwajaʒe] §38 *intr* to travel

voya·geur [vwajaʒœr] **-geuse** [ʒøz] *mf* traveler; passenger

voyance [vwajɑ̃s] *f* clairvoyance

voyant [vwajɑ̃] **voyante** [vwajɑ̃t] *adj* loud, gaudy ǁ *mf* clairvoyant ǁ *m* signal; (aut) gauge ǁ *f* fortuneteller

voyelle [vwajel] *f* vowel

voyeur [vwajœr] **voyeuse** [vwajøz] *mf* voyeur || *m* Peeping Tom

voyou [vwaju] **voyoute** [vwajut] *adj* gutter (*e.g., language*) || *mf* gutter-snipe; brat; hoodlum

vrac [vrak]—**en vrac** unpacked, loose; in bulk; in disorder

vrai vraie [vrɛ], [vrɛ] *adj* true, real, genuine || *m* truth; **à vrai dire** to tell the truth; **pour vrai** (coll) for good

vraiment [vrɛmã] *adv* truly, really

vraisemblable [vrɛsãblabl] *adj* probable, likely; true to life, realistic (*play, novel*)

vraisemblance [vrɛsãblãs] *f* probability, likelihood; realism

vrille [vrij] *f* drill; (aer) spin; (bot) tendril

vriller [vrije] *tr* to bore || *intr* to go into a tailspin

vrombir [vrɔ̃bir] *intr* to throb; to buzz; to hum, to purr (*said of motor*)

vu vue [vy] *adj* seen, regarded; **bien vu de** in favor with; **mal vu de** out of favor with || *m*—**au vu de** upon presentation of; **au vu et au su de tout le monde** openly || *f* view; sight; eyesight; **avoir à vue** to have in mind; **à vue** in sight; (com) on demand; **à vue de nez** at first sight; **à vue d'œil** visibly; quickly; **de vue** by sight; **en vue** in evidence; in sight; **en vue de** in order to; **garder à vue** to keep under observation, to keep locked up; **perdre qn de vue** to lose sight of s.o.; to get out of touch with s.o.; **vue à vol d'oiseau** bird's-eye view; **vues sur** designs on || **vu** *prep* considering, in view of; **vu que** whereas

vulcaniser [vylkanize] *tr* to vulcanize

vulgaire [vylgɛr] *adj* common, vulgar; ordinary, everyday; vernacular || *m* common herd; vernacular

vulgariser [vylgarize] *tr* to popularize; to make vulgar

vulgarité [vylgarite] *f* vulgarity

vulnérable [vylnerabl] *adj* vulnerable

Vve *abbr* (**veuve**) widow

W

W, w [dublǝve] *m invar* twenty-third letter of the French alphabet

wagon [vagɔ̃] *m* (rr) car, coach; (coll) big car; **un wagon** (coll) a lot; **wagon à bagages** baggage car; **wagon à bestiaux** cattle car; **wagon couvert** boxcar; **wagon de marchandises** freight car; **wagon frigorifique** or **réfrigérant** refrigerator car; **wagon plat** flat car

wagon-bar [vagɔ̃bar] *m* (*pl* **wagons-bars**) club car

wagon-citerne [vagɔ̃sitern] *m* (*pl* **wagons-citernes**) tank car

wagon-lit [vagɔ̃li] *m* (*pl* **wagons-lits**) sleeping car

wagon-poste [vagɔ̃pɔst] *m* (*pl* **wagons-poste**) mail car

wagon-réservoir [vagɔ̃rezervwar] *m* (*pl* **wagons-réservoirs**) tank car

wagon-restaurant [vagɔ̃rɛstǝrã] *m* (*pl* **wagons-restaurants**) dining car.

wagon-salon [vagɔ̃salɔ̃] *m* (*pl* **wagons-salons**) parlor car

wagon-tombereau [vagɔ̃tɔ̃bro] *m* (*pl* **wagons-tombereaux**) dump truck

wallace [valas] *f* drinking fountain

wal•lon [walɔ̃] **wal•lonne** [walɔn] *adj* Walloon || *m* Walloon (*dialect*) || (*cap*) *mf* Walloon

warrant [warã], [varã] *m* receipt

water-polo [waterpolo] *m* water polo

waterproof [waterpruf] *adj invar* waterproof || *m invar* raincoat

waters [water], [vater] *mpl* toilet

watt [wat] *m* watt

watt-heure [watœr] *m* (*pl* **watts-heures**) watt-hour

wattman [watman] *m* motorman

wattmètre [watmetr] *m* wattmeter

week-end [wikɛnd] *m* (*pl* -**ends**) week-end

whisky [wiski] *m* whiskey; **whisky écossais** Scotch

wolfram [vɔlfram] *m* wolfram

X

X, x [iks], *[iks] *m invar* twenty-fourth letter of the French alphabet

Xavier [gzavje] *m* Xavier

xénon [ksenɔ̃] *m* xenon

xénophobe [ksenɔfɔb] *adj* xenophobic || *mf* xenophobe

Xérès [keres], [gzeres] *m* Jerez; sherry

Xerxès [gzerses] *m* Xerxes

xylophone [ksilɔfɔn] *m* xylophone

Y

Y, y [igrek], *[igrek] *m invar* twenty-fifth letter of the French alphabet

y [i] *pron pers* §87 to it, to them; at it, at them; in it, in them; by it, by them; of it, of them, e.g., **j'y pense** I am thinking of it or them; (untranslated with certain verbs), e.g., **je n'y vois pas** I don't see; e.g., **il s'y connaît** (coll) he's an expert, he knows what he's talking about; him, her, e.g., **je m'y fie** I trust him; **allez-y!** go ahead!, start!; **ça y est!** that's it!; **je n'y suis pour personne** I am not at home for anybody; **je n'y suis pour rien** I have nothing to do with it; **j'y suis!** I've got it! || *adv* there; here, in, e.g., **Monsieur votre père y est-il?** is your father here?, is your father in?

yacht [jɔt], [jak] *m* yacht; **yacht à glace** iceboat

yacht-club [jɔtklœb] *m* yacht club

yankee [jɑ̃ki] *adj masc* Yankee || (cap) *mf* Yankee

yèble [jebl] *f* (bot) elder; **l'yèble** the elder

yeoman [jɔman] *m* yeoman

yeuse [jøz] *f* holm oak; **l'yeuse** the holm oak

yeux [jø] *mpl* see **œil**

yé-yé [jeje] (*pl* **-yés**) *adj & mf* jitterbug

yiddish [jidiʃ] *adj invar & m* Yiddish

yogourt [jɔgur] *m* yogurt

yole [jɔl] *f* yawl

Yonne [jɔn] *f* Yonne; **l'Yonne** the Yonne

yougoslave [jugɔslav] *adj* Yugoslav || (cap) *mf* Yugoslav

Yougoslavie [jugɔslavi] *f* Yugoslavia; **la Yougoslavie** Yugoslavia

youyou [juju] *m* dinghy

Z

Z, z [zed] *m invar* twenty-sixth letter of the French alphabet

za·zou -zoue [zazu] *adj* (coll) jazzy || *m* (coll) zoot suiter

zèbre [zebr] *m* zebra; (slang) guy

zébrer [zebre] §10 *tr* to stripe; **le soleil zèbre** the sun casts streaks of light on

zébrure [zebryr] *f* stripe

zéla·teur -trice [tris] *mf* zealot

zèle [zel] *m* zeal

zénith [zenit] *m* zenith

zéphyr [zefir] *m* zephyr

zeppelin [zeplɛ̃] *m* zeppelin

zéro [zero] *m* zero

zest [zɛst] *m*—**entre le zist et le zest** (coll) betwixt and between || *interj* tush!

zeste [zɛst] *m* peel (*of citrus fruit*); dividing membrane (*of nut*); **pas un zeste** (fig) not a particle of difference

Zeus [zøs] *m* Zeus

zézaiement [zezemɑ̃] *m* lisp

zézayer [zezeje] §49 *intr* to lisp

zibeline [ziblin] *f* sable

zieuter [zjøte] *tr* (slang) to get a load of

zigzag [zigzag] *m* zigzag

zigzaguer [zigzage] *intr* to zigzag

zinc [zɛ̃g] *m* zinc; (coll) bar

zizanie [zizani] *f* wild rice; tare; **semer la zizanie** to sow discord

zodiaque [zɔdjak] *m* zodiac

zone [zon] *f* zone; **zone bleu** center city with limited parking

zoo [zoo] *m* zoo

zoologie [zɔɔlɔʒi] *f* zoology

zoologique [zɔɔlɔʒik] *adj* zoologic(al)

zouave [zwav] *m* Zouave; **faire le zouave** (coll) to play the fool

zut [zyt] *interj* heck!, hang it!

PART TWO

Anglais-Français

La prononciation de l'anglais

Les signes suivants représentent à peu près tous les sons de la langue anglaise.

VOYELLES

SIGNE	SON	EXEMPLE
[æ]	Plus fermé que a dans **patte**.	hat [hæt]
[ɑ]	Comme a dans **pâte**.	father ['fɑðər] proper ['prɑpər]
[ɛ]	Comme e dans **sec**.	met [mɛt]
[e]	Comme e dans **récit**. Surtout en position finale, [e] se prononce comme s'il était suivi de [ɪ].	fate [fet] they [ðe]
[ə]	C'est e muet, par ex., e dans **gouvernement**.	heaven ['hevən] pardon ['pɑrdən]
[i]	Comme i dans **mine**.	she [ʃi] machine [məˈʃin]
[ɪ]	Moins fermé que i dans **mirage**.	fit [fɪt] beer [bɪr]
[o]	Comme au dans **haut**. Surtout en position finale, [o] se prononce comme s'il était suivi de [ʊ].	nose [noz] road [rod] row [ro]
[ɔ]	Un peu plus fermé que o dans **donne**.	bought [bɔt] law [lɔ]
[ʌ]	Plus ou moins comme eu dans **peur**.	cup [kʌp] come [kʌm] mother ['mʌðər]
[ʊ]	Moins fermé que ou dans **doublage**.	pull [pʊl] book [bʊk] wolf [wʊlf]
[u]	Comme ou dans **doublage**.	move [muv] tomb [tum]

DIPHTONGUES

SIGNE	SON	EXEMPLE
[aɪ]	Comme aï dans **aïl**.	night [naɪt] eye [aɪ]
[aʊ]	Comme aou dans **caoutchouc**.	found [faʊnd] cow [kaʊ]
[ɔɪ]	Comme oy dans **boy**.	voice [vɔɪs] oil [ɔɪl]

CONSONNES

SIGNE	SON	EXEMPLE
[b]	Comme b dans **bébé**.	bed [bɛd] robber ['rʌbər]
[d]	Comme d dans **don**.	dead [dɛd] add [æd]

3

SIGNE	SON	EXEMPLE
[dʒ]	Comme dj dans djinn.	gem [dʒem] jail [dʒel]
[ð]	Comme la consonne castillane d intervocalique de moda.	this [ðɪs] father ['faðər]
[f]	Comme f dans fin.	face [fes] phone [fon]
[g]	Comme g dans gallois.	go [go] get [get]
[h]	Comme la consonne allemande h de Haus ou comme la consonne espagnole j de jota mais moins aspiré.	hot [hat] alcohol ['ælkə,hɔl]
[j]	Comme i dans hier ou comme y dans yod.	yes [jes] unit ['junɪt]
[k]	Comme k dans kiosque ou comme c dans cote, mais accompagné d'une aspiration.	cat [kæt] chord [kɔrd] kill [kɪl]
[l]	Comme l ou ll dans pulluler.	late [let] allow [ə'lau]
[m]	Comme m dans mère.	more [mor] command [kə'mænd]
[n]	Comme n dans note.	nest [nest] manner ['mænər]
[ŋ]	Comme ng dans parking.	king [kɪŋ] conquer ['kaŋkər]
[p]	Comme p dans père, mais accompagné d'une aspiration.	pen [pen] cap [kæp]
[r]	Le r le plus commun dans une grande partie de l'Angleterre et dans la plus grande partie des États-Unis et du Canada, c'est le r rétroflexe, une semi-voyelle dont l'articulation se produit par la pointe de la langue élevée vers la voûte du palais. Cette consonne est très faible dans la position intervocalique ou à la fin de la syllabe et, par conséquent, elle y est très peu audible. L'articulation de cette consonne tend à colorier le son des voyelles voisines.	run [rʌn] far [far] art [art] carry ['kærɪ]
	Le r, précédé des sons [ʌ] ou [ə], donne sa propre couleur à ces sons et disparaît complètement en tant que son consonant.	burn [bʌrn] learn [lʌrn] weather ['wɛðər]
[s]	Comme ss dans classe.	send [send] cellar ['selər]
[ʃ]	Comme ch dans chose.	shall [ʃæl] machine [mə'ʃin] nation ['neʃən]
[t]	Comme t dans table, mais accompagné d'une aspiration.	ten [ten] dropped [drapt]
[tʃ]	Comme tch dans caoutchouc.	child [tʃaɪld] much [mʌtʃ] nature ['netʃər]
[θ]	Comme la consonne castillane c de cinco.	think [θɪŋk] truth [truθ]
[v]	Comme v dans veuve.	vest [vest] over ['ovər] of [ʌv]
[w]	Comme w dans watt; comme le [w] produit en prononçant le mot bois.	work [wʌrk] tweed [twid] queen [kwin]
[z]	Comme s dans rose ou comme z dans zèbre.	zeal [zil] busy ['bɪzɪ] his [hɪz] winds [wɪndz]
[ʒ]	Comme j dans jardin.	azure ['eʒər] measure ['meʒər]

L'accent tonique principal, indiqué par le signe graphique ˈ , et l'accent secondaire, indiqué par le signe graphique ˌ , précèdent la syllabe à laquelle ils s'appliquent, par ex., **fascinate** [ˈfæsɪ ˌnet].

La prononciation des mots composés

Dans la partie anglais-français du Dictionnaire la prononciation figurée de tous les mots anglais simples est indiquée selon une nouvelle adaptation de la méthode de l'Association phonétique internationale, et placée entre crochets à la suite du mot-souche.

Il y a trois genres de mots composés en anglais: (1) les mots dont les éléments composants sont soudés en un mot simple, par ex., **steamboat** vapeur, (2) les mots dont les éléments composants sont reliés entre eux par un trait d'union, par ex., **short-circuit** court-circuiter, et (3) les mots dont les éléments composants restent graphiquement indépendants, par ex., **post card** carte postale. La prononciation des mots composés anglais n'est pas indiquée dans ce Dictionnaire lorsque celle des éléments composants a déjà été indiquée à la suite de ces éléments là où ils apparaissent comme mots-souches. Néanmoins, les accents principaux et secondaires sont indiqués dans l'écriture de ces mots composés, ex.: **steamˈboatˈ, shortˈ-cirˈcuit, postˈ cardˈ, eyeˈ of the mornˈing.**

En ce qui concerne les éléments composants qui se terminent par **-ing** [ɪŋ] dans les mots composés, l'accent seul est précisé lorsque ces éléments se présentent également comme mots-souches suivis de la prononciation figurée, par ex., **playˈing cardˈ.**

Dans les noms dans lesquels les éléments composants **-man** et **-men** portent l'accent secondaire, les voyelles de ces éléments se prononcent comme dans les mots simples **man** et **men**, par ex., **mailman** [ˈmel ˌmæn] et **mailmen** [ˈmel ˌmen]. Dans les noms dans lesquels ces éléments composants sont inaccentués, les voyelles se prononcent dans les deux formes comme e muet, par ex., **policeman** [pəˈlismən] et **policemen** [pəˈlismən]. Il y a des noms dans lesquels ces éléments composants se prononcent des deux façons, c'est-à-dire, avec l'accent secondaire ou sans accent, par ex., **doorman** [ˈdor ˌmæn] ou [ˈdormən] et **doormen** [ˈdor ˌmen] ou [ˈdormən]. Dans ce Dictionnaire la transcription phonétique de ces mots est omise si le premier élément composant se présente ailleurs comme mot-souche suivi de la prononciation figurée. Cependant, l'accentuation de ces mots est indiquée dans le mot-souche même:

> mailˈmanˈ s (pl -men')
> policeˈman s (pl -men)
> doorˈmanˈ or doorˈman s (pl -men' or -men)

La prononciation des participes passés

Lorsqu'un mot a pour désinence **-ed** (ou **-d** après un e muet), et une prononciation conforme aux principes énoncés plus bas, celle-ci ne figurera pas dans ce Dictionnaire, si elle est indiquée quand la forme du mot sans cette désinence se présente comme mot-souche.

La désinence **-ed** (ou **-d** après un e muet) du prétérit, du participe passé, et de certains adjectifs possède trois prononciations différentes selon le son de la dernière consonne du radical.

5

1) Si le radical se termine par le son d'une consonne sonore (sauf [d]), que voici: [b], [g], [l], [m], [n], [ŋ], [r], [v], [z], [ð], [ʒ], ou [dʒ] ou par le son d'une voyelle, -ed se prononce [d].

SON DU RADICAL	INFINITIF	PRÉTÉRIT ET PARTICIPE PASSÉ
[b]	ebb [ɛb]	ebbed [ɛbd]
	rob [rɑb]	robbed [rɑbd]
	robe [rob]	robed [robd]
[g]	egg [ɛg]	egged [ɛgd]
	sag [sæg]	sagged [sægd]
[l]	mail [mel]	mailed [meld]
	scale [skel]	scaled [skeld]
[m]	storm [stɔrm]	stormed [stɔrmd]
	bomb [bɑm]	bombed [bɑmd]
	name [nem]	named [nemd]
[n]	tan [tæn]	tanned [tænd]
	sign [saɪn]	signed [saɪnd]
	mine [maɪn]	mined [maɪnd]
[ŋ]	hang [hæŋ]	hanged [hæŋd]
[r]	fear [fɪr]	feared [fɪrd]
	care [ker]	cared [kerd]
[v]	rev [rɛv]	revved [rɛvd]
	save [sev]	saved [sevd]
[z]	buzz [bʌz]	buzzed [bʌzd]
	fuse [fjuz]	fused [fjuzd]
[ð]	smooth [smuð]	smoothed [smuðd]
	bathe [beð]	bathed [beðd]
[ʒ]	massage [məˈsɑʒ]	massaged [məˈsɑʒd]
[dʒ]	page [pedʒ]	paged [pedʒd]
son de voyelle	key [ki]	keyed [kid]
	sigh [saɪ]	sighed [saɪd]
	paw [pɔ]	pawed [pɔd]

2) Si le radical se termine par le son d'une consonne sourde (sauf [t]), que voici: [f], [k], [p], [s], [θ], [ʃ], ou [tʃ], -ed se prononce [t].

SON DU RADICAL	INFINITIF	PRÉTÉRIT ET PARTICIPE PASSÉ
[f]	loaf [lof]	loafed [loft]
	knife [naɪf]	knifed [naɪft]
[k]	back [bæk]	backed [bækt]
	bake [bek]	baked [bekt]
[p]	cap [kæp]	capped [kæpt]
	wipe [waɪp]	wiped [waɪpt]
[s]	hiss [hɪs]	hissed [hɪst]
	mix [mɪks]	mixed [mɪkst]
[θ]	lath [læθ]	lathed [læθt]
[ʃ]	mash [mæʃ]	mashed [mæʃt]
[tʃ]	match [mætʃ]	matched [mætʃt]

3) Si le radical se termine par le son d'une dentale, que voici: [t] ou [d], -ed se prononce [ɪd] ou [əd].

SON DU RADICAL	INFINITIF	PRÉTÉRIT ET PARTICIPE PASSÉ
[t]	wait [wet]	waited [ˈwetɪd]
	mate [met]	mated [ˈmetɪd]
[d]	mend [mɛnd]	mended [ˈmɛndɪd]
	wade [wed]	waded [ˈwedɪd]

6

Notez que le redoublement orthographique de la consonne finale après une voyelle simple accentuée n'altère pas la prononciation de la désinence -ed: **batted** ['bætɪd], **dropped** [drɑpt], **robbed** [rɑbd].

Ces règles s'appliquent aussi aux adjectifs composés qui se terminent par -ed. On n'indique que l'accent de ces adjectifs lorsque les éléments composants (le dernier, bien entendu, sans la désinence -ed) se présentent ailleurs comme motssouches suivis de la prononciation figurée, par ex., **flat′-nosed′**.

Cependant, le -ed de quelques adjectifs formés sur un radical qui se termine par un son consonantique en plus de ceux qui se terminent par [d] et [t], est prononcé [ɪd] et cette irrégularité s'indique en donnant la prononciation figurée complète, par ex., **blessed** ['blɛsɪd], **crabbed** ['kræbɪd].

ANGLAIS—FRANÇAIS

A

A, a [e] *s* Ière lettre de l'alphabet
a *art indef* un
aback [ə'bæk] *adv* avec le vent dessus;
taken aback déconcerté
abandon [ə'bændən] *s* abandon *m* ‖ *tr*
abandonner
abase [ə'bes] *tr* abaisser, humilier
abasement [ə'besmənt] *s* abaissement *m*
abash [ə'bæʃ] *tr* décontenancer
abashed *adj* confus, confondu
abate [ə'bet] *tr* diminuer, réduire; (*part
of price*) rabattre ‖ *intr* se calmer;
(*said of wind*) tomber
abbess ['æbɪs] *s* abbesse *f*
abbey ['æbi] *s* abbaye *f*
abbot ['æbət] *s* abbé *m*
abbreviate [ə'brivɪ,et] *tr* abréger
abbreviation [ə,brivɪ'eʃən] *s* abréviation *f*
A B C's [,e,bi'siz] *spl* (letterword)
a b c m
abdicate ['æbdɪ,ket] *tr & intr* abdiquer
abdomen ['æbdəmən], [æb'domən] *s*
abdomen *m*
abduct [æb'dʌkt] *tr* enlever, ravir
abeam [ə'bim] *adv* par le travers
abed [ə'bed] *adv* au lit
abet [ə'bet] *v* (*pret & pp* **abetted**; *ger*
abetting) *tr* encourager
abettor [ə'betər] *s* complice *mf*
abeyance [ə'beəns] *s* suspension *f*; **in
abeyance** en suspens
ab·hor [æb'hɔr] *v* (*pret & pp* **-horred**;
ger **-horring**) *tr* abhorrer, détester
abhorrent [æb'hɑrənt], [æb'hɔrənt] *adj*
détestable, répugnant
abide [ə'baɪd] *v* (*pret & pp* **abode** or
abided) *tr* attendre ‖ *intr* demeurer,
continuer, persister; **to abide by** s'en
tenir à; rester fidèle à
abili·ty [ə'bɪlɪti] *s* (*pl* **-ties**) capacité
f, habileté *f*; talent *m*
abject [æb'dʒekt] *adj* abject
ablative ['æblətɪv] *adj & s* ablatif *m*
ablaut ['æblaut] *s* apophonie *f*
ablaze [ə'blez] *adj* enflammé; (*colorful*) resplendissant ‖ *adv* en feu
able ['ebəl] *adj* capable, habile; **to be
able to** pouvoir
a'ble-bod'ied *adj* robuste, vigoureux,
(*seaman*) breveté
abloom [ə'blum] *adj & adv* en fleur
abnormal [æb'nɔrməl] *adj* anormal
abnormali·ty [,æbnɔr'mælɪti] *s* (*pl*
-ties) anomalie *f*, irrégularité *f*; (*of
body*) difformité *f*
aboard [ə'bord] *adv* à bord; **all
aboard!** en voiture!; **to go aboard**
s'embarquer ‖ *prep* à bord de
abode [ə'bod] *s* demeure *f*, résidence *f*

abolish [ə'bɑlɪʃ] *tr* abolir
A-bomb ['e,bɑm] *s* bombe *f* atomique
abomination [ə,bɑmɪ'neʃən] *s* abomination *f*
aborigines [,æbə'rɪdʒɪ,niz] *spl* abori-
gènes *mpl*
abort [ə'bɔrt] *intr* avorter
abortion [ə'bɔrʃən] *s* avortement *m*
abound [ə'baund] *intr* abonder
about [ə'baut] *adv* à la ronde, tout
autour; (*almost*) presque; (*here and
there*) çà et là; **to be about to** être
sur le point de ‖ *prep* autour de, aux
environs de; (*approximately*) environ; au sujet de; vers, e.g., **about six
o'clock** vers six heures; **it is about
. . .** il s'agit de . . .
about'-face' or **about'-face!** *s* volte-
face *f*; (mil) demi-tour *m* ‖ **about'-
face!** *intr* faire volte-face
above [ə'bʌv] *adv* en haut; au-dessus,
ci-dessus ‖ *prep* au-dessus de; plus
que, outre; (*another point on the
river*) en amont de; **above all** surtout
above'-men'tioned *adj* susmentionné
abrasive [ə'bresɪv], [ə'brezɪv] *adj & s*
abrasif *m*
abreast [ə'brest] *adj & adv* de front;
three abreast par rangs de trois; **to
be abreast of** or **with** être en ligne
avec; **to keep abreast of** se tenir au
courant de
abridge [ə'brɪdʒ] *tr* abréger
abridgment [ə'brɪdʒmənt] *s* abrégé *m*,
résumé *m*; réduction *f*
abroad [ə'brɔd] *adv* au loin; (*in foreign parts*) à l'étranger
abrogate ['æbrə,get] *tr* abroger
abrupt [ə'brʌpt] *adj* (*steep; impolite*)
abrupt; (*hasty*) brusque, précipité
abscess ['æbses] *s* abcès *m*
abscond [æb'skand] *intr* s'enfuir, déguerpir; **to abscond with** lever le pied
avec
absence ['æbsəns] *s* absence *f*
absent ['æbsənt] *adj* absent ‖ [æb-
'sent] *tr*—**to absent oneself** s'absenter
absentee [,æbsən'ti] *s* absent *m*
ab'sent-mind'ed *adj* absent, distrait
absolute ['æbsə,lut] *adj & s* absolu *m*
absolutely ['æbsə,lutli] *adv* absolument ‖ [,æbsə'lutli] *adv* (coll) absolument
absolve [æb'salv] *tr* absoudre
absorb [æb'sɔrb] *tr* absorber; **to be or
become absorbed in** s'absorber dans
absorbent [æb'sɔrbənt] *adj* absorbant;
(*cotton*) hydrophile ‖ *s* absorbant *m*
absorbing [æb'sɔrbɪŋ] *adj* absorbant
abstain [æb'sten] *intr* s'abstenir

abstemious [æb'stimɪ·əs] *adj* abstinent, sobre

abstinent ['æbstɪnənt] *adj* abstinent

abstract ['æbstrækt] *adj* abstrait ‖ *s* abrégé *m*, résumé *m* ‖ *tr* résumer ‖ [æb'strækt] *tr* abstraire; (*to remove*) soustraire

abstractedly [æb'stræktɪdli] *adv* d'un œil distrait

abstruse [æb'strus] *adj* abstrus

absurd [æb'sʌrd], [æb'zʌrd] *adj* absurde

absurdi·ty [æb'sʌrdɪti], [æb'zʌrdɪti] *s* (*pl* **-ties**) absurdité *f*

abundance [ə'bʌndəns] *s* abondance *f*

abundant [ə'bʌndənt] *adj* abondant

abuse [ə'bjus] *s* abus *m*; (*mistreatment*) maltraitement *m*; (*insulting words*) insultes *fpl* ‖ [ə'bjuz] *tr* abuser de; maltraiter; insulter

abusive [ə'bjusɪv] *adj* (*insulting*) injurieux; (*wrong*) abusif

abut [ə'bʌt] *v* (*pret & pp* **abutted**; *ger* **abutting**) *intr*—**to abut on** border, confiner

abutment [ə'bʌtmənt] *s* (*of wall*) contrefort *m*; (*of bridge*) culée *f*; (*of arch*) pied-droit *m*

abyss [ə'bɪs] *s* abîme *m*

A.C. ['e'si] *s* (letterword) (**alternating current**) courant *m* alternatif

academic [,ækə'dɛmɪk] *adj* académique; théorique ‖ *s* étudiant *m* or professeur *m* de l'université

academical [,ækə'dɛmɪkəl] *adj* académique; théorique ‖ **academicals** *spl* costume *m* académique

academician [ə,kædə'mɪʃən] *s* académicien *m*

acade·my [ə'kædəmi] *s* (*pl* **-mies**) académie *f*; (*preparatory school*) collège *m*

accede [æk'sid] *intr* acquiescer; **to accede to** accéder à; (*the throne*) monter sur

accelerate [æk'sɛlə,ret] *tr & intr* accélérer

accelerator [æk'sɛlə,retər] *s* accélérateur *m*

accent ['æksɛnt] *s* accent *m* ‖ ['æksɛnt], [æk'sɛnt] *tr* accentuer

accentuate [æk'sɛntʃʊ,et] *tr* accentuer

accept [æk'sɛpt] *tr* accepter

acceptable [æk'sɛptəbəl] *adj* acceptable

acceptance [æk'sɛptəns] *s* acceptation *f*; (*approval*) approbation *f*

acceptation [,æksɛp'teʃən] *s* acceptation *f*; (*meaning*) acception *f*

access ['æksɛs] *s* accès *m*

accessible [æk'sɛsɪbəl] *adj* accessible

accession [æk'sɛʃən] *s* accession *f*

accesso·ry [æk'sɛsəri] *adj* accessoire ‖ *s* (*pl* **-ries**) accessoire *m*; (*to a crime*) complice *mf*

ac'cess route' *s* voie *f* de raccordement, bretelle *f*

accident ['æksɪdənt] *s* accident *m*; **by accident** par accident

accidental [,æksɪ'dɛntəl] *adj* accidentel ‖ *s* (mus) accident *m*

ac'cident-prone' *adj* prédisposé aux accidents

acclaim [ə'klem] *tr* acclamer

acclimate ['æklɪ,mɛt] *tr* acclimater

accommodate [ə'kʌmə,det] *tr* accommoder; (*to oblige*) rendre service à; (*to lodge*) loger

accommodating [ə'kʌmə,detɪŋ] *adj* accommodant, serviable

accommodation [ə,kʌmə'deʃən] *s* accommodation *f*; **accommodations** commodités *fpl*; (*in a train*) place *f*; (*in a hotel*) chambre *f*; (*room and board*) le vivre et le couvert

accompaniment [ə'kʌmpənɪmənt] *s* accompagnement *m*

accompanist [ə'kʌmpənɪst] *s* accompagnateur *m*

accompa·ny [ə'kʌmpəni] *v* (*pret & pp* **-nied**) *tr* accompagner

accomplice [ə'kɑmplɪs] *s* complice *mf*

accomplish [ə'kɑmplɪʃ] *tr* accomplir

accomplishment [ə'kɑmplɪmənt] *s* accomplissement *m*, réalisation *f*; (*thing itself*) œuvre *f* accomplie; **accomplishments** arts *mpl* d'agrément, talents *mpl*

accord [ə'kɔrd] *s* accord *m*; **in accord** d'accord; **of one's own accord** de son plein gré ‖ *tr* accorder ‖ *intr* se mettre d'accord

accordance [ə'kɔrdəns] *s* accord *m*; **in accordance with** conformément à

according [ə'kɔrdɪŋ] *adj*—**according as** selon que; **according to** selon, d'après, suivant; **according to expert advice** au dire d'experts

accordingly [ə'kɔrdɪŋli] *adv* en conséquence

accordion [ə'kɔrdɪ·ən] *s* accordéon *m*

accost [ə'kɔst], [ə'kɑst] *tr* accoster

account [ə'kaunt] *s* compte *m*; profit *m*, calcul *m*; (*narration*) récit *m*; (*report*) compte rendu; (*explanation*) explication *f*; **of no account** sans importance; **on account of** à cause de; **on no account** en aucune façon; **to call to account** demander des comptes à ‖ *intr*—**to account for** expliquer; (*money*) rendre compte de

accountable [ə'kauntəbəl] *adj* responsable; (*explainable*) explicable

accountant [ə'kauntənt] *s* comptable *mf*

account' book' *s* registre *m* de comptabilité

accounting [ə'kauntɪŋ] *s* règlement *m* de comptes; (*profession*) comptabilité *f*

accouterments [ə'kutərmənts] *spl* équipement *m*

accredit [ə'krɛdɪt] *tr* accréditer

accretion [ə'kriʃən] *s* accroissement *m*

accrue [ə'kru] *intr* s'accroître; **to accrue from** dériver de; **to accrue to** échoir à

accumulate [ə'kjumjə,let] *tr* accumuler ‖ *intr* s'accumuler

accuracy ['ækjərəsi] *s* exactitude *f*

accurate ['ækjərɪt] *adj* exact; (*aim*) juste; (*translation*) fidèle

accursed [ə'kʌrsɪd], [ə'kʌrst] *adj* maudit

accusation [,ækjə'zeʃən] *s* accusation *f*

accusative [ə'kju:zətɪv] *adj & s* accusatif *m*

accuse [ə'kju:z] *tr* accuser

accused *s* accusé *m*, inculpé *m*

accustom [ə'kʌstəm] *tr* accoutumer; **to become accustomed** s'accoutumer

ace [es] *s* as *m*; **to have an ace up one's sleeve** avoir un atout dans la manche

acetate ['æsɪ,tet] *s* acétate *m*

ace/tic ac/id [ə'si:tɪk] *s* acide *m* acétique

acetone ['æsɪ,ton] *s* acétone *f*

acet/ylene torch/ [ə'setɪ,lin] *s* chalumeau *m* oxyacétylénique

ache [ek] *s* douleur *f* || *intr* faire mal; **my head aches** j'ai mal à la tête; **to be aching to** (coll) brûler de

achieve [ə't/i:v] *tr* accomplir, atteindre; **(a victory)** remporter

achievement [ə't/i:vmənt] *s* accomplissement *m*, réalisation *f*; **(thing itself)** œuvre *f* remarquable, réussite *f*; **(heroic deed)** exploit *m*

Achil/les' heel/ [ə'kɪliz] *s* talon *m* d'Achille

acid ['æsɪd] *adj & s* acide *m*

acidi·ty [ə'sɪdɪti] *s* (*pl* -ties) acidité *f*

ac/id test/ *s* (fig) épreuve *f* définitive

acknowledge [æk'nɑlɪdʒ] *tr* reconnaître; **to acknowledge receipt of** accuser réception de

acknowledgment [æk'nɑlɪdʒmənt] *s* reconnaissance *f*; **(of a letter)** accusé *m* de réception; **(receipt)** récépissé *m*

acme ['ækmi] *s* comble *m*, sommet *m*

acolyte ['ækə,laɪt] *s* enfant *m* de chœur; **(priest)** acolyte *m*; assistant *m*

acorn ['ekɔrn], ['ekərn] *s* gland *m*

acoustic [ə'ku:stɪk] *adj* acoustique || **acoustics** *s & spl* acoustique *f*

acquaint [ə'kwent] *tr* informer; **to be acquainted** se connaître; **to be acquainted with** connaître

acquaintance [ə'kwentəns] *s* connaissance *f*

acquiesce [,ækwɪ'es] *intr* acquiescer

acquiescence [,ækwɪ'esəns] *s* acquiescement *m*, consentement *m*

acquire [ə'kwaɪr] *tr* acquérir; **(friends; a reputation)** s'acquérir

acquirement [ə'kwaɪrmənt] *s* acquisition *f*

acquisition [,ækwɪ'zɪ/ən] *s* acquisition *f*

acquisitive [ə'kwɪzɪtɪv] *adj* âpre au gain, avide

acquit [ə'kwɪt] *v* (*pret & pp* **acquitted**; *ger* **acquitting**) *tr* acquitter; **to acquit oneself** se comporter

acquittal [ə'kwɪtəl] *s* acquittement *m*

acre ['ekər] *s* acre *f*

acrid ['ækrɪd] *adj* âcre

acrimonious [,ækrɪ'monɪ·əs] *adj* acrimonieux

acrobat ['ækrə,bæt] *s* acrobate *mf*

acrobatic [,ækrə'bætɪk] *adj* acrobatique || **acrobatics** *s* (*profession*) acrobatie *f*; **acrobatics** *spl* (*stunts*) acrobaties

acronym ['ækrənɪm] *s* sigle *m*

acropolis [ə'krɑpəlɪs] *s* acropole *f*

across [ə'krɔs], [ə'krɑs] *adv* en travers, à travers; **(sidewise)** en largeur || *prep* en travers de; **(e.g., the street)** de l'autre côté de; **across country** à travers champs; **to come across** rencontrer par hasard; **to go across** traverser

acrostic [ə'krɑstɪk], [ə'krɑstɪk] *s* acrostiche *m*

act [ækt] *s* action *f*, acte *m*; **(circus, rad, telv)** numéro *m*; **(govt)** loi *f*; **(law, theat)** acte; **(coll)** allure *f* affectée, comédie *f*; **in the act** sur le fait, en flagrant délit || *tr* jouer; **to act the fool** faire le pitre || *intr* agir; se conduire; **(theat)** jouer; **to act as** servir de; **to act on** influer sur

acting ['æktɪŋ] *adj* intérimaire || *s* **(actor's art)** jeu *m*; **(profession)** théâtre *m*

action ['æk/ən] *s* action *f*; **(law)** acte *m*; **(mach)** jeu *m*; **(theat)** intrigue *f*; **out of action** hors de service; **to go into action** (mil) aller au feu; **to suit the action to the word** joindre le geste à la parole; **to take action** prendre des mesures

activate ['æktɪ,vet] *tr* activer

active ['æktɪv] *adj* actif

activi·ty [æk'tɪvɪti] *s* (*pl* -ties) activité *f*

actor ['æktər] *s* acteur *m*

actress ['æktrɪs] *s* actrice *f*

actual ['ækt/u·əl] *adj* véritable, réel, effectif

actually ['ækt/u·əli] *adv* réellement, en réalité, effectivement

actuar·y ['ækt/u,eri] *s* (*pl* -les) actuaire *m*

actuate ['ækt/u,et] *tr* actionner; **(to motivate)** animer

acuity [ə'kju·ɪti] *s* acuité *f*

acumen [ə'kjumən] *s* finesse *f*

acute [ə'kjut] *adj* aigu; (fig) avisé

acutely [ə'kjutli] *adv* profondément

A.D. ['e'di] *adj* (letterword) **(Anno Domini)** ap. J.-C.

ad [æd] *s* (coll) annonce *f*

adage ['ædɪdʒ] *s* adage *m*

Adam ['ædəm] *s* Adam *m*; **I don't know him from Adam** (coll) je ne le connais ni d'Ève ni d'Adam

adamant ['ædəmənt] *adj* inflexible

Ad/am's ap/ple *s* pomme *f* d'Adam

adapt [ə'dæpt] *tr* adapter

adaptation [,ædæp'te/ən] *s* adaptation *f*

adapter [ə'dæptər] *s* adaptateur *m*, raccord *m*; **(phot)** bague *f* porte-objectif

add [æd] *tr* ajouter; **to add up** additionner || *intr* additionner; **to add up to** s'élever à

adder ['ædər] *s* (zool) vipère *f*

addict ['ædɪkt] *s* toxicomane *mf*; **(sports)** fanatique *mf* || [ə'dɪkt] *tr* atteindre de toxicomanie; **to be addicted to** (to enjoy) s'adonner à

addiction [ə'dɪk/ən] *s* toxicomanie *f*; **addiction to** penchant *m* pour

add/ing machine/ *s* machine *f* à calculer, additionneuse *f*

addition [ə'dɪʃən] s addition f; **in addition to** en plus de

additive ['ædɪtɪv] adj & s additif m

addle ['ædəl] tr brouiller

address [ə'dres], ['ædres] s adresse f ‖ [ə'dres] s discours m; **to deliver an address** prononcer un discours ‖ tr adresser; s'adresser à; (*an audience*) faire un discours à

address' book s carnet m d'adresses

addressee [ˌædre'si] s destinataire mf

adduce [ə'd(j)us] tr alléguer; (*proof*) fournir

adenoids ['ædəˌnɔɪdz] spl végétations fpl adénoïdes

adept [ə'dept] adj habile ‖ s adepte mf

adequate ['ædɪkwɪt] adj suffisant, adéquat; **adequate to** à la hauteur de, proportionné à

adhere [æd'hɪr] intr adhérer

adherence [æd'hɪrəns] s adhérence f

adherent [æd'hɪrənt] adj & s adhérent m

adhesion [æd'hiʒən] s adhésion f; (pathol) adhérence f

adhesive [æd'hisɪv], [æd'hizɪv] adj & s adhésif m

adhe'sive tape' s sparadrap m

adieu [ə'd(j)u] s (pl **adieus** or **adieux**) adieu m ‖ interj adieu!

ad infinitum [ˌæd ˌɪnfɪ'naɪtəm] adv sans fin

adjacent [ə'dʒesənt] adj adjacent

adjective ['ædʒɪktɪv] adj & s adjectif m

adjoin [ə'dʒɔɪn] tr avoisiner ‖ intr être contigu

adjoining [ə'dʒɔɪnɪŋ] adj contigu

adjourn [ə'dʒʌrn] tr (*to postpone*) remettre, reporter; (*a meeting, a session*) lever; (*sine die; for resumption at another time or place*) ajourner ‖ intr s'ajourner; lever la séance

adjournment [ə'dʒʌrnmənt] s suspension f de séance

adjudge [ə'dʒʌdʒ] tr adjuger; (*a criminal*) condamner

adjudicate [ə'dʒudɪˌket] tr & intr juger

adjunct ['ædʒʌŋkt] adj & s adjoint m; **adjuncts** accessoires mpl

adjust [ə'dʒʌst] tr ajuster ‖ intr s'adapter

adjustable [ə'dʒʌstəbəl] adj réglable

adjustment [ə'dʒʌstmənt] s ajustage m, réglage m; (*arrangement*) ajustement m, règlement m; (telv) mise f au point

adjutant ['ædʒətənt] s adjutant m

ad-lib [ˌæd'lɪb] adj improvisé ‖ v (*pret* & *pp* **-libbed**; *ger* **-libbing**) tr & intr improviser (en cascade)

administer [æd'mɪnɪstər] tr administrer; **to administer an oath** faire prêter serment ‖ intr—**to administer to** pourvoir à, aider, assister

administration [ædˌmɪnɪs'treʃən] s administration f; gouvernement m

administrator [æd'mɪnɪsˌtretər] s administrateur m

admiral ['ædmɪrəl] s amiral m

admiral·ty ['ædmɪrəlti] s (pl **-ties**) amirauté f; ministère m de la marine

admiration [ˌædmɪ'reʃən] s admiration f

admire [æd'maɪr] tr admirer

admirer [æd'maɪrər] s admirateur m; (*suitor*) soupirant m

admission [æd'mɪʃən] s admission f; (*price*) entrée f; (*confession*) aveu m

ad·mit [æd'mɪt] v (*pret* & *pp* **-mitted**; *ger* **-mitting**) tr admettre; (*e.g., a mistake*) avouer; **admit bearer** laisser passer

admittance [æd'mɪtəns] s entrée f

admittedly [æd'mɪtɪdli] adv manifestement

admonish [æd'monɪʃ] tr admonester

ad nauseam [æd'nɔ/ɪ·əm], [æd'nɔsɪ·əm] adv jusqu'au dégoût

ado [ə'du] s agitation f; **much ado about nothing** beaucoup de bruit pour rien; **without further ado** sans plus de façons

adolescence [ˌædə'lesəns] s adolescence f

adolescent [ˌædə'lesənt] adj & s adolescent m

adopt [ə'dapt] tr adopter

adoption [ə'dapʃən] s adoption f

adoptive [ə'daptɪv] adj adoptif

adorable [ə'dorəbəl] adj adorable

adoration [ˌædə'reʃən] s adoration f

adore [ə'dor] tr adorer

adorn [ə'dɔrn] tr orner, parer

adornment [ə'dɔrnmənt] s parure f

adre'nal glands' [ə'drinəl], [æ'drinəl] spl (capsules) surrénales fpl

adrenalin [ə'drenəlɪn] s adrénaline f

Adriatic [ˌedrɪ'ætɪk], [ˌædrɪ'ætɪk] adj & s Adriatique f

adrift [ə'drɪft] adj & adv à la dérive

adroit [ə'drɔɪt] adj adroit, habile

adulate ['ædʒəˌlet] tr aduler

adult [ə'dʌlt], ['ædʌlt] adj & s adulte mf

adulterate [ə'dʌltəˌret] tr frelater

adulteration [əˌdʌltə'reʃən] s frelatage m

adulterer [ə'dʌltərər] s adultère m

adulteress [ə'dʌltərɪs] s adultère f

adulterous [ə'dʌltərəs] adj adultère

adulter·y [ə'dʌltəri] s (pl **-ies**) adultère m

adumbrate [æd'ʌmbret], ['ædəmˌbret] tr ébaucher; (*to foreshadow*) présager

advance [æd'væns], [æd'vɑns] s avance f; **advances** propositions fpl; propositions malhonnêtes; **in advance** d'avance; en avance ‖ tr avancer ‖ intr avancer, s'avancer; (*said of prices*) augmenter; (*said of stocks*) monter

advancement [æd'vænsmənt], [æd'vɑnsmənt] s avancement m

advance' pay'ment s versement m anticipé

advantage [æd'væntɪdʒ], [æd'vɑntɪdʒ] s avantage m; **to take advantage of** profiter de

advent ['ædvent] s venue f; **Advent** (eccl) Avent m

adventitious [ˌædven'tɪʃəs] adj adventice

adventure [æd'vent/ər] *s* aventure *f*

adventurer [æd'vent/ərər] *s* aventurier *m*

adventuress [æd'vent/əris] *s* aventurière *f*

adventurous [æd'vent/ərəs] *adj* aventureux

adverb ['ædvʌrb] *s* adverbe *m*

adversary ['ædvər,seri] *s* (*pl* **-ies**) adversaire *mf*

adverse [æd'vʌrs], ['ædvʌrs] *adj* adverse

adversity [æd'vʌrsiti] *s* (*pl* **-ties**) adversité *f*

advertise ['ædvər,taiz], [,ædvər'taiz] *tr* & *intr* annoncer

advertisement [,ædvər'taizmənt], [æd-'vʌrtizmənt] *s* annonce *f*

advertiser ['ædvər,taizər], [,ædvər-'taizər] *s* annonceur *m*

advertising ['ædvər,taiziŋ] *s* réclame *f*

ad'vertising a'gency *s* agence *f* de publicité

ad'vertising man' *s* entrepreneur *m* de publicité

advice [æd'vais] *s* conseil *m*; conseils; **a piece of advice** un conseil

advisable [æd'vaizəbəl] *adj* opportun, recommandable

advise [æd'vaiz] *tr* conseiller; (*to inform*) aviser; **to advise against** déconseiller; **to advise s.o. to** + *inf* conseiller à qn de + *inf*

advisedly [æd'vaizidli] *adv* en connaissance de cause

advisement [æd'vaizmənt] *s* conseils *mpl*; **to take under advisement** mettre en délibération

adviser [æd'vaizər] *s* conseiller *m*

advisory [æd'vaizəri] *adj* consultatif

advocacy ['ædvəkəsi] *s* plaidoyer *m*

advocate ['ædvə,ket] *s* partisan *m*; (*lawyer*) avocat *m* || *tr* préconiser

Aege'an Sea' [i'dʒi-ən] *s* mer *f* Égée, mer de l'Archipel

aegis ['idʒis] *s* égide *f*

aerate ['eret] *tr* aérer

aerial ['eri-əl] *adj* aérien || *s* antenne *f*

aerodynamic [,erodai'næmik] *adj* aérodynamique || **aerodynamics** *s* aérodynamique *f*

aeronautic [,ero'nɔtik] *adj* aéronautique || **aeronautics** *s* aéronautique *f*

aerosol ['erə,sol] *s* aérosol *m*

aerospace ['erə,spes] *adj* aérospatial

Aeschylus ['eskiləs] *s* Eschyle *m*

aesthete ['esθit] *s* esthète *mf*

aesthetic [es'θetik] *adj* esthétique || **aesthetics** *s* esthétique *f*

afar [ə'far] *adv* au loin

affable ['æfəbəl] *adj* affable

affair [ə'fer] *s* affaire *f*; (*of lovers*) affaire de cœur

affect [ə'fekt] *tr* affecter

affectation [,æfek'te/ən] *s* affectation *f*

affected *adj* affecté, maniéré

affection [ə'fek/ən] *s* affection *f*

affectionate [ə'fek/ənit] *adj* affectueux

affidavit [,æfi'devit] *s* déclaration *f* sous serment

affiliate [ə'fili,et] *s* (com) société *f* affiliée || *tr* affilier || *intr* s'affilier

affinity [ə'finiti] *s* (*pl* **-ties**) affinité *f*; (*inlawry*) alliance *f*

affirm [ə'fʌrm] *tr* & *intr* affirmer

affirmative [ə'fʌrmətiv] *adj* affirmatif || *s* affirmative *f*

affix ['æfiks] *s* affixe *m* || [ə'fiks] *tr* annexer; (*a signature*) apposer; (*guilt*) attribuer; (*on the wall*) afficher

afflict [ə'flikt] *tr* affliger

affliction [ə'flik/ən] *s* (*sorrow*) affliction *f*; (*disorder*) infirmité *f*

affluence ['æflu-əns] *s* affluence *f* de biens, richesse *f*

afford [ə'ford] *tr* fournir; se permettre, avoir de quoi payer

affront [ə'frʌnt] *s* affront *m* || *tr* insulter

Afghanistan [æf'gæni,stæn] *s* l'Afghanistan *m*

afire [ə'fair] *adj* & *adv* en feu

aflame [ə'flem] *adj* & *adv* en flammes

afloat [ə'flot] *adj* & *adv* à flot; (*rumor*) en circulation; **to keep afloat on the water** se tenir sur l'eau

afoot [ə'fut] *adj* & *adv* à pied; (*underway*) en œuvre

aforesaid [ə'for,sed] *adj* susdit; ci-dessus mentionné

afraid [ə'fred] *adj* effrayé; **to be afraid** avoir peur

afresh [ə'fre/] *adv* à nouveau

Africa ['æfrikə] *s* Afrique *f*; l'Afrique

African ['æfrikən] *adj* africain || *s* Africain *m*

after ['æftər], ['aftər] *adj* suivant, postérieur || *adv* après, plus tard || *prep* après, à la suite de; (*in the manner or style of*) d'après; (*not translated in expressions of time*), e.g., **eight minutes after ten** dix heures huit || *conj* après que

af'ter-din'ner *adj* d'après dîner

af'ter-effect' *s* contrecoup *m*; **after-effects** (pathol) séquelles *fpl*

af'ter-glow' *s* lueur *f* du coucher

af'ter-im'age *s* image *f* consécutive

af'ter-life' *s* survie *f*

aftermath ['æftər,mæθ], ['aftər,mæθ] *s* conséquences *fpl* sérieuses, suites *fpl*; (agr) regain *m*

af'ter-noon' *s* après-midi *m* & *f*; **good afternoon!** bonjour!

af'ter-shav'ing lo'tion *s* eau *f* de Cologne pour la barbe

af'ter-taste' *s* arrière-goût *m*

af'ter-thought' *s* réflexion *f* après coup

afterward ['æftərwərd], ['aftərwərd] *adv* après, ensuite

again [ə'gen] *adv* encore, de plus; de nouveau, encore une fois; **now and again** de temps en temps

against [ə'genst] *prep* contre; **against the grain** à rebrousse-poil; **over against** en face de; par contraste avec

age [edʒ] *s* âge *m*; (*about a hundred years*) siècle *m*; **for ages** depuis longtemps; **of age** majeur; **to come of age** atteindre sa majorité; **under age** mineur || *tr* & *intr* vieillir

aged [edʒd] *adj* (*wine, cheese, etc.*)

vieilli; (of the age of) âgé de ||
['edʒɪd] adj âgé, vieux

agen·cy ['edʒənsɪ] s (pl **-cies**) agence
f; (means) action f

agenda [ə'dʒɛndə] s ordre m du jour

agent ['edʒənt] s agent m; (means)
moyen m; (com) commissionnaire m

agglomeration [ə‚glɑmə'reʃən] s agglomération f

aggrandizement [ə'grændɪzmənt] s
agrandissement m

aggravate ['ægrə‚vet] tr aggraver;
(coll) exaspérer

aggregate ['ægrɪ‚get] adj global || s
agrégat m || tr rassembler; (coll)
s'élever à

aggression [ə'grɛʃən] s agression f

aggressive [ə'grɛsɪv] adj agressif; (live-
wire) entreprenant

aggressor [ə'grɛsər] s agresseur m

aghast [ə'gæst], [ə'gɑst] adj abasourdi

agile ['ædʒɪl] adj agile

agility [ə'dʒɪlɪtɪ] s agilité f

agitate ['ædʒɪ‚tet] tr agiter

agitator ['ædʒɪ‚tetər] s agitateur m

aglow [ə'glo] adj & adv rougeoyant

agnostic [æg'nɑstɪk] adj & s agnostique mf

ago [ə'go] adv il y a, e.g., **two days
ago** il y a deux jours

agog [ə'gɑg] adj & adv en émoi

agonizing ['ægə‚naɪzɪŋ] adj angoissant

ago·ny ['ægənɪ] s (pl **-nies**) angoisse f;
(death struggle) agonie f

agrarian [ə'grɛrɪ‚ən] adj agraire; (law)
agrairien || s agrairien m

agree [ə'gri] intr être d'accord, s'accorder; **agreed!** d'accord!; **to agree
to consentir à**

agreeable [ə'gri‚əbəl] adj agréable,
sympathique; (consenting) d'accord

agreement [ə'grimənt] s accord m;
contrat m

agriculture ['ægrɪ‚kʌltʃər] s agriculture f

aground [ə'graʊnd] adj (naut) échoué
|| adv—**to run aground** échouer

ague ['egju] s fièvre f intermittente;
accès m de frisson

ahead [ə'hɛd] adj & adv en avant;
ahead of avant; devant; **straight
ahead** tout droit; **to get ahead of**
devancer

ahem [ə'hɛm] interj hum!

ahoy [ə'hɔɪ] interj—**ship ahoy!** ohé
du navire!

aid [ed] s (assistance) aide f; (assist-
ant) aide mf || tr aider

aide-de-camp ['edə‚kæmp] s (pl
aides-de-camp) officier m d'ordonnance, aide m de camp

ail [el] tr affliger; **what ails you?**
qu'avez-vous? || intr être souffrant

ailment ['elmənt] s indisposition f,
maladie f

aim [em] s but m, objectif m; (of gun)
pointage m || tr diriger; (a blow) al-
longer; (a telescope, cannon, etc.)
pointer, viser || intr viser

air [ɛr] s air m; **on the air** à la radio,
à la télévision, à l'antenne; **to put on
airs** prendre des airs; **to put on the**
air radiodiffuser; **to walk on air** ne
pas toucher terre; **up in the air** con-
fondu, sidéré; (angry) très monté ||
tr aérer; (a question) ventiler; (feelings) donner libre cours à

air-borne ['ɛr‚bɔrn] adj aéroporté

air' brake' s frein m à air comprimé

air'-condi'tion tr climatiser

air' condi'tioner s climatiseur m

air' condi'tioning s climatisation f

air'craft' s aéronef m, appareil m
d'aviation

air'craft car'rier s porte-avions m

air'drop' s parachutage m || tr para-
chuter

air'field' s terrain m d'aviation, aéro-
drome m

air' force' s forces fpl aériennes

air' gap' s (elec) entrefer m

air' let'ter s aérogramme m

air'lift' s pont m aérien

air'line' s ligne f aérienne

air'line pi'lot s pilote m de ligne

air'li'ner s avion m de transport

air'mail' adj aéropostal || s poste f
aérienne; **by airmail** par avion

air'plane' s avion m

air' pock'et s trou m d'air

air' pollu'tion s pollution f de l'air

air'port' s aéroport m

air' raid' s attaque f aérienne

air'-raid drill' s exercice m d'alerte
aérienne

air'-raid shel'ter s abri m

air'-raid ward'en s chef m d'îlot

air'-raid warn'ing s alarme f aérienne

air'sick' adj atteint du mal de l'air

air'sick'ness s mal m de l'air

air' sleeve' or **sock'** s manche f à air

air'strip' s piste f

air' term'inal s aérogare f

air'tight' adj hermétique

air'waves' spl ondes fpl radiophoniques

air'way' s route f aérienne

air·y ['ɛrɪ] adj (comp **-ier**; super **-lest**)
aérien; gracieux; (coll) maniéré

aisle [aɪl] s (through rows of seats)
passage m central, allée f; (in a
train) couloir m; (long passageway
in a church) nef f latérale

ajar [ə'dʒɑr] adj entrebâillé

akimbo [ə'kɪmbo] adj & adv—**with
arms akimbo** les poings sur les
hanches

akin [ə'kɪn] adj apparenté

alabaster ['ælə‚bæstər], ['ælə‚bɑstər]
s albâtre m

alacrity [ə'lækrɪtɪ] s vivacité f, empressement m

alarm [ə'lɑrm] s alarme f; (of clock)
sonnerie f || tr alarmer

alarm' clock' s réveille-matin m, réveil
m

alarming [ə'lɑrmɪŋ] adj alarmant

alas [ə'læs], [ə'lɑs] interj hélas!

Albanian [æl'benɪ‚ən] adj albanais || s
(language) albanais m; (person)
Albanais

albatross ['ælbə‚trɔs], ['ælbə‚trɑs] s
albatros m

albi·no [æl'baɪno] adj albinos || s (pl
-nos) albinos m

album ['ælbəm] s album m

albumen [æl'bjumən] s albumen m

alchemy ['ælkɪmɪ] s alchimie f

alcohol ['ælkə,hɔl], ['ælkə,hɑl] s alcool m

alcoholic [,ælkə'hɔlɪk], [,ælkə'hɑlɪk] adj & s alcoolique mf

alcove ['ælkov] s niche f; (for a bed) alcôve f

alder ['ɔldər] s aune m

alder-man ['ɔldərmən] s (pl -men) conseiller m municipal

ale [el] s ale f

alembic [ə'lembɪk] s alambic m; (fig) creuset m

alert [ə'lʌrt] adj & s alerte f || tr alerter

alfalfa [æl'fælfə] s luzerne f

algebra ['ældʒɪbrə] s algèbre f

Algeria [æl'dʒɪrɪə] s Algérie f

Algerian [æl'dʒɪrɪən] adj (of Algeria) algérien; (of Algiers, the Barbary state) algérois || s Algérien m; Algérois m

Algiers [æl'dʒɪrz] s Alger m

alias ['elɪəs] s nom m d'emprunt f || adv alias, autrement dit

ali-bi ['ælɪ,baɪ] s (pl -bis) excuse f; (law) alibi m

alien ['eljən], ['elɪ-ən] adj & s étranger m

alienate ['eljə,net], ['elɪ-ə,net] tr s'aliéner; (to transfer) aliéner

alight [ə'laɪt] adj allumé || v (pret & pp alighted or alit [ə'lɪt]) intr descendre, se poser; (aer) (on land) atterrir; (aer) (on sea) amerrir

align [ə'laɪn] tr aligner || intr s'aligner

alike [ə'laɪk] adj pareils, e.g., these books are alike ces livres sont pareils; to look alike se ressembler || adv de la même façon

alimony ['ælɪ,monɪ] s pension f alimentaire après divorce

alive [ə'laɪv] adj vivant; vif; alive to sensible à

alka-li ['ælkə,laɪ] s (pl -lis or -lies) alcali m

alkaline ['ælkə,laɪn], ['ælkəlɪn] adj alcalin

all [ɔl] adj indef tout; tout le || s tout m || pron indef tout; tous; all of tout le; first of all tout d'abord; is that all? c'est tout?; (ironically) c'est ça?; not at all pas du tout || adv tout; all at once tout à coup; all but presque; all in (coll) éreinté; all in all à tout prendre; all off (slang) abandonné; all right bon, ça va, très bien; all's well! (naut) bon quart!; all the better tant mieux; all told en tout; fifteen (thirty, etc.) all (tennis) égalité à quinze (trente, etc.); to be all for ne demander mieux que

allay [ə'le] tr apaiser

all'-clear' s fin f d'alerte

allege [ə'ledʒ] tr alléguer; déclarer sous serment; affirmer sans preuve

alleged adj présumé, prétendu, censé

allegedly [ə'ledʒɪdlɪ] adv prétendument, censément

allegiance [ə'lidʒəns] s allégeance f

allegoric(al) [,ælɪ'gɑrɪk(əl)], [,ælɪ'gɔrɪk(əl)] adj allégorique

allego·ry ['ælɪ,gorɪ] s (pl -ries) allégorie f

aller·gy ['ælərdʒɪ] s (pl -gies) allergie f

alleviate [ə'livɪ,et] tr soulager, alléger

alley ['ælɪ] s ruelle f; this is up my alley (slang) cela est dans mes cordes

al'ley cat' s chat m de gouttière

alliance [ə'laɪəns] s alliance f

alligator ['ælɪ,getər] s alligator m

al'ligator pear' s poire f d'avocat

al'ligator wrench' s clef f à mâchoires dentées

alliteration [ə,lɪtə're∫ən] s allitération f

all'-know'ing adj omniscient

allocate ['ælə,ket] tr allouer, assigner

allot [ə'lɑt] v (pret & pp allotted; ger allotting) tr répartir

allotment [ə'lɑtmənt] s allocation f; (from social security) prestation f

all'-out' adj total

allow [ə'laʊ] tr permettre; (a fact; a privilege) accorder; (as an allocation) allouer || intr—to allow for tenir compte de

allowance [ə'laʊ-əns] s allocation f, indemnité f; concession f; tolérance f

alloy ['ælɔɪ], [ə'lɔɪ] s alliage m || [ə'lɔɪ] tr allier

all' right' interj bon!, très bien!, ça va!; (agreed!) c'est entendu!, d'accord!

all'-round' adj (athlete) complet; (man) universel; total, global

All' Saints'' Day' s la Toussaint

All' Souls'' Day' s la fête des Morts

all'spice' s (plant) quatre-épices f; (berry) toute-épice f; piment m

all'-time' adj record

allude [ə'lud] intr—to allude to faire allusion à

allure [ə'lʊr] tr séduire, tenter

allurement [ə'lʊrmənt] s charme m

alluring [ə'lʊrɪŋ] adj séduisant

all' wet' adj (coll) fichu, erroné

al·ly ['ælaɪ], [ə'laɪ] s (pl -lies) allié m || [ə'laɪ] v (pret & pp -lied) tr allier

almanac ['ɔlmə,næk] s almanach m

almighty [ɔl'maɪtɪ] adj omnipotent

almond ['amənd], ['æmənd] s amande f

al'mond tree' s amandier m

almost ['ɔlmost], [ɔl'most] adv presque; I almost fell j'ai failli tomber

alms [amz] s & spl aumône f

alms'house' s hospice m

aloe ['ælo] s aloès m

aloft [ə'lɔft], [ə'lɑft] adv en l'air; (aer) en vol; (naut) en haut

alone [ə'lon] adj seul, e.g., my arm alone suffices mon bras seul suffit; e.g., the metropolis alone la seule métropole; let alone . . . sans compter . . . ; to leave alone laisser tranquille || adv seulement

along [ə'lɔŋ], [ə'laŋ] adv avec; all along tout le temps; come along! venez donc!; to get along s'en aller; se porter, faire des progrès || prep le long de; sur

along'side' adv à côté || prep à côté de

aloof [ə'luːf] *adj* isolé, peu abordable ‖ *adv* à l'écart, à distance

aloud [ə'laud] *adv* à haute voix

alpenstock ['ælpən‚stɑk] *s* bâton *m* ferré

alphabet ['ælfə‚bet] *s* alphabet *m*

alpine ['ælpaɪn] *adj* alpin

Alps [ælps] *spl*—**the Alps** les Alpes *fpl*

already [ɔl'redɪ] *adv* déjà

Alsatian [æl'seʃən] *adj* alsacien ‖ *s* (*dialect*) alsacien *m*; (*person*) Alsacien *m*

also ['ɔlso] *adv* aussi, également

altar ['ɔltər] *s* autel *m*

al'tar boy' *s* enfant *m* de chœur

al'tar cloth' *s* nappe *f* d'autel

al'tar‑piece' *s* rétable *m*

al'tar rail' *s* grille *f* du chœur

alter ['ɔltər] *tr* altérer; (*a suit of clothes*) retoucher, faire des retouches à; (*an animal*) châtrer ‖ *intr* se modifier

alteration [‚ɔltə'reʃən] *s* altération *f*; (*in a building*) modification *f*; **alterations** (*in clothing*) retouches *fpl*

alternate ['ɔltərnɪt], ['æltərnɪt] *adj* alternatif; (*angle*) alterne; (*rhyme*) croisé ‖ ['ɔltər‚net], ['æltər‚net] *tr* faire alternance à ‖ *intr* alterner

al'ternating cur'rent *s* courant *m* alternatif

alternative [ɔl'tɑrnətɪv], [æl'tɑrnətɪv] *adj & s* alternatif *m*

although [ɔl'ðo] *conj* bien que, quoique

altitude ['æltɪ‚t(j)ud] *s* altitude *f*

al‑to ['ælto] *s* (*pl* **-tos**) alto *m*

altogether [‚ɔltə'geðər] *adv* ensemble, entièrement; tout compris

altruist ['æltru‑ɪst] *adj & s* altruiste *mf*

alum ['æləm] *s* alun *m*

aluminum [ə'lumɪnəm] *s* aluminium *m*

alum‑nus [ə'lʌmnəs] *s* (*pl* **-ni** [naɪ]) diplômé *m*, ancien étudiant *m*

alveo‑lus [æl'vi‑ələs] *s* (*pl* **-li** [‚laɪ]) alvéole *m*

always ['ɔlwɪz], ['ɔlwez] *adv* toujours

A.M. ['e'em] *adv* (letterword) (**ante meridiem**) du matin

amalgam [ə'mælgəm] *s* amalgame *m*

amalgamate [ə'mælgə‚met] *tr* amalgamer ‖ *intr* s'amalgamer

amass [ə'mæs] *tr* amasser

amateur ['æmət/ər] *adj & s* amateur *m*

amaze [ə'mez] *tr* étonner

amazing [ə'mezɪŋ] *adj* étonnant

amazon ['æmə‚zɑn], ['æməzən] *s* amazone *f*; **Amazon** Amazone *f*; (*river*) fleuve *m* des Amazones

ambassador [æm'bæsədər] *s* ambassadeur *m*

ambassadress [æm'bæsədrɪs] *s* ambassadrice *f*, ambassadeur *m*

amber ['æmbər] *adj* ambré ‖ *s* ambre *m* jaune, ambre succin

ambidextrous [‚æmbɪ'dekstrəs] *adj* ambidextre

ambigui‑ty [‚æmbɪ'gju‑ɪti] *s* (*pl* **-ties**) ambiguïté *f*

ambition [æm'bɪʃən] *s* ambition *f*

ambitious [æm'bɪʃəs] *adj* ambitieux

amble ['æmbəl] *s* amble *m* ‖ *intr* (*to stroll*) déambuler; (equit) ambler

ambulance ['æmbjələns] *s* ambulance *f*

am'bulance corps' *s* service *m* sanitaire

am'bulance driv'er *s* ambulancier *m*

ambulatory ['æmbjələ‚tori] *adj* ambulatoire

ambush ['æmbuʃ] *s* embuscade *f* ‖ *tr* embusquer

ameliorate [ə'miljə‚ret] *tr* améliorer ‖ *intr* s'améliorer

amen ['e'men], ['ɑ'men] *s* amen *m* ‖ *interj* ainsi soit-il!

amenable [ə'minəbəl], [ə'menəbəl] *adj* docile; **amenable to** (*a court*) justiciable de; (*a fine*) passible de; (*a law*) soumis à; (*persuasion*) disposé à; (*a superior*) responsable envers

amend [ə'mend] *tr* amender ‖ *intr* s'amender

amendment [ə'mendmənt] *s* amendement *m*

amends [ə'mendz] *spl* dédommagement *m*; **to make amends to** dédommager

ameni‑ty [ə'minɪti], [ə'menɪti] *s* (*pl* **-ties**) aménité *f*; **amenities** agréments *mpl*; civilités *fpl*

America [ə'merɪkə] *s* Amérique *f*; l'Amérique

American [ə'merɪkən] *adj* américain *f*; *s* Américain *m*

Amer'ican Eng'lish *s* anglais *m* d'Amérique, américain *m*

Amer'ican In'dian *s* amérindien *m*

Americanism [ə'merɪkə‚nɪzəm] *s* (*word*) américanisme *m*; patriotisme *m* américain

Amer'ican plan' *s* pension *f* complète

Amer'ican way of life' *s* mode *m* de vie américain

amethyst ['æmɪθɪst] *s* améthyste *f*

amiable ['emɪ‑əbəl] *adj* aimable

amicable ['æmɪkəbəl] *adj* amical

amid [ə'mɪd] *prep* au milieu de

amid'ships *adv* au milieu du navire

amidst [ə'mɪdst] *prep* au milieu de

amiss [ə'mɪs] *adj* détraqué; **not amiss** pas mal; **something amiss** quelque chose qui manque, quelque chose qui cloche ‖ *adv* de travers; **to take amiss** prendre en mauvaise part

ami‑ty ['æmɪti] *s* (*pl* **-ties**) amitié *f*

ammeter ['æm‚mitər] *s* ampèremètre *m*

ammonia [ə'monɪ‑ə] *s* (*gas*) ammoniac *m*; (*gas dissolved in water*) ammoniaque *f*

ammunition [‚æmjə'nɪʃən] *s* munitions *fpl*

amnesia [æm'niʒɪ‑ə], [æm'niʒə] *s* amnésie *f*

amnes‑ty ['æmnɪsti] *s* (*pl* **-ties**) amnistie *f* ‖ *v* (*pret & pp* **-tied**) *tr* amnistier

amoeba [ə'mibə] *s* amibe *f*

among [ə'mʌŋ] *prep* entre, parmi

amorous ['æmərəs] *adj* amoureux

amorphous [ə'mɔrfəs] *adj* amorphe

amortize ['æmər‚taɪz] *tr* amortir

amount [ə'maunt] *s* montant *m*, quantité *f* ‖ *intr*—**to amount to** s'élever à

ampere ['æmpɪr] *s* ampère *m*

amphibian [æm'fɪbɪ·ən] *adj & s* amphibie *mf*; amphibien *m*

amphibious [æm'fɪbɪ·əs] *adj* amphibie

amphitheater ['æmfɪ,θɪ·ətər] *s* amphithéâtre *m*

ample ['æmpəl] *adj* ample; (*speech*) satisfaisant; (*reward*) suffisant

amplifier ['æmplɪ,faɪ·ər] *s* amplificateur *m*

ampli·fy ['æmplɪ,faɪ] *v* (*pret & pp* -fied) *tr* amplifier

amplitude ['æmplɪ,t(j)ud] *s* amplitude *f*

am/plitude modula/tion *s* modulation *f* d'amplitude

amputate ['æmpjə,tet] *tr* amputer

amputee [,æmpjə'ti] *s* amputé *m*

amuck [ə'mʌk] *adv*—**to run amuck** s'emballer

amulet ['æmjəlɪt] *s* amulette *f*

amuse [ə'mjuz] *tr* amuser

amusement [ə'mjuzmənt] *s* amusement *m*

amusing [ə'mjuzɪŋ] *adj* amusant

an [æn], [ən] *art indef* (devant un son vocalique) un

anachronism [ə'nækrə,nɪzəm] *s* anachronisme *m*

analogous [ə'næləgəs] *adj* analogue

analo·gy [ə'nælədʒɪ] *s* (*pl* -gies) analogie *f*

analy·sis [ə'nælɪsɪs] *s* (*pl* -ses [,siz]) analyse *f*

analyst ['ænəlɪst] *s* analyste *mf*

analytic(al) [,ænə'lɪtɪk(əl)] *adj* analytique

analyze ['ænə,laɪz] *tr* analyser

anarchist ['ænərkɪst] *s* anarchiste *mf*

anarchy ['ænərkɪ] *s* anarchie *f*

anathema [ə'næθɪmə] *s* anathème *m*

anatomic(al) [,ænə'tɑmɪk(əl)] *adj* anatomique

anato·my [ə'nætəmɪ] *s* (*pl* -mies) anatomie *f*

ancestor ['ænsestər] *s* ancêtre *m*

ances·try ['ænsestrɪ] *s* (*pl* -tries) ancêtres *mpl*, aïeux *mpl*; (*line*) ascendance *f*

anchor ['æŋkər] *s* ancre *f*; **anchors aweigh!** ancres levées!; **to cast anchor** jeter l'ancre, mouiller l'ancre; **to weigh anchor** lever l'ancre || *tr & intr* ancrer

ancho·vy ['æntʃovi] *s* (*pl* -vies) anchois *m*

ancient ['enʃənt] *adj* ancien

and [ænd] *conj* et; **and/or** et/ou; **and so forth** et ainsi de suite

andiron ['ænd,aɪ·ərn] *s* chenet *m*

anecdote ['ænɪk,dot] *s* anecdote *f*

anemia [ə'nimɪ·ə] *s* anémie *f*

anesthesia [,ænɪs'θiʒə] *s* anesthésie *f*

anesthetic [,ænɪs'θetɪk] *adj & s* anesthésique *m*

anesthetist [æ'nesθɪtɪst] *s* anesthésiste *mf*

anesthetize [æ'nesθɪ,taɪz] *tr* anesthésier

aneurysm ['ænjə,rɪzəm] *s* anévrisme *m*

anew [ə'n(j)u] *adv* à (or de) nouveau

angel ['endʒəl] *s* ange *m*; (*financial backer*) (coll) bailleur *m* de fonds

angelic(al) [æn'dʒelɪk(əl)] *adj* angélique

anger ['æŋgər] *s* colère *f* || *tr* mettre en colère, fâcher

angina pectoris [æn'dʒaɪnə'pektərɪs] *s* angine *f* de poitrine

angle ['æŋgəl] *s* angle *m* || *tr* (journ) présenter sous un certain angle || *intr* pêcher à la ligne; **to angle for** essayer d'attraper; (*a compliment*) quêter

angler ['æŋglər] *s* pêcheur *m* à la ligne; (*schemer*) intrigant *m*

an·gry ['æŋgri] *adj* (*comp* -grier; *super* -griest) fâché; **angry at** fâché de; **angry with** fâché contre; **to become angry** se mettre en colère

anguish ['æŋgwɪʃ] *s* angoisse *f*

angular ['æŋgjələr] *adj* angulaire; (*features*) anguleux

animal ['ænɪməl] *adj & s* animal *m*

animate ['ænɪmɪt] *adj* animé ['ænɪ,met] *tr* animer

an/imated cartoon/ *s* dessins *mpl* animés

animation [,ænɪ'meʃən] *s* animation *f*

animosi·ty [,ænɪ'mɑsɪtɪ] *s* (*pl* -ties) animosité *f*

animus ['ænɪməs] *s* animosité *f*; intention *f*

anion ['æn,aɪ·ən] *s* anion *m*

anise ['ænɪs] *s* anis *m*

aniseed ['ænɪ,sid] *s* graine *f* d'anis

ankle ['æŋkəl] *s* cheville *f*

anklet ['æŋklɪt] *s* socquette *f*; bracelet *m* de cheville

annals ['ænəlz] *spl* annales *fpl*

anneal [ə'nil] *tr* recuire, détremper

annex ['æneks] *s* annexe *f* || [ə'neks] *tr* annexer, rattacher

annexation [,æneks'eʃən] *s* annexion *f*, rattachement *m*

annihilate [ə'naɪ·ɪ,let] *tr* annihiler

annihilation [ə,naɪ·ɪ'leʃən] *s* anéantissement *m*

anniversa·ry [,ænɪ'vʌrsərɪ] *adj* anniversaire || *s* (*pl* -ries) anniversaire *m*

annotate ['ænə,tet] *tr* annoter

announce [ə'nauns] *tr* annoncer

announcement [ə'naunsmənt] *s* annonce *f*, avis *m*

announcer [ə'naunsər] *s* annonceur *m*; (rad) présentateur *m*, speaker *m*

annoy [ə'nɔɪ] *tr* ennuyer, tourmenter

annoyance [ə'nɔɪ·əns] *s* ennui *m*

annoying [ə'nɔɪ·ɪŋ] *adj* ennuyeux

annual ['ænju·əl] *adj* annuel || *s* annuaire *m*; plante *f* annuelle

annui·ty [ə'n(j)u·ɪtɪ] *s* (*pl* -ties) (*annual payment*) annuité *f*; (*of a retired person*) pension *f* de retraite, pension viagère

an·nul [ə'nʌl] *v* (*pret & pp* -nulled; *ger* -nulling) *tr* annuler; abolir

anode ['ænod] *s* anode *f*

anodyne ['ænə,daɪn] *adj & s* anodin *m*

anoint [ə'nɔɪnt] *tr* oindre

anon [ə'nɑn] *adv* tout à l'heure

anonymity [,ænə'nɪmɪtɪ] *s* anonymat *m*

anonymous [ə'nɑnɪməs] *adj* anonyme

another [ə'nʌðər] *adj & pron indef* un autre; (*an additional*) encore un; **many another** beaucoup d'autres

answer ['ænsər], ['ɑnsər] s réponse f; (math) solution f || tr (e.g., yes or no) répondre; (a question, a letter) répondre à || intr répondre; **to answer for** répondre de
an'swer book' s livre m du maître
an'swering ser'vice s (telp) service m des abonnés absents
ant [ænt] s fourmi f
antagonism [æn'tægə‚nɪzəm] s antagonisme m
antagonize [æn'tægə‚naɪz] tr contrarier; (a friend) s'aliéner
Antarctic [ænt'ɑrktɪk] adj & s Antarctique f
Antarctica [ænt'ɑrktɪkə] s l'Antarctique f
Antarc'tic O'cean s Océan m glacial antarctique
ante ['ænti] s mise f || tr miser || intr miser, caver; **ante up!** misez!
anteater ['ænt‚itər] s fourmilier m
antecedent [‚ænti'sidənt] adj & s antécédent m
antechamber ['ænti‚tʃembər] s antichambre f
antelope ['ænti‚lop] s antilope f
antenna [æn'tenə] s (pl -nae [ni]) (ent) antenne f || s (pl -nas) (rad) antenne f
antepenult [‚ænti'pinʌlt] s antépénultième f
anterior [æn'tɪrɪ‚ər] adj antérieur
anthem ['ænθəm] s hymne m; (eccl) antienne f, hymne f
ant' hill' s fourmilière f
anthology [æn'θɑlədʒi] s (pl -gies) anthologie f
anthropoid ['ænθro‚pɔɪd] adj & s anthropoïde m
antiaircraft [‚ænti'er‚kræft], [‚ænti-'er‚krɑft] adj antiaérien, contre-avions
antibiotic [‚æntibaɪ'ɑtɪk] adj & s antibiotique m
antibody ['ænti‚bɑdi] s (pl -ies) anticorps m
anticipate [æn'tɪsɪ‚pet] tr anticiper; (to expect) s'attendre à
anticipation [æn‚tɪsɪ'peʃən] s anticipation f
anticlimax [‚ænti'klaɪmæks] s chute f dans le trivial, désillusion f
antics ['æntɪks] spl bouffonnerie f
antidote ['ænti‚dot] s antidote m
antifreeze [‚ænti'friz] s antigel m
antiglare [‚ænti'gler] adj antiaveuglant
antiknock [‚ænti'nɑk] adj & s antidétonant m
an'timis'sile mis'sile [‚ænti'mɪsəl] s missile m antimissile
antimony ['ænti‚moni] s antimoine m
antipathy [æn'tɪpəθi] s (pl -thies) antipathie f
antiperspirant [‚ænti'pʌrspərənt] s antitranspirant m
antiphon ['ænti‚fɑn] s antienne f
antiquated ['ænti‚kwetɪd] adj vieilli, démodé
antique [æn'tik] s antique; ancien || s (piece of furniture) original m; **antiques** meubles mpl d'époque

antique' deal'er s antiquaire m
antique' shop' s magasin m d'antiquités, maison f de meubles d'époque
antiquity [æn'tɪkwɪti] s (pl -ties) antiquité f; (oldness) ancienneté f
anti-Semitic [‚æntɪsɪ'mɪtɪk] adj antisémite, antisémitique
antiseptic [‚ænti'septɪk] adj & s antiseptique m
an'titank' gun' [‚ænti'tæŋk] s canon m antichar
antithesis [æn'tɪθɪsɪs] s (pl -ses [‚siz]) antithèse f
antitoxin [‚ænti'tɑksɪn] s antitoxine f
antiwar [‚ænti'wɔr] adj antimilitariste
antler ['æntlər] s andouiller m
antonym ['æntənɪm] s antonyme m
anvil ['ænvɪl] s enclume f
anxiety [æŋ'zaɪ‚əti] s (pl -ties) anxiété f, inquiétude f
anxious ['æŋkʃəs] adj inquiet, soucieux; **to be anxious to** avoir envie de, tenir beaucoup à
any ['eni] adj indef quelque, du; aucun; **any day** n'importe quel jour; **any place** n'importe où; **any time** n'importe quand, à tout moment; **any way** n'importe comment, de toute façon || pron indef quiconque; quelques-uns §81; **not . . . any** ne . . . aucun, ne . . . en . . . pas, e.g., **I will not give him any** je ne lui en donnerai pas || adv un peu
an'ybod'y pron indef quelqu'un §81; n'importe qui; **not . . . anybody** ne . . . personne
an'yhow' adv en tout cas; cependant
an'yone' pron indef quelqu'un §81; n'importe qui; quiconque; **not . . . anyone** ne . . . personne, ne . . . pas, e.g., **I don't see anyone** je ne vois personne
an'ything' pron indef quelque chose; n'importe quoi; **anything at all** quoi que se soit, si peu que ce soit; **anything but** rien moins que; **anything else?** et avec ça?, ensuite?; **not . . . anything** ne . . . rien
an'yway' adv en tout cas
an'ywhere' adv n'importe où; **not . . . anywhere** ne . . . nulle part
aorta [e'ɔrtə] s (pl -tas or -tae [ti]) aorte f
apace [ə'pes] adv vite, rapidement
apache [ə'pɑʃ], [ə'pæʃ] s apache m || **Apache** [ə'pætʃi] s apache m
apart [ə'pɑrt] adj séparé || adv à part, à l'écart; **apart from** en dehors de
apartment [ə'pɑrtmənt] s appartement m
apart'ment house' s maison f de rapport, immeuble m d'habitation
apathetic [‚æpə'θetɪk] adj apathique
apathy ['æpəθi] s (pl -thies) apathie f
ape [ep] s singe m || tr singer
aperture ['æpərt/ər] s ouverture f; (phonet) aperture f
apex ['epeks] s (pl apexes or apices ['æpɪ‚siz]) sommet m; (astr) apex m
aphid ['efɪd], ['æfɪd] s puceron m
aphorism ['æfə‚rɪzəm] s aphorisme m
aphrodisiac [‚æfrə'dɪzɪ‚æk] adj & s aphrodisiaque m

apiar·y ['epɪ ˌeri] s (pl -ies) rucher m

apiece [ə'pis] adv la pièce, chacun

apish ['epɪʃ] adj simiesque; (fig) imitateur

aplomb [ə'plɑm], [ə'plɔm] s aplomb m

apocalyptic(al) [ə ˌpɑkə'lɪptɪk(əl)] adj apocalyptique

Apocrypha [ə'pɑkrɪfə] s apocryphes mpl

apogee ['æpə ˌdʒi] s apogée m

Apollo [ə'pɑlo] s Apollon m

apologetic [ə ˌpɑlə'dʒetɪk] adj prêt à s'excuser, humble, penaud

apologize [ə'pɑlə ˌdʒaɪz] intr faire des excuses, s'excuser

apolo·gy [ə'pɑlədʒi] s (pl -gies) excuse f; (makeshift) semblant m, prétexte m; (apologia) apologie f

A.P.O. number ['e'pi'o ˌnʌmbər] s (letterword) (Army Post Office) secteur m postal

apoplectic [ˌæpə'plektɪk] adj & s apoplectique m

apoplexy ['æpə ˌpleksi] s apoplexie f

apostle [ə'pɑsəl] s apôtre m

Apos'tles' Creed' s symbole m des apôtres

apos'tle-ship' s apostolat m

apostrophe [ə'pɑstrəfi] s apostrophe f

apothecar·y [ə'pɑθɪ ˌkeri] s (pl -ies) apothicaire m

appall [ə'pɔl] tr épouvanter, effrayer, consterner

appalling [ə'pɔlɪŋ] adj épouvantable

appara·tus [ˌæpə'retəs], [ˌæpə'rætəs] s (pl -tus or -tuses) appareil m, dispositif m

appar·el [ə'pærəl] s (equipment; clothes) appareil m; (clothes) habillement m ‖ v (pret & pp -eled or -elled; ger -eling or -elling) tr habiller, vêtir; parer

apparent [ə'pærənt], [ə'perənt] adj apparent; (heir) présomptif

apparition [ˌæpə'rɪʃən] s apparition f

appeal [ə'pil] s appel m, recours m; charme m, attrait m; (law) pourvoi m ‖ tr (a case) faire appeler ‖ intr séduire, charmer; s'adresser, recourir; (law) appeler, pourvoir en cassation

appealing [ə'pilɪŋ] adj séduisant, attrayant, sympathique

appear [ə'pɪr] intr (to come into view; to be published; to seem) paraître; (to come into view) apparaître

appearance [ə'pɪrəns] s (look) apparence f, aspect m; (act of showing up) apparition f; (in print) parution f; **to all appearances** selon toute vraisemblance; **to make one's appearance** faire acte de présence

appease [ə'piz] tr apaiser

appeasement [ə'pizmənt] s apaisement m

appeaser [ə'pizər] s conciliateur m, pacificateur m

appel'late court' [ə'pelɪt], [ə'pelet] s tribunal m d'appel; **highest appellate court** cour f de cassation

append [ə'pend] tr apposer, ajouter

appendage [ə'pendɪdʒ] s dépendance f, accessoire m

appendecto·my [ˌæpən'dektəmi] s (pl -mies) appendicectomie f

appendicitis [ə ˌpendɪ'saɪtɪs] s appendicite f

appen·dix [ə'pendɪks] s (pl -dixes or -dices [dɪ ˌsiz]) appendice m

appertain [ˌæpər'ten] intr se rapporter

appetite ['æpɪ ˌtaɪt] s appétit m

appetizer ['æpɪ ˌtaɪzər] s apéritif m

appetizing ['æpɪ ˌtaɪzɪŋ] adj appétissant

applaud [ə'plɔd] tr applaudir; (to approve) applaudir à; **to applaud s.o. for** applaudir qn de ‖ intr applaudir

applause [ə'plɔz] s applaudissements mpl

apple ['æpəl] s pomme f; (tree) pommier m

ap'ple-jack' s calvados m

ap'ple of the eye' s prunelle f des yeux

ap'ple or'chard s pommeraie f, verger m à pommes

ap'ple pie' s tarte f aux pommes

ap'ple pol'isher s (coll) chien m couchant, flagorneur m

ap'ple-sauce' s compote f de pommes; (slang) balivernes fpl

ap'ple tree' s pommier m

ap'ple turn'over s chausson m (aux pommes)

appliance [ə'plaɪ·əns] s appareil m; application f; **appliances** accessoires mpl

applicable ['æplɪkəbəl] adj applicable

applicant ['æplɪkənt] s candidat m, postulant m

application [ˌæplɪ'keʃən] s application f; (for a job) demande f, sollicitation f

applica'tion blank' s formule f

applied' arts' spl arts mpl industriels

ap·ply [ə'plaɪ] v (pret & pp -plied) tr appliquer ‖ intr s'appliquer; **to apply for** solliciter, postuler; **to apply to s.o.** s'adresser à qn

appoint [ə'pɔɪnt] tr nommer, désigner; (obs) équiper

appointed adj désigné; (time) convenu, dit

appointment [ə'pɔɪntmənt] s (engagement) rendez-vous m; (to a position) désignation f, nomination f; **appointments** (of a room) aménagements mpl; **by appointment** sur rendez-vous

apportion [ə'porʃən] tr répartir; (com) ventiler

appraisal [ə'prezəl] s appréciation f, estimation f, évaluation f; (by an appraiser) expertise f

appraise [ə'prez] tr priser, estimer, évaluer; faire l'expertise de

appraiser [ə'prezər] s priseur m, estimateur m, évaluateur m; expert m, commissaire-priseur m

appreciable [ə'priʃɪ·əbəl] adj appréciable, sensible

appreciate [ə'priʃɪ ˌet] tr apprécier; (to be grateful for) reconnaître; (to be aware of) être sensible à, s'apercevoir de ‖ intr augmenter, hausser

appreciation [əˌpriʃɪ'eʃən] s appréciation f; reconnaissance f, gratitude f; (rise in value) plus-value f

appreciative [ə'priʃɪˌetɪv] adj reconnaissant

apprehend [ˌæprɪ'hend] tr comprendre; (to seize; to fear) appréhender

apprehension [ˌæprɪ'henʃən] s appréhension f

apprehensive [ˌæprɪ'hensɪv] adj craintif

apprentice [ə'prentɪs] s apprenti m

appren'tice-ship' s apprentissage m

apprise [ə'praɪz] tr prévenir, informer, mettre au courant

approach [ə'protʃ] s approche f; **to make approaches to** faire des avances à || tr approcher, approcher de, s'approcher de || intr approcher, s'approcher

approachable [ə'protʃəbəl] adj abordable, accessible

approbation [ˌæprə'beʃən] s approbation f

appropriate [ə'propri·ɪt] adj approprié || [ə'propri·et] tr (to take for oneself) s'approprier; (to assign) affecter

appropriation [əˌpropri'eʃən] s appropriation f; (assigning) affectation f; (govt) crédit m budgétaire

approval [ə'pruvəl] s approbation f, consentement m; **on approval** à l'essai, à condition

approve [ə'pruv] tr approuver || intr être d'accord; **to approve of** approuver

approximate [ə'praksɪmɪt] adj approximatif || [ə'praksɪˌmet] tr se rapprocher de

appurtenance [ə'pʌrtɪnəns] s appartenance f; attirail m; **appurtenances** dépendances fpl

apricot ['eprɪˌkat], ['æprɪˌkat] s abricot m; (tree) abricotier m

April ['eprɪl] s avril m

A'pril fool' s (joke) poisson m d'avril; (victim) dupe f, dindon m

A'pril Fools'' Day' s le jour du poisson d'avril

apron ['eprən] s tablier m; (aer) aire f de manœuvre

apropos [ˌæprə'po] adj opportun || adv opportunément; **apropos of** quant à, à l'égard de

apse [æps] s abside f

apt [æpt] adj apte; bien à propos; **apt to** enclin à, porté à

aptitude ['æptɪˌt(j)ud] s aptitude f

aquacade ['ækwəˌked] s féerie f sur l'eau, spectacle m aquatique

aqualung ['ækwəˌlʌŋ] s scaphandre m autonome

aquamarine [ˌækwəmə'rin] s aigue-marine f

aquaplane ['ækwəˌplen] s aquaplane m

aquari·um [ə'kwɛrɪ·əm] s (pl -ums or -a [ə]) aquarium m

aquatic [ə'kwætɪk], [ə'kwatɪk] adj aquatique || **aquatics** spl sports mpl nautiques

aqueduct ['ækwəˌdʌkt] s aqueduc m

aquiline ['ækwɪˌlaɪn] adj aquilin

Arab ['ærəb] adj arabe || s (horse) arabe m; (person) Arabe mf

Arabian [ə'rebɪ·ən] adj arabe || s Arabe mf

Arabic ['ærəbɪk] adj arabique || s (language) arabe m

Ar'abic nu'meral s chiffre m arabe

arbiter ['arbɪtər] s arbitre m

arbitrary ['arbɪˌtreri] adj arbitraire

arbitrate ['arbɪˌtret] tr & intr arbitrer

arbitration [ˌarbɪ'treʃən] s arbitrage m

arbitrator ['arbɪˌtretər] s arbitre m; (law) amiable compositeur m

arbor ['arbər] s berceau m, charmille f; (mach) arbre m

arbore·tum [ˌarbə'ritəm] s (pl -tums or -ta [tə]) jardin m botanique d'arbres

arbutus [ar'bjutəs] s arbousier m

arc [ark] s (elec, geom) arc m

arcade [ar'ked] s arcade f; galerie f

arcane [ar'ken] adj mystérieux

arch [artʃ] adj insigne; espiègle || s (of a building, cathedral, etc.) arc m; (of bridge) arche f; (of vault) voûte f || tr voûter; (the back) arquer || intr se voûter; s'arquer

archaic [ar'ke·ɪk] adj archaïque

archaism ['arkeˌɪzəm], ['arkɪˌɪzəm] s archaïsme m

archangel ['arkˌendʒəl] s archange m

arch'bish'op s archevêque m

arch'duke' s archiduc m

arched [artʃt] adj voûté, courbé, arqué

archeologist [ˌarkɪ'alədʒɪst] s archéologue m

archeology [ˌarkɪ'alɪdʒɪ] s archéologie f

archer ['artʃər] s archer m

archery ['artʃəri] s tir m à l'arc

archetype ['arkɪˌtaɪp] s archétype m

archipela·go [ˌarkɪ'peləgo] s (pl -gos or -goes) archipel m

architect ['arkɪˌtekt] s architecte m

architecture ['arkɪˌtektʃər] s architecture f

archives ['arkaɪvz] spl archives fpl

arch'priest' s archiprêtre m

arch'way' s voûte f, arcade f

Arctic ['arktɪk] adj & s (ocean) Arctique m; (region) Arctique f

arc' weld'ing s soudure f à l'arc

ardent ['ardənt] adj ardent

ardor ['ardər] s ardeur f

arduous ['ardʒʊ·əs], ['ardju·əs] adj ardu, difficile

area ['ɛrɪ·ə] s aire f, surface f; territoire m; (mil) secteur m, zone f

arena [ə'rinə] s arène f

Argentina [ˌardʒən'tinə] s Argentine f; l'Argentine

argue ['argju] tr (a question) discuter; (a case) plaider; (a point) soutenir; (to imply) arguer; **to argue s.o. into** + ger persuader à qn de + inf || intr discuter, argumenter; plaider

argument ['argjəmənt] s (proof; reason; theme) argument m; discussion f, argumentation f; dispute f

argumentative [ˌargjə'mentətɪv] adj disposé à argumenter, raisonneur

aria ['arɪ·ə], ['ɛrɪ·ə] s aria f

arid ['ærɪd] *adj* aride

aridity [ə'rɪdɪti] *s* aridité *f*

arise [ə'raɪz] *v* (*pret* **arose** [ə'roz]; *pp* **arisen** [ə'rɪzən]) *intr* (*to rise*) se lever; (*to originate*) provenir, prendre naissance; (*to occur*) se produire; (*to be raised, as objections*) s'élever

aristocra•cy [,ærɪs'tɑkrəsi] *s* (*pl* -cies) aristocratie *f*

aristocrat [ə'rɪstə,kræt] *s* aristocrate *mf*

aristocratic [ə,rɪstə'krætɪk] *adj* aristocrate

Aristotle ['ærɪ,stɑtəl] *s* Aristote *m*

arithmetic [ə'rɪθmətɪk] *s* arithmétique *f*

arithmetician [ə,rɪθmə'tɪʃən] *s* arithméticien *m*

ark [ɑrk] *s* arche *f*

arm [ɑrm] *s* bras *m*; (*mil*) arme *f*; **arm in arm** bras dessus bras dessous; **at arm's length** à bout de bras; **under my (your, etc.) arm** sous mon (ton, etc.) aisselle; **up in arms** en rébellion ouverte ‖ *tr* armer ‖ *intr* s'armer

armada [ɑr'mɑdə], [ɑr'medə] *s* armada *f*, grande flotte *f*

armadil•lo [,ɑrmə'dɪlo] *s* (*pl* -los) tatou *m*

armament ['ɑrməmənt] *s* armement *m*

armature ['ɑrmə,tʃər] *s* (*elec*) induit *m*

arm/band/ *s* brassard *m*

arm/chair/ *s* fauteuil *m*

Armenian [ɑr'mɪni·ən] *adj* arménien ‖ *s* (*language*) arménien *m*; (*person*) Arménien

armful ['ɑrm,fʊl] *s* brassée *f*

arm/hole/ *s* emmanchure *f*, entournure *f*

armistice ['ɑrmɪstɪs] *s* armistice *m*

armor ['ɑrmər] *s* (*personal*) armure *f*; (*on ships, tanks, etc.*) cuirasse *f*, blindage *m* ‖ *tr* cuirasser, blinder ‖ *intr* se mettre l'armure

ar/mored car/ *s* fourgon *m* blindé

ar/mor plate/ *s* plaque *f* de blindage

ar/mor-plate/ *tr* cuirasser, blinder

armor•y ['ɑrməri] *s* (*pl* -ies) ateliers *mpl* d'armes, salle *f* d'armes

arm/pit/ *s* aisselle *f*

arm/rest/ *s* appui-bras *m*, accoudoir *m*

arms/ race/ *s* course *f* aux armements

ar•my ['ɑrmi] *adj* militaire ‖ *s* (*pl* -mies) armée *f*

aroma [ə'romə] *s* arôme *m*

aromatic [,ærə'mætɪk] *adj* aromatique

around [ə'raʊnd] *adv* autour, alentour; de tous côtés ‖ *prep* autour de; **around 1950** (coll) vers 1950

arouse [ə'raʊz] *tr* éveiller; (*from sleep*) réveiller

arpeg•gio [ɑr'pedʒo] *s* (*pl* -gios) arpège *m*

arraign [ə'ren] *tr* accuser; (law) mettre en accusation

arrange [ə'rendʒ] *tr* arranger ‖ *intr* s'arranger

arrangement [ə'rendʒmənt] *s* arrangement *m*

array [ə're] *s* ordre *m*; (*display*) étalage *m*; (*adornment*) parure *f*; (*mil*) rangée *f*, rangs *mpl* ‖ *tr* ranger, disposer; (*to adorn*) parer

arrearage [ə'rɪrɪdʒ] *s* arriéré *m*

arrears [ə'rɪrz] *spl* arriéré *m*; **in arrears** arriéré

arrest [ə'rest] *s* (*capture*) arrestation *f*; (*halt*) arrêt *m* ‖ *tr* arrêter; fixer; (*attention*) retenir

arrival [ə'raɪvəl] *s* arrivée *f*; (*of goods or ships*) arrivage *m*

arrive [ə'raɪv] *intr* arriver

arrogance ['ærəgəns] *s* arrogance *f*

arrogant ['ærəgənt] *adj* arrogant

arrogate ['ærə,get] *tr*—**to arrogate to oneself** s'arroger

arrow ['æro] *s* flèche *f*

ar/row•head/ *s* tête *f* de flèche; (bot) sagittaire *m*

arsenal ['ɑrsənəl] *s* ateliers *mpl* d'armes; manufacture *f* d'armes

arsenic ['ɑrsɪnɪk] *s* arsenic *m*

arson ['ɑrsən] *s* incendie *m* volontaire

arsonist ['ɑrsənɪst] *s* incendiaire *mf*

art [ɑrt] *s* art *m*

arterial [ɑr'tɪrɪ·əl] *adj* artériel

arteriosclerotic [ɑr,tɪrɪ·oskli'rɑtɪk] *adj* artérioscléreux

arter•y ['ɑrtəri] *s* (*pl* -ies) artère *f*

arte/sian well/ [ɑr'tiʒən] *s* puits *m* artésien

artful ['ɑrtfəl] *adj* ingénieux; (*crafty*) artificieux, sournois; artificiel

arthritis [ɑr'θraɪtɪs] *s* arthrite *f*

artichoke ['ɑrtɪ,tʃok] *s* artichaut *m*

article ['ɑrtɪkəl] *s* article; **article of clothing** objet *m* d'habillement

articulate [ɑr'tɪkjəlɪt] *adj* articulé; (*expressing oneself clearly*) clair, expressif; (*speech*) intelligible; (*creature*) doué de la parole ‖ [ɑr'tɪkjə,let] *tr* articuler ‖ *intr* s'articuler

artifact ['ɑrtɪ,fækt] *s* artefact *m*

artifice ['ɑrtɪfɪs] *s* artifice *m*

artificial [,ɑrtɪ'fɪʃəl] *adj* artificiel

artificiali•ty [,ɑrtɪ,fɪʃɪ'ælɪti] *s* (*pl* -ties) manque *m* de naturel

artillery [ɑr'tɪləri] *s* artillerie *f*

artil/lery•man *s* (*pl* -men) artilleur *m*

artisan ['ɑrtɪzən] *s* artisan *m*

artist ['ɑrtɪst] *s* artiste *mf*

artistic [ɑr'tɪstɪk] *adj* artistique, artiste

artistry ['ɑrtɪstri] *s* art *m*, habileté *f*

artless ['ɑrtlɪs] *adj* naturel; ingénu, naïf; sans art

arts/ and crafts/ *spl* arts et métiers *mpl*

Aryan ['ɛrɪ·ən], ['ɑrjən] *adj* aryen ‖ *s* (*person*) Aryen *m*

as [æz], [əz] *pron rel* que, e.g., **the same as** le même que ‖ *adv* aussi, e.g., **as . . . as** aussi . . . que; **as for** quant à; **as is** tel quel; **as of** (*a certain date*) en date du; **as regards** en ce qui concerne; **as soon as** aussitôt que; **as though** comme si; **as yet** jusqu'ici ‖ *prep* comme ‖ *conj* puisque; comme; que

asbestos [æs'bɛstəs] *s* amiante *m*, asbeste *m*

ascend [ə'sɛnd] *tr* (*a ladder*) monter à; (*a mountain*) gravir; (*a river*) remonter ‖ *intr* monter, s'élever

ascendancy [ə'sɛndənsi] *s* supériorité *f*, domination *f*

ascension [ə'sɛnʃən] *s* ascension *f*

Ascen/sion Day/ *s* Ascension *f*

ascent [ə'sent] s ascension f

ascertain [,æsər'ten] tr vérifier

ascertainment [,æsər'tenmənt] s constatation f

ascetic [ə'setɪk] adj ascétique || s ascète mf

asceticism [ə'setɪ,sɪzəm] s ascétisme m, ascèse f

ascorbic ac'id [ə'skɔrbɪk] s acide m ascorbique

ascribe [ə'skraɪb] tr attribuer, imputer

aseptic [ə'septɪk], [e'septɪk] adj aseptique

ash [æʃ] s cendre f; (tree) frêne m

ashamed [ə'ʃemd] adj honteux; to be ashamed avoir honte

ash'can' s poubelle f

ashen [æʃən] adj cendré

ashore [ə'ʃor] adv à terre; to go ashore débarquer

ash'tray' s cendrier m

Ash' Wednes'day s le mercredi des Cendres

Asia ['eʒə], ['eʃə] s Asie f; l'Asie

A'sia Mi'nor s Asie f Mineure; l'Asie Mineure

aside [ə'saɪd] s aparté m || adv de côté, à part; (aloof, at a distance) à l'écart; aside from en dehors de, à part; to step aside s'écarter; (fig) quitter la partie

asinine ['æsɪ,naɪn] adj stupide

ask [æsk], [ɑsk] tr (a favor; one's way) demander; (a question) poser; to ask s.o. about s.th. interroger qn au sujet de q.ch.; to ask s.o. for s.th. demander q.ch. à qn; to ask s.o. to + inf demander à qn de + inf, prier qn de + inf || intr—to ask about s'enquérir de; to ask for (a package; a porter) demander; (to inquire about) demander après; you asked for it (you're in for it) (coll) c'est bien fait pour vous

askance [ə'skæns] adv de côté; to look askance at regarder de travers

askew [ə'skju] adj & adv de travers, en biais, de biais

asleep [ə'slip] adj endormi; to fall asleep s'endormir

asp [æsp] s aspic m

asparagus [ə'spærəgəs] s asperge f; (stalks and tips used as food) des asperges

aspect ['æspekt] s aspect m

aspen ['æspən] s tremble m

aspersion [ə'spʌrʒən], [ə'spʌrʃən] s (sprinkling) aspersion f; (slander) calomnie f

asphalt ['æsfɔlt], ['æsfælt] s asphalte m

asphyxiate [æs'fɪksɪ,et] tr asphyxier

aspirate ['æspɪrɪt] adj & s (phonet) aspiré m || ['æspɪ,ret] tr aspirer

aspire [ə'spaɪr] intr—to aspire to aspirer à

aspirin ['æspɪrɪn] s aspirine f

ass [æs] s âne m

assail [ə'sel] tr assaillir

assailant [ə'selənt] s assaillant m

assassin [ə'sæsɪn] s assassin m

assassinate [ə'sæsɪ,net] tr assassiner

assassination [ə,sæsɪ'neʃən] s assassinat m

assault [ə'sɔlt] s assaut m; (rape) viol m; (law) voie f de fait || tr assaillir

assault' and bat'tery s (law) voies fpl de fait

assay [ə'se], ['æse] s essai m; métal m titré || [ə'se] tr essayer; titrer

assayer [ə'se.ər] s essayeur m

assemblage [ə'semblɪdʒ] s assemblage m

assemble [ə'sembl] tr assembler || intr s'assembler, se réunir

assem•bly [ə'sembli] s (pl -blies) (meeting) assemblée f, réunion f; (assembling) assemblage m, montage m

assem'bly hall' s salle f de conférences; (educ) grand amphithéâtre m

assem'bly line' s chaîne f de fabrication, chaîne de montage

assem'bly room' s salle f de réunion; (mach) atelier m de montage

assent [ə'sent] s assentiment m || intr assentir

assert [ə'sʌrt] tr affirmer; (one's rights) revendiquer; to assert oneself imposer le respect, s'imposer

assertion [ə'sʌrʃən] s assertion f

assess [ə'ses] tr (damages, taxes, etc.) évaluer; (value of property) coter; (property for tax purposes) grever

assessment [ə'sesmənt] s évaluation f; cote f; charge f, taxe f

assessor [ə'sesər] s répartiteur m d'impôts

asset ['æset] s avantage m; possession f; assets biens mpl, avoirs mpl, actif m

assiduous [ə'sɪdʒu.əs], [ə'sɪdju.əs] adj assidu

assign [ə'saɪn] tr assigner; (mil) affecter

assignation [,æsɪg'neʃən] s assignation f; rendez-vous m illicite

assignment [ə'saɪnmənt] s attribution f; (schoolwork) devoirs mpl; (law) assignation f, transfer m; (mil) affectation f

assimilate [ə'sɪmɪ,let] tr assimiler || intr s'assimiler

assimilation [ə,sɪmɪ'leʃən] s assimilation f

assist [ə'sɪst] tr assister, aider, secourir || intr être assistant

assistance [ə'sɪstəns] s assistance f, aide f, secours m

assistant [ə'sɪstənt] adj & s assistant m, adjoint m

assizes [ə'saɪzɪz] spl assises fpl

associate [ə'soʃɪ.ɪt] adj associé || s associé m || [ə'soʃɪ,et] tr associer || intr s'associer

association [ə,soʃɪ'eʃən] s association f

assonance ['æsənəns] s assonance f

assort [ə'sɔrt] tr assortir || intr s'associer

assorted adj assorti

assortment [ə'sɔrtmənt] s assortiment m

assuage [ə'swedʒ] tr assouvir; soulager, apaiser

assume [ə's(j)um] tr supposer; (various

forms) affecter; (*a fact*) présumer; (*a name*) emprunter; (*duties*) assumer, se charger de

assumed *adj* supposé; (*borrowed*) d'emprunt, emprunté; (*feigned*) feint

assumed′ name′ *s* nom *m* d'emprunt, nom de guerre

assuming [ə's(j)umɪŋ] *adj* prétentieux

assumption [ə'sʌmpʃən] *s* présomption *f*, hypothèse *f*; (*of virtue*) affectation *f*; (*of power*) appropriation *f*; **Assumption** (eccl) Assomption *f*

assurance [ə'ʃurəns] *s* assurance *f*, confiance *f*; promesse *f*

assure [ə'ʃur] *tr* assurer, garantir

astatine ['æstə,tin] *s* astate *m*

aster ['æstər] *s* aster *m*; (*China aster*) reine-marguerite *f*

asterisk ['æstə,rɪsk] *s* astérisque *m*

astern [ə'stʌrn] *adv* à l'arrière

asthma ['æzmə], ['æsmə] *s* asthme *m*

astonish [ə'stɑnɪʃ] *tr* étonner

astonishing [ə'stɑnɪʃɪŋ] *adj* étonnant

astonishment [ə'stɑnɪʃmənt] *s* étonnement *m*

astound [ə'staund] *tr* stupéfier, ahurir, étonner

astounding [ə'staundɪŋ] *adj* étonnant, abasourdissant; (*success*) foudroyant

astraddle [ə'strædəl] *adv* à califourchon

astray [ə'stre] *adv*—**to go astray** s'égarer; **to lead astray** égarer

astride [ə'straɪd] *adv* à califourchon || *prep* à califourchon sur

astrologer [ə'strɑlədʒər] *s* astrologue *m*

astrology [ə'strɑlədʒɪ] *s* astrologie *f*

astronaut ['æstrə,nɔt] *s* astronaute *mf*

astronautics [,æstrə'nɔtɪks] *s* astronautique *f*

astronomer [ə'strɑnəmər] *s* astronome *m*

astronomic(al) [,æstrə'nɑmɪk(əl)] *adj* astronomique

as′tronom′ical year′ *s* année *f* solaire, année tropique

astronomy [ə'strɑnəmɪ] *s* astronomie *f*

astute [ə'st(j)ut] *adj* astucieux, fin

asunder [ə'sʌndər] *adj* séparé || *adv* en deux

asylum [ə'saɪləm] *s* asile *m*

at [æt], [ət] *prep* à, e.g., **at Paris** à Paris; chez, e.g., **at John's** chez Jean; en, e.g., **at the same time** en même temps

atheism ['eθɪ,ɪzəm] *s* athéisme *m*

atheist ['eθɪ-ɪst] *s* athée *mf*

atheistic [,eθɪ'ɪstɪk] *adj* athée

Athens ['æθɪnz] *s* Athènes *f*

athlete ['æθlit] *s* athlète *m*, sportif *m*

ath′lete's foot′ *s* pied *m* d'athlète

athletic [æθ'lɛtɪk] *adj* athlétique || **athletics** *s* athlétisme *m*

athwart [ə'θwɔrt] *adv* par le travers

Atlantic [æt'læntɪk] *adj & s* Atlantique *m*

atlas ['ætləs] *s* atlas *m*

atmosphere ['ætməs,fɪr] *s* atmosphère *f*

atmospheric [,ætməs'fɛrɪk] *adj* atmosphérique || **atmospherics** *spl* parasites *mpl* atmosphériques

atom ['ætəm] *s* atome *m*

atomic [ə'tɑmɪk] *adj* atomique

atom′ic bomb′ *s* bombe *f* atomique

atom′ic nuc′leus *s* noyau *m* d'atome

atom′ic pile′ *s* pile *f* atomique

atom′ic struc′ture *s* édifice *m* atomique

atomize ['ætə,maɪz] *tr* atomiser

atomizer ['ætə,maɪzər] *s* atomiseur *m*, vaporisateur *m*

atone [ə'ton] *intr*—**to atone for** expier

atonement [ə'tonmənt] *s* expiation *f*

atrocious [ə'troʃəs] *adj* atroce

atrocity [ə'trɑsɪti] *s* (*pl* -ties) atrocité *f*

atrophy ['ætrəfɪ] *s* atrophie *f* || *v* (*pret & pp* -phied) *tr* atrophier || *intr* s'atrophier

attach [ə'tætʃ] *tr* attacher; (*property*) saisir; (*salary*) mettre opposition sur; **to be attached to** s'attacher à

attachment [ə'tætʃmənt] *s* attache *f*; (*of the sentiments*) attachement *m*; (law) opposition *f*, saisie-arrêt *f*

attack [ə'tæk] *s* attaque *f* || *tr* attaquer; s'attaquer à || *intr* attaquer

attacker [ə'tækər] *s* assaillant *m*

attain [ə'ten] *tr* atteindre

attainment [ə'tenmənt] *s* acquisition *f*, réalisation *f*; **attainments** connaissances *fpl*

attar ['ætər] *s* essence *f*

attempt [ə'tempt] *s* tentative *f*, essai *m*; (*assault*) attentat *m* || *tr* tenter; (*s.o.'s life*) attenter à

attend [ə'tend] *tr* (*a performance*) assister à; (*a sick person*) soigner; (*a person*) servir; **to attend classes** suivre des cours || *intr*—**to attend to** vaquer à, s'occuper de

attendance [ə'tendəns] *s* assistance *f*; présence *f*; (med) soins *mpl*

attendant [ə'tendənt] *adj* concomitant || *s* assistant *m*; (*to royalty*) serviteur *m*; **attendants** suite *f*

attention [ə'tenʃən] *s* attention *f*; **attention: Mr. Doe** à l'attention de M. Dupont; **attentions** égards *mpl* || *interj* attention!; (mil) garde à vous!

attentive [ə'tentɪv] *adj* attentif

attenuate [ə'tenju,et] *tr* amincir; (*words; bacteria*) atténuer

attest [ə'test] *tr* attester || *intr*—**to attest to** attester

Attic ['ætɪk] *adj* attique || (*l.c.*) *s* mansarde *f*, grenier *m*, soupente *f*

attire [ə'taɪr] *s* vêtement *m*, parure *f* || *tr* habiller, vêtir; parer

attitude ['ætɪ,t(j)ud] *s* attitude *f*

attorney [ə'tʌrnɪ] *s* avoué *m*, avocat *m*

attor′ney gen′eral *s* procureur *m* général, ministre *m* de justice

attract [ə'trækt] *tr* attirer

attraction [ə'trækʃən] *s* attraction *f*; attrait *m*, attirance *f*

attractive [ə'træktɪv] *adj* attirant, attrayant; (*said, e.g., of a force*) attractif

attribute ['ætrɪ,bjut] *s* attribut *m* || [ə'trɪbjut] *tr* attribuer

attrition [ə'trɪʃən] *s* attrition *f*, usure *f*

attune [ə't(j)un] *tr* accorder

auburn ['ɔbərn] *adj* auburn, brun rougeâtre

auction ['ɔkʃən] s vente f aux enchères ‖ tr vendre aux enchères

auctioneer [,ɔkʃən'ɪr] s adjudicateur m, commissaire-priseur m ‖ tr & intr vendre aux enchères

audacious [ɔ'deʃəs] adj audacieux

audacity [ɔ'dæsɪti] s audace f

audience ['ɔdɪ·əns] s (hearing; formal interview) audience f; (assembly of hearers or spectators) assistance f, salle f, auditoire m; (those who follow what one says or writes) public m

au'dio fre'quency ['ɔdɪ,o] s audio-fréquence f

audiometer [,ɔdɪ'amɪtər] s audiomètre m

audit ['ɔdɪt] s apurement m ‖ tr apurer; **to audit a class** assister à la classe en auditeur libre

audition [ɔ'dɪʃən] s audition f ‖ tr & intr auditionner

auditor ['ɔdɪtər] s (com) comptable m agréé, expert comptable m; (educ) auditeur m libre

auditorium [,ɔdɪ'torɪ·əm] s auditorium m, salle f, amphithéâtre m

auditory ['ɔdɪ,tori] adj auditif

auger ['ɔgər] s tarière f

aught [ɔt] s zéro m ‖ pron indef—**for aught I know** autant que je sache ‖ adv du tout

augment [ɔg'ment] tr & intr augmenter

augur ['ɔgər] s augure m ‖ tr & intr augurer; **to augur well** être de bon augure

augu·ry ['ɔgjəri] s (pl -ries) augure m

august [ɔ'gʌst] adj auguste ‖ **August** ['ɔgəst] s août m

auk [ɔk] s guillemot m

aunt [ænt], [ɑnt] s tante f

aureomycin [,ɔri·o'maɪsɪn] s (pharm) auréomycine f

auricle ['ɔrɪkəl] s auricule f, oreillette f

aurora [ə'rɔrə] s aurore f

auscultate ['ɔskəl,tet] tr ausculter

auspices ['ɔspɪsɪz] spl auspices mpl

auspicious [ɔs'pɪʃəs] adj propice, favorable

austere [ɔs'tɪr] adj austère

Australia [ɔ'streljə] s Australie f; l'Australie

Australian [ɔ'streljən] adj australien ‖ s (person) Australien m

Austria ['ɔstri·ə] s Autriche f; l'Autriche

Austrian ['ɔstrɪ·ən] adj autrichien ‖ s (person) Autrichien m

authentic [ɔ'θentɪk] adj authentique

authenticate [ɔ'θentɪ,ket] tr authentifier, constater l'authenticité de

author ['ɔθər] s auteur m

authoress ['ɔθərɪs] s femme f auteur

authoritarian [ə,θɔrɪ'terɪ·ən], [ə,θɑrɪ'terɪ·ən] adj autoritaire ‖ s homme m autoritaire

authoritative [ə'θɔrɪ,tetɪv], [ə'θɑrɪ,tetɪv] adj autorisé; (dictatorial) autoritaire

authori·ty [ə'θɔrɪti], [ə'θɑrɪti] s (pl -ties) autorité f; **on good authority** de bonne part

authorize ['ɔθə,raɪz] tr autoriser

au'thor·ship's paternité f

au·to ['ɔto] s (pl -tos) (coll) auto f, voiture f

autobiogra·phy [,ɔtobaɪ'ɑgrəfi], [,ɔtobɪ'ɑgrəfi] s (pl -phies) autobiographie f

autocrat ['ɔtə,kræt] s autocrate mf

autocratic(al) [,ɔtə'krætɪk(əl)] adj autocratique

autograph ['ɔtə,græf], ['ɔtə,grɑf] s autographe m ‖ tr écrire l'autographe sur, dédicacer

au'tographed cop'y s exemplaire m dédicacé

au'to·intox'ica'tion s auto-intoxication f

automat ['ɔtə,mæt] s restaurant m libre service

automate ['ɔtə,met] tr automatiser

automatic [,ɔtə'mætɪk] adj automatique ‖ s revolver m

automat'ic transmis'sion s changement m de vitesse automatique

automation [,ɔtə'meʃən] s automatisation f, automation f

automa·ton [ɔ'tɑmə,tɑn] s (pl -tons or -ta [tə]) automate m

automobile [,ɔtəmo'bil], [,ɔtə'mobil] s automobile f

automobile' show' s salon m de l'automobile

automotive [,ɔtə'motɪv] adj automobile; automoteur

autonomous [ɔ'tɑnəməs] adj autonome

autonomy [ɔ'tɑnəmi] s autonomie f

autop·sy ['ɔtɑpsi] s (pl -sies) autopsie f

autumn ['ɔtəm] s automne m

autumnal [ɔ'tʌmnəl] adj automnal, d'automne

auxilia·ry [ɔg'zɪljəri] adj auxiliaire ‖ s (pl -ries) auxiliaire mf; **auxiliaries** (mil) troupes fpl auxiliaires

avail [ə'vel] s utilité f ‖ tr profiter à; **to avail oneself of** avoir recours à, profiter de ‖ intr être utile, servir

available [ə'veləbəl] adj disponible; (e.g., train) accessible; **to make available to** mettre à la disposition de

avalanche ['ævə,læntʃ], ['ævə,lɑntʃ] s avalanche f

avarice ['ævərɪs] s avarice f

avaricious [,ævə'rɪʃəs] adj avaricieux

avenge [ə'vendʒ] tr venger

avenger [ə'vendʒər] s vengeur m

avenue ['ævə,n(j)u] s avenue f

aver [ə'vʌr] v (pret & pp averred; ger averring) tr avérer, affirmer

average ['ævərɪdʒ] adj moyen ‖ s moyenne f; **on the average** en moyenne ‖ tr prendre la moyenne de ‖ intr atteindre une moyenne

averse [ə'vʌrs] adj—**averse to** hostile à, opposé à, ennemi de

aversion [ə'vʌrʒən] s aversion f

avert [ə'vʌrt] tr détourner, écarter; empêcher, éviter

aviar·y ['evi,eri] s (pl -ies) volière f

aviation [,evi'eʃən] s aviation f

aviator ['evi,etər] s aviateur m

avid ['ævɪd] adj avide; **avid for** avide de

avidity [ə'vıdıti] s avidité f
avoca·do [ˌævo'kɑdo] s (pl -dos) avocat m
avocation [ˌævə'keʃən] s occupation f, profession f; distraction f
avoid [ə'vɔıd] tr éviter
avoidable [ə'vɔıdəbəl] adj évitable
avoidance [ə'vɔıdəns] s dérobade f
avow [ə'vau] tr avouer
avowal [ə'vau·əl] s aveu m
avowedly [ə'vau·ıdlı] adv ouvertement, franchement
await [ə'wet] tr attendre
awake [ə'wek] adj éveillé ‖ v (pret & pp awoke [ə'wok] or awaked) tr éveiller ‖ intr s'éveiller
awaken [ə'wekən] tr éveiller, réveiller ‖ intr se réveiller
awakening [ə'wekənıŋ] s réveil m; (disillusionment) désabusement m
award [ə'word] s prix m; (law) dommages et intérêts mpl ‖ tr décerner; accorder
aware [ə'wer] adj conscient; to become aware of se rendre compte de
awareness [ə'wernıs] s conscience f
away [ə'we] adj absent ‖ adv au loin, loin; away from éloigné de, loin de; to do away with abolir; to get away s'absenter; (to escape) échapper; to go away s'en aller; to make away with (to steal) dérober; to run away se sauver; to send away renvoyer; to take away enlever ‖ interj hors d'ici!; away with! à bas!
awe [ə] s crainte f révérentielle ‖ tr inspirer de la crainte à

awesome ['ɔsəm] adj impressionnant
awful ['ɔfəl] adj terrible; (coll) terrible, affreux
awfully ['ɔfəlı] adv terriblement; (coll) joliment, rudement
awhile [ə'hwaıl] adv quelque temps, un peu, un moment
awkward ['ɔkwərd] adj gauche, maladroit; (moment) embarrassant
awl [ɔl] s alène f
awning ['ɔnıŋ] s tente f; (in front of store) banne f
A.W.O.L. ['e'dʌbəlˌju'o'el] (letterword ['ewɔl] (acronym) s (absent without leave) absence f illégale; to be A.W.O.L. être absent sans permission
awry [ə'raı] adv de travers
ax [æks] s hache f
axiom ['æksı·əm] s axiome m
axiomatic [ˌæksı·ə'mætık] adj axiomatique
axis ['æksıs] s (pl axes ['æksiz]) axe m
axle ['æksəl] s essieu m
axle grease s cambouis m
ay or **aye** [aı] s oui m; **aye aye, sir!** oui, commandant!, bien, capitaine!; the ayes have it les oui l'emportent ‖ [e] adv toujours
azalea [ə'zeljə] s azalée f
azimuth ['æzıməθ] s azimut m
Azores [ə'zorz], ['ezorz] spl Açores fpl
Aztecs ['æzteks] spl Aztèques mpl
azure ['æʒər], ['eʒər] adj azuré, d'azur ‖ s azur m ‖ tr azurer

B

B, b [bi] s IIᵉ lettre de l'alphabet
babble ['bæbəl] s babil m ‖ tr (secrets) dire à tort et à travers ‖ intr babiller; (said of birds) jaser; (said of brook) murmurer
babbling ['bæblıŋ] adj (gossiper) babillard; (brook) murmurant ‖ s babillage m
babe [beb] s bébé m, bambin m; (naive person) (coll) enfant mf; (pretty girl) (coll) pépée f, môme f
babel ['bebəl] s brouhaha m, vacarme m
baboon [bæ'bun] s babouin m
ba·by ['bebı] s (pl -bies) bébé m; (youngest child) cadet m, benjamin m; baby! (honey!) (coll) ma choute! ‖ v (pret & pp -bied) tr traiter en bébé, dorloter; (e.g., a machine) traiter avec soin
baby carriage s voiture f d'enfant, poussette f; (with hood) landau m
baby grand s piano m demi-queue
baby-sit·ter s gardienne f d'enfants, garde-bébé mf
baby talk s babil m enfantin

baby teeth spl dents fpl de lait
baccalaureate [ˌbækə'lɔrı·ıt] s baccalauréat m
bacchanal ['bækənəl] adj bachique ‖ s bacchanale f; (person) noceur m
bachelor ['bætʃələr] s célibataire m; (graduate) bachelier m
bachelor apartment s garçonnière f
bachelor girl s garçonne f
bachelor·hood s célibat m
bachelor's-but·ton s (bot) bluet m, barbeau m
bachelor's degree s baccalauréat m
bacil·lus [bə'sıləs] s (pl -li [laı]) bacille m
back [bæk] adj postérieur ‖ s dos m; (of house; of head or body) derrière m; (of house; of car) arrière m; (of room) fond m; (of fabric) envers m; (of seat) dossier m; (of medal; of hand) revers m; (of page) verso m; (sports) arrière; **back to back** dos à dos; **with one's back to the wall** poussé au pied du mur, aux abois ‖ adv en arrière, à l'arrière; **as far back as** déjà en, dès; **back and forth**

de long en large; **back of** derrière; **back to front** sens devant derrière; **in back** par derrière; **some weeks back** il y a quelques semaines; **to be back** être de retour; **to come back** revenir; **to go back** retourner; **to go back home** rentrer; **to go back on** (coll) abandonner; **to go back to** (*to hark back to*) remonter à; **to make one's way back** s'en retourner || *tr* faire faire marche arrière à; (*e.g., a car*) faire reculer; (*to support*) appuyer, soutenir; (*to reinforce*) renforcer; (*e.g., a racehorse*) parier pour; **to back s.o. up** soutenir qn; **to back water** nager à culer || *intr* reculer; faire marche arrière; **to back down** (fig) se rétracter, se retirer; **to back out of** (*e.g., an agreement*) se dédire de, se soustraire à; **to back up** reculer

back'ache' *s* mal m de dos
back'bite' *v* (pret **-bit**; pp **-bitten** or **bit**) *tr* médire de || *intr* médire
back'bit'er *s* médisant m
back'bone' *s* colonne *f* vertébrale, épine *f* dorsale, échine *f*; (*of a fish*) grande arête *f*; (*of an enterprise*) colonne *f*, appui m; (fig) caractère m, cran m; **to have no backbone** (fig) avoir l'échine souple
back'break'ing *adj* éreintant, dur
back'door' *adj* (fig) secret, clandestin
back' door' *s* porte *f* de derrière; (fig) petite porte
back'down' *s* (coll) palinodie *f*
back'drop' *s* toile *f* de fond
backer ['bækər] *s* (*of team, party, etc.*) supporter m; (com) bailleur m de fonds, commanditaire m
back'fire' *s* retour m de flamme, pétarade *f*; (*for firefighting*) contre-feu m; (mach) contre-allumage m || *intr* donner des retours de flamme; (fig) produire un résultat imprévu
backgammon ['bæk,gæmən], [,bæk-'gæmən] *s* trictrac m, jacquet m
back'ground' *s* fond m; (*of person*) origines *fpl*, éducation *f*; (*music, sound effects, etc.*) fond sonore
back'hand' *s* (tennis) revers m
back'hand'ed *adj* de revers; (*compliment*) à rebours, équivoque
backing ['bækɪŋ] *s* (*support*) appui m, soutien m; (*reinforcement*) renforcement m; (*backing up*) recul m
back' in'terest m arrérage m; arrérages *mpl*
back'lash' *s* contrecoup m
back'light'ing *s* contre-jour m
back'log' *s* arriéré m, accumulation *f*
back' num'ber *s* (*of newspaper, magazine*) vieux numéro m; (coll) vieux jeu m
back' pay' *s* salaire m arriéré; (mil) arriéré m de solde
back' pay'ment *s* arriéré m
back' scratch'er *s* gratte-dos m; (slang) lèche-bottes m
back' seat' *s* banquette *f* arrière; **to take a back seat** (fig) aller au second plan

back'side' *s* derrière m, postérieur m
back'slide' *intr* récidiver
back'slid'er *s* récidiviste *mf*, relaps m
back'space key' *s* rappel m de chariot
back'spac'er *s* rappel m de chariot
back'spin' *s* (*of ball*) coup m en bas, effet m
back'stage' *adv* dans les coulisses
back'stairs' *adj* caché, indirect
back' stairs' *spl* escalier m de service
back'stitch' *s* point m arrière
back'stop' *s* (baseball) attrapeur m || *v* (pret & pp **-stopped**; ger **-stopping**) *tr* (coll) soutenir
back'stroke' *s* (*of piston*) course *f* de retour; (swimming) brasse *f* sur le dos
back'swept wing' *s* aile *f* en flèche
back' talk' *s* réplique *f* impertinente
back' tax'es *spl* impôts *mpl* arriérés
back'track' *intr* rebrousser chemin
back'up' *s* appui m, soutien m
back'up light' *s* phare m de recul
backward ['bækwərd] *adj* (*in direction*) en arrière, rétrograde; (*in time*) en retard; (*in development*) arriéré, attardé || *adv* en arrière; (*opposite to the normal*) à rebours; (*walking*) à reculons; (*flowing*) à contre-courant; (*stroking of the hair*) à contre-poil; **backward and forward** de long en large; **to go backward and forward** aller et venir
back'ward-and-for'ward mo'tion *s* va-et-vient m
backwardness ['bækwərdnɪs] *s* retard m, lenteur *f*
backwards ['bækwərdz] *adv* var of **backward**
back'wash' *s* remous m
back'wa'ter *s* (*of river*) bras m mort; (*e.g., of water wheel*) remous m; (fig) endroit m isolé, trou m
back' wheel' *s* roue *f* arrière
back'woods' *spl* forêts *fpl* de l'intérieur; bled m, brousse *f*
back'woods'man *s* (pl **-men**) défricheur m de forêts, coureur m des bois
back'yard' *s* derrière m (de la maison)
bacon ['bekən] *s* lard m, bacon m; (slang) butin m; **to bring home the bacon** (coll) remporter la timbale
bacteria [bæk'tɪrɪ·ə] *spl* bactéries *fpl*
bacteriology [bæk,tɪrɪ'ɑlədʒɪ] *s* bactériologie *f*
bacteri·um [bæk'tɪrɪ·əm] *s* (pl **-a** [ə]) bactérie *f*
bad [bæd] *adj* mauvais §91; (*wicked*) méchant; (*serious*) grave; **from bad to worse** de mal en pis; **too bad!** c'est dommage!
bad' breath' *s* haleine *f* forte
bad' com'pany *s* mauvaises fréquentations *fpl*
bad' debt' *s* mauvaise créance *f*
bad' egg' *s* (slang) mauvais sujet m
bad' exam'ple *s* exemple m pernicieux
badge [bædʒ] *s* insigne m, plaque *f*
badger ['bædʒər] *s* blaireau m || *tr* harceler, ennuyer
bad' lot' *s* voyous *mpl*, racaille *f*

badly ['bædlɪ] *adv* mal §91; (*seriously*) gravement; **to want badly** avoir grande envie de

bad'man' *s* (*pl* **-men'**) bandit *m*

badness ['bædnɪs] *s* mauvaise qualité *f*; (*of character*) méchanceté *f*

bad'-tem'pered *adj* susceptible, méchant; (*e.g., horse*) vicieux, rétif

baffle ['bæfəl] *s* déflecteur *m*, chicane *f* || *tr* déconcerter, confondre

baffling ['bæflɪŋ] *adj* déconcertant

bag [bæg] *s* sac *m*; (*suitcase*) valise *f*; (*of game*) chasse *f* || *v* (*pret & pp* **bagged**; *ger* **bagging**) *tr* ensacher, mettre en sac; (*game*) abattre, tuer || *intr* (*said of clothing*) faire poche

bagful ['bæg,ful] *s* sachée *f*

baggage ['bægɪdʒ] *s* bagage *m*, bagages

bag'gage car' *s* (rr) fourgon *m* à bagages

bag'gage check' *s* bulletin *m* de bagages

bag'gage room' *s* bureau *m* de gare expéditeur; (*checkroom*) consigne *f*

bag'gage truck' *s* chariot *m* à bagages; (*hand truck*) diable *m*

bag-gy ['bægɪ] *adj* (*comp* **-gier**; *super* **-giest**) bouffant

bag' of tricks' *s* sac *m* à malice

bag'pipe' *s* cornemuse *f*

bail [bel] *s* caution *f*; **to be out on bail** être libre sous caution; **to put up bail** se porter caution || *tr* cautionner; **to bail out** se porter caution pour; (*a boat*) écoper || *intr*—**to bail out** (aer) sauter en parachute

bailiff ['belɪf] *s* (*of a court*) huissier *m*, bailli *m*; (*on a farm*) régisseur *m*

bailiwick ['belɪwɪk] *s* bailliage *m*, rayon *m*; (fig) domaine *m*

bait [bet] *s* appât *m*, amorce *f* || *tr* appâter, amorcer; (*to harass*) harceler

bake [bek] *tr* faire cuire au four; **to bake bread** boulanger, faire le pain || *intr* cuire au four

baked' pota'toes *spl* pommes *fpl* de terre au four

bakelite ['bekə,laɪt] *s* bakélite *f*

baker ['bekər] *s* boulanger *m*

bak'er's doz'en *s* treize *m* à la douzaine

baker-y ['bekərɪ] *s* (*pl* **-ies**) boulangerie *f*

baking ['bekɪŋ] *s* cuisson *f* au four

bak'ing pow'der *s* levure *f* anglaise

bak'ing so'da *s* bicarbonate *m* de soude

balance ['bæləns] *s* balance *f*, équilibre *m*; (*scales*) balance *f*; (*what is left*) reste *m*; (com) solde *m*, report *m* || *tr* balancer; (*an account*) solder || *intr* se balancer; se solder

bal'ance of pay'ments *s* balance *f* des comptes

bal'ance of pow'er *s* équilibre *m* politique

bal'ance of trade' *s* balance du commerce

bal'ance sheet' *s* bilan *m*

bal'ance wheel' *s* balancier *m*

balancing ['bælənsɪŋ] *s* balancement

m; équilibrage *m*; ajustement *m*; (com) règlement *m* des comptes

balco-ny ['bælkənɪ] *s* (*pl* **-nies**) balcon *m*; (*in a theater*) galerie *f*

bald [bɔld] *adj* chauve; (*fact, statement, etc.*) simple, net, carré

balderdash ['bɔldər,dæʃ] *s* galimatias *m*, fatras *m*

baldness ['bɔldnɪs] *s* calvitie *f*

bale [bel] *s* balle *f* || *tr* emballer

Balear'ic Is'lands [,bælɪ'ærɪk] *spl* Baléares *fpl*

baleful ['belfəl] *adj* funeste, fatal; triste

balk [bɔk] *s* déception *f*, contretemps *m*; (*beam*) poutre *f*; (agr) billon *m* || *tr* frustrer || *intr* regimber

Balkan ['bɔlkən] *adj* balkanique

balk-y ['bɔkɪ] *adj* (*comp* **-ier**; *super* **-iest**) regimbé, rétif

ball [bɔl] *s* balle *f*; (*in billiards; in bearings*) bille *f*; (*spherical body*) boule *f*; (*dance*) bal *m*; (sports) ballon *m*; **to be on the ball** (slang) être toujours là pour le coup; **to have s.th. on the ball** (slang) avoir q.ch. dans le ventre; **to play ball** jouer au ballon; (slang) coopérer; (*to be in cahoots*) (slang) être en tandem || *tr*—**to ball up** (slang) bousiller, embrouiller

ballad ['bæləd] *s* (*song*) romance *f*, complainte *f*; (*poem*) ballade *f*

ball' and chain' *s* boulet *m*; (slang) femme *f*, épouse *f*

ball'-and-sock'et joint' *s* joint *m* à rotule

ballast ['bæləst] *s* (aer, naut) lest *m*; (rr) ballast *m* || *tr* lester; ballaster

ball' bear'ing *s* bille *f*, roulement *m* à billes

ball' cock' *s* robinet *m* à flotteur

ballerina [,bælə'rinə] *s* ballerine *f*

ballet ['bæle] *s* ballet *m*

ballistic [bə'lɪstɪk] *adj* balistique || **ballistics** *s* balistique *f*

ballis'tic mis'sile *s* engin *m* balistique

balloon [bə'lun] *s* ballon *m* || *tr* ballonner || *intr* ballonner, se ballonner

ballot ['bælət] *s* scrutin *m*; (*individual ballot*) bulletin *m* || *intr* scrutiner, voter

bal'lot box' *s* urne *f*; **to stuff the ballot boxes** bourrer les urnes

balloting ['bælətɪŋ] *s* scrutin *m*

ball'-point pen' *s* stylo *m* à bille

ball'room' *s* salon *m* de bal, salle *f* de danse

ballyhoo ['bælɪ,hu] *s* publicité *f* tapageuse || *tr* faire de la réclame pour

balm [bɑm] *s* baume *m* || *tr* parfumer

balm-y ['bɑmɪ] *adj* (*comp* **-ier**; *super* **-iest**) embaumé; (slang) toqué

baloney [bə'lonɪ] *s* (culin) mortadelle *f*; (slang) fadaises *fpl*

balsam ['bɔlsəm] *s* baume *m*

bal'sam fir' *s* sapin *m* baumier

bal'sam pop'lar *s* peuplier *m* baumier

Balt [bɔlt] *s* Balte *mf*

Bal'timore o'riole ['bɔltɪ,mor] *s* loriot *m* de Baltimore

baluster ['bæləstər] *s* balustre *m*

balustrade [ˌbæləsˈtred] s balustrade f, rampe f

bamboo [bæmˈbu] s bambou m

bamboozle [bæmˈbuzəl] tr (slang) mystifier

ban [bæn] s ban m, interdiction f; bans bans mpl || v (pret & pp banned; ger banning) tr mettre au ban

banal [ˈbenəl], [bəˈnæl] adj banal

banali·ty [bəˈnælɪti] s (pl -ties) banalité f

banana [bəˈnænə] s banane f

banan/a tree/ s bananier m

band [bænd] s bande f, lien m; musique f, fanfare f; (dance band) orchestre m; (strip of color) raie f; **to beat the band** (slang) sans pareille; (hastily) vivement || tr entourer de bandes; (a bird) marquer de bandes || intr—**to band together** se grouper

bandage [ˈbændɪdʒ] s (dressing) pansement m; (holding the dressing in place) bandage m || tr panser; bander

band/box/ s carton m de modiste

bandit [ˈbændɪt] s bandit m

band/mas·ter s chef m de musique

band/ saw/ s scie f à ruban

band/stand/ s kiosque m

band/wag·on s char m de la victoire; **to jump on the bandwagon** suivre la majorité victorieuse

ban·dy [ˈbændi] adj tortu || v (pret & pp -died) tr renvoyer, échanger; **to bandy words** se renvoyer des paroles || intr se disputer

ban/dy-leg/ged adj bancal

bane [ben] s poison m; ruine f

baneful [ˈbenfəl] adj funeste, nuisible

bang [bæŋ] s coup m; (of a door) claquement m; (of fireworks; of a gun) détonation f; bangs frange f; **to go off with a bang** détoner; (slang) réussir || tr frapper; (a door) faire claquer; **to bang down** (e.g., a lid) abattre violemment; **to bang up** (slang) rosser, cogner || intr claquer avec fracas; **to bang against** cogner; **to bang on** frapper à || interj pan!; pom!

bang/-up/ adj (slang) de premier ordre, à la hauteur

banish [ˈbænɪʃ] tr bannir, exiler

banishment [ˈbænɪʃmənt] s bannissement m

banister [ˈbænɪstər] s balustre m; banisters balustrade f, rampe f

bank [bæŋk] s banque f; (of river) rive f, bord m; (shoal) banc m; (slope) talus m, terrasse f; (in a gambling game) cave f; (aer) virage m incliné; **to break the bank** faire sauter la banque || tr terrasser; (money) déposer; (an airplane) incliner || intr (aer) virer, virer sur l'aile, s'incliner; **to bank on** compter sur

bank/ account/ s compte m en banque

bank/book/ s carnet m de banque

banked adj incliné

banker [ˈbæŋkər] s banquier m

banking [ˈbæŋkɪŋ] adj bancaire

bank/ note/ s billet m de banque

bank/roll/ s paquet m de billets, liasse f de billets

bankrupt [ˈbæŋkrʌpt] adj & s failli m; (with guilt) banqueroutier m; **to go bankrupt** faire banqueroute || tr mettre en faillite

bankrupt·cy [ˈbæŋkrʌptsi] s (pl -cies) banqueroute f

bank/ vault/ s chambre f forte

banner [ˈbænər] s bannière f

ban/ner cry/ s cri m de guerre

ban/ner year/ s année f record

banquet [ˈbæŋkwɪt] s banquet m || intr banqueter

bantam [ˈbæntəm] adj nain || s poulet m nain, poulet de Bantam

ban/tam-weight/ s poids m bantam

banter [ˈbæntər] s badinage m || tr & intr badiner

bantering [ˈbæntərɪŋ] adj railleur, goguenard

baptism [ˈbæptɪzəm] s baptême m

baptismal [bæpˈtɪzməl] adj baptismal

baptis/mal certif/icate s extrait m baptême, bulletin m de naissance

baptis/mal font/ s fonts mpl baptismaux

Baptist [ˈbæptɪst] s baptiste mf

baptister·y [ˈbæptɪstəri] s (pl -ies) baptistère m

baptize [bæpˈtaɪz], [ˈbæptaɪz] tr baptiser

bar [bɑr] s barre f, barreau m; (obstacle) barrière f, empêchement m; (barroom; counter) bar m; (profession of law) barreau; (of public opinion) tribunal m; (of chocolate) tablette f; (mus) mesure f; (phys) bar; **behind bars** sous les barreaux || prep —**bar none** sans exception || v (pret & pp barred; ger barring) tr barrer

barb [bɑrb] s barbillon m; dent f d'une flèche; (in metalwork) barbe f || tr garnir de barbillons

Barbados [bɑrˈbedoz] s la Barbade

barbarian [bɑrˈberi·ən] adj & s barbare mf

barbaric [bɑrˈbærɪk] adj barbare

barbarism [ˈbɑrbə ˌrɪzəm] s barbarie f; (in speech or writing) barbarisme m

barbari·ty [bɑrˈbærɪti] s (pl -ties) barbarie f

barbarous [ˈbɑrbərəs] adj barbare

barbecue [ˈbɑrbɪ ˌkju] s grillade f en plein air || tr griller à la sauce piquante

bar/becue pit/ s rôtisserie f en plein air

barbed adj barbelé, pointu

barbed/ wire/ s fil m de fer barbelé

barbed/-wire entan/glement s réseau m de barbelés

barber [ˈbɑrbər] s coiffeur m; (who shaves) barbier m

bar/ber pole/ s enseigne f de barbier

bar/ber-shop/ s salon m de coiffeur

bar/ber-shop quartet/ s ensemble m harmonique de chanteurs amateurs

barbiturate [bɑrˈbɪtʃə ˌret], [ˌbɑrbɪˈtjuret] adj & s barbiturique m

bard [bɑrd] s barde m

bare [ber] adj nu; découvert; simple || tr mettre à nu

bare'back' *adv* à nu
bare'faced' *adj* éhonté, effronté, sans déguisement
bare'foot' *adj* nu-pieds
bare'head'ed *adj* nu-tête
bare'leg'ged *adj* nu-jambes
barely ['bɛrli] *adv* à peine
bareness ['bɛrnɪs] *s* nudité *f*, dénuement *m*; (*of style*) pauvreté *f*
bar'fly' *s* (*pl* -flies) (slang) pilier *m* de cabaret
bargain ['bɑrgɪn] *s* (*deal*) marché *m*, affaire *f*; (*cheap purchase*) solde *m*, occasion *f*; into the bargain par-dessus le marché || *tr*—to bargain away vendre à perte || *intr* entrer en négociations; she gave him more than he bargained for (fig) elle lui a donné du fil à retordre; to bargain over marchander; to bargain with traiter avec
bar'gain count'er *s* rayon *m* des soldes
bar'gain sale' *s* vente *f* de soldes
barge [bɑrdʒ] *s* barge *f*, chaland *m*, péniche *f* || *intr*—to barge into entrer sans façons
baritone ['bærɪ,ton] *adj* de baryton || *s* baryton *m*
barium ['bɛrɪ·əm] *s* baryum *m*
bark [bɑrk] *s* (*of tree*) écorce *f*; (*of dog*) aboiement *m*; (*boat*) trois-mâts *m*; his bark is worse than his bite il fait plus de bruit que de mal || *tr*—to bark out dire d'un ton sec || *intr* aboyer; to bark up the wrong tree suivre une mauvaise piste
bar'keep'er *s* barman *m*
barker ['bɑrkər] (coll) *s* bonimenteur *m*, barnum *m*
barley ['bɑrli] *s* orge *f*
bar'maid' *s* fille *f* de comptoir, demoiselle *f* de comptoir, serveuse *f*
barn [bɑrn] *s* (*for grain*) grange *f*; (*for horses*) écurie *f*; (*for livestock*) étable *f*
barnacle ['bɑrnəkəl] *s* (*on a ship*) anatife *m*, patelle *f*; (*goose*) bernacle *f*
barn' owl' *s* (*Tyto alba*) effraie *f*
barn'storm' *intr* aller en tournée
barn'yard' *s* basse-cour *f*
barometer [bə'rɑmɪtər] *s* baromètre *m*
barometric [,bærə'mɛtrɪk] *adj* barométrique
baron ['bærən] *s* baron *m*; (*of steel, coal, lumber*) (coll) magnat *m*
baroness ['bærənɪs] *s* baronne *f*
baroque [bə'rok] *adj & s* baroque *m*
bar'rack-room' *adj* (*humor; manners*) soldatesque, de caserne || *s* chambrée *f*
barracks ['bærəks] *spl* caserne *f*
barrage [bə'rɑʒ] *s* barrage *m*
barred *adj* barré; (*excluded*) exclu
barrel ['bærəl] *s* tonneau *m*, fût *m*; large barrel barrique *f*; small barrel baril *m*, baricaut *m*, tonnelet *m*
bar'rel or'gan *s* orgue *m* de Barbarie
barren ['bærən] *adj* stérile; (*bare*) nu; (*of style*) aride, sec
barricade [,bærɪ'ked] *s* barricade *f* || *tr* barricader

barrier ['bærɪ·ər] *s* barrière *f*
bar'rier reef' *s* récif-barrière *m*
barring ['bɑrɪŋ] *prep* sauf
barrister ['bærɪstər] *s* (Brit) avocat *m*
bar'room' *s* cabaret *m*, bar *m*, bistrot *m*
bar'tend'er *s* barman *m*
barter ['bɑrtər] *s* échange *m*, troc *m* || *tr* échanger
ba'sal metab'olism ['bɛsəl] *s* métabolisme *m* basal
basalt [bə'sɔlt], ['bæsɔlt] *s* basalte *m*
base [bes] *adj* bas, vil || *s* base *f*; fondement *m*, ligne *f* d'appui, principe *m*; (*pedestal*) socle *m* || *tr* baser; fonder
base'ball' *s* base-ball *m*
base'board' *s* moulure *f* de base
basement ['besmənt] *s* sous-sol *m*, cave *f*
base'ment win'dow *s* soupirail *m*
bash [bæʃ] *tr* cogner, assommer
bashful ['bæʃfəl] *adj* timide
basic ['besɪk] *adj* fondamental, de base, essentiel; (*alkaline*) basique
basil ['bæzəl] *s* basilic *m*
basilica [bə'sɪlɪkə] *s* basilique *f*
basin ['besɪn] *s* bassin *m*; (*washbasin*) cuvette *f*; (*bowl*) bol *m*
ba·sis ['besɪs] *s* (*pl* -ses [siz]) base *f*, fondement *m*; on the basis of sur la base de
bask [bæsk], [bɑsk] *intr* se chauffer
basket ['bæskɪt], ['bɑskɪt] *s* panier *m*; (*with a handle*) corbeille *f*; (*carried on the back*) hotte *f*
bas'ket-ball' *s* basket-ball *m*, basket *m*
bas'ket lunch' *s* panier-repas *m*
bas'ket-mak'er *s* vannier *m*
bas'ket-work' *s* vannerie *f*
Basque [bæsk] *adj* basque || *s* (*language*) basque *m*; (*person*) Basque *mf*
bass [bes] *adj* grave, bas || *s* (mus) basse *f* || [bæs] *s* (ichth) bar *m*
bass' drum' [bes] *s* grosse caisse *f*
bassinet [,bæsɪ'nɛt], ['bæsɪ,nɛt] *s* bercelonnette *f*
bassoon [bə'sun] *s* basson *m*
bass viol ['bes'vaɪ·əl] *s* basse *f* de viole
basswood ['bæs,wʊd] *s* tilleul *m*
bastard ['bæstərd] *adj & s* bâtard *m*
baste [best] *tr* (*to thrash*) rosser; (*to scold*) éreinter; (culin) arroser; (sewing) faufiler, baguer, bâtir
bastion ['bæstʃən], ['bæstɪ·ən] *s* bastion *m*
bat [bæt] *s* bâton *m*; (*for cricket*) bat *m*; (sports) batte *f*; (zool) chauve-souris *f*; (*blow*) (coll) coup *m*; to be at bat tenir la batte; to go to bat for (coll) intervenir au profit de; to have bats in the belfry (coll) avoir une araignée dans le plafond || *v* (*pret & pp* batted; *ger* batting) *tr* battre
batch [bætʃ] *s* (*of papers*) liasse *f*; (coll) fournée *f*, lot *m*
bated ['betɪd] *adj*—with bated breath en baissant la voix, dans un souffle
bath [bæθ], [bɑθ] *s* bain *m*; (*bathroom*) salle *f* de bains; to take a bath prendre un bain, se baigner
bathe [beð] *tr* baigner || *intr* se baigner

bather ['beðər] s baigneur m
bath'house' s établissement m de bains; (at the seashore) cabine f
bath'ing suit' s costume m de bain
bath'ing trunks' s slip m de bain
bath' mat' s tapis m de bain
bath'robe' s peignoir m
bath'room' s salle f de bains
bath'room fix'tures spl appareils mpl sanitaires
bath'room scale' s pèse-personne m
bath' tow'el s serviette f de bain
bath'tub' s baignoire f
baton [bæ'tɑn], ['bætən] s baguette f, bâton m de chef d'orchestre
battalion [bə'tæljən] s bataillon m
batten ['bætən] tr—**to batten down the hatches** condamner les panneaux
batter ['bætər] s (culin) pâte f; (sports) batteur m || tr battre
bat'tering ram' s bélier m
batter•y ['bætəri] s (pl -ies) (elec, mil, mus) batterie f; (primary cell) pile f; (secondary cell or cells) accumulateur m, accu m
battle ['bætəl] s bataille f; **to do battle** livrer combat || tr & intr combattre
bat'tle-ax' s hache f d'armes; (shrew) (slang) harpie f, mégère f
bat'tle cruis'er s croiseur m de bataille
bat'tle cry' s cri m de guerre
bat'tle-field' s champ m de bataille
bat'tle-front' s front m de bataille
bat'tle line' s ligne f de feu
battlement ['bætəlmənt] s créneau m; **battlements** parapet m, rempart m
bat'tle roy'al s mêlée f générale
bat'tle-ship' s cuirassé m, navire m de guerre
bat•ty ['bæti] adj (comp -tier; super -tiest) (slang) dingo, maboul, braque
bauble ['bɔbəl] s babiole f, bagatelle f; (of jester) marotte f
Bavaria [bə'vɛri-ə] s la Bavière
Bavarian [bə'vɛri-ən] adj bavarois || s Bavarois m
bawd•y ['bɔdi] adj (comp -ier; super -iest) obscène, impudique
bawl [bɔl] tr—**to bawl out** (slang) engueuler || intr gueuler; (to cry) sangloter
bawl'ing out' s (slang) engueulade f
bay [be] adj & s baie f; **at bay** aux abois || intr aboyer, hurler
bay'ber'ry s (pl -ries) baie f
bay'berry tree' s laurier m
bayonet ['be-ənɪt] s baïonnette f || tr percer d'un coup de baïonnette
bayou ['baɪ-u], ['baɪ-o] s anse f
bay' rum' s eau f de toilette au laurier
bay' win'dow s fenêtre f en saillie; (slang) bedaine f, gros ventre m
bazaar [bə'zɑr] s bazar m; (social event) kermesse f
B.C. ['bi'si] adv (letterword) (before Christ) av. J.-C.
be [bi] v (pres am [æm], is [ɪz], are [ɑr]; pret was [wɑz] or [wʌz], were [wʌr]; pp been [bɪn]) intr être; avoir, e.g., **to be five years old** avoir cinq ans; e.g., **to be ten feet long** avoir dix pieds de long; e.g., **what is the matter with you?** qu'avez-vous?; **here is** or **here are** voici; **how are you?** comment allez-vous?, ça va?, comment vous portez-vous?; **how much is that?** combien coûte cela?, c'est combien ça?; **so be it** ainsi soit-il; **there is** or **there are** il y a; (in directing the attention) voilà; for expressions like **it is warm** il fait chaud or **I am cold** j'ai froid, see the noun || aux (to form the passive voice) être, e.g., **he is loved by every-body** il est aimé de tout le monde; (progressive not expressed in French), e.g., **he is eating** il mange; **to be to** + inf devoir + inf, e.g., **I am to give a speech** je dois prononcer un discours
beach [bitʃ] s plage f, bord m de la mer; grève f, rivage m || tr & intr échouer
beach'comb'er s batteur m de grève
beach'head' s (mil) tête f de pont
beach' umbrel'la s parasol m de plage
beacon ['bikən] s signal m, phare m || tr éclairer || intr briller
bead [bid] s perle f, grain m; (of a gun) guidon m; **beads** collier m; (of sweat) gouttes fpl; (eccl) chapelet m; **to draw a bead on** viser; **to tell one's beads** égrener son chapelet
beadle ['bidəl] s bedeau m, appariteur m
beagle ['bigəl] s beagle m, briquet m
beak [bik] s bec m; (nose) (slang) pif m; (slang) grand nez m crochu
beaker ['bikər] s coupe f, vase m à bec, verre m à expérience
beam [bim] s poutre f, (plank) madrier m; (of roof) solive f; (of ship) bau m, barrot m; (of light; of hope) rayon m; (rad) faisceau m; **on the beam** (slang) sur la bonne piste; **to be off the beam** (slang) faire fausse route || tr (light, waves, etc.) émettre; **to beam a broadcast** faire une émission || intr rayonner
bean [bin] s haricot m; fève f; (slang) caboche f; **to spill the beans** (coll) vendre la mèche
beaner•y ['binəri] s (pl -ies) (slang) gargote f
bean'pole' s perche f à fèves; (person) (slang) asperge f
bean'stalk' s tige f de fève, tige de haricot
bear [bɛr] s ours m; (in the stock market) baissier m || v (pret bore [bor]; pp borne [born]) tr porter; (a child) enfanter; (interest on money) rapporter; (to put up with) souffrir, supporter; **to bear the market** jouer à la baisse || intr porter; **to bear down** appuyer; **to bear up against** résister à; **to bear upon** avoir du rapport à; **to bring to bear** mettre en jeu
bearable ['bɛrəbəl] adj supportable
bear' cub' s ourson m
beard [bɪrd] s barbe f || tr braver, narguer
bearded adj barbu

beardless ['bɪrdlɪs] *adj* imberbe, sans barbe

bearer ['berər] *s* porteur *m*

bearing ['berɪŋ] *s* port *m*, maintien *m*; (mach) roulement *m*, coussinet *m*; (naut) relèvement *m*; **to get one's bearings** se retrouver; **to have a bearing on** s'appliquer à; **to take bearings** (naut) faire le point

bear' mar'ket *s* marché *m* à la baisse

bear'skin' *s* peau *f* d'ours; colback *m*

beast [bist] *s* bête *f*, animal *m*; (person) brute *f*, animal *m*

beast·ly ['bistli] *adj* (comp -lier; super -liest) brutal, bestial; (coll) abominable, détestable

beast' of bur'den *s* bête *f* de somme, bête de charge

beat [bit] *s* battement *m*; (of policeman) ronde *f*; (mus) mesure *f*, temps *m* ‖ *v* (pret beat; pp beat or beaten) *tr* battre; (to defeat) vaincre, battre; **that beats me!** (slang) ça me dépasse!; **to beat back** or **down** rabattre; **to beat in** enfoncer; **to beat it** (slang) filer, décamper; **to beat s.o. hollow** (coll) battre qn à plate couture; **to beat s.o. out of money** (slang) escroquer qn; **to beat time** battre la mesure; **to beat up** (slang) rosser ‖ *intr* battre; **to beat around the bush** (coll) tourner autour du pot

beater ['bitər] *s* batteur *m*; (culin) fouet *m*

beati·fy [bɪ'ætɪ,faɪ] *v* (pret & pp -fied) *tr* béatifier

beating ['bitɪŋ] *s* battement *m*; (blows) bastonnade *f*, rossée *f*; (defeat) (coll) raclée *f*

beatitude [bɪ'ætɪ,t(j)ud] *s* béatitude *f*

beau [bo] *s* (pl beaus or beaux [boz]) beau *m*, galant *m*

beautician [bju'tɪʃən] *s* coiffeur *m*, coiffeuse *f*, esthéticienne *f*

beautiful ['bjutɪfəl] *adj* beau

beautifully ['bjutɪfəli] *adv* admirablement

beauti·fy ['bjutɪ,faɪ] *v* (pret & pp -fied) *tr* embellir

beau·ty ['bjuti] *s* (pl -ties) beauté *f*

beau'ty con'test *s* concours *m* de beauté

beau'ty par'lor or **beau'ty shop'** *s* salon *m* or institut *m* de beauté

beau'ty queen' *s* reine *f* de beauté

beau'ty sleep' *s* sommeil *m* avant minuit

beau'ty spot' *s* (place) coin *m* délicieux; (on face) grain *m* de beauté

beaver ['bivər] *s* castor *m*

becalm [bɪ'kɑm] *tr* calmer, apaiser; (naut) abriter

because [bɪ'kɔz] *conj* parce que; **because of** à cause de, par suite de

beck [bek] *s*—**to be at s.o.'s beck and call** obéir à qn au doigt et à l'œil

beckon ['bekən] *tr* faire signe à, appeler ‖ *intr* appeler

be·come [bɪ'kʌm] *v* (pret -came; pp -come) *tr* convenir à, aller à, seoir à ‖ *intr* devenir; se faire, e.g., **to become a doctor** se faire médecin; e.g., **to become known** se faire connaître;

to become accustomed s'accoutumer; **to become old** vieillir; **what has become of him?** qu'est-ce qu'il est devenu?

becoming [bɪ'kʌmɪŋ] *adj* convenable, seyant

bed [bed] *s* lit *m*; couche *f*; **to go to bed** se coucher; **to put to bed** coucher

bed' and board' *s* le vivre et le couvert

bed'bug' *s* punaise *f* (des lits)

bed'clothes' *spl* couvertures *fpl* et draps *mpl*

bedding ['bedɪŋ] *s* literie *f*

bedeck [bɪ'dek] *tr* parer, orner, chamarrer; **to bedeck oneself** s'attifer

bed'fast' *adj* cloué au lit

bed'fel'low *s* camarade *m* de lit

bedizen [bɪ'daɪzən], [bɪ'dɪzən] *tr* attifer, chamarrer

bed'jack'et *s* liseuse *f*

bedlam ['bedləm] *s* pétaudière *f*, tumulte *m*

bed'lamp' *s* lampe *f* de chevet

bed' lin'en *s* literie *f*, draps *mpl* en toile de fil

bed'pan' *s* bassin *m* (de lit)

bed'post' *s* pied *m* de lit

bedraggled [bɪ'dræɡəld] *adj* crotté, échevelé

bedridden ['bed,rɪdən] *adj* alité, cloué au lit

bed'rock' *s* roche *f* de fond; tuf *m*; (fig) fondement *m*

bed'room' *s* chambre *f* à coucher

bed'room lamp' *s* lampe *f* de chevet

bed'side' *s* bord *m* du lit, chevet *m*

bed'side book' *s* livre *m* de chevet

bed'sore' *s* escarre *f*

bed'spread' *s* dessus-de-lit *m*

bed'spring' *s* sommier *m*

bed'stead' *s* bois *m* de lit

bed' tick' *s* coutil *m*

bed'time' *s* l'heure *f* du coucher

bed' warm'er *s* chauffe-lit *m*

bed'wet'ting *s* énurésie *f*

bee [bi] *s* abeille *f*; (get-together) réunion *f*; (contest) concours *m*

beech [bitʃ] *s* hêtre *m*

beech' mar'ten *s* (zool) fouine *f*

beech'nut' *s* faîne *f*

beef [bif] *s* bœuf *m* ‖ *tr*—**to beef up** (coll) renforcer ‖ *intr* (slang) rouspéter

beef' cat'tle *s* bœufs *mpl* de boucherie

beef'steak' *s* bifteck *m*

beef' stew' *s* ragoût *m* de bœuf

bee'hive' *s* ruche *f*

bee'keep'er *s* apiculteur *m*

bee'keep'ing *s* apiculture *f*

bee'line' *s*—**to make a beeline for** aller en droite ligne à

beer [bɪr] *s* bière *f*

beer' bot'tle *s* canette *f* (de bière)

bees'wax' *s* cire *f* d'abeille

beet [bit] *s* betterave *f*

beetle ['bitəl] *s* scarabée *m*, escarbot *m*

bee'tle-browed' *adj* à sourcils épais, à sourcils fournis

be·fall [bɪ'fɔl] *v* (pret -fell; pp -fallen) *tr* arriver à ‖ *intr* arriver

befitting [bɪ'fɪtɪŋ] *adj* convenable, seyant

before [bɪ'for] *adv* avant, auparavant ‖ *prep* avant; (*in front of*) devant; **before** + *ger* avant de + *inf* ‖ *conj* avant que

before'hand' *adv* d'avance, préalablement, auparavant

befriend [bɪ'frend] *tr* venir en aide à

befuddle [bɪ'fʌdəl] *tr* embrouiller

beg [beg] *v* (*pret & pp* **begged**; *ger* **begging**) *tr* mendier; (*to entreat*) prier ‖ *intr* mendier; (*said of dog*) faire le beau; **I beg of you** je vous en prie; **to beg for** solliciter; **to beg off** s'excuser; **to go begging** (fig) rester pour compte

be-get [bɪ'get] *v* (*pret* **-got**; *pp* **-gotten** or **-got**; *ger* **-getting**) *tr* engendrer

beggar ['begər] *s* mendiant *m*

beggarly ['begərli] *adj* chétif, misérable

be-gin [bɪ'gɪn] *v* (*pret* **-gan** ['gæn]; *pp* **-gun** ['gʌn]; *ger* **-ginning**) *tr & intr* commencer; **beginning with** à partir de; **to begin to** commencer à

beginner [bɪ'gɪnər] *s* débutant *m*, commençant *m*; (*tyro*) blanc-bec *m*, novice *m*, béjaune *m*; (mil) bleu *m*

beginning [bɪ'gɪnɪŋ] *s* commencement *m*, début *m*

begrudge [bɪ'grʌdʒ] *tr* donner à contrecœur; **to begrudge s.o. s.th.** envier q.ch. à qn

beguile [bɪ'gaɪl] *tr* charmer, tromper

behalf [bɪ'hæf], [bɪ'hɑf] *s*—**on behalf of** de la part de, au nom de

behave [bɪ'hev] *intr* se comporter, se conduire; se comporter bien

behavior [bɪ'hevjər] *s* comportement *m*, conduite *f*

behead [bɪ'hed] *tr* décapiter

beheading [bɪ'hedɪŋ] *s* décapitation *f*

behest [bɪ'hest] *s* ordre *m*, demande *f*

behind [bɪ'haɪnd] *s* derrière *m* ‖ *adv* derrière, par derrière; to be behind être en retard; **to fall behind** traîner en arrière ‖ *prep* derrière; en arrière de; **behind the back of** dans le dos de; **behind time** en retard

be-hold [bɪ'hold] *v* (*pret & pp* **-held** ['held]) *tr* contempler ‖ *interj* voyez!, voici!

behoove [bɪ'huv] *impers*—**it behooves him to** il lui appartient de; **it does not behoove him to** mal lui sied de

being ['bi·ɪŋ] *adj*—**for the time being** pour le moment ‖ *s* être *m*

belabor [bɪ'lebər] *tr* rosser, (fig) trop insister sur

belated [bɪ'letɪd] *adj* attardé, tardif

belch [beltʃ] *s* éructation *f*; rot *m* (slang) ‖ *tr & intr* éructer

bel-fry ['belfri] *s* (*pl* **-fries**) beffroi *m*, clocher *m*

Belgian ['beldʒən] *adj* belge ‖ *s* Belge *mf*

Belgium ['beldʒəm] *s* Belgique *f*; la Belgique

be-lie [bɪ'laɪ] *v* (*pret & pp* **-lied** ['laɪd]; *ger* **-lying** ['laɪ·ɪŋ]) *tr* démentir

belief [bɪ'lif] *s* croyance *f*

believable [bɪ'livəbəl] *adj* croyable

believe [bɪ'liv] *tr & intr* croire; **to believe in** croire à or en; **to make believe** faire semblant, feindre

believer [bɪ'livər] *s* croyant *m*

belittle [bɪ'lɪtəl] *tr* rabaisser

bell [bel] *s* cloche *f*; (*of a clock or gong*) timbre *m*; (*small bell*) sonnette *f*, clochette *f*; (*big bell*) bourdon *m*; (*on animals*) grelot *m*, clarine *f*, sonnaille *f*; (*of a trumpet*) pavillon *m*; **bells** sonnerie *f* ‖ *tr* attacher un grelot à

belladonna [ˌbelə'dɑnə] *s* belladone *f*

bell'-bot'tom trou'sers *spl* pantalon *m* à pattes d'éléphant

bell'boy' *s* chasseur *m*, garçon *m* d'hôtel

bell' glass' *s* globe *m*, garde-poussière *m*

bell'hop' *s* chasseur *m*, garçon *m* d'hôtel

bellicose ['belɪˌkos] *adj* belliqueux

belligerent [bə'lɪdʒərənt] *adj & s* belligérant *m*

bell' jar' *s var of* bell glass

bellow ['belo] *s* mugissement *m*; **bellows** (*of camera; of fireplace*) soufflet *m*; (*of organ; of forge*) soufflerie *f* ‖ *intr* mugir, beugler

bell'pull' *s* cordon *m* de sonnette

bell' ring'er *s* sonneur *m*; carillonneur *m*

bell'-shaped' *adj* en forme de cloche

bell' tow'er *s* clocher *m*, campanile *m*

bellwether ['belˌweðər] *s* sonnailler *m*

bel-ly ['beli] *s* (*pl* **-lies**) ventre *m* ‖ *v* (*pret & pp* **-lied**) *intr*—**to belly out** s'enfler

bel'ly-ache' *s* (coll) mal *m* de ventre ‖ *intr* (slang) rouspéter

bel'ly-but'ton *s* (coll) nombril *m*

bel'ly dance' *s* (coll) danse *f* du ventre

bel'ly flop' *s* plat ventre *m* (acrobatique)

bellyful ['belɪˌful] *s* (slang) ventrée *f*

bel'ly-land' *intr* (aer) aterrir sur le ventre

belong [bɪ'lɔŋ], [bɪ'lɑŋ] *intr* (*to have the proper qualities*) aller bien; **to belong in** devoir être dans, e.g., **this chair belongs in that corner** cette chaise doit être dans ce coin-là; **to belong to** appartenir à; **to belong together** aller ensemble

belongings [bɪ'lɔŋɪŋz], [bɪ'lɑŋɪŋz] *spl* biens *mpl*, effets *mpl*

beloved [bɪ'lʌvɪd], [bɪ'lʌvd] *adj & s* bien-aimé *m*

below [bɪ'lo] *adv* dessous, au-dessous, en bas; (*as follows, following*) ci-dessous, ci-après ‖ *prep* sous, au-dessous de; (*another point on the river*) en aval de

belt [belt] *s* ceinture *f*; zone *f*; (*of a machine*) courroie *f*; **to tighten one's belt** se serrer la ceinture ‖ *tr* ceindre; (slang) cogner

belt' buck'le *s* boucle *f* de ceinturon

belt' convey'or *s* tapis *m* roulant

belted *adj* à ceinture

belt'way' *s* route *f* de ceinture, boulevard *m* périphérique

bemoan [bɪ'mon] *tr* déplorer
bemuse [bɪ'mjuz] *tr* stupéfier, hébéter
bench [bentʃ] *s* banc *m*; (law) siège *m*
bench' mark' *s* repère *m*
bend [bend] *s* courbure *f*; (of road) tournant *m*; (of river) sinuosité *f*; (of caissons) || *v* (pret & pp **bent** [bent]) *tr* courber; (the elbow; a person to one's will) plier; (the knee) fléchir || *intr* courber; plier; **do not bend** (label) ne pas plier; **to bend down** se courber
bender ['bendər] *s*—**to go on a bender** (slang) faire la bombe
beneath [bɪ'niθ] *adv* dessous, au-dessous, en bas || *prep* sous, au-dessous de
benediction [,benɪ'dɪkʃən] *s* bénédiction *f*
benefactor ['benɪ,fæktər], [,benɪ'fæktər] *s* bienfaiteur *m*
beneficence [bɪ'nefɪsəns] *s* bienfaisance *f*
beneficent [bɪ'nefɪsənt] *adj* bienfaisant
beneficial [,benɪ'fɪʃəl] *adj* profitable, avantageux; (remedy) salutaire
beneficiar•y [,benɪ'fɪʃɪ,eri] *s* (pl **-ies**) bénéficiaire *mf*, ayant droit *m*
benefit ['benɪfɪt] *s* profit *m*; (theat) bénéfice *m*; **benefits** bienfaits *mpl*, avantages *mpl*; **for the benefit of** au profit de || *tr* profiter (with *dat*) || *intr* bénéficier
ben'efit soci'ety *s* société *f* de prévoyance
benevolent [bɪ'nevələnt] *adj* bienveillant, bienfaisant, bénévole
benign [bɪ'naɪn] *adj* bénin
bent [bent] *adj* courbé, plié; (person's back) voûté; (determined) résolu; **bent over** (shoulders) voûté; (figure, person) courbé; **to be bent on** être acharné à || *s* penchant *m*; **to have a bent for** avoir du goût pour
benzene [ben'zin] *s* (chem) benzène *m*
benzine [ben'zin] *s* benzine *f*
bequeath [bɪ'kwið], [bɪ'kwiθ] *tr* léguer
bequest [bɪ'kwest] *s* legs *m*
berate [bɪ'ret] *tr* gronder
be•reave [bɪ'riv] *v* (pret & pp **-reaved** or **-reft** ['reft]) *tr* priver; (to cause sorrow to) affliger
bereavement [bɪ'rivmənt] *s* privation *f*; (sorrow) deuil *m*, affliction *f*
Berlin [bər'lɪn] *adj* berlinois || *s* Berlin *m*
Berliner [bər'lɪnər] *s* berlinois *m*
Bermuda [bər'mjudə] *s* les Bermudes *fpl*
ber•ry ['beri] *s* (pl **-ries**) baie *f*; (seed) grain *m*
berserk [bər'sʌrk], [bər'zʌrk] *adv* frénétiquement; **to go berserk** frapper à tort et à travers
berth [bʌrθ] *s* couchette *f*; (at a dock) emplacement *m*; (space to move about) évitage *m*; (fig) poste *m*, situation *f* || *tr* (a ship) accoster
beryllium [bə'rɪli•əm] *s* béryllium *m*
be•seech [bɪ'sitʃ] *v* (pret & pp **-sought** ['sɔt] or **-seeched**) *tr* supplier

be•set [bɪ'set] *v* (pret & pp **-set**; ger **-setting**) *tr* assiéger, assaillir
beside [bɪ'saɪd] *prep* à côté de, auprès de; **to be beside oneself** être hors de soi; **to be beside oneself with** (e.g., joy) être transporté de
besides [bɪ'saɪdz] *adv* en outre, de plus; (otherwise) d'ailleurs || *prep* en sus de, en plus de, outre
besiege [bɪ'sidʒ] *tr* assiéger
besmear [bɪ'smɪr] *tr* barbouiller
besmirch [bɪ'smʌrtʃ] *tr* souiller
best [best] *adj super* (le) meilleur §91 || *s* (le) meilleur *m*; **at best** au mieux; **to do one's best** faire de son mieux; **to get the best of it** avoir le dessus; **to make the best of** s'accommoder de || *adv super* (le) mieux §91 || *tr* l'emporter sur
bestial ['bestjəl], ['bestʃəl] *adj* bestial, brutal
best' man' *s* garçon *m* d'honneur
bestow [bɪ'sto] *tr* accorder, conférer
bestowal [bɪ'sto•əl] *s* don *m*, dispensation *f*
best' sell'er *s* livre *m* à succès, succès *m* de librairie
bet [bet] *s* pari *m*, gageure *f*; **make your bets!** faites vos jeux! || *v* (pret & pp **bet** or **betted**; ger **betting**) *tr & intr* parier; **you bet!** (slang) je vous croisl, tu parles!
be•take [bɪ'tek] *v* (pret **-took**; pp **-taken**) *tr*—**to betake oneself** se rendre
betray [bɪ'tre] *tr* trahir
betrayal [bɪ'tre•əl] *s* trahison *f*
betrayer [bɪ'tre•ər] *s* traître *m*
betroth [bɪ'troð], [bɪ'troθ] *tr*—**to be betrothed** se fiancer
betrothal [bɪ'troðəl], [bɪ'troθəl] *s* fiançailles *fpl*
better ['betər] *adj comp* meilleur §91; **better than** meilleur que || *adv comp* mieux §91; **better than** mieux que; (followed by numeral) plus de; **it is better to** il vaut mieux de; **so much the better** tant mieux; **to be better** (in better health) aller mieux; **to be better** to valoir mieux; **to get better** s'améliorer; **to get the better of** l'emporter sur; **to think better** se raviser || *tr* améliorer || *intr* s'améliorer
bet'ter half' *s* (coll) chère moitié *f*
bet'ting odds' *spl* cote *f* (des paris)
bettor ['betər] *s* parieur *m*, gageur *m*
between [bɪ'twin] *adv* au milieu; dans l'intervalle || *prep* entre; **between friends** dans l'intimité
between'-decks' *s* (naut) entrepont *m*
bev•el ['bevəl] *adj* biseauté, taillé en biseau || *s* (instrument) équerre *f*; (sloping part) biseau *m* || *v* (pret & pp **-eled** or **-elled**; ger **-eling** or **-elling**) *tr* biseauter, chanfreiner, équerrer
beverage ['bevərɪdʒ] *s* boisson *f*
bev•y ['bevi] *s* (pl **-ies**) bande *f*
bewail [bɪ'wel] *tr* lamenter, pleurer
beware [bɪ'wer] *tr* se bien garder de || *intr* prendre garde; **to beware of**

prendre garde à || *interj* gare!, prenez garde!

bewilder [bɪ'wɪldər] *tr* confondre, ahurir

bewilderment [bɪ'wɪldərmənt] *s* confusion *f*, ahurissement *m*

bewitch [bɪ'wɪtʃ] *tr* ensorceler

bewitching [bɪ'wɪtʃɪŋ] *adj* enchanteur

beyond [bɪ'jɑnd] *s*—**the beyond** l'audelà *m* || *adv* au-delà || *prep* au-delà de; **beyond a doubt** hors de doute; **it's beyond me** (coll) je n'y comprends rien; **to go beyond** dépasser

biannual [baɪ'ænjʊ·əl] *adj* semi-annuel

bias ['baɪ·əs] *adj* biais || *s* biais *m*; (fig) prévention *f*, préjugé *m* || *tr* prédisposer, prévenir, rendre partial

bib [bɪb] *s* bavette *f*

Bible ['baɪbəl] *s* Bible *f*

Biblical ['bɪblɪkəl] *adj* biblique

bibliographer [,bɪblɪ'ɑgrəfər] *s* bibliographe *m*

bibliography [,bɪblɪ'ɑgrəfi] *s* (*pl* -phies) bibliographie *f*

biceps ['baɪseps] *s* biceps *m*

bicker ['bɪkər] *intr* se quereller, se chamailler

bickering ['bɪkərɪŋ] *s* bisbille *f*

bicuspid [baɪ'kʌspɪd] *s* prémolaire *f*

bicycle ['baɪsɪkəl] *s* bicyclette *f*, vélo *m* || *intr* faire de la bicyclette, aller à bicyclette

bi'cycle path' *s* piste *f* cyclable

bicyclist ['baɪsɪklɪst] *s* cycliste *mf*

bid [bɪd] *s* enchère *f*, offre *f*, mise *f*; (e.g., *to build a school*) soumission *f*; (cards) demande *f* || *v* (*pret* **bad** [bæd] *or* **bid**; *ger* **bidden** ['bɪdən]) *tr* inviter; (*to order*) commander; (cards) demander; **to bid ten thousand on** mettre une enchère de dix mille sur || *intr*—**to bid on** mettre une enchère sur

bidder ['bɪdər] *s* enchérisseur *m*, offrant *m*; (*person who submits an estimate*) soumissionnaire *mf*

bidding ['bɪdɪŋ] *s* enchères *fpl*; **at s.o.'s bidding** aux ordres de qn

bide [baɪd] *tr*—**to bide one's time** attendre l'heure or le bon moment

biennial [baɪ'ɛnɪ·əl] *adj* biennal

bier [bɪr] *s* (*frame or stand*) catafalque *m*; (*coffin*) cercueil *m*

biff [bɪf] *s* (slang) gnon *m*, beigne *f* || *tr* (slang) gifler, cogner

bifocal [baɪ'fokəl] *adj* bifocal || **bifocals** *spl* lunettes *fpl* bifocales

big [bɪg] *adj* (*comp* **bigger**; *super* **biggest**) gros, grand; (*man*) de grande taille || *adv*—**to grow big** grandir; **to talk big** (slang) se vanter

bigamist ['bɪgəmɪst] *s* bigame *mf*

bigamous ['bɪgəməs] *adj* bigame

bigamy ['bɪgəmi] *s* bigamie *f*

big'-boned' *adj* ossu, à gros os

big' busi'ness *s* (pej) les grosses affaires *fpl*

Big' Dip'per *s* Grande Ourse *f*

big' game' *s* fauves *mpl*, gros gibier *m*

big'-heart'ed *adj* généreux, cordial

big'mouth' *s* (slang) gueulard *m*

bigot ['bɪgət] *s* bigot *m*

bigoted ['bɪgətɪd] *adj* bigot

bigot·ry ['bɪgətri] *s* (*pl* -ries) bigoterie *f*

big' shot' *s* (slang) grand manitou *m*, gros bonnet *m*

big' splash' *s* (slang) sensation *f* à tout casser

big' stiff' *s* (slang) personnage *m* guindé

big' talk' *s* (slang) vantardise *f*

big'-time' op'erator *s* (slang) gros trafiquant *m*

big' toe' *s* orteil *m*, gros orteil

big' top' *s* (circus tent) chapiteau *m*

big' wheel' *s* (slang) gros bonnet *m*, grand manitou *m*, grosse légume *f*

big'wig' *s* (coll) gros bonnet *m*, grand manitou *m*, grosse légume *f*

bike [baɪk] *s* (coll) bécane *f*, vélo *m*

bile [baɪl] *s* bile *f*

bilge [bɪldʒ] *s* sentine *f*, cale *f*

bilge' wa'ter *s* eau *f* de cale

bilingual [baɪ'lɪŋgwəl] *adj* bilingue

bilious ['bɪljəs] *adj* bilieux

bilk [bɪlk] *s* tromperie *f*, escroquerie *f* || *tr* tromper, escroquer

bill [bɪl] *s* (*invoice*) facture *f*, mémoire *m*; (*in a hotel*) note *f*; (*in a restaurant*) addition *f*; (*currency*) billet *m*; (*of a bird*) bec *m*; (*posted*) affiche *f*, placard *m*, écriteau *m*; (*in a legislature*) projet *m* de loi; **post no bills** (*public sign*) défense d'afficher; **to head the bill** (theat) avoir la vedette || *tr* facturer

bill'board' *s* tableau *m* d'affichage, panneau *m* d'affichage

billet ['bɪlɪt] *s* (*order*) billet *m* de logement; (*of metal or wood*) billette *f* || *tr* loger, cantonner

bill'fold' *s* portefeuille *m*

bil'liard ball' *s* bille *f*

billiards ['bɪljərdz] *s* & *spl* billard *m*

bil'liard ta'ble *s* billard *m*

billion ['bɪljən] *s* (U.S.A.) milliard *m*; (Brit) billion *m*

billionaire [,bɪljən'ɛr] *s* milliardaire *mf*

bill' of exchange' *s* lettre *f* de change, traite *f*

bill' of fare' *s* carte *f* du jour

bill' of health' *s* patente *f* de santé

bill' of lad'ing *s* connaissement *m*

bill' of rights' *s* déclaration *f* des droits de l'homme

bill' of sale' *s* acte *m* de vente

billow ['bɪlo] *s* flot *m*, grosse vague *f* || *intr* onduler

billowy ['bɪlo·i] *adj* onduleux, ondoyant

bill'post'er *s* colleur *m* d'affiches, afficheur *m*

bil·ly ['bɪli] *s* (*pl* -lies) bâton *m*

bil'ly goat' *s* (coll) bouc *m*

bimonthly [baɪ'mʌnθli] *adj* bimestriel

bin [bɪn] *s* huche *f*, coffre *m*

binary ['baɪnəri] *adj* binaire

binaural [baɪ'nɔrəl], [bɪn'ɔrəl] *adj* stéréophonique; à deux oreilles

bind [baɪnd] *v* (*pret* & *pp* **bound** [baʊnd]) *tr* lier, attacher; (*a book*) relier; (*s.o. to an agreement*) obliger

binder ['baɪndər] s (person) lieur m; (of books) relieur m; (agreement) conventions fpl; (mach) lieuse f
binder·y ['baɪndəri] s (pl -ies) atelier m de reliure
binding ['baɪndɪŋ] adj obligatoire; (med) astringent; **binding on all concerned** solidaire ‖ s reliure f
bind'ing post' s (elec) borne f
binge [bɪndʒ] s (coll) noce f, bombe f
bingo ['bɪŋgo] s loto m
binocular [bɪ'nɑkjələr] adj & s binoculaire m; **binoculars** jumelles fpl
binomial [baɪ'nomɪ·əl] adj & s binôme m
biochemistry [ˌbaɪ·o'kemɪstri] s biochimie f
biographer [baɪ'ɑgrəfər] s biographe mf
biographic(al) [ˌbaɪ·ə'græfɪk(əl)] adj biographique
biogra·phy [baɪ'ɑgrəfi] s (pl -phies) biographie f
biologist [baɪ'ɑlədʒɪst] s biologiste mf
biology [baɪ'ɑlədʒi] s biologie f
biophysics [ˌbaɪ·ə'fɪzɪks] s biophysique f
biop·sy ['baɪ·ɑpsi] s (pl -sies) biopsie f
bipartisan [baɪ'pɑrtɪzən] adj bipartite
bipartite [baɪ'pɑrtaɪt] adj biparti
biped ['baɪped] adj & s bipède m
biplane ['baɪˌplen] s biplan m
birch [bʌrtʃ] s bouleau m; (for whipping) verges fpl ‖ tr battre à coups de verges
birch' rod' s verges fpl
bird [bʌrd] s oiseau m; (slang) type m, individu m; **a bird in the hand is worth two in the bush** un "tiens" vaut mieux que deux "tu l'auras"; **to give s.o. the bird** (slang) envoyer qn promener; **to kill two birds with one stone** faire d'une pierre deux coups
bird' bath' s baignoire f pour oiseaux, bain m pour oiseaux
bird' cage' s cage f d'oiseau
bird' call' s appeau m, pipeau m
bird' dog' s chien m pour la plume
bird' fan'cier s oiselier m
birdie ['bʌrdi] s oiselet m, oisillon m
bird' lime' s glu f
bird' of pas'sage s oiseau m de passage
bird' of prey' s oiseau m de proie
bird' seed' s alpiste m, chènevis m
bird's'-eye' s (pattern) œil-de-perdrix m
bird's'-eye view' s vue f à vol d'oiseau, tour m d'horizon, vue d'ensemble
biretta [bɪ'retə] s barette f
birth [bʌrθ] s naissance f; **by birth** de naissance; **to give birth to** donner naissance à
birth' certif'icate s acte m de naissance, bulletin m de naissance
birth' control' s contrôle m des naissances, procréation f dirigée
birth'day' s anniversaire m; **happy birthday!** heureux anniversaire!
birth'day cake' s gâteau m d'anniversaire
birth'day pres'ent s cadeau m d'anniversaire

birth'mark' s tache f, envie f
birth'place' s lieu m de naissance
birth' rate' s natalité f, taux m de natalité
birth'right' s droit m de naissance; droit d'aînesse
biscuit ['bɪskɪt] s petit pain m, crêpe f au beurre, gâteau m feuilleté
bisect [baɪ'sekt] tr couper en deux, diviser en deux
bisexual [baɪ'sek∫ʊ·əl] adj bissexuel
bishop ['bɪ∫əp] s évêque m; (chess) fou m
bishopric ['bɪ∫əprɪk] s évêché m
bison ['baɪsən], ['baɪzən] s bison m
bisulfate [baɪ'sʌlfet] s bisulfate m
bisulfite [baɪ'sʌlfaɪt] s bisulfite m
bit [bɪt] s morceau m, bout m, brin m; (of a bridle) mors m; (of a drill) mèche f; **bit by bit** petit à petit
bitch [bɪt∫] s (dog) chienne f; (fox) renarde f; (wolf) louve f; (vulgar) vache f
bite [baɪt] s (of food) bouchée f; (by an animal) morsure f; (by an insect) piqûre f; (by a fish on a hook) touche f ‖ v (pret bit [bɪt]; pp bit or bitten ['bɪtən]) tr mordre; (said of an insect or snake) piquer
biting ['baɪtɪŋ] adj mordant; (cold) piquant; (wind) coupant
bit' play'er s figurant m
bitter ['bɪtər] adj amer; (cold) âpre, noir; (fight) acharné; (style) mordant ‖ **bitters** spl bitter m
bit'ter end' s—**to the bitter end** jusqu'au bout
bit'ter-end'er s (coll) intransigeant m, jusqu'au-boutiste mf
bitterness ['bɪtərnɪs] s amertume f; (of winter) âpreté f; (fig) aigreur f
bit'ter·sweet' adj aigre-doux ‖ s douce-amère f
bitumen [bɪ't(j)umən] s bitume m
bivou·ac ['bɪvʊˌæk], ['bɪvwæk] s bivouac m, cantonnement m ‖ v (pret & pp -acked; ger -acking) intr bivouaquer
biweekly [baɪ'wikli] adj bimensuel ‖ adv bimensuellement
biyearly [baɪ'jɪrli] adj semestriel ‖ adv semestriellement
bizarre [bɪ'zɑr] adj bizarre
blab [blæb] v (pret & pp blabbed; ger blabbing) tr ébruiter ‖ intr jaser
blabber ['blæbər] intr jaser
blab'ber·mouth' s (slang) jaseur m
black [blæk] adj & s noir m ‖ tr noircir; **to black out** faire le black-out dans
black'-and-blue' adj meurtri
black'-and-white' adj en blanc et noir
black'ball' tr blackbouler
black'ber'ry s (pl -ries) mûre f, mûre de ronce
black'berry bush' s mûrier m sauvage
black'bird' s (Turdus merula) merle m
black'board' s tableau m noir
black'board eras'er s éponge f, chiffon m
black' cur'rant s cassis m
black' damp' s mofette f

blacken ['blækən] *tr* noircir
black' eye' *s* œil *m* poché; **to give s.o. a black eye** pocher l'œil à qn; (fig) ruiner la réputation de qn
black'-eyed Su'san ['suzən] *s* marguerite *f* américaine
blackguard ['blægərd] *s* vaurien *m*, salaud *m*
black'head' *s* comédon *m*, tanne *f*
black'-headed gull' *s* mouette *f* rieuse
blacking ['blækɪŋ] *s* cirage *m* noir
blackish ['blækɪʃ] *adj* noirâtre
black'jack' *s* assommoir *m*; (cards) vingt-et-un *m* ‖ *tr* assommer
black' lead' [lɛd] *s* mine *f* de plomb
black' let'ter *s* caractère *m* gothique
black' list' *s* liste *f* noire
black'-list' *tr* mettre à l'index, mettre en quarantaine
black' lo'cust *s* (bot) faux acacia *m*
black' mag'ic *s* magie *f* noire
black'mail' *s* chantage *m* ‖ *tr* faire chanter ‖ *intr* faire du chantage
blackmailer ['blæk,melər] *s* maître *m* chanteur
black' mark' *s* (of censure) tache *f*
black' mar'ket *s* marché *m* noir
black' marketeer' [,mɑrkɪ'tɪr] *s* trafiquant *m* du marché noir
black'out' *s* black-out *m*; (of aviator) cécité *f* temporaire
black' pep'per *s* poivre *m* noir
black' sheep' *s* (fig) brebis *f* galeuse
black'smith' *s* forgeron *m*, maréchal-ferrant *m*
bladder ['blædər] *s* vessie *f*
bladderwort ['blædər,wʌrt] *s* utriculaire *f*
blade [bled] *s* lame *f*; (of grass) brin *m*; (of propeller) aile *f*, pale *f*; (of oar) plat *m*; (young man) gaillard *m*; (mach) ailette *f*, palette *f*, aube *f*
blah [blɑ] *s* (slang) sornettes *fpl*, fadaises *fpl*, bêtises *fpl*
blah-blah ['blɑ'blɑ] *s* baratin *m*
blamable ['blemabəl] *adj* blâmable, coupable
blame [blem] *s* blâme *m*; reproches *mpl* ‖ *tr* blâmer; reprocher; **s'en prendre à**
blameless ['blemlɪs] *adj* sans reproche
blame'wor'thy *adj* blâmable
blanch [blæntʃ], [blɑntʃ] *tr & intr* blanchir
bland [blænd] *adj* doux, suave; (with dissimulation) narquois
blandish ['blændɪʃ] *tr* flatter, cajoler
blandishment ['blændɪʃmənt] *s* flatterie *f*; attrait *m*, charme *m*
blank [blæŋk] *adj* blanc; (check; form) en blanc; (mind) confondu, déconcerté ‖ *s* blanc *m*; trou *m*, vide *m*, lacune *f*; (metal mold) flan *m*; (form to be filled out) fiche *f*, formule *f*, feuille *f*; (space to be filled in) tiret *m* ‖ *tr*—**to blank out** effacer ‖ *intr*—**to blank out** (coll) s'évanouir
blank' check' *s* chèque *m* en blanc; (fig) chèque en blanc
blanket ['blæŋkɪt] *adj* général *f* ‖ *s* couverture *f* ‖ *tr* envelopper; traiter sous une rubrique générale

blank' verse' *s* vers *mpl* blancs
blare [blɛr] *s* bruit *m*; (of trumpet) sonnerie *f* ‖ *tr* faire retentir; (like a trumpet) sonner ‖ *intr* retentir
blarney ['blɑrni] *s* (coll) flagornerie *f* ‖ *tr* (coll) flagorner
blaspheme [blæs'fim] *tr & intr* blasphémer
blasphemous ['blæsfɪməs] *adj* blasphématoire, blasphémateur
blasphe•my ['blæsfɪmi] *s* (pl -mies) blasphème *m*
blast [blæst], [blɑst] *s* rafale *f*, souffle *m*; explosion *f*; (of dynamite) charge *f*; (of whistle) coup *m*; (of trumpet) sonnerie *f*; **at full blast** à toute allure ‖ *tr* (to blow up) faire sauter; (hopes) ruiner; (a plant) flétrir ‖ *intr* (said of plant) se faner; **to blast off** (said of rocket) se mettre à feu
blast' fur'nace *s* haut fourneau *m*
blasting ['blæstɪŋ], ['blɑstɪŋ] *s* abattage *m* à la poudre; (of hopes) anéantissement *m*; (coll) abattage *m*, verte semonce *f*
blast'ing cap' *s* capsule *f* fulminante
blast'off' *s* mise *f* à feu
blatant ['bletənt] *adj* criard; (injustice) criant
blaze [blez] *s* flamme *f*, flambée *f*; (e.g., blazing house) incendie *m*; **to run like blazes** (slang) courir furieusement ‖ *tr*—**to blaze the trail** frayer la piste ‖ *intr* flamboyer, s'embraser
blazing ['blezɪŋ] *adj* embrasé, en feu; (sun) flamboyant
blazon ['blezən] *s* (heral) blason *m* ‖ *tr* célébrer; exalter; (heral) blasonner; **to blazon out** proclamer
bleach [blitʃ] *s* décolorant *m*, eau *f* de Javel; (for hair) eau oxygénée *f* ‖ *tr* blanchir, décolorer
bleachers ['blitʃərz] *spl* gradins *mpl*, tribune *f*
bleak [blik] *adj* froid, morne, nu
blear-eyed ['blɪr'aɪd] *adj* chassieux, larmoyant; (dull) d'un esprit épais
blear•y ['blɪri] *adj* (comp -ier; super -iest) (eyes) chassieux; (prospect) voilé, incertain
bleat [blit] *s* bêlement *m* ‖ *intr* bêler, béguer
bleed [blid] *v* (pret & pp bled [bled]) *tr & intr* saigner; **to bleed white** saigner à blanc
bleeding ['blidɪŋ] *adj* saignant ‖ *s* saignement *m*; (bloodletting) saignée *f*
blemish ['blɛmɪʃ] *s* défaut *m*, tache *f* ‖ *tr* défigurer; (a reputation) tacher
blench [blɛntʃ] *intr* pâlir; (to draw back) broncher
blend [blɛnd] *s* mélange *m* ‖ *v* (pret & pp blended or blent [blɛnt]) *tr* mêler, mélanger; fondre, marier ‖ *intr* se fondre, se marier
bless [blɛs] *tr* bénir
blessed ['blɛsɪd] *adj* béni, saint; (happy) bienheureux
blessing ['blɛsɪŋ] *s* bénédiction *f*; (at meals) bénédicité *m*

blight [blaɪt] s rouille f, nielle f; (of peaches) cloque f; (of potatoes; of vines) brunissure f; (fig) flétrissure f || tr rouiller, nieller; (hopes, aspirations) flétrir, frustrer

blimp [blɪmp] s vedette f (aérienne)

blind [blaɪnd] adj aveugle; **blind by birth** aveugle-né; **blind in one eye** borgne; **blind person** aveugle m || s store m; (for hunting) guet-apens m, (fig) feinte f; (cards) talon m || tr aveugler; (by dazzling) éblouir

blind′ al′ley s cul-de-sac m, impasse f

blinder ['blaɪndər] s œillère f

blind′ flight′ s vol m à l'aveuglette

blind′ fly′ing s (aer) pilotage m sans visibilité

blind′fold adj les yeux bandés || s bandeau m || tr bander les yeux de

blindly ['blaɪndli] adv aveuglément

blind′ man′ s aveugle m

blind′man's buff′ s colin-maillard m

blindness ['blaɪndnɪs] s cécité f; (fig) aveuglement m

blind′ spot′ s côté m faible

blink [blɪŋk] s clignotement m || tr faire clignoter || intr clignoter

blinker ['blɪŋkər] s feu m clignotant; (for horses) œillère f; (for signals) projecteur m clignotant

blink′er light′ s feu m à éclipses

blip [blɪp] s spot m

bliss [blɪs] s félicité f, béatitude f

blissful ['blɪsfəl] adj bienheureux

blister ['blɪstər] s ampoule f, bulle f || tr couvrir d'ampoules; (paint) boursoufler || intr se couvrir d'ampoules; se boursoufler

blithe [blaɪð], [blaɪθ] adj gai, joyeux

blitzkrieg ['blɪts,krig] s guerre f éclair

blizzard ['blɪzərd] s tempête f de neige

bloat [blot] tr boursoufler, enfler || intr se boursoufler, enfler

blob [blab] s motte f; (of color) tache f; (of ink) pâté m

block [blak] s bloc m; (toy) cube m; (of shares) tranche f; (of houses) pâté m, îlot m || tr (a project) contrecarrer; (a wall) condamner, murer; **to block up** boucher, bloquer

blockade [bla'ked] s blocus m; **to run the blockade** forcer le blocus || tr bloquer

block′ and tac′kle s palan m

block′head′ s sot m, niais m

blond [bland] adj & s blond m

blonde [bland] adj & s blonde f

blood [blʌd] s sang m; parenté f, race f; **in cold blood** de sang-froid; **to put new blood into** infuser un sang nouveau à

blood′ and guts′ spl sang m et tripes

blood′ bank′ s banque f du sang

blood′ count′ s numération f globulaire

blood′curd′ling adj horripilant

blood′hound′ s limier m

bloodless ['blʌdlɪs] adj exsangue; (revolution) sans effusion de sang

bloodletting ['blʌd,letɪŋ] s saignée f; (fig) effusion f de sang

blood′ or′ange s sanguine f

blood′ plas′ma s plasma m sanguin

blood′ poi′soning s septicémie f, empoisonnement m du sang

blood′ pres′sure s tension f artérielle

blood′shed′ s effusion f de sang

blood′shot′ adj injecté, éraillé

blood′ spec′imen s prise f de sang

blood′stained′ adj taché de sang

blood′stream′ s circulation f du sang

blood′suck′er s sangsue f

blood′ test′ s examen m du sang

blood′thirst′y adj sanguinaire

blood′ transfu′sion s transfusion f de sang, transfusion sanguine

blood′ type′ s groupe m de sang

blood′ ves′sel s vaisseau m sanguin

blood·y ['blʌdi] adj (comp -ier; super -iest) sanglant

bloom [blum] s fleur f; fraîcheur f; (of a fruit) velouté m, duvet m; **in bloom** en fleur || intr fleurir

bloomers ['blumərz] spl culotte f de femme

blooper ['blupər] s (coll) gaffe f, bévue f; (rad) poste m brouilleur

blossom ['blɑsəm] s fleur f; **in blossom** en fleur || intr fleurir; **to blossom out** s'épanouir

blot [blat] s tache f; (of ink) pâté m || v (pret & pp blotted; ger blotting) tr tacher, barbouiller; (ink) sécher; **to blot out** rayer || intr (said of ink) boire

blotch [blatʃ] s tache f; (on face) pustule f || tr couvrir de taches; (the skin) marbrer

blotch·y ['blatʃi] adj (comp -ier; super -iest) brouillé, tacheté

blotter ['blatər] s buvard m

blot′ting pa′per s papier m buvard

blouse [blaus] s corsage m; (children's) chemise f; (mil) vareuse f

blow [blo] s coup m; **to come to blows** en venir aux coups || v (pret blew [blu]; pp blown) tr souffler; **to blow one's nose** se moucher; **to blow out** (a candle) éteindre; **to blow up** faire sauter; (a photograph) agrandir; (a balloon) gonfler || intr souffler; (slang) décamper en vitesse; **to blow out** (said of a tire) éclater; **to blow over** passer; **to blow up** éclater; (slang) se mettre en colère

blower ['blo·ər] s soufflerie f; (mach) ventilateur m

blow′fly′ s (pl -flies) mouche f à viande

blow′gun′ s sarbacane f

blow′hard′ s (slang) hâbleur m

blow′hole′ s (of tunnel) ventilateur m; (of whale) évent m

blowing ['blo·ɪŋ] s soufflage m; (of the wind) soufflement m

blow′out′ s (of a tire) éclatement m; (orgy) (slang) gueuleton m

blow′pipe′ s chalumeau m

blow′torch′ s lampe f à souder

blubber ['blʌbər] s graisse f de baleine || tr bredouiller || intr pleurer comme un veau

bludgeon ['blʌdʒən] s matraque f || tr assommer

blue [blu] adj bleu; **to be blue** (coll) broyer du noir, avoir le cafard || s

bleu *m*; **from out of the blue** du ciel, à l'improviste; **the blues** le cafard, l'humeur *f* noire || *tr* bleuir
blue′bell′ *s* jacinthe *f* des bois
blue′ber′ry *s* (*pl* **-ries**) myrtille *f*
blue′bird′ *s* oiseau *m* bleu
blue′-black′ *adj* noir tirant sur le bleu
blue′ blood′ *s* sang *m* royal; aristocrate *mf*
blue′bot′tle *s* bluet *m*, barbeau *m*
blue′ cheese′ *s* roquefort *m* américain
blue′ chip′ *s* valeur-vedette *f*, valeur *f* de tout repos
blue′-gray′ *adj* gris bleuté, gris-bleu
blue′jay′ *s* geai *m* bleu
blue′ jeans′ *spl* blue-jean *m*
blue′ moon′ *s*—**once in a blue moon** tous les trente-six du mois
blue′nose′ *s* puritain *m*, collet *m* monté
blue′-pen′cil *v* (*pret & pp* **-ciled** or **-cilled;** *ger* **-ciling** or **-cilling**) *tr* corriger au crayon bleu; couper, censurer
blue′print′ *s* dessin *m* négatif, photocalque *m*; (*fig*) plan *m*, schéma *m* || *tr* planifier
blue′stock′ing *s* (coll) bas-bleu *m*
bluff [blʌf] *adj* abrupt; (*cliff*) accore, escarpé; (*person*) brusque || *s* (*cliff*) falaise *f*, cap *m* à pic; (*deception*) bluff *m*; **to call s.o.'s bluff** relever un défi || *tr & intr* bluffer
bluffer [′blʌfər] *s* bluffeur *m*
bluish [′bluˑɪʃ] *adj* bleuté, bleuâtre
blunder [′blʌndər] *s* bévue *f*, gaffe *f* || *intr* faire une bévue, gaffer; **to blunder into** se heurter contre; **to blunder upon** découvrir par hasard; tomber sur
blunt [blʌnt] *adj* (*blade*) émoussé; (*point*) épointé; (*person*) brusque || *tr* émousser; épointer
bluntly [′blʌntli] *adv* brusquement, sans façons; carrément, sans ménagements
blur [blʌr] *s* barbouillage *m* || *v* (*pret & pp* **blurred;** *ger* **blurring**) *tr* embrouiller, voiler
blurb [blʌrb] *s* annonce *f*; publicité *f* au protège-livre
blurt [blʌrt] *tr*—**to blurt out** laisser échapper, lâcher
blush [blʌʃ] *s* rougeur *f*; **at first blush** au premier abord || *intr* rougir
bluster [′blʌstər] *s* rodomontade *f*, fanfaronnade *f* || *intr* (*of wind*) souffler en rafales; (*of person*) faire du fracas
blustery [′blʌstəri] *adj* (*wind*) orageux; (*person*) bravache, fanfaron
boar [bor] *s* (*male swine*) verrat *m*; (*wild hog*) sanglier *m*
board [bord] *s* planche *f*; (e.g., *of directors*) conseil *m*, commission *f*; (*meals*) le couvert; **above board** cartes sur table; **on board** à bord || *tr* (*a ship*) monter à bord de; (*paying guests*) nourrir || *intr* monter à bord; (*said of paying guest*) prendre pension
board′ and room′ *s* pension *f* et chambre *f*
boarder [′bordər] *s* pensionnaire *mf*; (*student*) interne *mf*

board′ing-house′ *s* pension *f* (de famille)
board′ of direc′tors *s* conseil *m* d'administration, gérance *f*
board′ of trade′ *s* association *f* des industriels et commerçants
board′ of trustees′ *s* comité *m* administrateur (e.g., *of a university*)
board′walk′ *s* promenade *f* planchéiée au bord de la mer; (*over mud*) caillebotis *m*
boast [bost] *s* vanterie *f* || *intr* se vanter
boastful [′bostfəl] *adj* vantard
boasting [′bostɪŋ] *s* jactance *f*
boat [bot] *s* bateau *m*; (*small boat*) embarcation *f*; **to miss the boat** (coll) manquer le coche
boat′ hook′ *s* gaffe *f*
boat′house′ *s* hangar *m* à bateaux or à canots
boating [′botɪŋ] *s* canotage *m*; **to go boating** faire du canotage
boat′load′ *s* batelée *f*
boat′man *s* (*pl* **-men**) batelier *m*
boat′ race′ *s* régate *f*
boatswain [′bosən], [′bot‚swen] *s* maître *m* d'équipage
bob [bab] *s* plomb *m*; (*of hair*) chignon *m* || *v* (*pret & pp* **bobbed;** *ger* **bobbing**) *intr* s'agiter, danser
bobbin [′babɪn] *s* bobine *f*
bob′by pin′ *s* épingle *f* à cheveux
bob′by-socks′ *spl* (coll) socquettes *fpl*, chaussettes *fpl* basses
bobbysoxer [′babɪ‚saksər] *s* (coll) zazou *m*, jeune lycéenne *f*
bob′sled′ *s* bobsleigh *m*
bob′tail′ *adj* à queue écartée || *tr* couper court
bode [bod] *tr & intr* présager
bodily [′badɪli] *adj* corporel, physique || *adv* corporellement, en corps
bod·y [′badi] *s* (*pl* **-ies**) corps *m*; (*dead body*) cadavre *m*; (*solidity*) consistance *f*; (*flavor of wine*) sève *f*, générosité *f*; (aer) fuselage *m*; (aut) carrosserie *f*; **to come in a body** venir en corps
bod′y-guard′ *s* garde *m* du corps; (*group*) garde *f* du corps
bog [bag] *s* marécage *m*, fondrière *f* || *v* (*pret & pp* **bogged;** *ger* **bogging**) *intr*—**to bog down** s'enliser
bogey·man [′bogi‚mæn] *s* (*pl* **-men**) croque-mitaine *m*
bogus [′bogəs] *adj* faux, simulé
Bohemia [boˈhimiˑə] *s* (*country*) Bohême *f*, la Bohême; (*of artistic world*) la bohème
Bohemian [boˈhimiˑən] *adj* bohémien; (*unconventional, arty*) bohème, de bohème || *s* (*person living in the country of Bohemia*) Bohémien *m*; (*artist*) bohème *mf*
boil [bɔɪl] *s* ébullition *f*; (*on the skin*) furoncle *m*, clou *m* || *tr* faire bouillir || *intr* bouillir
boiled′ din′ner *s* pot-au-feu *m*
boiled′ ham′ *s* jambon *m* d'York
boiled′ pota′toes *spl* pommes *fpl* bouillies, pommes vapeur

boiler ['bɔɪlər] s chaudière f
boil·ler·mak·er s chaudronnier m
boiling ['bɔɪlɪŋ] adj bouillonnant ‖ s ébullition f, bouillonnement m
boisterous ['bɔɪstərəs] adj bruyant, débordant
bold [bold] adj hardi, osé, téméraire; (headland) à pic; (look) assuré
bold/face/ s (typ) caractères mpl gras
bold/-faced/ adj (forward) effronté
boldness ['boldnɪs] s hardiesse f; effronterie f
boll/ wee/vil [bol] s anthonome m du coton, charançon m du coton
bologna [bə'lonə], [bə'lonjə] s mortadelle f, gros saucisson m
Bolshevik ['bal/əvɪk], ['bol/əvɪk] adj bolcheviste, bolchevique ‖ s Bolcheviste mf, Bolchevique mf
bolster ['bolstər] s traversin m ‖ tr soutenir
bolt [bolt] s verrou m; (with a thread at one end) boulon m; (of cloth) rouleau m ‖ tr verrouiller; (food) gober; (e.g., a political party) lâcher ‖ intr décamper
bomb [bam] s bombe f ‖ tr bombarder
bombard [bam'bard] tr bombarder
bombardier [,bambər'dɪr] s bombardier m
bombardment [bam'bardmənt] s bombardement m
bombast ['bambæst] s boursouflure f
bombastic [bam'bæstɪk] adj boursouflé
bomb/ bay/ s (aer) soute f à bombes
bomb/ cra/ter s entonnoir m, trou m d'obus
bomber ['bamər] s avion m de bombardement, bombardier m
bombing ['bamɪŋ] s bombardement m
bomb/proof/ adj à l'épreuve des bombes
bomb/shell/ s obus m; to fall like a bombshell tomber comme une bombe
bomb/ shel/ter s abri m à l'épreuve des bombes
bomb/sight/ s viseur m de lancement
bona fide ['bonə,faɪd] adj & adv de bonne foi
bonanza [bo'nænzə] s aubaine f, filon m
bonbon ['ban,ban] s bonbon m
bond [band] s lien m; (com) obligation f; in bond en entrepôt ‖ tr (com) entreposer, mettre en entrepôt
bondage ['bandɪdʒ] s esclavage m
bond/hold/er s obligataire mf
bone [bon] s os m; (of a fish) arête f; to have a bone to pick avoir maille à partir ‖ tr (meat or fish) désosser ‖ intr—to bone up on (a subject) (slang) potasser, piocher
bone/head/ s (slang) ignorant m
boneless ['bonlɪs] adj sans os; sans arêtes
bone/ of conten/tion s pomme f de discorde
boner ['bonər] s (coll) bourde f
bonfire ['ban,faɪr] s feu m de joie; (for burning trash) feu de jardin

bonnet ['banɪt] s bonnet m; chapeau m à brides; (fig) chapeau
bonus ['bonəs] s boni m, prime f
bon·y ['boni] adj (comp -ier; super -iest) osseux; (thin) décharné
boo [bu] s huée f, sifflement m; not to say boo ne pas souffler mot ‖ tr & intr huer, siffler
boob [bub] s (coll) emplâtre m
boo·by ['bubi] s (pl -bies) (coll) nigaud m
boo/by hatch/ s (slang) asile m d'aliénés; (prison) (slang) violon m
boo/by prize/ s fiche f de consolation
boo/by trap/ s engin m piégé; (fig) attrape-nigaud m
boo/by-trap/ v (pret & pp -trapped; ger -trapping) tr piéger
book [buk] s livre m; (of tickets) carnet m; (libretto) livret m; by the book d'après le texte, selon les règles; to make book (sports) inscrire les paris ‖ tr (a seat or room) retenir, réserver
book/bind/er s relieur m
book/bind·er·y s (pl -ies) atelier m de reliure
book/bind/ing s reliure f
book/case/ s bibliothèque f, étagère f
book/ end/ s serre-livres m, appui-livres m
booking ['bukɪŋ] s réservation f; (theat) location f
bookish ['bukɪ/] adj livresque; (person) studieux
book/keep/er s comptable mf, teneur m de livres
book/keep/ing s comptabilité f
book/ learn/ing s science f livresque
booklet ['buklɪt] s livret m; (notebook) cahier m; (pamphlet) brochure f
book/lov/er s bibliophile mf
book/mark/ s signet m
bookmobile ['bukmo,bil] s bibliobus m
book/plate/ s ex-libris m
book/rack/ s étagère f
book/ review/ s compte m rendu
book/sell/er s libraire mf
book/shelf/ s (pl -shelves) rayon m, étagère f
book/stand/ s étalage m de livres; (in a station) bibliothèque f
book/store/ s librairie f
book/ val/ue s (com) valeur f comptable
book/worm/ s ciron m; (fig) rat m de bibliothèque
boom [bum] s retentissement m, grondement m; (rapid rise or growth) vague f de prospérité, boom m; (naut) bout-dehors m ‖ intr retentir; (com) prospérer ‖ interj boum!
boomerang ['bumə,ræŋ] s boomerang m
boom/ town/ s ville f champignon
boon [bun] s bienfait m, avantage m; (archaic) don m, faveur f
boon/ compan/ion s joyeux compagnon m
boor [bur] s rustre m, goujat m
boost [bust] s relèvement m; (help)

aide *f* ‖ *tr* soulever par derrière; (prices) hausser; (to praise) faire la réclame pour

booster ['bustər] *s* (enthusiastic backer) réclamiste *mf*; (go-getter) homme *m* d'expédition, lanceur *m* d'affaires; (elec) survolteur *m*; (rok) booster *m*, propulseur *m*

boost'er rock'et *s* fusée *f* de lancement

boost'er shot' *s* piqûre *f* de rappel

boot [but] *s* botte *f*, bottine *f*; **to boot** en sus; **to lick s.o.'s boots** (coll) lécher les bottes à qn ‖ *tr* botter

boot'black' *s* cireur *m* de bottes

booth [buθ] *s* (at fair) baraque *f*; (e.g., for telephoning) cabine *f*

boot'leg' *adj* (slang) clandestin, de contrebande ‖ *v* (pret & pp -legged; ger -legging) *tr* (slang) faire la contrebande de ‖ *intr* (slang) faire la contrebande

bootlegger ['but,lɛgər] *s* (slang) contrebandier *m*; (slang) contrebandier *m* d'alcool, bootlegger *m*

boot'leg'ging *s* contrebande *f*

boot'lick' *tr* (coll) lécher les bottes à

boo·ty ['buti] *s* (pl -ties) butin *m*

booze [buz] *s* (coll) boisson *f* alcoolique ‖ *intr* (coll) s'adonner à la boisson

border ['bɔrdər] *s* bord *m*, bordure *f*; (of field and forest; of a piece of cloth) lisière *f*; (of a road) marge *f*; (of a country) frontière *f*; (edging) galon *m*, bordé *m* ‖ *tr* border; (a handkerchief) liserer ‖ *intr*—**to border on** confiner à, toucher à; (a color) tirer sur

bor'der-line' *adj* indéterminé ‖ *s* ligne *f* de démarcation

bore [bor] *s* trou *m*; (of gun) calibre *m*; (of cannon) âme *f*; (of cylinder) alésage *m*; (nuisance) ennui *m*; (person) raseur *m* ‖ *tr* percer; (a cylinder) aléser; (to annoy) ennuyer

boreal ['bɔri·əl] *adj* boréal

boredom ['bordəm] *s* ennui *m*

boring ['bɔrɪŋ] *adj* ennuyeux, rasant, rasoir ‖ *s* perçage *m*, percement *m*

born [bɔrn] *adj* né; **to be born** naître

borough ['bʌro] *s* (town) bourg *m*; circonscription *f* électorale

borrow ['baro], ['bɔro] *tr* emprunter; **to borrow from** emprunter à

borrower ['baro·ər], ['bɔro·ər] *s* emprunteur *m*

bor'rower's card' *s* bulletin *m* de prêt

borrowing ['baro·ɪŋ], ['bɔro·ɪŋ] *s* emprunt *m*

borzoi ['bɔrzɔɪ] *s* lévrier *m* russe

bosom ['buzəm] *s* sein *m*, poitrine *f*; (of the Church) giron *m*

boss [bɔs], [bas] *s* patron *m*, chef *m*; (foreman) contremaître *m* ‖ *tr* diriger

boss·y ['bɔsi], ['basi] *adj* (comp -ier; super -iest) autoritaire; **to be bossy** jordonner

botanical [bə'tænɪkəl] *adj* botanique

botanist ['batənɪst] *s* botaniste *mf*

botany ['batəni] *s* botanique *f*

both [boθ] *adj* deux, e.g., **with both hands** à deux mains; les deux, e.g.,

both books les deux livres ‖ *pron* les deux, tous les deux ‖ *conj* à la fois; **both . . . and** aussi bien . . . que, e.g., **both in England and France** aussi bien en Angleterre qu'en France

bother ['baðər] *s* ennui *m* ‖ *tr* ennuyer, déranger ‖ *intr* se déranger

bothersome ['baðərsəm] *adj* importun

bottle ['batəl] *s* bouteille *f* ‖ *tr* mettre en bouteille, embouteiller

bot'tle cap' *s* capsule *f*

bot'tled gas' *s* gaz *m* en cylindre

bot'tle·neck' *s* goulot *m*; (fig) embouteillage *m*

bot'tle o'pener *s* ouvre-bouteilles *m*

bottler ['batlər] *s* metteur *m* en bouteilles

bottling ['batlɪŋ] *s* mise *f* en bouteilles

bottom ['batəm] *s* fond *m*; **at the bottom of** au fond de; (the page) en bas de; **to reach the bottom of the barrel** (coll) être à fond de cale

bot'tom dol'lar *s* dernier sou *m*

bottomless ['batəmlɪs] *adj* sans fond

bough [bau] *s* rameau *m*

boulder ['boldər] *s* bloc *m*, rocher *m*

boulevard ['bulə,vard] *s* boulevard *m*

bounce [bauns] *s* (elasticity) bond *m*; (of a ball) rebond *m* ‖ *tr* faire rebondir; (slang) flanquer à la porte ‖ *intr* rebondir

bouncer ['baunsər] *s* (in night club) (coll) videur *m*, gorille *m*

bound [baund] *adj* (tied) lié; (obliged) obligé, tenu; **bound for** en partance pour ‖ *s* bond *m*, saut *m*; **bounds** bornes *fpl*, limites *fpl*; **out of bounds** hors jeu; (prohibited) défendu ‖ *tr* borner, limiter ‖ *intr* bondir

bounda·ry ['baundəri] *s* (pl -ries) borne *f*, limite *f*

boun'dary stone' *s* borne *f*

boundless ['baundlɪs] *adj* sans bornes

boun·ty ['baunti] *s* (pl -ties) largesse *f*; (award) prime *f*

bouquet [bu'ke], [bo'ke] *s* bouquet *m*

bout [baut] *s* rencontre *f*; (e.g., of fever) accès *m*; (sports) match *m*

bow [bau] *s* inclination *f*, révérence *f*; (of ship) avant *m*, proue *f* ‖ *tr* incliner, courber ‖ *intr* s'incliner, se courber; **to bow down** se prosterner; **to bow out** se retirer; **to bow to** saluer ‖ [bo] *s* (weapon) arc *m*; (bowknot) nœud *m*; (of violin) archet *m* ‖ *intr* (mus) tirer l'archet

bowdlerize ['baudlə,raɪz] *tr* expurger

bowel ['bau·əl] *s* intestin *m*, boyau *m*; **bowels** entrailles *fpl*

bow'el move'ment *s* selle *f*; **to have a bowel movement** aller à la selle

bower ['bau·ər] *s* berceau *m*, tonnelle *f*

bow'ie knife' ['bo·ɪ], ['bu·i] *s* couteau-poignard *m*

bowknot ['bo,nat] *s* nœud *m* en forme de rose, rosette *f*

bowl [bol] *s* bol *m*, jatte *f*; (of pipe) fourneau *m*; (of spoon) cuilleron *m*; **bowls** (sports) boules *fpl* ‖ *tr* rouler, lancer; **to bowl over** (to overturn) (coll) renverser; (slang) déconcerter

‖ *intr*—**to bowl along** rouler rapidement
bowlegged ['bo,lɛgd], ['bo,lɛgɪd] *adj* aux jambes arquées
bowler ['bolər] *s* (*hat*) chapeau *m* melon; (*in cricket*) lanceur *m*; (*in bowling*) joueur *m* de boules
bowling ['bolɪŋ] *s* jeu *m* de boules, jeu de quilles
bowl/ing al'ley *s* boulodrome *m*
bowl/ing green' *s* boulingrin *m*
bowl/ing pin' *s* quille *f*
bowsprit ['bausprɪt], ['bosprɪt] *s* beaupré *m*
bow' tie' [bo] *s* nœud *m* papillon
box [baks] *s* boîte *f*; (*law*) barre *f*; (*theat*) loge *f*, baignoire *f*; **box on the ear** claque *f* ‖ *tr* emboîter; (*to hit*) boxer; **to box the compass** réciter la rose des vents ‖ *intr* (*sports*) boxer
box'car' *s* (rr) wagon *m* couvert
boxer ['baksər] *s* (*person*) boxeur *m*; (*dog*) boxer *m*
boxing ['baksɪŋ] *s* emboîtage *m*; (*sports*) boxe *f*
box' of'fice *s* bureau *m* de location
box'-office flop' *s* (slang) four *m*
box'-office hit' *s* pièce *f* à succès
box'wood' *s* buis *m*
boy [bɔɪ] *s* garçon *m*; (*little boy*) garçonnet *m*
boycott ['bɔɪkat] *s* boycottage *m* ‖ *tr* boycotter
boy' friend' *s* ami *m*, camarade *m*; (*of a girl*) bon ami *m*
boyhood ['bɔɪhud] *s* enfance *f*, jeunesse *f*, adolescence *f*
boyish ['bɔɪ,ɪʃ] *adj* de garçon
boy' scout' *s* boy-scout *m*
bra [bra] *s* (coll) soutien-gorge *m*
brace [bres] *s* attache *f*, lien *m*; (*of game birds*) couple *f*; (*of pistols*) paire *f*; (*to impart a rotary movement to a bit*) vilebrequin *m*; (aer, aut) entretoise *f*; (mus, typ) accolade *f* ‖ *tr* ancrer, entretoiser; (*to tone up*) fortifier, remonter ‖ *intr*—**to brace up** prendre courage
brace' and bit' *s* vilebrequin *m*
bracelet ['breslɪt] *s* bracelet *m*
bracer ['bresər] *s* tonique *m*
bracing ['bresɪŋ] *adj* tonique, fortifiant
bracket ['brækɪt] *s* console *f*; (*grouping*) niveau *m*; (*mach*) chaise *f*; (*typ*) crochet *m* ‖ *tr* grouper; (*typ*) mettre entre crochets
brackish ['brækɪʃ] *adj* saumâtre
brad [bræd] *s* semence *f*, clou *m* (sans tête)
brag [bræg] *s* (*pret & pp* bragged; *ger* bragging) *intr* se vanter
braggadoci•o [,brægə'doʃɪ,o] *s* (*pl* -os) fanfaronnade *f*; (*person*) fanfaron *m*
braggart ['brægərt] *s* vantard *m*
bragging ['brægɪŋ] *s* vanterie *f*
Brah•man ['bramən] *s* (*pl* -mans) brahmane *m*
braid [bred] *s* tresse *f*, passement *m*; (*mil*) galon *m*; **to trim with braid** soutacher ‖ *tr* passementer; (*the hair*) tresser

braille [brel] *s* braille *m*
brain [bren] *s* cerveau *m*; **brains** cervelle *f*; (*fig*) intelligence *f*, cerveau; **to rack one's brains** se creuser la cervelle ‖ *tr* casser la tête à
brain' child' *s* idée *f* de génie
brainless ['brenlɪs] *adj* sans cervelle
brain'storm' *s* accès *m* de folie; (coll) confusion *f* mentale; (coll) trouvaille *f*, bonne idée *f*
brain'wash' *tr* (*by use of torture, drugs, etc.*) faire un lavage de cerveau à; (*by means of commercials, sales talk, etc.*) bourrer le crâne de
brain'wash'ing *s* lavage *m* de cerveau; bourrage *m* de crâne
brain'work' *s* travail *m* intellectuel
brain•y ['brenɪ] *adj* (*comp* -ier; *super* -iest) (coll) intelligent, à l'esprit vif
braise [brez] *tr* braiser, endauber
brais/ing pan' *s* braisière *f*
brake [brek] *s* frein *m*; **to put on the brakes** serrer les freins ‖ *tr & intr* freiner
brake' drum' *s* tambour *m* de frein
brake' light' *s* (aut) feu *m* de freinage
brake' lin'ing *s* garniture *f* de frein
brake'man *s* (*pl* -men) serre-freins *m*
brake' ped'al *s* pédale *f* de frein
brake' shoe' *s* sabot *m* de frein
bramble ['bræmbəl] *s* ronce *f*
bran [bræn] *s* son *m*, bran *m*
branch [bræntʃ] *s* branche *f*; (*of tree*) rameau *m*, branche; (*of a business*) succursale *f*, filiale *f* ‖ *intr*—**to branch off** s'embrancher, se bifurquer; **to branch out** se ramifier
branch' line' *s* embranchement *m*
branch' of'fice *s* succursale *f*; bureau *m* de quartier
branch' road' *s* embranchement *m*
brand [brænd] *s* (*trademark*) marque *f*; (*torch*) brandon *m*; (*coal*) tison *m*; (*on a criminal*) flétrissure *f*; (*on cattle*) marque ‖ *tr* marquer au fer rouge, flétrir
brand/ing i'ron *s* fer *m* à flétrir
brandish ['brændɪʃ] *tr* brandir
brand'-new' *adj* tout neuf, flambant neuf
bran•dy ['brændɪ] *s* (*pl* -dies) eau-de-vie *f*
brash [bræʃ] *adj* impertinent
brass [bræs], [bras] *s* laiton *m*; (mil) (coll) officiers *mpl* supérieurs, galonnard *m*; (slang) toupet *m*, culot *m*; **big brass** (slang) grosses légumes *fpl*; **the brasses** (mus) les cuivres
brass' band' *s* fanfare *f*, musique *f*
brassiere [brə'zɪr] *s* soutien-gorge *m*
brass' knuck'les *spl* coup-de-poing *m*
brass' tack' *s* semence *f* (de tapissier); **to get down to brass tacks** (coll) en venir aux faits
brat [bræt] *s* (coll) gamin *m*, gosse *mf*
brava•do [brə'vado] *s* (*pl* -does or -dos) bravade *f*
brave [brev] *adj* brave ‖ *s* guerrier *m* peau-rouge ‖ *tr* braver
bravery ['brevərɪ] *s* bravoure *f*
bra•vo ['bravo] *s* (*pl* -vos) bravo *m* ‖ *interj* bravo!

brawl [brɔl] *s* bagarre *f*, querelle *f* ‖ *intr* se bagarrer, se quereller

brawler ['brɔlər] *s* bagarreur *m*

brawn [brɔn] *s* muscle *m*; muscles bien développés; (culin) fromage *m* de cochon

brawn·y ['brɔni] *adj* (*comp* -ier; *super* -iest) bien découplé, musclé

bray [bre] *s* braiment *m* ‖ *intr* braire

braze [brez] *tr* braser

brazen ['brezən] *adj* effronté ‖ *tr*—to **brazen** through mener à bonne fin avec une effronterie audacieuse

Brazil [brə'zɪl] *s* le Brésil

Brazilian [brə'zɪljən] *adj* brésilien ‖ *s* (*person*) Brésilien *m*

Brazil' nut' *s* noix *f* du Brésil

breach [britʃ] *s* (*in a wall*) brèche *f*; (*violation*) infraction *f* ‖ *tr* ouvrir une brèche dans

breach' of con'tract *s* rupture *f* de contrat

breach' of prom'ise *s* rupture *f* de fiançailles

breach' of the peace' *s* attentat *m* contre l'ordre public

breach' of trust' *s* abus *m* de confiance

bread [brɛd] *s* pain *m* ‖ *tr* paner, gratiner

bread' and but'ter *s* (fig) gagne-pain *m*

bread'bas'ket *s* panier *m* à pain, corbeille *f* à pain

bread'board' *s* planche *f* à pain

bread' crumbs' *spl* chapelure *f*

breaded *adj* (culin) au gratin

bread'ed veal' cut'let *s* escalope *f* panée de veau

bread'fruit' *s* fruit *m* à pain; (*tree*) arbre *m* à pain, jacquier *m*

bread' knife' *s* couteau *m* à pain

breadth [brɛdθ] *s* largeur *f*

bread'win'ner *s* soutien *m* de famille

break [brek] *s* rupture *f*; (*of an object*) brisure *f*, cassure *f*; (*in time or space*) trou *m*, pause *f*; (slang) chance *f* ‖ *v* (*pret* broke [brok]; *pp* broken) *tr* rompre, briser, casser; (*a law*) violer; (*the heart*) fendre; (*one's word*) manquer à; (*a will*; *a soldier by reducing his rank*) casser; **to break bread** rompre le pain; **to break down** (*for analysis*) analyser; **to break in** (*a door*) enfoncer; (*a new car*) roder ‖ *intr* rompre, briser, se briser; (*said of clouds*) se dissiper; (*said of waves*) déferler; **to break down** avoir une panne

breakable ['brekəbəl] *adj* fragile

breakage ['brekɪdʒ] *s* casse *f*

break'down' *s* (*stoppage*) arrêt *m*; (*disaster*) débâcle *f*; (*of health*) épuisement *m*; (*of negotiations*) rupture *f*; (*for analysis*) analyse *f*, ventilation *f*; (mach) panne *f*

breaker ['brekər] *s* brisant *m*

breakfast ['brɛkfəst] *s* petit déjeuner *m* ‖ *intr* prendre le petit déjeuner

break'fast food' *s* céréales *fpl* (pour le petit déjeuner)

break'neck' *adj* vertigineux; **at breakneck speed** à tombeau ouvert

break' of day' *s* point *m* du jour

break'through' *s* (mil) percée *f*; (fig) découverte *f* sensationnelle

break'up' *s* dissolution *f*; écroulement *m*; (*in health*) abattement *m*

break'wa'ter *s* digue *f*, brise-lames *m*

breast [brɛst] *s* sein *m*; (*of cooked chicken*) blanc *m*; **to make a clean breast of it** se déboutonner

breast'bone' *s* sternum *m*; (*of fowl*) bréchet *m*

breast' feed'ing *s* allaitement *m*

breast'plate' *s* (*of high priest*) pectoral *m*; (*of armor*) plastron *m*

breast'stroke' *s* brasse *f*

breast'work' *s* (mil) parapet *m*

breath [brɛθ] *s* haleine *f*, souffle *m*; **last breath** dernier soupir *m*; **out of breath** hors d'haleine

breathe [brið] *tr & intr* respirer, souffler; **not to breathe a word** ne pas souffler mot

breathing ['briðɪŋ] *s* souffle *m*

breath'ing space' *s* répit *m*

breathless ['brɛθlɪs] *adj* haletant, hors d'haleine; inanimé

breath'tak'ing *adj* émouvant, sensationnel

breech [britʃ] *s* culasse *f*

breech'es bu'oy *s* (naut) bouée-culotte *f*

breed [brid] *s* race *f* ‖ *v* (*pret & pp* bred [brɛd]) *tr* engendrer; (*e.g., cattle*) élever ‖ *intr* se reproduire

breeder ['bridər] *s* éleveur *m*

breeding ['bridɪŋ] *s* (*of animals*) élevage *m*; **good breeding** savoir-vivre *m*

breeze [briz] *s* brise *f*

breez·y ['brizi] *adj* (*comp* -ier; *super* -iest) aéré; (coll) désinvolte, dégagé

brethren ['brɛðrɪn] *spl* frères *mpl*

Breton ['brɛtən] *adj* breton ‖ *s* (*language*) breton *m*; (*person*) Breton *m*

breviar·y ['brivɪ,ɛri], ['brɛvɪ,ɛri] *s* (*pl* -ies) (eccl) bréviaire *m*

brevi·ty ['brɛvɪti] *s* (*pl* -ties) brièveté *f*

brew [bru] *s* breuvage *m*, infusion *f* ‖ *tr* infuser; (*beer*) brasser ‖ *intr* s'infuser

brewer ['bru·ər] *s* brasseur *m*

brew'er's yeast' *s* levure *f* de bière

brewer·y ['bru·əri] *s* (*pl* -ies) brasserie *f*

brewing ['bru·ɪŋ] *s* brassage *m*

bribe [braɪb] *s* pot-de-vin *m* ‖ *tr* corrompre, suborner, soudoyer

briber·y ['braɪbəri] *s* (*pl* -ies) corruption *f*, subornation *f*

brick [brɪk] *s* brique *f* ‖ *tr* briqueter

brick'bat' *s* brocard *m*; **to hurl brickbats** lancer des brocards

brick'lay'er *s* briqueteur *m*

brick'work' *s* briquetage *m*

brick'yard' *s* briqueterie *f*

bridal ['braɪdəl] *adj* nuptial

bride [braɪd] *s* (nouvelle) mariée *f*

bride'groom' *s* (nouveau) marié *m*

brides'maid' *s* demoiselle *f* d'honneur

bride'-to-be' *s* future femme *f*

bridge [brɪdʒ] *s* pont *m*; (cards, dentistry) bridge *m*; (naut) passerelle *f*; **to burn one's bridges** couper les ponts ‖ *tr* construire un pont sur; **to bridge a gap** combler une lacune

bridge′head′ *s* (mil) tête *f* de pont

bridle [′braɪdəl] *s* bride *f*; (fig) frein *m* || *tr* brider; (fig) freiner || *intr* se raidir

bri′dle path′ *s* piste *f* cavalière

brief [brif] *adj* bref || *s* résumé *m*; (law) dossier *m*; **briefs** slip *m*; **to hold a brief for** plaider pour || *tr* mettre au courant

brief′ case′ *s* serviette *f*

briefing [′brifɪŋ] *s* briefing *m*, renseignements *mpl* tactiques

briefly [′brifli] *adv* bref, brièvement, en substance

brier [′braɪ-ər] *s* ronce *f*

brig [brɪg] *s* prison *f* navale; (ship) brick *m*

brigade [brɪ′ged] *s* brigade *f*

brigadier [‚brɪgə′dɪr] *s* général *m* de brigade

brigand [′brɪgənd] *s* brigand *m*

brigantine [′brɪgən‚tin], [′brɪgən‚taɪn] *s* brigantin *m*

bright [braɪt] *adj* brillant; (day) clair; (color) vif; (person) (fig) brillant

brighten [′braɪtən] *tr* faire briller; égayer, réjouir || *intr* s′éclaircir

bright′ ide′a *s* (coll) idée *f* lumineuse

brightness [′braɪtnɪs] *s* éclat *m*, clarté *f*; (of mind) vivacité *f*

brilliance [′brɪljəns] **or brilliancy** [′brɪljənsi] *s* brillant *m*, éclat *m*

brilliant [′brɪljənt] *adj & s* brillant *m*

brim [brɪm] *s* bord *m* || *v* (pret & pp **brimmed**; ger **brimming**) *intr*—to **brim over** (with) déborder (de)

brimful [′brɪm‚ful] *adj* à ras bords

brim′ stone′ *s* soufre *m*

brine [braɪn] *s* saumure *f*

bring [brɪŋ] *v* (pret & pp **brought** [brɔt]) *tr* apporter; (a person) amener, conduire; **to bring back** rapporter; (a person) ramener; **to bring down** (baggage) descendre; (with a gun) abattre; **to bring in** entrer, introduire; **to bring out** faire ressortir; (e.g., a book) publier; **to bring together** réunir; **to bring to pass** causer, opérer; **to bring up** éduquer, élever; (baggage) monter

bring′ing-up′ *s* éducation *f*

brink [brɪŋk] *s* bord *m*

brisk [brɪsk] *adj* vif, actif, animé

brisket [′brɪskɪt] *s* (culin) poitrine *f*

bristle [′brɪsəl] *s* soie *f*; (of brush) poil *m* || *tr* hérisser || *intr* se hérisser

bristling [′brɪslɪŋ] *adj* hérissé

Bris′tol board′ [′brɪstəl] *s* bristol *m*

Britain [′brɪtən] *s* Grande-Bretagne *f*; la Grande-Bretagne

British [′brɪtɪʃ] *adj* britannique || **the British** les Britanniques

Britisher [′brɪtɪʃər] *s* Britannique *mf*

Briton [′brɪtən] *s* Britannique *mf*

Brittany [′brɪtəni] *s* Bretagne *f*; la Bretagne

brittle [′brɪtəl] *adj* fragile, cassant

broach [brotʃ] *s* broche *f*; (for tapping casks) mèche *f* à percer || *tr* (e.g., a keg of beer) mettre en perce; (a subject) entamer

broad [brɔd] *adj* (wide) large; (immense) vaste; (mind, views) libéral, tolérant; (accent) fort, prononcé; (use, sense) répandu, général; (daylight) plein; (joke, story) grossier, salé

broad′-backed′ *adj* d′une belle carrure

broad′ brimmed′ *adj* à larges bords

broad′cast′ *adj* diffusé; (rad) radiodiffusé || *s* (rad) radiodiffusion *f*, émission *f* || *v* (pret & pp -**cast**) *tr* diffuser, répandre || (pret & pp -**cast** or -**casted**) *tr* radiodiffuser || *intr* (rad) émettre

broad′casting sta′tion *s* station *f* d′émission

broad′cloth′ *s* popeline *f*

broaden [′brɔdən] *tr* élargir || *intr* s′élargir

broad′-gauge′ *adj* à voie large

broad′ jump′ *s* saut *m* en longueur

broad′-mind′ed *adj* à l′esprit large

broad′side′ *s* bordée *f*; (typ) placard *m*

brocade [bro′ked] *s* brocart *m* || *tr* brocher

broccoli [′brɑkəli] *s* brocoli *m*

brochure [bro′ʃur] *s* brochure *f*

brogue [brog] *s* accent *m* irlandais; (shoe) soulier *m* grossier

broil [brɔɪl] *s* grillade *f*; (quarrel) rixe *f* || *tr & intr* griller

broiler [′brɔɪlər] *s* gril *m*

broke [brok] *adj* (slang) fauché

broken [′brokən] *adj* brisé, cassé; (promise; ranks; beam) rompu

brok′en-down′ *adj* délabré; en panne

bro′ken-heart′ed *adj* au cœur brisé

broker [′brokər] *s* courtier *m*

brokerage [′brokərɪdʒ] *s* courtage *m*

bromide [′bromaɪd] *s* bromure *m*; (coll) platitude *f*

bromine [′bromin] *s* brome *m*

bronchial [′brɑŋkɪ-əl] *adj* bronchique

bron′chial tube′ *s* bronche *f*

bronchitis [brɑŋ′kaɪtɪs] *s* bronchite *f*

bron·co [′brɑŋko] *s* (pl -**cos**) cheval *m* sauvage

bronze [brɑnz] *adj* bronzé || *s* bronze *m* || *tr* bronzer || *intr* se bronzer

brooch [brotʃ], [brutʃ] *s* broche *f*

brood [brud] *s* couvée *f*; (of children) nichée *f* || *intr* couver; (to sulk) broyer du noir; **to brood over** songer sombrement à

brood′ hen′ *s* couveuse *f*

brood′ mare′ *s* poulinière *f*

brook [bruk] *s* ruisseau *m* || *tr*—to **brook no** ne pas tolérer

brooklet [′bruklɪt] *s* ruisseau *m*

broom [brum], [brum] *s* balai *m*; (bot) genêt *m*

broom′ stick′ *s* manche *m* à balai

broth [brɔθ], [brɑθ] *s* bouillon *m*, consommé *m*

brothel [′brɑθəl], [′brɑðəl] *s* bordel *m*

brother [′brʌðər] *s* frère *m*

broth′er-hood′ *s* fraternité *f*

broth′er-in-law′ *s* (pl **brothers-in-law**) beau-frère *m*

brotherly [′brʌðərli] *adj* fraternel || *adv* fraternellement

brow [brau] *s* (forehead) front *m*;

(*eyebrow*) sourcil *m*; **to knit one's brow** froncer le sourcil

brow/beat/ *v* (*pret* **-beat**; *pp* **-beaten**) *tr* rabrouer, brusquer

brown [braun] *adj* marron; (*paper*) gris; (*bread*) bis; (*shoes*) jaune; (*butter*) roux, noir; (*hair*) brun, châtain ‖ *tr* brunir; (*culin*) rissoler, dorer

brownish ['braunɪʃ] *adj* brunâtre

brown/ stud/y *s*—**in a brown study** absorbé dans des méditations

brown/ sug/ar *s* cassonade *f*, sucre *m* brut

browse [brauz] *intr* (*said of animals*) brouter; (*said of booklovers*) butiner; (*said of customers for secondhand books*) bouquiner

bruise [bruz] *s* (*on body or fruit*) meurtrissure *f*; (*on body*) contusion *f* ‖ *tr* meurtrir, contusionner

bruiser ['bruzər] *s* (coll) costaud *m*

bruit [brut] *tr* ébruiter; **to bruit about** répandre

brunette [bru'nɛt] *adj* & *s* brune *f*, brunette *f*

brunt [brʌnt] *s* choc *m*, assaut *m*; **to bear the brunt of** (fig) faire tous les frais de

brush [brʌʃ] *s* brosse *f*; (*countryside*) brousse *f*; (elec) balai *m* ‖ *tr* brosser; **to brush aside** écarter ‖ *intr*—**to brush against** frôler; **to brush up on** repasser, rafraîchir

brush/-off/ *s* (slang) affront *m*; **to give a brush-off to** (slang) expédier avec rudesse

brush/wood/ *s* broussailles *fpl*, brindilles *fpl*

brusque [brʌsk] *adj* brusque

Brussels ['brʌsəlz] *s* Bruxelles *f*

Brus/sels sprouts/ *mpl* chou *m* de Bruxelles

brutal ['brutəl] *adj* brutal

brutal·i·ty [bru'tælɪti] *s* (*pl* **-ties**) brutalité *f*

brute [brut] *adj* brutal ‖ *s* bête *f*, animal *m*; (*person*) brute *f*, animal *m*

brutish ['brutɪʃ] *adj* grossier, brut, brutal

bubble ['bʌbəl] *s* bulle *f* ‖ *intr* bouillonner; (*said of drink*) pétiller; **to bubble over** déborder

bub/ble gum/ *s* gomme *f* à claquer

bub·bly ['bʌbli] *adj* (*comp* **-blier**; *super* **-bliest**) bouillonnant, gazeux

bubon/ic plague/ [bju'bɑnɪk] *s* peste *f* bubonique

buccaneer [,bʌkə'nɪr] *s* boucanier *m*

buck [bʌk] *s* (*red deer*) cerf *m*; (*fallow deer*) daim *m*; (*roebuck*) chevreuil *m*; (slang) dollar *m*; the male of many animals such as: (*goat*) bouc *m*; (*rabbit*) lapin *m*; (*hare*) lièvre *m*; **to pass the buck** (coll) renvoyer la balle ‖ *tr*—**to buck off** (*a rider*) désarçonner; **to buck up** (coll) remonter le courage de ‖ *intr*—**to buck up** (coll) reprendre courage

bucket ['bʌkɪt] *s* seau *m*; **to kick the bucket** (slang) casser sa pipe

buck/et seat/ *s* siège *m* baquet

buckle ['bʌkəl] *s* boucle *f* ‖ *tr* boucler ‖ *intr* arquer, gauchir; **to buckle down** s'appliquer

buck/ pri/vate *s* simple soldat *m*

buckram ['bʌkrəm] *s* bougran *m*

buck/saw/ *s* scie *f* à bûches

buck/shot/ *s* gros plomb *m*

buck/tooth/ *s* (*pl* **-teeth**) dent *f* saillante

buck/wheat/ *s* sarrasin *m*

buck/wheat cake/ *s* crêpe *f* de sarrasin

bud [bʌd] *s* bouton *m*, bourgeon *m* ‖ *v* (*pret* & *pp* **budded**; *ger* **budding**) *intr* boutonner, bourgeonner

Buddhism ['budɪzəm] *s* bouddhisme *m*

Buddhist ['budɪst] *adj* & *s* bouddhiste *mf*

budding ['bʌdɪŋ] *adj* en bouton; (*beginning*) en germe, naissant

bud·dy ['bʌdi] *s* (*pl* **-dies**) (coll) copain *m*

budge [bʌdʒ] *tr* faire bouger ‖ *intr* bouger

budget ['bʌdʒɪt] *s* budget *m* ‖ *tr* comptabiliser, inscrire au budget

budgetary ['bʌdʒɪ,tɛri] *adj* budgétaire

buff [bʌf] *adj* (*color*) chamois ‖ *s* (coll) fanatique *mf*, enthousiaste *mf* ‖ *tr* polir, émeuler

buffa·lo ['bʌfə,lo] *s* (*pl* **-loes** *or* **-los**) bison *m*; (*water buffalo*; *Cape buffalo*) buffle *m*

buffer ['bʌfər] *s* (mach) brunissoir *m*; (rr) (*on cars*) tampon *m*; (rr) (*at end of track*) butoir *m*

buff/er state/ *s* état *m* tampon

buf/fer zone/ *s* zone *f* tampon

buffet [bu'fe] *s* buffet *m* ‖ ['bʌfɪt] *tr* frapper (violemment)

buffet/ lunch/ [bu'fe] *s* lunch *m*

buffoon [bə'fun] *s* bouffon *m*

buffooner·y [bə'funəri] *s* (*pl* **-ies**) bouffonnerie *f*

bug [bʌg] *s* insecte *m*; (germ) microbe *m*; (*in a mechanical device*) vice *m*, défaut *m*; (coll) idée *f* fixe, lutin *m*; (Brit) punaise *f*; **he's a bug for . . .** (coll) il est fou de . . . ‖ *v* (*pret* & *pp* **bugged**; *ger* **bugging**) *tr* (slang) installer une table d'écoute dans; installer un microphone dans; (*to annoy*) (slang) embêter, emmerder

bug/bear/ *s* épouvantail *m*, croque-mitaine *m*; (*pet peeve*) bête *f* noire

bug/-eyed/ *adj* (slang) aux yeux saillants

bug·gy ['bʌgi] *adj* (*comp* **-gier**; *super* **-giest**) infesté d'insectes; infesté; (slang) fou ‖ *s* (*pl* **-gies**) buggy *m* à quatre roues; (*two-wheeled*) buggy, boguet *m*

bug/house/ *s* (slang) cabanon *m*

bugle ['bjugəl] *s* (bot) bugle *f*; (mus) clairon *m* ‖ *tr* & *intr* claironner

bu/gle call/ *s* sonnerie *f* de clairon

bugler ['bjuglər] *s* clairon *m*

build [bɪld] *s* structure *f*; (*of human body*) taille *f*, charpente *f* ‖ *v* (*pret* & *pp* **built** [bɪlt]) *tr* bâtir, construire

builder ['bɪldər] *s* constructeur *m*; (*of bridges, roads, etc.*) entrepreneur *m*

building ['bɪldɪŋ] s immeuble m, bâtiment m, édifice m

build'ing and loan' associa'tion s société f de prêt à la construction

build'ing lot' s terrain m à bâtir

builtʼ-inʼ adj incorporé

builtʼ-upʼ adj agglomérié; (heel) renforcé; (land) bâti

bulb [bʌlb] s bulbe m; (of vaporizer) poire f; (bot) oignon m; (elec) ampoule f

bulbous ['bʌlbəs] adj bulbeux

Bulgaria [bʌl'gɛrɪ-ə] s Bulgarie f; la Bulgarie

Bulgarian [bʌl'gɛrɪ-ən] adj bulgare || s (language) bulgare m; (person) Bulgare mf

bulge [bʌldʒ] s bosse f, bombement m; (mil) saillant m || tr bourrer, gonfler || intr faire une bosse, bomber

bulk [bʌlk] s masse f, volume m; in bulk en bloc; (com) en vrac || tr entasser (en vrac) || intr tenir de la place; **to bulk large** devenir important

bulk'head' s (naut) cloison f

bulk·y ['bʌlki] adj (comp -ier; super -iest) volumineux

bull [bul] s taureau m; (on the stock exchange) haussier m, spéculateur m à la hausse; (eccl) bulle f; (policeman) (slang) flic m, vache f; (exaggeration) (slang) blague f, boniment m, chiqué m; **like a bull in a china shop** comme un éléphant dans un magasin de porcelaine; **to take the bull by the horns** (fig) prendre le taureau par les cornes || tr—**to bull the market** jouer à la hausse

bull'dog' s bouledogue m

bull'doze' tr passer au bulldozer; (coll) intimider

bulldozer ['bul,dozər] s chasse-terre m, bulldozer m

bullet ['bulɪt] s balle f

bulletin ['bulətɪn] s bulletin m; (e.g., of a university) annuaire m

bul'letin board' s tableau m d'affichage

bul'let-proof' adj à l'épreuve des balles || tr blinder

bul'let-proof vest' s gilet m pare-balles

bull'fight' s course f de taureaux

bull'fight'er s torero m

bull'fight'ing s tauromachie f

bull'finch' s bouvreuil m

bull'frog' s grenouille f d'Amérique

bull'head' s (ichth) chabot m, cabot m; (miller's-thumb) meunier m, cabot

bull'head'ed adj entêté

bullion ['buljən] s (of gold) or m; (of silver) argent m; encaisse f métallique, lingots mpl d'or, lingots d'argent; (on uniform) cordonnet m d'or, cordonnet d'argent

bull' mar'ket s marché m à la hausse

bullock ['bulək] s bœuf m

bull' pen' s toril m; (jail) poste m de détention préventive

bull'ring' s arène f, arène pour les courses de taureaux

bull's'-eye' s mouche f; **to hit the bull's-eye** faire mouche

bull's'-eye win'dow s œil-de-bœuf m

bull'ter'rier s bull-terrier m

bul·ly ['buli] adj (coll) épatant || s (pl -lies) brute f, brutal m; (at school) brimeur m, tyranneau m || v (pret & pp -lied) tr brutaliser, malmener; (at school) brimer, tyranniser

bulrush ['bul,rʌʃ] s jonc m des marais

bulwark ['bulwərk] s rempart m; (naut) pavois m || tr garnir de remparts; (fig) protéger

bum [bʌm] adj (slang) moche, de camelote || s (slang) clochard m || v (pret & pp bummed; ger bumming) tr & intr (slang) écornifler

bumble ['bʌmbəl] tr bâcler || intr (to stumble) trébucher; (in speaking) bafouiller; (said of bee) bourdonner

bum'ble-bee' s bourdon m

bump [bʌmp] s choc m; (protuberance) bosse f; (of car on rough road) cahot m || tr cogner, tamponner, heurter; **to bump off** (to kill) (slang) buter || intr se cogner; **to bump along** (said of car) cahoter; **to bump into** buter contre, choquer

bumper ['bʌmpər] adj exceptionnel || s (aut) pare-chocs m; (rr) tampon m

bumpkin ['bʌmpkɪn] s péquenot m, rustre m

bumptious ['bʌmpʃəs] adj outrecuidant

bump·y ['bʌmpi] adj (comp -ier; super -iest) bosselé f; (road) cahoteux

bun [bʌn] s brioche f, petit pain m; (hair) chignon m

bunch [bʌntʃ] s botte f; (of bananas) régime m; (of flowers) bouquet m; (of grapes) grappe f; (of keys) trousseau m; (of people) groupe m, bande f; (of ribbons) flot m; (of twigs) paquet m; (on body) bosse f || tr grouper || intr se serrer

buncombe ['bʌŋkəm] s (coll) baliverne fpl, sornettes fpl

bundle ['bʌndəl] s paquet m; (of banknotes, papers, etc.) liasse f || tr empaqueter, mettre en paquet; **to bundle up** (in warm clothing) emmitoufler || intr—**to bundle up** s'emmitoufler

bung [bʌŋ] s bonde f || tr mettre une bonde à

bungalow ['bʌŋgə,lo] s bungalow m

bung'hole' s bonde f

bungle ['bʌŋgəl] s gâchis m, bousillage m || tr saboter, bousiller || intr saboter

bungler ['bʌŋglər] s gâcheur m, bousilleur m

bungling ['bʌŋglɪŋ] adj gauche, maladroit || s maladresse f

bunion ['bʌnjən] s oignon m (au pied)

bunk [bʌŋk] s couchette f; (slang) balivernes fpl, sornettes fpl || intr (coll) se coucher

bunk' bed' s (naut) cadre m

bunker ['bʌŋkər] s (golf) banquette f; (naut) soute f

bun·ny ['bʌni] s (pl -nies) petit lapin m

bunting ['bʌntɪŋ] s drapeaux mpl; (cloth) étamine f; (orn) bruant m

buoy [bɔɪ], ['bu-i] s bouée f || tr—**to buoy up** faire flotter; (fig) soutenir

buoyancy ['bɔɪ.ənsɪ], ['bujənsɪ] s flottabilité f

buoyant ['bɔɪ.ənt], ['bujənt] adj flottant; (cheerful) plein d'allant, plein de ressort

bur [bʌr] s (of chestnut) bogue f; (ragged metal edge) bavure f, barbe f

burble ['bʌrbəl] s murmure m || intr murmurer

burden ['bʌrdən] s fardeau m, charge f; (mus) refrain m || tr charger

burdensome ['bʌrdənsəm] adj onéreux

burdock ['bʌrdɑk] s bardane f

bureau ['bjuro] s commode f, chiffonier m; (office) bureau m

bureaucracy [bju'rɑkrəsɪ] s (pl -cies) bureaucratie f

bureaucrat ['bjurə,kræt] s bureaucrate mf

bureaucratic [,bjurə'krætɪk] adj bureaucratique

bu'reau of vi'tal statis'tics s bureau m de l'état civil

burg [bʌrg] s (coll) hameau m, patelin m; (coll) ville f

burglar ['bʌrglər] s cambrioleur m

bur'glar alarm' s signalisateur m antivol, sonnette f d'alarme

burglarize ['bʌrglə,raɪz] tr cambrioler

bur'glar-proof' adj incrochetable

burglary ['bʌrgləri] s (pl -ies) cambriolage m

Burgundian [bər'gʌndɪ.ən] adj bourguignon || s (dialect) bourguignon m; (person) Bourguignon m

Burgundy ['bʌrgəndɪ] s Bourgogne f; la Bourgogne || **burgun·dy** s (-dies) (wine) bourgogne m

burial ['berɪ.əl] s enterrement m, inhumation f

bur'ial ground' s cimetière m

burlap ['bʌrlæp] s toile f d'emballage, serpillière f

burlesque [bər'lesk] adj & s burlesque m || tr parodier

burlesque' show' s music-hall m

burly ['bʌrlɪ] adj (comp -lier; super -liest) solide, costaud

Burma ['bʌrmə] s Birmanie f; la Birmanie

Bur·mese [bər'miz] adj birman || s (pl -mese) (language) birman m; (person) Birman m

burn [bʌrn] s brûlure f || v (pret & pp burned or burnt [bʌrnt]) tr & intr brûler; **to burn out** (elec) griller

burner ['bʌrnər] s brûleur m; (using gas) bec m; (of a stove) feu m

burning ['bʌrnɪŋ] adj brûlant; (in flames) en feu || s brûlure f; (fire) incendie m

burnish ['bʌrnɪʃ] tr brunir, polir

burrow ['bʌro] s terrier m || tr creuser || intr se terrer

bursar ['bʌrsər] s économe m

burst [bʌrst] s éclat m, explosion f || v (pret & pp burst) tr faire éclater; (a balloon) crever; (a boiler; one's buttons) faire sauter || intr éclater, exploser; (said of tire) crever; **to burst into tears** fondre en larmes; **to burst out laughing** éclater de rire

bury ['berɪ] v (pret & pp -ied) tr enterrer, ensevelir; (e.g., pirate treasure) enfouir

bus [bʌs] s (pl busses or buses) autobus m; (interurban or sightseeing) car m, autocar m || v (pret & pp bused or bussed) ger busing or bussing) tr transporter en autobus

bus'boy' s aide-serveur m

bush [buʃ] s buisson m; (shrub) arbuste m; (in Africa and Australia) brousse f; **to beat around the bush** tourner autour du pot, tortiller

bushed [buʃt] adj (coll) éreinté

bushel ['buʃəl] s boisseau m

bushing ['buʃɪŋ] s manchon m, douille f, bague f, coussinet m

bushy ['buʃɪ] adj (comp -ier; super -iest) (countryside) buissonneux; (hair) touffu; (eyebrows) broussailleux

business ['bɪznɪs] adj commercial || s affaires fpl; (subject) sujet m; (theat) jeux mpl de scène; **it's none of your business** cela ne vous regarde pas; **mind your own business!** occupez-vous de vos affaires!, faites votre métier!; **to mean business** (coll) ne pas plaisanter; **to send about one's business** envoyer paître

busi'ness dis'trict s quartier m commerçant

busi'ness hours' s heures fpl d'ouverture

busi'ness house' s maison f de commerce

busi'ness-like' adj pratique; (manner, transaction) sérieux

busi'ness-man' s (pl -men') homme m d'affaires; **big businessman** grand industriel m, chef m d'industrie

busi'ness man'ager s directeur m commercial

busi'ness reply' card' s carte f postale avec réponse payée

busi'ness suit' s complet m veston

busi'ness-wom'an s (pl -wom'en) femme f d'affaires

buskin ['bʌskɪn] s brodequin m

bus' sta'tion s gare f routière

bus' stop' s arrêt m d'autobus

bust [bʌst] s buste m; (of woman) gorge f, buste m; (slang) faillite f || tr (mil) limoger; (slang) casser || intr (slang) échouer

busting ['bʌstɪŋ] s (mil) cassation f

bustle ['bʌsəl] s remue-ménage m, affairement m, branle-bas m || intr se remuer, s'affairer

bustling ['bʌslɪŋ] adj affairé

busy ['bɪzɪ] adj (comp -ier; super -iest) occupé || v (pret & pp -ied) tr —**to busy oneself with** s'occuper de

bus'y-bod'y s (pl -ies) officieux m

bus'y sig'nal s (telp) signal m de ligne occupée

but [bʌt] adv seulement; **ne . . . que,** e.g., **he has nothing but trouble** n'avoir que des ennuis; **but for** sans; **but for that** à part cela || prep sauf, excepté; **all but** presque || conj mais

butcher ['butʃər] s boucher m || tr (an

animal for meat) abattre, dépecer; (*to massacre; to bungle*) massacrer

butch′er knife′ *s* couperet *m*, coutelas *m* (de boucher)

butch′er shop′ *s* boucherie *f*

butler [ˈbʌtlər] *s* maître *m* d'hôtel, intendant *m*

butt [bʌt] *s* bout *m*; (*cask*) futaille *f*; (*of a gun*) crosse *f*; (*of a cigarette*) mégot *m*; (*of a joke*) souffre-douleur *m*, plastron *m*; (*blow*) coup *m* de tête, coup de corne; (*slang*) postérieur *m*, derrière *m* ‖ *tr* (*like a goat*) donner un coup de corne à ‖ *intr*—**to butt up against** buter contre; **to butt in** (coll) intervenir sans façon

butte [bjut] *s* butte *f*, tertre *m*, puy *m*

butt′ end′ *s* gros bout *m*

butter [ˈbʌtər] *s* beurre *m* ‖ *tr* beurrer; **to butter up** (coll) passer de la pommade à, pateliner

but′ter-cup′ *s* renoncule *f*, bouton-d'or *m*

but′ter dish′ *s* beurrier *m*, beurrière *f*

but′ter-fat′ *s* crème *f*

but′ter-fin′gered *adj* maladroit

but′ter-fin′gers *s* brise-tout *mf*

but′ter-fly′ *s* (*pl* **-flies**) papillon *m*

but′ter knife′ *s* couteau *m* à beurre

but′ter-milk′ *s* babeurre *m*

but′ter-scotch′ *s* caramel *m* au beurre

buttocks [ˈbʌtəks] *spl* fesses *fpl*

button [ˈbʌtən] *s* bouton *m* ‖ *tr* boutonner

but′ton-hole′ *s* boutonnière *f* ‖ *tr* (coll) retenir (*qqn*) par le pan de sa veste

but′ton-hook′ *s* tire-bouton *m*

buttress [ˈbʌtrɪs] *s* contrefort *m* ‖ *tr* arc-bouter; (fig) étayer

buxom [ˈbʌksəm] *adj* plantureuse

buy [baɪ] *s*—**a good buy** (coll) une bonne affaire ‖ *v* (*pret & pp* **bought** [bɔt]) *tr* acheter; (*a ticket*) prendre; **to buy a drink for** payer un verre à; **to buy back** racheter; **to buy from** acheter à or de; **to buy out** (*a part-*

ner) désintéresser; **to buy s.o. off** se débarrasser de qn, racheter qn; **to buy up** accaparer

buyer [ˈbaɪ-ər] *s* acheteur *m*

buzz [bʌz] *s* bourdonnement *m*; **to give s.o. a buzz** (*on the telephone*) (coll) passer un coup de fil à ‖ *tr* (aer) survoler à basse altitude ‖ *intr* bourdonner

buzzard [ˈbʌzərd] *s* buse *f*

buzz′ bomb′ *s* bombe *f* volante

buzzer [ˈbʌzər] *s* trembleur *m*

buzz′ saw′ *s* scie *f* circulaire

by [baɪ] *adv* près, auprès; (*aside*) de côté; **by and by** tout à l'heure, sous peu; **by and large** généralement parlant ‖ *prep* par; (*near*) près de; **by a head** (*taller*) d'une tête; **by day** pendant la journée; **by far** de beaucoup; **by Monday** d'ici à lundi; **by profession** de profession; **by the way** à propos; **by** être suivi (aimé, etc.) de

by-and-by [ˈbaɪ-ən'baɪ] *s* proche avenir *m*; **in the sweet by-and-by** à la Saint-Glinglin

by′gone′ *adj* d'autrefois, passé

by′law′ *s* ordonnance *f*, règlement *m*

by′-line′ *s* signature *f* de journaliste

by′-pass′ *s* déviation *f*; (elec) dérivation *f* ‖ *tr* éviter, contourner; (mach) amener or placer en dérivation

by′-play′ *s* (theat) jeu *m* en aparté

by′-prod′uct *s* sous-produit *m*

by′-road′ *s* chemin *m* détourné

bystander [ˈbaɪ ˌstændər] *s* spectateur *m*, assistant *m*

by′way′ *s* chemin *m* écarté, voie *f* indirecte

by′word′ *s* dicton *m*, proverbe *m*; objet *m* de dérision

Byzantine [ˈbɪzən.tin], [bɪˈzæntin] *adj* & *s* byzantin *m*

Byzantium [bɪˈzænʃɪ-əm], [bɪˈzæntɪ-əm] *s* Byzance *f*

C

C, c [si] *s* IIIᵉ lettre de l'alphabet

cab [kæb] *s* taxi *m*; (*of locomotive or truck*) cabine *f*; (*hansom*) fiacre *m*, cab *m*

cabaret [ˌkæbə're] *s* boîte *f* de nuit, cabaret *m*

cabbage [ˈkæbɪdʒ] *s* chou *m*

cab′driv′er *s* chauffeur *m* de taxi

cabin [ˈkæbɪn] *s* case *f*, cabane *f*; (*of ship or airplane*) cabine *f*

cab′in boy′ *s* (naut) mousse *m*

cabinet [ˈkæbɪnɪt] *s* cabinet *m*; (*cupboard; radio cabinet*) meuble *m*; meuble à tiroirs; (*of professional men*) étude *m*, cabinet; (*of officers*) cabinet, bureau *m* directoire, comité *m*, conseil *m*

cab′inet-mak′er *s* ébéniste *m*, menuisier *m*

cab′inet mem′ber *s* ministre *m*

cable [ˈkebəl] *s* câble *m* ‖ *tr* & *intr* câbler

ca′ble car′ *s* funiculaire *m*, téléférique *m*

ca′ble-gram′ *s* câblogramme *m*

ca′ble ship′ *s* câblier *m*

ca′ble's length′ *s* encablure *f*

caboose [kə'bus] *s* (naut) coquerie *f*; (rr) fourgon *m* de queue, wagon *m* du personnel

cab′stand′ *s* station *f* de taxi

cache [kæʃ] *s* cachette *f*, cache *f* ‖ *tr* mettre dans une cachette, cacher

cachet [kæ'ʃe] *s* cachet *m*

cackle ['kækəl] s caquet m || intr caqueter; (said of goose) cacarder

cacopho•ny [kə'kafəni] s (pl -nies) cacophonie f

cac•tus ['kæktəs] s (pl -tuses or -ti [taɪ]) cactus m

cad [kæd] s malotru m

cadaver [kə'dævər] s cadavre m

cad•dy ['kædɪ] s (pl -dies) boîte f à thé; (person) cadet m, caddie m

cadence ['kedəns] s cadence f

cadet [kə'dɛt] s cadet m

cadmium ['kædmɪ-əm] s cadmium m

Caesar'ean opera'tion [sɪ'zɛrɪ-ən] s césarienne f

café [kæ'fe] s cabaret m; café-restaurant m

ca'fé soci'ety s gens mpl chic des cabarets à la mode

cafeteria [,kæfə'tɪrɪ-ə] s cafétéria f, restaurant m de libre-service

caffeine [kæ'fin], ['kæfin], ['kæfi-ɪn] s caféine f

cage [kedʒ] s cage f || tr mettre en cage

ca•gey ['kedʒi] adj (comp -gier; super -giest) (coll) rusé, fin

cahoots [kə'huts] s—in cahoots (slang) de mèche

Cain [ken] s Caïn m; to raise Cain (coll) faire le diable à quatre

Cairo ['kaɪro] s Le Caire

caisson ['kesən] s caisson m

cais'son disease' s maladie f des caissons

cajole [kə'dʒol] tr cajoler, enjôler

cajoler•y [kə'dʒoləri] s (pl -ies) cajolerie f, enjôlement m

cake [kek] s gâteau m; (one-layer cake) galette f; (pastry) pâtisserie f; (of soap, wax) pain m; (of ice) bloc m; (crust) croûte f; to sell like hot cakes (coll) se vendre comme des petits pains; to take the cake (coll) être la fin des haricots || tr couvrir d'une croûte || intr s'agglutiner, faire croûte

calabash ['kælə,bæʃ] s calebasse f; (tree) calebassier m

calaboose ['kælə,bus] s (coll) violon m, tôle f

calamitous [kə'læmɪtəs] adj calamiteux

calami•ty [kə'læmɪti] s (pl -ties) calamité f

calci•fy ['kælsɪ,faɪ] v (pret & pp -fied) tr calcifier || intr se calcifier

calcium ['kælsɪ-əm] s calcium m

calculate ['kælkjə,let] tr & intr calculer

calculating ['kælkjə,letɪŋ] adj calculateur

calculation [,kælkjə'leʃən] s calcul m

calcu•lus ['kælkjələs] s (pl -luses or -li [,laɪ]) (math, pathol) calcul m

caldron ['koldrən] s (culin) chaudron m; (mach) chaudière f

calendar ['kæləndər] s calendrier m

cal'endar year' s année f civile

calender ['kæləndər] s calandre f || tr calandrer, cylindrer

calf [kæf], [kɑf] s (pl calves [kævz], [kɑvz]) veau m; (of leg) mollet m

calf'skin' s veau m, peau f de veau

calf's' liv'er s foie m de veau

caliber ['kælɪbər] s calibre m

calibrate ['kælɪ,bret] tr calibrer

cal•ico ['kælɪ,ko] s (pl -coes or -cos) calicot m; indienne f

California [,kælɪ'fɔrnɪ-ə] s Californie f; la Californie

calipers ['kælɪpərz] spl compas m à calibrer

caliph ['kelɪf], ['kælɪf] s calife m

caliphate ['kælɪ,fet] s califat m

calisthenic [,kælɪs'θɛnɪk] adj callisthénique || **calisthenics** spl callisthénie f

calk [kok] s crampon m à glace || tr calfater

call [kol] s appel m; (cry) cri m; (visit) visite f; (at a port) escale f; to have no call to n'avoir aucune raison de || tr appeler; (e.g., the doctor) faire venir; (a meeting) convoquer; to call aside prendre à part; to call back rappeler; to call down (from upstairs) faire descendre; (the wrath of the gods) invoquer; (to scold) (coll) gronder; to call off (a dog) rappeler; (coll) annuler, décommander; to call the roll faire l'appel; to call to mind rappeler; to call to order rappeler à l'ordre; to call up (coll) passer un coup de fil à; (mil) mobiliser || intr appeler; crier; (to visit) faire une visite; (naut) faire escale; to call upon faire appel à; to call upon s.o. to speak inviter qn à prendre la parole

call' bell' s sonnette f

call' box' s guérite f téléphonique

call' boy' s (in a hotel) chasseur m; (theat) avertisseur m

caller ['kolər] s visiteur m

call' girl' s call-girl f

calling ['kolɪŋ] s vocation f, profession f; (of a meeting) convocation f

cal'ling card' s carte f de visite

call' let'ter s (telg, rad) indicatif m d'appel

call' mon'ey s prêts mpl au jour le jour

callous ['kæləs] adj (foot, hand, etc.) calleux; (unfeeling) endurci, insensible

callow ['kælo] adj inexpérimenté, novice

cal'low youth' s blanc-bec m

callus ['kæləs] s (on skin) cal m, durillon m, callosité f; (bot) cal m

calm [kɑm] adj & s calme m || tr calmer; to calm down pacifier || intr —to calm down se calmer; (said of wind or sea) calmir

calorie ['kæləri] s calorie f

calum•ny ['kæləmni] s (pl -nies) calomnie f

calva•ry ['kælvəri] s (pl -ries) calvaire m; Calvary le Calvaire

calve [kæv], [kɑv] intr vêler

cam [kæm] s came f

cambric ['kembrɪk] s batiste f

camel ['kæməl] s chameau m

camellia [kə'miljə] s camélia m

came•o ['kæmi,o] s (pl -os) camée m

camera ['kæmərə] *s* appareil *m* (photographique)

cam'era-man' *s* (*pl* -men') photographe *m*

camouflage ['kæmə,flɑʒ] *s* camouflage *m* ‖ *tr* camoufler

camp [kæmp] *s* camp *m* ‖ *intr* camper; **to go camping** faire du camping

campaign [kæm'pen] *s* campagne *f* ‖ *intr* faire campagne

campaigner [kæm'penər] *s* propagandiste *mf*; vétéran *m*

camp' bed' *s* lit *m* de camp, lit de sangle

camp' chair' *s* chaise *f* pliante

camper ['kæmpər] *s* campeur *m*

camp'fire' *s* feu *m* de camp

camp'ground' *s* camping *m*

camphor ['kæmfər] *s* camphre *m*

camping ['kæmpɪŋ] *s* camping *m*

camp'stool' *s* pliant *m*

campus ['kæmpəs] *s* campus *m*, terrain *m* universitaire

cam'shaft' *s* arbre *m* à cames

can [kæn] *s* boîte *f*; (*e.g., for gasoline*) bidon *m* ‖ *v* (*pret & pp* **canned**; *ger* **canning**) *tr* mettre en boîte, conserver; (*to dismiss*) (slang) dégommer ‖ *v* (*pret & cond* **could** [kʊd]) *aux*—**Albert can't do it** Albert ne peut (pas) le faire; **can he swim?** sait-il nager?

Canada ['kænədə] *s* le Canada

Canadian [kə'nedɪ·ən] *adj* canadien ‖ *s* (*person*) Canadien *m*

canal [kə'næl] *s* canal *m*

canary [kə'nerɪ] *s* (*pl* -ies) canari *m*, serin *m*

can-cel ['kænsəl] *v* (*pret & pp* -celed *or* -celled; *ger* -celing *or* -celling) *tr* annuler; (*a word*) biffer, rayer; (*a contract*) résilier; (*a postage stamp*) oblitérer; **to cancel an invitation** décommander les invités; **to cancel each other out** s'annuler, se détruire

cancellation [,kænsə'le/ən] *s* annulation *f*; (*of postage stamp*) oblitération *f*; (*of contract*) résiliation *f*

cancer ['kænsər] *s* cancer *m*

cancerous ['kænsərəs] *adj* cancéreux

candela-brum [,kændə'lebrəm] *s* (*pl* -bra [brə] *or* -brums) candélabre *m*

candid ['kændɪd] *adj* franc

candida-cy ['kændɪdəsɪ] *s* (*pl* -cies) candidature *f*

candidate ['kændɪ,det] *s* candidat *m*

candied *adj* candi

candied' fruit' *s* fruit *m* candi

candle ['kændəl] *s* bougie *f*; (*of tallow*) chandelle *f*; (eccl) cierge *m*

can'dle-hold'er *s* bougeoir *m*

can'dle-light' *s* lumière *f* de bougie

can'dle-pow'er *s* (phys) bougie *f*

can'dle-stick' *s* chandelier *m*, bougeoir *m*

can'dle ta'ble *s* guéridon *m*

candor ['kændər] *s* franchise *f*, loyauté *f*

candy ['kændɪ] *s* (*pl* -dies) confiserie *f*, bonbons *mpl*; **candies** douceurs *fpl*; **piece of candy** bonbon *m* ‖ *v* (*pret & pp* -died) *tr* glacer, faire candir ‖ *intr* se candir

can'dy box' *s* boîte *f* à bonbons

can'dy corn' *s* grains *mpl* de maïs soufflés et sucrés

can'dy dish' *s* bonbonnière

can'dy store' *s* confiserie *f*

cane [ken] *s* canne *f*; (bot) canne ‖ *tr* canner, rempailler

cane' chair' *s* chaise *f* cannée

cane' sug'ar *s* sucre *m* de canne

canine ['kenaɪn] *adj* canin ‖ *s* (*tooth*) canine *f*

canister ['kænɪstər] *s* boîte *f* métallique; (mil) boîte à mitraille

canker ['kæŋkər] *s* chancre *m*; (*in fruit; in society*) ver *m* rongeur ‖ *tr* ronger; (*society*) corrompre

canned' goods' *spl* conserves *fpl*, aliments *mpl* conservés

canned' mu'sic *s* (coll) musique *f* enregistrée

canner-y ['kænərɪ] *s* (*pl* -ies) conserverie *f*

cannibal ['kænɪbəl] *adj & s* cannibale *mf*

canning ['kænɪŋ] *s* conservation *f*

can'ning fac'tory *s* conserverie *f*

cannon ['kænən] *s* canon *m*

cannonade [,kænə'ned] *s* canonnade *f* ‖ *tr* canonner

can'non-ball' *s* boulet *m* (de canon)

can'non fod'der *s* chair *f* à canon

can-ny ['kænɪ] *adj* (*comp* -nier; *super* -niest) prudent, circonspect; rusé, malin

canoe [kə'nu] *s* canoë *m*

canoeist [kə'nu·ɪst] *s* canoéiste *mf*

canon ['kænən] *s* canon *m*

canonical [kə'nɑnɪkəl] *adj* canonique, canonial ‖ **canonicals** *spl* vêtements *mpl* sacerdotaux

canonize ['kænə,naɪz] *tr* canoniser

can' o'pener *s* ouvre-boîtes *m*

cano-py ['kænəpɪ] *s* (*pl* -pies) dais *m*; (*over an entrance*) marquise *f*

cant [kænt] *s* cant *m*, cafardise *f*; (*argot*) jargon *m* ‖ *tr* (*to tip*) incliner ‖ *intr* (*to tip*) s'incliner; (*to be hypocritical*) papelarder

cantaloupe ['kæntə,lop] *s* cantaloup *m*

cantankerous [kæn'tæŋkərəs] *adj* revêche, acariâtre

cantata [kən'tɑtə] *s* cantate *f*

canteen [kæn'tin] *s* (*shop*) cantine *f*; (*water flask*) bidon *m*; (*service club*) foyer *m* du soldat, du marin, etc.

canter ['kæntər] *s* petit galop *m* ‖ *intr* aller au petit galop

canticle ['kæntɪkəl] *s* cantique *m*, hymne *f*

cantilever ['kæntɪ,livər] *adj & s* cantilever *m*

can'tilever bridge' *s* pont *m* cantilever, pont à consoles

canton [kæn'tɑn] *s* canton *m*

canvas ['kænvəs] *s* (*cloth*) canevas *m*; (*picture*) toile *f*

canvass ['kænvəs] *s* enquête *f*, sondage *m*; (pol) tournée *f* électorale ‖ *tr* (*a voter*) solliciter la voix de; (*a district*) faire une tournée électorale dans; (com) prospecter ‖ *intr* (com) faire la place; **to canvass for** (*a can-*

didate) faire une campagne électorale en faveur de

canyon [ˈkænjən] *s* cañon *m*

cap [kæp] *s* (*with visor*) casquette *f*; (*without brim*) bonnet *m*; (*to wear with academic gown*) toque *f*, mortier *m*; (*of bottle*) capsule *f*; (*of cartridge*) amorce *f*, capsule; (*of fountain pen*) capuchon *m*, chapeau *m*; (*of valve; to cover photographic lens*) chapeau; **to set one's cap for** chercher à captiver ‖ *v* (*pret & pp* **capped;** *ger* **capping**) *tr* coiffer; (*a bottle*) capsuler; (*a cartridge*) amorcer; (*a success*) couronner; (*to outdo*) (coll) surpasser

cap. *abbr* (**capital letter**) maj.

capable [ˈkepəbəl] *adj* capable

capacious [kəˈpeʃəs] *adj* spacieux, vaste, ample

capaci·ty [kəˈpæsɪti] *s* (*pl* **-ties**) capacité *f*; **filled to capacity** comble; **in the capacity of** en tant que, en qualité de, à titre de

cap′ and gown′ *s* costume *m* académique, toge *f* et mortier *m*; **in cap and gown** en toque et en toge

cape [kep] *s* (*clothing*) cape *f*, pèlerine *f*; (geog) cap *m*, promontoire *m*

Cape′ of Good Hope′ *s* Cap *m* de Bonne Espérance

caper [ˈkepər] *s* cabriole *f*, gambade *f*; (bot) câpre *f* ‖ *tr* cabrioler, gambader

Cape′town′ *s* Le Cap

capital [ˈkæpɪtəl] *adj* capital; excellent ‖ *s* (*city*) capitale *f*; (archit) chapiteau *m*; (com) capital *m*; (typ) majuscule *f*, capitale; **small capital** petite capitale

cap′ital and la′bor *spl* le capital et le travail

capitalism [ˈkæpɪtəˌlɪzəm] *s* capitalisme *m*

capitalist [ˈkæpɪtəlɪst] *adj & s* capitaliste *mf*

capitalize [ˈkæpɪtəˌlaɪz] *tr & intr* capitaliser; (typ) écrire avec une majuscule; **to capitalize on** miser sur, tourner à son profit, tirer parti de

cap′ital let′ter *s* majuscule *f*

cap′ital pun′ishment *s* peine *f* capitale

capitol [ˈkæpɪtəl] *s* capitole *m*

capitulate [kəˈpɪtʃəˌlet] *intr* capituler

capon [ˈkepən] *s* chapon *m*

caprice [kəˈpris] *s* caprice *m*

capricious [kəˈprɪʃəs] *adj* capricieux

capsize [ˈkæpsaɪz] *tr* faire chavirer ‖ *intr* chavirer, capoter

capstan [ˈkæpstən] *s* cabestan *m*

capsule [ˈkæpsəl] *s* capsule *f*; (bot, rok) capsule

captain [ˈkæptən] *s* capitaine *m*; chef *m*; (sports) chef d'équipe *m* ‖ *tr* commander, diriger

captain·cy [ˈkæptənsi] *s* (*pl* **-cies**) direction *f*, commandement *m*; grade *m* de capitaine

caption [ˈkæpʃən] *s* légende *f*; (mov) sous-titre *m* ‖ *tr* intituler, donner un sous-titre à

captious [ˈkæpʃəs] *adj* pointilleux, chicaneux; (*insidious*) captieux

captivate [ˈkæptɪˌvet] *tr* captiver

captive [ˈkæptɪv] *adj & s* captif *m*

captivi·ty [kæpˈtɪvɪti] *s* (*pl* **-ties**) captivité *f*

captor [ˈkæptər] *s* ravisseur *m*; (naut) auteur *m* d'une prise

capture [ˈkæptʃər] *s* capture *f*, prise *f* ‖ *tr* capturer

car [kɑr] *s* auto *f*, voiture *f*; (*of elevator*) cabine *f*; (rr) wagon *m*, voiture; (*for mail, baggage, etc.*) (rr) fourgon *m*

carafe [kəˈræf] *s* carafe *f*

caramel [ˈkærəməl], [ˈkɑrməl] *s* caramel *m*

carat [ˈkærət] *s* carat *m*

caravan [ˈkærəˌvæn] *s* caravane *f*

caravansa·ry [ˌkærəˈvænsəri] *s* (*pl* **-ries**) caravansérail *m*

caraway [ˈkærəˌwe] *s* carvi *m*

car′away seed′ *s* graine *f* de carvi

car′barn′ *s* dépôt *m* de tramways

carbide [ˈkɑrbaɪd] *s* carbure *m*

carbine [ˈkɑrbaɪn] *s* carabine *f*

carbol′ic ac′id [kɑrˈbɑlɪk] *s* acide *m* phénique

carbon [ˈkɑrbən] *s* (*chemical element*) carbone *m*; (*part of arc light or battery*) charbon *m*; (*in auto cylinder*) calamine *f*; papier *m* carbone

car′bonated wa′ter [ˈkɑrbəˌnetɪd] *s* eau *f* gazeuse, soda *m*

car′bon cop′y *s* double *m* au carbone; (fig) calque *m*; (*person*) (fig) sosie *m*

car′bon diox′ide *s* gaz *m* carbonique

car′bon monox′ide *s* oxyde *m* de carbone

car′bon pa′per *s* papier *m* carbone

carbuncle [ˈkɑrbʌŋkəl] *s* furoncle *m*

carburetor [ˈkɑrbəˌretər] *s* carburateur *m*

carcass [ˈkɑrkəs] *s* (*dead body*) cadavre *m*; (*without offal*) carcasse *f*

card [kɑrd] *s* carte *f*; (*for filing*) fiche *f*; (*for carding*) carde *f*; (coll) original *m*, numéro *m*, type *m*; **to put one's cards on the table** jouer cartes sur table ‖ *tr* carder, peigner

card′board′ *s* carton *m*

card′ case′ *s* porte-cartes *m*

card′ cat′alogue *s* fichier *m*

cardiac [ˈkɑrdɪˌæk] *adj* cardiaque ‖ *s* (*patient*) (coll) cardiaque *mf*

cardinal [ˈkɑrdɪnəl] *adj & s* cardinal *m*

card′ in′dex *s* fichier *m*

cardiogram [ˈkɑrdɪoˌgræm] *s* cardiogramme *m*

card′sharp′ *s* tricheur *m*

card′ ta′ble *s* table *f* de jeu

card′ trick′ *s* tour *m* de cartes

care [ker] *s* (*attention*) soin *m*; (*anxiety*) souci *m*; (*responsibility*) charge *f*; (*upkeep*) entretien *m*; **in care of** aux bons soins de, à l'attention de; **take care!** faites attention!; **to take care not to** se garder de; **to take care of** se charger de; (*a sick person*) soigner; **to take care to** avoir soin de ‖ *intr*—**I don't care** ça m'est égal; **to care about** se soucier de, se préoccuper de; **to care for** (*s.o.*) avoir de la sympathie pour; (*s.th.*) trouver plaisir à; (*a sick person*) soigner; **to care to** désirer, vouloir

careen [kə'rin] *tr* faire coucher sur le côté || *intr* donner de la bande, s'incliner

career [kə'rɪr] *s* carrière *f*

care'free' *adj* sans souci, insouciant

careful ['kɛrfəl] *adj* soigneux, attentif; **be careful!** soyez prudent!

careless ['kɛrlɪs] *adj* (*neglectful*) négligent; (*nonchalant*) insouciant

carelessness ['kɛrlɪsnɪs] *s* négligence *f*

caress [kə'rɛs] *s* caresse *f* || *tr* caresser

caret ['kærət] *s* guidon *m* de renvoi

care'tak'er *s* concierge *mf*, gardien *m*

care'taker gov'ernment *s* gouvernement *m* intérimaire

care'worn' *adj* rongé par les soucis

car'fare' *s* prix *m* du trajet, place *f*; **to pay carfare** payer le parcours

car-go ['kɑrgo] *s* (*pl* **-goes** or **-gos**) cargaison *f*

car' heat'er *s* chauffage *m* de voiture

Car-ib'be-an Sea' [,kærɪ'bi-ən], [kə-'rɪbɪ-ən] *s* Mer *f* des Caraïbes, Mer des Antilles

caricature ['kærɪkət/ər] *s* caricature *f* || *tr* caricaturer

caricaturist ['kærɪkət/ərɪst] *s* caricaturiste *mf*

caries ['kɛriz], ['kɛrɪ ,iz] *s* carie *f*

carillon ['kærɪ ,lɑn], [kə'rɪljən] *s* carillon *m* || *tr* & *intr* carillonner

car'load' *s* voiturée *f*

carnage ['kɑrnɪdʒ] *s* carnage *m*

carnal ['kɑrnəl] *adj* charnel; sexuel

car'nal sin' *s* péché *m* de la chair

carnation [kɑr'neʃən] *s* œillet *m*

carnival ['kɑrnɪvəl] *s* carnaval *m*; fête *f*

car-ol ['kærəl] *s* chanson *f*, cantique *m*; (*Christmas carol*) noël *m* || *v* (*pret* & *pp* **-oled** or **-olled**; *ger* **-oling** or **-olling**) *tr* & *intr* chanter

carom ['kærəm] *s* carambolage *m* || *intr* caramboler

carouse [kə'rauz] *intr* faire la bombe

carp [kɑrp] *s* carpe *f* || *intr* se plaindre

carpenter ['kɑrpəntər] *s* charpentier *m*; (*joiner*) menuisier *m*

carpentry ['kɑrpəntri] *s* charpenterie *f*

carpet ['kɑrpɪt] *s* tapis *m* || *tr* recouvrir d'un tapis

car'pet sweep'er *s* balai *m* mécanique

car'port' *s* abri *m* pour auto

car'-rent'al serv'ice *s* entreprise *f* de location de voitures

carriage ['kærɪdʒ] *s* voiture *f*; (*used to transport royalty*) carrosse *m*; (*bearing*) port *m*, maintien *m*; (*cost of transport*) frais *mpl* de port; (*of typewriter*; *of rocket*) chariot *m*; (*of gun*) affût *m*

carrier ['kærɪ-ər] *s* (*person*) porteur *m*; (*e.g., a teamster*) camionneur *m*, voiturier *m*; (*vehicle*) transporteur *m*

car'rier pig'eon *s* pigeon *m* voyageur

car'rier wave' *s* onde *f* porteuse

carrion ['kærɪ-ən] *s* charogne *f*

carrot ['kærət] *s* carotte *f*

carrousel [,kærə'zɛl] *s* (*merry-go-round*) manège *m* de chevaux de bois; (*hist*) carrousel *m*

car-ry ['kæri] *v* (*pret* & *pp* **-ried**) *tr* porter; (*in adding numbers*) retenir; **to be carried** (parl) être voté, être adopté; **to be carried away** (*e.g., with enthusiasm*) être entraîné, s'importer; **to carry away** or **off** emporter, enlever; **to carry back** rapporter; **to carry down** descendre; **to carry forward**; (bk) reporter; **to carry on** continuer; (*e.g., a conversation*) soutenir; **to carry oneself straight** se tenir droit; **to carry out** (*a plan*) exécuter; **to carry over** (bk) reporter; **to carry through** mener à bonne fin; **to carry up** monter; **to carry with one** (*e.g., an audience*) entraîner || *intr* (*said of voice or sound*) porter; **to carry on** continuer; (*in a ridiculous manner*) (coll) faire des espiègleries; (*angrily*) (coll) s'emporter

car' sick'ness *s* mal *m* de la route

cart [kɑrt] *s* charrette *f*; **to put the cart before the horse** mettre la charrue devant les bœufs || *tr* charrier; (*to truck*) camionner

cartel [kɑr'tɛl] *s* cartel *m*

cartilage ['kɑrtɪlɪdʒ] *s* cartilage *m*

cartographer [kɑr'tɑgrəfər] *s* cartographe *m*

carton ['kɑrtən] *s* carton *m*, boîte *f*

cartoon [kɑr'tun] *s* dessin *m* humoristique; caricature *f*; (*comic strip*) bande *f* dessinée; (*mov*) dessin animé || *tr* caricaturer

cartoonist [kɑr'tunɪst] *s* caricaturiste *mf*

cartridge ['kɑrtrɪdʒ] *s* cartouche *f*; capsule *f* enregistreuse de pick-up

car'tridge belt' *s* cartouchière *f*

car'tridge case' *s* cartouchière *f*

cart'wheel' *s* roue *f*; **to turn cartwheels** faire la roue

carve [kɑrv] *tr* & *intr* sculpter; (culin) découper

carver ['kɑrvər] *s* sculpteur *m*; (culin) découpeur *m*

carv'ing knife' *s* couteau *m* à découper

cascade [kæs'ked] *s* cascade *f* || *intr* cascader

case [kes] *s* (*instance, example*) cas *m*; (*for packing; of clock or piano*) caisse *f*; (*for cigarettes, eyeglasses, cartridges*) étui *m*; (*for jewels, silver, etc.*) écrin *m*; (*for watch*) boîtier *m*; (*for pillow*) taie *f*; (*for surgical instruments*) trousse *f*; (*for sausage*) peau *f*; (*showcase*) vitrine *f*; (*covering*) enveloppe *f*, couverture *f*; (law) cause *f*; (typ) casse *f*; **as the case may be** selon le cas; **in any case** en tout cas; **in case** au cas où; **in case of emergency** en cas d'imprévu; **in no case** en aucun cas; **just in case** à tout hasard; **to win one's case** avoir gain de cause || *tr* (*to put into a case*) encaisser; (*to package*) envelopper; (*to observe*) (slang) observer, épier

case′hard′en tr aciérer, cémenter; (fig) endurcir

casein [′kesɪˌɪn] s caséine f

casement [′kesmənt] s croisée f

cash [kæʃ] s espèces fpl; **cash down** argent comptant; **cash offer** offre f réelle; **cash on delivery** livraison contre remboursement; **cash on hand** fonds mpl en caisse; **in cash** en numéraire ‖ tr toucher, encaisser ‖ intr —**to cash in on** (coll) tirer parti de

cash′ and car′ry s achat m au comptant et à emporter

cash′ bal′ance s solde m de caisse

cash′ dis′count s escompte m au comptant

cashew [′kæʃu] s noix f d'acajou, anacarde m; (tree) anacardier m

cash′ew nut′ s noix f d'acajou

cashier [kæ′ʃɪr] s caissier m

cashmere [′kæʒmɪr] s cachemire m

cash′ reg′ister s caisse f enregistreuse

casing [′kesɪŋ] s enveloppe f, chemise f, coffrage m; (of door or window) chambranle m

cask [kæsk], [kɑsk] s tonneau m, fût m

casket [′kæskɪt], [′kɑskɪt] s (for jewels) écrin m, cassette f; (for interment) cercueil m

casserole [′kæsəˌrol] s terrine f

cassock [′kæsək] s soutane f

cast [kæst], [kɑst] s (mold) moule m; (of metal) fonte f; (of fish line) lancer m; (throw) jet m; (for broken limb) plâtre m; (squint) léger strabisme m; (theat) distribution f ‖ v (pret & pp cast) tr fondre, jeter en moule; (to throw) lancer; (a glance) jeter; (a play) distribuer les rôles de; **to be cast in one piece** venir de fonte avec; **to cast aside** mettre de côté; **to cast lots** tirer au sort; **to cast off** rejeter; **to cast out** mettre à la porte; (a spell) exorciser ‖ intr (fishing) lancer la canne; **to cast about for** chercher; **to cast off** (naut) larguer les amarres

castanets [ˌkæstə′nets] spl castagnettes fpl

cast′away′ adj & s naufragé m

caste [kæst], [kɑst] s caste f

caster [′kæstər], [′kɑstər] s (wheel) roulette f; (cruet stand) huilier m; (shaker) saupoudreuse f

castigate [′kæstɪˌget] tr châtier, corriger

Castile [kæs′til] s Castille f; la Castille

Castilian [kæs′tɪljən] adj castillan ‖ s (language) castillan m; (person) Castillan m

casting [′kæstɪŋ] s fonte f; (thing cast) pièce f fondue; (act) lancement m; (fishing) pêche f au lancer; (theat) distribution f

cast′ing rod′ s canne f à lancer

cast′ i′ron s fonte f

cast′-i′ron adj en fonte

cast′-iron stom′ach s estomac m d'autruche

castle [′kæsəl], [′kɑsəl] s château m; (fortified castle) château fort; (chess) tour f ‖ tr & intr (chess) roquer

cast′ off′ adj & s rejeté m

cas′tor oil′ [′kæstər], [′kɑstər] s huile f de ricin

castrate [′kæstret] tr castrer

casual [′kæʒuˌəl] adj casuel; (indifferent) insouciant, désinvolte

casually [′kæʒuˌəli] adv nonchalamment, avec désinvolture; (by chance) fortuitement

casual·ty [′kæʒuˌəlti] s (pl -ties) accident m; (person) accidenté m; **casualties** (mil) pertes fpl

cas′ualty list′ s état m des pertes

cat [kæt] s (tomcat) chat m; (female cat) chatte f; (naut) capon m; (shrew) (coll) cancanière f, chipie f; **a cat may look at a queen** un chien regarde bien un évêque; **to let the cat out of the bag** (coll) vendre or éventer la mèche; **to rain cats and dogs** (coll) pleuvoir à seaux

cataclysm [′kætəˌklɪzəm] s cataclysme m

catacombs [′kætəˌkomz] spl catacombes fpl

catalogue [′kætəˌlɔg], [′kætəˌlɑg] s catalogue m; (of university) annuaire m ‖ tr cataloguer, classer

Catalonia [ˌkætə′lonɪ·ə] s Catalogne f; la Catalogne

catalyst [′kætəlɪst] s catalyseur m

catapult [′kætəˌpʌlt] s catapulte f ‖ tr catapulter

cataract [′kætəˌrækt] s cataracte f

catarrh [kə′tɑr] s catarrhe m

catastrophe [kə′tæstrəfi] s catastrophe f

cat′call′ s huée f; (theat) coup m de sifflet ‖ tr & intr (theat) siffler

catch [kætʃ] s prise f; (on door) loquet m; (on buckle) ardillon m; (caught by fisherman) pêche f; (mach) cliquet m, chien m; **there's a catch to it** (coll) c'est une attrape ‖ v (pret & pp caught [kɔt]) tr attraper; (a train; a fish; fire) prendre; (a word or sound) saisir; (e.g., one's coat) accrocher; **caught like a rat in a trap** fait comme un rat; **to catch hold of** saisir, s'accrocher à; **to catch s.o. in the act** prendre qn sur le fait; **to catch up** (in a mistake) surprendre ‖ intr prendre; (said of fire) s'allumer, s'enflammer, se prendre; **to catch on** (a nail, thorn, etc.) s'accrocher à; (to understand) (coll) comprendre; (to become popular) (coll) devenir célèbre, devenir populaire; **to catch up** se rattraper; **to catch up with** rattraper

catch′all′ s débarras m, fourre-tout m

catching [′kætʃɪŋ] adj contagieux; (e.g., smile) communicatif

catch′ ques′tion s (coll) colle f

catch′word′ s mot m de ralliement, slogan m; (cliché) rengaine f, scie f; (at the bottom of page) réclame f; (theat) réplique f; (typ) mot-souche m

catch·y [′kætʃi] adj (comp -ier; super -iest) (tune) facile à retenir, entraînant; (question) insidieux, à traquenard

catechism [′kætɪˌkɪzəm] s catéchisme m

categorical [ˌkætɪˈɡɑrɪkəl], [ˌkætɪˈɡɔrɪkəl] *adj* catégorique

catego·ry [ˈkætɪˌɡori] *s* (*pl* -ries) catégorie *f*

cater [ˈketər] *tr* (e.g., *a wedding*) fournir le buffet de ‖ *intr* être fournisseur; **to cater to** pourvoir à; (*to favor*) entourer de prévenances

cat'er-cor'nered [ˈkætərˌkɔrnərd] *adj* diagonal ‖ *adv* diagonalement

caterer [ˈketərər] *s* fournisseur *m*, traiteur *m*

caterpillar [ˈkætərˌpɪlər] *s* chenille *f*

cat'erpillar trac'tor *s* autochenille *f*

cat'fish' *s* poisson-chat *m*

cat'gut' *s* boyau *m* de chat; (*string*) corde *f* à boyau, boyau; (*surg*) cat-gut *m*

cathedral [kəˈθidrəl] *s* cathédrale *f*

catheter [ˈkæθɪtər] *s* (med) cathéter *m*

catheterization [ˌkæθɪtərɪˈzeʃən] *s* (surg) cathétérisme *m*

cathode [ˈkæθod] *s* cathode *m*

catholic [ˈkæθəlɪk] *adj* (*universal*) catholique; tolérant, large, e.g., **he has a catholic mind** il a l'esprit large, il est fort tolérant ‖ (*cap*) *adj & s* catholique *m*

Catholicism [kəˈθɑlɪˌsɪzəm] *s* catholicisme *m*

catholicity [ˌkæθəˈlɪsɪti] *s* catholicité *f*, universalité *f*; (*tolerance*) largeur *f* d'esprit, tolérance *f*

catkin [ˈkætkɪn] *s* (bot) chaton *m*

cat'nap' *s* petit somme *m*

cat'nip *s* herbe-aux-chats *f*, cataire *f*

cat-o'-nine-tails [ˈkætəˈnaɪnˌtelz] *s* chat *m* à neuf queues

cat's'-paw' *s* (naut) risée *f*; (coll) dupe *f*

catsup [ˈkætsəp], [ˈketʃəp] *s* sauce *f* tomate

cattle [ˈkætəl] *s* bœufs *mpl*; (*including horses*) gros bétail *m*, bestiaux *mpl*

cat'tle car' *s* fourgon *m* à bestiaux

cat'tle cross'ing *s* passage *m* de troupeaux

cat'tle·man *s* (*pl* -men) éleveur *m* de bétail

cat'tle thief' *s* voleur *m* de bétail

cat·ty [ˈkæti] *adj* (*comp* -tier; *super* -tiest) (coll) cancanier, méchant

cat'ty-cor'ner *adj* (coll) diagonal ‖ *adv* (coll) diagonalement

cat'walk' *s* passerelle *f*

Caucasian [kɔˈkeʒən], [kɔˈkeʃən] *adj* caucasien ‖ *s* Caucasien *m*

caucus [ˈkɔkəs] *s* comité *m* électoral ‖ *intr* se grouper en comité électoral

cauliflower [ˈkɔlɪˌflauˌər] *s* chou-fleur *m*

caulk [kɔk] *tr* calfater

cause [kɔz] *s* cause *f*; **to have cause to** avoir lieu de ‖ *tr* causer; **to cause to** + *inf* faire + *inf*, e.g., **he caused him to stumble** il l'a fait trébucher

cause'way' *s* chaussée *f*

caustic [ˈkɔstɪk] *adj* caustique

cauterize [ˈkɔtəˌraɪz] *tr* cautériser

caution [ˈkɔʃən] *s* prudence *f*, précaution *f*; (*warning*) avertissement *m* ‖ *tr* mettre en garde, avertir

cautious [ˈkɔʃəs] *adj* prudent, circonspect

cavalcade [ˌkævəlˈked], [ˈkævəlˌked] *s* cavalcade *f*

cavalier [ˌkævəˈlɪr] *adj & s* cavalier *m*

caval·ry [ˈkævəlri] *s* (*pl* -ries) cavalerie *f*

cav'alry·man or **cav'alry·man** *s* (*pl* -men or -men) cavalier *m*

cave [kev] *s* caverne *f* ‖ *intr*—**to cave in** s'effondrer

cave'-in' *s* effondrement *m*

cavern [ˈkævərn] *s* caverne *f*

caviar [ˈkævɪˌɑr], [ˈkɑvɪˌɑr] *s* caviar *m*

cav·il [ˈkævɪl] *v* (*pret & pp* -iled or -illed; *ger* -iling or -illing) *intr* ergoter, chicaner

cavi·ty [ˈkævɪti] *s* (*pl* -ties) cavité *f*

cavort [kəˈvɔrt] *intr* gambader, caracoler

caw [kɔ] *s* croassement *m* ‖ *intr* croasser, crailler

cease [sis] *s* cessation *f*; **without cease** sans cesse ‖ *tr & intr* cesser; **to cease fire** cesser le feu

cease'-fire' *s* cessez-le-feu *m*

ceaseless [ˈsislɪs] *adj* incessant, continuel

cedar [ˈsidər] *s* cèdre *m*

cede [sid] *tr & intr* céder

cedilla [sɪˈdɪlə] *s* cédille *f*

ceiling [ˈsilɪŋ] *s* plafond *m*; **to hit the ceiling** (coll) sortir de ses gonds

ceil'ing lamp' *s* plafonnier *m*

ceil'ing price' *s* prix *m* maximum

celebrant [ˈsɛlɪbrənt] *s* (eccl) célébrant *m*

celebrate [ˈsɛlɪˌbret] *tr* célébrer

celebrated *adj* célèbre

celebration [ˌsɛlɪˈbreʃən] *s* célébration *f*, fête *f*

celebri·ty [sɪˈlɛbrɪti] *s* (*pl* -ties) célébrité *f*; (e.g., *movie star*) vedette *f*

celery [ˈsɛləri] *s* céleri *m*

celestial [sɪˈlɛstʃəl] *adj* céleste

celiba·cy [ˈsɛlɪbəsi] *s* (*pl* -cies) célibat *m*

celibate [ˈsɛliˌbet], [ˈsɛlɪbɪt] *adj & s* célibataire *mf*

cell [sɛl] *s* cellule *f*; (*of electric battery*) élément *m*

cellar [ˈsɛlər] *s* (*basement; wine cellar*) cave *f*; (*often partly above ground*) sous-sol *m*

cellist or **'cellist** [ˈtʃɛlɪst] *s* violoncelliste *mf*

cel·lo or **'cel·lo** [ˈtʃɛlo] *s* (*pl* -los) violoncelle *m*

cellophane [ˈsɛləˌfɛn] *s* cellophane *f*

celluloid [ˈsɛljəˌlɔɪd] *s* celluloïd *m*

Celt [sɛlt], [kɛlt] *s* Celte *mf*

Celtic [ˈsɛltɪk], [ˈkɛltɪk] *adj* celte, celtique ‖ *s* celtique *m*

cement [sɪˈmɛnt] *s* ciment *m* ‖ *tr* cimenter

cement' mix'er *s* bétonnière *f*

cemeter·y [ˈsɛmɪˌtɛri] *s* (*pl* -ies) cimetière *m*

censer [ˈsɛnsər] *s* encensoir *m*

censor [ˈsɛnsər] *s* censeur *m* ‖ *tr* censurer

cen·sor·ship ['sen(ər)] s censure f
censure ['sen(ər)] s blâme m || tr blâmer
census ['sensəs] s recensement m, dénombrement m; (in Roman Empire)
cens m
cen'sus tak'er s recenseur m; (in ancient Rome) censeur m
cent [sent] s cent m; not to have a red
cent to one's name n'avoir pas un
sou vaillant
centaur ['sentər] s centaure m
centenarian [,sentɪ'nerɪ·ən] s centenaire mf
centennial [sen'tenɪ·əl] adj centennal ||
s centenaire m
center ['sentər] s central m; centre
m; (middle) milieu m || tr centrer
|| intr—to center on concentrer sur
centering ['sentərɪŋ] s centrage m;
(phot) cadrage m
cen'ter·piece' s surtout m; milieu m de
table
centigrade ['sentɪ,gred] adj & s centigrade m
centimeter ['sentɪ,mitər] s centimètre
m
centipede ['sentɪ,pid] s mille-pattes m,
myriapodes mpl
central ['sentrəl] adj & s central m
Cen'tral Amer'ica s l'Amérique f centrale
Cen'tral Intel'ligence s la Sûreté, la
Sûreté nationale
centralize ['sentrə,laɪz] tr centraliser ||
intr se centraliser
centrifugal [sen'trɪfjʊgəl] adj centrifuge
centrifuge ['sentrɪ,fjudʒ] s essoreuse f
|| tr essorer
centu·ry ['sentʃəri] s (pl -ries) siècle m
cen'tury-old' adj séculaire
ceramic [sɪ'ræmɪk] adj céramique ||
ceramics (art) céramique f; spl (objects) céramiques
cereal ['sɪrɪ·əl] adj céréalier || s (grain)
céréale f; (oatmeal) flocons mpl
d'avoine; (cornflakes) flocons de
maïs; (cooked cereal) bouillie f,
gruau m
cerebral ['serɪbrəl] adj cérébral
ceremonial [,serɪ'monɪ·əl] adj cérémo-
nial; (e.g., tribal rites) cérémoniel ||
s cérémonial m
ceremonious [,serɪ'monɪ·əs] adj cérémonieux
ceremo·ny ['serɪ,moni] s (pl -nies)
cérémonie f; to stand on ceremony
faire des cérémonies
certain ['sʌrtən] adj certain; a certain
certain; certain people certains; for
certain pour sûr, à coup sûr; to make
certain of s'assurer de
certainly ['sʌrtənli] adv certainement
certain·ty ['sʌrtənti] s (pl -ties) certitude f
certificate [sər'tɪfɪkɪt] s certificat m;
(of birth, of marriage, etc.) bulletin
m, acte m, extrait m; (proof) attestation f
cer'tified cop'y s extrait m; (formula
used on documents) pour copie conforme

cer'tified pub'lic account'ant s expert-
comptable m, comptable m agréé
certi·fy ['sʌrtɪ,faɪ] v (pret & pp -fied)
tr certifier
cervix ['sʌrvɪks] s (pl cervices [sər-
'vaɪsɪz]) nuque f
cessation [se'seʃən] s cessation f, cesse f
cesspool ['ses,pul] s fosse f d'aisance,
cloaque m
Ceylon [sɪ'lɑn] s Ceylan m
Ceylo·nese [,sɪlə'niz] adj cingalais || s
(pl -nese) Cingalais m
chafe [tʃef] tr écorcher, irriter || intr
s'écorcher, s'irriter
chaff [tʃæf], [tʃɑf] s balle f; (banter)
raillerie f || tr railler, persifler
chaf'ing dish' s réchaud m de table,
chauffe-plats m
chagrin [ʃə'grɪn] s mortification f,
humiliation f || tr mortifier, humilier
chain [tʃen] s chaîne f || tr enchaîner
chain' gang' s forçats mpl à la chaîne
chain' reac'tion s (phys) réaction f en
chaîne
chain' smok'er s fumeur m à la file
chain'stitch' s point m de chaînette
chain' store' s magasin m à succursales
multiples, économat m
chair [tʃer] s chaise f; (held by university professor) chaire f; (of presiding officer; presiding officer himself) fauteuil m; to take a chair prendre un siège, s'asseoir; to take the
chair occuper le fauteuil, présider une
assemblée || tr présider
chair' lift' s télé-siège m
chair'man s (pl -men) président m
chair'man·ship' s présidence f
chair'wom'an s (pl -wom'en) présidente f
chalice ['tʃælɪs] s calice m
chalk [tʃɔk] s craie f; a piece of chalk
une craie, un morceau de craie || tr
marquer avec de la craie, écrire à la
craie
chalk·y ['tʃɔki] adj (comp -ier; super
-iest) crayeux
challenge ['tʃælɪndʒ] s défi m; (objection) contestation f; (mil) qui-vive
m; (sports) challenge m || tr défier;
(to question) mettre en question, contester; (mil) crier qui-vive
chamber ['tʃembər] s chambre f
chamberlain ['tʃembərlɪn] s chambellan m
cham'ber·maid' s femme f de chambre
cham'ber mu'sic s musique f de chambre
Cham'ber of Com'merce s syndicat m
d'initiative
chameleon [kə'milɪ·ən] s caméléon m
chamfer ['tʃæmfər] s chanfrein m || tr
chanfreiner
cham·ois ['ʃæmi] s (pl -ois) chamois m
champ [tʃæmp] s mâchonnement m ||
tr mâcher bruyamment; to champ the
bit ronger le frein
champagne [ʃæm'pen] s champagne m
|| (cap) adj champenois || (cap) s
Champagne f; la Champagne
champion ['tʃæmpɪ·ən] s champion m
|| tr se faire le champion de, défendre

cham/pion·ship/ s championnat m
chance [tʃæns], [tʃɑns] adj fortuit, de rencontre || s hasard m; risque m; (opportunity) occasion f; **by chance** par hasard, fortuitement; **chances** chances fpl, sort m; **to take a chance** encourir un risque; acheter un billet de loterie; **to take chances** jouer gros jeu || tr hasarder, risquer || intr—**to chance** to venir à, avoir l'occasion de; **to chance upon** rencontrer par hasard
chancel [ˈtʃænsəl], [ˈtʃɑnsəl] s chœur m, sanctuaire m
chanceller·y [ˈtʃænsələri], [ˈtʃɑnsələri] s (pl -ies) chancellerie f
chancellor [ˈtʃænsələr], [ˈtʃɑnsələr] s chancelier m, ministre m
chancre [ˈʃæŋkər] s chancre m
chandelier [ˌʃændəˈlɪr] s lustre m
change [tʃendʒ] s changement m; (coins) monnaie f; **change in the wind** saute f de vent; **change of address** changement de domicile; **change of clothes** vêtements mpl de rechange; **for a change** comme distraction; pour changer || tr changer; changer de, e.g., **to change religions** changer de culte; **to change sides** tourner casaque || intr changer; (said of voice at puberty) muer; **to change over** (e.g., from one system to another) passer
changeable [ˈtʃendʒəbəl] adj changeable; (weather) variable; (character) changeant, mobile
changeless [ˈtʃendʒlɪs] adj immuable
change/ of life/ s retour m d'âge
change/ of voice/ s mue f
change/o/ver s changement m, renversement m, relève f
change/ purse/ s porte-monnaie m
chan·nel [ˈtʃænəl] s (body of water joining two others) canal m; (bed of river) chenal m; (means of communication) voie f, canal; (passage) conduit m; (groove) cannelure f; (strait) bras m de mer; (for trade) débouché m; (rad) canal; (rad, telv) chaîne f; (telv) canal (Canad); **through channels** par la voie hiérarchique || v (pret & pp -neled or -nelled; ger -neling or -nelling) tr creuser, canneler
Chan/nel Is/lands spl îles fpl Anglo-Normandes
chant [tʃænt], [tʃɑnt] s chant m; (song sung in a monotone) plain-chant m, psalmodie f || tr & intr psalmodier
chanter [ˈtʃæntər], [ˈtʃɑntər] s chantre m
chantey [ˈʃænti], [ˈtʃænti] s chanson f de bord
chaos [ˈke·ɑs] s chaos m
chaotic [keˈɑtɪk] adj chaotique
chap [tʃæp] s crevasse f, gerçure f; (coll) type m, individu m || v (pret & pp chapped; ger chapping) tr crevasser, gercer || intr se crevasser, se gercer
chapel [ˈtʃæpəl] s chapelle f; (in a house) oratoire m; (Protestant chapel) temple m

chaperon [ˈʃæpəˌron] s chaperon m, duègne f || tr chaperonner
chaplain [ˈtʃæplɪn] s aumônier m
chaplet [ˈtʃæplɪt] s chapelet m
chapter [ˈtʃæptər] s chapitre m; (of an association) bureau m régional
char [tʃɑr] v (pret & pp charred; ger charring) tr & intr charbonner; **to become charred** se charbonner, se carboniser
character [ˈkærɪktər] s caractère m; (theat) personnage m; (coll) type m, sujet m
char/acter ac/tor s acteur m de genre
characteristic [ˌkærɪktəˈrɪstɪk] adj & s caractéristique f
characterize [ˈkærɪktəˌraɪz] tr caractériser
char/acter ref/erence s certificat m de moralité
char/coal/ s charbon m de bois
char/coal burn/er s charbonnier m
char/coal pen/cil s charbon m, crayon m de fusain
charge [tʃɑrdʒ] s charge f; prix m; (against a defendant) chef m d'accusation; (made to a jury) résumé m; **on a charge of** sous l'inculpation de; **to reverse the charges** téléphoner en p.c.v.; **to take charge of** se charger de; **without charge** gratis || tr charger; **to charge s.o. s.th. for s.th.** prendre or demander q.ch. à qn pour q.ch.; **to charge to s.o.'s account** mettre sur le compte de qn || intr (mil) charger; **to charge down on** foncer sur
charge/ account/ s compte m courant
charger [ˈtʃɑrdʒər] s cheval m de bataille; (elec) chargeur m
chariot [ˈtʃærɪ·ət] s char m
charitable [ˈtʃærɪtəbəl] adj charitable
char·i·ty [ˈtʃærɪti] s (pl -ties) charité f; (alms) bienfaisance f, aumônes fpl; (institution) société f or œuvre f de bienfaisance; **for charity's sake** par charité
charlatan [ˈʃɑrlətən] s charlatan m
charm [tʃɑrm] s charme m; (e.g., on a bracelet) breloque f, porte-bonheur m || tr charmer
charming [ˈtʃɑrmɪŋ] adj charmeur, charmant
charnel [ˈtʃɑrnəl] adj de charnier || s charnier m, ossuaire m
chart [tʃɑrt] s (map) carte f; (graph) dessin m graphique; (diagram) diagramme m; (table) tableau m || tr inscrire sur un dessin graphique; (naut) porter sur une carte, dresser la carte de
charter [ˈtʃɑrtər] s charte f; (of bank) privilège m; (naut) affrètement m || tr accorder une charte à; (a ship) affréter, noliser; (a bus) louer
char/ter mem/ber s membre m fondateur
char/wom/an s (pl -wom/en) nettoyeuse f

chase [tʃes] s chasse f, poursuite f; (for printing) châssis m ‖ tr chasser; (a gem) enchâsser; (gold) ciseler; (metal) repousser; **to chase away** chasser ‖ intr—**to chase after** pourchasser, poursuivre

chaser ['tʃesər] s chasseur m; (of women) (coll) coureur m; (taken after an alcoholic drink) (coll) rince-gueule m

chasm ['kæzəm] s abîme m

chas·sis ['tʃæsi] s (pl -sis [siz]) châssis m

chaste [tʃest] adj chaste

chasten ['tʃesən] tr châtier

chastise [tʃæs'taɪz] tr châtier, corriger

chastisement ['tʃæstɪzmənt], [tʃæs-'taɪzmənt] s châtiment m

chastity ['tʃæstɪti] s chasteté f

chat [tʃæt] s causerie f, causette f ‖ v (pret & pp chatted; ger chatting) intr causer, bavarder

chattel ['tʃætəl] s bien m meuble, objet m mobiliaire

chatter ['tʃætər] s bavardage m, caquetage m ‖ intr bavarder, caqueter; (said of teeth) claquer

chat·ter·box s bavard m, babillard m

chauffeur ['ʃofər], [ʃo'fʌr] s chauffeur m

chauvinistic [ˌʃovɪ'nɪstɪk] adj chauvin

cheap [tʃip] adj bon marché; (coll) honteux; **to get off cheap** (coll) en être quitte à bon compte

cheapen ['tʃipən] tr baisser le prix de; diminuer la valeur de

cheap/skate/ s (slang) rat m

cheat [tʃit] s tricheur m, fraudeur m ‖ tr tricher, frauder ‖ intr (e.g., at cards) tricher; (e.g., in an examination) frauder

cheating ['tʃitɪŋ] s tricherie f, fraude f

check [tʃek] s (stopping) arrêt m; (brake) frein m; (supervision) contrôle m, vérification f; (in a restaurant) addition f; (drawn on a bank) chèque m; (e.g., of a chessboard) carreau m; (of the king in chess) échec m; (for baggage) bulletin m; (pass-out check) contremarque f; (chip, counter) jeton m; **in check** en échec ‖ tr arrêter, freiner; contrôler, vérifier; (baggage) faire enregistrer; (e.g., one's coat) mettre au vestiaire; (the king in chess) faire échec à; **to check off** pointer, cocher ‖ intr s'arrêter; **to check in** (at a hotel) s'inscrire sur le registre; **to check out** (of a hotel) régler sa note; **to check up on** contrôler, examiner

check/book/ s carnet m de chèques, chéquier m

checked adj (checkered) à carreaux; (syllable) entravé

checker ['tʃekər] s (inspector) contrôleur m; (piece used in game) pion m; (square of checkerboard) carreau m; **checkers** jeu m de dames ‖ tr quadriller; (to divide in squares) quadriller; (to scatter here and there) diaprer

check/er·board/ s damier m

checkered adj (divided into squares) quadrillé, à carreaux; (varied) varié, accidenté; (career, life) plein de vicissitudes, mouvementé

check/ girl/ s préposée f au vestiaire

check/ing account/ s compte m en banque

check/ list/ s liste f de contrôle

check/ mark/ s trait m de repère, repère m, coche f

check/mate/ s échec et mat m; (fig) échec m ‖ tr faire échec et mat à, mater ‖ intr faire échec et mat, mater ‖ interj échec et mat!

check/-out count/er s caisse f de supermarché

check/point/ s contrôle m de police

check/room/ s (cloakroom) vestiaire m; (baggage room) consigne f

check/up/ s vérification f, examen m

cheek [tʃik] s joue f; (coll) aplomb m, toupet m

cheek/bone/ s pommette f

cheep [tʃip] intr piauler

cheer [tʃɪr] s bonne humeur f, gaieté f; encouragement m, e.g., **word of cheer** parole f d'encouragement; **cheers** acclamations fpl, bravos mpl, vivats mpl; **three cheers for ...!** vive ...!; **to give three cheers** pousser trois hourras ‖ tr (to cheer up) encourager, égayer; (to applaud) acclamer, applaudir ‖ intr pousser les vivats, applaudir; **cheer up!** courage!

cheerful ['tʃɪrfəl] adj de bonne humeur, gai; (place) d'aspect agréable

cheerfully ['tʃɪrfəli] adv gaiement; (willingly) de bon cœur

cheer/lead/er s chef m de claque

cheerless ['tʃɪrlɪs] adj morne, triste

cheese [tʃiz] s fromage m ‖ tr—**cheese it, the cops!** (slang) vingt-deux, les flics!

cheese/cake/ s (slang) les pin up fpl

cheese/ cake/ s soufflé m au fromage, tarte f au fromage

cheese/cloth/ s gaze f

chees·y ['tʃizi] adj (comp -ier; super -iest) caséeux; (slang) miteux

cheetah ['tʃita] s guépard m

chef [ʃef] s chef m de cuisine, maître queux m

chemical ['kemɪkəl] adj chimique ‖ s produit m chimique

chemist ['kemɪst] s chimiste mf

chemistry ['kemɪstri] s chimie f

cherish ['tʃerɪʃ] tr chérir; (an idea) nourrir; (a hope) caresser

cher·ry ['tʃeri] s (pl -ries) cerise f; (tree) cerisier m

cher/ry or/chard s cerisaie f

cher/ry tree/ s cerisier m

cher·ub ['tʃerəb] s (pl -ubim [əbɪm]) chérubin m ‖ s (pl -ubs) (fig) chérubin m

chess [tʃes] s échecs mpl; **to play chess** jouer aux échecs

chess/board/ s échiquier m

chess/man/ s (pl -men/) pièce f du jeu d'échecs

chess/ set/ s échecs mpl

chest [tʃest] s caisse f; (of drawers)

commode *f*; (anat) poitrine *f*; **to get s.th. off one's chest** (coll) se déboutonner, dire ce qu'on a sur le cœur

chestnut ['tʃɛsnət] *adj (color)* châtain ‖ *s (color)* châtain *m*; *(nut)* châtaigne *f*; *(tree)* châtaignier *m*

chest' of drawers' *s* commode *f*, chiffonnier *m*

cheval' glass' [ʃə'væl] *s* psyché *f*

chevron ['ʃɛvrən] *s* chevron *m*

chew [tʃu] *tr* mâcher; *(tobacco)* chiquer

chewing ['tʃu·ɪŋ] *s* mastication *f*

chew'ing gum' *s* gomme *f* à mâcher, chewing-gum *m*

chicaner·y [ʃɪ'kenəri] *s (pl -ies)* truc *m*, ruse *f*, artifice *m*

chick [tʃɪk] *s* poussin *m*; *(girl)* (slang) tendron *m*

chickadee ['tʃɪkə‚di] *s (Parus atricapillus)* mésange *f* boréale

chicken ['tʃɪkən] *s* poulet *m*; **to be chicken** (slang) avoir la frousse ‖ *intr*—**to chicken out** (slang) caner

chick'en coop' *s* poulailler *m*

chick'en-heart'ed *adj* froussard, poltron

chick'en pox' *s* varicelle *f*

chick'en stew' *s* poule-au-pot *m*

chick'en wire' *s* treillis *m* métallique

chick'pea' *s* pois *m* chiche

chico·ry ['tʃɪkəri] *s (pl -ries)* chicorée *f*

chide [tʃaɪd] *v (pret* **chided** *or* **chid** [tʃɪd]; *pp* **chided, chid,** *or* **chidden** ['tʃɪdən]) *tr & intr* gronder

chief [tʃif] *adj* principal, en chef ‖ *s* chef *m*; *(boss)* (coll) patron *m*

chief' exec'utive *s* chef de l'exécutif

chief' jus'tice *s* président *m* de la Cour suprême

chiefly ['tʃifli] *adv* principalement

chief' of police' *s* préfet de police

chief' of staff' *s* chef de d'état-major

chief' of state' *s* chef *m* d'État

chieftain ['tʃiftən] *s* chef *m*

chiffon [ʃɪ'fɑn] *s* mousseline *f* de soie

chiffonier [‚ʃɪfə'nɪr] *s* chiffonnier *m*

chilblain ['tʃɪl‚blen] *s* engelure *f*

child [tʃaɪld] *s (pl* **children** ['tʃɪldrən]) enfant *mf*; **with child** enceinte

child'birth' *s* accouchement *m*

child'hood' *s* enfance *f*

childish ['tʃaɪldɪʃ] *adj* enfantin, puéril

child'like' *adj* enfantin, d'enfant

child' la'bor *s* travail *m* des enfants

child's' play' *s* jeu *m* d'enfant; **it's child's play** c'est l'enfance de l'art

child' wel'fare *s* protection *f* de l'enfance

Chile ['tʃɪli] *s* le Chili

chili pep'per ['tʃɪli] *s* piment *m*

chill [tʃɪl] *adj & s* froid *m*; **sudden chill** saisissement *m*, coup *m* de froid; **to take the chill off** faire tiédir ‖ *tr* refroidir; *(a person)* transir, faire frissonner; *(wine)* frapper

chill·y ['tʃɪli] *adj (comp* **-ier;** *super* **-iest)** froid; *(sensitive to cold)* frileux; **it is chilly** il fait frisquet

chime [tʃaɪm] *s* coup *m* de son; **chimes** *(at doorway)* sonnerie *f*; *(in bell tower)* carillon *m* ‖ *tr & intr* carillonner

chimera [kaɪ'mɪrə], [kɪ'mɪrə] *s* chimère *f*

chiming ['tʃaɪmɪŋ] *s* carillonnement *m*, sonnerie *f*

chimney ['tʃɪmni] *s* cheminée *f*; *(of lamp)* verre *m*

chim'ney pot' *s* abat-vent *m*, mitre *f*

chim'ney sweep' *s* ramoneur *m*

chimpanzee [tʃɪm'pænzi], [‚tʃɪmpæn-'zi] *s* chimpanzé *m*

chin [tʃɪn] *s* menton *m*

china ['tʃaɪnə] *s* porcelaine *f* de Chine; **China** Chine *f*; la Chine

chi'na clos'et *s* vitrine *f*

chi'na·ware' *s* porcelaine *f*

Chi·nese [tʃaɪ'niz] *adj*—chinois ‖ *s (language)* chinois *m* ‖ *s (pl -nese)* Chinois *m (person)*

Chi'nese lan'tern *s* lanterne *f* vénitienne, lampion *m*

chink [tʃɪŋk] *s* fente *f*, crevasse *f*; **chink in one's armor** (coll) défaut *m* de la cuirasse

chin' strap' *s* sous-mentonnière *f*, jugulaire *f*

chip [tʃɪp] *s* copeau *m*, éclat *m*; *(in gambling)* jeton *m*; **to be a chip off the old block** (coll) chasser de race, être un rejeton de la vieille souche ‖ *v (pret & pp* **chipped;** *ger* **chipping)** *tr* enlever un copeau à ‖ *intr* s'écailler; **to chip in** contribuer

chipmunk ['tʃɪp‚mʌŋk] *s* tamias *m* rayé

chipper ['tʃɪpər] *adj* (coll) en forme, guilleret

chiropodist [kaɪ'rɑpədɪst], [kɪ'rɑpə-dɪst] *s* pédicure *mf*

chiropractor ['kaɪrə‚præktər] *s* chiropracteur *m*

chirp [tʃʌrp] *s* gazouillis *m*, pépiement *m* ‖ *intr* gazouiller, pépier

chis·el ['tʃɪzəl] *s* ciseau *m* ‖ *v (pret & pp* **-eled** *or* **-elled;** *ger* **-eling** *or* **-el-ling)** *tr* ciseler; *(a person)* (slang) escroquer; **to chisel s.o. out of s.th.** (slang) escroquer q.ch. à qn

chiseler ['tʃɪzələr] *s* ciseleur *m*; (slang) escroc *m*

chit [tʃɪt] *s* note *f*, ticket *m*; (coll) gamin *m*

chit'-chat' *s* bavardage *m*

chivalrous ['ʃɪvəlrəs] *adj* honorable, courtois; *(lit)* chevaleresque

chivalry ['ʃɪvəlri] *s (of Middle Ages)* chevalerie *f*; *(politeness)* courtoisie *f*, galanterie *f*

chive [tʃaɪv] *s* ciboulette *f*, civette *f*

chloride ['klɔraɪd] *s* chlorure *m*

chlorinate ['klɔrɪ‚net] *tr (water)* verduniser

chlorination [‚klɔrɪ'neʃən] *s* verdunisation *f*

chlorine ['klɔrin] *s* chlore *m*

chloroform ['klɔrə‚fɔrm] *s* chloroforme *m* ‖ *tr* chloroformer

chlorophyll ['klɔrəfɪl] *s* chlorophylle *f*

chock [tʃɑk] *s* cale *f*; (naut) poulie *f* ‖ *tr* caler

chock'-full' *adj* bondé, comble, bourré

chocolate ['tʃɔkəlɪt], ['tʃɑkəlɪt] *adj & s* chocolat *m*

choc′olate bar′ *s* tablette *f* de chocolat
choice [tʃɔɪs] *adj* de choix, choisi ‖ *m* choix *m*; **by choice** par goût, volontairement
choir [kwaɪr] *s* chœur *m*
choir′boy′ *s* enfant *m* de chœur
choir′mas′ter *s* chef *m* de chœur; (eccl) maître *m* de chapelle
choir′ robe′ *s* soutanelle *f*
choke [tʃok] *s* (aut) starter *m* ‖ *tr* étouffer; (*to obstruct*) obstruer, boucher; **to choke back, down,** or **off** étouffer; **to choke up** obstruer, engorger ‖ *intr* étouffer; **to choke up** (*e.g., with tears*) étouffer
choke′ coil′ *s* (elec) bobine *f* de réactance
choker [′tʃokər] *s* (*scarf*) foulard *m*; (*necklace*) collier *m* court
choking [′tʃokɪŋ] *s* étouffement *m*
cholera [′kɑlərə] *s* choléra *m*
choleric [′kɑlərɪk] *adj* coléreux
cholesterol [kə′lɛstə‚rol], [kə′lɛstə‚rɑl] *s* cholestérol *m*
choose [tʃuz] *v* (*pret* chose [tʃoz]; *pp* chosen [′tʃozən]) *tr* & *intr* choisir
choos·y [′tʃuzi] *adj* (*comp* -ier; *super* -iest) (coll) difficile à plaire, chipoteur
chop [tʃɑp] *s* coup *m* de hache; (culin) côtelette *f*; **to lick one's chops** (coll) se lécher or s'essuyer les babines ‖ *v* (*pret* & *pp* chopped; *ger* chopping) *tr* hacher, couper; **to chop down** abattre; **to chop off** trancher, couper; **to chop up** couper en morceaux, hacher ‖ *intr* (*said of waves*) clapoter
chopper [′tʃɑpər] *s* (*of butcher*) couperet *m*; (coll) hélicoptère *m*; **choppers** (slang) les dents *fpl*
chop′ping block′ *s* billot *m*, hachoir *m*
chop·py [′tʃɑpi] *adj* (*comp* -pier; *ger* -piest) agité; (*waves*) clapoteux
chop′stick′ *s* baguette *f*, bâtonnet *m*
choral [′korəl] *adj* choral
chorale [ko′rɑl] *s* choral *m*
cho′ral soci′ety *s* chorale *f*
chord [tʃord] *s* accord *m*; (geom) corde *f*
chore [tʃor] *s* devoir *m*; (*burdensome chore*) corvée *f*, besogne *f*
choreography [‚korɪ′ɑgrəfi] *s* chorégraphie *f*
chorister [′kɑrɪstər], [′kɔrɪstər] *s* choriste *mf*
chortle [′tʃortəl] *intr* glousser
chorus [′korəs] *s* chœur *m*, chorale *f*; (*of song*) refrain *m*; (*of protest*) concert *m* ‖ *tr* répéter en chœur, faire chorus
cho′rus boy′ *s* boy *m*
cho′rus girl′ *s* girl *m*
cho′sen few′ [′tʃozən] *s* élite *f*
chow [tʃaʊ] *s* (*dog*) chow-chow *m*; (mil) boustifaille *f*, mangeaille *f*
chow′-chow′ *s* (culin) macédoine *f* assaisonnée
chowder [′tʃaʊdər] *s* soupe *f* au poisson
Christ [kraɪst] *s* Christ *m*; le Christ
christen [′krɪsən] *tr* baptiser
Christendom [′krɪsəndəm] *s* chrétienté *f*

christening [′krɪsənɪŋ] *s* baptême *m*
Christian [′krɪstʃən] *adj* & *s* chrétien *m*
Christianity [‚krɪstʃɪ′æniti] *s* christianisme *m*
Christianize [′krɪstʃə‚naɪz] *tr* christianiser
Christ′ian name′ *s* nom *m* de baptême
Christmas [′krɪsməs] *adj* de Noël ‖ *s* Noël *m*; **Merry Christmas!** Joyeux Noël!
Christ′mas card′ *s* carte *f* de Noël
Christ′mas car′ol *s* chanson *f* de Noël, chant *m* de Noël; (eccl) cantique *m* de Noël
Christ′mas Day′ *s* le jour de Noël
Christ′mas Eve′ *s* la veille de Noël
Christ′mas gift′ *s* cadeau *m* de Noël
Christ′mas tree′ *s* arbre *m* de Noël
Christ′mas tree lights′ *spl* guirlandes *fpl*
chromatic [kro′mætɪk] *adj* chromatique
chrome [krom] *adj* acier *m* chromé; (*color*) jaune *m*; (chem) chrome *m* ‖ *tr* chromer
chromium [′kromɪəm] *s* chrome *m*
chromosome [′kromə‚som] *s* chromosome *m*
chronic [′krɑnɪk] *adj* chronique
chronicle [′krɑnɪkəl] *s* chronique *f* ‖ *tr* faire la chronique de
chronicler [′krɑnɪklər] *s* chroniqueur *m*
chronologic(al) [‚krɑnə′lɑdʒɪk(əl)] *adj* chronologique
chronolo·gy [krə′nɑlədʒi] *s* (*pl* -gies) chronologie *f*
chronometer [krə′nɑmɪtər] *s* chronomètre *m*
chrysanthemum [krɪ′sænθɪməm] *s* chrysanthème *m*
chub·by [′tʃʌbi] *adj* (*comp* -bier; *super* -biest) joufflu, potelé, dodu
chuck [tʃʌk] *s* (*tap, blow, etc.*) petite tape *f*; (*under the chin*) caresse *f* sous le menton; (*of lathe*) mandrin *m*; (*bottom chuck and chuck rib*) paleron *m*; (*top chuck roast and chuck rib*) entrecôte *f* ‖ *tr* tapoter; **to chuck away** jeter
chuckle [′tʃʌkəl] *s* gloussement *m*, petit rire *m* ‖ *intr* glousser, rire tout bas
chum [tʃʌm] *s* (coll) copain *m* ‖ *v* (*pret* & *pp* chummed; *ger* chumming) *intr*—**to chum around with** (coll) fraterniser avec
chum·my [′tʃʌmi] *adj* (*comp* -mier; *super* -miest) intime, familier
chump [tʃʌmp] *s* (slang) ballot *m*, lourdaud *m*
chunk [tʃʌŋk] *s* gros morceau *m*; (*e.g., of wood*) bloc *m*
church [tʃɑrtʃ] *s* église *f*
church′go′er *s* pratiquant *m*
church′man *s* (*pl* -men) (*clergyman*) ecclésiastique *m*; (*layman*) membre *m* d'une église, fidèle *mf*, paroissien *m*
church′ mem′ber *s* fidèle *mf*
church′ ser′vice *s* office *m*, culte *m*
church′yard′ *s* cimetière *m*
churlish [′tʃɑrlɪʃ] *adj* rustre, grossier; (*out of sorts*) grincheux
churn [tʃɑrn] *s* baratte *f* ‖ *tr* (*cream*)

baratter; (e.g., water) agiter; **to churn butter** battre le beurre || intr bouillonner

chute [ʃut] s glissière f; parachute m; (of river) rapide m, chute f d'eau

Cicero ['sisə,ro] s Cicéron m

cider ['saɪdər] s cidre m

cigar [sɪ'gɑr] s cigare m

cigarette [,sɪgə'rɛt] s cigarette f

cigarette' butt' s mégot m

cigarette' case' s étui m à cigarettes

cigarette' fiend' s fumeur m enragé

cigarette' hold'er s fume-cigarette m

cigarette' light'er s briquet m

cigar' hold'er s fume-cigare m

cigar' store' s bureau m de tabac

cinch [sɪntʃ] s (of saddle) sangle f; **it's a cinch** (coll) c'est couru d'avance || tr sangler; (to make sure of) (slang) assurer

cinder ['sɪndər] s cendre f || tr cendrer

Cinderella [,sɪndə'rɛlə] s la Cendrillon f

cin'der track' s piste f cendrée

cinema ['sɪnəmə] s cinéma m

cinnamon ['sɪnəmən] s cannelle f

cipher ['saɪfər] s zéro m; (code) chiffre m; **in cipher** en chiffres || tr & intr chiffrer

circle ['sʌrkəl] s cercle m; (coterie) milieu m, monde m; **to have circles around the eyes** avoir les yeux cernés || tr ceindre, entourer; (to travel around) faire le tour de

circuit ['sʌrkɪt] s circuit m; (of judge) tournée f

cir'cuit break'er s (elec) disjoncteur m

cir'cuit court' s cour f d'assises

circuitous [sər'kju·ɪtəs] adj détourné, indirect

circular ['sʌrkjələr] adj & s circulaire f

circulate ['sʌrkjə,let] tr faire circuler || intr circuler

circulation [,sʌrkjə'leʃən] s circulation f; (of newspaper) tirage m

circumcise ['sʌrkəm,saɪz] tr circoncire

circumcision [,sʌrkəm'sɪʒən] s circoncision f

circumference [sər'kʌmfərəns] s circonférence f

circumflex ['sʌrkəm,flɛks] adj & s circonflexe m

circumlocution [,sʌrkəmlo'kjuʃən] s circonlocution f

circumscribe [,sʌrkəm'skraɪb] tr circonscrire

circumspect ['sʌrkəm,spɛkt] adv circonspect

circumstance ['sʌrkəm,stæns] s circonstance f; (pomp) cérémonie f; **in easy circumstances** aisé; **under no circumstance** sous aucun prétexte; **under the circumstances** dans ces conditions

circumstantial [,sʌrkəm'stænʃəl] adj (derived from circumstances) circonstanciel; (detailed) circonstancié

cir'cumstan'tial ev'idence s preuves fpl indirectes

circumvent [,sʌrkəm'vɛnt] tr circonvenir

circus ['sʌrkəs] s cirque m; (Brit) rond-point m

cirrhosis [sɪ'rosɪs] s cirrhose f

cistern ['sɪstərn] s citerne f

citadel ['sɪtədəl] s citadelle f

citation [saɪ'teʃən] s citation f; (award) présentation f, mention f

cite [saɪt] tr citer

cither ['sɪθər] s cithare f

citified ['sɪtɪ,faɪd] adj urbain

citizen ['sɪtɪzən] s citoyen m

citizen·ry ['sɪtɪzənri] s (pl -ries) citoyens mpl

cit'izen·ship' s citoyenneté f

citric ['sɪtrɪk] adj citrique

citron ['sɪtrən] s cédrat m; (tree) cédratier m

citronella [,sɪtrə'nɛlə] s citronnelle f

cit'rus fruit' ['sɪtrəs] s agrumes mpl

cit·y ['sɪti] s (pl -ies) ville f; **the City** (district within ancient boundaries) la Cité

cit'y coun'cil s conseil m municipal

cit'y hall' s hôtel m de ville

cit'y plan'ner s urbaniste mf

cit'y plan'ning s urbanisme m

civ'et cat' ['sɪvɪt] s civette f

civic ['sɪvɪk] adj civique; **civics** instruction f civique

civies ['sɪviz] spl (coll) vêtements mpl civils; **in civies** en civil, en bourgeois

civil ['sɪvɪl] adj civil; (courteous) poli

civ'il defense' s protection f civile

civ'il engineer'ing s génie m civil

civilian [sɪ'vɪljən] adj & s civil m

civ'il life' s vie f civile

civili·ty [sɪ'vɪlɪti] s (pl -ties) civilité f

civilization [,sɪvɪlɪ'zeʃən] s civilisation f

civilize ['sɪvɪ,laɪz] tr civiliser

civ'il rights' spl droits mpl civiques, droits politiques

civ'il serv'ant s fonctionnaire mf

civ'il serv'ice s fonction f publique

civ'il war' s guerre f civile; **Civil War** (of the United States) Guerre de Sécession

clack [klæk] s claquement m || intr claquer

clad [klæd] adj vêtu, habillé

claim [klem] s demande f; (to a right) revendication f; (in prospecting) concession f || tr (a right) réclamer, revendiquer; (to require) exiger, demander; **to claim that ...** prétendre que ...; **to claim to** prétendre

claimant ['klemənt] s prétendant m, ayant droit m

clairvoyance [klɛr'vɔɪ·əns] s voyance f, seconde vue f; (keen insight) clairvoyance f

clairvoyant [klɛr'vɔɪ·ənt] adj clairvoyant || s voyante f; voyant m

clam [klæm] s palourde f || v (pret & pp clammed; ger clamming) intr—**to clam up** (slang) se taire

clam'bake' s pique-nique m aux palourdes

clamber ['klæmbər] intr grimper; **to clamber over** ou **up** escalader

clam·my ['klæmi] adj (comp -mier; super -miest) moite; (clinging) collant

clamor ['klæmər] s clameur f || intr vociférer; **to clamor for** réclamer

clamorous ['klæmərəs] *adj* bruyant
clamp [klæmp] *s* crampon *m*, agrafe *f*; (med) clamp *m* || *tr* fixer, attacher; **to clamp together** cramponner || *intr* —**to clamp down on** (coll) visser
clan [klæn] *s* clan *m*
clandestine [klæn'dɛstɪn] *adj* clandestin
clang [klæŋ] *s* bruit *m* métallique, choc *m* retentissant, cliquetis *m* || *tr* faire résonner || *intr* résonner
clank [klæŋk] *s* bruit *m* sec, bruit métallique, cliquetis *m* || *tr* faire résonner || *intr* résonner
clannish ['klænɪʃ] *adj* partisan
clap [klæp] *s* coup *m*; (with hand) tape *f*; (with the hands) battement *m* || *v* (pret & pp **clapped**; ger **clapping**) *tr* battre; (into jail) (coll) fourrer; **to clap the hands** claquer or battre les mains || *intr* applaudir, claquer
clapper ['klæpər] *s* applaudisseur *m*; (of bell) battant *m*
claque [klæk] *s* (paid clappers) claque *f*; (crush hat) claque *m*
claret ['klærɪt] *s* bordeaux *m*
clari·fy ['klærɪ,faɪ] *v* (pret & pp **-fied**) *tr* clarifier
clarinet [,klærɪ'nɛt] *s* clarinette *f*
clarity ['klærɪtɪ] *s* clarté *f*
clash [klæʃ] *s* choc *m*; (conflict) dispute *f*; (of colors) disparate *f* || *intr* se heurter, s'entre-choquer; (said of colors) former una disparate
clasp [klæsp], [klɑsp] *s* agrafe *f*, fermoir *m*; (embrace) étreinte *f* || *tr* agrafer; (to embrace) étreindre
clasp' knife' *s* couteau *m* pliant
class [klæs], [klɑs] *s* classe *f* || *tr* classer
classic ['klæsɪk] *adj* & *s* classique *m*
classical ['klæsɪkəl] *adj* classique
classicism ['klæsɪ,sɪzəm] *s* classicisme *m*
classicist ['klæsɪsɪst] *s* classique *mf*
classification [,klæsɪfɪ'ke/ən] *s* classification *f*, classement *m*
classified *adj* classifié, classé; (documents) secret, confidentiel
clas'sified advertise'ments *spl* petites annonces *fpl*
classi·fy ['klæsɪ,faɪ] *v* (pret & pp **-fied**) *tr* classifier
class'mate' *s* camarade *mf* de classe
class'room' *s* salle *f* de classe, classe *f*
class·y ['klæsɪ] *adj* (comp **-ier**; super **-iest**) (slang) chic
clatter ['klætər] *s* fracas *m* || *intr* faire un fracas
clause [klɔz] *s* clause *f*, article *m*; (gram) proposition *f*
clavicle ['klævɪkəl] *s* clavicule *f*
claw [klɔ] *s* (of animal) griffe *f*; (of crab) pince *f*; (of hammer) panne *f* fendue || *tr* griffer, déchirer
clay [kle] *s* argile *f*, glaise *f*
clay' pig'eon *s* pigeon *m* d'argile
clay' pipe' *s* pipe *f* en terre
clay' pit' *s* argilière *f*, glaisière *f*
clean [klin] *adj* propre; (precise) net || *adv* net; tout à fait || *tr* nettoyer; (fish) vider; (streets) balayer; **to clean out** curer; (a person) (slang)

mettre à sec, décaver; **to clean up** nettoyer || *intr* faire le nettoyage
clean'-cut' *adj* bien délimité, net; (e.g., athlete) bien découplé
cleaner ['klinər] *s* nettoyeur *m*, dégraisseur *m*; **to be taken to the cleaners** (slang) se faire rincer
cleaning ['klinɪŋ] *s* nettoyage *m*
clean'ing wom'an *s* femme *f* de ménage
cleanliness ['klɛnlɪnɪs] *s* propreté *f*, netteté *f*
cleanse [klɛnz] *tr* nettoyer, écurer; (e.g., a wound) assainir; (e.g., one's thoughts) purifier
cleanser ['klɛnzər] *s* produit *m* de nettoyage; (soap) détersif *m*
clean'-shav'en *adj* rasé de frais
cleans'ing cream' *s* crème *f* de démaquillage
clean'up' *s* nettoiement *m*
clear [klɪr] *adj* clair; (sharp) net; (free) dégagé, libre; (unmortgaged) franc d'hypothèque; **to become clear** s'éclaircir; **to keep clear of** éviter || *tr* (to brighten) éclaircir; (e.g., a fence) franchir; (obstacles) dégager; (land) défricher; (goods in customs) dédouaner; (an account) solder; **to clear away** écarter, enlever; **to clear oneself** se disculper; **to clear out** (e.g., a garden) jardiner; **to clear the table** desservir, enlever le couvert, ôter la nappe; **to clear up** éclaircir || *intr* (said of weather) s'éclaircir; **to clear out** (coll) filer, se sauver
clearance ['klɪrəns] *s* permis *m*, laissez-passer *m*, autorisation *f*; (between two objects) espace *m* libre; (com) compensation *f*; (mach) espace *m* mort, jeu *m*
clear'ance sale' *s* vente *f* de soldes
clear'-cut' *adj* net, tranché; (case) absolu
clear'-head'ed *adj* lucide, perspicace
clearing ['klɪrɪŋ] *s* (in clouds) éclaircie *f*; (in forest) clairière *f*, trouée *f*
clear'ing house' *s* (com) comptoir *m* de règlement, chambre *f* de compensation
clearness ['klɪrnɪs] *s* clarté *f*, netteté *f*
clear'-sight'ed *adj* perspicace, clairvoyant
cleat [klit] *s* taquet *m*
cleavage ['klivɪdʒ] *s* clivage *m*
cleave [kliv] *v* (pret & pp **cleft** [klɛft] or **cleaved**) *tr* fendre || *intr* se fendre; **to cleave to** s'attacher à, adhérer à
cleaver ['klivər] *s* couperet *m*, hachoir *m*
clef [klɛf] *s* (mus) clef *f*
cleft [klɛft] *adj* fendu || *s* fente *f*, crevasse *f*
cleft' pal'ate *s* palais *m* fendu, fissure *f* palatine
clemen·cy ['klɛmənsɪ] *s* (pl **-cies**) clémence *f*
clement ['klɛmənt] *adj* clément
clench [klɛntʃ] *tr* serrer, crisper
cler·gy ['klɜrdʒɪ] *s* (pl **-gies**) (members) clergé *m*; (profession) clergie *f*
cler'gy·man *s* (pl **-men**) ecclésiastique *m*, clerc *m*

cleric ['klerɪk] s clerc m, ecclésiastique m

clerical ['klerɪkəl] adj clerical; de bureau || s clerical m; **clericals** habit m ecclésiastique

clerical er'ror s faute f de copiste, faute de sténographe

clerical work' s travail m de bureau

clerk [klɑrk] s (clerical worker) employé m de bureau, commis m; (in lawyer's office) clerc m; (in store) vendeur m; (in bank) comptable mf; (of court) greffier m; (eccl) clerc

clever ['klevər] adj habile, adroit

cliché [kli'ʃe] s cliché m, expression f consacrée

click [klɪk] s cliquetis m, clic m; (of heels) bruit m sec; (of tongue) claquement m; (of a machine) déclic m || intr cliqueter, faire un déclic; (to succeed) (coll) réussir; (to get along well) (coll) s'entendre à merveille

client ['klaɪ·ənt] s client m

clientele [ˌklaɪ·ən'tɛl] s clientèle f

cliff [klɪf] s falaise f, talus m raide

climate ['klaɪmɪt] s climat m

climax ['klaɪmæks] s point m culminant, comble m

climb [klaɪm] s montée f, ascension f || tr & intr monter, gravir; grimper; **to climb down** descendre

climber ['klaɪmər] s grimpeur m; (bot) plante f grimpante; (social climber) parvenu m, arriviste mf

climbing ['klaɪmɪŋ] s montée f, escalade f

clinch [klɪntʃ] s crampon m, rivet m; (boxing) corps-à-corps m || tr river; (a bargain) boucler || intr se prendre corps à corps

clincher ['klɪntʃər] s (coll) argument m sans réplique

cling [klɪŋ] v (pret & pp clung [klʌŋ]) intr s'accrocher, se cramponner; **to cling to** (a person) se serrer contre; (a belief) adhérer à

cling'stone peach' s alberge f

clinic ['klɪnɪk] s clinique f

clinical ['klɪnɪkəl] adj clinique

clinician [klɪ'nɪʃən] s clinicien m

clink [klɪŋk] s cliquetis m; (e.g., of glasses) tintement m, choc m || tr (glasses, in a toast) choquer; **to clink glasses with** trinquer avec || intr tinter, cliqueter

clip [klɪp] s attache f; (brooch) agrafe f, clip m; (of gun) chargeur m; (blow) (coll) taloche f; (fast pace) (coll) pas m rapide || v (pret & pp clipped) ger clipping) tr (to fasten) attacher; (hair) rafraîchir; (sheep) tondre; (one's words) avaler

clipper ['klɪpər] s (aer) clipper m; (naut) voilier m de course; **clippers** tondeuse f

clipping ['klɪpɪŋ] s tondage m; (of sheep) tonte f; (of one's hair) taille f; (of newspaper) coupure f (de presse); **clippings** (cuttings, shavings, etc.) rognures fpl, chutes fpl

clip'ping ser'vice s argus m

clique [klik] s coterie f, clan m, chapelle f

cloak [klok] s manteau m || tr masquer

cloak'-and-dag'ger adj (e.g., story) de cape et d'épée

cloak'room' s vestiaire m; (rr) consigne f

clock [klɑk] s pendule f; (e.g., in a tower) horloge f; **to turn back the clock** retarder l'horloge; (fig) revenir en arrière || tr chronométrer

clock'mak'er s horloger m

clock'tow'er s tour f de l'horloge

clock'wise' adj & adv dans le sens des aiguilles d'une montre

clock'work' s mouvement m d'horlogerie; **like clockwork** (coll) comme une horloge

clod [klɑd] s motte f; (person) rustre mf

clod'hop'per s cul-terreux m; (shoe) godillot m

clog [klɑg] s (shoe) galoche f, socque m; (hindrance) entrave f || v (pret & pp clogged) ger clogging) tr (e.g., a pipe) boucher; (e.g., traffic) entraver || intr se boucher

cloister ['klɔɪstər] s cloître m || tr cloîtrer

close [klos] adj proche, tout près; (game) weave; formation, order) serré; (friend) intime; (friendship) étroit; (room) renfermé, étouffant; (translation) fidèle; **close to** près de || adv près, de près || [kloz] s (enclosure) clos m; (end) fin f; (closing) fermeture f || tr fermer; (to end) conclure, terminer; (an account) régler, clôturer; (ranks) serrer, resserrer; (a meeting) lever; **close quotes** fermez les guillemets; **to close in** enfermer; **to close out** (com) liquider, solder || intr se fermer; finir, se terminer; (on certain days) (theat) faire relâche; **to close in on** (the enemy) aborder

close' call' [klos] s—**to have a close call** (coll) l'échapper belle

close-cropped ['klos'krɑpt] adj coupé ras

closed [klozd] adj fermé; (road) barré; (e.g., pipe) obturé, bouché; (ranks) serré; (public sign in front of theater) relâche; **with closed eyes** les yeux clos

closed' car' s conduite f intérieure

closed'-cir'cuit tel'evision s télévision f en circuit fermé

closed' sea'son s fermeture f de la chasse, fermeture de la pêche

closefisted ['klos'fɪstəd] adj ladre, avare

close-fitting ['klos'fɪtɪŋ] adj collant, ajusté, qui moule le corps

close-grained ['klos'grend] adj serré

closely ['klosli] adv (near) de près, étroitement; (exactly) exactement

close-mouthed ['klos'mauðd] adj peu communicatif, économe de mots

closeness ['klosnɪs] s (nearness) proximité f; (accuracy) exactitude f; (stinginess) avarice f; (of weather) lourdeur f; (of air) manque m d'air

close′ shave′ [klos] *s*—to have a close shave se faire raser de près; (coll) échapper à un cheveu près

closet [′klɑzɪt] *s* placard *m*

clos′et dra′ma *s* spectacle *m* dans un fauteuil

close-up [′klos‚ʌp] *s* premier plan *m*, gros plan

closing [′klozɪŋ] *adj* dernier, final ‖ *s* fermeture *f*; (*of account; of meeting*) clôture *f*

clos′ing-out′ sale′ *s* soldes *mpl* des fins de séries

clos′ing price′ *s* dernier cours *m*

clot [klɑt] *s* caillot *m* ‖ *v* (*pret & pp* clotted; *ger* clotting) *tr* cailler ‖ *intr* se cailler

cloth [klɔθ], [klɑθ] *s* étoffe *f*; (*fabric*) tissu *m*; (*of wool*) drap *m*; (*of cotton or linen*) toile *f*; **cloths** (*for cleaning*) chiffons *mpl*, torchons *mpl*, linge *m*; **the cloth** le clergé

clothe [kloð] *v* (*pret & pp* clothed or clad [klæd]) *tr* habiller, vêtir; (*e.g., with authority*) revêtir, investir

clothes [kloz], [kloðz] *spl* vêtements *mpl*, habits *mpl*; (*underclothes, shirts, etc.; wash*) linge *m*; **in plain clothes** en civil; **to put on one's clothes** s'habiller; **to take off one's clothes** se déshabiller

clothes′bas′ket *s* panier *m* à linge

clothes′brush′ *s* brosse *f* à habits

clothes′ clos′et *s* garde-robe *f*, penderie *f*, placard *m*

clothes′ dry′er *s* séchoir *m* à linge

clothes′ hang′er *s* cintre *m*

clothes′horse′ *s* séchoir-chevalet *m*

clothes′line′ *s* corde *f* à linge, étendoir *m*

clothes′ moth′ *s* gerce *f*

clothes′pin′ *s* pince *f* à linge

clothes′ rack′ *s* patère *f*

clothier [′kloðjər] *s* confectionneur *m*, marchand *m* de confections

clothing [′kloðɪŋ] *s* vêtements *mpl*

cloud [klaud] *s* nuage *m*; (*heavy cloud; multitude*) nuée *f*; **in the clouds** dans les nues ‖ *tr* couvrir de nuages; (*phot*) voiler ‖ *intr* (phot) se voiler; **to cloud over** or **up** se couvrir de nuages

cloud′burst′ *s* averse *f*, rafale *f* de pluie

cloud′ cham′ber *s* (phys) chambre *f* d'ionisation

cloudless [′klaudlɪs] *adj* sans nuages

cloud-y [′klaudi] *adj* (*comp* -ier; *super* -iest) nuageux; (phot) voilé

clout [klaut] *s* (coll) gifle *f* ‖ *tr* (coll) gifler

clove [klov] *s* clou *m* de girofle, girofle *m*; (*of garlic*) gousse *f*; (bot) giroflier *m*

clove′ hitch′ *s* demi-clef *f* à capeler

clo′ven hoof′ [′kloven] *s* pied *m* fourchu; **to show the cloven hoof** (coll) montrer le bout de l'oreille

clover [′klovər] *s* trèfle *m*; **to be in clover** (coll) être sur le velours

clo′ver-leaf′ *s* (*pl* -leaves) feuille *f* de trèfle; (*intersection*) croisement *m* en trèfle, saut-de-mouton *m*

clown [klaun] *s* clown *m*, pitre *m*, bouffon *m* ‖ *intr* faire le pitre

clownish [′klaunɪʃ] *adj* bouffon; (*clumsy*) empoté, rustre

cloy [klɔɪ] *tr* rassasier

club [klʌb] *s* massue *f*, gourdin *m*, assommoir *m*; cercle *m*, amicale *f*, club *m*; (cards) trèfle *m*; (golf) crosse *f*, club *m* ‖ *v* (*pret & pp* clubbed; *ger* clubbing) *tr* (*to strike*) assommer; (*to pool*) mettre en commun ‖ *intr*—**to club together** s'associer; se cotiser

club′ car′ *s* voiture-salon *f*

club′foot′ *s* (*pl* -feet) pied *m* équin, pied bot

club′foot′ed *adj*—**to be clubfooted** avoir le pied bot, être pied-bot

club′house′ *s* club *m*, cercle *m*

club′man *s* (*pl* -men) clubman *m*

club′room′ *s* salle *f* de réunion

club′ steak′ *s* aloyau *m* de bœuf

club′wom′an *s* (*pl* -wom′en) cercleuse *f*

cluck [klʌk] *s* gloussement *m* ‖ *intr* glousser

clue [klu] *s* indice *m*, indication *f*; **to find the clue** trouver la clef; **to give s.o. a clue** mettre qn sur la piste; **to have the clue** tenir le bout du fil

clump [klʌmp] *s* (*of earth*) bloc *m*, masse *f*; (*of trees*) bouquet *m*; (*of shrubs or flowers*) massif *m*; (*gait*) pas *m* lourd ‖ *intr*—**to clump along** marcher lourdement

clum·sy [′klʌmzi] *adj* (*comp* -sier; *super* -siest) (*worker*) maladroit, gauche; (*work*) bâclé, grossier

cluster [′klʌstər] *s* bouquet *m*, massif *m*; (*of grapes*) grappe *f*; (*of pears*) glane *f*; (*of bananas*) régime *m*; (*of diamonds*) épi *m*, nœud *m*; (*of stars*) amas *m* ‖ *tr* grouper ‖ *intr*—**to cluster around** se rassembler; **to cluster together** se conglomérer

clutch [klʌtʃ] *s* (*grasp, grip*) griffe *f*, serre *f*; (aut) embrayage *m*; (aut) pédale *f* d'embrayage; **to fall into the clutches of** tomber sous la patte de; **to let in the clutch** embrayer; **to throw out the clutch** débrayer ‖ *tr* saisir, empoigner ‖ *intr*—**to clutch at** se raccrocher à

clutter [′klʌtər] *s* encombrement *m* ‖ *tr*—**to clutter up** encombrer

Co. *abbr* (**Company**) Cie

c/o *abbr* (**in care of**) a/s (aux soins de)

coach [kotʃ] *s* coche *m*, carrosse *f*; (*bus*) autocar *m*, car *m*; (*two-door sedan*) coche *m*; (rr) voiture *f*; (sports) entraîneur *m*, moniteur *m* ‖ *tr* donner des leçons particulières à; entraîner; (*for an exam*) préparer à un examen, chauffer; (*an actor*) faire répéter

coach′-and-four′ *s* carrosse *f* à quatre chevaux

coach′ box′ *s* siège *m* du cocher

coach′ house′ *s* remise *f*

coaching [′kotʃɪŋ] *s* leçons *fpl* particulières, chauffage *m*, répétitions *fpl*; (sport) entraînement *m*

coach′man *s* (*pl* -men) cocher *m*

coagulate [koˈægjəˌlet] *tr* coaguler || *intr* se coaguler

coal [kol] *adj* charbonnier, houiller || *s* houille *f*, charbon *m*; **coals** (*embers*) tisons *mpl*, charbons ardents; **to carry coals to Newcastle** porter de l'eau à la rivière

coal′bin′ *s* coffre *m* à charbon

coal′ bunk′er *s* soute *f* à charbon

coal′ car′ *s* wagon-tombereau *m*

coal′ deal′er *s* charbonnier *m*

coalesce [ˌko‧əˈles] *intr* s'unir, se combiner, fusionner

coal′ field′ *s* bassin *m* houiller

coalition [ˌko‧əˈlɪʃən] *s* coalition *f*; **to form a coalition** se coaliser

coal′ mine′ *s* houillère *f*

coal′ oil′ *s* pétrole *m* lampant

coal′ scut′tle *s* seau *m* à charbon

coal′ tar′ *s* goudron *m* de houille

coal′yard′ *s* charbonnerie *f*

coarse [kors] *adj* (*in manners*) grossier; (*composed of large particles*) gros; (*hair, skin*) rude

coarse′-grained′ *adj* à gros grain; (*wood*) à gros fil

coarseness [ˈkorsnɪs] *s* grossièreté *f*; (*of hair, skin*) rudesse *f*

coast [kost] *s* côte *f*; **the coast is clear** la route est libre || *intr* caboter; (*said of automobile*) aller au débrayé; (*said of bicycle*) aller en roue libre; **to coast along** continuer sur sa lancée

coastal [ˈkostəl] *adj* côtier

coaster [ˈkostər] *s* dessous-de-verre *m*, sous-verre *m*; (*naut*) caboteur *m*

coast′er brake′ *s* frein *m* à contre-pédalage

coast′ guard′ *s* service *m* de guet le long des côtes

coast′-guard cut′ter *s* garde-côte *m*

coast′guards′man *s* (*pl* **-men**) soldat *m* chargé de la garde des côtes

coasting [ˈkostɪŋ] *s* (*e.g., on a cycle*) descente *f* en roue libre

coast′ing trade′ *s* cabotage *m*

coast′line′ *s* littoral *m*

coast′wise′ *adj* côtier || *adv* le long de la côte

coat [kot] *s* (*jacket*) veste *f*; (*suitcoat*) veston *m*; (*topcoat*) manteau *m*; (*of an animal*) robe *f*, pelage *m*, livrée *f*; (*of paint*) couche *f* || *tr* enduire; (*with chocolate*) enrober; (*a pill*) dragéifier

coat′ hang′er *s* cintre *m*, portemanteau *m*

coating [ˈkotɪŋ] *s* enduit *m*, couche *f*

coat′ of arms′ *s* écu *m* armorial; (*bearings*) blason *m*, armoiries *fpl*

coat′ of mail′ *s* cotte *f* de mailles

coat′rack′ *s* portemanteau *m*

coat′room′ *s* vestiaire *m*

coat′tail′ *s* basque *f*

coauthor [koˈɔθər] *s* coauteur *m*

coax [koks] *tr* cajoler, amadouer

cob [kab] *s* (*of corn*) épi *m* de maïs; (*horse*) bidet *m*; (*swan*) cygne *m* mâle

cobalt [ˈkobɔlt] *s* cobalt *m*

cobbler [ˈkablər] *s* cordonnier *m*; (*cake*) tourte *f* aux fruits; (*drink*) boisson *f* glacée

cobble‧stone [ˈkabəlˌston] *s* pavé *m*

cob′web′ *s* toile *f* d'araignée

cocaine [koˈken] *s* cocaïne *f*

cock [kak] *s* coq *m*; (*faucet*) robinet *m*; (*of gun*) chien *m* || *tr* (*one's ears*) dresser, redresser; (*one's hat*) mettre sur l'oreille, retrousser; (*a rifle*) armer

cockade [kaˈked] *s* cocarde *f*

cock-a-doodle-doo [ˈkakəˌdudəlˈdu] *interj* cocorico!

cock′-and-bull′ sto′ry *s* coq-à-l'âne *m*

cock′crow′ *s* cocorico *m*

cocked′ hat′ *s* chapeau *m* à cornes; **to knock into a cocked hat** (slang) démolir, aplatir

cock′er span′iel [ˈkakər] *s* cocker *m*

cock′eyed′ *adj* (coll) de travers, de biais; (slang) insensé

cock′fight′ *s* combat *m* de coqs

cockle [ˈkakəl] *s* (bot) nielle *f*; (zool) bucarde *f*, clovisse *f*

cock′pit′ *s* (aer) cockpit *m*, carlingue *f*

cock′roach′ *s* blatte *f*, cafard *m*

cockscomb [ˈkaksˌkom] *s* crête *f* de coq; (bot) crête-de-coq *f*

cock′sure′ *adj* (coll) sûr et certain

cock′tail dress′ *s* robe *f* de cocktail

cock′tail par′ty *s* cocktail *m*

cock′tail shak′er *s* shaker *m*

cock‧y [ˈkaki] *adj* (comp **-ier**; super **-iest**) (coll) effronté, suffisant

cocoa [ˈkoko] *s* cacao *m*; (*drink*) chocolat *m*

co′coa bean′ *s* cacao *m*

coconut [ˈkokəˌnʌt] *s* noix *f* de coco, coco *m*

co′conut palm′ *s* cocotier *m*

cocoon [kəˈkun] *s* cocon *m*

cod [kad] *s* (ichth) morue *f*

C.O.D. [ˈsiˈoˈdi] *s* (letterword) (**Collect on Delivery**) C.R., contre remboursement, e.g., **send it to me C.O.D.** envoyez-le-moi C.R.

coddle [ˈkadəl] *tr* dorloter, gâter

code [kod] *s* code *m*; (*secret code*) chiffre *m* || *tr* chiffrer

code′ word′ *s* mot *m* convenu

codex [ˈkodeks] *s* (*pl* **codices** [ˈkodɪˌsiz], [ˈkadɪˌsiz]) manuscrit *m* ancien

cod′fish′ *s* morue *f*

codger [ˈkadʒər] *s*—**old codger** (coll) vieux bonhomme *m*

codicil [ˈkadɪsɪl] *s* (*of will*) codicille *m*; (*of contract, treaty, etc.*) avenant *m*

codi‧fy [ˈkadɪˌfaɪ], [ˈkodɪˌfaɪ] *v* (*pret & pp* **-fied**) *tr* codifier

cod′-liver oil′ *s* huile *f* de foie de morue

coed [ˈkoˌed] *s* collégienne *f*, étudiante *f* universitaire

coeducation [ˌko‧edʒəˈkeʃən] *s* co-éducation *f*

co′educa′tional school′ [ˌko‧edʒəˈkeʃənəl] *s* école *f* mixte

coefficient [ˌko‧ɪˈfɪʃənt] *s* coefficient *m*

coerce [koˈʌrs] *tr* contraindre, forcer

coercion [koˈʌrʃən] *s* coercition *f*

coexist [ˌko·ɪgˈzɪst] *intr* coexister
coexistence [ˌko·ɪgˈzɪstəns] *s* coexistence *f*
coffee [ˈkɔfi], [ˈkɑfi] *s* café *m*; **black coffee** café noir, café nature; **ground coffee** café moulu; **roasted coffee** café brûlé, café torréfié
coffee and rolls *s* café *m* complet
coffee bean *s* grain *m* de café
coffee break *s* pause-café *f*
coffee-cake *s* gimblette *f* (qui se prend avec le café)
coffee cup *s* tasse *f* à café
coffee grinder *s* moulin *m* à café
coffee grounds *spl* marc *m* de café
coffee maker *s* percolateur *m*
coffee mill *s* moulin *m* à café
coffee plantation *s* caféière *f*
coffeepot *s* cafetière *f*; *(for pouring)* verseuse *f*
coffee roaster *s* brûloir *m*
coffee shop *s* *(of hotel)* hôtel-restaurant *m*; *(in station)* buffet *m*
coffee tree *s* caféier *m*
coffer [ˈkɔfər], [ˈkɑfər] *s* coffre *m*, caisse *f*; *(archit)* caisson *m*; **coffers** trésor *m*, fonds *mpl*
cofferdam *s* coffre *m*, bâtardeau *m*
coffin [ˈkɔfɪn], [ˈkɑfɪn] *s* cercueil *m*, bière *f*
cog [kɑg] *s* dent *f*; *(cogwheel)* roue *f* dentée; **to slip a cog** (coll) avoir des absences
cogency [ˈkodʒənsi] *s* force *f* (de persuasion)
cogent [ˈkodʒənt] *adj* puissant, convaincant
cogitate [ˈkadʒɪˌtet] *tr & intr* méditer
cognac [ˈkonjæk], [ˈkɑnjæk] *s* cognac *m*
cognate [ˈkagnet] *adj* congénère, apparenté || *s* congénère *mf*; *(word)* mot *m* apparenté
cognizance [ˈkagnɪzəns], [ˈkɑnɪzəns] *s* connaissance *f*
cognizant [ˈkagnɪzənt], [ˈkɑnɪzənt] *adj* informé
cogwheel *s* roue *f* dentée
cohabit [koˈhæbɪt] *intr* cohabiter
coheir [koˈɛr] *s* cohéritier
cohere [koˈhɪr] *intr* s'agglomérer, adhérer; *(said of reasoning or style)* se suivre logiquement, correspondre
coherent [koˈhɪrənt] *adj* cohérent
cohesion [koˈhiʒən] *s* cohésion *f*
coiffeur [kwaˈfʌr] *s* coiffeur *m* pour dames
coiffure [kwaˈfjur] *s* coiffure *f* || *tr* coiffer
coil [kɔɪl] *s* *(something wound in a spiral)* rouleau *m*; *(single turn of spiral)* tour *m*; *(of a still)* serpentin *m*; *(of hair)* boucle *f*; (elec) bobine *f*; **coils** *(of snake)* nœuds *mpl* || *tr* enrouler; (naut) lover, gléner || *intr* s'enrouler; *(said of snake or stream)* serpenter
coil spring *s* ressort *m* en spirale, ressort à boudin
coin [kɔɪn] *s* monnaie *f*; *(single coin)* pièce *f* de monnaie; *(wedge)* coin *m*; **in coin** en espèces, en numéraire; **to**

pay back s.o. in his own coin rendre à qn la monnaie de sa pièce; **to toss a coin** jouer à pile ou face || *tr* *(a new word; a story or lie)* forger, inventer; **to coin money** frapper de la monnaie; (coll) faire des affaires d'or, s'enrichir à vue d'œil
coinage [ˈkɔɪnɪdʒ] *s* monnayage *m*; (fig) invention *f*
coincide [ˌko·ɪnˈsaɪd] *intr* coïncider
coincidence [koˈɪnsɪdəns] *s* coïncidence *f*
coition [koˈɪʃən] or **coitus** [ˈko·ɪtəs] *s* coït *m*
coke [kok] *s* coke *m* || *tr* cokéfier || *intr* se cokéfier
colander [ˈkʌləndər], [ˈkɑləndər] *s* passoire *f*
cold [kold] *adj* froid; **it is cold** *(said of weather)* il fait froid; **to be cold** *(said of person)* avoir froid || *s* froid *m*; *(indisposition)* rhume *m*; **to be left out in the cold** (slang) rester en carafe; **to catch a cold** attraper un rhume, s'enrhumer
cold blood *s*—**in cold blood** de sang-froid
cold-blooded *adj* insensible; *(sensitive to cold)* frileux; (zool) à sang froid
cold chisel *s* ciseau *m* à froid
cold comfort *s* maigre consolation *f*
cold cream *s* cold-cream *m*
cold cuts *spl* viandes *fpl* froides, assiette *f* anglaise
cold feet [fit] *spl*—**to have cold feet** (coll) avoir froid aux yeux
cold front *s* front *m* froid
cold-hearted *adj* au cœur dur, insensible
coldness [ˈkoldnɪs] *s* froideur *f*; *(in the air)* froidure *f*
cold shoulder *s*—**to give s.o. the cold shoulder** (coll) battre froid à qn
cold snap *s* coup *m* de froid
cold storage *s* entrepôt *m* frigorifique; **in cold storage** en glacière
cold-storage *adj* frigorifique
cold war *s* guerre *f* froide
cold wave *s* vague *f* de froid
coleslaw [ˈkolˌslɔ] *s* salade *f* de chou
colic [ˈkalɪk] *s* colique *f*
coliseum [ˌkalɪˈsi·əm] *s* colisée *m*
collaborate [kəˈlæbəˌret] *intr* collaborer
collaborationist [kəˌlæbəˈreʃənɪst] *s* collaborationniste *mf*
collaborator [kəˈlæbəˌretər] *s* collaborateur *m*
collapse [kəˈlæps] *s* écroulement *m*, effondrement *m*; *(of prices; of government)* chute *f*; *(of prices; of a beam)* fléchissement *m*; (pathol) collapsus *m* || *intr* s'écrouler, s'effondrer; *(said of government)* tomber; *(said of structure or prices)* s'effondrer; *(said of balloon)* se dégonfler
collapsible [kəˈlæpsɪbəl] *adj* démontable, rabattable, pliant
collar [ˈkalər] *s* *(of dress, shirt)* collet *m*, col *m*; *(worn by dog; on pigeon)* collier *m*; (mach) collier || *tr* colleter; (coll) empoigner

col·lar·band' *s* pied *m* de col (d'une chemise)

col·lar·bone' *s* clavicule *f*

collate [kə'let], ['kalet] *tr* collationner, conférer

collateral [kə'lætərəl] *adj* accessoire; correspondant; (*kin*) collatéral ‖ *s* (*kin*) collatéral *m*; (*com*) nantissement *m*

collation [kə'leʃən] *s* collation *f*

colleague ['kalig] *s* collègue *mf*

collect ['kalɛkt] *s* (eccl) collecte *f* ‖ [kə'lɛkt] *tr* rassembler; (*taxes*) percevoir, lever; (*stamps, antiques*) collectionner; (*eggs*; *classroom papers*; *tickets*) ramasser; (*mail*) faire la levée de; (*debts*) recouvrir; (*gifts, money*) collecter; (*one's thoughts, anecdotes*) recueillir; **to collect oneself** se reprendre, se remettre ‖ *intr* (*for the poor*) quêter; (*to gather together*) se rassembler, se réunir; (*to pile up*) s'amasser ‖ *adv* en p.c.v., e.g., **to telephone collect** téléphoner en p.c.v.

collect' call' *s* (telp) communication *f* P.C.V.

collected *adj* recueilli, maître de soi

collection [kə'lɛkʃən] *s* collection *f*; (*of taxes*) perception *f*, levée *f*, recouvrement *m*; (*of mail*) levée *f*; (*of verses*) recueil *m*

collec'tion plate' *s* plateau *m* de quête

collective [kə'lɛktɪv] *adj* collectif

collector [kə'lɛktər] *s* (*of stamps, antiques*) collectionneur *m*; (*of taxes*) percepteur *m*, receveur *m*, collecteur *m*; (*of tickets*) contrôleur *m*

college ['kalɪdʒ] *s* (*of cardinals, electors, etc.*) collège *m*; (*school in a university*) faculté *f*; (U.S.A.) école *f* des arts et sciences

collegian [kə'lidʒɪ·ən] *s* étudiant *m*

collegiate [kə'lidʒɪ·ɪt] *adj* collégial, de l'université, universitaire

collide [kə'laɪd] *intr* se heurter, tamponner; **to collide with** se heurter à contre, heurter contre

collier ['kaljər] *s* houilleur *m*; (*ship*) charbonnier *m*

collier·y ['kaljəri] *s* (*pl* **-ies**) houillère *f*

collision [kə'lɪʒən] *s* collision *f*

collocate ['kalo͵ket] *tr* disposer en rapport; (*creditors*) colloquer

colloid ['kalɔɪd] *adj* colloïdal ‖ *s* colloïde *m*

colloquial [kə'lokwɪ·əl] *adj* familier

colloquialism [kə'lokwɪ·ə͵lɪzəm] *s* expression *f* familière

collo·quy ['kaləkwi] *s* (*pl* **-quies**) colloque *m*

collusion [kə'luʒən] *s* collusion *f*; **to be in collusion with** être d'intelligence avec

cologne [kə'lon] *s* eau *f* de Cologne

Colombia [kə'lʌmbɪ·ə] *s* Colombie *f*; la Colombie

colon ['kolən] *s* (anat) côlon *m*; (gram) deux points *mpl*

colonel ['kʌrnəl] *s* colonel *m*

colonial [kə'lonɪ·əl] *adj* & *s* colonial *m*

colonist ['kalənɪst] *s* colon *m*

colonize ['kalə͵naɪz] *tr* & *intr* coloniser

colonnade [͵kalə'ned] *s* colonnade *f*

colo·ny ['kaləni] *s* (*pl* **-nies**) colonie *f*

colophon ['kalə͵fan] *s* colophon *m*

color ['kʌlər] *s* couleur *f*; **the colors** les couleurs, le drapeau; **to call to the colors** appeler sous les drapeaux; **to give** or **lend color to** colorer; (fig) rendre vraisemblable; **to show one's true colors** se révéler sous son vrai jour; **under color of** sous couleur de; **with flying colors** enseignes déployées ‖ *tr* colorer; (*e.g., a drawing*) colorier; (*to exaggerate*) donner de l'éclat à, imager; (*to dye*) teindre ‖ *intr* se colorer; (*to blush*) rougir

col'or·bear'er *s* porte-drapeau *m*

col'or-blind' *adj* daltonien, aveugle des couleurs

colored *adj* coloré; (*person*) de couleur; (*drawing*) colorié

colorful ['kʌlərfəl] *adj* (*striking*) coloré; (*unusual*) pittoresque

col'or guard' *s* garde *f* d'honneur du drapeau

coloring ['kʌlərɪŋ] *adj* colorant ‖ *s* colorant *m*; (*of painting, complexion, style*) coloris *m*

colorless ['kʌlərlɪs] *adj* incolore

col'or photog'raphy *s* photographie *f* en couleurs

col'or salute' *s* (mil) salut *m* au drapeau, salut aux couleurs

col'or ser'geant *s* sergent-chef *m*, sergent-major *m*

col'or tel'evision *s* télévision *f* en couleurs

colossal [kə'lasəl] *adj* colossal

colossus [kə'lasəs] *s* colosse *m*

colt [kolt] *s* poulain *m*

Columbus [kə'lʌmbəs] *s* Colomb *m*

column ['kaləm] *s* colonne *f*; (journ) rubrique *f*, chronique *f*, courrier *m*; (mil) colonne

columnar [kə'lʌmnər] *adj* en colonne

columnist ['kaləmnɪst] *s* chroniqueur *m*, courriériste *mf*

coma ['komə] *s* (pathol) coma *m*

comb [kom] *s* peigne *m*; (currycomb) étrille *f*; (*of rooster; of wave*) crête *f*; (*filled with honey*) rayon *m* ‖ *tr* peigner; explorer minutieusement, fouiller; **to comb out** démêler ‖ *intr* (*said of waves*) déferler

com·bat ['kambæt] *s* combat *m* ‖ ['kambæt], [kəm'bæt] *v* (*pret* & *pp* **-bated** or **-batted**; *ger* **-bating** or **-batting**) *tr* & *intr* combattre

combatant ['kambətənt] *adj* & *s* combattant *m*

com'bat du'ty *s* service *m* de combat, service au front

combination [͵kambɪ'neʃən] *s* combinaison *f*

combine ['kambaɪn] *s* trust *m*, combinaison *f* financière, entente *f* industrielle; (agr) moissonneuse-batteuse *f* ‖ [kəm'baɪn] *tr* combiner ‖ *intr* se liguer, fusionner; (chem) se combiner

combin'ing form' *s* élément *m* de composition

combo ['kɑmbo] s (of four musicians) quartette f
combustible [kəm'bʌstɪbəl] adj & s combustible m
combustion [kəm'bʌstʃən] s combustion f
come [kʌm] v (pret came [kem]; pp come) intr venir; come in! entrez!; to come after succéder à, suivre; (to come to get) venir chercher; to come apart se séparer, se défaire; (to come around) (to snap back) se rétablir; (to give in) céder; to come at (to attack) se jeter sur; to come back revenir; (coll) revenir en vogue; to come before précéder; (e.g., a legislature) se mettre devant; to come between s'interposer entre; to come by (to get) obtenir; (to pass) passer; to come down descendre; to come downstairs descendre (en bas); to come down with tomber malade avec; to come for venir chercher; to come from provenir de, dériver de; (said of wind) chasser de; to come in entrer; entrer dans; (said of tide) monter; (said of style) entrer en vogue; to come in for avoir part à; (e.g., an inheritance) succéder à; (e.g., sympathy) s'attirer; to come off se détacher; (to take place) avoir lieu; en sortir, e.g., to come off victorious en sortir vainqueur; to come out sortir; (said of sun, stars; said of book) paraître; (said of buds) éclore; (said of news) se divulguer; (said of debutante) débuter; to come out for se prononcer pour; to come over se laisser persuader; arriver, e.g., what's come over him? qu'est-ce qui lui est arrivé?; to come through (e.g., fields) passer par, passer à travers; (e.g., a wall) pénétrer; (an illness) surmonter; se tirer indemne; to come to revenir à soi; to come together s'assembler, se réunir; to come true se réaliser; to come up monter; (to occur) se présenter; to come upstairs monter (en haut); to come up to monter jusqu'à, venir à; to come up with proposer
come'-and-go' s va-et-vient m
come'back' s (of style) (coll) retour m en vogue; (of statesman) (coll) retour m au pouvoir; (slang) réplique f, riposte f; to stage a comeback (coll) se réhabiliter, faire une belle remontée
comedian [kə'midɪ-ən] s comique m; (on the legitimate stage) comédien m; auteur m comique
comedienne [kə,midɪ'ɛn] s comédienne f
come'down' s humiliation f, déchéance f
come·dy ['kɑmədi] s (pl -dies) comédie f
come·ly ['kʌmli] adj (comp -lier; super -liest) (attractive) avenant, gracieux; (decorous) convenable, bienséant
come'-on' s (slang) leurre m, attrape f
comet ['kɑmɪt] s comète f
comfort ['kʌmfərt] s confort m; consolation f; (person) consolateur m;

comforts commodités fpl, agréments mpl ‖ tr consoler, réconforter
comfortable ['kʌmfərtəbəl] adj confortable; (in a state of comfort) bien; (well-off) à l'aise
comforter ['kʌmfərtər] s consolateur m; (bedcover) couvre-pieds m piqué; (of wool) cache-nez m; (for baby) tétine f, sucette f
comforting ['kʌmfərtɪŋ] adj consolateur, réconfortant
com'fort sta'tion s châlet m de nécessité, lieux mpl d'aisances, toilette f
comic ['kɑmɪk] adj & s comique m; comics (cartoons) dessins mpl humoristiques
com'ic op'era s opéra m bouffe
com'ic strip' s bande f humoristique
coming ['kʌmɪŋ] adj qui vient; (future) ·d'avenir, de demain ‖ s arrivée f, venue f; comings and goings allées et venues
com'ing out' s (of stocks, bonds, etc.) émission f; (of a book) parution f; (of a young lady) début m
comma ['kɑmə] s virgule f; (in French a period or sometimes a small space is used to mark the divisions of whole numbers) point m
command [kə'mænd], [kə'mɑnd] s (leadership) gouvernement m; (order, direction) commandement m, ordre m; (e.g., of a foreign language) maîtrise f; to be at s.o.'s command être aux ordres de qn; to have a command of (a language) posséder; to have at one's command avoir à sa disposition ‖ tr commander, ordonner; (respect) inspirer; (to look out over) dominer; (a language) connaître ‖ intr (mil) commander, donner les ordres
commandant [,kɑmən'dænt], [,kɑmən'dɑnt] s commandant m
commandeer [,kɑmən'dɪr] tr réquisitionner
commander [kə'mændər], [kə'mɑndər] s commandant m
comman'der in chief' s commandant m en chef
commanding [kə'mændɪŋ], [kə'mɑndɪŋ] adj imposant; (in charge) d'autorité
commemorate [kə'mɛməret] tr commémorer, célébrer
commence [kə'mɛns] tr & intr commencer
commencement [kə'mɛnsmənt] s commencement m; (educ) jour m de la distribution des prix, jour de la collation des grades
commence'ment ex'ercise s cérémonie f de remise des diplômes
commend [kə'mɛnd] tr (to praise) louer; (to entrust) confier, recommander
commendable [kə'mɛndəbəl] adj louable
commendation [,kɑmən'deʃən] s louange f, éloge m; (mil) citation f
comment ['kɑmɛnt] s remarque f, observation f, commentaire m ‖ intr

faire des observations; **to comment on** commenter

commentar·y ['kamən,teri] *s* (*pl* -**ies**) commentaire *m*

commentator ['kamən,tetər] *s* commentateur *m*

commerce ['kamərs] *s* commerce *m*, négoce *m*

commercial [kə'mʌrʃəl] *adj* commercial, commerçant || *s* annonce *f* publicitaire

commercialize [kə'mʌrʃə,laɪz] *tr* commercialiser

commiserate [kə'mɪzə,ret] *intr*—**to commiserate with** compatir aux malheurs de

commiseration [kə,mɪzə'reʃən] *s* commisération *f*

commissar [,kamɪ'sar] *s* commissaire *m*

commissar·y ['kamɪ,seri] *s* (*pl* -**ies**) (*person*) commissaire *m*; (*canteen*) cantine *f*

commission [kə'mɪʃən] *s* commission *f*; (*board, council*) conseil *m*; (*com*) guelte *f*; (*mil*) brevet *m*; **out of commission** hors de service; (*naut*) désarmé || *tr* commissionner; (*mil*) promouvoir

commis'sioned of'ficer *s* breveté *m*

commissioner [kə'mɪʃənər] *s* commissaire *m*

com·mit [kə'mɪt] *v* (*pret & pp* -**mitted**; *ger* -**mitting**) *tr* (*an error, crime, etc.*) commettre; (*one's soul, one's money, etc.*) confier; (*one's word*) engager; (*to a mental hospital*) interner; **to commit to memory** apprendre par cœur; **to commit to prison** envoyer en prison; **to commit to writing** coucher par écrit

commitment [kə'mɪtmənt] *s* (*act of committing*) perpétration *f*; (*to a mental institution*) internement *m*; (*to prison*) emprisonnement *m*; (*to a cause*) engagement *m*

committal [kə'mɪtəl] *s* (*of a crime*) perpétration *f*; (*of a task*) délégation *f*; **committal to prison** mise en prison

commit'tal ser'vice *s* (*eccl*) prières *fpl* au bord de la tombe

committee [kə'mɪti] *s* comité *m*, commission *f*

commode [kə'mod] *s* (*toilet*) chaise *f* percée; (*dressing table*) grande table *f* de nuit

commodious [kə'modɪ·əs] *adj* spacieux, confortable

commodi·ty [kə'madɪti] *s* (*pl* -**ties**) denrée *f*, marchandise *f*

common ['kamən] *adj* commun || *s* terrain *m* communal; **commons** communaux *mpl*; (*of school*) réfectoire *m*; **the Commons** (Brit) les communes *fpl*

com'mon car'rier *s* entreprise *f* de transports

commoner ['kamənər] *s* homme *m* du peuple, roturier *m*; (Brit) membre *m* de la Chambre des communes

com'mon law' *s* droit *m* coutumier, coutume *f*

com'mon-law mar'riage *s* union *f* libre, collage *m*

Com'mon Mar'ket *s* Marché *m* Commun

com'mon noun' *s* nom *m* commun

com'mon-place *adj* banal || *s* banalité *f*

com'mon sense' *s* sens *m* commun

com'mon-sense' *adj* sensé

com'mon stock' *s* action *f* ordinaire, actions ordinaires

commonweal ['kamən,wil] *s* bien *m* public

com'mon-wealth *s* état *m*, république *f*

commotion [kə'moʃən] *s* commotion *f*

commune [kə'mjun] *intr* s'entretenir; (*eccl*) communier

communicant [kə'mjunɪkənt] *s* informateur *m*; (*eccl*) communiant *m*

communicate [kə'mjunɪ,ket] *tr & intr* communiquer

communicating [kə'mjunɪ,ketɪŋ] *adj* communicant

communication [kə,mjunɪ'keʃən] *s* communication *f*

communicative [kə'mjunɪ,ketɪv] *adj* communicatif

communion [kə'mjunjən] *s* communion *f*; **to take communion** communier

communism ['kamjə,nɪzəm] *s* communisme *m*

communist ['kamjənɪst] *adj & s* communiste *mf*

communi·ty [kə'mjunɪti] *s* (*pl* -**ties**) (*locality*) voisinage *m*; (*group of people living together*) communauté *f*

commu'nity chest' *s* caisse *f* de secours

commutation [,kamjə'teʃən] *s* commutation *f*

commuta'tion tick'et *s* carte *f* d'abonnement

commutator ['kamjə,tetər] *s* (elec) collecteur *m*

commute [kə'mjut] *tr* échanger; (*e.g., a prison term*) commuer || *intr* s'abonner au chemin de fer; voyager avec carte d'abonnement

commuter [kə'mjutər] *s* abonné *m* au chemin de fer

compact [kəm'pækt] *adj* compact || ['kampækt] *s* (*agreement*) pacte *m*; (*for cosmetics*) poudrier *m*, boîte *f* à poudre

companion [kəm'pænjən] *s* compagnon *m*; (*female companion*) compagne *f*

companionable [kəm'pænjənəbəl] *adj* sociable

compan'ion-ship' *s* camaraderie *f*

compan'ion-way' *s* escalier *m* des cabines

compa·ny ['kʌmpəni] *s* (*pl* -**nies**) compagnie *f*; (com) société *f*, compagnie; (naut) équipage *m*; (theat) troupe *f*; **to have company** avoir du monde; **to keep bad company** fréquenter la mauvaise compagnie; **to keep company** sortir ensemble; **to keep s.o. company** tenir compagnie à qn; **to part company** se séparer

comparative [kəm'pærətɪv] *adj* comparatif; (*anatomy, literature, etc.*) comparé || *s* comparatif *m*

compare [kəm'per] *s*—**beyond compare** incomparablement, sans égal ‖ *tr* comparer; **compared to** en comparaison de; **to be compared to** se comparer à

comparison [kəm'pærɪsən] *s* comparaison *f*

compartment [kəm'partmənt] *s* compartiment *m*

compass ['kʌmpəs] *s* (*for showing direction*) boussole *f*; (*range, reach*) portée *f*; (*for drawing circles*) compas *m*; **the rose des vents** ‖ *tr*—**to compass about** entourer

com'pass card' *s* rose *f* des vents

compassion [kəm'pæʃən] *s* compassion *f*

compassionate [kəm'pæʃənɪt] *adj* compatissant

compatibility [kəm,pætɪ'bɪlɪti] *s* compatibilité *f*, convenance *f*

com-pel [kəm'pel] *v* (*pret & pp* -**pelled**; *ger* -**pelling**) *tr* contraindre, obliger; (*respect, silence*) imposer

compelling [kəm'pelɪŋ] *adj* irrésistible; (*motive*) impérieux

compendious [kəm'pendɪ·əs] *adj* abrégé, succinct

compensate ['kʌmpən,set] *tr* compenser; **to compensate s.o. for** dédommager qn de ‖ *intr*—**to compensate for** compenser

compensation [,kʌmpən'seʃən] *s* compensation *f*

compete [kəm'pit] *intr* concourir

competence ['kʌmpɪtəns] *or* **competency** ['kʌmpɪtənsi] *s* compétence *f*

competent ['kʌmpɪtənt] *adj* compétent

competition [,kʌmpɪ'tɪʃən] *s* concurrence *f*, compétition *f*; (*contest*) concours *m*; (*sports*) compétition, épreuve *f*

competitive [kəm'petɪtɪv] *adj* compétitif

compet'itive exam'ination *s* concours *m*

competitor [kəm'petɪtər] *s* concurrent *m*

compilation [,kʌmpɪ'leʃən] *s* compilation *f*

compile [kəm'paɪl] *tr* compiler

complacency [kəm'plesənsi] *s* complaisance *f*; (*self-satisfaction*) suffisance *f*

complacent [kəm'plesənt] *adj* complaisant; content de soi, suffisant

complain [kəm'plen] *intr* se plaindre

complainant [kəm'plenənt] *s* plaignant *m*

complaint [kəm'plent] *s* plainte *f*; (*grievance*) grief *m*; (*illness*) maladie *f*, mal *m*

complaisant [kəm'plezənt], ['kʌmplɪ,zænt] *adj* complaisant

complement ['kʌmplɪmənt] *s* complément *m*; (*mil*) effectif *m* ‖ ['kʌmplɪ,ment] *tr* compléter

complete [kəm'plit] *adj* complet ‖ *tr* compléter

complex [kəm'pleks], ['kʌmpleks] *adj* complexe ‖ ['kʌmpleks] *s* complexe *m*

complexion [kəm'plekʃən] *s* (*texture*

of skin, especially of face) teint *m*; (*general aspect*) caractère *m*; (*constitution*) complexion *f*

compliance [kəm'plaɪ·əns] *s* complaisance *f*; soumission *f*, conformité *f*; **in compliance with** conformément à

complicate ['kʌmplɪ,ket] *tr* compliquer

complicated *adj* compliqué

complication [,kʌmplɪ'keʃən] *s* complication *f*

complici-ty [kəm'plɪsɪti] *s* (*pl* -**ties**) complicité *f*

compliment ['kʌmplɪmənt] *s* compliment *m*; **compliments** (*kind regards*) civilités *fpl*; **to pay a compliment to** faire un compliment à; **with the compliments of the author** hommage de l'auteur ‖ *tr* complimenter

com'plimen'tary cop'y [,kʌmplɪ'mentəri] *s* exemplaire *m* en hommage; **to give a complimentary copy of a book** faire hommage d'un livre

com'plimen'tary tick'et *s* billet *m* de faveur

com-ply [kəm'plaɪ] *v* (*pret & pp* -**plied**) *intr*—**to comply with** se conformer à, acquiescer à

component [kəm'ponənt] *adj* composant ‖ *s* (*chem*) composant *m*; (*mech, math*) composante *f*

comportment [kəm'portmənt] *s* comportement *m*

compose [kəm'poz] *tr* composer; **to be composed of** se composer de; **to compose oneself** se calmer

composed *adj* paisible, tranquille

composer [kəm'pozər] *s* compositeur *m*

compos'ing stick' *s* compositeur *m*

composite [kəm'pazɪt] *adj & s* composé *m*

composition [,kʌmpə'zɪʃən] *s* composition *f*

compositor [kəm'pazɪtər] *s* compositeur *m*

compost ['kʌmpost] *s* compost *m*

composure [kəm'poʒər] *s* calme *m*, sang-froid *m*

compote ['kʌmpot] *s* (*stewed fruits*) compote *f*; (*dish*) compotier *m*

compound ['kʌmpaund] *adj* composé ‖ *s* composé *m*; (*gram*) mot *m* composé; (*math*) complexe *m*; (*mil*) enceinte *f* ‖ [kəm'paund] *tr* composer, combiner; (*interest*) capitaliser

comprehend [,kʌmprɪ'hend] *tr* comprendre

comprehensible [,kʌmprɪ'hensɪbəl] *adj* compréhensible

comprehension [,kʌmprɪ'henʃən] *s* compréhension *f*

comprehensive [,kʌmprɪ'hensɪv] *adj* compréhensif, étendu; (*study, view, measure*) d'ensemble

compress ['kʌmpres] *s* (*med*) compresse *f* ‖ [kəm'pres] *tr* comprimer

compression [kəm'preʃən] *s* compression *f*

comprise [kəm'praɪz] *tr* comprendre, renfermer

compromise ['kʌmprə,maɪz] *s* compromis m; (with one's conscience) transaction f; rough compromise cote f mal taillée || tr (e.g., one's honor) compromettre || intr (to make concessions) transiger

comptroller [kən'trolər] s vérificateur m, contrôleur m

compulsive [kəm'pʌlsɪv] adj obligatoire; (psychol) compulsif

compulsory [kəm'pʌlsəri] adj obligatoire, forcé

compute [kəm'pjut] tr computer, calculer, supputer || intr calculer

computer [kəm'pjutər] s ordinateur m

comrade ['kɑmræd], ['kɑmrɪd] s camarade mf

com'rade in arms' s compagnon m d'armes

com'rade-ship' s camaraderie f

con [kɑn] s contre m || v (pret & pp conned; ger conning) tr étudier; (naut) gouverner; (slang) escroquer

concave ['kɑnkev], [kɑn'kev] adj concave

conceal [kən'sil] tr dissimuler

concealment [kən'silmənt] s dissimulation f; (place) cachette f

concede [kən'sid] tr & intr concéder

conceit [kən'sit] s (vanity) vanité f; (witty expression) saillie f, mot m; conceits concetti mpl

conceited adj vaniteux, vain

conceivable [kən'sivəbəl] adj concevable

conceive [kən'siv] tr & intr concevoir

concentrate ['kɑnsən‚tret] tr concentrer || intr se concentrer

concentra'tion camp' [‚kɑnsən'treʃən] s camp m de concentration

concentric [kən'sentrɪk] adj concentrique

concept ['kɑnsept] s concept m

conception [kən'sepʃən] s conception f

concern [kən'sʌrn] s (business establishment) maison f, compagnie f; (worry) inquiétude f; (relation, reference) intérêt m; (matter) affaire f || tr concerner; as concerns quant à; persons concerned intéressés mpl; to be concerned être inquiet; to be concerned about se préoccuper de; to concern oneself with s'intéresser à; to whom it may concern à qui de droit

concerning [kən'sʌrnɪŋ] prep concernant, en ce qui concerne, touchant

concert ['kɑnsərt] s concert m; in concert de concert || [kən'sʌrt] tr concerter || intr se concerter

con'cert-mas'ter s premier violon m soliste

concer-to [kən'tʃɛrto] s (pl -tos or -ti [ti]) concerto m

concession [kən'seʃən] s concession f

conciliate [kən'sɪlɪ‚et] tr concilier

conciliatory [kən'sɪlɪ-ə‚tori] adj conciliatoire

concise [kən'saɪs] adj concis

conclude [kən'klud] tr & intr conclure

conclusion [kən'kluʒən] s conclusion f

conclusive [kən'klusɪv] adj concluant

concoct [kən'kɑkt] tr confectionner; (a story) inventer; (a plan) machiner

concoction [kən'kɑkʃən] s confection f; (mixture) mélange m; (pej) drogue f

concomitant [kən'kɑmɪtənt] adj concomitant || s accompagnement m

concord ['kɑŋkɔrd] s concorde f; (gram) concordance f; (mus) accord m

concordance [kən'kɔrdəns] s concordance f

concourse ['kɑŋkɔrs] s (of people) concours m, foule f; (road) boulevard m; (of railroad station) hall m, salle f des pas perdus

concrete ['kɑnkrit], [kɑn'krit] adj concret; de béton || s concret m; (for construction) béton m || tr (a sidewalk) bétonner

con'crete block' s parpaing m

con'crete mix'er s bétonnière f

concubine ['kɑŋkjə‚baɪn] s concubine f

con-cur [kən'kʌr] v (pret & pp -curred; ger -curring) intr (said of events) concourir; (said of persons) s'accorder

concurrence [kən'kʌrəns] s concours m

concurrent [kən'kʌrənt] adj concourant

concussion [kən'kʌʃən] s secousse f, ébranlement m; (pathol) commotion f

condemn [kən'dem] tr condamner

condemnation [‚kɑndem'neʃən] s condamnation f

condense [kən'dens] tr condenser || intr se condenser

condenser [kən'densər] s condenseur m; (elec) condensateur m

condescend [‚kɑndɪ'send] intr condescendre

condescending [‚kɑndɪ'sendɪŋ] adj condescendant

condescension [‚kɑndɪ'senʃən] s condescendance f

condiment ['kɑndɪmənt] s condiment m

condition [kən'dɪʃən] s condition f; on condition that à condition que || tr conditionner

conditional [kən'dɪʃənəl] adj & s conditionnel m

condole [kən'dol] intr—to condole with offrir ses condoléances à

condolence [kən'doləns] s condoléances fpl

condone [kən'don] tr pardonner, tolérer

conducive [kən'd(j)usɪv] adj favorable

conduct ['kɑndʌkt] s conduite f, comportement m || [kən'dʌkt] tr conduire

conductor [kən'dʌktər] s (on bus or streetcar) receveur m; (mus) chef m d'orchestre; (rr) chef de train; (elec, phys) conducteur m; (elec, phys) (in predicate after to be, it may be translated by an adjective) conducteur, e.g., metals are good conductors of electricity les métaux sont bons conducteurs de l'électricité

conduit ['kɑndɪt], ['kɑndu‚ɪt] s conduit m; (elec) caniveau m

cone [kon] *s* cône *m*; (*for popcorn, ice cream*) cornet *m*, plaisir *m*

confection [kənˈfekʃən] *s* confiserie *f*

confectioner [kənˈfekʃənər] *s* confiseur *m*

confec′tioners′ sug′ar *s* sucre *m* glace

confection·y [kənˈfekʃəˌneri] *s* (*pl* -ies) confiserie *f*

confedera·cy [kənˈfedərəsi] *s* (*pl* -cies) confédération *f*; (*for unlawful purposes*) conspiration *f*, entente *f*

confederate [kənˈfedərɪt] *adj* confédéré || *s* complice *mf*; **Confederate** (hist) Confédéré *m* || [kənˈfedəˌret] *tr* fédérer || *intr* se confédérer

con·fer [kənˈfʌr] *v* (*pret & pp* -ferred; *ger* -ferring) *tr & intr* conférer

conference [ˈkɑnfərəns] *s* conférence *f*; (*interview*) entretien *m*; (*sports*) groupement *m* (d'équipes)

conferment [kənˈfʌrmənt] *s* (*of degrees*) collation *f*

confess [kənˈfes] *tr* confesser || *intr* se confesser

confession [kənˈfeʃən] *s* confession *f*

confessional [kənˈfeʃənəl] *s* confessional *m*

confessor [kənˈfesər] *s* confesseur *m*

confidant [ˌkɑnfɪˈdænt], [ˈkɑnfɪˌdænt] *s* confident *m*

confide [kənˈfaɪd] *tr* confier || *intr*—**to confide in** se confier à

confidence [ˈkɑnfɪdəns] *s* confiance *f*; (*secret*) confidence *f*; **in strict confidence** sous toute réserve; **to have confidence in** se confier à

confident [ˈkɑnfɪdənt] *adj* confiant || *s* confident *m*

confidential [ˌkɑnfɪˈdenʃəl] *adj* confidentiel

confiden′tial sec′retary *s* secrétaire *m* particulier, secrétaire *f* particulière

confine [ˈkɑnfaɪn] *s* (obs) confinement *m*; **the confines** les confins *mpl* || [kənˈfaɪn] *tr* confiner, enfermer; (*to keep within limits*) limiter; **to be confined** (*said of woman*) accoucher; **to be confined to bed** être alité

confinement [kənˈfaɪnmənt] *s* limitation *f*; (*in prison*) emprisonnement *m*; (*in childbirth*) accouchement *m*

confirm [kənˈfʌrm] *tr* confirmer

confirmed *adj* (*reassured*) confirmé; (*bachelor*) endurci; (*drunkard*) fieffé; (*drinker*) invétéré; (*smoker*) émérite

confiscate [ˈkɑnfɪsˌket] *tr* confisquer

conflagration [ˌkɑnfləˈgreʃən] *s* conflagration *f*, incendie *m*

conflict [ˈkɑnflɪkt] *s* conflit *m* || [kənˈflɪkt] *intr* être en contradiction, se heurter

conflicting [kənˈflɪktɪŋ] *adj* contradictoire; (*events, class hours, etc.*) incompatible

con′flict of in′terest *s* conflit *m* d'intérêts, conflit des intérêts

conform [kənˈfɔrm] *tr* conformer || *intr* se conformer, s'accommoder

conformist [kənˈfɔrmɪst] *s* conformiste *mf*

conformi·ty [kənˈfɔrmɪti] *s* (*pl* -ties)

conformité *f*; **in conformity with** conformément à

confound [kɑnˈfaund] *tr* confondre || [ˈkɑnˈfaund] *tr* maudire; **confound it!** diable!

confounded *adj* confus; (*damned*) sacré

confrere [ˈkɑnfrer] *s* confrère *m*

confront [kənˈfrʌnt] *tr* (*to face boldly*) affronter, faire face à; (*witnesses; documents*) confronter; **to be confronted by** se trouver en face de

confuse [kənˈfjuz] *tr* confondre; **to get confused** devenir confus, s'embrouiller

confusing [kənˈfjuzɪŋ] *adj* déroutant, embrouillant

confusion [kənˈfjuʒən] *s* confusion *f*

confute [kənˈfjut] *tr* réfuter

congeal [kənˈdʒil] *tr* congeler || *intr* se congeler

congenial [kənˈdʒinjəl] *adj* sympathique, agréable; compatible; **congenial to** ou **with** apparenté à, conforme au tempérament de

congenital [kənˈdʒenɪtəl] *adj* congénital

con′ger eel′ [ˈkɑŋgər] *s* congre *m*, anguille *f* de mer

congest [kənˈdʒest] *tr* congestionner || *intr* se congestionner

congestion [kənˈdʒestʃən] *s* congestion *f*

conglomeration [kənˌglɑməˈreʃən] *s* conglomération *f*

congratulate [kənˈgrætʃəˌlet] *tr* féliciter, congratuler; **to congratulate s.o. for** féliciter qn de ou pour; **to congratulate s.o. for** + *ger* féliciter qn de + *inf*

congratulations [kənˌgrætʃəˈleʃənz] *spl* félicitations *fpl*

congregate [ˈkɑŋgrɪˌget] *tr* rassembler || *intr* se rassembler

congregation [ˌkɑŋgrɪˈgeʃən] *s* rassemblement *m*; (*parishioners*) fidèles *mfpl*; (*Protestant parishioners; committee of Roman Catholic prelates*) congrégation *f*

congress [ˈkɑŋgrɪs] *s* congrès *m*

congressional [kənˈgreʃənəl] *adj* parlementaire

con′gress·man *s* (*pl* -men) congressiste *m*, parlementaire *m*

con′gress·wom′an *s* (*pl* -wom′en) congressiste *f*, parlementaire *f*

congruent [ˈkɑŋgru·ənt] *adj* (math) congru

conical [ˈkɑnɪkəl] *adj* conique

conjecture [kənˈdʒektʃər] *s* conjecture *f* || *tr & intr* conjecturer

conjugal [ˈkɑndʒəgəl] *adj* conjugal

conjugate [ˈkɑndʒəˌget] *tr* conjuguer

conjugation [ˌkɑndʒəˈgeʃən] *s* conjugaison *f*

conjunction [kənˈdʒʌŋkʃən] *s* conjonction *f*

conjuration [ˌkɑndʒəˈreʃən] *s* conjuration *f*

conjure [kənˈdʒʊr] *tr* (*to appeal to solemnly*) conjurer || [ˈkɑndʒər], [ˈkʌndʒər] *tr* (*to exorcise, drive away*) conjurer; **to conjure up** évoquer || *intr* faire de la sorcellerie

connect [kə'nɛkt] *tr* relier, joindre; (*e.g.*, *two parties on the telephone*) mettre en communication; (*a pipe, an electrical device*) brancher, connecter ‖ *intr* se lier, se joindre; **to connect with** (*said of train*) correspondre avec

connected *adj* (*related*) connexe; (*logical*) suivi

connecting [kə'nɛktɪŋ] *adj* de liaison; (*wire*) de connexion; (*pipe*) de raccord; (*street*) communiquant

connect'ing rod' *s* bielle *f*

connection [kə'nɛkʃən] *s* connexion *f*, liaison *f*; (*between two causes*) connexité *f*; (*in families*) parenté *f*, parent *m*; (*by telephone*) communication *f*; (*of trains*) correspondance *f*; (elec) connexion; **connections** (*in the business world*) clientèle *f*, relations *fpl*; (*in families*) alliés *mpl*, consanguins *mpl*; **in connection with** à propos de

con'ning tow'er [ˈkɑnɪŋ] *s* (*e.g.*, *on battleship*) poste *m* or tourelle *f* de commandement; (*on sub*) kiosque *m*

conniption [kə'nɪpʃən] *s* (coll) rogne *f*

connive [kə'naɪv] *intr* être de connivence, être complice

connote [kə'not] *tr* (*to signify*) signifier, vouloir dire; (*to imply*) suggérer, sous-entendre

connubial [kə'n(j)ubɪ.əl] *adj* conjugal

conquer [ˈkɑŋkər] *tr* conquérir

conqueror [ˈkɑŋkərər] *s* conquérant *m*

conquest [ˈkɑŋkwɛst] *s* conquête *f*

conscience [ˈkɑnʃəns] *s* conscience *f*; **in all conscience** en conscience; **to have on one's conscience** avoir sur la conscience

conscientious [ˌkɑnʃɪ'ɛnʃəs] *adj* consciencieux

conscien'tious objec'tor [əb'dʒɛktər] *s* objecteur *m* de conscience

conscious [ˈkɑnʃəs] *adj* conscient; **to be conscious** (*not unconscious*) avoir connaissance; **to be conscious of** avoir conscience de

consciousness [ˈkɑnʃəsnɪs] *s* (*not sleep or coma*) connaissance *f*; (*awareness*) conscience *f*

conscript [ˈkɑnskrɪpt] *s* (mil) conscrit *m*; (nav) inscrit *m* maritime ‖ [kən'skrɪpt] *tr* (mil) enrôler; (nav) inscrire

conscription [kən'skrɪpʃən] *s* conscription *f*

consecrate [ˈkɑnsɪ‚kret] *tr* consacrer; (*e.g.*, *bread*) bénir; (*a king or bishop*) sacrer

consecration [ˌkɑnsɪ'kreʃən] *s* consécration *f*; (*to a task*) dévouement *m*; (*of a king or bishop*) sacre *m*

consecutive [kən'sɛkjətɪv] *adj* de suite, consécutif

consensus [kən'sɛnsəs] *s* consensus *m*

consent [kən'sɛnt] *s* consentement *m*; **by common consent** d'un commun accord ‖ *intr* consentir

consequence [ˈkɑnsɪ‚kwɛns] *s* conséquence *f*

consequential [ˌkɑnsɪ'kwɛnʃəl] *adj* conséquent, logique

consequently [ˈkɑnsɪ‚kwɛntli] *adv* conséquemment, par conséquent

conservation [ˌkɑnsər've ʃən] *s* conservation *f*

conservatism [kən'sʌrvə‚tɪzəm] *s* conservatisme *m*

conservative [kən'sʌrvətɪv] *adj* & *s* conservateur *m*; **at a conservative estimate** au bas mot, au moins

conservatory [kən'sʌrvə‚tori] *s* (*pl* **-ries**) (*of music*) conservatoire *m*; (*greenhouse*) serre *f*

conserve [kən'sʌrv] *tr* conserver

consider [kən'sɪdər] *tr* considérer

considerable [kən'sɪdərəbəl] *adj* considérable

considerate [kən'sɪdərɪt] *adj* prévenant, plein d'égards

consideration [kən‚sɪdə'reʃən] *s* considération *f*; (*remuneration*) rétribution *f*; (*favor*) indulgence *f*; **to take into consideration** tenir compte de; **under consideration** à l'étude

considering [kən'sɪdərɪŋ] *prep* eu égard à; **considering that** vu que

consign [kən'saɪn] *tr* consigner

consignee [ˌkɑnsaɪ'ni] *s* consignataire *m*

consignment [kən'saɪnmənt] *s* consignation *f*, livraison *f*

consist [kən'sɪst] *intr*—**to consist in** consister dans or en; **to consist in** + *ger* consister à + *inf*; **to consist of** consister dans or en

consistency [kən'sɪstənsi] *s* (*pl* **-cies**) (*logical connection*) conséquence *f*; (*firmness, amount of firmness*) consistance *f*

consistent [kən'sɪstənt] *adj* (*agreeing with itself or oneself*) conséquent; (*holding firmly together*) consistant; **consistent with** compatible avec

consistory [kən'sɪstəri] *s* (*pl* **-ries**) consistoire *m*

consolation [ˌkɑnsə'leʃən] *s* consolation *f*

console [ˈkɑnsol] *s* console *f* ‖ [kən'sol] *tr* consoler

con'sole ta'ble *s* console *f*

consolidate [kən'sɑlɪ‚det] *tr* consolider

consonant [ˈkɑnsənənt] *adj* (*in sound*) consonant; **consonant with** d'accord avec ‖ *s* consonne *f*

consort [ˈkɑnsɔrt] *s* compagnon *m*; (*husband*) conjoint *m*; (*wife*) conjointe *f*; **prince** *m* **consort**; (*convoy*) conserve *f* ‖ [kən'sɔrt] *tr* unir ‖ *intr* s'associer; (*to harmonize*) s'accorder; **to consort with** s'associer à or avec

conspicuous [kən'spɪkju.əs] *adj* apparent, frappant; (*attracting special attention*) voyant; **to make oneself conspicuous** se faire remarquer

conspiracy [kən'spɪrəsi] *s* (*pl* **-cies**) conspiration *f*, conjuration *f*

conspirator [kən'spɪrətər] *s* conspirateur *m*, conjuré *m*

conspire [kən'spaɪr] *intr* conspirer

constable [ˈkɑnstəbəl], [ˈkʌnstəbəl] *s* garde *m* champêtre; juge *m* de paix

constancy ['kɑnstænsɪ] *s* constance *f*

constant ['kɑnstənt] *adj* constant ‖ *s* constante *f*

constantly ['kɑnstəntlɪ] *adv* constamment

constellation [ˌkɑnstə'leʃən] *s* constellation *f*

constipate ['kɑnstɪˌpet] *tr* constiper

constipation [ˌkɑnstɪ'peʃən] *s* constipation *f*

constituen‧cy [kən'stɪtʃ∪·ənsɪ] *s* (*pl* -cies) électeurs *mpl*, commettants *mpl*; circonscription *f* électorale

constituent [kən'stɪtʃ∪·ənt] *adj* constituant, constitutif ‖ *s* élément *m*, constituant *m*; (*voter, client*) électeur *m*, commettant *m*

constitute ['kɑnstɪˌt(j)ut] *tr* constituer

constitution [ˌkɑnstɪ't(j)uʃən] *s* constitution *f*

constrain [kən'stren] *tr* contraindre

constraint [kən'strent] *s* contrainte *f*; (*restraint*) retenue *f*; (*uneasiness*) gêne *f*

constrict [kən'strɪkt] *tr* resserrer

construct [kən'strʌkt] *tr* construire

construction [kən'strʌkʃən] *s* construction *f*; interprétation *f*

constructive [kən'strʌktɪv] *adj* constructif, constructeur

construe [kən'stru] *tr* expliquer, interpréter; (*gram*) construire

consul ['kɑnsəl] *s* consul *m*

consular ['kɑns(j)ələr] *adj* consulaire

consulate ['kɑns(j)əlɪt] *s* consulat *m*

consult [kən'sʌlt] *tr* consulter ‖ *intr* consulter; se consulter

consultant [kən'sʌltənt] *s* conseiller *m*, consultant *m*

consultation [ˌkɑnsəl'teʃən] *s* consultation *f*; (*eccl, law*) consulte *f*

consume [kən's(j)um] *tr* (*to make use of, use up*) consommer; (*to use up entirely; to destroy*) consumer, épuiser

consumer [kən's(j)umər] *s* consommateur *m*; (*of gas, electricity, etc.*) abonné *m*

consum'er goods' *spl* denrées *fpl* de consommation

consummate [kən'sʌmɪt] *adj* consommé ‖ ['kɑnsəˌmet] *tr* consommer

consumption [kən'sʌmpʃən] *s* consommation *f*; (*pathol*) tuberculose *f* pulmonaire

consumptive [kən'sʌmptɪv] *adj* destructeur; (*pathol*) poitrinaire ‖ *s* (*pathol*) poitrinaire *mf*

contact ['kɑntækt] *s* contact *m*; **to put in contact** mettre en contact ‖ *tr* (*coll*) prendre contact avec, contacter ‖ *intr* prendre contact

con'tact lens' *s* verre *m* de contact, lentille *f* de contact

contagion [kən'tedʒən] *s* contagion *f*

contagious [kən'tedʒəs] *adj* contagieux

contain [kən'ten] *tr* contenir; (*one's sorrow*) apprivoiser

container [kən'tenər] *s* boîte *f*, contenant *m*, récipient *m*

containment [kən'tenmənt] *s* refoulement *m*, retenue *f*

contaminate [kən'tæmɪˌnet] *tr* contaminer

contamination [kənˌtæmɪ'neʃən] *s* contamination *f*

contemplate ['kɑntəmˌplet] *tr & intr* contempler; (*e.g., a trip*) projeter; **to contemplate** + *ger* penser + *inf*

contemplation [ˌkɑntəm'pleʃən] *s* contemplation *f*

contemporaneous [kənˌtempə'renɪ·əs] *adj* contemporain

contemporar‧y [kən'tempəˌrerɪ] *adj* contemporain ‖ *s* (*pl* -ies) contemporain *m*

contempt [kən'tempt] *s* mépris *m*, nargue *f*; (*law*) contumace *f*; **to hold in contempt** mépriser

contemptible [kən'temptɪbəl] *adj* méprisable

contempt' of court' *s* outrage *m* à la justice

contemptuous [kən'temptʃ∪·əs] *adj* méprisant

contend [kən'tend] *tr* prétendre ‖ *intr* combattre; **to contend with** lutter contre

contender [kən'tendər] *s* concurrent *m*, compétiteur *m*

content [kən'tent] *adj & s* content *m* ‖ ['kɑntent] *s* contenu *m*; **contents** contenu; (*of table of contents*) matières *fpl* ‖ [kən'tent] *tr* contenter

contented [kən'tentɪd] *adj* content, satisfait

contention [kən'tenʃən] *s* (*strife*) dispute *f*, différend *m*; (*point argued for*) point *m* discuté, argument *m*; (*law*) contentieux *m*

contentious [kən'tenʃəs] *adj* contentieux

contentment [kən'tentmənt] *s* contentement *m*

contest ['kɑntest] *s* (*struggle, fight*) lutte *f*, dispute *f*; (*competition*) concours *m*, compétition *f* ‖ [kən'test] *tr & intr* contester

contestant [kən'testənt] *s* concurrent *m*

context ['kɑntekst] *s* contexte *m*

contiguous [kən'tɪgjʊ·əs] *adj* contigu

continence ['kɑntɪnəns] *s* continence *f*

continent ['kɑntɪnənt] *adj & s* continent *m*

continental [ˌkɑntɪ'nentəl] *adj* continental

contingen‧cy [kən'tɪndʒənsɪ] *s* (*pl* -cies) contingence *f*

contingent [kən'tɪndʒənt] *adj & s* contingent *m*

continual [kən'tɪnjʊ·əl] *adj* continuel

continuation [kənˌtɪnjʊ'eʃən] *s* continuation *f*; (*e.g., of a story*) suite *f*

continue [kən'tɪnjʊ] *tr & intr* continuer; **continued on page two (three, etc.)** suite page deux (trois, etc.); **to be continued** à suivre

continui‧ty [ˌkɑntɪ'n(j)u·ɪtɪ] *s* (*pl* -ties) continuité *f*; (*mov, rad, telv*) découpage *m*, scénario *m*

continuous [kən'tɪnjʊ·əs] *adj* continu

contin'uous show'ing *s* (*mov*) spectacle *m* permanent

contin′uous waves′ spl ondes fpl entretenues

contortion [kən′tɔrʃən] s contorsion f

contour [′kɑntur] s contour m ‖ tr contourner

con′tour line′ s courbe f de niveau

contraband [′kɑntrə‚bænd] adj contrebandier ‖ s contrebande f

contrabass [′kɑntrə‚bes] s contrebasse f

contraceptive [‚kɑntrə′septɪv] adj & s contraceptif m

contract [′kɑntrækt] s contrat m ‖ [′kɑntrækt], [kən′trækt] tr contracter ‖ [kən′trækt] intr se contracter

contraction [kən′trækʃən] s contraction f

contractor [kən′træktər] s entrepreneur m

contradict [‚kɑntrə′dɪkt] tr contredire

contradiction [‚kɑntrə′dɪkʃən] s contradiction f

contradictory [‚kɑntrə′dɪktəri] adj contradictoire

contral·to [kən′trælto] s (pl -tos) contralto m

contraption [kən′træpʃən] s (coll) machin m, truc m

contra·ry [′kɑntreri] adj contraire ‖ adv contrairement ‖ [kən′treri] adj (coll) obstiné, têtu ‖ [′kɑntreri] s (pl -ries) contraire m; **on the contrary** au contraire, par contre

contrast [′kɑntræst] s contraste m ‖ [kən′træst] tr & intr contraster

contravene [‚kɑntrə′vin] tr contredire; (a law) contrevenir (with dat)

contribute [kən′trɪbjut] tr (e.g., a sum of money) contribuer pour ‖ intr contribuer; (to a newspaper, conference, etc.) collaborer

contribution [‚kɑntrɪ′bjuʃən] s contribution f, apport m; (e.g., for charity) souscription f; (to a newspaper, conference, etc.) collaboration f

contributor [kən′trɪbjutər] s (donor) donneur m; (e.g., to a charitable cause) souscripteur m; (to a newspaper, conference, etc.) collaborateur m

contrite [kən′traɪt] adj contrit

contrition [kən′trɪʃən] s contrition f

contrivance [kən′traɪvəns] s invention f, expédient m; (gadget) dispositif m

contrive [kən′traɪv] tr inventer ‖ intr s'arranger; **to contrive to** trouver moyen de

con·trol [kən′trol] s direction f, autorité f; (mastery) maîtrise f; (surveillance) contrôle m; **controls** commandes fpl ‖ v (pret & pp -trolled; ger -trolling) tr diriger; maîtriser; (to give surveillance to) contrôler; (to handle the controls of) commander; **to control oneself** se contrôler

controller [kən′trolər] s contrôleur m, appareil m de contrôle; (elec) controller m

control′ pan′el s (aer) planche f de bord, tableau m de bord

control′ stick′ s (aer) manche m à balai

control′ tow′er s poste-vigie m, tourelle f de commandement

controversial [‚kɑntrə′vʌrʃəl] adj controversable

controver·sy [′kɑntrə‚vʌrsi] s (pl -sies) controverse f; dispute f, querelle f

controvert [′kɑntrə‚vʌrt], [‚kɑntrə′vʌrt] tr controverser; contredire

contumacious [‚kɑnt(j)u′meʃəs] adj rebelle, récalcitrant

contume·ly [′kɑnt(j)umɪli] s (pl -lies) injure f, outrage m, mépris m

contusion [kən′t(j)uʒən] s contusion f

conundrum [kə′nʌndrəm] s devinette f, énigme f

convalesce [‚kɑnvə′les] intr guérir, se remettre, se rétablir

convalescence [‚kɑnvə′lesəns] s convalescence f

convalescent [‚kɑnvə′lesənt] adj & s convalescent m

convales′cent home′ s maison f de repos

convene [kən′vin] tr assembler, convoquer ‖ intr s'assembler

convenience [kən′vinjəns] s commodité f; (e.g., in the home) confort m; **at your earliest convenience** aussitôt que possible

convent [′kɑnvent] s couvent m (de religieuses)

convention [kən′venʃən] s assemblée f, congrès m; (agreement) convention f; (accepted usage) convention sociale; **conventions** convenances fpl, bienséances fpl

conventional [kən′venʃənəl] adj conventionnel; (in conduct) respectueux des convenances; (everyday) usuel; (model, type) traditionnel

converge [kən′vʌrdʒ] intr converger

conversant [kən′vʌrsənt] adj familier, versé

conversation [‚kɑnvər′seʃən] s conversation f

conversational [‚kɑnvər′seʃənəl] adj de conversation

converse [′kɑnvʌrs] adj & s contraire m, inverse m, réciproque f ‖ [kən′vʌrs] intr converser

conversion [kən′vʌrʒən] s conversion f

convert [′kɑnvʌrt] s converti m ‖ [kən′vʌrt] tr convertir ‖ intr se convertir

converter [kən′vʌrtər] s convertisseur m

convertible [kən′vʌrtɪbəl] adj (person) convertissable; (thing; security) convertible; (aut) décapotable ‖ s (aut) décapotable f

convex [′kɑnveks], [kɑn′veks] adj convexe, bombé

convey [kən′ve] tr transporter; (e.g., a message) communiquer; (e.g., property) transmettre; (law) céder

conveyance [kən′ve·əns] s transport m; (vehicle) moyen m de transport, voiture f; (of message) communication f; (transfer) transmission f; (law) transfert m, cession f

conveyor [kən′ve·ər] s transporteur m, convoyeur m

convey′or belt′ s tapis m roulant

convict [′kɑnvɪkt] s condamné m, forçat *m* ‖ [kən'vɪkt] *tr* condamner, convaincre

conviction [kən'vɪkʃən] *s* condamnation *f*; (*certainty*) conviction *f*

convince [kən'vɪns] *tr* convaincre

convincing [kən'vɪnsɪŋ] *adj* convaincant

convivial [kən'vɪvɪ-əl] *adj* jovial, plein d'entrain

convocation [ˌkɑnvə'keʃən] *s* (*calling together*) convocation *f*; (*meeting*) assemblée *f*

convoke [kən'vok] *tr* convoquer

convolution [ˌkɑnvə'luʃən] *s* (*of brain*) circonvolution *f*

convoy ['kɑnvɔɪ] *s* convoi *m*, conserve *f*, e.g., **to sail in convoy** naviguer de conserve ‖ *tr* convoyer

convulse [kən'vʌls] *tr* convulsionner, convulser; **to be convulsed with laughter** se tordre de rire

coo [ku] *intr* roucouler

cooing ['ku·ɪŋ] *s* roucoulement *m*

cook [kʊk] *s* cuisinier *m*, chef *m*; (*female cook*) cuisinière *f* ‖ *tr* cuisiner, faire cuire; **to cook up** (*a plot*) machiner, tramer ‖ *intr* faire la cuisine, cuisiner; (*said of food*) cuire

cook/book/ *s* livre *m* de cuisine

cooker ['kʊkər] *s* réchaud *m*, cuisinière *f*

cookery ['kʊkəri] *s* cuisine *f*

cookie ['kʊki] *s* var of **cooky**

cooking ['kʊkɪŋ] *s* cuisine *f*; (*e.g., of meat*) cuisson *f*

cook/ing uten/sils *spl* batterie *f* de cuisine

cook/stove/ *s* cuisinière *f*

cook·y ['kʊki] *s* (*pl* -ies) biscuit *m*, gâteau *m* sec

cool [kul] *adj* frais; (*e.g., to an idea*) indifférent; **it is cool out** il fait frais; **to keep cool** tenir au frais; se tenir tranquille ‖ *s* fraîcheur *f* ‖ *tr* rafraîchir, refroidir; **to cool one's heels** (coll) se morfondre ‖ *intr* se refroidir, se rafraîchir; **to cool down** se calmer; **to cool off** se refroidir

cooler ['kulər] *s* frigorifique *m*; (*prison*) (slang) violon *m*, tôle *f*

cool/-head/ed *adj* imperturbable, de sang-froid

coolness ['kulnɪs] *s* fraîcheur *f*; (*of disposition*) sang-froid *m*, calme *m*; (*stand-offishness*) froideur *f*

coon [kun] *s* raton *m* laveur

coop [kup] *s* poulailler *m*; **to fly the coop** (slang) débiner, décamper ‖ *tr* enfermer dans un poulailler; **to coop up** claquemurer

co-op ['ko·ɑp], [ko'ɑp] *s* entreprise *f* coopérative

cooper ['kʊpər] *s* tonnelier *m*

cooperate [ko'ɑpəˌret] *intr* coopérer; (*to be helpful*) faire preuve de bonne volonté

cooperation [koˌɑpə'reʃən] *s* coopération *f*

cooperative [ko'ɑpəˌretɪv] *adj* coopératif

coordinate [ko'ɔrdɪnɪt] *adj* coordonné

‖ *s* coordonnée *f* ‖ [ko'ɔrdɪˌnet] *tr* coordonner

coot [kut] *s* foulque *f*; **old coot** (coll) vieille baderne *f*

cootie ['kuti] *s* (slang) pou *m*

cop [kɑp] *s* (slang) flic *m* ‖ *v* (*pret* & *pp* **copped**; *ger* **copping**) *tr* (slang) dérober

copartner [ko'pɑrtnər] *s* coassocié *m*, coparticipant *m*; (*in crime*) complice *mf*

cope [kop] *intr*—**to cope with** faire face à, tenir tête à

cope/stone/ *s* couronnement *m*

copier ['kɑpɪ·ər] *s* (*person who copies*) copiste *mf*, imitateur *m*; (*apparatus*) appareil *m* à copier

copilot ['ko·ˌpaɪlət] *s* copilote *m*

coping ['kopɪŋ] *s* faîte *m*, comble *m*; (*of bridge*) chape *f*

copious ['kopɪ·əs] *adj* copieux

copper ['kɑpər] *adj* de cuivre, en cuivre; (*color*) cuivré ‖ *s* cuivre *m*; (*coin*) petite monnaie *f*; (slang) flic *m*

cop/per·smith/ *s* chaudronnier *m*

coppery ['kɑpəri] *adj* cuivreux

coppice ['kɑpɪs] *s* taillis *m*

copulate ['kɑpjəˌlet] *intr* s'accoupler

copulation [ˌkɑpjə'leʃən] *s* copulation *f*, accouplement *m*

cop·y ['kɑpi] *s* (*pl* -ies) copie *f*; (*of a book*) exemplaire *m*; (*of a magazine*) numéro *m*; (*for printer*) original *m*; **to make copies** exécuter des doubles ‖ *v* (*pret* & *pp* -ied) *tr* & *intr* copier

cop/y·book/ *s* cahier *m*

cop/y·cat/ *s* (coll) imitateur *m*, singe *m*

cop/y·right/ *s* propriété *f* artistique or littéraire, droit *m* de l'artiste or de l'auteur, copyright *m*; (*formula on printed matter*) dépôt *m* légal ‖ *tr* réserver les droits de publication de

cop/y·right/ed *adj* (formula used on printed material) droits de reproduction réservés

cop/y·writ/er *s* rédacteur *m* d'annonces publicitaires

co·quet [ko'kɛt] *v* (*pret* & *pp* **-quetted**; *ger* **-quetting**) *intr* coqueter

coquet·ry ['kokətri], [ko'kɛtri] *s* (*pl* -ries) coquetterie *f*

coquette [ko'kɛt] *s* coquette *f* ‖ *intr* coqueter

coquettish [ko'kɛtɪʃ] *adj* coquet

coral ['kɑrəl], ['kɔrəl] *adj* de corail, en corail ‖ *s* corail *m*

cor/al reef/ *s* récif *m* de corail

cord [kɔrd] *s* corde *f*; (*string*) ficelle *f*; (*attached to a bell*) cordon *m*; (elec) fil *m* ‖ *tr* corder

cordage ['kɔrdɪdʒ] *s* cordage *m*

cordial ['kɔrdʒəl] *adj* & *s* cordial *m*

cordiali·ty [kɔr'dʒælɪti] *s* (*pl* -ties) cordialité *f*

corduroy ['kɔrdəˌrɔɪ] *s* velours *m* côtelé; **corduroys** pantalon *m* en velours côtelé

core [kor] *s* cœur *m*; (elec) noyau *m*; **rotten to the core** pourri à la base ‖ *tr* vider

corespondent [ˌkorɪs'pɑndənt] *s* complice *mf* d'adultère

cork [kɔrk] *s* liège *m*; (*of bottle*) bouchon *m*; **to take the cork out of** déboucher || *tr* boucher
corking ['kɔrkɪŋ] *adj* (coll) épatant
cork' oak' *s* chêne-liège *m*
cork'screw' *s* tire-bouchon *m*
cork'-tipped' *adj* à bout de liège
cormorant ['kɔrmərənt] *s* cormoran *m*
corn [kɔrn] *s* (in U.S.A.) maïs *m*; (in England) blé *m*; (in Scotland) avoine *f*; (*single seed*) grain *m*; (*on foot*) cor *m*, durillon *m*; (*whiskey*) (coll) eau-de-vie *f* de grain; (slang) platitude *f*, banalité *f*
corn' bread' *s* pain *m* de maïs
corn'cob' *s* épi *m* de maïs; (*without the grain*) rafle *f*
corn'cob pipe' *s* pipe *f* en rafle de maïs
corn'crib' *s* dépôt *m* de maïs
cornea ['kɔrnɪ·ə] *s* cornée *f*
corned' beef' *s* bœuf *m* salé
corner ['kɔrnər] *adj* cornier || *s* coin *m*, angle *m*; (*of room*) encoignure *f*; (*of lips*) commissure *f*; **around the corner** au tournant; **in a corner** (fig) au pied du mur, à l'accul; **to cut a corner close** prendre un virage à la corde; **to cut corners** (in spending) rogner les dépenses; (in work) bâcler un travail || *tr* coincer, acculer; (*the market*) accaparer
cor'ner cup'board *s* encoignure *f*
cor'ner room' *s* pièce *f* d'angle
cor'ner-stone' *s* pierre *f* angulaire
cornet [kɔr'nɛt] *s* cornet *m*; (*head-dress*) cornette *f*; (mil) cornette *m*; (mus) cornet à pistons
corn' exchange' *s* bourse *f* des céréales
corn'field' *s* (in U.S.A.) champ *m* de maïs; (in England) champ de blé; (in Scotland) champ d'avoine
corn'flakes' *spl* paillettes *fpl* de maïs
corn' flour' *s* farine *f* de maïs
corn'flow'er *s* bluet *m*, barbeau *m*
corn' frit'ter *s* crêpes *fpl* de maïs
corn'husk' *s* enveloppe *f* de l'épi de maïs
cornice ['kɔrnɪs] *s* corniche *f*
corn' meal' *s* farine *f* de maïs
corn' on the cob' *s* maïs *m* en épi
corn' pad' *s* bourrelet *m* coricide
corn' pone' *s* pain *m* de maïs
corn' pop'per *s* appareil *m* pour faire éclater le maïs
corn' remov'er *s* coricide *m*
corn' silk' *s* barbe *f* de maïs
corn'stalk' *s* tige *f* de maïs
corn'starch' *s* fécule *f* de maïs
cornucopia [,kɔrnə'kopɪ·ə] *s* corne *f* d'abondance
Cornwall ['kɔrn,wɔl], ['kɔrnwəl] *s* la Cornouailles
corn•y ['kɔrni] *adj* (*comp* -ier; *super* -iest*) (slang) banal, trivial, fade
corollar•y ['kɔrə,lɛri], ['kɔrə,lɛri] *s* (*pl* -ies) corollaire *m*
coronary ['kɔrə,nɛri], ['kɔrə,nɛri] *adj* coronaire
coronation [,kɔrə'neʃən], [,kɔrə'neʃən] *s* couronnement *m*, sacre *m*
cor'oner's in'quest ['kɔrənərz], ['kɔrənərz] *s* enquête *f* judiciaire par-devant jury (en cas de mort violente ou suspecte)
coronet ['kɔrə,net], ['kɔrə,net] *s* diadème *m*; (*worn by members of nobility*) couronne *f*; (*worn by earl or baron*) tortil *m*
corporal ['kɔrpərəl] *adj* corporel || *s* (mil) caporal *m*
corporate ['kɔrpərɪt] *adj* incorporé
corporation [,kɔrpə'reʃən] *s* société *f* anonyme, compagnie *f* anonyme
corporeal [kɔr'porɪ·əl] *adj* corporel, matériel
corps [kor] *s* (*pl* **corps** [korz]) corps *m*; (mil) corps d'armée
corpse [kɔrps] *s* cadavre *m*
corps'man *s* (*pl* -men) (mil) infirmier *m*
corpulent ['kɔrpjələnt] *adj* corpulent
corpuscle ['kɔrpəsəl] *s* (phys) corpuscule *m*; (physiol) globule *m*
corpus delicti ['kɔrpəsdɪ'lɪktaɪ] *s* (law) corps *m* du délit
cor·ral [kə'ræl] *s* corral *m*, enclos *m* || *v* (*pret & pp* -ralled; *ger* -ralling) *tr* enfermer dans un corral; (fig) saisir
correct [kə'rɛkt] *adj* correct || *tr* corriger
correction [kə'rɛkʃən] *s* correction *f*
corrective [kə'rɛktɪv] *adj & s* correctif *m*
correc'tive lens'es *spl* verres *mpl* correcteurs
correctness [kə'rɛktnɪs] *s* correction *f*
correlate [kara,let], ['kɔrə,let] *tr* mettre en corrélation || *intr* correspondre; **to correlate with** correspondre à
correlation [,karə'leʃən], [,kɔrɪ'leʃən] *s* corrélation *f*
correspond [,karɪ'spand], [,kɔrɪ'spand] *intr* correspondre
correspondence [,karɪ'spandəns], [,kɔrɪ'spandəns] *s* correspondance *f*
correspondent [,karɪ'spandənt], [,kɔrɪ'spandənt] *adj & s* correspondant *m*
corresponding [,karɪ'spandɪŋ], [,kɔrɪ'spandɪŋ] *adj* correspondant
corridor ['karɪdər], ['kɔrɪdər] *s* corridor *m*, couloir *m*
corroborate [kə'rabə,ret] *tr* corroborer
corrode [kə'rod] *tr* corroder || *intr* se corroder
corrosion [kə'roʒən] *s* corrosion *f*
corrosive [kə'rosɪv] *adj & s* corrosif *m*
corrugated ['karə,getɪd], ['kɔrə,getɪd] *adj* ondulé
corrupt [kə'rʌpt] *adj* corrompu || *tr* corrompre
corruption [kə'rʌpʃən] *s* corruption *f*
corsage [kɔr'saʒ] *s* bouquet *m*
corsair ['kɔr,sɛr] *s* corsaire *m*
corset ['kɔrsɪt] *s* corset *m*
Corsica ['kɔrsɪkə] *s* Corse *f*; la Corse
Corsican ['kɔrsɪkən] *adj* corse || *s* (*dialect*) corse *m*; (*person*) Corse *mf*
cortege [kɔr'teʒ] *s* cortège *m*
cor·tex ['kɔr,tɛks] *s* (*pl* -tices [tɪ,siz]) cortex *m*
cortisone ['kɔrtɪ,son] *s* cortisone *f*
coruscate ['karəs,ket], ['kɔrəs,ket] *intr* scintiller

cosmetic [kɑz'metɪk] adj & s cosmétique m

cosmic ['kɑzmɪk] adj cosmique

cosmonaut ['kɑzmə‚nɔt] s cosmonaute mf

cosmopolitan [‚kɑzmə'pɑlɪtən] adj & s cosmopolite mf

cosmos ['kɑzməs] s cosmos m

Cossack [kɑ‚sæk] adj cosaque ‖ s Cosaque mf

cost [kɔst], [kɑst] s coût m; (price) prix m; **at all costs** à tout prix, coûte que coûte; **at cost** au prix coûtant; **costs** frais mpl; (law) dépens mpl ‖ v (pret & pp **cost**) intr coûter

cost′ account′ing s comptabilité f industrielle

costliness ['kɔstlɪnɪs], ['kɑstlɪnɪs] s cherté f, haut prix m

cost·ly ['kɔstli], ['kɑstli] adj (comp -lier; super -liest) coûteux, cher

cost′ of liv′ing s coût m de la vie

cost′ price′ s prix m coûtant; (net price) prix de revient

costume ['kɑst(j)um] s costume m

cos′tume ball′ s bal m costumé

cos′tume jew′elry s bijoux mpl en toc

costumer [kɑs't(j)umər] s costumier m

cot [kɑt] s lit m de sangle

coterie ['kotəri] s coterie f

cottage ['kɑtɪdʒ] s chalet m, cabanon m, villa f; (with a thatched roof) chaumière f

cot′tage cheese′ s lait m caillé, caillé m, jonchée f

cot′ter pin′ ['kɑtər] s goupille f fendue, clavette f

cotton ['kɑtən] adj cotonnier, de coton ‖ s coton m ‖ intr—**to cotton up to** (coll) éprouver de la sympathie pour

cot′ton bat′ting s coton m or ouate f hydrophile

cot′ton field′ s cotonnerie f

cot′ton gin′ s égreneuse f

cot′ton mill′ s filature f de coton, cotonnerie f

cot′ton pick′er s cotonnier m

cot′ton pick′ing s récolte f du coton

cot′ton·seed′ s graine f de coton

cot′tonseed oil′ s huile f de coton

cot′ton waste′ s déchets mpl or bourre f de coton

cot′ton·wood′ s peuplier m de Virginie

cottony ['kɑtəni] adj cotonneux

couch [kautʃ] s (without back) divan m; (with back) sofa m, canapé m ‖ tr (a demand, a letter) rédiger ‖ intr (to lie in wait) se tapir

cougar ['kugər] s couguar m, cougouar m

cough [kɔf], [kɑf] s toux f ‖ tr—**to cough up** cracher en toussant; (slang) (money) cracher ‖ intr tousser

cough′ drop′ s pastille f pectorale, pastille pour la toux

cough′ syr′up s sirop m pectoral, sirop contre la toux

could [kud] aux—**he could not come** il ne pouvait pas venir; **he couldn't do it** il n'a (pas) pu le faire; **he couldn't do it if he wanted to** il ne pourrait

(pas) le faire s'il le voulait, il ne saurait (pas) le faire s'il le voulait

council ['kaunsəl] s conseil m; (eccl) concile m

coun′cil·man s (pl -men) conseiller m municipal

councilor ['kaunsələr] s conseiller m

coun·sel ['kaunsəl] s conseil m, avis m; (lawyer) avocat m ‖ v (pret & pp -seled or -selled; ger -seling or -selling) tr & intr conseiller; **to counsel s.o. to** + inf conseiller à qn de + inf

counselor ['kaunsələr] s conseiller m, conseil m; (lawyer) avocat m

count [kaunt] s compte m; (nobleman) comte m ‖ tr compter; **to count the votes** dépouiller le scrutin ‖ intr compter; **count off!** (mil) comptez-vous!; **to count for** valoir; **to count on** (to have confidence in) compter sur (s.o. or s.th.); **to count on** + ger compter + inf

countable ['kauntəbəl] adj comptable

count′down′ s compte m à rebours

countenance ['kauntɪnəns] s mine f, contenance f; **to give countenance** appuyer; **to keep one's countenance** garder son sérieux; **to lose countenance** perdre contenance ‖ tr soutenir, approver

counter ['kauntər] adj contraire ‖ s compteur m; (piece of wood or metal for keeping score) jeton m; (board in shop over which business is transacted) comptoir m; (in a bar or café) zinc m; **under the counter** en dessous de table, sous le comptoir, sous cape ‖ adv contrairement; en sens inverse; **to run counter to** aller à l'encontre de ‖ tr contrarier, contrecarrer; (a move, e.g., in chess) contrer; (an opinion) prendre le contre-pied de ‖ intr parer le coup, parer un coup; **to counter with** riposter par

coun′ter·act′ tr contrebalancer

coun′ter·attack′ s contre-attaque f ‖ **coun′ter·attack′** tr contre-attaquer

coun′ter·bal′ance s contrepoids m ‖ **coun′ter·bal′ance** tr contrebalancer

coun′ter·clock′wise′ adj & adv en sens inverse des aiguilles d'une montre

coun′ter·cur′rent s contre-courant m

coun′ter·es′pionage s contre-espionnage m

counterfeit ['kauntərfɪt] adj contrefait; (beauty) sophistiqué ‖ s contrefaction f, contrefaçon f; (money) fausse monnaie f ‖ tr contrefaire; (e.g., an illness) feindre

counterfeiter ['kauntər‚fɪtər] s contrefacteur m; (of money) faux-monnayeur m

coun′terfeit mon′ey s fausse monnaie f, faux billets mpl

coun′ter·ir′ritant adj & s révulsif m

countermand ['kauntər‚mænd] ['kauntər‚mand] s contre-ordre m ‖ tr contremander

coun′ter·march′ s contremarche f ‖ intr faire une contremarche

coun′ter·meas′ure s contre-mesure f

coun′ter·offen′sive s contre-offensive f

coun'ter·pane' s courtepointe f

coun'ter·part' s contrepartie f, homologue m

coun'ter·point' s contrepoint m

coun'ter·poise' s contrepoids m || tr faire équilibre à

coun'ter·rev'olu'tionar·y adj contre-révolutionnaire || s (pl -ies) contre-révolutionnaire mf

coun'ter·sign' s contremarque f; (signature) contreseing m; (mil) mot m d'ordre || tr contresigner

coun'ter·sig'nature s contreseing m

coun'ter·sink' s fraise f || v (pret & pp -sunk) tr fraiser

coun'ter·spy' s (pl -spies) contre-espion m

coun'ter·stroke' s contrecoup m

coun'ter·weight' s contrepoids m

countess ['kauntɪs] s comtesse f

countless ['kauntlɪs] adj innombrable

countrified ['kʌntrɪˌfaɪd] adj provincial, compagnard

coun·try ['kʌntri] s (pl -tries) (territory of a nation) pays m; (land of one's birth) patrie f; (region) contrée f; (not the city) campagne f

coun'try club' s club m privé situé hors des agglomérations

coun'try estate' s domaine m

coun'try·folk' s campagnards mpl

coun'try gen'tleman s châtelain m, propriétaire m d'un château

coun'try house' s maison f de campagne

coun'try·man s (pl -men) (of the same country) compatriote mf; (rural) compagnard m

coun'try·side' s paysage m, campagne f

coun'try town' s petite ville f de province

coun'try·wide' adj national

coun'try·wom'an s (pl -wom'en) (of the same country) compatriote f; (rural) campagnarde f

coun·ty ['kaunti] s (pl -ties) comté m

coun'ty seat' s chef-lieu m de comté

coupé [kupe] s coupé m

couple ['kʌpəl] s (man and wife; male and female; friends) couple m, paire f; (of eggs, cakes, etc.) couple f; (elec, mech) couple m || tr coupler, accoupler; (mach) embrayer || intr s'accoupler

coupler ['kʌplər] s (mach) coupleur m

coupling ['kʌplɪŋ] s accouplement m; (mach) couplage m

coupon ['k(j)upɑn] s coupon m, bon m

courage ['kʌrɪdʒ] s courage m

courageous [kə'redʒəs] adj courageux

courier ['kʌrɪˌər], ['kurɪˌər] s courrier m; (on horseback) estafette f

course [kors] s cours m; carrière f, voie f, course f; (of a meal) service m, plat m; (of a stream) parcours m, cours m; (direction) route f, chemin m; in due course en temps voulu; in the course of au cours de; in the course of time avec le temps; of course! naturellement!, bien entendu!; to give a course faire un cours; to set a course for (naut) mettre le cap sur; to take a course suivre un cours || tr & intr courir

court [kort] s cour f; (of law) tribunal m, cour; (sports) terrain m, court m; out of court à l'amiable || tr courtiser, faire la cour à; (favor, votes) briguer, solliciter; (danger) aller audevant de

courteous ['kʌrtɪˌəs] adj poli, courtois

courtesan ['kʌrtɪzən], ['kɔrtɪzən] s courtisane f

courte·sy ['kʌrtɪsi] s (pl -sies) politesse f, courtoisie f; through the courtesy of avec la gracieuse permission de

court'house' s palais m de justice

courtier ['kortɪˌər] s courtisan m

court' jest'er s bouffon m du roi

court·ly ['kortli] adj (comp -lier; super -liest) courtois, élégant

court'-mar'tial s (pl courts-martial) conseil m de guerre || v (pret & pp -tialed or -tialled; ger -tialing or -tialling) tr traduire en conseil de guerre; to be court-martialed passer en conseil de guerre

court' plas'ter s taffetas m gommé, sparadrap m

court'room' s salle f du tribunal

court'ship' s cour f

court'yard' s cour f

cousin ['kʌzɪn] s cousin m

cove [kov] s anse f, crique f

covenant ['kʌvənənt] s contrat m, accord m, pacte m; (Bib) alliance f

cover ['kʌvər] s couverture f; (lid) couvercle m; (for furniture) housse f; (of wild game) remise f, gîte m; (com) couverture f, provision f, marge f; (mach) chape f; (phila) enveloppe f; from cover to cover de la première page à la dernière; to take cover se mettre à l'abri; under cover (e.g., of trees) sous les couverts; (safe from harm) à couvert; under cover of sous le couvert de, dissimulé dans; under separate cover sous pli distinct || tr couvrir; (a certain distance) parcourir; (a newspaper story) faire le reportage de; (one's tracks) brouiller; (with, e.g., chocolate) enrober; to cover up recouvrir || intr se couvrir; (to brood) couver

coverage ['kʌvərɪdʒ] s (amount or space covered) portée f; (of news) reportage m; (insurance) assurance f, couverture f d'assurance

co'ver·alls' spl salopette f, bleus mpl

cov'er charge' s couvert m

cov'ered wag'on s chariot m couvert

cov'er girl' s cover-girl f, pin up f

covering ['kʌvərɪŋ] s couverture f, recouvrement m

covert ['kʌvərt] adj couvert, caché

cov'er-up' s subterfuge m; (reply) réponse f évasive

covet ['kʌvɪt] tr convoiter

covetous ['kʌvɪtəs] adj cupide, avide

covetousness ['kʌvɪtəsnɪs] s convoitise f, cupidité f

covey [ˈkʌvi] s couvée f; (in flight) volée f

cow [kau] s vache f; (of seal, elephant) femelle f || tr intimider

coward [ˈkau·ərd] s lâche mf

cowardice [ˈkau·ərdɪs] s lâcheté f

cowardly [ˈkau·ərdli] adj lâche || adv lâchement, peureusement

cow'bell' s grelot m, clarine f

cow'boy' s cow-boy m

cow'catch'er s (rr) chasse-bestiaux m

cower [ˈkau·ər] intr se tapir

cow'herd' s vacher m, bouvier m

cow'hide' s vache f, peau f de vache; fouet m || tr fouetter

cowl [kaul] s capuchon m, cagoule f; (of chimney) chapeau m; (aer, aut) capot m

cow'lick' s mèche f rebelle

cow'pox' s (pathol) vaccine f

coxcomb [ˈkaks‚kom] s (conceited person) petit-maître m, fat m; (bot) crête-de-coq f

coxswain [ˈkaksən], [ˈkak‚swen] s patron m de chaloupe; (rowing) barreur m

coy [kɔɪ] adj réservé, modeste

co·zy [ˈkozi] adj (comp -zier; super -ziest) douillet, intime || s (pl -zies) couvre-théière m

C.P.A. [ˈsi‚piˈe] s (letterword) (certified public accountant) expert-comptable m, comptable m agréé

crab [kræb] s crabe m; (grouch) grincheux m || v (pret & pp crabbed; ger crabbing) intr (coll) se plaindre

crab' ap'ple s pomme f sauvage

crabbed [ˈkræbɪd] adj acariâtre; (handwriting) de chat; (author) hermétique; (style) entortillé

crab·by [ˈkræbi] adj (comp -bier; super -biest) (coll) revêche, grognon

crack [kræk] adj (troops) d'élite; (coll) expert, de premier ordre || s (noise) bruit m sec, craquement m; (of whip) claquement m; (fissure) fente f; (e.g., in a dish) fêlure f; (e.g., in a wall) lézarde f; (in skin) gerçure f; (joke) bon mot m; **crack of dawn** pointe f du jour || tr (one's fingers; petroleum) faire craquer; (a whip) claquer; (to split) fendre; (e.g., a dish) fêler; (e.g., a wall) lézarder; (the skin) gercer; (nuts) casser; **to crack a joke** (slang) faire or lâcher une plaisanterie; **to crack up** (to praise) (coll) vanter, prôner; (to crash) (coll) écraser || intr (to make a noise) craquer; (said of whip) claquer; (to be split) se fendre; (said of dish) se fêler; (said of wall) se lézarder; (said of skin) se gercer; **to crack up** (to crash) (coll) s'écraser; (to break down) (coll) craquer, s'effondrer

crack'-brained' adj timbré; **to be crack-brained** avoir le cerveau fêlé

crack'down' s (coll) répression f

cracked [krækt] adj (split) fendu, fêlé; (foolish) (coll) timbré, toqué, cinglé

cracker [ˈkrækər] s biscuit m sec

crack'er-bar'rel adj (coll) en chambre, au petit pied

crack'er-jack' adj (slang) expérimenté, remarquable || s (slang) crack m

cracking [ˈkrækɪŋ] s (of petroleum) cracking m

crackle [ˈkrækəl] s crépitation f || intr crépiter, pétiller

crack'le-ware' s porcelaine f craquelée

crackling [ˈkræklɪŋ] s crépitement m, pétillement m; (culin) couenne f rissolée; **cracklings** cretons pl

crack'pot' adj & s (slang) original m, excentrique mf

crack' shot' s (coll) fin tireur m

crack'-up' s (collision) (coll) écrasement m; (breakdown) (coll) effondrement m

cradle [ˈkredəl] s berceau m || tr bercer

cra'dle-song' s berceuse f

craft [kræft], [kraft] s métier m; (trickery) artifice m; (naut) embarcation f, barque f

craftiness [ˈkræftɪnɪs], [ˈkraftɪnɪs] s ruse f, astuce f

crafts'man s (pl -men) artisan m

crafts'man-ship' s habileté f technique; exécution f

craft·y [ˈkræfti], [ˈkrafti] adj (comp -ier; super -iest) rusé

crag [kræg] s rocher m escarpé

cram [kræm] v (pret & pp crammed; ger cramming) tr (with food) bourrer, gaver; (with people) bonder; (for an exam) (coll) chauffer || intr se bourrer, se gaver; (for an exam) (coll) potasser

cramp [kræmp] s (metal bar; clamp) crampon m; (in a muscle) crampe f; (carpentry) serre-joint m || tr cramponner, agrafer; presser, serrer; (one's movements, style, or manner of living) gêner

cranber·ry [ˈkræn‚beri] s (pl -ries) (Vaccinium oxycoccus or V. uliginosum) canneberge f, airelle f canneberge

crane [kren] s (mach, orn) grue f || tr (one's neck) allonger, tendre || intr allonger le cou

crani·um [ˈkreni·əm] s (pl -a [ə]) crâne m

crank [kræŋk] s manivelle f; (person) (coll) excentrique mf || tr (a motor) faire partir à la manivelle

crank'case' s carter m

crank'shaft' s vilebrequin m

crank·y [ˈkræŋki] adj (comp -ier; super -iest) revêche, grincheux; (not working well) détraqué; (queer) excentrique

cran·ny [ˈkræni] s (pl -nies) fente f, crevasse f; (corner) coin m

crape [krep] s crêpe m

crape'hang'er s (slang) rabat-joie m

craps [kræps] s (slang) jeu m de dés; **to shoot craps** (slang) jouer aux dés

crash [kræʃ] s fracas m, écroulement m; (of thunder) coup m; (of airplane) écrasement m; (e.g., on stock market) krach m || tr briser, fracasser; (e.g., an airplane) écraser || intr retentir; (said of airplane) s'écraser; (to fail) craquer; **to crash into** emboutir, tamponner; **to crash through** enfoncer

crash′ dive′ s brusque plongée f

crash′ hel′met s casque m

crash′-land′ing s crash m, atterrissage m violent

crass [kræs] adj grossier; (ignorance) crasse

crate [kret] s caisse f à claire-voie, cageot m ‖ tr emballer dans une caisse à claire-voie

crater [′kretər] s cratère m

cravat [krə′væt] s cravate f

crave [krev] tr désirer ardemment; implorer; requérir, e.g., **the problem craves serious consideration** le problème requiert une considération sérieuse; **to crave s.o.'s pardon** demander pardon à qn ‖ intr—**to crave for** désirer ardemment; implorer

craven [′krevən] adj & s poltron m

craving [′kreviŋ] s désir m ardent, désir obsédant

craw [krɔ] s jabot m

crawl [krɔl] s rampement m; (swimming) crawl m ‖ intr ramper; **to be crawling with** fourmiller de, grouiller de; **to crawl along** se traîner; **to crawl on one's hands and knees** aller à quatre pattes; **to crawl over** escalader; **to crawl up** grimper

crayon [′kre·ən] s crayon m de pastel, pastel m ‖ tr crayonner

craze [krez] s manie f, toquade f ‖ tr rendre fou

cra·zy [′krezi] adj (comp -zier; super -ziest) fou; (rickety) délabré; **to be crazy about** (coll) être fou de, être toqué de; **to drive crazy** rendre fou, affoler

cra′zy bone′ s nerf m du coude

cra′zy quilt′ s courtepointe f multicolore

creak [krik] s cri m, grincement m ‖ intr crier, grincer

creak·y [′kriki] adj (comp -ier; super -iest) criard

cream [krim] s crème f; **creams** (with chocolate coating) chocolats mpl fourrés ‖ tr écrémer; (butter and sugar together) mélanger ‖ intr crémer

cream′ cheese′ s fromage m à la crème, fromage blanc, petit suisse m

creamer·y [′kriməri] s (pl -ies) laiterie f; compagnie f laitière

cream′ of tar′tar s crème f de tartre

cream′ pitch′er s crémière f

cream′ puff′ s chou m à la crème

cream′ sep′arator [′sepə‚retər] s écrémeuse f

cream·y [′krimi] adj (comp -ier; super -iest) crémeux

crease [kris] s pli m, faux pli m ‖ tr & intr plisser

create [kri′et] tr créer

creation [kri′e·ən] s création f

creative [kri′etiv] adj créateur, inventif

creator [kri′etər] s créateur m

creature [′krit/ər] s créature f

credence [′kridəns] s créance f, croyance f, foi f

credentials [kri′den/əlz] spl papiers mpl, pièces fpl justificatives, lettres fpl de créance

credibility [‚kredɪ′bɪlɪti] s crédibilité f

credible [′kredɪbəl] adj croyable, digne de foi

credit [′kredɪt] s crédit m; (belief; claim) créance f; **on credit** à crédit; **to be a credit to** faire honneur à; **to take credit for** s'attribuer le mérite de ‖ tr croire, ajouter foi à; (com) créditer, porter au crédit

creditable [′kredɪtəbəl] adj estimable, honorable

cred′it card′ s carte f de crédit

creditor [′kredɪtər] s créditeur m, créancier m

cre·do [′krido], [′kredo] s (pl -dos) credo m

credulous [′kredʒələs] adj crédule

creed [krid] s credo m; (denomination) foi f

creek [krik] s ruisseau m

creep [krip] v (pret & pp **crept** [krept]) intr ramper; (stealthily) se glisser; (slowly) se traîner, se couler; (to climb) grimper; (with a sensation of insects) fourmiller; **to creep up on s.o.** s'approcher de qn à pas lents

creeper [′kripər] s plante f rampante

creeping [′kripiŋ] adj lent, traînant; (plant) rampant ‖ s rampement m

creep·y [′kripi] adj (comp -ier; super -iest) (coll) mystérieux; **to feel creepy** fourmiller

cremate [′krimet] tr incinérer

cremation [krɪ′me/ən] s crémation f, incinération f

cremato·ry [′krimə‚tori] adj crématoire ‖ s (pl -ries) crématoire m, four m crématoire

Creole [′kri·ol] adj créole ‖ s (language) créole m; (person) Créole mf

crepe [krep] s crêpe m; (pancake) crêpe f

crepe′ pa′per s papier m crêpe

crescent [′kresənt] s croissant m

cress [kres] s cresson m

crest [krest] s crête f

crested [′krestɪd] adj à crête; (with feathers) huppé

crest′fall′en adj abattu, découragé

Cretan [′kritən] adj crétois ‖ s Crétois m

Crete [krit] s Crète f; **la Crète**

cretin [′kritən] s crétin m

crevice [′krevɪs] s crevasse f, fente f

crew [kru] s équipe f; (of a ship) équipage m; (group, especially of armed men) bande f, troupe f

crew′ cut′ s cheveux mpl en brosse

crew′ mem′ber s équipier m

crib [krɪb] s lit m d'enfant; crèche f, mangeoire f; (for grain) coffre m; (student's pony) corrigé m employé subrepticement ‖ v (pret & pp **cribbed**; ger **cribbing**) tr & intr (coll) copier à la dérobée

cricket [′krɪkɪt] s (ent) grillon m; (sports) cricket m; (coll) franc jeu m, jeu loyal; **to be cricket** être de bonne guerre

crier ['kraɪ·ər] s crieur m
crime [kraɪm] s crime m; (misdemeanor) délit m
criminal ['krɪmɪnəl] adj & s criminel m
crim′inal code′ s code m pénal
crim′inal court′ s cour f d'assises
crim′inal law′ s loi f pénale
crimp [krɪmp] s (in cloth) pli m; (in hair) frisure f; (recruiter) racoleur m; **to put a crimp in** (coll) mettre obstacle à || tr (cloth) plisser; (hair) friser, crêper; (metal) onduler
crimson ['krɪmzən] adj & s cramoisi m
cringe [krɪndʒ] intr s'humilier, s'abaisser
cringing ['krɪndʒɪŋ] adj craintif, servile || s crainte f, servilité f
crinkle ['krɪŋkəl] s pli m, ride f || tr froisser, plisser || intr se froisser
cripple ['krɪpəl] s estropié m; (lame person) boiteux m || tr estropier; (a machine) disloquer; (business or industry) paralyser; (a ship) désemparer
cri·sis ['kraɪsɪs] s (pl -ses [siz]) crise f
crisp [krɪsp] adj croustillant; (tone) tranchant, brusque; (air) vif, frais
crisscross ['krɪs‚krɔs], ['krɪs‚krɑs] adj entrecroisé, treillissé || s entrecroisement m; (e.g., of wires) enchevêtrement m || adv en forme de croix || tr entrecroiser || intr s'entrecroiser
criteri·on [kraɪˈtɪrɪ·ən] s (pl -a [ə] or -ons) critère m
critic ['krɪtɪk] s critique mf; (faultfinder) critiqueur m, désapprobateur m
critical ['krɪtɪkəl] adj critique
critically ['krɪtɪkəli] adv en critique; **critically ill** gravement malade
criticism ['krɪtɪ‚sɪzəm] s critique f
criticize ['krɪtɪ‚saɪz] tr & intr critiquer
croak [krok] s (of raven) croassement m; (of frog) coassement m || intr (said of raven) croasser; (said of frog) coasser; (to die) (slang) mourir
Croat ['kro·æt] s (language) croate m; (person) Croate mf
Croatian [kro'eʃən] adj croate || s (language) croate m; (person) Croate mf
cro·chet [kro'ʃe] s crochet m || v (pret & pp -cheted ['ʃed]; ger -cheting ['ʃe·ɪŋ]) tr & intr tricoter au crochet
crochet′ nee′dle s crochet m
crock [krɑk] s pot m de terre
crockery ['krɑkəri] s faïence f, poterie f
crocodile ['krɑkə‚daɪl] s crocodile m
croc′odile tears′ spl larmes fpl de crocodile
crocus ['krokəs] s crocus m
crone [kron] s vieille femme f au visage parcheminé
cro·ny ['kroni] s (pl -nies) copain m
crook [kruk] s (hook) croc m; (of shepherd) houlette f; (of bishop) crosse f; (in road) courbure f; (person) (coll) escroc m || tr courber || intr se courber
crooked ['krukɪd] adj courbé, crochu; (path; conduct) tortueux; (tree; nose; legs) tortu; (person) (coll) malhonnête, fourbe

croon [krun] intr chanter des chansons sentimentales
crooner ['krunər] s chanteur m de charme
crop [krɑp] s récolte f; (head of hair) cheveux mpl ras; (of bird) jabot m; (whip) fouet m; (of whip) manche m; (of appointments, promotions, heroes, discoveries) moisson f || v (pret & pp cropped; ger cropping) tr tondre; (head of hair) couper, tailler; (ears of animal) essoriller || intr—**crop up** (coll) surgir, s'élever brusquement
croquet [kro'ke] s croquet m
crosier ['kroʒər] s crosse f
cross [krɔs], [krɑs] adj transversal, oblique; (breed) croisé; (ill-humored) maussade || s croix f; (of races or breeds; of roads) croisement m || tr croiser; (the sea; a street) traverser; (breeds) croiser, métisser; (the threshold) franchir; (said of one road with respect to another) couper; (the letter t) barrer; (e.g., s.o.'s plans) (coll) contrecarrer; **to cross oneself** (eccl) se signer; **to cross out** biffer, rayer || intr se croiser, passer; **to cross over** passer de l'autre côté
cross′ bones′ spl tibias mpl croisés
cross′ bow′ s arbalète f
cross′-breed′ v (pret & pp -bred) tr croiser, métisser
cross′-coun′try adj à travers champs
cross′ cur′rent s contre-courant m; tendance f contraire
cross′-exami-na′tion s contre-interrogatoire m
cross′-exam′ine tr contre-interroger, contre-examiner
cross′-eyed′ adj louche
crossing ['krɔsɪŋ], ['krɑsɪŋ] s croisement m; (of ocean) traversée f; (of river, mountain, etc.) passage m; (rr) passage m à niveau
cross′ing gate′ s barrière f d'un passage à niveau
cross′patch′ s (coll) grincheux m, grognon m
cross′piece′ s entretoise f
cross′ ref′erence s renvoi m
cross′road′ s voie f transversale, chemin m de traverse; **crossroads** carrefour m, croisement m
cross′ sec′tion s coupe f transversale; (e.g., of building) section f; (of opinion) sondage m, groupe m représentatif; tranche f de vie
cross′-sec′tion tr couper transversalement
cross′ street′ s rue f de traverse, rue transversale
cross′wise′ adv en croix, en sautoir
cross′word puz′zle s mots mpl croisés
crotch [krɑtʃ] s (forked piece) fourche f; (between legs) entrejambe f, enfourchure f
crotchet ['krɑtʃɪt] s (mus) noire f; (coll) lubie f
crotchety ['krɑtʃɪti] adj capricieux, fantasque

crouch [krautʃ] s accroupissement m
|| intr s'accroupir, se blottir
croup [krup] s (of horse) croupe f;
(pathol) croup m
croupier ['krupɪ·ər] s croupier m
crouton ['krutɑn] s croûton m
crow [kro] s corbeau m; (rook) corneille f, freux m; as the crow flies à
vol d'oiseau; to eat crow (coll) avaler
des couleuvres || intr (said of cock)
chanter; (said of babies) gazouiller;
to crow over chanter victoire sur,
triompher bruyamment de
crow'bar' s levier m; (for forcing
doors) pince-monseigneur f
crowd [kraud] s foule f; (large flock
of people) affluence f, presse f; (mob,
common people) populace f, vulgaire
m; (clique, set) bande f, monde m; a
crowd (of people) du monde, beau-
coup de monde || tr serrer, entasser;
(to push) pousser; (a debtor) presser;
to crowd out ne pas laisser de place
à || intr affluer, s'amasser; to crowd
around se presser autour de; to
crowd in s'attrouper
crowded adj encombré, bondé
crow'foot' s renoncule f, bouton m
d'or
crowing ['kro·ɪŋ] s chant m de coq,
cocorico m; (of babies) gazouillement m
crown [kraun] s couronne f; (of hat)
calotte f || tr couronner, sacrer;
(checkers) damer; to crown s.o.
(slang) flanquer un coup sur la tête
à qn
crowning ['kraunɪŋ] s couronnement
m
crown' prince' s prince m héritier
crown' prin'cess s princesse f héritière
crow's'-foot' s (pl -feet) patte-d'oie f
crow's'-nest s (naut) nid m de pie, tonneau m de vigie
crucial ['kru·əl] adj crucial
crucible ['krusɪbəl] s creuset m
crucifix ['krusɪfɪks] s crucifix m, christ
m
crucifixion [ˌkrusɪ'fɪkʃən] s crucifixion f
cruci·fy ['krusɪˌfaɪ] v (pret & pp -fied)
tr crucifier
crude [krud] adj (raw, unrefined) cru,
brut; (lacking culture) fruste, grossier; (unfinished) informe, grossier,
mal développé; (oil) brut
crudi·ty ['krudɪti] s (pl -ties) crudité
f; (of person) grossièreté f
cruel ['kru·əl] adj cruel
cruel·ty ['kru·əlti] s (pl -ties) cruauté f
cruet ['kru·ɪt] s burette f
cru'et stand' s huilier m
cruise [kruz] s croisière f || intr croiser
cruiser ['kruzər] s croiseur m
cruising ['kruzɪŋ] adj en croisière;
(taxi) en maraude
cruis'ing range' s autonomie f
cruis'ing speed' s vitesse f de route
cruller ['krʌlər] s beignet m
crumb [krʌm] s miette f; (soft part of
bread) mie f || tr (cutlets, etc.) paner
crumble ['krʌmbəl] tr émietter, ré-

duire en miettes; (e.g., stone) effriter
|| intr s'émietter; s'effriter; (to fall
to pieces) s'écrouler
crum·my ['krʌmi] adj (comp -mier;
super -miest) (slang) sale, minable
crumple ['krʌmpəl] tr friper, froisser;
(a fender) mettre en accordéon ||
intr se friper, se froisser
crunch [krʌntʃ] tr croquer, broyer ||
intr (said of snow) craquer
crupper ['krʌpər] s croupière f
crusade [kru'sed] s croisade f || intr se
croiser, prendre part à une croisade
crush [krʌʃ] s écrasement m; (of people) presse f, foule f; to have a crush
on (slang) avoir un béguin pour || tr
écraser; (e.g., stone) broyer, concasser; (to oppress, grieve) accabler,
aplatir
crush' hat' s claque m, gibus m
crust [krʌst] s croûte f
crustacean [krʌs'teʃən] s crustacé m
crust·y ['krʌsti] adj (comp -ier; super
-iest) croustillant; (said of person)
bourru, hargneux
crutch [krʌtʃ] s béquille f
crux [krʌks] s nœud m
cry [kraɪ] s (pl cries) cri m; (of wolf)
hurlement m; (of bull) mugissement
m; to cry one's eyes out pleurer à
chaudes larmes; to have a good cry
donner libre cours aux larmes || v
(pret & pp cried) tr crier; to cry out
crier || intr crier; (to weep) pleurer;
to cry for crier à; to cry for joy
pleurer de joie; to cry out pousser
des cris, s'écrier; to cry out against
crier à
cry'ba'by s (pl -bies) pleurard m
crypt [krɪpt] s crypte f
cryptic(al) ['krɪptɪk(əl)] adj secret,
occulte; (silence) énigmatique
crystal ['krɪstəl] s cristal m
crys'tal ball' s boule f de cristal
crystalline ['krɪstəlɪn], ['krɪstəˌlaɪn]
adj cristallin
crystallize ['krɪstəˌlaɪz] tr cristalliser;
(sugar) candir || intr cristalliser; (said
of sugar) se candir; (said of one's
thoughts) (fig) se cristalliser
cub [kʌb] s petit m; (of bear) ourson
m; (of fox) renardeau m; (of lion)
lionceau m; (of wolf) louveteau m
Cuban ['kjubən] adj cubain || s Cubain
m
cubbyhole ['kʌbɪˌhol] s retraite f; (in
wall) placard m; (in furniture) case f
cube [kjub] adj & s cube m; in cubes
(said of sugar) en morceaux || tr
cuber
cube' root' s racine f cubique
cubic ['kjubɪk] adj cubique, cube
cu'bic me'ter s mètre m cube
cub' report'er s reporter m débutant
cub' scout' s louveteau m
cuckold ['kʌkəld] adj & s cocu m, cor-
nard m || tr cocufier
cuckoo ['kuku] adj (slang) niais, be-
nêt || s coucou m
cuck'oo clock' s coucou m
cucumber ['kjukəmbər] s concombre m

cud [kʌd] *s* bol *m* alimentaire; **to chew the cud** ruminer

cuddle ['kʌdəl] *tr* serrer doucement dans les bras ‖ *intr* (*said of lovers*) s'étreindre; **to cuddle up** se pelotonner

cudg·el ['kʌdʒəl] *s* gourdin *m*, trique *f*; **to take up the cudgels for** prendre fait et cause pour ‖ *v* (*pret & pp* **-eled** *or* **-elled**; *ger* **-eling** *or* **-elling**) *tr* bâtonner, rosser

cue [kju] *s* avis *m*; (*hint*) mot *m*; (*rod used in billiards; persons in line*) queue *f*; (*theat*) réclame *f* de rentrée; (*theat*) réclame *f*; **to give s.o. the cue** faire la leçon à qn, donner le mot à qn; **to take one's cue from** se conformer à

cuff [kʌf] *s* (*of shirt*) poignet *m*, manchette *f*; (*of coat or trousers*) parement *m*; (*blow*) taloche *f*, manchette *f* ‖ *tr* talocher, flanquer une taloche à

cuff′ link′ *s* bouton *m* de manchette

cuirass [kwɪ'ræs] *s* cuirasse *f*

cuisine [kwɪ'zin] *s* cuisine *f*

culinary ['kjulɪ‚nɛri] *adj* culinaire

cull [kʌl] *tr* choisir; (*to gather, pluck*) cueillir; **to cull from** recueillir dans

culm [kʌlm] *s* chaume *m*; (*coal dust*) charbonnaille *f*

culminate ['kʌlmɪ‚net] *intr* (*astr*) culminer; **to culminate in** finir par, se terminer en

culmination [‚kʌlmɪ'neʃən] *s* point *m* culminant; (*astr*) culmination *f*

culottes [k(j)u'lɑts] *spl* pantalon *m* de plage

culpable ['kʌlpəbəl] *adj* coupable

culprit ['kʌlprɪt] *s* coupable *mf*; (*accused*) accusé *m*, prévenu *m*

cult [kʌlt] *s* culte *m*

cultivate ['kʌltɪ‚vet] *tr* cultiver

cultivation [‚kʌltɪ've/ən] *s* culture *f*

cultivator ['kʌltɪ‚vetər] *s* (*person*) cultivateur *m*, exploitant *m* agricole; (*mach*) cultivateur *m*, scarificateur *m*

cultural ['kʌltʃərəl] *adj* culturel

culture ['kʌltʃər] *s* culture *f* ‖ *tr* cultiver

cultured *adj* (*learned*) cultivé, lettré

cul′tured pearl′ *s* perle *f* de culture

culvert ['kʌlvərt] *s* ponceau *m*, cassis *m*

cumbersome ['kʌmbərsəm] *adj* incommode, encombrant; (*clumsy*) lourd, difficile à manier

cummerbund ['kʌmər‚bʌnd] *s* ceinture *f* d'étoffe

cumulative ['kjumjə‚letɪv] *adj* croissant, cumulatif

cunning ['kʌnɪŋ] *adj* (*sly*) astucieux, rusé; (*clever*) habile, fin; (*attractive*) gentil ‖ *s* (*slyness*) astuce *f*, ruse *f*; (*cleverness*) habileté *f*, finesse *f*

cup [kʌp] *s* tasse *f*; (*of metal*) gobelet *m*, timbale *f*; (*bot, eccl*) calice *m*; (*mach*) godet *m* graisseur; (*sports*) coupe *f* ‖ *v* (*pret & pp* **cupped**; *ger* **cupping**) *tr* (*surg*) ventouser

cupboard ['kʌbərd] *s* armoire *f*; (*in wall*) placard *m*

Cupid ['kjupɪd] *s* Cupidon *m*

cupidity [kju'pɪdɪti] *s* cupidité *f*

cupola ['kjupələ] *s* coupole *f*

cur [kʌr] *s* chien *m* métis, roquet *m*; (*despicable person*) mufle *m*

curate ['kjurɪt] *s* vicaire *m*

curative ['kjurətɪv] *adj* curatif

curator [kju'retər] *s* conservateur *m*

curb [kʌrb] *s* bordure *f* de pavés, bord *m* de trottoir; (*of well*) margelle *f*; (*of bit*) gourmette *f*; (*market*) coulisse *f*; (*check, restraint*) frein *m* ‖ *tr* (*a horse*) gourmer; (*passions, anger, desires*) réprimer, refréner; **curb your dog** (*public sign*) faites faire votre chien dans le ruisseau

curb′ serv′ice *s* restoroute *m*

curb′stone′ *s* garde-pavé *m*; **curbstones** bordure *f* de pavés

curd [kʌrd] *s* caillé *m*; **curds** caillebotte *f* ‖ *tr* cailler, caillebotter ‖ *intr* se cailler, se caillebotter

curdle ['kʌrdəl] *tr* cailler; (*the blood*) figer ‖ *intr* se cailler; se figer

curds′ and whey′ *spl* lait *m* caillé sucré

cure [kjur] *s* guérison *f*; (*treatment*) cure *f*; (*remedy*) remède *m* ‖ *tr* guérir; (*meat; leather*) saler; (*a pipe*) culotter

cure′-all′ *s* panacée *f*

curfew ['kʌrfju] *s* couvre-feu *m*

curi·o ['kjurɪ‚o] *s* (*pl* **-os**) bibelot *m*

curiosi·ty [‚kjurɪ'ɑsɪti] *s* (*pl* **-ties**) curiosité *f*

curious ['kjurɪ·əs] *adj* curieux

curl [kʌrl] *s* boucle *f*, frisure *f*; (*spiral-shaped*) volute *f*; (*of smoke*) spirale *f* ‖ *tr* boucler, friser; (*to coil, to roll up*) enrouler, tire-bouchonner; **to curl one's lip** faire la moue ‖ *intr* boucler, friser; (*said of smoke*) s'élever en spirales; (*said of waves*) onduler, déferler; **to curl up** (*said of leaves, paper, etc.*) se recroqueviller; (*in bed*) se rouler en boule

curlew ['kʌrl(j)u] *s* courlis *m*

curlicue ['kʌrlɪ‚kju] *s* paraphe *m*

curl′ing i′ron *s* fer *m* à friser

curl′pa′per *s* papillote *f*

curl·y ['kʌrli] *adj* (*comp* **-ier**; *super* **-iest**) bouclé, frisé

curmudgeon [kər'mʌdʒən] *s* (*crosspatch*) bourru *m*, sale bougre *m*; (*miser*) ladre *mf*

currant ['kʌrənt] *s* groseille *f*

curren·cy ['kʌrənsi] *s* (*pl* **-cies**) circulation *f*; (*legal tender*) monnaie *f*, devises *fpl*; **to give currency to** donner cours à

current ['kʌrənt] *adj* courant; (*month*) en cours; (*accepted*) admis, reçu; (*present-day*) actuel ‖ *s* courant *m*; (*stream*) courant, cours *m*

cur′rent account′ *s* compte *m* courant

cur′rent events′ *spl* actualités *fpl*

cur′rent fail′ure *s* panne *f* de secteur

cur′rent is′sue *s* dernier numéro *m*

curricu·lum [kə'rɪkjələm] *s* (*pl* **-lums** *or* **-la** [lə]) programme *m* scolaire, plan *m* d'études

cur·ry ['kʌri] *s* (*pl* **-ries**) cari *m* ‖ *v* (*pret & pp* **-ried**) *tr* (*a horse*) étriller; (*culin*) apprêter au cari; **to curry favor with** faire la cour à

cur′ry·comb′ *s* étrille *f* ‖ *tr* étriller

cur'ry pow'der *s* cari *m*

curse [kʌrs] *s* malédiction *f*; (*oath*) juron *m* ‖ *tr* maudire ‖ *intr* jurer, sacrer

cursed ['kʌrsɪd], [kʌrst] *adj* maudit, exécrable, sacré

cursive ['kʌrsɪv] *adj* cursif ‖ *s* cursive *f*

cursory ['kʌrsəri] *adj* superficiel, précipité

curt [kʌrt] *adj* brusque, court

curtail [kər'tel] *tr* amoindrir, diminuer; (*expenses*) restreindre; (*rights*) enlever

curtailment [kʌr'telmənt] *s* diminution *f*; (*of expenses*) restriction *f*; (*of rights*) privation *f*

curtain ['kʌrtən] *s* rideau *m* ‖ *tr* garnir de rideaux; (*to hide*) cacher sous des rideaux; **to curtain off** séparer par un rideau

cur'tain call' *s* rappel *m*

cur'tain rais'er *s* (*play*) lever *m* de rideau

cur'tain ring' *s* anneau *m* de rideau

cur'tain rod' *s* tringle *f* de rideau

curt·sy ['kʌrtsi] *s* (*pl* **-sies**) révérence *f* ‖ *v* (*pret* & *pp* **-sied**) *intr* faire la révérence

curvature ['kʌrvətʃər] *s* courbure *f*; (*of spine*) déviation *f*

curve [kʌrv] *s* courbe *f*; (*of road*) virage *m*; (*curvature*) courbure *f* ‖ *tr* courber ‖ *intr* se courber

curved *adj* courbe, courbé

cushion ['kʊʃən] *s* coussin *m* ‖ *tr* (*a chair*) rembourrer; (*a shock*) amortir

cuspidor ['kʌspɪˌdɔr] *s* crachoir *m*

cuss [kʌs] *s* (*person*) (coll) vaurien *m*, chenapan *m* ‖ *tr* (coll) maudire ‖ *intr* (coll) jurer, sacrer

cuss'word' *s* (coll) juron *m*

custard ['kʌstərd] *s* flan *m*, œufs *mpl* au lait, crème *f* caramel

custodian [kəs'todɪ·ən] *s* gardien *m*, concierge *mf*

custo·dy ['kʌstədɪ] *s* (*pl* **-dies**) garde *f*; emprisonnement *m*; **in custody** en sûreté; **to take into custody** mettre en état d'arrestation

custom ['kʌstəm] *s* coutume *f*; (*customers*) clientèle *f*; **customs** douane *f*; (*duties*) droits *mpl* de douane

customary ['kʌstəˌmɛri] *adj* coutumier, ordinaire, habituel

custom-built ['kʌstəm'bɪlt] *adj* hors série, fait sur commande

customer ['kʌstəmər] *s* client *m*, chaland *m*; (coll) individu *m*, type *m*; **customers** clientèle *f*, achalandage *m*

cus'tom·house' *adj* douanier ‖ *s* douane *f*

custom-made ['kʌstəm'med] *adj* fait sur commande; (*clothes*) sur mesure

cus'toms clear'ance *s* expédition *f* douanière

cus'toms of'ficer *s* douanier *m*

cus'toms un'ion *s* union *f* douanière

cus'tom tai'lor *s* tailleur *m* à façon

cut [kʌt] *adj* coupé; **cut out** taillé, e.g., **he is not cut out for that** il n'est pas taillé pour cela; e.g., **your work is cut out for you** voilà votre besogne

taillée ‖ *s* coupe *f*; (*piece cut off*) tranche *f*, morceau *m*; (*slash*) coupure *f*; (*with knife, whip, etc.*) coup *m*; (*in prices, wages, etc.*) réduction *f*, baisse *f*; (*of a garment*) coupe; (typ) gravure *f*, planche *f*; (*absence from school*) (coll) séchage *m*; (*in winnings, earnings, etc.*) (slang) part *f*; **the cheap cuts** les bas morceaux *mpl* ‖ *v* (*pret* & *pp* **cut**; *ger* **cutting**) *tr* couper; (*meat, bread*) trancher; (*prices*) réduire, baisser; (e.g., *a hole*) pratiquer; (*glass, diamonds*) tailler; (*fingernails*) rogner; (*an article, play, speech*) sabrer, faire des coupures à; (*a phonograph record*) enregistrer; (*a class*) (coll) sécher; **to cut down** faucher, abattre; (*expenses*) réduire; **to cut off, out,** or **up** découper, couper; **to cut short** couper court à ‖ *intr* couper; trancher; **to cut in** (*a conversation*) s'immiscer dans; (coll) enlever la danseuse d'un autre; **to cut off** (*debate*) clore; **to cut up** (slang) faire le pitre

cut'-and-dried' *adj* décidé d'avance, tout fait; monotone, rasoir

cutaneous [kju'teni·əs] *adj* cutané

cut'away' *s* frac *m*

cut'back' *s* réduction *f*; (mov) retour *m* en arrière

cute [kjut] *adj* (coll) mignon; (*shrewd*) (coll) rusé

cut' glass' *s* cristal *m* taillé

cuticle ['kjutɪkəl] *s* cuticule *f*

cutlass ['kʌtləs] *s* coutelas *m*

cutlery ['kʌtləri] *s* coutellerie *f*

cutlet ['kʌtlɪt] *s* côtelette *f*; (*without bone*) escalope *f*

cut'off' *s* point *m* de coupure; (*road*) raccourci *m*; (*of river*) bras *m* mort; (*of cylinder*) obturateur *m*

cut'out' *s* (aut) échappement *m* libre; (elec) coupe-circuit *m*; (mov) décor *m* découpé

cut'-rate' *adj* à prix réduit

cutter ['kʌtər] *s* (naut) cotre *m*

cut'throat' *s* coup-jarret *m*

cutting ['kʌtɪŋ] *adj* tranchant; (*tone, remark*) mordant, cinglant ‖ *s* coupe *f*; (*from a newspaper*) coupure *f*; (e.g., *of prices*) réduction *f*; (hort) bouture *f*; (mov) découpage *m*

cuttlefish ['kʌtəlˌfɪʃ] *s* seiche *f*

cut'wa'ter *s* (naut) étrave *f*; (*of bridge*) bec *m*

cyanamide [saɪ'ænəˌmaɪd] *s* cyanamide *f*

cyanide ['saɪ·əˌnaɪd] *s* cyanure *m*

cyanosis [ˌsaɪ·ə'nosɪs] *s* cyanose *f*

cycle ['saɪkəl] *s* cycle *m*; (*of internal-combustion engine*) temps *m*; (phys) période *f* ‖ *intr* faire de la bicyclette

cyclic(al) ['saɪklɪk(əl)], ['sɪklɪk(əl)] *adj* cyclique

cyclist ['saɪklɪst] *s* cycliste *mf*

cyclone ['saɪklon] *s* cyclone *m*

cyclops ['saɪklɒps] *s* cyclope *m*

cyclotron ['saɪkloˌtrɑn], ['sɪkloˌtrɑn] *s* cyclotron *m*

cylinder ['sɪlɪndər] *s* cylindre *m*; (*of revolver*) barillet *m*

cyl'inder block' s cylindre m
cyl'inder bore' s alésage m
cyl'inder head' s culasse f
cylindric(al) [sɪ'lɪndrɪk(əl)] adj cylindrique
cymbal ['sɪmbəl] s cymbale f
cynic ['sɪnɪk] adj & s cynique m
cynical ['sɪnɪkəl] adj cynique
cynicism ['sɪnɪ,sɪzəm] s cynisme m
cynosure ['saɪnə,ʃʊr], ['sɪnə,ʃʊr] s guide m, exemple m, norme f; (center of attention) clou m; (astr) cynosure f
cypress ['saɪprəs] s cyprès m

Cyprus ['saɪprəs] s Chypre f
Cyrillic [sɪ'rɪlɪk] adj cyrillique
cyst [sɪst] s kyste m; (on the skin) vésicule f
czar [zar] s tsar m, czar m
czarina [za'rinə] s tsarine f, czarine f
Czech [tʃɛk] adj tchèque ‖ s (language) tchèque m; (person) Tchèque mf
Czecho-Slovak ['tʃɛko'slovæk] adj tchécoslovaque ‖ s Tchécoslovaque mf
Czecho-Slovakia [,tʃɛkoslo'vækɪ·ə] s Tchécoslovaquie f; la Tchécoslovaquie

D

D, d [di] s IVᵉ lettre de l'alphabet
dab [dæb] s touche f; (of ink) tache f; (of butter) petit morceau m ‖ v (pret & pp **dabbed**; ger **dabbing**) tr essuyer légèrement; (to pat) tapoter
dabble ['dæbəl] tr humecter ‖ intr barboter; **to dabble in** se mêler de; **to dabble in the stock market** boursicoter
dad [dæd] s (coll) papa m
dad·dy ['dædɪ] s (pl -dies) papa m
dad'dy-long'legs' s (pl -legs) faucheux m
daffodil ['dæfədɪl] s jonquille f des prés, narcisse m des bois
daff·y ['dæfɪ] adj (comp -ier; super -iest) (coll) timbré, toqué
dagger ['dægər] s poignard m, dague f; (typ) croix f, obel m; **to look daggers at** foudroyer du regard
dahlia ['dæljə] s dahlia m
dai·ly ['delɪ] adj quotidien, journalier ‖ s (pl -lies) quotidien m ‖ adv journellement
dain·ty ['dentɪ] adj (comp -tier; super -tiest) délicat ‖ s (pl -ties) friandise f
dair·y ['derɪ] s (pl -ies) laiterie f; (shop) crémerie f; (farm) vacherie f
dair'y farm' s vacherie f
dair'y-man s (pl -men) laitier m
dais ['de·ɪs] s estrade f
dai·sy ['dezɪ] s (pl -sies) marguerite f
dal·ly ['dælɪ] v (pret & pp -lied) intr badiner; (to delay) s'attarder
dam [dæm] s barrage m; (female quadruped) mère f ‖ v (pret & pp **dammed**; ger **damming**) tr contenir, endiguer
damage ['dæmɪdʒ] s dommage m, dégâts mpl; (to engine, ship, etc.) avaries fpl; (to one's reputation) tort m; **damages** (law) dommages-intérêts mpl ‖ tr endommager; (merchandise; a machine) avarier; (a reputation) faire du tort à
damaging ['dæmɪdʒɪŋ] adj dommageable, préjudiciable
damascene ['dæmə,sin], [,dæmə'sin]

adj damasquiné ‖ s damasquinage m ‖ tr damasquiner
Damascus [də'mæskəs] s Damas f
dame [dem] s dame f; (coll) jupon m
damn [dæm] s juron m, gros mot m; **I don't give a damn** (slang) je m'en fiche; **that's not worth a damn** (slang) ça ne vaut pas un pet de lapin, ça ne vaut pas chipette ‖ tr condamner; (to criticize harshly) éreinter; (to curse) maudire; **damn it!** oh, la vache!; **to damn with faint praise** assommer avec des fleurs ‖ intr maudire
damnation [dæm'neʃən] s damnation f
damned [dæmd] adj damné m ‖ s—**the damned** les damnés ‖ adv (slang) diablement, bigrement
damp [dæmp] adj humide, moite ‖ s humidité f; (firedamp) grisou m ‖ tr (to dampen) humecter, mouiller; (a furnace) étouffer; (sound; electromagnetic waves) amortir
dampen ['dæmpən] tr humecter; (enthusiasm) refroidir; (to muffle) amortir
damper ['dæmpər] s (of chimney) registre m; (of stovepipe) soupape f de réglage; (of piano) étouffoir m; **to put a damper on** (fig) jeter un froid sur
damsel ['dæmzəl] s demoiselle f
dance [dæns], [dɑns] s danse f; bal m, soirée f dansante ‖ tr & intr danser
dance' band' s orchestre m de danse
dance' floor' s piste f de danse
dance' hall' s dancing m, salle f de danse
dance' pro'gram s carnet m de bal
dancer ['dænsər], ['dɑnsər] s danseur m
danc'ing part'ner s danseur m
dandelion ['dændɪ,laɪ·ən] s pissenlit m
dandruff ['dændrəf] s pellicules fpl
dan·dy ['dændɪ] adj (comp -dier; super -diest) (coll) chic, chouette ‖ s (pl -dies) dandy m, élégant m
Dane [den] s Danois m
danger ['dendʒər] s danger m

dangerous ['deɪdʒərəs] *adj* dangereux

dangle ['dæŋgəl] *tr* faire pendiller || *intr* pendiller

Danish ['denɪʃ] *adj & s* danois *m*

dank [dæŋk] *adj* humide, moite

Danube ['dænjub] *s* Danube *m*

dapper ['dæpər] *adj* fringant, élégant

dappled ['dæpəld] *adj* tacheté; (*sky*) pommelé; (*horse*) moucheté, miroité

dare [der] *s* défi *m*; **to take a dare** relever un défi || *tr* défier; oser; **to dare s.o. to** + *inf* défier qn de + *inf* || *intr* oser; **to dare** + *inf* oser + *inf*

dare'dev'il *s* risque-tout *mf*

daring ['derɪŋ] *adj* audacieux, hardi || *s* audace *f*, hardiesse *f*

dark [dɑrk] *adj* sombre, obscur; (*color*) foncé; (*complexion*) basané, brun; **it is dark** il fait noir, il fait nuit || *s* obscurité *f*, ténèbres *fpl*

Dark' Ag'es *spl* âge *m* des ténèbres

darken ['dɑrkən] *tr* assombrir; (*the complexion*) brunir; (*a color*) foncer || *intr* s'assombrir; (*said of forehead*) se rembrunir

dark' horse' *s* (pol) candidat *m* obscur; (sports) outsider *m*

darkly ['dɑrklɪ] *adv* obscurément; (*mysteriously*) ténébreusement; (*threateningly*) d'un air menaçant

dark' meat' *s* viande *f* brune; (*of game*) viande noire

darkness ['dɑrknɪs] *s* obscurité *f*

dark'room' *s* (phot) chambre *f* noire

darling ['dɑrlɪŋ] *adj & s* chéri *m*, bienaimé *m*; **my darling** mon chou

darn [dɑrn] *s* reprise *f*, raccommodage *m* || *tr* repriser, raccommoder || *interj* zut!

darn'ing egg' *s* œuf *m* à repriser

darn'ing nee'dle *s* aiguille *f* à repriser

dart [dɑrt] *s* dard *m*; (*small missile used in a game*) fléchette *f* || *intr* se précipiter, aller comme une flèche

dash [dæʃ] *s* trait *m*; (*small amount*) soupçon *m*, petit brin *m*; (*of color*) pointe *f*, touche *f*; (*splash*) choc *m*, floc *m*; (*spirit*) élan *m*, fougue *f*; (*in printing, writing*) tiret *m*; (*in telegraphy*) trait *m*, longue *f* || *tr* (*quickly*) précipiter; (*violently*) heurter; (*hopes*) abattre; **to dash off** écrire d'un trait, esquisser; **to dash to pieces** fracasser || *intr* se précipiter; **to dash against** se heurter contre; **to dash by** filer à grand train; **to dash in** entrer en trombe; **to dash off** or **out** s'élancer, s'élancer dehors

dash'board' *s* tableau *m* de bord

dashing ['dæʃɪŋ] *adj* impétueux, fougueux; (*elegant*) fringant

dastard ['dæstərd] *adj & s* lâche *mf*

data ['detə], ['dætə] *spl* données *fpl*

da'ta proc'essing *s* analyse *f* des renseignements, étude *f* des données

date [det] *s* (*time*) date *f*; (*on books, on coins*) millésime *m*; (*palm*) dattier *m*; (*fruit*) datte *f*; (*of note, of loan*) terme *m*, échéance *f*; (*appointment*) rendez-vous *m*; **out of date** suranné, périmé; **to date** à ce jour; **up to date** à la page, au courant || *tr* dater;

(e.g., *a work of art*) assigner une date à; (coll) fixer un rendez-vous avec || *intr* (*to be outmoded*) dater; **to date from** dater de, remonter à

date' line' *s* ligne *f* de changement de date

date' palm' *s* dattier *m*

dative ['detɪv] *s* datif *m*

daub [dɔb] *s* barbouillage *m* || *tr* barbouiller

daughter ['dɔtər] *s* fille *f*

daugh'ter-in-law' *s* (*pl* **daughters-in-law**) belle-fille *f*, bru *f*

daunt [dɔnt] *tr* intimider, abattre

dauntless ['dɔntlɪs] *adj* intrépide

dauphin ['dɔfɪn] *s* dauphin *m*

davenport ['dævən‚pɔrt] *s* canapé-lit *m*

daw [dɔ] *s* choucas *m*

dawdle ['dɔdəl] *intr* flâner, muser

dawn [dɔn] *s* aube *f*, aurore *f* || *intr* poindre; **to dawn on** venir à l'esprit à

day [de] *adj* (*work*) diurne; (*worker*) de journée || *s* jour *m*; (*of travel, work, worry*) journée *f*; (*of the month*) quantième *m*; **a day** (*per day*) par jour; **by the day** à la journée; **day by day** au jour le jour, jour par jour; **every day** tous les jours, chaque jour; **every other day** tous les deux jours; **from day to day** de jour en jour; **good old days** bon vieux temps; **in less than a day** du jour au lendemain; **in these days** de nos jours; **in those days** à ce moment-là, à cette époque; **one fine day** un beau jour; **the day after** le lendemain; le lendemain de; **the day after tomorrow** après-demain; l'après-demain *m*; **the day before** la veille; la veille de; **the day before yesterday** avant-hier; l'avant-hier *m*

day' bed' *s* canapé-lit *m*

day'break' *s* pointe *f* du jour, lever *m* du jour; **at daybreak** au jour levant

day' coach' *s* (rr) voiture *f*

day'dream' *s* rêvasserie *f*, rêverie *f* || *intr* rêvasser, rêver creux

day'dream'er *s* songe-creux *m*, songeur *m*

day'dream'ing *s* rêvasserie *f*

day' la'borer *s* journalier *m*

day'light' *s* jour *m*; **in broad daylight** en plein jour; **to see daylight** (coll) comprendre; (coll) voir la fin d'une tâche difficile

day'light-sav'ing time' *s* heure *f* d'été

day' lil'y *s* lis *m* jaune, belle-d'un-jour *f*

day' nurs'ery *s* garderie *f* d'enfants, crèche *f*

day' off' *s* jour *m* de congé, jour chômé

day' of reck'oning *s* jour *m* de règlement; (*last judgment*) jour d'expiation

day' shift' *s* équipe *f* de jour

day' stu'dent *s* externe *mf*

day'time' *s* jour *m*, journée *f*

daze [dez] *s* étourdissement *m*; **in a daze** hébété || *tr* étourdir

dazzle ['dæzəl] *s* éblouissement *m* || *tr* éblouir

dazzling ['dæzlɪŋ] *adj* éblouissant

D.C. ['di'si'] *s* (letterword) (**District of**

Columbia) le district de Columbia; (direct current) le courant continu

D'-day' *s* le jour J

deacon ['dikən] *s* diacre *m*

deaconess ['dikənɪs] *s* diaconesse *f*

dead [dɛd] *adj* mort; (*tired*) épuisé; (*color*) terne; (*business*) stagnant; (*sleep*) profond; (*calm*) plat; (*loss*) sec; (*typewriter key*) immobile; **on a dead level** à franc niveau ‖ *s*—**in the dead of night** au milieu de la nuit; **the dead** les morts; **the dead of winter** le cœur de l'hiver ‖ *adv* absolument; **to stop dead** s'arrêter net

dead'beat' *s* (slang) écornifleur *m*

dead' bolt' *s* pêne *m* dormant

dead' calm' *s* calme *m* plat

dead' cen'ter *s* point *m* mort

dead'-drunk' *adj* ivre mort

deaden ['dɛdən] *tr* amortir; (*sound*) assourdir

dead' end' *s* cul-de-sac *m*, impasse *f*

dead' latch' *s* pêne *m* dormant

dead'-let'ter of'fice *s* bureau *m* des rebuts

dead'line' *s* dernier délai *m*, date *f* limite

dead'lock' *s* serrure *f* à pêne dormant; (fig) impasse *f* ‖ *tr* faire aboutir à une impasse

dead·ly ['dɛdli] *adj* (*comp* **-lier**; *super* **-liest**) mortel; (*sin*) capital

dead' pan' *s* (slang) visage *m* sans expression

dead' reck'oning *s* estime *f*; (*position*) point *m* d'estime

dead' ring'er *s* (coll) portrait *m* vivant

dead' sol'dier *s* (*bottle*) (slang) cadavre *m*

dead' weight' *s* poids *m* lourd

dead'wood' *s* bois *m* mort; (fig) objet *m* ou individu *m* inutile

deaf [dɛf] *adj* sourd; **to turn a deaf ear** faire la sourde oreille

deaf'-and-dumb' *adj* sourd-muet

deafen ['dɛfən] *tr* assourdir

deafening ['dɛfənɪŋ] *adj* assourdissant

deaf'-mute' *adj & s* sourd-muet *m*

deafness ['dɛfnɪs] *s* surdité *f*

deal [dil] *s* affaire *f*; (*cards*) main *f*, donne *f*; **a good deal (of)** or **a great deal (of)** beaucoup (de); **to think a great deal of s.o.** estimer qn ‖ *v* (*pret & pp* **dealt** [dɛlt]) *tr* (*a blow*) donner, porter; (*cards*) donner, distribuer; **to deal out** (*e.g., gifts*) distribuer, répartir; (*alms*) dispenser; (*justice*) rendre ‖ *intr* négocier; (*cards*) faire la donne; **to deal in** faire le commerce de; **to deal with** (*a person*) traiter avec; (*a subject*) traiter de

dealer ['dilər] *s* marchand *m*, négociant *m*; (*of cards*) donneur *m*; (*middleman, e.g., in selling automobiles*) concessionnaire *m*, stockiste *m*

dean [din] *s* doyen *m*

dean'ship *s* doyenné *m*, décanat *m*

dear [dɪr] *adj* cher; **dear me!** mon Dieu!; **Dear Sir** (*salutation in a letter*) Monsieur ‖ *s* chéri *m*

dearie ['dɪri] *s* (coll) petite, chérie *f*

dearth [dʌrθ] *s* disette *f*, pénurie *f*

death [dɛθ] *s* mort *f*; **at death's door** à deux doigts de la mort; **to bore to death** raser; **to put to death** mettre à mort; **to starve to death** mourir de faim

death'bed' *s* lit *m* de mort

death'blow' *s* coup *m* mortel

death' certif'icate *s* constatation *f* de décès, extrait *m* mortuaire

death' house' *s* quartier *m* de la mort

death' knell' *s* glas *m* funèbre

deathless ['dɛθlɪs] *adj* immortel

deathly ['dɛθli] *adj* mortel ‖ *adv* mortellement, comme la mort

death' mask' *s* masque *m* mortuaire

death' pen'alty *s* peine *f* capitale

death' rate' *s* mortalité *f*, taux *m* de mortalité

death' rat'tle *s* râle *m* de la mort

death' war'rant *s* ordre *m* d'exécution

death'watch' *s* veillée *f* funèbre

deb [dɛb] *s* (slang) débutante *f*

debacle [de'bakəl] *s* débâcle *m*

de·bar [dɪ'bɑr] *v* (*pret & pp* **-barred**; *ger* **-barring**) *tr* exclure; empêcher

debark [dɪ'bɑrk] *tr & intr* débarquer

debarkation [,dɪbɑr'keʃən] *s* débarquement *m*

debase [dɪ'bes] *tr* avilir, abaisser; (*e.g., money*) altérer

debatable [dɪ'betəbəl] *adj* discutable

debate [dɪ'bet] *s* débat *m*; **under debate** en discussion ‖ *tr & intr* discuter

debauch [dɪ'bɔtʃ] *s* débauche *f* ‖ *tr* débaucher, corrompre

debauchee [,dɛbə'ʃi], [,dɛbə'tʃi] *s* débauché *m*

debauch·ery [dɪ'bɔtʃəri] *s* (*pl* **-ies**) débauche *f*

debenture [dɪ'bɛntʃər] *s* (*bond*) obligation *f*; (*voucher*) reçu *m*

debilitate [dɪ'bɪlɪ,tet] *tr* débiliter

debili·ty [dɪ'bɪlɪti] *s* (*pl* **-ties**) débilité *f*

debit ['dɛbɪt] *s* débit *m*; (*entry on debit side*) article *m* au débit ‖ *tr* débiter, porter au débit

deb'it bal'ance *s* solde *m* débiteur

debonair [,dɛbə'nɛr] *adj* gai, jovial; élégant, charmant

debris [də'bri], ['debri] *s* débris *mpl*, détritus *m*; (*from ruined buildings*) décombres *mpl*

debt [dɛt] *s* dette *f*; **to run into debt** s'endetter

debtor ['dɛtər] *s* débiteur *m*

debut [de'bju], ['debju] *s* début *m* ‖ *intr* débuter

debutante [,dɛbju'tɑnt], ['dɛbjə,tænt] *s* débutante *f*

decade ['dɛked] *s* décennie *f*, décade *f*

decadence [dɪ'kedəns] *s* décadence *f*

decadent [dɪ'kedənt] *adj & s* décadent *m*

decal ['dikæl], [dɪ'kæl], ['dɛkəl] *s* décalcomanie *f*

decamp [dɪ'kæmp] *intr* décamper

decanter [dɪ'kæntər] *s* carafe *f*

decapitate [dɪ'kæpɪ,tet] *tr* décapiter

decay [dɪ'ke] *s* (*rotting*) pourriture *f*; (*decline*) décadence *f*; (*falling to pieces*) délabrement *m*; (*of teeth*) carie f || tr pourrir; (teeth) carier || intr pourrir, se gâter; (said of teeth) se carier; tomber en décadence or ruine; délabrer

decease [dɪ'sis] s décès m || intr décéder

deceit [dɪ'sit] s tromperie f

deceitful [dɪ'sitfəl] adj trompeur

deceive [dɪ'siv] tr & intr tromper

decelerate [dɪ'selə‚ret] tr & intr ralentir

December [dɪ'sembər] s décembre m

decen•cy ['disənsi] s (pl -cies) décence f; decencies convenances fpl

decent ['disənt] adj décent

decentralize [di'sentrə‚laɪz] tr décentraliser

deception [dɪ'sepʃən] s tromperie f

deceptive [dɪ'septɪv] adj trompeur

decide [dɪ'saɪd] tr décider; (the outcome) décider de || intr décider, se décider; to decide to + inf décider de + inf, se décider à + inf; to decide upon a day fixer un jour

deciduous [dɪ'sɪdʒu‑əs], [dɪ'sɪdju‑əs] adj caduc

decimal ['desɪməl] adj décimal || s décimale f

dec'imal point' s (in French the comma is used to separate the decimal fraction from the integer) virgule f

decimate ['desɪ‚met] tr décimer

decipher [dɪ'saɪfər] tr déchiffrer

decision [dɪ'sɪʒən] s décision f

decisive [dɪ'saɪsɪv] adj décisif

deck [dek] s (of cards) jeu m, paquet m; (of ship) pont m; between decks (naut) dans l'entrepont || tr—to deck out parer, orner

deck' chair' s transatlantique m, transat m, chaise f longue de bord

deck' hand' s matelot m de pont

deck'-land' intr apponter

deck'-land'ing s appontage m

declaim [dɪ'klem] tr & intr déclamer

declaration [‚deklə'reʃən] s déclaration f

declarative [dɪ'klærətɪv] adj déclaratif

declare [dɪ'kler] tr & intr déclarer

declension [dɪ'klenʃən] s (gram) déclinaison f

declination [‚deklɪ'neʃən] s (astr, geog) déclinaison f

decline [dɪ'klaɪn] s déclin m, décadence f; (in prices) baisse f || tr & intr décliner

declivi•ty [dɪ'klɪvɪti] s (pl -ties) déclivité f, pente f

decode [dɪ'kod] tr décoder, déchiffrer

decompose [‚dikəm'poz] tr décomposer || intr se décomposer

decomposition [‚dikampə'zɪʃən] s décomposition f

decompression [‚dikəm'preʃən] s décompression f

decontamination [‚dikən‚tæmɪ'neʃən] s décontamination f

decorate ['dekə‚ret] tr décorer

decoration [‚dekə'reʃən] s décoration f

decorator ['dekə‚retər] s décorateur m

decorous ['dekərəs], [dɪ'korəs] adj convenable, correct, bienséant

decorum [dɪ'korəm] s décorum m

decrease ['dikris], [dɪ'kris] s diminution f || [dɪ'kris] tr & intr diminuer

decree [dɪ'kri] s décret m, arrêté m; (of divorce) ordonnance f || tr décréter, arrêter, ordonner

decrepit [dɪ'krepɪt] adj décrépit

de•cry [dɪ'kraɪ] v (pret & pp -cried) tr décrier, dénigrer

dedicate ['dedɪ‚ket] tr dédier

dedication [‚dedɪ'keʃən] s consécration f; (e.g., in a book) dédicace f

dedicatory ['dedɪkə‚tori] adj dédicatoire

deduce [dɪ'd(j)us] tr déduire, inférer

deduct [dɪ'dʌkt] tr déduire

deduction [dɪ'dʌkʃən] s déduction f

deed [did] s action f, acte m; (law) acte, titre m, contrat m; deed of valor haut fait m; good deed bonne action; in deed dans le fait || tr transférer par un acte

deem [dim] tr estimer, juger, croire || intr penser

deep [dip] adj profond; (sound) grave; (color) foncé; de profondeur, e.g., to be twenty feet deep avoir vingt pieds de profondeur; deep in debt criblé de dettes; deep in thought plongé dans la méditation || adv profondément; deep into the night très avant dans la nuit

deepen [dipən] tr approfondir || intr s'approfondir

deep'-freeze' v (pret -froze; pp -frozen) tr congeler à basse température

deep'-laid' adj habilement ourdi

deep' mourn'ing s grand deuil m

deep'-root'ed adj profondément enraciné

deep'-sea fish'ing s grande pêche f au large, pêche maritime

deer [dɪr] s (red deer) cerf m; (fallow deer) daim m; (roe deer) chevreuil m

deer'skin' s peau f de daim

deface [dɪ'fes] tr défigurer

de facto [di'fækto] adv de fait, de facto

defamation [‚defə'meʃən], [‚difə'meʃən] s diffamation f, injures fpl

defame [dɪ'fem] tr diffamer

default [dɪ'fɔlt] s manque m, défaut m; (on an obligation) carence f; by default par défaut; (sports) par forfait; in default of à défaut de || tr (a debt) manquer de s'acquitter || intr ne pas tenir ses engagements; (sports) perdre par forfait

defeat [dɪ'fit] s défaite f; unexpected defeat contre-performance f || tr vaincre, battre, défaire

defeatism [dɪ'fitɪzəm] s défaitisme m

defeatist [dɪ'fitɪst] adj & s défaitiste mf

defecate ['defɪ‚ket] intr déféquer

defect ['difekt], ['difekt] s défaut m, imperfection f, vice m || [dɪ'fekt] intr faire défection, déserter

defection [dɪˈfɛkʃən] *s* défection *f*

defective [dɪˈfɛktɪv] *adj* défectueux, vicieux; (gram) défectif

defend [dɪˈfɛnd] *tr* défendre

defendant [dɪˈfɛndənt] *s* (law) défendeur *m*, intimé *m*

defense [dɪˈfɛns] *s* défense *f*

defenseless [dɪˈfɛnslɪs] *adj* sans défense

defensive [dɪˈfɛnsɪv] *adj* défensif ‖ *s* défensive *f*

de·fer [dɪˈfʌr] *v* (pret & pp -ferred; ger -ferring) *tr* différer; (mil) mettre en sursis ‖ *intr*—**to defer to** déférer à

deference [ˈdɛfərəns] *s* déférence *f*

deferential [ˌdɛfəˈrɛnʃəl] *adj* déférent

deferment [dɪˈfʌrmənt] *s* ajournement *m*, remise *f*; (extension of time) délai *m*; (mil) sursis *m* d'appel

defiance [dɪˈfaɪəns] *s* défi *m*, provocation *f*, nargue *f*; **in defiance of** au mépris de, en dépit de

defiant [dɪˈfaɪənt] *adj* provocant, hostile, de défi

deficien·cy [dɪˈfɪʃənsi] *s* (pl -cies) déficience *f*, insuffisance *f*; (of vitamins or minerals) carence *f*; (com) déficit *m*

deficient [dɪˈfɪʃənt] *adj* déficient, insuffisant

deficit [ˈdɛfɪsɪt] *adj* déficitaire ‖ *s* déficit *m*

defile [dɪˈfaɪl], [ˈdifaɪl] *s* défilé *m* ‖ [dɪˈfaɪl] *tr* souiller ‖ *intr* défiler

defilement [dɪˈfaɪlmənt] *s* souillure *f*

define [dɪˈfaɪn] *tr* définir

definite [ˈdɛfɪnɪt] *adj* défini; (opinions, viewpoints) décidé

definitely [ˈdɛfɪnɪtli] *adv* décidément, nettement

definition [ˌdɛfɪˈnɪʃən] *s* définition *f*

definitive [dɪˈfɪnɪtɪv] *adj* définitif

deflate [dɪˈflet] *tr* dégonfler; (currency) amener la déflation de ‖ *intr* se dégonfler

deflation [dɪˈfleʃən] *s* dégonflement *m*; (of prices) déflation *f*

deflect [dɪˈflɛkt] *tr* & *intr* dévier

deflower [dɪˈflaʊər] *tr* déflorer; (to strip of flowers) défleurir

deforest [diˈfɑrɪst], [diˈfɔrɪst] *tr* déboiser

deform [dɪˈfɔrm] *tr* déformer

deformed *adj* contrefait, difforme

deformi·ty [dɪˈfɔrmɪti] *s* (pl -ties) difformité *f*

defraud [dɪˈfrɔd] *tr* frauder

defray [dɪˈfre] *tr* payer, supporter

defrost [diˈfrɔst], [diˈfrɑst] *tr* décongeler, dégivrer

defroster [diˈfrɔstər], [diˈfrɑstər] *s* dégivreur *m*, dégivrage *m*

defrosting [diˈfrɔstɪŋ], [diˈfrɑstɪŋ] *s* dégèlement *m*, dégivrage *m*

deft [dɛft] *adj* adroit, habile; (hand) exercé, preste

defunct [dɪˈfʌŋkt] *adj* défunt; (practice, style, etc.) tombé en désuétude

de·fy [dɪˈfaɪ] *v* (pret & pp -fied) *tr* défier, braver, porter un défi à

degeneracy [dɪˈdʒɛnərəsi] *s* dégénérescence *f*

degenerate [dɪˈdʒɛnərɪt] *adj* & *s* dégénéré *m* ‖ [dɪˈdʒɛnəˌret] *intr* dégénérer

degrade [dɪˈgred] *tr* dégrader

degrading [dɪˈgredɪŋ] *adj* dégradant

degree [dɪˈgri] *s* degré *m*; (from a university) grade *m*; (of humidity) titre *m*; **to take a degree** obtenir ses diplômes, obtenir ses titres universitaires

dehumidi·fy [ˌdihjuˈmɪdɪˌfaɪ] *v* (pret & pp -fied) *tr* déshumidifier

dehydrate [diˈhaɪdret] *tr* déshydrater; (the body) dessécher

deice [diˈaɪs] *tr* déglacer, dégivrer

deicer [diˈaɪsər] *s* dégivreur *m*, antigivrant *m*

dei·fy [ˈdi·ɪˌfaɪ] *v* (pret & pp -fied) *tr* déifier

dei·ty [ˈdi·ɪti] *s* (pl -ties) divinité *f*; (mythol) déité *f*; **the Deity** Dieu *m*

dejected [dɪˈdʒɛktɪd] *adj* abattu, découragé

dejection [dɪˈdʒɛkʃən] *s* abattement *m*

delay [dɪˈle] *s* retard *m*; (postponement) sursis *m*, remise *f*; **without delay** sans délai; **without further delay** sans plus tarder ‖ *tr* retarder; (to put off) remettre, différer ‖ *intr* tarder, s'attarder

delayed'-ac'tion *adj* à action différée

delayed'-ac'tion switch' *s* minuterie *f* d'escalier

delayed'-time' switch' *s* coupe-circuit *m* à action différée

dele [ˈdili] *s* (typ) deleatur *m*

delectable [dɪˈlɛktəbəl] *adj* délectable

delegate [ˈdɛlɪˌget], [ˈdɛlɪgɪt] *s* délégué *m*; (at a convention) congressiste *mf*, délégué *f* ‖ [ˈdɛlɪˌget] *tr* déléguer

delegation [ˌdɛlɪˈgeʃən] *s* délégation *f*

delete [dɪˈlit] *tr* supprimer

deletion [dɪˈliʃən] *s* suppression *f*; (the deleted part) passage *m* supprimé

deliberate [dɪˈlɪbərɪt] *adj* (premeditated) délibéré, réfléchi; (cautious) circonspect; (slow) lent ‖ [dɪˈlɪbəˌret] *tr* & *intr* délibérer

deliberately [dɪˈlɪbərɪtli] *adv* (on purpose) exprès, de propos délibéré; (without hurrying) posément, sans hâte

deliberation [dɪˌlɪbəˈreʃən] *s* délibération *f*; (slowness) lenteur *f*

delica·cy [ˈdɛlɪkəsi] *s* (pl -cies) délicatesse *f*; (choice food) friandise *f*, gourmandise *f*

delicate [ˈdɛlɪkɪt] *adj* délicat

delicatessen [ˌdɛlɪkəˈtɛsən] *s* charcuterie *f*

delicious [dɪˈlɪʃəs] *adj* délicieux

delight [dɪˈlaɪt] *s* délice *m*, délices *fpl*, plaisir *m* ‖ *tr* enchanter, ravir ‖ *intr*—**to delight in** se délecter à

delighted *adj* enchanté, ravi, content

delightful [dɪˈlaɪtfəl] *adj* délicieux, ravissant, enchanteur

delineate [dɪˈlɪnɪˌet] *tr* esquisser

delinquen·cy [dɪˈlɪŋkwənsi] *s* (pl -cies) délit *m*, faute *f*; (e.g., of juveniles) délinquance *f*

delinquent [dɪ'lɪŋkwənt] adj négligent, coupable; (in payment) arriéré; (in guilt) délinquant || s délinquant m; créancier m en retard

delirious [dɪ'lɪrɪ-əs] adj délirant

deliri·um [dɪ'lɪrɪ-əm] s (pl -ums or -a [ə]) délire m

deliver [dɪ'lɪvər] tr délivrer; (e.g., laundry) livrer; (mail) distribuer; (a blow) asséner; (an opinion) exprimer; (a speech) prononcer; (energy) débiter, fournir; **to be delivered of a child** accoucher d'un enfant

deliver·y [dɪ'lɪvərɪ] s (pl -ies) s remise f; (e.g., of a package) livraison f; (of mail) distribution f; (of a speech; of electricity) débit m; (of a woman in childbirth) accouchement m, délivrance f; **free delivery** livraison franco

deliv'ery·man s (pl -men) livreur m

deliv'ery room' s salle f d'accouchement, salle de travail

deliv'ery truck' s fourgon m à livraison

dell [del] s vallon m

delouse [di'laus], [di'lauz] tr épouiller

delphinium [del'fɪnɪ-əm] s dauphinelle f, pied-d'alouette m

delta [ˈdɛltə] s delta m

delude [dɪ'lud] tr duper, tromper

deluge [ˈdɛljudʒ] s déluge m || tr inonder

delusion [dɪ'luʒən] s illusion f, tromperie f; **delusions** (psychopathol) hallucinations fpl; **delusions of grandeur** folie f des grandeurs

delusive [dɪ'lusɪv] or **delusory** [dɪ'lusərɪ] adj trompeur

de luxe [dɪ'lʊks], [dɪ'lʌks] adj & adv de luxe

delve [delv] intr—**to delve into** fouiller dans, approfondir

demagnetize [di'mægnɪ,taɪz] tr démagnétiser, désaimanter

demagogue [ˈdɛmə,gɑg] s démagogue mf

demand [dɪ'mænd], [dɪ'mɑnd] s exigence f; (of the buying public) demande f; **demands** exigences; **in great demand** très recherché; **on demand** sur demande || tr exiger

demanding [dɪ'mændɪŋ], [dɪ'mɑndɪŋ] adj exigeant

demarcate [dɪ'mɑrket], [ˈdimɑr,ket] tr délimiter

demean [dɪ'min] tr dégrader; **to demean oneself** se conduire

demeanor [dɪ'minər] s conduite f, tenue f

demented [dɪ'mɛntɪd] adj aliéné, fou

demerit [di'mɛrɪt] s démérite m

demigod [ˈdɛmɪ,gɑd] s demi-dieu m

demijohn [ˈdɛmɪ,dʒɑn] s dame-jeanne f

demilitarize [di'mɪlɪtə,raɪz] tr démilitariser

demise [dɪ'maɪz] s décès m

demitasse [ˈdɛmɪ,tæs], [ˈdɛmɪ,tɑs] s petite tasse f à café; (contents) café m noir

demobilize [di'mobɪ,laɪz] tr démobiliser

democra·cy [dɪ'mɑkrəsɪ] s (pl -cies) démocratie f

democrat [ˈdɛmə,kræt] s démocrate mf

democratic [,dɛmə'krætɪk] adj démocratique

demolish [dɪ'mɑlɪʃ] tr démolir

demolition [,dɛmə'lɪʃən], [,dimə'lɪʃən] s démolition f

demon [ˈdimən] s démon m

demoniac [dɪ'monɪ,æk] adj & s démoniaque mf

demonic [dɪ'mɑnɪk] adj démoniaque

demonstrate [ˈdɛmən,stret] tr démontrer || intr (to show feelings in public gatherings) manifester

demonstration [,dɛmən'streʃən] s démonstration f; (public show of feeling) manifestation f

demonstrative [dɪ'mɑnstrətɪv] adj démonstratif

demonstrator [ˈdɛmən,stretər] s (salesman) démonstrateur m; (agitator) manifestant m

demoralize [dɪ'mɑrə,laɪz], [dɪ'mɔrə,laɪz] tr démoraliser

demote [dɪ'mot] tr rétrograder

demotion [dɪ'moʃən] s rétrogradation f

de·mur [dɪ'mʌr] v (pret & pp -murred; ger -murring) intr faire des objections

demure [dɪ'mjur] adj modeste, posé

demurrage [dɪ'mʌrɪdʒ] s (naut) surestarie f

den [den] s (of animals; of thieves) repaire m, retraite f; (of wild beasts) antre m; (of lions) tanière f; (room in a house) cabinet m de travail, fumoir m; (Cub Scouts) sizaine f

denaturalize [di'nætʃərə,laɪz] tr dénaturaliser

denial [dɪ'naɪ-əl] s (contradiction) dénégation f, démenti m; (refusal) refus m, déni m

denim [ˈdɛnɪm] s coutil m

denizen [ˈdɛnɪzən] s habitant m

Denmark [ˈdɛnmɑrk] s le Danemark

denomination [dɪ,nɑmɪ'neʃən] s dénomination f; (of coin or stamp) valeur f; (eccl) secte f, confession f, communion f

denote [dɪ'not] tr dénoter

denounce [dɪ'nauns] tr dénoncer

dense [dens] adj dense; (stupid) bête

densi·ty [ˈdɛnsɪtɪ] s (pl -ties) densité f

dent [dent] s marque f de coup, creux m; (in a knife; in a fortune) brèche f; **to make a dent in** faire une brèche à || tr ébrécher

dental [ˈdɛntəl] adj dentaire; (phonet) dental || s dentale f

den'tal floss' s fil m dentaire

den'tal sur'geon s chirurgien-dentiste m

dentifrice [ˈdɛntɪfrɪs] s dentifrice m

dentist [ˈdɛntɪst] s dentiste mf

dentistry [ˈdɛntɪstrɪ] s odontologie f

denture [ˈdɛntʃər] s (set of teeth) denture f; (set of artificial teeth) dentier m, râtelier m

denunciation [dɪ,nʌnsɪ'eʃən], [dɪ,nʌnʃɪ'eʃən] s dénonciation f

de·ny [dɪ'naɪ] v (pret & pp -nied) tr nier, démentir; **to deny oneself** se refuser, se priver

deodorant [di'odərənt] *adj & s* désodorisant *m*

deodorize [di'odə,raiz] *tr* désodoriser

depart [di'part] *intr* partir; **to depart from** se départir de

departed *adj* (*dead*) mort, défunt

department [di'partmənt] *s* département *m*; (*of hospital*) service *m*; (*of agency*) bureau *m*; (*of store*) rayon *m*, comptoir *m*; (*of university*) section *f*

Depart'ment of State' *s* ministère *m* des affaires étrangères

depart'ment store' *s* grands magasins *mpl*, galerie *f*

departure [di'partʃər] *s* départ *m*

depend [di'pend] *intr* dépendre; **to depend on** or **upon** dépendre de

dependable [di'pendəbəl] *adj* sûr; (*person*) digne de confiance

dependence [di'pendəns] *s* dépendance *f*; **dependence on** dépendance de; (*trust in*) confiance en

dependen·cy [di'pendənsi] *s* (*pl* **-cies**) dépendance *f*; (*country, territory*) possession *f*, colonie *f*

dependent [di'pendənt] *adj* dépendant; **dependent on** dépendant de; (*s.o. for family support*) à la charge de || *s* charge *f* de famille

depend'ent clause' *s* proposition *f* subordonnée

depict [di'pikt] *tr* dépeindre, décrire

depiction [di'pikʃən] *s* peinture *f*

deplete [di'plit] *tr* épuiser

depletion [di'pliʃən] *s* épuisement *m*

deplorable [di'plorəbəl] *adj* déplorable

deplore [di'plor] *tr* déplorer

deploy [di'plɔɪ] *tr* (mil) déployer || *intr* (mil) se déployer

deployment [di'plɔɪmənt] *s* (mil) déploiement *m*

depolarize [di'polə,raiz] *tr* dépolariser

depopulate [di'papjə,let] *tr & intr* dépeupler

deport [di'port] *tr* déporter; **to deport oneself** se comporter

deportation [,dipor'teʃən] *s* déportation *f*

deportee [,dipor'ti] *s* déporté *m*

deportment [di'portmənt] *s* comportement *m*, tenue *f*, manières *fpl*

depose [di'poz] *tr & intr* déposer

deposit [di'pazit] *s* dépôt *m*; (*as pledge*) cautionnement *m*, arrhes *fpl*, gage *m*; **no deposit** (*bottle*) perdu; **to pay a deposit** verser une provision, un acompte, or une caution; **with deposit** (*on a bottle*) consigné || *tr* déposer; laisser comme provision

depos'it account' *s* compte *m* courant

depositor [di'pazitər] *s* déposant *m*

deposito·ry [di'pazi,tori] *s* (*pl* **-ries**) dépôt *m*; (*person*) dépositaire *mf*

depot ['dipo], ['dɛpo] *s* dépôt *m*; (rr) gare *f*

depraved [di'prevd] *adj* dépravé

depravi·ty [di'præviti] *s* (*pl* **-ties**) dépravation *f*

deprecate ['dɛpri,ket] *tr* désapprouver

depreciate [di'priʃi,et] *tr* déprécier || *intr* se déprécier

depreciation [di,priʃi'eʃən] *s* dépréciation *f*

depredation [,dɛpri'deʃən] *s* déprédation *f*

depress [di'pres] *tr* déprimer; (*prices*) abaisser

depressing [di'prɛsɪŋ] *adj* attristant

depression [di'prɛʃən] *s* dépression *f*

deprive [di'praiv] *tr* priver

depth [dɛpθ] *s* profondeur *f*; (*in sound*) gravité *f*; **depths** abîme *m*; **in the depth of winter** en plein hiver; **to go beyond one's depth** perdre pied; sortir de sa compétence

depth' bomb' *s* bombe *f* sous-marine

depth' charge' *s* grenade *f* sous-marine

deputation [,dɛpjə'teʃən] *s* députation *f*

deputize ['dɛpjə,taiz] *tr* députer

depu·ty ['dɛpjəti] *s* (*pl* **-ties**) député *m*

derail [di'rel] *tr* faire dérailler || *intr* dérailler

derailment [di'relmənt] *s* déraillement *m*

derange [di'rendʒ] *tr* déranger

derangement [di'rendʒmənt] *s* dérangement *m*; (*of mind*) aliénation *f*

der·by ['dɑrbi] *s* (*pl* **-bies**) (*race*) derby *m*; (*hat*) chapeau *m* melon

derelict ['dɛrilikt] *adj* abandonné, délaissé; (*in one's duty*) négligent || *s* épave *f*

dereliction [,dɛri'likʃən] *s* abandon *m*, renoncement *m*

deride [di'raid] *tr* tourner en dérision, ridiculiser

derision [di'riʒən] *s* dérision *f*

derisive [di'raisiv] *adj* dérisoire

derivation [,dɛri've∫ən] *s* dérivation *f*

derivative [di'rivətiv] *adj & s* dérivé *m*

derive [di'raiv] *tr & intr* dériver

dermatology [,dɑrmə'talədʒi] *s* dermatologie *f*

derogatory [di'rɑgə,tori] *adj* péjoratif

derrick ['dɛrik] *s* grue *f*; (*for extracting oil*) derrick *m*

dervish ['dʌrvi∫] *s* derviche *m*

desalinization [di,selini'zeʃən] *s* dessalement *m*

desalt [di'sɔlt] *tr* dessaler

descend [di'sɛnd] *tr* descendre || *intr* descendre; (*said of rain*) tomber; **to be descended from** descendre de; **to descend on** s'abattre sur

descendant [di'sɛndənt] *adj & s* descendant *m*

descendent [di'sɛndənt] *adj* descendant

descent [di'sɛnt] *s* descente *f*; (*drop in temperature*) chute *f*; (*lineage*) descendance *f*, naissance *f*

describe [di'skraib] *tr* décrire

description [di'skripʃən] *s* description *f*

descriptive [di'skriptiv] *adj* descriptif

de·scry [di'skrai] *v* (*pret & pp* **-scried**) *tr* découvrir, apercevoir

desecrate ['dɛsi,kret] *tr* profaner

desegregate [di'sɛgri,get] *intr* supprimer la ségrégation raciale

desegregation [di,sɛgri'geʃən] *s* déségrégation *f*

desensitize [di'sɛnsi,taiz] *tr* désensibiliser

desert ['dɛzərt] *adj & s* désert *m* ‖ [dɪ'zʌrt] *s* mérite *m*; **to get one's just deserts** recevoir son salaire, recevoir sa juste punition ‖ *tr & intr* déserter

deserted *adj* (*person*) abandonné; (*place*) désert, nu

deserter [dɪ'zʌrtər] *s* déserteur *m*

desertion [dɪ'zʌrʃən] *s* désertion *f*

deserve [dɪ'zʌrv] *tr & intr* mériter

deservedly [dɪ'zʌrvidli] *adv* à juste titre, dignement

deserving [dɪ'zʌrvɪŋ] *adj* méritoire, digne

design [dɪ'zaɪn] *s* (*combination of details; art of designing; work of art*) dessin *m*; (*plan, scheme*) dessein *m*, projet *m*, plan *m*; (*model, outline*) modèle *m*, type *m*, grandes lignes *fpl*; **to have designs on** avoir des desseins sur ‖ *tr* inventer, projeter; (*e.g., a dress*) dessiner; (*a secret plan*) combiner; **designed for** destiné à

designate ['dɛzɪg,net] *tr* désigner

designer [dɪ'zaɪnər] *s* dessinateur *m*

designing [dɪ'zaɪnɪŋ] *adj* artificieux, intrigant ‖ *s* dessin *m*

desirable [dɪ'zaɪrəbəl] *adj* désirable

desire [dɪ'zaɪr] *s* désir *m* ‖ *tr* désirer

desirous [dɪ'zaɪrəs] *adj* désireux

desist [dɪ'zɪst] *intr* cesser

desk [dɛsk] *s* bureau *m*; (*in schoolroom*) pupitre *m*; (*of cashier*) caisse *f*

desk' blot'ter *s* sous-main *m*

desk' clerk' *s* réceptionnaire *mf*

desk' set' *s* écritoire *f*

desolate ['dɛsəlɪt] *adj* désert; (*sad*) désolé; (*alone*) abandonné ‖ ['dɛsə,let] *tr* désoler

desolation [,dɛsə'leʃən] *s* désolation *f*

despair [dɪ'spɛr] *s* désespoir *m*, désespérance *f* ‖ *intr* désespérer

despairing [dɪ'spɛrɪŋ] *adj* désespéré

desperado [,dɛspə'redo], [,dɛspə'rado] *s* (*pl* **-does** *or* **-dos**) hors-la-loi *m*

desperate ['dɛspərɪt] *adj* capable de tout, poussé à bout; (*bitter, excessive*) acharné, à outrance; (*hopeless*) désespéré; (*remedy*) héroïque

desperation [,dɛspə'reʃən] *s* désespoir *m*; (*recklessness*) témérité *f*

despicable ['dɛspɪkəbəl] *adj* méprisable, mesquin

despise [dɪ'spaɪz] *tr* mépriser, dédaigner

despite [dɪ'spaɪt] *prep* en dépit de, malgré

despoil [dɪ'spɔɪl] *tr* dépouiller

desponden•cy [dɪ'spandənsi] *s* (*pl* **-cies**) abattement *m*, accablement *m*

despondent [dɪ'spandənt] *adj* abattu, accablé, déprimé

despot ['dɛspat] *s* despote *m*, tyran *m*

despotic [dɛs'patɪk] *adj* despotique

despotism ['dɛspə,tɪzəm] *s* despotisme *m*

dessert [dɪ'zʌrt] *s* dessert *m*

dessert' spoon' *s* cuiller *f* à dessert

destination [,dɛstɪ'neʃən] *s* destination *f*

destine ['dɛstɪn] *tr* destiner

destiny ['dɛstɪni] *s* (*pl* **-nies**) destin *m*, destinée *f*

destitute ['dɛstɪ,t(j)ut] *adj* indigent; dépourvu

destitution [,dɛstɪ't(j)uʃən] *s* dénuement *m*, indigence *f*

destroy [dɪ'strɔɪ] *tr* détruire

destroyer [dɪ'strɔɪ•ər] *s* destructeur *m*; (*nav*) destroyer *m*

destruction [dɪ'strʌkʃən] *s* destruction *f*

destructive [dɪ'strʌktɪv] *adj* destructeur, destructif

desultory ['dɛsəl,tori] *adj* décousu, sans suite; (*conversation*) à bâtons rompus

detach [dɪ'tætʃ] *tr* détacher

detachable [dɪ'tætʃəbəl] *adj* détachable, démontable; (*collar*) faux

detached *adj* détaché

detachment [dɪ'tætʃmənt] *s* détachement *m*

detail [dɪ'tel], ['ditel] *s* détail *m*; (*mil*) extrait *m* de l'ordre du jour; (*mil*) détachement *m* ‖ [dɪ'tel] *tr* détailler

detailed' state'ment *s* bordereau *m*

detain [dɪ'ten] *tr* retenir, retarder; (*in prison*) détenir

detect [dɪ'tɛkt] *tr* déceler, détecter

detection [dɪ'tɛkʃən] *s* détection *f*

detective [dɪ'tɛktɪv] *adj* (*device*) détecteur; (*film, novel*) policier ‖ *s* détective *m*, agent *m* de la sûreté

detec'tive sto'ry *s* roman *m* policier

detector [dɪ'tɛktər] *s* détecteur *m*

detention [dɪ'tɛnʃən] *s* détention *f*

de•ter [dɪ'tʌr] *v* (*pret & pp* **-terred**; *ger* **-terring**) *tr* détourner

detergent [dɪ'tʌrdʒənt] *adj & s* détersif *m*

deteriorate [dɪ'tɪrɪ•ə,ret] *tr* détériorer ‖ *intr* se détériorer

determination [dɪ,tʌrmɪ'neʃən] *s* détermination *f*

determine [dɪ'tʌrmɪn] *tr* déterminer

determined *adj* déterminé, résolu

deterrent [dɪ'tʌrənt] *adj & s* préventif *m*

detest [dɪ'tɛst] *tr* détester

dethrone [dɪ'θron] *tr* détrôner

detonate ['dɛtə,net], ['ditə,net] *tr* faire détoner, faire éclater ‖ *intr* détoner

detour ['ditur], [dɪ'tur] *s* déviation *f*; (*indirect manner*) détour *m* ‖ *tr & intr* dévier

detract [dɪ'trækt] *tr* diminuer ‖ *intr—* **to detract from** amoindrir

detractor [dɪ'træktər] *s* détracteur *m*

detriment ['dɛtrɪmənt] *s* détriment *m*

detrimental [,dɛtrɪ'mɛntəl] *adj* préjudiciable, nuisible

deuce [d(j)us] *s* deux *m*; **what the deuce!** (*coll*) diantre!, que diable!

devaluate [di'vælju,et] *tr* dévaluer

devaluation [di,vælju'eʃən] *s* dévaluation *f*

devastate ['dɛvəs,tet] *tr* dévaster

devastating ['dɛvəs,tetɪŋ] *adj* dévastateur; (*coll*) écrasant, accablant

devastation [,dɛvəs'teʃən] *s* dévastation *f*

develop [dɪ'vɛləp] *tr* développer; (*a mine*) exploiter; (*e.g., a fever*) contracter; (phot) révéler, développer ‖ intr se développer; (to become evident) se produire, se manifester

developer [dɪˈvɛləpər] s entrepreneur m; (builder) maître m d'œuvre; (phot) révélateur m

development [dɪˈvɛləpmənt] s développement m; (event) événement m récent; (of housing) cité f, grand ensemble m

deviate [ˈdivɪˌet] s perverti m ‖ tr faire dévier ‖ intr dévier

deviation [ˌdivɪˈeʃən] s déviation f

device [dɪˈvaɪs] s appareil m, dispositif m; (trick) stratagème m, ruse f; (motto) emblème m, devise f; to leave s.o. to his own devices abandonner qn à ses propres moyens

dev·il [ˈdɛvəl] s diable m; speak of the devil! (coll) je vois un loup!; to be between the devil and the deep blue sea (coll) se trouver entre l'enclume et le marteau; to raise the devil (slang) faire le diable à quatre ‖ v (pret & pp -iled or -illed; ger -iling or -illing) tr épicer fortement; (coll) tourmenter

devilish [ˈdɛvəlɪʃ] adj diabolique; (roguish) coquin

dev'il-may-care' adj insouciant, étourdi

devilment [ˈdɛvəlmənt] s (mischief) diablerie f; (evil) méchanceté f

devil·try [ˈdɛvəltri] s (pl -tries) méchanceté f, cruauté f; (mischief) espièglerie f

devious [ˈdivɪəs] adj (straying) détourné, dévié; (roundabout; shifty) tortueux

devise [dɪˈvaɪz] tr combiner, inventer; (law) léguer

devoid [dɪˈvɔɪd] adj dépourvu, vide, dénué

devolve [dɪˈvɑlv] intr—to devolve on, to, or upon échoir à

devote [dɪˈvot] tr consacrer

devoted adj dévoué; **devoted to** voué à, dévoué à, attaché à

devotee [ˌdɛvəˈti] s dévot m, adepte mf; (sports) fervent m, fanatique mf

devotion [dɪˈvoʃən] s dévotion f; (to study, work, etc.) dévouement m; **devotions** dévotions, prières fpl

devour [dɪˈvaʊr] tr dévorer

devout [dɪˈvaʊt] adj dévot, pieux

dew [d(j)u] s rosée f

dew'drop' s goutte f de rosée

dew'lap' s fanon m, double menton m

dew·y [ˈd(j)u·i] adj (comp -ier; super -iest) couvert de rosée

dexterity [dɛksˈtɛriti] s dextérité f, adresse f

diabetes [ˌdaɪ·əˈbitɪs], [ˌdaɪ·əˈbitiz] s diabète m

diabetic [ˌdaɪ·əˈbɛtɪk], [ˌdaɪ·əˈbitik] adj & s diabétique mf

diabolic(al) [ˌdaɪ·əˈbɑlɪk(əl)] adj diabolique

diacritical [ˌdaɪ·əˈkritikəl] adj diacritique

diadem [ˈdaɪ·əˌdɛm] s diadème m

diaere·sis [daɪˈɛrɪsɪs] s (pl -ses [ˌsiz]) diérèse f; (mark) tréma m

diagnose [ˌdaɪ·əgˈnos], [ˌdaɪ·əgˈnoz] tr diagnostiquer

diagno·sis [ˌdaɪ·əgˈnosɪs] s (pl -ses [ˌsiz]) diagnostic m

diagonal [daɪˈægənəl] adj diagonal ‖ s diagonale f

dia·gram [ˈdaɪ·əˌgræm] s diagramme m, croquis m coté ‖ v (pret & pp -gramed or -grammed; ger -graming or -gramming) tr représenter schématiquement

di·al [ˈdaɪ·əl], [daɪl] s cadran m ‖ v (pret & pp -aled or -alled; ger -aling or -alling) tr (a telephone number) composer ‖ intr faire un numéro

dialect [ˈdaɪ·əˌlɛkt] s dialecte m

dialing [ˈdaɪ·əlɪŋ] s (telp) composition f du numéro

dialogue [ˈdaɪ·əˌlɔg], [ˈdaɪ·əˌlag] s dialogue m

di'al tel'ephone s téléphone m automatique, automatique m

di'al tone' s (telp) tonalité f

diameter [daɪˈæmɪtər] s diamètre m

diametric(al) [ˌdaɪ·əˈmɛtrɪk(əl)] adj diamétral

diamond [ˈdaɪmənd] s diamant m; (figure of a rhombus) losange m; (baseball) petit champ m; (cards) carreau m

diaper [ˈdaɪ·əpər] s lange m, couche f ‖ tr (to variegate) diaprer

diaphanous [daɪˈæfənəs] adj diaphane

diaphragm [ˈdaɪ·əˌfræm] s diaphragme m

diarrhea [ˌdaɪ·əˈri·ə] s diarrhée f

dia·ry [ˈdaɪ·əri] s (pl -ries) journal m

diastole [daɪˈæstəli] s diastole f

diathermy [ˈdaɪ·əˌθɑrmi] s diathermie f

diatribe [ˈdaɪ·əˌtraɪb] s diatribe f

dice [daɪs] spl dés mpl; **no dice!** (slang) pas moyen!; **to load the dice** piper les dés ‖ tr couper en cubes

dice'box' s cornet m à dés

dichoto·my [daɪˈkɑtəmi] s (pl -mies) dichotomie f

dictaphone [ˈdɪktəˌfon] s (trademark) dictaphone m

dictate [ˈdɪktet] s précepte m, règle f ‖ tr & intr dicter

dictation [dɪkˈteʃən] s dictée f; **to take dictation from** écrire sous la dictée de

dictator [ˈdɪktetər], [dɪkˈtetər] s dictateur m

dic'tator·ship' s dictature f

diction [ˈdɪkʃən] s diction f

dictionar·y [ˈdɪkʃənˌɛri] s (pl -ies) dictionnaire m

dic·tum [ˈdɪktəm] s (pl -ta [tə]) dicton m; (law) opinion f, arrêt m

didactic(al) [daɪˈdæktɪk(əl)], [dɪˈdæktɪk(əl)] adj didactique

die [daɪ] s (pl dice [daɪs]) dé m; **the die is cast** le dé en est jeté ‖ s (pl dies) (for stamping coins, medals, etc.) coin m; (for cutting threads) filière f; (key pattern) jeu m ‖ v (pret & pp died; ger dying) intr mourir; **to be dying** se mourir; **to be dying to** (coll) mourir d'envie de; **to die away**

s'éteindre; **to die laughing** (coll) mourir de rire

die'hard' adj intransigeant || s intransigeant m, jusqu'au-boutiste mf

die'sel en'gine [dizəl] s diesel m, moteur m diesel

die'sel oil' s gas-oil m

die'stock' s porte-filière m

diet ['daɪ·ət] s nourriture f; (congress; abstention from food) diète f; (special menu) régime m || intr être ou se mettre au régime, suivre un régime

dietetic [,daɪ·ə'tɛtɪk] adj diététique || **dietetics** s diététique f

dietician [,daɪ·ə'tɪʃən] s diététicien m

differ ['dɪfər] intr différer; **to differ with** être en désaccord avec

difference ['dɪfərəns] s différence f; (controversy) différend m; **to make no difference** ne rien faire; **to split the difference** partager le différend

different ['dɪfərənt] adj différent

differential [,dɪfə'rɛnʃəl] adj différentiel || s (mach) différentiel m; (math) différentielle f

differentiate [,dɪfə'rɛnʃɪ,et] tr différencier || intr se différencier

difficult ['dɪfɪ,kʌlt] adj difficile

difficul·ty ['dɪfɪ,kʌltɪ] s (pl -ties) difficulté f

diffident ['dɪfɪdənt] adj défiant, timide

diffuse [dɪ'fjus] adj diffus || [dɪ'fjuz] tr diffuser || intr se diffuser

dig [dɪg] s—**to give s.o. a dig** (coll) lancer un trait à qn || v (pret & pp dug [dʌg]; ger digging) tr bêcher, creuser; **to dig up** déterrer || intr bêcher

digest ['daɪdʒɛst] s abrégé m, résumé m; (publication) digest m, sélection f; (law) digeste m || [dɪ'dʒɛst], [daɪ'dʒɛst] tr & intr digérer

digestible [dɪ'dʒɛstɪbəl], [daɪ'dʒɛstɪbəl] adj digestible

digestion [dɪ'dʒɛstʃən], [daɪ'dʒɛstʃən] s digestion f

digestive [dɪ'dʒɛstɪv], [daɪ'dʒɛstɪv] adj digestif

diges'tive tract' s appareil m digestif

digit ['dɪdʒɪt] s chiffre m; (finger) doigt m; (toe) doigt du pied

digitalis [,dɪdʒɪ'tælɪs], [,dɪdʒɪ'telɪs] s (bot) digitale f; (pharm) digitaline f

dignified adj distingué; (air) digne

digni·fy ['dɪgnɪ,faɪ] v (pret & pp -fied) tr glorifier, honorer

dignitar·y ['dɪgnɪ,tɛri] s (pl -ies) dignitaire mf

digni·ty ['dɪgnɪti] s (pl -ties) dignité f; **to stand on one's dignity** rester sur son quant-à-soi, le prendre de haut

digress [dɪ'grɛs], [daɪ'grɛs] intr faire une digression

digression [dɪ'grɛʃən], [daɪ'grɛʃən] s digression f

dihedral [daɪ'hidrəl] adj & s dièdre m

dike [daɪk] s digue f

dilapidated [dɪ'læpɪ,detɪd] adj délabré, déglingué

dilate [daɪ'let] tr dilater || intr se dilater

dilatory ['dɪlə,tori] adj lent, tardif; (strategy, answer) dilatoire

dilemma [dɪ'lɛmə] s dilemme m

dilettan·te [,dɪlə'tænti] adj dilettante || s (pl -tes or -ti [ti]) dilettante mf

diligence ['dɪlɪdʒəns] s diligence f

diligent ['dɪlɪdʒənt] adj diligent

dill [dɪl] s fenouil m bâtard, aneth m

dillydal·ly ['dɪli,dæli] v (pret & pp -lied) intr traînasser

dilute [dɪ'lut], [daɪ'lut] adj dilué || [dɪ'lut] tr diluer, délayer

dilution [dɪ'luʃən] s dilution f

dim [dɪm] adj faible, indistinct; (forebodings) obscur; (memory) effacé; (color) terne; (idea of what is going on) obtus, confus; **to take a dim view of** envisager sans enthousiasme || v (pret & pp dimmed; ger dimming) tr affaiblir, obscurcir; (beauty) ternir; (the headlights) baisser, mettre en code || intr s'affaiblir, s'obscurcir; (said of color, beauty, etc.) se ternir

dime [daɪm] s monnaie f de dix cents américains

dimension [dɪ'mɛnʃən] s dimension f

diminish [dɪ'mɪnɪʃ] tr & intr diminuer

diminutive [dɪ'mɪnjətɪv] adj & s diminutif m

dimi·ty ['dɪmɪti] s (pl -ties) basin m, brillanté m

dimly ['dɪmli] adv indistinctement

dimmers ['dɪmərz] spl (aut) feux mpl code, feux de croisement; **to put on the dimmers** se mettre en code

dimple ['dɪmpəl] s fossette f

dim'wit' s (slang) sot m, niais m

din [dɪn] s tapage m, fracas m || v (pret & pp dinned; ger dinning) tr assourdir; répéter sans cesse || intr sonner bruyamment

dine [daɪn] tr fêter par un dîner || intr dîner; **to dine out** dîner en ville

diner ['daɪnər] s dîneur m; (short-order restaurant) plats-cuisinés m; (rr) wagon-restaurant m

dinette [daɪ'nɛt] s coin-repas m

ding-dong ['dɪŋ,dɔŋ], ['dɪŋ,dɑŋ] s tintement m, digue-din-don m

din·ghy ['dɪŋgi] s (pl -ghies) canot m, youyou m

din·gy ['dɪndʒi] adj (comp -gier; super -giest) défraîchi, terne

din'ing car' s wagon-restaurant m

din'ing hall' s salle f à manger; (of university) réfectoire m

din'ing room' s salle f à manger

din'ing-room suite' s salle f à manger

dinner ['dɪnər] s dîner m

din'ner coat' s smoking m

din'ner dance' s dîner m suivi de bal

din'ner guest' s convive mf, invité m

din'ner jack'et s smoking m

din'ner pail' s potager m

din'ner set' s service m de table

din'ner time' s heure f du dîner

dinosaur ['daɪnə,sɔr] s dinosaure m

dint [dɪnt] s—**by dint of** s force de

diocese ['daɪ·ə,sis], ['daɪ·əsɪs] s diocèse m

diode ['daɪ·od] s diode f

dioxide [daɪ'ɑksaɪd] s bioxyde m

dip [dɪp] *s* (*immersion*) plongeon *m*; (*swim*) baignade *f*; (*slope*) pente *f*; (*of magnetic needle*) inclinaison *f* || *v* (*pret & pp* **dipped;** *ger* **dipping**) *tr* plonger; (*a flag*) marquer || *intr* plonger; (*said of magnetic needle*) incliner; (*said of scale*) pencher; **to dip into** (*a book*) feuilleter; (*one's capital*) prendre dans

diphtheria [dɪf'θɪrɪ-ə] *s* diphtérie *f*

diphthong ['dɪfθɔŋ], ['dɪfθaŋ] *s* diphtongue *f*

diphthongize ['dɪfθɔŋ ,gaɪz], ['dɪfθaŋ ,gaɪz] *tr* diphtonguer || *intr* se diphtonguer

diploma [dɪ'plomə] *s* diplôme *m*

diploma·cy [dɪ'ploməsi] *s* (*pl* **-cies**) diplomatie *f*

diplomat ['dɪplə ,mæt] *s* diplomate *mf*

diplomatic [,dɪplə'mætɪk] *adj* diplomatique, diplomate

dip'lomat'ic pouch' *s* valise *f* diplomatique

dipper ['dɪpər] *s* louche *f*, cuiller *f* à pot

dip'stick' *s* jauge *f*

dire [daɪr] *adj* affreux, terrible

direct [dɪ'rekt], [daɪ'rekt] *adj* direct; franc, sincère || *tr* diriger; (*to order*) ordonner; (*a letter, question, etc.*) adresser; (*to point out*) indiquer; (*theat*) mettre en scène

direct' cur'rent *s* courant *m* continu

direct' di'aling *s* (telp) automatique *m* interurbain

direct' hit' *s* coup *m* or tir *m* direct

direction [dɪ'rekʃən], [daɪ'rekʃən] *s* direction *f*; (*e.g., of a street*) sens *m*; (theat) mise *f* en scène; **directions** instructions *fpl*; (*for use*) mode *m* d'emploi

directional [dɪ'rekʃənəl], [daɪ'rekʃən-əl] *adj* directionnel

direc'tional sig'nal *s* clignotant *m*

directive [dɪ'rektɪv], [daɪ'rektɪv] *s* ordre *m*, avis *m*

direct' ob'ject *s* (gram) complément *m* direct

director [dɪ'rektər], [daɪ'rektər] *s* directeur *m*, administrateur *m*, chef *m*; (*of a board*) membre *m* du conseil, votant *m*; (theat) metteur *m* en scène

direc'tor-ship' *s* direction *f*, directorat *m*

directo·ry [dɪ'rektəri], [daɪ'rektəri] *s* (*pl* **-ries**) (*board of directors*) conseil *m* d'administration; (*e.g., of telephone*) annuaire *m*; (*e.g., of genealogy*) almanach *m*; (eccl) directoire *m*

dirge [dʌrdʒ] *s* hymne *f* or chant *m* funèbre

dirigible ['dɪrɪdʒɪbəl] *adj* & *s* dirigeable *m*

dirt [dʌrt] *s* saleté *f*, ordure *f*; (*on clothes, skin, etc.*) crasse *f*; (mire) crotte *f*, boue *f*; (earth) terre *f*

dirt'-cheap' *adj* vendu à vil prix

dirt' road' *s* chemin *m* de terre

dirt·y ['dʌrti] *adj* (*comp* **-ier;** *super* **-iest**) sale, malpropre; (*clothes, skin, etc.*) crasseux; (muddy) crotté, boueux; (mean) méchant, vilain

dir'ty lin'en *s* linge *m* sale; **don't wash your dirty linen in public** il faut laver son linge sale en famille

dir'ty trick' *s* (slang) sale tour *m*

disabili·ty [,dɪsə'bɪlɪti] *s* (*pl* **-ties**) incapacité *f*, invalidité *f*

disabil'ity pen'sion *s* pension *f* d'invalidité

disable [dɪs'ebəl] *tr* rendre incapable, mettre hors de combat; (*to hurt the limbs of*) estropier, mutiler

disabled *adj* (*serviceman*) invalide; (ship) désemparé

disa'bled vet'eran *s* invalide *m*, réformé *m*

disabuse [,dɪsə'bjuz] *tr* désabuser

disadvantage [,dɪsəd'væntɪdʒ], [,dɪs-əd'vantɪdʒ] *s* désavantage *m* || *tr* désavantager

disadvantageous [dɪs ,ædvən'tedʒəs] *adj* désavantageux

disagree [,dɪsə'gri] *intr* différer; **to disagree with** (*to cause discomfort to*) ne pas convenir à; (*to dissent from*) donner tort à

disagreeable [,dɪsə'gri-əbəl] *adj* désagréable; (*mood, weather, etc.*) maussade

disagreement [,dɪsə'grimənt] *s* désaccord *m*, différend *m*

disallow [,dɪsə'lau] *tr* désapprouver, rejeter

disappear [,dɪsə'pɪr] *intr* disparaître; (phonet) s'amuïr

disappearance [,dɪsə'pɪrəns] *s* disparition *f*; (phonet) amuïssement *m*

disappoint [,dɪsə'pɔɪnt] *tr* décevoir, désappointer

disappointed *adj* déçu

disappointment [,dɪsə'pɔɪntmənt] *s* déception *f*, désappointement *m*

disapproval [,dɪsə'pruvəl] *s* désapprobation *f*

disapprove [,dɪsə'pruv] *tr* & *intr* désapprouver

disarm [dɪs'arm] *tr* & *intr* désarmer

disarmament [dɪs'arməmənt] *s* désarmement *m*

disarming [dɪs'armɪŋ] *adj* désarmant

disarray [,dɪsə're] *s* désarroi *m*, désordre *m*; **in disarray** (*said of apparel*) à demi vêtu || *tr* mettre en désarroi

disassemble [,dɪsə'sembəl] *tr* démonter, désassembler

disassociate [,dɪsə'soʃɪ ,et] *tr* dissocier

disaster [dɪ'zæstər], [dɪ'zastər] *s* désastre *m*

disastrous [dɪ'zæstrəs], [dɪ'zastrəs] *adj* désastreux

disavow [,dɪsə'vau] *tr* désavouer

disavowal [,dɪsə'vau·əl] *s* désaveu *m*

disband [dɪs'bænd] *tr* licencier, congédier || *intr* se débander, se disperser

dis·bar [dɪs'bar] *v* (*pret & pp* **-barred;** *ger* **-barring**) *tr* (law) rayer du barreau

disbelief [,dɪsbɪ'lif] *s* incroyance *f*

disbelieve [,dɪsbɪ'liv] *tr* & *intr* ne pas croire

disburse [dɪs'bʌrs] *tr* débourser

disbursement [dɪs'bʌrsmənt] *s* déboursement *m*; **disbursements** débours *mpl*

disc [dɪsk] *s* disque *m*

discard [dɪs'kɑrd] *s* rebut *m*; (cards) écart *m*; **discards** marchandises *fpl* de rebut ‖ *tr* mettre de côté, jeter; (cards) écarter ‖ *intr* (cards) se défausser

discern [dɪ'zʌrn], [dɪ'sʌrn] *tr* discerner, percevoir

discernible [dɪ'zʌrnɪbəl], [dɪ'sʌrnɪbəl] *adj* discernable

discerning [dɪ'zʌrnɪŋ], [dɪ'sʌrnɪŋ] *adj* judicieux, pénétrant, éclairé

discernment [dɪ'zʌrnmənt], [dɪ'sʌrnmənt] *s* discernement *m*

discharge [dɪs't ʃɑrdʒ] *s* décharge *f*; (of a prisoner) élargissement *m*; (from a job) congé *m*, renvoi *m*; (from the armed forces) libération *f*; (from the armed forces for unfitness) réforme *f*; (from a wound) suppuration *f* ‖ *tr* décharger; (a prisoner) élargir; (an employee) congédier, renvoyer, licencier; (a soldier) libérer, réformer ‖ *intr* se décharger; (pathol) suppurer

disciple [dɪ'saɪpəl] *s* disciple *m*

disciplinarian [,dɪsɪplɪ'nɛrɪ·ən] *s* partisan *m* d'une forte discipline; personne *f* qui impose une forte discipline

disciplinary ['dɪsɪplɪ‚nɛri] *adj* disciplinaire

discipline ['dɪsɪplɪn] *s* discipline *f* ‖ *tr* discipliner

disclaim [dɪs'klem] *tr* désavouer, renier

disclaimer [dɪs'klemər] *s* désaveu *m*

disclose [dɪs'kloz] *tr* découvrir, révéler

disclosure [dɪs'kloʒər] *s* découverte *f*, révélation *f*

discolor [dɪs'kʌlər] *tr* décolorer ‖ *intr* se décolorer

discoloration [dɪs‚kʌlə'reʃən] *s* décoloration *f*

discomfit [dɪs'kʌmfɪt] *tr* décontenancer, bafouer

discomfiture [dɪs'kʌmfɪt/ər] *s* déconfiture *f*, déconvenue *f*

discomfort [dɪs'kʌmfərt] *s* malaise *f*; (inconvenience) gêne *f* ‖ *tr* gêner

disconcert [,dɪskən'sʌrt] *tr* déconcerter

disconnect [,dɪskə'nɛkt] *tr* désunir, séparer; (a mechanism) débrayer; (a plug) débrancher; (current) couper

disconsolate [dɪs'kɑnsəlɪt] *adj* désolé, inconsolable

discontent [,dɪskən'tɛnt] *adj* mécontent ‖ *s* mécontentement *m* ‖ *tr* mécontenter

discontented *adj* mécontent

discontinue [,dɪskən'tɪnju] *tr* discontinuer

discontinuous [,dɪskən'tɪnju·əs] *adj* discontinu

discord ['dɪskɔrd] *s* discorde *f*, désaccord *m*; (mus) discordance *f*

discordance [dɪs'kɔrdəns] *s* discordance *f*

discotheque ['dɪskə‚tɛk] *s* discothèque *f*

discount ['dɪskaunt] *s* escompte *m*, remise *f*, rabais *m* ‖ ['dɪskaunt], [dɪs'kaunt] *tr* escompter, rabattre

dis'count rate' *s* taux *m* d'escompte

discourage [dɪs'kʌrɪdʒ] *tr* décourager

discouragement [dɪs'kʌrɪdʒmənt] *s* découragement *m*

discourse ['dɪskors], [dɪs'kors] *s* discours *m* ‖ [dɪs'kors] *intr* discourir

discourteous [dɪs'kʌrtɪ·əs] *adj* impoli, discourtois

discourte·sy [dɪs'kʌrtəsi] *s* (*pl* -sies) impolitesse *f*, discourtoisie *f*

discover [dɪs'kʌvər] *tr* découvrir

discoverer [dɪs'kʌvərər] *s* découvreur *m*

discover·y [dɪs'kʌvəri] *s* (*pl* -ies) découverte *f*

discredit [dɪs'krɛdɪt] *s* discrédit *m* ‖ *tr* discréditer

discreditable [dɪs'krɛdɪtəbəl] *adj* déshonorant, peu honorable

discreet [dɪs'krit] *adj* discret

discrepan·cy [dɪs'krɛpənsi] *s* (*pl* -cies) désaccord *m*, différence *f*

discretion [dɪs'krɛʃən] *s* discrétion *f*

discriminate [dɪs'krɪmɪ‚net] *tr* & *intr* discriminer; **to discriminate against** défavoriser

discrimination [dɪs‚krɪmɪ'neʃən] *s* discrimination *f*

discriminatory [dɪs'krɪmɪnə‚tori] *adj* discriminatoire

discus ['dɪskəs] *s* (sports) disque *m*, palet *m*

discuss [dɪs'kʌs] *tr* & *intr* discuter

discussion [dɪs'kʌ/ən] *s* discussion *f*

disdain [dɪs'den] *s* dédain *m* ‖ *tr* dédaigner

disdainful [dɪs'denfəl] *adj* dédaigneux

disease [dɪ'ziz] *s* maladie *f*

diseased *adj* malade

disembark [,dɪsɛm'bɑrk] *tr* & *intr* débarquer

disembarkation [dɪs‚ɛmbɑr'keʃən] *s* débarquement *m*

disembow·el [,dɪsɛm'bau·əl] *v* (*pret* & *pp* -eled or -elled; *ger* -eling or -elling) *tr* éventrer

disenchant [,dɪsɛn't ʃænt], [,dɪsɛn-'t ʃɑnt] *tr* désenchanter

disenchantment [,dɪsɛn't ʃæntmənt], [,dɪsɛn't ʃɑntmənt] *s* désenchantement *m*

disengage [,dɪsɛn'gedʒ] *tr* dégager; (toothed wheels) désengrener; (a motor) débrayer ‖ *intr* se dégager

disengagement [,dɪsɛn'gedʒmənt] *s* dégagement *m*, détachement *m*

disentangle [,dɪsɛn'tæŋgəl] *tr* démêler, débrouiller

disentanglement [,dɪsɛn'tæŋgəlmənt] *s* démêlage *m*, débrouillement *m*

disestablish [,dɪsɛs'tæblɪʃ] *tr* (the Church) séparer de l'État

disfavor [dɪs'fevər] *s* défaveur *f* ‖ *tr* défavoriser

disfigure [dɪs'fɪgjər] *tr* défigurer, enlaidir

disfigurement [dɪs'fɪgjərmənt] *s* défiguration *f*

disfranchise [dɪsˈfræntʃaɪz] *tr* priver de ses droits civiques

disgorge [dɪsˈgɔrdʒ] *tr & intr* dégorger

disgrace [dɪsˈgres] *s* déshonneur *m* || *tr* déshonorer; (*to deprive of favor*) disgracier; **to disgrace oneself** se déshonorer

disgraceful [dɪsˈgresfəl] *adj* déshonorant, honteux

disgruntled [dɪsˈgrʌntəld] *adj* contrarié, de mauvaise humeur

disguise [dɪsˈgaɪz] *s* déguisement *m* || *tr* déguiser

disgust [dɪsˈgʌst] *s* dégoût *m* || *tr* dégoûter

disgusting [dɪsˈgʌstɪŋ] *adj* dégoûtant

dish [dɪʃ] *s* plat *m*; (*food*) mets *m*, plat; **to wash the dishes** faire la vaisselle || *tr*—**to dish up** servir

dish' clos'et *s* étagère *f* à vaisselle

dish'cloth' *s* lavette *f*

dishearten [dɪsˈhɑrtən] *tr* décourager

dishev-el [dɪˈʃevəl] *v* (*pret & pp* -**eled** or -**elled**; *ger* -**eling** or -**elling**) *tr* écheveler

dishonest [dɪsˈɑnɪst] *adj* malhonnête, déloyal

dishones-ty [dɪsˈɑnɪsti] *s* (*pl* -**ties**) malhonnêteté *f*, déloyauté *f*, improbité *f*

dishonor [dɪsˈɑnər] *s* déshonneur *m* || *tr* déshonorer

dishonorable [dɪsˈɑnərəbəl] *adj* déshonorant

dish'pan' *s* bassine *f*

dish' rack' *s* égouttoir *m*

dish'rag' *s* lavette *f*

dish'tow'el *s* torchon *m*

dish'wash'er *s* machine *f* à laver la vaisselle, lave-vaisselles *f*; (*person*) plongeur *m*

dish'wa'ter *s* eau *f* de vaisselle

disillusion [ˌdɪsɪˈluʒən] *s* désillusion *f* || *tr* désillusionner

disillusionment [ˌdɪsɪˈluʒənmənt] *s* désillusionnement *m*

disinclination [dɪsˌɪnkləˈneʃən] *s* répugnance *f*, aversion *f*

disinclined [ˌdɪsɪnˈklaɪnd] *adj* indisposé

disinfect [ˌdɪsɪnˈfekt] *tr* désinfecter

disinfectant [ˌdɪsɪnˈfektənt] *adj & s* désinfectant *m*

disingenuous [ˌdɪsɪnˈdʒenju·əs] *adj* insincère, sans franchise

disinherit [ˌdɪsɪnˈherɪt] *tr* déshériter

disintegrate [dɪsˈɪntɪˌgret] *tr* désagréger; (nucl) désintégrer || *intr* se désagréger; (nucl) se désintégrer

disintegration [dɪsˌɪntɪˈgreʃən] *s* désagrégation *f*; (nucl) désintégration *f*

disin-ter [ˌdɪsɪnˈtʌr] *v* (*pret & pp* -**terred**; *ger* -**terring**) *tr* déterrer

disinterested [dɪsˈɪntəˌrestɪd], [dɪsˈɪntrɪstɪd] *adj* désintéressé

disjointed [dɪsˈdʒɔɪntɪd] *adj* désarticulé; (*e.g.*, *style*) décousu

disjunctive [dɪsˈdʒʌŋktɪv] *adj* disjonctif; (*pronoun*) tonique

disk [dɪsk] *s* disque *m*

disk' jock'ey *s* présentateur *m* de disques

dislike [dɪsˈlaɪk] *s* aversion *f*; **to take a dislike for** prendre en aversion || *tr* ne pas aimer

dislocate [ˈdɪsloˌket] *tr* disloquer; (*a joint*) luxer

dislodge [dɪsˈlɑdʒ] *tr* déplacer; (*e.g.*, *the enemy*) déloger

disloyal [dɪsˈlɔɪ·əl] *adj* déloyal

disloyal-ty [dɪsˈlɔɪ·əlti] *s* (*pl* -**ties**) déloyauté *f*

dismal [ˈdɪzməl] *adj* sombre, triste

dismantle [dɪsˈmæntəl] *tr* démanteler; (*a machine*) démonter; (*a ship*) désarmer

dismay [dɪsˈme] *s* consternation *f* || *tr* consterner

dismember [dɪsˈmembər] *tr* démembrer

dismiss [dɪsˈmɪs] *tr* congédier; (*a servant*) renvoyer; (*an employee*) licencier; (*a government official*) destituer; (*a class in school*) terminer

dismissal [dɪsˈmɪsəl] *s* congédiement *m*; (*from a job*) congé *m*, renvoi *m*; (*of an appeal*) (law) rejet *m*

dismount [dɪsˈmaunt] *tr* démonter || *intr* descendre

disobedience [ˌdɪsəˈbidɪ·əns] *s* désobéissance *f*

disobedient [ˌdɪsəˈbidɪ·ənt] *adj* désobéissant

disobey [ˌdɪsəˈbe] *tr* désobéir (with *dat*); **to be disobeyed** être désobéi || *intr* désobéir

disorder [dɪsˈɔrdər] *s* désordre *m* || *tr* désordonner

disorderly [dɪsˈɔrdərli] *adj* désordonné, déréglé; (*crowd*) turbulent, effervescent

disor'derly con'duct *s* conduite *f* désordonnée

disor'derly house' *s* maison *f* de prostitution; maison de jeu

disorganize [dɪsˈɔrgəˌnaɪz] *tr* désorganiser

disoriented [dɪsˈɔrɪˌentɪd] *adj* désorienté

disown [dɪsˈon] *tr* désavouer, renier

disparage [dɪˈspærɪdʒ] *tr* dénigrer, déprécier

disparagement [dɪˈspærɪdʒmənt] *s* dénigrement *m*, dépréciation *f*

disparate [ˈdɪspərɪt] *adj* disparate

dispari-ty [dɪˈspærɪti] *s* (*pl* -**ties**) disparité *f*

dispassionate [dɪsˈpæʃənɪt] *adj* calme; impartial

dispatch [dɪˈspætʃ] *s* dépêche *f*; (*shipment*) envoi *m*, expédition *f*; (*promptness*) promptitude *f* || *tr* dépêcher; (coll) expédier

dis-pel [dɪˈspel] *v* (*pret & pp* -**pelled**; *ger* -**pelling**) *tr* dissiper, disperser

dispensa-ry [dɪˈspensəri] *s* (*pl* -**ries**) dispensaire *m*

dispensation [ˌdɪspenˈseʃən] *s* (*dispensing*) dispensation *f*; (*exemption*) dispense *f*

dispense [dɪˈspens] *tr* dispenser, distribuer || *intr*—**to dispense with** se passer de; se défaire de

dispenser [dɪˈspensər] *s* dispensateur *m*; (*automatic*) distributeur *m*

disperse [dɪ'spʌrs] *tr* disperser || *intr* se disperser

dispersion [dɪ'spʌrʒən], [dɪ'spʌrʃən] *s* dispersion *f*

dispirit [dɪ'spɪrɪt] *tr* décourager

displace [dɪs'ples] *tr* déplacer; *(to take the place of)* remplacer

displaced/ per'son *s* personne *f* déplacée

displacement [dɪs'plesmənt] *s* déplacement *m*; *(substitution)* remplacement *m*

display [dɪ'sple] *s* exposition *f*, étalage *m*; *(of emotion)* manifestation *f* || *tr* exposer, étaler; *(anger, courage, etc.)* manifester; *(ignorance)* révéler

display/ cab'inet *s* vitrine *f*

display/ win'dow *s* vitrine *f*, devanture *f*

displease [dɪs'pliz] *tr* déplaire (with *dat*)

displeasing [dɪs'plizɪŋ] *adj* déplaisant

displeasure [dɪs'pleʒər] *s* déplaisir *m*, mécontentement *m*

disposable [dɪ'spozəbəl] *adj* (*available*) disponible; (*made to be disposed of*) à jeter; (*container*) perdu, e.g., **dis-posable bottle** verre perdu

disposal [dɪ'spozəl] *s* disposition *f*; (*of a question*) résolution *f*; (*of trash, garbage, etc.*) destruction *f*

dispose [dɪ'spoz] *tr* disposer || *intr* dis-poser; **to dispose of** se défaire de; (*to get rid of*) se défaire de; (*a question*) résoudre, trancher

disposed *adj*—**to be disposed to** se dis-poser à, être porté à

disposition [,dɪspə'zɪʃən] *s* disposition *f*; (*mental outlook*) naturel *m*; (*mil*) dispositif *m*

dispossess [,dɪspə'zes] *tr* déposséder; expulser

disproof [dɪs'pruf] *s* réfutation *f*

disproportionate [,dɪsprə'porʃənɪt] *adj* disproportionné

disprove [dɪs'pruv] *tr* réfuter

dispute [dɪs'pjut] *s* dispute *f*; **beyond dispute** incontestable || *tr* disputer || *intr* se disputer

disquali·fy [dɪs'kwɑlɪ,faɪ] *v* (*pret & pp* **-fied**) *tr* disqualifier

disquiet [dɪs'kwaɪ·ət] *s* inquiétude *f* || *tr* inquiéter

disquisition [,dɪskwɪ'zɪʃən] *s* essai *m*, traité *m* considérable

disregard [,dɪsrɪ'gɑrd] *s* indifférence *f*; **disregard for** manque *m* d'égards en-vers || *tr* ne pas faire cas de, passer sous silence

disrepair [,dɪsrɪ'per] *s* délabrement *m*

disreputable [dɪs'repjətəbəl] *adj* dés-honorant, suspect; (*shabby*) débraillé, râpé

disrepute [,dɪsrɪ'pjut] *s* discrédit *m*

disrespect [,dɪsrɪ'spekt] *s* irrévérence *f*; manque *m* de respect, irrespect *m*

disrespectful [,dɪsrɪ'spektfəl] *adj* irré-vérencieux, irrespectueux; **to be dis-respectful to** manquer de respect à

disrobe [dɪs'rob] *tr* déshabiller || *intr* se déshabiller

disrupt [dɪs'rʌpt] *tr* rompre; (*to throw into disorder*) bouleverser

disruption [dɪs'rʌpʃən] *s* rupture *f*; (*disorganization*) bouleversement *m*

dissatisfaction [,dɪssætɪs'fækʃən] *s* mécontentement *m*

dissatisfied *adj* mécontent

dissatis·fy [dɪs'sætɪs,faɪ] *v* (*pret & pp* **-fied**) *tr* mécontenter

dissect [dɪ'sekt] *tr* disséquer

dissection [dɪ'sekʃən] *s* dissection *f*

dissemble [dɪ'sembəl] *tr & intr* dis-simuler

disseminate [dɪ'semɪ,net] *tr* dissémi-ner

dissension [dɪ'senʃən] *s* dissension *f*

dissent [dɪ'sent] *s* dissentiment *m*; (*nonconformity*) dissidence *f* || *intr* différer

dissenter [dɪ'sentər] *s* dissident *m*

dissertation [,dɪsər'teʃən] *s* disserta-tion *f*; (*for a degree*) thèse *f*; (*speech*) discours *m*

disservice [dɪ'sʌrvɪs] *s* mauvais service *m*, tort *m*

dissidence ['dɪsɪdəns] *s* dissidence *f*

dissident ['dɪsɪdənt] *adj & s* dissident *m*

dissimilar [dɪ'sɪmɪlər] *adj* dissemblable

dissimilate [dɪ'sɪmɪ,let] *tr* (*phonet*) dissimiler

dissimulate [dɪ'sɪmjə,let] *tr & intr* dis-simuler

dissipate ['dɪsɪ,pet] *tr* dissiper; (*en-ergy, heat, etc.*) disperser || *intr* se dissiper

dissipated *adj* dissipé; débauché

dissipation [,dɪsɪ'peʃən] *s* dissipation *f*; (*of energy, heat, etc.*) dispersion *f*

dissociate [dɪ'soʃɪ,et] *tr* dissocier || *intr* se dissocier

dissolute ['dɪsə,lut] *adj* dissolu

dissolution [,dɪsə'luʃən] *s* dissolution *f*

dissolve [dɪ'zɑlv] *tr* dissoudre || *intr* se dissoudre

dissonance ['dɪsənəns] *s* dissonance *f*

dissuade [dɪ'swed] *tr* dissuader

distaff ['dɪstæf], ['dɪstɑf] *s* quenouille *f*

dis'taff side' *s* côté *m* maternel

distance ['dɪstəns] *s* distance *f*; **at a distance** à distance; **in the distance** au loin, dans le lointain || *tr* distancer

distant ['dɪstənt] *adj* distant; (*uncle, cousin, etc.*) éloigné

distaste [dɪs'test] *s* dégoût *m*, aversion *f*

distasteful [dɪs'testfəl] *adj* dégoûtant, répugnant

distemper [dɪs'tempər] *s* (*of dog*) rou-pie *f*; (*painting*) détrempe *f* || *tr* pein-dre en détrempe

distend [dɪ'stend] *tr* distendre || *intr* se distendre

distension [dɪ'stenʃən] *s* distension *f*

distill [dɪ'stɪl] *tr* distiller

distillation [,dɪstɪ'leʃən] *s* distillation *f*

distiller·y [dɪs'tɪləri] *s* (*pl* **-ies**) distil-lerie *f*

distinct [dɪs'tɪŋkt] *adj* distinct; (*un-usual*) insigne

distinction [dɪs'tɪŋkʃən] *s* distinction *f*

distinctive [dɪs'tɪŋktɪv] *adj* distinctif

distinguish [dɪs'tɪŋgwɪʃ] *tr* distinguer; **to distinguish oneself** se distinguer, se faire remarquer

distinguished *adj* distingué

distort [dɪs'tɔrt] *tr* déformer

distortion [dɪs'tɔrʃən] *s* déformation *f*; (*of meaning*) sens *m* forcé; (phot, rad) distorsion *f*

distract [dɪ'strækt] *tr* (*to amuse*) distraire; (*to bewilder*) bouleverser

distracted *adj* bouleversé, éperdu

distraction [dɪ'strækʃən] *s* (*amusement*) distraction *f*; (*madness*) folie *f*

distraught [dɪ'strɔt] *adj* bouleversé

distress [dɪ'stres] *s* détresse *f* ‖ *tr* affliger

distress′ call′ *s* signal *m* de détresse

distressing [dɪ'stresɪŋ] *adj* affligeant, pénible

distribute [dɪ'strɪbjut] *tr* distribuer

distribution [ˌdɪstrə'bjuʃən] *s* distribution *f*

distributor [dɪ'strɪbjətər] *s* distributeur *m*; (*for a product*) concessionnaire *mf*

district [ˈdɪstrɪkt] *s* contrée *f*, région *f*; (*of a city*) quartier *m*; (*administrative division*) district *m*, circonscription *f* ‖ *tr* diviser en districts

dis′trict attor′ney *s* procureur *m* de la République, procureur général

distrust [dɪs'trʌst] *s* défiance *f*, méfiance *f* ‖ *tr* se défier de, se méfier de

distrustful [dɪs'trʌstfəl] *adj* défiant

disturb [dɪ'stʌrb] *tr* déranger, troubler; (*the peace*) perturber

disturbance [dɪ'stʌrbəns] *s* dérangement *m*, trouble *m*; (*riot*) bagarre *f*, émeute *f*; (*in the atmosphere or magnetic field*) perturbation *f*

disuse [dɪs'jus] *s* désuétude *f*

ditch [dɪtʃ] *s* fossé *m*; **to the last ditch** jusqu'à la dernière extrémité ‖ *tr* fossoyer; (slang) se défaire de ‖ *intr* (aer) faire un amerrissage forcé

ditch′ reed′ *s* (bot) laîche *m*

dither [ˈdɪðər] *s* agitation *f*; **to be in a dither** (coll) s'agiter sans but

dit·to [ˈdɪto] *s* (*pl* **-tos**) le même; (*on a duplicating machine*) copie *f*, duplicata *m* ‖ *adv* dito, de même, idem ‖ *tr* copier, reproduire

dit·ty [ˈdɪti] *s* (*pl* **-ties**) chansonnette *f*; **old ditty** (coll) vieux refrain *m*

diva [ˈdivə] *s* diva *f*

divan [ˈdarvæn], [dɪ'væn] *s* divan *m*

dive [darv] *s* plongeon *m*; (*of a submarine*) plongée *f*; (aer) piqué *m*; (coll) gargote *f*, cabaret *m* borgne ‖ *v* (*pret & pp* **dived** *or* **dove** [dov]) *intr* plonger; (*said of submarine*) plonger, effectuer une plongée; (aer) piquer; **to dive for** (*e.g., pearls*) pêcher; **to dive into** (coll) piquer une tête dans

dive′-bomb′ *tr & intr* bombarder en piqué

dive′ bomb′er *s* bombardier *m* à piqué

dive′ bomb′ing *s* bombardement *m* en piqué, piqué *m*

diver [ˈdarvər] *s* plongeur *m*; (*person who works under water*) scaphandrier *m*; (orn) plongeon *m*

diverge [dɪ'vʌrdʒ], [dar'vʌrdʒ] *intr* diverger

divers [ˈdarvərz] *adj* divers

diverse [dɪ'vʌrs], [dar'vʌrs], [ˈdarvʌrs] *adj* divers

diversi·fy [dɪ'vʌrsɪˌfar], [dar'vʌrsɪˌfar] *v* (*pret & pp* **-fied**) *tr* diversifier ‖ *intr* se diversifier

diversion [dɪ'vʌrʒən], [dar'vʌrʒən] *s* diversion *f*

diversi·ty [dɪ'vʌrsɪti], [dar'vʌrsɪti] *s* (*pl* **-ties**) diversité *f*

divert [dɪ'vʌrt], [dar'vʌrt] *tr* détourner; (*to entertain*) distraire, divertir

diverting [dɪ'vʌrtɪŋ], [dar'vʌrtɪŋ] *adj* divertissant

divest [dɪ'vest], [dar'vest] *tr* dépouiller; **to divest oneself of** se défaire de; (*property, holdings*) se déposséder de

divide [dɪ'vard] *s* (geog) ligne *f* de partage ‖ *tr* diviser ‖ *intr* se diviser

dividend [ˈdɪvɪˌdend] *s* dividende *m*

dividers [dɪ'vardərz] *spl* compas *m* de mesure

dividing [dɪ'vardɪŋ] *s* division *f*; **dividing up** répartition *f*, partage *m*

divination [ˌdɪvɪ'neʃən] *s* divination *f*

divine [dɪ'varn] *adj* divin ‖ *s* ecclésiastique *mf* ‖ *tr* deviner

diviner [dɪ'varnər] *s* devin *m*

diving [ˈdarvɪŋ] *s* plongeon *m*

div′ing bell′ *s* cloche *f* à plongeur

div′ing board′ *s* plongeoir *m*, tremplin *m*

div′ing suit′ *s* scaphandre *m*

divin′ing rod′ [dɪ'varnɪŋ] *s* baguette *f* divinatoire

divini·ty [dɪ'vɪnɪti] *s* (*pl* **-ties**) divinité *f*; (*subject of study*) théologie *f*; **the Divinity** Dieu *m*

divisible [dɪ'vɪzɪbəl] *adj* divisible

division [dɪ'vɪʒən] *s* division *f*

divisor [dɪ'varzər] *s* diviseur *m*

divorce [dɪ'vors] *s* divorce *m*; **to get a divorce** divorcer; **to get a divorce from** (*husband or wife*) divorcer d'avec ‖ *tr* (*the married couple*) divorcer; (*husband or wife*) divorcer d'avec ‖ *intr* divorcer

divorcee [dɪvor'si] *s* divorcée *f*

divulge [dɪ'vʌldʒ] *tr* divulguer

dizziness [ˈdɪzɪnɪs] *s* vertige *m*

diz·zy [ˈdɪzi] *adj* (*comp* **-zier**; *super -ziest*) vertigineux; (coll) étourdi, farfelu; **to feel dizzy** avoir le vertige; **to make dizzy** étourdir

do [du] *v* (3d *pers* **does** [dʌz]; *pret* **did** [dɪd]; *pp* **done** [dʌn]; *ger* **doing** [ˈduˑɪŋ]) *tr* faire; (*homage*) rendre; *a good turn*) rendre; **to do over** refaire; **to do up** emballer, envelopper ‖ *intr* faire; **how do you do?** enchanté de faire votre connaissance; comment allez-vous?; **that will do** c'est bien; **en voilà assez**; **that will never do** cela n'ira jamais; **to do away with** supprimer; **to do without** se passer de; **will I do?** suis-je bien comme ça?; **will it do?** ça va-t-il comme ça? ‖ *aux* used in English but not specifically expressed in French: 1) in questions, e.g., **do you speak French?** parlez-vous français?; 2) in negative sentences, e.g., **I do not speak French**

je ne parle pas français; 3) as a substitute for another verb in an elliptical question, e.g., **I saw him. Did you?** je l'ai vu. L'avez-vous vu?; 4) for emphasis, e.g., **I do believe what you told me** je crois bien ce que vous m'avez dit; 5) in inversions after certain adverbs, e.g., **hardly did we finish when** . . . à peine avions-nous fini que . . . ; 6) in an imperative entreaty, e.g., **do come in!** entrez donc!

do. *abbr* (**ditto**) d°

docile ['dɑsɪl] *adj* docile

dock [dɑk] *s* embarcadère *m*, quai *m*; *(area including piers and waterways)* bassin *m*, dock *m*; *(bot)* oseille *f*, patience *f*; *(law)* banc *m* des prévenus ‖ *tr* faire entrer au bassin; *(an animal)* couper la queue à; *(s.o.'s salary)* retrancher ‖ *intr* (naut) s'amarrer au quai

docket ['dɑkɪt] *s* (law) rôle *m*; **on the docket** pendant, non jugé; **to put on the docket** (coll) prendre en main

dock/hand/ *s* docker *m*

docking ['dɑkɪŋ] *s* (rok) arrimage *m*

dock/work/er *s* docker *m*

dock/yard/ *s* chantier *m*

doctor ['dɑktər] *s* docteur *m*; *(woman)* femme *f* docteur; *(med)* docteur, médecin *m*; *(med)* doctoresse *f*; **Doctor Curie** *(professor, Ph.D., etc.)* Monsieur Curie; Madame Curie ‖ *tr* soigner; *(e.g., a chipped vase)* réparer; *(e.g., the facts)* falsifier ‖ *intr* pratiquer la médecine; (coll) être en traitement; (coll) prendre des médicaments

doctorate ['dɑktərɪt] *s* doctorat *m*

Doc/tor of Laws/ *s* docteur *m* en droit

doctrine ['dɑktrɪn] *s* doctrine *f*

document ['dɑkjəmənt] *s* document *m* ‖ ['dɑkjə,mɛnt] *tr* documenter

documenta.ry [,dɑkjə'mɛntəri] *adj* documentaire ‖ *s* (*pl* -**ries**) documentaire *m*

documentation [,dɑkjəmən'te/ən] *s* documentation *f*

doddering ['dɑdərɪŋ] *adj* tremblotant, gâteux

dodge [dɑdʒ] *s* écart *m*, esquive *f*; (coll) ruse *f*, truc *m* ‖ *tr* esquiver; *(a question)* éluder ‖ *intr* s'esquiver

do-do ['dodo] *s* (*pl* -**dos** or -**does**) (orn) dronte *m*, dodo *m*; (coll) vieux fossile *m*, innocent *m*

doe [do] *s* *(of fallow deer)* daine *f*; *(hind)* biche *f*; *(roe doe)* chevrette *f*; *(of hare)* hase *f*; *(of rabbit)* lapine *f*

doe/skin/ *s* peau *f* de daim

doff [dɑf], [dɔf] *tr* ôter

dog [dɔg], [dɑg] *s* chien *m*; **let sleeping dogs lie** il ne faut pas réveiller le chat qui dort; **to go to the dogs** (coll) se débaucher; *(said of business)* (coll) aller à vau-l'eau; **to put on the dog** (coll) faire de l'épate ‖ *v* (*pret & pp* **dogged**; *ger* **dogging**) *tr* poursuivre

dog/catch/er *s* employé *m* de la fourrière

dog/ days/ *spl* canicule *f*

doge [dodʒ] *s* doge *m*

dog/face/ *s* (slang) troufion *m*

dog/fight/ *s* (aer) combat *m* aérien tournoyant et violent; (coll) bagarre *f*

dogged ['dɔgɪd], ['dɑgɪd] *adj* tenace, obstiné

doggerel ['dɔgərəl], ['dɑgərəl] *s* vers *mpl* de mirliton

dog-gy ['dɔgi], ['dɑgi] *adj* (*comp* -**gier**; *super* -**giest**) canin, de chien ‖ *s* (*pl* -**gies**) toutou *m*

dog/house/ *s* niche *f* à chien; **in the doghouse** (slang) en disgrâce

dog/ in the man/ger *s* chien *m* du jardinier

dog/ Lat/in *s* latin *m* de cuisine

dogma ['dɔgmə], ['dɑgmə] *s* dogme *m*

dogmatic [dɔg'mætɪk], [dɑg'mætɪk] *adj* dogmatique ‖ **dogmatics** *s* dogmatique *f*

dog/ pound/ *s* fourrière *f*

dog/ rac/ing *s* courses *fpl* de lévriers

dog/ rose/ *s* rose *f* des haies

dog's/-ear/ *s* corne *f* ‖ *tr* corner

dog/ show/ *s* exposition *f* canine

dog/ sled/ or **dog/ sledge/** *s* traîneau *m* à chiens

dog's/ life/ *s* vie *f* de chien

Dog/ Star/ *s* Canicule *f*

dog/ tag/ *s* (mil) plaque *f* d'identité

dog/-tired/ *adj* éreinté, fourbu

dog/tooth/ *s* (*pl* -**teeth**) dent *f* de chien, canine *f*; (archit, bot, mach) dent-de-chien *f*

dog/tooth vi/olet *s* dent-de-chien *f*

dog/trot/ *s* petit-trot *m*

dog/watch/ *s* (naut) petit quart *m*

dog/wood/ *s* cornouiller *m*

doi-ly ['dɔɪli] *s* (*pl* -**lies**) napperon *m*; *(underplate)* garde-nappe *m*

doings ['du.ɪŋz] *spl* actions *fpl*, œuvres *fpl*, faits et gestes *mpl*

do-it-yourself [,du.ɪt/ər'sɛlf] *adj* de bricolage ‖ *s* bricolage *m*

doldrums ['doldrəmz], ['dɑldrəmz] *spl* marasme *m*; (naut) zone *f* des calmes

dole [dol] *s* aumône *f*; indemnité *f* de chômage ‖ *tr*—**to dole out** distribuer parcimonieusement

doleful ['dolfəl] *adj* dolent

doll [dɑl] *s* poupée *f* ‖ *tr*—**to be dolled up** (coll) être tiré à quatre épingles ‖ *intr*—**to doll up** (coll) se parer, s'endimancher

dollar ['dɑlər] *s* dollar *m*

dol-ly ['dɑli] *s* (*pl* -**lies**) *(low movable frame)* chariot *m*; *(hand truck)* diable *m*; *(child's doll)* poupée *f*; *(mov, telv)* travelling *m*

dolphin ['dɑlfɪn] *s* dauphin *m*

dolt [dolt] *s* nigaud *m*, lourdaud *m*

doltish ['doltɪ/] *adj* nigaud, lourdaud

domain [do'men] *s* domaine *m*; *(private estate)* terres *fpl*, propriété *f*

dome [dom] *s* dôme *m*, coupole *f*

dome/ light/ *s* (aut) plafonnier *m*

domestic [də'mɛstɪk] *adj & s* domestique *mf*

domesticate [də'mɛstɪ,ket] *tr* domestiquer

domesticity [ˌdɔmesˈtɪsɪtɪ] s caractère m casanier; vie f familiale

domicile [ˈdɔmɪsɪl], [ˈdɔmɪˌsaɪl] s domicile m ‖ tr domicilier

dominance [ˈdɑmɪnəns] s prédominance f; (genetics) dominance f

dominant [ˈdɑmɪnənt] adj prédominant, dominant ‖ s (mus) dominante f

dominate [ˈdɑmɪˌnet] tr & intr dominer

dominating [ˈdɑmɪˌnetɪŋ] adj dominateur

domination [ˌdɑmɪˈneʃən] s domination f

domineer [ˌdɑmɪˈnɪr] intr se montrer tyrannique

domineering [ˌdɑmɪˈnɪrɪŋ] adj tyrannique, autoritaire

dominion [dəˈmɪnjən] s domination f; (of British Commonwealth) dominion m

domi•no [ˈdɑmɪˌno] s (pl -noes or -nos) domino m; **dominoes** sg (game) les dominos

don [dɑn] s (tutor) précepteur m ‖ v (pret & pp **donned**; ger **donning**) tr mettre, enfiler

donate [ˈdonet] tr faire un don de

donation [doˈneʃən] s don m, cadeau m

done [dʌn] adj fait; **are you done?** en avez-vous fini?; **it is done** (it is finished) c'en est fait; **to be done** (e.g., beefsteak) être cuit; **to have done with** en finir avec; **well done!** très bien!, bravo!, à la bonne heure!

done′ for′ adj (tired out) (coll) fourbu; (ruined) (coll) abattu; (out of the running) (coll) hors de combat; (dead) (coll) estourbi

donkey [ˈdɑŋkɪ], [ˈdʌŋkɪ] s âne m, baudet m

donor [ˈdonər] s donneur m; (law) donateur m

doodle [ˈdudəl] tr & intr griffonner

doom [dum] s condamnation f; destin m funeste ‖ tr condamner

dooms′day′ s jugement m dernier

door [dor] s porte f; (of a carriage or automobile) portière f; (one part of a double door) battant m; **behind closed doors** à huis clos; **to see to the door** conduire à la porte; **to show s.o. the door** éconduire qn, mettre qn à la porte

door′bell′ s timbre m, sonnette f

door′bell transform′er s transformateur m de sonnerie

door′bell wire′ s fil m sonnerie

door′ check′ s arrêt m de porte

door′frame′ s chambranle m, huisserie f, dormant m

door′head′ s linteau m

door′jamb′ s jambage m

door′knob′ s bouton m de porte

door′knock′er s heurtoir m, marteau m de porte

door′ latch′ s loquet m

door′man′ s (pl -men) portier m

door′mat′ s essuie-pieds m, paillasson m

door′nail′ s clou m de porte; **dead as a doornail** (coll) bien mort

door′post′ s montant m de porte

door′ scrap′er [ˈskrepər] s décrottoir m, grattepieds m

door′sill′ s seuil m, traverse f

door′step′ s seuil m, pas m

door′stop′ s entrebâilleur m, butoir m

door′-to-door′ adj porte-à-porte

door′way′ s porte f, portail m

dope [dop] s enduit m; (slang) narcotique m, stupéfiant m; (information) (slang) renseignements mpl; (fool) (slang) cornichon m ‖ tr enduire; (slang) doper, stupéfier; **to dope out** (slang) deviner, déchiffrer

dope′ fiend′ s (slang) toxicomane mf

dope′ ped′dler s trafiquant m de stupéfiants

dormant [ˈdɔrmənt] adj endormi, assoupi; latent; **to lie dormant** dormir

dor′mer win′dow [ˈdɔrmər] s lucarne f

dormi•to•ry [ˈdɔrmɪˌtori] s (pl -ries) (room) dortoir m; (building) pavillon m des étudiants, maison f de résidence

dor′mitory com′plex s cité f universitaire

dor•mouse [ˈdɔrˌmaus] s (pl -mice) loir m

dosage [ˈdosɪdʒ] s dosage m

dose [dos] s dose f ‖ tr donner en doses; donner un médicament à

dossier [ˈdɑsɪˌe] s dossier m

dot [dɑt] s point m; **on the dot** (coll) à l'heure tapante; pile, e.g., **at noon on the dot** à midi pile ‖ v (pret & pp **dotted**; ger **dotting**) tr (to make with dots) pointiller; **to dot one's i's** mettre les points sur les i

dotage [ˈdotɪdʒ] s radotage m

dotard [ˈdotərd] s gâteux m, gaga m

dote [dot] intr radoter; **to dote on** raffoler de

doting [ˈdotɪŋ] adj radoteur; (loving to excess) qui aime follement

dots′ and dash′es spl (telg) points et traits mpl

dot′ted line′ s ligne f pointillée, ligne hachée; **to sign on the dotted line** signer aveuglément

double [ˈdʌbəl] adj & adv double, en deux, deux fois ‖ s double m; (cards) contre m; (stunt man) (mov) cascadeur m; **doubles** (tennis) double; **on the double!** (coll) dare-dare!, au trot! ‖ tr doubler; (cards) contrer; **to double up** plier en deux ‖ intr doubler; (cards) contrer; **to double back** faire un crochet; **to double up** se plier, se tordre

dou′ble-act′ing adj à double effet

dou′ble-bar′reled adj (gun) à deux coups

dou′ble bass′ [bes] s contrebasse f

dou′ble bed′ s grand lit m, lit à deux places

dou′ble boil′er s bain-marie m

dou′ble-breast′ed adj croisé

dou′ble chin′ s double menton m

dou′ble cross′ s (slang) entourloupette f, double jeu m

dou′ble-cross′ tr (coll) doubler, rouler, faire une entourloupette à

dou'ble-cross'er *s* (slang) personne *f* double, faux jeton *m*

dou'ble date' *s* partie *f* carrée, sortie *f* à quatre

dou'ble-deal'er *s* personne *f* double, homme *m* à deux visages

dou'ble-deal'ing *adj* hypocrite ‖ *s* duplicité *f*

dou'ble-deck'er *s* (bed) lits *mpl* superposés, lits gigognes, lit à deux étages; (bus) autobus *m* à deux étages; (sandwich) double sandwich *m*; (aer, naut) deux-ponts *m*

dou'ble-edged' *adj* à deux tranchants, à double tranchant

double entendre ['dubələn'tandrə] *s* expression *f* à double entente, mot *m* à double sens

dou'ble-en'try *adj* en partie double

dou'ble-faced' *adj* à double face

dou'ble fea'ture *s* (mov) deux grands films *mpl*, double programme *m*

dou'ble-joint'ed *adj* désarticulé

dou'ble-lock' *tr* fermer à double tour

dou'ble-park' *tr* faire stationner en double file ‖ *intr* stationner en double file

dou'ble room' *s* chambre *f* à deux lits

dou'ble-spaced' *adj* à l'interligne

dou'ble stand'ard *s* code *m* de morale à deux aspects; **to have a double standard** avoir deux poids et deux mesures

doublet ['dʌblɪt] *s* (close-fitting jacket) pourpoint *m*; (counterfeit stone; each of two words having the same origin) doublet *m*

dou'ble-talk' *s* (coll) non-sens *m*; (coll) paroles *fpl* creuses or ambiguës, mots *mpl* couverts

dou'ble time' *s* (for work) salaire *m* double; (mil) pas *m* redoublé

doubleton ['dʌbəltən] *s* deux cartes *fpl* d'une couleur

dou'ble track' *s* double piste *f*

doubling ['dʌblɪŋ] *s* doublement *m*

doubly ['dʌbli] *adv* doublement

doubt [daut] *s* doute *m*; **beyond a doubt** à n'en pas douter; **no doubt** sans doute ‖ *tr* douter de; **to doubt that** douter que; **to doubt whether** douter si ‖ *intr* douter

doubter ['dautər] *s* douteur *m*

doubtful ['dautfəl] *adj* douteux; indécis, hésitant

doubtless ['dautlɪs] *adv* sans doute

douche [duʃ] *s* douche *f*; (instrument) seringue *f* à lavement ‖ *tr* doucher ‖ *intr* se doucher

dough [do] *s* pâte *f*; (slang) fric *m*; **big dough** (slang) grosse galette *f*

dough'boy' *s* (coll) troufion *m*, biffin *m*; (in the first World War) poilu *m*

dough'nut' *s* beignet *m*

dough•ty ['dauti] *adj* (comp -tier; super -tiest) vaillant, preux

dough•y ['do·i] *adj* (comp -ier; super -iest) pâteux

dour [daur], [dur] *adj* (severe) austère; (obstinate) buté; (gloomy) mélancolique

douse [daus] *tr* tremper, arroser; (slang) éteindre

dove [dʌv] *s* colombe *f*

dovecote ['dʌv‚kot] *s* pigeonnier *m*, colombier *m*

Dover ['dovər] *s* Douvres

dove'tail' *s* queue-d'aronde *f*, adent *m* ‖ *tr* assembler à queue-d'aronde, adenter; (fig) raccorder, opérer le raccord entre ‖ *intr* se raccorder

dove'tailed' *adj* à queue-d'aronde

dowager ['dau·ədʒər] *s* douairière *f*

dow•dy ['daudi] *adj* (comp -dier; super -diest) gauche, fagoté, mal habillé

dow•el ['dau·əl] *s* goujon *m* ‖ *v* (pret & pp -eled or -elled; ger -eling or -elling) *tr* goujonner

dower ['dau·ər] *s* (widow's portion) douaire *m*; (marriage portion) dot *f*; (natural gift) don *m* ‖ *tr* assigner un douaire à; doter

down [daun] *adj* bas; (train) descendant; (storage battery) épuisé; (tire) à plat; (sun) couché; (wind, sea, etc.) calmé; (blinds; prices) baissé; (stocks) en moins-value; (sad) abattu, triste ‖ *s* duvet *m*; (sand hill) dune *f* ‖ *adv* en bas, au bas, vers les bas; à terre; (south) au sud; **down!** (in elevator) on descend!, pour la descente!; **down from** du haut de; **down there** là-bas; **down to** jusqu'à; **down under** aux antipodes; **down with . . . !** à bas . . . !; for expressions like **to go down** descendre or **to pay down** payer comptant, see the verb ‖ *prep* en bas de; (along) le long de; (a stream) en descendant ‖ *tr* descendre, abattre; (to swallow) (coll) avaler

down'-and-out' *adj* décavé

down'beat' *s* (mus) temps *m* fort, frappé *m*, premier accent *m*

down'cast' *adj* abattu, baissé

down'fall' *s* chute *f*, ruine *f*

down'grade' *adj* (coll) descendant ‖ *s* descente *f*; **to be on the downgrade** déchoir ‖ *adv* en déclin ‖ *tr* déclasser

down'heart'ed *adj* abattu, découragé

down'hill' *adj* descendant ‖ *adv*—**to go downhill** aller en descendant; (fig) décliner

down' pay'ment *s* acompte *m*

down'pour' *s* déluge *m*, averse *f*

down'right' *adj* absolu, véritable ‖ *adv* tout à fait, absolument

down'stairs' *s* rez-de-chaussée *m* ‖ *adv* en bas; **to go downstairs** descendre

down'stream' *adv* en aval

down'stroke' *s* (of piston) course *f* descendante; (in writing) jambage *m*

down'town' *adj* du centre ‖ *s* centre *m* ‖ *adv* en ville

down'trend' *s* tendance *f* à la baisse

downtrodden ['daun‚tradən] *adj* opprimé

downward ['daunwərd] *adj* descendant ‖ *adv* en bas, en descendant

downwards ['daunwərdz] *adv* en bas, en descendant

down'wash' *s* (aer) air *m* déplacé

down•y ['dauni] *adj* (comp -ier; super

-iest) duveteux; (velvety) velouté; (soft) mou, moelleux

dow·ry ['dauri] s (pl -ries) dot f

dowser ['dauzər] s sourcier m, hydroscope m

doze [doz] s petit somme m || intr sommeiller; **to doze off** s'assoupir

dozen ['dʌzən] s douzaine f; **a dozen . . .** une douzaine de . . . ; **by the dozen** à la douzaine

D.P. abbr (**displaced person**) personne f déplacée

Dr. abbr (**Doctor**) Dr

drab [dræb] adj (comp **drabber**; super **drabbest**) gris || s gris m

drach·ma ['drækmə] s (pl -mas or -mae [mi]) drachme f

draft [dræft], [draft] s courant m d'air; (pulling; current of air in chimney) tirage m; (sketch, outline) ébauche f; (of a letter, novel, etc.) brouillon m, premier jet m; (of a bill in Congress) projet m; (of a law) avant-projet m; (drink) trait m, gorgée f; (com) mandat m, traite f; (mil) conscription f; (naut) tirant m d'eau; **drafts** (game) dames fpl; **on draft** à la pression; **to be exempted from the draft** être exempté du service militaire || tr (a document) rédiger, faire le brouillon de; (a bill in Congress) dresser; (a recruit) appeler sous les drapeaux; **to be drafted** être appelé sous les drapeaux

draft′ beer′ s bière f pression

draft′ board′ s conseil m de révision; commission f locale des conscriptions

draft′ call′ s appel m sous les drapeaux

draft′ dodg′er ['dadʒər] s embusqué m

draftee [,dræf'ti], [,draf'ti] s appelé m (sous les drapeaux), conscrit m

draft′ horse′ s cheval m de trait

drafting ['dræftiŋ], ['draftiŋ] s dessin m industriel

draft′ing room′ s bureau m d'études

drafts′man s (pl -men) dessinateur m; (man who draws up documents) rédacteur m

draft·y ['dræfti], ['drafti] adj (comp -ier; super -iest) plein de courants d'air

drag [dræg] s (net) drège f; (sledge or sled) traîneau m; (stone drag) fardier m; (brake) enrayure f; (impediment) entrave f; (aer) résistance f à l'avancement || v (pret & pp **dragged**); ger **dragging**) tr (anything); (one's feet) traînasser; (a net) draguer; (a field) herser; **to drag down** entraîner; **to drag in** introduire de force; **to drag out** faire sortir de force || intr traîner à terre; se traîner

drag′net′ s traîneau m, chalut m

dragon ['drægən] s dragon m

drag′on-fly′ s (pl -flies) demoiselle f, libellule f

dragoon [drə'gun] s dragon m || tr tyranniser; forcer, contraindre

drain [dren] s (sewer) égout m; (pipe) tuyau m d'égout; (ditch) tranchée f d'écoulement; (source of continual expense) saignée f; (med) drain m ||

tr (wet ground) drainer; (a glass or cup) vider entièrement; (a crankcase) vidanger; (s.o. of strength) épuiser; (med) drainer || intr s'égoutter, s'écouler

drainage ['drenidʒ] s drainage m

drain′board′ s égouttoir m

drain′ cock′ s purgeur m

drain′pipe′ s tuyau m d'écoulement, drain m

drain′ plug′ s bouchon m de vidange

drake [drek] s canard m mâle

dram [dræm] s (weight) drachme m; (drink) petit verre m, goutte f

drama ['dramə], ['dræmə] s drame m

dra′ma crit′ic s chroniqueur m dramatique

dra′ma review′ s avant-première f

dramatic [drə'mætik] adj dramatique || **dramatics** s dramaturgie f, art m dramatique

dramatist ['dræmətist] s auteur m dramatique, dramaturge mf

dramatize ['dræmə,taiz] tr dramatiser

drape [drep] s rideau m; (hang of a curtain, skirt, etc.) drapement m || tr draper, tendre; se draper dans

draper·y ['drepəri] s (pl -ies) draperie f; **draperies** rideaux mpl, tentures fpl

drastic ['dræstik] adj énergique, radical; (laxative) drastique

draught [dræft], [draft] s (of fish) coup m de filet; (drink) trait m, gorgée f; (naut) tirant m d'eau; **draughts** (game) dames fpl; **on draught** à la pression

draught′ beer′ s bière f pression

draught′board′ s damier m

draw [drɔ] s tirage m; (in a game or other contest) partie f nulle, match m nul || v (pret **drew** [dru]; pp **drawn** [drɔn]) tr tirer; (a crowd) attirer; (a design) dessiner; (a card) tirer; (trumps) faire tomber; (a bow) bander, tendre; (water) puiser; **to draw a conclusion** tirer une conséquence; **to draw aside** prendre à l'écart; **to draw blood** faire saigner; **to draw interest** porter intérêt; **to draw lots** tirer au sort; **to draw off** (e.g., a liquid) soutirer; **to draw out** (a person) faire parler; (an activity) prolonger, traîner; **to draw up** (a list) dresser; (a plan) rédiger; (naut) jauger || intr tirer; dessiner; faire partie nulle, faire match nul; **to draw away** s'éloigner; **to draw back** reculer, se retirer; **to draw near** approcher; s'approcher de

draw′back′ s désavantage m, inconvénient m

draw′bridge′ s pont-levis m

drawee [,drɔ'i] s tiré m, accepteur m

drawer ['drɔ·ər] s dessinateur m; (com) tireur m || [drɔr] s tiroir m; **drawers** caleçon m

drawing ['drɔ·iŋ] s dessin m; (in a lottery) tirage m

draw′ing board′ s planche f à dessin

draw′ing card′ s attrait m, attraction f

draw′ing room′ s salon m

draw′knife′ s (pl -knives) plane f

drawl [drɔl] s voix f traînante ‖ tr dire d'une voix traînante ‖ intr traîner la voix en parlant

drawn/ but/ter [drɔn] s beurre m fondu; sauce f blanche

drawn/ work/ s broderie f à fils tirés

dray [dre] s haquet m, charrette f; (sledge) fardier m, schlitte f

drayage ['dre-ɪdʒ] s charriage m, charroi m; frais mpl de transport

dray/ horse/ s cheval m de trait

dray/man s (pl -men) haquetier m

dread [drɛd] adj redoutable, terrible ‖ s terreur f, crainte f ‖ tr & intr redouter, craindre

dreadful ['drɛdfəl] adj épouvantable

dream [drim] s rêve m, songe m; (fancy, illusion) rêverie f, songerie f ‖ v (pret & pp **dreamed** or **dreamt** [drɛmt]) tr—to dream up rêver ‖ intr rêver, songer; **to dream of** (future plans) rêver à; (s.o.) rêver de

dreamer ['drimər] s rêveur m

dream/land/ s pays m des songes

dream/ world/ s monde m des rêves

dream·y ['drimi] adj (comp -ier; super -iest) rêveur; (slang) épatant

drear·y ['drɪri] adj (comp -ier; super -iest) triste, morne; monotone

dredge [drɛdʒ] s drague f ‖ tr draguer

dredger ['drɛdʒər] s dragueur m; (mach) drague f

dredging ['drɛdʒɪŋ] s dragage m

dregs [drɛgz] spl lie f

drench [drɛntʃ] tr tremper, inonder

dress [drɛs] s habillement m, costume m; (woman's attire) toilette f, mise f; (woman's dress) robe f ‖ tr habiller, vêtir; (to apply a dressing to) panser; (culin) garnir; **to dress down** (coll) passer un savon à, chapitrer; **to dress up** parer; (ranks) (mil) aligner; **to get dressed** s'habiller ‖ intr s'habiller, se vêtir; (mil) s'aligner; **to dress up** se parer

dress/ ball/ s bal m paré

dress/ cir/cle s corbeille f, premier balcon m

dress/ coat/ s frac m

dresser ['drɛsər] s coiffeuse f; commode f à miroir; (sideboard) dressoir m; **to be a good dresser** être recherché dans sa mise

dress/ form/ s mannequin m

dress/ goods/ spl étoffes fpl pour costumes

dressing ['drɛsɪŋ] s toilette f; (for food) assaisonnement m, sauce f; (stuffing for fowl) farce f; (fertilizer) engrais m; (for a wound) pansement m

dress/ing down/ s (coll) savon m, verte réprimande f, algarade f

dress/ing gown/ s peignoir m, robe f de chambre

dress/ing room/ s cabinet m de toilette; (theat) loge f

dress/ing sta/tion s poste m de secours

dress/ing ta/ble s coiffeuse f, toilette f

dress/mak/er s couturière f

dress/mak/ing s couture f

dress/making estab/lishment s maison f de couture

dress/ rehear/sal s répétition f en costume; **final dress rehearsal** répétition générale

dress/ shield/ s dessous-de-bras m

dress/ shirt/ s chemise f à plastron

dress/ shop/ s magasin m de modes

dress/ suit/ s habit m de cérémonie, tenue f de soirée

dress/ tie/ s cravate f de smoking, cravate-plastron f

dress/ u/niform s (mil) grande tenue f

dress·y ['drɛsi] adj (comp -ier; super -iest) (coll) élégant, chic

dribble ['drɪbəl] s dégouttement m; (of child) bave f; (sports) dribble m ‖ tr (sports) dribbler ‖ intr dégoutter; (said of child) baver; (sports) dribbler

driblet ['drɪblɪt] s chiquet m; **in driblets** au compte-gouttes

dried/ ap/ple [draɪd] s pomme f tapée

dried/ beef/ s viande f boucanée

dried/ fig/ s figue f sèche

dried/ fruit/ s fruit m sec

dried/ pear/ s poire f tapée

drier ['draɪər] s (for clothes) séchoir m, sécheuse f; (for paint) siccatif m; (mach) sécheur m

drift [drɪft] s dérive f; (of sand, snow) amoncellement m; (of meaning) sens m, direction f ‖ intr aller à la dérive; (said of snow) s'amonceler; (aer, naut) dériver; (fig) se laisser aller, flotter

drift/ ice/ s glaces fpl flottantes

drift/wood/ s bois m flotté

drill [drɪl] s foret m; (machine) perforatrice f; (fabric) coutil m, treillis m; (furrow) sillon m; (agricultural implement) semoir m; (in school; on the drill ground) exercice m ‖ tr instruire; (e.g., students) former, entraîner; (mach) forer; (mil) faire faire l'exercice à; **to drill s.th. into s.o.** seriner q.ch. à qn ‖ intr faire l'exercice; forer

driller ['drɪlər] s foreur m

drill/ field/ or **drill/ ground/** s terrain m d'exercice

drill/mas/ter s moniteur m; (mil) instructeur m

drill/ press/ s foreuse f à colonnes

drink [drɪŋk] s boisson f, breuvage m; boire m, e.g., **food and drink** le boire et le manger ‖ v (pret **drank** [dræŋk]; pp **drunk** [drʌŋk]) tr boire; (e.g., with a meal) prendre; **to drink down** boire d'un trait ‖ intr boire; **to drink out of** (a glass) boire dans; (a bottle) boire à; **to drink to the health of** boire à la santé de

drinkable ['drɪŋkəbəl] adj buvable, potable

drinker ['drɪŋkər] s buveur m

drink/ing cup/ s tasse f à boire, gobelet m

drink/ing foun/tain s fontaine f à boire, borne-fontaine f

drink/ing song/ s chanson f à boire

drink/ing trough/ s abreuvoir m

drink'ing wa'ter s eau f potable

drip [drɪp] s (drop) goutte f; (dripping) égout m, dégouttement m; (person) (slang) cornichon m || v (pret & pp dripped; ger dripping) intr dégoutter, goutter

drip' cof'fee s café-filtre m

drip' cof'fee mak'er s cafetière f à filtre

drip'-dry' adj à séchage rapide; (label on shirt) repassage inutile

dripolator ['drɪpə‚letər] s filtre m à café

drip' pan' s égouttoir m

dripping ['drɪpɪŋ] s ruissellement m; **drippings** graisse f de rôti

drive [draɪv] s (in an automobile) promenade f; (road) chaussée f; (vigor) énergie f, initiative f; (fund-raising) campagne f; (push forward) propulsion f; (aut) (point of power application to roadway) traction f; (golf) crossée f; (mach) transmission f; **to go for a drive** faire une promenade en auto || v (pret drove [drov]; pp driven ['drɪvən]) tr (an automobile, locomotive, etc.; an animal; a person in an automobile) conduire; (a nail) enfoncer; (a bargain) conclure; (the ball in a game) renvoyer, chasser; (to push, force) pousser, forcer; (to overwork) surmener; **to drive away** chasser; **to drive back** repousser; (e.g., in a car) reconduire; **to drive crazy** rendre fou; **to drive in** enfoncer; **to drive out** chasser; **to drive to despair** conduire au désespoir || intr conduire; **drive slowly** (public sign) marcher au pas; **to drive away** partir, démarrer; **to drive back** rentrer en auto; **to drive on** continuer sa route; **to drive out** sortir

drive'-in' s (motion-picture theater) cinéma m auto; (restaurant) restoroute m

driv·el ['drɪvəl] s (slobber) bave f; (nonsense) bêtises fpl || v (pret -eled or -elled; ger -eling or -elling) intr baver; (to talk nonsense) radoter

driver ['draɪvər] s chauffeur m, conducteur m; (of a carriage) cocher m; (of a locomotive) mécanicien m; (of pack animals) toucheur m

driv'er's li'cense s permis m de conduire

drive' shaft' s arbre m d'entraînement

drive'way' s voie f de garage, sortie f de voiture

drive' wheel' s roue f motrice, roue de transmission

driv'ing school' s auto-école f

drizzle ['drɪzəl] s pluie f fine, bruine f || intr bruiner, brouillasser

droll [drol] adj drôle, drolatique

dromedar·y ['drɑmə‚deri] s (pl -ies) dromadaire m

drone [dron] s bourdonnement m; (of plane or engine) vrombissement m, ronron m; fainéant m; (aer) avion m téléguidé, avion sans pilote; (ent) faux bourdon m || intr bourdonner, ronronner

drool [drul] intr baver

droop [drup] s inclinaison f || intr se baisser; (to lose one's pep) s'alanguir; (bot) languir

drooping ['drupɪŋ] adj languissant

drop [drɑp] s goutte f; (fall) chute f; (slope) précipice m; (depth of drop) hauteur f de chute; (in price; in temperature) baisse f; (lozenge) pastille f; (of supplies from an airplane) droppage m; **a drop in the bucket** une goutte d'eau dans la mer || v (pret & pp dropped; ger dropping) tr laisser tomber; (a curtain; the eyes, voice) baisser; (from an airplane) lâcher; (e.g., a name from a list) omettre, supprimer; (a remark) glisser; (a conversation; relations; negotiations) cesser; (anchor) jeter, mouiller; (an idea, a habit, etc.) renoncer à; **to drop off** déposer || intr tomber; se laisser tomber; baisser; cesser; **to drop in** entrer en passant; **to drop in on** faire une visite au chez; to **drop off** se détacher; s'endormir; **to drop out of** (to quit) renoncer à, abandonner

drop' cur'tain s rideau m d'entracte

drop' ham'mer s marteau-pilon m

drop' kick' s coup m tombé

drop' leaf' s abattant m

drop'light' s lampe f suspendue

drop'out' s raté m; **to become a drop-out** abandonner les études

dropper ['drɑpər] s compte-gouttes m

dropsy ['drɑpsi] s hydropisie f

drop' ta'ble s table f à abattants

dross [drɔs], [drɑs] s scories mpl, écume f

drought [draut] s sécheresse f

drove [drov] s troupeau m; (multitude) foule f, flots mpl; **in droves** par bandes

drover ['drovər] s bouvier m

drown [draun] tr noyer; **to drown out** couvrir || intr se noyer

drowse [drauz] intr somnoler, s'assoupir

drow·sy ['drauzi] adj (comp -sier; super -siest) somnolent

drub [drʌb] v (pret & pp drubbed; ger drubbing) tr flanquer une raclée à, rosser

drudge [drʌdʒ] s homme m de peine, piocheur m; **harmless drudge** (e.g., who compiles dictionaries) gratte-papier m inoffensif

drudger·y ['drʌdʒəri] s (pl -ies) corvée f, travail m pénible

drug [drʌg] s drogue f, stupéfiant m, produit m pharmaceutique; **drug on the market** rossignol m || v (pret & pp drugged; ger drugging) tr (a person) donner un stupéfiant à, stupéfier; (food or drink) ajouter un stupéfiant à

drug' ad'dict s toxicomane mf

drug' addic'tion s toxicomanie f

druggist ['drʌgɪst] s pharmacien m

drug' hab'it s toxicomanie f, vice m des stupéfiants

drug'store' s pharmacie-bazar f, pharmacie f

drug' traf'fic s trafic m des stupéfiants

druid ['dru·ɪd] s druide m

drum [drʌm] s (cylinder; instrument of percussion) tambour m; (container for oil, gasoline, etc.) bidon m; to play the drum battre du tambour || v (pret & pp drummed; ger drumming) tr (e.g., a march) tambouriner; rassembler au son du tambour; to drum into fourrer dans; to drum up customers racoler des clients || intr jouer du tambour; (with the fingers) tambouriner; (on the piano) pianoter

drum' and bu'gle corps' s clairons et tambours mpl, clique f

drum' beat' s coup m de tambour

drum'fire' s (mil) tir m nourri, feu m roulant

drum'head' s peau f de tambour; (naut) noix f

drum' ma'jor s tambour-major m

drummer ['drʌmər] s tambour m; (salesman) (coll) commis m voyageur

drum'stick' s baguette f de tambour; (of chicken) (coll) cuisse f, pilon m

drunk [drʌŋk] adj ivre, soûl; to get drunk s'enivrer; to get s.o. drunk enivrer qn || s (person) (coll) ivrogne m; (state) ivresse f; to go on a drunk se soûler

drunkard ['drʌŋkərd] s ivrogne m

drunken ['drʌŋkən] adj enivré

drunk'en driv'ing s conduite f en état d'ivresse

drunkenness ['drʌŋkənnɪs] s ivresse f

dry [draɪ] adj (comp drier; super driest) sec; (thirsty) assoiffé; (boring) aride || s (pl drys) (prohibitionist) antialcoolique mf || v (pret & pp dried) tr sécher; (the dishes) essuyer || intr sécher; to dry up se dessécher; (slang) se taire

dry' bat'tery s pile f sèche; (number of dry cells) batterie f de piles

dry' cell' s pile f sèche

dry'-clean' tr nettoyer à sec

dry' clean'er s nettoyeur m à sec, teinturier m

dry' clean'er's s teinturerie f

dry' clean'ing s nettoyage m à sec

dry' dock' s cale f sèche, bassin m de radoub

dry'-eyed' adj d'un œil sec

dry' goods' spl tissus mpl, étoffes fpl

dry' ice' s glace f sèche

dry' land' s terre f ferme

dry' meas'ure s mesure f à grains

dryness ['draɪnɪs] s sécheresse f; (e.g., of a speaker) aridité f

dry' nurse' s nourrice f sèche

dry' rot' s carie f sèche

dry' run' s exercice m simulé, répétition f, examen m blanc

dry' sea'son s saison f sèche

dry' wash' s blanchissage m sans repassage

dual ['d(j)u·əl] adj double || s duel m

dub [dʌb] s (slang) balourd m || v (pret & pp dubbed; ger dubbing) tr (to nickname) donner un sobriquet à; (to

knight) donner l'accolade à, adouber; (a tape recording or movie film) doubler

dubbing ['dʌbɪŋ] s (mov) doublage m

dubious ['d(j)ubɪ·əs] adj (undecided) hésitant; (questionable) douteux

ducat ['dʌkət] s ducat m

duchess ['dʌtʃɪs] s duchesse f

duch·y ['dʌtʃi] s (pl -ies) duché m

duck [dʌk] s canard m; (female) cane f; (motion) esquive f; ducks (trousers) pantalon m de coutil || tr (the head) baisser || intr se baisser; to duck out (coll) s'esquiver

ducking ['dʌkɪŋ] s plongeon m, bain m forcé

duckling ['dʌklɪŋ] s caneton m; (female) canette f

ducks' and drakes' s—to play at ducks and drakes faire des ricochets sur l'eau; (fig) jeter son argent par les fenêtres

duck'-toed' adj qui marche en canard

duct [dʌkt] s conduit m, canal m

duct'less glands' ['dʌktlɪs] spl glandes fpl closes

duct'work' s tuyauterie f, canalisation f

dud [dʌd] s (slang) obus m qui a raté; (slang) raté m, navet m; duds (clothes) (coll) frusques fpl, nippes fpl

dude [d(j)ud] s poseur m, gommeux m

dude' ranch' s ranch m d'opérette

due [d(j)u] adj dû; (note) échéant; (bill) exigible; (train, bus, person) attendu; due to par suite de; in due form en bonne forme, en règle; to fall due venir à l'échéance; when is the train due? à quelle heure doit arriver le train? || s dû m; dues cotisation f; to pay one's dues cotiser || adv droit vers, e.g., due north droit vers le nord

due' date' s échéance f

duel ['d(j)u·əl] s duel m; to fight a duel se battre en duel || v (pret & pp dueled or duelled; ger dueling or duelling) intr se battre en duel

duelist or **duellist** ['d(j)u·əlɪst] s dueliste m

duenna [d(j)u'ɛnə] s duègne f

dues'-pay'ing adj cotisant

duet [d(j)u'ɛt] s duo m

duke [d(j)uk] s duc m

dukedom ['d(j)ukdəm] s duché m

dull [dʌl] adj (not sharp) émoussé; (color) terne; (sound; pain) sourd; (stupid) lourd; (business) lent; (boring) ennuyeux; (flat) fade, insipide; to become dull s'émousser; (said of senses) s'engourdir || tr (a knife) émousser; (color) ternir; (sound; pain) amortir; (spirits) hébéter, engourdir || intr s'émousser; se ternir; s'amortir; s'engourdir

dullard ['dʌlərd] s lourdaud m, hébété m

dullness ['dʌlnɪs] s (of knife) émoussement m; (e.g., of wits) lenteur f

duly ['d(j)uli] adv dûment, justement

dumb [dʌm] adj (lacking the power to speak) muet; (coll) gourde, imbécile;

completely dumb (coll) bouché à l'émeri; **to play dumb** (coll) feindre l'innocence

dumb′bell′ s (sports) haltère m; (slang) gourde f, imbécile mf

dumb′ crea′ture s animal m, brute f

dumb′wait′er s monte-plats m; (serving table) table f roulante

dumfound ['dʌm‚faʊnd] tr abasourdir, ébahir

dum·my ['dʌmi] adj faux, factice ǁ s (pl -mies) (dress form) mannequin; (in card games) mort m; (figurehead, straw man) prête-nom m, homme m de paille; (skeleton copy of a book or magazine) maquette f; (object put in place of the real thing) simulacre m; (slang) bêta m, ballot m

dump [dʌmp] s (pile of rubbish) amas m, tas m; (place) dépotoir m; (mil) dépôt m; (slang) taudis m; **to be down in the dumps** (coll) avoir le cafard ǁ tr décharger, déverser; (on rubbish pile) jeter au rebut; (com) vendre en faisant du dumping

dumping ['dʌmpɪŋ] s (com) dumping m

dumpling ['dʌmplɪŋ] s dumpling m, boulette f

dump′ truck′ s tombereau m

dump·y ['dʌmpi] adj (comp -ier; super -iest) (short and fat) courtaud, trapu; (shabby) râpé, minable

dun [dʌn] adj isabelle ǁ s créancier m importun; (demand for payment) demande f pressante ǁ v (pret & pp dunned; ger dunning) tr (for payment) importuner, poursuivre

dunce [dʌns] s âne m, cancre m

dunce′ cap′ s bonnet m d'âne

dune [d(j)un] s dune f

dung [dʌŋ] s fumier m

dungarees [‚dʌŋgə'riz] spl pantalon m de treillis, treillis m, bleu m

dungeon ['dʌndʒən] s cachot m, cul-de-basse-fosse m; (keep of castle) donjon m

dung′hill′ s tas m de fumier

dunk [dʌŋk] tr & intr tremper

du·o ['d(j)u·o] s (pl -os) duo m

duode·num [‚d(j)u·ə'dinəm] s (pl -na [nə]) duodénum m

dupe [d(j)up] s dupe f, dindon m de la farce ǁ tr duper

duplex ['d(j)upleks] adj double, duplex ǁ s maison f double

du′plex house′ s maison f double

duplicate ['d(j)uplɪkɪt] adj double ǁ s duplicata m, polycopie f; **in duplicate** en double, en duplicata ǁ ['d(j)uplɪ‚ket] tr faire le double de, reproduire; (on a machine) polycopier, ronéocopier

du′plicating machine′ s duplicateur m

duplici·ty [d(j)u'plɪsɪti] s (pl -ties) duplicité f

durable ['d(j)urəbəl] adj durable

duration [d(j)u'reʃən] s durée f

duress ['d(j)ures], [d(j)u'res] s contrainte f; emprisonnement m

during ['d(j)urɪŋ] prep pendant

dusk [dʌsk] s crépuscule m; **at dusk** entre chien et loup

dust [dʌst] s poussière f ǁ tr (to free of dust) épousseter; (to sprinkle with dust) saupoudrer; **to dust off** épousseter

dust′ bowl′ s région f dénudée

dust′cloth′ s chiffon m à épousseter

dust′ cloud′ s nuage m de poussière

duster ['dʌstər] s (made of feathers) plumeau m; (made of cloth) chiffon m; (overgarment) cache-poussière m

dust′ jack′et s protège-livre m, couvre-livre m, liseuse f

dust′pan′ s pelle f à ordures

dust′ rag′ s chiffon m à épousseter

dust·y ['dʌsti] adj (comp -ier; super -iest) poussiéreux; (color) cendré

Dutch [dʌtʃ] adj hollandais, néerlandais; (slang) allemand ǁ s (language) hollandais m, néerlandais m; (slang) allemand m; **in Dutch** (slang) en disgrâce; **the Dutch** les Hollandais mpl, les Néerlandais mpl; (slang) les Allemands mpl; **we will go Dutch** (coll) chacun paiera son écot

Dutch′man s (pl -men) Hollandais m, Néerlandais m; (slang) Allemand m

Dutch′ treat′ s—**to have a Dutch treat** (coll) faire suisse, payer son écot

dutiable ['d(j)utɪ·əbəl] adj soumis aux droits de douane

dutiful ['d(j)utɪfəl] adj respectueux, soumis, plein d'égards

du·ty ['d(j)uti] s (pl -ties) devoir m; duties fonctions fpl; (taxes, customs) droits mpl; **to be off duty** ne pas être de service, avoir quartier libre; **to be on duty** être de service, être de garde

du′ty-free′ adj exempt de droits

dwarf [dwɔrf] adj & s nain m ǁ tr & intr rapetisser

dwell [dwel] v (pret & pp dwelled or dwelt [dwelt]) intr demeurer; **to dwell on** appuyer sur

dwelling ['dwelɪŋ] s demeure f, habitation f

dwell′ing house′ s maison f d'habitation

dwindle ['dwɪndəl] intr diminuer; **to dwindle away** s'affaiblir

dye [daɪ] s teinture f ǁ v (pret & pp dyed; ger dyeing) tr teindre

dyed′-in-the-wool′ adj intransigeant

dyeing ['daɪ·ɪŋ] s teinture f

dyer ['daɪ·ər] s teinturier m

dying ['daɪ·ɪŋ] adj mourant, moribond

dynamic [daɪ'næmɪk], [dɪ'næmɪk] adj dynamique ǁ **dynamics** s dynamique f

dynamite ['daɪnə‚maɪt] s dynamite f ǁ tr dynamiter

dyna·mo ['daɪnə‚mo] s (pl -mos) dynamo f

dynast ['daɪnæst] s dynaste m

dynas·ty ['daɪnəsti] s (pl -ties) dynastie f

dysentery ['dɪsən‚teri] s dysenterie f

dyspepsia [dɪs'pepsɪ·ə], [dɪs'pep/ə] s dyspepsie f

E

E, e [i] *s* Ve lettre de l'alphabet

each [it/] *adj indef* chaque || *pron indef* chacun; **each other** nous, se; l'un l'autre; **to each other** l'un à l'autre || *adv* chacun; (*apiece*) pièce, la pièce

eager ['igər] *adj* ardent, empressé; **eager for** avide de; **to be eager to** brûler de, désirer ardemment

ea'ger bea'ver *s* bûcheur *m*, mouche *f* du coche

eagerness ['igərnıs] *s* ardeur *f*, empressement *m*

eagle ['igəl] *s* aigle *m*

ea'gle-eyed' *adj* à l'œil d'aigle

ea'gle ray' *s* (ichth) aigle *m* de mer

eaglet ['iglıt] *s* aiglon *m*

ear [ır] *s* oreille *f*; (*of corn or wheat*) épi *m*; **to box s.o.'s ears** frotter les oreilles à qn; **to prick up one's ears** dresser l'oreille; **to turn a deaf ear** faire la sourde oreille || *intr* (*said of grain*) épier

ear'ache' *s* douleur *m* d'oreille

ear'drop' *s* pendant *m* d'oreille

ear'drum' *s* tympan *m*

ear'flap' *s* lobe *m* de l'oreille; (*on a cap*) protège-oreilles *m*

earl [ʌrl] *s* comte *m*

earldom ['ʌrldəm] *s* comté *m*

ear-ly ['ʌrli] (*comp* -lier; *super* -liest) *adj* primitif; (*first in a series*) premier; (*occurring in the near future*) prochain; (*in the morning*) matinal; (*ahead of time*) en avance; **at an early age** dès l'enfance || *adv* de bonne heure, tôt; anciennement; **as early as** dès

ear'ly bird' *s* matinal *m*

ear'ly mass' *s* première messe *f*

ear'ly-morn'ing *adj* matinal

ear'ly ris'er *s* matinal *m*

ear'ly-ris'ing *adj* matineux, matinal

ear'mark' *s* marque *f*, cachet *m* || *tr* (*animals*) marquer à l'oreille; (*e.g., money*) spécialiser; **to earmark for** affecter à, assigner à

ear'muff' *s* couvre-oreille *m*

earn [ʌrn] *tr* gagner; (*to get as one's due*) mériter; (*interest*) rapporter

earnest ['ʌrnıst] *adj* sérieux; **in earnest** sérieusement || *s* gage *m*; (com) arrhes *fpl*

earnings ['ʌrnıŋz] *spl* (*wages*) gages *mpl*; (*profits*) profit *m*, bénéfices *mpl*

ear'phone' *s* écouteur *m*; **earphones** casque *m*, écouteurs

ear'ring' *s* boucle *f* d'oreille

ear'split'ting *adj* assourdissant

earth [ʌrθ] *s* terre *f*; **to come down to earth** retomber des nues; **where on earth . . . ?** où diable . . . ?

earthen ['ʌrθən] *adj* de terre, en terre

ear'then-ware' *s* faïence *f*

earthly ['ʌrθli] *adj* terrestre

earth'man' *or* **earth'man** *s* (*pl* **men'** *or* **men**) terrien *m*

earth'quake' *s* tremblement *m* de terre

earth'work' *s* terrassement *m*

earth'worm' *s* lombric *m*, ver *m* de terre

earth-y ['ʌrθi] *adj* (*comp* -ier; *super* -iest) terreux; (*worldly*) mondain; (*unrefined*) grossier, terre à terre

ear' trum'pet *s* cornet *m* acoustique

ease [iz] *s* aise *f*; (*readiness, naturalness*) désinvolture *f*; (*comfort, well-being*) bien-être *m*, tranquillité *f*; **at ease** tranquille; (mil) au repos; **to take one's ease** prendre ses aises; **with ease** facilement || *tr* faciliter; (*a burden*) alléger; (*e.g., one's mind*) calmer, apaiser; (*to let up on*) ralentir || *intr* se calmer, s'apaiser

easel ['izəl] *s* chevalet *m*

easement ['izmənt] *s* (law) servitude *f*

easily ['izɪli] *adv* facilement, aisément; (*certainly*) sans doute

easiness ['izınıs] *s* facilité *f*; (*of manner*) désinvolture *f*, insouciance *f*

east [ist] *adj & s* est *m* || *adv* à l'est, vers l'est

Easter ['istər] *s* Pâques *m*; **Happy Easter!** Joyeuses Pâques!

East'er egg' *s* œuf *m* de Pâques

East'er Mon'day *s* lundi *m* de Pâques

eastern ['istərn] *adj* oriental, de l'est

East'ern Stand'ard Time' *s* l'heure *f* de l'Est

East'ern Town'ships *spl* (*in Canada*) Cantons *mpl* de l'Est

eastward ['istwərd] *adv* vers l'est

eas-y ['izi] *adj* (*comp* -ier; *super* -iest) facile; (*easygoing*) aisé, désinvolte || *adv* (coll) facilement; (coll) lentement; **to take it easy** (coll) en prendre à son aise

eas'y chair' *s* fauteuil *m*, bergère *f*

eas'y-go'ing *adj* insouciant, nonchalant, commode à vivre

eas'y mark' *s* jobard *m*

eas'y pay'ments *spl* facilités *fpl* de paiement

eat [it] *v* (*pret* **ate** [et]; *pp* **eaten** ['itən]) *tr* manger; **to eat away** ronger || *intr* manger

eatable ['itəbəl] *adj* comestible

eaves [ivz] *spl* avant-toits *mpl*

eaves'drop' *v* (*pret & pp* -**dropped**; *ger* -**dropping**) *intr* écouter à la porte

ebb [ɛb] *s* reflux *m*, baisse *f* || *intr* refluer, baisser; **to ebb and flow** monter et baisser, fluer et refluer

ebb' and flow' *s* flux et reflux *m*

ebb' tide' *s* marée *f* descendante, jusant *m*

ebon-y ['ɛbəni] *s* (*pl* -ies) ébène *f*; (*tree*) ébénier *m*

ebullient [ɪ'bʌljənt] *adj* bouillonnant; (fig) enthousiaste, exubérant

eccentric [ɛk'sɛntrɪk] *adj* excentrique || *s* (*odd person*) excentrique *mf*; (*device*) excentrique *m*

eccentrici·ty [ˌeksen'trɪsɪti] *s* (*pl* -ties) excentricité *f*

ecclesiastic [ɪˌkliːzɪ'æstɪk] *adj & s* ecclésiastique *m*

echelon ['eʃəˌlɑn] *s* échelon *m* ‖ *tr* (mil) échelonner

ech·o ['ekoʊ] *s* (*pl* -oes) écho *m* ‖ *tr* répéter ‖ *intr* faire écho

eclectic [ɛk'lektɪk] *adj & s* éclectique *mf*

eclipse [ɪ'klɪps] *s* éclipse *f* ‖ *tr* éclipser

eclogue ['eklɔg], ['eklɑg] *s* églogue *f*

ecology [ɪ'kɑlədʒi] *s* écologie *f*

economic [ˌikə'nɑmɪk], [ˌekə'nɑmɪk] *adj* économique ‖ **economics** *s* économique *f*

economical [ˌikə'nɑmɪkəl], [ˌekə'nɑmɪkəl] *adj* économe

economize [ɪ'kɑnəˌmaɪz] *tr & intr* économiser

econo·my [ɪ'kɑnəmi] *s* (*pl* -mies) économie *f*

ecsta·sy ['ekstəsi] *s* (*pl* -sies) extase *f*

ecstatic [ek'stætɪk] *adj & s* extatique *mf*

Ecuador ['ekwəˌdɔr] *s* l'Équateur *m*

ecumenic(al) [ˌekjə'menɪk(əl)] *adj* œcuménique

eczema ['eksɪmə], [eg'zimə] *s* eczéma *m*

ed·dy ['edi] *s* (*pl* -dies) tourbillon *m* ‖ *v* (*pret & pp* -died) *intr* tourbillonner

edelweiss ['edəlˌvaɪs] *s* edelweiss *m*, fleur *f* de neige

Eden ['idən] *s* (fig) éden *m*

edge [edʒ] *s* bord *m*; (*of a knife, sword, etc.*) fil *m*, tranchant *m*; (*of a field, forest, etc.*) lisière *f*; (*of a strip of cloth*) lisière *f*; (slang) avantage *m*; **on edge** de chant; (*nervous*) énervé, crispé; **to be on edge** avoir les nerfs à fleur de peau; **to have the edge on** (coll) enfoncer; **to set the teeth on edge** agacer les dents ‖ *tr* border; (*to sharpen*) affiler, aiguiser ‖ *intr* s'avancer de biais; **to edge away** s'écarter peu à peu; **to edge in** se glisser parmi or dans

edge·ways *adv* de côté, de biais

edging ['edʒɪŋ] *s* bordure *f*

edg·y ['edʒi] *adj* (*comp* -ier; *super* -iest) (*nervous*) crispé, irritable

edible ['edɪbəl] *adj* comestible

edict ['idɪkt] *s* édit *m*

edification [ˌedɪfɪ'keʃən] *s* édification *f*

edifice ['edɪfɪs] *s* édifice *m*

edi·fy ['edɪˌfaɪ] *v* (*pret & pp* -fied) *tr* édifier

edifying ['edɪˌfaɪɪŋ] *adj* édifiant

edit ['edɪt] *tr* préparer la publication de; (*e.g., a newspaper*) diriger, rédiger; (*a text*) éditer

edition [ɪ'dɪʃən] *s* édition *f*

editor ['edɪtər] *s* (*of newspaper or magazine*) rédacteur *m*; (*of manuscript*) éditeur *m*; (*of feature or column*) chroniqueur *m*, courriériste *mf*

editorial [ˌedɪ'tɔrɪəl] *adj & s* éditorial *m*

editor·ial of·fice *s* rédaction *f*

edito·rial pol·icy *s* ligne *f* politique

edito·rial staff· *s* rédaction *f*

ed·itor in chief· *s* rédacteur *m* en chef

educate ['edʒʊˌket] *tr* instruire, éduquer

educated *adj* cultivé, instruit

education [ˌedʒʊ'keʃən] *s* éducation *f*, instruction *f*

educational [ˌedʒʊ'keʃənəl] *adj* éducatif, éducateur

educator ['edʒʊˌketər] *s* éducateur *m*

eel [il] *s* anguille *f*

ee·rie or **ee·ry** ['ɪri] *adj* (*comp* -rier; *super* -riest) mystérieux, spectral

efface [ɪ'fes] *tr* effacer

effect [ɪ'fekt] *s* effet *m*; **in effect** en fait, effectivement; **to be in effect** être en vigueur; **to feel the effects of** se ressentir de; **to go into effect, to take effect** prendre effet; (*said of law*) entrer en vigueur ‖ *tr* effectuer, mettre à exécution

effective [ɪ'fektɪv] *adj* efficace; (*actually in effect*) en vigueur; (*striking*) impressionnant; **to become effective** produire son effet; (*to go into effect*) entrer en vigueur

effectual [ɪ'fektʃʊəl] *adj* efficace

effectuate [ɪ'fektʃʊˌet] *tr* effectuer

effeminacy [ɪ'femɪnəsi] *s* effémination *f*

effeminate [ɪ'femɪnɪt] *adj* efféminé; **to become effeminate** s'efféminer

effervesce [ˌefər'ves] *intr* être en effervescence

effervescent [ˌefər'vesənt] *adj* effervescent

effete [ɪ'fit] *adj* stérile, épuisé

efficacious [ˌefɪ'keʃəs] *adj* efficace

efficacy ['efɪkəsi] *s* efficacité *f*

efficien·cy [ɪ'fɪʃənsi] *s* (*pl* -cies) efficacité *f*; (*of business*) efficience *f*; (*of machine*) rendement *m*; (*of person*) compétence *f*

effi·ciency ex·pert *s* ingénieur *m* en organisation

efficient [ɪ'fɪʃənt] *adj* efficace; (*of machine*) efficient, de bon rendement; (*of person*) efficient, compétent

effi·gy ['efɪdʒi] *s* (*pl* -gies) effigie *f*

effort ['efərt] *s* effort *m*

effronter·y [ɪ'frʌntəri] *s* (*pl* -ies) effronterie *f*

effusion [ɪ'fjuʒən] *s* effusion *f*

effusive [ɪ'fjusɪv] *adj* démonstratif; **to be effusive in** se répandre en

e.g. *abbr* (Lat: **exempli gratia** for example) par ex., ex.

egg [eg] *s* œuf *m* ‖ *tr*—**to egg on** pousser, inciter

egg·beat·er *s* fouet *m*, batteur *m* à œufs

egg·cup· *s* coquetier *m*

egg·head· *s* (slang) intellectuel *m*

eggnog ['eg,nɑg] *s* lait *m* de poule

egg·plant· *s* aubergine *f*

egg· poach·er *s* pocheuse *f*

egg·shell· *s* coquille *f* d'œuf

egg· white· *s* blanc *m* d'œuf

egoism ['ego,ɪzəm], ['igo,ɪzəm] *s* égoïsme *m*

egoist ['ego·ɪst], ['igo·ɪst] s égoïste mf

egotism ['ego·ˌtɪzəm], ['igo·ˌtɪzəm] s égotisme m

egotist ['ɛgotɪst], ['igotɪst] s égotiste mf

egregious [ɪ'gridʒəs] adj insigne, notoire

egress ['igres] s sortie f, issue f

egret ['igret] s aigrette f

Egypt ['idʒɪpt] s Égypte f; l'Égypte

Egyptian [ɪ'dʒɪpʃən] adj égyptien || s Égyptien m

ei'der down' s édredon m

ei'der duck' s eider m

eight [et] adj & pron huit s huit m; (group of eight) huitaine f; about eight une huitaine de; eight o'clock huit heures

eight'ball' s—behind the eightball (coll) dans le pétrin

eighteen ['et'tin] adj, pron, & s dix-huit m

eighteenth ['et'tinθ] adj & pron dix-huitième (masc, fem); the Eighteenth dix-huit, e.g., John the Eighteenth Jean dix-huit || s dix-huitième m; the eighteenth (in dates) le dix-huit

eighth [etθ] adj & pron huitième (masc, fem); the Eighth huit, e.g., John the Eighth Jean huit || s huitième m; the eighth (in dates) le huit

eightieth ['eti·ɪθ] adj & pron quatre-vingtième (masc, fem) || s quatre-vingtième m

eigh·ty ['eti] adj & pron quatre-vingts || s (pl -ties) quatre-vingts m

eight'y-first' adj & pron quatre-vingt-unième (masc, fem) || s quatre-vingt-unième m

eight'y-one' adj, pron, & s quatre-vingt-un m

either ['iðər], ['aɪðər] adj & pron indef l'un ou l'autre; l'un et l'autre; on either side de chaque côté || adv—not either non plus || conj—either . . . or ou . . . ou, soit . . . soit, ou bien . . . ou bien

ejaculate [ɪ'dʒækjə·ˌlet] tr & intr crier; (physiol) éjaculer

eject [ɪ'dʒɛkt] tr éjecter; (to evict) expulser, chasser

ejection [ɪ'dʒɛkʃən] s éjection f; (eviction) expulsion f

ejec'tion seat' s (aer) siège m éjectable

eke [ik] tr—to eke out gagner avec difficulté

elaborate [ɪ'læbərɪt] adj élaboré, soigné; (ornate) orné, travaillé; (involved) compliqué, recherché || [ɪ'læbə·ˌret] tr élaborer || intr—to elaborate on or upon donner des détails sur

elapse [ɪ'læps] intr s'écouler

elastic [ɪ'læstɪk] adj & s élastique m

elasticity [ɪ·læs'tɪsɪti], [ˌilæs'tɪsɪti] s élasticité f

elated [ɪ'letɪd] adj transporté, exalté

elation [ɪ'leʃən] s transport m, exultation f

elbow ['ɛlbo] s coude m; at one's elbow à portée de la main; to rub

elbows with coudoyer || tr coudoyer; to elbow one's way se frayer un chemin à coups de coude || intr jouer des coudes

el'bow grease' s (coll) huile f de coude

el'bow·room' s espace m; to have elbowroom avoir ses coudées franches

elder ['ɛldər] adj aîné, plus âgé || s aîné m; (senior) doyen m; (bot) sureau m; (eccl) ancien m

el'der·ber'ry s (pl -ries) sureau m; (berry) baie f de sureau

elderly ['ɛldərli] adj vieux, âgé

eld'er states'man s vétéran m de la politique

eldest ['ɛldɪst] adj (l')aîné, (le) plus âgé

elect [ɪ'lɛkt] adj élu || s—the elect les élus mpl || tr élire

election [ɪ'lɛkʃən] s élection f

electioneer [ɪ·ˌlɛkʃə'nɪr] intr faire la campagne électorale, solliciter des voix

elective [ɪ'lɛktɪv] adj électif; (optional) facultatif || s matière f à option

elec'toral col'lege [ɪ'lɛktərəl] s collège m électoral

electorate [ɪ'lɛktərɪt] s corps m électoral, électeurs mpl, votants mpl

electric(al) [ɪ'lɛktrɪk(əl)] adj électrique

elec'trical engineer' s ingénieur m électricien

elec'trical engineer'ing s technique f électrique

elec'tric blan'ket s couverture f chauffante

elec'tric chair' s chaise f électrique

elec'tric clothes' dri'er s séchoir m électrique

elec'tric eel' s gymnote m

elec'tric eye' s cellule f photo-électrique

elec'tric fan' s ventilateur m électrique

elec'tric heat'er s radiateur m électrique

electrician [ɪ·ˌlɛk'trɪʃən], [ˌɛlɛk'trɪʃən] s électricien m

electricity [ɪ·ˌlɛk'trɪsɪti], [ˌɛlɛk'trɪsɪti] s électricité f

elec'tric light' s lampe f électrique

elec'tric me'ter s compteur m de courant

elec'tric mix'er s batteur m électrique

elec'tric per'colator s cafetière f électrique

elec'tric range' s cuisinière f électrique

elec'tric shav'er s rasoir m électrique

elec'tric shock' treat'ment s (med) électrochoc m

electri·fy [ɪ'lɛktrɪ·ˌfaɪ] v (pret & pp -fied) tr (to provide with electric power) électrifier; (to communicate electricity to; to thrill) électriser

elec·tro [ɪ'lɛktro] s (pl -tros) électro-type m

electrocute [ɪ'lɛktrə·ˌkjut] tr électrocuter

electrode [ɪ'lɛktrod] s électrode f

electrolysis [ɪ·ˌlɛk'trɑlɪsɪs], [ˌɛlɛk'trɑlɪsɪs] s électrolyse f

electrolyte [ɪ'lɛktrə·ˌlaɪt] s électrolyte m

electromagnet [ɪ·ˌlɛktrə'mægnɪt] s électro-aimant m

electromagnetic [ɪ͵lektrəmæg'netɪk] *adj* électromagnétique

electron [ɪ'lektran] *s* électron *m*

elec'tron gun' *s* canon *m* à électrons

electronic [ɪ͵lek'tranɪk], [͵elek'tranɪk] *adj* électronique || **electronics** *s* électronique *f*

elec'tron mi'croscope *s* microscope *m* électronique

electroplate [ɪ'lektrə͵plet] *tr* galvaniser

electrotype [ɪ'lektrə͵taɪp] *s* électrotype *m* || *tr* électrotyper

elegance ['elɪgəns] *s* élégance *f*

elegant ['elɪgənt] *adj* élégant

elegiac [͵elɪ'dʒaɪ͵æk] [ɪ'lidʒɪ͵æk] *adj* élégiaque

ele•gy ['elɪdʒɪ] *s* (*pl* **-gies**) élégie *f*

element ['elɪmənt] *s* élément *m*

elementary [͵elɪ'mentərɪ] *adj* élémentaire

elephant ['elɪfənt] *s* éléphant *m*

elevate ['elɪ͵vet] *tr* élever

elevated *adj* élevé; (*style*) soutenu; (*train, railway, etc*) aérien

el'evated rail'way *s* métro *m* aérien

elevation [͵elɪ'veʃən] *s* élévation *f*

elevator ['elɪ͵vetər] *s* ascenseur *m*; (*for freight*) monte-charge *m*; (*for hoisting grain*) élévateur *m*; (*warehouse for storing grain*) silo *m* à céréales; (*aer*) gouvernail *m* d'altitude, gouvernail de profondeur

eleven [ɪ'levən] *adj & pron* onze || *s* onze *m*; **eleven o'clock** onze heures

eleventh [ɪ'levənθ] *adj & pron* onzième (*masc, fem*); **the Eleventh** onze, e.g., **John the Eleventh** Jean onze || *s* onzième *m*; **the eleventh** (*in dates*) le onze

elev'enth hour' *s* dernier moment *m*

elf [elf] *s* (*pl* **elves** [elvz]) elfe *m*

elicit [ɪ'lɪsɪt] *tr* (*e.g., a smile*) provoquer, faire sortir; (*e.g., help*) obtenir

elide [ɪ'laɪd] *tr* élider

eligible ['elɪdʒɪbəl] *adj* éligible; (*e.g., bachelor*) sortable

eliminate [ɪ'lɪmɪ͵net] *tr* éliminer

elision [ɪ'lɪʒən] *s* élision *f*

elite [e'lit] *s* élite *f*

elk [elk] *s* élan *m*

ellipse [ɪ'lɪps] *s* (geom) ellipse *f*

ellip•sis [ɪ'lɪpsɪs] *s* (*pl* **-ses** [siz]) ellipse *f*; (*punctuation*) points *mpl* de suspension

elliptic(al) [ɪ'lɪptɪk(əl)] *adj* elliptique

elm [elm] *s* orme *m*

elongate [ɪ'lɔŋget], [ɪ'laŋget] *tr* allonger, prolonger

elope [ɪ'lop] *intr* s'enfuir avec un amant

elopement [ɪ'lopmənt] *s* enlèvement *m* consenti

eloquence ['eləkwəns] *s* éloquence *f*

eloquent ['eləkwənt] *adj* éloquent

else [els] *adj*—**nobody else** personne d'autre; **nothing else** rien d'autre; **somebody else** quelqu'un d'autre, un autre; **something else** autre chose; **what else** quoi encore; **who else** qui encore; **who's else** de qui d'autre || *adv* d'une autre façon, autrement; **how(ever) else** de toute autre façon;

nowhere else nulle part ailleurs; **or else** sinon, ou bien, sans quoi; **somewhere else** ailleurs, autre part; **when else** quand encore; **where else** où encore

else'where' *adv* ailleurs, autre part

elucidate [ɪ'lusɪ͵det] *tr* élucider

elude [ɪ'lud] *tr* éluder, se soustraire à; (*a pursuer*) échapper à

elusive [ɪ'lusɪv] *adj* évasif, fuyant; (*baffling*) insaisissable, déconcertant

emaciated [ɪ'meʃɪ͵etɪd] *adj* émacié; **to become emaciated** s'émacier

emanate ['emə͵net] *intr* émaner

emancipate [ɪ'mænsɪ͵pet] *tr* émanciper

embalm [em'bam] *tr* embaumer

embalming [em'bamɪŋ] *s* embaumement *m*

embankment [em'bæŋkmənt] *s* (*of river*) digue *f*; (*of road*) remblai *m*

embar•go [em'bargo] *s* (*pl* **-goes**) embargo *m* || *tr* mettre un embargo sur

embark [em'bark] *intr* s'embarquer

embarkation [͵embar'keʃən] *s* embarquement *m*

embarrass [em'bærəs] *tr* faire honte à; (*to make difficult*) embarrasser

embarrassment [em'bærəsmənt] *s* honte *f*; (*difficulty*) embarras *m*

embas•sy ['embəsi] *s* (*pl* **-sies**) ambassade *f*

em•bed [em'bed] *v* (*pret & pp* **-bedded**; *ger* **-bedding**) *tr* encastrer

embellish [em'belɪʃ] *tr* embellir

embellishment [em'belɪʃmənt] *s* embellissement *m*

ember ['embər] *s* tison *m*; **embers** braise *f*

Em'ber days' *spl* quatre-temps *mpl*

embezzle [em'bezəl] *tr* détourner, s'approprier || *intr* commettre des détournements

embezzler [em'bezlər] *s* détourneur *m* de fonds

embitter [em'bɪtər] *tr* aigrir

emblazon [em'blezən] *tr* embellir; exalter, célébrer

emblem ['embləm] *s* emblème *m*

emblematic(al) [͵emblə'mætɪk(əl)] *adj* emblématique

embodiment [em'badɪmənt] *s* personnification *f*, incarnation *f*

embod•y [em'badi] *v* (*pret & pp* **-ied**) *tr* personnifier, incarner; (*to include*) incorporer

embolden [em'boldən] *tr* enhardir

embolism ['embə͵lɪzəm] *s* embolie *f*

emboss [em'bɔs], [em'bas] *tr* (*to raise in relief*) graver en relief; (*metal*) bosseler; (*e.g., leather*) gaufrer, repousser

embouchure [͵ɑmbu'ʃur] *s* embouchure *f*; (mus) position *f* des lèvres

embrace [em'bres] *s* étreinte *f*, embrassement *m* || *tr* étreindre, embrasser || *intr* s'étreindre, s'embrasser

embroider [em'brɔɪdər] *tr* broder

embroider•y [em'brɔɪdəri] *s* (*pl* **-ies**) broderie *f*

embroil [em'brɔɪl] *tr* (*to throw into confusion*) embrouiller; (*to involve in contention*) brouiller

embroilment [em'broilmənt] *s* embrouillage *m*, brouillamini *m*, imbroglio *m*

embry·o ['embrı͵o] *s* (*pl* -os) embryon *m*

embryology [͵embrı'alədʒı] *s* embryologie *f*

embryonic [͵embrı'anık] *adj* embryonnaire

emend [ı'mend] *tr* corriger

emendation [͵imen'de/ən] *s* correction *f*

emerald ['emərəld] *s* émeraude *f*

emerge [ı'mʌrdʒ] *intr* émerger

emergence [ı'mʌrdʒəns] *s* émergence *f*

emergen·cy [ı'mʌrdʒənsı] *adj* urgent, d'urgence; (*exit*) de secours ‖ *s* (*pl* -cies) cas *m* urgent

emer'gency brake' *s* frein *m* de secours

emer'gency ex'it *s* sortie *f* de secours

emer'gency land'ing *s* atterrissage *m* forcé

emer'gency opera'tion *s* (med) opération *f* à chaud

emer'gency ra'tions *spl* vivres *mpl* de réserve

emer'gency ward' *s* salle *f* d'urgence

emeritus [ı'merıtəs] *adj* honoraire, d'honneur

emersion [ı'mʌrʒən], [ı'mʌr/ən] *s* émersion *f*

emery ['emərı] *s* émeri *m*

em'ery cloth' *s* toile *f* d'émeri

em'ery wheel' *s* meule *f* en émeri

emetic [ı'metık] *adj* & *s* émétique *m*

emigrant ['emıgrənt] *adj* & *s* émigrant *m*

emigrate ['emı͵gret] *intr* émigrer

eminence ['emınəns] *s* éminence *f*

eminent ['emınənt] *adj* éminent; **most eminent** (eccl) éminentissime

emissar·y ['emı͵serı] *s* (*pl* -ies) émissaire *m*

emit [ı'mıt] *v* (*pret* & *pp* emitted; *ger* emitting) *tr* émettre; (*a gas, an odor, etc.*) exhaler

emolument [ı'maljəmənt] *s* émoluments *mpl*

emotion [ı'mo/ən] *s* émotion *f*

emotional [ı'mo/ənəl] *adj* émotif, émotionnable

emperor ['empərər] *s* empereur *m*

empha·sis ['emfəsıs] *s* (*pl* -ses [͵sız]) accentuation *f*, mise *f* en relief; énergie *f*, force *f*; (*on word or phrase*) accent *m* d'insistance; **to place emphasis on** insister vivement sur; **with emphasis on** en insistant particulièrement sur

emphasize ['emfə͵saız] *tr* accentuer, mettre en relief; appuyer sur, souligner

emphatic [em'fætık] *adj* accentué, énergique

emphysema [͵emfı'simə] *s* emphysème *m*

empire ['empaır] *s* empire *m*

empiric(al) [em'pırık(əl)] *adj* empirique

empiricist [em'pırısıst] *s* empirique *m*

emplacement [em'plesmənt] *s* emplacement *m*

employ [em'plɔı] *s* service *m* ‖ *tr* employer

employee [em'plɔı·i], [͵emplɔı'i] *s* employé *m*

employer [em'plɔı·ər] *s* employeur *m*, patron *m*, chef *m*

employment [em'plɔımənt] *s* emploi *m*

employ'ment a'gency *s* bureau *m* de placement

empower [em'pau·ər] *tr* autoriser

empress ['emprıs] *s* impératrice *f*

emptiness ['emptınıs] *s* vide *m*

emp·ty ['emptı] *adj* (*comp* -tier; *super* -tiest) vide; (*hollow*) creux, vain; (coll) affamé ‖ *v* (*pret* & *pp* -tied) *tr* vider ‖ *intr* se vider; (*said of river*) se jeter; (*said of auditorium*) se dégarnir

emp·ty-hand'ed *adj* & *adv* les mains vides

emp·ty-head'ed *adj* écervelé

empye·ma [͵empı'imə] *s* (*pl* -mata [mətə]) empyème *m*

empyrean [͵empı'ri·ən] *s* empyrée *m*

emu ['imju] *s* (zool) émeu *m*

emulate ['emjə͵let] *tr* chercher à égaler, imiter ‖ *intr* rivaliser

emulator ['emjə͵letər] *s* émule *mf*

emulsi·fy [ı'mʌlsı͵faı] *v* (*pret* & *pp* -fied) *tr* émulsionner

emulsion [ı'mʌl/ən] *s* émulsion *f*

enable [en'ebəl] *tr*—**to enable to** rendre capable de, mettre à même de

enact [en'ækt] *tr* (*to decree*) décréter, arrêter; (theat) représenter

enactment [en'æktmənt] *s* loi *f*; (*establishing*) établissement *m*; (govt) promulgation *f*; (law) décret *m*; (theat) représentation *f*

enam·el [ı'næməl] *s* émail *m* ‖ *v* (*pret* & *pp* -eled or -elled; *ger* -eling or -elling) *tr* émailler

enameling [ı'næməlıŋ] *s* émaillage *m*

enam'el·ware' *s* ustensiles *mpl* en fer émaillé

enamor [en'æmər] *tr* rendre amoureux; **to become enamored with** s'énamourer de

encamp [en'kæmp] *tr* & *intr* camper

encampment [en'kæmpmənt] *s* campement *m*

encase [en'kes] *tr* mettre en caisse; enfermer, envelopper

encephalitis [en͵sefə'laıtıs] *s* encéphalite *f*

enchain [en't/en] *tr* enchaîner

enchant [en't/ænt], [en't/ant] *tr* enchanter

enchanting [en't/æntıŋ], [en't/antıŋ] *adj* charmant, ravissant; (*casting a spell*) enchanteur

enchantment [en't/æntmənt], [en't/antmənt] *s* enchantement *m*

enchantress [en't/æntrıs], [en't/antrıs] *s* enchanteresse *f*

encircle [en'sʌrkəl] *tr* encercler, cerner; (*a word*) entourer d'un cercle

enclitic [en'klıtık] *adj* & *s* enclitique *m*

enclose [en'kloz] *tr* enclore, entourer; (*in a letter*) inclure, joindre

enclosed *adj* (*in a letter*) ci-joint, ci-inclus

enclosure [en'kloʒər] *s* clôture *f*, enceinte *f*, enclos *m*; (*e.g., in a letter*) pièce *f* jointe, pièce annexée

encomi•um [en'komɪ•əm] *s* (*pl* -**ums** or -**a** [ə]) panégyrique *m*, éloge *m*

encompass [en'kʌmpəs] *tr* entourer, renfermer

encore ['ɑnkor] *s* rappel *m*, bis *m* ‖ *tr* bisser ‖ *interj* bis!

encounter [en'kauntər] *s* rencontre *f* ‖ *tr* rencontrer ‖ *intr* se rencontrer, combattre

encourage [en'kʌrɪdʒ] *tr* encourager

encouragement [en'kʌrɪdʒmənt] *s* encouragement *m*

encroach [en'krotʃ] *intr*—**to encroach on** or **upon** empiéter sur; abuser de

encumber [en'kʌmbər] *tr* encombrer, embarrasser; (*with debts*) grever

encumbrance [en'kʌmbrəns] *s* encombrement *m*, embarras *m*; (*law*) charge *f*

encyclical [en'sɪklɪkəl], [en'saɪklɪkəl] *adj & s* encyclique *f*

encyclopedia [en‚saɪklə'pidɪ•ə] *s* encyclopédie *f*

encyclopedic [en‚saɪklə'pidɪk] *adj* encyclopédique

end [end] *s* (*in time*) fin *f*; (*in space*; *small piece*) bout *m*; (*purpose*) but *m*; (*end of set period of time*) terme *m*; **at loose ends** en pagaille; **at the end, in the end** à la fin; **to be at the end of one's rope** être au bout de son rouleau; **to bring to an end** mettre fin à; **to come to an end** prendre fin; **to make both ends meet** joindre les deux bouts; **to stand on end** (*said of hair*) se dresser; **to this end** à cet effet ‖ *tr* achever, terminer ‖ *intr* s'achever, se terminer; **to end up by** finir par

endanger [en'dendʒər] *tr* mettre en danger

endear [en'dɪr] *tr* faire aimer; **to endear oneself to** se faire aimer de

endeavor [en'devər] *s* effort *m*, tentative *f* ‖ *intr*—**to endeavor to** s'efforcer de, tâcher de

endemic [en'demɪk] *adj* endémique

ending ['endɪŋ] *s* fin *f*, terminaison *f*; (*gram*) désinence *f*

endive ['endarv] *s* (*blanched type*) endive *f*; (*Cichorium endivia*) chicorée *f* frisée

endless ['endlɪs] *adj* sans fin

end'most' *adj* extrême

endocrine ['endo‚kraɪn], ['endokrɪn] *adj* endocrine

endorse [en'dɔrs] *tr* endosser; (*a candidate*) appuyer; (*a plan*) souscrire à

endorsement [en'dɔrsmənt] *s* endos *m*, endossement *m*; (*approval*) appui *m*, approbation *f*

endorser [en'dɔrsər] *s* endosseur *m*

endow [en'dau] *tr* doter, fonder

endowment [en'daumənt] *s* dotation *f*, fondation *f*; (*talent*) don *m*

endow'ment fund' *s* caisse *f* de dotation

end' pa'per *s* pages *fpl* de garde

endurance [en'd(j)urəns] *s* endurance *f*

endur'ance test' *s* épreuve *f* d'endurance

endure [en'd(j)ur] *tr* endurer ‖ *intr* durer

enduring [en'd(j)urɪŋ] *adj* durable

enema ['enəmə] *s* lavement *m*

ene•my ['enəmi] *adj* ennemi ‖ *s* (*pl* -**mies**) ennemi *m*

en'emy al'ien *s* étranger *m* ennemi

energetic [‚enər'dʒetɪk] *adj* énergique

ener•gy ['enərdʒi] *s* (*pl* -**gies**) énergie *f*

en'ergy bal'ance *s* (nucl) bilan *m* énergétique

enervate ['enər‚vet] *tr* énerver

enfeeble [en'fibəl] *tr* affaiblir

enfold [en'fold] *tr* envelopper, enrouler; (*to embrace*) embrasser

enforce [en'fors] *tr* (*a law*) faire exécuter, mettre en vigueur; (*one's rights, one's point of view*) faire valoir, appuyer; (*e.g., obedience*) imposer

enforcement [en'forsmənt] *s* contrainte *f*; (*of a law*) exécution *f*, mise *f* en vigueur

enfranchise [en'fræntʃaɪz] *tr* affranchir; donner le droit de vote à

engage [en'gedʒ] *tr* engager; (*to hire*) engager, embaucher; (*to reserve*) retenir, réserver, louer; (*s.o.'s attention*) fixer, attirer; (*the clutch*) embrayer; (*toothed wheels*) engrener; **to be engaged in** s'occuper de; **to be engaged to be married** être fiancé; **to engage s.o. in conversation** entamer une conversation avec qn ‖ *intr* s'engager; (mach) engrener; **to engage in** s'embarquer dans, entrer en or dans

engaged *adj* (*to be married*) fiancé; (*busy*) occupé, pris; (mach) en prise; (mil) aux prises, aux mains

engagement [en'gedʒmənt] *s* engagement *m*; (*betrothal*) fiançailles *fpl*; (*appointment*) rendez-vous *m*; (mach) embrayage *m*, engrenage *m*; (mil) engagement, combat *m*

engage'ment ring' *s* bague *f* or anneau *m* de fiançailles

engaging [en'gedʒɪŋ] *adj* engageant, attirant

engender [en'dʒendər] *tr* engendrer

engine ['endʒɪn] *s* machine *f*; (*of automobile*) moteur *m*

engineer [‚endʒə'nɪr] *s* ingénieur *m*; (*engine driver*) mécanicien *m* ‖ *tr* diriger or construire en qualité d'ingénieur; (coll) manigancer, machiner

engineering [‚endʒə'nɪrɪŋ] *s* génie *m*

en'gine house' *s* dépôt *m* de pompes à incendie

en'gine-man' or **en'gine-man** *s* (*pl* -**men'** or -**men**) mécanicien *m*

en'gine room' *s* chambre *f* des machines

en'gine-room tel'egraph *s* (naut) transmetteur *m* d'ordres

en'gine trou'ble *s* panne *f* de moteur

England ['ɪŋglənd] *s* Angleterre *f*; l'Angleterre

English ['ɪŋglɪʃ] *adj* anglais ‖ *s* (*language*) anglais *m*; (billiards) effet *m*; **the English** les Anglais

Eng'lish Chan'nel *s* Manche *f*

Eng/lish dai/sy *s* marguerite *f* des champs
Eng/lish horn/ *s* cor *m* anglais
Eng/lish-man *s* (*pl* -men) Anglais *m*
Eng/lish-speak/ing *adj* anglophone, d'expression anglaise; (*country*) de langue anglaise
Eng/lish-wom/an *s* (*pl* -wom/en) Anglaise *f*
engraft [en'græft], [en'grɑft] *tr* greffer; (fig) implanter
engrave [en'grev] *tr* graver
engraver [en'grevər] *s* graveur *m*
engraving [en'greviŋ] *s* gravure *f*
engross [en'gros] *tr* absorber, occuper; (*a document*) grossoyer
engrossing [en'grosiŋ] *adj* absorbant
engulf [en'gʌlf] *tr* engouffrer, engloutir
enhance [en'hæns], [en'hɑns] *tr* rehausser, relever
enhancement [en'hænsmənt], [en'hɑnsmənt] *s* rehaussement *m*
enigma [ɪ'nɪgmə] *s* énigme *f*
enigmatic(al) [ˌɪnɪg'mætɪk(əl)] *adj* énigmatique
enjoin [en'dʒɔɪn] *tr* enjoindre; (*to forbid*) interdire
enjoy [en'dʒɔɪ] *tr* jouir de; **to enjoy +** *ger* prendre plaisir à + *inf*; **to enjoy oneself** s'amuser, se divertir
enjoyable [en'dʒɔɪ-əbəl] *adj* agréable, plaisant; (*show, party, etc.*) divertissant
enjoyment [en'dʒɔɪmənt] *s* (*pleasure*) plaisir *m*; (*pleasurable use*) jouissance *f*
enkindle [en'kɪndəl] *tr* allumer
enlarge [en'lɑrdʒ] *tr* agrandir, élargir; (phot) agrandir || *intr* s'agrandir, s'élargir; **to enlarge on** or **upon** discourir longuement sur, amplifier
enlargement [en'lɑrdʒmənt] *s* agrandissement *m*
enlighten [en'laɪtən] *tr* éclairer
enlightenment [en'laɪtənmənt] *s* éclaircissements *mpl*; **the Enlightenment** le siècle des lumières
enlist [en'lɪst] *tr* enrôler || *intr* s'enrôler, s'engager
enlist/ed man/ *s* homme *m* de troupe
enlistment [en'lɪstmənt] *s* enrôlement *m*, engagement *m*
enliven [en'laɪvən] *tr* animer, égayer
enmesh [en'mɛʃ] *tr* prendre dans les rets; (*e.g., in an evil design*) empêtrer; (mach) engrener
enmi-ty ['enmɪti] *s* (*pl* -ties) inimitié *f*
ennoble [en'nobəl] *tr* ennoblir; (*to confer a title of nobility upon*) anoblir
ennui ['ɑnwi] *s* ennui *m*
enormous [ɪ'nɔrməs] *adj* énorme
enormously [ɪ'nɔrməsli] *adv* énormément
enough [ɪ'nʌf] *adj, s, & adv* assez; **more than enough** plus qu'il n'en faut; **that's enough!** en voilà assez!; **to be intelligent enough** être assez intelligent; **to have enough to live on** avoir de quoi vivre || *interj* assez!, ça suffit!
enounce [ɪ'naʊns] *tr* énoncer

enrage [en'redʒ] *tr* faire enrager, rendre furieux; **to be enraged** enrager
enrapture [ən'ræptʃər] *tr* ravir, transporter
enrich [en'rɪtʃ] *tr* enrichir
enrichment [en'rɪtʃmənt] *s* enrichissement *m*
enroll [en'rol] *tr* enrôler; (*a student*) inscrire; (*to wrap up*) enrouler || *intr* s'enrôler; (*said of student*) prendre ses inscriptions, se faire inscrire
enrollment [en'rolmənt] *s* enrôlement *m*; (*of a student*) inscription *f*; (*wrapping up*) enroulement *m*
ensconce [en'skɑns] *tr* cacher; **to ensconce oneself** s'installer
ensemble [ɑn'sɑmbəl] *s* ensemble *m*
ensign ['ensaɪn] *s* enseigne *f* || ['en-sən], ['ensaɪn] *s* (nav) enseigne *m* de deuxième classe
ensilage ['ensɪlɪdʒ] *s* fourrage *m* d'un silo américain || *tr* ensiler
enslave [en'slev] *tr* asservir, réduire en esclavage
enslavement [en'slevmənt] *s* asservissement *m*
ensnare [en'snɛr] *tr* prendre au piège, attraper
ensue [en's(j)u] *intr* s'ensuivre, résulter
ensuing [en's(j)u-ɪŋ] *adj* suivant
ensure [en'ʃʊr] *tr* assurer, garantir
entail [en'tel] *tr* occasionner, entraîner
entangle [en'tæŋgəl] *tr* embrouiller
entanglement [en'tæŋgəlmənt] *s* embrouillement *m*, embarras *m*
enter ['entər] *tr* (*a room, a house, etc.*) entrer dans; (*a school, the army, etc.*) entrer à; (*e.g., a period of convalescence*) entrer en; (*a highway, a public square, etc.*) déboucher sur; (*e.g., a club*) devenir membre de; (*a request*) enregistrer, consigner par écrit; (*a student, a contestant, etc.*) admettre, faire inscrire; (*in the customhouse*) déclarer; (*to make a record of*) inscrire, porter; **to enter one's name for** se faire inscrire à or pour || *intr* entrer; (theat) entrer en scène; **to enter into** entrer à, dans, or en; (*to be an ingredient of*) entrer pour; **to enter on** or **upon** entreprendre, débuter dans
enterprise ['entər‚praɪz] *s* (*undertaking*) entreprise *f*; (*spirit, push*) esprit *m* d'entreprise, allant *m*, entrain *m*
enterprising ['entər‚praɪzɪŋ] *adj* entreprenant
entertain [‚entər'ten] *tr* (*to distract*) amuser, divertir; (*to show hospitality to*) recevoir; (*at a meal*) régaler; (*a hope*) entretenir, nourrir; (*an idea*) concevoir || *intr* recevoir
entertainer [‚entər'tenər] *s* (*host*) hôte *m*, amphitryon *m*; amuseur *m*; (*comedian*) comique *mf*
entertaining [‚entər'tenɪŋ] *adj* amusant, divertissant
entertainment [‚entər'tenmənt] *s* (*distraction*) amusement *m*, divertissement *m*; (*show*) spectacle *m*; (*as a guest*) accueil *m*, hospitalité *f*

en/tertain/ment tax/ s taxe f sur les spectacles

enthrall [ɛn'θrɔl] tr (to charm) captiver, charmer; (to enslave) asservir, rendre esclave

enthrone [ɛn'θron] tr introniser

enthuse [ɛn'θ(j)uz] tr (coll) enthousiasmer || intr (coll) s'enthousiasmer

enthusiasm [ɛn'θ(j)uzɪ͟ɑ ɑezəm] s enthousiasme m

enthusiast [ɛn'θ(j)uzɪ ɑest] s enthousiaste mf; (camera fiend, sports fan, etc.) fanatique mf, enragé m

enthusiastic [ɛn ͵θ(j)uzɪ'ɑestɪk] adj enthousiaste; (for sports, music, a hobby) fanatique, enragé

entice [ɛn'taɪs] tr attirer, séduire; (to evil) tenter, chercher à séduire

enticement [ɛn'taɪsmənt] s attrait m, appât m; tentation f, séduction f

entire [ɛn'taɪr] adj entier

entirely [ɛn'taɪrli] adv entièrement, en entier; (absolutely) tout à fait, absolument

entire·ty [ɛn'taɪrti] s (pl -ties) totalité f, entier m; in its entirety dans sa totalité

entitle [ɛn'taɪtəl] tr (to name) intituler; (to qualify) donner le droit à; to be entitled to avoir droit à

enti·ty ['ɛntɪti] s (pl -ties) entité f

entomb [ɛn'tum] tr ensevelir

entombment [ɛn'tummənt] s ensevelissement m

entomology [͵ɛntə'mɑlədʒi] s entomologie f

entourage [͵ɑntu'rɑʒ] s entourage m

entrails ['ɛntrelz], ['ɛntrəlz] spl entrailles fpl

entrain [ɛn'tren] tr faire prendre le train, embarquer; (to carry along) entraîner || intr embarquer, s'embarquer

entrance ['ɛntrəns] s entrée f; (theat) entrée en scène; **entrance to . . .** (public sign) accès à . . . || [ɛn'træns], [ɛn'trɑns] tr enchanter, ensorceler; **to be entranced** s'extasier

en/trance examina/tion s examen m d'entrée

en/trance fee/ s droits mpl d'entrée

entrancing [ɛn'trænsɪŋ], [ɛn'trɑnsɪŋ] adj enchanteur, ensorceleur

entrant ['ɛntrənt] s inscrit m; (in a competition) concurrent m, participant m

en·trap [ɛn'træp] v (pret & pp -trapped; ger -trapping) tr attraper

entreat [ɛn'trit] tr supplier, prier, conjurer

entreat·y [ɛn'triti] s (pl -ies) supplication f, prière f

entree ['ɑntre] s (entrance; course preceding the roast) entrée f; (main dish) plat m de résistance

entrench [ɛn'trɛntʃ] tr retrancher; **to be entrenched** se retrancher || intr— to entrench on or upon empiéter sur

entrust [ɛn'trʌst] tr—to entrust s.o. with s.th., to entrust s.th. to s.o. confier q.ch. à qn

en·try ['ɛntri] s (pl -tries) entrée f; (in a dictionary) article m, entrée; (on a register) inscription f; (in a competition) concurrent m, participant m; (thing entered for judging in a competition) objet m exposé

en/try blank/ s feuille f d'inscription

entwine [ɛn'twaɪn] tr entrelacer, enlacer || intr s'entrelacer, s'enlacer

enumerate [ɪ'n(j)umə͵ret] tr énumérer

enunciate [ɪ'nʌnʃi͵et], [ɪ'nʌnʃi͵et] tr énoncer, déclarer; (to articulate) articuler, prononcer

envelop [ɛn'vɛləp] tr envelopper

envelope ['ɛnvə͵lop], ['ɑnvə͵lop] s enveloppe f; **in an envelope** sous enveloppe, sous pli

envenom [ɛn'vɛnəm] tr envenimer, empoisonner

enviable ['ɛnvɪ·əbəl] adj enviable, digne d'envie

envious ['ɛnvɪ·əs] adj envieux

environment [ɛn'vaɪrənmənt] s environnement m, milieu m

environs [ɛn'vaɪrənz] spl environs mpl

envisage [ɛn'vɪzɪdʒ] tr envisager

envoi ['ɛnvɔɪ] s envoi m

envoy ['ɛnvɔɪ] s envoyé m, émissaire m; (of poem) envoi m

en·vy ['ɛnvi] s (pl -vies) envie f || v (pret & pp -vied) tr envier

enzyme ['ɛnzaɪm], ['ɛnzɪm] s enzyme m & f

epaulet ['ɛpə͵let] s épaulette f

epergne [ɪ'pʌrn], [e'pɛrn] s surtout m

ephemeral [ɪ'fɛmərəl] adj éphémère

epic ['ɛpɪk] adj épique || s épopée f

epicure ['ɛpɪ͵kjur] s gourmet m, gastronome m

epidemic [͵ɛpɪ'dɛmɪk] adj épidémique || s épidémie f

epidemiology [͵ɛpɪ͵dimɪ'ɑlədʒi] s épidémiologie f

epidermis [͵ɛpɪ'dʌrmɪs] s épiderme m

epiglottis [͵ɛpɪ'glɑtɪs] s épiglotte f

epigram ['ɛpɪ͵græm] s épigramme f

epilepsy ['ɛpɪ͵lɛpsi] s épilepsie f

epileptic [͵ɛpɪ'lɛptɪk] adj & s épileptique mf

epilogue ['ɛpɪ͵lɔg], ['ɛpɪ͵lɑg] s épilogue m

episcopal [ɪ'pɪskəpəl] adj épiscopal

Episcopalian [ɪ͵pɪskə'pelɪ·ən] adj épiscopal || s épiscopal m

episode ['ɛpɪ͵sod] s épisode m

episodic [͵ɛpɪ'sɑdɪk] adj épisodique

epistle [ɪ'pɪsəl] s épître f

epitaph ['ɛpɪ͵tæf] s épitaphe f

epithet ['ɛpɪ͵θɛt] s épithète f

epitome [ɪ'pɪtəmi] s (abridgment) épitomé m; (representative of a class) modèle m, personnification f

epitomize [ɪ'pɪtə͵maɪz] tr abréger; personnifier

epoch ['ɛpək], ['ipɑk] s époque f

epochal ['ɛpəkəl] adj mémorable

ep/och-mak/ing adj qui fait époque

Ep/som salts/ ['ɛpsəm] spl epsomite f, sels mpl d'Epsom

equable ['ɛkwəbəl], ['ikwəbəl] adj uniforme, égal; tranquille

equal ['ikwəl] adj égal; **to be equal to** égaler, valoir; (e.g., the occasion) être à la hauteur de; **to be equal to** + ger être de force à + inf, être à même de + inf; **to get equal with** (coll) se venger de ǁ s égal m, pareil m ǁ v (pret & pp **equaled** or **equalled**; ger **equaling** or **equalling**) tr égaler

equali·ty [ɪˈkwɑlɪti] s (pl **-ties**) égalité f

equalize [ˈikwəˌlaiz] tr égaliser

equally [ˈikwəli] adv également

equanimity [ˌikwəˈnimiti] s équanimité f, égalité f d'âme

equate [iˈkwet] tr égaliser, mettre en équation

equation [iˈkweʒən], [iˈkweʃən] s équation f

equator [iˈkwetər] s équateur m

equatorial [ˌikwəˈtori·əl] adj équatorial

equestrian [ɪˈkwɛstri·ən] adj équestre ǁ s cavalier m, écuyer m

equilateral [ˌikwiˈlætərəl] adj équilatéral

equilibrium [ˌikwiˈlibri·əm] s équilibre m

equinoctial [ˌikwiˈnɑkʃəl] adj équinoxial

equinox [ˈikwiˌnɑks] s équinoxe m

equip [ɪˈkwip] v (pret & pp **equipped**; ger **equipping**) tr équiper, outiller; **to equip with** munir de

equipment [ɪˈkwipmənt] s équipement m, matériel m

equipoise [ˈikwiˌpɔiz], [ˈɛkwiˌpɔiz] s équilibre m ǁ tr équilibrer

equitable [ˈɛkwitəbəl] adj équitable

equi·ty [ˈɛkwiti] s (pl **-ties**) équité f; (com) part f résiduaire

equivalent [ɪˈkwivələnt] adj & s équivalent m

equivocal [ɪˈkwivəkəl] adj équivoque

equivocate [ɪˈkwivəˌket] intr équivoquer

equivocation [ɪˌkwivəˈkeʃən] s tergiversation f, équivoque f

era [ˈirə], [ˈirə] s ère f, époque f

eradicate [ɪˈrædiˌket] tr déraciner, extirper

erase [ɪˈres] tr effacer, biffer

eraser [ɪˈresər] s gomme f à effacer; brosse f

erasure [ɪˈreʃər] s effacement m, rature f

ere [er] prep (poetic) avant ǁ conj (poetic) avant que

erect [ɪˈrekt] adj droit, debout ǁ tr (to set in an upright position) dresser, élever; (a building) ériger, édifier; (a machine) monter

erection [ɪˈrekʃən] s érection f

erg [ʌrg] s erg m

ermine [ˈʌrmin] s hermine f

erode [ɪˈrod] tr éroder

erosion [ɪˈroʒən] s érosion f

erotic [ɪˈratik] adj érotique

err [ʌr] intr se tromper, faire erreur, errer; (to do wrong) s'égarer, pécher

errand [ˈɛrənd] s commission f, course f; **to go on** or **to run an errand** faire une course

er'rand boy' s coursier m, garçon de courses

erratic [ɪˈrætik] adj variable; capricieux, excentrique

erroneous [ɪˈroni·əs] adj erroné

error [ˈɛrər] s erreur f

erudite [ˈɛr(j)uˌdait] adj érudit

erudition [ˌɛr(j)uˈdiʃən] s érudition f

erupt [ɪˈrʌpt] intr faire éruption

eruption [ɪˈrʌpʃən] s éruption f

escalate [ˈɛskəˌlet] tr escalader

escalation [ˌɛskəˈleʃən] s escalade f

escalator [ˈɛskəˌletər] s escalator m, escalier m mécanique or roulant

escallop [ɛsˈkæləp] s coquille f Saint-Jacques, peigne m, pétoncle m; (culin) coquille au gratin ǁ tr (the edges) denteler, découper; (culin) gratiner et cuire au four et à la crème

escapade [ˈɛskəˌped] s fredaine f, frasque f; (getting away) escapade f

escape [ɛsˈkep] s (getaway) évasion f, fuite f; (from responsibilities, duties, etc.) évasion, escapade f; (of gas, liquid, etc.) échappement m, fuite; (of a clock) échappement m; **to have a narrow escape** l'échapper belle; **to make one's escape** se sauver, s'échapper ǁ tr échapper à, éviter ǁ intr échapper, s'échapper, s'évader; **to escape from** échapper à

escape' clause' s échappatoire f

escapee [ˌɛskəˈpi] s évadé m, échappé m

escape' hatch' s (aer) sas m d'évacuation

escape' lit'erature s littérature f d'évasion

escapement [ɛsˈkepmənt] s issue f, débouché m; (mach) échappement m

escape' wheel' s roue f de rencontre

escarole [ˈɛskəˌrol] s scarole f

escarpment [ɛsˈkarpmənt] s escarpement m

eschew [ɛsˈtʃu] tr éviter, s'abstenir de

escort [ˈɛskɔrt] s escorte f; (gentleman escort) cavalier m ǁ [ɛsˈkɔrt] tr escorter

escutcheon [ɛsˈkʌtʃən] s écusson m

Eski·mo [ˈɛskiˌmo] adj eskimo, esquimau ǁ s (pl **-mos** or **-mo**) (language; dog) esquimau m; (person) Eskimo m, Esquimau m

Es'kimo wom'an s Esquimaude f, femme f esquimau

esopha·gus [iˈsɑfəgəs] s (pl **-gi** [ˌdʒaɪ]) œsophage m

esoteric [ˌɛsoˈtɛrɪk] adj ésotérique

especial [ɛsˈpeʃəl] adj spécial

especially [ɛsˈpeʃəli] adv surtout, particulièrement

espionage [ˈɛspi·əˌnidʒ], [ˌɛspi·əˈnaʒ] s espionnage m

espousal [ɛsˈpauzəl] s épousailles f; **espousal of** (a cause) adoption de, adhésion à

espouse [ɛsˈpauz] tr épouser; (to advocate, adopt) adopter, embrasser

Esq. abbr (**Esquire**)—**John Smith, Esq.** Monsieur Jean Smith

esquire [ɛsˈkwair], [ˈɛskwair] s (hist) écuyer m

essay [ˈɛse] s essai m ǁ tr essayer

essayist [ˈɛse·ist] s essayiste mf

essence ['esəns] s essence f
essential [e'senʃəl] adj & s essentiel m
establish [es'tæblıʃ] tr établir
establishment [es'tæblıʃmənt] s établissement m
estate [es'tet] s (landed property) domaine m, propriété f, terres fpl; (a person's possessions) biens mpl, possessions fpl; (left by a decedent) héritage m, succession f; (social status) rang m, condition f; (hist) état m
esteem [es'tim] s estime f || tr estimer
esthete ['esθit] s esthète m f
esthetic [es'θetɪk] adj esthétique || esthetics s esthétique f
estimable ['estıməbəl] adj estimable
estimate ['estı,met], ['estımıt] s évaluation f, appréciation f; (appraisal) estimation f || ['estı,met] tr (to judge, deem) apprécier, estimer; (the cost) estimer, évaluer
estimation [,estı'meʃən] s (opinion) jugement m; (esteem) estime f; (appraisal) estimation f; in my estimation à mon avis
Estonia [es'tonıə] s Estonie f; l'Estonie
estrangement [es'trendʒmənt] s éloignement m; (a becoming unfriendly) désaffection f
estuar·y ['estʃʊ,eri] s (pl -ies) estuaire m
etch [etʃ] tr & intr graver à l'eau-forte
etcher ['etʃər] s aquafortiste m
etching ['etʃıŋ] s eau-forte f
eternal [ı'tʌrnəl] adj éternel
eterni·ty [ı'tʌrnıtı] s (pl -ties) éternité f
ether ['iθər] s éther m
ethereal [ı'θırıəl] adj éthéré
ethical ['eθıkəl] adj éthique
ethics ['eθıks] s (branch of philosophy) étique f, morale f; spl (one's conduct, one's moral principles) morale
Ethiopia [,iθı'opıə] s Éthiopie f; l'Éthiopie
Ethiopian [,iθı'opıən] adj éthiopien || s (language) éthiopien m; (person) Éthiopien m
ethnic(al) ['eθnık(əl)] adj ethnique
ethnography [eθ'nagrəfı] s ethnographie f
ethnology [eθ'nalədʒı] s ethnologie f
ethyl ['eθıl] s éthyle m
ethylene ['eθı,lin] s éthylène m
etiquette ['etı,ket] s étiquette f
etymolo·gy [,etı'malədʒı] s (pl -gies) étymologie f
ety·mon ['etı,man] s (pl -mons or -ma [mə]) étymon m
eucalyp·tus [,jukə'lıptəs] s (pl -tuses or -ti [taı]) eucalyptus m
Eucharist ['jukərıst] s Eucharistie f
euchre ['jukər] s euchre m || tr (coll) l'emporter sur
eulogize ['jula,dʒaız] tr faire l'éloge de
eulo·gy ['julədʒı] s (pl -gies) éloge m
eunuch ['junək] s eunuque m
euphemism ['jufı,mızəm] s euphémisme m
euphemistic [,jufı'mıstık] adj euphémique

euphonic [ju'fanık] adj euphonique
eupho·ny ['jufənı] s (pl -nies) euphonie f
euphoria [ju'forıə] s euphorie f
euphuism ['jufju,ızəm] s euphuisme m; préciosité f
Europe ['jurəp] s Europe f; l'Europe
European [,jurə'piən] adj européen || s Européen m
euthanasia [,juθə'neʒə] s euthanasie f
evacuate [ı'vækju,et] tr évacuer || intr s'évacuer
evade [ı'ved] tr échapper à, éviter, esquiver || intr s'évader
evaluate [ı'vælju,et] tr évaluer
Evangel [ı'vændʒəl] s évangile m
evangelic(al) [,ıvæn'dʒelık(əl)], [,evən'dʒelık(əl)] adj évangélique
evangelist [ı'vændʒəlıst] s évangéliste m
evaporate [ı'væpə,ret] tr évaporer || intr s'évaporer
evasion [ı'veʒən] s évasion f; subterfuge m, détour m
evasive [ı'vesıv] adj évasif
eve [iv] s veille f, (poetic) soir m; on the eve of à la veille de; Eve Ève f
even ['ivən] adj (smooth) uni; (number) pair; (equal, uniform) égal; (temperament) calme, rassis, égal; even with à fleur de; to be even être quitte; (cards, sports) être manche à manche or point à point; to get even with (coll) rendre la pareille à || adv même; even + comp encore + comp, e.g., even better encore mieux; even so quand même || tr aplanir, égaliser
evening ['ivnıŋ] adj du soir || s soir m; all evening toute la soirée; every evening tous les soirs; in the evening le soir; the evening before la veille au soir
eve'ning clothes' s tenue f de soirée; (for women) toilette f de soirée; (for men) habit m de soirée
eve'ning damp' s serein m
eve'ning prim'rose s onagraire f
eve'ning star' s étoile f du soir, étoile du berger
eve'ning wrap' s sortie f de soirée
e'ven-song' s (eccl) vêpres fpl
event [ı'vent] s événement m; at all events or in any event en tout cas; in the event that dans le cas où
eventful [ı'ventfəl] adj mouvementé; mémorable
eventual [ı'ventʃʊ,əl] adj final
eventuali·ty [ı,ventʃʊ'ælıtı] s (pl -ties) éventualité f
eventually [ı'ventʃʊ,əlı] adv finalement, à la longue
eventuate [ı'ventʃʊ,et] intr—to eventuate in se terminer par, aboutir à
ever ['evər] adv (at all times) toujours; (at any time) jamais; ever since dès lors, depuis; for ever and ever à tout jamais; hardly ever presque jamais
ev'er·glade' s région f marécageuse
ev'er·green' adj toujours vert || s arbre m vert; evergreens plantes fpl vertes, verdure f décorative

ev'er·last'ing adj éternel; (continual) sempiternel, perpétuel

ev'er·more' adv toujours; **for evermore** à jamais

every ['evri] adj tous les; (each) chaque, tout; (coll) tout, e.g., **every bit as good as** tout aussi bon que; **every man for himself** sauve qui peut; **every now and then** de temps en temps; **every once in a while** de temps à autre; **every other day** tous les deux jours; **every other one** un sur deux; **every which way** (coll) de tous côtés; (coll) en désordre

ev'ery·bod'y pron indef tout le monde

ev'ery·day' adj de tous les jours

ev'ery·man' s Monsieur Tout-le-monde

ev'ery·one' or **ev'ery one'** pron indef chacun, tous, tout le monde

ev'ery·thing' pron indef tout

ev'ery·where' adv partout, de toutes parts; partout où; **everywhere else** partout ailleurs

evict [ɪ'vɪkt] tr évincer, expulser

eviction [ɪ'vɪkʃən] s éviction f

evidence ['evɪdəns] s évidence f; (proof) preuve f, témoignage m || tr manifester, démontrer

evident ['evɪdənt] adj évident

evidently ['evɪdəntli], [ˌevɪ'dɛntli] adv évidemment

evil ['ivəl] adj mauvais, méchant || s mal m, méchanceté f

evildoer ['ivəlˌdu·ər] s malfaisant m, méchant m

e'vil·do'ing s malfaisance f

e'vil eye' s mauvais œil m

e'vil-mind'ed adj malintentionné, malin

E'vil One' s Esprit m malin

evince [ɪ'vɪns] tr montrer, manifester

evocative [ɪ'vɑkətɪv] adj évocateur

evoke [ɪ'vok] tr évoquer

evolution [ˌevə'luʃən] s évolution f

evolve [ɪ'vɑlv] tr développer, élaborer || intr évoluer

ewe [ju] s brebis f

ewer ['ju·ər] s aiguière f

exact [eg'zækt] adj exact || tr exiger

exacting [eg'zæktɪŋ] adj exigeant

exactly [eg'zæktli] adv exactement; (sharp, on the dot) précisément, justement

exactness [eg'zæktnɪs] s exactitude f

exaggerate [eg'zædʒə·ret] tr exagérer

exalt [eg'zɔlt] tr exalter

exam [eg'zæm] s (coll) examen m

examination [egˌzæmɪ'neʃən] s examen m; **to take an examination** se présenter à, passer, or subir un examen

examine [eg'zæmɪn] tr examiner

examiner [eg'zæmɪnər] s inspecteur m, vérificateur m; (in a school) examinateur m

example [eg'zæmpəl], [eg'zɑmpəl] s exemple m; **for example** par exemple

exasperate [eg'zæspə·ret] tr exaspérer

exasperation [egˌzæspə're∫ən] s exaspération f

excavate ['ekskə·vet] tr excaver

exceed [ek'sid] tr excéder

exceedingly [ek'sidɪŋli] adv extrêmement

excel [ek'sel] v (pret & pp -celled; ger -celling) tr surpasser || intr exceller; **to excel in** exceller dans; **to excel in** + ger exceller à + inf

excellence ['ekselens] s excellence f

excellen·cy ['ekselensi] s (pl -cies) excellence f; **Your Excellency** Votre Excellence

excelsior [ek'selsɪ·ər] s copeaux mpl d'emballage

except [ek'sept] adv—**except for** excepté; **except that** excepté que || prep excepté || tr excepter

exception [ek'sepʃən] s exception f; **to take exception to** trouver à redire à; **with the exception of** à l'exception de

exceptional [ek'sepʃənəl] adj exceptionnel

excerpt ['eksʌrpt], [ek'sʌrpt] s extrait m, citation f || [ek'sʌrpt] tr extraire

excess ['ekses], [ek'ses] adj excédentaire || [ek'ses] s (amount or degree) excédent m, excès m; (excessive amount; immoderate indulgence) excès m; **in excess of** en plus de

ex'cess bag'gage s excédent m de bagages

ex'cess fare' s supplément m

excessive [ek'sesɪv] adj excessif

ex'cess-prof'its tax' s contribution f sur les bénéfices extraordinaires

ex'cess weight' s excédent m de poids

exchange [eks'tʃendʒ] s échange m; (barter) troc m; (com) bourse f; (telp) central m || tr échanger; (to barter) troquer; **to exchange compliments** échanger des politesses; **to exchange for** échanger contre, échanger pour

exchequer [eks'tʃekər], ['ekstʃekər] s trésor m public; ministère m des finances; (hist) échiquier m

excise [ek'saɪz], ['eksaɪz] s contributions fpl indirectes || tr effacer, rayer; (surg) exciser

excitable [ek'saɪtəbəl] adj excitable

excite [ek'saɪt] tr exciter

excitement [ek'saɪtmənt] m agitation f, excitation f

exciting [ek'saɪtɪŋ] adj émotionnant, entraînant, passionnant

exclaim [eks'klem] tr s'écrier, e.g., **"All is lost!"** he exclaimed "Tout est perdu!" s'écria-t-il || intr s'exclamer, se récrier

exclamation [ˌeksklə'meʃən] s exclamation f

exclama'tion mark' s point m d'exclamation

exclude [eks'klud] tr exclure

excluding [eks'kludɪŋ] prep à l'exclusion de, sans compter

exclusion [eks'kluʒən] s exclusion f

exclusive [eks'klusɪv] adj exclusif; (expensive; fashionable) (coll) choisi, select; **exclusive of** à l'exclusion de

exclu'sive rights' spl exclusivité f

exclu'sive show'ing s (public sign in front of a theater) en exclusivité

excommunicate [ˌekskə'mjunɪˌket] tr excommunier

excommunication [ˌɛkskəˌmjunɪˈke-ʃən] s excommunication f

excoriate [ɛksˈkorɪˌet] tr (fig) vitupérer

excrement [ˈɛkskrəmənt] s excrément m

excruciating [ɛksˈkru/ɪˌetɪŋ] adj affreux, atroce

exculpate [ˈɛkskʌl.pet], [ɛksˈkʌlpet] tr disculper

excursion [ɛksˈkʌrʒən], [ɛksˈkʌr/ən] s excursion f

excusable [ɛksˈkjuzəbəl] adj excusable

excuse [ɛksˈkjus] s excuse f || [ɛksˈkjuz] tr excuser; **excuse me!** pardon!, je m'excuse!, **to excuse oneself** s'excuser

execrate [ˈɛksɪˌkret] tr exécrer; (to curse) maudire

execute [ˈɛksɪˌkjut] tr exécuter

execution [ˌɛksɪˈkju/ən] s exécution f

executioner [ˌɛksɪˈkju/ənər] s bourreau m

executive [ɛgˈzɛkjətɪv] adj (powers) exécutif; (position) administratif || s exécutif m; (of school, business, etc.) directeur m, administrateur m

Exec′utive Man′sion s (U.S.A.) demeure f du Président

executor [ɛgˈzɛkjətər] s exécuteur m testamentaire

executrix [ɛgˈzɛkjətrɪks] s exécutrice f testamentaire

exemplary [ɛgˈzɛmpləri], [ˈɛgzəm-ˌpleri] adj exemplaire

exempli·fy [ɛgˈzɛmplɪˌfaɪ] v (pret & pp -fied) tr démontrer par des exemples; (to be a model of) servir d'exemple à

exempt [ɛgˈzɛmpt] adj exempt || tr exempter

exemption [ɛgˈzɛmp/ən] s exemption f; **exemptions** (from taxes) déductions fpl

exercise [ˈɛksərˌsaɪz] s exercice m; **exercises** cérémonies fpl || tr exercer || intr s'exercer, s'entraîner

exert [ɛgˈzʌrt] tr exercer; **to exert oneself** faire des efforts

exertion [ɛgˈzʌr/ən] s effort m; (e.g., of power) exercice m

exhalation [ˌɛks·hə′le/ən] s (of air) expiration f; (of gas, vapors, etc.) exhalaison f

exhale [ɛksˈhel], [ɛgˈzel] tr (air from lungs) expirer; (gas, vapor) exhaler || intr expirer; s'exhaler

exhaust [ɛgˈzost] s échappement m; gaz mpl d'échappement || tr épuiser; faire le vide dans

exhaust′ fan′ s ventilateur m aspirant

exhaustion [ɛgˈzost/ən] s épuisement m

exhaustive [ɛgˈzostɪv] adj exhaustif

exhaust′ man′ifold s tuyauterie f or collecteur m d'échappement

exhaust′ pipe′ s tuyau m d'échappement

exhaust′ valve′ s soupape f d'échappement

exhibit [ɛgˈzɪbɪt] s exhibition f; (of art) exposition f; (law) document m à l'appui, pièce f à conviction || tr

exhiber; (e.g., pictures) exposer || intr faire une exposition

exhibition [ˌɛksɪˈbɪ/ən] s exhibition f

exhibitor [ɛgˈzɪbɪtər] s exposant m

exhilarate [ɛgˈzɪləˌret] tr égayer, animer

exhort [ɛgˈzort] tr exhorter

exhume [ɛksˈhjum], [ɛgˈzjum] tr exhumer

exigen·cy [ˈɛksɪdʒənsi] s (pl -cies) exigence f

exigent [ˈɛksɪdʒənt] adj exigeant

exile [ˈɛgzaɪl], [ˈɛksaɪl] s exil m; (person) exilé m || tr exiler

exist [ɛgˈzɪst] intr exister

existence [ɛgˈzɪstəns] s existence f

exit [ˈɛgzɪt], [ˈɛksɪt] s sortie f || intr sortir

exodus [ˈɛksədəs] s exode m

exonerate [ɛgˈzɑnəˌret] tr (to free from blame) disculper; (to free from an obligation) exonérer, dispenser

exorbitant [ɛgˈzorbɪtənt] adj exorbitant

exorcize [ˈɛksorˌsaɪz] tr exorciser

exotic [ɛgˈzɑtɪk] adj exotique

expand [ɛksˈpænd] tr (a gas, metal, etc.) dilater; (to enlarge, develop) élargir, développer; (to unfold, stretch out) étendre, déployer; (the chest) gonfler; (math) développer || intr se dilater; s'élargir, se développer; s'étendre, se déployer; se gonfler

expanse [ɛksˈpæns] s étendue f

expansion [ɛksˈpæn/ən] s expansion f

expan′sion joint′ s joint m de dilatation thermique

expansive [ɛksˈpænsɪv] adj expansif; (broad) large, étendu

expatiate [ɛksˈpe/ɪˌet] intr discourir, s'étendre

expatriate [ɛksˈpetrɪ·ɪt] adj & s expatrié m || [ɛksˈpetrɪˌet] tr expatrier

expect [ɛksˈpɛkt] tr (to await the coming of) attendre; (to look for as likely) s'attendre à; **to expect it** s'y attendre; **to expect s.o. to** + inf s'attendre à ce que qn + subj; **to expect to** + inf s'attendre à + inf

expectan·cy [ɛksˈpɛktənsi] s (pl -cies) attente f, expectative f

expect′ant moth′er [ɛksˈpɛktənt] s future mère f

expectation [ˌɛkspɛkˈte/ən] s expectative f, espérance f

expectorate [ɛksˈpɛktəˌret] tr & intr expectorer

expedien·cy [ɛksˈpidɪ·ənsi] s (pl -cies) convenance f, opportunité f; opportunisme m, débrouillage m

expedient [ɛksˈpidɪ·ənt] adj expédient; (looking out for oneself) débrouillard || s expédient m

expedite [ˈɛkspɪˌdaɪt] tr expédier

expedition [ˌɛkspɪˈdɪ/ən] s expédition f; célérité f, promptitude f

expeditionary [ˌɛkspɪˈdɪ/ənˌɛri] adj expéditionnaire

expeditious [ˌɛkspɪˈdɪ/əs] adj expéditif

ex·pel [ɛksˈpɛl] v (pret & pp -pelled; ger -pelling) tr expulser; (from school) renvoyer

expend [eks'pend] *tr* (*to pay out*) dépenser; (*to use up*) consommer

expendable [eks'pendəbəl] *adj* non récupérable; (*soldier*) sacrifiable

expenditure [eks'pendɪt/ər] *s* dépense *f*; consommation *f*

expense [eks'pens] *s* dépense *f*; **at the expense of** aux dépens de; **expenses** frais *mpl*; (*for which a person will be reimbursed*) indemnité *f*; **to meet expenses** faire face aux dépenses

expense' account' *s* état *m* de frais, note *f* de frais

expensive [eks'pensɪv] *adj* cher, couteux; (*tastes*) dispendieux

experience [eks'pɪrɪ·əns] *s* expérience *f* || *tr* éprouver

experienced *adj* expérimenté

experiment [eks'perɪmənt] *s* expérience *f* || [eks'perɪ‚ment] *intr* faire des expériences, expérimenter

expert ['ekspərt] *adj & s* expert *m*

expertise [‚ekspər'tiz] *s* maîtrise *f*

expiate ['ekspɪ‚et] *tr* expier

expire [eks'paɪr] *tr & intr* expirer

expired *adj* (*lease; passport*) expiré; (*note; permit*) périmé; (*e.g., driver's license*) suranné; (*insurance policy*) déchu

explain [eks'plen] *tr* expliquer; **to explain oneself** s'expliquer || *intr* expliquer

explainable [eks'plenəbəl] *adj* explicable

explanation [‚eksplə'ne/ən] *s* explication *f*

explanatory [eks'plænə‚tori] *adj* explicatif

explicit [eks'plɪsɪt] *adj* explicite

explode [eks'plod] *tr* faire sauter; (*a theory, opinion, etc.*) discréditer || *intr* exploser, éclater, sauter

exploit [eks'plɔɪt], ['eksplɔɪt] *s* exploit *m* || [eks'plɔɪt] *tr* exploiter

exploitation [‚eksplɔɪ'te/ən] *s* exploitation *f*

exploration [‚eksplə're/ən] *s* exploration *f*

explore [eks'plor] *tr* explorer

explorer [eks'plorər] *s* explorateur *m*; (*boy scout*) routier *m*

explosion [eks'ploʒən] *s* explosion *f*

explosive [eks'plosɪv] *adj* explosif; (*mixture*) explosible || *s* explosif *m*

exponent [eks'ponənt] *s* interprète *mf*; (*math*) exposant *m*

export ['eksport] *s* exportation *f* || [eks'port], ['eksport] *tr & intr* exporter

exportation [‚ekspor'te/ən] *s* exportation *f*

exporter ['eksportər], [eks'portər] *s* exportateur *m*

expose [eks'poz] *tr* exposer; (*to unmask*) démasquer, dévoiler; (*phot*) impressionner

exposé [‚ekspo'ze] *s* dévoilement *m*, révélation *f*, mise *f* en lumière

exposition [‚ekspə'zɪ/ən] *s* exposition *f*

expostulate [eks'past/ə‚let] *intr* faire des remontrances; **to expostulate with** faire des remontrances à

exposure [eks'poʒər] *s* exposition *f*; (*unmasking*) dévoilement *m*; (*phot*) exposition *f*; (*phot*) durée *f* d'exposition

expound [eks'paund] *tr* exposer

express [eks'pres] *adj* exprès, formel; (*train; gun*) express || *s* (*merchandise*) messagerie *f*; (*train*) express *m*, rapide *m*; **by express** (rr) en grande vitesse || *adv* (rr) en grande vitesse || *tr* exprimer; (*merchandise*) envoyer en grande vitesse; (*through the express company*) expédier par les messageries; **to express oneself** s'exprimer

express' com'pany *s* messageries *fpl*

express' high'way *s* autoroute *f*

expression [eks'pre/ən] *s* expression *f*

expressive [eks'presɪv] *adj* expressif

expressly [eks'presli] *adv* exprès

express'man *s* (*pl* -men) entrepreneur *m* de messageries; facteur *m*, agent *m* d'un service de messageries

express' train' *s* train *m* express

express'way' *s* autoroute *f*

expropriate [eks'propri‚et] *tr* exproprier

expulsion [eks'pʌl/ən] *s* expulsion *f*; (*from schools*) renvoi *m*

expunge [eks'pʌndʒ] *tr* effacer, supprimer, rayer

expurgate ['ekspər‚get] *tr* expurger

exquisite ['ekskwɪzɪt], [eks'kwɪzɪt] *adj* exquis

ex-service·man [‚eks'sʌrvɪs‚mæn] *s* (*pl* -men') ancien combattant *m*

extant ['ekstənt], [eks'tænt] *adj* existant, subsistant

extemporaneous [eks‚tempə'reni·əs] *adj* improvisé, impromptu

extemporaneously [eks‚tempə'reni·əsli] *adv* à l'impromptu, d'abondance

extempore [eks'tempəri] *adj* improvisé || *adv* d'abondance, à l'impromptu

extemporize [eks'tempə‚raɪz] *tr & intr* improviser

extend [eks'tend] *tr* étendre; (*a period of time; a street; a line*) prolonger; (*a treaty; a session; a right; a due date*) proroger; (*a helping hand*) tendre || *intr* s'étendre

extended *adj* étendu, prolongé

extension [eks'ten/ən] *s* extension *f*; prolongation *f*; (*board for a table*) rallonge *f*; (*to building*) annexe *f*; (*telp*) poste *m*

exten'sion cord' *s* cordon *m* prolongateur, prolongateur *m*

exten'sion lad'der *s* échelle *f* à coulisse

exten'sion ta'ble *s* table *f* à rallonges

extensive [eks'tensɪv] *adj* vaste, étendu

extent [eks'tent] *s* étendue *f*; **to a certain extent** dans une certaine mesure; **to a great extent** en grande partie, considérablement; **to the full extent** dans toute la mesure

extenuate [eks'tenju‚et] *tr* atténuer; minimiser

exterior [eks'tɪrɪ·ər] *adj & s* extérieur *m*

exterminate [eks'tʌrmɪ‚net] *tr* exterminer

external [eks'tʌrnəl] *adj* extérieur; (pharm, med) externe || **externals** *spl* dehors *mpl*, apparences *fpl*; (*superficialities*) choses *fpl* secondaires

extinct [eks'tɪŋkt] *adj* (*volcano*) éteint; disparu; tombé en désuétude

extinction [eks'tɪŋk/ən] *s* extinction *f*

extinguish [eks'tɪŋgwɪ/] *tr* éteindre

extinguisher [eks'tɪŋgwɪ/ər] *s* (*for candles*) éteignoir *m*; (*for fires*) extincteur *m*

extirpate ['ekstər‚pet], [eks'tʌrpet] *tr* extirper

ex•tol [eks'tol], [eks'tal] *v* (*pret & pp* -tolled; *ger* -tolling) *tr* exalter, vanter

extort [eks'tort] *tr* extorquer

extortion [eks'tor/ən] *s* extorsion *f*

extortionist [eks'tor/ənɪst] *s* extorqueur *m*

extra ['ekstrə] *adj* supplémentaire; (*of high quality*) extra, extra-fin; (*spare*) de rechange || *s* extra *m*; (*of a newspaper*) édition *f* spéciale; (mov, theat) figurant *m* || *adv* en plus, en sus; (*not on the bill*) non compris

ex'tra board' *s* (*for extension table*) rallonge *f*

ex'tra charge' *s* supplément *m*

extract ['ekstrækt] *s* extrait *m* || [eks'trækt] *tr* extraire

extraction [eks'træk/ən] *s* extraction *f*

extracurricular [‚ekstrəkə'rɪkjələr] *adj* extra-scolaire

extradite ['ekstrə‚daɪt] *tr* extrader

extradition [‚ekstrə'dɪ/ən] *s* extradition *f*

ex'tra-dry' *adj* (*champagne*) très sec

ex'tra fare' *s* supplément *m* de billet

extramural [‚ekstrə'mjurəl] *adj* à l'extérieur de la ville; à l'extérieur de l'université

extraneous [eks'treni‐əs] *adj* étranger

extraordinary [eks'trordɪ‚neri], [‚ekstrə'ordɪ‚neri] *adj* extraordinaire

extrapolate [eks'træpə‚let] *tr & intr* extrapoler

extrasensory [‚ekstrə'sensəri] *adj* extrasensoriel

ex'tra-spe'cial *adj* extra

extravagance [eks'trævəgəns] *s* (*lavishness*) prodigalité *f*, gaspillage *m*; (*folly*) extravagance *f*

extravagant [eks'trævəgənt] *adj* (*person*) dépensier, prodigue; (*price*) exorbitant; (*e.g., praise*) outré; (*e.g., claims*) exagéré, extravagant

extreme [eks'trim] *adj & s* extrême *m*; **in the extreme, to extremes** à l'extrême

extremely [eks'trimli] *adv* extrêmement

extreme' unc'tion *s* extrême-onction *f*

extremist [eks'trimɪst] *adj & s* extrémiste *mf*

extremi•ty [eks'tremɪti] *s* (*pl* -ties) extrémité *f*; **extremities** extrémités

extricate ['ekstrɪ‚ket] *tr* dégager; (*a gas*) libérer; **to extricate oneself from** se tirer de, se dépêtrer de

extrinsic [eks'trɪnsɪk] *adj* extrinsèque

èxtrovert ['ekstrə‚vʌrt] *adj & s* extraverti *m*

extrude [eks'trud] *intr* faire saillie, dépasser

exuberant [eg'z(j)ubərənt] *adj* exubérant

exude [eg'zud], [ek'sud] *tr & intr* exsuder

exult [eg'zʌlt] *intr* exulter

exultant [eg'zʌltənt] *adj* triomphant

eye [aɪ] *s* œil *m*; (*of needle*) chas *m*, trou *m*; (*of optical instrument*) oculaire *m*; **to catch s.o.'s eye** tirer l'œil à qn; **to lay eyes on** jeter les yeux sur; **to make eyes at** (coll) faire les yeux doux à; **to see eye to eye with s.o.** voir les choses du même œil que qn; **with an eye to** en vue de; **without batting an eye** (coll) sans sourciller || *v* (*pret & pp* eyed; *ger* eying or eyeing) *tr* toiser, reluquer

eye'ball' *s* globe *m* oculaire

eye' bank' *s* banque *f* des yeux

eye'bolt' *s* boulon *m* à œil

eye'brow' *s* sourcil *m*

eye'cup' *s* œillère *f*

eye' drops' *spl* collyre *m*

eyeful ['aɪful] *s* vue *f*, coup *m* d'œil; **to get an eyeful** (coll) s'en mettre plein la vue, se rincer l'œil

eye'glass' *s* (*of optical instrument*) oculaire *m*; (*eyecup*) œillère *f*; **eyeglasses** lunettes *fpl*

eye'lash' *s* cil *m*; (*fringe of hair*) cils

eyelet ['aɪlɪt] *s* œillet *m*; (*of sail*) œil *m* de pie

eye'lid' *s* paupière *f*

eye' of the morn'ing *s* astre *m* du jour

eye' o'pener ['opənər] *s* révélation *f*; (coll) goutte *f* de bonne heure

eye'piece' *s* oculaire *m*

eye'shade' *s* visière *f*, abat-jour *m*

eye'shad'ow *s* fard *m* à paupière

eye'shot' *s* portée *f* de la vue

eye'sight' *s* vue *f*; (*eyeshot*) portée *f* de la vue

eye' sock'et *s* orbite *f* de l'œil

eye'sore' *s* objet *m* déplaisant

eye'strain' *s* fatigue *f* des yeux; **to suffer from eyestrain** avoir les yeux fatigués

eye'-test chart' *s* tableau *m* de lecture pour la vision

eye'tooth' *s* (*pl* -teeth) dent *f* œillère or canine; **to cut one's eyeteeth** (coll) ne pas être un blanc-bec; **to give one's eyeteeth for** (coll) donner la prunelle de ses yeux pour

eye'wash' *s* collyre *m*; (slang) de l'eau bénite de cour, de la poudre aux yeux

eye'wit'ness *s* témoin *m* oculaire

ey•rie or ey•ry ['eri] *s* (*pl* -ries) aire *f* (de l'aigle); (fig) nid *m* d'aigle

F

F, f [ef] *s* VI⁰ lettre de l'alphabet
fable ['febəl] *s* fable *f*
fabric ['fæbrɪk] *s* tissu *m*, étoffe *f*
fabricate ['fæbrɪ,ket] *tr* fabriquer
fabrication [,fæbrɪ'keʃən] *s* fabrication *f*; (*lie*) mensonge *m*
fabulous ['fæbjələs] *adj* fabuleux
façade [fə'sad] *s* façade *f*
face [fes] *s* visage *m*, figure *f*; (*side*) face *f*; (*of the earth*) surface *f*; (*appearance, expression*) mine *f*, physionomie *f*; **about face!** (mil) demitour! **to keep a straight face** montrer un front sérieux; **to lose face** perdre la face; **to make a face** faire une grimace; **to set one's face against** faire front à || *tr* faire face à; (*a wall*) revêtir; (*a garment*) mettre un revers à || *intr—to face about* faire demi-tour; **to face up to** faire face à, affronter
face′ card′ *s* figure *f*
face′ lift′ing *s* ridectomie *f*
face′ pow′der *s* poudre *f* de riz
facet ['fæsɪt] *s* facette *f*
facetious [fə'siʃəs] *adj* plaisant
face′ tow′el *s* serviette *f* de toilette
face′ val′ue *s* valeur *f* faciale, valeur nominale
facial ['feʃəl] *adj* facial || *s* massage *m* esthétique
fa′cial tis′sue *s* serviette *f* à démaquiller
facilitate [fə'sɪlɪ,tet] *tr* faciliter
facili-ty [fə'sɪlɪti] *s* (*pl* -ties) facilité *f*; **facilities** installations *fpl*
facing ['fesɪŋ] *s* revêtement *m*; (*of garment*) revers *m*
facsimile [fæk'sɪmɪlɪ] *s* fac-similé *m*
fact [fækt] *s* fait *m*; **in fact** en fait, de fait; **the fact is that** c'est que
faction ['fækʃən] *s* faction *f*
factor ['fæktər] *s* facteur *m* || *tr* résoudre ou décomposer en facteurs
facto-ry ['fæktəri] *s* (*pl* -ries) usine *f*, fabrique *f*
fac′tory price′ *s* prix *m* de facture
factual ['fæktʃʊ-əl] *adj* vrai, réel
facul-ty ['fækəltɪ] *s* (*pl* -ties) faculté *f*; (*teaching staff*) corps *m* enseignant
fad [fæd] *s* mode *f*, marotte *f*; **latest fad** dernier cri *m*
fade [fed] *tr* déteindre, décolorer || *intr* déteindre, se décolorer; (*to lose vigor, freshness*) se faner; **to fade in** apparaître graduellement; **to fade out** disparaître graduellement
fade′-in′ *s* (mov) apparition *f* en fondu
fade′-out′ *s* (mov) fondu *m*
fag [fæg] *s* (slang) cibiche *f* || *v* (*pret & pp* **fagged**; *ger* **fagging**) *tr*—**to fag out** éreinter
fagot ['fægət] *s* fagot *m*; (*for filling up trenches*) fascine *f* || *tr* fagoter
fail [fel] *s*—**without fail** sans faute || *tr* manquer à; (*a student*) refuser; (*an examination*) échouer à or dans

|| *intr* manquer, faire défaut; (*to not succeed*) échouer, rater; (*said of motor*) tomber en panne; (*to weaken*) baisser, faiblir; **to fail in** faillir à; **to fail to** manquer de, faillir à; **to fail to do or to keep** faillir à
failing ['felɪŋ] *adj* défaillant || *s* défaut *m* || *prep* à défaut de
failure ['feljər] *s* insuccès *m*, échec *m*; (*lack*) manque *m*, défaut *m*; (*person*) raté *m*; (com) faillite *f*
faint [fent] *adj* faible; **to feel faint** se sentir mal || *s* évanouissement *m* || *intr* s'évanouir
faint′-heart′ed *adj* timide, peureux
fair [fɛr] *adj* juste, équitable; (*honest*) loyal, honnête; (*average*) moyen, passable; (*clear*) clair; (*beautiful*) beau; (*pleasing*) agréable, plaisant; (*of hair*) blond; (*complexion*) blanc; **to be fair** (*to be just*) être de bonne guerre || *s* foire *f*, fête *f*; (*bazaar*) kermesse *f* || *adv* impartialement; **to bid fair to** avoir des chances de; **to play fair** jouer franc jeu
fair′ cop′y *s* copie *f* au net
fair′ground′ *s* champ *m* de foire
fairly ['ferlɪ] *adv* impartialement, loyalement; assez
fair′-mind′ed *adj* impartial
fairness ['fernɪs] *s* impartialité *f*, justice *f*; (*of complexion*) clarté *f*
fair′ play′ *s* franc jeu *m*
fair′ sex′ *s* beau sexe *m*
fair′way′ *s* (golf) parcours *m* normal; (naut) chenal *m*
fair′-weath′er *adj* (e.g., *friend*) des beaux jours
fair-y ['ferɪ] *adj* féerique || *s* (*pl* -ies) fée *f*; (*homosexual*) (coll) tante *f*
fair′y god′mother *s* marraine *f* fée; (coll) marraine gâteau
fair′y-land′ *s* royaume *m* des fées
fair′y tale′ *s* conte *m* de fées
faith [feθ] *s* foi *f*; **to break faith with** manquer de foi à; **to keep faith with** tenir ses engagements envers; **to pin one's faith on** mettre tout son espoir en
faithful ['feθfəl] *adj* fidèle || *s*—**the faithful** les fidèles *mpl*
faithless ['feθlɪs] *adj* infidèle
fake [fek] *adj* (coll) faux || *s* faux *m*, article *m* truqué || *tr* truquer
faker ['fekər] *s* truqueur *m*
falcon ['fɔkən], ['fɔlkən] *s* faucon *m*
falconer ['fɔkənər], ['fɔlkənər] *s* fauconnier *m*
fall [fɔl] *adj* automnal || *s* chute *f*; (*of prices*) baisse *f*; (*season*) automne *m & f*; **falls** chute d'eau || *v* (*pret* **fell** [fel]; *pp* **fallen** ['fɔlən]) *intr* tomber; (*said of prices*) baisser; **fall in!** (mil) rassemblement!; **fall out!** (mil) rompez les rangs!; **to fall down** (*said of person*) tomber par terre; (*said of building*) s'écrouler; **to fall for** (coll)

se laisser prendre à; *(to fall in love with)* (coll) tomber amoureux de; **to fall in** s'effondrer; (mil) former des rangs; **to fall into the trap** donner dans le piège; **to fall off** tomber de; *(to decline)* baisser, diminuer; **to fall out** *(to disagree)* se brouiller; **to fall over oneself** to (coll) se mettre en quatre pour

fallacious [fə'leʃəs] *adj* fallacieux

falla·cy ['fæləsi] *s (pl* **-cies)** erreur *f*, fausseté *f*

fall' guy' *s* (slang) tête *f* de Turc

fallible ['fælɪbəl] *adj* faillible

fall'ing star' *s* étoile *f* filante

fall'out' *s* pluies *fpl* radioactives, retombées *fpl* radioactives

fall'out shel'ter *s* abri *m* antiatomique

fallow ['fælo] *adj* en friche, en jachère || *s* friche *f*, jachère *f* || *tr* laisser en friche ou en jachère

false [fɔls] *adj* faux; artificiel, simulé; *(hair)* postiche || *adv* faussement; **to play false** tromper

false' alarm' *s* fausse alerte *f*

false' bot'tom *s* double fond *m*

false' cog'nate *s* faux ami *m*

false' eye'lashes *spl* cils *mpl* postiches

false' face' *s* masque *m*

false'-heart'ed *adj* perfide, traître

false'hood *s* mensonge *m*

false' pretens'es *spl* faux-semblants *mpl*

false' return' *s* fausse déclaration *f* d'impôts

false' step' *s* faux-pas *m*

false' teeth' ['tiθ] *spl* fausses dents *fpl*

falset·to [fɔl'seto] *s (pl* **-tos)** fausset *m*, voix *f* de tête; *(person)* fausset *m*

falsi·fy ['fɔlsɪˌfaɪ] *v (pret & pp* **-fied)** *tr* falsifier, fausser

falsi·ty ['fɔlsɪti] *s (pl* **-ties)** fausseté *f*

falter ['fɔltər] *s* vacillation *f*, hésitation *f*; *(of speech)* balbutiement *m* || *intr* vaciller, hésiter; balbutier

fame [fem] *s* renom *m*, renommée *f*

famed *adj* renommé, célèbre

familiar [fə'mɪljər] *adj & s* familier *m*; **to become familiar with** se familiariser avec

familiari·ty [fəˌmɪlɪ'ærɪti] *s (pl* **-ties)** familiarité *f*

familiarize [fə'mɪljəˌraɪz] *tr* familiariser

fami·ly ['fæmɪli] *adj* familial; **in a or the family way** (coll) dans une position intéressante; (coll) en famille (Canad) || *s (pl* **-lies)** famille *f*

fam'ily man' *s (pl* **men')** père *m* de famille; *(stay-at-home)* homme *m* casanier, pantouflard *m*

fam'ily name' *s* nom *m* de famille

fam'ily physi'cian *s* médecin *m* de famille

fam'ily tree' *s* arbre *m* généalogique

famine ['fæmɪn] *s* famine *f*

famish ['fæmɪʃ] *tr* affamer, priver de vivres || *intr* souffrir de la faim

famished *adj* affamé, famélique; **to be famished** (coll) mourir de faim

famous ['feməs] *adj* renommé, célèbre

fan [fæn] *s* éventail *m*; (mach) ventilateur *m*; (coll) fanatique *mf*, enragé *m* || *v (pret & pp* **fanned**; *ger* **fanning)** *tr* éventer; *(to winnow)* vanner; *(e.g., passions)* exciter || *intr*—**to fan out** se déployer en éventail

fanatic [fə'nætɪk] *adj & s* fanatique *mf*

fanatical [fə'nætɪkəl] *adj* fanatique

fanaticism [fə'nætɪˌsɪzəm] *s* fanatisme *m*

fan' belt' *s* (aut) courroie *f* de ventilateur

fancied *adj* imaginaire, supposé

fanciful ['fænsɪfəl] *adj* fantaisiste, capricieux

fan·cy ['fænsi] *adj (comp* **-cier;** *super* **-ciest)** ornemental; *(goods, clothes, bread)* de fantaisie; *(high-quaity)* fin, extra, de luxe || *s (pl* **-cies)** fantaisie *f*, caprice *m*; **to take a fancy to** prendre du goût pour; *(a loved one)* prendre en affection || *v (pret & pp* **-cied)** *tr* s'imaginer, se figurer; **to fancy oneself** s'imaginer; **to fancy that** imaginer que

fan'cy dress' *s* costume *m* de fantaisie, travesti *m*

fan'cy dress' ball' *s* bal *m* costumé, bal travesti

fan'cy foods' *spl* comestibles *mpl* de fantaisie

fan'cy-free' *adj* libre, gai, sans amour

fan'cy jew'elry *s* bijouterie *f* de fantaisie

fan'cy skat'ing *s* patinage *m* de fantaisie

fan'cy-work' *s* broderie *f*, ouvrage *m* d'agrément

fanfare ['fænfer] *s* fanfare *f*

fang [fæŋ] *s* croc *m*; *(of snake)* crochet *m*

fantastic(al) [fæn'tæstɪk(əl)] *adj* fantastique

fanta·sy ['fæntəzi], ['fæntəsi] *s (pl* **-sies)** fantaisie *f*

far [fɑr] *adj* lointain; **on the far side of** à l'autre côté de || *adv* loin; **as far as** autant que; *(up to)* jusqu'à; **as far as I am concerned** quant à moi; **as far as I know** pour autant que je sache; **by far** de beaucoup; **far and wide** partout; **far away** au loin; **far from** loin de; **far from it** tant s'en faut; **far into the night** fort avant dans la nuit; **far into the woods** avant dans le bois; **far off** au loin; **how far?** jusqu'où?; **how far is it from . . . ?** combien y a-t-il de . . . ?; **in so far as** dans la mesure où; **so far or thus far** jusqu'ici; **to go far to** contribuer pour beaucoup à

far'away' *adj* éloigné, distant

farce [fɑrs] *s* farce *f*

farcical ['fɑrsɪkəl] *adj* grotesque, ridicule

fare [fer] *s* prix *m*, tarif *m*; *(cost of taxi)* course *f*; *(passenger in taxi)* client *m*; *(passenger in bus)* voyageur *m*; *(culin)* chère *f*, ordinaire *m*; **fares, please!** vos places, s'il vous plaît! || *intr* se porter; **how did you fare?** comment ça s'est-il passé?

Far' East' *s* Extrême-Orient *m*

fare′well′ s adieu m; **to bid s.o. fare-well** dire adieu à qn

far′-fetched′ adj tiré par les cheveux

far-flung [ˈfɑrˈflʌŋ] adj étendu, vaste, d'une grande envergure

farm [fɑrm] s ferme f; (sharecropper's farm) métairie f ‖ tr cultiver, exploiter; **to farm out** donner à ferme; (work) donner en exploitation à l'extérieur ‖ intr faire de la culture

farmer [ˈfɑrmər] s fermier m

farm′ hand′ s valet m de ferme

farm′house′ s ferme f, maison f de ferme

farming [ˈfɑrmɪŋ] s agriculture f, exploitation f agricole

farm′yard′ s cour f de ferme

Far′ North′ s Grand Nord m

far′-off′ adj lointain, éloigné

far′-reach′ing adj à longue portée

far′sight′ed adj prévoyant; (physiol) presbyte

farther [ˈfɑrðər] adj plus éloigné ‖ adv plus loin

farthest [ˈfɑrðɪst] adj (le) plus éloigné ‖ adv le plus loin; au plus

farthing [ˈfɑrðɪŋ] s liard m

fascinate [ˈfæsɪˌnet] tr fasciner

fascinating [ˈfæsɪˌnetɪŋ] adj fascinateur, fascinant

fascism [ˈfæʃɪzəm] s fascisme m

fascist [ˈfæʃɪst] adj & s fasciste mf

fashion [ˈfæʃən] s mode f, vogue f; (manner) façon f, manière f; **after a fashion** tant bien que mal; **in fashion** à la mode, en vogue; **out of fashion** démodé ‖ tr façonner

fashionable [ˈfæʃənəbəl] adj à la mode, élégant, chic

fash′ion design′ing s haute couture f

fash′ion plate′ s gravure f de mode; (person) (coll) élégant m

fash′ion show′ s présentation f de collection

fast [fæst], [fɑst] adj rapide; (fixed) solide, fixe; (clock) en avance; (friend) fidèle; (color) grand, bon, e.g., **fast color** grand teint, bon teint; (person) (slang) dévergondé; **to make fast** fixer, fermer ‖ s jeûne m; **to break one's fast** rompre le jeûne ‖ adv vite, rapidement; (firmly) solidement, ferme; (asleep) profondément; **to hold fast** tenir bon; **to live fast** (coll) faire la noce, mener la vie à grandes guides; **to stand fast against** tenir tête à ‖ intr jeûner

fast′ day′ s jour m de jeûne, jour maigre

fasten [ˈfæsən], [ˈfɑsən] tr attacher, fixer; (e.g., a belt) ajuster ‖ intr s'attacher, se fixer

fastener [ˈfæsənər], [ˈfɑsənər] s attache f, agrafe f

fastidious [fæsˈtɪdɪ·əs] adj délicat, dégoûté, difficile

fasting [ˈfæstɪŋ], [ˈfɑstɪŋ] s jeûne m

fat [fæt] adj (comp **fatter**; super **fattest**) (plump; greasy) gras; (large) gros; (soil) riche; (spark) nourri; **to get fat** engraisser ‖ s graisse f; (of meat) gras m

fatal [ˈfetəl] adj fatal

fatalism [ˈfetəˌlɪzəm] s fatalisme m

fatalist [ˈfetəlɪst] s fataliste mf

fatali·ty [fəˈtælɪti] s (pl -ties) fatalité f; (in accidents, war, etc.) mort f, accident m mortel

fate [fet] s sort m, destin m; **the Fates** les Parques fpl

fated adj destiné, voué

fateful [ˈfetfəl] adj fatal; (prophetic) fatidique

fat′head′ s (coll) crétin m, sot m

father [ˈfɑðər] s père m; **Father** (salutation given a priest) Monsieur l'abbé ‖ tr servir de père à; (to beget) engendrer; (an idea, project) inventer

fa′ther-hood′ s paternité f

fa′ther-in-law′ s (pl **fathers-in-law**) beau-père m

fa′ther-land′ s patrie f

fatherless [ˈfɑðərlɪs] adj sans père, orphelin de père

fatherly [ˈfɑðərli] adj paternel

Fa′ther Time′ s le Temps

fathom [ˈfæðəm] s brasse f ‖ tr sonder

fathomless [ˈfæðəmlɪs] adj insondable

fatigue [fəˈtig] s fatigue f; **fatigues** (mil) bleus mpl

fatigue′ clothes′ spl tenue f de corvée

fatigue′ du′ty s (mil) corvée f

fatten [ˈfætən] tr & intr engraisser

fat·ty [ˈfæti] adj (comp **-tier**; super **-tiest**) gras, graisseux; (tissue) adipeux; (chubby) (coll) potelé, dodu ‖ s (pl **-ties**) (coll) boule m de gras

fatuous [ˈfætʃʊ·əs] adj sot, idiot

faucet [ˈfɔsɪt] s robinet m

fault [fɔlt] s faute f; (geol) faille f; **to a fault** à l'excès; **to find fault with** trouver à redire à

fault′find′er s critiqueur m, éplucheur m

fault′find′ing adj chicaneur ‖ s chicanerie f, critique f

faultless [ˈfɔltlɪs] adj sans défaut

fault·y [ˈfɔlti] adj (comp **-ier**; super **-iest**) fautif, défectueux

faun [fɔn] s faune m

fauna [ˈfɔnə] s faune f

favor [ˈfevər] s faveur f; **do me the favor to** faites-moi le plaisir de; **to be in favor of** être partisan de; **to be in favor with** jouir de la faveur de; **to decide in s.o.'s favor** donner gain de cause à qn ‖ tr favoriser; (to look like) (coll) tenir de; (e.g., a sore leg) (coll) ménager

favorable [ˈfevərəbəl] adj favorable

favorite [ˈfevərɪt] adj & s favori m

fawn [fɔn] adj (color) fauve ‖ s faon m ‖ intr—**to fawn upon** (said of dog) faire des caresses à; (said of person) faire le chien couchant auprès de

faze [fez] tr (coll) affecter, troubler

FBI [ˌɛfˌbiˈaɪ] s (letterword) (**Federal Bureau of Investigation**) Sûreté f nationale, Sûreté (the French equivalent)

fear [fɪr] s crainte f, peur f ‖ tr craindre, avoir peur de ‖ intr craindre, avoir peur

fearful [ˈfɪrfəl] adj (frightened) peureux, effrayé; (*frightful*) effrayant; (coll) énorme, effrayant

fearless ['fɪrlɪs] *adj* sans peur

feasible ['fizɪbəl] *adj* faisable

feast [fist] *s* festin *m*, régal *m* || *tr* régaler || *intr* faire bonne chère; **to feast on** se régaler de

feast' day' *s* fête *f*, jour *m* de fête

feat [fit] *s* exploit *m*, haut fait *m*

feather ['fɛðər] *s* plume *f*; **feather in one's cap** (coll) fleuron *m* à sa couronne; **in fine feather** (coll) plein d'entrain || *tr* emplumer; (*an oar*) ramener à plat; **to feather one's nest** (coll) faire son beurre

feath'er•bed' *s* lit *m* de plumes, couette *f*

feath'er•bed'ding *s* emploi *m* de plus d'ouvriers qu'il n'en faut

feath'er•brained' *adj* braque, étourdi

feath'er dust'er *s* plumeau *m*

feath'er•edge' *s* (*of board*) biseau *m*; (*of tool*) morfil *m*

feath'er•weight' *s* poids-plume *m*

feathery ['fɛðəri] *adj* plumeux

feature ['fitʃər] *s* trait *m*, caractéristique *f*; (mov) long métrage *m*, grand film *m* || *tr* caractériser; offrir comme attraction principale

fea'ture writ'er *s* rédacteur *m*

February ['fɛbru,ɛri] *s* février *m*

feces ['fisiz] *spl* fèces *fpl*

feckless ['fɛklɪs] *adj* veule, faible

federal ['fɛdərəl] *adj* & *s* fédéral *m*

federate ['fɛdə,ret] *adj* fédéré || *tr* fédérer || *intr* se fédérer

federation [,fɛdə'reʃən] *s* fédération *f*

fedora [fɪ'dɔrə] *s* chapeau *m* mou

fed' up' [fɛd] *adj*—**to be fed up** (coll) en avoir marre; **to be fed up with** (coll) avoir plein le dos de

fee [fi] *s* honoraires *mpl*, cachet *m*; **for a nominal fee** pour une somme symbolique

feeble ['fibəl] *adj* faible

fee'ble-mind'ed *adj* imbécile; obtus, à l'esprit lourd

feed [fid] *s* nourriture *f*, pâture *f*; (mach) alimentation *f*; (slang) grand repas *m* || *v* (*pret & pp* fed [fɛd]) *tr* nourrir, donner à manger à; (*a machine*) alimenter || *intr* manger; **to feed upon** se nourrir de

feed'back' *s* réalimentation *f*, régénération *f*, contre-réaction *f*

feed' bag' *s* musette-mangeoire *f*; **to put on the feed bag** (slang) casser la croûte

feeder ['fidər] *s* alimenteur *m*; (elec) canal *m* d'amenée

feed' pump' *s* pompe *f* d'alimentation

feed' trough' *s* mangeoire *f*, auge *f*

feed' wire' *s* (elec) fil *m* d'amenée

feel [fil] *s* sensation *f* || *v* (*pret & pp* felt [fɛlt]) *tr* sentir, éprouver; (*the pulse*) tâter; (*to examine*) palper; **to feel one's way** avancer à tâtons || *intr* (*sick, tired, etc.*) se sentir; **to feel for** tâtonner, chercher à tâtons; (*to sympathize with*) (coll) être plein de pitié pour; **to feel like** avoir envie de

feeler ['filər] *s* (ent) antenne *f*; **to put out a feeler** (coll) tâter le terrain

feeling ['filɪŋ] *s* (*with senses*) toucher *m*, tact *m*; (*with hands*) tâtage *m*; (*impression, emotion*) sentiment *m*; **feelings** sensibilité *f*

feign [fen] *tr & intr* feindre

feint [fent] *s* feinte *f* || *intr* feinter

feldspar ['fɛld,spar] *s* feldspath *m*

felicitate [fə'lɪsɪ,tet] *tr* féliciter

felicitous [fə'lɪsɪtəs] *adj* heureux, à propos

fell [fɛl] *adj* cruel, féroce || *tr* abattre

felloe ['fɛlo] *s* jante *f*

fellow ['fɛlo] *s* (*of a society*) membre *m*; (*holder of a fellowship*) boursier *m*; (*friend, neighbor, etc.*) homme *m*, compagnon *m*; (coll) type *m*, bonhomme *m*, gars *m*; **poor fellow!** (coll) pauvre garçon!

fel'low cit'izen *s* concitoyen *m*

fel'low coun'tryman *s* compatriote *mf*

fel'low crea'ture *s* semblable *mf*

fel'low•man' *s* (*pl* **-men'**) semblable *m*, prochain *m*

fel'low mem'ber *s* confrère *m*

fel'low•ship' *s* camaraderie *f*; (*scholarship*) bourse *f*; (*organization*) association *f*

fel'low stu'dent *s* condisciple *m*

fel'low trav'eler *s* compagnon *m* de voyage; (pol) compagnon de route

felon ['fɛlən] *s* criminel *m*; (pathol) panaris *m*

felo•ny ['fɛləni] *s* (*pl* **-nies**) crime *m*

felt [fɛlt] *s* feutre *m* || *tr* feutrer

female ['fimel] *adj* (sex) féminin; (*animal, plant, piece of a device*) femelle || *s* (*person*) femme *f*; (*plant, animal*) femelle *f*

feminine ['fɛmɪnɪn] *adj* & *s* féminin *m*

feminism ['fɛmɪ,nɪzəm] *s* féminisme *m*

fen [fɛn] *s* marécage *m*

fence [fɛns] *s* barrière *f*, clôture *f*; palissade *f*; (*for stolen goods*) receleur *m*; **on the fence** (coll) indécis, en balance || *tr* clôturer || *intr* faire de l'escrime

fencing ['fɛnsɪŋ] *s* (*enclosure*) clôture *f*; (sports) escrime *f*

fenc'ing acad'emy *s* salle *f* d'armes

fenc'ing mas'ter *s* maître *m* d'armes

fenc'ing match' *s* assaut *m* d'armes

fend [fɛnd] *tr*—**to fend off** parer || *intr*—**to fend for oneself** (coll) se débrouiller, se tirer d'affaire

fender ['fɛndər] *s* (*mudguard*) aile *f*, garde-boue *m*; (*of locomotive*) chasse-pierres *m*; (*of fireplace*) garde-feu *m*

fennel ['fɛnəl] *s* fenouil *m*

ferment ['fʌrmɛnt] *s* ferment *m* || [fər'mɛnt] *tr* faire fermenter; (*wine*) cuver || *intr* fermenter

fern [fʌrn] *s* fougère *f*

ferocious [fə'roʃəs] *adj* féroce

feroci•ty [fə'rasɪti] *s* (*pl* **-ties**) férocité *f*

ferret ['fɛrɪt] *s* furet *m* || *tr*—**to ferret out** dénicher || *intr* fureter

Fer'ris wheel' ['fɛrɪs] *s* grande roue *f*

fer•ry ['fɛri] *s* (*pl* **-ries**) bac *m*; (*to transport trains*) ferry-boat *m* || *v* (*pret* & *pp* **-ried**) *tr* & *intr* passer en bac

fer′ry-boat′ *s* bac *m*; (*to transport trains*) ferry-boat *m*

fer′ry-man *s* (*pl* **-men**) passeur *m*

fertile [ˈfʌrtɪl] *adj* fertile, fécond

fertilize [ˈfʌrtɪˌlaɪz] *tr* fertiliser; (*to impregnate*) féconder

fertilizer [ˈfʌrtɪˌlaɪzər] *s* engrais *m*, amendement *m*; (*bot*) fécondateur *m*

fervent [ˈfʌrvənt] *adj* fervent

fervid [ˈfʌrvɪd] *adj* fervent

fervor [ˈfʌrvər] *s* ferveur *f*

fester [ˈfɛstər] *s* ulcère *m* ‖ *tr* ulcérer ‖ *intr* s'ulcérer

festival [ˈfɛstɪvəl] *adj* de fête ‖ *s* fête *f*; (*mov, mus*) festival *m*

festive [ˈfɛstɪv] *adj* de fête, gai

festivi•ty [fɛsˈtɪvɪti] *s* (*pl* **-ties**) festivité *f*

festoon [fɛsˈtun] *s* feston *m* ‖ *tr* festonner

fetch [fɛtʃ] *tr* aller chercher; (*a certain price*) se vendre à

fetching [ˈfɛtʃɪŋ] *adj* (*coll*) séduisant

fete [fet] *s* fête *f* ‖ *tr* fêter

fetish [ˈfɛtɪʃ], [ˈfitɪʃ] *s* fétiche *m*

fetlock [ˈfɛtlɑk] *s* boulet *m*; (*tuft of hair*) fanon *m*

fetter [ˈfɛtər] *s* lien *m*; **fetters** fers *mpl*, chaînes *fpl* ‖ *tr* enchaîner, entraver

fettle [ˈfɛtəl] *s* condition *f*, état *m*; **in fine fettle** en pleine forme

fetus [ˈfitəs] *s* fœtus *m*

feud [fjud] *s* querelle *f*, vendetta *f* ‖ *intr* quereller, être à couteaux tirés

feudal [ˈfjudəl] *adj* féodal

feudalism [ˈfjudəˌlɪzəm] *s* féodalisme *m*

fever [ˈfivər] *s* fièvre *f*

fe′ver blis/ter *s* bouton *m* de fièvre

feverish [ˈfivərɪʃ] *adj* fiévreux

few [fju] *adj* peu de; **a few** . . . quelques . . . ; **quite a few** pas mal de; **the few** . . . les rares . . . ‖ *pron indef* peu; **a few** quelques-uns §81; **quite a few** beaucoup

fiancé [ˌfi·ɑnˈse] *s* fiancé *m*

fiancée [ˌfi·ɑnˈse] *s* fiancée *f*

fias•co [fiˈæsko] *s* (*pl* **-cos** or **-coes**) fiasco *m*, échec *m*

fiat [ˈfaɪ·ət], [ˈfaɪ·æt] *s* ordonnance *f*, autorisation *f*

fib [fɪb] *s* (*coll*) petit mensonge *m*, blague *f* ‖ *v* (*pret* & *pp* **fibbed**; *ger* **fibbing**) *intr* (*coll*) blaguer

fiber [ˈfaɪbər] *s* fibre *f*

fibrous [ˈfaɪbrəs] *adj* fibreux

fickle [ˈfɪkəl] *adj* inconstant, volage

fiction [ˈfɪkʃən] *s* fiction *f*; (*branch of literature*) ouvrages *mpl* d'imagination, romans *mpl*

fictional [ˈfɪkʃənəl] *adj* romanesque, d'imagination

fictionalize [ˈfɪkʃənəˌlaɪz] *tr* romancer

fictitious [fɪkˈtɪʃəs] *adj* fictif

fiddle [ˈfɪdəl] *s* violon *m* ‖ *tr*—**to fiddle away** (*coll*) gaspiller ‖ *intr* jouer du violon; **to fiddle around** or **with** (*coll*) tripoter

fiddler [ˈfɪdlər] *s* (*coll*) violoneux *m*

fid′dle•stick′ *s* (*coll*) archet *m*; **fiddlesticks!** (*coll*) quelle blague!

fiddling [ˈfɪdlɪŋ] *adj* (*coll*) musard

fideli•ty [faɪˈdɛlɪti], [fɪˈdɛlɪti] *s* (*pl* **-ties**) fidélité *f*

fidget [ˈfɪdʒɪt] *intr* se trémousser; **to fidget with** tripoter

fidgety [ˈfɪdʒɪti] *adj* nerveux

fiduciar•y [fɪˈd(j)uʃɪˌɛri] *adj* fiduciaire ‖ *s* (*pl* **-ies**) fiduciaire *m*

fie [faɪ] *interj* fi!; **fie on** . . . ! nargue de . . . !

field [fild] *s* champ *m*; (*area, activity*) domaine *m*, aire *f*; (*aer, sports*) terrain *m*; (*elec*) champ; (*of motor or dynamo*) (*elec*) inducteur *m*; (*mil*) aire *f*, théâtre *m*

field′ day′ *s* (*cleanup*) (*mil*) manœuvres *fpl* de garnison; (*sports*) manifestation *f* sportive

fielder [ˈfildər] *s* (*baseball*) chasseur *m*, homme *m* de champ

field′ glass′es *spl* jumelles *fpl*

field′ hock′ey *s* hockey *m* sur gazon

field′ hos/pital *s* ambulance *f*, formation *f* sanitaire

field′ mag/net *s* aimant *m* inducteur

field′ mar/shal *s* maréchal *m*

field′ mouse′ *s* mulot *m*

field′piece′ *s* pièce *f* de campagne

fiend [find] *s* démon *m*; (*mischief-maker*) (*coll*) espiègle *mf*; (*enthusiast*) (*coll*) mordu *m*; (*addict*) (*coll*) toxicomane *mf*

fiendish [ˈfindɪʃ] *adj* diabolique

fierce [firs] *adj* féroce, farouche; (*wind*) furieux; (*coll*) très mauvais

fierceness [ˈfirsnɪs] *s* férocité *f*

fier•y [ˈfaɪri], [ˈfaɪ·əri] *adj* (*comp* **-ier**; *super* **-iest**) ardent; (*speech*) enflammé; (*horse, person, etc.*) fougueux

fife [faɪf] *s* fifre *m*

fifteen [ˈfɪfˈtin] *adj*, *pron*, & *s* quinze *m*; **about fifteen** une quinzaine de

fifteenth [ˈfɪfˈtinθ] *adj* & *pron* quinzième (*masc, fem*); **the Fifteenth** quinze, e.g., **John the Fifteenth** Jean quinze ‖ *s* quinzième *m*; **the fifteenth** (*in dates*) le quinze

fifth [fɪfθ] *adj* & *pron* cinquième (*masc, fem*); **the Fifth** cinq, e.g., **John the Fifth** Jean cinq ‖ *s* cinquième *m*; (*mus*) quinte *f*; **the fifth** (*in dates*) le cinq

fifth′ col/umn *s* cinquième colonne *f*

fiftieth [ˈfɪftɪ·ɪθ] *adj* & *pron* cinquantième (*masc, fem*) ‖ *s* cinquantième *m*

fif•ty [ˈfɪfti] *adj* & *pron* cinquante ‖ *s* (*pl* **-ties**) cinquante *m*; **about fifty** une cinquantaine *f*; **fifties** (*years of the decade*) années *fpl* cinquante

fif′ty-fif′ty *adv*—**to go fifty-fifty** (*coll*) être de moitié, être en compte à demi

fig [fɪg] *s* figue *f*; (*tree*) figuier *m*; **a fig for** . . . ! (*coll*) nargue de . . . !

fight [faɪt] *s* combat *m*, bataille *f*; (*spirit*) cœur *m*; **to pick a fight with** chercher querelle à ‖ *v* (*pret* & *pp* **fought** [fɔt]) *tr* combattre, se battre contre; **to fight off** repousser ‖ *intr* combattre, se battre; **to fight shy of** se défier de

fighter ['faɪtər] s combattant m; (*game person*) batailleur m; (aer) chasseur m, avion m de chasse

fight′er pi′lot s chasseur m

fig′ leaf′ s feuille f de figuier; (*on statues*) feuille de vigne

figment ['fɪgmənt] s fiction f, invention f

figurative ['fɪgjərətɪv] adj figuratif; (*meaning*) figuré

figure ['fɪgjər] s figure f; (*bodily form*) taille f; (math) chiffre m; **to be good at figures** être bon en calcul; **to have a good figure** avoir de la ligne; **to keep one's figure** garder sa ligne ‖ tr figurer; (*to embellish*) orner de motifs; (*to imagine*) se figurer, s'imaginer; **to figure out** calculer; (coll) déchiffrer ‖ intr figurer; **to figure on** compter sur

fig′ured bass′ [bes] s (mus) basse f chiffrée

fig′ured silk′ s soie f à dessin

fig′ure-head′ s prête-nom m, homme m de paille; (naut) figure f de proue

fig′ure of speech′ s figure f de rhétorique

fig′ure skat′ing s patinage m de fantaisie

filament ['fɪləmənt] s filament m

filbert ['fɪlbərt] s noisette f, aveline f; (*tree*) noisetier m, avelinier m

filch [fɪltʃ] tr chaparder, chiper

file [faɪl] s (*tool*) lime f; (*for papers*) classeur m; (*for cards*) fichier m; (*personal record*) dossier m; (*line*) file f; **in single file** en file indienne, à la queue leu leu; **to form single file** dédoubler les rangs ‖ tr limer; classer, ranger; (*a petition*) déposer; **to file down** enlever à la lime ‖ intr—**to file off** défiler; **to file out** sortir un à un

file′ case′ s fichier m

file′ clerk′ s employé m, commis m

file′ num′ber s (e.g., *used in answering a letter*) référence f

filial ['fɪlɪ-əl], ['fɪljəl] adj filial

filiation [,fɪlɪ'eʃən] s filiation f

filibuster ['fɪlɪ,bʌstər] s (*use of delaying tactics*) obstruction f; (*legislator*) obstructionniste mf; (*pirate*) flibustier m ‖ tr (*in legislation*) obstruer ‖ intr faire de l'obstruction

filigree ['fɪlɪ,gri] adj filigrané ‖ s filigrane m ‖ tr filigraner

filing ['faɪlɪŋ] s (*of documents*) classement m; (*with a tool*) limage m; **filings** limaille f, grains mpl de limaille

fil′ing cab′inet s classeur m

fil′ing card′ s fiche f

Filipi·no [,fɪlɪ'pino] adj philippin ‖ s (pl **-nos**) Philippin m

fill [fɪl] s suffisance f; (*earth, stones, etc.*) remblai m; **to have one's fill of** avoir tout son soûl de ‖ tr remplir; (*a prescription*) exécuter; (*a tooth*) plomber; (*a cylinder with gas*) charger; (*a hollow or gap*) combler; (*a job*) occuper; **to fill in** remblayer,

combler; **to fill out** (*a questionnaire*) remplir ‖ intr se remplir; **to fill out** se gonfler; (*said of sail*) s'enfler; **to fill up** se combler; (*to fill the tank full*) faire le plein

filler ['fɪlər] s remplissage m; (*of cigar*) tripe f; (*sizing*) apprêt m, mastic m; (*in notebook*) papier m; (journ) pesée f

fillet ['fɪlɪt] s bande f; (*for hair*) bandeau m; (archit) moulure f ‖ ['fɪle], ['fɪlɪt] s (culin) filet m ‖ tr couper en filets

filling ['fɪlɪŋ] adj (*food*) rassasiant ‖ s (*of job*) occupation f; (*of tooth*) plombage m; (*e.g., of turkey*) farce f; (*of cigar*) tripe f

fill′ing sta′tion s poste m d'essence

fill′ing-station attend′ant s pompiste mf

fillip ['fɪlɪp] s tonique m, stimulant m; (*with finger*) chiquenaude f ‖ tr donner une chiquenaude à

fil·ly ['fɪlɪ] s (pl **-lies**) pouliche f; (coll) fillette f

film [fɪlm] s film m; (*in a roll*) pellicule f, film m ‖ tr filmer

filming ['fɪlmɪŋ] s filmage m

film′ li′brary s cinémathèque f

film′ mak′er s cinéaste mf

film′ star′ s vedette f du cinéma

film′strip′ s film m fixe

film·y ['fɪlmɪ] adj (comp **-ier**; super **-iest**) diaphane, voilé

filter ['fɪltər] s filtre m ‖ tr & intr filtrer

filtering ['fɪltərɪŋ] s filtrage m; (*of water*) filtration f

fil′ter pa′per s papier-filtre m

fil′ter tip′ s (*a*) à bout-filtre ‖ s bout-filtre m, bout-filtrant m

filth [fɪlθ] s saleté f, ordure f; (fig) obscénité f

filth·y ['fɪlθɪ] adj (comp **-ier**; super **-iest**) sale, immonde

filth′y lu′cre ['lukər] s (coll) lucre m

fin [fɪn] s nageoire f

final ['faɪnəl] adj final; (*last in a series*) ultime, définitif ‖ s examen m final; (sports) finale f

finale [fɪ'nɑli] s (mus) final m

finalist ['faɪnəlɪst] s finaliste mf

finally ['faɪnəlɪ] adv finalement, enfin

finance [fɪ'næns], ['faɪnæns] s finance f ‖ tr financer

financial [fɪ'næn(ə)l], [faɪ'næn(ə)l] adj financier; (*interest; distress*) pécuniaire

financier [,fɪnən'sɪr], [,faɪnən'sɪr] s financier m

financing [fɪ'nænsɪŋ], ['faɪnænsɪŋ] s financement m

finch [fɪntʃ] s pinson m

find [faɪnd] s trouvaille f ‖ v (pret & pp **found** [faʊnd]) tr trouver; **to find out** apprendre ‖ intr (law) déclarer; **to find out** (*about*) se renseigner (sur), se mettre au courant (de); **find out!** à vous de trouver!

finder ['faɪndər] s (*of camera*) viseur m; (*of optical instrument*) chercheur m

finding ['faɪndɪŋ] s découverte f; (law) décision f; **findings** conclusions fpl

fine [faɪn] adj fin; (weather) beau; (person, manners, etc.) distingué, excellent; **that's fine!** bien!, parfait! || s amende f || tr mettre à l'amende

fine′ arts′ spl beaux-arts mpl

fineness ['faɪnɪs] s finesse f; (of metal) titre m

fine′ print′ s petits caractères mpl

finer·y ['faɪnərɪ] s (pl -ies) parure f

finespun ['faɪn,spʌn] adj ténu; (fig) subtil

finesse [fɪ'nɛs] s finesse f; (in bridge) impasse f; **to use finesse** finasser || tr faire l'impasse à

fine′-toothed comb′ s peigne m aux dents fines, peigne fin

finger ['fɪŋgər] s doigt m; (slang) mouchard m, indicateur m; **not to lift a finger** (fig) ne pas remuer le petit doigt; **to burn one's fingers** (fig) se faire échauder; **to put one's finger on the spot** (fig) mettre le doigt dessus; **to slip between the fingers** glisser entre les doigts; **to snap one's fingers at** (fig) faire la figue à, narguer; **to twist around one's little finger** (coll) mener par le bout du nez, faire tourner comme un toton || tr toucher du doigt, manier; (mus) doigter; (slang) espionner; (slang) identifier

fin′ger board′ s (of guitar) touche f; (of piano) clavier m

fin′ger bowl′ s rince-doigts m

fin′ger dexter′ity s (mus) doigté m

fingering ['fɪŋgərɪŋ] s maniement m; (mus) doigté m

fin′ger-nail′ s ongle m

fin′gernail pol′ish s brillant m

fin′ger-print′ s empreinte f digitale || tr prendre les empreintes digitales de

fin′ger-tip′ s bout m du doigt; **to have at one's fingertips** tenir sur le bout du doigt

finicky ['fɪnɪkɪ] adj méticuleux

finish ['fɪnɪʃ] s (perfection) achevé m, fini m; (elegance) finesse f; (conclusion) fin f; (gloss, coating, etc.) fini m || tr & intr finir; **to finish** + ger finir de + inf; **to finish by** + ger finir par + inf

fin′ishing touch′ s dernière main f

finite ['faɪnaɪt] adj & s fini m

Finland ['fɪnlənd] s Finlande f; **la Finlande**

Finlander ['fɪnləndər] s Finlandais m

Finn [fɪn] s (member of a Finnish-speaking group of people) Finnois m; (native or inhabitant of Finland) Finlandais m

Finnish ['fɪnɪʃ] adj & s finnois m

fir [fʌr] s sapin m

fire [faɪr] s feu m; (destructive burning) incendie m; **to catch fire** prendre feu; **to set on fire** mettre le feu à || tr mettre le feu à; (e.g., passions) enflammer; (a weapon) tirer; (a rocket) lancer; (an employee) (coll) renvoyer || interj (warning) au feu!; (command to fire) feu!

fire′ alarm′ s avertisseur m d'incendie; (box) poste m avertisseur d'incendie

fire′ arm′ s arme f à feu

fire′ ball′ s globe m de feu; (mil) grenade f incendiaire

fire′ bird′ s loriot m d'Amérique

fire′ boat′ s bateau-pompe m

fire′ box′ s boîte f à feu; (rr) foyer m

fire′ brand′ s tison m; (coll) brandon m de discorde

fire′ break′ s tranchée f garde-feu, pare-feu m

fire′ brick′ s brique f réfractaire

fire′ brigade′ s corps m de sapeurs-pompiers

fire′ bug′ s (coll) incendiaire mf

fire′ chief′ s capitaine m des pompiers

fire′ com′pany s corps m de sapeurs-pompiers; (insurance company) compagnie f d'assurance contre l'incendie

fire′ crack′er s pétard m

fire′ damp′ s grisou m

fire′ depart′ment s service m des incendies, sapeurs-pompiers mpl

fire′ dog′ s chenet m, landier m

fire′ drill′ s exercices mpl de sauvetage en cas d'incendie

fire′ en′gine s pompe f à incendie

fire′ escape′ s échelle f de sauvetage, escalier m de secours

fire′ extin′guisher s extincteur m

fire′ fly′ s (pl -flies) luciole f

fire′ guard′ s (before hearth) pare-étincelles m; (in forest) pare-feu m

fire′ hose′ s manche f d'incendie

fire′house′ s caserne f de pompiers, poste m de pompiers

fire′ hy′drant s bouche f d'incendie

fire′ insur′ance s assurance f contre l'incendie

fire′ i′rons spl garniture f de foyer

fire′less cook′er ['faɪrlɪs] s marmite f norvégienne

fire′man s (pl -men) (man who stokes fires) chauffeur m; (man who extinguishes fires) sapeur-pompier m, pompier m

fire′place′ s cheminée f, foyer m

fire′plug′ s bouche f d'incendie

fire′ pow′er s puissance f de feu

fire′proof′ adj ignifuge; (dish) apyre || tr ignifuger

fire′ sale′ s vente f après incendie

fire′ screen′ s écran m de cheminée, garde-feu m

fire′ ship′ s brûlot m

fire′ shov′el s pelle f à feu

fire′side′ s coin m du feu

fire′trap′ s édifice m qui invite l'incendie

fire′ wall′ s coupe-feu m

fire′ward′en s garde m forestier, vigie f

fire′ wa′ter s (slang) gnole f, whisky m

fire′wood′ s bois m de chauffage

fire′works′ spl feu m d'artifice

firing ['faɪrɪŋ] s (of furnace) chauffe f; (of bricks, ceramics, etc.) cuite f; (of gun) tir m, feu m; (by a group of soldiers) fusillade f; (of an internal-combustion engine) allumage m; (of an employee) (coll) renvoi m

fir'ing line' s ligne f de feu, chaîne f de combat

fir'ing or'der s rythme m d'allumage

fir'ing pin' s percuteur m, aiguille f

fir'ing squad' s peloton m d'exécution; (*for ceremonies*) piquet m d'honneurs funèbres

firm [fʌrm] *adj* & *adv* ferme; **to stand firm** tenir bon ‖ s maison f de commerce, firme f

firmament ['fʌrməmənt] s firmament m

firm' name' s nom m commercial

firmness ['fʌrmnɪs] s fermeté f

first [fʌrst] *adj, pron,* & s premier m; **at first** au commencement, au début; **first come first served** les premiers vont devant; **from the first** depuis le premier jour; **John the First** Jean premier ‖ *adv* premièrement, d'abord; **first and last** en tout et pour tout; **first of all, first off** tout d'abord, de prime abord

first' aid' s premiers soins mpl, premiers secours mpl

first'-aid' kit' s boîte f à pansements, trousse f de première urgence

first'-aid' sta'tion s poste m de secours

first'-born' *adj* & s premier-né m

first'-class' *adj* de première classe, de premier ordre ‖ *adv* en première classe

first' cous'in s cousin m germain

first' draft' s brouillon m, premier jet m

first' fin'ger s index m

first' floor' s rez-de-chaussée m

first' fruits' spl prémices fpl

first'hand' *adj* & *adv* de première main

first' lieuten'ant s lieutenant m en premier

firstly ['fʌrstli] *adv* en premier lieu, d'abord

first' mate' s (naut) second m

first' name' s prénom m, petit nom m

first' night' s (theat) première f

first-nighter [,fʌrst'naɪtər] s (theat) habitué m des premières

first' offend'er s délinquant m primaire

first' offi'cer s (naut) officier m en second

first' prize' s (*in a lottery*) gros lot m; **to win first prize** remporter le prix

first' quar'ter s (*of the moon*) premier quartier m

first'-rate' *adj* de premier ordre, de première qualité; (coll) excellent ‖ *adv* (coll) très bien, à merveille

first'-run mov'ie s film m en exclusivité

fiscal ['fɪskəl] *adj* fiscal

fis'cal year' s exercice m budgétaire

fish [fɪʃ] s poisson m; **to be like a fish out of water** être comme un poisson sur la paille; **to be neither fish nor fowl** être ni chair ni poisson; **to drink like a fish** boire comme un trou; **to have other fish to fry** avoir d'autres chiens à fouetter ‖ *tr* pêcher; (rr) éclisser; **to fish out** *or* **up** repêcher ‖ *intr* pêcher; **to fish for compliments** quêter des compliments; **to go fishing** aller à la pêche; **to take fishing** emmener à la pêche

fish'bone' s arête f

fish'bowl' s bocal m

fisher ['fɪʃər] s pêcheur m; (zool) martre f

fish'er·man s (pl -men) pêcheur m

fisher·y ['fɪʃəri] s (pl -ies) (*activity; business*) pêche f; (*grounds*) pêcherie f

fish' hawk' s aigle m pêcheur

fish'hook' s hameçon m

fishing ['fɪʃɪŋ] *adj* pêcheur, de pêche ‖ s pêche f

fish'ing ground' s pêcherie f

fish'ing reel' s moulinet m

fish'ing rod' s canne f à pêche

fish'ing tack'le s attirail m de pêche

fish'line' s ligne f de pêche

fish' mar'ket s poissonnerie f

fish'plate' s (rr) éclisse f

fish'pool' s vivier m

fish' spear' s foène f, fouëne f

fish' sto'ry s hâblerie f, blague f

fish'tail' s queue f de poisson; (aer) embardée f ‖ *intr* (aer) embarder

fish'wife' s (pl -wives') poissonnière f; (*foul-mouthed woman*) poissarde f

fish'worm' s asticot m

fish·y ['fɪʃi] *adj* (comp -ier; super -iest) (*eyes*) (coll) vitreux; (coll) véreux, louche

fission ['fɪʃən] s (biol) scission f; (nucl) fission f

fissionable ['fɪʃənəbəl] *adj* fissible, fissile

fissure ['fɪʃər] s fissure f, fente f ‖ *tr* fissurer ‖ *intr* se fissurer

fist [fɪst] s poing m; (typ) petite main f; **to shake one's fist at** menacer du poing

fist'fight' s combat m à coup de poings

fistful ['fɪstful] s poignée f

fisticuffs ['fɪstɪ,kʌfs] spl empoignade f *or* rixe f à coups de poing; (sports) boxe f

fit [fɪt] *adj* (comp fitter; super fittest) bon, convenable; capable, digne; (*in good health*) en forme, sain; **fit to be tied** (coll) en colère; **fit to drink** buvable; **fit to eat** mangeable; **to feel fit** être frais et dispos ‖ s ajustement m; (*of clothes*) coupe f, façon f; (*of fever, rage, coughing*) accès m; **by fits and starts** par accès; **fit of coughing** quinte f de toux ‖ v (pret & pp fitted; ger fitting) *tr* ajuster; (*s.th. in s.th*) emboîter; **to fit for** (e.g., *a task*) préparer à; **to fit out** *or* **up** aménager; **to fit out with** garnir de ‖ *intr* s'emboîter; **to fit in with** s'accorder avec, convenir à

fitful ['fɪtfəl] *adj* intermittent

fitness ['fɪtnɪs] s convenance f; (*for a task*) aptitude f; (*good shape*) bonne forme f

fitter ['fɪtər] s ajusteur m; (*of machinery*) monteur m; (*of clothing*) essayeur m

fitting ['fɪtɪŋ] *adj* convenable, approprié, à propos ‖ s ajustage m; (*of a garment*) essayage m; **fittings** aménagements mpl; (*of metal*) ferrures fpl

five [faɪv] adj & pron cinq || s cinq m; **five o'clock** cinq heures

five'-year plan' s plan m quinquennal

fix [fɪks] s (coll) mauvais pas m; **to be in a fix** (coll) être dans le pétrin || tr réparer; (e.g., a date; a photographic image; prices; one's eyes) fixer; (slang) donner son compte à

fixedly [ˈfɪksɪdli] adv fixement

fixing [ˈfɪksɪŋ] s fixation f; (phot) fixage m; **fixings** (slang) collation f, des mets mpl

fix'ing bath' s bain m de fixage, fixateur m

fixture [ˈfɪkstʃər] s accessoire m, garniture f; **fixtures** meubles mpl à demeure

fizz [fɪz] s pétillement m || intr pétiller

fizzle [ˈfɪzəl] s (coll) avortement m || intr (coll) avorter; **to fizzle out** (coll) tomber à l'eau, échouer

flabbergasted [ˈflæbərˌgæstɪd] adj (coll) éberlué, épaté

flab·by [ˈflæbi] adj (comp **-bier**; super **-biest**) mou, flasque

flag [flæg] s drapeau m || v (pret & pp **flagged**; ger **flagging**) tr—**to flag s.o.** transmettre des signaux à qn en agitant un fanion || intr faiblir, se relâcher

flag' cap'tain s (nav) capitaine m de pavillon

flag'man s (pl **-men**) signaleur m; (rr) garde-voie m

flag' of truce' s drapeau m parlementaire

flag'pole' s hampe f de drapeau; (naut) mât m de pavillon; (surv) jalon m

flagrant [ˈflegrənt] adj scandaleux; (e.g., injustice) flagrant

flag'ship' s (nav) vaisseau m amiral

flag'staff' s hampe f de drapeau

flag'stone' s dalle f

flag' stop' s (rr) halte f, arrêt m facultatif

flag'-wav'ing adj cocardier || s patriotisme m de façade

flail [flel] s fléau m || tr (agr) battre au fléau; (fig) éreinter

flair [fler] s flair m; aptitude f

flak [flæk] s tir m contre-avions

flake [flek] s (of snow; of cereal) flocon m; (of soap; of mica) paillette f; (of paint) écaille f || intr tomber en flocons; **to flake off** s'écailler

flak·y [ˈfleki] adj (comp **-ier**; super **-iest**) floconneux, lamelleux

flamboyant [flæmˈbɔɪənt] adj fleuri, orné, coloré; (archit) flamboyant

flame [flem] s flamme f; (coll) amant m, amante f || tr flamber || intr flamber, flamboyer

flamethrower [ˈflemˌθroˌər] s lance-flammes m

flaming [ˈflemɪŋ] adj flambant

flamin·go [fləˈmɪŋgo] s (pl **-gos** or **-goes**) flamant m

flammable [ˈflæməbəl] adj inflammable

Flanders [ˈflændərz] s Flandre f; la Flandre

flange [flændʒ] s rebord m, saillie f; (of wheel) jante f; (of rail) patin m

flank [flæŋk] s flanc m || tr flanquer

flannel [ˈflænəl] s flanelle f

flap [flæp] s (part that can be folded under) rabat m; (fold in clothing) pan m; (of a cap) couvre-nuque m; (of a pocket; of an envelope) patte f; (of wings) coup m, battement m; (of a table) battant m; (of a sail, flag, etc.) claquement m; (slap) tape f; (aer) volet m || v (pret & pp **flapped**; ger **flapping**) tr (wings, arms, etc.) battre; (to slap) taper || intr battre; (said of sail, flag, etc.) claquer; (said of curtain) voltiger; (to hang down) pendre

flap'jack' s (coll) crêpe f

flare [fler] s éclat m vif; (e.g., of skirt; of pipe or funnel) évasement m; (for signaling) fusée f éclairante || tr évaser || intr flamboyer; (to spread outward) s'évaser; **to flare up** s'enflammer; (to reappear) se produire de nouveau; (to become angry) s'emporter

flare'-up' s flambée f soudaine; (of illness) recrudescence f; (of anger) accès m de colère

flash [flæʃ] s éclair m; (of hope) lueur f, rayon m; (of wit) trait m; (of genius) éclair; (brief moment) instant m; (ostentation) (coll) tape-à-l'œil m; (last-minute news) (coll) nouvelle f éclair; **flash in the pan** (coll) feu m de paille; **in a flash** en un clin d'œil || tr projeter; (a gem) faire étinceler; (to show off) faire parade de; (a message) répandre, transmettre || intr jeter des éclairs; (said of gem, eyes, etc.) étinceler; **to flash by** passer comme un éclair

flash'back' s (mov) retour m en arrière, rappel m

flash' bulb' s ampoule f flash, flash m

flash' flood' s crue f subite

flashing [ˈflæʃɪŋ] adj éclatant; (light) à éclats; (signal) clignotant || s bande f de solin

flash'light' s lampe f torche, lampe de poche; (phot) lampe éclair

flash'light bat'tery s pile f torche

flash·y [ˈflæʃi] adj (comp **-ier**; super **-iest**) (coll) tapageur, criard

flask [flæsk] s (flosk) s flacon m, gourde f; (in lab) ballon m, flacon

flat [flæt] adj (comp **flatter**; super **flattest**) plat, uni; (nose) aplati; (refusal) net; (beer) éventé; (tire) dégonflé; (dull, tasteless) fade, terne; (mus) bémol || s appartement m; (flat tire) crevaison f; (of sword) plat m; (mus) bémol m; (theat) châssis m || adv (outright) (coll) nettement, carrément; **to fall flat** tomber à plat; (fig) manquer son effet; **to sing flat** chanter faux

flat'boat' s plate f

flat-broke [ˈflætˈbrok] adj (coll) complètement fauché, à la côte

flat'car' s plate-forme f

flat'foot' s (slang) flic m

flat'-foot'ed adj aux pieds plats; (coll) franc, brutal

flat'i'ron s fer m à repasser

flatly ['flætli] adv net, platement

flat'-nosed' adj camard, camus

flatten ['flætən] tr aplatir, aplanir; (metallurgy) laminer || intr s'aplatir, s'aplanir; **to flatten out** (aer) se redresser

flatter ['flætər] tr & intr flatter

flatterer ['flætərər] s flatteur m

flattering ['flætərɪŋ] adj flatteur

flatter·y ['flætəri] s (pl -ies) flatterie f

flat' tire' s pneu m dégonflé, à plat, or crevé, crevaison f

flat'top' s (nav) porte-avions m

flatulence ['flætʃələns] s boursouflure f; (pathol) flatulence f

flat'ware' s couverts mpl; (plates) assiettes fpl

flaunt [flɔnt], [flɑnt] tr faire étalage de

flautist ['flɔtɪst] s flûtiste mf

flavor ['flevər] s saveur f, goût m; (of ice cream) parfum m || tr assaisonner, parfumer

flavoring ['flevərɪŋ] s assaisonnement m; (lemon, rum, etc.) parfum m

flaw [flɔ] s défaut m, tache f; (crack) fêlure f; (in metal) paille f; (in diamond) crapaud m

flawless ['flɔlɪs] adj sans défaut, sans tache

flax [flæks] s lin m

flaxen ['flæksən] adj de lin, blond

flax'seed' s graine f de lin

flay [fle] tr écorcher; (to criticize) rosser, fustiger

flea [fli] s puce f

flea'bite' s piqûre f de puce; (trifle) vétille f

fleck [flɛk] s tache f; (particle) particule f || tr tacheter

fledgling ['fledʒlɪŋ] adj (lawyer, teacher) en herbe, débutant || s oisillon m; (novice) débutant m, béjaune m

flee [fli] v (pret & pp fled [fled]) tr & intr fuir

fleece [flis] s toison f || tr tondre; (to strip of money) (coll) écorcher, plumer

fleec·y ['flisi] adj (comp -ier; super -iest) laineux; (snow, wool) floconneux; (hair) moutonneux; (clouds) moutonné

fleet [flit] adj rapide || s flotte f

fleet'-foot'ed adj au pied léger

fleeting ['flitɪŋ] adj passager, fugitif

Fleming ['flemɪŋ] s Flamand m

Flemish ['flemɪʃ] adj & s flamand m

flesh [flɛʃ] s chair f; **in the flesh** en chair et en os; **to lose flesh** perdre de l'embonpoint; **to put on flesh** prendre de l'embonpoint, s'empâter

flesh' and blood' s nature f humaine; (relatives) famille f, parenté f

flesh'-col'ored adj couleur f de chair, carné

flesh'pot' s (pot for cooking meat) pot-au-feu m; (fleshpots (high living) luxe m, grande chère f; (evil places) maisons fpl de débauche, mauvais lieux mpl

flesh' wound' [wund] s blessure f en séton, blessure superficielle

flesh·y ['fleʃi] adj (comp -ier; super -iest) charnu

flex [flɛks] tr & intr fléchir

flexible ['flɛksɪbəl] adj flexible

flick [flɪk] s (with finger) chiquenaude f; (with whip) petit coup m; **flicks** (coll) ciné m || tr faire une chiquenaude à; (a whip) faire claquer

flicker ['flɪkər] s petite lueur f vacillante; (of eyelids) battement m; (of emotion) frisson m || intr trembloter, vaciller; (said of eyelids) ciller

flier ['flaɪər] s aviateur m; (rr) rapide m; (handbill) (coll) prospectus m

flight [flaɪt] s fuite f; (of airplane) vol m; (of birds) volée f; (of stairs) volée; (of fancy) élan m; **to put to flight** mettre en fuite; **to take flight** prendre la fuite

flight' deck' s (nav) pont m d'envol

flight' record'er s enregistreur m en vol

flight·y ['flaɪti] adj (comp -ier; super -iest) volage, léger; braque, écervelé

flim-flam ['flɪm,flæm] s (coll) baliverne f; (fraud) (coll) escroquerie f || v (pret & pp -flammed; ger -flamming) tr (coll) escroquer

flim·sy ['flɪmzi] adj (comp -sier; super -siest) léger; (e.g., cloth) fragile; (e.g., excuse) frivole

flinch [flɪntʃ] intr reculer, fléchir; **without flinching** sans broncher, sans hésiter

fling [flɪŋ] s jet m; **to go on a fling** faire la noce; **to have a fling at** tenter; **to have one's fling** jeter sa gourme || v (pret & pp flung [flʌŋ]) tr lancer; (on the floor, out the window; in jail) jeter; **to fling open** ouvrir brusquement

flint [flɪnt] s silex m; (of lighter) pierre f

flint'lock' s fusil m à pierre

flint·y ['flɪnti] adj (comp -ier; super -iest) siliceux; (heart) de pierre, insensible

flip [flɪp] adj (comp flipper; super flippest) (coll) mutin, moqueur || s chiquenaude f; (somersault) culbute f; (aer) petit tour m de vol || v (pret & pp flipped; ger flipping) tr donner une chiquenaude à; (a page) tourner rapidement; **to flip a coin** jouer à pile ou face; **to flip over** (a phonograph record) retourner

flippancy ['flɪpənsi] s désinvolture f

flippant ['flɪpənt] adj désinvolte

flipper ['flɪpər] s nageoire f

flirt [flʌrt] s flirteur m, flirt m || intr flirter; (said only of a man) conter fleurette

flit [flɪt] v (pret & pp flitted; ger flitting) intr voleter; **to flit away** passer rapidement; **to flit here and there** voltiger

float [flot] s (raft) radeau m; (on fish line; in carburetor; on seaplane) flotteur *m*; (*on fish line or net*) flotte *f*; (*of mason*) aplanissoire *f*; (*in parade*) char *m* de cavalcade, char de Carnaval ‖ *tr* faire flotter; (*a loan*) émettre, contracter ‖ *intr* flotter, nager; (*on one's back*) faire la planche

floater ['flotər] *s* vagabond *m*; (*illegal voter*) faux électeur *m*

floating ['flotɪŋ] *adj* flottant; (*free*) libre ‖ *s* flottement *m*; (*of loan*) émission *f*

float′ing is′land *s* (culin) œufs *mpl* à la neige

flock [flɑk] *s* (*of birds*) volée *f*; (*of sheep*) troupeau *m*; (*of nonsense*) foule *f*, bande *f*; (*of nonsense*) tas *m*; (*of faithful*) ouailles *fpl* ‖ *intr* s'assembler; **to flock in** entrer en foule; **to flock together** s'attrouper

floe [flo] *s* banquise *f*; (*floating piece of ice*) glaçon *m* flottant

flog [flɑg] *v* (*pret & pp* **flogged**; *ger* **flogging**) *tr* fouetter, flageller

flogging ['flɑgɪŋ] *s* fouet *m*

flood [flʌd] *s* inondation *f*; (*caused by heavy rain*) déluge *m*; (*sudden rise of river*) crue *f*; (*of tide*) flot *m*; (*of words, tears, light*) flots *mpl*, déluge ‖ *tr* inonder; (*to overwhelm*) submerger, inonder; (*a carburetor*) noyer ‖ *intr* (*said of river*) déborder; (*aut*) se noyer

flood′gate′ *s* (*of a dam*) vanne *f*; (*of a canal*) porte *f* d'écluse

flood′light′ *s* phare *m* d'éclairage, projecteur *m* de lumière ‖ *tr* illuminer par projecteurs

flood′ tide′ *s* marée *f* montante, flux *m*

floor [flor] *s* (*inside bottom surface of room*) plancher *m*, parquet *m*; (*story of building*) étage *m*; (*of swimming pool, the sea, etc.*) fond *m*; (*of assembly hall*) enceinte *f*, parquet; (*of the court*) prétoire *m*, parquet; (naut) varangue *f*; **to ask for the floor** réclamer la parole; **to give s.o. the floor** donner la parole à qn; **to have the floor** avoir la parole; **to take the floor** prendre la parole ‖ *tr* parqueter; (*an opponent*) terrasser; (*to disconcert*) (coll) désarçonner

flooring ['florɪŋ] *s* planchéiage *m*, parquetage *m*

floor′ lamp′ *s* lampe *f* à pied, lampadaire *m*

floor′ mop′ *s* brosse *f* à parquet

floor′ show′ *s* spectacle *m* de cabaret

floor′ tim′ber *s* (naut) varangue *f*

floor′walk′er *s* chef *m* de rayon

floor′ wax′ *s* cire *f* à parquet, encaustique *f*

flop [flɑp] *s* (coll) insuccès *m*, échec *m*; (*literary work or painting*) (coll) navet *m*; (*play*) (coll) four *m*; **to take a flop** (coll) faire patapouf ‖ *v* (*pret & pp* **flopped**; *ger* **flopping**) *intr* tomber lourdement; (*to fail*) (coll) échouer, rater

flora ['florə] *s* flore *f*

floral ['florəl] *adj* floral

florescence [flo'rɛsəns] *s* floraison *f*

florid ['flɑrɪd], ['flɔrɪd] *adj* fleuri, flamboyant; (*complexion*) rubicond

Florida ['flɑrɪdə], ['flɔrɪdə] *s* Floride *f*; la Floride

Flor′ida Keys′ *spl* Cayes *fpl* de la Floride

floss [flɔs], [flɑs] *s* bourre *f*; (*of corn*) barbe *f*

floss′ silk′ *s* bourre *f* de soie, filoselle *f*

floss•y ['flɔsi], ['flɑsi] *adj* (*comp* **-ier**; *super* **-iest**) soyeux; (slang) pimpant, tapageur

flotsam ['flɑtsəm] *s* épave *f*

flot′sam and jet′sam *s* choses *fpl* de flot et de mer, épaves *fpl*

flounce [flauns] *s* volant *m* ‖ *tr* garnir de volants ‖ *intr* s'élancer avec emportement

flounder ['flaundər] *s* flet *m*; (*plaice*) carrelet *m*, plie *f* ‖ *intr* patauger

flour [flaur] *s* farine *f* ‖ *tr* fariner

flourish ['flʌrɪʃ] *s* fioriture *f*; (*on a signature*) paraphe *m*; (*of trumpets*) fanfare *m*; (*brandishing*) brandissement *m* ‖ *tr* brandir; (*to wave*) agiter ‖ *intr* fleurir, prospérer

flourishing ['flʌrɪʃɪŋ] *adj* florissant

flour′ mill′ *s* moulin *m*, minoterie *f*

floury ['flauri] *adj* farineux

flout [flaut] *tr* se moquer de, narguer ‖ *intr* se moquer

flow [flo] *s* écoulement *m*; (*of tide, blood, words*) flot *m*, flux *m*; (*of blood to the head*) afflux *m*; (*rate of flow*) débit *m*; (*current*) courant *m* ‖ *intr* écouler; (*said of tide*) monter; (*said of blood in the body*) circuler; (fig) couler; **to flow into** déboucher dans, se verser dans; **to flow over** déborder

flower ['flau•ər] *s* fleur *f* ‖ *tr & intr* fleurir

flow′er bed′ *s* plate-bande *f*, parterre *m*; (*round flower bed*) corbeille *f*

flow′er gar′den *s* jardin *m* de fleurs, jardin d'agrément

flow′er girl′ *s* bouquetière *f*; (*at a wedding*) fille *f* d'honneur

flow′er-pot′ *s* pot *m* à fleurs

flow′er shop′ *s* boutique *f* de fleuriste

flow′er show′ *s* exposition *f* horticole, floralies *fpl*

flow′er stand′ *s* jardinière *f*

flowery ['flau•əri] *adj* fleuri

flu [flu] *s* (coll) grippe *f*

fluctuate ['flʌktʃu‚et] *intr* fluctuer

flue [flu] *s* tuyau *m*

fluency ['flu•ənsi] *s* facilité *f*

fluent ['flu•ənt] *adj* disert, facile; (*flowing*) coulant

fluently ['flu•əntli] *adv* couramment

fluff [flʌf] *s* (*velvety cloth*) peluche *f*; (*tuft of fur, dust, etc.*) duvet *m*; (*boner made by actor*) (coll) loup *m* ‖ *tr* lainer, rendre pelucheux; (*one's entrance*) (coll) louper; (*one's lines*) (coll) bouler ‖ *intr* pelucher

fluff•y ['flʌfi] *adj* (*comp* **-ier**; *super* **-iest**) duveteux; (*hair*) flou

fluid ['flu•ɪd] *adj & s* fluide *m*

fluke [fluk] *s* (*of anchor*) patte *f*; (billiards) raccroc *m*, coup *m* de veine

flume [flum] s canalisation *f*; ravin *m*

flunk [flʌŋk] *tr* (*a student*) (coll) recaler, coller; (*an exam*) rater ‖ *intr* être recalé, se faire coller

flunk·y [ˈflʌŋkɪ] s (*pl* **-ies**) laquais *m*

fluorescent [ˌfluˈrɛsənt] *adj* fluorescent

fluoridate [ˈflorɪˌdet], [ˈflurɪˌdet] *tr* & *intr* fluorider

fluoridation [ˌflorɪˈdeʃən], [ˌflurɪˈdeʃən] s fluoridation *f*

fluoride [ˈfluəˌraɪd] s fluorure *m*

fluorine [ˈfluəˌrin] s fluor *m*

fluoroscopy [ˌfluəˈrɑskəpɪ] s radioscopie *f*

fluorspar [ˈfluəˌspɑr] s spath *m* fluor

flur·ry [ˈflʌrɪ] s (*pl* **-ries**) agitation *f*; (*of wind, snow, etc.*) rafale *f* ‖ *v* (*pret & pp* **-ried**) *tr* agiter

flush [flʌʃ] *adj* (*level*) à ras; (*well-provided*) bien pourvu; (*healthy*) vigoureux; **flush with** au ras de, au niveau de ‖ s (*of light*) éclat *m*; (*in the cheeks*) rougeur *f*; (*of toilet*) chasse *f* d'eau; (*in poker*) flush *m*; **in the first flush of** dans l'ivresse or le premier éclat de ‖ *adv* à ras, de niveau; (*directly*) droit ‖ *tr* (*a bird*) lever; **to flush a toilet** tirer la chasse d'eau; **to flush out** (*e.g., a drain*) laver à grande eau ‖ *intr* (*to blush*) rougir

flush′ switch′ s interrupteur *m* encastré

flush′ tank′ s réservoir *m* de chasse

flush′ toi′let s water-closet *m* à chasse d'eau

fluster [ˈflʌstər] s agitation *f*; **in a fluster** en émoi ‖ *tr* agiter

flute [flut] s flûte *f* ‖ *tr* (*a column*) canneler; (*a dress*) tuyauter

flutist [ˈflutɪst] s flûtiste *mf*

flutter [ˈflʌtər] s battement *m*; **all of a flutter** (coll) tout agité ‖ *intr* voleter; (*said of pulse*) battre fébrilement; (*said of heart*) palpiter

flux [flʌks] s flux *m*; (*for fusing metals*) acide *m* à souder; **to be in flux** être dans un état indécis

fly [flaɪ] s (*pl* **flies**) mouche *f*; (*for fishing*) mouche artificielle; (*of trousers*) braguette *f*; (*of tent*) auvent *m*; **flies** (theat) cintres *mpl*; **fly in the ointment** (fig) ombre *f* au tableau; **on the fly** au vol ‖ *v* (*pret* **flew** [flu]; *pp* **flown** [flon]) *tr* (*a kite*) faire voler; (*an airplane*) piloter; (*freight or passengers*) transporter en avion; (*e.g. the Atlantic*) survoler; (*to flee from*) fuir ‖ *intr* voler; (*to flee*) fuir; (*said of flag*) flotter; **to fly blind** voler à l'aveuglette; **to fly by** voler; **to fly in the face of** porter un défi à; **to fly off** s'envoler; **to fly off the handle** (coll) sortir de ses gonds; **to fly open** s'ouvrir brusquement; **to fly over** survoler

fly′blow′ s œufs *mpl* de mouche

fly′-by-night′ *adj* mal financé, indigne de confiance ‖ s financier *m* qui lève le pied

fly′ cast′ing s pêche *f* à la mouche noyée

fly′catch′er s attrape-mouches *m*; (bot) dionée *f*, attrape-mouches; (orn) gobe-mouches *m*

fly′-fish′ *intr* pêcher à la mouche

flying [ˈflaɪɪŋ] *adj* volant; rapide; court, passager ‖ s aviation *f*; vol *m*

fly′ing but′tress s arc-boutant *m*

fly′ing col′ors—**with flying colors** drapeau *m* déployé; brillamment

fly′ing field′ s champ *m* d'aviation

fly′ing-fish′ s poisson *m* volant

fly′ing sau′cer s soucoupe *f* volante

fly′ing start′ s départ *m* lancé

fly′ing time′ s heures *fpl* de vol

fly′leaf′ s (*pl* **-leaves**) feuille *f* de garde, garde *f*

fly′ net′ s (*for a bed*) moustiquaire *f*; (*for a horse*) chasse-mouches *m*

fly′pa′per s papier *m* tue-mouches

fly′ rod′ s canne *f* à mouche

fly′speck′ s chiure *f*, chiasse *f*

fly′ swat′ter [ˌswatər] s chasse-mouches *m*, émouchoir *m*

fly′trap′ s attrape-mouches *m*

fly′wheel′ s volant *m*

foal [fol] s poulain *m* ‖ *intr* mettre bas

foam [fom] s écume *f*; (*on beer*) mousse *f* ‖ *intr* écumer, mousser

foam′ rub′ber s caoutchouc *m* mousse

foam·y [ˈfomɪ] *adj* (*comp* **-ier**; *super* **-iest**) écumeux, mousseux

fob [fɑb] s (*pocket*) gousset *m*; (*ornament*) breloque *f* ‖ *v* (*pret & pp* **fobbed**; *ger* **fobbing**) *tr*—**to fob off s.th. on s.o.** refiler q.ch. à qn

f.o.b. or **F.O.B.** [ˌɛfˌoˈbi] *adv* (letter-word) (**free on board**) franco de bord, départ usine

focal [ˈfokəl] *adj* focal

fo·cus [ˈfokəs] s (*pl* **-cuses** or **-ci** [saɪ]) foyer *m*; **in focus** au point; **out of focus** non réglé, hors du point focal ‖ *v* (*pret & pp* **-cused** or **-cussed**; *ger* **-cusing** or **-cussing**) *tr* mettre au point, faire converger; (*a beam of electrons*) focaliser; (*e.g., attention*) concentrer ‖ *intr* converger; **to focus on** se concentrer sur

fodder [ˈfɑdər] s fourrage *m*

foe [fo] s ennemi *m*, adversaire *mf*

fog [fɑg], [fɔg] s brouillard *m*; (naut) brume *f*; (phot) voile *m* ‖ *v* (*pret & pp* **fogged**; *ger* **fogging**) *tr* embrumer; (phot) voiler ‖ *intr* s'embrumer; (phot) se voiler

fog′ bank′ s banc *m* de brume

fog′ bell′ s cloche *f* de brume

fog′bound′ *adj* arrêté par le brouillard, pris dans le brouillard

fog·gy [ˈfɑgɪ], [ˈfɔgɪ] *adj* (*comp* **-gier**; *super* **-giest**) brumeux; (phot) voilé; (fig) confus, flou; **it is foggy** il fait du brouillard

fog′horn′ s sirène *f*, corne *f*, or trompe *f* de brume

foible [ˈfɔɪbəl] s faible *m*, marotte *f*

foil [fɔɪl] s (*thin sheet of metal*) feuille *f*, lame *f*; (*of mirror*) tain *m*; (*sword*) fleuret *m*; (*person whose personality sets off another's*) repoussoir *m* ‖ *tr* déjouer, frustrer

foil′-wrapped′ *adj* ceint de papier d'argent

foist [fɔɪst] *tr*—**to foist oneself upon** s'imposer chez; **to foist s.th. on s.o.** imposer q.ch. à qn

fold [fold] *s* pli *m*, repli *m*; (*for sheep*) parc *m*, bergerie *f*; (*of fat*) bourrelet *m*; (*of the faithful*) bercail *m* ‖ *tr* plier, replier; (*one's arms*) se croiser; **to fold in** (culin) incorporer; **to fold up** replier ‖ *intr* se replier; **to fold up** (theat) faire four; (coll) s'effondrer

folder [′foldər] *s* (*covers for holding papers*) chemise *f*; (*pamphlet*) dépliant *m*; (*person folding newspapers*) plieur *m*

folderol [′faldə‚ral] *s* sottise *f*; (*piece of foolishness*) bagatelle *f*

folding [′foldɪŋ] *adj* pliant, repliant, rabattable

fold′ing cam′era *s* appareil *m* pliant

fold′ing chair′ *s* chaise *f* pliante, chaise brisée

fold′ing cot′ *s* lit *m* pliant or escamotable

fold′ing door′ *s* porte *f* à deux battants

fold′ing rule′ *s* mètre *m* pliant

fold′ing screen′ *s* paravent *m*

fold′ing seat′ *s* strapontin *m*

foliage [′folɪ‚ɪdʒ] *s* feuillage *m*, feuillu *m*

foli·o [′folɪ‚o] *adj* in-folio ‖ *s* (*pl* -os) (*sheet*) folio *m*; (*book*) in-folio *m* ‖ *tr* folioter, paginer

folk [fok] *adj* populaire, traditionnel, du peuple ‖ *s* (*pl* folk or folks) peuple *m*, race *f*; **folks** (coll) gens *mpl*, personnes *fpl*; **my folks** (coll) les miens *mpl*, ma famille

folk′ dance′ *s* danse *f* folklorique

folk′lore′ *s* folklore *m*

folk′ mu′sic *s* musique *f* populaire

folk′ song′ *s* chanson *f* du terroir

folk·sy [′foksi] *adj* (*comp* -sier; *super* -siest) (coll) sociable, liant; (*like common people*) (coll) du terroir

folk′ways′ *spl* coutumes *fpl* traditionnelles

follicle [′falɪkəl] *s* follicule *m*

follow [′falo] *tr* suivre; (*to come after*) succéder (with *dat*); (*to understand*) comprendre; (*a profession*) embrasser; **to follow up** poursuivre; (*e.g., a success*) exploiter ‖ *intr* suivre; (*one after the other*) se suivre; **as follows** comme suit; **it follows that** il s'ensuit que

follower [′falo‚ər] *s* suivant *m*, partisan *m*, disciple *m*

following [′falo‚ɪŋ] *adj* suivant ‖ *s* (*of a prince*) suite *f*; (*followers*) partisans *mpl*, disciples *mpl*

fol′low the lead′er *s* jeu *m* de la queue leu leu

fol′low-up′ *adj* de continuation, complémentaire; (*car*) suiveur ‖ *s* soins *mpl* post-hospitaliers

fol·ly [′fali] *s* (*pl* -lies) sottise *f*; (*madness*) folie *f*; **follies** spectacle *m* de music-hall, folies *fpl*

foment [fo′ment] *tr* fomenter

fond [fand] *adj* affectueux, tendre; **to become fond of** s'attacher à

fondle [′fandəl] *tr* caresser

fondness [′fandnɪs] *s* affection *f*, tendresse *f*; (*appetite*) goût *m*, penchant *m*

font [fant] *s* source *f*; (*for holy water*) bénitier *m*; (*for baptism*) fonts *mpl*; (typ) fonte *f*

food [fud] *adj* alimentaire ‖ *s* nourriture *f*, aliments *mpl*; **food for thought** matière *f* à réflexion; **good food** bonne cuisine *f*

food′ and cloth′ing *s* le vivre et le vêtement

food′ and drink′ *s* le boire et le manger

food′stuffs′ *spl* denrées *fpl* alimentaires, vivres *mpl*

fool [ful] *s* sot *m*; (*jester*) fou *m*; (*person imposed on*) innocent *m*, niais *m*; **to make a fool of** se moquer de; **to play the fool** faire le pitre ‖ *tr* mystifier, abuser; **to fool away** gaspiller sottement ‖ *intr* faire la bête; **to fool around** (coll) gâcher son temps; **to fool with** (coll) tripoter

fooler·y [′fuləri] *s* (*pl* -ies) sottise *f*, ânerie *f*

fool′har′dy *adj* (*comp* -dier; *super* -diest) téméraire

fooling [′fulɪŋ] *s* tromperie *f*; **no fooling!** sans blague!

foolish [′fulɪʃ] *adj* sot, niais; ridicule, absurde

fool′proof′ *adj* à toute épreuve; infaillible

fools′cap′ *s* papier *m* ministre

fool′s′ er′rand *s*—**to go on a fool's errand** y aller pour des prunes

foot [fut] *s* (*pl* feet [fit]) pied *m*; (*of cat, dog, bird*) patte *f*; **on foot** à pied; **to drag one's feet** aller à pas de tortue; **to have one foot in the grave** avoir un pied dans la tombe; **to put one's best foot forward** (coll) partir du bon pied; **to put one's foot down** faire acte d'autorité; **to put one's foot in it** (coll) mettre les pieds dans le plat; **to stand on one's own feet** voler de ses propres ailes; **to tread under foot** fouler aux pieds ‖ *tr* (*the bill*) payer; **to foot it** aller à pied

footage [′futɪdʒ] *s* (mov, telv) (*in French* métrage *m*, i.e., *length of film in meters*) longueur *f* d'un film en pieds

foot′-and-mouth′ disease′ *s* (vet) fièvre *f* aphteuse

foot′ball′ *s* football *m* américain; (*ball*) ballon *m*

foot′ brake′ *s* frein *m* à pédale

foot′bridge′ *s* passerelle *f*

foot′fall′ *s* pas *m* léger, bruit *m* de pas

foot′hills′ *spl* contreforts *mpl*, collines *fpl* basses

foot′hold′ *s*—**to gain a foothold** prendre pied

footing [′futɪŋ] *s* équilibre *m*; (archit) empattement *m*, base *f*, socle *m*; **to be on a friendly footing** être en bons termes; **to be on an equal footing**

être sur un pied d'égalité; **to lose one's footing** perdre pied

foot/lights/ spl (theat) rampe f

foot/lock/er s (mil) cantine f

foot/loose/ adj libre, sans entraves

foot/man s (pl -men) valet m de pied

foot/mark/ s empreinte f de pied

foot/note/ s note f au bas de la page

foot/pad/ s voleur m de grand chemin

foot/path/ s sentier m pour piétons

foot/print/ s empreinte f de pas, trace f

foot/ race/ s course f à pied

foot/rest/ s cale-pied m, repose-pied m

foot/ sol/dier s fantassin m

foot/sore/ adj aux pieds endoloris, éclopé

foot/step/ s pas m; **to follow in s.o.'s footsteps** suivre les traces de qn

foot/stone/ s pierre f tumulaire (au pied d'une tombe); (archit) première pierre

foot/stool/ s tabouret m

foot/ warm/er s chauffe-pieds m

foot/wear/ s chaussures fpl

foot/work/ s jeu m de jambes

foot/worn/ adj usé; (person) aux pieds endoloris

fop [fɑp] s petit-maître m, bellâtre m

for [fɔr], [fər] prep pour; de, e.g., **to thank s.o. for** remercier qn de; e.g., **time for dinner** l'heure du dîner; e.g., **to cry for joy** pleurer de joie; e.g., **request for money** demande d'argent, à, e.g., **for sale** à vendre; e.g., **to sell for a high price** vendre à un prix élevé; e.g., **it is for you to decide** c'est à vous de décider; par, e.g., **famous for** célèbre par; e.g., **for example** par exemple; e.g., **for pity's sake** par pitié; contre, e.g., **a remedy for** un remède contre; as for quant à; **for** + ger pour + perf inf, e.g., **he was punished for stealing** il fut puni pour avoir volé; **for all that** malgré tout cela; **for short** en abrégé; **he has been in Paris for a week** il est à Paris depuis une semaine, il y a une semaine qu'il est à Paris; **he was in Paris for a week** il était à Paris pendant une semaine; **to be for** (to be in favor of) être en faveur de, être partisan de or pour; **to use s.th. for s.th.** employer q.ch. comme q.ch.; e.g., **to use coal for fuel** employer le charbon comme combustible ‖ conj car, parce que

forage ['fɑrɪdʒ], ['fɔrɪdʒ] s fourrage m ‖ tr & intr fourrager

foray ['fɑre], ['fɔre] s incursion f ‖ tr saccager, fourrager ‖ intr faire une incursion

for·bear [fɔr'bɛr] v (pret -bore; pp -borne) tr s'abstenir de ‖ intr se montrer patient

forbearance [fɔr'bɛrəns] s abstention f; patience f

for·bid [fɔr'bɪd] v (pret -bade or -bad ['bæd]; pp -bidden; ger -bidding) tr défendre, interdire; **God forbid!** qu'à Dieu ne plaise!; **to forbid s.o. s.th.** défendre q.ch. à qn; **to forbid s.o. to** défendre à qn de

forbidden [fɔr'bɪdən] adj défendu

forbidding [fɔr'bɪdɪŋ] adj rebutant, rébarbatif, sinistre

force [fɔrs] s force f; (of a word) signification f, valeur f; **in force** en vigueur; **in full force** en force; **the allied forces** les puissances alliées ‖ tr forcer; **to force back** repousser; (air; water) refouler; **to force in** (e.g., a door) enfoncer; **to force one's way into** (e.g., a house) pénétrer de force dans; **to force s.o.'s hand** forcer la main à qn; **to force s.o. to** + inf forcer qn à or de + inf; **to force s.th. into s.th.** faire entrer q.ch. dans q.ch.; **to force up** (e.g., prices) faire monter

forced/ draft/ s tirage m forcé

forced/ land/ing s atterrissage m forcé

forced/ march/ s marche f forcée

force/-feed/ tr (pret & pp -fed) gaver, suralimenter

force/-feed/ing s suralimentation f

forceful ['fɔrsfəl] adj énergique

for·ceps ['fɔrseps] s (pl -ceps or -cipes [sɪ,piz]) (dent, surg) pince f; (obstet) forceps m

force/ pump/ s pompe f foulante

forcible ['fɔrsɪbəl] adj énergique, vigoureux; (convincing) convaincant; (imposed) forcé

ford [fɔrd] s gué m ‖ tr franchir à gué

fore [fɔr] adj antérieur; (naut) de l'avant ‖ s (naut) avant m; **to the fore** en vue, en vedette ‖ adv à l'avant ‖ interj (golf) gare devant!

fore/and aft/ adv de l'avant à l'arrière

fore/arm/ s avant-bras m ‖ **fore·arm/** tr prémunir; (to warn) avertir

fore/bear/ s ancêtre m

foreboding [fɔr'bodɪŋ] s (sign) présage m; (feeling) pressentiment m

fore/cast/ s prévision f ‖ v (pret & pp -cast or -casted) tr pronostiquer

forecastle ['foksəl], ['for,kæsəl], ['for,kɑsəl] s gaillard m d'avant

fore·close/ tr exclure; (law) forclore; **to foreclose the mortgage** saisir l'immeuble hypothéqué

foreclosure [fɔr'kloʒər] s saisie f, forclusion f

fore·doom/ tr condamner par avance

fore/ edge/ s (bb) tranche f

fore/fa/ther s aïeul m, ancêtre m

fore/fin/ger s index m

fore/foot/ s (pl -feet) patte f de devant

fore/front/ s premier rang m; **in the forefront** en première ligne

fore·go/ v (pret -went; pp -gone) tr (to give up) renoncer à

foregoing ['fɔr,goɪŋ], [fɔr'goɪŋ] adj précédent, antérieur; (facts, text, etc. already cited) déjà cité, ci-dessus

fore/gone/ adj inévitable; (anticipated) décidé d'avance, prévu

fore/ground/ s premier plan m

fore/hand/ed adj prévoyant; (thrifty) ménager

forehead ['fɑrɪd], ['fɔrɪd] s front m

foreign ['fɑrɪn], ['fɔrɪn] adj étranger

for/eign affairs/ spl affaires fpl étrangères

foreigner ['fɑrɪnər], ['fɒrɪnər] s étranger m
for'eign exchange' s change m étranger; (currency) devises fpl
for'eign min'ister s ministre m des affaires étrangères
for'eign of'fice s ministère m des affaires étrangères
for'eign serv'ice s (dipl) service m diplomatique; (mil) service m à l'étranger
for'eign trade' s commerce m extérieur
fore'leg' s jambe f de devant
fore'lock' s mèche f sur le front; (of horse) toupet m; **to take time by the forelock** saisir l'occasion par les cheveux
fore'man s (pl -men) chef m d'équipe; (in machine shop, factory) contremaître m; (of jury) premier juré m
foremast ['formɑst], ['for,mæst], ['for,mɑst] s mât m de misaine
fore'most' adj premier, principal || adv au premier rang
fore'noon' s matinée f
fore'part' s avant m, devant m, partie f avant
fore'paw' s patte f de devant
fore'quar'ter s quartier m de devant
fore'run'ner s précurseur m, avant-coureur m; (sign) signe m avant-coureur
foresail ['forsəl], ['for,sel], s misaine f, voile f de misaine
fore•see' v (pret -saw; pp -seen) tr prévoir
foreseeable [for'si•əbəl] adj prévisible
fore•shad'ow tr présager, préfigurer
fore•short'en tr dessiner en raccourci
fore•short'ening s raccourci m
fore'sight' s prévision f, prévoyance f
fore'sight'ed adj prévoyant
fore'skin' s prépuce m
forest ['fɑrɪst], ['fɒrɪst] adj forestier || s forêt f
fore'stage' s (theat) avant-scène f
fore•stall' tr anticiper, devancer
for'est rang'er s garde m forestier
forestry ['fɑrɪstri], ['fɒrɪstri] s sylviculture f
fore'taste' s avant-goût m
fore•tell' v (pret & pp -told) tr prédire
fore'thought' s prévoyance f; (law) préméditation f
for•ev'er adv pour toujours, à jamais
fore•warn' tr avertir, prévenir
fore'word' s avant-propos m, avis m au lecteur
forfeit ['fɔrfɪt] adj perdu || s (pledge) dédit m, gage m; (fine) amende f; **to play at forfeits** jouer aux gages || tr être déchu de, être privé de
forfeiture ['fɔrfɪtʃər] s perte f; (fine) amende f, confiscation f
forge [fordʒ] s forge f || tr forger; (e.g., documents) contrefaire, falsifier
forger ['fordʒər] s forgeur m; (e.g., of documents) faussaire m
forger•y ['fordʒəri] s (pl -ies) contrefaçon f; (of a document, a painting, etc.) faux m
for•get [fər'gɛt] v (pret -got; pp -got or

-gotten; ger -getting) tr & intr oublier; **forget it!** n'y pensez plus!; **to forget to** + inf oublier de + inf
forgetful [fər'gɛtfəl] adj oublieux
forget'-me-not' s myosotis m, ne-m'oubliez-pas m
forgivable [fər'gɪvəbəl] adj pardonnable
for•give [fər'gɪv] v (pret -gave; pp -given) tr & intr pardonner
forgiveness [fər'gɪvnɪs] s pardon m
forgiving [fər'gɪvɪŋ] adj indulgent, miséricordieux
for•go [fɔr'go] v (pret -went; pp -gone) tr renoncer à, s'abstenir de
fork [fork] s fourche f; (of road, tree, stem) fourche f, bifurcation f; (at table) fourchette f || tr & intr fourcher, bifurquer
forked adj fourchu
forked' light'ning s éclairs mpl en zig-zag
fork'lift truck' s chariot m élévateur
forlorn [fɔr'lɔrn] adj (destitute) abandonné; (hopeless) désespéré; (wretched) misérable
forlorn' hope' s tentative f désespérée
form [form] s forme f; (paper to be filled out) formule f, fiche f, feuille f; (construction to give shape to cement) coffrage m || tr former || intr se former
formal ['fɔrməl] adj cérémonieux, officiel; (formalistic) formaliste; (superficial) formel, de pure forme
for'mal attire' s tenue f de cérémonie
for'mal call' s visite f de politesse
for'mal din'ner s dîner m de cérémonie, dîner prié
formali•ty [fɔr'mælɪti] s (pl -ties) formalité f; (stiffness) raideur f; (polite conventions) cérémonie f, étiquette f
for'mal par'ty s soirée f de gala
for'mal speech' s discours m d'apparat
format ['fɔrmæt] s format m
formation [fɔr'meʃən] s formation f
former ['fɔrmər] adj antérieur, précédent; (long past) ancien; (first of two things mentioned) premier || pron—**the former** celui-ci m §84; le premier
formerly ['fɔrmərli] adv autrefois, anciennement, jadis
form'fit'ting adj ajusté, moulant
formidable ['fɔrmɪdəbəl] adj formidable
formless ['fɔrmlɪs] adj informe
form' let'ter s lettre f circulaire
formu•la ['fɔrmjələ] s (pl -las or -lae [,li]) formule f
formulate ['fɔrmjə,let] tr formuler
for•sake [fɔr'sek] v (pret -sook ['suk]; pp -saken ['sekən]) tr abandonner, délaisser
fort [fort] s fort m, forteresse f; **hold the fort!** (coll) je vous confie la maison!
forte [fort] s fort m
forth [forθ] adv en avant; **and so forth** et ainsi de suite; **from this day forth** à partir de ce jour; **to go forth** sortir, se mettre en route
forth'com'ing adj à venir, à paraître

forth'right' *adj* net, direct || *adv* droit, carrément; (*immediately*) tout de suite

forth'with' *adv* sur-le-champ

fortieth ['fɔrtɪ·ɪθ] *adj & pron* quarantième (*masc, fem*) || *s* quarantième *m*

fortification [ˌfɔrtɪfɪ'keʃən] *s* fortification *f*

forti·fy ['fɔrtɪˌfaɪ] *v* (*pret & pp* **-fied**) *tr* fortifier; (*wine*) viner

fortitude ['fɔrtɪˌt(j)ud] *s* force *f* d'âme

fortnight ['fɔrt͵naɪt], ['fɔrtnɪt] *s* quinze jours *mpl*, quinzaine *f*

fortress ['fɔrtrɪs] *s* forteresse *f*

fortuitous [fɔr't(j)u·ɪtəs] *adj* (*accidental*) fortuit; (*lucky*) fortuné

fortunate ['fɔrtʃənɪt] *adj* heureux

fortune ['fɔrtʃən] *s* fortune *f*; **to make a fortune** faire fortune; **to tell s.o. his fortune** dire la bonne aventure à qn

for'tune hunt'er *s* coureur *m* de dots

for'tune-tel'ler *s* diseuse *f* de bonne aventure

for·ty ['fɔrtɪ] *adj & pron* quarante || *s* (*pl* **-ties**) quarante *m*; **about forty** une quarantaine

fo·rum ['forəm] *s* (*pl* **-rums** or **-ra** [rə]) forum *m*; (*e.g., of public opinion*) tribunal *m*; **open forum** tribune *f* libre

forward ['fɔrwərd] *adj* de devant; (*precocious*) avancé, précoce; (*bold*) audacieux, effronté || *s* (*sports*) avant *m* || *adv* en avant; **to bring forward** (bk) reporter; **to come forward** s'avancer; **to look forward to** compter sur, se faire une fête de || *tr* envoyer, expédier; (*a letter*) faire suivre; (*a project*) avancer, favoriser

for'warding address' *s* adresse *f* d'expédition, adresse d'envoi

fossil ['fɑsɪl] *adj & s* fossile *m*

foster ['fɑstər], ['fɔstər] *adj* de lait, nourricier || *tr* encourager, entretenir

fos'ter broth'er *s* frère *m* de lait

fos'ter fa'ther *s* père *m* nourricier

foul [faʊl] *adj* immonde; (*air*) vicié; (*wind*) contraire; (*weather*) gros, sale; (*breath*) fétide; (*language*) ordurier; (*water*) bourbeux; (*ball*) hors jeu || *s* (baseball) faute *f*; (boxing) coup *m* bas || *adv* déloyalement || *tr* (sports) commettre une faute contre || *intr* (*said of anchor, propeller, rope, etc.*) s'engager

foul-mouthed ['faʊl'maʊðd], ['faʊl-'maʊθt] *adj* mal embouché

foul' play' *s* malveillance *f*; (sports) jeu *m* déloyal

found [faʊnd] *tr* fonder, établir; (*metal*) fondre

foundation [faʊn'deʃən] *s* (*basis; masonry support*) fondement *m*; (*act of endowing*) dotation *f*; (*endowment*) fondation *f*

founder ['faʊndər] *s* fondateur *m*; (*in foundry*) fondeur *m* || *intr* (*said of horse*) boiter bas; (*said of building*) s'effondrer; (*said of ship*) (naut) sombrer

foundling ['faʊndlɪŋ] *s* enfant *m* trouvé

found'ling hos'pital *s* hospice *m* des enfants trouvés

found·ry ['faʊndrɪ] *s* (*pl* **-ries**) fonderie *f*

found'ry·man *s* (*pl* **-men**) fondeur *m*

fount [faʊnt] *s* source *f*

fountain ['faʊntən] *s* fontaine *f*

foun'tain-head' *s* source *f*, origine *f*

Foun'tain of Youth' *s* fontaine *f* de Jouvence

foun'tain pen' *s* stylo *m*

four [for] *adj & pron* quatre || *s* quatre *m*; **four o'clock** quatre heures; **on all fours** à quatre pattes

four'-cy'cle *adj* (mach) à quatre temps

four'-cyl'inder *adj* (mach) à quatre cylindres

four'-flush' *intr* (coll) bluffer, faire le fanfaron

fourflusher ['for͵flʌʃər] *s* (coll) bluffeur *m*

four'-foot'ed *adj* quadrupède

four' hun'dred *adj & pron* quatre cents || *s* quatre cents *m*; **the Four Hundred** la haute société; le Tout Paris

four'-in-hand' *s* (tie) cravate-plastron *f*; (*team*) attelage *m* à quatre

four'-lane' *adj* à quatre voies

four'-leaf clo'ver *s* trèfle *m* à quatre feuilles

four'-motor plane' *s* quadrimoteur *m*

four'-o'clock' *s* (*Mirabilis jalapa*) belle-de-nuit *f*

four' of a kind' *s* (cards) un carré

four'-post'er *s* lit *m* à colonnes

four'score' *adj* quatre-vingts

foursome ['forsəm] *s* partie *f* double

fourteen ['for'tin] *adj, pron, & s* quatorze *m*

fourteenth ['for'tinθ] *adj & pron* quatorzième (*masc, fem*); **the Fourteenth** quatorze, e.g., **John the Fourteenth** Jean quatorze || *s* quatorzième *m*; **the fourteenth** (*in dates*) le quatorze

fourth [forθ] *adj & pron* quatrième (*masc, fem*); **the Fourth** quatre, e.g., **John the Fourth** Jean quatre || *s* quatrième *m*; (*in fractions*) quart *m*; **the fourth** (*in dates*) le quatre

fourth' estate' *s* quatrième pouvoir *m*

fowl [faʊl] *s* volaille *f*

fox [fɑks] *s* renard *m* || *tr* (coll) mystifier

fox'glove' *s* digitale *f*

fox'hole' *s* renardière *f*; (mil) gourbi *m*, abri *m* de tranchée

fox'hound' *s* fox-hound *m*

fox' hunt' *s* chasse *f* au renard

fox' ter'rier *s* fox-terrier *m*

fox' trot' *s* (*of animal*) petit trot *m*; (*dance*) fox-trot *m*

fox·y ['fɑksɪ] *adj* (*comp* **-ier**; *super* **-iest**) rusé, madré

foyer ['fɔɪ·ər] *s* (*lobby*) foyer *m*; (*entrance hall*) vestibule *m*

fracas ['frekəs] *s* bagarre *f*, rixe *f*

fraction ['frækʃən] *s* fraction *f*

fractional ['frækʃənəl] *adj* fractionnaire

frac'tional cur'rency *s* monnaie *f* divisionnaire

fracture ['fræktʃər] *s* fracture *f*; **to set**

a fracture réduire une fracture || tr fracturer

fragile ['frædʒɪl] adj fragile

fragment ['frægmənt] s fragment m || tr fragmenter

fragrance ['fregrəns] s parfum m

fragrant ['fregrənt] adj parfumé

frail [frel] adj frêle; (e.g., virtue) fragile, faible || s (basket) couffe f

frail·ty ['frelti] s (pl -ties) fragilité f; (weakness) faiblesse f

frame [frem] s (of picture, mirror) cadre m; (of glasses) monture f; (of window, car) châssis m; (of window, motor) bâti m; (support, stand) armature f; (structure) charpente f; (for embroidering) métier m; (of comic strip) cadre, dessin m; (mov, telv) image f || tr former, charpenter; (a picture) encadrer; (film) cadrer; (an answer) formuler; (slang) monter une accusation contre

frame' house' s maison f en bois

frame' of mind' s disposition f d'esprit

frame'-up' s (slang) coup m monté

frame'work' s charpente f, squelette m

framing ['fremɪŋ] s (mov, phot) cadrage m

France [fræns], [frɑns] s France f; la France

franchise ['fræntʃaɪz] s concession f, privilège m; droit m de vote

frank [fræŋk] adj franc || s franchise f postale; **Frank** (medieval German person) Franc m; (masculine name) François m || tr affranchir

frankfurter ['fræŋkfərtər] s saucisse f de Francfort

frankincense ['fræŋkɪn‚sens] s oliban m

Frankish ['fræŋkɪʃ] adj franc || s francique m

frankness ['fræŋknɪs] s franchise f

frantic ['fræntɪk] adj frénétique

fraternal [frə'tʌrnəl] adj fraternel

fraterni·ty [frə'tʌrnɪti] s (pl -ties) fraternité f; (association) confrérie f; (at a university) club m d'étudiants, amicale f estudiantine

fraternize ['frætər‚naɪz] intr fraterniser

fraud [frɔd] s fraude f; (person) imposteur m, fourbe mf

fraudulent ['frɔdjələnt] adj frauduleux, en fraude

fraught [frɔt] adj—**fraught with** chargé de

fray [fre] s bagarre f || tr érailler || intr s'érailler

freak [frik] s (sudden fancy) caprice m; (anomaly) curiosité f; (person, animal) monstre m

freakish ['frikɪʃ] adj capricieux; bizarre; (grotesque) monstrueux

freckle ['frekəl] s tache f de rousseur, éphélide f

freckly ['frekli] adj couvert de taches de rousseur

free [fri] adj (comp freer ['fri·ər]; super freest ['fri·ɪst]) libre; (without charge) gratuit; (without extra charge) franc, exempt; (e.g., end of a rope) dégagé; (with money, advice, etc.) libéral, généreux; (manner, speech, etc.) franc, ouvert; **to set free** libérer, affranchir || adv franco, gratis, gratuitement; (naut) largue, e.g., **running free** courant largue || v (pret & pp **freed** [frid]; ger **freeing** ['fri·ɪŋ]) tr libérer; (a prisoner) affranchir, élargir; (to disengage) dégager; (from an obligation) exempter

free' and eas'y adj désinvolte, dégagé

freebooter ['fri‚butər] s flibustier m, maraudeur m

free' com'peti'tion s libre concurrence f

freedom ['fridəm] s liberté f

free'dom of speech' s liberté f de la parole

free'dom of the press' s liberté f de la presse

free'dom of the seas' s liberté f des mers

free'dom of thought' s liberté f de la pensée

free'dom of wor'ship s liberté f du culte, libre pratique f

free'-for-all' s foire f d'empoigne, mêlée f

free' hand' s carte f blanche

free'-hand draw'ing s dessin m à main levée

free'hand'ed adj libéral, généreux

free'hold' s (law) propriété f foncière perpétuelle; (hist) franc-alleu m

free' lance' s franc-tireur m

free'man s (pl -men) homme m libre; (citizen) citoyen m

Free'ma'son s franc-maçon m

Free'ma'sonry s franc-maçonnerie f

free' of charge' adj & adv gratis, exempt de frais

free' on board' adv franco de bord, départ usine

free' port' s port m franc

free' speech' s liberté f de la parole

free'-spo'ken adj franc; **to be free-spoken** avoir son franc-parler

free'think'er s libre penseur m

free' thought' s libre pensée f

free' tick'et s billet m de faveur

free' trade' s libre-échange m

free' trad'er s libre-échangiste mf

free'way' s autoroute f

free'will' adj volontaire, de plein gré

free' will' s libre arbitre m; **of one's own free will** de son propre gré

freeze [friz] s congélation f || v (pret **froze** [froz]; pp **frozen**) tr geler, congeler; (assets, credits, etc.) geler, bloquer; (e.g., meat) congeler || intr geler; **it is freezing** il gèle

freezer ['frizər] s (for making ice cream) sorbetière f; (for foods) congélateur m

freight [fret] s fret m, chargement m; (cost) fret, prix m du transport; **by freight** (rr) en petite vitesse || tr transporter; (a ship, truck, etc.) charger

freight' car' s wagon m de marchandises, wagon à caisse

freighter ['fretər] s cargo m

freight' plat'form s quai m de déchargement

freight' sta'tion s gare f de marchandises

freight' train' s train m de marchandises

freight' yard' s (rr) cour f de marchandises

French [frɛntʃ] adj français ‖ s (language) français m; **the French** les Français

French' Cana'dian s Franco-Canadien m

French'-Cana'dian adj franco-canadien

French' chalk' s craie f de tailleur, stéatite f

French' cuff' s poignet m mousquetaire

French' door' s porte-fenêtre f

French' dress'ing s vinaigrette f

French' fries' spl frites fpl

French' horn' s (mus) cor m d'harmonie

French' horse'power s (735 watts) cheval-vapeur m, cheval m

French' leave' s—**to take French leave** filer à l'anglaise

French'man s (pl -men) Français m

French' roll' s petit pain m

French'-speak'ing adj francophone; (country) de langue française

French' tel'ephone s combiné m

French' toast' s pain m perdu

French' win'dow s porte-fenêtre f

French'wom'an s (pl -wom'en) Française f

frenzied ['frɛnzid] adj frénétique

fren·zy ['frɛnzi] s (pl -zies) frénésie f

frequen·cy ['frikwənsi] s (pl -cies) fréquence f

fre'quency modula'tion s modulation f de fréquence

frequent ['frikwənt] adj fréquent ‖ [frɪ'kwɛnt], ['frikwənt] tr fréquenter

frequently ['frikwəntli] adv fréquemment

fres·co ['frɛsko] s (pl -coes or -cos) fresque f ‖ tr peindre à fresque

fresh [frɛʃ] adj frais; (water) doux; (e.g., idea) nouveau; (wound) saignant; (cheeky) (coll) osé, impertinent; **fresh paint!** (public sign) attention, peinture fraîche! ‖ adv nouvellement; **fresh in** (coll) récemment arrivé; **fresh out** (coll) récemment épuisé

freshen ['frɛʃən] tr rafraîchir ‖ intr se rafraîchir; (said of wind) fraîchir

freshet ['frɛʃɪt] s crue f

fresh'man s (pl -men) étudiant m de première année, bizut m

freshness ['frɛʃnɪs] s fraîcheur f; (sauciness) impudence f, impertinence f

fresh'-wa'ter adj d'eau douce

fret [frɛt] s (interlaced design) frette f; (uneasiness) inquiétude f; (mus) touchette f ‖ v (pret & pp fretted; ger fretting) tr ajourer ‖ intr s'inquiéter, geindre

fretful ['frɛtfəl] adj irritable, boudeur

fret'work' s ajour m, ornementation f ajourée

Freudianism ['frɔɪdɪ-ə‚nɪzəm] s freudisme m

friar ['fraɪ-ər] s moine m

fricassee [‚frɪkə'si] s fricassée f

friction ['frɪkʃən] s friction f

fric'tion tape' s chatterton m, ruban m isolant

Friday ['fraɪdi] s vendredi m

fried [fraɪd] adj frit

fried' egg' s œuf m sur le plat

friend [frɛnd] s ami m; **to make friends with** se lier d'amitié avec

friend·ly ['frɛndli] adj (comp -lier; super -liest) amical, sympathique

friendship ['frɛndʃɪp] s amitié f

frieze [friz] s (archit) frise f

frigate ['frɪgɪt] s frégate f

fright [fraɪt] s frayeur f, effroi m; (grotesque or ridiculous person) (coll) épouvantail m; **to take fright at** s'effrayer de

frighten ['fraɪtən] tr effrayer; **to frighten away** effaroucher, faire fuir

frightful ['fraɪtfəl] adj effroyable; (coll) affreux; (huge) (coll) énorme

frigid ['frɪdʒɪd] adj frigide; (zone) glacial

frigidity [frɪ'dʒɪdɪti] s frigidité f

frill [frɪl] s (on shirt front) jabot m; (frippery) falbala m

fringe [frɪndʒ] s frange f; (border) bordure f; (opt) frange; **on the fringe of** en marge de ‖ tr franger

fringe' ben'efits spl supplément m de solde, bénéfices mpl marginaux

fripper·y ['frɪpəri] s (pl -ies) (flashiness) clinquant m; (inferior goods) camelote f

frisk [frɪsk] tr (slang) fouiller, palper ‖ intr—**to frisk about** gambader, folâtrer

frisk·y ['frɪski] adj (comp -ier; super -iest) vif, folâtre; (horse) fringant

fritter ['frɪtər] s beignet m ‖ tr—**to fritter away** gaspiller

frivolous ['frɪvələs] adj frivole

frizzle ['frɪzəl] s frisure f ‖ tr frisotter; (culin) faire frire ‖ intr frisotter; (culin) grésiller

friz·zly ['frɪzli] adj (comp -zlier; super -zliest) crépu, crépelu

fro [fro] adv—**to and fro** de long en large; **to go to and fro** aller et venir

frock [frɑk] s robe f; (overalls, smock) blouse f; (eccl) froc m

frock' coat' s redingote f

frog [frɑg], [frɔg] s grenouille f; (in throat) chat m

frog'man s (pl -men') homme-grenouille m

frogs'' legs' spl cuisses fpl de grenouille

frol·ic ['frɑlɪk] s gaieté f, ébat m ‖ v (pret & pp -icked; ger -icking) intr s'ébattre, folâtrer

frolicsome ['frɑlɪksəm] adj folâtre

from [frʌm], [frɑm], [frəm] prep de; de la part de, e.g., **greetings from your friend** compliments de la part de votre ami; contre, e.g., **a shelter from the rain** un abri contre la pluie; **from a certain angle** sous un certain angle; **from . . . to** depuis . . .

jusqu'à; **from what I hear** d'après ce que j'apprends; **the flight from** le vol en provenance de; **to drink from** (*a glass*) boire dans; (*a bottle*) boire à; **to learn from a book** apprendre dans un livre; **to steal from** voler à

front [frʌnt] *adj* antérieur, de devant ‖ *s* devant *m*; (*first place*) premier rang *m*; (aut) avant *m*; (geog, mil, pol) front *m*; (*figurehead*) (coll) prête-nom *m*; **in front** par devant; **in front of** en face de, devant; **to put up a bold front** (coll) faire bonne contenance ‖ *tr* (*to face*) donner sur; (*to confront*) affronter ‖ *intr*—**to front on** donner sur

frontage ['frʌntɪdʒ] *s* façade *f*; (*along a street, lake, etc.*) largeur *f*

front' door' *s* porte *f* d'entrée

front' drive' *s* (aut) traction *f* avant

frontier [frʌn'tɪr] *adj* frontalier ‖ *s* frontière *f*; (hist) front *m* de colonisation, front pionnier

frontiers'man *s* (*pl* -**men**) frontalier *m*, broussard *m*

frontispiece ['frʌntɪs‚pis] *s* frontispice *m*; (archit) façade *f* principale

front' lines' *spl* avant-postes *mpl*

front' mat'ter *s* (*of book*) feuilles *fpl* liminaires

front' of'fice *s* direction *f*

front' porch' *s* porche *m*

front' room' *s* chambre *f* sur la rue

front' row' *s* premier rang *m*

front' seat' *s* siège *m* avant; (aut) banquette *f* avant

front' steps' *spl* perron *m*

front' view' *s* vue *f* de face

front' yard' *s* devant *m* de la maison

frost [frɔst], [frast] *s* (*freezing*) gelée *f*; (*frozen dew*) givre *m* ‖ *tr* (*to freeze*) geler; (*to cover with frost*) givrer; (culin) glacer

frost'bite' *s* engelure *f*

frost'ed glass' *s* verre *m* dépoli

frosting ['frɔstɪŋ], ['frastɪŋ] *s* (*on glass*) dépolissage *m*; (culin) fondant *m*

frost·y ['frɔsti], ['frasti] *adj* (*comp* -**ier**; *super* -**iest**) couvert de givre; (*reception, welcome*) glacé, glacial

froth [frɔθ], [fraθ] *s* écume *f*; (*on soap, beer, chocolate*) mousse *f*; (*frivolity*) futilité *f* ‖ *intr* mousser; (*at the mouth*) écumer

froth·y ['frɔθi], ['fraθi] *adj* (*comp* -**ier**; *super* -**iest**) écumeux; (*soap, beer, chocolate*) mousseux; (*frivolous*) creux, futile

froward ['frowərd] *adj* obstiné, revêche

frown [fraun] *s* froncement *m* de sourcils ‖ *intr* froncer les sourcils; **to frown at** or **on** être contraire à, désapprouver

frows·y or **frowz·y** ['frauzi] *adj* (*comp* -**ier**; *super* -**iest**) malpropre, négligé, peu soigné; (*smelling bad*) malodorant

fro'zen as'sets ['frozən] *spl* fonds *mpl* gelés

fro'zen foods' *spl* aliments *mpl* surgelés

frugal ['frugəl] *adj* sobre, modéré; (*meal*) frugal

fruit [frut] *adj* fruitier ‖ *s* fruit *m*; les fruits, e.g., **I like fruit** j'aime les fruits

fruit' cake' *s* cake *m*

fruit' cup' *s* coupe *f* de fruits

fruit' fly' *s* mouche *f* du vinaigre

fruitful ['frutfəl] *adj* fructueux, fécond

fruition [fru'ɪʃən] *s* réalisation *f*; **to come to fruition** fructifier

fruit' juice' *s* jus *m* de fruits

fruitless ['frutlɪs] *adj* stérile, vain

fruit' sal'ad *s* macédoine *f* de fruits, salade *f* de fruits

fruit' stand' *s* étalage *m* de fruits

fruit' store' *s* fruiterie *f*

frumpish ['frʌmpɪʃ] *adj* fagoté, négligé

frustrate ['frʌstret] *tr* frustrer

fry [fraɪ] *s* (*pl* **fries**) (culin) friture *f*; (ichth) fretin *m* ‖ *v* (*pret* & *pp* **fried**) *tr* faire frire; (*to sauté*) faire sauter ‖ *intr* frire

fry'ing pan' *s* poêle *f* à frire; **to jump from the frying pan into the fire** sauter de la poêle dans le feu

fudge [fʌdʒ] *s* fondant *m* de chocolat; (*humbug*) blague *f*

fuel ['fjuəl] *s* combustible *m*; (aut) carburant *m*; (fig) aliment *m* ‖ *v* (*pret* & *pp* **fueled** or **fuelled**) *ger* **fueling** or **fuelling**) *tr* pourvoir en combustible

fu'el gauge' *s* jauge *f* de combustible

fu'el line' *s* conduite *f* de combustible

fu'el oil' *s* mazout *m*, fuel-oil *m*, fuel *m*

fu'el tank' *s* réservoir *m* de carburant; (aut) réservoir à essence

fugitive ['fjudʒɪtɪv] *adj* & *s* fugitif *m*

ful·crum ['fʌlkrəm] *s* (*pl* -**crums** or -**cra** [krə]) point *m* d'appui

fulfill [ful'fɪl] *tr* accomplir; (*an obligation*) s'acquitter de, remplir

fulfillment [ful'fɪlmənt] *s* accomplissement *m*

full [ful] *adj* plein; (*dress, garment*) ample, bouffant; (*schedule*) chargé; (*lips*) gros, fort; (*brother, sister*) germain; (*having no more room*) complet; **full to overflowing** plein à déborder ‖ *s* plein *m*; in full intégralement, entièrement; (*to spell in full*) en toutes lettres; **to the full** complètement ‖ *adv* complètement; **full in the face** en pleine figure; **full many a** bien des; **full well** parfaitement ‖ *tr* (*cloth*) fouler

full' blast' *adv* (coll) en pleine activité

full'-blood'ed *adj* robuste; (*thoroughbred*) pur sang

full-blown ['ful'blon] *adj* achevé, développé; en pleine fleur

full'-bod'ied *adj* (e.g., *wine*) corsé

full' dress' *s* grande tenue *f*

full'-dress' coat' *s* frac *m*

full'-faced' *adj* (*portrait*) de face

full-fledged ['ful'fledʒd] *adj* véritable, rien moins que

full-grown ['ful'gron] *adj* (*plant*) mûr; (*tree*) de haute futaie; (*person*) adulte

full′ house′ s (poker) main f pleine; (theat) salle f comble
full′-length′ adj (portrait) en pied
full′-length mir′ror s psyché f
full′-length mov′ie s long métrage m
full′ load′ s plein chargement m
full′ meas′ure s mesure f comble
full′ moon′ s pleine lune f
full′ name′ s nom m et prénoms mpl
full′ pow′ers spl pleins pouvoirs mpl
full′ rest′ s (mus) pause f
full′ sail′ adv toutes voiles dehors
full′ ses′sion s assemblée f plénière
full′-sized′ adj de grandeur nature
full′ speed′ s toute vitesse f
full′ stop′ s (gram) point m final; **to come to a full stop** s'arrêter net
full′ swing′ s—**in full swing** en pleine activité, en train
full′ tilt′ adv à toute vitesse
full′ time′ adv à pleines journées
full′-time′ adj à temps plein
full′ view′ s—**in full view** à la vue de tous
full′ weight′ s poids m juste
fully ['fuli], ['fulli] adv entièrement, pleinement
fulsome ['fulsəm], ['fʌlsəm] adj écœurant, bas, servile
fumble ['fʌmbəl] tr manier maladroitement; (the ball) ne pas attraper, laisser tomber || intr tâtonner
fume [fjum] s (bad humor) rage f; **fumes** fumées fpl, vapeurs fpl || tr & intr fumer
fumigate ['fjumɪ,get] tr fumiger
fun [fʌn] s amusement m, gaieté f; (badinage) plaisanterie f; **in fun** pour rire; **to have fun** s'amuser; **to make fun of** se moquer de
function ['fʌŋkʃən] s fonction f; (meeting) cérémonie f || intr fonctionner; **to function as** faire fonction de
functional ['fʌŋk/ənəl] adj fonctionnel
functionar·y ['fʌŋk/ə,neri] s (pl -ies) fonctionnaire mf
fund [fʌnd] s fonds m; **funds** fonds mpl || tr (a debt) consolider
fundamental [,fʌndə'mentəl] adj fondamental || s principe m, base f
fundamentalist [,fʌndə'mentəlɪst] s (rel) scripturaire m
funeral ['fjunərəl] adj (march, procession, ceremony) funèbre; (expenses) funéraire || s funérailles fpl
fu′neral direc′tor s entrepreneur m de pompes funèbres
fu′neral home′ or **par′lor** s chapelle f mortuaire; salon m mortuaire (Canad); (business) entreprise f de pompes funèbres
fu′neral proces′sion s convoi m funèbre, enterrement m, deuil m
fu′neral serv′ice s office m des morts
funereal [fju'nɪriəl] adj funèbre
fungus ['fʌŋgəs] s (pl **funguses** or **fungi** ['fʌndʒaɪ]) (bot) champignon m; (pathol) fongus m
funicular [fju'nɪkjələr] adj & s funiculaire m
funk [fʌŋk] s (coll) frousse f

fun·nel ['fʌnəl] s entonnoir m; (smokestack) cheminée f; (tube for ventilation) tuyau m || v (pret & pp -neled or -nelled; ger -neling or -nelling) tr verser avec un entonnoir; (to channel) concentrer
funnies ['fʌniz] spl pages fpl comiques
fun·ny ['fʌni] adj (comp -nier; super -niest) comique; amusant, drôle; (coll) bizarre, curieux; **to strike s.o. as funny** paraître drôle à qn
fun′ny pa′per s pages fpl comiques
fur [fʌr] s fourrure f; (on tongue) empâtement m; **furs** pelleteries fpl
furbish ['fʌrbɪʃ] tr fourbir; **to furbish up** remettre à neuf
furious ['fjurɪ·əs] adj furieux
furl [fʌrl] tr (naut) ferler
fur′-lined′ adj doublé de fourrure
furlough ['fʌrlo] s permission f; **on furlough** en permission || tr donner une permission à
furnace ['fʌrnɪs] s (to heat a house) calorifère m; (to produce steam) chaudière f; (e.g., to smelt ores) fourneau m; (rr) foyer m; (fig) fournaise f
furnish ['fʌrnɪʃ] tr fournir; (a house) meubler
fur′nished apart′ment s garni m, appartement m meublé
furnishings ['fʌrnɪʃɪŋz] spl ameublement m; (things to wear) articles mpl d'habillement
furniture ['fʌrnɪtʃər] s meubles mpl; **a piece of furniture** un meuble; **a suite of furniture** un mobilier
fur′niture deal′er s marchand m de meubles
fur′niture pol′ish s encaustique f
fur′niture store′ s maison f d'ameublement
fur′niture ware′house s garde-meuble m
furor ['fjuror] s fureur f
furrier ['fʌrɪ·ər] s fourreur m, pelletier m
furrow ['fʌro] s sillon m || tr sillonner
fur·ry ['fʌri] adj (comp -rier; super -riest) fourré, à fourrure
further ['fʌrðər] adj additionnel, supplémentaire || adv plus loin; (besides) en outre, de plus || tr avancer, favoriser
furtherance ['fʌrðərəns] s avancement m
fur′ther·more′ adv de plus, d'ailleurs
furthest ['fʌrðɪst] adj (le) plus éloigné || adv le plus loin
furtive ['fʌrtɪv] adj furtif
fu·ry ['fjuri] s (pl -ries) furie f
furze [fʌrz] s genêt m épineux, ajonc m d'Europe
fuse [fjuz] s (tube or wick filled with explosive material) étoupille f, mèche f; (device for exploding a bomb or projectile) fusée f; (elec) fusible m, plomb m de sûreté, plomb fusible; **to burn** or **blow out a fuse** faire sauter un plomb || tr fondre; étoupiller || intr se fondre
fuse′ box′ s boîte f à fusibles

fuselage ['fjuzəlɪdʒ], [,fjuzə'laʒ] *s* fuselage *m*

fusible ['fjuzɪbəl] *adj* fusible

fusillade [,fjuzɪ'led] *s* fusillade *f*

fusion ['fjuʒən] *s* fusion *f*

fuss [fʌs] *s* fracas *m*; (*dispute*) bagarre *f*; **to kick up a fuss** (coll) faire un tas d'histoires; **to make a fuss over** faire grand cas de ‖ *intr* faire des embarras, simagrées, or chichis; **to fuss over** être aux petits soins auprès de

fuss·y ['fʌsi] *adj* (*comp* **-ier**; *super* **-lest**) tracassier, tatillon; (*in dress*) pomponné

fustian ['fʌstʃən] *s* (*cloth*) futaine *f*; (*bombast*) grandiloquence *f*

futile ['fjutɪl] *adj* futile

future ['fjutʃər] *adj* futur, d'avenir ‖ *s* avenir *m*; (gram) futur *m*; **futures** (com) valeurs *fpl* négociées à terme; **in the future** à l'avenir; **in the near future** à brève échéance

fuzz [fʌz] *s* (*on a peach*) duvet *m*; (*on a blanket*) peluche *f*; (*in pockets and corners*) bourre *f*

fuzz·y ['fʌzi] *adj* (*comp* **-ier**; *super* **-iest**) pelucheux; (*hair*) crépelu; (*indistinct*) flou

G

G, g [dʒi] *s* VIIᵉ lettre de l'alphabet

gab [gæb] *s* (coll) bavardage *m*, langue *f* ‖ *v* (*pret & pp* **gabbed**; *ger* **gabbing**) *intr* (coll) bavarder

gabardine ['gæbər,din] *s* gabardine *f*

gabble ['gæbəl] *s* jacasserie *f* ‖ *intr* jacasser

gable ['gebəl] *s* (*of roof*) pignon *m*; (*over a door or window*) gable *m*

ga/ble end/ *s* pignon *m*

ga/ble roof/ *s* comble *m* sur pignon, toit *m* à deux pentes

gad [gæd] *v* (*pret & pp* **gadded**; *ger* **gadding**) *intr*—**to gad about** courir la prétantaine, vadrouiller

gad/about/ *s* vadrouilleur *m*

gad/fly/ *s* (*pl* **-flies**) taon *m*

gadget ['gædʒɪt] *s* dispositif *m*; (*unnamed article*) machin *m*, truc *m*

Gaelic ['gelɪk] *adj & s* gaélique *m*

gaff [gæf] *s* gaffe *f*; **to stand the gaff** (slang) ne pas broncher

gaffer ['gæfər] *s* (coll) vieux bonhomme *m*

gag [gæg] *s* bâillon *m*; (*interpolation by an actor*) gag *m*; (*joke*) blague *f* ‖ *v* (*pret & pp* **gagged**; *ger* **gagging**) *tr* bâillonner ‖ *intr* avoir des haut-le-cœur

gage [gedʒ] *s* (*pledge*) gage *m*; (*challenge*) défi *m*

gaie·ty ['ge·ɪti] *s* (*pl* **-ties**) gaîeté *f*

gaily ['geli] *adv* gaiement

gain [gen] *s* gain *m*; (*increase*) accroissement *m* ‖ *tr* gagner; (*to reach*) atteindre, gagner ‖ *intr* gagner du terrain; (*said of invalid*) s'améliorer; (*said of watch*) avancer; **to gain on** prendre de l'avance sur

gainful ['genfəl] *adj* profitable

gain/say/ *v* (*pret & pp* **-said** [,sed], [,sɛd]) (*tr*) (*to deny*) nier; (*to contradict*) contredire; **not to gainsay** ne pas disconvenir de

gait [get] *s* démarche *f*, allure *f*

gaiter ['getər] *s* guêtre *f*

gala ['gælæ], ['gelə] *adj* de gala ‖ *s* gala *m*

galax·y ['gæləksi] *s* (*pl* **-ies**) galaxie *f*

gale [gel] *s* gros vent *m*; **gales of laughter** éclats *mpl* de rire; **to weather a gale** étaler un coup de vent

gall [gɔl] *s* bile *f*, fiel *m*; (*something bitter*) (fig) fiel *m*, amertume *f*; (*audacity*) (coll) toupet *m* ‖ *tr* écorcher par le frottement; (fig) irriter

gallant ['gælənt] *adj* (*spirited, daring*) vaillant, brave; (*stately, grand*) fier, noble; (*showy, gay*) élégant, superbe, de fête ‖ ['gælænt], [gə'lænt] *adj* galant ‖ *s* galant *m*; vaillant *m* ‖ [gə'lænt] *intr* faire le galant

gallant·ry ['gæləntri] *s* (*pl* **-ries**) galanterie *f*; (*bravery*) vaillance *f*

gall/ blad/der *s* vésicule *f* biliaire

gall/ duct/ *s* conduit *m* biliaire

galleon ['gælɪ·ən] *s* (naut) galion *m*

galler·y ['gæləri] *s* (*pl* **-ies**) galerie *f*; (*cheapest seats in theater*) poulailler *m*; **to play to the gallery** poser pour la galerie

galley ['gæli] *s* (*ship*) galère *f*; (*ship's kitchen*) coquerie *f*; (typ) galée *f*

gal/ley proof/ *s* placard *m*; épreuve *f* en placard

Gallic ['gælɪk] *adj* gaulois

Gal/lic wit/ *s* esprit *m* gaulois

galling ['gɔlɪŋ] *adj* irritant, blessant

gallivant ['gælɪ,vænt] *intr* courailler

gall/nut/ *s* noix *f* de galle

gallon ['gælən] *s* gallon *m* américain

galloon [gə'lun] *s* galon *m*

gallop ['gæləp] *s* galop *m* ‖ *tr* faire galoper ‖ *intr* galoper

gal·lows ['gæloz] *s* (*pl* **-lows** or **-lowses**) gibet *m*, potence *f*

gal/lows bird/ *s* (coll) gibier *m* de potence

gall/stone/ *s* calcul *m* biliaire

galore [gə'lor] *adv* à foison, à gogo

galoshes [gə'laʃɪz] *spl* caoutchoucs *mpl*

galvanize ['gælvə,naɪz] *tr* galvaniser

gal/vanized i/ron *s* tôle *f* galvanisée

gambit ['gæmbɪt] *s* gambit *m*

gamble ['gæmbəl] *s* risque *m*, affaire *f* de chance ‖ *tr* jouer; **to gamble away**

perdre au jeu ‖ *intr* jouer; jouer à la Bourse; (fig) prendre des risques

gambler ['gæmblər] *s* joueur *m*

gambling ['gæmblɪŋ] *s* jeu *m*

gam'bling den' *s* tripot *m*

gam'bling house' *s* maison *f* de jeu

gam'bling ta'ble *s* table *f* de jeu

gam·bol ['gæmbəl] *s* gambade *f* ‖ *v* (*pret & pp* **-boled** or **-bolled**; *ger* **-boling** or **-bolling**) *intr* gambader

gambrel ['gæmbrəl] *s* (*hock*) jarret *m*; (*in butcher shop*) jambier *m*

gam'brel roof' *s* toit *m* en croupe

game [gem] *adj* crâne, résolu; (*leg*) boiteux ‖ *s* jeu *m*; (*contest*) match *m*; (*score necessary to win*) partie *f*; (*animal or bird*) gibier *m*; **to make game of** tourner en dérision

game'bag' *s* carnassière *f*, gibecière *f*

game' bird' *s* oiseau *m* que l'on chasse

game'cock' *s* coq *m* de combat

game'keep'er *s* garde-chasse *m*

game' of chance' *s* jeu *m* de hasard

game' preserve' *s* chasse *f* gardée

game' war'den *s* garde-chasse *m*

gamut ['gæmət] *s* gamme *f*

gam·y ['gemi] *adj* (*comp* **-ier**; *super* **-iest**) (*having flavor of uncooked game*) faisandé; (*plucky*) crâne

gander ['gændər] *s* jars *m*

gang [gæŋ] *adj* multiple ‖ *s* (*of work-men*) équipe *f*, brigade *f*; (*of thugs*) bande *f*; (*of wrongdoers*) séquelle *f*, clique *f* ‖ *intr*—**to gang up** se concerter; **to gang up on** se liguer contre

gangling ['gæŋglɪŋ] *adj* dégingandé

gangli·on ['gæŋglɪ·ən] *s* (*pl* **-ons** or **-a** [ə]) ganglion *m*

gang'plank' *s* passerelle *f*, planche *f* de débarquement

gangrene ['gæŋgrin] *s* gangrène *f* ‖ *tr* gangrener ‖ *intr* se gangrener

gangster ['gæŋstər] *s* bandit *m*, gangster *m*

gang'way' *s* (*passageway*) passage *m*, coursive *f*; (*gangplank*) planche *f* de débarquement; (*in ship's side*) coupée *f* ‖ *interj* rangez-vous!, dégagez!

gan·try ['gæntri] *s* (*pl* **-tries**) (*for bar-rels*) chantier *m*; (*for crane*) portique *m*; (*rr*) pont *m* à signaux

gan'try crane' *s* grue *f* à portique

gap [gæp] *s* lacune *f*; (*in wall*) brèche *f*; (*between mountains*) col *m*, gorge *f*; (*between two points of view*) abîme *m*, gouffre *m*

gape [gep], [gæp] *s* ouverture *f*, brèche *f*; (*yawn*) bâillement *m*; (*look of astonishment*) badauderie *f* ‖ *intr* (*to yawn*) bâiller; (*to look with aston-ishment*) badauder; **to gape at** re-garder bouche bée

garage [gə'rɑʒ] *s* garage *m*

garb [gɑrb] *s* costume *m* ‖ *tr* vêtir

garbage ['gɑrbɪdʒ] *s* ordures *fpl*

gar'bage can' *s* poubelle *f*

gar'bage collec'tor *s* boueur *m*

gar'bage dispos'al *s* destruction *f* des ordures ménagères

gar'bage truck' *s* benne *f* à ordures

garble ['gɑrbəl] *tr* mutiler, tronquer

garden ['gɑrdən] *s* jardin *m*; (*of vege-tables*) potager *m*; (*of flowers*) par-terre *m* ‖ *intr* jardiner

gardener ['gɑrdnər] *s* jardinier *m*

gardening ['gɑrdnɪŋ] *s* jardinage *m*

gar'den par'ty *s* garden-party *f*

gargle ['gɑrgəl] *s* gargarisme *m* ‖ *intr* se gargariser

gargoyle ['gɑrgɔɪl] *s* gargouille *f*

garish ['gerɪʃ], ['gærɪʃ] *adj* cru, ruti-lant, criard

garland ['gɑrlənd] *s* guirlande *f* ‖ *tr* guirlander

garlic ['gɑrlɪk] *s* ail *m*

garment ['gɑrmənt] *s* vêtement *m*

gar'ment bag' *s* housse *f* à vêtements

garner ['gɑrnər] *tr* (*to gather, collect*) amasser; (*cereals*) engranger

garnet ['gɑrnɪt] *adj & s* grenat *m*

garnish ['gɑrnɪʃ] *s* garniture *f* ‖ *tr* garnir; (*law*) effectuer une saisie-arrêt sur

garret ['gærɪt] *s* grenier *m*; (*dormer room*) mansarde *f*

garrison ['gærɪsən] *s* garnison *f* ‖ *tr* (*troops*) mettre en garnison; (*a city*) mettre des troupes en garnison dans

garrote [gə'rɑt], [gə'rot] *s* (*method of execution*) garrotte *f*; (*iron collar used for such an execution*) garrot *m* ‖ *tr* garrotter

garrulous ['gær(j)ələs] *adj* bavard

garter ['gɑrtər] *s* jarretelle *f*, jarre-tière *f*; (*for men's socks*) support-chaussette *m*, fixe-chaussette *m*

garth [gɑrθ] *s* cour *f* intérieure d'un cloître

gas [gæs] *s* gaz *m*; (*coll*) essence *f*; (*empty talk*) (*coll*) bavardage *m*; **out of gas** en panne sèche ‖ *v* (*pret & pp* **gassed**; *ger* **gassing**) *tr* gazer, as-phyxier ‖ *intr* dégager des gaz; (*to talk nonsense*) (*coll*) bavarder

gas'bag' *s* enveloppe *f* à gaz; (*coll*) blagueur *m*, baratineur *m*

gas' burn'er *s* bec *m* de gaz

gas' cham'ber *s* chambre *f* à gaz

Gascony ['gæskəni] *s* Gascogne *f*; la Gascogne

gas' en'gine *s* moteur *m* à gaz

gaseous ['gæsɪ·əs] *adj* gazeux

gas' gen'erator *s* gazogène *m*

gash [gæʃ] *s* entaille *f*; (*on face*) bala-fre *f* ‖ *tr* entailler; balafrer

gas' heat' *s* chauffage *m* au gaz

gas' heat'er *s* (*for hot water*) chauffe-eau *m* à gaz; (*for house heat*) calori-fère *m* à gaz

gas'hold'er *s* gazomètre *m*

gasi·fy ['gæsɪ‚faɪ] *v* (*pret & pp* **-fied**) *tr* gazéifier ‖ *intr* se gazéifier

gas' jet' *s* bec *m* de gaz

gasket ['gæskɪt] *s* joint *m*

gas'light' *s* éclairage *m* au gaz

gas' main' *s* conduite *f* de gaz

gas' mask' *s* masque *m* à gaz

gas' me'ter *s* compteur *m* à gaz

gasoline ['gæsə‚lin], [‚gæsə'lin] *s* es-sence *f*

gas'oline can' *s* bidon *m* d'essence

gas'oline gauge' *s* voyant *m* d'essence

gas'oline pump' *s* pompe *f* à essence

gasp [gæsp], [gɑsp], s halètement m; (of surprise; of death) hoquet m ǁ tr —to gasp out (a word) dire dans un souffle ǁ intr haleter

gas′ pipe′ s conduite f de gaz

gas′ produc′er s gazogène m

gas′ range′ s fourneau m à gaz, cuisinière f à gaz

gas′ sta′tion s poste m d'essence

gas′ stove′ s cuisinière f à gaz, réchaud m à gaz

gas′ tank′ s gazomètre m; (aut) réservoir m d'essence

gastric ['gæstrɪk] adj gastrique

gastronomy [gæs'trɑnəmi] s gastronomie f

gas′works′ spl usine f à gaz

gate [get] s porte f; (in fence or wall) grille f; (main gate) portail f; (of sluice) vanne f; (number paying admission; amount paid) entrée f; (rr) barrière f; **to crash the gate** resquiller

gate-crasher ['get,kræʃər] s (coll) resquilleur m

gate′keep′er s portier m; (rr) garde-barrière mf

gate′-leg ta′ble s table f à abattants

gate′post′ s montant m

gate′way′ s passage m, entrée f; (main entrance) portail m

gather ['gæðər] tr amasser, rassembler; (the harvest) rentrer; (fruits, flowers, etc.) cueillir, ramasser; (one's thoughts) recueillir; (sewing) froncer; (to deduce) (fig) conclure; **to gather dust** s'encrasser; **to gather oneself together** se ramasser ǁ intr se réunir, s'assembler; (said of clouds) s'amonceler

gathering ['gæðərɪŋ] s réunion m, rassemblement m; (of harvest) récolte f; (of fruits, flowers, etc.) cueillette f; (bb) assemblage m; (sewing) froncis m

gaud·y ['gɔdi] adj (comp -ier; super -iest) criard, voyant

gauge [gedʒ] s jauge f, calibre m; (of liquid in a container) niveau m; (of gasoline, oil, etc.) indicateur m; (of carpenter) trusquin m; (rr) écartement m ǁ tr jauger, calibrer; (a person; s.o.'s capacities; a distance) juger de, jauger

gauge′ glass′ s indicateur m de niveau

Gaul [gɔl] s Gaule f; la Gaule

Gaulish ['gɔlɪʃ] adj & s gaulois m

gaunt [gɔnt], [gɑnt] adj décharné, étique, efflanqué

gauntlet ['gɔntlɪt], ['gɑntlɪt] s gantelet m; **to run the gauntlet** passer par les baguettes; **to take up the gauntlet** relever le gant; **to throw down the gauntlet** jeter le gant

gauze [gɔz] s gaze f

gavel ['gævəl] s marteau m

gawk [gɔk] s (coll) godiche mf ǁ intr (coll) bayer aux corneilles; **to gawk at** (coll) regarder bouche bée

gawk·y ['gɔki] adj (comp -ier; super -iest) godiche

gay [ge] adj gai

gay′ blade′ s (coll) joyeux drille m

gaze [gez] s regard m fixe ǁ intr regarder fixement

gazelle [gə'zel] s gazelle f

gazette [gə'zet] s gazette f; journal m officiel

gazetteer [,gæzə'tɪr] s dictionnaire m géographique

gear [gɪr] s attirail m, appareil m; (of transmission, steering, etc.) mécanisme m; (adjustment of automobile transmission) marche f, vitesse f; (two or more toothed wheels meshed together) engrenage m; **out of gear** débrayé); **to throw into gear** embrayer; **to throw out of gear** débrayer; (fig) disloquer ǁ tr & intr engrener

gear′box′ s (aut) boîte f de vitesses

gear′shift′ s changement m de vitesse

gear′shift lev′er s levier m de changement de vitesse

gear′wheel′ s roue f d'engrenage

gee [dʒi] interj sapristi!; (to the right) hue!; **gee up!** hue!

Gei′ger count′er ['gaɪgər] s compteur m de Geiger

gel [dʒel] s (chem) gel m

gelatine ['dʒelətɪn] s gélatine f

geld [geld] v (pret & pp gelded or gelt [gelt]) tr châtrer

gelding ['geldɪŋ] s hongre m

gem [dʒem] s gemme f; (fig) bijou m

gender ['dʒendər] s (gram) genre m; (coll) sexe m

gene [dʒin] s (biol) gène m

genealo·gy [,dʒeni'ælədʒi], [,dʒini-'ælədʒi] s (pl -gies) généalogie f

general ['dʒenərəl] adj & s général m; **in general** en général

gen′eral deliv′ery s poste f restante

generalissi·mo [,dʒenərə'lɪsɪmo] s (pl -mos) généralissime m

generali·ty [,dʒenə'rælɪti] s (pl -ties) généralité f

generalize ['dʒenərə,laɪz] tr & intr généraliser

generally ['dʒenərəli] adv généralement

gen′eral practi′tioner s médecin m de médecine générale

gen′eral-ship′ s tactique f; (office) généralat m

gen′eral staff′ s état-major m

generate ['dʒenə,ret] tr générer; (to beget) engendrer; (geom) engendrer

gen′erating sta′tion s usine f génératrice, centrale f

generation [,dʒenə'reʃən] s génération f

generator ['dʒenə,retər] s (chem) gazogène m; (elec) génératrice f

generic [dʒɪ'nerɪk] adj générique

generosi·ty [,dʒenə'rɑsɪti] s (pl -ties) générosité f

generous ['dʒenərəs] adj généreux; abondant

gene·sis ['dʒenɪsɪs] s (pl -ses [,siz]) genèse f; **Genesis** (Bib) La Genèse

genetic [dʒɪ'netɪk] adj génétique ǁ **genetics** s génétique f

Geneva [dʒɪ'nivə] s Genève f

genial ['dʒinɪ-əl] adj affable

genie ['dʒini] s génie m

genital ['dʒenɪtəl] *adj* génital ‖ **genitals** *spl* organes *mpl* génitaux

genitive ['dʒenɪtɪv] *s* génitif *m*

genius ['dʒinjəs], ['dʒini·əs] *s* (*pl* **geniuses**) génie *m* ‖ *s* (*pl* **genii** ['dʒini,aɪ]) génie *m*

Genoa ['dʒeno·ə] *s* Gênes *f*

genocide ['dʒenə,saɪd] *s* génocide *m*

genteel [dʒen'til] *adj* distingué, de bon ton; élégant, chic

gentian ['dʒenʃən] *s* gentiane *f*

gentile ['dʒentaɪl] *s* non-juif *m*, chrétien *m*

gentili·ty [dʒen'tɪlɪti] *s* (*pl* **-ties**) (*birth*) naissance *f* distinguée; (*breeding*) politesse *f*

gentle ['dʒentəl] *adj* doux; (*in birth*) noble, bien né; (*e.g., tap on the shoulder*) léger

gen'tle-folk' *s* gens *mpl* de bonne naissance

gen'tle-man' *s* (*pl* **-men**) monsieur *m*; (*man of independent means*) rentier *m*; (*hist*) gentilhomme *m*

gentlemanly ['dʒentəlmənli] *adj* bien élevé, de bon ton

gen'tleman's agree'ment *s* engagement *m* sur parole, contrat *m* verbal

gen'tle sex' *s* sexe *m* faible

gentry ['dʒentri] *s* gens *mpl* de bonne naissance; (*birth*) petite noblesse *f*

genuine ['dʒenju·ɪn] *adj* véritable, authentique; (*person*) sincère, franc

genus ['dʒinəs] *s* (*pl* **genera** ['dʒenərə] *or* **genuses**) genre *m*

geogra·phy [dʒɪ'agrəfi] *s* (*pl* **-phies**) géographie *f*

geologic(al) [,dʒiə'ladʒɪk(əl)] *adj* géologique

geolo·gy [dʒɪ'alədʒi] *s* (*pl* **-gies**) géologie *f*

geometric(al) [,dʒiə'metrɪk(əl)] *adj* géométrique

geome·try [dʒɪ'amitri] *s* (*pl* **-tries**) géométrie *f*

geophysics [,dʒiə'fɪzɪks] *s* géophysique *f*

geopolitics [,dʒiə'palɪtɪks] *s* géopolitique *f*

George [dʒɔrdʒ] *s* Georges *m*

geranium [dʒɪ'reni·əm] *s* géranium *m*

geriatrics [,dʒerɪ'ætrɪks] *s* gériatrie *f*

germ [dʒʌrm] *s* germe *m*

German ['dʒʌrmən] *adj* allemand ‖ *s* (*language*) allemand *m*; (*person*) Allemand *m*

germane [dʒʌr'men] *adj* à propos, pertinent; **germane to** se rapportant à

Ger'man mea'sles *s* rubéole *f*

Ger'man sil'ver *s* maillechort *m*, argentan *m*

Germa·ny ['dʒʌrməni] *s* (*pl* **-nies**) Allemagne *f*; l'Allemagne

germicidal [,dʒʌrmɪ'saɪdəl] *adj* germicide

germicide ['dʒʌrmɪ,saɪd] *s* germicide *m*

germinate ['dʒʌrmɪ,net] *intr* germer

germ' war'fare *s* guerre *f* bactériologique

gerontology [,dʒerən'talədʒi] *s* gérontologie *f*

gerund ['dʒerənd] *s* gérondif *m*

gestation [dʒes'teʃən] *s* gestation *f*

gesticulate [dʒes'tɪkjə,let] *intr* gesticuler

gesture ['dʒestʃər] *s* geste *m* ‖ *intr* faire des gestes; **to gesture to** faire signe à

get [gɛt] *v* (*pret* **got** [gat]; *pp* **got** *or* **gotten** ['gɑtən]; *ger* **getting**) *tr* obtenir, procurer; (*to receive*) avoir, recevoir; (*to catch*) attraper; (*to seek*) chercher, aller chercher; (*to reach*) atteindre; (*to find*) trouver, rencontrer; (*to obtain and bring*) prendre; (*e.g., dinner*) faire; (*rad*) avoir, prendre, accrocher; (*to understand*) (coll) comprendre; **to get across** faire accepter; faire comprendre; **to get a kick out of** (coll) prendre plaisir à; **to get back** ravoir, se faire rendre; **to get down** descendre; (*to swallow*) avaler; **to get in** rentrer; **to get s.o. to** + *inf* persuader à qn de + *inf*; **to get s.th. done** faire faire q.ch. ‖ *intr* (*to become*) devenir, se faire; (*to arrive*) arriver, parvenir; **get up!** (*said to an animal*) huel; **to get about** (*said of news*) se répandre; (*said of convalescent*) se de nouveau sur pied; **to get accustomed to** se faire à; **to get across** traverser; **to get along** circuler; **to get along** (*to succeed*) se tirer d'affaire; **to get along without** se passer de; **to get angry** se fâcher; **to get away** s'évader; **to get away with** s'en aller avec; (coll) s'en tirer avec; **to get back** reculer; (*to return*) rentrer; **to get back at** (coll) rendre la pareille à, se venger sur; **to get by** passer; (*to manage, to shift*) (coll) s'en tirer sans peine; **to get dark** faire nuit; **to get down** descendre; **to get going** se mettre en marche; **to get in** *or* **into** entrer dans; **to get off with** en être quitte pour; **to get on** monter sur; (*a car*) monter dans; (*to succeed*) faire des progrès; **to get out** sortir; **to get rid of** se défaire de; **to get to** arriver à; (*to have an opportunity to*) avoir l'occasion de; **to get up** se lever; **to not get over it** (coll) ne pas en revenir

get'away' *s* démarrage *m*; (*flight*) fuite *f*

get'-togeth'er *s* réunion *f*

get'up' *s* (*style*) (coll) présentation *f*; (*outfit*) (coll) affublement *m*

geyser ['gaɪzər] *s* geyser *m* ‖ ['gizər] *s* (Brit) chauffe-eau *m* à gaz

ghast·ly ['gæstli], ['gɑstli] *adj* (*comp* **-lier**; *super* **-liest**) livide, blême; horrible, affreux

Ghent [gent] *s* Gand *m*

gherkin ['gʌrkɪn] *s* cornichon *m*

ghet·to ['geto] *s* (*pl* **-tos**) ghetto *m*

ghost [gost] *s* revenant *m*; (*shade, semblance*) ombre *f*; **not the ghost of a chance** pas la moindre chance; **to give up the ghost** rendre l'âme, rendre l'esprit

ghost·ly ['gostli] *adj* (*comp* **-lier**; *super* **-liest**) spectral, fantomatique

ghost' sto'ry *s* histoire *f* de revenants

ghost′ town′ s ville f morte

ghost′ writ′er s nègre m

ghoul [gul] s goule f; (body snatcher) déterreur m de cadavres

ghoulish [′gulɪʃ] adj vampirique

GI [′dʒi′aɪ] (letterword) (General Issue) adj fourni par l′armée ‖ s (pl GI′s) soldat m américain, simple soldat

giant [′dʒaɪ-ənt] adj & s géant m

giantess [′dʒaɪ-əntɪs] s géante f

gibberish [′dʒɪbərɪʃ], [′gɪbərɪʃ] s baragouin m

gibbet [′dʒɪbɪt] s gibet m, potence f

gibe [dʒaɪb] s raillerie f, moquerie f ‖ tr & intr railler; to gibe at se moquer de, railler

giblets [′dʒɪblɪts] spl abattis m, abats mpl

gid·dy [′gɪdi] adj (comp -dier; super -diest) étourdi; (height) vertigineux; (foolish) léger, frivole

Gideon [′gɪdɪ-ən] s (Bib) Gédéon m

gift [gɪft] s cadeau m; (natural ability) don m, talent m ‖ tr douer

gifted adj doué

gift′ horse′ s—never look a gift horse in the mouth à cheval donné on ne regarde pas à la bride

gift′ of gab′ s (coll) bagou m, faconde f

gift′ shop′ s boutique f de souvenirs, magasin m de nouveautés

gift′-wrap′ v (pret & pp -wrapped; ger -wrapping) tr faire un paquet cadeau de

gigantic [dʒaɪ′gæntɪk] adj gigantesque

giggle [′gɪgəl] s petit rire m ‖ intr pousser de petits rires, glousser

gigo·lo [′dʒɪgə‚lo] s (pl -los) gigolo m

GI Joe [′dʒi‚aɪ′dʒo] s le troufion

gild [gɪld] v (pret & pp gilded or gilt [gɪlt]) tr dorer

gilding [′gɪldɪŋ] s dorure f

gill [gɪl] s (of cock) fanon m; gills (of fish) ouïes fpl, branchies fpl

gilt [gɪlt] adj & s doré m

gilt′-edged′ adj (e.g., book) doré sur tranche; (securities) de premier ordre, de tout repos

gimcrack [′dʒɪm‚kræk] adj de pacotille, de camelote ‖ s babiole f

gimlet [′gɪmlɪt] s vrille f, perçoir m

gimmick [′gɪmɪk] s (coll) truc m, machin m; (trick) tour m

gin [dʒɪn] s (alcoholic liquor) gin m, genièvre m; (for cotton, corn, etc.) égreneuse f; (snare) trébuchet m ‖ v (pret & pp ginned; ger ginning) tr égrener

ginger [′dʒɪndʒər] s gingembre m; (fig) entrain m, allant m

gin′ger ale′ s boisson f gazeuse au gingembre

gin′ger·bread′ s pain m d′épice; ornement m de mauvais goût

gingerly [′dʒɪndʒərlɪ] adj précautionneux ‖ adv tout doux, avec précaution

gin′ger·snap′ s gâteau m sec au gingembre

gingham [′gɪŋəm] s guingan m

giraffe [dʒɪ′ræf], [dʒɪ′rɑf] s girafe f

gird [gʌrd] v (pret & pp girt [gʌrt] or girded) tr ceindre; to gird on se ceindre de; to gird oneself for se préparer à

girder [′gʌrdər] s poutre f

girdle [′gʌrdəl] s ceinture f ‖ tr ceindre, entourer

girl [gʌrl] s jeune fille f; (little girl) petite fille; (servant) bonne f

girl′ friend′ s (sweetheart) petite amie f, bonne amie f; (female friend) amie f, camarade f

girl′hood s enfance f, jeunesse f d′une femme

girlish [′gʌrlɪʃ] adj de jeune fille, de petite fille

girl′ scout′ s éclaireuse f, guide f

girls′ school′ s école f de filles

girth [gʌrθ] s (band) sangle f; (measure around) circonférence f; (of person) tour m de taille

gist [dʒɪst] s fond m, essence f

give [gɪv] s élasticité f ‖ v (pret gave [gev]; pp given [′gɪvən]) tr donner; (a speech, a lecture, a class; a smile) faire; to give away donner, distribuer; révéler; to give back rendre, remettre; to give forth or off émettre; to give oneself up se rendre; to give up renoncer à, abandonner ‖ intr donner; to give in se rendre; to give out manquer; (to become exhausted) s′épuiser; to give way faire place, reculer

give′-and-take′ s compromis m; échange m de propos plaisants

give′away′ s (coll) révélation f involontaire; (coll) trahison f; to play giveaway jouer à qui perd gagne

given [′gɪvən] adj donné m; given that vu que, étant donné que

giv′en name′ s prénom m

giver [′gɪvər] s donneur m, donateur m

gizzard [′gɪzərd] s gésier m

glacial [′gleʃəl] adj glacial; (chem) en cristaux; (geol) glaciaire

glacier [′gleʃər] s glacier m

glad [glæd] adj (comp gladder; super gladdest) content, heureux; to be glad to être content or heureux de

gladden [′glædən] tr réjouir

glade [gled] s clairière f, éclaircie f

glad′ hand′ s (coll) accueil m chaleureux

gladiator [′glædɪ‚etər] s gladiateur m

gladiola [‚glædɪ′olə], [glə′daɪ-ələ] s glaïeul m

gladly [′glædlɪ] adv volontiers, avec plaisir

gladness [′glædnɪs] s joie f, plaisir m

glad′ rags′ spl (slang) frusques fpl des grands jours

glamorous [′glæmərəs] adj ravissant, éclatant

glamour [′glæmər] s charme m, éclat m

glam′our girl′ s ensorceleuse f

glance [glæns], [glɑns] s coup m d′œil; at a glance d′un seul coup d′œil; at first glance à première vue ‖ intr jeter un regard; to glance at jeter un coup d′œil sur; to glance off ricocher, dévier; to glance through a book feuilleter un livre; **to glance up** lever les yeux

gland [glænd] *s* glande *f*

glanders ['glændərz] *spl* (vet) morve *f*

glare [gler] *s* lumière *f* éblouissante; (*look*) regard *m* irrité ‖ *intr* éblouir, briller; **to glare at** lancer un regard méchant à, foudroyer du regard

glare/ ice/ *s* verglas *m*

glaring ['glerɪŋ] *adj* éblouissant; (*mistake, fact*) évident, qui saute aux yeux; (*blunder, abuse*) grossier, scandaleux

glass [glæs], [glas] *s* verre *m*; (*mirror*) glace *f*; **glasses** lunettes *fpl*

glass/ blow/er ['blo·ər] *s* verrier-souffleur *m*

glass/ case/ *s* vitrine *f*

glass/ cut/ter *s* (*tool*) diamant *m*; (*workman*) vitrier *m*

glass/ door/ *s* porte *f* vitrée

glassful ['glæsfʊl], ['glasfʊl] *s* verre *m*

glass/ house/ *s* serre *f*; (fig) maison *f* de verre

glass/ware/ *s* verrerie *f*

glass/ wool/ *s* laine *f* de verre

glass/works/ *s* verrerie *f*, glacerie *f*

glass·y ['glæsi], ['glasi] *adj* (*comp* -**ier**; *super* -**iest**) vitreux; (*smooth*) lisse

glaze [glez] *s* (*ceramics*) vernis *m*; (culin) glace *f*; (tex) lustre *m* ‖ *tr* (*to cover with a glossy coating*) glacer; (*to fit with glass*) vitrer

glazier ['glezər] *s* vitrier *m*

gleam [glim] *s* rayon *m*; (*of hope*) lueur *f* ‖ *intr* rayonner, reluire

glean [glin] *tr* glaner

glee [gli] *s* allégresse *f*, joie *f*

glee/ club/ *s* orphéon *m*, société *f* chorale

glen [glɛn] *s* vallon *m*, ravin *m*

glib [glɪb] *adj* (*comp* **glibber**; *super* **glibbest**) facile; (*tongue*) délié

glide [glaɪd] *s* glissement *m*; (aer) vol *m* plané; (mus) port *m* de voix; (phonet) son *m* transitoire ‖ *intr* glisser, se glisser; (aer) planer

glider ['glaɪdər] *s* (*porch seat*) siège *m* à glissière; (aer) planeur *m*

glimmer ['glɪmər] *s* faible lueur *f* ‖ *intr* jeter une faible lueur

glimmering ['glɪmərɪŋ] *adj* faible, vacillant ‖ *s* faible lueur *f*, miroitement *m*; soupçon *m*, indice *m*

glimpse [glɪmps] *s* aperçu *m*; **to catch a glimpse of** entrevoir, aviser ‖ *tr* entrevoir

glint [glɪnt] *s* reflet *m*, éclair *m* ‖ *intr* jeter un reflet, étinceler

glisten ['glɪsən] *s* scintillement *m* ‖ *intr* scintiller

glitter ['glɪtər] *s* éclat *m*, étincellement *m* ‖ *intr* étinceler

gloaming ['glomɪŋ] *s* crépuscule *m*, jour *m* crépusculaire

gloat [glot] *intr* éprouver un malin plaisir; **to gloat over** faire des gorges chaudes de; (*e.g., one's victim*) couver du regard

global ['globəl] *adj* sphérique; mondial

globe [glob] *s* globe *m*

globe/-trot/ter *s* globe-trotter *m*

globule ['globjʊl] *s* globule *m*

gloom [glum] *s* obscurité *f*, ténèbres *fpl*; tristesse *f*

gloom·y ['glumi] *adj* (*comp* -**ier**; *super* -**iest**) sombre, lugubre; (*ideas*) noir

glori·fy ['glorɪ,faɪ] *v* (*pret & pp* -**fied**) *tr* glorifier

glorious ['glori·əs] *adj* glorieux

glo·ry ['glori] *s* (*pl* -**ries**) gloire *f*; **to be in one's glory** être aux anges; **to go to glory** (slang) aller à la ruine ‖ *v* (*pret & pp* -**ried**) *intr*—**to glory in** se glorifier de

gloss [glɔs], [glas] *s* lustre *m*; (*on cloth*) cati *m*; (*on floor*) brillant *m*; (*note, commentary*) glose *f*; **to take off the gloss from** décatir ‖ *tr* lustrer; **to gloss over** maquiller, farder

glossa·ry ['glasəri] *s* (*pl* -**ries**) glossaire *m*

gloss·y ['glɔsi], ['glasi] *adj* (*comp* -**ier**; *super* -**iest**) lustré, brillant

glot/tal stop/ ['glatəl] *s* coup *m* de glotte

glottis ['glatɪs] *s* glotte *f*

glove [glʌv] *s* gant *m* ‖ *tr* ganter

glove/ compart/ment *s* boîte *f* à gants

glow [glo] *s* rougeoiement *m* ‖ *intr* rougeoyer

glower ['glau·ər] *s* grise mine *f* ‖ *intr* avoir l'air renfrogné

glowing ['glo·ɪŋ] *adj* rougeoyant, incandescent; (*healthy*) rayonnant; (*cheeks*) vermeil; (*reports*) enthousiaste, élogieux

glow/worm/ *s* ver *m* luisant

glucose ['glukos] *s* glucose *m*

glue [glu] *s* colle *f* ‖ *tr* coller

glue/pot/ *s* pot *m* à colle

gluey ['glu·i] *adj* (*comp* **gluier**; *super* **gluiest**) gluant

glum [glʌm] *adj* (*comp* **glummer**; *super* **glummest**) maussade, renfrogné

glut [glʌt] *s* surabondance *f*; (*on the market*) engorgement *m* ‖ *v* (*pret & pp* **glutted**; *ger* **glutting**) *tr* (*with food*) rassasier; (*the market*) inonder, engorger

glutton ['glʌtən] *s* glouton *m*

gluttonous ['glʌtənəs] *adj* glouton

glutton·y ['glʌtəni] *s* (*pl* -**ies**) gloutonnerie *f*

glycerine ['glɪsərɪn] *s* glycérine *f*

G.M.T. *abbr* (**Greenwich mean time** *temps moyen de Greenwich*) T.U., temps *m* universel

gnarl [narl] *s* (bot) nœud *m* ‖ *tr* tordre ‖ *intr* grogner

gnarled *adj* noueux

gnash [næʃ] *tr*—**to gnash the teeth** grincer des dents or les dents

gnat [næt] *s* moucheron *m*, moustique *m*

gnaw [nɔ] *tr* ronger

gnome [nom] *s* gnome *m*

go [go] *s* (*pl* **goes**) aller *m*; **a lot of go** (slang) beaucoup d'allant; **it's no go** (coll) ça ne marche pas, pas mèche; **to have a go at** (coll) essayer; **to make a go of** (coll) réussir à ‖ *v* (*pret* went [wɛnt]; *pp* **gone** [gɔn], [gɑn]) *tr*—to go it alone le faire tout seul || *intr* aller; (*to work, operate*) marcher; y aller, e.g., **did you go?** y êtes-vous allé?; devenir, e.g., **to go crazy** devenir fou; faire, e.g., **to go quack-quack** faire couin-couin; **going, going, gone!** une fois, deux fois, adjugé!; **go to it!** allez-y!; **to be going to** or **to go to** + *inf* aller + *inf*, e.g., **I am going to the store to buy some shoes** je vais au magasin acheter des souliers; (to express futurity from the point of view of the present or past) aller + *inf*, e.g., **he is going to get married** il va se marier; e.g., **he was going to get married** il allait se marier; **to go** (*to take out*) (coll) à emporter; **to go against** contrarier; **to go ahead of** dépasser; **to go away** s'en aller; **to go back** retourner; (*to return home*) rentrer; (*to back up*) reculer; (*to date back*) remonter; **to go by** passer; (*a rule, model, etc.*) agir selon; **to go down** descendre; (*said of sun*) se coucher; (*said of ship*) sombrer; **to go fishing** aller à la pêche; **to go for** or **to go get** aller chercher; **to go in** entrer; **to go into** entrer dans; (*to fit into*) tenir dans; **to go in for** se consacrer à; **to go in with** s'associer à or avec, se joindre à; **to go off** (*said of bomb, gun, etc.*) partir; **to go on** + *ger* continuer à + *inf*; **to go out** sortir; (*said of light, fire, etc.*) s'éteindre; **to go over** (*to examine*) parcourir, repasser; **to go through** (*e.g., a door*) passer par; (*e.g., a city*) traverser; (*a fortune*) dissiper, dilapider; **to go together** (*said, e.g., of colors*) s'assortir; (*said of lovers*) être très liés; **to go under** suceomber; (*said, e.g., of submarine*) plonger; (*a false name*) être connu sous; **to go up** monter; **to go with** accompagner; (*a color, dress, etc.*) s'assortir avec; **to go without** se passer de; **to let go of** lâcher

goad [god] *s* aiguillon *m* || *tr* aiguillonner

go'-ahead' *adj* (coll) entreprenant || *s* (coll) signal *m* d'aller en avant

goal [gol] *s* but *m*

goal'keep'er *s* goal *m*, gardien *m* de but

goal' line' *s* ligne *f* de but

goal' post' *s* montant *m*, poteau *m* de but

goat [got] *s* chèvre *f*; (*male goat*) bouc *m*; (coll) dindon *m*; **to get the goat of** (slang) exaspérer, irriter

goatee [go'ti] *s* barbiche *f*

goat'herd' *s* chevrier *m*

goat'skin' *s* peau *f* de chèvre

goat'suck'er *s* (orn) engoulevent *m*

gob [gɑb] *s* (coll) grumeau *m*; (coll) marin *m*

gobble ['gɑbəl] *s* glouglou *m* || *tr* engloutir, bâfrer || *intr* bâfrer; (*said of turkey*) glouglouter

gobbledegook ['gɑbəldı ˌgʊk] *s* (coll) palabre *m* & *f*, charabia *m*

go'-between' *s* intermédiaire *mf*; (*in shady love affairs*) entremetteur *m*

goblet ['gɑblɪt] *s* verre *m* à pied

goblin ['gɑblın] *s* lutin *m*

go'-by' *s* (coll) affront *m*; **to give s.o. the go-by** (coll) brûler la politesse à qn

go'cart' *s* chariot *m*; (*baby carriage*) poussette *f*; (*handcart*) charrette *f* à bras

god [gɑd] *s* dieu *m*; **God forbid** qu'à Dieu ne plaise; **God grant** plût à Dieu; **God willing** s'il plaît à Dieu

god'child' *s* (*pl* -chil'dren) filleul *m*

god'daugh'ter *s* filleule *f*

goddess ['gɑdıs] *s* déesse *f*

god'fa'ther *s* parrain *m*

God'-fear'ing *adj* dévot, pieux

God'forsak'en *adj* abandonné de Dieu; (coll) perdu, misérable

god'head' *s* divinité *f*; **Godhead** Dieu *m*

godless ['gɑdlıs] *adj* athée, impie

god'ly ['gɑdlı] *adj* (*comp* -lier; *super* -liest*) dévot, pieux

god'moth'er *s* marraine *f*

God's' a'cre *s* le champ de repos

god'send' *s* aubaine *f*

god'son' *s* filleul *m*

God'speed' *s* bonne chance *f*, bon voyage *m*

go-getter ['go ˌgɛtər] *s* (coll) homme *m* d'expédition, lanceur *m* d'affaires

goggle ['gɑgəl] *intr* rouler de gros yeux; (*to open the eyes wide*) écarquiller les yeux

gog'gle-eyed' *adj* aux yeux saillants

goggles ['gɑgəlz] *spl* lunettes *fpl* protectrices

going ['go-ıŋ] *adj* en marche; **going on two o'clock** presque deux heures || *s* départ *m*; **good going!** bien joué!

go'ing concern' *s* maison *f* en pleine activité

go'ings on' *spl* (coll) chahut *m*, tapage *m*; (coll) événements *mpl*

goiter ['gɔıtər] *s* goitre *m*

gold [gold] *adj* d'or, en or || *s* or *m*

gold'beat'er *s* batteur *m* d'or

gold'beater's skin' *s* baudruche *f*

gold'crest' *s* roitelet *m* à tête dorée

golden ['goldən] *adj* d'or; (*gilt*) doré; (*hair*) d'or, d'un blond doré; (*opportunity*) favorable, magnifique

gold'en age' *s* âge *m* d'or

gold'en calf' *s* veau *m* d'or

Gold'en Fleece' *s* Toison *f* d'or

gold'en mean' *s* juste-milieu *m*

gold'en plov'er *s* pluvier *m* doré

gold'en-rod' *s* solidage *f*, gerbe *f* d'or

gold'en rule' *s* règle *f* de la charité chrétienne

gold'en wed'ding *s* noces *fpl* d'or, jubilé *m*

gold'-filled' *adj* (*tooth*) aurifié

gold'finch' *s* chardonneret *m*

gold'fish' *s* poisson *m* rouge

goldilocks ['goldı ˌlaks] *s* jeune fille *f* aux cheveux d'or

gold' leaf' *s* feuille *f* d'or

gold' mine' *s* mine *f* d'or; **to strike a gold mine** (fig) dénicher le bon filon, faire des affaires d'or

gold' plate' s vaisselle f d'or
gold'-plate' tr plaquer d'or
gold' rush' s ruée f vers l'or
gold'smith's s orfèvre m
gold' stan'dard s étalon-or m
golf [galf] s golf m || intr jouer au golf
golf' club' s crosse f de golf, club m;
  (association) club m de golf
golfer ['galfər] s joueur m de golf
golf' links' spl terrain m de golf
gondola ['gandələ] s gondole f
gondolier [,gandə'lɪr] s gondolier m
gone [gɔn], [gɑn] adj parti, disparu;
  (used up) épuisé; (ruined) ruiné,
  fichu; (dead) mort; **far gone** avancé;
  gone on (in love with) (coll) entiché
  de, épris de
gong [gɔŋ], [gɑŋ] s gong m
gonorrhea [,gɑnə'ri·ə] s blennorragie f
goo [gu] s (slang) matière f collante
good [gud] adj (comp **better**; super
  best) bon §91; (child) sage; (meals)
  soigné; **good for you!** bien joué!; **to
  be good at** être fort en, être expert à;
  to make good prospérer; (a loss)
  compenser; (a promise) tenir; **will
  you be good enough to** voulez-vous
  être assez aimable de || s bien m; **for
  good** pour de bon, définitivement;
  goods biens mpl; (com) marchandises
  fpl; **to catch with the goods** (slang)
  prendre la main dans le sac; **to the
  good** de gagné, e.g., **all or so much
  to the good** autant de gagné || interj
  bon!, bien!, à la bonne heure!; **very
  good!** parfait!
good' after'noon' s bonjour m
good'-by' or **good'-bye'** s adieu m ||
  interj au revoir!; (before a long journey) adieu!
good' cit'izenship s civisme m
good' day' s bonjour m
good' deed' s bonne action f
good' egg' s (slang) chic type m
good' eve'ning s bonsoir m
good' fel'low s brave garçon m, brave
  type m
good' fel'lowship s camaraderie f
good'-for-noth'ing adj inutile m || s
  bon m à rien
Good' Fri'day s le Vendredi saint
good' grac'es spl bonnes grâces fpl
good'-heart'ed adj au cœur généreux
good'-hu'mored adj de bonne humeur
good'-look'ing adj beau, joli
good' looks' spl belle mine f
good' luck' s bonne chance f
good·ly ['gudli] adj (comp **-lier**; super
  -liest) considérable, important; (quality) bon; (appearance) beau
good' morn'ing s bonjour m
good'-na'tured adj aimable, accommodant
goodness ['gudnis] s bonté f; **for goodness' sake!** pour l'amour de Dieu!;
  goodness knows Dieu seul sait ||
  interj mon Dieu!
good' night' s bonne nuit f
good' sense' s bon sens m
good'-sized' adj de grandeur moyenne,
  assez grand

good' speed' s succès m, bonne chance f
good'-tem'pered de caractère facile, d'humeur égale
good' time' s bon temps m; **to have a
  good time** prendre du bon temps,
  bien s'amuser; **to make good time**
  arriver en peu de temps
good' turn' s bienfait m, service m
good' will' s bonne volonté f; (com)
  achalandage m
good' works' spl bonnes œuvres fpl
good·y ['gudi] adj (coll) d'une piété
  affectée || s (pl **-ies**) (coll) petit saint
  m; **goodies** friandises fpl || interj
  chouette!, chic!
gooey ['gu·i] adj (comp **gooier**; super
  gooiest) (slang) gluant; (sentimental)
  (slang) à l'eau de rose
goof [guf] s (slang) toqué m || intr—
  to goof off (slang) tirer au flanc
goof·y ['gufi] adj (comp **-ier**; super
  -iest) (slang) toqué, maboul
goon [gun] s (roughneck) (coll) dur m;
  (coll) terroriste m professionnel;
  (slang) niais m
goose [gus] s (pl **geese** [gis]) oie f;
  **to kill the goose that lays the golden
  eggs** tuer la poule aux œufs d'or || s
  (pl **gooses**) (of tailor) carreau m
goose'ber'ry s (pl **-ries**) groseille f
  verte
goose' egg' s œuf m d'oie; (slang) zéro
  m
goose' flesh' s chair f de poule
goose'neck' s col m de cygne
goose' pim'ples spl chair f de poule
goose' step' s (mil) pas m de l'oie
goose'-step' v (pret & pp **-stepped**; ger
  -stepping) intr marcher au pas de
  l'oie
gopher ['gofər] s citelle m
gore [gor] s (blood) sang m caillé;
  (sewing) soufflet m || tr percer d'un
  coup de corne; (sewing) tailler en
  pointe
gorge [gɔrdʒ] s gorge f || tr gorger ||
  intr se gorger
gorgeous ['gɔrdʒəs] adj magnifique
gorilla [gə'rɪlə] s gorille m
gorse [gɔrs] s (bot) genêt m épineux
gor·y ['gori] adj (comp **-ier**; super
  -iest) ensanglanté, sanglant
gosh [gaʃ] interj (coll) sapristi!, mon
  Dieu!
goshawk ['gas,hɔk] s autour m
gospel ['gaspəl] s évangile m; **Gospel**
  Évangile
gos'pel truth' s parole f d'Évangile
gossamer ['gasəmər] adj ténu || s toile
  f d'araignée, fils mpl de la Vierge;
  (gauze) gaze f
gossip ['gasɪp] s commérage m, cancan
  m; (person) commère f; **piece of gos-
  sip** potin m, racontar m || intr can-
  caner
gos'sip col'umnist s échotier m
Gothic ['gaθɪk] adj & s gothique m
gouge [gaudʒ] s gouge f || tr gouger;
  (to swindle) empiler
goulash ['gulaʃ] s goulasch m & f
gourd [gord], [gurd] s gourde f

gourmand ['gurmənd] *s* gourmand *m*; (*glutton*) glouton *m*

gourmet ['gurme] *s* gourmet *m*

gout [gaut] *s* goutte *f*

govern ['gʌvərn] *tr* gouverner; (*gram*) régir ‖ *intr* gouverner

governess ['gʌvərnɪs] *s* institutrice *f*, gouvernante *f*

government ['gʌvərnmənt] *s* gouvernement *m*

governmental [‚gʌvərn'mentəl] *adj* gouvernemental

governor ['gʌvərnər] *s* gouverneur *m*; (*mach*) régulateur *m*

gown [gaun] *s* robe *f*

grab [græb] *s* prise *f*; (*coll*) vol *m*, coup *m* ‖ *v* (*pret & pp* grabbed; *ger* grabbing) *tr* empoigner, saisir ‖ *intr* —to grab at s'agripper à

grab' bag' *s* sac *m* à surprises

grace [gres] *s* grâce *f*; (*prayer at table before meals*) bénédicité *m*; (*prayer at table after meals*) grâces; (*extension of time*) délai *m* de grâce ‖ *tr* orner; honorer

graceful ['gresfəl] *adj* gracieux

grace' note' *s* note *f* d'agrément, appoggiature *f*

gracious ['greʃəs] *adj* gracieux; (*compassionate*) miséricordieux

grackle ['grækəl] *s* (*myna*) mainate *m*; (*purple grackle*) quiscale *m*

gradation [gre'deʃən] *s* gradation *f*

grade [gred] *s* (*rank*) grade *m*; (*of oil*) grade; qualité *f*; (*school class*) classe *f*, année *f*; (*mark in school*) note *f*; (*slope*) pente *f*; **to make the grade** réussir ‖ *tr* classer; (*a school paper*) noter; (*land*) niveler

grade' cross'ing *s* (rr) passage *m* à niveau

grade' school' *s* école *f* primaire

gradient ['gredɪənt] *adj* montant ‖ *s* pente *f*; (*phys*) gradient *m*

gradual ['grædʒuəl] *adj & s* graduel *m*

gradually ['grædʒuəli] *adv* graduellement, peu à peu

graduate ['grædʒuˌet] *s* diplômé *m* ‖ ['grædʒuˌet] *tr* conférer un diplôme à, décerner des diplômes à; (*to mark with degrees*) graduer ‖ *intr* recevoir son diplôme

grad'uate school' *s* faculté *f* des hautes études

grad'uate stu'dent *s* étudiant *m* avancé, étudiant de maîtrise, de doctorat

grad'uate work' *s* études *fpl* avancées

grad'uat'ing class' *s* classe *f* sortante

graduation [‚grædʒu'eʃən] *s* collation *f* des grades; (*e.g., marking on beaker*) graduation *f*

graft [græft], [graft] *s* (hort, surg) greffe *f*; (*coll*) gratte *f*, grattage *m* ‖ *tr & intr* (hort, surg) greffer; (*coll*) gratter

grafter ['græftər], ['graftər] *s* (hort) greffeur *m*; (*coll*) homme *m* véreux, concussionnaire *mf*

gra'ham bread' ['gre·əm] *s* pain *m* entier

gra'ham flour' *s* farine *f* entière

grain [gren] *s* (*small seed; tiny particle of sand, etc.; small unit of weight; small amount*) grain *m*; (*cereal seeds*) grains *mpl*, céréales *fpl*; (*in stone*) fil *m*; (*in wood*) fibres *fpl*; **against the grain** à contre-fil, à rebrousse-poil ‖ *tr* grener; (*wood, etc.*) veiner

grain' el'evator *s* dépôt *m* et élévateur *m* à grains

grain' field' *s* champ *m* de blé

graining ['grenɪŋ] *s* grenage *m*; (*of painting*) veinage *m*

gram [græm] *s* gramme *m*

grammar ['græmər] *s* grammaire *f*

grammarian [grə'merɪ·ən] *s* grammairien *m*

gram'mar school' *s* école *f* primaire

grammatical [grə'mætɪkəl] *adj* grammatical

granary ['grænəri] *s* (*pl* -ries) grenier *m*

grand [grænd] *adj* magnifique; (*person*) grand; (*coll*) formidable

grand'aunt' *s* grand-tante *f*

grand'child' *s* (*pl* -chil'dren) petit-fils *m*; petite-fille *f*; **grandchildren** petits-enfants *mpl*

grand'daugh'ter *s* petite-fille *f*

grand' duch'ess *s* grande-duchesse *f*

grand' duch'y *s* grand-duché *m*

grand' duke' *s* grand-duc *m*

grandee [græn'di] *s* grand *m* d'Espagne

grand'fa'ther *s* grand-père *m*

grand'father's clock' *s* pendule *f* à gaine, horloge *f* comtoise

grandiose ['grændɪˌos] *adj* grandiose; pompeux

grand' ju'ry *s* jury *m* d'accusation

grand' lar'ceny *s* grand larcin *m*

grand' lodge' *s* grand orient *m*

grandma ['grænd‚ma], ['græm‚ma], ['græmə] *s* (*coll*) grand-maman *f*

grand'moth'er *s* grand-mère *f*

grand'neph'ew *s* petit-neveu *m*

grand'niece' *s* petite-nièce *f*

grand' op'era *s* grand opéra *m*

grandpa ['grænd‚pa], ['græn‚pa], ['græmpa] *s* (*coll*) grand-papa *m*

grand'par'ent *s* grand-père *m*; grand-mère *f*; **grandparents** grands-parents *mpl*

grand' pian'o *s* piano *m* à queue

grand' slam' *s* grand chelem *m*

grand'son' *s* petit-fils *m*

grand'stand' *s* tribune *f*, gradins *mpl*

grand' to'tal *s* total *m* global

grand'un'cle *s* grand-oncle *m*

grand' vizier' *s* grand vizir *m*

grange [grendʒ] *s* ferme *f*; syndicat *m* d'agriculteurs

granite ['grænɪt] *s* granite *m*, granit *m*

granny ['græni] *s* (*pl* -nies) (*coll*) grand-mère *f*

gran'ny knot' *s* nœud *m* de vache

grant [grænt], [grant] *s* concession *f*; (*subsidy*) subvention *f*; (*scholarship*) bourse *f* ‖ *tr* concéder, accorder; (*a wish*) exaucer; (*e.g., a charter*) octroyer; (*a degree*) décerner; **to take for granted** escompter, tenir pour évident; traiter avec indifférence

grantee [græn'ti], [gran'ti] *s* donataire *mf*

grantor [græn'tər], [gran'tər] s donateur *m*

granular ['grænjələr] *adj* granulaire

granulate ['grænjə‚let] *tr* granuler ‖ *intr* se granuler

gran'ulated sug'ar s sucre *m* cristallisé

granule ['grænjʊl] s granule *m*, granulé *m*

grape [grep] s (*fruit*) raisin *m*; (*vine*) vigne *f*; (*single grape*) grain *m* de raisin

grape' ar'bor s treille *f*

grape'fruit' s (*fruit*) pamplemousse *m* & *f*; (*tree*) pamplemoussier *m*

grape' juice' s jus *m* de raisin

grape'shot' s mitraille *f*

grape'vine' s vigne *f*; (*chain of gossip*) source *f* de canards

graph [græf], [graf] s graphique *m*; (*gram*) graphie *f*

graphic(al) ['græfɪk(əl)] *adj* graphique; (*fig*) vivant, net

graphite ['græfaɪt] s graphite *m*

graph' pa'per s papier *m* quadrillé

grapnel ['græpnəl] s grappin *m*

grapple ['græpəl] s grappin *m*; (*fight*) corps à corps *m* ‖ *tr* saisir au grappin; (*a person*) empoigner à bras le corps ‖ *intr* (*to fight*) lutter corps à corps; **to grapple with** en venir aux prises avec, s'attaquer à

grap'pling i'ron s grappin *m*

grasp [græsp], [grasp] s prise *f*; **to have a good grasp of** avoir une profonde connaissance de; **within one's grasp** à sa portée ‖ *tr* saisir ‖ *intr*— **to grasp at** tâcher de saisir; saisir avidement

grasping ['græspɪŋ], ['graspɪŋ] *adj* avide, rapace

grass [græs], [gras] s herbe *f*; (*pasture*) herbage *m*; (*lawn*) gazon *m*; **keep off the grass** (public sign) ne marchez pas sur le gazon; **to go to grass** (fig) s'étaler par terre

grass'hop'per s sauterelle *f*

grass'-roots' *adj* populaire, du peuple

grass' seed' s graine *f* fourragère; (*for lawns*) graine *f* pour gazon

grass' snake' s (*Tropidonotus natrix*) couleuvre *f* à collier

grass' wid'ow s demi-veuve *f*

grass·y ['græsi], ['grasi] *adj* (*comp* -**ier;** *super* -**iest**) herbeux

grate [gret] s grille *f*, grillage *m* ‖ *tr* (*to put a grate on*) griller; (*e.g., cheese*) râper; **to grate the teeth** grincer des dents ‖ *intr* grincer; **to grate on** écorcher

grateful ['gretfəl] *adj* reconnaissant, agréable; **to be grateful for** être reconnaissant de or pour

grater ['gretər] s râpe *f*

grati·fy ['grætɪ‚faɪ] *v* (*pret.* & *pp* -**fied**) *tr* faire plaisir à, satisfaire

gratifying ['grætɪ‚faɪ·ɪŋ] *adj* agréable, satisfaisant

grating ['gretɪŋ] *adj* grinçant ‖ s grillage *m*, grille *f*

gratis ['grætɪs], ['grætɪs] *adj* gratuit, gracieux ‖ *adv* gratis, gratuitement

gratitude ['grætɪ‚t(j)ud] s gratitude *f*,

reconnaissance *f*; **gratitude for** reconnaissance de or pour

gratuitous [grə't(j)u·ɪtəs] *adj* gratuit

gratui·ty [grə't(j)u·ɪti] s (*pl* -**ties**) gratification *f*, pourboire *m*

grave [grev] *adj* grave ‖ s fosse *f*, tombe *f*

gravedigger ['grev‚dɪgər] s fossoyeur *m*

gravel ['grævəl] s gravier *m*; (pathol) gravelle *f*

grav'en im'age ['grevən] s image *f* taillée

grave'stone' s pierre *f* tombale

grave'yard' s cimetière *m*

gravitate ['grævɪ‚tet] *intr* graviter

gravitation [‚grævɪ'teʃən] s gravitation *f*

gravi·ty ['grævɪti] s (*pl* -**ties**) gravité *f*; (phys) pesanteur *f*, gravité

gra·vy ['grevi] s (*pl* -**vies**) (*juice from cooking meat*) jus *m*; (*sauce made with this juice*) sauce *f*; (slang) profit *m* facile, profit supplémentaire

gra'vy boat' s saucière *f*

gra'vy train' s (slang) assiette *f* au beurre

gray [gre] *adj* gris; (*gray-haired*) gris, chenu; **to turn gray** grisonner ‖ s gris *m* ‖ *intr* grisonner

gray'beard' s barbon *m*, ancien *m*

gray'-haired' *adj* gris, chenu

gray'hound' s lévrier *m*; (*female*) levrette *f*

grayish ['gre·ɪʃ] *adj* grisâtre

gray' mat'ter s substance *f* grise

graze [grez] *tr* (*to touch lightly*) frôler, effleurer; (*to scratch lightly in passing*) érafler; (*to pasture*) faire paître ‖ *intr* paître

grease [gris] s graisse *f* ‖ [gris], [griz] *tr* graisser

grease' cup' [gris] s godet *m* graisseur

grease' gun' [gris] s graisseur *m*, seringue *f* à graisse

grease' paint' [gris] s fard *m*, grimage *m*

greas·y ['grisi], ['grizi] *adj* (*comp* -**ier;** *super* -**iest**) graisseux, gras

great [gret] *adj* grand; (coll) excellent, formidable; **a great deal, a great many** beaucoup

great'-aunt' s grand-tante *f*

Great' Bear' s Grande Ourse *f*

Great' Brit'ain s Grande Bretagne *f*; la Grande Bretagne

great'coat' s capote *f*

Great' Dane' s danois *m*

Great'er Lon'don s le Grand Londres

Great'er New' York' s le Grand New York

great'-grand'child' s (*pl* -**chil'dren**) arrière-petit-fils *m*; arrière-petite-fille *f*; **great-grandchildren** arrière-petits-enfants *mpl*

great'-grand'daugh'ter s arrière-petite-fille *f*

great'-grand'fa'ther s arrière-grand-père *m*, bisaïeul *m*

great'-grand'moth'er s arrière-grand-mère *f*, bisaïeule *f*

great'-grand'par'ents *spl* arrière-grands-parents *mpl*

great'-grand'son *s* arrière-petit-fils *m*

greatly ['gretli] *adv* grandement, fort, beaucoup

great'-neph'ew *s* petit-neveu *m*

greatness ['gretnis] *s* grandeur *f*

great'-niece' *s* petite-nièce *f*

great'-un'cle *s* grand-oncle *m*

Great' War' *s* Grande Guerre *f*

Grecian ['griʃən] *adj* grec || *s* (*person*) Grec *m*

Greece [gris] *s* Grèce *f*; la Grèce

greed [grid] *s* avidité *f*

greed·y ['gridi] *adj* (*comp* -ier; *super* -iest) avide

Greek [grik] *adj* grec || *s* (*language*) grec *m*; (*unintelligible language*) (coll) hébreu *m*, e.g., **it's Greek to me** (coll) c'est de l'hébreu pour moi; (*person*) Grec *m*

Greek' fire' *s* feu *m* grégeois

green [grin] *adj* vert; inexpérimenté, novice || *s* vert *m*; (*lawn*) gazon *m*; (*golf*) pelouse *f* d'arrivée; **greens** légumes *mpl* verts

green'back' *s* (U.S.A.) billet *m* de banque

greener·y ['grinəri] *s* (*pl* -ies) verdure *f*

green'-eyed' *adj* aux yeux verts; (*envious*) jaloux

green'gage' *s* (bot) reine-claude *f*

green'gro'cer·y *s* (*pl* -ies) fruiterie *f*

green'horn' *s* blanc-bec *m*, bleu *m*

green'house' *s* serre *f*

greenish ['griniʃ] *adj* verdâtre

Greenland ['grinlənd] *s* le Groënland

green' light' *s* feu *m* vert, voie *f* libre

greenness ['grinnis] *s* verdure *f*; (*unripeness*) verdeur *f*; inexpérience *f*, naïveté *f*

green' pep'per *s* poivron *m* vert

green'room' *s* (theat) foyer *m*

greensward ['grin,sword] *s* pelouse *f*

green' thumb' *s*—**to have a green thumb** avoir la main verte

greet [grit] *tr* saluer; (*to welcome*) accueillir

greeting ['gritɪŋ] *s* salutation *f*; (*welcome*) accueil *m*; **greetings** (*on greeting card*) vœux *mpl* || **greetings** *interj* salut!

greet'ing card' *s* carte *f* de vœux

gregarious [grɪ'gɛrɪ·əs] *adj* grégaire

Gregorian [grɪ'gori·ən] *adj* grégorien

grenade [grɪ'ned] *s* grenade *f*

grey [gre] *adj*, *s*, & *intr* var of **gray**

grey'hound' *s* var of **grayhound**

grid [grid] *s* (*of storage battery and vacuum tube*) grille *f*; (*on map*) quadrillage *m*; (culin) gril *m*

griddle ['gridəl] *s* plaque *f* chauffante

grid'dle-cake' *s* crêpe *f*

grid'i'ron *s* gril *m*; (sports) terrain *m* de football

grid' leak' *s* résistance *f* de fuite de la grille

grid' line' *s* ligne *f* de quadrillage

grief [grif] *s* chagrin *m*, affliction *f*; **to come to grief** finir mal

grief'-strick'en *adj* affligé, navré

grievance ['grivəns] *s* grief *m*

grieve [griv] *tr* chagriner, affliger || *intr* se chagriner, s'affliger

grievous ['grivəs] *adj* grave, douloureux

griffin ['grɪfɪn] *s* griffon *m*

grill [grɪl] *s* gril *m*; (*grating*) grille *f* || *tr* griller; (*an accused person*) (coll) cuisiner

grille [grɪl] *s* grille *f*; (aut) calandre *f*

grilled' beef'steak *s* châteaubriand *m*

grill'room' *s* grill-room *m*

grim [grɪm] *adj* (*comp* grimmer; *super* grimmest) (*fierce*) menaçant; (*repellent*) macabre; (*unyielding*) implacable; (*stern-looking*) lugubre

grimace ['grɪməs], [grɪ'mes] *s* grimace *f* || *intr* grimacer

grime [graɪm] *s* crasse *f*, saleté *f*

grim·y ['graɪmi] *adj* (*comp* -ier; *super* -iest) crasseux, sale

grin [grɪn] *s* grimace *f*; (*smile*) large sourire *m* || *v* (*pret* & *pp* grinned; *ger* grinning) *intr* avoir un large sourire, rire à belles dents

grind [graɪnd] *s* (*of coffee*) mouture *f*; (*job*) (coll) boulot *m*, collier *m*; (*student*) (coll) bûcheur *m*; **daily grind** (coll) train-train *m* quotidien || *v* (*pret* & *pp* ground [graund]) *tr* (*coffee, flour*) moudre; (*food*) broyer; (*meat*) hacher; (*a knife*) aiguiser; (*the teeth*) grincer; (*valves*) roder || *intr* grincer; **to grind away at** (coll) bûcher

grinder ['graɪndər] *s* (*for coffee, pepper, etc.*) moulin *m*, broyeur *m*; (*for meat*) hachoir *m*; (*for tools*) repasseur *m*; (*back tooth*) molaire *f*

grind'stone' *s* meule *f*, pierre *f* à aiguiser

grip [grɪp] *s* prise *f*; (*with hand*) poigne *f*; (*handle*) poignée *f*; (*handbag*) sac *m* de voyage; (*understanding*) compréhension *f*; **to come to grips** en venir aux prises; **to lose one's grip** lâcher prise || *v* (*pret* & *pp* gripped; *ger* gripping) *tr* serrer, saisir fortement; (*e.g., a theater audience*) empoigner

gripe [graɪp] *s* (coll) rouspétance *f* || *intr* (coll) rouspéter, ronchonner

grippe [grɪp] *s* grippe *f*

gripping ['grɪpɪŋ] *adj* passionnant

gris·ly ['grɪzli] *adj* (*comp* -lier; *super* -liest) horrible, macabre

grist [grɪst] *s* blé *m* à moudre

gristle ['grɪsəl] *s* cartilage *m*

gris·tly ['grɪsli] *adj* (*comp* -tlier; *super* -tliest) cartilagineux

grist'mill' *s* moulin *m* à blé

grit [grɪt] *s* grès *m*, sable *m*; (*courage*) cran *m*; **grits** gruau *m* || *v* (*pret* & *pp* gritted; *ger* gritting) *tr* (*one's teeth*) grincer

grit·ty ['grɪti] *adj* (*comp* -tier; *super* -tiest) sablonneux; (fig) plein de cran

griz·zly ['grɪzli] *adj* (*comp* -zlier; *super* -zliest) grisonnant || *s* (*pl* -zlies) ours *m* gris

griz'zly bear' *s* ours *m* gris

groan [gron] *s* gémissement *m* || *intr* gémir

grocer ['grosər] s épicier m

grocer·y ['grosəri] s (pl -ies) épicerie f; **groceries** denrées fpl

gro'cery store' s épicerie f

grog [grɑg] s grog m

grog·gy ['grɑgi] adj (comp -gier; super -giest) (coll) vacillant; (shaky, e.g., from a blow) (coll) étourdi; (drunk) (coll) gris, ivre

groin [grɔɪn] s (anat) aine f; (archit) arête f

groom [grum] s (bridegroom) marié m; (stableboy) palefrenier m || tr soigner, astiquer; (horses) panser; (a politician, a starlet, etc.) dresser, préparer

grooms'man s (pl -men) garçon m d'honneur

groove [gruv] s rainure f; (of pulley) gorge f; (of phonograph record) sillon m; (mark left by wheel) ornière f; (of window, door, etc.) feuillure f; **in the groove** (coll) comme sur des roulettes; **to get into a groove** (coll) devenir routinier || tr rainer, canneler

grope [grop] intr tâtonner; **to grope for** chercher à tâtons

gropingly ['gropɪŋli] adv à tâtons

grosbeak ['gros,bik] s gros-bec m

gross [gros] adj gros; (fat, burly) gras, épais; (crass, vulgar) grossier; (weight; receipts) brut; (displacement) global || s invar recette f brute; (twelve dozen) grosse f || tr produire en recette brute, produire brut, e.g., **the business grossed a million dollars** l'entreprise a produit un million de dollars, brut

gross' na'tional prod'uct s produit m national brut

grotesque [gro'tɛsk] adj grotesque || s grotesque m; (ornament) grotesque f

grot·to ['grɑto] s (pl -toes or -tos) grotte f

grouch [grautʃ] s (coll) humeur f grognon; (person) (coll) grognon m || intr (coll) grogner

grouch·y ['grautʃi] adj (comp -ier; super -iest) (coll) grognon, maussade

ground [graund] s terre f; (piece of land) terrain m; (basis, foundation) fondement m, base f; (reason) motif m, cause f; (elec) terre f; (body of automobile corresponding to ground) (elec) masse f; **ground for complaint** grief m; **grounds** parc m, terrain; fondement, cause; (of coffee) marc m; **on the ground of** pour raison de, sous prétexte de; **to be losing ground** être en recul; **to break ground** donner le premier coup de pioche; **to have grounds for** avoir matière à; **to stand one's ground** tenir bon or ferme; **to yield ground** lâcher pied || tr fonder, baser; (elec) mettre à terre; **grounded** (aer) interdit de vol, gardé au sol; **to ground s.o. in s.th.** enseigner à fond q.ch. à qn

ground' connec'tion s prise f de terre

ground' crew' s équipe f au sol, personnel m rampant

ground' floor' s rez-de-chaussée m

ground' glass' s verre m dépoli

ground' hog' s marmotte f d'Amérique

grounding ['graundɪŋ] s (aer) interdiction f de vol; (elec) mise f à la masse

ground' installa'tions spl (aer) infrastructure f

ground' lead' ['lid] s (elec) conduite f à terre

groundless ['graundlɪs] adj sans fondement

ground' meat' s viande f hachée

ground' plan' s plan m de base; (archit) plan horizontal

ground' speed' s (aer) vitesse f par rapport au sol

ground' swell' s lame f de fond

ground' troops' spl (mil) effectifs mpl terrestres

ground' wire' s (elec) fil m de terre, fil de masse

ground'work' s fondement m, fond m

group [grup] s groupe m || tr grouper || intr se grouper

grouse [graus] s coq m de bruyère || intr (slang) grogner

grove [grov] s bocage m, bosquet m

grov·el ['grɑvəl], ['grʌvəl] v (pret & pp -eled or -elled; ger -eling or -elling) intr se vautrer; (before s.o.) ramper

grow [gro] v (pret grew [gru]; pp grown [gron]) tr cultiver, faire pousser; (a beard) laisser pousser || intr croître; (said of plants) pousser; (said of seeds) germer; (to become) devenir; **to grow angry** se mettre en colère; **to grow old** vieillir; **to grow out of** se développer de; (e.g., a suit of clothes) devenir trop grand pour; **to grow up** grandir, profiter

growl [graul] s grondement m, grognement m || tr & intr gronder, grogner

grown-up' adj adulte || s (pl grownups) adulte mf; **grown-ups** grandes personnes fpl

growth [groθ] s croissance f, développement m; (increase) accroissement m; (of trees, grass, etc.) pousse f; (pathol) excroissance f, grosseur f

grub [grʌb] s asticot m; (person) homme m de peine; (food) (coll) boustifaille f || v (pret & pp grubbed; ger grubbing) tr défricher || intr fouiller

grub·by ['grʌbi] adj (comp -bier; super -biest) sale, malpropre

grudge [grʌdʒ] s rancune f; **to have a grudge against** garder rancune à || tr donner à contre-cœur

grudgingly ['grʌdʒɪŋli] adv à contre-cœur

gruel ['gruəl] s gruau m, bouillie f

grueling ['gruəlɪŋ] adj éreintant

gruesome ['grusəm] adj macabre

gruff [grʌf] adj bourru, brusque; (voice) rauque, gros

grumble ['grʌmbəl] s grognement m || intr grogner, grommeler

grump·y ['grʌmpi] adj (comp -ier; super -iest) maussade, grognon

grunt [grʌnt] s grognement m || intr grogner

G′-string′ s (*loincloth*) pagne m; (*worn by women entertainers*) cache-sexe m; (*mus*) corde f de sol

guarantee [ˌgærənˈti] s garantie f; (*guarantor*) garant m, répondant m; (*security*) caution f || tr garantir

guarantor [ˈgærənˌtɔr] s garant m

guaran·ty [ˈgærənti] s (pl **-ties**) garantie f || v (*pret & pp* **-tied**) tr garantir

guard [gɑrd] s garde f; (*person*) garde m; **on guard** en garde; (*on duty*) de garde; (*mil*) en faction, de faction; **on one's guard** sur ses gardes; **to mount guard** monter la garde; **under guard** gardé à vue || tr garder || intr être de faction; **to guard against** se garder de

guard′ du′ty s service m de garde

guarded adj (*remark*) prudent

guard′house′ s guérite f, corps-de-garde m; prison f militaire

guardian [ˈgɑrdɪ·ən] adj gardien || s gardien m; (*of a ward*) tuteur m

guard′ian an′gel s ange m gardien, ange tutélaire

guard′ian·ship′ s garde f; (*law*) tutelle f

guard′rail′ s garde-fou m, parapet m

guard′room′ s corps-de-garde m, salle f de police; (*prison*) bloc m, tôle f

guards′man s (pl **-men**) garde m

Guatemala [ˌgwɑtəˈmɑlən] adj guatémaltèque || s Guatémaltèque m

guava [ˈgwɑvə] s goyave f; (*tree*) goyavier m

guerrilla [gəˈrɪlə] s guérillero m; **guerrillas** (*band*) guérilla f

guerril′la war′fare s guérilla f

guess [gɛs] s conjecture f || tr & intr conjecturer; (*a secret, riddle, etc.*) deviner; (*coll*) supposer, penser; **I guess so** je crois que oui; **to guess right** bien deviner

guess′work′ s supposition f; **by guesswork** au jugé

guest [gɛst] s invité m, hôte mf; (*in a hotel*) client m, hôte

guest′ room′ s chambre f d'ami

guest′ speak′er s orateur m de circonstance

guffaw [gəˈfɔ] s gros rire m || tr dire avec un gros rire || intr rire bruyamment

Guiana [gɪˈɑnə], [gɪˈænə] s Guyane f; la Guyane

guidance [ˈgaɪdəns] s gouverne f; (*guiding*) conduite f; (*in choosing a career*) orientation f; (*of rocket*) guidage m; **for your guidance** pour votre gouverne

guide [gaɪd] s guide m || tr guider

guide′book′ s guide m

guid′ed mis′sile s engin m téléguidé

guide′ dog′ s chien m d'aveugle

guide′ line′ s (*fig*) norme f, règle f; **guide lines** (*for writing straight lines*) transparent m, guide-âne m

guide′post′ s poteau m indicateur

guide′ word′ s lettrine f

guild [gɪld] s association f, corporation f; (*eccl*) confrérie f; (*hist*) guilde f

guild′hall′ s hôtel m de ville

guile [gaɪl] s astuce f, artifice m

guileful [ˈgaɪlfəl] adj astucieux, artificieux

guileless [ˈgaɪllɪs] adj candide, innocent

guillotine [ˈgɪləˌtin] s guillotine f || tr guillotiner

guilt [gɪlt] s culpabilité f

guiltless [ˈgɪltlɪs] adj innocent

guilt·y [ˈgɪlti] adj (*comp* **-ier**; *super* **-iest**) coupable; **found guilty** reconnu coupable

guimpe [gɪmp], [gæmp] s empièce-ment m

guinea [ˈgɪni] s guinée f; **Guinea** Guinée; la Guinée

guin′ea fowl′ or **hen′** s poule f de Guinée, pintade f

guin′ea pig′ s cobaye m

guise [gaɪz] s apparences fpl, déguisement m; **under the guise of** sous un semblant de, sous le masque de

guitar [gɪˈtɑr] s guitare f

guitarist [gɪˈtɑrɪst] s guitariste mf

gulch [gʌltʃ] s ravin m

gulf [gʌlf] s golfe m; (*fig*) gouffre m

Gulf′ of Mex′ico s Golfe m du Mexique

Gulf′ Stream′ s Courant m du Golfe

gull [gʌl] s mouette f, goéland m; (*coll*) gogo m, jobard m || tr escroquer, duper

gullet [ˈgʌlɪt] s gosier m

gullible [ˈgʌlɪbəl] adj crédule, naïf

gul·ly [ˈgʌli] s (pl **-lies**) ravin m; (*channel*) rigole f

gulp [gʌlp] s gorgée f, lampée f; **at one gulp** d'un trait || tr—**to gulp down** avaler à grandes bouchées, lamper; (*e.g., tears*) ravaler, refouler || intr avoir la gorge serrée

gum [gʌm] s gomme f; (*on eyelids*) chassie f; (*anat*) gencive f || v (*pret & pp* **gummed**; *ger* **gumming**) tr gommer; **to gum up** encrasser; (*coll*) bousiller

gum′ ar′abic s gomme f arabique

gum′boil′ s phlegmon m, fluxion f

gum′ boot′ s botte f de caoutchouc

gum′drop′ s boule f de gomme, pâte f de fruits

gum·my [ˈgʌmi] adj (*comp* **-mier**; *super* **-miest**) gommeux; (*eyelids*) chassieux

gumption [ˈgʌmpʃən] s (*coll*) initiative f, cran m

gum′shoe′ s caoutchouc m; (*coll*) détective m || intr rôder en tapinois, marcher furtivement

gun [gʌn] s fusil m; (*for spraying*) pistolet m; **to stick to one's guns** (*coll*) ne pas en démordre || v (*pret & pp* **gunned**; *ger* **gunning**) tr—**to gun down** tuer d'un coup de fusil; **to gun the engine** (*slang*) appuyer sur le champignon || intr—**to gun for** (*game*) chasser; (*an enemy*) pourchasser

gun′ bar′rel s canon m

gun′boat′ s cannonière f

gun′ car′riage s affût m de canon

gun′cot′ton s fulmicoton m

gun′ crew′ s peloton m de pièce, servants mpl de canon

gun′fire′ s canonnade f, coups mpl de feu

gun′man s (pl -men) s bandit m

gun′ met′al s métal m bleui

gunner ['gʌnər] s canonnier m, artilleur m; (aer) mitrailleur m

gunnery ['gʌnəri] s tir m, canonnage m

gunnysack ['gʌni,sæk] s sac m de serpillière

gun′pow′der s poudre f à canon

gun′run′ning s contrebande f d'armes

gun′shot′ s coup m de feu, coup de fusil

gun′smith′ s armurier m

gun′stock′ s fût m

gunwale ['gʌnəl] s (naut) plat-bord m

gup-py ['gʌpi] s (pl -pies) guppy m

gurgle ['gʌrgəl] s glouglou m, gargouillement m || intr glouglouter, gargouiller

gush [gʌʃ] s jaillissement m || intr jaillir; **to gush over** (coll) s'attendrir sur

gusher ['gʌʃər] s puits m jaillissant

gush•y ['gʌʃi] adj (comp -ier; super -iest) (coll) démonstratif, expansif

gusset ['gʌsɪt] s (in garment) soufflet m; (mach) gousset m

gust [gʌst] s bouffée f, coup m

gusto ['gʌsto] s goût m, entrain m

gust•y ['gʌsti] adj (comp -ier; super -iest) venteux; (wind) à rafales

gut [gʌt] s boyau m; **guts** (coll) cran m || v (pret & pp gutted; ger gutting) tr raser à l'intérieur; (to take out the guts of) vider

gutter ['gʌtər] s (on side of road) caniveau m; (in street) ruisseau m; (of roof) gouttière f; (ditch formed by rain water) rigole f

gut′ter•snipe′ s (coll) voyou m

guttural ['gʌtərəl] adj guttural || s gutturale f

guy [gaɪ] s câble m tenseur; (naut) hauban m; (coll) type m, gars m || tr haubaner; (coll) se moquer de

guy′ wire′ s câble m tenseur; (naut) hauban m

guzzle ['gʌzəl] tr & intr boire avidement

guzzler ['gʌzlər] s soiffard m

gym [dʒɪm] s (coll) gymnase m

gymnasi•um [dʒɪm'nezɪ•əm] s (pl -ums or -a [ə]) gymnase m

gymnast ['dʒɪmnæst] s gymnaste mf

gynecology [,gaɪnə'kɑlədʒi], [,dʒaɪnə-'kɑlədʒi] s gynécologie f

gyp [dʒɪp] s (slang) escroquerie f; (person) (slang) aigrefin m || v (pret & pp gypped; ger gypping) tr (slang) tirer une carotte à, refaire, gruger

gypsum ['dʒɪpsəm] s gypse m

gyp•sy ['dʒɪpsi] adj bohémien || s (pl -sies) bohémien m; **Gypsy** (language) tsigane m, romanichel m; (person) gitan m, tsigane mf, romanichel m

gyp′sy moth′ s zigzag m

gyrate ['dʒaɪret] intr tournoyer

gyrocompass ['dʒaɪro,kʌmpəs] s gyrocompas m

gyroscope ['dʒaɪrə,skop] s gyroscope m

H

H, h [etʃ] s VIIIᵉ lettre de l'alphabet

haberdasher ['hæbər,dæʃər] s chemisier m

haberdasher•y ['hæbər,dæʃəri] s (pl -ies) chemiserie f, confection f pour hommes

habit ['hæbɪt] s habitude f; (dress) habit m, costume m; **to get into the habit of** s'habituer à

habitual [hə'bɪtʃʊ•əl] adj habituel

habituate [hə'bɪtʃʊ,et] tr habituer

hack [hæk] s (notch) entaille f; (cough) toux f sèche; (hackney) voiture f de louage; (old nag) rosse f; (writer) écrivassier m || tr hacher

hackney ['hækni] s voiture f de louage

hackneyed ['hæknid] adj banal, battu

hack′saw′ s scie f à métaux

haddock ['hædək] s églefin m

hag [hæg] s (ugly woman) guenon f; (witch) sorcière f; **old hag** vieille fée f

haggard ['hægərd] adj décharné, hâve; (wild-looking) hagard, farouche

haggle ['hægəl] intr marchander; **to haggle over** marchander

Hague [heg] s—**The Hague** La Haye

hail [hel] s (frozen rain) grêle f; **within hail** à portée de la voix || tr saluer; (a ship, taxi, etc.) héler || intr grêler; **to hail from** venir de || interj salut!

Hail′ Mar′y s Ave Maria m

hail′stone′ s grêlon m

hail′storm′ s tempête f de grêle

hair [her] s poil m; (of person) cheveu m; (head of human hair) cheveux mpl; **against the hair** à rebrousse-poil, à contre-poil; **hairs** cheveux; **to a hair** à un cheveu près; **to get in s.o.'s hair** (slang) porter sur les nerfs à qn; **to let one's hair down** (slang) en prendre à son aise; **to make s.o.'s hair stand on end** faire dresser les cheveux à qn; **to not turn a hair** ne pas tiquer; **to split hairs** fendre or couper les cheveux en quatre

hair′breadth′ s épaisseur f d'un cheveu; **to escape by a hairbreadth** l'échapper belle

hair′brush′ s brosse f à cheveux

hair′cloth′ s thibaude f; (for furniture) tissu-crin m

hair′ curl′er [ˌkʌrlər] s frisoir m; (pin) bigoudi m

hair′cut′ s coupe f de cheveux; **to get a haircut** se faire couper les cheveux

hair′do′ s (pl -dos) coiffure f

hair′dress′er s coiffeur m pour dames; coiffeuse f

hair′dress′ing s cosmétique m

hair′ dri′er s sèche-cheveux m, séchoir m à cheveux

hair′ dye′ s teinture f des cheveux

hair′line′ s (on face of type) délié m; (along the upper forehead) naissance f des cheveux, plantation f des cheveux

hair′ net′ s résille f

hair′pin′ s épingle f à cheveux

hair′pin turn′ s lacet m

hair′-rais′ing adj (coll) horripilant

hair′ rib′bon s ruban m à cheveux

hair′ set′ s mise f en plis

hair′ shirt′ s haire f, cilice m

hair′split′ting adj vétilleux, trop subtil || s ergotage m

hair′ spray′ s (for setting hair) laque f, fixatif m

hair′spring′ s spiral m

hair′ style′ s coiffure f

hair′ ton′ic s lotion f capillaire

hair′ trig′ger s détente f douce

hair-y [ˈheri] adj (comp -ier; super -iest) poilu, velu; (on head) chevelu

Haiti [ˈheti] s Haïti f

Haitian [ˈhetɪ-ən], [ˈheʃən] adj haïtien || s Haïtien m

halberd [ˈhælbərd] s hallebarde f

hal′cyon days′ [ˈhælsɪ-ən] spl jours mpl alcyoniens, jours sereins

hale [hel] adj vigoureux, sain; **hale and hearty** frais et gaillard || tr haler

half [hæf], [hɑf] adj demi || s (pl **halves** [hævz], [hɑvz]) moitié f, la moitié; (of the hour) demi m; **by half** de moitié, à demi; **half an hour** une demi-heure; **in half** en deux; **to go halves** être de moitié || adv moitié, à moitié; **half . . . half** moitié . . . moitié; **half past** et demie, e.g., **half past three** trois heures et demie

half′-and-half′ adj & adv moitié l'un moitié l'autre, en parties égales || s (for coffee) mélange m de lait et de crème; (beer) mélange de bière et porter

half′back′ s (football) demi-arrière m, demi m

half′-baked′ adj à moitié cuit; (person) inexpérimenté; (plan) prématuré, incomplet

half′ bind′ing s (bb) demi-reliure f à petit coins

half′-blood′ s métis m; demi-frère m

half′ boot′ s demi-botte f

half′-bound′ adj (bb) en demi-reliure à coins

half′-breed′ s métis m, sang-mêlé m; (e.g., horse) demi-sang m

half′ broth′er s demi-frère m

half′-cocked′ adv (coll) avec trop de hâte

half′-day′ s demi-journée f

half′-doz′en s demi-douzaine f

half′ fare′ s demi-tarif m, demi-place f

half′-full′ adj à moitié plein

half′-heart′ed adj sans entrain, hésitant

half′-hol′iday s demi-congé m

half′ hose′ s chaussettes fpl

half′-hour′ s demi-heure f; **every half-hour on the half-hour** toutes les demi-heures à la demi-heure juste; **on the half-hour** à la demie

half′ leath′er s (bb) demi-reliure f à petit coins

half′-length′ s demi-longueur f

half′-length por′trait s portrait m en buste

half′-light′ s demi-jour m

half′-mast′ s—**at half-mast** en berne, à mi-mât

half′-moon′ s demi-lune f

half′ mourn′ing s demi-deuil m

half′ note′ s (mus) blanche f

half′ pay′ s demi-solde f

halfpen·ny [ˈhepəni], [ˈhepni] s (pl -nies) demi-penny m; (fig) sou m

half′ pint′ s demi-pinte f; (little runt) (slang) petit culot m

half′-seas o′ver adj—**to be half-seas over** avoir du vent dans les voiles

half′ shell′ s (either half of a bivalve) écaille f; **on the half shell** dans sa coquille

half′ sis′ter s demi-sœur f

half′ sole′ s demi-semelle f

half′-staff′ s—**at half-staff** à mi-mât

half′-tim′bered adj à demi-boisage

half′ time′ s (sports) mi-temps f

half′-time′ adj à demi-journée

half′tone′ s (painting, phot) demi-teinte f; (typ) similigravure f

half′ tone′ s (mus) demi-ton m

half′-track′ s semi-chenillé m

half′-truth′ s demi-vérité f

half′turn′ s demi-tour m; (of wheel) demi-révolution f

half′way′ adj & adv à mi-chemin; **halfway through** à moitié de; **halfway up** à mi-côte; **to meet s.o. halfway** couper la poire en deux avec qn

half′-wit′ted adj à moitié idiot

halibut [ˈhælɪbət] s flétan m

halitosis [ˌhælɪˈtosɪs] s mauvaise haleine f

hall [hɔl] s (passageway) corridor m, couloir m; (entranceway) entrée f, vestibule m; (large meeting room) salle f, hall m; (assembly room of a university) amphithéâtre m; (building of a university) bâtiment m

halleluiah or **hallelujah** [ˌhælɪˈlujə] s alléluia m || interj alléluia!

hall′mark′ s estampille f, poinçon m; (fig) cachet m, marque f

hal-lo [həˈlo] s (pl -los) holà m || intr huer || interj holà!, ohé!; (hunting) taïaut!

hallow [ˈhælo] tr sanctifier

hallowed adj sanctifié, saint

Halloween or **Hallowe'en** [ˌhæloˈin] s la veille de la Toussaint

hallucination [həˌlusɪˈneʃən] s hallucination f

hall/way/ s corridor m, couloir m

ha·lo ['helo] s (pl -los or -loes) (meteo) auréole f, halo m; (around a head) auréole f

halogen ['hælədʒən] s halogène m

halt [hɔlt] adj boiteux, estropié || s halte f, arrêt m; **to come to a halt** faire halte || tr faire faire halte à || intr faire halte || interj halte!; (mil) halte-là!

halter ['hɔltər] s licou m; (noose) corde f

halting ['hɔltɪŋ] adj boiteux; hésitant

halve [hæv], [hɑv] tr diviser or partager en deux; réduire de moitié

halyard ['hæljərd] s (naut) drisse f

ham [hæm] s (part of leg behind knee) jarret m; (thigh and buttock) fesse f; (culin) cuisse f; (cured) (culin) jambon m; (rad) radio amateur m; (theat) cabotin m; **hams** fesses

hamburger ['hæm,bʌrgər] s sandwich m à la hambourgeoise, hamburger m; (Hamburg steak) biftek m haché

hamlet ['hæmlɪt] s hameau m

hammer ['hæmər] s marteau m; (of gun) chien m, percuteur m || tr marteler; **to hammer out** étendre au marteau; (to resolve) résoudre || intr—**to hammer away at** (e.g., a job) travailler d'arrache-pied à

hammock ['hæmək] s hamac m

hamper ['hæmpər] s manne f || tr embarrasser, gêner, empêcher

hamster ['hæmstər] s hamster m

ham/string/ v (pret & pp -strung) tr couper le jarret à; (fig) couper les moyens à

hand [hænd] adj à main, à la main, manuel || s main f; (workman) manœuvre m, ouvrier m; (way of writing) écriture f; (clapping of hands) applaudissements mpl; (of clock or watch) aiguille f; (a round of play) coup m, partie f, main; (of God) doigt m; (measure) palme m; (cards) jeu m; **at hand** sous la main; (said of approaching event) proche, prochain; **by hand** à la main; **hands off!** n'y touchez pas!; **hands up!** haut les mains!; **hand to hand** corps à corps; **on every hand** de toutes parts, de tous côtés; **on the one hand . . . on the other hand** d'une part . . . d'autre part; **to live from hand to mouth** vivre au jour le jour; **to shake hands with** serrer la main à; **to wait on hand and foot** être aux petits soins pour; **to win hands down** gagner dans un fauteuil; **under the hand and seal of** signé et scellé de || tr donner, présenter; (e.g., food at table) passer; **to hand down** (e.g., property) léguer; (a verdict) prononcer; **to hand in** remettre; **to hand on** transmettre; **to hand out** distribuer; **to hand over** céder, livrer

hand/bag/ s sac m à main

hand/ bag/gage s menus bagages mpl

hand/ball/ s pelote f; (game) handball m

hand/bill/ s prospectus m

hand/book/ s manuel m

hand/ brake/ s frein m à main

hand/car/ s (rr) draisine f

hand/cart/ s voiture f à bras

hand/clasp/ s poignée f de main

hand/ control/ s commande f à la main

hand/cuff/ s menotte f || tr mettre les menottes à

handful ['hænd,fʊl] s poignée f

hand/ glass/ s miroir m à main; (magnifying glass) loupe f à main

hand/ grenade/ s grenade f à main

handi·cap ['hændɪ,kæp] s handicap m || v (pret & pp -capped; ger -capping) tr handicaper

handicraft ['hændɪ,kræft], ['hændɪ,krɑft] s habileté f manuelle; métier m; **handicrafts** produits mpl d'artisanat

handiwork ['hændɪ,wʌrk] s ouvrage m, travail m manuel; (fig) œuvre f

handkerchief ['hæŋkərt/ɪf], ['hæŋkər,t/if] s mouchoir m

handle ['hændəl] s (of basket, crock, pitcher) anse f; (of shovel, broom, knife) manche m; (of umbrella, sword, door) poignée f; (of frying pan) queue f; (of pump) brimbale f; (of handcart) brancard m; (of wheelbarrow) bras m; (opportunity, pretext) prétexte m; (mach) manivelle f, manette f; **to fly off the handle** (coll) sortir de ses gonds || tr manier; (with one's hands) palper, tâter; **handle with care** (shipping label) fragile; **to handle roughly** malmener || intr—**to handle well** (mach) avoir de bonnes réactions

han/dle·bars/ spl guidon m

handler ['hændlər] s (sports) entraîneur m

handling ['hændlɪŋ] s (e.g., of tool) maniement m; (e.g., of person) traitement m; (of merchandise) manutention f

hand/made/ adj fait à la main

hand/maid/ or **hand/maid/en** s servante f; (fig) auxiliaire mf

hand/-me-down/ s (coll) vêtement m de seconde main

hand/ or/gan s orgue m de Barbarie

hand/out/ s (notes) (coll) documentation f; (slang) aumône f

hand/-picked/ adj trié sur le volet

hand/rail/ s main f courante, rampe f

hand/saw/ s égoïne f, scie f à main

hand/set/ s combiné m

hand/shake/ s poignée f de main

handsome ['hænsəm] adj beau; (e.g., fortune) considérable

hand/spring/ s—**to do a handspring** prendre appui sur les mains pour faire la culbute

hand/-to-hand/ adj corps-à-corps

hand/-to-mouth/ adj—**to lead a hand-to-mouth existence** vivre au jour le jour

hand/ truck/ s bard m, diable m

hand/work/ s travail m à la main

hand/writ/ing s écriture f

handwritten ['hænd,rɪtən] adj manuscrit, autographe

hand·y ['hændi] *adj* (*comp* **-ier**; *super* **-iest**) (*easy to handle*) maniable; (*within easy reach*) accessible, sous la main; (*skillful*) adroit, habile; **to come in handy** être très à propos

hand'y-man' *s* (*pl* **-men'**) homme *m* à tout faire, bricoleur *m*

hang [hæŋ] *s* (*of dress, curtain, etc.*) retombé *f*, drapé *m*; (*skill; insight*) adresse *f*, sens *m*; **I don't give a hang!** (coll) je m'en moque pas mal!; **to get the hang** (coll) saisir le truc, attraper le chic ‖ *v* (*pret & pp* **hung** [hʌŋ]) *tr* pendre; (*laundry*) étendre; (*wallpaper*) coller; (*one's head*) baisser; **hang it all!** zut alors!; **to hang up** suspendre, accrocher; (telp) raccrocher ‖ *intr* pendre, être accroché; **to hang around** flâner, rôder; **to hang on** se cramponner à, s'accrocher à; (*to depend on*) dépendre de; (*to stay put*) tenir bon; **to hang out** pendre dehors; (slang) percher, loger; **to hang over** (*to threaten*) peser sur, menacer; **to hang together** rester unis; **to hang up** (telp) raccrocher ‖ *v* (*pret & pp* **hung** or **hanged**) *tr* (*to execute by hanging*) pendre ‖ *intr* se pendre

hangar ['hæŋər], ['hæŋgər] *s* hangar *m*

hang'dog' *adj* (*look*) patibulaire

hanger ['hæŋər] *s* crochet *m*; (*coathanger*) cintre *m*, portemanteau *m*

hang'er-on' *s* (*pl* **hangers-on**) parasite *m*, pique-assiette *m*

hanging ['hæŋɪŋ] *adj* pendant, suspendu ‖ *s* pendaison *f*; **hangings** tentures *fpl*

hang'man *s* (*pl* **-men**) bourreau *m*

hang'nail' *s* envie *f*

hang'out' *s* (coll) repaire *m*

hang'o'ver *s* (coll) gueule *f* de bois

hank [hæŋk] *s* écheveau *m*

hanker ['hæŋkər] *intr*—**to hanker after** or **for** désirer vivement, être affamé de

Hannibal ['hænɪbəl] *s* Annibal *m*

haphazard [,hæp'hæzərd] *adj* fortuit, imprévu; au petit bonheur ‖ *adv* à l'aventure, au hasard

hapless ['hæplɪs] *adj* malheureux, malchanceux

happen ['hæpən] *intr* arriver, se passer; (*to be the case by chance*) survenir; **happen what may** advienne que pourra; **how does it happen that . . . ?** comment se fait-il que . . . ?, d'où vient-il que . . . ?; **to happen upon** tomber sur; **to happen to** + *inf* se trouver + *inf*, venir à + *inf*

happening ['hæpənɪŋ] *s* événement *m*

happily ['hæpɪli] *adv* heureusement

happiness ['hæpɪnɪs] *s* bonheur *m*

hap·py ['hæpi] *adj* (*comp* **-pier**; *super* **-piest**) heureux; (*pleased*) content; (*hour*) propice; **to be happy to** être heureux or content de

hap'py-go-luck'y *adj* sans souci, insouciant ‖ *adv* (archaic) à l'aventure

hap'py me'dium *s* juste-milieu *m*

Hap'py New' Year' *interj* bonne année!

harangue [hə'ræŋ] *s* harangue *f* ‖ *tr & intr* haranguer

harass ['hærəs], [hə'ræs] *tr* harceler; tourmenter

harbinger ['harbɪndʒər] *s* avant-coureur *m*, précurseur *m*

harbor ['harbər] *s* port *m*; ‖ *tr* héberger, donner asile à; (*a criminal, stolen goods, etc.*) receler; (*suspicions; a hope*) entretenir, nourrir; (*a grudge*) garder

har'bor mas'ter *s* capitaine *m* de port

hard [hard] *adj* dur; (*difficult*) difficile; (*water*) cru, calcaire; (*work*) assidu, dur; **to be hard on** (*to treat severely*) être dur or sévère envers; (*to wear out fast*) user ‖ *adv* dur, fort; (*firmly*) ferme; **hard upon** de près, tout contre; **to rain hard** pleuvoir fort; **to try hard** bien essayer

hard'-and-fast' *adj* strict, inflexible, établi

hard-bitten ['hard'bɪtən] *adj* tenace, dur à cuire

hard'-boiled' *adj* (*egg*) dur; (coll) dur, inflexible

hard' can'dy *s* bonbons *mpl*; **piece of hard candy** bonbon *m*

hard' cash' *s* espèces *fpl* sonnantes

hard' ci'der *s* cidre *m*

hard' coal' *s* houille *f* éclatante, anthracite *m*

hard' drink' *s* boissons *fpl* alcooliques, liqueurs *fpl* fortes

hard' drink'er *s* grand buveur *m*

hard'-earned' *adj* péniblement gagné

harden ['hardən] *tr* durcir, endurcir ‖ *intr* se durcir, s'endurcir

hardening ['hardənɪŋ] *s* durcissement *m*; (fig) endurcissement *m*

hard' fact' *s* fait *m* brutal; **hard facts** réalités *fpl*

hard-fought ['hard'fɔt] *adj* acharné, chaudement disputé

hard'-head'ed *adj* positif, à la tête froide

hard'-heart'ed *adj* dur, sans compassion

hardihood ['hardi,hʊd] *s* endurance *f*; courage *m*; audace *f*

hardiness ['hardɪnɪs] *s* vigueur *f*

hard' la'bor *s* travaux *mpl* forcés

hard' luck' *s* guigne *f*, malchance *f*

hardly ['hardli] *adv* guère; à peine, ne . . . guère, e.g., **he hardly thinks of anything else** à peine pense-t-il à autre chose, il ne pense guère à autre chose; **hardly ever** presque jamais

hardness ['hardnɪs] *s* dureté *f*

hard' of hear'ing *adj* dur d'oreille

hard'-pressed' *adj* aux abois, gêné

hard' rub'ber *s* caoutchouc *m* durci, ébonite *f*

hard'-shell' *adj* (*clam*) à carapace dure; (coll) opiniâtre

hard'ship' *s* peine *f*; **hardships** privations *fpl*; fatigues *fpl*

hard'tack' *s* biscuit *m*, biscotin *m*

hard' times' *spl* difficultés *fpl*, temps *mpl* difficiles

hard' to please' *adj* difficile à contenter, exigeant

hard' up' *adj* (coll) à court d'argent; **to be hard up for** (coll) être à court de

hard'ware' *s* quincaillerie *f*; (*trimmings*) ferrure *f*

hard'ware'man *s* (*pl* -men) quincaillier *m*

hard'ware store' *s* quincaillerie *f*

hard-won ['hard,wʌn] *adj* chèrement disputé, conquis de haute lutte

hard'wood' *s* bois *m* dur; arbre *m* de bois dur

hard'wood floor' *s* parquet *m*

har·dy ['hardi] *adj* (*comp* -dier; *super* -diest) vigoureux, robuste; (*rash*) hardi; (*hort*) résistant

hare [her] *s* lièvre *m*

hare'brained' *adj* écervelé, farfelu

hare'lip' *s* bec-de-lièvre *m*

harem ['herəm] *s* harem *m*

hark [hark] *intr* écouter; **to hark back to** en revenir à || *interj* écoutez!

harken ['harkən] *intr*—to harken to écouter

harlequin ['harləkwin] *s* arlequin *m*

harlot ['harlət] *s* prostituée *f*, fille *f* publique

harm [harm] *s* mal *m*, dommage *m* || *tr* nuire (with *dat*), faire du mal (with *dat*)

harmful ['harmfəl] *adj* nuisible

harmless ['harmlis] *adj* inoffensif

harmonic [har'manik] *adj* harmonique

harmonica [har'manikə] *s* harmonica *m*

harmonious [har'moni·əs] *adj* harmonieux

harmonize ['harmə,naiz] *tr* harmoniser || *intr* s'harmoniser

harmo·ny ['harmoni] *s* (*pl* -nies) harmonie *f*

harness ['harnis] *s* harnais *m*, harnachement *m*; **to die in the harness** (coll) mourir sous le harnais, mourir debout; **to get back in the harness** (coll) reprendre le collier || *tr* harnacher; (*e.g., a river*) aménager, capter

har'ness ma'ker *s* bourrelier *m*, harnacheur *m*

har'ness race' *s* course *f* attelée

harp [harp] *s* harpe *f* || *intr*—to harp on rabâcher

harpist ['harpist] *s* harpiste *mf*

harpoon [har'pun] *s* harpon *m* || *tr* harponner

harpsichord ['harpsi,kord] *s* clavecin *m*

har·py ['harpi] *s* (*pl* -pies) harpie *f*

harrow ['hæro] *s* (agr) herse *f* || *tr* tourmenter; (agr) herser

harrowing ['hæro·iŋ] *adj* horripilant

har·ry ['hæri] *v* (*pret* & *pp* -ried) *tr* harceler; (*to devastate*) ravager

harsh [harʃ] *adj* (*life, treatment, etc.*) sévère, dur; (*to the touch*) rude; (*to the taste*) âpre; (*to the ear*) discordant

harshness ['harʃnis] *s* dureté *f*, rudesse *f*; âpreté *f*

hart [hart] *s* cerf *m*

harum-scarum ['herəm'skerəm] *adj* & *s* écervelé || *adv* en casse-cou

harvest ['harvist] *s* récolte *f*; (*of grain*) moisson *f* || *tr* récolter, moissonner || *intr* faire la récolte or moisson

harvester ['harvistər] *s* moissonneur *m*; (mach) moissonneuse *f*

har'vest home' *s* fin *f* de la moisson; fête *f* de la moisson

har'vest moon' *s* lune *f* des moissons

has-been ['hæz,bin] *s* (coll) vieille croûte *f*

hash [hæʃ] *s* hachis *m* || *tr* hacher

hash' house' *s* (slang) gargote *f*

hashish ['hæʃiʃ] *s* hachisch *m*

hasp [hæsp], [hasp] *s* moraillon *m*

hassle ['hæsəl] *s* (coll) querelle *f*, accrochage *m*

hassock ['hæsək] *s* pouf *m*

haste [hest] *s* hâte *f*; **in haste** à la hâte; **to make haste** se hâter

hasten ['hesən] *tr* hâter || *intr* se hâter

hast·y ['hesti] *adj* (*comp* -ier; *super* -lest) hâtif, précipité; (*rash*) inconsidéré, emporté

hat [hæt] *s* chapeau *m*; **hat in hand** chapeau bas; **hats off to . . . !** chapeau bas devant . . . !; **to keep under one's hat** (coll) garder strictement pour soi; **to talk through one's hat** (coll) parler à tort et à travers; **to throw one's hat in the ring** (coll) descendre dans l'arène

hat'band' *s* ruban *m* de chapeau

hat' block' *s* forme *f* à chapeaux

hat'box' *s* carton *m* à chapeaux

hatch [hætʃ] *s* (*brood*) éclosion *f*; (*trap door*) trappe *f*; (*lower half of door*) demi-porte *f*; (*opening in ship's deck*) écoutille *f*; (*hood over hatchway*) capot *m*; (*lid for opening in ship's deck*) panneau *m* de descente || *tr* (*eggs*) couver, faire éclore; (*a plot*) ourdir, manigancer; (*to hachure*) hachurer || *intr* éclore; (*said of chicks*) sortir de la coquille

hat'check girl' *s* préposée *f* au vestiaire

hatchet ['hætʃit] *s* hachette *f*; **to bury the hatchet** faire la paix

hatch'way' *s* écoutille *f*

hate [het] *s* haine *f* || *tr* haïr, détester; **to hate to** haïr de

hateful ['hetfəl] *adj* haïssable

hat'pin' *s* épingle *f* à chapeau

hat'rack' *s* porte-chapeaux *m*

hatred ['hetrid] *s* haine *f*

hat' shop' *s* chapellerie *f*

hatter ['hætər] *s* chapelier *m*

haughtiness ['hotinis] *s* hauteur *f*

haugh·ty ['hoti] *adj* (*comp* -tier; *super* -tiest) hautain, altier

haul [hol] *s* (*pull, tug*) effort *m*; (*amount caught*) coup *m* de filet, prise *f*; (*distance covered*) parcours *m*, distance *f* de transport || *tr* (*to tug*) tirer; (com) transporter

haulage ['holidʒ] *s* transport *m*; (*cost*) frais *m* de transport

haunch [hontʃ], [hantʃ] *s* (*hip*) hanche *f*; (*hind quarter of an animal*) quartier *m*; (*leg of animal used for food*) cuissot *m*

haunt [hont], [hant] *s* lieu *m* fréquenté, rendez-vous *m*; (*e.g., of criminals*) repaire m || tr (to obsess) hanter; (to frequent) fréquenter

haunt'ed house' s maison f hantée par les fantômes

Havana [həˈvænə] s La Havane

have [hæv] s—the haves and the have-nots les riches et les pauvres || v (3d pers has [hæz]; pret & pp had [hæd]) tr avoir; to have + inf faire + inf, e.g., I shall have him go je le ferai aller; to have + pp faire + inf, e.g., I am going to have a suit made je vais faire faire un complet; to have nothing to do with n'avoir rien à voir avec; to have on (clothing) porter; to have s.th. to + inf avoir q.ch. à + inf, e.g., I have a lot of work to do j'ai beaucoup de travail à faire || intr—to have to avoir à; devoir; falloir, e.g., I have to go il me faut aller; falloir que. e.g., I have to read him the letter il faut que je lui lise la lettre || aux (to form compound past tenses) avoir, e.g., I have run too fast j'ai couru trop vite; (to form compound past tenses with some intransitive verbs and all reflexive verbs) être, e.g., they have arrived elles sont arrivées; to have just + pp venir de + inf, e.g., they have just returned ils viennent de rentrer; e.g., they had just returned ils venaient de rentrer

have'lock s couvre-nuque m

haven [ˈhevən] s havre m, asile m

haversack [ˈhævərˌsæk] s havresac m

havoc [ˈhævək] s ravage m; to play havoc with causer des dégâts à

haw [hɔ] s (bot) cenelle f || tr & intr tourner à gauche || interj dia!, à gauche!

Hawaiian [həˈwaɪjən] adj hawaïen || s Hawaïen m

Hawai'ian Is'lands spl îles fpl Hawaii

haw'-haw' s rire m bête || intr rire bêtement || interj heu!

hawk [hɔk] s faucon m; (mortarboard) taloche f; (sharper) (coll) vautour m || colporter; to hawk up expectorer || intr chasser au faucon; (to hawk up phlegm) graillonner

hawker [ˈhɔkər] s colporteur m

hawk' owl' s chouette f épervière

hawks'bill tur'tle s caret m, caouane f

hawse [hɔz] s (hole) écubier m; (prow) nez m; (distance) évitage m

hawse'hole' s écubier m

hawser [ˈhɔzər] s haussière f

haw'thorn' s aubépine f

hay [he] s foin m; to hit the hay (slang) aller au plumard; to make hay faire les foins

hay' fe'ver s rhume m des foins

hay'field' s pré m à foin

hay'fork' s fourche f à foin

hay'loft' s fenil m, grenier m à foin

hay'mak'er s (boxing) coup m de poing en assommoir

haymow [ˈheˌmaʊ] s fenil m; approvisionnement m de foin

hay'rack' s râtelier m

hay'ride' s promenade f en charrette de foin

hay'seed' s graine f de foin; (coll) culterreux m

hay'stack' s meule f de foin

hay'wire' adj (slang) en pagaille; to go haywire (slang) perdre la boussole || s fil m de fer à lier la foin

hazard [ˈhæzərd] s risque m, danger m; (golf) obstacle m; at all hazards à tout hasard || tr hasarder, risquer

hazardous [ˈhæzərdəs] adj hasardé

haze [hez] s brume f; (fig) obscurité f || tr brimer

hazel [ˈhezəl] adj couleur de noisette, brun clair || s (tree) noisetier m, avelinier m

ha'zel-nut' s noisette f, aveline f

hazing [ˈhezɪŋ] s brimade f; (at university) bizutage m

ha-zy [ˈhezi] adj (comp -zier; super -ziest) brumeux; (notion) nébuleux, vague

H'-bomb' s bombe f H

he [hi] pron pers il §87; lui §85; ce §82B; he who celui qui §83

head [hed] s tête f; (of bed) chevet m; (of boil) tête; (on glass of beer) mousse f; (of drum) peau f; (of cane) pomme f; (of coin) face f; (of barrel, cylinder, etc.) fond m; (of cylinder of automobile engine) culasse f; (of celery) pied m; (of ship) avant m; (of spear, ax, etc.) fer m; (of arrow) pointe f; (of business, department, etc.) chef m, directeur m; (of school) directeur, principal m; (of stream) source f; (of lake; of the table) bout m, haut bout; (caption) titre m; (decisive point) point m culminant, crise f; at the head of à la tête de; from head to foot des pieds à la tête; head downwards la tête en bas; head of cattle bœuf m; head over heels in love (with) éperdument amoureux (de); heads or tails pile ou face; over one's head (beyond reach) hors de la portée de qn; (going to a higher authority) sans tenir compte de qn; to be out of one's head (coll) être timbré or fou; to go to one's head monter à la tête de qn; to keep one's head garder son sang-froid; to keep one's head above water se tenir à flot; to not make head or tail of it n'y comprendre rien; to put heads together prendre conseil; to take it into one's head to avoir l'idée de, se mettre en tête de; to win by a head gagner d'une tête || tr (to direct) diriger; (a procession) conduire, mener; (an organization; a class in school) être en tête de; (a list) venir en tête de; to head off détourner || intr (said of grain) épier; to head for or towards se diriger vers

head'ache' s mal m de tête

head'band' s bandeau m

head'board' s panneau m de tête

head'cheese' s fromage m de tête

head' cold' s rhume m de cerveau

head'dress' s coiffure f

head'first' adv la tête la première; (*impetuously*) précipitamment

head'frame' s (min) chevalement m

head'gear' s garniture f de tête, couvre-chef m; (*for protection*) casque m

head'hunt'er s chasseur m de têtes

heading ['hɛdɪŋ] s titre m; (*of letter*) en-tête m; (*of chapter*) tête f

headland ['hɛdlənd] s promontoire m

headless ['hɛdlɪs] adj sans tête; (*leaderless*) sans chef

head'light' s (aut) phare m; (naut) fanal m; (rr) feu m d'avant

head'line' s (*of newspaper*) manchette f; (*of article*) titre m; **to make the headlines** apparaître aux premières pages des journaux || tr mettre en vedette

head'lin'er s (slang) tête f d'affiche

head'long' adj précipité || adv précipitamment

head'man' s (pl **-men'**) chef m

head'mas'ter s principal m, directeur m

head'most' adj de tête, premier

head' of'fice s bureau m central; (*director's office*) direction f; (*of a corporation*) siège m social

head' of hair' s chevelure f

head'-on' adj & adv de front, face à face

head'phones' spl écouteurs mpl, casque m

head'piece' s (*any covering for head*) casque m; (*headset*) écouteur m; (*brains, judgment*) tête f, caboche f; (typ) vignette f, en-tête m

head'quar'ters s bureau m central; commissariat m de police; (mil) quartier m général; (*staff headquarters*) (mil) état-major m

head'rest' s appui-tête m

head'set' s casque m, écouteurs mpl

heads'man s (pl **-men**) bourreau m

head'stone' s pierre f tumulaire (à la tête d'une tombe); (*cornerstone*) pierre angulaire

head'strong' adj têtu, entêté

head'wait'er s maître m d'hôtel, steward m

head'wa'ters spl cours m supérieur d'une rivière

head'way' s progrès m, marche f avant; (*between buses*) intervalle m; (naut) erre f; **to make headway** progresser, aller de l'avant

head'wear' s garniture f de tête

headwind ['hɛd,wɪnd] s vent m contraire, vent debout

head'work' s travail m mental, travail de tête

head·y ['hɛdi] adj (comp **-ier**; super **-iest**) (*wine*) capiteux; (*conduct*) emporté; (*news*) excitant; (*perfume*) entêtant

heal [hil] tr guérir; (*a wound*) cicatriser || intr guérir

healer ['hilər] s guérisseur m

healing ['hilɪŋ] s guérison f

health [hɛlθ] s santé f; **to be in good health** se porter bien, être en bonne santé; **to be in poor health** se porter mal, être en mauvaise santé; **to**

drink to the health of boire à la santé de; **to enjoy radiant health** avoir une santé florissante; **to your health!** à votre santé!

healthful ['hɛlθfəl] adj sain; (*air, climate, etc.*) salubre; (*recreation, work, etc.*) salutaire

health·y ['hɛlθi] adj (comp **-ier**; super **-iest**) sain; (*air, climate, etc.*) salubre; (*person*) bien portant; (*appetite*) robuste

heap [hip] s tas m, amas m || tr entasser, amasser; **to heap** (*honors, praise, etc.*) **on s.o.** combler qn de; **to heap** (*insults*) **on s.o.** accabler qn de

hear [hɪr] v (*pret & pp* **heard** [hʌrd]) tr entendre, ouïr; **to hear it said** l'entendre dire; **to hear s.o. sing,** to **hear s.o. singing** entendre chanter qn, entendre qn qui chante; **to hear s.th. sung** entendre chanter q.ch. || intr entendre; **hear! hear!** très bien!, bravo!; **hear ye!** oyez!; **to hear about** entendre parler de; **to hear from** avoir des nouvelles de; **to hear of** entendre parler de; **to hear tell of** (coll) entendre parler de; **to hear that** entendre dire que

hearer ['hɪrər] s auditeur m; **hearers** auditoire m

hearing ['hɪrɪŋ] s (*sense*) l'ouïe f; (*act; opportunity to be heard*) audition f; (law) audience f; **in the hearing of** en la présence de, devant; **within hearing** à portée de la voix

hear'ing aid' s sonotone m, microvibrateur m, appareil m de correction auditive

hear'say' s ouï-dire m

hear'say ev'idence s simples ouï-dire mpl

hearse [hʌrs] s corbillard m, char m funèbre

heart [hɑrt] s cœur m; (cards) cœur; **after one's heart** selon son cœur; **at heart** au fond; **by heart** par cœur; **heart and soul** corps et âme; **lift your hearts!** haut les cœurs!; **to break the heart of** fendre le cœur à; **to die of a broken heart** mourir de chagrin; **to eat one's heart out** se ronger le cœur; **to eat to one's heart's content** manger tout son soûl; **to get to the heart of the matter** entrer dans le vif de la question; **to have one's heart in one's work** avoir le cœur à l'ouvrage; **to have one's heart in the right place** avoir le cœur bien placé; **to lose heart** perdre courage; **to open one's heart to** épancher son cœur à; **to take heart** prendre courage; **to take to heart** prendre à cœur; **to wear one's heart on one's sleeve** avoir le cœur sur les lèvres; **with a heavy heart** le cœur gros; **with all one's heart** de tout son cœur; **with one's heart in one's mouth** le gosier serré

heart'ache' s peine f de cœur

heart' attack' s crise f cardiaque

heart'beat' s battement m du cœur

heart'break' s crève-cœur m

heartbroken ['hɑrt,brokən] adj navré, chagriné
heart' burn' s pyrosis m
heart' cher'ry s guigne f
heart' disease' s maladie f de cœur
hearten ['hɑrtən] tr encourager
heart' fail'ure s arrêt m du cœur
heartfelt ['hɑrt,fɛlt] adj sincère, cordial, bien senti
hearth [hɑrθ] s foyer m, âtre m
hearth'stone' s pierre f de cheminée
heartily ['hɑrtɪli] adv de bon cœur, sincèrement
heartless ['hɑrtlɪs] adj sans cœur
heart' of stone' s (fig) cœur m de bronze
heart'-rend'ing adj désolant, navrant
heart'sick' adj désolé, chagrin
heart'strings' spl fibres fpl, replis mpl du cœur
heart'-to-heart' adj franc, ouvert; sérieux || adv à cœur ouvert
heart' trans'plant s greffe f du cœur, transplantation f cardiaque
heart' trou'ble s maladie f de cœur
heart'wood' s bois m de cœur
heart-y ['hɑrti] adj (comp -ier; super -iest) cordial, sincère; (meal) copieux; (laugh) sonore; (eater) gros
heat [hit] s chaleur f; (heating) chauffage m; (rut of animals) rut m; (in horse racing) éliminatoire f; **in heat** en rut || tr échauffer; (e.g., a house) chauffer || intr s'échauffer; **to heat up** chauffer
heated adj chauffé; (fig) chaud, échauffé
heater ['hitər] s (for food) réchaud m; (for heating house) calorifère m
heath [hiθ] s bruyère f
hea·then ['hiðən] adj païen || s (pl -then or -thens) païen m
heathendom ['hiðəndəm] s paganisme m
heather ['hɛðər] s bruyère f
heating ['hitɪŋ] adj échauffant || s chauffage m
heat' light'ning s éclairs mpl de chaleur
heat' shield' s (rok) bouclier m contre la chaleur, bouclier antithermique
heat'stroke' s insolation f, coup m de chaleur
heat' wave' s vague f de chaleur; (phys) onde f calorifique
heave [hiv] s soulèvement m; heaves (vet) pousse f || v (pret & pp heaved or hove [hov]) tr soulever; (to throw) lancer; (a sigh) pousser; (the anchor) lever || intr se soulever; faire des efforts pour vomir; (said of bosom) palpiter
heaven ['hɛvən] s ciel m; **for heaven's sake** pour l'amour de Dieu; **Heaven** le ciel; **heavens** cieux mpl, ciel
heavenly ['hɛvənli] adj céleste
heav'enly bod'y s corps m céleste
heav·y ['hɛvi] adj (comp -ier; super -iest) lourd, pesant; (heart; crop; eater; baggage; rain, sea, weather) gros; (meal) copieux; (sleep) profond; (work) pénible; (book, reading, etc.) indigeste; (parts) (theat) tra-

gique, sombre || adv lourd, lourdement; **to hang heavy on** peser sur
heav'y drink'er s fort buveur m
heav'y-du'ty adj extra-fort
heav'y-heart'ed adj au cœur lourd
heav'y-set' adj de forte carrure, costaud
heav'y-weight' s (boxing) poids m lourd
Hebraist ['hibre-ɪst] s hébraïsant m
Hebrew ['hibru] adj hébreu, hébraïque || s (language) hébreu m, langue f hébraïque; (man) Hébreu m; (woman) Juive f
hecatomb ['hɛkə,tom] s hécatombe f
heckle ['hɛkəl] tr interrompre bruyamment, chahuter; (on account of trifles) asticoter, harceler
heckler ['hɛklər] s interrupteur m impertinent, interpellateur m
hectic ['hɛktɪk] adj fou, bouleversant
hedge [hɛdʒ] s haie f || tr entourer d'une haie; **to hedge in** entourer de tous côtés || intr chercher des échappatoires, hésiter; (com) faire la contrepartie
hedge'hog' s hérisson m; (porcupine) porc-épic m
hedge'hop' v (pret & pp -hopped; ger -hopping) intr (aer) voler en rasemottes
hedgerow ['hɛdʒ,ro] s bordure f de haies, haie f vive
heed [hid] s attention f, soin m; **to take heed** prendre garde || tr faire attention à, prendre garde à || intr faire attention, prendre garde
heedful ['hidfəl] adj attentif
heedless ['hidlɪs] adj inattentif
heehaw ['hi,hɔ] s hi-han m || intr pousser des hi-hans
heel [hil] s talon m; (slang) goujat m; **to be down at the heel** traîner la savate; **to cool one's heels** (coll) croquer le marmot, faire le pied de grue
heft·y ['hɛfti] adj (comp -ier; super -iest) costaud; (heavy) pesant
heifer ['hɛfər] s génisse f
height [haɪt] s hauteur f; (e.g., of folly) comble m
height·en ['haɪtən] tr rehausser; (to increase the amount of) augmenter; (to set off, bring out) relever || intr se rehausser; augmenter
heinous ['henəs] adj odieux, atroce
heir [ɛr] s héritier m; **to become the heir of** hériter de
heir' appar'ent s (pl heirs apparent) héritier m présomptif
heiress ['ɛrɪs] s héritière f
heir'loom' s meuble m, bijou m, or souvenir m de famille
Helen ['hɛlən] s Hélène f
helicopter ['hɛlɪ,kɑptər] s hélicoptère m
heliport ['hɛlɪ,pɔrt] s héliport m
helium ['hilɪ-əm] s hélium m
helix ['hilɪks] s (pl helixes or helices ['hɛlɪ,siz]) hélice f; (anat) hélix m
hell [hɛl] s enfer m
hell'bent' adj (slang) hardi; **hellbent on** (slang) acharné en diable à

hell′cat′ s *(bad-tempered woman)* harpie f; *(witch)* sorcière f
Hellene ['helin] s Hellène mf
Hellenic [he'lenɪk], [he'linɪk] adj hellène
hell′fire′ s feu m de l'enfer
hellish ['helɪʃ] adj infernal
hel·lo [he'lo] s *(pl* -los) bonjour m || *interj* bonjour!; *(on telephone)* allô!
helm [helm] s gouvernail m
helmet ['helmɪt] s casque m
helms′man s *(pl* -men) homme m de barre
help [help] s aide f, secours m; *(workers)* main-d'œuvre f; *(office workers)* employés mpl; *(domestic servants)* domestiques mfpl; **help wanted** *(public sign)* offres d'emploi, embauche; **there's no help for it** il n'y a pas de remède || *tr* aider, secourir; **so help me God!** que Dieu me juge!; **to help down** aider à descendre; **to help oneself** se défendre; *(to food)* se servir; **to not be able to help** ne pouvoir s'empêcher de || *intr* aider || *interj* au secours!
helper ['helpər] s aide mf, assistant m
helpful ['helpfəl] adj utile; *(person)* serviable, secourable
helping ['helpɪŋ] s *(of food)* portion f
helpless ['helplɪs] adj *(weak)* faible; *(powerless)* impuissant; *(penniless)* sans ressource; *(confused)* désemparé; *(situation)* sans recours
helter-skelter ['heltər'skeltər] adj désordonné || s débandade f || adv pêle-mêle
hem [hem] s ourlet m, bord m || v *(pret & pp* hemmed; *ger* hemming) *tr* ourler, border; **to hem in** entourer, cerner || *intr* faire un ourlet; **to hem and haw** ânonner; *(fig)* tourner autour du pot || *interj* hum!
hemisphere ['hemɪ,sfɪr] s hémisphère m
hemistich ['hemɪ,stɪk] s hémistiche m
hem′line′ s ourlet m de la jupe
hem′lock′ s *(Tsuga canadensis)* sapin m du Canada, pruche f; *(herb and poison)* ciguë f
hemoglobin [,hemə'globɪn], [,himə'globɪn] s hémoglobine f
hemophilia [,hemə'fɪl·ə], [,himə'fɪl·ə] s hémophilie f
hemorrhage ['hemərɪdʒ] s hémorragie f
hemorrhoids ['hemə,rɔɪdz] spl hémorroïdes fpl
hemostat ['hemə,stæt], ['himə,stæt] s hémostatique m
hemp [hemp] s chanvre m
hem′stitch′ s ourlet m à jour || *tr* ourler à jour || *intr* faire un ourlet à jour
hen [hen] s poule f
hence [hens] adv d'ici; *(therefore)* d'où, donc
hence′forth′ adv désormais, dorénavant
hench·man ['hentʃmən] s *(pl* -men) partisan m, acolyte m, complice mf
hen′coop′ s cage f à poules, épinette f
hen′house′ s poulailler m

henna ['henə] s henné m || *tr* teindre au henné
hen′peck′ *tr* mener par le bout du nez
Henry ['henrɪ] s Henri m
hep [hep] adj *(slang)* à la page, dans le train; **to be hep to** *(slang)* être au courant de
her [hʌr] adj poss son §88 || *pron pers* elle §85; la §87; lui §87
herald ['herəld] s héraut m; *(fig)* avant-coureur m || *tr* annoncer; **to herald in** introduire
herald·ry ['herəldrɪ] s *(pl* -ries) héraldique f, blason m
herb [ʌrb], [hʌrb] s herbe f; *(pharm)* herbe médicinale or officinale f; **herbs for seasoning** fines herbes
herculean [hʌr'kjulɪ·ən], [,hʌrkju'li·ən] adj herculéen
herd [hʌrd] s troupeau m || *tr* rassembler en troupeau || *intr*—**to herd together** s'attrouper
herds′man s *(pl* -men) pâtre m; *(of sheep)* berger m; *(of cattle)* bouvier m
here [hɪr] adv ici; **from here to there** d'ici là; **here and there** çà et là, par-ci par-là; **here below** ici-bas; **here is** or **here are** voici; **here lies** ci-gît; **that's neither here nor there** ça n'a rien à y voir || *interj* tenez!; *(answering roll call)* présent!
hereabouts ['hɪrə,bauts] adv près d'ici
here·af′ter s—**the hereafter** l'autre monde || adv désormais, à l'avenir; *(farther along)* ci-après
here·by′ adv par ce moyen, par ceci; *(in legal language)* par les présentes
hereditary [hɪ'redɪ,terɪ] adj héréditaire
heredi·ty [hɪ'redɪtɪ] s *(pl* -ties) hérédité f
here·in′ adv ici; *(on this point)* en ceci; *(in this writing)* ci-inclus
here·of′ adv de ceci, à ce sujet
here·on′ adv là-dessus
here·sy ['herəsɪ] s *(pl* -sies) hérésie f
heretic ['herətɪk] adj & s hérétique f
heretical [hɪ'retɪkəl] adj hérétique
heretofore [,hɪrtu'for] adv jusqu'ici
here·upon′ adv là-dessus
here·with′ adv ci-joint, avec ceci
heritage ['herɪtɪdʒ] s héritage m
hermetic(al) [hʌr'metɪk(əl)] adj hermétique
hermit ['hʌrmɪt] s ermite m
hermitage ['hʌrmɪtɪdʒ] s ermitage m
herni·a ['hʌrnɪ·ə] s *(pl* -as or -ae [,i]) hernie f
he·ro ['hɪro] s *(pl* -roes) héros m
heroic [hɪ'ro·ɪk] adj héroïque f; **heroics** spl *(verse)* vers m héroïque; *(language)* grandiloquence f
heroin ['hero·ɪn] s héroïne f
heroine ['hero·ɪn] s héroïne f
heroism ['hero,ɪzəm] s héroïsme m
heron ['herən] s héron m
herring ['herɪŋ] s hareng m
her′ring-bone′ s *(in fabrics)* point m de chausson; *(in hardwood floors)* parquet m à batons rompus; *(in design)* arête f de hareng
hers [hʌrz] pron poss le sien §89

her·self' *pron pers* elle §85; soi §85; elle-même §86; se §87

hesitan·cy ['hɛzɪtənsɪ] *s* (*pl* **-cies**) hésitation *f*

hesitant ['hɛzɪtənt] *adj* hésitant

hesitate ['hɛzɪ‚tet] *intr* hésiter

hesitation [‚hɛzɪ'teʃən] *s* hésitation *f*

heterodox ['hɛtərə‚dɑks] *adj* hétérodoxe

heterodyne ['hɛtərə‚daɪn] *adj* hétérodyne

heterogeneous [‚hɛtərə'dʒɪnɪ·əs] *adj* hétérogène

hew [hju] *v* (*pret* **hewed**; *pp* **hewed** or **hewn**) *tr* tailler, couper; **to hew down** abattre || *intr*—**to hew close to the line** (coll) agir dans les règles, être très méticuleux

hex [hɛks] *s* porte-guigne *m* || *tr* porter la guigne à

hey [he] *interj* hé!; attention!

hey'day' *s* meilleure période *f*, fleur *f*

hi [haɪ] *interj* salut!

hia·tus [haɪ'etəs] *s* (*pl* **-tuses** or **-tus**) (*gap*) lacune *f*; (*in a text; in verse*) hiatus *m*

hibernate ['haɪbər‚net] *intr* hiberner

hibiscus [hɪ'bɪskəs], [haɪ'bɪskəs] *s* hibiscus *m*, ketmie *f*

hiccough or **hiccup** ['hɪkəp] *s* hoquet *m* || *intr* hoqueter

hick [hɪk] (coll) *adj & s* rustaud *m*

hicko·ry ['hɪkərɪ] *s* (*pl* **-ries**) hickory *m*

hidden ['hɪdən] *adj* caché, dérobée; (*mysterious*) occulte

hide [haɪd] *s* peau *f*, cuir *m* || *v* (*pret* **hid** [hɪd]; *pp* **hid** or **hidden** ['hɪdən]) *tr* cacher; **to hide s.th. from** cacher q.ch. à || *intr* se cacher; **to hide from** se cacher à

hide'-and-seek' *s* cache-cache *m*

hide'bound' *adj* à l'esprit étroit

hideous ['hɪdɪ·əs] *adj* hideux

hide'-out' *s* repaire *m*, planque *f*

hiding ['haɪdɪŋ] *s* dissimulation *f*; (*punishment*) (coll) raclée *f*, rossée *f*; **in hiding** caché

hid'ing place' *s* cachette *f*

hierar·chy ['haɪ·ə‚rɑrkɪ] *s* (*pl* **-chies**) hiérarchie *f*

hieroglyphic [‚haɪ·ərə'glɪfɪk] *adj* hiéroglyphique || *s* hiéroglyphe *m*

hi-fi ['haɪ'faɪ] *adj* (coll) de haute fidélité || *s* (coll) haute fidélité *f*

hi'-fi' fan' *s* (coll) fanatique *mf* de la haute fidélité

high [haɪ] *adj* haut; (*river, price, rate, temperature, opinion*) élevé; (*fever, wind*) fort; (*sea, wind*) gros; (*cheekbones*) saillant; (*sound*) aigu; (coll) gris; (culin) avancé; **high and dry** à sec; **high and mighty** prétentieux; **to be high** (coll) avoir son pompon || *s* (aut) prise *f* directe; **on high** en haut, dans le ciel || *adv* haut; à un prix élevé; **high and low** partout; **to aim high** viser haut; **to come high** se vendre cher

high' al'tar *s* maître-autel *m*

high'ball' *s* whisky *m* à l'eau

high' blood' pres'sure *s* hypertension *f*

high'born' *adj* de haute naissance

high'boy' *s* chiffonnier *m* semainier *m*

high'brow' *adj & s* (slang) intellectuel *m*

high' chair' *s* chaise *f* d'enfant

high' command' *s* haut commandement *m*

high' cost of liv'ing *s* cherté *f* de la vie

high'er educa'tion ['haɪ·ər] *s* enseignement *m* supérieur

high'er-up' *s* (coll) supérieur *m* hiérarchique

high'est bid'der ['haɪ·ɪst] *s* dernier enchérisseur *m*

high' explo'sive *s* haut explosif *m*, explosif puissant

highfalutin [‚haɪfə'lutən] *adj* (coll) pompeux, ampoulé

high' fidel'ity *s* haute fidélité *f*

high' fre'quen·cy *s* haute fréquence *f*

high' gear' *s* (aut) prise *f* directe

high'-grade' *adj* de qualité supérieure

high'-hand'ed *adj* autoritaire, arbitraire

high' hat' *s* chapeau *m* haut de forme

high'-hat' *adj* (coll) snob, poseur || **high'-hat'** *v* (*pret & pp* **-hatted**; *ger* **-hatting**) *tr* (coll) traiter de haut en bas

high'-heeled' *adj* à talons hauts

high' horse' *s* raideur *f* hautaine; **to get up on one's high horse** monter sur ses grands chevaux

high' jinks' [‚dʒɪŋks] *s* (slang) clownerie *f*, drôlerie *f*

high' jump' *s* saut *m* en hauteur

high'-key' *adj* (phot) lumineux

highland ['haɪlənd] *s* pays *m* de montagne; **highlands** hautes terres *fpl*

high' life' *s* grand monde *m*

high'light' *s* (big moment) clou *m*; **highlights** (in a picture) clairs *mpl* || *tr* mettre en vedette

highly ['haɪlɪ] *adv* hautement; (very) extrêmement, fort; haut, e.g., **highly colored** haut en couleur; **to think highly of** avoir une bonne opinion de

High' Mass' *s* grand-messe *f*

high'-mind'ed *adj* magnanime, noble

highness ['haɪnɪs] *s* hauteur *f*; **Highness** Altesse *f*

high' noon' *s* plein midi *m*

high'-oc'tane *adj* à indice d'octane élevé

high'-pitched' *adj* aigu; (roof) à forte pente

high'-powered' *adj* de haute puissance

high'-pres'sure *adj* à haute pression; (fig) dynamique, persuasif || *tr* (coll) gonfler à bloc

high'-priced' *adj* de prix élevé

high' priest' *s* grand prêtre *m*; (fig) pontife *m*

high'road' *s* grand-route *f*; (fig) bonne voie *f*

high' school' *s* école *f* secondaire publique; (in France) lycée *m*

high'-school stu'dent *s* lycéen *m*; collégien *m*

high' sea' *s* houle *f*, grosse mer *f*; **high seas** haute mer

high' soci'ety *s* la haute société, le beau monde

high′-sound′ing adj pompeux, prétentieux

high′-speed′ adj à grande vitesse

high′-spir′ited adj fougueux, plein d'entrain

high′ spir′its spl gaieté f, entrain m

high′ stakes′ spl—to play for high stakes jouer gros jeu

high-strung [′haɪ′strʌŋ] adj tendu, nerveux

high′-test′ gas′oline s supercarburant m

high′ tide′ s marée f haute, haute marée

high′ time′ s heure f, e.g., it is high time for you to go c'est certainement l'heure de votre départ; (slang) bombance f, bombe f

high′ trea′son s haute trahison f

high′ volt′age s haute tension f

high wa′ter s marée f haute, hautes eaux fpl

high′way′ s grand-route f

high′way commis′sion s administration f des ponts et chaussées

high′way man s (pl -men) voleur m de grand chemin

high′way map′ s carte f routière

hijack [′haɪ‚dʒæk] tr (coll) arrêter et voler sur la route; (coll) saisir de force; (an airplane) (coll) détourner

hijacker [′haɪ‚dʒækər] s (coll) bandit m, bandit de grand chemin; (coll) pirate m de l'air, pirate aérien

hijacking [′haɪ‚dʒækɪŋ] s (coll) piraterie f aérienne, détournement m

hike [haɪk] s excursion f à pied, voyage m pédestre; (e.g., in rent) hausse f ‖ tr hausser, faire monter ‖ intr faire de longues promenades à pied

hiker [′haɪkər] s excursionniste mf à pied, touriste mf pédestre

hilarious [hɪ′lerɪ·əs], [haɪ′lerɪ·əs] adj hilare, gai; (joke) hilarant

hill [hɪl] s colline f, coteau m; (incline) côte f; (mil) cote f; over hill and dale par monts et par vaux ‖ tr (a plant) butter, chausser

hill′bil′ly s (pl -lies) montagnard m rustique

hillock [′hɪlək] s tertre m, butte f

hill′side′ s versant m, coteau m

hill·y [′hɪli] adj (comp -ier; super -iest) montueux, accidenté; (steep) en pente, à fortes pentes

hilt [hɪlt] s poignée f; up to the hilt jusqu'à la garde

him [hɪm] pron pers lui §85, §87; le §87

him·self′ pron lui §85; soi §85; lui-même §86; se §87

hind [haɪnd] adj postérieur, de derrière ‖ s biche f

hinder [′hɪndər] tr empêcher

hind′most′ adj dernier, ultime

hind′quar′ter s arrière-train m, train m de derrière; (of horse) arrière-main m

hindrance [′hɪndrəns] s empêchement m

hind′sight′ s (of firearm) hausse f; compréhension f tardive

Hindu [′hɪndu] adj hindou ‖ s Hindou m

hinge [hɪndʒ] s charnière f, gond m; (of mollusk) charnière; (bb) onglet m ‖ intr—to hinge on axer sur, dépendre de

hin·ny [′hɪni] s (pl -nies) bardot m

hint [hɪnt] s insinuation f; (small quantity) soupçon m; to take the hint comprendre à demi-mot, accepter le conseil ‖ tr insinuer ‖ intr procéder par insinuation; to hint at laisser entendre

hinterland [′hɪntər‚lænd] s arrière-pays m

hip [hɪp] adj (slang) à la page, dans le train; to be hip to (slang) être au courant de ‖ s hanche f; (of roof) arête f

hip′bone′ s os m coxal, os de la hanche

hipped adj—to be hipped on (coll) avoir la manie de

hippety-hop [′hɪpɪti′hɑp] adv (coll) en sautillant

hip·po [′hɪpo] s (pl -pos) (coll) hippopotame m

hippopota·mus [‚hɪpə′pɑtəməs] s (pl -muses or -mi [‚maɪ]) hippopotame m

hip′ roof′ s toit m en croupe

hire [haɪr] s (salary) gages mpl; (renting) louage m; for hire à louer; in the hire of aux gages de ‖ tr (a person) engager, embaucher; (to rent) louer, prendre en location ‖ intr—to hire out (said of person) se louer, entrer en service

hired′ girl′ s servante f, servante de ferme

hired′ man′ s (pl men′) s (coll) valet m de ferme, garçon m de ferme

hireling [′haɪrlɪŋ] adj & s mercenaire m

hiring [′haɪrɪŋ] s embauchage m

his [hɪz] adj poss son §88 ‖ pron poss le sien §89

Hispanic [hɪs′pænɪk] adj hispanique

Hispanist [′hɪspənɪst], [hɪs′pænɪst] s hispanisant m

hiss [hɪs] s sifflement m ‖ tr & intr siffler

hist [hɪst] interj psitt!, pst!

histology [hɪs′tɑlədʒi] s histologie f

historian [hɪs′tɔrɪ·ən] s historien m

historic(al) [hɪs′tɑrɪk(əl)], [hɪs′tɔrɪk(əl)] adj historique

histo·ry [′hɪstəri] s (pl -ries) histoire f

histrionic [‚hɪstrɪ′ɑnɪk] adj théâtral ‖ histrionics s art m du théâtre; (fig) attitude f spectaculaire

hit [hɪt] s coup m; (blow that hits its mark) coup au but, coup heureux; (sarcastic remark) coup de patte, trait m satirique; (on the hit parade) tube m; (baseball) coup de batte; (theat) succès m, spectacle m très couru; (coll) réussite f; to make a hit (coll) faire sensation ‖ v (pret & pp hit; ger hitting) tr frapper; (the mark) atteindre; (e.g., a car) heurter, heurter contre; (to move the emotions of) toucher; to hit it off (coll) s'entendre, se trouver d'accord ‖ *intr* frapper; **to hit on** tomber sur, trouver

hit/-and-run/ driv/er *s* chauffard *m* qui abandonne la scène d'un accident, qui prend la fuite

hitch [hɪtʃ] *s* saccade *f*, secousse *f*; obstacle *m*, difficulté *f*; (*knot*) nœud *m*, e.g., **timber hitch** nœud de bois; **without a hitch** sans accroc ‖ *tr* accrocher; (*naut*) nouer; **to hitch up** (*e.g., a horse*) atteler

hitch/hike/ *intr* (coll) faire de l'auto-stop

hitch/hik/er *s* auto-stoppeur *m*

hitch/hik/ing *s* auto-stop *m*

hitch/ing post/ *s* poteau *m* d'attache

hither ['hɪðər] *adv* ici; **hither and thither** çà et là

hith/er-to/ *adv* jusqu'ici, jusqu'à présent

hit/-or-miss/ *adj* capricieux, éventuel

hit/ parade/ *s* (coll) chansons *fpl* populaires du moment

hit/ rec/ord *s* (coll) disque *m* à succès

hive [haɪv] *s* ruche *f*; **hives** (pathol) urticaire *f*

hoard [hord] *s* entassement *m*, trésor *m* ‖ *tr* accumuler secrètement, thésauriser ‖ *intr* accumuler, entasser, thésauriser

hoarding ['hordɪŋ] *s* accumulation *f* secrète, thésaurisation *f*

hoarfrost ['hor,frɔst] *s* givre *m*, gelée *f* blanche

hoarse [hors] *adj* enroué, rauque

hoarseness ['horsnɪs] *s* enrouement *m*

hoar·y ['hori] *adj* (*comp* **-ier**; *super* **-iest**) chenu, blanchi

hoax [hoks] *s* mystification *f*, canard *m* ‖ *tr* mystifier

hob [hɑb] *s* (*of fireplace*) plaque *f*; **to play hob** (coll) causer des ennuis; **to play hob with** (coll) bouleverser

hobble ['hɑbəl] *s* (*limp*) boitillement *m*; (*rope used to tie legs of animal*) entrave *f* ‖ *tr* faire boiter; (*e.g., a horse*) entraver ‖ *intr* boiter, clocher

hob·by ['hɑbɪ] *s* (*pl* **-bies**) distraction *f*, violon *m* d'Ingres; (orn) hobereau *m*; **to ride one's hobby** enfourcher son dada

hob/by·horse/ *s* cheval *m* de bois

hob/gob/lin *s* lutin *m*; (*bogy*) épouvantail *m*

hob/nail/ *s* caboche *f*

hob·nob ['hɑb,nɑb] *v* (*pret & pp* **-nobbed**; *ger* **-nobbing**) *intr* trinquer ensemble; **to hobnob with** être à tu et à toi avec

ho·bo ['hobo] *s* (*pl* **-bos** or **-boes**) chemineau *m*, vagabond *m*

hock [hɑk] *s* (*of horse*) jarret *m*; (*wine*) vin *m* du Rhin; (*pawn*) (coll) gage *m*; **in hock** (coll) au clou; (*in prison*) (coll) au bloc ‖ *tr* couper le jarret à; (*to pawn*) (coll) mettre en gage, mettre au clou

hockey ['hɑkɪ] *s* hockey *m*

hock/shop/ *s* (slang) mont-de-piété *m*, clou *m*

hocus-pocus ['hokəs'pokəs] *s* tour *m* de passe-passe; (*meaningless formula*) abracadabra *m*

hod [hɑd] *s* oiseau *m*, auge *f*

hod/ car/rier *s* aide-maçon *m*

hodgepodge ['hɑdʒ,pɑdʒ] *s* salmigondis *m*, méli-mélo *m*

hoe [ho] *s* houe *f*, binette *f* ‖ *tr* houer, biner

hog [hɑg], [hɔg] *s* pourceau *m*, porc *m*; (*pig*) cochon ‖ *v* (*pret & pp* **hogged**; *ger* **hogging**) *tr* (slang) s'emparer de, saisir avidement

hog/back/ *s* dos *m* d'âne

hoggish ['hɑgɪʃ], ['hɔgɪʃ] *adj* glouton

hogs/head/ *s* barrique *f*

hog/wash/ *s* eaux *fpl* grasses; vinasse *f*; (fig) boniments *mpl* à la noix de coco

hoist [hɔɪst] *s* monte-charge *m*, grue *f*; (*shove*) poussée *f* vers le haut ‖ *tr* lever, guinder; (*a flag, sail, boat, etc.*) hisser

hoity-toity ['hɔɪtɪ'tɔɪtɪ] *adj* hautain; **to be hoity-toity** le prendre de haut

hokum ['hokəm] *s* (coll) boniments *mpl*, fumisterie *f*

hold [hold] *s* prise *f*; (*handle*) poignée *f*, manche *m*; (*domination*) pouvoir *m*, autorité *f*; (mus) point *m* d'orgue; (naut) cale *f*; **hold for arrival** (formula on envelope) garder jusqu'à l'arrivée; **to take hold of** empoigner, saisir ‖ *v* (*pret & pp* **held** [held]) *tr* tenir; (*one's breath; s.o.'s attention*) retenir; (*to contain*) contenir; (*a job; a title*) avoir, posséder; (*e.g., a university chair*) occuper; (*a fort*) défendre; (*a note*) (mus) tenir, prolonger; **to be held to be . . .** passer pour . . .; **to hold back or in** retenir; **to hold one's own** rivaliser, se défendre; **to hold out** tendre, offrir; **to hold over** continuer, remettre; **to hold s.o. to be . . .** tenir qn pour . . .; **to hold s.o. to his word** obliger qn à tenir sa promesse; **to hold up** (*to delay*) retarder; (*to keep from falling*) retenir, soutenir; (*to rob*) (coll) voler à main armée ‖ *intr* (*to hold good*) rester valable, rester en vigueur; **hold on!** (telp) restez en ligne!; **to hold back** se retenir, hésiter; **to hold forth** disserter; **to hold off** se tenir à distance; **to hold on or out** tenir bon; **to hold on to** s'accrocher à, se cramponner à; **to hold out for** insister pour

holder ['holdər] *s* possesseur *m*; (*of stock*) porteur *m*; (*of stock; of a record*) détenteur *m*; (*of degree, fellowship, etc.*) impétrant *m*; (*for a cigarette*) porte-cigarettes *m*; (*for a post, a right, etc.*) titulaire *mf*; (*for holding, e.g., a hot dish*) poignée *f*

holding ['holdɪŋ] *s* possession *f*; **holdings** valeurs *fpl*; (*of an investor*) portefeuille *m*; (*of a landlord*) propriétés *fpl*

hold/ing com/pany *s* holding trust *m*, holding *m*

hold/up/ *s* (*stop, delay*) arrêt *m*; (coll) attaque *f* à main armée, hold-up *m*; **what's the holdup?** (coll) qu'est-ce qu'on attend?

hole [hol] *s* trou *m*; **in the hole** (coll)

dans l'embarras; **to burn a hole in s.o.'s pocket** (coll) brûler la poche à qn; **to get s.o. out of a hole** (coll) tirer qn d'un mauvais pas; **to pick holes in** (coll) trouver à redire à, démolir; **to wear holes in** (e.g., a garment) trouer || intr—**to hole up** se terrer

holiday ['halɪ ˌde] s jour m de fête, jour férié; (vacation) vacances fpl

holiness ['holɪnɪs] s sainteté f; **His Holiness** Sa Sainteté

holla ['hala], [həˈla] interj holà!

Holland ['halənd] s Hollande f; **la Hollande**

Hollander ['haləndər] s Hollandais m

hollow ['halo] adj & s creux m || adv —**to beat all hollow** (coll) battre à plate couture || tr creuser

hol•ly ['halɪ] s (pl -lies) houx m

hol•ly•hock ['halɪ ˌhɑk] s primerose f, rose f trémière

holm' oak' [hom] s yeuse f

holocaust ['halə ˌkɔst] s (sacrifice) holocauste m; (disaster) sinistre m

holster ['holstər] s étui m; (on saddle) fonte f

ho•ly ['holɪ] adj (comp -lier; super -liest) saint; (e.g., water) bénit

Ho'ly Ghost' s Saint-Esprit m

ho'ly or'ders spl ordres mpl sacrés

Ho'ly Scrip'ture s l'Écriture f Sainte

Ho'ly See' s Saint-Siège m

Ho'ly Sep'ulcher s Saint Sépulcre m

ho'ly wa'ter s eau f bénite

Ho'ly Writ' s l'Écriture f Sainte

homage ['hamɪdʒ], ['amɪdʒ] s hommage m

home [hom] adj domestique; national, natal || s foyer m, chez-soi m, domicile m; (house) maison f; (of the arts; native land) patrie f; (for the sick, poor, etc.) asile m, foyer, hospice m; **at home** à la maison; (at ease) à l'aise; **make yourself at home** faites comme chez vous || adv à la maison; **to see s.o.** home raccompagner qn jusqu'à chez lui; **to strike home** frapper juste, toucher au vif

home' address' s adresse f personnelle

home•bod•y s (pl -ies) casanier m, pantouflard m

homebred ['hom ˌbred] adj élevé à la maison; du pays, indigène

home' brew' s boisson f faite à la maison

home'com'ing s retour m au foyer; (at university, church, etc.) journée f or semaine f des anciens

home' coun'try s pays m natal

home' deliv'ery s livraison f à domicile

home' econom'ics s économie f domestique; (instruction) enseignement m ménager

home' front' s théâtre m d'opérations à l'intérieur du pays

home'land' s patrie f, pays m natal

homeless ['homlɪs] adj sans foyer

home' life' s vie f familiale

home'like' adj familial, comme chez soi

home'-lov'ing adj casanier

home•ly ['homlɪ] adj (comp -lier; super -liest) (not good-looking) laid, vilain; (not elegant) sans façons

home'made' adj fait à la maison, de ménage

home'mak'er s maîtresse f de maison, ménagère f

home' of'fice s siège m social

homeopathy [ˌhomɪˈapəθɪ], [ˌhamɪˈapəθɪ] s homéopathie f

home'own'er s propriétaire mf

home' plate' s (baseball) marbre m (Canad)

home' port' s port m d'attache

home' rule' s autonomie f, gouvernement m autonome

home'sick' adj nostalgique; **to be homesick** avoir le mal du pays

home'sick'ness s mal m du pays, nostalgie f

homespun ['hom ˌspʌn] adj filé à la maison; (fig) simple, sans apprêt

home'stead' s bien m de famille, ferme f

home'stretch' s fin f de course, dernière étape f

home' team' s locaux mpl, équipe f qui reçoit

home'town' s ville f natale

homeward ['homwərd] adj de retour || adv vers la maison; vers son pays

home'work' s travail m à la maison; devoirs mpl

homey ['homɪ] adj (comp homier; super homiest) (coll) familial, intime

homicidal [ˌhamɪˈsaɪdəl] adj homicide

homicide ['hamɪ ˌsaɪd] s (act) homicide m; (person) homicide mf

homi•ly ['hamɪlɪ] s (pl -lies) homélie f

hom'ing head' s (of missile) tête f chercheuse

hom'ing pi'geon s pigeon m voyageur

hominy ['hamɪnɪ] s semoule f de maïs

homogeneous [ˌhoməˈdʒinɪ·əs], [ˌhaməˈdʒinɪ·əs] adj homogène

homogenize [həˈmadʒə ˌnaɪz] tr homogénéiser

homonym ['hamənɪm] s homonyme m

homonymous [həˈmanɪməs] adj homonyme

homosexual [ˌhoməˈsɛkʃʊ·əl] adj & s homosexuel m

hone [hon] s pierre f à aiguiser || tr aiguiser, affiler

honest ['anɪst] adj honnête; (money) honnêtement acquis

honesty ['anɪstɪ] s honnêteté f; (bot) monnaie f du pape

hon•ey ['hʌnɪ] s miel m || v (pret & pp -eyed or -ied) tr emmieller

hon'ey•bee' s abeille f à miel

hon'ey•comb' s rayon m, gâteau m de cire; (anything like a honeycomb) nid m d'abeilles || tr cribler

honeyed adj emmiellé

hon'ey•moon' s lune f de miel; voyage m de noces || intr passer la lune de miel

hon'ey•suck'le s chèvrefeuille m

honk [haŋk], [hɔŋk] s (aut) klaxon m || tr (the horn) sonner || intr klaxonner

honkytonk ['haŋkɪ,taŋk], ['hɔŋkɪ-,taŋk] s (slang) boui-boui m

honor ['anər] s honneur m; (award) distinction f; **honors** honneurs || tr honorer

honorable ['anərəbəl] adj honorable

hon'orable dis'charge s (mil) démobilisation f honorable

honorari·um [,anə'rɛrɪ·əm] s (pl -ums or -a [ə]) s honoraires mpl

honorary ['anə,rɛri] adj honoraire

honorific [,anə'rɪfɪk] adj honorifique || s formule f de politesse

hood [hʊd] s capuchon m, chaperon m; (of chimney) hotte f; (academic hood) capuce m; (aut) capot m; (slang) gangster m || tr capoter

hoodlum ['hʊdləm] s (coll) chenapan m

hoodoo ['hudu] s (bad luck) guigne f; (rites) vaudou m || tr porter la guigne à

hood'wink' tr tromper, abuser

hooey ['hu·i] s (slang) blague f

hoof [huf], [hʊf] s sabot m; **on the hoof** sur pied || tr—**to hoof it** (coll) aller à pied

hoof'beat' s pas m de cheval

hook [hʊk] s crochet m; (for fishing) hameçon m; (to join two things) croc m; (boxing) crochet m; **by hook or by crook** (coll) de bric ou de broc, coûte que coûte; **hook line and sinker** (coll) tout à fait, avec tout le bataclan; **to get one's hooks on to** (coll) mettre le grappin sur || tr accrocher; (e.g., a dress) agrafer; (e.g., a boat) crocher, gaffer; (slang) amorcer, attraper; **to hook up** agrafer; (e.g., a loudspeaking system) monter || intr s'accrocher

hookah ['hʊkə] s narguilé m

hook' and eye' s agrafe f et porte f

hook' and lad'der s camion m équipé d'une échelle d'incendie

hooked' rug' s tapis m à points noués

hook'up' s (diagram) (rad, telv) montage m; (network) (rad, telv) chaîne f

hook'worm' s ankylostome m

hooky ['hʊki] s—**to play hooky** (coll) faire l'école buissonnière

hooligan ['hulɪgən] s voyou m

hooliganism ['hulɪgən,ɪzəm] s voyouterie f

hoop [hup], [hʊp] s cerceau m; (of cask) cercle m || tr cercler, entourer

hoop' skirt' s crinoline f

hoot [hut] s huée f; (of owl) ululement m || tr huer || intr huer; (said of owl) ululer; **to hoot at** huer

hoot' owl' s chat-huant m, hulotte f

hop [hap] s saut m; (dance) (coll) sauterie f, surboum m; (coll) vol m en avion, étape f; **hops** (bot) houblon m || v (pret & pp hopped; ger hopping) tr sauter, franchir; (e.g., a taxi) (coll) prendre || intr sauter, sautiller; **to hop on the foot** sauter à cloche-pied; **to hop over** sauter

hope [hop] s (feeling of hope) espérance f; (instance of hope) espoir m; (person or thing one puts one's hope in) espérance, espoir || tr & intr

espérer; **to hope for** espérer; **to hope to** + inf espérer + inf

hope' chest' s trousseau m

hopeful ['hopfəl] adj (feeling hope) plein d'espoir; (giving hope) prometteur

hopeless ['hoplɪs] adj sans espoir

hopper ['hapər] s (funnel-shaped container) trémie f; (of blast furnace) gueulard m

hop'per car' s wagon-trémie m

hop'scotch' s marelle f

horde [hɔrd] s horde f

horehound ['hor,haʊnd] s (bot) marrube m

horizon [hə'raɪzən] s horizon m

horizontal [,harɪ'zantəl], [,hɔrɪ'zantəl] adj horizontal || s horizontale f

hor'izon'tal hold' s (telv) commande f de stabilité horizontale

hormone ['hɔrmon] s hormone f

horn [hɔrn] s (bony projection on head of certain animals) corne f; (of anvil) bigorne f; (of auto) klaxon m; (of snail; of insect) antenne f; (mus) cor m; (French horn) (mus) cor d'harmonie; **horns** (of deer) bois m; **to blow one's own horn** (coll) se vanter, exalter son propre mérite; **to draw in one's horns** (fig) rentrer les cornes; **to toot the horn** corner || intr—**to horn in** (slang) intervenir sans façon

horn'beam' s (bot) charme m

horned' owl' s duc m

hornet ['hɔrnɪt] s frelon m

hor'net's nest' s guêpier m

horn' of plen'ty s corne f d'abondance

horn'pipe' s chalumeau m; (dance) matelote f

horn'rimmed glas'ses spl lunettes fpl à monture en corne

horn·y ['hɔrni] adj (comp -ier; super -iest) corné, en corne; (callous) calleux; (horned) cornu

horoscope ['harə,skop], ['hɔrə,skop] s horoscope m; **to cast s.o.'s horoscope** tirer l'horoscope de qn

horrible ['harɪbəl], ['hɔrɪbəl] adj horrible; (coll) horrible, détestable

horrid ['harɪd], ['hɔrɪd] adj affreux; (coll) affreux, très désagréable

horri·fy ['harɪ,faɪ], ['hɔrɪ,faɪ] v (pret & pp -fied) tr horrifier

horror ['harər], ['hɔrər] s horreur f; **to have a horror of** avoir horreur de

hors d'oeuvre [ɔr'dʌrv] s (pl **hors d'oeuvres** [ɔr'dʌrvz]) hors-d'œuvre m

horse [hɔrs] s cheval m; (of carpenter) chevalet m; **hold your horses!** (coll) arrêtez un moment!; **to back the wrong horse** (coll) miser sur le mauvais cheval; **to be a horse of another color** (coll) être une autre paire de manches; **to eat like a horse** (coll) manger comme un ogre; **to ride a horse** monter à cheval || intr—**to horse around** (slang) muser, se baguenauder

horse'back' s—**on horseback** à cheval || adv—**to ride horseback** monter à cheval

horse′back rid′ing *s* équitation *f*, exercice *m* à cheval
horse′ blan′ket *s* couverture *f* de cheval
horse′ break′er *s* dompteur *m* de chevaux
horse′car′ *s* tramway *m* à chevaux
horse′ chest′nut *s* (*tree*) marronnier *m* d'Inde; (*nut*) marron *m* d'Inde
horse′cloth′ *s* housse *f*
horse′ col′lar *s* collier *m* de cheval
horse′ deal′er *s* marchand *m* de chevaux
horse′ doc′tor *s* (*coll*) vétérinaire *m*
horse′ fly′ *s* (*pl* **flies**) taon *m*
horse′hair′ *s* crin *m*
horse′hide′ *s* peau *f* or cuir *m* de cheval
horse′laugh′ *s* gros rire *m* bruyant
horse′less car′riage [′hɔrslıs] *s* voiture *f* sans chevaux
horse′man *s* (*pl* **-men**) cavalier *m*; (*at race track*) turfiste *m*
horsemanship [′hɔrsmənˌʃɪp] *s* équitation *f*
horse′ meat′ *s* viande *f* de cheval
horse′ op′era *s* (*coll*) western *m*
horse′ pis′tol *s* pistolet *m* d'arçon
horse′play′ *s* jeu *m* de mains, clownerie *f*
horse′pow′er *s* (*746 watts*) cheval-vapeur anglais
horse′ race′ *s* course *f* de chevaux
horse′rad′ish *s* raifort *m*
horse′ sense′ *s* (*coll*) gros bon sens *m*
horse′shoe′ *s* fer *m* à cheval
horse′shoe′ing *s* ferrure *f*, ferrage *m*
horse′shoe mag′net *s* aimant *m* en fer à cheval
horse′ show′ *s* exposition *f* de chevaux, concours *m* hippique
horse′tail′ *s* queue *f* de cheval; (bot) prêle *f*
horse′ thief′ *s* voleur *m* de chevaux
horse′ trad′er *s* maquignon *m*
horse′ trad′ing *s* maquignonnage *m*
horse′whip′ *s* cravache *f* ‖ *v* (*pret* & *pp* **-whipped**; *ger* **-whipping**) *tr* cravacher
horse′wom′an *s* (*pl* **-wom′en**) cavalière *f*, amazone *f*
hors·y [′hɔrsi] *adj* (*comp* **-ier**; *super* **-iest**) chevalin; (*coll*) hippomane; (*awkward in appearance*) (*coll*) maladroit
horticultural [ˌhɔrtı′kʌltʃərəl] *adj* horticole
horticulture [′hɔrtıˌkʌltʃər] *s* horticulture *f*
hose [hoz] *s* (*flexible tube*) tuyau *m* ‖ *s* (*pl* **hose**) (*stocking*) bas *m*; (*sock*) chaussette *f*
hosier [′hoʒər] *s* bonnetier *m*
hosiery [′hoʒəri] *s* la bonneterie; (*stockings*) les bas *mpl*
hospice [′hɑspɪs] *s* hospice *m*
hospitable [′hɑspɪtəbəl], [hɑs′pɪtəbəl] *adj* hospitalier
hospital [′hɑspɪtəl] *s* hôpital *m*, clinique *f*, maison *f* de santé
hospitali·ty [ˌhɑspɪ′tælɪti] *s* (*pl* **-ties**) hospitalité *f*

hospitalize [′hɑspɪtəˌlaɪz] *tr* hospitaliser
hos′pital plane′ *s* avion *m* sanitaire
hos′pital ship′ *s* navire-hôpital *m*
hos′pital train′ *s* train *m* sanitaire
host [host] *s* hôte *m*; (*who entertains dinner guests*) amphitryon *m*; (*multitude*) foule *f*, légion *f*; (*army*) armée *f*; **Host** (*eccl*) hostie *f*
hostage [′hɑstɪdʒ] *s* otage *m*
hostel [′hɑstəl] *s* hôtellerie *f*; (*youth hostel*) auberge *f* de la jeunesse
hostel·ry [′hɑstəlri] *s* (*pl* **-ries**) hôtellerie *f*
hostess [′hostɪs] *s* hôtesse *f*; (*taxi dancer*) entraîneuse *f*
hostile [′hɑstɪl] *adj* hostile
hostili·ty [hɑs′tɪlɪti] *s* (*pl* **-ties**) hostilité *f*
hostler [′hɑslər], [′ɑslər] *s* palefrenier *m*, valet *m* d'écurie
hot [hɑt] *adj* (*comp* **hotter**; *super* **hottest**) chaud; (*spicy*) piquant; (*fight, pursuit, etc.*) acharné; (*in rut*) en chaleur; (*radioactive*) (*coll*) fortement radioactif; **hot off** (*e.g., the press*) (*coll*) sortant tout droit de; **to be hot** (*said of person*) avoir chaud; (*said of weather*) faire chaud; **to get hot under the collar** (*coll*) s'emporter; **to make it hot for** (*coll*) rendre la vie intenable à, harceler
hot′ air′ *s* (*slang*) hâblerie *f*, discours *mpl* vides
hot′-air′ fur′nace *s* calorifère *m* à air chaud
hot′ and cold′ run′ning wa′ter *s* eau *f* courante chaude et froide
hot′bed′ *s* (hort) couche *f*, couche de fumier; (*e.g., of vice*) foyer *m*; (*e.g., of intrigue*) officine *f*
hot′-blood′ed *adj* au sang fougueux
hot′box′ *s* (rr) coussinet *m* échauffé
hot′ cake′ *s* crêpe *f*; **to sell like hot cakes** (*coll*) se vendre comme des petits pains
hot′ dog′ *s* saucisse *f* de Francfort, saucisse chaude
hotel [ho′tel] *adj* hôtelier ‖ *s* hôtel *m*
hotel′keep′er *s* hôtelier *m*
hot′foot′ *adv* (*coll*) à toute vitesse ‖ *tr* **—to hotfoot it after** (*coll*) s'élancer à la poursuite de
hot′head′ed *adj* exalté, fougueux
hot′house′ *s* serre *f* chaude
hot′ pad′ *s* (*for plates at table*) garde-nappe *m*, dessous-de-plat *m*
hot′ pep′per *s* piment *m* rouge
hot′ plate′ *s* réchaud *m*
hot′ rod′ *s* (slang) bolide *m*
hot′ rod′der *s* (slang) bolide *m*, casse-cou *m*
hot′ springs′ *spl* sources *fpl* thermales
hot′-tem′pered *adj* coléreux, irascible
hot′ wa′ter *s* (*coll*) mauvaise passe *f*; **to be in hot water** (*coll*) être dans le pétrin
hot′-wa′ter boil′er *s* chaudière *f* à eau chaude
hot′-wa′ter bot′tle *s* bouillotte *f*
hot′-wa′ter heat′er *s* calorifère *m* à eau

chaude; (*with instantaneous delivery of hot water*) chauffe-eau *m*

hot/-wa/ter heat/ing *s* chauffage *m* par eau chaude

hot/-wa/ter tank/ *s* réservoir *m* d'eau chaude, bâche *f*

hound [haund] *s* chien *m* de chasse, chien courant; **to follow the hounds** or **to ride to hounds** chasser à courre || *tr* poursuivre avec ardeur, pourchasser

hour [aur] *s* heure *f*; **by the hour** à l'heure; **on the hour** à l'heure sonnante; **to keep late hours** se coucher tard

hour/glass/ *s* sablier *m*

hour/-glass fig/ure *s* taille *f* de guêpe

hour/ hand/ *s* petite aiguille *f*, aiguille des heures

hourly ['aurli] *adj* à l'heure, horaire || *adv* toutes les heures; (*hour by hour*) d'heure en heure

house [haus] *s* (*pl* **houses** ['hauzɪz]) maison *f*; (*legislative body*) chambre *f*; (*theat*) salle *f*, e.g., **full house** salle comble; **to be on the house** (coll) être au frais du patron; **to bring down the house** (theat) faire crouler la salle sous les applaudissements; **to keep house** for tenir la maison de; **to put one's house in order** (fig) mettre de l'ordre dans ses affaires || [hauz] *tr* loger, abriter

house/ arrest/ *s*—**under house arrest** en résidence surveillée

house/boat/ *s* bateau-maison *m*

house/boy/ *s* boy *m*

house/break/er *s* cambrioleur *m*

house/break/ing *s* effraction *f*, cambriolage *m*

housebroken ['haus,brokən] *adj* (*dog or cat*) dressé à la propreté

house/ clean/ing *s* grand nettoyage *m* de la maison

house/coat/ *s* peignoir *m*

house/ cur/rent *s* courant *m* de secteur, secteur *m*

house/fly/ *s* (*pl* **-flies**) mouche *f* domestique

houseful ['haus,ful] *s* pleine maison *f*

house/ fur/nishings *spl* ménage *m*

house/hold/ *adj* domestique, du ménage || *s* ménage *m*, maisonnée *f*

house/hold/er *s* chef *m* de famille, maître *m* de maison

house/ hunt/ing *s* chasse *f* aux appartements

house/keep/er *s* ménagère *f*; (*employee*) femme *f* de charge; (*for a bachelor*) gouvernante *f*

house/keep/ing *s* le ménage, l'économie *f* domestique; **to set up housekeeping** se mettre en ménage

house/maid/ *s* bonne *f*

house/moth/er *s* maîtresse *f* d'internat

house/ of cards/ *s* château *m* de cartes

House/ of Com/mons *s* Chambre *f* des communes

house/ of ill/ repute/ *s* maison *f* mal famée, maison borgne

House/ of Represen/tatives *s* Chambre *f* des Représentants

house/ paint/er *s* peintre *m* en bâtiments

house/ physi/cian *s* (*in hospital*) interne *m*; (*e.g., in hotel*) médecin *m*

house/top/ *s* toit *m*; **to shout from the housetops** (coll) crier sur les toits

house/ trail/er *s* caravane *f*

house/warm/ing *s*—**to have a house-warming** pendre la crémaillère

house/wife/ *s* (*pl* **-wives**) maîtresse *f* de maison, ménagère *f*

house/work/ *s* travaux *mpl* ménagers; **to do the housework** faire le ménage

housing ['hauzɪŋ] *s* logement *m*, habitation *f*; (*horsecloth*) housse *f*; (*mach*) enchâssure *f*, carter *m*

hous/ing devel/opment *s* (*houses*) grand ensemble *m*, habitations *fpl* neuves; (*apartments*) cité *f*

hous/ing short/age *s* crise *f* du logement

hovel ['hʌvəl], ['hɑvəl] *s* bicoque *f*, masure *f*; (*shed for cattle, tools, etc.*) appentis *m*, cabane *f*

hover ['hʌvər], ['hɑvər] *intr* planer, voltiger; (*to move to and fro near a person*) papillonner; (*to hang around threateningly*) rôder; (*said of smile on lips*) errer; hésiter

how [hau] *s* comment *m*; **the how, the when, and the wherefore** (coll) tous les détails || *adv* comment; **how** + *adj* quel + *adj*, e.g., **how beautiful a morning!** quelle belle matinée!; **comme** + **c'est** + *adj*, e.g., **how beautiful it is!** comme c'est beau!; **que** + **c'est** + *adj*, e.g., **how beautiful it is!** que c'est beau!; **how are you?** comment allez-vous?, ça va?; **how early** quand, à quelle heure; **how else** de quelle autre manière; **how far** jusqu'où; à quelle distance, e.g., **how far is it?** à quelle distance est-ce?; **how long** (*in time*) jusqu'à quand, combien de temps; **how long is the stick?** quelle est la longueur du bâton?; **how many** combien; **how much** combien; (*at what price*) à combien; **how often** combien de fois; **how old are you?** quel âge avez-vous?; **how soon** quand, à quelle heure; **to know how** to savoir

how-do-you-do ['haudəjə'du] *s*—**that's a fine how-do-you-do!** (coll) en voilà une affaire!

how-ev/er *adv* cependant, pourtant, toutefois; **however little it may be** si peu que ce soit; **however much** or **many it may be** autant que ce soit; **however pretty she may be** quelque jolie qu'elle soit; **however that may be** quoi qu'il en soit || *conj* comme, e.g., **do it however you want** faites-le comme vous voudrez

howitzer ['hau·ɪtsər] *s* obusier *m*

howl [haul] *s* hurlement *m* || *tr* hurler; **to howl down** faire taire en poussant des huées || *intr* hurler; (*said of wind*) mugir

howler ['haulər] *s* hurleur *m*; (coll) grosse gaffe *f*, bourde *f*, bévue *f*

hoyden ['hɔɪdən] *s* petite coquine *f*

H.P. or **hp** abbr (**horsepower**) CV
hub [hʌb] s moyeu m; (fig) centre m
hubbub ['hʌbəb] s vacarme m, tumulte m
hub'cap' s enjoliveur m, chapeau m de roue
huckster ['hʌkstər] s (peddler) camelot m; (adman) publicitaire mf
huddle ['hʌdəl] s (coll) conférence f secrète; **to go into a huddle** (coll) entrer en conclave ‖ intr s'entasser, se presser
hue [hju] s teinte f, nuance f
hue' and cry' s clameur f de haro; **with hue and cry** à cor et à cri
huff [hʌf] s accès m de colère; **in a huff** vexé, offensé
hug [hʌg] s étreinte f ‖ v (pret & pp **hugged**; ger **hugging**) tr étreindre; (e.g., the coast) serrer; (e.g., the wall) raser ‖ intr s'étreindre
huge [hjudʒ] adj énorme, immense
huh [hʌ] interj hein!, hé!
hulk [hʌlk] s (body of an old ship) carcasse f; (old ship used as warehouse, prison, etc.) ponton m; (heavy, unwieldy person) mastodonte m
hull [hʌl] s (of certain vegetables) cosse f; (of nuts) écale f; (of ship or hydroplane) coque f ‖ tr (e.g., peas) écosser; (e.g., almonds) écaler
hullabaloo ['hʌləbə,lu], [,hʌləbə'lu] s (coll) boucan m, brouhaha m
hum [hʌm] s (e.g., of bee) bourdonnement m; (e.g., of motor) vrombissement m; (of singer) fredonnement m ‖ v (pret & pp **hummed**; ger **humming**) tr (a melody) fredonner, chantonner ‖ intr (said of bee) bourdonner; (said of machine) vrombir; (said of singer) fredonner, chantonner; (to be active) (coll) aller rondement ‖ interj hum!
human ['hjumən] adj humain
hu'man be'ing s être m humain
humane [hju'men] adj humain, compatissant
humanist ['hjumənɪst] adj & s humaniste m
humanitarian [hju,mænɪ'terɪ-ən] adj & s humanitaire mf
humani·ty [hju'mænɪti] s (pl -ties) humanité f; **humanities** (Greek and Latin classics) humanités classiques; (belles-lettres) humanités modernes
hu'man·kind' s genre m humain
humble ['hʌmbəl], ['ʌmbəl] adj humble ‖ tr humilier; **to humble oneself** s'humilier
hum'ble pie' s—**to eat humble pie** faire amende honorable, s'humilier
hum'bug' s blague f; (person) imposteur m ‖ v (pret & pp **-bugged**; ger **-bugging**) tr mystifier
hum'drum' adj monotone, banal
humer·us ['hjumərəs] s (pl -i [,aɪ]) humérus m
humid ['hjumɪd] adj humide, moite
humidifier [hju'mɪdɪ,faɪ·ər] s humidificateur m
humidi·fy [hju'mɪdɪ,faɪ] v (pret & pp **-fied**) tr humidifier

humidity [hju'mɪdɪti] s humidité f
humiliate [hju'mɪlɪ,et] tr humilier
humiliating [hju'mɪlɪ,etɪŋ] adj humiliant
humili·ty [hju'mɪlɪti] s (pl -ties) humilité f
hum'ming·bird' s oiseau-mouche m, colibri m
humor ['hjumər], ['jumər] s (comic quality) humour m; (frame of mind; fluid) humeur f; **out of humor** maussade, grognon; **to be in the humor to** être d'humeur à ‖ tr ménager, satisfaire; (s.o.'s fancies) se plier à, accéder à
humorist ['hjumərɪst], ['jumərɪst] s humoriste mf, comique mf
humorous ['hjumərəs], ['jumərəs] adj humoristique; (writer) humoriste
hump [hʌmp] s bosse f
hump'back' s bossu m; (whale) mégaptère m
humus ['hjuməs] s humus m
hunch [hʌntʃ] s bosse f; (premonition) (coll) pressentiment m ‖ tr arrondir, voûter ‖ intr s'accroupir
hunch'back' s bossu m
hundred ['hʌndrəd] adj cent ‖ s cent m, centaine f; **about a hundred** une centaine; **a hundred or one hundred** cent; une centaine; **by the hundreds** par centaines
hun'dred·fold' adj & s centuple m; **to increase a hundredfold** centupler ‖ adv au centuple
hundredth ['hʌndrədθ] adj, pron, & s centième m
hun'dred·weight' s quintal m
Hungarian [hʌŋ'gerɪ·ən] adj hongrois ‖ s (language) hongrois m; (person) Hongrois m
Hungary ['hʌŋgəri] s Hongrie f; la Hongrie
hunger ['hʌŋgər] s faim f ‖ intr avoir faim; **to hunger for** être affamé de
hun'ger march' s marche f de la faim
hun'ger strike' s grève f de la faim
hun·gry ['hʌŋgri] adj (comp -grier; super -griest) affamé; **to be hungry** avoir faim
hunk [hʌŋk] s gros morceau m
hunt [hʌnt] s (act of hunting) chasse f; (hunting party) équipage m de chasse; **on the hunt for** à la recherche de ‖ tr chasser; (to seek, look for) chercher; **to hunt down** donner la chasse à, traquer; **to hunt out** faire la chasse à ‖ intr chasser; (with dogs) chasser à courre; **to go hunting** aller à la chasse; **to hunt for** chercher; **to take hunting** emmener à la chasse
hunter ['hʌntər] s chasseur m
hunting ['hʌntɪŋ] adj de chasse ‖ s chasse f
hunt'ing dog' s chien m de chasse
hunt'ing ground' s terrain m de chasse, chasse f
hunt'ing horn' s cor m de chasse
hunt'ing jack'et s paletot m de chasse
hunt'ing knife' s couteau m de chasse

hunt'ing li'cense s permis m de chasse
hunt'ing lodge' s pavillon m de chasse
hunt'ing sea'son s saison f de la chasse
huntress ['hʌntrɪs] s chasseuse f
hunts'man s (pl -men) chasseur m
hurdle ['hʌrdəl] s (hedge over which horses jump) haie f; (wooden frame over which runners jump) barrière f; (fig) obstacle m; hurdles course f d'obstacles || tr sauter
hur'dle race' s course f d'obstacles; (turf) course de haies
hurdy-gur'dy ['hʌrdi'gɑrdi] s (pl -dies) orgue m de Barbarie
hurl [hʌrl] s lancée f || tr lancer; to hurl back repousser, refouler
hurrah [hʌ'rɑ] or hurray [hʊ're] s hourra m || interj hourra!; hurrah for . . . ! vive . . . !
hurricane ['hʌrɪ‚ken] s ouragan m, hurricane m
hurried ['hʌrɪd] adj pressé, précipité; (hasty) hâtif, fait à la hâte
hur-ry ['hʌri] s (pl -ries) hâte f; to be in a hurry être pressé || v (pret & pp -ried) tr hâter, presser || intr se hâter, se presser; to hurry after courir après; to hurry away s'en aller bien vite; to hurry back revenir vite; to hurry over venir vite; to hurry up se dépêcher
hurt [hʌrt] adj blessé || s blessure f; (pain) douleur f || v (pret & pp hurt) tr faire mal à || intr faire mal, e.g., does that hurt? ça fait mal?; avoir mal, e.g., my head hurts j'ai mal à la tête
hurtful ['hʌrtfəl] adj nuisible
hurtle ['hʌrtəl] intr se précipiter
husband ['hʌzbənd] s mari m, époux m || tr ménager, économiser
hus'band·man s (pl -men) cultivateur m
husbandry ['hʌzbəndri] s agriculture f; (raising of livestock) élevage m
hush [hʌʃ] s silence m, calme m || tr faire taire; to hush up (e.g., a scandal) étouffer || intr se taire || interj chut!
hushaby ['hʌʃə‚baɪ] interj fais dodo!
hush'-hush' adj très secret
hush' mon'ey s prix m du silence
husk [hʌsk] s peau f; (of certain vegetables) cosse f, gousse f; (of nuts) écale f; (of corn) enveloppe f; (of oats) balle f; (of onion) pelure f || tr (grain) vanner; (vegetables) éplucher; (peas) écosser; (nuts) écaler
husk'ing bee' s réunion f pour l'épluchage du maïs
husk·y ['hʌski] adj (comp -ier; super -iest) costaud; (voice) enroué || s (pl -ies) (dog) chien m esquimau
hus·sy ['hʌzi], ['hʌsi] s (pl -sies) (coll) garce f; (coll) coquine f
hustle ['hʌsəl] s (coll) bousculade f, énergie f, allant m || tr pousser, bousculer || intr se dépêcher, se presser; (to work hard) (coll) se démener, s'activer
hustler ['hʌslər] s (go-getter) homme m d'action; (swindler) (slang) filou

m; (streetwalker) (slang) traînée f, grue f
hut [hʌt] s hutte f, cabane f; (mil) baraque f
hutch [hʌtʃ] s (for rabbits) clapier m; (used by baker) huche f, pétrin m
hyacinth ['haɪ‚əsɪnθ] s (stone) hyacinthe f; (flower) jacinthe f
hybrid ['haɪbrɪd] adj & s hybride m
hy·dra ['haɪdrə] s (pl -dras or -drae [dri]) hydre f
hydrant ['haɪdrənt] s prise f d'eau; (faucet) robinet m; (fire hydrant) bouche f d'incendie
hydrate ['haɪdret] s hydrate m || tr hydrater || intr s'hydrater
hydraulic [haɪ'drɔlɪk] adj hydraulique || hydraulics s hydraulique f
hydrau'lic ram' s bélier m hydraulique
hydrocarbon [‚haɪdrə'kɑrbən] s hydrocarbure m
hy'drochlo'ric ac'id [‚haɪdrə'klorɪk] s acide m chlorhydrique
hydroelectric [‚haɪdro·ɪ'lektrɪk] adj hydro-électrique
hydrofoil ['haɪdrə‚fɔɪl] s hydrofoil m
hydrogen ['haɪdrədʒən] s hydrogène m
hy'drogen bomb' s bombe f à hydrogène
hy'drogen perox'ide s eau f oxygénée
hy'drogen sul'fide s hydrogène m sulfuré
hydrometer [haɪ'drɑmɪtər] s aréomètre m, hydromètre m
hydrophobia [‚haɪdrə'fobɪ·ə] s hydrophobie f
hydroplane ['haɪdrə‚plen] s hydravion m
hydroxide [haɪ'drɑksaɪd] s hydroxyde m
hyena [haɪ'inə] s hyène f
hygiene ['haɪdʒin], ['haɪdʒɪ‚in] s hygiène f
hygienic [‚haɪdʒɪ'enɪk], [haɪ'dʒinɪk] adj hygiénique
hymn [hɪm] s hymne m; (eccl) hymne f, cantique m
hymnal ['hɪmnəl] s livre m d'hymnes
hyperacidity [‚haɪpərə'sɪdɪti] s hyperacidité f
hyperbola [haɪ'pʌrbələ] s hyperbole f
hyperbole [haɪ'pʌrbəli] s hyperbole f
hypersensitive [‚haɪpər'sensɪtɪv] adj hypersensible, hypersensitif
hypertension [‚haɪpər'tenʃən] s hypertension f
hyphen ['haɪfən] s trait m d'union
hyphenate ['haɪfə‚net] tr joindre avec un trait d'union
hypno·sis [hɪp'nosɪs] s (pl -ses [siz]) hypnose f
hypnotic [hɪp'nɑtɪk] adj & s hypnotique m
hypnotism ['hɪpnə‚tɪzəm] s hypnotisme m
hypnotist ['hɪpnətɪst] s hypnotiseur m
hypnotize ['hɪpnə‚taɪz] tr hypnotiser
hypochondriac [‚haɪpə'kɑndrɪ‚æk], [‚haɪpə'kɑndrɪ‚æk] adj & s hypocondriaque mf

hypocri·sy [hɪ'pɑkrəsi] s (pl **-sies**) hypocrisie f
hypocrite ['hɪpəkrɪt] s hypocrite mf
hypocritical [ˌhɪpə'krɪtɪkəl] adj hypocrite
hypodermic [ˌhaɪpə'dʌrmɪk] adj hypodermique
hyposulfite [ˌhaɪpə'sʌlfaɪt] s hyposulfite f
hypotenuse [haɪ'pɑtɪˌn(j)us] s hypoténuse f

hypothe·sis [haɪ'pɑθɪsɪs] s (pl **-ses** [ˌsiz]) hypothèse f
hypothetic(al) [ˌhaɪpə'θɛtɪk(əl)] adj hypothétique
hysteria [hɪs'tɪrɪ·ə] s agitation f, frénésie f; (pathol) hystérie f
hysteric [hɪs'tɛrɪk] adj hystérique || **hysterics** spl crise f de nerfs, crise de larmes, fou rire m
hysterical [hɪs'tɛrɪkəl] adj hystérique

I

I, i [aɪ] s IXᵉ lettre de l'alphabet
I pron je §87; moi §85
iambic [aɪ'æmbɪk] adj iambique
Iberian [aɪ'bɪrɪ·ən] adj ibérien, ibérique || s Ibérien m
ibex ['aɪbɛks] s (pl **ibexes** or **ibices** ['ɪbɪˌsiz]) bouquetin m
ice [aɪs] s glace f; **to break the ice** (fig) rompre la glace; **to cut no ice** (coll) ne rien casser, ne pas prendre; **to skate on thin ice** (coll) s'engager sur un terrain dangereux || tr glacer; (e.g., champagne) frapper; (e.g., melon) rafraîchir || intr geler; **to ice up** (said of windshield, airplane wings, etc.) se givrer
ice′ age′ s époque f glaciaire
ice′ bag′ s sac m à glace
ice′ bank′ s banquise f
iceberg ['aɪsˌbʌrg] s banquise f, iceberg m; (person) (coll) glaçon m
ice′ boat′ s (icebreaker) brise-glace m; (for sport) bateau m à patins
icebound ['aɪsˌbaʊnd] adj pris dans les glaces
ice′ box′ s glacière f
ice′ break′er s brise-glace m
ice′ cap′ s calotte f glaciaire
ice′ cream′ s glace f
ice′-cream′ cone′ s cornet m de glace, glace f en cornet
ice′-cream′ freez′er s sorbetière f
ice′ cube′ s glaçon m
ice′-cube′ tray′ s bac m à glaçons
iced′ tea′ s thé m glacé
ice′ floe′ s banquise f
ice′ hock′ey s hockey m sur glace
ice′ jam′ s embâcle m
Iceland ['aɪslənd] s Islande f; l'Islande
Icelander ['aɪsˌlændər], ['aɪsləndər] s Islandais m
Icelandic [aɪs'lændɪk] adj & s islandais m
ice′ man′ s (pl **-men′**) glacier m
ice′ pack′ s (pack ice) embâcle m; (med) vessie f de glace
ice′ pail′ s seau m à glace
ice′ pick′ s poinçon m à glace; (of mountain climber) piolet m
ice′ skate′ s patin m à glace
ice′ wa′ter s eau f glacée f

ichthyology [ˌɪkθɪ'ɑlədʒi] s ichtyologie f
icicle ['aɪsɪkəl] s glaçon m, chandelle f de glace
icing ['aɪsɪŋ] s (on cake) glaçage m; (aer) givrage m
icon ['aɪkɑn] s icône f
iconoclast [aɪ'kɑnəˌklæst] s iconoclaste mf
iconoclastic [aɪˌkɑnə'klæstɪk] adj iconoclaste
iconoscope [aɪ'kɑnəˌskop] s (trademark) iconoscope m
icy ['aɪsi] adj (comp **icier**; super **iciest**) glacé; (slippery) glissant; (fig) froid, glacial
idea [aɪ'di·ə] s idée f; **the very idea!** par exemple!
ideal [aɪ'di·əl] adj & s idéal m
idealist [aɪ'di·əlɪst] adj & s idéaliste mf
idealistic [aɪˌdi·əl'ɪstɪk] adj idéaliste
idealize [aɪ'di·ə ˌlaɪz] tr idéaliser
identic(al) [aɪ'dɛntɪk(əl)] adj identique
identification [aɪˌdɛntɪfɪ'keʃən] s identification f
identifica′tion card′ s carte f d'identité
identifica′tion tag′ s plaque f d'identité
identi·fy [aɪ'dɛntɪˌfaɪ] v (pret & pp **-fied**) tr identifier
identi·ty [aɪ'dɛntɪti] s (pl **-ties**) identité f
ideolo·gy [ˌaɪdɪ'ɑlədʒi], [ˌɪdɪ'ɑlədʒi] s (pl **-gies**) idéologie f
ides [aɪdz] spl ides fpl
idio·cy ['ɪdɪ·əsi] s (pl **-cies**) idiotie f
idiom ['ɪdɪ·əm] s (phrase, expression) idiotisme m; (language, style) idiome m
idiomatic [ˌɪdɪ·ə'mætɪk] adj idiomatique || tr—**to speak idiomatic**
idiosyncra·sy [ˌɪdɪ·ə'sɪnkrəsi] s (pl **-sies**) idiosyncrasie f
idiot ['ɪdɪ·ət] s idiot m
idiotic [ˌɪdɪ'ɑtɪk] adj idiot
idle ['aɪdəl] adj oisif, désœuvré; (futile) oiseux; **to run idle** marcher au ralenti || tr—**to idle away** (time) passer à ne rien faire || intr fainéanter; (mach) tourner au ralenti
idleness ['aɪdəlnɪs] s oisiveté f
idler ['aɪdlər] s oisif m
idling ['aɪdlɪŋ] s (of motor) ralenti m

idol ['aɪdəl] s idole f

idola•try [aɪ'dɑlətrɪ] s (pl -tries) idolâtrie f

idolize ['aɪdə,laɪz] tr idolâtrer

idyll ['aɪdəl] s idylle f

idyllic [aɪ'dɪlɪk] adj idyllique

if [rf] s—ifs and buts des si et des mais || conj si; even if quand même; if it is true that si tant est que; if not sinon; if so dans ce cas, s'il en est ainsi

ignis fatuus ['ɪgnɪs'fætʃʊ•əs] s (pl ignes fatui ['ɪgnɪz'fætʃʊ,aɪ]) feu m follet

ignite [ɪg'naɪt] tr allumer || intr prendre feu

ignition [ɪg'nɪʃən] s ignition f; (aut) allumage m

igni'tion coil' s (aut) bobine f d'allumage

igni'tion switch' s (key) (aut) clé f de contact; (button) (aut) bouton m de contact

ignoble [ɪg'nobəl] adj ignoble

ignominious [,ɪgnə'mɪnɪ•əs] adj ignominieux

ignoramus [,ɪgnə'reməs] s ignorant m

ignorance ['ɪgnərəns] s ignorance f

ignorant ['ɪgnərənt] adj ignorant; to be ignorant of ignorer

ignore [ɪg'nor] tr ne pas tenir compte de, ne pas faire attention à; (a suggestion) passer outre à; (to snub) faire semblant de ne pas voir, ignorer à dessein

ilk [ɪlk] s espèce f; of that ilk de cet acabit

ill [ɪl] adj (comp worse [wʌrs]; super worst [wʌrst]) malade, souffrant || adv mal; to take ill prendre en mauvaise part; (to get sick) tomber malade

ill'-advised' adj (person) malavisé; (action) peu judicieux

ill' at ease' adj mal à l'aise

ill-bred [ɪl'brɛd] adj mal élevé

ill'-consid'ered adj peu réfléchi, hâtif

ill'-disposed' adj mal disposé, malintentionné

illegal [ɪ'ligəl] adj illégal

illegible [ɪ'lɛdʒɪbəl] adj illisible

illegitimate [,ɪlɪ'dʒɪtɪmɪt] adj illégitime

ill'-famed' adj mal famé

ill'-fat'ed adj malheureux, infortuné

ill-gotten ['ɪl'gɑtən] adj mal acquis

ill' health' s mauvaise santé f

ill'-hu'mored adj de mauvaise humeur, maussade

illicit [ɪ'lɪsɪt] adj illicite

illitera•cy [ɪ'lɪtərəsɪ] s (pl -cies) ignorance f; analphabétisme m

illiterate [ɪ'lɪtərɪt] adj (uneducated) ignorant, illettré; (unable to read or write) analphabète || s analphabète mf

ill'-man'nered adj malappris, mal élevé

ill'-na'tured adj désagréable, méchant

illness ['ɪlnɪs] s maladie f

illogical [ɪ'lɑdʒɪkəl] adj illogique

ill-spent ['ɪl'spɛnt] adj gaspillé

ill'-starred' adj néfaste, de mauvais augure

ill'-tem'pered adj désagréable, de mauvais caractère

ill'-timed' adj intempestif, mal à propos

ill'-treat' tr maltraiter, rudoyer

illuminate [ɪ'lumɪ,net] tr illuminer; (a manuscript) enluminer

illu'minating gas' s gaz m d'éclairage

illumination [ɪ'lumɪ'neʃən] s illumination f; (in manuscript) enluminure f

illusion [ɪ'luʒən] s illusion f

illusive [ɪ'lusɪv] adj illusoire, trompeur

illusory [ɪ'lusərɪ] adj illusoire

illustrate ['ɪləs,tret], [ɪ'lʌstret] tr illustrer

illustration s [,ɪləs'treʃən] s illustration f; (explanation) explication f, éclaircissement m

illustrative [ɪ'lʌstrətɪv] adj explicatif, éclairant

illustrator ['ɪləs,tretər] s illustrateur m, dessinateur m

illustrious [ɪ'lʌstrɪ•əs] adj illustre

ill' will' s rancune f

image ['ɪmɪdʒ] s image f

image•ry ['ɪmɪdʒrɪ], ['ɪmɪdʒərɪ] s (pl -ries) images fpl

imaginary [ɪ'mædʒɪ,nerɪ] adj imaginaire

imagination [ɪ,mædʒɪ'neʃən] s imagination f

imagine [ɪ'mædʒɪn] tr imaginer, s'imaginer || intr imaginer; imagine! figurez-vous!

imbecile ['ɪmbɪsɪl] adj & s imbécile mf

imbecil•ity [,ɪmbɪ'sɪlɪtɪ] s (pl -ties) imbécillité f

imbibe [ɪm'baɪb] tr absorber || intr boire, lever le coude

imbue [ɪm'bju] tr imprégner, pénétrer; imbued with imbu de

imitate ['ɪmɪ,tet] tr imiter

imitation [,ɪmɪ'teʃən] adj d'imitation || s imitation f

imitator ['ɪmɪ,tetər] s imitateur m

immaculate [ɪ'mækjəlɪt] adj immaculé

immaterial [,ɪmə'tɪrɪ•əl] adj immatériel; (pointless) sans conséquence; it's immaterial to me cela m'est égal

immature [,ɪmə'tjʊr] adj pas mûr, peu mûr; pas adulte

immeasurable [ɪ'mɛʒərəbəl] adj immensurable

immediacy [ɪ'midɪ•əsɪ] s caractère m immédiat, imminence f

immediate [ɪ'midɪ•ɪt] adj immédiat

immediately [ɪ'midɪ•ɪtlɪ] adv immédiatement

immemorial [,ɪmɪ'morɪ•əl] adj immémorial

immense [ɪ'mɛns] adj immense

immerse [ɪ'mʌrs] tr immerger, plonger

immersion [ɪ'mʌrʃən], [ɪ'mʌrʒən] s immersion f

immigrant ['ɪmɪgrənt] adj & s immigrant m

immigrate ['ɪmɪ,gret] intr immigrer

immigration [,ɪmɪ'greʃən] s immigration f

imminent ['ɪmɪnənt] adj imminent, très prochain

immobile [ɪˈmobɪl], [ɪˈmobɪl] adj immobile

immobilize [ɪˈmobɪˌlaɪz] tr immobiliser

immoderate [ɪˈmɑdərɪt] adj immodéré

immodest [ɪˈmɑdɪst] adj impudique

immoral [ɪˈmɑrəl], [ɪˈmɔrəl] adj immoral

immortal [ɪˈmɔrtəl] adj & s immortel m

immortalize [ɪˈmɔrtəˌlaɪz] tr immortaliser

immune [ɪˈmjun] adj dispensé, exempt; (med) immunisé

immunize [ˈɪmjəˌnaɪz], [ɪˈmjunaɪz] tr immuniser

imp [ɪmp] s suppôt m du diable; (child) diablotin m, polisson m

impact [ˈɪmpækt] s impact m

impair [ɪmˈper] tr endommager, affaiblir; (health, digestion) délabrer

impan·el [ɪmˈpænəl] v (pret & pp -eled or -elled; ger -eling or -elling) tr appeler à faire partie de; (a jury) dresser la liste de

impart [ɪmˈpɑrt] tr imprimer, communiquer; (to make known) communiquer

impartial [ɪmˈpɑrʃəl] adj impartial

impassable [ɪmˈpæsəbəl], [ɪmˈpɑsəbəl] adj (road) impraticable; (mountain) infranchissable

impassible [ɪmˈpæsɪbəl] adj impassible

impassioned [ɪmˈpæʃənd] adj passionné

impassive [ɪmˈpæsɪv] adj insensible; (look, face) impassible, composé

impatience [ɪmˈpeʃəns] s impatience f

impatient [ɪmˈpeʃənt] adj impatient

impeach [ɪmˈpitʃ] tr accuser; (s.o.'s honor, veracity) attaquer

impeachment [ɪmˈpitʃmənt] s accusation f; (of honor, veracity) attaque f

impeccable [ɪmˈpekəbəl] adj impeccable

impecunious [ˌɪmpɪˈkjuniˑəs] adj besogneux, impécunieux

impede [ɪmˈpid] tr entraver, empêcher

impediment [ɪmˈpedɪmənt] s obstacle m, empêchement m

im·pel [ɪmˈpel] v (pret & pp -pelled; ger -pelling) tr pousser, forcer

impending [ɪmˈpendɪŋ] adj imminent

impenetrable [ɪmˈpenətrəbəl] adj impénétrable

impenitent [ɪmˈpenɪtənt] adj impénitent m

imperative [ɪmˈperɪtɪv] adj & s impératif m

imperceptible [ˌɪmpərˈseptɪbəl] adj imperceptible

imperfect [ɪmˈpɑrfɪkt] adj & s imparfait m

imperfection [ˌɪmpərˈfek/ən] s imperfection f

imperial [ɪmˈpɪriˑəl] adj impérial

imperialist [ɪmˈpɪriˑəlɪst] adj & s impérialiste mf

imper·il [ɪmˈperɪl] v (pret & pp -iled or -illed; ger -iling or -illing) tr mettre en péril, exposer au danger

imperious [ɪmˈpɪriˑəs] adj impérieux

imperishable [ɪmˈperɪʃəbəl] adj impérissable

impersonal [ɪmˈpʌrsənəl] adj impersonnel

impersonate [ɪmˈpʌrsəˌnet] tr contrefaire, singer; jouer le rôle de

impertinent [ɪmˈpʌrtɪnənt] adj impertinent

impetuous [ɪmˈpetʃʊˑəs] adj impétueux

impetus [ˈɪmpɪtəs] s impulsion f; (mech) force f impulsive; (fig) élan m

imple·ty [ɪmˈpaɪˑəti] s (pl -ties) impiété f

impinge [ɪmˈpɪndʒ] intr—to impinge on or upon empiéter sur; (to violate) enfreindre

impious [ˈɪmpiˑəs] adj impie

impish [ˈɪmpɪʃ] adj espiègle

implant [ɪmˈplænt] tr implanter

implement [ˈɪmplɪmənt] s outil m, ustensile m || tr mettre en œuvre, réaliser; (to provide with implements) outiller

implicate [ˈɪmplɪˌket] tr impliquer

implicit [ɪmˈplɪsɪt] adj implicite

implied [ɪmˈplaɪd] adj implicite, sousentendu

implore [ɪmˈplor] tr implorer, supplier, solliciter

im·ply [ɪmˈplaɪ] v (pret & pp -plied) tr impliquer

impolite [ˌɪmpəˈlaɪt] adj impoli

import [ˈɪmpɔrt] s importance f; (meaning) sens m, signification f; (extent) portée f; (com) article m d'importation; imports importations fpl || [ɪmˈpɔrt], [ˈɪmpɔrt] tr importer; (to mean) signifier, vouloir dire

importance [ɪmˈpɔrtəns] s importance f

important [ɪmˈpɔrtənt] adj important

importer [ɪmˈpɔrtər] s importateur m

importune [ˌɪmpɔrˈt(j)un] tr importuner, harceler

impose [ɪmˈpoz] tr imposer || intr—to impose on or upon en imposer à, abuser de

imposing [ɪmˈpozɪŋ] adj imposant

imposition [ˌɪmpəˈzɪʃən] s (laying on of a burden or obligation) imposition f; (rudeness, taking unfair advantage) abus m

impossible [ɪmˈpasɪbəl] adj impossible

impostor [ɪmˈpɑstər] s imposteur m

imposture [ɪmˈpɑstʃər] s imposture f

impotence [ˈɪmpətəns] s impuissance f

impotent [ˈɪmpətənt] adj impuissant

impound [ɪmˈpaʊnd] tr confisquer, saisir; (a dog, an auto, etc.) mettre en fourrière

impoverish [ɪmˈpɑvərɪʃ] tr appauvrir

impracticable [ɪmˈpræktɪkəbəl] adj impraticable, inexécutable

impractical [ɪmˈpræktɪkəl] adj peu pratique; (plan) impraticable

impregnable [ɪmˈpregnəbəl] adj imprenable, inexpugnable

impregnate [ɪmˈpregnet] tr imprégner; (to make pregnant) féconder

impresari·o [ˌɪmprɪˈsɑriˌo] s (pl -os) imprésario m

impress [ɪmˈpres] tr (to have an effect

on the mind or emotions of) impressionner; (to mark by using pressure) imprimer; (on the memory) graver; (mil) enrôler de force; **to impress s.o. with** pénétrer qn de

impression [ɪmˈpreʃən] s impression f

impressive [ɪmˈpresɪv] adj impressionnant

imprint [ˈɪmprɪnt] s empreinte f; (typ) rubrique f, griffe f ‖ [ɪmˈprɪnt] tr imprimer

imprison [ɪmˈprɪzən] tr emprisonner

imprisonment [ɪmˈprɪzənmənt] s emprisonnement m

improbable [ɪmˈprɑbəbəl] adj improbable

impromptu [ɪmˈprɑmpt(j)u] adj & adv impromptu ‖ s (mus) impromptu m

impromp′tu speech′ s improvisation f, discours m improvisé

improper [ɪmˈprɑpər] adj (not the right) impropre; (contrary to good taste or decency) inconvenant

improve [ɪmˈpruv] tr améliorer, perfectionner ‖ intr s'améliorer, se perfectionner

improvement [ɪmˈpruvmənt] s amélioration f, perfectionnement m

improvident [ɪmˈprɑvɪdənt] adj imprévoyant

improvise [ˈɪmprə‚vaɪz] tr & intr improviser

imprudent [ɪmˈprudənt] adj imprudent

impudent [ˈɪmpjədənt] adj impudent, effronté

impugn [ɪmˈpjun] tr contester, mettre en doute

impulse [ˈɪmpʌls] s impulsion f

impulsive [ɪmˈpʌlsɪv] adj impulsif

impunity [ɪmˈpjunɪti] s impunité f

impure [ɪmˈpjʊr] adj impur

impuri‧ty [ɪmˈpjʊrɪti] s (pl -ties) impureté f

impute [ɪmˈpjut] tr imputer

in [ɪn] adv en dedans, à l'intérieur; (at home) à la maison, chez soi; (pol) au pouvoir; **all in** (tired) (coll) éreinté; **in here** ici, par ici; **in there** là-dedans, là ‖ prep dans; en; (inside) en dedans de, à l'intérieur de; (in ratios) sur, e.g., **one in a hundred** un sur cent; **in that** du fait que ‖ s (coll) entrée f, e.g., **to have an in with** avoir ses entrées chez

inability [‚ɪnəˈbɪlɪti] s incapacité f, impuissance f

inaccessible [‚ɪnækˈsesɪbəl] adj inaccessible

inaccura‧cy [ɪnˈækjərəsi] s (pl -cies) inexactitude f, infidélité f

inaccurate [ɪnˈækjərɪt] adj inexact, infidèle

inaction [ɪnˈækʃən] s inaction f

inactive [ɪnˈæktɪv] adj inactif

inactivity [‚ɪnækˈtɪvɪti] s inactivité f

inadequate [ɪnˈædɪkwɪt] adj insuffisant

inadvertent [‚ɪnədˈvɑrtənt] adj distrait, étourdi; commis par inadvertance

inadvisable [‚ɪnədˈvaɪzəbəl] adj imprudent, peu sage

inane [ɪnˈen] adj inepte, absurde

inanimate [ɪnˈænɪmɪt] adj inanimé

inappropriate [‚ɪnəˈproprɪ‧ɪt] adj inapproprié; (word) impropre

inarticulate [‚ɪnɑrˈtɪkjəlɪt] adj inarticulé; (person) muet, incapable de s'exprimer

inartistic [‚ɪnɑrˈtɪstɪk] adj peu artistique; (person) peu artiste

inasmuch as [‚ɪnəzˈmʌtʃ ‚æz] conj attendu que, vu que

inattentive [‚ɪnəˈtentɪv] adj inattentif

inaudible [ɪnˈɔdɪbəl] adj inaudible

inaugural [ɪnˈɔgjərəl] adj inaugural ‖ s discours m d'inauguration

inaugurate [ɪnˈɔgjə‚ret] tr inaugurer

inauguration [ɪn‚ɔgjəˈreʃən] s inauguration f; (investiture) installation f

inborn [ˈɪn‚bɔrn] adj inné, infus

in′breed′ing s croisement m consanguin

Inc. abbr (**Incorporated**) S.A.

incandescent [‚ɪnkənˈdesənt] adj incandescent

incapable [ɪnˈkepəbəl] adj incapable

incapacitate [‚ɪnkəˈpæsɪ‚tet] tr rendre incapable

incarcerate [ɪnˈkɑrsə‚ret] tr incarcérer

incarnate [ɪnˈkɑrnɪt], [ɪnˈkɑrnet] adj incarné ‖ [ɪnˈkɑrnet] tr incarner

incarnation [‚ɪnkɑrˈneʃən] s incarnation f

incendiar‧y [ɪnˈsendɪ‚ɛri] adj incendiaire ‖ s (pl -ies) incendiaire mf

incense [ˈɪnsens] s encens m ‖ tr (to burn incense before) encenser ‖ [ɪnˈsens] tr exaspérer, irriter

in′cense burn′er s brûle-parfum m

incentive [ɪnˈsentɪv] adj & s stimulant m

inception [ɪnˈsepʃən] s début m

incessant [ɪnˈsesənt] adj incessant

incest [ˈɪnsest] s inceste m

incestuous [ɪnˈsestʃʊ‧əs] adj incestueux

inch [ɪntʃ] s pouce m; **by inches** peu à peu, petit à petit; **not to give way an inch** ne pas reculer d'une semelle; **within an inch of** à deux doigts de ‖ intr—**to inch along** se déplacer imperceptiblement; **to inch forward** avancer peu à peu

incidence [ˈɪnsɪdəns] s incidence f; (range of occurrence) portée f

incident [ˈɪnsɪdənt] adj & s incident m

incidental [‚ɪnsɪˈdentəl] adj accidentel, fortuit; (expenses) accessoire ‖ **incidentals** spl faux frais mpl

incidentally [‚ɪnsɪˈdentəli] adv incidemment, à propos

incinerate [ɪnˈsɪnə‚ret] tr incinérer

incipient [ɪnˈsɪpɪənt] adj naissant

incision [ɪnˈsɪʒən] s incision f

incisive [ɪnˈsaɪsɪv] adj incisif

incisor [ɪnˈsaɪzər] s incisive f

incite [ɪnˈsaɪt] tr inciter

inclement [ɪnˈklemənt] adj inclément

inclination [‚ɪnkləˈneʃən] s inclination f; (slope) inclinaison f

incline [ˈɪnklaɪn], [ɪnˈklaɪn] s inclinaison f, pente f ‖ [ɪnˈklaɪn] tr incliner ‖ intr s'incliner

include [ɪnˈklud] tr comprendre, comporter; (to contain) renfermer; (e.g., in a letter) inclure

including [ɪnˈkludɪŋ] prep y compris;

up to and including page ten jusqu'à la page dix incluse

inclusive [ɪnˈklusɪv] *adj* global; *(including everything)* tout compris; **from Wednesday to Saturday inclusive** de mercredi à samedi inclus; **inclusive of . . .** qui comprend . . . ‖ *adv* inclusivement

incogni•to [ɪnˈkɑgnɪˌto] *adj & adv* incognito ‖ *s (pl -tos)* incognito *m*

incoherent [ˌɪnkoˈhɪrənt] *adj* incohérent

incombustible [ˌɪnkəmˈbʌstɪbəl] *adj* incombustible

income [ˈɪnkʌm] *s* revenu *m*, revenus; *(annual income)* rentes *fpl*

in'come tax' *s* impôt *m* sur le revenu

in'come-tax return' *s* déclaration *f* de revenus

in'com'ing *adj* entrant, rentrant; *(tide)* montant ‖ *s* arrivée *f*

incomparable [ɪnˈkɑmpərəbəl] *adj* incomparable

incompatible [ˌɪnkəmˈpætɪbəl] *adj* incompatible

incompetent [ɪnˈkɑmpɪtənt] *adj & s* incompétent *m*, incapable *mf*

incomplete [ˌɪnkəmˈplit] *adj* incomplet

incomprehensible [ˌɪnkɑmprɪˈhensɪbəl] *adj* incompréhensible

inconceivable [ˌɪnkənˈsivəbəl] *adj* inconcevable

inconclusive [ˌɪnkənˈklusɪv] *adj* peu concluant, non concluant

incongruous [ɪnˈkɑŋgru·əs] *adj* incongru, impropre; disparate

inconsequential [ɪnˌkɑnsɪˈkwenʃəl] *adj* sans importance

inconsiderate [ˌɪnkənˈsɪdərɪt] *adj* inconsidéré

inconsisten•cy [ˌɪnkənˈsɪstənsi] *s (pl -cies)* *(lack of coherence; instability)* inconsistance *f*; *(lack of logical connection or uniformity)* inconséquence *f*

inconsistent [ˌɪnkənˈsɪstənt] *adj* *(lacking coherence of parts; unstable)* inconsistant; *(not agreeing with itself or oneself)* inconséquent

inconspicuous [ˌɪnkənˈspɪkju·əs] *adj* peu apparent; peu impressionnant

inconstant [ɪnˈkɑnstənt] *adj* inconstant

incontinent [ɪnˈkɑntɪnənt] *adj* incontinent

incontrovertible [ˌɪnkɑntrəˈvʌrtɪbəl] *adj* incontestable

inconvenience [ˌɪnkənˈvinɪ·əns] *s* incommodité *f* ‖ *tr* incommoder, gêner

inconvenient [ˌɪnkənˈvinɪ·ənt] *adj* incommode, gênant; *(time)* inopportun

incorporate [ɪnˈkɔrpəˌret] *tr* incorporer; *(com)* constituer en société anonyme ‖ *intr* s'incorporer; *(com)* se constituer en société anonyme

incorporation [ɪnˌkɔrpəˈreʃən] *s* incorporation *f*; *(of company)* constitution *f* en société anonyme; *(of town)* érection *f* en municipalité

incorrect [ˌɪnkəˈrekt] *adj* incorrect

increase [ˈɪnkris] *s* augmentation *f*; **on the increase** en voie d'accroissement ‖ [ɪnˈkris] *tr & intr* augmenter

increasingly [ɪnˈkrisɪŋli] *adv* de plus en plus

incredible [ɪnˈkredɪbəl] *adj* incroyable

incredulous [ɪnˈkredʒələs] *adj* incrédule

increment [ˈɪnkrɪmənt] *s* augmentation *f*

incriminate [ɪnˈkrɪmɪˌnet] *tr* incriminer

incrust [ɪnˈkrʌst] *tr* incruster

incubate [ˈɪnkjəˌbet] *tr* incuber, couver ‖ *intr* couver

incubator [ˈɪnkjəˌbetər] *s* incubateur *m*

inculcate [ɪnˈkʌlket], [ˈɪnkʌlˌket] *tr* inculquer

incumben•cy [ɪnˈkʌmbənsi] *s (pl -cies)* charge *f*; période *f* d'exercice

incumbent [ɪnˈkʌmbənt] *adj*—**to be incumbent on** incomber (with *dat*) ‖ *m* titulaire *mf*

incunabula [ˌɪnkjuˈnæbjələ] *spl* origines *fpl*; *(books)* incunables *mpl*

in•cur [ɪnˈkʌr] *v (pret & pp -curred; ger -curring)* *tr* encourir, s'attirer; *(a debt)* contracter

incurable [ɪnˈkjurəbəl] *adj & s* incurable *mf*, inguérissable *mf*

incursion [ɪnˈkʌrʒən], [ɪnˈkʌrʃən] *s* incursion *f*

indebted [ɪnˈdetɪd] *adj* endetté; **indebted to s.o. for** redevable à qn de

indecen•cy [ɪnˈdisənsi] *s (pl -cies)* indécence *f*, impudeur *f*

indecent [ɪnˈdisənt] *adj* indécent, impudique

inde'cent expo'sure *s* attentat *m* à la pudeur

indecisive [ˌɪndɪˈsaɪsɪv] *adj* indécis

indeclinable [ˌɪndɪˈklaɪnəbəl] *adj* *(gram)* indéclinable

indeed [ɪnˈdid] *adv* en effet; *(truly)* en vérité ‖ *interj* vraiment!

indefatigable [ˌɪndɪˈfætɪgəbəl] *adj* infatigable

indefensible [ˌɪndɪˈfensɪbəl] *adj* indéfendable

indefinable [ˌɪndɪˈfaɪnəbəl] *adj* indéfinissable

indefinite [ɪnˈdefɪnɪt] *adj* indéfini

indelible [ɪnˈdelɪbəl] *adj* indélébile

indelicate [ɪnˈdelɪkɪt] *adj* indélicat

indemnification [ɪnˌdemnɪfɪˈkeʃən] *s* indemnisation *f*

indemni•fy [ɪnˈdemnɪˌfaɪ] *v (pret & pp -fied)* *tr* indemniser

indemni•ty [ɪnˈdemnɪti] *s (pl -ties)* indemnité *f*

indent [ɪnˈdent] *tr* denteler; *(to recess)* renfoncer; *(typ)* mettre en alinéa, rentrer ‖ *intr* *(typ)* faire un alinéa

indentation [ˌɪndenˈteʃən] *s* dentelure *f*; *(notch)* entaille *f*; *(recess)* renfoncement *m*; *(typ)* alinéa *m*

indented *adj* *(typ)* en alinéa

indenture [ɪnˈdentʃər] *s* contrat *m* d'apprentissage ‖ *tr* mettre en apprentissage

independence [ˌɪndɪˈpendəns] *s* indépendance *f*

independen•cy [ˌɪndɪˈpendənsi] *s (pl -cies)* indépendance *f*; nation *f* indépendante

independent [ˌɪndɪ'pendənt] *adj & s* indépendant *m*

indescribable [ˌɪndɪ'skraɪbəbəl] *adj* indescriptible, indicible

indestructible [ˌɪndɪ'strʌktɪbəl] *adj* indestructible

index ['ɪndɛks] *s* (*pl* **indexes** or **indices** ['ɪndɪˌsiz]) index *m*; (*of prices*) indice *m*; (*typ*) main *f*; **Index** Index ‖ *tr* répertorier; (*a book*) faire un index à

in'dex card' *s* fiche *f*

in'dex fin'ger *s* index *m*

in'dex tab' *s* onglet *m*

India ['ɪndɪ·ə] *s* Inde *f*; l'Inde

In'dia ink' *s* encre *f* de Chine

Indian ['ɪndɪ·ən] *adj* indien ‖ *s* Indien *m*

In'dian club' *s* mil *m*, massue *f*

In'dian corn' *s* maïs *m*

In'dian file' *s* file *f* indienne ‖ *adv* en file indienne, à la queue leu leu

In'dian O'cean *s* mer *f* des Indes, océan *m* Indien

In'dian sum'mer *s* été *m* de la Saint-Martin

In'dia rub'ber *s* caoutchouc *m*, gomme *f*

indicate ['ɪndɪˌket] *tr* indiquer

indication [ˌɪndɪ'keʃən] *s* indication *f*

indicative [ɪn'dɪkətɪv] *adj & s* indicatif *m*

indicator ['ɪndɪˌketər] *s* indicateur *m*

indict [ɪn'daɪt] *tr* (law) inculper

indictment [ɪn'daɪtmənt] *s* inculpation *f*, mise *f* en accusation

indifferent [ɪn'dɪfərənt] *adj* indifférent; (*poor*) médiocre

indigenous [ɪn'dɪdʒɪnəs] *adj* indigène

indigent ['ɪndɪdʒənt] *adj* indigent

indigestible [ˌɪndɪ'dʒɛstɪbəl] *adj* indigeste

indigestion [ˌɪndɪ'dʒɛstʃən] *s* indigestion *f*

indignant [ɪn'dɪgnənt] *adj* indigné

indignation [ˌɪndɪg'neʃən] *s* indignation *f*

indigni·ty [ɪn'dɪgnɪti] *s* (*pl* -ties) indignité *f*

indi·go ['ɪndɪˌgo] *adj* indigo ‖ *s* (*pl* -gos or -goes) indigo *m*

indirect [ˌɪndɪ'rɛkt], [ˌɪndaɪ'rɛkt] *adj* indirect

in'direct dis'course *s* discours *m* indirect, style *m* indirect

indiscreet [ˌɪndɪs'krit] *adj* indiscret

indispensable [ˌɪndɪs'pɛnsəbəl] *adj* indispensable

indispose [ˌɪndɪs'poz] *tr* indisposer

indisposed *adj* indisposé; (*disinclined*) peu enclin, peu disposé

indissoluble [ˌɪndɪ'saljəbəl] *adj* indissoluble

indistinct [ˌɪndɪ'stɪŋkt] *adj* indistinct

individual [ˌɪndɪ'vɪdʒʊ·əl] *adj* individuel ‖ *s* individu *m*

individuali·ty [ˌɪndɪˌvɪdʒʊ'ælɪti] *s* (*pl* -ties) individualité *f*

indivisible [ˌɪndɪ'vɪzɪbəl] *adj* indivisible

Indochina ['ɪndo'tʃaɪnə] *s* Indochine *f*; l'Indochine

indoctrinate [ɪn'dɑktrɪˌnet] *tr* endoctriner, catéchiser

Indo-European ['ɪndo'jʊrə'pi·ən] *adj* indo-européen ‖ *s* (*language*) indo-européen *m*; (*person*) Indo-Européen *m*

indolent ['ɪndələnt] *adj* indolent

Indonesia [ˌɪndo'niʒə], [ˌɪndo'niʒə] *s* Indonésie *f*; l'Indonésie

Indonesian [ˌɪndo'niʃən], [ˌɪndo'niʒən] *adj* indonésien ‖ *s* (*language*) indonésien *m*; (*person*) Indonésien *m*

indoor [ɪn'dor] *adj* d'intérieur; (*homeloving*) casanier; (*tennis*) couvert; (*swimming pool*) fermé

indoors ['ɪn'dorz] *adv* à l'intérieur

induce [ɪn'd(j)us] *tr* induire; (*to bring about*) provoquer; **to induce s.o. to** porter qn à

induced *adj* provoqué; (elec) induit

inducement [ɪn'd(j)usmənt] *s* encouragement *m*, mobile *m*, invite *f*

induct [ɪn'dʌkt] *tr* installer; (mil) incorporer

inductee [ɪn'dʌkti] *s* appelé *m*

induction [ɪn'dʌkʃən] *s* installation *f*; (elec, logic) induction *f*; (mil) incorporation *f*

induc'tion coil' *s* bobine *f* d'induction

indulge [ɪn'dʌldʒ] *tr* favoriser; (*s.o.'s desires*) donner libre cours à; (*a child*) tout passer à ‖ *intr* (coll) boire; (coll) fumer; **to indulge in** se livrer à

indulgence [ɪn'dʌldʒəns] *s* indulgence *f*; **indulgence in** jouissance de

indulgent [ɪn'dʌldʒənt] *adj* indulgent

industrial [ɪn'dʌstrɪ·əl] *adj* industriel

industrialist [ɪn'dʌstrɪ·əlɪst] *s* industriel *m*

industrialize [ɪn'dʌstrɪ·əˌlaɪz] *tr* industrialiser

industrious [ɪn'dʌstrɪ·əs] *adj* industrieux, appliqué, assidu

indus·try ['ɪndəstri] *s* (*pl* -tries) industrie *f*; (*zeal*) assiduité *f*

inebriation [ɪnˌibrɪ'eʃən] *s* ébriété *f*

inedible [ɪn'ɛdɪbəl] *adj* incomestible

ineffable [ɪn'ɛfəbəl] *adj* ineffable

ineffective [ˌɪnɪ'fɛktɪv] *adj* inefficace; (*person*) incapable

ineffectual [ˌɪnɪ'fɛktʃʊ·əl] *adj* inefficace

inefficient [ˌɪnɪ'fɪʃənt] *adj* inefficace; (*person*) incapable

ineligible [ɪn'ɛlɪdʒɪbəl] *adj* inéligible

inept [ɪn'ɛpt] *adj* inepte

inequali·ty [ˌɪnɪ'kwɑlɪti] *s* (*pl* -ties) inégalité *f*

inequi·ty [ɪn'ɛkwɪti] *s* (*pl* -ties) injustice *f*

inertia [ɪn'ʌrʃə] *s* inertie *f*

inescapable [ˌɪnɛs'kepəbəl] *adj* inéluctable

inevitable [ɪn'ɛvɪtəbəl] *adj* inévitable

inexact [ˌɪnɛg'zækt] *adj* inexact

inexcusable [ˌɪnɛks'kjuzəbəl] *adj* inexcusable

inexhaustible [ˌɪnɛg'zɔstɪbəl] *adj* inexhaustible, inépuisable

inexorable [ɪn'ɛksərəbəl] *adj* inexorable

inexpedient [ˌɪnekˈspidɪˌənt] *adj* inopportun, peu expédient

inexpensive [ˌɪnekˈspensɪv] *adj* pas cher, bon marché

inexperience [ˌɪnekˈspɪriˌəns] *s* inexpérience *f*

inexperienced *adj* inexpérimenté

inexplicable [ɪnˈeksplɪkəbəl] *adj* inexplicable

inexpressible [ˌɪnekˈspresɪbəl] *adj* inexprimable, indicible

infallible [ɪnˈfælɪbəl] *adj* infaillible

infamous [ˈɪnfəməs] *adj* infâme

infa·my [ˈɪnfəmi] *s* (*pl* **-mies**) infamie *f*

infan·cy [ˈɪnfənsi] *s* (*pl* **-cies**) première enfance *f*; (fig) enfance

infant [ˈɪnfənt] *adj* infantile; (*in the earliest stage*) (fig) débutant ‖ *s* nourrisson *m*, bébé *m*; enfant *mf* en bas âge

infantile [ˈɪnfənˌtaɪl], [ˈɪnfəntɪl] *adj* infantile; (*childish*) enfantin

in'fantile paral'ysis *s* paralysie *f* infantile

infan·try [ˈɪnfəntri] *s* (*pl* **-tries**) infanterie *f*

in'fantry·man *s* (*pl* **-men**) militaire *m* de l'infanterie, fantassin *m*

infatuated [ɪnˈfætʃuˌetɪd] *adj* entiché, épris; **infatuated with oneself** infatué; **to be infatuated** s'engouer

infect [ɪnˈfekt] *tr* infecter

infection [ɪnˈfekʃən] *s* infection *f*

infectious [ɪnˈfekʃəs] *adj* infectieux; (*laughter*) communicatif, contagieux

in·fer [ɪnˈfʌr] *v* (*pret* & *pp* **-ferred**; *ger* **-ferring**) *tr* inférer

inferior [ɪnˈfɪriˌər] *adj* & *s* inférieur *m*

inferiority [ɪnˌfɪriˈɑrɪti] *s* infériorité *f*

inferior'ity com'plex *s* complexe *m* d'infériorité

infernal [ɪnˈfʌrnəl] *adj* infernal

infest [ɪnˈfest] *tr* infester

infidel [ˈɪnfɪdəl] *adj* & *s* infidèle *mf*

infideli·ty [ˌɪnfɪˈdelɪti] *s* (*pl* **-ties**) infidélité *f*

in'field' *s* (baseball) petit champ *m*

infiltrate [ɪnˈfɪltret], [ˈɪnfɪlˌtret] *tr* s'infiltrer dans, pénétrer; (*with conspirators*) noyauter ‖ *intr* s'infiltrer

infinite [ˈɪnfɪnɪt] *adj* & *s* infini *m*

infinitely [ˈɪnfɪnɪtli] *adv* infiniment

infinitive [ɪnˈfɪnɪtɪv] *adj* & *s* infinitif *m*

infini·ty [ɪnˈfɪnɪti] *s* (*pl* **-ties**) infinité *f*; (math) infini *m*

infirm [ɪnˈfʌrm] *adj* infirme, maladif

infirma·ry [ɪnˈfʌrməri] *s* (*pl* **-ries**) infirmerie *f*

infirmi·ty [ɪnˈfʌrmɪti] *s* (*pl* **-ties**) infirmité *f*

in'fix *s* infixe *m*

inflame [ɪnˈflem] *tr* enflammer ‖ *intr* s'enflammer

inflammable [ɪnˈflæməbəl] *adj* inflammable

inflammation [ˌɪnfləˈmeʃən] *s* inflammation *f*

inflammatory [ɪnˈflæməˌtori] *adj* incendiaire, provocateur; (pathol) inflammatoire

inflate [ɪnˈflet] *tr* gonfler ‖ *intr* se gonfler

inflation [ɪnˈfleʃən] *s* gonflement *m*; (com) inflation *f*

inflationary [ɪnˈfleʃənˌeri] *adj* inflationniste

inflect [ɪnˈflekt] *tr* infléchir; (*e.g., a noun*) décliner; (*a verb*) conjuguer; (*the voice*) moduler

inflection [ɪnˈflekʃən] *s* inflexion *f*

inflexible [ɪnˈfleksɪbəl] *adj* inflexible

inflict [ɪnˈflɪkt] *tr* infliger

influence [ˈɪnfluˌəns] *s* influence *f* ‖ *tr* influencer, influer sur

in'fluence ped'dling *s* trafic *m* d'influence

influential [ˌɪnfluˈenʃəl] *adj* influent

influenza [ˌɪnfluˈenzə] *s* influenza *f*

in'flux' *s* afflux *m*

inform [ɪnˈfɔrm] *tr* informer, renseigner; **keep me informed** tenez-moi au courant ‖ *intr*—**to inform on** informer contre, dénoncer

informal [ɪnˈfɔrməl] *adj* sans cérémonie; (*person; manners*) familier; (*unofficial*) officieux

infor'mal dance' *s* sauterie *f*

informant [ɪnˈfɔrmənt] *s* informateur *m*; (*in, e.g., language study*) source *f* d'informations

information [ˌɪnfərˈmeʃən] *s* information *f*, renseignement *mpl*; (telp) service *m* des renseignements téléphoniques; **piece of information** information, renseignement

informational [ˌɪnfərˈmeʃənəl] *adj* instructif, documentaire; (comp) informatique

informa'tion bu'reau *s* bureau *m* de renseignements

informative [ɪnˈfɔrmətɪv] *adj* instructif, édifiant

informed' sour'ces *spl* sources *fpl* bien informées

informer [ɪnˈfɔrmər] *s* délateur *m*, dénonciateur *m*; (*police spy*) indicateur *m*, mouchard *m*

infraction [ɪnˈfrækʃən] *s* infraction *f*

infrared [ˌɪnfrəˈred] *adj* & *s* infrarouge *m*

infrequent [ɪnˈfrikwənt] *adj* peu fréquent, rare

infringe [ɪnˈfrɪndʒ] *tr* enfreindre; (*a patent*) contrefaire ‖ *intr*—**to infringe on** empiéter sur, enfreindre

infringement [ɪnˈfrɪndʒmənt] *s* infraction *f*; (*on patent rights*) contrefaçon *f*

infuriate [ɪnˈfjʊriˌet] *tr* rendre furieux

infuse [ɪnˈfjuz] *tr* infuser

infusion [ɪnˈfjuʒən] *s* infusion *f*

ingenious [ɪnˈdʒinjəs] *adj* ingénieux

ingenui·ty [ˌɪndʒɪˈn(j)uˌɪti] *s* (*pl* **-ties**) ingéniosité *f*

ingenuous [ɪnˈdʒenjuˌəs] *adj* ingénu, naïf

ingenuousness [ɪnˈdʒenjuˌəsnɪs] *s* ingénuité *f*, naïveté *f*

ingest [ɪnˈdʒest] *tr* ingérer

ingot [ˈɪngət] *s* lingot *m*

in·grained' *adj* imprégné; (*habit*) invétéré; (*prejudice*) enraciné

ingrate [ˈɪngret] *adj* & *s* ingrat *m*

ingratiate [ɪnˈgreʃɪˌet] *tr*—**to ingratiate oneself (with)** se faire bien voir (de)

ingratiating [ɪnˈgreʃɪˌetɪŋ] *adj* insinuant, persuasif

ingratitude [ɪnˈgrætɪˌt(j)ud] *s* ingratitude *f*

ingredient [ɪnˈgridɪ‧ənt] *s* ingrédient *m*

in′growing nail′ *s* ongle *m* incarné

ingulf [ɪnˈgʌlf] *tr* engouffrer

inhabit [ɪnˈhæbɪt] *tr* habiter

inhabitant [ɪnˈhæbɪtənt] *s* habitant *m*

inhale [ɪnˈhel] *tr* inhaler, aspirer; (*smoke*) avaler ‖ *intr* (*while smoking*) avaler

inherent [ɪnˈhɪrənt] *adj* inhérent

inherit [ɪnˈhɛrɪt] *tr* (*e.g., money*) hériter; (*e.g., money to become the heir or successor of*) hériter de; **to inherit s.th. from s.o.** hériter q.ch. de qn

inheritance [ɪnˈhɛrɪtəns] *s* héritage *m*

inher′itance tax′ *s* droits *mpl* de succession

inheritor [ɪnˈhɛrɪtər] *s* héritier *m*

inhibit [ɪnˈhɪbɪt] *tr* inhiber

inhibition [ˌɪnɪˈbɪʃən] *s* inhibition *f*

inhospitable [ɪnˈhɑspɪtəbəl], [ˌɪnhɑsˈpɪtəbəl] *adj* inhospitalier

inhuman [ɪnˈhjumən] *adj* inhumain

inhumane [ˌɪnhjuˈmen] *adj* inhumain, insensible

inhumani‧ty [ˌɪnhjuˈmænɪti] *s* (*pl* -**ties**) inhumanité *f*

inimical [ɪnˈnɪmɪkəl] *adj* inamical

iniqui‧ty [ɪˈnɪkwɪti] *s* (*pl* -**ties**) iniquité *f*

ini′tial [ɪˈnɪʃəl] *adj* initial ‖ *s* initiale *f*; **initials** parafe *m*, initiales ‖ *v* (*pret* -**tialed** or -**tialled**; *ger* -**tialing** or -**tialling**) *tr* signer de ses initiales, parafer

initiate [ɪˈnɪʃɪˌet] *s* initié *m* ‖ *tr* initier; (*a project*) commencer

initiation [ɪˌnɪʃɪˈeʃən] *s* initiation *f*

initiative [ɪˈnɪʃɪ‧ətɪv], [ɪˈnɪʃətɪv] *s* initiative *f*

inject [ɪnˈdʒɛkt] *tr* injecter; (*a remark or suggestion*) introduire

injection [ɪnˈdʒɛkʃən] *s* injection *f*

injudicious [ˌɪndʒuˈdɪʃəs] *adj* peu judicieux

injunction [ɪnˈdʒʌŋkʃən] *s* injonction *f*; (*law*) mise *f* en demeure

injure [ˈɪndʒər] *tr* (*to harm*) nuire (with *dat*); (*to wound*) blesser; (*to offend*) faire tort à, léser

injurious [ɪnˈdʒʊrɪ‧əs] *adj* nuisible, préjudiciable; (*offensive*) blessant, injurieux

inju‧ry [ˈɪndʒəri] *s* (*pl* -**ries**) blessure *f*, lésion *f*; (*harm*) tort *m*; injure *f*, offense *f*

injustice [ɪnˈdʒʌstɪs] *s* injustice *f*

ink [ɪŋk] *s* encre *f* ‖ *tr* encrer

ink′ blot′ *s* pâté *m*, macule *f*

inkling [ˈɪŋklɪŋ] *s* soupçon *m*, pressentiment *m*

ink′ pad′ *s* tampon *m* encreur

ink′stand′ *s* encrier *m*

ink′well′ *s* encrier *m* de bureau

ink‧y [ˈɪŋki] *adj* (*comp* -**ier**; *super* -**iest**) noir foncé; taché d'encre

inlaid [ˈɪnˌled], [ˌɪnˈled] *adj* incrusté

inland [ˈɪnlənd] *adj & s* intérieur *m* ‖ *adv* à l'intérieur, vers l'intérieur

in′-law′ *s* (*coll*) parent *m* par alliance; **the in-laws** (*coll*) la belle-famille, les beaux-parents *mpl*

in‧lay [ˈɪnˌle] *s* incrustation *f* ‖ [ɪnˈle], [ˈɪnˌle] *v* (*pret & pp* -**laid**) *tr* incruster

in′let *s* bras *m* de mer, crique *f*; (*e.g., of air*) arrivée *f*

in′mate *s* habitant *m*; (*of an institution*) pensionnaire *mf*

inn [ɪn] *s* auberge *f*

innate [ɪˈnet], [ˈɪnet] *adj* inné, infus

inner [ˈɪnər] *adj* intérieur; (*e.g., ear*) interne; intime, secret

in′ner‧spring mat′tress *s* sommier *m* à ressorts internes

in′ner tube′ *s* chambre *f* à air

inning [ˈɪnɪŋ] *s* manche *f*, tour *m*

inn′keep′er *s* aubergiste *mf*

innocence [ˈɪnəsəns] *s* innocence *f*

innocent [ˈɪnəsənt] *adj & s* innocent *m*

innocuous [ɪˈnɑkjʊ‧əs] *adj* inoffensif

innovate [ˈɪnəˌvet] *tr & intr* innover

innovation [ˌɪnəˈveʃən] *s* innovation *f*

innuen‧do [ˌɪnjuˈendo] *s* (*pl* -**does**) allusion *f*, sous-entendu *m*

innumerable [ɪˈn(j)umərəbəl] *adj* innombrable

inoculate [ɪnˈɑkjəˌlet] *tr* inoculer

inoculation [ɪnˌɑkjəˈleʃən] *s* inoculation *f*

inoffensive [ˌɪnəˈfɛnsɪv] *adj* inoffensif

inopportune [ɪnˌɑpərˈt(j)un] *adj* inopportun, mal choisi

inordinate [ɪnˈɔrdɪnɪt] *adj* désordonné, déréglé; (*unrestrained*) démesuré

inorganic [ˌɪnɔrˈgænɪk] *adj* inorganique

in′put′ *s* consommation *f*; (elec) prise *f*, entrée *f*

inquest [ˈɪnkwɛst] *s* enquête *f*

inquire [ɪnˈkwaɪr] *tr* s'informer de, e.g., **to inquire the price of** s'informer du prix de ‖ *intr* s'enquérir; **to inquire about** s'enquérir de, se renseigner sur; **to inquire into** faire des recherches sur

inquir‧y [ɪnˈkwaɪri], [ˈɪnkwɪri] *s* (*pl* -**ies**) investigation *f*, enquête *f*; (*question*) demande *f*; **to make inquiries** s'informer

inquisition [ˌɪnkwɪˈzɪʃən] *s* inquisition *f*

inquisitive [ɪnˈkwɪzɪtɪv] *adj* curieux, questionneur

in′road′ *s* incursion *f*, empiètement *m*

ins′ and outs′ *spl* tours et détours *mpl*

insane [ɪnˈsen] *adj* dément, fou; (*unreasonable*) insensé, insane

insane′ asy′lum *s* asile *m* d'aliénés

insani‧ty [ɪnˈsænɪti] *s* (*pl* -**ties**) démence *f*, aliénation *f*

insatiable [ɪnˈseʃəbəl] *adj* insatiable

inscribe [ɪnˈskraɪb] *tr* inscrire; (*a book*) dédier

inscription [ɪnˈskrɪpʃən] *s* inscription *f*; (*of a book*) dédicace *f* inscrutable [ɪn'skrutəbəl] adj impénétrable, fermé

insect ['ɪnsekt] s insecte m

insecticide [ɪn'sektɪ,saɪd] adj & s insecticide m

insecure [,ɪnsɪ'kjʊr] adj peu sûr; (nervous) inquiet

insensitive [ɪn'sensɪtɪv] adj insensible

inseparable [ɪn'sepərəbəl] adj inséparable

insert ['ɪnsʌrt] s (sewing) incrustation f; (typ) hors-texte m, encart m || [ɪn-'sʌrt] tr insérer, introduire; (typ) encarter

insertion [ɪn'sʌrʃən] s insertion f; (sewing) incrustation f

in•set ['ɪn,set] s (map, picture, etc.) médaillon m; (sewing) incrustation f; (typ) hors-texte m, encart m || [ɪn'set], ['ɪn,set] v (pret & pp -set; ger -setting) tr insérer; (a page or pages) encarter

in'shore' adj côtier || adv près de la côte

in'side' adj d'intérieur, interne; secret || s intérieur m, dedans m; insides (coll) entrailles fpl || adv à l'intérieur; inside and out au-dedans et au-dehors; inside of à l'intérieur de; inside out à l'envers; to turn inside out (e.g., a coat) retourner || prep à l'intérieur de, dans

in'side infor'mation s tuyau m, tuyaux

insider [ɪn'saɪdər] s initié m

in'side track' s—to have the inside track prendre à la corde; (fig) avoir un avantage

insidious [ɪn'sɪdɪ·əs] adj insidieux

in'sight' s pénétration f; (psychol) défoulement m

insignia [ɪn'sɪgnɪ·ə] s (pl -a or -as) insigne m

insignificant [,ɪnsɪg'nɪfɪkənt] adj insignifiant

insincere [,ɪnsɪn'sɪr] adj insincère, peu sincère

insinuate [ɪn'sɪnju,et] tr insinuer

insipid [ɪn'sɪpɪd] adj insipide

insist [ɪn'sɪst] intr insister; to insist on insister sur; to insist on + ger insister pour + inf

insofar as [,ɪnso'farəz] conj pour autant que, dans la mesure où

insolence ['ɪnsələns] s insolence f

insolent ['ɪnsələnt] adj insolent

insoluble [ɪn'saljəbəl] adj insoluble

insolven•cy [ɪn'salvənsi] s (pl -cies) insolvabilité f

insolvent [ɪn'salvənt] adj insolvable

insomnia [ɪn'samnɪ·ə] s insomnie f

insomuch [,ɪnso'mʌtʃ] adv—insomuch as vu que; insomuch that à tel point que

inspect [ɪn'spekt] tr inspecter

inspection [ɪn'spekʃən] s inspection f

inspector [ɪn'spektər] s inspecteur m

inspiration [,ɪnspɪ'reʃən] s inspiration f

inspire [ɪn'spaɪr] tr inspirer

inspiring [ɪn'spaɪrɪŋ] adj inspirant

install [ɪn'stɔl] tr installer

installment [ɪn'stɔlmənt] s installation f; (delivery) livraison f; (serial story) feuilleton m; (partial payment) acompte m, versement m; in installments par acomptes, par tranches

install'ment plan' s vente f à tempérament or à crédit; on the installment plan avec facilités de paiement

instance ['ɪnstəns] s cas m, exemple m; for instance par exemple

instant ['ɪnstənt] adj imminent, immédiat; on the fifth instant le cinq courant || s instant m, moment m

instantaneous [,ɪnstən'tenɪ·əs] adj instantané

instantly ['ɪnstəntli] adv à l'instant

instead [ɪn'sted] adv plutôt, au contraire; à ma (votre, sa, etc.) place; instead of au lieu de

in'step' s cou-de-pied m

instigate ['ɪnstɪ,get] tr inciter

instigation [,ɪnstɪ'geʃən] s instigation f

instill [ɪn'stɪl] tr instiller

instinct ['ɪnstɪŋkt] s instinct m

instinctive [ɪn'stɪŋktɪv] adj instinctif

institute ['ɪnstɪ,t(j)ut] s institut m || tr instituer

institution [,ɪnstɪ't(j)uʃən] s institution f

instruct [ɪn'strʌkt] tr instruire

instruction [ɪn'strʌkʃən] s instruction f

instructive [ɪn'strʌktɪv] adj instructif

instructor [ɪn'strʌktər] s instructeur m

instrument ['ɪnstrəmənt] s instrument m || ['ɪnstrə,ment] tr instrumenter

instrumental [,ɪnstrə'mentəl] adj instrumental; to be instrumental in contribuer à

instrumentalist [,ɪnstrə'mentəlɪst] s instrumentiste mf

instrumentali•ty [,ɪnstrəmən'tælɪti] s (pl -ties) intermédiaire m, intervention f

in'strument board' s tableau m de bord

in'strument fly'ing s radio-navigation f, vol m aux instruments

in'strument land'ing s atterrissage m aux instruments

in'strument pan'el s tableau m de bord

insubordinate [,ɪnsə'bɔrdɪnɪt] adj insubordonné

insufferable [ɪn'sʌfərəbəl] adj insupportable, intolérable

insufficient [,ɪnsə'fɪʃənt] adj insuffisant

insular ['ɪnsələr], ['ɪnsjʊlər] adj insulaire

insulate ['ɪnsə,let] tr insoler

in'sulating tape' s ruban m isolant, chatterton m

insulation [,ɪnsə'leʃən] s isolation f

insulator ['ɪnsə,letər] s isolant m

insulin ['ɪnsəlɪn] s insuline f

insult ['ɪnsʌlt] s insulte f || [ɪn'sʌlt] tr insulter

insulting [ɪn'sʌltɪŋ] adj insultant, injurieux

insurance [ɪn'ʃʊrəns] s assurance f

insure [ɪn'ʃʊr] tr assurer

insurer [ɪn'ʃʊrər] s assureur m

insurgent [ɪn'sʌrdʒənt] adj & s insurgé m

insurmountable [ˌɪnsər'maʊntəbəl] *adj* insurmontable

insurrection [ˌɪnsə'rek/ən] *s* insurrection *f*

intact [ɪn'tækt] *adj* intact

in'take' *s* (*place*) entrée *f*; (*act or amount*) prise *f*; (*mach*) admission *f*

in'take man'ifold *s* tubulure *f* d'admission, collecteur *m* d'admission

in'take valve' *s* soupape *f* d'admission

intangible [ɪn'tændʒɪbəl] *adj* intangible

integer ['ɪntɪdʒər] *s* nombre *m* entier

integral ['ɪntɪgrəl] *adj* intégral; (*part*) intégrant; **integral with** solidaire de ǁ *s* intégrale *f*

integrate ['ɪntɪ,gret] *tr* intégrer

integration [ˌɪntɪ'gre/ən] *s* intégration *f*

integrity [ɪn'tegrɪti] *s* intégrité *f*

intellect ['ɪntə,lekt] *s* intellect *m*; (*person*) intelligence *f*

intellectual [ˌɪntə'lekt/ʊ·əl] *adj & s* intellectuel *m*

intelligence [ɪn'telɪdʒəns] *s* intelligence *f*

intel'ligence bu'reau *s* deuxième bureau *m*, service *m* de renseignements

intel'ligence quo'tient *s* quotient *m* intellectuel

intel'ligence test' *s* test *m* d'habileté mentale

intelligent [ɪn'telɪdʒənt] *adj* intelligent

intelligible [ɪn'telɪdʒɪbəl] *adj* intelligible

intemperate [ɪn'tempərɪt] *adj* intempérant

intend [ɪn'tend] *tr* destiner; signifier, vouloir dire; **to intend to** avoir l'intention de, penser; **to intend to become** se destiner à

intended *adj & s* (coll) futur *m*

intense [ɪn'tens] *adj* intense

intensi·fy [ɪn'tensɪ,faɪ] *v* (*pret & pp* -fied) *tr* intensifier ǁ *intr* s'intensifier

intensi·ty [ɪn'tensɪti] *s* (*pl* -ties) intensité *f*

intensive [ɪn'tensɪv] *adj* intensif

intent [ɪn'tent] *adj* attentif; (*look, gaze*) fixe, intense; **intent on** résolu à ǁ *s* intention *f*; **to all intents and purposes** en fait, pratiquement

intention [ɪn'ten/ən] *s* intention *f*

intentional [ɪn'ten/ənəl] *adj* intentionnel, délibéré

intentionally [ɪn'ten/ənəli] *adv* exprès, à dessein

in·ter [ɪn'tʌr] *v* (*pret & pp* -terred; *ger* -terring) *tr* enterrer

interact [ˌɪntər'ækt] *intr* agir réciproquement

interaction [ˌɪntər'æk/ən] *s* interaction *f*

inter·breed [ˌɪntər'brid] *v* (*pret & pp* -bred) *tr* croiser ǁ *intr* se croiser

intercalate [ɪn'tʌrkə,let] *tr* intercaler

intercede [ˌɪntər'sid] *intr* intercéder

intercept [ˌɪntər'sept] *tr* intercepter

interceptor [ˌɪntər'septər] *s* intercepteur *m*

interchange ['ɪntər,t/endʒ] *s* échange *m*, permutation *f*; (*transfer point*) correspondance *f*; (*on highway*)

échangeur *m* ǁ [ˌɪntər't/endʒ] *tr* échanger, permuter ǁ *intr* permuter

intercollegiate [ˌɪntərkə'lidʒɪ·ɪt] *adj* interuniversitaire, entre universités

intercom ['ɪntər,kɑm] *s* (coll) interphone *m*

intercourse ['ɪntər,kors] *s* relations *fpl*, rapports *mpl*; (*copulation*) copulation *f*, coït *m*

intercross ['ɪntər,krɑs], [ˌɪntər'krɑs] *tr* entrecroiser ǁ *intr* s'entrecroiser

interdict ['ɪntər,dɪkt] *s* interdit *m* ǁ [ˌɪntər'dɪkt] *tr* interdire; **to interdict s.o. from** + *ger* interdire à qn de + *inf*

interest ['ɪntərɪst], ['ɪntrɪst] *s* intérêt *m*; **the interests** les gens influents; **to pay back with interest** rendre avec usure ǁ ['ɪntərɪst], ['ɪntrɪst], ['ɪntə,rest] *tr* intéresser

interested *adj* intéressé; **to be interested in** s'intéresser à or dans

interesting ['ɪntrɪstɪŋ], ['ɪntə,restɪŋ] *adj* intéressant

interfere [ˌɪntər'fɪr] *intr* (*to meddle*) s'ingérer; (*phys*) interférer; **to interfere with** intervenir dans, se mêler de; (*to come into opposition with*) gêner, entraver; **to interfere with each other** interférer (entre eux)

interference [ˌɪntər'fɪrəns] *s* interférence *f*, intervention *f*; (*phys*) interférence; (*jamming*) (rad) brouillage *m*

interim ['ɪntərɪm] *adj* provisoire, par intérim ǁ *s* intérim *m*

interior [ɪn'tɪrɪ·ər] *adj & s* intérieur *m*

inte'rior dec'orator *s* décorateur *m* d'intérieurs

interject [ˌɪntər'dʒekt] *tr* interposer; (*questions*) lancer

interjection [ˌɪntər'dʒek/ən] *s* intervention *f*; (gram) interjection *f*

interlard [ˌɪntər'lɑrd] *tr* entrelarder

interline [ˌɪntər'laɪn] *tr* interligner

interlining ['ɪntər,laɪnɪŋ] *s* doublure *f* intermédiaire

interlock [ˌɪntər'lɑk] *tr* emboîter, engager ǁ *intr* s'emboîter, s'engager

interloper [ˌɪntər'lopər] *s* intrus *m*

interlude ['ɪntər,lud] *s* (mov, mus, telv) interlude *m*; (theat, fig) intermède *m*

intermediar·y [ˌɪntər'midɪ,ɛri] *adj* intermédiaire ǁ *s* (*pl* -ies) intermédiaire *mf*

intermediate [ˌɪntər'midɪ·ɪt] *adj* intermédiaire

interment [ɪn'tʌrmənt] *s* enterrement *m*, sépulture *f*

interminable [ɪn'tʌrmɪnəbəl] *adj* interminable

intermingle [ˌɪntər'mɪŋgəl] *tr* entremêler ǁ *intr* s'entremêler

intermission [ˌɪntər'mɪ/ən] *s* relâche *m*, pause *f*; (theat) entracte *m*

intermittent [ˌɪntər'mɪtənt] *adj* intermittent

intermix [ˌɪntər'mɪks] *tr* entremêler ǁ *intr* s'entremêler

intern ['ɪntʌrn] *s* interne *mf* ǁ [ɪn'tʌrn] *tr* interner

internal [ɪn'tʌrnəl] *adj* interne
inter'nal-combus'tion en'gine *s* moteur *m* à explosion
inter'nal rev'enue *s* recettes *fpl* fiscales
international [,ɪntər'næʃənəl] *adj* international; (*exposition*) universel
in'terna'tional date' line' *s* ligne *f* de changement de date
in'terna'tional time' zone' *s* fuseau *m* horaire international
internecine [,ɪntər'nisin] *adj* domestique, intestin; (*war*) sanguinaire, d'extermination
intersee [,ɪntʌr'ni] *s* interné *m*
internment [ɪn'tʌrnmənt] *s* internement *m*
in'tern·ship' *s* internat *m*
interpellate [,ɪntər'pelet], [ɪn'tʌrpɪ,let] *tr* interpeller
interplanetary [,ɪntər'plænə,teri] *adj* interplanétaire
interplan'etary trav'el *s* voyages *mpl* interplanétaires
interplay ['ɪntər,ple] *s* interaction *f*
interpolate [ɪn'tʌrpə,let] *tr* interpoler
interpose [,ɪntər'poz] *tr* interposer
interpret [ɪn'tʌrprɪt] *tr* interpréter
interpretation [ɪn,tʌrprɪ'teʃən] *s* interprétation *f*
interpreter [ɪn'tʌrprɪtər] *s* interprète *mf*
interrogate [ɪn'terə,get] *tr* interroger
interrogation [ɪn,terə'geʃən] *s* interrogation *f*
interroga'tion mark' *s* point *m* d'interrogation
interrupt [,ɪntə'rʌpt] *tr* interrompre
interruption [,ɪntə'rʌpʃən] *s* interruption *f*
intersect [,ɪntər'sekt] *tr* entrecouper || *intr* s'entrecouper
intersection [,ɪntər'sekʃən] *s* intersection *f*
intersperse [,ɪntər'spʌrs] *tr* entremêler
interstellar [,ɪntər'stelər] *adj* interstellaire
interstice [ɪn'tʌrstɪs] *s* interstice *m*
intertwine [,ɪntər'twaɪn] *tr* entrelacer || *intr* s'entrelacer
interval ['ɪntərvəl] *s* intervalle *m*
intervene [,ɪntər'vin] *intr* intervenir
intervening [,ɪntər'vinɪŋ] *adj* (*period*) intermédiaire; (*party*) intervenant
intervention [,ɪntər'venʃən] *s* intervention *f*
interview ['ɪntər,vju] *s* entrevue *f*; (*journ*) interview *f* || *tr* avoir une entrevue avec; (*journ*) interviewer
inter·weave [,ɪntər'wiv] *v* (*pret* -wove or -weaved; *pp* -wove, woven or weaved) *tr* entrelacer; (*to intermingle*) entremêler
intestate [ɪn'testet], [ɪn'testɪt] *adj & s* intestat *m*
intestine [ɪn'testɪn] *adj & s* intestin *m*
intima·cy ['ɪntɪməsi] *s* (*pl* -cies) intimité *f*; rapports *mpl* sexuels
intimate ['ɪntɪmɪt] *adj & s* intime *mf* || ['ɪntɪ,met] *tr* donner à entendre
intimation [,ɪntɪ'meʃən] *s* suggestion *f*, insinuation *f*
intimidate [ɪn'tɪmɪ,det] *tr* intimider

into ['ɪntu], ['ɪntu] *prep* dans, en
intolerant [ɪn'talərənt] *adj* intolérant
intonation [,ɪnto'neʃən] *s* intonation *f*
intone [ɪn'ton] *tr* (*to begin to sing*) entonner; (*to sing or recite in a monotone*) psalmodier || *intr* psalmodier
intoxicant [ɪn'taksɪkənt] *s* boisson *f* alcoolique
intoxicate [ɪn'taksɪ,ket] *tr* enivrer; (*to poison*) intoxiquer
intoxication [ɪn,taksɪ'keʃən] *s* ivresse *f*; (*poisoning*) intoxication *f*; (*fig*) enivrement *m*
intractable [ɪn'træktəbəl] *adj* intraitable
intransigent [ɪn'trænsɪdʒənt] *adj* intransigeant
intransitive [ɪn'trænsɪtɪv] *adj* intransitif
intravenous [,ɪntrə'vinəs] *adj* intraveineux
intrepid [ɪn'trepɪd] *adj* intrépide
intricate ['ɪntrɪkɪt] *adj* compliqué
intrigue [ɪn'trig], ['ɪntrig] *s* intrigue *f* || [ɪn'trig] *tr & intr* intriguer
intrinsic(al) [ɪn'trɪnsɪk(əl)] *adj* intrinsèque
introduce [,ɪntrə'd(j)us] *tr* introduire; (*to make acquainted*) présenter
introduction [,ɪntrə'dʌkʃən] *s* introduction *f*; (*of one person to another or others*) présentation *f*
introductory [,ɪntrə'dʌktəri] *adj* préliminaire; (*text*) liminaire; (*speech, letter, etc.*) de présentation
introduc'tory of'fer *s* offre *f* de présentation
introspective [,ɪntrə'spektɪv] *adj* introspectif; (*person*) méditatif
introvert ['ɪntrə,vʌrt] *adj & s* introverti *m*
intrude [ɪn'trud] *intr* s'ingérer, s'immiscer; **to intrude on s.o.** déranger qn
intruder [ɪn'trudər] *s* intrus *m*
intrusion [ɪn'truʒən] *s* intrusion *f*
intrusive [ɪn'trusɪv] *adj* importun
intuition [,ɪnt(j)u'ɪʃən] *s* intuition *f*
inundate ['ɪnən,det] *tr* inonder
inundation [,ɪnən'deʃən] *s* inondation *f*
inure [ɪn'jur] *tr* aguerrir, endurcir || *intr* entrer en vigueur; **to inure to** rejaillir sur
invade [ɪn'ved] *tr* envahir
invader [ɪn'vedər] *s* envahisseur *m*
invalid [ɪn'vælɪd] *adj* invalide, nul || ['ɪnvəlɪd] *adj & s* malade *mf*, invalide *mf*
invalidate [ɪn'vælɪ,det] *tr* invalider
invalidity [,ɪnvə'lɪdɪti] *s* invalidité *f*
invaluable [ɪn'vælju·əbəl] *adj* inappréciable, inestimable
invariable [ɪn'verɪ·əbəl] *adj* invariable
invasion [ɪn'veʒən] *s* invasion *f*
invective [ɪn'vektɪv] *s* invective *f*
inveigh [ɪn'veɪ] *intr*—**to inveigh against** invectiver contre
inveigle [ɪn'vegəl], [ɪn'vigəl] *tr* séduire, enjôler; **to inveigle s.o. into + ger** entraîner qn à *+ inf*
invent [ɪn'vent] *tr* inventer
invention [ɪn'venʃən] *s* invention *f*

inventive [ɪn'vɛntɪv] *adj* inventif
inventiveness [ɪn'vɛntɪvnɪs] *s* esprit *m* inventif
inventor [ɪn'vɛntər] *s* inventeur *m*
invento•ry ['ɪnvən,tori] *s* (*pl* -ries) inventaire *m* || *v* (*pret* & *pp* -ried) *tr* inventorier
inverse [ɪn'vʌrs] *adj* & *s* inverse *m*
inversion [ɪn'vʌrʒən], [ɪn'vʌrʃən] *s* interversion *f*, inversion *f*
invert [ɪn'vʌrt] *adj* & *s* inverti *m* || [ɪn'vʌrt] *tr* inverser; (*an image*) invertir
inver•tebrate [ɪn'vʌrtɪ,bret], [ɪn'vʌrtɪbrɪt] *adj* & *s* invertébré *m*
invest [ɪn'vɛst] *tr* investir; (*money*) investir, placer; **to invest with** investir de || *intr* investir or placer de l'argent
investigate [ɪn'vɛstɪ,get] *tr* examiner, rechercher
investigation [ɪn,vɛstɪ'geʃən] *s* investigation *f*
investigator [ɪn'vɛstɪ,getər] *s* investigateur *m*, chercheur *m*
investment [ɪn'vɛstmənt] *s* investissement *m*, placement *m*; (*with an office or dignity*) investiture *f*; (*siege*) investissement
investor [ɪn'vɛstər] *s* capitaliste *mf*
inveterate [ɪn'vɛtərɪt] *adj* invétéré
invidious [ɪn'vɪdɪ·əs] *adj* odieux
invigorate [ɪn'vɪgə,ret] *tr* vivifier, fortifier
invigorating [ɪn'vɪgə,retɪŋ] *adj* vivifiant, fortifiant
invincible [ɪn'vɪnsɪbəl] *adj* invincible
invisible [ɪn'vɪzɪbəl] *adj* invisible
invis'ible ink' *s* encre *f* sympathique
invitation [,ɪnvɪ'teʃən] *s* invitation *f*
invite [ɪn'vaɪt] *tr* inviter
inviting [ɪn'vaɪtɪŋ] *adj* invitant
invoice ['ɪnvɔɪs] *s* facture *f*; **as per invoice** suivant facture || *tr* facturer
invoke [ɪn'vok] *tr* invoquer
involuntary [ɪn'vɑlən,tɛri] *adj* involontaire
involve [ɪn'vɑlv] *tr* impliquer, entraîner, engager
invulnerable [ɪn'vʌlnərəbəl] *adj* invulnérable
inward ['ɪnwərd] *adj* intérieur || *adv* intérieurement, en dedans
Iodide ['aɪ·ə,daɪd] *s* iodure *m*
iodine ['aɪ·ə,din] *s* (chem) iode *m* || ['aɪ·ə,daɪn] *s* (pharm) teinture *f* d'iode
ion ['aɪ·ən], ['aɪ·ɑn] *s* ion *m*
ionize ['aɪ·ə,naɪz] *tr* ioniser
I.O.U. ['aɪ,o'ju] *s* (letterword) (**I owe you**) reconnaissance *f* de dette
I.Q. ['aɪ'kju] *s* (letterword) (**intelligence quotient**) quotient *m* intellectuel
Iran [ɪ'rɑn], [aɪ'ræn] *s* l'Iran *m*
Iranian [aɪ'reni·ən] *adj* iranien || *s* (*language*) iranien *m*; (*person*) Iranien *m*
Iraq [ɪ'rɑk] *s* l'Irak *m*
Ira•qi [ɪ'rɑki] *adj* irakien || *s* (*pl* -qis) Irakien *m*
irate ['aɪret], [aɪ'ret] *adj* irrité
ire [aɪr] *s* courroux *m*, colère *f*

Ireland ['aɪrlənd] *s* Irlande *f*; l'Irlande *f*
iris ['aɪrɪs] *s* iris *m*
Irish ['aɪrɪʃ] *adj* irlandais || *s* (*language*) irlandais *m*; **the Irish** les Irlandais
I'rish•man *s* (*pl* -men) Irlandais *m*
I'rish stew' *s* ragoût *m* irlandais
I'rish•wom'an *s* (*pl* -wom'en) Irlandaise *f*
irk [ʌrk] *tr* ennuyer, fâcher
irksome ['ʌrksəm] *adj* ennuyeux
iron ['aɪ·ərn] *s* fer *m*; (*for pressing clothes*) fer à repasser; **irons** (*fetters*) fers; **to have too many irons in the fire** courir deux lièvres à la fois; **to strike while the iron is hot** battre le fer tant qu'il est chaud || *tr* (*clothes*) repasser; **to iron out** (*a difficulty*) aplanir
i'ron and steel' in'dustry *s* sidérurgie *f*
i'ron-bound' *adj* cerclé; (*unyielding*) inflexible; (*rock-bound*) plein de récifs
ironclad ['aɪ·ərn,klæd] *adj* blindé, cuirassé; (*e.g., contract*) infrangible
i'ron cur'tain *s* rideau *m* de fer
i'ron diges'tion *s* estomac *m* d'autruche
i'ron horse' *s* coursier *m* de fer
ironic(al) [aɪ'rɑnɪk(əl)] *adj* ironique
ironing ['aɪ·ərnɪŋ] *s* repassage *m*
i'roning board' *s* planche *f* à repasser
i'ron lung' *s* poumon *m* d'acier
i'ron ore' *s* minerai *m* de fer
i'ron•ware' *s* quincaillerie *f*, ferblanterie *f*
i'ron will' *s* volonté *f* inflexible
i'ron•work' *s* ferrure *f*, ferronnerie *f*
i'ron•work'er *s* ferronnier *m*
iro•ny ['aɪrəni] *s* (*pl* -nies) ironie *f*
irradiate [ɪ'redɪ,et] *tr* & *intr* irradier
irrational [ɪ'ræʃənəl] *adj* irrationnel
irredeemable [,ɪrɪ'dimabəl] *adj* irrémédiable; (*bonds*) non remboursable
irrefutable [,ɪrɪ'fjutəbəl], [ɪ'rɛfjutəbəl] *adj* irréfutable
irregular [ɪ'rɛgjələr] *adj* & *s* irrégulier *m*
irrelevant [ɪ'rɛləvənt] *adj* non pertinent, hors de propos
irreligious [,ɪrɪ'lɪdʒəs] *adj* irréligieux
irremediable [,ɪrɪ'midɪ·əbəl] *adj* irrémédiable
irreparable [ɪ'rɛpərəbəl] *adj* irréparable
irreplaceable [,ɪrɪ'plesəbəl] *adj* irremplaçable
irrepressible [,ɪrɪ'prɛsɪbəl] *adj* irrépressible, irrésistible
irreproachable [,ɪrɪ'protʃəbəl] *adj* irréprochable
irresistible [,ɪrɪ'zɪstɪbəl] *adj* irrésistible
irrespective [,ɪrɪ'spɛktɪv] *adj*—**irrespective of** indépendant de
irresponsible [,ɪrɪ'spɑnsɪbəl] *adj* irresponsable
irretrievable [,ɪrɪ'trivəbəl] *adj* irréparable; (*lost*) irrécupérable
irreverent [ɪ'rɛvərənt] *adj* irrévérencieux
irrevocable [ɪ'rɛvəkəbəl] *adj* irrévocable
irrigate ['ɪrɪ,get] *tr* irriguer

irrigation [ˌɪrɪˈgeʃən] s irrigation f
irritant [ˈɪrɪtənt] adj & s irritant m
irritate [ˈɪrɪˌtet] tr irriter
irritation [ˌɪrɪˈteʃən] s irritation f
irruption [ɪˈrʌpʃən] s irruption f
Isaiah [aɪˈzeˌə] s Isaïe m
isinglass [ˈaɪzɪŋˌglæs], [ˈaɪzɪŋˌglɑs]
　s gélatine f, colle f de poisson; (min-
　eral) mica m
Islam [ˈɪsləm], [ɪsˈlɑm] s l'Islam m
island [ˈaɪlənd] adj insulaire || s île f
islander [ˈaɪləndər] s insulaire mf
isle [aɪl] s îlot m; (poetic) île f
isolate [ˈaɪsəˌlet], [ˈaɪsəˌlet] tr isoler
isolation [ˌaɪsəˈleʃən], [ˌɪsəˈleʃən] s
　isolement m
isolationist [ˌaɪsəˈleʃənɪst], [ˌɪsəˈle-
　ʃənɪst] adj & s isolationniste mf
isosceles [aɪˈsɑsəˌliz] adj isocèle
isotope [ˈaɪsəˌtop] s isotope m
Israel [ˈɪzrɪˌəl] s Israël m
Israe·li [ɪzˈreli] adj israélien || s (pl
　-lis [liz]) Israélien m
Israelite [ˈɪzrɪˌə, laɪt] adj israélite || s
　Israélite mf
issuance [ˈɪʃu·əns] s émission f
issue [ˈɪʃu] s (way out) sortie f, issue
　f; (outcome) issue; (of a magazine)
　numéro m; (offspring) descendance
　f; (of banknotes, stamps, etc.) émis-
　sion f; (under discussion) point m à
　discuter; (pathol) écoulement m; at
　issue en jeu, en litige; to take issue
　with être en désaccord avec; with-
　out issue sans enfants || tr (a book,
　a magazine) publier; (banknotes,
　stamps, etc.) émettre; (a summons)
　lancer; (an order) donner; (a procla-

mation) faire; (a verdict) rendre ||
　intr sortir, déboucher
isthmus [ˈɪsməs] s isthme m
it [ɪt] pron pers ce §82B, §85; lui §85;
　il §87; le §87; y §87; en §87
Italian [ɪˈtæljən] adj italien || s (lan-
　guage) italien m; (person) Italien m
italic [ɪˈtælɪk] adj (typ) italique; Italic
　italique || italics spl italique m
italicize [ɪˈtælɪˌsaɪz] tr mettre en itali-
　que
Italy [ˈɪtəli] s Italie f; l'Italie
itch [ɪtʃ] s démangeaison f; (pathol)
　gale f || tr démanger (with dat) || intr
　(said of part of body) démanger;
　(said of person) avoir une déman-
　geaison; to itch to (fig) avoir une
　démangeaison de
itch·y [ˈɪtʃi] adj (comp -ier; super
　-iest) piquant; (pathol) galeux
item [ˈaɪtəm] s article m; (in a list)
　point m; (piece of news) nouvelle f
itemize [ˈaɪtəˌmaɪz] tr spécifier, énu-
　mérer
itinerant [aɪˈtɪnərənt], [ɪˈtɪnərənt] adj
　& s itinérant m
itinerar·y [aɪˈtɪnəˌreri], [ɪˈtɪnəˌreri]
　adj itinéraire || s (pl -ies) itinéraire m
its [ɪts] adj poss son §88 || pron poss
　le sien §89
it·self' pron pers soi §85; lui-même §86;
　se §87
ivied [ˈaɪvɪd] adj couvert de lierre
ivo·ry [ˈaɪvəri] adj d'ivoire, en ivoire ||
　s (pl -ries) ivoire m; to tickle the
　ivories (slang) taquiner l'ivoire
i'vory tow'er s (fig) tour f d'ivoire
ivy [ˈaɪvi] s (pl ivies) lierre m

J

J, j [dʒe] s Xᵉ lettre de l'alphabet
jab [dʒæb] s (with a sharp point; with
　a penknife; with the elbow) coup m;
　(with a needle) piqûre f; (with the
　fist) coup sec || v (pret & pp jabbed;
　ger jabbing) tr donner un coup de
　coude à; piquer; donner un coup sec
　à; (a knife) enfoncer
jabber [ˈdʒæbər] tr & intr jaboter
jack [dʒæk] s (aut) cric m; (cards)
　valet m; (elec) jack m, prise f; (coll)
　fric m; Jack Jeannot m || tr—to
　jack up soulever au cric; (prices)
　faire monter
jackal [ˈdʒækəl] s chacal m
jack'ass' s baudet m
jack'daw' s choucas m
jacket [ˈdʒækɪt] s (of a woman; of a
　book) jaquette f; (of a man's suit)
　veston m; (metal casing) chemise f
Jack' Frost' s le Bonhomme Hiver
jack'-in-the-box' s diable m à ressort,
　boîte f à surprise
jack'knife' s (pl -knives) couteau m de
　poche, couteau pliant; (fancy dive)
　saut m de carpe
jack'-of-all'-trades' s bricoleur m

jack-o'-lantern [ˈdʒækə ˌlæntərn] s po-
　tiron m lumineux
jack'pot' s gros lot m, poule f; to hit
　the jackpot décrocher la timbale
jack' rab'bit s lièvre m des prairies
Jacob [ˈdʒekəb] s Jacques m
jade [dʒed] s (stone; color) jade m;
　(horse) haridelle f; (woman) coquine
　f, friponne f
jaded adj éreinté, excédé; blasé
jag [dʒæg] s dentelure f; to have a
　jag on (slang) être paf
jagged [ˈdʒægɪd] adj dentelé
jaguar [ˈdʒægwər] s jaguar m
jail [dʒel] s prison f || tr emprisonner
jail'bird' s cheval m de retour
jailer [ˈdʒelər] s geôlier m
jalop·y [dʒəˈlɑpi] s (pl -ies) bagnole f,
　tacot m, guimbarde f, clou m
jam [dʒæm] s confiture f; to be in a
　jam (coll) être dans le pétrin || v (pret
　& pp jammed; ger jamming) tr coin-
　cer || intr se coincer
jamboree [ˌdʒæmbəˈri] s (of boy
　scouts) jamboree m; (slang) bom-
　bance f
James [dʒemz] s Jacques m

jamming ['dʒæmɪŋ] s (rad) brouillage m

Jane [dʒen] s Jeanne f

jangle ['dʒæŋgəl] s cliquetis m || tr faire cliqueter; (nerves) mettre en boule || intr cliqueter

janitor ['dʒænɪtər] s concierge m

janitress ['dʒænɪtrɪs] s concierge f

January ['dʒænju ˌɛri] s janvier m

ja·pan [dʒə'pæn] s laque m du Japon; **Japan** le Japon || v (pret & pp -panned; ger -panning) tr laquer

Japa·nese [ˌdʒæpə'niz] adj japonais || s (language) japonais m || s (pl -nese) (person) Japonais m

Jap′anese bee′tle s cétoine f

Jap′anese lan′tern s lanterne f vénitienne

jar [dʒɑr] s pot m, bocal m; secousse f || v (pret & pp jarred; ger jarring) tr ébranler, secouer § intr trembler, vibrer; (said of sounds, colors, opinions) discorder; **to jar on the nerves** taper sur les nerfs

jargon ['dʒɑrgən] s jargon m

jasmine ['dʒæsmɪn], ['dʒæzmɪn] s jasmin m

jasper ['dʒæspər] s jaspe m

jaundice ['dʒɔndɪs], ['dʒɑndɪs] s jaunisse f, ictère m

jaundiced adj ictérique; (fig) amer

jaunt [dʒɔnt], [dʒɑnt] s excursion f

jaun·ty ['dʒɔnti], ['dʒɑnti] adj (comp -tier; super -tiest) vif, dégagé; (smart) chic

javelin ['dʒævlɪn], ['dʒævəlɪn] s javelot m

jaw [dʒɔ] s mâchoire f; (of animal) gueule f; **jaws** (e.g., of death) griffes fpl || tr (slang) engueuler || intr (to gossip) (slang) bavarder

jaw′bone′ s mâchoire f, maxillaire m

jay [dʒe] s geai m

jay′walk′ intr traverser la rue en dehors des clous

jay′walk′er s piéton m distrait

jazz [dʒæz] s jazz m || tr—**to jazz up** (coll) animer, égayer

jazz′ band′ s orchestre m de jazz

jazz′ sing′er s chanteur m de rythme

jealous ['dʒɛləs] adj jaloux

jealous·y ['dʒɛləsi] s (pl -ies) jalousie f

jean [dʒin] s treillis m; **Jean** Jeanne f; **jeans** pantalon m de treillis

jeep [dʒip] s jeep f

jeer [dʒɪr] s raillerie f || intr railler; **to jeer at** se moquer de

Jehovah [dʒɪ'hovə] s Jéhovah m

jell [dʒɛl] s gelée f || intr se convertir en gelée; (to take hold) prendre forme, se préciser

jel·ly ['dʒɛli] s (pl -lies) gelée f || v (pret & pp -lied) tr convertir en gelée § intr se convertir en gelée

jel′ly·fish′ s méduse f; (person) chiffe f

jeopardize ['dʒɛpər ˌdaɪz] tr mettre en danger, compromettre

jeopardy ['dʒɛpərdi] s danger m

jerk [dʒʌrk] s saccade f, secousse f;

(slang) mufle m || tr tirer brusquement, secouer || intr se mouvoir brusquement

jerk′water town′ s trou m, petite ville f de province

jerk′water train′ s tortillard m

jerk·y ['dʒʌrki] adj (comp -ier; super -iest) saccadé

Jerome [dʒə'rom] s Jérôme m

jersey ['dʒʌrzi] s jersey m

Jerusalem [dʒɪ'rusələm] s Jérusalem f

jest [dʒɛst] s plaisanterie f; **in jest** en plaisantant || intr plaisanter

jester ['dʒɛstər] s plaisantin m; (medieval clown) bouffon m

Jesuit ['dʒɛzjʊ ˌɪt], ['dʒɛzjʊ ˌɪt] adj jésuite, jésuitique || s Jésuite m

Jesus ['dʒizəs] s Jésus m

Je′sus Christ′ s Jésus-Christ m

jet [dʒɛt] s (color; mineral) jais m; (of water, gas, etc.) jet m; avion m à réaction || v (pret & pp jetted; ger jetting) intr gicler, jaillir; voyager en jet

jet′-black′ adj noir de jais

jet′ en′gine s moteur m à réaction

jet′ fight′er s chasseur m à réaction

jet′ fu′el s carburéacteur m

jet′lin′er s avion m de ligne à réaction

jet′ plane′ s avion m à réaction

jet′ propul′sion s propulsion f par réaction

jetsam ['dʒɛtsəm] s marchandise f jetée à la mer

jettison ['dʒɛtɪsən] s jet m à la mer || tr jeter à la mer; (fig) mettre au rebut, rejeter

jet·ty ['dʒɛti] s (pl -ties) (wharf) appontement m; (breakwater) jetée f

Jew [dʒu] s Juif m; (rel) juif m

jewel ['dʒu·əl] s joyau m, bijou m; (of a watch) rubis m; (person) bijou

jew′el case′ s écrin m

jeweler or jeweller ['dʒu·ələr] s horloger-bijoutier m, bijoutier m

jewelry ['dʒu·əlri] s joaillerie f

jew′elry store′ s bijouterie f; (for watches) horlogerie f

Jewess ['dʒu·ɪs] s Juive f; (rel) juive f

Jewish ['dʒu·ɪʃ] adj juif, judaïque

jews′-harp or jew′s-harp ['dʒuz ˌhɑrp] s guimbarde f

jib [dʒɪb] s (mach) flèche f; (naut) foc m

jibe [dʒaɪb] s moquerie f || intr (coll) concorder; **to jibe at** se moquer de

jif·fy ['dʒɪfi] s (pl -fies)—**in a jiffy** (coll) en un clin d'œil

jig [dʒɪg] s (dance) gigue f; **the jig is up** (slang) il n'y a pas mèche, tout est dans le lac

jigger ['dʒɪgər] s mesure f qui contient une once et demie; (for fishing) leurre m; (tackle) palan m; (flea) puce f; (for separating ore) crible m; (naut) tapecul m; (gadget) (coll) machin m

jiggle ['dʒɪgəl] s petite secousse f || tr agiter, secouer || intr se trémousser

jig′saw′ tr chantourner

jig′ saw′ s scie f à chantourner

jig·saw puz·zle s casse-tête m chinois, puzzle m

jilt [dʒɪlt] tr lâcher, repousser

jim·my ['dʒɪmi] s (pl -mies) pince-monseigneur f ‖ v (pret & pp -mied) tr forcer à l'aide d'une pince-monseigneur

jingle ['dʒɪŋgəl] s (small bell) grelot m; (sound) grelottement m; (poem) rimes fpl enfantines; slogan m à rimes; (rad) réclame f chantée ‖ tr faire grelotter ‖ intr grelotter

jin·go ['dʒɪŋgo] adj chauvin ‖ s (pl -goes) chauvin m; by jingo! (coll) sapristi!

jingoism ['dʒɪŋgo‚ɪzəm] s chauvinisme m

jinx [dʒɪŋks] s guigne f ‖ tr (coll) porter la guigne à

jitters ['dʒɪtərz] spl (coll) frousse f, trouille f; to give the jitters to (coll) flanquer la trouille à

jittery ['dʒɪtəri] adj froussard

Joan [dʒon] s Jeanne f

job [dʒab] s (piece of work) travail m; (chore) besogne f, tâche f; (employment) emploi m; (work done by contract) travail à forfait; (slang) vol m; bad job (fig) mauvaise affaire f; by the job à la pièce; on the job faisant un stage; (slang) attentif; soft job (coll) filon m, fromage m; to be out of a job être en chômage; to lie down on the job (slang) tirer au flanc

jobber ['dʒabər] s grossiste m; (pieceworker) ouvrier m à la tâche; (dishonest official) agioteur m

job'hold'er s employé m; (in the government) fonctionnaire m

job' lot' s solde m de marchandises

job' print'ing s bilboquet m

jockey ['dʒaki] s jockey m ‖ tr (coll) manœuvrer

jockstrap ['dʒak‚stræp] s suspensoir m

jocose [dʒo'kos] adj jovial, joyeux

jocular ['dʒakjələr] adj facétieux

jog [dʒag] s saccade f ‖ v (pret & pp jogged; ger jogging) tr secouer; (the memory) rafraîchir ‖ intr—to jog along aller au petit trot

John [dʒan] s Jean m; john (slang) toilettes fpl

John' Bull' s l'Anglais m typique

John' Doe' s M. Dupont, M. Durand

Johnny ['dʒani] s (coll) Jeannot m

john'ny-cake' s galette f de farine de maïs

John'ny-come'-late'ly s (coll) nouveau venu m

join [dʒɔɪn] tr joindre; (to meet) rejoindre; (a club, a church) se joindre à, entrer dans; (a political party) s'affilier à; (the army) s'engager dans; to join s.o. in + ger se joindre à qn pour + inf ‖ intr se joindre

joiner ['dʒɔɪnər] s menuisier m; (coll) clubiste m

joint [dʒɔɪnt] adj joint, combiné ‖ s joint m; (culin) rôti m; (slang) boîte f; out of joint disloqué; (fig) de travers

joint' account' s compte m indivis

joint' commit'tee s commission f mixte

joint' own'er s copropriétaire mf

joint'-stock' com'pany s société f par actions

joist [dʒɔɪst] s solive f, poutre f

joke [dʒok] s plaisanterie f; to play a joke on faire une attrape à ‖ intr plaisanter

joker ['dʒokər] s farceur m, blagueur m; (cards) joker m, fou m; (coll) clause f ambiguë

jol·ly ['dʒali] adj (comp -lier; super -liest) joyeux, enjoué ‖ adv (coll) rudement

jolt [dʒolt] s cahot m, secousse f ‖ tr cahoter, secouer ‖ intr cahoter

Jonah ['dʒonə] s Jonas m

jonquil ['dʒaŋkwɪl] s jonquille f

Jordan ['dʒɔrdən] s (country) Jordanie f; la Jordanie; (river) Jourdain m

josh [dʒaʃ] tr & intr (coll) blaguer

jostle ['dʒasəl] tr bousculer ‖ intr se bousculer

jot [dʒat] s—not a jot pas un iota ‖ v (pret & pp jotted; ger jotting) tr—to jot down prendre note de

journal ['dʒʌrnəl] s journal m; (magazine) revue f; (mach) tourillon m; (naut) journal de bord

jour'nal box' s boîte f d'essieu

journalism ['dʒʌrnə‚lɪzəm] s journalisme m

journalist ['dʒʌrnəlɪst] s journaliste mf

journey ['dʒʌrni] s voyage m; trajet m, parcours m ‖ intr voyager

jour'ney·man s (pl -men) compagnon m

joust [dʒʌst], [dʒust], [dʒaust] s joute f ‖ intr jouter

Jove [dʒov] s Jupiter m; by Jove! parbleu!

jovial ['dʒovɪ·əl] adj jovial

jowl [dʒaul] s bajoue f

joy [dʒɔɪ] s joie f

joyful ['dʒɔɪfəl] adj joyeux

joyless ['dʒɔɪlɪs] adj sans joie

joyous ['dʒɔɪ·əs] adj joyeux

joy' ride' s (coll) balade f en auto

joy' stick' s manche m à balai

Jr. abbr (junior) fils, e.g., Mr. Martin, Jr. M. Martin fils

jubilant ['dʒubɪlənt] adj jubilant

jubilee ['dʒubɪ‚li] s jubilé m

Judaism ['dʒude‚ɪzəm] s judaïsme m

judge [dʒʌdʒ] s juge m ‖ tr & intr juger; judging by à en juger par

judge' ad'vocate s commissaire m du gouvernement

judgment ['dʒʌdʒmənt] s jugement m

judg'ment day' s jour m du jugement dernier

judicial [dʒu'dɪʃəl] adj judiciaire; (legal) juridique

judiciar·y [dʒu'dɪʃɪ‚eri] adj judiciaire ‖ s (pl -ies) pouvoir m judiciaire; (judges) judicature f

judicious [dʒu'dɪʃəs] s judicieux

jug [dʒʌg] s (of earthenware) cruche f; (of metal) broc m; (jail) (slang) bloc m

juggle ['dʒʌgəl] *tr* jongler avec; **to juggle away** escamoter ‖ *intr* jongler

juggler ['dʒʌglər] *s* jongleur *m*; imposteur *m*, mystificateur *m*

jugglery ['dʒʌgləri] or **juggling** ['dʒʌglɪŋ] *s* jonglerie *f*; (*trickery*) passe-passe *m*

Jugoslavia ['jugo'slɑvɪ-ə] *s* Yougoslavie *f*; **la Yougoslavie**

jugular ['dʒʌgjələr], ['dʒugjələr] *adj & s* jugulaire *f*

juice [dʒus] *s* jus *m*; (coll) courant *m* électrique

juic·y ['dʒusi] *adj* (*comp* **-ier**; *super* **-iest**) juteux; (fig) savoureux

jukebox ['dʒuk,bɑks] *s* pick-up *m* électrique à sous, distributeur *m* de musique

July [dʒu'laɪ] *s* juillet *m*

jumble ['dʒʌmbəl] *s* fouillis *m*, enchevêtrement *m* ‖ *tr* brouiller

jumbo ['dʒʌmbo] *adj* (coll) géant

jump [dʒʌmp] *s* saut *m*, bond *m*; (*nervous start*) sursaut *m*; (sports) saut *m*; (sports) obstacle *m* ‖ *tr* sauter; **to jump ship** tirer une bordée; **to jump the gun** démarrer trop tôt; **to jump the track** dérailler ‖ *intr* sauter, bondir; **to jump at the chance** sauter sur l'occasion

jump' ball' *s* (sports) entre-deux *m*

jump'ing jack' *s* pantin *m*

jump' rope' *s* corde *f* à sauter

jump' seat' *s* strapontin *m*

jump·y ['dʒʌmpi] *adj* (*comp* **-ier**; *super* **-iest**) nerveux

junction ['dʒʌŋkʃən] *s* jonction *f*; (*of railroads, roads*) embranchement *m*

juncture ['dʒʌŋktʃər] *s* jointure *f*; (*occasion*) conjoncture *f*; **at this juncture** en cette occasion

June [dʒun] *s* juin *m*

jungle ['dʒʌŋgəl] *s* jungle *f*

jun'gle war'fare *s* guerre *f* de la brousse

junior ['dʒunjər] *adj* cadet; **Bobby Watson, Junior** le jeune Bobby Watson; **Martin, Junior** Martin fils ‖ *s*

cadet *m*; (educ) étudiant *m* de troisième année

jun'ior of'ficer *s* officier *m* subalterne

juniper ['dʒunɪpər] *s* genévrier *m*

ju'niper ber'ry *s* genièvre *m*

junk [dʒʌŋk] *s* (*old metal*) ferraille *f*; (*worthless objects*) bric-à-brac *m*; (*cheap merchandise*) camelote *f*, pacotille *f*; (coll) gnognote *f*; (naut) jonque *f* ‖ *tr* mettre au rebut

junk' deal'er *s* fripier *m*; marchand *m* de ferraille

junket ['dʒʌŋkɪt] *s* excursion *f*; voyage *m* officiel aux frais de la princesse

junk'man' *s* (*pl* **-men'**) ferrailleur *m*; chiffonnier *m*

junk' shop' *s* boutique *f* de bric-à-brac et friperie; bric-à-brac *m*

junk'yard' *s* cimetière *m* de ferraille

jurisdiction [,dʒurɪs'dɪkʃən] *s* juridiction *f*; **within the jurisdiction of** du ressort de

jurist ['dʒurɪst] *s* légiste *m*

juror ['dʒurər] *s* juré *m*

ju·ry ['dʒuri] *s* (*pl* **-ries**) jury *m*

just [dʒʌst] *adj* juste ‖ *adv* seulement; justement; **just as** à l'instant où; (*in the same way that*) de même que; **just as it is** tel quel; **just out** vient de paraître; **to have just** venir de

justice ['dʒʌstɪs] *s* justice *f*; (*judge*) juge *m*

jus'tice of the peace' *s* juge *m* de paix

justi·fy ['dʒʌstɪ,faɪ] *v* (*pret & pp* **-fied**) *tr* justifier

justly ['dʒʌstli] *adv* justement

jut [dʒʌt] *v* (*pret & pp* **jutted**; *ger* **jutting**) *intr*—**to jut out** faire saillie

jute [dʒut] *s* jute *m*

juvenile ['dʒuvənɪl], ['dʒuvə,naɪl] *adj* juvénile, adolescent; (*e.g., books*) pour la jeunesse ‖ *s* adolescent *m*

ju'venile delin'quency *s* délinquance *f* juvénile

ju'venile delin'quent *s* délinquant *m* juvénile; **juvenile delinquents** jeunes délinquants *mpl*

juxtapose [,dʒʌkstə'poz] *tr* juxtaposer

K

K, k [ke] *s* XIᵉ lettre de l'alphabet

kale [kel] *s* chou *m* frisé

kaleidoscope [kə'laɪdə,skop] *s* kaléidoscope *m*

kangaroo [,kæŋgə'ru] *s* kangourou *m*

kan'garoo court' *s* tribunal *m* à bidon

Kashmir ['kæʃmɪr] *s* le Cachemire

kash'mir shawl' *s* châle *m* de cachemire

keel [kil] *s* quille *f* ‖ *intr*—**to keel over** (naut) chavirer; (coll) tomber dans les pommes

keen [kin] *adj* (*having a sharp edge*) aiguisé, affilé; (*sharp, cutting*) mordant, pénétrant; (*sharp-witted*) perçant, perspicace; (*eager, much interested*) enthousiaste, vif; (slang) formidable; **keen on** engoué de, passionné de

keep [kip] *s* entretien *m*; (*of medieval castle*) donjon *m*; **for keeps** (*for good*) (coll) pour de bon; (*forever*) (coll) à tout jamais; **to earn one's keep** (coll) gagner sa nourriture, gagner sa vie; **to play for keeps** (coll) jouer le tout pour le tout ‖ *v* (*pret & pp* **kept** [kept]) *tr* garder, conserver; (*one's word or promise; accounts, a diary*) tenir; (*animals*) élever; (*a garden*) cultiver; (*a hotel, a school, etc.*) diriger; (*an appointment*) ne pas manquer à; (*a holiday*) observer; (*a person*) avoir à sa charge, entretenir; **keep it up!** ne flanchez pas!, continuez!; **to keep away** éloigner; **to keep back** retenir; **to keep down** baisser; (*prices*) maintenir bas; (*a revolt*) réprimer; **to keep in** retenir; (*a student after school*) garder en retenue; (*dust, fire, etc.*) entretenir; **to keep off** éloigner; **to keep out** tenir éloigné, empêcher d'entrer; **to keep quiet** faire taire; **to keep running** laisser marcher; **to keep score** marquer les points; **to keep servants** avoir des domestiques; **to keep s.o. busy** occuper qn; **to keep s.o. clean (cool, warm, etc.)** tenir qn propre (au frais, au chaud, etc.); **to keep s.o. or s.th. from** + *ger* empêcher qn or q.ch. de + *inf*; **to keep s.o. informed about** mettre or tenir qn au courant de; **to keep s.o. waiting** faire attendre qn; **to keep up** maintenir; (*e.g., all night*) faire veiller ‖ *intr* rester, se tenir; (*in good shape*) demeurer, se conserver; (*e.g., from rotting*) se garder; **keep out** (public sign) entrée interdite; **that can keep** (coll) ça peut attendre; **to keep** + *ger* continuer à + *inf*; **to keep away** s'éloigner, se tenir à l'écart; **to keep from** + *ger* s'abstenir de + *inf*; **to keep in** rester avec; **to keep in with** rester en bons termes avec; **to keep on** + *ger* continuer à + *inf*; **to keep out** rester dehors; **to keep out of** ne pas se mêler de; **to keep quiet** rester tranquille, se taire; **to keep to** (*e.g., the right*) garder (*e.g., la droite*); **to keep up** tenir bon, tenir ferme; **to keep up with** aller de pair avec

keeper ['kipər] *s* gardien *m*, garde *m*; (*of a game preserve*) garde forestier; (*of a horseshoe magnet*) armature *f*

keeping ['kipiŋ] *s* garde *f*, surveillance *f*; (*of a holiday*) observance *f*; **in keeping with** en accord avec; **in safe keeping** sous bonne garde; **out of keeping with** en désaccord avec

keep′sake′ *s* souvenir *m*, gage *m* d'amitié

keg [keg] *s* tonnelet *m*; (*of herring*) caque *f*

ken [ken] *s*—**beyond the ken of** hors de la portée de

kennel ['kenəl] *s* chenil *m*

kep·i ['kepi], ['kepi] *s* (*pl* -**is**) képi *m*

kept′ wom′an [kept] *s* (*pl* **wom′en**) femme *f* entretenue

kerchief ['kʌrtʃif] *s* fichu *m*

kernel ['kʌrnəl] *s* (*inner part of a nut or fruit stone*) amande *f*; (*of wheat or corn*) grain *m*; (fig) noyau *m*, cœur *m*

kerosene ['kerə,sin], [,kerə'sin] *s* kérosène *m*, pétrole *m* lampant

ker′osene lamp′ *s* lampe *f* à pétrole

kerplunk [,kʌr'plʌŋk] *interj* patatras!

ketchup ['ketʃəp] *s* sauce *f* tomate, ketchup *m*

kettle ['ketəl] *s* chaudron *m*, marmite *f*; (*teakettle*) bouilloire *m*

ket′tle·drum′ *s* timbale *f*

key [ki] *adj* clef, clé ‖ *s* clef *f*, clé *f*; (*of piano, typewriter, etc.*) touche *f*; (*wedge or cotter used to lock parts together*) cheville *f*, clavette *f*; (*reef or low island*) caye *f*; (*answer book*) livre *m* du maître; (*tone of voice*) ton *m*; (*to a map*) légende *f*; (bot) samare *f*; (mus) tonalité *f*; (telg) manipulateur *m*; **key to the city** droit *m* de cité; **off key** faux; **on key** juste ‖ *tr* claveter, coincer; **to be keyed up** être surexcité, être tendu

key′board′ *s* clavier *m*

key′hole′ *s* trou *m* de la serrure; (*of clock*) trou de clef

key′man′ *s* (*pl* -**men**) pivot *m*, homme *m* indispensable

key′note′ *s* (mus) tonique *f*; (fig) dominante *f*

key′note speech′ *s* discours *m* d'ouverture

key′punch′ *s* (mach) perforatrice *f*

key′ ring′ *s* porte-clefs *m*

key′ sig′nature *s* (mus) armature *f* de la clé

key′stone′ *s* clef *f* de voûte

key′word′ *s* mot-clé *m*

kha·ki ['kɑki], ['kæki] *adj* kaki ‖ *s* (*pl* -**kis**) kaki *m*

khan [kɑn] *s* khan *m*

kibitz ['kɪbɪts] *intr* (coll) faire la mouche du coche

kibitzer ['kɪbɪtsər] *s* (coll) casse-pieds *mf*, curieux *m*

kick [kɪk] *s* coup *m* de pied; (*e.g., of a horse*) ruade *f*; (*of a gun*) recul *m*; (*complaint*) (slang) plainte *f*; (*thrill*) (slang) effet *m*, frisson *m*; **to get a kick out of** (slang) s'en payer une tranche de ‖ *tr* donner un coup de pied à; (*a ball*) botter; **to kick out** (coll) chasser à coups de pied; **to kick s.o. in the pants** (coll) botter le derrière à qn; **to kick the bucket** (coll) casser sa pipe, passer l'arme à gauche; **to kick up a row** (slang) déclencher un chahut ‖ *intr* donner un coup de pied; (*said of gun*) reculer; (*said of horse*) ruer; (sports) botter; **to kick against** regimber contre; **to kick off** (football) donner le coup d'envoi

kick′back′ *s* contrecoup *m*; (slang) ristourne *f*

kick′off′ *s* (sports) coup *m* d'envoi

kid [kɪd] *s* chevreau *m*; (coll) gosse *mf*, mioche *mf* ‖ *v* (*pret & pp* **kidded**; *ger* **kidding**) *tr & intr* (slang) blaguer; **to kid oneself** (slang) se faire des illusions

kidder ['kɪdər] *s* (slang) blagueur *m*

kidding ['kɪdɪŋ] *s* (slang) blague *f*; **no kidding!** (slang) sans blague!

kid′ gloves′ *spl* gants *mpl* de chevreau; **to handle with kid gloves** traiter avec douceur, ménager

kid′nap′ *v* (*pret & pp* **-naped** or **-napped**; *ger* **-naping** or **-napping**) *tr* kidnapper

kidnaper or **kidnapper** ['kɪdnæpər] *s* kidnappeur *m*

kidnaping or **kidnapping** [ˈkɪdnæpɪŋ] s kidnappage m

kidney [ˈkɪdni] s rein m; (culin) rognon m

kid′ney bean′ s haricot m de Soissons

kid′ney-shaped′ adj réniforme

kid′ney stone′ s calcul m rénal

kill [kɪl] s mise f à mort; (bag of game) gibier m tué ‖ tr tuer; (an animal) abattre; (a bill, amendment, etc.) mettre son veto à, faire échouer

killer [ˈkɪlər] s assassin m

kill′er whale′ s épaulard m, orque f

killing [ˈkɪlɪŋ] adj meurtrier; (exhausting; ridiculous) crevant ‖ s tuerie f; **to make a killing** (coll) réussir un beau coup

kill′-joy′ s rabat-joie m, trouble-fête mf

kiln [kɪl], [kɪln] s four m

kil·o [ˈkɪlo], [ˈkilo] s (pl -os) kilo m, kilogramme m; kilomètre m

kilocycle [ˈkɪlə‚saɪkəl] s kilocycle m

kilogram [ˈkɪlə‚græm] s kilogramme m

kilometer [ˈkɪlə‚mitər], [kɪˈlɑmɪtər] s kilomètre m

kilowatt [ˈkɪlə‚wɑt] s kilowatt m

kilowatt-hour [ˈkɪlə‚wɑtˈaur] s (pl -hours) kilowatt-heure m

kilt [kɪlt] s kilt m

kilter [ˈkɪltər] s—**to be out of kilter** (coll) être détraqué

kimo·no [kɪˈmonə], [kɪˈmono] s (pl -nos) kimono m

kin [kɪn] s (family relationship) parenté f; (relatives) les parents mpl; **of kin** apparenté; **the next of kin** le plus proche parent, les plus proches parents

kind [kaɪnd] adj bon, bienveillant; **kind to** bon pour; **to be so kind as to** être aussi aimable pour ‖ s espèce f, genre m, sorte f, classe f; **all kinds of** (coll) quantité de; **kind of** (coll) plutôt, en quelque sorte; **of a kind** semblable, de même nature; **to pay in kind** payer en nature

kindergarten [ˈkɪndər‚gɑrtən] s jardin m d'enfants

kindergartner [ˈkɪndər‚gɑrtnər] s élève mf de jardin d'enfants; (teacher) jardinière f

kind′-heart′ed adj bon, bienveillant

kindle [ˈkɪndəl] tr allumer ‖ intr s'allumer

kindling [ˈkɪndlɪŋ] s allumage m; (wood) bois m d'allumage

kin′dling wood′ s bois m d'allumage

kind·ly [ˈkaɪndli] adj (comp -lier; super -liest) (kind-hearted) bon, bienveillant; (e.g., climate) doux; (e.g., terrain) favorable ‖ adv avec bonté, avec bienveillance; **to take kindly** prendre en bonne part; **to take kindly to** prendre en amitié

kindness [ˈkaɪndnɪs] s bonté f, obligeance f

kindred [ˈkɪndrɪd] adj apparenté, de même nature ‖ s parenté f, famille f; parenté, ressemblance f

kinescope [ˈkɪnɪ‚skop] s (trademark) kinescope m

kinetic [kɪˈnetɪk], [kaɪˈnetɪk] adj cinétique ‖ **kinetics** s cinétique f

kinet′ic en′ergy s énergie f cinétique

king [kɪŋ] s roi m; (cards, chess, & fig) roi; (checkers) pion m doublé, dame f ‖ tr (checkers) damer

king′bolt′ s cheville f maîtresse

kingdom [ˈkɪŋdəm] s royaume m; (one of three divisions of nature) règne m

king′fish′er s martin-pêcheur m

king·ly [ˈkɪŋli] adj (comp -lier; super -liest) royal, de roi, digne d'un roi ‖ adv en roi, de roi, comme un roi

king′pin′ s cheville f ouvrière; (bowling) quille f du milieu; (coll) ponte m, pontife m

king′ post′ s poinçon m

kingship [ˈkɪŋʃɪp] s royauté f

king′-size′ adj grand format, géant

king′s′ ran′som s rançon f de roi

kink [kɪŋk] s (twist, e.g., in a rope) nœud m; (in a wire) faux pli m; (in hair) frisette f, bouclette f; (soreness in neck) torticolis m; (flaw, difficulty) point m faible; (mental twist) lubie f; (naut) coque f ‖ tr nouer, entortiller ‖ intr se nouer, s'entortiller

kink·y [ˈkɪŋki] adj (comp -ier; super -iest) crépu, bouclé

kinsfolk [ˈkɪnz‚fok] spl parents mpl

kin′ship s parenté f

kins·man [ˈkɪnzmən] s (pl -men) parent m

kins·woman [ˈkɪnz‚wumən] s (pl -wom′en) parente f

kipper [ˈkɪpər] s kipper m ‖ tr saurer

kiss [kɪs] s baiser m ‖ tr embrasser, donner un baiser à ‖ intr s'embrasser

kit [kɪt] s nécessaire m; (tub) tonnelet m; (of traveler) trousse f de voyage; (mil) équipement m, sac m; **the whole kit and caboodle** (coll) tout le saint-frusquin

kitchen [ˈkɪtʃən] s cuisine f

kitch′en cup′board s vaisselier m

kitchenette [‚kɪtʃəˈnet] s petite cuisine f

kitch′en gar′den s jardin m potager

kitch′en-maid′ s fille f de cuisine

kitch′en police′ s (mil) corvée f de cuisine

kitch′en range′ s cuisinière f

kitch′en sink′ s évier m

kitch′en-ware′ s ustensiles mpl de cuisine

kite [kaɪt] s cerf-volant m; (orn) milan m; **to fly a kite** lancer or enlever un cerf-volant

kith′ and kin′ [kɪθ] spl amis et parents mpl, cousinage m

kitten [ˈkɪtən] s chaton m, petit chat m

kittenish [ˈkɪtənɪʃ] adj enjoué, folâtre; (woman) coquette, dame f

kit·ty [ˈkɪti] s (pl -ties) minet m, minou m; (in card games) cagnotte f, poule f; **kitty, kitty, kitty!** minet, minet, minet!

kleptomaniac [‚kleptəˈmeni‚æk] adj & s kleptomane mf

knack [næk] s adresse f, chic m

knapsack ['næp,sæk] *s* sac *m* à dos, havresac *m*

knave [nev] *s* fripon *m*; (cards) valet *m*

knaver·y ['nevəri] *s* (*pl* -ies) friponnerie *f*

knead [nid] *tr* pétrir; (*to massage*) masser

knee [ni] *s* genou *m*; **to bring s.o. to his knees** mettre qn à genoux; **to go down on one's knees** se mettre à genoux

knee' breech'es *spl* culotte *f* courte

knee'cap' *s* rotule *f*; (*protective covering*) genouillère *f*

knee'-deep' *adj* jusqu'aux genoux

knee'-high' *adj* à la hauteur du genou

knee'hole' *s* trou *m*, évidement *m* pour l'entrée des genoux

knee' jerk' *s* réflexe *m* rotulien

kneel [nil] *v* (*pret & pp* **knelt** [nɛlt] or **kneeled**) *intr* s'agenouiller, **se mettre à genoux**

knee'pad' *s* genouillère *f*

knee'pan' *s* rotule *f*

knee' swell' *s* (*of organ*) genouillère *f*

knell [nɛl] *s* glas *m*; **to toll the knell of** sonner le glas de || *intr* sonner le glas

knickers ['nɪkərz] *spl* pantalons *mpl* de golf, knickerbockers *mpl*

knickknack ['nɪk,næk] *s* colifichet *m*

knife [naɪf] *s* (*pl* **knives** [naɪvz]) couteau *m*; (*of paper cutter or other instrument*) couperet *m*, lame *f*; **to go under the knife** (coll) monter or passer sur le billard || *tr* poignarder

knife' sharp'ener *s* fusil *m*, affiloir *m*

knife' switch' *s* (elec) interrupteur *m* à couteau

knight [naɪt] *s* chevalier *m*; (chess) cavalier *m* || *tr* créer or faire chevalier

knight-errant ['naɪt'ɛrənt] *s* (*pl* **knights-errant**) chevalier *m* errant

knighthood ['naɪthʊd] *s* chevalerie *f*

knightly ['naɪtli] *adj* chevaleresque

knit [nɪt] *v* (*pret & pp* **knitted** or **knit**; *ger* **knitting**) *tr* tricoter; (*one's brows*) froncer; **to knit together** lier, unir || *intr* tricoter; (*said of bones*) se souder

knit' goods' *spl* tricot *m*, bonneterie *f*

knitting ['nɪtɪŋ] *s* (*action*) tricotage *m*; (*product*) tricot *m*

knit'ting machine' *s* tricoteuse *f*

knit'ting nee'dle *s* aiguille *f* à tricoter

knit'wear' *s* tricot *m*

knob [nɑb] *s* (*lump*) bosse *f*; (*of a door, drawer, etc.*) bouton *m*, poignée *f*; (*of a radio*) bouton *m*

knock [nɑk] *s* coup *m*, heurt *m*; (*of an internal-combustion engine*) cognement *m*; (slang) éreintement *m*, dénigrement *m* || *tr* frapper; (*repeatedly*) cogner à, contre, or sur; (slang) éreinter, dénigrer; **to knock about** bousculer; **to knock against** heurter contre; **to knock down** (*with a blow, punch, etc.*) renverser; (*to the highest bidder*) adjuger; **to knock in** enfoncer; **to knock off** faire tomber; **to knock out** faire sortir en cognant; (boxing) mettre knock-out; (*to fatigue*) (coll) claquer, fatiguer || *intr*

frapper; (*said of internal-combustion engine*) cogner; **to knock about** vagabonder, se balader; **to knock against** se heurter contre; **to knock at** or **on** (*e.g., a door*) heurter à, frapper à; **to knock off** (*to stop working*) (coll) débrayer

knock'down' *adj* (*dismountable*) démontable || *s* (*blow*) coup *m* d'assommoir; (*discount*) escompte *m*

knocked' out' *adj* éreinté; (boxing) knock-out

knocker ['nɑkər] *s* (*on a door*) heurtoir *m*, marteau *m*; (*critic*) (coll) éreinteur *m*

knock-kneed ['nɑk,nid] *adj* cagneux

knock'out' *s* (boxing) knock-out *m*; (*person*) (coll) type *m* renversant; (*thing*) (coll) chose *f* sensationnelle

knock'out drops' *spl* (slang) narcotique *m*

knoll [nol] *s* mamelon *m*, tertre *m*

knot [nɑt] *s* nœud *m*; (*e.g., of people*) groupe *m*; (naut) nœud *m*, mille *m* marin à l'heure; (*loosely*) (naut) mille marin; **to tie a knot** faire un nœud; **to the knot** (coll) prononcer le conjungo || *v* (*pret & pp* **knotted**; *ger* **knotting**) *tr* nouer; **to knot one's brow** froncer le sourcil || *intr* se nouer

knot'hole' *s* trou *m* de nœud

knot·ty ['nɑti] *adj* (*comp* **-tier**; *super* **-tiest**) noueux; (*e.g., question*) épineux

know [no] *s*—**to be in the know** (coll) être au courant, être à la page || *v* (*pret* **knew** [n(j)u]; *pp* **known**) *tr & intr* (*by reasoning or learning*) savoir; (*by the senses or by perception, through acquaintance or recognition*) connaître; **as far as I know** autant que je sache; **to know about** être informé de, savoir; **to know best** être le meilleur juge; **to know how to +** *inf* savoir + *inf*; **to let s.o. know about** faire part à qn de; **you ought to know better** vous devriez avoir honte; **you ought to know better than to . . .** vous devriez vous bien garder de . . . ; **you wouldn't know s.o. from . . .** on prendrait qn pour . . .

knowable ['no·əbəl] *adj* connaissable

know'-how' *s* technique *f*, savoir-faire *m*

knowing ['no·ɪŋ] *adj* avisé; (*look, smile*) entendu

knowingly ['no·ɪŋli] *adv* sciemment, en connaissance de cause; (*on purpose*) exprès

know'-it-all' *adj* (coll) omniscient || *s* (coll) Monsieur Je-sais-tout *m*

knowledge ['nɑlɪdʒ] *s* (*faculty*) science *f*, connaissances *fpl*, savoir *m*; (*awareness, familiarity*) connaissance *f*; **not to my knowledge** pas que je sache; **to have a thorough knowledge of** posséder une connaissance approfondie de; **to my knowledge, to the best of my knowledge** à ma connaissance, autant que je sache; **without my knowledge** à mon insu

knowledgeable ['nɑlɪdʒəbəl] *adj* (coll) intelligent, bien informé

know'-noth'ing *s* ignorant *m*

knuckle ['nʌkəl] *s* jointure *f* or articulation *f* du doigt; (*of a quadruped*) jarret *m*; (*mach*) joint *m* en charnière; **knuckle of ham** jambonneau *m*; **to rap s.o. over the knuckles** donner sur les doigts or ongles à qn ‖ *intr*—**to knuckle down** se soumettre; (*to work hard*) s'y mettre sérieusement

knurl [nʌrl] *s* molette *f* ‖ *tr* moleter

k.o. ['ke'o] (letterword) (**knockout**) *s* k.o. *m* ‖ *tr* mettre k.o.

Koran [ko'ran], [ko'ræn] *s* Coran *m*

Korea [ko'ri·ə] *s* Corée *f*; la Corée

Korean [ko'ri·ən] *adj* coréen ‖ *s* (*language*) coréen; (*person*) Coréen *m*

kosher ['koʃər] *adj* casher, cawcher; (coll) convenable

kowtow ['kau'tau], ['ko'tau] *intr* se prosterner à la chinoise; **to kowtow to** faire des courbettes à or devant

K.P. ['ke'pi] *s* (letterword) (**kitchen police**) (mil) corvée *f* de cuisine; **to be on K.P. duty** (mil) être de soupe

kudos ['k(j)udas] *s* (coll) gloire *f*, éloges *mpl*, flatteries *fpl*

L

L, l [el] *s* XIIe lettre de l'alphabet

la·bel ['lebəl] *s* étiquette *f*; (*brand*) marque *f*; (*in a dictionary*) rubrique *f*, référence *f* ‖ *v* (*pret & pp* **-beled** or **-belled**; *ger* **-beling** or **-belling**) *tr* étiqueter

labial ['lebɪ·əl] *adj* labial ‖ *s* labiale *f*

labor ['lebər] *adj* ouvrier ‖ *s* travail *m*; (*toil*) labeur *m*, peine *f*; (*job, task*) tâche *f*, besogne *f*; (*manual work involved in an undertaking; the wages for such work*) main-d'œuvre *f*; (*wage-earning worker as contrasted with capital and management*) le salariat, le travail; (*childbirth*) couches *fpl*, travail; **to be in labor** être en couches ‖ *tr* (*a point, subject, etc.*) insister sur; (*one's style*) travailler, élaborer ‖ *intr* travailler; (*to toil*) travailler dur, peiner; (*to exert oneself*) s'efforcer; (*said of ship*) fatiguer, bourlinguer; **to labor under** être victime de; **to labor up** (*a hill, slope, etc.*) gravir; **to labor uphill** peiner en côte; **to labor with child** être en travail d'enfant

la'bor and man'agement *spl* la classe ouvrière et le patronat

laborato·ry ['læbərə,tori] *s* (*pl* **-ries**) laboratoire *m*

lab'oratory class' *s* classe *f* de travaux pratiques

labored ['lebərd] *adj* travaillé, trop élaboré; (*e.g., breathing*) pénible

laborer ['lebərər] *s* travailleur *m*, ouvrier *m*; (*unskilled worker*) journalier *m*, manœuvre *m*

laborious [lə'borɪ·əs] *adj* laborieux

la'bor move'ment *s* mouvement *m* syndicaliste

la'bor un'ion *s* syndicat *m*, syndicat ouvrier

Labourite ['lebə,raɪt] *adj & s* (Brit) travailliste *mf*

La'bour Par'ty ['lebər] *adj* (Brit) travailliste ‖ *s* parti *m* travailliste

Labrador ['læbrə,dər] *s* le Labrador

laburnum [lə'bʌrnəm] *s* cytise *m*

labyrinth ['læbɪrɪnθ] *s* labyrinthe *m*

lace [les] *s* dentelle *f*; (*string to tie shoe, corset, etc.*) lacet *m*, cordon *m*; (*braid*) broderies *fpl* ‖ *tr* garnir or border de dentelles; (*shoes, corset, etc.*) lacer; (*to braid*) entrelacer; (coll) flanquer une rossée à, rosser

lace' trim'ming *s* passementerie *f*

lace'work' *s* dentelles *fpl*, passementerie *f*

lachrymose ['lækrɪ,mos] *adj* larmoyant

lacing ['lesɪŋ] *s* lacet *m*, cordon *m*; (*trimming*) galon *m*, passement *m*; (coll) rossée *f*

lack [læk] *s* manque *m*, défaut *m*; (*lack of necessities*) pénurie *f*; **for lack of** faute de ‖ *tr* manquer de, être dépourvu de ‖ *intr* (*to be lacking*) manquer

lackadaisical [,lækə'dezɪkəl] *adj* languissant, apathique

lackey ['læki] *s* laquais *m*

lacking ['lækɪŋ] *prep* dépourvu de, dénué de

lack'lus'ter *adj* terne, fade

laconic [lə'kɑnɪk] *adj* laconique

lacquer ['lækər] *s* laque *m & f* ‖ *tr* laquer

lac'quer ware' *s* laques *mpl*, objets *mpl* d'art en laque

lacrosse [lə'krɔs], [lə'krɑs] *s* crosse *f*, jeu *m* de crosse; **to play lacrosse** jouer à la crosse

lacu·na [lə'kjunə] *s* (*pl* **-nas** or **-nae** [ni]) lacune *f*

lac·y ['lesi] *adj* (*comp* **-ier**; *super* **-iest**) de dentelle; (fig) fin, léger

lad [læd] *s* garçon *m*, gars *m*

ladder ['lædər] *s* échelle *f*; (*stepping stone*) (fig) marchepied *m*, échelon *m*; (*stepladder*) marchepied, escabeau *m*; (*run in stocking*) (Brit) démaillage *m*; (*stairway*) (naut) escalier *m*

lad'der truck' *s* fourgon-pompe *m* à échelle

la'dies' room' *s* toilettes *fpl* pour dames, lavabos *mpl* pour dames

ladle [ˈledəl] *s* louche *f* || *tr* servir à la louche

la·dy [ˈledi] *s* (*pl* **-dies**) dame *f*; **ladies** (public sign) dames; **ladies and gentlemen!** (formula used in addressing an audience) mesdames, mesdemoiselles, messieurs!; messieurs dames! (coll)

la'dy·bird' or **la'dy·bug'** *s* cocinelle *f*, bête *f* à bon Dieu

la'dy·fin'ger *s* biscuit *m* à la cuiller

la'dy-in-wait'ing *s* (*pl* **ladies-in-waiting**) demoiselle *f* d'honneur

la'dy-kil'ler *s* bourreau *m* des cœurs, tombeur *m* de femmes

la'dy·like' *adj* de bon ton, de dame

la'dy·love' *s* bien-aimée *f*, dulcinée *f*

la'dy of the house' *s* maîtresse *f* de maison

la'dy's maid' *s* camériste *f*

la'dy's man' *s* homme *m* à succès

lag [læg] *s* retard *m* || *v* (*pret & pp* **lagged**; *ger* **lagging**) *intr* traîner; **to lag behind** rester en arrière

la'ger beer' [ˈlagər] *s* bière *f* de fermentation basse, lager *m*

laggard [ˈlægərd] *adj* tardif || *s* traînard *m*

lagoon [ləˈgun] *s* lagune *f*

laid' pa'per [led] *s* papier *m* vergé

laid' up' *adj* mis en réserve; (naut) mis en rade; (coll) alité, au lit

lair [ler] *s* tanière *f*; (fig) repaire *m*

laity [ˈle·ɪti] *s* profanes *mfpl*; (eccl) laïques *mfpl*

lake [lek] *adj* lacustre || *s* lac *m*

lamb [læm] *s* agneau *m*

lambaste [læmˈbest] *tr* (*to thrash*) (coll) flanquer une rossée à; (*to reprimand harshly*) (coll) passer un savon à

lamb' chop' *s* côtelette *f* d'agneau

lambkin [ˈlæmkɪn] *s* agnelet *m*

lamb'skin' *s* peau *f* d'agneau; (*dressed with its wool*) mouton *m*, agnelin *m*

lame [lem] *adj* boiteux; (*sore*) endolori; (*e.g., excuse*) faible, piètre || *tr* estropier, rendre boiteux

lament [ləˈment] *s* lamentation *f*; (*dirge*) complainte *f* || *tr* déplorer || *intr* lamenter, se lamenter

lamentable [ˈlæməntəbəl] *adj* lamentable

lamentation [ˌlæmənˈteʃən] *s* lamentation *f*

laminate [ˈlæmɪˌnet] *tr* laminer

lamp [læmp] *s* lampe *f*

lamp'black' *s* noir *m* de fumée

lamp' chim'ney *s* verre *m* de lampe

lamp'light' *s* lumière *f* de lampe

lamp'light'er *s* allumeur *m* de réverbères

lampoon [læmˈpun] *s* libelle *m*, pasquinade *f* || *tr* faire des libelles contre

lamp'post' *s* réverbère *m*, poteau *m* de réverbère

lamprey [ˈlæmpri] *s* lamproie *f*

lamp'shade' *s* abat-jour *m*

lamp'wick' *s* mèche *f* de lampe

lance [læns], [lɑns] *s* lance *f*; (surg) lancette *f*, bistouri *m* || *tr* percer d'un coup de lance; (surg) donner un coup de lancette or bistouri à

lancet [ˈlænsɪt], [ˈlɑnsɪt] *s* (surg) lancette *f*, bistouri *m*

land [lænd] *adj* terrestre, de terre || *s* terre *f*; **land of milk and honey** pays de cocagne; **to make land** toucher terre; **to see how the land lies** sonder or tâter le terrain || *tr* débarquer, mettre à terre; (*an airplane*) atterrir; (*a fish*) amener à terre; (*e.g., a job*) (coll) décrocher; (*a blow*) (coll) flanquer || *intr* débarquer, descendre à terre; (*said of air plane*) atterrir; **to land on one's feet** retomber sur ses pieds; **to land on the moon** alunir; **to land on the water** amerrir

land' breeze' *s* brise *f* de terre

landed *adj* (*owning land*) terrien; (*real-estate*) immobilier

land'ed prop'erty *s* propriété *f* foncière

land'fall' *s* (*sighting land*) abordage *m*; (*landing of ship or plane*) atterrissage *m*; (*landslide*) glissement *m* de terrain

landing [ˈlændɪŋ] *s* (*of plane*) atterrissage *m*; (*of ship*) mise *f* à terre, débarquement *m*; (*place where passengers and goods are landed*) débarcadère *m*; (*of stairway*) palier *m*; (*on the moon*) alunissage *m*

land'ing bea'con *s* (aer) radiophare *m* d'atterrissage

land'ing craft' *s* (nav) péniche *f* de débarquement

land'ing field' *s* (aer) terrain *m* d'atterrissage

land'ing force' *s* (nav) détachement *m* de débarquement

land'ing gear' *s* (aer) train *m* d'atterrissage

land'ing par'ty *s* (nav) détachement *m* de débarquement

land'ing stage' *s* débarcadère *m*

land'ing strip' *s* (aer) piste *f* d'atterrissage

land'la'dy *s* (*pl* **-dies**) (*e.g., of an apartment*) logeuse *f*, propriétaire *f*; (*of a lodging house*) patronne *f*; (*of an inn*) aubergiste *f*

land'locked' *adj* entouré de terre

land'lord' *s* (*e.g., of an apartment*) logeur *m*, propriétaire *m*; (*of a lodging house*) patron *m*; (*of an inn*) aubergiste *m*

landlubber [ˈlændˌlʌbər] *s* marin *m* d'eau douce

land'mark' *s* point *m* de repère, borne *f*; (*important event*) étape *f* importante; (naut) amer *m*

land' of'fice *s* bureau *m* du cadastre

land'own'er *s* propriétaire *m* foncier

landscape [ˈlændˌskep] *s* paysage *m* || *tr* aménager en jardins

land'scape ar'chitect *s* architecte *m* paysagiste

land'scape gar'dener *s* jardinier *m* paysagiste

land'scape paint'er *s* paysagiste *mf*

landscapist [ˈlændˌskepɪst] *s* paysagiste *mf*

land′slide′ s glissement m de terrain, éboulement m; (*in an election*) raz m de marée

landward ['lændwərd] adv du côté de la terre, vers la terre

land′ wind′ ['wɪnd] s vent m de terre

lane [len] s (*narrow street or passage*) ruelle f; (*in the country*) sentier m; (*of an automobile highway*) voie f; (*line of cars*) file f; (*of an air or ocean route*) route f de navigation

langsyne ['læŋ'saɪn] s (Scotch) le temps jadis || adv (Scotch) au temps jadis

language ['læŋgwɪdʒ] s langage m; (*e.g., of a nation*) langue f

languid ['læŋgwɪd] adj languissant

languish ['læŋgwɪʃ] intr languir

languor ['læŋgər] s langueur f

languorous ['læŋgərəs] adj langoureux

lank [læŋk] adj efflanqué, maigre; (*hair*) plat, e.g., **lank hair** cheveux plats

lank·y ['læŋki] adj (comp **-ier**; super **-iest**) grand et maigre

lanolin ['lænəlɪn] s lanoline f

lantern ['læntərn] s lanterne f

lan′tern slide′ s diapositive f

lanyard ['lænjərd] s (*around the neck*) cordon m; (arti) tire-feu m; (naut) ride f

lap [læp] s (*of human body or clothing*) genoux mpl, giron m; (*of garment*) genoux, pan m; (*with the tongue*) coup m de langue; (*of the waves*) clapotis m; (*in a race*) (sports) tour m; **last lap** dernière étape f || v (pret & pp **lapped**; ger **lapping**) tr (*with the tongue*) laper; **to lap up** laper; (coll) gober || intr laper; (*said of waves*) clapoter; **to lap over** déborder

lap′ dog′ s bichon m, chien m de manchon

lapel [lə'pɛl] s revers m

Lap′land′ s Laponie f; la Laponie

Laplander ['læp,lændər] s Lapon m

Lapp [læp] s (*language*) lapon m; (*person*) Lapon m

lap′ robe′ s couverture f de voyage

lapse [læps] s (*passing of time*) laps m; (*slipping into guilt or error*) faute f, écart m; (*fall, decline*) chute f; (e.g., *of an insurance policy*) expiration f, échéance f; (*of memory*) absence f, défaillance f || intr (*to elapse*) s'écouler, passer; (*to err*) manquer à ses devoirs; (*to decline*) déchoir; (*said, e.g., of a right*) périmer, tomber en désuétude; (*said, e.g., of a legacy*) devenir caduc; (*said, e.g., of an insurance policy*) cesser d'être en vigueur

lap′wing′ s (orn) vanneau m huppé

larce·ny ['larsəni] s (pl **-nies**) larcin m, vol m

larch [lartʃ] s (bot) mélèze m

lard [lard] s saindoux m || tr larder

larder ['lardər] s garde-manger m

large [lardʒ] adj grand; **at large** en liberté

large′ intes′tine s gros intestin m

largely ['lardʒli] adv principalement

largeness ['lardʒnɪs] s grandeur f

large′-scale′ adj sur une large échelle, de grande envergure

lariat ['lærɪ·ət] s (*for catching animals*) lasso m; (*for tying grazing animals*) longe f

lark [lark] s alouette f; (*prank*) espièglerie f; **to go on a lark** (coll) faire la bombe

lark′spur′ s (*rocket larkspur*) pied-d'alouette m; (*field larkspur*) consoude f royale

lar·va ['larvə] s (pl **-vae** [vi]) larve f

laryngeal [lə'rɪndʒɪ·əl], [,lærɪn'dʒi·əl] adj laryngé, laryngien

laryngitis [,lærɪn'dʒaɪtɪs] s laryngite f

laryngoscope [lə'rɪŋgə,skop] s laryngoscope m

larynx ['lærɪŋks] s (pl **larynxes** or **larynges** [lə'rɪndʒiz]) larynx m

lascivious [lə'sɪvɪ·əs] adj lascif

lasciviousness [lə'sɪvɪ·əsnɪs] s lasciveté f

laser ['lezər] s (acronym) (light amplification by stimulated emission of radiation) laser m

lash [læʃ] s (*cord on end of whip*) mèche f; coup m; (*splatter of rain on window*) fouettement m; (*eyelash*) cil m || tr fouetter, cingler; (*to bind, tie*) lier; (naut) amarrer || intr fouetter; **to lash out** at cingler

lashing ['læʃɪŋ] s fouettée f; (*rope*) amarre f; (naut) amarrage m

lass [læs] s jeune fille f, jeunesse f; bonne amie f

lassitude ['læsɪ,t(j)ud] s lassitude f

las·so ['læso], [læ'su] s (pl **-sos** or **-soes**) lasso m

last [læst], [last] adj (*in a series*) dernier (before noun), e.g., **the last week of the war** la dernière semaine de la guerre; (*just elapsed*) dernier (after noun), e.g., **last week** la semaine dernière; **before last** avant-dernier, e.g., **the time before last** l'avant-dernière fois; **the last two** les deux derniers || s dernier m; (*the end*) fin f, bout m; (*for holding shoe*) forme f; **at last** enfin, à la fin; **at long last** à la fin des fins; **the last of the month** la fin du mois; **to the last** jusqu'à la fin, jusqu'au bout || intr durer; (*to hold out*) tenir

last′ eve′ning adv hier soir

lasting ['læstɪŋ], ['lastɪŋ] adj durable

lastly ['læstli], ['lastli] adv pour finir, en dernier lieu, enfin

last′-minute news′ s nouvelles fpl de dernière heure

last′ name′ s nom m, nom de famille

last′ night′ adv hier soir; cette nuit

last′ quar′ter s dernier quartier m

last′ sleep′ s sommeil m de la mort

last′ straw′ s—that's **the last straw!** c'est le comble!

Last′ Sup′per s (eccl) Cène f

last will′ and test′ament s testament m, acte m de dernière volonté

last′ word′ s dernier mot m; (*latest style*) (coll) dernier cri m

latch [læt∫] s loquet m ‖ tr fermer au loquet

latch′key′ s clef f de porte d'entrée

latch′string′ s cordon m de loquet

late [let] adj (happening after the usual time); (person; train, bus, etc.) en retard; (e.g., art) de la dernière époque; (events) dernier, récent; (news) de la dernière heure; (incumbent of an office) ancien; (deceased) défunt, feu; **at a late hour in** (the night, the day) bien avant dans, à une heure avancée de; **in the late seventeenth century (eighteenth century, etc.)** vers la fin du dix-septième siècle (dix-huitième siècle, etc.); **it is late** il est tard; **of late** dernièrement, récemment, depuis peu; **to be late** être en retard; **to be late in** + ger tarder à + inf ‖ adv tard, tardivement; (after the appointed time) en retard; **late in** (the afternoon, the season, the week, the month) vers la fin de; **late in life** sur le tard; **very late in** (the night, the day) bien avant dans, à une heure avancée de

late-comer ['let,kʌmər] s (newcomer) nouveau venu m; (one who arrives late) retardataire mf

lateen′ sail′ [læ'tin] s voile f latine

lateen′ yard′ s antenne f

lately ['letli] adv dernièrement, récemment, depuis peu

latency ['letənsi] s latence f

latent ['letənt] adj latent

later ['letər] adj comp plus tard, plus tardif; (event) subséquent, plus récent; (kings, luminaries, etc.) derniers en date; **later than** postérieur à ‖ adv comp plus tard; **later on** plus tard, par la suite; **see you later** (coll) à tout à l'heure

lateral ['lætərəl] adj latéral

lath [læθ], [lɑθ] s latte f ‖ tr latter

lathe [leð] s (mach) tour m; **to turn on a lathe** façonner au tour

lather ['læðər] s (of soap) mousse f; (of horse) écume f ‖ tr savonner ‖ intr (said of soap) mousser; (said of horse) être couvert d'écume

lathing ['læθɪŋ], ['lɑθɪŋ] s lattage m

Latin ['lætɪn], ['lætən] adj latin ‖ s (language) latin m; (person) Latin m

Lat′in Amer′ica s l'Amérique f latine

Lat′in-Amer′ican adj latino-américain ‖ s Latino-américain m

latitude ['lætɪ,t(j)ud] s latitude f

latrine [lə'trin] s latrines fpl

latter ['lætər] adj dernier; **the latter part of** (e.g., a century) la fin de ‖ pron—**the latter** celui-ci §84; le dernier

lattice ['lætɪs] adj treillissé ‖ s treillis m ‖ tr treillisser

lat′tice gird′er s poutre f à croisillons

lat′tice-work′ s treillis m, grillage m

laud [lɔd] tr louer

laudable ['lɔdəbəl] adj louable

laudanum ['lɔdənəm], ['lɔdnəm] s laudanum m

laudatory ['lɔdə,tori] adj laudatif, élogieux

laugh [læf], [lɑf] s rire m ‖ tr—**to laugh away** chasser en riant; **to laugh off** tourner en plaisanterie ‖ intr rire; **to laugh at** rire de

laughable ['læfəbəl], ['lɑfəbəl] adj risible

laughing ['læfɪŋ], ['lɑfɪŋ] adj riant, rieur; **it's no laughing matter** il n'y a pas de quoi rire ‖ s rire m

laugh′ing gas′ s gaz m hilarant

laugh′ing-stock′ s risée f, fable f

laughter ['læftər], ['lɑftər] s rire m

launch [lɔnt∫], [lɑnt∫] s (open motorboat) canot m automobile, vedette f; (naut) chaloupe f ‖ tr lancer; (an attack) déclencher ‖ intr—**to launch into, to launch out on** se lancer dans

launching ['lɔnt∫ɪŋ], ['lɑnt∫ɪŋ] s lancement m

launch′ing pad′ s rampe f de lancement, aire f de lancement

launder ['lɔndər], ['lɑndər] tr blanchir

launderer ['lɔndərər], ['lɑndərər] s blanchisseur m, buandier m

laundering ['lɔndərɪŋ], ['lɑndərɪŋ] s blanchissage m

laundress ['lɔndrɪs], ['lɑndrɪs] s blanchisseuse f, buandière f

laun·dry ['lɔndri], ['lɑndri] s (pl -dries) linge m à blanchir, lessive f; (room) buanderie f; (business) blanchisserie f

laun′dry·man s (pl -men) blanchisseur m, buandier m

laun′dry room′ s buanderie f

laun′dry·wom′an s (pl -wom′en) blanchisseuse f, buandière f

laureate ['lɔrɪ·ɪt] adj & s lauréat m

lau·rel ['lɔrəl], ['lɑrəl] s laurier m; **to rest on one's laurels** s'endormir sur ses lauriers ‖ v (pret & pp -reled or -relled; ger -reling or -relling) tr couronner de lauriers

lava ['lɑvə], ['lævə] s lave f

lavaliere [,lævə'lɪr] s pendentif m

lavato·ry ['lævə,tori] s (pl -ries) (room equipped for washing hands and face; bowl with running water) lavabo m; (toilet) lavabos

lavender ['lævəndər] s lavande f

lav′ender wa′ter s eau f de lavande

lavish ['lævɪ∫] adj prodigue; (reception, dinner, etc.) somptueux, magnifique ‖ tr prodiguer

law [lɔ] s (of man, of nature, of science) loi f; (branch of knowledge concerned with law; body of laws; study of law, profession of law) droit m; **to go to law** recourir à la justice; **to go to law with** s.o. citer qn en justice; **to lay down the law** faire la loi; **to practice law** exercer le droit; **to read law** étudier le droit, faire son droit

law′-abid′ing adj soumis aux lois, respectueux des lois

law′ and or′der s ordre m public; **to maintain law and order** maintenir or faire régner l'ordre

law′break′er s transgresseur m de la loi

law′ court′ s cour f de justice, tribunal m

lawful ['lɔfəl] *adj* légal, légitime

lawless ['lɔlɪs] *adj* sans loi; (*unbridled*) sans frein, déréglé

law'mak'er *s* législateur *m*

lawn [lɔn] *s* pelouse *f*, gazon *m*; (*fabric*) batiste *f*, linon *m*

lawn' mow'er *s* tondeuse *f* de gazon

law' of'fice *s* étude *f* (d'avocat)

law' of na'tions *s* loi *f* des nations

law' of the jun'gle *s* loi *f* de la jungle

law' stu'dent *s* étudiant *m* en droit

law'suit' *s* procès *m*

lawyer ['lɔjər] *s* avocat *m*

lax [læks] *adj* (*in morals, discipline, etc.*) relâché, négligent; (*loose, not tense*) lâche; (*vague*) vague, flou

laxative ['læksətɪv] *adj* & *s* laxatif *m*

lay [le] *adj* (*not belonging to clergy*) laïc or laïque; (*not having special training*) profane ‖ *s* situation *f*; (*poem*) lai *m* ‖ *v* (*pret* & *pp* **laid** [led]) *tr* poser, mettre; (*a trap*) tendre; (*eggs*) pondre; (*e.g., bricks*) ranger; (*a foundation*) jeter, établir; (*a cable*) poser; (*a mine*) (naut) mouiller; **to be laid in Rome (in France, etc.**) (*said, e.g., of scene*) se passer à Rome (en France, etc.); **to lay aside, away,** or **by** mettre de côté; **to lay down** (*one's life*) sacrifier; (*one's weapons*) déposer; (*conditions*) imposer; **to lay down the law to s.o.** (coll) rappeler qn à l'ordre; **to lay in** (*supplies*) faire provision de; **to lay into s.o.** (coll) sauter dessus qn; **to lay it on thick** (coll) y aller fort; **to lay low** (*to overwhelm*) abattre, terrasser; **to lay off** (*an employee*) congédier; (*to mark the boundaries of*) tracer; (*to stop bothering*) (coll) laisser tranquille; **to lay on** (*paint*) appliquer; (*hands; taxes*) imposer; **to lay open** mettre à nu; **to lay out** arranger; (*to display*) étaler; (*to outline*) tracer; (*money*) débourser; (*a corpse*) faire la toilette de; (*a garden*) aménager; **to lay up** (*to stock up on*) amasser; (*to injure*) aliter; (*a boat*) mettre en rade ‖ *intr* (*said of hen*) pondre; **to lay about** frapper de tous côtés; **to lay for** être à l'affût de, guetter; **to lay in** (to slang) rosser, battre; **to lay off** (coll) cesser; **to lay off smoking** (coll) renoncer au tabac; **to lay over** faire escale; **to lay to** (naut) se mettre à la cape

lay' broth'er *s* frère *m* lai, frère convers

layer ['le·ər] *s* couche *f*; (hen) pondeuse *f* ‖ *tr* (hort) marcotter

lay'er cake' *s* gâteau *m* sandwich

layette [le'ɛt] *s* layette *f*

lay' fig'ure *s* mannequin *m*

laying ['le·ɪŋ] *s* pose *f*; (*of foundation*) assise *f*; (*of eggs*) ponte *f*

lay'man *s* (*pl* **-men**) (*person who is not a clergyman*) laïc *m* or laïque *m*; (*person who has no special training*) profane *m*

lay'off' *s* (*discharge*) renvoi *m*; (*unemployment*) chômage *m*

lay' of the land' *s* configuration *f* du terrain; (fig) aspect *m* de l'affaire

lay'out' *s* plan *m*, dessin *m*, tracé *m*; (*of tools*) montage *m*; (*organization*) disposition *f*; (*banquet*) (coll) festin *m*

lay'o'ver *s* arrêt *m* en cours de route

lay' sis'ter *s* sœur *f* laie, sœur converse

laziness ['lezɪnɪs] *s* paresse *f*

la·zy ['lezi] *adj* (*comp* **-zier;** *super* **-ziest**) paresseux

la'zy-bones' *s* (coll) flemmard *m*, fainéant *m*

lb. *abbr* (**pound**) livre *f*

lea [li] *s* (*meadow*) pâturage *m*, prairie *f*

lead [led] *adj* en plomb, de plomb ‖ [led] *s* plomb *m*; (*of lead pencil*) mine *f* (de plombagine); (*for sounding depth*) (naut) sonde *f*; (typ) interligne *f* ‖ [led] *v* (*pret* & *pp* **leaded; ger leading**) *tr* plomber; (typ) interligner ‖ [lid] *s* (*foremost place*) avance *f*; (*guidance*) direction *f*, conduite *f*; (*leash*) laisse *f*; (*of a newspaper article*) article *m* de fond; (*leading role*) premier rôle *m*; (*leading man*) jeune premier *m*; (elec) câble *m* de canalisation, conducteur *m*; (elec, mach) avance; (min) filon *m*; **to follow s.o.'s lead** suivre l'exemple de qn; **to have the lead** (cards) avoir la main; **to return the lead** (cards) rejouer la couleur; **to take the lead** prendre le pas ‖ [lid] *v* (*pret* & *pp* **led** [led]) *tr* conduire, mener; (*to command*) commander, diriger; (*to be foremost in*) être à la tête de; (*e.g., an orchestra*) diriger; (*a good or bad life*) mener; (*a certain card*) attaquer de; (*a certain card suit*) attaquer; (elec, mach) canaliser; **to lead away** or **off** emmener; **to lead off** (*to start*) commencer; **to lead on** encourager; **to lead s.o. to believe** mener qn à croire ‖ *intr* aller devant, tenir la tête; (cards) avoir la main; **to lead to** conduire à, mener à; (*another street, a certain result, etc.*) aboutir à; **to lead up to** (*a great work*) préluder à (un grand ouvrage); (*a subject*) amener (un sujet)

leaden ['ledən] *adj* (*of lead; like lead*) de plomb, en plomb; (*heavy as lead*) pesant; (*sluggish*) alangui; (*complexion*) plombé

leader ['lidər] *s* chef *m*, guide *mf*; (*ringleader*) tête *f*; chef d'orchestre; (*in a dance; among animals*) meneur *m*; (*in a newspaper*) article *m* de fond; (*of a reel of tape or film*) amorce *f*; (*bargain*) article réclame; (*vein of ore*) filon *m*

leadership ['lidər‚ʃɪp] *s* direction *f*; don *m* de commandement

leading ['lidɪŋ] *adj* principal, premier

lead'ing edge' *s* (aer) bord *m* d'attaque

lead'ing la'dy *s* vedette *f*, étoile *f*, jeune première *f*

lead'ing man' *s* (*pl* **men'**) jeune premier *m*

lead'ing ques'tion *s* question *f* tendancieuse

lead'-in wire' ['lid‚ɪn] *s* (rad, telv) fil *m* d'amenée

lead′ pen′cil [lɛd] s crayon m (à mine de graphite)
lead′ poi′soning [lɛd] s saturnisme m
leaf [lif] s (pl **leaves** [livz]) feuille f; (inserted leaf of table) rallonge f; (hinged leaf of door or table top) battant m; **to shake like a leaf** trembler comme une feuille; **to turn over a new leaf** tourner la page, faire peau neuve ‖ intr—**to leaf through** feuilleter
leafless [′liflɪs] adj sans feuilles, dénudé
leaflet [′liflɪt] s dépliant m, papillon m, feuillet m; (bot) foliole f
leaf′stalk′ s (bot) pétiole m
leaf·y [′lifi] adj (comp -ier; super -iest) feuillu, touffu
league [lig] s (unit of distance) lieue f; (association, alliance) ligue f ‖ tr liguer ‖ intr se liguer
League′ of Na′tions s Société f des Nations
leak [lik] s fuite f; (in a ship) voie f d'eau; (of electricity, heat, etc.) perte f, fuite; (of news, secrets, money, etc.) fuite; **to spring a leak** avoir une fuite; (naut) faire une voie d'eau ‖ tr faire couler; (gas, steam; secrets, news) laisser échapper ‖ intr fuire, s'écouler; (naut) faire eau; **to leak away** se perdre; **to leak out** (said of news, secrets, etc.) transpirer, s'ébruiter
leakage [′likɪdʒ] s fuite f; (elec) perte f
leak·y [′liki] adj (comp -ier; super -iest) percé, troué; qui a des fuites; (shoes) qui prennent l'eau; (coll) indiscret
lean [lin] adj maigre; (gasoline mixture) pauvre ‖ s inclinaison f; (of meat) maigre m ‖ v (pret & pp **leaned** or **leant** [lɛnt]) tr incliner; **to lean s.th. against s.th.** appuyer q.ch. contre q.ch. ‖ intr s'incliner, pencher; **to lean against** s'appuyer contre; **to lean forward** s'incliner or se pencher en avant; **to lean out of** (e.g., a window) se pencher par; **to lean over** se pencher; (e.g., s.o.'s shoulder) se pencher sur; **to lean toward** (fig) incliner à or vers, pencher pour or vers
leaning [′linɪŋ] adj penché ‖ s inclinaison f; (fig) inclination f, penchant m
lean′-to′ s (pl -tos) appentis m
lean′ years′ spl années fpl maigres
leap [lip] s saut m, bond m; **by leaps and bounds** par sauts et par bonds; **leap in the dark** saut m à l'aveuglette ‖ v (pret & pp **leaped** or **leapt** [lɛpt]) tr sauter, franchir ‖ intr sauter, bondir; **to leap across** or **over** sauter; **to leap up** sursauter; (said, e.g., of flame) jaillir
leap′ day′ s jour m intercalaire
leap′frog′ s saute-mouton m
leap′ year′ s année f bissextile
learn [lʌrn] v (pret & pp **learned** or **learnt** [lʌrnt]) tr apprendre ‖ intr apprendre; **to learn to** apprendre à
learned [′lʌrnɪd] adj savant, érudit

learn′ed jour′nal s revue f d'une société savante
learn′ed profes′sion s profession f libérale
learn′ed soci′ety s société f savante
learn′ed word′ s mot m savant
learner [′lʌrnər] s élève mf; (beginner) débutant m, apprenti m
learn′er's per′mit s (aut) permis m de conduire (d'un élève chauffeur)
learning [′lʌrnɪŋ] s (act and time devoted) étude f; (scholarship) savoir m, érudition f, science f
lease [lis] s bail m; **to give a new lease on life** donner un regain de vie ‖ tr (in the role of landlord) donner or louer à bail; (in the role of tenant) prendre à bail
lease′hold′ adj tenu à bail ‖ s tenure f à bail
leash [liʃ] s laisse f; **on the leash** en laisse, à l'attache; **to strain at the leash** (fig) ruer dans les brancards ‖ tr tenir en laisse
least [list] adj super (le) moindre §91 ‖ s (le) moins m; **at least** du moins; **at the very least** tout au moins; **not in the least** pas le moins du monde, nullement ‖ adv super (le) moins §91
leather [′lɛðər] s cuir m
leath′er·back′ tur′tle s luth m
leath′er·neck′ s (slang) fusilier m marin
leathery [′lɛðəri] adj (e.g., steak) (coll) coriace
leave [liv] s permission f; **by your leave** ne vous en déplaise; **on leave** en congé; (mil) en permission; **to give leave to s.o.** permettre or accorder à qn de; **to take leave (of)** prendre congé (de), faire ses adieux (à) ‖ v (pret & pp **left** [lɛft]) tr (to let stay; to stop, give up; to disregard) laisser; (to go away from) partir de, quitter; (to bequeath) léguer, laisser; (a wife) quitter, abandonner; **to be left** rester, e.g., **the letter was left unanswered** la lettre est restée sans réponse; e.g., **there are three dollars left** il reste trois dollars; **to be left for s.o.** to être à qn de; **to be left over** rester; **to leave about** (without putting away) laisser traîner; **to leave alone** laisser tranquille; **to leave it up to** s'en remettre à, s'en rapporter à; **to leave no stone unturned** faire flèche de tout bois, mettre tout en œuvre; **to leave off** (a piece of clothing) ne pas mettre; (a passenger) déposer; **to leave off** + ger cesser de + inf, renoncer à + inf; **to leave out** omettre ‖ intr partir, s'en aller; **where did we leave off?** où en sommes-nous restés?
leaven [′lɛvən] s levain m ‖ tr faire lever; (fig) transformer, modifier
leavening [′lɛvənɪŋ] adj transformateur ‖ s levain m
leave′ of ab′sence s congé m
leave′-tak′ing s congé m, adieux mpl
leavings [′livɪŋz] spl restes mpl, reliefs mpl
Leba·nese [,lɛbə′niz] adj libanais ‖ s (pl -nese) Libanais m

Lebanon ['lɛbənən] *s* le Liban
lecher ['lɛtʃər] *s* débauché *m*, libertin *m* ‖ *intr* vivre dans la débauche
lecherous ['lɛtʃərəs] *adj* lubrique, lascif
lechery ['lɛtʃəri] *s* lubricité *f*, lasciveté *f*
lectern ['lɛktərn] *s* lutrin *m*
lecture ['lɛktʃər] *s* conférence *f*; (*tedious reprimand*) sermon *m* ‖ *tr* faire une conférence à; (*to rebuke*) sermonner ‖ *intr* faire une conférence or des conférences
lecturer ['lɛktʃərər] *s* conférencier *m*
ledge [lɛdʒ] *s* saillie *f*, corniche *f*; (*projection in a wall*) corniche *f*
ledger ['lɛdʒər] *s* (*slab*) pierre *f* tombale; (com) grand livre *m*
ledg′er line′ *s* (mus) ligne *f* supplémentaire
lee [li] *s* (*shelter*) (naut) abri *m*; (*quarter toward which wind blows*) côté *m* sous le vent; **lees lie** *f*
leech [litʃ] *s* sangsue *f*; **to stick like a leech** to s.o. s'accrocher à qn
leek [lik] *s* poireau *m*
leer [lɪr] *s* regard *m* lubrique, œillade *f* ‖ *intr* lancer or jeter une œillade; **to leer at** lorgner
leer·y ['lɪri] *adj* (comp **-ier**; super **-iest**) (coll) soupçonneux, méfiant
leeward ['liwərd], ['lu·ərd] *adj & adv* sous le vent ‖ *s* côté *m* sous le vent; **to pass to leeward of** passer sous le vent de
Lee′ward Is′lands ['liwərd] *spl* îles *fpl* Sous-le-Vent
lee′way′ *s* (aer, naut) dérive *f*; (*of time, money*) (coll) marge *f*; (*for action*) (coll) champ *m*, liberté *f*
left [lɛft] *adj* gauche; (*left over*) de surplus ‖ *s* (*left hand*) gauche *f*; (boxing) gauche *m*; **on the left, to the left** à gauche; **the Left** (pol) la gauche; **to make a left** tourner à gauche ‖ *adv* à gauche
left′ field′ *s* (baseball) gauche *f* du grand champ
left′-hand′ drive′ *s* conduite *f* à gauche
left′-hand′ed *adj* gaucher; (*clumsy*) gauche; (*counterclockwise*) à gauche, en sens inverse des aiguilles d'une montre; (*e.g., compliment*) douteux, ambigu
leftish ['lɛftɪʃ] *adj* gauchisant
leftism ['lɛftɪzəm] *s* gauchisme *m*
leftist ['lɛftɪst] *adj & s* gauchiste *mf*
left′o′ver *adj* de surplus, restant ‖ **leftovers** *spl* restes *mpl*
left′-wing′ *adj* gauchiste, gauchisant
left-winger ['lɛft'wɪŋər] *s* (coll) gauchiste *mf*
left·y ['lɛfti] *adj* (coll) gaucher ‖ *s* (*pl* **-ies**) (coll) gaucher *m*
leg [lɛg] *s* jambe *f*; (*of boot or stocking*) tige *f*; (*of fowl; of frogs*) cuisse *f*; (*of journey*) étape *f*; **to be on one's last legs** n'avoir plus de jambes; **to pull the leg of** (coll) se payer la tête de, faire marcher
lega·cy ['lɛgəsi] *s* (*pl* **-cies**) legs *m*
legal ['ligəl] *adj* légal; (*practice*) juridique
le′gal hol′iday *s* jour *m* férié

legali·ty [lɪ'gæliti] *s* (*pl* **-ties**) légalité *f*
legalize ['ligə‚laɪz] *tr* légaliser
le′gal ten′der *s* cours *m* légal, monnaie *f* libératoire
legate ['lɛgit] *s* ambassadeur *m*, envoyé *m*; (eccl) légat *m*
legatee [‚lɛgə'ti] *s* légataire *mf*
legation [lɪ'geʃən] *s* légation *f*
legend ['lɛdʒənd] *s* légende *f*
legendary ['lɛdʒən‚dɛri] *adj* légendaire
legerdemain [‚lɛdʒərdɪ'men] *s* escamotage *m*, passe-passe *m*
leggings ['lɛgɪŋz] *spl* jambières *fpl*, guêtres *fpl*, leggings *fpl*
leg·gy ['lɛgi] *adj* (comp **-gier**; super **-giest**) (*awkward*) dégingandé; (*attractive*) aux longues jambes élégantes
leg′horn′ *s* (*hat*) chapeau *m* de paille d'Italie; (*chicken*) leghorn *f*, **Leghorn** Livourne *f*
legibility [‚lɛdʒɪ'brilɪti] *s* lisibilité *f*
legible ['lɛdʒɪbəl] *adj* lisible
legion ['lidʒən] *s* légion *f*
legislate ['lɛdʒɪs‚let] *tr* imposer à force de loi ‖ *intr* faire des lois, légiférer
legislation [‚lɛdʒɪs'leʃən] *s* législation *f*
legislative ['lɛdʒɪs‚letɪv] *adj* législatif
legislator ['lɛdʒɪs‚letər] *s* législateur *m*
legislature ['lɛdʒɪs‚letʃər] *s* assemblée *f* législative, législature *f*
legitimacy [lɪ'dʒɪtɪməsi] *s* légitimité *f*
legitimate [lɪ'dʒɪtɪmɪt] *adj* légitime ‖ [lɪ'dʒɪtɪ‚met] *tr* légitimer
legit′imate dra′ma *s* théâtre *m* régulier
legitimize [lɪ'dʒɪtɪ‚maɪz] *tr* légitimer
leg′ of lamb′ *s* gigot *m* d'agneau
leg′ of mut′ton *s* gigot *m*
leg′-of-mut′ton sleeve′ *s* manche *f* gigot
legume ['lɛgjum], [lɪ'gjum] *s* (*pod*) légume *m*; (bot) légumineuse *f*
leisure ['liʒər], ['lɛʒər] *s* loisir *m*; **at leisure** à loisir; **in leisure moments** à temps perdu
lei′sure class′ *s* désœuvrés *mpl*, rentiers *mpl*
lei′sure hours′ *spl* heures *fpl* de loisir
leisurely ['liʒərli], ['lɛʒərli] *adj* tranquille, posé ‖ *adv* posément, sans hâte
lemon ['lɛmən] *s* citron *m*; (*e.g., worthless car*) (coll) clou *m*
lemonade [‚lɛmə'ned] *s* citronnade *f*
lem′on squeez′er *s* presse-citron *m*
lem′on tree′ *s* citronnier *m*
lem′on verbe′na [vər'binə] *s* verveine *f* citronnelle
lend [lɛnd] *v* (*pret & pp* **lent** [lɛnt]) *tr* prêter
lender ['lɛndər] *s* prêteur *m*
lend′ing li′brary *s* bibliothèque *f* de prêt
length [lɛŋθ] *s* longueur *f*; (*e.g., of string*) bout *m*, morceau *m*; (*of time*) durée *f*; **at length** longuement, en détail; (*finally*) enfin, à la fin; **in length** de longueur; **to go to any length** to ne reculer devant rien pour; **to keep at arm's length** tenir à distance

lengthen ['lɛŋθən] tr allonger, rallonger ‖ intr s'allonger

length/wise/ adj longitudinal ‖ adv en longueur, dans le sens de la longueur

length·y ['lɛŋθi] adj (comp -ier; super -iest) prolongé, assez long

leniency ['lini·ənsi] s douceur f, clémence f

lenient ['lini·ənt] adj doux, clément

lens [lɛnz] s lentille f; (anat) cristallin m

Lent [lɛnt] s le Carême

Lenten ['lɛntən] adj de carême

lentil ['lɛntəl] s lentille f

leopard ['lɛpərd] s léopard m

leper ['lɛpər] s lépreux m

lep/er house/ s léproserie f

leprosy ['lɛprəsi] s lèpre f

leprous ['lɛprəs] adj lépreux

lesbian ['lɛzbi·ən] adj érotique; Lesbian lesbien ‖ s (female homosexual) lesbienne f; Lesbian Lesbien m

lesbianism ['lɛzbi·ə‚nɪzəm] s saphisme m

lese majesty ['liz'mædʒɪsti] s crime m de lèse-majesté

lesion ['liʒən] s lésion f

less [lɛs] adj comp moindre §91 ‖ s moins m ‖ adv comp moins §91; less and less de moins en moins; less than moins que; (followed by numeral) moins de; the less . . . the less (or the more) moins . . . moins (or plus)

lessee [lɛs'i] s preneur m; (e.g., of house) locataire mf; (e.g., of gasoline station) concessionnaire mf

lessen ['lɛsən] tr diminuer, amoindrir ‖ intr se diminuer, s'amoindrir

lesser ['lɛsər] adj comp moindre §91

lesson ['lɛsən] s leçon f

lessor ['lɛsər] s bailleur m

lest [lɛst] conj de peur que, de crainte que

let [lɛt] v (pret & pp let; ger letting) tr laisser; (to rent) louer; let + inf que, e.g., let him come in qu'il entre; let alone sans parler de, sans compter; let well enough alone le mieux est souvent l'ennemi du bien; let us eat, work, etc. mangeons, travaillons, etc.; to be let off with en être quitte pour; to let s louer, e.g., house to let maison à louer; to let alone, to let be laisser tranquille; to let by laisser passer; to let down baisser, descendre; (one's hair) dénouer, défaire; (e.g., a garment) allonger; (to leave in the lurch) laisser en panne, faire faux bond à; to let fly décocher; to let go laisser partir; to let have laisser, e.g., he let Robert have it for three dollars il l'a laissé à Robert pour trois dollars; to let in laisser entrer; to let in the clutch (aut) embrayer; to let into admettre dans; to let loose lâcher; to let off laisser partir; (e.g., steam from a boiler) laisser échapper, lâcher; (e.g., a culprit) pardonner à; to let oneself go se laisser aller; to let on that (coll) faire croire que; to let out faire ou laisser sortir; (e.g., a

dress) élargir; (a cry; a secret; a prisoner) laisser échapper; (to reveal) révéler, divulguer; to let out on bail relâcher sous caution; to let out the clutch débrayer; to let slip laisser tomber; to let s.o. + inf permettre à qn de + inf; laisser qn + inf, e.g., he let Mary go to the theater il a laissé Marie aller au théâtre; to let s.o. in on (a secret) (coll) confier à qn; (e.g., a racing tip) (coll) tuyauter qn sur; to let s.o. know s.th. faire savoir q.ch. à qn, mettre qn au courant de q.ch.; to let s.o. off faire grâce à qn de; to let stand laisser, e.g., let the errors stand il a laissé les fautes; to let s.th. go for (a low price) laisser q.ch. pour; to let through laisser passer; to let up laisser monter ‖ intr (said of house, apartment, etc.) se louer; to let down (coll) ralentir; to let go of lâcher prise de; to let out (said of class, school, etc.) finir, se terminer; to let up (coll) ralentir, se diminuer; (on discipline; on a person) devenir moins sévère

let/down/ s diminution f; (disappointment) déception f

lethal ['liθəl] adj mortel; (weapon) meurtrier

lethargic [lɪ'θɑrdʒɪk] adj léthargique

lethar·gy ['lɛθərdʒi] s (pl -gies) léthargie f

Lett [lɛt] s Letton m

letter ['lɛtər] s lettre f; to the letter à la lettre, au pied de la lettre ‖ tr marquer avec des lettres

let/ter box/ s boîte f aux lettres

let/ter car/rier s facteur m

let/ter drop/ s passe-lettres m, fente f (dans la porte pour le courrier)

lettered adj (person) lettré

let/ter file/ s classeur m de lettres

let/ter·head/ s en-tête m

lettering ['lɛtərɪŋ] s (action) lettrage m; (title) inscription f

let/ter of cred/it s lettre f de crédit

let/ter o/pener s coupe-papier m

let/ter pa/per s papier m à lettres

let/ter·per/fect adj correct; sûr

let/ter press/ s presse f à copier

let/ter press/ s impression f typographique; (in distinction to illustrations) texte m

let/ter scales/ spl pèse-lettre m

let/ter·word/ s sigle m

Lettish ['lɛtɪʃ] adj & s letton m

lettuce ['lɛtɪs] s laitue f

let/up/ s accalmie f, pause f; without letup sans relâche

leucorrhea [‚lukə'ri·ə] s leucorrhée f

leukemia [lu'kimi·ə] s leucémie f

Levant [lɪ'vænt] s Levant m

Levantine ['lɛvən‚tin], [lɪ'væntin] adj levantin ‖ s Levantin m

levee ['lɛvi] s (embankment) levée f, digue f; réception f royale

lev·el ['lɛvəl] adj de niveau, (flat) égal, uni; (spoonful) arasé; level with de niveau avec, à fleur de ‖ s niveau m; on a level with au niveau du; to be

on the level (coll) être de bonne foi; **to find one's level** trouver son niveau ‖ v (pret & pp **-eled** or **-elled**; ger **-eling** or **-elling**) tr niveler; (to smooth, flatten out) aplanir, araser; (to bring down) raser; (a gun) braquer; (accusations, sarcasm) lancer, diriger; **to level out** égaliser; **to level up** (aer) redresser ‖ intr (aer) redresser; **to level with** (coll) parler franchement à

lev•el-head/ed adj équilibré, pondéré

lev/eling rod/ s (surv) jalon-mire m, jalon m d'arpentage

lever ['livər], ['lɛvər] s levier m ‖ tr soulever or ouvrir au moyen d'un levier

leverage ['livərɪdʒ], ['lɛvərɪdʒ] s puissance f or force f de levier; (fig) influence f, avantage m

leviathan [lɪ'vaɪ-əθən] s léviathan m

levitation [,lɛvɪ'teʃən] s lévitation f

levi•ty ['lɛvɪti] s (pl -ties) légèreté f

lev•y ['lɛvi] s (pl -ies) levée f ‖ v (pret & pp -ied) tr lever; (a fine) imposer

lewd [lud] adj luxurieux, lubrique

lewdness ['ludnɪs] s luxure f, lubricité f

lexical ['lɛksɪkəl] adj lexical

lexicographer [,lɛksɪ'kɑgrəfər] s lexicographe mf

lexicographic(al) [,lɛksɪkə'græfɪk(əl)] adj lexicographique

lexicography [,lɛksɪ'kɑgrəfi] s lexicographie f

lexicology [,lɛksɪ'kɑlədʒi] s lexicologie f

lexicon ['lɛksɪkən] s lexique m

liabili•ty [,laɪ-ə'bɪlɪti] s (pl -ties) responsabilité f; (e.g., to disease) prédisposition f; **liabilities** obligations fpl, dettes fpl

liabil/ity insur/ance s assurance f tous risques

liable ['laɪ-əbəl] adj sujet; **liable for** (a debt, fine, etc.) passible de, responsable de; **we** (**you, etc.**) **are liable to** + inf (coll) il se peut que nous (vous, etc.) + pres subj; (coll) il est probable que nous (vous, etc.) + pres ind

liaison ['li-ə,zɑn], [li'ezɑn] s liaison f

liar ['laɪ-ər] s menteur m

libation [laɪ'beʃən] s libation f

li•bel ['laɪbəl] s diffamation f, calomnie f; (in writing) écrit m diffamatoire ‖ v (pret & pp -beled or -belled; ger -beling or -belling) tr diffamer, calomnier

libelous ['laɪbələs] adj diffamatoire, calomnieux

liberal ['lɪbərəl] adj libéral; (share, supply, etc.) libéral, généreux, copieux; (ideas) large ‖ s libéral m

liberali•ty [,lɪbə'rælɪti] s (pl -ties) libéralité f; (breadth of mind) largeur f de vues

lib/eral-mind/ed adj tolérant

liberate ['lɪbə,ret] tr libérer

liberation [,lɪbə're/ən] s libération f

liberator ['lɪbə,retər] s libérateur m

libertine ['lɪbər,tin] adj & s libertin m

liber•ty ['lɪbərti] s (pl -ties) liberté f; **at liberty** en liberté; **at liberty to** libre de; **to take the liberty to** se permettre de, prendre la liberté de

libidinous [lɪ'bɪdɪnəs] adj libidineux

libido [lɪ'bido], [lɪ'baɪdo] s libido f

librarian [laɪ'brɛrɪ-ən] s bibliothécaire mf

librar•y ['laɪ,brɛri], ['laɪbrəri] s (pl -ies) bibliothèque f

li/brary num/ber s cote f

libret•to [lɪ'brɛto] s (pl -tos) livret m, libretto m

license ['laɪsəns] s permis m, licence f; (to drive) permis de conduire ‖ tr accorder un permis à, autoriser

li/cense num/ber s numéro m d'immatriculation; (aut) numéro m minéralogique

li/cense plate/ or tag/ s plaque f d'immatriculation, plaque minéralogique

licentious [laɪ'sɛn/əs] adj licencieux

lichen ['laɪkən] s lichen m

lick [lɪk] s coup m de langue; (salt lick) terrain m salifère; (blow) (coll) coup m; **at full lick** (coll) à plein gaz; **to give a lick and a promise to** (coll) nettoyer à la six-quatre-deux; (coll) faire un brin de toilette à ‖ tr lécher; (e.g., the fingers) se lécher; (to beat, thrash) (coll) enfoncer les côtes à, rosser; (to beat, surpass, e.g., in a sporting event) (coll) battre, enfoncer; (e.g., a problem) (coll) venir à bout de; **to lick into shape** (coll) dégrossir; **to lick up** lécher

licking ['lɪkɪŋ] s léchage m; (drubbing) (coll) raclée f

licorice ['lɪkərɪs] s réglisse f

lid [lɪd] s couvercle m; (eyelid) paupière f; (hat) (slang) couvre-chef m

lie [laɪ] s mensonge m; **to give the lie to** donner le démenti à ‖ v (pret & pp lied; ger lying) tr—**to lie one's way out** se tirer d'affaire par des mensonges ‖ intr mentir ‖ v (pret lay; pp lain [len]; ger lying) intr être couché; (to be located) se trouver; (e.g., in the grave) gésir, e.g., **here lies** ci-gît; **to lie down** se coucher

lie/ detec/tor s détecteur m de mensonges

lien [lin], ['li-ən] s privilège m, droit m de rétention

lieu [lu] s—**in lieu of** au lieu de

lieutenant [lu'tɛnənt] s lieutenant m; (nav) lieutenant m de vaisseau

lieuten/ant colo/nel s lieutenant-colonel m

lieuten/ant comman/der s (nav) capitaine m de corvette

lieuten/ant gov/ernor s (U.S.A.) vice-gouverneur m; (Brit) lieutenant-gouverneur m

lieuten/ant jun/ior grade/ s (nav) enseigne m de première classe

life [laɪf] s (pl lives [laɪvz]) vie f; (of light bulb, lease, insurance policy) durée f; **bigger than life** plus grand que nature; **for dear life** de toutes ses forces; **for life** à vie, pour la vie, à perpétuité; **for the life of me!** (coll) de ma vie!; **lives lost** morts *mpl*; **long life** longévité *f*; **never in my life!**, **not on your life!** jamais de la vie!; **run for your life!** sauve qui peut!; **such is life!** c'est la vie!; **taken from life** pris sur le vif; **to come to life** revenir à la vie; **to depart this life** quitter ce monde; **to risk life and limb** risquer sa peau

life′ annu′ity *s* viagère

life′ belt′ *s* ceinture *f* de sauvetage

life′blood′ *s* sang *m*; (fig) vie *f*

life′boat′ *s* chaloupe *f* de sauvetage; *(for shore-based rescue services)* canot *m* de sauvetage

life′ buoy′ *s* bouée *f* de sauvetage

life′ float′ *s* radeau *m* de sauvetage

life′ guard′ *s* (mil) garde *f* du corps

life′guard′ *s* sauveteur *m*, maître nageur *m*

life′ impris′onment *s* emprisonnement *m* à vie

life′ insur′ance *s* assurance *f* sur la vie, assurance-vie *f*

life′ jack′et *s* gilet *m* de sauvetage

lifeless [′laɪflɪs] *adj* sans vie, inanimé; *(colors)* embu, terne

life′like′ *adj* vivant, ressemblant

life′ line′ *s* ligne *f* or corde *f* de sauvetage

life′long′ *adj* de toute la vie, perpétuel

life′ mem′ber *s* membre *m* à vie

life′ of lei′sure *s* vie *f* de château

Life′ of Ri′ley [′raɪlɪ] *s* (slang) joyeuse vie *f*, vie oisive

life′ of the par′ty *s* (coll) boute-entrain *m*

life′ preserv′er [prɪ′zʌrvər] *s* appareil *m* de sauvetage

lifer [′laɪfər] *s* (slang) condamné *m* à perpétuité

life′ raft′ *s* radeau *m* de sauvetage

lifesaver [′laɪf,sevər] *s* sauveteur *m*; (fig) planche *f* de salut

life′sav′ing *s* sauvetage *m*

life′ sen′tence *s* condamnation *f* à perpétuité

life′-size′ *adj* de grandeur nature

life′time′ *adj* à vie || *s* vie *f*, toute une vie; **in his lifetime** de son vivant

life′work′ *s* travail *m* de toute une vie

lift [lɪft] *s* haussement *m*, levée *f*; aide *f*; (aer) poussée *f*; (Brit) ascenseur *m*; *(of dumbbell or weight)* arraché *m*; **to give a lift to** *(by offering a ride)* conduire d'un coup de voiture, faire monter dans la voiture; *(an aid)* donner un coup de main à; ranimer || *tr* lever, soulever; *(heart, mind, etc.)* élever, ranimer; *(a sail)* soulager; *(an embargo)* lever; *(e.g., passages from a book)* démarquer, plagier; *(to rob)* (slang) dérober; **to lift up** *(the hands)* lever; *(the head)* relever; *(the voice)* élever || *intr* se lever, se soulever; *(said of clouds, fog, etc.)* se lever, se dissiper

lift′ bridge′ *s* pont *m* levant, pont-levis *m*

lift′off′ *s* (rok) montée verticale, chandelle *f*

lift′ truck′ *s* chariot *m* élévateur

ligament [′lɪgəmənt] *s* ligament *m*

ligature [′lɪgətʃər] *s* ligature *f*

light [laɪt] *adj* léger; *(having illumination)* éclairé; *(color, complexion, hair)* clair; *(beer)* blond; *(wine)* léger; **to make light of** faire peu de cas de || *s* lumière *f*; *(to control traffic)* feu *m*; *(window or other opening in a wall)* jour *m*; *(example, shining figure)* lumière; *(headlight of automobile)* phare *m*; du feu, e.g., **do you have a light?** *(e.g., to light a cigarette)* avez-vous du feu?; **according to one's lights** selon ses lumières, dans la mesure de son intelligence; **against the light** à contre-jour; **in a false light** sous un faux jour; **in a new light** sous un jour nouveau; **in the same light** sous le même aspect; **it is light (out)** il fait jour; **lights** *(navigation lights; parking lights)* feux *mpl*; *(of sheep, calf, etc.)* mou *m*; **lights out** (mil) l'extinction *f* des feux; **to bring to light** mettre au jour; **to come to light** se révéler; **to shed or throw light on** éclairer; **to strike a light** allumer || *adv* à vide; **to run light** *(said of engine)* aller haut le pied || *v* (*pret* & *pp* **lighted** or **lit** [lɪt]) *tr* *(to furnish with illumination)* éclairer, illuminer; *(to set afire, ignite)* allumer; **to light the way for** éclairer; **to light up** illuminer || *intr* s'éclairer, s'illuminer; allumer; *(to perch)* se poser; **to light from** or **off** *(an auto, carriage, etc.)* descendre de; **to light into** *(to attack; to berate)* (slang) tomber sur; **to light out** *(to skedaddle)* (slang) décamper; **to light up** s'éclairer, s'illuminer; **to light upon** *(by happenstance)* tomber sur, trouver par hasard

light′ bulb′ *s* ampoule *f* électrique, lampe *f* électrique

light′ complex′ion *s* teint *m* clair

lighten [′laɪtən] *tr* *(to make lighter in weight)* alléger, soulager; *(to provide more light)* éclairer, illuminer; *(to give a lighter or brighter hue to)* éclaircir; *(grief, punishment, etc.)* adoucir || *intr* *(to become less dark or sorrowful)* s'éclaircir; *(to give off flashes of lightning)* faire des éclairs; *(to becomes less weighty)* s'alléger

lighter [′laɪtər] *s* *(to light cigarette)* briquet *m*; *(flat-bottomed barge)* chaland *m*, péniche *f*

light′-fin′gered *adj* à doigts agiles

light′-foot′ed *adj* au pied léger

light′-head′ed *adj* étourdi

light′-heart′ed *adj* joyeux, allègre, au cœur léger

light′house′ *s* phare *m*

lighting [′laɪtɪŋ] *s* allumage *m*, éclairage *m*

light′ing fix′tures *spl* appareils *mpl* d'éclairage

light′ me′ter *s* posemètre *m*

lightness [′laɪtnɪs] *s* *(in weight)* légèreté *f*; *(in illumination; of complexion)* clarté *f*

light·ning ['laɪtnɪŋ] s (electric discharge) foudre f; (light produced by this discharge) éclairs mpl || v (ger -ning) intr faire des éclairs
light'ning arrest'er [ə,rɛstər] s parafoudre m
light'ning bug' s luciole f
light'ning rod' s paratonnerre m
light' op'era s opérette f
light' read'ing s livres mpl d'agrément; lecture f légère ou amusante
light'ship' s bateau-feu m
light-struck ['laɪt,strʌk] adj (phot) voilé
light' wave' s onde f lumineuse
light'weight' adj léger || s (sports) poids m léger
light'weight coat' s surtout m de demi-saison
light'-year' s année-lumière f
likable ['laɪkəbəl] adj sympathique
like [laɪk] adj (alike) pareils, semblables; pareil à, semblable à; (typical of) caractéristique de; (poles of a magnet) (elec) de même nom; **like father like son** tel père tel fils; **that is like him** il n'en fait pas d'autres || s pareil m, semblable m; **likes** (desires) goût m, inclinations fpl; **the likes of him** son pareil || adv—**like enough** probablement; **like mad** comme un fou || prep comme; **like that** de la sorte || conj (coll) de la même manière que, comme || tr aimer, aimer bien, trouver bon; plaire (with dat), e.g., **I like milk** le lait me plaît; se plaire, e.g., **I like it in the country** je me plais à la campagne || intr vouloir; **as you like** comme vous voudrez; **if you like** si vous voulez
likelihood ['laɪklɪ,hud] s probabilité f, vraisemblance f
like·ly ['laɪklɪ] adj (comp -lier; super -liest) probable, vraisemblable; **to be likely to** + inf être probable que + ind, e.g., **Mary is likely to come to see us tomorrow** il est probable que Marie viendra nous voir demain || adv probablement, vraisemblablement
like'-mind'ed adj du même avis
liken ['laɪkən] tr comparer, assimiler
likeness ['laɪknɪs] s (picture or image) portrait m; (similarity) ressemblance f
like'wise' adv également, de même; **to do likewise** en faire autant
liking ['laɪkɪŋ] s sympathie f, penchant m; **to one's liking** à souhait; **to take a liking to** (a thing) accueillir avec sympathie; (a person) montrer de la sympathie à, se prendre d'amitié pour
lilac ['laɪlək] adj & s lilas m
Lilliputian [,lɪlɪ'pjuʃən] adj & s lilliputien m
lilt [lɪlt] s cadence f
lil·y ['lɪlɪ] s (pl -ies) lis m, lis blanc; (royal arms of France) fleur f de lis; **to gild the lily** orner la beauté même
lil'y of the val'ley s muguet m
lil'y pad' s feuille f de nénuphar

lil'y-white' adj blanc comme le lis, lilial
Li'ma bean' ['laɪmə] s (Phaseolus limensis) haricot m de Lima
limb [lɪm] s (arm or leg) membre m; (of a tree) branche f; (of a cross; of the sea) bras m; (astr, bot) limbe m; **to be out on a limb** (coll) être sur la corde raide
limber ['lɪmbər] adj souple, flexible || intr—**to limber up** se dégourdir
lim·bo ['lɪmbo] s (pl -bos) limbes mpl
lime [laɪm] s (calcium oxide) chaux f; (linden tree) tilleul m; (Citrus aurantifolia) citron m; **sweet lime** (Citrus limetta) lime f
lime'kiln' s four m à chaux
lime'light' s—**to be in the limelight** être sous les feux de la rampe
limerick ['lɪmərɪk] s poème m humoristique en cinq vers
lime'stone' adj calcaire || s calcaire m, pierre f à chaux
limit ['lɪmɪt] s limite f, borne f; **to be the limit** (to be exasperating) (coll) être le comble; (to be bizarre) (coll) être impayable; **to go the limit** aller jusqu'au bout || tr limiter, borner
limitation [,lɪmɪ'teʃən] s limitation f
lim'ited-ac'cess high'way s autoroute f
lim'ited mon'archy s monarchie f constitutionnelle
limitless ['lɪmɪtlɪs] adj sans bornes, illimité
limousine ['lɪmə,zin], [,lɪmə'zin] s (aut) limousine f
limp [lɪmp] adj mou, flasque, souple || s boiterie f || intr boiter
limpid ['lɪmpɪd] adj limpide
linchpin ['lɪntʃ,pɪn] s cheville f d'essieu, esse f
linden ['lɪndən] s tilleul m
line [laɪn] s ligne f; (of poetry) vers m; (rope, string) cordage m, corde f; (wrinkle) ride f; (dash) trait m; (bar) barre f; (lineage) lignée f; (trade) métier m; (of merchandise) article m; (of traffic) file f; (mil) rang m; (of the spectrum) (phys) raie f; **hold the line!** (telp) ne quittez pas!; **in line** aligné, en rang; **in line with** conforme à, d'accord avec; **on the line** (telp) au bout du fil; **out of line** désaligné; en désaccord; **to bring into line with** mettre d'accord avec; **to drop s.o. a line** envoyer un mot à qn; **to fall into line** se mettre en ligne, s'aligner; **to hand s.o. a line** (slang) faire du baratin à qn, bourrer le crâne de qn; **to have a line on** (coll) se tuyauter sur; **to learn one's lines** apprendre son texte ou rôle; **to read between the lines** lire entre les lignes; **to stand or wait in line** faire la queue; **to toe the line** se mettre au pas || tr aligner; (a face) rider; (a suit, coat, etc.) doubler; (brakes) fourrer; **to be lined with** (e.g., trees) être bordé de || intr—**to line up** s'aligner, se mettre en ligne; faire la queue
lineage ['lɪnɪ·ɪdʒ] s lignée f, race f

lineal ['lɪnɪ·əl] adj linéal; (succession) en ligne directe

lineaments ['lɪnɪ·əmənts] spl linéaments mpl

linear ['lɪnɪ·ər] adj linéaire

lined' pa'per s papier m rayé

line'man s (pl -men) (elec) poseur m de lignes; (rr) garde-ligne m

linen ['lɪnən] adj de lin ‖ s (fabric) toile f de lin; (yarn) fil m de lin; (sheets, tablecloths, underclothes, etc.) linge m, lingerie f; **pure linen** pur fil

lin'en clos'et s lingerie f

line' of fire' s (mil) ligne f de tir

line' of sight' s ligne f de mire

liner ['laɪnər] s (naut) paquebot m

line'-up' s mise f en rang; personnel m; (arrangement) disposition f; (of prisoners) défilé m de détenus, alignement m de suspects; (sports) composition f

linger ['lɪŋgər] intr s'attarder; (said of hope, doubt, etc.) persister; **to linger on** traîner; **to linger over** s'attarder sur

lingerie [,læŋʒə'rɪ] s lingerie f fine pour dames, lingerie de dame

lingering ['lɪŋgərɪŋ] adj prolongé, lent

lingual ['lɪŋgwəl] adj lingual ‖ s (consonant) linguale f

linguist ['lɪŋgwɪst] s (person skilled in several languages) polyglotte mf; (specialist in linguistics) linguiste mf

linguistic [lɪŋ'gwɪstɪk] adj linguistique ‖ **linguistics** s linguistique f

liniment ['lɪnɪmənt] s liniment m

lining ['laɪnɪŋ] s (of a coat) doublure f; (of a hat) coiffe f; (of auto brake) garniture f; (of furnace, wall, etc.) revêtement m

link [lɪŋk] s maillon m, chaînon m; (fig) lien m; **links** terrain m de golf ‖ tr enchaîner; lier ‖ intr—**to link in, on,** or **up** se lier

linnet ['lɪnɪt] s (orn) linotte f

linoleum [lɪ'nolɪ·əm] s linoléum m

linotype ['laɪnə,taɪp] (trademark) s linotype f ‖ tr & intr composer à la lino

lin'otype op'erator s linotypiste mf

linseed ['lɪn,sid] s linette f, graine f de lin

lin'seed oil' s huile f de lin

lint [lɪnt] s bourre f, filasse f; (used to dress wounds) charpie f

lintel ['lɪntəl] s linteau m

lion ['laɪ·ən] s lion m; (fig) lion m; **to put one's head in the lion's mouth** se fourrer dans la gueule du loup or du lion

lioness ['laɪ·ənɪs] s lionne f

li'on-heart'ed adj au cœur de lion

lionize ['laɪ·ə,naɪz] tr faire une célébrité de, traiter en vedette

li'ons' den' s (Bib) fosse f aux lions

li'on's share' s part f du lion

lip [lɪp] s lèvre f; (edge) bord m; (slang) impertinence f; **to hang on the lips of** être suspendu aux lèvres de; **to smack one's lips** se lécher les babines

lip'read' v (pret & pp -read [,rɛd]) tr & intr lire sur les lèvres

lip' read'ing s lecture f sur les lèvres

lip' serv'ice s dévotion f des lèvres

lip'stick' s bâton m de rouge à lèvres

lique·fy ['lɪkwɪ,faɪ] v (pret & pp -fied) tr liquéfier

liqueur [lɪ'kʌr] s liqueur f

liquid ['lɪkwɪd] adj liquide ‖ s liquide m; (consonant) liquide f

liq'uid as'sets spl valeurs fpl disponibles

liquidate ['lɪkwɪ,det] tr & intr liquider

liquidity [lɪ'kwɪdɪtɪ] s liquidité f

liquor ['lɪkər] s boisson f alcoolique, spiritueux m; (culin) jus m, bouillon m

Lisbon ['lɪzbən] s Lisbonne f

lisle [laɪl] s fil m d'Écosse, fil retors de coton

lisp [lɪsp] s zézayement m, blésement m ‖ intr zézayer, bléser

lissome ['lɪsəm] adj souple, flexible; (nimble) agile, leste

list [lɪst] s liste f; (selvage) lisière f; (naut) bande f; **to enter the lists** entrer en lice; **to have a list** (naut) donner de la bande ‖ tr cataloguer, enregistrer ‖ intr (naut) donner de la bande

listen ['lɪsən] intr écouter; **to listen in** rester à l'écoute; **to listen to** écouter; **to listen to reason** entendre raison

listener ['lɪsənər] s auditeur m; (educ) auditeur libre

listening ['lɪsənɪŋ] s écoute f

lis'tening post' s poste m d'écoute

listless ['lɪstlɪs] adj apathique, inattentif

list' price' s prix m courant, cote f

lita·ny ['lɪtənɪ] s (pl -nies) litanie f

liter ['litər] s litre m

literal ['lɪtərəl] adj littéral; (person) prosaïque

literary ['lɪtə,rɛrɪ] adj littéraire

literate ['lɪtərɪt] adj qui sait lire et écrire; (well-read) lettré ‖ s personne f qui sait lire et écrire; lettré m, érudit m

literati [,lɪtə'ratɪ] spl littérateurs mpl

literature ['lɪtərət∫ər] s littérature f; (com) documentation f

lithe [laɪð] adj souple, flexible

lithia ['lɪθɪ·ə] s (chem) lithine f

lithium ['lɪθɪ·əm] s (chem) lithium m

lithograph ['lɪθə,græf], ['lɪθə,grɑf] s lithographie f ‖ tr lithographier

lithographer [lɪ'θagrəfər] s lithographe mf

lithography [lɪ'θagrəfɪ] s lithographie f

Lithuania [,lɪθɪu'enɪ·ə] s Lituanie f; la Lituanie

Lithuanian [,lɪθɪu'enɪ·ən] adj lituanien ‖ s (language) lituanien m; (person) Lituanien m

litigant ['lɪtɪgənt] adj plaidant ‖ s plaideur m

litigate ['lɪtɪ,get] tr mettre en litige ‖ intr plaider

litigation [,lɪtɪ'ge∫ən] s litige m

lit′mus pa′per ['lɪtməs] *s* papier *m* de tournesol

litter ['lɪtər] *s* fouillis *m*; (*things strewn about*) jonchée *f*; (*scattered rubbish*) ordures *fpl*; (*young brought forth at one birth*) portée *f*; (*bedding for animals*) litière *f*; (*vehicle carried by men or animals*) palanquin *m*; (*stretcher*) civière *f* ‖ *tr* joncher ‖ *intr* (*to bring forth young*) mettre bas

lit′ter-bug′ *s* souillon *m*, malpropre *m*, personne *f* qui dépose des ordures et des papiers dans la rue

littering ['lɪtərɪŋ] *s*—**no littering** (*public sign*) défense de déposer des ordures

little ['lɪtəl] *adj* petit; (*in amount*) peu de, e.g., **little money** peu d'argent; **a little** un peu de, e.g., **a little money** un peu d'argent ‖ *s* peu *m*; **a little** un peu; **to make little of, to think little** of faire peu de cas de; **wait a little** attendez un petit moment, attendez quelques instants ‖ *adv* peu §91; ne . . . guère §90, e.g., **she little thinks that** elle ne se doute guère que; **little by little** peu à peu, petit à petit

Lit′tle Bear′ *s* Petite Ourse *f*

Lit′tle Dip′per *s* Petit Chariot *m*

lit′tle fin′ger *s* petit doigt *m*, auriculaire *m*; **to twist around one's little finger** mener par le bout du nez

lit′tle-neck′ *s* coque *f* de Vénus

littleness ['lɪtəlnɪs] *s* petitesse *f*

lit′tle owl′ *s* (*Athene noctua*) chouette *f* chevêche, chevêche *f*

lit′tle peo′ple *spl* (*fairies*) fées *fpl*; (*common people*) menu peuple *m*

Lit′tle Red Rid′ing-hood′ *s* le Petit Chaperon rouge

lit′tle slam′ *s* (bridge) petit chelem *m*

liturgic(al) [lɪ′tʌrdʒɪk(əl)] *adj* liturgique

litur·gy ['lɪtərdʒi] *s* (*pl* **-gies**) liturgie *f*

livable ['lɪvəbəl] *adj* (*house*) habitable; (*life, person*) supportable

live [laɪv] *adj* vivant, vif; (*coals; flame*) ardent; (elec) sous tension; (telv) en direct ‖ [lɪv] *tr* vivre; **to live down** faire oublier ‖ *intr* vivre; (*in a certain locality*) demeurer, habiter; **live and learn** qui vivra verra; **to live high** mener grand train; **to live in** (*e.g., a city*) habiter; **to live on** continuer à vivre; (*e.g., meat*) vivre de; (*a benefactor*) vivre aux crochets de; (*one's capital*) manger; **to live up to** (*e.g., one's reputation*) faire honneur à

live′ coal′ [laɪv] *s* charbon *m* ardent

livelihood ['laɪvlɪ,hʊd] *s* vie *f*; **to earn one's livelihood** gagner sa vie

livelong ['lɪv,lɔŋ], ['lɪv,lɑŋ] *adj*—**all the livelong day** toute la sainte journée

live·ly ['laɪvli] *adj* (*comp* **-lier**; *super* **-liest**) animé, vivant, plein d'entrain; (*merry*) enjoué, gai; (*active, keen*) vif; (*resilient*) élastique

liven ['laɪvən] *tr* animer ‖ *intr* s'animer

liver ['lɪvər] *s* vivant *m*; (*e.g., in cities*) habitant *m*; (anat) foie *m*

liver·y ['lɪvəri] *s* (*pl* **-ies**) livrée *f*

liv′ery-man *s* (*pl* **-men**) loueur *m* de chevaux

liv′ery sta′ble *s* écurie *f* de louage

live′ show′ [laɪv] *s* (telv) prise *f* de vues en direct

live′stock′ [laɪv] *s* bétail *m*, bestiaux *mpl*, cheptel *m*

live′ tel′evision broad′cast [laɪv] *s* prise *f* de vues en direct

live′ wire′ [laɪv] *s* fil *m* sous tension; (slang) type *m* dynamique

livid ['lɪvɪd] *adj* livide

living ['lɪvɪŋ] *adj* vivant, en vie ‖ *s* vie *f*; **to earn** or **to make a living** gagner sa vie

liv′ing quar′ters *spl* appartements *mpl*, habitations *fpl*

liv′ing room′ *s* salle *f* de séjour, salon *m*

liv′ing space′ *s* espace *m* vital

liv′ing wage′ *s* salaire *m* suffisant pour vivre, salaire *m* de base

lizard ['lɪzərd] *s* lézard *m*

load [lod] *s* charge *f*; **loads (of)** (coll) énormément (de); **to get a load of** (slang) observer, écouter; **to have a load on** (slang) avoir son compte ‖ *tr* charger ‖ *intr* charger; se charger

loaded *adj* chargé; (*very drunk*) (slang) soûl; (*very rich*) (slang) huppé

load′ed dice′ *spl* dés *mpl* pipés

load′stone′ *s* pierre *f* d'aimant; (fig) aimant *m*

loaf [lof] *s* (*pl* **loaves** [lovz]) pain *m* ‖ *intr* flâner

loafer ['lofər] *s* flâneur *m*

loam [lom] *s* terre *f* franche, glaise *f*; (*mixture used in making molds*) potée *f*

loamy ['lomi] *adj* franc, glaiseux

loan [lon] *s* prêt *m*, emprunt *m* ‖ *tr* prêter

loan′ shark′ *s* usurier *m*

loan′ word′ *s* mot *m* d'emprunt

loath [loθ] *adj*—**loath to** peu enclin à

loathe [loð] *tr* détester

loathing ['loðɪŋ] *s* dégoût *m*

loathsome ['loðsəm] *adj* dégoûtant

lob [lab] *s* (tennis) lob *m* ‖ *v* (*pret* & *pp* **lobbed**; *ger* **lobbing**) *tr* frapper en hauteur, lober

lob·by ['labi] *s* (*pl* **-bies**) vestibule *m*; (*e.g., in a theater*) foyer *m*; (*pressure group*) groupe *m* de pression, lobby *m* ‖ *v* (*pret* & *pp* **-bied**) *intr* faire les couloirs

lobbying ['labɪ,ɪŋ] *s* intrigues *fpl* de couloir

lobbyist ['labɪ,ɪst] *s* intrigant *m* de couloir

lobe [lob] *s* lobe *m*

lobster ['labstər] *s* (*spiny lobster*) langouste *f*; (*Homarus*) homard *m*

lob′ster pot′ *s* casier *m* à homards

local ['lokəl] *adj* local ‖ *s* (*of labor union*) succursale *f*; (journ) informations *fpl* régionales; (rr) train *m* omnibus

locale [lo′kæl] *s* lieu *m*, milieu *m*; scène *f*

locali·ty [lo'kælɪtɪ] s (pl -ties) localité f

localize ['lokə,laɪz] tr localiser

lo'cal supply' cir'cuit s secteur m

locate [lo'ket], ['loket] tr (to discover the location of) localiser; (to place, to settle) placer, installer; (to ascribe a particular location to) situer; **to be located** se trouver ‖ intr se fixer, s'établir

location [lo'keʃən] s (place, position) situation f, emplacement m; (act of placing) établissement m; (act of finding) localisation f, détermination f; (of a railroad line) tracé m; **on location** (mov) en extérieur

loca'tion shot' s (mov) extérieur m

lock [lak] s serrure f; (of a canal) écluse f; (of hair) mèche f, boucle f; (of a firearm) platine f; (wrestling) clef f; **lock, stock, and barrel** tout le bataclan, tout le fourbi; **under lock and key** sous clé ‖ tr fermer à clef; (to key) caler, bloquer; (a boat) écluser, sasser; (a switch) (rr) verrouiller; **to be locked in each other's arms** être enlacés; **to lock in** enfermer à clef; **to lock out** fermer la porte à ou sur; (workers) fermer les ateliers contre; **to lock up** fermer à clef, mettre sous clé; (e.g., a prisoner) boucler, enfermer; (a form) (typ) serrer ‖ intr (said of door) fermer à clef; (said of brake, wheel, etc.) se bloquer; **to lock into** s'engrener dans

locker ['lakər] s armoire f, coffre m de sûreté (in a station) compartiment m individuel

lock'er room' s vestiaire m à cases individuelles

locket ['lakɪt] s médaillon m

lock'jaw' s trisme m

lock' nut' s contre-écrou m

lock'out' s lock-out m

lock'smith' s serrurier m

lock' step' s—**to march in lock step** emboîter le pas

lock' stitch' s point m indécousable

lock'ten'der s éclusier m

lock'up' s (prison) (coll) bloc m, violon m

lock' wash'er s rondelle f Grower, rondelle à ressort

locomotive [,lokə'motɪv] s locomotive f

lo·cus ['lokəs] s (pl -ci [saɪ]) lieu m; (math) lieu géométrique

locust ['lokəst] s (Pachytylus) (ent) criquet m migrateur, locuste f; (Cicada) (ent) cigale f; (bot) faux acacia m

lode [lod] s filon m, veine f

lode'star' s (astr) étoile f polaire; (fig) pôle m d'attraction

lodge [ladʒ] s (of gatekeeper; of animal; of Mason) loge f; (residence, e.g., for hunting) pavillon m; (hotel) relais m, hostellerie f ‖ tr loger; **to lodge a complaint with** porter plainte auprès de ‖ intr loger; (said of arrow, bullet) se loger

lodger ['ladʒər] s locataire mf, pensionnaire mf

lodging ['ladʒɪŋ] s logement m; (of a complaint) déposition f

loft [lɔft], [laft] s (attic) grenier m, soupente f; (hayloft) fenil m; (in theater or church) tribune f; (in store or office building) atelier m

loft·y ['lɔftɪ], ['laftɪ] adj (comp -ier; super -iest) (towering; sublime) élevé, exalté; (haughty) hautain

log [lɔg], [lag] s bûche f, rondin m; (record book) registre m de travail; (aer) livre m de vol; (record book) (naut) journal m de bord; (chip log) (naut) loch m; (rad) carnet m d'écoute; **to sleep like a log** dormir comme une souche ‖ v (pret & ger logged; ger logging) tr (wood) tronçonner; (an event) porter au journal; (a certain distance) (naut) filer ‖ intr (to cut wood) couper des rondins

logarithm ['lɔgə,rɪðəm], ['lagə,rɪðəm] s logarithme m

log'book' s (aer) livre m de vol; (naut) journal m de bord, livre de loch

log' cab'in s cabane f en rondins

log' chip' s (naut) flotteur m de loch

log' driv'er s flotteur m

log' driv'ing s flottage m

logger ['lɔgər], ['lagər] s bûcheron m; (loader) (mach) grue f de chargement; (mach) tracteur m

log'ger-head' s tête f de bois; **at loggerheads** en bisbille, aux prises

logic ['ladʒɪk] s logique f

logical ['ladʒɪkəl] adj logique

logician [lo'dʒɪʃən] s logicien m

logistic(al) [lo'dʒɪstɪk(əl)] adj logistique

logistics [lo'dʒɪstɪks] s logistique f

log'jam' s embâcle m de bûches; (fig) bouchon m, embouteillage m

log' line' s (naut) ligne f de loch

log'roll' intr faire trafic de faveurs politiques

log'wood' s bois m de campêche; (tree) campêche m

loin [lɔɪn] s (of beef) aloyau m; (of veal) longe f; (of pork) échine f; **to gird up one's loins** se ceindre les reins

loin'cloth' s pagne m

loiter ['lɔɪtər] tr—**to loiter away** perdre en flânant ‖ intr flâner

loiterer ['lɔɪtərər] s flâneur m

loll [lall] intr se prélasser, s'allonger, s'affaler

lollipop ['lalɪ,pap] s sucette f

Lom'bardy pop'lar ['lambərdɪ] s peuplier m noir

London ['lʌndən] adj londonien ‖ s Londres m

Londoner ['lʌndənər] s Londonien m

lone [lon] adj solitaire, seul; (sole, single) unique

loneliness ['lonlɪnɪs] s solitude f

lone·ly ['lonlɪ] adj (comp -lier; super -liest) solitaire, isolé

lonesome ['lonsəm] adj solitaire, seul

lone' wolf' s (fig) solitaire mf, ours m

long [lɔŋ], [laŋ] (comp **longer** ['lɔŋgər], ['lɔŋgər]; *super* **longest** ['lɔŋ-gɪst], ['lɑŋgɪst]) *adj* long; de long, de longueur, e.g., **two meters long** deux mètres de long or de longueur ‖ *adv* longtemps; **as long as** aussi long-temps que; (*provided that*) tant que; **before long** sous peu; **how long?** combien de temps?, depuis combien de temps?, depuis quand?; **long ago** il y a longtemps; **long before** longtemps avant; **longer** plus long; **long since** depuis longtemps; **no longer** ne . . . plus longtemps; ne . . . plus, e.g., **I could no longer see him** je ne pouvais plus le voir; **so long!** (coll) à bientôt!; **so long as** tant que; **to be long in** tarder à ‖ *intr*—**to long for** soupirer pour or après

long/boat/ *s* chaloupe *f*

long/ dis/tance *s* (telp) l'interurbain *m*; **to call s.o. long distance** appeler qn par l'interurbain

long/-dis/tance call/ *s* (telp) appel *m* interurbain

long/-dis/tance flight/ *s* (aer) vol *m* au long cours, raid *m* aérien

long/-drawn/-out/ *adj* prolongé; (*story*) délayé

longevity [lɑn'dʒɛvɪti] *s* longévité *f*

long/ face/ *s* (coll) triste figure *f*

long/hair/ *adj & s* intellectuel *m*; fanatique *mf* de la musique classique

long/hand/ *s* écriture *f* ordinaire; **in longhand** à la main

longing ['lɔŋɪŋ], ['lɑŋɪŋ] *adj* ardent ‖ *s* désir *m* ardent

longitude ['lɑndʒɪ‚t(j)ud] *s* longitude *f*

long/ jump/ *s* saut *m* en longueur

long-lived ['lɔŋ'laɪvd], ['lɔŋ'lɪvd], ['lɑŋ'laɪvd], ['lɑŋ'lɪvd] *adj* à longue vie; persistant

long/-play/ing rec/ord *s* disque *m* de longue durée

long/ prim/er ['prɪmər] *s* (typ) philosophie *f*

long/-range/ *adj* à longue portée; (*e.g., plan*) à long terme

long/shore/man *s* (*pl* -men) arrimeur *m*, débardeur *m*

long/-stand/ing *adj* de longue date

long/-suf/fering *adj* patient, endurant

long/ suit/ *s* (cards) couleur *f* longue, longue *f*; (fig) fort *m*

long/-term/ *adj* à longue échéance

long/-wind/ed ['wɪndɪd] *adj* interminable; (*person*) intarissable

look [lʊk] *s* (*appearance*) aspect *m*; (*glance*) regard *m*; **looks** apparence *f*, mine *f*; **to take a look at** jeter un coup d'œil sur or à ‖ *tr* regarder; (*e.g., one's age*) paraître; **to look daggers at** lancer un regard furieux à; **to look the part** avoir le physique de l'emploi; **to look up** (*e.g., in a dictionary*) chercher, rechercher; (*to visit*) aller voir, venir voir ‖ *intr* regarder; (*to seek*) chercher; **it looks like rain** le temps est à la pluie; **look here!** dites donc!; **look out!** gare!, attention!; **to look after** s'occuper de; (*e.g., an invalid*) soigner; **to look at** regarder; **to look away** détourner

les yeux; **to look back** regarder en arrière; **to look down on** mépriser; **to look for** chercher; (*to expect*) s'attendre à; **to look forward to** s'attendre à, attendre avec impatience; **to look ill** avoir mauvaise mine; **to look in on** passer voir; **to look into** examiner, vérifier; **to look like** (*s.o. or s.th.*) ressembler à; (*to give promise of*) avoir l'air de; **to look out** faire attention; (*e.g., the window*) regarder par; **to look out on** donner sur; **to look through** (*a window*) regarder par; (*a telescope*) regarder dans; (*a book*) feuilleter; **to look toward** regarder du côté de; **to look up** lever les yeux; **to look up to** respecter; **to look well** avoir bonne mine

looker-on [‚lʊkər'ɑn], [‚lʊkər'ɔn] *s* (*pl* **lookers-on**) spectateur *m*, assistant *m*

look/ing glass/ *s* miroir *m*

look/out/ *s* guet *m*; (*person*) guetteur *m*; (*place*) poste *m* d'observation; (*person or place*) (naut) vigie *f*; **that's his lookout** (coll) ça, c'est son affaire; **to be on the lookout for** être à l'affût de

loom [lum] *s* métier *m* ‖ *intr* apparaî-tre indistinctement; s'élever; mena-cer, paraître imminent

loon [lun] *s* lourdaud *m*, sot *m*; (orn) plongeon *m*

loon-y ['luni] *adj* (*comp* -**ier**; *super* -**iest**) (slang) toqué ‖ *s* (*pl* -**ies**) (slang) toqué *m*

loop [lup] *s* boucle *f*; (*for fastening a button*) bride *f*; (*circular route*) boulevard *m* périphérique; (*in skating*) croisé *m*; **to loop the loop** (aer) boucler la boucle ‖ *tr & intr* boucler

loop/hole/ *s* meurtrière *f*; (fig) échap-patoire *f*

loop/-the-loop/ *s* looping *m*

loose [lus] *adj* lâche; (*stone, tooth*) branlant; (*screw*) desserré; (*pulley, wheel*) fou; (*rope*) mou, détendu; (*coat, dress*) vague, ample; (*earth, soil*) meuble, friable; (*bowels*) re-lâché; (*style*) décousu; (*translation*) libre, peu exact; (*life, morals*) re-lâché, dissolu; (*woman*) facile; (*un-packaged*) en vrac; (*unbound, e.g., pages*) détaché; **to become loose** se détacher; **to break loose** (*from captivity*) s'évader; (fig) se déchaîner; **to let loose** lâcher, lâcher la bride à ‖ *s*—**to be on the loose** (*to debauch*) (coll) courir la prétentaine; (*to be out of work*) (coll) être sans occupa-tion ‖ *tr* lâcher; (*to untie*) détacher

loose/ end/ *s* (fig) affaire *f* pendante; **at loose ends** désœuvré, indécis

loose/-leaf note/book *s* cahier *m* à feuilles mobiles

loosen ['lusən] *tr* lâcher, relâcher; (*a screw*) desserrer ‖ *intr* se relâcher

looseness ['lusnɪs] *s* relâchement *m*; (*of garment*) ampleur *f*; (*play of screw*) jeu *m*, desserrage *m*

loose/strife/ *s* (*common yellow type*)

chasse-bosse *f*, grande lysimaque *f*; (*spiked-purple type*) salicaire *f*

loose'-tongued' *adj*—to be loose-tongued avoir la langue déliée

loot [lut] *s* butin *m*, pillage *m* ‖ *tr* piller, saccager

lop [lɑp] *v* (*pret & pp* lopped; *ger* lopping) *tr*—to lop off abattre, trancher; (*a tree, a branch*) élaguer ‖ *intr* pendre

lope [lop] *s* galop *m* lent ‖ *intr*—to lope along aller doucement

lop'sid'ed *adj* déjeté, bancal

loquacious [lo'kweʃəs] *adj* loquace

lord [lɔrd] *s* seigneur *m*; (*hum & poetic*) époux *m*; (*Brit*) lord *m* ‖ *tr*—to lord it over dominer despotiquement

lord·ly ['lɔrdli] *adj* (*comp* -lier; *super* -liest) de grand seigneur, majestueux; (*arrogant*) hautain, altier

Lord's' Day' *s* jour *m* du Seigneur

lordship ['lɔrd/ɪp] *s* seigneurie *f*

Lord's' Prayer' *s* oraison *f* dominicale

Lord's' Sup'per *s* communion *f*, cène *f*; Cène

lore [lor] *s* savoir *m*, science *f*; tradition *f* populaire

lorgnette [lɔrn'jɛt] *s* (*eyeglasses*) face-à-main *m*; (*opera glasses*) lorgnette *f*

lor·ry ['lɑri], ['lɔri] *s* (*pl* -ries) lorry *m*, wagonnet *m*; (*truck*) (Brit) camion *m*; (*wagon*) (Brit) fardier *m*

lose [luz] *v* (*pret & pp* lost [lɔst], [lɑst]) *tr* perdre; (*a patient who dies*) ne pas réussir à sauver; (*several minutes, as a timepiece does*) retarder de; **to lose oneself in** s'absorber dans; **to lose one's way** s'égarer ‖ *intr* perdre; (*said of timepiece*) retarder

loser ['luzər] *s* perdant *m*

losing ['luzɪŋ] *adj* perdant ‖ **losings** *spl* pertes *fpl*

loss [lɔs], [lɑs] *s* perte *f*; **to be at a loss** ne savoir que faire; **to be at a loss to** avoir de la peine à, être bien embarrassé pour; **to sell at a loss** vendre à perte

loss' of face' *s* perte *f* de prestige

lost [lɔst], [lɑst] *adj* perdu; **lost in thought** perdu or absorbé dans ses pensées; **lost to** perdu pour

lost'-and-found' depart'ment *s* bureau *m* des objets trouvés

lost' sheep' *s* brebis *f* perdue, brebis égarée

lot [lɑt] *s* lot *m*; (*for building*) lotissement *m*, lot; (*fate*) sort *m*, lot; **a bad lot** (coll) un mauvais sujet, de la mauvaise graine; **a lot of or lots of** (coll) un tas de; **a queer lot** (coll) un drôle de numéro; **in a lot** en bloc; **to cast or to throw in one's lot with** tenter la fortune avec; **to draw or to cast lots** tirer au sort; **such a lot of** tellement de; **what a lot of . . .** que de . . . !

lotion ['loʃən] *s* lotion *f*

lotter·y ['lɑtəri] *s* (*pl* -ies) loterie *f*

lotto ['lɑto] *s* loto *m*

lotus ['lotəs] *s* lotus *m*

loud [laud] *adj* haut, fort; (*noisy*) bruyant; (*voice*) fort; (*showy*) voyant ‖ *adv* fort; (*noisily*) bruyamment; **out loud** à haute voix

loud-mouthed ['laud,mauθt], ['laud,mauðd] *adj* au verbe haut

loud'speak'er *s* haut-parleur *m*

Louisiana [lu,izɪ'ænə] *s* Louisiane *f*, la Louisiane

lounge [laundʒ] *s* divan *m*, sofa *m*; (*room*) petit salon *m*, salle *f* de repos; (*in a hotel*) hall *m* ‖ *intr* flâner; (*e.g., in a chair*) se vautrer

lounge' liz'ard *s* (slang) gigolo *m*

louse [laus] *s* (*pl* lice [lais]) pou *m*; (slang) salaud *m* ‖ *tr*—to louse up (slang) bâcler

lous·y ['lauzi] *adj* (*comp* -ier; *super* -iest) pouilleux; (*mean; ugly*) (coll) moche; (*bungling*) (coll) maladroit, gauche; **lousy with** (slang) chargé de

lout [laut] *s* lourdaud *m*, balourd *m*

louver ['luvər] *s* abat-vent *m*; (aut) auvent *m*

lovable ['lʌvəbəl] *adj* aimable, sympathique

love [lʌv] *s* amour *m*; affection *f*; (tennis) zéro *m*; **in love with** amoureux de; **love at first sight** le coup de foudre; **love to all!** vives amitiés à tous!; **not for love or money** pour rien au monde; **to make love to** faire la cour à; **with much love!** avec mes affectueuses pensées! ‖ *tr & intr* aimer

love' affair' *s* affaire *f* de cœur

love'birds' *spl* inséparables *mpl*; nouveaux mariés *mpl*

love' child' *s* enfant *mf* de l'amour

love' feast' *s* (eccl) agape *f*

love' game' *s* (tennis) jeu *m* blanc

love' knot' *s* lacs *m* d'amour

loveless ['lʌvlɪs] *adj* sans amour; (*feeling no love*) insensible à l'amour

love' let'ter *s* billet *m* doux

lovelorn ['lʌv,lɔrn] *adj* délaissé d'amour; éperdu d'amour

love·ly ['lʌvli] *adj* (*comp* -lier; *super* -liest) beau; (*adorable*) charmant, gracieux; (*enjoyable*) (coll) agréable, aimable

love' match' *s* mariage *m* d'amour

love' po'tion *s* philtre *m* d'amour

lover ['lʌvər] *s* amoureux *m*, amant *m*; (*of hunting, sports, music, etc.*) amateur *m*, fanatique *mf*

love' seat' *s* causeuse *f*

love'sick' *adj* féru d'amour

love'sick'ness *s* mal *m* d'amour

love' song' *s* romance *f*, chanson *f* d'amour

loving ['lʌvɪŋ] *adj* aimant, affectueux; affectionné, e.g., **your loving daughter** votre fille affectionnée

lov'ing cup' *s* coupe *f* de l'amitié; trophée *m*

lov'ing-kind'ness *s* bonté *f* d'âme

low [lo] *adj* bas; (*speed; price*) bas; (*speed; price; number; light*) faible; (*opinion*) défavorable; (*dress*) décolleté; (*sound, note*) bas, grave; (*fever*) lent; (*bow*) profond; **to lay low** étendre, terrasser; **to lie low** se tenir coi ‖ *s* bas *m*; (*moo of cow*) meuglement *m*; (aut) première vitesse *f*; (meteo) dépression *f* ‖ *adv* bas; **to speak low** parler à voix basse ‖ *intr* (*said of cow*) meugler

low′born′ *adj* de basse naissance

low′boy′ *s* commode *f* basse

low′brow′ *adj* (coll) peu intellectuel ‖ *s* (coll) ignorant *m*

low′-cost′ hous′ing *s* habitations *fpl* à loyer modéré or à bon marché

Low′ Coun′tries *spl* Pays-Bas *mpl*

low′-down′ *adj* (coll) bas, vil ‖ **low′-down′** *s* (slang) faits *mpl* véritables; **to give s.o. the low-down on** (slang) tuyauter qn sur

lower [′lo·ər] *adj* inférieur, bas ‖ *tr & intr* baisser ‖ [′laυ·ər] *intr* se renfrogner, regarder de travers

low′er berth′ [′lo·ər] *s* couchette *f* inférieure

low′er case′ [′lo·ər] *s* (typ) bas *m* de casse

low′er mid′dle class′ [′lo·ər] *s* petite bourgeoisie *f*

lowermost [′lo·ər‚most] *adj* (le) plus bas

low′-fre′quency *adj* à basse fréquence

low′ gear′ *s* première vitesse *f*

lowland [′loland] *s* plaine *f* basse; **Lowlands** (*in Scotland*) Basse-Écosse *f*

low·ly [′loli] *adj* (*comp* **-lier;** *super* **-liest**) humble, modeste; (*in growth or position*) bas, infime

Low′ Mass′ *s* messe basse *f*, petite messe

low′-mind′ed *adj* d'esprit vulgaire

low′ neck′ *s* décolleté *m*

low′-necked′ *adj* décolleté

low′-pitched′ *adj* (*sound*) grave; (*roof*) à faible inclinaison

low′-pres′sure *adj* à basse pression

low′-priced′ *adj* à bas prix

low′ shoe′ *s* soulier *m* bas

low′-speed′ *adj* à petite vitesse

low′-spir′ited *adj* abattu

low′ spir′its *spl* abattement *m*, accablement *m*

low′ tide′ *s* marée *f* basse

low′ vis′ibil′ity *s* (aer) mauvaise visibilité *f*

low′-warp′ *adj* (tex) de basse lice

low′ wa′ter *s* (*of river*) étiage *m*; (*of sea*) niveau *m* des basses eaux; marée *f* basse

loyal [′lɔɪ·əl] *adj* loyal

loyalist [′lɔɪ·əlɪst] *s* loyaliste *mf*

loyal·ty [′lɔɪ·əlti] *s* (*pl* **-ties**) loyauté *f*

lozenge [′lazɪndʒ] *s* (*candy cough drop*) pastille *f*; (geom) losange *m*

LP [′εl′pi] *s* (letterword) (trademark) (**long-playing**) disque *m* de longue durée

lubricant [′lubrɪkənt] *adj & s* lubrifiant *m*

lubricate [′lubrɪ‚ket] *tr* lubrifier

lubricous [′lubrɪkəs] *adj* (*slippery*) glissant; (*lewd*) lubrique; inconstant

lucerne [lu′sʌrn] *s* luzerne *f*

lucid [′lusɪd] *adj* lucide

luck [lʌk] *s* (*good or bad*) chance *f*;

(*good*) chance, bonne chance; **to be down on one's luck, to be out of luck** avoir de la malchance, être dans la déveine; **to be in luck** avoir de la chance, avoir de la veine; **to bring luck** porter bonheur; **to try one's luck** tenter la fortune, tenter l'aventure; **worse luck!** tant pis!, pas de chance!

luckily [′lʌkɪli] *adv* heureusement, par bonheur

luckless [′lʌklɪs] *adj* malheureux, malchanceux

luck·y [′lʌki] *adj* (*comp* **-ier;** *super* **-iest**) heureux, fortuné; (*supposed to bring luck*) porte-bonheur; **how lucky!** quelle chance!; **to be lucky** avoir de la chance

luck′y charm′ *s* porte-bonheur *m*

luck′y find′ *s* (coll) trouvaille *f*

luck′y hit′ *s* (coll) coup *m* de bonheur

lucrative [′lukrətɪv] *adj* lucratif

ludicrous [′ludɪkrəs] *adj* ridicule, risible

lug [lʌg] *s* oreille *f*; (*pull, tug*) saccade *f* ‖ *v* (*pret & pp* **lugged;** *ger* **lugging**) *tr* traîner, tirer; (*to bring up irrelevantly*) (coll) ressortir, amener de force

luggage [′lʌgɪdʒ] *s* bagages *mpl*

lug′gage car′rier *s* porte-bagages *m*

lugubrious [lu′g(j)ubrɪ·əs] *adj* lugubre

lukewarm [′luk‚wɔrm] *adj* tiède

lull [lʌl] *s* accalmie *f* ‖ *tr* bercer, endormir, calmer

lulla·by [′lʌlə‚baɪ] *s* (*pl* **-bies**) berceuse *f*

lumbago [lʌm′bego] *s* lumbago *m*

lumber [′lʌmbər] *s* bois *m* de charpente, bois de construction ‖ *intr* se traîner lourdement

lum′ber·jack′ *s* bûcheron *m*

lum′ber jack′et *s* canadienne *f*

lum′ber·man *s* (*pl* **-men**) (*dealer*) exploitant *m* forestier, propriétaire *m* forestier; (*man who cuts down lumber*) bûcheron *m*

lum′ber raft′ *s* train *m* de flottage

lum′ber room′ *s* fourre-tout *m*, débarras *m*

lum′ber·yard′ *s* chantier *m* de bois, dépôt *m* de bois de charpente

luminar·y [′lumɪ‚nεri] *s* (*pl* **-ies**) corps *m* lumineux; (astr) luminaire *m*; (*person*) (fig) lumière *f*

luminescent [‚lumɪ′nεsənt] *adj* luminescent

luminous [′lumɪnəs] *adj* lumineux

lummox [′lʌməks] *s* (coll) lourdaud *m*

lump [lʌmp] *s* masse *f*; (*of earth*) motte *f*; (*of sugar*) morceau *m*; (*of salt, flour, porridge, etc.*) grumeau *m*; (*swelling*) bosse *f*; (*of ice, stone, etc.*) bloc *m*; **in the lump** en bloc; **to get a lump in one's throat** avoir un serrement de gorge ‖ *tr* réunir; **to lump together** prendre en bloc, englober ‖ *intr*—**to lump along** marcher d'un pas lourd

lumpish [′lʌmpɪʃ] *adj* balourd

lump′ sug′ar *s* sucre *m* en morceaux

lump′ sum′ *s* somme *f* globale

lump·y ['lʌmpi] adj (comp **-ier**; super **-iest**) grumeleux; (covered with lumps) couvert de bosses; (sea) clapoteux

luna·cy ['lunəsi] s (pl **-cies**) folie f

lu'nar land'ing s alunissage m

lu'nar mod'ule s (rok) module m lunaire

lunatic ['lunətɪk] adj & s fou m

lu'natic asy'lum s maison f de fous

lu'natic fringe' s minorité f fanatique

lunch [lʌntʃ] s (midday meal) déjeuner m; (light meal) collation f, petit repas m ‖ intr déjeuner; (to snack) casser la croûte, manger sur le pouce

lunch' bas'ket s panier m à provisions

lunch' cloth' s nappe f à thé

lunch' coun'ter s snack m, buffet m

luncheon ['lʌntʃən] s déjeuner m

luncheonette [ˌlʌntʃə'nɛt] s brasserie f, café-restaurant m

lunch'room' s brasserie f, café-restaurant m

lunch'time' s heure f du déjeuner

lung [lʌŋ] s poumon m

lunge [lʌndʒ] s mouvement m en avant; (with a sword) botte f ‖ intr se précipiter en avant; (with a sword) se fendre; **to lunge at** porter une botte à

lurch [lʌrtʃ] s embardée f; (of person) secousse f; **to leave in the lurch** laisser en plan ‖ intr faire une embardée; (said of person) vaciller

lure [lur] s (decoy) leurre m, amorce f; (fig) attrait m ‖ tr leurrer; **to lure away** détourner

lurid ['lurɪd] adj sensationnel; (gruesome) terrible, macabre; (fiery) rougeoyant; (livid) blafard

lurk [lʌrk] intr se cacher; (to prowl) rôder

luscious ['lʌʃəs] adj délicieux, succulent; luxueux, somptueux

lush [lʌʃ] adj plein de sève; (abundant) luxuriant; opulent, luxueux

lust [lʌst] s désir m ardent; (greed)

convoitise f, soif f; (strong sexual appetite) luxure f

luster ['lʌstər] s lustre m

lus'ter·ware' s poterie f lustrée, poterie à reflets métalliques

lustful ['lʌstfəl] adj luxurieux, lascif

lustrous ['lʌstrəs] adj lustré, chatoyant

lust·y ['lʌsti] adj (comp **-ier**; super **-iest**) robuste, vigoureux

lute [lut] s (mus) luth m; (substance used to close or seal a joint) (chem) lut m

Lutheran ['luθərən] adj luthérien ‖ s Luthérien m

Luxemburg ['lʌksəmˌbʌrg] s le Luxembourg

luxuriant [lʌg'ʒuri·ənt], [lʌk'ʃuri·ənt] adj luxuriant; (overornamented) surchargé

luxurious [lʌg'ʒuri·əs], [lʌk'ʃuri·əs] adj luxueux, somptueux

luxu·ry ['lʌkʃəri], ['lʌgʒəri] s (pl **-ries**) luxe m

lux'ury i'tem s produit m de luxe

lux'ury tax' s impôt m somptuaire

lyceum [laɪ'si·əm] s lycée m

lye [laɪ] s lessive f

lying ['laɪ·ɪŋ] adj menteur ‖ s le mensonge

ly'ing-in' hos'pital s maternité f, clinique f d'accouchement

lymph [lɪmf] s lymphe f

lymphatic [lɪm'fætɪk] adj lymphatique

lynch [lɪntʃ] tr lyncher

lynching ['lɪntʃɪŋ] s lynchage m

lynx [lɪŋks] s lynx m

Lyons ['laɪ·ənz] s Lyon m

lyre [laɪr] s (mus) lyre f

lyric ['lɪrɪk] adj lyrique ‖ s poème m lyrique; **lyrics** (of song) paroles fpl; (theat) chansons fpl du livret

lyrical ['lɪrɪkəl] adj lyrique

lyricism ['lɪrɪˌsɪzəm] s lyrisme m

lyricist ['lɪrɪsɪst] s poète m lyrique; (writer of words for songs) parolier m

M

M, m [ɛm] XIIIᵉ lettre de l'alphabet

ma'am [mæm], [mɑm] s (coll) madame f

macadam [mə'kædəm] s macadam m

macadamize [mə'kædəˌmaɪz] tr macadamiser

macaroon [ˌmækə'run] s macaron m

macaw [mə'kɔ] s (orn) ara m

mace [mes] s masse f

mace'bear'er s massier m

machination [ˌmækɪ'neʃən] s machination f

machine [mə'ʃin] s machine f; (of a political party) noyau m directeur, leviers mpl de commande ‖ tr usiner, façonner

machine' gun' s mitrailleuse f

ma·chine'-gun' v (pret & pp **-gunned**; ger **-gunning**) tr mitrailler

ma·chine'-made' adj fait à la machine

machiner·y [mə'ʃinəri] s (pl **-ies**) machinerie f, machines fpl; (of a watch; of government) mécanisme m; (in literature) merveilleux m

machine' screw' s vis f à métaux

machine' shop' s atelier m d'usinage

machine' tool' s machine-outil f

machine' transla'tion s traduction f automatique

machinist [mə'ʃinɪst] s mécanicien m

mackerel ['mækərəl] s maquereau m

mack'erel sky' s ciel m pommelé or moutonné

mad [mæd] adj (comp **madder**; super

maddest) fou; (*dog*) enragé; (coll) fâché, irrité; **as mad as a hatter** fou à lier; **like mad** (coll) comme un fou, éperdument; **to be mad about** (coll) être fou or passionné de; **to drive mad** rendre fou

madam ['mædəm] s madame f; (*of a brothel*) (slang) tenancière f

mad'cap' adj & s écervelé m, étourdi m

madden ['mædən] tr rendre fou || intr devenir fou

made-to-order ['medtə'ɔrdər] adj fait sur demande; (*clothing*) fait sur mesure

made'-up' adj inventé; (*artificial*) postiche; (*face*) maquillé

mad'house' s maison f de fous

mad'man' s (pl -men') fou m

madness ['mædnɪs] s folie f; (*of dog*) rage f

Madonna [mə'dɑnə] s madone f; (eccl) Madone

maelstrom ['melstrəm] s maelstrom m, tourbillon m

magazine ['mægə,zin], [,mægə'zin] s (*periodical*) revue f, magazine m; (*warehouse; for cartridges of gun or camera; for munitions or powder*) magasin m; (naut) soute f

mag'azine' rack' s casier m à revues

Magdalen ['mægdələn] s Madeleine f

Maggie ['mægi] s (coll) Margot f

maggot ['mægət] s asticot m

Magi ['medʒaɪ] spl mages mpl

magic ['mædʒɪk] adj magique || s magie f; **as if by magic** comme par enchantement

magician [mə'dʒɪʃən] s magicien m

magisterial [,mædʒɪs'tɪrɪ·əl] adj magistral

magistrate ['mædʒɪs,tret] s magistrat m

Magna Charta ['mægnə'kɑrtə] s la Grande Charte f

magnanimous [mæg'nænɪməs] adj magnanime

magnate ['mægnet] s magnat m

magnesium [mæg'niʃ/ɪ·əm], [mæg'niʒɪ·əm] s magnésium m

magnet ['mægnɪt] s aimant m

magnetic [mæg'nɛtɪk] adj magnétique; (fig) attrayant, séduisant

magnetism ['mægnɪ,tɪzəm] s magnétisme m

magnetize ['mægnɪ,taɪz] tr aimanter

magne·to [mæg'nito] s (pl -tos) magnéto f

magnificent [mæg'nɪfɪsənt] adj magnifique

magni·fy ['mægnɪ,faɪ] v (pret & pp -fied) tr grossir; (opt) grossir

mag'nifying glass' s loupe f

magnitude ['mægnɪ,t(j)ud] s grandeur f; (astr) magnitude f

magpie ['mæg,paɪ] s (orn, fig) pie f

mahlstick ['mɑl,stɪk], ['mɔl,stɪk] s appui-main m

mahoga·ny [mə'hɑgəni] s (pl -nies) acajou m

Mahomet [mə'hɑmɪt] s Mahomet m

mahout [mə'haʊt] s cornac m

maid [med] s (*servant*) bonne f; (*young girl*) jeune fille f, demoiselle f

maiden ['medən] s jeune fille f, demoiselle f

maid'en·hair' s (bot) capillaire m

maid'en·head' s hymen m

maid'en·hood' s virginité f

maid'en la'dy s demoiselle f, célibataire f

maidenly ['medənli] adj virginal, de jeune fille

maid'en name' s nom m de jeune fille

maid'en voy'age s premier voyage m

maid'-in-wait'ing s (pl maids-in-waiting) fille f d'honneur, dame f d'honneur

maid' of hon'or s demoiselle f d'honneur

maid'serv'ant s fille f de service, servante f

mail [mel] adj postal || s courrier m; (*system*) poste f; (*armor*) mailles fpl, cotte f de mailles; **by return mail** par retour du courrier; **mails** poste || tr mettre à la poste, envoyer par la poste

mail'bag' s sac m postal

mail'boat' s paquebot m, bateau-poste m

mail'box' s boîte f aux lettres

mail' car' s fourgon m postal, bureau m ambulant, wagon-poste m

mail' car'rier s facteur m

mail' clerk' s postier m; (mil, nav) vaguemestre m; (rr) convoyeur m des postes

mailing ['melɪŋ] s envoi m

mail'ing list' s liste f d'adresses; (*of subscribers*) liste d'abonnés

mail'ing per'mit s (label on envelopes) dispensé du timbrage

mail'man' s (pl -men') facteur m

mail' or'der s commande f par la poste

mail'-order house' s établissement m de vente par correspondance or de vente sur catalogue; comptoir m postal (Canad)

mail'-order sell'ing s vente f par correspondance

mail'plane' s avion m postal

mail' train' s train-poste m

maim [mem] tr mutiler, estropier

main [men] adj principal || s égout m collecteur, canalisation f or conduite f principale; **in the main** en général, pour la plupart

main' clause' s proposition f principale

main' course' s (culin) plat m principal, pièce f de résistance

main' deck' s pont m principal

main' floor' s rez-de-chaussée m

mainland ['men,lænd], ['menlənd] s terre f ferme, continent m

main' line' s (rr) grande ligne f

mainly ['menli] adv principalement

mainmast ['menməst], ['men,mæst], ['men,mast] s grand mât m

mainsail ['mensəl], ['men,sel] s grand-voile f

main'spring' s (of watch) ressort m moteur, grand ressort; (fig) mobile m essentiel, principe m

main'stay' s (naut) étai m de grand mât; (fig) point m d'appui

main' street' s rue f principale

maintain [men'ten] tr maintenir; (e.g., a family) entretenir, faire subsister

maintenance ['mentinəns] s entretien m, maintien m; (department entrusted with upkeep) services mpl d'entretien, maintenance f

maître d'hôtel [‚metərdo'tel] s maître m d'hôtel

maize [mez] s maïs m

majestic [mə'dʒestɪk] adj majestueux

majes·ty ['mædʒɪstɪ] s (pl -ties) majesté f

major ['medʒər] adj majeur || s (person of full legal age) majeur m; (educ) spécialisation f; (mil) commandant m || intr (educ) se spécialiser

Majorca [mə'dʒɔrkə] s Majorque f; île f de Majorque

Majorcan [mə'dʒɔrkən] adj majorquin || s Majorquin m

ma'jor gen'eral s général m de division

majori·ty [mə'dʒɑrɪtɪ] , [mə'dʒɔrɪtɪ] adj majoritaire || s (pl -ties) majorité f; (mil) grade m de commandant; **the majority of** la plupart de

major'ity vote' s scrutin m majoritaire

make [mek] s fabrication f; (brand name) marque f; modèle m || v (pret & pp made [med]) tr faire; rendre, e.g., **to make sick** rendre malade; (money) gagner; (the cards) battre; (a train) attraper; **to make into** transformer en; **to make known** faire savoir; **to make out** déchiffrer, distinguer; (a bill, receipt, check) écrire; (a list) dresser; **to make s.o. + inf** faire + inf + qn, e.g., **I will make my uncle talk** je ferai parler mon oncle || intr être, e.g., **to make sure** être sûr; **to make believe** feindre; **to make good** réussir; **to make off** filer, décamper

make'-believe' adj simulé || s faux-semblant m, feinte f

maker ['mekər] s fabricant m

make'shift' adj de fortune, de circonstance || s expédient m; (person) bouche-trou m

make'-up' s arrangement m, composition f; (cosmetic) maquillage m; (typ) mise f en pages, imposition f

make'-up man' s (theat) maquilleur m; (typ) metteur m en pages, imposeur m

make'weight' s complément m de poids

making ['mekɪŋ] s fabrication f; (of a dress; of a cooked dish) confection f; **makings** éléments mpl constitutifs; (money) recettes fpl; **to have the makings of** avoir l'étoffe de

maladjusted [‚mælə'dʒʌstɪd] adj inadapté

maladjustment [‚mælə'dʒʌstmənt] s inadaptation f

mala·dy ['mælədɪ] s (pl -dies) maladie f

malaise [mæ'lez] s malaise m

malaria [mə'lɛrɪ·ə] s malaria f, paludisme m

Malay ['mele], [mə'le] adj malais || s (language) malais m; (person) Malais m

Malaya [mə'le·ə] s Malaisie f; la Malaisie

malcontent ['mælkən‚tent] adj & s mécontent m

male [mel] adj & s mâle m

malediction [‚mælɪ'dɪk/ən] s malédiction f

malefactor ['mælɪ‚fæktər] s malfaiteur m

male' nurse' s infirmier m

malevolent [mə'levələnt] adj malveillant

malfeasance [‚mæl'fizəns] s prévarication f, trafic m

malice ['mælɪs] s méchanceté f

malicious [mə'lɪ/əs] adj méchant

malign [mə'laɪn] adj pernicieux; malveillant || tr calomnier

malignan·cy [mə'lɪgnənsɪ] s (pl -cies) malignité f

malignant [mə'lɪgnənt] adj méchant, malin

malinger [mə'lɪŋgər] intr faire le malade

malingerer [mə'lɪŋgərər] s simulateur m

mall [mɔl], [mæl] s mail m

mallard ['mælərd] s (orn) col-vert m

malleable ['mælɪ·əbəl] adj malléable

mallet ['mælɪt] s maillet m

mallow ['mælo] s (bot) mauve f

malnutrition [‚mæln(j)u'trɪ/ən] s sous-alimentation f, malnutrition f

malodorous [mæl'odərəs] adj malodorant

malpractice [mæl'præktɪs] s incurie f; méfait m

malt [mɔlt] s malt m

maltreat [mæl'trit] tr maltraiter

mamma ['mɑmə], [mə'mɑ] s maman f

mammal ['mæməl] s mammifère m

mammalian [mæ'melɪ·ən] adj & s mammifère m

mammoth ['mæməθ] adj énorme, colossal || s mammouth m

man [mæn] s (pl men [men]) s homme m; (servant) domestique m; (worker) ouvrier m, employé m; (checkers) pion m; (chess) pièce f; **a man on**, e.g., **what can a man do?** qu'est-ce qu'on peut faire?; **every man for himself!** sauve qui peut!; **man alive!** (coll) tiens!; fichtre!; **man and wife** mari et femme; **men at work** (public sign) travaux en cours || v (pret & pp manned; ger manning) tr (a ship) équiper; (a fort) garnir; (a cannon, the pumps, etc.) armer; (a battery) servir

man' about town' s boulevardier m, coureur m de cabarets

manacle ['mænəkəl] s manilla f; **manacles** menottes fpl || tr mettre les menottes à

manage ['mænɪdʒ] tr gérer, diriger; (to handle) manier || intr se débrouiller; **how did you manage to . . . ?** comment avez-vous fait pour . . . ?; **to manage to** s'arranger pour

manageable ['mænɪdʒəbəl] adj maniable

management ['mænɪdʒmənt] s direction f, gérance f; (group who manage) direction, administration f; (in contrast to labor) patronat m; **under new management** (public sign) changement de propriétaire

manager ['mænədʒər] s directeur m, gérant m; (e.g., of a department) chef m; (impresario) manager m

managerial [‚mænə'dʒɪrɪ·əl] adj patronal

man'aging ed'itor s rédacteur m gérant

Manchuria [mæn'tʃurɪ·ə] s Mandchourie f; la Mandchourie

man'darin or'ange ['mændərɪn] s mandarine f

mandate ['mændet] s mandat m ‖ tr placer sous le mandat de

mandatory ['mændə‚tori] adj obligatoire

mandolin ['mændəlɪn] s mandoline f

mandrake ['mændrek] s mandragore f

mane [men] s crinière f

maneuver [mə'nuvər] s manœuvre m ‖ tr & intr manœuvrer

manful ['mænfəl] adj viril, hardi

manganese ['mæŋgə‚nis], ['mæŋgə‚niz] s manganèse m

mange [mendʒ] s gale f

manger ['mendʒər] s mangeoire f, crèche f

mangle ['mæŋgəl] s calandre f ‖ tr lacérer, mutiler; (to press) calandrer

man·gy ['mendʒi] adj (comp -gier; super -giest) galeux; (dirty, squalid) miteux

man'han'dle tr malmener

man'hole' s trou m d'homme, regard m

manhood ['mænhud] s virilité f; humanité f

man'hunt' s chasse f à l'homme; chasse au mari

mania ['menɪ·ə] s manie f

maniac ['menɪ‚æk] adj & s maniaque mf

maniacal [mə'naɪ·əkəl] adj maniaque

manicure ['mænɪ‚kjur] s soins mpl esthétiques des mains et des ongles; (person) manucure mf ‖ tr manucurer

manicurist ['mænɪ‚kjurɪst] s manucure mf

manifest ['mænɪ‚fest] adj manifeste ‖ s (naut) manifeste m ‖ tr & intr manifester

manifestation [‚mænɪfes'teʃən] s manifestation f

manifes·to [‚mænɪ'festo] s (pl -toes) manifeste m

manifold ['mænɪ‚fold] adj multiple, nombreux ‖ s (aut) tuyauterie f, collecteur m

manikin ['mænɪkɪn] s mannequin m; (dwarf) nabot m

man' in the moon' s homme m dans la lune

man' in the street' s homme m de la rue

manipulate [mə'nɪpjə‚let] tr manipuler

man'kind' s le genre humain, l'humanité f ‖ **man'kind'** s le sexe fort, les hommes mpl

manliness ['mænlɪnɪs] s virilité f

man·ly ['mænli] adj (comp -lier; super -liest) viril, masculin

manna ['mænə] s manne f

manned' space'craft s vaisseau m spatial habité

mannequin ['mænɪkɪn] s mannequin m

manner ['mænər] s manière f; **by all manner of means** certainement; **by no manner of means** en aucune manière; **in a manner of speaking** pour ainsi dire; **in the manner of** à la, e.g., **in the manner of the French, in the French manner** à la manière française, à la française; **manners** manières; **manners of the time** mœurs fpl de l'époque; **to the manner born** créé et mis au monde pour ça

mannerism ['mænə‚rɪzm] s maniérisme m

mannish ['mænɪʃ] adj hommasse

man' of let'ters s homme m de lettres, bel esprit m

man' of parts' s homme m de talent

man' of straw' s homme m de paille

man' of the world' s homme m du monde

man-of-war [‚mænəv'wɔr] s (pl men-of-war) navire m de guerre

manor ['mænər] s seigneurie f

man'or house' s château m, manoir m

man' o'verboard' interj un homme à la mer!

man'pow'er s main-d'œuvre f; (mil) effectifs mpl

manse [mæns] s maison f du pasteur

man'serv'ant s (pl men'serv'ants) valet m

mansion ['mænʃən] s hôtel m particulier; château m, manoir m

man'slaugh'ter s (law) homicide m involontaire

mantel ['mæntəl] s manteau m de cheminée

man'tel·piece' s manteau m de cheminée; dessus m de cheminée

mantilla [mæn'tɪlə] s mantille f

mantle ['mæntəl] s manteau m, mante f; (of gaslight) manchon m ‖ tr envelopper d'une mante; couvrir, revêtir; (to hide) voiler ‖ intr (said of face) rougir

manual ['mænju·əl] adj manuel ‖ s (book) manuel m; (of arms) (mil) maniement m; (mus) clavier m d'orgue

man'ual dexter'ity s habileté f manuelle

man'ual train'ing s apprentissage m manuel

manufacture [‚mænjə'fæktʃər] s fabrication f; (thing manufactured) produit m fabriqué ‖ tr fabriquer

manufacturer [‚mænjə'fæktʃərər] s fabricant m

manure [mə'n(j)ur] s fumier m ‖ tr fumer

manuscript ['mænjə‚skrɪpt] adj & s manuscrit m

many ['meni] adj beaucoup de; **a good many** bien des, maintes; **how many** combien de; **many another** bien d'autres; **many more** beaucoup d'autres;

so many tant de; **too many** trop de; **twice as many** deux fois autant de ‖ *pron* adj; **as many as** autant de; jusqu'à, e.g., **as many as twenty** jusqu'à vingt; **how many** combien; **many a** maint; **many another** bien d'autres; **many more** beaucoup d'autres; **so many** tant; **too many** trop; **twice as many** deux fois autant

man'y-sid'ed adj polygonal; *(having many interests or capabilities)* complexe

map [mæp] s carte f; *(of a city)* plan m ‖ v *(pret & pp* **mapped**; *ger* **mapping)** tr faire la carte de; **to map out** tracer le plan de; **to put on the map** (coll) faire connaître, mettre en vedette

maple ['mepəl] s érable m

ma'ple sug'ar s sucre m d'érable

mar [mɑr] v *(pret & pp* **marred**; *ger* **marring)** tr défigurer, gâcher

marathon ['mærə‚θɑn] s marathon m

maraud [mə'rɔd] tr piller ‖ *intr* marauder

marauder [mə'rɔdər] s maraudeur m

marauding [mə'rɔdɪŋ] adj maraudeur ‖ s maraude f

marble ['mɑrbəl] s marbre m; *(little ball of glass)* bille f; **marbles** (game) jeu m de billes ‖ tr marbrer; *(the edge of a book)* jasper

march [mɑrtʃ] s marche f; **March** mars m; **to steal a march on** prendre de l'avance sur ‖ tr faire marcher ‖ *intr* marcher

marchioness ['mɑrʃənɪs] s marquise f

mare [mɛr] s *(female horse)* jument f; *(female donkey)* ânesse f

Margaret ['mɑrgərɪt] s Marguerite f

margarine ['mɑrdʒərɪn] s margarine f

margin ['mɑrdʒɪn] s marge f; *(border)* bord m; (com) acompte m

marginal ['mɑrdʒɪnəl] adj marginal

mar'gin release' s déclenche-marge f

mar'gin stop' s margeur m

marigold ['mærɪ‚gold] s *(Calendula)* souci m; *(Tagetes)* œillet m d'Inde

marihuana or **marijuana** [‚mærɪ-'hwɑnə] s marihuana f or marijuana f

marinate ['mærɪ‚net] tr mariner

marine [mə'rin] adj marin, maritime ‖ s flotte f; (nav) fusilier m marin; **tell it to the marines!** (coll) à d'autres!

Marine' Corps' s infanterie f de marine

mariner ['mærɪnər] s marin m

marionette [‚mærɪ‚ə'nɛt] s marionnette f

marital ['mærɪtəl] adj matrimonial

mar'ital sta'tus s état m civil

maritime ['mærɪ‚taɪm] adj maritime

marjoram ['mɑrdʒərəm] s marjolaine f; origan m

mark [mɑrk] s marque f, signe m; *(of punctuation)* point m; *(in an examination)* note f; *(spot, stain)* tache f, marque; *(monetary unit)* mark m; *(starting point in a race)* ligne f de départ; **as a mark of** en témoignage de; **Mark Marc** m; **on your mark!** à vos marques!; **to hit the mark** mettre dans le mille, atteindre le but; **to**

leave one's mark laisser son empreinte; **to make one's mark** se faire un nom, marquer; **to miss the mark** manquer le but; **to toe the mark** se conformer au mot d'ordre ‖ tr marquer; *(a student; an exam)* donner une note à; *(e.g., one's approval)* témoigner; **to mark down** noter; (com) démarquer; **to mark off** distinguer; **to mark up** (com) majorer

mark'down' s rabais m

marker ['mɑrkər] s marqueur m; *(of boundary)* borne f; *(landmark)* repère m

market ['mɑrkɪt] s marché m; **to bear the market** jouer à la baisse; **to bull the market** jouer à la hausse; **to play the market** jouer à la bourse; **to put on the market** lancer, vendre, or mettre sur le marché ‖ tr commercialiser

marketable ['mɑrkɪtəbəl] adj vendable

mar'ket bas'ket s panier m à provisions

marketing ['mɑrkɪtɪŋ] s marché m; *(of a product)* commercialisation f, exploitation f

mar'ket-place' s place f du marché

mar'ket price' s cours m du marché, prix m courant

mark'ing gauge' s trusquin m

marks·man ['mɑrksmən] s *(pl* -men) tireur m

marks'man·ship' s habileté f au tir, adresse f au tir

mark'up' s *(profit)* marge f bénéficiaire; *(price increase)* majoration f de prix

marl [mɑrl] s marne f ‖ tr marner

marmalade ['mɑrmə‚led] s marmelade f

maroon [mə'run] adj & s *(color)* lie f de vin, rouge m violacé ‖ tr abandonner, isoler

marquee [mɑr'ki] s marquise f

marquis ['mɑrkwɪs] s marquis m

marquise [mɑr'kiz] s marquise f

marriage ['mærɪdʒ] s mariage m

marriageable ['mærɪdʒəbəl] adj mariable

mar'riage certif'icate s acte m de mariage

mar'riage por'tion s dot f

mar'riage rate' s taux m de nuptialité

mar'ried life' ['mærɪd] s vie f conjugale

marrow ['mæro] s moelle f

mar·ry ['mærɪ] v *(pret & pp* -ried) tr *(to join in wedlock)* marier; *(to take in marriage)* se marier avec; **to get married to** se marier avec; **to marry off** marier ‖ *intr* se marier

Mars [mɑrz] s Mars m

Marseilles [mɑr'selz] s Marseille f

marsh [mɑrʃ] s marais m, marécage m

mar·shal ['mɑrʃəl] s maître m des cérémonies; *(policeman)* shérif m; (mil) maréchal m ‖ v *(pret & pp* -shaled or -shalled; *ger* -shaling or -shalling) tr conduire; *(one's reasons, arguments, etc.)* ranger, rassembler

marsh'mal'low s (bot) guimauve f

marsh'mal'low s *(candy)* pâte f de guimauve; bonbon m à la guimauve

marsh·y ['marʃi] adj (comp -ier; super -iest) marécageux

mart [mart] s marché m, foire f

marten ['martən] s (pine marten) martre f; (beech marten) fouine f

Martha ['marθə] s Marthe f

martial ['marʃəl] adj martial

mar'tial law' s loi f martiale

martin ['martɪn] s (orn) martinet m

martinet [,martɪ'net], ['martɪ,net] s pêtesec m

martyr ['martər] s martyr m || tr martyriser

martyrdom ['martərdəm] s martyre m

mar·vel ['marvəl] s merveille f || v (pret & pp -veled or -velled; ger -veling or -velling) intr s'émerveiller; **to marvel at** s'émerveiller de

marvelous ['marvələs] adj merveilleux

Marxist ['marksɪst] adj & s marxiste mf

Maryland ['merələnd] s le Maryland

marzipan ['marzɪ,pæn] s massepain m

mascara [mæs'kærə] s rimmel m

mascot ['mæskət] s mascotte f

masculine ['mæskjəlɪn] adj & s masculin m

mash [mæʃ] s (crushed mass) bouillie f; (to form wort) fardeau m || tr écraser; (malt, in brewing) brasser

mashed' pota'toes spl purée f de pommes de terre

masher ['mæʃər] s (device) broyeur m; (slang) tombeur m

mask [mæsk], [mask] s masque m; (phot) cache m || tr masquer; (phot) poser un cache à || intr se masquer

masked' ball' s bal m masqué

mason ['mesən] s maçon m; **Mason** Maçon

mason·ry ['mesənri] s (pl -ries) maçonnerie f; **Masonry** Maçonnerie

masquerade [,mæskə'red], [,maskə'red] s mascarade f || intr se déguiser; **to masquerade as** se faire passer pour

mass [mæs] s masse f; (eccl) messe f || tr masser || intr se masser

massacre ['mæsəkər] s massacre m || tr massacrer

massage [mə'saʒ] s massage m || tr masser

mass' arrest' s rafle f

masseur [mə'sʌr] s masseur m

masseuse [mə'suz] s masseuse f

massive ['mæsɪv] adj massif

mass' me'dia ['midɪ·ə] spl communication f de masse

mass' meet'ing s meeting m monstre, rassemblement m

mass' produc'tion s fabrication f en série

mast [mæst], [mast] s mât m; (food for swine) gland m, faîne f; **before the mast** comme simple matelot

master ['mæstər], ['mastər] s maître m; (employer) chef m, patron m; (male head of household) maître de maison; (title of respect) Monsieur m; (naut) commandant m || tr maîtriser; (a subject) connaître à fond, posséder

mas'ter bed'room s chambre f du maître

mas'ter build'er s entrepreneur m de bâtiments

masterful ['mæstərfəl], ['mastərfəl] adj magistral, expert; impérieux, en maître

mas'ter key' s passe-partout m

masterly ['mæstərli], ['mastərli] adj magistral, de maître || adv magistralement

mas'ter mechan'ic s maître m mécanicien

mas'ter-mind' s organisateur m, cerveau m || tr organiser, diriger

mas'ter of cer'emonies s maître m des cérémonies; (in a night club, on television, etc.) animateur m

mas'ter·piece' s chef-d'œuvre m

mas'ter stroke' s coup m de maître

mas'ter·work' s chef-d'œuvre m

master·y ['mæstəri], ['mastəri] s (pl -ies) maîtrise f

mast'head' s (of a newspaper) en-tête m; (naut) tête f de mât

masticate ['mæstɪ,ket] tr mastiquer

mastiff ['mæstɪf], ['mastɪf] s mâtin m

masturbate ['mæstər,bet] tr masturber || intr se masturber

mat [mæt] s (for floor) natte f; (for a cup, vase, etc.) dessous m de plat; (before a door) paillasson m || v (pret & pp matted; ger matting) tr (to cover with matting) couvrir de nattes; (hair) emmêler; (with blood) coller || intr s'emmêler

match [mætʃ] s allumette f; (wick) mèche f; (counterpart) égal m, pair m; (suitable partner in marriage) parti m; (suitably associated pair) assortiment m; (game, contest) match m, partie f; **to be a match for** être de la force de, être à la hauteur de; **to meet one's match** trouver son pareil || tr égaler; (objects) faire pendant à, assortir || intr s'assortir

match'box' s boîte f d'allumettes, porte-allumettes m

matchless ['mætʃlɪs] adj incomparable, sans pareil

match'mak'er s marieur m

mate [met] s compagnon m; (husband) conjoint m; (wife) conjointe f; (to a female) mâle m; (to a male) femelle f; (checkmate) mat m; (naut) officier m en second, second maître m || tr marier; (zool) accoupler || intr se marier; s'accoupler

material [mə'tɪrɪ·əl] adj matériel; important || s matériel m; (what a thing is made of) matière f; (cloth, fabric) étoffe f; (archit) matériau m; **materials** matériaux mpl

materialist [mə'tɪrɪ·əlɪst] s matérialiste mf

materialistic [mə,tɪrɪ·ə'lɪstɪk] adj matérialiste, matériel

materialize [mə'tɪrɪə,laɪz] intr se matérialiser; (to be realized) se réaliser

matériel [mə,tɪrɪ'el] s matériel m

maternal [mə'tʌrnəl] adj maternel

maternity [məˈtʌrnɪti] s maternité f
mater′nity hos′pital s maternité f
mater′nity room′ s salle f d'accouchement
mater′nity ward′ s salle f des accouchées
math [mæθ] s (coll) math fpl
mathematical [ˌmæθɪˈmætɪkəl] adj mathématique
mathematician [ˌmæθɪməˈtɪʃən] s mathématicien m
mathematics [ˌmæθɪˈmætɪks] s mathématiques fpl
matinée [ˌmætɪˈne] s matinée f
mat′ing sea′son s saison f des amours
matins [ˈmætɪnz] spl matines fpl
matriarch [ˈmetrɪˌark] s matrone f
matriar·chy [ˈmetrɪˌarki] s (pl -chies) matriarcat m
matricide [ˈmetrɪˌsaɪd], [ˈmætrɪˌsaɪd] s (person) matricide mf; (action) matricide m
matriculate [məˈtrɪkjəˌlet] tr immatriculer ‖ intr s'inscrire à l'université, prendre ses inscriptions
matriculation [məˌtrɪkjəˈleʃən] s inscription f, immatriculation f
matrimonial [ˌmætrɪˈmonɪˌəl] adj matrimonial
matrimo·ny [ˈmætrɪˌmoni] s (pl -nies) mariage m, vie f conjugale
ma·trix [ˈmetrɪks], [ˈmætrɪks] s (pl -trices [trɪˌsiz] or -trixes) matrice f
matron [ˈmetrən] s (woman no longer young, and of good standing) matrone f; intendante f, surveillante f
matronly [ˈmetrənli] adj de matrone, digne, respectable
matter [ˈmætər] s matière f; (pathol) pus m; **a matter of** affaire de, une question de; **for that matter** à vrai dire; **it doesn't matter** cela ne fait rien; **no matter when** n'importe quand; **no matter where** n'importe où; **no matter who** n'importe qui; **what is the matter?** qu'y a-t-il?; **what is the matter with you?** qu'avez-vous? ‖ intr importer
mat′ter of course′ s chose f qui va de soi
mat′ter of fact′ s—**as a matter of fact** en réalité, effectivement, de fait
matter-of-fact [ˈmætərəvˈfækt] adj prosaïque, terre à terre
mattock [ˈmætək] s pioche f
mattress [ˈmætrɪs] s matelas m
mature [məˈtjʊr], [məˈtur] adj mûr; (due) échu ‖ tr faire mûrir ‖ intr mûrir; (to become due) échoir
maturity [məˈtjʊrɪti], [məˈturɪti] s maturité f; (com) échéance f
maudlin [ˈmɔdlɪn] adj larmoyant
maul [mɔl] tr malmener; (to split) fendre au coin
maulstick [ˈmɔlˌstɪk] s appui-main m
Maun′dy Thurs′day [ˈmɔndi] s jeudi m saint
mausole·um [ˌmɔsəˈli·əm] s (pl -ums or -a [ə]) mausolée m
maw [mɔ] s (of birds) jabot m; (of fish) poche f d'air

mawkish [ˈmɔkɪʃ] adj à l'eau de rose; (sickening) écœurant
maxim [ˈmæksɪm] s maxime f
maximum [ˈmæksɪməm] adj & s maximum m
May [me] s mai m ‖ (l.c.) v (pret & cond might [maɪt]) aux—**it may be** il ne peut; **may I?** vous permettez?; **may I + inf** puis-je + inf, est-ce que je peux + inf; **may I** (may we, etc.) **+ inf** peut-on + inf; **may you be happy!** puissiez-vous être heureux!
maybe [ˈmebi] adv peut-être
May′ Day′ s le premier mai m
mayhem [ˈmehem], [ˈme·əm] s mutilation f
mayonnaise [ˌme·əˈnez] s mayonnaise f
mayor [ˈme·ər], [mer] s maire m
May′pole′ s mai m
May′ queen′ s reine f du premier mai
maze [mez] s labyrinthe m, dédale m
me [mi] pron moi §85, §87; me §87
meadow [ˈmedo] s prairie f, pré m
mead′ow·land′ s herbage m, prairie f
meager [ˈmigər] adj maigre
meal [mil] s repas m; (grain) farine f; **to miss a meal** serrer la ceinture d'un cran
meal′ tick′et s ticket-repas m; (job) gagne-pain m
meal′time′ s heure f du repas
meal·y [ˈmili] adj (comp -ier; super -iest) farineux
mean [min] adj (intermediate) moyen; (low in station or rank) bas, humble; (shabby) vil, misérable; (stingy) mesquin; (small-minded) bas, vilain, méprisable; (vicious) sauvage, mal intentionné; **no mean** fameux, excellent ‖ s milieu m, moyen terme m; (math) moyenne f; **by all means** de toute façon, je vous en prie; **by means of** au moyen de; **by no means** en aucune façon; **means** ressources fpl, fortune f; (agency) moyen m; **means to an end** moyens d'arriver à ses fins; **not by any means!** jamais de la vie! ‖ v (pret & pp meant [ment]) tr vouloir dire, signifier; (to intend) entendre; (to entail) entraîner; **to mean s.th. for s.o.** destiner q.ch. à qn; **to mean** to avoir l'intention de, compter ‖ intr —**to mean well** avoir de bonnes intentions
meander [mɪˈændər] s méandre m ‖ intr faire des méandres
meaning [ˈminɪŋ] s signification f, sens m; intention f
meaningful [ˈminɪŋfəl] adj significatif
meaningless [ˈminɪŋlɪs] adj sans signification, dénué de sens
meanness [ˈminnɪs] s bassesse f, vilenie f; (stinginess) mesquinerie f
mean′time′ s—**in the meantime** dans l'intervalle, sur ces entrefaites ‖ adv entre-temps, en attendant
mean′while′ s & adv var of meantime
measles [ˈmizəlz] s rougeole f; (German measles) rubéole f
mea·sly [ˈmizli] adj (comp -slier; super -sliest) rougeoleux; (slang) piètre, insignifiant

measurable [ˈmɛʒərəbəl] *adj* mesurable
measure [ˈmɛʒər] *s* mesure *f*; (*step, procedure*) mesure, démarche *f*; (*legislative bill*) projet *m* de loi; (*mus, poetic*) mesure; **in a large measure** en grande partie; **in a measure** dans une certaine mesure; **to take measures** prendre des mesures pour; **to take s.o.'s measure** (fig) prendre la mesure de qn ‖ *tr* mesurer; **to measure out** distribuer ‖ *intr* mesurer
measurement [ˈmɛʒərmənt] *s* mesure *f*; **to take s.o.'s measurements** prendre les mesures de qn
meas′uring cup′ *s* verre *m* gradué
meat [mit] *s* viande *f*; (*food in general*) nourriture *f*; (*gist*) moelle *f*, substance *f*
meat′ball′ *s* boulette *f* de viande
meat′hook′ *s* croc *m*, allonge *f*
meat′ mar′ket *s* boucherie *f*
meat′ pie′ *s* tourte *f* à la viande, pâté *m* en croûte
meat-y [ˈmiti] *adj* (*comp* **-ier**; *super* **-iest**) charnu; (fig) plein de substance, étoffé
Mecca [ˈmɛkə] *s* La Mecque
mechanic [məˈkænɪk] *s* mécanicien *m*; **mechanics** mécanique *f*
mechanical [məˈkænɪkəl] *adj* mécanique; (fig) mécanique, machinal
mechan′ical draw′ing *s* dessin *m* industriel
mechan′ical engineer′ *s* ingénieur *m* mécanicien
mechan′ical toy′ *s* jouet *m* mécanique
mechanics [mɪˈkænɪks] *s* mécanique *f*
mechanism [ˈmɛkəˌnɪzəm] *s* mécanisme *m*
mechanize [ˈmɛkəˌnaɪz] *tr* mécaniser
medal [ˈmɛdəl] *s* médaille *f*
medallion [mɪˈdæljən] *s* médaillon *m*
meddle [ˈmɛdəl] *intr* s'ingérer; **to meddle in or with** se mêler de, s'immiscer dans
meddler [ˈmɛdlər] *s* intrigant *m*, touche-à-tout *m*
meddlesome [ˈmɛdəlsəm] *adj* intrigant
median [ˈmidɪ-ən] *adj* médian ‖ *s* médiane *f*
me′dian strip′ *s* bande *f* médiane
mediate [ˈmidɪˌet] *tr* procurer par médiation, négocier ‖ *intr* s'entremettre, s'interposer
mediation [ˌmidɪˈeʃən] *s* médiation *f*
mediator [ˈmidɪˌetər] *s* médiateur *m*
medical [ˈmɛdɪkəl] *adj* médical
med′ical stu′dent *s* étudiant *m* en médecine
medicinal [məˈdɪsɪnəl] *adj* médicinal
medicine [ˈmɛdɪsɪn] *s* (*science and art*) médecine *f*; (pharm) médicament *m*
med′icine cab′inet *s* armoire *f* à pharmacie
med′icine kit′ *s* pharmacie *f* portative
med′icine man′ *s* (*pl* **men′**) sorcier *m* indien; (*mountebank*) charlatan *m*
medi-co [ˈmɛdɪˌko] *s* (*pl* **-cos**) (slang) carabin *m*, morticole *m*
medieval [ˌmidɪˈivəl], [ˌmɛdɪˈivəl] *adj* médiéval

medievalist [ˌmidɪˈivəlɪst], [ˌmɛdɪˈivəlɪst] *s* médiéviste *mf*
mediocre [ˈmidɪˌokər], [ˌmidɪˈokər] *adj* médiocre
mediocri-ty [ˌmidɪˈɑkrɪti] *s* (*pl* **-ties**) médiocrité *f*
meditate [ˈmɛdɪˌtet] *tr* & *intr* méditer
meditation [ˌmɛdɪˈteʃən] *s* méditation *f*
Mediterranean [ˌmɛdɪtəˈreni-ən] *adj* méditerranéen ‖ *s* Méditerranée *f*
medi-um [ˈmidɪ-əm] *adj* moyen; (culin) à point ‖ *s* (*pl* **-ums** or **-a** [ə]) milieu *m*; (*means*) moyen *m*; (*in spiritualism*) médium *m*; (journ) organe *m*; **through the medium of** par l'intermédiaire de
me′dium of exchange′ *s* agent *m* monétaire
me′dium-range′ *adj* à portée moyenne
me′dium-sized′ *adj* de grandeur moyenne
medlar [ˈmɛdlər] *s* (*fruit*) nèfle *f*; (*tree*) néflier *m*
medley [ˈmɛdli] *s* mélange *m*; (mus) pot-pourri *m*
medul-la [mɪˈdʌlə] *s* (*pl* **-lae** [li]) moelle *f*
Medusa [məˈduzə] *s* Méduse *f*
meek [mik] *adj* doux, humble
meekness [ˈmiknɪs] *s* douceur *f*, humilité *f*
meerschaum [ˈmɪrʃəm], [ˈmɪrʃəm] *s* écume *f* de mer; pipe *f* d'écume de mer
meet [mit] *adj*—**it is meet that** il convient que ‖ *s* (sports) meeting *m* ‖ *v* (*pret* & *pp* **met** [mɛt]) *tr* rencontrer; (*to make the acquaintance of*) faire la connaissance de; (*to go to meet*) aller au-devant de; (*a car in the street; a person on the sidewalk*) croiser; (*by appointment*) retrouver, rejoindre; (*difficulties; expenses*) faire face à; (*one's debts*) honorer; (*one's death*) trouver; (*a need*) satisfaire à; (*an objection*) réfuter; (*the ear*) frapper; **meet my wife** (my friend, etc.) je vous présente ma femme (mon ami, etc.) ‖ *intr* se rencontrer; se retrouver, se rejoindre; (*to assemble*) se réunir; (*to join, touch*) se joindre, se toucher; (*said of rivers*) confluer; (*said of roads; said of cars, persons, etc.*) se croiser; **till we meet again** au revoir; **to meet with** se rencontrer avec, rencontrer; (*difficulties, an affront, etc.*) subir
meeting [ˈmitɪŋ] *s* rencontre *f*; (*session*) séance *f*; (*assemblage*) réunion *f*, assemblée *f*; (*of two rivers*) confluent *m*; (*of two cars; of two roads*) croisement *m*
meet′ing of the minds′ *s* bonne entente *f*
meet′ing place′ *s* rendez-vous *m*
megacycle [ˈmɛgəˌsaɪkəl] *s* mégacycle *m*
megaphone [ˈmɛgəˌfon] *s* mégaphone *m*, porte-voix *m*
megohm [ˈmɛgˌom] *s* mégohm *m*

melancholia [ˌmɛlənˈkolɪ·ə] s mélancolie f

melanchol·y [ˈmɛlənˌkɑli] adj mélancolique ‖ s (pl -ies) mélancolie f

melee [ˈmele], [ˈmele] s mêlée f

mellow [ˈmelo] adj moelleux; enjoué, débonnaire; (ripe) mûr ‖ tr rendre moelleux, mûrir

melodic [mɪˈlɑdɪk] adj mélodique

melodious [mɪˈlodɪ·əs] adj mélodieux

melodramatic [ˌmɛlədrəˈmætɪk] adj mélodramatique

melo·dy [ˈmelədɪ] s (pl -dies) mélodie f

melon [ˈmelən] s melon m

melt [melt] tr & intr fondre; **to melt into** (e.g., tears) fondre en

melt'ing pot' s creuset m

member [ˈmɛmbər] s membre m

mem'ber·ship' s membres mpl; (in a club, etc.) association f

membrane [ˈmembren] s membrane f

memen·to [mɪˈmento] s (pl -tos or -toes) mémento m

mem·o [ˈmemo] s (pl -os) (coll) note f, rappel m

mem'o book' s calepin m, mémento m

memoir [ˈmemwɑr] s biographie f; **memoirs** mémoires mpl

mem'o pad' s bloc-notes m, bloc m

memoran·dum [ˌmeməˈrændəm] s (pl -dums or -da [də]) memorandum m; note f, rappel m

memorial [mɪˈmorɪ·əl] adj commémoratif ‖ s mémorial m; pétition f, mémoire m

memo'rial arch' s arc m de triomphe

Memo'rial Day' s la journée du Souvenir

memorialize [mɪˈmorɪ·əˌlaɪz] tr commémorer

memorize [ˈmeməˌraɪz] tr apprendre par cœur

memo·ry [ˈmeməri] s (pl -ries) mémoire f; **from memory** de mémoire; **in memory of** en souvenir de, à la mémoire de

menace [ˈmenɪs] s menace f ‖ tr & intr menacer

menagerie [məˈnæʒərɪ], [məˈnædʒəri] s ménagerie f

mend [mend] s raccommodage m, reprise f ‖ tr réparer; (to patch) raccommoder; (stockings) repriser; (to reform) améliorer ‖ intr s'améliorer, s'amender

mendacious [menˈdeʃəs] adj mensonger

mendicant [ˈmendɪkənt] adj & s mendiant m

mending [ˈmendɪŋ] s raccommodage m; (of stockings) reprisage m

menfolk [ˈmenˌfok] spl hommes mpl

menial [ˈminɪ·əl] adj servile ‖ s domestique mf

menses [ˈmensiz] spl menstrues fpl

men's' fur'nishings spl confection f pour hommes

men's' room' s toilettes fpl pour hommes, lavabos mpl pour messieurs

menstruate [ˈmenstruˌet] intr avoir ses règles

mental [ˈmentəl] adj mental

men'tal arith'metic s calcul m mental

men'tal defec'tive s débile mf

men'tal ill'ness s maladie f mentale

mentali·ty [menˈtæliti] s (pl -ties) mentalité f

men'tal reserva'tion s arrière-pensée f

men'tal test' s test m psychologique

mention [ˈmenʃən] s mention f ‖ tr mentionner; **don't mention it** il n'y a pas de quoi, je vous en prie

menu [ˈmenju], [ˈmenju] s menu m, carte f

meow [mɪˈau] s miaou m ‖ intr miauler

Mephistophelian [ˌmefistəˈfilɪ·ən] adj méphistophélique

mercantile [ˈmʌrkənˌtil], [ˈmʌrkənˌtail] adj commercial, commerçant

mercenar·y [ˈmʌrsəˌneri] adj mercenaire ‖ s (pl -ies) mercenaire mf

merchandise [ˈmʌrtʃənˌdaɪz] s marchandise f

merchant [ˈmʌrtʃənt] adj & s marchand m

mer'chant·man s (pl -men) navire m marchand

mer'chant marine' s marine f marchande

mer'chant ves'sel s navire m marchand

merciful [ˈmʌrsɪfəl] adj miséricordieux

merciless [ˈmʌrsɪlɪs] adj impitoyable

mercurial [mɛrˈkjurɪ·əl] adj inconstant, versatile; (lively) vif

mercu·ry [ˈmʌrkjeri] s (pl -ries) mercure m

mer·cy [ˈmʌrsi] s (pl -cies) miséricorde f, pitié f; **at the mercy of** à la merci de

mere [mɪr] adj simple, pur; seul, e.g., **at the mere thought of it** à la seule pensée de cela; rien que, e.g., **to shudder at the mere thought of it** frissonner rien que d'y penser

meretricious [ˌmerɪˈtrɪʃəs] adj factice, postiche; de courtisane

merge [mʌrdʒ] tr fusionner ‖ intr fusionner; (said of two roads) converger; **to merge into** se fondre dans

merger [ˈmʌrdʒər] s fusion f

meridian [məˈrɪdɪ·ən] adj & s méridien m

meringue [məˈræŋ] s meringue f

merit [ˈmerɪt] s mérite m ‖ tr mériter

meritorious [ˌmerɪˈtorɪ·əs] adj méritoire; (person) méritant

merlin [ˈmʌrlɪn] s (orn) émerillon m

mermaid [ˈmʌrˌmed] s sirène f

merriment [ˈmerɪmənt] s gaieté f, réjouissance f

mer·ry [ˈmeri] adj (comp -rier; super -riest) gai, joyeux; **to make merry** se divertir

Mer'ry Christ'mas s Joyeux Noël m

mer'ry-go-round' s chevaux mpl de bois, manège m forain

mer'ry-mak'er s noceur m, fêtard m

mesh [meʃ] s (network) réseau m; (each open space of net) maille f; (net) filet m; (engagement of gears) engrenage m; **meshes** rets m, filets *mpl* || *tr* (mach) engrener || *intr* s'engrener

mesmerize ['mɛsmə,raɪz] *tr* magnétiser

mess [mɛs] *s* gâchis *m*; (*refuse*) saleté *f*; (*meal*) (mil) ordinaire *m*; (*for officers*) (mil) mess *m*; **to get into a mess** se mettre dans le pétrin; **to make a mess of** gâcher || *tr*—**to mess up** (*to botch*) gâcher; (*to dirty*) salir || *intr*—**to mess around** (*to putter*) (coll) bricoler; (*to waste time*) (coll) lambiner

message ['mɛsɪdʒ] *s* message *m*

messenger ['mɛsəndʒər] *s* messager *m*; (*one who goes on errands*) commissionnaire *m*

mess' hall' *s* cantine *f*; (*for officers*) mess *m*

Messiah [mə'saɪə] *s* Messie *m*

mess' kit' *s* gamelle *f*

mess'mate' *s* camarade *mf* de table; (nav) camarade de plat

mess' of pot'tage ['pɑtɪdʒ] *s* (Bib) plat *m* de lentilles

Messrs. ['mɛsərz] *pl* of **Mr.**

mess·y ['mɛsi] *adj* (*comp* **-ier**; *super* **-iest**) en désordre; (*dirty*) sale, poisseux

metal ['mɛtəl] *s* métal *m*

metallic [mɪ'tælɪk] *adj* métallique

metallurgy ['mɛtə,lʌrdʒi] *s* métallurgie *f*

met'al pol'ish *s* brillant *m* à métaux

met'al·work' *s* serrurerie *f*, travail *m* des métaux

metamorpho·sis [,mɛtə'mɔrfəsɪs] *s* (*pl* **-ses** [,siz]) métamorphose *f*

metaphony [mə'tæfəni] *s* métaphonie *f*, inflexion *f*

metaphor ['mɛtəfər], ['mɛtə,fɔr] *s* métaphore *f*

metaphorical [,mɛtə'fɑrɪkəl], [,mɛtə'fɔrɪkəl] *adj* métaphorique

metathe·sis [mɪ'tæθɪsɪs] *s* (*pl* **-ses** [,siz]) métathèse *f*

mete [mit] *tr*—**to mete out** distribuer

meteor ['mitɪ·ər] *s* étoile *f* filante; (*atmospheric phenomenon*) météore *m*

meteoric [,mitɪ'ɑrɪk], [,mitɪ'ɔrɪk] *adj* météorique; (fig) fulgurant

meteorite ['mitɪ·ə,raɪt] *s* météorite *m* & *f*

meteorology [,mitɪ·ə'rɑlədʒi] *s* météorologie *f*

meter ['mitər] *s* (*unit of measurement; verse*) mètre *m*; (*instrument for measuring gas, electricity, water*) compteur *m*; (mus) mesure *f*

me'ter read'er *s* releveur *m* de compteurs

methane ['mɛθen] *s* méthane *m*

method ['mɛθəd] *s* méthode *f*

methodic(al) [mɪ'θɑdɪk(əl)] *adj* méthodique

Methodist ['mɛθədɪst] *adj* & *s* méthodiste *mf*

Methuselah [mɪ'θuzələ] *s* Mathusalem *m*

meticulous [mɪ'tɪkjələs] *adj* méticuleux

metric(al) ['mɛtrɪk(əl)] *adj* métrique

metrics ['mɛtrɪks] *s* métrique *f*

metronome ['mɛtrə,nom] *s* métronome *m*

metropolis [mɪ'trɑpəlɪs] *s* métropole *f*

metropolitan [,mɛtrə'pɑlɪtən] *adj* & *s* métropolitain *m*

mettle ['mɛtəl] *s* ardeur *f*, fougue *f*; **to be on one's mettle** se piquer au jeu

mettlesome ['mɛtəlsəm] *adj* ardent, vif, fougueux

mew [mju] *s* miaulement *m* || *intr* miauler

Mexican ['mɛksɪkən] *adj* mexicain || *s* Mexicain *m*

Mexico ['mɛksɪ,ko] *s* le Mexique

Mex'ico Cit'y *s* Mexico

mezzanine ['mɛzə,nin] *s* entresol *m*; (theat) mezzanine *m* & *f*, corbeille *f*

mica ['maɪkə] *s* mica *m*

microbe ['maɪkrob] *s* microbe *m*

microbiology [,maɪkrəbaɪ'alədʒi] *s* microbiologie *f*

microfilm ['maɪkrə,fɪlm] *s* microfilm *m* || *tr* microfilmer

microgroove ['maɪkrə,gruv] *adj* & *s* microsillon *m*

mi'crogroove rec'ord *s* disque *m* à microsillons

microphone ['maɪkrə,fon] *s* microphone *m*

microscope ['maɪkrə,skop] *s* microscope *m*

microscopic [,maɪkrə'skɑpɪk] *adj* microscopique

microwave ['maɪkrə,wev] *s* microonde *f*

mid [mɪd] *adj*—**in mid course** à michemin

mid'day' *s* midi *m*

middle ['mɪdəl] *adj* moyen, du milieu || *s* milieu *m*; **in the middle of** au milieu de

mid'dle age' *s* âge *m* moyen; **Middle Ages** moyen-âge *m*

middle-aged ['mɪdəl,edʒd] *adj* d'un âge moyen

mid'dle class' *s* classe *f* moyenne, bourgeoisie *f*

mid'dle-class' *adj* bourgeois

Mid'dle East' *s* Moyen-Orient *m*

Mid'dle Eng'lish *s* moyen anglais *m*

mid'dle fin'ger *s* majeur *m*, doigt *m* du milieu

mid'dle·man' *s* (*pl* **-men'**) intermédiaire *mf*

middling ['mɪdlɪŋ] *adj* moyen, assez bien, passable || *adv* (coll) assez bien, passablement

mid·dy ['mɪdi] *s* (*pl* **-dies**) (coll) aspirant *m*

mid'dy blouse' *s* marinière *f*

midget ['mɪdʒɪt] *s* nain *m*, nabot *m*

midland ['mɪdlənd] *adj* de l'intérieur || *s* centre *m* du pays

mid'night' *adj* de minuit; **to burn the midnight oil** pâlir sur les livres, se crever les livres || *s* minuit *m*

midriff ['mɪdrɪf] *s* diaphragme *m*

mid'ship·man *s* (*pl* **-men**) aspirant *m*

midst [mɪdst] *s* centre *m*; **in our** (*your*, etc.) **midst** parmi nous (vous, etc.); **in the midst of** au milieu de

mid′stream′ s—**in midstream** au milieu du courant

mid′sum′mer s milieu m de l'été

mid′way′ adj & adv à mi-chemin || **mid′way′** s fête f foraine

mid′week′ s milieu m de la semaine

mid′wife′ s (pl **-wives′**) sage-femme f

mid′win′ter s milieu m de l'hiver

mid′year′ s mi-année f

mien [min] s mine f, aspect m

miff [mɪf] s (coll) fâcherie f || tr (coll) fâcher

might [maɪt] s puissance f, force f; **with might and main, with all one's might** de toute sa force || aux used to form the potential mood, e.g., **she might not be able to come** il se pourrait qu'elle ne puisse pas venir

mightily [′maɪtɪli] adv puissamment; (coll) énormément

might·y [′maɪti] adj (comp **-ier**; super **-iest**) puissant; (of great size) grand, vaste || adv (coll) rudement, diablement

mignonette [,mɪnjə′nɛt] s réséda m

migraine [′maɪgren] s migraine f

migrate [′maɪgret] intr émigrer

migratory [′maɪgrə,tori] adj migratoire

milch [mɪltʃ] adj laitier

mild [maɪld] adj doux

mildew [′mɪl,d(j)u] s moisissure f; (on vine) mildiou m, blanc m

mildness [′maɪldnɪs] s douceur f

mile [maɪl] s mille m

mileage [′maɪlɪdʒ] s distance f en milles; (charge) tarif m au mille

mile′post′ s borne f milliaire

mile′stone′ s borne f milliaire; (fig) jalon m

militancy [′mɪlɪtənsi] s esprit m militant

militant [′mɪlɪtənt] adj & s militant m

militarism [′mɪlɪtə,rɪzəm] s militarisme m

militarize [′mɪlɪtə,raɪz] tr militariser

military [′mɪlɪ,tɛri] adj & s militaire m

mil′itary police′man s (pl **-men**) agent m de la police militaire

militate [′mɪlɪ,tet] intr militer

militia [mɪ′lɪʃə] s milice f

mili′tia·man s (pl **-men**) milicien m

milk [mɪlk] adj laitier || s lait m || tr traire; abuser de, exploiter; **to milk s.th. from s.o.** soutirer q.ch. à qn

milk′ can′ s pot m à lait, berthe f

milk′ car′ton s boîte f de lait, berlingot m

milk′ di′et s régime m lacté

milk′maid′ s laitière f

milk′man′ s (pl **-men′**) laitier m, crémier m

milk′ pail′ s seau m à lait

milk′sop′ s poule f mouillée

milk′ tooth′ s dent f de lait

milk′weed′ s laiteron m

milk·y [′mɪlki] adj (comp **-ier**; super **-iest**) laiteux

Milk′y Way′ s Voie f Lactée

mill [mɪl] s moulin m; (factory) fabrique f, usine f; millième m de dollar; **to put through the mill** (coll)

faire passer au laminoir || tr moudre, broyer; (a coin) créneler; (gears) fraiser; (steel) laminer; (ore) bocarder; (chocolate) faire mousser || intr —**to mill around** circuler

millennial [mɪ′lɛnɪəl] adj millénaire

millenni·um [mɪ′lɛnɪəm] s (pl **-ums** or **-a** [ə]) millénaire m

miller [′mɪlər] s meunier m

millet [′mɪlɪt] s millet m

milligram [′mɪlɪ,græm] s milligramme m

millimeter [′mɪlɪ,mitər] s millimètre m

milliner [′mɪlɪnər] s modiste f

mil′linery shop′ [′mɪlɪ,nɛri], [′mɪlɪnəri] s boutique f de modiste

milling [′mɪlɪŋ] s (of grain) mouture f

mill′ing machine′ s fraiseuse f

million [′mɪljən] adj million de || s million m

millionaire [,mɪljən′ɛr] s millionnaire mf

millionth [′mɪljənθ] adj & pron millionième (masc, fem) || s millionième m

mill′pond′ s retenue f, réservoir m

mill′race′ s bief m

mill′stone′ s meule f; (fig) boulet m

mill′wheel′ s roue f de moulin

mill′work′ s ouvrage m de menuiserie

mime [maɪm] s mime mf || tr & intr mimer

mimeograph [′mɪmɪə,græf], [′mɪmɪə,graf] s ronéo f || tr ronéocopier, ronéotyper

mim·ic [′mɪmɪk] s mime mf, imitateur m || v (pret & pp **-icked**; ger **-icking**) tr mimer, imiter

mimic·ry [′mɪmɪkri] s (pl **-ries**) mimique f, imitation f

minaret [′mɪnə′rɛt], [′mɪnə,rɛt] s minaret m

mince [mɪns] tr (meat) hacher menu || intr minauder

mince′meat′ s hachis m de viande et de fruits aromatisés; **to make mincemeat of** (coll) mettre en marmelade

mind [maɪnd] s esprit m; **to be of one mind** être d'accord; **to change one's mind** changer d'avis; **to have a mind to** avoir envie de; **to have in mind** avoir en vue; **to lose one's mind** perdre la raison; **to make up one's mind** to prendre le parti de; **to slip one's mind** échapper à qn; **to speak one's mind** donner son avis || tr (to take care of) garder; (to obey) obéir (with dat); (to be troubled by) s'inquiéter de; (e.g., one's manners) faire attention à; (e.g., a dangerous step) prendre garde à; **mind your own business!** occupez-vous de vos affaires! || intr —**do you mind?** cela ne vous ennuie pas?, cela ne vous gêne pas?; **if you don't mind** si cela ne vous fait rien, si cela vous est égal; **never mind!** n'importe!

mindful [′maɪndfəl] adj attentif; **mindful of** attentif à, soigneux de

mind′ read′er s liseur m de la pensée

mind′ read′ing s lecture f de la pensée

mine [maɪn] s mine f || pron poss le mien §89; à moi §85 A, 10 || tr (coal, *minerals, etc.*) extraire; (*to under-mine; to lay mines in*) miner

mine'field' s champ m de mines

mine'lay'er s poseur m de mines

miner ['maɪnər] s mineur m

mineral ['mɪnərəl] *adj & s* minéral m

mineralogy [,mɪnə'rɑlədʒɪ] s minéralogie f

min'eral wool' s laine f minérale, laine de scories

mine'sweep'er s dragueur m de mines

mingle ['mɪŋgəl] *tr* mêler, mélanger || *intr* se mêler, se mélanger

miniature ['mɪnɪ-ət/ər], ['mɪnɪt/ər] s miniature f

miniaturization [,mɪnɪ-ət/ərɪ'zefən], [,mɪnɪt/ərɪ'zefən] s miniaturisation f

miniaturize ['mɪnɪ-ət/ə ,raɪz], ['mɪnɪt/ə ,raɪz] *tr* miniaturiser

minimal ['mɪnɪməl] *adj* minimum

minimize ['mɪnə ,maɪz] *tr* minimiser

minimum ['mɪnɪməm] *adj* minimum; (*temperature*) minimal || s minimum m

min'imum wage' s salaire m minimum, minimum m vital

mining ['maɪnɪŋ] *adj* minier || s exploitation f des mines; (nav) pose f de mines

minion ['mɪnjən] s favori m; (*henchman*) séide m

miniskirt ['mɪnɪ ,skʌrt] s minijupe f

minister ['mɪnɪstər] s ministre m; (eccl) pasteur m || *intr*—**to minister to** (*the needs of*) subvenir à; (*a person*) soigner; (*a parish*) desservir

ministerial [,mɪnɪs'tɪrɪ-əl] *adj* ministériel

minis·try ['mɪnɪstrɪ] s (pl **-tries**) ministère m; (eccl) clergé m; (eccl) pastorat m

mink [mɪŋk] s vison m

minnow ['mɪno] s vairon m

minor ['maɪnər] *adj & s* mineur m

Minorca [mɪ'nɔrkə] s Minorque f; île f de Minorque

minori·ty [mɪ'nɑrɪtɪ], [mɪ'nɔrɪtɪ] *adj* minoritaire || s (pl **-ties**) minorité f

minstrel ['mɪnstrəl] s (*in a minstrel show*) interprète m de chants nègres; (hist) ménestrel m

mint [mɪnt] s hôtel m des Monnaies, Monnaie f; (bot) menthe f; (fig) mine f || *tr* frapper, monnayer; (fig) forger

minuet [,mɪnju'et] s menuet m

minus ['maɪnəs] *adj* négatif || s moins m || *prep* moins; (coll) sans, dépourvu de

minute [maɪ'n(j)ut] *adj* (*tiny*) minime; (*meticulous*) minutieux || ['mɪnɪt] s minute f; **minutes** compte m rendu, procès-verbal m de séance; (*often omitted in expressions of time*), e.g., **ten after two, ten minutes after two** deux heures dix; **up to the minute** de la dernière heure; à la dernière mode; au courant

min'ute hand' ['mɪnɪt] s grande aiguille f

min'ute steak' ['mɪnɪt] s entrecôte f minute

minutiae [mɪ'n(j)u/ɪ ,i] *spl* minuties fpl

minx [mɪŋks] s effrontée f

miracle ['mɪrəkəl] s miracle m

mir'acle play' s miracle m

miraculous [mɪ'rækjələs] *adj* miraculeux

mirage [mɪ'rɑʒ] s mirage m

mire [maɪr] s fange f

mirror ['mɪrər] s miroir m, glace f || *tr* refléter

mirth [mʌrθ] s joie f, gaieté f

mir·y ['maɪrɪ] *adj* (*comp* **-ier**; *super* **-iest**) fangeux

misadventure [,mɪsəd'vent/ər] s mésaventure f

misanthrope ['mɪsən ,θrop] s misanthrope mf

misapprehension [,mɪsæprɪ'hen/ən] s fausse idée f, malentendu m

misappropriation [,mɪsə ,proprɪ'efən] s détournement m de fonds

misbehave [,mɪsbɪ'hev] *intr* se conduire mal

misbehavior [,mɪsbɪ'hevɪ·ər] s mauvaise conduite f

miscalculation [,mɪskælkjə'lefən] s mécompte m

miscarriage [mɪs'kærɪdʒ] s fausse couche f; (e.g., *of letter*) perte f; (*of justice*) déni m, mal-jugé m; (fig) avortement m, insuccès m

miscar·ry [mɪs'kærɪ] v (*pret & pp* **-ried**) *intr* faire une fausse couche; (*said, e.g., of letter*) s'égarer; (fig) avorter, échouer

miscellaneous [,mɪsə'lenɪ·əs] *adj* divers, mélangé

miscella·ny ['mɪsə ,lenɪ] s (pl **-nies**) miscellanées fpl

mischief ['mɪst/ɪf] s (*harm*) tort m; (*disposition to annoy*) méchanceté f; (*prankishness*) espièglerie f

mis'chief-mak'er s brandon m de discorde

mischievous ['mɪst/ɪvəs] *adj* (*harmful*) nuisible; (*mean*) méchant; (*prankish*) espiègle

misconception [,mɪskən'sep/ən] s conception f erronée

misconduct [mɪs'kɑndʌkt] s inconduite f; (e.g., *of a business*) mauvaise administration f || [,mɪskən'dʌkt] *tr* mal administrer; **to misconduct oneself** se conduire mal

misconstrue [,mɪskən'stru], [mɪs'kɑnstru] *tr* mal interpréter

miscount [mɪs'kaunt] s erreur f de calcul || *tr & intr* mal compter

miscue [mɪs'kju] s fausse queue f; (*blunder*) bévue f || *intr* faire fausse queue; (theat) se tromper de réplique

mis·deal ['mɪs ,dil] s maldonne f, mauvaise donne f || [mɪs'dil] v (*pret & pp* **-dealt**) *tr* mal distribuer || *intr* faire maldonne

misdeed [mɪs'did], ['mɪs ,did] s méfait m

misdemeanor [,mɪsdɪ'minər] s mauvaise conduite f; (law) délit m correctionnel

misdirect [ˌmɪsdɪˈrekt], [ˌmɪsdaɪˈrekt] *tr* mal diriger

misdoing [mɪsˈduːɪŋ] *s* méfait *m*

miser [ˈmaɪzər] *s* avare *mf*

miserable [ˈmɪzərəbəl] *adj* misérable

miserly [ˈmaɪzərli] *adj* avare

miser·y [ˈmɪzəri] *s* (*pl* -ies) misère *f*, détresse *f*

misfeasance [mɪsˈfiːzəns] *s* (law) abus *m* de pouvoir

misfire [mɪsˈfaɪr] *s* raté *m* ‖ *intr* rater

mis·fit [mɪsˈfɪt] *s* (*clothing*) vêtement *m* manqué; (*thing*) laissé-pour-compte *m*; (fig) inadapté *m* ‖ [mɪsˈfɪt] *v* (*pret & pp* -fitted; *ger* -fitting) *tr* mal aller (with *dat*) ‖ *intr* mal aller

misfortune [mɪsˈfɔrtʃən] *s* infortune *f*, malheur *m*

misgiving [mɪsˈgɪvɪŋ] *s* pressentiment *m*, appréhension *f*, soupçon *m*

misgovern [mɪsˈgʌvərn] *tr* mal gouverner

misguidance [mɪsˈgaɪdəns] *s* mauvais conseils *mpl*

misguided [mɪsˈgaɪdɪd] *adj* mal placé, hors de propos; (*e.g., youth*) dévoyé

mishap [ˈmɪshæp], [mɪsˈhæp] *s* contretemps *m*, mésaventure *f*

misinform [ˌmɪsɪnˈfɔrm] *tr* mal renseigner

misinterpret [ˌmɪsɪnˈtʌrprɪt] *tr* mal interpréter

misjudge [mɪsˈdʒʌdʒ] *tr & intr* mal juger

mis·lay [mɪsˈle] *v* (*pret & pp* -laid), *tr* égarer, perdre

mis·lead [mɪsˈliːd] *v* (*pret & pp* -led) *tr* égarer; corrompre

misleading [mɪsˈliːdɪŋ] *adj* trompeur

mismanagement [mɪsˈmænɪdʒmənt] *s* mauvaise administration *f*

misnomer [mɪsˈnomər] *s* faux nom *m*

misplace [mɪsˈples] *tr* mal placer; (*to mislay*) (coll) égarer, perdre

misprint [ˈmɪsˌprɪnt] *s* erreur *f* typographique, coquille *f* ‖ [mɪsˈprɪnt] *tr* imprimer incorrectement

mispronounce [ˌmɪsprəˈnauns] *tr* mal prononcer

misquote [mɪsˈkwot] *tr* citer à faux, citer inexactement

misrepresent [ˌmɪsreprɪˈzent] *tr* représenter sous un faux jour; (*e.g., facts*) dénaturer, travestir

miss [mɪs] *s* coup *m* manqué; Miss Mademoiselle *f*, Mlle; (*winner of beauty contest*) Miss *f* ‖ *tr* manquer; (*to feel the absence of*) regretter; (*not to run into*) ne pas voir, ne pas rencontrer; (*e.g., one's way*) se tromper de; **he misses you very much** vous lui manquez beaucoup ‖ *intr* manquer

missal [ˈmɪsəl] *s* missel *m*

misshapen [mɪsˈʃepən] *adj* difforme, contrefait

missile [ˈmɪsɪl] *s* projectile *m*; (*guided missile*) missile *m*

mis·sile launch·er *s* lance-fusées *m*

missing [ˈmɪsɪŋ] *adj* manquant, absent; perdu; **missing in action** (mil) porté disparu; **to be missing** manquer, e.g., **three are missing** il en manque trois

miss·ing per·sons *spl* disparus *mpl*

mission [ˈmɪʃən] *s* mission *f*

missionar·y [ˈmɪʃənˌeri] *adj* missionnaire *s* (*pl* -ies) missionnaire *m*

missis [ˈmɪsɪz] *s*—**the missis** (coll) votre femme *f*

missive [ˈmɪsɪv] *adj & s* missive *f*

mis·spell [mɪsˈspel] *v* (*pret & pp* -spelled or -spelt) *tr & intr* écrire incorrectement

misspelling [mɪsˈspelɪŋ] *s* faute *f* d'orthographe

misspent [mɪsˈspent] *adj* gaspillé; dissipé

misstatement [mɪsˈstetmənt] *s* rapport *m* inexact, erreur *f* de fait

misstep [mɪsˈstep] *s* faux pas *m*

miss·y [ˈmɪsi] *s* (*pl* -ies) (coll) mademoiselle *f*

mist [mɪst] *s* brume *f*, buée *f*; (*fine spray*) vapeur *f*; (*of tears*) voile *m*

mis·take [mɪsˈtek] *s* faute *f*; **by mistake** par erreur, par méprise; **to make a mistake** se tromper ‖ *v* (*pret* -took; *pp* -taken) *tr* (*to misunderstand*) mal comprendre; (*to be wrong about*) se tromper de; **to mistake s.o. for s.o. else** prendre qn pour qn d'autre

mistaken [mɪsˈtekən] *adj* erroné, faux; (*person*) dans l'erreur

mistak·en iden·tity *s* erreur *f* d'identité, erreur sur la personne

mistakenly [mɪsˈtekənli] *adv* par erreur

mister [ˈmɪstər] *s*—**the mister** (coll) votre mari *m* ‖ *interj* (slang & pej) Jules!, mon petit bonhomme!

mistletoe [ˈmɪsəlˌto] *s* gui *m*

mistreat [mɪsˈtrit] *tr* maltraiter

mistreatment [mɪsˈtritmənt] *s* mauvais traitement *m*

mistress [ˈmɪstrɪs] *s* maîtresse *f*

mistrial [mɪsˈtraɪəl] *s* (law) procès *m* entaché de nullité

mistrust [mɪsˈtrʌst] *s* méfiance *f* ‖ *tr* se méfier de ‖ *intr* se méfier

mistrustful [mɪsˈtrʌstfəl] *adj* méfiant

mist·y [ˈmɪsti] *adj* (*comp* -ier; *super* -iest) brumeux; vague, indistinct

misunder·stand [ˌmɪsʌndərˈstænd] *v* (*pret & pp* -stood) *tr* mal comprendre

misunderstanding [ˌmɪsʌndərˈstændɪŋ] *s* malentendu *m*

misuse [mɪsˈjus] *s* mauvais usage *m*, abus *m*; (*of words*) emploi *m* abusif ‖ [mɪsˈjuz] *tr* faire mauvais usage de, abuser de; (*a person*) maltraiter

misword [mɪsˈwʌrd] *tr* mal rédiger, mal exprimer

mite [maɪt] *s* (*small contribution*) obole *f*; (*small amount*) brin *m*, bagatelle *f*; (ent) mite *f*

miter [ˈmaɪtər] *s* (*carpentry*) onglet *m*; (eccl) mitre *f* ‖ *tr* tailler à onglet

mi·ter box· *s* boîte *f* à onglets

mitigate [ˈmɪtɪˌget] *tr* adoucir, atténuer

mitt [mɪt] *s* (*fingerless glove*) mitaine *f*; (*mitten*) moufle *f*; (baseball) gant *m* de prise; (*hand*) (slang) main *f*

mitten ['mɪtən] s moufle f
mix [mɪks] tr mélanger, mêler; (cement; a cake) malaxer; (the cards; the salad) touiller; **to mix up** (to confuse) confondre || intr se mélanger, se mêler; **to mix with** s'associer à or avec
mixed adj mélangé; (races; style; colors) mêlé; (feelings; marriage; school; doubles) mixte; (candy) assorti; (salad, vegetables, etc.) panaché; (number) fractionnaire
mixed' drink' s boisson f mélangée
mixer ['mɪksər] s (device) mélangeur m; (for, e.g., concrete) malaxeur m; **to be a good mixer** (coll) avoir le don de plaire
mix'ing fau'cet s robinet m mélangeur
mixture ['mɪkstʃər] s mélange m
mix'-up' s embrouillage m
mizzen ['mɪzən] s artimon m
moan [mon] s gémissement m || intr gémir
moat [mot] s fossé m
mob [mab] s populace f; (crush of people) cohue f grouillante; (crowd bent on violence) foule f en colère, ameutement m || v (pret & pp **mobbed**; ger **mobbing**) tr s'attrouper autour de; fondre sur, assaillir
mobile ['mobɪl], ['mobɪl] adj & s mobile m
mobility [mo'bɪlɪti] s mobilité f
mobilization [,mobɪlɪ'zefən] s mobilisation f
mobilize ['mobɪ,laɪz] tr & intr mobiliser
mob' rule' s loi f de la populace
mobster ['mabstər] s (slang) gangster m
moccasin ['makəsɪn] s mocassin m
Mo'cha cof'fee ['mokə] s moka m
mock [mak] adj simulé, contrefait || s moquerie f || tr se moquer de, moquer; (to imitate) contrefaire, singer; (to deceive) tromper || intr se moquer; **to mock at** se moquer de; **to mock up** construire une maquette de
mock' elec'tion s élection f blanche
mocker·y ['makəri] s (pl -ies) moquerie f; (subject of derision) objet m de risée; (poor imitation) parodie f; (e.g., of justice) simulacre m
mockingbird ['makɪŋ,bʌrd] s moqueur m, oiseau m moqueur
mock' or'ange s seringa m
mock' tur'tle soup' s potage m à la tête de veau
mock'-up' s maquette f
mode [mod] s (kind) mode m; (fashion) mode f; (gram, mus) mode m
mod·el ['madəl] adj modèle || s modèle m; (for dressmaker or artist; at a fashion show) mannequin m; (of a statue) maquette f || v (pret & pp -eled or -elled; ger -eling or -elling) tr modeler || intr dessiner des modèles; servir de modèle, poser
mod'el air'plane s aéromodèle m
mod'el-air'plane build'er s aéromodéliste mf
mod'el-air'plane build'ing s aéromodélisme m

moderate ['madərɪt] adj modéré || ['madə,ret] tr modérer; (a meeting) présider || intr se modérer; présider
moderator ['madə,retər] s (over an assembly) président m; (mediator; substance used for slowing down neutrons) modérateur m
modern ['madərn] adj moderne
modernize ['madər,naɪz] tr moderniser
mod'ern lan'guages spl langues fpl vivantes
modest ['madɪst] adj modeste
modes·ty ['madɪsti] s (pl -ties) modestie f
modicum ['madɪkəm] s petite quantité f
modifier ['madɪ,faɪ·ər] s (gram) modificateur m
modi·fy ['madɪ,faɪ] v (pret & pp -fied) tr modifier
modish ['modɪʃ] adj à la mode, élégant
modulate ['madʒə,let] tr & intr moduler
modulation [,madʒə'lefən] s modulation f
mohair ['mo,her] s mohair m
Mohammedan [mo'hæmɪdən] adj mahométan || s mahométan m
Mohammedanism [mo'hæmɪdə,nɪzəm] s mahométisme m
moist [mɔɪst] adj humide; (e.g., skin) moite
moisten ['mɔɪsən] tr humecter || intr s'humecter
moisture ['mɔɪstʃər] s humidité f
molar ['molər] adj & s molaire f
molasses [mə'læsɪz] s mélasse f
mold [mold] s moule m; (fungus) moisi m, moisissure f; (agr) humus m, terreau m; (fig) trempe f || tr mouler; (to make moldy) moisir || intr moisir, se moisir
molder ['moldər] s mouleur m || intr tomber en poussière
molding ['moldɪŋ] s moulage m; (cornice, shaped strip of wood, etc.) moulure f
mold·y ['moldi] adj (comp -ier; super -iest) moisi
mole [mol] s (breakwater) môle m; (inner harbor) bassin m; (spot on skin) grain m de beauté; (small mammal) taupe f
molecule ['malɪ,kjul] s molécule f
mole'hill' s taupinière f
mole'skin' s (fur) taupe f; (fabric) moleskine f
molest [mə'lest] tr déranger, inquiéter; molester, rudoyer
moll [mal] s (slang) femme f du Milieu
molli·fy ['malɪ,faɪ] v (pret & pp -fied) tr apaiser, adoucir
mollusk ['maləsk] s mollusque m
mollycoddle ['malɪ,kadəl] s poule f mouillée || tr dorloter
molt [molt] s mue f || intr muer
molten ['moltən] adj fondu
molybdenum [mə'lɪbdɪnəm], [,malɪb'dinəm] s molybdène m
moment ['momənt] s moment m; at

any moment d'un moment à l'autre; **at that moment** à ce moment-là; **at this moment** en ce moment; **in a moment** dans un instant; **of great moment** d'une grande importance; **one moment please!** (telp) ne quittez pas!

momentary ['momən,teri] *adj* momentané

momentous [mo'mentəs] *adj* important, d'importance

momen-tum [mo'mentəm] *s* (*pl* **-tums** or **-ta** [tə]) élan *m*; (mech) force *f* d'impulsion, quantité *f* de mouvement

monarch ['manərk] *s* monarque *m*

monarchic(al) [mə'nɑrkɪk(əl)] *adj* monarchique

monar-chy ['manərki] *s* (*pl* **-chies**) monarchie *f*

monaster-y ['manɛs,teri] *s* (*pl* **-ies**) monastère *m*

monastic [mə'næstɪk] *adj* monastique

monasticism [mə'næstɪ,sɪzəm] *s* monachisme *m*

Monday ['mʌndi] *s* lundi *m*

monetary ['manɪ,teri] *adj* (*pertaining to coinage*) monétaire; (*pertaining to money*) pécuniaire

money ['mʌni] *s* argent *m*; (*legal tender of a country*) monnaie *f*; **to get one's money's worth** en avoir pour son argent; **to make money** gagner de l'argent

mon'ey-bag' *s* sacoche *f*; **moneybags** (*wealth*) (coll) sac *m*; (*wealthy person*) (coll) richard *m*

mon'ey belt' *s* ceinture *f* porte-monnaie

moneychanger ['mʌni,tʃendʒər] *s* changeur *m*, cambiste *m*

moneyed ['mʌnid] *adj* possédant

mon'ey-lend'er *s* bailleur *m* de fonds

mon'ey-mak'er *s* amasseur *m* d'argent; (fig) source *f* de gain

mon'ey or'der *s* mandat *m* postal

Mongol ['maŋgəl], ['maŋgal] *adj* mongol || *s* (*language*) mongol *m*; (*person*) Mongol *m*

mon-goose ['maŋgus] *s* (*pl* **-gooses**) mangouste *f*

mongrel ['mʌŋgrəl], ['maŋgrəl] *adj* & *s* métis *m*

monitor ['manɪtər] *s* contrôleur *m*; (*at school*) pion *m*, moniteur *m* || *tr* contrôler; (rad) écouter

monk [mʌŋk] *s* moine *m*

monkey ['mʌŋki] *s* singe *m*; (*female*) guenon *f*; **to make a monkey of** tourner en ridicule || *intr*—**to monkey around** tripoter; **to monkey around with** tripoter; **to monkey with** (*to tamper with*) tripatouiller

mon'key-shine' *s* (slang) singerie *f*

mon'key wrench' *s* clé *f* anglaise

monks'hood *s* (bot) napel *m*

monocle ['manəkəl] *s* monocle *m*

monogamy [mə'nagəmi] *s* monogamie *f*

monogram ['manə,græm] *s* monogramme *m*

monograph ['manə,græf], ['manə,grɑf] *s* monographie *f*

monolithic [,manə'lɪθɪk] *adj* monolithique

monologue ['manə,lɔg], ['manə,lag] *s* monologue *m*

monomania [,manə'meni-ə] *s* monomanie *f*

monomial [mə'nomɪ-əl] *s* monôme *m*

monoplane ['manə,plen] *s* monoplan *m*

monopolize [mə'napə,laiz] *tr* monopoliser

monopo-ly [mə'napəli] *s* (*pl* **-lies**) monopole *m*

monorail ['manə,rel] *s* monorail *m*

monosyllable ['manə,sɪləbəl] *s* monosyllabe *m*

monotheist ['manə,θi-ɪst] *adj* & *s* monothéiste *mf*

monotonous [mə'natənəs] *adj* monotone

monotony [mə'natəni] *s* monotonie *f*

monotype ['manə,taɪp] *s* monotype *m*; (*machine to set type*) monotype *f*

monoxide [mə'naksaɪd] *s* oxyde *m*, e.g., **carbon monoxide** oxyde *m* de carbone

monsignor [man'sinjər] *s* (*pl* **monsignors** or **monsignori** [,mɔnsi'njori]) (eccl) monseigneur *m*

monsoon [man'sun] *s* mousson *f*

monster ['manstər] *adj* & *s* monstre *m*

monstrance ['manstrəns] *s* ostensoir *m*

monstrous ['manstrəs] *adj* monstrueux

month [mʌnθ] *s* mois *m*

month-ly ['mʌnθli] *adj* mensuel || *s* (*pl* **-lies**) revue *f* mensuelle; **monthlies** (coll) règles *fpl* || *adv* mensuellement

monument ['manjəmənt] *s* monument *m*

moo [mu] *s* meuglement *m* || *intr* meugler

mood [mud] *s* humeur *f*, disposition *f*; (gram) mode *m*; **moods** accès *mpl* de mauvaise humeur

mood-y ['mudi] *adj* (*comp* **-ier**; *super* **-iest**) d'humeur changeante; (*melancholy*) maussade

moon [mun] *s* lune *f* || *intr*—**to moon about** musarder; (*to daydream about*) rêver à

moon'beam' *s* rayon *m* de lune

moon'light' *s* clair *m* de lune

moon'light'ing *s* deuxième emploi *m*

moon'shine' *s* clair *m* de lune; (*idle talk*) baliverne *f*; (coll) alcool *m* de contrebande

moon' shot' *s* tir *m* à la lune

moor [mur] *s* lande *f*, bruyère *f*; **Moor** Maure *m* || *tr* amarrer || *intr* s'amarrer

Moorish ['murɪʃ] *adj* mauresque

moose [mus] *s* (*pl* **moose**) élan *m* du Canada, orignal *m*; (*European elk*) élan *m*

moot [mut] *adj* discutable

mop [map] *s* balai *m* à franges; (*of hair*) tignasse *f* || *v* (*pret* & *pp* **mopped**; *ger* **mopping**) *tr* nettoyer avec un balai à franges; (*e.g., one's brow*) s'essuyer; **to mop up** (mil) nettoyer

mope [mop] *intr* avoir le cafard

moral ['marəl], ['mɔrəl] *adj* moral || *s* (*of a fable*) morale *f*; **morals** mœurs *fpl*

morale [mə'ræl], [mə'rɑl] s moral m

morali·ty [mə'rælti] s (pl **-ties**) moralité f

morass [mə'ræs] s marais m

moratori·um [ˌmɔrə'tɔri·əm], [ˌmɑrə‐'tɔri·əm] s (pl **-ums** or **-a** [ə]) moratoire m, moratorium m

morbid ['mɔrbɪd] adj morbide

mordacious [mɔr'deʃəs] adj mordant

mordant ['mɔrdənt] adj & s mordant m

more [mor] adj comp plus de §91; plus nombreux; de plus, e.g., **one minute more** une minute de plus; **more than** plus que; (followed by numeral) plus de ‖ s plus m; **all the more so** d'autant plus; **what is more** qui plus est; **what more do you need?** que vous faut-il de plus? ‖ pron indef plus, davantage ‖ adv comp plus §91; davantage; **more and more** de plus en plus; **more or less** plus ou moins; **more than** plus que, davantage que; (followed by numeral) plus de; **neither more nor less** ni plus ni moins; **never more** jamais plus, plus jamais; **no more ne . . . plus** §90; **once more** une fois de plus; **the more . . . the more** (or **the less**) plus . . . plus (or moins)

more·o'ver adv de plus, du reste

Moresque [mo'resk] adj mauresque

morgue [mɔrg] s institut m médico-légal, morgue f; (journ) archives fpl

Mormon ['mɔrmən] adj & s mormon m

morning ['mɔrnɪŋ] adj matinal, du matin ‖ s matin m; (time between sunrise and noon) matinée f, matin; **in the morning** le matin; **the morning after** le lendemain matin; (coll) le lendemain de bombe

morn'ing coat' s jaquette f

morn'ing-glo'ry s (pl **-ries**) belle-de-jour f

morn'ing sick'ness s des nausées fpl

morn'ing star' s étoile f du matin

Moroccan [mə'rɑkən] adj marocain ‖ s Marocain m

morocco [mə'rɑko] s (leather) maroquin m; **Morocco** le Maroc

moron ['mɔrɑn] s arriéré m; (coll) minus mf, minus habens mf

morose [mə'ros] adj morose

morphine ['mɔrfin] s morphine f

morphology [mɔr'fɑlədʒi] s morphologie f

morrow ['mɑro], ['mɔro] s—**on the morrow** (of) le lendemain (de)

Morse' code' [mɔrs] s alphabet m morse

morsel ['mɔrsəl] s morceau m

mortal ['mɔrtəl] adj & s mortel m

mortality [mɔr'tælti] s mortalité f

mortar ['mɔrtər] s mortier m

mor'tar-board' s bonnet m carré; (of mason) taloche f

mortgage ['mɔrgɪdʒ] s hypothèque f ‖ tr hypothéquer

mortgagee [ˌmɔrgɪ'dʒi] s créancier m hypothécaire

mortgagor ['mɔrgɪdʒər] s débiteur m hypothécaire

mortician [mɔr'tɪʃən] s entrepreneur m de pompes funèbres

morti·fy ['mɔrtɪˌfaɪ] v (pret & pp **-fied**) tr mortifier

mortise ['mɔrtɪs] s mortaise f ‖ tr mortaiser

mortuar·y ['mɔrtʃu·ˌɛri] adj mortuaire ‖ s (pl **-ies**) morgue f; chapelle f mortuaire

mosaic [mo'ze·ɪk] adj & s mosaïque f

Moscow ['mɑskau], ['mɑsko] s Moscou m

Moses ['moziz], ['mozis] s Moïse m

Mos·lem ['mazləm], ['masləm] adj musulman ‖ s (pl **-lems** or **-lem**) musulman m

mosque [mask] s mosquée f

mosqui·to [məs'kito] s (pl **-toes** or **-tos**) moustique m

mosqui'to net' s moustiquaire f

moss [mɔs], [mas] s mousse f

moss·y ['mɔsi], ['masi] adj (comp **-ier**; super **-iest**) moussu

most [most] adj super (le) plus de §91, (la) plupart de; **for the most part** pour la plupart ‖ s (le) plus, (la) plupart; **at the most** au plus, tout au plus; **most of** la plupart de; **to make the most of** tirer le meilleur parti possible de ‖ pron indef la plupart ‖ adv super (le) plus §91, e.g., **what I like** (the) most ce que j'aime le plus; **the** (or **his,** etc.) **most** + adj le (or son, etc.) plus + adj ‖ adv très, bien, fort, des plus

mostly ['mostli] adv pour la plupart, principalement

motel [mo'tɛl] s motel m

moth [mɔθ], [maθ] s teigne f, papillon m nocturne; (clothes moth) mite f

moth'ball' s boule f antimite, boule de naphtaline

moth-eaten ['mɔθˌitən], ['maθˌitən] adj mité

mother ['mʌðər] s mère f ‖ tr servir de mère à; (to coddle) dorloter

Moth'er Goose's Nurs'ery Rhymes' spl les Contes de ma mère l'oie

moth'er-hood' s maternité f

moth'er-in-law' s (pl **mothers-in-law**) belle-mère f

motherless ['mʌðərlɪs] adj orphelin de mère

motherly ['mʌðərli] adj maternel

mother-of-pearl ['mʌðərəv'pʌrl] adj de nacre, en nacre ‖ s nacre f

Moth'er's Day' s fête f des mères

moth'er supe'rior s mère f supérieure

moth'er tongue' s langue f maternelle

moth'er wit' s bon sens m, esprit m

moth' hole' s trou m de mite

moth'proof' adj antimite ‖ tr rendre antimite

moth·y ['mɔθi], ['maθi] adj (comp **-ier**; super **-iest**) mité, plein de mites

motif [mo'tif] s motif m

motion ['moʃən] s mouvement m; (gesture) geste m; (in a deliberating assembly) motion f, proposition f ‖ intr—**to motion to** faire signe à

motionless ['moʃənlɪs] adj immobile

mo'tion pic'ture s film m; **motion pictures** cinéma m

mo′tion-pic′ture *adj* cinématographi-que

mo′tion-pic′ture the′ater *s* cinéma *m*

motivate [′motɪ‚vet] *tr* motiver

motive [′motɪv] *adj* moteur ‖ *s* mobile *m*, motif *m*

mo′tive pow′er *s* force *f* motrice

motley [′matlɪ] *adj* bigarré; (mixed) mélangé

motor [′motər] *adj & s* moteur *m* ‖ *intr* aller en voiture

mo′tor-bike′ *s* vélomoteur *m*

mo′tor-boat′ *s* canot *m* automobile

mo′tor-bus′ *s* autocar *m*

motorcade [′motər‚ked] *s* défilé *m* de voitures

mo′tor-car′ *s* automobile *f*

mo′tor-cy′cle *s* moto *f*

motorist [′motərɪst] *s* automobiliste *mf*

motorize [′motə‚raɪz] *tr* motoriser

mo′tor launch′ *s* chaloupe *f* à moteur

mo′tor-man *s* (pl -men) conducteur *m*, wattman *m*

mo′tor pool′ *s* parc *m* automobile

mo′tor scoot′er *s* scooter *m*

mo′tor ship′ *s* navire *m* à moteurs

mo′tor truck′ *s* camion *m* automobile

mo′tor ve′hicle *s* véhicule *m* automobile

mottle [′matəl] *tr* marbrer, tacheter

mot-to [′mato] *s* (pl -toes or -tos) devise *f*

mound [maund] *s* monticule *m*

mount [maunt] *s* montage *m*; (hill, mountain) mont *m*; (horse for riding) monture *f* ‖ *tr & intr* monter

mountain [′mauntɪn] *s* montagne *f*

moun′tain climb′ing *s* alpinisme *m*

mountaineer [‚mauntɪ′nɪr] *s* montagnard *m*; (climber) alpiniste *mf*

mountainous [′mauntənəs] *adj* montagneux

moun′tain range′ *s* chaîne *f* de montagnes

mountebank [′mauntɪ‚bæŋk] *s* saltimbanque *mf*

mounting [′mauntɪŋ] *s* montage *m*

mourn [morn] *tr & intr* pleurer

mourner [′mornər] *s* affligé *m*; (woman hired as mourner) pleureuse *f*; pénitent *m*; **mourners** deuil *m*

mourn′er's bench′ *s* banc *m* des pénitents

mournful [′mornfəl] *adj* lugubre

mourning [′mornɪŋ] *s* deuil *m*

mouse [maus] *s* (pl mice [maɪs]) souris *f*

mouse′hole′ *s* trou *m* de souris

mouser [′mauzər] *s* souricier *m*

mouse′trap′ *s* souricière *f*

moustache [məs′tæʃ], [məs′taʃ] *s* moustache *f*

mouth [mauθ] *s* (pl mouths [mauðz]) bouche *f*; (of gun; of, e.g., wolf) gueule *f*; (of river) embouchure *f*; **by mouth** par voie buccale; **to make s.o.'s mouth water** faire venir l'eau à la bouche à qn

mouthful [′mauθ‚ful] *s* bouchée *f*

mouth′ or′gan *s* harmonica *m*

mouth′piece′ *s* embouchure *f*; (person) porte-parole *m*

mouth′wash′ *s* rince-bouche *m*, eau *f* dentifrice

movable [′muvəbəl] *adj* mobile

move [muv] *s* mouvement *m*; démarche *f*; (from one house to another) déménagement *m*; **on the move** en mouvement ‖ *tr* remuer; (to excite the feelings of) émouvoir; **to move that** (parl) proposer que; **to move up** (a date) avancer ‖ *intr* remuer; (to stir) se remuer; (said of traffic, crowd, etc.) circuler; (e.g., to another city) déménager; **don't move!** ne bougez pas!; **to move away** or **off** s'éloigner; **to move back** reculer; **to move in** emménager

movement [′muvmənt] *s* mouvement *m*

movie [′muvi] *s* (coll) film *m*; **movies** (coll) cinéma *m*

mov′ie cam′era *s* caméra *f*

movie-goer [′muvi‚go·ər] *s* (coll) amateur *m* de cinéma

mov′ie house′ *s* (coll) cinéma *m*, salle *f* de spectacles

moving [′muvɪŋ] *adj* mouvant, en marche; (touching) émouvant; (force) moteur ‖ *s* mouvement *m*; (from one house to another) déménagement *m*

mov′ing pic′ture *s* film *m*; **moving pictures** cinéma *m*

mov′ing-pic′ture the′ater *s* cinéma *m*

mov′ing spir′it *s* âme *f*

mov′ing stair′way *s* escalier *m* mécanique, escalier roulant

mov′ing van′ *s* voiture *f* de déménagement

mow [mo] *v* (pret mowed; pp mowed or mown) *tr* faucher; (a lawn) tondre; **to mow down** faucher

mower [′mo·ər] *s* faucheur *m*; (mach) faucheuse *f*; (for lawns) (mach) tondeuse *f*

m.p.h. [′em′pi′etʃ] *spl* (letterword) (miles per hour—six tenths of a mile equaling approximately one kilometer).km/h

Mr. [′mɪstər] *s* Monsieur *m*, M.

Mrs. [′mɪsɪz] *s* Madame *f*, Mme

much [mʌtʃ] *adj* beaucoup de, e.g., **much time** beaucoup de temps; bien de + *art*, e.g., **much trouble** bien du mal ‖ *pron indef* beaucoup; **too much** trop ‖ *adv* beaucoup, bien §91; **however much** pour autant que; **how much** combien; **much less** encore moins; **too much** trop; **very much** beaucoup

mucilage [′mjusɪlɪdʒ] *s* colle *f* de bureau; (gummy secretion in plants) mucilage *m*

muck [mʌk] *s* fange *f*

muck′rake′ *intr* (coll) dévoiler des scandales

mucous [′mjukəs] *adj* muqueux

mu′cous lin′ing *s* (anat) muqueuse *f*

mucus [′mjukəs] *s* mucus *m*, mucosité *f*

mud [mʌd] *s* boue *f*; **to sling mud at** couvrir de boue

muddle [′mʌdəl] *s* confusion *f*, fouillis *m* ‖ *tr* embrouiller ‖ *intr—to muddle through** se débrouiller

mud′dle·head′ s brouillon m

mud·dy ['mʌdi] adj (comp **-dier;** super **-diest**) boueux; (clothes) crotté || v (pret & pp **-died**) tr salir; (clothes) crotter; (a liquid) troubler; (fig) embrouiller

mud′guard′ s garde-boue m

mud′hole′ s bourbier m

mudslinger ['mʌd,slɪŋər] s (fig) calomniateur m

muff [mʌf] s manchon m; (failure) coup m raté || tr rater, louper

muffin ['mʌfɪn] s petit pain m rond, muffin m

muffle ['mʌfəl] tr (a sound) assourdir; (the face) emmitoufler

muffler ['mʌflər] s (scarf) cache-nez m; (aut) pot m d'échappement, silencieux m

mufti ['mʌfti] s vêtement m civil; **in mufti** en civil, en pékin, en bourgeois

mug [mʌg] s timbale f, gobelet m; (tankard) chope f; (slang) gueule f, museau m || v (pret & pp **mugged;** ger **mugging**) tr (e.g., a suspect) (slang) photographier; (a victim) (slang) saisir à la gorge || intr (slang) faire des grimaces

mug·gy ['mʌgi] adj (comp **-gier;** super **-giest**) lourd, étouffant

mulat·to [mju'læto], [mə'læto] s (pl **-toes**) mulâtre m

mulber·ry ['mʌl,beri] s (pl **-ries**) mûre f; (tree) mûrier m

mulct [mʌlkt] tr (a person) priver, dépouiller; (money) carotter, extorquer

mule [mjul] s (female mule; slipper) mule f; (male mule) mulet m

muleteer [,mjulə'tɪr] s muletier m

mulish ['mjulɪʃ] adj têtu, entêté

mull [mʌl] tr chauffer avec des épices; (to muddle) embrouiller || intr—to **mull over** réfléchir sur, remâcher

mullion ['mʌljən] s meneau m

multigraph ['mʌlti,græf], ['mʌlti,graf] s (trademark) ronéo f || tr ronéotyper, polycopier

multilateral [,mʌltɪ'lætərəl] adj multilatéral

multiple ['mʌltɪpəl] adj & s multiple m

multiplici·ty [,mʌltɪ'plɪsɪti] s (pl **-ties**) multiplicité f

multi·ply ['mʌlti,plaɪ] v (pret & pp **-plied**) tr multiplier || intr se multiplier

multitude ['mʌlti,t(j)ud] s multitude f

mum [mʌm] adj silencieux; **mum's the word!** motus!, bouche cousue!; **to keep mum** about ne souffler mot de

mumble ['mʌmbəl] tr & intr marmotter

mummer·y ['mʌməri] s (pl **-ies**) momerie f

mum·my ['mʌmi] s (pl **-mies**) momie f; (slang) maman f

mumps [mʌmps] s oreillons mpl

munch [mʌntʃ] tr mâchonner

mundane ['mʌnden] adj mondain

municipal [mju'nɪsɪpəl] adj municipal

municipali·ty [mju,nɪsɪ'pælɪti] s (pl **-ties**) municipalité f

munificent [mju'nɪfɪsənt] adj munificent

munition [mju'nɪʃən] s munition f || tr approvisionner de munitions

muni′tion dump′ s dépôt m de munitions

mural ['mjurəl] adj mural || s peinture f murale

murder ['mʌrdər] s assassinat m, meurtre m || tr assassiner; (a language, proper names, etc.) (coll) estropier, écorcher

murderer ['mʌrdərər] s meurtrier m, assassin m

murderess ['mʌrdərɪs] s meurtrière f

murderous ['mʌrdərəs] adj meurtrier

murk·y ['mʌrki] adj (comp **-ier;** super **-iest**) ténébreux, nébuleux

murmur ['mʌrmər] s murmure m || tr & intr murmurer

muscle ['mʌsəl] s muscle m

muscular ['mʌskjələr] adj musclé, musculeux; (system, tissue, etc.) musculaire

muse [mjuz] s muse f; **the Muses** les Muses || intr méditer; **to muse on** méditer

museum [mju'zi·əm] s musée m

muse′um piece′ s pièce f de musée

mush [mʌʃ] s bouillie f; (coll) sentimentalité f de guimauve

mush′room′ s champignon m || intr pousser comme un champignon

mush′room cloud′ s champignon m atomique

mush·y ['mʌʃi] adj (comp **-ier;** super **-iest**) mou; (ground) détrempé; (coll) à la guimauve, sentimental

music ['mjuzɪk] s musique f; **to face the music** (coll) affronter les opposants; **to set to music** mettre en musique

musical ['mjuzɪkəl] adj musical

mu′sical com′edy s comédie f musicale

musicale [,mjuzɪ'kæl] s soirée f musicale; matinée f musicale

mu′sic box′ s boîte f à musique

mu′sic cab′inet s casier m à musique

mu′sic hall′ s salle f de musique; (Brit) music-hall m

musician [mju'zɪʃən] s musicien m

mu′sic lov′er s mélomane mf

musicology [,mjuzɪ'kalədʒi] s musicologie f

mu′sic rack′ or **mu′sic stand′** s pupitre m à musique

musk [mʌsk] s musc m

musk′ deer′ s porte-musc m

musketeer [,mʌskɪ'tɪr] s mousquetaire m

musk′mel′on s melon m; cantaloup m

musk′rat′ s rat m musqué, ondatra m

Mus·lim ['mʌzlɪm] adj musulman || s (pl **-lims** or **-lim**) musulman m

muslin ['mʌzlɪn] s mousseline f

muss [mʌs] tr (the hair) ébouriffer; (the clothing) froisser

Mussulman ['mʌsəlmən] adj & s musulman m

muss·y ['mʌsi] adj (comp **-ier;** super **-iest**) en désordre, froissé

must [mʌst] s moût m; nécessité f absolue || aux used to express 1) necessity, e.g., **he must go away** il doit s'en aller; 2) conjecture, e.g., **he must be ill** il doit être malade; **he must have been ill** il a dû être malade

mustache [məsˈtæʃ], [məsˈtɑ/], [ˈmʌstæʃ] *s* moustache *f*

mustard [ˈmʌstərd] *s* moutarde *f*

mus/tard plas/ter *s* sinapisme *m*

muster [ˈmʌstər] *s* rassemblement *m*; (mil) revue *f*; **to pass muster** être porté à l'appel; (fig) être acceptable ‖ *tr* rassembler; **to muster in** enrôler; **to muster out** démobiliser; **to muster up courage** prendre son courage à deux mains

mus/ter roll/ *s* feuille *f* d'appel

mus•ty [ˈmʌsti] *adj* (*comp* -tier; *super* -tiest) (*moldy*) moisi; (*stale*) renfermé; (*antiquated*) désuet

mutation [mjuˈteʃən] *s* mutation *f*

mute [mjut] *adj* muet ‖ *s* muet *m*; (mus) sourdine *f* ‖ *tr* amortir; (mus) mettre une sourdine à

mutilate [ˈmjutɪˌlet] *tr* mutiler

mutineer [ˌmjutɪˈnɪr] *s* mutin *m*

mutinous [ˈmjutɪnəs] *adj* mutiné

muti•ny [ˈmjutɪni] *s* (*pl* -nies) mutinerie *f* ‖ *v* (*pret & pp* -nied) *intr* se mutiner

mutt [mʌt] *s* (*dog*) (slang) cabot *m*; (*person*) (slang) nigaud *m*

mutter [ˈmʌtər] *tr & intr* marmonner

mutton [ˈmʌtən] *s* mouton *m*

mut/ton-chop/ *s* côtelette *f* de mouton; **muttonchops** favoris *mpl* en côtelette

mutual [ˈmjut/ʊ-əl] *adj* mutuel

mu/tual aid/ *s* entraide *f*

mu/tual fund/ *s* mutuelle *f*

muzzle [ˈmʌzəl] *s* (*projecting part of head of animal*) museau *m*; (*device to keep animal from biting*) muselière *f*; (*of firearm*) gueule *f* ‖ *tr* museler

my [maɪ] *adj poss* mon §88

myriad [ˈmɪrɪ-əd] *adj* innombrable ‖ *s* myriade *f*

myrrh [mɪr] *s* myrrhe *f*

myrtle [ˈmʌrtəl] *s* myrte *m*; (*periwinkle*) pervenche *f*

my•self/ *pron pers* moi §85; moi-même §86; me §87

mysterious [mɪsˈtɪrɪ-əs] *adj* mystérieux

myster•y [ˈmɪstəri] *s* (*pl* -ies) mystère *m*

mystic [ˈmɪstɪk] *adj & s* mystique *mf*

mystical [ˈmɪstɪkəl] *adj* mystique

mysticism [ˈmɪstɪˌsɪzəm] *s* mysticisme *m*

mystification [ˌmɪstɪfɪˈkeʃən] *s* mystification *f*

mysti•fy [ˈmɪstɪˌfaɪ] *v* (*pret & pp* -fied) *tr* mystifier

myth [mɪθ] *s* mythe *m*

mythical [ˈmɪθɪkəl] *adj* mythique

mythological [ˌmɪθəˈlɑdʒɪkəl] *adj* mythologique

mytholo•gy [mɪˈθɑlədʒi] *s* (*pl* -gies) mythologie *f*

N

N, n [en] *s* XIVe lettre de l'alphabet

nab [næb] *v* (*pret & pp* nabbed; *ger* nabbing) *tr* (slang) happer; (*to arrest*) (slang) pincer, harponner

nag [næg] *s* bidet *m* ‖ *v* (*pret & pp* nagged; *ger* nagging) *tr & intr* gronder constamment; **to nag at** gronder constamment

nail [nel] *s* (*of finger*) ongle *m*; (*to be hammered*) clou *m*; **to bite one's nails** se ronger les ongles; **to hit the nail on the head** mettre le doigt dessus, frapper juste ‖ *tr* clouer; (*a lie*) mettre à découvert; (coll) saisir, attraper

nail/brush/ *s* brosse *f* à ongles

nail/ clip/pers *spl* coupe-ongles *m*

nail/ file/ *s* lime *f* à ongles

nail/ pol/ish *s* vernis *m* à ongles

nail/ scis/sors *s & spl* ciseaux *mpl* à ongles

nail/ set/ *s* chasse-clou *m*

naïve [nɑˈiv] *adj* naïf

naked [ˈnekɪd] *adj* nu; **to strip naked** se mettre tout nu; mettre tout nu; **with the naked eye** à l'œil nu

namby-pamby [ˈnæmbiˈpæmbi] *adj* minaudier

name [nem] *s* nom *m*; (*reputation*) renom *m*; **by name** de nom; **by the**

name of sous le nom de; **to call names** traiter de tous les noms; **what is your name?** comment vous appelez-vous? ‖ *tr* nommer; (*a price*) fixer, indiquer

name/ day/ *s* fête *f*

nameless [ˈnemlɪs] *adj* sans nom, anonyme; (*horrid*) odieux

namely [ˈnemli] *adv* à savoir, nommément

name/sake/ *s* homonyme *m*

nan•ny [ˈnæni] *s* (*pl* -nies) nounou *f*

nan/ny goat/ *s* (coll) chèvre *f*, bique *f*

nap [næp] *s* (*short sleep*) somme *m*, sieste *f*; (*of cloth*) poil *m*, duvet *m*; **to take a nap** faire un petit somme ‖ *v* (*pret & pp* napped; *ger* napping) *intr* faire un somme; manquer de vigilance; **to catch napping** prendre au dépourvu

napalm [ˈnepam] *s* (mil) napalm *m*

nape [nep] *s* nuque *f*

naphtha [ˈnæfθə] *s* naphte *m*

napkin [ˈnæpkɪn] *s* serviette *f*

nap/kin ring/ *s* rond *m* de serviette

Napoleonic [nəˌpolɪˈɑnɪk] *adj* napoléonien

narcissus [nɑrˈsɪsəs] *s* narcisse *m*; **Narcissus** Narcisse

narcotic [nɑr'kɑtɪk] *adj* & *s* narcotique *m*

narrate [næ'ret] *tr* narrer, raconter

narration [næ're/ən] *s* narration *f*

narrative ['nærətɪv] *adj* narratif ‖ *s* narration *f*, récit *m*

narrator [næ'retər] *s* narrateur *m*

narrow ['næro] *adj* étroit; (*e.g., margin of votes*) faible ‖ **narrows** *spl* détroit *m*, goulet *m* ‖ *tr* rétrécir ‖ *intr* se rétrécir

nar'row escape' s—to have a narrow escape l'échapper belle

nar'row gauge' s voie *f* étroite

nar'row-mind'ed *adj* à l'esprit étroit, intolérant

nasal ['nezəl] *adj* nasal; (*sound, voice*) nasillard ‖ *s* (phonet) nasale *f*

nasalize ['nezə,laɪz] *tr* & *intr* nasaliser

nasturtium [nə'stʌr/əm] *s* capucine *f*

nas•ty ['næsti], ['nɑsti] *adj* (*comp -tier; super -tiest*) mauvais, sale, dégoûtant; féroce, farouche; désagréable

nation ['ne/ən] *s* nation *f*

national ['næ/ənəl] *adj* & *s* national *m*

na'tional an'them *s* hymne *m* national

nationalism ['næ/ənə,lɪzəm] *s* nationalisme *m*

nationali•ty [,næ/ən'ælɪti] *s* (*pl -ties*) nationalité *f*

nationalize ['næ/ənə,laɪz] *tr* nationaliser, étatiser

na'tion-wide' *adj* de toute la nation

native ['netɪv] *adj* natif; (*land, language*) natal; **native of** originaire de ‖ *s* natif *m*; (*original inhabitant*) naturel *m*, indigène *mf*, autochtone *mf*

na'tive land' *s* pays *m* natal

nativi•ty [nə'tɪvɪti] *s* (*pl -ties*) naissance *f*; (astrol) nativité *f*; **Nativity** Nativité *f*

NATO ['neto] *s* (acronym) (**North Atlantic Treaty Organization**) l'O.T.A.N. *f*, l'OTAN *f*

nat•ty ['næti] *adj* (*comp -tier; super -tiest*) coquet, élégant, soigné

natural ['næt/ərəl] *adj* naturel ‖ *s* (mus) bécarre *m*; (mus) touche *f* blanche; **a natural** (coll) juste ce qu'il faut

naturalism ['næt/ərə,lɪzəm] *s* naturalisme *m*

naturalist ['næt/ərəlɪst] *s* naturaliste *mf*

naturalization [,næt/ərəlɪ'ze/ən] *s* naturalisation *f*

naturaliza'tion pa'pers *spl* déclaration *f* de naturalisation

naturalize ['næt/ərə,laɪz] *tr* naturaliser

nature ['net/ər] *s* nature *f*

naught [nɔt] *s* zéro *m*; rien *m*; **to come to naught** n'aboutir à rien

naugh•ty ['nɔti] *adj* (*comp -tier; super -tiest*) méchant, vilain; (*story*) risqué

nausea ['nɔ/ɪ·ə], ['nɔsɪ·ə] *s* nausée *f*

nauseate ['nɔ/ɪ,et], ['nɔsɪ,et] *tr* donner la nausée à ‖ *intr* avoir des nausées

nauseating ['nɔ/ɪ,etɪŋ], ['nɔsɪ,etɪŋ] *adj* nauséabond

nauseous ['nɔ/ɪ·əs], ['nɔsɪ·əs] *adj* nauséeux

nautical ['nɔtɪkəl] *adj* nautique; naval, marin

naval ['nevəl] *adj* naval

na'val acad'emy *s* école *f* navale

na'val of'ficer *s* officier *m* de marine

na'val sta'tion *s* station *f* navale

nave [nev] *s* (*of a church*) nef *f*, vaisseau *m*; (*of a wheel*) moyeu *m*

navel ['nevəl] *s* nombril *m*

na'vel or'ange *s* orange *f* navel

navigable ['nævɪgəbəl] *adj* (*river*) navigable; (*aircraft*) dirigeable; (*ship*) bon marcheur

navigate ['nævɪ,get] *tr* gouverner, conduire; (*the sea*) naviguer sur ‖ *intr* naviguer

navigation [,nævɪ'ge/ən] *s* navigation *f*

navigator ['nævɪ,getər] *s* navigateur *m*

na•vy ['nevi] *adj* bleu marine ‖ *s* (*pl -vies*) marine *f* militaire, marine de guerre; (*color*) bleu *m* marine

na'vy bean' *s* haricot *m* blanc

na'vy blue' *s* bleu *m* marine

na'vy yard' *s* chantier *m* naval

nay [ne] *adv* non; voire, même ‖ *s* non *m*; (parl) vote *m* négatif

Nazarene [,næzə'rin] *adj* nazaréen ‖ *s* (*person*) Nazaréen *m*

Nazi ['nɑtsi], ['nætsi] *adj* & *s* nazi *m*

n.d. *abbr* (**no date**) s.d.

Ne'apol'itan ice' cream' [,ni·ə'pɑlɪtən] *s* glace *f* panachée

neap' tide' [nip] *s* morte-eau *f*

near [nɪr] *adj* proche, prochain; d'imitation; **near at hand** tout près; **near side** (*of horse*) côté *m* de montoir ‖ *adv* près, de près; presque; **to come near** s'approcher ‖ *prep* près de; **auprès de** ‖ *tr* s'approcher de

near'by' *adj* proche ‖ *adv* tout près

Near' East' s—the Near East le Proche Orient

nearly ['nɪrli] *adv* presque, de près; faillir, manquer de, e.g., **I nearly fell** j'ai failli tomber

near'-sight'ed *adj* myope

near'-sight'edness *s* myopie *f*

neat [nit] *adj* soigné, rangé; concis; (*clever*) adroit; (*liquor*) nature; (slang) chouette

neat's'-foot oil' *s* huile *f* de pied de bœuf

nebu•la ['nebjələ] *s* (*pl -lae* [,li] or *-las*) nébuleuse *f*

nebulous ['nebjələs] *adj* nébuleux

necessarily [,nesɪ'serɪli] *adv* nécessairement, forcément

necessary ['nesɪ,seri] *adj* nécessaire

necessitate [nɪ'sesɪ,tet] *tr* nécessiter, exiger

necessi•ty [nɪ'sesɪti] *s* (*pl -ties*) nécessité *f*

neck [nek] *s* cou *m*; (*of bottle*) col *m*, goulot *m*; (*of land*) cap *m*; (*of tooth*) collet *m*; (*of violin*) manche *m*, collet; (*strait*) étroit *m*; **neck and neck** manche à manche; **to break one's neck** (coll) se rompre le cou; **to stick one's neck out** prêter le flanc; **to win**

by a neck gagner par une encolure || *intr* (slang) se peloter
neck/band/ s tour m de cou
neckerchief ['nekərt/ıf] s foulard m
necking ['nekıŋ] s (slang) pelotage m
necklace ['neklıs] s collier m
neck/piece/ s col m de fourrure
neck/tie/ s cravate f
neck/tie pin/ s épingle f de cravate
necrolo·gy [ne'krɑlədʒı] s (pl -gies) nécrologie f
nectar ['nektər] s nectar m
nectarine [ˌnektə'rin] s brugnon m
nee [ne] adj née
need [nid] s besoin m; (*want, poverty*) besoin, indigence f, nécessité f; **if need be** au besoin, s'il le faut || *tr* avoir besoin de, falloir, e.g., **he needs money** il a besoin d'argent, il lui faut de l'argent; demander, e.g., **the motor needs oil** le moteur demande de l'huile || *aux* devoir
needful ['nidfəl] adj nécessaire
needle ['nidəl] s aiguille f || *tr* (*to prod*) aiguillonner; (coll) taquiner; (*a drink*) (coll) corser
nee/dle-point/ s broderie f sur canevas; (*lace*) dentelle f à l'aiguille
needless ['nidlıs] adj inutile
nee/dle-work/ s ouvrage m à l'aiguille
need·y ['nidı] adj (comp -ier; super -iest) nécessiteux || s—**the needy** les nécessiteux
ne'er-do-well ['nerduˌwel] adj propre à rien || s vaurien m
nefarious [nı'ferıˌəs] adj scélérat
negate ['neget], [nı'get] tr invalider; nier
negation [nı'ge/ən] s négation f
negative ['negatıv] adj négatif || s (*opinion*) négative f; (gram) négation f; (phot) négatif m
neglect [nı'glekt] s négligence f || tr négliger; **to neglect to** négliger de
négligee or **negligee** [ˌneglı'ʒe] s négligé m, robe f de chambre
negligence ['neglıdʒəns] s négligence f
negligent ['neglıdʒənt] adj négligent
negligible ['neglıdʒıbəl] adj négligeable
negotiable [nı'goʃıˌəbəl] adj négociable
negotiate [nı'goʃıˌet] tr & intr négocier
negotiation [nıˌgoʃı'eʃən] s négociation f
negotiator [nı'goʃıˌetər] s négociateur m
Ne·gro ['nigro] adj noir, nègre || s (pl -groes) noir m, nègre m
neigh [ne] s hennissement m || *intr* hennir
neighbor ['nebər] adj voisin || s voisin m; (fig) prochain m || tr avoisiner || *intr* être voisin
neigh/bor·hood/ s voisinage m; **in the neighborhood of** aux environs de; (*approximately, about*) (coll) environ
neighborliness ['nebərlınıs] s bon voisinage m
neighborly ['nebərlı] adj bon voisin
neither ['niðər], ['naıðər] adj indef ni, e.g., **neither one of us** ni l'un ni

l'autre || pron indef ni, e.g., **neither** ni l'un ni l'autre || conj ni; ni . . . non plus, e.g., **neither do I** ni moi non plus; **neither . . . nor** ni . . . ni
neme·sis ['nemısıs] s (pl -ses [ˌsiz]) juste châtiment m; Nemesis Némésis f
neologism [nı'ɑləˌdʒızəm] s néologisme m
neon ['niˌɑn] s néon m
ne/on lamp/ s lampe f au néon
ne/on sign/ s réclame f lumineuse
neophyte ['niˌəˌfaıt] s néophyte mf
nephew ['nefju], ['nevju] s neveu m
neptunium [nep't(j)unıˌəm] s neptunium m
Nero ['nıro] s Néron m
nerve [nɜrv] adj nerveux || s nerf m; audace f; **to get on s.o.'s nerves** porter sur les nerfs à qn; **to have a lot of nerve** avoir du toupet; **to have nerves of steel** avoir du nerf; **to lose one's nerve** avoir le trac
nerve/ cen/ter s nœud m vital; (anat) centre m nerveux
nerve/-rack/ing adj énervant, agaçant
nervous ['nɜrvəs] adj nerveux
ner/vous break/down s épuisement m nerveux, dépression f nerveuse
nerv·y ['nɜrvı] adj (comp -ier; super -iest) nerveux, musclé; (coll) audacieux, culotté; (slang) dévergondé
nest [nest] s nid m; (*set of things fitting together*) jeu m || intr se nicher
nest/ egg/ s nichet m; (fig) boursicot m, bas m de laine
nestle ['nesəl] intr se blottir, se nicher
nest/ of ta/bles s table f gigogne
net [net] adj net || s filet m; (*for fishing; for catching birds*) nappe f; (tex) tulle m || v (pret & pp netted; ger netting) tr (*a profit*) réaliser
Netherlander ['neðərˌlændər], ['neðərləndər] s Néerlandais m
Netherlands ['neðərləndz] s—**The Netherlands** les Pays-Bas mpl
nettle ['netəl] s ortie f || tr piquer au vif
net/work/ s réseau m; (rad, telv) chaîne f, réseau
neuralgia [n(j)ʊ'rældʒə] s névralgie f
neuro·sis [n(j)ʊ'rosıs] s (pl -ses [siz]) névrose f
neurotic [n(j)ʊ'rɑtık] adj & s névrosé m
neuter ['n(j)utər] adj & s neutre m
neutral ['n(j)utrəl] adj neutre || s neutre m; (gear) point m mort
neutrality [n(j)u'trælıtı] s neutralité f
neutralize ['n(j)utrəˌlaız] tr neutraliser
neutron ['n(j)utrɑn] s neutron m
neu/tron bomb/ s bombe f à neutrons
never ['nevər] adv jamais **§90B**; **ne . . . jamais §90**, e.g., **he never talks** il ne parle jamais
nev/er-more/ adv ne . . . plus jamais || interj jamais plus!, plus jamais!
nev/er-the-less/ adv néanmoins
new [n(j)u] adj (*unused*) neuf; (*other, additional, different*) nouveau (before noun); (*recent*) nouveau (after noun); (*inexperienced*) novice; (*wine*)

jeune; **what's new?** quoi de nouveau?, quoi de neuf?

new'born' adj nouveau-né

new'born child' s nouveau-né m

New'cas'tle s—to carry coals to Newcastle porter de l'eau à la rivière

newcomer ['nju̇ˌkʌmər] s nouveau venu m

New' Cov'enant s (Bib) nouvelle alliance f

newel ['nju̇əl] s (of winding stairs) noyau m; (post at end of stair rail) pilastre m

New' Eng'land s Nouvelle-Angleterre f; la Nouvelle-Angleterre

newfangled ['nju̇ˌfæŋgəld] adj à la dernière mode, du dernier cri

Newfoundland ['nju̇fənd,lænd] s Terre-Neuve f; **in or to Newfoundland** à Terre-Neuve || [nju̇'faʊndlənd] s (dog) terre-neuve m

newly ['nju̇li] adv nouvellement

new'ly-wed' s nouveau marié m

new' moon' s nouvelle lune f

newness ['nju̇nɪs] s nouveauté f

New' Or'leans ['ɔrlɪˌənz] s la Nouvelle-Orléans

news [n(j)uz] s nouvelles fpl; **a news item** un fait-divers; **a piece of news** une nouvelle

news' a'gency s agence f d'information, agence de presse; agence à journaux

news'beat' s exclusivité f

news'boy' s vendeur m de journaux

news' bul'letin s bulletin m d'actualités

news'cast' s journal m parlé; journal télévisé

news'cast'er s reporter m de la radio

news' con'ference s conférence f de presse

news' cov'erage s reportage m

news'deal'er s marchand m de journaux

news' ed'itor s rédacteur m publicitaire

news'let'ter s circulaire f publicitaire

news'man' s (pl -men') journaliste m; (dealer) marchand m de journaux

New' South' Wales' s la Nouvelle-Galles du Sud

news'pa'per adj journalistique || s journal m

news'paper clip'ping s coupure f de presse

news'paper-man' s (pl -men') journaliste m; (dealer) marchand m de journaux

news'paper rack' s casier m à journaux

news'paper se'rial s feuilleton m

news'print' s papier m journal

news'reel' s actualités fpl

news'room' s salle f de rédaction

news'stand' s kiosque m

news'week'ly s (pl -lies) hebdomadaire m

news'wor'thy adj d'actualité

New' Tes'tament s Nouveau Testament m

New' Year's' Day' s le jour de l'An

New' Year's' Eve' s la Saint-Sylvestre

New' Year's' greet'ings spl souhaits mpl de nouvel An

New' Year's' resolu'tion s résolution f de nouvel An

New' York' [jɔrk] adj newyorkais || s New York m

New' York'er ['jɔrkər] s newyorkais m

next [nɛkst] adj (in time) prochain, suivant; (in place) voisin; (first in the period which follows) prochain (before noun), e.g., **the next time** la prochaine fois; (following the present time) prochain (after noun), e.g., **next week** la semaine prochaine; **next to** à côté de || adv après, ensuite; la prochaine fois; **who comes next?** à qui le tour? || interj au premier de ces messieurs!, au suivant!

next'-door' adj d'à côté, voisin || **next'-door'** adv à côté; **next-door to** à côté de; à côté de chez

next' of kin' s (pl next of kin) proche parent m

Niag'ara Falls' [naɪˈægərə] s la Cataracte du Niagara

nib [nɪb] s pointe f; (of pen) bec m

nibble ['nɪbəl] s grignotement m; (on fish line) touche f; (fig) morceau m || tr & intr grignoter

nice [naɪs] adj agréable, gentil, aimable; (distinction) subtil, fin; (weather) beau; **nice and . . .** (coll) très; **not nice** (coll) vilain

nicely ['naɪsli] adv bien; avec délicatesse

nice·ty ['naɪsəti] s (pl -ties) précision f; (subtlety) finesse f

niche [nɪtʃ] s niche f; (job, position) place f, poste m

nick [nɪk] s (e.g., on china) brèche f; **in the nick of time** à point nommé, à pic || tr ébrécher; (for money, favors) (slang) cramponner

nickel ['nɪkəl] s (metal) nickel m; (coin) pièce f de cinq sous || tr nickeler

nick'el plate' s nickelure f

nick'el-plate' tr nickeler

nicknack ['nɪkˌnæk] s colifichet m

nick'name' s sobriquet m, surnom m || tr donner un sobriquet à, surnommer

nicotine ['nɪkəˌtin] s nicotine f

niece [nis] s nièce f

nif·ty ['nɪfti] adj (comp -tier; super -tiest) (slang) coquet, pimpant

niggard ['nɪgərd] adj & s avare mf

night [naɪt] s nuit f; (evening) soir m; **last night** (night that has just passed) cette nuit; (last evening) hier soir; **night before last** avant-hier soir

night'cap' s bonnet m de nuit, casque m à mèche; (drink) posset m

night' club' s boîte f de nuit

night'fall' s tombée f de la nuit

night'gown' s chemise f de nuit

night'hawk' s noctambule mf; (orn) engoulevent m

nightingale ['naɪtənˌgel] s rossignol m

night'latch' s serrure f à ressort

night' light' s veilleuse f

night'long' adj de toute la nuit || adv pendant toute la nuit

nightly ['naɪtli] adj nocturne; de chaque nuit || *adv* nocturnement; chaque nuit

night/mare/ *s* cauchemar *m*

nightmarish [ˈnaɪtˌmɛrɪʃ] *adj* (coll) cauchemardeux

night/ owl/ *s* (coll) noctambule *mf*

night/ school/ *s* cours *mpl* du soir

night/shade/ *s* morelle *f*

night/ shift/ *s* équipe *f* de nuit

night/ watch/man *s* (*pl* **-men**) veilleur *m* de nuit

nihilism [ˈnaɪ·ɪˌlɪzəm] *s* nihilisme *m*

nil [nɪl] *s* rien *m*

Nile [naɪl] *s* Nil *m*

nimble [ˈnɪmbəl] *adj* agile, leste; (*mind*) délié

nim·bus [ˈnɪmbəs] *s* (*pl* **-buses** or **-bi** [baɪ]) nimbe *m*, auréole *f*; (meteo) nimbus *m*

nincompoop [ˈnɪnkəmˌpup] *s* nigaud *m*

nine [naɪn] *adj & pron* neuf || *s* neuf *m*; **nine o'clock** neuf heures

nine/pins/ *s* quilles *fpl*

nineteen [ˈnaɪnˈtin] *adj & pron* dix-neuf *m*

nineteenth [ˈnaɪnˈtinθ] *adj & pron* dix-neuvième (*masc, fem*); **the Nineteenth** dix-neuf, e.g., **John the Nineteenth** Jean dix-neuf || *s* dix-neuvième *m*; **the nineteenth** (*in dates*) le dix-neuf

ninetieth [ˈnaɪntɪ·ɪθ] *adj & pron* quatre-vingt-dixième (*masc, fem*) || *s* quatre-vingt-dixième *m*

nine·ty [ˈnaɪntɪ] *adj & pron* quatre-vingt-dix || *s* (*pl* **-ties**) quatre-vingt-dix *m*

nine/ty-first/ *adj & pron* quatre-vingt-onzième (*masc, fem*) || *s* quatre-vingt-onzième *m*

nine/ty-one/ *adj, pron, & s* quatre-vingt-onze *m*

ninth [naɪnθ] *adj & pron* neuvième (*masc, fem*); **the Ninth** neuf, e.g., **John the Ninth** Jean neuf || *s* neuvième *m*; **the ninth** (*in dates*) le neuf

nip [nɪp] *s* pincement *m*, petite morsure *f*; (*of cold weather*) morsure; (*of liquor*) goutte *f* || *v* (*pret & pp* **nipped**; *ger* **nipping**) *tr* pincer, donner une petite morsure à; **to nip in the bud** tuer dans l'œuf || *intr* (coll) biberonner, picoler

nipple [ˈnɪpəl] *s* mamelon *m*; (*of nursing bottle*) tétine *f*; (mach) raccord *m*

nip·py [ˈnɪpɪ] *adj* (*comp* **-pier**; *super* **-piest**) piquant; (*cold*) vif; (Brit) leste, rapide

nirvana [nɪrˈvɑnə] *s* le nirvâna

nit [nɪt] *s* pou *m*; (*egg*) lente *f*

niter [ˈnaɪtər] *s* nitrate *m* de potasse; nitrate de soude

nitrate [ˈnaɪtret] *s* azotate *m*, nitrate *m*; (*fertilizer*) engrais *m* nitraté *f* || *tr* nitrater

nitric [ˈnaɪtrɪk] *adj* azotique, nitrique

nitrogen [ˈnaɪtrədʒən] *s* azote *m*

nitroglycerin [ˌnaɪtrəˈglɪsərɪn] *s* nitroglycérine *f*

nitrous [ˈnaɪtrəs] *adj* azoteux

ni/trous ox/ide *s* oxyde *m* azoteux, protoxyde *m* d'azote

nit/wit/ *s* (coll) imbécile *mf*

no [no] *adj indef* aucun, nul, pas de §90B; **no admittance** entrée *f* interdite; **no answer** pas de réponse; **no comment!** rien à dire!; **no go** or **no soap** (coll) pas mèche *f*; **no kidding** (coll) blague *f* à part; **no littering** défense *f* de déposer des ordures; **no loitering** vagabondage *m* interdit; **no parking** stationnement *m* interdit; **no place** nulle part; **no place else** nulle part ailleurs; **no shooting** chasse *f* réservée; **no smoking** défense de fumer; **no thoroughfare** circulation *f* interdite, passage *m* interdit; **no use** inutile; **with no** sans || *s* non *m* || *adv* non; **no good** vil; **no longer** ne . . . plus §90, e.g., **he no longer works here** il ne travaille plus ici; **no more** ne . . . plus §90, e.g., **he has no more** il n'en a plus; **no more . . .** (or *comp* in **-er**) **than** ne . . . pas plus . . . que, e.g., **she is no happier than he** elle n'est pas plus heureuse que lui

No/ah's Ark/ [ˈno·əz] *s* l'arche *f* de Noé

nobili·ty [noˈbɪlɪtɪ] *s* (*pl* **-ties**) noblesse *f*

noble [ˈnobəl] *adj & s* noble *mf*

no/ble·man *s* (*pl* **-men**) noble *m*

nobleness [ˈnobəlnɪs] *s* noblesse *f*

nobod·y [ˈnoˌbɑdi], [ˈnobədi] *s* (*pl* **-ies**) nullité *f* || *pron indef* personne; ne . . . personne §90, e.g., **I see nobody there** je n'y vois personne; personne ne, nul ne §90, e.g., **nobody knows** it personne ne le sait, nul ne le sait

nocturnal [nɑkˈtʌrnəl] *adj* nocturne

nocturne [ˈnɑktʌrn] *s* nocturne *m*

nod [nɑd] *s* signe *m* de tête; (*greeting*) inclination *f* de tête || *v* (*pret & pp* **nodded**; *ger* **nodding**) *tr* (*the head*) incliner; **to nod assent** faire un signe d'assentiment || *intr* (*with sleep*) dodeliner de la tête; (*to greet*) incliner la tête

node [nod] *s* nœud *m*

noise [nɔɪz] *s* bruit *m* || *tr* (*a rumor*) ébruiter

noiseless [ˈnɔɪzlɪs] *adj* silencieux

nois·y [ˈnɔɪzi] *adj* (*comp* **-ier**; *super* **-iest**) bruyant

nomad [ˈnomæd] *adj & s* nomade *mf*

no/ man's/ land/ *s* région *f* désolée; (mil) zone *f* neutre

nominal [ˈnɑmɪnəl] *adj* nominal

nominate [ˈnɑmɪˌnet] *tr* désigner; (*to appoint*) nommer

nomination [ˌnɑmɪˈneʃən] *s* désignation *f*, investiture *f*

nominative [ˈnɑmɪnətɪv] *adj & s* nominatif *m*

nominee [ˌnɑmɪˈni] *s* désigné *m*, candidat *m*

nonbelligerent [ˌnɑnbəˈlɪdʒərənt] *adj & s* non-belligérant *m*

nonbreakable [nɑnˈbrekəbəl] *adj* incassable

nonchalant [ˈnɑnʃələnt], (ˌnɑnʃəˈlɑnt) adj nonchalant

noncom [ˈnɑnˌkɑm] s (coll) sous-off m

noncombatant [nɑnˈkɑmbətənt] adj & s non-combattant m

noncommissioned [ˌnɑnkəˈmɪʃənd] adj non breveté

non-commis'sioned of'ficer s sous-officier m

noncommittal [ˌnɑnkəˈmɪtəl] adj évasif, réticent

nonconductor [ˌnɑnkənˈdʌktər] s non-conducteur m, mauvais conducteur m

nonconformist [ˌnɑnkənˈfɔrmɪst] adj & s non-conformiste mf

nondenominational [ˌnɑndɪˌnɑmɪˈneʃənəl] adj indépendant, qui ne fait partie d'aucune secte religieuse; (school) laïque

nondescript [ˈnɑndɪˌskrɪpt] adj indéfinissable, inclassable

none [nʌn] pron indef aucun §90B; (nobody) personne, nul §90B; ne . . aucun, ne . . nul §90; n'en . . pas, e.g., **I have none** je n'en ai pas; (as a response on the blank of an official form) néant ‖ adv—to be none the wiser ne pas en être plus sage

nonenti-ty [nɑnˈentɪti] s (pl -ties) nullité f

none'such' s nonpareil m; (apple) nonpareille f; (bot) lupuline f, minette f

nonfiction [nɑnˈfɪkʃən] s littérature f autre que le roman

nonfulfillment [ˌnɑnfʊlˈfɪlmənt] s inaccomplissement m

nonintervention [ˌnɑnɪntərˈvenʃən] s non-intervention f

nonmetal [ˈnɑnˌmetəl] s métalloïde m

nonpartisan [nɑnˈpɑrtɪzən] adj neutre, indépendant

nonpayment [nɑnˈpemənt] s non-paiement m

non-plus [ˈnɑnplʌs], [nɑnˈplʌs] s perplexité f ‖ v (pret & pp -plused or -plussed; ger -plusing or -plussing) tr déconcerter, dérouter

nonresident [nɑnˈrezɪdənt] adj & s non-résident m

nonresidential [nɑnˌrezɪˈdenʃəl] adj commercial

nonreturnable [ˌnɑnrɪˈtʌrnəbəl] adj (bottle) perdu

nonscientific [nɑnˌsaɪ-ənˈtɪfɪk] adj anti-scientifique

nonsectarian [ˌnɑnsəkˈterɪ-ən] adj non-sectaire; qui ne fait partie d'aucune secte religieuse; (education) laïque

nonsense [ˈnɑnsens] s bêtise f, nonsens m

nonskid [ˈnɑnˈskɪd] adj antidérapant

nonstop [ˈnɑnˈstɑp] adj & adv sans arrêt; sans escale

nonviolence [nɑnˈvaɪ-ələns] s non-violence f

noodle [ˈnudəl] s nouille f; (fool) (slang) niais m; (head) (slang) tronche f

nook [nʊk] s coin m, recoin m

noon [nun] s midi m

no' one' or **no'-one'** pron indef personne §90B; ne . . personne §90, e.g., **I see no one there** je n'y vois personne; personne ne, nul ne §90B, e.g., **no one knows it** personne ne le sait, nul ne le sait; **no one else** personne d'autre

noon'time' s midi m

noose [nus] s nœud m coulant; (for hanging) corde f, hart f

nor [nɔr] conj ni

norm [nɔrm] s norme f

normal [ˈnɔrməl] adj normal

Norman [ˈnɔrmən] adj normand ‖ s (dialect) normand m; (person) Normand m

Normandy [ˈnɔrməndi] s Normandie f; la Normandie

Norse [nɔrs] adj & s norrois m

Norse'man s (pl -men) Norrois m

north [nɔrθ] adj & s nord m ‖ adv au nord, vers le nord

North' Af'rican adj nord-africain ‖ s Nord-Africain m

north'east' adj & s nord-est m

north'east'er s vent m du nord-est

northern [ˈnɔrðərn] adj septentrional, du nord

North' Kore'a s Corée f du Nord; la Corée du Nord

North' Kore'an adj nord-coréen ‖ s (person) Nord-Coréen m

North' Pole' s pôle m Nord

northward [ˈnɔrθwərd] adv vers le nord

north'west' adj & s nord-ouest m

north' wind' s bise f

Norway [ˈnɔrwe] s Norvège f; la Norvège

Norwegian [nɔrˈwidʒən] adj norvégien ‖ s (language) norvégien m; (person) Norvégien m

nose [noz] s nez m; (of certain animals) museau m; **to blow one's nose** se moucher; **to have a nose for** avoir le flair de; **to keep one's nose to the grindstone** travailler sans relâche, buriner; **to lead by the nose** mener par le bout du nez; **to look down one's nose at** faire un nez à; **to thumb one's nose at** faire un pied de nez à; **to turn up one's nose at** faire la nique à; **under the nose of** à la barbe de ‖ tr flairer, sentir; **to nose out** flairer, dépister ‖ intr—**to nose about** fouiner; **to nose over** capoter

nose' bag' s musette f

nose'bleed' s saignement m de nez

nose' cone' s ogive f

nose' dive' s piqué m

nose'-dive' intr descendre en piqué

nose' drops' spl instillations fpl nasales

nose'gay' s bouquet m

nose' glass'es spl pince-nez m

nostalgia [nɑˈstældʒə] s nostalgie f

nostalgic [nɑˈstældʒɪk] adj nostalgique

nostril [ˈnɑstrɪl] s narine f; (of horse, cow, etc.) naseau m

nostrum [ˈnɑstrəm] s (quack and his medicine) orviétan m; panacée f

nos-y [ˈnozi] adj (comp -ier; super -iest) fureteur, indiscret

not [nɑt] *adv* ne §87, §90C; ne . . . pas §90, e.g., **he is not here** il n'est pas ici; non, non pas; **not at all** pas du tout; **not much** peu de chose; **not one** pas un; **not that** non pas que; **not yet** pas encore; **to think not** croire que non

notable [ˈnotəbəl] *adj & s* notable *m*

notarize [ˈnotəˌraɪz] *tr* authentiquer

notarized *adj* authentique

nota•ry [ˈnotəri] *s* (*pl* **-ries**) notaire *m*

notation [noˈteʃən] *s* notation *f*

notch [nɑtʃ] *s* coche *f*, entaille *f*; (*of a belt*) cran *m*; (*of a wheel*) dent *f*; (*gap in a mountain*) brèche *f* ‖ *tr* encocher, entailler

note [not] *s* note *f*; (*short letter*) billet *m*; **notes** commentaires *mpl*; (*of a speech*) feuillets *mpl*; **note to the reader** avis *m* au lecteur ‖ *tr* noter; **to note down** prendre note de

note′book′ *s* cahier *m*; (*bill book, memo pad, etc.*) carnet *m*, calepin *m*

note′book cov′er *s* protège-cahier *m*

noted [ˈnotɪd] *adj* éminent, distingué, connu

note′ pad′ *s* bloc-notes *m*

note′wor′thy *adj* notable, remarquable

nothing [ˈnʌθɪŋ] *s* rien *m* ‖ *pron indef* rien §90B; ne . . . rien §90, e.g., **I have nothing** je n'ai rien; **nothing at all** rien du tout; **nothing doing!** (*slang*) pas mèche! ‖ *adv*—**nothing less than** rien moins que

nothingness [ˈnʌθɪŋnɪs] *s* néant *m*

notice [ˈnotɪs] *s* (*warning; advertisement*) avis *m*; (*in a newspaper*) annonce *f*; (*observation*) attention *f*; (*of dismissal*) congé *m*; **at short notice** à bref délai; **to take notice of** faire attention à; **until further notice** jusqu'à nouvel ordre ‖ *tr* s'apercevoir de, remarquer

noticeable [ˈnotɪsəbəl] *adj* apparent, perceptible

notification [ˌnotɪfɪˈkeʃən] *s* notification *f*, avertissement *m*

noti•fy [ˈnotɪˌfaɪ] *v* (*pret & pp* **-fied**) *tr* aviser, avertir

notion [ˈnoʃən] *s* notion *f*; intention *f*; **notions** mercerie *f*; **to have a notion to** avoir dans l'idée, avoir envie de

notorie•ty [ˌnotəˈraɪɪti] *s* (*pl* **-ties**) renom *m* déshonorant, triste notoriété *f*

notorious [noˈtorɪ•əs] *adj* insigne, mal famé; (*person*) d'une triste notoriété

no′-trump′ *adj & s* sans-atout *m*

notwithstanding [ˌnɑtwɪðˈstændɪŋ], [ˌnɑtwɪθˈstændɪŋ] *adv* nonobstant, néanmoins ‖ *prep* malgré ‖ *conj* quoique

nought [nɔt] *s var of* **naught**

noun [naun] *s* nom *m*

nourish [ˈnʌrɪʃ] *tr* nourrir

nourishment [ˈnʌrɪʃmənt] *s* nourriture *f*, alimentation *f*

Nova Scotia [ˈnovəˈskoʃə] *s* Nouvelle-Écosse *f*; la Nouvelle-Écosse

novel [ˈnɑvəl] *adj* nouveau; original, bizarre ‖ *s* roman *m*

novelette [ˌnɑvəlˈɛt] *s* nouvelle *f*, bluette *f*

novelist [ˈnɑvəlɪst] *s* romancier *m*

novel•ty [ˈnɑvəlti] *s* (*pl* **-ties**) nouveauté *f*; **novelties** bibelots *mpl*, souvenirs *mpl*

November [noˈvɛmbər] *s* novembre *m*

novice [ˈnɑvɪs] *s* novice *mf*

novitiate [noˈvɪʃɪ•ɪt] *s* noviciat *m*

novocaine [ˈnovəˌken] *s* novocaïne *f*

now [nau] *adv* maintenant; **just now** tout à l'heure, naguère; **now and again** de temps en temps ‖ *interj* allez-y!

nowadays [ˈnau•əˌdez] *adv* de nos jours

no′way′ *or* **no′ways′** *adv* en aucune façon

no′where′ *adv* nulle part; ne . . . nulle part; **nowhere else** nulle autre part, nulle part ailleurs

noxious [ˈnɑkʃəs] *adj* nocif

nozzle [ˈnɑzəl] *s* (*of hose*) ajutage *m*; (*of fire hose*) lance *f*; (*of sprinkling can*) pomme *f*; (*of candlestick*) douille *f*; (*of pitcher; of gas burner*) bec *m*; (*of carburetor*) buse *f*; (*of vacuum cleaner*) suceur *m*; (*nose*) (*slang*) museau *m*

nth [ɛnθ] *adj* énième, nième; **for the nth time** pour la énième fois; **the nth power** la énième puissance

nuance [njuˈɑns], [ˈnju•ɑns] *s* nuance *f*

nub [nʌb] *s* protubérance *f*; (*piece*) petit morceau *m*; (*slang*) nœud *m*

nuclear [ˈn(j)uklɪ•ər] *adj* nucléaire

nu′clear pow′er plant′ *s* centrale *f* nucléaire

nu′clear test′ ban′ *s* interdiction *f* des essais nucléaires

nucleolus [n(j)uˈkli•ələs] *s* nucléole *m*

nucleon [ˈn(j)ukli•ɑn] *s* nucléon *m*

nucle•us [ˈn(j)ukli•əs] *s* (*pl* **-i** [ˌaɪ] *or* **-uses**) noyau *m*

nude [n(j)ud] *adj* nu ‖ *s* nu *m*; **in the nude** nu, sans vêtements

nudge [nʌdʒ] *s* coup *m* de coude ‖ *tr* pousser du coude

nudist [ˈn(j)udɪst] *adj & s* nudiste *mf*

nudity [ˈn(j)udɪti] *s* nudité *f*

nugget [ˈnʌgɪt] *s* pépite *f*

nuisance [ˈn(j)usəns] *s* ennui *m*; (*person*) peste *f*

null [nʌl] *adj indef* nul

null′ and void′ *adj* nul et non avenu

nulli•fy [ˈnʌlɪˌfaɪ] *v* (*pret & pp* **-fied**) *tr* annuler

numb [nʌm] *adj* engourdi; **to grow numb** s'engourdir ‖ *tr* engourdir

number [ˈnʌmbər] *s* numéro *m*, chiffre *m*; (*quantity*) nombre *m*; **wrong number** faux numéro ‖ *tr* numéroter; nombrer; (*to amount to*) s'élever à, compter; **to number among** compter parmi

numberless [ˈnʌmbərlɪs] *adj* innombrable

numbness [ˈnʌmnɪs] *s* engourdissement *m*

numeral [ˈn(j)umərəl] *adj* numéral ‖ *s* numéro *m*, chiffre *m*

numeration [ˌn(j)uməˈreʃən] s numération f
numerical [n(j)uˈmerɪkəl] adj numérique
numerous [ˈn(j)umərəs] adj nombreux
numismatic [ˌn(j)umɪzˈmætɪk] adj numismatique || **numismatics** s numismatique f
numskull [ˈnʌmˌskʌl] s (coll) sot m
nun [nʌn] s religieuse f, nonne f
nunci·o [ˈnʌnʃɪˌo] s (pl -os) nonce m
nuptial [ˈnʌpʃəl] adj nuptial || **nuptials** spl noces fpl
nurse [nʌrs] s infirmière f; (male nurse) infirmier m; (wet nurse) nourrice f; (practical nurse) garde-malade mf; (children's nurse) bonne f d'enfant, nurse f || tr soigner; (hopes; plants; a baby) nourrir
nurse′maid′ s bonne f d'enfant
nurser·y [ˈnʌrsəri] s (pl -ies) chambre f des enfants; (for day care) crèche f, pouponnière f; (hort) pépinière f
nurs′ery·man s (pl -men) pépiniériste m
nurs′ery school′ s maternelle f
nursing [ˈnʌrsɪŋ] s soins mpl; (profession) métier m d'infirmière; (by mother) nourriture f
nurs′ing bot′tle s biberon m
nurs′ing home′ s maison f de repos, maison f de santé
nursling [ˈnʌrslɪŋ] s nourrisson m

nurture [ˈnʌrtʃər] s éducation f; nourriture f || tr élever; (to nurse) nourrir
nut [nʌt] s noix f, e.g., **Brazil nut** noix du Brésil; (of walnut tree) noix; (of filbert) noisette f; (to screw on a bolt) écrou m; (slang) extravagant m; **to be nuts about** (slang) être follement épris de
nut′crack′er s casse-noisettes m, casse-noix m; (orn) casse-noix
nut′hatch′ s sittelle f
nut′meat′ s graine f de fruit sec, graine de noix
nutmeg [ˈnʌtˌmeg] s (seed or spice) noix f muscade, muscade f; (tree) muscadier m
nutriment [ˈn(j)utrɪmənt] s nourriture f
nutrition [n(j)uˈtrɪʃən] s nutrition f
nutritious [n(j)uˈtrɪʃəs] adj nutritif
nut′shell′ s coquille f de noix; **in a nutshell** en un mot
nut·ty [ˈnʌti] adj (comp -tier; super -tiest) à goût de noisette, à goût de noix; (slang) cinglé
nuzzle [ˈnʌzəl] tr fouiller du groin || intr fouiller du groin; s'envelopper chaudement; **to nuzzle up to** se pelotonner contre
nylon [ˈnaɪlɑn] s nylon m; **nylons** bas mpl de nylon, bas nylon
nymph [nɪmf] s nymphe f

O

O, o [o] s XVᵉ lettre de l'alphabet
oaf [of] s lourdaud m, rustre m
oak [ok] s chêne m
oaken [ˈokən] adj de chêne, en chêne
oakum [ˈokəm] s étoupe f
oar [or], [ɔr] s rame f, aviron m
oar′lock′ s tolet m
oars′man s (pl -men) rameur m
oa·sis [oˈesɪs] s (pl -ses [siz]) oasis f
oat [ot] s avoine f; **oats** (edible grain) avoine; **to feel one's oats** être imbu de sa personne; **to sow one's wild oats** (coll) jeter sa gourme
oath [oθ] s (pl oaths [oðz]) serment m; (swearword) juron m; **to administer an oath** to (law) faire prêter serment à; **to take an oath** prêter serment
oat′meal′ s farine f d'avoine; (breakfast food) flocons mpl d'avoine
obbligato [ˌɑblɪˈgɑto] s accompagnement m à volonté
obdurate [ˈɑbdjərɪt] adj obstiné, endurci
obedience [oˈbidɪ·əns] s obéissance f
obedient [oˈbidɪ·ənt] adj obéissant
obeisance [oˈbesəns], [oˈbisəns] s hommage m; (greeting) révérence f
obelisk [ˈɑbəlɪsk] s obélisque m
obese [oˈbis] adj obèse
obesity [oˈbisɪti] s obésité f

obey [əˈbe] tr obéir (with dat); **to be obeyed** être obéi || intr obéir
obfuscate [ɑbˈfʌsket], [ˈɑbfəsˌket] tr offusquer
obituar·y [oˈbɪtʃu·ˌeri] adj nécrologique || s (pl -ies) nécrologie f
object [ˈɑbdʒɪkt] s objet m || [əbˈdʒekt] tr objecter, rétorquer || intr faire des objections; **to object to** s'opposer à, avoir des objections contre
objection [əbˈdʒekʃən] s objection f
objectionable [əbˈdʒekʃənəbəl] adj répréhensible; répugnant, désagréable
objective [əbˈdʒektɪv] adj & s objectif m
obligate [ˈɑblɪˌget] tr obliger
obligation [ˌɑblɪˈgeʃən] s obligation f
obligatory [ˈɑblɪgəˌtori], [əˈblɪgəˌtori] adj obligatoire
oblige [əˈblaɪdʒ] tr obliger; **much obliged** bien obligé, très reconnaissant; **to be obliged to** être obligé de
obliging [əˈblaɪdʒɪŋ] adj accommodant, obligeant
oblique [əˈblik], [əˈblaɪk] adj oblique
obliterate [əˈblɪtəˌret] tr effacer, oblitérer
oblivion [əˈblɪvɪ·ən] s oubli m
oblivious [əˈblɪvɪ·əs] adj oublieux
oblong [ˈɑblɔŋ], [ˈɑblɑŋ] adj oblong

obnoxious [əb'nakʃəs] *adj* odieux, désagréable

oboe ['obo] *s* hautbois *m*

oboist ['obo·ıst] *s* hautboïste *mf*

obscene [ab'sin] *adj* obscène

obsceni·ty [ab'seniti], [ab'siniti] *s* (*pl* -ties) obscénité *f*

obscure [əb'skjur] *adj* obscur; (*vowel*) relâché, neutre

obscuri·ty [əb'skjuriti] *s* (*pl* -ties) obscurité *f*

obsequies ['absikwiz] *spl* obsèques *fpl*

obsequious [əb'sikwı·əs] *adj* obséquieux

observance [əb'zʌrvəns] *s* observance *f*

observant [əb'zʌrvənt] *adj* observateur

observation [,abzər'veʃən] *s* observation *f*

observato·ry [əb'zʌrvə,tori] *s* (*pl* -ries) observatoire *m*

observe [əb'zʌrv] *tr* observer; (*silence*) garder; (*a holiday*) célébrer; dire, remarquer

observer [əb'zʌrvər] *s* observateur *m*

obsess [ab'ses] *tr* obséder

obsession [ab'seʃən] *s* obsession *f*

obsolescent [,absə'lesənt] *adj* vieillissant

obsolete ['absəlit] *adj* désuet, vieilli, (*gram*) obsolète

obstacle ['abstəkəl] *s* obstacle *m*

ob'stacle course' *s* champ *m* d'obstacles, piste *f* d'obstacles

obstetrical [ab'stetrikəl] *adj* obstétrique

obstetrics [ab'stetriks] *spl* obstétrique *f*

obstina·cy ['abstinəsi] *s* (*pl* -cies) obstination *f*, entêtement *m*

obstinate ['abstinit] *adj* obstiné

obstreperous [əb'strepərəs] *adj* turbulent

obstruct [əb'strʌkt] *tr* obstruer; (*movements*) empêcher, entraver

obstruction [əb'strʌkʃən] *s* obstruction *f*; (*on railroad tracks*) obstacle *m*; (*to movement*) empêchement *m*, entrave *f*

obtain [əb'ten] *tr* obtenir, se procurer || *intr* prévaloir

obtrusive [əb'trusıv] *adj* importun, intrus

obtuse [əb't(j)us] *adj* obtus

obviate ['abvı,et] *tr* obvier (with *dat*)

obvious ['abvı·əs] *adj* évident

occasion [ə'keʒən] *s* occasion *f*; **on occasion** en différentes occasions || *tr* occasionner

occasional [ə'keʒənəl] *adj*. fortuit, occasionnel; (*verses*) de circonstance; (*showers*) épars; (*chair*) volant

occasionally [ə'keʒənəli] *adv* de temps en temps, occasionnellement

occident ['aksidənt] *s* occident *m*

occidental [,aksə'dentəl] *adj* & *s* occidental *m*

occlusion [ə'kluʒən] *s* occlusion *f*

occlusive [ə'klusıv] *adj* occlusif || *s* occlusive *f*

occult [ə'kʌlt], ['akʌlt] *adj* occulte

occupancy ['akjəpənsi] *s* occupation *f*, habitation *f*

occupant ['akjəpənt] *s* occupant *m*

occupation [,akjə'peʃən] *s* occupation *f*

occupational [,akjə'peʃənəl] *adj* professionnel; de métier

oc'cupa'tional ther'apy *s* thérapie *f* rééducative, réadaptation *f* fonctionnelle

occu·py ['akjə,paɪ] *v* (*pret & pp* -pied) *tr* occuper; **to be occupied with** s'occuper de

oc·cur [ə'kʌr] *v* (*pret & pp* -curred; *ger* -curring) *intr* arriver, avoir lieu; (*to be found; to come to mind*) se présenter; **it occurs to me that** il me vient à l'esprit que

occurrence [ə'kʌrəns] *s* événement *m*; cas *m*, exemple *m*; **everyday occurrence** fait *m* journalier

ocean ['oʃən] *s* océan *m*

oceanic [,oʃı'ænık] *adj* océanique

o'cean lin'er *s* paquebot *m* transocéanique

ocher ['okər] *s* ocre *f*

o'clock [ə'klak] *adv*—**it is one o'clock** il est une heure; **it is two o'clock** il est deux heures

octane ['akten] *s* octane *m*

oc'tane num'ber *s* indice *m* d'octane

octave ['aktıv], ['aktev] *s* octave *f*

October [ak'tobər] *s* octobre *m*

octo·pus ['aktəpəs] *s* (*pl* -puses or -pi [,paɪ]) pieuvre *f*, poulpe *m*

octoroon [,aktə'run] *s* octavon *m*

ocular ['akjələr] *adj* & *s* oculaire *m*

oculist ['akjəlıst] *s* oculiste *mf*

odd [ad] *adj* (*number*) impair; (*that doesn't match*) dépareillé, déparié; (*queer*) bizarre, étrange; (*occasional*) divers; quelque, e.g., **three hundred odd horses** quelque trois cents chevaux; et quelques || **odds** *spl* chances *fpl*; (*disparity*) inégalité *f*; (*on a horse*) cote *f*; **at odds** en désaccord, en bisbille; **by all odds** sans aucun doute; **to be at odds with** être mal avec; **to give odds to** donner de l'avance à; **to set at odds** brouiller

oddi·ty ['aditi] *s* (*pl* -ties) bizarrerie *f*

odd' jobs' *spl* bricolage *m*, petits travaux *mpl*

odd' man' out' *s*—**to be odd man out** être en trop

odds' and ends' *spl* petits bouts *mpl*, bribes *fpl*; (*trinkets*) bibelots *mpl*; (*food*) restes *mpl*

ode [od] *s* ode *f*

odious ['odı·əs] *adj* odieux

odor ['odər] *s* odeur *f*; **to be in bad odor** être mal vu

odorless ['odərlıs] *adj* inodore

Odyssey ['adisi] *s* Odyssée *f*

Oedipus ['edıpəs], ['idıpəs] *s* Œdipe *m*

of [ʌv], [ʌv], [əʌ] *prep* de; à, e.g., **to think of** penser à; e.g., **to ask s.th. of s.o.** demander q.ch. à qn; en, e.g., **a doctor of medicine** un docteur en médecine; moins, à., e.g., **a quarter of two** deux heures moins le quart; entre, e.g., **he of all people** lui entre tous; d'entre, e.g., **five of them** cinq d'entre eux; par, e.g., **of necessity** par nécessité; en or de, e.g., **made of**

wood en bois, de bois; (not translated), e.g., **the fifth of March** le cinq mars; e.g., **we often see her of a morning** nous la voyons souvent le matin

off [ɔf], [ɑf] adj mauvais, e.g., **off day** (bad day) mauvaise journée; libre, e.g., **off day** journée libre; de congé, e.g., **off day** jour de congé; (account, sum) inexact; (meat) avancé; (electric current) coupé; (light) éteint; (radio; faucet) fermé; (street) secondaire, transversal; (distant) éloigné, écarté ‖ adv loin; à . . . de distance, e.g., **three kilometers off** à trois kilomètres de distance; parti, e.g., **they're off!** les voilà partis! bas, e.g., **hats off!** chapeaux bas!; (naut) au large; (theat) à la cantonade ‖ prep de; (at a distance from) éloigné de, écarté de; (naut) au large de, à la hauteur de; **from off** de dessous de

offal ['ɑfəl], ['ɔfəl] s (of butchered meat) abats mpl; (refuse) ordures fpl

off′ and on′ adv de temps en temps, par intervalles

off′beat′ adj (slang) insolite, rare

off′ chance′ s chance f improbable

off′-col′or adj décoloré; (e.g., story) grivois, vert

offend [ə'fɛnd] tr offenser; **to be offended** s'offenser ‖ intr—**to offend against** enfreindre

offender [ə'fɛndər] s offenseur m; (criminal) délinquant m, coupable mf

offense [ə'fɛns] s offense f; (law) délit m; **to take offense (at)** s'offenser (de)

offensive [ə'fɛnsɪv] adj offensant, blessant; (mil) offensif ‖ s offensive f

offer ['ɔfər], ['ɑfər] s offre f ‖ tr offrir; (excuses; best wishes) présenter; (prayers) adresser ‖ intr—**to offer to** faire l'offre de; faire mine de, e.g., **he offered to fight** il a fait mine de se battre

offering ['ɔfərɪŋ], ['ɑfərɪŋ] s offre f; (eccl) offrande f

off′hand′ adj improvisé; brusque ‖ adv au pied levé; brusquement

office ['ɔfɪs], ['ɑfɪs] s fonction f, office m; (in business, school, government) bureau m; (national agency) office m; (of lawyer) étude f; (of doctor) cabinet m; **elective office** poste m électif; **good offices** bons offices; **to run for office** se présenter aux élections

of′fice boy′ s coursier m, commissionnaire m de bureau

of′fice-desk′ s bureau m

of′fice-hold′er s fonctionnaire mf

of′fice hours′ spl heures fpl de bureau; (of doctor, counselor, etc.) heures de consultation

officer ['ɔfɪsər], ['ɑfɪsər] s (of a company) administrateur m, dirigeant m; (of army, an order, a society, etc.) officier m; (police officer) agent m de police, officier de police; **officer of the day** (mil) officier de service

of′ficer can′didate s élève-officier m

of′fice seek′er s solliciteur m

of′fice supplies′ spl fournitures fpl de bureau, articles mpl de bureau

of′fice work′ s travail m de bureau

official [ə'fɪʃəl] adj officiel; (e.g., stationery) réglementaire ‖ s fonctionnaire mf, officiel m; **officials** cadres mpl; (executives) dirigeants mpl

offi′cial board′ s comité m directeur

officialese [ə,fɪʃə'liz] s jargon m administratif

officiate [ə'fɪʃɪ,et] intr (eccl) officier; **to officiate as** exercer les fonctions de

officious [ə'fɪʃəs] adj trop empressé; **to be officious** faire l'officieux

offing ['ɔfɪŋ], ['ɑfɪŋ] s—**in the offing** au large; (fig) en perspective

off′-lim′its adj défendu; (public sign) défense d'entrer, entrée interdite; (mil) interdit aux troupes

off′-peak heat′er s thermosiphon m à accumulation

off′print′ s tiré m à part

off′-seas′on s morte-saison f

off′set′ s compensation f; (typ) offset m ‖ **off′set′** v (pret & pp -set; ger -setting) tr compenser

off′shoot′ s rejeton m

off′shore′ adj éloigné de la côte, du côté de la terre; (wind) de terre ‖ adv au large, vers la haute mer

off′side′ adv (sports) hors jeu

off′spring′ s descendance f; (descendant) rejeton m, enfant mf; (result) conséquence f

off′stage′ adj dans les coulisses ‖ adv à la cantonade

off′-the-cuff′ adj (coll) impromptu

off′-the-rec′ord adj confidentiel

often ['ɔfən], ['ɑfən] adv souvent; **how often?** combien de fois?; tous les combien?; **not often** rarement; **once too often** une fois de trop

ogive ['odʒaɪv], [o'dʒaɪv] s ogive f

ogle ['ogəl] tr lancer une œillade à; (to stare at) dévisager

ogre ['ogər] s ogre m

ohm [om] s ohm m

oil [ɔɪl] s huile f; (painting) huile, peinture f à l'huile; **holy oil** huile sainte, saintes huiles; **to pour oil on troubled waters** calmer la tempête, verser de l'huile sur les plaies de qn; **to smell of midnight oil** sentir l'huile; **to strike oil** atteindre une nappe pétrolifère; (fig) trouver le filon ‖ tr huiler; (to bribe) graisser la patte à ‖ intr (naut) faire le plein de mazout

oil′ burn′er s réchaud m à pétrole

oil′ can′ s bidon m d'huile, burette f d'huile

oil′cloth′ s toile f cirée

oil′ com′pany s société f pétrolière

oil′cup′ s (mach) godet m graisseur

oil′ drum′ s bidon m d'huile

oil′ field′ s gisement m pétrolifère

oil′ gauge′ s jauge f de niveau d'huile

oil′ lamp′ s lampe f à huile, lampe à pétrole

oil′man′ s (pl -men′) (retailer) huilier m; (operator) pétrolier m

oil′ pump′ s pompe f à huile

oil′ stove′ s poêle m à mazout, fourneau m à pétrole

oil′ tank′er s pétrolier m, tanker m

oil′ well′ s puits m à pétrole

oil·y [′ɔɪli] adj (comp -ier; super -iest) huileux, oléagineux; (fig) onctueux

ointment [′ɔɪntmənt] s onguent m, pommade f

O.K. [′o′ke] (letterword) adj (coll) très bien, parfait ‖ s (coll) approbation f ‖ adv (coll) très bien ‖ v (pret & pp O.K.'d; ger O.K.'ing) tr (coll) approuver ‖ interj O.K.!, ça colle!

okra [′okrə] s gombo m, ketmie f comestible

old [old] adj vieux; (of former times) ancien; (wine) vieux; **any old** n'importe, e.g., **any old time** n'importe quand; quelconque, e.g., **any old book** un livre quelconque; **at . . . years old** à l'âge de . . . ans; **how old is . . . ?** quel âge a . . . ?; **of old** d'autrefois, de jadis; **to be . . . years old** avoir . . . ans

old′ age′ s vieillesse f, âge m avancé

old′-clothes′man′ s (pl -men′) fripier m

old′ coun′try s mère patrie f

Old′ Cov′enant s (Bib) ancienne alliance f

old′-fash′ioned adj démodé, suranné; (literary style) vieillot

old′ fo′gey or **old′ fo′gy** [′fogi] s (pl -gies) vieux bonhomme m, grime m

Old′ French′ s ancien français m

Old′ Glo′ry s le drapeau des États-Unis

old′ hag′ s vieille fée f

old′ hand′ s vieux routier m

old′ lad′y s vieille dame f; (coll) grand-mère f

old′ maid′ s vieille fille f

old′ mas′ter s grand maître m; œuvre f d'un grand maître

old′ moon′ s Lune f à son décours

old′ peo′ple's home′ s hospice m de vieillards

old′ salt′ s loup m de mer

old′ school′ s vieille école f, vieille roche f

oldster [′oldstər] s vieillard m, vieux m

Old′ Tes′tament s Ancien Testament m

old′-time′ adj du temps jadis, d'autrefois

old′-tim′er s (coll) vieux m de la vieille, vieux routier m

old′ wives′ tale′ s conte m de bonne femme

Old Wom′an who lived′ in a shoe′ s mère f Gigogne

Old′ World′ s vieux monde m

old′-world′ adj de l'ancien monde; du vieux monde

oleander [′oli′ændər] s laurier-rose m

olfactory [ɑl′fæktəri] adj olfactif

oligar·chy [′ɑlɪ‚gɑrki] s (pl -chies) oligarchie f

olive [′ɑlɪv] adj olive; (complexion) olivâtre ‖ s olive f; (tree) olivier m

ol′ive branch′ s rameau m d'olivier

ol′ive grove′ s olivaie f

ol′ive oil′ s huile f d'olive

Oliver [′ɑlɪvər] s Olivier m

ol′ive tree′ s olivier m

olympiad [o′lɪmpɪˌæd] s olympiade f

Olympian [o′lɪmpɪˌən] adj olympien

Olympic [o′lɪmpɪk] adj olympique ‖ **Olympics** spl jeux mpl olympiques

omelet [′ɑmə‚let], [′ɑmlɪt] s omelette f

omen [′omən] s augure m, présage m

ominous [′ɑmɪnəs] adj de mauvais augure

omission [o′mɪʃən] s omission f

omit [o′mɪt] v (pret & pp omitted; ger omitting) tr omettre

omnibus [′ɑmnɪ‚bʌs], [′ɑmnɪbəs] adj & s omnibus m

omnipotent [ɑm′nɪpətənt] adj omnipotent

omniscient [ɑm′nɪʃənt] adj omniscient

omnivorous [ɑm′nɪvərəs] adj omnivore

on [ɑn], [ɔn] adj (light, radio) allumé; (faucet) ouvert; (machine, motor) en marche; (electrical appliance) branché; (brake) serré; (steak, chops, etc.) dans la poêle; (game, program, etc.) commencé ‖ adv—**and so on et** ainsi de suite; **come on!** (coll) allons donc!; **farther on** plus loin; **from this day on** à dater de ce jour; **later on** plus tard; **move on!** circulez!; **to be on** (theat) être en scène; **to be on to s.o.** (coll) voir clair dans le jeu de qn; **to have on** être vêtu de, porter; **to . . . on** continuer à + inf, e.g., **to sing on** continuer à chanter; **well on** avancé, e.g., **well on in years** d'un âge avancé ‖ prep sur; (at the time of) lors de; à, e.g., **on foot** à pied; e.g., **on my arrival** à mon arrivée; e.g., **on page three** à la page trois; e.g., **on the first floor** au rez-de-chaussée; e.g., **on the right** à droite; en, e.g., **on a journey** en voyage; e.g., **on arriving** en arrivant; e.g., **on fire** en feu; e.g., **on sale** en vente; e.g., **on the** or **an average** en moyenne; e.g., **on the top of** en dessus de; dans, e.g., **on a farm** dans une ferme; e.g., **on the jury** dans le jury; e.g., **on the street** dans la rue; e.g., **on the train** dans le train; par, e.g., **he came on the train** il est venu par le train; e.g., **on a fine day** par un beau jour; de, e.g., **on good authority** de source certaine, de bonne part; e.g., **on the north** du côté du nord; e.g., **on the one hand . . . on the other hand** d'une part . . . d'autre part; e.g., **on this side of** de ce côté-ci; e.g., **to have pity on** avoir pitié de; e.g., **to live on bread and water** vivre de pain et d'eau; sous, e.g., **on a charge of** sous l'inculpation de; e.g., **on pain of death** sous peine de mort; (not translated), e.g., **on Tuesday** mardi; e.g., **on Tuesdays** le mardi, tous les mardis; e.g., **on July fourteenth** le quatorze juillet; contre, e.g., **an attack on** une attaque contre; **it's on me** (*it's my turn to pay*) (coll) c'est ma tournée; **it's on the house** (coll) c'est la tournée du patron; **on examination** après examen; **on it** y, e.g., **there is the shelf; put the book on it** voilà l'étagère; mettez-y le livre; **on or about** (*a certain date*) aux environs de; **on or after** (*a certain date*) à partir de; **on tap** en perce, à la pression; **on the spot** (*immediately*) sur-le-champ; (*there*) sur place; (slang) en danger imminent; **to be on the committee** faire partie du comité; **to march on a city** marcher sur une ville

on' **and on'** *adv* continuellement, sans fin

once [wʌns] *s*—**this once** pour cette fois-ci ‖ *adv* une fois; (*formerly*) autrefois; **all at once** (*all together*) tous à la fois; (*suddenly*) tout à coup; **at once** tout de suite, sur-le-champ; (*at the same time*) à la fois, en même temps; **for once** pour une fois; **once and for all** une bonne fois, une fois pour toutes; **once in a while** de temps en temps; **once more** encore une fois; **once or twice** une ou deux fois; **once upon a time there was** il était une fois ‖ *conj* une fois que, dès que

once'-o'ver *s* (slang) examen *m* rapide; travail *m* hâtif; **to give the once-over to** (slang) jeter un coup d'œil à

one [wʌn] *adj* & *pron* un; un certain, e.g., **one Dupont** un certain Dupont; un seul, e.g., **with one voice** d'une seule voix; unique, e.g., **one price** prix unique; (not translated when preceded by an adjective), e.g., **the red pencil and the blue one** le crayon rouge et le bleu; **not one** pas un; **one and all** tous; **one and only** unique, e.g., **the one and only closet in the house** l'armoire unique de la maison; seul et unique, e.g., **my one and only umbrella** mon seul et unique parapluie; **one another** l'un l'autre; les uns les autres; **one by one** un à un; **that one** celui-là; **the one that** celui que, celui qui; **this one** celui-ci; **to become one** s'unir, se marier ‖ *s* un *m*; **one o'clock** une heure ‖ *pron indef* on §87, e.g., **one cannot go there alone** on ne peut pas y aller seul; **one's** son, e.g., **one's son** son fils

one'-horse' *adj* à un cheval, (coll) provincial, insignifiant

one'-horse town' *s* (coll) trou *m*

onerous ['ɑnərəs] *adj* onéreux

one·self' *pron* soi §85; soi-même §86; se §87, e.g., **to cut oneself** se couper; **to be oneself** se conduire sans affectation

one'-sid'ed *adj* à un côté, à une face; (*e.g., decision*) unilatéral; (*unfair*) partial, injuste

one'-track' *adj* à une voie; (coll) routinier

one'-way' *adj* à sens unique

one'-way tick'et *s* billet *m* d'aller, billet simple

onion ['ʌnjən] *s* oignon *m*; **to know one's onions** (coll) connaître son affaire

on'ion·skin' *s* papier *m* pelure

on'look'er *s* assistant *m*, spectateur *m*

only ['onli] *adj* seul, unique; (*child*) unique ‖ *adv* seulement; ne . . . que, e.g., **I have only two** je n'en ai que deux; réservé, e.g., **staff only** (public sign) réservé au personnel ‖ *conj* mais, si ce n'était que

on'rush' *s* ruée *f*

on'set' *s* attaque *f*; **at the onset** de prime abord, au premier abord

onslaught ['ɑn‚slɔt], ['ɔn‚slɔt] *s* assaut *m*

on'-the-job' *adj* (*training*) en stage; (coll) alerte

onus ['onəs] *s* charge *f*, fardeau *m*

onward ['ɑnwərd] *or* **onwards** ['ɑnwərdz] *adv* en avant

onyx ['ɑnɪks] *s* onyx *m*

ooze [uz] *s* suintement *m*; (*mud*) vase *f*, limon *m* ‖ *tr* filtrer ‖ *intr* suinter, filtrer; **to ooze out** s'écouler

opal ['opəl] *s* opale *f*

opaque [o'pek] *adj* opaque; (*style*) obscur

open ['opən] *adj* ouvert; (*personality*) franc, sincère; (*job, position*) vacant; (*hour*) libre; (*automobile*) découvert; (*market; trial*) public; (*question*) pendant, indécis; (*wound*) béant; (*to attack, to criticism, etc.*) exposé; (sports) international; **to break or crack open** éventrer; **to throw open the door** ouvrir la porte toute grande ‖ *s* ouverture *f*; (*in the woods*) clairière *f*; **in the open** au grand air, à ciel ouvert; (*in the open country*) en rase campagne; (*in the open sea*) en pleine mer; (*without being hidden*) découvert; (*openly*) ouvertement ‖ *tr* ouvrir; (*a canal lock*) lâcher; **to open fire** déclencher le feu ‖ *intr* ouvrir, s'ouvrir; (*said, e.g., of a play*) commencer, débuter; **to open into** aboutir à, déboucher sur; **to open on** donner sur; **to open up** s'épanouir, s'ouvrir

o'pen-air' *adj* en plein air, au grand air

o'pen-eyed' *adj* les yeux écarquillés

o'pen-hand'ed *adj* libéral, la main ouverte

o'pen-heart'ed *adj* ouvert, franc

o'pen-heart' sur'gery *s* chirurgie *f* à cœur ouvert

o'pen house' *s* journée *f* d'accueil; **to keep open house** tenir table ouverte

opening ['opənɪŋ] *s* ouverture *f*; (*in the woods*) clairière *f*; (*vacancy*) vacance *f*, poste *m* vacant; (*chance to say something*) occasion *f* favorable

o'pening night' *s* première *f*

o'pening num'ber *s* ouverture *f*

o'pening price' *s* cours *m* de début

o'pen-mind'ed *adj* à l'esprit ouvert, sans parti pris

o'pen se'cret *s* secret *m* de Polichinelle

o'pen shop' *s* atelier *m* ouvert aux non-syndiqués

o/pen•work/ s ouvrage m à jour, ajours mpl

opera ['apərə] s opéra m

op/era glass/es spl jumelles fpl de spectacle

op/era hat/ s claque m, gibus m

op/era house/ s opéra m

operate ['apə‚ret] tr actionner, faire marcher; exploiter ‖ intr fonctionner; s'opérer; (surg) opérer; to operate on (surg) opérer

operatic [‚apə'rætɪk] adj d'opéra

opera/ting expen/ses spl (overhead) frais mpl généraux, frais d'exploitation

op/erating room/ s salle f d'opération

op/erating ta/ble s table f d'opération, billard m

operation [‚apə're/ən] s opération f; (of a business, of a machine, etc.) fonctionnement m; (med) intervention f chirurgicale, opération

operative ['apə‚retɪv], ['apə‚rɪtɪv] adj opératif; (surg) opératoire ‖ s (workman) ouvrier m; (spy) agent m, espion m

operator ['apə‚retər] s opérateur m; (e.g., of a machine) propriétaire m exploitant; (of an automobile) conducteur m; téléphoniste mf, standardiste mf; (slang) chevalier m d'industrie, aigrefin m

operetta [‚apə'retə] s opérette f

opiate ['opɪ‚ɪt], ['opɪ‚et] adj opiacé ‖ s médicament m opiacé; (coll) narcotique m

opinion [ə'pɪnjən] s opinion f; in my opinion à mon avis

opinionated [ə'pɪnjə‚netɪd] adj fier de ses opinions, dogmatique

opium ['opɪ‚əm] s opium m

o/pium den/ s fumerie f

o/pium pop/py s œillette f

opossum [ə'pasəm] s opossum m, sarigue f

opponent [ə'ponənt] s adversaire mf, opposant m

opportune [‚apər't(j)un] adj opportun, convenable

opportunist [‚apər't(j)unɪst] s opportuniste mf

opportuni•ty [‚apər't(j)unɪti] s (pl -ties) occasion f; chance f

oppose [ə'poz] tr s'opposer à

opposite ['apəsɪt] adj opposé, contraire; d'en face, e.g., the house opposite la maison d'en face ‖ s opposé m, contraire m ‖ adv en face, vis-à-vis ‖ prep en face de, à l'opposite de

op/posite num/ber s (fig) homologue mf

opposition [‚apə'zɪ/ən] s opposition f

oppress [ə'pres] tr opprimer; (to weigh heavily upon) oppresser

oppression [ə'pre/ən] s oppression f

oppressive [ə'presɪv] adj oppressif; (stifling) étouffant, accablant

oppressor [ə'presər] s oppresseur m

opprobrious [ə'probrɪ•əs] adj infamant, injurieux, honteux

opprobrium [ə'probrɪ•əm] s opprobre m

optic ['aptɪk] adj optique ‖ optics s optique f

optical ['aptɪkəl] adj optique

op/tical illu/sion s illusion f d'optique

optician [ap'tɪ/ən] s opticien m

optimism ['aptɪ‚mɪzəm] s optimisme m

optimist ['aptɪmɪst] s optimiste mf

optimistic [‚aptɪ'mɪstɪk] adj optimiste

option ['ap/ən] s option f

optional ['ap/ənəl] adj facultatif

optometrist [ap'tamɪtrɪst] s opticien m; optométriste mf (Canad)

opulent ['apjələnt] adj opulent

or [ɔr] conj ou

oracle ['arəkəl], ['ɔrəkəl] s oracle m

oracular [o'rækjələr] adj d'oracle; dogmatique, sentencieux; (ambiguous) équivoque

oral ['orəl] adj oral

orange ['arɪndʒ], ['ɔrɪndʒ] adj orangé, orange ‖ s (color) orangé m, orange m; (fruit) orange f

orangeade [‚arɪndʒ'ed], [‚ɔrɪndʒ'ed] s orangeade f

or/ange blos/som s fleur f d'oranger

or/ange grove/ s orangeraie f

or/ange juice/ s jus m d'orange

or/ange squeez/er s presse-fruits m

or/ange tree/ s oranger m

orang-outang [o'ræŋu‚tæŋ] s orang-outan m

oration [o're/ən] s discours m

orator ['arətər], ['ɔrətər] s orateur m

oratorical [‚arə'tarɪkəl], [‚ɔrə'tɔrɪkəl] adj oratoire

oratori•o [‚arə'torɪ‚o], [‚ɔrə'tɔrɪ‚o] s (pl -os) oratorio m

orato•ry ['arə‚tori], ['ɔrə‚tori] s (pl -ries) art m oratoire; (eccl) oratoire m

orb [ɔrb] s orbe m

orbit ['ɔrbɪt] s orbite f; in orbit sur orbite ‖ tr (e.g., the sun) tourner autour de; (e.g., a rocket) mettre en orbite, satelliser ‖ intr se mettre en orbite

orchard ['ɔrt/ərd] s verger m

orchestra ['ɔrkɪstrə] s orchestre m

orchestrate ['ɔrkɪ‚stret] tr orchestrer

orchid ['ɔrkɪd] s orchidée f

ordain [or'den] tr destiner; (eccl) ordonner; to be ordained (eccl) recevoir les ordres

ordeal [or'dil], [or'di•əl] s épreuve f; (hist) ordalie f

order ['ɔrdər] s ordre m; (of words) ordonnance f; (for merchandise, a meal, etc.) commande f; (military formation) ordre; (law) arrêt m, arrêté m; in order en ordre; in order of appearance (theat) dans l'ordre d'entrée en scène; in order that pour que, afin que; in order to + inf pour + inf, afin de + inf; on order en commande, commandé; order! à l'ordre!; orders (eccl) les ordres; (mil) la consigne; pay to the order of (com) payez à l'ordre de; to get s.th. out of order détraquer q.ch.; to put in order mettre en règle ‖ tr ordonner; (com) commander; to order around

faire aller et venir; **to order s.o. to** +
inf ordonner à qn de + *inf*

or′der blank′ *s* bon *m* de commande,
bulletin *m* de commande

order·ly [′ɔrdərli] *adj* ordonné; (*life*)
réglé; **to be orderly** avoir de l'ordre ‖
s (*pl* **-lies**) (med) ambulancier *m*, infirmier *m*; (mil) planton *m*

ordinal [′ɔrdɪnəl] *adj & s* ordinal *m*

ordinance [′ɔrdɪnəns] *s* ordonnance *f*

ordinary [′ɔrdɪn‚eri] *adj* ordinaire; **out
of the ordinary** exceptionnel

ordination [‚ɔrdɪn′eʃən] *s* ordination *f*

ordnance [′ɔrdnəns] *s* artillerie *f*;
(*branch of an army*) service *m* du
matériel

ore [or] *s* minéral *m*

oregano [ə′regə‚no] *s* origan *m*

organ [′ɔrgən] *s* (anat, journ) organe
m; (mus) orgue *m*

organdy [′ɔrgəndi] *s* organdi *m*

or′gan grind′er *s* joueur *m* d'orgue

organic [ɔr′gænɪk] *adj* organique

organism [′ɔrgə‚nɪzəm] *s* organisme *m*

organist [′ɔrgənɪst] *s* organiste *m*

organization [‚ɔrgənɪ′zeʃən] *s* organisation *f*

organize [′ɔrgə‚naɪz] *tr* organiser

organizer [′ɔrgə‚naɪzər] *s* organisateur
m

or′gan loft′ *s* tribune *f* d'orgue

orgasm [′ɔrgæzəm] *s* orgasme *m*

or·gy [′ɔrdʒi] *s* (*pl* **-gies**) orgie *f*

orient [′ɔri‚ɛnt] *s* orient *m*; **Orient**
Orient ‖ [′ɔri‚ɛnt] *tr* orienter

oriental [‚ɔri′ɛntəl] *adj* oriental ‖
(*cap*) *s* Oriental *m*

orientate [′ɔri‚ɛn‚tet] *tr* orienter

orientation [‚ɔri‚ɛn′teʃən] *s* orientation *f*

orifice [′ɑrɪfɪs], [′ɔrɪfɪs] *s* orifice *m*

origin [′ɑrədʒɪn], [′ɔrədʒɪn] *s* origine *f*

original [ə′rɪdʒɪnəl] *adj* (*new, not
copied; inventive*) original; (*earliest*)
originel, primitif; (*first*) originaire,
premier ‖ *s* original *m*

originality [ə‚rɪdʒɪ′næləti] *s* originalité *f*

originate [ə′rɪdʒə‚net] *tr* faire naître,
créer ‖ *intr* prendre naissance; **to
originate from** provenir de

oriole [′ɔri‚ol], [′ɔri‚ol] *s* loriot *m*

ormolu [′ɔrmə‚lu] *s* bronze *m* doré;
(*powdered gold for gilding*) or *m*
moulu; (*alloy of zinc and copper*)
similor *m*

ornament [′ɔrnəmənt] *s* ornement *m* ‖
[′ɔrnə‚ment] *tr* ornementer, orner

ornamental [‚ɔrnə′mentəl] *adj* orne-
mental

ornate [ɔr′net], [′ɔrnet] *adj* orné, fleuri

ornery [′ɔrnəri] *adj* (coll) acariâtre,
intraitable

ornithology [‚ɔrnɪ′θɑlədʒi] *f* ornithologie *f*

orphan [′ɔrfən] *adj & s* orphelin *m*

orphanage [′ɔrfənɪdʒ] *s* (*asylum*) orphelinat *m*; (*orphanhood*) orpheli-
nage *m*

Orpheus [′ɔrfjus], [′ɔrfi‚əs] *s* Orphée
m

orthodox [′ɔrθə‚dɑks] *adj* orthodoxe

orthogra·phy [ɔr′θɑgrəfi] *s* (*pl* **-phies**)
orthographe *f*

oscillate [′ɑsɪ‚let] *intr* osciller

osier [′oʒər] *s* osier *m*

osmosis [ɑz′mosɪs], [ɑs′mosɪs] *s* osmose *f*

osprey [′ɑspri] *s* aigle *m* pêcheur

ossi·fy [′ɑsɪ‚faɪ] *v* (*pret & pp* **-fied**) *tr*
ossifier ‖ *intr* s'ossifier

ostensible [ɑs′tensɪbəl] *adj* prétendu,
apparent, soi-disant

ostentatious [‚ɑsten′teʃəs] *adj* ostenta-
tieux, fastueux

osteopathy [‚ɑsti′ɑpəθi] *s* ostéopathie *f*

ostracism [′ɑstrə‚sɪzəm] *s* ostracisme *m*

ostracize [′ɑstrə‚saɪz] *tr* frapper d'ostracisme

ostrich [′ɑstrɪtʃ] *s* autruche *f*

other [′ʌðər] *adj* autre; **every other
day** tous les deux jours; **every other
one** un sur deux ‖ *pron indef* autre
‖ *adv*—**other than** autrement que

otherwise [′ʌðər‚waɪz] *adv* autrement,
à part cela ‖ *conj* sinon, e.g., **come
at once, otherwise it will be too late**
venez tout de suite, sinon il sera trop
tard; sans cela, e.g., **thanks, otherwise I'd have forgotten** merci, sans
cela j'aurais oublié

otter [′ɑtər] *s* loutre *f*

Ottoman [′ɑtəmən] *adj* ottoman ‖
(*l.c.*) *s* (*corded fabric*) ottomane *m*;
(*divan*) ottomane *f*; (*footstool*) pouf
m; **Ottoman** (*person*) Ottoman *m*

ouch [aʊtʃ] *interj* aïe!

ought [ɔt] *s* zéro *m*; **for ought I know**
pour autant que je sache ‖ *aux* used
to express obligation, e.g., **he ought
to go away** il devrait s'en aller; e.g.,
he ought to have gone away il aurait
dû s'en aller

ounce [aʊns] *s* once *f*

our [aʊr] *adj poss* notre §88

ours [aʊrz] *pron poss* le nôtre §89

our·selves [aʊr′selvz] *pron pers* nous-mêmes §86;
nous §85, §87

oust [aʊst] *tr* évincer, chasser

out [aʊt] *adj* extérieur; absent; (*fire*)
éteint; (*secret*) divulgué; (*tide*) bas;
(*flower*) épanoui; (*rope*) filé; (*lease*)
expiré; (*gear*) débrayé; (*unconscious
person*) évanoui; (*boxer*) knockouté;
(*book, magazine, etc.*) paru, publié;
(*out of print, out of stock*) épuisé;
(*a ball*) (sports) hors jeu; (*a player*)
(sports) éliminé ‖ *s* (*pretext*) échappatoire *f*; **to be on the outs with** être
brouillé avec ‖ *adv* dehors, au dehors; (*outdoors*) en plein air; **out and
out** complètement; **out for** en quête
de; **out for lunch** parti déjeuner; **out
of** (*cash*) démuni de; (*a glass, cup,
etc.*) dans; (*a bottle*) à; (*the window,
curiosity, friendship, respect, etc.*)
par; (*range, sight*) hors de; de, e.g.,
to cry out of joy pleurer de joie; e.g.,
made out of fait de; sur, e.g., **nine
times out of ten** neuf fois sur dix; **out
with it!** allez, dites-le!; **to be out** (*to
be absent*) être sorti; faire, e.g., **the
sun is out** il fait du soleil; **to be out**

of bounds (sports) être hors jeu ‖ *prep* par ‖ *interj* hors d'ici!, ouste!

out′ and away′ *adv* de beaucoup, de loin

out′-and-out′ *adj* vrai; (*fanatic*) intransigeant; (*liar*) achevé

out′-and-out′er *s* (coll) intransigeant *m*

out′bid′ *v* (*pret* -bid; *pp* -bid or -bidden; *ger* -bidding) *tr* enchérir sur; (fig) renchérir sur ‖ *intr* surenchérir

out′board mo′tor *s* moteur *m* hors-bord

out′break′ *s* déchaînement *m*; (*of hives; of anger; etc.*) éruption *f*; (*of epidemic*) manifestation *f*; (*insurrection*) révolte *f*

out′build′ing *s* annexe *f*, dépendance *f*

out′burst′ *s* explosion *f*; (*of anger*) accès *m*; (*of laughter*) éclat *m*; (*e.g., of generosity*) élan *m*

out′cast′ *adj* & *s* banni *m*, proscrit *m*

out′caste′ *adj* hors caste ‖ *s* hors-caste *mf*

out′come′ *s* résultat *m*, dénouement *m*

out′cry′ *s* (*pl* -cries) clameur *f*; (*of indignation*) levée *f* de boucliers

out-dat′ed *adj* démodé, suranné

out′dis′tance *tr* dépasser; (sports) distancer

out′do′ *v* (*pret* -did; *pp* -done) *tr* surpasser, l'emporter sur; **to outdo oneself** se surpasser

out′door′ *adj* au grand air; (sports) de plein air

out′door grill′ *s* rôtisserie *f* en plein air

out′doors′ *s* rase campagne *f*, plein air *m* ‖ *adv* au grand air, en plein air; en plein air; (*outside of the house*) hors de la maison; (*at night*) à la belle étoile

out′door swim′ming pool′ *s* piscine *f* à ciel ouvert

outer [′aʊtər] *adj* extérieur, externe

out′er space′ *s* cosmos *m*, espace *m* cosmique

out′field′ *s* (baseball) grand champ *m*

out′fit′ *s* équipement *m*, attirail *m*; (*caseful of implements*) trousse *f*, nécessaire *m*; (*ensemble*) costume et accessoires *mpl*; (*of a bride*) trousseau *m*; (*team*) équipe *f*; (*group of soldiers*) unité *f*; (com) compagnie *f* ‖ *v* (*pret* & *pp* -fitted; *ger* -fitting) *tr* équiper

out′go′ing *adj* en partance, partant; (*officeholder*) sortant; (*friendly*) communicatif, sympathique

out′grow′ *v* (*pret* -grew; *pp* -grown) *tr* devenir plus grand que; (*e.g., childhood clothes, activities, etc.*) devenir trop grand pour; abandonner, se défaire de

out′growth′ *s* excroissance *f*; (fig) résultat *m*, conséquence *f*

outing [′aʊtɪŋ] *s* excursion *f*, sortie *f*

outlandish [aʊt′lændɪʃ] *adj* bizarre, baroque

out′last′ *tr* durer plus longtemps que; survivre (with *dat*)

out′law′ *s* hors-la-loi *m*, proscrit *m* ‖ *tr* mettre hors la loi, proscrire

out′lay′ *s* débours *mpl*, dépenses *fpl* ‖ **out′lay′** *v* (*pret* & *pp* -laid) *tr* débourser, dépenser

out′let′ *s* sortie *f*, issue *f*; (*escape valve*) déversoir *m*; (*for, e.g., pent-up emotions*) exutoire *m*; (com) débouché *m*; (elec) prise *f* de courant; **no outlet** (public sign) rue sans issue

out′line′ *s* (*profile*) contour *m*; (*sketch*) esquisse *f*; (*summary*) aperçu *m*; (*of a work in preparation*) plan *m*; (*main points*) grandes lignes *fpl* ‖ *tr* esquisser; (*a work in preparation*) ébaucher

out′live′ *tr* survivre (with *dat*)

out′lived′ *adj* caduc, désuet

out′look′ *s* perspective *f*, point *m* de vue

out′ly′ing *adj* éloigné, écarté, isolé

outmoded [,aʊt′modɪd] *adj* démodé

out′num′ber *tr* surpasser en nombre

out′-of-date′ *adj* démodé, suranné

out′-of-door′ *adj* au grand air

out′-of-doors′ *adj* au grand air ‖ *s* rase campagne *f*, plein air *m* ‖ *adv* au grand air, hors de la maison

out′ of or′der *adj* en panne; **to be out of order** (*to be out of sequence*) ne pas être dans l'ordre

out′ of print′ *adj* épuisé

out′ of tune′ *adj* désaccordé ‖ *adv* faux, e.g., **to sing out of tune** chanter faux

out′ of work′ *adj* en chômage

out′pa′tient *s* malade *mf* de consultation externe

out′patient clin′ic *s* consultation *f* externe

out′post′ *s* avant-poste *m*, antenne *f*

out′put′ *s* rendement *m*, débit *m*; (*of a mine; of a worker*) production *f*

out′rage *s* outrage *m*; (*wanton violence*) atrocité *f*, attentat *m* honteux ‖ *tr* faire outrage à, outrager; (*a woman*) violer

outrageous [aʊt′redʒəs] *adj* outrageux; (*intolerable*) insupportable

out′rank′ *tr* dépasser en grade, dépasser en rang

out′rid′er *s* explorateur *m*; cow-boy *m*; (*mounted attendant*) piqueur *m*

outrigger [′aʊt,rɪgər] *s* (*outboard framework*) balancier *m*; (*oar support*) porte-en-dehors *m*

out′right′ *adj* pur, absolu; (*e.g., manner*) franc, direct ‖ **out′right′** *adv* complètement; (*frankly*) franchement; (*at once*) sur le coup

out′set′ *s* début *m*, commencement *m*

out′side′ *adj* du dehors, d'extérieur ‖ **out′side′** *s* dehors *m*, extérieur *m*; surface *f*; **at the outside** tout au plus, au maximum ‖ **out′side′** *adv* dehors, à l'extérieur; (*outdoors*) en plein air; **outside of** en dehors de, à l'extérieur de; (*except for*) sauf ‖ **out′side′** or **out′side′** *prep* en dehors de, à l'extérieur de

outsider [,aʊt′saɪdər] *s* étranger *m*; (*intruder*) intrus *m*; (*uninitiated*) profane *mf*; (*dark horse*) outsider *m*

out′size′ *adj* hors série

out'skirts' *spl* approches *fpl*, périphérie *f*

out'spo'ken *adj* franc; **to be outspoken** avoir son franc-parler

out'stand'ing *adj* saillant; (*eminent*) hors pair, hors ligne; (*debts*) à recouvrer, impayé

outward ['autwərd] *adj* extérieur; (*apparent*) superficiel; (*direction*) en dehors || *adv* au dehors, vers le dehors

out'weigh' *tr* peser plus que; (*in value*) l'emporter en valeur sur

out'wit' *v* (*pret & pp* **-witted;** *ger* **-witting**) *tr* duper, déjouer; (*a pursuer*) dépister

oval ['ovəl] *adj & s* ovale *m*

ova·ry ['ovəri] *s* (*pl* **-ries**) ovaire *m*

ovation [o've/ən] *s* ovation *f*

oven ['ʌvən] *s* four *m*; (*fig*) fournaise *f*

over ['ovər] *adj* fini, passé; (*additional*) en plus; (*excessive*) en excès; plus, e.g., **eight and over** huit et plus || *adv* au-dessus, dessus; (*on the other side of*) de l'autre côté; (*again*) de nouveau; (*on the reverse side of sheet of paper*) au verso; (*finished*) passé, achevé; **all over** (*everywhere*) partout; (*finished*) fini; (*completely*) jusqu'au bout des ongles; **I'll be right over** (*coll*) j'arrive tout de suite; **over!** (*turn the page!*) voir au verso!, tournez!; (*rad*) à vous!; **over again** de nouveau, encore une fois; **over against** en face de; (*compared to*) auprès de; **over and above** en plus de; **over and out!** (*rad*) terminé!; **over and over** à coups répétés, à plusieurs reprises; **over here** ici, de ce côté; **over there** là-bas; **to be over** (*an illness*) s'être remis de; **to hand over** remettre || *prep* au-dessus de; (*on top of*) sur, par-dessus; (*with motion*) par-dessus, e.g., **to jump over a fence** sauter par-dessus une barrière; (*a period of time*) pendant, au cours de; (*near*) près de; (*a certain number or amount*) plus de, au-dessus de; (*concerning*) à propos de, au sujet de; (*on the other side of*) au delà de, de l'autre côté de; à, e.g., **over the telephone** au téléphone; (*while doing s.th.*) tout en prenant, e.g., **over a cup of coffee** tout en prenant une tasse de café; **all over** répandu sur; **over and above** en sus de, en plus de; **to fall over** (*e.g., a cliff*) tomber du haut de; **to reign over** régner sur

o'ver·all' *adj* hors tout, complet; général, total || **overalls** *spl* combinaison *f* d'homme, cotte *f*, salopette *f*

o'ver·awe' *tr* impressionner, intimider

o'ver·bear'ing *adj* impérieux, tranchant, autoritaire

o'ver·board' *adv* par-dessus bord; **man overboard!** un homme à la mer!; **to throw overboard** jeter par-dessus le bord; (*fig*) abandonner

o'ver·cast' *adj* obscurci, nuageux || *s* ciel *m* couvert || *v* (*pret & pp* **-cast**) *tr* obscurcir, couvrir

o'ver·charge' *s* prix *m* excessif, majoration *f* excessive; (*elec*) surcharge *f* || **o'ver·charge'** *tr* (*e.g., an account*) majorer; (*elec*) surcharger; **to overcharge s.o. for s.th.** faire payer trop cher q.ch. à qn

o'ver·coat' *s* pardessus *m*

o'ver·come' *v* (*pret* **-came;** *pp* **-come**) *tr* vaincre; (*difficulties*) surmonter

o'ver·con'fidence *s* témérité *f*, confiance *f* exagérée

o'ver·con'fident *adj* téméraire, excessivement confiant

o'ver·cooked' *adj* trop cuit

o'ver·crowd' *tr* bonder; (*a town, region, etc.*) surpeupler

o'ver·do' *v* (*pret* **-did;** *pp* **-done**) *tr* exagérer; **overdone** (*culin*) trop cuit || *intr* se surmener

o'ver·dose' *s* dose *f* excessive

o'ver·draft' *s* découvert *m*, solde *m* débiteur

o'ver·draw' *v* (*pret* **-drew;** *pp* **-drawn**) *tr* tirer à découvert || *intr* excéder son crédit

o'ver·drive' *s* (*aut*) surmultiplication *f*

o'ver·due' *adj* en retard; (*com*) échu, arriéré

o'ver·eat' *v* (*pret* **-ate;** *pp* **-eaten**) *tr & intr* trop manger

o'ver·exer'tion *s* surmenage *m*

o'ver·expose' *tr* surexposer

o'ver·expo'sure *s* surexposition *f*

o'ver·flow' *s* débordement *m*; (*pipe*) trop-plein *m* || **o'ver·flow'** *tr & intr* déborder

o'ver·fly' *v* (*pret* **-flew;** *pp* **-flown**) *tr* survoler

o'ver·grown' *adj* démesuré; (*e.g., child*) trop grand pour son âge; **overgrown with** (*e.g., weeds*) envahi par, recouvert de

o'ver·hang' *v* (*pret & pp* **-hung**) *tr* surplomber, faire saillie au-dessus de; (*to threaten*) menacer || *intr* (*to jut out*) faire saillie

o'ver·haul' *s* remise *f* en état || **o'ver·haul'** *tr* remettre en état; (*to catch up to*) rattraper

o'ver·head' *adj* élevé; aérien, surélevé || *s* (*overpass*) pont-route *m*; (*com*) frais *mpl* généraux || **o'ver·head'** *adv* au-dessus de la tête, en haut

o'ver·head valve' *s* soupape *f* en tête

o'ver·hear' *v* (*pret & pp* **-heard**) *tr* entendre par hasard; (*a conversation*) surprendre

o'ver·heat' *tr* surchauffer

overjoyed [‚ovər'dʒɔɪd] *adj* ravi, transporté de joie

overland ['ovər‚lænd] *adj & adv* par terre, par voie de terre

o'ver·lap' *v* (*pret & pp* **-lapped;** *ger* **-lapping**) *tr* enchevaucher || *intr* chevaucher

o'ver·lap'ping *s* recouvrement *m*, chevauchement *m*; (*of functions, offices, etc.*) double emploi *m*

o'ver·load' *s* surcharge *f*; **sudden overload** (*elec*) coup *m* de collier || **o'ver·load'** *tr* surcharger o/ver·look/ *tr* donner sur, avoir vue sur; (*to ignore*) fermer les yeux sur, passer sous silence; (*to neglect*) oublier, négliger

o/ver·lord/ *s* suzerain *m* || o/ver·lord/ *tr* dominer, tyranniser

overly ['ovərli] *adv* (coll) trop, à l'excès

o/ver·night/ *adv* toute la nuit; du jour au lendemain; **to stay overnight** passer la nuit

o/ver·night/ bag/ *s* sac *m* de nuit

o/ver·pass/ *s* passage *m* supérieur, pont-route *m*

o/ver·pay/ment *s* surpaye *f*, rétribution *f* excessive

o/ver·pop/u·la/tion *s* surpeuplement *m*, surpopulation *f*

o/ver·pow/er *tr* maîtriser; **overpowered with grief** accablé de douleur

o/ver·pow/er·ing *adj* accablant, irrésistible

o/ver·pro·duc/tion *s* surproduction *f*

o/ver·rate/ *tr* surestimer

o/ver·reach/ *tr* dépasser

o/ver·ripe/ *adj* blet, trop mûr

o/ver·rule/ *tr* décider contre; (*to set aside*) annuler, casser

o/ver·run/ *v* (*pret* -ran; *pp* -run; *ger* -running) *tr* envahir; (*to flood*) inonder; (*limits, boundaries, etc.*) dépasser || *intr* déborder

o/ver·sea/ or o/ver·seas/ *adj* d'outre-mer || o/ver·sea/ or o/ver·seas/ *adv* outre-mer

o/ver·see/ *v* (*pret* -saw; *pp* -seen) *tr* surveiller

o/ver·se/er *s* surveillant *m*, inspecteur *m*

o/ver·shad/ow *tr* ombrager; (fig) éclipser

o/ver·shoes/ *spl* caoutchoucs *mpl*

o/ver·sight/ *s* inadvertance *f*, étourderie *f*

o/ver·sleep/ *v* (*pret* & *pp* -slept) *intr* dormir trop longtemps

o/ver·step/ *v* (*pret* & *pp* -stepped; *ger* -stepping) *tr* dépasser, outrepasser

o/ver·stock/ *tr* surapprovisionner

o/ver·stuffed/ *adj* rembourré

o/ver·sup·ply/ *s* (*pl* -plies) excédent *m*, abondance *f* || o/ver·sup·ply/ *v* (*pret* & *pp* -plied) *tr* approvisionner avec excès

overt ['ovərt], [o'vʌrt] *adj* ouvert, manifeste; (*intentional*) prémédité

o/ver·take/ *v* (*pret* -took; *pp* -taken) *tr* rattraper; (*a runner*) dépasser; (*an automobile*) doubler; (*to surprise*) surprendre

o/ver·tax/ *tr* surtaxer; (*to tire*) surmener, excéder

o/ver·the·coun/ter *adj* vendu directement à l'acheteur

o/ver·throw/ *s* renversement *m* || o/ver·throw/ *v* (*pret* -threw; *pp* -thrown) *tr* renverser

o/ver·time/ *adj* & *adv* en heures supplémentaires || *s* heures *fpl* supplémentaires

o/ver·tone/ *s* (mus) harmonique *m*; (fig) signification *f*, sous-entendu *m*

o/ver·trump/ *tr* surcouper

overture ['ovərtʃər] *s* ouverture *f*

o/ver·turn/ *tr* renverser, chavirer || *intr* chavirer; (aer, aut) capoter

overweening [,ovər'winɪŋ] *adj* arrogant, outrecuidant

o/ver·weight/ *adj* au-dessus du poids normal; (*fat*) obèse || *s* excédent *m* de poids

overwhelm [,ovər'hwɛlm] *tr* accabler, écraser; (*with favors, gifts, etc.*) combler

o/ver·work/ *s* surmenage *m*, excès *m* de travail || o/ver·work/ *tr* surmener, surcharger; abuser de, trop employer || *intr* se surmener

Ovid ['ɑvɪd] *s* Ovide *m*

ow [au] *interj* aïe!

owe [o] *tr* devoir || *intr* avoir des dettes; **to owe for** avoir à payer, devoir

owing ['o·ɪŋ] *adj* dû, redû; **owing to** à cause de, en raison de

owl [aul] *s* (*Asio*) hibou *m*; (*Strix*) chouette *f*, hulotte *f*; (*Tyto alba*) effraie *f*

own [on] *adj* propre, e.g. **my own brother** mon propre frère || *s*—**all its own** spécial, authentique, e.g., **an aroma all its own** un parfum spécial, un parfum authentique; (**my own** (**your own**, etc.) le mien (le vôtre, etc.) §89; **of my own** (of their own, etc.) bien à moi (bien à eux, etc.); **on one's own** à son propre compte, de son propre chef; **to come into one's own** entrer en possession de son bien; (*to win out*) obtenir des succès; (*to receive due praise*) recevoir les honneurs qu'on mérite; **to hold one's own** se maintenir, se défendre || *tr* posséder; être propriétaire de; (*to acknowledge*) reconnaître || *intr*—**to own to** convenir de, reconnaître; **to own up** (coll) faire des aveux; **to own up to** (coll) faire l'aveu de, avouer

owner ['onər] *s* propriétaire *mf*, possesseur *m*

ownership ['onər,ʃɪp] *s* propriété *f*, possession *f*

own/er's li/cense *s* carte *f* grise

ox [ɑks] *s* (*pl* oxen ['ɑksən] bœuf *m*

ox/cart/ *s* char *m* à bœufs

oxfords ['ɑksfərdz] *spl* richelieus *mpl*

oxide ['ɑksaɪd] *s* oxyde *m*

oxidize ['ɑksɪ,daɪz] *tr* oxyder || *intr* s'oxyder

oxygen ['ɑksɪdʒən] *s* oxygène *m*

oxygenate ['ɑksɪdʒə,net] *tr* oxygéner

ox/ygen tent/ *s* tente *f* à oxygène

oxytone ['ɑksɪ,ton] *adj* & *s* oxyton *m*

oyster ['ɔɪstər] *adj* huîtrier || *s* huître *f*

oys/ter bed/ *s* huîtrière *f*, banc *m* d'huîtres

oys/ter cock/tail *s* huîtres *fpl* écaillées aux condiments

oys/ter farm/ *s* parc *m* à huîtres, clayère *f*

oys/ter fork/ *s* fourchette *f* à huîtres

oys/ter knife/ *s* couteau *m* à huîtres

oys'ter·man *s* (*pl* **-men**) écailler *m*
oys'ter op'ener *s* (*person*) écailler *m*; (*implement*) ouvre-huîtres *m*
oys'ter plant' *s* salsifis *m*

oys'ter shell' *s* coquille *f* d'huître
oys'ter stew' *s* soupe *f* à huîtres
ozone ['ozon] *s* ozone *m*; (coll) air *m* frais

P

P, p [pi] *s* XVIᵉ lettre de l'alphabet
pace [pes] *s* pas *m*; **to keep pace with** marcher de pair avec; **to put through one's paces** mettre à l'épreuve; **to set the pace** mener le train ‖ *tr* arpenter; **to pace off** mesurer au pas ‖ *intr* aller au pas
pace'mak'er *s* meneur *m* de train
pacific [pə'sɪfɪk] *adj* pacifique ‖ Pacific *adj* & *s* Pacifique *m*
pacifier ['pæsɪ,faɪ·ər] *s* pacificateur *m*; (*teething ring*) sucette *f*
pacifism ['pæsɪ,fɪzəm] *s* pacifisme *m*
pacifist ['pæsɪfɪst] *adj* & *s* pacifiste *mf*
paci·fy ['pæsɪ,faɪ] *v* (*pret* & *pp* **-fied**) *tr* pacifier
pack [pæk] *s* paquet *m*; (*of peddler*) ballot *m*; (*of soldier*) paquetage *m*, sac *m*; (*of beast of burden*) bât *m*; (*of hounds*) meute *f*; (*of evildoers; of wolves*) bande *f*; (*of lies*) tissu *m*; (*of playing cards*) jeu *m*; (*of cigarettes*) paquet; (*of floating ice*) banquise *f*; (*of troubles*) foule *f*; (*of fools*) tas *m*; (med) enveloppement *m* ‖ *tr* emballer, empaqueter; mettre en boîte; (*e.g., earth*) tasser; (*to stuff*) bourrer; **to send packing** (coll) envoyer promener ‖ *intr* faire ses bagages
package ['pækɪdʒ] *s* paquet *m* ‖ *tr* empaqueter
pack'age plan' *s* voyage *m* à forfait
pack' an'imal *s* bête *f* de somme
packet ['pækɪt] *s* paquet *m*; (naut) paquebot *m*; (pharm) sachet *m*
pack'ing box' *or* **case'** *s* caisse *f* d'emballage
pack'ing house' *s* conserverie *f*
pack'sad'dle *s* bât *m*
pack'thread' *s* ficelle *f*
pack'train' *s* convoi *m* de bêtes de somme
pact [pækt] *s* pacte *m*
pad [pæd] *s* bourrelet *m*; (*of writing paper*) bloc *m*; (*for inking*) tampon *m*; (*of an aquatic plant*) feuille *f*; (*for launching a rocket*) rampe *f*; (*sound of footsteps*) pas *m* ‖ *v* (*pret* & *pp* **padded**; *ger* **padding**) *tr* rembourrer; (*to expand unnecessarily*) délayer ‖ *intr* aller à pied
pad'ded cell' *s* cellule *f* matelassée, cabanon *m*
paddle ['pædəl] *s* (*of a canoe*) pagaie *f*; (*for table tennis*) raquette *f*; (*of a wheel*) aube *f*; (*for beating*) palette *f* ‖ *tr* pagayer; (*to spank*) fesser ‖ *intr* pagayer; (*to splash*) barboter
pad'dle wheel' *s* roue *f* à aubes

paddock ['pædək] *s* enclos *m*; (*at race track*) paddock *m*
pad'dy wag'on ['pædɪ] *s* (slang) panier *m* à salade
pad'lock' *s* cadenas *m* ‖ *tr* cadenasser
pagan ['pegən] *adj* & *s* païen *m*
paganism ['pegə,nɪzəm] *s* paganisme *m*
page [pedʒ] *s* (*of a book*) page *f*; (*boy attendant*) page *m*; (*in a hotel or club*) chasseur *m* ‖ *tr* (*a book*) paginer; appeler, demander, e.g., **you are being paged** on vous demande
pageant ['pædʒənt] *s* parade *f* à grand spectacle
pageant·ry ['pædʒəntri] *s* (*pl* **-ries**) grand apparat *m*; vaines pompes *fpl*
page' proof' *s* seconde épreuve *f*; (journ) morasse *f*
paginate ['pædʒɪ,net] *tr* paginer
paging ['pedʒɪŋ] *s* mise *f* en pages
paid' in full' [ped] *adj* (formula stamped on bill) pour acquit
paid' vaca'tion *s* congé *m* payé
pail [pel] *s* seau *m*
pain [pen] *s* douleur *f*; **on pain of** sous peine de; **to take pains** se donner de la peine ‖ *tr* faire mal (with *dat*); **it pains me to** il me coûte de ‖ *intr* faire mal
painful ['penfəl] *adj* douloureux
pain'kil'ler *s* (coll) calmant *m*
painless ['penlɪs] *adj* sans douleur
pains'tak'ing *adj* soigneux; (*work*) soigné
paint [pent] *s* peinture *f*; **wet paint** peinture fraîche; (public sign) attention à la peinture! ‖ *tr* & *intr* peindre
paint'box' *s* boîte *f* de couleurs
paint'brush' *s* pinceau *m*
paint' buck'et *s* camion *m*
painter ['pentər] *s* peintre *mf*
painting ['pentɪŋ] *s* peinture *f*
paint' remov'er *s* décapant *m*
pair [per] *s* paire *f*; (*of people*) couple *m* ‖ *tr* accoupler ‖ *intr* s'accoupler
pair' of scis'sors *s* ciseaux *mpl*
pair' of trou'sers *s* pantalon *m*
pajamas [pə'dʒɑməz], [pə'dʒæməz], *spl* pyjama *m*, pyjamas
Pakistan [,pɑkɪ'stɑn] *s* le Pakistan
Pakista·ni [,pɑkɪ'stɑni] *adj* pakistanais ‖ *s* (*pl* **-nis**) Pakistanais *m*
pal [pæl] *s* copain *m* ‖ *v* (*pret* & *pp* **palled**; *ger* **palling**) *intr* (coll) être de bons copains; **to pal with** être copain de
palace ['pælɪs] *s* palais *m*
palatable ['pælətəbəl] *adj* savoureux; (*acceptable*) agréable

palatal ['pælətəl] *adj* palatal ‖ *s* palatale *f*

palate ['pælɪt] *s* palais *m*

pale [pel] *adj* pâle ‖ *s* pieux *m*; limites *fpl* ‖ *intr* pâlir

pale'face' *s* visage *m* pâle

palette ['pælɪt] *s* palette *f*

palfrey ['pɔlfri] *s* palefroi *m*

palisade [,pælɪ'sed] *s* palissade *f*; (*line of cliffs*) falaise *f*

pall [pɔl] *s* poêle *m*, drap *m* mortuaire; (*to cover chalice*) pale *f*; (*vestment*) pallium *m* ‖ *intr* devenir fade; **to pall on** rassasier

pall'bear'er *s* porteur *m* d'un cordon du poêle

pallet ['pælɪt] *s* grabat *m*

palliate ['pælɪ,et] *tr* pallier

pallid ['pælɪd] *adj* pâle, blême

pallor ['pælər] *s* pâleur *f*

palm [pam] *s* (*of the hand*) paume *f*; (*measure*) palme *m*; (*leaf*) palme *f*; (*tree*) palmier *m*; **to carry off the palm** remporter la palme; **to grease the palm of** (slang) graisser la patte à ‖ *tr* (*a card*) escamoter; **to palm off s.th. on s.o.** refiler q.ch. à qn

palmet·to [pæl'meto] *s* (*pl* **-tos** or **-toes**) palmier *m* nain

palmist ['pamɪst] *s* chiromancien *m*

palmistry ['pamɪstri] *s* chiromancie *f*

palm' leaf' *s* palme *f*

palm' oil' *s* huile *f* de palme

Palm' Sun'day *s* le dimanche des Rameaux

palm' tree' *s* palmier *m*

palpable ['pælpabəl] *adj* palpable

palpitate ['pælpɪ,tet] *intr* palpiter

pal·sy ['pɔlzi] *s* (*pl* **-sies**) paralysie *f* ‖ *v* (*pret & pp* **-sied**) *tr* paralyser

pal·try ['pɔltri] *adj* (*comp* **-trier**; *super* **-triest**) misérable

pamper ['pæmpər] *tr* choyer, gâter

pamphlet ['pæmflɪt] *s* brochure *f*

pan [pæn] *s* casserole *f*; (*basin; scale of a balance*) bassin *m*; (slang) binette *f*; **Pan** Pan *m* ‖ *v* (*pret & pp* **panned**; *ger* **panning**) *tr* (*gold*) laver à la batée; (coll) débiner, éreinter ‖ *intr* laver à la batée; (mov) panoramiquer; **to pan out well** (coll) réussir

panacea [,pænə'si·ə] *s* panacée *f*

Panama ['pænə,ma], [,pænə'ma] *s* le Panama

Pan'ama Canal' *s* canal *m* de Panama

Pan'ama Canal' Zone' *s* zone *f* canal du Panama

Pan'ama hat' *s* panama *m*

Pan-American [,pænə'merɪkən] *adj* panaméricain

pan'cake' *s* crêpe *f* ‖ *intr* (aer) descendre à plat, se plaquer

pan'cake land'ing *s* atterrissage *m* plaqué, sur le ventre, or à plat

panchromatic [,pænkro'mætɪk] *adj* panchromatique

pancreas ['pænkrɪ·əs] *s* pancréas *m*

pander ['pændər] *s* entremetteur *m* ‖ *intr* servir d'entremetteur; **to pander to** se prêter à; encourager

pane [pen] *s* carreau *m*, vitre *f*

pan·el ['pænəl] *s* panneau *m*; (*on wall*) lambris *m*; liste *f*, tableau *m*; groupe *m* de discussion ‖ *v* (*pret & pp* **-eled** or **-elled**; *ger* **-eling** or **-elling**) *tr* (*a room*) garnir de boiseries; (*a wall*) lambrisser

pan'el discus'sion *s* colloque *m*

panelist ['pænəlɪst] *s* membre *m* d'un groupe de discussion

pang [pæŋ] *s* élancement *m*, angoisse *f*

pan'han·dle ['pæn,hændəl] *s* queue *f* de la poêle; (geog) projection *f* d'un territoire dans un autre ‖ *intr* (slang) mendigoter

pan'han'dler *s* (slang) mendigot *m*

pan·ic ['pænɪk] *adj & s* panique *f* ‖ *v* (*pret & pp* **-icked**; *ger* **-icking**) *tr* semer la panique dans ‖ *intr* être pris de panique

pan'ic-strick'en *adj* pris de panique

pano·ply ['pænəpli] *s* (*pl* **-plies**) panoplie *f*

panorama [,pænə'ræmə], [,pænə'ramə] *s* panorama *m*

pan·sy ['pænzi] *s* (*pl* **-sies**) pensée *f*; (slang) tapette *f*

pant [pænt] *s* halètement *m*; **pants** pantalon *m*; **to wear the pants** (coll) porter la culotte ‖ *intr* haleter, panteler

pantheism ['pænθɪ,ɪzəm] *s* panthéisme *m*

pantheon ['pænθɪ,an], ['pænθɪ·ən] *s* panthéon *m*

panther ['pænθər] *s* panthère *f*

panties ['pæntiz] *spl* culotte *f*

pantomime ['pæntə,maɪm] *s* pantomime *f*

pan·try ['pæntri] *s* (*pl* **-tries**) office *m & f*, dépense *f*

pap [pæp] *s* bouillie *f*

papa ['papə], [pə'pa] *s* papa *m*

papa·cy ['pepəsi] *s* (*pl* **-cies**) papauté *f*

paper ['pepər] *s* papier *m*; (*newspaper*) journal *m*; (*of needles*) carte *f* ‖ *tr* tapisser

pa'per·back' *s* livre *m* broché; (*pocketbook*) livre de poche

pa'per·boy' *s* vendeur *m* de journaux

pa'per clip' *s* attache *f*, trombone *m*

pa'per cone' *s* cornet *m* de papier

pa'per cup' *s* verre *m* en carton, gobelet *m* de papier

pa'per cut'ter *s* coupe-papier *m*

pa'per hand'kerchief *s* mouchoir *m* à jeter, mouchoir en papier

pa'per·hang'er *s* tapissier *m*

pa'per knife' *s* coupe-papier *m*

pa'per mill' *s* papeterie *f*

pa'per mon'ey *s* papier-monnaie *m*

pa'per nap'kin *s* serviette *f* en papier

pa'per plate' *s* assiette *f* en carton, assiette de papier

pa'per tape' *s* bande *f* de papier

pa'per tow'el *s* serviette *f* de toilette en papier

pa'per·weight' *s* presse-papiers *m*

pa'per work' *s* travail *m* de bureau

papier-mâché [,pepərma'ʃe] *s* papier-pierre *m*, papier *m* mâché

paprika [pæ'prikə], ['pæprɪkə] *s* paprika *m*

papy·rus [pə'paɪrəs] s (pl **-ri** [raɪ]) papyrus m

par [pɑr] s pair m; (golf) normale f du parcours; **at par** au pair; **to be on a par with** aller de pair avec

parable ['pærəbəl] s parabole f

parabola [pə'ræbələ] s parabole f

parachute ['pærə‚ʃut] s parachute m || tr & intr parachuter

par'achute jump' s saut m en parachute

parachutist ['pærə‚ʃutɪst] s parachutiste mf

parade [pə'red] s défilé m; (ostentation) parade f; (mil) parade || tr faire parade de || intr défiler; parader

paradise ['pærə‚daɪs] s paradis m

paradox ['pærə‚dɑks] s paradoxe m

paradoxical [‚pærə'dɑksɪkəl] adj paradoxal

paraffin ['pærəfɪn] s paraffine f || tr paraffiner

paragon ['pærə‚gɑn] s parangon m

paragraph ['pærə‚græf], ['pærə‚grɑf] s paragraphe m

Paraguay ['pærə‚gwe], ['pærə‚gwaɪ] s le Paraguay

Paraguayan [‚pærə'gwe·ən], [‚pærə‚'gwaɪ·ən] adj paraguayen || s Paraguayen m

parakeet ['pærə‚kit] s perruche f

paral·lel ['pærə‚lɛl] adj parallèle || s (line) parallèle f; (latitude; declination; comparison) parallèle m; (parallels (typ) barres fpl; **without parallel** sans pareil || v (pret & pp -leled or -lelled; ger -leling or -lelling) tr mettre en parallèle; entrer en parallèle avec, égaler

par'allel bars' spl barres fpl parallèles

paraly·sis [pə'rælɪsɪs] s (pl -ses [‚siz]) paralysie f

paralytic [‚pærə'lɪtɪk] adj & s paralytique mf

paralyze ['pærə‚laɪz] tr paralyser

paramount ['pærə‚maunt] adj suprême, capital

paranoiac [‚pærə'nɔɪ·æk] adj & s paranoïaque mf

parapet ['pærə‚pet] s parapet m

paraphernalia [‚pærəfər'nelɪ·ə] spl effets mpl personnels; attirail m

paraphrase ['pærə‚frez] s remaniement m || tr remanier

parasite ['pærə‚saɪt] s parasite m

parasitic(al) [‚pærə'sɪtɪk(əl)] adj parasite

parasol ['pærə‚sɔl], ['pærə‚sɑl] s parasol m, ombrelle f

paratrooper ['pærə‚trupər] s parachutiste m

parboil ['pɑr‚bɔɪl] tr faire cuire légèrement; (vegetables) blanchir

par·cel ['pɑrsəl] s colis m, paquet m || v (pret & pp -celed or -celled; ger -celing or -celling) tr morceler; **to parcel out** répartir

par'cel post' s colis mpl postaux

parch [pɑrtʃ] tr dessécher; (beans, grain, etc.) griller

parchment ['pɑrtʃmənt] s parchemin m

pardon ['pɑrdən] s pardon m; (remis-

sion of penalty by the state) grâce f; **I beg your pardon** je vous demande pardon || tr pardonner; pardonner (with dat); (a criminal) gracier; **to pardon s.o. for s.th.** pardonner q.ch. à qn

pardonable ['pɑrdənəbəl] adj pardonnable

pare [per] tr (potatoes, fruit, etc.) éplucher; (the nails) rogner; (costs) réduire

parent ['perənt] s père m or mère f; origine f, base f; **parents** parents mpl, père et mère

parentage ['perəntɪdʒ] s paternité f or maternité f; naissance f, origine f

parenthe·sis [pə'rɛnθɪsɪs] s (pl -ses [‚siz]) parenthèse f; **in parentheses** entre parenthèses

parenthood ['perənt‚hud] s paternité f or maternité f

pariah [pə'raɪ·ə], ['pɑrɪ·ə] s paria m

par'ing knife' s couteau m à éplucher

Paris ['pærɪs] s Paris m

parish ['pærɪʃ] adj paroissien || s paroisse f

parishioner [pə'rɪʃənər] s paroissien m

Parisian [pə'rɪʒən], [pə'rɪʒən] adj & s parisien m

parity ['pærɪti] s parité f

park [pɑrk] s parc m || tr garer, parquer || intr stationner

parked adj en stationnement

parking ['pɑrkɪŋ] s parcage m; (e.g., in a city street) stationnement m; **no parking** (public sign) stationnement interdit

park'ing lights' spl (aut) feux mpl de stationnement, feux de position

park'ing lot' s parking m, parc m à autos

park'ing me'ter s parcomètre m

park'ing tick'et s contravention f, papillon m

park'way' s route f panoramique; (turnpike) autoroute f

parley ['pɑrli] s pourparlers mpl || intr parlementer

parliament ['pɑrlɪmənt] s parlement m

parliamentarian [‚pɑrlɪmen'terɪ·ən] s expert m en usages parlementaires

parlor ['pɑrlər] s salon m; (in an institution) parloir m

par'lor car' s (rr) wagon-salon m

par'lor game' s jeu m de société

Parnassus [pɑr'næsəs] s le Parnasse

parochial [pə'rokɪ·əl] adj paroissial; (attitude) provincial

paro'chial school' s école f confessionnelle, école libre

paro·dy ['pærədi] s (pl -dies) parodie f || v (pret & pp -died) tr parodier

parole [pə'rol] s parole f d'honneur; liberté f sur parole || tr libérer sur parole

par·quet [pɑr'ke], [pɑr'ket] s parquet m; (theat) premiers rangs mpl du parterre || v (pret & pp -queted ['ked], -ketted ['ketɪd]; ger -queting ['ke·ɪŋ], ['ketɪŋ]) tr parqueter

parricide ['pærɪ‚saɪd] s (act) parricide m; (person) parricide mf

parrot ['pærət] s perroquet m ‖ tr répéter or imiter comme un perroquet

par·ry ['pæri] s (pl -ries) parade f ‖ v (pret & pp -ried) tr parer; (a question) éluder

parse [pɑrs] tr faire l'analyse grammaticale de

parsimonious [ˌpɑrsɪ'monɪ·əs] adj parcimonieux, regardant

parsley ['pɑrslɪ] s persil m

parsnip ['pɑrsnɪp] s panais m

parson ['pɑrsən] s curé m; pasteur m protestant

parsonage ['pɑrsənɪdʒ] s presbytère m

part [pɑrt] s partie f; (share) part f; (of a machine) organe m, pièce f; (of the hair) raie f; (theat) rôle m; **for my part** pour ma part; **for the most part** pour la plupart; **in part** en partie; **in these parts** dans ces parages; **on the part of** de la part de; **parts** qualités fpl; parties (génitales) fpl; **to be or form part of** faire partie de; **to be part and parcel of** faire partie intégrante de; **to do one's part** faire son devoir; **to live a part** (theat) entrer dans la peau d'un personnage; **to look the part** avoir le physique de l'emploi; **to take part in** prendre part à; **to take the part of** prendre parti pour; jouer le rôle de ‖ adv partiellement, en partie; **part . . . part** moitié . . . moitié ‖ tr séparer; **to part the hair** se faire une raie ‖ intr se séparer; (said, e.g., of road) diverger; (to break) rompre; **to part with** se défaire de; se dessaisir de

par·take [pɑr'tek] v (pret -took; pp -taken) intr—**to partake in** participer à; **to partake of** (e.g., a meal) prendre; (e.g., joy) participer de

partial ['pɑrʃəl] adj partiel; (prejudiced) partial

participant [pɑr'tɪsɪpənt] adj & s participant m

participate [pɑr'tɪsɪˌpet] intr participer

participation [pɑrˌtɪsɪ'peʃən] s participation f

participle ['pɑrtɪˌsɪpəl] s participe m

particle ['pɑrtɪkəl] s particule f

particular [pər'tɪkjələr] adj particulier; difficile, exigeant; méticuleux; **a particular . . .** un certain . . . ‖ s détail m

particularize [pər'tɪkjələˌraɪz] tr & intr individualiser, particulariser

parting ['pɑrtɪŋ] s séparation f

partisan ['pɑrtɪzən] adj & s partisan m

partition [pɑr'tɪʃən] s partage m; (wall) paroi f, cloison f ‖ tr partager; **to partition off** séparer par des cloisons

partner ['pɑrtnər] s partenaire mf; (husband) conjoint m; (wife) conjointe f; (in a dance) cavalier m; (in business) associé m

part'ner·ship' s association f; (com) société f

part' of speech' s partie f du discours

part' own'er s copropriétaire mf

partridge ['pɑrtrɪdʒ] s perdrix m

part'-time' adj & adv à mi-temps

par·ty ['pɑrtɪ] adj de gala ‖ s (pl -ties) fête f, soirée f; (diversion of a group of persons; individual named in contract or lawsuit) partie f; (with whom one is conversing) interlocuteur m; (mil) détachement m, peloton m; (pol) parti m; (telp) correspondant m; (coll) individu m; **to be a party to** être complice de

party-goer ['pɑrtɪˌgo·ər] s invité m; (nightlifer) noceur m

par'ty line' s (between two properties) limite f; (telp) ligne f à postes groupés ‖ **par'ty line'** s ligne du parti; (of communist party) directives fpl du parti

par'ty pol'itics s politique f de parti

par'ty wall' s mur m mitoyen

pass [pæs], [pɑs] s (navigable channel; movement of hands of magician; in sports) passe f; (straits) pas m; (in mountains) col m, passage m; (document) laissez-passer m; difficulté f; (mil) permission f; (rr) permis m de circulation; (theat) billet m de faveur ‖ tr passer; (an exam) réussir à; (e.g., a student) recevoir; (a law) adopter, voter; (a red light) brûler; (to get ahead of) dépasser; (a car going in the same direction) doubler; (s.o. or s.th. coming toward one) croiser; (a certain place) passer devant; **to pass around** faire circuler; **to pass oneself off as** se faire passer pour; **to pass out** distribuer; **to pass over** passer sous silence; (to hand over) transmettre; **to pass s.th. off on s.o.** repasser or refiler q.ch. à qn ‖ intr passer; (educ) être reçu; **to bring to pass** réaliser; **to come to pass** se passer; **to pass as or for** passer pour; **to pass away** disparaître; (to die out) s'éteindre; (to die) mourir; **to pass by** passer devant; **to pass out** sortir; (slang) s'évanouir; **to pass over** passer sur; (an obstacle) franchir; (said of storm) s'éloigner; (to pass through) traverser; **to pass over to** (e.g., the enemy) passer à

passable ['pæsəbəl], ['pɑsəbəl] adj passable; (road, river, etc.) franchissable

passage ['pæsɪdʒ] s passage m; (of time) cours m; (of a law) adoption f

pass'book' s carnet m de banque

passenger ['pæsəndʒər] adj (e.g., train) de voyageurs; (e.g., pigeon) de passage ‖ s voyageur m, passager m

passer-by ['pæsər'baɪ], ['pɑsər'baɪ] s (pl passers-by) passant m

passing ['pæsɪŋ], ['pɑsɪŋ] adj passager m; (act of passing) dépassement m; (death) trépas m; (of time) écoulement m; (of a law) adoption f; (in an examination) la moyenne; une mention passable

passion ['pæʃən] s passion f

passionate ['pæʃənɪt] adj passionné

passive ['pæsɪv] adj & s passif m

pass'key' s passe-partout m

pass'-out' check' s contremarque f

Pass'o'ver s Pâque f
pass'port' s passeport m
pass'word' s mot m de passe
past [pæst], [pɑst] adj passé, dernier; (e.g., president) ancien ‖ s passé m ‖ prep au-delà de, passé; plus de; hors de, e.g., **past all understanding** hors de toute compréhension; **it's twenty past five** il est cinq heures vingt; **it's past three o'clock** il est trois heures passées
paste [pest] s (glue) colle f de pâte; (jewelry) strass m; (culin) pâte f ‖ tr coller
paste'board' s carton m
pastel [pæs'tel] adj & s pastel m
pasteurize ['pæstə,raɪz] tr pasteuriser
pastime ['pæs,taɪm], ['pɑs,taɪm] s passe-temps m
past' mas'ter s expert m en la matière, passé maître
pastor ['pæstər], ['pɑstər] s pasteur m
pastoral ['pæstərəl], ['pɑstərəl] adj pastoral ‖ s pastorale f
pastorate ['pæstərɪt], ['pɑstərɪt] s pastorat m
pas·try ['pestri] s (pl -tries) pâtisserie f
pas'try cook' s pâtissier m
pas'try shop' s pâtisserie f
pasture ['pæstʃər], ['pɑstʃər] s pâturage m, pâture f ‖ tr faire paître ‖ intr paître
past·y ['pesti] adj (comp -ier; super -iest) pâteux; (face) terreux
pat [pæt] adj à propos; (e.g., excuse) tout prêt ‖ s petite tape f; caresse f; (of butter) coquille f ‖ v (pret & pp patted; ger patting) tr tapoter; caresser; **to pat on the back** encourager, complimenter
patch [pætʃ] s (e.g., of cloth) pièce f, raccommodage m; (of land) parcelle f; (of ice) plaque f; (of inner tube) rustine f; (e.g., of color) tache f; (beauty spot) mouche f ‖ tr rapiécer; **to patch up** rapetasser; (e.g., a quarrel) arranger, raccommoder
patent ['petənt] adj patent ‖ ['pætənt] adj breveté ‖ s brevet m d'invention; **patent applied for** une demande de brevet a été déposée ‖ tr breveter
pat'ent leath'er ['pætənt] s cuir m verni
pat'ent med'icine ['pætənt] s spécialité f pharmaceutique
pat'ent rights' ['pætənt] spl propriété f industrielle
paternal [pə'tʌrnəl] adj paternel
paternity [pə'tʌrnɪti] s paternité f
path [pæθ], [pɑθ] s sentier m; (in garden) allée f; (of bullet, heavenly body, etc.) trajectoire f; (for, e.g., riding horses) piste f; **to beat a path** frayer un chemin
pathetic [pə'θɛtɪk] adj pathétique
path'find'er s pionnier m
pathology [pə'θɑlədʒi] s pathologie f
pathos ['peθɑs] s pathétique m
path'way' s sentier m; (fig) voie f
patience ['peʃəns] s patience f
patient ['peʃənt] adj patient ‖ s malade mf; (undergoing surgery) patient m

pati·o ['pɑtɪ,o] s (pl -os) patio m
patriarch ['petrɪ,ɑrk] s patriarche m
patrician [pə'trɪʃən] adj & s patricien m
patricide ['pætrɪ,saɪd] s (act) parricide m; (person) parricide mf
Patrick ['pætrɪk] s Patrice m
patrimo·ny ['pætrɪ,moni] s (pl -nies) patrimoine m
patriot ['petrɪ·ət], ['pætrɪ·ət] s patriote mf
patriotic [,petrɪ'ɑtɪk], [,pætrɪ'ɑtɪk] adj patriotique, patriote
patriotism ['petrɪ·ə,tɪzəm], ['pætrɪ·ə,tɪzəm] s patriotisme m
pa·trol [pə'trol] s patrouille f ‖ v (pret & pp -trolled; ger -trolling) tr faire la patrouille dans ‖ intr patrouiller
patrol'man s (pl -men) agent m de police
patrol' wag'on s voiture f cellulaire
patron ['petrən], ['pætrən] adj patron ‖ s protecteur m; (com) client m
patronage ['petrənɪdʒ], ['pætrənɪdʒ] s patronage m, clientèle f
patronize ['petrə,naɪz], ['pætrə,naɪz] tr patronner, protéger; traiter avec condescendance; (com) acheter chez
pa'tron saint' s patron m
patter ['pætər] s petit bruit m; (of rain) fouettement m; (of magician, peddler, etc.) boniment m ‖ intr (said of rain) fouetter; (said of little feet) trottiner
pattern ['pætərn] s patron m; modèle m
pat·ty ['pæti] s (pl -ties) petit pâté m
paucity ['pɑsɪti] s rareté f; manque m, disette f
paunch [pɔntʃ] s panse f
paunch·y ['pɔntʃi] adj (comp -ier; super -iest) ventru
pauper ['pɔpər] s indigent m
pause [pɔz] s pause f; (mus) point m d'orgue; **to give pause to** faire hésiter ‖ intr faire une pause; hésiter
pave [pev] tr paver
pavement ['pevmənt] s pavé m; (surface) chaussée f
pavilion [pə'vɪljən] s pavillon m
paw [pɔ] s patte f; (coll) main f ‖ tr donner un coup de patte à ‖ intr (said of horse) piaffer
pawl [pɔl] s cliquet m d'arrêt
pawn [pɔn] s (in chess) pion m; (security, pledge) gage m; (tool of another person) jouet m ‖ tr mettre en gage; **to pawn s.th. off on s.o.** (coll) refiler q.ch. à qn
pawn'bro'ker s prêteur m sur gages
pawn'shop' s mont-de-piété m, crédit m municipal
pawn' tick'et s reconnaissance f du mont-de-piété
pay [pe] s paye f; (mil) solde f ‖ v (pret & pp paid [ped]) tr payer; (mil) solder; (a compliment; a visit; attention) faire; **to pay back** payer de retour; **to pay down** payer comptant; **to pay off** (a debt) acquitter; (a mortgage) purger; (a creditor) rembourser; **to pay s.o. for s.th.**

payer qn de q.ch., payer q.ch. à qn ||
intr payer, rapporter; **to pay for**
payer; **to pay off** (coll) avoir du succès; **to pay up** se libérer par un
paiement

payable ['pe·əbəl] *adj* payable
pay/ boost/ *s* augmentation *f*
pay/ check/ *s* paye *f*
pay/ day/ *s* jour *m* de paye
pay/ dirt/ *s* alluvion *f* exploitable; (coll)
source *f* d'argent
payee [pe'i] *s* bénéficiaire *mf*
pay/ en/velope *s* sachet *m* de paye;
paye *f*
payer ['pe·ər] *s* payeur *m*
pay/ load/ *s* charge *f* payante; (aer)
poids *m* utile
pay/ mas/ter *s* payeur *m*
payment ['pemənt] *m* paiement *m*; (*installment, deposit, etc.*) versement *m*
pay/ phone/ *s* taxiphone *m*
pay/ roll/ *s* bulletin *m* de paye; (*for officers*) état *m* de solde; (*for enlisted
men*) feuille *f* de prêt
pay/ sta/tion *s* téléphone *m* public
pea [pi] *s* pois *m*; **green peas** petits
pois
peace [pis] *s* paix *f*
peaceable ['pisəbəl] *adj* pacifique
peaceful ['pisfəl] *adj* paisible, pacifique
peace/ mak/er *s* pacificateur *m*
peace/ of mind/ *s* tranquillité *f* d'esprit
peace/ pipe/ *s* calumet *m* de paix
peach [pitʃ] *s* pêche *f*; (slang) bijou *m*
peach/ tree/ *s* pêcher *m*
peach·y ['pit/i] *adj* (comp **-ier**; super
-iest) (slang) chouette
pea/ coat/ *s* (naut) caban *m*
pea/ cock/ *s* paon *m*
pea/ hen/ *s* paonne *f*
peak [pik] *s* cime *f*, sommet *m*; (*mountain; mountain top*) pic *m*; (*of beard*)
pointe *f*; (*of a cap*) visière *f*; (elec)
pointe
peak/ hour/ *s* heure *f* de pointe
peak/ load/ *s* (elec) charge *f* maximum
peak/ vol/tage *s* tension *f* de crête
peal [pil] *s* retentissement *m*; (*of bells*)
carillon *m* || *intr* carillonner
peal/ of laugh/ter *s* éclat *m* de rire
peal/ of thun/der *s* coup *m* de tonnerre
pea/nut/ *s* cacahuète *f*; (bot) arachide *f*
pea/nut but/ter *s* beurre *m* de caca-
huètes or d'arachide
pear [per] *s* poire *f*
pearl [pʌrl] *s* perle *f*
pearl/ oys/ter *s* huître *f* perlière
pear/ tree/ *s* poirier *m*
peasant ['pezənt] *adj* & *s* paysan *m*
pea/shoot/er *s* sarbacane *f*
pea/ soup/ *s* (culin, fig) purée *f* de pois
peat [pit] *s* tourbe *f*
pebble ['pebəl] *s* caillou *m*; (*on seashore*) galet *m*
pebbled *adj* (*leather*) grenu
peck [pek] *s* coup *m* de bec; (*eight
quarts*) picotin *m*; (*kiss*) (coll) baiser
m d'oiseau, bécot *m*; (coll) tas *m*
|| *tr* becqueter || *intr* picorer; **to peck
at** picorer; (*food*) pignocher
peculation [ˌpekjəˈleʃən] *s* péculat *m*,
détournement *m* de fonds

peculiar [pɪˈkjuljər] *adj* particulier;
(*strange*) bizarre
pedagogue ['pedəˌgag] *s* pédagogue *mf*
pedagogy ['pedəˌgodʒi], ['pedəˌgadʒi]
s pédagogie *f*
ped·al ['pedəl] *s* pédale *f* || *v* (pret &
pp **-aled** or **-alled**; ger **-aling** or
-alling) *tr* actionner les pédales de ||
intr pédaler
pedant ['pedənt] *s* pédant *m*
pedantic [pɪˈdæntɪk] *adj* pédant
pedant·ry ['pedəntri] *s* (pl **-ries**) pédanterie *f*
peddle ['pedəl] *tr* & *intr* colporter
peddler ['pedlər] *s* colporteur *m*
pedestal ['pedɪstəl] *s* piédestal *m*
pedestrian [pɪˈdestrɪ·ən] *adj* (*style*)
prosaïque || *s* piéton *m*
pediatrics [ˌpidiˈætrɪks], [ˌpedɪˈæ-
trɪks] *s* pédiatrie *f*
pedigree ['pedɪˌgri] *s* généalogie *f*;
(*table*) arbre *m* généalogique; (*of
animal*) pedigree *m*
pediment ['pedɪmənt] *s* fronton *m*
peek [pik] *s* coup *m* d'œil furtif || *intr*
—**to peek at** regarder furtivement
peel [pil] *s* pelure *f*; (*of lemon*) zeste
m || *tr* peler; **to peel off** enlever ||
intr se peler; (*said of paint*) s'écailler
peep [pip] *s* regard *m* furtif; (*of, e.g.,
chickens*) piaulement *m* || *intr* piau-
ler; **to peep at** regarder furtivement
peep/hole/ *s* judas *m*
peer [pɪr] *s* pair *m* || *intr* regarder avec
attention; **to peer at** or **into** scruter
peerless ['pɪrlɪs] *adj* sans pareil
peeve [piv] *s* (coll) embêtement *m* || *tr*
(coll) irriter, embêter, fâcher
peevish ['pivɪʃ] *adj* maussade
peg [peg] *s* cheville *f*; (*for tent*) piquet
m; **to take down a peg** (coll) rabattre
le caquet de || *v* (pret & pp **pegged**;
ger **pegging**) *tr* cheviller; (*e.g., prices*)
indexer, fixer; (*points*) marquer ||
intr piocher; **to peg away at** travailler
ferme à
Pegasus ['pegəsəs] *s* Pégase *m*
peg/ leg/ *s* jambe *f* de bois
peg/ top/ *s* toupie *f*; **peg tops** pantalon
m fuseau
Pekin·ese [ˌpikɪˈniz] *adj* pékinois || *s*
(pl **-ese**) Pékinois *m*
Peking ['piˈkɪŋ] *s* Pékin *m*
pelf [pelf] *s* (pej) lucre *m*
pelican ['pelɪkən] *s* pélican *m*
pellet ['pelɪt] *s* boulette *f*; (*bullet*)
grain *m* de plomb; (pharm) pilule *f*
pell-mell ['pel'mel] *adj* confus || *adv*
pêle-mêle
pelt [pelt] *s* peau *m*; coup *m* violent;
(*of stones, insults, etc.*) grêle *f* || *tr*
cribler; (*e.g., stones*) lancer || *intr*
tomber à verse
pen [pen] *s* plume *f*; (*fountain pen*)
stylo *m*; (*corral*) enclos *m*; (fig)
plume; (*prison*) (slang) bloc *m* || *v*
(pret & pp **penned**; ger **penning**) *tr*
écrire || *v* (pret & pp **penned** or **pent**
[pent]; ger **penning**) *tr* parquer
penalize ['pinəˌlaɪz] *tr* (*an action*)
sanctionner; (*a person*) punir;
(sports) pénaliser

penal·ty ['penəlti] s (pl **-ties**) peine f; (for late payment; in a game) pénalité f; **under penalty of** sous peine de

penance ['penəns] s pénitence f

penchant ['penʃənt] s penchant m

pen·cil ['pensəl] s crayon m; (of light) faisceau m || v (pret & pp **-ciled** or **-cilled**; ger **-ciling** or **-cilling**) tr crayonner

pen'cil sharp'ener s taille-crayon m

pendent ['pendənt] adj pendant || s pendant m, pendentif m; (of chandelier) pendeloque f

pending ['pendɪŋ] adj pendant || prep en attendant

pendulum ['pendʒələm] s pendule m

pen'dulum bob' s lentille f

penetrate ['penɪ‚tret] tr & intr pénétrer

penguin ['pengwɪn] s manchot m

pen'hold'er s porte-plume m; (rack) pose-plumes m

penicillin [‚penɪ'sɪlɪn] s pénicilline f

peninsula [pə'nɪnsələ] s presqu'île f; (large peninsula like Spain or Italy) péninsule f

peninsular [pə'nɪnsələr] adj péninsulaire

penitence ['penɪtəns] s pénitence f

penitent ['penɪtənt] adj & s pénitent m

pen'knife' s (pl **-knives**) canif m

penmanship ['penmən‚ʃɪp] s calligraphie f; (person's handwriting) écriture f

pen' name' s pseudonyme m

pennant ['penənt] s flamme f; (sports) banderole f du championnat

penniless ['penɪlɪs] adj sans le sou

pen·ny ['penɪ] s (pl **-nies**) (U.S.A.) centime m; **not a penny** pas un sou || s (pl **pence** [pens]) (Brit) penny m

pen'ny-pinch'ing adj regardant

pen'ny-weight' s poids m de 24 grains

pen' pal' s (coll) correspondant m

pen'point' s bec m de plume

pension ['penʃən] s pension f || tr pensionner

pensioner ['penʃənər] s pensionné m

pensive ['pensɪv] adj pensif

Pentagon ['pentə‚gɑn] s Pentagone m

Pentecost ['pentɪ‚kɔst], ['pentɪ‚kɑst] s la Pentecôte

penthouse ['pent‚haus] s toit m en auvent, appentis m; appartement m sur toit, maison f à terrasse

pent-up ['pent‚ʌp] adj renfermé, refoulé

penult ['pinʌlt] s pénultième f

penum·bra [pɪ'nʌmbrə] s (pl **-brae** [bri] or **-bras**) pénombre f

penurious [pɪ'nurɪ‚əs] adj (stingy) mesquin, parcimonieux; (poor) pauvre

penury ['penjərɪ] s indigence f, misère f

pen'wip'er s essuie-plume m

peo·ny ['pi‚ənɪ] s (pl **-nies**) pivoine f

people ['pipəl] spl gens mpl, personnes fpl; **many people** beaucoup de monde; **my people** ma famille, mes parents; **people say** on dit || s (pl **peoples**) peuple m, nation f || tr peupler

pep [pep] s (coll) allant m || v (pret & pp **pepped**; ger **pepping**) tr—**to pep up** (coll) animer

pepper ['pepər] s (spice) poivre m; (fruit) grain m de poivre; (plant) poivrier m; (plant or fruit of the hot or red pepper) piment m rouge; (plant or fruit of the sweet or green pepper) piment doux, poivron m vert || tr poivrer; (e.g., with bullets) cribler

pep'per-box' s poivrière f

pep'per-mill' s moulin m à poivre

pep'per-mint' s menthe f poivrée; (lozenge) pastille f de menthe

per [pʌr] prep par; **as per** suivant

perambulator [pər'æmbjə‚letər] s voiture f d'enfant

per capita [pər'kæpɪtə] par tête, par personne

per cent or **percent** [pər'sent] pour cent

percentage [pər'sentɪdʒ] s pourcentage m; **to get a percentage** (slang) avoir part au gâteau

perceptible [pər'septəbəl] adj perceptible, sensible, appréciable

perception [pər'sepʃən] s perception f; compréhension f, pénétration f

perch [pʌrtʃ] s perchoir m; (ichth) perche f || tr percher || intr percher, se percher

percolate ['pʌrkə‚let] tr & intr filtrer

percolator ['pʌrkə‚letər] s cafetière f à filtre

percussion [pər'kʌʃən] s percussion f

percus'sion cap' s capsule f fulminante

per diem [pər'daɪ‚əm] par jour

perdition [pər'dɪʃən] s perdition f

perennial [pə'renɪ‚əl] adj perpétuel; (bot) vivace || s plante f vivace

perfect ['pʌrfɪkt] adj & s parfait m || [pər'fekt] tr perfectionner

perfidious [pər'fɪdɪ‚əs] adj perfide

perfi·dy ['pʌrfɪdɪ] s (pl **-dies**) perfidie f

perforate ['pʌrfə‚ret] tr perforer

per'forated line' s pointillé m

perforation [‚pʌrfə're‚ʃən] s perforation f; (of postage stamp) dentelure f

perforce [pər'fors] adv forcément

perform [pər'form] tr exécuter; (surg) faire; (theat) représenter || intr jouer; (said of machine) fonctionner

performance [pər'forməns] s exécution f; (production) rendement m; (of a machine) fonctionnement m; (sports) performance f; (theat) représentation f

performer [pər'formər] s artiste mf

perform'ing arts' spl arts mpl du spectacle

perfume ['pʌrfjum] s parfum m || [pər'fjum] tr parfumer

perfunctory [pər'fʌŋktərɪ] adj superficiel; négligent

perhaps [pər'hæps] adv peut-être; **perhaps not** peut-être que non

per hour' à l'heure

peril ['perəl] s péril m
perilous ['perıləs] adj périlleux
period ['pırıəd] s période f; (in school) heure f de cours; (gram) point m; (sports) division f
pe'riod cos'tume s costume m d'époque
pe'riod fur'niture s meubles d'époque
periodic [,pırı'adık] adj périodique
periodical [,pırı'adıkəl] adj périodique || s publication f périodique
peripheral [pə'rıfərəl] adj périphérique
peripher·y [pə'rıfəri] s (pl -ies) périphérie f
periscope ['perı,skop] s périscope m
perish ['perıʃ] intr périr
perishable ['perıʃəbəl] adj périssable
perjure ['pʌrdʒər] tr—to perjure oneself se parjurer
perju·ry ['pʌrdʒəri] s (pl -ries) parjure m
perk [pʌrk] tr—to perk up (the head) redresser; (the ears) dresser; (the appetite) ravigoter || intr—to perk up se ranimer
permanence ['pʌrmənəns] s permanence f
permanent ['pʌrmənənt] adj permanent || s permanente f
per'manent address' s domicile m fixe
per'manent ten'ure s inamovibilité f
per'manent wave' s ondulation f permanente
per'manent way' s (rr) matériel m fixe
permeate ['pʌrmı,et] tr & intr pénétrer
permissible [pər'mısıbəl] adj permis
permission [pər'mıʃən] s permission f
per-mit ['pʌrmıt] s permis m; (com) passavant m || [pər'mıt] v (pret & pp -mitted; ger -mitting) tr permettre; to permit s.o. to permettre à qn de
permute [pər'mjut] tr permuter
pernicious [pər'nıʃəs] adj pernicieux
pernickety [pər'nıkıti] adj (coll) pointilleux
perox'ide blonde' [pər'aksaıd] s blonde f décolorée
perpendicular [,pʌrpən'dıkjələr] adj & s perpendiculaire f
perpetrate ['pʌrpı,tret] tr perpétrer
perpetual [pər'petʃʊ·əl] adj perpétuel
perpetuate [pər'petʃʊ,et] tr perpétuer
perplex [pər'pleks] tr rendre perplexe
perplexed [pər'plekst] adj perplexe
perplexi·ty [pər'pleksıti] s (pl -ties) perplexité f
persecute ['pʌrsı,kjut] tr persécuter
persecution [,pʌrsı'kjuʃən] s persécution f
persevere [,pʌrsı'vır] intr persévérer
Persian ['pʌrʒən] adj persan || s (language) persan m; (person) Persan m
Per'sian blind' s persienne f
Per'sian Gulf' s Golfe m Persique
Per'sian rug' s tapis m de Perse
persimmon [pər'sımən] s plaquemine f; (tree) plaqueminier m
persist [pər'sıst], [pər'zıst] intr persister; to persist in persister dans; + ger persister à + inf
persistent [pər'sıstənt], [pər'zıstənt] adj persistant

person ['pʌrsən] s personne f; no person personne; per person par personne, chacun
personage ['pʌrsənıdʒ] s personnage m
personal ['pʌrsənəl] adj personnel || s (journ) note f dans la chronique mondaine
personali·ty [,pʌrsə'nælıti] s (pl -ties) personnalité f
per'sonal prop'erty s biens mpl mobiliers
personi·fy [pər'sanı,faı] v (pret & pp -fied) tr personnifier
personnel [,pʌrsə'nel] s personnel m
per'son-to-per'son tel'ephone call' s communication f avec préavis
perspective [pər'spektıv] s perspective f
perspicacious [,pʌrspı'keʃəs] adj perspicace
perspiration [,pʌrspı'reʃən] s transpiration f
perspire [pər'spaır] intr transpirer
persuade [pər'swed] tr persuader; to persuade s.o. of s.th. persuader q.ch. à qn, persuader qn de q.ch.; to persuade s.o. to persuader à qn de
persuasion [pər'sweʒən] s persuasion f; (faith) (coll) croyance f
pert [pʌrt] adj effronté; (sprightly) animé
pertain [pər'ten] intr—to pertain to avoir rapport à
pertinacious [,pʌrtı'neʃəs] adj obstiné, persévérant
pertinent ['pʌrtınənt] adj pertinent
perturb [pər'tʌrb] tr perturber
Peru [pə'ru] s le Pérou
peruse [pə'ruz] tr lire; lire attentivement
Peruvian [pə'ruvı·ən] adj péruvien || s Péruvien m
pervade [pər'ved] tr pénétrer, s'infiltrer dans
perverse [pər'vʌrs] adj pervers; obstiné; capricieux
perversion [pər'vʌrʒən] s perversion f
perversi·ty [pər'vʌrsıti] s (pl -ties) perversité f; obstination f
pervert ['pʌrvʌrt] s pervers m, perverti m || [pər'vʌrt] tr pervertir
pes·ky ['peski] adj (comp -kier; super -kiest) (coll) importun
pessimism ['pesı,mızəm] s pessimisme m
pessimist ['pesımıst] s pessimiste mf
pessimistic [,pesı'mıstık] adj pessimiste
pest [pest] s insecte m nuisible; (pestilence) peste f; (annoying person) raseur m
pester ['pestər] tr casser la tête à, importuner
pest'house' s lazaret m
pesticide ['pestı,saıd] s pesticide m
pestiferous [pes'tıfərəs] adj pestiféré; (coll) ennuyeux
pestilence ['pestıləns] s pestilence f
pestle ['pesəl] s pilon m
pet [pet] s animal m favori; familial m; (child) enfant m gâté; (anger) accès m de mauvaise humeur || v (pret &

pp **petted**; *ger* **petting**) *tr* choyer; (*e.g., an animal's fur*) caresser ‖ *intr* (slang) se bécoter

petal ['petəl] *s* pétale *m*

pet′cock′ *s* robinet *m* de purge

Peter ['pitər] *s* Pierre *m*; **to rob Peter to pay Paul** découvrir saint Pierre pour habiller saint Paul ‖ (*l.c.*) *intr* —**to peter out** (coll) s'épuiser, s'en aller en fumée

petition [pɪ'tɪʃən] *s* pétition *f* ‖ *tr* adresser or présenter une pétition à

pet′ name′ *s* mot *m* doux, nom *m* d'amitié

Petrarch ['pitrɑrk] *s* Pétrarque *m*

petri·fy ['petrɪ,faɪ] *v* (*pret & pp* **-fied**) *tr* pétrifier ‖ *intr* se pétrifier

petrol ['petrəl] *s* (Brit) essence *f*

petroleum [pɪ'trolɪ·əm] *s* pétrole *m*

pet′ shop′ *s* boutique *f* aux petites bêtes; (*for birds*) oisellerie *f*

petticoat ['petɪ,kot] *s* jupon *m*

pet·ty ['petɪ] *adj* (*comp* **-tier**; *super* **-tiest**) insignifiant, petit; (*narrow*) mesquin; intolérant

pet′ty cash′ *s* petite caisse *f*

pet′ty expen′ses *s* menus frais *mpl*

pet′ty lar′ceny *s* vol *m* simple

pet′ty of′ficer *s* (naut) officier *m* marinier

petulant ['petjələnt] *adj* irritable, boudeur

pew [pju] *s* banc *m* d'église

pewter ['pjutər] *s* étain *m*

Pfc. ['pi'ef'si] *s* (letterword) (*private first class*) soldat *m* de première

phalanx ['felæŋks], ['fælæŋks] *s* phalange *f*

phantasm ['fæntæzəm] *s* fantasme *m*

phantom ['fæntəm] *s* fantôme *m*

Pharaoh ['fero] *s* Pharaon *m*

pharisee ['færɪ,si] *s* pharisien *m*; **Pharisee** Pharisien *m*

pharmaceutical [,fɑrmə'sutɪkəl] *adj* pharmaceutique

pharmacist ['fɑrməsɪst] *s* pharmacien *m*

pharma·cy ['fɑrməsi] *s* (*pl* **-cies**) pharmacie *f*

pharynx ['færɪŋks] *s* pharynx *m*

phase [fez] *s* phase *f*; **out of phase** (*said of motor*) décalé ‖ *tr* mettre en phase; développer en phases successives; (coll) inquiéter; **to phase out** faire disparaître peu à peu

pheasant ['fezənt] *s* faisan *m*

phenobarbital [,fino'bɑrbɪ,tæl] *s* phénobarbital *m*

phenomenal [fɪ'nɑmɪ,nəl] *adj* phénoménal

phenome·non [fɪ'nɑmɪ,nɑn] *s* (*pl* **-na** [nə]) phénomène *m*

phial ['faɪ·əl] *s* fiole *f*

philanderer [fɪ'lændərər] *s* coureur *m*, galant *m*

philanthropist [fɪ'lænθrəpɪst] *s* philanthrope *mf*

philanthro·py [fɪ'lænθrəpi] *s* (*pl* **-pies**) philanthropie *f*

philatelist [fɪ'lætəlɪst] *s* philatéliste *mf*

philately [fɪ'lætəli] *s* philatélie *f*

Philippine ['fɪlɪ,pin] *adj* philippin ‖ **Philippines** *spl* Philippines *fpl*

Philistine [fɪ'lɪstin], ['fɪlɪ,stin], ['fɪlɪ,staɪn] *adj & s* philistin *m*

philologist [fɪ'lɑlədʒɪst] *s* philologue *mf*

philology [fɪ'lɑlədʒi] *s* philologie *f*

philosopher [fɪ'lɑsəfər] *s* philosophe *mf*

philosophic(al) [,frlə'sɑfɪk(əl)] *adj* philosophique

philoso·phy [fɪ'lɑsəfi] *s* (*pl* **-phies**) philosophie *f*

philter ['fɪltər] *s* philtre *m*

phlebitis [flɪ'baɪtɪs] *s* phlébite *f*

phlegm [flem] *s* flegme *m*; **to cough up phlegm** cracher des glaires, tousser gras

phlegmatic(al) [fleg'mætɪk(əl)] *adj* flegmatique

phobia ['fobɪ·ə] *s* phobie *f*

Phoebe ['fibi] *s* Phébé *f*

Phoenicia [fɪ'nɪʃə], [fɪ'niʃə] *s* Phénicie *f*; la Phénicie

Phoenician [fɪ'nɪʃən], [fɪ'niʃən] *adj* phénicien ‖ *s* Phénicien *m*

phoenix ['finɪks] *s* phénix *m*

phone [fon] *s* (coll) téléphone *m* ‖ *tr & intr* (coll) téléphoner

phone′ call′ *s* coup *m* de téléphone, coup de fil

phonetic [fo'netɪk] *adj* phonétique ‖ **phonetics** *s* phonétique *f*

phonograph ['fonə,græf], ['fonə,grɑf] *s* phonographe *m*

phonology [fə'nɑlədʒi] *s* phonologie *f*

pho·ny ['foni] *adj* (*comp* **-nier**; *super* **-niest**) faux, truqué ‖ *s* (*pl* **-nies**) charlatan *m*

pho′ny war′ *s* drôle *f* de guerre

phosphate ['fɑsfet] *s* phosphate *m*

phosphorescent [,fɑsfə'resənt] *adj* phosphorescent

phospho·rus ['fɑsfərəs] *s* (*pl* **-ri** [,raɪ]) phosphore *m*

pho·to ['foto] *s* (*pl* **-tos**) (coll) photo *f*

photoengraving [,foto·en'grevɪŋ] *s* photogravure *f*

pho′to fin′ish *s* photo-finish *f*

photogenic [,foto'dʒenɪk] *adj* photogénique

photograph ['fotə,græf], ['fotə,grɑf] *s* photographie *f* ‖ *tr* photographier ‖ *intr*—**to photograph well** être photogénique

photographer [fə'tɑgrəfər] *s* photographe *mf*

photography [fə'tɑgrəfi] *s* photographie *f*

photostat ['fotə,stæt] *s* (trademark) photostat *m* ‖ *tr & intr* photocopier

phrase [frez] *s* locution *f*, expression *f*; (mus) phrase *f* ‖ *tr* exprimer, rédiger; (mus) phraser

phrenology [frɪ'nɑlədʒi] *s* phrénologie *f*

phys·ic ['fɪzɪk] *s* médicament *m*; (*laxative*) purgatif *m* ‖ *v* (*pret & pp* **-icked**; *ger* **-icking**) *tr* purger

physical ['fɪzɪkəl] *adj* physique

phys′ical de′fect *s* vice *m* de conformation

physician [fɪ'zɪʃən] *s* médecin *m*

physicist ['fɪzɪsɪst] *s* physicien *m*

physics ['fɪzɪks] s physique f
physiogno·my [,fɪzɪ'ɑgnəmɪ], [,fɪzɪ-'ɑnəmɪ] s (pl -mies) physionomie f
physiological [,fɪzɪ·ə'lɑdʒɪkəl] adj physiologique
physiology [,fɪzɪ'ɑlədʒɪ] s physiologie f
physique [fɪ'zik] s physique m
pi [paɪ] s (math) pi m; (typ) pâté m || v (pret & pp pied; ger piing) tr (typ) mettre en pâte
pianist [pɪ'ænɪst], ['pi·ənɪst] s pianiste mf
pian·o [pɪ'æno] s (pl -os) piano m
pian/o stool/ s tabouret m de piano
picayune [,pɪkə'jun] adj mesquin
picco·lo ['pɪkəlo] s (pl -los) piccolo m
pick [prk] s (tool) pic m, pioche f; (choice) choix m; (choicest) élite f, fleur f || tr choisir; (flowers) cueillir; (fibers) effiler; (one's teeth, nose, etc.) se curer; (a scab) gratter; (a fowl) plumer; (a bone) ronger; (a lock) crocheter; (the ground) piocher; (e.g., guitar strings) toucher; (a quarrel; flaws) chercher; to pick off enlever; (to shoot) descendre; to pick out trier; to pick pockets voler à la tire; to pick to pieces (coll) éplucher; to pick up ramasser; (one's strength) reprendre; (speed) accroître; (a passenger) prendre; (a man overboard) recueillir; (an anchor; a stitch; a fallen child) relever; (information; a language) apprendre; (the scent) retrouver; (rad) capter || intr (said of birds) picorer; to pick at (to scold) (coll) gronder; to pick at one's food manger du bout des dents; to pick on choisir; (coll) gronder; to pick up (coll) se rétablir
pick/ax/ s pioche f
picket ['pɪkɪt] s (stake, pale) pieu m; (of strikers; of soldiers) piquet m || tr entourer de piquets de grève || intr faire le piquet
pick/et fence/ s palis m
pick/et line/ s piquet m de grève
pickle ['pɪkəl] s cornichon m; (brine) marinade f, saumure f; (coll) gâchis m || tr conserver dans du vinaigre
pick/lock/ s crochet m; (person) crocheteur m
pick/-me-up/ s (coll) remontant m
pick/pock/et s voleur m à la tire
pick/up/ s chargement m; passager m; (of a motor) reprise f; (truck; phonograph cartridge) pick-up m; (woman) (coll) racoleuse f
pick/up arm/ s bras m de pick-up
pick/up truck/ s camionnette f
pic·nic ['pɪknɪk] s pique-nique m || v (pret & pp -nicked; ger -nicking) intr pique-niquer
pictorial [pɪk'torɪ·əl] adj & s illustré m
picture ['pɪktʃər] s tableau m; image f; photographie f; (painting) peinture f; (engraving) gravure f; (mov) film m; (screen) (mov, telv) écran m; the very picture of le portrait de, l'image de; to receive the picture (telv) capter l'image || tr dépeindre, représenter; to picture to oneself s'imaginer

pic/ture gal/lery s musée m de peinture
pic/ture post/ card/ s carte f postale illustrée
pic/ture show/ s exhibition f de peinture; (mov) cinéma m
pic/ture sig/nal s signal m vidéo
picturesque [,pɪktʃə'rɛsk] adj pittoresque
pic/ture tube/ s tube m de l'image
pic/ture win/dow s fenêtre f panoramique
piddling ['pɪdlɪŋ] adj insignifiant
pie [paɪ] s pâté m; (dessert) tarte f; (bird) pie f
piece [pis] s (of music; of bread) morceau m; (cannon, coin, chessman, pastry, clothing) pièce f; (of land) parcelle f; (e.g., of glass) éclat m; a piece of advice un conseil; a piece of furniture un meuble; to break into pieces mettre en pièces, mettre en morceaux; to give s.o. a piece of one's mind (coll) dire son fait à qn; to go to pieces se désagréger; (to be hysterical) avoir ses nerfs; to pick to pieces (coll) éplucher || tr rapiécer; to piece together rassembler, coordonner
piece/meal/ adv pièce à pièce
piece/work/ s travail m à la tâche
piece/work/er s ouvrier m à la tâche
pied [paɪd] adj bigarré, panaché; (typ) tombé en pâte
pier [pɪr] s quai m; (of a bridge) pile f; (of a harbor) jetée f; (wall between two openings) (archit) trumeau m
pierce [pɪrs] tr & intr percer
piercing ['pɪrsɪŋ] adj perçant; (sharp) aigu
pier/ glass/ s grand miroir m
pie·ty ['paɪ·ətɪ] s (pl -ties) piété f
piffle ['pɪfəl] s (coll) futilités fpl, sottises fpl
pig [pɪg] s cochon m, porc m
pigeon ['pɪdʒən] s pigeon m
pi/geon·hole/ s boulin m; (in desk) case f || tr caser; mettre au rancart
pi/geon house/ s pigeonnier m
piggish ['pɪgɪʃ] adj goinfre
piggyback ['pɪgɪ,bæk] adv sur le dos, sur les epaules; en auto-couchette
pig/gy bank/ ['pɪgɪ] s tirelire f, grenouille f
pig/-head/ed adj cabochard, têtu
pig/ i/ron s gueuse f
piglet ['pɪglɪt] s cochonnet m
pigment ['pɪgmənt] s pigment m
pig/pen/ s porcherie f
pig/skin/ s peau f de porc; (coll) ballon m du football
pig/sty/ s (pl -sties) porcherie f
pig/tail/ s queue f, natte f; (of tobacco) carotte f
pike [paɪk] s pique f; autoroute f à péage; (fish) brochet m
piker ['paɪkər] s (slang) rat m
pile [paɪl] s tas m; (stake) pieu m; (of rug) poil m; (of building) masse f; (elec, phys) pile f; (coll) fortune f
piles (pathol) hémorroïdes fpl || tr empiler || intr s'empiler
pile/ dri/ver s sonnette f

pilfer ['pɪlfər] *tr & intr* chaparder
pilgrim ['pɪlgrɪm] *s* pèlerin *m*
pilgrimage ['pɪlgrɪmɪdʒ] *s* pèlerinage *m*
pill [pɪl] *s* pilule *f*; (*something unpleasant*) pilule; (*coll*) casse-pieds *m*
pillage ['pɪlɪdʒ] *s* pillage *m* || *tr & intr* piller
pillar ['pɪlər] *s* pilier *m*
pillory ['pɪləri] *s* (*pl* -ries) pilori *m* || *v* (*pret & pp* -ried) *tr* clouer au pilori
pillow ['pɪlo] *s* oreiller *m*
pil'low-case' *or* **pil'low-slip'** *s* taie *f* d'oreiller
pilot ['paɪlət] *s* pilote *m*; (*of gas range*) veilleuse *f* || *tr* piloter
pi'lot en'gine *s* locomotive-pilote *f*
pi'lot light' *s* veilleuse *f*
pimp [pɪmp] *s* entremetteur *m*
pimple ['pɪmpəl] *s* bouton *m*
pim·ply ['pɪmpli] *adj* (*comp* -plier; *super* -pliest) boutonneux
pin [pɪn] *s* épingle *f*; (*of wearing apparel*) agrafe *f*; (*bowling*) quille *f*; (*mach*) clavette *f*, cheville *f*, goupille *f*; **to be on pins and needles** être sur les chardons ardents || *v* (*pret & pp* pinned; *ger* pinning) *tr* épingler; (*mach*) cheviller, goupiller; **to pin down** fixer, clouer
pinafore ['pɪnə,for] *s* tablier *m* d'enfant
pin'ball' *s* billard *m* américain
pincers ['pɪnsərz] *s & spl* pinces *fpl*
pinch [pɪntʃ] *s* pinçade *f*; (*of salt*) pincée *f*; (*of tobacco*) prise *f*; (*of hunger*) morsure *f*; (*trying time*) moment *m* critique; (*slang*) arrestation *f*; **in a pinch** au besoin || *tr* pincer; (*to press tightly on*) serrer; (*e.g., one's finger in a door*) se prendre; (*to arrest*) (*slang*) pincer; (*to steal*) (*slang*) chiper || *intr* (*said, e.g., of shoe*) gêner; (*to save*) lésiner
pinchers ['pɪntʃərz] *s & spl* pinces *fpl*
pin'cush'ion *s* pelote *f* d'épingles
pine [paɪn] *s* pin *m* || *intr* languir; **to pine for** soupirer après
pine'ap'ple *s* ananas *m*
pine' cone' *s* pomme *f* de pin
pine' nee'dle *s* aiguille *f* de pin
ping [pɪŋ] *s* sifflement *m*; (*in a motor*) cognement *m* || *intr* siffler; cogner
pin'head' *s* tête *f* d'épingle; (*coll*) crétin *m*
pink [pɪŋk] *adj* rose || *s* rose *m*; (*bot*) œillet *m*; **to be in the pink** se porter à merveille
pin' mon'ey *s* argent *m* de poche
pinnacle ['pɪnəkəl] *s* pinacle *m*
pin'point' *adj* exact *f* || *tr* situer avec précision
pin'prick' *s* piqûre *f* d'épingle
pint [paɪnt] *s* chopine *f*
pin'up girl' *s* pin up *f*
pin'wheel' *s* (*fireworks*) soleil *m*; (*child's toy*) moulinet *m*
pioneer [,paɪə'nɪr] *s* pionnier *m* || *tr* défricher || *intr* faire œuvre de pionnier
pious ['paɪ·əs] *adj* pieux, dévot
pip [pɪp] *s* (*in fruit*) pépin *m*; (*on cards, dice, etc.*) point *m*; (*rad*) top *m*; (*vet*) pépie *f*
pipe [paɪp] *s* tuyau *m*, tube *m*, conduit *m*; (*to smoke tobacco*) pipe *f*; (*of an organ*) tuyau; (*mus*) chalumeau *m* || *tr* canaliser || *intr* jouer du chalumeau; **pipe down!** (*slang*) boucle-la!
pipe' clean'er *s* cure-pipe *m*
pipe' dream' *s* rêve *m*, projet *m* illusoire
pipe' line' *s* pipe-line *m*; (*of information*) tuyau *m*
pipe' or'gan *s* grandes orgues *fpl*
piper ['paɪpər] *s* joueur *m* de chalumeau; (*bagpiper*) cornemuseur *m*; **to pay the piper** payer les violons
pipe' wrench' *s* clef *f* à tubes
piping ['paɪpɪŋ] *s* tuyauterie *f*; (*sewing*) passepoil *m*
pippin ['pɪpɪn] *s* (*apple*) reinette *f*; (*highly admired person or thing*) bijou *m*
piquancy ['pɪkənsi] *s* piquant *m*
piquant ['pɪkənt] *adj* piquant
pique [pik] *s* pique *f* || *tr* piquer; **to pique oneself on** se piquer de
pira·cy ['paɪrəsi] *s* (*pl* -cies) piraterie *f*
Piraeus [paɪ'ri·əs] *s* Le Pirée
pirate ['paɪrɪt] *s* pirate *m* || *tr* piller || *intr* pirater
pirouette [,pɪru'ɛt] *s* pirouette *f* || *intr* pirouetter
pistol ['pɪstəl] *s* pistolet *m*
piston ['pɪstən] *s* piston *m*
pis'ton ring' *s* segment *m* de piston
pis'ton rod' *s* tige *f* de piston
pis'ton stroke' *s* course *f* de piston
pitch [pɪtʃ] *s* (*black sticky substance*) poix *f*; (*throw*) lancement *m*, jet *m*; (*of a boat*) tangage *m*; (*of a roof*) degré *m* de pente; (*of, e.g., a screw*) pas *m*; (*of a tone, of the voice, etc.*) hauteur *f*; (*coll*) boniment *m*, tam-tam *m*; **to such a pitch that** à tel point que || *tr* lancer, jeter; (*hay*) fourcher; (*a tent*) dresser; enduire de poix; (*mus*) donner le ton de || *intr* (*said of boat*) tanguer; **to pitch in** (*coll*) se mettre à la besogne; (*coll*) commencer à manger; **to pitch into** s'attaquer à
pitch' ac'cent *s* accent *m* de hauteur
pitcher ['pɪtʃər] *s* broc *m*, cruche *f*; (*baseball*) lanceur *m*
pitch'fork' *s* fourche *f*; **to rain pitchforks** pleuvoir à torrents
pitch' pipe' *s* diapason *m* de bouche
pit'fall' *s* trappe *f*; (*fig*) écueil *m*, pierre *f* d'écueil
pith [pɪθ] *s* moelle *f*; (*fig*) suc *m*
pith·y ['pɪθi] *adj* (*comp* -ier; *super* -iest) moelleux; (*fig*) plein de suc
pitiful ['pɪtɪfəl] *adj* pitoyable

pitiless ['pɪtɪlɪs] adj impitoyable
pit·y ['pɪti] s (pl -ies) pitié f; **for pity's sake!** par pitié!; **what a pity!** quel dommage! || v (pret & pp -ied) tr avoir pitié de, plaindre
pivot ['pɪvət] s pivot m || tr faire pivoter || intr pivoter
placard ['plækərd] s placard m, affiche f || tr placarder
placate ['pleket] tr apaiser
place [ples] s endroit m; (job) poste m, emploi m; (seat) place f; (rank) rang m; **everything in its place** chaque chose à sa place; **in no place** nulle part; **in place of** au lieu de; **in your place** à votre place; **out of place** déplacé; **to change places** changer de place; **to keep one's place** (fig) tenir ses distances; **to take place** avoir lieu || tr mettre, placer; (to find a job for; to invest) placer; (to recall) remettre, se rappeler; (to set down) poser || intr (turf) finir placé
place·bo [plə'sibo] s (pl -bos or -boes) remède m factice
place′ card′ s marque-place f, carton m marque-place
place′ mat′ s garde-nappe m
placement ['plesmənt] s placement m; (location) emplacement m
place′ment exam′ s examen m probatoire
place′-name′ s nom m de lieu, toponyme m
placid ['plæsɪd] adj placide
plagiarism ['pledʒə‚rɪzəm] s plagiat m
plagiarize ['pledʒə‚raɪz] tr plagier
plague [pleg] s peste f; (great public calamity) fléau m || tr tourmenter
plaid [plæd] s plaid m
plain [plen] adj clair; simple; (e.g., answer) franc; (color) uni; (ugly) sans attraits || s plaine f
plain′ clothes′ spl—**in plain clothes** en civil, en bourgeois
plain′-clothes′man′ s (pl -men′) agent m en civil
plain′ cook′ing s cuisine f bourgeoise
plain′ om′elet s omelette f nature
plain′ speech′ s franc-parler m
plaintiff ['plentɪf] s (law) demandeur m, plaignant m
plaintive ['plentɪv] adj plaintif
plan [plæn] s plan m, projet m; (drawing, diagram) plan, dessein m || v (pret & pp planned; ger planning) tr projeter; **to plan to** se proposer de || intr faire des projets
plane [plen] adj plan, plat || s (aer) avion m; (bot) platane m; (carpentry) rabot m; (geom) plan m || tr raboter
plane′ sick′ness s mal m de l'air
planet ['plænɪt] s planète f
plane′ tree′ s platane m
plan′ing mill′ s atelier m de rabotage
plank [plæŋk] s planche f; (pol) article m d'une plate-forme électorale
plant [plænt], [plɑnt] s (factory) usine f; (building and equipment) installation f; (bot) plante f || tr planter

plantation [plæn'teʃən] s plantation f
planter ['plæntər] s planteur m
plant′ louse′ s puceron m
plasma ['plæzmə] s plasma m
plaster ['plæstər], ['plɑstər] s plâtre m; (poultice) emplâtre m || tr plâtrer; (a bill, poster) coller; (slang) griser
plas′ter cast′ s plâtre m
plas′ter of Par′is s plâtre m à mouler
plastic ['plæstɪk] adj plastique || s (substance) plastique m; (art) plastique f
plas′tic bomb′ s plastic m
plas′tic sur′gery s chirurgie f esthétique, chirurgie f plastique
plate [plet] s (dish) assiette f; (platter) plateau m; (sheet of metal) tôle f, plaque f; vaisselle f d'or ou d'argent; (anat, elec, phot, rad, zool) plaque; (typ) planche f || tr plaquer; (elec) galvaniser; (typ) clicher
plateau [plæ'to] s plateau m, massif m
plate′ glass′ s verre m cylindré
platen ['plætən] s rouleau m
platform ['plæt‚fɔrm] s plate-forme f; (for arrivals and departures) quai m; (of a speaker) estrade f; (political program) plate-forme
plat′form car′ s (rr) plate-forme f
platinum ['plætɪnəm] s platine m
plat′inum blonde′ s blonde f platinée
platitude ['plætɪ‚t(j)ud] s platitude f
Plato ['pleto] s Platon m
platoon [plə'tun] s section f
platter ['plætər] s plat m; (slang) disque m
plausible ['plɔzɪbəl] adj plausible
play [ple] s jeu m; (drama) pièce f; (mach) jeu; **to give full play to** donner libre cours à || tr jouer; (e.g., the fool) faire; (cards; e.g., football) jouer à; (an instrument) jouer de; **to play back** (a tape) faire repasser; **to play down** diminuer; **to play hooky** faire l'école buissonnière; **to play off** (sports) rejouer; **to play out** s'épuiser || intr jouer; **to play out** s'épuiser; **to play safe** prendre des précautions; **to play sick** faire semblant d'être malade; **to play up to** passer de la pommade à
play′back′ s (device) lecteur m; (reproduction) lecture f
play′back head′ s tête f de lecture
play′bill′ s programme m; (poster) affiche f
play′er pian′o ['ple-ər] s piano m mécanique
playful ['plefəl] adj enjoué, badin
playgoer ['ple‚go-ər] s amateur m de théâtre
play′ground′ s terrain m de jeu
play′house′ s théâtre m; (dollhouse) maison f de poupée
play′ing card′ s carte f à jouer
play′ing field′ s terrain m de sports
play′mate′ s compagnon m de jeu
play′-off′ s finale f, match m d'appui
play′ on words′ s jeu m de mots
play′pen′ s parc m d'enfants
play′room′ s salle f de jeux
play′thing′ s jouet m

play'time' s recréation f
playwright ['ple_raɪt] s auteur m dramatique, dramaturge mf
play'writ'ing s dramaturgie f
plea [pli] s requête f, appel m; prétexte m; (law) défense f
plead [plid] v (pret & pp **pleaded** or **pled** [pled]) tr & intr plaider; **to plead not guilty** plaider non coupable
pleasant ['plezənt] adj agréable
pleasant·ry ['plezəntri] s (pl -ries) plaisanterie f
please [pliz] tr plaire (with dat); **it pleases him to** il lui plaît de; **please** + inf veuillez + inf; **to be pleased with** être content ou satisfait de || intr plaire; **as you please** comme vous voulez; **if you please** s'il vous plaît
pleasing ['plizɪŋ] adj agréable
pleasure ['plezər] s plaisir m; **at the pleasure of** au gré de; **what is your pleasure?** qu'y a-t-il pour votre service?, que puis-je faire pour vous?
pleas'ure car' s voiture f de tourisme
pleas'ure trip' s voyage m d'agrément
pleat [plit] s pli m || tr plisser
plebe [plib] s élève m de première année
plebeian [plɪ'bi·ən] adj & s plébéien m
plebiscite ['plebɪ_saɪt] s plébiscite m
pledge [pledʒ] s gage m; engagement m d'honneur, promesse f || tr mettre en gage; **(one's word)** engager
plentiful ['plentɪfəl] adj abondant
plenty ['plenti] s abondance f; **plenty of** beaucoup de || adv (coll) largement
pleurisy ['plʊrɪsi] s pleurésie f
pliable ['plaɪ·əbəl] adj pliable; docile, maniable
pliers ['plaɪ·ərz] s & spl pinces fpl, tenailles fpl
plight [plaɪt] s embarras m; (promise) engagement m || tr engager; **to plight one's troth** promettre fidélité
plod [plad] v (pret & pp **plodded**; ger **plodding**) tr parcourir lourdement et péniblement || intr cheminer; travailler laborieusement
plot [plat] s complot m; (of a play or novel) intrigue f; (of ground) lopin m, parcelle f; (map) tracé m, plan m; (of vegetables) carré m || v (pret & pp **plotted**; ger **plotting**) tr comploter, tramer; (a tract of land) faire le plan de; (a point) relever; (lines) tracer || intr comploter; **to plot to** + inf comploter de + inf
plough [plaʊ] s, tr & intr var of **plow**
plover ['plʌvər], ['plovər] s pluvier m
plow [plaʊ] s charrue f; (for snow) chasse-neige m || tr labourer; (the sea; the forehead) sillonner; (snow) déblayer; **to plow back** (com) affecter aux investissements || intr labourer; **to plow through** avancer péniblement dans
plow'man s (pl -men) laboureur m
plow'share' s soc m de charrue
pluck [plʌk] s cran m; (tug) saccade f || tr arracher; (flowers) cueillir; (a fowl) plumer; (one's eyebrows)

épiler; (e.g., the strings of a guitar) pincer || intr—**to pluck at** arracher d'un coup sec; **to pluck up** reprendre courage
pluck·y ['plʌki] adj (comp **-ier**; super **-iest**) courageux, crâne
plug [plʌg] s tampon m, bouchon m; (of sink, bathtub, etc.) bonde f; (of tobacco) chique f; (aut) bougie f; (on wall) (elec) prise f; (prongs) (elec) fiche f, prise; (old horse) (coll) rosse f; (hat) (coll) haut-de-forme m; (slang) annonce f publicitaire || v (pret & pp **plugged**; ger **plugging**) tr boucher; (a melon) entamer; **to plug in** (elec) brancher || intr—**to plug away** (coll) persévérer
plum [plʌm] s prune f; (tree) prunier m; (slang) fromage m
plumage ['plumɪdʒ] s plumage m
plumb [plʌm] adj d'aplomb; (coll) pur || s plomb m; **out of plumb** hors d'aplomb || adv d'aplomb; (coll) en plein; (coll) complètement || tr sonder
plumb' bob' s plomb m
plumber ['plʌmər] s plombier m
plumbing ['plʌmɪŋ] s plomberie f
plumb' line' s fil m à plomb
plume [plum] s aigrette f; (of a hat, of smoke, etc.) panache m || tr orner de plumes; (feathers) lisser; **to plume oneself on** se piquer de
plummet ['plʌmɪt] s plomb m || intr tomber d'aplomb, se précipiter
plump [plʌmp] adj grassouillet, potelé, dodu; brusque || s (coll) chute f lourde; (coll) bruit m sourd || adv en plein; brusquement || tr jeter brusquement; **to plump oneself down** s'affaler || intr tomber lourdement
plunder ['plʌndər] s pillage m; (booty) butin m || tr piller
plunge [plʌndʒ] s plongeon m; (pitching movement) tangage m || tr plonger || intr plonger; se précipiter; (fig) se plonger; (naut) tanguer; (slang) risquer de grosses sommes
plunger ['plʌndʒər] s plongeur m; (slang) risque-tout m
plunk [plʌŋk] adv d'un coup sec; (squarely) carrément || tr jeter bruyamment || intr tomber raide
plural ['plʊrəl] adj & s pluriel m
plus [plʌs] adj positif || s (sign) plus m; quantité f positive || prep plus
plush [plʌʃ] s en peluche; (coll) rupin || s peluche f
plush·y ['plʌʃi] adj (comp **-ier**; super **-iest**) pelucheux; (coll) rupin
plus' sign' s signe m plus
Plutarch ['plutark] s Plutarque m
Pluto ['pluto] s Pluton m
plutonium [plu'toni·əm] s plutonium m
ply [plaɪ] s (pl **plies**) (e.g., of a cloth) pli m; (of rope, wool, etc.) brin m || v (pret & pp **plied**; ger **plying**) tr manier; (a trade) exercer; **to ply s.o. with** presser qn de || intr faire la navette
ply'wood' s bois m de placage, contreplaqué m

P.M. ['pi'em] *adv* (letterword) (*post meridiem*) de l'après-midi, du soir

pneumatic-[n(j)u'mætɪk] *adj* pneumatique

pneumat'ic drill' *s* foreuse *f* à air comprimé

pneumonia [n(j)u'monɪ'ə] *s* pneumonie *f*

P.O. ['pi'o] *s* (letterword) (*post office*) poste *f*

poach [potʃ] *tr* (*eggs*) pocher ‖ *intr* (*hunting*) braconner

poached' egg' *s* œuf *m* poché

poacher ['potʃər] *s* braconnier *m*

pock [pɑk] *s* pustule *f*

pocket ['pɑkɪt] *s* poche *f*; (billiards) blouse *f*; (aer) trou *m* d'air ‖ *tr* empocher; (*a billiard ball*) blouser; (*insults*) avaler

pock'et-book' *s* portefeuille *m*; (*small book*) livre *m* de poche

pock'et hand'kerchief *s* mouchoir *m* de poche

pock'et-knife' *s* (*pl* -knives) couteau *m* de poche, canif *m*

pock'et mon'ey *s* argent *m* de poche

pock'mark' *s* marque *f* de la petite vérole

pock'marked' *adj* grêlé

pod [pɑd] *s* cosse *f*, gousse *f*

poem ['po·ɪm] *s* poème *m*

poet ['po·ɪt] *s* poète *m*

poetess ['po·ɪtɪs] *s* poétesse *f*

poetic ['po·ɛtɪk] *adj* poétique ‖ **poetics** *s* poétique *f*

poetry ['po·ɪtri] *s* poésie *f*

pogrom ['pogrəm] *s* pogrom *m*

poignancy ['pɔɪnənsi] *s* piquant *m*

poignant ['pɔɪnənt] *adj* poignant

point [pɔɪnt] *s* (*spot, dot, score, etc.*) point *m*; (*tip*) pointe *f*; (*of pen*) bec *m*; (*of conscience*) cas *m*; (*of a star*) rayon *m*; (*of a joke*) piquant *m*; (*of, e.g., grammar*) question *f*; (geog, naut) pointe *f*; (typ) point *m*; **beside the point**, **off the point** hors de propos; **on the point of** sur le point de; (*death*) à l'article de; **on this point** à cet égard, à ce propos; **point of a compass** aire *f* de vent; **point of order** rappel *m* au règlement; **points** (aut) vis *f* platinées; **to carry one's point** avoir gain de cause; **to come to the point** venir au fait; **to have one's good points** avoir ses qualités; **to make a point of** se faire un devoir de ‖ *tr* (*a gun, telescope, etc.*) braquer, pointer; (*a finger*) tendre; (*the way*) indiquer; (*a wall*) jointoyer; (*to sharpen*) tailler en pointe; **to point out** signaler, faire remarquer ‖ *intr* pointer; (*said of hunting dog*) tomber en arrêt; **to point at** montrer du doigt

point'-blank' *adj & adv* (*fired straight at the mark*) à bout portant; (*straightforward*) à brûle-pourpoint

pointed *adj* pointu; (*remark*) mordant

pointer ['pɔɪntər] *s* (*stick*) baguette *f*; (*of a dial*) aiguille *f*; (*dog*) chien *m* d'arrêt, pointeur *m*

poise [pɔɪz] *s* équilibre *m*; (*assurance*)

---

aplomb *m* ‖ *tr* tenir en équilibre ‖ *intr* être en équilibre; (*in the air*) planer

poison ['pɔɪzən] *s* poison *m* ‖ *tr* empoisonner

poi'son gas' *s* gaz *m* asphyxiant

poi'son i'vy *s* sumac *m* vénéneux

poisonous ['pɔɪzənəs] *adj* toxique; (*plant*) vénéneux; (*snake*) venimeux

poke [pok] *s* poussée *f*; (*with elbow*) coup *m* de coude; (coll) traînard *m* ‖ *tr* pousser; (*the fire*) tisonner; **to poke fun at** se moquer de; **to poke one's nose into** (coll) fourrer son nez dans; **to poke s.th. into** fourrer q.ch. dans ‖ *intr* aller sans se presser; **to poke about** fureter

poker ['pokər] *s* tisonnier *m*; (cards) poker *m*

pok'er face' *s* visage *m* impassible

pok·y ['poki] *adj* (*comp* -ier; *super* -iest) (coll) lambin, lent

Poland ['poland] *s* Pologne *f*; la Pologne

polar ['polər] *adj* polaire

po'lar bear' *s* ours *m* blanc

polarize ['polə,raɪz] *tr* polariser

pole [pol] *s* (*long rod or staff*) perche *f*; (*of flag*) hampe *f*; (*upright support*) poteau *m*; (astr, biol, elec, geog, math) pôle *m*; **Pole** (*person*) Polonais *m* ‖ *tr* pousser à la perche

pole'cat' *s* putois *m*

pole'star' *s* étoile *f* polaire

pole' vault' *s* saut *m* à la perche

police [pə'lis] *s* police *f* ‖ *tr* maintenir l'ordre dans

police' brutal'ity *s* brutalité *f* policière

police' commis'sioner *s* préfet *m* de police

police'man *s* (*pl* -men) agent *m* de police

police' pre'cinct *s* commissariat *m* de police

police' state' *s* régime *m* policier

police' sta'tion *s* poste *m* de police, commissariat *m*

police'wom'an *s* (*pl* -wom'en) femme *f* agent

pol·i·cy ['pɑlɪsi] *s* (*pl* -cies) politique *f*; (ins) police *f*

polio ['polɪ,o] *s* (coll) polio *f*

polish ['pɑlɪʃ] *s* poli *m*; (*for household uses*) cire *f*; (*for shoes*) cirage *m*; (fig) politesse *f*, vernis *m* ‖ *tr* polir; (*shoes, floor, etc.*) cirer; (*one's nails*) vernir; **to polish off** (coll) expédier; (*e.g., a meal*) (slang) engloutir ‖ **Polish** ['polɪʃ] *adj & s* polonais *m*

polite [pə'laɪt] *adj* poli

politeness [pə'laɪtnɪs] *s* politesse *f*

politic ['pɑlɪtɪk] *adj* (*prudent*) diplomatique, politique; (*shrewd*) rusé

political [pə'lɪtɪkəl] *adj* politique

politician [,pɑlɪ'tɪʃən] *s* politicien *m*

politics ['pɑlɪtɪks] *s & spl* politique *f*

poll [pol] *s* liste *f* électorale; (*vote*) scrutin *m*; (*head*) tête *f*; sondage *m* d'opinion; **to go to the polls** aller aux urnes; **to take a poll** faire une enquête par sondage ‖ *tr* (*e.g., a dele-*

gation) dépouiller le scrutin de; *(a certain number of votes)* recevoir

pollen ['palən] *s* pollen *m*

poll'ing booth' ['polɪŋ] *s* isoloir *m*

polliwog ['palɪ,wag] *s* têtard *m*

pol'liwog initia'tion *s* baptême *m* de la ligne

poll' tax' *s* taxe *f* par tête

pollute [pə'lut] *tr* polluer

pollution [pə'luʃən] *s* pollution *f*

polo ['polo] *s* polo *m*

polonium [pə'lonɪ-əm] *s* polonium *m*

polygamist [pə'lɪgəmɪst] *s* polygame *mf*

polygamous [pə'lɪgəməs] *adj* polygame

polyglot ['palɪ,glat] *adj & s* polyglotte *mf*

polygon ['palɪ,gan] *s* polygone *m*

polynomial [,palɪ'nomɪ-əl] *s* polynôme *m*

polyp ['palɪp] *s* polype *m*

polytheist ['palɪ,θi-ɪst] *s* polythéiste *mf*

polytheistic [,palɪθi'ɪstɪk] *adj* polythéiste

pomade [pə'med], [pə'mad] *s* pommade *f*

pomegranate ['pam,grænɪt] *s (shrub)* grenadier *m*; *(fruit)* grenade *f*

pom-mel ['pʌmǝl], ['paməl] *s* pommeau *m* ‖ *v (pret & pp* -meled or -melled; *ger* -meling or -melling) *tr* rosser

pomp [pamp] *s* pompe *f*

pompous ['pampəs] *adj* pompeux

pon-cho ['pantʃo] *s (pl* -chos) poncho *m*

pond [pand] *s* étang *m*, mare *f*

ponder ['pandər] *tr* peser ‖ *intr* méditer; **to ponder over** réfléchir sur

ponderous ['pandərəs] *adj* pesant

poniard ['panjərd] *s* poignard *m* ‖ *tr* poignarder

pontiff ['pantɪf] *s* pontife *m*

pontifical [pan'tɪfɪkəl] *adj (e.g., air)* de pontife

pontoon [pan'tun] *s* ponton *m*

po·ny ['poni] *s (pl* -nies) poney *m*; *(for drinking liquor)* petit verre *m*; *(coll)* aide-mémoire *m* illicite

poodle ['pudǝl] *s* caniche *m*

pool [pul] *s (small puddle)* mare *f*; *(for swimming)* piscine *f*; *(game)* billard *m*; *(in certain games)* poule *f*; *(of workers)* équipe *f*; *(combine)* pool *m*; *(com)* fonds *m* commun ‖ *tr* mettre en commun

pool'room' *s* salle *f* de billard

pool' ta'ble *s* table *f* de billard

poop [pup] *s* poupe *f*; *(deck)* dunette *f* ‖ *tr (slang)* casser la tête à

poor [pur] *adj* pauvre; *(mediocre)* piètre; *(unfortunate)* pauvre *(before noun)*; *(without money)* pauvre *(after noun)*

poor' box' *s* tronc *m* des pauvres

poor'house' *s* asile *m* des indigents

poorly ['purlɪ] *adj* souffrant ‖ *adv* mal

pop [pap] *s* bruit *m* sec; *(soda)* boisson *f* gazeuse ‖ *v (pret & pp* popped; *ger* popping) *tr (corn)* faire éclater ‖ *intr*

(said, e.g., of balloon) crever; *(said of cork)* sauter

pop'corn' *s* maïs *m* éclaté, grains *mpl* de maïs soufflés, pop-corn *m*

pope [pop] *s* pape *m*

pop'-eyed' *adj* aux yeux saillants

pop'gun' *s* canonnière *f*

poplar ['paplər] *s* peuplier *m*

pop·py ['papɪ] *s (pl* -pies) pavot *m*; *(corn poppy)* coquelicot *m*

pop'py-cock' *s (coll)* fadaises *fpl*

populace ['papjəlɪs] *s* peuple *m*, populace *f*

popular ['papjələr] *adj* populaire

popularize ['papjələ,raɪz] *tr* populariser, vulgariser

populate ['papjə,let] *tr* peupler

population [,papjə'leʃən] *s* population *f*

populous ['papjələs] *adj* populeux

porcelain ['pɔrsəlɪn], ['pɔrslɪn] *s* porcelaine *f*

porch [pɔrtʃ] *s (portico)* porche *m*; *(enclosed)* véranda *f*

porcupine ['pɔrkjə,paɪn] *s* porc-épic *m*

pore [pɔr] *s* pore *m* ‖ *intr*—**to pore over** examiner avec attention, s'absorber dans

pork [pɔrk] *s* porc *m*

pork' and beans' *spl* fèves *fpl* au lard

pork'chop' *s* côtelette *f* de porc

pornography [pɔr'nagrəfi] *s* pornographie *f*

porous ['pɔrəs] *adj* poreux

porphy·ry ['pɔrfɪri] *s (pl* -ries) porphyre *m*

porpoise ['pɔrpəs] *s* marsouin *m*

porridge ['parɪdʒ], ['pɔrɪdʒ] *s* bouillie *f*, porridge *m*

port [pɔrt] *s* port *m*; *(opening in ship's side)* hublot *m*, sabord *m*; *(left side of ship or airplane)* bâbord *m*; *(wine)* porto *m*; *(mach)* orifice *m*

portable ['pɔrtəbǝl] *adj* portatif

portage ['pɔrtɪdʒ] *s* transport *m*; portage *m*

portal ['pɔrtəl] *s* portail *m*

portcullis [pɔrt'kʌlɪs] *s* herse *f*

portend [pɔr'tend] *tr* présager

portent ['pɔrtent] *s* présage *m*

portentous [pɔr'tentəs] *adj* extraordinaire; de mauvais augure

porter ['pɔrtər] *s (doorkeeper)* portier *m*, concierge *m*; *(in hotels and trains)* porteur *m*

portfoli·o [pɔrt'folɪ,o] *s (pl* -os) portefeuille *m*

port'hole' *s* hublot *m*

porti·co ['pɔrtɪ,ko] *s (pl* -coes or -cos) portique *m*

portion ['pɔrʃən] *s* portion *f*; *(dowry)* dot *f* ‖ *tr*—**to portion out** partager, répartir

port·ly ['pɔrtlɪ] *adj (comp* -lier; *super* -liest) corpulent

port' of call' *s* port *m* d'escale

portrait ['pɔrtret], ['pɔrtrɪt] *s* portrait *m*; **to sit for one's portrait** se faire faire son portrait

portray [pɔr'tre] *tr* faire le portrait de; dépeindre, décrire; *(theat)* jouer le rôle de

portrayal [por'tre·əl] *s* représentation *f*; description *f*

Portugal ['portʃəgəl] *s* le Portugal

Portu·guese ['portʃə,giz] *adj* portugais ‖ *s* (*language*) portugais *m* ‖ *s* (*pl* -guese) (*person*) Portugais *m*

port' wine' *s* porto *m*

pose [poz] *s* pose *f* ‖ *tr & intr* poser; **to pose as** se poser comme

posh [paʃ] *adj* (slang) chic, élégant

position [pə'zɪʃən] *s* position *f*; (*job*) poste *m*; **in position** en place; **in your position** à votre place

positive ['pazɪtɪv] *adj & s* positif *m*

possess [pə'zɛs] *tr* posséder

possession [pə'zɛʃən] *s* possession *f*; **to take possession of** s'emparer de

possible ['pasɪbəl] *adj* possible

possum ['pasəm] *s* opossum *m*; **to play possum** (coll) faire le mort

post [post] *s* (*upright*) poteau *m*; (*job, position*) poste *m*; (*post office*) poste *f*; (mil) poste *m* ‖ *tr* (*a notice, placard, etc.*) afficher, placarder; (*a letter*) poster, mettre à la poste; (*a sentinel*) poster; (*with news*) tenir au courant; **post no bills** (public sign) défense d'afficher

postage ['postɪdʒ] *s* port *m*, affranchissement *m*

post'age due' *s* port *m* dû, affranchissement *m* insuffisant

post'age me'ter *s* affranchisseuse *f* à compteur

post'age stamp' *s* timbre-poste *m*

postal ['postəl] *adj* postal

post'al card' *s* carte *f* postale

post'al clerk' *s* postier *m*

post'al mon'ey or'der *s* mandat-poste *m*

post'al per'mit *s* franchise *f* postale, dispensé *m* du timbrage

post'al sav'ings bank' *s* caisse *f* d'épargne postale

post' card' *s* carte *f* postale

post'date' *s* postdate *f* ‖ **post'date'** *tr* postdater

poster ['postər] *s* affiche *f*

posterity [pas'terɪti] *s* postérité *f*

postern ['postərn] *s* poterne *f*

post'haste' *adv* en toute hâte

posthumous ['pastʃuməs] *adj* posthume

post'man *s* (*pl* -men) facteur *m*

post'mark' *s* cachet *m* d'oblitération, timbre *m* ‖ *tr* timbrer

post'mas'ter *s* receveur *m* des postes, administrateur *m* du bureau de postes

post'master gen'eral *s* ministre *m* des Postes et Télécommunications

post-mortem [,post'mortəm] *adj* après décès, (fig) après le fait ‖ *s* autopsie *f*; discussion *f* après le fait

post' of'fice *s* bureau *m* de poste

post'-office box' *s* case *f* postale, boîte *f* postale

post'paid' *adv* port payé, franc de port, franco de port

postpone [post'pon] *tr* remettre, différer; (*a meeting*) ajourner

postponement [post'ponmənt] *s* remise *f*, ajournement *m*

postscript ['post,skrɪpt] *s* post-scriptum *m*

posture ['pastʃər] *s* posture *f* ‖ *intr* prendre une posture

post'war' *adj* d'après-guerre

po·sy ['pozi] *s* (*pl* -sies) fleur *f*; bouquet *m*

pot [pat] *s* pot *m*; (in gambling) mise *f*; **to go to pot** (slang) s'en aller à vau-l'eau

potash ['pat,æʃ] *s* potasse *f*

potassium [pə'tæsɪəm] *s* potassium *m*

pota·to [pə'teto] *s* (*pl* -toes) pomme *f* de terre; (*sweet potato*) patate *f*

pota'to chips' *spl* pommes *fpl* chips, croustelle *f* (Canad)

potbellied ['pat,belɪd] *adj* ventru

poten·cy ['potənsi] *s* (*pl* -cies) puissance *f*, virilité *f*

potent ['potənt] *adj* puissant, fort; (*effective*) efficace

potentate ['potən,tet] *s* potentat *m*

potential [pə'tenʃəl] *adj & s* potentiel *m*

pot'hang'er *s* crémaillère *f*

pot'herb' *s* herbe *f* potagère

pot'hold'er *s* poignée *f*

pot'hole' *s* nid *m* de poule

pot'hook' *s* croc *m*

potion ['poʃən] *s* potion *f*

pot'luck' *s*—**to take potluck** manger à la fortune du pot

pot' shot' *s* coup *m* tiré à courte distance

potter ['patər] *s* potier *m* ‖ *intr*—**to potter around** s'occuper de bagatelles, bricoler

pot'ter's clay' *s* terre *f* à potier

pot'ter's field' *s* fosse *f* commune

pot'ter's wheel' *s* roue *f* or tour *m* de potier

potter·y ['patəri] *s* (*pl* -ies) poterie *f*

pouch [pautʃ] *s* poche *f*, petit sac *m*; (*of kangaroo*) poche *f* ventrale; (*for tobacco*) blague *f*

poultice ['poltɪs] *s* cataplasme *m*

poultry ['poltri] *s* volaille *f*

poul'try·man *s* (*pl* -men) éleveur *m* de volailles; (*dealer*) volailleur *m*

pounce [pauns] *intr*—**to pounce on** fondre sur, s'abattre sur

pound [paund] *s* (*weight*) livre *f*; (*for automobiles, stray animals, etc.*) fourrière *f* ‖ *tr* battre; (*to pulverize*) piler, broyer; (*to bombard*) pilonner; (*e.g., an animal*) mettre en fourrière; (*e.g., the sidewalk*) (fig) battre ‖ *intr* battre

pound' ster'ling *s* livre *f* sterling

pour [por] *tr* verser; (*tea*) servir; **to pour off** décanter ‖ *intr* écouler; (*said of rain*) tomber à verse; **to pour out** of sortir à flots

pout [paut] *s* moue *f* ‖ *intr* faire la moue

poverty ['pavərti] *s* pauvreté *f*

POW ['pi'o'dʌb'l,ju] *s* (letterword) (prisoner of war) P.G.

powder ['paudər] *s* poudre *f* ‖ *tr* réduire en poudre; (*to sprinkle with powder*) poudrer ‖ *intr* se poudrer

pow'dered sug'ar *s* sucre *m* de confiseur

pow'der puff' *s* houppe *f*

pow′der room′ s toilettes fpl pour dames
powdery [ˈpaʊdəri] adj (like powder) poudreux; (sprinkled with powder) poussiéreux; (crumbly) friable
power [ˈpaʊ·ər] s pouvoir m; (influential nation; energy, force, strength; of a machine, microscope, number) puissance f; (talent, capacity, etc.) faculté f; **the powers that be** les autorités fpl; **to seize power** saisir le pouvoir ‖ tr actionner
pow′er brake′ s (aut) servo-frein m
pow′er dive′ s piqué m à plein gaz
pow′er-dive′ intr piquer à plein gaz
powerful [ˈpaʊ·ərfəl] adj puissant
pow′er-house′ s usine f centrale; (coll) foyer m d'énergie
pow′er lawn′mower s tondeuse f à gazon à moteur
powerless [ˈpaʊ·ərlɪs] adj impuissant
pow′er line′ s secteur m de distribution
pow′er mow′er s tondeuse f à gazon à moteur; motofaucheuse f
pow′er of attorn′ey s procuration f, mandat m
pow′er pack′ s (rad) unité f d'alimentation
pow′er plant′ s (powerhouse) centrale f électrique; (aer, aut) groupe m motopropulseur
pow′er steer′ing s (aut) servo-direction f
practicable [ˈpræktɪkəbəl] adj praticable
practical [ˈpræktɪkəl] adj pratique
prac′tical joke′ s farce f, attrape f
prac′tical jok′er s fumiste m
practically [ˈpræktɪkəli] adv pratiquement; (more or less) à peu près
prac′tical nurse′ s garde-malade mf
practice [ˈpræktɪs] s pratique f; (of a profession) exercice m; (of a doctor) clientèle f; **in practice** en pratique, pratiquement; (well-trained) en forme; **out of practice** rouillé ‖ tr pratiquer; (a profession) exercer, pratiquer; (e.g., the violin) s'exercer à; **to practice what one preaches** prêcher d'exemple ‖ intr faire des exercices, s'exercer; (said of doctor, lawyer, etc.) exercer
practiced adj expert
practitioner [prækˈtɪʃənər] s praticien m
prairie [ˈprɛri] s steppes fpl; **the prairie** les Prairies fpl
praise [prez] s louange f ‖ tr louer
praise′wor′thy adj louable
pram [præm] s voiture f d'enfant
prance [præns], [prɑns] intr caracoler, cabrioler
prank [præŋk] s espièglerie f
prate [pret] intr bavarder, papoter
prattle [ˈprætəl] s bavardage m, papotage m ‖ intr bavarder, papoter; (said of children) babiller
prawn [prɔn] s crevette f rose, bouquet m
pray [pre] tr & intr prier
prayer [prer] s prière f
prayer′ book′ s livre m de prières

pray′ing man′tis [ˈmæntɪs] s mante f religieuse
preach [pritʃ] tr & intr prêcher
preacher [ˈpritʃər] s prédicateur m
preamble [ˈpriˌæmbəl] s préambule m
precarious [prɪˈkɛri·əs] adj précaire
precaution [prɪˈkɔʃən] s précaution f
precede [prɪˈsid] tr & intr précéder
precedent [ˈprɛsɪdənt] s précédent m
precept [ˈprisɛpt] s précepte m
precinct [ˈprisɪŋkt] s enceinte f; circonscription f électorale
precious [ˈprɛʃəs] adj précieux ‖ adv— **precious little** (coll) très peu
precipice [ˈprɛsɪpɪs] s précipice m
precipitate [prɪˈsɪpɪˌtet] adj & s précipité m ‖ tr précipiter ‖ intr se précipiter
precipitous [prɪˈsɪpɪtəs] adj escarpé; (hurried) précipité
precise [prɪˈsaɪs] adj précis
precision [prɪˈsɪʒən] s précision f
preclude [prɪˈklud] tr empêcher
precocious [prɪˈkoʃəs] adj précoce
preconceived [ˌprikənˈsivd] adj préconçu
predatory [ˈprɛdəˌtori] adj rapace; (zool) prédateur
predicament [prɪˈdɪkəmənt] s situation f difficile
predict [prɪˈdɪkt] tr prédire
prediction [prɪˈdɪkʃən] s prédiction f
predispose [ˌpridɪsˈpoz] tr prédisposer
predominant [prɪˈdɑmɪnənt] adj prédominant
preeminent [prɪˈɛmɪnənt] adj prééminent
preempt [prɪˈɛmpt] tr s'approprier
preen [prin] tr lisser; **to preen oneself** se bichonner; être fier, se piquer
prefabricated [priˈfæbrɪˌketɪd] adj préfabriqué
preface [ˈprɛfɪs] s préface f ‖ tr préfacer
pre-fer [prɪˈfʌr] v (pret & pp -ferred; ger -ferring) tr préférer
preferable [ˈprɛfərəbəl] adj préférable
preference [ˈprɛfərəns] s préférence f
preferred′ stock′ s actions f privilégiées
prefix [ˈprifɪks] s préfixe m ‖ tr préfixer
pregnan·cy [ˈprɛgnənsi] s (pl -cies) grossesse f
pregnant [ˈprɛgnənt] adj enceinte, grosse; (fig) gros
prehistoric [ˌprihɪsˈtɑrɪk], [ˌprihɪsˈtɔrɪk] adj préhistorique
prejudice [ˈprɛdʒədɪs] s préjugé m; (detriment) préjudice m ‖ tr prévenir, prédisposer; (to harm) porter préjudice à
prejudicial [ˌprɛdʒəˈdɪʃəl] adj préjudiciable
prelate [ˈprɛlɪt] s prélat m
preliminar·y [prɪˈlɪmɪˌnɛri] adj préliminaire ‖ s (pl -ies) préliminaire m
prelude [ˈprɛljud], [ˈprɪlud] s prélude m ‖ tr introduire; préluder à; (a piece of music) préluder par
premature [ˌpriməˈt(j)ʊr] adj prématuré; (plant) hâtif
premeditate [prɪˈmɛdɪˌtet] tr préméditer

premier [prɪˈmɪr], [ˈprimɪ·ər] s premier ministre *m*
première [prəˈmjɛr], [prɪˈmɪr] s première *f*; (*actress*) vedette *f*
premise [ˈprɛmɪs] s prémisse *f*; **on the premises** sur les lieux; **premises** local *m*, locaux *mpl*
premium [ˈprimɪ·əm] s prime *f*
premonition [ˌpriməˈnɪʃən] s prémonition *f*
preoccupation [prɪˌɑkjəˈpeʃən] s préoccupation *f*
preoccu·py [prɪˈɑkjəˌpaɪ] v (*pret & pp* -**pied**) *tr* préoccuper
prepaid [prɪˈped] *adj* payé d'avance; (*letter*) affranchi
preparation [ˌprɛpəˈreʃən] s préparation *f*; **preparations** (*for a trip; for war*) préparatifs *mpl*
preparatory [prɪˈpærəˌtori] *adj* préparatoire
prepare [prɪˈpɛr] *tr* préparer || *intr* se préparer
preparedness [prɪˈpɛrɪdnɪs], [prɪˈpɛrdnɪs] s préparation *f*; armement *m* préventif
pre·pay [prɪˈpe] v (*pret & pp* -**paid**) *tr* payer d'avance
preponderant [prɪˈpɑndərənt] *adj* prépondérant
preposition [ˌprɛpəˈzɪʃən] s préposition *f*
prepossessing [ˌpripəˈzɛsɪŋ] *adj* avenant, agréable
preposterous [prɪˈpɑstərəs] *adj* absurde, extravagant
prep′ school′ [prɛp] s école *f* préparatoire
prerecorded [ˌprirɪˈkɔrdɪd] *adj* (rad, telv) différé
prerequisite [priˈrɛkwɪzɪt] s préalable *m*; (educ) cours *m* préalable
prerogative [prɪˈrɑgətɪv] s prérogative *f*
presage [ˈprɛsɪdʒ] s présage *m*; (*foreboding*) pressentiment *m* || [prɪˈsedʒ] *tr* présager; pressentir
Presbyterian [ˌprɛzbɪˈtɪrɪ·ən] *adj & s* presbytérien *m*
prescribe [prɪˈskraɪb] *tr* prescrire || *intr* faire une ordonnance
prescription [prɪˈskrɪpʃən] s prescription *f*; (*pharm*) ordonnance *f*
presence [ˈprɛzəns] s présence *f*
present [ˈprɛzənt] *adj* (*at this time*) actuel; (*at this place or time*) présent; **to be present at** assister à || s cadeau *m*, présent *m*; (*present time or tense*) présent; **at present** à présent || [prɪˈzɛnt] *tr* présenter
presentable [prɪˈzɛntəbəl] *adj* présentable, sortable
presentation [ˌprɛzənˈteʃən], [ˌprizənˈteʃən] s présentation *f*
presenta′tion cop′y s exemplaire *m* offert à titre d'hommage
presentiment [prɪˈzɛntɪmənt] s pressentiment *m*
presently [ˈprɛzəntli] *adv* tout à l'heure; (*now*) à présent
preserve [prɪˈzɜrv] s confiture *f*; (*for game*) chasse *f* gardée || *tr* préserver, conserver; (*to can*) conserver

pre-shrunk [prɪˈʃrʌŋk] *adj* irrétrécissable
preside [prɪˈzaɪd] *intr* présider; **to preside over** présider
presiden·cy [ˈprɛzɪdənsi] s (*pl* -**cies**) présidence *f*
president [ˈprɛzɪdənt] s président *m*; (*of a university*) recteur *m*
presidential [ˌprɛzɪˈdɛnʃəl] *adj* présidentiel
press [prɛs] s presse *f*; (e.g., *for wine*) pressoir *m*; (*pressure*) pression *f*; (*for clothes*) armoire *f*; (*in weight lifting*) développé *m*; **in press** (*said of clothes*) lisse et net; (*said of book being published*) sous presse; **to go to press** être mis sous presse || *tr* presser; (e.g., *a button*) appuyer sur, presser; (*clothes*) donner un coup de fer à, repasser || *intr* presser; **to press against** se serrer contre; **to press forward, to press on** presser le pas
press′ a′gent s agent *m* de publicité
press′ box′ s tribune *f* des journalistes
press′ card′ s coupe-file *m* d'un journaliste
press′ con′ference s conférence *f* de presse
press′ gal′lery s tribune *f* de la presse
pressing [ˈprɛsɪŋ] *adj* pressé, pressant
press′ release′ s communiqué *m* de presse
pressure [ˈprɛʃər] s pression *f*
pres′sure cook′er s autocuiseur *m*, cocotte *f* minute
pressurize [ˈprɛʃəˌraɪz] *tr* pressuriser
prestige [prɛsˈtiʒ], [ˈprɛstɪdʒ] s prestige *m*
presumably [prɪˈz(j)uməbli] *adv* probablement
presume [prɪˈz(j)um] *tr* présumer; **to presume to** présumer à || *intr* présumer; **to presume on** or **upon** abuser de
presumption [prɪˈzʌmpʃən] s présomption *f*
presumptuous [prɪˈzʌmptʃu·əs] *adj* présomptueux
presuppose [ˌprisəˈpoz] *tr* présupposer
pretend [prɪˈtɛnd] *tr* feindre; **to pretend to** + *inf* feindre de + *inf* || *intr* feindre; **to pretend to** (e.g., *the throne*) prétendre à
pretender [prɪˈtɛndər] s prétendant *m*; (*imposter*) simulateur *m*
pretense [prɪˈtɛns], [ˈpritɛns] s prétention *f*; feinte *f*; **under false pretenses** par des moyens frauduleux; **under pretense of** sous prétexte de
pretension [prɪˈtɛnʃən] s prétention *f*
pretentious [prɪˈtɛnʃəs] *adj* prétentieux
pretext [ˈpritɛkst] s prétexte *m*
pretonic [prɪˈtɑnɪk] *adj* prétonique
pret·ty [ˈprɪti] *adj* (*comp* -**tier**; *super* -**tiest**) joli; (coll) considérable || *adv* assez; très
prevail [prɪˈvel] *intr* prévaloir, régner; **to prevail on** or **upon** persuader
prevailing [prɪˈvelɪŋ] *adj* prédominant; (*wind*) dominant; (*fashion*) en vogue
prevalent [ˈprɛvələnt] *adj* commun, courant

prevaricate [prɪ'værɪˌket] *intr* mentir
prevent [prɪ'vent] *tr* empêcher
prevention [prɪ'venʃən] *s* empêchement *m*; (*e.g., of accidents*) prévention *f*
preventive [prɪ'ventɪv] *adj & s* préventif *m*
preview ['pri,vju] *s* (*of something to come*) amorce *f*; (*private showing*) (mov) avant-première *f*; (*show of brief scenes for advertising*) film *m* annonce
previous ['privɪ·əs] *adj* précédent, antérieur; (*notice*) préalable; (coll) pressé || *adv*—previous to antérieurement à
prewar [prɪ,wɔr] *adj* d'avant-guerre
prey [pre] *s* proie *f*; to be a prey to être en proie à || *intr*—to prey on or upon faire sa proie de; (*e.g., a sea-coast*) piller; (*e.g., the mind*) ronger, miner
price [praɪs] *s* prix *m* || *tr* mettre un prix à, tarifer; s'informer du prix de
price' control' *s* contrôle *m* des prix
price' cut'ting *s* rabais *m*, remise *f*
price' fix'ing *s* stabilisation *f* des prix
price' freez'ing *s* blocage *m* des prix
priceless ['praɪslɪs] *adj* sans prix; (coll) impayable, absurde
price' list' *s* liste *f* de prix, tarif *m*
price' war' *s* guerre *f* des prix
prick [prɪk] *s* piqûre *f*; (*spur; sting of conscience*) aiguillon *m* || *tr* piquer; to prick up (*the ears*) dresser
prick·ly ['prɪklɪ] *adj* (*comp* -lier; *super* -liest) épineux
prick'ly heat' *s* lichen *m* vésiculaire, miliaire *f*
prick'ly pear' *s* figue *f* de Barbarie; (*plant*) figuier *m* de Barbarie
pride [praɪd] *s* orgueil *m*; (*satisfaction*) fierté *f*; to take pride in être fier de || *tr*—to pride oneself on or upon s'enorgueillir de
priest [prist] *s* prêtre *m*
priestess ['pristɪs] *s* prêtresse *f*
priesthood ['prist·hʊd] *s* sacerdoce *m*
priest·ly ['pristlɪ] *adj* (*comp* -lier; *super* -liest) sacerdotal
prig [prɪg] *s* poseur *m*, pédant *m*
prim [prɪm] *adj* (*comp* primmer; *super* primmest) compassé, guindé
prima·ry ['praɪˌmerɪ], ['praɪmərɪ] *adj* primaire || *s* (*pl* -ries) élection *f* primaire; (elec) primaire *m*
primate ['praɪmet] *s* (eccl) primat *m*; (zool) primate *m*
prime [praɪm] *adj* premier, principal; (*of the best quality*) de première qualité, (le) meilleur; (math) prime || *s* fleur *f*, perfection *f*; commencement *m*, premiers jours *mpl*; prime of life fleur *m* ou force de l'âge || *tr* amorcer; (*a surface to be painted*) appliquer une couche de fond à; (*to supply with information*) mettre au courant
prime' min'ister *s* premier ministre *m*
primer ['prɪmər] *s* premier livre *m* de lecture; manuel *m* élémentaire || ['praɪmər] *s* (*for paint*) couche *f* de fond, impression *f*; (mach) amorce *f*

primeval [praɪ'mivəl] *adj* primitif
primitive ['prɪmɪtɪv] *adj & s* primitif *m*
primordial [praɪ'mɔrdɪ·əl] *adj* primordial
primp [prɪmp] *tr* bichonner, pomponner || *intr* se bichonner, se pomponner
prim'rose' *s* primevère *f*
prim'rose path' *s* chemin *m* de velours
prince [prɪns] *s* prince *m*
prince·ly ['prɪnslɪ] *adj* (*comp* -lier; *super* -liest) princier
Prince' of Wales' *s* prince *m* de Galles
princess ['prɪnsɪs] *s* princesse *f*
principal ['prɪnsɪpəl] *adj & s* principal *m*
principali·ty [ˌprɪnsɪ'pælɪtɪ] *s* (*pl* -ties) principauté *f*
principle ['prɪnsɪpəl] *s* principe *m*
print [prɪnt] *s* empreinte *f*; (*printed cloth*) imprimé *m*; (*design in printed cloth*) estampe *f*; (*lettering*) lettres *fpl* moulées; (*act of printing*) impression *f*; (phot) épreuve *f*; out of print épuisé; small print petits caractères *mpl* || *tr* imprimer; écrire en lettres moulées; publier; (*an edition; a photographic negative*) tirer
print'ed mat'ter *s* imprimés *mpl*
printer ['prɪntər] *s* imprimeur *m*
prin'ter's dev'il *s* apprenti *m* imprimeur
prin'ter's er'ror *s* faute *f* d'impression, coquille *f*
prin'ter's ink' *s* encre *f* d'imprimerie
prin'ter's mark' *s* nom *m* de l'imprimeur
printing ['prɪntɪŋ] *s* imprimerie *f*; (*act*) impression *f*; (*by hand*) écriture *f* en caractères d'imprimerie; édition *f*; tirage *m*; (phot) tirage
print'ing frame' *s* (phot) châssis-presse *m*
print'ing of'fice *s* imprimerie *f*
prior ['praɪ·ər] *adj* antérieur || *s* prieur *m* || *adv* antérieurement; prior to avant; avant de
priori·ty [praɪ'ɑrɪtɪ], [praɪ'ɔrɪtɪ] *s* (*pl* -ties) priorité *f*
prism ['prɪzəm] *s* prisme *m*
prison ['prɪzən] *s* prison *f* || *tr* emprisonner
prisoner ['prɪzənər], ['prɪznər] *s* prisonnier *m*
pris'on van' *s* voiture *f* cellulaire
pris·sy ['prɪsɪ] *adj* (*comp* -sier; *super* -siest) (coll) bégueule
priva·cy ['praɪvəsɪ] *s* (*pl* -cies) intimité *f*; secret *m*
private ['praɪvɪt] *adj* privé, particulier; confidentiel, secret; (*public sign*) défense d'entrer || *s* simple soldat *m*; in private dans l'intimité, en particulier; privates parties *fpl*
pri'vate cit'izen *s* simple particulier *m*, simple citoyen *m*
pri'vate first' class' *s* soldat *m* de première
pri'vate hos'pital *s* clinique *f*
pri'vate sec'retary *s* secrétaire *m* particulier
privet ['prɪvɪt] *s* troène *m*

privilege ['prɪvɪlɪdʒ] *s* privilège *m*
priv·y ['prɪvi] *adj* privé; **privy to** averti de || *s* (*pl* -**ies**) cabinets *mpl* au fond du jardin
prize [praɪz] *s* prix *m*; (*something captured*) prise *f* || *tr* faire cas de, estimer
prize′ fight′ *s* match *m* de boxe
prize′ fight′er *s* boxeur *m* professionnel
prize′ ring′ *s* ring *m*
prize′ win′ner *s* lauréat *m*; **prizewinners** (*list*) palmarès *m*
pro [pro] *s* (*pl* **pros**) vote *m* affirmatif; (*professional*) (coll) pro *m*; **the pros and the cons** le pour et le contre || *prep* en faveur de
probabili·ty [ˌprɑbə'bɪlɪti] *s* (*pl* -**ties**) probabilité *f*
probable ['prɑbəbəl] *adj* probable
probably ['prɑbəbli] *adv* probablement
probate ['probet] *s* homologation *f* || *tr* homologuer
probation [pro'beʃən] *s* liberté *f* surveillée; (*on a job*) stage *m*
probe [prob] *s* sondage *m*; (*instrument*) sonde *f*; (rok) échos *mpl*; (rok) engin *m* exploratoire || *tr* sonder
problem ['prɑbləm] *s* problème *m*
prob′lem child′ *s* enfant *mf* terrible
procedure [pro'sidʒər] *s* procédé *m*
proceed ['prosid] *s*—**proceeds** produit *m*, bénéfices *mpl* || [pro'sid] *intr* avancer, continuer; continuer à parler; **to proceed from** procéder de; **to proceed to** se mettre à; (*to go to*) se diriger à
proceeding [pro'sidɪŋ] *s* procédé *m*; **proceedings** actes *mpl*
process ['prɑses] *s* (*technique*) procédé *m*; (*development*) processus *m*; **in the process of** en train de || *tr* soumettre à un procédé, traiter
procession [pro'seʃən] *s* cortège *m*, défilé *m*, procession *f*
pro′cess serv′er *s* huissier *m* exploitant
proclaim [pro'klem] *tr* proclamer
proclitic [pro'klɪtɪk] *adj* & *s* proclitique *m*
procommunist [pro'kɑmjənɪst] *adj* & *s* procommuniste *mf*
procrastinate [pro'kræstɪˌnet] *tr* différer || *intr* remettre les affaires à plus tard
proctor ['prɑktər] *s* surveillant *m*
procure [pro'kjur] *tr* obtenir, se procurer; (*a woman*) entraîner à la prostitution || *intr* faire du proxénétisme
procurement [pro'kjurmənt] *s* obtention *f*, acquisition *f*
procurer [pro'kjurər] *s* proxénète *mf*
prod [prɑd] *s* poussée *f*; (*stick*) aiguillon *m* || *v* (*pret* & *pp* **prodded**; *ger* **prodding**) *tr* aiguillonner
prodigal ['prɑdɪgəl] *adj* & *s* prodigue *mf*
prodigious [pro'dɪdʒəs] *adj* prodigieux
prodi·gy ['prɑdɪdʒi] *s* (*pl* -**gies**) prodige *m*
produce ['prɑd(j)us] *s* produit *m*; (*eatables*) denrées *fpl* || [pro'd(j)us] *tr* produire; (*a play*) mettre en scène; (geom) prolonger

producer [pro'd(j)usər] *s* producteur *m*
product ['prɑdəkt] *s* produit *m*
production [pro'dʌkʃən] *s* production *f*
profane [pro'fen] *adj* profane; (*language*) impie, blasphématoire || *s* profane *mf*; impie *mf* || *tr* profaner
profani·ty [pro'fænɪti] *s* (*pl* -**ties**) blasphème *m*
profess [pro'fes] *tr* professer
profession [pro'feʃən] *s* profession *f*
professor [pro'fesər] *s* professeur *m*
proffer ['prɑfər] *s* offre *f* || *tr* offrir, tendre
proficient [pro'fɪʃənt] *adj* compétent, expert
profile ['profaɪl] *s* profil *m*; courte biographie *f* || *tr* profiler; **to be profiled against** se profiler sur
profit ['prɑfɪt] *s* bénéfice *m*, profit *m* || *tr* profiter (with *dat*) || *intr* profiter; **to profit from** profiter à, de, or en
profitable ['prɑfɪtəbəl] *adj* profitable
prof′it-and-loss′ account′ *s* compte *m* de profits et pertes
profiteer [ˌprɑfɪ'tɪr] *s* profiteur *m* || *intr* faire des bénéfices excessifs
prof′it tak′ing *s* prise *f* de bénéfices
profligate ['prɑflɪgɪt] *adj* & *s* débauché *m*
pro′ for′ma in′voice [ˌpro'fɔrmə] *s* facture *f* simulée
profound [pro'faʊnd] *adj* profond
pro-French *adj* francophile
profuse [pro'fjuz] *adj* abondant; (*extravagant*) prodigue
proge·ny ['prɑdʒəni] *s* (*pl* -**nies**) progéniture *f*
progno·sis [prɑg'nosɪs] *s* (*pl* -**ses** [siz]) pronostic *m*
prognosticate [prɑg'nɑstɪˌket] *tr* pronostiquer
pro·gram ['progræm] *s* programme *m* || *v* (*pret* & *pp* -**gramed** or -**grammed**; *ger* -**graming** or -**gramming**) *tr* programmer
programmer ['progræmər] *s* (comp) programmeur *m*; (mov, rad, telv) programmateur *m*
programming ['progræmɪŋ] *s* programmation *f*
progress ['prɑgres] *s* progrès *m*; cours *m*, e.g., **work in progress** travaux en cours; **to make progress** faire des progrès || [prə'gres] *intr* progresser
progressive [prə'gresɪv] *adj* progressif; (pol) progressiste || *s* (pol) progressiste *mf*
prohibit [pro'hɪbɪt] *tr* prohiber, interdire
prohibition [ˌpro·ə'bɪʃən] *s* prohibition *f*
project ['prɑdʒekt] *s* projet *m* || [prə'dʒekt] *tr* projeter || *intr* (*to jut out*) saillir; (theat) passer la rampe
projectile [prə'dʒektɪl] *s* projectile *m*
projection [prə'dʒekʃən] *s* projection *f*; (*something jutting out*) saillie *f*
projec′tion booth′ *s* (mov) cabine *f* de projection
projector [prə'dʒektər] *s* projecteur *m*

proletarian [,prolɪ'terɪ·ən] *adj* proléta-
rien ‖ *s* prolétaire *m*
proletariat [,prolɪ'terɪ·ət] *s* prolétariat *m*
proliferate [prə'lɪfə ,ret] *intr* proliférer
prolific [prə'lɪfɪk] *adj* prolifique
prolix ['prolɪks], [pro'lɪks] *adj* prolixe
prologue ['prolɔg], ['prolɑg] *s* prologue *m*
prolong [pro'lɔŋ], [pro'lɑŋ] *tr* prolonger
promenade [,pramɪ'ned], [,pramɪ-
'nad] *s* promenade *f*; bal *m* d'apparat; (theat) promenoir *m* ‖ *intr* se
promener
prom'enade/ deck/ *s* (naut) pont-promenade *m*
prominent ['pramɪnənt] *adj* proémi-
nent; (*well-known*) éminent
promiscuity [,pramɪs'kju·əti] *s* promiscuité *f*
promise ['pramɪs] *s* promesse *f* ‖ *tr* &
intr promettre; **to promise s.o.** to
promettre à qn de; **to promise s.th.
to s.o.** promettre q.ch. à qn
prom'issory note/ ['pramɪ ,sori] *m* billet *m* à ordre
promonto•ry ['pramən ,tori] *s* (*pl* -ries)
promontoire *m*
promote [prə'mot] *tr* promouvoir
promoter [prə'motər] *s* promoteur *m*
promotion [prə'moʃən] *s* promotion *f*
prompt [prampt] *adj* prompt; ponctuel
‖ *tr* inciter; (theat) souffler son rôle à
prompter ['pramptər] *s* (theat) souffleur *m*
promp'ter's box/ *s* (theat) trou *m* du
souffleur
promptness ['pramptnɪs] *s* promptitude *f*
promulgate ['praməl ,get], [pro'mʌl-
get] *tr* promulguer
prone [pron] *adj* à plat ventre, prostré; **prone to** enclin à
prong [prɔŋ], [praŋ] *s* dent *f*
pronoun ['pronaun] *s* pronom *m*
pronounce [prə'nauns] *tr* prononcer
pronouncement [prə'naunsmənt] *s* déclaration *f*
pronunciation [prə ,nʌnsɪ'eʃən], [prə-
,nʌn/ɪ'eʃən] *s* prononciation *f*
proof [pruf] *adj*—**proof against** à
l'épreuve de, résistant à ‖ *s* preuve
f; (phot, typ) épreuve *f*; **to read
proof** corriger les épreuves
proof'read'er *s* correcteur *m*
prop [prap] *s* appui *m*; (*to hold up a
plant*) tuteur *m*; **props** (theat) accessoires *mpl* ‖ *v* (*pret & pp* **propped**;
ger **propping**) *tr* appuyer; (hort)
tuteurer
propaganda [,prapə'gændə] *s* propagande *f*
propagate ['prapə ,get] *tr* propager
pro•pel [prə'pel] *v* (*pret & pp* -**pelled**;
ger -**pelling**) *tr* propulser
propeller [prə'pelər] *s* hélice *f*
propensi•ty [prə'pensɪti] *s* (*pl* -ties)
propension *f*
proper ['prapər] *adj* propre; (*fitting,
correct*) convenable, comme il faut

prop'erty ['prapərti] *s* (*pl* -ties) propriété *f*; **properties** (theat) accessoires *mpl*
prop'erty own'er *s* propriétaire *mf*
prop'erty tax/ *s* impôt *m* foncier
prophe•cy ['prafɪsi] *s* (*pl* -cies) prophétie *f*
prophe•sy ['prafɪ ,saɪ] *v* (*pret & pp*
-sied) *tr* prophétiser
prophet ['prafɪt] *s* prophète *m*
prophetess ['prafɪtɪs] *s* prophétesse *f*
prophylactic [,profɪ'læktɪk] *adj* prophylactique ‖ *s* médicament *m* prophylactique
propitiate [prə'pɪʃɪ ,et] *tr* apaiser
propitious [prə'pɪʃəs] *adj* propice
prop'jet/ *s* turbopropulseur *m*
proportion [prə'porʃən] *s* proportion *f*;
in proportion as à mesure que; **in
proportion to** en proportion de, en
raison de; **out of proportion** hors de
proportion ‖ *tr* proportionner
proportionate [prə'porʃənɪt] *adj* proportionné
proposal [prə'pozəl] *s* proposition *f*;
demande *f* en mariage
propose [prə'poz] *tr* proposer ‖ *intr*
faire sa déclaration; **to propose to**
demander sa main à; (*to decide to*) se
proposer de
proposition [,prapə'zɪʃən] *s* proposition *f* ‖ *tr* faire des propositions malhonnêtes à
propound [prə'paund] *tr* proposer
proprietor [prə'praɪ·ətər] *s* propriétaire
mf
proprietress [prə'praɪ·ətrɪs] *s* propriétaire *f*
proprie•ty [prə'praɪ·əti] *s* (*pl* -ties)
propriété *f*; (*of conduct*) bienséance
f; **proprieties** convenances *fpl*
propulsion [prə'pʌlʃən] *s* propulsion *f*
prorate [pro'ret] *tr* partager au prorata
prosaic [pro'ze·ɪk] *adj* prosaïque
proscenium [pro'sini·əm] *s* avant-
scène *f*
proscribe [pro'skraɪb] *tr* proscrire
prose [proz] *adj* en prose ‖ *s* prose *f*
prosecute ['prasɪ ,kjut] *tr* poursuivre
prosecutor ['prasɪ ,kjutər] *s* (*lawyer*)
procureur *m*; (*plaintiff*) plaignant *m*
proselyte ['prasɪ ,laɪt] *s* prosélyte *mf*
prose/ writ'er *s* prosateur *m*
prosody ['prasədi] *s* prosodie *f*
prospect ['praspekt] *s* perspective *f*;
(*future*) avenir *m*; (com) client *m*
éventuel ‖ *tr & intr* prospecter; **to
prospect for** (*e.g., gold*) chercher
prospector ['praspektər] *s* prospecteur
m
prospectus [prə'spektəs] *s* prospectus
m
prosper ['praspər] *intr* prospérer
prosperity [pras'periti] *s* prospérité *f*
prosperous ['praspərəs] *adj* prospère
prostitute ['prastɪ ,t(j)ut] *s* prostituée
f ‖ *tr* prostituer
prostrate ['prastret] *adj* prosterné; (*exhausted*) prostré ‖ *tr* abattre; **to prostrate oneself** se prosterner
prostration [pras'treʃən] *s* prostration
f; (*abasement*) prosternation *f*

protagonist [pro'tægənɪst] *s* protagoniste *m*
protect [prə'tɛkt] *tr* protéger
protection [prə'tɛkʃən] *s* protection *f*
protein ['proti·ɪn], ['protɪn] *s* protéine *f*
pro-tempore [pro'tɛmpə ‚ri] *adj* intérimaire, par intérim
protest ['protɛst] *s* protestation *f* [pro'tɛst] *tr* protester de; protester || *intr* protester
Protestant ['pratɪstənt] *adj & s* protestant *m*
protocol ['protə ‚kal] *s* protocole *m*
proton ['protan] *s* proton *m*
protoplasm ['protə ‚plæzəm] *s* protoplasme *m*
prototype ['protə ‚taɪp] *s* prototype *m*
protozoan [‚protə'zo·ən] *s* protozoaire *m*
protract [pro'trækt] *tr* prolonger
protrude [pro'trud] *intr* saillir
protuberance [pro't(j)ubərəns] *s* protubérance *f*
proud [praud] *adj* fier; (*vain*) orgueilleux
proud/ flesh/ *s* chair *f* fongueuse
prove [pruv] *v* (*pret* **proved**; *pp* **proved** or **proven** ['pruvən]) *tr* prouver; (*to put to the test*) éprouver || *intr* se montrer, se trouver; **to prove to be** se révéler, s'avérer
proverb ['pravərb] *s* proverbe *m*
provide [prə'vaɪd] *tr* pourvoir, fournir; **to provide s.th. for s.o.** fournir q.ch. à qn || *intr*—**to provide for** pourvoir à; (*e.g., future needs*) prévoir
provided *conj* pourvu que, à condition que
providence ['pravɪdəns] *s* providence *f*; (*prudence*) prévoyance *f*
providential [‚pravɪ'dɛnʃəl] *adj* providentiel
providing [prə'vaɪdɪŋ] *conj* pourvu que, à condition que
province ['pravɪns] *s* province *f*; (*sphere*) compétence *f*
prov/ing ground/ *s* terrain *m* d'essai
provision [prə'vɪʒən] *s* (*supplying*) fourniture *f*; clause *f*; **provisions** provisions *fpl*
provi·so [prə'vaɪzo] *s* (*pl* **-sos** or **-soes**) condition *f*, stipulation *f*
provocative [prə'vakətɪv] *adj* provocant
provoke [prə'vok] *tr* provoquer; fâcher, contrarier
provoking [prə'vokɪŋ] *adj* contrariant
prow [prau] *s* proue *f*
prowess ['prau·ɪs] *s* prouesse *f*
prowl [praul] *intr* rôder
prowler ['praulər] *s* rôdeur *m*
proximity [prak'sɪmɪti] *s* proximité *f*
prox·y ['praksi] *s* (*pl* **-ies**) mandat *m*; (*agent*) mandataire *mf*; **by proxy** par procuration
prude [prud] *s* prude *mf*
prudence ['prudəns] *s* prudence *f*
prudent ['prudənt] *adj* prudent
pruder·y ['prudəri] *s* (*pl* **-ies**) pruderie *f*
prudish ['prudɪʃ] *adj* prude
prune [prun] *s* pruneau *m* || *tr* élaguer

Prussian ['prʌʃən] *adj* prussien || *s* Prussien *m*
pry [praɪ] *v* (*pret & pp* **pried**) *tr*—**to pry open** forcer avec un levier; **to pry s.th. out of s.o.** extorquer, soutirer q.ch. à qn || *intr* fureter; **to pry into** fourrer son nez dans
P.S. ['pi'ɛs] *s* (letterword) (postscript) P.-S.
psalm [sam] *s* psaume *m*
Psalter ['sɔltər] *s* psautier *m*
pseudo ['s(j)udo] *adj* faux, supposé, feint, factice
pseudonym ['s(j)udənɪm] *s* pseudonyme *m*
psyche ['saɪki] *s* psyché *f*
psychiatrist [saɪ'kaɪ·ətrɪst] *s* psychiatre *mf*
psychiatry [saɪ'kaɪ·ətri] *s* psychiatrie *f*
psychic ['saɪkɪk] *adj* psychique; médiumnique || *s* médium *m*
psychoanalysis [‚saɪko·ə'nælɪsɪs] *s* psychanalyse *f*
psychoanalyze [‚saɪko'ænə ‚laɪz] *tr* psychanalyser
psychologic(al) [‚saɪko'ladʒɪk(əl)] *adj* psychologique
psychologist [saɪ'kalədʒɪst] *s* psychologue *mf*
psychology [saɪ'kalədʒi] *s* psychologie *f*
psychopath ['saɪkə ‚pæθ] *s* psychopathe *mf*
psycho·sis [saɪ'kosɪs] *s* (*pl* **-ses** [siz]) psychose *f*
psychotic [saɪ'katɪk] *adj & s* psychotique *mf*
ptomaine ['tomen] *s* ptomaïne *f*
pub [pʌb] *s* (Brit) bistrot *m*, café *m*
puberty ['pjubərti] *s* puberté *f*
public ['pʌblɪk] *adj & s* public *m*
publication [‚pʌblɪ'keʃən] *s* publication *f*
publicity [pʌb'lɪsɪti] *s* publicité *f*
public/ity stunt/ *s* canard *m* publicitaire
publicize ['pʌblɪ ‚saɪz] *tr* publier
pub/lic li/brary *s* bibliothèque *f* municipale
pub/lic-opin/ion poll/ *s* sondage *m* de l'opinion, enquête *f* par sondage
pub/lic school/ *s* (U.S.A.) école *f* primaire; (Brit) école privée
pub/lic serv/ant *s* fonctionnaire *mf*
pub/lic speak/ing *s* art *m* oratoire, éloquence *f*
pub/lic toi/let *s* chalet *m* de nécessité
pub/lic util/ity *s* entreprise *f* de service public; **public utilities** actions *fpl* émises par les entreprises de service public
publish ['pʌblɪʃ] *tr* publier
publisher ['pʌblɪʃər] *s* éditeur *m*
pub/lishing house/ *s* maison *f* d'édition
puck [pʌk] *s* palet *m*
pucker ['pʌkər] *s* fronce *m*, faux pli *m* || *tr* froncer || *intr* se froncer
pudding ['pudɪŋ] *s* entremets *m* sucré au lait, crème *f*
puddle ['pʌdəl] *s* flaque *f* || *tr* puddler
pudg·y ['pʌdʒi] *adj* (*comp* **-ier**; *super* **-iest**) bouffi, rondouillard
puerile ['pju·ərɪl] *adj* puéril

puerili·ty [ˌpjuːəˈrɪlɪti] s (pl -ties) puérilité f
Puerto Rican [ˈpwɛrtoˈrikən] adj portoricain || s Portoricain m
puff [pʌf] s souffle m; (of smoke) bouffée f; (in clothing) bouillon m; (in sleeve) bouffant m; (for powder) houppette f; (swelling) bouffissure f; (praise) battage m; (culin) moule m de pâte feuilletée fourré à la crème, à la confiture, etc. || tr lancer des bouffées de; to puff oneself up se rengorger; to puff out souffler; to puff up gonfler || intr souffler; (to swell) gonfler, se gonfler; to puff at or on (a pipe) tirer sur
puff′ paste′ s pâte f feuilletée
pugilism [ˈpjudʒɪˌlɪzəm] s science f pugilistique, boxe f
pugilist [ˈpjudʒɪlɪst] s pugiliste m
pugnacious [pʌɡˈneʃəs] adj pugnace
pug′-nosed′ adj camus
puke [pjuk] s (slang) dégobillage m || tr & intr (slang) dégobiller
pull [pʊl] s secousse f, coup m; (handle of door) poignée f; (slang) piston m, appuis mpl || tr tirer; (a muscle) tordre; (the trigger) appuyer sur; (a proof) (typ) tirer; to pull about tirailler; to pull away arracher; to pull down baisser; (e.g., a house) abattre; (to degrade) abaisser; to pull in rentrer; to pull off enlever; (fig) réussir; to pull on (a garment) mettre; to pull oneself together se ressaisir; to pull out sortir; (a tooth) arracher || intr tirer; bouger lentement, bouger avec effort; to pull at tirer sur; to pull for (slang) plaider en faveur de; to pull in rentrer; (said of train) entrer en gare; to pull out partir; (said of train) sortir de la gare; to pull through se tirer d'affaire; (to get well) se remettre
pull′ chain′ s chasse f d'eau
pullet [ˈpʊlɪt] s poulette f
pulley [ˈpʊli] s poulie f
pulmonary [ˈpʌlməˌnɛri] adj pulmonaire
pulp [pʌlp] s pulpe f; (to make paper) pâte f; (of tooth) bulbe m; to beat to a pulp (coll) mettre en bouillie
pulp′ fic′tion s romans mpl à sensation; le roman de la concierge
pulpit [ˈpʊlpɪt] s chaire f
pulsate [ˈpʌlset] intr palpiter; vibrer
pulsation [pʌlˈseʃən] s pulsation f
pulse [pʌls] s pouls m; to feel or take the pulse of tâter le pouls à
pulverize [ˈpʌlvəˌraɪz] tr pulvériser
pu′mice stone′ [ˈpʌmɪs] s pierre f ponce
pum·mel [ˈpʌməl] v (pret & pp -meled or -melled; ger -meling or -melling) tr bourrer de coups
pump [pʌmp] s pompe f; (slipperlike shoe) escarpin m || tr pomper; (coll) tirer les vers du nez à; to pump up pomper; (a tire) gonfler || intr pomper
pump′han′dle s bras m de pompe

pumpkin [ˈpʌmpkɪn], [ˈpʌŋkɪn] s citrouille f, potiron m
pun [pʌn] s calembour m, jeu m de mots || v (pret & pp punned; ger punning) intr faire des jeux de mots
punch [pʌntʃ] s coup m de poing; (to pierce metal) mandrin m; (to drive a nail or bolt) poinçon m; (for tickets) pince f, emporte-pièce m; (drink; blow) punch m; (mach) poinçonneuse f; (energy) (coll) allant m, punch; to pull no punches parler carrément || tr donner un coup de poing à; poinçonner
punch′ bowl′ s bol m à punch
punch′ card′ s carte f perforée
punch′ clock′ s horloge f de pointage
punch′-drunk′ adj abruti de coups; (coll) abruti, étourdi
punched′ tape′ s bande f enregistreuse perforée
punch′ing bag′ s punching-ball m; (fig) tête f de Turc
punch′ line′ s point m final, phrase f clé
punctilious [pʌŋkˈtɪlɪəs] adj pointilleux, minutieux
punctual [ˈpʌŋktʃuəl] adj ponctuel
punctuate [ˈpʌŋktʃuˌet] tr & intr ponctuer
punctuation [ˌpʌŋktʃuˈeʃən] s ponctuation f
punctua′tion mark′ s signe m de ponctuation
puncture [ˈpʌŋktʃər] s perforation f; (of a tire) crevaison f; (med) ponction f || tr perforer; (a tire) crever; (med) ponctionner
punc′ture-proof′ adj increvable
pundit [ˈpʌndɪt] s pandit m; (savant) mandarin m; (pej) pontife m
pungent [ˈpʌndʒənt] adj piquant
punish [ˈpʌnɪʃ] tr & intr punir
punishment [ˈpʌnɪʃmənt] s punition f; (for a crime) peine f; (severe handling) mauvais traitements mpl
punk [pʌŋk] adj (slang) moche, fichu; to feel punk (slang) être mal fichu || s amadou m; mèche f d'amadou; (decayed wood) bois m pourri; (slang) voyou m, mauvais sujet m
punster [ˈpʌnstər] s faiseur m de calembours
pu·ny [ˈpjuni] adj (comp -nier; super -niest) chétif, malingre
pup [pʌp] s chiot m
pupil [ˈpjupəl] s élève mf; (of the eye) pupille f, prunelle f
puppet [ˈpʌpɪt] s marionnette f; (person controlled by another) fantoche m, pantin m
pup′pet gov′ernment s gouvernement m fantoche
pup′pet show′ s spectacle m de marionnettes, marionnettes fpl
pup·py [ˈpʌpi] s (pl -pies) petit chien m
pup′py love′ s premières amours fpl
pup′ tent′ s tente-abri f
purchase [ˈpʌrtʃəs] s achat m; (leverage) point m d'appui, prise f || tr acheter
pur′chasing pow′er s pouvoir m d'achat

pure [pjur] adj pur

purgative ['pʌrgətɪv] adj & s purgatif m

purgato·ry ['pʌrgə͵tori] s (pl -ries) purgatoire m

purge [pʌrdʒ] s purge f || tr purger

puri·fy ['pjurɪ͵faɪ] v (pret & pp -fied) tr purifier

puritan ['pjurɪtən] adj & s puritain m; **Puritan** puritain

purity ['pjurɪti] s pureté f

purloin [pər'lɔɪn] tr & intr voler

purple ['pʌrpəl] adj pourpre || s (violescent) pourpre m; (deep red, crimson) pourpre f; **born to the purple** né dans la pourpre

purport ['pʌrport] s sens m, teneur f; (intention) but m, objet m || [pər'port] tr signifier, vouloir dire

purpose ['pʌrpəs] s intention f, dessein m; (goal) but m, objet m, fin f; **for all purposes** à tous usages; pratiquement; **for the purpose of, with the purpose of** dans le dessein de, dans le but de; **for this purpose** à cet effet; **for what purpose?** à quoi bon?, à quelle fin?; **on purpose** exprès, à dessein; **to good purpose**, **to some purpose** utilement; **to no purpose** vainement; **to serve the purpose** faire l'affaire

purposely ['pʌrpəsli] adv exprès, à dessein, de propos délibéré

purr [pʌr] s ronron m || intr ronronner

purse [pʌrs] s bourse f, porte-monnaie m; (handbag) sac m à main || tr (one's lips) pincer

purser ['pʌrsər] s commissaire m

purse' snatch'er ['snæt/ər] s voleur m à la tire

purse' strings' spl cordons mpl de bourse

pursue [pər's(j)u] tr poursuivre; (a profession) suivre

pursuit [pər's(j)ut] s poursuite f; profession f

pursuit' plane' s chasseur m, avion m de chasse

purvey [pər've] tr fournir

pus [pʌs] s pus m

push [puʃ] s poussée f || tr pousser; (a button) appuyer sur, presser; **to push around** (coll) rudoyer; **to push aside** écarter; **to push away** or **back** repousser; **to push in** enfoncer; **to push over** faire tomber; **to push through** amener à bonne fin; (a resolution, bill, etc.) faire adopter || intr pousser; **to push forward** or **on** avancer; **to push off** se mettre en route; (naut) pousser au large

push' but'ton s bouton m électrique, poussoir m

push'-but'ton war'fare s guerre f presse-bouton

push'cart' s voiture f à bras

pushing ['puʃɪŋ] adj entreprenant; indiscret; agressif

pusillanimous [͵pjusɪ'læniməs] adj pusillanime

puss [pus] s minet m; (slang) gueule f; **sly puss** (girl) (coll) futée f || interj minet!

Puss' in Boots' s Chat m botté

puss' in the cor'ner s les quatre coins mpl

puss·y ['pusi] s (pl -ies) minet m || interj minet!

puss'y wil'low s saule m nord-américain aux chatons très soyeux

put [put] v (pret & pp put; ger putting) tr mettre, placer; (to throw) lancer; (a question) poser; **to put across** passer; faire accepter; **to put aside** mettre de côté; **to put away** ranger; (to jail) mettre en prison; **to put back** remettre; retarder; **to put down** poser; (e.g., a name) noter; (a revolution) réprimer; (to lower) baisser; **to put off** renvoyer; (to mislead) dérouter; **to put on** (clothes) mettre; (a play) mettre en scène, monter; (a brake) serrer; (a light, radio, etc.) allumer; (to feign) feindre, simuler; **to put oneself out** se déranger; **to put on sale** mettre en vente; mettre en solde; **to put out** (the hand) étendre; (the fire, light, etc.) éteindre; (s.o.'s eyes) crever; (e.g., a book) publier; (to show to the door) mettre dehors; (to vex) contrarier; **to put over** (coll) faire accepter; **to put s.o. through s.th.** faire subir q.ch. à qn; **to put through** passer; (a resolution, bill, etc.) faire adopter; **to put up** lever; (a house) construire, faire construire; (one's collar, hair, etc.) relever; (a picture) accrocher; (a notice) afficher; (a tent) dresser; (an umbrella) ouvrir; (the price) augmenter; (money as an investment) fournir; (resistance) offrir; (an overnight guest) loger; (fruit, vegetables, etc.) conserver; (coll) pousser, inciter || intr se diriger; **to put on** feindre; **to put up** loger; **to put up with** tolérer

put'-out' adj ennuyeux, fâcheux

putrid ['pjutrɪd] adj putride

putter ['pʌtər] intr—**to putter around** s'occuper de bagatelles

put·ty ['pʌti] s (pl -ties) mastic m || (pret & pp -tied) tr mastiquer

put'ty knife' s (pl knives) couteau m à mastiquer

put'-up' adj (coll) machiné à l'avance, monté

puzzle ['pʌzəl] s énigme f || tr intriguer; **to puzzle out** déchiffrer || intr —**to puzzle over** se creuser la tête pour comprendre

puzzler ['pʌzlər] s énigme f, colle f

puzzling ['pʌzlɪŋ] adj énigmatique

PW ['pi'dʌbəl͵ju] s (letterword) (prisoner of war) P.G.

pyg·my ['pɪgmi] adj pygméen || s (pl -mies) pygmée m

pylon ['paɪlɑn] s pylône m

pyramid ['pɪrəmɪd] *s* pyramide *f* || *tr* augmenter graduellement || *intr* pyramider

pyre [paɪr] *s* bûcher *m* funéraire

Pyrenees ['pɪrɪ ‚niz] *spl* Pyrénées *fpl*

pyrites [paɪ'raɪtiz], ['paɪraɪts] *s* pyrite *f*

pyrotechnical [‚paɪrə'teknɪkəl] *adj* pyrotechnique

pyrotechnics [‚paɪrə'teknɪks] *spl* pyrotechnie *f*

python ['paɪθɑn], ['paɪθən] *s* python *m*

pythoness ['paɪθənɪs] *s* pythonisse *f*

pyx [pɪks] *s* (eccl) ciboire *m*; (for carrying Eucharist to sick) (eccl) pyxide *f*; (at a mint) boîte *f* des monnaies

Q

Q, q [kju] *s* XVIIe lettre de l'alphabet

quack [kwæk] *adj* frauduleux, de charlatan || *s* charlatan *m* || *intr* cancaner, faire couin-couin

quacker·y ['kwækərɪ] *s* (pl -ies) charlatanisme *m*

quadrangle ['kwɑd‚ræŋgəl] *s* plan *m* quadrangulaire; cour *f* carrée

quadrant ['kwɑdrənt] *s* (instrument) quart *m* de cercle, secteur *m*; (math) quadrant *m*

quadroon [kwɑd'run] *s* quarteron *m*

quadruped ['kwɑdrə‚ped] *adj & s* quadrupède *m*

quadruple ['kwɑdrupəl] *or* [kwɑd'rupəl] *adj & s* quadruple *m* || *tr & intr* quadrupler

quadruplets ['kwɑdru‚plets], [kwɑd'ruplets] *spl* quadruplés *mpl*

quaff [kwɑf], [kwæf] *s* lampée *f* || *tr & intr* boire à longs traits

quagmire ['kwæg‚maɪr] *s* bourbier *m*, fondrière *f*

quail [kwel] *s* caille *f* || *intr* fléchir

quaint [kwent] *adj* pittoresque, bizarre

quake [kwek] *s* tremblement *m*; (earthquake) tremblement de terre || *intr* trembler

Quaker ['kwekər] *adj & s* quaker *m*

Quak′er meet′ing *s* réunion *f* de quakers; (coll) réunion où il y a très peu de conversation

quali·fy ['kwɑlɪ‚faɪ] *v* (pret & pp -fied) *tr* qualifier; (e.g., a recommendation) apporter des réserves à, modifier; **to qualify oneself for** se préparer à, se rendre apte à || *intr* se qualifier

quali·ty ['kwɑlɪtɪ] *s* (pl -ties) qualité *f*; (of a sound) timbre *m*

qualm [kwɑm] *s* scrupule *m*; (remorse) remords *m*; (nausea) soulèvement *m* de cœur

quanda·ry ['kwɑndərɪ] *s* (pl -ries) incertitude *f*, impasse *f*

quanti·ty ['kwɑntɪtɪ] *s* (pl -ties) quantité *f*

quan·tum ['kwɑntəm] *adj* quantique || *s* (pl -ta [tə]) quantum *m*

quan′tum the′ory *s* théorie *f* des quanta

quarantine ['kwɑrən‚tin], ['kwɑrən‚tin] *s* quarantaine *f* || *tr* mettre en quarantaine

quar·rel ['kwɑrəl], ['kwɔrəl] *s* querelle *f*, dispute *f*; **to have no quarrel with** n'avoir rien à redire à; **to pick a quarrel with** chercher querelle à || *v* (pret & pp -reled or -relled; ger -reling or -relling) *intr* se quereller, se disputer; **to quarrel over** contester sur, se disputer

quarrelsome ['kwɑrəlsəm], ['kwɔrəlsəm] *adj* querelleur

quar·ry ['kwɑrɪ], ['kwɔrɪ] *s* (pl -ries) carrière *f*; (hunted animal) proie *f* || *v* (pret & pp -ried) *tr* extraire || *intr* exploiter une carrière

quart [kwɔrt] *s* quart *m* de gallon, pinte *f*

quarter ['kwɔrtər] *s* quart *m*; (American coin) vingt-cinq cents *mpl*; (of a year) trimestre *m*; (of town; of beef; of moon; of shield) quartier *m*; **a quarter after one** une heure et quart; **a quarter of an hour** un quart d'heure; **a quarter to one** une heure moins le quart; **at close quarters** corps à corps; **quarters** (mil) quartiers *mpl*, cantonnement *m* || *tr & intr* (mil) loger, cantonner

quar′ter-deck′ *s* gaillard *m* d'arrière

quar′ter-hour′ *s* quart *m* d'heure; **every quarter-hour on the quarter-hour** tous les quarts d'heure au quart d'heure juste

quarter·ly ['kwɔrtərlɪ] *adj* trimestriel || *s* (pl -lies) publication *f* ou revue *f* trimestrielle || *adv* trimestriellement, par trimestre

quar′ter-mas′ter *s* (mil) quartier-maître *m*, intendant *m* militaire

Quar′ter-master Corps′ *s* Intendance *f*, service *m* de l'Intendance

quar′ter note′ *s* (mus) noire *f*

quar′ter rest′ *s* (mus) soupir *m*

quar′ter tone′ *s* (mus) quart *m* de ton

quartet [kwɔr'tet] *s* quatuor *m*

quartz [kwɔrts] *s* quartz *m*

quasar ['kwesɑr] *s* (astr) quasar *m*

quash [kwɑʃ] *tr* étouffer; (to set aside) annuler, invalider

quatrain ['kwɑtren] *s* quatrain *m*

quaver ['kwevər] *s* tremblement *m*; (in the singing voice) trémolo *m*; (mus) croche *f* || *intr* trembloter

quay [ki] *s* quai *m*, débarcadère *m*

queen [kwin] *s* reine *f*; (cards, chess) reine

queen' bee' s reine f des abeilles
queen' dow'ager s reine f douairière
queen•ly ['kwinli] adj (comp -lier; super -liest) de reine, digne d'une reine
queen' moth'er s reine f mère
queen' post' s faux poinçon m
queer [kwɪr] adj bizarre, drôle; (suspicious) (coll) suspect; (homosexual) (coll) pervers, inverti; **to feel queer** (coll) se sentir indisposé || s excentrique mf; (homosexual) (coll) tapette f, inverti m || tr (slang) faire échouer, déranger
quell [kwɛl] tr étouffer, réprimer; (pain, sorrow, etc.) calmer
quench [kwɛntʃ] tr (the thirst) étancher; (a rebellion) étouffer; (a fire) éteindre
que•ry ['kwɪri] s (pl -ries) question f; doute m; (question mark) point m d'interrogation || v (pret & pp -ried) tr questionner; mettre en doute; (to affix a question mark) marquer d'un point d'interrogation
quest [kwɛst] s quête f; **in quest of** en quête de
question ['kwɛstʃən] s question f; doute m; **beyond question** indiscutable, incontestable; **it is a question of** il s'agit de; **out of the question** impossible, impensable; **to ask s.o. a question** poser une question à qn; **to beg the question** faire une pétition de principe; **to call into question** mettre en question; **to move the previous question** (parl) demander la question préalable; **without question** sans aucun doute || tr interroger, questionner; (to cast doubt upon) douter de, contester
questionable ['kwɛstʃənəbəl] adj discutable, douteux
ques'tion mark' s point m d'interrogation
questionnaire [,kwɛstʃən'ɛr] s questionnaire m
queue [kju] s queue f || intr—**to queue up** faire la queue
quibble ['kwɪbəl] intr chicaner, ergoter
quibbling ['kwɪblɪŋ] s chicane f
quick [kwɪk] adj rapide, vif || s—**the quick and the dead** les vivants et les morts; **to cut to the quick** piquer au vif
quicken ['kwɪkən] tr accélérer; (e.g., the imagination) animer || intr s'accélérer; s'animer
quick'lime' s chaux f vive
quick' lunch' s casse-croûte m, repas m léger
quickly ['kwɪkli] adv vite, rapidement
quick'sand' s sable m mouvant
quick'sil'ver s vif-argent m, mercure m
quick'-tem'pered adj coléreux
quiet ['kwaɪ•ət] adj (still) tranquille, silencieux; (person) modeste, discret; (market) (com) calme; **be quiet!** taisez-vous!; **to keep quiet** rester tranquille; (to not speak) se taire || s tranquillité f; (rest) repos m; **on the quiet** en douce, à la dérobée ||

tr calmer, tranquilliser; (a child) faire taire || intr—**to quiet down** se calmer
quill [kwɪl] s plume f d'oie; (hollow part) tuyau m (de plume); (of hedgehog, porcupine) piquant m
quilt [kwɪlt] s courtepointe f || tr piquer
quince [kwɪns] s coing m; (tree) cognassier m
quinine ['kwaɪnaɪn] s quinine f
quinsy ['kwɪnzi] s angine f
quintessence [kwɪn'tɛsəns] s quintessence f
quintet [kwɪn'tɛt] s quintette m
quintuplets ['kwɪntu,plɛts], [kwɪn-'tʌplɛts], [kwɪn't(j)uplɛts] spl quintuplés mpl
quip [kwɪp] s raillerie f, quolibet m || v (pret & pp quipped; ger quipping) tr dire sur un ton railleur || intr railler
quire [kwaɪr] s main f
quirk [kwʌrk] s excentricité f; (subterfuge) faux-fuyant m; **quirk of fate** caprice m du sort
quit [kwɪt] adj quitte; **to be quits** être quitte; **to call it quits** cesser, s'y renoncer; **we are quits** nous voilà quittes || v (pret & pp quit or quitted; ger quitting) tr (e.g., a city) quitter; (one's work, a pursuit, etc.) cesser; **to quit** + ger s'arrêter de + inf || intr partir; (coll) lâcher la partie
quite [kwaɪt] adv tout à fait; **quite a story** (coll) toute une histoire
quitter ['kwɪtər] s défaitiste m, lâcheur m
quiver ['kwɪvər] s tremblement m; (to hold arrows) carquois m || intr trembler
quixotic [kwɪks'ɑtɪk] adj de don Quichotte; visionnaire, exalté
quiz [kwɪz] s (pl quizzes) interrogation f, colle f || v (pret & pp quizzed; ger quizzing) tr examiner, interroger
quiz' sec'tion s classe f d'exercices
quiz' show' s émission-questionnaire f
quizzical ['kwɪzɪkəl] adj curieux; (laughable) risible; (mocking) railleur
quoin [kɔɪn], [kwɔɪn] s angle m; (cornerstone) pierre f d'angle; (wedge) coin m, cale f || tr coincer, caler
quoit [kwɔɪt], [kɔɪt] s palet m; **to play quoits** jouer au palet
quondam ['kwɑndæm] adj ci-devant, d'autrefois
quorum ['kwɔrəm] s quorum m
quota ['kwotə] s quote-part f; (e.g., of immigration) quota m, contingent m
quotation [kwo'teʃən] s (from a book) citation f; (of prices) cours m, cote f
quota'tion marks' spl guillemets mpl
quote [kwot] s (from a book) citation f; (of prices) cours m, cote f; **in quotes** (coll) entre guillemets || tr (from a book) citer; (values) coter || intr tirer des citations; **to quote out of context** citer hors contexte || interj je cite
quotient ['kwoʃənt] s quotient m

R, r [ɑr] *s* XVIIIᵉ lettre de l'alphabet
rabbet ['ræbɪt] *s* feuillure *f* ‖ *tr* feuiller
rab·bi ['ræbaɪ] *s* (*pl* **-bis** or **-bies**) rabbin *m*
rabbit ['ræbɪt] *s* lapin *m*
rab/bit stew/ *s* lapin *m* en civet
rabble ['ræbəl] *s* canaille *f*
rab/ble-rous/er *s* fomentateur *m*, agitateur *m*
rabies ['rebiz], ['rebɪˌiz] *s* rage *f*
raccoon [ræ'kun] *s* raton *m* laveur
race [res] *s* race *f*; (*contest*) course *f*; (*channel to lead water*) bief *m*; (*rapid current*) raz *m* ‖ *tr* lutter de vitesse avec; (*e.g., a horse*) faire courir; (*a motor*) emballer ‖ *intr* faire une course, courir; (*said of motor*) s'emballer
race/ horse/ *s* cheval *m* de course
race/ ri/ot *s* émeute *f* raciale
race/ track/ *s* champ *m* de courses, hippodrome *m*
racial ['refəl] *adj* racial
rac/ing car/ *s* automobile *f* de course
rac/ing odds/ *spl* cote *f*
rack [ræk] *s* (*shelf*) étagère *f*; (*to hang clothes*) portemanteau *m*; (*for baggage*) porte-bagages *m*; (*for guns; for fodder*) râtelier *m*; (*for torture*) chevalet *m*; (*bar made to gear with a pinion*) crémaillère *f*; **to go to rack and ruin** aller à vau-l'eau ‖ *tr* (*with hunger, remorse, etc.*) tenailler; (*one's brains*) se creuser
racket ['rækɪt] *s* raquette *f*; (*noise*) vacarme *m*; (*slang*) racket *m*; **to make a racket** faire du tapage
racketeer [ˌrækɪ'tɪr] *s* racketter *m* ‖ *intr* pratiquer l'escroquerie
rack/ rail/way *s* chemin *m* de fer à crémaillère
rac·y ['resi] *adj* (*comp* **-ier**; *super* **-iest**) plein de verve, vigoureux; parfumé; (*off-color*) sale, grivois
radar ['redar] *s* (*acronym*) (**radio detecting and ranging**) radar *m*
ra/dar sta/tion *s* poste *m* radar
radiant ['redɪ·ənt] *adj* radieux, rayonnant; (*astr & phys*) radiant
radiate ['redɪˌet] *tr* rayonner; (*e.g., happiness*) répandre ‖ *intr* rayonner
radiation [ˌredɪ'e/ən] *s* rayonnement *m*, radiation *f*
radia/tion sick/ness *s* mal *m* des rayons
radiator ['redɪˌetər] *s* radiateur *m*
ra/diator cap/ *s* bouchon *m* de radiateur
radical ['rædɪkəl] *adj & s* radical *m*
radi·o ['redɪˌo] *s* (*pl* **-os**) radio *f* ‖ *tr* radiodiffuser
radioactive [ˌredɪ·o'æktɪv] *adj* radioactif
ra/dio am/ateur *s* sans-filiste *mf*
ra/dio announ/cer *s* speaker *m*
ra/dio·broad/cast/ing *s* radiodiffusion *f*
ra/dio·fre/quency *s* radiofréquence *f*

radiogram ['redɪ·oˌgræm] *s* radiogramme *m*
ra/dio lis/tener *s* auditeur *m* de la radio
radiology [ˌredɪ'ɑledʒi] *s* radiologie *f*
ra/dio net/work *s* chaîne *f* de radiodiffusion
ra/dio news/cast *s* journal *m* parlé, radio-journal *m*
ra/dio receiv/er *s* récepteur *m* de radio
radioscopy [ˌredɪ'ɑskəpi] *s* radioscopie *f*
ra/dio set/ *s* poste *m* de radio
ra/dio sta/tion *s* poste *m* émetteur
ra/dio tube/ *s* lampe *f* de radio
radish ['redɪʃ] *s* radis *m*
radium ['redɪ·əm] *s* radium *m*
radi·us ['redɪ·əs] *s* (*pl* **-i** [ˌaɪ] or **-uses**) rayon *m*; (anat) radius *m*; **within a radius of** dans un rayon de, à . . . à la ronde
raffish ['ræfɪʃ] *adj* bravache; (*flashy*) criard
raffle ['ræfəl] *s* tombola *f* ‖ *tr* mettre en tombola
raft [ræft], [rɑft] *s* radeau *m*; **a raft of** (coll) un tas de
rafter ['ræftər], ['rɑftər] *s* chevron *m*
rag [ræg] *s* chiffon *m*; **in rags** en haillons; **to chew the rag** (slang) tailler une bavette
ragamuffin ['rægəˌmʌfɪn] *s* gueux *m*, va-nu-pieds *m*; (*urchin*) gamin *m*
rag/ doll/ *s* poupée *f* de chiffon
rage [redʒ] *s* rage *f*; **to be all the rage** faire fureur; **to fly into a rage** entrer en fureur ‖ *intr* faire rage
rag/ fair/ *s* marché *m* aux puces
ragged ['rægɪd] *adj* en haillons; (*edge*) hérissé
ragpicker ['rægˌpɪkər] *s* chiffonnier *m*
rag/time/ *s* rythme *m* syncopé du jazz; musique *f* syncopée du jazz
rag/weed/ *s* ambroisie *f*
ragwort ['rægˌwʌrt] *s* (*Senecio vulgaris*) séneçon *m*; (*S. jacobaea*) jacobée *f*
raid [red] *s* incursion *f*, razzia *f*; (*by police*) descente *f*; (mil) raid *m* ‖ *tr* razzier; faire une descente dans
rail [rel] *s* rail *m*; (*railing*) balustrade *f*; (*of stairway*) rampe *f*; (*of, e.g., a bridge*) garde-fou *m*; (orn) râle *m*; **by rail** par chemin de fer ‖ *intr* invectiver; **to rail at** invectiver
rail/ fence/ *s* palissade *f* à claire-voie
rail/head/ *s* tête *f* de ligne
railing ['relɪŋ] *s* balustrade *f*
rail/road/ *adj* ferroviaire ‖ *s* chemin *m* de fer ‖ *tr* (*a bill*) faire voter en vitesse; (coll) emprisonner à tort
rail/road cros/sing *s* passage *m* à niveau
railroader ['relˌrodər] *s* cheminot *m*
rail/road sta/tion *s* gare *f*
rail/way/ *adj* ferroviaire ‖ *s* chemin *m* de fer
raiment ['remənt] *s* habillement *m*
rain [ren] *s* pluie *f*; **in the rain** sous la pluie ‖ *tr* faire pleuvoir ‖ *intr* pleu-

voir; **it is raining cats and dogs** il
pleut à seaux

rainbow ['ren ‚bo] s arc-en-ciel m

rain′coat′ s imperméable m

rain′fall′ s chute f de pluie

rain′proof′ adj imperméable

rain′ wa′ter s eau f de pluie

rain·y ['reni] adj (comp **-ier**; super
-iest) pluvieux

raise [rez] s augmentation f; (in poker)
relance f || tr augmenter; (plants,
animals, children; one's voice; a
number to a certain power) élever;
(an army, a camp, a siege; anchor;
game) lever; (an objection, questions,
etc.) soulever; (doubts; a hope; a
storm) faire naître; (a window) relever; (one's head, one's voice; prices;
the land) hausser; (a flag) arborer;
(the dead) ressusciter; (money) se
procurer; (the ante) relancer; **to raise
up** soulever, dresser

raisin ['rezən] s raisin m sec, grain m
de raisin sec

rake [rek] s râteau m; (person) dé-
bauché m || tr ratisser; **to rake to-
gether** râteler

rake′-off′ s (coll) gratte f

rakish ['rekiʃ] adj gaillard; dissolu

ral·ly ['ræli] s (pl **-lies**) ralliement m;
réunion f politique; (in a game) re-
prise f; (auto race) rallye m || v (pret
& pp **-lied**) tr rallier || intr se rallier;
(from illness) se remettre; (sports) se
reprendre; **to rally to the side of** se
rallier à

ram [ræm] s bélier m || v (pret & pp
rammed; ger **ramming**) tr tampon-
ner; **to ram down or in** enfoncer ||
intr se tamponner; **to ram into** tamponner

ramble ['ræmbəl] s flânerie f || intr flâ-
ner, errer à l'aventure; (to talk aimlessly) divaguer

rami·fy ['ræmɪ ‚faɪ] v (pret & pp **-fied**)
tr ramifier || intr se ramifier

ramp [ræmp] s rampe f

rampage ['ræmpedʒ] s tempête f; **to go
on a rampage** se déchaîner

rampart ['ræmpart] s rempart m

ram′rod′ s écouvillon m

ram′shack′le adj délabré

ranch [rænt∫] s ranch m, rancho m

rancid ['rænsɪd] adj rance

rancor ['ræŋkər] s rancœur f

random ['rændəm] adj fortuit; **at random** au hasard

range [rendʒ] s (row) rangée f; (scope)
portée f; (mountains) chaîne f;
(stove) cuisinière f; (for rifle practice) champ m de tir; (of colors, musical notes, prices, speeds, etc.)
gamme f; (of words) répartition f;
(of voice) tessiture f; (of vision, of
activity, etc.) champ m; (for pasture)
grand pâturage m; **within range of** à
portée de || tr ranger || intr se ranger;
to range from s'échelonner entre, varier entre; **to range over** parcourir

range′ find′er s télémètre m

rank [ræŋk] adj fétide, rance; (injus-
tice) criant; (vegetation) luxuriant ||

s rang m || tr ranger || intr occuper
le premier rang; **to rank above** être
supérieur à; **to rank with** aller de pair
avec

rank′ and file′ s hommes mpl de
troupe; commun m des mortels; (of
the party, union, etc.) commun m

rankle ['ræŋkəl] tr ulcérer; irriter ||
intr s'ulcérer

ransack ['rænsæk] tr fouiller, fouiller
dans; mettre à sac

ransom ['rænsəm] s rançon f || tr ran-
çonner

rant [rænt] intr tempêter

rap [ræp] s tape f; (noise) petit coup
m sec; (slang) éreintement m; **to not
care a rap** (slang) s'en ficher; **to take
the rap** (slang) se laisser châtier || v
(pret & pp **rapped**; ger **rapping**) tr &
intr frapper d'un coup sec

rapacious [rə'pe∫əs] adj rapace

rape [rep] s viol m || tr violer

rapid ['ræpɪd] adj rapide || **rapids** spl
rapides mpl

rap′id-fire′ adj à tir rapide

rapidity [rə'pɪdətɪ] s rapidité f

rapier ['repɪ‚ər] s rapière f

rapt [ræpt] adj ravi; absorbé

rapture ['ræpt∫ər] s ravissement m

rare [rer] adj rare; (meat) saignant;
(amusing) (coll) impayable

rare′ bird′ s merle m blanc

rarely ['rerli] adv rarement

rascal ['ræskəl] s coquin m

rash [ræ∫] adj téméraire || s éruption f

rasp [ræsp], [rɑsp] s crissement m;
(tool) râpe f || tr râper || intr crisser

raspber·ry ['ræz‚beri], ['rɑz‚beri] s (pl
-ries) framboise f

rasp′berry bush′ s framboisier m

rat [ræt] s rat m; (false hair) (coll)
postiche m; (deserter) (slang) lâcheur
m; (informer) (slang) mouchard m;
(scoundrel) (slang) cochon m; **rats!**
zut!; **to smell a rat** (coll) soupçonner
anguille sous roche

ratchet ['ræt∫ɪt] s encliquetage m

rate [ret] s taux m; (for freight, mail, a
subscription) tarif m; **at any rate** en
tout cas; **at the rate of** à raison de ||
tr évaluer; mériter || intr (coll) être
favori

rate′ of exchange′ s cours m

rather ['ræðər], ['rɑðər] adv plutôt;
(fairly) assez; **rather than** plutôt que
|| interj je vous crois!

rathskeller ['ræts‚kelər] s caveau m

rati·fy ['rætɪ‚faɪ] v (pret & pp **-fied**)
tr ratifier

rating ['retɪŋ] s classement m, cote f

ra·tio ['re∫o], ['re∫ɪ‚o] s (pl **-tios**)
raison f, rapport m

ration ['re∫ən], ['ræ∫ən] s ration f || tr
rationner

rational ['ræ∫ənəl] adj rationnel

ra′tion book′ s tickets mpl de rationnement

ra′tion card′ s carte f de ravitaillement

rat′ poi′son s mort m aux rats

rat′-tail file′ s queue-de-rat f

rattan [ræ'tæn] s rotin m

rattle ['rætəl] s (*number of short, sharp sounds*) bruit *m* de ferraille, cliquetis *m*; (*noisemaking device*) crécelle *f*; (*child's toy*) hochet *m*; (*in the throat*) râle *m* || *tr* agiter; (*to confuse*) (coll) affoler; **to rattle off** débiter comme un moulin || *intr* cliqueter; (*said of windows*) trembler

rat′tle·snake′ s serpent *m* à sonnettes

rat′trap′ s ratière *f*

raucous ['rɔkəs] *adj* rauque

ravage ['rævɪdʒ] s ravage *m*; **ravages** (*of time*) injure *f* || *tr* ravager

rave [rev] s (coll) éloge *m* enthousiaste || *intr* délirer; **to rave about** or **over** s'extasier devant or sur

raven ['revən] s corbeau *m*

ravenous ['rævənəs] *adj* vorace

rave′ review′ s article *m* dithyrambique

ravine [rə'vin] s ravin *m*

ravish ['rævɪʃ] *tr* ravir

ravishing ['rævɪʃɪŋ] *adj* ravissant

raw [rɔ] *adj* cru; (*sugar, metal*) brut; (*silk*) grège; (*wound*) vif; (*wind*) aigre; (*weather*) humide et froid; novice, inexpérimenté

raw′boned′ *adj* décharné

raw′ deal′ s (slang) mauvais tour *m*

raw′hide′ s cuir *m* vert

raw′ mate′rial s matière *f* première, matières premières, matière brute

ray [re] s (*of light*) rayon *m*; (*fish*) raie *f*

rayon ['re·ɑn] s rayonne *f*

raze [rez] *tr* raser

razor ['rezər] s rasoir *m*

ra′zor blade′ s lame *f* de rasoir

ra′zor strop′ s cuir *m* à rasoir

razz [ræz] *tr* (slang) mettre en boîte

reach [ritʃ] s portée *f*; **out of reach (of)** hors d'atteinte (de), hors de portée (de); **within reach of** à portée de || *tr* atteindre; arriver à; **to reach out** (*a hand*) tendre; (*an arm*) allonger || *intr* s'étendre

react [rɪ'ækt] *intr* réagir

reaction [rɪ'ækʃən] s réaction *f*

reaction·a·ry [rɪ'ækʃənˌɛri] *adj* réactionnaire & s (*pl* -**ies**) réactionnaire *mf*

reactor [rɪ'æktər] s réacteur *m*

read [rid] *v* (*pret* & *pp* **read** [red]) *tr* lire; **to read over** parcourir || *intr* lire; (*said of passage, description, etc.*) se lire; (*said, e.g., of thermometer*) marquer; **to read on** continuer à lire; **to read up on** étudier

reader ['ridər] s lecteur *m*; livre *m* de lecture

readily ['rɛdɪli] *adv* (*willingly*) volontiers; (*easily*) facilement

reading ['ridɪŋ] s lecture *f*

read′ing desk′ s pupitre *m*

read′ing glass′ s loupe *f*; **reading glasses** lunettes *fpl* pour lire

read′ing lamp′ s lampe *f* de bureau

read′ing room′ s salle *f* de lecture

read·y ['rɛdi] *adj* (*comp* -**ier**; *super* -**iest**) prêt; (*quick*) vif; (*money*) comptant || *v* (*pret* & *pp* -**ied**) *tr* préparer || *intr* se préparer

read′y cash′ s argent *m* comptant

read′y-made′ suit′ s (*for men*) complet *m* de confection; (*for women*) costume *m* de confection

ready-to-eat ['rɛditə'it] *adj* prêt à servir

ready-to-wear ['rɛditə'wɛr] *adj* prêt à porter || s prêt-à-porter *m*

reaffirm [ˌri·ə'fʌrm] *tr* réaffirmer

reagent [rɪ'edʒənt] s (chem) réactif *m*

real ['ri·əl] *adj* vrai, réel

re′al estate′ s biens *mpl* immobiliers

re′al-estate′ *adj* immobilier

realism ['ri·ə ˌlɪzəm] s réalisme *m*

realist ['ri·əlɪst] s réaliste *mf*

realistic [ˌri·ə'lɪstɪk] *adj* réaliste

reali·ty [ri'ɛlti] s (*pl* -**ties**) réalité *f*

realize ['ri·əˌlaɪz] *tr* se rendre compte de, s'apercevoir de; (*hopes, profits, etc.*) réaliser

really ['ri·əli] *adv* vraiment

realm [rɛlm] s royaume *m*; (*field*) domaine *m*

realtor ['ri·əlˌtɔr], ['ri·əltər] s agent *m* immobilier

ream [rim] s rame *f*; **reams** (coll) masses *fpl* || *tr* aléser

reap [rip] *tr* moissonner; (*to gather*) recueillir

reaper ['ripər] s moissonneur *m*; (mach) moissonneuse *f*

reappear [ˌri·ə'pɪr] *intr* réapparaître

reappearance [ˌri·ə'pɪrəns] s réapparition *f*

reapportionment [ˌri·ə'pɔrʃənmənt] s nouvelle répartition *f*

rear [rɪr] *adj* arrière, d'arrière, de derrière || s derrière *m*; (*of a car, ship, etc.; of an army*) arrière *m*; (*of a row*) queue *f*; **to the rear!** (mil) demitour à droite! || *tr* élever || *intr* (*said of animal*) se cabrer

rear′ ad′miral s contre-amiral *m*

rear′-axle assem′bly s (*pl* -**blies**) pont *m* arrière

rear′ drive′ s traction *f* arrière

rearmament [ri'ɑrməmənt] s réarmement *m*

rearrange [ˌri·ə'rendʒ] *tr* arranger de nouveau

rear′-view mir′ror s rétroviseur *m*

rear′ win′dow s (aut) lunette *f* arrière

reason ['rizən] s raison *f*; **by reason of** à cause de; **for good reason** pour cause; **to listen to reason** entendre raison; **to stand to reason** être de toute évidence || *tr* & *intr* raisonner

reasonable ['rizənəbəl] *adj* raisonnable

reassessment [ˌri·ə'sɛsmənt] s réévaluation *f*

reassure [ˌri·ə'ʃʊr] *tr* rassurer

reawaken [ˌri·ə'wekən] *tr* réveiller || *intr* se réveiller

rebate ['ribet], [rɪ'bet] s rabais *m*, escompte *m*; ristourne *f*, bonification *f* || *tr* faire un rabais sur

rebel ['rɛbəl] *adj* & s rebelle *mf* || **re·bel** [rɪ'bɛl] *v* (*pret* & *pp* -**belled**; *ger* -**belling**) *intr* se rebeller

rebellion [rɪ'bɛljən] s rébellion *f*

rebellious [rɪ'bɛljəs] *adj* rebelle

re·bind [ri'baɪnd] *v* (*pret* & *pp* -**bound**) *tr* (bb) relier à neuf

rebirth ['ribʌrθ] s renaissance f
rebore [ri'bor] tr rectifier
rebound ['ri,baund], [ri'baund] s re-
bondissement m || [ri'baund] intr
rebondir
rebroad·cast [ri'brɔd,kæst], [ri'brɔd-
,kɑst] s retransmission f || v (pret &
pp -cast or -casted) tr retransmettre
rebuff [ri'bʌf] s rebuffade f || tr mal
accueillir
re·build [ri'bild] v (pret & pp -built)
tr reconstruire
rebuke [ri'bjuk] s réprimande f || tr
réprimander
re·but [ri'bʌt] v (pret & pp -butted;
ger -butting) tr réfuter, repousser
rebuttal [ri'bʌtəl] s réfutation f
recall [ri'kɔl], ['rikɔl] s rappel m ||
[ri'kɔl] tr rappeler; se rappeler de
recant [ri'kænt] tr rétracter || intr se
rétracter
re·cap ['ri,kæp], [ri'kæp] v (pret & pp
-capped; ger -capping) tr rechaper
recapitulation [,rikə,pɪt[ə'leʃən] s récapitulation f
re·cast ['ri,kæst], ['ri,kɑst] s refonte
f || [ri'kæst], [ri'kɑst] v (pret & pp
-cast) tr (metal; a play, novel, etc.)
refondre; (the actors of a play) re-
distribuer
recede [ri'sid] intr reculer; (said of
forehead, chin, etc.) fuir; (said of
sea) se retirer
receipt [ri'sit] s (for goods) récépissé
m; (for money) récépissé, reçu m;
(recipe) recette f; receipts recettes; to
acknowledge receipt of accuser récep-
tion de || tr acquitter
receive [ri'siv] tr recevoir; (stolen
goods) recéler; (a station) (rad)
capter; received payment pour acquit
|| intr recevoir
receiver [ri'sivər] s (of letter) destinataire mf; (in bankruptcy) syndic m,
liquidateur m; (telp) récepteur m
receiv'ing set' s poste m récepteur
recent ['risənt] adj récent
recently ['risəntli] adv récemment
receptacle [ri'septəkəl] s récipient m;
(elec) prise f femelle
reception [ri'sepʃən] s réception f;
(welcome) accueil m
recep'tion desk' s réception f
receptionist [ri'sepʃənist] s préposé m
à la réception
receptive [ri'septiv] adj réceptif
recess [ri'ses], ['rises] s (of court,
legislature, etc.) ajournement m; (at
school) récréation f; (in a wall) niche
f || [ri'ses] tr ajourner; (s.th., e.g., in
a wall) encastrer || intr s'ajourner
recession [ri'seʃən] s récession f
recipe ['resi,pi] s recette f
recipient [ri'sipi·ənt] s (person) bénéficiaire mf; (of a degree, honor, etc.)
récipiendaire m; (of blood) receveur
m
reciprocal [ri'siprəkəl] adj réciproque
reciprocity [,resi'prasiti] s réciprocité f
recital [ri'saitəl] s récit m; (of music
or poetry) récital m

recite [ri'sait] tr réciter; narrer
reckless ['reklis] adj téméraire, imprudent, insouciant
reckon ['rekən] tr calculer; considérer;
(coll) supposer, imaginer || intr cal-
culer; to reckon on compter sur; to
reckon with tenir compte de
reclaim [ri'klem] tr récupérer; (e.g.,
waste land) mettre en valeur; (a person) réformer
reclamation [,reklə'meʃən] s récupération f; (e.g., of waste land) mise f
en valeur; (of a person) réforme f
recline [ri'klain] tr appuyer, reposer ||
intr s'appuyer, se reposer
recluse [ri'klus], ['reklus] adj & s re-
clus m
recognition [,rekəg'niʃən] s reconnaissance f
recognize ['rekəg,naiz] tr reconnaître;
(parl) donner la parole à
recoil [ri'kɔil] s répugnance f; (of,
e.g., firearm) recul m || intr reculer
recollect [,rekə'lekt] tr se rappeler
recollection [,rekə'lekʃən] s souvenir m
recommend [,rekə'mend] tr recommander
recompense ['rekəm,pens] s récom-
pense f || tr récompenser
reconcile ['rekən,sail] tr réconcilier;
to reconcile oneself to se résigner à
reconnaissance [ri'kanisəns] s reconnaissance f
reconnoiter [,rekə'nɔitər], [,rikə'nɔi-
tər] tr & intr reconnaître
reconquer [ri'kaŋkər] tr reconquérir
reconquest [ri'kaŋkwest] s reconquête f
reconsider [,rikən'sidər] tr reconsidérer
reconstruct [,rikən'strʌkt] tr reconstruire; (a crime) reconstituer
reconversion [,rikən'vʌrʒən], [,rikən-
'vʌrʃən] s reconversion f
record ['rekərd] s enregistrement m,
registre m; (to play on the phonograph) disque m; (mil) état m de
service; (sports) record m; off the
record en confidence; records archives
fpl; to break the record battre
le record; to have a good record être
bien noté; (at school) avoir de bon-
nes notes || [ri'kɔrd] tr enregistrer
rec'ord chang'er s tourne-disque m
automatique
recorder [ri'kɔrdər] s appareil m enregistreur; (law) greffier m; (mus) flûte
f à bec
rec'ord hold'er s recordman m
recording [ri'kɔrdiŋ] adj enregistreur
|| s enregistrement m
record'ing tape' s ruban m magnétique
rec'ord li'brary s discothèque m
rec'ord play'er s électrophone m
recount ['ri,kaunt] s nouveau dépouil-
lement m du scrutin || [ri'kaunt] tr
(to count again) recompter || [ri-
'kaunt] tr (to tell) raconter
recoup [ri'kup] tr recouvrer; to recoup
s.o. for dédommager qn de
recourse ['rikors], ['rikɔrs] s recours
m; to have recourse to recourir à
recover [ri'kʌvər] tr (to get back) re-

couvrer; (*to cover again*) recouvrir ‖ *intr* (*to get well*) se rétablir

recover•y [rɪ'kʌvəri] *s* (*pl* -**ies**) récupération *f*, recouvrement *m*; (*e.g., of health*) rétablissement *m*

recreant ['rɛkrɪ-ənt] *adj* & *s* lâche *mf*; traître *m*; apostat *m*

recreation [,rɛkrɪ'eʃən] *s* récréation *f*

recruit [rɪ'krut] *s* recrue *f* ‖ *tr* recruter; **to be recruited** se recruter

rectangle ['rɛk,tæŋgəl] *s* rectangle *m*

rectifier ['rɛktə,faɪ-ər] *s* rectificateur *m*; (elec) redresseur *m*

recti•fy ['rɛktɪ,faɪ] *v* (*pret* & *pp* -**fied**) *tr* rectifier; (elec) redresser

rec•tum ['rɛktəm] *s* (*pl* -**ta** [tə]) rectum *m*

recumbent [rɪ'kʌmbənt] *adj* couché

recuperate [rɪ'kjupə,ret] *tr* & *intr* récupérer

re•cur [rɪ'kʌr] *v* (*pret* & *pp* -**curred**; *ger* -**curring**) *intr* revenir, se reproduire; revenir à la mémoire de

recurrent [rɪ'kʌrənt] *adj* récurrent

red [rɛd] *adj* (*comp* **redder**; *super* **reddest**) rouge ‖ *s* (*color*) rouge *m*; **in the red** en déficit; **Red** (*communist*) rouge *mf*; (*nickname*) Rouquin *m*

red′bait′ *tr* taxer de communiste

red′bird′ *s* cardinal *m* d'Amérique, tangara *m*

red′-blood′ed *adj* vigoureux

red′breast′ *s* rouge-gorge *m*

red′cap′ *s* porteur *m*; (Brit) soldat *m* de la police militaire

red′ cell′ *s* globule *m* rouge

Red′ Cross′ *s* Croix-Rouge *f*

redden ['rɛdən] *tr* & *intr* rougir

redeem [rɪ'dim] *tr* racheter; (*a pawned article*) dégager; (*a promise*) remplir; (*a debt*) s'acquitter de, acquitter

redeemer [rɪ'dimər] *s* rédempteur *m*

redemption [rɪ'dɛmpʃən] *s* rachat *m*; (rel) rédemption *f*

red′-haired′ *adj* roux

red′-hand′ed *adj* & *adv* sur le fait, en flagrant délit

red′head′ *s* (*woman*) rousse *f*

red′ her′ring *s* hareng *m* saur; (fig) faux-fuyant *m*

red′-hot′ *adj* chauffé au rouge; ardent; (*news*) tout frais

rediscount [ri'dɪskaunt] *s* réescompte *m* ‖ *tr* réescompter

rediscover [,ridɪs'kʌvər] *tr* redécouvrir

red′-let′ter day′ *s* jour *m* mémorable

red′ light′ *s* feu *m* rouge; **to go through a red light** brûler un feu rouge

red′-light′ dis′trict *s* quartier *m* réservé

red′ man′ *s* (*pl* **men′**) Peau-Rouge *m*

re•do ['ri'du] *v* (*pret* -**did**; *pp* -**done**) *tr* refaire

redolent ['rɛdələnt] *adj* parfumé; **redolent of** exhalant une senteur de; qui fait penser à

redoubt [rɪ'daut] *s* redoute *f*

redound [rɪ'daund] *intr* contribuer; **to redound to** tourner à

red′ pep′per *s* piment *m* rouge

redress [rɪ'drɛs], ['ridrɛs] *s* redressement *m* ‖ [rɪ'drɛs] *tr* redresser

Red′ Rid′ing-hood′ *s* Chaperon rouge *m*

red′skin′ *s* Peau-Rouge *mf*

red′ tape′ *s* paperasserie *f*, chinoiseries *fpl* administratives

reduce [rɪ'd(j)us] *tr* réduire ‖ *intr* maigrir

reduc′ing ex′ercises *spl* exercices *mpl* amaigrissants

reduction [rɪ'dʌkʃən] *s* réduction *f*

redundant [rɪ'dʌndənt] *adj* redondant

red′ wine′ *s* vin *m* rouge

red′wing′ *s* (orn) mauvis *m*

red′wood′ *s* séquoia *m*

reed [rid] *s* (*of instrument*) anche *f*; (bot) roseau *m*; **reeds** (mus) instruments *mpl* à anche

reedit [ri'ɛdɪt] *tr* rééditer

reef [rif] *s* récif *m*; (*of sail*) ris *m* ‖ *tr* (naut) prendre un ris dans

reefer ['rifər] *s* caban *m*; (slang) cigarette *f* à marijuana

reek [rik] *intr* fumer; **to reek of** or **with** empester, puer

reel [ril] *s* bobine *f*; (*of film*) rouleau *m*, bobine; (*of fishing rod*) moulinet *m*; (*sway*) balancement *m*; **off the reel** (coll) d'affilée ‖ *tr* bobiner; **to reel off** dévider; (coll) réciter d'un trait ‖ *intr* chanceler

reelection [,ri·ɪ'lɛkʃən] *s* réélection *f*

reenlist [,ri·ɛn'lɪst] *tr* engager ‖ *intr* rengager, se rengager

reenlistment [,ri·ɛn'lɪstmənt] *s* rengagement *m*; (*person*) engagé *m*

reen•try [rɪ'ɛntri] *s* (*pl* -**tries**) rentrée *f*; (rok) retour *m* à la Terre

reexamination [,ri·ɛg,zæmɪ'neʃən] *s* réexamen *m*

re•fer [rɪ'fʌr] *v* (*pret* & *pp* -**ferred**; *ger* -**ferring**) *tr* renvoyer ‖ *intr*—**to refer to** se référer à

referee [,rɛfə'ri] *s* arbitre *m* ‖ *tr* & *intr* arbitrer

reference ['rɛfərəns] *s* référence *f*

ref′erence room′ *s* bibliothèque *f* de consultation

referen•dum [,rɛfə'rɛndəm] *s* (*pl* -**da** [də]) référendum *m*

refill ['rifɪl] *s* recharge *f* ‖ [rɪ'fɪl] *tr* remplir à nouveau

refine [rɪ'faɪn] *tr* raffiner

refinement [rɪ'faɪnmənt] *s* raffinage *m*; (*e.g., of manners*) raffinement *m*

refiner•y [rɪ'faɪnəri] *s* (*pl* -**ies**) raffinerie *f*

reflect [rɪ'flɛkt] *tr* réfléchir ‖ *intr* (*to meditate*) réfléchir; **to reflect on** or **upon** réfléchir à or sur; nuire à la réputation de

reflection [rɪ'flɛkʃən] *s* (*e.g., of light; thought*) réflexion *f*; (*reflected light; image*) reflet *m*; **to cast reflections on** faire des réflexions à

reflex ['riflɛks] *adj* & *s* réflexe *m*

reforestation [,rifɔrɪs'teʃən], [,rifɔrɪs-'teʃən] *s* reboisement *m*

reform [rɪ'fɔrm] *s* reforme *f* ‖ *tr* réformer ‖ *intr* se réformer

reformation [,rɛfər'meʃən] *s* réformation *f*; **the Reformation** la Réforme

reformato·ry [rɪ'fɔrmə ˌtori] s (pl -ries) maison f de correction

reformer [rɪ'fɔrmər] s réformateur m

reform′ school′ s maison f de correction

refraction [rɪ'frækʃən] s réfraction f

refrain [rɪ'fren] s refrain m ‖ intr s'abstenir

refresh [rɪ'freʃ] tr rafraîchir ‖ intr se rafraîchir

refreshing [rɪ'freʃɪŋ] adj rafraîchissant

refreshment [rɪ'freʃmənt] s rafraîchissement m

refresh′ment bar′ s buvette f

refrigerate [rɪ'frɪdʒə ˌret] tr réfrigérer

refrigerator [rɪ'frɪdʒə ˌretər] s (icebox) glacière; réfrigérateur m; (condenser) congélateur m

refrig′erator car′ s (rr) wagon m frigorifique

re-fuel [rɪ'fjul] v (pret & pp -fueled or -fuelled; ger -fueling or -fuelling) tr ravitailler en carburant ‖ intr se ravitailler en carburant

refuge ['refjudʒ] s refuge m; **to take refuge (in)** se réfugier (dans)

refugee [ˌrefju'dʒi] s réfugié m

refund ['rifʌnd] s remboursement m ‖ [rɪ'fʌnd] tr (to pay back) rembourser ‖ [rɪ'fʌnd] tr (to fund again) consolider

refurnish [rɪ'fʌrnɪʃ] tr remeubler

refusal [rɪ'fjuzəl] s refus m

refuse ['refjus] s ordures fpl, détritus mpl ‖ [rɪ'fjuz] tr & intr refuser

refute [rɪ'fjut] tr réfuter

regain [rɪ'gen] tr regagner; (consciousness) reprendre

regal ['rigəl] adj royal

regale [rɪ'gel] tr régaler

regalia [rɪ'geli·ə] spl atours mpl, ornements mpl; (of an office) insignes mpl

regard [rɪ'gard] s considération f; (esteem) respect m; (look) regard m; **in or with regard to** à l'égard de; **regards** sincères amitiés fpl ‖ tr considérer, estimer; **as regards** quant à

regarding [rɪ'gardɪŋ] prep au sujet de, touchant

regardless [rɪ'gardlɪs] adj inattentif ‖ adv (coll) coûte que coûte; **regardless of** sans tenir compte de

regatta [rɪ'gætə] s régates fpl

regen·cy ['ridʒənsi] s (pl -cies) régence f

regenerate [rɪ'dʒenə ˌret] tr régénérer ‖ intr se régénérer

regent ['ridʒənt] s régent m

regicide ['redʒɪ ˌsaɪd] s (act) régicide m; (person) régicide mf

regime [re'ʒim] s régime m

regiment ['redʒɪmənt] s régiment m ‖ ['redʒɪ ˌment] tr enrégimenter, régenter

regimental [ˌredʒɪ'mentəl] adj régimentaire ‖ **regimentals** spl tenue f militaire

region ['ridʒən] s région f

register ['redʒɪstər] s registre m ‖ tr enregistrer; (a student; an automobile) immatriculer; (a letter) recommander ‖ intr s'inscrire

reg′istered let′ter s lettre f recommandée

reg′istered mail′ s envoi m en recommandé

reg′istered nurse′ s infirmière f diplômée

registrar ['redʒɪs ˌtrar] s archiviste mf, secrétaire mf

registration [ˌredʒɪs'treʃən] s enregistrement m; immatriculation f, inscription f; (of mail) recommandation f

registra′tion blank′ s fiche f d'inscription

registra′tion fee′ s frais mpl d'inscription

registra′tion num′ber s (of soldier or student) numéro m matricule

re-gret [rɪ'gret] s regret m; **regrets** excuses fpl ‖ v (pret & pp -gretted; ger -gretting) tr regretter

regrettable [rɪ'gretəbəl] adj regrettable

regular ['regjələr] adj & s régulier m

reg′ular fel′low s (coll) chic type m

regularity [ˌregjə'lɛrɪti] s régularité f

regularize ['regjələ ˌraɪz] tr régulariser

regulate ['regjə ˌlet] tr régler; (to control) réglementer

regulation [ˌregjə'leʃən] s régulation f; (rule) règlement m

rehabilitate [ˌrihə'bɪlɪ ˌtet] tr réadapter; (in reputation, standing, etc.) réhabiliter

rehearsal [rɪ'hʌrsəl] s répétition f

rehearse [rɪ'hʌrs] tr & intr répéter

reign [ren] s règne m ‖ intr régner

reimburse [ˌri·ɪm'bʌrs] tr rembourser

rein [ren] s rêne f; **to give free rein to** donner libre cours à ‖ tr contenir, freiner

reincarnation [ˌri·ɪnkar'neʃən] s réincarnation f

rein′deer′ s renne m

reinforce [ˌri·ɪn'fors] tr renforcer; (concrete) armer

reinforcement [ˌri·ɪn'forsmənt] s renforcement m

reinstate [ˌri·ɪn'stet] tr rétablir

reiterate [ri'ɪtə ˌret] tr réitérer

reject ['ridʒekt] s pièce f or article m de rebut; **rejects** rebuts mpl ‖ [rɪ'dʒekt] tr rejeter

rejection [rɪ'dʒekʃən] s rejet m, refus m

rejoice [rɪ'dʒoɪs] intr se réjouir

rejoin [rɪ'dʒoɪn] tr rejoindre

rejoinder [rɪ'dʒoɪndər] s réplique f; (law) réponse f à une réplique

rejuvenation [rɪ ˌdʒuvɪ'neʃən] s rajeunissement m

rekindle [ri'kɪndəl] tr rallumer

relapse [rɪ'læps] s rechute f ‖ intr rechuter

relate [rɪ'let] tr (to narrate) relater; (e.g., two events) établir un rapport entre; **to be related** être apparenté

relation [rɪ'leʃən] s relation f; récit m, relation; (relative) parent m; (kinship) parenté f; **in relation to** or **with** par rapport à; **relations** (of a sexual nature) rapports mpl

relationship [rɪ'leʃən ˌʃɪp] s (connection) rapport m; (kinship) parenté f

relative ['relətɪv] *adj* relatif ‖ *s* parent *m*

relativity [,relə'tɪvəti] *s* relativité *f*

relax [rɪ'læks] *tr* détendre; **to be relaxed** être décontracté or détendu ‖ *intr* se détendre

relaxation [,rɪlæks'eʃən] *s* détente *f*, délassement *m*

relaxing [rɪ'læksɪŋ] *adj* tranquillisant, apaisant; (*diverting*) délassant

relay ['rile], [rɪ'le] *s* relais *m* ‖ *v* (*pret & pp* **-layed**) *tr* relayer; (rad, telg, telp, telv) retransmettre ‖ [rɪ'le] *v* (*pret & pp* **-laid**) *tr* tendre de nouveau

re'lay race' *s* course *f* de relais

release [rɪ'lis] *s* délivrance *f*; (*from jail*) mise *f* en liberté; (*permission*) autorisation *f*; (aer) lâchage *m*; (mach) déclenchement *m* ‖ *tr* délivrer; (*from jail*) mettre en liberté; autoriser; (*a bomb*) lâcher

relegate ['reli,get] *tr* reléguer

relent [rɪ'lent] *intr* se laisser attendrir, s'adoucir

relentless [rɪ'lentlɪs] *adj* implacable

relevant ['relɪvənt] *adj* pertinent

reliable [rɪ'laɪ·əbəl] *adj* digne de confiance, digne de foi

reliance [rɪ'laɪ·əns] *s* confiance *f*

relic ['relɪk] *s* (rel) relique *f*; (fig) vestige *m*

relief [rɪ'lif] *s* soulagement *m*; (*projection of figures; elevation*) relief *m*; (*aid*) secours *m*; (*welfare program*) aide *f* sociale; (mil) relève *f*; **in relief** en relief

relieve [rɪ'liv] *tr* soulager; (*to aid*) secourir; (*to release from a post; to give variety to*) relever; (mil) relever

religion [rɪ'lɪdʒən] *s* religion *f*

religious [rɪ'lɪdʒəs] *adj* religieux

relinquish [rɪ'lɪŋkwɪʃ] *tr* abandonner

relish ['relɪʃ] *s* goût *m*; (*condiment*) assaisonnement *m*; **relish for** penchant pour ‖ *tr* goûter, apprécier

reluctance [rɪ'lʌktəns] *s* répugnance *f*; **with reluctance** à contrecœur

reluctant [rɪ'lʌktənt] *adj* hésitant, peu disposé

re·ly [rɪ'laɪ] *v* (*pret & pp* **-lied**) *intr*—**to rely on** compter sur, se fier à

remain [rɪ'men] *s*—**remains** restes *mpl*; œuvres *fpl* posthumes ‖ *intr* rester

remainder [rɪ'mendər] *s* reste *m*; **remainders** bouillons *mpl* ‖ *tr* solder

re·make [rɪ'mek] *v* (*pret & pp* **-made**) *tr* refaire

remark [rɪ'mɑrk] *s* remarque *f*, observation *f* ‖ *tr & intr* remarquer, observer; **to remark on** faire des remarques sur

remarkable [rɪ'mɑrkəbəl] *adj* remarquable

remar·ry [rɪ'mæri] *v* (*pret & pp* **-ried**) *tr* remarier; se remarier avec ‖ *intr* se remarier

reme·dy ['remɪdi] *s* (*pl* **-dies**) remède *m* ‖ *v* (*pret & pp* **-died**) *tr* remédier (*with dat*)

remember [rɪ'membər] *tr* se souvenir de, se rappeler; **remember me to** rappelez-moi au bon souvenir de ‖ *intr* se souvenir, se rappeler

remembrance [rɪ'membrəns] *s* souvenir *m*

remind [rɪ'maɪnd] *tr* rappeler

reminder [rɪ'maɪndər] *s* note *f* de rappel, mémento *m*

reminisce [,remɪ'nɪs] *intr* se livrer au souvenirs, raconter ses souvenirs

remiss [rɪ'mɪs] *adj* négligent

remission [rɪ'mɪʃən] *s* rémission *f*

re·mit [rɪ'mɪt] *v* (*pret & pp* **-mitted**; *ger* **-mitting**) *tr* remettre ‖ *intr* se calmer

remittance [rɪ'mɪtəns] *s* remise *f*, envoi *m*

remnant ['remnənt] *s* reste *m*; (*of cloth*) coupon *m*; (*at reduced price*) solde *m*

remod·el [rɪ'mɑdəl] *v* (*pret & pp* **-eled** or **-elled**; *ger* **-eling** or **-elling**) *tr* modeler de nouveau, remanier; (*a house*) transformer

remonstrance [rɪ'mɑnstrəns] *s* remontrance *f*

remonstrate [rɪ'mɑnstret] *intr* protester; **to remonstrate with** faire des remontrances à

remorse [rɪ'mɔrs] *s* remords *m*

remorseful [rɪ'mɔrsfəl] *adj* contrit, repentant, plein de remords

remote [rɪ'mot] *adj* éloigné

remote' control' *s* commande *f* à distance, télécommande *f*

removable [rɪ'muvəbəl] *adj* amovible

removal [rɪ'muvəl] *s* enlèvement *m*; (*from house*) déménagement *m*; (*dismissal*) révocation *f*

remove [rɪ'muv] *tr* enlever, ôter; éloigner; (*furniture*) déménager; (*to dismiss*) révoquer ‖ *intr* se déplacer; déménager

remuneration [rɪ,mjunə'reʃən] *s* rémunération *f*

renaissance [,renə'sɑns], [rɪ'nesəns] *s* renaissance *f*

rend [rend] *v* (*pret & pp* **rent** [rent]) *tr* déchirer; (*to split*) fendre; (*the air; the heart*) fendre

render ['rendər] *tr* rendre; (*a piece of music*) interpréter; (*lard*) fondre

rendez·vous ['rɑndə,vu] *s* (*pl* **-vous** [,vuz]) rendez-vous *m* ‖ *v* (*pret & pp* **-voused** [,vud]; *ger* **-vousing** [,vuɪŋ]) *intr* se rencontrer

rendition [ren'dɪʃən] *s* (*translation*) traduction *f*; (mus) interprétation *f*

renegade ['renɪ,ged] *s* renégat *m*

renege [rɪ'nɪg] *s* renonce *f* ‖ *intr* renoncer; (coll) se dédire, ne pas tenir sa parole

renew [rɪ'n(j)u] *tr* renouveler ‖ *intr* se renouveler

renewable [rɪ'n(j)u·əbəl] *adj* renouvelable

renewal [rɪ'n(j)u·əl] *s* renouvellement *m*

renounce [rɪ'nauns] *s* renonce *f* ‖ *tr* renoncer (*with dat*) ‖ *intr* renoncer

renovate ['renə,vet] *tr* renouveler; (*a room, a house, etc.*) mettre à neuf, rénover, transformer

renown [rɪ'naun] *s* renom *m*

renowned [rɪ'naund] *adj* renommé

rent [rent] *adj* déchiré || *s* loyer *m*, location *f*; (*tear, slit*) déchirure *f*; **for rent** à louer || *tr* louer || *intr* se louer

rental ['rentəl] *s* loyer *m*, location *f*

rent'al a'gen•cy *s* (*pl* **-cies**) agence *f* de location

rent'ed car' *s* voiture *f* de louage, voiture de location; (*chauffeur-driven limousine*) voiture de grande remise

renter ['rentər] *s* locataire *mf*

renunciation [rɪ,nʌnsɪ'eʃən] *s* renonciation *f*

reopen [rɪ'opən] *tr* & *intr* rouvrir

reopening [rɪ'opənɪŋ] *s* réouverture *f*; (*of school*) rentrée *f*

reorganize [rɪ'ɔrgə,naɪz] *tr* réorganiser || *intr* se réorganiser

repair [rɪ'per] *s* réparation *f*; **in good repair** en bon état || *tr* réparer || *intr* se rendre

repaper [rɪ'pepər] *tr* retapisser

reparation [,repə'reʃən] *s* réparation *f*

repartee [,repar'ti] *s* repartie *f*

repast [rɪ'pæst], [rɪ'pɑst] *s* repas *m*

repatriate [rɪ'petrɪ,et] *tr* rapatrier

re•pay [rɪ'pe] *v* (*pret* & *pp* **-paid**) *tr* rembourser; récompenser

repayment [rɪ'pemənt] *s* remboursement *m*; récompense *f*

repeal [rɪ'pil] *s* révocation *f*, abrogation *f* || *tr* révoquer, abroger

repeat [rɪ'pit] *s* répétition *f* || *tr* & *intr* répéter

re•pel [rɪ'pel] *v* (*pret* & *pp* **-pelled**; *ger* **-pelling**) *tr* repousser; dégoûter

repent [rɪ'pent] *tr* se repentir de || *intr* se repentir

repentance [rɪ'pentəns] *s* repentir *m*

repentant [rɪ'pentənt] *adj* repentant

repercussion [,ripər'kʌʃən] *s* répercussion *f*, contrecoup *m*

reperto•ry ['repər,tori] *s* (*pl* **-ries**) répertoire *m*

repetition [,repɪ'tɪʃən] *s* répétition *f*

replace [rɪ'ples] *tr* (*to put back*) remettre en place; (*to take the place of*) remplacer

replaceable [rɪ'plesəbəl] *adj* remplaçable, amovible

replacement [rɪ'plesmənt] *s* replacement *m*; (*substitution*) remplacement *m*; (*substitute part*) pièce *f* de rechange; (*person*) remplaçant *m*

replenish [rɪ'plenɪʃ] *tr* réapprovisionner; remplir

replete [rɪ'plit] *adj* rempli, plein

replica ['replɪkə] *s* reproduction *f*, réplique *f*

re•ply [rɪ'plaɪ] *s* (*pl* **-plies**) réponse *f*, réplique *f* || *v* (*pret* & *pp* **-plied**) *tr* & *intr* répondre, répliquer

reply' cou'pon *s* coupon-réponse *m*

report [rɪ'port] *s* rapport *m*; (*rumor*) bruit *m*; (*e.g., of firearm*) détonation *f* || *tr* rapporter; dénoncer; **it is reported that** le bruit court que; **reported missing** porté manquant || *intr* faire un rapport; (*to show up*) se présenter

report' card' *s* bulletin *m* scolaire

reportedly [rɪ'portɪdli] *adv* au dire de tout le monde

reporter [rɪ'portər] *s* reporter *m*

reporting [rɪ'portɪŋ] *s* reportage *m*

repose [rɪ'poz] *s* repos *m* || *tr* reposer; (*confidence*) placer || *intr* reposer

reprehend [,reprɪ'hend] *tr* reprendre

represent [,reprɪ'zent] *tr* représenter

representation [,reprɪzen'teʃən] *s* représentation *f*

representative [,reprɪ'zentətɪv] *adj* représentatif || *s* représentant *m*

repress [rɪ'pres] *tr* réprimer; (*psychoanal*) refouler

repression [rɪ'preʃən] *s* répression *f*; (*psychoanal*) refoulement *m*

reprieve [rɪ'priv] *s* sursis *m* || *tr* surseoir à l'exécution de

reprimand ['reprɪ,mænd], ['reprɪ,mɑnd] *s* réprimande *f* || *tr* réprimander

reprint ['ri,prɪnt] *s* (*book*) réimpression *f*; (*offprint*) tiré *m* à part || [ri-'prɪnt] *tr* réimprimer

reprisal [rɪ'praɪzəl] *s* représailles *fpl*

reproach [rɪ'protʃ] *s* reproche *m*; opprobre *m* || *tr* reprocher; couvrir d'opprobre; **to reproach s.o. for s.th.** reprocher q.ch. à qn

reproduce [,riprə'd(j)us] *tr* reproduire || *intr* se reproduire

reproduction [,riprə'dʌkʃən] *s* reproduction *f*

reproof [rɪ'pruf] *s* reproche *m*

reprove [rɪ'pruv] *tr* réprimander

reptile ['reptɪl] *s* reptile *m*

republic [rɪ'pʌblɪk] *s* république *f*

republican [rɪ'pʌblɪkən] *adj* & *s* républicain *m*

repudiate [rɪ'pjudɪ,et] *tr* répudier

repugnant [rɪ'pʌgnənt] *adj* répugnant

repulse [rɪ'pʌls] *s* refus *m*; (*setback*) échec *m* || *tr* repousser

repulsive [rɪ'pʌlsɪv] *adj* répulsif

reputation [,repjə'teʃən] *s* réputation *f*

repute [rɪ'pjut] *s* réputation *f*; **of ill repute** mal famé || *tr*—**to be reputed to be** être réputé

reputedly [rɪ'pjutɪdli] *adv* suivant l'opinion commune

request [rɪ'kwest] *s* demande *f*; **on request** sur demande || *tr* demander

Requiem ['rikwɪ,em], ['rekwɪ,em] *s* Requiem *m*

require [rɪ'kwaɪr] *tr* exiger

requirement [rɪ'kwaɪrmənt] *s* exigence *f*; besoin *m*

requisite ['rekwɪzɪt] *adj* requis || *s* chose *f* nécessaire; condition *f* nécessaire

requisition [,rekwɪ'zɪʃən] *s* réquisition *f* || *tr* réquisitionner

requital [rɪ'kwaɪtəl] *s* récompense *f*; (*retaliation*) revanche *f*

requite [rɪ'kwaɪt] *tr* récompenser; (*to avenge*) venger

re•read [ri'rid] *v* (*pret* & *pp* **-read** ['red]) *tr* relire

resale ['ri,sel], [ri'sel] *s* revente *f*

rescind [rɪ'sɪnd] *tr* abroger

rescue ['reskju] *s* sauvetage *m*; **to the**

rescue au secours, à la rescousse || *tr* sauver, secourir

res′cue par′ty *s* équipe *f* de secours

research [rɪ′sʌrtʃ], [′risʌrtʃ] *s* recherche *f* || *intr* faire des recherches

re·sell [ri′sel] *v* (*pret & pp* **-sold**) *tr* revendre

resemblance [rɪ′zembləns] *s* ressemblance *f*

resemble [rɪ′zembəl] *tr* ressembler (with *dat*); **to resemble one another** se ressembler

resent [rɪ′zent] *tr* s′offenser de

resentful [rɪ′zentfəl] *adj* offensé

resentment [rɪ′zentmənt] *s* ressentiment *m*

reservation [,rezər′veʃən] *s* location *f*, réservation *f*; (*Indian land*) réserve *f*; **without reservation** sans réserve

reserve [rɪ′zʌrv] *s* réserve *f* || *tr* réserver

reservist [rɪ′zʌrvɪst] *s* réserviste *m*

reservoir [′rezər,vwar] *s* réservoir *m*

re·set [ri′set] *v* (*pret & pp* **-set**; *ger* **-setting**) *tr* remettre; (*a gem*) remonter

re·ship [ri′ʃɪp] *v* (*pret & pp* **-shipped**; *ger* **-shipping**) *tr* réexpédier; (*on a ship*) rembarquer || *intr* se rembarquer

reshipment [ri′ʃɪpmənt] *s* réexpédition *f*; (*on a ship*) rembarquement *m*

reside [rɪ′zaɪd] *intr* résider, demeurer

residence [′rezɪdəns] *s* résidence *f*, domicile *m*

resident [′rezɪdənt] *adj & s* habitant *m*

residential [,rezɪ′denʃəl] *adj* résidentiel

residue [′rezɪ,d(j)u] *s* résidu *m*

resign [rɪ′zaɪn] *tr* démissionner de, résigner; **to resign oneself to** se résigner à || *intr* démissionner; se résigner; **to resign from** démissionner de

resignation [,rezɪg′neʃən] *s* (*from a job, etc.*) démission *f*; (*submissive state*) résignation *f*

resin [′rezɪn] *s* résine *f*

resist [rɪ′zɪst] *tr* résister (with *dat*); **to resist** + *ger* s′empêcher de + *inf* || *intr* résister

resistance [rɪ′zɪstəns] *s* résistance *f*

resole [ri′sol] *tr* ressemeler

resolute [′rezə,lut] *adj* résolu

resolution [rezə′luʃən] *s* résolution *f*

resolve [rɪ′zɔlv] *s* résolution *f* || *tr* résoudre || *intr* résoudre, se résoudre

resonance [′rezənəns] *s* résonance *f*

resort [rɪ′zɔrt] *s* station *f*, e.g., **health resort** station climatique; (*for help or support*) recours *m*; **as a last resort** en dernier ressort || *intr*—**to resort to** recourir à

resound [rɪ′zaund] *intr* résonner

resource [′risors], [′risɔrs] *s* ressource *f*

resourceful [rɪ′sorsfəl] *adj* débrouillard

respect [rɪ′spekt] *s* respect *m*; **in many respects** à bien des égards; **in this respect** sous ce rapport; **to pay one′s respects (to)** présenter ses respects (à); **with respect to** par rapport à || *tr* respecter

respectable [rɪ′spektəbəl] *adj* respectable; considérable

respectful [rɪ′spektfəl] *adj* respectueux

respectfully [rɪ′spektfəli] *adv* respectueusement; **respectfully yours** (complimentary close) veuillez agréer l′assurance de mes sentiments très respectueux

respective [rɪ′spektɪv] *adj* respectif

res′piratory tract′ [′respɪrə,tori], [rɪ′spaɪrə,tori] *s* appareil *m* respiratoire

respite [′respɪt] *s* répit *m*; **without respite** sans relâche

resplendent [rɪ′splendənt] *adj* resplendissant

respond [rɪ′spand] *intr* répondre

response [rɪ′spans] *s* réponse *f*

responsibili·ty [rɪ,spansɪ′bɪlɪti] *s* (*pl* **-ties**) responsabilité *f*

responsible [rɪ′spansɪbəl] *adj* responsable; (*person*) digne de confiance; (*job, position*) de confiance; **responsible for** responsable de; **responsible to** responsable envers

responsive [rɪ′spansɪv] *adj* sensible, réceptif; prompt à sympathiser

rest [rest] *s* repos *m*; (*lack of motion*) pause *f*; (*what remains*) reste *m*; (*mus*) silence *m*; **at rest** en repos; (*dead*) mort; **the rest** les autres; (*the remainder*) le restant; **the rest of us** nous autres; **to come to rest** s′immobiliser; **to lay to rest** enterrer || *tr* reposer || *intr* reposer, se reposer; **to rest on** reposer sur, s′appuyer sur

restaurant [′restərənt], [′restə,rɑnt] *s* restaurant *m*

rest′ cure′ *s* cure *f* de repos

restful [′restfəl] *adj* reposant; (*calm*) tranquille, paisible

rest′ing place′ *s* lieu *m* de repos, gîte *m*; (*of the dead*) dernière demeure *f*

restitution [,restɪ′t(j)uʃən] *s* restitution *f*

restive [′restɪv] *adj* rétif

restless [′restlɪs] *adj* agité, inquiet; sans repos

restock [ri′stak] *tr* réapprovisionner; (*with fish or game*) repeupler

restoration [,restə′reʃən] *s* restauration *f*

restore [rɪ′stor] *tr* restaurer; (*health*) rétablir; (*to give back*) restituer

restrain [rɪ′stren] *tr* retenir, contenir

restraint [rɪ′strent] *s* restriction *f*, contrainte *f*

restrict [rɪ′strɪkt] *tr* restreindre

restriction [rɪ′strɪkʃən] *s* restriction *f*

rest′ room′ *s* cabinet *m* d′aisance

result [rɪ′zʌlt] *s* résultat *m*; **as a result of** par suite de || *intr* résulter; **to result in** aboutir à

resume [rɪ′z(j)um] *tr & intr* reprendre

résumé [,rez(j)u′me] *s* résumé *m*

resumption [rɪ′zʌmpʃən] *s* reprise *f*

resurface [ri′sʌrfɪs] *tr* refaire le revêtement de || *intr* (*said of submarine*) faire surface

resurrect [,rezə′rekt] *tr & intr* ressusciter

resurrection [ˌrezəˈrekʃən] s résurrection f

resuscitate [rɪˈsʌsɪˌtet] tr & intr ressusciter

retail [ˈritel] adj & adv au détail ‖ s vente f au détail ‖ tr vendre au détail, détailler ‖ intr se vendre au détail

retailer [ˈritelər] s détaillant m

retain [rɪˈten] tr retenir; engager

retaliate [rɪˈtælɪˌet] intr prendre sa revanche, user de représailles

retaliation [rɪˌtælɪˈeʃən] s représailles fpl

retard [rɪˈtɑrd] s retard m ‖ tr retarder

retch [retʃ] tr vomir ‖ intr avoir un haut-le-cœur

retching [ˈretʃɪŋ] s haut-le-cœur m

reticence [ˈretɪsəns] s réserve f

reticent [ˈretɪsənt] adj réservé

retina [ˈretɪnə] s rétine f

retinue [ˈretɪˌn(j)u] s suite f, cortège m

retire [rɪˈtaɪr] tr mettre à la retraite ‖ intr se retirer

retired adj en retraite

retirement [rɪˈtaɪrmənt] s retraite f

retire′ment pro′gram s programme m de prévoyance

retiring [rɪˈtaɪrɪŋ] adj (shy) effacé; (e.g., congressman) sortant

retort [rɪˈtɔrt] s riposte f, réplique f; (chem) cornue f ‖ tr & intr riposter

retouch [ritˈʌtʃ] tr retoucher

retrace [rɪˈtres] tr retracer; (one's steps) revenir sur

retract [rɪˈtrækt] tr rétracter ‖ intr se rétracter

retractable [rɪˈtræktəbəl] adj (aer) escamotable

re-tread [ˈriˌtred] s pneu m rechapé ‖ [riˈtred] v (pret & pp -treaded) tr rechaper ‖ v (pret -trod; pp -trod or -trodden) tr & intr repasser

retreat [rɪˈtrit] s retraite f; **to beat a retreat** battre en retraite ‖ intr se retirer

retrench [rɪˈtrentʃ] tr restreindre ‖ intr faire des économies

retribution [ˌretrɪˈbjuʃən] s rétribution f

retrieve [rɪˈtriv] tr retrouver, recouvrer; (a fortune, a reputation, etc.) rétablir; (game) rapporter ‖ intr (said of hunting dog) rapporter

retriever [rɪˈtrivər] s retriever m

retroactive [ˌretroˈæktɪv] adj rétroactif

retrogress [ˌretroˈgres] intr rétrograder

retrorocket [ˈretroˌrɑkɪt] s rétrofusée f

retrospect [ˈretroˌspekt] s—**to consider in retrospect** jeter un coup d'œil rétrospectif à

retrospective [ˌretroˈspektɪv] adj rétrospectif

re-try [riˈtraɪ] v (pret & pp -tried) tr essayer de nouveau; (law) juger à nouveau

return [rɪˈtʌrn] adj de retour; **by return mail** par retour du courrier ‖ s retour m; (profit) bénéfice m; (yield) rendement m; (unwanted merchandise) rendu m; (of ball) renvoi m; (of income tax) déclaration f; **in return**

(for) en retour (de); **returns** (profits) recettes fpl; (of an election) résultats mpl ‖ tr rendre; (to put back) remettre; (to bring back) rapporter; (e.g., a letter) retourner ‖ intr (to go back) retourner; (to come back) revenir; (to get back home) rentrer; **to return empty-handed** revenir bredouille

return′ address′ s adresse f de l'expéditeur

return′ bout′ s revanche f

return′ game′ or **match′** s match m retour

return′ tick′et s aller et retour m

return′ trip′ s voyage m de retour

reunification [riˌjunɪfɪˈkeʃən] s réunification f

reunion [riˈjunjən] s réunion f

reunite [ˌrijuˈnaɪt] tr réunir ‖ intr se réunir

rev [rev] s (coll) tour m ‖ v (pret & pp revved; ger revving) tr (coll) accélérer; (to race) (coll) emballer ‖ intr (coll) s'accélérer

revamp [riˈvæmp] tr refaire

reveal [rɪˈvil] tr révéler

reveille [ˈrevəli] s réveil m

rev-el [ˈrevəl] s fête f; **revels** ébats mpl, orgie f ‖ v (pret & pp -eled or -elled; ger -eling or -elling) intr faire la fête, faire la bombe; **to revel in** se délecter à

revelation [ˌrevəˈleʃən] s révélation f; **Revelation** (Bib) Apocalypse f

revel-ry [ˈrevəlri] s (pl -ries) réjouissances fpl, orgie f

revenge [rɪˈvendʒ] s vengeance f; **to take revenge on s.o. for s.th.** se venger de q.ch. sur qn ‖ tr venger

revengeful [rɪˈvendʒfəl] adj vindicatif

revenue [ˈrevəˌn(j)u] s revenu m

rev′enue cut′ter s garde-côte m, vedette f

rev′enue stamp′ s timbre m fiscal

reverberate [rɪˈvʌrbəˌret] intr résonner

revere [rɪˈvɪr] tr révérer

reverence [ˈrevərəns] s révérence f ‖ tr révérer

reverend [ˈrevərənd] adj & s révérend m

reverent [ˈrevərənt] adj révérenciel

reverie [ˈrevəri] s rêverie f

reversal [rɪˈvʌrsəl] s renversement m

reverse [rɪˈvʌrs] adj contraire ‖ s contraire m; (of medal; of fortune) revers m; (of page) verso m; (aut) marche f arrière ‖ tr renverser; (a sentence) (law) révoquer ‖ intr renverser; (said of motor) faire machine arrière; (aut) faire marche arrière

reverse′ lev′er s levier m de renvoi

reverse′ side′ s revers m, dos m

reversible [rɪˈvʌrsəbəl] adj réversible

revert [rɪˈvʌrt] intr revenir, faire retour

review [rɪˈvju] s revue f; (of a book) compte m rendu; (of a lesson) révision f ‖ tr revoir; (a book) faire la critique de; (a lesson) réviser, revoir; (past events; troops) passer en revue ‖ intr faire des révisions

revile [rɪˈvaɪl] tr injurier, outrager

revise [rɪˈvaɪz] s révision f; (typ)

épreuve *f* de révision || *tr* réviser; (*a book*) revoir

revised' edi'tion *s* édition *f* revue et corrigée

revision [rɪ'vɪʒən] *s* révision *f*

revisionist [rɪ'vɪʒənɪst] *adj* & *s* révisionniste *mf*

revival [rɪ'vaɪvəl] *s* retour *m* à la vie; (*of learning*) renaissance *f*; (rel) réveil *m*; (theat) reprise *f*

reviv'al meet'ings *spl* (rel) réveils *mpl*

revive [rɪ'vaɪv] *tr* ranimer; (*a victim*) ressusciter; (*a memory*) réveiller; (*a play*) reprendre || *intr* reprendre; se ranimer

revoke [rɪ'vok] *tr* révoquer

revolt [rɪ'volt] *s* révolte *f* || *tr* révolter || *intr* se révolter

revolting [rɪ'voltɪŋ] *adj* dégoûtant, repoussant; rebelle, révolté

revolution [ˌrɛvə'luʃən] *s* révolution *f*

revolutionar•y [ˌrɛvə'luʃəˌnɛri] *adj* révolutionnaire || *s* (*pl* -ies) révolutionnaire *mf*

revolve [rɪ'valv] *tr* faire tourner; (*in one's mind*) retourner || *intr* tourner

revolver [rɪ'valvər] *s* revolver *m*

revolv'ing book'case *s* bibliothèque *f* tournante

revolv'ing door' *s* porte *f* à tambour, tambour *m* cylindrique

revolv'ing fund' *s* fonds *m* de roulement

revolv'ing stage' *s* scène *f* tournante

revue [rɪ'vju] *s* (theat) revue *f*

revulsion [rɪ'vʌlʃən] *s* aversion *f*, répugnance *f*; (*change of feeling*) revirement *m*

reward [rɪ'wɔrd] *s* récompense *f* || *tr* récompenser

rewarding [rɪ'wɔrdɪŋ] *adj* rémunérateur; (*experience*) enrichissant

re•wind [ri'waɪnd] *v* (*pret & pp* -wound*) *tr* (*film, tape, etc.*) renverser la marche de; (*a typewriter ribbon*) embobiner de nouveau; (*a clock*) remonter

rewire [ri'waɪr] *tr* (*a building*) refaire l'installation électrique dans

re•write [ri'raɪt] *v* (*pret* -wrote*; *pp* -written*) *tr* récrire

rhapso•dy ['ræpsədi] *s* (*pl* -dies) *s* rhapsodie *f*

rheostat ['ri•əˌstæt] *s* rhéostat *m*

rhetoric ['rɛtərɪk] *s* rhétorique *f*

rhetorical [rɪ'tɑrɪkəl], [rɪ'tɔrɪkəl] *adj* rhétorique

rheumatic [ru'mætɪk] *adj* rhumatismal; (*person*) rhumatisant || *s* rhumatisant *m*

rheumatism ['rumə ˌtɪzəm] *s* rhumatisme *m*

Rhine [raɪn] *s* Rhin *m*

Rhineland ['raɪn ˌlænd] *s* Rhénanie *f*

rhine'stone' *s* faux diamant *m*

rhinoceros [raɪ'nɑsərəs] *s* rhinocéros *m*

rhubarb ['rubɑrb] *s* rhubarbe *f*

rhyme [raɪm] *s* rime *f*; **in rhyme** en vers || *tr* & *intr* rimer

rhythm ['rɪðəm] *s* rythme *m*

rhythmic(al) ['rɪðmɪk(əl)] *adj* rythmique

rib [rɪb] *s* côte *f*; (*of umbrella*) baleine *f*; (*archit, biol, mach*) nervure *f* || *v* (*pret & pp* ribbed*; *ger* ribbing*) *tr* garnir de nervures; (slang) taquiner

ribald ['rɪbəld] *adj* grivois

ribbon ['rɪbən] *s* ruban *m*

rice [raɪs] *s* riz *m*

rice' field' *s* rizière *f*

rice' pud'ding *s* riz *m* au lait

rich [rɪtʃ] *adj* riche; (*voice*) sonore; (*wine*) généreux; (*funny*) (coll) impayable; (coll) ridicule; **to get rich** s'enrichir; **to strike it rich** trouver le bon filon || **riches** *spl* richesses *fpl*

rickets ['rɪkɪts] *s* rachitisme *m*

rickety ['rɪkɪti] *adj* (*object*) boiteux, délabré; (*person*) chancelant; (*suffering from rickets*) rachitique

rickshaw ['rɪkˌʃɔ] *s* pousse-pousse *m*

rid [rɪd] *v* (*pret & pp* rid*; *ger* ridding*) *tr* débarrasser; **to get rid of** se débarrasser de

riddance ['rɪdəns] *s* débarras *m*; **good riddance!** bon débarras!

riddle ['rɪdəl] *s* devinette *f*, énigme *f* || *tr*—**to riddle with** cribler de

ride [raɪd] *s* promenade *f*; **to take a ride** faire une promenade (en auto, à cheval, à motocyclette, etc.); **to take s.o. for a ride** (*to dupe s.o.*) (slang) faire marcher qn; (*to murder s.o.*) (slang) descendre qn || *v* (*pret* rode [rod]; *pp* ridden ['rɪdən]) *tr* monter à; (coll) se moquer de; **ridden down**, dominé; **to ride out** (*e.g., a storm*) étaler à || *intr* monter à cheval (à bicyclette, etc.); **to let ride** (coll) laisser courir

rider ['raɪdər] *s* (*on horseback*) cavalier *m*; (*on a bicycle*) cycliste *mf*; (*in a vehicle*) voyageur *m*; (*to a document*) annexe *f*

ridge [rɪdʒ] *s* arête *f*, crête *f*; (*of a fabric*) grain *m*

ridge'pole' *s* faîtage *m*

ridicule ['rɪdɪˌkjul] *s* ridicule *m* || *tr* ridiculiser

ridiculous [rɪ'dɪkjələs] *adj* ridicule

rid'ing acad'emy *s* école *f* d'équitation

rid'ing boot' *s* botte *f* de cheval, botte à l'écuyère

rid'ing hab'it *s* habit *m* d'amazone

rife [raɪf] *adj* répandu; **rife with** abondant en

riffraff ['rɪf ˌræf] *s* racaille *f*

rifle ['raɪfəl] *s* fusil *m*; (*spiral groove*) rayure *f* || *tr* piller; (*a gun barrel*) rayer

rift [rɪft] *s* fente *f*, crevasse *f*; (*disagreement*) désaccord *m*

rig [rɪg] *s* équipement *m*; (*carriage*) équipage *m*; (naut) gréement *m*; (*getup*) (coll) accoutrement *m* || *v* (*pret & pp* rigged*; *ger* rigging*) *tr* équiper; (*to falsify*) truquer; (naut) gréer; **to rig out with** (coll) accoutrer de

rigging ['rɪgɪŋ] *s* gréement *m*; (*fraud*) truquage *m*

right [raɪt] *adj* droit; (*change, time, etc.*) exact; (*statement, answer, etc.*) correct; (*conclusion, word, etc.*)

juste; (*name*) vrai; (*moment, house, road, etc.*) bon, e.g., **it's not the right road** ce n'est pas la bonne route; qu'il faut, e.g., **it's not the right village** (*spot, boy, etc.*) ce n'est pas le village (endroit, garçon, etc.) qu'il faut; **to be all right** aller très bien; **to be right** avoir raison || *s* (*justice*) droit *m*; (*reason*) raison *f*; (*right hand*) droite *f*; (*fist or blow in boxing*) droit; **all rights reserved** tous droits réservés; **by right of** à titre de; **by rights** de plein droit; **by the right!** (mil) guide à droite!; **on the right** à droite; **right and wrong** le bien et le mal; **rights** droits; **to be in the right** avoir raison || *adv* directement; correctement; complètement; bien, en bon état; (*to the right*) à droite; (coll) très; même, e.g., **right here** ici même; **all right!** d'accord!; **right and left** à droite et à gauche; **right away** tout de suite; **to put right** mettre bon ordre à, mettre en état || *tr* faire droit à; (*to correct*) corriger; (*to set up-right*) redresser || *intr* se redresser || *interj* parfait!

right′ about′ face′ *s* volte-face *f* || *interj* (mil) demi-tour à droite!

righteous ['raɪtʃəs] *adj* juste; vertueux

right′ field′ *s* (baseball) champ *m* droit

rightful ['raɪtfəl] *adj* légitime

right′-hand drive′ *s* conduite *f* à droite

right-hander ['raɪt'hændər] *s* droitier *m*

right′-hand man′ *s* bras *m* droit

rightist ['raɪtɪst] *adj* & *s* droitier *m*

rightly ['raɪtli] *adv* à bon droit, à juste titre; correctement, avec sagesse; **rightly or wrongly** à tort ou à raison

right′ of assem′bly *s* liberté *f* de réunion

right′ of way′ *s* droit *m* de passage; **to yield the right of way** céder le pas

rights′ of man′ *spl* droits *mpl* de l'homme

right to work ['raɪttə'wʌrk] *s* liberté *f* du travail des ouvriers non syndiqués

right′-wing *adj* de droite

right-winger ['raɪt'wɪŋər] *s* (coll) droitier *m*

rigid ['rɪdʒɪd] *adj* rigide

rigmarole ['rɪgmə͵rol] *s* galimatias *m*

rigor ['rɪgər] *s* rigueur *f*; (pathol) rigidité *f*

rigorous ['rɪgərəs] *adj* rigoureux

rile [raɪl] *tr* (coll) exaspérer

rill [rɪl] *s* ruisselet *m*

rim [rɪm] *s* bord *m*, rebord *m*; (*of spectacles*) monture *f*; (*of wheel*) jante *f*

rind [raɪnd] *s* écorce *f*; (*of cheese*) croûte *f*; (*of bacon*) couenne *f*

ring [rɪŋ] *s* anneau *m*; (*for the finger*) bague *f*, anneau; (*for some sport or exhibition*) piste *f*; (*for boxing*) ring *m*; (*for bullfight*) arène *f*; (*of a group of people*) cercle *m*; (*of evildoers*) gang *m*; (*under the eyes*) cerne *m*; (*sound*) son *m*; (*of bell, clock, telephone, etc.*) sonnerie *f*; (*of a small bell; in the ears; of the glass of glassware*) tintement *m*; (*to summon a*

person) coup *m* de sonnette; (*quality*) timbre *m*; (telp) coup de téléphone || *v* (*pret & pp* **ringed**) *tr* cerner || *intr* décrire des cercles || *v* (*pret* **rang** [ræŋ]; *pp* **rung** [rʌŋ]) *tr* sonner; **to ring up** (telp) donner un coup de téléphone à || *intr* sonner; (*said, e.g., of ears*) tinter; **to ring out** résonner

ring′bolt′ *s* piton *m*

ring′dove′ *s* (orn) ramier *m*

ring′ fin′ger *s* annulaire *m*

ringing ['rɪŋɪŋ] *adj* résonnant, retentissant || *s* sonnerie *f*; (*in the ears*) tintement *m*

ring′lead′er *s* meneur *m*

ringlet ['rɪŋlɪt] *s* bouclette *f*

ring′mas′ter *s* maître *m* de manège, chef *m* de piste

ring′side′ *s* premier rang *m*

ring′snake′ *s* (*Tropidonotus natrix*) couleuvre *f* à collier

ring′worm′ *s* teigne *f*

rink [rɪŋk] *s* patinoire *f*

rinse [rɪns] *s* rinçage *m* || *tr* rincer

riot ['raɪət] *s* émeute *f*; (*of colors*) orgie *f*; **to run riot** se déchaîner; (*said of plants or vines*) pulluler || *intr* émeuter

rioter ['raɪətər] *s* émeutier *m*

rip [rɪp] *s* déchirure *f* || *v* (*pret & pp* **ripped**; *ger* **ripping**) *tr* déchirer; **to rip away or off** arracher; **to rip open** or **up** découdre; (*a letter, package, etc.*) ouvrir en le déchirant || *intr* se déchirer

rip′ cord′ *s* (*of parachute*) cordelette *f* de déclenchement

ripe [raɪp] *adj* mûr; (*cheese*) fait; (*olive*) noir

ripen ['raɪpən] *tr* & *intr* mûrir

ripple ['rɪpəl] *s* ride *f*; (*sound*) murmure *m* || *tr* rider || *intr* se rider; murmurer

rise [raɪz] *s* hausse *f*, augmentation *f*; (*of ground; of the voice*) élévation *f*; (*of a heavenly body; of the curtain*) lever *m*; (*in one's employment, in one's fortunes*) ascension *f*; (*of water*) montée *f*; (*of a source of water*) naissance *f*; **to get a rise out of** (slang) se payer la tête de; **to give rise to** donner naissance à || *v* (*pret* **rose** [roz]; *pp* **risen** ['rɪzən]) *intr* s'élever, monter; (*to get out of bed; to stand up; to ascend in the heavens*) se lever; (*to revolt*) se soulever; (*said, e.g., of a danger*) se montrer; (*said of a fluid*) jaillir; (*in someone's esteem*) grandir; (*said of river*) prendre sa source; **to rise above** dépasser; (*unfortunate events, insults, etc.*) se montrer supérieur à; **to rise to** (e.g., *the occasion*) se montrer à la hauteur de

riser ['raɪzər] *s* (*of staircase*) contre-marche *f*; (*of gas or water*) colonne *f* montante; **to be a late riser** faire la grasse matinée; **to be an early riser** être matinal

risk [rɪsk] *s* risque *m* || *tr* risquer

risk·y ['rɪski] *adj* (*comp* **-ier**; *super* **-lest**) dangereux, hasardeux, risqué

risqué [rɪs'ke] adj risqué, osé

rite [raɪt] s rite m; **last rites** derniers sacrements mpl

ritual ['rɪt/ʊ·əl] adj & s rituel m

ri·val ['raɪvəl] adj & s rival m || v (pret & pp -valed or -valled; ger -valing or -valling) tr rivaliser avec

rival·ry ['raɪvəlrɪ] s (pl -ries) rivalité f

river ['rɪvər] adj fluvial || s fleuve m; (tributary) rivière f; (stream) cours m d'eau; **down the river** en aval; **up the river** en amont

riv'er bas/in s bassin m fluvial

riv'er·bed' s lit m de rivière

riv'er·front' s rive f d'un fleuve

riv'er·side' adj riverain || s rive f

rivet ['rɪvɪt] s rivet m || tr river

riv'et gun' s riveuse f pneumatique

rivulet ['rɪvjəlɪt] s ruisselet m

R.N. ['ar'en] s (letterword) (registered nurse) infirmière f diplômée

roach [rotʃ] s (ent) blatte f, cafard m; (ichth) gardon m

road [rod] s route f, chemin m; (naut) rade f; **road under construction** (public sign) travaux

road'bed' s assiette f; (rr) infrastructure f

road'block' s barrage m

road' hog' s écraseur m, chauffard m

road'house' s guinguette f au bord de la route

road' map' s carte f routière

road' serv'ice s secours m routier

road'side' s bord m de la route

road' sign' s poteau m indicateur

road'stead' s rade f

road'way' s chaussée f

roam [rom] tr parcourir; (the seas) sillonner || intr errer, rôder

roar [ror] s rugissement m; (of cannon, engine, etc.) grondement m; (of crowd) hurlement m; (of laughter) éclat m || intr rugir; gronder; hurler

roast [rost] s rôti m; (of coffee) torréfaction f || tr rôtir; (coffee) torréfier; (chestnuts) griller || intr se rôtir; se torréfier

roast' beef' s rosbif m, rôti m de bœuf

roaster ['rostər] s (appliance) rôtissoire f; (for coffee) brûloir m; (fowl) volaille f à rôtir

roast' pork' s porc m rôti

rob [rab] v (pret & pp robbed; ger robbing) tr & intr voler; **to rob s.o. of s.th.** voler q.ch. à qn

robber ['rabər] s voleur m

robber·y ['rabərɪ] s (pl -ies) vol m

robe [rob] s robe f; (of a professor, judge, etc.) toge f; (dressing gown) robe f de chambre; (for lap in a carriage) couverture f || tr revêtir d'une robe || intr revêtir sa robe

robin ['rabɪn] s (Erithacus rubecula) rouge-gorge m; (Turdus migratorius) grive f migratoire

robot ['robat] s robot m

robust [ro'bʌst] adj robuste

rock [rak] s roche f; (eminence) roc m, rocher m; (sticking out of water) rocher; (one that is thrown) pierre f; (slang) diamant m; **on the rocks**

(coll) fauché, à sec; (said of liquor) (coll) sur glace || tr balancer; (to rock to sleep) bercer || intr se balancer; se bercer

rock'-bot'tom adj (le) plus bas || s (le) fin fond m

rock' can'dy s candi m

rock' crys'tal s cristal m de roche

rocker ['rakər] s bascule f; (chair) chaise f à bascule; **to go off one's rocker** (slang) perdre la boussole

rock'er arm' s culbuteur m

rocket ['rakɪt] s fusée f; (arti, bot) roquette f || intr monter en chandelle; (said of prices) monter en flèche

rock'et bomb' s bombe f volante, fusée f

rock'et launch'er s lance-fusées m; (arti) lance-roquettes m

rock'et ship' s fusée f interplanétaire, fusée interstellaire

rock' gar'den s jardin m de rocaille

rock'ing chair' s fauteuil m à bascule

rock'ing horse' s cheval m à bascule

Rock' of Gibral'tar [dʒɪ'brɔltər] s rocher m de Gibraltar

rock' salt' s sel m gemme

rock' wool' s laine f minérale, laine de verre

rock·y ['rakɪ] adj (comp -ier; super -iest) rocheux, rocailleux

Rock'y Moun'tains spl Montagnes fpl Rocheuses

rod [rad] s baguette f; (for punishment) verge f; (of the retina; elongated microorganism) bâtonnet m; (of authority) main f; (of curtain) tringle f; (for fishing) canne f; (Bib) lignée f, race f; (mach) bielle f; (surv) jalon m; (revolver) (slang) pétard m; **rod and gun** la chasse et la pêche

rodent ['rodənt] adj & s rongeur m

roe [ro] s (deer) chevreuil m; (of fish) œufs mpl

roger ['radʒər] interj O.K.!; (rad) message reçu!

rogue [rog] s coquin m

rogues'/ gal'lery s fichier m de la police de portraits de criminels

roguish ['rogɪʃ] adj espiègle, coquin

roister ['rɔɪstər] intr faire du tapage

role or rôle [rol] s rôle m

roll [rol] s rouleau m; (of thunder, drums, etc.) roulement m; (roll call) appel m; (list) rôle m; (of film) rouleau; (of paper money) liasse f; (of dice) coup m; (of a boat) roulis m; (of fat) bourrelet m; (culin) petit pain m; **to call the roll** faire l'appel || tr rouler; **to roll over** retourner; **to roll up** enrouler || intr rouler; (said of thunder) gronder; (to sway) se balancer; (to overturn) faire panache; (said of ship) rouler; **to roll over** se retourner; **to roll up** se rouler

roll'back' s repoussement m; (com) baisse f de prix

roll' call' s appel m; (vote) appel nominal

roller ['rolər] s rouleau m; (of a skate) roulette f; (wave) lame f de houle

roll′er bear′ing s coussinet m à rouleaux

roll′er coast′er s montagnes fpl russes

roll′er skate′ s patin m à roulettes

roll′er-skate′ intr patiner sur des roulettes

roll′er-skating rink′ s skating m

roll′er tow′el s essuie-mains m à rouleau, serviette f sans fin

roll′ing mill′ s usine f de laminage; (set of rollers) laminoir m

roll′ing pin′ s rouleau m

roll′ing stock′ s (rr) matériel m roulant

roll′-top desk′ s bureau m à cylindre

roly-poly [′roli′poli] adj rondelet

romaine [ro′men] s romaine f

roman [′romən] adj & s (typ) romain m; **Roman** Romain m

Ro′man can′dle s chandelle f romaine

Ro′man Cath′olic adj & s catholique mf

Romance [′romæns], [ro′mæns] adj roman || (l.c.) [ro′mæns], [′romæns] s roman m de chevalerie; (made-up story) conte m bleu; (love affair) idylle f; (mus) romance f || (l.c.) [ro′mæns] intr exagérer, broder

Romanesque [,romən′ɛsk] adj & s roman m

Ro′man nose′ s nez m aquilin

Ro′man nu′meral s chiffre m romain

romantic [ro′mæntɪk] adj (genre; literature; scenery) romantique; (imagination) romanesque

romanticism [ro′mæntɪ,sɪzəm] s romantisme m

romanticist [ro′mæntɪsɪst] s romantique mf

romp [rɑmp] intr s'ébattre

rompers [′rɑmpərz] spl barboteuse f

roof [ruf], [rʊf] s toit m; (of the mouth) palais m; **to raise the roof** (slang) faire un boucan de tous les diables

roofer [′rufər], [′rʊfər] s couvreur m

roof′ garden s terrasse f avec jardin, pergola f

rook [rʊk] s (chess) tour f, corneille f || tr (coll) rouler; **to rook s.o. out of s.th.** (coll) filouter q.ch. à qn

rookie [′rʊki] s (slang) bleu m

room [rum], [rʊm] s pièce f; (especially bedroom) chambre f; (where people congregate) salle f; (space) place f; **to make room for** faire place à || intr vivre en garni; **to room with** partager une chambre avec

room′ and board′ s le vivre et le couvert

room′ clerk′ s employé m à la réception

roomer [′rumər], [′rʊmər] s locataire mf

roomette [ru′met] s chambrette f de sleeping

room′ing house′ s maison f meublée, maison garnie

room′mate′ s camarade mf de chambre

room·y [′rumi], [′rʊmi] adj (comp -ier; super -iest) spacieux, ample

roost [rust] s perchoir m; (coll) logis m, demeure f; **to rule the roost** (coll) faire la loi || intr se percher, percher

rooster [′rustər] s coq m

root [rut], [rʊt] s racine f; **to get to the root of** approfondir; **to take root** prendre racine || tr fouiller; **to root out** déraciner || intr s'enraciner; **to root around in** fouiller dans; **to root for** (coll) applaudir, encourager

rooter [′rutər], [′rʊtər] s (coll) fanatique mf, fana mf

rope [rop] s corde f; (lasso) corde à nœud coulant; **to jump rope** sauter à la corde; **to know the ropes** (slang) connaître les ficelles || tr (corder; (cattle) prendre au lasso; **to rope in** (slang) entraîner

rope′ lad′der s échelle f de corde

rope′ walk′er s funambule mf, danseur m de corde

rosa·ry [′rozəri] s (pl -ries) rosaire m

rose [roz] adj rose || s (color) rose m; (bot) rose f

rose′ bee′tle s cétoine f dorée

rose′bud′ s bouton m de rose

rose′bush′ s rosier m

rose′-col′ored adj rosé, couleur de rose; **to see everything through rose-colored glasses** voir tout en rose

rose′ gar′den s roseraie f

rosemar·y [′roz,meri] s (pl -ies) romarin m

rose′ of Shar′on [′ʃɛrən] s rose f de Saron

rosette [ro′zet] s rosette f; (archit, elec) rosace f

rose′ win′dow s rosace f, rose f

rose′wood′ s bois m de rose, palissandre m

rosin [′rɑzɪn] s colophane f

roster [′rɑstər] s liste f, appel m; (educ) heures fpl de classe; (mil) tableau m de service; (naut) rôle m

rostrum [′rɑstrəm] s tribune f

ros·y [′rozi] adj (comp -ier; super -iest) rosé; (complexion) vermeil; (fig) riant

rot [rɑt] s pourriture f; (slang) sottise f || v (pret & pp rotted; ger rotting) tr & intr pourrir

ro′tary press′ [′rotəri] s rotative f

rotate [′rotet], [ro′tet] tr & intr tourner; (agr) alterner

rotation [ro′teʃən] s rotation f; **in rotation** à tour de rôle

rote [rot] s routine f; **by rote** par cœur, machinalement

rot′gut′ s (slang) tord-boyaux m

rotisserie [ro′tɪsəri] s rôtissoire f

rotogravure [,rotəgrə′vjʊr], [,rotə-′grevjʊr] s rotogravure f

rotten [′rɑtən] adj pourri

rotund [ro′tʌnd] adj rond, arrondi; (e.g., language) ampoulé

rotunda [ro′tʌndə] s rotonde f

rouge [ruʒ] s fard m, rouge m || tr farder || intr se farder, se mettre du rouge

rough [rʌf] adj rude; (uneven) inégal; (coarse) grossier; (unfinished) brut; (road) raboteux; (game) brutal; (sea) agité; (guess) approximatif || tr—**to**

rough it faire du camping, coucher sur la dure; **to rough up** malmener

rough' draft' s ébauche f, avant-projet m, brouillon m

rough'house' s boucan m, chahut m || intr faire du boucan, chahuter

rough' ide'a s aperçu m

roughly ['rʌfli] adv grossièrement; brutalement; approximativement

rough'neck' s (coll) canaille f

roulette [ru'let] s roulette f

round [raund] adj rond; (rounded) arrondi, rond; (e.g., shoulders) voûté; **three (four, etc.) feet round** trois (quatre, etc.) pieds de tour || s rond m; (inspection) ronde f; (of golf; of drinks; of postman, doctor, etc.) tournée f; (of applause) salve f; (of ammunition) cartouche f; (of veal) noix f; (boxing) round m; **to go the rounds** faire le tour || adv à la ronde; **round about** aux alentours; **the year round** pendant toute l'année; **to pass round** faire circuler, passer la ronde || prep autour de || tr (to make round) arrondir; (e.g., a corner) tourner, prendre; (a cape) doubler; **to round off** or **out** arrondir; (to finish) achever; **to round up** rassembler; (suspects) cueillir || intr s'arrondir

roundabout ['raundə,baut] adj indirect || s détour m; (carrousel) (Brit) manège m; (traffic circle) (Brit) rond-point m

rounder ['raundər] s (coll) fêtard m

round'house' s (rr) rotonde f

round'-shoul'dered adj voûté

round' steak' s gîte m à la noix

round' ta'ble s table f ronde; **Round Table** Table ronde

round'-trip' tick'et s billet m d'aller et retour

round'up' s (of cattle) rassemblement m; (of suspects) rafle f

rouse [rauz] tr réveiller || intr se réveiller

rout [raut] s déroute f || tr mettre en déroute

route [rut], [raut] s route f; (of, e.g., bus) ligne f, parcours m || tr acheminer

routine [ru'tin] adj routinier || s routine f

rove [rov] intr errer, vagabonder

rover ['rovər] s vagabond m

row [rau] s (coll) altercation f, prise f de bec; **to raise a row** (coll) faire du boucan || [ro] s rang m; (of, e.g., houses) rangée f; (boat ride) promenade f en barque; **in a row** à la file; (without interruption) de suite; **in rows** par rangs || intr ramer

rowboat ['ro,bot] s bateau m à rames, canot m

row'dy ['raudi] adj (comp **-dier**; super **-diest**) tapageur || s (pl **-dies**) tapageur m

rower ['ro·ər] s rameur m

rowing ['ro·ɪŋ] s nage f, canotage m, sport m de l'aviron

royal ['rɔɪ·əl] adj royal

royalist ['rɔɪ·əlɪst] adj & s royaliste mf

royal·ty ['rɔɪ·əlti] s (pl **-ties**) royauté f; droit m d'auteur; redevance f, droit d'inventeur

r.p.m. ['ɑr'pi'em] spl (letterword) (**revolutions per minute**) tours mpl à la minute

rub [rʌb] s frottement m; **there's the rub** (coll) voilà le hic || v (pret & pp **rubbed**; ger **rubbing**) tr frotter; **to rub elbows with** coudoyer; **to rub out** effacer; (slang) descendre, liquider || intr se frotter; (said, e.g., of moving parts) frotter; **to rub off** s'enlever, disparaître

rubber ['rʌbər] s caoutchouc m; (eraser) gomme f à effacer; (in bridge) robre m; **rubbers** (overshoes) caoutchoucs

rub'ber band' s élastique m

rubberize ['rʌbə,raɪz] tr caoutchouter

rub'ber·neck' s (coll) badaud m || intr (coll) badauder

rub'ber plant' s figuier m élastique, caoutchoutier m; (tree) arbre m à caoutchouc, hévéa m

rub'ber stamp' s tampon m; (coll) béni-oui-oui m

rub'ber-stamp' tr apposer le tampon sur; (with a person's signature) estampiller; (coll) approuver à tort et à travers

rub'bing al'cohol s alcool m pour les frictions

rubbish ['rʌbɪʃ] s détritus m, rebut m; (coll) imbécillités fpl

rubble ['rʌbəl] s (broken stone) décombres mpl; (used in masonry) moellons mpl

rub'down' s friction f

rubric ['rubrɪk] s rubrique f

ru·by ['rubi] adj (lips) vermeil || s (pl **-bies**) rubis m

rucksack ['rʌk,sæk] s sac-à-dos m

rudder ['rʌdər] s gouvernail m

rud·dy ['rʌdi] adj (comp **-dier**; super **-diest**) rougeaud, coloré

rude [rud] adj (rough, rugged) rude; (discourteous) impoli, grossier

rudeness ['rudnɪs] s rudesse f; impolitesse f

rudiment ['rudɪmənt] s rudiment m

rue [ru] tr regretter amèrement

rueful ['rufəl] adj lamentable; triste

ruffian ['rʌfɪ·ən] s brute f

ruffle ['rʌfəl] s (in water) rides fpl; (of drum) roulement m; (sewing) jabot m plissé || tr (to crease; to vex) froisser; (the water) rider; (its feathers) hérisser; (one's hair) ébouriffer

rug [rʌg] s tapis m, carpette f

rugged ['rʌgɪd] adj rude, sévère; (road, country, etc.) raboteux; (person) robuste; (e.g., machine) résistant à toute épreuve

ruin ['ru·ɪn] s ruine f || tr ruiner

rule [rul] s règle f; autorité f; (reign) règne m; (law) décision f; **as a rule** en général; **by rule of thumb** empiriquement, à vue de nez || tr gouverner; (to lead) diriger, guider; (one's passions) contenir; (with lines) régler; (law) décider; **to rule out** écarter, éliminer || *intr* gouverner; (*to be the rule*) prévaloir; **to rule over** régner sur

ruler ['rulər] *s* dirigeant *m*; souverain *m*; (*for ruling lines*) règle *f*

ruling ['rulɪŋ] *adj* actuel; (*e.g., classes*) dirigeant; (*quality, trait, etc.*) dominant || *s* (*of paper*) réglage *m*; (*law*) décision *f*

rum [rʌm] *s* rhum *m*

Rumanian [ru'menɪ·ən] *adj* roumain || *s* (*language*) roumain *m*; (*person*) Roumain *m*

rumble ['rʌmbəl] *s* (*of thunder*) grondement *m*; (*of a cart*) roulement *m*; (*of intestines*) gargouillement *m*; (*slang*) rixe *f* entre gangs || *intr* gronder, rouler

ruminate ['rumɪ‚net] *tr & intr* ruminer

rummage ['rʌmɪdʒ] *intr* fouiller

rum'mage sale' *s* vente *f* d'objets usagés

rumor ['rumər] *s* rumeur *f* || *tr*—**it is rumored that** le bruit court que

rump [rʌmp] *s* (*of animal*) croupe *f*; (*of bird*) croupion *m*; (*cut of meat*) culotte *f*; (*buttocks*) postérieur *m*

rumple ['rʌmpəl] *s* faux pli *m* || *tr* (*paper, cloth, etc.*) froisser, chiffonner; (*one's hair*) ébouriffer

rump' steak' *s* romsteck *m*

rumpus ['rʌmpəs] *s* (coll) chahut *m*; (*argument*) (coll) prise *f* de bec; **to raise a rumpus** (coll) déclencher un chahut; faire une scène violente

rum'pus room' *s* salle *f* de jeux

run [rʌn] *s* course *f*; (*e.g., of good or bad luck*) suite *f*; (*on a bank by depositors*) descente *f*; (*of salmon*) remonte *f*; (*of, e.g., a bus*) parcours *m*; (*in a stocking*) échelle *f*, démaillage *m*; (*cards*) séquence *f*; (*mus*) roulade *f*; **in the long run** à la longue; **on the run** à la débandade, en fuite; **run of bad luck** série *f* noire; **the general run** la généralité; **to give free run to** donner libre carrière à; **to give s.o. a run for his money** en donner à qn pour son argent; **to have a long run** (theat) tenir longtemps l'affiche; **to have the run of** avoir libre accès à or dans; **to keep s.o. on the run** ne laisser aucun répit à qn; **to make a run in** (*a stocking*) démailler || *v* (*pret* **ran** [ræn]; *pp* **run**; *ger* **running**) *tr* (*the streets; a race; a risk*) courir; (*a motor, machine, etc.*) faire marcher; (*an organization, project, etc.*) diriger; (*a business, factory, etc.*) exploiter; (*a blockade*) forcer; (*a line*) tracer; (turf) faire courir; **to run aground** échouer; **to run down** (*to knock down*) renverser; (*to find*) dépister; (*game*) mettre aux abois; (*to disparage*) (coll) dénigrer; **to run in** (*a motor*) roder; **to run off** (*a liquid*) faire écouler; (*copies, pages, etc.*) tirer; **to run through** (*e.g., with a sword*) transpercer; **to run up** (*a flag*) hisser; (*a debt*) (coll) laisser accumuler || *intr* courir; (*said, e.g., of water;*

said of fountain pen, nose, etc.) couler; (*said of stockings*) se démailler; (*said of salmon*) faire la montaison; (*said of colors*) s'étaler, se déteindre; (*said of sore*) suppurer; (*said of rumor, news, etc.*) circuler, courir; (*for office*) se présenter; (mach) fonctionner, marcher; (theat) rester à l'affiche, se jouer; **run along!** filez!; **to run across** (*to meet by chance*) rencontrer par hasard; **to run along** (*border, longer*) (*to go*) s'en aller; **to run at** se jeter sur; **to run away** se sauver, s'enfuir; (*said of horse*) s'emballer, s'emporter; **to run away with** enlever; **to run down** (*e.g., a hill*) descendre en courant; (*said of spring*) se détendre; (*said of watch*) s'arrêter (faute d'être remonté); (*said of storage battery*) se décharger, s'épuiser; **to run for** (*an office*) poser sa candidature pour; **to run in the family** tenir de famille; **to run into** heurter; (*to meet*) (coll) rencontrer; **to run off** se sauver, s'enfuir; (*said of liquid*) s'écouler; **to run out** (*said of passport, lease, etc.*) expirer; **to run out of** être à court de; **to run over** (*said of a liquid*) déborder; (*an article, a text, etc.*) parcourir; (*s.th. in the road*) passer sur; (*e.g., a pedestrian*) écraser; **to run through** (*an article, text, etc.*) parcourir; (*a fortune*) gaspiller

run'away' *adj* fugitif; (*horse*) emballé || *s* fugitif *m*; cheval *m* emballé

run'down' *s* compte rendu *m*, récit *m*

run'-down' *adj* délabré; (*person; battery*) épuisé, à plat; (*clock spring*) détendu

rung [rʌŋ] *s* (*of ladder or chair*) barreau *m*; (*of wheel*) rayon *m*

runner ['rʌnər] *s* (*person*) coureur *m*; (*messenger*) courrier *m*; (*of ice skate or sleigh*) patin *m*; (*narrow rug*) rampe *f* d'escalier; (*strip of cloth for table top*) chemin *m* de table; (*in stockings*) démaillage *m*; (bot) coulant *m*

run'ner-up' *s* (*pl* **runners-up**) bon second *m*, premier accessit *m*

running ['rʌnɪŋ] *adj* (*person; water; expenses*) courant; (*stream; knot; style*) coulant; (*sore*) suppurant; (*e.g., motor*) en marche || *s* (*of man or animal*) course *f*; (*of water*) écoulement *m*; (*of machine*) fonctionnement *m*, marche *f*; (*of business*) direction *f*

run'ning board' *s* marchepied *m*

run'ning com'mentar'y *s* (*pl* **-ies**) (rad, telv) reportage *m* en direct

run'ning head' *s* titre *m* courant

run'ning start' *s* départ *m* lancé

run'off elec'tion *s* scrutin *m* de ballottage

run'proof' *adj* indémaillable

runt [rʌnt] *s* avorton *m*

run'way' *s* piste *f*, rampe *f*

rupture ['rʌptʃər] *s* rupture *f*; (pathol) hernie *f* || *tr* rompre; (*a ligament,* *blood vessel, etc.*) se rompre ‖ *intr* se rompre

rural ['rʊrəl] *adj* rural

ru′ral free′ deliv′ery *s* distribution *f* gratuite par le facteur rural

ru′ral police′man *s* garde *m* champêtre

ruse [ruz] *s* ruse *f*

rush [rʌʃ] *adj* urgent ‖ *s* course *f* précipitée, ruée *f*; précipitation *f*; (bot) jonc *m*; (formula on envelope or letterhead) urgent; **to be in a rush to** être pressé de ‖ *tr* pousser vivement; (*e.g., to the hospital*) transporter d'urgence; (*a piece of work*) exécuter d'urgence; (*e.g., a girl*) (slang) insister auprès de; **to rush through** (*e.g., a law*) faire passer à la hâte ‖ *intr* se précipiter, se ruer; **to rush about** courir ça et là; **to rush headlong** foncer tête baissée; **to rush into** (*e.g., a room*) faire irruption dans; (*an affair*) se jeter dans; **to rush out** sortir précipitamment; **to rush through** (*one's lessons, prayers, etc.*) expédier; (*e.g., a town*) traverser à toute vitesse; (*a tourist attraction*) visiter au pas de course; (*a book*) lire à la hâte; **to rush to** s'empresser de; **to rush to**

one's face (*said of blood*) monter au visage à qn

rush′-bot′tomed chair′ *s* chaise *f* à fond de paille

rush′ hours′ *spl* heures *fpl* d'affluence or de pointe

rush′ or′der *s* commande *f* urgente

russet ['rʌsɪt] *adj* roussâtre, roux

Russia ['rʌʃə] *s* Russie *f*; la Russie

Russian ['rʌʃən] *adj* russe ‖ *s* (*language*) russe *m*; (*person*) Russe *mf*

rust [rʌst] *s* rouille *f* ‖ *tr* rouiller ‖ *intr* se rouiller

rustic ['rʌstɪk] *adj* rustique; simple, net; (pej) rustaud ‖ *s* paysan *m*, villageois *m*

rustle ['rʌsəl] *s* bruissement *m*; (*of, e.g., a dress*) froufrou *m* ‖ *tr* faire bruire; (*cattle*) (coll) voler ‖ *intr* bruire; (*said, e.g., of a dress*) froufrouter; **to rustle around** (coll) se démener

rust′proof′ *adj* inoxydable

rust·y ['rʌsti] *adj* (*comp* **-ier;** *super* **-iest**) rouillé

rut [rʌt] *s* ornière *f*; (zool) rut *m*

ruthless ['ruθlɪs] *adj* impitoyable

rye [raɪ] *s* seigle *m*; whisky *m* de seigle

S

S, s [es] *s* XIXᵉ lettre de l'alphabet

Sabbath ['sæbəθ] *s* sabbat *m*; dimanche *m*

sabbat′ical year′ [sə'bætɪkəl] *s* année *f* de congé

saber ['sebər] *s* sabre *m* ‖ *tr* sabrer

sable ['sebəl] *adj* noir ‖ *s* (*animal, fur*) zibeline *f*; noir *m*; **sables** vêtements *mpl* de deuil

sabotage ['sæbə,taʒ] *s* sabotage *m* ‖ *tr* & *intr* saboter

saccharin ['sækərɪn] *s* saccharine *f*

sachet [sæ'ʃe] *s* sachet *m* (à parfums)

sack [sæk] *s* sac *m*; (wine) xérès *m* ‖ *tr* mettre en sac; (mil) saccager; (coll) saquer, congédier

sack′cloth′ *s* grosse toile *f* d'emballage, serpillière *f*; (*worn for penitence*) cilice *m*; **in sackcloth and ashes** sous le sac et la cendre

sacrament ['sækrəmənt] *s* sacrement *m*

sacramental [,sækrə'mɛntəl] *adj* sacramentel

sacred ['sekrəd] *adj* sacré

sa′cred cow′ *s* (fig) monstre *m* sacré

sacrifice ['sækrɪ,faɪs] *s* sacrifice *m*; **at a sacrifice** à perte ‖ *tr* & *intr* sacrifier

sacrilege ['sækrɪlɪdʒ] *s* sacrilège *m*

sacrilegious [,sækrɪ'lɪdʒəs], [,sækrɪ'lidʒəs] *adj* sacrilège

sacristan ['sækrɪstən] *s* sacristain *m*

sad [sæd] *adj* (*comp* **sadder;** *super* **saddest**) triste

sadden ['sædən] *tr* attrister ‖ *intr* s'attrister

saddle ['sædəl] *s* selle *f* ‖ *tr* seller; **to saddle with** charger de, encombrer de

sad′dle·bag′ *s* sacoche *f* (de selle)

saddlebow ['sædəl,bo] *s* arçon *m* de devant

saddler ['sædlər] *s* sellier *m*

sad′dle·tree′ *s* arçon *m*

sadist ['sædɪst], ['sedɪst] *s* sadique *mf*

sadistic [sæ'dɪstɪk], [se'dɪstɪk] *adj* sadique

sadness ['sædnɪs] *s* tristesse *f*

sad′ sack′ *s* (slang) bidasse *mf*

safe [sef] *adj* (*from danger*) sûr; (*unhurt*) sauf; (*margin*) certain; **safe and sound** sain et sauf; **safe from** à l'abri de ‖ *s* coffre-fort *m*, caisse *f*

safe′-con′duct *s* sauf-conduit *m*

safe′-depos′it box′ *s* coffre *m* à la banque; coffret de sûreté (Canad)

safe′guard′ *s* sauvegarde *f* ‖ *tr* sauvegarder

safe′keep′ing *s* bonne garde *f*

safe·ty ['sefti] *adj* de sûreté ‖ *s* (*pl* **-ties**) (*state of being safe*) sécurité *f*, sûreté *f*; (*avoidance of danger*) salut *m*

safe′ty belt′ *s* ceinture *f* de sécurité

safe′ty match′ *s* allumette *f* de sûreté

safe′ty pin′ *s* épingle *f* de sûreté

safe′ty ra′zor *s* rasoir *m* de sûreté

safe′ty valve′ *s* soupape *f* de sûreté

saffron ['sæfrən] *adj* safrané ‖ *s* safran *m*

sag [sæg] *s* affaissement *m* ‖ *v* (*pret* &

pp **sagged**; ger **sagging**) intr s'affaisser

sagacious [sə'geʃəs] adj sagace

sage [sedʒ] adj sage ‖ s sage mf; (plant) sauge f

sage'brush' s armoise f

sail [sel] s voile f; (sails) voilure f; (of windmill) aile f; **full sail** toutes voiles dehors; **to set sail** mettre les voiles; **to take a sail** faire une promenade à la voile; **to take in sail** baisser pavillon ‖ tr (a ship) gouverner, commander; (to travel over) naviguer sur ‖ intr naviguer; **to sail along the coast** côtoyer; **to sail into** (coll) assaillir

sail'boat' s bateau m à voiles

sail'cloth' s toile f à voile

sailing ['selɪŋ] s navigation f; (working of ship) manœuvre f; (of pleasure craft) voile f

sail'ing ves'sel s voilier m

sail'mak'er s voilier m

sailor ['selər] s marin m; (simple crewman) matelot m

saint [sent] adj & s saint m

saint'hood s sainteté f

saintliness ['sentlɪnɪs] s sainteté f

Saint' Vi'tus's dance' ['vaɪtəsəz] s (pathol) danse f de Saint-Guy

sake [sek] s—**for the sake of** pour l'amour de, dans l'intérêt de; **for your sake** pour vous

salable ['seləbəl] adj vendable

salacious [sə'leʃəs] adj lubrique

salad ['sæləd] s salade f

sal'ad bowl' s saladier m

sala•ry ['sæləri] s (pl -ries) salaire m

sale [sel] s vente f; **for sale** en vente; **on sale** en solde, en réclame

sales' clerk' s vendeur m

sales'girl' s vendeuse f, demoiselle f de magasin

sales'la'dy s (pl -dies) vendeuse f

sales'man s (pl -men) vendeur m, commis m

sales'man•ship' s l'art m de vendre

sales' promo'tion s stimulation f de la vente

sales'room' s salle f de vente

sales' talk' s raisonnements mpl destinés à convaincre le client

sales' tax' s taxe f sur les ventes, impôt m indirect

saliva [sə'laɪvə] s salive f

sallow ['sælo] adj olivâtre

sal•ly ['sæli] s (pl -lies) saillie f; (mil) sortie f ‖ v (pret & pp -lied) intr faire une sortie

salmon ['sæmən] adj & s saumon m

saloon [sə'lun] s cabaret m, estaminet m, bistrot m; (naut) salon m

salt [sɔlt] s sel m ‖ tr saler; **to salt away** (coll) économiser, mettre de côté

salt'cel'lar s salière f

salt' lick' s terrain m salifère

salt'pe'ter s (potassium nitrate) salpêtre m; (sodium nitrate) nitrate m du Chili

salt' pork' s salé m

salt'sha'ker s salière f

salt•y ['sɔlti] adj (comp -ier; super -iest) salé

salute [sə'lut] s salut m ‖ tr saluer

salvage ['sælvɪdʒ] s sauvetage m; biens mpl sauvés ‖ tr sauver; récupérer

salvation [sæl'veʃən] s salut m

Salva'tion Ar'my s Armée f du Salut

salve [sæv], [sɑv] s onguent m, pommade f; baume m ‖ tr appliquer un onguent sur; (fig) apaiser

sal•vo ['sælvo] s (pl -vos or -voes) salve f

Samaritan [sə'mærɪtən] adj samaritain ‖ s Samaritain m

same [sem] adj & pron indef même (before noun); **at the same time** en même temps, au même moment, à la fois; **it's all the same to me** ça m'est égal; **just the same, all the same** malgré tout, quand même; **the same ... as** le même ... que

sameness ['semnɪs] s monotonie f

sample ['sæmpəl] s échantillon m ‖ tr échantillonner; essayer

sam'ple cop'y s (pl -ies) numéro m spécimen

sancti•fy ['sæŋktɪ,faɪ] v (pret & pp -fied) tr sanctifier

sanctimonious [,sæŋktɪ'moni•əs] adj papelard, bigot

sanction ['sæŋkʃən] s sanction f ‖ tr sanctionner

sanctuar•y ['sæŋktʃu,eri] s (pl -ies) sanctuaire m; refuge m, asile m

sand [sænd] s sable m ‖ tr sablonner

sandal ['sændəl] s sandale f

san'dal•wood' s santal m

sand'bag' s sac m de sable

sand' bar' s banc m de sable

sand'blast' s jet m de sable; (apparatus) sableuse f ‖ tr sabler

sand'box' s (rr) sablière f

sand'glass' s sablier m

sand'pa'per s papier m de verre ‖ tr polir au papier de verre

sand'pi'per s bécasseau m

sand'stone' s grès m

sand'storm' s tempête f de sable

sandwich ['sændwɪtʃ] s sandwich m ‖ tr intercaler

sand'wich man' s homme-affiche m

sand•y ['sændi] adj (comp -ier; super -iest) sablonneux; (hair) blond roux

sane [sen] adj sain, équilibré; (principles) raisonnable

sanguine ['sæŋgwɪn] adj confiant, optimiste; (countenance) sanguin

sanitary ['sænɪ,teri] adj sanitaire

san'itary nap'kin s serviette f hygiénique

sanitation [,sænɪ'teʃən] s hygiène f, salubrité f; (drainage) assainissement m

sanity ['sænɪti] s santé f mentale; bon sens m

Santa Claus ['sæntə,klɔz] s le père Noël

sap [sæp] s sève f; (mil) sape f; (coll) poire f, nigaud m ‖ v (pret & pp sapped; ger sapping) tr tirer la sève de; (to weaken) affaiblir; (mil) saper

sapling ['sæplɪŋ] *s* jeune arbre *m*; jeune homme *m*

sapphire ['sæfaɪr] *s* saphir *m*

Saracen ['særəsən] *adj* sarrasin ‖ *s* Sarrasin *m*

sarcasm ['sɑrkæzəm] *s* sarcasme *m*

sardine [sɑr'din] *s* sardine *f*; **packed in like sardines** serrés comme des harengs

Sardinia [sɑr'dɪnɪ·ə] *s* Sardaigne; la Sardaigne

Sardinian [sɑr'dɪnɪ·ən] *adj* sarde ‖ *s* (*language*) sarde *m*; (*person*) Sarde *mf*

sarsaparilla [,sɑrsəpə'rɪlə] *s* salsepareille *f*

sash [sæʃ] *s* ceinture *f*; (*of window*) châssis *m*

sash' win'dow *s* fenêtre *f* à guillotine

sas·sy ['sæsɪ] *adj* (*comp* **-sier;** *super* **-siest**) (coll) impudent, effronté

satchel ['sætʃəl] *s* sacoche *f*; (*of schoolboy*) carton *m*

sate [set] *tr* soûler

sateen [sæ'tin] *s* satinette *f*

satellite ['sætə,laɪt] *adj & s* satellite *m*

sat'ellite coun'try *s* pays *m* satellite

satiate ['seʃɪ,et] *adj* rassasié ‖ *tr* rassasier

satin ['sætɪn] *s* satin *m*

satire ['sætaɪr] *s* satire *f*

satiric(al) [sə'tɪrɪk(əl)] *adj* satirique

satirize ['sætɪ,raɪz] *tr* satiriser

satisfaction [,sætɪs'fækʃən] *s* satisfaction *f*

satisfactory [,sætɪs'fæktərɪ] *adj* satisfaisant

satis·fy ['sætɪs,faɪ] *v* (*pret & pp* **-fied**) *tr* satisfaire; (*a requirement, need, etc.*) satisfaire (with *dat*) ‖ *intr* satisfaire

saturate ['sætʃə,ret] *tr* saturer

Saturday ['sætərdɪ] *s* samedi *m*

Saturn ['sætərn] *s* Saturne *m*

sauce [sɔs] *s* sauce *f*; (coll) insolence *f*, toupet *m* ‖ *tr* assaisonner [sɔs], [sæs] *tr* (coll) parler avec impudence à

sauce'pan' *s* casserole *f*

saucer ['sɔsər] *s* soucoupe *f*

sau·cy ['sɔsɪ] *adj* (*comp* **-cier;** *super* **-ciest**) impudent, effronté

sauerkraut ['saʊr,kraʊt] *s* choucroute *f*

saunter ['sɔntər] *s* flânerie *f* ‖ *intr* flâner

sausage ['sɔsɪdʒ] *s* saucisse *f*, saucisson *m*

sauté [so'te] *tr* sauter, faire sauter

savage ['sævɪdʒ] *adj & s* sauvage *mf*

savant ['sævənt] *s* savant *m*, érudit *m*

save [sev] *prep* sauf, excepté ‖ *tr* sauver; (*money*) épargner; (*time*) gagner ‖ *intr* économiser

saving ['sevɪŋ] *adj* économe ‖ **savings** *spl* épargne *f*, économies *fpl*

sav'ings account' *s* dépôt *m* d'épargne

sav'ings and loan' associa'tion *s* caisse *f* d'épargne et de prêt

sav'ings bank' *s* caisse *f* d'épargne

sav'ings book' *s* livret *m* de caisse d'épargne

savior ['sevjər] *s* sauveur *m*

Saviour ['sevjər] *s* Sauveur *m*

savor ['sevər] *s* saveur *f* ‖ *tr* savourer ‖ *intr*—**to savor of** avoir un goût de

savor·y ['sevərɪ] *adj* (*comp* **-ier;** *super* **-iest**) (*taste*) savoureux; (*smell*) odorant ‖ *s* (*pl* **-ies**) (bot) sariette *f*

saw [sɔ] *s* scie *f*; (*proverb*) dicton *m* ‖ *tr* scier

saw'dust' *s* sciure *f* de bois

saw'horse' *s* chevalet *m*

saw'mill' *s* scierie *f*

Saxon ['sæksən] *adj* saxon ‖ *s* (*language*) saxon *m*; (*person*) Saxon *m*

saxophone ['sæksə,fon] *s* saxophone *m*

say [se] *s* mot *m*; **to have one's say** avoir son mot à dire ‖ *v* (*pret & pp* **said** [sed]) *tr* dire; **I should say not!** absolument pas!; **I should say so!** je crois bien!; **it is said** on dit; **no sooner said than done** sitôt dit, sitôt fait; **that is to say** c'est-à-dire; **to go without saying** aller sans dire; **you said it!** (coll) et comment!, tu parles!

saying ['se·ɪŋ] *s* proverbe *m*

scab [skæb] *s* croûte *f*; (*strikebreaker*) jaune *m*; canaille *f*

scabbard ['skæbərd] *s* fourreau *m*

scab·by ['skæbɪ] *adj* (*comp* **-bier;** *super* **-biest**) croûteux; (coll) vil

scabrous ['skæbrəs] *adj* scabreux; (*uneven*) rugueux

scads [skædz] *spl* (slang) des tas *mpl*

scaffold ['skæfəld] *s* échafaud *m*; (*used in construction*) échafaudage *m*

scaffolding ['skæfəldɪŋ] *s* échafaudage *m*

scald [skɔld] *tr* échauder

scale [skel] *s* (*of thermometer, map, salaries, etc.*) échelle *f*; (*for weighing*) plateau *m*; (*incrustation*) tartre *m*; (bot, zool) écaille *f*; (mus) échelle; **on a large scale** sur une grande échelle; **scales** balance *f*; **to tip the scales** faire pencher la balance ‖ *tr* escalader; **to scale down** réduire l'échelle de

scallop ['skɑləp], ['skæləp] *s* coquille *f* Saint-Jacques, peigne *m*, pétoncle *m*; (*thin slice of meat*) escalope *f*; (*on edge of cloth*) feston *m* ‖ *tr* (*the edges*) denteler, découper; (culin) gratiner et cuire au four et à la crème

scalp [skælp] *s* cuir *m* chevelu; (*Indian trophy*) scalp *m* ‖ *tr* scalper; (*tickets*) (coll) faire le trafic de; (*to hoodwink*) (slang) abuser de

scalpel ['skælpəl] *s* scalpel *m*

scal·y ['skelɪ] *adj* (*comp* **-ier;** *super* **-iest**) écailleux

scamp [skæmp] *s* garnement *m*

scamper ['skæmpər] *intr* courir allégrement; **to scamper away or off** détaler

scan [skæn] *v* (*pret & pp* **scanned;** *ger* **scanning**) *tr* scruter; (*e.g., a page*) jeter un coup d'œil sur; (*verses*) scander; (telv) balayer

scandal ['skændəl] *s* scandale *m*

scandalize ['skændə,laɪz] *tr* scandaliser

scandalous ['skændələs] *adj* scandaleux

Scandinavian [,skændɪ'nevɪ·ən] *adj*

scandinave ‖ s (*language*) scandinave m; (*person*) Scandinave mf

scanning ['skænɪŋ] s (telv) balayage m

scant [skænt] adj maigre; (*attire*) léger, sommaire ‖ tr réduire; lésiner sur

scant•y ['skænti] adj (comp -ier; super -iest) rare, maigre; léger

scapegoat ['skep,got] s bouc m émissaire

scar [skɑr] s cicatrice f; (*on face*) balafre f ‖ v (pret & pp scarred; ger scarring) tr balafrer

scarce [skers] adj rare, peu abondant

scarcely ['skersli] adv à peine, presque pas; ne . . . guère §90; scarcely ever rarement

scarci•ty ['skersɪti] s (pl -ties) manque m, pénurie f

scare [sker] s panique f, effroi m ‖ tr épouvanter, effrayer; to scare away or off effaroucher; to scare up (coll) procurer ‖ intr s'effaroucher

scare'crow' s épouvantail m

scarf [skɑrf] s (pl scarfs or scarves [skɑrvz]) foulard m, écharpe f

scarlet ['skɑrlɪt] adj & s écarlate f

scar'let fe'ver s scarlatine f

scar•y ['skeri] adj (comp -ier; super -iest) (*easily frightened*) (coll) peureux, ombrageux; (*causing fright*) (coll) effrayant

scathing ['skeðɪŋ] adj cinglant

scatter ['skætər] tr éparpiller; (*a mob*) disperser ‖ intr se disperser

scat'ter-brained' adj (coll) étourdi

scenari•o [sɪ'nerɪ,o], [sɪ'nɑrɪ,o] s (pl -os) scénario m

scene [sin] s scène f; (*landscape*) paysage m; behind the scenes dans les coulisses; to make a scene faire une scène

scener•y ['sinəri] s (pl -ies) paysage m; (theat) décor m, décors m

scene'shifter ['sin,ʃɪftər] s (theat) machiniste m

scenic ['sinɪk], ['senɪk] adj pittoresque; spectaculaire; (theat) scénique

sce'nic rail'way s chemin m de fer en miniature des parcs d'attraction

scent [sent] s odeur f; parfum m; (*trail*) piste f ‖ tr parfumer; (*an odor*) renifler; (*game as a dog does; a trap*) flairer

scepter ['septər] s sceptre m

sceptic ['skeptɪk] adj & s sceptique mf

sceptical ['skeptɪkəl] adj sceptique

scepticism ['skeptɪ,sɪzəm] s scepticisme m

schedule ['skedʒʊl] s (*of work*) plan m; (*of things to do*) emploi m du temps; (*of prices*) barème m; (rr) horaire m; on schedule selon l'horaire; selon les prévisions ‖ tr classer; inscrire au programme, à l'horaire, etc.; scheduled to speak prévu comme orateur

scheme [skim] s projet m; machination f, truc m ‖ tr projeter ‖ intr ruser

schemer ['skimər] s faiseur m de projets; intrigant m

schism ['sɪzəm] s schisme m, scission f

scholar ['skɑlər] s (*pupil*) écolier m;

(*learned person*) érudit m, savant m; (*holder of scholarship*) boursier m

scholarly ['skɑlərli] adj érudit, savant ‖ adv savamment

schol'ar•ship' s érudition f; (*award*) bourse f

scholasticism [skə'læstɪ,sɪzəm] s scolastique f

school [skul] adj scolaire; school zone (public sign) ralentir école ‖ s école f; (*of a university*) faculté f; (*of fish*) banc m ‖ tr instruire, discipliner

school' board' s conseil m de l'instruction publique

school'book' s livre m de classe, livre scolaire

school'boy' s écolier m

school'girl' s écolière f

school'house' s maison f d'école

schooling ['skulɪŋ] s instruction f, enseignement m; discipline f; frais mpl de l'éducation

schoolmarm ['skul,mɑrm] s maîtresse f d'école, institutrice f

school'mas'ter s maître m d'école, instituteur m

school'mate' s camarade mf d'école, condisciple m

school'room' s classe f, salle f de classe

school'teach'er s enseignant m, instituteur m

school'yard' s cour f de récréation

school' year' s année f scolaire

schooner ['skunər] s schooner m, goélette f

sciatica [saɪ'ætɪkə] s (pathol) sciatique f

science ['saɪ•əns] s science f

sci'ence fic'tion s science-fiction f

scientific [ˌsaɪ•ən'tɪfɪk] adj scientifique

scientist ['saɪ•əntɪst] s homme m de science, savant m

scimitar ['sɪmɪtər] s cimeterre m

scintillate ['sɪntɪ,let] intr scintiller, étinceler

scion ['saɪ•ən] s héritier m; (hort) scion m

scissors ['sɪzərz] s & spl ciseaux mpl

scis'sors-grind'er s rémouleur m; (orn) engoulevent m

scoff [skɔf], [skɑf] s raillerie f ‖ intr —to scoff at se moquer de

scold [skold] s harpie f ‖ tr & intr gronder

scolding ['skoldɪŋ] s gronderie f

scoop [skup] s pelle f à main; (*for coal*) seau m; (*kitchen utensil*) louche f; (*of dredge*) godet m; (journ) nouvelle f sensationnelle; (naut) écope f ‖ tr creuser; to scoop out excaver à la pelle; (*water*) écoper

scoot [skut] intr (coll) détaler

scooter ['skutər] s trottinette f, patinette f

scope [skop] s (*field*) domaine m, étendue f; (*reach*) portée f, envergure f; to give free scope to donner libre carrière à

scorch [skɔrtʃ] tr roussir; flétrir, dessécher

scorched'-earth' pol'icy s politique f de la terre brûlée

scorching ['skɔrtʃɪŋ] adj brûlant; caustique, mordant

score [skor] s compte m, total m; (twenty) vingtaine f; (notch) entaille f; (on metal) rayure f, éraflure f; (mus) partition f; (sports) score m, marque f; **on that score** à cet égard; **to keep score** compter les points || tr (to notch) entailler; (to criticize) blâmer; (metal) rayer, érafler; (a success) remporter; (e.g., a goal) marquer; (mus) orchestrer

score'board' s tableau m

score'keep'er s marqueur m

scorn [skɔrn] s mépris m, dédain m || tr mépriser, dédaigner || intr—to scorn to dédaigner de

scorpion ['skɔrpɪ·ən] s scorpion m

Scot [skɑt] s Écossais m

Scotch [skɑtʃ] adj écossais; (slang) avare, chiche || s (dialect) écossais m; whisky m écossais; **the Scotch** les Écossais || (l.c.) s (wedge) cale f; (notch) entaille f || tr caler; entailler; (a rumor) étouffer

Scotch'man s (pl -men) Écossais m

Scotch' pine' s pin m sylvestre

Scotch' tape' s (trademark) ruban m cellulosique, adhésif m scotch

Scotland ['skɑtlənd] s Écosse f; l'Écosse

Scottish ['skɑtɪʃ] adj écossais || s (dialect) écossais m; **the Scottish** les Écossais

scoundrel ['skaʊndrəl] s coquin m, fripon m, canaille f

scour [skaʊr] tr récurer; (e.g., the countryside) parcourir

scourge [skʌrdʒ] s nerf m de bœuf, discipline f; (fig) fléau m || tr fouetter, flageller

scout [skaʊt] adj scout || s éclaireur m; (boy scout) scout m, éclaireur; **a good scout** (coll) un brave gars || tr reconnaître; (to scoff at) repousser avec dédain || intr aller en reconnaissance

scouting ['skaʊtɪŋ] s scoutisme m

scout'ing par'ty s (pl -ties) (mil) détachement m de reconnaissance

scout'mas'ter s chef m de troupe

scowl [skaʊl] s renfrognement m || intr se renfrogner

scram [skræm] v (pret & pp scrammed; ger scramming) intr (coll) ficher le camp; **scram!** (coll) fiche-moi le camp!

scramble ['skræmbəl] s bousculade f || tr brouiller || intr se disputer; grimper à quatre pattes

scram'bled eggs' spl œufs mpl brouillés

scrap [skræp] s ferraille f; (little bit) petit morceau m; (fight) (coll) chamaillerie f || v (pret & pp scrapped; ger scrapping) tr mettre au rebut || intr (coll) se chamailler

scrap'book' s album m de découpures

scrape [skrep] s grincement m; (coll) mauvaise affaire f || tr gratter, râcler

scrap' heap' s tas m de rebut

scrap' i'ron s ferraille f

scrap' pa'per s bloc-notes m; (refuse) papier m de rebut

scratch [skrætʃ] s égratignure f; **to start from scratch** partir de rien || tr gratter, égratigner

scratch' pad' s bloc-notes m, brouillon m

scratch' pa'per s bloc-notes m

scrawl [skrɔl] s griffonnage m || tr & intr griffonner

scraw·ny ['skrɔni] adj (comp -nier; super -niest) décharné, mince

scream [skrim] s cri m perçant; (slang) personne f ridicule; (slang) chose f ridicule || tr & intr pousser des cris, crier

screech [skritʃ] s cri m perçant || intr jeter des cris perçants

screech' owl' s chat-huant m; (barn owl) effraie f

screen [skrin] s écran m; grillage m en fil de fer, treillis m métallique; (for sifting) crible m || tr abriter; (candidates) trier; (mov) porter à l'écran

screen' grid' s (electron) grille f blindée

screen'play' s scénario m; drame m filmé

screen' test' s bout m d'essai

screw [skru] s vis f; (naut) hélice f; **to have a screw loose** (coll) être toqué || tr visser; **to screw off** dévisser; **to screw tight** visser à bloc; **to screw up** (one's courage) rassembler || intr se visser

screw'ball' adj & s (slang) extravagant m, loufoque m

screw'driv'er s tournevis m

screw' eye' s vis f à œil

screw' press' s cric m à vis

screw' pro'pel·ler s hélice f

screw·y ['skru·i] adj (comp -ier; super -iest) (slang) loufoque

scrib'al er'ror ['skraɪbəl] s faute f de copiste

scribble ['skrɪbəl] s griffonnage m || tr & intr griffonner

scribe [skraɪb] s scribe m

scrimmage ['skrɪmɪdʒ] s mêlée f

scrimp [skrɪmp] tr lésiner sur || intr lésiner

scrip [skrɪp] s monnaie f scripturale, script m

script [skrɪpt] s manuscrit m, original m; (handwriting) écriture f; (mov) scénario m; (typ) script m

scriptural ['skrɪptʃərəl] adj biblique

scripture ['skrɪptʃər] s citation f tirée de l'Écriture; **Scripture** l'Écriture f; **the Scriptures** les Écritures

script'writ'er s scénariste mf

scrofula ['skrɑfjələ] s scrofule f

scroll [skrol] s rouleau m; (archit) volute f

scroll'work' s ornementation f en volute

scro·tum ['skrotəm] s (pl -ta [tə] or -tums) scrotum m, bourses fpl

scrub [skrʌb] adj rabougri || s arbuste m rabougri; personne f malingre; (sports) joueur m novice || v (pret &

pp scrubbed; *ger* scrubbing) *tr* frotter, nettoyer, récurer

scrub'bing brush' *s* brosse *f* de chiendent

scrub'wom'an *s* (*pl* -wom'en) nettoyeuse *f*

scruff [skrʌf] *s* nuque *f*

scruple ['skrupəl] *s* scrupule *f*

scrupulous ['skrupjələs] *adj* scrupuleux

scrutinize ['skruti͵naɪz] *tr* scruter

scruti-ny ['skrutɪnɪ] *s* (*pl* -nies) examen *m* minutieux

scuff [skʌf] *s* usure *f* || *tr* érafler

scuffle ['skʌfəl] *s* bagarre *f* || *intr* se bagarrer

scull [skʌl] *s* (*stern oar*) godille *f*; aviron *m* de couple || *tr* godiller || *intr* ramer en couple

sculler-y ['skʌləri] *s* (*pl* -ies) arrière-cuisine *f*

scul'lery maid' *s* laveuse *f* de vaisselle

scullion ['skʌljən] *s* marmiton *m*

sculptor ['skʌlptər] *s* sculpteur *m*

sculptress ['skʌlptrɪs] *s* femme *f* sculpteur

sculpture ['skʌlptʃər] *s* sculpture *f* || *tr & intr* sculpter

scum [skʌm] *s* écume *f*; (*of society*) canaille *f* || *v* (*pret & pp* scummed; *ger* scumming) *tr & intr* écumer

scum-my ['skʌmi] *adj* (*comp* -mier; *super* -miest) écumeux; (fig) vil

scurrilous ['skʌrɪləs] *adj* injurieux, grossier, outrageant

scur-ry ['skʌri] *v* (*pret & pp* -ried) *intr* —to scurry around galoper; to scurry away or off déguerpir

scur-vy ['skʌrvi] *adj* (*comp* -vier; *super* -viest) méprisable, vil || *s* scorbut *m*

scuttle ['skʌtəl] *s* (*bucket for coal*) seau *m* à charbon; (*trap door*) trappe *f*; (*run*) course *f* précipitée; (naut) écoutillon *m* || *tr* saborder || *intr* filer, déguerpir

scut'tle-butt' *s* (coll) on-dit *m*

scythe [saɪð] *s* faux *f*

sea [si] *s* mer *f*; at sea en mer; (fig) désorienté; by sea au bord de la mer; to put to sea prendre le large

sea'board' *s* littoral *m*

sea' breeze' *s* brise *f* de mer

sea'coast' *s* côte *f*, littoral *m*

seafarer ['si͵ferər] *s* marin *m*; voyageur *m* par mer

sea'food' *s* fruits *mpl* de mer, marée *f*

seagoing ['si͵go·ɪŋ] *adj* de haute mer, au long cours

sea' gull' *s* mouette *f*, goéland *m*

seal [sil] *s* sceau *m*; (zool) phoque *m* || *tr* sceller

sea' legs' *spl* pied *m* marin

sea' lev'el *s* niveau *m* de la mer

seal'ing wax' *s* cire *f* à cacheter

seal'skin' *s* peau *f* de phoque

seam [sim] *s* couture *f*; (*of metal*) joint *m*; (geol) fissure *f*; (min) couche *f*

sea'man *s* (*pl* -men) marin *m*

sea' mile' *s* mille *m* marin

seamless ['simlɪs] *adj* sans couture; (mach) sans soudure

seamstress ['simstrɪs] *s* couturière *f*

seam-y ['simi] *adj* (*comp* -ier; *super* -iest) plein de coutures; vil, vilain

séance ['se·ɑns] *s* séance *f* de spiritisme

sea'plane' *s* hydravion *m*

sea'port' *s* port *m* de mer

sea' pow'er *s* puissance *f* maritime

sear [sɪr] *adj* desséché || *s* cicatrice *f* de brûlure || *tr* dessécher; marquer au fer rouge

search [sʌrtʃ] *s* recherche *f*; in search of à la recherche de || *tr & intr* fouiller; to search for chercher

searching ['sʌrtʃɪŋ] *adj* pénétrant, scrutateur

search'light' *s* projecteur *m*

search' war'rant *s* mandat *m* de perquisition

seascape ['si͵skep] *s* panorama *m* marin; (*painting*) marine *f*

sea' shell' *s* coquille *f* de mer

sea'shore' *s* bord *m* de la mer

sea'sick'—to be seasick avoir le mal de mer

sea'sick'ness *s* mal *m* de mer

season ['sizən] *s* saison *f* || *tr* assaisonner; (*troops*) aguerrir; (*wood*) sécher

seasonal ['sizənəl] *adj* saisonnier

seasoning ['sizənɪŋ] *s* assaisonnement *m*

sea'son's greet'ings *spl* meilleurs souhaits *mpl*, tous mes vœux *mpl*

sea'son tick'et *s* carte *f* d'abonnement

seat [sit] *s* place *f*, siège *m*; (*of trousers*) fond *m*; have a seat asseyez-vous donc; keep your seat restez assis || *tr* asseoir; (*a number of persons*) contenir; to be seated (*to sit down*) s'asseoir; (*to be in sitting posture*) être assis

seat' belt' *s* ceinture *f* de sécurité

seat' cov'er *s* (aut) housse *f*

SEATO ['sito] *s* (acronym) (Southeast Asia Treaty Organization) OTASE *f*

sea' wall' *s* digue *f*

sea'way' *s* voie *f* maritime; (*of ship*) sillage *m*; (*rough sea*) mer *f* dure

sea'weed' *s* algue *f* marine; plante *f* marine

sea'wor'thy *adj* en état de naviguer

secede [sɪ'sid] *intr* se séparer, faire sécession

secession [sɪ'sɛʃən] *s* sécession *f*

seclude [sɪ'klud] *tr* tenir éloigné; (*to shut up*) enfermer

secluded *adj* retiré, écarté

seclusion [sɪ'kluʒən] *s* retraite *f*

second ['sɛkənd] *adj & pron* deuxième (*masc, fem*), second; the Second deux, e.g., **John the Second** Jean deux; to be second in command commander en second; to be second to none ne le céder à personne || *s* deuxième *m*, second *m*; (*in time; musical interval; of angle*) seconde *f*; (*in a duel*) témoin *m*, second *m*; (com) article *m* de deuxième qualité; the second (*in dates*) le deux || *adv* en second lieu || *tr* affirmer; (*to back up*) seconder

secondar-y ['sɛkən͵dɛri] *adj* secondaire || *s* (*pl* -ies) (elec) secondaire *m*

sec'ond best' s pis-aller m
sec'ond-best' adj (everyday) de tous les jours; **to come off second-best** être battu
sec'ond-class' adj de second ordre; (rr) de seconde classe
sec'ond hand' s trotteuse f
sec'ond-hand' adj d'occasion, de seconde main
sec'ond-hand book' dealer s bouquiniste mf
sec'ond lieuten'ant s sous-lieutenant m
sec'ond mate' s (naut) second maître m
sec'ond-rate' adj de second ordre
sec'ond sight' s seconde vue f
sec'ond wind' s—**to get one's second wind** reprendre haleine
secre•cy ['sikrəsi] s (pl -cies) secret m; **in secrecy** en secret
secret ['sikrɪt] adj & s secret m; **in secret** en secret
secretar•y ['sεkrɪ‚teri] s (pl -ies) secrétaire mf; (desk) secrétaire m
se'cret bal'lot s scrutin m secret
secrete [sɪ'krit] tr cacher; (physiol) sécréter
secretive [sɪ'kritɪv] adj cachottier
se'cret serv'ice s deuxième bureau m
sect [sεkt] s secte f
sectarian [sεk'tεri‚ən] adj sectaire; (school) confessionnel || sectaire mf
section ['sεk/ən] s section f
sectionalism ['sεk/ənə‚lɪzəm] s régionalisme m
sec'tion hand' s cantonnier m
sector ['sεktər] s secteur m; (instrument) compas m de proportion
secular ['sεkjələr] adj (worldly, of this world) séculier; (century-old) séculaire || s séculier m
secularism ['sεkjələ‚rɪzəm] s laïcisme m, mondanité f
secure [sɪ'kjur] adj sûr || tr obtenir; (to make fast) fixer
securi•ty [sɪ'kjuriti] s (pl -ties) sécurité f; (pledge) garantie f; (person) garant m; **securities** valeurs fpl
sedan [sɪ'dæn] s (aut) conduite f intérieure
sedan' chair' s chaise f à porteurs
sedate [sɪ'det] adj calme, discret
sedation [sɪ'de/ən] s sédation f
sedative ['sεdətɪv] adj & s sédatif m
sedentary ['sεdən‚teri] adj sédentaire
sedge [sεdʒ] s (Carex) laîche f
sediment ['sεdɪmənt] s sédiment m
sedition [sɪ'dɪ/ən] s sédition f
seditious [sɪ'dɪ/əs] adj séditieux
seduce [sɪ'd(j)us] tr séduire
seducer [sɪ'd(j)usər] s séducteur m
seduction [sɪ'dʌk/ən] s séduction f
seductive [sɪ'dʌktɪv] adj séduisant
sedulous ['sεdʒələs] adj assidu
see [si] s (eccl) siège m || v (pret saw [sɔ]; pp seen [sin]) tr voir; **see other side** (turn the page) voir au dos; **to see s.o. play, to see s.o. playing** voir jouer qn, voir qn qui joue; **to see s.th. played** voir jouer q.ch. || intr voir; **to see through s.o.** (fig) voir venir qn
seed [sid] s graine f, semence f; sperme m; (in fruit) pépin m; (fig) germe m; **to go to seed** monter en graine || tr semer, ensemencer
seed'bed' s semis m
seeder ['sidər] s (mach) semeuse f
seedling ['sidlɪŋ] s semis m
seed•y ['sidi] adj (comp -ier; super -iest) (coll) râpé, miteux
seeing ['si‚ɪŋ] adj voyant || s vue f || conj vu que
See'ing Eye' dog' s chien m d'aveugle
seek [sik] v (pret & pp sought [sɔt]) tr chercher || intr chercher; **to seek after** rechercher; **to seek to** chercher à
seem [sim] intr sembler
seemingly ['simɪŋli] adv en apparence
seem•ly ['simli] adj (comp -lier; super -liest) gracieux; (correct) bienséant
seep [sip] intr suinter
seer [sɪr] s prophète m, voyant m
see'saw' s balançoire f, bascule f; (motion) va-et-vient m || intr basculer, balancer
seethe [sið] intr bouillonner
segment ['sεgmənt] s segment m
segregate ['sεgrɪ‚get] tr mettre à part, isoler
segregation [‚sεgrɪ'ge/ən] s ségrégation f
segregationist [‚sεgrɪ'ge/ənɪst] s ségrégationniste mf
seismograph ['saɪzmə‚græf], ['saɪzmə‚grɑf] s sismographe m
seismology [saɪz'mɑlədʒi] s sismologie f
seize [siz] tr saisir
seizure ['siʒər] s prise f; (law) saisie f; (pathol) attaque f
seldom ['sεldəm] adv rarement
select [sɪ'lεkt] adj choisi || tr choisir, sélectionner
selection [sɪ'lεk/ən] s sélection f
selective [sɪ'lεktɪv] adj sélectif
self [sεlf] adj de même || s (pl selves [sεlvz]) moi m, être m; **all by one's self** tout seul; **one's better self** notre meilleur côté || pron—**payable to self** payable à moi-même
self'-addressed en'velope s enveloppe f adressée à l'envoyeur
self'-cen'tered adj égocentrique
self'-con'fidence s confiance f en soi
self'-con'fident adj sûr de soi
self'-con'scious adj gêné, embarrassé
self'-control' s sang-froid m, maîtrise f de soi
self'-defense' s autodéfense f; **in self-defense** en légitime défense
self'-deni'al s abnégation f
self'-deter'mina'tion s autodétermination f
self'-dis'cipline s discipline f personnelle
self'-ed'ucated adj autodidacte
self'-employed' adj indépendant
self'-esteem' s amour-propre m
self'-ev'ident adj évident aux yeux de tout le monde
self'-explan'ator'y adj qui s'explique de soi-même
self'-gov'ernment s autonomie f; maîtrise f de soi

self'-impor'tant adj suffisant, présomptueux

self'-indul'gence s faiblesse f envers soi-même, intempérance f

self'-in'terest s intérêt m personnel

selfish ['selfɪʃ] adj égoïste

selfishness ['selfɪʃnɪs] s égoïsme m

selfless ['selflɪs] adj désintéressé

self'-love' s égoïsme m

self'-made man' s (pl men') fils m de ses œuvres

self'-por'trait s autoportrait m

self'-possessed' adj maître de soi

self'-preser'va'tion s conservation f de soi-même

self'-reli'ant adj sûr de soi, assuré

self'-respect'ing adj correct, honorable

self'-right'eous adj pharisaïque

self'-sac'rifice' s abnégation f

self'same' adj identique

self'-sat'isfied' adj content de soi

self'-seek'ing adj égoïste, intéressé

self'-serv'ice s libre-service m

self'-serv'ice laun'dry s (pl -dries) laverie f libre-service, laverie automatique

self'-start'er s démarreur m automatique

self'-styled' adj soi-disant

self'-taught' adj autodidacte

self'-tim'er s (phot) retardateur m

self'-willed' adj obstiné, entêté

self'-wind'ing adj à remontage automatique

sell [sɛl] v (pret & pp sold [sold]) tr vendre; **to sell out** solder; (to betray) vendre ∥ intr vendre; **to sell for** (e.g., ten dollars) se vendre à

seller ['selər] s vendeur m

Selt'zer wa'ter ['seltsər] s eau f de Seltz

selvage ['selvɪdʒ] s (of fabric) lisière f; (of lock) gâche f

semantic [sɪ'mæntɪk] adj sémantique ∥ **semantics** s sémantique f

semaphore ['semə,for] s sémaphore m

semblance ['sembləns] s semblant m

semen ['simen] s sperme m, semence f

semester [sɪ'mestər] adj semestriel ∥ s semestre m

semicircle ['semɪ,sʌrkəl] s demi-cercle m

semicolon ['semɪ,kolən] s point-virgule m

semiconductor [,semɪkən'dʌktər] s semi-conducteur m

semiconscious [,semɪ'kɑnʃəs] adj à demi conscient

semifinal [,semɪ'faɪnəl] adj avant-dernière ∥ s demi-finale f

semilearned [,semɪ'lʌrnɪd] adj à moitié savant

seminar ['semɪ,nɑr] s séminaire m

seminar·y ['semɪ,neri] s (pl -ies) séminaire m

semiprecious [,semɪ'preʃəs] adj fin, semi-précieux

Semite ['semaɪt], ['simaɪt] s Sémite m f

Semitic [sɪ'mɪtɪk] adj (e.g., language) sémitique; (person) sémite

semitrailer ['semɪ,trelər] s semi-remorque f

senate ['senɪt] s sénat m

senator ['senətər] s sénateur m

send [send] v (pret & pp sent [sent]) tr envoyer; (rad, telv) émettre; **to send back** renvoyer; **to send out** envoyer; **to send s.o. for s.th.** or **s.o.** envoyer qn chercher q.ch. or qn; **to send s.o. to** + inf envoyer qn + inf ∥ intr (rad, telv) émettre; **to send for** envoyer chercher

sender ['sendər] s expéditeur m; (telg) transmetteur m

send'-off' s manifestation f d'adieu

senile ['sinaɪl], ['sinɪl] adj sénile

senility [sɪ'nɪlɪti] s sénilité f

senior ['sinjər] adj aîné; (clerk, partner, etc.) principal; (rank) supérieur; père, e.g., **Maurice Laporte, Senior** Maurice Laporte père ∥ s aîné m, doyen m; (U.S. upperclassman) étudiant m de dernière année

sen'ior cit'izens spl les vieilles gens fpl

seniority [sin'jɑrɪti], [sin'jɔrɪti] s ancienneté f, doyenneté f

sen'ior staff' s personnel m hors classe

sensation [sen'seʃən] s sensation f

sensational [sen'seʃənəl] adj sensationnel

sense [sens] s sens m; (wisdom) bon sens; (e.g., of pain) sensation f; **to make sense out of** arriver à comprendre ∥ tr percevoir, sentir

senseless ['senslɪs] adj (lacking perception) insensible; (unconscious) sans connaissance; (unreasonable) insensé

sense' of guilt' s remords m

sense' or'gans spl organes mpl des sens

sensibili·ty [,sensɪ'bɪlɪti] s (pl -ties) sensibilité f; susceptibilité f

sensible ['sensɪbəl] adj sensible; (endowed with good sense) sensé, raisonnable

sensitive ['sensɪtɪv] adj sensible; (touchy) susceptible, sensitif

sensitize ['sensɪ,taɪz] tr sensibiliser

sensory ['sensəri] adj sensoriel

sensual ['senʃu·əl] adj sensuel

sensuous ['senʃu·əs] adj sensuel

sentence ['sentəns] s (gram) phrase f; (law) sentence f ∥ tr condamner

sentiment ['sentɪmənt] s sentiment m

sentimental [,sentɪ'mentəl] adj sentimental

sentinel ['sentɪnəl] s sentinelle f; **to stand sentinel** être en sentinelle

sen·try ['sentri] s (pl -tries) sentinelle f

sen'try box' s guérite f

separate ['sepərɪt] adj séparé ∥ ['sepə,ret] tr séparer ∥ intr se séparer

separation [,sepə'reʃən] s séparation f

September [sep'tembər] s septembre m

septic ['septɪk] adj septique

sepulcher ['sepəlkər] s sépulcre m

sequel ['sikwəl] s conséquence f; (something following) suite f

sequence ['sikwəns] s succession f, ordre m; (cards, mov) séquence f; (of tenses) (gram) concordance f

sequester [sɪ'kwestər] tr séquestrer

sequin ['sikwın] s paillette f

ser-aph ['seræf] s (pl -aphs or -aphim [əf ɪm]) séraphin m

Serb [sʌrb] adj serbe || s Serbe mf

sere [sɪr] adj sec, desséché

serenade [,serə'ned] s sérénade f || tr donner une sérénade à || intr donner des sérénades

serene [sɪ'rin] adj serein

serenity [sɪ'renɪti] s sérénité f

serf [sʌrf] s serf m

serfdom ['sʌrfdəm] s servage m

serge [sʌrdʒ] s serge f

sergeant ['sʌrdʒənt] s sergent m

ser'geant-at-arms' s (pl sergeants-at-arms) huissier m, sergent m d'armes

ser'geant ma'jor s (pl sergeant majors) sergent-major m

serial ['sɪrɪ-əl] adj de série || s roman-feuilleton m

serially ['sɪrɪ-əli] adv en série; (in installments) en feuilleton

se'rial num'ber s numéro m d'ordre; (mil) numéro m matricule

se-ries ['sɪriz] s (pl -ries) série f; in series en série

serious ['sɪrɪ-əs] adj sérieux

seriousness ['sɪrɪ-əsnɪs] s sérieux m, gravité f

sermon ['sʌrmən] s sermon m

sermonize ['sʌrmə,naız] tr & intr sermonner

serpent ['sʌrpənt] s serpent m

se-rum ['sɪrəm] s (pl -rums or -ra [rə]) sérum m

servant ['sʌrvənt] s domestique mf; (civil servant) fonctionnaire m; (housemaid) bonne f; (humble servant) (fig) serviteur m

serv'ant girl' s servante f

serv'ant prob'lem s crise f domestique

serve [sʌrv] tr servir; to serve s.o. as servir à qn de; to serve time purger une peine || intr servir; to serve as (to function as) servir de; (to be useful for) servir à

service ['sʌrvɪs] s service m; (eccl) office m; the services (mil) les forces fpl armées || tr entretenir, réparer

serviceable ['sʌrvɪsəbəl] adj utile, pratique; résistant

serv'ice club' s foyer m du soldat

serv'ice·man' s (pl -men') réparateur m; (mil) militaire m

serv'ice rec'ord s état m de service

serv'ice sta'tion s station-service f

serv'ice stripe' s chevron m, galon m

servile ['sʌrvɪl] adj servile

servitude ['sʌrvɪ,t(j)ud] s servitude f

sesame ['sesəmi] s sésame m; open sesame! sésame, ouvre-toi!

session ['se/ən] s session f; to be in session siéger

set [set] adj (rule) établi; (price) fixe; (time) fixé; (smile; locution) figé || s ensemble f m; (of dishes, linen, etc.) assortiment m; (of dishes) service m; (of kitchen utensils) batterie f; (of pans; of weights; of tickets) série f; (of tools, chessmen, oars, etc.) jeu m; (of books) collection f; (of diamonds) parure f; (of tennis)

set m; (of cement) prise f; (of a garment) tournure f; (group of persons) coterie f; (mov) plateau m; (rad) poste m; (theat) mise f en scène; set of false teeth dentier m; set of teeth denture f || v (pret & pp set; ger setting) tr mettre, placer, poser; (a date, price, etc.) fixer; (a gem) monter; (a trap) tendre; (a timepiece) mettre à l'heure, régler; (the hair) mettre en plis; (a bone) remettre; to set aside mettre de côté; annuler; to set going mettre en marche; to set off mettre en valeur; (e.g., a rocket) lancer, tirer || intr se figer; (said of sun, moon, etc.) se coucher; (said of hen) couver; (said of garment) tomber; to set about, to set out to se mettre à; to set upon attaquer

set'back' s revers m, échec m

set'screw' s vis f de pression

settee [se'ti] s canapé m; (for two) canapé à deux places, causeuse f

setting ['setɪŋ] s cadre m; (of a gem) monture f; (of cement) prise f; (of sun) coucher m; (of a bone) recollement m; (of a watch) réglage m; (adjustment) ajustage m; (theat) mise f en scène

set'ting-up' ex'ercises spl gymnastique f rythmique, gymnastique suédoise

settle ['setəl] tr établir; (a region) coloniser; (a dispute, account, debt, etc.) régler; (a problem) résoudre; (doubts, fears, etc.) calmer || intr se coloniser; se calmer; (said of weather) se mettre au beau; (said of building) se tasser; (said of sediment, dust, etc.) se déposer; (said of liquid) se clarifier; to settle down s'établir; (to be less wild) se ranger; to settle down to (a task) s'appliquer à; to settle on se décider pour

settlement ['setəlmənt] s établissement m, colonie f; (of an account, dispute, etc.) règlement m; (of a debt) liquidation f; (settlement house) œuvre f sociale

settler ['setlər] s colon m

set'up' s port m, maintien m; (of the parts of a machine) installation f; (coll) organisation f

seven ['sevən] adj & pron sept || s sept m; seven o'clock sept heures

seventeen ['sevən'tin] adj, pron, & s dix-sept

seventeenth ['sevən'tinθ] adj & pron dix-septième (masc, fem); the Seventeenth dix-sept, e.g., John the Seventeenth Jean dix-sept || s dix-septième m; the seventeenth (in dates) le dix-sept

seventh ['sevənθ] adj & pron septième (masc, fem); the Seventh sept, e.g., John the Seventh Jean sept || s septième m; the seventh (in dates) le sept

seventieth ['sevəntɪ·ɪθ] adj & pron soixante-dixième (masc, fem) || s soixante-dixième m

seven-ty ['sevənti] adj & pron soixante-dix || s (pl -ties) soixante-dix m

sev′enty-first′ *adj & pron* soixante et onzième (*masc, fem*) ‖ *s* soixante et onzième *m*

sev′enty-one′ *adj, pron, & s* soixante et onze *m*

sever [′sɛvər] *tr* séparer; (*relations*) rompre ‖ *intr* se séparer

several [′sɛvərəl] *adj & pron indef* plusieurs

severance [′sɛvərəns] *s* séparation *f*; (*of relations*) rupture *f*; (*of communications*) interruption *f*

sev′erance pay′ *s* indemnité *f* pour cause de renvoi

severe [sɪ′vɪr] *adj* sévère; (*weather*) rigoureux; (*pain*) aigu; (*illness*) grave

sew [so] *v* (*pret sewed*; *pp sewed or sewn*) *tr & intr* coudre

sewage [′s(j)u·ɪdʒ] *s* eaux *fpl* d'égouts

sewer [′s(j)u·ər] *s* égout *m* ‖ [′so·ər] *s* (*one who sews*) couseur *m*

sewerage [′s(j)u·ərɪdʒ] *s* (*removal*) vidange *f*; (*system*) système *m* d'égouts; (*sewage*) eaux *fpl* d'égouts

sew′ing bas′ket *s* nécessaire *m* de couture

sew′ing machine′ *s* machine *f* à coudre

sex [sɛks] *s* sexe *m*; **the fair sex** le beau sexe; **the sterner sex** le sexe fort; **to have sex with** (coll) avoir des rapports avec

sex′ appeal′ *s* sex-appeal *m*

sextant [′sɛkstənt] *s* sextant *m*

sextet [sɛks′tɛt] *s* sextuor *m*

sexton [′sɛkstən] *s* sacristain *m*

sexual [′sɛkʃu·əl] *adj* sexuel

sex·y [′sɛksi] *adj* (*comp* -ier; *super* -iest) (slang) aguichant, grivois; (*story*) érotique

sh [ʃ] *interj* chut!

shab·by [′ʃæbi] *adj* (*comp* -bier; *super* -biest) râpé, usé; (*mean*) mesquin; (*house*) délabré

shack [ʃæk] *s* cabane *f*, case *f*

shackle [′ʃækəl] *s* boucle *f*; **shackles** entraves *fpl* ‖ *tr* entraver

shad [ʃæd] *s* alose *f*

shade [ʃed] *s* ombre *f*; (*of lamp*) abat-jour *m*; (*of window*) store *m*; (*slight difference*) nuance *f*; (*little bit*) soupçon *m* ‖ *tr* ombrager; (*to make gradual changes in*) nuancer

shadow [′ʃædo] *s* ombre *f* ‖ *tr* ombrager; (*to spy on*) filer, pister

shad′ow gov′ernment *s* gouvernement *m* fantôme

shadowy [′ʃædo·i] *adj* ombreux, sombre; (fig) vague, obscur

shad·y [′ʃedi] *adj* (*comp* -ier; *super* -iest) ombreux, ombragé; (coll) louche

shaft [ʃæft], [ʃɑft] *s* (*of mine; of elevator*) puits *m*; (*of feather*) tige *f*; (*of arrow*) bois *m*; (*of column*) fût *m*, tige *f*; (*of flag*) mât *m*; (*of wagon*) brancard *m*, limon *m*; (*of motor*) arbre *m*; (*of light*) rayon *m*; (*to make fun of s.o.*) trait *m*

shag·gy [′ʃægi] *adj* (*comp* -gier; *super* -giest) poilu, à longs poils

shag′gy dog′ sto′ry *s* (*pl* -ries) histoire *f* sans queue ni tête

shake [ʃek] *s* secousse *f* ‖ *v* (*pret shook* [ʃuk]; *pp shaken*) *tr* secouer; (*the head*) hocher, secouer; (*one's hand*) serrer; **to shake down** faire tomber; (*a thermometer*) secouer; (slang) escroquer; **to shake off** secouer; (*to get rid of*) se débarrasser de; **to shake up** (*a liquid*) agiter, (fig) ébranler ‖ *intr* trembler

shake′down′ *s* (slang) exaction *f*, concussion *f*

shaker [′ʃekər] *s* (*for salt*) salière *f*; (*for cocktails*) shaker *m*

shake′up′ *s* bouleversement *m*; (*reorganization*) remaniement *m*

shak·y [′ʃeki] *adj* (*comp* -ier; *super* -iest) tremblant, chancelant; (*hand; writing*) tremblé; (voice) tremblotant

shall [ʃæl] *v* (*cond should* [ʃud]) *aux* used to express 1) the future indicative, e.g., **I shall arrive** j'arriverai; 2) the future perfect indicative, e.g., **I shall have arrived** je serai arrivé; 3) the potential mood, e.g., **what shall he do?** que doit-il faire?

shallow [′ʃælo] *adj* peu profond; (*dish*) plat; (fig) creux, superficiel ‖ **shallows** *spl* haut-fond *m*

sham [ʃæm] *adj* feint, simulé ‖ *s* feinte *f*, simulacre *m*; (*person*) imposteur *m* ‖ *v* (*pret & pp shammed*) *ger shamming*) *tr & intr* feindre, simuler

sham′ bat′tle *s* combat *m* simulé

shambles [′ʃæmbəlz] *spl* boucherie *f*; ravage *m*, ruine *f*; (*disorder*) pagaille *f*

shame [ʃem] *s* honte *f*; **shame on you! for shame!** quelle honte!; **what a shame!** quel dommage! ‖ *tr* faire honte à

shame′faced′ *adj* penaud

shameful [′ʃemfəl] *adj* honteux

shameless [′ʃemlɪs] *adj* éhonté

shampoo [ʃæm′pu] *s* shampooing *m* ‖ *tr* (*the hair*) laver; (*a person*) faire un shampooing à

shamrock [′ʃæmrɑk] *s* trèfle *m* d'Irlande

Shanghai [′ʃæɲhaɪ], [ʃæɲ′haɪ] *s* Changhaï *f* (*l.c.*) *tr* (coll) racoler

Shangri-la [ˌʃæɲgrɪ′lɑ] *s* le pays de Cocagne

shank [ʃæɲk] *s* jambe *f*, tibia *m*; (*of horse*) canon *m*; (*of anchor*) verge *f*; (culin) manche *m*; (*of a column*) fût *m*

shan·ty [′ʃænti] *s* (*pl* -ties) masure *f*, bicoque *f*

shan′ty-town′ *s* bidonville *m*

shape [ʃep] *s* forme *f*; **in bad shape** (coll) mal en point; **out of shape** déformé ‖ *tr* former ‖ *intr* se former; **to shape up** prendre forme; avancer

shapeless [′ʃeplɪs] *adj* informe

shape·ly [′ʃepli] *adj* (*comp* -lier; *super* -liest) bien proportionné, bien fait, svelte

share [ʃer] *s* part *f*; (*of stock in a company*) action *f* ‖ *tr* partager ‖ *intr*— **to share in** prendre part à, participer à

sharecropper [′ʃɛrˌkrɑpər] *s* métayer *m*

share′hold′er *s* actionnaire *mf*

shark [ʃɑrk] *s* requin *m*; (*swindler*) escroc *m*; (slang) as *m*, expert *m*

sharp [ʃɑrp] *adj* aigu; (*wind, cold, pain, fight, criticism, edge, trot, mind*) vif; (*knife*) tranchant; (*point; tongue*) acéré; (*slope*) raide; (*curve*) prononcé; (*turn*) brusque; (*photograph*) net; (*hearing*) fin; (*step, gait*) rapide; (*taste*) piquant; (*reprimand*) vert; (*keen*) éveillé; (*cunning*) rusé, fin; (mus) dièse; (*stylish*) (coll) chic; **sharp features** traits *mpl* accentués || *adv* vivement; brusquement; précis, sonnant, tapant, e.g., **at four o'clock sharp** à quatre heures précises, sonnantes, or tapantes; **to stop short** s'arrêter net or pile || *s* (mus) dièse *m* || *tr* (mus) diéser

sharpen [ʃɑrpən] *tr* aiguiser; (*a pencil*) tailler || *intr* s'aiguiser

sharpener [ʃɑrpənər] *s* aiguisoir *m*

sharper [ʃɑrpər] *s* filou *m*, tricheur *m*

sharp'shoot'er *s* tireur *m* d'élite

shatter [ʃætər] *tr* fracasser, briser || *intr* se fracasser, se briser

shat'ter-proof' *adj* de sécurité

shave [ʃev] *s*—**to get a shave** se faire raser, se faire faire la barbe; **to have a close shave** (coll) l'échapper belle || *tr* (*hair, beard, etc.*) raser; (*a person*) faire la barbe à, raser; (*e.g., wood*) doler; (*e.g., expenses*) rogner || *intr* se raser, se faire la barbe

shaving [ʃevɪŋ] *s* rasage *m*; **shavings** rognures *fpl*, copeaux *mpl*

shav'ing brush' *s* blaireau *m*

shav'ing soap' *s* savon *m* à barbe

shawl [ʃɔl] *s* châle *m*, fichu *m*

she [ʃi] *s* femelle *f* || *pron pers* elle §85, §87; ce §82B; **she who** celle qui §83

sheaf [ʃif] *s* (*pl* **sheaves** [ʃivz]) gerbe *f*; (*of papers*) liasse *f*

shear [ʃɪr] *s* lame *f* de ciseau; **shears** ciseaux *mpl*; (*to cut metal*) cisaille *f* || *v* (*pret* **sheared**; *pp* **sheared** or **shorn** [ʃɔrn]) *tr* (*sheep*) tondre; (*velvet*) ciseler; (*metal*) cisailler; **to shear off** couper

sheath [ʃiθ] *s* (*pl* **sheaths** [ʃiðz]) gaine *f*, fourreau *m*

sheathe [ʃið] *tr* envelopper; (*a sword*) rengainer

shed [ʃɛd] *s* hangar *m*; (*for, e.g., tools*) remise *f*; (*line from which water flows in two directions*) ligne *f* de faîte || *v* (*pret* & *pp* **shed**; *ger* **shedding**) *tr* répandre, verser; (*e.g., leaves*) perdre; (*e.g., light; skin*) jeter

sheen [ʃin] *s* lustre *m*, brillant *m*

sheep [ʃip] *s* (*pl* **sheep**) mouton *m*; (*ewe*) brebis *f*

sheep'dog' *s* chien *m* de berger

sheep'fold' *s* bergerie *f*

sheepish [ʃipɪʃ] *adj* penaud; timide

sheep'skin' *s* (*undressed*) peau *f* de mouton; (*dressed*) basane *f*; (*diploma*) (coll) peau d'âne

sheep'skin jack'et *s* canadienne *f*

sheer [ʃɪr] *adj* transparent; léger; (*stocking*) extra-fin; (*steep*) à pic; (fig) pur; (fig) vif, e.g., **by sheer force** de vive force || *intr* faire une embardée

sheet [ʃit] *s* (*e.g., for the bed*) drap *m*; (*of paper*) feuille *f*; (*of metal*) tôle *f*, lame *f*; (*of water*) nappe *f*; (*of ice*) couche *f*; (naut) écoute *f*; **white as a sheet** blanc comme un linge

sheet' light'ning *s* fulguration *f*, éclairs *mpl* en nappe

sheet' met'al *s* tôle *f*

sheet' mu'sic *s* morceaux *mpl* de musique

sheik [ʃik] *s* cheik *m*; (coll) tombeur *m* de femmes

shelf [ʃelf] *s* (*pl* **shelves** [ʃelvz]) tablette *f*, planche *f*; (*of cupboard; of library*) rayon *m*; (geog) plateau *m*; **on the shelf** au rancart, laissé à l'écart

shell [ʃel] *s* coque *f*, coquille *f*; (*of nut*) écale *f*, coque; (*of pea*) cosse *f*; (*of oyster, clam, etc.*) écaille *f*; (*of building, ship, etc.*) carcasse *f*; (*cartridge*) cartouche *f*; (*projectile*) obus *m*; (*long, narrow racing boat*) yole *f* || *tr* écaler, écosser; (mil) bombarder, pilonner; **to shell out** (coll) débourser || *intr*—**to shell out** (coll) casquer

shel·lac [ʃəˈlæk] *s* laque *f*, gomme *f* laque *f* || *v* (*pret* & *pp* **-lacked**; *ger* **-lacking**) *tr* laquer; (slang) tabasser

shell'fish' *s* fruits *mpl* de mer, coquillages *mpl*

shell' hole' *s* entonnoir *m*, trou *m* d'obus

shell' shock' *s* commotion *f* cérébrale

shelter [ʃeltər] *s* abri *m* || *tr* abriter

shelve [ʃelv] *tr* (*a book*) ranger; (*merchandise*) entreposer; (*a project, a question, etc., by putting it aside*) enterrer, classer; (*to provide with shelves*) garnir de tablettes, rayons, or planches

shepherd [ʃepərd] *s* berger *m*; (fig) pasteur *m* || *tr* veiller sur, guider

shep'herd dog' *s* berger *m*, chien *m* de berger

shepherdess [ʃepərdɪs] *s* bergère *f*

sherbet [ʃɑrbət] *s* sorbet *m*

sheriff [ʃerɪf] *s* shérif *m*

sher·ry [ʃeri] *s* (*pl* **-ries**) xérès *m*

shield [ʃild] *s* bouclier *m*; (elec) blindage *m*; (heral, hist) écu *m*, écusson *m* || *tr* protéger; (elec) blinder

shift [ʃift] *s* changement *m*; (*in wind, temperature, etc.*) saute *f*; (*group of workmen*) équipe *f* de relais; (fig) expédient *m* || *tr* changer; (*the blame, the guilt, etc.*) rejeter; **to shift gears** changer de vitesse || *intr* changer; changer de place; changer de direction; **to shift for oneself** se débrouiller tout seul

shift' key' *s* touche *f* majuscules

shiftless [ʃɪftlɪs] *adj* mollasse, peu débrouillard

shift·y [ʃɪfti] *adj* (*comp* **-ier**; *super* **-iest**) roublard; (*look*) chafouin; (*eye*) fuyant

shimmer [ʃɪmər] *s* chatoiement *m*, miroitement *m* || *intr* chatoyer, miroiter shin [ʃɪn] s tibia m; (culin) jarret m ‖ v (pret & pp shinned; ger shinning) intr—to shin up grimper

shin'bone' s tibia m

shine [ʃaɪn] s brillant m; (of cloth, clothing, etc.) luisant m; (on shoes) coup m de cirage; to take a shine to (slang) s'enticher de ‖ v (pret & pp shined) tr faire briller, faire reluire; (shoes) cirer ‖ v (pret & pp shone [ʃon]) intr briller, reluire

shiner ['ʃaɪnər] s (slang) œil m poché

shingle ['ʃɪŋɡəl] s bardeau m; (of doctor, lawyer, etc.) (coll) enseigne f; shingles (pathol) zona m

shining ['ʃaɪnɪŋ] adj brillant, luisant

shin·y ['ʃaɪni] adj (comp -ier; super -iest) brillant, reluisant; (from much wear) lustré

ship [ʃɪp] s navire m; (steamer, liner) paquebot m; (aer) appareil m; (nav) bâtiment m ‖ v (pret & pp shipped; ger shipping) tr expédier; (a cargo; water) embarquer; (oars) armer, rentrer ‖ intr s'embarquer

ship'board' s bord m; on shipboard à bord

ship'build'er s constructeur m de navires

ship'build'ing s construction f navale

ship'mate' s compagnon m de bord

shipment ['ʃɪpmənt] s expédition f; (goods shipped) chargement m

ship'own'er s armateur m

shipper ['ʃɪpər] s expéditeur m

shipping ['ʃɪpɪŋ] s embarquement m, expédition f; (naut) transport m maritime

ship'ping clerk' s expéditionnaire mf

ship'ping mem'o s connaissement m

ship'ping room' s salle f d'expédition

ship'shape' adj & adv en bon ordre

ship's' pa'pers spl papiers mpl de bord

ship's' time' s heure f locale du navire

ship'-to-shore' ra'di·o ['ʃɪptə'ʃor] s (pl -os) liaison f radio maritime

ship'wreck' s naufrage m ‖ tr faire naufrager ‖ intr faire naufrage

ship'yard' s chantier m de construction navale or maritime

shirk [ʃʌrk] tr manquer à, esquiver ‖ intr négliger son devoir

shirred' eggs' [ʃʌrd] spl œufs mpl pochés à la crème

shirt [ʃʌrt] s chemise f; keep your shirt on! (slang) ne vous emballez pas!; to lose one's shirt perdre jusqu'à son dernier sou

shirt'band' s encolure f

shirt' front' s plastron m de chemise

shirt' sleeve' s manche f de chemise; in shirt sleeves en bras de chemise

shirt'tails' spl pans mpl de chemise

shirt'waist' s chemisier m

shiver ['ʃɪvər] s frisson m ‖ intr frissonner

shoal [ʃol] s banc m, bas-fond m

shock [ʃɑk] s (bump, clash) choc m, heurt m; (upset, misfortune; earthquake tremor) secousse f; (of grain) gerbe f, moyette f; (of hair) tignasse f; (elec) commotion f, choc m; to die of

shock mourir de saisissement ‖ tr choquer; (elec) commotionner, choquer

shock' absorb'er [æb,sɔrbər] s amortisseur m

shocking ['ʃɑkɪŋ] adj choquant, scandaleux

shock' troops' spl troupes fpl de choc

shod·dy ['ʃɑdi] adj (comp -dier; super -diest) inférieur, de pacotille

shoe [ʃu] s soulier m; to be in the shoes of être dans la peau de; to put one's shoes on se chausser; to take one's shoes off se déchausser ‖ v (pret & pp shod [ʃɑd]) tr chausser; (a horse) ferrer

shoe'black' s cireur m de bottes

shoe'horn' s chausse-pied m

shoe'lace' s lacet m, cordon m de soulier

shoe'mak'er s cordonnier m

shoe' pol'ish s cirage m de chaussures

shoe'shine' s cirage m

shoe' store' s magasin m de chaussures

shoe'string' s lacet m, cordon m de soulier; on a shoestring avec de minces capitaux

shoe'tree' s embauchoir m, forme f

shoo [ʃu] tr chasser ‖ interj ch!, filez!

shoot [ʃut] s (sprout, twig) rejeton m, pousse f; (for grain, sand, etc.) goulotte f; (contest) concours m de tir; (hunting party) partie f de chasse ‖ v (pret & pp shot [ʃɑt]) tr tirer; (a person) tuer d'un coup de fusil; (to execute with a discharge of rifles) fusiller; (with a camera) photographier; (a scene; a motion picture) tourner, roder; (the sun) prendre la hauteur de; (dice) jeter; to shoot down abattre; to shoot up (slang) cribler de balles ‖ intr tirer; s'élancer, se précipiter; (said of pain) lanciner; (said of star) filer; to shoot at faire feu sur; (to strive for) viser; to shoot up (said of plant) pousser; (said of plant) pousser; (said of flame) jaillir; (said of prices) augmenter

shooting ['ʃutɪŋ] s tir m; (phot) prise f de vues

shoot'ing gal'ler·y s (pl -ies) stand m de tir, tir m

shoot'ing match' s concours m de tir

shoot'ing script' s découpage m

shoot'ing star' s étoile f filante

shop [ʃɑp] s (store) boutique f; (workshop) atelier m; to talk shop parler boutique, parler affaires ‖ v (pret & pp shopped; ger shopping) intr faire des emplettes, faire des courses; magasiner (Canad) ‖ to go shopping faire des emplettes, faire des courses; to shop around être à l'affût de bonnes occasions; to shop for chercher à acheter

shop'girl' s vendeuse f

shop'keep'er s boutiquier m

shoplifter ['ʃɑp,lɪftər] s voleur m à l'étalage

shopper ['ʃɑpər] s acheteur m

shopping ['ʃɑpɪŋ] s achat m; (purchases) achats mpl, emplettes fpl

shop'ping bag' s sac m à provisions

shop'ping cen'ter s centre m commercial

shop'ping dis'trict s quartier m commerçant

shop' stew'ard s délégué m d'atelier

shop' win'dow s vitrine f, devanture f

shop'worn' adj défraîchi

shore [ʃor] s rivage m, rive f, bord m; (sandy beach) plage f; **shores** (poetic) pays m ‖ tr—to shore up étayer

shore' din'ner s dîner m de marée

shore' leave' s (nav) descente f à terre

shore'line' s ligne f de côte

shore' patrol' s patrouille f de garde-côte; (police) (nav) police f militaire de la marine

short [ʃort] adj court; (person) petit; (temper) brusque; (phonet) bref; **in short** en somme; **short of breath** poussif; **to be short for** (coll) être le diminutif de; **to be short of** être à court de ‖ s (elec) court-circuit m; (mov) court-métrage m; **shorts** culotte f courte, culotte de sport ‖ adv court, de court; **to run short of** être à court de, à manquer de; **to sell short** (com) vendre à découvert; **to stop short** s'arrêter net ‖ tr (elec) court-circuiter ‖ intr (elec) se mettre en court-circuit

shortage [ˈʃortɪdʒ] s manque m, pénurie f; crise f, e.g., **housing shortage** crise du logement; (com) déficit m; **shortages** manquants mpl

short'cake' s gâteau m recouvert de fruits frais m

short'-change' tr ne pas rendre assez de monnaie à; (to cheat) (coll) rouler

short' cir'cuit s court-circuit m

short'-cir'cuit tr court-circuiter

short'com'ing s défaut m

short'cut' s raccourci m

shorten [ˈʃortən] tr raccourcir ‖ intr se raccourcir

shortening [ˈʃortənɪŋ] s raccourcissement m; (culin) saindoux m

short'hand' adj sténographique ‖ s sténographie f; **to take down in shorthand** sténographier

short'hand notes' spl sténogramme m

short'hand typ'ist s sténodactylo m f

short-lived [ˈʃortˈlaɪvd], [ˈʃortˈlɪvd] adj de courte durée, bref

shortly [ˈʃortli] adv tantôt, sous peu; brièvement; (curtly) sèchement; **shortly after** peu après

short'-range' adj à courte portée

short' sale' s vente f à découvert

short'-sight'ed adj myope; **to be short-sighted** (fig) avoir la vue courte

short' sto'ry s nouvelle f, conte m

short'-tem'pered adj vif, emporté

short'-term' adj à court terme

short'wave' adj aux petites ondes, aux ondes courtes ‖ s petite onde f, onde courte

short' weight' s poids m insuffisant

shot [ʃat] adj (silk) changeant; (e.g., chances) (coll) réduit à zéro; (drunk) (slang) paf ‖ s coup m de feu, décharge f; (marksman) tireur m; (pellets) petits plombs mpl; (of a rocket into space) lancement m, tir m; (in certain games) shoot m; (snapshot) instantané m; (mov) plan m; (hypodermic injection) (coll) piqûre f; (drink of liquor) (slang) verre m d'alcool; **a long shot** un gros risque, une chance sur mille; **to fire a shot at** tirer sur; **to start like a shot** partir comme un trait

shot'gun' s fusil m de chasse

shot'-put' s (sports) lancement m du poids

should [ʃʊd] aux used to express 1) the present conditional, e.g., **if I waited for him, I should miss the train** si je l'attendais, je manquerais le train; 2) the past conditional, e.g., **if I had waited for him, I should have missed the train** si je l'avais attendu, j'aurais manqué le train; 3) the potential mood, e.g., **he should go at once** il devrait aller aussitôt; e.g., **he should have gone at once** il aurait dû aller aussitôt; 4) a softened affirmation, e.g., **I should like a drink** je prendrais bien quelque chose à boire; e.g., **I should have thought that you would have known better** j'aurais cru que vous auriez été plus avisé

shoulder [ˈʃoldər] s épaule f; (of a road) accotement m; **across the shoulder** en bandoulière, en écharpe; **shoulders** (of a garment) carrure f ‖ tr (a gun) mettre sur l'épaule; **to shoulder aside** pousser de l'épaule

shoul'der blade' s omoplate f

shoul'der strap' s (of underwear) épaulette f; (mil) bandoulière f

shout [ʃaʊt] s cri m ‖ tr crier; **to shout down** huer ‖ intr crier

shove [ʃʌv] s poussée f, bourrade f ‖ tr pousser, bousculer ‖ intr pousser; **to shove off** pousser au large; (slang) filer, décamper

shov'el [ˈʃʌvəl] s pelle f ‖ v (pret & pp -eled or -elled; ger -eling or -elling) tr pelleter; (e.g., snow) balayer

show [ʃo] s exposition f; apparence f; (display) étalage m; (of hands) levée f; (each performance) séance f; (mov) film m; (theat) spectacle m; **to make a show of** faire parade de ‖ v (pret showed; pp shown [ʃon] or showed) tr montrer; (one's passport) présenter; (a film) projeter; (e.g., to the door) conduire; **to show off** faire étalage de; **to show up** (coll) démasquer ‖ intr se montrer; **to show through** transparaître; **to show up** (against a background) ressortir; (coll) faire son apparition

show' bill' s affiche f

show'boat' s bateau-théâtre m

show' busi'ness s l'industrie f du spectacle

show'case' s vitrine f

show'down' s cartes fpl sur table, moment m critique; **to come to a showdown** en venir au fait

shower [ˈʃaʊər] s averse f, ondée f; (of blows, bullets, kisses, etc.) pluie *f*; *(bath)* douche *f* || *tr* faire pleuvoir; **to shower with** combler de || *intr* pleuvoir à verse

show′er bath′ *s* douche *f*

show′ girl′ *s* girl *f*

show′man *s* (*pl* **-men**) impresario *m*; **he's a great showman** c'est un as pour la mise en scène

show′-off′ *s* (coll) m'as-tu-vu *m*

show′piece′ *s* pièce *f* maîtresse

show′place′ *s* lieu *m* célèbre

show′room′ *s* salon *m* d'exposition

show′ win′dow *s* vitrine *f*

show•y [′ʃo•i] *adj* (*comp* **-ier**; *super* **-iest**) fastueux; *(gaudy)* voyant

shrapnel [′ʃræpnəl] *s* shrapnel *m*, obus *m* à mitraille; éclat *m* d'obus

shred [ʃrɛd] *s* morceau *m*, lambeau *f*; **not a shred of** pas l'ombre de; **to tear to shreds** mettre en lambeaux || *v* (*pret & pp* **shredded** or **shred**; *ger* **shredding**) *tr* mettre en lambeaux, déchiqueter

shrew [ʃru] *s* *(nagging woman)* mégère *f*; (zool) musaraigne *f*

shrewd [ʃrud] *adj* sagace, fin

shriek [ʃrik] *s* cri *m* perçant || *intr* pousser un cri perçant

shrike [ʃraɪk] *s* pie-grièche *f*

shrill [ʃrɪl] *adj* aigu, perçant

shrimp [ʃrɪmp] *s* crevette *f*; *(insignificant person)* gringalet *m*

shrine [ʃraɪn] *s* tombeau *m* de saint; *(reliquary)* châsse *f*; *(holy place)* lieu *m* saint, sanctuaire *m*

shrink [ʃrɪŋk] *v* (*pret* **shrank** [ʃræŋk] or **shrunk** [ʃrʌŋk]; *pp* **shrunk** or **shrunken**) *tr* rétrécir || *intr* se rétrécir; **to shrink away** or **back from** reculer devant

shrinkage [′ʃrɪŋkɪdʒ] *s* rétrécissement *m*

shriv•el [′ʃrɪvəl] *v* (*pret & pp* **-eled** or **-elled**; *ger* **-eling** or **-elling**) *tr* ratatiner, recroqueviller || *intr* se ratatiner, se recroqueviller

shroud [ʃraʊd] *s* linceul *m*; *(veil)* voile *m*; **shrouds** (naut) haubans *mpl* || *tr* ensevelir; voiler

Shrove′ Tues′day [ʃrov] *s* mardi *m* gras

shrub [ʃrʌb] *s* arbuste *m*

shrubber•y [′ʃrʌbəri] *s* (*pl* **-ies**) bosquet *m*

shrug [ʃrʌg] *s* haussement *m* d'épaules || *v* (*pret & pp* **shrugged**; *ger* **shrugging**) *tr* (*one's shoulders*) hausser; **to shrug off** minimiser; ne tenir aucun compte de || *intr* hausser les épaules

shudder [′ʃʌdər] *s* frisson *m*, frémissement *m* || *intr* frissonner, frémir

shuffle [′ʃʌfəl] *s* (*of cards*) battement *m*, mélange *m*; *(of feet)* frottement *m*; *(change of place)* déplacement *m* || *tr* (*cards*) battre; (*the feet*) traîner; *(to mix up)* mêler, brouiller || *intr* battre les cartes; traîner les pieds

shuf′fle-board′ *s* jeu *m* de palets

shun [ʃʌn] *v* (*pret & pp* **shunned**; *ger* **shunning**) *tr* éviter, fuir

shunt [ʃʌnt] *tr* garer, manœuvrer; (elec) shunter, dériver

shut [ʃʌt] *adj* fermé || *v* (*pret & pp* **shut**; *ger* **shutting**) *tr* fermer; **to shut in** enfermer; **to shut off** couper; **to shut up** enfermer; (coll) faire taire || *intr* se fermer; **shut up!** (slang) taistoi!, ferme-la!

shut′down′ *s* fermeture *f*

shutter [′ʃʌtər] *s* volet *m*, contrevent *m*; *(over store window)* rideau *m*; (phot) obturateur *m*

shuttle [′ʃʌtəl] *s* navette *f* || *intr* faire la navette

shut′tle train′ *s* navette *f*

shy [ʃaɪ] *adj* (*comp* **shyer** or **shier**; *super* **shyest** or **shiest**) timide, sauvage; *(said of horse)* ombrageux; **I am shy a dollar** il me faut un dollar; **to be shy of** se méfier de || *v* (*pret & pp* **shied**) *intr* (*said of horse*) faire un écart; **to shy away from** éviter

shyster [′ʃaɪstər] *s* (coll) avocat *m* marron

Sia•mese [‚saɪ•ə′miz] *adj* siamois || *s* (*pl* **-mese**) Siamois *m*

Si′amese twins′ *spl* frères *mpl* siamois

Siberian [saɪ′bɪrɪ•ən] *adj* sibérien || *s* Sibérien *m*

sibyl [′sɪbɪl] *s* sibylle *f*

sic [sɪk], [sɪk] *adv* sic || [sɪk] *v* (*pret & pp* **sicked**; *ger* **sicking**) *tr*—**sic 'em!** (coll) pille!; **to sic on** lancer après

Sicilian [sɪ′sɪljən] *adj* sicilien || *s* Sicilien *m*

Sicily [′sɪsɪli] *s* Sicile *f*; la Sicile

sick [sɪk] *adj* malade; **to be sick and tired of** (coll) en avoir plein le dos de, en avoir marre de; **to be sick at** or **to one's stomach** avoir mal au cœur, avoir des nausées; **to take sick** tomber malade

sick′bed′ *s* lit *m* de malade

sicken [′sɪkən] *tr* rendre malade || *intr* tomber malade; *(to be disgusted)* être écœuré

sickening [′sɪkənɪŋ] *adj* écœurant, dégoûtant

sickle [′sɪkəl] *s* faucille *f*

sick′ leave′ *s* congé *m* de maladie

sick•ly [′sɪkli] *adj* (*comp* **-lier**; *super* **-liest**) maladif, débile

sickness [′sɪknɪs] *s* maladie *f*; nausée *f*

side [saɪd] *adj* latéral, de côté || *s* côté *m*; *(of phonograph)* face *f*; *(of team, government, etc.)* camp *m*, parti *m*, côté; **this side up** (*on package*) haut || *intr*—**to side with** prendre le parti de

side′ arms′ *spl* armes *fpl* de ceinturon

side′board′ *s* buffet *m*, desserte *f*

side′burns′ *spl* favoris *mpl*

side′ dish′ *s* plat *m* d'accompagnement

side′ door′ *s* porte *f* latérale, porte *f* de service

side′ effect′ *s* effet *m* secondaire

side′ en′trance *s* entrée *f* latérale

side′ glance′ *s* regard *m* de côté

side′ is′sue *s* question *f* d'intérêt secondaire

side′line′ *s* occupation *f* secondaire; **on the sidelines** sans y prendre part

sidereal [saɪ'dɪrɪ‧əl] adj sidéral
side' road' s chemin m de traverse
side'sad'dle adv en amazone
side' show' s spectacle m forain; (fig) événement m secondaire
side'slip' s glissade f sur l'aile
side'split'ting adj désopilant
side' step' s écart m
side'-step' v (pret & pp -stepped; ger -stepping) tr éviter || intr faire un pas de côté
side'stroke' s nage f sur le côté
side'track' s voie f de garage || tr écarter, dévier; (rr) aiguiller sur une voie de garage
side' view' s vue f de profil
side'walk' s trottoir m
side'walk café' s terrasse f de café
sideward ['saɪdwərd] adj latéral || adv latéralement, de côté
side'ways' adj latéral || adv latéralement, de côté
side' whisk'ers spl favoris mpl
side'wise' adj latéral || adv latéralement, de côté
siding ['saɪdɪŋ] s (rr) voie f d'évitement, voie de garage
sidle ['saɪdəl] intr avancer de biais; to sidle up se couler auprès de
siege [sidʒ] s siège m; to lay siege to mettre le siège devant
siesta [si'estə] s sieste f; to take a siesta faire la sieste
sieve [sɪv] s crible m, tamis m || tr passer au crible, au tamis
sift [sɪft] tr passer au crible, passer au tamis; (flour) tamiser; (fig) examiner soigneusement
sigh [saɪ] s soupir m || intr soupirer
sight [saɪt] s vue f; (of firearm) mire f; (of telescope, camera, etc.) viseur m; chose f digne d'être vue; a sight of (coll) énormément de; at sight à vue; à livre ouvert; by sight de vue; in sight of à la vue de; sad sight spectacle m navrant; sights curiosités fpl; to catch sight of apercevoir; what a sight you are! comme vous voilà fait! || tr & intr viser
sight' draft' s (com) effet m à vue
sight'-read' v (pret & pp -read [ˌred]) tr & intr lire à livre ouvert; (mus) déchiffrer
sight' read'er s déchiffreur m
sight'see'ing s tourisme m; to go sightseeing visiter les curiosités
sightseer ['saɪtˌsi‧ər] s touriste mf, excursionniste mf
sign [saɪn] s signe m; (on a store) enseigne f || tr signer; to sign up engager, embaucher || intr signer; to sign off (rad) terminer l'émission; to sign up for (coll) s'inscrire à
sig‧nal ['sɪɡnəl] adj signalé, insigne || s signal m || v (pret & pp -naled or -nalled; ger -naling or -nalling) tr faire signe à, signaler || intr faire des signaux
sig'nal tow'er s tour f de signalisation
signature ['sɪɡnət/ər] s signature f; (mus) armature f; (rad) indicatif m
sign'board' s panneau m d'affichage

signer ['saɪnər] s signataire mf
sig'net ring' ['sɪɡnɪt] s chevalière f
significance [sɪɡ'nɪfɪkəns] s importance f; (meaning) signification f
significant [sɪɡ'nɪfəkənt] adj important; significatif
signi‧fy ['sɪɡnɪˌfaɪ] v (pret & pp -fied) tr signifier
sign'post' s poteau m indicateur
silence ['saɪləns] s silence m || tr faire taire, réduire au silence
silent ['saɪlənt] adj silencieux
sil'ent mov'ie s film m muet
silhouette [ˌsɪlu'et] s silhouette f || tr silhouetter
silicon ['sɪlɪkən] s silicium m
silicone ['sɪlɪˌkon] s silicone f
silk [sɪlk] s soie f
silk'-cotton tree' s fromager m
silken ['sɪlkən] adj soyeux
silk' hat' s haut-de-forme m
silk'-stock'ing adj aristocratique || s aristocrate mf
silk'worm' s ver m à soie
silk‧y ['sɪlki] adj (comp -ier; super -iest) soyeux
sill [sɪl] s (of window) rebord m; (of door) seuil m; (of walls) sablière f
sil‧ly ['sɪli] adj (comp -lier; super -liest) sot, niais
si‧lo ['saɪlo] s (pl -los) silo m || tr ensiler
silt [sɪlt] s vase f
silver ['sɪlvər] s argent m || tr argenter; (a mirror) étamer
sil'ver-fish' s (ent) poisson m d'argent
sil'ver foil' s feuille f d'argent
sil'ver lin'ing s beau côté m, côté brillant
sil'ver plate' s argenterie f
sil'ver screen' s écran m
sil'ver-smith' s orfèvre m
sil'ver spoon' s—born with a silver spoon in one's mouth né coiffé
sil'ver-tongued' adj à la langue dorée, éloquent
sil'ver-ware' s argenterie f
similar ['sɪmɪlər] adj semblable
similari‧ty [ˌsɪmɪ'lærɪti] s (pl -ties) ressemblance f, similitude f
simile ['sɪmɪli] s comparaison f
simmer ['sɪmər] tr mijoter || intr mijoter; to simmer down s'apaiser
Simon ['saɪmən] s Simon m; Simon says . . . (game) Caporal a dit . . .
simper ['sɪmpər] s sourire m niais || intr sourire bêtement
simple ['sɪmpəl] adj & s simple m
sim'ple-mind'ed adj simple, naïf; niais
simpleton ['sɪmpəltən] s niais m
simpli‧fy ['sɪmplɪˌfaɪ] v (pret & pp -fied) tr simplifier
simulate ['sɪmjəˌlet] tr simuler
simultaneous [ˌsaɪməl'teni‧əs], [ˌsɪməl'teni‧əs] adj simultané
sin [sɪn] s péché m || v (pret & pp sinned; ger sinning) intr pécher
since [sɪns] adv & prep depuis || conj depuis que; (inasmuch as) puisque
sincere [sɪn'sɪr] adj sincère
sincerity [sɪn'serɪti] s sincérité f
sine [saɪn] s (trig) sinus m

sinecure ['saɪn,kjur], ['sɪnɪ,kjur] s
sinécure f

sinew ['sɪnju] s tendon m; (fig) nerf
m, force f

sinful ['sɪnfəl] adj (person) pécheur;
(act, intention) coupable

sing [sɪŋ] v (pret sang [sæŋ] or sung
[sʌŋ]; pp sung) tr & intr chanter

singe [sɪndʒ] v (ger singeing) tr roussir; (poultry) flamber

singer ['sɪŋər] s chanteur m

single ['sɪŋgəl] adj seul, unique; (unmarried) célibataire; (e.g., room in a
hotel) à un lit; (bed) à une place;
(e.g., devotion) simple, honnête || tr
—to single out distinguer, choisir

sin'gle bless'edness ['blɛsɪdnɪs] s le
bonheur m du célibat

sin'gle-breast'ed adj droit

sin'gle-en'try adj (bk) en partie simple

sin'gle-en'try book'keeping s comptabilité f simple

sin'gle file' s—in single file en file
indienne, à la file

sin'gle-hand'ed adj sans aide, tout seul

sin'gle life' s vie f de célibataire

sin'gle room' s chambre f à un lit

sin'gle-track' adj (rr) à voie unique;
(coll) d'une portée limitée

sing'song' adj monotone || s mélopée f

singular ['sɪŋgjələr] adj & s singulier f

sinister ['sɪnɪstər] adj sinistre

sink [sɪŋk] s évier m; (drain) égout m
|| v (pret sank [sæŋk] or sunk
[sʌŋk]; pp sunk) tr enfoncer; (a
ship) couler, faire sombrer; (a well)
creuser; (money) immobiliser || intr
s'enfoncer, s'affaisser; (under the water) couler, sombrer; (said of heart)
se serrer; (said of health, prices, sun,
etc.) baisser; to sink into plonger
dans; (an armchair) s'effondrer dans

sink'ing fund' s caisse f d'amortissement

sinless ['sɪnlɪs] adj sans péché

sinner ['sɪnər] s pécheur m

sintering ['sɪntərɪŋ] s (metallurgy)
frittage m

sinuous ['sɪnju·əs] adj sinueux

sinus ['saɪnəs] s sinus m

sip [sɪp] s petite gorgée f, petit coup m
|| v (pret & pp sipped; ger sipping)
tr boire à petits coups, siroter

siphon ['saɪfən] s siphon m || tr
siphonner

si'phon bot'tle s siphon m

sir [sʌr] s monsieur m; (British title)
Sir m; Dear Sir Monsieur

sire [saɪr] s sire m; (of a quadruped)
père m || tr engendrer

siren ['saɪrən] s sirène f

sirloin ['sʌrlɔɪn] s aloyau m

sirup ['sɪrəp], ['sʌrəp] s sirop m

sis·sy ['sɪsi] s (pl -sies) efféminé m;
fillette f; (cowardly fellow) poule f
mouillée

sister ['sɪstər] adj (fig) jumeau || s
sœur f

sis'ter-in-law' s (pl sisters-in-law) belle-
sœur f

sit [sɪt] v (pret & pp sat [sæt]; ger
sitting) intr s'asseoir; être assis; (said

of hen on eggs) couver; (for a portrait) poser; (said of legislature,
court, etc.) siéger; to sit down s'asseoir; to sit still ne pas bouger; to sit
up se redresser; se tenir droit; to sit
up and beg (said of dog) faire le beau

sit'-down strike' s grève f sur le tas

site [saɪt] s site m

sitting ['sɪtɪŋ] s séance f

sit'ting duck' s (coll) cible f facile

sit'ting room' s salon m

situate ['sɪt/u,et] tr situer

situation [,sɪt/u'e/ən] s situation f;
poste m, emploi m

sitz' bath' [sɪts] s bain m de siège

six [sɪks] adj & pron six || s six m; at
sixes and sevens de travers, en désaccord; six o'clock six heures

sixteen ['sɪks'tin] adj, pron, & s seize m

sixteenth ['sɪks'tinθ] adj & pron seizième (masc, fem); the Sixteenth
seize, e.g., John the Sixteenth Jean
seize || s seizième m; the sixteenth
(in dates) le seize

sixth [sɪksθ] adj & pron sixième (masc,
fem); the Sixth six, e.g., John the
Sixth Jean six || s sixième m; the
sixth (in dates) le six

sixtieth ['sɪkstɪ·ɪθ] adj & pron soixan-
tième (masc, fem) || s soixantième m

six·ty ['sɪksti] adj & pron soixante;
about sixty une soixantaine de || s
(pl -ties) soixante m; (age of) soixan-
taine f

sizable ['saɪzəbəl] adj assez grand, considérable

size [saɪz] s grandeur f; dimensions
fpl; (of a person or garment) taille
f; (of a shoe, glove, or hat) pointure
f; (of a shirt collar) encolure f; (of a
book or box) format m; (to fill a
porous surface) apprêt m; what size
hat do you wear? du combien coiffez-
vous?; what size shoes do you wear?
du combien chaussez-vous? || tr clas-
ser; (wood to be painted) coller; to
size up juger

sizzle ['sɪzəl] s grésillement m || intr
grésiller

skate [sket] s patin m; (ichth) raie f;
good skate (slang) brave homme m ||
intr patiner; to go skating faire du
patin

skat'ing rink' s patinoire f

skein [sken] s écheveau m

skeleton ['skɛlɪtən] s squelette m

skel'eton key' s crochet m

skeptic ['skɛptɪk] adj & s sceptique mf

skeptical ['skɛptɪkəl] adj sceptique

skepticism ['skɛptɪ,sɪzəm] s scepticisme m

sketch [skɛt/] s esquisse f; (pen or pencil drawing) croquis m, esquisse; (lit)
aperçu m; (theat) sketch m || tr es-
quisser || intr croquer

sketch'book' s album m de croquis

skew [skju] adj & s biais m || intr
biaiser

skewer ['skju·ər] s brochette f || tr em-
brocher

ski [ski] s ski m || intr skier; to go
skiing faire du ski

ski' boots' *spl* chaussures *fpl* de ski

skid [skɪd] *s* (*sidewise*) dérapage *m*; (*forward*) patinage *m*; (*of wheel*) sabot *m*, patin *m* ‖ *v* (*pret & pp* **skidded**; *ger* **skidding**) *tr* enrayer, bloquer ‖ *intr* (*sidewise*) déraper; (*forward*) patiner

skid' row' [ro] *s* quartier *m* mal famé

skier ['ski·ər] *s* skieur *m*

skiff [skɪf] *s* skiff *m*, esquif *m*

skiing ['ski·ɪŋ] *s* ski *m*

ski' jack'et *s* anorak *m*

ski' jump' *s* (*place to jump*) tremplin *m*; (*act of jumping*) saut *m* en skis

ski' lift' *s* remonte-pente *m*, téléski *m*

skill [skɪl] *s* habilité *f*, adresse *f*; (*job*) métier *m*

skilled *adj* habile, adroit

skillet ['skɪlɪt] *s* casserole *f*; (*frying pan*) poêle *f*

skillful ['skɪlfəl] *adj* habile, expert

skim [skɪm] *v* (*pret & pp* **skimmed**; *ger* **skimming**) *tr* (*milk*) écrémer; (*molten metal*) écumer; (*to graze*) raser ‖ *intr* —to skim over passer légèrement sur

ski' mask' *s* passe-montagne *m*

skimmer ['skɪmər] *s* écumoire *f*; (*straw hat*) canotier *m*

skim' milk' *s* lait *m* écrémé

skimp [skɪmp] *tr* bâcler ‖ *intr* lésiner; **to skimp on** lésiner sur

skimp·y ['skɪmpi] *adj* (*comp* **-ier**; *super* **-iest**) maigre; (*garment*) étriqué; avare, mesquin

skin [skɪn] *s* peau *f*; **by the skin of one's teeth** de justesse, par un cheveu; **soaked to the skin** trempé jusqu'aux os; **to strip to the skin** se mettre à poil ‖ *v* (*pret & pp* **skinned**; *ger* **skinning**) *tr* écorcher, dépouiller; (*e.g., an elbow*) s'écorcher; **to skin alive** (*coll*) écorcher vif

skin'-deep' *adj* superficiel; (*beauty*) à fleur de peau

skin' div'er *s* plongeur *m* autonome

skin'flint' *s* grippe-sou *m*

skin' game' *s* (*slang*) escroquerie *f*

skin' graft'ing *s* greffe *f* cutanée, autoplastie *f*

skin·ny ['skɪni] *adj* (*comp* **-nier**; *super* **-niest**) maigre, décharné

skip [skɪp] *s* saut *m* ‖ *v* (*pret & pp* **skipped**; *ger* **skipping**) *tr* sauter; **skip it!** ça suffit!, laisse tomber!; **to skip rope** sauter à la corde ‖ *intr* sauter; **to skip out** or **off** filer

ski' pole' *s* bâton *m* de skis

skipper ['skɪpər] *s* patron *m* ‖ *tr* commander, conduire

skirmish ['skʌrmɪʃ] *s* escarmouche *f* ‖ *intr* escarmoucher

skirt [skʌrt] *s* jupe *f*; (*woman*) (*slang*) jupe ‖ *tr* côtoyer, longer; éviter

ski' run' *s* descente *f* en skis

ski' stick' *s* bâton *m* de skis

skit [skɪt] *s* sketch *m*

skittish ['skɪtɪʃ] *adj* capricieux; timide; (*e.g., horse*) ombrageux

skulduggery [skʌl'dʌgəri] *s* (*coll*) fourberie *f*, ruse *f*, cuisine *f*

skull [skʌl] *s* crâne *m*

skull' and cross'bones *s* tibias *mpl* croisés et tête *f* de mort

skull'cap' *s* calotte *f*

skunk [skʌŋk] *s* mouffette *f*; (*person*) (*coll*) salaud *m*

sky [skaɪ] *s* (*pl* **skies**) ciel *m*; **to praise to the skies** porter aux nues

sky'div'er *s* parachutiste *mf*

sky'div'ing *s* parachutisme *m*, saut *m* en chute libre

sky'lark' *s* (*Alauda arvensis*) alouette *f*, alouette des champs ‖ *intr* (*coll*) batifoler

sky'light' *s* lucarne *f*

sky'line' *s* ligne *m* d'horizon; (*of city*) profil *m*

sky'rock'et *s* fusée *f* volante ‖ *intr* monter en flèche

sky'scrap'er *s* gratte-ciel *m*

slab [slæb] *s* (*of stone*) dalle *f*; (*slice*) tranche *f*

slack [slæk] *adj* lâche, mou; négligent ‖ *s* mou *m*; (*slowdown*) ralentissement *m*; **slacks** pantalon *m* ‖ *tr* relâcher; (*lime*) éteindre; **to slack off** larguer ‖ *intr*—**to slack off** or **up** se relâcher

slacken ['slækən] *tr* relâcher; (*to slow down*) ralentir ‖ *intr* se relâcher; se ralentir

slacker ['slækər] *s* flemmard *m*; (*mil*) tire-au-flanc *m*, embusqué *m*

slack' hours' *spl* heures *fpl* creuses

slag [slæg] *s* scorie *f*

slake [slek] *tr* apaiser, étancher; (*lime*) éteindre

slalom ['slɑləm] *s* slalom *m*

slam [slæm] *s* claquement *m*; (*cards*) chelem *m*; (*coll*) critique *f* sévère ‖ *v* (*pret & pp* **slammed**; *ger* **slamming**) *tr* claquer; (*coll*) éreinter; **to slam down on** flanquer sur ‖ *intr* claquer

slander ['slændər] *s* calomnie *f* ‖ *tr* calomnier

slanderous ['slændərəs] *adj* calomnieux

slang [slæŋ] *s* argot *m*

slant [slænt] *s* pente *f*; (*bias*) point *m* de vue ‖ *tr* mettre en pente, incliner; donner un biais spécial à ‖ *intr* être en pente, s'incliner

slap [slæp] *s* tape *f*, claque *f*; (*in the face*) soufflet *m*, gifle *f* ‖ *v* (*pret & pp* **slapped**; *ger* **slapping**) *tr* taper, gifler

slap'dash' *adj*—**in a slapdash manner** à la va-comme-je-te-pousse ‖ *adv* à la six-quatre-deux

slap'stick' *adj* bouffon ‖ *s* bouffonnerie *f*

slash [slæʃ] *s* entaille *f* ‖ *tr* taillader; (*e.g., prices*) réduire beaucoup

slat [slæt] *s* latte *f*

slate [slet] *s* ardoise *f*; (*of candidates*) liste *f* ‖ *tr* couvrir d'ardoises; inscrire sur la liste, désigner

slate' pen'cil *s* crayon *m* d'ardoise

slate' roof' *s* toit *m* d'ardoise

slattern ['slætərn] *s* (*slovenly woman*) marie-salope *f*; (*slut*) voyoute *f*, gueuse *f*

slaughter ['slɔtər] *s* boucherie *f* ‖ *tr* abattre; massacrer

slaught′er-house′ s abattoir m
Slav [slɑv], [slæv] adj slave ‖ s (language) slave m; (person) Slave mf
slave [slev] adj & s esclave mf ‖ intr besogner, trimer
slave′ driv′er s (hist, fig) négrier m
slavery [′slevəri] s esclavage m; (institutition of keeping slaves) esclavagisme m
slave′ ship′ s négrier m
slave′ trade′ s traite f des noirs
Slavic [′slɑvɪk], [′slævɪk] adj & s slave m
slavish [′slevɪʃ] adj servile
slay [sle] v (pret slew [slu]; pp slain [slen]) tr tuer, massacrer
slayer [′sle·ər] s meurtrier m
sled [sled] s luge f ‖ v (pret & pp sledded; ger sledding) intr faire de la luge, luger
sledge′ ham′mer [sledʒ] s massette f, masse f
sleek [slik] adj lisse, luisant ‖ tr lisser
sleep [slip] s sommeil m; to go to sleep s'endormir; to put to sleep endormir ‖ v (pret & pp slept [slept]) tr—to sleep it over, to sleep on it prendre conseil de son oreiller; to sleep off (a hangover, headache, etc.) faire passer en dormant ‖ intr dormir; (e.g., with a woman) coucher; to sleep late faire la grasse matinée; to sleep like a log dormir comme un loir
sleeper [′slipər] s dormeur m; (girder) poutre f horizontale; (tie) (rr) traverse f
sleep′ing bag′ s sac m de couchage
sleep′ing car′ s wagon-lit m
sleep′ing pill′ s somnifère m
sleepless [′slɪplɪs] adj sans sommeil
sleep′less night′ s nuit f blanche
sleep′walk′er s somnambule mf
sleep-y [′slipi] adj (comp -ier; super -iest) endormi, somnolent; to be sleepy avoir sommeil
sleep′y-head′ s endormi m, grand dormeur m
sleet [slit] s grésil m ‖ intr grésiller
sleeve [sliv] s manche f; (mach) manchon m, douille f; to laugh in or up one's sleeve rire sous cape
sleigh [sle] s traîneau m ‖ intr aller en traîneau
sleigh′ bell′ s grelot m
sleigh′ ride′ s promenade f en traîneau
sleight′ of hand′ [slaɪt] s prestidigitation f, tours mpl de passe-passe
slender [′slendər] adj svelte, mince, élancé; (resources) maigre
sleuth [sluθ] s limier m, détective m
slew [slu] s (coll) tas m, floppée f
slice [slaɪs] s tranche f ‖ tr trancher
slick [slɪk] adj lisse; (appearance) élégant; (coll) rusé ‖ s tache f, e.g., oil slick tache d'huile ‖ tr lisser; to slick up (coll) mettre en ordre
slicker [′slɪkər] s ciré m, imper m; (coll) enjôleur m
slide [slaɪd] s (sliding) glissade f, glissement m; (sliding place) glissoire m; (of microscope) plaque f; (of trombone) coulisse f; (on a slide rule) curseur m; (piece that slides) glissière f; (phot) diapositive f ‖ v (pret & pp slid [slɪd]) tr glisser ‖ intr glisser; to let slide ne faire aucun cas de, laisser aller
slide′ fas′tener s fermeture f éclair
slide′ rule′ s règle f à calcul
slide′ valve′ s soupape f à tiroir
slid′ing con′tact s curseur m
slid′ing door′ s porte f à coulisse
slid′ing scale′ s échelle f mobile
slight [slaɪt] adj léger; (slender; insignificant) mince; (e.g., effort) faible ‖ s affront m ‖ tr faire peu de cas de, dédaigner; (a person) méconnaître
slim [slɪm] adj (comp slimmer; super slimmest) mince, svelte; (chance, excuse) mauvais; (resources) maigre
slime [slaɪm] s limon m, vase f; (of snakes, fish, etc.) bave f
slim-y [′slaɪmi] adj (comp -ier; super -iest) limoneux, vaseux
sling [slɪŋ] s (to shoot stones) fronde f; (to hold up a broken arm) écharpe f; (shoulder strap) bretelle f, bandoulière f ‖ v (pret & pp slung [slʌŋ]) tr lancer; passer en bandoulière
sling′shot′ s fronde f
slink [slɪŋk] v (pret & pp slunk [slʌŋk]) intr—to slink away s'esquiver
slip [slɪp] s glissade f, glissement m; bout m de papier; (for indexing, filing, etc.) fiche f; (cutting from plant) bouture f; (piece of underclothing) combinaison f; (blunder) faux pas m, bévue f; (naut) cale f; to give the slip to échapper à ‖ v (pret & pp slipped; ger slipping) tr glisser; to slip off (a garment) enlever, ôter; to slip on (a garment, shoes, etc.) enfiler; to slip one's mind sortir de l'esprit, échapper à qn ‖ intr glisser; (to blunder) faire un faux pas; to let slip laisser échapper; to slip away or off s'échapper, se dérober; to slip by s'échapper; (said of time) s'écouler; to slip up se tromper
slip′cov′er s housse f
slipper [′slɪpər] s pantoufle f
slippery [′slɪpəri] adj glissant; (deceitful) rusé
slip′-up′ s (coll) erreur f, bévue f
slit [slɪt] s fente f, fissure f ‖ v (pret & pp slit; ger slitting) tr fendre; (e.g., pages) couper; to slit the throat of égorger
slob [slɑb] s (slang) rustaud m
slobber [′slɑbər] s bave f; (fig) sentimentalité f ‖ intr baver
sloe [slo] s (shrub) prunellier m; (fruit) prunelle f
slogan [′slogən] s mot m d'ordre, devise f; (com) slogan m
sloop [slup] s sloop m
slop [slɑp] s lavure f, rinçure f ‖ v (pret & pp slopped; ger slopping) tr répandre ‖ intr se répandre; to slop over déborder
slope [slop] s pente f; (of a roof) inclinaison f; (of a region, mountain,

etc.) versant *m* ‖ *tr* pencher, incliner ‖ *intr* se pencher, s'incliner

slop·py ['slapi] *adj* (*comp* **-pier**; *super* **-piest**) mouillé; (*dress*) négligé, mal ajusté; (*work*) bâclé

slot [slɑt] *s* entaille *f*, rainure *f*; (*e.g., in a coin telephone*) fente *f*

sloth [sloθ], [slɔθ] *s* paresse *f*; (zool) paresseux *m*

slot′ machine′ *s* (*for gambling*) appareil *m* à sous; (*for vending*) distributeur *m* automatique

slouch [slaʊtʃ] *s* démarche *f* lourde; (*person*) lourdaud *m* ‖ *intr* ne pas se tenir droit; (*e.g., in a chair*) se vautrer; **to slouch along** traîner le pas

slouch′ hat′ *s* chapeau *m* mou

slough [slaʊ] *s* bourbier *m* ‖ [slʌf] (*of snake*) dépouille *f*; (pathol) escarre *f* ‖ *tr*—**to slough off** se débarrasser de ‖ *intr* muer, se dépouiller

Slovak ['slovæk], [slo'væk] *adj* slovaque ‖ *s* (*language*) slovaque *m*; (*person*) Slovaque *mf*

sloven·ly ['slʌvənli] *adj* (*comp* **-lier**; *super* **-liest**) négligé, malpropre

slow [slo] *adj* lent; (*sluggish*) traînard; (*clock, watch*) en retard; (*in understanding*) lourdaud ‖ *adv* lentement ‖ *tr* & *intr* ralentir; **SLOW** (*public sign*) ralentir; **to slow down** ralentir

slow′down′ *s* grève *f* perlée

slow′ mo′tion *s* ralenti *m*; **in slow motion** au ralenti, en ralenti

slow′poke′ *s* (coll) lambin *m*, traînard *m*

slug [slʌg] *s* (*used as coin*) jeton *m*; (*of linotype*) ligne-bloc *f*; (zool) limace *f*; (*blow*) (coll) bon coup *m*; (*drink*) (coll) gorgée *f* ‖ *v* (*pret* & *pp* **slugged**; *ger* **slugging**) *tr* (coll) flanquer un coup à

sluggard ['slʌgərd] *s* paresseux *m*

sluggish ['slʌgɪʃ] *adj* traînard

sluice [slus] *s* canal *m*; (*floodgate*) écluse *f*; (*dam; flume*) bief *m*

sluice′ gate′ *s* vanne *f*

slum [slʌm] *s* bas quartiers *mpl* ‖ *v* (*pret* & *pp* **slummed**; *ger* **slumming**) *intr*—**to go slumming** aller visiter les taudis

slumber ['slʌmbər] *s* sommeil *m*, assoupissement *m* ‖ *intr* sommeiller

slum′ dwell′ing *s* taudis *m*

slump [slʌmp] *s* affaissement *m*; (com) crise *f*, baisse *f* ‖ *intr* s'affaisser; (*said of prices, stocks, etc.*) dégringoler, s'effondrer

slur [slʌr] *s* (*in pronunciation*) mauvaise articulation *f*; (*insult*) affront *m*; (mus) liaison *f*; **to cast a slur on** porter atteinte à ‖ *v* (*pret* & *pp* **slurred**; *ger* **slurring**) *tr* (*a sound, a syllable*) mal articuler; (*a person*) déprécier; (mus) lier; **to slur over** glisser sur

slush [slʌʃ] *s* fange *f*, boue *f* liquide; (*gush*) sensiblerie *f*

slut [slʌt] *s* chienne *f*; (*slovenly woman*) marie-salope *f*

sly [slaɪ] *adj* (*comp* **slyer** or **slier**; *super*

slyest or **sliest**) rusé, sournois; (*mischievous*) espiègle, futé; **on the sly** furtivement, en cachette

smack [smæk] *s* claquement *m*; (*with the hand*) gifle *f*, claque *f*; (*trace, touch*) soupçon *m*; (*kiss*) (coll) gros baiser *m* ‖ *adv* en plein ‖ *tr* claquer ‖ *intr*—**to smack of** sentir; avoir un goût de

small [smɔl] *adj* petit §91; (*income*) modique; (*short in stature*) court; (*petty*) mesquin; (typ) minuscule

small′ arms′ *spl* armes *fpl* portatives

small′ beer′ *s* petite bière *f*; (slang) petite bière

small′ busi′ness *s* petite industrie *f*

small′ cap′ital *s* (typ) petite capitale *f*

small′ change′ *s* petite monnaie *f*, menue monnaie

small′ fry′ *s* menu fretin *m*

small′ intes′tine *s* intestin *m* grêle

small′-mind′ed *adj* mesquin, étriqué, étroit

small′ of the back′ *s* chute *f* des reins, bas *m* du dos

smallpox ['smɔl‚pɑks] *s* variole *f*

small′ print′ *s* petits caractères *mpl*

small′ talk′ *s* ragots *mpl*, papotage *m*

small′-time′ *adj* de troisième ordre, insignifiant, petit

small′-town′ *adj* provincial

smart [smɑrt] *adj* intelligent, éveillé; (*pace*) vif; (*person, clothes*) élégant, chic; (*pain*) cuisant; (*saucy*) impertinent ‖ *s* douleur *f* cuisante ‖ *intr* brûler, cuire; (*said of person with hurt feelings*) être cinglé

smart′ al′eck ['ælɪk] *s* (coll) fat *m*, présomptueux *m*

smart′ set′ *s* monde *m* élégant, gens *mpl* chic

smash [smæʃ] *s* fracassement *m*, fracas *m*; (coll) succès *m* ‖ *tr* fracasser ‖ *intr* se fracasser; **to smash into** emboutir, écraser

smash′ hit′ *s* (coll) succès *m*, (coll) pièce *f* à succès

smash′-up′ *s* collision *f*; débâcle *f*, culbute *f*

smattering ['smætərɪŋ] *s* légère connaissance *f*, teinture *f*

smear [smɪr] *s* tache *f*; (*vilification*) calomnie *f*; (med) frottis *m* ‖ *tr* tacher; calomnier; (*to coat*) enduire

smear′ campaign′ *s* campagne *f* de calomnies

smell [smel] *s* odeur *f*; (*aroma*) parfum *m*, senteur *f*; (*sense*) odorat *m* ‖ *v* (*pret* & *pp* **smelled** or **smelt** [smelt]) *tr* & *intr* sentir; **to smell of** sentir

smell′ing salts′ *spl* sels *mpl* volatils

smell·y ['smeli] *adj* (*comp* **-ier**; *super* **-iest**) malodorant, puant

smelt [smelt] *s* (*fish*) éperlan *m* ‖ *tr* & *intr* fondre

smile [smaɪl] *s* sourire *m* ‖ *intr* sourire; **to smile at** sourire à

smirk [smʌrk] *s* minauderie *f* ‖ *intr* minauder

smite [smaɪt] *v* (*pret* **smote** [smot]; *pp* **smitten** ['smɪtən] or **smit** [smɪt]) *tr* frapper; **to smite down** abattre

smith [smɪθ] s forgeron m

smith·y ['smɪθi] s (pl -ies) forge f

smitten ['smɪtən] adj frappé, affligé; (coll) épris, amoureux

smock [smɑk] s blouse f; (of artists) sarrau m; (buttoned in back) tablier m

smock' frock' s sarrau m

smog [smɑg] s (coll) brouillard m fumeux

smoke [smok] s fumée f; (coll) cigarette f; **to go up in smoke** s'en aller en fumée || tr & intr fumer

smoked' glass'es spl verres mpl fumés

smoke'-filled room' s tabagie f

smoke'less pow'der ['smoklɪs] s poudre f sans fumée

smoker ['smokər] s fumeur m; (room) fumoir m; (meeting) réunion f de fumeurs; (rr) compartiment m pour fumeurs

smoke' rings' spl ronds mpl de fumée

smoke' screen' s rideau m de fumée

smoke'stack' s cheminée f

smoking ['smokɪŋ] s le fumer m; **no smoking** (public sign) défense de fumer

smok'ing car' s voiture f de fumeurs

smok'ing jack'et s veston m d'intérieur

smok'ing room' s fumoir m

smok·y ['smoki] adj (comp -ier; super -iest) fumeux, enfumé

smolder ['smoldər] s fumée f épaisse; feu m qui couve || intr brûler sans flamme; (said of fire, anger, rebellion, etc.) couver

smooch [smutʃ] intr (coll) se bécoter

smooth [smuð] adj uni, lisse; (gentle, mellow) doux, moelleux; (operation) doux, régulier; (style) facile || tr unir, lisser; **to smooth away** (e.g., obstacles) aplanir, enlever; **to smooth down** (to calm) apaiser, calmer; **to smooth out** défroisser

smooth'-faced' adj imberbe

smooth-shaven ['smuð'ʃevən] adj rasé de près

smooth·y ['smuði] s (pl -ies) (coll) chattemite f, flagorneur m

smother ['smʌðər] tr suffoquer, étouffer; (culin) recouvrir

smudge [smʌdʒ] s tache f; (smoke) fumée f épaisse || tr tacher; (agr) fumiger

smudge' pot' s fumigène m

smug [smʌg] adj (comp smugger; super smuggest) fat, suffisant

smuggle ['smʌgəl] tr introduire en contrebande, faire la contrebande de || intr faire la contrebande

smuggler ['smʌglər] s contrebandier m

smuggling ['smʌglɪŋ] s contrebande f

smut [smʌt] s tache f de suie; (obscenity) ordure f; (agr) nielle f

smut·ty ['smʌti] adj (comp -tier; super -tiest) taché de suie, noirci; (obscene) ordurier; (agr) niellé

snack [snæk] s casse-croûte m; **to have a snack** casser la croûte

snack' bar' s snack-bar m, snack m

snag [snæg] s (of tree; of tooth) chicot m; **to hit a snag** se heurter à un obs-

---

tacle || v (pret & pp snagged; ger snagging) tr (a stocking) faire un accroc à

snail [snel] s escargot m; **at a snail's pace** à pas de tortue, comme un escargot

snake [snek] s serpent m || intr serpenter

snake' in the grass' s serpent m caché sous les fleurs; ami m perfide, traître m, individu m louche

snap [snæp] s (breaking) cassure f; (crackling sound) bruit m sec; (of the fingers) chiquenaude f; (bite) coup m de dents; (cookie) biscuit m croquant; (catch or fastener) bouton-pression m, fermoir m; (phot) instantané m; (slang) jeu m d'enfant, coup facile; **cold snap** coup m de froid; **it's a snap!** (slang) c'est du tout cuit! || v (pret & pp snapped; ger snapping) tr casser net; (one's fingers, a whip, etc.) faire claquer; (a picture, a scene) prendre un instantané de; **to snap up** happer, saisir || intr casser net; faire un bruit sec; (from fatigue) s'effondrer; **to snap at** donner un coup de dents à; (to speak sharply to) rembarrer; (an opportunity) saisir; **to snap out of it** (slang) se secouer; **to snap shut** se fermer avec un bruit sec

snap' course' s (slang) cours m tout mâché

snap'drag'on s (bot) gueule-de-loup f

snap' fas'tener s bouton-pression m

snap' judg'ment s décision f prise sans réflexion

snap·py ['snæpi] adj (comp -pier; super -piest) mordant, acariâtre; (quick, sudden) vif; **make it snappy!** (slang) grouillez-vous!

snap'shot' s instantané m

snare [sner] s collet m; (trap) piège m; (of a drum) timbre m, corde f de timbre || tr prendre au collet, prendre au piège

snare' drum' s caisse f claire

snarl [snɑrl] s (sound) grognement m; (intertwining) enchevêtrement m || tr dire en grognant; enchevêtrer || intr grogner; s'enchevêtrer

snatch [snætʃ] s arrachement m; petit moment m; (bit, scrap) bribe f, fragment m; (in weight lifting) arraché m || tr saisir brusquement, arracher; **to snatch from** arracher à; **to snatch up** ramasser vivement || intr—**to snatch at** saisir au vol

sneak [snik] adj furtif || s chipeur m, mauvais type m f tr (e.g., a drink) prendre à la dérobée; glisser furtivement; (coll) chiper || intr se glisser furtivement; **to sneak into** se faufiler dans; **to sneak out** s'esquiver

sneaker ['snikər] s espadrille f

sneak' thief' s chipeur m, voleur m à la tire

sneak·y ['sniki] adj (comp -ier; super -iest) furtif, sournois

sneer [snɪr] s ricanement m || intr ricaner; **to sneer at** se moquer de

sneeze [sniz] *s* éternuement *m* ‖ *intr* éternuer; **it's not to be sneezed at** (coll) il ne faut pas cracher dessus

snicker ['snɪkər] *s* rire *m* bête; (*sneer*) rire narquois; (*in response to smut*) petit rire grivois ‖ *intr* rire bêtement; **to snicker at** se moquer de

sniff [snɪf] *s* reniflement *m*; (*odor*) parfum *m*; (*e.g., of air*) bouffée *f* ‖ *tr* renifler; (*e.g., fresh air*) humer; (*e.g., a scandal*) flairer; **to sniff up** renifler ‖ *intr* renifler; **to sniff at** flairer; (*to disdain*) cracher sur

sniffle ['snɪfəl] *s* reniflement *m*; **to have the sniffles** être enchifrené ‖ *intr* renifler

snip [snɪp] *s* (*e.g., of cloth*) petit bout *m*; (*cut*) coup *m* de ciseaux; (*coll*) personne *f* insignifiante ‖ *v* (*pret & pp* snipped; *ger* snipping) *tr* couper; **to snip off** enlever, détacher

snipe [snaɪp] *s* (orn) bécassine *f* ‖ *intr* —to snipe at canarder

sniper ['snaɪpər] *s* tireur *m* embusqué

snippet ['snɪpɪt] *s* petit bout *m*, bribe *f*; personne *f* insignifiante

snip•py ['snɪpɪ] *adj* (*comp* -pier; *super* -piest) hautain, brusque

snitch [snɪtʃ] *tr* (coll) chaparder ‖ *intr* (coll) moucharder; **to snitch on** (coll) moucharder

sniv•el ['snɪvəl] *s* pleurnicherie *f*; (*mucus*) morve *f* ‖ *v* (*pret & pp* -eled or -elled; *ger* -eling or -elling) *intr* pleurnicher; (*to have a runny nose*) être morveux

snob [snɑb] *s* snob *m*

snobbery ['snɑbərɪ] *s* snobisme *m*

snobbish ['snɑbɪʃ] *adj* snob

snoop [snup] *s* (coll) curieux *m* ‖ *intr* (coll) fouiner, fureter

snoop•y ['snupɪ] *adj* (*comp* -ier; *super* -iest) (coll) curieux

snoot [snut] *s* (slang) nez *m*

snoot•y ['snutɪ] *adj* (*comp* -ier; *super* -iest) (slang) snob, hautain

snooze [snuz] *s* (coll) petit somme *m* ‖ *intr* (coll) sommeiller

snore [snor] *s* ronflement *m* ‖ *intr* ronfler

snort [snɔrt] *s* ébrouement *m*; (*of person, horse, etc.*) reniflement *m* ‖ *tr* dire en reniflant, grogner ‖ *intr* s'ébrouer, renifler bruyamment

snot [snɑt] *s* (slang) morve *f*

snot•ty ['snɑtɪ] *adj* (*comp* -tier; *super* -tiest) (coll) morveux; (slang) snob, hautain

snout [snaʊt] *s* museau *m*; (*of pig*) groin *m*; (*of bull*) mufle *m*; (*something shaped like the snout of an animal*) bec *m*, tuyère *f*

snow [sno] *s* neige *f* ‖ *intr* neiger; **it is snowing** il neige; **to shovel snow** balayer la neige

snow'ball' *s* boule *f* de neige ‖ *tr* lancer des boules de neige à ‖ *intr* faire boule de neige

snow' blind'ness *s* cécité *f* des neiges

snow'-capped' *adj* couronné de neige

snow'-clad' *adj* enneigé

snow'drift' *s* congère *f*

snow'fall' *s* chute *f* de neige; (*amount*) enneigement *m*

snow'flake' *s* flocon *m* de neige

snow' flur'ry *s* (*pl* -ries) bouffée *f* de neige

snow' line' *s* limite *f* des neiges éternelles

snow'man' *s* (*pl* -men') bonhomme *m* de neige

snow'plow' *s* chasse-neige *m*

snow'shoe' *s* raquette *f*

snow'slide' *s* avalanche *f*

snow'storm' *s* tempête *f* de neige

snow' tire' *s* pneu *m* à neige

snow'white' *adj* blanc comme la neige ‖ **Snowwhite** *s* Blanche-Neige *f*

snow•y ['sno-ɪ] *adj* (*comp* -ier; *super* -iest) neigeux

snow'y owl' *s* chouette *f* blanche

snub [snʌb] *s* affront *m*, rebuffade *f* ‖ *v* (*pret & pp* snubbed; *ger* snubbing) *tr* traiter avec froideur, rabrouer

snub•by ['snʌbɪ] *adj* (*comp* -bier; *super* -biest) trapu; (*nose*) camus

snub'-nosed' *adj* camard

snuff [snʌf] *s* tabac *m* à priser; (*of a candlewick*) mouchure *f*; **to be up to snuff** (*to be shrewd*) (slang) être dessalé; (*to be up to par*) (slang) être dégourdi ‖ *tr* priser; (*a candle*) moucher; **to snuff out** éteindre

snuff'box' *s* tabatière *f*

snuffers ['snʌfərz] *spl* mouchettes *fpl*

snug [snʌg] *adj* (*comp* snugger; *super* snuggest) confortable; (*garment*) être ajusté; (*bed*) douillet; (*sheltered*) abrité; (*hidden*) caché; **snug and warm** bien au chaud; **snug as a bug in a rug** comme un poisson dans l'eau

snuggle ['snʌgəl] *tr* serrer dans ses bras ‖ *intr* se pelotonner; **to snuggle up to** se serrer tout près de

so [so] *adv* si, tellement; ainsi; donc, par conséquent, aussi; **or so** plus ou moins; **so as to** afin de, pour; **so far** jusqu'ici; **so long!** (coll) à bientôt!; **so many** tant; **tant de**; **so much** tant; tant de; **so that** pour que, afin que; de sorte que; **so to speak** pour ainsi dire; **so what?** (slang) et alors?; **to hope so** espérer bien; **to think so** croire que oui ‖ *conj* (coll) de sorte que

soak [sok] *s* trempage *m*; (slang) sac *m* à vin, soûlard *m* ‖ *tr* tremper; (*to swindle*) (slang) estamper; **to soak to the skin** tremper jusqu'aux os ‖ *intr* tremper

so'-and-so' *s* (*pl* -sos) (pej) triste individu *m*, mauvais sujet *m*; **Mr. So-and-So** Monsieur un tel

soap [sop] *s* savon *m* ‖ *tr* savonner

soap'box' *s* caisse *f* à savon; (fig) plateforme *f*

soap'box or'ator *s* orateur *m* de carrefour

soap' bub'ble *s* bulle *f* de savon

soap' dish' *s* plateau *m* à savon

soap' fac'to•ry *s* (*pl* -ries) savonnerie *f*

soap' flakes' *spl* savon *m* en paillettes

soap' op'era *s* mélo *m*

soap' pow'der *s* savon *m* en poudre

soap'stone' s pierre f de savon; craie f de tailleur

soap'suds' spl mousse f de savon, eau f de savon

soap·y ['sopɪ] adj (comp **-ier**; super **-iest**) savonneux

soar [sor] intr planer dans les airs; prendre l'essor, monter subitement

sob [sɑb] s sanglot m || v (pret & pp **sobbed**; ger **sobbing**) intr sangloter

sober ['sobər] adj sobre; (expression) grave; (truth) simple; (not drunk) pas ivre; (no longer drunk) dégrisé || tr calmer; **to sober up** dégriser || intr— **to sober up** se dégriser

sobriety [so'braɪ·ətɪ] s sobriété f

sob' sis'ter s (slang) journaliste f larmoyante

sob' sto'ry s (pl **-ries**) (slang) lamentation f, jérémiade f

so'-called' adj dit; soi-disant, prétendu; ainsi nommé

soccer ['sɑkər] s football m

sociable ['soʃəbəl] adj sociable

social ['soʃəl] adj social || s réunion f sans cérémonie

so'cial climb'er s parvenu m, arriviste mf

so'cial events' spl mondanités fpl

socialism ['soʃə‚lɪzəm] s socialisme m

socialist ['soʃəlɪst] s socialiste mf

socialite ['soʃə‚laɪt] s (coll) membre m de la haute société

so'cial reg'ister s annuaire m de la haute société

so'cial secu'rity s sécurité f sociale, assistance f familiale

so'cial serv'ice s assistance f sociale, aide f sociale, aide familiale

so'cial stra'ta [‚streɪtə], [‚stræte] spl couches fpl sociales

so'cial work'er s assistant m social, travailleuse f familiale

socie·ty [sə'saɪ·ətɪ] s (pl **-ties**) société f

soci'ety col'umn s carnet m mondain

soci'ety ed'itor s chroniqueur m mondain

sociology [‚sosɪ'ɑlədʒɪ], [‚soʃɪ'ɑlədʒɪ] s sociologie f

sock [sɑk] s chaussette f; (slang) coup m de poing || tr (slang) donner un coup de poing à

socket ['sɑkɪt] s (of bone) cavité f, glène f; (of candlestick) tube m; (of caster) sabot m; (of eye) orbite f; (of tooth) alvéole m; (elec) douille f

sock'et joint' s joint m à rotule

sock'et wrench' s clé f à tube

sod [sɑd] s gazon m; motte f de gazon || v (pret & pp **sodded**; ger **sodding**) tr gazonner

soda ['sodə] s (soda water) soda m; (chem) soude f

so'da crack'er s biscuit m soda

so'da wa'ter s soda m

sodium ['sodɪ·əm] s sodium m

sofa ['sofə] s canapé m, sofa m

soft [sɔft], [sɑft] adj (yielding) mou; (mild) doux; (weak in character) faible; **to go soft** (coll) perdre la boule

soft'-boiled egg' s œuf m à la coque

soft' coal' s houille f grasse

soft' drink' s boisson f non-alcoolisée

soften ['sɔfən], ['sɑfən] tr amollir; (e.g., noise) atténuer; (one's voice) adoucir; (one's moral fiber) affaiblir; **to soften up** amollir || intr s'amollir; s'adoucir; s'affaiblir

soft' land'ing s (rok) arrivée f en douceur

soft' ped'al s (mus) pédale f sourde

soft'-ped'al v (pret & pp **-aled** or **-alled**; ger **-aling** or **-alling**) tr (coll) atténuer, modérer

soft' soap' s savon m mou, savon noir; (coll) pommade f

soft'-soap' tr (coll) passer de la pommade à

sog·gy ['sɑgɪ] adj (comp **-gier**; super **-giest**) saturé, détrempé

soil [sɔɪl] s sol m, terroir m || tr salir, souiller || intr se salir

soil' pipe' s tuyau m de descente

sojourn ['sodʒʌrn] s séjour m || ['so-dʒʌrn], [so'dʒʌrn] intr séjourner

solace ['sɑlɪs] s consolation f || tr consoler

solar ['solər] adj solaire

so'lar bat'tery s photopile f

sold [sold] adj—**sold out** (no more room) complet; (no more merchandise) épuisé; **to be sold on** (coll) raffoler de || interj (to the highest bidder) adjugé!

solder ['sɑdər] s soudure f || tr souder

sol'dering i'ron s fer m à souder

soldier ['soldʒər] s soldat m

sole [sol] adj seul, unique || s (of shoe) semelle f; (of foot) plante f; (fish) sole f || tr ressemeler

solemn ['sɑləm] adj sérieux, grave; (ceremony) solennel

solicit [sə'lɪsɪt] tr solliciter || intr quêter; (with immoral intentions) racoler

solicitor [sə'lɪsɪtər] s solliciteur m; agent m, représentant m; (com) démarcheur m; (law) procureur m; (Brit) avoué m

solicitous [sə'lɪsɪtəs] adj soucieux

solid ['sɑlɪd] adj solide; (clouds) dense; (gold) massif; (opinion) unanime; (color) uni; (hour, day, week) entier; (e.g., three days) d'affilée || s solide m

sol'id geom'etry s géométrie f dans l'espace

solidity [sə'lɪdɪtɪ] s solidité f, consistance f

solilo·quy [sə'lɪləkwɪ] s (pl **-quies**) soliloque m

solitaire ['sɑlɪ‚ter] s solitaire m; (cards) patience f, réussite f; **to play solitaire** faire une réussite

solitar·y ['sɑlɪ‚terɪ] adj solitaire || s (pl **-ies**) solitaire m

solitude ['sɑlɪ‚t(j)ud] s solitude f

so·lo ['solo] adj solo || s (pl **-los**) solo m

soloist ['solo·ɪst] s soliste mf

solstice ['sɑlstɪs] s solstice m

soluble ['sɑljəbəl] adj soluble

solution [sə'luʃən] s solution f
solvable ['salvəbəl] adj soluble
solve [salv] tr résoudre
solvency ['salvənsi] s solvabilité f
solvent ['salvənt] adj (substance) solu-
bilisant; (person or business) solvable
|| s (of a substance) solvant m
somber ['sambər] adj sombre
some [sʌm] adj indef quelque, du;
some way or other d'une manière ou
d'une autre || pron indef certains,
quelques-uns §81; en §87 || adv un
peu, passablement, assez; environ;
quelque, e.g., **some two hundred
soldiers** quelque deux cents soldats
some'bod'y pron indef quelqu'un §81;
somebody else quelqu'un d'autre || s
(pl -ies) (coll) quelqu'un m
some'day' adv un jour
some'how' adv dans un sens, je ne sais
comment; **somehow or other** d'une
manière ou d'une autre
some'one' pron indef quelqu'un §81
somersault ['sʌmər‚salt] s saut m périlleux
some'thing s (coll) quelque chose m ||
pron indef quelque chose (masc) ||
adv quelque peu, un peu
some'time' adj ancien, ci-devant || adv
un jour; un de ces jours
some'times' adv quelquefois, de temps
en temps; **sometimes . . . sometimes**
tantôt . . . tantôt
some'way' adv d'une manière ou d'une
autre
some'what' adv un peu, assez
some'where' adv quelque part; **somewhere else** ailleurs, autre part
somnambulist [sam'næmbjəlɪst] s somnambule mf
somnolent ['samnələnt] adj somnolent
son [sʌn] s fils m
sonata [sə'natə] s sonate f
song [sɔŋ], [saŋ] s chanson f; (of
praise) hymne m; **to buy for a song**
(coll) acheter pour une bouchée de
pain
song'bird' s oiseau m chanteur
song'book' s recueil m de chansons
Song' of Songs' s (Bib) Cantique m
des Cantiques
song' thrush' s grive f musicienne
song'writ'er s chansonnier m
sonic ['sanɪk] adj sonique
son'ic boom' s double bang m
son'-in-law' s (pl sons-in-law) gendre
m, beau fils m
sonnet ['sanɪt] s sonnet m
son-ny ['sʌni] s (pl -nies) fiston m
soon [sun] adv bientôt; (early) tôt; **as
soon as** aussitôt que, dès que, sitôt
que; **as soon as possible** le plus tôt
possible; **how soon** quand; **no sooner
said than done** sitôt dit sitôt fait;
soon after tôt après; **sooner** plus tôt;
(rather) (coll) plutôt; **sooner or later**
tôt ou tard; **so soon** si tôt; **too soon**
trop tôt
soot [sut], [sut] s suie f || tr—**soot
up** encrasser de suie || intr s'encras-
ser
soothe [suð] tr calmer, apaiser; flatter

soothsayer ['suθ‚se·ər] s devin m
soot-y ['suti], ['suti] adj (comp -ier;
super -iest) (color; flame) fuligineux;
couvert de suie
sop [sap] s morceaux m trempé; (fig)
os m à ronger, cadeau m || v (pret &
pp sopped; ger sopping) tr tremper,
faire tremper; **to sop up** absorber
sophisticated [sə'fɪstɪ‚ketɪd] adj mondain, sceptique; complexe
sophistication [sə‚fɪstɪ'keʃən] s mondanité f
sophomore ['safə‚mor] s étudiant m de
deuxième année
sophomoric [‚safə'mɔrɪk] adj naïf, suffisant, présomptueux
sopping ['sapɪŋ] adj détrempé, trempé
|| adv—**sopping wet** trempé comme
une soupe
sopran-o [sə'præno], [sə'prano] adj de
soprano || s (pl -os) soprano f; (boy)
soprano m
sorcerer ['sɔrsərər] s sorcier m
sorceress ['sɔrsərɪs] s sorcière f
sorcer-y ['sɔrsəri] s (pl -ies) sorcellerie f
sordid ['sɔrdɪd] adj sordide
sore [sor] adj douloureux, enflammé;
(coll) fâché || s plaie f, ulcère m
sore'head' s (coll) rouspéteur m, grincheux m
sorely ['sorli] adv gravement, grièvement; cruellement
soreness ['sornɪs] s douleur f, sensibilité f
sore' throat' s—to have a sore throat
avoir mal à la gorge
sorori-ty [sə'rarɪti], [sə'rorɪti] s (pl
-ties) club m d'étudiantes universitaires
sorrow ['saro], ['soro] s chagrin m,
peine f, affliction f, tristesse f || intr
s'affliger, avoir du chagrin; être en
deuil; **to sorrow for** s'affliger de
sorrowful ['sarəfəl], ['sɔrəfəl] adj (person) affligé, attristé; (news) affligeant
sor-ry ['sari], ['sɔri] adj (comp -rier;
super -riest) désolé, navré, fâché;
(appearance) piteux, misérable; (situation) triste; **to be or feel sorry** regretter; **to be or feel sorry for** regretter (q.ch.); plaindre (qn); **to be sorry
to + inf** regretter de + inf || interj
pardon!
sort [sɔrt] s sorte f, espèce f, genre m;
a sort of une espèce de; **out of sorts**
de mauvaise humeur || tr classer; **to
sort out** trier
so'-so' adj (coll) assez bon, passable,
supportable || adv assez bien, comme
ci comme ça
sot [sat] s ivrogne mf
soul [sol] s âme f; **not a soul** (coll) pas
un chat; **upon my soul!** par ma foi!
sound [saund] adj sain; solide, en bon
état; (sleep) profond || s son m;
(probe) sonde f; (geog) goulet m,
détroit m, bras m de mer || adv
(asleep) profondément || tr sonner;
(to take a sounding of) sonder; **to
sound out** sonder; **to sound the horn**
klaxonner, corner || intr sonner; son-

der; **to sound off** parler haut; **to sound strange** sembler bizarre

sound/ bar/rier *s* mur *m* du son

sound/ film/ *s* film *m* sonore

sound/ hole/ *s* (*of a violin*) ouïe *f*

soundly ['saʊndli] *adj* sainement; profondément; (*hard*) bien

sound/ post/ *s* (*of a violin*) âme *f*

sound/proof/ *adj* insonorisé, insonore || *tr* insonoriser

sound/ track/ *s* piste *f* sonore

sound/ wave/ *s* onde *f* sonore

soup [sup] *s* potage *m*, bouillon *m*; (*with vegetables*) soupe *f*; **in the soup** (*coll*) dans le pétrin or la mélasse

soup/ kitch/en *s* soupe *f* populaire

soup/ spoon/ *s* cuiller *f* à soupe

soup/ tureen/ *s* soupière *f*

sour [saʊr] *adj* aigre; (*grapes*) vert; (*apples*) sur; (*milk*) tourné || *tr* rendre aigre || *intr* tourner, s'aigrir

source [sɔrs] *s* source *f*

source/ lan/guage *s* langue *f* source

source/ mate/rial *s* sources *fpl* originales

sour/ cher/ry *s* (*pl* **-ries**) griotte *f*; (*tree*) griottier *m*

sour/ grapes/ *interj* ils sont trop verts!

sour/puss/ *s* (*slang*) grincheux *m*

south [saʊθ] *adj & s* sud *m*; **the South** (*of France, Italy, etc.*) le Midi; (*of U.S.A.*) le Sud || *adv* au sud, vers le sud

South/ Af/rica *s* la République sud-africaine

South/ Amer/ica *s* Amérique *f* du Sud; l'Amérique du Sud

South/ Amer/ican *adj* sud-américain || *s* (*person*) Sud-Américain *m*

south/east/ *adj & s* sud-est *m*

southern ['sʌðərn] *adj* du sud, méridional

southerner ['sʌðərnər] *s* Méridional *m*; (*U.S.A.*) sudiste *mf*

South/ Kore/a *s* Corée *f* du Sud; la Corée du Sud

South/ Kore/an *adj* sud-coréen || *s* (*person*) Sud-Coréen *m*

south/paw/ *adj & s* (*coll*) gaucher *m*

South/ Pole/ *s* pôle *m* Sud

South/ Vietnam•ese/ [vɪ ˌetnə'miz] *adj* sud-vietnamien || *s* (*pl* **-ese**) Sud-Vietnamien *m*

southward ['saʊθwərd] *adv* vers le sud

south/west/ *adj & s* sud-ouest *m*

souvenir [ˌsuvə'nɪr] *s* souvenir *m*

sovereign ['savrɪn], ['sʌvrɪn] *adj* souverain || *s* (*king; coin*) souverain *m*; (*queen*) souveraine *f*

sovereign•ty ['savrɪnti], ['sʌvrɪnti] *s* (*pl* **-ties**) souveraineté *f*

soviet ['sovɪ ˌet], [ˌsovɪ'et] *adj* soviétique || *s* soviet *m*; **Soviet** (*person*) Soviétique *mf*

So/viet Rus/sia *s* la Russie *f* soviétique

So/viet Un/ion *s* Union *f* soviétique

sow [saʊ] *s* truie *f*; [so] *v* (*pret* **sowed**; *pp* **sown** or **sowed**) *tr* (*seed; a field*) semer; (*a field*) ensemencer

soybean ['sɔɪ ˌbin] *s* soya *m*, soja *m*

spa [spa] *s* ville *f* d'eau, station *f* thermale, bains *mpl*

space [spes] *s* espace *m*; (*typ*) espace *f* || *tr* espacer

space/ age/ *s* âge *m* de l'exploration spatiale

space/ bar/ *s* barre *f* d'espacement

space/craft/ *s* astronef *f*

space/ flight/ *s* voyage *m* spatial, vol *m* spatial

space/ heat/er *s* chaufferette *f*

space/ hel/met *s* casque *m* de cosmonaute

space/man or **space/man** *s* (*pl* **-men/** or **-men**) homme *m* de l'espace, astronaute *m*, cosmonaute *m*

space/ probe/ *s* coup *m* de sonde dans l'espace; (*rocket*) fusée *f* sonde

spacer ['spesər] *s* (*of typewriter*) barre *f* d'espacement

space/ship/ *s* vaisseau *m* spatial, astronef *m*

space/ sta/tion *s* station *f* orbitale

space/ suit/ *s* (rok) scaphandre *m* des cosmonautes

space/ walk/ *s* promenade *f* dans l'espace

spacious ['speʃəs] *adj* spacieux

spade [sped] *s* bêche *f*; (*cards*) pique *m*; **to call a spade a spade** (coll) appeler un chat un chat

spade/work/ *s* gros travail *m*, défrichage *m*

spaghetti [spə'geti] *s* spaghetti *m*

Spain [spen] *s* Espagne *f*; l'Espagne

span [spæn] *s* portée *f*; (*of time*) durée *f*; (*of hand*) empan *m*; (*of wing*) envergure *f*; (*of bridge*) travée *f* || *v* (*pret & pp* **spanned**; *ger* **spanning**) *tr* couvrir, traverser

spangle ['spæŋgəl] *s* paillette *f* || *tr* orner de paillettes

Spaniard ['spænjərd] *s* Espagnol *m*

spaniel ['spænjəl] *s* épagneul *m*

Spanish ['spænɪʃ] *adj* espagnol || *s* (*language*) espagnol *m*; **the Spanish** (*persons*) les Espagnols *mpl*

Span/ish-Amer/ican *adj* hispano-américain || *s* Hispano-Américain *m*

Span/ish broom/ *s* genêt *m* d'Espagne

Span/ish fly/ *s* cantharide *f*

Span/ish Main/ *s* Terre *f* ferme; mer *f* des Antilles

Span/ish moss/ *s* tillandsie *f*

spank [spæŋk] *tr* fesser

spanking ['spæŋkɪŋ] *adj* (Brit) de premier ordre; **at a spanking pace** à toute vitesse || *s* fessée *f*

spar [spar] *s* (*mineral*) spath *m*; (naut) espar *m* || *v* (*pret & pp* **sparred**; *ger* **sparring**) *intr* s'entraîner à la boxe; se battre

spare [sper] *adj* (*thin*) maigre; (*available*) disponible; (*interchangeable*) de rechange; (*left over*) en surnombre || *tr* (*to save*) épargner, économiser; (*one's efforts*) ménager; (*a person*) faire grâce à, traiter avec indulgence; (*time, money, etc.*) disposer de; (*something*) se passer de

spare/ parts/ *spl* pièces *fpl* détachées, pièces de rechange

spare/rib/ *s* côte *f* découverte de porc, plat *m* de côtes

spare' room' s chambre f d'ami
spare' tire' s pneu m de rechange
spare' wheel' s roue f de secours
sparing ['spɛrɪŋ] adj économe, frugal
spark [spark] s étincelle f
spark' coil' s bobine f d'allumage
spark' gap' s (of induction coil) éclateur m; (of spark plug) entrefer m
sparkle ['sparkəl] s étincellement m, éclat m || intr étinceler
sparkling ['sparklɪŋ] adj étincelant; (wine) mousseux; (soft drink) gazeux
spark' plug' s bougie f
sparrow ['spæro] s moineau m
spar'row hawk' s épervier m
sparse [spars] adj clairsemé, rare; peu nombreux
Spartan ['spartən] adj spartiate || s Spartiate m
spasm ['spæzəm] s spasme m
spasmodic [spæz'madɪk] adj intermittent, irrégulier; (pathol) spasmodique
spastic ['spæstɪk] adj spasmodique
spat [spæt] s (coll) dispute f, prise f de bec; **spats** demi-guêtres fpl || v (pret & pp **spatted**; ger **spatting**) intr se disputer
spatial ['spe/əl] adj spatial, de l'espace
spatter ['spætər] s éclaboussure f || tr éclabousser
spatula ['spætʃələ] s spatule f
spawn [spɔn] s frai m || tr engendrer || intr frayer
spay [spe] tr châtrer
speak [spik] v (pret **spoke** [spok]; pp **spoken**) tr (a word, one's mind, the truth) dire; (a language) parler || intr parler; **so to speak** pour ainsi dire; **speaking!** à l'appareil!; **to speak out** or **up** parler plus haut, élever la voix; (fig) parler franc
speak'-eas'y s (pl -ies) bar m clandestin
speaker ['spikər] s parleur m; (person addressing a group) conférencier m; (presiding officer) speaker m, président m; (rad) haut-parleur m
spear [spɪr] s lance f || tr percer d'un coup de lance
spear'head' s fer m de lance; (mil) pointe f, avancée f || tr (e.g., a campaign) diriger
spear'mint' s menthe f verte
special ['spe/əl] adj spécial, particulier || s train m spécial
spe'cial-deliv'ery let'ter s lettre f exprès
specialist ['spe/əlɪst] s spécialiste mf
specialize ['spe/ə,laɪz] tr spécialiser || intr se spécialiser
special-ty ['spe/əlti] s (pl -ties) spécialité f
specie ['spisi] s—**in specie** en espèces
spe-cies ['spisiz] s (pl -cies) espèce f
specific [spɪ'sɪfɪk] adj & s spécifique m
specif'ic grav'ity s poids m spécifique
speci-fy ['spɛsɪ,faɪ] v (pret & pp -fied) tr spécifier
specimen ['spɛsɪmən] s spécimen m; (coll) drôle m de type
specious ['spi/əs] adj spécieux
speck [spɛk] s (on fruit, face, etc.) tache f; (in the distance) point m;

(small quantity) brin m, grain m, atome m || tr tacheter
speckle ['spɛkəl] s petite tache f || tr tacheter, moucheter
spectacle ['spɛktəkəl] s spectacle m; **spectacles** lunettes fpl
spec'tacle case' s étui m à lunettes
spectator ['spɛktetər], [spɛk'tetər] s spectateur m
specter ['spɛktər] s spectre m
spec-trum ['spɛktrəm] s (pl -tra [trə] or -trums) spectre m
speculate ['spɛkjə,let] intr spéculer
speculator ['spɛkjə,letər] s spéculateur m, boursicotier m
speech [spit/] s discours m; (language) langage m; (of a people or region) parler m; (power of speech) parole f; (theat) tirade f; **to make a speech** prononcer un discours
speech' clin'ic s centre m de rééducation de la parole
speech' correc'tion s rééducation f de la parole
speechless ['spit/lɪs] adj sans parole, muet; (fig) sidéré, stupéfié
speed [spid] s vitesse f; **at full speed** à toute vitesse || v (pret & pp **speeded** or **sped** [spɛd]) tr dépêcher, hâter || intr se dépêcher; **to speed up** aller plus vite
speeding ['spidɪŋ] s excès m de vitesse
speed' king' s as m du volant
speed' lim'it s vitesse f maximum
speedometer [spi'damɪtər] s indicateur m de vitesse
speed' rec'ord s record m de vitesse
speed'-up' s accélération f
speed'way' s (racetrack) piste f d'autos; (highway) autoroute f
speed-y ['spidi] adj (comp -ier; super -iest) rapide, vite, prompt
speed' zone' s zone f de vitesse surveillée
spell [spɛl] s sortilège m; intervalle m; (attack) accès m || v (pret & pp **spelled** or **spelt** [spɛlt]) tr (orally) épeler; (in writing) orthographier, écrire; **to spell out** (coll) expliquer en détail || v (pret & pp **spelled**) tr (to relieve) remplacer, relever, relayer
spell'bind'er s orateur m fascinant, orateur entraînant
spell'bound' adj fasciné
spelling ['spɛlɪŋ] s orthographe f
spell'ing bee' s concours m d'orthographe
spelunker [spɪ'lʌŋkər] s spéléo m
spend [spɛnd] v (pret & pp **spent** [spɛnt]) tr dépenser; (a period of time) passer
spender ['spɛndər] s dépensier m
spend'ing mon'ey s argent m de poche pour les menues dépenses
spend'thrift' s prodigue mf, grand dépensier m
sperm [spʌrm] s sperme m
sperm' whale' s cachalot m
spew [spju] tr & intr vomir
sphere [sfɪr] s sphère f; corps m céleste
spherical ['sfɛrɪkəl] adj sphérique

sphinx [sfɪŋks] *s* (*pl* **sphinxes** or **sphinges** [ˈsfɪndʒiz]) sphinx *m*

spice [spaɪs] *s* épice *f*; (fig) sel *m*, piquant *m* || *tr* épicer

spick-and-span [ˈspɪkəndˈspæn] *adj* brillant comme un sou neuf; tiré à quatre épingles

spic·y [ˈspaɪsi] *adj* (*comp* **-ier**; *super* **-iest**) épicé, aromatique; (*e.g., gravy*) relevé; (*conversation, etc.*) épicé, salé, piquant, grivois

spider [ˈspaɪdər] *s* araignée *f*

spi′der·web′ *s* toile *f* d'araignée

spiff·y [ˈspɪfi] *adj* (*comp* **-ier**; *super* **-iest**) (slang) épatant, élégant

spigot [ˈspɪgət] *s* robinet *m*

spike [spaɪk] *s* pointe *f*; (*nail*) clou *m* à large tête; (bot) épi *m*; (rr) crampon *m* || *tr* clouer; ruiner, supprimer; (*a drink*) (coll) corser à l'alcool || *intr* (bot) former des épis

spill [spɪl] *s* chute *f*, culbute *f* || *v* (*pret & pp* **spilled** or **spilt** [spɪlt]) *tr* renverser; (*a liquid*) répandre; (*a rider*) désarçonner; (*passengers*) verser || *intr* se répandre, s'écouler

spill′way′ *s* déversoir *m*

spin [spɪn] *s* tournoiement *m*, rotation *f*; (*on a ball*) effet *m*; (aer) vrille *f*; **to go for a spin** (coll) se balader en voiture; **to go into a spin** (aer) descendre en vrille || *v* (*pret & pp* **spun** [spʌn]; *ger* **spinning**) *tr* filer; faire tournoyer || *intr* filer; tournoyer

spinach [ˈspɪnɪtʃ], [ˈspɪnɪdʒ] *s* épinard *m*; (*leaves used as food*) des épinards

spinal [ˈspaɪnəl] *adj* spinal

spi′nal col′umn *s* colonne *f* vertébrale

spi′nal cord′ *s* moelle *f* épinière

spindle [ˈspɪndəl] *s* fuseau *m*

spin′-dri′er *s* essoreuse *f*

spin′-dry′ *v* (*pret & pp* **-dried**) *tr* essorer

spine [spaɪn] *s* épine *f* dorsale, échine *f*; (*quill, fin*) épine; (*ridge*) arête *f*; (*of book*) dos *m*; (fig) courage *m*

spineless [ˈspaɪnlɪs] *adj* sans épines; (*weak*) mou; **to be spineless** (fig) avoir l'échine souple

spinet [ˈspɪnɪt] *s* épinette *f*

spinner [ˈspɪnər] *s* fileur *m*; machine *f* à filer

spinning [ˈspɪnɪŋ] *adj* tournoyant || *s* (*act*) filage *m*; (*art*) filature *f*

spin′ning wheel′ *s* rouet *m*

spinster [ˈspɪnstər] *s* célibataire *f*, vieille fille *f*

spiraea [spaɪˈriə] *s* spirée *f*

spi·ral [ˈspaɪrəl] *adj* spiral, en spirale || *s* spirale *f* || *v* (*pret & pp* **-raled** or **-ralled**; *ger* **-raling** or **-ralling**) *intr* tourner en spirale; (aer) vriller

spi′ral stair′case *s* escalier *m* en colimaçon

spire [spaɪr] *s* aiguille *f*; (*of clock tower*) flèche *f*

spirit [ˈspɪrɪt] *s* esprit *m*; (*enthusiasm*) feu *m*; (*temper, genius*) génie *m*; (*ghost*) esprit, revenant *m*; **high spirits** joie *f*, abandon *m*; **spirits** (*alcoholic liquor*) esprit *m*, spiritueux *m*; **to raise the spirits of** remonter le courage de || *tr*—**to spirit away** enlever, faire disparaître mystérieusement

spirited *adj* animé, vigoureux

spiritless [ˈspɪrɪtlɪs] *adj* sans force, abattu, déprimé

spir′it lev′el *s* niveau *m* à bulle

spiritual [ˈspɪrɪt/u·əl] *adj* spirituel || *s* chant *m* religieux populaire

spiritualism [ˈspɪrɪt/u·ə,lɪzəm] *s* spiritisme *m*

spiritualist [ˈspɪrɪt/u·əlɪst] *s* spirite *mf*; (philos) spiritualiste *mf*

spir′ituous bev′erages [ˈspɪrɪt/u·əs] *spl* boissons *fpl* spiritueuses

spit [spɪt] *s* salive *f*; (culin) broche *f* || *v* (*pret & pp* **spat** [spæt]) or **spit**; *ger* **spitting**) *tr* & *intr* cracher

spite [spaɪt] *s* dépit *m*, rancune *f*; **in spite of** en dépit de, malgré || *tr* dépiter, contrarier

spiteful [ˈspaɪtfəl] *adj* rancunier

spit′fire′ *s* mégère *f*

spit′ting im′age *s* (coll) portrait *m* craché

spittoon [spɪˈtun] *s* crachoir *m*

splash [splæʃ] *s* éclaboussure *f*; (*of waves*) clapotis *m*; **to make a splash** (coll) faire sensation || *tr* & *intr* éclabousser

splash′down′ *s* (rok) amerrissage *m*

spleen [splin] *s* rate *f*; (fig) maussaderie *f*, mauvaise humeur *f*; **to vent one's spleen on** décharger sa bile sur

splendid [ˈsplɛndɪd] *adj* splendide; (coll) admirable, superbe

splendor [ˈsplɛndər] *s* splendeur *f*

splice [splaɪs] *s* (*in rope*) épissure *f*; (*in wood*) enture *f* || *tr* (*rope*) épisser; (*wood*) enter; (*film*) réparer, coller; (slang) marier

splint [splɪnt] *s* éclisse *f* || *tr* éclisser

splinter [ˈsplɪntər] *s* éclat *m*, éclisse *f*; (*lodged under the skin*) écharde *f* || *tr* briser en éclats || *intr* voler en éclats

splin′ter group′ *s* minorité *f* dissidente, groupe *m* fragmentaire

split [splɪt] *adj* fendu; (pea) cassé; (*skirt*) déchiré || *s* fente *f*, fissure *f*; (*quarrel*) rupture *f*; (*one's share*) part *f*; (*bottle*) quart *m*, demi *m*; (gymnastics) grand écart *m* || *v* (*pret & pp* **split**; *ger* **splitting**) *tr* fendre; (money; work; ticket) partager; (*in two*) couper; (*a hide*) dédoubler; **to split hairs** couper les cheveux en quatre; **to split one's sides laughing** se tenir les côtes de rire; **to split the difference** couper la poire en deux || *intr* se fendre; **to split away (from)** se séparer (de)

split′ fee′ *s* (*between doctors*) dichotomie *f*

split′ personal′ity *s* personnalité *f* dédoublée

split′ tick′et *s* (pol) panachage *m*

splitting [ˈsplɪtɪŋ] *adj* violent; (*headache*) atroce || *s* fendage *m*; (*of the atom*) désintégration *f*; (*of the personality*) dédoublement *m*

splotch [splɑtʃ] *s* tache *f* || *tr* tacher, barbouiller

splurge [splʌrdʒ] s (coll) épate f || intr (coll) se payer une fête; (to show off) (coll) faire de l'épate

splutter ['splʌtər] s crachement m || tr —to splutter out bredouiller || intr cracheter; (said of candle, grease, etc.) grésiller

spoil [spɔɪl] s (object of plunder) prise f, proie f; **spoils** (booty) butin m, dépouilles fpl; (emoluments, especially of public office) assiette f au beurre, part f du gâteau || v (pret & pp spoiled or spoilt [spɔɪlt]) tr gâter, abîmer || intr se gâter, s'abîmer; to be spoiling for (coll) brûler du désir de

spoilage ['spɔɪlɪdʒ] s déchet m

spoiled adj gâté

spoil'sport' s rabat-joie m

spoils' sys'tem s système m des postes aux petits copains

spoke [spok] s rai m, rayon m; (of a ladder) échelon m

spokes'man s (pl -men) porte-parole m

sponge [spʌndʒ] s éponge f || tr éponger; (a meal) (coll) écornifler || intr (coll) écornifler; to sponge on (coll) vivre aux crochets de

sponge' cake' s gâteau m de Savoie, gâteau mousseline

sponger ['spʌndʒər] s écornifleur m, pique-assiette f

sponge' rub'ber s caoutchouc m mousse

spon·gy ['spʌndʒi] adj (comp -gier; super -giest) spongieux

sponsor ['spɑnsər] s patron m; (godfather) parrain m; (godmother) marraine f; (law) garant m; (rad, telv) commanditaire m || tr patronner; (law) se porter garant de; (rad, telv) commanditer

spon·sor·ship' s patronnage m

spontaneous [spɑn'teni·əs] adj spontané

spoof [spuf] s (slang) mystification f; (slang) parodie f || tr (slang) mystifier; (slang) blaguer || intr (slang) blaguer

spook [spuk] s (coll) revenant m, spectre m

spool [spul] s bobine f

spoon [spun] s cuiller f; to be born with a silver spoon in one's mouth (coll) être né coiffé || tr prendre dans une cuiller; to spoon off enlever avec la cuiller || intr (coll) se faire des mamours

spooner ['spunər] s (coll) peloteur m

spoonerism ['spunə,rɪzəm] s contrepèterie f

spoon'-feed' v (pret & pp -fed) tr nourrir à la cuiller; (an industry) subventionner; (coll) mâcher la besogne à

spoonful ['spun,ful] s cuillerée f

spoon·y ['spuni] adj (comp -ier; super -iest) (coll) peloteur

sporadic(al) [spə'rædɪk(əl)] adj sporadique

spore [spor] s spore f

sport [sport] adj sportif, de sport || s sport m; amusement m, jeu m; (biol) mutation f; (coll) chic type m; **a good**

sport un bon copain; (a good loser) un beau joueur; **in sport** par plaisanterie; **to make sport of** tourner en ridicule || tr faire parade de, arborer || intr s'amuser, jouer

sport' clothes' spl vêtements mpl de sport

sport'ing goods' spl articles mpl de sport

sports'cast'er s radioreporter m sportif

sports' ed'itor s rédacteur m sportif

sports' fan' s fanatique mf, enragé m des sports

sports'man s (pl -men) sportif m

sports'man-like' adj sportif

sports'man-ship' s sportivité f

sports'wear' s vêtements mpl sport

sports'writ'er s reporter m sportif

sport·y ['sporti] adj (comp -ier; super -iest) (coll) sportif; (smart in dress) (coll) chic; (flashy) (coll) criard, voyant; (coll) dissolu, libertin

spot [spɑt] s tache f; (place) endroit m, lieu m; **on the spot** sur place; (slang) dans le pétrin; **spots** (before eyes) mouches fpl || v (pret & pp spotted; ger spotting) tr tacher; (coll) repérer, détecter || intr se tacher

spot' cash' s argent m comptant

spot' check' s échantillonnage m

spot'-check' tr échantillonner

spotless ['spɑtlɪs] adj sans tache

spot'light' s spot m; (aut) projecteur m auxiliaire orientable; to hold the spotlight (fig) être en vedette || tr diriger les projecteurs sur; (fig) mettre en vedette

spot' remov'er [rɪ,muvər] s détachant m

spot' weld'ing s soudage m par points

spouse [spauz], [spaus] s (man) époux m, conjoint m; (woman) épouse f, conjointe f

spout [spaut] s tuyau m de décharge; (e.g., of teapot) bec m; (of sprinkling can) col m, queue f; (of water) jet m || tr faire jaillir; (e.g., insults) (coll) déclamer || intr jaillir; to spout off (coll) déclamer

sprain [spren] s foulure f, entorse f || tr fouler, se fouler

sprawl [sprɔl] intr s'étaler, se carrer

spray [spre] s (of ocean) embruns mpl; (branch) rameau m; (for insects) liquide m insecticide; (for weeds) produit m herbicide; (for spraying insects or weeds) pulvérisateur m; (for spraying perfume) vaporisateur m || tr pulvériser; (with a vaporizer) vaporiser; (hort) désinfecter par pulvérisation d'insecticide; to spray paint on peindre au pistolet || intr— to spray out gicler

sprayer ['spre·ər] s vaporisateur m, pulvérisateur m

spray' gun' s pulvérisateur m; (for paint) pistolet m; (hort) seringue f

spread [spred] adj étendu, écarté, ouvert || s étendue f, rayonnement m; (on bed) dessus-de-lit m, couvre-lit m; (on sandwich) pâte f; (buffet lunch) collation f || v (pret & pp spread) *tr* étendre, étaler; (*news*) répandre; (*disease*) propager; (*the wings*) déployer; (*a piece of bread*) tartiner ‖ *intr* s'étendre, s'étaler; se répandre, rayonner

spree [sprī] *s* bombance *f*, orgie *f*; to go on a spree (coll) faire la bombe

sprig [sprɪg] *s* brin *m*, brindille *f*

spright·ly ['spraɪtli] *adj* (*comp* -lier; *super* -liest) vif, enjoué

spring [sprɪŋ] *adj* printanier ‖ *s* (*of water*) source *f*; (*season*) printemps *m*; (*jump*) saut *m*, bond *m*; (*elastic device*) ressort *m*; (*quality*) élasticité *f* ‖ *v* (*pret* sprang [spræŋ] *or* sprung [sprʌŋ]; *pp* sprung) *tr* (*the frame of a car*) faire déjeter; (*a lock*) faire jouer; (*a leak*) contracter; (*a question*) proposer à l'improviste; (*a prisoner*) (coll) faire sortir de prison ‖ *intr* sauter, bondir; (*said of oil, water, etc.*) jaillir; to spring up se lever; naître

spring'-and-fall' *adj* (*coat*) de demi-saison

spring'board' *s* tremplin *m*

spring' fe'ver *s* (hum) malaise *m* des premières chaleurs, flemme *f*

spring'like' *adj* printanier

spring'time' *s* printemps *m*

sprinkle ['sprɪŋkəl] *s* pluie *f* fine; (culin) pincée *f* ‖ *tr* (*with water*) asperger, arroser; (*with powder*) saupoudrer; (*to strew*) parsemer ‖ *intr* tomber en pluie fine

sprinkler ['sprɪŋklər] *s* arrosoir *m*

sprinkling ['sprɪŋklɪŋ] *s* aspersion *f*, arrosage *m*; (*with holy water*) aspersion; (*with powder*) saupoudrage *m*; (*of knowledge*) bribes *fpl*, notions *fpl*; (*of persons*) petit nombre *m*

sprin'kling can' *s* arrosoir *m*

sprint [sprɪnt] *s* course *f* de vitesse, sprint *m* ‖ *intr* faire une course de vitesse, courir à toute vitesse

sprite [spraɪt] *s* lutin *m*

sprocket ['sprɑkɪt] *s* dent *f* de pignon; (*wheel*) pignon *m* de chaîne

sprock'et wheel' *s* pignon *m* de chaîne

sprout [spraʊt] *s* pousse *f*, rejeton *m*; (*of seed*) germe *m* ‖ *intr* (*said of plant*) pousser, pointer; (*said of seed*) germer

spruce [sprus] *adj* pimpant, tiré à quatre épingles ‖ *s* sapin `m`; (*Norway spruce*) épicéa *m* commun ‖ *intr* —to spruce up se faire beau, se pomponner

spry [spraɪ] *adj* (*comp* spryer *or* sprier; *super* spryest *or* spriest) vif, alerte

spud [spʌd] *s* (*chisel*) bédane *f*; (agr) arrache-racines *m*; (coll) pomme *f* de terre, patate *f*

spun' glass' [spʌn] *s* coton *m* de verre

spunk [spʌŋk] *s* (coll) cran *m*, courage *m*

spur [spʌr] *s* éperon *m*; (*of rooster*) ergot *m*; (*stimulant*) aiguillon *m*, stimulant *m*; (rr) embranchement *m*; on the spur of the moment sous l'impulsion du moment ‖ *v* (*pret* & *pp*

spurred; *ger* spurring) *tr* éperonner; to spur on aiguillonner, stimuler

spurious ['spjʊrɪ·əs] *adj* faux; (*sentiments*) simulé, feint; (*document*) apocryphe

spurn [spʌrn] *tr* repousser avec mépris, faire fi de

spurt [spʌrt] *s* jaillissement *m*, giclée *f*, jet *m*; (*of enthusiasm*) élan *m*; effort *m* soudain ‖ *intr* jaillir; to spurt out gicler

sputnik ['sputnɪk], ['spʌtnɪk] *s* spoutnik *m*

sputter ['spʌtər] *s* (*manner of speaking*) bredouillement *m*; (*of candle*) grésillement *m*; (*of fire*) crachement *m* ‖ *tr* (*words*) débiter en lançant des postillons ‖ *intr* postillonner; (*said of candle*) grésiller; (*said of fire*) cracher, pétiller

spu·tum ['spjutəm] *s* (*pl* -ta [tə]) crachat *m*

spy [spaɪ] *s* (*pl* spies) espion *m* ‖ *v* (*pret* & *pp* spied) *tr* (*to catch sight of*) entrevoir; to spy out découvrir par ruse ‖ *intr* espionner; to spy on épier, guetter

spy'glass' *s* longue-vue *f*

spying ['spaɪ·ɪŋ] *s* espionnage *m*

spy' ring' *s* réseau *m* d'espionnage

squabble ['skwɑbəl] *s* chamaillerie *f* ‖ *intr* se chamailler

squad [skwɑd] *s* escouade *f*, peloton *m*; (*of detectives*) brigade *f*

squadron ['skwɑdrən] *s* (aer) escadrille *f*; (mil) escadron *m*; (nav) escadre *f*

squalid ['skwɑlɪd] *adj* sordide

squall [skwɔl] *s* bourrasque *f*, rafale *f*; (*cry*) braillement *m*; (coll) grabuge *m* ‖ *intr* souffler en bourrasque; brailler

squalor ['skwɑlər] *s* saleté *f*; misère *f*

squander ['skwɑndər] *tr* gaspiller

square [skwɛr] *adj* carré; (*honest*) loyal, franc; (*real*) véritable; (*conventional*) (slang) formaliste; nine (ten, etc.) inches square de neuf (dix, etc.) pouces en carré; nine (ten, etc.) square inches neuf (dix, etc.) pouces carrés; to get square with (coll) régler ses comptes avec; we'll call it square (coll) nous sommes quittes ‖ *s* carré *m*; (*of checkerboard or chessboard*) case *f*; (*city block*) pâté *m* de maisons; (*open area in town or city*) place *f*; (*of carpenter*) équerre *f*; to be on the square (coll) jouer franc jeu ‖ *adv* carrément ‖ *tr* carrer; (*a number*) élever au carré; (*wood, marble, etc.*) équarrir; (*a debt*) régler; (bk) balancer ‖ *intr*—to square off (coll) se mettre en posture de combat; to square with (*to tally with*) s'accorder avec; régler ses comptes avec

square' dance' *s* quadrille *m* américain

square' deal' *s* (coll) procédé *m* loyal

square' meal' *s* repas *m* copieux

square' root' *s* racine *f* carrée

squash [skwɑʃ] *s* écrasement *m*; (bot) courge *f*; (sports) squash *m* ‖ *tr* écraser ‖ *intr* s'écraser

squash·y ['skwaʃi] *adj* (*comp* **-ier**; *super* **-iest**) mou et humide; (*fruit*) à pulpe molle

squat [skwɑt] *adj* accroupi; (*heavyset*) trapu, ramassé || *s* position *f* accroupie || *v* (*pret & pp* **squatted**; *ger* **squatting**) *intr* s'accroupir; (*to settle*) s'installer sans titre légal

squatter ['skwɑtər] *s* squatter *m*

squaw [skwɔ] *s* femme *f* peau-rouge

squawk [skwɔk] *s* cri *m* rauque; (slang) protestation *f*, piaillerie *f* || *intr* pousser un cri rauque; (slang) protester, piailler

squeak [skwik] *s* grincement *m*; (*of living being*) couic *m*, petit cri *m* || *intr* grincer; pousser des petits cris, couiner

squeal [skwil] *s* cri *m* aigu || *intr* piailler; (slang) manger le morceau; **to squeal on** (slang) moucharder

squealer ['skwilər] *s* (coll) cafard *m*

squeamish ['skwimɪʃ] *adj* trop scrupuleux; prude; sujet aux nausées

squeeze [skwiz] *s* pression *f*; (coll) extorsion *f*; **it's a tight squeeze** (coll) ça tient tout juste || *tr* serrer; (*fruit*) presser; **to squeeze from** (coll) extorquer à; **to squeeze into** faire entrer de force dans || *intr* se blottir; **to squeeze through** se frayer un passage à travers

squeezer ['skwizər] *s* presse *f*, presse-fruits *m*

squelch [skweltʃ] *s* (coll) remarque *f* écrasante || *tr* écraser, réprimer

squid [skwɪd] *s* calmar *m*

squill [skwɪl] *s* (bot) scille *f*; (zool) squille *f*

squint [skwɪnt] *s* coup *m* d'œil furtif; (pathol) strabisme *m* || *tr* fermer à moitié || *intr* loucher; **to squint at** regarder furtivement

squint'-eyed' *adj* bigle, strabique; malveillant

squire [skwaɪr] *s* écuyer *m*; (*lady's escort*) cavalier *m* servant; (*property owner*) propriétaire *m* terrien; juge *m* de paix || *tr* escorter

squirm [skwʌrm] *s* tortillement *m* || *intr* se tortiller; **to squirm out of** se tirer de

squirrel ['skwʌrəl] *s* écureuil *m*

squirt [skwʌrt] *s* giclée *f*, jet *m*; (*syringe*) seringue *f*; (coll) morveux *m* || *tr* faire gicler || *intr* gicler, jaillir

stab [stæb] *s* coup *m* de poignard, de couteau; (*wound*) estafilade *f*; (coll) coup d'essai; **to make a stab at** (coll) s'essayer à || *v* (*pret & pp* **stabbed**; *ger* **stabbing**) *tr* poignarder

stabilize ['stebəl‚aɪz] *tr* stabiliser

stab' in the back' *s* coup *m* de Jarnac, coup de traître

stable ['stebəl] *adj* stable || *s* (*for cows*) étable *f*; (*for horses*) écurie *f*

stack [stæk] *s* tas *m*, pile *f*; (*of hay, straw, etc.*) meule *f*; (*of sheaves*) gerbier *m*; (*e.g., of rifles*) faisceau *m*; (*of ship or locomotive*) cheminée *f*; (*of fireplace*) souche *f*; **stacks** (*in library*) rayons *mpl* || *tr* entasser, em-

piler; mettre en meule, en gerbier, or en faisceau; (*a deck of cards*) truquer, donner un coup de pouce à; **to stack arms** former les faisceaux

stadi·um ['stedɪ‚əm] *s* (*pl* **-ums** or **-a** [ə]) stade *m*

staff [stæf], [stɑf] *s* bâton *m*; (*of pilgrim*) bourdon *m*; (*of flag*) hampe *f*; (*of newspaper*) rédaction *f*; (*employees*) personnel *m*; (*servants*) domestiques *mfpl*; (*support*) soutien *m*; (mil) état-major *m*; (mus) portée *f* || *tr* fournir, pourvoir de personnel; nommer le personnel pour

staff' head'quarters *spl* (mil) état-major *m*

staff' of'ficer *s* officier *m* d'état-major

stag [stæg] *adj* exclusivement masculin; **to go stag** aller sans compagne || *s* homme *m*; (zool) cerf *m*

stage [stedʒ] *s* stade *m*, étape *f*, phase *f*; (*of rocket*) étage *m*; (*stagecoach*) diligence *f*; (*scene*) champ *m* d'action, scène *f*; (*staging*) échafaudage *m*; (*platform*) estrade *f*; (*of microscope*) platine *f*; (theat) scène; **by easy stages** par petites étapes; **by successive stages** par échelons; **to go on the stage** monter sur les planches || *tr* (*a play, demonstration, riot, etc.*) monter; (*a play*) mettre en scène

stage'coach' *s* diligence *f*, coche *m*

stage'craft' *s* technique *f* de la scène

stage' door' *s* entrée *f* des artistes

stage'-door' John'ny *s* (*pl* **-nies**) coureur *m* de girls

stage' effect' *s* effet *m* scénique

stage' fright' *s* trac *m*

stage'hand' *s* machiniste *m*

stage' left' *s* côté *m* jardin

stage' man'ager *s* régisseur *m*

stage' name' *s* nom *m* de théâtre

stage' prop'erties *spl* accessoires *mpl*

stage' right' *s* côté *m* cour

stage'-struck' [strʌk] *adj* entiché de théâtre

stage' whis'per *s* aparté *m*

stagger ['stægər] *tr* ébranler; (*to surprise*) étonner; (*to arrange*) disposer en chicane, en zigzag; (*hours of work, train schedules, etc.*) échelonner || *intr* chanceler, tituber

staggering ['stægərɪŋ] *adj* chancelant; (*amazing*) étonnant

staging ['stedʒɪŋ] *s* échafaudage *m*; (theat) mise *f* en scène

stagnant ['stægnənt] *adj* stagnant

stag' par'ty *s* (*pl* **-ties**) (coll) réunion *f* entre hommes, réunion d'hommes seuls

staid [sted] *adj* posé, sérieux

stain [sten] *s* tache *f*, souillure *f* || *tr* tacher, souiller; (*to tint*) teindre || *intr* se tacher

stained' glass' *s* vitre *f* de couleur

stained'-glass win'dow *s* vitrail *m*

stain'less steel' ['stenlɪs] *s* acier *m* inoxydable

stair [ster] *s* escalier *m*; (*step of a series*) marche *f*, degré *m*; **stairs** escalier *m*

stair'case' *s* escalier *m*

stair′way′ s escalier m
stair′well′ s cage f d'escalier
stake [stek] s pieu m, poteau m; (of tent) piquet m; (marker) jalon m; (for burning condemned persons) bûcher m; (in a game of chance) mise f, enjeu m; **at stake** en jeu; **to pull up stakes** (coll) déménager ‖ tr (a road) bornoyer; (plants) échalasser, ramer; (money) risquer; (to back financially) (slang) fournir aux besoins de; **to stake all** mettre tout en jeu; **to stake off** or **out** jalonner, piqueter
stale [stel] adj (bread) rassis; (wine or beer) éventé; (air) confiné; (joke) vieux; (check) proscrit; (subject) rabattu; (news) défloré, défraîchi; **to smell stale** (said of room) sentir le renfermé
stale′mate′ s (chess) pat m; (fig) impasse f; **in stalemate** pat ‖ tr (chess) faire pat; (fig) paralyser
stalk [stɔk] s tige f; (of flower or leaf) queue f ‖ tr traquer, suivre à la piste ‖ intr marcher fièrement, marcher à grandes enjambées
stall [stɔl] s stalle f; (at a market) étal m, échoppe f; (slang) prétexte m ‖ tr mettre dans une stalle; (a car) caler; (an airplane) mettre en perte de vitesse; **to stall off** (coll) différer sous prétexte ‖ intr (said of motor) se bloquer; **to stall for time** (slang) temporiser
stallion [′stæljən] s étalon m
stalwart [′stɔlwərt] adj robuste; vaillant ‖ s partisan m loyal
stamen [′stemən] s étamine f
stamina [′stæmɪnə] s vigueur f, résistance f
stammer [′stæmər] s bégaiement m, balbutiement m ‖ tr & intr bégayer, balbutier
stammerer [′stæmərər] s bègue mf
stamp [stæmp] s empreinte f; (for postage) timbre m; (for stamping) poinçon m ‖ tr (mail) affranchir; (money; leather; a medal) frapper, estamper; (a document) timbrer; (a passport) viser; **to stamp one's feet** trépigner; **to stamp one's foot** frapper du pied; **to stamp out** (e.g., a rebellion) écraser, étouffer
stampede [stæm′pid] s débandade f; (rush) ruée f; (of people) sauve-quipeut m ‖ tr provoquer la ruée de ‖ intr se débander
stamped′ self′-addressed′ en′velope s enveloppe f timbrée par l'expéditeur
stamp′ing grounds′ spl—**to be on one's stamping grounds** (slang) être sur son terrain, être dans son domaine
stamp′ pad′ s tampon m encreur
stamp′-vend′ing machine′ s distributeur m automatique de timbres-poste
stance [stæns] s attitude f, posture f
stanch [stɑntʃ] adj ferme, solide; vrai, loyal; (watertight) étanche ‖ tr étancher
stand [stænd] s résistance f; position f; (of a merchant) étal m, éventaire m;

(of a speaker) tribune f, estrade f; (of a horse) aplombs mpl; (piece of furniture) guéridon m, console f; (to hold music, papers) pupitre m; (stands tribune f, stand m ‖ v (pret & pp stood [stud]) tr mettre, placer, poser; (the cold) supporter; (a shock; an attack) soutenir; (a round of drinks) (coll) payer; **to stand off** repousser; **to stand up** (to keep waiting) (coll) poser un lapin à ‖ intr se lever, se mettre debout; se tenir debout, être debout; en être, e.g., **how does it stand?** où en est-il?; **to stand aloof** or **aside** se tenir à l'écart; **to stand by** se tenir prêt; (e.g., a friend) rester fidèle à; **to stand fast** tenir bon; **to stand for** (to mean) signifier; (to affirm) soutenir; (to allow) tolérer; **to stand in for** doubler, remplacer; **to stand in line** faire la queue; **to stand out** sortir, saillir; **to stand up** se lever, se mettre debout; se tenir debout, être debout; **to stand up against** or **to** tenir tête à; **to stand up for** prendre fait et cause pour
standard [′stændərd] adj (product, part, unit) standard, de série, normal; (current) courant; (author, book, work) classique; (edition) définitif; (keyboard of typewriter) universel; (coinage) au titre ‖ s norme f, mesure f, règle f, pratique f; (of quantity, weight, value) standard m; (banner) étendard m; (of lamp) support m; (of wires) pylône m; (of coinage) titre m; (for a monetary system) étalon m; (fig) degré m, niveau m; **standards** critères mpl; **up to standard** suivant la norme
stand′-bear′er s porte-drapeau m
stand′ard gauge′ s voie f normale
standardize [′stændər‚daɪz] tr standardiser
stand′ard of liv′ing s niveau m de vie
stand′ard time′ s heure f légale
standee [stæn′di] s voyageur m debout; (theat) spectateur m debout
stand′-in′ s (mov, theat) doublure f, remplaçant m; (coll) appuis mpl, piston m
standing [′stændɪŋ] adj (upright) debout; (statue) en pied; (water) stagnant; (army; committee) permanent; (price; rule; rope) fixe; (custom) établi, courant; (jump) à pieds joints ‖ s standing m, position f, importance f; **in good standing** estimé, accrédité; **of long standing** de longue date
stand′ing ar′my s armée f permanente
stand′ing room′ s places fpl debout
stand′ing vote′ s vote m par assis et levé
stand′pat′ adj & s (coll) immobiliste mf
stand′pat′ter s (coll) immobiliste mf
stand′point′ s point m de vue
stand′still′ s arrêt m, immobilisation f; **to come to a standstill** s'arrêter court
stanza [′stænzə] s strophe f
staple [′stepəl] adj principal ‖ s (product) produit m principal; (for hold-

ing papers together) agrafe *f*; (bb) broche *f*; **staples** denrées *fpl* principales || *tr* agrafer; (*books*) brocher

stapler ['steplər] *s* agrafeuse *f*; (bb) brocheuse *f*

star [star] *s* astre *m*; (*heavenly body except sun and moon; figure that represents a star*) étoile *f*; (*of stage or screen*) vedette *f* || *v* (*pret & pp* **starred**; *ger* **starring**) *tr* étoiler, consteller; (mov, rad, telv, theat) mettre en vedette; (*typ*) marquer d'un astérisque || *intr* apparaître comme vedette

starboard ['starbərd], ['star‚bord] *adj* de tribord || *s* tribord *m* || *adv* à tribord

star′ board′er *s* (coll) pensionnaire *mf* de prédilection

starch [start∫] *s* amidon *m*; (*for fabrics*) empois *m*; (*formality*) raideur *f*; (bot, culin) fécule *f*; (coll) force *f*, vigueur *f* || *tr* empeser

starch·y ['start∫i] *adj* (*comp* **-ier**; *super* **-iest**) empesé; (*foods*) féculent; (*manner*) raide, guindé

stare [ster] *s* regard *m* fixe || *tr*—to **stare s.o. in the face** dévisager qn; (*to be obvious to s.o.*) sauter aux yeux de qn || *intr* regarder fixement; **to stare at** regarder fixement, dévisager

star′ fish′ *s* étoile *f* de mer

star′ gaze′ *intr* regarder les étoiles; rêvasser, être dans la lune

stark [stark] *adj* pur; rigide; désert, solitaire || *adv* entièrement

stark′ na′ked *adj* tout nu

star′ light′ *s* lumière *f* des étoiles

starling ['starlɪŋ] *s* étourneau *m*

star·ry ['stari] *adj* (*comp* **-rier**; *super* **-riest**) étoilé

Stars′ and Stripes′ *spl* bannière *f* étoilée

Star′-Spangled Ban′ner *s* bannière *f* étoilée

start [start] *s* commencement *m*, début *m*; (*sudden start*) sursaut *m*, haut-le-corps *m* || *tr* commencer; (*a car, a motor, etc.*) mettre en marche, démarrer; (*a conversation*) entamer; (*a hare*) lever; (*a deer*) lancer; **to start + ger** se mettre à + *inf* || *intr* commencer, débuter; démarrer; (*to be startled*) sursauter; **starting from** or **with** à partir de; **to start after** sortir à la recherche de; **to start out** se mettre en route

starter ['startər] *s* initiateur *m*; (aut) démarreur *m*; (sports) starter *m*

start′ ing point′ *s* point *m* de départ

startle ['startəl] *tr* faire tressaillir || *intr* tressaillir

startling ['startlɪŋ] *adj* effrayant; (*event*) sensationnel; (*resemblance*) saisissant

starvation [star've∫ən] *s* inanition *f*, famine *f*

starva′ tion di′ et *s* diète *f* absolue

starva′ tion wag′ es *spl* salaire *m* de famine

starve [starv] *tr* affamer; faire mourir

de faim; **to starve out** réduire par la faim || *intr* être affamé; être dans la misère; mourir de faim; (coll) mourir de faim

state [stet] *s* état *m*; (*pomp*) apparat *m*; **to lie in state** être exposé solennellement || *tr* affirmer, déclarer; (*an hour or date*) régler, fixer; (*a problem*) poser

stateless ['stetlɪs] *adj* apatride

state·ly ['stetli] *adj* (*comp* **-lier**; *super* **-liest**) majestueux, imposant

statement ['stetmənt] *s* énoncé *m*, exposé *m*; (*account, report*) compte rendu *m*, rapport *m*; (*of an account*) (com) relevé *m*

state′ of mind′ *s* état *m* d'esprit, état d'âme

state′ room′ *s* (naut) cabine *f*; (rr) compartiment *m*

states′ man *s* (*pl* **-men**) homme *m* d'État

static ['stætɪk] *adj* statique; (rad) parasite || *s* (rad) parasites *mpl*

station ['ste∫ən] *s* station *f*; (*for police; for selling gasoline; for broadcasting*) poste *m*; (*of bus, subway, rail line, taxi; for observation*) station; (rr) gare *f* || *tr* poster, placer

sta′ tion a′ gent *s* chef *m* de gare

stationary ['ste∫ən‚eri] *adj* stationnaire

sta′ tion break′ *s* (rad) pause *f*

stationer ['ste∫ənər] *s* papetier *m*

stationery ['ste∫ən‚eri] *s* papeterie *f*, fournitures *fpl* de bureau

sta′ tionery store′ *s* papeterie *f*

sta′ tion house′ *s* commissariat *m* de police

sta′ tion identifica′ tion *s* (rad) indicatif *m*

sta′ tion-mas′ ter *s* chef *m* de gare

sta′ tion wag′ on *s* familiale *f*, break *m*

statistical [stə'tɪstɪkəl] *adj* statistique

statistician [‚stætɪs'tɪ∫ən] *s* statisticien *m*

statistics [stə'tɪstɪks] *s* (*science*) statistique *f* || *spl* (*data*) statistique, statistiques

statue ['stæt∫u] *s* statue *f*

Stat′ ue of Lib′ erty *s* Liberté *f* éclairant le monde

statuesque [‚stæt∫u'esk] *adj* sculptural

stature ['stæt∫ər] *s* stature *f*, taille *f*; caractère *m*, stature

status ['stetəs] *s* condition *f*; rang *m*, standing *m*

sta′ tus quo′ [kwo] *s* statu quo *m*

sta′ tus seek′ er *s* obsédé *m* du standing

sta′ tus sym′ bol *s* symbole *m* du rang social

statute ['stæt∫ʊt] *s* statut *m*

statutory ['stæt∫ʊ‚tori] *adj* statutaire

staunch [stɔnt∫], [stant∫] *adj & tr* var of **stanch**

stave [stev] *s* bâton *m*; (*of barrel*) douve *f*; (*of ladder*) échelon *m*; (mus) portée *f* || *v* (*pret & pp* **staved** or **stove** [stov]) *tr*—to **stave in** défoncer, crever; **to stave off** détourner, éloigner

stay [ste] *s* (*visit*) séjour *m*; (*prop*) étai *m*; (*of a corset*) baleine *f*; (*of execution*) sursis *m*; (fig) soutien *m* ||

tr arrêter ‖ *intr* rester; séjourner; (*at a hotel*) descendre; **to stay put** ne pas bouger; **to stay up** veiller

stay'-at-home' *adj & s* casanier *m*

stead [sted] *s*—**in s.o.'s stead** à la place de qn; **to stand s.o. in good stead** être fort utile à qn

stead'fast' *adj* ferme; constant

stead·y ['stedi] *adj* (*comp* **-ier**; *super* **-iest**) ferme, solide; régulier; (*market*) soutenu ‖ *v* (*pret & pp* **-ied**) *tr* raffermir ‖ *intr* se raffermir

steak [stek] *s* (*slice*) tranche *f*; bifteck *m*

steal [stil] *s* (coll) vol *m*; (*bargain*) (coll) occasion *f* ‖ *v* (*pret* **stole** [stol]; *pp* **stolen**) *tr* voler; **to steal s.th. from s.o.** voler q.ch. à qn ‖ *intr* voler; **to steal away** se dérober; **to steal into** se glisser dans; **to steal upon** s'approcher en tapinois de

stealth [stelθ] *s*—**by stealth** en tapinois, à la dérobée

steam [stim] *s* vapeur *f*; (*e.g., on a window*) buée *f*; **full steam ahead!** en avant à toute vapeur!; **to get up steam** faire monter la pression; **to let off steam** lâcher la vapeur; (fig) s'épancher ‖ *tr* passer à la vapeur; (culin) cuire à la vapeur; **to steam up** (*e.g., a window*) embuer ‖ *intr* dégager de la vapeur, fumer; s'évaporer; **to steam ahead** avancer à la vapeur; (fig) faire des progrès rapides; **to steam up** s'embuer

steam'boat' *s* vapeur *m*

steam' chest' *s* boîte *f* à vapeur

steam' en'gine *s* machine *f* à vapeur

steamer ['stimər] *s* vapeur *m*

steam' heat' *s* chauffage *m* à la vapeur

steam' roll'er *s* rouleau *m* compresseur; (fig) force *f* irrésistible

steam'ship' *s* vapeur *m*

steam' shov'el *s* pelle *f* à vapeur

steam' ta'ble *s* table *f* à compartiments chauffés à la vapeur

steed [stid] *s* coursier *m*

steel [stil] *adj* (*industry*) sidérurgique ‖ *s* acier *m*; (*for striking fire from flint*) briquet *m*; (*for sharpening knives*) fusil *m* ‖ *tr* aciérer; **to steel oneself against** se cuirasser contre

steel' wool' *s* laine *f* d'acier, paille *f* de fer

steel'works' *spl* aciérie *f*

steelyard ['stil,jɑrd], ['stiljərd] *s* romaine *f*

steep [stip] *adj* raide, abrupt; (*cliff*) escarpé; (*price*) (coll) exorbitant ‖ *tr* tremper; (*e.g., tea*) infuser; **steeped in** saturé de; (*ignorance*) pétri de; (*the classics*) nourri de

steeple ['stipəl] *s* clocher *m*; (*spire*) flèche *f*

stee'ple·chase' *s* course *f* d'obstacles

steer [stɪr] *s* bouvillon *m* ‖ *tr* diriger, conduire; (naut) gouverner ‖ *intr* se diriger; (naut) se gouverner; **to steer clear of** (coll) éviter

steerage ['stɪrɪdʒ] *s* entrepont *m*

steer'age pas'senger *s* passager *m* d'entrepont

steer'ing wheel' *s* volant *m*; (naut) roue *f* de gouvernail

stellar ['stelər] *adj* stellaire; (*rôle*) de vedette

stem [stem] *s* (*of plant; of key*) tige *f*; (*of column; of tree*) fût *m*, tige; (*of fruit*) queue *f*; (*of pipe; of feather*) tuyau *m*; (*of goblet*) pied *m*; (*of watch*) remontoir *m*; (*of word*) radical *m*, thème *m*; (naut) étrave *f*; **from stem to stern** de l'étrave à l'étambot, d'un bout à l'autre ‖ *v* (*pret & pp* **stemmed**; *ger* **stemming**) *tr* (*e.g., grapes*) égrapper; (*e.g., the flow of blood*) étancher; (*the tide*) lutter contre, refouler; (*to check*) arrêter, endiguer ‖ *intr*—**to stem from** provenir de

stem'-wind'er *s* montre *f* à remontoir

stench [stentʃ] *s* puanteur *f*

sten·cil ['stensəl] *s* pochoir *m*; (*work produced by it*) travail *m* au pochoir; (*for reproducing typewriting*) stencil *m* ‖ *v* (*pret & pp* **-ciled** or **-cilled**; *ger* **-ciling** or **-cilling**) *tr* passer au pochoir; tirer au stencil

stenographer [stə'nɑɡrəfər] *s* sténo *f*, sténographe *mf*

stenography [stə'nɑɡrəfi] *s* sténographie *f*

step [step] *s* pas *m*; (*of staircase*) marche *f*, degré *m*; (*footprint*) trace *f*; (*of carriage*) marchepied *m*; (*of ladder*) échelon *m*; (*procedure*) démarche *f*; **in step with** au pas avec; **step by step** pas à pas; **watch your step!** prenez garde de tomber!; (fig) évitez tout faux pas! ‖ *v* (*pret & pp* **stepped**; *ger* **stepping**) *tr* échelonner; **to step off** mesurer au pas ‖ *intr* faire un pas; marcher; (coll) aller en toute hâte; **to step aside** s'écarter; **to step back** reculer; **to step in** entrer; **to step on it** (coll) mettre tous les gaz; **to step on the starter** appuyer sur le démarreur

step'broth'er *s* demi-frère *m*

step'child' *s* (*pl* **-child'ren**) beau-fils *m*; belle-fille *f*

step'daugh'ter *s* belle-fille *f*

step'fa'ther *s* beau-père *m*

step'lad'der *s* échelle *f* double, marche-pied *m*, escabeau *m*

step'moth'er *s* belle-mère *f*

steppe [step] *s* steppe *f*

step'ping stone' *s* pierre *f* de passage; (fig) marchepied *m*

step'sis'ter *s* demi-sœur *f*

step'son' *s* beau-fils *m*

stere·o ['sterɪ,o], ['stɪrɪ,o] *adj* (coll) stéréo, stéréophonique; (coll) stéréoscopique ‖ *s* (*pl* **-os**) (coll) disque *m* stéréo; (coll) émission *f* en stéréophonie; (coll) photographie *f* stéréoscopique

stereotyped ['sterɪ·ə,taɪpt], ['stɪrɪ·ə,taɪpt] *adj* stéréotypé

sterile ['sterɪl] *adj* stérile

sterilize ['sterɪ,laɪz] *tr* stériliser

sterling ['stɜrlɪŋ] *adj* de bon aloi ‖ *s* livres *fpl* sterling; argent *m* au titre; vaisselle *f* d'argent

stern [stʌrn] *adj* sévère, austère; *(look)* rébarbatif ǁ *s* poupe *f*

stethoscope ['steθə‚skop] *s* stéthoscope *m*

stevedore ['stivə‚dor] *s* arrimeur *m*

stew [st(j)u] *s* ragoût *m* ǁ *tr* mettre en ragoût ǁ *intr* (coll) être dans tous ses états

steward ['st(j)u‚ərd] *s* régisseur *m*, intendant *m*; maître d'hôtel; (aer, naut) steward *m*

stewardess ['st(j)u‚ərdɪs] *s* (aer) hôtesse *f* de l'air; (naut) stewardesse *f*

stewed′ fruit′ *s* compote *f*

stewed′ toma′toes *spl* purée *f* de tomates

stick [stɪk] *s* bâtonnet *m*, bâton *m*; *(rod)* verge *f*; *(wand; drumstick)* baguette *f*; *(of chewing gum; of dynamite)* bâton; *(firewood)* bois *m* sec; *(walking stick)* canne *f*; (naut) mât *m*; (typ) composteur *m* ǁ *v (pret & pp* stuck [stʌk]) *tr* piquer, enfoncer; *(to fasten in position)* clouer, ficher, planter; *(to glue)* coller; *(a pig)* saigner; (coll) confondre; **stick 'em up!** (slang) haut les mains!; **to be stuck** être pris; *(e.g., in the mud)* s'enliser; *(to be unable to continue)* (coll) être en panne; **to stick it out** (coll) tenir jusqu'au bout; **to stick out** *(one's tongue)* tirer; *(one's head)* passer; *(one's chest)* bomber; **to stick up** *(in order to rob)* (slang) voler à main armée ǁ *intr* se piquer, s'enfoncer; se ficher, se planter; *(to be jammed)* être pris, se coincer; *(to adhere)* coller; *(to remain)* continuer, rester; **to stick out** saillir, dépasser; *(to be evident)* sauter aux yeux; **to stick up for** (coll) prendre la défense de

sticker ['stɪkər] *s* étiquette *f* gommée; *(difficult question)* (coll) colle *f*

stick′pin′ *s* épingle *f* de cravate

stick′-up′ *s* (slang) attaque *f* à main armée, hold-up *m*

stick·y ['stɪki] *adj (comp* -ier; *super* -iest) gluant, collant; *(hands)* poisseux; *(weather)* étouffant; *(question)* épineux; *(unaccommodating)* tatillon

stiff [stɪf] *adj* raide; difficile, ardu; *(joint)* ankylosé; *(brush; batter)* dur; *(style, manner)* guindé, empesé; *(drink)* fort; *(price)* (coll) salé, exagéré ǁ *s (corpse)* (slang) macchabée *m*

stiff′ col′lar *s* col *m* empesé

stiffen ['stɪfən] *tr* raidir, tendre; (culin) épaissir ǁ *intr* se raidir

stiff′ neck′ *s* torticolis *m*

stiff′-necked′ *adj* obstiné, entêté

stiff′ shirt′ *s* chemise *f* empesée, chemise à plastron

stifle ['staɪfəl] *tr & intr* étouffer

stig·ma ['stɪgmə] *s (pl* -mas *or* -mata [mətə]) stigmate *m*

stigmatize ['stɪgmə‚taɪz] *tr* stigmatiser

stilet·to [stɪ'leto] *s (pl* -tos) stylet *m*

still [stɪl] *adj* tranquille, calme; immobile; silencieux; *(wine)* non mousseux ǁ *s* alambic *m*; (phot) image *f*; (mov) photogramme *m*; (poetic) silence *m* ǁ *adv (yet)* encore, toujours ǁ *conj* cependant, pourtant ǁ *tr* calmer, apaiser; *(to silence)* faire taire ǁ *intr* se calmer, s'apaiser; se taire

still′born′ *adj* mort-né

still′ life′ *s (pl* still lifes *or* still lives) nature *f* morte

stilt [stɪlt] *s* échasse *f*; *(in the water)* pilotis *m*

stilted *adj* guindé; (archit) surhaussé

stimulant ['stɪmjələnt] *adj & s* stimulant *m*

stimulate ['stɪmjə‚let] *tr* stimuler

stimu·lus ['stɪmjələs] *s (pl* -li [‚laɪ]) stimulant *m*, aiguillon *m*; (physiol) stimulus *m*

sting [stɪŋ] *s* piqûre *f*; *(stinging organ)* aiguillon *m*, dard *m* ǁ *v (pret & pp* stung [stʌŋ]) *tr & intr* piquer

stin·gy ['stɪndʒi] *adj (comp* -gier; *super* -giest) avare, pingre

stink [stɪŋk] *s* puanteur *f* ǁ *v (pret* stank [stæŋk]; *pp* stunk [stʌŋk]) *tr* —**to stink up** empester, empuantir ǁ *intr* puer, empester; **to stink of** puer, empester

stinker ['stɪŋkər] *s* (slang) peau *f* de vache, chameau *m*

stint [stɪnt] *s* tâche *f*, besogne *f*; **without stint** sans réserve, sans limite ǁ *tr* limiter, réduire; **to stint oneself** se priver ǁ *intr* lésiner, être chiche

stipend ['staɪpənd] *s* traitement *m*, honoraires *mpl*

stipulate ['stɪpjə‚let] *tr* stipuler

stir [stʌr] *s* remuement *m*, agitation *f*; *(prison)* (slang) bloc *m*; **to create a stir** faire sensation ǁ *v (pret & pp* stirred; *ger* stirring) *tr* remuer, agiter; **to stir up** *(trouble)* fomenter ǁ *intr* remuer, s'agiter, bouger

stirring ['stʌrɪŋ] *adj* entraînant

stirrup ['stʌrəp], ['stɪrəp] *s* étrier *m*

stitch [stɪtʃ] *s* point *m*; *(in knitting)* maille *f*; (surg) point de suture; **not a stitch of** (coll) pas un brin de; **stitch in the side** point de côté; **to be in stitches** (coll) se tenir les côtes ǁ *tr* coudre; (bb) brocher; (surg) suturer ǁ *intr* coudre

stock [stak] *s* approvisionnement *m*, stock *m*; *(assortment)* assortiment *m*; capital *m*, fonds *m*; *(shares)* valeurs *fpl*, actions *fpl*; *(of meat)* bouillon *m*; *(of a tree)* tronc *m*; *(of an anvil)* billot *m*; *(of a rifle)* crosse *f*; *(of a tree; of a family)* souche *f*; *(livestock)* bétail *m*, bestiaux *mpl*; *(handle)* poignée *f*; *(for dies)* tourne-à-gauche *m*; (hort) ente *f*; **in stock** en magasin; **on the stocks** (fig) sur le métier; **out of stock** épuisé; **stocks** *(for punishment)* pilori *m*; (naut) chantier *m*; **to take stock** faire le point; **to take stock in** (coll) faire grand cas de; **to take stock of** faire l'inventaire de ǁ *tr* approvisionner; garder en magasin; *(a forest or lake)* peupler; *(a farm)* monter en bétail; *(a pool)* empoissonner

stockade [stɑˈked] *s* palanque *f*, palissade *f* || *tr* palissader

stock′breed′er *s* éleveur *m* de bestiaux

stock′breed′ing *s* élevage *m*

stock′bro′ker *s* agent *m* de change, courtier *m* de bourse

stock′ car′ *s* (aut) voiture *f* de série; (rr) wagon *m* à bestiaux

stock′ com′pany *s* (com) société *f* anonyme; (theat) troupe *f* à demeure

stock′ div′idend *s* action *f* gratuite

stock′ exchange′ *s* bourse *f*

stock′hold′er *s* actionnaire *mf*

stocking [ˈstɑkɪŋ] *s* bas *m*

stock′ mar′ket *s* bourse *f*, marché *m* des valeurs; **to play the stock market** jouer à la bourse

stock′pile′ *s* stocks *mpl* de réserve || *tr & intr* stocker

stock′ rais′ing *s* élevage *m*

stock′room′ *s* magasin *m*

stock-y [ˈstɑki] *adj* (*comp* -ier; *super* -iest) trapu, costaud

stock′yard′ *s* parc *m* à bétail

stoic [ˈstoˑɪk] *adj & s* stoïque; **Stoic** stoïcien *m*

stoke [stok] *tr* (*a fire*) attiser; (*a furnace*) alimenter, charger

stoker [ˈstokər] *s* chauffeur *m*; (mach) stoker *m*

stolid [ˈstɑlɪd] *adj* flegmatique, impassible, lourd

stomach [ˈstʌmək] *s* estomac *m* || *tr* digérer; (coll) digérer, avaler

stom′ach ache′ *s* mal *m* d'estomac

stone [ston] *s* pierre *f*; (*of fruit*) noyau *m*; (pathol) calcul *m*; (typ) marbre *m* || *tr* lapider; (*fruit*) dénoyauter

stone′-broke′ *adj* (coll) complètement fauché, raide

stone′-deaf′ *adj* sourd comme un pot

stone′ma′son *s* maçon *m*

stone′ quar′ry *s* (*pl* -ries) carrière *f*

stone's′ throw′ *s*—**within a stone's throw** à un jet de pierre

ston-y [ˈstoni] *adj* (*comp* -ier; *super* -iest) pierreux; (fig) dur, endurci

stooge [studʒ] *s* (theat) compère *m*; (slang) homme *f* de paille, acolyte *m*

stool [stul] *s* tabouret *m*, escabeau *m*; (*bowel movement*) selles *fpl*

stool′ pi′geon *s* appeau *m*; (slang) mouchard *m*, mouton *m*

stoop [stup] *s* courbure *f*, inclinaison *f*; (*porch*) véranda *f* || *intr* se pencher; se tenir voûté; (*to debase oneself*) s'abaisser

stoop′-shoul′dered *adj* voûté

stop [stɑp] *s* arrêt *m*; (*in telegrams*) stop *m*; (*full stop*) point *m*; (*of a guitar*) touche *f*; (mus) jeu *m* d'orgue; (*public sign*) stop; **to put a stop to** mettre fin à || *v* (*pret & pp* stopped; *ger* stopping) *tr* arrêter; (*a check*) faire opposition à; **to stop up** boucher || *intr* s'arrêter, arrêter; **to stop + ger** cesser de + *inf*, s'arrêter de + *inf*; **to stop off** descendre en passant; **to stop off at** s'arrêter un moment à; **to stop over** (aer, naut) faire escale

stop′cock′ *s* robinet *m* d'arrêt

stop′gap′ *adj* provisoire || *s* bouche-trou *m*

stop′light′ *s* signal *m* lumineux; (aut) feu *m* stop, stop *m*

stop′o′ver *s* arrêt *m* en cours de route, étape *f*

stoppage [ˈstɑpɪdʒ] *s* arrêt *m*; (*of payments*) suspension *f*; (*of wages*) retenue *f*; obstruction *f*; (pathol) occlusion *f*

stopper [ˈstɑpər] *s* bouchon *m*, tampon *m*

stop′ sign′ *s* signal *m* d'arrêt

stop′ thief′ *interj* au voleur!

stop′watch′ *s* chronomètre *m* à déclic, compte-secondes *m*

storage [ˈstorɪdʒ] *s* emmagasinage *m*, entreposage *m*; **to put in storage** entreposer

stor′age bat′ter-y *s* (*pl* -ies) (elec) accumulateur *m*, accu *m*

store [stor] *s* magasin *m*, boutique *f*; approvisionnement *m*; (*warehouse*) (Brit) entrepôt *m*; stores matériel *m*; vivres *mpl*; **to set great store by** faire grand cas de || *tr* emmagasiner; (*to warehouse*) entreposer; (*to supply or stock*) approvisionner; **to store away** or up accumuler

store′house′ *s* magasin *m*, entrepôt *m*; (*of information*) mine *f*

store′keep′er *s* boutiquier *m*

store′room′ *s* dépense *f*, office *f*; (*for furniture*) garde-meuble *m*; (naut) soute *f*

stork [stɔrk] *s* cigogne *f*

storm [stɔrm] *s* orage *m*; (mil) assaut *m*; (fig) tempête *f*; **to take by storm** prendre d'assaut || *tr* livrer l'assaut à || *intr* faire de l'orage; (fig) tempêter

storm′ cloud′ *s* nuage *m* orageux; (fig) nuage noir

storm′ door′ *s* contre-porte *f*

storm′ pet′rel [ˈpetrəl] *s* oiseau *m* des tempêtes

storm′ sash′ *s* contre-fenêtre *f*

storm′ troops′ *spl* troupes *fpl* d'assaut

storm′ win′dow *s* contre-fenêtre *f*

storm-y [ˈstɔrmi] *adj* (*comp* -ier; *super* -iest) orageux

sto-ry [ˈstori] *s* (*pl* -ries) histoire *f*; (*tale*) conte *m*; (*plot*) intrigue *f*; (*floor*) étage *m*; (coll) mensonge *m*, histoire

sto′ry-tel′ler *s* conteur *m*; (*fibber*) menteur *m*

stout [staut] *adj* corpulent, gros; vaillant; ferme, résolu; (*strong*) fort || *s* stout *m*

stout′-heart′ed *adj* au cœur vaillant

stove [stov] *s* (*for heating a house or room*) poêle *m*; (*for cooking*) fourneau *m* de cuisine, cuisinière *f*

stove′pipe′ *s* tuyau *m* de poêle; (*hat*) (coll) huit-reflets *m*, tuyau de poêle

stow [sto] *tr* mettre en place, ranger; (naut) arrimer; **to stow with** remplir de || *intr*—**to stow away** s'embarquer clandestinement

stowage [ˈstoˑɪdʒ] *s* arrimage *m*; (*costs*) frais *mpl* d'arrimage

stow′away′ *s* passager *m* clandestin

straddle ['strædəl] *tr* enfourcher, chevaucher || *intr* se mettre à califourchon; (coll) répondre en normand

strafe [straf], [stref] *s* (slang) bombardement *m*, marmitage *m* || *tr* (slang) bombarder, marmiter

straggle ['strægəl] *intr* traîner; (*to be scattered*) s'éparpiller; **to straggle along** marcher sans ordre

straggler ['stræglər] *s* traînard *m*

straight [stret] *adj* droit; direct; loyal, honnête; correct, en ordre; (*hair*) raide; (*whiskey*) sec; (*candid*) franc; (*hanging straight*) d'aplomb; **to set s.o. straight** faire la leçon à qn || *s* (poker) séquence *f* || *adv* droit; directement; loyalement, honnêtement; (*without interruption*) de suite; **straight ahead** tout droit; **straight out** franchement, sans detours; **straight through** de part en part; (*d'un bout à l'autre*); **to go straight** (coll) vivre honnêtement

straighten ['stretən] *tr* redresser; mettre en ordre || *intr* se redresser

straight' face' *s*—**to keep a straight face** montrer un front sérieux

straight'for'ward *adj* franc, direct; loyal

straight' off' *adv* sur-le-champ, d'emblée

straight' ra'zor *s* rasoir *m* à main

straight'way' *adv* sur-le-champ, d'emblée

strain [stren] *s* tension *f*; (*of a muscle*) foulure *f*; (*descendants*) lignée *f*; (*ancestry; type of virus*) souche *f*; (*trait*) héritage *m*, tendance *f*; (*vein*) ton *m*, sens *m*; (*bit*) trace *f*; (coll) grand effort *m*; **mental strain** surmenage *m* intellectuel; **strains** (*of, e.g., the Marseillaise*) accents *mpl*; **sweet strains** doux accords *mpl* || *tr* forcer; (*e.g., a wrist*) se fouler; (*e.g., one's eyes*) se fatiguer; (*e.g., part of a machine*) déformer; (*e.g., a liquid*) filtrer, tamiser; **to strain oneself** se surmener || *intr* s'efforcer; filtrer, tamiser; (*to trickle*) suinter; (*said of beam, ship, motor, etc.*) fatiguer; **to strain at** (*a leash, rope, etc.*) tirer sur; (*to balk at*) reculer devant

strained *adj* (*smile*) forcé; (*friendship*) tendu

strainer ['strenər] *s* passoire *f*, filtre *m*

strait [stret] *s* détroit *m*; **straits** détroit; **to be in dire straits** être dans la plus grande gêne

strait' jack'et *s* camisole *f* de force

strait'-laced' *adj* prude, collet monté, puritain

Straits' of Do'ver *spl* Pas *m* de Calais

strand [strænd] *s* (*beach*) plage *f*, grève *f*; (*of rope or cable*) toron *m*; (*of thread*) brin *m*; (*of pearls*) collier *m*; (*of hair*) cheveu *m* || *tr* toronner; **to undo strands of** décorder; (*a ship*) échouer

stranded *adj* abandonné; (*lost*) égaré; (*ship*) échoué; (*rope or cable*) à torons; **to leave s.o. stranded** laisser qn en plan

strange [strendʒ] *adj* étrange; (*unfamiliar*) inconnu, étranger; (*unaccustomed*) inhabituel

stranger ['strendʒər] *s* étranger *m*; visiteur *m*

strangle ['stræŋgəl] *tr* étrangler, étouffer || *intr* s'étrangler

strap [stræp] *s* (*of leather, rubber, etc.*) courroie *f*; (*of cloth, metal, leather, etc.*) bande *f*; (*to sharpen a razor*) cuir *m* à rasoir; (*of, e.g., a harness*) sangle *f* || *v* (*pret & pp* strapped; *ger* strapping) *tr* attacher avec une courroie, sangler; (*a razor*) repasser sur le cuir

strap'hang'er *s* (coll) voyageur *m* debout

strapping ['stræpɪŋ] *adj* bien découplé, robuste; (coll) énorme, gros

stratagem ['strætədʒəm] *s* stratagème *m*

strategic(al) [strə'tidʒɪk(əl)] *adj* stratégique

strategist ['strætɪdʒɪst] *s* stratège *m*

strate·gy ['strætɪdʒɪ] *s* (*pl* -gies) stratégie *f*

strati·fy ['strætɪ,faɪ] *v* (*pret & pp* -fied) *tr* stratifier || *intr* se stratifier

stratosphere ['strætə,sfɪr], ['stretə,sfɪr] *s* stratosphère *f*

stra·tum ['stretəm], ['strætəm] *s* (*pl* -ta [tə] *or* -tums) couche *f*; (*e.g., of society*) classe *f*, couche

straw [strɔ] *s* paille *f*; (*for drinking*) chalumeau *m*, paille; **it's the last straw!** c'est le bouquet!

straw'ber'ry *s* (*pl* -ries) fraise *f*; (*plant*) fraisier *m*

straw'hat' *s* chapeau *m* de paille; (*skimmer*) canotier *m*

straw' man' *s* (*pl* men') (*figurehead*) homme *m* de paille; (*scarecrow*) épouvantail *m*; (*red herring*) canard *m*, diversion *f*

straw' mat'tress *s* paillasse *f*

straw' vote' *s* vote *m* d'essai

stray [stre] *adj* égaré; (*bullet*) perdu; (*scattered*) épars || *s* animal *m* égaré || *intr* s'égarer

streak [strik] *s* raie *f*, rayure *f*, bande *f*; (*of light*) trait *m*, filet *m*; (*of lightning*) éclair *m*; (*layer*) veine *f*; (*bit*) trace *f*; **like a streak** comme un éclair; **streak of luck** filon *m* || *tr* rayer, strier, zébrer || *intr* faire des raies; passer comme un éclair

stream [strim] *s* ruisseau *m*; (*steady flow of current*) courant *m*; (*of people, abuse, light, etc.*) flot *m*; (*of, e.g., automobiles*) défilé *m* || *intr* couler; (*said of blood*) ruisseler; (*said of light*) jaillir; (*said of flag*) flotter; **to stream out** sortir à flots

streamer ['strimər] *s* banderole *f*

stream'lined' *adj* aérodynamique, caréné; (fig) abrégé, concis

stream'lin'er *s* train *m* caréné de luxe

street [strit] *s* rue *f*; (*surface of the street*) chaussée *f*

street' Ar'ab *s* gamin *m* des rues

street'car' *s* tramway *m*

street' clean'er *s* balayeur *m*; (mach) balayeuse *f*

street' clothes' *spl* vêtements *mpl* de ville

street' floor' *s* rez-de-chaussée *m*

street'light' *s* réverbère *m*

street' sprink'ler *s* arroseuse *f*

street' u'rinal *s* vespasienne *f*, édicule *m*, urinoir *m*

street'walk'er *s* racoleuse *f*, fille *f* des rues

strength [strɛŋθ] *s* force *f*; intensité *f*; *(of a fabric)* solidité *f*; *(of spirituous liquors)* degré *m*, titre *m*; *(com)* tendance *f* à la hausse; *(mil)* effectif *m*; **on the strength of** sur la foi de

strengthen ['strɛŋθən] *tr* fortifier, renforcer; consolider ‖ *intr* se fortifier, se renforcer

strenuous ['strɛnjʊ·əs] *adj* actif, énergique; *(work)* ardu; *(effort)* acharné; *(objection)* vigoureux

stress [strɛs] *s* tension *f*, force *f*; *(mach)* stress *m*, tension *f*; *(phonet)* accent *m* d'intensité; **to lay stress on** insister sur ‖ *tr (e.g., a beam)* charger; *(a syllable)* accentuer; insister sur, appuyer sur

stress' ac'cent *s* accent *m* d'intensité

stretch [strɛtʃ] *s* allongement *m*; *(of the arm, of the meaning)* extension *f*; *(of the imagination)* effort *m*; *(distance in time or space)* intervalle *m*; *(section of road)* section *f*; *(section of country, water, etc.)* étendue *f*; **at a stretch** d'un trait; **in one stretch** d'une seule traite; **to do a stretch** (slang) faire de la taule ‖ *tr* tendre; *(the sense of a word)* forcer; *(a sauce)* allonger; **to stretch oneself** s'étirer; **to stretch out** allonger, étendre; *(the hand)* tendre ‖ *intr* s'étirer; *(said of shoes, gloves, etc.)* s'élargir; **to stretch out** s'allonger, s'étendre

stretcher ['strɛtʃər] *s (for gloves, trousers, etc.)* tendeur *m*; *(for a painting)* châssis *m*; *(to carry sick or wounded)* civière *f*, brancard *m*

stretch'er-bear'er *s* brancardier *m*

strew [stru] *v (pret strewed; pp strewed or strewn)* *tr* semer, éparpiller; *(e.g., with flowers)* joncher, parsemer

stricken ['strɪkən] *adj* frappé; *(e.g., with grief)* affligé; *(crossed out)* rayé; **stricken with** atteint de

strict [strɪkt] *adj* strict; *(exacting)* sévère

stricture ['strɪktʃər] *s* critique *f* sévère; *(pathol)* rétrécissement *m*

stride [straɪd] *s* enjambée *f*; **to hit one's stride** attraper la cadence; **to make great (or rapid) strides** avancer à grands pas; **to take in one's stride** faire sans le moindre effort ‖ *v (pret strode* [strod]; *pp stridden* ['strɪdən]) *tr* parcourir à grandes enjambées; *(to straddle)* enfourcher ‖ *intr* **—to stride across or over** enjamber; **to stride along** marcher à grandes enjambées

strident ['straɪdənt] *adj* strident

strife [straɪf] *s* lutte *f*

strike [straɪk] *s (blow)* coup *m*; *(stopping of work)* grève *f*; *(discovery of*

ore, oil, etc.) rencontre *f*; *(baseball)* coup du batteur; **to go on strike** se mettre en grève ‖ *v (pret & pp struck* [strʌk]) *tr* frapper; *(coins)* frapper; *(a match)* frotter; *(a bargain)* conclure; *(camp)* lever; *(the sails; the colors)* amener; *(the hour)* sonner; *(root; a pose)* prendre; **how does he strike you?** quelle impression vous fait-il?; **to strike it rich** trouver le filon; **to strike out** rayer; **to strike up** *(a song, piece of music, etc.)* attaquer, entonner; *(an acquaintance, conversation, etc.)* lier ‖ *intr* frapper; *(said of clock)* sonner; *(said of workers)* faire la grève; *(mil)* donner l'assaut; **to strike out** se mettre en route

strike'break'er *s* briseur *m* de grève, jaune *m*

striker ['straɪkər] *s* frappeur *m*; *(on door)* marteau *m*; *(worker on strike)* gréviste *mf*

striking ['straɪkɪŋ] *adj* frappant, saisissant; *(workers)* en grève

strik'ing pow'er *s* force *f* de frappe

string [strɪŋ] *s* ficelle *f*; *(of onions or garlic; of islands; of pearls; of abuse)* chapelet *m*; *(of words, insults)* enfilade *f*, kyrielle *f*; *(e.g., of cars)* file *f*; *(of beans)* fil *m*; *(for shoes)* lacet *m*; *(mus)* corde *f*; **strings** instruments *mpl* à cordes; **to pull strings** (fig) tirer les ficelles; **with no strings attached** (coll) sans restriction ‖ *v (pret & pp strung* [strʌŋ]) *tr* mettre une ficelle à, garnir de cordes; *(e.g., a violin)* mettre les cordes à; *(a bow)* bander; *(a tennis racket)* corder; *(beads, sentences, etc.)* enfiler; *(a cord, a thread, a wire, etc.)* tendre; *(to tune)* monter; **to string along** (slang) lanterner, faire marcher; **to string up** (coll) pendre ‖ *intr* **—to string along with** (slang) collaborer avec, suivre

string' bean' *s* haricot *m* vert

stringed' in'strument *s* instrument *m* à cordes

stringent ['strɪndʒənt] *adj* rigoureux; *(tight)* tendu; *(convincing)* convaincant

string' quartet' *s* quatuor *m* à cordes

stringy ['strɪŋi] *adj (comp -ier; super -iest)* fibreux, filandreux

strip [strɪp] *s (of paper, cloth, land)* bande *f*; *(of metal)* lame *f*, ruban *m* ‖ *v (pret & pp stripped; ger stripping)* *tr* dépouiller; *(to strip bare)* mettre à nu; *(the bed)* défaire; *(a screw)* arracher le filet de, faire foirer; *(tobacco)* écoter; **to strip down** *(e.g., a motor)* démonter; **to strip off** enlever; *(e.g., bark)* écorcer ‖ *intr* se déshabiller

stripe [straɪp] *s* raie *f*, bande *f*; *(on cloth)* rayure *f*; *(flesh wound)* marque *f*; *(mil, nav)* chevron *m*, galon *m*; **to win one's stripes** gagner ses galons ‖ *tr* rayer

strip' min'ing *s* exploitation *f* minière à ciel ouvert

strip'tease' s strip-tease m, déshabillage m suggestif

stripteaser ['strɪp,tizər] s effeuilleuse f, strip-teaseuse f

strive [straɪv] v (pret strove [strov]; pp striven ['strɪvən]) intr s'efforcer; to strive after rechercher; to strive against lutter contre; to strive to s'efforcer à, s'évertuer à

stroke [strok] s coup m; (of pen; of wit) trait m; (of arms in swimming) brassée f; (caress with hand) caresse f de la main; (of a piston) course f; (of lightning) foudre f; (pathol) attaque f d'apoplexie; at the stroke of sonnant, e.g., at the stroke of five à cinq heures sonnantes; to not do a stroke of work ne pas en ficher une ramée || tr caresser de la main

stroll [strol] s promenade f; to take a stroll aller faire un tour || intr se promener

stroller ['strolər] s promeneur m; (for babies) poussette f

strong [strɔŋ], [strɑŋ] adj (comp stronger ['strɔŋgər], ['strɑŋgər]; super strongest ['strɔŋgɪst], ['strɑŋgɪst]) fort; (stock market) ferme; (musical beat) marqué; (spicy) piquant; (rancid) rance

strong'box' s coffre-fort m

strong' drink' s boissons fpl spiritueuses

strong'hold' s place f forte

strong' man' s (pl men') (e.g., in a circus) hercule m forain; (leader, good planner) animateur m; (dictator) chef m autoritaire

strong'-mind'ed adj résolu, décidé; (woman) hommasse

strontium ['strɑn/ɪ-əm] s strontium m

strop [strɑp] s cuir m à rasoir || v (pret & pp stropped; ger stropping) tr repasser sur le cuir

strophe ['strofi] s strophe f

structure ['strʌkt/ər] s structure f; (building) édifice m

struggle ['strʌgəl] s lutte f || intr lutter; to struggle along avancer péniblement; to struggle for exist'ence s lutte f pour la vie

strum [strʌm] v (pret & pp strummed; ger strumming) tr (an instrument) gratter de; (a tune) tapoter || intr jouailler; to strum on plaquer des arpèges sur

strumpet ['strʌmpɪt] s putain f

strut [strʌt] s (brace, prop) étai m, support m, entretoise f; démarche f orgueilleuse || v (pret & pp strutted; ger strutting) intr se pavaner

strychnine ['strɪknaɪn], ['strɪknɪn] s strychnine f

stub [stʌb] s (fragment) tronçon m; (of a tree) souche f; (of a pencil; of a cigar, cigarette) bout m; (of a check) talon m, souche || v (pret & pp stubbed; ger stubbing) tr—to stub one's toe se cogner le bout du pied

stubble ['stʌbəl] s éteule f, chaume m; (of beard) poil m court et raide

stubborn ['stʌbərn] adj obstiné; (head-

strong) têtu; (resolute) acharné; (fever) rebelle; (soil) ingrat

stuc·co ['stʌko] s (pl -coes or -cos) stuc m || tr stuquer

stuck [stʌk] adj coincé, pris; (glued) collé; (unable to continue) en panne; stuck on (coll) entiché de

stuck'-up' adj (coll) hautain, prétentieux

stud [stʌd] s clou m à grosse tête; (ornament) clou doré; (on shirt) bouton m; (studhorse) étalon m; (horse farm) haras m; (bolt) goujon m; (archit) montant m || v (pret & pp studded; ger studding) tr clouter; studded with jonché de, parsemé de

stud' bolt' s goujon m

student ['st(j)udənt] adj estudiantin || s étudiant m; (researcher) chercheur m

stu'dent bod'y s étudiants mpl

stu'dent cen'ter s foyer m d'étudiants, centre m social des étudiants

stu'dent nurse' s élève f infirmière

stud' farm' s haras m

stud'horse' s étalon m

studied ['stʌdid] adj prémédité; recherché

studi·o ['st(j)udɪ,o] s (pl -os) studio m, atelier m

studious ['st(j)udɪ-əs] adj studieux, appliqué

stud·y ['stʌdi] s (pl -ies) étude f; rêverie f; cabinet m || v (pret & pp -ied) tr & intr étudier

stuff [stʌf] s matière f; chose f; to know one's stuff (coll) s'y connaître || tr bourrer; (with food) gaver; (furniture) rembourrer; (an animal) empailler; (culin) farcir; to stuff up boucher || intr se gaver

stuffed' shirt' s collet m monté

stuffing ['stʌfɪŋ] s rembourrage m; (culin) farce f

stuff·y ['stʌfi] adj (comp -ier; super -iest) mal ventilé; (tedious) ennuyeux; (pompous) collet monté; to smell stuffy sentir le renfermé

stumble ['stʌmbəl] intr trébucher; (in speaking) hésiter

stum'bling block' s pierre f d'achoppement

stump [stʌmp] s (of tree) souche f; (e.g., of arm) moignon m; (of tooth) chicot m || v (pret & pp stumped) tr (a design) estomper; (coll) embarrasser, coller; (a state, district, region) (coll) faire une tournée électorale en, dans, or à || intr clopiner

stump' speak'er s orateur m de carrefour

stump' speech' s harangue f électorale improvisée

stun [stʌn] v (pret & pp stunned; ger stunning) tr étourdir

stunning ['stʌnɪŋ] adj (coll) étourdissant, épatant

stunt [stʌnt] s atrophie f; (underdeveloped creature) avorton m; (coll) tour m de force, acrobatie f || tr atrophier || intr (coll) faire des acrobaties

stunted *adj* rabougri

stunt′ fly′ing *s* vol *m* de virtuosité, acrobatie *f* aérienne

stunt′ man′ *s* (*pl* **men′**) cascadeur *m*, doublure *f*

stupe·fy [′st(j)upɪ‚faɪ] *v* (*pret & pp* **-fied**) *tr* stupéfier

stupendous [st(j)u′pɛndəs] *adj* prodigieux, formidable

stupid [′st(j)upɪd] *adj* stupide

stupor [′st(j)upər] *s* stupeur *f*

stur·dy [′stʌrdɪ] *adj* (*comp* **-dier;** *super* **-diest**) robuste, vigoureux; (*resolute*) ferme, hardi

sturgeon [′stʌrdʒən] *s* esturgeon *m*

stutter [′stʌtər] *s* bégaiement *m* ‖ *tr & intr* bégayer

sty [staɪ] *s* (*pl* **sties**) porcherie *f*; (*pathol*) orgelet *m*

style [staɪl] *s* style *m*; (*fashion*) mode *f*; (*elegance*) ton *m*, chic *m*; **to live in great style** mener grand train ‖ *tr* appeler, dénommer; **to style oneself** s'intituler

stylish [′staɪlɪʃ] *adj* à la mode, élégant, chic

sty·mie [′staɪmɪ] *v* (*pret & pp* **-mied;** *ger* **-mieing**) *tr* contrecarrer

styp′tic pen′cil [′stɪptɪk] *s* crayon *m* styptique

suave [swɑv], [swev] *adj* suave; (*person*) affable; (*manners*) doucereux

sub [sʌb] *s* (coll) sous-marin *m*

subconscious [səb′kɑnʃəs] *adj & s* subconscient *m*

sub′divide′ or **sub′divide′** *tr* subdiviser ‖ *intr* se subdiviser

subdue [səb′d(j)u] *tr* subjuguer, vaincre, asservir; (*color, light, sound*) adoucir, amortir; (*passions, feelings*) dompter

sub′head′ *s* sous-titre *m*

subject [′sʌbdʒɪkt] *adj* sujet, assujetti, soumis ‖ *s* sujet *m*; (*e.g., in school*) matière *f* ‖ [səb′dʒɛkt] *tr* assujettir, soumettre

subjection [səb′dʒɛkʃən] *s* sujétion *f*, soumission *f*

subjective [səb′dʒɛktɪv] *adj* subjectif

sub′ject mat′ter *s* matière *f*

subjugate [′sʌbdʒə‚get] *tr* subjuguer

subjunctive [səb′dʒʌŋktɪv] *adj & s* subjonctif *m*

sub′lease′ *s* sous-location *f* ‖ **sub′lease′** *tr* sous-louer

sub·let [səb′lɛt], [′sʌb‚lɛt] *v* (*pret & pp* **-let;** *ger* **-letting**) *tr* sous-louer

sub′machine′ gun′ *s* mitraillette *f*

sub′marine′ *adj & s* sous-marin *m*

sub′marine chas′er *s* chasseur *m* de sous-marins

submerge [səb′mʌrdʒ] *tr* submerger ‖ *intr* (*said of submarine*) plonger

submersion [səb′mʌrʒən], [səb′mʌr‚ʃən] *s* submersion *f*

submission [səb′mɪʃən] *s* soumission *f*; (*delivery*) présentation *f*

submissive [səb′mɪsɪv] *adj* soumis

sub·mit [səb′mɪt] *v* (*pret & pp* **-mitted;** *ger* **-mitting**) *tr* soumettre ‖ *intr* se soumettre

subordinate [səb′ɔrdɪnɪt] *adj & s*

subordonné *m* ‖ [səb′ɔrdɪ‚net] *tr* subordonner

subpoena [sʌb′pinə], [sə′pinə] *s* assignation *f*, citation *f* ‖ *tr* citer

subscribe [səb′skraɪb] *tr* souscrire ‖ *intr*—**to subscribe to** (*an opinion; a charity; a loan; a newspaper*) souscrire à; (*a newspaper*) s'abonner à

subscriber [səb′skraɪbər] *s* abonné *m*

subscription [səb′skrɪpʃən] *s* souscription *f*; (*to newspaper or magazine*) abonnement *m*; (*to club*) cotisation *f*; **to take out a subscription for s.o.** abonner qn; **to take out a subscription to** s'abonner à

subsequent [′sʌbsɪkwənt] *adj* subséquent, suivant

subservient [səb′sʌrvɪ·ənt] *adj* asservi, subordonné

subside [səb′saɪd] *intr* (*said of water, ground, etc.*) s'abaisser; (*said of storm, excitement, etc.*) s'apaiser

subsidiar·y [səb′sɪdɪ‚ɛri] *adj* subsidiaire ‖ *s* (*pl* **-ies**) filiale *f*

subsidize [′sʌbsɪ‚daɪz] *tr* subventionner; suborner

subsi·dy [′sʌbsɪdɪ] *s* (*pl* **-dies**) subside *m*, subvention *f*

subsist [səb′sɪst] *intr* subsister

subsistence [səb′sɪstəns] *s* (*supplies*) subsistance *f*; existence *f*

sub′soil′ *s* sous-sol *m*

substance [′sʌbstəns] *s* substance *f*

sub·stand′ard *adj* inférieur au niveau normal

substantial [səb′stænʃəl] *adj* substantiel; (*wealthy*) aisé, cossu

substantiate [səb′stænʃɪ‚et] *tr* établir, vérifier

substantive [′sʌbstəntɪv] *adj & s* substantif *m*

sub′sta′tion *s* (*of post office*) bureau *m* auxiliaire; (elec) sous-station *f*

substitute [′sʌbstɪ‚t(j)ut] *s* (*person*) remplaçant *m*, suppléant *m*, substitut *m*; (*e.g., for coffee*) succédané *m* ‖ *tr* remplacer, e.g., **they substituted copper for silver** ils ont remplacé l'argent par le cuivre; substituer, e.g., **a hind was substituted for Iphigenia** une biche fut substituée à Iphigénie ‖ *intr* servir de remplaçant; **to substitute for** remplacer, suppléer

substitution [‚sʌbstɪ′t(j)uʃən] *s* substitution *f*

sub′stra′tum *s* (*pl* **-ta** [tə] or **-tums**) substrat *m*

subterfuge [′sʌbtər‚fjudʒ] *s* subterfuge *m*, faux-fuyant *m*

subterranean [‚sʌbtə′reni·ən] *adj* souterrain

sub′ti′tle *s* sous-titre *m*

subtle [′sʌtəl] *adj* subtil

subtle·ty [′sʌtəlti] *s* (*pl* **-ties**) subtilité *f*

subtract [səb′trækt] *tr* soustraire

subtraction [səb′trækʃən] *s* soustraction *f*

suburb [′sʌbʌrb] *s* ville *f* de la banlieue; **the suburbs** la banlieue

suburban [sə′bʌrbən] *adj* suburbain

suburbanite [sə′bʌrbə‚naɪt] *s* banlieusard *m*

subvention [səb'vɛnʃən] s subvention f || tr subventionner

subversive [səb'vʌrsɪv] adj subversif || s factieux m

subvert [səb'vʌrt] tr corrompre; renverser

sub'way' s métro m; (tunnel for pedestrians) souterrain m

sub'way car' s voiture f de métro

sub'way sta'tion s station f de métro

succeed [sək'sid] tr succéder (with dat); **to succeed one another** se succéder || intr réussir; **to succeed in** + ger réussir à + inf; **to succeed to** (the throne; a fortune) succéder à

success [sək'sɛs] s succès m, réussite f; **to be a success** avoir du succès

successful [sək'sɛsfəl] adj réussi; heureux, prospère

succession [sək'sɛʃən] s succession f; **in succession** de suite

successive [sək'sɛsɪv] adj successif

succor ['sʌkər] s secours m || tr secourir

succotash ['sʌkə,tæʃ] s plat m de fèves et de maïs

succumb [sə'kʌm] intr succomber

such [sʌtʃ] adj & pron indef tel, pareil, semblable; **such a** un tel; **such and such** tel et tel; **such as** tel que

suck [sʌk] s—**to give suck to** allaiter || tr sucer; (a nipple) téter; **to suck in** aspirer; (to absorb) sucer || intr sucer; téter

sucker ['sʌkər] s suceur m; (sucking organ) suçoir m, ventouse f; (bot) drageon m; (ichth) rémora m; (gullible person) (coll) gogo m; (lollipop) (coll) sucette f

suckle ['sʌkəl] tr allaiter

suck'ling pig' s cochon m de lait

suction ['sʌkʃən] s succion f

suc'tion cup' s ventouse f

suc'tion pump' s pompe f aspirante

sudden ['sʌdən] adj brusque, soudain; **all of a sudden** tout à coup

suddenly ['sʌdənlɪ] adv tout à coup

suds [sʌdz] spl eau f savonneuse; mousse f de savon

sue [s(j)u] tr poursuivre en justice || intr intenter un procès

suede [swed] s suède m; (for shoes) daim m

suet ['s(j)u·ɪt] s graisse f de rognon

suffer ['sʌfər] tr souffrir; (to allow) permettre; (a defeat) essuyer, subir || intr souffrir

sufferance ['sʌfərəns] s tolérance f

suffering ['sʌfərɪŋ] adj souffrant || s souffrance f

suffice [sə'faɪs] tr suffire (with dat) || intr suffire; **it suffices to** + inf il suffit de + inf

sufficient [sə'fɪʃənt] adj suffisant

suffix ['sʌfɪks] s suffixe m

suffocate ['sʌfə,ket] tr & intr suffoquer, étouffer

suffrage ['sʌfrɪdʒ] s suffrage m

suffragist ['sʌfrədʒɪst] s partisan m du droit de vote des femmes

suffuse [sə'fjuz] tr baigner, saturer

sugar ['ʃugər] s sucre m || tr sucrer;

(a cake) saupoudrer de sucre; (a pill) recouvrir de sucre || intr former du sucre

sug'ar beet' s betterave f sucrière, betterave à sucre

sug'ar bowl' s sucrier m

sug'ar cane' s canne f à sucre

sug'ar-coat' tr dragéifier; (fig) dorer

sug'ar dad'dy s (pl -dies) papa m gâteau

sug'ar ma'ple s érable m à sucre

sug'ar pea' s mange-tout m

sug'ar tongs' spl pince f à sucre

sugary ['ʃugəri] adj sucré; (fig) doucereux

suggest [səg'dʒɛst] tr suggérer

suggestion [səg'dʒɛstʃən] s suggestion f; nuance f, pointe f, soupçon m

suggestive [səg'dʒɛstɪv] adj suggestif

suicidal [,s(j)u·ɪ'saɪdəl] adj suicidaire

suicide ['s(j)u·ɪ,saɪd] s (act) suicide m; (person) suicidé m; **to commit suicide** se suicider

suit [s(j)ut] s costume m; (men's) complet m, costume; (women's) costume tailleur, tailleur m; (lawsuit) procès m; (plea) requête f; (cards) couleur f; **to follow suit** jouer la couleur; (fig) en faire autant || tr adapter; convenir (with dat), e.g., **does that suit him?** cela lui convient?; aller (with dat), seoir (with dat), e.g., **the dress suits her well** la robe lui va bien, la robe lui sied bien || intr convenir, aller

suitable ['s(j)utəbəl] adj convenable, à propos; compétent

suit'case' s valise f

suite [swit] s suite f || [s(j)ut] s (of furniture) ameublement m, mobilier m

suiting ['s(j)utɪŋ] s étoffe f pour complets

suit' of clothes' s complet-veston m

suitor ['s(j)utər] s prétendant m, soupirant m

sul'fa drugs' ['sʌlfə] spl sulfamides mpl

sulfide ['sʌlfaɪd] s sulfure m

sulfur ['sʌlfər] adj soufré || s soufre m || tr soufrer

sulfuric [sʌl'fjurɪk] adj sulfurique

sul'fur mine' s soufrière f

sulk [sʌlk] s bouderie f || intr bouder

sulk·y ['sʌlki] adj (comp -ier; super -iest) boudeur, maussade

sullen ['sʌlən] adj maussade, rébarbatif

sul·ly ['sʌli] v (pret & pp -lied) tr souiller

sulphur ['sʌlfər] adj, s & tr var of **sulfur**

sultan ['sʌltən] s sultan m

sul·try ['sʌltri] adj (comp -trier; super -triest) étouffant, suffocant

sum [sʌm] s somme f; tout m, total m; **in sum** somme toute || v (pret & pp summed; ger summing) tr—**to sum up** résumer

sumac or **sumach** ['ʃumæk], ['sumæk] s sumac m

summarize ['sʌmə,raɪz] tr résumer

summa·ry ['sʌməri] adj sommaire || s (pl -ries) sommaire m

summer ['sʌmər] *adj* estival || *s* été *m* || *intr* passer l'été

sum'mer resort' *s* station *f* estivale

sum'mer school' *s* cours *m* d'été, cours de vacances

summery ['sʌməri] *adj* estival, d'été

summit ['sʌmɪt] *s* sommet *m*

sum'mit con'ference *s* conférence *f* au sommet

summon ['sʌmən] *tr* appeler, convoquer; (law) sommer, citer, assigner

summons ['sʌmənz] *s* appel *m*; (law) citation *f*, assignation *f*, exploit *m*

sumptuous ['sʌmptʃʊ·əs] *adj* somptueux

sun [sʌn] *s* soleil *m* || *v* (*pret & pp* sunned; *ger* sunning) *tr* exposer au soleil || *intr* prendre le soleil

sun' bath' *s* bain *m* de soleil

sun'beam' *s* rayon *m* de soleil

sun'bon'net *s* capeline *f*

sun'burn' *s* coup *m* de soleil || *v* (*pret & pp* -burned or -burnt) *tr* hâler, basaner || *intr* se basaner

sun'burned' *adj* brûlé par le soleil

sundae ['sʌndi] *s* coupe *f* de glace garnie de fruits

Sunday ['sʌndi] *adj* dominical || *s* dimanche *m*

Sun'day best' *s* (coll) habits *mpl* du dimanche

Sun'day driv'er *s* chauffeur *m* du dimanche

Sun'day school' *s* école *f* du dimanche

sunder ['sʌndər] *tr* séparer, rompre

sun'di'al *s* cadran *m* solaire, gnomon *m*

sun'down' *s* coucher *m* du soleil

sundries ['sʌndriz] *spl* articles *mpl* divers

sundry ['sʌndri] *adj* divers

sun'fish' *s* poisson-lune *m*

sun'flow'er *s* soleil *m*, tournesol *m*

sun'glass'es *spl* lunettes *fpl* de soleil, verres *mpl* fumés

sunken ['sʌŋkən] *adj* creux, enfoncé; (*rock*) noyé; (*ship*) sous-marin

sun' lamp' *s* lampe *f* à rayons ultraviolets

sun'light' *s* lumière *f* du soleil

sun·ny ['sʌni] *adj* (*comp* -nier; *super* -niest) ensoleillé; (*happy*) enjoué; **it is sunny** il fait du soleil

sun'ny side' *s* côté *m* exposé au soleil; (fig) bon côté

sun' par'lor *s* véranda *f*

sun'rise' *s* lever *m* du soleil

sun'set' *s* coucher *m* du soleil

sun'shade' *s* (*over door*) banne *f*; parasol *m*; abat-jour *m*, visière *f*

sun'shine' *s* clarté *f* du soleil, soleil *m*; (fig) gaieté *f* rayonnante; **in the sunshine** en plein soleil

sun'spot' *s* tache *f* solaire

sun'stroke' *s* insolation *f*

sun' tan' *s* hâle *m*

sun'-tan oil' *s* huile *f* solaire

sun'up' *s* lever *m* du soleil

sun' vi'sor *s* abat-jour *m*

sup [sʌp] *v* (*pret & pp* supped; *ger* supping) *intr* souper

super ['sʌpər] *adj* (slang) superbe, formidable || *s* (theat) figurant *m*; (slang) concierge *mf*

superannuated [,supər'ænju,etɪd] *adj* (*person*) retraité; (*thing*) suranné

superb [sʊ'pʌrb], [sə'pʌrb] *adj* superbe

su'per-car'go *s* (*pl* -goes or -gos) subrécargue *m*

su'per-charge' *s* surcompression *f* || *tr* surcomprimer

supercilious [,supər'stɪli·əs] *adj* sourcilleux, hautain, arrogant

superficial [,supər'fɪʃəl] *adj* superficiel

superfluous [sʊ'pʌrflu·əs] *adj* superflu

su'per-high'way' *s* autoroute *f*

su'per-hu'man *adj* surhumain

su'per-impose' *tr* superposer

su'per-intend' *tr* surveiller; diriger

superintendent [,supərin'tendənt] *s* directeur *m*, directeur en chef; (*of a building*) concierge *mf*

superior [sə'pɪrɪ·ər], [sʊ'pɪrɪ·ər] *adj & s* supérieur *m*

superiority [sə,pɪrɪ'arɪti], [sʊ,pɪrɪ·ariti] *s* supériorité *f*

superlative [sə'pʌrlətɪv], [sʊ'pʌrlətɪv] *adj & s* superlatif *m*

su'per-man' *s* (*pl* -men') surhomme *m*

su'per-mar'ket *s* supermarché *m*

su'per-nat'ural *adj & s* surnaturel *m*

supersede [,supər'sid] *tr* remplacer

su'per-sen'sitive *adj* hypersensible

su'per-son'ic *adj* supersonique

superstition [,supər'stɪʃən] *s* superstition *f*

superstitious [,supər'stɪʃəs] *adj* superstitieux

supervene [,supər'vin] *intr* survenir

supervise ['supər,vaɪz] *tr* surveiller; diriger

supervision [,supər'vɪʒən] *s* surveillance *f*; direction *f*

supervisor ['supər,vaɪzər] *s* surveillant *m*, inspecteur *m*; directeur *m*

supper ['sʌpər] *s* souper *m*

sup'per-time' *s* heure *f* du souper

supplant [sə'plænt] *tr* supplanter

supple ['sʌpəl] *adj* souple, flexible

supplement ['sʌplɪmənt] *s* supplément *m* || ['sʌplɪ,ment] *tr* ajouter à

suppliant ['sʌplɪ·ənt] *adj & s* suppliant *m*

supplicant ['sʌplɪkənt] *s* suppliant *m*

supplicate ['sʌplɪ,ket] *tr* supplier

supplier [sə'plaɪ·ər] *s* fournisseur *m*, pourvoyeur *m*

sup·ply [sə'plaɪ] *s* (*pl* -plies) fourniture *f*, provision *f*; (mil) approvisionnement *m*; **supplies** fournitures; (*of food*) vivres *mpl* || *v* (*pret & pp* -plied) *tr* fournir; (*a person, a city, a fort*) pourvoir, munir; (*a need*) répondre à; (*what is lacking*) suppléer; (mil) approvisionner

supply' and demand' *spl* l'offre *f* et la demande

support [sə'port] *s* soutien *m*, appui *m*; ressources *fpl*, de quoi vivre *m*; (*pillar*) support *m* || *tr* soutenir, appuyer; (*e.g., a wife*) entretenir, soutenir; (*to* hold up; to corroborate; to tolerate) supporter; **to support oneself** gagner sa vie

supporter [sə'pɔrtər] s partisan m, supporter m; (for part of body) suspensoir m

suppose [sə'poz] tr supposer; s'imaginer; **I suppose so** probablement; **suppose that . . .** à supposer que . . . ; **suppose we take a walk?** si nous faisions une promenade?; **to be supposed to** + inf devoir + inf; (to be considered to be) être censé + inf

supposedly [sə'pozidli] adv censément

supposition [ˌsʌpə'zɪʃən] s supposition f

supposito·ry [sə'pɑzɪˌtori] s (pl -ries) suppositoire m

suppress [sə'prɛs] tr supprimer; (rebellion; anger) réprimer, contenir; (a yawn) étouffer, empêcher

suppression [sə'prɛʃən] s suppression f; (of a rebellion) subjugation f, répression f; (of a yawn) empêchement m

suppurate ['sʌpjəˌret] intr suppurer

supreme [sə'prim], [su'prim] adj suprême

supreme' court' s cour f de cassation

surcharge ['sʌrˌtʃɑrdʒ] s surcharge f || [ˌsʌr'tʃɑrdʒ], ['sʌrˌtʃɑrdʒ] tr surcharger

sure [ʃur] adj sûr, certain; (e.g., hand) ferme; **for sure** à coup sûr, pour sûr; **to be sure to** + inf ne pas manquer de + inf; **to make sure** s'assurer || adv (coll) certainement; **sure enough** (coll) effectivement, assurément || interj (slang) mais oui!, bien sûr!, entendu!

sure'-foot'ed adj au pied sûr

sure·ty ['ʃurti], ['ʃuriti] s (pl -ties) sûreté f

surf [sʌrf] s barre f, ressac m, brisants mpl

surface ['sʌrfɪs] adj superficiel || s surface f; (area) superficie f; **on the surface** à la surface, en apparence; **to float under the surface** nager entre deux eaux || tr polir la surface de; (a road) recouvrir, revêtir || intr (said of submarine) faire surface

sur'face mail' s courrier m par voie ordinaire

surf'board' s planche f pour le surf, surfboard m

surfeit ['sʌrfɪt] s satiété f || tr rassasier || intr se rassasier

surf'rid'ing s surfing m, planking m

surge [sʌrdʒ] s houle f; (elec) surtension f || intr être houleux; se répandre; **to surge up** s'enfler, s'élever

surgeon ['sʌrdʒən] s chirurgien m

surger·y ['sʌrdʒəri] s (pl -ies) chirurgie f; salle f d'opération

surgical ['sʌrdʒɪkəl] adj chirurgical

sur·ly ['sʌrli] adj (comp -lier; super -liest) hargneux, maussade, bourru

surmise [sər'maɪz], ['sʌrmaɪz] s conjecture f || [sər'maɪz] tr & intr conjecturer

surmount [sər'maunt] tr surmonter

surname ['sʌrˌnem] s nom m de famil-

le; surnom m || tr donner un nom de famille à; surnommer

surpass [sər'pæs], [sər'pɑs] tr surpasser

surplice ['sʌrplɪs] s surplis m

surplus ['sʌrpləs] adj excédent, excédentaire, en excédent || s surplus m, excédent m

sur'plus bag'gage s excédent m de bagages

surprise [sər'praɪz] adj à l'improviste, brusqué, inopiné || s surprise f, étonnement m; **to take by surprise** prendre à l'improviste, prendre au dépourvu || tr surprendre; **to be surprised at** être surpris de

surprise' attack' s attaque f brusquée

surprise' pack'age s surprise f, pochette f surprise

surprise' par'ty s (pl -ties) réunion f à l'improviste

surprising [sər'praɪzɪŋ] adj surprenant

surrealism [sə'ri·əˌlɪzəm] s surréalisme m

surrender [sə'rɛndər] s reddition f, soumission f; (e.g., of prisoners, goods) remise f; (e.g., of rights, property) cession f || tr rendre, céder || intr se rendre

surren'der val'ue s valeur f de rachat

surreptitious [ˌsʌrɛp'tɪʃəs] adj subreptice

surround [sə'raund] tr entourer

surrounding [sə'raundɪŋ] adj entourant, environnant || **surroundings** spl environs mpl, alentours mpl; entourage m, milieu m

surtax ['sʌrˌtæks] s surtaxe f || tr surtaxer

surveillance [sər'vel(j)əns] s surveillance f

survey ['sʌrve] s (for verification) contrôle m; (for evaluation) appréciation f, évaluation f; (report) expertise f, aperçu m; (of a whole) vue f d'ensemble, tour m d'horizon; (measured plan or drawing) levé m, plan m; (surv) lever m or levé des plans; **to make a survey** (to map out) lever un plan; (to poll) effectuer un contrôle par sondage || [sʌr've], ['sʌrve] tr contrôler; apprécier, évaluer, faire l'expertise de; (as a whole) jeter un coup d'œil sur; (to poll) sonder; (e.g., a farm) arpenter, faire l'arpentage de; (e.g., a city) faire le levé de

sur'vey course' s cours m général

surveying [sʌr've·ɪŋ] s arpentage m, géodésie f, levé m des plans

surveyor [sər've·ər] s arpenteur m

survival [sər'vaɪvəl] s survivance f; (after death) survie f

survive [sər'vaɪv] tr survivre (with dat) || intr survivre

surviving [sər'vaɪvɪŋ] adj survivant

survivor [sər'vaɪvər] s survivant m

survivorship [sər'vaɪvərˌʃɪp] s (law) survie f

susceptible [sə'sɛptɪbəl] adj (capable) susceptible; (liable, subject) sensible; (to love) facilement amoureux

suspect ['sʌspɛkt], [səs'pɛkt] adj & s

suspect *m* || [səs'pekt] *tr* soupçonner || *intr* s'en douter

suspend [səs'pend] *tr* suspendre

suspenders [səs'pendərz] *spl* bretelles *fpl*

suspense [səs'pens] *s* suspens *m*

suspension [səs'penʃən] *s* suspension *f*; suspension of driver's license retrait *m* de permis

suspen'sion bridge' *s* pont *m* suspendu

suspicion [səs'pɪʃən] *s* soupçon *m*

suspicious [səs'pɪʃəs] *adj* (*inclined to suspect*) soupçonneux; (*subject to suspicion*) suspect

sustain [səs'ten] *tr* soutenir; (*a loss, injury, etc.*) éprouver

sustenance ['sʌstɪnəns] *s* subsistance *f*; (*food*) nourriture *f*

swab [swab] *s* écouvillon *m*; (*naut*) faubert *m*; (*surg*) tampon *m* || *v* (*pret & pp* swabbed; *ger* swabbing) *tr* écouvillonner

swaddle ['swadəl] *tr* emmailloter

swad'dling clothes' *spl* maillot *m*

swagger ['swægər] *s* fanfaronnade *f* || *intr* faire des fanfaronnades

swain [swen] *s* garçon *m*; jeune berger *m*; soupirant *m*

swallow ['swalo] *s* gorgée *f*; (*orn*) hirondelle *f* || *tr & intr* avaler

swal'low-tailed coat' *s* frac *m*

swamp [swamp] *s* marécage *m* || *tr* submerger, inonder

swampy ['swampi] *adj* (*comp* -ier; *super* -iest) marécageux

swan [swan] *s* cygne *m*

swan' dive' *s* saut *m* de l'ange

swank [swæŋk] *adj* (*slang*) élégant, chic

swan' knight' *s* chevalier *m* au cygne

swan'-down' *s* cygne *m*, duvet *m* de cygne

swan' song' *s* chant *m* du cygne

swap [swap] *s* (*coll*) troc *m* || *v* (*pret & pp* swapped; *ger* swapping) *tr & intr* troquer

swarm [swarm] *s* essaim *m* || *intr* essaimer; (*fig*) fourmiller

swarthy ['swɔrði], ['swɔrθi] *adj* (*comp* -ier; *super* -iest) basané, brun, noiraud

swashbuckler ['swaʃ‚bʌklər] *s* rodomont *m*, bretteur *m*

swat [swat] *s* (*coll*) coup *m* violent || *v* (*pret & pp* swatted; *ger* swatting) *tr* (*coll*) frapper; (*a fly*) écraser

sway [swe] *s* balancement *m*; (*domination*) empire *m* || *tr* balancer || *intr* se balancer; (*to hesitate*) balancer

swear [swer] *v* (*pret* swore [swor]; *pp* sworn [sworn]) *tr* jurer; to swear in faire prêter serment à; to swear off jurer de renoncer à || *intr* jurer; to swear at injurier; to swear by (*e.g., a remedy*) préconiser; to swear to déclarer sous serment; jurer de + *inf*

swear' words' *spl* gros mots *mpl*

sweat [swet] *s* sueur *f* || *v* (*pret & pp* sweat or sweated) *tr* (*e.g., blood*) suer; (*slang*) faire suer; to sweat it out (*slang*) en baver jusqu'à la fin || *intr* suer

sweater ['swetər] *s* chandail *m*

sweat' shirt' *s* maillot *m* de sport

sweaty ['sweti] *adj* (*comp* -ier; *super* -iest) suant

Swede [swid] *s* Suédois *m*

Sweden ['swidən] *s* Suède *f*; la Suède

Swedish ['swidɪʃ] *adj & s* suédois *m*

sweep [swip] *s* balayage *m*; étendue *f*; (*curve*) courbe *f*; (*of wind*) souffle *m*; (*of well*) chadouf *m*; at one sweep d'un seul coup; to make a clean sweep of faire table rase de; (*to win all of*) rafler || *v* (*pret & pp* swept [swept]) *tr* balayer; (*the chimney*) ramoner; (*for mines*) draguer || *intr* balayer; s'étendre

sweeper ['swipər] *s* balayeur *m*; (*mach*) balai *m* mécanique

sweeping ['swipɪŋ] *adj* (*movement*) vigoureux; (*statement*) catégorique || *s* balayage *m*; sweepings balayures *fpl*

sweep'-sec'ond *s* trotteuse *f* centrale

sweep'stakes' *s* or *spl* loterie *f*; (*turf*) sweepstake *m*

sweet [swit] *adj* doux; sucré; (*perfume, music, etc.*) suave; (*sound*) mélodieux; (*milk*) frais; (*person*) charmant, gentil; (*dear*) cher; to be sweet on (*coll*) avoir un béguin pour; to smell sweet sentir bon || sweets *spl* sucreries *fpl*

sweet'bread' *s* ris *m* de veau

sweet'bri'er *s* églantier *m*

sweeten ['switən] *tr* sucrer; purifier; (*fig*) adoucir || *intr* s'adoucir

sweet'heart' *s* petite amie *f*, chérie *f*; sweethearts amoureux *mpl*

sweet' mar'joram *s* marjolaine *f*

sweet'meats' *spl* sucreries *fpl*

sweet' pea' *s* gesse *f* odorante, pois *m* de senteur

sweet' pep'per *s* piment *m* doux, poivron *m*

sweet' pota'to *s* patate *f* douce

sweet'-scent'ed *adj* parfumé

sweet'-toothed' *adj* friand de sucreries

sweet' wil'liam *s* œillet *m* de poète

swell [swel] *adj* (*coll*) élégant; (*slang*) épatant || *s* gonflement *m*; (*of sea*) houle *f*; (*mus*) crescendo *m*; (*pathol*) enflure *f*; (*coll*) rupin *m* || *v* (*pret* swelled; *pp* swelled or swollen ['swolən]) *tr* gonfler, enfler || *intr* se gonfler, s'enfler; (*said of sea*) se soulever; (*fig*) augmenter

swell'head'ed *adj* suffisant, vaniteux

swelter ['sweltər] *intr* étouffer de chaleur

swept'back' wing' *s* aile *f* en flèche

swerve [swʌrv] *s* écart *m*, déviation *f*; (*aut*) embardée *f* || *tr* faire dévier || *intr* écarter, dévier; (*aut*) faire une embardée

swift [swɪft] *adj* rapide || *adv* vite || *s* (*orn*) martinet *m*

swig [swɪg] *s* (*coll*) lampée *f*, trait *m* || *v* (*pret & pp* swigged; *ger* swigging) *tr & intr* lamper

swill [swɪl] *s* eaux *fpl* grasses, ordures *fpl*; (*drink*) lampée *f* || *tr & intr* lamper

swim [swɪm] *s* nage *f*; **to be in the swim** (coll) être dans le train || *v* (*pret* **swam** [swæm]; *pp* **swum** [swʌm]; *ger* **swimming**) *tr* nager || *intr* nager; (*said of head*) tourner; **to swim across** traverser à la nage; **to swim under water** nager entre deux eaux

swimmer ['swɪmər] *s* nageur *m*

swimming ['swɪmɪŋ] *s* natation *f*, nage *f*

swim'ming pool' *s* piscine *f*

swim'ming suit' *s* maillot *m* de bain

swim'ming trunks' *spl* slip *m* de bain

swindle ['swɪndəl] *s* escroquerie *f* || *tr* escroquer

swine [swaɪn] *s* (*pl* **swine**) cochon *m*, pourceau *m*, porc *m*

swing [swɪŋ] *s* balancement *m*, oscillation *f*; (*device used for recreation*) escarpolette *f*; (*trip*) tournée *f*; (*boxing, mus*) swing *m*; **in full swing** en pleine marche || *v* (*pret & pp* **swung** [swʌŋ]) *tr* balancer, faire osciller; (*the arms*) agiter; (*a sword*) brandir; (*e.g., an election*) mener à bien || *intr* se balancer; (*said of pendulum*) osciller; (*said of door*) pivoter; (*said of bell*) branler; **to swing open** s'ouvrir tout d'un coup

swing'ing door' *s* porte *f* va-et-vient

swinish ['swaɪnɪʃ] *adj* cochon

swipe [swaɪp] *s* (coll) coup *m* à toute volée || *tr* (coll) frapper à toute volée; (*to steal*) (slang) chiper

swirl [swʌrl] *s* remous *m*, tourbillon *m* || *tr* faire tourbillonner || *intr* tourbillonner

swish [swɪʃ] *s* (*e.g., of a whip*) sifflement *m*; (*of a dress*) froufrou *m*; (*e.g., of water*) susurrement *m* || *tr* (*a whip*) faire siffler; (*its tail*) battre || *intr* siffler; froufrouter; susurrer

Swiss [swɪs] *adj* suisse || *s* Suisse *m*; **the Swiss** les Suisses *mpl*

Swiss' chard' [tʃɑrd] *s* bette *f*, poirée *f*

Swiss' cheese' *s* emmenthal *m*, gruyère *m*

Swiss' Guard' *s* suisse *m*

switch [swɪtʃ] *s* (*stick*) badine *f*; (*exchange*) échange *m*; (*hairpiece*) postiche *m*; (*elec*) interrupteur *m*; (rr) aiguille *f* || *tr* cingler; (*places*) échanger; (rr) aiguiller; **to switch off** couper; (*a light*) éteindre; **to switch on** mettre en circuit; (*a light*) allumer || *intr* changer de place

switch'back' *s* chemin *m* en lacet

switch'board' *s* tableau *m* de distribution; standard *m* téléphonique

switch'board op'erator *s* standardiste *mf*

switch'ing en'gine *s* locomotive *f* de manœuvre

switch'man *s* (*pl* **-men**) aiguilleur *m*

switch' tow'er *s* poste *m* d'aiguillage

switch'yard' *s* gare *f* de triage

Switzerland ['swɪtsərlənd] *s* Suisse *f*; la Suisse

swiv·el ['swɪvəl] *s* pivot *m*; (*link*) émerillon *m* || *v* (*pret & pp* **-eled** or **-elled**; *ger* **-eling** or **-elling**) *tr* faire pivoter || *intr* pivoter

swiv'el chair' *s* fauteuil *m* tournant

swoon [swun] *s* évanouissement *m* || *intr* s'évanouir

swoop [swup] *s* attaque *f* brusque; **at one fell swoop** d'un seul coup || *intr* foncer, fondre; **to swoop down on** s'abattre sur

sword [sord] *s* épée *f*; **to cross swords with** croiser le fer avec; **to put to the sword** passer au fil de l'épée

sword' belt' *s* ceinturon *m*

sword'fish' *s* espadon *m*

swords'man *s* (*pl* **-men**) épéiste *m*

sword' swal'lower ['swɑlo·ər] *s* avaleur *m* de sabres

sword' thrust' *s* coup *m* de pointe, coup d'épée

sworn [sworn] *adj* (*enemy*) juré; **sworn in** assermenté

sycophant ['sɪkəfənt] *s* flagorneur *m*

syllable ['sɪləbəl] *s* syllabe *f*

sylla·bus ['sɪləbəs] *s* (*pl* **-bi** [,baɪ] or **-buses**) programme *m*

syllogism ['sɪlə,dʒɪzəm] *s* syllogisme *m*

sylph [sɪlf] *s* sylphe *m*

sylvan ['sɪlvən] *adj* sylvestre

symbol ['sɪmbəl] *s* symbole *m*

symbolic(al) [sɪm'balɪk(əl)] *adj* symbolique

symbolism ['sɪmbə,lɪzm] *s* symbolisme *m*

symbolize ['sɪmbə,laɪz] *tr* symboliser

symmetric(al) [sɪ'metrɪk(əl)] *adj* symétrique

symme·try ['sɪmɪtri] *s* (*pl* **-tries**) symétrie *f*

sympathetic [,sɪmpə'θetɪk] *adj* compatissant; bien disposé; (anat, physiol) sympathique

sympathize ['sɪmpə,θaɪz] *intr*—**to sympathize with** compatir à; comprendre

sympa·thy ['sɪmpəθi] *s* (*pl* **-thies**) sympathie *f*; (*shared sorrow*) compassion *f*; **to be in sympathy with** être en sympathie avec; **to extend one's sympathy to** offrir ses condoléances à

sym'pathy strike' *s* grève *f* de solidarité

sympho·ny ['sɪmfəni] *s* (*pl* **-nies**) symphonie *f*

symposi·um [sɪm'pozɪ·əm] *s* (*pl* **-a** [ə]) colloque *m*, symposium *m*

symptom ['sɪmptəm] *s* symptôme *m*

synagogue ['sɪnə,gɔg], ['sɪnə,gag] *s* synagogue *f*

synchronize ['sɪŋkrə,naɪz] *tr* synchroniser

synchronous ['sɪŋkrənəs] *adj* synchrone

syncopation [,sɪŋkə'peʃən] *s* syncope *f*

syncope ['sɪŋkə,pi] *s* syncope *f*

syndicate ['sɪndɪkɪt] *s* syndicat *m* || ['sɪndɪ,ket] *tr* syndiquer || *intr* se syndiquer

synonym ['sɪnənɪm] *s* synonyme *m*

synonymous [sɪ'nɑnɪməs] *adj* synonyme

synop·sis [sɪ'nɑpsɪs] *s* (*pl* **-ses** [siz]) abrégé *m*, résumé *m*; (mov) synopsis *m & f*

syntax ['sɪntæks] *s* syntaxe *f*

synthe·sis ['sɪnθɪsɪs] *s* (*pl* **-ses** [,siz]) synthèse *f*

synthesize ['sɪnθɪ,saɪz] *tr* synthétiser

synthetic(al) [sɪn'θetɪk(əl)] *adj* synthétique
syphilis ['sɪfɪlɪs] *s* syphilis *f*
Syria ['sɪrɪ·ə] *s* Syrie *f*; la Syrie
Syrian ['sɪrɪ·ən] *adj* syrien || *s* (*language*) syrien *m*; (*person*) Syrien *m*
syringe [sɪ'rɪndʒ], ['sɪrɪndʒ] *s* seringue *f* || *tr* seringuer

syrup ['sɪrəp], ['sʌrəp] *s* sirop *m*
system ['sɪstəm] *s* système *m*; (*of lines, wires, pipes, roads*) réseau *m*
systematic(al) [‚sɪstə'mætɪk(əl)] *adj* systématique
systematize ['sɪstəmə‚taɪz] *tr* systématiser
systole ['sɪstəli] *s* systole *f*

T

T, t [ti] *s* XXe lettre de l'alphabet
tab [tæb] *s* patte *f*; (*label*) étiquette *f*; **to keep tab on** (coll) garder à l'œil; **to pick up the tab** (coll) payer l'addition
tab-by ['tæbi] *s* (*pl* **-bies**) chat *m* moucheté; (*female cat*) chatte *f*; (*old maid*) vieille fille *f*; (*spiteful female*) vieille chipie *f*
tabernacle ['tæbər‚nækəl] *s* tabernacle *m*
table ['tebəl] *s* table *f*; (*tableland*) plateau *m*; (*list, chart*) tableau *m*, table; **to clear the table** ôter le couvert; **to set the table** mettre le couvert || *tr* ajourner la discussion de
tab-leau ['tæblo] *s* (*pl* **-leaux** or **-leaus** [loz]) tableau *m* vivant
ta'ble-cloth' *s* nappe *f*
table d'hôte ['tabəl'dot] *s* repas *m* à prix fixe
ta'ble-land' *s* plateau *m*
ta'ble lin'en *s* nappage *m*, linge *m* de table
ta'ble man'ners *spl*—**to have good table manners** bien se tenir à table
tab'le-mate' *s* commensal *m*
ta'ble of con'tents *s* table *f* des matières
ta'ble-spoon' *s* cuiller *f* à soupe
tablespoonful ['tebəl‚spun‚ful] *s* cuillerée *f* à soupe or à bouche
tablet ['tæblɪt] *s* (*writing pad*) bloc-notes *m*, bloc *m*; (*lozenge*) pastille *f*, comprimé *m*; plaque *f* commémorative
ta'ble talk' *s* propos *mpl* de table
ta'ble ten'nis *s* tennis *m* de table
ta'ble-top' *s* dessus *m* de table
ta'ble-ware' *s* ustensiles *mpl* de table
ta'ble wine' *s* vin *m* ordinaire
tabloid ['tæblɔɪd] *adj* (*press, article, etc.*) à sensation || *s* journal *m* de petit format à l'affût du sensationnel
taboo [tə'bu] *adj* & *s* tabou *m* || *tr* déclarer tabou
tabular ['tæbjələr] *adj* tabulaire
tabulate ['tæbjə‚let] *tr* disposer en forme de table or en tableaux, dresser un tableau de, aligner en colonnes
tabulator ['tæbjə‚letər] *s* tabulateur *m*
tacit ['tæsɪt] *adj* tacite
taciturn ['tæsɪtərn] *adj* taciturne
tack [tæk] *s* (*nail*) semence *f*; (*plan*) voie *f*, tactique *f*; (*of sail*) amure *f*; (*naut*) bordée *f*; (*sewing*) point *m* de

bâti || *tr* clouer; (*sewing*) bâtir || *intr* louvoyer
tackle ['tækəl] *s* attirail *m*; (*for lifting*) treuil *m*; (*football*) plaquage *m*; (*naut*) palan *m* || *tr* empoigner, saisir; (*a problem, job, etc.*) chercher à résoudre, attaquer; (*football*) plaquer
tack-y ['tæki] *adj* (*comp* **-ier**; *super* **-iest**) collant; (coll) râpé, minable
tact [tækt] *s* tact *m*
tactful ['tæktfəl] *adj* plein de tact; **to be tactful** avoir du tact
tactical ['tæktɪkəl] *adj* tactique
tactician [tæk'tɪʃən] *s* tacticien *m*
tactics ['tæktɪks] *spl* tactique *f*
tactless ['tæktlɪs] *adj* sans tact
tadpole ['tæd‚pol] *s* têtard *m*
taffeta ['tæfɪtə] *s* taffetas *m*
taffy ['tæfi] *s* pâte *f* à berlingots; (coll) flagornerie *f*
tag [tæg] *s* (*label*) étiquette *f*; (*of shoelace*) ferret *m*; (*game*) chat *m* perché || *v* (*pret* & *pp* **tagged**; *ger* **tagging**) *tr* étiqueter; (*in the game of tag*) attraper || *intr* (coll) suivre de près; **to tag along behind s.o.** (coll) traîner derrière qn
tag' day' *s* jour *m* de collecte publique
tag' end' *s* queue *f*; (*remnant*) coupon *m*
Tagus ['tegəs] *s* Tage *m*
tail [tel] *s* queue *f*; (*of shirt*) pan *m*; **tails** (*of a coin*) pile *f*; (coll) frac *m*; **to turn tail** tourner les talons || *tr* (coll) suivre de tout près || *intr*—**to tail after** marcher sur les talons de; **to tail off** s'éteindre, disparaître
tail' assem'bly *s* (*pl* **-blies**) (aer) empennage *m*
tail' end' *s* queue *f*, fin *f*
tail'light' *s* feu *m* arrière
tailor ['telər] *s* tailleur *m* || *tr* (*a suit*) faire || *intr* être tailleur
tailoring ['telərɪŋ] *s* métier *m* de tailleur
tai'lor-made suit' *s* (*men's*) costume *m* sur mesure, complet *m* sur mesure; (*women's*) costume tailleur, tailleur *m*
tai'lor shop' *s* boutique *f* de tailleur
tail'piece' *s* queue *f*; (*of stringed instrument*) cordier *m*
tail'race' *s* canal *m* de fuite
tail'spin' *s* chute *f* en vrille
tail'wind' *s* (aer) vent *m* arrière; (naut) vent en poupe

taint [tent] *s* tache *f* || *tr* tacher; (*food*) gâter

take [tek] *s* prise *f*; (*mov*) prise de vues; (*slang*) recette *f* || *v* (*pret* took [tʊk]; *pp* taken) *tr* prendre; (*a walk; a trip*) faire; (*a course; advice*) suivre; (*an examination*) passer; (*a person on a trip*) emmener; (*the occasion*) profiter de; (*a photograph*) prendre; (*a newspaper*) être abonné à; (*a purchase*) garder; (*a certain amount of time*) falloir, e.g., **it takes an hour to walk there** il faut une heure pour y aller à pied; (*to lead*) conduire, mener; (*to tolerate, stand*) supporter; (*a seat*) prendre, occuper, e.g., **this seat is taken** cette place est prise ou occupée; **do you take that to be important?** tenez-vous cela pour important?; **I take it that je** suppose que; **take it easy!** (coll) allez-y doucement!; **to be taken ill** tomber malade; **to take amiss** prendre mal; **to take away** enlever; emmener; (*to subtract*) soustraire, retrancher; **to take down** descendre; (*a building*) démolir; (*in writing*) noter; **to take in** (*a roomer*) recevoir; (*laundry*) prendre à faire à la maison; (*the harvest*) rentrer; (*a seam*) reprendre; (*to include*) embrasser; (*to deceive*) (coll) duper; **to take off** ôter, enlever; (*from the price*) rabattre; (*to imitate*) (coll) singer; **to take on** (*passengers*) prendre; (*a responsibility*) prendre sur soi; (*workers*) embaucher, prendre; **to take out** sortir; (*a bullet from a wound; a passage from a text; an element from a compound*) extraire; (*public sign*) à emporter; **to take place** avoir lieu; **to take s.th. from s.o.** enlever, ôter, ou prendre q.ch. à qn; **to take up** (*to carry up*) monter; (*to remove*) enlever; (*a dress*) raccourcir; (*an idea, method, etc.*) adopter; (*a profession*) embrasser, prendre; (*a question, a study, etc.*) aborder || *intr* prendre; **to not take to** (*a person*) prendre en grippe; **to take after** ressembler à; (*to chase*) poursuivre; **to take off** s'en aller; (aer) décoller; **to take to** (*flight; the woods*) prendre; (*a bad habit*) se livrer à; (*a person*) se prendre d'amitié avec; (*to like*) s'adonner à; **to take to + inf** se mettre à + *inf*; **to take up with s.o.** (coll) se lier avec qn

take'-off' *s* (aer) décollage *m*; (coll) caricature *f*

tal'cum pow'der ['tælkəm] *s* poudre *f* de talc

tale [tel] *s* conte *m*; mensonge *m*; (*gossip*) raconter *m*, histoire *f*

tale'bear'er *s* rapporteur *m*

talent ['tælənt] *s* talent *m*; gens *mpl* de talent

talented ['tæləntɪd] *adj* doué, talentueux

tal'ent scout' *s* dénicheur *m* de vedettes

tal'ent show' *s* crochet *m* radiophonique, radio-crochet *m*

talk [tɔk] *s* paroles *fpl*; (*gossip*) raconters *mpl*, dires *mpl*; (*lecture*) conférence *f*, causerie *f*; **to cause talk** défrayer la chronique; **to have a talk with** s'entretenir avec || *tr* parler; **to talk over** discuter; **to talk up** vanter || *intr* parler; (*to chatter, gossip, etc.*) bavarder, jaser; **to talk back** répliquer; **to talk on** continuer à parler

talkative ['tɔkətɪv] *adj* bavard

talker ['tɔkər] *s* parleur *m*; **a great talker** (coll) un causeur, un hâbleur

talkie ['tɔki] *s* (coll) film *m* parlant

talk'ing doll' ['tɔkɪŋ] *s* poupée *f* parlante

talk'ing pic'ture *s* film *m* parlant

tall [tɔl] *adj* haut, élevé; (*person*) grand; (coll) exagéré

tallow ['tælo] *s* suif *m*

tal·ly ['tæli] *s* (*pl* -lies) compte *m*, pointage *m* || *v* (*pret & pp* -lied) *tr* pointer, contrôler || *intr* s'accorder

tallyho ['tæli,ho] *interj* taïaut!

tal'ly sheet' *s* feuille *f* de pointage, bordereau *m*

talon ['tælən] *s* serre *f*

tamarack ['tæmə,ræk] *s* mélèze *m* d'Amérique

tambourine [,tæmbə'rin] *s* tambour *m* de basque

tame [tem] *adj* apprivoisé; (*e.g., lion*) dompté; (*e.g., style*) fade, terne || *tr* apprivoiser; (*e.g., a lion*) dompter

tamp [tæmp] *tr* bourrer; (*e.g., a hole in the ground*) damer

tamper ['tæmpər] *intr*—**to tamper with** se mêler de; (*a lock*) fausser; (*a document*) falsifier; (*a witness*) suborner

tampon ['tæmpɑn] *s* (surg) tampon *m* || *tr* (surg) tamponner

tan [tæn] *adj* jaune; (*e.g., skin*) bronzé, hâlé || *v* (*pret & pp* tanned; *ger* tanning) *tr* tanner; (*e.g., the skin*) bronzer, hâler || *intr* se hâler

tandem ['tændəm] *adj & adv* en tandem, en flèche || *s* tandem *m*

tang [tæŋ] *s* goût *m* vif, saveur *f*; (*ringing sound*) tintement *m*

tangent ['tændʒənt] *adj* tangent || *s* tangente *f*; **to fly off at or on a tangent** changer brusquement de sujet

tangerine [,tændʒə'rin] *s* mandarine *f*

tangible ['tændʒɪbəl] *adj* tangible

Tangier [tæn'dʒɪr] *s* Tanger *m*

tangle ['tæŋgəl] *s* enchevêtrement *m* || *tr* enchevêtrer || *intr* s'enchevêtrer

tank [tæŋk] *s* réservoir *m*; (mil) char *m*

tank' car' *s* (rr) wagon-citerne *m*

tanker ['tæŋkər] *s* (ship) bateau-citerne *m*; (*truck*) camion-citerne *m*; (*plane*) ravitailleur *m*

tank' truck' *s* camion-citerne *m*

tanner ['tænər] *s* tanneur *m*

tanner·y ['tænəri] *s* (*pl* -ies) tannerie *f*

tantalize ['tæntə,laɪz] *tr* tenter, allécher

tantamount ['tæntə,maunt] *adj* équivalent

tantrum ['tæntrəm] *s* accès *m* de colère; **in a tantrum** en rogne

tap [tæp] *s* petit coup *m*; (*faucet*) robinet *m*; (elec) prise *f*; (mach) taraud *m*; **on tap** au tonneau, en perce;

(*available*) (coll) disponible; **taps** (mil) l'extinction *f* des feux || *v* (*pret & pp* **tapped**; *ger* **tapping**) *tr* taper; (*a cask*) mettre en perce; (*a tree*) entailler; (*a telephone*) passer à la table d'écoute; (*a nut*) tarauder; (*resources, talent, etc.*) drainer; (elec) brancher sur || *intr* taper

tap′ dance′ *s* danse *f* à claquettes

tap′-dance′ *intr* danser les claquettes, faire les claquettes

tap′ dan′cer *s* danseur *m* à claquettes

tape [tep] *s* ruban *m* || *tr* (*an electric wire*) guiper; (*land*) mesurer au cordeau; (*to tape-record*) enregistrer sur ruban

tape′ meas′ure *s* mètre-ruban *m*, centimètre *m*

taper ['tepər] *s* (*for lighting candles*) allumette-bougie *f*; (eccl) cierge *m* || *tr* effiler || *intr* s'effiler

tape′-record′ *tr* enregistrer sur ruban magnétique ou au magnétophone

tape′ record′er *s* magnétophone *m*

tapes·try ['tæpɪstri] *s* (*pl* **-tries**) tapisserie *f* || *v* (*pret & pp* **-tried**) *tr* tapisser

tape′worm′ *s* ver *m* solitaire

tappet ['tæpɪt] *s* (mach) taquet *m*

tap′room′ *s* débit *m* de boissons, buvette *f*

tap′ wa′ter *s* eau *f* du robinet

tap′ wrench′ *s* taraudeuse *f*

tar [tar] *s* goudron *m*; (coll) marin *m* || *v* (*pret & pp* **tarred**; *ger* **tarring**) *tr* goudronner; **to tar and feather** enduire de goudron et de plumes

tar·dy ['tardi] *adj* (*comp* **-dier**; *super* **-diest**) lent; retardataire, en retard

tare [ter] *s* (*weight*) tare *f*; (Bib) ivraie *f* || *tr* tarer

target ['targɪt] *s* cible *f*; (*goal*) but *m*; (mil) objectif *m*; (*butt*) (fig) cible

tar′get ar′ea *s* zone *f* de tir

tar′get lan′guage *s* langue *f* cible

tar′get prac′tice *s* tir *m* à la cible

tariff ['tærɪf] *s* (*duties*) droits *mpl* de douane; (*rates in general*) tarif *m*

tarnish ['tarnɪʃ] *s* ternissure *f* || *tr* ternir ‖ *intr* se ternir

tar′ pa′per *s* papier *m* goudronné

tarpaulin [tar'pɔlɪn] *s* bâche *f*, prélart *m*

tarragon ['tærəgən] *s* estragon *m*

tar·ry ['tari] *adj* (*comp* **-rier**; *super* **-riest**) goudronneux ‖ ['tæri] *v* (*pret & pp* **-ried**) *intr* tarder; (*to stay*) rester, demeurer

tart [tart] *adj* aigrelet; (*reply*) mordant ‖ *s* tarte *f*; (slang) grue *f*, poule *f*

tartar ['tartər] *adj* (*sauce*) tartare; **Tartar** tartare ‖ *s* (*on teeth*) tartre *m*; **Tartar** Tartare *mf*

task [tæsk], [task] *s* tâche *f*; **to bring or take to task** prendre à partie

task′ force′ *s* (mil) groupement *m* stratégique mixte

task′mas′ter *s* chef *m* de corvée; (fig) tyran *m*

tassel ['tæsəl] *s* gland *m*; (*on corn*) barbe *f*; (*on nightcap*) mèche *f*; (bot) aigrette *f*

---

taste [test] *s* goût *m*, saveur *f*; (*sense of what is fitting*) goût, bon goût || *tr* goûter; (*to sample*) goûter à; (*to try out*) goûter de ‖ *intr* goûter; **to taste like** avoir le goût de; **to taste of** avoir un goût de

taste′ bud′ *s* papille *f* gustative

tasteless ['testlɪs] *adj* sans saveur, fade; (*in bad taste*) de mauvais goût

tast·y ['testi] *adj* (*comp* **-ier**; *super* **-iest**) (coll) savoureux; (coll) de bon goût

tatter ['tætər] *s* lambeau *m* || *tr* mettre en lambeaux

tatterdemalion [ˌtætərdɪ'meljən], [ˌtætərdɪ'mæljən] *s* loqueteux *m*

tattered *adj* en lambeaux, en loques

tattle ['tætəl] *s* bavardage *m*; (*gossip*) cancan *m* ‖ *intr* bavarder; cancaner

tat′tle·tale′ *adj* révélateur ‖ *s* rapporteur *m*, cancanier *m*

tattoo [tæ'tu] *s* tatouage *m*; (mil) retraite *f* ‖ *tr* tatouer

taunt [tɔnt], [tant] *s* sarcasme *m* || *tr* bafouer

taut [tɔt] *adj* tendu

tavern ['tævərn] *s* café *m*, bar *m*, bistrot *m*; (*inn*) taverne *f*

taw·dry ['tɔdri] *adj* (*comp* **-drier**; *super* **-driest**) criard, voyant

taw·ny ['tɔni] *adj* (*comp* **-nier**; *super* **-niest**) fauve; (*skin*) basané

tax [tæks] *s* impôt *m*; **to reduce the tax on** dégrever || *tr* imposer; (*e.g., one's patience*) mettre à l'épreuve; **to tax s.o. with** (*e.g., laziness*) taxer qn de

taxable ['tæksəbəl] *adj* imposable

taxation [tæk'seʃən] *s* imposition *f*; charges *fpl* fiscales, impôts *mpl*

tax′ collec′tor *s* percepteur *m*

tax′ cut′ *s* dégrèvement *m* d'impôt

tax′ eva′sion *s* fraude *f* fiscale

tax′-exempt′ *adj* net d'impôt, exempt d'impôts

tax·i ['tæksi] *s* (*pl* **-is**) taxi *m* || *v* (*pret & pp* **-ied**; *ger* **-ling** or **-ying**) *tr* (aer) rouler au sol ‖ *intr* aller en taxi; (aer) rouler au sol ‖ *interj* hep taxi!

tax′i-cab′ *s* taxi *m*

tax′i danc′er *s* taxi-girl *f*

taxidermy ['tæksɪˌdɑrmi] *s* taxidermie *f*

tax′i driv′er *s* chauffeur *m* de taxi

tax′i-plane′ *s* avion-taxi *m*

tax′i stand′ *s* station *f* de taxis

tax′pay′er *s* contribuable *mf*

tax′ rate′ *s* taux *m* de l'impôt

tea [ti] *s* thé *m*; (*medicinal infusion*) tisane *f*

tea′ bag′ *s* sachet *m* de thé

tea′ ball′ *s* boule *f* à thé

tea′cart′ *s* table *f* roulante

teach [titʃ] *v* (*pret & pp* **taught** [tɔt]) *tr* enseigner; **to teach s.o. s.th.** enseigner q.ch. à qn; **to teach s.o. to +** *inf* enseigner à qn à + *inf* ‖ *intr* enseigner

teacher ['titʃər] *s* instituteur *m*, enseignant *m*; (*such as adversity*) (fig) maître *m*

teach′er's pet′ *s* élève *m* gâté

teaching ['titʃɪŋ] *s* enseignement *m*

teach′ing aids′ *spl* matériel *m* auxiliaire d'enseignement

teach′ing staff′ *s* corps *m* enseignant

tea′cup′ *s* tasse *f* à thé

tea′ dance′ *s* thé dansant

teak [tik] *s* teck *m*

tea′ket′tle *s* bouilloire *f*

team [tim] *s* (*of horses, oxen, etc.*) attelage *m*; (*sports*) équipe *f* ‖ *tr* atteler ‖ *intr*—**to team up with** faire équipe avec

team′mate′ *s* équipier *m*

teamster [′timstər] *s* (*of horses*) charretier *m*; (*of a truck*) camionneur *m*

team′work′ *s* travail *m* en équipe; (*spirit*) esprit *m* d'équipe

tea′pot′ *s* théière *f*

tear [tɪr] *s* larme *f*; **to burst into tears** fondre en larmes ‖ [tɛr] *s* déchirure *f* ‖ [tɛr] *v* (*pret* **tore** [tor]; *pp* **torn** [torn]) *tr* déchirer; **to tear away, down, off,** or **out** arracher; **to tear up** (*e.g., a letter*) déchirer ‖ *intr* se déchirer; **to tear along** filer précipitamment, aller à fond de train

tear′ bomb′ [tɪr] *s* bombe *f* lacrymogène

tear′ duct′ [tɪr] *s* conduit *m* lacrymal

tearful [′tɪrfəl] *adj* larmoyant, éploré

tear′ gas′ [tɪr] *s* gaz *m* lacrymogène

tear-jerker [′tɪr‚dʒʌrkər] *s* (slang) comédie *f* larmoyante

tea′room′ *s* salon *m* de thé

tease [tiz] *tr* taquiner

tea′spoon′ *s* cuiller *f* à café

teaspoonful [′ti‚spun‚ful] *s* cuillerée *f* à café

teat [tit] *s* tétine *f*

tea′time′ *s* l'heure *f* du thé

technical [′tɛknɪkəl] *adj* technique

technical·i·ty [‚tɛknɪ′kælɪtɪ] *s* (*pl* **-ties**) technicité *f*; (*fine point*) subtilité *f*

technician [tɛk′nɪʃən] *s* technicien *m*

technique [tɛk′nik] *s* technique *f*

ted′dy bear′ [′tɛdɪ] *s* ours *m* en peluche

tedious [′tidɪ·əs], [′tidʒəs] *adj* ennuyeux, fatigant

teem [tim] *intr* fourmiller; **to teem with** abonder en, fourmiller de

teeming [′timɪŋ] *adj* fourmillant; (*rain*) torrentiel

teen-ager [′tin‚edʒər] *s* adolescent *m* de 13 à 19 ans

teens [tinz] *spl* numéros anglais qui se terminent en -teen (de 13 à 19); adolescence *f* de 13 à 19 ans; **to be in one's teens** être adolescent

tee·ny [′tini] *adj* (*comp* **-nier;** *super* **-niest**) (coll) minuscule, tout petit

teeter [′titər] *s* branlement *m*; balançoire *f* ‖ *intr* se balancer, chanceler

teethe [tið] *intr* faire ses dents

teething [′tiðɪŋ] *s* dentition *f*

teeth′ing ring′ *s* sucette *f*

teetotaler [ti′totələr] *s* antialcoolique *mf* (*qui s'abstient totalement de boissons alcooliques*)

tele·cast [′tɛlɪ‚kæst], [′tɛlɪ‚kɑst] *s* émission *f* télévisée ‖ *v* (*pret & pp* **-cast** or **-casted**) *tr & intr* téléviser

telegram [′tɛlɪ‚græm] *s* télégramme *m*

telegraph [′tɛlɪ‚græf], [′tɛlɪ‚grɑf] *s* télégraphe *m* ‖ *tr & intr* télégraphier

telegrapher [tɪ′lɛgrəfər] *s* télégraphiste *mf*

tel′egraph pole′ *s* poteau *m* télégraphique

telemeter [tɪ′lɛmɪtər] *s* télémètre *m*

telepathy [tɪ′lɛpəθɪ] *s* télépathie *f*

telephone [′tɛlɪ‚fon] *s* téléphone *m* ‖ *tr & intr* téléphoner

tel′ephone booth′ *s* cabine *f* téléphonique

tel′ephone call′ *s* appel *m* téléphonique

tel′ephone direc′tory *s* annuaire *m* du téléphone

tel′ephone exchange′ *s* central *m* téléphonique

tel′ephone op′erator *s* standardiste *mf*, téléphoniste *f*

tel′ephone receiv′er *s* récepteur *m* de téléphone

tel′ephoto lens′ [′tɛlɪ‚foto] *s* téléobjectif *m*

teleprinter [′tɛlɪ‚prɪntər] *s* téléimprimeur *m*

telescope [′tɛlɪ‚skop] *s* télescope *m* ‖ *tr* télescoper ‖ *intr* se télescoper

telescopic [‚tɛlɪ′skɑpɪk] *adj* télescopique

teletype [′tɛlɪ‚taɪp] *s* (trademark) télétype *m*

tel′etype′writ′er *s* téléscripteur *m*

teleview [′tɛlɪ‚vju] *tr & intr* voir à la télévision

televiewer [′tɛlɪ‚vju·ər] *s* téléspectateur *m*

televise [′tɛlɪ‚vaɪz] *tr* téléviser

television [′tɛlɪ‚vɪʒən] *adj* télévisuel ‖ *s* télévision *f*

tel′evision screen′ *s* écran *m* de télévision, petit écran

tel′evision set′ *s* téléviseur *m*

tell [tɛl] *v* (*pret & pp* **told** [told]) *tr* dire; (*a story*) raconter; (*to count*) compter; (*to recognize as distinct*) distinguer; **tell me another!** (coll) à d'autres!; **to tell off** compter; (coll) dire son fait à; **to tell s.o. to** + *inf* dire à qn de + *inf* ‖ *intr* produire un effet; **do tell!** (coll) vraiment!; **to tell on** influer sur; (coll) dénoncer; **who can tell?** qui sait?

teller [′tɛlər] *s* narrateur *m*; (*of a bank*) caissier *m*; (*of votes*) scrutateur *m*

temper [′tɛmpər] *s* humeur *f*, caractère *m*; (*of steel, glass, etc.*) trempe *f*; **to keep one's temper** retenir sa colère; **to lose one's temper** se mettre en colère ‖ *tr* tremper ‖ *intr* se tremper

temperament [′tɛmpərəmənt] *s* tempérament *m*

temperamental [‚tɛmpərə′mɛntəl] *adj* constitutionnel; capricieux, instable

temperance [′tɛmpərəns] *s* tempérance *f*

temperate [′tɛmpərɪt] *adj* tempéré; (*in food or drink*) tempérant

temperature [′tɛmpərətʃər] *s* température *f*

tempest [′tɛmpɪst] *s* tempête *f*; **tempest in a teapot** tempête dans un verre d'eau tempestuous [tem'pestʃʊ·əs] adj tempétueux

temple ['tempəl] s temple m; (side of forehead) tempe f; (of spectacles) branche f

templet ['templɪt] s gabarit m

tem·po ['tempo] s (pl -pos or -pi [pi]) tempo m

temporal ['tempərəl] adj temporel; (anat) temporal

temporary ['tempə‚reri] adj temporaire

temporize ['tempə‚raɪz] intr temporiser

tempt [tempt] tr tenter

temptation [temp'teʃən] s tentation f

tempter ['temptər] s tentateur m

tempting ['temptɪŋ] adj tentant

ten [ten] adj & pron dix; about ten une dizaine de || s dix m; ten o'clock dix heures

tenable ['tenəbəl] adj soutenable

tenacious [tɪ'neʃəs] adj tenace

tenacity [tɪ'næsɪti] s ténacité f

tenant ['tenənt] s locataire mf

ten'ant farm'er s métayer m

tend [tend] tr soigner; (sheep) garder; (a machine) surveiller || intr—to tend to (to be disposed to) tendre à; (to attend to) vaquer à; to tend towards tendre vers or à

tenden·cy ['tendənsi] s (pl -cies) tendance f

tender ['tendər] adj tendre || s offre f; (aer, naut) ravitailleur m; (rr) tender m || tr offrir

ten'der-heart'ed adj au cœur tendre

ten'der-loin' s filet m

tenderness ['tendərnɪs] s tendresse f; (of, e.g., the skin) sensibilité f; (of, e.g., meat) tendreté f

tendon ['tendən] s tendon m

tendril ['tendrɪl] s vrille f

tenement ['tenɪmənt] s maison f d'habitation

ten'ement house' s maison f de rapport; (in the slums) taudis m

tenet ['tenɪt] s doctrine f, principe m

tennis ['tenɪs] s tennis m

ten'nis court' s court m de tennis

tenor ['tenər] s teneur f, cours m; (mus) ténor m

tense [tens] adj tendu || s (gram) temps m

tension ['tenʃən] s tension f

tent [tent] s tente f

tentacle ['tentəkəl] s tentacule m

tentative ['tentətɪv] adj provisoire; (hesitant) timide

tenth [tenθ] adj & pron dixième (masc, fem); the Tenth dix, e.g., John the Tenth Jean dix || s dixième m; the tenth (in dates) le dix

tent' pole' s montant m de tente

tenuous ['tenjʊ·əs] adj ténu

tenure ['tenjər] s (possession) tenure f; (of an office) occupation f; (protection from dismissal) inamovibilité f

tepid ['tepɪd] adj tiède

term [tʌrm] s terme m; (of imprisonment) temps m; (of office) mandat m; (of the school year) semestre m; terms conditions fpl || tr appeler, qualifier

termagant ['tʌrməgənt] s mégère f

terminal ['tʌrmɪnəl] adj terminal || s (elec) borne f; (rr) terminus m

terminate ['tʌrmɪ‚net] tr terminer || intr se terminer

termination [‚tʌrmɪ'neʃən] s conclusion f; (extremity) bout m; (of word) désinence f

terminus ['tʌrmɪnəs] s bout m, extrémité f; (boundary) borne f; (rr) terminus m

termite ['tʌrmaɪt] s termite m

term' pa'per s dissertation f

terrace ['terəs] s terrasse f || tr disposer en terrasse

terra firma ['terə'fʌrmə] s terre f ferme

terrain [te'ren] s terrain m

terrestrial [tə'restrɪ·əl] adj terrestre

terrible ['terɪbəl] adj terrible; (extremely bad) atroce

terrific [tə'rɪfɪk] adj terrible, terrifiant; (coll) formidable

terri·fy ['terɪ‚faɪ] v (pret & pp -fied) tr terrifier

territo·ry ['terɪ‚tori] s (pl -ries) territoire m

terror ['terər] s terreur f

terrorize ['terə‚raɪz] tr terroriser

ter'ry cloth' ['teri] s tissu-éponge m

terse [tʌrs] adj concis, succinct

tertiary ['tʌrʃɪ‚eri], ['tʌrʃəri] adj tertiaire

test [test] s épreuve f; (exam) examen m; (trial) essai m; (e.g., of intelligence) test m || tr éprouver, mettre à l'épreuve; examiner, tester

testament ['testəmənt] s testament m

test' ban' s interdiction f des essais nucléaires

test' flight' s vol m d'essai

testicle ['testɪkəl] s testicule m

testi·fy ['testɪ‚faɪ] v (pret & pp -fied) tr déclarer || intr déposer; to testify to témoigner de

testimonial [‚testɪ'monɪ·əl] s attestation f

testimo·ny ['testɪ‚moni] s (pl -nies) témoignage m

test' pat'tern s (telv) mire f

test' pi'lot s pilote m d'essai

test' tube' s éprouvette f

tes·ty ['testi] adj (comp -tier; super -tiest) susceptible

tetanus ['tetənəs] s tétanos m

tether ['teðər] s attache f; at the end of one's tether à bout de ressources || tr mettre à l'attache

tetter ['tetər] s (pathol) dartre f

text [tekst] s texte m

text'book' s manuel m scolaire, livre m de classe

textile ['tekstɪl], ['tekstaɪl] adj & s textile m

textual ['tekstʃʊ·əl] adj textuel

texture ['tekstʃər] s texture f; (woven fabric) tissu m

Thai [tɑ·i], [taɪ] adj thaï, thaïlandais || s (language) thaï m; (person)

Thaïlandais *m*; **the Thai** les Thaïlandais

Thailand ['tailənd] *s* Thaïlande *f*; la Thaïlande

Thames [temz] *s* Tamise *f*

than [ðæn] *conj* que; (*before a numeral*) de, e.g., **more than three** plus de trois

thank [θæŋk] *adj* (*e.g., offering*) de reconnaissance ‖ **thanks** *spl* remerciements *mpl*; **thanks to** grâce à ‖ **thanks** *interj* merci!; **no thanks!** merci ‖ **thank** *tr* remercier; **thank you je vous remercie; thank you for** merci de or pour; **thank you for** + *ger* merci de + *inf*; **to thank s.o. for** remercier qn de or pour; **to thank s.o. for** + *ger* remercier qn de + *inf*

thankful ['θæŋkfəl] *adj* reconnaissant

thankless ['θæŋklɪs] *adj* ingrat

Thanksgiv'ing Day' *s* le jour d'action de grâces

that [ðæt] *adj dem* (*pl* **those**) ce §82; **that one** celui-là §84 ‖ *pron dem* (*pl* **those**) celui §83; celui-là §84 ‖ *pron rel* qui; que ‖ *pron neut* cela, ça; **that is** c'est-à-dire; **that's all** voilà tout; **that will do** cela suffit ‖ *adv* tellement, si, aussi; **that far** si loin, aussi loin; **that much, that many** tant ‖ *conj* que; (*in order that*) pour que, afin que; **in that** en ce que

thatch [θætʃ] *s* chaume *m* ‖ *tr* couvrir de chaume

thatched' cot'tage *s* chaumière *f*

thaw [θɔ] *s* dégel *m* ‖ *tr & intr* dégeler

the [ðə], [ðɪ], [ði] *art def* le §77 ‖ *adv* d'autant plus, e.g., **she will be the happier for it** elle en sera d'autant plus heureuse; **the more . . . the more** plus . . . plus

theater ['θiətər] *s* théâtre *m*

the'ater club' *s* association *f* des spectateurs

the'ater-go'er *s* habitué *m* du théâtre

the'ater page' *s* chronique *f* théâtrale

theatrical [θɪ'ætrɪkəl] *adj* théâtral

thee [ði] *pron pers* (archaic, poetic, Bib) toi §85; te §87

theft [θɛft] *s* vol *m*

their [ðɛr] *adj poss* leur §88

theirs [ðɛrz] *pron poss* le leur §89

them [ðɛm] *pron pers* eux §85; les §87; leur §87; **of them** en §87; **to them** leur §87; y §87

theme [θim] *s* thème *m*; (*essay*) composition *f*; (mus) thème

theme' song' *s* leitmotiv *m*; (rad) indicatif *m*

them-selves' *pron pers* soi §85; eux-mêmes §86; se §87; eux §85

then [ðɛn] *adv* alors; (*next*) ensuite, puis; (*therefore*) donc; **by then** d'ici là; **from then on**, since then depuis lors, dès lors; **then and there** séance tenante; **till then** jusque-là; **what then?** et après?

thence [ðɛns] *adv* de là; (*from that fact*) pour cette raison

thence'forth' *adv* dès lors

theolo-gy [θi'ɑlədʒi] *s* (*pl* -gies) théologie *f*

theorem ['θiərəm] *s* théorème *m*

theoretical [,θiə'rɛtɪkəl] *adj* théorique

theo-ry ['θi·əri] *s* (*pl* -ries) théorie *f*

therapeutic [,θɛrə'pjutɪk] *adj* thérapeutique ‖ **therapeutics** *spl* thérapeutique *f*

thera-py ['θɛrəpi] *s* (*pl* -pies) thérapie *f*

there [ðɛr] *adv* là; y §87; **down there, over there** là-bas; **from there** de là; **en** §87; **in there** là-dedans; **on there** là-dessus; **there is or there are** il y a; (*pointing out*) voilà; **under there** là-dessous; **up there** là-haut

there'abouts' *adv* aux environs, près de là; (*approximately*) à peu près

there'af'ter *adv* par la suite

there'by' *adv* par là; de cette manière

therefore ['ðɛr,for] *adv* par conséquent, donc

there'in' *adv* dedans, là-dedans

there'of' *adv* de cela; en §87

there'upon' *adv* là-dessus §85A; sur cela

there'with' *adv* avec cela

thermal ['θʌrməl] *adj* (*waters*) thermal; (*capacity*) thermique

thermocouple ['θʌrmo,kʌpəl] *s* thermocouple *m*

thermodynamic [,θʌrmodai'næmɪk] *adj* thermodynamique ‖ **thermodynamics** *spl* thermodynamique *f*

thermometer [θər'mɑmɪtər] *s* thermomètre *m*

thermonuclear [,θʌrmo'n(j)uklɪ·ər] *adj* thermonucléaire

Thermopylae [θər'mɑpɪ,li] *s* les Thermopyles *fpl*

ther'mos bot'tle ['θʌrməs] *s* thermos *m & f*, bouteille *f* thermos

thermostat ['θʌrmə,stæt] *s* thermostat *m*

thesau-rus [θɪ'sɔrəs] *s* (*pl* -ri [rai]) trésor *m*; dictionnaire *m* analogique

these [ðiz] *adj dem pl* ces §82 ‖ *pron dem pl* ceux §83; ceux-ci §84

the-sis ['θisɪs] *s* (*pl* -ses [siz]) thèse *f*

they [ðe] *pron pers* ils §87; eux §85; on §87, e.g., **they say** on dit; ce §82B

thick [θɪk] *adj* épais; (*pipe, rod, etc.*) gros; (*forest, eyebrows, etc.*) touffu; (*grass, grain, etc.*) dru; (*voice*) pâteux; (*gravy*) court; (coll) stupide, obtus; (coll) intime ‖ *s* (*of thumb, leg, etc.*) gras *m*; **the thick of** (*e.g., a crowd*) le milieu de; (*e.g., a battle*) le fort de; **through thick and thin** contre vents et marées

thicken ['θɪkən] *tr* épaissir ‖ *intr* s'épaissir; (*said, e.g., of plot*) se corser

thicket ['θɪkɪt] *s* fourré *m*, maquis *m*

thick'-head'ed *adj* à la tête dure

thick'-lipped' *adj* lippu

thick'-set' *adj* trapu

thief [θif] *s* (*pl* **thieves** [θivz]) voleur *m*

thieve [θiv] *intr* voler

thiever-y ['θivəri] *s* (*pl* -ies) volerie *f*

thigh [θai] *s* cuisse *f*

thigh'bone' *s* fémur *m*

thimble ['θɪmbəl] *s* dé *m*

thin [θɪn] *adj* (*comp* **thinner**; *super* **thinnest**) mince; (*person*) élancé, maigre; (*hair*) rare; (*soup*) clair;

(gravy) long; (voice) grêle; (excuse) faible || v (pret & pp thinned; ger thinning) tr amincir; (colors) délayer; **to thin out** éclaircir || intr s'amincir; **to thin out** s'éclaircir

thine [ðaɪn] adj poss (archaic, poetic, Bib) ton §88 || pron poss (archaic, poetic, Bib) le tien §89

thing [θɪŋ] s chose f; **for another thing** d'autre part; **for one thing** en premier lieu; **of all things!** par exemple!; **to be the thing** être le dernier cri; **to see things** avoir des hallucinations

thingumbob ['θɪŋəm,bab] s (coll) truc m, machin m

think [θɪŋk] v (pret & pp thought [θɔt]) tr penser; (to deem, consider) estimer; **to think of** (to have as an opinion of) penser de || intr penser, songer; **to think fast** avoir l'esprit alerte; **to think of** (to direct one's thoughts toward) penser à, songer à; **to think of it or them** y penser, y songer; **to think so** croire que oui

thinker ['θɪŋkər] s penseur m

third [θʌrd] adj & pron troisième (masc, fem); **the Third** trois, e.g., **John the Third** Jean trois || s troisième m; (in fractions) tiers m; **the third** (in dates) le trois

third' degree' s (coll) passage m à tabac, cuisinage m

third' fin'ger s annulaire m

third' rail' s (rr) rail m de contact; rail conducteur

third'-rate' adj de troisième ordre

thirst [θʌrst] s soif f || intr avoir soif; **to thirst for** avoir soif de

thirst'-quench'ing adj désaltérant

thirst-y ['θʌrsti] adj (comp -ier; super -iest) altéré, assoiffé; **to be thirsty** avoir soif

thirteen ['θʌr'tin] adj, pron, & s treize m

thirteenth ['θʌr'tinθ] adj & pron treizième (masc, fem); **the Thirteenth** treize, e.g., **John the Thirteenth** Jean treize || s treizième m; **the thirteenth** (in dates) le treize

thirtieth ['θʌrtɪ-ɪθ] adj & pron trentième (masc, fem) || s trentième m; **the thirtieth** (in dates) trente

thir-ty ['θʌrti] adj & pron trente; **about thirty** une trentaine de || s (pl -ties) trente m; **the thirties** les années fpl trente

this [ðɪs] adj dem (pl these) ce §82; **this one** celui-ci §84 || pron dem (pl these) celui §83; celui-ci §84 || pron neut ceci §83; celui-ci §84 || pron neut ceci || adv tellement, si, aussi; **this far** si loin, aussi loin; **this much,** this many tant

thistle ['θɪsəl] s chardon m

thither ['θɪðər], ['ðɪðər] adv là, de ce côté là

thong [θɔŋ], [θɑŋ] s courroie f

tho-rax ['θoræks] s (pl -raxes or -races [rə,siz]) thorax m

thorn [θɔrn] s épine f

thorn-y ['θɔrni] adj (comp -ier; super -iest) épineux

thorough ['θʌro] adj approfondi, complet; consciencieux, minutieux

thor'ough-bred' adj de race, racé; (horse) pur sang || s personne f racée; (horse) pur-sang m

thor'ough-fare' s voie f de communication; **no thoroughfare** (public sign) rue barrée

thor'ough-go'ing adj parfait; consciencieux

thoroughly ['θʌroli] adv à fond

those [ðoz] adj dem pl ces §82 || pron dem pl ceux §83; ceux-là §84

thou [ðaʊ] pron pers (archaic, poetic, Bib) tu §87 || tr & intr tutoyer

though [ðo] adv cependant || conj (although) bien que, quoique; (even if) même si; **as though** comme si

thought [θɔt] s pensée f

thought' control' s asservissement m des consciences

thoughtful ['θɔtfəl] adj pensif; (considerate) prévenant, attentif; (serious) profond

thoughtless ['θɔtlɪs] adj étourdi, négligent; inconsidéré

thousand ['θaʊzənd] adj & pron mille; mil, e.g., **the year one thousand nineteen hundred and eighty-one** l'an mil neuf cent quatre-vingt-un || s mille m; **a thousand** un millier de, mille

thousandth ['θaʊzəndθ] adj & pron millième (masc, fem) || s millième m

thrash [θræʃ] tr rosser; (agr) battre; **to thrash out** débattre || intr s'agiter; (agr) battre le blé

thread [θrɛd] s fil m; (bot) filament m; (mach) filet m; **to hang by a thread** ne tenir qu'à un fil; **to lose the thread of** perdre le fil de || tr enfiler; (mach) fileter

thread'bare' adj élimé, râpé; (tire) usé jusqu'à la corde

threat [θrɛt] s menace f

threaten ['θrɛtən] tr & intr menacer

threatening ['θrɛtənɪŋ] adj menaçant

three [θri] adj & pron trois || s trois m; **three o'clock** trois heures; **three of a kind** (cards) un fredon

three'-cor'nered adj triangulaire; (hat) tricorne

three'-ply' adj à trois épaisseurs; (e.g., wool) à trois fils

three' R's' [ɑrz] spl la lecture, l'écriture et l'arithmétique, premières notions fpl

three'score' adj soixante

threno-dy ['θrɛnədi] s (pl -dies) thrène m

thresh [θrɛʃ] tr (agr) battre; **to thresh out** (a problem) débattre || intr s'agiter; (agr) battre le blé

thresh'ing floor' s aire f

thresh'ing machine' s batteuse f

threshold ['θrɛʃold] s seuil m; **to cross the threshold** franchir le seuil

thrice [θraɪs] adv trois fois

thrift [θrɪft] s économie f, épargne f

thrift-y ['θrɪfti] adj (comp -ier; super -iest) économe, ménager, frugal; prospère

thrill [θrɪl] *s* frisson *m* || *tr* faire frémir || *intr* frémir

thriller ['θrɪlər] *s* roman *m*, film *m*, or pièce *f* à sensation

thrilling ['θrɪlɪŋ] *adj* émouvant, passionnant

thrive [θraɪv] *v* (*pret* **thrived** or **throve** [θrov]; *pp* **thrived** or **thriven** ['θrɪvən]) *intr* prospérer; (*said of child, plant, etc.*) croître, se développer

throat [θrot] *s* gorge *f*; **to clear one's throat** s'éclaircir le gosier; **to have a sore throat** avoir mal à la gorge

throb [θrab] *s* palpitation *f*, battement *m*; (*of motor*) vrombissement *m* || *v* (*pret & pp* **throbbed**; *ger* **throbbing**) *intr* palpiter, battre fort; (*said of motor*) vrombir

throes [θroz] *spl* (*of childbirth*) douleurs *fpl*; (*of death*) affres *fpl*; **in the throes of** luttant avec

throne [θron] *s* trône *m*

throng [θrɔŋ], [θraŋ] *s* foule *f*, affluence *f* || *intr* affluer

throttle ['θratəl] *s* (*of steam engine*) régulateur *m*; (*aut*) étrangleur *m* || *tr* régler; étrangler

through [θru] *adj* direct; (*finished*) fini; (*traffic*) prioritaire || *adv* à travers; complètement || *prep* au travers de, par; grâce à, par le canal de

through-out/ *adv* d'un bout à l'autre || *prep* d'un bout à l'autre de; (*during*) pendant tout

through/ **street**/ *s* rue *f* à circulation prioritaire

through/**way**/ *s* autoroute *f*

throw [θro] *s* jet *m*, lancement *m*; (*scarf*) châle *m* || *v* (*pret* **threw** [θru]; *pp* **thrown**) *tr* jeter, lancer; (*a glance; the dice*) jeter; (*e.g., a baseball*) lancer; (*e.g., a shadow*) jeter; (*blame; responsibility*) rejeter; (*a rider*) désarçonner; (*a game, career, etc.*) perdre à dessein; **to throw away** jeter; **to throw back** renvoyer; **to throw in** ajouter; **to throw out** expulser, chasser; (*e.g., an odor*) répandre; (*one's chest*) bomber; **to throw over** abandonner; **to throw up** jeter en l'air; vomir; (*one's hands*) lever; (*e.g., one's claims*) renoncer à || *intr* jeter, lancer; jeter les dés; **to throw up** vomir

throw/**back**/ *s* recul *m*; (*setback*) échec *m*; (*reversion*) retour *m* atavique

thrum [θrʌm] *v* (*pret & pp* **thrummed**; *ger* **thrumming**) *intr* pianoter

thrush [θrʌʃ] *s* grive *f*

thrust [θrʌst] *s* poussée *f*; (*with a weapon*) coup *m* de pointe; (*with a sword*) coup d'estoc; (*jibe*) trait *m*; (*rok*) poussée *f*; **thrust and parry the botte et la parade** || *v* (*pret & pp* **thrust**) *tr* pousser; (*e.g., a dagger*) enfoncer; **to thrust oneself on** s'imposer à

thud [θʌd] *s* bruit *m* sourd || *v* (*pret & pp* **thudded**; *ger* **thudding**) *tr* & *intr* frapper avec un son mat

thug [θʌg] *s* bandit *m*, assassin *m*

thumb [θʌm] *s* pouce *m*; **all thumbs** (*coll*) maladroit; **to twiddle one's thumbs** se tourner les pouces; **under the thumb of** sous la coupe de || *tr* tripoter; (*a book*) feuilleter; **to thumb a ride** faire de l'auto-stop; **to thumb one's nose at** (*coll*) faire un pied de nez à

thumb/ **in**/**dex** *s* onglet *m*, encoche *f*

thumb/**print**/ *s* marque *f* de pouce

thumb/**screw**/ *s* papillon *m*, vis *f* à ailettes

thumb/**tack**/ *s* punaise *f*

thump [θʌmp] *s* coup *m* violent || *tr* cogner || *intr* tomber avec un bruit sourd; (*said, e.g., of marching feet*) sonner lourdement; (*said of heart*) battre fort

thumping ['θʌmpɪŋ] *adj* (*coll*) énorme

thunder ['θʌndər] *s* tonnerre *m* || *tr* fulminer || *intr* tonner; **to thunder at** tonner contre, tempêter contre

thun/**der-bolt**/ *s* foudre *f*; (*disaster*) coup *m* de foudre

thun/**der-clap**/ *s* coup *m* de tonnerre

thunderous ['θʌndərəs] *adj* orageux; (*voice; applause*) tonnant

thun/**der-show**/**er** *s* pluie *f* d'orage

thun/**der-storm**/ *s* orage *m*

thunderstruck ['θʌndər,strʌk] *adj* foudroyé

Thursday ['θʌrzdɪ] *s* jeudi *m*

thus [ðʌs] *adv* ainsi; (*therefore*) donc; **thus far** jusqu'ici

thwack [θwæk] *s* coup *m* || *tr* flanquer un coup à

thwart [θwɔrt] *adj* transversal || *adv* en travers || *tr* déjouer, frustrer

thy [ðaɪ] *adj poss* (archaic, poetic, Bib) ton §88

thyme [taɪm] *s* thym *m*

thyroid ['θaɪrɔɪd] *s* thyroïde *f*; (*pharm*) extrait *m* thyroïde

thyself [ðaɪ'self] *pron* (archaic, poetic, Bib) toi-même §86; te §87

tiara [taɪ'ærə], [taɪ'ɛrə] *s* tiare *f*; (*woman's headdress*) diadème *m*

tic [tɪk] *s* (pathol) tic *m*

tick [tɪk] *s* tic-tac *m*; (*e.g., of pillow*) taie *f*; (*e.g., of mattress*) housse *f* de coutil; (ent) tique *f*; **on tick** à crédit || *tr*—**to tick off** (*to check off*) pointer || *intr* tictaquer; (*said of heart*) battre

ticker ['tɪkər] *s* téléimprimeur *m*; (*watch*) (slang) toquante *f*; (*heart*) (slang) cœur *m*

tick/**er tape**/ *s* bande *f* de téléimprimeur

ticket ['tɪkɪt] *s* billet *m*; (*of bus, subway, etc.*) ticket *m*; (*of baggage checkroom*) bulletin *m*; (*of cloakroom*) numéro *m*; (*for boat trip*) passage *m*; (*of a political party*) liste *f* électorale; (*for violation*) (coll) papillon *m* de procès-verbal, contravention *f*; **that's the ticket** (coll) c'est bien ça, à la bonne heure; **tickets, please!** vos places, s'il vous plaît!

tick/**et a**/**gent** *s* guichetier *m*

tick/**et collec**/**tor** *s* contrôleur *m*

tick/**et of**/**fice** *s* guichet *m*; (theat) bureau *m* de location

tick′et scalp′er [,skælpər] s trafiquant m de billets de théâtre

tick′et win′dow s guichet m

ticking ['tɪkɪŋ] s coutil m

tickle ['tɪkəl] s chatouillement m || tr chatouiller; amuser; plaire (with dat) || intr chatouiller

ticklish ['tɪklɪʃ] adj chatouilleux; (touchy) susceptible; (subject, question) épineux, délicat

tick′-tack-toe′ s morpion m

ticktock ['tɪk,tɑk] s tic-tac m || intr faire tic-tac

tid′al wave′ ['taɪdəl] s raz m de marée; (e.g., of popular indignation) vague f

tidbit ['tɪd,bɪt] s bon morceau m

tiddlywinks ['tɪdli,wɪŋks] s jeu m de puce

tide [taɪd] s marée f; **against the tide** à contre-marée; **to go with the tide** suivre le courant || tr—**to tide over** dépanner, remettre à flot; (a difficulty) venir à bout de

tide′land′ s terres fpl inondées aux grandes marées

tide′wa′ter s eaux fpl de marée; bord m de la mer

tide′water pow′er plant′ s usine f marémotrice

tidings ['taɪdɪŋz] spl nouvelles fpl

ti-dy ['taɪdi] adj (comp -dier; super -diest) propre, net, bien tenu; (considerable) (coll) joli, fameux || s (pl -dies) voile m de fauteuil || v (pret & pp -died) tr mettre en ordre, nettoyer || intr—**to tidy up** faire un brin de toilette

tie [taɪ] s lien m, attache f; (knot) nœud m; (necktie) cravate f; (in games) match m nul; (mus) liaison f; (rr) traverse f || v (pret & pp tied; ger tying) tr lier; (a knot, a necktie, etc.) nouer; (shoelaces; a knot; one's apron) attacher; (an artery) ligaturer; (a competitor) être à égalité avec; (mus) lier; **tied up** (busy) occupé; **to tie down** assujettir; **to tie up** attacher; (a package) ficeler; (a person) ligoter; (a wound) bander; (funds) immobiliser; (traffic, a telephone line) embouteiller || intr (sports) faire match nul, égaliser

tie′back′ s embrasse f

tie′pin′ s épingle f de cravate

tier [tɪr] s étage m; (of stadium) gradin m

tiger ['taɪgər] s tigre m

ti′ger lil′y s lis m tigré

tight [taɪt] adj serré, juste; (e.g., rope) tendu; (clothes) ajusté; (container) étanche; (game) serré; (money) rare; (miserly) (coll) chiche; (drunk) (coll) rond, noir || **tights** spl collant m, maillot m || adv fermement, bien; **to hold tight** tenir serré; se tenir, se cramponner; **to sit tight** (coll) tenir bon

tighten ['taɪtən] tr (a knot, a bolt) serrer, resserrer; (e.g., a rope) tendre || intr se serrer; se tendre

tight-fisted ['taɪt'fɪstɪd] adj dur à la détente, serré

tight′-fit′ting adj collant, ajusté

tight′rope′ s corde f raide

tight′rope walk′er s funambule mf

tight′ squeeze′ s (coll) situation f difficile, embarras m

tight′wad′ s (coll) grippe-sou m

tigress ['taɪgrɪs] s tigresse f

tile [taɪl] s (for roof) tuile f; (for floor) carreau m || tr (e.g., a house) couvrir de tuiles; (a floor) carreler

tile′ roof′ s toit m de tuiles

till [tɪl] s tiroir-caisse m || prep jusqu'à || conj jusqu'à ce que || tr labourer

tilt [tɪlt] s pente f, inclinaison f; (contest) joute f; **full tilt** à fond de train || tr pencher, incliner; **to tilt back** renverser en arrière; **to tilt up** redresser || intr se pencher, s'incliner; (with lance) jouter; (naut) donner de la bande; **to tilt at** attaquer, critiquer; **to tilt back** se renverser en arrière

timber ['tɪmbər] s bois m de construction; (trees) bois m de haute futaie; (rafter) poutre f

tim′ber-land′ s bois m pour exploitation forestière

tim′ber line′ s limite f de la végétation forestière

timbre ['tɪmbər] s (phonet, phys) timbre m

time [taɪm] s temps m; heure f, e.g., **what time is it?** quelle heure est-il?; fois, e.g., **five times** cinq fois; e.g., **five times two is ten** cinq fois deux font dix; (period of payment) délai m; (phot) temps d'exposition; **at that time** à ce moment-là; à cette époque; **at the present time** à l'heure actuelle; **at the same time** en même temps; **at times** parfois; **behind the times** en retard sur son époque; **between times** entre-temps; **full time** plein temps; **in due time** en temps et lieu; **in no time** en moins de rien; **on time** à l'heure, à temps; **several times** à plusieurs reprises; **time and time again** maintes fois; **to beat time** (mus) battre la mesure; **to do time** (coll) faire son temps; **to have a good time** s'amuser bien, se divertir; **to lose time** (said of timepiece) retarder; **to mark time** marquer le pas; **to play for time** (coll) chercher à gagner du temps || tr mesurer la durée de; (sports) chronométrer

time′ bomb′ s bombe f à retardement

time′ card′ s registre m de présence

time′ clock′ s horloge f enregistreuse

time′ expo′sure s (phot) pose f

time′ fuse′ s fusée f fusante

time′-hon′ored adj consacré par l'usage

time′keep′er s pointeur m, chronométreur m; pendule f; montre f

timeless ['taɪmlɪs] adj sans fin, éternel

time-ly ['taɪmli] adj (comp -lier; super -liest) opportun, à propos

time′piece′ s pendule f; montre f

timer ['taɪmər] s (person) chronométreur m; (of an electrical appliance) minuterie f

time′ sheet′ s feuille f de présence

time′ sig′nal s signal m horaire

time'ta'ble s horaire m; (rr) indicateur m

time'work' s travail m à l'heure

time'worn' adj usé par le temps; (venerable) séculaire

time' zone' s fuseau m horaire

timid ['tɪmɪd] adj timide

timing ['taɪmɪŋ] s chronométrage m; choix m du moment propice; (of an electrical appliance) minuterie f; (aut, mach) réglage m; (sports) chronométrage; (theat) tempo m

tim'ing gears' spl engrenage m de distribution

timorous ['tɪmərəs] adj timoré, peureux

tin [tɪn] s (element) étain m; (tin plate) fer-blanc m; (cup, box, etc.) boîte f || v (pret & pp tinned; ger tinning) tr étamer; (to can) (Brit) mettre en boîte

tin' can' s boîte f en fer-blanc, boîte de conserve

tincture ['tɪŋktʃər] s teinture f

tin' cup' s timbale f

tinder ['tɪndər] s amadou m

tin'der-box' s briquet m à amadou; (fig) foyer m de l'effervescence

tin' foil' s feuille f d'étain, papier m d'argent

ting-a-ling ['tɪŋə,lɪŋ] s drelin m

tinge [tɪndʒ] s teinte f, nuance f || v (ger tingeing or tinging) tr teinter, nuancer

tingle ['tɪŋgəl] s picotement m, fourmillement m || intr picoter, fourmiller; (e.g., with enthusiasm) tressaillir

tin' hat' s (coll) casque m en acier

tinker ['tɪŋkər] s chaudronnier m ambulant; (bungler) bousilleur m || intr bricoler; **to tinker with** tripatouiller

tinkle ['tɪŋkəl] s tintement m || tr faire tinter || intr tinter

tin' plate' s fer-blanc m

tin'-plate' tr étamer

tin' roof' s toit m de fer-blanc

tinsel ['tɪnsəl] s clinquant m; (for a Christmas tree) paillettes fpl, guirlandes fpl clinquantes

tin'smith' s ferblantier m

tin' sol'dier s soldat m de plomb

tint [tɪnt] s teinte f || tr teinter

tin'type' s ferrotypie f

tin'ware' s ferblanterie f

ti-ny ['taɪni] adj (comp -nier; super -niest) minuscule

tip [tɪp] s bout m, pointe f; (slant) inclinaison f; (fee to a waiter) pourboire m; (secret information) (slang) tuyau m || v (pret & pp tipped; ger tipping) tr incliner; (the scales) faire pencher; (a waiter) donner un pourboire à, donner la pièce à; **to tip off** (slang) tuyauter; **to tip over** renverser || intr se renverser; donner un pourboire

tip'cart' s tombereau m

tip'-in' s (bb) hors-texte m

tip'-off' s (coll) tuyau m

tipped'-in' adj (bb) hors texte

tipple ['tɪpəl] intr biberonner

tip'staff' s verge f d'huissier; huissier m à verge

tip·sy ['tɪpsi] adj (comp -sier; super -siest) gris, grisé

tip'toe' s pointe f des pieds || v (pret & pp -toed; ger -toeing) intr marcher sur la pointe des pieds

tirade ['taɪred] s diatribe f

tire [taɪr] s pneu m || tr fatiguer || intr se fatiguer

tire' chain' s chaîne f antidérapante

tired [taɪrd] adj fatigué, las

tire' gauge' s manomètre m

tire' i'ron s démonte-pneu m

tireless ['taɪrlɪs] adj infatigable

tire' pres'sure s pression f des pneus

tire' pump' s gonfleur m pour pneus

tiresome ['taɪrsəm] adj fatigant, ennuyeux

tissue ['tɪʃu] s tissu m; (thin paper) papier m de soie; (toilet tissue) papier hygiénique; (paper handkerchief) mouchoir m à jeter

tis'sue pa'per s papier m de soie

tit [tɪt] s téton m; (orn) mésange f; **tit for tat** le chat bon rat

titanium [taɪ'teni·əm], [tɪ'teni·əm] s titane m

tithe [taɪð] s dixième m; (rel) dîme f || tr soumettre à la dîme; payer la dîme sur

Titian ['tɪʃən] s le Titien m

Ti'tian red' s blond m vénitien

title ['taɪtəl] s titre m || tr intituler

ti'tle deed' s titre m de propriété

ti'tle-hold'er s tenant m du titre

ti'tle page' s page f de titre

ti'tle role' s rôle m principal

tit'mouse' s (pl -mice) (orn) mésange f

titter ['tɪtər] s rire m étouffé || intr rire en catimini

titular ['tɪtʃələr] adj titulaire

to [tu], [tʊ], [tə] adv—**to and fro** de long en large || prep à; (towards) vers; (in order to) afin de, pour; envers, pour, e.g., **good to her** bon envers elle, bon pour elle; jusqu'à, e.g., **to this day** jusqu'à ce jour; e.g., **to count to a hundred** compter jusqu'à cent; moins, e.g., **a quarter to eight** huit heures moins le quart; contre, e.g., **seven to one** sept contre un; dans, e.g., **to a certain extent** dans une certaine mesure; en, e.g., **from door to door** de porte en porte; e.g., **I am going to France** je vais en France; de, e.g., **to try to + inf** essayer de + inf; **to him** lui §87

toad [tod] s crapaud m

toad'stool' s agaric m; champignon m vénéneux

to-and-fro ['tu·ənd'fro] adj de va-et-vient

toast [tost] s pain m grillé; (with a drink) toast m || tr griller; porter un toast à, boire à la santé de

toaster ['tostər] s grille-pain m

toast'mas'ter s préposé m aux toasts

tobac·co [tə'bæko] s (pl -cos) tabac m

tobac'co pouch' s blague f

toboggan [tə'bɑgən] s toboggan m

tocsin ['tɑksɪn] *s* tocsin *m*; (*bell*) cloche *f* qui sonne le tocsin

today [tʊ'de] *s & adv* aujourd'hui *m*

toddle ['tɑdəl] *s* allure *f* chancelante ‖ *intr* marcher à petits pas chancelants

toddler ['tɑdlər] *s* tout-petit *m*

tod-dy ['tɑdi] *s* (*pl* -dies) grog *m*

to-do [tə'du] *s* (*pl* -dos) embarras *mpl*, chichis *mpl*, façons *fpl*

toe [to] *s* doigt *m* du pied, orteil *m*; (*of shoe, of stocking*) bout *m* ‖ *v* (*pret & pp* toed; *ger* toeing) *tr*—to toe the line or the mark s'aligner, se mettre au pas

toe'nail' *s* ongle *m* du pied

tog [tɑg] *v* (*pret & pp* togged; *ger* togging) *tr*—to tog out or up attifer, fringuer ‖ togs *spl* fringues *fpl*

together [tʊ'gɛðər] *adv* ensemble; (*at the same time*) en même temps, à la fois

tog'gle switch' ['tɑgəl] *s* (elec) interrupteur *m* à culbuteur ou à bascule

toil [tɔɪl] *s* travail *m* dur; toils filet *m*, piège *m* ‖ *intr* travailler dur

toilet ['tɔɪlɪt] *s* toilette *f*; (*rest room*) cabinet *m* de toilette

toi'let ar'ticles *spl* objets *mpl* de toilette

toi'let bowl' *s* cuvette *f*

toi'let pa'per *s* papier *m* hygiénique

toi'let seat' *s* siège *m* des toilettes

toi'let set' *s* nécessaire *m* de toilette

toi'let soap' *s* savonnette *f*

toi'let wa'ter *s* eaux *fpl* de toilette

token ['tokən] *adj* symbolique ‖ *s* signe *m*, marque *f*; (*keepsake*) souvenir *m*; (*used as money*) jeton *m*; by the same token de plus; in token of en témoignage de

tolerance ['tɑlərəns] *s* tolérance *f*

tolerate ['tɑlə,ret] *tr* tolérer

toll [tol] *s* (*of bells*) glas *m*; (*payment*) droit *m* de passage, péage *m*; (*number of victims*) mortalité *f*; (telp) tarif *m* ‖ *tr* tinter; (*to ring the knell for*) sonner le glas de ‖ *intr* sonner le glas

toll' bridge' *s* pont *m* à péage

toll' call' *s* appel *m* interurbain

toll'gate' *s* barrière *f* à péage

toll' road' *s* autoroute *f* à péage

toma-to [tə'meto], [tə'mɑto] *s* (*pl* -toes) tomate *f*

tomb [tum] *s* tombeau *m*

tomboy ['tɑm,bɔɪ] *s* garçon *m* manqué

tomb'stone' *s* pierre *f* tombale

tomcat ['tɑm,kæt] *s* matou *m*

tome [tom] *s* tome *m*

tomorrow [tʊ'mɑro], [tʊ'mɔro] *adj*, *s*, & *adv* demain *m*; tomorrow morning demain matin; until tomorrow à demain

tom-tom ['tɑm,tɑm] *s* tam-tam *m*

ton [tʌn] *s* tonne *f*

tone [ton] *s* ton *m* ‖ *tr* accorder; to tone down atténuer; to tone up renforcer; (*e.g., the muscles*) tonifier ‖ *intr*—to tone down se modérer

tone' po'em *s* poème *m* symphonique

tongs [tɔŋz], [tɑŋz] *spl* pincettes *fpl*; (*e.g., for sugar*) pince *f*; (*of blacksmith*) tenailles *fpl*

tongue [tʌŋ] *s* (*language; part of body*) langue *f*; (*of wagon*) timon *m*; (*of buckle*) ardillon *m*; (*of shoe*) languette *f*; to hold one's tongue se mordre la langue

tongue-tied ['tʌŋ,taɪd] *adj* bouche cousue

tongue' twist'er *s* phrase *f* à décrocher la mâchoire

tonic ['tɑnɪk] *adj & s* tonique *m*

tonight [tʊ'naɪt] *adj & s* ce soir

tonsil ['tɑnsəl] *s* amygdale *f*

tonsillitis [,tɑnsɪ'laɪtɪs] *s* amygdalite *f*

ton-y ['toni] *adj* (*comp* -ier; *super* -iest) (slang) élégant, chic

too [tu] *adv* (*also*) aussi; (*more than enough*) trop; (*moreover*) d'ailleurs; I did too! mais si; too bad! dommage!; too many, too much trop, trop de

tool [tul] *s* outil ‖ *tr* (*a piece of metal*) usiner; (*leather*) repousser; (bb) dorer ‖ *intr*—to tool along rouler; to tool up s'outiller

tool'box' *s* trousse *f* à outils

tool'mak'er *s* taillandier *m*

toot [tut] *s* son *m* du cor; (*of auto*) coup *m* de klaxon; (*of locomotive*) coup *m* de sifflet ‖ *tr* sonner ‖ *intr* corner; (aut) klaxonner

tooth [tuθ] *s* (*pl* teeth [tiθ]) dent *f*; to grit, grind, or gnash the teeth grincer des dents, crisser des dents

tooth'ache' *s* mal *m* de dents

tooth'brush' *s* brosse *f* à dents

toothless ['tuθlɪs] *adj* édenté

tooth'paste' *s* pâte *f* dentifrice

tooth'pick' *s* cure-dent *m*

tooth' pow'der *s* poudre *f* dentifrice

top [tɑp] *adj* premier, de tête ‖ *s* sommet *m*, cime *f*, faîte *m*; (*of a barrel, table, etc.*) dessus *m*; (*of a page*) haut *m*; (*of a box*) couvercle *m*; (*of a carriage or auto*) capote *f*; (*toy*) toupie *f*; (naut) hune *f*; at the top of en haut de; (*e.g., one's class*) à la tête de; at the top of one's voice à tue-tête; from top to bottom de haut en bas, de fond en comble; on top of sur; (*in addition to*) en plus de; tops (*e.g., of carrots*) fanes *fpl*; to sleep like a top dormir comme un sabot ‖ *v* (*pret & pp* topped; *ger* topping) *tr* couronner, surmonter; (*to surpass*) dépasser; (*a tree, plant, etc.*) écimer

topaz ['topæz] *s* topaze *f*

top' bill'ing *s* tête *f* d'affiche

top'coat' *s* surtout *m* de demi-saison

toper ['topər] *s* soiffard *m*

top' hat' *s* haut-de-forme *m*

top'-heav'y *adj* trop lourd du haut

topic ['tɑpɪk] *s* sujet *m*

top'knot' *s* chignon *m*

top'mast' *s* mât *m* de hune

top'most' *adj* (le) plus haut

top'notch' *adj* (coll) d'élite

topogra-phy [tə'pɑgrəfi] *s* (*pl* -phies) topographie *f*

topple ['tɑpəl] *tr & intr* culbuter

topsoil ['tɑpsəl], ['tɑp,səl] *s* (naut) hunier *m*

top'soil' *s* couche *f* arable

topsy-turvy ['tɑpsi'tʌrvi] *adj & adv* sens dessus dessous

torch [tɔrʧ] *s* torche *f*, flambeau *m*; (Brit) lampe *f* torche; (slang) **to carry the torch for** (slang) avoir un amour sans retour pour

torch·bear'er *s* porte-flambeau *m*; (fig) défenseur *m*

torch'light *s* lueur *f* des flambeaux

torch'light proces'sion *s* défilé *m* aux flambeaux

torch' song' *s* chanson *f* de l'amour non partagé

torment ['tɔrmənt] *s* tourment *m* ‖ [tɔr'mɛnt] *tr* tourmenter

torna·do [tɔr'nedo] *s* (*pl* **-does** or **-dos**) tornade *f*

torpe·do [tɔr'pido] *s* (*pl* **-does**) torpille *f* ‖ *tr* torpiller

torpe'do-boat destroy'er *s* contre-torpilleur *m*

torpid ['tɔrpɪd] *adj* engourdi

torque [tɔrk] *s* effort *m* de torsion, couple *m* de torsion

torrent ['tɑrənt], ['tɔrənt] *s* torrent *m*

torrid ['tɑrɪd], ['tɔrɪd] *adj* torride

tor·so ['tɔrso] *s* (*pl* **-sos**) torse *m*

tort [tɔrt] *s* (law) acte *m* dommageable sauf rupture de contrat ou abus de confiance

tortoise ['tɔrtəs] *s* tortue *f*

tor'toise shell' *s* écaille *f*

torture ['tɔrʧər] *s* torture *f* ‖ *tr* torturer

toss [tɔs], [tɑs] *s* lancement *m*; (*of the head*) mouvement *m* dédaigneux ‖ *tr* lancer; (*one's hand*) relever dédaigneusement; (*a rider*) démonter; (*a coin*) jouer à pile et face avec; **to toss about** agiter, ballotter; **to toss off** (*e.g., work*) expédier; (*in one gulp*) lamper; **to toss up** jeter en l'air ‖ *intr* s'agiter; **to toss and turn** se tourner et retourner

toss'up' *s* (coll) coup *m* de pile ou face; chances *fpl* égales

tot [tɑt] *s* bambin *m*, tout petit *m* ‖ *v* (*pret & pp* **totted**; *ger* **totting**) *tr*—**to tot up** additionner

to·tal ['totəl] *adj & s* total *m*; **as a total** au total ‖ *v* (*pret & pp* **-taled** or **-talled**; *ger* **-taling** or **-talling**) *tr* additionner, totaliser; (*to amount to*) s'élever à

totalitarian [to‚tælɪ'terɪ·ən] *adj & mf* totalitaire

totem ['totəm] *s* totem *m*

totter ['tɑtər] *intr* chanceler

touch [tʌʧ] *s* (*act*) attouchement *m*; (*e.g., of color; with a brush*) touche *f*; (*sense; of pianist*) toucher *m*; (*of typist*) frappe *f*; (*little bit*) pointe *f*, brin *m*; **in touch** in communication; **to get in touch with** prendre contact avec ‖ *tr* toucher; (*for a loan*) (slang) taper; **to touch off** déclencher; **to touch up** retoucher ‖ *intr* se toucher; **to touch on** toucher à

touched *adj* touché; (*crazy*) timbré

touching ['tʌʧɪŋ] *adj* touchant, émouvant ‖ *prep* touchant, concernant

touch·y ['tʌʧi] *adj* (*comp* **-ier;** *super* **-iest**) susceptible, irritable

tough [tʌf] *adj* dur, coriace; (*tenacious*) résistant; (*task*) difficile ‖ *s* voyou *m*

toughen ['tʌfən] *tr* endurcir ‖ *intr* s'endurcir

tough' luck' *s* déveine *f*

tour [tur] *s* tour *m*; (*e.g., of inspection*) tournée *f*; **on tour** en tournée ‖ *tr* faire le tour de; (*e.g., a country*) voyager en; (theat) faire une tournée de, en, or dans ‖ *intr* voyager

tour'ing car' *s* voiture *f* de tourisme

tourist ['turɪst] *adj & s* touriste *mf*

tournament ['turnəmənt], ['tʌrnəmənt] *s* tournoi *m*

tourney ['turni], ['tʌrni] *s* tournoi *m* ‖ *intr* tournoyer

tourniquet ['turnɪ‚ket], ['tʌrnɪ‚ke] *s* (surg) garrot *m*, tourniquet *m*

tousle ['tauzəl] *tr* ébouriffer; tirailler, maltraiter

tow [to] *s* remorque *f*; (*e.g., of hemp*) filasse *f*; **to take in tow** prendre en remorque; (fig) se charger de ‖ *tr* remorquer

towage ['to·ɪʤ] *s* remorquage *m*; droits *mpl* de remorquage

toward(s) [tord(z)], [tə'word(z)] *prep* vers; (*in regard to*) envers

tow'boat' *s* remorqueur *m*

tow·el ['tau·əl] *s* serviette *f*, essuie-main *m* ‖ *v* (*pret & pp* **-eled** or **-elled**; *ger* **-eling** or **-elling**) *tr* essuyer avec une serviette

tow'el rack' *s* porte-serviettes *m*

tower ['tau·ər] *s* tour *f* ‖ *intr* s'élever

towering ['tau·ərɪŋ] *adj* élevé, géant; (*e.g., ambition*) sans bornes

tow'er-man *s* (*pl* **-men**) (aer, rr) aiguilleur *m*

tow'ing serv'ice ['to·ɪŋ] *s* service *m* de dépannage

tow'line' *s* câble *m* de remorque

town [taun] *s* ville *f*; **in town** en ville

town' clerk' *s* secrétaire *m* de mairie

town' coun'cil *s* conseil *m* municipal

town' cri'er *s* crieur *m* public

town' hall' *s* hôtel *m* de ville

town' plan'ning *s* urbanisme *m*

towns'folk' *spl* citadins *mpl*

town'ship *s* commune *f*; (U.S.A.) circonscription *f* administrative de six milles carrés

towns'man ['taunzmən] *s* (*pl* **-men**) citadin *m*

towns'peo'ple *spl* citadins *mpl*

town' talk' *s* sujet *m* du jour

tow'path' *s* chemin *m* de halage

tow'rope' *s* corde *f* de remorque

tow' truck' *s* dépanneuse *f*, voiture *f* de dépannage

toxic ['tɑksɪk] *adj & s* toxique *m*

toy [tɔɪ] *adj* petit; d'enfant ‖ *s* jouet *m*, joujou *m*; (*trifle*) bagatelle *f* ‖ *intr* jouer, s'amuser; **to toy with** (*a person*) badiner avec; (*an idea*) caresser

toy' dog' *s* chien *m* de manchon

toy' sol'dier *s* soldat *m* de plomb

trace [tres] *s* trace *f*; (*of harness*) trait *m* ‖ *tr* tracer; (*the whereabouts of* *s.o. or s.th.*) pister; (*e.g., an influence*) retrouver les traces de; (*a design seen through thin paper*) calquer; **to trace back** remonter jusqu'à l'origine de

tracer ['tresər] *s* traceur *m*

trac′er bul′let *s* balle *f* traçante

trache·a ['treki·ə] *s* (*pl* **-ae** [ˌi]) trachée *f*

tracing ['tresɪŋ] *s* tracé *m*

trac′ing tape′ *s* cordeau *m*

track [træk] *s* (*of foot or vehicle*) trace *f*; (*of an animal; in a stadium*) piste *f*; (*of a boat*) sillage *m*; (*of a railroad*) voie *f*; (*of an airplane, of a hurricane*) trajet *m*; (*of a tractor*) chenille *f*; (*course followed*) chemin *m* tracé; (sports) la course et le saut de barrières; (sports) athlétisme *m*; **off the beaten track** hors des sentiers battus; **on the right track** sur la bonne voie; **to be on the wrong track** faire fausse route; **to have an inside track** tenir la corde; **to keep track of** ne pas perdre de vue; **to make tracks** (coll) filer || *tr* traquer; laisser des traces de pas dans; **to track down** dépister

tracking ['trækɪŋ] *s* (*of spaceship*) repérage *m*

track′ing sta′tion *s* poste *m* de repérage

track′less trol′ley *s* trolleybus *m*

track′ meet′ *s* concours *m* de courses et de sauts, épreuve *f* d'athlétisme

track′walk′er *s* garde-voie *m*

tract [trækt] *s* (*of land*) étendue *f*; (*leaflet*) tract *m*; (anat) voie *f*

traction ['trækʃən] *s* traction *f*

trac′tion com′pany *s* entreprise *f* de transports urbains

tractor ['træktər] *s* tracteur *m*

trade [tred] *s* commerce *m*, négoce *m*; clientèle *f*; (*calling, job*) métier *m*; (*exchange*) échange *m*; (*in slaves*) traite *f*; **to take in trade** reprendre en compte || *tr* échanger; **to trade in** (*e.g., a used car*) donner en reprise || *intr* commercer; **to trade in** faire le commerce de; **to trade on** exploiter

trade′-in′ *s* reprise *f*

trade′mark′ *s* marque *f* déposée

trade′ name′ *s* raison *f* sociale

trader ['tredər] *s* commerçant *m*

trade′ school′ *s* école *f* des arts et métiers

trades′man *s* (*pl* **-men**) commerçant *m*; (*shopkeeper*) boutiquier *m*; (Brit) artisan *m*

trades′ un′ion or **trade′ un′ion** *s* syndicat *m* ouvrier

trade′ winds′ *spl* vents *mpl* alizés

trad′ing post′ ['tredɪŋ] *s* factorerie *f*

trad′ing stamp′ *s* timbre-prime *m*

tradition [trə'dɪʃən] *s* tradition *f*

traditional [trə'dɪʃənəl] *adj* traditionnel

traf·fic ['træfɪk] *s* (*commerce*) négoce *m*; (*in the street*) circulation *f*; (*illegal*) trafic *m*; (*in, e.g., slaves*) traite *f*; (naut, rr) trafic || *v* (*pret & pp* **-ficked**; *ger* **-ficking**) *intr* trafiquer

traf′fic cir′cle *s* rond-point *m*

traf′fic cop′ *s* agent *m* de la circulation

traf′fic court′ *s* tribunal *m* de simple police (pour les contraventions au code de la route)

traf′fic jam′ *s* embouteillage *m*

traf′fic light′ *s* feu *m* de circulation

traf′fic sign′ *s* panneau *m* de signalisation, poteau *m* indicateur

traf′fic sig′nal *s* signal *m* routier

traf′fic tick′et *s* contravention *f*

traf′fic vi′olator *s* contrevenant *m*

tragedian [trə'dʒidi·ən] *s* tragédien *m*

trage·dy ['trædʒidi] *s* (*pl* **-dies**) tragédie *f*

tragic ['trædʒɪk] *adj* tragique

trail [trel] *s* trace *f*, piste *f*; (*e.g., of smoke*) traînée *f* || *tr* traîner; (*to look for*) pister || *intr* traîner; (*said of a plant*) grimper; **to trail off** se perdre

trailer ['trelər] *s* remorque *f*; (*for vacationing*) remorque de plaisance, caravane *f*; (mov) film-annonce *m*

trail′er court′ *s* camp *m* pour caravanes

trail′er home′ *s* caravane *f*

train [tren] *s* (*of railway cars*) train *m*; (*of dress*) traîne *f*; (*of thought*) enchaînement *m*; (*streak*) traînée *f* || *tr* entraîner, former; (*plants*) palisser; (*a gun; a telescope*) pointer || *intr* s'entraîner

trained′ an′imals *spl* animaux *mpl* savants

trained′ nurse′ *s* infirmière *f* diplômée

trainer ['trenər] *s* (*of animals*) dresseur *m*; (sports) entraîneur *m*

training ['trenɪŋ] *s* entraînement *m*; instruction *f*; (*of animals*) dressage *m*

train′ing school′ *s* école *f* technique; (*reformatory*) maison *f* de correction

train′ing ship′ *s* navire-école *m*

trait [tret] *s* trait *m*

traitor ['tretər] *s* traître *m*

traitress ['tretrɪs] *s* traîtresse *f*

trajecto·ry [trə'dʒektəri] *s* (*pl* **-ries**) trajectoire *f*

tramp [træmp] *s* vagabond *m*; bruit *m* de pas lourds || *tr* parcourir à pied; (*the street*) battre || *intr* vagabonder; marcher lourdement; **to tramp on** marcher sur

trample ['træmpəl] *tr* fouler, piétiner || *intr*—**to trample on** or **upon** fouler, piétiner

trampoline ['træmpəˌlin] *s* tremplin *m* de gymnase

tramp′ steam′er *s* tramp *m*

trance [træns], [trɑns] *s* transe *f*; **in a trance** en transe

tranquil ['træŋkwɪl] *adj* tranquille

tranquilize ['træŋkwɪˌlaɪz] *tr* tranquilliser

tranquilizer ['træŋkwɪˌlaɪzər] *s* tranquillisant *m*

tranquillity [træn'kwɪlɪti] *s* tranquillité *f*

transact [træn'zækt], [træns'ækt] *tr* traiter, négocier || *intr* faire des affaires

transaction [træn'zækʃən], [træns'ækʃən] *s* transaction *f*; (*of business*) conduite f; **transactions** (of a society) actes mpl

transatlantic [ˌtrænsət'læntɪk] adj & s transatlantique m

transcend [træn'sɛnd] tr transcender ‖ intr se transcender

transcribe [træn'skraɪb] tr transcrire

transcript ['trænskrɪpt] s copie f; (of a meeting) procès-verbal m; (educ) livret m scolaire

transcription [træn'skrɪpʃən] s transcription f

transept ['trænsɛpt] s transept m

trans·fer ['trænsfər] s (e.g., of stock, property, etc.) transfert m; (from one place to the other) translation f; (from one job to the other) mutation f; (of a design) décalque m; (for bus or subway) billet m de correspondance; (public sign) correspondance ‖ [træns'fʌr], ['trænsfər] v (pret & pp -ferred; ger -ferring) tr transférer; transporter; (e.g., a civil servant) déplacer; (a design) décalquer ‖ intr se déplacer; changer de train (de l'autobus, etc.)

transfix [træns'fɪks] tr transpercer

transform [træns'fɔrm] tr transformer ‖ intr se transformer

transformer [træns'fɔrmər] s transformateur m

transfusion [træns'fjuʒən] s transfusion f

transgress [træns'grɛs] tr & intr transgresser

transgression [træns'grɛʃən] s transgression f

transient ['trænʃənt] adj transitoire, passager; (e.g., guest) de passage ‖ s hôte mf de passage

transistor [træn'sɪstər] s transistor m

transit ['trænsɪt], ['trænzɪt] s transit m

transition [træn'zɪʃən] s transition f

transitional [træn'zɪʃənəl] adj transitoire, de transition

transitive ['trænsɪtɪv] adj transitif ‖ s verbe m transitif

transitory ['trænsɪˌtori] adj transitoire

translate ['trænslet], ['trænslet] tr traduire

translation [træns'leʃən] s traduction f; (transfer) translation f

translator [træns'letər] s traducteur m

transliterate [træns'lɪtəˌret] tr translitérer

translucent [træns'lusənt] adj translucide, diaphane

transmission [træns'mɪʃən] s transmission f; (gear change) changement m de vitesse; (housing for gears) boîte f de vitesses

transmis'sion-gear' box' s boîte f de vitesses

trans·mit [træns'mɪt] v (pret & pp -mitted; ger -mitting) tr & intr transmettre; (rad) émettre

transmitter [træns'mɪtər] s (telg, telp) transmetteur m; (rad) émetteur m

transmit'ting sta'tion s poste m émetteur

transmute [træns'mjut] tr transmuer

transom ['trænsəm] s (crosspiece) linteau m; (window over door) imposte f, vasistas m; (of ship) barre f d'arcasse

transparen·cy [træns'pɛrənsi] s (pl -cies) transparence f; (phot) diapositive f

transparent [træns'pɛrənt] adj transparent

transpire [træns'paɪr] intr se passer; (to leak out) transpirer

transplant ['træns,plænt], ['træns,plænt] s (organ or tissue) greffon m; (operation) greffe f ‖ [træns'plænt], [træns'plænt] tr transplanter; (e.g., a heart) greffer

transport ['trænsport] s transport m ‖ [træns'port] tr transporter

transportation [ˌtrænspor'teʃən] s transport m; billet m de train, de bateau, or d'avion; (deportation) transportation f

transport'er bridge' [træns'portər] s transbordeur m

trans'port work'er s employé m des entreprises de transport

transpose [træns'poz] tr transposer

trans·ship [træns'ʃɪp] v (pret & pp -shipped; ger -shipping) tr transborder

transshipment [træns'ʃɪpmənt] s transbordement m

trap [træp] s piège m; (pitfall) trappe f; (double-curved pipe) siphon m; **traps** (mus) batterie f de jazz ‖ v (pret & pp trapped; ger trapping) tr prendre au piège, attraper

trap' door' s trappe f

trapeze [trə'piz] s trapèze m

trapezoid ['træpɪˌzɔɪd] s trapèze m

trapper ['træpər] s trappeur m

trappings ['træpɪŋz] spl (adornments) atours mpl; (of horse's harness) harnachement m

trap'shoot'ing s tir m au pigeon

trash [træʃ] s déchets mpl, rebuts mpl; (junk) camelote f; (nonsense) ineptie f; (worthless people) racaille f

trash' can' s poubelle f

travail [trə'vel] s labeur m; douleur f de l'enfantement

trav·el ['trævəl] s voyages mpl; (mach) course f ‖ v (pret & pp -eled or -elled; ger -eling or -elling) tr parcourir ‖ intr voyager; (mach) se déplacer

trav'el bu'reau s agence f de voyages

traveler ['trævələr] s voyageur m

trav'eler's check' s chèque m de voyage

trav'eling expen'ses spl frais mpl de voyage

trav'eling sales'man s (pl -men) commis m voyageur

traverse [trə'vʌrs] tr parcourir, traverser

traves·ty ['trævɪsti] s (pl -ties) s travestissement m ‖ v (pret & pp -tied) tr travestir

trawl [trɔl] s chalut m ‖ tr traîner ‖ intr pêcher au chalut

trawler ['trɔlər] s chalutier m

tray [tre] s plateau m; (of refrigerator) bac f; (chem, phot) cuvette f

treacherous ['tretʃərəs] *adj* traître

treacher·y ['tretʃəri] *s* (*pl* -ies) trahison *f*

tread [tred] *s* (*step; sound of steps*) pas *m*; (*gait*) allure *f*; (*of stairs*) giron *m*; (*of tire*) chape *f*; (*of shoe*) semelle *f*; (*of egg*) cicatricule *f* ‖ *v* (*pret* **trod** [trɑd]; *pp* **trodden** ['trɑdən] *or* **trod**) *tr* marcher sur, piétiner ‖ *intr* marcher

treadle ['tredəl] *s* pédale *f*

tread'mill' *s* trépigneuse *f*; (*futile drudgery*) besogne *f* ingrate

treason ['trizən] *s* trahison *f*

treasonable ['trizənəbəl] *adj* traître

treasure ['treʒər] *s* trésor *m* ‖ *tr* garder soigneusement; (*to prize*) tenir beaucoup à

treasurer ['treʒərər] *s* trésorier *m*

treasur·y ['treʒəri] *s* (*pl* -ies) trésorerie *f*; trésor *m*

treat [trit] *s* régal *m*, plaisir *m* ‖ *tr* traiter; régaler; (*to a drink*) payer à boire à ‖ *intr* traiter

treatise ['tritɪs] *s* traité *m*

treatment ['tritmənt] *s* traitement *m*

trea·ty ['triti] *s* (*pl* -ties) traité *m*

treble ['trebəl] *adj* (*threefold*) triple; (*mus*) de soprano ‖ *s* soprano *mf*; (*voice*) soprano *m* ‖ *tr* & *intr* tripler

tre'ble clef' [klef] *s* clef *f* de sol

tree [tri] *s* arbre *m*

tree' farm' *s* taillis *m*

treeless ['trilɪs] *adj* sans arbres

tree'top' *s* cime *f* d'un arbre

trellis ['trelɪs] *s* treillis *m*, treillage *m*; (*summerhouse*) tonnelle *f* ‖ *tr* treillager

tremble ['trembəl] *s* tremblement *m* ‖ *intr* trembler

tremendous [trɪ'mendəs] *adj* terrible; (*coll*) formidable

tremor ['tremər], ['trimər] *s* tremblement *m*

trench [trentʃ] *s* tranchée *f*

trenchant ['trentʃənt] *adj* tranchant

trench' mor'tar *s* lance-bombes *m*

trend [trend] *s* tendance *f*, cours *m*

trespass ['trespəs] *s* entrée *f* sans permission; délit *m*, offense *f* ‖ *intr* entrer sans permission; **no trespassing** (*public sign*) défense d'entrer; **to trespass against** offenser; **to trespass on** empiéter sur; (*s.o.'s patience*) abuser de

trespasser ['trespəsər] *s* intrus *m*

tress [tres] *s* tresse *f*; **tresses** chevelure *f*

trestle ['tresəl] *s* tréteau *m*; (*bridge*) pont *m* en treillis

trial ['traɪəl] *s* essai *m*; (*difficulty*) épreuve *f*; (*law*) procès *m*; **on trial** à titre d'essai; (*law*) en jugement; **to bring to trial** faire passer en jugement

tri'al and er'ror *s*—**by trial and error** par tâtonnements

tri'al balloon' *s* ballon *m* d'essai

tri'al by ju'ry *s* jugement *m* par jury

tri'al ju'ry *s* jury *m* de jugement

tri'al or'der *s* commande *f* d'essai

tri'al run' *s* course *f* d'essai

triangle ['traɪ‚ængəl] *s* triangle *m*

tribe [traɪb] *s* tribu *f*

tribunal [trɪ'bjunəl], [traɪ'bjunəl] *s* tribunal *m*

tribune ['trɪbjun] *s* tribune *f*

tributar·y ['trɪbjə‚teri] *adj* tributaire ‖ *s* (*pl* -ies) tributaire *m*

tribute ['trɪbjut] *s* tribut *m*; éloge *m*, compliment *m*; **to pay tribute to** (*e.g., merit*) rendre hommage à

trice [traɪs] *s*—**in a trice** en un clin d'œil

trick [trɪk] *s* tour *m*; (*prank*) farce *f*; (*artifice*) ruse *f*; (*cards in one round*) levée *f*; (*habit*) manie *f*; (*girl*) (coll) belle *f*; **to be up to one's old tricks again** faire encore des siennes; **to play a dirty trick on** faire un vilain tour à; **tricks of the trade** trucs *mpl* du métier ‖ *tr* duper

tricker·y ['trɪkəri] *s* (*pl* -ies) tromperie *f*

trickle ['trɪkəl] *s* filet *m* ‖ *intr* dégoutter

trickster ['trɪkstər] *s* fourbe *mf*

trick·y ['trɪki] *adj* (*comp* -ier; *super* -iest) rusé; (*difficult*) compliqué, délicat

tricolor ['traɪ‚kʌlər] *adj* & *s* tricolore *m*

tried [traɪd] *adj* loyal, éprouvé

trifle ['traɪfəl] *s* bagatelle *f* ‖ *tr*—**trifle away** gaspiller ‖ *intr* badiner

trifling ['traɪflɪŋ] *adj* frivole; insignifiant

trifocals [traɪ'fokəlz] *spl* lunettes *fpl* à trois foyers

trigger ['trɪgər] *s* (*of gun*) détente *f*; (*of any device*) déclencheur *m*; **to pull the trigger** appuyer sur la détente ‖ *tr* déclencher

trig'ger-hap'py *adj*—**to be trigger-happy** (coll) avoir la gâchette facile

trigonometry [‚trɪgə'nɑmɪtri] *s* trigonométrie *f*

trill [trɪl] *s* trille *m* ‖ *tr* & *intr* triller

trillion ['trɪljən] *s* (U.S.A.) billion *m*; (Brit) trillion *m*

trilo·gy ['trɪlədʒi] *s* (*pl* -gies) trilogie *f*

trim [trɪm] *adj* (*comp* **trimmer**; *super* **trimmest**) ordonné, coquet ‖ *s* état *m*; ornement *m*; (*of sails*) orientation *f* ‖ *v* (*pret* & *pp* **trimmed**; *ger* **trimming**) *tr* enguirlander; (*a Christmas tree*) orner; (*hat, dress, etc.*) garnir; (*the hair*) rafraîchir; (*a candle or lamp*) moucher; (*trees, plants*) tailler; (*the edges of a book*) rogner; (*the sails*) orienter; (coll) battre

trimming ['trɪmɪŋ] *s* (*of clothes, hat, etc.*) garniture *f*; (*of hedges*) taille *f*; (*of sails*) orientation *f*; **to get a trimming** (coll) essuyer une défaite

trini·ty ['trɪnɪti] *s* (*pl* -ties) trinité *f*; **Trinity** Trinité

trinket ['trɪŋkɪt] *s* colifichet *m*; (*trifle*) babiole *f*

tri·o ['tri·o] *s* (*pl* -os) trio *m*

trip [trɪp] *s* voyage *m*; trajet *m*, parcours *m*; (*stumble; blunder*) faux pas *m*; (*act of causing a person to stumble*) croc-en-jambe *m* ‖ *v* (*pret* & *pp* **tripped**; *ger* **tripping**) *tr* faire trébucher; **to trip up** donner un croc-en-jambe à; prendre en défaut ‖ *intr* trébucher

tripartite [traɪ'pɑrtart] *adj* tripartite

tripe [traɪp] *s* tripe *f*; (slang) fatras *m*

trip′ham′mer *s* marteau *m* à bascule

triple ['trɪpəl] *adj* & *s* triple *m* ‖ *tr* & *intr* tripler

triplet ['trɪplɪt] *s* (offspring) triplet *m*; (stanza) tercet *m*; (mus) triolet *m*; **triplets** (offspring) triplés *mpl*

triplicate ['trɪplɪkɪt] *adj* triple ‖ *s* triplicata *m*; **in triplicate** en trois exemplaires

tripod ['traɪpɑd] *s* trépied *m*

triptych ['trɪptɪk] *s* triptyque *m*

trite [traɪt] *adj* banal, rebattu

triumph ['traɪ-əmf] *s* triomphe *m* ‖ *intr* triompher; **to triumph over** triompher de

trium′phal arch′ [traɪ'ʌmfəl] *s* arc *m* de triomphe

triumphant [traɪ'ʌmfənt] *adj* triomphant

trivia ['trɪvɪ-ə] *spl* vétilles *fpl*

trivial ['trɪvɪ-əl] *adj* trivial, insignifiant

triviali·ty [,trɪvɪ'ælɪtɪ] *s* (pl -ties) trivialité *f*, insignifiance *f*

Trojan ['trodʒən] *adj* troyen ‖ *s* Troyen *m*

Tro′jan Horse′ *s* cheval *m* de Troie

Tro′jan war′ *s* guerre *f* de Troie

troll [trol] *tr* & *intr* pêcher à la cuiller

trolley ['trɑlɪ] *s* trolley *m*; (streetcar) tramway *m*

trol′ley car′ *s* tramway *m*

trol′ley pole′ *s* perche *f*

trolling ['trolɪŋ] *s* pêche *f* à la cuiller

trollop ['trɑləp] *s* souillon *f*; (prostitute) traînée *f*

trombone ['trɑmbon] *s* trombone *m*

troop [trup] *s* troupe *f*; **troops** (mil) troupes *fpl* ‖ *tr* (the colors) présenter ‖ *intr* s'attrouper

trooper ['trupər] *s* cavalier *m*; membre *m* de la police montée; **to swear like a trooper** jurer comme un charretier

tro·phy ['trofɪ] *s* (pl -phies) trophée *m*; (sports) coupe *f*

tropic ['trɑpɪk] *adj* & *s* tropique *m*; **tropics** tropiques, zone *f* tropicale

tropical ['trɑpɪkəl] *adj* tropical

trot [trɑt] *s* trot *m* ‖ *v* (pret & pp **trotted**; ger **trotting**) *tr* faire trotter; **to trot out** (slang) exhiber ‖ *intr* trotter

troth [trɔθ], [troθ] *s* foi *f*; **in troth** en vérité; **to plight one's troth** promettre fidélité; donner sa promesse de mariage

trouble ['trʌbəl] *s* dérangement *m*; (illness) trouble *m*; **that's not worth the trouble** cela ne vaut pas la peine; **that's the trouble** voilà le hic; **the trouble is that . . .** la difficulté c'est que . . . ; **to be in trouble** avoir des ennuis; (said of a woman) (coll) faire Pâques avant les Rameaux; **to be looking for trouble** chercher querelle; **to get into trouble** se créer des ennuis, s'attirer une mauvaise affaire;

to take the trouble to se donner la peine de; **with very little trouble** à peu de frais ‖ *tr* déranger; affliger; **to be troubled about** se tourmenter au sujet de; **to trouble oneself** s'inquiéter ‖ *intr* se déranger; **to trouble** to se donner la peine de

trou′ble light′ *s* lampe *f* de secours

trou′ble-mak′er *s* fomentateur *m*, perturbateur *m*

troubleshooter ['trʌbəl,ʃutər] *s* dépanneur *m*; (in disputes) arbitre *m*

trou′ble-shoot′ing *s* dépannage *m*; (of disputes) composition *f*, arbitrage *m*

troublesome ['trʌbəlsəm] *adj* ennuyeux

trou′ble spot′ *s* foyer *m* de conflit

trough [trɔf], [traf] *s* (e.g., to knead bread) pétrin *m*; (for water for animals) abreuvoir *m*; (for feeding animals) auge *f*; (under the eaves) chéneau *m*; (between two waves) creux *m*

troupe [trup] *s* troupe *f*

trouper ['trupər] *s* membre *m* de la troupe; vieil acteur *m*; vieux routier *m*

trousers ['trauzərz] *spl* pantalon *m*

trous·seau [tru'so], ['truso] *s* (pl -seaux or -seaus) trousseau *m*

trout [traut] *s* truite *f*

trowel ['trau-əl] *s* truelle *f*; (for gardening) déplantoir *m*

Troy [trɔɪ] *s* Troie *f*

truant ['tru-ənt] *s*—**to play truant** faire l'école buissonnière

truce [trus] *s* trêve *f*

truck [trʌk] *s* camion *m*, poids *m* lourd; (for baggage) diable *m*; légumes *mpl*; (coll) rapports *mpl* ‖ *tr* camionner

truck′driv′er *s* camionneur *m*

truck′ farm′ing *s* culture *f* maraîchère

truck′ gar′den *s* jardin *m* maraîcher

trucking ['trʌkɪŋ] *s* camionnage *m*

truculent ['trʌkjələnt], ['trukjələnt] *adj* truculent

trudge [trʌdʒ] *intr* cheminer

true [tru] *adj* vrai; loyal; (exact) juste; (copy) conforme; **to come true** se réaliser ‖ *tr* rectifier, dégauchir

true′ cop′y *s* (pl -ies) copie *f* conforme

true′-heart′ed *adj* au cœur sincère

true′love′ *s* bien-aimé *m*

truffle ['trʌfəl], ['trufəl] *s* truffe *f*

truism ['tru-ɪzm] *s* truisme *m*

truly ['trulɪ] *adv* vraiment; sincèrement; **yours truly** (complimentary close) veuillez agréer, Monsieur (Madame, etc.), l'assurance de mes sentiments distingués

trump [trʌmp] *s* atout *m*; brave garçon *m*, brave fille *f*; **no trump** sans atout ‖ *tr* couper; **to trump up** inventer ‖ *intr* couper

trumpet ['trʌmpɪt] *s* trompette *f* ‖ *tr* & *intr* trompeter

trumpeter ['trʌmpətər] *s* trompette *m*

truncheon ['trʌntʃən] *s* matraque *f*; (of policeman) bâton *m*

trunk [trʌŋk] *s* tronc *m*; (chest for clothes) malle *f*; (of elephant) trompe *f*; (aut) coffre *m*; **trunks** slip *m*

truss [trʌs] *s* (framework) armature *f*; (med) bandage *m* herniaire ‖ *tr* armer; (culin) trousser

trust [trʌst] *s* confiance *f*; (*hope*) espoir *m*; (*duty*) charge *f*; (*safekeeping*) dépôt *m*; (com) trust *m*, cartel *m* || *tr* se fier à; (*to entrust*) confier; (com) faire crédit à || *intr* espérer; **to trust in** avoir confiance en

trust′ com′pany *s* crédit *m*, société *f* de banque

trustee [trʌs′ti] *s* administrateur *m*; (*of a university*) régent *m*; (*of an estate*) fidéicommissaire *mf*

trusteeship [trʌs′tiʃɪp] *s* tutelle *f*

trustful [′trʌstfəl] *adj* confiant

trust′wor′thy *adj* digne de confiance

trust·y [′trʌsti] *adj* (*comp* -**ier**; *super* -**iest**) sûr, loyal || *s* (*pl* -**ies**) forçat *m* bien noté

truth [truθ] *s* vérité *f*; **in truth** en vérité

truthful [′truθfəl] *adj* véridique

try [traɪ] *s* (*pl* **tries**) essai *m* || *v* (*pret & pp* **tried**) *tr* mettre à l'épreuve; (law) juger; **to try on** or **out** essayer || *intr* essayer; **to try to** essayer de

trying [′traɪ·ɪŋ] *adj* pénible

tryst [trɪst], [traɪst] *s* rendez-vous *m*

T′-shirt′ *s* gilet *m* de peau avec manches

tub [tʌb] *s* cuvier *m*, baquet *m*; (*clumsy boat*) (coll) rafiot *m*

tube [t(j)ub] *s* tube *m*; tunnel *m*; (aut) chambre *f* à air; (*subway*) (Brit) métro *m*

tuber [′t(j)ubər] *s* tubercule *m*

tubercle [′t(j)ubərkəl] *s* tubercule *m*

tuberculosis [t(j)u‚bʌrkjə′losɪs] *s* tuberculose *f*

tuck [tʌk] *s* pli *m*, rempli *m* || *tr* plisser, remplier; **to tuck away** reléguer; **to tuck in** rentrer; **to tuck in bed** border; **to tuck up** retrousser

tucker [′tʌkər] *tr*—**tucker out** (coll) fatiguer

Tuesday [′t(j)uzdi] *s* mardi *m*

tuft [tʌft] *s* touffe *f* || *tr* garnir de touffes || *intr* former une touffe

tug [tʌg] *s* tiraillement *m*, effort *m*; (*boat*) remorqueur *m* || *v* (*pret & pp* **tugged**; *ger* **tugging**) *tr* tirer fort; (*a boat*) remorquer || *intr* tirer fort

tug′boat′ *s* remorqueur *m*

tug′ of war′ *s* lutte *f* à la corde (de traction)

tuition [t(j)u′ɪʃən] *s* enseignement *m*; (*fees*) frais *mpl* de scolarité

tulip [′t(j)ulɪp] *s* tulipe *f*

tumble [′tʌmbəl] *s* chute *f*; (sports) culbute *f* || *tr* culbuter || *intr* tomber, culbuter; (sports) faire des culbutes; (*to catch on*) (slang) comprendre; **tumble down** dégringoler

tum′ble·down′ *adj* croulant, délabré

tumbler [′tʌmblər] *s* gobelet *m*, verre *m*; acrobate *m*; (*self-righting toy*) poussah *m*, ramponneau *m*

tumor [′t(j)umər] *s* tumeur *f*

tumult [′t(j)umʌlt] *s* tumulte *m*

tun [tʌn] *s* tonne *f*

tuna [′tunə] *s* thon *m*

tune [t(j)un] *s* air *m*; (*manner of acting or speaking*) ton *m*; **in tune** (mus) accordé; (rad) en syntonie; **out of tune** (mus) désaccordé; **to change**

one's tune (coll) changer de disque || *tr* accorder; (*a radio or television set*) régler; **to tune in** (rad) syntoniser; **to tune up** régler

tungsten [′tʌŋstən] *s* tungstène *m*

tunic [′t(j)unɪk] *s* tunique *f*

tuning [′t(j)unɪŋ] *s* réglage *m*; (rad) syntonisation *f*

tun′ing coil′ *s* bobine *f* de syntonisation

tun′ing fork′ *s* diapason *m*

tun·nel [′tʌnəl] *s* tunnel *m*; (min) galerie *f* || *v* (*pret & pp* -**neled** or -**nelled**; *ger* -**neling** or -**nelling**) *tr* percer un tunnel dans or sous

turban [′tʌrbən] *s* turban *m*

turbid [′tʌrbɪd] *adj* trouble

turbine [′tʌrbɪn], [′tʌrbaɪn] *s* turbine *f*

turbojet [′tʌrbo‚dʒɛt] *s* turboréacteur *m*; avion *m* à turboréacteur

turboprop [′tʌrbo‚prɑp] *s* turbopropulseur *m*; avion *m* à turbopropulseur

turbulent [′tʌrbjələnt] *adj* turbulent

tureen [t(j)u′rin] *s* soupière *f*

turf [tʌrf] *s* gazon *m*; (*sod*) motte *f* de gazon; (*peat*) tourbe *f*; **the turf** le turf

turf′man *s* (*pl* -**men**) turfiste *mf*

Turk [tʌrk] *s* Turc *m*

turkey [′tʌrki] *s* dindon *m*; (culin) dinde *f*; (*flop*) (slang) four *m*; **Turkey** Turquie *f*; **la Turquie**

Turkish [′tʌrkɪʃ] *adj & s* turc *m*

Turk′ish delight′ *s* loukoum *m*

Turk′ish tow′el *s* serviette *f* éponge

turmoil [′tʌrmɔɪl] *s* agitation *f*

turn [tʌrn] *s* tour *m*; (*change of direction*) virage *m*; (*bend*) tournant *m*; (*of events; of an expression*) tournure *f*; (*in a wire*) spire *f*; (coll) coup *m*, choc *m*; **at every turn** à tout propos; **by turns** tour à tour; **in turn** à tour de rôle; **to a turn** (culin) à point; **to do a good turn** rendre un service; **to take turns** alterner; **to wait one's turn** prendre son tour; **whose turn is it?** à qui le tour? || *tr* tourner; **to turn about** or **around** retourner; **to turn aside** or **away** détourner; **to turn back** renvoyer; (*an attack*) repousser; (*a clock*) retarder; **to turn down** (*a collar*) rabattre; (*e.g., the gas*) baisser; (*an offer*) refuser; **to turn from** détourner de; **to turn in** replier; (*a wrongdoer*) dénoncer; **to turn into** changer en; **to turn off** (*the water, the gas, etc.*) fermer; (*the light, the radio, etc.*) éteindre; (*a road*) quitter; **to turn on** (*the water, the gas, etc.*) ouvrir; (*the light, the radio, the gas, etc.*) allumer; **to turn out** mettre dehors; (*to manufacture*) produire; (*e.g., the light*) éteindre; **to turn over and over** tourner et retourner; **to turn up** (*a collar*) relever; (*one's sleeves*) retrousser; (*to unearth*) déterrer || *intr* tourner; se tourner; (*said of milk*) tourner; (*to toss and turn*) se retourner; (*to be dizzy*) tourner, e.g., **his head is turning** la tête lui tourne; **to turn about** or **around** se retourner, se tourner; **to turn aside** or **away** se détourner; **to turn back** rebrousser chemin; **to turn down** se rabattre; **to turn in** (coll) aller se coucher; **to turn into** tourner à or en; **to turn on** se jeter sur; (*to depend on*) dépendre de; **to turn out to be** se trouver être; **to turn out well** tourner bien; **to turn over** se retourner; (*said of auto*) capoter; **to turn up** se relever; se présenter, arriver

turn'coat' *s* transfuge *m*

turn'down' *adj* rabattu || *s* refus *m*

turn'ing point' *s* moment *m* décisif

turnip ['tʌrnɪp] *s* navet *m*; (*big watch*) (slang) bassinoire *f*; (slang) tête *f* de bois

turn'key' *s* geôlier *m*

turn' of life' *s* retour *m* d'âge

turn' of mind' *s* inclination *f* naturelle

turn'out' *s* (*gathering*) assistance *f*; (*output*) rendement *m*; (*equipment*) attelage *m*

turn'o'ver *s* renversement *m*; (com) chiffre *m* d'affaires

turn'pike' *s* autoroute *f* à péage

turn'spit' *s* tournebroche *m*

turnstile ['tʌrn‚staɪl] *s* tourniquet *m*

turn'stone' *s* (orn) tourne-pierre *m*

turn'ta'ble *s* (*of phonograph*) plateau *m* porte-disque; (rr) plaque *f* tournante

turpentine ['tʌrpən‚taɪn] *s* térébenthine *f*

turpitude ['tʌrpɪ‚t(j)ud] *s* turpitude *f*

turquoise ['tʌrkɔɪz], ['tʌrkwɔɪz] *s* turquoise *f*

turret ['tʌrɪt] *s* tourelle *f*

turtle ['tʌrtəl] *s* tortue *f*

tur'tle-dove' *s* tourterelle *f*

tur'tle-neck' *s* col *m* roulé; chandail *m* à col roulé

Tuscan ['tʌskən] *adj & s* toscan *m*

Tuscany ['tʌskəni] *s* Toscane *f*; la Toscane

tusk [tʌsk] *s* défense *f*

tussle ['tʌsəl] *s* bagarre *f* || *intr* se bagarrer

tutor ['t(j)utər] *s* précepteur *m*, répétiteur *m* || *tr* donner des leçons particulières à || *intr* donner des leçons particulières

tuxe·do [tʌk'sido] *s* (*pl* -**dos**) smoking *m*

TV ['ti'vi] *s* (letterword) (television) tévé *f*, télé *f*

twaddle ['twadəl] *s* fadaises *fpl* || *intr* dire des fadaises

twang [twæŋ] *s* (*of musical instrument*) son *m* vibrant; (*of voice*) ton *m* nasillard || *tr* faire résonner; dire en nasillant || *intr* nasiller

twang·y ['twæŋi] *adj* (*comp* -**ier**; *super* -**iest**) (*nasal*) nasillard; (*resonant*) vibrant

tweed [twid] *s* tweed *m*

tweet [twit] *s* pépiement *m* || *intr* pépier

tweeter ['twitər] *s* (rad) tweeter *m*

tweezers ['twizərz] *spl* brucelles *fpl*; pince *f* à épiler

twelfth [twelfθ] *adj & pron* douzième (*masc, fem*); **the Twelfth** douze, e.g., **John the Twelfth** Jean douze || *s*

douzième *m*; **the twelfth** (*in dates*) le douze

twelve [twelv] *adj & pron* douze; **about twelve** une douzaine de || *s* douze *m*; **twelve o'clock** (*noon*) midi *m*; (*midnight*) minuit *m*

twentieth ['twentɪ·ɪθ] *adj & pron* vingtième (*masc, fem*); **the Twentieth** vingt, e.g., **John the Twentieth** Jean vingt || *s* vingt *m*; **the twentieth** (*in dates*) le vingt

twen·ty ['twenti] *adj & pron* vingt; **about twenty** une vingtaine de || *s* (*pl* -**ties**) vingt *m*; **the twenties** les années *fpl* vingt

twen'ty-first' *adj & pron* vingt et unième (*masc, fem*); **the Twenty-first** vingt et un, e.g., **John the Twenty-first** Jean vingt et un || *s* vingt et unième *m*; **the twenty-first** (*in dates*) le vingt et un

twen'ty-one' *adj & pron* vingt et un || *s* vingt et un *m*; (*cards*) vingt-et-un

twen'ty-sec'ond *adj & pron* vingt-deuxième (*masc, fem*); **the Twenty-second** vingt-deux, e.g., **John the Twenty-second** Jean vingt-deux || *s* vingt-deuxième *m*; **the twenty-second** (*in dates*) le vingt-deux

twen'ty-two' *adj, pron, & s* vingt-deux *m*

twice [twaɪs] *adv* deux fois; **twice over** à deux reprises

twiddle ['twɪdəl] *tr* tourner, jouer avec; (*e.g., one's moustache*) tortiller

twig [twɪg] *s* brindille *f*

twilight ['twaɪ‚laɪt] *adj* crépusculaire || *s* crépuscule *m*

twill [twɪl] *s* croisé *m* || *tr* croiser

twin [twɪn] *adj & s* jumeau *m* || *v* (*pret & pp* **twinned**; *ger* **twinning**) *tr* jumeler

twin' beds' *spl* lits *mpl* jumeaux

twine [twaɪn] *s* ficelle *f* || *tr* enrouler || *intr* s'enrouler

twinge [twɪndʒ] *s* élancement *m* || *intr* élancer

twin'jet' plane' *s* biréacteur *m*

twinkle ['twɪŋkəl] *s* scintillement *m*; (*of the eye*) clignotement *m* || *intr* scintiller; clignoter

twin'-screw' *adj* à hélices jumelles

twirl [twʌrl] *s* tournoiement *m* || *tr* faire tournoyer; (*e.g., a cane*) faire des moulinets avec || *intr* tournoyer

twist [twɪst] *s* torsion *f*; (*strand*) cordon *m*; (*of the wrist, of rope, etc.*) tour *m*; (*of the road, river, etc.*) coude *m*; (*of tobacco*) rouleau *m*; (*of the ankle*) entorse *f*; (*of mind or disposition*) prédisposition *f* || *tr* tordre, tortiller || *intr* se tordre, se tortiller; **to twist and turn** (*said, e.g., of road*) serpenter; (*said of sleeper*) se tourner et se retourner

twister ['twɪstər] *s* (coll) tornade *f*

twit [twɪt] *v* (*pret & pp* **twitted**; *ger* **twitting**) *tr* taquiner

twitch [twɪtʃ] *s* crispation *f* || *intr* se crisper

twitter ['twɪtər] *s* gazouillement *m* || *intr* gazouiller

two [tu] *adj & pron* deux ‖ *s* deux *m*;
to put two and two together raisonner juste; two o'clock deux heures
two'-cy'cle *adj* (mach) à deux temps
two'-cyl'inder *adj* (mach) à deux cylindres
two'-edged' *adj* à deux tranchants
two' hun'dred *adj, pron, & s* deux
cents *m*
twosome ['tusəm] *s* paire *f*; jeu *m* à
deux joueurs
two'-time' *tr* (slang) tromper
tycoon [taɪ'kun] *s* (coll) magnat *m*
type [taɪp] *s* type *m* ‖ *tr* typer; (*to
typewrite*) taper; (*a sample of blood*)
chercher le groupe sanguin sur ‖ *intr*
taper
type'face' *s* œil *m*
type'script' *s* manuscrit *m* dactylogra-
phié
typesetter ['taɪp,setər] *s* compositeur
m, typographe *mf*; machine *f* à composer

type'write' *v* (*pret* -wrote; *pp* -written)
tr & intr taper à la machine
type'writ'er *s* machine *f* à écrire
type'writer rib'bon *s* ruban *m* encreur
type'writ'ing *s* dactylographie *f*
ty'phoid fe'ver ['taɪfɔɪd] *s* fièvre *f*
typhoïde
typhoon [taɪ'fun] *s* typhon *m*
typical ['tɪpɪkəl] *adj* typique
typi·fy ['tɪpɪ,faɪ] *v* (*pret & pp* -fied)
tr symboliser; être le type de
typ'ing er'ror *s* faute *f* de frappe
typist ['taɪpɪst] *s* dactylo *f*
typographic(al) [,taɪpə'græfɪk(əl)] *adj*
typographique
typograph'ical er'ror *s* erreur *f* typographique
typography [taɪ'pɑgrəfi] *s* typographie *f*
tyrannic(al) [tɪ'rænɪk(əl)], [taɪ'rænɪk-
(əl)] *adj* tyrannique
tyran·ny ['tɪrəni] *s* (*pl* -nies) tyrannie *f*
tyrant ['taɪrənt] *s* tyran *m*
ty·ro ['taɪro] *s* (*pl* -ros) novice *mf*

U

U, u [ju] *s* XXIᵉ lettre de l'alphabet
ubiquitous [ju'bɪkwɪtəs] *adj* ubiquiste,
omniprésent
udder ['ʌdər] *s* pis *m*
ugliness ['ʌglɪnɪs] *s* laideur *f*
ug·ly ['ʌgli] *adj* (*comp* -lier; *super*
-liest) laid; (*disagreeable; mean*)
vilain
Ukraine ['jukren], [ju'kren] *s* Ukraine
f; l'Ukraine
Ukrainian [ju'krenɪ·ən] *adj* ukrainien ‖
s (*language*) ukrainien *m*; (*person*)
Ukrainien *m*
ulcer ['ʌlsər] *s* ulcère *m*
ulcerate ['ʌlsə,ret] *tr* ulcérer ‖ *intr*
s'ulcérer
ulterior [ʌl'tɪrɪ·ər] *adj* ultérieur; secret,
inavoué
ultimate ['ʌltɪmɪt] *adj* ultime, final,
définitif
ultima·tum [,ʌltɪ'metəm] *s* (*pl* -tums
or -ta [tə]) ultimatum *m*
ultrashort [,ʌltrə'ʃɔrt] *adj* (electron)
ultra-court
ultraviolet [,ʌltrə'vaɪ·əlɪt] *adj & s*
ultraviolet *m*
umbil'ical cord' [ʌm'bɪlɪkəl] *s* cordon
m ombilical
umbrage ['ʌmbrɪdʒ] *s*—to take umbrage at prendre ombrage de
umbrella [ʌm'brelə] *s* parapluie *m*;
(mil) ombrelle *f* de protection
umbrel'la stand' *s* porte-parapluies *m*
umlaut ['umlaut] *s* métaphonie *f*, inflexion *f* vocalique; (*mark*) tréma *m*
‖ *tr* changer le timbre de; écrire avec
un tréma
umpire ['ʌmpaɪr] *s* arbitre *m* ‖ *tr &
intr* arbitrer

UN ['ju'en] *s* (letterword) (United Nations) ONU *f*
unable [ʌn'ebəl] *adj* incapable; to be
unable to être incapable de
unabridged [,ʌnə'brɪdʒd] *adj* intégral
unaccented [ʌn'æksentɪd], [,ʌnæk-
'sentɪd] *adj* inaccentué
unacceptable [,ʌnək'septəbəl] *adj* inac-
ceptable
unaccountable [,ʌnə'kauntəbəl] *adj*
inexplicable; irresponsable
unaccounted-for [,ʌnə'kauntɪd,fɔr] *adj*
inexpliqué, pas retrouvé
unaccustomed [,ʌnə'kʌstəmd] *adj* inaccoutumé
unafraid [,ʌnə'fred] *adj* sans peur
unaligned [,ʌnə'laɪnd] *adj* non-engagé
unanimity [,junə'nɪmɪti] *s* unanimité *f*
unanimous [ju'nænɪməs] *adj* unanime
unanswerable [ʌn'ænsərəbəl] *adj* incontestable, sans réplique; (*argument*) irréfutable
unappreciative [,ʌnə'priʃɪ,etɪv] *adj* ingrat, peu reconnaissant
unapproachable [,ʌnə'protʃəbəl] *adj*
inabordable; (fig) incomparable
unarmed [ʌn'ɑrmd] *adj* sans armes
unascertainable [ʌn,æsər'tenəbəl] *adj*
non vérifiable
unasked [ʌn'æskt], [ʌn'ɑskt] *adj* non
invité; to do s.th. unasked faire q.ch.
spontanément
unassembled [,ʌnə'sembəld] *adj* dé-
monté
unassuming [,ʌnə's(j)umɪŋ] *adj* modeste, sans prétentions
unattached [,ʌnə'tæt/t] *adj* indépendant; (*loose*) détaché; (*not engaged
to be married*) seul; (mil, nav) en disponibilité

unattainable [ˌʌnəˈtenəbəl] *adj* inaccessible

unattractive [ˌʌnəˈtræktɪv] *adj* peu attrayant, peu séduisant

unavailable [ˌʌnəˈveləbəl] *adj* non disponible

unavailing [ˌʌnəˈvelɪŋ] *adj* inutile

unavoidable [ˌʌnəˈvɔɪdəbəl] *adj* inévitable

unaware [ˌʌnəˈwer] *adj* ignorant; **to be unaware of** ignorer || *adv* à l'improviste; à mon (son, etc.) insu

unawares [ˌʌnəˈwerz] *adv* (*unexpectedly*) à l'improviste; (*unknowingly*) à mon (son, etc.) insu

unbalanced [ʌnˈbælənst] *adj* non équilibré; (*mind*) déséquilibré; (*bank account*) non soldé

unbandage [ʌnˈbændɪdʒ] *tr* débander

un·bar [ʌnˈbɑr] *v* (*pret & pp* **-barred**; *ger* **-barring**) *tr* débarrer

unbearable [ʌnˈberəbəl] *adj* insupportable

unbeatable [ʌnˈbitəbəl] *adj* imbattable

unbecoming [ˌʌnbɪˈkʌmɪŋ] *adj* déplacé, inconvenant; (*dress*) peu seyant

unbelievable [ˌʌnbɪˈlivəbəl] *adj* incroyable

unbeliever [ˌʌnbɪˈlivər] *s* incroyant *m*

unbending [ʌnˈbendɪŋ] *adj* inflexible

unbiased [ʌnˈbaɪ·əst] *adj* impartial

un·bind [ʌnˈbaɪnd] *v* (*pret & pp* **-bound**) *tr* délier

unbleached [ʌnˈblitʃt] *adj* écru

unbolt [ʌnˈbolt] *tr* (*a gun; a door*) déverrouiller; (*a machine*) déboulonner

unborn [ʌnˈbɔrn] *adj* à naître, futur

unbosom [ʌnˈbuzəm] *tr* découvrir; **to unbosom oneself** ouvrir son cœur

unbound [ʌnˈbaʊnd] *adj* non relié

unbreakable [ʌnˈbrekəbəl] *adj* incassable

unbroken [ʌnˈbrokən] *adj* intact; ininterrompu; (*spirit*) indompté; (*horse*) non rompu

unbuckle [ʌnˈbʌkəl] *tr* déboucler

unburden [ʌnˈbʌrdən] *tr* alléger; **to unburden oneself of** se soulager de

unburied [ʌnˈberid] *adj* non enseveli

unbutton [ʌnˈbʌtən] *tr* déboutonner

uncalled-for [ʌnˈkɔld‚fɔr] *adj* déplacé; (*e.g., insult*) gratuit

uncanny [ʌnˈkæni] *adj* inquiétant, mystérieux; rare, remarquable

uncared-for [ʌnˈkerd‚fɔr] *adj* négligé; peu soignée

unceasing [ʌnˈsisɪŋ] *adj* incessant

unceremonious [ˌʌnserɪˈmoni·əs] *adj* sans façon

uncertain [ʌnˈsʌrtən] *adj* incertain

uncertain·ty [ʌnˈsʌrtənti] *s* (*pl* **-ties**) incertitude *f*

unchain [ʌnˈtʃen] *tr* désenchaîner

unchangeable [ʌnˈtʃendʒəbəl] *adj* immuable

uncharted [ʌnˈtʃɑrtɪd] *adj* inexploré

unchecked [ʌnˈtʃɛkt] *adj* sans frein, non contenu; non vérifié

uncivilized [ʌnˈsɪvɪ‚laɪzd] *adj* incivilisé

unclad [ʌnˈklæd] *adj* déshabillé

unclaimed [ʌnˈklemd] *adj* non réclamé; (*mail*) au rebut

unclasp [ʌnˈklæsp], [ʌnˈklɑsp] *tr* dégrafer; (*one's hands*) desserrer

unclassified [ʌnˈklæsɪ‚faɪd] *adj* non classé; (*documents, information, etc.*) pas secret

uncle [ˈʌŋkəl] *s* oncle *m*

unclean [ʌnˈklin] *adj* sale, immonde

un·clog [ʌnˈklɑg] *v* (*pret & pp* **-clogged**; *ger* **-clogging**) *tr* dégager, désobstruer

unclouded [ʌnˈklaʊdɪd] *adj* clair, dégagé

uncollectible [ˌʌnkəˈlektɪbəl] *adj* irrécouvrable

uncomfortable [ʌnˈkʌmfərtəbəl] *adj* (*causing discomfort*) inconfortable; (*feeling discomfort*) mal à l'aise

uncommitted [ˌʌnkəˈmɪtɪd] *adj* nonengagé

uncommon [ʌnˈkɑmən] *adj* peu commun

uncompromising [ʌnˈkɑmprə‚maɪzɪŋ] *adj* intransigeant

unconcerned [ˌʌnkənˈsʌrnd] *adj* indifférent

unconditional [ˌʌnkənˈdɪʃənəl] *adj* inconditionnel

uncongenial [ˌʌnkənˈdʒini·əl] *adj* peu sympathique; incompatible; désagréable

unconquerable [ʌnˈkɑŋkərəbəl] *adj* invincible

unconquered [ʌnˈkɑŋkərd] *adj* invaincu, indompté

unconscious [ʌnˈkɑnʃəs] *adj* inconscient; (*temporarily deprived of consciousness*) sans connaissance || *s*— **the unconscious** l'inconscient *m*

unconsciousness [ʌnˈkɑnʃəsnɪs] *s* inconscience *f*; perte *f* de connaissance, évanouissement *m*

unconstitutional [ˌʌnkɑnstɪˈt(j)uʃənəl] *adj* inconstitutionnel

uncontrollable [ˌʌnkənˈtroləbəl] *adj* ingouvernable; (*e.g., desires*) irrésistible; (*e.g., laughter*) inextinguible

unconventional [ˌʌnkənˈvenʃənəl] *adj* original, peu conventionnel; (*person*) non-conformiste

uncork [ʌnˈkɔrk] *tr* déboucher

uncouple [ʌnˈkʌpəl] *tr* désaccoupler

uncouth [ʌnˈkuθ] *adj* gauche, sauvage; (*language*) grossier

uncover [ʌnˈkʌvər] *tr* découvrir

unction [ˈʌŋkʃən] *s* onction *f*

unctuous [ˈʌŋktʃu·əs] *adj* onctueux

uncultivated [ʌnˈkʌltɪ‚vetɪd] *adj* inculte

uncultured [ʌnˈkʌltʃərd] *adj* inculte, sans culture

uncut [ʌnˈkʌt] *adj* non coupé; (*stone, diamond*) brut; (*crops*) sur pied; (*book*) non rogné

undamaged [ʌnˈdæmɪdʒd] *adj* indemne

undaunted [ʌnˈdɔntɪd] *adj* pas découragé; sans peur

undecided [ˌʌndɪˈsaɪdɪd] *adj* indécis

undefeated [ˌʌndɪˈfitɪd] *adj* invaincu

undefended [ˌʌndɪˈfendɪd] *adj* sans défense

undefiled [ˌʌndɪˈfaɪld] *adj* sans tache

undeniable [ˌʌndɪˈnaɪ·əbəl] *adj* indéniable

under [ˈʌndər] *adj* (*lower*) inférieur; (*underneath*) de dessous ‖ *adv* dessous; **to go under** sombrer; **to keep under** tenir dans la soumission ‖ *prep* sous, au-dessous de, dessous; moins de, e.g., **under forty** moins de quarante ans; dans, e.g., **under the circumstances** dans les circonstances; en, e.g., **under treatment** en traitement; e.g., **under repair** en voie de réparation; à, e.g., **under the microscope** au microscope; e.g., **under examination** à l'examen; e.g., **under the terms of** aux termes de; e.g., **under the word** (*in dictionary*) au mot; **to serve under** servir sous les ordres de

un′der·age′ *adj* mineur

un′der·arm pad′ *s* dessous-de-bras *m*

un′der·bid′ *v* (*pret & pp* -**bid**; *ger* -**bidding**) *tr* offrir moins que

un′der·brush′ *s* broussailles *fpl*

un′der·car′riage *s* (aer) train *m* d'atterrissage; (aut) dessous *m*

un′der·clothes′ *spl* sous-vêtements *mpl*

un′der·con·sump′tion *s* sous-consommation *f*

un′der·cov′er *adj* secret

un′der·cur′rent *s* courant *m* de fond; (fig) vague *f* de fond

un′der·devel′oped *adj* sous-développé

un′der·dog′ *s* opprimé *m*; (sports) parti *m* non favori, outsider *m*

underdone [ˈʌndər ˌdʌn] *adj* pas assez cuit

un′der·es′timate *tr* sous-estimer

un′der·gar′ment *s* sous-vêtement *m*

un′der·go′ *v* (*pret* -**went**; *pp* -**gone**) *tr* subir, éprouver, souffrir

un′der·grad′uate *adj & s* non diplômé *m*

un′der·ground′ *adj* souterrain; (fig) clandestin ‖ *s* (*subway*) métro *m*; résistance *f*, maquis *m* ‖ *adv* sous terre; **to go underground** (fig) entrer dans la clandestinité, prendre le maquis

un′der·growth′ *s* sous-bois *m*; (*underbrush*) broussailles *fpl*

un′der·hand′ed *adj* sournois, dissimulé

un′der·line′ or **un′der·line′** *tr* souligner

underling [ˈʌndərlɪŋ] *s* sous-ordre *m*, sous-fifre *m*

un′der·mine′ *tr* miner, saper

underneath [ˌʌndərˈniθ] *adj* de dessous; (*lower*) inférieur ‖ *s* dessous *m* ‖ *adv* dessous, en dessous ‖ *prep* sous, au-dessous de

un′der·nour′ished *adj* sous-alimenté

un′der·nour′ishment *s* sous-alimentation *f*

underpaid [ˌʌndərˈped] *adj* mal rétribué

un′der·pass′ *s* passage *m* souterrain

un′der·pin′ *v* (*pret & pp* -**pinned**; *ger* -**pinning**) *tr* étayer

un′der·priv′ileged *adj* déshérité

un′der·rate′ *tr* sous-estimer

un′der·score′ *tr* souligner

un′der·sea′ *adj* sous-marin ‖ **un′der·sea′** *adv* sous la surface de la mer

un′der·sec′retar′y *s* (*pl* -**ies**) sous-secrétaire *m*

un′der·sell′ *v* (*pret & pp* -**sold**) *tr* vendre à meilleur marché que; (*for less than the actual value*) solder

un′der·shirt′ *s* gilet *m*, maillot *m* de corps

un′der·signed′ *adj* soussigné

un′der·skirt′ *s* jupon *m*

un′der·stand′ *v* (*pret & pp* -**stood**) *tr & intr* comprendre, entendre

understandable [ˌʌndərˈstændəbəl] *adj* compréhensible; **that's understandable** cela se comprend

un′der·stand′ing *adj* compréhensif ‖ *s* compréhension *f*; (*intellectual faculty, mind*) entendement *m*; (*agreement*) accord *m*, entente *f*; **on the understanding that** à condition que; **to come to an understanding** arriver à un accord

un′der·stud′y *s* (*pl* -**ies**) doublure *f* ‖ *v* (*pret & pp* -**ied**) *tr* (*an actor*) doubler

un′der·take′ *v* (*pret* -**took**; *pp* -**taken**) *tr* entreprendre; (*to agree to perform*) s'engager à faire; **to undertake to** s'engager à

undertaker [ˈʌndər ˌtekər] *s* (*mortician*) entrepreneur *m* de pompes funèbres

undertaking [ˌʌndərˈtekɪŋ] *s* entreprise *f*; (*commitment*) engagement *m* ‖ [ˈʌndər ˌtekɪŋ] *s* service *m* des pompes funèbres

un′der·tone′ *s* ton *m* atténué; (*background sound*) fond *m* obscur; **in an undertone** à voix basse

un′der·tow′ *s* (*countercurrent below surface*) courant *m* de fond; (*on beach*) ressac *m*

un′der·wear′ *s* sous-vêtements *mpl*

un′der·world′ *s* (*criminal world*) basfonds *mpl*, pègre *f*; (*pagan world of the dead*) enfers *mpl*

un′der·write′ or **un′der·write′** *v* (*pret* -**wrote**; *pp* -**written**) *tr* souscrire; (ins) assurer

un′der·writ′er *s* souscripteur *m*; (ins) assureur *m*

undeserved [ˌʌndɪˈzɜrvd] *adj* immérité

undesirable [ˌʌndɪˈzaɪrəbəl] *adj* peu désirable; (*e.g., alien*) indésirable ‖ *s* indésirable *mf*

undetachable [ˌʌndɪˈtætʃəbəl] *adj* inséparable

undeveloped [ˌʌndɪˈveləpt] *adj* (*land*) inexploité; (*country*) sous-développé

undigested [ˌʌndɪˈdʒɛstɪd] *adj* indigeste

undignified [ʌnˈdɪgnɪˌfaɪd] *adj* sans dignité, peu digne

undiscernible [ˌʌndɪˈzɜrnɪbəl], [ˌʌndɪˈsɜrnəbəl] *adj* imperceptible

undisputed [ˌʌndɪsˈpjutɪd] *adj* incontesté

undo [ʌnˈdu] *v* (*pret* -**did**; *pp* -**done**) *tr* défaire; (fig) ruiner

undoing [ʌnˈdu·ɪŋ] *s* perte *f*, ruine *f*

undone [ʌnˈdʌn] *adj* défait; (*omitted*) inaccompli; **to come undone** se défaire; **to leave nothing undone** ne rien négliger

undoubtedly [ʌn'dautɪdli] *adv* sans aucun doute, incontestablement

undramatic [ˌʌndrə'mætɪk] *adj* peu dramatique

undress ['ʌn ˌdres], [ʌn'dres] *s* déshabillé *m*; (*scanty dress*) petite tenue *f* || [ʌn'dres] *tr* déshabiller || *intr* se déshabiller

undrinkable [ʌn'drɪŋkəbəl] *adj* imbuvable

undue [ʌn'd(j)u] *adj* indu

undulate ['ʌndjə ˌlet] *intr* onduler

unduly [ʌn'd(j)uli] *adv* indûment

undying [ʌn'daɪ·ɪŋ] *adj* impérissable

un'earned in'come ['ʌn ˌɜrnd] *s* rente *f*, revenu *m* d'un bien

un'earned in'crement *s* plus-value *f*

unearth [ʌn'ɜrθ] *tr* déterrer

unearthly [ʌn'ɜrθli] *adj* surnaturel, spectral; bizarre; (*hour*) indu

uneasy [ʌn'izi] *adj* inquiet; contraint, gêné

uneatable [ʌn'itəbəl] *adj* immangeable

uneconomic(al) [ˌʌnikə'nɑmɪk(əl)], [ˌʌnekə'nɑmɪk(əl)] *adj* peu économique; (*person*) peu économe

uneducated [ʌn'edʒə ˌketɪd] *adj* ignorant, sans instruction

unemployed [ˌʌnem'plɔɪd] *adj* en chômage, sans travail || *spl* chômeurs *mpl*, sans-travail *mfpl*

unemployment [ˌʌnem'plɔɪmənt] *s* chômage *m*

un'employ'ment insur'ance *s* assurance-chômage *f*

unending [ʌn'endɪŋ] *adj* interminable

unequal [ʌn'ikwəl] *adj* inégal; **to be unequal to** (*a task*) ne pas être à la hauteur de

unequaled *or* **unequalled** [ʌn'ikwəld] *adj* sans égal, sans pareil

unerring [ʌn'ʌrɪŋ], [ʌn'erɪŋ] *adj* infaillible

UNESCO [ju'nesko] *s* (acronym) (**United Nations Educational, Scientific, and Cultural Organization**) l'Unesco *f*

unessential [ˌʌne'senʃəl] *adj* non essentiel

uneven [ʌn'ivən] *adj* inégal; (*number*) impair

uneventful [ˌʌnɪ'ventfəl] *adj* sans incident, peu mouvementé

unexceptionable [ˌʌnek'sepʃənəbəl] *adj* irréprochable

unexpected [ˌʌnek'spektɪd] *adj* inattendu, imprévu

unexplained [ˌʌnek'splend] *adj* inexpliqué

unexplored [ˌʌnek'splord] *adj* inexploré

unexposed [ˌʌnek'spozd] *adj* (*phot*) vierge

unfading [ʌn'fedɪŋ] *adj* immarcescible

unfailing [ʌn'felɪŋ] *adj* infaillible; (*inexhaustible*) intarissable

unfair [ʌn'fer] *adj* injuste, déloyal

unfaithful [ʌn'feθfəl] *adj* infidèle

unfamiliar [ˌʌnfə'mɪljər] *adj* étranger, peu familier

unfasten [ʌn'fæsən], [ʌn'fɑsən] *tr* défaire, détacher

unfathomable [ʌn'fæðəməbəl] *adj* insondable

unfavorable [ʌn'fevərəbəl] *adj* défavorable

unfeeling [ʌn'filɪŋ] *adj* insensible

unfilled [ʌn'fɪld] *adj* vide; (*post*) vacant

unfinished [ʌn'fɪnɪʃt] *adj* inachevé

unfit [ʌn'fɪt] *adj* impropre, inapte

unfold [ʌn'fold] *tr* déplier || *intr* se déplier

unforeseeable [ˌʌnfor'si·əbəl] *adj* imprévisible

unforeseen [ˌʌnfor'sin] *adj* imprévu

unforgettable [ˌʌnfər'getəbəl] *adj* inoubliable

unforgivable [ˌʌnfər'gɪvəbəl] *adj* impardonnable

unfortunate [ʌn'fɔrtʃənɪt] *adj & s* malheureux *m*

un-freeze [ʌn'friz] *v* (*pret* -froze; *pp* -frozen) *tr* dégeler

unfriend-ly [ʌn'frendli] *adj* (*comp* -lier; *super* -liest) inamical

unfruitful [ʌn'frutfəl] *adj* infructueux

unfulfilled [ˌʌnfəl'fɪld] *adj* inaccompli

unfurl [ʌn'fʌrl] *tr* déployer

unfurnished [ʌn'fʌrnɪʃt] *adj* non meublé

ungain-ly [ʌn'genli] *adj* gauche, disgracieux

ungentlemanly [ʌn'dʒentəlmənli] *adj* mal élevé, impoli

ungird [ʌn'gɑrd] *tr* déceindre

ungodly [ʌn'gɑdli] *adj* impie; (*dreadful*) (coll) atroce

ungracious [ʌn'greʃəs] *adj* malgracieux

ungrammatical [ˌʌngrə'mætɪkəl] *adj* peu grammatical

ungrateful [ʌn'gretfəl] *adj* ingrat

ungrudgingly [ʌn'grʌdʒɪŋli] *adj* de bon cœur, libéralement

unguarded [ʌn'gɑrdɪd] *adj* sans défense; (*moment*) d'inattention; (*card*) sec

unguent ['ʌŋgwənt] *s* onguent *m*

unhandy [ʌn'hændi] *adj* maladroit; (*e.g., tool*) incommode, pas maniable

unhap-py [ʌn'hæpi] *adj* (*comp* -pier; *super* -piest) malheureux, triste; (*unlucky*) malheureux, malencontreux; (*fateful*) funeste

unharmed [ʌn'hɑrmd] *adj* indemne

unharness [ʌn'hɑrnɪs] *tr* dételer

unheal-thy [ʌn'helθi] *adj* (*comp* -thier; *super* -thiest) malsain; (*person*) maladif

unheard-of [ʌn'hɑrd ˌʌv] *adj* inouï

unhinge [ʌn'hɪndʒ] *tr* (fig) détraquer

unhitch [ʌn'hɪtʃ] *tr* décrocher; (*e.g., a horse*) dételer

unho-ly [ʌn'holi] *adj* (*comp* -lier; *super* -liest) profane; (coll) affreux

unhook [ʌn'huk] *tr* décrocher; (*e.g., a dress*) dégrafer

unhoped-for [ʌn'hopt ˌfər] *adj* inespéré

unhorse [ʌn'hɔrs] *tr* désarçonner

unhurt [ʌn'hʌrt] *adj* indemne

unicorn ['juni ˌkɔrn] *s* unicorne *m*

unification [ˌjunifɪ'keʃən] *s* unification *f*

uniform ['juni ˌfɔrm] *adj & s* uniforme

m ‖ *tr* uniformiser; vêtir d'un uniforme

uniformi·ty [ˌjuni'fɔrmiti] *s* (*pl* -ties) uniformité *f*

uni·fy ['juni ˌfai] *v* (*pret & pp* -fied) unifier

unilateral [ˌjuni'lætərəl] *adj* unilatéral

unimpeachable [ˌʌnim'pitʃəbəl] *adj* irrécusable

unimportant [ˌʌnim'pɔrtənt] *adj* peu important, sans importance

uninhabited [ˌʌnin'hæbitid] *adj* inhabité

uninspired [ˌʌnin'spaird] *adj* sans inspiration, sans vigueur

unintelligent [ˌʌnin'telidʒənt] *adj* inintelligent

unintelligible [ˌʌnin'telidʒibəl] *adj* inintelligible

uninterested [ʌn'intristid], [ʌn'intəˌrestid] *adj* indifférent

uninteresting [ʌn'intristiŋ], [ʌn'intəˌrestiŋ] *adj* peu intéressant

uninterrupted [ˌʌnintə'rʌptid] *adj* ininterrompu

union ['junjən] *adj* (*leader, scale, card, etc.*) syndical ‖ *s* union *f*; (*of workmen*) syndicat *m*

unionize ['junjə ˌnaiz] *tr* syndiquer ‖ *intr* se syndiquer

un'ion shop' *s* atelier *m* syndical

un'ion suit' *s* sous-vêtement *m* d'une seule pièce

unique [ju'nik] *adj* unique

unison ['junisən], ['junizən] *s* unisson *m*; **in unison (with)** à l'unisson (de)

unit ['junit] *adj* unitaire ‖ *s* unité *f*; (elec, mach) groupe *m*

unite [ju'nait] *tr* unir ‖ *intr* s'unir

united [ju'naitid] *adj* uni

Unit'ed King'dom *s* Royaume-Uni *m*

Unit'ed Na'tions *spl* Nations *fpl* Unies

Unit'ed States' *adj* des États-Unis, américain ‖ *s*—**the United States** les États-Unis *mpl*

uni·ty ['juniti] *s* (*pl* -ties) unité *f*

universal [ˌjuni'vʌrsəl] *adj & s* universel *m*

u'niversal joint' *s* joint *m* articulé, cardan *m*

universe ['juni ˌvʌrs] *s* univers *m*

universi·ty [ˌjuni'vʌrsiti] *adj* universitaire ‖ *s* (*pl* -ties) université *f*

unjust [ʌn'dʒʌst] *adj* injuste

unjustified [ʌn'dʒʌsti ˌfaid] *adj* injustifié

unkempt [ʌn'kempt] *adj* dépeigné; mal tenu, négligé

unkind [ʌn'kaind] *adj* désobligeant; (*pitiless*) impitoyable, dur

unknowable [ʌn'no·əbəl] *adj* inconnaissable

unknowingly [ʌn'no·iŋli] *adv* inconsciemment

unknown [ʌn'non] *adj* inconnu; (*not yet revealed*) inédit; **unknown to** à l'insu de ‖ *s* inconnu *m*; (math) inconnue *f*

un'known quan'tity *s* (math, fig) inconnue *f*

Un'known Sol'dier *s* Soldat *m* inconnu

unlace [ʌn'les] *tr* délacer

unlatch [ʌn'lætʃ] *tr* lever le loquet de

unlawful [ʌn'lɔfəl] *adj* illégal, illicite

unleash [ʌn'liʃ] *tr* lâcher

unleavened [ʌn'levənd] *adj* azyme

unless [ʌn'les] *prep* sauf ‖ *conj* à moins que

unlettered [ʌn'letərd] *adj* illettré

unlike [ʌn'laik] *adj* (*not alike*) dissemblables; différent de; (*not typical of*) pas caractéristique de; (*poles of a magnet*) (elec) de noms contraires ‖ *prep* (*contrary to*) à la différence de

unlikely [ʌn'laikli] *adj* peu probable

unlimited [ʌn'limitid] *adj* illimité

unlined [ʌn'laind] *adj* (*coat*) non fourré; (*paper*) non rayé; (*face*) sans rides

unload [ʌn'lod] *tr* décharger; (*a gun*) désarmer; (coll) se décharger de ‖ *intr* décharger

unloading [ʌn'lodiŋ] *s* déchargement *m*

unlock [ʌn'lak] *tr* ouvrir; (*a bolted door*) déverrouiller; (*the jaws*) desserrer

unloose [ʌn'lus] *tr* lâcher; (*to undo*) délier; (*a mighty force*) déchaîner

unloved [ʌn'lʌvd] *adj* peu aimé, haï

unlovely [ʌn'lʌvli] *adj* disgracieux

unluck·y [ʌn'lʌki] *adj* (*comp* -ier; *super* -iest) malchanceux, malheureux

un·make [ʌn'mek] *v* (*pret & pp* -made) *tr* défaire

unmanageable [ʌn'mænidʒəbəl] *adj* difficile à manier, ingouvernable

unmanly [ʌn'mænli] *adj* indigne d'un homme, poltron; efféminé

unmannerly [ʌn'mænərli] *adj* impoli, mal élevé

unmarketable [ʌn'markitəbəl] *adj* invendable

unmarriageable [ʌn'mæridʒəbəl] *adj* non mariable

unmarried [ʌn'mærid] *adj* célibataire

unmask [ʌn'mæsk] *tr* démasquer ‖ *intr* se démasquer

unmatched [ʌn'mætʃt] *adj* sans égal, incomparable; (*unpaired*) désassorti, dépareillé

unmerciful [ʌn'mʌrsifəl] *adj* impitoyable

unmesh [ʌn'meʃ] *tr* (mach) désengrener ‖ *intr* (mach) se désengrener

unmindful [ʌn'maindfəl] *adj* oublieux

unmistakable [ˌʌnmis'tekəbəl] *adj* évident, facilement reconnaissable

unmitigated [ʌn'miti ˌgetid] *adj* parfait, fieffé

unmixed [ʌn'mikst] *adj* sans mélange

unmoor [ʌn'mur] *tr* désamarrer

unmoved [ʌn'muvd] *adj* impassible

unmuzzle [ʌn'mʌzəl] *tr* démuseler

unnatural [ʌn'nætʃərəl] *adj* anormal, dénaturé; maniéré; artificiel

unnecessary [ʌn'nesə ˌseri] *adj* inutile

unnerve [ʌn'nʌrv] *tr* démonter, décontenancer, bouleverser

unnoticeable [ʌn'notisəbəl] *adj* imperceptible

unnoticed [ʌn'notist] *adj* inaperçu

unobserved [ˌʌnəb'zʌrvd] *adj* inobservé, inaperçu

unobtainable [ˌʌnəb'tenəbəl] adj introuvable

unobtrusive [ˌʌnəb'trusɪv] adj discret, effacé

unoccupied [ʌn'akjəˌpaɪd] adj libre, inoccupé

unofficial [ˌʌnə'fɪʃəl] adj officieux, non officiel

unopened [ʌn'opənd] adj fermé; (letter) non décacheté

unopposed [ˌʌnə'pozd] adj sans opposition; (candidate) unique

unorthodox [ʌn'ɔrθəˌdaks] adj peu orthodox

unpack [ʌn'pæk] tr déballer

unpalatable [ʌn'pælətəbəl] adj fade, insipide

unparalleled [ʌn'pærəˌleld] adj sans précédent, sans pareil

unpardonable [ʌn'pardənəbəl] adj impardonnable

unpatriotic [ˌʌnpetrɪ'atɪk], [ˌʌnpætrɪ'atɪk] adj antipatriotique

unperceived [ˌʌnpər'sivd] adj inaperçu

unperturbable [ˌʌnpər'tʌrbəbəl] adj imperturbable

unpleasant [ʌn'plezənt] adj désagréable, déplaisant

unpopular [ʌn'papjələr] adj impopulaire

unpopularity [ʌnˌpapjə'lærɪti] s impopularité f

unprecedented [ʌn'presɪˌdentɪd] adj sans précédent, inédit

unprejudiced [ʌn'predʒədɪst] adj sans préjugés, impartial

unpremeditated [ˌʌnpri'medɪˌtetɪd] adj non prémédité

unprepared [ˌʌnprɪ'perd] adj sans préparation; (e.g., speech) improvisé

unprepossessing [ˌʌnpripə'zesɪŋ] adj peu engageant

unpresentable [ˌʌnprɪ'zentəbəl] adj peu présentable

unpretentious [ˌʌnprɪ'tenʃəs] adj sans prétentions, modeste

unprincipled [ʌn'prɪnsɪpəld] adj sans principes, sans scrupules

unproductive [ˌʌnprə'dʌktɪv] adj improductif

unprofitable [ʌn'prafɪtəbəl] adj peu profitable, inutile

unpronounceable [ˌʌnprə'naʊnsəbəl] adj imprononçable

unpropitious [ˌʌnprə'pɪʃəs] adj défavorable

unpublished [ʌn'pʌblɪʃt] adj inédit

unpunished [ʌn'pʌnɪʃt] adj impuni

unqualified [ʌn'kwalɪˌfaɪd] adj incompétent; parfait, fieffé

unquenchable [ʌn'kwentʃəbəl] adj inextinguible

unquestionable [ʌn'kwestʃənəbəl] adj indiscutable

unrav•el [ʌn'rævəl] v (pret & pp -eled or -elled; ger -eling or -elling) tr effiler; (fig) débrouiller ‖ intr s'effiler; (fig) se débrouiller

unreachable [ʌn'ritʃəbəl] adj inaccessible

unreal [ʌn'riəl] adj irréel

unreality [ˌʌnrɪ'ælɪti] s (pl -ties) irréalité f

unreasonable [ʌn'rizənəbəl] adj déraisonnable

unrecognizable [ʌn'rekəgˌnaɪzəbəl] adj méconnaissable

unreel [ʌn'ril] tr dérouler ‖ intr se dérouler

unrelenting [ˌʌnrɪ'lentɪŋ] adj implacable

unreliable [ˌʌnrɪ'laɪ•əbəl] adj peu fidèle, instable, sujet à caution

unremitting [ˌʌnrɪ'mɪtɪŋ] adj incessant, infatigable

unrented [ʌn'rentrd] adj libre, sans locataires

unrepentant [ˌʌnrɪ'pentənt] adj impénitent

un'requit'ed love' [ˌʌnrɪ'kwaɪtɪd] s amour m non partagé

unresponsive [ˌʌnrɪ'spansɪv] adj peu sensible, froid, détaché

unrest [ʌn'rest] s agitation f, trouble m; inquiétude f

un•rig [ʌn'rɪg] v (pret & pp -rigged; ger -rigging) tr (naut) dégréer

unrighteous [ʌn'raɪtʃəs] adj inique, injuste

unripe [ʌn'raɪp] adj vert, pas mûr; précoce

unrivaled or **unrivalled** [ʌn'raɪvəld] adj sans rival

unroll [ʌn'rol] tr dérouler ‖ intr se dérouler

unromantic [ˌʌnro'mæntɪk] adj peu romanesque, terre à terre

unruffled [ʌn'rʌfəld] adj calme, serein

unruly [ʌn'ruli] adj indiscipliné, ingouvernable

unsaddle [ʌn'sædəl] tr (a horse) desseller; (a horseman) désarçonner

unsafe [ʌn'sef] adj dangereux

unsaid [ʌn'sed] adj—to leave unsaid passer sous silence

unsalable [ʌn'seləbəl] adj invendable

unsanitary [ʌn'sænɪˌteri] adj peu hygiénique

unsatisfactory [ʌnˌsætɪs'fæktəri] adj peu satisfaisant

unsatisfied [ʌn'sætɪsˌfaɪd] adj insatisfait, inassouvi

unsavory [ʌn'sevəri] adj désagréable; (fig) équivoque, louche

unscathed [ʌn'skeðd] adj indemne

unscientific [ˌʌnsaɪ•ən'tɪfɪk] adj antiscientifique

unscrew [ʌn'skru] tr dévisser

unscrupulous [ʌn'skrupjələs] adj sans scrupules

unseal [ʌn'sil] tr desceller

unsealed adj (mail) non clos

unseasonable [ʌn'sizənəbəl] adj hors de saison; (untimely) inopportun

unseemly [ʌn'simli] adj inconvenant

unseen [ʌn'sin] adj invisible

unselfish [ʌn'selfɪʃ] adj désintéressé

unsettled [ʌn'setəld] adj instable; (region) non colonisé; (question) en suspens; (weather) variable; (bills) non réglé

unshackle [ʌn'ʃækəl] tr désentraver

unshaken [ʌn'ʃekən] adj inébranlé

unshapely [ʌnˈʃepli] *adj* difforme, informe

unshaven [ʌnˈʃevən] *adj* non rasé

unsheathe [ʌnˈʃið] *tr* dégainer

unshod [ʌnˈʃad] *adj* déchaussé; (*horse*) déferré

unshrinkable [ʌnˈʃrɪŋkəbəl] *adj* irrétrécissable

unsightly [ʌnˈsaɪtli] *adj* laid, hideux

unsinkable [ʌnˈsɪŋkəbəl] *adj* insubmersible

unskilled [ʌnˈskɪld] *adj* inexpérimenté; de manœuvre

un/skilled la/borer *s* manœuvre *m*

unskillful [ʌnˈskɪlfəl] *adj* maladroit

unsnarl [ʌnˈsnarl] *tr* débrouiller

unsociable [ʌnˈsoʃəbəl] *adj* insociable

unsold [ʌnˈsold] *adj* invendu

unsolder [ʌnˈsadər] *tr* dessouder

unsophisticated [ˌʌnsəˈfɪstɪˌ ketɪd] *adj* ingénu, naïf, simple

unsound [ʌnˈsaund] *adj* peu solide; (*false*) faux; (*decayed*) gâté; (*mind*) dérangé; (*sleep*) léger

unspeakable [ʌnˈspikəbəl] *adj* indicible; (*disgusting*) sans nom

unsportsmanlike [ʌnˈsportsmən ˌlaɪk] *adj* antisportif

unstable [ʌnˈstebəl] *adj* instable

unsteady [ʌnˈstedi] *adj* chancelant, tremblant, vacillant

unstinted [ʌnˈstɪntɪd] *adj* abondant, sans bornes

unstitch [ʌnˈstɪtʃ] *tr* découdre

un-stop [ʌnˈstap] *v* (*pret & pp* -stopped; *ger* -stopping) *tr* déboucher

unstressed [ʌnˈstrest] *adj* inaccentué

unstrung [ʌnˈstrʌŋ] *adj* détraqué; (*necklace*) défilé; (*mus*) sans cordes

unsuccessful [ˌʌnsəkˈsesfəl] *adj* non réussi; **to be unsuccessful** ne pas réussir

unsuitable [ʌnˈs(j)utəbəl] *adj* impropre; (*time*) inopportun; **unsuitable for** peu fait pour, inapte à

unsuspected [ˌʌnsəsˈpektɪd] *adj* insoupçonné

unswerving [ʌnˈswʌrvɪŋ] *adj* ferme, inébranlable

unsympathetic [ˌʌnsɪmpəˈθetɪk] *adj* peu compatissant

unsystematic(al) [ˌʌnsɪstəˈmætɪk(əl)] *adj* non systématique, sans méthode

untactful [ʌnˈtæktfəl] *adj* indiscret, indélicat

untamed [ʌnˈtemd] *adj* indompté

untangle [ʌnˈtæŋgəl] *tr* démêler, débrouiller

untenable [ʌnˈtenəbəl] *adj* insoutenable

unthankful [ʌnˈθæŋkfəl] *adj* ingrat

unthinkable [ʌnˈθɪŋkəbəl] *adj* impensable

unthinking [ʌnˈθɪŋkɪŋ] *adj* irréfléchi

untidy [ʌnˈtaɪdi] *adj* désordonné, débraillé

un-tie [ʌnˈtaɪ] *v* (*pret & pp* -tied; *ger* -tying) *tr* délier, dénouer

until [ʌnˈtɪl] *prep* jusqu'à || *conj* jusqu'à ce que, en attendant que

untimely [ʌnˈtaɪmli] *adj* inopportun; (*premature*) prématuré

untiring [ʌnˈtaɪrɪŋ] *adj* infatigable

untold [ʌnˈtold] *adj* incalculable; (*suffering*) inouï; (*joy*) indicible; (*tale*) non raconté

untouchable [ʌnˈtʌtʃəbəl] *adj & s* intouchable *mf*

untouched [ʌnˈtʌtʃt] *adj* intact; indifférent; non mentionné

untoward [ʌnˈtord] *adj* malencontreux

untrained [ʌnˈtrend] *adj* inexpérimenté; (*animal*) non dressé

untrammeled or **untrammelled** [ʌnˈtræməld] *adj* sans entraves

untried [ʌnˈtraɪd] *adj* inéprouvé

untroubled [ʌnˈtrʌbəld] *adj* calme, insoucieux

untrue [ʌnˈtru] *adj* faux; infidèle

untrustworthy [ʌnˈtrʌstˌwʌrði] *adj* indigne de confiance

untruth [ʌnˈtruθ] *s* mensonge *m*

untruthful [ʌnˈtruθfəl] *adj* mensonger

untwist [ʌnˈtwɪst] *tr* détordre || *intr* se détordre

unused [ʌnˈjuzd] *adj* inutilisé, inemployé; **unused to** [ʌnˈjuzdtʊ], [ʌnˈjustʊ] peu accoutumé à

unusual [ʌnˈjuʒʊəl] *adj* insolite, inusité, inhabituel

unutterable [ʌnˈʌtərəbəl] *adj* indicible, inexprimable

unvanquished [ʌnˈvæŋkwɪʃt] *adj* invaincu

unvarnished [ʌnˈvarnɪʃt] *adj* non verni; (*fig*) sans fard, simple

unveil [ʌnˈvel] *tr* dévoiler; (*e.g., a statue*) inaugurer || *intr* se dévoiler

unveiling [ʌnˈvelɪŋ] *s* dévoilement *m*

unventilated [ʌnˈventɪˌletɪd] *adj* sans aération

unvoice [ʌnˈvɔɪs] *tr* dévoiser, assourdir

unwanted [ʌnˈwɑntɪd] *adj* non voulu

unwarranted [ʌnˈwɑrəntɪd] *adj* injustifié; sans garantie

unwary [ʌnˈweri] *adj* imprudent

unwavering [ʌnˈwevərɪŋ] *adj* constant, ferme, résolu

unwelcome [ʌnˈwelkəm] *adj* (*e.g., visitor*) importun; (*e.g., news*) fâcheux

unwell [ʌnˈwel] *adj* indisposé, souffrant; (*menstruating*) indisposée

unwholesome [ʌnˈholsəm] *adj* malsain, insalubre

unwieldy [ʌnˈwildi] *adj* peu maniable

unwilling [ʌnˈwɪlɪŋ] *adj* peu disposé

unwillingly [ʌnˈwɪlɪŋli] *adv* à contre-cœur

un-wind [ʌnˈwaɪnd] *v* (*pret & pp* -wound) *tr* dérouler || *intr* se dérouler

unwise [ʌnˈwaɪz] *adj* peu judicieux, malavisé

unwished-for [ʌnˈwɪʃtˌfɔr] *adj* non souhaité

unwittingly [ʌnˈwɪtɪŋli] *adv* inconsciemment, sans le savoir

unwonted [ʌnˈwʌntɪd] *adj* inaccoutumé, peu commun

unworldly [ʌnˈwʌrldli] *adj* peu mondain; simple, naïf

unworthy [ʌnˈwʌrði] *adj* indigne

un-wrap [ʌnˈræp] *v* (*pret & pp* -wrapped; *ger* -wrapping) *tr* dépaqueter, désenvelopper

unwrinkled [ʌn'rɪŋkəld] *adj* uni, lisse, sans rides

unwritten [ʌn'rɪtən] *adj* non écrit; oral; *(blank)* vierge, blanc

unwrit'ten law' s droit m coutumier

unyielding [ʌn'jildɪŋ] *adj* ferme, solide; inébranlable

unyoke [ʌn'jok] *tr* dételer

up [ʌp] *adj* montant, ascendant; *(raised)* levé; *(standing)* debout; *(time)* expiré; *(blinds)* relevé; **up in arms** soulevé, indigné ‖ *adv* haut, en haut; **to be up against** se heurter à; **to be up against it** avoir la déveine; **to be up to** être capable de, être à la hauteur de; être à, e.g., **to be up to you (me, etc.)** être à vous (moi, etc.); **up and down** de haut en bas; *(back and forth)* de long en large; **up there** là-haut; **up to** jusqu'à; *(at the level of)* au niveau de, à la hauteur de; **up to and including** jusques et y compris; **what's up?** qu'est-ce qui se passe?; for expressions like **to go up** monter and **to get up** se lever, see the verb ‖ *prep* en haut de, vers le haut de; *(a stream)* en montant ‖ *v (pret & pp* **upped;** *ger* **upping)** *tr* (coll) faire monter; *(prices, wages)* (coll) élever ‖ *interj* debout!

up-and-coming ['ʌpən'kʌmɪŋ] *adj* (coll) entreprenant

up-and-doing ['ʌpən'du·ɪŋ] *adj* (coll) entreprenant, alerte, énergique

up-and-up ['ʌpən'ʌp] s—**to be on the up-and-up** (coll) être en bonne voie; (coll) être honnête

up'braid' *tr* réprimander, reprendre

upbringing ['ʌp‚brɪŋɪŋ] s éducation f

up'coun'try *adv* (coll) à l'intérieur du pays ‖ s (coll) intérieur m du pays

up·date' *tr* mettre à jour

upheaval [ʌp'hivəl] s soulèvement m

up'hill' *adj* montant; difficile, pénible ‖ **up'hill'** *adv* en montant

up·hold' *v (pret & pp* **-held)** *tr* soutenir, maintenir

upholster [ʌp'holstər] *tr* tapisser

upholsterer [ʌp'holstərər] s tapissier m

upholster·y [ʌp'holstəri] s (*pl* **-ies**) tapisserie f

up'keep' s entretien m; *(expenses)* frais mpl d'entretien

upland ['ʌplənd], ['ʌp‚lænd] *adj* élevé ‖ s région f montagneuse; **uplands** hautes terres fpl

up'lift' s élévation f; *(moral improvement)* édification f ‖ **up·lift'** *tr* soulever, élever

upon [ə'pɑn] *prep* sur; à, e.g., **upon my arrival** à mon arrivée; **upon** + *ger* en + *ger*, e.g., **upon arriving** en arrivant

upper ['ʌpər] *adj* supérieur; haut; *(first)* premier ‖ s *(of shoe)* empeigne f

up'per berth' s couchette f du haut, couchette supérieure

up'per-case' *adj* (typ) du haut de casse

up'per clas'ses spl hautes classes fpl

up'per hand' s dessus m, haute main f

up'per mid'dle class' s haute bourgeoisie f

up'per·most' *adj* (le) plus haut, (le) plus élevé; (le) premier ‖ *adv* en dessus

uppish ['ʌpɪʃ] *adj* (coll) suffisant, arrogant

up·raise' *tr* lever

up'right' *adj & adv* droit ‖ s montant m

uprising [ʌp'raɪzɪŋ], ['ʌp‚raɪzɪŋ] s soulèvement m, insurrection f

up'roar' s tumulte m, vacarme m

uproarious [ʌp'rorɪ·əs] *adj* tumultueux; *(funny)* comique, impayable

up·root' *tr* déraciner

ups' and downs' spl vicissitudes fpl

up·set' or **up'set'** *adj (overturned)* renversé; *(disturbed)* bouleversé; *(stomach)* dérangé ‖ **up'set'** s *(overturn)* renversement m; *(of emotions)* bouleversement m ‖ **up·set'** *v (pret & pp* **-set;** *ger* **-setting)** *tr* renverser; bouleverser ‖ *intr* se renverser

up'set price' s prix m de départ

upsetting [ʌp'setɪŋ] *adj* bouleversant, inquiétant

up'shot' s résultat m; point m essentiel

up'side down' *adv* sens dessus dessous; **to turn upside down** renverser; se renverser; *(said of carriage)* verser

up'stage' *adj & adv* au second plan, à l'arrière-plan; **to go upstage** remonter ‖ s arrière-plan m ‖ **up'stage'** *tr* (coll) prendre un air dédaigneux envers

up'stairs' *adj* d'en haut ‖ s l'étage m supérieur ‖ *adv* en haut; **to go upstairs** monter, monter en haut

up'stand'ing *adj* droit; *(vigorous)* gaillard; *(sincere)* honnête, probe

up'start' *adj & s* parvenu m

up'stream' *adj* d'amont ‖ *adv* en amont

up'stroke' s *(in writing)* délié m; *(mach)* course f ascendante

up'surge' s poussée f

up'swing' s mouvement m de montée; (com) amélioration f

up-to-date ['ʌptə'det] *adj* à la page; *(e.g., account books)* mis à jour

up-to-the-minute ['ʌptəðə'mɪnɪt] *adj* de la dernière heure

up'trend' s tendance f à la hausse

up'turn' s hausse f, amélioration f

up'turned' *adj (e.g., eyes)* levé; *(part of clothing)* relevé; *(nose)* retroussé

upward ['ʌpwərd] *adj* ascendant ‖ *adv* vers le haut; **upward of** plus de

Ural ['jurəl] *adj* Ouralien ‖ s Oural m; **Urals** Oural

uranium [ju'renɪ·əm] s uranium m

urban ['ʌrbən] *adj* urbain

urbane [ʌr'ben] *adj* urbain, courtois

urbanite ['ʌrbə‚naɪt] s citadin m, habitant m d'une ville

urbanity [ʌr'bænɪti] s urbanité f

urbanize ['ʌrbə‚naɪz] *tr* urbaniser

ur'ban renew'al s renouveau m urbain

urchin ['ʌrtʃɪn] s gamin m, galopin m

ure·thra [ju'riθrə] s (*pl* **-thras** or **-thrae** [θri]) urètre m

urge [ʌrdʒ] s impulsion f ‖ *tr & intr* presser

urgen·cy ['ʌrdʒənsi] s (*pl* **-cies**) urgence f; insistance f, sollicitation f

urgent ['ʌrdʒənt] *adj* urgent, pressant; (*insistent*) pressant, importun
urinal ['jurɪnəl] *s* (*small building or convenience for men*) urinoir *m*, vespasienne *f*; (*for bed*) urinal *m*
urinary ['jurɪ,neri] *adj* urinaire
urinate ['jurɪ,net] *tr & intr* uriner; pisser (coll)
urine ['jurɪn] *s* urine *f*
urn [ʌrn] *s* urne *f*; (*for tea, coffee, etc.*) fontaine *f*
urology [ju'ralədʒi] *s* urologie *f*
us [ʌs] *pron pers* nous §85, §87
U.S.A. ['ju'es'e] *s* (letterword) (**United States of America**) E.-U.A. *mpl* or U.S.A. *mpl*
usable ['juzəbəl] *adj* utilisable
usage ['jusɪdʒ], ['juzɪdʒ] *s* usage *m*
use [jus] *s* emploi *m*, usage *m*; (*usefulness*) utilité *f*; **in use** occupé; **of what use is it?** à quoi cela sert-il?; **out of use** hors de service; **to be of no use** ne servir à rien; **to have no use for s.o.** tenir qn en mauvaise estime; **to make use of** se servir de; **what's the use?** à quoi bon? ‖ [juz] *tr* employer, se servir de, user de; **to use up** épuiser, user ‖ *intr*—**I used to visit my friend every evening** je visitais mon ami tous les soirs
used [juzd] *adj* usagé, usé; d'occasion, e.g., **used car** voiture *f* d'occasion; **to be used** (*to be put into use*) être usité, être employé; **to be used as** servir de; **to be used to** (*to be useful for*) servir à; **used to** ['justu] accoutumé à; **used up** épuisé
useful ['jusfəl] *adj* utile
usefulness ['jusfəlnɪs] *s* utilité *f*

useless ['juslɪs] *adj* inutile
user ['juzər] *s* usager *m*; (*of a machine, of gas, etc.*) utilisateur *m*
usher ['ʌʃər] *s* placeur *m*; ouvreuse *f*; (*doorkeeper*) huissier *m* ‖ *tr*—**to usher in** inaugurer; (*a person*) introduire
U.S.S.R. ['ju'es'es'ar] *s* (letterword) (**Union of Soviet Socialist Republics**) U.R.S.S. *f*
usual ['juʒu-əl] *adj* usuel; **as usual** comme d'habitude
usually ['juʒu-əli] *adv* usuellement, d'habitude, d'ordinaire
usurp [ju'zʌrp] *tr* usurper
usu-ry ['juʒəri] *s* (*pl* -**ries**) usure *f*
utensil [ju'tensɪl] *s* ustensile *m*
uter-us ['jutərəs] *s* (*pl* -**i** [,aɪ]) utérus *m*
utilitarian [,jutɪlɪ'terɪ-ən] *adj* utilitaire
utili-ty [ju'tɪlɪti] *s* (*pl* -**ties**) utilité *f*; service *m* public; **utilities** services en commun (*gaz, transports, etc.*)
utilize ['jutɪ,laɪz] *tr* utiliser
utmost ['ʌt,most] *adj* extrême; plus grand; plus éloigné ‖ *s*—**the utmost** l'extrême *m*, le comble *m*; **to do one's utmost** faire tout son possible; **to the utmost** jusqu'au dernier point
utopia [ju'topɪ-ə] *s* utopie *f*
utopian [ju'topɪ-ən] *adj* utopique ‖ *s* utopiste *mf*
utter ['ʌtər] *adj* complet, total, absolu ‖ *tr* proférer, émettre; (*a cry*) pousser
utterance ['ʌtərəns] *s* expression *f*, émission *f*; (*gram*) énoncé *m*; **to give utterance to** exprimer
utterly ['ʌtərli] *adj* complètement, tout à fait, totalement

V

V, v [vi] *s* XXIIᵉ lettre de l'alphabet
vacan-cy ['vekənsi] *s* (*pl* -**cies**) (*emptiness; gap, opening*) vide *m*; (*unfilled position or job*) vacance *f*; (*in a building*) appartement *m* disponible; (*in a hotel*) chambre *f* de libre; **no vacancy** (public sign) complet
vacant ['vekənt] *adj* (*empty*) vide; (*having no occupant; untenanted*) vacant, libre, disponible; (*expression, look*) distrait, vague
va'cant lot' *s* terrain *m* vague
vacate ['veket] *tr* quitter, évacuer ‖ *intr* (*to move out*) déménager
vacation [ve'keʃən] *s* vacances *fpl*; **on vacation** en vacances ‖ *intr* prendre ses vacances, passer les vacances
vacationist [ve'keʃənɪst] *s* vacancier *m*
vaca'tion with pay' *s* congé *m* payé
vaccinate ['væksɪnet] *tr* vacciner
vaccination [,væksɪ'neʃən] *s* vaccination *f*
vaccine [væk'sin] *s* vaccin *m*
vacillate ['væsɪ,let] *intr* vaciller

vacui-ty [væ'kju-ɪti] *s* (*pl* -**ties**) vacuité *f*
vacu-um ['vækju-əm] *s* (*pl* -**ums** or -**a** [ə]) vacuum *m*, vide *m* ‖ *tr* passer à l'aspirateur, dépoussiérer
vac'uum clean'er *s* aspirateur *m*
vac'uum pump' *s* pompe *f* à vide
vac'uum tube' *s* tube *m* à vide
vagabond ['vægə,band] *adj & s* vagabond *m*
vagar-y [və'geri] *s* (*pl* -**ies**) caprice *m*
vagran-cy ['vegrənsi] *s* (*pl* -**cies**) vagabondage *m*
vague [veg] *adj* vague
vain [ven] *adj* vain; **in vain** en vain
vainglorious [ven'glorɪ-əs] *adj* vaniteux
valance ['væləns] *s* cantonnière *f*, lambrequin *m*
vale [vel] *s* vallon *m*
valedicto-ry [,vælɪ'dɪktəri] *s* (*pl* -**ries**) discours *m* d'adieu
valence ['veləns] *s* (chem) valence *f*
valentine ['vælən,taɪn] *s* (*sweetheart*)

valentin m; (*card*) carte f de la Saint-Valentin

Val′entine Day′ s la Saint-Valentin

vale′ of tears′ s vallée f de larmes

valet ['vælɪt], ['væle] s valet m

valiant ['væljənt] adj vaillant

valid ['vælɪd] adj valable, valide

validate ['vælɪ‚det] tr valider; (sports) homologuer

validation [‚vælɪ'deʃən] s validation f; (sports) homologation f

validi·ty [və'lɪdɪti] s (pl -ties) validité f

valise [və'lis] s mallette f

valley ['væli] s vallée f, vallon m; (of roof) corniére f

valor ['vælər] s valeur f, vaillance f

valorous ['vælərəs] adj valeureux

valuable ['vælju‚əbəl], ['væljəbəl] adj précieux, de valeur || **valuables** spl objets mpl de valeur

value ['vælju] s valeur f; (bargain) affaire f, occasion f; **to set a value on** estimer, évaluer || tr (to think highly of) priser, estimer; (to set a price for) estimer, évaluer; **if you value your life** si vous tenez à la vie

val′ue-added tax′ s taxe f à la valeur ajoutée, T.V.A.

valueless ['væljulɪs] adj sans valeur

valve [vælv] s soupape f; (of mollusk; of fruit; of tire) valve f; (of heart) valvule f; (mus) clé f

valve′ cap′ s chapeau m, bouchon m

valve′ gears′ spl (of gas engine) engrenages mpl de distribution; (of steam engine) mécanisme m de distribution

valve′-in-head′ en′gine s moteur m à soupapes en tête, moteur à culbuteurs

valve′ seat′ s siège m de soupape

valve′ spring′ s ressort m de soupape

valve′ stem′ s tige f de soupape

vamp [væmp] s (of shoe) empeigne f; (patchwork) rapiéçage m; (woman who preys on man) (coll) femme f fatale, vamp f || tr (a shoe) mettre une empeigne à; (to piece together) rapiécer; (a susceptible man) (coll) vamper; (an accompaniment) (coll) improviser

vampire ['væmpaɪr] s vampire m; femme f fatale, vamp f

van [væn] s camion m, voiture f de déménagement; (mil, fig) avant-garde f; (railway car) (Brit) fourgon m

vandal ['vændəl] adj & s vandale m || (cap) adj vandale || (cap) s Vandale mf

vandalism ['vændə‚lɪzəm] s vandalisme m

vane [ven] s (weathervane) girouette f; (of windmill) aile f; (of propeller or turbine) ailette f; (of feather) lame f

vanguard ['væn‚gɑrd] s (mil, fig) avant-garde f; **in the vanguard** à l'avant-garde

vanilla [və'nɪlə] s vanille f

vanish ['vænɪʃ] intr s'évanouir, disparaître

van′ishing cream′ s crème f de jour

vani·ty ['vænɪti] s (pl -ties) vanité f; (dressing table) table f de toilette, coiffeuse f; (vanity case) poudrier m

van′ity case′ s poudrier m, nécessaire m de toilette

vanquish ['væŋkwɪʃ] tr vaincre

van′tage point′ ['væntɪdʒ] s position f avantageuse

vapid ['væpɪd] adj insipide

vapor ['vepər] s vapeur f

vaporize ['vepə‚raɪz] tr vaporiser || intr se vaporiser

va′por trail′ s (aer) sillage m de fumée

variable ['vɛrɪ‚əbl] adj & s variable f

variance ['vɛrɪ‚əns] s différence f, variation f; **at variance with** en désaccord avec

variant ['vɛrɪ‚ənt] adj variant || s variante f

variation [‚vɛrɪ'eʃən] s variation f

varicose ['værɪ‚kos] adj variqueux

var′icose veins′ spl (pathol) varice f

varied ['vɛrɪd] adj varié

variegated ['vɛrɪ‚ə‚getɪd], ['vɛrɪ‚getɪd] adj varié; (spotted) bigarré, bariolé

varie·ty [və'raɪ‚ɪti] s (pl -ties) variété f

vari′ety show′ s spectacle m de variétés

various ['vɛrɪ‚əs] adj divers, différent; (several) plusieurs; (variegated) bigarré

varnish ['vɑrnɪʃ] s vernis m || tr vernir; (e.g., the truth) farder, embellir

varsi·ty ['vɑrsɪti] adj (sports) universitaire || s (pl -ties) (sports) équipe f universitaire principale

var·y ['vɛri] v (pret & pp -ied) tr & intr varier

vase [ves], [vez] s vase m

vaseline ['væsə‚lin] s (trademark) vaseline f

vassal ['væsəl] adj & s vassal m

vast [væst] adj vaste

vastness ['væstnɪs], ['vɑstnɪs] s vaste étendue f, immensité f

vat [væt] s cuve f, bac m

Vatican ['vætɪkən] adj vaticane || s Vatican m

vaudeville ['vodvɪl], ['vodəvɪl] s spectacle m de variétés, music-hall m; (light theatrical piece interspersed with songs) vaudeville m

vault [vɔlt] s (underground chamber) souterrain m; (of a bank) chambre f forte; (burial chamber) caveau m; (leap) saut m; (anat, archit) voûte f || tr & intr sauter

vaunt [vɔnt], [vɑnt] s vantardise f || tr vanter || intr se vanter

veal [vil] s veau m

veal′ chop′ s côtelette f de veau

veal′ cut′let s escalope f de veau

veer [vɪr] s virage m || tr faire virer || intr virer

vegetable ['vedʒɪtəbəl] adj végétal || s (plant) végétal m; (edible part of plant) légume m

veg′etable gar′den s potager m

veg′etable soup′ s potage m aux légumes

vegetarian [‚vedʒɪ'tɛrɪ‚ən] adj & s végétarien m

vegetate ['vedʒɪ‚tet] intr végéter

vehemence ['vi‚ɪməns] s véhémence f

vehement ['vi‚ɪmənt] adj véhément

vehicle ['vi·ɪkəl] *s* véhicule *m*

veil [vel] *s* voile *m*; **to take the veil** prendre le voile || *tr* voiler || *intr* se voiler

vein [ven] *s* veine *f* || *tr* veiner

velar ['vilər] *adj* & *s* vélaire *f*

vellum ['veləm] *s* vélin *m*; papier *m* vélin

veloci·ty [vɪ'lɑsɪti] *s* (*pl* -ties) vitesse *f*

velvet ['velvɪt] *s* velours *m*

velveteen [,velvɪ'tin] *s* velvet *m*

velvety ['velvɪti] *adj* velouté

vend [vend] *tr* vendre, colporter

vend′ing machine′ *s* distributeur *m* automatique

vendor ['vendər] *s* vendeur *m*

veneer [və'nɪr] *s* placage *m*; (fig) vernis *m* || *tr* plaquer

venerable ['venərəbəl] *adj* vénérable

venerate ['venə,ret] *tr* vénérer

venereal [vɪ'nɪrɪ·əl] *adj* vénérien

Venetian [vɪ'niʃən] *adj* vénitien || *s* Vénitien *m*

Vene′tian blind′ *s* jalousie *f*, store *m* vénitien

vengeance ['vendʒəns] *s* vengeance *f*; **with a vengeance** furieusement, à outrance; (*to the utmost limit*) tant que ça peut

vengeful ['vendʒfəl] *adj* vengeur

Venice ['venɪs] *s* Venise *f*

venison ['venɪsən], ['venɪzən] *s* venaison *f*

venom ['venəm] *s* venin *m*

venomous ['venəməs] *adj* venimeux

vent [vent] *s* orifice *m*; (*for air*) ventouse *f*; **to give vent to** donner libre cours à || *tr* décharger

ventilate ['ventɪ,let] *tr* ventiler

ventilator ['ventɪ,letər] *s* ventilateur *m*

ventricle ['ventrɪkəl] *s* ventricule *m*

ventriloquism [ven'trɪlə,kwɪzəm] *s* ventriloquie *f*

ventriloquist [ven'trɪləkwɪst] *s* ventriloque *mf*

venture ['ventʃər] *s* entreprise *f* risquée; **at a venture** à l'aventure || *tr* aventurer || *intr* s'aventurer; **to venture on** hasarder

venturesome ['ventʃərsəm] *adj* aventureux

venturous ['ventʃərəs] *adj* aventureux

venue ['venju] *s* (law) lieu *m* du jugement; **change of venue** (law) renvoi *m*

Venus ['vinəs] *s* Vénus *f*

veracious [vɪ're·əs] *adj* véridique

veraci·ty [vɪ'ræsɪti] *s* (*pl* -ties) véracité *f*

veranda *or* **verandah** [və'rændə] *s* véranda *f*

verb [vʌrb] *adj* verbal || *s* verbe *m*

verbalize ['vʌrbə,laɪz] *tr* exprimer par des mots; (gram) changer en verbe || *intr* être verbeux

verbatim [vər'betɪm] *adj* textuel || *adv* textuellement

verbiage ['vʌrbɪ·ɪdʒ] *s* verbiage *m*

verbose [vər'bos] *adj* verbeux

verdant ['vʌrdənt] *adj* vert; naïf, candide

verdict ['vʌrdɪkt] *s* verdict *m*

verdigris ['vʌrdɪ,grɪs] *s* vert-de-gris *m*

verdure ['vʌrdʒər] *s* verdure *f*

verge [vʌrdʒ] *s* bord *m*, limite *f*; **on the verge of** sur le point de || *intr*—**to verge on** *or* **upon** toucher à; (*bad faith; the age of forty; etc.*) friser

verification [,verɪfɪ'keʃən] *s* vérification *f*

veri·fy ['verɪ,faɪ] *v* (*pret* & *pp* -fied) *tr* vérifier

verily ['verɪli] *adv* en vérité

veritable ['verɪtəbəl] *adj* véritable

vermilion [vər'mɪljən] *adj* & *s* vermillon *m*

vermin ['vʌrmɪn] *s* (*objectionable person*) vermine *f* || *spl* (*objectionable animals or persons*) vermine

vermouth [vər'muθ], ['vʌrmuθ] *s* vermout *m*

vernacular [vər'nækjələr] *adj* vernaculaire || *s* langue *f* vernaculaire; (*everyday language*) langage *m* vulgaire; (*language peculiar to a class or profession*) jargon *m*

versatile ['vʌrsətɪl] *adj* aux talents variés; (*e.g., mind*) universel, souple

verse [vʌrs] *s* vers *mpl*; (*stanza*) strophe *f*; (Bib) verset *m*

versed [vʌrst] *adj*—**versed in** versé dans; spécialiste de

versification [,vʌrsɪfɪ'keʃən] *s* versification *f*

versi·fy ['vʌrsɪ,faɪ] *v* (*pret* & *pp* -fied) *tr* & *intr* versifier

version ['vʌrʒən] *s* version *f*

ver·so ['vʌrso] *s* (*pl* -sos) (*e.g., of a coin*) revers *m*; (typ) verso *m*

versus ['vʌrsəs] *prep* contre

verte·bra ['vʌrtɪbrə] *s* (*pl* -brae [,bri] *or* -bras) vertèbre *f*

vertebrate ['vʌrtɪ,bret] *adj* & *s* vertébré *m*

ver·tex ['vʌrteks] *s* (*pl* -texes *or* -tices [tɪ,siz]) sommet *m*

vertical ['vʌrtɪkəl] *adj* vertical || *s* verticale *f*

ver′tical hold′ *s* (telv) commande *f* de stabilité verticale

ver′tical rud′der *s* gouvernail *m* de direction

verti·go ['vʌrtɪ,go] *s* (*pl* -gos *or* -goes) vertige *m*

very ['veri] *adj* véritable; même, e.g., **at this very moment** à cet instant même || *adv* très, e.g., **I am very hungry** j'ai très faim; bien, e.g., **you are very nice** vous êtes bien gentil; tout, e.g., **the very first** le tout premier; e.g., **my very best** tout mon possible; **for my very own** pour moi tout seul; **very much** beaucoup

vesicle ['vesɪkəl] *s* vésicule *f*

vespers ['vespərz] *spl* vêpres *fpl*

vessel ['vesəl] *s* bâtiment *m*, navire *m*; (*container*) vase *m*; (anat, bot, zool) vaisseau *m*

vest [vest] *s* gilet *m*; **to play it close to the vest** (coll) jouer serré || *tr* vêtir; **to vest with** investir de, revêtir de

vest′ed in′terests *spl* classes *fpl* dirigeantes

vestibule ['vestɪ,bjul] *s* vestibule *m*

ves'tibule car' s (rr) wagon m à soufflets

vestige ['vɛstɪdʒ] s vestige m

vestment ['vɛstmənt] s vêtement m sacerdotal

vest'-pock'et adj de poche, de petit format

ves-try ['vɛstri] s (pl -tries) sacristie f; (committee) conseil m paroissial

ves'try-man s (pl -men) marguillier m

Vesuvius [vɪ's(j)uvɪ-əs] s le Vésuve

vetch [vɛtʃ] s vesce f; (Lathyrus sativus) gesse f

veteran ['vɛtərən] s vétéran m

veterinarian [,vɛtərɪ'nɛrɪ-ən] s vétérinaire mf

veterinar•y ['vɛtərɪ,nɛri] adj vétérinaire ‖ s (pl -ies) vétérinaire f

ve•to ['vito] s (pl -toes) veto m ‖ tr mettre son veto à

vex [vɛks] tr vexer, contrarier

vexation [vɛk'seʃən] s vexation f

via ['vaɪ-ə] prep via

viaduct ['vaɪ-ə,dʌkt] s viaduc m

vial ['vaɪ-əl] s fiole f

viand ['vaɪ-ənd] s mets m

vibrate ['vaɪbret] intr vibrer

vibration [vaɪ'breʃən] s vibration f

vicar ['vɪkər] s vicaire m; (in Church of England) curé m

vicarage ['vɪkərɪdʒ] s presbytère m; (duties of vicar) cure f

vicarious [vaɪ'kɛrɪ-əs], [vɪ'kɛrɪ-əs] adj substitut; (punishment) souffert pour autrui; (power, authority) délégué; (enjoyment) partagé

vice [vaɪs] s vice m; (device) étau m

vice'-ad'miral s vice-amiral m

vice'-pres'ident s vice-président m

viceroy ['vaɪsrɔɪ] s vice-roi m

vice' squad' s brigade f des mœurs

vice versa ['vaɪsə'vʌrsə], ['vaɪs'vʌrsə] adv vice versa

vicin•ity [vɪ'sɪnɪti] s (pl -ties) voisinage m; environs mpl, e.g., **New York and vicinity** New York et ses environs

vicious ['vɪ-əs] adj vicieux; (mean) méchant; (ferocious) féroce

vicissitude [vɪ'sɪsɪ,t(j)ud] s vicissitude f

victim ['vɪktɪm] s victime f; (e.g., of a collision, fire) accidenté m

victimize ['vɪktɪ,maɪz] tr prendre pour victime; (to swindle) duper

victor ['vɪktər] s vainqueur m

victorious [vɪk'torɪ-əs] adj victorieux

victo•ry ['vɪktəri] s (pl -ries) victoire f

victuals ['vɪtəlz] spl victuailles fpl

vid'eo sig'nal ['vɪdɪ,o] s signal m d'image

vid'eo tape' s bande f magnétique vidéo

vid'eo tape' record'er s magnétoscope m

vid'eo tape' record'ing s magnétoscope m

vie [vaɪ] v (pret & pp **vied**; ger **vying**) intr rivaliser, lutter

Vienna [vɪ'ɛnə] s Vienne f

Vien•nese [,vi-ə'niz] adj viennois ‖ s (pl -nese) Viennois m

Vietnam [,vɪ-ɛt'nɑm] s le Vietnam

Vietnam•ese [vɪ,ɛtnə'miz] adj vietnamien ‖ s (pl -ese) Vietnamien m

view [vju] s vue f; **in my view** à mon avis, selon mon opinion; **in view** en vue; **in view of** étant donné, vu; **on view** exposé; **with a view to** en vue de ‖ tr voir, regarder; considérer, examiner

viewer ['vju-ər] s spectateur m; (for film, slides, etc.) visionneuse f; (telv) téléspectateur m

view'find'er s viseur m

view'point' s point m de vue

vigil ['vɪdʒɪl] s veille f; (eccl) vigile f; **to keep a vigil** veiller

vigilance ['vɪdʒɪləns] s vigilance f

vigilant ['vɪdʒɪlənt] adj vigilant

vignette [vɪn'jɛt] s vignette f

vigor ['vɪgər] s vigueur f

vigorous ['vɪgərəs] adj vigoureux

vile [vaɪl] adj vil; (smell) infect; (weather) sale; (disgusting) détestable

vili•fy ['vɪlɪ,faɪ] v (pret & pp **-fied**) tr diffamer, dénigrer

villa ['vɪlə] s villa f

village ['vɪlɪdʒ] s village m

villager ['vɪlɪdʒər] s villageois m

villain ['vɪlən] s scélérat m; (of a play) traître m

villainous ['vɪlənəs] adj vil, infame

villain•y ['vɪləni] s (pl -ies) vilenie f, infamie f

vim [vɪm] s énergie f, vigueur f

vinaigrette' sauce' [,vɪnə'grɛt] s vinaigrette f

vindicate ['vɪndɪ,ket] tr justifier, défendre

vindictive [vɪn'dɪktɪv] adj vindicatif

vine [vaɪn] s plante f grimpante; (grape plant) vigne f

vinegar ['vɪnɪgər] s vinaigre m

vinegary ['vɪnɪgəri] adj aigre; acariâtre

vine' grow'er [,gro-ər] s viticulteur m

vine' stock' s cep m

vineyard ['vɪnjərd] s vignoble m, vigne f

vintage ['vɪntɪdʒ] s vendange f; (year) année f, cru m; (coll) classe f, catégorie f

vin'tage wine' s bon cru m

vin'tage year' s grande année f

vintner ['vɪntnər] s négociant m en vins; (person who makes wine) vigneron m

vinyl ['vaɪnɪl], ['vɪnɪl] s vinyle m

viola [vaɪ'olə], [vɪ'olə] s alto m

violate ['vaɪ-ə,let] tr violer

violation [,vaɪ-ə'leʃən] s violation f

violence ['vaɪ-ələns] s violence f

violent ['vaɪ-ələnt] adj violent

violet ['vaɪ-əlɪt] adj violet ‖ s (color) violet m; (bot) violette f

violin [,vaɪ-ə'lɪn] s violon m

violinist [,vaɪ-ə'lɪnɪst] s violoniste mf

violoncel•lo [,vaɪ-ələn't(ʃ)elo], [,vi-ələn't(ʃ)elo] s (pl -los) violoncelle m

viper ['vaɪpər] s vipère f

vira•go [vɪ'rego] s (pl -goes or -gos) mégère f

virgin ['vɑrdʒɪn] adj vierge ‖ s vierge f; (male virgin) puceau m

Virgin'ia creep'er [vər'dʒɪnɪ-ə] s vigne f vierge

virginity [vər'dʒɪnɪti] s virginité f
virility [vɪ'rɪlɪti] s virilité f
virology [vaɪ'rɑlədʒi] s virologie f
virtual ['vʌrtʃʊ·əl] adj véritable, effectif; (mech, opt, phys) virtuel
virtue ['vʌrtʃu] s vertu f; mérite m, avantage m
virtuosi·ty [,vʌrtʃu'ɑsɪti] s (pl -ties) virtuosité f
virtuo·so [,vʌrtʃu'oso] s (pl -sos or -si [si]) virtuose mf
virtuous ['vʌrtʃu·əs] adj vertueux
virulence ['vɪrjələns] s virulence f
virulent ['vɪrjələnt] adj virulent
virus ['vaɪrəs] s virus m
visa ['viza] s visa m || tr viser
visage ['vɪzɪdʒ] s visage m
vis-à-vis [,viza'vi] adj face à face || s & adv vis-à-vis m || prep vis-à-vis de, vis-à-vis
viscera ['vɪsərə] spl viscères mpl
viscount ['vaɪkaunt] s vicomte m
viscountess ['vaɪkauntɪs] s vicomtesse f
viscous ['vɪskəs] adj visqueux
vise [vaɪs] s étau m
visible ['vɪzɪbəl] adj visible
vision ['vɪʒən] s vision f
visionar·y ['vɪʒə,nɛri] adj visionnaire || s (pl -ies) visionnaire m
visit ['vɪzɪt] s visite f || tr visiter; (e.g., a person) rendre visite à || intr faire des visites
visitation [,vɪzɪ'teʃən] s visite f; justice f du ciel; clémence f du ciel; (e.g., in a séance) apparition f; **Visitation** (eccl) Visitation f
vis′iting card′ s carte f de visite
vis′iting hours′ spl heures fpl de visite
vis′iting nurse′ s infirmière f visiteuse
vis′iting profes′sor s visiting m
visitor ['vɪzɪtər] s visiteur m
visor ['vaɪzər] s visière f
vista ['vɪstə] s perspective f
visual ['vɪʒu·əl] adj visuel
visualize ['vɪʒu·ə,laɪz] tr (in one's mind) se faire une image mentale de, se représenter; (to make visible) visualiser
vital ['vaɪtəl] adj vital || **vitals** spl organes mpl vitaux
vitality [vaɪ'tælɪti] s vitalité f
vitalize ['vaɪtə,laɪz] tr vitaliser
vitamin ['vaɪtəmɪn] s vitamine f
vitiate ['vɪʃɪ,et] tr vicier
vitreous ['vɪtrɪ·əs] adj vitreux
vitriolic [,vɪtrɪ'ɑlɪk] adj (chem) vitriolique; (fig) trempé dans du vitriol
vituperate [vaɪ't(j)upə,ret] tr vitupérer
viva ['vivə] s vivat m || interj vive!
vivacious [vɪ'veʃəs], [vaɪ'veʃəs] adj vif, animé
vivaci·ty [vɪ'væsɪti], [vaɪ'væsɪti] s (pl -ties) vivacité f
viva voce ['vaɪvə'vosi] adv de vive voix
vivid ['vɪvɪd] adj vif; (description) vivant; (recollection) vivace
vivi·fy ['vɪvɪ,faɪ] v (pret & pp -fied) tr vivifier
vivisection [,vɪvɪ'sɛkʃən] s vivisection f

vixen ['vɪksən] s mégère f; (zool) renarde f
viz. abbr (Lat: **videlicet** namely, to wit) c.-à-d., à savoir
vizier [vɪ'zɪr], ['vɪzjər] s vizir m
vocabular·y [vo'kæbjə,lɛri] s (pl -ies) vocabulaire m
vocal ['vokəl] adj vocal; (inclined to express oneself freely) communicatif, démonstratif
vocalist ['vokəlɪst] s chanteur m
vocalize ['vokə,laɪz] tr vocaliser || intr vocaliser; (phonet) se vocaliser
vocation [vo'keʃən] s vocation f; profession f, métier m
voca′tional guid′ance [vo'keʃənəl] s orientation f professionnelle
voca′tional school′ s école f professionnelle
vocative ['vɑkətɪv] s vocatif m
vociferate [vo'sɪfə,ret] intr vociférer
vociferous [vo'sɪfərəs] adj vociférant, criard
vogue [vog] s vogue f; **in vogue** en vogue
voice [vɔɪs] s voix f; **in a loud voice** à voix haute; **in a low voice** à voix basse; **with one voice** unanimement || tr exprimer; (a consonant) voiser, sonoriser || intr se voiser
voiced adj (phonet) voisé, sonore
voiceless ['vɔɪslɪs] adj sans voix; (consonant) sourd
void [vɔɪd] adj vide; (law) nul; **void of** dénué de || s vide m || tr vider; (the bowels) évacuer; (law) rendre nul || intr évacuer, excréter
voile [vɔɪl] s voile m
volatile ['vɑlətɪl] adj (solvent) volatil; (disposition) volage; (temper) vif
volatilize ['vɑlətə,laɪz] tr volatiliser || intr se volatiliser
volcanic [vɑl'kænɪk] adj volcanique
volca·no [vɑl'keno] s (pl -noes or -nos) volcan m
volition [və'lɪʃən] s volition f, volonté f; **of one's own volition** de son propre gré
volley ['vɑli] s volée f || tr lancer à la volée; (sports) reprendre de volée || intr lancer une volée
vol′ley·ball′ s volley-ball m
volplane ['vɑl,plen] s vol m plané || intr descendre en vol plané
volt [volt] s volt m
voltage ['voltɪdʒ] s voltage m; **high voltage** haute tension f
volt′age drop′ s perte f de charge
volte-face [volt'fɑs] s volte-face f
volt′me′ter s voltmètre m
voluble ['vɑljəbəl] adj volubile
volume ['vɑljəm] s volume m; **to speak volumes** en dire long
vol′ume num′ber s tomaison f
voluminous [və'lumɪnəs] adj volumineux
voluntar·y ['vɑlən,tɛri] adj volontaire || s (pl -ies) (mus) morceau m d'orgue improvisé
volunteer [,vɑlən'tɪr] adj & s volontaire mf || tr offrir volontairement ||

intr (mil) s'engager; **to volunteer to** + *inf* s'offrir à + *inf*

voluptuar·y [vəˈlʌptʃʊˌeri] *adj* voluptuaire || *s* (*pl* -ies) voluptueux *m*

voluptuous [vəˈlʌptʃu·əs] *adj* voluptueux

vomit [ˈvɑmɪt] *s* vomissure *f* || *tr* & *intr* vomir

voodoo [ˈvudu] *adj* & *s* vaudou *m*

voracious [vəˈreʃəs] *adj* vorace

voraci·ty [vəˈræsɪti] *s* (*pl* -ties) voracité *f*

vor·tex [ˈvɔrteks] *s* (*pl* -texes or -tices [trˌsiz]) vortex *m*, tourbillon *m*

vota·ry [ˈvotəri] *s* (*pl* -ries) fidèle *mf*

vote [vot] *s* vote *m*; **by popular vote** au suffrage universel; **to put to the vote** mettre aux voix; **to tally the votes** dépouiller le scrutin; **vote by show of hands** vote à main levée || *tr* voter; **to vote down** repousser; **to vote in** élire || *intr* voter; **to vote for** voter; **to vote on** passer au vote

voter [ˈvotər] *s* votant *m*, électeur *m*

vot′ing booth′ *s* isoloir *m*

vot′ing machine′ *s* machine *f* électorale

votive [ˈvotɪv] *adj* votif

vouch [vautʃ] *tr* affirmer, garantir || *intr*—**to vouch for** répondre de

voucher [ˈvautʃər] *s* garant *m*; (*certificate*) récépissé *m*, pièce *f* comptable

vouch·safe′ *tr* octroyer || *intr*—**to vouchsafe to** + *inf* daigner + *inf*

vow [vau] *s* vœu *m*; **to take vows** entrer en religion || *tr* (*e.g., revenge*) jurer || *intr* faire un vœu; **to vow to** faire vœu de

vowel [ˈvau·əl] *s* voyelle *f*

voyage [ˈvɔɪ·ɪdʒ] *s* (*by air or sea*) traversée *f*; (*any journey*) voyage *m* || *tr* traverser || *intr* voyager

voyager [ˈvɔɪ·ɪdʒər] *s* voyageur *m*

vs. *abbr* (*versus*) contre

vulcanize [ˈvʌlkəˌnaɪz] *tr* vulcaniser

vulgar [ˈvʌlgər] *adj* grossier; (*popular, common; vernacular*) vulgaire

vulgari·ty [vʌlˈgærɪti] *s* (*pl* -ties) grossièreté *f*, vulgarité *f*

Vul′gar Lat′in *s* latin *m* vulgaire

vulnerable [ˈvʌlnərəbəl] *adj* vulnérable

vulture [ˈvʌltʃər] *s* vautour *m*

W

W, w [ˈdʌbəlˌju] *s* XXIIIe lettre de l'alphabet

wad [wɑd] *s* (*of cotton*) tampon *m*; (*of papers*) liasse *f*; (*in a gun*) bourre *f* || *v* (*pret* & *pp* wadded; *ger* wadding) *tr* bourrer

waddle [ˈwɑdəl] *s* dandinement *m* || *intr* se dandiner

wade [wed] *tr* traverser à gué || *intr* marcher dans l'eau, patauger; **to wade into** (coll) s'attaquer à; **to wade through** (coll) avancer péniblement dans

wad′ing bird′ *s* (orn) échassier *m*

wafer [ˈwefər] *s* (*thin, crisp cake*) gaufrette *f*; (*pill*) cachet *m*; (*for sealing letters*) pain *m* à cacheter; (eccl) hostie *f*

waffle [ˈwɑfəl] *s* gaufre *f*

waf′fle i′ron *s* gaufrier *m*

waft [wæft], [wɑft] *tr* porter; (*a kiss*) envoyer || *intr* flotter

wag [wæg] *s* (*of head*) hochement *m*; (*of tail*) frétillement *m*; (*jester*) farceur *m* || *v* (*pret* & *pp* wagged; *ger* wagging) *tr* (*the head*) hocher; (*the tail*) remuer || *intr* frétiller

wage [wedʒ] *s* salaire *m*; **wages** gages *mpl*, salaire *m*; (fig) salaire, récompense *f* || *tr*—**to wage war** faire la guerre

wage′ earn′er [ˌʌrnər] *s* salarié *m*

wage′-price′ freeze′ *s* blocage *m* des prix et des salaires

wager [ˈwedʒər] *s* pari *m*; **to lay a wager** faire un pari || *tr* & *intr* parier

wage′work′er *s* salarié *m*

waggish [ˈwægɪʃ] *adj* plaisant, facétieux

wagon [ˈwægən] *s* charrette *f*; (*Conestoga wagon; plaything*) chariot *m*; (mil) fourgon *m*; **to be on the wagon** (slang) s'abstenir de boissons alcooliques

wag′tail′ *s* hochequeue *m*, bergeronnette *f*

waif [wef] *s* (*foundling*) enfant *m* trouvé; *animal m* égaré or abandonné; (*stray child*) voyou *m*

wail [wel] *s* lamentation *f*, plainte *f* || *intr* se lamenter, gémir

wain·scot [ˈwenskət], [ˈwenskɑt] *s* lambris *m* || *v* (*pret* & *pp* -scoted or -scotted; *ger* -scoting or -scotting) *tr* lambrisser

waist [west] *s* (*of human body; corresponding part of garment*) taille *f*, ceinture *f*; (*garment*) corsage *m*, blouse *f*

waist′band′ *s* ceinture *f*

waist′cloth′ *s* pagne *m*

waistcoat [ˈwest,kot], [ˈweskət] *s* gilet *m*

waist′-deep′ *adj* jusqu'à la ceinture

waist′line′ *s* taille *f*, ceinture *f*; **to keep or watch one's waistline** garder or soigner sa ligne

wait [wet] *s* attente *f*; **to lie in wait for** guetter || *tr*—**to wait one's turn** attendre son tour || *intr* attendre; **to wait for** attendre; **to wait on** (*customers; dinner guests*) servir

wait′-and-see′ pol′icy *s* attentisme *m*

waiter [ˈwetər] *s* garçon *m*; (*tray*) plateau *m*

wait′ing list′ *s* liste *f* d'attente

wait'ing room' s salle f d'attente; (of a doctor) antichambre f

waitress ['wetris] s serveuse f; **waitress!** mademoiselle!

waive [wev] tr renoncer (with dat); (to defer) différer

waiver ['wevər] s renonciation f, abandon m

wake [wek] s (watch by the body of a dead person) veillée f mortuaire; (of a boat or other moving object) sillage m; **in the wake of** dans le sillage de, à la suite de ‖ v (pret **waked** or **woke** [wok]; pp **waked**) tr réveiller ‖ intr —**to wake to** se rendre compte de; **to wake up** se réveiller

wakeful ['wekfəl] adj éveillé

wakefulness ['wekfəlnɪs] s veille f

waken ['wekən] tr éveiller, réveiller ‖ intr s'éveiller, se réveiller

wale [wel] s zébrure f ‖ tr zébrer

Wales [welz] s le pays de Galles

walk [wɔk] s (act) promenade f; (distance) marche f; (way of walking, bearing) démarche f; (of a garden) allée f; (calling) métier m; **to fall into a walk** (said of horse) se mettre au pas; **to go for a walk** faire une promenade ‖ tr promener; (a horse) promener au pas ‖ intr aller à pied, marcher; (to stroll) se promener; **to walk away** s'en aller à pied; **to walk off with** (a prize) gagner; (a stolen object) décamper avec; **to walk out** sortir, partir subitement; (to go on strike) se mettre en grève; **to walk out on** abandonner; quitter en colère

walk'away' s (coll) victoire f facile

walker ['wɔkər] s marcheur m, promeneur m; (pedestrian) piéton m; (gocart) chariot m d'enfant

walkie-talkie ['wɔki'tɔki] s (rad) émetteur-récepteur m portatif, parle-en-marche m

walk'ing pa'pers spl—**to give s.o. his walking papers** (coll) congédier qn

walk'ing stick' s canne f

walk'-on' s (actor) figurant m, comparse m; (role) figuration f

walk'out' s (coll) grève f improvisée

walk'o'ver s (coll) victoire f dans un fauteuil

walk'-up' s appartement m sans ascenseur

wall [wɔl] s mur m; (between rooms; of a pipe, boiler, etc.) paroi f; (of a fortification) muraille f; **to go to the wall** succomber; perdre la partie ‖ tr entourer de murs; **to wall up** murer

wall'board' s panneau m or carreau m de revêtement

wall' clock' s pendule f murale

wallet ['wɑlɪt] s portefeuille m

wall'flow'er s (bot) ravenelle f, giroflée f; **to be a wallflower** (coll) faire tapisserie

wall' lamp' s applique f

wall' map' s carte f murale

Walloon [wɑ'lun] adj wallon f ‖ s (dialect) wallon m; (person) Wallon m

wallop ['wɑləp] s (coll) coup m, gnon m; **with a wallop** (fig) à grand fracas ‖ tr (coll) tanner le cuir à, rosser; (a ball) (coll) frapper raide; (to defeat) (coll) battre

wallow ['wɑlo] s souille f ‖ intr se vautrer; (e.g., in wealth) nager

wall'pa'per s papier m peint ‖ tr tapisser

walnut ['wɔlnət] s noix f; (tree and wood) noyer m

walrus ['wɔlrəs], ['wɑlrəs] s morse m

Walter ['wɔltər] s Gautier m

waltz [wɔlts] s valse f ‖ tr & intr valser

wan [wɑn] adj (comp **wanner**; super **wannest**) pâle, blême; (weak) faible

wand [wɑnd] s baguette f; (emblem of authority) bâton m, verge f

wander ['wɑndər] tr vagabonder sur, parcourir ‖ intr errer, vaguer; (said of one's mind) vagabonder

wanderer ['wɑndərər] s vagabond m

wan'der·lust' s manie f des voyages, bougeotte f

wane [wen] s déclin m; (of moon) décours m ‖ intr décliner; (said of moon) décroître

wangle ['wæŋgəl] tr (to obtain by scheming) (coll) resquiller; (accounts) (coll) cuisiner; (e.g., a leave of absence) (coll) carotter; **to wangle one's way out of** (coll) se débrouiller de ‖ intr (coll) pratiquer le système D

want [wɑnt], [wɔnt] s (need; misery) besoin m; (lack) manque m; **for want of** faute de, à défaut de; **to be in want** être dans la gêne ‖ tr vouloir; (to need) avoir besoin de; **to want s.o. to +** inf vouloir que qn + subj; **to want to +** inf avoir envie de + inf, vouloir + inf ‖ intr être dans le besoin; **to be wanting** manquer

want'ad' spl petites annonces fpl

wanton ['wɑntən] adj déréglé; (e.g., cruelty) gratuit; (e.g., child) espiègle; (e.g., woman) impudique

war [wɔr] s guerre f; **to go to war** se mettre en guerre; (as a soldier) aller à la guerre; **to wage war** faire la guerre ‖ v (pret & pp **warred**; ger **warring**) intr faire la guerre; **to war on** faire la guerre contre

warble ['wɔrbəl] s gazouillement m ‖ intr gazouiller

warbler ['wɔrblər] s (orn) fauvette f

war' cloud' s menace f de guerre

war' correspon'dent s correspondant m de guerre

war' cry' s (pl **cries**) cri m de guerre

ward [wɔrd] s (person, usually a minor under protection of another) pupille mf; (guardianship) tutelle f; (of a city) circonscription f électorale, quartier m; (of a hospital) salle f; (of a lock) gardes fpl ‖ tr—**to ward off** parer

war' dance' s danse f guerrière

warden ['wɔrdən] s gardien m; (of a jail) directeur m; (of a church) marguillier m; (gamekeeper) garde-chasse m

ward'heel'er s politicailleur m servile

ward'robe' s garde-robe f

ward/robe trunk/ s malle-armoire f
ward/room/ s (nav) carré m des officiers
ware [wer] s faïence f; **wares** articles mpl de vente, marchandises fpl
ware/house/ s entrepôt m
ware/house/man s (pl **-men**) gardemagasin m, magasinier m
war/fare/ s guerre f
war/head/ s charge f creuse
war/-horse/ s cheval m de bataille; (coll) vétéran m
warily ['werɪlɪ] adv prudemment
war/like/ adj guerrier
war/ loan/ s emprunt m de guerre
war/ lord/ s seigneur m de la guerre
warm [wɔrm] adj chaud; (welcome, thanks, friend, etc.) chaleureux; (heart) généreux; **it is warm** (said of weather) il fait chaud; **to be warm** (said of person) avoir chaud; **to keep s.th. warm** tenir q.ch. au chaud; **you're getting warm!** (you've almost found it!) vous brûlez! || tr chauffer, faire chauffer; **to warm up** se réchauffer || intr se réchauffer; **to warm up** se réchauffer, chauffer, se chauffer; (said of speaker, discussion, etc.) s'animer, s'échauffer
warm/-blood/ed adj passionné, ardent; (animals) à sang chaud
war/ memor/ial s monument m aux morts de la guerre
warmer ['wɔrmər] s (culin) réchaud m
warm/-heart/ed adj au cœur généreux
warm/ing pan/ s bassinoire f
warmonger ['wɔr,mʌŋgər] s belliciste mf
war/ moth/er s marraine f de guerre
warmth [wɔrmθ] s chaleur f
warm/-up/ s exercices mpl d'assouplissement; mise f en condition
warn [wɔrn] tr prévenir; **to warn s.o. to** avertir qn de
warning ['wɔrnɪŋ] s avertissement m; **without warning** par surprise
warn/ing shot/ s coup m de semonce
war/ of attri/tion s guerre f d'usure
warp [wɔrp] s (of a fabric) chaîne f; (of a board) gauchissement m; (naut) touée f || tr gauchir; (the mind, judgment, etc.) fausser; (naut) touer || intr se gauchir; (naut) se touer
war/path/ s—**to be on the warpath** être sur le sentier de la guerre; (to be out of sorts) (coll) être d'une humeur de dogue
war/plane/ s avion m de guerre
warrant ['wɔrənt], ['wɑrənt] s garantie f; certificat m; (for arrest) mandat m d'arrêt || tr garantir; certifier, justifier
war/rant of/ficer s (mil) sous-officier m breveté; (nav) premier maître m
warran·ty ['wɔrəntɪ], ['wɑrəntɪ] s (pl **-ties**) garantie f; autorisation f
warren ['wɔrən], ['wɑrən] s garenne f
warrior ['wɔrjər], ['wɑrjər] s guerrier m
Warsaw ['wɔrsɔ] s Varsovie f
war/ship/ s navire m de guerre

wart [wɔrt] s verrue f
war/time/ s temps m de guerre
war/-torn/ adj dévasté par la guerre
war·y ['werɪ] adj (comp **-ier**; super **-iest**) prudent, avisé
wash [wɑʃ], [wɔʃ] s lavage m; (clothes washed or to be washed) lessive f; (dirty water) lavure f; (place where the surf breaks; broken water behind a moving ship) remous m; (aer) souffle m || tr laver; (one's hands, face, etc.) se laver; (dishes, laundry, etc.) faire; (e.g., a seacoast) baigner; **to wash away** enlever; (e.g., a bank) affouiller, ronger || intr se laver; faire la lessive
washable ['wɑʃəbəl], ['wɔʃəbəl] adj lavable
wash/-and-wear/ adj de repassage superflu, de séchage rapide
wash/ba/sin s (basin) cuvette f; (fixture) lavabo m
wash/bas/ket s corbeille f à linge
wash/board/ s planche f à laver
wash/bowl/ s (basin) cuvette f; (fixture) lavabo m
wash/cloth/ s gant m de toilette
wash/day/ s jour m de lessive
washed/-out/ adj délavé, déteint; (coll) flapi, vanné
washed/-up/ adj (coll) hors de combat, ruiné
washer ['wɑʃər], ['wɔʃər] s laveur m; (machine) laveuse f, lessiveuse f; (ring of metal) rondelle f; (ring of rubber) rondelle de robinet
wash/er-wom/an s (pl **-wom/en**) blanchisseuse f
wash/ goods/ spl tissus mpl grand teint
washing ['wɑʃɪŋ], ['wɔʃɪŋ] s lavage m; (act of washing clothes) blanchissage m; (clothes washed or to be washed) lessive f; **washings** lavures fpl
wash/ing machine/ s machine f à laver, laveuse f automatique
wash/ing so/da s cristaux mpl de soude
wash/out/ s affouillement m; (person) (coll) raté m; **to be a washout** (coll) faire fiasco, faire four
wash/rag/ s gant m de toilette, torchon m
wash/room/ s cabinet m de toilette, lavabo m
wash/ sale/ s (com) lavage m des titres
wash/stand/ s lavabo m
wash/tub/ s baquet m, cuvier m
wash/ wa/ter s lavure f
wasp [wɑsp] s guêpe f
wasp/ waist/ s taille f de guêpe
waste [west] adj (land) inculte; (material) de rebut || s gaspillage m; (garbage) déchets mpl; (wild region) région f inculte; (of time) perte f; (for wiping machinery) chiffons mpl de nettoyage, effiloche f de coton; **to lay waste** dévaster; **wastes** déchets; excrément m || tr gaspiller, perdre || intr—**to waste away** dépérir, maigrir
waste/bas/ket s corbeille f à papier
wasteful ['westfəl] adj gaspilleur
waste/pa/per s papier m de rebut

waste′ pipe′ s tuyau m d'écoulement, vidange f

waste′ prod′ucts spl déchets mpl

wastrel ['westrəl] s gaspilleur m, prodigue mf

watch [wɑtʃ] s montre f; (lookout) garde f, guet m; (naut) quart m; to be on the watch for guetter; to be on watch (naut) être de quart; to keep watch over surveiller || tr (to look at) observer; (to oversee) surveiller || intr être aux aguets; (to keep awake) veiller; to watch for guetter; to watch out faire attention; to watch out for faire attention à; to watch over surveiller; watch out! attention!, gare!

watch′case′ s boîtier m de montre

watch′ chain′ s chaîne f de montre

watch′ charm′ s breloque f

watch′ crys′tal s verre m de montre

watch′dog′ s chien m de garde; gardien m vigilant

watch′dog′ commit′tee s comité m de surveillance

watchful ['wɑtʃfəl] adj vigilant

watchfulness ['wɑtʃfəlnɪs] s vigilance f

watch′mak′er s horloger m

watch′man s (pl -men) gardien m

watch′ night′ s réveillon m du jour de l'an

watch′ pock′et s gousset m

watch′ strap′ s bracelet m d'une montre

watch′tow′er s tour f de guet

watch′word′ s mot m d'ordre, mot de passe; devise f

water ['wɔtər], ['wɑtər] s eau f; of the first water de premier ordre; (diamond) de première eau; to back water (naut) culer; reculer; to be in hot water (coll) être dans le pétrin; to fish in troubled waters pêcher en eau trouble; to hold water (coll) tenir debout, être bien fondé; to make water (to urinate) uriner; (naut) faire eau; to pour or throw cold water on (fig) jeter une douche froide sur, refroidir; to swim under water nager entre deux eaux; to tread water nager debout || tr (e.g., plants) arroser; (horses, cattle, etc.) abreuver; (wine) couper; to water down atténuer || intr (said of horses, cattle, etc.) s'abreuver; (said of locomotive, ship, etc.) faire de l'eau; (said of eyes) se mouiller, larmoyer

wa′ter buf′fa·lo s (pl -loes or -los) buffle m

wa′ter car′rier s porteur m d'eau

wa′ter clos′et s water-closet m, waters mpl

wa′ter·col′or s aquarelle f

wa′ter-cooled′ adj à refroidissement d'eau

wa′ter·course′ s cours m d'eau; (of a stream) lit m

wa′ter·cress′ s cresson m de fontaine

wa′ter cure′ s cure f des eaux

wa′ter·fall′ s chute f d'eau

wa′ter·front′ s terrain m sur la rive

wa′ter gap′ s percée f, trouée f, gorge f

wa′ter ham′mer s (in pipe) coup m de bélier

wa′ter heat′er s chauffe-eau m, chauffe-bain m

wa′ter ice′ s boisson f à demi glacée

wa′tering can′ s arrosoir m

wa′tering place′ s (for cattle) abreuvoir m; (for tourists) ville f d'eau

wa′tering pot′ s arrosoir m

wa′tering trough′ s abreuvoir m

wa′ter jack′et s chemise f d'eau

wa′ter lil′y s nénuphar m

wa′ter line′ s ligne f de flottaison; niveau m d'eau

wa′ter-logged′ adj détrempé

wa′ter main′ s conduite f principale

wa′ter·mark′ s (in paper) filigrane m; (naut) laisse f

wa′ter·mel′on s pastèque f, melon m d'eau

wa′ter me′ter s compteur m à eau

wa′ter pipe′ s conduite f d'eau

wa′ter po′lo s water-polo m

wa′ter pow′er s force f hydraulique, houille f blanche

wa′ter-proof′ adj & s imperméable m

wa′ter rights′ spl droits mpl de captation d'eau, droits d'irrigation

wa′ter·shed′ s ligne f de partage des eaux

wa′ter ski′ing s ski m nautique

wa′ter span′iel s (zool) barbet m

wa′ter·spout′ s descente f d'eau, gouttière f; (funnel of wet air) trombe f

wa′ter-supply sys′tem s service m des eaux; réseau m de conduites d'eau

wa′ter ta′ble s (geol) nappe f phréatique

wa′ter-tight′ adj étanche; (argument) inattaquable; (law) sans clause échappatoire

wa′ter tow′er s château m d'eau

wa′ter wag′on s—to be on the water wagon (coll) s'abstenir de boissons alcooliques

wa′ter·way′ s voie f navigable

wa′ter wheel′ s roue f hydraulique; roue à aubes or à palettes; roue-turbine f

wa′ter wings′ spl flotteur m de natation

wa′ter·works′ s (system) canalisations fpl d'eau; (pumping station) usine f de distribution des eaux

watery ['wɔtəri], ['wɑtəri] adj aqueux; (eyes) larmoyant; (food) insipide, fade

watt [wɑt] s watt m

wattage ['wɑtɪdʒ] s puissance f en watts

watt′-hour′ s (pl watt-hours) watt-heure m

wattle ['wɑtəl] s (of bird) caroncule f; (of fish) barbillon m

watt′me′ter s wattmètre m

wave [wev] s onde f, vague f; (in hair) ondulation f; geste m de la main; (of heat or cold; of people; of the future) vague f; (phys) onde || tr (a handkerchief) agiter; (the hair) onduler; (a hat, newspaper, cane) brandir; to wave aside écarter d'un geste;

to wave good-bye faire un signe d'adieu; to wave one's hand faire un geste de la main || *intr* s'agiter; (*said of a flag*) ondoyer; to wave to faire signe à

wave/length/ *s* longueur *f* d'onde

wave/ mo'tion *s* mouvement *m* ondulatoire

waver ['wevər] *intr* vaciller

wav·y ['wevi] *adj* (*comp* -ier; *super* -iest) onduleux, ondoyant; (*hair; road surface*) ondulé; (*line*) tremblé, onduleux

wax [wæks] *s* cire *f* || *tr* cirer || *intr*— to wax and wane croître et décroître; to wax indignant s'indigner

wax/ bean/ *s* haricot *m* beurre

wax/ pa'per *s* papier *m* paraffiné

wax/ ta'per *s* allumette-bougie *f*

wax/wing/ *s* (orn) jaseur *m*

wax/works/ *s* musée *m* de cire

way [we] *s* voie *f*; (*road*) chemin *m*; (*direction*) côté *m*, sens *m*; (*manner*) façon *f*, manière *f*; (*means*) moyen *m*; (*habit, custom*) manière, habitude *f*, usage *m*; across the way en face; all the way jusqu'au bout; by the way à propos; by way of par; comme; get out of the way! ôter-vous de là!; in a way en un certain sens; in every way à tous les égards; in my (his, etc.) own way à ma (sa, etc.) façon or manière; in no way en aucune façon; in some ways par certains côtés; in such a way that de sorte que; in that way de la sorte; in this way de cette façon; on the way chemin faisant; on the way to en route pour; out of the way écarté; that way par là; the wrong way le mauvais sens, la mauvaise route; (*the wrong manner*) la mauvaise façon; (*when brushing hair*) à contrepoil; this way par ici; to be in the way être encombrant; to feel one's way avancer à tâtons; to get out of the way s'écarter; to get (*s.th. or s.o.*) out of the way se débarrasser de (*q.ch. or qn*); to give way céder; to go one's own way faire bande à part; to go one's way passer son chemin; to go out of one's way faire un détour; (fig) se déranger; to have one's way avoir le dernier mot, l'emporter; to keep out of s.o.'s way se tenir à l'écart de qn; to know one's way around connaître son affaire, être à la coule; to lead the way montrer le chemin; to make one's way se frayer un chemin; to make way for faire place à; to mend one's ways s'amender; to see one's way to trouver moyen de; to stand in the way of barrer le chemin à; under way en marche, en cours; way down descente *f*; way in entrée *f*; way out sortie *f*; ways (*for launching a ship*) couette *f*, anguilles *fpl*; way through passage *m*; way up montée *f*; which way? par où?

way/bill/ *s* feuille *f* de route, lettre *f* de voiture

wayfarer ['we,ferər] *s* voyageur *m*, vagabond *m*

way/lay/ *v* (*pret & pp* -laid) *tr* embusquer; (*to buttonhole*) arrêter au passage

way/ of life/ *s* manière *f* de vivre, genre *m* de vie, train *m* de vie

way/side/ *s* bord *m* de la route; to fall by the wayside rester en chemin

wayward ['wewərd] *adj* capricieux, rebelle

we [wi] *pron pers* nous §85, §87; nous autres, e.g., we Americans nous autres américains

weak [wik] *adj* faible

weaken ['wikən] *tr* affaiblir || *intr* faiblir, s'affaiblir

weakling ['wiklɪŋ] *s* chétif *m*, malingre *mf*; (*in character*) mou *m*

weak/-mind'ed *adj* irrésolu, d'esprit faible; (*feeble-minded*) débile

weakness ['wiknɪs] *s* faiblesse *f*

weal [wil] *s* papule *f*; (archaic) bien *m*

wealth [welθ] *s* richesse *f*

wealth·y ['welθi] *adj* (*comp* -ier; *super* -iest) riche, opulent

wean [win] *tr* sevrer; to wean away from détacher de

weapon ['wepən] *s* arme *f*

weaponry ['wepənri] *s* armement *m*

wear [wer] *s* (*use*) usage *m*; (*wasting away from use*) usure *f*; (*clothing*) vêtements *mpl*, articles *mpl* d'habillement; for evening wear pour le soir; for everyday wear pour tous les jours || *v* (*pret* wore [wor]; *pp* worn [worn]) *tr* porter; (*to put on*) mettre; to wear down or out user; (*e.g., one's patience*) épuiser || *intr* s'user; to wear off s'effacer; to wear on s'écouler, s'avancer; to wear out s'user; to wear well durer

wearable ['werəbəl] *adj* mettable

wear/ and tear/ [ter] *s* usure *f*

weariness ['wɪrɪnɪs] *s* lassitude *f*, fatigue *f*; ennui *m*

wear/ing appar'el ['werɪŋ] *s* vêtements *mpl*, habits *mpl*

wearisome ['wɪrɪsəm] *adj* lassant, ennuyeux

wea·ry ['wɪri] *adj* (*comp* -rier; *super* -riest) las || *v* (*pret & pp* -ried) *tr* lasser || *intr* se lasser

weasel ['wizəl] *s* (zool) belette *f*; (slang) mouchard *m*

wea/sel words/ *spl* mots *mpl* ambigus

weather ['weðər] *s* temps *m*; to be under the weather (coll) se sentir patraque; (*from drinking*) (coll) avoir mal aux cheveux; what's the weather like? quel temps fait-il? || *tr* altérer; (*e.g., difficulties*) survivre à, étaler || *intr* s'altérer

weath/er balloon/ *s* ballon *m* atmosphérique

weath/er-beat'en *adj* usé par les intempéries

weath/er bu'reau *s* bureau *m* météorologique, météo *f*

weath/er-cock/ *s* girouette *f*; (fig) girouette, caméléon *m*

weath′er fore′cast s bulletin m météorologique

weath′er fore′casting s prévision f du temps

weath′er·man′ s (pl -men′) météorologue mf, météorologiste mf

weath′er report′ s bulletin m de la météo

weath′er strip′ping s bourrelet m

weath′er vane′ s girouette f

weave [wiv] v (pret **wove** [wov] or **weaved**; pp **wove** or **woven** ['wovən]) tr tisser; **to weave one's way through** se faufiler à travers, se faufiler entre || intr tisser; serpenter, zigzaguer

weaver ['wivər] s tisserand m

web [wɛb] s (piece of cloth) tissu m; (roll of newsprint) rouleau m; (of spider) toile f; (between toes of birds and other animals) palmure f; (of an iron rail) âme f; (fig) trame f

web′-foot′ed adj palmé, palmipède

wed [wɛd] v (pret & pp **wed** or **wedded**; ger **wedding**) tr (to join in wedlock) marier; (to take in marriage) épouser || intr épouser, se marier

wedding ['wɛdɪŋ] adj nuptial || s mariage m, noces fpl

wed′ding ban′quet s repas m de noce

wed′ding cake′ s gâteau m de mariage

wed′ding cer′emo·ny s (pl -nies) cérémonie f nuptiale

wed′ding day′ s jour m des noces; anniversaire m du mariage

wed′ding dress′ s robe f nuptiale, robe de noce

wed′ding march′ s marche f nuptiale

wed′ding night′ s nuit f de noces

wed′ding pres′ent s cadeau m de mariage; **wedding presents** corbeille f de mariage

wed′ding ring′ s anneau m nuptial, alliance f

wedge [wɛdʒ] s coin m || tr coincer

wedlock ['wɛdlɑk] s mariage m

Wednesday ['wɛnzdi] s mercredi m

wee [wi] adj tout petit

weed [wid] s mauvaise herbe f; **the weed** (coll) le tabac; **weeds** vêtements mpl de deuil || tr & intr désherber, sarcler; **to weed out** éliminer, extirper

weed′ing hoe′ s sarcloir m

weed′ kill′er s herbicide m

week [wik] s semaine f; **a week from today** d'aujourd'hui en huit; **week in week out** d'un bout de la semaine à l'autre

week′day′ s jour m de semaine, jour ouvrable

week′end′ s fin f de semaine, week-end m || intr passer le week-end

week′ly ['wikli] adj hebdomadaire || s (pl -lies) hebdomadaire m || adv tous les huit jours

weep [wip] v (pret & pp **wept** [wɛpt]) tr pleurer || intr pleurer; (to drip) suinter; **to weep for** pleurer; (joy) pleurer de

weep′ing wil′low s saule m pleureur

weep·y ['wipi] adj (comp -ier; super -iest) (coll) pleurnicheur

weevil ['wivəl] s charançon m

weft [wɛft] s (yarns running across warp) trame f; (fabric) tissu m

weigh [we] tr peser; (anchor) lever; **to weigh down** faire pencher; **to weigh in one's hand** soupeser || intr peser; **to weigh heavily with** avoir du poids auprès de; **to weigh in** (sports) se faire peser

weight [wet] s poids m; **to gain weight** prendre du poids; **to lift weights** faire des haltères; **to lose weight** perdre du poids; **to throw one's weight around** (coll) s'imposer || tr charger; (statistically) pondérer; **to weight down** alourdir

weightless ['wetlɪs] adj sans pesanteur

weightlessness ['wetlɪsnɪs] s apesanteur f

weight′ lift′er s [ˌlɪftər] s (sports) haltérophile m

weight′ lift′ing s poids et haltères mpl

weight·y ['weti] adj (comp -ier; super -iest) pesant, lourd; (troublesome) grave; important, puissant

weir [wɪr] s (dam) barrage m; (trap) filet m à poissons

weird [wɪrd] adj surnaturel; étrange

welcome ['wɛlkəm] adj bienvenu; (change, news, etc.) agréable; **to be welcome to** + inf être libre de + inf; **you are welcome!** (i.e., gladly received) soyez le bienvenu!; (in response to thanks) de rien!, je vous en prie!, il n'y a pas de quoi!; **you are welcome to it** c'est à votre disposition; (ironically) je ne vous envie pas || s bienvenue f, bon accueil m || tr souhaiter la bienvenue à, faire bon accueil à, accueillir; **to welcome coldly** faire mauvais accueil à, accueillir froidement

weld [wɛld] s soudure f autogène; (bot) gaude f, réséda m || tr souder à l'autogène

welder ['wɛldər] s soudeur m; (mach) soudeuse f

welding ['wɛldɪŋ] s soudure f autogène

welfare ['wɛl‚fɛr] s bien-être m; (for underprivileged) aide f sociale

wel′fare state′ s état-providence m

wel′fare work′ s assistance f sociale

well [wɛl] adj bien (enjoying good health) bien, bien portant; **all's well** tout est bien; **it would be just as well to** il serait bon de; **to be well** aller bien || s puits m; (natural source of water) source f, fontaine f; (of stairway) cage f || adv bien; **as well** aussi; **as well as** aussi bien que; **well and good!** à la bonne heure! || intr—**to well up** jaillir || interj alors!, tiens!

well′-behaved′ adj de bonne conduite; (child) sage

well′-be′ing s bien-être m

well′born′ adj bien né

well-bred ['wɛl'brɛd] adj bien élevé

well′-disposed′ adj bien disposé

well-done ['wɛl'dʌn] adj bien fait; (culin) bien cuit

well'-dressed' *adj* bien vêtu
well'-fixed' *adj* (coll) bien renté, riche
well'-formed' *adj* bien conformé
well'-found'ed *adj* bien fondé
well'-groomed' *adj* paré, soigné
well'-heeled' *adj* (coll) huppé, riche
well'-informed' *adj* bien informé
well'-inten'tioned *adj* bien intentionné
well-kept ['wel'kept] *adj* bien tenu; (*secret*) bien gardé
well-known ['wel'non] *adj* bien connu, notoire
well'-matched' *adj* bien assortis
well'-mean'ing *adj* bien intentionné
well'-nigh' *adv* presque
well'-off' *adj* fortuné, prospère
well'-preserved' *adj* bien conservé
well-read ['wel'red] *adj* qui a beau-coup de lecture
well-spent ['wel'spent] *adj* bien employé
well'spring' *s* source *f*, source intarissable
well'sweep' *s* chadouf *m*
well'-thought'-of' *adj* de bonne réputation
well'-timed' *adj* opportun
well-to-do ['weltə'du] *adj* aisé, cossu
well-wisher ['wel'wɪʃər] *s* partisan *m*, ami *m* fidèle
well'-worn' *adj* usé; (*subject*) rebattu
Welsh [welʃ] *adj* gallois || *s* (*language*) gallois *m*; **the Welsh** les Gallois *mpl* || (*l.c.*) *intr* (slang) manquer à sa parole, manquer à ses obligations; **to welsh on s.o.** (slang) manquer à qn
Welsh'man *s* (*pl* **-men**) Gallois *m*
Welsh' rab'bit or **rare'bit** ['rerbɪt] *s* fondue *f* au fromage et à la bière sur canapé
welt [welt] *s* zébrure *f*; (*border*) bordure *f*; (*of shoe*) trépointe *f*
welter ['weltər] *s* confusion *f*, fouillis *m* || *intr* se vautrer
wel'ter-weight' *s* (*boxing*) poids *m* mi-moyen
wen [wen] *s* kyste *m* sébacé, loupe *f*
wench [wentʃ] *s* jeune fille *f*, jeune femme *f*
wend [wend] *tr*—**to wend one's way (to)** diriger ses pas (vers)
west [west] *adj* & *s* ouest *m* || *adv* à l'ouest, vers l'ouest
western ['westərn] *adj* occidental, de l'ouest || *s* (*mov*) western *m*
westerner ['westərnər] *s* habitant *m* de l'ouest, Occidental *m*
West' Ger'many *s* Allemagne *f* de l'Ouest, l'Allemagne de l'Ouest
West' In'dies ['ɪndiz] *spl* Indes *fpl* occidentales, Antilles *fpl*
westward ['westwərd] *adv* vers l'ouest
wet [wet] *adj* (*comp* **wetter**; *super* **wettest**) mouillé; (*damp*) humide; (*rainy*) pluvieux; (*paint*) frais; (coll) antiprohibitionniste; **all wet** (slang) fichu, erroné || *s* antiprohibitionniste *mf* || *v* (*pret* & *pp* **wet** or **wetted**; *ger* **wetting**) *tr* mouiller || *intr* se mouiller
wet' bat'ter·y *s* (*pl* **-ies**) pile *f* à liquide

wet' blan'ket *s* trouble-fête *mf*, rabat-joie *m*
wet' nurse' *s* nourrice *f*
wet' paint' (*public sign*) peinture *f* fraîche; (*public sign*) attention à la peinture
whack [hwæk] *s* (coll) coup *m*, gnon *m*; (*try*) (coll) tentative *f*; **to have a whack at** (coll) s'attaquer à || *tr* (coll) cogner
whale [hwel] *s* baleine *f*; (*sperm whale*) cachalot *m*; **to have a whale of a time** (coll) s'amuser follement || *tr* (coll) rosser
whale'bone' *s* baleine *f*, fanon *m* de baleine
whaler ['hwelər] *s* baleinier *m*
wharf [hwɔrf] *s* (*pl* **wharves** [hwɔrvz] or **wharfs**) quai *m*, débarcadère *m*
what [hwɑt] *adj interr* quel §80, e.g., **what time is it?** quelle heure est-il?; e.g., **what is his occupation?** quel est son métier? || *adj rel* ce qui, e.g., **I'll give you what water I have left** je vous donnerai ce qui me reste d'eau; ce que, e.g., **I know what drink you want** je sais ce que vous voulez comme boisson || *pron interr* qu'est-ce qui, e.g., **what happened?** qu'est-ce qui s'est passé?; que, e.g., **what are you doing?** que faites-vous?; qu'est-ce que, e.g., **what are you doing?** qu'est-ce que vous faites?; comment, e.g., **what is he like?** comment est-il?; combien, e.g., **what is two and two?** combien font deux et deux?; **what** (*did you say*)? comment?; **what else?** quoi d'autre?, quoi encore; **what for?** pourquoi donc?; **what if** si, e.g., **what if I were to die?** si je venais à mourir?; **what if I did?**, **what of it?**, **so what?** qu'importe?; **what is it?** qu'est-ce que c'est?, qu'est-ce qu'il y a?; **what now?** alors?; **what's that?** qu'est-ce que c'est que cela?; **what then?** et après? || *pron rel* ce qui, ce que; ce dont §79, e.g., **I have what you need** j'ai ce dont vous avez besoin; ce à quoi, e.g., **I know what you are thinking of** je sais ce à quoi vous pensez; (*sometimes untranslated*), e.g., **he asked them what time it was** il leur a demandé l'heure; **to know what's what** (coll) s'y connaître, être au courant || *interj* comment!; **what a lot of people!** que de monde!; **what a pity!** quel dommage!
what·ev'er *adj* quel que §80; moindre or quelconque, e.g., **is there any hope whatever?** y a-t-il le moindre espoir?, y a-t-il un espoir quelconque? || *pron* tout ce qui; tout ce que, e.g., **tell him whatever you like** dites-lui tout ce que vous voudrez; quoi que, e.g., **whatever you do** quoi que vous fassiez; **whatever comes** à tout hasard
what'not' *s* étagère *f*
what's'-his-name' *s* (coll) Monsieur un tel
wheal [wil] *s* papule *f*

wheat [hwit] s blé m

wheedle ['hwidəl] tr enjôler

wheel [hwil] s roue f; at the wheel au volant || tr (to turn) faire pivoter; (a wheelbarrow, table, etc.) rouler || intr pivoter; (said, e.g., of birds in the sky) tournoyer; to wheel about or around faire demi-tour

wheelbarrow ['hwil,bæro] s brouette f

wheel'base' s (aut) empattement m

wheel'chair' s fauteuil m roulant pour malade, voiture f d'infirme

wheel' horse' s (horse) timonier m; (person) bûcheur m

wheelwright ['hwil,rait] s charron m

wheeze [hwiz] s respiration f sifflante; (pathol) cornage m || intr respirer avec peine, souffler

whelp [hwelp] s petit m || tr & intr mettre bas

when [hwen] adv quand || conj quand, lorsque; (on which, in which) où; (whereas) alors que

whence [hwens] adv & conj d'où

when•ev'er conj chaque fois que, quand

where [hwer] adv & conj où; from where d'où

whereabouts ['hwerə,bauts] s—the whereabouts of l'endroit où se trouve || adv & conj où donc

whereas [hwer'æz] conj tandis que, attendu que || s considérant m

where•by' conj par lequel

wherefore ['hwerfor] s & adv pourquoi m || conj à cause de quoi

where•from' adv d'où

where•in' adv d'où; en quoi || conj où

where•of' adv de quoi || conj dont §79

where•up•on' adv sur quoi, sur ce

wherever [hwer'evər] conj partout où; où que, n'importe où

wherewithal ['hwerwɪð,ɔl] s ressources fpl, moyens mpl

whet [hwet] v (pret & pp whetted; ger whetting) tr aiguiser

whether ['weðər] conj si; que, e.g., it is doubtful whether you can finish il est douteux que vous puissiez finir; e.g., whether he is rich or poor qu'il soit riche ou qu'il soit pauvre; whether or no de toute façon; whether or not qu'il en soit ainsi ou non

whet'stone' s pierre f à aiguiser

whew [hwju] interj ouf!

whey [hwe] s petit lait m

which [hwɪt/] adj interr quel §80, e.g., which university do you prefer? quelle université préférez-vous?; which one? lequel? || adj rel le . . . que, e.g., choose which road you prefer choisissez le chemin que vous préférez || pron interr lequel §78; which is which? lequel des deux est-ce?; which of them? lequel d'entre eux? || pron rel qui; que; dont §79

which•ev'er adj rel n'importe quel || pron rel n'importe lequel

whiff [hwɪf] s bouffé f; to get a whiff of flairer

while [hwaɪl] s temps m, moment m; a

long while longtemps; a (little) while ago tout à l'heure; in a little while sous peu, tout à l'heure || conj pendant que; (as long as) tant que; (although) quoique || tr—to while away tuer, faire passer

whim [hwɪm] s caprice m, lubie f

whimper ['hwɪmpər] s pleurnicherie f || tr dire en pleurnichant || intr pleurnicher

whimsical ['hwɪmzɪkəl] adj capricieux, lunatique

whine [hwaɪn] s geignement m; (of siren) hurlement m || intr geindre; (said of siren) hurler

whin•ny ['hwɪni] s (pl -nies) hennissement m || v (pret & pp -nied) intr hennir

whip [hwɪp] s fouet m || v (pret & pp whipped or whipt; ger whipping) tr fouetter; (to defeat) battre; (the end of a rope) surlier; to whip out (e.g., a gun) sortir brusquement; to whip up (e.g., a supper) (coll) préparer à l'improviste; (e.g., enthusiasm) (coll) stimuler

whip'cord' s corde f à fouet

whip' hand' s main f du fouet; (upper hand) avantage m, dessus m

whip'lash' s mèche f de fouet

whipped' cream' s crème f fouettée, chantilly m

whipper-snapper ['hwɪpər,snæpər] s freluquet m, paltoquet m

whip'ping boy' s tête f de Turc

whip'ping post' s poteau m des condamnés au fouet

whippoorwill [,hwɪpər'wɪl] s (Caprimulgus vociferus) engoulevent m américain

whir [hwʌr] s ronflement m || v (pret & pp whirred; ger whirring) intr ronfler

whirl [hwʌrl] s tourbillon m; (of events, parties, etc.) succession f ininterrompue || tr faire tourbillonner || intr tourbillonner; his head whirls la tête lui tourne

whirligig ['hwʌrlɪ,gɪg] s tourniquet m; (ent) gyrin m, tourniquet

whirl'pool' s tourbillon m, remous m

whirl'wind' s tourbillon m

whirlybird ['hwʌrli,bʌrd] s (coll) hélicoptère m

whisk [hwɪsk] s coup m léger; (broom) époussette f; (culin) fouet m || tr balayer; (culin) fouetter; to whisk out of sight escamoter || intr aller comme un trait

whisk' broom' s époussette f

whiskers ['hwɪskərz] spl barbe f, poils mpl de barbe; (on side of face) favoris mpl; (of cat) moustaches fpl

whiskey ['hwɪski] s whisky m

whisper ['hwɪspər] s chuchotement m || tr chuchoter, dire à l'oreille || intr chuchoter

whispering ['hwɪspərɪŋ] s chuchotement m

whist [hwɪst] s whist m

whistle ['hwɪsəl] s (sound) sifflement

m; (device) sifflet m; **to wet one's whistle** (coll) s'humecter le gosier || tr siffler, siffloter || intr siffler; **to whistle for** siffler; attendre en vain, se voir obligé de se passer de

whis'tle stop' s arrêt m facultatif

whit [hwɪt] s—not a whit pas un brin; **to not care a whit** s'en moquer

white [hwaɪt] adj blanc || s blanc m; blanc d'œuf; **whites** (pathol) pertes fpl blanches

white'caps' spl moutons mpl

white' coal' s houille f blanche

white'-col'lar adj de bureau

white' feath'er s—**to show the white feather** lâcher pied, flancher, caner

white'fish' s poisson m blanc, merlan m

white' goods' spl vêtements mpl blancs; tissus mpl de coton, cotonnade f; (appliances) appareils mpl électroménagers

white'-haired' adj aux cheveux blancs, chenu; (coll) favori

white'-hot' adj chauffé à blanc

white' lead' [led] s céruse f, blanc m de céruse

white' lie' s mensonge m pieux

white' meat' s blanc m

whiten ['hwaɪtən] tr & intr blanchir

whiteness ['hwaɪtnɪs] s blancheur f

white' slav'ery s traite f des blanches

white' tie' s cravate f blanche; tenue f de soirée

white'wash' s blanc m de chaux, badigeon m; (cover-up) couverture f || tr blanchir à la chaux; (e.g., a guilty person, a scandal) blanchir

whither ['hwɪðər] adv & conj où, là où

whitish ['hwaɪtɪʃ] adj blanchâtre

whitlow ['hwɪtlo] s panaris m

Whitsuntide ['hwɪtsən,taɪd] s saison f de la Pentecôte

whittle ['hwɪtəl] tr tailler au couteau; **to whittle away** or **down** amenuiser

whiz or **whizz** [hwɪz] s sifflement m; (slang) prodige m || v (pret & pp **whizzed**; ger **whizzing**) intr—**to whiz by** passer en sifflant, passer comme le vent

who [hu] pron interr qui; quel §80; **who else?** qui d'autre?; qui encore?; **who is there?** (mil) qui vive? || pron rel qui; celui qui §83

whoa [hwo] interj holà!, doucement!

who·ev'er pron rel quiconque; celui qui §83; qui que, e.g., **whoever you are** qui que vous soyez

whole [hol] adj entier || s tout m, totalité f, ensemble m; **on the whole** somme toute, à tout prendre

whole'heart'ed adj sincère, de bon cœur

whole' note' s (mus) ronde f

whole' rest' s (mus) pause f

whole'sale' adj & adv en gros; (e.g., slaughter) en masse || s gros m, vente f en gros || tr & intr vendre en gros

whole'sale price' s prix m de gros

wholesaler ['hol,selər] s commerçant m en gros, grossiste mf

whole'sale trade' s commerce m de gros

wholesome ['holsəm] adj sain

wholly ['holɪ] adv entièrement

whom [hum] pron interr qui || pron rel que; lequel §78; celui que §83; **of whom** dont, de qui §79

whom·ev'er pron rel celui que §83; tous ceux que; (with a preposition) quiconque

whoop [hup], [hwup] s huée f; (cough) quinte f || tr—**to whoop it up** (slang) pousser des cris || intr huer

whoop'ing cough' ['hupɪŋ], ['hwupɪŋ] s coqueluche f

whopper ['hwapər] s (coll) chose f énorme; (lie) (coll) gros mensonge m

whopping ['hwapɪŋ] adj (coll) énorme

whore [hor] s putain f || intr—**to whore around** courir la gueuse

whortleber·ry ['hwʌrtəl,beri] s (pl -ries) myrtille f

whose [huz] pron interr à qui, e.g., **whose pen is that?** à qui est ce stylo? || pron rel dont, de qui §79; duquel §78

why [hwaɪ] s (pl **whys** [hwaɪz]) pourquoi m; **the why and the wherefore** le pourquoi et le comment || adv pourquoi; **why not?** pourquoi pas? || interj tiens!; **why, certainly!** mais bien sûr!; **why, yes!** mais oui!

wick [wɪk] s mèche f

wicked ['wɪkɪd] adj méchant, mauvais

wicker ['wɪkər] adj en osier || s osier m

wicket ['wɪkɪt] s guichet m; (croquet) arceau m

wide [waɪd] adj large; (range) vaste, étendu; (spread, angle, etc.) grand; large de, e.g., **eight feet wide** large de huit pieds || adv loin, partout; **open wide!** ouvrez bien!

wide'-an'gle adj grand-angulaire

wide'-awake' adj bien éveillé

widen ['waɪdən] tr élargir || intr s'élargir

wide'-o'pen adj grand ouvert

wide'spread' adj (arms, wings) étendu; répandu, universel

widow ['wɪdo] s veuve f || tr—**to be widowed** devenir veuf

widower ['wɪdo·ər] s veuf m

widowhood ['wɪdo,hʊd] s veuvage m

wid'ow's mite' s obole f

wid'ow's weeds' spl deuil m de veuve

width [wɪdθ] s largeur f; (of cloth) lé m

wield [wild] tr (sword, pen) manier; (power) exercer

wife [waɪf] s (pl **wives** [waɪvz]) femme f, épouse f

wig [wɪg] s perruque f

wiggle ['wɪgəl] s tortillement m || tr agiter || intr tortiller, se tortiller

wig'wag' s télégraphie f optique || v (pret & pp **-wagged**; ger **-wagging**) tr transmettre à bras avec fanions || intr signaler à bras avec fanions

wigwam ['wɪgwam] s wigwam m

wild [waɪld] adj sauvage; (untamed) sauvage, fauve; (frantic, mad) frénétique; (hair; dance; dream) échevelé; (passion; torrent; night) tumultueux;

(idea, plan) insensé, extravagant; *(life)* déréglé; *(blows, bullet, shot)* perdu; **wild about** or **for** fou de || **wilds** *spl* régions *fpl* sauvages || *adv* **—to run wild** dépasser toutes les bornes; *(said of plants)* pousser librement

wild/ boar/ *s* sanglier *m*

wild/ card/ *s* mistigri *m*

wild/ cat/ *s* chat *m* sauvage; lynx *m*; *(well)* sondage *m* d'exploration

wild/ cat strike/ *s* grève *f* sauvage, grève spontanée

wild/ cher/ry *s (pl -ries)* merise *f*; *(tree)* merisier *m*

wilderness ['wɪldərnɪs] *s* désert *m*

wild/ fire/ *s* feu *m* grégeois; feu *m* follet; éclairs *mpl* en nappe; like wildfire comme une traînée de poudre

wild/ flow/er *s* fleur *f* des champs

wild/ goose/ *s* oie *f* sauvage

wild/-goose/ chase/ *s*—to go on a wild-goose chase faire buisson creux

wild/ life/ *s* animaux *mpl* sauvages

wild/ oats/ *spl*—to sow one's wild oats jeter sa gourme

wile [waɪl] *s* ruse *f* || *tr*—to wile away tuer, faire passer

will [wɪl] *s* volonté *f*; *(law)* testament *m*; against one's will à contre-cœur; at will à volonté; with a will de bon cœur || *tr* vouloir; *(to bequeath)* léguer || *intr* vouloir; do as you will faites comme vous voudrez || *v (pret & cond* would [wʊd]) *aux* used to express 1) the future indicative, e.g., he will arrive early il arrivera de bonne heure; 2) the future perfect indicative, e.g., he will have arrived before I leave il sera arrivé avant que je parte; 3) the present indicative denoting habit or custom, e.g., after breakfast he will go out for a walk every morning après le petit déjeuner il fait une promenade tous les matins

willful ['wɪlfəl] *adj* volontaire; *(stubborn)* obstiné

willfulness ['wɪlfəlnɪs] *s* entêtement *m*

William ['wɪljəm] *s* Guillaume *m*

willing ['wɪlɪŋ] *adj* disposé, prêt; to be willing to vouloir bien; willing or unwilling bon gré mal gré

willingly ['wɪlɪŋli] *adv* volontiers

willingness ['wɪlɪŋnɪs] *s* bonne volonté *f*, consentement *m*

will-o'-the-wisp ['wɪləðə'wɪsp] *s* feu *m* follet; *(fig)* chimère *f*

willow ['wɪlo] *s* saule *m*

willowy ['wɪlo·i] *adj* souple, agile; svelte, élancé; couvert de saules

will/ pow/er *s* force *f* de volonté

willy-nilly ['wɪli'nɪli] *adv* bon gré mal gré

wilt [wɪlt] *tr* flétrir || *intr* se flétrir

wil-y ['waɪli] *adj (comp -ier; super -lest)* rusé, astucieux

wimple ['wɪmpəl] *s* guimpe *f*

win [wɪn] *s (coll)* victoire *f* || *v (pret & pp* won [wʌn]; *ger* winning) *tr* gagner; *(a victory, a prize)* remporter; to win back regagner; to win over gagner, convaincre || *intr* ga-

gner; convaincre; to win out *(coll)* réussir

wince [wɪns] *s*—without a wince sans sourciller || *intr* tressaillir

winch [wɪntʃ] *s* treuil *m*; *(handle, crank)* manivelle *f*

wind [wɪnd] *s* vent *m*; *(breath)* haleine *f*, souffle *m*; to break wind lâcher un vent, faire un pet; to get wind of avoir vent de; to sail close to the wind courir au plus près; to sail into the wind aller au lof, venir au lof || *tr* faire perdre le souffle à || *intr* flairer le gibier || [waɪnd] *s (pret & pp* wound [waʊnd]) *tr* enrouler; *(a timepiece)* remonter; *(yarn, thread, etc.)* pelotonner; to wind up enrouler; remonter; *(to finish)* (coll) terminer, régler || *intr* serpenter

windbag ['wɪnd,bæg] *s (of bagpipe)* outre *f*; *(coll)* moulin *m* à paroles

windbreak ['wɪnd,brek] *s* abrivent *m*

wind/ cone/ [wɪnd] *s (aer)* manche *f* à air

winded ['wɪndɪd] *adj* essoufflé

windfall ['wɪnd,fɔl] *s (fig)* aubaine *f*

wind/ ing road/ ['waɪndɪŋ] *s* route *f* en lacet

wind/ ing sheet/ *s* linceul *m*

wind/ ing stairs/ *spl* escalier *m* en colimaçon

wind/ in/strument [wɪnd] *s (mus)* instrument *m* à vent

windlass ['wɪndləs] *s* treuil *m*

windmill ['wɪnd,mɪl] *s* moulin *m* à vent; *(on a modern farm)* aéromoteur *m*; to tilt at windmills se battre contre des moulins à vent

window ['wɪndo] *s* fenêtre *f*; *(of ticket office)* guichet *m*; *(of store)* vitrine *f*; *(aut)* glace *f*

win/dow dress/er *s* étalagiste *mf*

win/dow dress/ing *s* art *m* de l'étalage; *(coll)* façade *f*

win/dow en/velope *s* enveloppe *f* à fenêtre

win/dow frame/ *s* châssis *m*, dormant *m*

win/dow-pane/ *s* vitre *f*, carreau *m*

win/dow screen/ *s* grillage *m*

win/dow shade/ *s* store *m*

win/dow-shop/ *v (pret & pp* -shopped; *ger* -shopping) *intr* faire du lèche-vitrines, lécher les vitrines

win/dow shut/ter *s* volet *m*

win/dow sill/ *s* rebord *m* de fenêtre

windpipe ['wɪnd,paɪp] *s* trachée-artère *f*

windshield ['wɪnd,ʃild] *s* pare-brise *m*

wind/shield wash/er *s* lave-glace *m*

wind/shield wip/er *s* essuie-glace *m*

windsock ['wɪnd,sak] *s* manche *f* à air

windstorm ['wɪnd,stɔrm] *s* tempête *f* de vent

wind/ tun/nel [wɪnd] *s* tunnel *m* aérodynamique

wind-up ['waɪnd,ʌp] *s* conclusion *f*, fin *f*

windward ['wɪndwərd] *adj & adv* au vent || *s* côté *m* du vent; to turn to windward louvoyer

wind·y ['wɪndɪ] adj (comp **-ier**; super **-iest**) venteux; (verbose) verbeux; **it is windy** il fait du vent

wine [waɪn] s vin m ‖ tr—**to wine and dine s.o.** fêter qn

wine/ cel/lar s cave f

wine/glass/ s verre m à vin

winegrower ['waɪnˌgroˌər] s viticulteur m

winegrowing ['waɪnˌgroˌɪŋ] s viticulture f

wine/ list/ s carte f des vins

wine/ press/ s pressoir m

winer·y ['waɪnərɪ] s (pl **-ies**) pressoir m

wine/skin/ s outre f à vin

wine/ stew/ard s sommelier m; (of prince, king) bouteiller m

winetaster ['waɪnˌtestər] s (person) dégustateur m; (pipette) taste-vin m

wing [wɪŋ] s aile f; (e.g., of hospital) pavillon m; (pol) parti m, faction f; **in the wings** (theat) dans la coulisse; **on the wing** au vol; **to take wing** prendre son essor ‖ tr (to wound) blesser; **to wing one's way** voler

wing/ chair/ s fauteuil m à oreilles

wing/ col/lar s col m rabattu

wing/ load/ s (aer) charge f alaire

wing/ nut/ s écrou m ailé

wing/spread/ s envergure f

wink [wɪŋk] s clin m d'œil; **to not sleep a wink** ne pas fermer l'œil; **to take forty winks** (coll) piquer un roupillon ‖ tr cligner ‖ intr cligner des yeux; **to wink at** cligner de l'œil à; (e.g., an abuse) fermer les yeux sur

winner ['wɪnər] s gagnant m, vainqueur m

winning ['wɪnɪŋ] adj gagnant; (attractive) séduisant ‖ **winnings** spl gains mpl

winnow ['wɪno] tr vanner, sasser; (e.g., the evidence) passer au crible

winsome ['wɪnsəm] adj séduisant

winter ['wɪntər] s hiver m ‖ intr passer l'hiver; (said of animals, troops, etc.) hiverner

win/ter·green/ s (oil) wintergreen m; (bot) gaulthérie f

win·try ['wɪntrɪ] adj (comp **-trier**; super **-triest**) hivernal, froid

wipe [waɪp] tr essuyer; **to wipe away** essuyer; **to wipe off** or **out** effacer; (to annihilate) anéantir; **to wipe up** nettoyer

wiper ['waɪpər] s torchon m; (elec) contact m glissant; (mach) came f

wire [waɪr] s fil m; télégramme m; **hold the wire!** (telp) restez à l'écoute!; **on the wire** (telp) au bout du fil; **reply by wire** réponse f télégraphique; **to get in under the wire** arriver juste à temps; terminer juste à temps; **to pull wires** (coll) tirer les ficelles ‖ tr attacher avec du fil de fer; (a message) télégraphier; (a house) canaliser ‖ intr télégraphier

wire/ cut/ter s coupe-fil m

wire/draw/ v (pret **-drew**; pp **-drawn**) tr tréfiler

wire/ entan/glement s réseau m de barbelés

wire/ gauge/ s calibre m or jauge f pour fils métalliques

wire/-haired/ adj à poil dur

wireless ['waɪrlɪs] adj sans fil

wire/ nail/ s clou m de Paris

wire/pho/to s (pl **-tos**) (trademark) (device) bélinographe m; (photo) bélinogramme m

wire/pull/ing s (coll) influences fpl secrètes, piston m

wire/ record/er s magnétophone m à fil d'acier

wire/tap/ s (device) table f d'écoute ‖ v (pret & pp **-tapped**; ger **-tapping**) tr passer à la table d'écoute

wiring ['waɪrɪŋ] s (e.g., of house) canalisation f; (e.g., of radio) montage m

wir·y ['waɪrɪ] adj (comp **-ier**; super **-iest**) nerveux; (hair) raide

wisdom ['wɪzdəm] s sagesse f

wis/dom tooth/ s dent f de sagesse

wise [waɪz] adj sage; (step, decision) judicieux, prudent; **to be wise to** (slang) voir clair dans le jeu de, percer le jeu de; **to get wise** (coll) se mettre au courant ‖ s—**in no wise** en aucune manière ‖ tr—**to wise up** (slang) avertir, désabuser

wiseacre ['waɪzˌekər] s fat m, fierot m

wise/crack/ s (coll) blague f, plaisanterie f ‖ intr (coll) blaguer, plaisanter

wise/ guy/ s (slang) type m goguenard

wish [wɪʃ] s souhait m, désir m; **best wishes** meilleurs vœux mpl; (formula used to close a letter) amitiés; **last wishes** dernières volontés fpl; **to make a wish** faire un vœu ‖ tr souhaiter, désirer; **to wish s.o. s.th.** souhaiter q.ch. à qn; **to wish s.o. to** + inf souhaiter que qn + subj; **to wish to** + inf vouloir + inf

wish/bone/ s fourchette f

wishful ['wɪʃfəl] adj désireux

wish/ful think/ing s optimisme m à outrance; **to indulge in wishful thinking** se forger des chimères

wish/ing well/ s puits m aux souhaits

wistful ['wɪstfəl] adj pensif, rêveur

wit [wɪt] s esprit m; (person) homme m d'esprit; **to be at one's wits' end** ne plus savoir que faire; **to keep one's wits about one** conserver toute sa présence d'esprit; **to live by one's wits** vivre d'expédients

witch [wɪtʃ] s sorcière f

witch/craft/ s sorcellerie f

witch/ doc/tor s sorcier m guérisseur

witch/es' Sab/bath s sabbat m

witch/ ha/zel s teinture f d'hamamélis; (bot) hamamélis m

witch/ hunt/ s chasse f aux sorcières

with [wɪð], [wɪθ] prep avec; (at the home of; in the case of) chez; (in spite of) malgré; à, e.g., **the girl with the blue eyes** la jeune fille aux yeux bleus; e.g., **coffee with milk** café au lait; e.g., **with open arms** à bras ouverts; e.g., **with these words . . .** à ces mots . . . ; de, e.g., **with a loud**

voice d'une voix forte; e.g., **with all his strength** de toutes ses forces; e.g., **to be satisfied with** être satisfait de; e.g., **to fill with** remplir de

with·draw′ v (pret **-drew**, pp **-drawn**) tr retirer || intr se retirer

withdrawal [wɪð'drɔ·əl], [wɪθ'drɔ·əl] s retrait m

wither ['wɪðər] tr faner || intr se faner

with·hold′ v (pret & pp **-held**) tr (money, taxes, etc.) retenir; (permission) refuser; (the truth) cacher

with·hold′ing tax′ s impôt m retenu à la source

with·in′ adv à l'intérieur; là-dedans §85A || prep à l'intérieur de; (in less than) en moins de; (within the limits of) dans; (in the bosom of) au sein de; (not exceeding a margin of error of) à . . . près, e.g., **I can tell you what time it is within five minutes** je peux vous dire l'heure à cinq minutes près; à portée de, e.g., **within reach** à portée de la main

with·out′ adv au-dehors, dehors || prep au dehors de; (lacking, not with) sans; **to do without** se passer de; **without** + ger sans + inf, e.g., **he left without seeing me** il est parti sans me voir; sans que + subj, e.g., **he left without anyone seeing him** il est parti sans que personne ne le voie

with·stand′ v (pret & pp **-stood**) tr résister à

witness ['wɪtnɪs] s témoin m; **in witness whereof** en foi de quoi; **to bear witness** rendre témoignage || tr (to be present at) être témoin de, assister à; (to attest) témoigner; (e.g., a contract) signer

wit′ness stand′ s barre f des témoins

witticism ['wɪtɪˌsɪzəm] s trait m d'esprit

wittingly ['wɪtɪŋli] adv sciemment

wit·ty ['wɪti] adj (comp **-tier**; super **-tiest**) spirituel

wizard ['wɪzərd] s sorcier m

wizardry ['wɪzərdri] s sorcellerie f

wizened ['wɪzənd] adj desséché

woad [wod] s guède f

wobble ['wɑbəl] intr chanceler; (said of table) branler; (said of voice) chevroter; vaciller

wob·bly ['wɑbli] adj (comp **-blier**; super **-bliest**) vacillant

woe [wo] s malheur m, affliction f; **woe is me!** pauvre de moi!

woebegone ['wobɪˌgɑn], ['wobɪˌgɔn] adj navré, abattu, désolé

woeful ['wofəl] adj triste, désolé; très mauvais

wolf [wʊlf] s (pl **wolves** [wʊlvz]) loup m; galant m, tombeur m de femmes; **to cry wolf** crier au loup; **to keep the wolf from the door** se mettre à l'abri du besoin, joindre les deux bouts || tr & intr engloutir

wolf′ cub′ s louveteau m

wolf′hound′ s chien-loup m

wolf′ pack′ s bande f de loups

wolfram ['wʊlfrəm] s (element) tungstène m; (mineral) wolfram m

wolf's′-bane′ or **wolfs′bane′** s tue-loup m, aconit m, napel m

woman ['wʊmən] s (pl **women** ['wɪmɪn]) femme f

wom′an doc′tor s femme f médecin, doctoresse f

womanhood ['wʊmənˌhʊd] s le sexe féminin; les femmes fpl

womanish ['wʊmənɪʃ] adj féminin; (effeminate) efféminé

wom′an·kind′ s le sexe féminin

wom′an la′borer s femme f manœuvre

woman·ly ['wʊmənli] adj (comp **-lier**; super **-liest**) féminin, femme

wom′an preach′er s femme f pasteur

womb [wum] s utérus m, matrice f; (fig) sein m

wonder ['wʌndər] s merveille f; (feeling of surprise) émerveillement m; (something strange) miracle m; **for a wonder** chose étonnante; **no wonder that . . .** rien d'étonnant que . . . ; **to work wonders** faire des merveilles || tr—**to wonder that** s'étonner que; **to wonder why, if, whether** se demander pourquoi, si || intr—**to wonder at** s'émerveiller de, s'étonner de

won′der drug′ s remède m miracle

wonderful ['wʌndərfəl] adj merveilleux, étonnant

won′der·land′ s pays m des merveilles

wonderment ['wʌndərmənt] s étonnement m

wont [wʌnt], [wɔnt] adj—**to be wont to** avoir l'habitude de || s—**his wont** son habitude

wonted adj habituel, accoutumé

woo [wu] tr courtiser

wood [wʊd] s bois m; (for wine) fût m; **out of the woods** (coll) hors de danger, hors d'affaire; **to take to the woods** se sauver dans la nature; **woods** bois m or mpl

woodbine ['wʊdˌbaɪn] s (honeysuckle) chèvrefeuille m; (Virginia creeper) vigne f vierge

wood′ carv′ing s sculpture f sur bois

wood′chuck′ s marmotte f d'Amérique

wood′cock′ s bécasse f

wood′cut′ s (typ) gravure f sur bois

wood′cut′ter s bûcheron m

wooded ['wʊdɪd] adj boisé

wooden ['wʊdən] adj en bois; (style, manners) guindé, raide

wood′ engrav′ing s (typ) gravure f sur bois

wood′en-head′ed adj (coll) stupide, obtus

wood′en leg′ s jambe f en bois

wood′en shoe′ s sabot m

wood′ grouse′ s grand tétras m, grand coq m de bruyère

woodland ['wʊdlənd] adj sylvestre || s pays m boisé

wood′land scene′ s (painting) paysage m boisé

wood′man s (pl **-men**) bûcheron m

woodpecker ['wʊdˌpɛkər] s pic m; (green woodpecker) pivert m, picvert m

wood′ pig′eon s (orn) ramier m

wood′pile′ s tas m de bois

wood′ screw′ s vis ƒ à bois
wood′shed′ s bûcher m
woods′man s (pl -men) bûcheron m; (trapper) trappeur m, chasseur m
wood′ tick′ s vrillette ƒ
wood′winds′ spl (mus) bois mpl
wood′work′ s (working in wood) menuiserie ƒ; (things made of wood) boiseries ƒpl
wood′work′er s menuisier m
wood′worm′ s (ent) artison m
wood·y [′wʊdɪ] adj (comp -ier; super -iest) boisé; (like wood) ligneux
wooer [′wu·ər] s prétendant m
woof [wuf] s trame ƒ; (fabric) tissu m
woofer [′wʊfər] s (rad) boomer m, woofer m
wool [wʊl] s laine ƒ
woolen [′wʊlən] adj de laine ‖ s tissu m de laine; **woolens** lainage m
wool′gath′ering s rêvasserie ƒ
woolgrower [′wʊl‚gro·ər] s éleveur m des bêtes à laine
wool·ly [′wʊli] adj (comp -lier; super -liest) laineux
word [wʌrd] s mot m; (promise, assurance) parole ƒ; **in other words** autrement dit; **in your own words** en vous propres termes; **my word!** ça alors!; **not a word!** motus!; **the Word** (eccl) le Verbe; **to break one's word** manquer à sa parole; **to have words with** échanger des propos désagréables avec; **to make s.o. eat his words** faire ravaler ses paroles à qn; **to put in a word** placer un mot; **to take s.o. at his word** prendre qn au mot, croire qn sur parole; **upon my word!** ma foi!; **without a word** sans mot dire; **words** (e.g., of song) paroles ‖ tr formuler, rédiger
word′-forma′tion s formation ƒ des mots
wording [′wʌrdɪŋ] s langage m
word′ or′der s ordre m des mots
word′-stock′ s vocabulaire m
word·y [′wʌrdi] adj (comp -ier; super -iest) verbeux
work [wʌrk] s travail m, ouvrage m; (production, book) œuvre ƒ, ouvrage; **at work** en œuvre; (not at home) au travail, au bureau, à l'usine; **out of work** sans travail, en chômage; **to shoot the works** (slang) mettre le paquet; **works** œuvres; mécanisme m; (of clock) mouvement m ‖ tr faire travailler; (to operate) faire fonctionner, faire marcher; (wood, iron) travailler; (mine) exploiter; **to work out** élaborer, résoudre; **to work up** préparer; stimuler ‖ intr travailler; (said of motor, machine, etc.) fonctionner, marcher; (said of remedy) faire de l'effet; (said of wine, beer) fermenter; **how will things work out?** à quoi tout cela aboutira-t-il?; **to work hard** travailler dur; **to work loose** se desserrer; **to work out** (sports) s'entraîner; **to work too hard** se surmener
workable [′wʌrkəbəl] adj (feasible)

réalisable; (that can be worked) ouvrable
work′bas′ket s corbeille ƒ à ouvrage
work′bench′ s établi m
work′book′ s manuel m; (notebook) carnet m; (for student) cahier m de devoirs
work′box′ s boîte ƒ à ouvrage; (for needlework) coffret m de travail
work′day′ adj de tous les jours; prosaïque, ordinaire ‖ s jour m ouvrable; (part of day devoted to work) journée ƒ
worked′-up′ adj préparé, ouvré; (excited) agité, emballé
worker [′wʌrkər] s travailleur m, ouvrier m, employé m
work′ force′ s main-d'œuvre ƒ; personnel m
work′horse′ s cheval m de charge; (tireless worker) vrai cheval m de labour
work′house′ s maison ƒ de correction; (Brit) asile m des pauvres
work′ing class′ s classe ƒ ouvrière
work′ing day′ s jour m ouvrable; (daily hours for work) journée ƒ
work′ing-girl′ s jeune ouvrière ƒ
work′ing hours′ spl heures ƒpl de travail
work′ing·man′ s (pl -men′) travailleur m
work′ing·wom′an s (pl -wom′en) ouvrière ƒ
work′man s (pl -men) ouvrier m
workmanship [′wʌrkmən‚ʃɪp] s habileté ƒ professionnelle, facture ƒ; (work executed) travail m
work′ of art′ s œuvre ƒ d'art
work′out′ s essai m, épreuve ƒ; (physical exercise) séance ƒ d'entraînement
work′room′ s atelier m; (for study) cabinet m de travail, cabinet d'études
work′shop′ s atelier m
work′ stop′page s arrêt m du travail
world [wʌrld] adj mondial ‖ s monde m; **a world of** énormément de; **for all the world** à tous les égards, exactement; **not for all the world** pour rien au monde; **since the world began** depuis que le monde est monde; **the other world** l'autre monde; **to bring into the world** mettre au monde; **to go around the world** faire le tour du monde; **to see the world** voir du pays; **to think the world of** estimer énormément, avoir une très haute opinion de
world′ affairs′ spl affaires ƒpl internationales
world′-fa′mous adj de renommée mondiale
world′ his′tory s histoire ƒ universelle
world·ly [′wʌrldli] adj (comp -lier; super -liest) mondain
world′ly-wise′ adj—**to be worldly-wise** savoir ce que c'est que la vie
world′ map′ s mappemonde ƒ
World′ Se′ries s championnat m mondial
world′s′ fair′ s exposition ƒ universelle
world′ war′ s guerre ƒ mondiale

world'-wide' adj mondial, universel

worm [wʌrm] s ver m || tr enlever les vers de; (a secret, money, etc.) soutirer; **to worm it out of him** lui tirer les vers du nez || intr se faufiler

worm-eaten ['wʌrm,itən] adj vermoulu

worm' gear' s engrenage m à vis sans fin

worm'wood' s (Artemisia) armoise f; (Artemisia absinthium) armoise absinthe; (something grievous) (fig) absinthe f

worm•y ['wʌrmi] adj (comp -ier; super -iest) véreux

worn [worn] adj usé, fatigué

worn'-out' adj épuisé, usé; éreinté

worrisome ['wʌrisəm] adj inquiétant; inquiet, anxieux

wor•ry ['wʌri] s (pl -ries) souci m, inquiétude f; (cause of anxiety) ennui m, tracas m || v (pret & pp -ried) tr inquiéter; (to harass, pester) ennuyer, tracasser; **to be worried** s'inquiéter || intr s'inquiéter; **don't worry!** ne vous en faites pas!

worse [wʌrs] adj comp pire, plus mauvais §91; **and to make matters worse** et par surcroît de malheur; **so much the worse** tant pis; **to make or get worse** empirer; **what's worse** qui pis est; **worse and worse** de pis en pis || adv comp pis, plus mal §91

worsen ['wʌrsən] tr & intr empirer

wor•ship ['wʌrʃip] s culte m, adoration f || v (pret & pp -shiped or -shipped; ger -shiping or -shipping) tr adorer || intr prier; (to go to church) aller au culte

worshiper or **worshipper** ['wʌrʃipər] s adorateur m, fidèle mf

worst [wʌrst] adj super pire §91; pis || s (le) pire, (le) pis; **to be hurt the worst** être le plus gravement atteint (blessé, etc.); **to get the worst of it** avoir le dessous || adv super pis §91

worsted ['wʊstid] adj de laine peignée || s peigné m, tissu m de laine peignée

wort [wʌrt] s (of beer) moût m

worth [wʌrθ] adj digne de; valant, e.g., **book worth three dollars** livre valant trois dollars; **to be worth** valoir; avoir une fortune de; **to be worth +** ger valoir la peine de + inf; **to be worth while** valoir la peine || s valeur f; **a dollar's worth of** pour un dollar de

worthless ['wʌrθlis] adj sans valeur; (person) bon à rien, indigne

worth'while' adj utile, de valeur

wor•thy ['wʌrði] adj (comp -thier; super -thiest) digne || s (pl -thies) notable mf; (hum, ironical) personnage m

would [wʊd] aux used to express 1) the past future, e.g., **he said he would come** il a dit qu'il viendrait; 2) the present conditional, e.g., **he would come if he could** il viendrait s'il pouvait; 3) the past conditional, e.g., **he would have come if he had been able (to)** il serait venu s'il avait pu; 4) the

potential mood, e.g., **would that I knew it!** plût à Dieu que je le sache!, je voudrais le savoir!; 5) the past indicative denoting habit or custom in the past, e.g., **he would visit us every day** il nous visitait tous les jours

would'-be' adj prétendu

wound [wund] s blessure f || tr blesser

wounded ['wundid] adj blessé || s— **the wounded les** blessés mpl

wow [wau] s (e.g., of phonograph record) distorsion f; (slang) succès m formidable || tr (slang) enthousiasmer || interj (slang) formidable!

wrack [ræk] s vestige m; (ruin) naufrage m; (bot) varech m

wraith [reθ] s apparition f

wrangle ['ræŋgəl] s querelle f || intr se quereller

wrap [ræp] s couverture f; (coat) manteau m || v (pret & pp wrapped; ger wrapping) tr envelopper, emballer

wrap'around' wind'shield' s pare-brise m panoramique

wrapper ['ræpər] s saut-de-lit m; (of newspaper or magazine) bande f; (of tobacco) robe f

wrap'ping pa'per s papier m d'emballage

wrath [ræθ], [rɑθ] s colère f

wrathful ['ræθfəl], ['rɑθfəl] adj courroucé, en colère

wreak [rik] tr assouvir

wreath [riθ] s (pl wreaths [riðz]) couronne f; (of smoke) volute f, panache m

wreathe [rið] tr enguirlander; (e.g., flowers) entrelacer || intr (said of smoke) s'élever en volutes

wreck [rek] s (shipwreck) naufrage m; (debris at sea or elsewhere) épave f; (of train) déraillement m; (of airplane) écrasement m; (of auto) accident m; (of one's hopes) naufrage; **to be a wreck** être une ruine || tr (a ship, one's hopes) faire échouer; (a train) faire dérailler; (one's health) ruiner

wreckage ['rekidʒ] s débris mpl, décombres mpl, ruines fpl

wrecker ['rekər] s (tow truck) dépanneuse f; (person) dépanneur m

wreck'ing car' s voiture f de dépannage

wreck'ing crane' s grue f de dépannage

wren [ren] s (orn) troglodyte m; (kinglet) (orn) roitelet m

wrench [rentʃ] s clef f; (pull) secousse f; (twist of a joint) foulure f || tr (e.g., one's ankle) se fouler; (to twist) tordre

wrest [rest] tr arracher violemment

wrestle ['resəl] s lutte f || intr lutter

wrestling ['resliŋ] s (sports) lutte f, catch m

wres'tling match' s rencontre f de catch

wretch [retʃ] s misérable mf

wretched ['retʃid] adj misérable

wriggle ['rigəl] s tortillement m || tr tortiller || intr se tortiller; **to wriggle out of** esquiver adroitement

wrig·gly ['rɪglɪ] adj (comp -glier; super -gliest) frétillant; évasif

wring [rɪŋ] v (pret & pp wrung [rʌŋ]) tr tordre; (one's hands) se tordre; (s.o.'s hand) serrer fortement; to wring out (clothes) essorer; (money, a secret, etc.) arracher

wringer ['rɪŋər] s essoreuse f

wrinkle ['rɪŋkəl] s (in skin) ride f; (in clothes) pli m, faux pli; (clever idea or trick) (coll) truc m || tr plisser || intr se plisser

wrin·kly ['rɪŋklɪ] adj (comp -klier; super -kliest) ridé, chiffonné

wrist [rɪst] s poignet m

wrist'band' s poignet m

wrist' watch' s montre-bracelet f

writ [rɪt] s (eccl) écriture f; (law) acte m judiciaire

write [raɪt] v (pret wrote [rot]; pp written ['rɪtən]) tr écrire; to write down consigner par écrit; baisser le prix de; to write in insérer; to write off (a debt) passer aux profits et pertes; to write up rédiger un compte rendu de; (to ballyhoo) faire l'éloge de || intr écrire; to write back répondre par écrit

writer ['raɪtər] s écrivain m

writ'er's cramp' s crampe f des écrivains

write'-up' s compte m rendu; (ballyhoo) battage m; (com) surestimation f

writhe [raɪð] intr se tordre

writing ['raɪtɪŋ] s l'écriture f; (something written) écrit m, œuvre f; (profession) métier m d'écrivain; at this writing au moment où j'écris; to put in writing mettre par écrit

writ'ing desk' s bureau m, écritoire f; (in schoolroom) pupitre m

writ'ing pa'per s papier m à lettres

wrong [rɔŋ], [rɑŋ] adj (unjust) injuste; (incorrect) erroné; (road, address, side, place, etc.) mauvais; ne pas . . . qu'il faut, e.g., **I arrived at the wrong city** je ne suis pas arrivé à la ville qu'il fallait; (word) impropre; qui ne marche pas, e.g., **something is wrong with the motor** il y a quelque chose qui ne marche pas dans le moteur; **to be wrong** (i.e., in error) avoir tort; (i.e., to blame) être le coupable || s mal m; injustice f; **to be in the wrong** être dans son tort, avoir tort; **to do wrong** faire du mal, faire du tort || adv mal; **to go wrong** faire fausse route; (said, e.g., of a plan) ne pas marcher; (said of one falling into evil ways) se dévoyer; **to guess wrong** se tromper || tr faire du tort à, être injuste envers

wrongdoer ['rɔŋ,du·ər], ['rɑŋ,du·ər] s malfaiteur m

wrong'do'ing s mal m, tort m; (misdeeds) méfaits mpl

wrong' num'ber s (telp) mauvais numéro m; **you have the wrong number** vous vous trompez de numéro

wrong' side' s (e.g., of material) revers m, envers m; (of the street) mauvais côté m; **to drive on the wrong side** circuler à contre-voie; **to get out of bed on the wrong side** se lever du pied gauche; **wrong side out** à l'envers; **wrong side up** sens dessus dessous

wrought' i'ron [rɔt] s fer m forgé

wrought'-up' adj excité, agité

wry [raɪ] adj (comp wrier; super wriest) tordu, de travers; forcé, ironique

wry'neck' s (orn) torcol m; (pathol) torticolis m

X

X, x [eks] s XXIVᵉ lettre de l'alphabet

Xavier ['zævɪ·ər], ['zevɪ·ər] s Xavier m

xenophobe ['zenə,fob] s xénophobe mf

Xerxes ['zʌrksiz] s Xerxès m

Xmas ['krɪsməs] adj de Noël || s Noël m

X' ray' s (photograph) radiographie f; **to have an X ray** passer à la radio; **X rays** rayons mpl X

X'-ray' adj radiographique || X'-ray' tr radiographier

X'-ray treat'ment s radiothérapie f

xylophone ['zaɪlə,fon] s xylophone m

Y

Y, y [waɪ] s XXVᵉ lettre de l'alphabet

yacht [jɑt] s yacht m

yacht' club' s yacht-club m

yah [jɑ] interj (in disgust) pouah!; (in derision) oh là là!

yam [jæm] s igname f; (sweet potato) patate f douce

yank [jæŋk] s (coll) secousse f || tr (coll) tirer d'un coup sec

Yankee ['jæŋkɪ] adj & s yankee mf

yap [jæp] *s* jappement *m*; (slang) criaillerie *f* || *v* (*pret & pp* **yapped**; *ger* **yapping**) *intr* japper; (slang) criailler; (slang) dégoiser

yard [jɑrd] *s* cour *f*; (*for lumber, for repairs, etc.*) chantier *m*; (*measure*) yard *m*; (naut) vergue *f*; (rr) gare *f* de triage

yard′arm′ *s* (naut) bout *m* de vergue

yard′mas′ter *s* (rr) chef *m* de dépôt

yard′stick′ *s* yard *m* en bois (en métal, etc.); (fig) unité *f* de comparaison

yarn [jɑrn] *s* fil *m*, filé *m*; (coll) histoire *f*

yarrow [′jæro] *s* mille-feuille *f*

yaw [jɔ] *s* (naut) embardée *f*; **yaws** (pathol) pian *m* || *intr* faire des embardées

yawl [jɔl] *s* yole *f*

yawn [jɔn] *s* bâillement *m* || *intr* bâiller; être béant

ye (old spelling of the [ðə]) *art* le, e.g., **ye olde shoppe** la vieille boutique *f* [ji] *pron* (obs) vous

yea [je] *s* oui *m*; vote *m* affirmatif || *adv* oui, voire

yeah [je] *adv* (coll) oui; **oh yeah?** (coll) de quoi?; **oh yeah!** (coll) ouais!

yean [jin] *intr* (*said of ewe*) agneler; (*said of goat*) chevreter

year [jɪr] *s* an *m*, année *f*; **to be . . . years old** avoir . . . ans; **year in year out** bon an mal an

year′book′ *s* annuaire *m*

yearling [′jɪrlɪŋ] *s* animal *m* d'un an; (*horse*) yearling *m*

yearly [′jɪrli] *adj* annuel || *adv* annuellement

yearn [jʌrn] *intr*—**to yearn for** soupirer après; **to yearn to** brûler de

yearning [′jʌrnɪŋ] *s* désir *m* ardent

yeast [jist] *s* levure *f*

yell [jel] *s* hurlement *m*; (*school yell*) cri *m* de ralliement || *tr & intr* hurler

yellow [′jelo] *adj* jaune; (*cowardly*) (coll) froussard; (*e.g., press*) à sensation; **to turn yellow** jaunir; (coll) avoir la frousse || *s* jaune *m* || *tr & intr* jaunir

yel′low-ham′mer *s* (orn) bruant *m* jaune

yellowish [′jelo.ɪʃ] *adj* jaunâtre

yel′low-jack′et *s* (ent) frelon *m*

yel′low streak′ *s* (coll) trait *m* de lâcheté

yelp [jelp] *s* glapissement *m*, jappement *m* || *intr* glapir, japper

yen [jen] *s*—**to have a yen to** or **for** (coll) avoir envie de

yeo·man [′jomən] *s* (*pl* **-men**) yeoman *m*; (*clerical worker*) (nav) commis *m* aux écritures

yeo′man of the guard′ *s* (Brit) hallebardier *m* de la garde du corps

yeo′man's serv′ice *s* effort *m* précieux

yes [jes] *s* oui *m* || *adv* oui; (to contradict a negative statement or question) si or pardon, e.g., **"You didn't know." "Yes, I did!"** "Vous ne le saviez pas." "Si!" || *v* (*pret & pp*

---

yessed; *ger* yessing) *tr* dire oui à || *intr* dire oui

yes′ man′ *s* (*pl* **men′**) (coll) M. Toujours; **to be a yes man** opiner du bonnet; **yes men** (coll) béni-oui-oui *mpl*

yesterday [′jestərdi], [′jestər,de] *adj*, *s*, & *adv* hier *m*; **yesterday morning** hier matin

yet [jet] *adv* encore; **as yet** jusqu'à présent; **not yet** pas encore || *conj* cependant

yew′ tree′ [ju] *s* if *m*

Yiddish [′jɪdɪʃ] *adj & s* yiddish *m*

yield [jild] *s* rendement *m*; (*crop*) produit *m*; (*income produced*) rapport *m*, revenu *m* || *tr* rendre, produire; (*a profit; a crop*) rapporter; (*to surrender*) céder || *intr* produire, rapporter; céder, se rendre; (public sign) céder (à droite; à gauche)

YMCA [′waɪ′em′si′e] *s* (letterword) (**Young Men's Christian Association**) Association *f* des jeunesses chrétiennes

yo·del [′jodəl] *s* tyrolienne *f* || *v* (*pret & pp* **-deled** or **-delled**; *ger* **-deling** or **-delling**) *tr & intr* jodler

yogurt [′jogurt] *s* yogourt *m*

yoke [jok] *s* (*pair of draft animals*) paire *f*; (*device to join a pair of draft animals*) joug *m*; (*of a shirt*) empiècement *m*; (elec) culasse *f*; (fig) joug; **to throw off the yoke** secouer le joug || *tr* accoupler

yokel [′jokəl] *s* rustaud *m*, manant *m*

yolk [jok] *s* jaune *m* d'œuf

yonder [′jɑndər] *adj* ce . . . -là là-bas || *adv* là-bas

yore [jor] *s*—**of yore** d'antan

you [ju] *pron pers* vous, toi §85; vous, tu §87; vous, te §87 || *pron indef* (coll) on §87, e.g., **you go in this way** on entre par ici

young [jʌŋ] *adj* (*comp* **younger** [′jʌŋgər]; *super* **youngest** [′jʌŋgɪst]) jeune || **the young** les jeunes; (*of animal*) les petits *mpl*; **to be with young** (*said of animal*) être pleine; **young and old** les grands et les petits

young′ la′dy *s* (*pl* **-dies**) jeune fille *f*; (*married*) jeune femme *f*; **young ladies** jeunes personnes *fpl*

young′ man′ *s* (*pl* **men′**) jeune homme *m*; **young men** jeunes gens *mpl*

young′ peo′ple *spl* jeunes gens *mpl*

youngster [′jʌŋstər] *s* gosse *mf*

your [jur] *adj poss* votre, ton §88

yours [jurz] *pron poss* le vôtre, le tien §89; **a friend of yours** un de vos amis; **cordially yours** (complimentary close) amitiés; **yours truly** or **sincerely yours** (complimentary close) veuillez agréer, Monsieur, l'expression de mes sentiments distingués

your·self [jur′self] *pron pers* (*pl* **-selves** [′selvz]) vous-même, toi-même §86; vous, te §87; vous, toi §85

youth [juθ] *s* (*pl* **youths** [juθs], [juðz]) jeunesse *f*; (*person*) jeune homme *m*; **youths** jeunes *mpl*

youthful [ˈjuθfəl] *adj* jeune, juvénile

yowl [jaʊl] *s* hurlement *m* ‖ *intr* hurler

Yugoslav [ˈjugoˈslɑv] *adj* yougoslave ‖ *s* Yougoslave *mf*

Yugoslavia [ˈjugoˈslɑvɪ·ə] *s* Yougoslavie *f*; la Yougoslavie

Yule′ log′ [jul] *s* bûche *f* de Noël

Yule′tide′ *s* les fêtes *fpl* de Noël

Z

Z, z [zi] or [zed] (Brit) *s* XXVIᵉ lettre de l'alphabet

za·ny [ˈzeni] *adj* (*comp* **-nier**; *super* **-niest**) bouffon, toqué ‖ *s* (*pl* **-nies**) bouffon *m*

zeal [zil] *s* zèle *m*

zealot [ˈzelət] *s* zélateur *m*, adepte *mf*

zealotry [ˈzelətrɪ] *s* fanatisme *m*

zealous [ˈzeləs] *adj* zélé

zebra [ˈzibrə] *s* zèbre *m*

zenith [ˈzinɪθ] *s* zénith *m*

zephyr [ˈzefər] *s* zéphyr *m*

zeppelin [ˈzepəlɪn] *s* zeppelin *m*

ze·ro [ˈzɪro] *s* (*pl* **-ros** or **-roes**) zéro *m* ‖ *intr*—**to zero in** (in mil) régler à la ligne de mire

ze′ro hour′ *s* heure *f* H

zest [zest] *s* enthousiasme *m*; (*agreeable and piquant flavor*) saveur *f*, piquant *m*

Zeus [zus] *s* Zeus *m*

zig-zag [ˈzɪɡˌzæɡ] *adj & adv* en zigzag ‖ *s* zigzag *m* ‖ *v* (*pret & pp* **-zagged**; *ger* **-zagging**) *intr* zigzaguer

zinc [zɪŋk] *s* zinc *m*

Zionism [ˈzaɪ·əˌnɪzəm] *s* sionisme *m*

zip [zɪp] *s* (coll) sifflement *m*; (coll) énergie *f* ‖ *v* (*pret & pp* **zipped**; *ger* **zipping**) *tr* fermer à fermeture éclair ‖ *intr* siffler; **to zip by** (coll) passer comme un éclair

zipper [ˈzɪpər] *s* fermeture *f* éclair

zither [ˈzɪθər] *s* cithare *f*

zodiac [ˈzodɪˌæk] *s* zodiaque *m*

zone [zon] *s* zone *f*

zon′ing or′dinance *s* réglementation *f* urbaine

zoo [zu] *s* zoo *m*

zoologic(al) [ˌzo·əˈlɑdʒɪk(əl)] *adj* zoologique

zoology [zoˈɑlədʒɪ] *s* zoologie *f*

zoom [zum] *s* vrombissement *m*; (aer) montée *f* en chandelle ‖ *intr* vrombir; **to zoom up** monter en chandelle

zoot′ suit′ [zut] *s* costume *m* zazou

Zu·lu [ˈzulu] *adj* zoulou ‖ *s* (*pl* **-lus**) Zoulou *m*

We Deliver!

And So Do These Bestsellers.

☐	22685	**THE COSMO REPORT** by Linda Wolfe $3.95
☐	22736	**A MANY SPLENDORED THING** by Han Suyin $3.95
☐	20922	**SHADOW OF CAIN** $3.95 V. Bugliosi & K. Hurwitz
☐	20230	**THE LAST MAFIOSO: The Treacherous** $3.95 **World of Jimmy Fratianno**
☐	20296	**THE COMING CURRENCY COLLAPSE** $3.95 by Jerome F. Smith
☐	20822	**THE GLITTER DOME** by Joseph Wambaugh $3.95
☐	20483	**WEALTH AND POVERTY** by George Gilder $3.95
☐	20198	**BOOK OF PREDICTIONS** $3.95 by Wallechinsky & Irving Wallace
☐	13101	**THE BOOK OF LISTS #2** by I. Wallace, $3.50 D. Wallechinsky, A. & S. Wallace
☐	05003	**THE GREATEST SUCCESS IN THE WORLD** $6.95 by Og Mandino (A Large Format Book)
☐	20558	**THE LORD GOD MADE THEM ALL** $3.95 by James Herriot
☐	20434	**ALL CREATURES GREAT AND SMALL** $3.95 by James Herriot
☐	14017	**THE SIMPLE SOLUTION TO RUBIK'S CUBE** $1.95 by Nourse
☐	20621	**THE PILL BOOK** by Dr. Gilbert Simon & $3.95 Dr. Harold Silverman
☐	01352	**THE PEOPLE'S ALMANAC #3** $10.95 by David Wallechinsky & Irving Wallace A Large Format Book
☐	20356	**GUINNESS BOOK OF WORLD RECORDS—** $3.95 **20th ed.** by McWhirter

Buy them at your local bookstore or use this handy coupon for ordering:

Bantam Books, Inc., Dept. NFB, 414 East Golf Road, Des Plaines, Ill. 60016

Please send me the books I have checked above. I am enclosing $_____
(please add $1.00 to cover postage and handling). Send check or money order
—no cash or C.O.D.'s please.

Mr/Mrs/Miss_____

Address_____

City_____ State/Zip_____

NFB—8/82

Please allow four to six weeks for delivery. This offer expires 2/83.

Facts at Your Fingertips!

☐ 20832	THE PUBLICITY HANDBOOK David Yale	$3.50
☐ 22573	THE BANTAM BOOK OF CORRECT LETTER WRITING	$3.50
☐ 20775	THE COMMON SENSE BOOK OF KITTEN AND CAT CARE	$2.95
☐ 14582	AMY VANDERBILT'S EVERYDAY ETIQUETTE	$3.50
☐ 14954	SOULE'S DICTIONARY OF ENGLISH SYNONYMS	$2.95
☐ 14483	DICTIONARY OF CLASSICAL MYTHOLOGY	$2.75
☐ 14080	THE BETTER HOMES AND GARDENS HANDYMAN BOOK	$3.95
☐ 20085	THE BANTAM NEW COLLEGE SPANISH & ENGLISH DICTIONARY	$2.75
☐ 20356	THE GUINNESS BOOK OF WORLD RECORDS 20th ed.	$3.95
☐ 20957	IT PAYS TO INCREASE YOUR WORD POWER	$2.95
☐ 14890	THE BANTAM COLLEGE FRENCH & ENGLISH DICTIONARY	$2.75
☐ 20298	THE FOOLPROOF GUIDE TO TAKING PICTURES	$3.50
☐ 22574	SCRIBNER/BANTAM ENGLISH DICTIONARY	$2.75
☐ 14090	WRITING AND RESEARCHING TERM PAPERS	$2.50

Ask for them at your local bookstore or use this handy coupon:

Bantam Books, Inc., Dept. RB, 414 East Golf Road, Des Plaines, Ill. 60016

Please send me the books I have checked above. I am enclosing $_____
(please add $1.00 to cover postage and handling). Send check or money order
—no cash or C.O.D.'s please.

Mr/Mrs/Miss_____

Address_____

_____ State/Zip_____

RB—8/82

llow four to six weeks for delivery. This offer expires 12/82.

<u>SAVE $2.00</u> ON YOUR NEXT BOOK ORDER!

BANTAM BOOKS 🐓
— Shop-at-Home —
Catalog

Now you can have a complete, up-to-date catalog of Bantam's inventory of over 1,600 titles—including hard-to-find books.

And, you can <u>save $2.00</u> on your next order by taking advantage of the money-saving coupon you'll find in this illustrated catalog. Choose from fiction and non-fiction titles, including mysteries, historical novels, westerns, cookbooks, romances, biographies, family living, health, and more. You'll find a description of most titles. Arranged by categories, the catalog makes it easy to find your favorite books and authors and to discover new ones.

So don't delay—send for this shop-at-home catalog and save money on your next book order.

Just send us your name and address and 50¢ to defray postage and handling costs.

BANTAM BOOKS, INC.
Dept. FC, 414 East Golf Road, Des Plaines, Ill. 60016

Mr./Mrs./Miss_____
_____(please print)_____
Address_____

City_____State_____Zip_____

Do you know someone who enjoys books? Just give us their names and addresses and we'll send them a catalog too at no extra cost!

Mr./Mrs./Miss_____
Address_____
City_____State_____Zip_____

Mr./Mrs./Miss_____
Address_____
City_____State_____Zip_____

FC—9/